THE
PULPIT COMMENTARY

Edited by

H. D. M. Spence

and

Joseph S. Exell

———————

Volume 16
MARK & LUKE

MACDONALD PUBLISHING COMPANY
MCLEAN, VIRGINIA 22102

ISBN 0-917006-32-1

ST. MARK

EXPOSITION BY

E. BICKERSTETH

HOMILETICS BY

J. R. THOMSON

HOMILIES BY VARIOUS AUTHORS

A. ROWLAND   J. J. GIVEN

A. F. MUIR   E. JOHNSON

R. GREEN

THE
GOSPEL ACCORDING TO ST. MARK

VOL. I.

INTRODUCTION

THE four living creatures mentioned in Ezekiel (i. 10), and which reappear in a modified form in the Apocalypse of St. John (iv. 7), are interpreted by very many Christian writers to signify the fourfold Gospel, the four faces representing the four evangelists. The face of a *man* is supposed to denote St. Matthew, who describes the actions of our Lord more especially as to his human nature. The face of an *eagle* is understood to indicate St. John, who soars at once into the highest heavens, and commences his Gospel with that magnificent declaration, "In the beginning was the Word, and the Word was with God, and the Word was God." Then the face of an *ox* symbolizes St. Luke, who commences his narrative with the priesthood of Zacharias. While, lastly, the face of a *lion* represents St. Mark, because he opens his Gospel with the trumpet voice, like the roaring of a lion, the loud call of the Baptist to repentance. These four carried the chariot of the gospel throughout the world, and subdued the nations to the obedience of Christ, the mighty Conqueror.

Other interesting interpretations have been suggested for these symbols; amongst them "the whole animate creation," the number four being understood to symbolize the material world, as the number three represents the Divine Being. But the former interpretation is largely supported by early Christian antiquity, and has been made familiar to us through the ages past in the representations of ancient art, both sculpture and painting.

If early testimony is to have its due weight, St. Mark wrote his Gospel in Greek, and at Rome, and apparently for Gentiles, certainly not exclusively, or in the first instance, for Jews. There are explanations given here and there in his Gospel which would be superfluous if it were written only for Jews. Jordan, when he first mentions it, is called "the river Jordan." It is true that many good authorities read "the river Jordan" in St. Matthew (iii. 6); but this may have been introduced to make his Gospel more clear to those who were unacquainted with the geography of Palestine. "John's disciples and the Pharisees used to fast" (ἦσαν νηστεύοντες); literally, "were fasting." This would have been unnecessary information for Jews. "The time of figs was not yet." Every inhabitant of Palestine would have known this. St. Mark alone preserves those words of our Lord, "The sabbath was made for man, and not man for the sabbath," (ch. ii. 27)—a great principle, belonging to all nations alike. He alone quotes the words (xi. 17), "of all nations," literally (πᾶσι τοῖς ἔθνεσιν), "for all the nations," in connection with our Lord's cleansing of the temple.

Early writers speak of St. Mark as the "interpreter" of St. Peter; by which expression it seems to be meant that he put down in writing, what he had heard orally from St. Peter, the things relating to the life of our Lord. It seems also plain that he must have had access to St. Matthew's Gospel. But he was not a mere copyist. He was an independent witness. He often supplies a sentence, detailing some little incident which he could only have received from an eye-witness, and which forms an additional link to the narrative, explaining something which had been left obscure, and filling up the picture. If we imagine St. Mark with St. Matthew's Gospel at hand, and with copious memoranda of the observations and graphic descriptions of St. Peter, together with his own peculiar gifts as a writer, and the unerring guidance of the Holy Spirit, we seem to see at once the sources of St. Mark's Gospel.

St. Mark's Gospel is the shortest of all the four Gospels; and yet there is a unity about it which, as has been well said, "quite excludes the notion that it is either a mere compendium of some richer, or an expansion of some briefer, Gospel" ('Speaker's Commentary'). The writer avails himself of all the information that he can procure; at the same time, he is an independent witness, giving, as all the sacred writers are permitted to do, the colouring of his own mind, his own "setting," so to speak, to those great truths and facts which the Holy Ghost moved him to communicate. His frequent use of the present for the aorist; his constant repetition of the word εὐθέως, "straightway" (carefully marked in the new Revision by the employment of the same English synonym, "straightway," throughout); his employment of diminutives, and his introduction of little details, imparting freshness and light to the whole narrative;—all these and many other circumstances give to St. Mark's Gospel a character of its own, distinct from, and yet in harmony with, the rest. It is a compendium of our blessed Lord's life upon earth; but it is a compendium with a peculiar richness and originality which differences it off from the other Gospels, making us feel that if we were called upon to part with any one of the four, we certainly could not spare that of St. Mark.

Another thought which is impressed upon us by the study of this Gospel is the shortness of the time within which the amazing mystery of our redemption was actually wrought out, and the marvellous activity of the earthly life of the Son of God. St. Mark's narrative, giving for the most part the salient facts and events, without the discourses and parables which enrich the other Gospels, presents us with a comprehensive conspectus, which is of special use in its relation to the other Gospels, in which we are led rather to dwell upon the details, and to linger over the Divine words, instructive as they are, until we almost lose sight of the grand outline of the history. St. Mark, by the structure of his narrative, helps us more readily to grasp the whole of the sublime and impressive record.

Take, for example, St. Mark's account of our Lord's ministry in Galilee. How it revolves around the familiar Lake of Gennesaret! A series of striking miracles at Capernaum and in that neighbourhood, commencing with the casting out of the "unclean spirit," excites the attention of the whole Jewish population, and exalts the fame of Jesus even amongst the heathen beyond the Jewish borders, so that they flock to him from every quarter. But the miracles were only intended to challenge attention to the words of Jesus; and therefore we find him continually preaching to the dense masses on the seashore, until they thronged him so that he was obliged to direct a boat to be always in attendance upon him, into which he might retreat, and which he might use as his pulpit when the pressure of the crowd became inconveniently great. Then there is the frequent crossing over the lake to and fro, from west to east, and back from east to west—the sea itself ministering to him, gathering into a storm at his bidding, and at his bidding becoming still. Then there are the miracles and the preaching on this side and on that, amongst a Jewish population here and a Gentile population there. And then there is the jealousy of the chief priests and scribes, sent purposely from Jerusalem to watch him, and to find grounds for accusation against him, while the mass of the people recognize him as the great Prophet that should come into the world. A few short chapters suffice to exhibit all this to us, and to present us with a striking and vivid illustration of the fulfilment of the prophecy quoted by St. Matthew (iv. 15, 16): "The land of Zabulon, and the land of Nephthali, by the way of the sea, beyond Jordan, Galilee of the Gentiles; the people which sat in darkness saw great light; and to them which sat in the region and shadow of death light is sprung up."

The connection of St. Peter with this Gospel has already been noticed; and, assuming the correctness of the supposition that St. Mark, in writing his Gospel, was to a great extent the "interpreter" of St. Peter, it is interesting to observe how the internal evidence supplied by this Gospel tends to confirm this view. Instead of being put prominently forward, as in the other Gospels, in this the Apostle Peter falls as much as possible into the background. When his name first occurs, it appears as Simon. It is not until the third chapter that he is spoken of as Peter, and then only in the simplest terms: "Simon he surnamed Peter" (ch. iii. 16). In the eighth chapter, while our Lord's severe rebuke of him is recorded, there is no mention of the noble confession which he had made just before. In the fourteenth chapter, while we are informed that our Lord sent two of his disciples to prepare the Passover, the names of the two are not given, although we know from another evangelist that they were Peter and John. In the same chapter, when they were in the Garden of Gethsemane, we read that our Lord singles out Peter as one who was heavy with sleep, and applies his remonstrance specially to him, addressing him as Simon, and saying, "Simon, sleepest thou?" The particulars of this apostle's denial of Christ are, as we might expect, given also with great minuteness. The only other notice that we find of him is that message sent to him by the angel after our Lord's resurrection, "Go tell his disciples and Peter, He goeth before you into Galilee"—a message which, while it would recall to him his sin, would also assure him of his forgiveness. Now, all this manifestly confirms the ancient traditions that St. Peter influenced the compilation of this Gospel. He had said (2 Pet. i. 15), "Moreover I will endeavour that ye may be able after my decease to have these things always in remembrance"—a sentence which shows his great anxiety that there should be a trustworthy record preserved for all future ages from the lips and pens of those who were eye-witnesses of Christ's majesty. Thus all that we read leads us to the conclusion that we have in St. Mark a faithful exponent of what St. Peter heard and saw and communicated to him; so that if we wanted another title for this Gospel, we might call it "The Gospel according to St. Peter."

I. The Life of St. Mark the Evangelist.

The name of Mark is by some supposed to be derived from the Latin "marcus," a hammer; not "marcellus," a little hammer, but "marcus," a strong hammer, able to crush the flinty rock, and thus indicative of the spiritual power wielded by the evangelist, and enabling him to break the stony hearts of the Gentiles, and to rouse them to penitence and faith and a holy life. The præ-nomen Marcus was in frequent use amongst the Romans, and often given to those who were the firstborn. Cicero was called Marcus Tullius Cicero, because he was the firstborn of his family. So St. Mark was in a spiritual sense the firstborn and well-beloved of St. Peter. "The Church that is at Babylon [literally, ἡ ἐν Βαβυλῶνι, 'she that is in Babylon'], elected together with you, saluteth you; and so doth Marcus my son" (1 Pet. v. 13). St. Mark drew his spirit and his ardour from St. Peter. St. Peter, as his father in Christ Jesus, impressed his wisdom and holiness upon him.

Who, then, was St. Mark? He appears to have been a Hebrew by nation and of the tribe of Levi. Bede says that he was a priest after the order of Aaron. There is very good reason to believe (although Grotius, Cornelius à Lapide, and others, think differently) that he is the same person who is mentioned in the Acts (xii. 12, 25) as "John whose surname is Mark." John was his original Jewish name; and Mark, his Roman prefix, was added afterwards, and gradually superseded the other name. We can trace the process of the change very clearly in the Acts and in the Epistles. We find John and John Mark in the earlier part of the Acts; but in Acts xv. 39 John disappears altogether, and in the Epistles he is always called Mark. His surname appears to have gradually taken the place of his other name, just as Paul takes the place of Saul. Then further we find him associated with St. Peter; which furnishes another evidence of his identity, as also does the fact that he was sister's son, or cousin (ἀνεψιὸς) to Barnabas, who was himself on terms of close fellowship with St. Peter. Moreover, the general consensus of the early Church identifies John Mark with the writer of this Gospel, which Eusebius informs us was written under the eye of St. Peter. The substitution of a Roman name for his family Jewish name was probably intentional, and designed to indicate his entrance upon a new life, and to prepare him for intercourse with Gentiles, especially Romans.

Assuming, then, that "John whose surname was Mark" was the writer of this Gospel, we have the following particulars respecting him:—He was the son of a certain Mary who dwelt in Jerusalem. She appears to have been well known, and to have been in a good position. Her house was open to the friends and disciples of our Lord. It is possible that hers may have been the house where our Lord "kept the Passover" with his disciples on the night of his betrayal; perhaps the house where the disciples were gathered together on the evening of the Resurrection; perhaps the house where they received the miraculous gifts on the day of Pentecost. It was certainly the house to which Peter betook himself when he was delivered out of prison; certainly the first great centre of Christian worship in Jerusalem after our Lord's ascension, and the site of the first Christian church in that city. It is probable that it was to the sacred intercourse of that home that John Mark owed his conversion, which may very probably have been delayed in consequence of his having been by birth of the family of the Jewish priesthood. It is more than probable that St. Mark, in ch. xiv. 51, 52, may have been relating what happened to himself. All the details fit in with this supposition. The action corresponds with what we know of his character, which appears to have been warm-hearted and earnest, but timid and impulsive. Moreover, the linen cloth, or *sindon*, cast about his body, answers to his position and circumstances. It would not have been worn by a person in very humble life. Indeed, nothing but the name is wanting to complete the evidence of the identity of "John whose surname was Mark" with Mark the writer of this Gospel. It will be remembered that St. John in his Gospel evidently speaks of himself more than once without mentioning his name, calling himself "another disciple." St. Mark, if the hypothesis be correct, speaks of himself as "a young man," probably because he was not yet a disciple.

We may assume, then, that the events of that terrible night and of the following day, followed by the great event of the Resurrection, so wrought upon the mind of John Mark, that they brought him to a full acceptance of Christ and his salvation. Hence we are not surprised to find that he was chosen at an early period in the history of the Acts of the Apostles (Acts xiii. 5) to accompany Paul and Barnabas as their minister, or attendant (ὑπηρέτης), on their first missionary journey. But we next read of him that when they reached Perga, in Pamphylia (Acts xiii. 13), John Mark left them and returned to Jerusalem. The sacred narrative does not give the reason for this defection. Pamphylia was a wild, rough district; and St. Paul and his companions may have encountered some dangers before reaching Perga, if Strabo's account of the Pamphylians is to be relied upon. Then John Mark may have felt a longing for his mother's home at Jerusalem; and some good opportunity for leaving them may have offered itself to him at Perga, which was not far from the sea. At all events, it is consistent with what we know of his character that he should have suddenly determined to leave the apostles. However, if any unworthy motive influenced him, he soon recovered himself; for not long after, we read of his having been again associated, not indeed with Paul, but with Barnabas, his cousin, in missionary labour. Indeed, Mark was the cause of a temporary estrangement between Paul and Barnabas, although, in the providence of him who is ever bringing good out of evil, this estrangement led to a still wider diffusion of the gospel.

The next notice that we have of Mark is in St. Paul's Epistle to the Colossians, written by him from Rome during his first imprisonment. At the close of that letter St. Paul writes (Col. iv. 10), "There saluteth you, . . . Marcus, sister's son to Barnabas, touching whom ye received commandments : if he come unto you, receive him." It is probable that these Christians at Colosse had heard of the temporary separation of Paul and Barnabas, and of its cause; and if so, there is something very pathetic in this allusion to Mark in this Epistle. It is as though the apostle said, "You may have heard of the separation between Barnabas and myself on account of Mark. You will therefore now rejoice to know that Mark is with me, and a comfort to me, and that he sends you Christian greetings by my hand. I have already given you directions concerning him: if he come unto you, receive him." (See Wordsworth, *in loc.*)

Nor is this all. Later on, in his Second Epistle to Timothy, written during his second imprisonment at Rome, St. Paul (iv. 11) desires his own son in the faith, Timothy, to come to him; and he adds, "Take Mark, and bring him with thee; for he is profitable to me for the ministry;" literally, "he is useful to me for ministering" (ἐστι γάρ μοι εὔχρηστος εἰς διακονίαν). It would seem as though these words had reference rather to Mark's useful qualities as an attendant (ὑπηρέτης), though possibly the higher service may be included. This is the latest notice that we have of Mark in the New Testament. But St. Peter, writing from Babylon, perhaps about five or six years before St. Paul sent this message to Timothy, alludes to Mark as having been with him there at that time, and calls him, "Marcus my son," as has already been noticed.

It will be seen, then, from hence that Mark had close and intimate relations with both St. Peter and St. Paul; and that he was with the one apostle at Babylon, and with the other at Rome. I am quite unable to accept the view that St. Peter, when mentioning Babylon, is referring mystically to Rome. This is not the place in which to look for figurative language. Nor is there anything remarkable in St. Peter, the apostle of the circumcision, having gone to Babylon, where we know there was a large colony of Jews, or in his having been accompanied thither by Mark himself, also a Jew of the family of Aaron. The whole is consistent with the idea that Mark wrote his Gospel under the direction of St. Peter. Ancient writers, as Irenæus, Tertullian, St. Jerome, and others, with one consent make him the interpreter of St. Peter. Eusebius, quoting from Papias, says, "Mark, being the interpreter of St. Peter, wrote down exactly whatever things he remembered, yet not in the order in which Christ either spoke or did them; for he was neither a hearer nor a follower of our Lord, but he was afterwards a follower of St. Peter." St. Jerome says, "St. Mark, the interpreter of the Apostle St. Peter, and the first bishop of the Church of Alexandria, related what things he heard his master preaching, rather according to the truth of the facts, than according to the order of the things that were done."

St. Augustine calls Mark the "breviator" of St. Matthew, not because he made an abridgment of St. Matthew's Gospel, but because he relates more briefly, according to what he had received from St. Peter, those things which St. Matthew relates more at length.

According to the testimony of St. Jerome, he wrote a short Gospel at Rome at the request of the brethren there; and St. Peter, when he had heard it, approved of it, and appointed it to be read in the churches by his authority. St. Jerome says, further, that St. Mark took this Gospel and went into Egypt; and, being the first preacher of Christ at Alexandria, established a Church with so much moderation of doctrine and of life, that he constrained all those who had opposed Christ to follow his example. Eusebius states that he became the first bishop of that Church, and that the catechetical school at Alexandria was founded under his authority. It is further stated that he ultimately died a martyr's death at Alexandria. But the evidence upon this latter point is not sufficiently trustworthy.

Tradition says that the body of St. Mark was translated by certain merchants from Alexandria to Venice, A.D. 827, where he was much honoured. The Venetian Senate adopted the emblem of St. Mark—the lion—for their crest; and when they directed anything to be done, they affirmed that it was by the order of St. Mark.

II. Observations on the Genuineness and Authenticity of the Last Twelve Verses of St. Mark's Gospel.

These verses have been admitted by the Revisers of 1881 into the text, but with a space between ver. 8 and ver. 9, to show that they have received them with some degree of caution and reserve, and not without having carefully weighed the evidence on both sides. The most important features in the evidence are the following:—

1. *The Evidence of Manuscripts.*

(1) Of the Uncial Manuscripts. The two oldest, namely, the Sinaitic and the Vatican, omit the whole passage, but under different conditions. The Sinaitic omits the passage absolutely. The Vatican omits it, but with a space left blank between the eighth verse of Mark xvi., and the beginning of St. Luke, just sufficient for its insertion; as though the writer of the manuscript, hesitating whether to omit or to insert the verses, thought it safest to leave a space for them.

But there is another and much later Uncial Manuscript (L), of about the eighth century. Of this manuscript it may be said that, although some four centuries later, it bears a strong family resemblance to the Sinaitic and the Vatican. This manuscript does not omit the passage, but it interpolates between it and the eighth verse an apocryphal addition, and then goes on with ver. 9. This addition is given at p. 538, second edition, of Dr. Scrivener's admirable work on the 'Criticism of the New Testament.'

It should be added here that there is a strong resemblance between the Sinaitic and Vatican manuscripts; so that practically the evidential value of these three manuscripts amounts to little more than one authority.

With these three exceptions, all the Uncial Manuscripts maintain the twelve verses in their integrity.

(2) The Cursive Manuscripts. The evidence of the Cursives is unanimous in favour of the disputed verses. It is true that some mark the passage as one of which the genuineness had been disputed. But against this there has to be set the fact that the verses are retained in all but two old manuscripts, and those two in all probability not independent. It has been clearly shown by Dean Burgon that the verses were read in the public services of the Church in the fourth century, and probably much earlier, as shown by the ancient Evangelisteria.

2. *Evidence of Ancient Versions.*

The most ancient versions, both of the Eastern and of the Western Churches, without a single exception, recognize this passage. Of the Eastern versions the evidence is very remarkable. The Peshito Syriac, which dates from the second century, bears witness to its genuineness; so does the Philoxenian; while the Curetonian Syriac, also very ancient, far earlier than the Sinaitic or Vatican manuscripts, bears a very singular testimony. In the only extant copy of that version, the Gospel of St. Mark is wanting, with the exception of one fragment only, and that fragment contains the last four of these disputed verses. The Coptic versions also recognize the passage.

The same may be said of the versions of the Western Church. The earlier version of the Vulgate, called the Old Italic, has it. Jerome, who used the best manuscript of the Old Italic when he prepared his Vulgate, felt himself obliged to admit this disputed passage, although he did not scruple to allege the objections to its reception, which were the same as those urged by Eusebius. The Gothic Version of Ulphilas (fourth century) has the passage from ver. 8 to ver. 12.

3. *Evidence of the Early Fathers.*

There are some expressions in the 'Shepherd of Hermas,' written in all probability not later than the middle of the second century, which are evidently taken from St. Mark (xvi. 16).

Justin Martyr (about A.D. 160) quotes the last two verses.

The evidence of Irenæus (A.D. 177) is yet more striking. In one of his books ('Adv. Hær.,' iii. 10) he quotes the beginning and the end of St. Mark's Gospel in the same passage, in the latter part of which he says, "But in the end of his Gospel Mark saith, 'And the Lord Jesus, after he had spoken unto them, was received into heaven, and sitteth at the right hand of God,' confirming what was said by the prophet, 'The Lord saith unto my Lord, Sit thou on my right hand, until I make thine enemies thy footstool.'"

This evidence of Irenæus is conclusive as to the fact that in his time there was no doubt as to the genuineness and authenticity of the passage in Asia Minor, in Gaul, or in Italy.

There yet remains the question of *internal evidence*.

Now, to begin with. If it is assumed that St. Mark's Gospel ended at the close of ver. 8, the abruptness of the conclusion is very striking in the English, and still more so in the Greek ($\dot{\epsilon}\phi o\beta o\hat{v}\nu\tau o$ $\gamma\acute{a}\rho$). It seems scarcely possible to suppose that it could have ended here. Renan says on this point, "On ne peut guére admettre que le texte primitif finit d'une maniere aussi abrupte."

On the other hand, having regard to the mode in which St. Mark opens his Gospel, we might suppose that he would condense at the close as he condenses at the beginning. The first year of our Lord's ministry is disposed of very briefly ; we might, therefore, expect a rapid and compendious conclusion. Two or three important evidences of our Lord's resurrection are concisely stated ; then, without any break, but where the reader must supply an interval, he is transported into Galilee. St. Mark had already recorded the words of Christ (xiv. 28), "But after that I am risen, I will go before you into Galilee." How natural, therefore, that he should refer in some way to our Lord's presence in Galilee after his resurrection ; which he does in the most effective manner by quoting the words which St. Matthew (xxvii. 16, etc.) tells us were spoken by him in Galilee. Then another stride from Galilee to Bethany, to the last earthly scene of all—the Ascension. The whole is eminently characteristic of St. Mark. His Gospel ends, as we might expect it to end, from the character of its beginning. On the whole, the evidence as to the genuineness and authenticity of this passage seems irresistible.

III. Analysis of Contents of St. Mark's Gospel.

IV. LITERATURE.

Papias; Irenæus; Tertullian; Origen; Clemens Alexandrinus; Eusebius; Jerome; Gregory; Augustine; Chrysostom; Cornelius à Lapide; the 'Catena Aurea' of Thomas Aquinas; Joseph Mede; Dr. John Lightfoot; Bengel's 'Gnomon;' Dean Alford; Bishop Wordsworth; Meyer; Stanley's 'Sinai and Palestine;' 'Speakers' Commentary;' Smith's 'Dictionary of the Bible;' Dr. Morison's 'Commentary on St. Mark' (3rd edit.); Dr. Scrivener on the Criticism of the New Testament; Dean Burgon on the last twelve verses of St. Mark's Gospel.

THE
GOSPEL ACCORDING TO ST. MARK

—◆—

EXPOSITION

CHAPTER I.

Ver. 1.—The beginning of the gospel of Jesus Christ. These words mean, not the title of the book, but the commencement of the narrative; and so they depend upon what follows, namely, "as it is written" (καθὼς for ὡς), "even as it is written." The words "the gospel of Jesus Christ" do not signify the book which St. Mark wrote, but the evangelical teaching of Jesus Christ. St. Mark means that the gospel announcement by Jesus Christ had such a beginning as had been predicted by Isaiah and Malachi, namely, the preaching of John the Baptist, and his testimony concerning Christ, to be fully laid open by the preaching and the death of Christ. The preaching of repentance by the Baptist was the preparation and the beginning of the evangelical preaching by Christ, of whom John was the forerunner. It has been well observed that St. Matthew and St. John begin their Gospels from Christ himself; but St. Matthew from the human, and St. John from the Divine, generation of Christ. St. Mark and St. Luke commence from John the Baptist; but St. Luke from his nativity, and St. John from his preaching. The words, **the Son of God,** are rightly retained in the Revised Version, although they are omitted by some ancient authorities.

Ver. 2.—Even as it is written in the prophets. The weight of evidence is here in favour of the reading "in Isaiah the prophet." Three of the most important uncials (א, B, and L), and twenty-six of the cursives, have the reading "Isaiah." With these agree the Italic, Coptic, and Vulgate versions. Of the Fathers, Irenæus quotes the passage three times, twice using the words "in the prophets," and once "in Isaiah the prophet."

Generally the Fathers agree that "Isaiah" is the received reading. The more natural reading would of course be "in the prophets," inasmuch as two prophets are quoted; but in deciding upon readings, it constantly happens that the less likely reading is the more probable. In the case before us we can hardly account for "Isaiah" being exchanged for "the prophets," although we can quite understand "the prophets" being interpolated for "Isaiah." Assuming, then, that St. Mark wrote "in Isaiah the prophet," we may ask why he mentions Isaiah only and not Malachi? The answer would seem to be this, that here the voice of Isaiah is the more powerful of the two. But in real truth, Malachi says the same thing that Isaiah says; for the messenger sent from God to prepare the way of Christ was none other than John, crying aloud and preaching repentance as a preparation for the receiving of the grace of Christ. The oracle of Malachi is, in fact, contained in the oracle of Isaiah; for what Malachi predicted, the same had Isaiah more clearly and concisely predicted in other words. And this is the reason why St. Mark here, and other evangelists elsewhere, when they cite two prophets, and two or more sentences from different places in the same connection, cite them as one and the same testimony, each sentence appearing to be not so much two, as one and the same declaration differently worded.

Ver. 4.—John came, and preached the baptism of repentance. John came, that is, that he might rouse the people to repentance, and prepare them, by the outward cleansing of their bodies, to receive the cleansing of their souls through Christ's baptism, which was to follow his. So that the baptism of John was the profession of their penitence. Hence they who were baptized with his baptism confessed their sins, and thus made the first step towards the forgiving mercy which was to be found in Christ; and the seal of his forgiveness they were to look for in his baptism, which is a baptism for the remission of sins to all true penitents and faithful believers. Christ's baptism was, therefore, the perfection and consummation of the baptism of John.

Ver. 6.—**Clothed with camel's hair.** This was a rough, coarse garment, characteristic of the doctrine which John taught, namely, penitence and contempt of the world. Camels abounded in Syria. **And a leathern girdle about his loins.** Not only the prophets, but the Jews and the inhabitants of Syria generally, used a girdle to keep the long flowing garment more closely about them, so as to leave them more free for journeying or for labour. Thus our Lord says (Luke xii. 35), "Let your loins be girded about, and your lamps burning." **And he did eat locusts and wild honey.** The insect called the locust (ἀκρίς) was permitted to be eaten (see Lev. xi. 22). It was used as food by the common people in Judæa. The Arabs eat them to this day; but they are considered as a common and inferior kind of food. They are a sign of temperance, poverty, and penitence. The wild honey (μέλι ἄγριον) was simply honey made by wild bees, either in the trees or in the hollows of the rocks. Isidorus says that it was of an inferior flavour. Both these kinds of food were consistent with the austere life and the solemn preaching of the Baptist.

Ver. 7.—**The latchet of whose shoes I am not worthy to stoop down and unloose.** This was the menial office of the slave, whose business it was to take off and put on the shoes of his master, stooping down with all humility and respect for this purpose. Thus John confessed that he was the servant of Christ, and that Christ was his Lord. In a mystical sense the shoes denote the humanity of Christ, which by its union with the Word became of the highest dignity and majesty. St. Bernard says, "The majesty of the Word was shod with the sandal of our humanity."

Ver. 8.—**I baptized you with water; but he shall baptize you with [or in] the Holy Ghost.** It is as though he said, "Christ will pour his Holy Spirit so abundantly upon you, that he will cleanse you from all your sins, and fill you with holiness and love and all his other excellent graces." Christ did this visibly on the day of Pentecost. And this he does invisibly in the sacrament of Holy Baptism, and in the rite of Confirmation, which is the completion of the sacrament of Baptism. John baptized with water only, but Christ with water and the Holy Spirit. John baptized the body only, Christ baptizes the soul. By how much, therefore, the Holy Spirit transcends the water, and the soul excels the body, by so much is Christ's baptism more excellent than that of John, which was only preparatory and rudimentary. If it be asked why it was needful that our Lord should be baptized with John's baptism, the best answer is that given by Christ himself, "Suffer it to be so now; for thus it becometh *us* to fulfil all righteousness;" it becometh us—me in receiving this baptism, and you in imparting it. Christ was sent to do the whole will of God; and as in his circumcision, so in his baptism, "he was made to be sin for us, who knew no sin."

Ver. 10.—**Straightway** (εὐθέως) **coming up out of the water, he saw the heavens opened** (σχιζομένους); literally, *rent asunder.* The word εὐθέως occurs more than forty times in this Gospel, and is so characteristic of St. Mark that, in the Revised Version, it is uniformly rendered by the same English synonym, "straightway." *He saw.* Elsewhere we are told (John i. 32) that St. John the Baptist saw this descent. The earliest heretics took advantage of this statement to represent this event as the descent of the eternal Christ upon the man Jesus for personal indwelling. Later critics have adopted this view. But it need hardly be said here that such an opinion is altogether inconsistent with all that we read elsewhere of the circumstances of the Incarnation, and of the intimate and indissoluble union of the Divine and human natures in the person of the one Christ, from the time of the "overshadowing of the Virgin Mary by the power of the Highest." The Spirit descending upon him at his baptism was not the descent of the eternal Christ upon the man Jesus. It was rather the conveyance to one who was already prepared for it as God and man, of office and authority as the great Prophet that should come into the world. St. Luke says particularly (iii. 21) that it was when Jesus had been baptized and was praying, that the Holy Spirit descended upon him; plainly showing us that it was not through the baptism of John, but through the meritorious obedience and the prayer of the Son of God, that the heavens were "rent asunder," and the Holy Spirit descended upon him.

Ver. 12.—**Driveth him** (ἐκβάλλει); literally, *driveth him forth.* That Holy Spirit, which not long before he had received at his baptism, impelled him with great energy; so that of his own accord he went forth, armed with Divine power, into the desert, that there, as in a wrestling-place, he might contend alone with Satan. There Christ and antichrist met, and entered upon the conflict upon the issue of which our salvation depended.

Ver. 13.—**Forty days tempted of Satan.** St. Mark gathers up the whole temptation into this one sentence; and the passage would seem to imply that the three temptations recorded by St. Matthew and St. Luke were not the only trials through which our Lord passed during those forty days, although they were no doubt the prominent and the most powerful assaults upon our Redeemer. **And he was with the wild beasts** (μετὰ τῶν θηρίων). This shows the extreme solitude of the place. It shows also the innocence of our Lord, that there, in that wild and desolate district, amongst lions, and wolves, and leopards, and serpents, he neither feared them nor was injured by them. He dwelt amongst them as Adam lived with them in his state of innocence in Paradise. These wild beasts recognized and revered their Creator and their Lord. **And the angels ministered unto him.** This, as we learn from St. Matthew (iv. 11), was after his temptation and victory. Some have thought that Jesus became known to the devil as the Son of God, by the reverence and adoration of the angels. Thus Jesus showed in his own person, when alone he had striven with Satan and had overcome him, that heavenly comfort and the ministry of angels are provided by God for those who overcome temptation.

Ver. 14.—**Now after that John was put in prison** (μετὰ τὸ παραδοθῆναι); literally, *was delivered up.* This was our Lord's second coming into Galilee. Galilee had been specially designated as the scene of the Divine manifestation (see Isa. ix. 1, 2). The land of Galilee, or of Zebulun and Naphtali, had the misfortune to be the first in the sad calamity which fell upon the Jewish nation through the Assyrian invasion; and, in order to console them under this grievous affliction, Isaiah assures them that, by way of recompense, they, above the rest of their brethren, should have the chief share in the presence and ministry of the future promised Messiah. It seems probable that our Lord remained some time in Judæa after his baptism. From thence he went, with Andrew and Peter, two of John's disciples, into Galilee, where he called Philip. And then it was that he turned the water into wine at the marriage feast in Cana. This was his first coming out of Judæa into Galilee, related by St. John (i. 43, etc.). But the Passover brought him back into Judæa, that he might present himself in the temple; and then occurred his first purging of the temple (John ii. 14). Then came the visit of Nicodemus to him by night; and then he began openly to preach and to baptize (John iii. 26), and thus incurred the envy of the scribes and Pharisees. Therefore he left Judæa, and departed again into Galilee; and this is the departure here recorded by St. Mark and by St. Matthew (iv. 12). Hence it came to pass that it was in Galilee that Christ called to himself four fishermen—Andrew and Peter, James and John.

Ver. 15.—**The time is fulfilled;** that is, the time for the coming of Messiah and of his kingdom. The kingdom which had been shut for so many ages was now to be re-opened by the preaching and the death of Christ. The time is very accurately indicated. St. Matthew tells us (iv. 12) that "when Jesus had heard that John was cast into prison, he departed into Galilee;" and then presently afterwards he adds, "From that time Jesus began to preach and to say, Repent, for the kingdom of God is at hand." The time and place are also accurately specified by St. Peter (Acts x. 36, 37), where he tells Cornelius that "the word of peace, preached by Jesus Christ, was published throughout all Judæa, and began from Galilee, after the baptism which John preached." It was necessary that these circumstances should be carefully detailed, because they were among the proofs of the Messiahship of Jesus. Elias must come first; and he had come in the person of the Baptist, although the prophecy probably awaits its full accomplishment in the actual reappearance of the great prophet of Israel before the second coming of our Lord. **Repent ye, and believe the gospel.** These words may be regarded as a summary of the method of salvation. Repentance and faith are the conditions of admission into the Christian covenant. Repentance has a special reference to God the Father, and faith, to Jesus Christ the eternal Son. It is in the gospel that Christ is revealed to us as a Saviour; and therefore we find Jesus Christ, as the object of our faith, distinguished from the Father as the object of our repentance. Repentance of itself is not sufficient—it makes no satisfaction for the Law which we have broken; and hence, over and above repentance, there is required from us faith in the Gospel, wherein Christ is revealed to us as a propitiation for sin, and as the only way of reconciliation with the Father. Without faith repentance becomes despair, and without repentance faith becomes only presumption. The two together, and the faithful soul is borne onwards, like a well-balanced vessel, to the haven where it would be.

Ver. 16.—**Now as he walked by the sea**

of Galilee; a better reading is (καὶ παράγων), *and passing along.* Our Lord came up from the south, passing through Samaria, till he reached Cana of Galilee. He then passed along by the seashore towards Capernaum; and on his way found the four disciples whom he had previously nominated, but who were now engaged in their calling of fishermen. St. Mark then relates the circumstances of their call in the exact words of St. Matthew, which were in all probability those of apostolical tradition ('Speaker's Commentary'). It will be seen that St. Mark's account, in this introductory portion of his Gospel, is very concise, and that there are many things to be supplied from the first chapter of St. John; as, for example, that after our Lord's baptism by John, and after his fasting and temptation in the desert, the Jews sent messengers to the Baptist, to inquire of him whether he were the Christ. John at once confessed that he was not the Christ, but that there was One even then among them, though they knew him not, who was indeed the Christ. And then, the very next day after, Jesus came to him, and John then said to those around him, "Behold the Lamb of God!" Upon this two of John's disciples at once betook themselves to Jesus. The first was Andrew, who forthwith brought his own brother Simon, afterwards called "Peter," to our Lord. Again, the day after this, our Lord called Philip, a fellow-citizen with Andrew and Peter, of Bethsaida. Then Philip brought Nathanael. Here, then, we have some more disciples nominated, who were with Jesus at the marriage in Cana of Galilee. Then Jesus returned again into Judæa; and those disciples "nominate," as we might call them, went back for a time to their occupation of fishermen. Meanwhile our Lord, while in Judæa, wrought miracles and preached, until the envy of the scribes and Pharisees constrained him to return again into Galilee. And then it was that he solemnly called Andrew and Peter, and James and John, as recorded by St. Mark here. So that St. John alone gives some account of the events of the first year of our Lord's ministry. The three synoptic Gospels give the narrative of his public ministry, commencing from the second year. **He saw Simon and Andrew, the brother of Simon, casting a net in the sea** (βάλλοντας ἀμφίβληστρον ἐν τῇ θαλάσσῃ). Such was the text underlying the Authorized Version; but a better reading is ἀμφιβάλλοντας ἐν τῇ θαλάσσῃ. St. Mark thinks it unnecessary to mention the net at all; though doubtless it was the ἀμφίβληστρον, or casting-net. When our Lord likens his gospel to a net, he uses the figure of the drag-net (σαγήνη). a net of a much larger size. But whether it be the casting-net or the drag-net, the comparison is a striking one. It is plain that, in the pursuit of his calling, the fisherman has no power to make any separation between the good fish and the worthless. He has little or no insight into what is going on beneath the surface of the water. So with the "fisher of men." He deals with the world spiritual and invisible; and how, then, can he be fully conscious of the results of his work? His work is pre-eminently a work of faith. It may be observed here that St. Mark, in this earlier part of his narrative, speaks of St. Peter as Simon, though afterwards (ch. iii. 16) he calls him Peter. We may also notice here, once for all, St. Mark's constant use of the word "straightway" (εὐθέως or εὐθὺς). This word occurs no less than ten times in this chapter. In the Authorized Version the word (εὐθέως) is rendered indifferently by various English synonyms, as "forthwith," "immediately," etc.; whereas in the Revised Version it has been thought fit to note this peculiarity or mannerism in St. Mark's Gospel by the use of the same English synonym, "straightway," throughout this Gospel. The Holy Spirit, while guiding the minds of those whom he moved to write these records, did not use an overpowering influence, so as to interfere with their own natural modes of expression. Each sacred writer, while guarded against error, has reserved to him his own peculiarities of style and expression.

Vers. 19, 20.—The calling of James and John, the sons of Zebedee. St. Mark here mentions that **they left their father Zebedee in the boat with the hired servants** (μετὰ τῶν μισθωτῶν). This mention of the "hired servants" is peculiar to St. Mark. He often follows the narrative of St. Matthew; but he adds little details such as this, here and there, which show that he knew St. Matthew's narrative to be true, and also that he was an independent witness. This circumstance here incidentally mentioned shows that there was a difference in position in life between Zebedee's family and that of Simon and Andrew. It appears that all Jews had free right of fishing in the sea of Galilee, which abounded in fish. Zebedee, therefore, whose home seems to have been at Jerusalem, had a fishing establishment in Galilee, probably managed by his partners, Andrew and Simon, during his absence. But he would naturally visit the establishment from time to time with his sons, and especially before the great festivals, when a larger supply of fish than usual would be required for the visitors crowding to Jerusalem at that time. (See 'Speaker's Commentary.')

Ver. 21.—**And they went into Caper-**

naum; literally, *they go into Capernaum* (εἰσπορεύονται). St. Mark is fond of the historical "present" tense, which often adds life and energy to his narrative. Who go into Capernaum? Our Lord and these four disciples, the elementary Church of God, the nucleus of that spiritual influence which is to spread wider and wider unto the perfect day. It does not follow that this going into Capernaum took place on the same day. They would not have been fishing on the sabbath day. The synagogue here spoken of was the gift of the good centurion of whom we read in St. Matthew (viii. 5) and St. Luke (vii. 2). Thus the first synagogue in which our Lord preached was the gift of a generous Gentile officer. It was an emblem of the union of Jews and Gentiles in one fold.

Ver. 22.—**They were astonished at his teaching** (ἐξεπλήσσοντο ἐπὶ τῇ διδαχῇ). The verb in the Greek is a very strong and expressive one; it is a very suitable word to express the first impressions of utter amazement produced by our Lord's "teaching." There were several things which caused his teaching (διδαχη) to differ from that of the scribes. There was no lack of self-assertion in their teaching; but their words did not carry weight. Their teaching was based chiefly on tradition; it dwelt much on the "mint and anise and cummin" of religion, but neglected "judgment and mercy and faith." Christ's teaching, on the contrary, was eminently spiritual. And then he practised what he taught. Not so the scribes.

Thus far St. Mark's narrative bears the character of brevity and conciseness, suitable to an introduction. From this point his record is rich in detail and in graphic description.

Ver. 23.—**And straightway there was in their synagogue a man with an unclean spirit.** According to the best authorities, the sentence in the Greek runs thus, Καὶ εὐθὺς ἦν ἐν τῇ συναγωγῇ αὐτῶν: *And straightway there was in their synagogue*, etc. This word "straightway" adds much force to the sentence. It marks the immediate effect of our Lord's preaching. *A man with an unclean spirit.* The words are literally, "a man in an unclean spirit" (ἐν πνεύματι ἀκαθάρτῳ); in his grasp, so to speak; possessed by him. There can be no reasonable doubt as to the personality of this unclean spirit (see ch. iv. 24; xii. 41). The man was so absolutely in the power of this evil spirit that he seemed to dwell in him; just as the world is said by St. John (1 Epist. v. 19) to lie "in the evil one" (ἐν τῷ πονηρῷ). **And he cried out.** Who cried out? Surely the unclean spirit, using the possessed man as his instrument. In the case of a true prophet, inspired by the Holy Spirit, he is

permitted to use his own gifts, his reason, and even his own particular manner of speech; whereas here a false and lying spirit usurps the organs of speech, and makes them his own.

Ver. 24.—The expression, Ἔα, incorrectly rendered **Let us alone**, has not sufficient authority to be retained here, though it is rightly retained in the parallel passage in St. Luke (iv. 34), where it is rendered in the Revised Version "Ah!" or "Ha!" If rendered, "Let us alone," or "Let alone," it must be assumed to be the imperative of ἐάω. It will be observed that this cry of the unclean spirit is spontaneous, before our Lord has addressed him. In real truth, the preaching of Jesus has already thrown the whole world of evil spirits into a state of excitement and alarm. The powers of darkness are beginning to tremble. They resent this intrusion into their domain. They feel that One greater than Satan has appeared, and they ask, **What have we to do with thee?** Wherein have we injured thee, that thou shouldest seek to drive us out of our possession? We have nothing to do with thee, thou Holy One of God; but we have a right to take possession of sinners. Bede says that the evil spirits, perceiving that "our Lord had come into the world, believed that they were about at once to be judged. They knew that dispossession would be their entrance upon a condition of torment, and therefore it is that they deprecate it." **I know thee who thou art, the Holy One of God.** St. Mark is very careful to bring out the hidden knowledge possessed by evil spirits, which enabled them at once to recognize the personality of Jesus (see ch. i. 34; iii. 11). It was given to them by him who has supreme power over the spiritual as well as the material world, to know as much as he saw fit that they should know; and he was pleased to make known as much as was needful. "But he made himself known to them, not as he makes himself known to the holy angels, who know him as the Word of God, and rejoice in his eternity, of which they partake. To the evil spirits he made himself known only so far as was requisite to strike with terror the beings from whose tyranny he was about to free those who were predestinated unto his kingdom and the glory of it" (see St. Augustine, 'City of God,' bk. ix. § 21).

Ver. 25.—**Hold thy peace, and come out of him.** It was necessary that our Lord should at once assert his absolute power over the evil spirits; and not only this, but also that he should show that he had nothing to do with them. Later on in his ministry it was objected to him that he cast out devils by the prince of the devils. Then, further, the time was not yet arrived when Christ was to be publicly proclaimed as the Son of God. This great truth was to be gradually unfolded, and the people were to be persuaded by many miracles. But at present they were not prepared for this, and therefore our Lord charged his apostles that they should not make him known.

Ver. 26.—**And when the unclean spirit had torn him, and cried with a loud voice, he came out of him** (καὶ σπαράξαν αὐτὸν). The Greek word σπαράσσω may be rendered in the passive *to be convulsed*. It is so used by medical writers, as Galen. It could hardly here mean physically "laceration," for St. Luke (iv. 35) is careful to say that "when the devil had thrown him down in the midst, he came out of him, having done him no hurt." At all events, the expression indicates the close union of the evil spirit with the possessed man's consciousness and with his physical frame. And the manner in which he departed showed his malignity, as though, being compelled by the supreme authority of Christ to leave the man, he would injure him as far as he was able to do so. But the power of Christ prevented him from doing any real injury. And all this was done (1) that there might be clear evidence that the man was actually possessed by the evil spirit; (2) that the anger and malice of the evil spirit might be shown; and (3) that it might be manifest that the unclean spirit came out, not of his own accord, but constrained and vanquished by Christ. We may observe also that the power of Christ restrained him from the use of any articulate words. While he was in possession he used the possessed man's organs of speech; but when he came out there was no articulate speech—it was nothing but a cry.

Ver. 27.—**What thing is this? what new doctrine is this?** The now generally approved text gives a different rendering, namely, *What is this? a new teaching!* (Τί ἐστὶ τοῦτο; διδαχη καινή). If this is the true reading—and there is excellent authority for it—it would mean that the bystanders inferred that this new and unexampled power indicated the accompanying gift of a "new teaching," a new revelation. Nay, more, it indicated that he who wrought these miracles must be the promised Messiah, the true God; for he alone by his power could rule the evil spirits.

Ver. 28.—**All the region round about Galilee**; more literally, *all the region of Galilee, round about;* and the best readings add "everywhere" (πανταχοῦ εἰς ὅλην τὴν περίχωρον τῆς Γαλιλαίας). This is, of course, said by anticipation.

Ver. 29.—**They came**; a better reading is, *he came* (ἦλθεν). St. Matthew and St. Luke speak of this house as the house of Simon Peter only; but St. Mark, writing probably under St. Peter's direction, includes Andrew as a joint owner with Simon Peter.

Vers. 30, 31.—**Lay sick of a fever** (κατέκειτο πυρέσσουσα). St. Luke (iv. 38) uses a stronger expression, "was holden with a great fever" (συνεχομένη πυρετῷ μεγάλῳ). There were marshes in that district; hence the prevalence of fevers of a malignant character. There is no mention of the wife of Peter by name in the New Testament. We may infer, from the fact that his wife's mother lived with him, that he was the head of the family. St. Paul (1 Cor. ix. 5) intimates that he was a married man, and that his wife accompanied him on his missionary tours. According to the testimony of Clement of Alexandria, and of Eusebius (iii. 30), she suffered martyrdom, and was led away to death in the sight of her husband, whose last words to her were, "Remember thou the Lord." St. Mark here tells us that Jesus **came and took** [Simon's wife's mother] **by the hand, and raised her up.** St. Luke (iv. 39) says that "he stood over her and rebuked the fever." **Immediately the fever left her.** The word "immediately" (εὐθέως), familiar as it is to St. Mark, is here omitted by the best authorities. But the omission is of no importance; for the fact that "the fever left her," and that she was at once strong enough to "minister to them," proves that it was not like an ordinary recovery from fever, which is wont to be slow and tedious.

Ver. 32.—**At even, when the sun did set.** It was the sabbath day; and, therefore, the sick were not brought to our Lord until six o'clock, when the sabbath ended. *When the sun did set* (ὅτε ἔδυ ὁ ἥλιος). St. Luke's phrase is (δύνοντος τοῦ ἡλίου), "When the sun was, so to speak, submerged *in the sea.*" So in Virgil, 'Æneid,' lib. vii. 100—

" . . . qua sol utrumque recurrens
Adspicit Oceanum;"

the popular idea being that, when the sun sets, it sinks into the ocean.

Vers. 33, 34.—**The whole city was gathered together at the door.** This would probably be the outer door in the wall, opening into the street; so that this need not be regarded as a hyperbolic statement. It is evidently the description of an eye-witness, or of one who had it from an eye-witness. He healed all that had need of healing, and he **suffered not the devils to speak,** for the reasons assigned at ver. 25.

Ver. 35.—**And in the morning, a great while before day, he rose up and went out, and departed into a desert place, and there prayed.** Our Lord thus prepared himself by prayer for his first departure on a missionary tour. This would be the morning of the first day of the week. A great while before day he left the scene of excitement. That was not a time for preaching the Gospel of the Kingdom. The miracles attracted attention to him, but they were not the object for which he came. They were necessary as means of stirring and awakening men's minds, and of fixing their attention upon him and upon the great salvation which he came to reveal. So he left the miracles to do their subordinate work; and he himself went into a desert place, that he might pray with more quiet and less distraction. He retired that he might escape the applause of men, which they were ready to lavish upon him after seeing so many miracles; that he might thus teach us to shun the praise of men. Let us learn from Christ to give the early morning to prayer, and to rise with the dawn of day, that we may have time for meditation, and give the firstfruits of the morning to God. The early morning is favourable for study; but it is specially dear to God and his angels.

Ver. 36.—**And Simon and they that were with him followed after him** (κατεδίωξαν); the word implies an "earnest pursuing." They that were with him would doubtless include Andrew and James and John, and probably others whose enthusiasm had been kindled by Simon Peter. St. Luke, in the parallel passage (iv. 42), tells us that "the multitudes sought after him, and came unto him, and would have stayed him, that he should not go from them."

Ver. 37.—**All are seeking thee.** The "thee" is here emphatic (πάντες ζητοῦσί σε).

Vers. 38, 39.—These two verses indicate the extent and duration of our Lord's first missionary journey. It must have been considerable. He preached in the synagogues. This would be on successive sabbaths. According to Josephus, Galilee was a densely populated district, with upwards of two hundred villages, each containing several thousand inhabitants.

Ver. 40.—The healing of the leper is recorded in all the three synoptic Gospels; but St. Mark gives more full details. From St. Matthew we learn that it took place after the sermon on the mount; and yet not at the very close of his missionary circuit. St. Luke (v. 12) says that the diseased man was "full of leprosy" (πλήρης λέπρας). The disorder was fully developed; it had spread over his whole body; he was leprous from head to foot. This leprosy was designed to be specially typical of the disease of sin. It was not infectious. It was not because it was either infectious or contagious that the leper was bidden under the Jewish Law to warn others off, in the words, "Unclean! un-

clean!" It was in some cases hereditary. It was a very revolting disease. It was a poisoning of the springs of life. It was a living death. It was incurable by any human art or skill. It was the awful sign of sin reaching unto death; and it was cured, as sin is cured, only by the mercy and favour of God. No wonder, then, that our Lord specially displayed his power over this terrible disease, that he might thus prove his power over the still worse malady of sin. St. Mark here tells us that this leper **knelt down** (καὶ γονυπετῶν). St. Matthew says (viii. 2) that he "worshipped him," (προσεκύνει αὐτῷ); St. Luke says (v. 12) that "he fell on his face" (πεσὼν ἐπὶ πρόσωπον). We thus see that the scriptural idea of worship is associated with some lowly posture of the body. But with this worship of the body, the leper offered also the homage of the soul. His prostration of himself before Christ was not merely a rendering of honour to an earthly being; it was a rendering of reverence to a Divine Being. For he does not say to him, "If thou wilt ask of God, he will give it thee;" but he says, "If thou wilt, thou canst make me clean." It is as though he said, "I know that thou art of equal power with the Father, and therefore supreme Lord over diseases; so that by thy word alone thou canst remove this leprosy from me. I ask, therefore, that thou wouldst be willing to do this, and then I know that the thing is done." The leper had faith in the Divine power of Christ, partly out of his own inward illumination, and partly by the evidence of the miracles which Christ had already wrought. **If thou wilt, thou canst.** Observe the hypothetic expression, "If thou wilt." He has no doubt as to Christ's power, but the words, "If thou wilt" show that his desire for healing was controlled by resignation to the will of God. For bodily diseases are often necessary for the health of the soul; and this God knows, though man knows it not. Therefore, in asking for earthly blessings, it behoves us to resign ourselves to the will and wisdom of God.

Ver. 41.—Observe in this verse that Jesus stretched forth his hand and touched the leper. Thus he showed that he was superior to the Law, which forbade contact with a leper. He touched him, knowing that he could not be defiled with the touch. He touched him that he might heal him, and that his Divine power of healing might be made manifest. "Thus," says Bede, "God stretched out his hand and touched the human nature in his incarnation, and restored to the Church those who had been cast out, that they might be able to offer their bodies a living sacrifice to him of whom it is said, 'Thou art a priest for ever after the order of Melchisedec.'" **I will; be** thou clean; literally, *be thou made clean* (καθαρίσθητι). It is well observed here by St. Jerome that our Lord aptly answers both the petitions of the leper. "If thou wilt;" "I will." "Thou canst make me clean;" "Be thou made clean." Indeed, Christ gives him more than he asks for. He makes him whole, not only in body, but in spirit. Thus Christ, in his loving-kindness, exceeds the wishes of his supplicants, that we may learn from him to do the same, and to enlarge our hearts, both towards God and towards our brethren.

Ver. 42.—**Straightway—St. Mark's favourite word—the leprosy departed from him.** There is no interval between the command and the work of Christ. "He spake, and it was done." His will is his omnipotence. By this act Christ showed that he came into the world as a great Physician, that he might cure all diseases, and cleanse us from all our defilements. The word "straightway" shows that Christ healed the leper, not by any natural means, but by a Divine power which works instantly. He is alike powerful both to command and to do. St. Matthew says here (viii. 3) that straightway "his leprosy was cleansed" (ἐκαθαρίσθη αὐτοῦ ἡ λέπρα). There is here what is called a "hypallage," or inversion of the meaning, which is, of course, that " he was cleansed from his leprosy."

Ver. 43.—**And he straitly charged him.** The Greek verb here (ἐμβριμησάμενος) has a tinge of severity in it, "he strictly [or *sternly*] charged him." Both word and action are severe. **He straightway sent him out** (ἐξέβαλεν αὐτὸν). It may be that he had incurred this rebuke by coming so near with his defilement to the holy Saviour. Christ thus showed not only his respect for the ordinances of the Jewish Law, but also how hateful sin is to the most holy God.

Ver. 44.—**See thou say nothing to any man.** St. Chrysostom says that our Lord gave him this charge, "to shun ostentation, and to teach us not to boast of our virtues, but to hide them." It is evident that he wished to draw the thoughts of men away from his miracles, and to fix them upon his doctrine. **Go thy way, show thyself to the priest;** *the* priest who in the order of his course presided over the rest. Our Lord sent him to the priest, that he might be seen to recognize their special office in cases of leprosy; and further, that the priest himself might have clear evidence that this leper was cleansed, not after the custom of the Law, but by the operation of grace.

Ver. 45.—**But he went out, and began to publish it much, and to spread abroad the matter.** It seems difficult to blame the man for doing what he thought must tend to the honour of his Healer; though, no doubt, it would have been better if he had humbly obeyed. And yet it was to be expected that the knowledge of our Lord's mighty works would be published by others. In this particular instance the effect of this man's conduct was probably unexpected by himself; for it led to the withdrawal of Christ from Capernaum. The crowds who were attracted to him by the fame of his miracles would have hampered him, so that he could not have exercised his ministry; for even in the desert places they sought him out, and came to him from every quarter.

It should be noticed here that this first chapter of St. Mark embraces, in a very condensed form, about twelve months of our Lord's public ministry, from his baptism by John. And it is a record of uninterrupted progress. The time had not then come for the opposition of the scribes and Pharisees and Herodians to show itself. It was, no doubt, wisely ordained that his gospel should take root and lay hold of the hearts and consciences of men, as it must have done in the minds of the Galilæans more especially, before it had to encounter the envy and malice of those who ultimately would bring him to his cross.

HOMILETICS.

Ver. 1.—*The beginning of the gospel.* "The beginning of the gospel of Jesus Christ the Son of God." The writers of the first four books of the New Testament are called evangelists, because they gathered up, put into writing, and published to the world the accounts of the Lord Jesus which were current among the first Christians, and which were constantly repeated by the first preachers of our religion. They did this under the guidance of the Holy Spirit, and their treatises come to us with Divine authority. Not only is the record credible; it is such that it claims our attention, and demands and justifies our faith. Of these four evangelists, Mark is one—doubtless the "John whose surname was Mark"—of whom we read in the Book of the Acts that his family resided in Jerusalem, and that he himself was a fellow-labourer with the Apostle Paul. It has generally been held that Mark was especially under the influence and guidance of Peter. The opening sentence of his Gospel is brief, striking, and full of meaning and of Divine truth.

I. Observe the SIGNIFICANCE OF THE BEGINNING OF THE GOSPEL. Matthew and Luke begin their narratives with a relation of the circumstances of the birth of our Lord; John commences with the pre-existence of the Word; Mark, whose treatise is the shortest, opens with the inauguration of our Lord's ministry. This second Gospel begins with Christ's baptism, and closes with his ascension. "The beginning" suggests *the time when the gospel was not*. Before the gospel was the Law. "The Law and the prophets," said Jesus, "were until John; since that time the kingdom of God is preached." What a different world it must have been to live in when there was no gospel!—at least in the full, the Christian, meaning of that term. "The beginning" suggests a *foretold and appointed time*. It was in the fulness of the time that the promised Messiah appeared, at the conjunction of national and of universal history foreseen by the Omniscient and indicated in prophecy. Accordingly the sacred historian at once appeals to the writings of Malachi and Isaiah to show the real continuity of sacred history. Nothing of God's appointment occurs haphazard; he sees the end from the beginning. "The beginning" points on to *the completion*. "Better," says the wise man, "is the end of a thing than the beginning;" yet the beginning is necessary to the end. It was so with the earthly ministry of Christ. It grew in solemnity and spiritual power as it approached its period; yet the earlier stages were preparatory for those which followed, and indispensable. That Christ's ministry dated—according to apostolic teaching—from the baptism of John, is apparent from Peter's language upon the occasion of the choice of a twelfth apostle, from his discourse before Cornelius, and from Paul's discourse at Antioch of Pisidia.

II. Observe the SIGNIFICANCE OF THE GOSPEL—the term by which the substance of the Christian record is here designated. The meaning, generally speaking, of the term is "good news," "glad, welcome tidings." But the Christian use of the term—which has absorbed all the meaning attaching to this glorious word—is special. The gospel is the designation of the facts and doctrines of Christianity. We look for these facts and doctrines in the writings of Mark and of the other three evangelists. The gospel was *spoken in words, e.g.* as here. The gospel was *embodied in deeds and sufferings, e.g.* in this record of Mark, the gospel of power. The gospel *came from God*, who alone was able to impart the blessings it promised. The gospel *came to men*—sinful, needy, helpless; who, without a gospel, must have remained in wretchedness. The gospel *proclaimed* pardon for sin, peace for the conscience, renewal for the whole nature, guidance and strength for the spiritual career, salvation, and life eternal.

III. Observe the SIGNIFICANCE OF THE APPELLATIONS HERE APPLIED TO HIM who is the Author, the Theme, the Substance of the gospel. 1. He is denominated *Jesus*—the name he bore as a human being, suggestive, therefore, of his humanity, yet in itself implying that he was the Salvation, the Help, of Jehovah. 2. He is denominated *Christ*—an official name, denoting his anointing and appointment by God to the discharge of the Messianic offices, as the Prophet, Priest, and King of men. (Note that the combined name, Jesus Christ, does not occur elsewhere in the first three Gospels.) 3. He is denominated *the Son of God*—a designation which impresses upon us his divinity and authority. Whereas Matthew opens his Gospel by showing that Jesus is the Son of David, a fact of special interest to the Hebrews, Mark takes a higher flight. These three appellations together present us with a full, delightful, instructive, and inspiriting representation of our Saviour's nature and mediatorial work and qualifications.

APPLICATION. 1. You need this gospel. 2. This gospel is sufficient for you. 3. This gospel is adapted to you. 4. This gospel alone can bless you. 5. This gospel is offered to you.

Vers. 2—8.—*The ministry of the forerunner*. This evangelist enters upon his treatise with no further preface than is to be found in the first verse. He has to tell the good news concerning Jesus Christ, the Son of God. And he begins his narrative at once, with an account of the ministry of that grand, heroic prophet, whose great distinction it was to be the herald of the Messiah, and whose greatness was in nothing more apparent than in this—he was willing to be superseded by his Lord, and to be lost in him: "He must increase, but I must decrease." In these verses we have—

I. A GLIMPSE OF THE FORERUNNER'S PERSON AND CHARACTER. 1. He was a *priest*. This we learn from St. Luke's narrative of his parentage and birth. John owed something of the respect and acceptance he met with to this fact. Yet his ministry was not sacerdotal, though his education and his associations must all have fitted him to testify to "the Lamb of God, who taketh away the sin of the world." 2. He was a *prophet*. As Christ himself bare witness, "a prophet, yea, and more than a prophet." He spoke forth the mind of God. He did not sacrifice for the people or reason with them; he declared to them the message he had received from heaven. 3. He was an *ascetic* in the wilderness. In his dress and mode of life he resembled Elijah the Tishbite. He lived in the wilderness of Judæa, and in the wilder parts of the valley of the Jordan. His raiment was of cloth woven from coarse camel's hair; his food was that of a child of the desert, "locusts and wild honey." He wore no soft raiment; he was no reed shaken by the wind. Independent alike of the luxuries of life and of the approval of his fellow-men, he lived apart. 4. He was a fearless, faithful *preacher*. He did not ask —Is this message what the people wish to hear? but—Is this the word of the living God? When the Divine commission was entrusted to him, no power on earth could prevent him from fulfilling it.

II. A STATEMENT THAT HIS MINISTRY WAS PROPHETICALLY FORETOLD. Mark quotes from Malachi, the last of the prophets, "Behold, I will send my messenger, and he will prepare my way before me." He quotes from Isaiah, "The voice of him that crieth in the wilderness, Prepare ye the way of the Lord, make straight in the desert a highway for our God." The forerunner was himself conscious of this; for, disclaiming Messiahship, he claimed to be the voice of the King's herald. Jesus, too, made the same assertion, "If ye will believe it, this is Elijah, which was to come." All was ordered and predicted beforehand by the wisdom of the Most High.

III. A VIEW OF HIS REMARKABLE SPIRITUAL MINISTRY. John did no miracles. But he spoke with a Divine authority; and he exercised an influence which was felt throughout the whole nation, and which was an historical and recognized fact. The elements of his ministry were these: 1. The *prediction* that the kingdom of God, or of heaven, was at hand. 2. An *appeal to repentance*, based upon the approach of the new kingdom. 3. The *administration of a rite* symbolical of spiritual purification.

IV. AN INSIGHT INTO THE REMARKABLE RESULTS OF THIS MINISTRY. 1. A general and profound impression was produced. 2. The most sinful classes shared in this moral awakening. 3. The religious leaders of the community were led to interest themselves in his message. 4. The political rulers of the land came to some extent under his influence. 5. The ardent and religious youth were at once attracted and awed by the presence and ministry of the prophet. The choice spirits of the generation rising up, the flower of the Hebrew youth, became his disciples. 6. There resulted a widespread conscience of sin, and a hope and desire for a great Saviour.

V. A DESCRIPTION OF HIS GREAT OFFICE AND FUNCTION. Above all, John was the forerunner and the herald of the Messianic King, even Jesus. Even before he met his cousin, before he administered baptism to him, he bore witness concerning him. He witnessed: 1. To his *personal* superiority, speaking of him as "One mightier than I." 2. And to his *ministerial* superiority; for while John's baptism was one with water unto repentance, that of Jesus was "with the Holy Spirit and with fire." Events proved the truth of this testimony.

APPLICATION. To receive the witness of John is to acknowledge the Messiahship of Jesus, to yield heart and life to the Saviour, seeking through him the forgiveness of sins, the renewal of the heart, and the consecration of the whole being.

Vers. 9—11.—*The baptism of Christ*. As this evangelist commences his treatise with what he terms "the beginning of the gospel of Jesus Christ," it is natural that our Lord should first be introduced by him as devoted to his ministry of benevolence in the rite of baptism; for this incident in our Saviour's life is justly held to have inaugurated his public work. What a hold the event has taken upon the Christian mind may be seen from the vast number of pictures in which the religious artists of all Christian countries have depicted the baptism. A striking scene for a painter, and a delightful theme for the preacher!

I. The baptism of our Saviour exhibits HIS RELATION TO THE FORERUNNER. The

ministry of the herald preceded that of the King.   Jesus was yet in the seclusion of
Nazareth when John was attracting multitudes of all classes, and from all parts of the
land, to his teaching and baptism in the Jordan valley.   When Jesus came to John it
seemed, to ordinary judgments, that the less came to the greater, the obscure to the
famous.   But it was not so.   To all around the relation between the two was unknown.
Nevertheless, to the two it was clear enough.   The forerunner knew that his mission
was temporary and introductory, and that " the coming One " should eclipse his light as
the sun extinguishes the bright morning star.   Hence the reluctance of the Baptist to do
anything which might seem to militate against the just dignity of the Being in whom he
recognized the Messiah.   " I have need to be baptized of thee, and comest thou to
me?"   This was the Person whose shoe's latchet he had declared himself unworthy to
unloose.   A slave would untie the thong of his master's sandals and bear them in his
hand; John deemed even such an office too honourable for himself to discharge for the
anointed King of mankind.   It was not only in the presence of Jesus that John felt
thus; the constant conviction of his mind was this, " I must decrease, but he must
increase."   But the witness was not all on one side.   Jesus also bore testimony to John.
In the very act of submitting to the baptism of the prophet, he acknowledged that
prophet's greatness and ratified his claims.   And he, in express words, testified to
John's unique position, as predicted by the ancient prophets, and of the man himself
and his character and work declared, " Of men born of women there hath not arisen a
greater than John the Baptist."

II. The baptism of our Saviour exhibits HIS RELATION TO THE HUMAN RACE.   There
seems to be no way of explaining and justifying this historical fact except by admitting
that Jesus was specially the representative man.   In endeavouring to explain, to account
for, the baptism of our Divine Saviour, we are met with a serious difficulty.   The
baptism of John was unto repentance and with a view to the remission of sins.   Men
came, and were invited to come, to receive the symbol of a cleansing which, being
spiritual, could only be wrought by a spiritual process.   The publicans, harlots, and
soldiers, whose conscience accused them of sin, in coming to John's baptism, confessed
their wrong doing and ill desert, and professed their desire, by repentance and reformation, to escape from the trammels of evil and to live a holier life.   They were warned
that mere feeling, mere conformity, mere profession, mere water baptism, were all insufficient, and, if alone, worthless; and they were directed to bring forth fruit meet for
repentance.   Now, in the case of such persons, and, we may add, in the case of all the
members of a sinful, guilty race, a moral purification was and is indispensably necessary.   But what reason, what appropriateness, what meaning, could there be in the
reception of a baptism such as this by the sinless Saviour of the world, the holy and
faultless and beloved Son of God ?   What need had he to confess and to ask pardon for
sin?   He had no sin to confess, no repentance to work out.   If he required no spiritual
purifying, to what purpose should he undergo the rite of lustration ?   The only answer
seems to be that Jesus did this, not as a personal, but as *an official and representative
act.*   The circumstances of Christ's life and death are not to be understood unless we
bear in mind that he acted and suffered as the second Adam, as the federal head and
representative of humanity, as the Son of man.   So regarded, we can to some extent
understand the answer of our Lord to the remonstrance of the baptizer. It became him,
as our Mediator, " to fulfil all righteousness."   He had mixed with the *sinful* population;
he was to live among and to minister unto the victims of sin; he was to be betrayed into
the hand of sinners; he was to be numbered, in his death, with the transgressors;
he was, in a word, made sin for us, though he knew no sin.   As, then, he had in infancy
been circumcised, though there was no sinful nature to be put away; as he was to be
put to death as a malefactor, though no fault was found in him; so he was baptized,
though he had personally no need of purification, no sins to wash away.   He was our
Representative in his birth and ministry, in his death and burial, and, none the less,
in his baptism by John in Jordan.

III. The baptism of our Saviour exhibits HIS RELATION TO THE DIVINE FATHER.
At the commencement of the ministry of Jesus it was appropriate that an attestation
of his mission should be given from above—not only for his own sake, but rather for the
sake, first of John, and then of those to whom in consequence John should bear witness.
Thus the forerunner was able to declare, " I have seen, and have borne witness that

this is the Son of God." There were probably no spectators of our Lord's baptism, and we are indebted to John himself for the record of what happened and of what became the accepted tradition among the early Christians. 1. Observe what was *seen*. It was as Jesus went up out of the river, and whilst he was praying, that the marvellous sign was given. The heavens were rent asunder and opened, indicating the interest taken in the Redeemer's career by the great God of heaven himself, and the Spirit, in the form and with the swift, gentle, hovering movement of a dove, descended upon Jesus. How beautiful an emblem of the Divine power of the ministry which was thus inaugurated, and solemnly, sacredly blessed from above! Surely it is significant that Christ should be represented as the Lamb of God, and the Holy Spirit as the Dove from heaven. A lesson as to the gentleness and grace characteristic of Christ's gospel. 2. Observe, further, what was *heard*. Language proceeded from the opened heavens, indicative of the Divine approval and complacency. Notice (1) the statement of relation and dignity, "Thou art my beloved Son;" and (2) the statement of satisfaction and approbation, "In thee I am well pleased."

APPLICATION. 1. Learn hence the Divine dignity of Emmanuel. 2. And, at the same time, his humility and condescension. 3. Let this marvellous combination of all mediatorial qualifications in the person of Christ encourage your faith in him and your devotion to his cause.

Vers. 12, 13.—*The temptation of Christ.* The portal by which our Lord entered upon his earthly ministry has two pillars—the baptism and the temptation. In his baptism the Saviour was visibly and audibly approved by God the Father. In his temptation he was manifestly put to the test by the power of evil. Consecration and probation were thus the two elements in the Redeemer's inauguration, by which he was dedicated to the earthly ministry of humiliation, obedience, and benevolence. Mark's narrative of the temptation is brief, but suggestive. I. The evangelist notes THE DIVINE IMPULSE which led Jesus to the place appointed for this spiritual encounter. The same Spirit who had just descended upon him like a dove now drove him forth, as with the impulse of a lion, as upon the wings of an eagle, to endure the great probation. The reason of this is to be found in the Divine intention that the Son of man should partake, not only in our human nature, but in our human experience. He did not shrink even from so keen a contest as that which awaited him. Led, driven, by the Spirit, the Divine Christ met his foe at the appointed spot, as the champion of humanity, in single combat, to submit to the fiercest assaults of Satan. II. In the fewest words is described THE SCENE of the temptation. We often encounter the tempter in the crowded streets and in the thronged assembly. Yet those who, like the monks of Egypt, have fled to the desert to escape his assaults and elude his wiles, have ever found their error. No place is secure from spiritual conflict or from sinful suggestion. But our great Leader chose to wrestle with the adversary alone, without the countenance of human virtue or the sympathy of human friendship to assist him. This was challenging the foe to do his worst. They met face to face. The only companions of Christ in the desert solitude were those wild beasts, whose presence emphasizes the awful loneliness of the spot. III. THE TEMPTER is mentioned by name. Satan was the foe with whom the Saviour engaged in this spiritual conflict. The tempter was brought into immediate contact with the Holy Being upon whom he exercised all his devices in vain. In ordinary cases the enemy of souls employs his emissaries, perhaps supernatural, certainly in many cases human. Scripture teaches us that our adversary is "as a roaring lion, going about seeking whom he may devour." We, as Christians, should not be ignorant of his devices. Sometimes he is transformed, as it were, into an angel of light. But let us not be deceived; the temptation betrays whence it comes, however it may be disguised by subtlety and craft. IV. The evangelist records THE PERIOD of our Lord's temptation. It lasted for forty days—a period agreeing with the term of very memorable events in the life of our Lord's illustrious predecessors, Moses and Elijah. A prolonged probation, repeated assaults, variety of spiritual warfare, and a decisive issue,—all were rendered possible by the protracted period to which this desert seclusion was extended. The several temptations which occupied this term are recorded in detail by the other evangelists, Matthew and Luke. 1. A temptation appealing to ordinary bodily wants. 2. A temptation appealing to spiritual pride. 3. A temptation appealing to ambition and the love of power.

V. St. Mark implies, what the other evangelists explicitly record, OUR SAVIOUR'S VICTORY. 1. It was gained by a *holy character*. The prince of this world came, and had nothing in him. 2. By a resolute and determined *opposition*. "Resist the devil, and he will flee from you." 3. By the use of the weapons of *Scripture*. If the devil quoted the Word, as he can for his purposes, Christ had ready the appropriate reply, couched in the words of inspiration. 4. It was a *complete* victory; for the tempter was foiled at every point. 5. Yet it was a victory which did not preserve the assailed from a renewal of attack. The devil left him for a season, only again to return to do his worst and again and finally to fail.

VI. The period of conflict and resistance was succeeded by ANGELIC MINISTRATIONS. The Son of God was encompassed by the services of these messengers from heaven, from his birth to his agony, and from his agony to his resurrection and ascension. How natural that those beings who minister to those who shall be heirs of salvation should minister to him who is salvation's Author and Giver! And it is instructive to find that, as the agency of temptation was not a human agency, so the ministrations which followed were not human ministrations. In what way the angels tended their Lord and did him service, we are not told; whether, as poetic fancy has feigned, by spreading for him a table in the wilderness, or by soothing his spirit by their sympathy as he emerged from the scene of unparalleled conflict and unparalleled victory.

PRACTICAL LESSONS. 1. Let every man expect temptation; it is the common lot, from which the Son of man himself was not exempt. 2. If temptation does not come in one form it will come in another; the tempter adapts himself to age and sex, temperament and education, position and character. 3. Let the Christian, when tempted, remember that he has the sympathy and may look for the succour of the High Priest, who was tempted as we are, though without sin. 4. Let the Saviour's mode of meeting and resisting the tempter be prayerfully pondered and copied; the Scriptures furnish the Christian's armoury, "The sword of the Spirit is the Word of God."

Vers. 14, 15.—*The Divine Preacher.* Christ was known as a Prophet before he was manifested as the Priest and the King of humanity. He came preaching. In these verses is related the fact of a ministry in Galilee. The occasion was the cessation of John's ministry; the place, that northern province which had been foretold as the scene of the Messiah's labours, and in which he had passed the years of his youth. We have here put upon record the substance of the Saviour's preaching.

I. CHRIST WAS A PREACHER. This fact seems to imply three things. 1. That Jesus *regarded men as intelligent, responsible beings*. He did not seek to awe or terrify them by portents. He did not attempt to cajole them by complying with their sinful tendencies and prejudices. He did not appeal to superstition. He treated men as beings having an understanding to be convinced, a heart to be affected, a moral nature rendering them susceptible to Divine motives and capable of willing obedience. 2. That Jesus had *confidence in his message*. It was not with that assumption of authority which disguises conscious weakness; it was not with the hesitation which betrays suspicion of the weakness of the cause; it was with the confidence of one who speaks forth words of truth and soberness,—that the great Teacher spoke. 3. That Jesus *had the assurance that his message would be accepted*. His was not a fruitless enterprise. He came with a Divine commission, which should not, could not, be frustrated. His words should not pass away; all should be fulfilled. And Christ's gospel is still to be promulgated in the same manner, in the same spirit. Christ's ministers are called upon to preach—to preach Christ crucified—to preach, whether men will hear or forbear. The religion of our Saviour is one which appeals to what is best and purest in human nature enlightened by the Spirit of God.

II. CHRIST, AS A PREACHER, MADE AN ANNOUNCEMENT. 1. An appointed time for a Divine visitation had now arrived. "Known unto God are all his works from the foundation of the world." There is a season for every step in the Divine procedure. That the advent of the Messiah, and the setting up of a spiritual kingdom, and the bringing in of an everlasting righteousness, were all foreseen and foretold, we are dis-

tinctly assured. This, the period of Christ's ministry, was "in the fulness of the time."
2. The kingdom of God was at hand. Not that the Most High had abdicated his
rightful throne; but he had long suffered the rebellion of men, and had not interfered
with the tyrant who had usurped dominion. The evils of this unjust tyranny had now
been made apparent. It was time, according to the counsels of God, that rightful
authority should be asserted and re-established. Little as the Prophet of Nazareth
seemed, to ordinary eyes, the Prince who should defeat the foe of God and man, this
was the character in which he came to earth, the work and warfare he came to accomplish. 3. Christ preached the gospel of God. Good news for mankind: an amnesty
for rebels, the favour of the Divine Sovereign, peace between heaven and earth, salvation for sinners, and eternal life for the dead,—such was the theme of this Messianic
proclamation. In preaching the gospel our Lord could not but preach himself, for he
not only brought the gospel—he *was* the gospel.

III. CHRIST ADDRESSED TO MEN AN EXHORTATION—A SUMMONS. A preacher has not
only truth to state, good news to proclaim, but he has counsel to offer, a requirement
to make. As here succinctly recorded, the preaching of Christ enjoined upon men two
precepts. 1. They were summoned to *repentance*. This is a universal condition of
entering into the benefits of Christ's kingdom. This change of heart, of thought, of
purpose, is a change indispensable to the highest privileges. It is the preparation
of spirit which, on the Divine side, is regeneration. "Except a man be born again
[afresh], he cannot see the kingdom of God." The condition of repentance is one binding
through all time. There are flagrant and notorious sinners, who must be brought to
penitence and contrition before they can receive the forgiveness which God has promised and which Christ has secured. There are unspiritual professors of Christianity,
who have the form of godliness without the power, who must be led to see the sandy
foundation upon which they build before they can seek and find their foundation
upon the Rock of Ages. There are backsliders, who have gone back religiously, who
have lost their first love, and have ceased to do their first works, who must repent
before they can enjoy the pleasures and privileges of religion. Christianity makes no
compromise with sin, has no flattery for sinners. Her voice rings through the wilderness and the city, and her demand is this—Repent! 2. They were summoned to
belief of the gospel. This is a condition which respects the relation and attitude of the
mind *towards God*. Those who credit God's promise alone can experience and enjoy
its fulfilment. Faith is ever represented in Scripture as the means of appropriating
what has been provided by Divine grace. A condition this both honourable to God
and spiritually profitable to the believer. Faith is the Divine path to acceptance and
pardon, to life and immortality. Christ demanded and deserved faith.

APPLICATION. This is a gospel *for sinners*. It is they who need a gospel, sunk as
they are in sin, exposed as they are to condemnation and destruction. This is a gospel
for you. Whoever you are, you need it; and, in your heart of hearts, you are well
aware that it is so. God sent his Son that *you* might be saved. Christ gave himself
for *you*. Unto *you* is the word of salvation sent. Christ has suffered that *you* might
escape, has died that *you* might live. In him there is for *you* pardon for the past and
strength for the present and hope for the future. "Believe in the Lord Jesus Christ,
and *thou* shalt be saved." This is a gospel *from God*. Only he could send news
adapted to the case of sinners, and he has sent such news. Here is the expression of
his deepest sympathy, his tenderest solicitude, his most fatherly love. Coming from
him, the gospel cannot be an illusion; it may be trusted. It is the wisdom of God
and the power of God unto salvation. Yet, what is this gospel to those who believe
not? Good news to those who reject it is all the same as bad news. There is every
reason, every motive, for believing it. Christ will be glorified, God will be rejoiced,
angels will sympathize and sing with gladness, and you will be saved. The gospel
is worthy of belief in itself, and it is exactly and perfectly adapted to you. Believe it,
and believe it now!

Vers. 16—20.—*Fishers of men.* It was an incident of great moment in the history
of Christianity and of the world—this, the calling by our Lord Jesus of his followers
and apostles. Christ did not make many converts; but the few he did make made
many, so that, in selecting and appointing them, he was sowing the seed of a great

and eternal harvest. He probably called these four more than once—first during the ministry of the forerunner, again as in the text, and a third time when he commissioned them formally to act as his apostles.

I. Observe WHO THE MEN WERE WHO WERE CALLED. 1. Their *position in life;* they were from the industrial classes. Not only did the Son of God choose himself to be born and brought up among the laborious and comparatively poor, he selected his immediate attendants, his personal friends, the promulgators of his religion, from the same rank of life. He took the form of a servant; he was known as "the carpenter's son;" it was asked concerning him, "Whence hath this man learning?" Luke indeed was a physician, and Paul a scholar, but the twelve seem to have been of lowly condition and surroundings. 2. Their *occupation;* they were fishermen. Theirs was, no doubt, a common calling among the dwellers by the shores of the Galilean lake. There may have been some moral qualities, such as reverence and simplicity, which fitted these men for their new calling and life. 3. In *relationship* they were united by family ties; for these four disciples were two pairs of brothers. Simon and Andrew, and likewise James and John, were not only called together, but seem to have been associated together in an evangelistic ministry, when our Lord sent his disciples forth "two and two." Natural kindred and affection were thus sanctified by community in Christian calling and service. The two pairs were friends, comrades, and associates in labour. 4. They were, at all events in some instances, specially *prepared for this calling.* Certainly some and probably all of these four were previously disciples of John the Baptist, who, in their hearing, had witnessed to Jesus as the Messiah. Jesus thus honoured his forerunner by receiving disciples from his training.

II. Regard THE CALL HERE RELATED. 1. The *Caller* was the Divine Christ. An inestimable privilege to hear from those lips a gracious summons such as this! It is a sacred responsibility to hear the voice of Christ speak to ourselves with words of invitation, command, or commission. 2. The *manner of the call* deserves attention; it was with authority. Simple and few were the words, but they were the words of One whose utterances carried with them their own authority—an authority acknowledged at once by the conscience of those to whom it was addressed. 3. The *import* of the call was most momentous—"Follow me!" This call seems to have been addressed to these men on more occasions than one. They were directed to follow Jesus that they might listen to his teaching and observe his mighty works, that they might be qualified for the solemn commission which was to be entrusted to them upon the Saviour's ascension.

III. Remark THE PROMISE GIVEN in connection with the call. These Galilean fishermen should become "fishers of men." Our Saviour here takes advantage of the deep resemblances between natural processes and human activities on the one hand, and spiritual realities on the other. The sea in which Christian ministers are called to toil is this world, is human society, with all its uncertainties, vicissitudes, and dangers. The fish they seek are human souls, oftentimes hard to find and to catch. The net which they let down at the Divine command is the gospel, fitted to include and to bring to safety all souls of men. The skill and patience and vigilance of the fishermen may well be studied and imitated by those who watch and labour for souls. To enclose within the net is to bring souls within the limits of the privileges and motives, the laws and hopes of the gospel. To land what is taken is to bring the rescued safely into the eternal security of heaven.

IV. The RESPONSE TO THE CALL is deserving of our observation. 1. There was cheerful *compliance.* No objection, no hesitation, no condition, not even an inquiry; but willing, contented obedience to a summons felt to be authoritative and binding. 2. This compliance was *immediate.* So should all respond whom Christ invites to come after him. Not a moment should be lost in choosing a lot so honourable, so desirable, so happy. 3. It was *self-sacrificing.* They left their nets, their kindred, their occupation, readily giving up all in order that they might follow Jesus. It was a condition which the Master now and again imposed, to prove the sincerity of his people's love, devotion, and zeal.

PRACTICAL LESSONS. 1. For preachers and teachers of the gospel. Remember what is the vocation with which you are called. Let this be the acknowledged end you set before you — to be fishers of men, to gain souls. 2. For hearers of the gospel.

Remember that Christ has called you and is calling you. The burden of his appeal is this—"Come ye after me!" And, when saved, seek that you may be the means of saving others. 3. For those who, hearing the voice of the Lord Christ, are disposed to obey his call. Bear in mind that he demands a complete surrender, that he will not be satisfied unless the heart is dedicated to him, unless, with the heart, all that we have is yielded to his service. There is sure to be something in the way of obeying the Divine and heavenly call. You will, like the fishermen of Galilee, have something to give up in following Christ. Be prepared for this, and count the cost. But, for your soul's sake and for the sake of your salvation, let nothing hinder you from faith and consecration. "Count all things but loss for the excellency of the knowledge of Christ Jesus our Lord."

Vers. 21, 22.—*Christ's authority in teaching.* This passage informs us of three circumstances connected with our Lord's early Galilean ministry. 1. It was exercised largely in Capernaum, a populous and busy town on the western shore of the Lake of Galilee. This fact exhibits Christ's resolve to mix with the people and to seek their enlightenment and welfare. 2. It was exercised specially on the sabbath days. In this Christ practically asserted his own principle, "The sabbath was made for man." Although a day of physical rest, it was stamped, by the Lord's action, as a day for spiritual activity and influence. 3. It was frequently exercised in the synagogues. These were not, indeed, of Mosaic institution, but had sprung up since the Captivity, and were especially connected with the professional labours of the scribes. They were a sign that the Hebrews cultivated an intellectual religion. The practice of regular religious instruction was sanctioned by the great Teacher, when he attended the synagogues, conformed to their usages, and took advantage of the assembling of congregations in them to exercise his ministry of teaching.

I. CHRIST FULFILLED HIS SPIRITUAL MINISTRY AMONG MEN LARGELY BY TEACHING. 1. This was a recognition of man's intelligent, rational nature. Our Lord did not appeal so much to men's fears as to their reason, their gratitude, their love. Instruction is the debt which every generation owes to its successor, and which the wise owe to the ignorant. The more the ministers of Christianity appeal to the intelligence of their hearers, the more do they follow the example of their Master. 2. It was an assertion of his own office. He claimed to be "the Light of the world." And this was in virtue of his very nature. He was "the Word of God," uttering the thought, expressing the mind, of God. There is something deeply affecting and truly encouraging in this representation of the incarnate Son of God, going about teaching the ignorant, the poor, the uncared for. 3. It was a revelation of Christ's own character. What condescension, gentleness, sympathy, were manifest in the quiet, patient manner in which the Lord frequented these lowly edifices and taught those simple congregations!

II. CHRIST'S TEACHING WAS RECOGNIZED AS AUTHORITATIVE. 1. In this it contrasted with the teaching of the scribes, who were the acknowledged and professional instructors in religion of the people of Israel. But they were expositors of the sacred books; they repeated and enforced the traditions of the elders. There was little or nothing original in their lessons; whereas Christ spoke from his own mind and heart, and acknowledged no master, no superior. 2. There was authority in our Lord's presence and manner. From the impression which his teaching made upon strangers, from their recorded testimony, it is clear that there was a Divine dignity in his aspect and his speech; "Never man spake like this man." 3. There was authority in the substance of his teaching. Truth has an authority of its own, an authority which is often, when questioned by the lips, confessed in the heart. Our Lord's revelations of the Father, his expositions of the spiritual nature of religion and morality, his insight into human nature, his predictions of the future,—all alike impressed his hearers with a sense of his special, unique authority. 4. This quality in our Lord's teaching was confessed by the conscience of men. It was not that the people were simply awed by his manner and language. What was best in their nature did homage to him. They could not question his wisdom, his justice, his insight, his compassion.

III. CHRIST'S AUTHORITATIVE TEACHING PRODUCED A PROFOUND IMPRESSION. This is described as astonishment, amazement. The novelty of the style, the tone, the matter, of our Lord's teaching, to some extent accounts for this. The unprecedented power of his discourse was, however, the chief cause of this general wonder. There were occasions when astonishment led to repugnance, and the people would fain shun the presence of One so awful; but there were instances in which astonishment glowed into admiration and kindled into faith. And this last is the proper and intended result. If we are to have a Teacher, let us welcome One who speaks with authority; if we are to have a Saviour, who so fit as One mighty to save? if we are to submit to a Lord, a King, may it be One whose right it is to reign!

Ver. 22.—"*Having authority.*" St. Mark's Gospel has been characterized as the Gospel for the Romans, as the Gospel of Power, as the Gospel of the Resurrection. The symbol denoting this second evangelist is the lion. There has always been a feeling that the dignity and majesty, the might and victory, of Emmanuel are in an especial manner set before the reader in this one of the four Gospels. Certainly the first chapter strikes the key-note of this strain. Jesus appears as the mysterious Lord, who with authority summons fishermen to forsake their nets and follow him; who teaches with authority in the synagogues, and awakens the amazement of his hearers; who with authority commands the unclean spirits, and they obey him; whose authority rebukes the fever and heals the leprosy; who by the magnetism of his power and love gathers the people from every quarter into his gracious presence, to hear his authoritative voice, and to receive a thousand blessings from his beneficent and powerful hands. In one word, he appears before us, at the very outset of his ministry, as "One that had authority."

I. How CHRIST'S AUTHORITY WAS ASSERTED. That we may understand that Christ claims authority, we must refer to the gospel narrative, in which his words are recorded, his character delineated, and his ministry related. Does he assert authority? Is he such a Being that his claims demand attention? Was his authority for a season only, or was it intended to subsist through all time and in eternity? Was his an authority local in its range, or universal as the presence of mankind on earth? That Christ possessed and exercised authority during his earthly ministry admits of no dispute or question. *Satan* himself confessed it; for Jesus spurned his assumptions, resisted his temptations, and sent him who claimed the lordship of the earth defeated and uncrowned from his holy and authoritative presence. *Angels* recognized it; for they came to minister to his wants, and stood in countless legions ready, at a word, to rescue and to honour him. *Demons* felt it, and quailed beneath his glance, did homage to his supremacy, and fled at his rebuke. *Nature* knew it; and the winds were hushed and the sea was calmed at his authoritative word, bread multiplied in his hand, and water at his bidding turned to wine, trees withered at his breath, the very grave gave up its dead at his command, and the gentle air floated his gracious form to heaven. His *enemies* were conscious of his superiority; for they were abashed and silenced by his reasoning, they fell backward at his look. *Men* generally acknowledged him to be other and higher than themselves; "Never man," said the officers sent to apprehend him—"never man spake like this man;" Pilate and Pilate's wife were under the mysterious spell of his Divine authority; and the Roman centurion was constrained to exclaim, "Truly this was the Son of God!" His *friends* were sensible that he was to them more than a friend; at his summons they forsook their callings and their homes, they attempted impossibilities with confidence, they consecrated their powers and they hazarded their lives for the mission to which he called them. But he had greater witness than that of man. The works which he performed, they testified to him. The seal of God was set upon his actions. The voice of God honoured the Holy One and Just; heaven itself was opened, and from the excellent glory came the attestation and the approval of the Most High, "This is my beloved Son, in whom I am well pleased!" and there was added the demand which sanctions the authority of Emmanuel over universal man, "Hear ye him!" The Jews sometimes felt that Jesus of Nazareth was laying claim to a special and unrivalled authority. His bold and thorough *cleansing of the temple* is a case in point. How came he to take upon himself so remarkable a function as this? Who was he that he should do what none of the great officials ventured upon? We cannot wonder that "the chief priests and the elders of the people came unto him as he was teaching, and said, By what authority doest thou these things, and who gave thee this authority?" The only explanation was that

Jesus was lord of the temple because he was the Son of God. And this lordship he asserted when he predicted the destruction of the material sanctuary, and when he, using it as a symbol of his body, foretold the rebuilding of the temple of God in three short days. Another case in point is his *assumption of the Divine prerogative of pardoning sin*. When Jesus publicly assured the believing paralytic that his sins were forgiven, this language aroused the indignation of the scribes and Pharisees. "This man blasphemeth! Who can forgive sins but God only?" The only reply of our Saviour to these insinuations was the performance of a miracle, that, as he phrased it, "they might know that the Son of man had power on earth to forgive sins."

II. UPON WHAT IS CHRIST'S AUTHORITY BASED? It is not all authority which the enlightened and the free, the honourable and the just, can regard with reverence. Much that bears the name may fairly be treated as usurpation. And even just authority may deserve only a partial reverence; it may be admitted, but admitted with reserve. Authority is of different kinds, for it rests on different bases. The authority of the tyrant over his subjects, of the conqueror over the vanquished, rests on force and fear; the authority of the priest over the devotee rests on superstition and assumption; but the authority of the teacher over the scholar is the authority of wisdom, and that of the parent over the child is the authority of care and love. There is authority which is natural, and authority which is conventional. Some authority it is virtue to recognize; other authority it is baseness and dishonour not to resist. Authority is excellent and admirable when there is a right to command, when there is an obligation to submit and to obey. To understand aright the authority of the Lord Jesus, we must divest our minds of their habitual notions of civil authority. Government is not only right, it is necessary, it is ordained of God. But it has regard only to human actions. It is not the business of the civil ruler to influence men's beliefs upon science, or philosophy, or religion, but to induce them to industry, independence, order, and peaceableness. And the sanctions governors employ are not so much moral as external and physical. Fine, imprisonment, death,—these are their weapons. Occasionally rewards, in the shape of distinctions and honours, may be added, but the system is mainly one of penalty. A submission to Christ's authority is nothing if it is not willing, cheerful, cordial. Too often human authority is asserted with harshness, is acknowledged with slavishness. None of our Redeemer's subjects bow the knee whilst the heart is unyielded, offer the homage of the voice whilst the spirit is in rebellion. Men may do this under some influences; but let them not be deceived; it is the authority of men to which they bow, not that of Christ! By virtue of what quality, of what possession, had Jesus Christ authority? For us there is one great and all-sufficient answer—*He was the Son of God*. It was upon this ground that he based his own claims. "I and my Father," said he, "are one." "Say ye of him whom the Father hath sanctified and sent into the world, Thou blasphemest! because I said, I am the Son of God?" "The works which My Father hath given me to do, bear witness of me that the Father hath sent me." In fact, Christ so often and so plainly asserted his unique authority that he came to refuse any further explanations or formal claims. He answered inquiry by inquiry, and boldly declared, "Neither tell I you by what authority I do these things.' Truth has authority over man's understanding, and Christ's words, his declarations and revelations, have the *authority of truth*. He claimed to have told them the truth which he had heard of God. Our nature is framed to recognize and to rest in truth; and, since Christ is "the Truth," he is exactly adapted to our mental necessities and desires, to afford them full and final satisfaction. Christ wields *the authority attaching to a holy and benevolent character*. The human heart always renders homage to goodness, though there may be motives which prevent that homage being manifested and expressed. We instinctively honour and reverence those whom we feel to be better than ourselves. Now, in the case of our Saviour, it was Divine, incarnate goodness which appeared before men and moved among them. A perfect man, he went about doing good; and, both by his pure and gentle character, and by his unselfish, compassionate life, he commanded the reverence and constrained the allegiance of men. An authority this far nobler and worthier than that derived from a splendid retinue and a glittering throne, a mighty army and a sounding name. The conscience of the Christian acknowledges the claims of the sinless Emmanuel. The heart confesses the unrivalled authority of his tender pity, his unselfish love. Power, apart from righteousness, enkindles resentment and arouses resistance. But goodness and benevolence, with the resources of Omnipotence at their command, summon our hearts to a willing surrender and our lives to a glad obedience. Our will, our whole nature, acknowledge the *authority of the Saviour's law.* When he was upon earth his disciples obeyed unquestioningly the mandates they could not always understand, and undertook with alacrity service for which they felt themselves utterly unqualified. And each awakened and enlightened hearer of the gospel gives utterance to his foremost and earnest desire in the words of the **trembling rabbi of Tarsus,** "Lord, what wilt thou have me to do?" When once we know ourselves and him, we feel that none other has the right to our loyalty, our love, our devotion. When we hear his voice, it carries with it its own authority to our heart.

III. OVER WHOM CHRIST'S AUTHORITY EXTENDS. The answer to this question is suggested by what has been already said regarding the instruments, so to speak, of the dominion of Jesus Christ. If truth and righteousness, love and sacrifice—spiritual influence, in a word—be the source of his authority, we feel at once that his reign is not primarily and chiefly one over actions and observances. It is far more deep-seated and efficient, far more adapted to the moral nature of man and the moral authority of God. Christ's authority is *over the spiritual nature of man, and it is supported by spiritual sanctions.* Not so much what men do, as what they are, and why they act, and how they feel, is of interest to the Lord of hearts. His appeal is to what is intellectual, to what is moral, in man. It is not his aim to induce men to wear one uniform, to utter one cry, but rather to share one spirit—his own, to live one life—that of God. He designs to bring every thought into captivity unto obedience to Jesus Christ. Yet it is important to remember that, constituted as man is, it is impossible that he should acknowledge an authority over his conscience and heart which will have no sway over the actions and habits of his life. The individual life will be cast into the mould of Christ's mind and will. Society will own practically the rightful and controlling sway of Jesus. "All power is given unto him."

IV. THE ADVANTAGES WHICH CHRIST'S AUTHORITY SECURES. Is it to be desired that the authority of the Saviour should be generally and indeed universally acknowledged? What are the fruits of obedience? what the influences of his reign? Are they such that we may look forward with hope and prayer to the submission and subjection of mankind to him whom we "call Master and Lord"? When the authority of the Saviour has been acknowledged by the soul, and when he is habitually exercising this authority over the whole nature, the results are most blessed. Happiness is not in wilfulness and unbridled licence, but in subjection to a Law, holy, approved, and willingly accepted. This is true liberty, when the soul finds an authority it can bow before and obey with the harmony of all its faculties. Christ's is the perfect law of liberty, and where this prevails and reigns there is peace and joy; for there freedom and obedience are one, yoked together by spiritual and most welcome bonds. The widespread and universal acknowledgment of the Redeemer's authority is the one hope for the world's future. No thoughtful man can look forward to a universal empire of force, to the prevalence of a supreme military authority. What, then, is to put an end to wars and fightings amongst men? They are not for ever to afflict and curse the world. It is only in the reign of righteousness and benevolence that the dreams of poets shall be realized, the forecastings of prophets fulfilled, and the prayers of saints shall be answered. "In the Name of Jesus every knee shall bow, and every tongue shall confess that he is Lord, to the glory of God the Father."

V. HOW THIS AUTHORITY OF CHRIST AFFECTS THOSE WHO HEAR THE GOSPEL. To some the authority of the Redeemer may be an unwelcome theme. They would rather hear of his grace than of his dominion. Yet it is well to see and feel that each is essential to the other in a perfect and Divine Saviour. Instruction, to be satisfactory, must be authoritative. Consolation comes most effectually from him who wields the sceptre of dominion, and who is able to rebuke and to master all our foes and to sanctify all our trials. Many hearers of the gospel in these days think little of the rightful and supreme authority of the Lord Christ. Preachers and writers of religious books are accustomed to lay great stress upon the love of the Redeemer, and to spend their energies in inducing sinful, weak, needy hearts to respond to Christ's love, and to accept his salvation. And this is quite right. But it is not right to overlook the just claim of Christ upon the faith and obedience of men, to keep out of sight the truth that men have no right to disbelieve and disobey the Son of God. No doubt it is for our interest and our happiness to be Christians. It is also our sin and our shame if we are not Christians. There have been parents among the poor who have thought that they were doing the teachers in Sunday schools a favour in sending their children to receive religious instruction; and this notion has arisen from the extreme and benevolent desire of teachers to bring the young into their classes. And in like manner it seems that there are many persons who think that they are quite at liberty to receive the Saviour or to reject him; that if they welcome the gospel and seek the fellowship of a Christian Church they will be bestowing an important favour upon those who present to them the invitations of the gospel. But, as the child renders no favour in doing his father's will, as the poor man renders no favour in accepting the bounty of his benefactor, as the subject renders no favour in obeying his country's laws, so the sinner, in listening to the gospel, obeying its summons and submitting to the Son of God, is far from rendering a favour. He is receiving a gift in his abject poverty; he is passing from the prison doors into light and liberty; he is acknowledging the just authority of an omnipotent Friend—a Saviour, not only gracious, but supreme, Divine!

Vers. 23—28.—*Christ's authority over spirits.* After a condensed narrative of the events introductory to our Lord's ministry, Mark proceeds to relate, in circumstantial detail, miracles performed in Capernaum and the neighbourhood, forming a cycle of the greatest importance; for by these miracles the interest of the population of Galilee was excited, whilst the hostility of the scribes and Pharisees was gradually aroused. Mark's is the Gospel of Power—his emblem is the lion. He tells the story of Christ's miraculous ministry with marvellous vigour and minuteness. The first miracle he records is the dispossession of a demon, impure and violent, yet unable to resist the authority of the Lord of the universe. This is well put in the forefront of the battle.

I. CHRIST'S AUTHORITY IS ACKNOWLEDGED BY THE SPIRIT. 1. Not willingly, but of constraint. The demon recognizes, in the great Healer and Master, the "Holy One of God," *i.e.* the Messiah. Shrinking from his presence—anxious to avoid the encounter— the evil spirit nevertheless cowers before the Lord. When multitudes of the race which Jesus came to save knew him not, neither confessed his rightful claim, this demon was compelled to cry, "I know thee who thou art!" Happy omen for humanity—the foe of God and man recognizes the irresistible Warrior and Conqueror! 2. There is an anticipation of the issue of the conflict, "Art thou come to destroy us?" What prescience is here! Scribes and Pharisees, Sadducees and Herodians, Jews and Romans, persuade themselves that they can destroy the Son of man. The demons know that the Son of man is their Destroyer! It is a just description of the Saviour's work—he comes to "destroy the works of the devil," to vanquish the foe, to cancel the sin, to release the sinner, to restore the captive of Satan to the liberty of the servant of the Lord.

II. CHRIST'S AUTHORITY IS ASSERTED AND EXERCISED BY HIMSELF. Salvation involves antagonism: the bondman can only be released by the defeat of the tyrant; the strong man must be bound that the spoil may be recovered. The Lord Jesus had met with and vanquished the prince of evil; he was now to contend with his servants. Accordingly, Christ, who rebuked the winds and the waves—elements producing discord in nature—rebukes also the evil and unclean spirit. It is a witness that the soul of man is not the fit and divinely ordered home and dwelling of the agents of the power of evil. Silence! Hence! Begone!—such is the bidding of Heaven to the emissaries of hell found encroaching upon the domain which is not theirs.

III. CHRIST'S AUTHORITY IS PRACTICALLY SHOWN AND PROVED. The unclean spirit is reluctant to quit his hold upon his prey. Satan cannot see his subjects liberated and his empire wane without resistance and resentment. But there is no withstanding the power of Emmanuel. The struggle is apparent in the convulsions with which the frame of the possessed is torn, and in the cry of anguish which is forced from his lips. But there is only one issue possible. The demon quails beneath the Master's eye, shudders at the Master's voice, and yields. Oh, happy omen of a great salvation! How often is this illustration of Christ's delivering power to be repeated in the Divine ministry, and through the dispensation of redemption and of grace!

IV. CHRIST'S AUTHORITY IS ADMITTED WITH AMAZEMENT. The rendering of the revisers is full of meaning and vivacity: "What is this? a new teaching!" or, as others read, "A new doctrine with authority!" The point is that miracle and doctrine are justly regarded as one and the same. The listeners to his discourses felt the authority of his words; the spectators of his miracles felt the authority of his works. We distinguish between the two, but Christ's contemporaries evidently saw the identity more clearly than the diversity. From his teaching they learned that the authority of his miracles was that of a wise and holy Being; from his beneficent miracles they inferred that all his Divine lessons were fraught with a heavenly energy, and proceeded from the mind of God. Their minds were evidently incited to inquiry, to consideration, to reflection. Who will not bow before an authority so just and so Divine as this?

V. CHRIST'S AUTHORITY BECAME THE THEME OF WIDESPREAD INTEREST AND FAME. Mark puts this dispossession of the demoniac forward as the first great miracle of this cycle, and represents it as the means of diffusing throughout Galilee an interest in the ministry of our Lord. Jesus thus became known as a Teacher, as a Saviour, as a Being of compassion and grace. Tidings of such a Prophet, of such a Benefactor, could not be other than a gospel to Israel and to mankind. What sacred and grateful and tender associations would mingle with the people's memories and thoughts and expectations regarding Jesus of Nazareth!

APPLICATION. 1. Behold a picture of the power of Satan and of sin over the nature of man. 2. Behold a proof of the authority of Christ, when he enters upon a struggle with the power of darkness dwelling in human spirits. 3. Learn a lesson of encouragement as to the personal and universal results of the great moral conflict of the world.

Vers. 29—31.—*Christ's domestic ministry.* Wherever Jesus went and amongst whomsoever, he took with him a heart sensitive to the appeal of human need, suffering, and sin; he took with him a hand open to give, stretched out to help and deliver. In city and country, among Jews and foreigners, with high and low, in the society of men, women, and children, he was always the same—the Helper, the Comforter, the Healer, the Friend of man. For the brief but pictorial and tender narrative in these verses we are doubtless indebted to the memory of the grateful Peter, himself a witness of the miracle, and one who profited by it in his own family and household.

I. THE DISCIPLES SOON REAP THE REWARD OF THEIR OBEDIENCE AND SELF-SACRIFICE. How readily had they responded to the Master's call, "Follow me"! How readily had they left their boats and fishing-nets, their daily occupations and their gains! So they had come into close relations with Jesus; so he became a guest in Simon's house. This led to the miracle here recorded, in which the Lord more than recompensed them for any loss they might have incurred. Christ often calls upon us for some self-denial and sacrifice; but he never does other than reward a hundredfold, even in this time, those who obey.

II. PETER LEARNS A LESSON OF HIS MASTER'S POWER AND WILLINGNESS TO SAVE. We know enough of Simon to understand that his nature was very receptive of impressions, very responsive to sympathy. What a lesson for him was this—which the Saviour vouchsafed to teach him so early in his discipleship—of the compassion and grace of his Lord! And what a preparation for the apostolate, yet so far in the future! First impressions are often the strongest. And we know that of all the twelve Peter was, in the course of the Lord's ministry, the first to confess his Divine dignity and Messiahship. Surely this was the maturity of the seed now sown at Capernaum.

III. CHRIST PROVES HIS SYMPATHY WITH HOME SUFFERINGS, AND BLESSES HOME LIFE. His ministry was indeed chiefly fulfilled in public; yet in the homes of Simon, of Levi, of Lazarus, he proved his interest in the domestic life of his friends. He entered into family feeling, and consecrated family life. It was sometimes said to him, "He whom thou lovest is sick." It was an appeal to which he was never indifferent. Christ is ever mindful of our family cares and anxieties, sorrows and joys. Let him "abide with us," and he will lighten our dwellings when they are clouded with trouble and with grief. When, like Simon's household, we "tell him" of the need and sorrow of those we love, his help is near.

IV. CHRIST EXERCISES HIS DIVINE POWER TO BANISH DISEASE. The action of our

Lord in performing this miracle deserves attention. He does not stand at a distance and utter words of exorcism, banishing the fever with an authoritative rebuke. Quite the reverse, he takes the sufferer by the hand and raises her up. An illustration of our Saviour's personal ministry, of the way in which he has ever come into contact with individual cases of need, of his tender and yet authoritative manner. It is not the religion of Christ, it is Christ himself who saves. And he ever saves by stretching forth the hand of help, and raising, elevating, the suppliant and penitent from the prostration and helplessness of sin. As the fever left this suffering woman, so all spiritual malady is banished at the bidding of a mighty, gracious Saviour.

V. AFFECTIONATE GRATITUDE PROMPTS TO PERSONAL SERVICE AND MINISTRATION. If our Lord made this house his home in Capernaum, Peter's mother-in-law must have had many opportunities of showing her thankfulness and love. Like many other devoted women, she took pleasure in showing how highly she honoured and how gratefully she loved her Lord. It is a law of moral life that those who are aided, healed, and pardoned shall love him to whom they owe so much ; and shall show their love by grateful ministrations. They may not have the opportunity of ministering to Christ in the body ; but the principle he propounds is this, " Inasmuch as ye did it unto one of the least of these my brethren, ye did it unto me."

PRACTICAL LESSONS. 1. Let us, like Simon, welcome Christ into our houses, our homes. 2. Let us, like this household, tell the Saviour of those members of the family who have special need of him. 3. Let us place all confidence in Christ's power and willingness to bless. 4. Let us, healed and pardoned by Christ's grace, take every opportunity of showing our gratitude, by engaging in his service; and, by ministering to his people, let us minister to him.

Vers. 32—34.—*The Healer of multitudes.* It was the hallowed evening of a memorable day The Lord Jesus had taught in the synagogue, consecrating the sabbath by worship and by spiritual instruction, and creating in the popular mind an impression of his unique authority. He had cast out the demon from a wretched sufferer; he had healed Simon's wife's mother of a raging fever;—all these instances of his power were related through the dwellings of Capernaum, and the popular excitement was great. No wonder that at sunset, when the sabbath was over, and it was lawful to do so, the multitude sought out the sick and maimed among their kindred and companions, and the miserable demoniacs; brought them to the house of Simon, where Jesus was staying ; and entreated the compassion and the succour of the Prophet of Nazareth.

I. In the sufferers brought to Jesus we have A REPRESENTATION OF THE WIDESPREAD AND VARIOUS ILLS THAT AFFLICT MANKIND. If all the diseased and mentally afflicted of any town were brought together to one spot, what a distressing scene would be exhibited ! When the sick and the demoniacs of Capernaum were gathered together on that sabbath evening, they may be said to have exemplified the state of our sin-stricken humanity. To him who looks below the surface, this human race, apart from Christ, offers a spectacle with which no hospital, no pest-house, could compare. Moral disorders, Satanic influences, display themselves in a thousand forms, each having its own loathsomeness, its own anguish, its own curse. " The whole head is sick, and the whole heart faint," etc. Fever, leprosy, palsy, possession,—each may indicate some special aspect of sin.

II. In the conduct of those who brought the sufferers to Christ we have A REPRESENTATION OF THE BENEVOLENT MINISTRATIONS OF THE CHURCH. There were those who had neither strength, knowledge, nor courage to come of themselves to Christ ; their pitying and thoughtful friends led or carried them into his sacred presence. So the Church, which cannot of itself save the world, may nevertheless bring the multitudes unto Christ, may, in a sense, bring Christ to the multitude. An honourable vocation this—to lead the morally disordered and distressed into the presence of the Divine Healer, of him who said, " The whole need not a physician, but those who are sick. I am come not to call the righteous, but sinners to repentance." Some by preaching, some by private ministrations, some by example, and some by precept,—all in the same spirit of compassion for perishing souls, may lead sinners to the Redeemer.

III. In the multitude we discern A FORECAST AND EARNEST OF THE APPROACH OF

SIN-STRICKEN HUMANITY TO THE SAVIOUR. What a sight—"all the city gathered together at the door" of Jesus! Men are learning the powerlessness of every other helper, the hopelessness of every other refuge and confidence. Heathenism and Mohammedanism are proving the futility of their claims; infidelity and atheism are showing that they can render no real service to mankind. At the same time, men are learning that, whilst there is salvation in no other, there is salvation in him. And they shall come, flocking like doves to his windows, like pilgrims from the east and from the west to his shrine, until this vast humanity shall gather into the presence, implore the aid, and know the power of the Divine Redeemer.

IV. In the cures effected we have AN EXEMPLIFICATION OF THE ACTUAL POWER OF THE SAVIOUR TO HEAL AND BLESS. The evangelist does not here dwell upon details, but he mentions two great classes of patients, the diseased and the demoniacs. Over sufferers in mind and body the Lord Jesus displayed his healing authority and grace. There was no case beyond his power. The faith of the applicants was rewarded, the report of their friends was justified, the authority of the Saviour was exemplified, the fame of his ministry was confirmed and extended. What happy households were to be found in Capernaum that night, which had long known pain, anxiety, and despondency! An encouragement surely, to all afflicted by the bondage and the curse of sin, to apply to Jesus for relief, for forgiveness, and for blessing. It does not matter what form your spiritual need and suffering have assumed; it does not matter for what length of time you have been the slave of sin; if you come to Christ you shall surely learn that "he is able to save to the uttermost all that come unto God by him." The purpose of our Saviour's advent and mediation includes all cases of sin and need. The power of the Redeemer is unlimited. The compassion of Jesus is unexhausted. As of old, "he has compassion on the multitudes." The promises of our Lord are large enough to include every case. "Come unto me, all ye," etc.

Vers. 35—39.—*Prayer and work.* We are told concerning our Divine Lord, that "it behoved him in all things to be made like unto his brethren." This indeed is implied in his designation, "Son of man." Our nature is both contemplative and active; the life of a religious man is distinguished alike by devout meditation and communion with God, and by consecrated and energetic labour in God's service. It was the same with our great Leader. The passage before us presents the Lord Jesus in both these aspects, both in prayer and in work.

I. CHRIST'S PRAYER. It is recorded that, at several crises in our Saviour's ministry, he prayed. 1. As to the *character* of Christ's prayers, we know that they were unlike ours in that they could not contain confession, contrition, and repentance; and they were like ours in containing thanksgivings, and also as expressing filial communion and uttering supplication. 2. As to the *occasion* of Christ's prayers, it is the fact that special mention is made of our Lord's appeals to the Father, in connection with the more solemn and significant acts of his ministry. So here, it was in the midst of publicity, of widespread interest, of strenuous labours, that Jesus prayed. 3. The *time* chosen is remarkable. Very early in the morning, before the stir and movement of daily life began, the early, waking, morning hour was consecrated to fellowship with the Father. 4. The *scene* of this prayer is observable. Jesus sought seclusion; he retired to a desert place. It is possible and it is desirable to pray in the assemblies of saints, and to pray in the crowded thoroughfares, to him who seeth in secret. Yet there is appropriateness in retirement and seclusion for special supplications in seasons of special need. The prayer offered on this occasion could not be put upon record, for it was offered in solitude. We know from the "intercessory prayer" recorded by John how fervently our Lord could pray. On this occasion he must have sought strength for the Galilean ministry, and a blessing upon the people, who were more ready to behold his miracles and to profit by them than they were to imbibe his spirit and receive his teaching.

II. CHRIST'S WORK. The prayer occupied the early morning, but the day was to be spent in toil. Our Lord's example gives no countenance to the practice of those who deem the beginning and the end of religion to consist in devotions. Prayer fits for work, and work necessitates prayer. 1. Christ's labours were *suggested by men's needs and entreaties.* What he had done had stirred up hope within the breasts of others, and "all men sought for him." Not always from the highest motives, yet with a faith and earnestness creditable to the suppliants, men sought Christ's help. 2. Christ's labours were regarded by him as *the fulfilment of Divine purpose.* "Therefore to this end came I forth." He did the will of the Father; this was his meat and drink. It gives dignity and happiness to our toil when we can regard it as the work which the Father has given us to do. 3. Christ's labours were prompted by a *universal and untiring benevolence.* There were "the next towns" to be visited; there was "all Galilee" to be evangelized. Only a large heart could take a survey so comprehensive, and cherish a compassion so vast. It was enough for him that sin and misery abounded; he had come "to seek and to save that which was lost." 4. Christ's works were *adapted to the many-sided nature and to the multiform needs of men.* Men were ignorant; he must teach them. Men were hopeless; he must cheer them with good tidings. Men were sick and suffering; he must relieve and heal them. Men were subject to Satanic sway; he must set them free. Men were sinful; he must pardon, cleanse, renew them.

III. THE CONNECTION BETWEEN PRAYER AND WORK. 1. It is a *divinely appointed* connection. There are those who would have Christians confine themselves to prayer, who think that to attempt to work for the Lord is the same as taking matters out of his hands, who tell us that the Lord will carry out his counsels without our help. That God *can* do so we believe, but that he *will* do so is contrary to all his Word. On the other hand, there are those who sneer at prayer as unreasonable and useless, and who preach the gospel of work—of prayerless work—of work without any reference to him who gives the power and who assigns the aim of labour. The Scriptures direct us to conjoin the two. Christ gives us in his own person an example of the harmonious conjunction of both. 2. By prayer may be *discovered the exact work which Providence entrusts to us.* There is no better prayer for the beginning of the day than this, "Lord, what wilt thou have me to do?" You may not clearly see what is the way of service in which the Lord would have you walk. There may open up before you two paths, and you may be uncertain which is that selected for you. In seeking to decide such questions, it is right to make use of your reason, and to take counsel of wise friends. Yet, whilst using human means, it is necessary to seek Divine guidance. "Commit thy way unto the Lord." A voice shall be heard saying, "This is the way; walk ye in it." Not by magic or miracle, but by clear indications of providence, the answer is given from above. 3. By prayer is gained *encouragement and strength for work.* The magnitude of the service may make us more conscious of the feebleness and ignorance of the servant. Our heart may sink within us as we contemplate our helplessness. But prayer can make the weakest strong. By prayer the impossible becomes the practicable. Prayer makes us feel that the power of Omnipotence is at our back. The fainting spirit is refreshed by communion with Heaven. The feeble arm is nerved for what seemed an unequal fight. The Holy Spirit—the Comforter, the Helper—is bestowed upon the suppliant, and his strength is no more his own, but God's. Then he exclaims, "I can do all things through Christ that strengtheneth me."

APPLICATION. 1. Let the hearers of the gospel remember that the work, the suffering, and the prayers of Christ were all for their salvation. 2. Let them imitate the spirit and conduct of those of whom we read that they sought Jesus: "All men seek for thee." If you wish to know the counsels of God, the preaching of Jesus will declare them to you. If you wish to experience the saving grace of God, you may through Christ find it for yourself. 3. Let the spirit of the Lord Jesus—his prayerfulness and his untiring zeal—serve as a model to every servant of his. Like him we must pray with sincerity, if like him we would work with diligence.

Ver. 37.—*Seeking Jesus.* "All are seeking thee." It is man's nature to seek. Men are seeking many things. Some things they seek and find, other things they seek in vain, whilst there are things they seek, first to find and then to lose again. The impulses of our constitution respond to the appeals made from without. There is a mysterious *personal* attraction which renders some men the object of the quest of their fellows. But none has ever so been sought as was and is the Lord Jesus. Men, when spiritually awakened, attracted by the promises of the gospel and influenced by the Holy Spirit, seek for Christ, and, when they find him, find all things in him.

I. WHAT IN MEN LEADS THEM TO SEEK CHRIST? There are many motives inducing to this inquiry and endeavour, just as when Jesus was on earth. 1. *Curiosity* leads men to seek him. During our Lord's ministry, especially the earlier ministry in Galilee, there occurred, now and again, a *rush* to Jesus. Crowds followed him even into the deserts and the mountains. They came from far and near. And not only the populace, but the leaders of the people, were curious to see the Prophet of Nazareth; and Pharisees invited him to dine with them, and asked their friends to meet him. The novelty of Christianity no longer acts amongst our population; but in regions where the gospel is for the first time preached, this motive operates, and many "inquirers" are drawn, simply by their desire for some new thing, to seek a knowledge of the Saviour. 2. *Admiration* leads men to seek him. Even sinful men confess the beauty of holiness, and the young and ardent and aspiring feel the marvellous attraction of a character with which no other can be compared. There is so much of meanness and selfishness in humanity, that the presence upon earth of one morally noble and perfectly benevolent charms some choice and fervent souls, and draws them to our Lord. 3. *Need and suffering* lead men to seek him. When Jesus was on earth there came to him the hungry to be fed, the sick to be healed, the suffering to be relieved, the ignorant to be taught, the anxious to secure his interposition on behalf of their friends and comrades. Human want is perennial; and there are wants which the world can never supply, hearts the world can never fill. Where Jesus is known as the Dispenser of Divine compassion and bounty to the souls of men, men will be drawn to him.

> " Far and wide, though all unknowing,
> Pants for thee each mortal breast;
> Human tears for thee are flowing,
> Human hearts in thee would rest."

4. *Sin and a sense of ill desert and need of pardon* lead men to seek him. Sinners, who were repelled from the formal and self-righteous, were attracted to the gracious and compassionate Redeemer. Often from his lips issued the merciful and authoritative words, "Thy sins be forgiven thee!" Sin has not ceased; its burden and its curse are still felt. And there is none but Christ who has power upon earth to forgive sins. No wonder that men come to him. In him the sinner meets with the pity of a tender heart and the authority of a Divine power.

II. WHAT IN CHRIST LEADS MEN TO SEEK HIM? 1. Foremost must be placed the fact that *he seeks them*. He came to seek and to save the lost. Had he not first come forth upon this quest, never would the needy and sinful children of men have gone forth to meet him. If "we love him because he first loved us," we have sought him because he first sought us. 2. *His invitations and promises*. He has both bidden men seek his help, and has assured them that they shall not seek in vain. "Come unto me" is his invitation; and the assurance is added, " Ye shall find rest unto your souls." 3. His *power to respond to their appeals*, and to satisfy their wants. They who seek and find not are discouraged from further quest. It is never thus with those who apply to Jesus. Here the words hold good, " Seek, and ye shall find." 4. His *benevolent disposition* renders it easy and congenial for those who seek good gifts to seek them here at the hands of Jesus; for in seeking him, the suppliant is seeking the gifts of his hands as well as the love of his heart. And our need and urgency are exceeded by his readiness to confer all real blessings.

APPLICATION. *How should men seek Christ?* 1. Sincerely and seriously. The sincere soul will seek, not his merely, but himself. 2. In faith, not as doubting whether he may now be found, but as assured of his spiritual nearness. 3. Seasonably, which is as much as to say, at once. "Now is the accepted time." We need him now, therefore we should seek him now. 4. Perseveringly, " watching daily at his gates." It is a life-long quest, and, though he be found to-day, none the less must he be sought to-morrow. The " seeking" must be continued, until we see him as he is.

Vers. 40—45.—*The leper healed.* Among the many miracles wrought by the Divine Physician upon the bodies and minds of suffering mankind, the evangelists have selected certain as types of the Saviour's spiritual work, as well as illustrations of his beneficent ministry. Every class of sufferers seems to represent some special aspect of sin and need, and every recorded miracle seems to convey some special lesson concerning the Healer's grace and power. Let this narrative be thus regarded, and we find here—

I. A SYMBOL OF HUMAN SIN AND MISERY. Leprosy was evidently so regarded among the Jews, and upon Divine authority, as is clear from the detailed directions given in Leviticus for its treatment by the priests. A loathsome, spreading, and generally incurable disease, leprosy was regarded with universal repugnance and disgust, and lepers were excluded from ordinary human society and banished from ordinary human dwellings. This disease, therefore, has always been regarded as emblematical of sin, which lays hold of man's moral nature, cripples and disables it, spreads to every department of his being, and is by human means altogether incurable. It renders the subject of it unfit for the society of holy beings, and unworthy of a place in the Church of the living God.

II. The conduct of this leper is AN EXAMPLE OF BELIEVING APPLICATION TO CHRIST. We observe: 1. *Approach* to the Saviour. Though lepers were not permitted to come into the neighbourhood of their fellow-men, this man drew near to Jesus, with the boldness inspired by necessity and hope. 2. There was *reverence*. He knelt, he fell on his face, he worshipped the Master; thus evincing his sense of inferiority and need, and his conviction of Christ's authority. 3. There was *faith*; for his language implies this, "Thou canst make me clean." Not perfect faith, but sincere and in accordance with what he had heard of the great Healer. 4. There was *entreaty*. He besought Jesus, as one who felt that here was his only hope, "Here I live, or here I die."

III. The record describes CHRIST'S POWER TO SAVE. The unusual fulness of the narrative gives us an insight into the movements and operations of Divine mercy. 1. Our Lord's action is traced to *compassion*, which stirred within his Divine heart—the source of all our salvation, the ground of all our hope. 2. *Contact* with the sufferer was the means and the symbol of healing. What Naaman expected Elisha to do to him, that Jesus did to this sufferer—laid his hands upon the place, and recovered the leper. How often is our Saviour represented as thus condescendingly and compassionately coming into personal contact with the wretched and sinful! It is the spiritual touch of the Redeemer that heals the sinner's maladies and banishes his woes. 3. Jesus *exercises his authority*, utters his will, pronounces the sentence of release, "I will; be thou clean!" What simplicity, majesty, authority, in the Saviour's language! It is thus that he addresses every believing suppliant, that he rewards the faith of every lowly applicant. No voice but that Divine voice can give this assurance and pronounce this sentence of liberty. 4. *The healing is effected* by him who is Lord of nature. No failure attended the Saviour's ministry of compassion. The leper's doubt, if he had any, was as to Christ's willingness, not as to his power. The result proved that there was no deficiency in either. The leprosy departed, and the man was cleansed. Christ's is ever a full and complete salvation; for he is "mighty to save."

IV. THE SAVIOUR HERE SANCTIONS THE OPEN EXPRESSION OF GRATITUDE. In bidding the cleansed leper go to the priest and present the customary offering, Jesus not only magnified the Law and conformed to custom, he also approved a grateful spirit, and commended the public acknowledgment of Divine mercy. It is well that we should "pay our vows unto the Most High," that we should "bring an offering, and come into his courts." He is the God who "healeth all our diseases," and every signal interposition on our behalf ought to be gratefully and publicly acknowledged.

V. We remark in this narrative the working of AN IMPULSE TO CELEBRATE AMONGST MEN THE MERCY OF GOD. Our Lord had reasons for enjoining silence upon this healed leper. Yet he would not be displeased with the grateful and benevolent spirit which led him to publish and blaze abroad the matter. Every Christian must exclaim, "The Lord hath done great things for me, whereof I am glad!" "Oh, taste and see that the Lord is good!"

VI. We see the issue of this miracle in THE INCREASING FAME OF CHRIST and the increasing number of applicants to him for relief and help. The tidings of this marvellous cure awakened such public attention to Christ's power and grace that he could not for a season fulfil his ministry in the crowded towns, but retired to secluded spots, where, however, he might well be sought and found by those who were drawn to him, not by an idle curiosity, but by a conviction of his power and grace, and by the urgency of conscious need.

Ver. 41.—" *Moved with compassion.*" There is something in human nature which draws men towards the great, the powerful, the prosperous—an impulse not altogether good. And there is something which attracts men towards the good and pure—a holy and admirable impulse. But there is yet another tendency, which impels souls towards the needy, the sorrowful, the sinful; and this is all Divine. For " God has gladness for those who are glad, and pity for those who are sad." We see this last-named impulse, in all its beauty and power, in the character and the ministry of Emmanuel.

I. THE IMPULSE OF COMPASSION WITHIN THE SOUL OF JESUS. 1. Observe what excited this emotion; it was ever the too familiar spectacle of human want and suffering, trouble and sin. *Passio* leads to *compassio.* Moving about among the people and accessible to all comers, Jesus could not but meet with innumerable cases of human misery, fitted to excite feelings of profoundest pity. The helpless babe, the untaught and neglected multitude, the powerless paralytic, the loathsome leper, the foaming lunatic, the furious demoniac, the crippled beggar, the blind, the deaf, the dumb, the bereaved widow, the mourning sister, the sinful woman, the dying thief,—all these alike were the objects of Christ's commiseration and sympathy. 2. Ponder the emotion itself. To some minds it seems that to attribute such feeling to Deity derogates from the dignity of God. But Christianity reveals to us something nobler, and worthier of our worship and our love, than an impassive and impersonal Law presiding over the destinies of the universe. If the Old Testament represents in words the long-suffering and tender mercy of Jehovah, in the New Testament God in Christ lives among men, susceptible to all their wants and woes, touched with a feeling of their infirmities. If the Old Testament astonishes us by the declaration concerning God, " In all their afflictions he was afflicted," the New Testament depicts one " moved with compassion," who asserts, " He that hath seen me hath seen the Father."

II. THE PRACTICAL EXPRESSION OF COMPASSION. Sentiment is divinely implanted in the human breast; but it is implanted as the root from which actions and habits corresponding with it are designed to grow. Those have been well denounced by the poet—

> " Who, nursed in mealy-mouthed philanthropies,
> Divorce the feeling from her mate, the deed."

Compassion is represented in the text as a principle of action. The Lord Jesus did feel, he did sigh over human sorrows, and groan over human unbelief, and weep over human ingratitude. But his feelings did not evaporate thus; they acted as the motive-power to deeds of charity and of helpfulness. When " moved with compassion," Jesus " stretched forth his hand," and healed, saved, and blessed the object of his gracious commiseration. He was not only tender to feel, he was mighty to save. The very names by which he is known are a monument of his practical compassion—he is the *Redeemer* and the *Saviour* of mankind.

III. THE HUMAN RESPONSE TO THE DIVINE COMPASSION OF CHRIST. A quality so beautiful in itself and so benignant in its operation cannot but exercise a mighty power over the whole nature of those for whose benefit it is displayed. Accordingly, we find that our Lord's pity has exercised such a power in two directions. 1. Christ's compassion becomes the spring of a new moral life in the hearts of his people. When Jesus brings to a soul gladness and peace, can it be matter of wonder that gratitude, love, and devotion become principles of a new nature, a new life? What more natural? " The love of Christ constraineth us." 2. Christ's compassion becomes the inspiration and the example of the compassion of his Church. It is not enough to admire; we are called to copy. Compassion is a " note " of the Christian life, a feeling to be cherished, a habit to be formed. Thus our Lord has introduced among men a new standard of virtue and a new type of character. If the influence of such parables as the Prodigal Son and the Good Samaritan has been great, what must have been the influence exercised by the incarnation and the sacrifice of Christ? The function and office of the redeemed Church of Emmanuel is, being moved with compassion, to minister unto mankind, and to bring the weary, the suffering, and the sinful unto him who never breaks the bruised reed nor quenches smoking flax.

HOMILIES BY VARIOUS AUTHORS.

Ver. 1.—" *The beginning of the gospel.*" Very simple and natural. There is hardly any preface. The narrator seems impatient to get into the very heart of his subject. This should ever be the instinct of the preacher. Ingenuously, yet with perfect inductive force, he shows that Christianity claims respect and acceptance as being connected with the highest aspirations and purest sentiments of morality.

I. THE SUBJECT STATED. "The gospel of Jesus Christ, the Son of God." This title, if title it ought to be called, is very full and felicitous. It is Jesus who is the great subject of the "gospel." The latter is used here in a transitional sense, *i.e.* not simply of "good news," or "glad tidings," but rather of "account," "history," of the great facts of salvation. 1. *The gospel concerns a great Personality.* His name, which was to be "as ointment poured forth," is twofold. Jesus is his ordinary human name; his official dignity is indicated by the term "Christ" or "the Christ," *i.e.* the Anointed. As Messiah, he occupied relations more than human, and therefore the addendum (supported by preponderating manuscript authority), "the Son of God." The Hope of Israel was, if prophetic language is subject to reasonable canons of interpretation, more than a saint or a seer; he was partaker of the Divine nature as truly as of the human, and thus fitted to mediate between the Father and his alienated children. 2. *The existence and gradual manifestation of this Person are of great and gladsome consequence to the world.* It is worth while to know what he was, did, and suffered, as thereby may be discovered the meaning and the method of salvation. For this reason the account of them is preserved and commended to men.

II. UNDER WHAT ASPECT IT IS REGARDED. As something coming into existence, beginning to be, in time. We are invited, so to speak, to consider how it grew. The greatest religions have not been sudden inventions. Christianity is no exception to the rule. The interest of the mind is excited by the prospect of tracing the genesis of so great and so remarkable a phenomenon, as one might seek to follow a river to its source, or speculate as to the origin of a world. One knows, must know, more about the nature of a thing when it is thus studied. But it would be easy to lose one's self in curious conjecture, in myth and legend of the prehistoric past, without any extension of actual knowledge. In the various ways in which the evangelists account for or trace out the origin of the gospel, there is always a use more or less apparent. In practical subjects speculative researches usually turn out to be aberrations. But Mark, who is the most realistic in his tendency of any of the New Testament writers, save perhaps James, contents himself with indicating proximate origins, but in such a way as to suggest in the strongest possible way the supernatural as the only possible explanation or key. 1. *It was foretold.* The coming of this Person was the chief burden of prophecy. He was the Hope of the ages. The many statements of the prophets are, however, passed over by Mark in favour of two, one being introductory (ver. 2) and the other of chief importance (ver. 3). It is said, "in Isaiah the prophet," because the attention of the writer went through and beyond the first quotation, which is from Malachi, and riveted itself upon the second, from Isaiah. That such words should have been spoken so long ago was a proof of the Divine character of Christ's mission. 2. *Moral preparation was needed for it.* John the Baptist's work was a preparatory one, upon the heart and conscience. As a whole it is termed, from its chief rite, "the baptism" of John; and its end was repentance. 3. *The personal preparation of its great subject was also essential.* His fulfilling of the Law in John's baptism, and his inward spiritual endowment and illumination, ensuring moral victory, spiritual maturity, and the fulness of the Messianic consciousness, are therefore described. All these are a very small portion of the whole gospel as given by Mark; he passes with light, firm touch over each, and then launches his readers upon the great river of Christ's doings and sayings, issuing inevitably, as he ever hints and suggests, in the tragedy of Golgotha. The fulness and intensity of the narrative sensibly increase as the great catastrophe is approached, and the end throws its light back upon the faintest and most obscure "beginning."—M.

Vers. 4—8.—*The ministry of John.* I. OF WHAT IT CONSISTED. In each Gospel the descriptions are very general, and look as if they had been foreshortened in order to give due prominence to the gospel narrative that had to follow. Yet a fairly complete impression may be received of his main doctrines and rules of discipline. Generally in his ministry there are four elements discoverable. 1. *Exhortation.* A direct appeal to the moral sense, the chief note of which was "Repent." It is a sharp word often repeated, refinement upon it being likely only to dull its edge. It meant, primarily, "to think after another," then "to change one's mind or opinion," the faculty addressed being that of moral reflection (*noûs*). Accordingly we read of repentance "unto acknowledgment of the truth" (2 Tim. ii. 25), "toward God" (Acts xx. 21), "from dead works" (Heb. vi. 1), and "unto life" (Acts xi. 18), or "unto salvation" (2 Cor. vii. 10). The two last expressions correspond with that of Mark, "unto remission of sins." The idea involved is intellectual as well as moral, thought being exercised as well as feeling. The mind is to be twisted back upon itself; spiritual resolution is demanded according to new principles. "Take a right view of sin—your sin—and quit it." John thus prepared men for Christ by making them prepare themselves, casting down every imagination and every high thing that stood in the way the coming King was to use for his glorious "progress." 2. *Ceremony.* There was but one rite—baptism; not created for the occasion, but simply adopted out of the multiform ceremonial of Judaism. Its use is explained by its symbolic suggestiveness of the spiritual change John sought to produce. The physical purifying set forth the spiritual, and was ineffectual without it. 3. *Example.* He himself was what he desired others to be. His habitat—the wilderness—was a protest against the corruption of the cities, and indeed of the whole social fabric. He dwelt apart, as being thus better able to seek God and serve him. His personality, too, was eloquent of the same truth. With clothing the coarsest and least comfortable, and food the simplest and cheapest, he maintained a strong, free, independent life, consecrated in Nazarite-like vows to God. 4. *Prophecy.* Not only a backward but also a forward look was implied in his teaching. It was by virtue of the coming of Another that all these moral acts were to be rendered valid and effectual. The atonement of Christ, as a prospective thing, is therefore the key-stone of all John's preaching. Not the baptism, the ascetic life, not even the "repentance," was in itself a saving principle. These only availed as they brought men to him who baptized not with water but with the Holy Spirit. His whole ministry did not confer, but simply prepared for, "the remission of sins."

II. ITS RELATIVE SIGNIFICANCE. It was, therefore, not of absolute or independent value, but only auxiliary to the advent of Christ. He stood midway between the Law and the Gospel. In this light, his recognition of the "Lamb of God, which taketh away the sin of the world" is at once the linking on of his ministry to Christ's, and its consummation and disappearance in it.

III. ITS RESULTS. Not substantive or permanent. A deep effect was produced upon Jewish life, but it did not last. Yet, in many instances, notably within the circle of the apostles, it was the preliminary stage, the "strait gate and narrow way," into the Divine life which Jesus brought. John's message exerted a far-reaching influence, thrilled the nation in all its classes and tribes, and then died away in ever fainter echoes, amidst the returning indifference or spiritual opposition to the Truth. It was not, therefore, useless; rather in the highest sense was it effectual only as it succeeded in making itself unnecessary for the further progress of those who received it. "He must increase, but I must decrease."—M.

Ver. 8.—*John's baptism and Christ's.* I. THE GRAND RELIGIOUS NEED OF MAN IS PURIFICATION. The existence of so many ceremonial religions is a presumption in favour of this. They all speak of offences in man which require expiation. But the knowledge of the true character of sin is revealed by the Law (Rom. iii. 19). Sin itself, of course, exists anterior to the knowledge of the Law of Moses, because of the "law of God written upon the heart." In Ps. xiv. the universal depravity of the Jews of the age in which the psalmist wrote is very absolutely declared; and St. Paul, in Rom. iii. 10, etc., quotes it freely, in proof that Jews as well as Gentiles are under the power of sin. "As his argument is at this point addressed particularly to the Jew, he reasons, not from the sense of sin or the voice of conscience, but from the Scriptures, whose authority the Jew acknowledged. The Jew would, of course, admit the inference as to the state of

the Gentile world" (Perowne). The first aim, therefore, of every real religion must be
the removal of sin, because: 1. *The sense of guilt estranges man from God.* Under this
feeling of alienation the heart hardens, and the tendency is to cast off the authority of
all Divine sanctions. 2. *Indwelling sin corrupts and perverts the moral nature.* The
vision of God is obscured, and as he is the Fountain of moral obligation and perception,
moral distinctions become uncertain and confused. Right and truth are not desired
for their own sakes; there is no genuine enthusiasm for them. On the contrary, the
heart is already biased and bribed on behalf of evil. "Evil, be thou my good,"
expresses the final stage to which the corruption of the heart may attain; and: 3. *Sinful
habit and inherited tendency enfeeble the will.* This moral weakness may coexist with
the clearest perceptions of right and wrong (Rom vii. 14—19).

II. RELIGIOUS MINISTRIES ARE TO BE TESTED BY THEIR POWER TO EFFECT THIS. 1. *It
is the general pretension which they make in common.* There may be supernatural
evidences, etc., to recommend them, but the practical ground upon which they base
their claim to reception is really that, in some way or other, they can settle the question
of sin between man and God. To judge them upon this point is not, therefore, to do
them an injustice. 2. *The standard is common and within human experience.* In the
measure in which they wean man from sin and reconcile him to the Divine Being,
they prove their ability to make good their pretension. A religion whose followers
have low moral ideas, or are not in the habit of practising what they profess, must be
discredited as a moral power. 3. *There are various respects in which this purifying
power may show itself:* (1) Spiritual rest. This arises from a sense of forgiveness and of
reconciliation with God. In other words, when the consciousness of guilt is removed
and the sanctions of righteousness have been honoured, the soul is satisfied and loses its
fear and dislike to God, trusting, and in time loving, him. (2) Moral inspiration. If
sin has truly been overcome, and the relations of the soul with God are satisfactory,
there will be hopefulness and vigour in the discharge of duty, resignation and patience
in suffering, and a disposition to do good. (3) Change of character and conduct. He
who did evil and delighted in it will then find his joy in righteousness and holiness.
There will be manifest "the fruits of the Spirit," and there will be "no fellowship with
the unfruitful works of darkness."

III. How THE SUPERIORITY OF THE CHRISTIAN RELIGION IN THIS RESPECT IS TO BE
EXPLAINED. 1. *Because it was spiritual and not ceremonial.* John anticipated the
explanation in his prophecy concerning Christ. He was not, like himself, to baptize
with water, but with the Holy Spirit. Now, John's baptism was most significant,
perhaps the most significant of the rites of the ceremonial law. Enforced by his moral
earnestness, it also exercised a powerful spiritual effect. But it did not produce that
which he preached, viz. repentance, in any inward and enduring manner. It was only
indirectly spiritual. Duty was powerfully suggested by the symbol, and, where spiritual
influence was at work, in many instances a moral change was produced. But there
was, so to speak, no command over that spiritual influence, no ensuring its operation
upon the heart. What was needed was something that would go directly to the heart,
and renew the moral nature. It is only in the communication of greater spiritual
power than existed before that this can take place. A strong moral nature like John's
was felt whilst it appealed to men, but, when its immediate influence was withdrawn,
the impulses and emotions to which it gave rise died down again. Christ, on the other
hand, furnished moral power in the communication of truth under vital and vivid
representations. From the fulness of his own spiritual life also there was a constant
overflowing of grace and strength. He spake as never man spake; his authority was
felt; his example inspired. It was the meaning and spirit of everything he revealed.
The conscience was strengthened, and the moral nature filled with new light and life.
"Lord, to whom shall we go? thou hast the words of eternal life. And we have believed
and know that thou art the Holy One of God" (John vi. 68). 2. *Because it was the
communication of Divine life and power.* He "baptized with the Holy Ghost." An
awful and mysterious expression. The Spirit of God was set free by the atoning work
of the Saviour to operate upon the heart and conscience of man. By purifying the
outward man John sought to impress men with the sense of their spiritual impurity,
and their need of forgiveness and inward cleansing. But only Christ could give purity
of heart. He gave life; he inspired. The inward man was renewed, "created after

God, in righteousness and true holiness." "I can do all things through Christ which strengtheneth me."—M.

Vers. 9—11.—*The baptism of Jesus.* One of many proofs of the wide influence of the Baptist's ministry. He came from Nazareth of Galilee. The multitudinous baptism of John was a fit occasion and background for the special and peculiar baptism of Jesus. The awakened national conscience represented for the nonce the general confession of sin by the individuals of mankind saved through the gospel. Christ's baptism was—

I. A FULFILMENT OF LEGAL RIGHTEOUSNESS. It was one ceremony of the Law taken as representative of the spirit and essence of the whole ceremonial system. Inasmuch as it involved a *confession of sin,* he by undergoing it (1) *humiliated himself;* and (2) *identified himself with the sinful nature of the race.* Whilst condemning in his pure spirit the sin of man, he yet takes his place with sinners, as one with them in their penalty and their hope.

II. A FULFILMENT OF SPIRITUAL CONSCIOUSNESS. 1. *Through plenary reception of the Holy Spirit.* This was the same Spirit in which he had already been living, but given now "without measure." Inspiration ensues upon conscious acts of obedience and righteousness; true spiritual baptism is given to those who submit willingly to the positive requirements of God's Law. This was (1) the completion of the Divine-human consciousness; and (2) the communion of God and man, of heaven and earth. The (violently and suddenly) rent heaven symbolized this. 2. *Through Divine attestation.* It was a voice to John, but much more to Jesus himself. Through this experience he realized that the attitude he had assumed, and the career upon which he was about to enter, were approved of his Father. The favour and acceptance therein declared were also, by implication, a recognition of his perfect personal purity. It was not as a sinner that he submitted to baptism, but as the sinner's Friend and intending Saviour.—M.

Vers. 12, 13.—*The temptation.* Great moral problems are suggested by the temptation. Mark does not describe the nature of it, but leaves the imagination and cognate experience of his readers to fill up the spaces, or, having a different object from the other evangelists, he, supposing the details furnished by them well known, contents himself with an epitome. But it is an epitome of a very vivid and pregnant kind. The salient points alluded to by him are—

I. THE PREDISPOSING CAUSE OF IT. The temptation, singularly enough, follows "straightway" upon the baptism, in such a way as to establish the fact of a close connection between the two events; and that Spirit which crowned with its descent the act of obedience is the direct cause of Christ's being tempted. Is not this inconsistent with what we learn of God from the Bible? He is not, we are told, tempted of evil, "neither tempteth he any man." 1. *It was necessary to the purpose of Christ's coming into the world that he should be tempted.* As a portion, therefore, of his mediatorial experience and perfecting, it was quite fitting that the Spirit, through whom he had come, should lead him forward to each chief point of trial in his career. It is conceivable that one should approach evil from the side of an evil heart already predisposed to yield. But it belongs to the virtue of Christ's position as one tempted that he was led into it by the Spirit. It was—to translate a part of the meaning of this into familiar speech—it was "from the highest motives" that he submitted to temptation. 2. *It was not the Spirit that tempted him, but it was through being in the condition induced by the indwelling of the Spirit that he became exposed to temptation in its most terrible forms.* It is only as being in a higher spiritual state than that to which one's circumstances correspond that they can be truly said to tempt him. The greatest temptations are revealed in the highest spiritual experience, even as darkness by light. We can never appreciate the power of Satan until we look at him from a state of holiness and devout illumination.

II. THE AGENT OF IT. Mark uses the peculiar word "Satan," instead of "the devil," as in the other Gospels. The choice of this term may have been determined by a desire to emphasize the special character of the devil as "the adversary" whom he was to overthrow, or simply by an instinctive sense that thereby the personality, and the identification of that personality with the historic Satanic principle of revelation, would be made clearer. It was with no secondary being that Jesus wrestled, but with the prince of darkness himself. In such an encounter the conflict must needs be a duel, and even then was it determined beforehand in favour of the Son of God. But the allurements employed were necessarily of the most subtle and grandly representative character. It was a final trial of strength, upon which the future of salvation depended.

III. THE ASSOCIATIONS OF IT. *The forty days in the wilderness* reminded men of the similar fasts of Moses and Elijah. *The wild beasts* may have been an unconscious reproduction of the conditions of the Paradisaic temptation. *The society of the wilderness* was of the most contrastive and representative character : the Spirit—Satan ; wild beasts—angels. As to the " wild beasts " (peculiar to Mark), Plumptre says, " In our Lord's time these might include the panther, the bear, the wolf, the hyena, possibly the lion." The implied thought is partly that their presence added to the terrors of the temptation, partly that in his being protected from them there was the fulfilment of the promise in the very psalm which furnished the tempter with his chief weapon, that the true child of God should trample underfoot " the lion and the adder," the " young lion and the dragon " (Ps. xci. 13). De Wette considers this to be " a mere pictorial embellishment." Lange holds that Christ's attitude " is a sovereign and peaceful one towards the beasts: they dare not hurt the Lord of creation, nor do they flee before him. Jesus takes away the curse also from the irrational creation (Rom. viii.)." As to the angels, we are not to regard them as assisting him in his conflict with Satan, but succouring him in his exhaustion after it. He holds his court, as it were, on the very battle-field. In token of his victory, heaven pours itself forth in its fairest and best on the spot that but a little before was the ante-chamber of hell.—M.

Vers. 16—20.—*The call of the disciples ;* or, *work and higher work.* I. THE ORDINARY WORK OF MEN AND THE EXTRAORDINARY ARE (HERE) PUT IN THE SAME LINE. It is no small presumption in favour of Christ's divinity that he chose common men—workmen—for his intimate disciples. What link could there be between the transcendent task of the apostleship and that mean calling in which they were engaged ? He alone saw a connection, and not a merely fanciful one. He indicated it and proceeded upon it. The idea was familiar to the prophets (*e.g.* Jer. xvi. 16), and to Greek literature (as in the ' Dialogues of Lucian,' etc.), but not in the same application. The resemblance he suggested is broad and deep. *It was while they were working* that he called them. What a practical, spiritual gain for all toilers is this revelation !

II. THEY ARE SHARPLY DISTINGUISHED AND ABSOLUTELY SEPARATED. As connected by analogy, it is implied that they are separated in fact. Not by confounding the sacred with the secular calling is either benefited. That they are not the same is shown by : 1. *A difference of object.* " For men." The means must therefore be different, and the entire method. Luke uses a word meaning " to catch alive." The fishers of men were not to snare them, but to win them to something worthy of them ; and not for selfish ends, but through love and Divine good will. So interpreted, how grand is this vocation ! 2. *A distinct call.* Christ asks—bids them " come after " him. Were there any previous inner witnessings which this endorsed and strengthened ? This call was no simply picturesque or accidental occurrence ; it was an essential condition of their assumption of apostolic service. The difference between their new duties and their old ones was so profound that only a distinct inward voice could warrant the transition from the one to the other. Christ spoke to the heart as well as to the ear, and his word was a determining one. 3. *Altered circumstances.* He would take them away for a time from the associations of the fish-net. They would have to cease looking at life as " making a living." As God's workmen, they would be his dependents. They would have to live by faith, that they might walk by faith. 4. *Special preparation.* " I will make." What they had done or learned would not qualify them for what they were to do. He alone could teach them the new craft ; and only as they drank in his spirit could they hope to succeed in it.

III. TO PASS FROM THE ONE TO THE OTHER IS ONLY POSSIBLE THROUGH OBEDIENCE, SELF-SACRIFICE, AND CLOSER FELLOWSHIP WITH CHRIST. Even as he calls them their preparation and discipline commence. It was a sharp trial, but salutary and wise. 1. *Obedience.* They were to go at once if at all, without question, and finally. 2.

Self-sacrifice. This was begun by "leaving all and following" Christ, as Peter phrased it. The will of the flesh, "the will to live," the whole self-life,—had to be renounced. 3. *But their life would be a fellowship with the Master.* This would compensate for every toil and trial. But it would also necessitate continual exercise of sympathy, spiritual insight, and resolute fidelity.—M.

Vers. 21—28.—*The authority of Jesus.* A note of Christ's work as a whole, which occasioned remark amongst his contemporaries. Not so much what he did, as how. A grandeur of nature and manner. Nothing is so difficult to define as authority, especially when it is a personal attribute.

I. How IT SHOWED ITSELF. 1. *From the outset of his career.* The Capernaum synagogue, where his boyhood had been passed, did not daunt him. The ordinary circumstances, which tend to dwarf even great men, did not detract from his greatness. 2. *It showed itself especially in two directions,* viz. teaching and spiritual healing. (1) Teaching. "He taught—spake—as one having authority." An indefinable yet absolute difference existed in this respect between him and the customary teachers of the people. They went back upon prescription and tradition, the sentences of the rabbis, the legal interpretations received in the schools. They would refer back to some great name, or some generally acknowledged opinion, as a lawyer collects his instances; but their own opinion was seldom or never forthcoming; if it was, it was tentative, unoriginal, and uninfluential. Now, Christ had quite a different tone. He referred to the sentences of the Jewish schools only to condemn them, and he did not hesitate to range himself alone against all the weight of tradition. "Ye have heard that it hath been said, . . . but *I* say unto you;" "Verily, verily, *I* say unto you;" "Heaven and earth shall pass away, but *my* words shall not pass away." (2) Action. Look at this special case, the man with the unclean spirit. He shows mastery from the very first. His word is a command, and there is no flinching or compromise. Nor is the order despised; he said, and it was done. 3. *It gave a character to his entire work.* "What is this? a new teaching! with authority he commandeth even the unclean spirits, and they obey him;" or, "A new teaching with authority (or power)! He commandeth," etc. In the whole round of duties, and undertakings connected with his mission, it is observable, and its effect is to draw attention and to impress.

II. To WHAT IT WAS DUE. This was the problem which presented itself, which was meant to present itself, to the men of his day. That it was no accident of manner or any mere assumption of superiority is shown by its results. And the general bearing of Christ was meekness itself. It was due to nature rather than office, to personal relation with God. 1. *To absolute spiritual insight.* He saw and knew what he was speaking about in its ground and essence. It was therefore unnecessary for him to sit at any man's feet, or to borrow wisdom of any teacher. 2. *To absolute trust in moral power.* This arose from his identifying himself with it. He did not only speak about truth; he was "the Way, the Truth, and the Life." "I and my Father are one." The display of superior physical strength did not appall him, nor was he discouraged by suffering or death.

III. WHAT IT ARGUED. 1. *His divinity.* This "unknown quantity" in Christ was as unmistakable as it was immeasurable. Out of the depth and fulness of his own spiritual life he must have spoken. The Divine element is therefore an inevitable inference. "Never *man* spake like this man." 2. *His power to save.* "Even the unclean spirits" obeyed him. It is the moral or subjective side of temptation on which the real weakness of man exists; and just there Christ is omnipotent. He can cure the sick soul and restore moral tone and energy. And his words are an unerring guidance and discipline for the soul: "Lord, to whom can we go? Thou hast the words of eternal life."—M.

Vers. 40—45.—*The leper's petition.* I. THE GENERAL WORK OF CHRIST, WHEN IT IS KNOWN, ENCOURAGES THE MOST FORLORN AND DESPERATE. (Cf. ver. 39.) The nature of leprosy and the law concerning it.

II. SINCERE FAITH, EVEN WHEN IMPERFECT, EVER MEETS WITH THE SYMPATHY AND HELP OF CHRIST. "If thou wilt, thou canst." He believed in his power, but was uncertain as to his willingness. The spirit of the Saviour was therefore concealed from him. Yet Christ answered his prayer. (There is no evidence that the leper identified the will with the power.)

III. CHRIST'S METHOD OF RESTORATION IS ADAPTED TO THE SPECIAL MORAL CONDITION OF THE SUBJECT OF HIS MERCY. It was his sympathy and willingness that had to be demonstrated to the poor leper. This is done by the *assurance*, " I will ; " and the *touch* (braving ceremonial defilement and physical repugnance). So, in saving men from their sins, their defects of character and experience are met by special revelations and mercies. A complete and perfect faith in Christ is the evidence and guarantee of perfect salvation.

IV. SPECIAL EXPERIENCES OF DIVINE GRACE DO NOT FREE FROM LESSER DUTIES, BUT RATHER INCREASE THEIR OBLIGATION. The Law was to be honoured. Civil and religious obligations were enjoined. There was a public use in the rules that were imposed, and it was well they should be observed.

V. MERCY MAY BE RECEIVED WITHOUT ITS OBLIGATIONS BEING FULLY REALIZED OR OBSERVED. The leper was cured, but not perfectly. He had not learned the obedience of faith. His inattention to Christ's request created a serious inconvenience and hindrance in prosecuting the work of salvation amongst others. Those who have received benefits from Christ should attend implicitly to all that he enjoins. " Ye are my friends, if ye do the things which I command you " (John xv. 14). The spiritual blessings of Christ are dependent on perfect subjection to his will.—M.

Ver. 24.—*Christ and the demons.* I. THE FEELINGS THE QUESTION BETRAYED. 1. *A sense of inevitable relation.* His presence at once discovers them ; there is no escape when he is near. Their true character is more strongly and unmistakably manifested, as darkness is revealed by light. A positive sense of relation to his person and work is called forth. How far may this have been a witness within themselves personally—in their own individual consciousness ? how far a merely constitutional instinct ? how far due to connection with the personality of the possessed ? That it was beyond their own control is evident. They were unwilling witnesses to his power, and their obedience was not due to loyalty or attachment. So whenever the truth is manifested, it addresses an instinct in intelligent nature which cannot be wholly indifferent to it. 2. *Conscious unlikeness and antagonism.* Being what they were, they could not acquiesce in what he was or did. His presence was judgment and torture to them. They had the keenest perception of his purity and sinlessness, without being attracted by it ; on the contrary, their opposition was only the more excited and extreme. The opposition was that of hell and heaven in their essential principles. 3. *Fear and apprehension.* A moral awe and dread attended the consciousness of such holiness, the awe which moral authority inspires. It is akin to what is felt towards God. But there was also " a fearful looking for of judgment and fiery indignation." Their empire was not only in jeopardy, it was already doomed. And they must stand or fall *together.* " Art thou come to destroy *us* ? " How ? By dismissing them to Hades. " But even in Hades Christ does not leave their empire to the demons. Thus it was by the destruction of their empire generally. Certainly it was by dismissing them to the Gehenna of torment (according to which the expression in Matt. [viii. 29], the Hades of torment, is to be explained) " (Meyer). In this the sinner is one with the demon.

II. THE ANSWER IT IMPLIED. The possessed one who asked the question knew it had but one answer. Christ had nothing whatever to do with the demons, and they had nothing whatever to do with him. *They had nothing to do with him* : 1. *As agents and representatives of evil.* At a later date he could say, " The prince of the world cometh : and he hath nothing in me " (John xiv. 30). None had ever convinced him of evil. So from the mouth of the demons themselves was the great calumny, afterwards so diligently promulgated, " He hath Beelzebub, and, By the prince of the devils casteth he out the devils " (ch. iii. 22), answered by anticipation. There is no key that will unlock the mystery of his devoted life save that of simplicity of purpose and infinite love. 2. *As moral beings.* There was the clearest knowledge of his character and dignity. " The demons who were in those possessed seem to have perceived sooner than the rest who Jesus was (*yea, sooner even than most of the men with whom he walked at that time*) " (Bengel). " *The Holy One of God* " (cf. Ps. xvi.)

was Christ's "concealed designation," a Messianic identification which implied spiritual insight or knowledge (John vi. 69; x. 36; Rev. iii. 7). *Knowledge without love.* How fruitless! They knew him as the Holy One of God, but not as their Saviour. Belief and obedience, but no salvation! So near, yet so far! How was this? (1) Because there was no inward loving acceptance of him as their moral Ruler. (2) This was probably due to the utter corruption of their moral nature. They had become wholly evil, even whilst they perceived the uselessness and misery of sin. They knew the good, but had lost the power to will it. *Even to this may any moral being come who continues in sin, or rather continues out of Christ.* There is no tenderness in Christ's tone to the demons, only rebuke. A day is coming when the blasphemer, the hypocrite, the liar too, will be silenced. It is from such a fate that Christ would save us whilst yet it might be said of us, "And this is *life eternal*, that they should know thee, the only true God, and him whom thou didst send, even **Jesus Christ**" (John xvii. 3).—M.

Ver. 28.—"*The region . . . round about.*" I. THE POSITION OF THE CHURCH. 1. *Centre of the world's life.* (1) This by virtue of what she is, the principles of righteousness which she inculcates and practises. These "doctrines of the cross" are keys to the chambers of power and authority. They are the true solution of the mysteries of human life. Questions of biography or of history, of individual lives or of eras, can only be understood from their underlying and determining spiritual principles—the relations of man to the Divine. Because of this connection of righteousness with the laws of the universe, Christian faith and virtue are the conditions of true possession and influence, whether in the region of the material or that of the spiritual. The beatitudes illustrate this truth. Only to the central principle does the world yield up its wealth. Herein, too, lies the reason of the Church's responsibility and stewardship. She holds what she has, not for herself alone, but for others. Her power is a moral one, as being guardian of the best interests of man. (2) This by virtue of her relation to Christ. He is the Centre of humanity, and in him all things are created and sustained. It is, however, only through doctrines and belief that vital connection with him is maintained. Being, so to speak, "in Christ," she is his representative in proportion to her faithfulness and vitality. It is as constituted of individual members, each believing in Christ and living in him, that this character belongs to her, and not from any mystic corporate prerogative. What is true, therefore, of the Church, is so because, in the first instance, it is true of individual believers. Christ himself is the great attractive force of the Church; "I, if I be lifted up, will draw all men unto me." (3) This by virtue of her present circumstances. Although not of the world, she is in it, sent into it, and kept there. The great reason of her institution is that she may influence—evangelize—her neighbourhood. For a season in the midst of the world, as Christ was in its midst, she is to radiate forth light and life upon mankind. The minster, "of the whole city centre," is typical of the spiritual temple in the midst of world-life. 2. *A moving centre.* Wherever our Saviour went he carried on his work in "the region round about," and "they came to him from every quarter" (ver. 45). In the same manner must it be with his followers. Like him, they must go about continually doing good. Christian work is not exclusively associated with a special place or building, a sacred day or an official service; it is inseparable from the individual personality of the believer, and must constantly proceed wherever he is. 3. *A multiplying centre.* The powers of the individual believer increase and multiply. His command of new truths, and attainment of fresh spiritual life, add to his facilities and capacities for usefulness. And every person added to the faith is a new evangelist, with a sphere and fitness of his own. It is the glory of Christianity thus to propagate itself. The "Society of Jesus" was described as "a sword, with the handle at Rome and the point everywhere." The ideal this represents is only realized in the spiritual society of Jesus—the Church saved through his blood, and in all her members, loyal and loving, carrying out the great commission, "Go ye into all the world, and preach the gospel to the whole creation" (ch. xvi. 15).

II. THE FIELD OF THE CHURCH. 1. *Always at hand.* The sphere of the Christian is described from himself as a centre. He can never escape it or be destitute of it. He ought to be always ready and furnished for his work, however poor or ignorant he may be; for "our sufficiency is of God." "Of whom are ye in Christ Jesus, who of God is made unto us wisdom, and righteousness, and sanctification, and redemption." Even the *one* talent is given for use and service. Men often lose themselves in vague dreams and extensive ideas. For this reason it may be, as Bishop Butler suggests, that we are first told to "love our neighbour"—a duty which develops into many graces. It is a bad sign when the immediate neighbourhood, the family, the servants, the friends, etc., of a professing Christian, are neglected. 2. *Practically infinite.* It is undefined save at its centre. Each region is a centre to others. The pressure of spiritual responsibility is as constant and necessary to the Christian's soul as that of the atmosphere in relation to his body. The ever-increasing and widening vistas of possible usefulness are occasions of inspiration and ennoblement to the earnest worker. 3. *Constantly varied.* New subjects of Christian solicitude present themselves, new adaptations of spiritual truth and agency. The adaptability, capacity, and sympathy of the Christian ought to be continually developing. And when "the region round about" has received its due labour and attention and prayer, there is ever some "region beyond" whither the hastening feet of the Saviour have already made a way.—M.

Ver. 35.—*The history of a prayer of Christ.* I. ITS IMMEDIATE OCCASION. 1. *To be found in connection with his work.* It was incessant. Fresh claims upon his attention and compassion were continually being made. Only the day before "all the city" had been "gathered together at the door." The exercise of his healing power was a drain upon his emotional and spiritual nature, and the fatigue of the work, which lasted from morning to night, must have been a severe tax upon the delicate organization of the Saviour. He needed rest. 2. *To be found in the excitement attaching to it.* He was at the beginning of his ministry, and it was full of novelty and uncertainty. As the supernatural power of Christ displayed itself, the people began to broach ideas of a temporal sovereignty. A profound impression was produced upon the public mind, and vast crowds attended him wherever he moved. The corruption and depravity of the human mind, too, must have become increasingly manifest to him. The problem of salvation never could have seemed more distressing or difficult. And, in the midst of his occupation, the contrary currents of worldly thought and human ambition must have been felt by him.

II. ITS ULTIMATE REASON. The circumstances of fatigue and excitement in themselves would not account for the anxiety displayed by Christ to secure opportunity for devotion; it is as associated with his unique personality and aim that they acquire significance. For it is only as arising from personal longing and necessity, that such a departure from the scene of his labours can be understood. We are not to suppose that it was done for an example; the whole proceeding would thereby be rendered too artificial and self-conscious. And yet the action itself was exemplary in the highest degree. Its value as a pattern for our imitation consists in its very absence of self-consciousness. We cannot help asking, "What was the place held by prayer in his spiritual life?" "How was the practice of devotion related to the inward needs-be of his nature?" It was not simply a reaction of overwrought feeling or an instinctive craving for emotional relief and variation. By his entire spiritual constitution he was intimately related to the Father. The filial bond was infinitely strong, tender, and intense. His true life was twofold—a giving forth of himself to man, and receiving from God; the latter was necessary to the efficiency of the former. He said, "I can of mine own self do nothing," and therefore he ever sought communion with his unseen Father: 1. *For restoration of spiritual power.* 2. *To maintain the elevation of his feeling and purpose.* 3. *For comfort and encouragement.*

III. HOW IT WAS PREPARED FOR. There is a climax in the text; an impression is thereby conveyed of inward trouble, leading to painstaking effort, which results in final relief and comfort. 1. *He sought the Father early.* "Very early, in the midst of the night," is the literal force of the words. His first impulse toward heavenly communion was obeyed. The thoughts which had kept the night wakeful were not corrupted by the new associations of another day. Are the first impressions of our minds on awaking Divine or human? of heaven or of earth? Do we earnestly seek to know first of all God's will, and strive to realize his presence? He who so prepares for the work and intercourse of the day will not be overtaken or surprised by evil. Better lose a little sleep than the restful communion of the Father. 2. *His departure was secret.* There was no consulting with flesh and blood. There are inward promptings and voices concerning which no earthly advice should be asked. It is possible that " Simon and they that were with him " were not a little disconcerted and annoyed that they had to seek for him ; but even their presence would have been a hindrance. The solemn yet fascinating individualism of true prayer is not realized as it might be. *Secret prayer* is the background of earnest and real *common prayer.* In this matter we have not only the example but the injunction of Christ (Matt. vi. 6). 3. *Not only the actual presence of men but human associations were avoided.* "He departed into a *desert place.*" Such a situation, as formerly the weird solitudes of the Quaritanian Desert, harmonized with his spiritual mood. Wide upland spaces, far withdrawn, brought him nearer to the Unseen and Eternal, afforded larger views, spiritual as well as physical, and favoured the ideality and inwardness that are essential to a great spirit.

> " The silence that is in the starry sky,
> The sleep that is among the lonely hills,"

were an anodyne to his fretted and troubled heart ; in nature he met God. Such a spot could only have been found at a distance, and this is further implied by the circumstance of the others following after him, and their message, " All are seeking thee." Lessons : (1) *Opportunities for secret prayer will be prized and even created by devout minds.* (2) *If the purest and grandest moral Being the world has seen needed such communion with his Father, how much more such as we ?* (3) *God must be sought diligently, and before all else, if he is to be sought effectually.* (4) *How difficult of access and realization is the oratory of the soul, where devotion may be free from earthliness, continuous and uninterrupted !*—M.

Vers. 14, 15.—*The ministry of mercy.* Our text reminds us of the significant fact that Jesus began his ministry in Galilee, and not in Jerusalem, as the Jews might have expected of their Messiah. In the city where the sacred temple stood there was far less of the earnestness and simplicity which our Lord sought for than among the rural peasants and fishermen. Hence his work was begun and was largely continued in a district which was poor and despised. This, however, was only in harmony with much that we know of God's methods; for "his ways are not as our ways." As the Creator of all things, he has placed some of the most beautiful products of nature in obscure spots. We find them in secluded dells, or in the depths of the earth and sea, or they are hidden under the curl of a leaf, or buried in a pool among the rocks. Some of the noblest Christians are to be found in quiet spheres of which the world knows nothing ; and some of the highest work has been done for our Lord in obscure villages, or in lands out of the range of tours and trades. Besides this, the selection of Galilee as the earliest scene of our Lord's ministry was an indication of its nature. It was a tacit rebuke to the carnal expectations current among the people concerning their Messiah ; and, in giving an opportunity to the degraded and despised provincials, it showed that he had come " to seek and save that which was lost." Several significant facts respecting his ministry are suggested by the text, namely—

I. THIS MINISTRY FOLLOWED UPON A TIME OF TERRIBLE TEMPTATION. The verse immediately preceding this puts in vivid contrast temptation in solitude and ministry in public. Loneliness of spirit is a fit preparation for publicity of life ; and our Lord, who was in all points made like unto his brethren, deigned to share this experience. Joseph was a solitary prisoner before he became a ruling prince. Moses passed from the splendours of Egypt to the quietude of Midian before he became a leader and lawgiver. David was a persecuted exile before he was ready for enthronement. Paul was three years in Arabia before he was the apostle to the Gentiles. Our Lord spoke of such inward preparation for outward work when he said to his disciples, " What I tell you in darkness, that speak ye in light ; and what ye hear in the ear, that preach ye upon the housetops." Public work is only safe when preceded by private prayer. True teaching can only come from those who are first taught of God. Without personal experience of inward struggles and victories, we shall never speak to others with power or sympathy. But if we would get the benefit of solitude, if we would achieve victory over self and sin in our own hour of temptation, we must be like our Lord, who was baptized before he was tempted, who was filled with the Holy Spirit before he fought with the evil spirit. Then out of such an experience we can speak lovingly and helpfully to others.

II. THIS MINISTRY SUCCEEDED THE SILENCING OF JOHN. Our text very pointedly suggests that the public appearance of the Lord occurred immediately after the ending and completion of the Baptist's work. The words are significant: "After that John was cast into prison, Jesus came." God will never let his work fall to the ground. If one noble witness to the truth is removed, another springs up in his place. If persecution silences one voice, another at once takes up the testimony. So when the disciples of John were most helpless and disheartened, and were beginning to scatter, suddenly the Lord of life stepped down into their midst, and rallying them round about himself, proved that he could do far more towards the victory than any fabled Achilles among his Greeks. Therefore let us reflect that when we or our fellow-workers fail or are removed, God can raise up others to accomplish his purpose ; and let us cheer ourselves with the thought that when heart and flesh fail he himself will appear amongst us. It was "when John was cast into prison" that "Jesus came."

III. THIS MINISTRY STRUCK THE KEY-NOTE OF MERCY. We must remember that our Lord came forth amongst the people as one humanly and divinely great, endued with power beyond all others. Yet by that wonderful self-restraint which always characterized him (Matt. xxvi. 53 ; John xviii. 36) he brought no immediate retribution on those who were foes both of God and man. Herod, for example, by his imprisonment of John, had done a wrong against conscience and against God, as well as against that faithful servant of the Most High. But Christ raised no revolt against the tyrant, which would have hurled him from the throne he desecrated ; nor did he threaten or curse him and his followers. He came preaching "the gospel," proclaiming the glad tidings, calling upon all—ay, even Herod himself—to repent and believe, and so receive salvation. This was the key-note of his ministry, and was heard throughout it, even to its last chord ; for on the cross he prayed, "Father, forgive them ; for they know not what they do."

IV. THIS MINISTRY PROCLAIMED THE ESTABLISHMENT OF A KINGDOM. "The time is fulfilled, and the kingdom of God is at hand." The long waiting for deliverance was over. God, in the person of his Son, had come to establish a kingdom, in which the Divine love and power and will would be revealed as never before. The forerunner had been making the way straight, and now the King had come and was ready to rule over all who would welcome him. This kingliness of Christ is one of the special characteristics of the revelation given to us through Mark. Matthew presents the Messiah who fulfilled ancient predictions ; Luke describes the Son of man in his pitifulness and graciousness ; John proclaims the Divine Word, who was in the beginning with God, and who himself was God ; but Mark, instructed possibly by Peter, who dwells so much on the kingdom in his Epistles, begins by announcing "the kingdom of God is at hand." Christ shall reign for ever, over all nations and kindreds and tongues ; and each one of us is invited to bow to his sceptre and submit ourselves to his gracious rule, that ours may be the bliss of those who shouted "Hosanna!" and not the curse of those who cried "Crucify him!" To enter that kingdom we are called upon to "repent and believe the gospel ;" to change our minds and ways, to turn from sin to God, from self to Christ, and to trust and follow him in whom the glad tidings are incarnate.—A. R.

Vers. 16, 17.—*Christ's call to busy men.* Simon and Andrew were just beginning their day's work by casting their net into the sea, and at that critical moment, when, if ever, delay would seem excusable, Christ called them to follow him. But he had already won their hearts, and they were only waiting for such a summons to come, "and straitway they forsook their nets, and followed him." In their daily work these fishermen had acquired devotion, patience, and enterprise, which were now to be consecrated to nobler service, when, as fishers of men, they would gather spoil from the restless, dreary sea of human life. A call coming to men in the midst of their daily business reminds us of the following truths :—

I. THAT HONEST WORK FITS FOR HIGHER DUTIES. Those who are indolent in the world are not of great use in the Church. If men are not fit for ordinary work, they seldom are fit for Christ's service. Our Lord does not call the indolent æsthetes, who would gaze on a lily for hours in a languid rapture, but he summons men with capacity, self-rule, vigour, and tact. God has ever chosen such. If he would have a lawgiver, he calls one who is as diligent among the sheepfolds in Midian as he had been in the schools of Egypt. If he would tell the world of his future kingdom, he inspires a statesman like Daniel, who already has upon him the cares of a great empire. If he would speak burning words to his people, he summons to his service the herdman who drives his cattle home in the gloaming down the hillside of Tekoa. So here, Christ calls Matthew from the receipt of custom, and these four fishers from their boats. In the daily plod, in the monotonous round of life, above the whirr of human traffic, a voice speaks, saying, "Come ye after me."

II. THAT DIGNITY AND BLESSING ARE TO BE FOUND IN DAILY TOIL. Toil, once a curse, has been transformed by Christ Jesus into work which is a source of blessing to the world. In nature we can only regain a wilderness to order and beauty by unremitting toil; and only by long labour do we repossess ourselves of rule. The exquisite flowers in the hothouse are signs of human skill as well as of God's gift. The rich harvest-fields, which whisper of abundance, are nature's response to work. Wherever idleness is supreme, fertile lands become the lairs of wild beasts, and man, who was appointed to regal right, starves amid profusion. Besides, work is good for society, as it was good for those disciples to be thrown together so as to share perils and successes, for thus mutual love and confidence arose. Society is most compact and stable when built upon a foundation of industry—every class recognizing its dependence on another, as stones in the living temple. That home is the happiest, too, in which self-indulgence is a stranger, and where mutual sympathy is felt in the efforts of all.

III. THAT IN ORDINARY OCCUPATIONS WE MAY REALIZE THE PRESENCE OF CHRIST. His sympathy with the busy none can question. He himself spent more time in ordinary work than in public teaching. He gave his presence to his disciples (both before his resurrection and after it) when they were on the lake working for a living. Still he is to be found, not in the dreams of the mystics or in the cell of the hermit, so much as in the heart of him who must be busy with the world's work and yet prays to be free from its spirit. Conscious of his nearness, we shall not do our work carelessly; we shall not lower the standard set before us in his Word; we shall never shrink from rebuking wrong-doing, even when it is customary; and there will be constant joy within our hearts amidst all turmoil, so that we can say, "I will bless the Lord at all times: his praise shall continually be in my mouth." Beware of going steadily on with work without any thought of Christ, as if self was your king and the world your home. You may prosper so greatly that others will envy your skill and "good luck;" but the day of reckoning will surely come; the law of retribution will not sleep. Reaping only what you have sown, your largest gain will prove your deepest loss.

IV. THAT CHRIST IS CALLING ALL TO LOFTIER SERVICE. It is necessary to labour for the supply of physical wants, but there are other and higher responsibilities resting upon us as parents, employers, teachers, and friends. With wonderful condescension our Lord describes the nature of his service, by figures drawn from the scenes with which his hearers were most familiar. If people followed him for the sake of the bread which perisheth, he spoke to them of the "Bread of life;" and if a woman was drawing water at the well, he spoke to her of "living water." He led the Magians to him by "a star;" and taught these fishermen by their fishing, telling them that hereafter they should "catch men," not, indeed, for death, but for life. This was a beautiful image for all time. The sea represents the wide world, which seems dark and deep as we stand on the fringe of its mystery, wonderingly. The fish are emblematic of those lost to the sight of some in the higher world, as they wander amid oozy weeds and treacherous rocks. The net pictures the truths and warnings of the gospel, which lay hold on men, and, gathering them together, raise them into a new element, in which they can only live when they have a new life. As "fishers of men," we want patience and hope, for we know little or nothing of the result of the toil as yet. We only know that the net is cast, but the draught is not yet counted upon the shore. It is ours to "mend" the net, to have it well in hand, to cast it in a likely place, and then to wait and watch and pray. Quote Keble's hymn beginning—

> "The livelong night we've toiled in vain ;
> But at thy gracious word
> I will let down the net again :
> Do thou thy will, O Lord."

A. R.

Ver. 29.—*The home and the synagogue.* This passage, which gives an account of a sabbath spent in Capernaum, shows us the manner in which many unmentioned sabbaths were spent by our Lord and his disciples. Whithersoever Jesus went we should follow him, translating into modern habits the principles which underlay his actions. Consider—

I. THE SYNAGOGUE WHICH JESUS ENTERED. Its worship, unlike that of the temple, was not specially ordained by the Mosaic code. It was the outcome of earlier and more habitual devotions, to which the tents of the patriarchs had not been strangers. Side by side with the ornate, national ritual that enshrined the spiritual truths which, as the Epistle to the Hebrews tells us, were fulfilled in the work of Jesus Christ, this more homely worship continued. Its form sometimes varied, yet it constantly ministered to the religious instruction of the people, and expressed their devotional feeling. In such services our Lord from his childhood took part, and his apostles used them for the propagation of Christian truth amongst their fellow-countrymen. As the synagogue represented the abiding religious worship of the people, we will consider what it was to our Lord and his disciples. 1. *It was a place of worship.* It is noteworthy that, so far as we know, Jesus Christ never neglected the ordinary worship in which the people united. If any might have found an excuse for doing so, it certainly was he. Self-sufficient in the fulness of his Divine life, he required no help from such extraneous means. With his spiritual insight he could see the formalism and unreality of many about him, and knew the terrible extent to which false teaching misrepresented the character and the ways of God. But he did not turn from the synagogue with contempt, nor did he make the place a scene of theological strife. He himself, the Sinless One, was present there amongst a sinful people, and he devoutly joined with them in prayer and praise. The remembrance of this should serve as a rebuke to those who, in our day, neglect the sanctuary. Their spirituality may be such that they can meditate profitably in their home or in the fields; their intelligence may be so great that no human teacher can help them; yet they do not surely compare with him who was the wisest Teacher and lived the loftiest life the world has ever known, and yet went into the synagogue every sabbath day, "as his custom was." 2. *It was a place for teaching.* During the service of the synagogue an opportunity was given to any worshipper present to speak a few words on the interpretation of the Scriptures (Acts xiii. 15). Of this liberty the apostles often availed themselves. In this they followed their Lord. It is stated in ver. 21 that Jesus "taught" on this sabbath, and we do not wonder that the people "were astonished at his teaching." He showed the spiritual significance of the events in Old Testament history, which were too often merely subjects of national boasting. He drew his illustrations, not from rabbinical books, but from the lake and the fields, from the housewife's employments and the merchant's trading. And as he spoke the weary found rest, the eager seekers had a revelation of God, the anxious lost their burdens, and a hush came over the assembly as if the peace of heaven was brooding there. 3. *It was a place of comfort.* Help and deliverance came even to the poor demoniac, whose obscene ravings and hideous shrieks disturbed the worship and, interrupted the teaching that day. He found that the synagogue was "the house of God and the gate of heaven" to his enslaved spirit. So has many a man, possessed by sin, had deliverance wrought for him where Jesus is. The disciples also knew that comfort was to be found in worship. Hence Simon Peter was there, although he had illness at home such as would detain many a Christian from public worship. What to some would be an excuse was to him a call to the house of God, as the place of rest for anxious hearts. There songs of praise may lift us up as on angels' wings, and Christian teaching may prove as the Bread of life to our hungering hearts.

II. THE HOME WHICH JESUS BLESSED — "the house of Simon and Andrew."

These two brethren appear to have removed from Bethsaida, possibly because of marriage connection with the place or for their convenience as fishermen. 1. *It was a home with ordinary associations.* There was nothing special or distinctive about it or about others which our Lord frequented, and in which he did some of his mightiest deeds and spoke some of his most weighty words. His presence gave sanctity to domestic associations from the time of his first miracle (John ii. 2) to the hour when he made himself known in the home of Emmaus (Luke xxiv. 29). We are not to sever ourselves from them—even Peter did not (ver. 30; 1 Cor. ix. 5)—but should rather seek to recognize and welcome Jesus amidst them. It is a happy thing when there is family peace and love such as seem to have prevailed in this home. A "wife's mother" would occupy a difficult and delicate position, but such had been her wisdom and gentleness, her sympathy and constancy, that she had now the love of all, and therefore, directly Jesus entered the home, her illness and need of help prompted the urgent and united prayer he so gladly answered. 2. *It was a home in lowly life.* A fisherman's house—not the stately palace of a Herod. In contrast with our Lord's humility and graciousness, how paltry seems the ambition of those who would make any sacrifice to get a stately establishment or to push their way into higher social circles! A palace often hides from the world aching hearts and wasted lives, while a cottage may be the home where love and peace are constant, because Jesus is in the midst. 3. *It was a home significant of higher fellowship.* The Christian Church sprang rather from the homes of the people than from the temple at Jerusalem. If it had originated in the temple, sacramentalism would have found more justification than it does in the New Testament. But the temple was not frequented by the great Teacher to the extent we might have expected. His Church met in the homes of Capernaum and Bethany. The relations between his disciples were to be those of brothers and sisters, bound together, not by law, but by love. Let us, then, try to make the Church a home, and thence the voice of our gracious Master will speak with effectual power to a weary world, saying, "Come unto me, all ye that labour and are heavy laden, and I will give you rest."—A. R.

Vers. 32, 33.—*Christ the Healer.* The healing of Peter's wife's mother, following on the cure of the demoniac in the synagogue, aroused the whole city of Capernaum. Believing that what this good Physician could do for one he could do for all, crowds of suppliants gathered around our Lord on the evening of the sabbath day. In this incident we see—

I. THE GRACIOUSNESS OF THE SAVIOUR. 1. *His accessibility.* Whether in the synagogue or in the house, whether in the glow of noonday or in the cool of eventide, he was always ready to meet a case of need where there was faith and expectancy. He was not like a popular physician, with whom the patient makes a previous appointment, in whose ante-chamber he waits till exhausted, and whose fee cripples his means. At any time, "without money and without price," Christ would heal the sick. He is "the same yesterday, to-day, and for ever." Even though the shadows of life's evening are falling around the sin-sick soul, it is not too late to offer the prayer, "Jesus, Master, have mercy upon me!" 2. *His consideration.* His varied methods of cure showed his readiness to meet the special circumstances of each. Thus, he took Peter's wife's mother "by the hand," perhaps because she was delirious and could not understand his words, or because she was weak and needed the confidence which that expectant hand-grasp would give. Similarly, he touched the eyes of the blind, and his disciples took the cripple by the hand (Acts iii. 7). Christ still adapts himself to men's peculiar necessities. To some a word of promise inspires hope, in others a word of warning awakens thought. A sermon may arouse to penitence, a mother's love may win to Christ, a grief may make serious, or a joy may bring a man on his knees in thankfulness. Happy is it when, in all of these or in any of these, Christ appears to the soul. 3. *His sympathy.* This was of the essence of his work. Matthew here appropriately applies to him the words of the prophet, "Himself took our infirmities and bare our sicknesses;" by which we understand that there was nothing perfunctory or mechanical in his healing work. He *felt* every case, and came in living contact with the soul he cured. His touch was not merely physical, it was an outgoing of soul. Hence he "sighed" when he cured the blind; he "felt virtue" going out of the hem of his garment; he "wept" and "groaned" at the grave of Lazarus;

and all this was not because the effort was great, but because the effort was needed. In harmony with this we read in ver. 41 that, when the leper came, Jesus being "moved with compassion, put forth his hand, and touched him." He did this although he knew that it involved him in ceremonial defilement; but he was willing to make the leper clean, even by contracting uncleanness himself. In that we have a sign of what St. Paul meant when he said, "He was made sin for us, who knew no sin, that we might be made the righteousness of God in him."

II. THE EAGERNESS OF THE SUPPLIANTS. She who was ill of fever in Peter's house could not plead for herself, and therefore others interceded for her, and not in vain. Encouraged by this, parents brought their children, sons their mothers, and "they brought unto him all that were diseased." 1. *Some were physically diseased.* Laid aside from activity, a burden instead of a support to others, suffering pain which made days and nights wearisome, invalids would be thankful to those who bore them in their strong arms to Jesus' feet. We may do the like for our sufferers, and if restoration to health is not given, serenity of heart will be. The voice of Christ will be heard amidst the storm of their trouble, saying, "It is I; be not afraid." Blessed by his presence, if they recover they will go back to the world as those who have been on the borders of heaven, or if they enter the dark valley, he will fulfil the promise, "I will come again, and receive you to myself." 2. *Some had spiritual disorders.* It was sin which lay at the root of all suffering. Christ came to put it away by the sacrifice of himself. By his removal of the effects he gave a sign of the removal of the cause. If we have those dear to us who are tied and bound by the chain of their sins, let us bring them to Jesus, earnestly, tenderly, patiently, hopefully. Those who through drink seem demon-possessed, those feverish with anxiety, those so morally stained that men of good repute avoid them as though they were leprous,—may all find hope and help in Christ. 3. *Some felt their own need of blessing.* They did not wait for others to bring them. The leper, for example, of his own accord came kneeling to Jesus, feeling that he could make him clean. The Law could only separate the leper from others and pronounce him clean after restoration; but Christ had purifying power, such as the Law never had. Similarly now, outward restrictions may check wrong-doing; the moral influence of friends may restrain us, and vows and resolves may prove of service; but the heart is only turned from sin when God answers the prayer, "Create within me a clean heart." It is just short of that acknowledgment and cry that many halt, though others have done for them all that they can; and Jesus waits for faith and prayer that he may say, "I will; be thou clean."—A. R.

Vers. 1—8.—*Glad tidings.* I. THEY ARE THE FULFILMENT OF LONG HOPES. Human nature is ideal; it is a creature of wishes and of hopes, and made for enjoyment. The love of the living God is at the root of all our instincts. Faith is our expression of the sense of this. It begets hope amidst suffering and sorrow, sustains the soul in patience. God seeking man, man in turn seeking God,—this is the secret life of Scripture and of history. History is sacred because it is the reflection of the vast spiritual struggle of man to apprehend God, of God to apprehend his creature. "I will not let thee go except thou bless me!" is the cry of man. "I am found of them that seek me!" is the answer of God.

II. HOPE DIES DOWN IN SIN AND MISERY, AND CAN ONLY BE REMOVED IN REPENTANCE. Pessimism and despondence spring from unfaithfulness. Men are not living the life which *begets* hope. Palestine was depressed, conquered and unhappy. John proposes no political change, but a moral change. Man can endure outward ills, and seek for their removal, if the hearts are only happy. The inward emancipation, the "remission of sins," is what we all need. No other "franchise" will really do much for us without this. In order to have the kingdom of God, there must be an energy in the soul to grasp it. The nerveless hand cannot raise the food to the lips. "In order to possess God, we must have something that is capable of possessing God." The *possibility* of repentance is itself glad tidings, virtually including all others.

III. SERIOUSNESS AND SOLEMNITY THE PROPER MOOD OF EXPECTATION. 1. This typified in the ascetic character of the Baptist. Thought and self-denial, prayer and fasting, low living and lofty aspiration,—this is the ground from which the fairest flowers of joy spring. Not upon any soil barren of thought are they found. 2. In the rite of baptism. It expressed the new will of the people—decision, renunciation of the old, the putting on of the white dress of purity in preparation for the Bridegroom. The confession of sin and the mercy of God are coincident. 3. In the attitude of reverent waiting. A mighty One is at hand. The mission of the Baptist was in itself incomplete. The symbolism of his apparel and way of life had a significance behind it. So had the outward baptism of water. To this mood the gospel would ever bring us. Revelation is inexhaustible. The secrets of history in the nation and the individual have not been all told. Every day is a new day, every morrow will bring its gladness to the soul that believes.—J.

Vers. 9—13.—*The consecration of Jesus.* I. THE GOOD OF CUSTOM. Honoured by his submission to baptism. This is an example. Custom is the sacred link between past and present. Old customs, sacred rites, should be kept up; only abandoned when they no longer teach truth, but more falsehood than truth. Rebellion against custom for rebellion's sake is vicious individualism. Compliance with the beauty of order is the mark of a loyal and loving spirit.

II. THE SYMBOL IS PRECIOUS, NOT FOR ITS FORM, BUT ITS CONTENTS. We speak of a " beautiful word," but it is the thought conveyed by it that shines. So of a " sacred rite ;" but the one sacred thing is the spiritual belief signified, the real union of the soul with God. Upon the meek spirit the gentleness of Heaven descends. The " meekness and gentleness " of Christ is the grace of the lowly and obedient heart. The delight of God is in those human traits which resemble and reflect Jesus.

III. TRIAL FOLLOWS CONSECRATION. The Spirit of God is given to prepare for service ; and the call to this is not long delayed. All trial is for good. There is no needless torment of the spirit in God's school. Only in conflict do we really learn reality.

> "When the fight begins within himself,
> A man's worth something. God stoops o'er his head,
> Satan looks up between his feet. Both try.
> He's left himself in the middle; the soul wakes
> And grows. Prolong that battle through his life!
> Never leave growing till the life to come!"

Solitude is a necessary element in trial. (See Robertson's sermon on the ' Loneliness of Christ.') Life is a drama on which angels and demons look with intensest interest. Evil is ever near ; succour never far off.—J.

Vers. 16—20.—*Call of disciples.* I. CALLING MEANS SEPARATION. We cannot prove any calling without separation. The merchant must separate himself from the easy-chair and the book, the student from society, the soldier from home. One main object is enough for most men. Few can properly pursue the ministry and business at the same time.

II. THE CALLING IMPLIES A CALLER. Not our fancy, whim, passion, but Divine will. To some that will is made known clearly and directly; they cannot mistake. To some not so directly. But need any mistake, if they make it a rule to be ever fulfilling the duty of the moment? It is a mistake to think too much on the point. True thought is God realizing himself in us. True action is God willing to do in and through us. Never resist a pure impulse; never turn from a voice that speaks to what is disinterested in you.

III. TO TAKE TO A HIGHER WAY OF LIFE ALWAYS MEANS THE GIVING UP OF A LOWER. God confounds our avarice by his generosity. We cling to all we can hold; want to keep incompatible things—to be learned but not poor; to have as much of the world as possible, yet not be worldly ; to live in self-indulgence, yet earn the reputation of saints. But God teaches us that our surrenders are no less profitable than our seeming gains. The provincial fisher becomes the apostle to the world. The things that are unseen are more than all that are seen.—J.

Vers. 21—28.—*Soul-emancipation.* I. BONDAGE OF BODY AND SOUL OUR NATURAL CONDITION. We are fettered and distressed in our fetters. Disease is a bond ; habitual ideas of one kind or another are bonds to every man. The mystery of evil possession we cannot fathom; what we *know* is that our imagination is a tyrant. "Fixed ideas" harshly govern us, irritate our passions. We long for freedom, yet cannot shake them off.

II. THIS RESTRAINT MUST BE PUT AN END TO BY DIVINE POWER. A tyrannous idea of sin or sorrow will only yield to a larger and stronger idea—to a new fact. A bad temper only to be driven out by the "expulsive force of a new affection." All conversion means this. The darkness is the absence of light, and the tyranny of dark beings is the absence of light in the soul. When we see and believe that the living God means our freedom by the truth, the fetters of the mind fall away. What was real in one way in connection with the local personal activity of Jesus, is universally true of the activity of God in the soul. Truth is one in all its forms: the truths of science, of morals, of art, of health. Reverently let us recognize all as works of God Incarnate, having authority over unclean spirits.—J.

Vers. 29—34.—*The progress of health.* I. IT IS IDENTICAL WITH THE PROGRESS OF CHRISTIANITY. For Christianity is the embodiment of the wisdom of the physician, the power of the Creator, the compassion of the God. These wonders are really revelations of law. Were the will of God the only factor in the case, we could hardly imagine how suffering could be. But there is our will also. The truth, so far as we may conjecture, seems to be that in the nature of things evil *cannot* be as a rule overcome without the co-operation of the individual free-will. On the other hand, without the operation of the living love of God, any removal of ill seems inconceivable.

II. CHRISTIANITY WILL NOT ADMIT ANY QUESTIONABLE AID IN THIS WORK. No recognition of evil powers, of compliments or testimonials from them. Christian work is vitiated when it courts bad alliances. Better to go on single-handed than in fellowship with those whose aims are not ours. One voice out of time spoils the chorus. One detected interest paralyzes the nerve of benevolent enterprise. Suffer not the demon of policy to speak in our councils.—J.

Vers. 40—45.—*The leper.* I. FOR THE WORST EVILS THERE IS A REMEDY. If not always in the physical, yet ever in the spiritual sphere. They are cured in effect when they are balanced by some weight of good in the soul.

II. IT IS HALF-WAY TO THE REMEDY TO KNOW WHERE IT LIES. The leper knew, and was not ashamed to seek it at the right quarter. Many know who or what will do them good, but are too proud to ask or ashamed to own their need.

III. CHRIST IS THE ALL-HELPFUL ONE. This is ever the representation of him. He wills, God wills, our recovery and our health. Do we then will it? It is an essential condition that we should.

IV. TRUE BENEVOLENCE AND TRUE GRATITUDE ARE UNOSTENTATIOUS. Christ is the example of the former; it is questionable whether the leper is the true type of the latter. He will not obey the word of his Deliverer. He cannot suppress the desire to talk. To prate about others' goodness may really spring from egotistic motives. It is pleasant to be the hero of a tale. Though the leper's conduct is not to be seriously blamed, it illustrates a certain frivolity of mind. And the lesson is taught that "still waters run deep," and thankfulness is best cultivated in silence.—J.

Vers. 1—8.—*The beginning of the gospel of Jesus Christ.* "The gospel" is a revelation of the Divine love; the "beginning" of it is therefore hidden in the depths of the eternal love of God. The whole gospel was buried, the end from the beginning, in the Divine purpose; and it was contained seminally in the first promise. Every Divine promise is equal to the event. But the manifestation of the gospel in time, or the historic "beginning of the gospel," is the theme of this prologue. Thought of within the limits of history, the "beginning" is a preparation. The messenger is sent to "prepare the way of the Lord." This preparation is twofold—historical and personal.

I. THE HISTORICAL PREPARATION IS A PREPARATION FOR THE ANNOUNCEMENT OF THE GOSPEL. The historic preparation must be traced from the moment when the first gentle word of promise mingled, half unheard, with the first words of judgment and condemnation, forwards to that moment in which "the time" was "fulfilled," and the word was heard, "The kingdom of God is at hand. Repent, and believe in the gospel."

The true disciple, always a listener and a learner, whose eyes are not holden, and who is not "slow of heart to believe," will gladly learn that "from Moses and from all the prophets, the things concerning" his Lord may be "interpreted;" and he will search "in all the Scriptures" for the hidden or open references to him. The preparation by the prophets was not the mere utterance of the word, "Make ye ready the way of the Lord, make his paths straight." Their denunciations of sin, their preaching of righteousness, their promises of forgiveness to a repentant Israel, their assurances of a restored prosperity rising into the delineation of a kingdom of holiness and peace, were elements of preparation. And the unique history of the holy nation, "beginning at Moses," and the concurrent histories of surrounding kingdoms, were parts of the same great preparation. And even before Moses, Abraham, through all the gloomy mist and the confusion of wild times, saw a day of peace and gladness and health, and, with largeness of heart and noble unselfishness, "rejoiced to see it," though he knew his sun would long have set ere that bright day arose. Yea, "he saw it and was glad," and by his testimomy against idolatry, by his avowal of the one true and living God, and by his sacrifice and obedience, he helped to "prepare the way," as did every seer and believer and righteous man, each in his measure, as far back as Abel. Thus "all the prophets and the Law prophesied until John," in whom the historic preparation was completed. He, than whom there had not "arisen a greater," cried, "Repent ye ; for the kingdom of heaven is at hand." So we humbly trace the Divine preparation by means of prophets and seers and righteous men, and also by a Divine overruling of the works of the wicked. The voice of the herald being ever sounded, if not ever heard, "Prepare ye the way of the Lord." But the gospel, which came to men by a prepared way, must be received by men in a prepared spirit.

II. THE PERSONAL PREPARATION IS A PREPARATION FOR THE RECEPTION OF THE GOSPEL. The external, historical preparation terminated in a word, a cry, a gracious preaching, "the voice of one" to whom "the Word of God came." Amid the dreary waste of the wilderness, where the signs of natural convulsion typified the needed moral upheaving, this man, rugged in speech as in dress, of few but earnest words, his tongue a burning flame, his fingers wetted for baptizing with the cooling waters of the brook, lifted up his voice and cried aloud his one message. It was a clear and definite cry, contained in the one word, "Repent." This was his one great demand of the ungodly around him. It is the one word now to be uttered in the hearing of all who have not entered the heavenly kingdom. It is the word which follows the awakening judgment, and precedes the comforting gospel. 1. Repentance, a change of mind leading to a change of life, follows upon reflection, and the deep Spirit-wrought conviction of the sinfulness and wrong of the past. St. Paul describes it as "toward God." No two words could better describe it. If the heart, the thoughts, the steps, have been toward evil, in repentance they turn "toward God." 2. Repentance is declared by confession of sins, a voluntary acknowledgment that the deeds of the past life have been evil. Of that past it is an open repudiation; it is a self-condemnation. 3. Repentance is attested by the beginning of a new life, by "the fruit worthy of repentance." 4. Repentance is sealed in baptism. This is a profession, a promise and pledge, of entering upon a new path. It is also the authorized seal and surety or earnest of the blessing the repentant one seeks. It is not that blessing, but it is the pledge and seal of it. Baptism is "unto repentance;" repentance is "unto remission of sins." When baptism is the true sign of the one, it is the certain pledge of the other; but it is not to be confounded with either, nor with the baptism of the Holy Spirit, which a mightier One will impart. Baptism does not bestow remission of sins or the baptism of fire, but it pledges the bestowment of both. So does John "prepare the way" for his Lord. (1) Let every one who is living in sin hear the authoritative cry, "Repent ye ;" and know that if the fire of the Spirit burn not up repented sins as chaff, it will burn into the conscience with its unquenchable flame. (2) And let every truly repentant one know that the outer sign is the indubitable pledge of admission into "the kingdom of God," and of participation in all the blessings of that kingdom. It is the seal of the Christian covenant. Then in him the gospel has had its true beginning. (3) The next duty for the repentant one, for which he by repentance is truly prepared, is to "believe the gospel," when he shall be baptized "with the Holy Ghost." But for this John must give place to Jesus, for whom he prepares the way in the hearts of his people. The preparation then, without and within, is complete. This is the true "beginning of the gospel of Jesus Christ." It is begun historically; it is begun personally.—G.

Vers. 9—13.—*The official preparation.* "The beginning of the gospel of Jesus Christ" embraces yet another element. The preparation of "the way" of the Lord is followed by the preparation of the Lord himself. This we must name — *The preparation of the Messiah, the Christ.*

I. The first step in this preparation is THE ASSUMPTION OF THE HUMAN NATURE. "The Word became flesh." "It behoved him," who "took hold of the seed of Abraham," with a view to raise it up, "to be made like unto" them whom he would call "his brethren." And "since they are sharers of flesh and blood, he also himself in like manner partook of the same." Never will the world exhaust the mystery of the Incarnation. No event in human history can equal the grandeur or significance of this. "He was made man" is a greater truth than "he suffered and was buried." It was an infinitely greater condescension to become man than to pass through the lowly shades of human history. The humble home, the toilsome endurance, the poverty, the suffering,—all fall below "Jesus was born in Bethlehem." This event is the most stupendous of all events in the history of the human race.

II. The second step in this preparation is THE PASSING THROUGH THE LOWLY CONDITIONS OF THE HUMAN LIFE. The words of the ninth verse turn our thoughts back to silent days of preparation going forward in the house of the carpenter at Nazareth of Galilee, wherein he passed into and passed through and honoured all the stages of human life from infancy to manhood, and where he sanctified the condition of helpless weakness, of ignorance, of submission, of toil, and of honest labour; sanctified the home and the workshop, and the relationships and intercourse of common village life; exalted the lowly lot, and thereby every lot. This was another element of that likeness to "his brethren" which it behoved him to assume. During this period the glory of his person was shrouded. Men had not yet been permitted to behold "the glory as of the only begotten from the Father," in which he was unlike his brethren. Yet he dwelt among men, the Incarnate Word, "full of grace and truth," though not yet "made manifest to Israel." In that tabernacle the true Shechinah was hidden. "He was in the world, and the world knew him not." A few who, with Simeon, "were looking for the redemption of Jerusalem," by prophetic intuition, saw in him the salvation "prepared before the face of all people; a light for revelation to the Gentiles, and the glory of thy people Israel." In Nazareth "he was subject unto" father and mother, the honoured mother keeping "all the sayings in her heart" that concerned him.

III. A third step in this preparation is THE SUBMITTING TO ALL THE ORDINANCES OF RIGHTEOUSNESS. Righteousness does not consist in an attendance upon ordinances, but consists not without it. John, who probably knew the character of Jesus better than any saving only Mary, hesitates when he presents himself for baptism; he even "hinders him" with the words, "'I have need to be baptized of thee,' so much better art thou, so much higher; and yet 'comest thou to me?'" He who though "separated from sinners," had daily mingled with them; who had submitted to every ordinance of the Lord for man's sake, "was circumcised the eighth day," was presented in the temple, that they might "do concerning him after the custom of the Law;" who at twelve years of age, and doubtless in succeeding years, "went up after the custom of the feast," would now "fulfil" this "righteousness" also. He passed through all in fellowship with the sinful, and for sinful ones, paying his tribute of duteous attendance on the Divine ordinance, leaving here "an example" that we should do as he had done. As one has said, "He who now comes to this baptism is not a sinner, but a righteous man, who needs neither repentance nor pardon. It is he who for us fulfils all righteousness, who, born of a woman and made under the Law which was given to the unrighteous, has already hitherto observed and performed all the commandments of the Lord to Israel, *and for that very reason* now subjects himself to that baptism which was ordained of God as the concluding commandment of the old covenant, through which is the transition to the new."[1]

IV. The fourth step in this preparation is THE PUBLIC AND OFFICIAL DESIGNATION OF

---

[1] Stier, 'Words of the Lord Jesus,' vol. i. p. 30.

MESSIAH. Yes, truly the transition; for now is the manifestation to Israel to be made, and the open, authoritative designation of him "who from the foundation of the world" had been in Heaven's counsels designated. When so suitable a time as when fulfilling all righteousness? Then, "coming up out of the water, he"—and, as we learn from St. John, the Baptist also—"saw the heavens rent asunder, and the Spirit as a dove descending upon him;" while a voice from heaven proclaims to him, and proclaims through him to all, "Thou art my beloved Son." Now is "Jesus of Nazareth anointed with the Holy Ghost and with power," officially called and set apart. Now the mystery of the Divine Name, in the historical development to the world of the triunity of the Godhead, is more fully than ever before disclosed. John, having seen, bears his "witness that this is the Son of God." Presently his works also will bear witness of him, that the Father hath sent him.

V. But meanwhile a yet further step in this preparation is needed. "To this end was the Son of God manifested, that he might destroy the works of the devil." Therefore must he be TEMPTED OF THE DEVIL. The devil is man's great adversary, Satan. All evil embodies itself in him. The Redeemer of men must taste—drink—this bitter cup; to a pure nature perhaps of all the bitterest. Full forty days he must needs fast in the wilderness. Oh, the buffetings of those days, of which three examples stand out prominently before us; when, lo! he is so bowed down that angels are sent to "minister to him." Then, "having been made perfect, he became unto all them that obey him the Author of eternal salvation."

From all may be learnt: 1. The perfectness of his human nature, with its experiences, its sympathy, and its example. 2. His perfect Divine nature. 3. His perfect fitness to be the Mediator, the Comforter, the Saviour of the world.—G.

Vers. 14—20.—*The fishers of men.* An interval of time elapses, the incidents of which, momentous in the great history, are recorded in the other Gospels, *e.g.* John's testimony to the Lamb of God (John i. 19—34), the gathering of the first disciples (John i. 35—51), the marriage at Cana (John ii. 1—12), the cleansing of the temple (John ii. 13—25), the conversation with Nicodemus (John iii. 1—21). "Now after that John was delivered up, Jesus came into Galilee, preaching the gospel of God, and saying, The time is fulfilled, and the kingdom of God is at hand: repent ye, and believe in the gospel." Truly a "beginning" is made. "All things are now ready;" and the Master himself cries aloud with his own voice, "Come." Oh, wondrous grace! The Divine call to the Divine feast! God calling men to himself, to receive mercy, blessing, life! Ever since and to the end will both "the Spirit and the bride say, Come." O Israel, "if thou hadst known in this day, even thou!" Simon and Andrew, James and John, already called to be disciples, but still pursuing, as should every disciple, their daily industry, are now called to be apostles, to forsake home, father, nets, avocations, and gain, to follow the young Rabbi with obedient steps and imitative carefulness, that he may "make" them "to become" (without which making of the Master none can become) "fishers of men." In this incident may be seen: 1. The greatness of this calling. 2. Its imperative demand. 3. An illustrious example of obedience.

I. THE GREATNESS OF THIS CALLING is not to be exaggerated. To "catch men"—by no trick, but by the Word of the Lord and by the aid of the Lord, who brings fishes to the nets of toilers on the sea—is to bring them up out of the deep wide sea, the world, into Christ's net, the Church, that they proving good may be gathered into vessels. It is to draw men from evil, to teach them heavenly truth, soul-renewing and saving truth, to guide them into the paths of peace, to encourage and help them in the maintenance of righteousness, to bind in bonds of brotherhood, to incite to holy charity, to build them up in knowledge and doctrine, and so to fit them for useful service on earth and for the felicities of the heavenly life on high. Oh, sacred calling! How immeasurably above all callings! How honourable the work! How honoured the men!—honoured, not by the distinctions that may be gained, but by the work itself. This toil is heavenly, often most heavenly when most hard, most fruitful when most despised and apparently least successful, as was that of the great Master.

II. For all time, and for the instruction of all apostles and servants who must, "for the kingdom of God's sake," forsake all and follow him, this simple incident, told in half a score lines, is ample. THE IMPERATIVE DEMAND is heard in the deep conscience, in the warm, pitiful sympathy of the obedient disciple, ready to lay down life and all for the Master's sake and in his cause; it is a call coming, not from the lips, but from the wretched, sinful lives of the wicked in the world around, or from the wilds of heathen darkness, superstition, and loss afar off; from the Church, that is quick to discern the signs of fitness, tender in feeling the claims of the needy, and watchful to behold the favouring conjunction of circumstances.   But the call, "Follow me," never comes from the lips of Jesus by way of the attractive position amongst men, of emolument, ease, or honour.   If the words are heard thence proceeding, they are simulated.   Let him who so hears beware!   The true call is imperative.   It cannot be relaxed even for the sake of "friends at home."   Nay, others must bury the "dead father" rather than the solemn "Follow me" be unheeded.

III. To illustrate this, the quick OBEDIENCE here so ILLUSTRIOUSLY EXEMPLIFIED is definitely expressed.   "They left their nets . . . they left their father Zebedee in the boat with the hired servants."   For ever *they left* must be the true test of sincere devotion.   If men leave a broken net for a whole one, and only to catch fishes, the world which has read this story knows the deceit, and does not acknowledge the Divine call. Generally the Church is pure.   The earthly gain is not great; the burden is heavy, Who follow this Master must cleave to his doctrine, and struggle to defend it, and bear the painfulness of maintaining the faith in presence of many difficulties and rude suggestions of doubt, and the severe treatment of men who do not intend to be cruel and wicked, but who severely try the hearts of humble believing servants with "doubtful disputations."   But the servant must stand by the Master; ah, and stand by his cause when he is not near; stand by it when it seems to be failing, as well as when it seems likely to prevail.   The true fitness to be a "fisher of men" is to "leave all;" for most truly here the Master saith, "Whosoever he be of you that renounceth not all that he hath, he cannot be," in the truest and best sense, "a fisher of men."   How cheering to these fishers must have been the prophetic testimony of the great ingatherings which rewarded the letting down the net "on the right side of the ship!"   Yet how much harder then to leave that net!—G.

Vers. 21—39.—*The illustrative example of Christ's work.*   No sooner is the great work begun than a strikingly illustrative example of its true character and beneficent power is presented.   It was in Capernaum, which, so far from being "exalted unto heaven," would hear the curse, "Thou shalt go down unto Hades."   And it was "the sabbath day;" therefore of a surety "he straightway . . . entered into the synagogue."   Now, in his "Father's house," he is doing the great work he came to do, "to bear witness of the truth."   Here are all Divine things—the Lord's day, the Lord's house, the Lord's Son, the Lord's Word.   Truly "the kingdom of God" is come. It is a typical example.   Here we learn that Christ's work is: 1. A work of teaching. 2. A conquest of the evil spirit.   3. A healing of human infirmities and sufferings. This threefold work finds its ample and beautiful illustration here.

I. In the synagogue he TAUGHT.   This is his chief, perhaps his greatest, work. His kingdom he will rule with truth; with truth he will wrest its alienated portions from the usurper.   This is his one weapon of antagonism against all evils.   He himself is "the Truth."   His was no second-hand, derived truth.   He was a perpetual spring of new truth—an authority in all matters of truth.   "Truth is in Jesus," and this his manner would betoken.   Well might the hearers stand "astonished."   Christ calmly spoke truth—the truth.   This was ever his sword.   By it the heart is pierced; men are convicted "in respect of sin" by it; the truth brings peace, for it brings the knowledge of salvation; the truth reveals the way of life; the truth unveils the future.   All truth he taught.   "Out of his mouth proceedeth a sharp sword, that with it he should smite the nations."   The wise soldiers of the cross to-day preach the Word; the wise servants scatter truth, for it is the only seed from which the kingdom of heaven will grow.

II. Following hard upon the utterance of truth is CONFLICT WITH THE SPIRIT OF EVIL, which, being a spirit of error, truth disturbs.   Then the great conflict is seen. The "unclean spirit" has nothing in common with Jesus, the pure One, as is declared in "What have we to do with thee, thou Jesus of Nazareth?"   No; these are mutually exclusive, mutually destructive.   The spirit of evil is revealed.   1. It is an "unclean" spirit.   2. It is a spirit of antagonism to truth.   3. It is a malignant spirit, "tearing" its victim till he cries aloud.   4. Till Jesus speaks, it dominates over the entire life of its victim.   5. But in his presence it is a conquered spirit.   "With authority he commandeth even the unclean spirits, and they obey him." There is no power, in earth or in Hades, above him.   Christ's word then, now, and always, casts out the evil spirit.

III. But men suffer many pains and sorrows. Ignorance, folly, mistake, sin,—all combine to expose the tender flesh to injury. It is the holy mission of the Son of man to HEAL HUMAN INFIRMITIES, to dry up the fount of human sorrow, to wipe the tears from human faces. The prostrate mother-in-law of his chief apostle is named to him as he leaves the synagogue, "and he came and took her by the hand, and raised her up; and the fever left her, and she ministered unto them." He has shown his relation to truth as its Fountain, to the evil spirit as its Conqueror, to disease as its Healer. Lo! the need of his presence and work is demonstrated. The cool of the day affords suitable time, and "they bring unto him all that were sick, and those that were possessed with devils." Of them, "he healed many that were sick with divers diseases, and cast out many devils." Oh, gracious visitation! Well might "all the city be gathered together at the door." What a holy excitement! What a day of grace! This but typifies the healing power of his word and doctrine. At once we learn that Christ stands opposed to human suffering. But disease is the natural consequence of broken law. It is the just retribution following disobedience. Is Christ opposed to law? No, he heals disease and casts out devils, as he commanded his disciples to do: 1. By his word and spirit bringing men to obedience to law. 2. By the sick being brought in penitent faith to him, when the moral end of the sickness is truly answered. 3. By ministrations of that charity which Christian teaching awakens and sustains. 4. By his own Divine word of blessing upon the efforts of men to learn and keep the laws of nature, which are his laws. Thus "the gospel of Jesus Christ" begins. For its end we wait. The seed-corn is cast into the earth. The harvest will follow.—G.

Vers. 40—45.—*The cleansing of the leper.* The work and wonders of the previous day created so great an excitement that he early rose, "a great while before day," for calmness and the refreshment of solitude and prayer, and finding "a desert place," he there "prayed." O hallowed ground! Simon and his companions follow, and finding him, say, "All are seeking thee." But he "came forth to preach," therefore he would go "elsewhere," and the marvellous account given is, "He went into their synagogues throughout all Galilee, preaching and casting out devils." In the course of his tour "there cometh to him" one of the many in whose bodily infirmity preachers and teachers have always seen the type of the spiritual sickness; "there cometh to him a leper." He is alone, for the multitude avoid him. Attention must not be diverted from these two—the *sufferer* and his *Saviour.*

I. THE SUFFERER AND HIS APPEAL. Leprosy is thus described: "The most terrible of all maladies, a living death, a poisoning of the springs, a corrupting of all the humours, of life; a dissolution little by little of the whole body, so that one limb after another actually decayed and fell away. The Jews called it 'the finger of God.'" They knew no cure for it. His "beseeching" cry is heard as he draws near, and ere he falls, kneeling, where so many afterwards knelt, at the feet of Jesus. He has heard of the fame of the Rabbi, for it has spread afar. With piteous words he cries, "If thou wilt, thou canst make me clean." What an inversion of this is much of the faith of to-day! The goodness of Jesus all acknowledge, but many deny his power to heal. This man knew only what had been reported to him—the power. He had not yet gazed into the tender eyes that beamed upon him. He had not yet heard the calm and gentle voice that breathed the tenderest love of the tenderest of all souls. But he will hear it. He had not felt the pressure of that hand of power; but, strange to say, he on whom no friendly hand has rested for long, will feel its healing touch. It needed not the cry to pierce to the heart of the great Healer; the sight was enough. But the words "thou canst" denote a faith which indicates the needed preparation. But the appealing "If," and "If thou wilt!" Oh, if all depended upon that alone, how many more would be healed! Once, it was said "If thou canst;" when the quick reply, "If thou canst," both rebuked the doubt (pardonable under the circumstances) and threw back upon the questioner the sense of weakness. Here is no doubt of the power; but "wilt" thou? So the unclean, corrupt, slow-dying sufferer appeals to the Lord of life, and love, and power.   It is not wrong to say " lf thou wilt."   It is a lower form of " Thy will be done."

II. The humble cry turns us from the sufferer to THE SAVIOUR, to learn his compassion, to see his touch, to hear his word of power, and to witness its instant effect. 1. Jesus was " moved with compassion."   What had not the world to hope from that " compassion " !   What may it not still hope from it !   We could hope much from compassion such as many good souls would show ; but what from his compassion ! What depth ; what tenderness ; what yearning ; and what power !   Happy he who commits himself to the compassion of Christ.   2. With quickness " he stretched forth his hand, and touched him."   There was comfort in that, for all others fled from him.   But it was a touch of acceptance and assurance, having many moral lessons.   " I do not despise thee."   His touch had compassion in it, perhaps more than power, though " power" went forth from him when others touched even his garments.   3. The true power, however, is in the word, " Be thou made clean."   It is a command to that body and to disease.   The disease, Christ's servant of judgment, obeys : " the leprosy departed from him ; " and the body obeys, putting on its new robes of health, the flesh as of a little child—" he was made clean."   Can faith desire more ?   He who would learn to have faith must stand near and see, and let the " works bear witness."   Faith is God's gift, like the dew of the morning, as silently, as wondrously given.   Again let it be said, if men would have faith they must come to the Word ; the air is full of blessing when the word of Christ is vibrating in it ; and it will distil as the dew upon the chill, sad heart.   How great a miracle ! yet typical of " greater works " yet to be done.   It is easier to say to the body, " Be thou made clean," than to say it to the soul.   But now a command, having within it a touch of sternness, " He strictly charged him, . . . Say nothing to any man : but go thy way, show thyself to the priest, and offer for thy cleansing the things which Moses commanded, for a testimony unto them."   Alas ! even gratitude could not conquer joy. His new life, his whole flesh, forbade silence, and he " began to publish it much."   It was almost excusable, yet not entirely.   For Christ's words must be obeyed at all cost. The Lord's ways are best, as is here proved.   Disobedience brings its inconvenience. The cities suffered by the man's error.   Ah, every city suffers by every man's error. Jesus could not " openly enter ; " he must hide " in desert places."   But " they came to him from every quarter."

Thus may all afflicted in body or soul learn : 1. To offer their cry to him, who, even if they err in their methods, will not despise their prayer.   2. That Christ willeth to heal all, and is able.   3. That his compassion is never unmoved in presence of human woe.   4. That the humble appeal to him will surely meet with a helpful response.   5. That the best return is to suppress their own inclination, and, even with crushed feelings, obey his minutest word ; for so is his purpose best answered.—G.

Vers. 1—8.   Parallel passages : Matt. iii. 1—12 ; Luke iii. 1—18.   *The ministry of John the Baptist.*   I. THE BEGINNING OF ST. MARK'S MEMOIR.   1. *The commencement.* It is a remarkable circumstance and a curious coincidence that the first words of this Gospel are an echo of Peter's confession.   In that confession, as recorded by St. Matthew, Peter expresses his belief in the very remarkable words, " Thou art *the Christ, the Son of* the living *God.*"   In nearly the same words St. Mark commences his narrative : " The beginning of the gospel of Jesus *Christ, the Son of God.*   2. *Difference of construction.*   The words of this first verse may be taken (1) as the title of the entire book ; or (2) in construction with the following verse, " The beginning of the gospel of Jesus Christ, the Son of God, was as it is written in the prophets ; " or (3) even in connection with the fourth verse, the second and third being parenthetic ; that is, " The beginning of the gospel . . . was John baptizing."   3. *Omissions.*   After a brief but indispensable introduction, touching the ministry of the Baptist, the evangelist hurries on to his concise but clear and comprehensive narrative of our Lord's public life, beginning with his baptism by John.   He passes over the four events of the Saviour's childhood—the circumcision and presentation in the temple, which are recorded by St. Luke, as also the visit of the Magi and the flight into Egypt, mentioned by St. Matthew.   He passes over the only recorded incident of his early days—the one event which constituted the dividing line between his childhood and youth, when, at his second appearance in the temple, he disputed with the doctors, and in connection with which we have his first recorded utterances, "How is it that ye sought me? wist ye not that I must be about my Father's business?" St. Mark also omits the lineage of our Lord, by which St. Matthew connects him with the seed of Abraham according to the flesh, and likewise that other genealogy, which St. Luke traces still higher up, connecting him with Adam and so with humanity itself, including Gentile as well as Jew. In the whole four Gospels there is only one single verse descriptive of our Lord's childhood, which reads as follows:—"The child grew and waxed strong in spirit, filled with wisdom [or rather, 'waxed strong, becoming filled with wisdom'] : and the grace of God was upon him;" while one other verse contains the record of his youth, "Jesus increased [rather, 'advanced'] in wisdom and stature, and in favour with God and man." All we know for certain of our Lord's life, up to the time of his manifestation to Israel, may be summed up in the few following facts:—Dutifulness to his earthly parents in childhood; diligence in business as a carpenter, like his fellow-men, in youth and early manhood; devotion to his heavenly Father all through his childhood, youth, and man-hood—from his earliest to his latest breath. St. Mark overleaps all the preceding period, and makes our Lord's entrance on ministerial life the starting-point of his Gospel. It is as though, impatient of delay, he hastened onward to the mighty issue. and acted on the well-known principle—

> "But to the grand event he speeds his course,
> And bears his readers with resistless force
> Into the midst of things."

4. *Practical observations.* (1) Long, laborious preparation is needed for the life-work, when that work is to be a noble one, and that life a real success. It was thus with Moses; it was thus with Jesus; it was so with Luther and other reformers; it has been so all down the centuries with the men who have blessed the world and benefited their race. (2) The example of our Lord dignifies honest industry and ennobles daily toil. (3) A spurious sentimentalism, like the apocryphal Gospels, is apt to busy itself more with the childhood and youth than with the manhood and ministry of the Saviour.

II. THE GOSPEL. 1. *Meaning of the term.* The original word rendered "gospel," or "good news," meant in Homeric times a reward given to the bearer of good news, or a sacrifice offered on account of good news; but in gospel days it signified the good news itself. 2. *Its embodiment.* This good news centres in a Saviour whose proper name is "Jesus"—indicating the nature of his work, "for he will save his people from their sins;" his official title is "Christ"—the Messiah, or Anointed One, promised to the fathers, and thus solemnly inaugurated in the high functions, prophetical, priestly, and kingly, which he was called to discharge; while his designation of "Son of God" implies his two-fold qualification, namely, dignity of nature and possession of power for the accom-plishment of the great redemption, God's remedy for sin. The good news is inseparable from the person of the Saviour—at once human and Divine, from the works he did, from the truths he taught, and from the sufferings he endured; and thus it is embodied in him. 3. *Its extent.* Its range is most extensive, including salvation for the lost, life for the dead, grace for the guilty, pardon for the penitent, bread of life for the hungry, and living water for the thirsty soul. Good news! no wonder the evangelist is in a hurry to make known such good news. 4. *Its essence.* The essence of the gospel may be expressed in a few sentences; its sum and substance may be compressed into the compass of a few short statements of Scripture; yea, the whole is contained in that single Scripture, "It is a faithful saying, and worthy of all acceptation, that Jesus Christ came into the world to save sinners;" or in that other Scripture, "The blood of Jesus Christ his Son cleanseth us from all sin;" or in that third Scripture, "The gift of God is eternal life through Jesus Christ our Lord." 5. *Its epithets.* The epithets applied to it are instructive, as indicating some of its many features. It is "the gospel of peace," for its contents proclaim "peace on earth and good will towards men," as well as "glory to God in the highest." It is called "the gospel of salvation," because it saves as well as sanctifies. It is styled "the glorious gospel," from its glorious influences—enlight-ening the understanding, purifying the heart, renewing the will, regenerating the soul, sanctifying the whole man—body, soul, and spirit; while at the same time it elevates the mind to God and heaven and eternal things. It is "the everlasting gospel," for it is still the same, though change and alteration are the very essence of this world; it remains the same amid all the ups and downs of time; and its blessed results are durable as eternity itself. It is "the gospel of Jesus Christ, the Son of God," for he is the Alpha and Omega of it; he is the Source from which all its benefits and blessings flow; he is the Guide to the ways and means by which we become partakers of the same. Whether, therefore, we consider it as the gospel of God, or the gospel of his grace, or the gospel of peace, or the gospel of salvation, or the glorious gospel, or the everlasting gospel, or the gospel of Jesus Christ, the Son of God, it justifies its claim to be the "godspell," or glad message, or good news, which the name implies. 6. *Its effects.* Good news, then, is the subject to which the evangelist, at the very outset, calls our attention. Good news! Oh, how the heart beats in the prospect of good news! How the pulse throbs in expectation of good news! How many a heart beats wildly when the post-man's knock comes to the door! How many a bright eye becomes still brighter when the precious little letter, which brings good news from friends abroad or friends at home, is put into the hand! Now, the best news that ever fell on the ear, or met the eye, or gladdened the heart, of mortal man, is this gospel of the Son of God. It has quickened many a dead soul; it has gladdened many a sad heart; it has filled many a drooping spirit with joy unspeakable; it has led many a pilgrim of earth onward and upward to the glories of heaven.

III. UNION OF THE OLD AND NEW TESTAMENT SCRIPTURES. In vers. 2, 3, the evangelist binds together as in one volume, and unites with better than clasps of gold, the Old Testament and the New. He brings into closest connection the canon of the former with that of the latter. They are, indeed, the twin lips of one and the same Divine oracle. Accordingly, he bridges over the chasm of four hundred years between the last prophet of the Old Testament and the first prophet, or rather precursor of the Saviour, in the New. The ministry of John and the mission of the Saviour had been expressly foretold by the prophets Isaiah and Malachi—the prediction of the former was *primary*, that of the latter *secondary* and subordinate. Consequently, treating Malachi's as prefatory and introductory, announcing the messenger and his function, he fixes attention mainly on that of Isaiah, as containing the message itself, and the actual ministry with which the forerunner was charged. The name of Malachi is therefore omitted, for the correct reading, as given by the critical editors is, no doubt, "in Isaiah the prophet."

IV. THE VOICE THE PROPHET HEARD. The prophet Isaiah, as we may picture his position, is looking away, with straining eyes, into the distant future of his people; he is listening, with outstretched neck and ears eagerly attentive, for any intimation of their redemption; but in vain. No vision is granted, no promise vouchsafed. He does not, however, despair; he keeps looking and listening and longing for something to strengthen his faith or encourage his hope. All is hushed around, and again he listens with bated breath; but hark! at length he hears a sound. It is a voice away in a distant desert land; it is waking the echoes of the wilderness. "It is the voice of one crying." It is just a voice, and seemingly nothing more—not unlike that bird of which the poet writes—

> "Shall I call thee bird,
> Or but a wandering voice? . . .
> Thrice welcome, darling of the spring!
> Even yet thou art to me
> No bird; but an invisible thing,
> A voice, a mystery."

We must not confound John with the voice, as those who translate the expression of the prophet, "a voice crying;" but understand the voice as his chief characteristic or main peculiarity, as in secular authors we read of the strength of Hercules, the virtue of Scipio, the wisdom of Lælius, or as when Cicero in a disparaging sense affirms that, on the removal of Catiline, he had nothing to fear from the drowsiness of Lentulus, or the corpulence of Cassius, or the mad rashness of Cethegus.

V. DISTRICT OF JOHN'S MINISTRY. Kings, when setting out to visit the remote provinces of their kingdoms, were usually preceded by heralds to announce their approach and pioneers to prepare the way—removing obstacles, clearing away impediments, and so making rough places smooth; bridging streams, filling up valleys, levelling hills, and so causing a straight, direct road to take the place of a circuitous and devious route. Some preparation like this was made for Alexander the Great when he marched to the Indus, and more so still for Semiramis in her progress through Media and Persia. Likewise in Vespasian's march to Galilee a detachment was appointed " to make the road even and straight, and, if it were anywhere rough and hard to be passed over, to plane it, and to cut down the woods that hindered their march." The necessity for such preparatory measures would be increased in a desert district without roads, or with roads so bad as to be almost impassable. When Jehovah restored the Hebrew exiles from Babylon to their own land, the region through which they had to pass was dreary and desolate, and in some places pathless. To the preparation of a way through the difficulties of such a district for the returning Hebrew exiles, with the great king at their head, the words of the prophet primarily referred. This, like other great events in the cycle of Jewish history, was, no doubt, typical of that moral waste in which the people were when Jehovah came again for their redemption in the person of Messiah. Very appropriately, therefore, did John choose for the scene of his ministry the wilderness of Judæa. This comprehended the eastern slope of the hills from Jerusalem and Hebron, down the Jordan valley to the western shore of the Dead Sea and the banks of Jordan—a wild region, in many places rough, rugged, and rocky, with sparse, if any, population, some spots of pasture-ground, and few or no trees. Here it was that the Baptist made his appearance ($\dot{\epsilon}\gamma\dot{\epsilon}\nu\epsilon\tau o$)—" comes forth " ($\pi a \rho a \gamma \dot{\iota} \nu \epsilon \tau a \iota$, St. Matthew). A difficult work awaits him in preparing Messiah's way : humble and contrite ones are to be elevated ; proud and lofty spirits to be brought low ; the crooked ways of crafty men to be made straight ; rough, untutored natures to be softened ; and moral obstacles of every kind to be removed, in order that, the way being thus prepared, the march of Prince Messiah might be unhindered.

VI. DISTINGUISHING RITE OF THE BAPTIST'S MINISTRY. 1. *Proselyte baptism.* In connection with the ceremonial law of the Jews, there were " divers washings." Such baptisms or ablutions were practised by them from the earliest period of their polity. Originally appointed by Divine authority, they were incorporated as part and parcel of the national religion. Their design was an important one, for they were intended to serve as symbols of that purity which was required in all true worshippers of Jehovah. On the eve of the giving of the Law to Israel, and of that people's gracious admission into covenant with God, a great national assembly took place—the various Hebrew tribes spreading over the desert and round the base of Sinai, the Lord directed Moses, saying, " Go unto the people, and sanctify them to-day and to-morrow, and let them *wash* their clothes, and be ready against the third day: for the third day the Lord will come down in the sight of all the people upon Mount Sinai ; " while, in consequence of and in obedience to this direction, " Moses went down from the mount unto the people, and sanctified the people ; and they washed their clothes." Further, when strangers from among the surrounding nations embraced the Jews' religion, they were washed as well as circumcised ; and that washing was called " baptizing unto Moses," or proselyte baptism. This rite, notwithstanding the assertion of some to the contrary, appears to have existed before our Saviour's time, and to be evidently implied in several passages of the New Testament. It was, moreover, a rite which sprang naturally out of the opinion commonly current among the Jews that all mankind were in an unclean condition, and so incapable of admission into the covenant of Israel, unless and until they were baptized or washed, in token of being purified from their state of moral uncleanness. 2. *Position of John's baptism.* But what, it is necessary to inquire, was the position occupied by the baptism of John ? What was its relation to other similar ablutions ? In reply we answer that the baptism of John was neither proselyte baptism on the one hand, nor Christian baptism on the other. It was *not proselyte baptism*, for that was administered only to proselytes, that is to say, converts to the Jewish faith, whereas John baptized Jews ; and this alone will account for the misgiving and alarm which the baptism of John caused to the Jewish authorities. Hence the question of the Pharisees, as recorded in John i. 25, " Why baptizest thou then, if thou be not that Christ, nor Elias, neither that prophet?" The prophet referred to, it may be remarked in passing, was probably Jeremiah, whose revivescence as a forerunner of Messiah the Jews expected, believing, according to an old legend, that he would restore, or reveal the hiding-place of, the ark of the covenant, the tabernacle, and the altar of incense, which he had hid in Pisgah, at whatever time God should gather his people together. The Pharisees could have readily understood the baptism of Gentile proselytes into the Jewish faith, and such baptism by John could have produced no uneasiness and caused no alarm. Instead of occasioning pain, it would have given them pleasure, as the admission of converts into the Jewish Church by such baptism would have contributed to their own ecclesiastical importance, and tended to augment the numerical power of their party. But the disquieting circumstance about it was that it was Jews whom John baptized; and what were they to make of that? What were these zealots for Judaism to think of the administration to Jews of a rite which had only been administered to Gentile proselytes; and the administration of which was either the formal introduction into a new faith or the first inauguration of a new dispensation? It was this that aroused their fears and excited their apprehensions. They saw clearly that John's baptism was the dawn of a new dispensation—a dispensation destined, as they rightly suspected, to subvert in a certain sense, or at least supersede, the old. In their alarm they accordingly ask, " If thou art not that Christ himself, who, we are taught to believe, will inaugurate a new dispensation; nor Elias, his forerunner; nor that prophet, be it Jeremiah or some other of the old prophets who shall reappear on earth at Messiah's advent;—why baptizest thou then, seeing it is not Gentile converts to Judaism, but Jews themselves, that are admitted to your baptism?" John's baptism, then, was not proselyte baptism. Neither was it *Christian baptism*, as we learn from Acts xix. at the beginning, where certain disciples at Ephesus, who had been baptized into John's baptism, were rebaptized into the name of the Lord Jesus. "Unto what then were ye baptized?" asks Paul. "And they said, Unto John's baptism. Then said Paul, John verily baptized with the baptism of repentance, saying unto the people, that they should believe on him which should come after him, that is, on Christ Jesus. When they heard this, they were baptized in the name of the Lord Jesus." With this agrees the sentiment of an ancient Greek Father, the purport of which is that John's baptism was more than Jewish baptism, for it involved repentance as well as water baptism; it was less than Christian, for it was not with the Spirit, as Christ's was.

VII. DOCTRINE PREACHED BY THE BAPTIST. The doctrine he preached was the doctrine of repentance for the remission of sins. He called their sins to mind, summoning them to confession and contrition; while this proper sense of, and sorrow for, sin showed them their need of a Saviour and prepared them for his salvation. In token of repentance commenced and to be continued, and of the power of him whose reign was now beginning, to cleanse the truly penitent from all sin, he baptized them with water unto repentance. Thus, while John proclaimed the advent of the new dispensation, he prepared for it and prefaced it by a most appropriate and significant rite. On this Theophylact comments as follows:—" But whither did this preaching of repentance lead? To the forgiveness of sins, that is, to the baptism of Christ which had the forgiveness of sins."

VIII. DRESS OF THE BAPTIST. Everything was in perfect keeping with the strange surroundings of the Baptist. His dress, his diet, and his discourse were all in harmony with the desert where he ministered. His dress was neither gorgeous nor gay like that of a king's herald; it was of the coarsest and roughest kind. His garment was made of cloth of rudest texture, woven out of camel's hair; he was girded not with the rich linen or highly ornamented girdle of the Oriental, but with a cincture of untanned hide, like the prophets' raiment of early times; just such as Elijah wore, and such as Zechariah speaks of when he refers to the rough garment as the proper prophetic costume, and as such assumed by false prophets in order to deceive.

IX. DIET OF THE BAPTIST. His diet was as plain as his dress. His food was not sumptuous, but of the simplest sort; scarce sufficient to keep soul and body together—the honey of the wild bee, which he found in the fissure of the rock or clefts of trees, and the locusts of the wilderness. The honey was not that which exuded from trees, but the veritable product of wild bees; nor were the locusts the sweet pods of the locust tree, but the real locusts still used for food by the Bedouin of the desert. "He also," says Thomson in 'The Land and the Book,' "dwelt in the desert where such food was and is still used; and therefore the text states the simple truth. His ordinary 'meat' was dried locusts—probably fried in butter and mixed with honey, as is still frequently done. The honey, too, was the article made by bees. . . . Wild honey is still gathered in large quantities from trees in the wilderness, and from rocks in the wadies, just where the Baptist sojourned, and where he came preaching the doctrine of repentance."

X. DISCOURSE OF THE BAPTIST TO THE COMING CROWDS. 1. *Audience addressed.* The persons who went out to John's ministry are described by St. Luke as crowds or multitudes (ὄχλοι); but they are distinguished by St. Matthew as comprehending two component parts, or two contending sects, namely, Pharisees and Sadducees, that together made up the main body of the nation. To the Gentiles, for whom St. Luke wrote, the distinction would have little meaning and no interest; to the Hebrew Christians, for whom St. Matthew wrote, it would convey the fact that the crowds that flocked to the Baptist's ministry were made up of the two religious sects of Judaism promiscuously. In his audience were Judæans and Jerusalemites—people from the country and the capital; and dwellers in all the region round about the Jordan (περίχωρος), Samaritans, Galileans, Peræans, and Gaulonites. 2. *His discourse denunciatory.* His discourse breathed the spirit of a reformer and evinced the power of a reformer. He denounced most scathingly the ritualistic Pharisee and the rationalistic Sadducee—traditionist and scripturist alike; high and low, rich and poor. He spared the shortcomings of no class, the iniquities of no rank, and the sins of no individual. The plea of ancient privilege and of pious ancestors he treated with scorn, telling such as resorted to those refuges that God could, and would if necessary, raise up children to Abraham out of the stones that lay scattered through the valley, or the shingle that strewed the strand of the Jordan, or those huge boulders—those memorial stones which Joshua had set up near the bank of that historic river. This expression, by the way, though apparently harsh, may allude to Isa. li. 1, 2, "Look unto the rock whence ye are hewn, and to the hole of the pit whence ye are digged. Look unto Abraham your father, and unto Sarah that bare you." 3. *His discourse menacing.* He threatened the vengeance of heaven on all who refused to repent and return to God. The woodman's axe was already brandished to fell the trees that continued barren. The axe was brought into unpleasant proximity to such trees—not to the branches merely, but was laid to the very root; in fact, lies at it (κεῖται). The fatal blow was ready to be struck at any moment. In view of anger so imminent, he urges all to flee from the wrath to come—to repent, and not only profess, but prove, their repentance real by fruits answerable to such profession; "If then (οὖν) you are as anxious as you seem to escape that storm of future wrath, bring forth fruit suitable to genuine penitence." 4. *His discourse effective.* The various classes that had resorted to his ministry were roused to a sense of danger. The terror of the alarmed multitudes took shape in the question, "What, then, shall we do?" Just as on the day of Pentecost, the men of Israel, pricked to the heart, addressed themselves to Peter and the rest of the apostles, asking, "Men and brethren, what shall we do?" And just as the Philippian jailor, in his wild alarm, trembling and falling down before Paul and Silas, cried out, "Sirs, what must I do to be saved?" 5. *Directions to different classes.* The reply in this case inculcated a lesson of charity and sympathy—the person who had two tunics or under garments (χιτῶνες), besides his outer garment (ἱμάτιον), was to impart to the poor starveling who had not even one. So with food of all forms and every kind (βρώματα), as well as raiment. Such were the directions addressed to the multitudes (ὄχλοι); while the difference between these directions and those addressed to the two following classes deserves notice. To the former (the multitudes) he said, "Do good;" to the latter (publicans and soldiers) he said, "Abstain from evil;" to the one the direction is positive, to the other negative. To the former he said, "Learn to do well;" and to the latter, "Cease to do evil." The publicans again, who were looked on as trading on their country's degradation, he forbade to continue their unjust exactions and dishonest dealings; while the soldiers on their march (στρατευόμενοι), whether those of Antipas marching against his father-in-law Aretas, or otherwise, he commanded, in reply to their numerous and earnest inquiries (ἐπηρώτων imperf.), to forbear extortions either by threats or false accusations—neither to concuss the poor by the former, nor force money out of the pockets of the rich by the latter: also to be content with their wages (ὀψωνίοις; literally, *boiled fish, rations, soldiers' pay*).

XI. FORMAL ANNOUNCEMENT OF MESSIAH. By this time the crowds assembled round the Baptist were on the tiptoe of expectation. At this period expectations of some great deliverer were rife both in Gentile lands and among Jewish people. It is not strange, then, that the multitudes who had listened to the instructions of the Baptist reasoned within themselves whether haply John himself were the Christ. He had already, it may be presumed, given a definite answer to the priests and Levites deputed by the Sanhedrin to ascertain his claims. But now he feels called on to make a more public announcement. 1. *Transition.* All along he never once lost sight of his office as harbinger or herald (κηρύσσων) calling attention to the coming One. Yet gradually the office of herald was merging in that of the evangelist; hence the employment of εὐηγγελίζετο in the parallel passage of Luke, at the eighteenth verse. Ever more and more John seeks to turn attention from himself to Jesus, to whom he acknowledges himself as inferior in rank as in office. The meanest slave that brought his master's sandals, or stooped down in lowliness to undo the latchet that bound them, stood to the mightiest earthly master in a higher relation than John to Jesus; while the work of the latter was proportionately superior. 2. *Superiority.* The one administered the symbol, the other the thing signified; the one baptized with water, the other with the Spirit; the one was a light as of a lamp (λύχνος) kindled by, and reflecting, a borrowed light, the other was that central source of light (φῶς); the one was the morning star, soon to wane, and wishing to wane, before the other, who was the sun himself going forth in his strength.

> "Where is the love the Baptist taught,
> The soul unswerving and the fearless tongue?
> The much-enduring wisdom, sought
> By lonely prayer the haunted rocks among?
> Who counts it gain
> His light should wane,
> So the whole world to Jesus throng!"

J. J. G.

Vers. 9—11. Parallel passages: Matt. iii. 13—17; Luke iii. 21—23. *The baptism of our Lord.* I. DIFFICULTY. There is something singular, to say the least, in the baptism of our Lord. In that solemn inauguration of the Saviour, as he entered on his public ministry, a difficulty is encountered. That difficulty respects the significance of the rite in relation to the spotless Son of God. Water, when applied to the person or used in the way of ablution, is employed as an element of cleansing. But the idea of cleansing necessarily carries along with it the notion of defilement. The thought of pollution, from whatever source derived, or in whatever way contracted, or in whatever it may consist, is inseparably connected with it. Cleansing has as its natural and necessary correlative uncleanness either expressed or implied.

II. INAPPLICABLE TO OUR LORD. Yet the Saviour was not only holy, harmless, and undefiled in life; but at his birth and in the very nature of his humanity, he was free from every taint and unsullied by the least stain of sin, as it is written, "Therefore also that holy thing which shall be born of thee shall be called the Son of God," or more literally, "Therefore also that which is born of thee, being holy, shall be called the Son of God." It is probable that the Baptist felt at once the awkwardness of his own position, and the incongruity of administering to One so perfectly pure and undefiled a rite which, as the symbol of cleansing, implied a previous condition or natural state of impurity and defilement.

III. THE BAPTIST'S RELUCTANCE. In view of the circumstance just mentioned, as well as of the overwhelming superiority of the Divine applicant, John expressed such extreme lothness to administer the rite. Nay more, that reluctance took the form of a somewhat firm refusal: "But John," we read, "forbad him, saying, I have need to be baptized of thee, and comest thou to me?" The imperfect διεκώλυεν may imply the *commencement*, that is, began to prevent, or be used *de conatu* of the endeavour to prevent, while the prepositional element imports activity and earnestness in the effort. It was only after a remonstrance on the part of the Saviour, and after he had pointed out to John the propriety of the course, that the Baptist yielded. The reason alleged by our Lord, while it was sufficient to overcome the scruples of the Baptist, is serviceable to us in inquiring into the nature of the ordinance then administered. True, that reason is expressed in somewhat general terms, as follows:—"Thus it becometh us to fulfil all righteousness;" but wherein this righteousness consisted, and how it was fulfilled, we proceed briefly to investigate.

IV. Priesthood of Christ. It will be borne in mind that our Lord, though a priest after the order of Melchisedec, and superior to that of Aaron, was nevertheless the great Antitype of the Aaronic priesthood. The priest of the Aaronic order was typical of the great High Priest of our profession. The rites of consecration in the one case may, therefore, be regarded as helpful in elucidating the mode of inauguration in the other.

V. Ceremonial of consecration. At the ceremonial of consecrating the Aaronic priest, there was (1) anointing with oil, and (2) washing with water. The oil was emblematical of the Spirit, the water of separation from all that would unfit for the service of the Holy One; the anointing with oil signified the bestowal of the needful endowments, the washing with water the impartation of the necessary moral qualities; the one has reference to the gifts, the other to the graces, required for the proper and efficient discharge of the priestly functions. It was thus with the type, while, in the case of the Antitype, the figure was realized in the fact; the sign gave place to the thing signified. In other words, the unction of the Spirit took the place of the anointing with oil; the washing with water, which in reference to the Levitical priest denoted the necessity for purity in the service of God, and entire separation from anything that would defile, implied, in relation to the Redeemer, the actual possession of that purity in its highest perfection, and of that separation from all possibility of defiling or contaminating influence.

VI. Reference to priestly character. 1. Accordingly, the baptism of our Lord had respect to the priestly character he sustained, not to any human imperfection that required to be repented of, or impurity that needed to be removed; so that the righteousness which it behoved to fulfil was conformity to the rite of priestly consecration; while the type merged in the antitype, and the figure gave place to fact. He was now about thirty years of age (the Levitical period) when he began (ἀρχόμενος) his ministry. 2. Another explanation solves the difficulty by giving prominence to the representative character of Christ. He came as the representative of a people guilty in God's sight, and morally unclean; and as he afterwards bore their sins in his own body on the tree in order to expiate their guilt, so now he was baptized vicariously because of their uncleanness, in token of his purpose to purge away their filth. "He was baptized," not as though in need of it himself, but on behalf of the human race; and such is the opinion of Justin Martyr. He was made in the likeness of sinful flesh—made sin for us, and so numbered with and treated as a transgressor. 3. Other explanations of the matter, still less probable, have been given, as for example (1) that it was the perfection and proof of humility; and (2) that it was for the purpose of being made manifest to the people, and that in presence of so great a concourse the Baptist might bear testimony to his Messiahship; which appears to be the view of Theophylact.

VII. The presence of the Trinity. At the baptism of our Lord the three Persons of the blessed Trinity were present or represented. The voice of the eternal Father came ringing down out of the cleaving heavens as they were rending asunder; the Holy Spirit in dove-like form descended; the beloved Son was the subject of the former, and the recipient of the latter. Thus Father, Son, and Holy Spirit inaugurated the Christian dispensation at its commencement; Father, Son, and Holy Spirit impart the grace and bestow the blessings of this dispensation during its continuance; while Father, Son, and Holy Spirit shall share the glory at its close. And so in the beautiful words of the *Te Deum*—

> "The holy Church throughout all the world doth acknowledge thee;
> The Father of an infinite majesty;
> Thine honourable, true, and only Son;
> Also the Holy Ghost, the Comforter."

VIII. Threefold testimony. Thrice during our Lord's public ministry a voice from heaven testified to his Messiahship—once at his baptism as just noticed; once on the Mount of Transfiguration; and once during Passion week, in the courts of the temple, as we read in the Gospel of St. John, xii. 28, "Father, glorify thy name. Then came there a voice from heaven, saying, I have both glorified it, and will glorify it again."

IX. TRIPLE RECORD. Again this acknowledgment of the Father puts honour on the Divine Word, for, from the three leading divisions of it—the Law, the Prophets, and the Psalms—that acknowledgment is taken. The words, "Thou art my Son," are taken from the second Psalm; from Genesis, the first book of the Law, xxii. 28, we have the expression, "My beloved Son;" while in the Prophets, namely, Isa. xlii. 1, we find the remaining clause, "In whom I am well pleased."

X. CHANGE IN THE BAPTIST'S PREACHING. The Galilean valley and the Judæan desert were far separate. Though closely allied by kinship, and more closely still by oneness of spirit, John and Jesus had grown up apart; their first actual contact was at the baptism of the latter. Personal acquaintance there had been none; or if there had, it did not contribute to the Baptist's recognition of his Messiah. Either by a conversation of which we have no record, or by direct revelation immediately before the baptism, the important fact was made known to the Baptist. Be this as it may, one very remarkable effect resulted from it. The style, and indeed the subject, of the Baptist underwent an entire change. Previously his manner had been denunciatory; subsequently it became conciliatory. Before he had borrowed his imagery from the harsh features of the surrounding desert—the rude rocks, the poisonous vipers, the barren tree; or from the rough ways and works of agricultural life, such as may have existed on the verge of the wilderness—the threshing-floor, the winnowing implement, and the worthless chaff. But now he tempers and softens his mode of speech with figures from the sanctuary and its service—the lamb slain, the sin sacrifice, and the expiation. We hear no more of viperous broods—vipers themselves and sprung from vipers; no more of fruitless trees, fit only for the fire; no more of *stones* taking the place of sons, that is, of *abanim* becoming *banim*; no more of the sifting and separating process by which the good grain would be garnered and the worthless residue gathered into heaps for burning. On the other hand, we read of the Lamb as the Sin-bearer, and salvation as the blessedness secured; in other words, we have the blessed truth first uttered by the Baptist's lips, "Behold, the Lamb of God, which taketh away the sin of the world!" The legal has given place to the evangelical. The first phase—equally needful and equally useful, it is true—of the Baptist's preaching is exhibited by the synoptists; the second—softer, sweeter, and superior in tone and tendency—by the penman of the fourth Gospel, the evangelist and beloved apostle John.

XI. THE BAPTIST'S FUNCTION THREEFOLD. The commission of the Baptist embraced three functions: 1. Herald-like, he was to prepare the way for the coming King by calling men to repentance. 2. He administered, on their full confession (ἐξομολογούμενοι, equivalent to making a clean breast of it), the rite which served as a pledge that their conviction of sin was real and their service sincere—that, in fact, they wished to act in conformity with such a direction as that of the prophet, "Wash you, make you clean, put away the evil of your doings from before my eyes." In all this, however, they might merely have an eye to the penal consequences of sin, and to that sweeping storm of coming wrath to which sin exposed them; and thus proceed no further than legal repentance. 3. But a yet higher office was to announce the kingdom of heaven as come down on earth, and point to the advent of its King; in other words, to direct the eye of *faith* to Messiah as the great Sin-sacrifice and the only Saviour. Repentance alone, especially of the legal kind referred to, could not merit the remission of sins; neither could baptism, nor yet the combination of both together: the real meritorious cause was the atoning sacrifice of the Son of God—the Lamb slain; while faith, that faith from which true evangelical repentance is never separate, was the link of union between the soul of the penitent and his Saviour. Thus John virtually preached faith as well as repentance; for his repentance-baptism derived its whole meaning and validity from faith in Christ. Evangelical repentance commences with Christ, the cross, Calvary, and is "the tear in the eye of faith" directed thereto, for, looking to him whom we have pierced, we mourn. Of this we have tolerably plain proof in the words of St. Paul (Acts xix. 4), "Then said Paul, John verily baptized with the baptism of repentance, saying unto the people, that they should believe on him which should come after him, that is, in Christ Jesus."—J. J. G.

Vers. 12, 13. Parallel passages: Matt. iv. 1—11; Luke iv. 1—13.—*The temptation.* I. THE REALITY OF THE TEMPTATION. The above passage of St. Mark, and the parallel passages of the other Gospels, contain the record of one of the most remarkable transactions in the Word of God. It records the temptation of the Son of God. It describes not a fiction but a fact—not a phantom scene, such as a poet's fancy delights to paint, nor a daydream that merely passed through the imagination of the Saviour, but a literal and historical reality. The whole is a narrative of a mysterious yet actual event. It is Satan, personally, that acts the part of the tempter; it is the Saviour, personally, who is tempted; it is the Word of God that is the armoury furnishing the celestial weapons by which the temptation is resisted and the tempter foiled.

II. THE FACT OF THE TEMPTATION AND ITS IMPORTANT BEARINGS. 1. *Proof of its reality.* That the event here recorded was an actual fact, a real transaction, is proved by the different expressions employed by the evangelists. Thus, St. Luke says he "was led by the Spirit;" St. Matthew, that he "was led up of the Spirit;" and St. Mark, that "the Spirit driveth him into the wilderness." Similarly Ezekiel, among the captives on the banks of the Chebar, says of himself, "The Spirit lifted me up, and took me away;" so Philip was caught away by the Spirit of the Lord; so also John was "in the Spirit on the Lord's day." 2. *The Saviour's first conflict.* The temptation was our Lord's first conflict with that enemy whom he came to contend with and to conquer. It was at the same time the last part of his preparation for his work and warfare. It made him aware of the dangerous devices of the adversary; of the mistakes that would certainly mar, and of the mismanagement which might possibly make his undertaking miscarry. His person, his work, his deportment, were all concerned. In his *person* identified with the human as well as the Divine, he was debarred from using the resources of the latter to raise him above the common wants and sinless weaknesses of the former; and in remembrance thereof he says, "*Man* shall not live by bread alone." Self-abnegation, not self-gratification, was the law of his life. In his *work* he behoved to stand aloof from the ways of the world, eschewing the plans and plots, and all those many means of questionable character, by which men have struggled for dominion and grasped at glory. The spirit of his work was non-conformity to this world; the nature of his kingdom was spiritual, not of this world; the way to reach it was self-sacrifice; the crown was to be gained, but only by the cross. In his *deportment* there was to be no ostentatious display of close kinship with the eternal Father, no proud presuming on that high relationship, no capricious exercise of Divine power. In due time he would be "declared" the Son of God with power. Accordingly he repels this assault with the strong language of intense abhorrence, if not indignation, saying, "Thou shalt not tempt out and out (ἐκπειράσεις) [to an extreme altogether intolerable] the Lord thy God." 3. *The weapon he wielded.* Once and again, moreover, the lesson of his childhood—the section of the Jewish Law that was written on the frontlet and thus familiar to every Hebrew youth—he called to his timely aid, and held up to the tempter as the old standing Scripture (γέγραπται, equivalent to "it stands written"), the ever-abiding truth never to be departed from. 4. *The key to the narrative.* The key to the entire narrative is contained in the words of the Epistle to the Hebrews, iv. 15, "We have not an high priest which cannot be touched with the feeling of our infirmities; but was in all points tempted like as we are, yet without sin;" and again in the same Epistle, ii. 18, "For in that he himself hath suffered being tempted, he is able to succour them that are tempted." From these Scriptures we learn that the design of Christ's mission to mankind was twofold; it was not only to make an expiation for our sins by his death, but to be a perfect example for our imitation in his life. He was tempted, therefore, in order that he might be an example to us when called to encounter temptation. He was tempted, moreover, in order that he might be able to sympathize with and succour us when tried and tempted; as the poet has beautifully as well as truly said of him—

> "Touched with a sympathy within,
> He knows our feeble frame;
> He knows what sore temptations mean,
> For he has felt the same.

Then let our humble faith address
His mercy and his power,
We shall obtain delivering grace
In every trying hour."

5. *Forewarned.* In the conflict of the Saviour with Satan, as narrated in the Gospels, we have the prototype of, and precedent for, the perfect believer, showing us what manner of adversary we have to contend with, how he fights, how he is resisted, how he is overcome; showing us also the arena on which we have to maintain the struggle, what weapons we must wield, how certain our victory will be when we use those weapons aright, as well as the true source of conquest and of triumph, on which we are to depend. Now, there is much truth in the old proverb, "Forewarned is forearmed;" and if this be true of conflicts where carnal weapons are employed, it is also true of that spiritual conflict which every Christian has to carry on with the great enemy of God and of goodness—of the soul and of salvation. Accordingly, the passage under consideration warns us of the adversary and of his devices, that we may not be ignorant of them; of the boldness of his assaults and the mode of his attacks; of what he did in a green tree; and of how much more powerful the fire of his temptation may be expected to be in a dry; of his repeated attacks on him of whom we read, "The prince of this world cometh, and hath nothing in me." How much more severe and repeated attacks of this great adversary may be expected by us, in whom a wicked heart within and a wicked world without combine to render temptation successful! For who among us has not felt the truth of the sentiment—

"A wicked heart and wicked world,
With Satan are combined;
Each acts a too successful part
In harassing my mind"?

6. *Forearmed.* Further, the lesson of the passage arms us with weapons of resistance and defence, which, if used duly, diligently, and dutifully, will enable us to resist the devil and force him to flee from us. It implies, moreover, the important duty incumbent on every Christian to guard against all appearance of evil, to check the first risings of evil in the heart, to resist the first suggestions of the evil one, to watch and pray, and apply God's Word, that we may not enter into temptation. And all this the more, that Satan's onsets are so daring and his designs so murderous; his arguments so specious and his schemes of ruin so subtle; his plan being our enslavement to himself and sin, while his purpose is to pay us the hard-earned wages of transgression. "What fruit had ye then," asks the apostle, "in those things whereof ye are now ashamed? for the end of those things is death."

III. THE FORMS OF THE TEMPTATION IN GENERAL. 1. *Striking similarity.* There is a remarkable and instructive similarity between the temptation of the first and that of the second Adam; and also a vast dissimilarity. The similarity consists in the means and manner of the temptation; but a world-wide difference is presented in the result. There are three powerful principles of human nature, of which Satan takes advantage, and to which he adapts his temptations. These principles are "the lust of the flesh, the lust of the eyes, and the pride of life" spoken of in Scripture. These have been called this world's Trinity. By means of these Satan tempted the first Adam, and succeeded; by the same means he attempted to ensnare the second Adam and failed. In tempting the first Adam he plied him with the lust of the *flesh*; for the tree of knowledge of good and evil, of which God had forbidden man to eat, was good for food, and so fitted to gratify the lust of the flesh and lead to the indulgence of carnal appetite. He tried him by the lust of the *eyes*; for the forbidden tree was pleasant to the eyes, and so adapted to gratify their lust and produce covetousness. He tried him by the *pride of life*; for it was a tree to be desired to make one wise—to make man as God, knowing good and evil, and so suited to the pride of life, prompting and fostering pride of heart. In all this Satan succeeded. He knew the baits to lay, and when and how to lay them. Besides, the first Adam was of the earth, earthy, and we, alas! have all borne his image; for "as by one man sin entered into the world, and death by sin, so death has passed upon all men for that all have sinned." Now, as Satan had been so successful with the first Adam, it is not to be wondered at that he should try the same mode of procedure in framing his temptation for the second Adam. Accordingly, he tries him first by the lust of the flesh, tempting him to change stones into bread, and so moving him to the indulgence of *appetite*. Next he tries him by the pride of life, tempting him to throw himself down from the temple's pinnacle, and so, in sight of the inhabitants of the holy city, to prove his deity and show forth his glory, employing the upbearing protection of glorious angelic hosts. Thus Satan does his best to move the Saviour to the sin of *pride*. Once more he tries him by the lust of the eyes, exhibiting to his vision a panoramic view of all the kingdoms of the world, or showing them to him stretched out before his eyes in widespread perspective. He offers him all these and all their glory, and so he endeavours to move him to *covetousness*. We have here followed the order in which the temptations occur in St. Matthew's narrative. 2. *Dissimilarity of sequel.* All Satan's temptations were in vain as regarded our Lord. The first Adam fell in Eden, a garden the fairest and loveliest ever planted on earth ; the second Adam overcame triumphantly on the bleak and dreary wild. A paradise of earthly glory was lost by the first ; the paradise of God was secured for us by the second. 3. *Special adaptations.* But not only did these temptations of our Lord correspond to the three forms of temptation which brought death into our world and all our woe ; they correspond to the three portions of man's composite nature, that is to say, body, soul, and spirit. The body needs bread to satisfy its natural cravings, and the temptation is to procure it independently of Providence. The soul is also appetitive, though in a different direction, and in its outlook contemplates a wide sweep and vast dominion ; the temptation is to secure all this at a single bound, overleaping the wearisome way of suffering and self-sacrifice. The middle place between the purely carnal and the purely spiritual is this visual illusion. The spirit rules in man over body and soul, and so liability to pride opens the way to temptation ; and here the temptation is to put to the test his eternal Sonship, and to prove by one splendid miracle the truth of his Messianic claims. Thus the appeal was to *appetite*, to *avarice* or aggrandizement, and to *ambition* ; in other words, to poverty, power, and pride ;—following, as we do here, the order of St. Luke's Gospel. 4. *Reason of this difference of arrangement.* But why is this difference of arrangement between St. Luke and St. Matthew, the former reversing the relative position of the second and the third temptations as recorded by the latter ? Why change the order ? Mill's solution is, perhaps, the right one ; at all events, it is very plausible and very probable. It is to the effect that while the flesh is the first avenue of assault in all men, the tempter varies his tactics in the case of the other two, and in accordance with the difference of temperament, leading some by the way of pride to ambition, but others, in reverse order, along the road of ambition to pride.

IV. THE FEATURES THAT DISTINGUISH EACH TEMPTATION IN PARTICULAR. 1. *Individual traits of the first temptation.* The exact gist of the first temptation is, " If thou art the Son of God, exercise thy lordship ; if the Son of God, prove thy possession of that power ; if the Son of God, what profit is there in this Sonship ? What good will this birthright do you ? " Now, a compliance with the suggestions of the tempter would have been practical denial of that very Sonship and virtual distrust of the Divine Fatherhood. While we do not and cannot dispense with bread, we must depend on God as Israel of old waited for the word that brought them food. This is in strict accord with the training of the Saviour's childhood as shadowed forth in that portion of Deuteronomy, namely, vi. 4—9, that formed the frontlet already mentioned, and in entire harmony with his own teaching in the sermon on the mount, where he says, " For your heavenly Father knoweth that ye have need of all these things." The evil one—at once Satan the adversary, and Diabolos the accuser—now puts forth all his power. The temptation had doubtless continued all those forty days of fasting (πειραζόμενος, present participle implying such continuance), but now it culminated. (1) *The scene suitable for Satan's purpose.* The scene of this first temptation is placed by some at Quarantana, but by others it is transferred to Sinai. The former is much the more probable. And so the scene was a district of country that lay eastward of Jerusalem, overlooking the valley of the Jordan, and not far from the place where Jesus had been baptized by John in the waters of that river. It was very wild and very dreary and very desolate. This much might be inferred from the name of " wilderness " by which it was designated, but especially from the additional circumstance supplied by St. Mark, that he was there " with the wild beasts," which laired, no doubt, in the thick brushwood along the banks, or among the caves of the neighbouring hills. In addition, therefore, to the natural horrors of the place, were those wild beasts with hungry jaws and glaring eyes and frightful cries, just waiting to seize him as their prey. Few, if any, human feet had trod this particular portion of that wild; no human habitation stood there; no village, or town, or city was to be found in its immediate vicinage. Consequently no supply of the necessaries of life was obtainable there; no food, no refreshment of any kind, was to be had there. Take in connection with all this that our Lord had fasted forty days and forty nights, and we must admit that such a place and such a time and such circumstances were the best possible for the success of such a temptation as that with which Satan first plied the Saviour. (2) *Possibilities.* No doubt it was *easy* for him who was "declared the Son of God" with power, who could multiply a few loaves and fishes into food for multitudes, who could transform the water-pots of Cana into vessels of wine, to turn the loaf-like stones of the wilderness into actual loaves (ἄρτοι) of wholesome bread. Further, it was but *natural* for him to do so when he was suffering such severe privation, when pained with the pangs of want, when distressed by hunger, which, as the old saying has it, "will break through stone walls." Moreover, was it not right to do this when no other way of relief appeared accessible, and when ordinary means of sustenance were out of reach? Not so, however. (3) *Things ever so plausible not therefore proper.* A thing may be ever so plausible in the eyes of man, and yet not proper in the sight of God. Notwithstanding all the plausibility of Satan's suggestion, had the Saviour yielded he would have been forestalling the providence of God; shown distrust in the provisions of that providence; renounced the exercise of patience; doubted the resources of that heavenly Father who had commissioned the voracious raven to bring flesh to his prophet, who long before had supplied his people's wants without their sowing or reaping, and that in a wilderness and for forty years, raining down bread from heaven every morning throughout that period round the camp of Israel. Still more, he would have been renouncing that abnegation of self—that poverty, humility, suffering, and sorrow, which were all, and more, included in the conditions of the covenant. He would have put aside the bitter cup of suffering without raising it to his lips, much less draining it to the dregs. He would have faltered at the first step, and so defeated the whole undertaking. Interests of greatest moment were at stake : the life or death of millions was in the balance; the weal or woe of countless human beings was depending on the decision of that moment; souls immortal were to be saved or sacrificed by the action of that hour. (4) *The Saviour victorious.* Angels, we doubt not, looked to see the issue, perhaps in terrible suspense; but it lasted not an instant. The conflict in this case is scarcely commenced, when the Son of God comes off the conqueror and Satan is repelled. The sword of the Spirit was the instrument of victory. The tempter is reminded that man is not dependent on bread alone; there are many other things called into existence by God for human food, and everything so appointed, be it root, or fruit, or berry, or tuber, or plant, or acorn, will, by the Divine blessing, serve the end. Besides, while the body is still craving and saying, "Give, give," there is another part of man, which must be supplied with spiritual nourishment, and which it is death to neglect. The soul lacks spiritual food. It feeds on the hidden and heavenly manna. (5) *Practical use of this first temptation.* (a) *To see the subtlety of Satan's snares.* We may now look at the practical bearing of this first temptation expressed in the words, "Speak a word of power in order that these stones may become bread or loaves—speak them by a word of power into bread;" though ἵνα with the subjunctive is not for the infinitive after εἰπὲ in the sense of command, but as Stolz translates, "Sprich ein Machtwort damit diese Steine Brod werden." If we reflect on the antecedents and the accompaniments of this temptation, we cannot conceive of anything more specious. The *time* was that moment when he began to be an hungered; when the sinless cravings of appetite began to be felt; when, in instructive parallelism with Moses at the promulgation of the Law from Sinai, and with Elias at its restoration on Carmel, the Saviour at the fulfilment of the Law and the introduction of the gospel fasted forty days and forty nights. By entering in this manner on the activities of his great mediatorial work, he teaches us, by the way, the importance of retiring for fasting, meditation, and prayer before commencing any very important duty in the service of God. The time was thus well chosen; for when the Saviour, being subject to all the sinless infirmities of humanity, began to feel the gnawings of hunger, just then Satan, who is as vigilant as he is malignant and murderous, took advantage of the moment at which appetite, after being so long whetted, had become keenest, and urged the change of stones into bread to meet the wants of nature. But the *place* as well as the time appeared to second the speciousness and seeming propriety of this suggestion. It was just such a place as that of which the Psalmist says, " They wandered in a wilderness in a solitary way . . . Hungry and thirsty, their soul fainted in them." Nothing eatable could be obtained; no esculent of any kind was to be met with. The *circumstances* also added to the speciousness of Satan's suggestion, and seemed to render the working of a miracle as proper as it was plausible. The Saviour had been declared and openly acknowledged as the Son of God. He is alone in a desert, hungry, without any possibility of supply, and yet " the Son of God with power." In such a case it was natural enough and reasonable enough to all human seeming for Satan to say, " If you really possess the power, why not exert it at a time when it is so much needed, and in a place where it is so indispensable, no suitable supply being otherwise procurable? If the Son of God, and in want, why not utter a creative word and relieve that want? If invested with sufficient ability, why not speak an omnific word and display that ability? If capable, why not work a miracle when it is so necessary, and when there can be nothing wrong in the act; for to turn stones into loaves of bread is in itself no more amiss than to turn water into wine?" Thus tempted Satan. Thus by plausible and powerful reasonings he backed his temptations. (*b*) *To shun those snares is the next practical use to be made of this temptation.* However specious and subtle, it is our interest as well as our duty to shun them; and the more specious and subtle they are, the more needful it is to be on our guard against them. Oh, how subtle the tempter is! He takes advantage of our circumstances, he takes occasion from our wants, he adapts his assaults to our weaknesses. The poor and needy he tempts to discontent, sometimes even to dishonesty. Are you poor? Then, says Satan, scruple not to supply the necessities of nature. Are you unable to rise in the world by fair means? Then use foul. Are you in low circumstances? Then try the tricks of trade. Are you necessitous? Then employ dishonesty in your dealings, or resort to fraud in some shape, or even have recourse to force. Are you given to appetite? Then Satan will tempt to excess in food, or drink, or both. " Use the world," says God. " Abuse it," says Satan. " Be temperate in all things," says God. " Never mind," says Satan, " live while live you can, ' eat, drink, and be merry, for to-morrow you die.'" His temptations too, as we have seen, are most plausible. He often seems to be urging us to what is good and proper, or even to what tends to promote the glory and honour of God. But the more plausible a temptation is, and the more appearance of good there is in it, the more dangerous generally it is, and the more destructive it may prove. In the temptation we are considering, had the Son of God yielded, and by miracle turned stones into bread, however justifiable the act at first sight appears, besides betraying distrust in Providence and disregard of the Divine will, he would have failed in the exercise of submission, and so in setting an *example* to his followers. God will have his children, when they are in want, to wait on him and wait for him; Satan tempts them to do neither. God assures his people that he is merciful and gracious—that he knows our frame, and will supply our wants in his own good time and way; Satan tempts to hard thoughts of God, and to doubt or distrust his paternal care. God witnesseth with our spirits that we are his children, just as he had done to the eternal Son; Satan strives to weaken that testimony, and tempts us to question our sonship. God tells us that afflictions not only consist with, but come from, his fatherly hand, for " whom he loveth he chasteneth; " Satan tempts us to regard them as evidences that God has forgotten or forsaken us. (*c*) *Scripture is the sword of the Spirit we must wield.* Now consider the Saviour's reply to this first temptation. He might have met the tempter with a positive declaration, " I am the Son of God." He might have asserted his lordship over him. He might have subdued him instantly by Almighty power. But in so doing he would only have left us an exhibition of omnipotence to astonish us, not an example to attract us. On the contrary, he takes away the ground of the temptation by appealing to the Divine Word. His answer was, " It is written [stands written], Man shall not live by bread alone, but by every word that proceedeth out of the mouth of God," or more simply, as in St. Luke, " by every word of God." Thus he put honour on the Divine Word, and at the same time put into our hand a weapon of greatest power for our individual defence. He shows, moreover, that, though man ordinarily lives by bread, yet that any word proceeding out of the mouth of God, anything created by God's word and by that same word commanded to be used for food, will serve the purpose. "He can either," says Bishop Hall in his 'Contemplations,' "sustain without bread, as he did Moses and Elias; or with a miraculous bread, as the Israelites with manna; or send ordinary means miraculously, as food to his prophet by the ravens; or miraculously multiply ordinary means, as the meal and oil to the Sareptan widow." Christ, therefore, needed not to turn stones into bread; he only needed to trust in his heavenly Father for a seasonable and suitable supply. Hence we learn that, while bread is the staff of life, God's blessing is the staff of bread. We may want bread, and yet be nourished by some other means; we may have bread, and not be satisfied. In our greatest abundance we must not think of living without God; in our greatest indigence we must learn to live upon God. Ordinary means of succour and support may fail or be cut off; the fig tree may not blossom, nor fruit be in the vines; the labour of the olive may fail, and the fields yield no meat; yet are we to rejoice in the Lord and joy in the God of our salvation. (d) *Spiritual life needs nourishment suited to it.* Bread, by the Divine blessing, supports the life of the body; but there is a higher style of life that needs for its sustenance more than bread, and which bread alone cannot maintain. There is the life of the soul, the life of the immortal spirit; that spiritual life depends for support on every word of God. "Thy words were found," says the prophet, "and I did eat them; and thy word was unto me the joy and rejoicing of mine heart;" and Job says, "I have esteemed the words of his mouth more than my necessary food;" while the Saviour himself says, in reference to the same life, "My meat is to do the will of him that sent me, and to finish his work." And if we would live this truer, higher, nobler life, we "must all eat the same spiritual meat," feeding on the Word of God and following the will of God.

2. *The special character of the second temptation.* This second temptation is an appeal to avarice or aggrandizement or covetousness. As Moses saw the land of promise from the top of Pisgah, so Satan brings the Saviour to "an exceeding high mountain." A mountain is still pointed out as the mount of the temptation. Its name is Quarantana, and its height nearly two thousand feet. "It is distinguished," says Kitto, "for its sere and desolate aspect even in this gloomy region of savage and dreary sights." From its summit Satan shows him "all the kingdoms of the world and the glory of them. Whether by "world" is to be understood the Holy Land, then divided into several petty principalities; or the Roman empire, comprising many conquered kingdoms as its provinces; or the world in its widest sense, we stop not to inquire. Neither do we attempt to explain what power of optics commanded such a prospect, or how the horizon widened and widened till the world, with its political divisions as well as physical features, spread out, before the two solitary spectators on yon mountain-top, like an unfolded chart; or how especially all this was accomplished in a moment or second (literally, *point*) of time. The Scripture states the fact, and we believe it; the *how* of it we are not curious to discover, nor do we think it necessary to define. Some think the whole subjective; we take the whole to be objective. Milton, it is true, speaks of the specular mount, and amplifies the scene descried from it, as a poet and a scholar; and yet there is good reason to believe that his realistic interpretation is in accordance with the Scripture representation, as he sings—

> "Here thou behold'st
> Assyria, and her empire's ancient bounds,
> Araxes and the Caspian lake; thence on
> As far as Indus east, Euphrates west,
> And oft beyond, to south the Persian bay,
> And inaccessible, the Arabian drouth."

(1) *Attempt to realize the stupendous spectacle.* The imaginings of the poet had their foundations in fact. Looking to the right, they saw the cities and countries peopled by the numerous children of the East—the once powerful empire of Persia, the equally powerful and still more ancient Babylonia, the distant India, and the remote Chinese. Looking northward, they saw the nomadic hordes of Scythia stretching far away towards the frozen arctic regions. Westward they saw the many provinces conquered by Roman valour and then subject to Roman rule, the sunny shores and isles of Greece, the amalga-

mated races that peopled the Italian peninsula, the savage tribes of Germany, the gallant men of Gaul, and the far-off inhabitants of Britain.   Southward they saw the unconquered Arabs, the polished Egyptians, the sunburnt dwellers of Ethiopia, the Lybians bordering on the desert, and other sable sons of Africa. " All these shall be yours at once, and without an effort on your part, if you fall down and worship me, or rather do homage before me." (2) *Satan's title.* What claim, we may well ask, had Satan on these kingdoms ?   What right dared he to assert over them ?   His claim was that of usurped dominion, for it is only by usurpation and for a little space that he is god of this world. No doubt he affirms, " It has been entrusted to me ; " and he is called " the prince of this world," and " the prince of the power of the air." His right is only, however, that which sinful men have given him—that of slaves to a tyrant master— conceded to him by those whom he leads captive at his will. " Those myriad idolaters are mine," he said. " Those unbelieving Jews are mine. Those sinners of every tribe, and race, and name are mine ; they are of their father the devil, and my bidding they are prompt and prepared to do." Thus spake, we may conceive, the usurper. Thank God ! his usurpation will one day end, his works shall be destroyed, he himself for ever bruised and his power broken.   But he presumed to add, " To thee will I give this power and all the *glory* of them." (3) *His disingenuousness.* He showed the fair side of all. He kept away in the background the foul ways and sinful means by which kingdoms often have been won, the bloody battles, the cruel massacres, the wicked plots, the diplomatic schemes, by which crowns have been gained ; the cares that attend them, the anxieties that perplex them, the thorns that line them, for often " uneasy rests the head that wears a crown." All this Satan is ready to give. But why act so disingenuously ? Why not state the drawbacks ? Ah ! this is never Satan's way. He shows the best part of the picture ; the darker background he keeps out of view. He exhibits the fascinations of sin ; he conceals its bitterness. He recounts its pleasures, not its pains ; its seductions, not its sorrows ; its allurements, not its sufferings and its sadness. Besides, his promises are lies. He never keeps his word ; he never means to do so ; he never performs his promise. (4) *The Saviour's indignant rejection of Satan's offer.* No wonder the Saviour, wearied of Satan's intrusions, of his impertinence, of his insolence, of his insults as well as assaults, repels him rudely, saying, " Get thee behind me, Satan ; for it is written, Thou shalt worship the Lord thy God, and him only shalt thou serve." (5) *Satan's dupes and dependants.*   Satan is, no doubt, a mighty prince ; his hosts are the world-rulers of the darkness of this age, his bait the love of power.   The world- rulers (κοσμοκράτορες), the Pharaohs, the Herods, the Cæsars, snatched at that bait, accepting the evil one as their master. And so he tempts the Saviour too, as though he said, " Why not be a king like other kings ? Let your kingdom be of this world ; I object not to its being the greatest and the mightiest ; otherwise I will oppose thee." Thus far Satan.   But the Holy One again repels the evil one by Scripture. Again he appeals to the lesson of his childhood—the words of the frontlet, recognizing the allegiance due to God. (6) *Practical lesson from the second temptation.* Satan is still lavish in his offers and liberal in pressing them on all. He offers the world, its praises, its profits, its pleasures ; but he must have a *quid pro quo,* a full equivalent. He insists on your making a return for his favours, on your reciprocating his benefactions.   He wants you to worship him. He will have you sacrifice your soul in his service. Disguise it as he may, he will have nothing else and will accept nothing less. Satan is proverbially good to his own ; but that goodness is only seeming, and even in its seeming short.   The way of duty is the way of safety. For though evil triumphed for a time, though the day of its downfall were far distant or not to be dreamt of, though there were no such thing as retribution, and though no period of redress appeared likely ; still to be guided by the Divine Word, to imitate the Saviour, and to render allegiance to God alone, will be found in the end the happiest, the wisest, and the best.

3. *Nature of the third temptation.* It is an appeal to ambition or pride. Some, how- ever, are of opinion that this is a temptation to an experiment in order to test whether the Divine presence or the Divine protection pertained to Sonship, rather than a tempta- tion to an effort in order to gain power and popularity with the people. In favour of this view is the history from which the tempter is answered. The people had called in question the Divine presence, saying, " Is the Lord among us or not ? " They required a supernatural proof to assure them of it. Similar conduct on the part of the Saviour to

that of Israel on the occasion referred to would have been sinful distrust. Here, as afterwards, he could have bidden to his side legions of angels; but in either case he forbore. Obedient trust in God and determined opposition to Satan were the principles that guided the conduct of the Saviour, and that ultimately gained the day. (1) *The acme of Satan's subtlety.* The pinnacle or battlement of the temple was, doubtless, the royal portico built by Herod and " overhanging the ravine of the Kedron." It stood on the very edge of the precipice and towered up to an immense height. From the top of this giddy eminence Josephus tells us that no eye could see the bottom. " Cast thyself down," said Satan, " and the Jews, who are on the look-out for a temporal prince, will take you at once, and make you their king, and render ready homage to thy sceptre. Cast thyself down, and other nations, who are all expecting some great potentate to appear in order to usher in an age of unexampled blessing, will all make common cause with them, and form one united and world-wide empire. Thus Jew and Gentile, in happy harmony, shall bind the diadem of royalty round thy brow, and so crown thee Lord and ruler of all. In any case," says Satan, " and whatever be the result, you lose nothing by the experiment. You run no risk by the attempt; for is it not written, ' He shall give his angels charge over thee to keep thee'?" (2) *Suppression of Scripture.* Ah! here is the masterpiece of the evil one. Here we see how he can adapt himself to the exigencies of every case. Here we see his skill in imitation. Here, after the example of the Saviour, he appeals to Scripture. " What," says an old divine quaintly, almost quizzically—" what is this I see? Satan himself, with a Bible under his arm and a text in his mouth." But then he misquotes by suppressing part of the sentence, and so altering the sense of the whole. Undoubtedly God had promised, " He shall give his angels charge over thee to keep thee *in all thy ways*;" but this latter clause Satan found it convenient to omit. Thereby we are taught that the way of duty is the way of safety; wisdom's ways are ways of pleasantness and paths of peace. When we walk in these ways God has promised to keep us safe. Off them we jeopardize ourselves every hour. " Not so," says Satan. " Go where you like, walk as you like, take my word for it, you are safe." Thus Satan misquotes, misinterprets, and misapplies. Thus he said to our first parents, in direct contravention of God's word, " Ye shall not surely die." Thus was he " a liar and a murderer from the beginning." Thus he continues to lead men blindfold to the brow of the precipice, and bids them cast themselves down, telling them there is no danger, and assuring them of safety. Thus he plunges men in misery. Thus he brings them to perdition. Thus he sinks them in the deep abyss. (3) *His tactics are still the same.* " Cast yourself down," he says to some; " sin is an easy and safe descent. The way of virtue is hard and uphill; don't trouble yourself about it. Cast yourself down, wallow in your beloved lust, take your fill of your besetting sin; God is too merciful to mind it, or at least to punish it. Cast yourself down before the god of gold, like Israel before the golden calf, that you may be elevated in worldly rank and be exalted among thy fellows." Again, to children of God he says, " Cast yourselves down. The gospel mystery of sanctification is slow work and a roundabout way; try penances, fastings, macerations, pilgrimages, will-worship, and thus expedite it." Perhaps he waxes bolder and says to another, " You are a child of grace: once in grace always in grace; you may indulge in sin with impunity, or that grace may abound, or that God may get glory and you more grace by repentance. Cast yourself down; the sin you dread is a trifle—is it not a little one?" These are only a few specimens of Satan's subtle snares and manifold devices. To those in high places he whispers, " Cast yourselves down. Place is before principle; expediency rather than consistency." To others again, "Cast yourselves down. Become slaves to luxury, or sensuality, or vice; your means warrant it, the circumstances justify it. Cast yourselves down. Thousands do worse, while few do better, and it will be all the same in the end." (4) *The third repulse.* That pinnacle was a *high place*, and high places are slippery places; they are difficult places; they are dangerous places. Comparing this temptation with the former, we are reminded of the wise man's words, " Give me neither poverty nor riches." Our Lord's reply repulsed Satan in this quarter also. It was, " Thou shalt not tempt [literally, *out and out*, or to an extreme] the Lord thy God." You are not to run unbidden into danger; you are not to run against the thick bosses of Jehovah's buckler; you are not to pray, " Lead me not into temptation," and then dash into it; you are not to venture into a perilous position, where neither necessity, nor Providence, nor duty calls you; you are not to plead the covenant of God while you disregard its conditions; you are not to appropriate promises that in no way apply to your character or conduct.

CONCLUDING REMARKS. 1. The battle of life is largely a *battle for daily bread*. In far northern regions it is extremely difficult; in the tropics it is exceedingly easy. It has been well remarked that neither extreme has conduced much to the world's progress; it is for the most part the dwellers in the temperate zones, where labour for the support of life is only ordinarily difficult—equally removed from the extremes of severity and facility, that have helped onward the march of civilization, of science, of art; in a word, human improvement and human culture. 2. As we are to watch as well as pray to avoid temptation, so we are *to labour* as well as pray for daily bread—labouring as if all depended on our work, praying as though work formed no factor in the process. 3. The first temptation tended to carnal appetite and distrust of Providence; the last, to ambition and proud presumption on the Father's protection. The first presupposes want; the last, abundance. The first teaches a lesson to the *poor*; the last, to the *rich*. And just as the wilderness was suitable to the first, so the world-famed city was a proper place for the last; for Jerusalem was the glory of Palestine, the pride of all the land, while "the temple was the glory of Jerusalem, the pinnacle the highest point of the temple." 4. Observe the *extremes* in Satan's temptations—the first was to despair and to distrust in Providence; the last, to pride and presumption. The tenor of the final suggestion was, "Cast thyself down. If thou art supported by his providence, thou wilt be sustained by his protection. Cast thyself down. When people see thee fling thyself from the high precipice and receive no hurt, all men will then own thy Godhead and acknowledge thy Divine commission. Jerusalem and the Jews will acknowledge it and admit thou art more than man—even 'the Messenger of the covenant,' coming suddenly and sublimely to his temple. The work of Messiahship shall be facilitated and shortened; while every one will be at once convinced of thy claims. Besides, when, or where, or how, could a better opportunity be had for declaring publicly and powerfully thy glory and thy Godhead, thy dignity and design?" And yet the arch-tempter was signally foiled and the Saviour gloriously victorious. He bruised Satan's head; and in Christ and through Christ we—even we shall, by Divine grace, be enabled to bruise Satan, and that speedily, under our feet. 5. Satan, having completed *every* temptation, that is, every typical form of temptation, as though all temptations are resolvable into one of the three, "departed from him," but only for a season, or rather *until an opportunity* (ἄχρι καιροῦ), that is to say, until another opportunity should occur or some new opportunity present itself, either by way of suffering or situation—negative endurance or positive enticement. 6. Angels ministered to him. The necessity for this arose from the desert district in which he found himself. The statement in St. Mark's narrative that "he was with the wild beasts" is generally understood to imply that the region was wild in the extreme, desolate, and full of terrors, like Virgil's "Vitam in sylvis inter deserta ferarum lustra domosque traho;" may it not rather, or also, assign a reason for the ministering of angels mentioned in the next clause, as rendered absolutely necessary from the total absence of all human help and distance from all the resources of civilized life?

INTERVAL. Between the temptation, according to St. Mark's brief record, and our Lord's Galilean ministry many things had taken place, as we learn from the evangelist John. Into that interval a Judæan ministry of rather uncertain duration and of much importance must be interjected. We are dependent entirely on the fourth Gospel for the narrative of that ministry. But, though unrecorded by the synoptists, it is nevertheless implied and referred to by them.

CONNECTING LINKS. In the intervening period the following circumstances transpired: —1. The testimony of the Baptist to Jesus, already referred to; the adhesion of two of John's disciples to Jesus, Andrew bringing his brother Simon to him; our Lord's return to Galilee, where Philip findeth Nathanael and bringeth him to Jesus; the marriage in Cana. 2. Our Lord's first Passover at Jerusalem as the Son of God, the Messiah promised to the fathers, together with the expulsion of the traders; his discourse with Nicodemus, who came to him by night; his leaving Jerusalem, but remaining some time longer in Judæa; further, a final testimony of the Baptist; his setting out for Galilee after John's imprisonment; his discourse with the woman of Samaria at Jacob's well, near Sychar, as he passed through Samaria on his way to Galilee; his return to Cana and cure of the nobleman's son at Capernaum; his rejection at Nazareth and settled abode at Capernaum.—J. J. G.

Vers. 14, 15. Parallel passages: Matt. iv. 17; Luke iv. 14, 15.—*The Galilean ministry.* I. HIS PREACHING BEGAN IN GALILEE. Though our Lord's public ministry may be regarded as having commenced at that Passover at Jerusalem to which reference has been already made, yet his public appearance as a preacher was in Galilee. The place, the date, the subject are all distinctly marked by St. Peter in the tenth chapter of the Acts, at the thirty-seventh verse, as we read, " That word which God sent unto the children of Israel, preaching the *gospel* [good tidings] *of peace* by Jesus Christ (he is Lord of all)—that saying ye yourselves know, which was published throughout all Judæa, beginning from *Galilee*, after the *baptism which John* preached."

II. A FAVOURABLE FIELD. Now commence our Lord's labours among the towns and villages of Galilee—a sphere of operation of the most promising kind at that period. Of the four provinces of Palestine in the time of Roman rule, while Judæa was south, Samaria central, and Peræa east, Galilee was in the north. Originally it comprehended only a limited circle or circuit, as the name *Galil* imports, round Kedesh-Naphtali, including the twenty towns which Solomon gave to Hiram, but it grew into much larger dimensions till it included the four northern tribes, Asher and Naphtali, Zebulun, and Issachar, embracing an oblong twenty-five miles from north to south and twenty-seven from east to west. It was divided into Lower and Upper Galilee; the former district consisted mainly of the plain of Esdraelon or Jezreel, and the latter, containing the district between the Upper Jordan and Phœnicia, was called Galilee of the Gentiles because of its mixed population—Greeks, Arabs, Phœnicians, as well as Jews. This northern province of the Holy Land in the days of our Lord was studded with towns and even cities, had a thriving population, and abounded in hives of busy industry. Speaking of our Lord selecting this district as the scene of his labours, the late Dean Stanley says, " It was no retired mountain-lake by whose shore he took up his abode, such as might have attracted the Eastern sage or Western hermit. It was to the Roman Palestine almost what the manufacturing districts are to England. Nowhere, except in the capital itself, could he have found such a sphere for his works and words of mercy." The husbandman that tilled the fields, the merchantman that traded in the towns or villages, the fisherman that plied his craft on the waters of the lake, and labourers standing in the market-place,—all these and many such abounded in this populous region; and while easily accessible, and willing to wait on our Lord's ministry, they were more free from prejudice—less bigoted and less exclusive than their brethren of the southern province.

III. THE DISTRICT POINTED OUT IN PROPHECY. Ancient prophecy had marked this region out as that where gospel light would shine most brightly. These northern tribes, Zebulun and Naphtali, had soonest sunk into idolatry through the influence of their idolatrous neighbours, the Phœnicians, on the west, and had suffered sorest from Assyrian invaders from the east, most of them having been carried captive by Tiglath-pileser and their land repeopled in large part by strangers. The prophet, however, in order to console and in some measure compensate, foretold a good time coming in Isa. ix. 1, 2, which rightly rendered reads thus: " There shall not hereafter be darkness in the land which was distressed; as in the former time he brought to shame the land of Zebulun and the land of Naphtali, so in the time to come he bringeth it to honour, even the tract by the sea [*i.e.* the western shore], the other side of Jordan [the eastern side], Galilee of the nations [*i.e.* district north of the sea]. The people that walked in darkness have seen a great light: they that dwell in the land of the shadow of death, upon them hath the light shined." Thus henceforth the scene of the Saviour's ministry lies by the Jordan, the Lake of Gennesaret, and in Galilee of the Gentiles—

> " What went ye out to see
> O'er the rude sandy lea,
> Where stately Jordan flows by many a palm,
> Or where Gennesaret's wave
> Delights the flowers to lave
> That o'er her western slope breathe airs of balm?

"Here may we sit and dream
Over the heavenly theme,
Till to our souls the former days return ;
Till on the grassy bed,
Where thousands once he fed,
The world's incarnate Maker we discern."

IV. The subjects of our Saviour's preaching. The precursor had been imprisoned in the castle of Machærus, some nine miles east of the Dead Sea, in the district of Peræa ; but the Prophet himself takes up the work. Thus it ever is. God buries his workmen, but carries on his work. The great theme of the Baptist, as we have seen, was repentance and correspondent reformation, yet with faith implied. The theme of repentance was resumed by Jesus, but with the other doctrine of faith not implicitly but explicitly taught. The doctrine of faith now comes into prominence—the doctrine of faith, and that not merely bare credence or simple assent to the good news, but faith in—reliance on the gospel as the great and only means of safety and salvation. He proclaims, moreover, the advent of Messiah's reign. That critical epoch had now come ; that greatest era in all human history had arrived.

V. Difference in the use of two synonymous terms. The kingdom is usually called by St. Matthew the "kingdom of heaven," and not "kingdom of God," lest the latter expression might confirm the Jews, for whom in the first instance the evangelist wrote, in their erroneous apprehension of it as a great kingdom of a worldly and temporal kind, as by a Hebrew idiom the name " God " is joined to anything excessively great or extremely grand ; thus, we read of the "river of God," of "the cedars of God," and other similar expressions. By St. Luke, on the other hand, it is called the "kingdom of God" and not the "kingdom of heaven," lest the Gentiles, for whom this evangelist specially wrote, should misapprehend the expression as countenancing local divinities, as they were accustomed to gods and goddesses of different localities or quarters of the universe, such as Naiads, Nereids, Dryads, Hamadryads ; gods of the ocean and of rivers ; deities of the ethereal and infernal regions. This kingdom had been foreshadowed by Daniel in his vision of the great world-powers.—J. J. G.

Vers. 16—20. Parallel passages : Matt. iv. 18—22 ; Luke v. 1—11.—*The call of the first four disciples*. I. Previous and less formal call. Our Lord now calls to his side the first four disciples—Andrew and John, Peter and James. With the former pair he had already made acquaintance when they were disciples of John the Baptist. The account which St. John in his Gospel gives of the matter is complementary, and throws light on it, enabling us to understand more clearly how it was that these two brethren showed such alacrity and readiness in now obeying the Saviour's *more formal* call, and in following him. Andrew was one of the two disciples whose attention the Baptist directed to Jesus as "the Lamb of God," and John was in all probability the other, though, with his usual reserve, he does not name himself in the narrative. These two were privileged to spend a day with Christ, by special invitation, from ten o'clock in the morning, if we adopt the modern reckoning ; otherwise from four p.m. Andrew was the means of bringing his brother Simon Peter to Christ, and John may have rendered the same signal service to his brother James. In the interval between the first and this more formal call, these disciples had returned to their daily duties, biding their time till the Master would require their more special and active services.

II. The missionary spirit of Andrew. The Christian spirit is in its very nature missionary. As soon as Andrew, with whom in one sense the Christian Church begins, got good for his own soul, he wished to share it with others ; soon as he found Christ for himself, he set about making him known to others. His charity, too, begins at home, for he does not rest satisfied with the great discovery he had been favoured with, nor does he selfishly keep it to himself, he immediately goes in quest of his own brother, to communicate to him the good news. But though charity in his case began at home, it did not confine itself to such narrow domestic limits. On two other occasions we find Andrew similarly employed in bringing persons to Christ. It was he that brought the lad with the five barley loaves and the two small fishes to Christ, as we read in John vi. 8. Not only so ; it was Andrew who, in company with his townsman Philip, introduced to the Saviour those Greeks who, having come up to worship at the feast, expressed their earnest wish for that interview, saying, "Sir, we would see Jesus." And now that Andrew, in the fulness of his brotherly affection, had brought Peter to Christ, Andrew and Peter were bound together ever after, in a dearer, because a double, bond of brotherhood. Here is an example worthy of imitation, and that not only by the brethren of the same family, but by dwellers in the same neighbourhood and members of the same community, who may have shared with us in the amusements of childhood or the employments of youth, or who still walk side by side with us in manhood on the journey of life. Nay, as far as in us lies, by proxy, if not in person, we must seek to be instrumental in bringing our fellow-creatures of every name and clime to the foot of the cross, and in thus winning the world for Christ.

III. THE EMPLOYMENT OF THESE DISCIPLES. While Andrew and Peter were brothers and joint-occupants of the same dwelling—as we learn from ver. 29, owing to St. Mark's attention to minute details—we are informed by St. Luke that James and John were partners in trade (κοινωνοί), i.e. in a sort of fishing firm, with Simon, and so sharers in the general profits of the little company. They were also fellow-workers, for they are called, some verses earlier in the same chapter, sharers in the work (μετόχοις). Diligence in business, whatever our employment may be, is an important duty, and one which God is sure to acknowledge and bless; while Satan is ever ready to find mischief for idle hands to do. Moses was keeping the flock of Jethro his father-in-law, the priest of Midian, when the angel of the Lord, appearing unto him in that bush that burned with fire and yet was not consumed, sent him to bring forth the children of Israel out of Egypt. Gideon was threshing wheat by the wine-press, to hide it, when he was summoned to save Israel from the hand of the Midianites. Saul was making search for the lost asses of his father, when he was taken by Samuel and anointed with oil to be captain over the Lord's inheritance. David was tending a few sheep in the wilderness, when God called him to the high office of shepherd of his people Israel. Elisha was "ploughing with twelve yoke of oxen before him, and he with the twelfth," when Elijah cast his mantle upon him in token of his becoming his assistant and successor in the prophetic office.

IV. THE PLACE OF THEIR WORK. 1. *Name of the lake.* "The Lake of Gennesaret," as St. Luke accurately calls this sheet of water so famous in sacred story, is termed "the Sea of Galilee" by St. Matthew and St. Mark, "the Sea of Tiberias" also by St. John, and in the Old Testament "the Sea of Chinnereth," i.e. *harp-like* in shape, of which "Gennesaret" may be a corruption, if the latter word be not derived from two Hebrew words meaning "gardens of princes" (*ganne sarim*) or "garden of Sharon" (*gan sharon*); while it gets the designation "of Galilee" from the province in which it is situated and that of "Tiberias" from the Roman emperor Tiberius, in compliment to whom the town Tiberias was so named by Herod Antipas, its founder. From this, too, comes the modern name by which the lake is sometimes named *Bahr-al-Tabariyeh.* 2. *The shape and size of the lake.* We have already referred to its shape as resembling a harp. It is somewhat oval, and very like a pear in form; while its length is twelve miles and a quarter by six and three quarters in breadth at its widest part. The depression of the lake is remarkable— between six hundred and seven hundred feet below the level of the Mediterranean Sea. Its waters, reflecting the blue of the sky above, are clear, transparent, and sweet to the taste; while all sorts of fish, largely contributed by the numerous streams that enter it, abound therein. 3. *Scenery and surroundings.* The margin of the lake is surrounded by a level beach, here covered with smooth sand or small shells, there strewn with coarser shingle, and discernible as a white line encompassing the lake. This beach (αἰγιαλός), so often mentioned in the Gospels, while laved on one side by the bright waters of the lake, is fringed on the other side in many parts by shrubs and oleanders with their rosy-red blossoms. From this shore-line rise gradually in most places the surrounding hills, though to no considerable height, with brown outline but ever-varying tints; while away in the distance are seen in white lines along the sky the snowy peaks of Hermon; also on the eastern side the undulating table-lands commencing in Gaulonitis run southward from Cæsarea Philippi down to the Yarmuck, and onward through Peræa. But coming close to the lake and commencing at Kerak, we proceed northward to the hot springs, near to which extend the ruins of Tiberias now Tabariyeh. This was the noble city where once "the Jewish pontiff fixed his throne," and where the Sanhedrin was established; where, moreover, existed for three centuries the metropolis and university of Judaism. Near this place are steep rocks and a mountain approaching the water's edge. Further north we reach Magdala, now a miserable village called *Mejdel*, where Mary Magdalene had her home. It is situated at the southern extremity of the plain of Gennesaret, now called *El Ghuweir*, "the little hollow." Here again the mountains recede, and this plain on the north-western shore of the lake is formed ; its extent is two miles and a half long and one mile broad. It is now covered with brushwood and some patches of corn, though once so celebrated for fertility and beauty. The description of it by Josephus has been often quoted ; it is as follows :—"One may call this place the ambition of nature, when it forces those plants that are naturally enemies to one another to agree together. It is a happy contention of the seasons, as if every one of them laid claim to this country ; for it not only nourishes different sorts of autumnal fruits beyond man's expectation, but preserves them a great while. It supplies man with its principal fruits, with grapes and figs continually during ten months of the year, and the rest of the fruits, as they become ripe together, through the whole year ; for besides the good temperature of the air, it is watered from a most fertile fountain." The abundant waters that irrigate this plain proceed from a large round basin of antique structure, called Ain-el-Medawara, or Round Fountain ; or according to others, from the fountain called Ain-et-Tabiga. At the other or northern extremity of the plain are the ruins of Khan Minyeh, marking, perhaps, the site of ancient Chinnereth, but wrongly identified by some with Capernaum Close to this is the Fountain of the Fig Tree, called Ain-et-Tin, with its rather indifferent water ; and a quarter of an hour further in the same direction brings us to the little bay and great spring of Tabiga, supposed, as we have seen, by some to be that of which Josephus speaks as watering the plain of Gennesaret. A mile and a half further northward we find the ruins of *Tell Hum*, rightly identified, as we think, with the ancient Capernaum, *Kefr-na-hum* being changed into Tell Hum by abridging the termination into *hum*, and substituting for *Kefr*, a village, *Tell*, a heap, when a heap of rubbish was all that remained of it. If Tell Hum be in reality Capernaum, then *Kerazeh*, two miles and a half from the lake, and about two miles north from Tell Hum, is Chorazin. Two miles further onward bring us to mounds and heaps of stones called Abu Zany, at the northern mouth of the Jordan, identified by the author of the 'Land and the Book' with Bethsaida of Galilee—the native place of Andrew and Peter and Philip ; while on the opposite bank are ruins which the same writer considers to be Bethsaida Julias. With the east side of the lake we have less to do, and the very few spots on that side of any importance have less interest for us. There is the very fertile and well-watered plain of Butaiha along the north-east shore of the lake, which bears a close resemblance to the plain of Gennesaret on the north-west shore. There are besides the ruins of *Khersa*, the ancient Gergesa, on the left bank of the Wady Semakh ; the remains of Gamala, on a hill near the Wady Fik ; and the ruins of *Um Keis*, the ancient Gadara, a long way southward. 4. *State of matters at present.* In the days of our Lord and his disciples the fisheries yielded a profitable revenue, while one, perhaps two, of the villages on its shores, viz. Western and Eastern Bethsaida, "house of fish," got their names therefrom. The white sails of vessels, amounting to some thousands, were seen in its waters, from the ship of war or merchantman down to the fishing-smack or pleasure-boat. Its surface was astir with life and energy and joy. Now a single miserable bark is all that furrows its waves, and even that is sometimes difficult to procure. The noise and bustle and activities of numerous villages and towns are hushed in unbroken silence. 5. *The sacredness of this district.* Here indeed is holy ground. "Five little towns," says Renan, "of which humanity will speak for ever as much as of Rome and of Athens, were, at the time of our Lord, scattered over the space that extends from the village of Mejdel to Tell Hum ;" the towns he refers to are Magdala, Dalmanutha, Capernaum, Bethsaida, and Chorazin. Elsewhere he says, " We have a fifth Gospel, lacerated, but still legible (*lacéré, mais lisible encore*)," in the harmony of the gospel narrative with the places therein described. It was here Jesus called his first disciples ; it was here he entered into a ship, and sat in the sea ; it was here from its deck he taught the pressing crowds that lined the shore ; it was here he walked upon the waters ; it was here he stilled the storm ; it was here, after his resurrection, he was known to the disciples by the great draught of fishes ; it was here he directed them to bring of the fish thus caught and "come and dine." "What," says Dr. Thomson in 'The Land and the Book,' "can be more interesting? A quiet ramble along the head of this sacred sea! The blessed feet of Emmanuel have hallowed every acre, and the eye of Divine love has gazed a thousand times upon this fair expanse of lake and land. Oh! it is surpassingly beautiful at this evening hour. Those western hills stretch their lengthening shadows over it, as loving mothers drop the gauzy curtains round the cradle of their sleeping babes. Cold must be the heart that throbs not with unwonted emotion. Son of God and Saviour of the world! with thee my thankful spirit seeks communion here on the threshold of thine earthly home." Still more beautiful and touching are the verses of the sainted McCheyne on the sea of Galilee, of which, though so well known, we venture to cite the three following :—

> "How pleasant to me thy deep blue wave,
>   O Sea of Galilee!
> For the glorious One who came to save
>   Hath often stood by thee.

> "Graceful around thee the mountains meet,
>   Thou calm reposing sea;
> But ah, far more! the beautiful feet
>   Of Jesus walked o'er thee.

> "O Saviour! gone to God's right hand!
>   Yet the same Saviour still,
> Graved on thy heart is this lovely strand
>   And every fragrant hill."

V. MANNER OF THEIR WORK AND ACTUAL ENGAGEMENT WHEN CALLED. Simon and Andrew were actually engaged in fishing when the Master called them; James and John were mending, or rather preparing ($\kappa\alpha\tau\alpha\rho\tau\acute{\iota}\zeta o\nu\tau\alpha s$), their nets. Here we are taught the right use and proper economy of time. When not actually engaged in the labours of our calling we may do much in preparing for it, either taking necessary rest and refreshment for our bodies, and so acquiring vigour by repose, or in getting our apparatus or equipments of whatever kind in readiness for the resumption of labour. *Different kinds of nets.* Three kinds of nets were used by the Galilean fishermen. There was the $\delta\acute{\iota}\kappa\tau\nu o\nu$, the most general name for any kind of net, and derived from $\delta\acute{\iota}\kappa\omega$, I cast, a word akin to $\delta\acute{\iota}\sigma\kappa os$, a quoit. It is sometimes used figuratively in the LXX., as $\pi\alpha\gamma\acute{\iota}s$ is in the Pauline Epistle in the New Testament. Nets of this sort John and James were repairing when they were summoned by the Saviour. There was the $\dot{\alpha}\mu\phi\acute{\iota}\beta\lambda\eta\sigma\tau\rho o\nu$, from $\dot{\alpha}\mu\phi\acute{\iota}$, around, and $\beta\alpha\lambda\lambda\acute{\omega}$, I cast—the casting-net spreading out in a circle when cast into the water, and sinking by weights attached. From its circular shape it enclosed whatever lay below it. There was also the $\sigma\alpha\gamma\acute{\eta}\nu\eta$, from $\sigma\acute{\alpha}\tau\tau\omega$, $\sigma\acute{\epsilon}\sigma\alpha\gamma\alpha$, I load, which was a sweep-net of wide reach, and included a wide extent of sea. Hence it is used, according to Trench, in a parable, "wherein our Lord is setting forth the wide reach and all-embracing character of his future kingdom," and where neither of the other two words would have suited as well or at all.

VI. READY AND UNRESERVED COMPLIANCE. No sooner had our Lord said, "Hither, after me," as the original words literally mean, than these four brethren, James and John, as well as Simon and Andrew, at once obeyed the summons. St. Mark's words here are very expressive—they *went away or off behind him*—and imply the completeness with which they separated themselves from previous connections and severed themselves from past pursuits, as also the entire devotion with which they joined their new Master and commenced their new calling. They do not seem to have entered into any worldly calculations as to their present maintenance or future prospects, or to have counted the cost of the sacrifice they were called to make; neither did they consult with flesh and blood, or take into account considerations such as carnal policy is apt to suggest. They left all at once and for ever. What if their boats and nets were comparatively of small value or little worth in the estimate of the rich? Still to these fishermen the sacrifice was great, for it involved their worldly all.

VII. THE GOODNESS OF THE MASTER. Hardly, if ever, does Christ give us a precept that he does not add a promise to encourage us to, and help us in, the performance. If he bids us come to him, however weary and worn, sad and suffering and sorrowful we may be, he promises to give us rest; if he bids us take his yoke upon us, he assures us it will be light; if he bids us seek, he promises we shall find; if he urges us to ask, he promises we shall receive; if he presses us to knock, he pledges his word that it shall be opened to us; and so of all the rest. Thus it is here, when he summons them to forsake their humble occupation of fishermen, he gives them the appropriate and characteristic promise to make them "fishers of men."

VIII. INSTRUCTIVE INCIDENT. True religion, instead of cutting the ties of kinship, as a rule consecrates them. Times of persecution, indeed, may separate us from the nearest relatives and dearest friends; for, unless we love Christ more than the nearest and dearest, we are unworthy of him. Still, such cases are exceptional. Here a beautiful circumstance is brought to our notice by St. Mark. John and James, when leaving their father Zebedee to follow their Master, were not forgetful of the claims of filial piety and natural affection. They did not leave their aged father helpless, but with "the hired servants." From this the obvious inference is that he would be still enabled to continue his ordinary business, and pursue his usual avocation as heretofore.

IX. INTERESTING INFERENCE. There is good reason to infer that, for his station in life, Zebedee was, as it is called, well to do. If not rich, he was not positively poor. He was in the happy mean which the wise man sought when he said, "Give me neither poverty nor riches; feed me with food convenient for me: lest I be full and deny thee, and say, Who is the Lord? or lest I be poor and steal, and take the name of my God in vain." The boats and nets and hired servants bespeak the possession of at least a competence for one in his humble position yet honest walk in life.—J. J. G.

Vers. 21—28. Parallel passage: Luke iv. 31—37.—*The healing of a demoniac in the synagogue of Capernaum.* I. SYNAGOGUE SERVICE. It was the sabbath, and our Lord was teaching in the synagogue of Capernaum. The service of the synagogue was simple. In addition to the prayers, there was the reading of the Divine Word. First came the *Parashah*, or lesson of the Law; then followed the *Haphtarah*, or prophetical section. Hence we read, in the account of our Lord standing up to read in the synagogue of Nazareth, that the roll of the Prophet Isaiah *was further* given him ($\epsilon\pi\epsilon\delta\delta\theta\eta$), that is, in addition to the lesson of the Law already read, he was handed the prophetical section, to be read as the second lesson. Any competent person might be invited by the ruler of the synagogue or elders to discharge this duty, and afterwards address "a word of exhortation to the people," as in Acts xiii. 15.

II. OUR LORD'S OBSERVANCE OF THE SABBATH. Our Lord honoured the Lord's day, the house of God, and the ordinance of preaching which God has appointed for the instruction and edification of his people, as also for the explanation and enforcement of his Holy Word.

III. HIS MODE OF TEACHING. He was teaching, and, as we are told, "with authority, and not as the scribes." His *method* of teaching differed from theirs. Instead of appealing to precedents or citing the traditions of ancient rabbis, our Lord taught with independence, originality, and freshness, enforcing what he taught by his own authority. The *matter* of his teaching also differed from theirs. Instead of subtle, useless distinctions, almost evanescent differences, and trifling puerilities, he expounded the great things of God—his kingdom, grace, and glory. Still more than the mode of teaching or the truth taught was the manifestation of *power* in proof of, or at least accompanying, his teaching. The power by which he confirmed, and the evidence which he adduced in attestation of the truth, was something new and strange and unequalled. Hence the subsequent question, "What new teaching with respect to power?" or, "What new and powerful teaching is this?" for so we must read with the critical editors rather than with the received text, "What thing is this? What new doctrine is this? for with authority commandeth he even the unclean spirits;" because "with authority" would regularly be $\epsilon\pi$' or $\mu\epsilon\tau$' $\epsilon\xi o\upsilon\sigma\iota\alpha\varsigma$, rather than $\kappa\alpha\tau$' $\epsilon\xi o\upsilon\sigma\iota\alpha\nu$. His teaching was accompanied with a novel exercise of power, not merely over the minds of men, but over beings of another race and belonging to a different sphere, even the spirits of evil. For one discharging the office of teacher to exercise such authority, and to put forth such power in commanding, coercing, and controlling such spiritual agencies, was unprecedented, and naturally enough led to the inquiry or exclamation we are considering. It may be observed that in some copies of the Italic Version the "and" in the clause "and not as the scribes" is omitted, but erroneously, for the copulative is used of things different rather than of opposites. In case of things not merely different, but opposite or contrary, the omission of the copula is admissible, as in the next chapter at ver. 27, "The sabbath was made for man, [and] not man for the sabbath," though the English Version inserts "and," and Tregelles reads the clause with καί. On this occasion, then, of our Lord's teaching in the synagogue, the healing of the demoniac was effected.

IV. REALITY OF DEMONIACAL POSSESSION. The subject of demoniacal possession has been so fully and frequently discussed that little remains to be said on it. Certain it is that, to any unprejudiced reader of the Gospels, such possession must appear an undeniable reality. This man in the power (ἐν) of an unclean spirit addresses Jesus, "What have we to do with thee, thou Jesus of Nazareth?" literally, "What is common [κοινόν understood] to us and to you?" In ch. v. Jesus commands the unclean spirit to come out of the man; and in the Gospel of St. Matthew (viii. 32) he suffers the demons to go away into the herd of swine. There can be no reasonable denial, then, of the actual personality of these evil spirits. Their presence and personality are distinctly and decidedly recognized in such Scriptures as those just mentioned.

V. NATURE OF THIS POSSESSION. The poor demoniac had, it would seem, a sort of double consciousness. His own will was dominated by a superior internal agent, who held him in terrible thrall. There was the human personality of the man possessed, as in the case of the Gadarene demoniac, who, when he had descried Jesus afar off, ran and worshipped him; there was the demoniac personality, or personality of the evil spirit, at the same time, which, employing the instrumentality of the man's organs of speech, cried with a loud voice, "I adjure thee by God, that thou torment me not." This possession was not disease, nor was it madness; it was not physical alone, nor mental alone; it was not corporeal merely, nor spiritual merely; but a strange and shocking combination of both.

VI. WHY WAS DEMONIAC POSSESSION CONFINED TO OUR SAVIOUR'S TIME OF SOJOURN ON EARTH? The most perplexing question perhaps in relation to this matter is, Why was it that such possession occurred just at the time of our Lord's ministry on earth— apparently neither before nor since? Several answers have been given to it, such as the prevalence of certain diseases, whether bodily or spiritual, at particular periods of the world's history; the climactic pitch which moral disintegration and social disorganization had reached at the time of Christ's appearance on earth; the check given to such possession by the introduction of Christianity; our ignorance of cases of the kind that may still exist. There may be an element of truth in each of these; still they are each and all inadequate as an answer to the difficult question propounded, and we must seek for a more satisfactory solution in some other direction.

VII. SATAN'S POWER. The discrowned archangel, called now *Diabolos* the accuser, again *Satan* the adversary, is the acknowledged head of these *daimonia* or *daimones*. He is still, as we have seen in connection with the temptation, the prince of the power of the air, and the prince of this world to a lamentable extent. His knowledge is immense, yet he is not omniscient; his power is enormous, yet he is not almighty; his presence is little short of ubiquitous—"going to and fro in the earth, and walking up and down in it"—yet he is not omnipresent; his resources for evil and for injury are amazing, yet they are not absolute. Happily, he is limited to some extent and restricted in some ways; he is not by any means infinite.

VIII. AN IMITATOR. With all his knowledge and power and resources, he is only an imitator at the best, and a destroyer at the worst. What God made he marred, as far as permitted to do so; what the Saviour does, he *imitates*. Accordingly, when the Son of God became incarnate, Satan or his subject-demons became incarnate too—at least, to the extent of entering and taking possession of the bodies of men. Again, when the dispensation became distinctly spiritual—when, after the Saviour's ascension, the Spirit was sent down—Satan confined himself also more to spiritual influences; that is to say, such influences as he still exercises over the spirits and minds of men.

IX. RECOGNITION AND CONFESSION OF THE SAVIOUR BY SATAN'S SUBJECTS. It need be no matter of surprise that, in person or by proxy, he is here found in the house of God, for such has been his practice from days of old. In the ancient time, when the sons of God came together and presented themselves before the Lord, Satan came among them and put in an appearance too. Nor can it be reasonably doubted that he continues his custom of frequenting the place of religious assemblies still. To the present hour he is sometimes with the preacher in the pulpit, sometimes with the hearer in the pew, though in neither case to help, but, whether with preacher or auditor, to hinder and to hurt. So in the instance before us.

X. THE SAVIOUR'S REFUSAL OF SUCH ACKNOWLEDGMENT. His acknowledgment of the Saviour is sternly rebuked. " Be muzzled (φιμώθητι) and come out of him ! " was our Lord's indignant command. The acknowledgment, we therefore conclude, was either the expression of fawning fear, or rather an effort of fiendish malice to compromise the Saviour's character, as though in league with Satanic power and the spirits of evil. If so, our Lord's acceptance of such acknowledgment would have tended to discredit his mission and to damage his work. Demons knew him, for Satan, their chief, had followed him on his mission of mercy to man. He had dogged his steps as if to find out his true relationship—if indeed he was the Son of God—and to foil and frustrate, as far as practicable, his redemptive work. He had encountered him in the wilderness, and by his own defeat had learnt with certainty that he was in truth the Holy One of God.

XI. A KNOWLEDGE THAT IS NOT SAVING. Though demons knew and confessed the Son of God, they had nothing to do with him, so that they could truly say, " What have we to do with thee?" Sad thought! These lost ones had nothing to expect at his hand but further, fuller, and final destruction. Alas! that any should know Christ as these evil spirits, acknowledge him, and yet have neither part nor lot in the matter! There is a knowledge that does not save, for it lodges in the head and never touches the heart; it makes itself known by profession, but never manifests itself in practice. There is a faith that only genders fear, but never gains forgiveness nor goes the length of favour; for devils believe and tremble. Blessed be God for the truth which, brought home to the understanding and heart and conscience by the Holy Spirit, saves the soul : " This is life eternal, that they might know thee, the only true God, and Jesus Christ, whom thou hast sent " !

XII. SATAN AND HIS SERVANTS EVERMORE EVIL. The unclean spirit was coerced into obedience. When reluctantly compelled to obey, he resolved to work all the mischief possible. He tore or convulsed (σπαράξαν) the man, " threw him (ῥίψαν) in the midst," as Luke informs us, but yet had no more that he could do, for he was obliged to come out without doing him any real or permanent bodily injury (μηδὲν βλάψαν). " It is much easier," says an old divine, " to keep him (Satan) out than to cast him out." And now heaven had acknowledged the Messiah; hell, as we have just seen, had to own him; while it remained for earth to confess its King.—J. J. G.

Vers. 29—34. Parallel passages : Matt. viii. 14—17; Luke iv. 38—41.—*The cure of Peter's wife's mother and others.* I. FEVER OF A VIRULENT TYPE. That St. Peter was a married man appears not only from this mention of his mother-in-law, but also from the reference of St. Paul (1 Cor. ix. 5), " Have we not power to lead about a sister, a wife, as well as other apostles, and as the brethren of the Lord, and Cephas?" But, near and dear as Peter was to the Saviour, he was not exempted from the common lot; his home was visited with sickness. Nor was it a mere slight indisposition. Fever of almost any type is a painful, wasting, and distressing malady. The present attack was one of no little severity, for St. Luke, a physician by profession, and so capable of accurate diagnosis, calls it a great or violent fever (πυρετῷ μεγάλῳ). " Anon they tell him of her." The persons who did so may have been Peter and Andrew, who had come to reside at Capernaum, and who, as St. Mark with his usual particularity here informs us, were joint-occupants of one house after they had removed from Bethsaida (" place of fishing "), their native place. Or it may have been the domestics; or rather, perhaps, the subject is left indeterminate. In any case, it was the right thing to do. At any time of sickness, and whatever be the nature of the disease, we should first go to God, then to the physician; first have recourse to prayer, then to the use of means. Similar in spirit is the injunction, " Is any sick among you? let him call for the elders of the Church; and let them pray over him, anointing him with oil in the name of the Lord."

II. THE MODE OF CURE. The cure was another manifestation of Divine power, as well as of human sympathy, on the part of our Lord. There are several graphic touches of a very interesting kind, especially in the description of the cure, by St. Mark. Our Lord approached the sufferer (προσελθών); St. Luke interjects the additional detail that he stood over her (ἐπιστὰς ἐπάνω); he raised her up (ἤγειρεν); he took hold of her by the hand (κρατήσας τῆς χειρὸς αὐτῆς). We cannot fail to be struck with the tenderness and compassion and sympathy of our blessed Lord with the poor sufferer. A word from him would have been quite as effectual. He did indeed rebuke the disease (ἐπετίμησε), but he did not stop there. Had he done so, there would have been apparently less of human interest, less of tender sensibility, and altogether less of that affectionate fellow-feeling that so touches the heart of suffering humanity.

III. THE EFFECTAL NATURE OF THE CURE. It was immediate. He had no sooner taken her by the hand than the fever left her. The cure was miraculous; not that the disease was incurable, or past the power of ordinary physicians, but from the manner of the cure—a touch of the hand, and its immediacy: "Immediately the fever left her." Still more, she was relieved of, or rather saved from, the prostration, often extreme, in consequence of fever. Her convalescence was instantaneous. No weary weeks of waiting for returning strength, no administering of restoratives to the exhausted frame, no slow or gradually perceptible increase of physical energy; at once, immediately, she arose and engaged in her usual routine of household duties.

IV. THE DUTY OF DEVOTING OUR RENEWED HEALTH AND RESTORED STRENGTH TO GOD'S SERVICE. She ministered unto them; that is, to Christ and his disciples. This is the great end and the sanctified use of affliction. When the visitation is removed, we are to employ ourselves with renewed zeal in the Divine service. We are to make some suitable return for the mercy experienced, and show our gratitude for the benefit bestowed. "Bless the Lord, O my soul, and forget not all his benefits: who forgiveth all thine iniquities; who healeth all thy diseases; who redeemeth thy life from destruction; who crowneth thee with loving-kindness and tender mercies."—J. J. G.

Vers. 32—39. Parallel passages: Matt. viii. 16, 17; iv. 23—25; Luke iv. 40—44.— *A Physician for both body and soul.* I. CURES OF DISEASED PERSONS AND DEMONIACS. 1. *The time specified.* It was now evening, and the sun had just set; and so the sabbath —for it was the sabbath day, as we know from ver. 21—was considered past. The people now felt at liberty, without encroaching on the sacred rest of that holy day, to bring their sick for healing. Another reason is assigned by some for delaying till evening, to the effect that the noontide heat was then over and the cool of evening come, and so the infirm could be brought with less risk and more convenience. *A motley group of invalids.* There was a general turn-out of the townspeople, so that the whole city seemed gathered together to the door of the dwelling, while they had brought with them all that were diseased and demoniac. What a motley multitude must have been there! The consumptive were there, with pale face or hectic flush; victims of incurable cancer were there; persons with the burning heat and the parched lips, or in the very delirium, of fever, were there; the palsied, the dropsical, the epileptic were there; patients having diseases of the heart, of the lungs, of the head, of the spine were there; the lame, the dumb, the blind, were there. Some were able to walk, some were on crutches, some were mounted on asses, and some carried on pallets by friends or neighbours. Demoniacs, too, were there, whether those whose souls were subject to demoniacal influence, like the "damsel possessed with a spirit of divination," of whom we read in Acts xvi. 16; or those whose bodies were inhabited by evil spirits; or those, as was generally the case, whose souls and bodies were both under the fearful control of the evil one. 2. *The number cured.* "He healed *many* that were sick," says St. Mark. Why not all? Theophylact answers the question by supposing that "he healed 'many' instead of 'all,' for the all were many;" but this would seem to require an article before πολλοὺς, and also one before κακῶς ἔχοντας, viz. the many that were diseased. Perhaps we may understand it of the limitation of time, that is to say, he healed all that there was time for, as it was already eventide when the process began; or perhaps we may suppose the restriction occasioned by the absence in some cases of the conditions of cure, just as we read of a certain place (ch. vi. 5) that "he could there do no mighty work." The parallel passages of the other two synoptic Gospels seem to favour the first explanation, as in St. Matthew we read that he "healed all that were sick," and in St. Luke that "he laid his hands on every one of them and healed them." 3. *Prohibition of demoniac testimony.* He had already rebuked an unclean spirit that volunteered his unwelcome testimony. He forbids their speaking at all, because they knew him—not as the margin has it, "to *say* that they knew him," which would require λέγειν instead of λαλεῖν—for one reason, lest he should appear to be in collusion with them, and lest countenance should thus be given to the calumny of the Pharisees, and also lest, if believed when happening to speak truly, they might be more readily credited when uttering the most fatal falsehoods. 4. *Origin and history of the name.* The history of the name *demons* is somewhat curious, and as follows:—Δαίμων—derived from δαήμων, skilful, and so implying superior knowledge, or from δαίω, I dispense, as if able to distribute destinies, and so superior in power—was at first nearly synonymous with θεός, except that the latter signified a particular god or person; while the former meant rather a deity with respect to power; then an inferior deity, or semi-god, an agency intermediate between God and man; in plural, departed spirits of the good, and so tutelary deities or lares; next, any departed spirits or manes. In the New Testament the term signifies, not the spirits of the departed, but those evil spirits or fallen angels "who kept not their first estate," who are distinguished from the elect angels, and of whom we read that "God spared not the angels that sinned." They are subject to Satan, but, like him, they can only act by permission of God, and in their operations they can neither contravene the laws of nature nor interfere with human freedom and responsibility. Powerful for evil as they undoubtedly are, leading men captive or working on the children of disobedience, they, like their head, have only such power over man as men themselves consent to or concede them. Hence Augustine says truly, "Consentientes tenet, non invitos cogit." Further, the violation of the rule of neuters plural being constructed with verbs singular in ᾔδεισαν, comes under the first of the two following exceptions, that is, when neuters imply persons, as τέλη, magistrates, and so individuality or plurality of persons is signified; or in case of inanimate objects, when individuality or plurality of parts is signified. 5. *Devotion of spirit.* To extraordinary diligence in business our Lord added singular devotion of spirit. After a fatiguing day in the synagogue, then with the sick who in such numbers resorted unto him, he at dawn of day next morning retires for secret devotion and spiritual communion with his heavenly Father. At daybreak, or "when it was day," as St. Luke expresses it, or more exactly, according to St. Mark, "early, while it was quite in the night" (πρωὶ ἔννυχον λίαν)—at that early hour, intermediate between night and day, before the light of day has fully dawned or the darkness of the night quite departed—he withdrew to some lone and barren spot in one of the ravines or mountains, or under some sheltering rock in the district of Capernaum, to be alone with God. There he *continued* in prayer (προσηύχετο, imperfect). How beautifully our Lord instructs us by his practice as well as his precept to enter our closet and shut to the door, and pray to our Father in secret! He further shows us the necessity of prayer to maintain the life of the soul and obtain the help of heaven, to prepare us for our daily duties and for faithful diligence in the discharge of those duties. At the same time he commends the early morning for this exercise of devotion, when the feelings are fresh, the spirits in the fittest frame, and the mind free from the distractions so common in the after-part of the day. 6. *Interruption.* But, early as was our Lord's matin-hour, he was not secure from interruption. The people (ὄχλοι, crowds) sought him, as St. Luke informs us, while Peter and his companions, as St. Mark tells us, with characteristic impetuosity and affectionate eagerness pursued him—actually pursued him, as though he had fled away and escaped from them. The word κατεδίωξαν is literally "hunted down" or "for;" that is, they pursued him closely, followed hard upon his tracks. But it is occasionally used in a good sense, as here; thus it is used in the Septuagint Version of Ps. xxiii. 6, "Surely goodness and mercy shall follow (καταδιώξει) me."

II. CIRCUIT THROUGH GALILEE. 1. *Evangelistic tour.* Peter and those with him were evidently proud of their Master's great and increasing popularity, for when they had found him they tell him gladly, perhaps with somewhat of exaggeration, "All men seek for thee;" or, as in St. Luke, "were earnestly seeking (ἐπιζήτουν) him, and tried to detain him (κατεῖχον)." They evidently wished to keep to themselves or to the city of their habitation a monopoly of their Lord's services. But he, unmoved by praise, uninfluenced by popularity, disabuses their minds of their narrowness in selfishly seeking to localize him in Capernaum, city though it was, calmly informing them of his purpose to itinerate throughout the villages or country towns of that then populous district. At once he puts his plan into execution, assuring them that the great object of his mission was not merely to plant the gospel in one spot or one solitary district, but to propagate it in all places, far off as well as near—"for therefore came I forth." This last expression is restricted by some to his coming out of the city of Capernaum, or out of the house, or out into the desert place, on the ground that, if the reference was to the general object of his mission, the verb would be simply ἐλήλυθα, not the compound which occurs here, or rather that παρὰ, or ἀπὸ, or ἐκ τοῦ Θεοῦ, would be employed, as in several passages of St. John's Gospel (e.g. viii. 42; xiii. 3; xvii. 8), to convey that meaning. The expression is, no doubt, somewhat indefinite, perhaps purposely indefinite, and so susceptible of either a more general or more specific sense; but by comparing the corresponding passage in St. Luke (i.e. "because unto this have I been sent") we are shut up to the larger and higher and inclusive sense. The whole of the sentence is more fully expressed by St. Luke, and is to the effect, "because to the rest of the cities also I must declare the glad tidings of the kingdom of God." Accordingly, in pursuance of his great object, he went forth "and came preaching into their synagogues, into the whole of Galilee, and casting out the demons," as the words (in the critical editions) are literally rendered. The number of such synagogues and the extent of the enterprise may be estimated from the statement of Josephus in relation to the great number of towns and villages with which Galilee was studded, and the exceeding populousness of the Galilean provinces in the days of our Lord. He writes ('Bel. Jud.,' iii. 3, 2), "Moreover, the cities lie here very thick; and the very many villages there are here are everywhere so full of people, by the richness of their soil, that the very least of them contain about fifteen thousand inhabitants." 2. *An important variant.* We may not, however, dismiss this part of the subject without drawing attention to a very interesting and important various reading which, on the authority of codices ℵ, B, C, L, Q, R, and of the Syriac and Coptic versions, substitutes Ἰουδαίας for Γαλιλαίας, as the Judæan ministry of our Lord, which is, no doubt, assumed and implied by the synoptists, is nowhere else *expressly* mentioned by them.—J. J. G.

Vers. 40—45. Parallel passages: Matt. viii. 2—4; Luke v. 12—16.—*The cure of a leper.* I. THE DISEASE OF LEPROSY REPRESENTS THE DISEASE OF SIN. Of all the diseases that have found their way into this world in consequence of sin, and which have afflicted the human race, there is, perhaps, none more dreadful than that of leprosy. It was peculiar to Egypt, and native in that country, but passed into Palestine, and prevailed over Syria and Arabia also. It was common among the Jews, as we learn from several passages of Scripture, thus, in the Gospel according to St. Luke we read, "Many lepers were in Israel in the time of Eliseus the prophet." The Hebrew name *tsaraath* is from a root which means to strike, smite, also to roughen; and thus it may mean either a stroke or a rough swelling; while the English name of leprosy, coming from the Greek λέπρα, and that from λέπις, a scale, signifies "the scaly disease." The two sure signs of leprosy were the whitening (where it reached) of the usually dark hair of the Oriental, and the deepening of the disease below the skin. It was usually denominated *nega*, stroke, or *hannega*, the stroke or wound; this implied that it was directly inflicted by and immediately proceeded from the hand of God; it was also always considered as a punishment for sin. It need scarcely be added that it was a disease of the most virulent kind, and was a striking emblem of sin. 1. *It was hereditary; so with sin.* That leprosy was hereditary, we may infer from the punishment of Gehazi, concerning which it is written, "The leprosy therefore of Naaman shall cleave unto thee and unto thy seed, for ever." So also we read of David's imprecation of leprosy on the descendants of Joab, on account of his murdering Abner, saying, "Let there not fail from the house of Joab one that hath an issue or is a leper." In like manner, the leprosy of sin has been inherited from the first parents of our race, and has continued hereditary throughout every succeeding generation. This remains true, whether we hold the doctrine of immediate and antecedent or mediate and consequent imputation in reference to the guilt of Adam's first sin; that is to say, whether we hold with the generality of the Reformed Churches that, in consequence of Adam having been the covenant head and representative of his descendants, the guilt or punishableness of his first sin was incurred by them, antecedently to their own actual transgressions, and that the corruption of their nature was the first part of that punishment—which is known as the doctrine of antenatal forfeiture ; or whethei we agree with Placæus and the New England root theory, which, denying the doctiine just stated, affirms that, while Adam was punished for his own sin, his descendants are not punishable for it, but derive from him corrupt natures by ordinary generation, and so, sinning after his example, are punished for their own sin, their progenitor's sin being thus punished " mediately through, and consequently to, their own sin in compliance with his example." Even this modified view refers the origin of man's sin to the natural descent from Adam, the organic root, so that, as the sap of a tree passes from the root along the trunk and through the branches and on to the smallest twigs, inherited corruption or derived inherent depravity is traceable, not as a penal consequence of Adam's sin, but a natural consequence of generation by or descent from him.   Even on this low ground, according to which the imputation of Adam's first sin is denied, it is admitted that original sin is the inherent hereditary corruption of nature or depravity derived from Adam, just as leprosy, its sorrowful but striking symbol, was hereditary to the fourth generation at least.   *An exceptional view*, it must be acknowledged, was held by Pelagius and his followers, who denied that man's moral character had suffered any injury from the Fall, or that men were born with less ability to do the will of God or discharge their duty to him than Adam ; and by consequence denied the necessity of Divine grace or any special Divine agency, except indeed to enable men to perform more easily what they could accomplish, though less easily, without it, being thus capable of and by themselves of attaining to a perfectly holy life.   Such doctrines, being evidently opposed to the whole scope and many plain statements of Scripture, were condemned by the Council of Ephesus, A.D. 431, having been vigorously combated and confuted by Augustine till his death in the preceding year, A.D. 430 ; and thenceforth they disappear till after the Reformation, when they were revived by the Socinians. But even the semi-Pelagians admitted original sin to the extent, at least, that man's moral nature is more or less corrupted by the Fall, and by consequence stands in need of special Divine assistance.   Two facts in connection with the introduction of sin, or the entrance of moral evil, into our world are undeniable : one is the painful fact that the leprous taint of sin is found more or less on every human being ; the other is equally unquestionable, namely, that man at his creation could not have had that taint, for a polluted creature could not have proceeded from the hands of a pure and holy God.   The truth of revelation, then, remains unassailable, when it teaches that man, by disobedience to his Maker, introduced sin, and by sin destroyed himself.   2. *The leprosy was* (according to some authorities) *fearfully contagious ; so is sin.*   It has not only passed, as already intimated, by inheritance from generation to generation, but it passes by contagion from one individual to another individual, or to a number of individuals, for one sinner destroys much good.   It spreads from family to family, from house to house, from one homestead to another, yea, from country to country ; for " evil communications corrupt good manners."   In its transmission through the generations from the Fall to the Flood, it propagated itself so rapidly, and spread so fast and so far that its violence became uncontrollable, and nothing could check or stay its virulence ; the only remedy that remained was to sweep away and swallow up in the waters of the Deluge that race of moral invalids, tainted as they were with this inveterate and deadly distemper.   And even the waters of the Flood were powerless to cleanse from this moral corruption, or to wash away the stain of this sin-leprosy.   Again, soon after this great catastrophe the taint of this old leprosy exhibited unmistakable symptoms, breaking out afresh, and reappearing even in the head of that privileged family which the ark had saved ; for Noah, we read, having planted a vineyard, " drank of the wine, and was drunken ; and he was uncovered within his tent."   We are aware that the contagious nature of leprosy is disputed by some, but we prefer the view commonly held on the subject.   3. *Leprosy was small at its first appearance ; so, too, is sin.*   Leprosy commenced with a rising in the skin of the flesh, or a single bright spot.   It was so small at the beginning as to be barely perceptible.   A few specks or reddish spots on the skin were all that appeared at the outset. These spots became more numerous; they grew larger, bleaching the hairs that came in their way ; they overspread the body, crusting it with leprous scurf or shining scales; sores and swellings ensued. For a long time it seemed only cutaneous. But it did not stop with the skin; it penetrated deep down. It ate its way to the bones, it attacked the joints, it reached the marrow. The blood is corrupt, portions of the extremities mortify and drop off, a wasting away supervenes, till the poor leper, mutilated and disfigured, presents a shocking sight—a hideous spectacle, when dissolution at last brings him to a welcome grave. How dreadful was all this! And yet how like the leprosy of sin! It also is little in its beginnings, but it makes gradual, sometimes rapid, progress. No one has become entirely vile all at once. At the first appearance of the leprosy of sin in childhood, it is a mere spot—a small speck. The beginning may be some slight evasion of parental authority, some trifling act of disobedience; or it may be some small departure from strict truth; or it may be, perhaps, a petty act of pilfering, an insignificant instance of dishonesty; or it may be a little outburst of childish passion. It appears so small a matter that the indulgent parent or guardian overlooks it as unworthy of notice—at all events, undeserving of punishment; or the kind friend laughs at it as a mere childish trick. But oh! let it never be forgotten that that trifling disobedience, or small fib, or petty theft, or little ebullition of passion is the first breaking out of a spiritual leprosy—the first manifestation 'of the plague-spot of sin. And who can set limits or bounds to a seemingly small transgression, once it has been repeated and repeated until it has grown into a habit? Who can tell where that single sin will end? Who can check its onward progress? What can resist its downward sweep when, like the rushing of the roaring torrent, or with more than the impetuosity of the mighty waterfall, it overbears and overcomes all resistance, hurrying its hapless victim downward to perdition? 4. *Leprosy separated those afflicted with it from society; so does sin.* As might be reasonably expected, leprosy, from its loathsomeness, the ceremonial uncleanness which it produced, as well as its infectious nature (if rightly judged to be so), excluded from society and rendered its victims a terror to all who saw or met or came near them. Thus we read in Lev. xiii. 45, "The leper in whom the plague is, his clothes shall be rent, and his head bare, and he shall put a covering upon his upper lip, and shall cry, *Tame, tame,* Unclean, unclean." Here there are four unmistakable signs, which, when combined, served as a sufficient deterrent to any wayfarer or unwary person that might through ignorance or inadvertence approach the leprous person, and thereby catch infection, or at least contract ceremonial defilement. The bare head, with locks dishevelled; the garment rent from the neck to the waist; the beard, man's ornament, covered in token of grief;—were the ordinary signs of mourning for the dead or any great calamity; while the bandaged chin, and muffled lips uttering in doleful accents the melancholy cry, "Unclean, unclean!" was a warning which the most unwary passers-by were not likely to neglect at the time or ever after to forget. But it is further added, "He shall dwell alone; without the camp shall his habitation be." From other passages of the Word of God, we learn that they were not only separated from intercourse with others, but dwelt in a separate house, companied together, and were cut off entirely from the house of God. What a dreadfully deserted condition! Their nearest relatives shunned them, their dearest friends dreaded them, the tenderest ties were sundered by this loathsome disease of leprosy. Their touch was feared and fled from, for it was the touch of contagion; their company was shunned, for it imparted uncleanness and defilement; their very breath was dreaded as the pestilence, for it was the breath of disease and death. Here, in all this, is a sad symbol of sin. It separates between us and our God; it excludes us from his presence and privileges, from his friendship and family; it shuts us out from the society of his saints, from their benefits and blessedness; and, unless cleansed in God's own way, it will shut us out at last finally and for ever from his heavenly temple, for "without are dogs, and sorcerers, and whoremongers, and murderers, and idolaters, and whosoever loveth and maketh a lie." When King Uzziah became leprous in the house of the Lord, "the priests thrust him out from thence, yea, himself hasted also to go out, because the Lord had smitten him." If we could suppose the possibility of an unrenewed sinner being admitted into heaven—if for a moment we might suppose the occurrence of a thing impossible, for the unclean shall never enter there—would not the pure spirits of that upper sanctuary rush upon that unholy one with deepest indignation, thrusting him out at once from thence, and hurling him over the high battlements of heaven? Yea, would not such a one himself, Uzziah-like, haste to get away from so pure a place, and to escape from such holy companionship? for heaven would not be heaven, and could not be heaven, to an unregenerate soul.   How terrible the sinner's condition, shunned as he is by the saintly, dreaded as he is by the pure and holy, separated from fellowship and communion with God on earth, shut out from the enjoyment and glory of God in heaven, secluded from all that is holy and happy both here and hereafter, and last of all and worst of all, shut up with the spirits of the lost—shut up with the filthy, the fearful, the unbelieving and abominable; shut up with the devil and his angels; shut up with companions in misery, whose very companionship, apart altogether from "the worm that dieth not and the fire that is unquenchable," would be in itself a hell! 5. *Leprosy was incurable by human power; sin is so likewise.* The disease of leprosy, as we have seen, proceeded immediately from the hand of God, and so it was the hand of God alone that could remove it.   No human power, no means that man might use, no medicines of any kind could avail aught, either for the relief or removal of this fatal malady.   This will, perhaps, account for the circumstance of St. Matthew giving such prominence to our Lord's cure of the leper by recording that miracle first.   The first miracle publicly performed by our Lord was the changing of water into wine, as we read, "This beginning of miracles did Jesus in Cana of Galilee." But St. Matthew, writing immediately for the Jews, records this miracle of our Lord's curing the leprosy *first* : though not first in the order of time, he gives it the precedence notwithstanding, because it was best calculated to impress his countrymen with the possession by Jesus of Divine power, and so of a Divine commission, since it was their fixed belief that none but God could effect a cure.   Hence the King of Israel said, "Am I God, to kill and to make alive, that this man doth send unto me to recover a man of his leprosy?"   In like manner the miracle which St. Luke, writing for the Gentiles, records *first*, was the cure of a demoniac, which proved the power of Jesus over those demons or deities which the Gentiles worshipped.   Hence, too, as may be observed in passing, it is that because the word *demon* was equivocal in its meaning among the Gentiles—sometimes denoting a good and sometimes an evil spirit—St. Luke restricts the meaning to the latter by the epithet " unclean " (ἀκαθάρτον) ; but St. Matthew never so employs it, and does not need to employ it, as the term had only the one sense of evil spirit among the Jews. Now, it is the same with the disease of sin.   It never gets cured of itself; no mortal man can recover himself from it ; no human being can restore the individual suffering from its pollution; no created power can heal this leprosy of the soul.   God alone can deliver from this spiritual disease; the blood of Christ alone can cleanse from its defilement.

II. THE CLEANSING OF LEPROSY REPRESENTS THE FORGIVENESS OF SIN.   There is a remarkable and instructive contrast between the cleansing of a leper, recorded in the Old Testament, and the cleansing of the leper mentioned in the Gospels.   That contrast holds both between the respective applicants and the different means of cure adopted.   Naaman's conduct—for his is the case referred to—presents a true picture of the natural heart proud and unhumbled.   Had he been commanded to do some great thing, he would have readily complied ; but the process prescribed by the prophet was too simple, the mode of cure too easy, and Naaman too proud to descend to it.   He became wroth, and went away.   The leper in the passage before us is determined to dare or die ; he defies the law of limitation which prohibited his approach or address to his fellow-men, and restricted him within certain bounds to prevent his contact with the living ; thus, breaking through the *cordon sanitaire*, he makes his way to Jesus.   Again, the prophet in the former case prescribed certain means, saying, " Go and wash in Jordan seven times." Here Jesus simply speaks the leper into health. 1. *The respectful application of the leper to our Lord.*   This is clearly seen when we combine the expressions in the different narratives.   St. Matthew states generally that he *worshipped* him (προσεκύνει).   The word employed, coming from a root which means to kiss, kiss the hand to, as a mark of respect and homage, conveys the idea of obeisance or reverence to one greatly superior.   St. Mark further informs us that he *fell on his knees* to him (γονυπετῶν) ; while from St. Luke we learn that, in his extremity and earnest entreaty, he *fell on his face* prostrate before him (πεσὼν ἐπὶ πρόσωπον).   With like humility, reverence, and earnestness must we come to Jesus.   Like the leper, we must come in humility, feeling that we are nothing and that Christ is all. We must come in earnest, feeling the desperate nature of our disease and our hopeless, perishing, and lost condition without him. The lepers of Samaria ventured at all hazards to fall into the host of the Syrians, "If they save us alive, we shall live; and if they kill us, we shall but die." We must also with like reverence and decision approach. It was an act of profound homage, as to a superior, on the part of the leper, not yet perhaps of worship in the higher sense as to a Divine being; but we, with superior knowledge of his claims, must acknowledge him as our Lord, worship him as our Messiah, bow in homage at his feet, and embrace him as our Saviour. Thus approaching him as lowly penitents, humble suppliants, and polluted transgressors, we, too, shall experience his power, and realize the preciousness of his salvation. 2. *The reception of the leper by our Lord.* St. Luke, with his customary medical exactness, tells us that this was a leper of no common kind, but one afflicted with the worst type of the disease, the sorest stage of it—he was full of leprosy ($\pi\lambda\eta\rho\eta s$ $\lambda\epsilon\pi\rho a s$). St. Mark, again, makes us acquainted with our Lord's deep feeling of compassion for this poor sufferer ($\sigma\pi\lambda a\gamma\chi\nu\iota\sigma\theta\epsilon\iota s$). "He stretched out his hand to him and touched him." By that touch he inspired the man with confidence, who believed in his power to cleanse, but doubted his willingness to risk contagion or ceremonial defilement; by that touch he proved himself "Lord of the Law," and exempt from its ritualistic restrictions; by that touch he broke through the ceremonialism which had usurped the place of true religion among the degenerate Jews of that time; by that touch, perhaps, he gave a sensible sign that healing virtue had already proceeded from him, and that the leper was virtually cleansed; by that touch he showed, as if by symbol, that he himself was made in the likeness of sinful flesh, and yet remained unsoiled by sin. 3. *The response of our Lord to the application of the leper.* The application of the leper shows (1) the prevalent opinion about this malady, that it was not a mere disease, but a defilement; and therefore he speaks of *cleansing* ($\kappa a\theta a\rho\iota\sigma a\iota$) rather than cure. But (2) the application implies faith in the Saviour's power. He did not question the Saviour's ability, he only doubted his willingness to exercise that ability on his behalf. He did not say, "If thou canst," but "If thou wilt, thou canst." The form of conditional sentence by which the leper expresses his mind of the matter is that of probable contingency ($\epsilon a\nu$ with the subjunctive), and so not a mere supposition. This unquestioning faith in Christ's power was faith of no ordinary kind; it was faith in his power as something more than human. This leper was painfully conscious of his disease; he knew that the "finger of God" had touched him; he must have been convinced that no earthly power could cleanse or cure him, and therefore, when he confessed his belief in Jesus' power to effect it, he must have attributed to him vastly more than human potency—in a word, not less than power Divine. The term of address, $K\upsilon\rho\iota\epsilon$, is more than respect —it is belief in his Messiahship. True, he doubted the will; he feared, and no wonder, lest the foulness of his disease, its loathsomeness, its extremely disgusting nature, its thorough repulsiveness, might act as a deterrent, and prevent the much-desired relief. But no, Jesus meets him on his own ground; he responds to him in his own chosen terms; he employs in reply the very words. And thus, by his hand outstretched in kindness, by the touch of tenderness, by the look of compassion, and now by the words he uses, and the tone, perhaps, in which he utters them, he at once reassures the sufferer, and at once and for ever removes his suffering. The leper had said, "If thou wilt;" Jesus replies, "I will." The leper had said, "Thou canst cleanse me;" Jesus responds, "Be cleansed." He spake the word, and healed him; he gave the command, and the leper was cleansed. The scales fell off, the swellings subsided, the sores were healed, the unnatural whiteness gave place to the hue of health, his skin became fresh as that of a chubby child. The words of Ambrose (3) have been often repeated; they are worth remembering, and are as follows:—" *Volo* dicit propter *Photinum; imperat* propter *Arium; tangit* propter *Manichæum;*" "Photinus held Christ to be a mere man; Arius maintained his inequality with the Father; and Manichæus asserted he was only a phantom without human flesh. 4. *Relation of this to ourselves.* In coming to Christ we must (1) have faith in his power. All we can expect from an earthly physician is that, with his knowledge of the healing art, he will do the best he can; that he will exert his medical skill to the utmost; that he will leave no means or medicines unapplied. But, with all his skilfulness and integrity of purpose and earnest desire to effect a cure, the appliances may be unavailing, the utmost exertions unsuccessful, and the disease may prove fatal. The soul's leprosy is beyond the power of any earthly physician; it baffles all human skill, and, if uncured, it ends in eternal death. We bless God there is one, though only one, Physician in heaven above or earth beneath that has power to cleanse and cure. In coming for cure we must (2) acknowledge our dependence on his sovereign will. We have no claim on him, nothing to recommend us to him, no merit to plead; we must refer all to his will, depend wholly on his mercy, trust his unlimited grace, cast ourselves at his feet, saying with the leper, "If thou wilt, thou canst." But (3) no one ever applied to him in this way whose application was in vain; no one ever came to him humbly and sincerely that was sent away uncured; no one ever came to him for cleansing that went unblest away. "Him that cometh unto me I will in no wise cast out." Once more, (4) while at the first we refer everything to the will of the Physician, we must ever after in everything yield obedience to that will and follow his directions, however mysterious or humbling they may be, whatever self-denial or self-sacrifice they may require. "See thou say nothing to any man; but go thy way, show thyself to the priest;" such is the direction given to the leper, now cleansed and cured. It has been well said, in reference to our Lord sending the leper to the priest, that "though as *God* he had just showed himself *above* the Law, yet as *man* he came to *fulfil* the Law." But why command him "to say nothing to any man"? To teach the avoidance of boasting and of ambition to his followers, according to Chrysostom; lest the crowd, attracted by and astonished at his miracles merely, should not allow sufficient opportunity for teaching, according to Beza; lest the report of the miracle might outrun him, and the priest, through ill will or envy, refuse to pronounce him cleansed, according to Grotius and others; other reasons have been assigned, *e.g.* the avoidance of tumult and excitement, or the subordinate place of miracles in his ministry; it was rather to lose no time in conversation about the cure, but to regard it of prime importance and claiming first attention to get his cleansing attested by the priest and to prove his gratitude by works rather than words, presenting the offering enjoined in the Law recorded in Lev. xiv. 4—10. "The customary salutations were formal and tedious, as they are now, particularly among Druses and other non-Christian sects, and consumed much valuable time. . . . Another propensity an Oriental can scarcely resist, no matter how urgent his business, is, that if he meets an acquaintance, he must stop and make an endless number of inquiries, and answer as many." But (5) the testimony desired was official proof of the reality of the man's cleansing by the scrutiny and certificate of the priest; or it was to prove the Saviour's reverence for the Law; or perhaps even for a testimony against the people, because of unbelief in not acknowledging his Messiahship, notwithstanding all his mighty works.

LESSONS. 1. No bodily disease is one-millionth part so terrible in its ravages as sin, of which leprosy is such a special and striking type; none so dreadful in its results, or so destructive in its consequences. It darkens that spirit in man that once reflected so purely and perfectly the image of the Creator; it defiles the fountain-head of thought and feeling; it destroys the health and happiness of the soul. 2. Our Lord is able to deliver from this disease and save from sin. This miracle, as a sort of acted parable, plainly and impressively teaches this. He spake the omnific word that cleansed the leper though the exercise of his volition was all that was needed, for he had already touched him, to show, perhaps, that the foul disease was gone. He is as willing as he is able, he is as ready as he is powerful, his love being great as his power. He is more willing to heal than we are to seek and accept the blessing. 3. He is not only willing, but waiting to bestow on us present and immediate blessings. Present pardon and purity and peace, immediate grace and instant loving-kindness, instantaneous spiritual health, as well as future everlasting happiness, are among the boons which he stands waiting to confer. 4. Present application is our duty as well as our privilege. The present is his accepted time; he is willing to receive us now, he is waiting to cleanse us now, he is ready to bless us now. Present opportunities may not return, present impressions may be effaced and never renewed; his spirit will not always strive, his salvation will not be offered evermore.—J. J. G.

EXPOSITION.

CHAPTER II.

Ver. 1.—The first sentence of this verse is better rendered thus: **And when he entered again** (εἰσελθὼν πάλιν) **into Capernaum after some days**; literally, *after days* (δι' ἡμερῶν). It is probable that a considerable interval had taken place since the events recorded in the former chapter. **It was noised that he was in the house** (ὅτι εἰς οἶκόν ἐστι); or, if the ὅτι be regarded as recitative, *it was noised, He is in the house, at home,* in his usual place of residence at Capernaum.

Ver. 2.—**Many were gathered together, so that there was no longer room** for them (ὥστε μηκέτι χωρεῖν), no, not even about the door. The description is very graphic. The house could not contain them, and even its court-yard and approaches were inconveniently thronged. This is one of the many examples of minute observation of details, observable in St. Mark's Gospel. **And he preached** (ἐλάλει)—more literally, *was speaking*—**the word unto them.** This little sentence indicates the great object of his ministry. The exercise of miraculous power was subordinated to this; the miracles being simply designed to fix the attention upon the Teacher as One sent from God.

Vers. 3, 4.—**And they come, bringing unto him a man sick of the palsy, borne of four.** Here again the minuteness of detail is very observable. It is also interesting to notice how the three writers of the synoptic Gospels supplement and illustrate one another. St. Matthew gives the outline, St. Mark and St. Luke fill up the picture. St. Luke (v. 18) tells us how they sought means to bring the paralytic into Christ's presence. They carried him on his bed up the flight of steps outside the house, and reaching to the roof; and then both St. Mark and St. Luke tell us how, having first removed a portion of the tiling and broken up the roof, they then let him down through the opening thus made into the midst before Jesus. The chamber into which he was thus abruptly lowered was most probably what is elsewhere called the "upper chamber," a large central room, convenient for the purpose of addressing both those who filled it and also the crowd that thronged the outer court below.

Ver. 5.—**Son, thy sins be forgiven thee;** literally, *thy sins are forgiven.* The word "son" is in the Greek the more endearing word (τέκνον) "child." St. Luke uses the word "man." St. Matthew adds the words "Be of good cheer." It is here to be carefully observed that the spiritual gift, the gift of forgiveness, is first conveyed; and

we must also notice the authoritative character of the address, "Thy sins are forgiven." Bede observes here that our Lord first forgives his sins, that he might show him that his suffering was ultimately due to sin. Bede also says that he was borne of four, to show that a man is carried onwards by four graces to the assured hope of healing, namely, by prudence, and courage, and righteousness, and temperance. **Jesus seeing their faith.** Some of the Fathers, as Jerome and Ambrose, think that this faith was in the bearers of the sick man, and in them only. But there is nothing in the words to limit them in this way. Indeed, it would seem far more natural to suppose that the paralytic must have been a consenting party. He must have approved of all that they did, otherwise we can hardly suppose that it would have been done. We may therefore more reasonably conclude, with St. Chrysostom, that it was alike their faith and his that our Lord crowned with his blessing. *Thy sins are forgiven.* These words of our Lord were not a mere wish only; they were this sick man's sentence of absolution. They were far more than the word of absolution which Christ's ambassadors are authorized to deliver to all those who "truly repent and unfeignedly believe." For Christ could read the heart, which they cannot do. And therefore his sentence is absolute, and not conditional only. It is not the announcement of a qualified gift, but the assertion of an undoubted fact. In his own name, and by his own inherent power, he there and then forgives the man his sins.

Vers. 6, 7.—The words, **Why doth this man thus speak blasphemies?** in accordance with the altered reading (βλασφημεῖ for βλασφημίας), should stand thus: *Why doth this man thus speak? he blasphemeth.* It is evident that the scribes, who were secretly amongst themselves finding fault with our Lord's words, understood that, by the use of these words, our Lord was assuming to himself a Divine attribute. And if he had been a mere man; if he had not really been, as he assumed to be, Divine, the only begotten Son of the Father,—then no doubt they would have been right in supposing that he blasphemed. But their error was that they could not perceive in him the glory of the only begotten Son. The light was shining in the darkness, and the darkness apprehended it not.

Vers. 8—11.—It does not clearly appear whether these murmurers communicated their thoughts audibly to one another. At all events, their words were evidently not heard beyond themselves. But Jesus perceived in his spirit their reasonings. He knew their thoughts, not by communication from another, as the prophets of old had things made known to them by revelation, but by his own Spirit pervading and penetrating all things. From this the Christian Fathers, against the Arians, infer the divinity of Christ, that he inspected the heart, which it is the prerogative of God alone to do. St. Chrysostom says, "Behold the evidences of the divinity of Christ. Observe that he knows the very secrets of your heart." Nor did Christ only perceive their thoughts. He perceived also the direction in which these thoughts were moving. Their feeling was no doubt this : "It is an easy thing to claim the power of forgiving sin, since this is a power which cannot be challenged by any outward sign." Now, it is to this form of unbelief that the next words of our Lord are the answer. It is as though he said, " You accuse me of blasphemy. You say that I am usurping the attributes of God when I claim the power of forgiving sin. You ask for the evidence that I really possess this power; and you say it is an easy thing to lay claim to a power which penetrates the spiritual world, and which is therefore beyond the reach of material proof. Be it so. I will now furnish that evidence. I will prove, by what I am now about to work upon the body, that what I have just said is effectual upon the spirit. I have just said to this paralytic, 'Thy sins are forgiven.' You challenge this power; you question my authority. I will now give you outward and sensible evidence that this is no fictitious or imaginary claim. You see this poor helpless, palsied man. I will say to him in presence of you all, 'Arise, take up thy bed, and go unto thy house.' And if simply at my bidding his nerves are braced, and his limbs gather strength, and he rises and walks, then judge ye whether I have a right to say to him, 'Thy sins are forgiven.' Thus, by doing that which is capable of proof, I will vindicate my power to do that which is beyond the reach of sensible evidence; and I will make manifest to you, by these visible tides of my grace, in what direction the deep under-current of my love is moving." (See Trench on the Miracles, p. 205.)

Ver. 12.—The words are spoken, and the paralytic arose, and straightway took up the bed (ἠγέρθη, καὶ εὐθὺς ἄρας) — such is the most approved reading — and went forth before them all. There is a spiritual application of this miracle which it is well to notice. The paralytic lifting up himself is a figure of him who, in the strength of Christ, has lifted himself up from the lethargy

of sin. He has first applied to Christ, perhaps by his own sense of his need, perhaps with the help of others. He may have had difficulty in approaching him. A multitude of sinful thoughts and cares may have thronged the door. But at length, whether alone or with the kind assistance of faithful friends, he has been brought to the feet of Jesus, and has heard those words of love and power, "Thy sins are forgiven thee." And then he will rise and walk. He will take up that whereon he lay. He will carry away those things whereon he has hitherto found satisfaction—his love of ease, his self-indulgence. His bed, whatever it may have been whereon he lay, becomes the proof of his cure. When the intemperate man becomes sober, the passionate man gentle, and the covetous man liberal, he takes up that whereon he lay. Thus does each penitent man begin a new life ; setting forward with new hopes and new powers towards his true home, eternal in the heavens.

We are not informed of the effect of this miracle upon the scribes and Pharisees. But it is too evident that, though they could not deny the fact, they would not acknowledge the power; while the mass of the people, more free from prejudice, and therefore more open to conviction, united in giving glory to God. Faith in Christ as sent by God was in fact increasing amongst the mass of the people ; while unbelief was working its deadly result of envy and malice amongst those who ought to have been their guides and instructors.

Vers. 13, 14.—It is probable that our Lord remained some time at Capernaum before he went forth again. The word "again" refers to his former going forth (see ch. i. 35). When he went forth on this occasion he appears to have travelled southwards along the sea-shore. There, not far from Capernaum, he saw Levi, the son of Alphæus, sitting at the receipt of custom (ἐπὶ τὸ τελώνιον); more literally, at the place of toll. This place would be in the direct line for traders from Damascus to Accho, and a convenient spot for the receipt of the duties on the shipping. It is observable that in St. Matthew's own Gospel (ix. 9) he describes himself as "a man named Matthew." St. Luke, like St. Mark, calls him Levi. The same person is no doubt meant. It is most likely that his original name was Levi, and that upon his call to be an apostle he received a new name, that of Matthew, or Mattathias, which, according to Gesenius, means "the gift of Jehovah." In his own Gospel he names himself Matthew, that he might proclaim the kindness and love of Christ towards him, in the spirit of St. Paul, where he says, "Christ Jesus came into the world to save sinners, of whom I am chief" (1 Tim. i. 15). **Follow me ;** me, that is, whom you have already heard preaching the gospel of the kingdom in Capernaum, and confirming it by many miracles, and especially by that conspicuous miracle spoken of by all, the healing of the paralytic. St. Chrysostom says that " our Lord called Matthew, who was already constrained by the report of his miracles." The condescension of Christ is shown in this, that he called Matthew the "publican," who on that account was odious to the Jews, not only to be a partaker of his grace, but to be one of his chosen followers, a friend, an apostle, and an evangelist.

It has been urged against the truth of Christianity, by Porphyry and others, that the first disciples followed Christ blindly, as though they would have followed without reason any one who called them. But they were not men who acted upon mere impulse and without reason. The miracles, no doubt, produced an impression upon them. And then we may reasonably suppose that their moral faculties perceived the majesty of Deity shining through the countenance of the Son of God. As the magnet attracts the iron, so Christ drew Matthew and others to himself ; and by this attractive power he communicated his graces and virtues to them, such as an ardent love of God, contempt of the world, and burning zeal for the salvation of souls.

Ver. 15.—**And it came to pass**—ἐγένετο seems the best reading—**as he was sitting at meat in his house.** This was the house of Matthew. St. Matthew (ix. 10) modestly says, " in *the* house," keeping himself as much as possible in the background. St. Luke, with greater fulness, says (v. 29) that " Levi made him a great feast in his house." From this it appears that Matthew at once marked the occasion of his call by inviting his associates, publicans and sinners, that they too, being won by the example and teaching of Christ, might be led in like manner to follow him. Good is ever diffusive of itself ; and Christian love prompts those who have experienced the love of Christ to draw others to the same fountain of mercy. We find **publicans and sinners** constantly associated together ; for, although there is nothing necessarily unlawful in the office of a tax-gatherer, yet, since men frequently followed that calling because it offered the opportunity for fraud and extortion, hence the "publicans" were, generally speaking, odious to the Jews, and regarded as nothing better than "sinners." Moreover the Jews of old maintained that they were Abraham's seed, and protested that as a people dedicated to God, they ought not to be subject to the Romans, who were

Gentiles and idolaters. They considered that it was contrary to the liberty and dignity of the children of God that they should pay tribute to them, a view which increased their prejudice against the tax-gatherers. And indeed this was one main cause of the rebellion of the Jews, which led finally to their overthrow by Titus and Vespasian.

Ver. 16.—According to the most approved readings, this verse should run thus : **And the scribes of the Pharisees, when they saw that he was eating with the sinners and publicans, said unto his disciples, He eateth and drinketh with publicans and sinners.** The words "publicans and sinners" are thus inverted in their order in the two clauses, as though they were convertible terms. Of course, the scribes and Pharisees had not sat down at this feast, but some of them had probably found their way into the chamber in which the feast was going on, where they would comment freely upon what they saw, and condemn our Lord's conduct as inconsistent with his character. It is as though they said, " By this conduct he transgresses the Law of God and the traditions of the elders. Why, then, do you follow him ? "

Ver. 17.—Jesus heard their murmurings, and his answer was, **They that are whole have no need of a physician, but they that are sick.** As the physician is not infected by the disease of the patient, but rather overcomes it and drives it from him, so it is no disgrace but rather an honour to the physician to associate himself with the sick, and so much the more, the greater the sickness. So that it is as though Christ said, " I who am sent from heaven by the Father, that I might be the Physician of the souls of sinners, am not defiled by their sins and spiritual diseases when I converse with them ; but rather I cure and heal them, which is alike for my glory and for their good, and so much the more, the greater their sins. For I am the physician of sinners, not their companion. But you, O scribes and Pharisees, are not the physicians but the companions of sinners, and so you are contaminated. Nevertheless, you desire to be thought righteous and holy ; and therefore I do not associate with you, (1) because the whole, such as you think yourselves to be, need not the spiritual Physician ; and (2) because your insincerity and hypocrisy are an offence to me."

Ver. 18.—The first sentence of this verse should be rendered thus : **And the disciples of John and the Pharisees were fasting** (ἦσαν νηστεύοντες). In all the synoptic Gospels we find this incident following closely upon what goes before. It is not improbable that the Pharisees and the disciples of John were fasting at the very time when Matthew gave his feast. This was not one of the fasts prescribed by the Law; had it been so, it would have been observed by our Lord. There were, however, fasts observed by the Pharisees which were not required by the Law; there were two in particular of a voluntary nature, mentioned by the Pharisee (Luke xviii. 12), where he says, "I fast twice in the week." It was a custom, observed by the stricter Pharisees, but not of legal obligation. It was not correct to say, **but thy disciples fast not.** They fasted, no doubt, but in a different spirit; they did not fast to be seen of men—they followed the higher teaching of their Master. It is remarkable to find the disciples of John here associated with the Pharisees. John was now in prison in the fort of Machærus. It is possible that jealousy of the increasing influence of Christ may have led John's disciples to associate themselves with the Pharisees. The point of this particular attack upon Christ was this: It is as though they said, "You claim to be a new teacher sent from God, a teacher of a more perfect religion. How is it, then, that we are fasting, while your disciples are eating and drinking?" The disciples of John more especially may have urged this out of zeal for their master. Such an unworthy zeal is too often seen in good men, who love to prefer their own leader to all others, forgetting the remonstrance of St. Paul, "While there is amongst you strife and contention, are ye not carnal, and walk after the manner of men?"

Ver. 19.—The Bridegroom here is Christ, because he espoused the human nature, and, through it, the Church to himself in his holy incarnation. This holy union he began by his grace on earth, and he will consummate it gloriously with his elect in heaven, when "the marriage of the Lamb shall have come, and his wife shall have made herself ready." Hence John the Baptist calls himself the friend of the Bridegroom, that is, of Christ. **The sons** (υἱοὶ) **of the bridechamber** are the special friends of the Bridegroom, those who are admitted into the closest fellowship with him. The expression is a Hebraism, like "the children of disobedience," and many other similar forms of expression. **So long, then, as the bridegroom is with them they cannot fast. But the days will come when the bridegroom shall be taken away from them, and then shall they fast.** It is as though our Lord said, "It is not surprising that they should not care to fast as long as they enjoy my presence; but when I am taken from them, then shall they fast."

Ver. 20.—This is the first occasion on which our Lord alludes to his removal from

them. **The bridegroom shall be taken away from them.** The Greek word (ἀπαρθῇ) conveys the idea of a painful severance. **And then will they fast in that day** (ἐν ἐκείνῃ τῇ ἡμέρᾳ). This is the true reading. After our Lord's death, his disciples frequently fasted as of necessity, and went through much privation and trial. And so it must be for the most part with all who will live godly in Christ Jesus, until he returns to take to himself his kingdom, when there will be a glad and everlasting festival.

Ver. 21.—**No man seweth a piece of new cloth**—the Greek is (ῥάκους ἀγνάφου) *undressed* cloth, cloth newly woven, and before it has been dressed by the fuller—**on an old garment.** The latter part of this verse is better rendered, as in the Revised Version, thus: **Else that which should fill it up taketh from it, the new from the old; and a worse rent is made.** The meaning of the words is this: An old garment, if it be torn, should be mended by a patch of old material; for if a patch of new material is used, its strength or fulness takes away from the old garment to which it is sewn; the old and the new do not agree, the new drags the old and tears it, and so a worse rent is made.

Ver. 22.—"Bottles" in this verse is better rendered literally *wine-skins* (ἀσκούς). **And no man putteth new wine** (οἶνον νέον) **into old wine-skins; else the new wine will burst the skins, and the wine perisheth, and the skins; but they put new wine into fresh wine-skins** (ἀσκοὺς καινούς). The sense is this: New wine, in the process of fermentation, will burst old bottles made of wine-skins not strong enough to resist the strength of the fermenting fluid; so that there is a twofold loss—both that of the bottles and that of the wine. And therefore new wine must be poured into bottles made of fresh wine-skins, which, by reason of their strength and toughness, shall be able to resist the fermenting energy of the new wine. And by these very apt illustrations our Lord teaches us that it is a vain thing to attempt to mingle together the spiritual freedom of the gospel with the old ceremonies of the Law. To attempt to engraft the living spiritual energy of the gospel upon the old legal ceremonial now about to pass away, would be as fatal a thing as to piece an old garment with new material, or to put new wine into old wine-skins. There is here, therefore, a valuable lesson for the Christian Church, namely, to treat new converts with gentleness and consideration.

Ver. 23.—If there is a rapid sequence in this part of the narrative, the fasting referred to in the last verses may have taken place the day before. St. Luke (vi. 1) here adds to St. Mark's account the words, "and did eat, rubbing them [that is, the ears of corn] in their hands;" an incidental evidence of a simple life, that they did not here eat prepared food, but the simple grains of wheat, which they separated from the chaff by rubbing the ears of corn in their hands. This passage marks with some nicety the time of the year. The corn in that district would be ripening about May. It would, therefore, be not long after the Passover. The difficult expression in St. Luke vi. 1, ἐν σαββάτῳ δευτεροπρώτῳ, and which is rendered in the Authorized Version "on the second sabbath after the first," is reduced by the Revisers of 1881 to the simple phrase (ἐν σαββάτῳ), "on a sabbath," there not being sufficient evidence to persuade them to retain the word δευτεροπρώτῳ. But other evidences seem to show that the incident occurred earlier than as recorded by St. Matthew. The Fathers are fond of spiritual applications of this rubbing of the ears of corn. Bede, in remarking upon the fact of the disciples plucking the ears of corn, and rubbing them until they get rid of the husks, and obtain the food itself, says that they do this who meditate upon the Holy Scriptures, and digest them, until they find in them the kernel, the quintessence of delight; and St. Augustine blames those who merely please themselves with the flowers of Holy Scripture, but do not rub out the grain by meditation, until they obtain the real nourishment of virtue.

Ver. 24.—**That which is not lawful.** The supposed unlawfulness was not the plucking of the ears of corn with the hand, which was expressly permitted by the Law (Deut. xxiii. 25), but the plucking and eating on the sabbath day.

Vers. 25, 26.—**David . . . and they that were with him.** This seems opposed to what we read in 1 Sam. xxi., where David is stated to have been alone. But the facts appear to have been these, that David, fleeing from Saul, went alone to Ahimelech the high priest, and sought and obtained five loaves of the "shewbread," which he carried away with him to his companions in flight, and shared with them; for he says (1 Sam. xxi. 2), "I have appointed my servants to such and such a place." This incident actually happened in the high priesthood of Ahimelech the father of Abiathar. Bede says that they were both present when David came in his distress and obtained the shewbread. But Ahimelech having been slain, together with eighty-six priests, by Saul, Abiathar fled to David, and became his companion in his exile. Moreover, when he succeeded to the high priesthood on the death of Ahimelech, he did far more good service than his father had done, and so was

worthy of being spoken of with this special commendation, and as though he was actually high priest, even though his father was then living. The words may properly mean "in the days when Abiathar was living who became high priest, and was more eminent than his father." **The shewbread;** literally, *the bread of the face*, that is, *of the Divine presence*, symbolizing the Divine Being who is the Bread of life. It was directed by the Law that within the sanctuary there should be a table of shittim (or acacia) wood; and every sabbath twelve newly baked loaves were placed upon it in two rows. These loaves were sprinkled with incense, and then remained there until the following sabbath. They were then replaced by twelve newly baked loaves, the old loaves being eaten by the priests in the holy place, from which it was unlawful to remove them. These twelve loaves corresponded to the twelve tribes. The force of our Lord's reasoning is this: David, a man after God's own heart, when sorely pressed by hunger, applied to the high priest and took some of these sacred loaves, loaves which under ordinary circumstances it was not lawful for the lay people to eat, because he wisely judged that a positive law, forbidding the laity to eat this bread, ought to yield to a law of necessity and of nature; which intimates to us that in a grave necessity of famine, life may be lawfully preserved by eating even sacred bread which has been dedicated to God. Therefore, in like manner, nay, much more, was it lawful for Christ and his disciples to pluck the ears of corn on the sabbath day, that by rubbing them in their hands they might pick out the good grain and satisfy their hunger.

Ver. 27.—The sabbath was instituted for the benefit of man, that he might refresh and renew his body, fatigued and worn by six days' labour, with the restful calm of the seventh; and that he might have leisure to apply his mind to the things which concern his everlasting salvation; to consider and meditate upon the Law of God; and rouse himself, by the remembrance of the Divine greatness and goodness, to true repentance, to gratitude, and to love. The force of the argument is this: The sabbath was made on account of man, not man on account of the sabbath. The sabbath, great and important as that institution is, is subordinate to man. If, then, the absolute rest of the sabbath becomes hurtful to man, a new departure must be taken, and some amount of labour must be undergone, that man may be benefited. Therefore was Christ justified in permitting to his disciples a little labour in plucking these ears of corn on the sabbath day, in order that they may appease their hunger. For it is better that the rest of the sabbath should be disturbed, though but a little, than that any one of those for whose sake the sabbath was instituted should perish.

Ver. 28.—**Therefore the Son of man is Lord also of the sabbath.** "The sabbath was made for man." It is the inferior institution, man being the higher, for whose sake the sabbath was appointed. But the Son of man is Lord of all men, and of all things that pertain to man's salvation; therefore he must of necessity be Lord even of the sabbath; so that when he sees fit he can relax or dispense with its obligations. It is true that for us Christians the first day of the week, the Lord's day, has taken the place of the ancient Jewish sabbath; but the principle here laid down by our Lord is applicable to the "first" day no less than to the "seventh;" and it teaches us that our own moral and religious advancement and that of our brethren is the object which we should all aim at in the manner of our observance of the Christian Sunday; while we strive to "stand fast in the liberty wherewith Christ has made us free."

HOMILETICS.

Vers. 1—12.—*Christ's authority to pardon.* Our Lord's miracles of healing were, upon the surface and obviously, designed to relieve from suffering and to restore to health. They, at the same time, directed the attention of both those benefited, and of spectators, to the supernatural power and to the benevolence of the Divine Physician. But no Christian can fail to see in them a moral significance. Disorders of the body were symbolical of spiritual disease. And the great Healer, who pitied and relieved physical suffering, nevertheless had regard to the more serious affections of the soul, and designed by his works of healing to direct attention to himself, to excite faith in himself, as able and willing to save sinners. It was in the miracle recorded in the passage before us that the Saviour first openly avowed the spiritual purpose of his ministry and the spiritual authority he possessed to pardon and to save.

I. The case in which this authority was exercised. A paralytic is in a condition both helpless and hopeless. Deprived by the disease of the command of his limbs, his case is one beyond the power of medical skill to deal with. This palsy may, therefore, be regarded as symbolical of the sinner's pitiable condition and gloomy prospects. With regard to the paralytic's state of mind, we are to presume that he was sensible of his sinfulness and of his need of pardon and acceptance; otherwise our Lord could never have treated him as he did. To the sufferer, his bodily malady was indeed afflictive; but he must have had such a "conscience of sin" as to regard his spiritual disorder as more oppressive and more pitiable still. The case, then, in which the Lord Jesus will exercise his prerogative of pardon, is the case of the sinner whose sin is a felt burden, and who brings that burden to the Divine Saviour.

II. The conditions present when Christ thus exercised his authority to pardon. There was a general interest and appreciation in the community; multitudes crowded to hear the Master's words, and many applicants were urgently seeking his healing mercy. There were sentiments of pity and kindliness on the part of the sufferer's friends, leading to practical interposition on his behalf. What these friends could do, they did; they brought the sufferer to Christ. There was faith, both in the paralytic and in his friends—faith, which took a practical form in the approach to Jesus, in the conjoined effort to bring the sufferer beneath the notice of the Healer, and especially in the perseverance so ingeniously and strikingly displayed. All these were conditions which the Saviour evidently regarded as peculiarly favourable to the public exercise of his prerogative to pardon.

III. The authoritative manner and language in which the assurance of pardon was given. There was no inquiry into the state of the paralytic's mind; for Jesus knew what was in man, and needed not to be told. There was no assertion of a delegated power; for the Son of man had authority on earth to forgive sins. There was no hesitation, or delay, or qualification. Nor was Christ's language a mere statement that the sins of the paralytic were forgiven; it was an actual pardon and absolution—nothing less. When Christ forgives, he forgives freely, fully, absolutely. He came to "save his people from their sins." He retains the same power still, and exercises it from the throne of his glory.

IV. The support and vindication of spiritual by miraculous authority. We can hardly wonder at the captious spirit in which Christ's claim was received, at the cavillings of unbelief. Unless they believed the speaker to be more than a prophet, more than human, they must have stumbled at his words. Their general principle was correct and sound: "Who can forgive sins, but God only?" What was passing in their minds was, in the circumstances, natural enough. "It is easy to *say*, 'Thy sins are forgiven;' but what assurance have we that the words are anything beyond words? This is ground upon which the speaker cannot be refuted, and yet upon which the hearers cannot be convinced." These reflections, which were passing in the minds of the scribes, were known to Christ. There was only one way of meeting the objection, of overcoming the difficulty. Jesus must descend to common ground, and appeal to the senses and the understanding of the bystanders. He accordingly wrought a miracle in support of his claims. In doing this, he both relieved the sufferer and vindicated his own authority in the spiritual realm. He bade the paralytic arise, take up his couch, and return home, sound and well.

V. The effect produced by this twofold exercise of power. The *patient* was at once pardoned and cured. With rejoicing heart, with restored powers of limb, he arose and departed to his house, free from burden of guilt, and free from the pains and infirmities of disease. The *scribes* were silenced; some may have been convinced, and few could have been unimpressed. The *witnesses* of the miracle were amazed at this exhibition of twofold authority by the Lord of nature and of spirits. They are recorded to have received the lessons aright; for they glorified God as the Author of healing and salvation in the person of his Son, and they recognized the unique authority entrusted to One human in form, in feeling, and in voice, but of authority supernatural, beneficent, Divine!

Application. 1. The sinner may learn from this narrative in what manner, and in what spirit, to come to Jesus. 2. And he may be encouraged by the representation here given of Christ's willingness and authority to save.

Vers. 13—17.—*Levi's discipleship and hospitality.* The story of Matthew illustrates the part of improbabilities in human life. Some would see in it the irony of fate; we would recognize the mystery of Providence. The evangelists tell us of a man who occupied the humble and even despised position of collector of Roman dues or customs by the shores of the little Lake of Gennesaret, who was summoned to leave this lowly occupation, for what seemed the yet humbler office of attendant and scholar to a peasant Teacher, but who, in course of time, became the chronicler of his Master's life and teachings, and thus the writer of a treatise which stands first in the New Testament—a volume which has been more widely circulated and read than any other composition in any language spoken by man! Looking back upon the call of Matthew, we can see in it an importance which none of the bystanders could possibly have surmised. The narrative yields instructive lessons, whether we consider the conduct of Levi himself, or study the action and the very memorable language used on this occasion by our Lord.

I. Taking first the conduct of this toll-taker or tax-gatherer of Gennesaret, we remark in him an instance of: 1. *A man forsaking a lucrative occupation in order to follow Christ.* Matthew had no doubt found time, amidst his many and exacting avocations, to resort to the Saviour's society and to listen to his public teaching. In this he furnishes us with an example of the effort and the self-denial which business men may find to be profitable to them, if they will, at some loss of time and gain, take advantage of opportunities of Christian fellowship and instruction. And when the time and the call came, the same spirit of self-sacrifice led this devout man to relinquish his secular occupation and emoluments, and to attend upon the Prophet of Nazareth, to learn his mind and to qualify for his service. Are none such called to a similar surrender to-day? See also: 2. *A man using his social influence to bring his companions under the teaching of the Saviour.* The feast to which Matthew invited his old associates was not merely complimentary or convivial. There can be no question that he was actuated by a high motive in inviting people of this class to meet Jesus. Probably it was the best, possibly it was the only, way in which this peculiar class could be brought into contact with the great Teacher. How well it is that those who have the means of doing so should use their hospitality for benevolent and truly Christian purposes—

should bring together those who need and those who are prepared to impart some spiritual blessing, and should thus instrumentally bring together the sinner and the Saviour!

II. But we have here also lessons derivable from THE CONDUCT OF CHRIST. 1. *Christ's disregard and defiance of public opinion.* This is evident (1) in *his selection of disciples and apostles.* He not only chose the lowly and the obscure; he, in this instance especially, chose the despised. The collectors of the Roman revenue were, among the Jews, the mark of general obloquy and contempt. The Son of man, who himself came from the despised Nazareth, selected his friends from the mean and unlettered; and in the case of Matthew he took a man from a sordid and repulsive calling to be an apostle of the greatest religion of the world. It is the wont of Divine wisdom to use "things which are not to bring to nought things which are." (2) *In his companionship and social intercourse.* That Jesus should eat and drink with publicans and sinners excited the surprise and the hatred of the "scribes of the Pharisees," who accounted the common people as accursed. But the rule of Jesus was to go where he could do the Father's will, and pluck men as brands from the burning. It is not well to be a "companion of fools," yet there are occasions upon which the mature and established Christian will do well to seek the society of the ignorant and debased, with the view of instructing and elevating them by the gospel of salvation. 2. *Christ's vindication of this disregard and defiance.* He had a reason for acting as he did. (1) *Jesus recognized men's spiritual need.* To the scribes, the guests at Levi's house were simply contemptible sinners, but to the holy Lord they were the spiritually sick; he saw upon them the marks of a dire disorder, the promise of approaching death. This is the just and Divine light in which to look at the misled and erring children of men. When we regard them thus, not contempt, but pity, will fill our hearts. (2) *Jesus asserted his own power to heal and save and bless.* He was the Divine Physician, in whom alone is help and hope for man. Bad as was the case of the "sinners," it was not beyond the power of his skill and kindness. He had purposes of mercy and power to save. And from the ranks of the sinners Jesus won over many to be soldiers of righteousness; from the pest-houses of the plague-stricken he drew forth many who, restored to spiritual health, became in turn amongst their sinful fellow-men, "ministers to minds diseased."

APPLICATION. 1. Let preachers and teachers of the gospel regard none as so base in condition, or so depraved in character, as to be beyond the power of Christ to save. 2. Let those who are humbled beneath a sense of sin and ill desert be encouraged to come to Jesus, who will both welcome them into his presence, and confer upon them all the priceless blessings of salvation and of eternal life.

Vers. 18—22.—*Christianity and asceticism.* Strange as it seems, it is unquestionable that the very humanity of Jesus, his truly broad and human sympathies, were an offence to the religious leaders of his time. The Pharisees fasted oft; John came neither eating nor drinking; Jesus, who came that he might live among men and who associated with them in all their innocent occupations and enjoyments, excited the displeasure and malice of those who were too superficial and ceremonial to understand his large-heartedness and spirituality. Accordingly, when our Lord joined the festive party at Levi's house, there arose questionings which issued in the explanations given in this passage of the relation between the old religion and its asceticism, and the new religion and its cheerfulness and Divine breadth.

I. A PERSONAL AND TEMPORARY REASON why the disciples of Jesus should not be ascetic. Like a true Leader and Master, Jesus defends his followers, whereinsoever their conduct admits of defence. The figure which he employs is one which John had already used, designating his Divine successor the Bridegroom who should possess the bride. The true *ground* of Christian joy is, in this passage, figuratively but beautifully explained. The Jewish wedding was an occasion for festivity, rejoicing, music, and society. The companions of the bridegroom—"children of the bride-chamber"—were his choicest and most trusted and beloved friends. They were happy in their friend's society, and rejoiced with him in his joy, and took a prominent part in the festivities appropriate to the occasion. The Lord Jesus honours his disciples by describing them as sustaining such a relationship to him, the Divine Bridegroom.

Whilst he was with them, how could they be sad? how could they fast? how could they refrain from holy mirth and pious songs? There is no ground of joy so just, so sacred, as the friendship of Jesus. To have him with us alway, to hear his voice, to be assured of his interest and love,—this is the purest satisfaction and the highest gladness known to human hearts. "I have," says he to his own—"I have called you friends." "Your sorrow shall be turned into joy." Christ's defence, then, is, that at the time and in the circumstances a joyful spirit was natural and blameless in his companions and disciples. And this was evidently, at this period at all events, the case. To the reader of the Gospels (although M. Renan has, no doubt, exaggerated the facts), it is clear that, in their earlier "progresses" through Galilee, our Lord and his followers led a cheerful, bright, and joyous existence. Time enough to mourn when their Lord, the Bridegroom, should be taken away from them. Then, at his approaching departure, sorrow filled their hearts. Yet this was but for a season; with his return at Pentecost, the joy of the Church returned.

II. A GENERAL AND ENDURING REASON WHY THE DISCIPLES OF JESUS SHOULD NOT BE ASCETIC. True, Christ has gone; so, if his personal presence alone restrained the disciples from mourning, sadness and fasting would be appropriate in the Church of the Redeemer, as the customary habit and sentiment. But the case is otherwise; our Lord himself has justified, in this passage, a lasting antagonism between his religion and practices of asceticism. Not that, under the Christian dispensation, fasting is unlawful; but that it should be rather exceptional and special than distinctive of the new life. The fact is, as Christ shows in these two parables, that there is a want of harmony between the old practices and the new faith, the old garment and the new cloth, the old skins and the new wine. 1. Christianity is a religion of *the spirit rather than of the form.* Our Lord teaches that it is better not to appear unto men to fast; it is better to humble ourselves in secret, because of our sins and the sins of our time, before our God. There is much danger of regarding fasting as in itself, because a mortification of the flesh, acceptable to God. This is a mistaken conception, as may be learned even from some passages of Old Testament Scripture. 2. Christianity is a religion *of love rather than of fear.* Those who are in dread of justice may seemingly be justified in their attitude of mind, when they so give way to sentiments of abject self-abasement that they cover themselves with sackcloth and ashes, and deprive themselves of necessary food. But those who are conscious that, through Christ, they are living in the enjoyment of the Divine favour, can scarcely be expected—at least, as an habitual exercise—to mourn and fast. They "rejoice evermore;" the "joy of the Lord is their strength;" his "statutes are their song in the house of their pilgrimage." For them, "perfect love casteth out fear." 3. Christianity is a religion *rather of hopefulness than of gloom.* It teaches us to look forward to the future with bright anticipation, ardently to desire the return of the Lord in triumph, and cheerfully to prepare for a glorious future. The Bridegroom will return and claim his own; how can the spiritual spouse do other than look forward, hopefully and joyfully, to the glad and festive day?

III. The general principle underlying our Lord's reply is this: THE FORM OF RELIGION, WITHOUT THE REALITY AND SPIRITUAL SUBSTANCE, IS ALTOGETHER VAIN. All religious observances have a tendency,—such is the weakness of human nature,—to harden into dead formalities. At first they are good, for they are the expression of sincere feeling and conviction. But by-and-by the spiritual disappears, and the mere ceremony remains. And the unspiritual mistake the form for the substance, and come to flatter themselves that they are religious and that it is well with them, when they are simply by ceremonial excuses justifying themselves for a heart and life profoundly irreligious. Thus it was with multitudes of the Jews, in the time of our Saviour and of the apostles. What stress they laid upon circumcision, upon sacrifices, upon ceremonial purity, upon tithes, upon alms, upon sabbath-keeping, upon observing sacred festivals, upon fasts appointed and traditional, upon the customs and superstitions received from their fathers! And how, at the same time, they neglected the weightier matters of the Law! Hence our Lord's frequent upbraidings of the scribes and Pharisees. They deceived themselves, they deluded others, they hindered the hearts of men from receiving the gospel. When Christianity was established, it was threatened by the same disastrous tendency. First, the Judaizers endeavoured to overlay the spirituality of the gospel with Jewish rites and customs. And afterwards, when

Christianity was in the act of vanquishing paganism, it submitted to assume much that was heathen. The great system of sacerdotalism, with its sacramentarianism, its saint-worship, and its mortifications and asceticism, was acquired from heathenism. And how much of this survives even to the present day, we have only to look around us that we may see. Now, Christ in his answer supplies the true corrective and safe-guard against the action of this evil tendency. Why should his disciples fast, when (as a matter of fact) they were happy and jubilant? It would have been mere formality and hypocrisy, than which nothing was more repugnant to his spiritual doctrines and the character of his religion.

APPLICATION. 1. Let those who fast, fast in spirit, and afflict the soul, and place no confidence in the flesh. 2. Let those who feast, feast as the children of God and the friends of Christ. 3. Let the demeanour of Christians be such, so glowing with sincere and hopeful cheerfulness, as to commend the glorious gospel.

Vers. 23—28.—*The sabbath.* The grounds upon which the Pharisees and scribes took offence at our Lord and his ministry were various. Some of these—as, *e.g.,* his claim to pardon sin—were very serious ; for in such a case Jesus was either an im-postor and blasphemer, or he was the Son of God. Others were very trivial, as, *e.g.,* his neglect of some unauthorized traditions, or his preference of moral duty to obser-vance of the ceremonial law. In this and in the following incident, the *sabbath* was the ground of misunderstanding, and Christ's preference of humanity to ceremonial compliance occasioned, on the part of his adversaries, hatred, enmity, and conspiracy. Still, the malice of Christ's foes furnished opportunities for the assertion of great religious principles. From this narrative we learn that *human need should take precedence of ceremony and tradition.* There is ever a danger lest the outward husk of religion should be mistaken for the precious kernel. Nowhere is this danger more stringently guarded against than in the conduct and the discourses of Christ. The principle is vindicated—

I. BY AN APPEAL TO OLD TESTAMENT HISTORY. It was a master-stroke of contro-versy on the part of the great Teacher to appeal to the Scriptures, which the Pharisees professed to hold in such reverence. The conduct of David, one of the great heroes and saints of their national history, was quoted in justification of the conduct of the disciples of Jesus. To eat is a necessity of human nature, and some kind of action, of rudimentary labour, is necessary in order to eating. The disciples of Jesus had plucked ears of corn, had rubbed the grain free from husk in their hands, and had eaten, in order to satisfy their hunger. Possibly in so doing they had violated the tradition of the elders, which maintained that anything approaching to labour on the sabbath day was an infraction of the Divine command. However, the Lord vindicated them by the example of David, who, for the purpose of providing food for himself and his com-panions, had not hesitated to take the shewbread of the sanctuary, which was reserved for the use of the priests alone ; and this probably also on the sabbath day. Punc-tiliousness of observance must give way before those necessities which the Creator has impressed upon our human nature.

II. BY THE ASSERTION THAT THE SABBATH IS THE MEANS TO WHICH HUMAN WELFARE IS THE END. How blessed an institution is the weekly day of rest ! The importance of the sabbath to man's bodily and spiritual welfare is very much overlooked by many advocates for the employment of labour on that day, and by many Christians who, in their zeal for men's instruction and salvation, labour seven days a week instead of six. Yet, as we are here taught, we are not to make an idol of even so precious an institu-tion. The day of rest was designed for man's good; and it must be maintained that man's good comes first, and the sabbath next. Thus it is allowable and it is required to perform " works of necessity and mercy " on the sabbath, and even on the Lord's day, which may be regarded as the higher sabbath of the Christian. Those who preach and teach, who visit the sick and the afflicted, although their doing these things may make them labour seven days in the week, may make them " sabbath-breakers," are held guiltless by the application of the great principle of the text.

III. BY THE CLAIM OF CHRIST TO LORDSHIP OVER THE SABBATH DAY. Christ is indeed Lord of all. He uses his lordship not so much to institute as to abrogate cere-monies, not so much to burden the religious life with observances as to set it free from

such trammels. He imparts the true sabbatic spirit ; he gives the rest of heart, which
is even more important than bodily repose. He sanctifies all days by his Spirit,
making every day to the Christian better and more sacred than the holiest festival or
the most solemn fast to the Jew of old. If the day be begun, continued, and ended in
him, and if all our works be done under his lordship and by his inspiration, life
itself will be a true sabbath, filled with the rest of his love and with the music of
his praise.

PRACTICAL LESSONS. 1. Guard against a merely external, ceremonial religion, which
is ever prone to degenerate into superstition. 2. Consider the preciousness of the
weekly day of rest ; it was given for our advantage ; it should be used for the glory of
God, in the welfare of those for whom Christ lived and died. 3. Think aright of him
who, without presumption, could claim a prerogative so lofty as lordship over the
sabbath. To be filled with his spirit, to yield ourselves to his authority,—this is the
best means of fulfilling the spiritual law of the God who is a Spirit, and who asks for
spiritual homage and service.

HOMILIES BY VARIOUS AUTHORS.

Vers. 1—12.—*Cure of the paralytic.* I. DIFFICULTIES ARE READILY OVERCOME WHERE
THERE IS FAITH. The house was probably a poor one, roofed with mud and shingle.
It would be easy, therefore, to dig a hole and obtain entrance in that way. But doing
it required a certain amount of ingenuity and effort, which proved that the man and
his friends were resolved to get to Jesus and obtain the cure. All this trouble and
thoughtfulness was the outcome of faith in Christ. Their boldness was the confidence
of faith. Where the heart is right, difficulties in the way of seeking or following the
Saviour will only call forth keener ingenuity and higher resolution.

II. FAITH EVER SECURES THE SYMPATHY AND ENCOURAGEMENT OF CHRIST. Christ's
first words were not chiding, but a welcome. He said, "Son [child], thy sins are forgiven." There would be tenderness and sympathy in the tone as well as in the
words. He spoke as a father or an elder brother. The sick man may have been
young. But in the midst of all the kindness the guilty past of the man is not forgotten. He had been a sinner, and probably his malady was but the fruit of his
misdoing. A thrill of wonder and fear, mingled with more hopeful feelings, would
pervade him as he listened. Here was one who knew all about him, and yet had
compassion on him ! The faith of the patient and his bearers (possibly relatives) was
thus rewarded beyond their hopes. A greater boon was conferred than they sought.
Christ is never satisfied with half measures. He goes at once to the root of the evil,
and seeks to save a man altogether, in soul as well as in body and fortune.

III. IN SHOWING MERCY CHRIST ASSUMES THE HIGHEST AUTHORITY. Whilst the
nature of the case before him demanded that the cure should be thus radical, the mere
utterance of the words, "Thy sins are forgiven," involved a claim which those looking
on were not ready to acknowledge. 1. *Faith in being taxed is rewarded.* The
believing men were required to believe more, and more definitely, than they had already
done. And to him chiefly concerned there were already inward witnesses in favour of
the new claim. That Christ should have divined the secret source of the bodily weakness and mental unrest was a presumption that he was what he professed implicitly
to be. Doubtless, with the rising of his spirit to the new duty of recognizing the
authority of Jesus, the sick man's conscience would receive sudden and unlooked-for
relief. The tide of life would turn again in the glad flush of peace and happiness.
Christ's demands upon men to believe more than they already do are intended as conditions of his bestowing greater blessings. 2. *In order to do all that he was sent to do,
Christ required to be Divine.* The argument was perfectly sound, which the scribes
carried on "in their hearts." Only God can, in the ultimate, forgive sins. Yet his
power is sometimes delegated according to fixed principles and appointments. But
probably they included in their reasoning the unspoken evidence given in Christ's
manner, that he forgave out of and from himself. The entire circumstances of the case
show that he must have done this. And so ever, when men come to him, it is that he

may exercise this authority and power. What they did not think of was the possibility of him whom they accused being " very God of very God."

IV. DIFFICULTIES ARE CREATED WHERE FAITH IS ABSENT. The simple soul of the paralytic grasped the secret of Divinity which escaped the subtlety of the scribes. Their very knowledge stood in their way, because it was not spiritually acquired and employed.

V. THE POWER OF CHRIST IS A PRACTICAL DEMONSTRATION OF HIS AUTHORITY. 1. Strictly speaking, healing the paralysis of the man was not, when taken by itself, on the same level with the forgiveness of his sins; but the two actions are distinctly declared to be in connection with one another. They both appealed to the same Divine power. If, therefore, the pretension to this power made in the former utterance was blasphemous, the ability to perform the consequent miracle would not have been forthcoming. It is also possible that the visible fact of the cure may have been meant as a making good of the invisible transaction declared in the first words. They were shown thereby not to be mere words. 2. And similarly, but even more cogently, is the proof of our Lord's divinity furnished by the spiritual experience of those whom he redeems. That they are forgiven is witnessed to in the subsequent power given to live righteously, and to continue in fellowship with a reconciled God. To those who are conscious of this inward result ("kept by the power of God through faith, unto salvation") there is no other evidence so conclusive.—M.

Vers. 13—22.—*Levi's feast : the moral questions it occasioned.* 1. (Vers. 13—17.) *Eating with publicans and sinners.* In calling Matthew (Levi) from the receipt of custom, our Saviour made him relinquish all his old pursuits and companions, and conferred upon him an unexpected honour. The feast given by him was, therefore, partly a farewell, partly a celebration. In overstepping the boundary line of Jewish religious and social etiquette, the Lord performed an act of great significance, which was sure to call forth remark.

I. SUPERFICIAL KNOWLEDGE, WHEN LINKED WITH MALICE, WILL PUT THE WORST CONSTRUCTION UPON THE BEST ACTIONS. Conventional morality was invoked to condemn Christ in mingling with the publicans. No trouble was taken to ascertain the true character of the feast. By their criticism the Pharisees exposed their own hollowness and unspirituality. They condemned themselves in seeking to condemn Christ. For such judgments men are responsible. The greatest care and most spiritual view should be taken ere judgment is passed upon the actions of others, especially when their character is known to be good.

II. IT IS THE MOTIVE WHICH IS THE TRUE KEY TO THE NATURE OF ACTIONS. 1. *This applies absolutely in the case of actions in themselves indifferent, or only conventionally forbidden ; but in all actions it is an indispensable canon of ultimate judgment.* Even where the external nature of an action is unmistakable, the utmost care should be taken in forming an opinion. Absolute and unqualified judgment is for God alone. 2. *When challenged for our conduct it is well to explain the principles upon which we act.* Christ at once makes known his motives, and with no anger. Yet in so doing he judged his accusers. They pretended to be whole, and so could not object to him doing good to those who required his aid. Why were they dissatisfied, if not from secret disquietude with their own condition and attitude? Irony proceeding from deepest spiritual discernment!

III. THE HOLIEST SOUGHT OUT AND COMPANIED WITH SINNERS THAT HE MIGHT MAKE THEM HOLY. It is only by sympathy, and by appeals to their highest nature, that sinful men can be won to God.—M.

Vers. 13—22.—*Levi's feast : the moral questions it occasioned.* 2. (Vers. 18—22.) *The rationale of fasting.* I. THE ORIGIN OF THE QUESTION. This seemed to be natural enough. A real perplexity was created which required to be removed. There is no malice or bitterness in the inquiry. Amongst spiritual associates all such difficulties ought to be frankly faced and kindly discussed. 1. *The feast of Levi was coincident with a traditional fast.* The Pharisees and the disciples of John both observed the fast, were observing it at the time the others were feasting. Now, within the band of Christ's disciples were two sections—one formerly wholly, and still to a great extent, identified with the doctrines and observances of John; the other following without question the spiritual guidance of Christ. The contrast would, therefore, be very marked. A schism seemed to discover itself within the circle of the brethren. 2. *The general life of the disciples of Christ was not so ascetic as that of John's, and the traditional fasts of Judaism were not so strictly observed by them.* The special occasion was only a striking instance of general divergence. In answering the question, then, the key would be given to the entire life which Christ desired men to lead.

II. Its solution. The answer was prompt and kindly, and it seemed to justify the question. It goes to the very root of the subject. No attention is given to the circumstance of fasting being a positive or conventional enactment. Its meaning and purpose are at once referred to, as alone determining the validity or otherwise of its claims to being observed. 1. *Subjective conditions and aims are stated to be of chief consequence in regard to such a question.* This was a new departure, a rationalizing of positive law and observance. Institutions and practices of religion are to stand or fall according to their spiritual adaptation to the needs of the human soul. 2. *Circumstances which determine spiritual states are, therefore, decisive as to the obligation or otherwise of fasting.* The Jews under the Law were without Christ; now he had come, and the spiritual experience of men who received him was wholly altered. Fasting would be out of keeping, because the mood of those who discerned and believed Christ (the Bridegroom) was festive and joyous. A feast rather than a fast was therefore the fitting ceremony. 3. *A fundamental distinction exists between Judaism and Christianity.* The one was old and ready to vanish away; the other was new and instinct with fresh, vigorous life. Any confusion of them would therefore be mutually injurious. This distinctive character of each is represented in two illustrations, viz. (1) The old garment and the new piece of cloth. It would be foolish to employ Christianity merely to make good the defects of Judaism. The combination would not only be motley; it would be disastrous, because of the difference of spiritual force in the two systems. Judaism was antiquated, full of holes and rottenness, and ready to vanish away. To patch it up with the gospel would, therefore, only hasten its destruction. Fasting was representative of the legalistic or external rites of Judaism ; Christianity was as new and " unfulled " cloth, which would shrink when put upon the old garment, and make the rent worse. This is one side of the truth; and in (2) the new wine and the old bottles, we have the other. Legal forms and observances are inadequate to contain and express the fresh, spiritual, ever-expanding life of the Christian. Spiritual truth and life must create their own ritual, and dictate their own ideal of morality.—M.

Vers. 23—28.—*The sabbath made for man.* I. The purpose of the sabbath is to be kept in view in interpreting its obligations.

II. Rules which do not have regard to this may violate what they profess to preserve. 1. The disciples were within the written permission of the Law. "To pluck and rub with the hand ears from the field of a neighbour was allowed; Moses forbade only the sickle (Deut. xxiii. 25). But the matter belonged to the thirty-nine chief classes (fathers), each of which had its subdivisions (daughters), in which the works forbidden on the sabbath were enumerated. This was their hypocritical way, to make of trifling things matters of sin and vexation to the conscience " (Braune). 2. "Men see that others neglect rules, when they see not their own violation of principles " (Godwin).

III. The best interests of man are to be served by the sabbath. 1. *" The sabbath was made for man, and not man for the sabbath."* This is proved by an incident from the life of David. As they revered David, the allusion was an *argumentum ad hominem* as well as an illustration of a general principle. By that occurrence it was shown that even the sanctities of the temple were subordinated to the welfare of God's anointed and his followers. If, then, these things bent to the highest interests of man, so must the sabbath. 2. *" The Son of man is Lord of the sabbath."* This is an inference from the foregoing principle. For Christ claimed this authority not merely as a man, but as "the Son of man in his inviolable holiness, and in his mysterious dignity (intimated in Daniel) as the holy Child and Head of humanity appearing in the name of God" (Lange). He summed up in his own person the highest interests of the race. And as Lord of the sabbath he uses it ever for the advancement of holiness and the development of spiritual freedom in his saints.—M.

Vers. 3—5.—*The pardon of the paralytic.* This miracle is recorded also by Matthew and Luke. The former indicates its chronological position as occurring after the return from Gadara. Our gracious Lord "again entered into Capernaum," so slow is he to leave the most undeserving. The news of his arrival quickly spread; indeed, whenever he enters a home or a heart, he cannot be hid. True love and eager faith will surely find him, and in this passage we find an example of that truth.

I. THE COMING OF THE PARALYTIC is full of teaching for those who are now seeking the Saviour. 1. *He had friends who helped him.* Powerless to move, he was peculiarly dependent on their kindness. A sufferer from palsy not only needs much patience and resignation himself, but creates a demand for it in others, and so may prove by his presence in the home to be a means of grace to those called on to minister to him. To serve and help those who are permanent invalids is a holy service, to which many are secretly called, who therein may prove themselves good and faithful servants of the Lord. Such ministration needs a gentle hand, a patient spirit, a courageous heart, and a noble self-forgetfulness. Above all, we should endeavour to bring our sick ones to the feet of Jesus, that they may rejoice in his pardoning love. Our counsels, our example, and our prayers may do for them what these people did for their paralyzed friend. 2. *He found difficulties in approaching Christ.* The crowd was impassable. They ascended the staircase outside (Matt. xxiv. 17), and so reached the flat roof. Then they broke up the covering of the roof and let down the bed on which the sick of the palsy lay. These obstacles tried their faith, proved and purified it. There are difficulties in the way of our approach to Christ; some of which may be removed by our friends, others of which can only be overcome by our own faith and courage. Prejudices, easily besetting sins, evil companions, are examples. 3. *The difficulties were victoriously surmounted.* The fact that they were so was a manifest proof of the faith which animated this man and his friends. Some way is always open to those eager for salvation, though it may be one that seems unusual to onlookers.

II. THE GRACIOUSNESS OF THE SAVIOUR. 1. *He knew the man's deepest wants.* Probably the paralytic was more troubled about his sin than about his sickness, although his friends did not know it. We ought to be more anxious about the soul than about the body. Christ Jesus reads our secret thoughts. "He knew what was in man." He noticed and exposed the unexpressed anger of his enemies (ver. 8). But while he discovers the secret sin, far more readily does he discern the silent longing for pardon. 2. *He was willing and waiting to bless.* There was no delay. The strange interruption to teaching was not resented but welcomed. At once he spoke the word of pardon for which the man's heart was hungering, although he foresaw the indignation and scorn which would follow on the declaration, "Thy sins be forgiven thee." Divine love is not to be restrained by human narrowness, whether in the Church or outside it. 3. *He showed himself ready and able to forgive.* Possibly our Lord saw a connection between this illness and some special sin. He guards us, however, against supposing that it is always so (Luke xiii. 15; John ix. 3). Perhaps the secret pangs of conscience were in the way of physical restoration here. Sometimes pardon was given after cure (Luke xvii. 19; John v. 14). The scribes were right in their declaration that none but God can forgive sins. The Levitical priests, under the old dispensation, were authorized to announce Divine forgiveness, as God's representatives, after the offering of appointed sacrifices; but the scribes very properly recognized that Jesus claimed to do far more than that. He admitted that it was so, and as the Son of man (Dan. vii. 13) he claimed the power they denied him, and at once gave a proof that the power was actually his. They might have argued that there was no evidence that the man's sins were forgiven; that Jesus was making a safe claim, which could not be tested. In order to meet this he said in effect, "I will now claim and exercise a power the result of which you can see; and it shall either brand me as an impostor, or else it shall be a sign that my former utterance had effect." Then said he to the sick of the palsy, "Arise, and take up thy bed, and go thy way into thine house." Like that man, may our recovered and redeemed powers be instantaneously used in obedience to Christ.—A. R.

Vers. 14, 15.—*Levi's call from dishonour to discipleship.* All the sacred Scriptures serve to show that God's redemption is meant for those who are conscious of their sin, however grievous have been their offences. *Promises* prove this. Isaiah's description of a people whose head was faint and whose heart was sick is followed by the invitation, "Come now, and let us reason together," etc., and this is intensified by the gracious words of Christ, "Come unto me, all ye that labour," etc. *Facts* suggest the same truth, *e.g.* God's dealing with Adam, the call of idolatrous Abram, and the pardon of Manasseh; and all such evidences are concentrated in Christ. Descended through Tamar, Rahab, Bathsheba, and David, he chose no spotless ancestry according to the flesh, but was from the first "numbered with the transgressors." His life-work touched the sinful—the woman who was a sinner, the adulteress of Samaria, the thief on the cross, etc. No wonder that his gospel was received by publicans and by sinners, in the house of Herod, in the court of Nero, among the idolatrous Ephesians and the profligate Corinthians. He came "not to call the righteous, but sinners to repentance." Levi the publican was an example of these. Let us consider—

I. THE POSITION LEVI OCCUPIED. "Levi" was the original name borne by the evangelist and apostle who was known in the Church as "Matthew," equivalent to "God's gift," he being so named because in him the Lord had a fulfilment of his own words, "All that the Father hath *given* me shall come to me, and him that cometh to me, I will in no wise cast out." Levi was a tax-gatherer, a rate collector, employed by the richer publicans (of whom Zacchæus was an example) to collect dues levied on the lake fishery or on the traffic passing through the district to Damascus; and consideration of what that involved may encourage the despondent. 1. *He was low in the social scale.* As a standing emblem of the authority of Roman tyranny, the tax-gatherer, especially when, like Levi, he was a renegade Jew, was intensely hated and despised; none of his fellow-countrymen would speak or eat with him. From the first Christ set himself against this prejudice and social distinction. As the "Son of man," as the King of men, he would have no narrow circle from which to draw his followers. His blessings were for the most despised and poor, as are God's air and sunshine. 2. *He was an outcast from religious men.* As patriots, the Jews hated him; as upholders of the ancient faith, they excommunicated him. Hence Matthew the apostle would seem to be a marvel of grace. The excommunicated man was to build up the communion of the Christian Church, the apostle was to become a pillar of Divine truth, the instrument of oppression was to proclaim true liberty, the byword was to become a burning and a shining light. God chose despised things to bring to nought those which were great and honoured. The Church's judgment is not always right, therefore "judge not, that ye be not judged." Christ saw in Levi one who was seeking higher things, and he said to him, "Follow me." 3. *He was subject to grievous temptations.* The bad reputation of the publicans was doubtless, to a large extent, deserved. The vicious system of raising revenue adopted by Rome, and still practised in Turkey, would tend to make men avaricious, hard, and unscrupulous. Large sums of money passed through their hands, and were loosely collected and accounted for; bribes were frequently offered and universally accepted, in order to obtain exemptions and privileges; and a publican, from the mere fact of being one, had no reputation to lose, so that if he had been more scrupulous than others he would get no credit for it. In that position Christ saw Levi and pitied him, and thence in his love he called him, teaching us that none are so low, or have circumstances so adverse, as to be beyond the reach of his pity and salvation.

II. THE SERVICE LEVI ATTEMPTED. 1. *He freely gave up all to follow Jesus.* It was a lucrative position, but he felt called to something nobler, for the sake of which any sacrifice should be made. Suggest certain trades and occupations which are now such a hindrance to the Divine life that for Christ's sake they ought to be abandoned by his followers. Indicate the call which sometimes comes to Christians to give up even innocent employments, for the higher work of preaching Christ. 2. *He invited others to see and hear his Master.* Luke (v. 27) speaks of this as a "great feast" which Levi made in honour of his Lord; to which he invited his old comrades, who like himself would be popularly ranked among "the publicans and sinners." The feast was an occasion for speaking his farewell, and giving reasons for the change in his life. He wished to show that he was about to serve One greater than Cæsar, and to do a nobler work. At his request Jesus became his guest. May that gracious Lord appear in our homes, at all our festive gatherings, and so show himself through us to those around us, that they too may find joy in his service!—A. R.

Vers. 18—20.—*On fasting.* Weak brethren too often do the work of evil men. The disciples of John, who were not hostile to our Lord, were made on this occasion the tools of the Pharisees, whose great object was to damage our Lord's reputation amongst the people, and to weaken the allegiance of his followers. The Baptist had never forbidden his disciples to observe the customary fasts, and his own ascetic life had taught them such lessons of self-denial that they readily observed them, especially at a time like this, when he was languishing in prison. Sore and sensitive in heart as they were, it was easy for the Pharisees to suggest that Jesus owed much to their teacher's testimony; that he had professedly been John's Friend and Fellow-worker; that he was doing nothing whatever to effect his deliverance; that he did not even fast for grief because of his imprisonment, but was enjoying social festivity in the house of a publican. But although the design of the Pharisees was to convict our Lord of disregard of national tradition and pious custom, and to condemn him for forgetfulness of his imprisoned friend, they only succeeded in educing a complete justification of his conduct, and the announcement of a noble principle which we have to consider, viz. *that religious observances are only acceptable to God when they are the natural outcome of the religious life of him who offers them.* In this passage we see the following facts:—

I. HYPOCRISY IS CONDEMNED. John's disciples were not guilty of this offensive sin. No doubt their fasting was, at this time, a true expression of inward grief; and was on other occasions used by them as a means of spiritual discipline. Our Lord does not imply that they were hypocritical, but asserts that his own disciples would be, if they outwardly joined in a fast which would be an untrue representation of their present feeling. Hopeful and jubilant in the presence of their Lord, his disciples could not fast, and would be wrong to do so. This tacitly condemns all fasts which arise from improper or untrue motives, or which are outwardly kept at the dictation of others. The principle, however, is of general application, teaching us that, under the new dispensation, no outward manifestation of devotion is acceptable to God, except as it is true to the inward feeling of the worshipper. The sin of unreality was often rebuked by the prophets, and still more vigorously by John the Baptist and by our Lord; indeed, the sternest words ever uttered by Christ were levelled against the unreal, insincere, and hypocritical Pharisees. From that sin he would save his disciples, and therefore asserted that as their inward condition did not lead them to fasting, a fast would at that time be unnatural and perilous. Be you who or what you may, be real and true before God and man. "If thine eye be single, thy whole body shall be full of light."

II. EXTERNALISM IS REBUKED. By externalism we mean the putting of external religious ceremonies in the place of spiritual acts of worship. We distinguish this decisively from hypocrisy, as the words are by no means interchangeable—some of the Pharisees, for example, being thoroughly sincere. But many rites enjoined under the old dispensation, which were meant to have spiritual significance and to give utterance to soul-longings, had become mere husks in which the kernel had rotted. Sacrifices were offered without sense of guilt; washings were frequent, even to absurdity, but did not express conscious uncleanness of soul; alms were largely given, but without generosity; fasts were observed without any humiliation of soul before God. Religion had become mechanical and soulless, and from that curse Christ would save his disciples. Hence he commended the mite of the widow, and not the large gifts of the wealthy; he chose his friends not from the priests in the temple, but from peasants in Galilee; he discerned faith not in the long prayers recited by the Pharisees, but in the secret petition of the trembling woman who only durst touch the hem of his garment. To him the unuttered sigh was a prayer, the generous purpose an alms-deed, and a holy aspiration was an evening sacrifice. So here he taught that fasting was not a rite of any value in itself, and that self-inflicted penance was not as such pleasing to God. (Apply this to what is similar in our days.)

III. FREEDOM IS PROCLAIMED. He who condemned fasting and all other rites and ceremonies, when put in a wrong place, allowed any of these to be used by his disciples when they naturally and truly expressed their inward spiritual life. When, for example, the Bridegroom was taken away, when the shadow of Calvary's cross rested on them, they fasted; for they had no heart to do anything else. But when the Resurrection morning dawned, and the gates of the grave were opened, and the Bridegroom came back to his waiting bride, to fulfil the promise, " I am with you always," then, and on the day of Pentecost, they could not fast. If now there are times when to our doubting minds the heavenly Bridegroom seems far away; if now we ever feel that temporary abstinence from food, or from pleasure, or from work, would help our spiritual life,—then let us fast; but even then let us do so in remembrance of the words, " Thou when thou fastest, anoint thy head, and wash thy face, that thou appear not unto *men* to fast." In regard to this and all other ceremonies, " Ye, brethren, are called unto liberty, only use not that liberty for an occasion to the flesh, but by love serve one another."

IV. JOYFULNESS IS INCULCATED. In this respect the practices of our Lord presented a striking contrast to those of John or of the Pharisees. Here he justifies his disciples, as formerly he had defended himself, against aspersions cast upon them for joining in social festivity. Appealing to the consciences of his questioners, and alluding to the last words of testimony their master had uttered concerning himself (John iii. 29), he asked, " Can the sons of the bridechamber mourn, while the bridegroom is with them?" We ought to be so glad because of our relation to Christ, because of his constant presence and undying love, that, like Paul, we can be "joyful in tribulations also," and sing God's praise in the darkness of a prison.— A. R.

Vers. 1—12.—*The paralytic.* I. THE PARALYTIC A TYPE OF HELPLESSNESS IN GENERAL. In this case both physical and moral. No malady is serious but that which attacks the freedom of the soul in its seat.

II. DIFFICULTIES ARE FOR THE TRIAL OF FAITH. The physical difficulty of getting to Christ's presence we may view as a parable or allegory of deeper moral difficulties. How hard to be a Christian—to reach the truth and live in the light of it! Argument breaks down; many gaps in our reasoning it is not easy to get over. But—

> " What if the breaks themselves should prove at last
> The most consummate of contrivances
> To train a man's eye, teach him what is faith?"

III. THE SEAT OF HEALTH OFTEN LIES IN THE IMAGINATION. A man has a dark picture of himself, his sin, his doom, etc., constantly before him. He cannot be well or happy. Reverse this picture, and the whole nature, physical and moral, recovers its healthy working. Christ will not suffer men to despond or despair of themselves. Believe yourself condemned, a life-failure, and you remain a paralytic. Believe in your Divine possibility and future; you can rise and walk. When the gospel is truly preached, men are not crushed, but uplifted; not discouraged, but heartened about themselves.

IV. THE GIFT OF SYMPATHY AND OF POWER. Here was a signal example of the *diagnosis* of Jesus. He *saw*, as we say, what was the matter. He *spoke* to the point; and his word was an idea and a power. Never is true sympathy disjoined from power. To love our fellows is to enjoy the noblest power.—J.

Vers. 15—22.—*Matthew's house.* I. THE SOCIALITY OF JESUS. He was found at ordinary dinner-parties and entertainments throughout his course, and to the last. He was a contrast in this to the ascetic Baptist. He was found in " questionable " company. But the company of Pharisees would have been as "questionable." With a clear conscience a man may go into the miscellany of people called " society." A free and open manner is certain to bring remark and censure upon him. But better to mix with others and be thought "no better" than they, than hold aloof and sour the heart with Pharisaic self-conceit. There is danger in general society, and danger in religious cliques.

II. LOVE; JUSTIFYING ALL ECCENTRICITIES. It was eccentric to mix with those common and tabooed people. The whole conduct of Jesus was eccentric, and brought about fatal consequences. To aim at singularity is a foppery; to follow love's impulse alone is graceful, generous, polite, refined. This *is* singular. Would there were more of such singularity!

III. NATURALNESS. The spirit of man is like the face of earth and sky. Clouds pass over it; the sun is hidden. Anon all is bright again, and birds sing. To follow the lead of joy is in the best sense natural. Let the face and manner reflect the inner mind; to reverse this is to act a part. The pure and lovely hypocrisy is that which tries to affect the mien of mirth, though the heart be heavy. To put on the mask of gloom for the sake of warning others is Pharisaic, not Christian. Jesus is the example of the perfect gentleman.

IV. The place and time of asceticism. It is the reaction of the mind against certain sorrows. We must be true again to feeling and to fancy. It would be a violence to natural taste to put on wedding garments when a friend has passed away, however logical it might seem. There is a natural homœopathy of grief. Speaking of it and representing it outwardly tends to its relief; but to mimic a grief we feel not is to do a violence to ourselves. Be true to yourself: this is the only secret of moral beauty, from the lowest to the highest moods, and is the lesson of Jesus.—J.

Vers. 23—28.—*Love greater than law.* I. Human life is more important than the means of living. All laws, ceremonial or otherwise, may be regarded as means towards ends. What end do we know higher than human weal and bliss? Christ points out that this is the real end of legislation—man, his education, his good, physical and spiritual.

II. It is a gross fallacy to put the means before the end. This the Pharisees did. They said, "Man for the sabbath." Christ said, "The sabbath for man." Ceremonies are all means of spiritual culture. Not so with moral ideals. They are our end.

III. Law is rooted in love. Christ is the representative of Divine love. If he by example or precept declares that a law is to be suspended or abrogated, this is in the interests of love. How absurd would it be, on a desert island, for a shipwrecked crew, almost starving, to refuse to avail themselves of food cast in their way, *e.g.* by a chance flight of birds, because it was a fast day! Analogous was the case mentioned by Christ (ver. 26). The sabbath had no meaning except as an expression of Divine love; and the rigid observance of it in defiance of love's dictates would be a mockery. Christ is Lord of love, and therefore Lord of law.—J.

Vers. 1—12.—*The sick of the palsy: the spiritual and physical healing.* The excitement having subsided, Jesus enters again into Capernaum. He, in the house, was teaching, "Pharisees and doctors of the Law sitting by," from all parts. The mighty "power of the Lord was with him to heal," as was made evident before, or as was to be proved by this event. It being "noised that he was in the house, many were gathered together," crowding "about the door." But attention is arrested by the bold deed of four men, who, carrying one sick of the palsy, and finding it impossible to get into the presence of Jesus, ascend to the low flat roof, "and let down the bed whereon the sick of the palsy lay," as men are wont to let down straw and other things to-day in similar houses. Instantly the whole event assumes a spiritual character, and Jesus, for all time, gives the spiritual its pre-eminence: "Jesus, seeing their faith." The *spiritual* must take precedence, the *material* must follow.

I. In order to spiritual healing a suitable condition is needful. Here and elsewhere that condition is expressed by the one word *faith.* Faith, though a simple act or condition of mind, is the result of many—consciousness of need, desire of relief, self-distrust, some knowledge of Christ, appreciative confidence leading to assured persuasion. In faith the soul is already at one with the Saviour; it has come to him; it is united to him. The faith of others besides that of the sick is a favourable condition. Here it first arrests attention: "Jesus, seeing their faith." How many are dependent for their salvation upon the faith and effort of others! By their deed they declared their faith. It said, "Thou canst;" if not also, "Thou wilt." Through their faith must be seen, however, that of the sufferer shining. For who urged them on to do even this for him? Would he have undergone the pain of this treatment had he not had faith? It is saying, as said another, "If I do but touch his garment, I shall be made whole." With the desire of the sufferer for relief the charity of his helpers mingled. Their acts of faith were so interwoven that they became one faith. It was this that Jesus saw.

II. Where the suitable spiritual condition is found the healing inevitably takes place. Yea, though the word declaring it be not uttered; and even when it is

uttered, men, "reasoning in their hearts," believe not. Where Jesus to-day sees faith
—and he is always on the look-out for it—there he heals. The faith of sufferers and
helpers must have respect to his promise and his power to heal, and not busy itself so
much with listening for the word which declares the healing to be done. "Jesus,
seeing their faith," and knowing there was the suitable condition for the reception of
spiritual blessing, even above and beyond that for which they asked, "saith, Son, thy
sins are forgiven." So is faith rewarded; so are spirituals put in their rightful place
before temporals; not really to hinder the temporal, but the better to prepare for it.

III. The opposition of antagonists is used by Christ for the greater confirmation of the believing ones; and, in mercy, also to awaken conviction in the
unbelieving heart. "Perceiving in his [own] spirit that they so reasoned" within the
dark chambers of their hearts, he graciously condescended to reason with them. "If
I can do the harder of two works, surely I can the easier. That ye will not doubt.
But 'whether is easier' in your view, to say, 'Thy sins are forgiven;' or to say, 'Arise,
take up thy bed and walk'? This must not only be said; to prove itself a real word
of power, it must be done. Of this ye can be judges. But that ye—even ye reasoning
and unbelieving ones—may know the unlimited power of the Son of man in the
spiritual realm, behold a proof of his power in the material! A word declares it. 'I
say unto thee, arise.'" A word of power indeed; for "he arose and took up the bed,
and went forth before them all"—a visible, undeniable testimony that the true kingdom of God had come, that the true King was amongst them; and they also were not
only amazed, but "they glorified God," and confessed, "We never saw it on this
fashion." So he who maketh "the wrath of man to praise him," maketh the thought
of evil to turn to the greater good of them whom he would bless.

IV. The wonderful power for the good of all that faith in the Son of man
calls into play. Therefore let every one who has faith use it: in faith bringing the
sin-stricken to Jesus; with strong faith encouraging all to seek him, to yield to him,
to follow, and to trust in him. And let every worker work in faith; for the faith of
the bearer of the sick is regarded. Let parents bring their children to Jesus in faith;
and pastors bring their flocks before him in faith; and friends, friends; and lovers of
men lay the world at his feet in lowly, loving, believing prayer. Unbelief stays the
strong arm of Christ, because it presents the unsuitable conditions before him who
always acts according to the "laws" of his own kingdom. Faith is not strength, but
acknowledged feebleness. We can aid the consciously feeble, but the presumptuously
strong put themselves beyond the power of men and the will of the Lord.—G.

Vers. 13—22.—*Fasting.* "By the sea side" the great Teacher is heard by a listening
multitude. Then passing near "the place of toll, his eye fell upon Levi, son of
Alphæus," whose service he imperatively claims. Levi, already called to be a disciple,
now called to be an apostle, with much sacrifice arises to follow his Lord and Master to
the end, so teaching for all future apostles and servants that the claims of the kingdom
of Heaven stand first in importance, and must first be met. The simple, brief, authoritative command, "Follow me," may seem to need an exposition and expansion. It is
the consummation, doubtless, of many words of instruction; and, perhaps, the outward
call corresponds to an inward conviction of duty and an inward preparedness for
the sacrifice. The story of compliance is almost as brief as that of the call, "And he
arose and followed him." But this does not shut out the possibility of the calm
adjustment by Levi of his affairs, as would be necessary before setting out upon a new
course of life. Only the impetuous need hurry lest they should change their minds.
Then, as it would seem in commemoration of the great change, when the new name
Matthew may have been assumed, he, called like Elisha, to the sacred office, like him
he makes his feast to his neighbours—his fellow tax-gatherers and friends—and his
sacrifice to his God. And Jesus and his disciples are there. Then the murmuring
voice of "the scribes of the Pharisees" must needs accuse him to his disciples: "He
eateth and drinketh with publicans and sinners." Ah, happily for them and us he doth.
He who did not always stoop to vindicate his ways, or tell wherefore or by "what
authority" he did such and such things, now, however, vouchsafes to declare his reason.
First parabolically: "The 'whole have no need of a physician, but they that are sick.'
If these are the sick and faulty, as your words imply, they indeed need me." But

the word applies itself. The really "sick" may be the carping complainers. Then, more precisely, he declares his mission: "'I came not to call the righteous, but sinners.' My dealings are with sinners. How can I reach them if I avoid them?" Let every self-conscious sinner who, bruised and sick, desires healing, hear this word of the Lord, the Lord who comes to "call" and to "eat with" the sinner that he may "heal" him. For all time he is to be known as the Seeker of the sinner and the Healer of the sick. But other murmurers are at hand. The feasting of Jesus and his disciples contrasts with the sadness and fasting of John—then in prison—and his disciples, now left alone; and with the punctilious fasting of the Pharisees. How is this? The reply from the lips of the Master is given in three parables, of which the first only, and but partially, is explained. The reply is not temporal and local merely, relating solely to the circumstances of that hour. The true parable has always within it a principle of universal application. The principle here embodied is—

The true purpose of fasting. This may be defined to be the honest expression of conditions proper to be represented by fasting. "There is a time to fast, and a time to feast;" and the outward ordinance must correspond with the inward spirit. The symbols of sorrow must not be assumed when the heart is merry. The song, not the sackcloth; the wine of joy, not the ashes,—is the more becoming. It is a lesson on *congruity, or the true harmony or fitness of things*; and the lesson is enforced by three parables. 1. "Can the sons of the bridechamber fast while the bridegroom is with them?" These words say, as plainly as words can, "Men must fast when there is occasion to fast." Is any sad? let the signs of sorrow appear; but if the heart within is merry, let him declare it in song. "Is any cheerful? let him sing praise." Fasting by order, whatever may be the state of the heart at the time, is not in accordance with Christ's teaching. It is not in harmony with itself. It becomes a species of hypocrisy. The day of loneliness and exposure and sadness will come; "and then will they fast in that day." 2. The patch upon the "old garment," while confirming the former lesson, declares the uselessness of patching up the old, dry, effete formalism with a piece of new, earnest, vigorous life. This would make the faults all the more obvious. Christ's work was not a patch upon the old; it was a new garment. How often men seem to be sewing a patch of Christian propriety on a faulty life—a mere mending of the torn and useless; and how impressively does this teach the need of a new garment altogether—the white robe of righteousness, an entire change of heart and life, a new birth! 3. But yet more forcibly Christ would teach by another parable the need there was for outward ordinances suited to the new spirit which he came to infuse. The fervent, vital evangelical spirit would certainly rend the dry, hard formalities of legalism. The words seem to refer to the more elastic organization which the expansive spirit would require. As to-day, when a new spirit enters the Churches, it demands not the rigid, unyielding methods of the past, but new ones. Even the good and useful that have long ministered to the spiritual comfort and joy of the fathers, must give place to others which the fresh, vigorous, inventive life of the children demands. "New skins" for "new wine." Yet they must be skins—that which is suitable to the holding of wine that it may be preserved. If changes be made in organizations or methods to suit the constantly fermenting times, they must be such as will conserve the true spirit of devotion and Christian brotherhood. What a striking comment on these words is found in the employment, by many even of the most rigid Churches in our day, of methods which the new spirit within them has demanded! Each may learn for himself: (1) The necessity for a strict correspondence between his outward religious performance and his inward religious state, and between all ordinances and the truths to which they relate. (2) The insufficiency of merely mending the old life of sin by a few patches of new manners. A whole new garment may be had for the asking. (3) The new reviving spirit should find its own appropriate means and ordinances, such as will preserve it from being dissipated and lost.—G.

Ver. 23—ch. iii. 6.—*The Lord and the law of the sabbath.* Jesus passed "through the cornfields," in the course of fulfilling his great mission of preaching, healing, and blessing. His "disciples began as they went" to pluck the ears of corn growing in abundance and probably lying across their path. It was the day of delights, a day hallowed and blessed. The plentifulness of the Divine beneficence, the quiet of the sabbath calm,

the glow of the bright light, would bring near to these self-sacrificing disciples thoughts
of him who now most truly must provide for them their daily bread, the firstfruits of
whose care they now gather.   Gladly the lynx-eyed Pharisees arrest the great Teacher
with their " Why do they on the sabbath day that which is not lawful?"   The direct
reply is reserved, and the inquirers thrown back upon themselves and their carelessness
in reading "what David did when he had need."   The reply rests upon this word
"need," and the following word "hungred," as in the second instance it rests upon " to
do good, and to save a life."   And we are reminded at once of the two classes of circumstances in which, as we have been accustomed to hear, the sabbath form may be
broken without infringing the sabbath law, yea, even when that is done which at
other times " it is not lawful " to do, viz. in works of necessity and works of charity.
But underlying and overarching the whole is the law which the " Lord of the sabbath "
now utters, a law wider in its application than the many details of sabbath observance
—" The sabbath was made for man."

I. Let us first learn that THE SABBATH WAS MADE.   It was a Divine institution.
It was ordained of God.   It was no mere accident that led men to mark the sabbath
day with a special sanctity.   From the many days, each laden with blessing, it pleased
God to choose each seventh day for rest.   To the toil-worn and weary how great an
addition of blessing is this !   The sabbath was not an imposition.   It was designed to
ease the heavily laden; to give time for song; to brighten the house by the presence of
the father, who from morn till night was torn from his family by the necessities of
labour; to minister to the demands of the higher nature; to bring all into closer alliance
with things spiritual, by reflection and by worship.   Truly this is to crowd it with
blessing.   It was not to be a dull day, for it was blessed; it was not to be a common
day, for it was hallowed.

II. BUT THE SABBATH WHICH WAS MADE, WAS MADE FOR MAN.   It was made in
his interests, to promote his weal.   Therefore, anything that can prove itself to be
"for man"—for man at large—is in harmony with sabbath law and the sabbath spirit.
And the strictest sabbath regulations must break down in presence of human necessities, provided they are indeed and of a truth necessities.   Yea, the need of the ox or
ass must be considered, whether it be the need of rest or deliverance from the pit.   It
is "lawful to do good," it is lawful "to save life," it is lawful to feed the hungry—even
the sacred temple bread yielding service to needy men.   The highest interest to be
considered is the interest of human life.   All must be sacrificed to it.   The temple
service itself must be stayed if the priest be needed to pluck one out of fire.

III. SINCE IT IS MADE FOR MAN, HE WHO, BEING SON OF ALL, IS LORD OF ALL, IS OF
NECESSITY AND RIGHT LORD OF MAN'S SABBATH.   Thus this great gift, the Divine
preservation of which was always a sign of blessing, and the removal of which a sign
of cursing,—this Lord's day and man's day, by the Lord's appointment and ordination,
must, if men would be wise, be observed in such a way as to promote the highest
interests of men, as they are interpreted by him who is Lord of them and Lord of
their day.   Oh, how well were it if the tight-laced, and the loose-laced also, would
consider this great law, and make the sabbath a day over which its true Lord rules !
Learn the sin of him who breaks the sabbath and who teaches men so.   1. He sins
against God who made it to be a sabbath.   2. And he sins against man who needs
it to be a sabbath, and for whom it was made.   Is it a sabbath if the son of toil, after
six long days of labour, is compelled to serve a seventh?   This is contrary to the Law
of the Lord.   Far less is it a sabbath if all opportunities for religious worship, for
spiritual refreshment, for family fellowship, are sacrificed ; and still less if the day be
spent in merely worldly amusements and pleasures; and least of all if it be devoted
to evil.   Then the day, designed for the good of body and soul, is spent to the injury
or ruin of both.   And so the Lord's day becomes the devil's day.—G.

Vers. 1—12.   Parallel passages: Matt. ix. 2—8 ; Luke v. 17—26.—*The cure of the
paralytic.*   I. THE POPULARITY OF OUR LORD.   After the cure of the leper, recorded at
the close of the preceding chapter, our Lord, to avoid tumult or undue excitement on the
part of the people, or an unseasonable precipitation of his plans, retired to and remained
some short time in unfrequented places ; but the crowds kept resorting (ἤρχοντο, imperfect) to him from all directions.   After an interval of some days (δι' ἡμερῶν) it was

reported that he was back in Capernaum—that, having previously arrived (εἰς), he was now in the house.   But what house?   Some say Peter's; others, as Euthymius, that it was simply a house (εἰς οἶκόν τινα); better perhaps understand it indefinitely of a house which he used as an inn or place of temporary abode, or to which as a sort of home he usually resorted.   The expression may thus, in a certain sense, be equivalent to the German *zu Hause.*

II. STRANGE METHOD OF APPROACH.   Again multitudes flocked to him; the humble dwelling was soon filled to overflowing, and still the crowd pressed on towards the door—even the parts next to it became so thronged that they could no longer contain or afford them room.   As was his wont, he was speaking, perhaps conversationally (ἐλάλει) *the word,* that is, of the kingdom or of his doctrine unto them.   Just then a novel and curious incident added a new feature to the scene.   On the outskirt of the crowd four men appeared, bearing a pallet between them, as St. Mark informs us—one at each corner probably; and on it lay a helpless invalid.   But so intently were all eyes fixed on, or all necks stretched out towards, the great Teacher that the crowd paid no attention to the invalid and his bearers, or at least showed no disposition to make way for them.   But, wherever there is a strong will, there is sure to be a way.   They were not to be deterred from their purpose, nor to be kept back from him whose presence they sought.   They mount the flat roof of the house, whether by steps outside or otherwise.   They remove a sufficient portion of the roof, or, as it is literally, they unroof the roof, digging out the tiling overlaid with earth, and so let down the couch on which the sick of the palsy lay, "into the midst before Jesus," as we learn from St. Luke.

III. ITS FEASIBILITY.   The objections of infidel writers, who have shown much ignorance and wasted much strength in attacking the plan resorted to in bringing the paralytic into the presence of the Saviour, are sufficiently and satisfactorily refuted by the following plain statements of facts in ' The Land and the Book ':—" Those (houses) of Capernaum, as is evident from the ruins, were, like those of modern villages in the same region, low, *very low*, with flat roofs, reached by a stairway from the yard or court. . . . Those who carried the paralytic . . . ascended to the roof, removed so much of it as was necessary, and let down their patient through the aperture.   Examine one of these houses, and you will see at once that the thing is natural, and easy to be accomplished.   The roof is only a few feet high, and by stooping down, and holding the corners of the couch—merely a thickly padded quilt, as at present in this region—they could let down the sick man without any apparatus of ropes or cords to assist them. . . . The whole affair was the extemporaneous device of plain peasants, accustomed to open their roofs, and let down grain, straw, and other articles, as they still do in this country. . . . The materials now employed are beams about three feet apart, across which short sticks are arranged close together, and covered with the thickly matted thorn bush called *bellan.*   Over this is spread a coat of stiff mortar, and then comes the marl or earth that makes the roof.   Now, it is easy to remove any part of this without injuring the rest. . . . They had merely to scrape back the earth from a portion of the roof over the *lewan,* take up the thorns and the short sticks, and let down the couch between the beams at the very feet of Jesus.   The end achieved, they could speedily restore the roof as it was before.   I have the impression, however," Dr. Thomson goes on to say, " that the covering at least of the *lewan* was not made of earth, but of materials more easily taken up.   It may have been merely of coarse matting, like the walls and roofs of Turkman huts; or it may have been made of boards, or even stone slabs (and such I have seen), that could be quickly removed.   All that is necessary, however, for us to know is, that the roof was flat, low, easily reached, and easily opened, so as to let down the couch of the sick man; and all these points are rendered intelligible by an acquaintance with modern houses in the villages of Palestine."   The frequency and force with which this portion of the miracle has been assailed must be our apology for quoting the above somewhat long extract.

IV. THE EVIDENCE OF THEIR FAITH.   The evangelist Matthew informs us that Jesus saw their faith, but makes no mention of the circumstances just referred to, which are so fully related by St. Luke, and with such particularity and minuteness of detail by St. Mark.   The singularity of the effort which they made to reach the Saviour afforded ocular demonstration of their belief in his power to help and heal.   The faith thus manifested was not restricted to the invalid, nor to those that bore him.   It was shared by both alike. They would not have engaged in the friendly office unless they had had faith in the probable result, nor would they have undertaken it against the will or wish of the invalid; neither would he have consented to allow himself to be conveyed, as he did, without believing in the power of him from whom he hoped relief.

V. NATURE OF FAITH, AS SEEN IN THIS TRANSACTION. Two things, the exact counterpart of each other, are the love of the Saviour and the faith of the sinner; they exactly and mutually correspond; the latter is the cheerful response to the former. The Saviour is waiting to be gracious; the sinner, in the exercise of faith, is ready to accept that grace. The Saviour offers the much-needed forgiveness; the sinner, by faith, stretches out his hand to receive the boon. The true *nature* of faith, moreover, is taught us here; it is not merely belief in a dogma, it is dependence on a person; it is not merely belief in a doctrine, it is reliance on a living Saviour; it is thus not only assent to a Divine testimony, it is trust in a Divine person. Accordingly, it is sometimes represented in Scripture as a coming to Christ; sometimes it is the receiving of Christ; again, it is a looking to Christ; also a fleeing to him for refuge. It is exhibited by other figures all of which imply not only implicit belief in what the Scriptures report of Christ, but actual trust in him as being all that Scripture represents him, and willing to do all that Scripture declares him to be able and willing to do.

VI. THE DISEASE AND ITS REMEDY. The sufferer was a paralytic, or rather, as St. Luke with his usual professional accuracy characterizes him more strictly, paralyzed or palsy-stricken ($\pi\alpha\rho\alpha\lambda\epsilon\lambda\upsilon\mu\acute{\epsilon}\nu\sigma$). This disease, which assumed a very aggravated form in the East, was attended with great suffering, besides leaving its victim altogether helpless. If leprosy was typical of pollution, and demoniac possession of passion, this form of disease was a type of utter prostration. The mode of cure adopted by our Lord in this case was somewhat unusual. Generally he administered relief to the body before restoring health to the soul; in the case of the paralytic the process is just the converse of this. Whether it was that sinful indulgence or evil excesses of some kind had weakened the nervous system of this man, and left him in this state of pain and prostration; or whether he felt with peculiar keenness the burden of sin pressing on his conscience; or whether some expression of penitence, though unrecorded, had escaped his lips; or whether it was only deep contrition of spirit of which our Lord alone was cognizant;—whichever of these it was, he first removed the soul disease. The expression, as recorded by St. Luke, is merely "man;" but both St. Matthew and St. Mark report the tenderer word of address, "son" or "child," more on the ground of affection than because of the youth of the sufferer; while St. Matthew alone adds the word of cheering—($\theta\acute{\alpha}\rho\sigma\epsilon\iota$), "Be of good cheer"—an expression so calculated to relieve the burthened spirit and ease the aching heart.

VII. GROUND OF ENCOURAGEMENT. But the ground of this encouragement is in the words, "Thy sins are forgiven thee;" not, observe, "be forgiven thee," for $\dot{\alpha}\phi\acute{\epsilon}\omega\nu\tau\alpha\iota$ is not for $\dot{\alpha}\phi\hat{\omega}\nu\tau\alpha\iota$, the aorist subjunctive in a precative sense, but for $\dot{\alpha}\phi\epsilon\hat{\iota}\nu\tau\alpha\iota$, perfect indicative in an affirmative sense—*have been forgiven thee.* The deed, in fact, was done, the blessing was bestowed, the sins of the man were, as the word implies, dismissed—sent away like the sins of Israel on the head of the scapegoat "into a land uninhabited," never again to return or be remembered.

VIII. HOSTILE ON-LOOKERS. In that surging crowd were some cold, unsympathetic hearts; there sat or stood there men who had come, if not as spies, yet through curiosity of a calculating, critical, sceptical kind. Not only had Galilee sent its contingent of such men from every village, but several had come all the way from the southern province, and even from its capital—an indirect evidence, by the way, of what is directly recorded by St. John of ministerial work carried on in these parts, and of attention roused by it. In the parallel portion of St. Luke where we read that "the power of the Lord was present to heal them ($\alpha\dot{\upsilon}\tau\sigma\acute{\upsilon}\varsigma$)"—that is, of course, those who sought or needed healing—there is a tolerably well-supported variant which reads the pronoun in the singular $\alpha\dot{\upsilon}\tau\acute{\sigma}\nu$ after $\aleph$, B, L, Ξ; the meaning in this case is, "the power of the Lord was in the direction of his healing," or more freely, "the power of the Lord [Jehovah] was present for his [work of] healing."

IX. A SECT AND A PROFESSION. St. Matthew and St. Mark both notice the presence of certain of the scribes. These were originally copyists, but afterwards textual critics, and subsequently expositors of the Law—in fact, the theologians of the nation. St.

Luke, however, gives us the additional information that "there were Pharisees and doctors of the Law sitting by." The latter had to do with the Law of the Old Testament, just as the scribes, but in the capacity of jurists. Hence the lawyers and scribes are commonly thought to have been identical. No doubt the same person might be both— a theologian and a jurist or ecclesiastical lawyer; while the Pharisees were the formalists—the religious sect that set such store by form and ceremony. The name is derived from *parash*, to separate, and thus signifies separatists. Now, these parties reasoned the matter out in their own minds (διαλογιζόμενοι), and were not long in coming to a conclusion that Jesus was guilty of a blasphemous assumption of an exclusively Divine attribute.

X. THE INTERPRETATION OF THEIR THOUGHTS. It was, "Why does this fellow thus speak blasphemies?" The "this" is contemptuous, and the "thus" implies "wickedly," or "as we have heard." If, however, we accept the text of the critical editors, Lachmann, Tischendorf, Tregelles, as well as that followed by the Revisers, it reads thus: "Why does this man thus speak? he blasphemeth." In the received text the plural denotes intensity, and is equivalent to "all this blasphemy;" or it refers to different expressions which they looked upon as blasphemous. It must be here observed that in Scripture language the word passes from the classical sense of speaking evil of or slandering a fellow-creature to the Hellenistic meaning of speaking impiously of God, or laying claim to a Divine attribute.

XI. DRIFT OF THEIR REASONING. "Who can forgive sins but one, that is, God, or God alone?" Such was the gist of their reasoning; the natural answer, of course, was that, unless in the exercise of delegated authority, or in a declarative sense, the thing transcended human power. God reserves to himself the power of pardon; Jesus, in his own name and by his own authority, claims to bestow forgiveness; therefore he blasphemeth, thus making himself equal to God. Both their premisses were correct and strictly logical; but the conclusion drawn from them was altogether erroneous—the very reverse of the fact. It should rather have been, not "he blasphemeth," arrogating to himself a Divine attribute, but, on the contrary, "he is truly Divine," really possessing Divine power.

XII. HELPS THEM TO THE RIGHT CONCLUSION. Our Lord knew at once and *well* (ἐπιγνοὺς) in his spirit their secret reasonings; for, though his soul was human, his spirit was Divine; while to the query latent in their minds, he accommodates the question which he addresses to them, as though he said, "Ye ask, What right have I to speak thus? I reply, What right have ye to reason thus? Which claim is easier to make—that of forgiving sins, or that of curing palsy?" But the nature of proof in each of the two cases is widely different: in the one case it is obvious, in the other it is obscure; in the one it is patent, in the other latent. But our Lord proceeds to put them in the position of coming to a correct conclusion. He gives them sufficient data to guide them: of what is cognizable by the senses he gives sensible proof; what is spiritual he leaves them to infer. "Up," he says to the paralytic, if we adopt the reading ἔγειρε, approved of by Lachmann and Tischendorf, and to be taken as a particle of excitement, like ἄγε or ἄνα, or *auf* in German, rather than with σεαυτὸν understood; or "Arise," if we read ἐγείρου, with Tregelles; or "Arise at once," if we adhere to ἔγειραι of the received text, though Fritzsche affirms that the middle voice signifies "to arouse or raise some one for one's self," while the passive is "to be aroused, raised up," and so "rise." Our Lord then adds, "Take up thy bed" (κράββατον, equivalent to the Latin *grabatum*, and equivalent to St. Luke's κλινίδιον, little bed, or mattress or pallet—every way appropriate, as well in sense as because the latter evangelist wrote for the Greeks, as St. Mark for the Romans, at least in the first instance), "and go into thy house."

XIII. STRANGE CONTRAST. Immediately the command was obeyed, and the man, who was carried on a bed by four into the Saviour's presence was now raised up (ἠγέρθη), and carried his bed on his back in presence of them all. As Bengel has finely expressed it, "Sweet saying! the bed hath borne the man: now the man bore the bed."

XIV. POWER OF FORGIVENESS. Thus our Lord, by this visible, palpable, and undeniable exercise of Divine power in relieving the body, proved that he possessed the power, and not only the power but the legitimate authority (ἐξουσίαν), to restore the soul from the disease of sin.

XV. THIS POWER POSSESSED ON EARTH. Of himself he speaks as the "Son of man."

This designation he applies no less than eighty times to himself; but it is only twice or thrice so applied by others, and in each instance of such application his exaltation is implied. He affirms that on earth the Son of man has power to forgive sins, how much more in heaven? In his humiliation, how much more in his exaltation? In his humiliation on earth, how much more in his glorification in heaven?

XVI. GOD GLORIFIED. No wonder the man himself, as St. Luke tells us, glorified God! And no wonder that the multitude (οἱ ὄχλοι according to St. Matthew, πάντας according to St. Mark) all likewise united with him in giving glory to God; while all, at the same time that they glorified God, expressed their own amazement in one way or other—some (as in St. Matthew) in reference to such power given unto men; others (according to St. Luke) because of the strange things—things beyond expectation (παράδοξα)—they had just seen; and some (as we read in St. Mark) because they had never seen it on this fashion.—J. J. G.

Vers. 13—22. Parallel passages: Matt. ix. 9—17; Luke v. 27—39.—*Call of Levi, Feasting, and Fasting.* I. THE CALL OF LEVI. 1. *Publicans, who were they?* The publicans proper, who paid a certain sum contracted for into the public treasury (*publicum*), were Roman knights, a wealthy class of citizens. These, again, had their agents who sublet, or acted as their own agents in subletting, the collection of the taxes, usually to natives of the country from which the taxes were to be collected. The correct name of these tax-collectors was *portitores*. 2. *Objects of public odium.* No class of men was so obnoxious to the Jews. They were looked on as unpatriotic, because they were in the service of a foreign government; they were regarded as irreligious, because they were engaged in an occupation suggestive of subjection to alien rule, and so derogatory to the high position of that people whom God had chosen for his peculiar possession and honoured with special privileges; in addition to all this, they were generally extortioners who by unjust exactions oppressed their countrymen. Thus regarded as traitors to their country and as apostates from the national faith, while at the same time they were exorbitant in their demands on their fellow-citizens, they were not without some reason subjects of odium and obloquy—men who had thus lost caste, both social and religious. 3. *St. Matthew originally a publican.* To this obnoxious class of men belonged the son of Alphæus, called Levi by St. Mark and St. Luke, but in the first Gospel named Matthew, which means "gift of Jehovah," nearly the same as Theodore, or Dositheus or Dorotheus, in Greek. That Levi was identical with the evangelist Matthew scarcely admits of any reasonable doubt. Busily employed in this obnoxious trade, he sat one day as usual at the custom-house or place of toll on the shore of the Lake of Gennesaret. 4. *His call.* Capernaum, now, as we have seen, probably *Tell Hum,* was then a busy mart of merchandise and a commercial centre, whence roads diverged, one to Damascus in the north-east; a second to Tyre in the north-west on the Mediterranean seaboard; a third ran southward to Jerusalem, the capital of the country; while a fourth led to Sepphoris or Dio-Cæsarea, the Roman capital of the province. It was exactly the kind of place where one would expect to find a custom-house for collecting the tolls of the lake, harbour dues, and duties on exports and imports, or other taxes. As our Lord went past, he fixed his eyes on (St. Luke, ἐθεάσατο, equivalent to observed) the tax-gatherer, who sat as usual at his post, not slothful in his business such as it was, and addressed to him the plain, direct invitation, "Follow me." Strange to say, that simple utterance had more than magic effect on this once unscrupulous, perhaps hardened custom-house officer. We are far from affirming that this was the first time that Levi had come in contact with Jesus. Gospel light had shined through all that once dark district; there can be little doubt that he had heard some of his discourses and listened to the gracious words that so often fell from his lips, or he had witnessed some of those works of wonder which he performed. Perhaps he had mingled in that crowd of the Capernaumites, which St. Mark reports in the preceding section of his Gospel, and had been a silent spectator when the poor paralytic had been so benefited and blessed in both body and soul. 5. *His love to Jesus.* Be this as it may, he, at all events, immediately accepted the invitation, and without demur or delay rose up at once—*left all,* as St. Luke tells us—and followed Jesus. Nor was this all; he shows his love to Jesus in another way—by an entertainment given in his honour. He made a great feast in his own house, as St. Luke further informs us. From this circumstance we naturally infer that his means were respectable ; that, if not very wealthy, he was at least in comfortable circumstances ; that by consequence the sacrifice he made for the Master was very considerable, and that his attachment was proportionately great. 6. *Further object of Levi's feast.* This complimentary feast to the Saviour was at the same time a farewell feast to his former associates, and a feast, moreover, by which he brought them into close contact with all that was spiritually good, in hope, no doubt, that they too might share the benefit and enjoy some measure of the same blessing which he himself had received. 7. *His humility.* Besides the self-sacrificing generosity of Levi who, no doubt, assumed the name of Matthew on his conversion, and his love to the Saviour as also to the souls of his brethren, he manifests a beautiful humility and an entire absence of ostentation. Acting on this principle, " Let another praise thee and not thine own lips," he makes no mention of the feast, more especially of the fact that it was himself, *in his own house* (so St. Luke), that gave at his own expense this great feast or reception (δοχὴν μεγάλην), as St. Luke terms it; while in the list of the names of the twelve apostles St. Mattthew alone, in his Gospel, speaks of himself as *the publican.* 8. *A seeming tautology.* In the fifteenth verse of this second chapter there appears to be a redundancy, for first we read that *many* publicans and sinners sat at meat, or reclined (συνανέκειντο), with Jesus and his disciples ; and then it is added, " for there were *many,* and they followed him." This seeming tautology is partially avoided by the reading οἳ καί of codex D, or by the rendering *qui* of the Italic and Vulgate ; while some understand the first part of the clause as a justification of the former statement about " many publicans and sinners," and a further affirmation of its being literally and exactly true, the expression " followed " being joined, as is done by some editors, to the next verse, that is, " And there followed him also scribes and Pharisees." These expedients are unnecessary, for if we take ἦσαν in the sense of παρῆσαν, which it some-times has, the words assign an appropriate reason, or account properly for the large number referred to ; thus, " Many publicans and sinners sat also together with Jesus and his disciples, for many were present [*i.e.* in Levi's house], and had followed Jesus [viz. thither]." 9. *Exception taken to such company.* " *How* is it that he eateth with publicans and sinners?" rather, " *Why* is it that he consorts with such?" the full expression being τί ἐστιν ὅτι, or τί γέγονεν ὅτι as in John xiv. 22. This complaint was addressed to the disciples, as though these separatists and sectaries still stood in salutary awe of the Master himself; but Jesus heard or *overheard* it, if the reading παρακούσας be admissible, and made reply by the aphorism, " They that are whole or strong," according to St. Matthew and St. Mark, but more precisely and perhaps professionally, according to St. Luke, " in sound health (ὑγιαίνοντες) " " have no need of the physician." He then applies the maxim to the particular case before him in the words, " I came not to call righteous [persons] but sinners to repentance." 10. *The objects of the Saviour's mission.* Theophylact understands by " the righteous " here those who think or speak of themselves as righteous, and imagines that our Lord terms them so by way of irony (κατ' εἰρωνείαν). This explanation of Theophylact, and others who hold with him, that by "righteous" in this passage are meant those who think themselves righteous, who are so in their own estimation, presents only one aspect of the matter. While there are many degrees in unrighteousness, self-righteousness is but one of those degrees, and, as such, is not a characteristic of the class, viz. the righteous which our Lord excludes from the objects of his mission. The meaning is rather that, as there is none by nature righteous—none righteous till made so by the Saviour himself, none really and perfectly righteous—the unrighteous (and all in their natural state are such, notwithstanding certain differences in degree) ; the sinful (and all belong to this category, for all have sinned though in vary-ing grades)—these are the very objects of his search and saving power. In a word, the morally unhealthy are those on whom the skill of the great Physician needs to be exer-cised, and who most require its exercise. Those that are such and feel themselves to be such are just the persons contemplated in his mission, and to whom on his errand of mercy he comes and calls. 11. *The Saviour's proper place.* Instead, then, of going out of his way, or his presence being found in the wrong place, our Lord, in consorting with publicans and sinners—sinners the vilest and the worst, as the objectors at least esteemed them—was just among those lost ones whom he came to seek and save, those sorely diseased ones whom he meant to restore to spiritual health and moral vigour. As in a hospital or lazar-house the physician's work is most abundant, so among such moral lazars the great Physician found the widest field of operation. We may not forget, however, that it is with much caution and certain restrictions that any mere man can so have intercourse with the degraded of his species; but Jesus, the God-man, ran no risk of moral taint, or of compromising character by associating freely and fully with such.

II. FASTING. 1. *Fasting.* In the former case just considered, the objectors shrank from directly assailing our Lord; they only took the disciples to task. Now, however, they have waxed bolder, and they attack the Master himself. The disciples of John imbibed the ascetic spirit of their master, who came neither eating nor drinking; the Pharisees, in addition to the one great annual fast appointed to be held on the Day of Atonement, and the four annual fasts observed after the Exile and enumerated by Zech. viii. 18 as "the fast of the fourth month, and the fast of the fifth, and the fast of the seventh, and the fast of the tenth" (held in the same month, and probably the same as that on the Day of Atonement), observed also the two weekly fasts which superstition or will-worship had superadded, namely, Thursday, the day on which, as was alleged, Moses reascended the mount, and Monday, on which he returned. Holding a common principle, the disciples of John and the Pharisees make common cause, and question our Lord about the laxity of his disciples in this regard—not fasting, while they themselves were so strict in such observances. 2. *The true nature of fasting.* This is made manifest by our Lord's reply. Nor do we find any new doctrine here; it is the restatement of an old truth or rather principle. As rending the garments was a token of grief, so fasting was at once an effect and evidence of grief. But if the reality were absent, the former was meaningless and the latter hypocritical; hence the prophet warned his countrymen to rend their hearts and not their garments, and turn truly unto the Lord. So here the disciples of Jesus had not as yet any cause of grief. Why, then, indulge in empty pretence, employing the sign when the thing signified was absent, and when, in fact, no occasion existed for either, and when from the time and the circumstances both were uncalled for? 3. *Allusion to an ancient custom.* John the Baptist had spoken (John ii. 29) of Jesus as the Church's Bridegroom; our Lord accepts the name John thus gave him, and adopts the figure, identifying himself with the bridegroom. In "the children of the bridechamber" we have an expression of Hebraistic impress, and equivalent to the more classical παράνυμφοι or νυμφαγωγοί, who were the friends of the bridegroom—the groomsmen—and who sat or went beside him to fetch the bride, and conduct her from her home, with merry music, gay procession, bright torches, and festive joy, to the house of her husband. Thus we read, in Judg. xiv. 10, 11, "So his father went down unto the woman: and Samson made there a feast; for so used the young men to do. And it came to pass, when they saw him, that they brought thirty companions to be with him." The allusion makes the meaning manifest. "Can," asks our Lord by a particle (μὴ) which usually implies a negative answer, "the children of the bridechamber fast, while the bridegroom is with them?" The answer was obvious. The presence of the bridegroom made it a time of feasting instead of fasting—of joy and not of grief; and so he returns answer to himself, "As long as they have the bridegroom with them, they cannot fast." Here the ancient Syriac Version omits this clause altogether, and substitutes for it the bare negative "no," as our Lord's reply to his own question. 4. *Our Lord's first intimation of his sufferings.* Yet he points to a time suited to fasting, and we can well imagine how a cloud shaded his benignant brow as he pronounced the darkly ominous words : "But," he says, "days shall come, yea, days when" (such is the import of the καὶ ὅταν of St. Luke) "the bridegroom shall be taken away from them; then will they fast in those days." The Revised Version renders perhaps more simply, though somewhat less significantly, we think, as follows:—"But the days will come; and *when* the bridegroom shall be taken away from them, then will they fast in those days." This is the first public intimation which our Lord gives of his future sufferings and death. He had indeed enigmatically hinted it to the Jewish rulers in the words, "Destroy this temple, and in three days I will raise it up" (John ii. 19); and he had dimly alluded to it in his private conversation with Nicodemus in the words, "Even so must the Son of man be lifted up" (John iii. 14). When that gloomy prospect should be realized, then it would be a time of real grief and consequently a suitable season for fasting. 5. *Maxim teaching the avoidance of things incongruous.* Our Lord takes occasion, from the notion of persons indulging sorrow when the occasion was festive and joyous, to enunciate a maxim of deep import and great significance, as also of far-reaching tendency and manifold applications. The new patch on an old garment is a sample of incongruity. The words in St. Mark read thus : " No man also seweth a piece of unfulled cloth on an old garment : else the new patch [or new piece that filled it up] taketh away *something* from the old, and the rent becomes worse ; " or the second clause may be rendered as follows : " Else the patch [or piece that filled up] takes away the new from the old." Also in the Gospel of St. Luke the words as commonly read are, " No man putteth a piece of new garment upon an old ; if otherwise, then both the new maketh a rent, and the piece that was *taken* out of the new agreeth not with the old ; " or if the reading (σχίσας) of א, A, B, D, L, Ξ, and the Syriac be adopted, the rendering may be, " No man having rent a piece from a new garment putteth it upon an old ; if otherwise, he will both rend the new garment [*i.e.* by taking the ἐπίβλημα, or patch, out of it] and the piece from the new garment will not agree with the old." The word " unfulled, " used by St. Mark, makes the meaning plainer, and implies that the unfulled patch, from its nature being stronger or more liable to shrink, works the mischief.   6. *Ill effects of such incongruity.*   The following ill effects are produced :—(1) The new garment is marred and rendered incomplete ; (2) the old is not made better, but worse, the rent becoming larger ; (3) the entire want of suitability or consistency ; in other words, obvious unseemliness, as well as unsuitability.   The Latins called a man " inept " (*ineptus*) who neglected what time, place, or circumstances demanded.   Even a thing which may be proper enough in itself, if done out of season, is spoiled.   On the contrary, everything that God makes is beautiful in its season ; and everything that man does should aim at and imitate the same.   Thus is it also when the proper requirements of place, and those of circumstances, are neglected.   7. *Variety of applications.*   This parable or proverbial representation is capable of a great variety of applications, all showing the necessity of duly attending to the fitness of things and the exceedingly inconvenient consequences sure to result from the opposite course.   (1) The old dispensation and the new may not be mixed up together.   Though they were one in essence, and though one vital principle pervaded them, yet the externals differed—the outward forms were distinct.   (2) The gospel was never meant to be used as a patch on the old threadbare garment of the Law.   The old economy was not to be repaired in this way ; it had to be renovated.   The legal dispensation was not to be patched up with gospel grace.   Christianity was never intended to be a patched-up Judaism ; the old had served its day and died, the new came in to take its place.   Nor is the new Christian life of individuals a purple patch here and there upon the old.   (3) More directly still to the present instance, the young life of new discipleship was not to be forced into conjunction and so crushed into conformity with Pharisaic asceticism, nor was their moral freedom to be hampered by such unnatural and unwelcome restrictions.   8. *A close connection.*   Again, as the incompatibility of fasting with a time of feasting, of sorrow with a season of gladness, is exhibited by the comparison of a wedding feast, the wedding feast naturally suggested the wedding garment, and again, by a similar association of ideas, the wine in use at a wedding.   Thus, too, the garment as an outer garb refers to externals, and the wine to something internal ; so the principles of true freedom infused by the gospel must burst through the narrowness of mere ceremonial swathing-bands.—J. J. G.

Vers. 23—28.   Parallel passages : Matt. xii. 1—8 ; Luke vi. 1—5.—*Sabbath observance.*   I. WORSHIP, NOT AMUSEMENT, SUITS THE SABBATH.   The common heading of this section in the Gospels is, "The disciples pluck the ears of corn on the sabbath day." On this occasion our Lord and his disciples were out walking on the sabbath ; but they were not walking for pleasure or even for health.   They were on their way to the house of God, as we learn from the parallel passage in St. Matthew, where we read that " when he was departed thence, he went into their synagogue."   The two main ideas associated with the sabbath are rest and worship ; the former held the first place in the old dispensation, the latter the second.   In the gospel dispensation their position seems reversed ; for, while never sundered and never to be separated, worship comes more to the front, holding a primary, while rest holds a secondary place.   On the sabbath our Lord and his disciples attended the usual place of Jewish worship ; on the sabbath the apostles, after our Lord's death and resurrection, met for the service of

God; on the sabbath, thenceforth the first day of the week, the Holy Spirit descended in Pentecostal power and plenty, while by means of St. Peter's sermon three thousand were converted that same day; on the sabbath the primitive Christians, taught by apostles and following apostolic example, met together to break bread, to read God's holy Word, or hear it preached, as also for prayer and praise, and to contribute for the necessities of the saints. Refreshment for the spirit and rest for the body went hand in hand; but worldly amusement found no place on the sabbath, and worldly pleasure formed no part of its service.

II. WORKS OF NECESSITY ALLOWABLE ON THE SABBATH. Stretches of corn-land abound in the fertile plain of Gennesaret. A pathway frequently ran through these unfenced fields, and on these pathways seed often fell and grain grew, as was the case with the wayside in the parable of the sower. Our Lord was passing by one of these, through the fields of corn (literally, *sown places*), alongside the grain. The disciples were "plucking and eating," as St. Matthew tells us, or, as St. Mark more graphically describes it, they "made a way" for themselves by plucking the stalks that had sprung up on what had previously been a path, and being an hungred, that is, in a state of hunger—for St. Matthew adds this important fact of their being hungry (ἐπείνασαν)— "they began to rub the ears of corn in their hand," as St. Luke informs us, and thus sought to appease the cravings of appetite. This was, of course, a work of necessity, and of urgent necessity, on the part of these hungry men. They had, however, only begun this operation (ἤρξαντο), when the Pharisees rudely checked them, administering the sharp rebuke recorded in this passage.

III. AN EXEGETICAL CONSIDERATION. The common English Version requires to make two assumptions in behoof of its rendering: 1. That ὁδὸν ποιεῖν is the same as ὁδὸν ποιεῖσθαι, though the former in reality is to make a path "*viam sternere* vel *munire—einen Weg machen*," as Fritzsche expresses it; while the latter is to go on one's way *iter facere* or *progredi*, which is the rendering of the Vulgate. 2. That the chief force here, as occasionally elsewhere, lies in the participle. In this way is reached (1) the usual free rendering, "His disciples began as they went to pluck the ears of corn;" but (2) the more correct translation is certainly that which is insisted on by the most accurate scholars, such as Fritzsche and Meyer, namely, "His disciples began to make a path [or way] plucking the ears." Though the Revised Version follows the ordinary rendering, it gives, in a note on this passage, an approximation to what we consider the right rendering, viz. "began to make their way plucking."

IV. THE RIGOROUS SABBATARIANISM OF THE PHARISEES. The question of the Pharisees is explained, or indeed translated, by some (1) as signifying, "Lo, what are they doing on the sabbath? That which is not lawful;" while by others it is rendered (2), "Lo, why are they doing on the sabbath what is not lawful?" In neither case can it properly mean that the thing was unlawful in itself, and still more unlawful because of its being done on the sabbath day. The superstitious sabbatarianism of the Pharisees suggests the real gist of the question. The action in itself was perfectly allowable, according to the Law as it stands written in Deut. xxiii. 25, "When thou comest into the standing corn of thy neighbour, then thou mayest pluck the ears with thine hand." The Pharisees, guided by oral tradition, interpreted the law of the sabbath so rigorously as to identify the plucking of the ears with reaping, and the rubbing of them in their hands with thrashing, so that the Law, as they explained it, was violated by both operations.

V. SABBATH DESECRATION FALSELY LAID TO THE CHARGE OF THE DISCIPLES. Our Lord undertakes the vindication of his disciples; he justifies their conduct by reminding their accusers of an incident in the life of David, when ceremonial observance yielded to moral necessity, and positive precept to the requirements of mercy. The occasion was that on which David found himself at Nob, a sacerdotal town to the north-east and within sight of Jerusalem, in a state of destitution—"he had need" (χρείαν ἔσχε), such is the general statement; and ready to perish with hunger—"was an hungred" (ἐπείνασεν), this is the particular specification. The "bread of the face" or presence, according to the Hebrew, or "the loaves of proposition," as rendered by the Vulgate, were twelve loaves— one for each tribe, placed in the presence of Jehovah as a symbol of the people's dependence on their heavenly Father for daily bread. None was permitted the use of these loaves but the priests; they were their perquisite. This rigid rule was relaxed in favour of David; and not only of David, whose eminence might be thought such as to entitle him to greater consideration, and sufficient to make his case exceptional, but in favour of those who were with him.   Our Lord adduces this instance of violating the letter of the Law, asking the Pharisees, according to a formula of their own, but with scornful irony, or rather in a tone of severe reproof, "Did ye never read?" or, as it is expressed in St. Luke, "Did ye not even read this?"—ye who are such sticklers for the Law and adepts in Scripture knowledge.

VI. SOLUTION OF A DIFFICULTY.   The name of Abiathar instead of Ahimelech has given trouble.   Of the many attempted solutions, such as in the *presence* of Abiathar, afterwards high priest, for it was Ahimelech, father of Abiathar, who really gave the shewbread to David and his men; or that he had *both names;* or that the deed was done by Ahimelech in the pontificate of Abiathar his son, as Theophylact explains it; or in the *section* or paragraph of Abiathar the high priest; or that the insertion of the article distinguishes the lifetime from the pontificate of Abiathar, according to Middleton;—of all these it must be said that they either involve error or have the appearance of mere shifts or evasions.   Of them all, Middleton's is perhaps best known, and has been adopted by not a few critical scholars.   Thus, in the first edition of Scrivener's 'Plain Introduction to the Criticism of the New Testament,' we find the following statement:—"In Mark ii. 26, ἐπὶ 'Αβ. ἀρχ., 'in the time that Abiathar was high priest,' would be historically incorrect; while ἐπὶ 'Αβ. τοῦ ἀρχ., 'in the days of Abiathar the high priest,' is suitable enough."   But this insertion of the article is a matter of dispute, for though it is found in four respectable uncials, including A and C, as also in the following cursives:—1, 33, and 69, of which 33 is known as the "Queen of the cursives;" yet it is absent in this place from ℵ, B, L, and many other uncials, and is rejected by most of the critical editors.   We cannot, therefore, build an argument on it.   We are inclined to Fritzsche's opinion, that the real removal of the difficulty appears to be effected by the position of the words ἐπὶ 'Αβ. ἀρχ., which implies that the transaction took place in the time of Abiathar, afterwards high priest; while ἐπὶ ἀρχ. 'Αβ. would restrict the occurrence to the actual time of his priesthood, though it is admitted that with a participle, as ἄρχοντος or βασιλεύοντος, for example, the position does not thus alter the sense. For the mention of Abiathar instead of Ahimelech several reasons might be assigned. He was more celebrated than his father, as also better known to the readers of Old Testament Scripture; besides, the mention of him as being present, and a consenting party to the transaction, would be calculated to obviate the possible retort which the Pharisees might otherwise make, namely, that Ahimelech paid the penalty of his profanation by his being slain.

VII. THE CHARGE OF SABBATH-BREAKING BY THE DISCIPLES FURTHER REFUTED. Additional arguments are found in the Gospel of St. Matthew to disprove the charge of sabbath profanation which these narrow, bigoted Pharisees urged against the disciples. The rather laborious service of the priests on the sabbath, in sacrificing, removing the shewbread, and other duties, was an apparent profanation of the sabbath; but in their case the Law was relaxed, or rather the principle of God's love to man, which lay at the foundation of the Law, and was the animating spirit of the Law, took precedence of the letter.   He taxes them with culpable and disgraceful, if not wilful, ignorance of such a plain Scripture as "I will have mercy and not sacrifice."   If, then, the necessity of David and his men prevailed over the letter of the Law; if the sabbath services of the priests made sabbath labour to some extent a duty; and if the claim of mercy be prior to and higher than that of sacrifice, our Lord claims exemption for his hungry disciples from the unbending rigour of the Law, or rather from the harsh, superstitious misinterpretation of it by those cold, heartless, cavilling, censorious Pharisees.

VIII. THE SABBATH DESIGNED TO BE SUBSERVIENT TO MAN.   Our Lord proceeds to take higher ground.   The sabbath was made for the sake of man, Gentile as well as Jew; it originated for his benefit; it is only the means to an end, and man's interests are that end; it owes its existence to man, and has the reason of its existence in man. It is a memorial of his creation, a remembrancer of his redemption, and a foretaste as well as pledge of his future and everlasting rest.   It is most valuable in its essential nature and right use; but if the circumstantial come into collision with the essential, or the ceremonial conflict with the moral, in either case the former, in the very nature of things, is bound to give place.

IX. THE SON OF MAN'S LORDSHIP WITH RESPECT TO THE SABBATH. The Son of man here mentioned is, in spite of all rationalistic quibbling, the Saviour, and he is Lord of the sabbath. In St. Mark and St. Luke καὶ stands before "sabbath;" it is likewise inserted in St. Matthew by some, but excluded by others. It may mean *even* or *also*. In the first of these two significations it implies that much as they valued the ordinance of the sabbath above all the other commandments of the Decalogue, and superstitious as was the veneration with which they regarded it, the Son of man was Lord even of the sabbath; and so he could make it elastic as the exigencies of any particular case might require; he could modify it according to any special emergency; he could determine the mode of its observance between the two limits of man's benefit on the one hand, and the Law's behest on the other. But if we take the meaning of the copulative to be *also*, then it signifies that, amid and in addition to his other lordships, the Son of man possesses this also—that he is Lord of the sabbath day. He is Lord of angels, for they worship him; he is the Lord from heaven, and all its hosts do acknowledge him; he is Lord of earth, for by him it was made, and through him it is upheld; he is the Lord of all creation, for he is the firstborn of every creature, that in all things he should have the pre-eminence; "he is Lord *also* of the sabbath." He vindicates his law from the lax observance of the worldling or pleasure-seeker on the one hand, and from the narrowness of Pharisaic superstition on the other. He manifests its true nature for the rest and refreshment—the physical, mental, moral, and spiritual blessing of mankind.

X. THE PERPETUAL OBLIGATION OF THE SABBATH. In proof of its perpetual obligation we may refer to its Divine appointment, so long prior to the division of Adam's family into the two great sections of Jew and Gentile—before the call of Abram and the existence of the Jewish nation; before the promulgation of the Law from Sinai and the establishment of the Jewish polity. We may trace the proof of its observance in the division of time into weeks among almost all nations and from the remotest antiquity; in certain incidental notices afforded by the history of the period between creation and the publishing of the Law; in the miraculous supply of a double portion of manna, which, even before the latter event, Israel received on the sixth day as a provision for the seventh; in the note of memory prefixed, implying at once its appointment and observance before the giving of the Law, and intimating not a new enactment merely national in its range, but the republication to a particular nation of an old one, that from the beginning had been binding on all. The latitude of its extent to the Gentile stranger, as well as to the Jew, may be argued from the terms of the command itself, "Nor the stranger that is within thy gates." Some importance, too, may be attached to its central position in the Decalogue, linking together the duties we owe our Father in heaven, and those which we owe our brother man on earth; while it blends, moreover, the joint memorials of creation and Calvary, and combines at the same time the creature's comfort and the Creator's glory in the words, "To you an holy day, a sabbath of rest to the Lord." We must have in recollection, besides, that it was written, as well as the other precepts of the moral law, by the finger of God on the stone tablet, in token, it would seem, of its durability. Further, we may observe the tense of the verb used in the last verse of this chapter, viz. "the Son of man *is* "—that is, continues—"Lord of the sabbath;" consequently Lord, not of an obsolete or decaying ordinance, but of a present, ever-abiding institution. Thus, indeed, it appears that "the sabbath was made for man," for the species, coeval and coextensive with the race—"for man," as has been well observed, "from the beginning; for man till the end; for man generally, at all times, in all countries, and under all circumstances." And when, we may ask, or where, or how was this original sabbath law either repealed or relaxed?— J. J. G.

EXPOSITION.

CHAPTER III.

This chapter begins with the record of another case of healing on the sabbath day; and it closes with the notice of a combi-nation of the Pharisees with the Herodians to bring about the destruction of the Saviour. We may observe that he again chose the sabbath for a new miracle, that he might again and again confute the error of the scribes and Pharisees with regard to the observance of the sabbath.

Ver. 1.—**He entered again into the synagogue.** St. Matthew (xii. 9) says, "their synagogue" (εἰς τὴν συναγωγὴν αὐτῶν). This would probably be on the next sabbath after that named at the close of the last chapter. **And there was a man there which had a withered hand** (ἐξηραμμένην ἔχων τὴν χεῖρα) ; literally, *which had his hand withered,* or *dried up.* **And they watched him** (παρετήρουν αὐτὸν) ; *kept watching him.* There were probably scribes sent for this purpose from Jerusalem. St. Jerome informs us that, in an apocryphal Gospel in use amongst the Nazarenes and Ebionites, the man whose hand was withered is described as a mason, and is said to have asked for help in the following terms :—" I was a mason, seeking my living by manual labour. I beseech thee, Jesus, to restore to me the use of my hand, that I may not be compelled to beg my bread." This is so far consistent with St. Mark's description (ἐξηραμμένην ἔχων τὴν χεῖρα) as to show that the malady was the result of disease or accident, and not congenital. St. Luke (vi. 6) informs us that it was the right hand. The disease probably extended through the whole arm according to the wider meaning of the Greek word χεὶρ. It seems to have been a kind of atrophy, causing a gradual drying up of the limb ; which in such a condition was beyond the reach of any mere human skill.

Ver. 2.—The scribes had already the evidence that our Lord had permitted his disciples to rub the ears of corn on the sabbath day. But this was the act of the disciples, not his. What he was now preparing to do was an act of miraculous power. And here the case was stronger, because work, which was prohibited under pain of death by the Law (Exod. xxxi. 14), was understood to include every act not absolutely necessary.

Vers. 3, 4.—**Stand forth.** The words in the original are Ἔγειραι εἰς τὸ μέσον, *Rise up into the midst.* In St. Matthew's account (xii. 10), the scribes and Pharisees here ask our Lord, "Is it lawful to heal on the sabbath day?" The two accounts are easily reconciled if we first suppose the scribes and Pharisees to ask this question of our Lord, and then our Lord to answer them by putting their own question to them in another form. **Is it lawful on the sabbath day to do good, or to do harm? to save a life, or to kill?** Our Lord's meaning appears to be this: "If any one, having it in his power, omits to do an act of mercy on the sabbath day for one grievously afflicted, as this man is, if he is able to cure him, as I Christ am able, he does him a wrong; for he denies

him that help which he owes him by the law of charity." Our Lord thus plainly signifies that not to do an act of kindness to a sick man on the sabbath day when you are able to do it, is really to do him a wrong. But it is never lawful to do a wrong; and therefore it is always lawful to do good, not excepting even the sabbath day, for that is dedicated to God and to good works. Whence it is a greater sin to do a wrong on the sabbath than on other days; for thus the sanctity of the sabbath is violated, just as it is all the more honoured and sanctified by doing good. In our Lord's judgment, then, to neglect to save, when you have it in your power to do so, is to destroy. **They held their peace.** They could not answer him. They are obstinate indeed in their infidelity, who, when they can say nothing against the truth, refuse to say anything for it.

Ver. 5.—**When he had looked round about on them with anger, being grieved** (συλλυπούμενος)—the word has a touch of "condolence" in it—**at the hardening of their heart.** All this is very characteristic of St. Mark, who is careful to notice the visible expression of our Lord's feelings in his looks. The account is evidently from an eye-witness, or from one who had it from an eye-witness. *He looked round about on them with anger.* He was indignant at their blindness of heart, and their unbelief, which led them to attack the miracles of mercy wrought by him on the sabbath day as though they were a violation of the law of the sabbath. We see here how plainly there were in Christ the passions and affections common to the human nature, only restrained and subordinated to reason. Here is the difference between the anger of fallen man and the anger of the sinless One. With fallen man, anger is the desire of retaliating, of punishing those by whom you consider yourself unjustly treated. Hence, in other men, anger springs from self-love; in Christ it sprang from the love of God. He loved God above all things; hence he was distressed and irritated on account of the wrongs done to God by sins and sinners. So that his anger was a righteous zeal for the honour of God; and hence it was mingled with grief, because, in their blindness and obstinacy, they would not acknowledge him to be the Messiah, but misrepresented his kindnesses wrought on the sick on the sabbath day, and found fault with them as evil. Thus our Lord, by showing grief and sorrow, makes it plain that his anger did not spring from the desire of revenge. He was indeed angry at the sin, while he grieved over and with the sinners, as those whom he loved, and for whose sake he came into the world that he might redeem and save them. **Stretch forth thy hand. And he stretched it forth: and his hand was restored.** The words "whole as the other" (ὑγιὴς ὡς ἡ ἄλλη) are not found in the best uncials. They were probably inserted from St. Matthew. In this instance our Lord performed no outward act. " He spake, and it was done." The Divine power wrought the miracle concurrently with the act of faith on the part of the man in obeying the command.

Ver. 6.—The Pharisees and the Herodians combine together against the Lord. This was a terrible crisis in his history, or rather in the history of those unbelieving men. They are now in this dilemma: they must either accept his teaching, or they must take steps against him as a sabbath-breaker. But what had he done? The miracle had been wrought by a word only. It would have been difficult, therefore, to have obtained a judgment against him. Therefore they secured some fresh allies. They had already gained to their side some of the disciples of John the Baptist (ch. ii. 18), now they associate with themselves the Herodians. This is the first mention that we find made of the Herodians. They were the natural opponents of the Pharisees; but here they seem to have found some common ground of agreement, though it is not very easy to say what it was, in combining against our Lord. But it is no uncommon thing to find coalitions of men, strangely opposed to one another on most points, but united to effect some particular object; and it is easy to see how the purity and spirituality of our Lord and of his doctrine would be opposed, on the one hand, to the ceremonial formality of the Pharisee, and on the other to the worldly and secular spirit of the Herodian.

Vers. 7, 8.—**Jesus with his disciples withdrew to the sea.** This shows that the miracle just recorded took place in the interior of Galilee, and not at Capernaum, which was close by the sea. The chief city in Galilee at that time was Sepphoris, which Herod Antipas had made his capital. There the Herodians would of course be numerous, and so too would the Pharisees; since that city was one of the five places where the five Sanhedrims met (see Reland, 'Palestine,' p. 100, referred to in the 'Speaker's Commentary,' *in loc.*). The remainder of these two verses should be read and pointed thus: **And a great multitude from Galilee followed: and from Judæa, and from Jerusalem, and from Idumæa, and beyond Jordan, and about Tyre and Sidon, a great multitude, hearing what great things he did, come unto him.** The meaning of the evangelist is this, that, in addition to the great multitude that followed him from the parts of Galilee which he had just been

visiting, there were vast numbers from other parts who had now heard of his fame, and flocked to him from every quarter. This description sets before us in a strikingly graphic manner the mixed character of the multitude who gathered around our Lord to listen to his teaching, and to be healed by him—as many, at least, as had need of healing.

Ver. 9.—**And he spake to his disciples, that a small ship** (πλοιάριον)—literally, *a little boat* — **should wait on him** (προσκαρτερῇ αὐτῷ)—literally, *should be in close attendance upon him*—**because of the multitude, lest they should throng him.** This shows in a very graphic manner how assiduously and closely the crowd pressed upon him, so that he was obliged to have a little boat always in readiness, in which he might take refuge when the pressure became too great, and so address them with greater freedom from the boat. St. Luke (v. 3) says, "He sat down, and taught the people out of the ship," making the boat, so to speak, his pulpit.

Ver. 10.—**As many as had plagues**—the Greek word is μάστιγας; literally, *scourges,* painful disorders—**pressed upon him** (ὥστε ἐπιπίπτειν αὐτῷ); literally, *fell upon him, clung to him,* hoping that the very contact with him might heal them. This expression, "scourges," reminds us that diseases are a punishment on account of our sins.

Ver. 11.—**And the unclean spirits, whensoever they beheld him, fell down before him, and cried, saying.** It is worthy of notice that the afflicted people fell upon him (ἐπίπιπτειν αὐτῷ); but the unclean spirits fell down before him (προσέπιπτεν αὐτῷ), and this not out of love or devotion, but out of abject fear, dreading lest he should drive them out of the " possessed," and send them before their time to their destined torment. It is just possible that this homage paid to our Lord may have been an act of cunning—a ruse, as it were, to lead the people to suppose that our Lord was in league with evil spirits. **Thou art the Son of God.** Did, then, the unclean spirits really know that Jesus was the Son of God? A voice from heaven at his baptism had proclaimed him to be the Son of God, and that voice must have vibrated through the spiritual world. Then, further, they must have known him to be the Son of God by the numerous and mighty miracles which he wrought, and which they must have seen to be real miracles, such as could only have been wrought by the supernatural power of God, and which were wrought by Christ for this very purpose, that they might prove him to be the promised Messiah, the only begotten Son of God. It may, however, be observed that they did not know this so clearly, but that, considering, on the other hand, the greatness of the mystery, they hesitated. It is probable that they were ignorant of the end and fruit of this great mystery, namely, that mankind were to be redeemed by the Incarnation, the Cross, and the Death of Christ; and so their own kingdom was to be overthrown, and the kingdom of God established. Blinded by their hatred of Jesus, whom they perceived to be a most holy Being, drawing multitudes to himself, they stirred up the passions of evil men against him, little dreaming that in promoting his destruction they were overthrowing their own kingdom.

Ver. 12.—(See notes on ch. i. 44.)

Ver. 13.—**Into a mountain**; literally, *into the mountain* (εἰς τὸ ὄρος). Similarly, St. Luke (vi. 12) says, " He went out into the mountain to pray." The use of the definite article might either point to some well-known eminence, or to the high table-land as distinguished from the plain, and in which there would be many recesses, which would explain the use of the preposition εἰς. Tradition indicates Mount Hatten as the place, about five miles to the west of the Sea of Galilee. The summit rises above a level space, where large numbers might stand within hearing. It is supposed, with good reason, that it was from thence that the sermon on the mount was delivered. It was at daybreak, as we learn from St. Luke (vi. 13), after this night of prayer, that **he called unto him whom he himself would** (οὓς ἤθελεν αὐτός): **and they went unto** him (καὶ ἀπῆλθον πρὸς); literally, *they went away to him*, the word implying that they forsook their former pursuits. His own will was the motive power: he called " whom he himself would;" but their will consented. "When thou saidst, Seek ye my face; my heart said unto thee, Thy face, Lord, will I seek."

Vers. 14, 15.—Out of those who thus came to him, **he ordained twelve** (ἐποίησε); literally, *he made or appointed twelve*. They were not solemnly ordained or consecrated to their office until after his resurrection. Their actual consecration (of all of them at least but one, namely, Judas Iscariot) took place when he breathed on them and said, " Receive ye the Holy Ghost " (John xx. 22). But from this time they were his apostles-" designate." They were henceforth to be with him as his attendants and disciples. They were to go forth and preach under his direction, and by his power they were to cast out devils. Several manuscripts add here that they were " to heal sicknesses," but the words are omitted in some of the oldest authorities. The authority over unclean spirits is more formally conveyed

later on (see ch. vi. 7), so that here St. Mark speaks by anticipation. But this shows how much importance was attached to this part of their mission ; for it recognizes the spiritual world, and the special purpose of the manifestation of the Son of God, namely, that he might "destroy the works of the devil." *He appointed twelve*. The number twelve symbolizes perfection and universality. The number three indicates what is Divine; and the number four, created things. Three multiplied by four gives twelve, the number of those who were to go forth as apostles into the four quarters of the world—called to the faith of the holy Trinity.

Vers. 16, 17.—**And Simon he surnamed Peter.** Our Lord had previously declared that Simon should be so called. But St. Mark avoids as much as possible the recognition of any special honour belonging to St. Peter; so he here simply mentions the fact of this surname having been given to him, a fact which was necessary in order that he might be identified. All the early Christian writers held that Peter was virtually the author of this Gospel. Simon, or Simeon, is from a Hebrew word, meaning " to hear." **James the son of Zebedee,** so called to distinguish him from the other James; **and John his brother.** In St. Matthew's list, Andrew is mentioned next after Peter, as his brother, and the first called. But here St. Mark mentions James and John first after Peter; these three, Peter and James and John, being the three leading apostles. Of James and John, James is mentioned first, as the eldest of the two brothers. **And them he surnamed Boanerges, which is, Sons of thunder.** " Boanerges " is the Aramaic pronunciation of the Hebrew *B'ne-ragesh*; *B'ne*, sons, and *ragesh*, thunder. The word was not intended as a term of reproach; although it fitly expressed that natural impetuosity and vehemence of character, which showed itself in their desire to bring down fire from heaven upon the Samaritan village, and in their ambitious request that they might have the highest places of honour in his coming kingdom. But their natural dispositions, under the Holy Spirit's influence, were gradually transformed so as to serve the cause of Christ, and their fiery zeal was transmuted into the steady flame of Christian earnestness and love, so as to become an element of great power in their new life as Christians. Christ called these men " Sons of thunder " because he would make their natural dispositions, when restrained and elevated by his grace, the great instruments of spreading his Gospel. He destined them for high service in his kingdom. By their holy lives they were to be as lightning, and by their preaching they were to be as thunder to rouse unbelievers, and to bring them to repentance and a holy life. It was no doubt on account of this zeal that James fell so early a victim to the wrath of Herod. A different lot was that which fell to St. John. Spared to a ripe old age, he influenced the early Church by his writings and his teaching. His Gospel begins as with the voice of thunder, "In the beginning was the Word, and the Word was with God, and the Word was God." Beza and others, followed by Dr. Morison, have thought that this distinctive name was given by our Lord to the two brothers on account of some deep-toned peculiarity of voice, which was of much service to them in impressing the message of the Gospel of the kingdom upon their hearers.

Vers. 18, 19.—**Andrew** is next mentioned after these eminent apostles, as the first called. The word is from the Greek, and means "manly." **Bartholomew**, that is, Bar-tolmai, the son of Tolmay. This is a patronymic, and not a proper name. It has been with good reason supposed that he is identical with Nathanael, of whom we first read in John i. 46, as having been found by Philip and brought to Christ. In the three synoptic Gospels we find Philip and Bartholomew enumerated together in the lists of the apostles; and certainly the mode in which Nathanael is mentioned in John xxi. 2 would seem to show that he was an apostle. His birthplace, too, Cana of Galilee, would point to the same conclusion. If this be so, then the name Nathanael, the "gift of God," would bear the same relation to Bartholomew that Simon does to Bar-jona. **Matthew.** In St Matthew's own list of the apostles (x. 3) the epithet "the publican" is added to his name, and he places himself after Thomas. This marks the humility of the apostle, that he does not scruple to place on record what he was before he was called. The word Matthew, a contraction of Mattathias, means the "gift of Jehovah," according to Gesenius, which in Greek would be "Theodore." **Thomas.** Eusebius says that his real name was Judas. It is possible that Thomas may have been a surname. The word is Hebrew meaning a twin, and it is so rendered in Greek in John xi. 16. **James the son of Alphæus,** or Clopas (not Cleophas): called "the Less," either because he was junior in age, or rather in his call, to James the Great, the brother of John. This James, the son of Alphæus, is called the brother of our Lord. St. Jerome says that his father Alphæus, or Clopas, married Mary, a sister of the blessed Virgin Mary, which would make him the cousin of our Lord. This view is confirmed by Bishop Pearson (Art. iii. on the Creed). He was the writer of the Epistle

which bears his name, and he became Bishop of Jerusalem. **Thaddæus,** called also Lebbæus and Judas; whence St. Jerome describes him as "trionimus," *i.e.* having three names. Judas would be his proper name. Lebbæus and Thaddæus have a kind of etymological affinity, the root of Lebbæus being "heart," and of Thaddæus, "breast." These names are probably recorded to distinguish him from Judas the traitor. **Simon the Canaanite.** The word in the Greek, according to the best authorities, is, both here and in St. Matthew (x. 4), Κανavaîos, from a Chaldean or Syriac word, *Kanean,* or *Kânenieh.* The Greek equivalent is Ζηλωτής, which we find preserved in St. Luke (vi. 15). It is possible, however, that Simon may have been born in Cana of Galilee. St. Jerome says that he was called a Cananæan or Zealot, by a double reference to the place of his birth and to his zeal. **Judas Iscariot.** *Iscariot.* The most probable derivation is from the Hebrew *Ish-Kerioth,* "a man of Kerioth," a city of the tribe of Judah. St. John (vi. 7) describes him as the son of Simon. If it be asked why our Lord should have chosen Judas Iscariot, the answer is that he chose him, although he knew that he would betray him, because it was his will that he should be betrayed by one that had been "his own familiar friend," and that had "eaten bread with him." Bengel says well here that "there is an election of grace from which men may fall." How far our Lord knew from the first the results of his choice of Judas belongs to the profound, unfathomable mystery of the union of the Godhead and the manhood in his sacred Person. We may notice generally, with regard to this choice by our Lord of his apostles, the germ of the principle of sending them forth by two and two. Here are Peter and Andrew, James and John, Philip and Bartholomew, and so on. Then, again, our Lord chose three pairs of brothers, Peter and Andrew, James and John, James the Less and Jude, that he might teach us how powerful an influence is brotherly love. We may also observe that Christ, in selecting his apostles, chose some of his kinsmen according to the flesh. When he took upon him our flesh, he recognized those who were near to him by nature, and he would unite them yet more closely by grace to his Divine nature. Three of the apostles took the lead, namely, Peter and James and John, who were admitted to be witnesses of his transfiguration, of one of his greatest miracles, and his passion.

Vers. 20, 21.—The last clause of ver. 19, **And they went into an house,** should form the opening sentence of a new paragraph, and should therefore become the first clause of ver. 20, as in the Revised Version. According to the most approved reading, the words are (ἔρχεται εἰς οἶκον), He cometh into an house, or, He cometh home. There is here a considerable gap in St. Mark's narrative. The sermon on the mount followed upon the call of the apostles, at all events so far as it affected them and their mission. Moreover, St. Matthew interposes here two miracles wrought by our Lord after his descent from the mount, and before his return to his own house at Capernaum. St. Mark seems anxious here to hasten on to describe the treatment of our Lord by his own near relatives at this important crisis in his ministry. So that they—i.e. our Lord and his disciples—could not so much as eat bread; such was the pressure of the crowd upon them. St. Mark evidently records this, in order to show the contrast between the zeal of the multitude and the very different feelings of our Lord's own connections. They, his friends, when they heard how he was thronged, went out to lay hold on him; for they said, He is beside himself. This little incident is mentioned only by St. Mark. When his friends saw him so bent upon his great mission as to neglect his bodily necessities, they considered that he was bereft of his reason, that too much zeal and piety had deranged his mind. His friends went out (ἐξῆλθον) to lay hold on him. They may probably have come from Nazareth. St. John (vii. 5) says that " even his brethren did not believe on him; " that is, they did not believe in him with that fulness of trust which is of the essence of true faith. Their impression was that he was in a condition requiring that he should be put under some restraint.

Ver. 22.—The scribes which came down from Jerusalem said, He hath Beelzebub, etc. These scribes had apparently been sent down by the Sanhedrim, on purpose to watch him, and, by giving their own opinion upon his claims, to undermine his influence. They gave as their authoritative judgment, " He hath Beelzebub." One of the most prominent characteristics of the public works of our Lord was the expulsion of evil spirits. There was no questioning the facts. Even modern scepticism is here at fault, and is constrained to admit the fact of sudden and complete cures of insanity. So the scribes were obliged to account for what they could not deny. " He hath Beelzebub," they say; that is, he is possessed by Beelzebub, or " the lord of the dwelling," as a source of supernatural power. They had heard it alleged against him, " He hath a devil; " and so they fall in with this popular error, and give it emphasis, by saying, Not only has he a devil, but he is possessed by the chief of the devils, and therefore has authority over inferior spirits. Observe the contrast be-

tween the thoughts of the multitude and of those who professed to be their teachers, the scribes and Pharisees. The multitude, free from prejudice, and using only their natural light of reason, candidly owned the greatness of Christ's miracles as wrought by a Divine power; whereas the Pharisees, filled with envy and malice, attributed these mighty works which he wrought by the finger of God, to the direct agency of Satan.

Vers. 23—27.—How can Satan cast out Satan? Observe here that our Lord distinctly affirms the personality of Satan, and a real kingdom of evil. But then he goes on to show that if this their allegation were true, namely, that he cast out devils by the prince of the devils, then it would follow that Satan's kingdom would be divided against itself. As a house divided against itself cannot stand, so neither could the kingdom of Satan exist in the world if one evil spirit was opposed to another for the purpose of dispossessing, the one the other, from the minds and bodies of men. Our Lord thus employs another argument to show that he casts out evil spirits, not by Beelzebub, but by the power of God. It is as though he said, " As he who invades the house of a strong man cannot succeed until he first binds the strong man; in like manner I, Christ Jesus, who spoil the kingdom of Satan, whilst I lead sinners who had been under his power to repentance and salvation, must first bind Satan himself, otherwise he would never suffer me to take his captives from him. Therefore he is my enemy, and not in league with me, not my ally in the casting out of evil spirits, as you falsely represent me to be. It behoves you, then, to understand that it is with the Spirit of God that I cast out devils, and that therefore the kingdom of God is come upon you."

Ver. 28.—All their sins shall be forgiven unto the sons of men, etc. St. Mark adds the words (ver. 30), " Because they said, [ἔλεγον, 'they were saying,'] He hath an unclean spirit." This helps us much to the true meaning of this declaration. Our Lord does not here speak of every sin against the Holy Spirit, but of blasphemy against the Holy Spirit. These words of St. Mark point to a sin of the tongue more especially, although not excluding thoughts and deeds against the Holy Spirit. Observe what these scribes and Pharisees did; they cavilled at works manifestly Divine—works wrought by God for the salvation of men, by which he confirmed his faith and truth. Now, when they spake against these, and knowingly and of malice ascribed them to the evil spirit, then they blasphemed against the Holy Ghost, dishonouring God by assigning his power to Satan. What could be more hateful than this? What greater blasphemy could be imagined? And surely they must be guilty of this sin who ascribe the fruits and actions of the Holy Spirit to an impure and unholy source, and so strive to mar his work and to hinder his influence in the hearts of men.

Ver. 29.—**Hath never forgiveness.** Not that any sinner need despair of forgiveness through the fear that he may have committed this sin; for his repentance shows that his state of mind has never been one of entire enmity, and that he has not so grieved the Holy Spirit as to have been entirely forsaken by him. **But is in danger of eternal damnation.** The Greek words, according to the most approved reading, are ἀλλ' ἔνοχός ἐστιν αἰωνίου ἁμαρτήματος: *but is guilty of an eternal sin*; thus showing that there are sins of which the effects and the punishment belong to eternity. He is bound by a chain of sin from which he can never be loosed. (See St. John ix. 41, "Therefore your sin remaineth.")

Vers. 31—33.—Our Lord's brethren and his mother had now arrived (see ver. 21) to look after him. He was in the house teaching; but the crowd was so great that they could not approach him. The multitude filled not only the room, but the courtyard and all the approaches. St. Luke (viii. 19) says, "they could not come at him for the crowd." **His brethren** here spoken of were in all probability his cousins, the sons of Mary, the wife of Alphæus or Clopas. But two of these, already chosen to be apostles, were most likely with him in the room, and of the number of those towards whom he stretched out his hand and said, "Behold, my mother and my brethren!" whilst Mary and the others had come (Mary, perhaps, induced by the others in the hope that the sight of his mother might the more move him) for the purpose of bringing him back to the quiet of Nazareth. We cannot suppose that the Virgin Mary came with any other feeling than that of a mother's anxiety in behalf of her Son. She may have thought that he was in danger, exposed to the fickle temper of a large multitude, who might at any moment have their passions stirred against him by

his enemies, the scribes and Pharisees; and so she was willingly persuaded to come and use her influence with him to induce him to escape from what appeared evidently to be a position of some danger. If so, this explains our Lord's behaviour on this occasion. The multitude was sitting about him, and he was teaching them; and then a message was brought to him from his mother and his brethren who were without, perhaps in the courtyard, perhaps beyond in the open street, calling for him. The interruption was untimely, not to say unseemly. And so he says, not without a little tone of severity in his words, **Who is my mother and my brethren?** Our Lord did not speak thus as denying his human relationship; as though he was not "very man," but a mere "phantom," as some early heretics taught; and still less as though he was ashamed of his earthly relationships; but partly perhaps because the messengers too boldly and inconsiderately interrupted him while he was teaching; and chiefly that he might show that his heavenly Father's business was more to him than the affection of his earthly mother, greatly as he valued it; and thus he preferred the spiritual relationship, in which there is neither male nor female, bond nor free, but all stand alike to Christ in the relationship of brother, sister, and mother. It is remarkable, and yet the reason for the omission is obvious, that our Lord does not mention "father" in this spiritual category.

Ver. 34.—**Looking round on them** (περιβλεψάμενος) **which sat round about him.** Here is one of the graphic touches of St. Mark, reproduced, it may be, from St. Peter. Our Lord's intellectual and loving eye swept the inner circle of his disciples. The twelve, of course, would be with him, and others with them. His enemies were not far off. But immediately about him were those who constituted his chosen ones. As man, he had his human affections and his earthly relationships; but as the Son of God, he knew no other relatives but God's children, to whom the performance of his will and the promotion of his glory are the first of all duties and the dominant principle of their lives.

HOMILETICS.

Vers. 1—5.—*The withered hand.* This incident serves to bring out the antagonism between the spiritual and benevolent ministry of the Lord Jesus, and the formalism, self-righteousness, and hard-heartedness of the religious leaders of the Jews. It serves to explain, not only the enmity of the Pharisees, but their resolve to league with whomsoever would help them in carrying out their purposes and plot against the very life of the Son of man. It serves to exhibit the mingled feelings of indignation and of pity with which Jesus regarded his enemies, whose hatred was directed, not only against his person, but against his works of mercy and healing. But the incident shall here be treated as a symbol of man's need and of Christ's authority and method as man's Saviour.

I. THE CONDITION OF THIS MAN IN THE SYNAGOGUE IS A SYMBOL OF THE STATE AND NEED OF MAN. He was a man "with a withered hand." 1. *The hand is the symbol of man's practical nature.* The husbandman, the mechanic, the painter, the musician, every craftsman of every grade, makes use of the hand in executing works of art or fulfilling the task of toil. The right hand may be regarded as the best bodily emblem of our active, energetic nature. It is our lot, not only to think and to feel, but to will and to do. 2. *The withering of the hand is symbolical of the effect of sin upon our practical nature.* As this man was rendered incapable of pursuing an industrial life, so the victim of sin is crippled for holy service, is both indisposed and incapacitated for Christian work. The withering of muscle, the paralysis of nerve, is no more disastrous to bodily effort than the blighting and enfeebling power of sin is destructive of all holy acceptable service unto God. 3. *The apparent hopelessness of this man's case is an emblem of the sinner's hopeless state.* This unhappy person was probably condemned by his misfortune to poverty, privation, neglect, and helplessness. He was aware of the inability of human skill to cure him. The case of the sinner is a case of inability and sometimes of despondency. Legislation and philosophy are powerless to deal with an evil so radical and so unmanageable. Unless God have mercy, the sinner is undone!

II. THE MIRACULOUS ACTION OF CHRIST SYMBOLIZES ONE ASPECT OF HIS REDEMPTIVE WORK. And this in two respects: 1. *He saves by the impartation of power.* Christ in the synagogue spoke with authority, both when addressing the spectators who cavilled, and when addressing the sufferer who doubtless welcomed his aid. Power accompanied his words—power from on high; healing virtue went forth from him. How grateful should we be that, when the Son of God came to earth with power, it was with power to heal and bless! He is "mighty to save." There was power in his person and presence, power in his words and works, power in his example and demeanour, power in his love and sacrifice. When he saves, he saves from sin and from sin's worst results. The spiritual inefficiency and helplessness, which is man's curse, gives place to a heavenly energy and activity. The redeemed sinner finds his right hand of service whole, restored, vigorous. Under the influence of new motives and new hopes, he consecrates his renewed nature of activity to the Lord who saved him. 2. *He saves with the concurrence of human effort.* Observe that the Lord Jesus addressed to this sufferer two commands. He bade him "Stand forth!" which he *could* do; and "Stretch forth thy hand!" which he *could not* do—or at least might, judging from the past, have felt and believed himself unable to do. Yet he believed that the Prophet and Healer, who spoke with such authority, and who was known to have healed many, was not uttering idle words. His faith was called forth, and his will was exercised. Without his obedience and concurrence, there is no reason to suppose that he would have been healed. So every sinner who would be saved by Christ must recognize the Divine authority of the Saviour, must avail himself of the Saviour's compassion, and in humble faith must obey the Saviour's command. It is not, indeed, faith which saves. It is Christ who saves, but he saves through faith; for it is by faith that the sinner lays hold upon the Saviour's might, and comes to rejoice in the Saviour's grace.

APPLICATION. 1. The first requisite for a sinner who would be saved is clearly to see, and deeply to feel, his need and helplessness. 2. The next requisite is to come into the presence of the Divine Saviour. 3. Yet again, it is requisite to exercise faith in him who is mighty and willing to save. 4. And every healed and restored sinner should consecrate all his active powers to the service of his Redeemer.

Vers. 6—12.—*Persecution and popularity.* The evangelist represents, in very graphic language, the crisis in the ministry of Jesus now reached. We learn what was the attitude towards Jesus, both of the populace and of the ruling classes. We see the scribes and Pharisees meeting with the Herodians, and plotting against the Benefactor of mankind. We see the multitudes thronging from every quarter to look upon, to listen to, the far-famed Prophet of Nazareth. It is a striking contrast. It may be to us an earnest of what was to come; of the malice that slew the Lord of glory, and of the praise that should encompass him from all lands; of the cross, and of the throne.

I. WE HAVE A PICTURE OF OUR LORD'S POPULARITY. 1. This passage furnishes the *evidence* of our Lord's popularity. The people left their cities and villages, their homes and occupations, in order to follow Jesus. From various parts of the province of Galilee, through which he had just been travelling upon an evangelistic tour, the people flocked to the neighbourhood of the lake. They came also from Jerusalem and Judæa, where successive miracles had made his name and person familiar to the inhabitants of the metropolis. Not only so, but from the east side of the Jordan, and Idumæa; and (strangest of all) from Phœnicia, far away in the north-west, multitudes, attracted by the great Prophet and Physician, found their way to Gennesaret. It is plain that an immense impression had been created by the ministry of our Lord, that he was becoming the chief figure in the land, succeeding to the prominence and the popularity of John the Baptist. 2. This same passage brings before us the *grounds* of our Lord's popularity. Wherever he had gone, he had so acted as to justify the name he gave himself, " the Son of man; " he had shown himself the universal Saviour and Friend. Some came grateful for healing virtue and for pardoning mercy, having themselves tasted and seen that the Lord was good. Some brought to him the maladies of themselves or their friends, hoping to experience his grace. The unclean spirits came, confessing him to be the Son of God, acknowledging his regal authority, prepared to flee at his bidding and to leave the sufferers free. Some came to see him of whom such great and delightful tidings had been spread abroad; and others hoping that they might witness some illus-trations of his saving might. His ministry of teaching attracted some, and the sequel tells us how richly such were rewarded by the incomparable discourses which were delivered at this period of Christ's career. And there were, doubtless, some few noble, devout, and ardent souls, who longed for the revelation of a spiritual kingdom, which should fulfil the promises of God and realize the ancient and prophetic visions. 3. The *consequences* of Christ's popularity are no less clearly related. It is plain that at this period our Lord was quite embarrassed by the excitement and eagerness of the crowds who thronged around him. It was this embarrassment that led him, first to withdraw to the lake, and then to request that a boat might be in readiness to receive him from the pressure of the crowd, and, if necessary, to take him to the near seclusion of the eastern shore. It was this embarrassment also which led him to direct those who par-took of the benefit of his compassion to refrain from celebrating his praise, and even to keep silence concerning what he had done for them. 4. But let us bear in mind that this popularity was but superficial. Jesus knew well that most who followed him did so either from curiosity or with selfish desires of benefiting from his ministry. He was not deceived by the popular interest and acclaim. He was aware that at any moment the tide might turn. At Nazareth it was proved how ungrateful and violent the people could be when once their passions were roused or their prejudices crossed. And his ministry closed amidst the clamour and the execration of the fickle multitude, upon whose minds the arts of crafty priests and politicians played, as the storm-wind plays upon the surface of the mighty sea.

II. WE HAVE A PICTURE OF OUR LORD'S PERSECUTORS, THEIR PLOTS AND PROJECTS. At the very time that multitudes were openly thronging around Christ, there was secret consultation among men of position and influence as to the means of effecting his ruin. We observe the *occasion* of this hostile attitude and action. For a while there had been no opposition, but rather a general interest and expectation. The change seems to have come about as a consequence of the violation by the Lord Jesus of the customs and traditions of the ceremonial rabbis or scribes. There were deep-seated *reasons* for the hostility cherished against the Prophet of Nazareth by the religious leaders—scribes and Pharisees. 1. His *conduct towards the common people* was a grave offence. The rabbis generally held the unlearned and lower class in great contempt; in their esteem those who knew not the Law were cursed. They would not associate with them or touch them. Now, the Lord Jesus made himself at home with all classes, and accepted invitations, not only from rulers and scholars, but from publicans, at whose table he met the worldly and the sinful. He even chose one from the despised class of tax-collectors to occupy a place among his own immediate friends and fol-lowers. He ate and drank with publicans and sinners, and, when he preached, encouraged such to draw near to him. "The common people heard him gladly." That an acknowledged rabbi should act in such a way was a scandal in the view of the self-righteous and ceremonious; it was conduct likely to lower the learned in the general esteem, to bring religion and the profession of the scribes into contempt. 2. We gather from the Gospel record that the chief cause of complaint against Jesus was his *neglect and violation of the ceremonial Law*. This Law was to the rabbis the breath of their nostrils; and our Lord and his disciples, doubtless under his influence, were very negligent of the observances upon which the ruling class laid such stress. The Pharisees fasted, Jesus feasted; the Pharisees performed innumerable ablutions, Jesus ate bread "with unwashen hands." 3. *The sabbath* was, however, the most important point of difference. Many of the rigid Jewish religionists held the most narrow opinions and cherished the most absurd and ridiculous scruples with regard to what was lawful and what unlawful upon the weekly day of rest. It was not possible that Jesus, with his views as to the spirituality of worship and as to the nature of holiness, should agree with these petty and childish notions; it was not possible that he should do other than violate traditional rules and shock formal prejudices. He encouraged his disciples to pluck and eat corn on the sabbath; he performed cures upon the day which he held to be made for man; he directed those who were healed to take up their couch and return home. In all these respects he both vindicated religious liberty and asserted himself "Lord of the sabbath." The rigid ceremonialism and ritualism of the rabbis was offended, alike with the superiority which the Lord claimed over all rules, and with the disdain he showed for their usages and traditions. They hated him, as narrow and formal religionists of all schools ever hate the teachers who place religion in the heart rather than in ceremonies and creeds, and who proclaim that newness of life is the one acceptable offering and sacrifice in the sight of the Divine Searcher of hearts. 4. Our Lord's *treatment of the scribes and Pharisees* was itself a cause of offence, an occasion of their enmity to him. Instead of treating them with deference, he defied their judgment, and (at a later period of his ministry) uttered denunciations and woes upon them for their hypocrisy. When about to heal the withered hand, Jesus "looked round about on them with anger, being grieved at the hardening of their heart." It was not thus that they were wont to be regarded and treated. If this treatment were continued, their influence must be undermined. 5. The cause of hostility just mentioned was a symptom of a deeper difference between Jesus and the rabbis: *the spiritual quality of his teaching* was such as to conflict with all their notions of religion. With them religion was an affair of the outward life alone; with him it was, first and foremost, an affair of the heart. And even with respect to outward actions there was this great difference: the rabbis thought of the attitude of prayer, Christ of the feeling and desire; the rabbis thought much of tithes and fasts, of sacrifices and services, Christ of the weightier matters of the Law; the rabbis thought much of what went as food into the man, Christ of the thoughts which expressed themselves in moral conduct. Observe the feeling that was aroused in the breasts of the Pharisees. Luke tells us "they were filled with madness," *i.e.* carried away by violent rage and hostility. What a revelation of human iniquity! The actions of the holy and gracious Redeemer excite the fury of those he came to benefit and save! And the hostility then felt grew and gathered as the months passed on, until it culminated in the successful plot against the Holy One and Just. Such feeling did not evaporate in words; it led to action. The enemies of Jesus retired to deliberate, to plot. There was more than indignation; there was malice, a resolve to avenge themselves upon One too holy, too authoritative, for them to bear with him. An unnatural alliance was formed between the rabbis, who represented the principles of rigid Judaism both in nationality and in religion; and the Herodians, who seem to have been Sadducees in religion, and in politics supporters of the house of Herod, and accordingly advocates of all possible independence upon Rome. It is not easy to understand this league. The Herodians themselves may not so much have hated Jesus as, from political motives, they desired to gain the favour of the powerful Pharisaic party, whose influence with the people generally was great, and who might be made the means of strengthening the supporters of Antipas. The aim which these confederates set before them was atrocious indeed; it was nothing less than the destruction of Jesus. Answer his reasoning they could not. Equally unable were they to find fault with his irreproachable character, his benevolent actions. Their only weapons were slander and craft and violence. How to work upon the fears of the secular authorities and the passions of the populace—this was their aim and endeavour.

Vers. 13—19.—*The twelve.* Some of these twelve had been "called" by the Master long ago, and had already been much in his company. Others had been, for a shorter time and less intimately, associated with him. This formal appointment and commission took place upon the mount, and immediately before the delivery of the ever-memorable sermon to the disciples and the multitude. The passage is suggestive of great general truths.

I. CHRIST THOUGHT FIT TO EMPLOY HUMAN AGENTS IN THE PROMULGATION OF HIS RELIGION. That he might have dispensed with all created agency, that he might have employed angelic ministers, we cannot doubt. But in becoming man—"the Son of man"—he contracted human sympathies and relationships, and undertook to work, with a Divine power indeed, yet by human means.

II. CHRIST SELECTED HIS AGENTS BY VIRTUE OF HIS OWN WISDOM AND AUTHORITY. He called "whom he himself would." The Lord Jesus is the absolute Monarch in his own kingdom. Having perfect knowledge, unerring wisdom, and unfailing justice, he is fitted for supreme, unshared rule.

III. CHRIST CHOSE HIS TRUSTED APOSTLES FROM A LOWLY POSITION OF SOCIETY. Only one of the band—and he the unworthy member—was from Judæa. All the others were Galileans; and the inhabitants of this northern province were comparatively rude, unlettered, unpolished. Some rabbis would fain have been received into the number, but the Lord would not encourage them. He preferred to deal with unsophisticated natures. Perhaps James and John and Levi were in fair circumstances; the rest were in all likelihood poor. The twelve were, in education, very different from such men as Luke and Paul. Christ chose, as he has often done since, "the weak things of the world to confound the mighty." He rejoiced and gave thanks because things, hidden from the wise and prudent, had been revealed unto babes.

IV. CHRIST APPOINTED AGENTS WITH VARIOUS GIFTS, QUALIFICATIONS, AND CHARACTER. The three leaders among the apostles were certainly men of ability. Peter's vigour of style was only one index to the great native force of his character; James was slain by Herod, as probably the most prominent representative of the early Christian community; and John's writings show him to have been both profound and imaginative as a thinker. Of the other apostles, James the Less was certainly a man of inflexible will and of vigorous administrative power. In disposition these twelve men differed marvellously from one another. Two were "sons of thunder," another—Thomas—was of a doubting, melancholy spirit, and Simon was ardent and impulsive. All but Iscariot were deeply attached to Jesus, and it was not without purpose that one avaricious and treacherous person was included in the number. What various instruments our Lord employs for accomplishing his own work!

V. CHRIST RECOGNIZED AND EMPLOYED THE SPECIAL GIFTS OF HIS DISCIPLES IN HIS OWN SERVICE. This passage brings this truth vividly before us. Simon was surnamed "The Rock"—a title to which his character especially entitled him; and the sons of Zebedee were designated "Sons of Thunder," doubtless from their ardent, impetuous zeal in the service of the Lord. There was a special work corresponding to the special endowments of each.

VI. CHRIST QUALIFIED THESE AGENTS BY KEEPING THEM IN HIS OWN SOCIETY AND BENEATH HIS OWN INFLUENCE. "That they might be with him." How simple, yet how profound these words! What a Companion! What lessons were to be learned from his character, his demeanour, his language, his mighty works! Nothing could so qualify these men for the service of coming years as this brief period of daily and close intimacy with a Being so gracious, so holy, so wise.

VII. CHRIST HIMSELF COMMISSIONED AND AUTHORIZED THESE AGENTS. They were to be "sent forth;" hence their designation, "apostles." They were to be his messengers, his heralds, his ambassadors. And what was their ministry? 1. To preach, to publish good tidings of salvation, righteousness, eternal life, through Christ. To this end it was evidently necessary that they should imbibe the Master's spirit, as well as know the Teacher's doctrine. It was necessary that, in due time, they should be witnesses of his resurrection and partakers of the Spirit poured out from on high. 2. To have authority to cast out demons, to carry on the work of the Lord, and to contend with the kingdom of Satan, and establish the reign of Christ, of light, of righteousness, of peace.

APPLICATION. 1. Christ's first call is to discipleship. We must first learn that we may teach; obey and serve that we may guide and aid others. 2. We are summoned to consecrate all our gifts and acquirements to the service and cause of Immanuel. 3. It is the highest honour and the purest happiness to be employed by Christ as his agents. 4. It is necessary to be much with Christ in order that we may be fitted efficiently to work for Christ.

Vers. 20—30.—*Blasphemy.* Great men are often misunderstood by reason of their very greatness. Aims higher than those of others need other methods than such as are commonly employed by ordinary persons. How much more must this have been the case with the Son of man! His mission was unique—was altogether his own. He could not fulfil his ministry and do the work of him who sent him, without stepping aside from the beaten tracks of conduct, and so courting criticism and obloquy. He could not well conciliate public opinion, for he came to condemn and to revolutionize it. For the most part he went his way, without noticing the misrepresentations and the calumnies of men. Yet there were occasions, like the present, when he paused to answer and to confute his adversaries.

I. THE BLASPHEMOUS CHARGE BROUGHT AGAINST JESUS. His friends charged him with madness; his enemies attributed his works to the power of evil. In the allegation of the former there may have been some sincerity; those of the latter were animated by malice and hatred. Probably these scribes were sent down into Galilee from the authorities at Jerusalem, to check the enthusiasm which was spreading throughout the northern province with regard to the Prophet of Nazareth. The same charges were brought against him in Jerusalem; so that there may have been an understanding as to the method to be adopted in opposing the great Teacher. The scribes discredited Jesus, first, by asserting that he was possessed by Beelzebub, the Syrian Satan; and secondly, by explaining his power to dispossess demons by the league between him and the lord of the demons, whose authority the inferior spirits could not but obey. There was no attempt to deny the fact that demoniacs were cured; this would have been so monstrously false that to take such a position would have been to ruin their own influence with the people.

II. THE REFUTATION OF THIS BLASPHEMY. 1. Our Lord's reply was on the ground of reason—of what might be called common sense. He used two parables, by which he showed the unreasonableness, the absurdity of the allegations in question. Suppose a house or a kingdom to be divided against itself, to be rent by internal discord and faction; what is the result? It comes to ruin. And can it be believed that the crafty prince of darkness will turn his arms against his own servants and minions? So, Satan would "have an end." 2. Having refuted their argument, our Lord proceeded with his own; gave his explanation of what was the spiritual significance of his ministry, especially as regarded the "possessed." So far from being in league with Satan, the Lord Jesus was Satan's one mighty Foe; he had already, in the temptation, overcome him, and was binding him, and now, behold! he was spoiling the house of his vanquished enemy, in expelling the demons from the wretched demoniacs of Galilee! He could not have done this had he been in league with Satan, had he not already vanquished Satan. Having effected this, he "spoiled principalities and powers."

III. THE CENSURE OF THIS BLASPHEMY. Our Lord first reasoned; then (as recorded from ver. 28) he spoke with authority, as One in the secrets of Heaven, with power to declare the principles of Divine judgment. There is, he declared, an eternal and unpardonable sin. If the scribes were not committing this, they were approaching it. The sin against the Holy Ghost, the confusion of truth with error, good with evil,—is a sin, not of ignorance, not of misunderstanding, but of wilfulness; a sin of the whole nature; a sin against the light without and the light within. Our Saviour, in condemning this sin, speaks as the rightful Lord, the authoritative Judge, of all mankind!

APPLICATION. "What think ye of Christ?" To think of him *with indifference* is unreasonable, and shows the most blameable insensibility to the great moral conflict of the universe, on one side of which Jesus is the Champion. To think of him *disparagingly* is blasphemy; for " he that honoureth the Son honoureth the Father," and he that honoureth not the Son honoureth not the Father. It is blasphemy to speak against the character or the authority of the Son of God. What remains, then? This:

to think and speak of him *with reverence and gratitude, faith, and love.* This is just and right; and though Christ does not need our homage and honour, he will accept it and reward it.

Vers. 31—35.—*Kindred of Christ.* The feeling with regard to Christ had, by this time, become extremely strong. On the one hand, the people generally were deeply interested in his teaching, were eager spectators of his mighty works, and in many cases were much attached to himself. Hence the crowd which thronged the house where Jesus was engaged in teaching—a crowd so dense that none from the outside could approach the Master. On the other hand, the opposition to the Prophet of Nazareth was growing and spreading among the scribes and Pharisees, some of whom from Jerusalem were now usually among the audience, anxiously on the watch for any utterance which they might use to the disadvantage of the bold and fearless Teacher. In these circumstances, the concern of the relatives of Jesus was natural enough. They saw that his labours were so arduous and protracted that he was in danger of exhaustion through weariness. And they feared that the attitude he was taking towards the hypocritical Pharisees was imperilling his liberty and safety. They accordingly professed to believe in his madness, and sought to lay hold on him. Hence the interruption recorded in this passage, which gave rise to this memorable and precious declaration of his spiritual affinity and kindred to all whose life is one of obedience to the Father.

I. THE FACT OF SPIRITUAL KINDRED BETWEEN CHRIST AND HIS PEOPLE. Earthly relationships were admitted and honoured by Jesus. Yet spiritual kindred was set above them. Under the gospel dispensation there are revealed emphatically the fatherhood of God, and the brotherhood of Christ. We are the children of God. Jesus, in his glory, " is not ashamed to call us brethren."

II. THE PROOF OF SPIRITUAL KINDRED WITH CHRIST. Who are they whom Jesus commends and admits to his fellowship and confidence? They who do his Father's will. Upon such he looks with approval. 1. His requirement is not intellectual or sentimental merely, but *practical.* Belief and feeling are necessary, but not sufficient. We are made to act, and in our life to carry out the Divine commands. Jesus asks the devotion of the heart, expressed in the service of the active nature. We are saved by grace, and works are the proofs of faith. Obedience proceeds from hearty confidence and sincere love. Indeed, the Lord himself has told us that this is the work of God, that we " believe on him whom he hath sent." And Christians are those who prove the sincerity of their love by a practical consecration. 2. It is the privilege of the Christian voluntarily to *obey a personal, Divine will.* He sees the Lawgiver behind the law. His life is not mere conformity to regulation—to some such abstract standard as " the fitness of things." It is subjection to a Being whose will enjoins a course of virtue and piety. Religion has too often, like law, like society, summoned men to do the will of man—of fallible, fickle man. Christ calls us all away from this endeavour to a far nobler and better aim—summons us to do the will, not of man, but of God! This is a standard with which no fault can be found, no dissatisfaction can be felt. 3. Jesus looks for, not a mechanical, but a *spiritual,* obedience. The description of the Christian life is, " doing the will of God from the heart." 4. Christ requires not servile but *filial* obedience. We know from personal experience the difference between doing the will of a master or a ruler and doing the will of a father. It is to this latter kind of obedience that we are called. It is much to believe in the personality and authority of God, but it is more to live under the sense of his fatherhood; for this involves his interest in us, his care for us, his love toward us; and all these are obviously considerations which make duty both delightful and easy. The motive is not merely moral, it becomes religious. The Christian acts as a child who brings before his mind, as a ruling consideration, " my Father's will." 5. Christ desires not occasional or fitful acts of obedience, but *habitual* service. One act is good, both in itself and also as making a second act easier. Obedience becomes a second nature, a law recognized and accepted; and perseverance is the one proof of true principle.

III. THE PRIVILEGE OF SPIRITUAL KINDRED ASSURED BY CHRIST. Men boast of eminent ancestors, distinguished connections, powerful kinsmen; but such boast is usually foolish and vain; whereas it is in the power of the humblest Christian to glory in the Lord. The friendship of Jesus surpasses that of the greatest and the best of human friends. It is closer and more delightful, it is more honourable and more certain and enduring than the intimacy of human kindred. 1. Participation in Christ's character. There is a family likeness; the Divine features are reproduced. 2. Enjoyment of the tender affection of Christ. 3. Intimate and confidential intercourse with Christ. These two are closely associated. This spiritual relationship involves a peculiar interest, each in the other. So far from indifference, there is mutual regard and concern. The honour of Christ is very near the Christian's heart, and Christ engraves his people "upon the palms of his hands." There is a special tenderness in these mutual regards, very different from the ceremonial or official respect attaching to some relations. "Ye are my friends," says the Saviour. Hymns and devotional books have sometimes exaggerated this side of piety; yet with many probably the danger lies on the other side. As there is a specially confidential tone in the intercourse of the several members of a family, so is there something like this in the fellowship of the Redeemer and his redeemed ones. "All things that I have heard of the Father," says he, "I have made known unto you;" and, on the other side, the follower of the Lord Jesus pours all his intimate thoughts and wishes into the ear of his heavenly Friend and Brother.

IV. The obligations of spiritual kindred. Of these may be mentioned: 1. Reverent regard for his honour. 2. Self-denying devotion to his cause. 3. Recognition of his brethren as ours.

Practical conclusion. Observe the liberality of the language of Jesus, the wide invitation virtually given in his declaration: "*Whosoever*," etc. This is not limited to the learned or the great; it is open to us all.

HOMILIES BY VARIOUS AUTHORS.

Vers. 1—6.—*The man with the withered hand; or, keeping the sabbath.* In the most sacred and joyous scenes there may be circumstances of pain and sorrow. There are often some in God's house who are hindered in their enjoyment by personal affliction. But even these may be of service in testing the spirit and disposition of God's professed people.

I. It is in spirit alone that the sabbath is truly kept. 1. *Outward observances are of value only as expressing and fostering this.* 2. *Evil hearts will fail to keep the day even whilst seemingly engaged in its special duties.* 3. *Institutions that were designed for the highest ends may be perverted to the worst.*

II. Works of mercy honour the sabbath. 1. *Because they are always urgent.* 2. *They exercise the holiest emotions and faculties of human nature.* 3. *They are the service of God.* 4. *They may be the means of others keeping the day and serving him.*

III. The true sabbatic spirit convicts and inflames the false. The hatred manifested is all but incredible. Yet it was already in their hearts. They had been condemned where they thought to have been judges. False religion (Pharisees) and worldliness (Herodians) are united in their hatred of the spirit and work of Christ, because they are both exposed by him.—M.

Ver. 4.—"*But they held their peace.*" "There is much silence that proceeds from the Spirit of God, but there is also a devilish silence," says Quesnel; and it is not difficult to pronounce upon the character of this.

I. What was intended by it. It was evasive. Christ had propounded a dilemma which those who watched him dared not answer, since, had they done so, they would either have compromised themselves or committed themselves to approval of his action. It was doubtless intended also to suggest that the problem was too difficult for them to solve, at any rate without due consideration.

II. What it showed. There was no concealing from his eyes its real meaning, which he at once denounced. The circumstances of it and the exposure it received made it evident that it was due: 1. *To unwillingness to be convinced.* The state called "hardness of heart" it is not easy to resolve into all its elements, but this is undoubtedly the chief one. These men had come into the synagogue with sinister designs against Christ, and so strong was their prejudice that they refused to assent to the most cogent evidence. The language used by their intended Victim conveys the impression that this "hardening" was in process whilst the scene lasted. It is impossible to dissociate religious opinion from character. Prejudice and malice incapacitate the mind for the reception of truth. Here the most cogent evidence was resisted; for they evidently expected that he would heal the man, and yet were unwilling to attach its due weight to the miracle as a proof of Christ's Divine mission. How much of modern scepticism is to be attributed to similar causes it is impossible to say; but that a large proportion of it is to be so explained cannot be doubted. The hesitation to reply is the more noticeable in this instance as the question is one turning, not upon material evidence, but upon moral considerations. 2. *To lack of sympathy.* The condition of the sufferer did not move them to compassion, even in the house of God. A touchstone of the religious professions of men may still be found in the poor, the suffering, etc. 3. *To dishonesty and cowardice.* They knew how the question ought to have been answered, but they feared the consequences. The question as to killing alarmed their own guilty consciences, for they knew that they had come thither not to worship but to compass the destruction of a fellow-creature. There is still a great deal of suppressed religious conviction amongst men; how are we to interpret it? When moral obligations are evaded, and scepticism is made an excuse for uncertainty of conduct and laxity of life, we are justified in attributing such behaviour to the same principles. There are circumstances that demand candour and outspokenness, and in which silence is dishonourable; we ought "to have the courage of our convictions:" occasions when it is wrong to be silent; when religious zeal is made a cloak for murder, cruelty, injustice, and licentiousness; when the difficulty of theological problems is made an excuse for compromise, or inaction, or moral indifference; when, in the face of the clearest evidence, a man says he "does not know."

III. WHAT IT EARNED. 1. *The anger of Christ.* His look must have searched their hearts and abashed them. There would be in it something of the awfulness of the judgment day. This moral indignation, in which there is surely an element of contempt, is still the sentence upon all similar conduct. 2. *Consciousness of guilt.* They were self-convicted, but the condemnation of one so pure and loving would seal their sense of unworthiness and dishonour. 3. *Exposure.* No one in that crowd was deceived as to their real motive. The same law still prevails; the moral obliquity which refuses to pronounce upon great questions of duty and righteousness will sooner or later be made evident to others. Just as there are circumstances which precipitate opinion, so there are circumstances in every life which call for decided action, and reveal the manner in which one has dealt with one's convictions. At such junctures the man who has been true to his best lights and sincere in following out his convictions, will be honest, fearless, chivalrous; the man who has not been truly in earnest, or disinterested in his attachment to truth, will be seen to shuffle, to shirk responsibility, and to shrink from sacrifice; or, worse still, he will yield to the lusts and tendencies of his baser nature, and act with unscrupulousness, inhumanity, and godlessness. It is the law that opinions determine character; and that, in the course of life, character must inevitably make itself known.—M.

Ver. 5.—"*Stretch forth thy hand!*" I. CHRIST SOMETIMES ENJOINS WHAT SEEMS TO BE IMPOSSIBLE.
II. FAITH IS SHOWN IN DOING WHAT HE COMMANDS, EVEN WHEN IT SEEMS TO BE IMPOSSIBLE.
III. WHERE THERE IS THE "OBEDIENCE OF FAITH," POWER WILL BE GRANTED.—M.

Vers. 13—19.—*The choosing of the apostles.* I. THE RELATION BETWEEN CHRIST AND HIS SERVANTS WAS DELIBERATELY ENTERED UPON AND VOLUNTARY IN ITS NATURE. 1. *It was formally commenced in retirement.* We may suppose a season of devotion. The absence of public excitement or external interference was evidently desired. 2. *The utmost freedom existed on both sides.* He called "whom he himself would: and they went unto him." There was no coercion. The highest principles and emotions were addressed. On the one hand, the teaching and the work of the Master were not dominated by the influence now associated with him; nor, on the other, was their service other than the fruit of enthusiasm, intelligent conviction, and willing sympathy.

II. Reputation was received from Christ by his servants, not conferred by them. The names are all of men in humble life, with no previous distinction of any kind. They were names common enough in Palestine. But their connection with Christ has immortalized them. How many have come to the Saviour in similar circumstances, and have received the reflected renown of his name ! He makes the best out of the poor materials of human nature, and bestows what human nature in its greatest circumstances and moods could never of itself have produced. Men are honoured in being made the servants of Christ.

III. The apostles were to be representative in office and character for all time. As his first disciples, and because of the marked variety and force of their individual natures as influenced by the gospel and developed in Christ's service; their names have wrought themselves into the very texture of the gospel, and we have received it with the impress of their varied natures and habits of thought. "He sent them forth to *preach*, and to have authority to cast out devils"—a fundamental work. Therefore are they called "the foundation of the apostles and prophets," of whom Jesus is the Corner-stone. In serving Christ they laid the world and the ages under inestimable obligation.—M.

Vers. 20, 21.—*Christ hindered by his friends.* I. Through ignorance. Owing (1) *to want of sympathy with him in his higher aims;* and (2) *consequent failure of spiritual perception.*

II. By charging him with madness. They had so little of the spirit of self-denial in themselves that they could not understand enthusiasm which would not admit of his attending to his own wants, "so much as to eat bread." 1. *They feared also the consequences which might arise from the presence of his enemies.* The scribes were there "from Jerusalem," on the alert to find accusation against him; and they must have been observed. 2. *But by this charge they discredited the character of his ministry.* Who should be supposed to know whether he was sane or not, if not his own family ? In attributing to maniacy the Divine works and words of Christ, they did him and all who might through him have life and peace, a cruel, irreparable wrong. So Paul was charged with being beside himself; and all who for Christ's sake try to live above the maxims and aims of the world will meet with similar judgment. The blow thus struck is not at an individual, but at the spiritual prospects and hopes of a whole race.

III. By unauthorized and untimely interference. 1. *A sin of presumption.* The judgment was hasty and mistaken; the action was unjustifiable, both foolish and wicked. 2. *Enmity to God.*—M.

Vers. 20—22.—*The Saviour judged by the world.* There were various opinions amongst the multitude. They cannot be indifferent to the work and teaching of Christ. "Some believed, and some believed not." Of those who did not believe all were in opposition to him. This circumstance was—

I. A tribute to the influence and importance of the gospel.

II. It illustrated the impotency of the carnal mind in spiritual questions.

III. It suggests the perils to which the carnal mind is exposed. "Lest haply ye be found to fight against God" (Acts v. 39).

IV. It suggests the duty under such circumstances of Christian testimony.—M.

Vers. 23—27.—*"How can Satan cast out Satan?" or, the logic of spiritual forces.* The spirit of Christ's answer to this malicious attack is calm, fearless, and full of light. He meets the charge with convincing and irrefutable logic.

I. The defence. There are two elements in his argument : 1. *A demonstration.* It is the familiar *reductio ad absurdum,* such as one might use with a schoolboy. It is so simple and trenchant that it straightway becomes an attack of the most powerful kind. He treats them as children in knowledge, and convicts them at the same time of diabolical malice. 2. *An inference.* Here the advantage is pushed beyond the point expected. He is not satisfied with a mere disclaimer; he comes to a further and higher deduction. If it was true that he did not cast out Satan by Satan, then it must also be true that he cast out Satan in spite of the latter; and that could only mean one thing. Satan,

" the strong man," must have been bound by the Son of man, else he would not suffer himself to be so " spoiled."　This is at once an assurance full of comfort to his friends and a warning to his enemies.

II. Positions assumed in it.　1. *The solidarity of evil.*　2. *The irreconcileableness of the kingdoms of light and darkness.*—M.

Vers. 28—30.—*The unforgivable sin.*　I. An actual offence.　It is not mentioned again in the Gospel, but the warning was called forth by the actual transgression.　There is no mere theorizing about it therefore.　It is an exposure and denunciation.　This gives us an idea of the fearful unbelief and bitter hatred of those who opposed him. The manifestation of light and love only strengthened the antagonism of some.　They consciously sinned against the light.

II. Why is it unforgivable ?　1. *Because of the majesty of the crime.*　It identifies the Representative and Son of God with the devil—the best with the worst.　2. *From the nature of the spiritual state induced.*　When a man deliberately falsifies his spiritual intuitions, and corrupts his conscience so that good is considered evil, there is no hope for him.　Such a condition can only be the result of long-continued opposition to God and determined hatred of his character.　The means of salvation are thereby robbed of their possibility to save.

III. The likelihood of its being repeated.　As it is an extreme and final degree of sin, there is little danger of its being committed without full consciousness and many previous warnings.　1. *It is therefore, a priori, improbable in any.*　Yet as increasing light and grace tend to throw into stronger opposition the spirit of evil, it must be regarded as : 2. *A possibility of every sinner.*　Necessity for self-examination and continual recourse to the cleansing and illuminating power of Christ.—M.

Vers. 31—35.—*The mother and the brethren of Jesus.*　The annoyance and hindrance of a moment are turned to eternal gain to the cause of truth.

I. Family influences may injure spiritual usefulness.　They are powerful either way.　They operate subtly and constantly.　A tendency to narrowness in the family tie, which requires to be checked.　Much of this influence which is adverse to Christian life is unconsciously so.　Yet the intensest forms of hatred to truth and goodness are exhibited within the family relation.　Hence the necessity for clear and forcible realization of the distinction between lower and higher obligations.　The child of God will have recourse to constant prayer for help and guidance, and for the conversion of relatives.

II. There are circumstances in which the natural must yield to the spiritual relationship.　This is so whenever they conflict, or when, both being of Divine obligation, the latter is manifestly more immediately impressed upon the conscience, and more evidently calculated for the good of men and the glory of God.

III. The nearest and only permanent relation to Christ is spiritual and not natural.　1. *An invitation to all.*　2. *An encouragement and inspiration to real disciples.* 3. *A forecast of the communion of saints.*—M.

Ver. 35.—*Divine relationships.*　1. How far resembling human relationships. 1. *In laying down the condition of Divine relationship, Christ does not absolutely displace human relationships.*　It would have been hard for him so to do, since men were being addressed, and the relationships sustained by them would depend upon the religious sanction they might possess for the measure of honour and faithful observance they would receive.　That the terms of human relationship were still employed showed that an analogy at least existed.　2. *The terms denoting the distinctions of natural relationships are used in speaking of the heavenly.*　The " brother " and " sister " and " mother," therefore, express a real distinction in the heavenly family.　And there are differences of mutual service and affection which must exist within the common " bond of charity," even as on earth.　In the case of those who believe in Christ, then, the beautiful variation which God has created in the affection of the domestic circle will have a use and fitness in fulfilling the duties and realizing the ideal of the Divine life.　The latter has its sphere for the sisterliness, the brotherliness, etc., even as the human life; and these are modes through which the Divine love will express itself.　Indeed, it may be said that the human affections of father, mother, etc., do not fully manifest or realize themselves in the merely human life; it is the Divine life in which the ideal of each is rendered possible.

II. IN WHAT RESPECTS DIFFERING FROM THESE. 1. *The affections characteristic of the human family will spring from a spiritual principle and express Divine love.* "The will of God," or "the will of the Father," will take the place of blind instinct or selfish gratification. Thus springing from a new source they will be transformed, purified, and freed from limitation and defect. "The will of God" will be the law according to which they will express themselves; but as that will has been interpreted as salvation and universal benevolence, so the distinctions of human affection will be brought into play in furthering the redemptive scheme of the Father amongst his sinful children; and through them phases of the Divine love will be realized that would otherwise find no expression. They will thus, also, be universalized and directed into channels of service and helpfulness. 2. *The Divine relationship is therefore based upon a new nature.* It is only those who are born of the Spirit who can do the will of God. It is the life of the Spirit in them that changes and adapts them for the unselfish affections of the family of God. 3. *The Divine relationship is a moral possibility of every one.* Every woman may become a sister, a mother, of Christ; every man his brother.—M.

Ver. 2.—*A miracle of healing.* The cure of the man with a withered hand was more obviously a supernatural work than sudden recovery from a fever, so that we need not wonder at the excitement it aroused. But it was only an example of many similar works, and as such we propose to consider it. I. THE MIRACLE WHICH JESUS DID. 1. *It was a removal of bodily infirmity.* Although the Son of God came from heaven to do a spiritual work, much of the time of his earthly ministry was spent in curing physical disorders. We might have supposed that, coming from a painless and sorrowless world he would have had sparse sympathy with such suffering; that he would have exhorted to fortitude and self-control, and expectation of a time when pain would be no more. It was not so, however. He sympathized with all sufferers, and, although he had before him a stupendous spiritual work, he by no means confined himself to it. Though sometimes he had "no leisure so much as to eat," he found time to heal many bodily diseases; and he did this without hurrying over it as if it were an inferior work, or as if it were necessitated by the hardness of the human heart; but he did it lovingly and constantly, as being an essential part of his mission. In some respects, no doubt, this was a lower work than preaching. The body is inferior to the soul, as the tent is to its inhabitant. The effects of cure were only transient, for none were promised exemption in the future from disease or death. Yet these lower and temporary blessings were generously bestowed by One who habitually stood in the light of eternity. Point out the ministry of mercy which the Church has yet to do, in Christ's name, for suffering humanity. 2. *It was a miracle with a moral purpose.* The supernatural works of Christ were not mainly intended to excite attention. When he was asked "for a sign" with that object, he resolutely refused it. Had this been his purpose, he would have flung snowy Hermon into the depths of the sea, instead of doing the kind of work which is more slowly done by human physicians. He had a better purpose than this. He healed disease because, as the Conqueror of sin, he would point out and abolish some of its effects. He rescued a man, if only for a time, from the evil that harassed him, to show that he was his Redeemer. And besides this, he appeared as the Representative of God, and therefore did what he is ever doing in more gradual methods. A modern writer has wisely said, "This, I think, is the true nature of miracles; they are an epitome of God's processes in nature, beheld in connection with their source." We are apt to forget God in the processes through which he ordinarily works, and this forgetfulness could not be better checked than by the miracles in which Christ did directly what is usually done indirectly. For example, when we eat our daily bread, we know all that man has done with the corn since the harvest, and seldom think of God who gave life to the seed, strength to the husbandman, and nutriment to the ground. But if we saw the processes condensed into one Divine act, as the multitude did on the hillside, when Jesus created bread, there would be a recognition of *God* which would afterwards find expression in the more ordinary events we saw. So with the healing of the diseased. Every such miracle revealed God as the Dispenser of health and the Giver of all blessings. 3. *It was a miracle having special significance for the spectators.* By means of it Christ taught more clearly the nature and design of the sabbath day. His foes had followed him from Jerusalem, with the resolute determination to destroy his influence and, if possible, to compass his death. Already they had detected his disciples in the violation of a rabbinical rule by rubbing corn in their hands on the sacred day. And the Lord had at once thrown over his followers the shield of his authority, as an Achilles would have done over the wounded Greeks, and had roundly declared that the " Son of man was Lord even of the sabbath day." They hoped now that he would publicly commit himself by some action in harmony with this declaration, and that so prejudice might be raised against his heresy. Show how bravely, wisely, and victoriously he met this, and taught for all generations that "it is lawful to do well on the sabbath day."

II. THE LESSONS JESUS TAUGHT. 1. *Neglecting opportunities for doing good is really doing evil.* Jesus Christ meant, by the alternative he put in the fourth verse, that if he did not do the good he was able to do for this poor sufferer, he did him a wrong. This is universally true. If at the judgment seat any appear who have done nothing for others and for their Lord, they will not be able to say, " We have done no harm ! " for they have injured themselves and others by neglect. The " wicked and slothful servant " was not condemned because he had done harm with his wealth and talent, but because he had done no good with them, having digged in the earth and hid his lord's money. 2. *Loving help is better than outward ritual.* The religious leaders of our Lord's day thought it of vital importance that the law of the Jewish sabbath— " Thou shalt do no manner of work "—should be observed with scrupulous exactness. But on that holy day Christ freely cured disease, and so taught the people the meaning of Jehovah's words, " I will have mercy, and not sacrifice." We are bound so to use our sacred day, associating acts of love and mercy with the services which sanctify its hours. 3. *Fear of personal consequences should never hinder the true servant of God.* What our Lord did on this occasion so aroused anger that we read in St. Luke's Gospel, " They were filled with madness ; " and " straightway they took counsel with the Herodians against him, how they might destroy him." Foreseeing this, he did not hesitate for a moment. May the fear of God in us also cast out all fear of man !—A. R.

Ver. 5 (first part).—*The Saviour's view of sin.* Describe the scene in the synagogue ; the wickedness of the plot formed by the Pharisees ; the compassion of our Lord, breaking through it as a mighty tide over a flimsy barrier ; the nobility of his teaching concerning the right use of the sabbath ; the healing of the man with the withered hand, etc. Our text graphically describes the feeling with which our Lord regarded his adversaries, and this deserves earnest consideration. At first the bold declaration, " He looked round about on them with anger," startles us ; for it seems in contradiction to his meekness and patience, which were perfect. But the explanation follows, " Being grieved for the hardness of their hearts." This shows the nature of his feeling. It reminds us of another occasion (Luke xiii. 34), when he spoke of Jerusalem in a tone of reproachful indignation ; but at once added the gentle words, " How often would I have gathered thy children together, as a hen doth gather her brood under her wings ! " On both occasions there was a blending of feelings which too often appear to us contradictory and incompatible. But it is possible to be " angry and sin not." Christ looked on the Pharisees, and was indignant at their hypocrisy and unscrupulous hatred ; but at once the feeling softened into pity as he thought of the insidious process of " hardening," which (as the Greek implies) was still going on, to end in hopeless callousness. With him warning was mingled with weeping ; as his disciple Paul afterwards spoke with tears of those who were " enemies of the cross of Christ " (Phil. iii. 18). In this, as in all things else, Christ has left us an example ; therefore we will endeavour first to—

I. UNDERSTAND THE COMPLEX FEELING HERE EXEMPLIFIED. We see in it two elements : 1. *Indignation against sin.* We are constantly coming in contact with the faults and sins of men. Our newspapers contain accounts of murders and cruelties, of thefts and treasons. Overreaching and fraud meet us in business ; slander and enmity lurk in society. Sensibility to such sins is not only not wrong, it is right and Christlike, and will become more keen as we grow in likeness to our Lord. It is an evil day for a man when he becomes callous even to those wickednesses which will never affect him personally; for this is distinctly contrary to the feeling which moved the Saviour to effect the world's redemption. As his disciples, we must never be good-naturedly easy about sin; we must not put on an air of worldly indifference; we must not attempt to hush feeling to rest, as if men were committed by a resistless fate to do "all these abominations" (Jer. vii. 10). The presence and prevalence of sin should stir within us strong moral indignation. 2. *Indignation tending to pity.* Anger should be swallowed up in grief. Indignation against wrong-doing, whether it affects ourselves or not, must not make us forget the deepest commiseration for the wrong-doer. Instead of this, too often, proud of our own virtue, we stand on our small moral pedestal, and look with scorn on those below it. Respected and honoured ourselves, with our robes to outward appearance unstained, we gather them about us, and sweep past some fallen brother or sister, and say, "Come not near unto me; for I am holier than thou!" The evil effects of this are manifold. We may drive others into deeper sin, because despair takes the place of hope in them; and we weaken ourselves in the service of our Lord. We can never benefit one whom we despise, or over whose fall we secretly exult; for nothing but love can so grasp the sinner as to lift him out of the horrible pit. Nor is it enough that we are indignant and angry with sin, so·that as passionate parents or denunciatory preachers we administer hasty reproof or indiscriminate punishment. Our faults will never conquer the faults of others. We must seek to deal with others as our Lord did. He loved the sinner, even when he hated the sin. His " gentleness hath made us great."

II. INCULCATION OF THE DUTIES HERE SUGGESTED. Let us point out a few considerations which may help us to cultivate the temper of mind we have discussed. 1. *Remember what sin is and what sin has done.* It caused the loss of Paradise; it brought about the sickness and sorrows we suffer; it made our work hard and unproductive; it created discord between man and his fellow, between man and his God; it seemed so woeful in itself and its results, to him who knows all things, that the Son of God gave himself as a sacrifice to save us from its power; it is so stupendous in its nature and awful in its issues that it is not a subject for selfish irritation, but one respecting which pity should blend with indignation. He who has done you a wanton wrong has injured himself far more than he can injure you. Therefore, beware of peevish anger and sinful revenge, remembering the words of the Master, "Blessed are the meek, . . . the merciful, . . . the peacemakers, . . . the persecuted for righteousness' sake." 2. *Reflect on what sin might have done for you.* How far character and reputation are affected by circumstances we cannot tell. But if we all have the same passions and evil propensities, our moral victory or defeat may depend largely on the degree of temptation which is permitted to assail us. We cherish a vindictive feeling against one who has offended his country's laws, but possibly our own criminality might have been as great but for the good providence of God. Certain classes of sin are so harshly and indiscriminately condemned that she who commits them is only left to plunge more deeply into sin and misery. But perhaps temptations were great, and home defences were few and frail, and the first wrong step was taken ignorantly; and then there seemed no going back. The story of the weeping penitent at our Saviour's feet is a rebuke to the want of pitifulness shown too often by the Christian Church. 3. *See the nobility of the feeling here portrayed.* To look with scorn, or with indifference, or with pleasure on sin, indicates a very low state of moral feeling. To burst forth with indignation against it is higher, but it is a sign of the youth of one's virtue, the manhood of which is seen in Jesus Christ. Forbearance and gentleness are among the higher Christian graces. We expect them of the cultured nation rather than of a savage horde, of a mature man than of a half-disciplined child. "He who ruleth his own spirit is greater than he that taketh a city." To control angry feeling within ourselves is the best means of helping us to control the evil deeds of others in our home and in the world.—A. R.

Ver. 5 (latter part).—"*Stretch forth thy hand!*" There was no kind of pain which Jesus could not relieve, no kind of grief he could not assuage. Those who were regarded as unclean were welcomed, and those whom none could cure he healed. Like the heavenly Father, of whom he was " the express Image," he was " kind to the unthankful and to the unworthy." We will regard the restoration of the man with the withered hand to health and soundness as a typical example of what our gracious Lord is ever doing. It reminds us of the following truths respecting him :—

I. OUR LORD GIVES STRENGTH FOR DAILY LABOUR. The apocryphal " Gospel according to the Hebrews " says that this sufferer was a mason by trade, and represents him as beseeching the Saviour to heal him in order that he might no longer be compelled to beg his daily bread. Be this as it may, he presented a piteous spectacle, for his limb was wasted, all power in it was gone as completely as if death had seized it, and he was without hope of cure. It was no small blessing to have that limb made in an instant "whole as the other ; " for henceforth honest industry was possible. We too may thank God if what we have has been sweetened by the toil which has made it our own. He gives us power to get wealth. It is his kindly providence which saves us from eating the bitter bread of charity and dependence.

II. THE LORD GIVES STRENGTH FOR CHRISTIAN SERVICE. Until we feel his touch and hear his voice, we are towards religious work what this man was towards daily work. Many in our congregations in this sense have their hand withered. Some cannot put forth their hand to give to the poor, to minister to the sick, to lead others to the Saviour, to "subscribe with their hands to the Lord," or even to lay hold on salvation. Their hand is withered. This paralysis or incapacity has its source in sin, in the selfishness which lives without love, in the pride which refuses to alter old habits, in the avarice which will hoard all it grasps, in the distrust of God that will make no venture. Only when God reveals the sin, and by his grace destroys it, can such be fit to serve him. But if Christ's voice is heard, there will come the stirring of new strength, the uprising of a new purpose in life, and the question will rise to heaven, " Lord, what wilt thou have me to do ? "

III. THE LORD OFTEN EFFECTS THIS IN HIS OWN HOUSE. As once Jesus was found in the synagogue, so now he is often found in the assembly of his people. After his resurrection he appeared amongst the praying disciples, and it was on those who had assembled together with one accord for prayer that the Holy Spirit came on the day of Pentecost. How often since, in our congregations, the power of the Lord has been present to heal us! Sin-laden souls have been relieved ; the perplexed have been guided aright; those morally weak have renewed their strength by waiting upon God ; hungry souls have been satisfied ; and those dead in trespasses and sins have been quickened to new life. Therefore, let us go to his house constantly, reverently, expectantly, and he will bless us "above all that we ask or think."

IV. THE LORD CONNECTS HIS HIGHER BLESSINGS WITH PROMPT AND FEARLESS OBEDIENCE TO HIS WORD. Directly Jesus saw the man with the withered hand, he said, " Stand forth ! " It was a simple command, but not easy under the circumstances to obey. Jesus was a comparative stranger ; the position of a crippled man, who was made the gazing-stock of a congregation, would be painful ; and the Pharisees might be angered by obedience. But on the man's part there was no hesitation. To the voice of authority he yielded at once, perhaps not without the stirring of new hope in his heart. This first act of obedience made the second more easy. After a few words to the Pharisees, our Lord spoke to him again, saying, " Stretch forth thy hand ! " He might have urged that it was impossible for him to do that, and that the attempt would only cover him with ridicule. But faith was growing fast and courage with it. He made the effort, and with the effort came the strength ; believing that through Christ he could do it, he did it, and his hand was restored "whole as the other." Many fail now through their want of this obedience of faith. They get no blessing because they neglect to obey the first command that comes to them. They want the assurance of salvation, the certain hope of heaven, and wonder that it does not come, though they have not obeyed the command. " Bow down in penitential prayer," or "give up the sin you love." Because they do not "stand forth in the midst," they do not hear the command, " Stretch forth thy hand ! " Be true to the impulse God gives, and then "to him that hath, to him shall be given yet more abundantly." In that synagogue Christ was both a Stone of stumbling and a sure Foundation, over which some stumbled and others rose to higher things. We too may leave his presence, like the Pharisees, hardened, or like this man who, believing and obeying, became ready for the work God gave him to do. Which shall it be ?—A. R.

Vers. 13, 14.—*The helpers of Jesus.*   Our Lord was fulfilling the prophecy Simeon had uttered concerning him.   From the cradle to the cross he was "set for the fall and rising again of many in Israel, . . . that the thoughts of many hearts may be revealed."   As a new element introduced into a chemical solution will detect and separate the elements already there, so did Christ appear in the moral world.   With growing distinctness his foes and friends became separate communities.   "He called unto him" those who were ready for service, while those who were hostile became more pronounced in their hatred.   The Pharisaic party, which began by the denial of his authority, tried next to disparage his character, and finally plotted his destruction. It is the tendency of sin thus to go onward toward deeper guilt.   He who "stands in the way of sinners" at last "sits in the seat of the scornful."   So unscrupulous had the Pharisees become that (ver. 6) they even took counsel with the Herodians to destroy him.   Professedly patriotic and orthodox, they united with the friends of the usurper; and (as so often since) priests and tyrants combined against the Christ.   See how Christ met this hostility.   He might have overwhelmed his foes by superhuman power, but he resolutely refused to use force against them (Matt. iv. 8—10; xxvi. 53, 54).   He might have defied them, and so hastened the crisis which ultimately came; but "his hour had not yet come," for he had a ministry yet to fulfil.   Hence he gave himself up to more private work, avoiding perils, although he never feared them, and labouring amongst the poor and obscure.   Around him he gathered a few faithful ones, "that they might be with him, and that he might send them forth to preach."   This text gives us some thoughts.

I. ON PREPARATION FOR SERVICE.   See how our Lord prepared himself and his disciples.   "He goeth up into a mountain"—an expression which in the Gospels implies the withdrawal of our Lord from the people for the purpose of prayer.   This preceded all his great deeds and sufferings, as was exemplified in the temptation and in the agony.   It was fitting that the disciples should be appointed in a place of prayer. Apart from the world and near to God, we are ready to hear our Master's words and receive his commission.   From the height of communion with God we should come down to our work (Isa. lii. 7).   His requirement of spiritual fitness for spiritual work is shown by his constant refusal of the testimony of demons (ver. 12): "He straitly charged *them* that they should not make him known."   This verse, immediately preceding our text, makes a suggestive contrast with it.   He recoiled from an ambiguous confession.   As the Holy One, he would not suffer the unclean to bear witness to him. The testimony was true, but the spirit that gave it was evil.   These disciples were "ordained," or more correctly (Revised Version) "appointed," that they might be with him, and that he might send them forth to preach.   The former was the preparation for the latter.   Only those who are in communion with Jesus can truly bear witness for him to the world.

II. ON ADVANTAGE IN FELLOWSHIP.   The Lord himself cared for the sympathy and co-operation of others.   Even in his direst agony he would not be without it (ch. xiv. 34).   Much more was it necessary for his disciples to be associated in a common brotherhood; the beauty of which appears again and again to those who study the Acts and the Epistles.   In the fellowship of the Church, one supplements the weakness of another; numbers increase enthusiasm and afford hope to the timid; intercourse with others removes one-sidedness of character, etc.   See the teaching of St. Paul about the "body of Christ," and "the temple of the Holy Spirit," in which Christians are living stones, mutually dependent, and all resting on Christ.

III. ON DIVERSITIES AMONG DISCIPLES.   Jesus chose "twelve" for special work—a number probably selected as a reminder that they were primarily commissioned to be ambassadors to the twelve tribes, and as a type of the perfection of the redeemed Church (Rev. vii.).   But even in that comparatively small company, what diversities of gifts!   Some of them are indicated even in the brief list of their names given here by St. Mark.   We see the Rock-man, Peter; "the beloved disciple," John; the fiery "sons of thunder;" the guileless Nathanael; the zealot Simon; and the traitor Judas. Each had his special gift and sphere.   And still there are "diversities of gifts" amongst the Lord's disciples.

IV. ON POSSIBILITIES OF PERIL.   Judas Iscariot lived with Jesus, was called by him, possessed miraculous gifts, preached the gospel to others; but he died a traitor and a suicide. To fill a spiritual office, and yet to be careless of our own spiritual life, is fatal. "Wherefore let him that thinketh he standeth take heed lest he fall." —A. R.

Vers. 7—35.—*Retirement.* In the calm and successful prosecution of his work, Jesus has excited various feelings in the minds of the different classes around him. He has wrought many miracles—all of them miracles of mercy; almost all, so far as recorded, miracles of healing. Of necessity his presence is hailed by the throngs of needy and suffering ones, and "his name is as ointment poured forth" to the multitudes who have proved his power to heal. These cannot be restrained from publishing his fame abroad, though he has begged them to be silent, for he sees but too plainly the hindrance to his usefulness which a blaze of popularity would cause. In the course of his teaching he has made the Pharisees to blush more than once; and the popular movement which he seems likely to excite has stirred up the fears or the jealousies of the court party—"the Herodians," who join their own political antagonists in their opposition to him, and they together plot his destruction. His relatives, "friends," including the highly honoured one, "his mother, and his brethren," are excited with fear that "he is beside himself," for he allows not himself time to "so much as eat bread." "Scribes from Jerusalem," learned in the Law, the trained expounders of its sacred truths, and the authoritative adjudicators in matters of dispute, pass their judgment and verdict in explanation of the astounding facts which they cannot or dare not deny. "He is possessed," they say, "by the very 'prince of the devils.' He is the tool, the agent of Beelzebub himself, and 'by the prince of the devils casteth he out the devils.'" This is truly a most ingenious though the most wicked of all explanations; a very blasphemy, ascribing the work of "the Holy Spirit" to "an unclean spirit," and placing Jesus in the lowest category of all—lower than the lowest. It affirms him to be the agent of the arch-demon, working his behests, the servant of the devil of devils. And if possession by an evil spirit is the consequence and punishment of evil work, as was the current opinion, he is surely the worst of the bad. All this needs adjustment. The anger of some, the timidity, the fears, the indiscreet zeal, the error, the false views, and the wickedness of others, must all be corrected. For this purpose he, "with his disciples," withdraws "to the sea," where, "because of the crowd, lest they should throng him," he orders that in future "a little boat should wait on him;" by which means he can escape the press, and either teach from the boat or sail away for rest and quiet. At even-tide "he goeth up into the mountain," where he continues "all night in prayer to God;" needful in the midst of so much pressure and excitement, and most fitting in anticipation of the great work of the morrow. Then, when the morning breaks, he calls his disciples to him, from whom he chooses twelve, "that they might be with him," for his own comfort and for purposes of training for future service in his kingdom, "and that he might send them forth to preach, and to have authority to cast out devils, and to heal all manner of disease, and all manner of sickness." These "he named apostles," and "appointed," and "sent forth," and "charged them." Then, with awful withering words, he silences the scribes, first by argument, showing that on their own ground the divided kingdom "hath an end;" then by pointing to the "eternal sin" which he committeth who thus "shall blaspheme against the Holy Spirit," and who "hath never forgiveness." And now, turning to his anxious relatives, he asks and answers the question, "Who is my mother and my brethren?" Breaking loose from the bonds of mere natural relationship, he declares that he holds the closest alliance with "whosoever shall do the will of God." From all which every true disciple treading in his Master's steps, and hearkening to his Master's teaching, may learn: 1. The wisdom of frequent with-drawal from the excitements of life into calm, quieting intercourse with God in prayer, to the cooling contemplation of the Divine works, and the humbling commu-nion with his own soul. 2. The sacredness of holy companionship; and, if he is called to teach great truths, the wisdom of gathering around him a few sympathetic spirits, and sharing with them his work and honour for the general good. 3. The necessity for keeping his mind sensitively alive to the teachings of the Holy Spirit, lest, resisting, he grieve him, and quench the only light by which the path of life may be found. 4. To learn the terrible peril to which he exposes himself who "puts darkness for light." 5. And joyfully to see the high calling which is of God, the close alliance with the

Lord Christ which is secured to him who keeps the commandments of God, concerning whom the Lord says, " The same is my brother, and sister, and mother."—G.

Vers. 1—6.—*Sabbath observance.* I. THE SABBATH MAY BE OBSERVED TO THE LETTER WHILE BROKEN IN THE SPIRIT. Here were men watching to see whether a man would *dare* to do a loving deed! The letter, which can never be more than the expression of the spirit, must be kept at all costs—except that of the literalists. There are pedants who will quarrel with a great writer because he departs from the "rules of grammar," forgetting that grammar is but a collection of observations of the best that has been written. So there are ritualists who will slander a good man because he neglects rites for the sake of going to the root of all rites.
II. CENSORIOUSNESS THE CERTAIN SYMPTOM OF SELF-DISCONTENT. Why do we want to find fault with others? Because we are not satisfied with ourselves. We must either feed on a good conscience or on the semblance of it. And it *seems* that we are better than others whenever we can put them in an unfavourable light.
III. EMULATION AND ENVY ARE NEAR AKIN. We are jealous of great successes. Jealousy is natural enough. It depends on the will whether the effects be good or evil on ourselves. A noble deed! let me seek to imitate it and share the blessedness of it: this is good. A noble deed! let me extinguish the author of it, who shames me: this of the devil, devilish; of hell, hellish. The ideal Christian and the ideal Pharisee are in eternal opposition. Goodness produces one of two effects in us—we long to embrace it and possess it, or to kill it.—J.

Vers. 7—12.—*Testimony of evil to goodness.* I. ITS SINCERITY. We see many coming to Christ who thought they could get an immediate good from him. Others kept aloof who doubted what good could come, what evil might come, from the intercourse. The devils, whether for good or evil, "rush to Jesus." Whenever there is such a " rush," something significant is stirring.
II. ITS IRRESISTIBLE CHARACTER. There are men, there are movements, which are advertised by the evil they elicit from the latent depths of the heart. Observe the man who is hated, and *by whom ;* observe the man who is loved, and *by whom.* Note the centre of attraction, and *for what sort of people ;* the centre of repulsion, and *for what sort of people ;* and you have a clue to important truths. Christ is illustrated by all these rules. Who were they who approached him in love then? who now? What were the instincts arrayed against him—then and now ?—J.

Vers. 13—19.—*The need of missionaries.* I. POPULARIZERS OF GREAT DOCTRINES ARE NECESSARY in every branch of science, art, literature, religion. Where would the sublime doctrine we call the gospel have been, as an influence, had there not been found men to make it "current coin "?
II. SECOND-HAND INSTRUMENTALITY PLAYS A LARGE PART IN THE SPIRITUAL WORLD. Few are the leaders or generals, many the officers, multitudinous the rank and file; but every soldier who is in living contact with the Leader's spirit may and will work marvels.
III. FEEBLENESS BECOMES STRENGTH WHEN INSPIRED BY ORIGINAL FORCE. These were humble men, yet their names live. They were reflections of Christ, as he was the Reflection of the power and love of God.
IV. THERE IS A MORAL MIXTURE IN EVERY RELIGIOUS MOVEMENT. A Judas among the apostles. Something of a Judas even in every apostle's heart. Light contends with darkness in the twilight before each great historical dawn. The characters of great religious reformers have often been mixed and dubious. There is a traitor in every camp, a doubtful element in every good man's life.—J.

Vers. 20—30.—*The sin against the Holy Spirit.* I. THE CHARGE AGAINST JESUS. He holds to Beelzebub, and by the chief of demons casts out demons. 1. It was absurd; but absurd arguments readily satisfy passion and hate and those who have no care for the truth. They accused the Saviour, in short, of a self-contradiction in thought and action, which was a moral impossibility. 2. It was wicked. It had the worst element of the lie in it—it denied the truth within them.

II. THE WORST DEGREE OF SIN. Sin has its scale, its climax. There are sins of instinct and of passion and of ignorance. When there is little light to be guided by there is little light to sin against. The next step in sin is where there is deliberation before the wrong is done. Last and worst is where not only the deliberate judgment is gone against, but the attempt is made to deny the principle of judgment in the soul itself. The hands of the watch move backwards; the lamp flags with the very abundance of oil; the man's soul dies. Over against the words "Repent! be forgiven!" stand these, "Irreclaimable! unforgivable!"—J.

Vers. 31—35.—*Kinship to Jesus.* I. FIRST THAT WHICH IS NATURAL, AFTERWARDS THAT WHICH IS SPIRITUAL. This is one order. Our spiritual being is built up on a natural basis. Slowly the bud of the higher being unfolds from the plant of earthly root. Through the home to the Church; by the love of mother and brother and sister, to the love of God and of all.

II. FIRST THE SPIRITUAL, AFTERWARDS THE NATURAL. This is the order in another way. The end of our being is in the spiritual; this is its dignity, its reflection of the Divine. It claims the first thought, other things being equal. When friends stand in the way of duty, between us and the light of truth, we must be true to the higher self. It may seem a stern rule, until we find that every low affection we renounced for the higher is given back to us bathed in a new glory.—J.

Vers. 1—6. Parallel passages: Matt. xii. 9—14; Luke vi. 6—11.—*The man with the withered hand.* I. THE NATURE OF THE DISEASE. It was a case of severe paralysis of the hand—the *right* hand, as St. Luke, with a physician's accuracy, informs us. The sinews were shrunken, and the hand shrivelled and dried up. And yet we owe to St. Mark's great particularity in narration and minuteness of detail a piece of information that one might rather have expected from the professional skill of "the beloved physician," Luke. St. Luke, as well as St. Matthew, uses an adjective (ξηρὰ, equivalent to dry) to describe, in a general way, the state of the diseased member; but St. Mark employs the participle of the perfect passive (ἐξηραμμένην, equivalent to having been dried up), which furnishes a hint as to the origin of the ailment. While from the expression of the former two evangelists we might conclude that the ailment was congenital—that the man was born with it; we are enabled, by the term made use of in the Gospel before us, to correct that conclusion, and to trace this defect of the hand as the result of disease or of accident.

II. VARIETY OF DISEASES. The multitude of "ills that flesh is heir to" is truly wonderful; the variety of diseases that afflict poor frail humanity is astonishing. Whatever be the place of our abode, or wherever we travel, we find our fellow-creatures subject to weakness, pains, physical defects, wasting disease, pining sickness, and bodily ailments, too many and too various to enumerate. No continent, no island, no zone of earth, is exempt. The greatest salubrity of climate, though it may somewhat diminish the number, does not do away with cases of the kind. Though our lot be cast amid the mildness of Southern climes, or under the clear bright sky of Eastern lands; though our dwelling-place be—

"Far from the winters of the West,
By every breeze and season blest;"

still we find ourselves within the reach of those infirmities that seem the common lot of man. We cannot read far in the Gospels, or trace the ministry of our Lord to much length, until we find him surrounded by and ministering to whole troops of invalids and impotent folk.

III. SOURCE OF ALL DISEASES. If there were no sin there would be no sorrow, and if there were no sin there would be no sickness. The effects of sin extend to both body and soul. Sin has brought disease as well as death into the world, as we read, "By one man sin entered into the world, and death by sin; and so death hath passed upon all men, for that all have sinned." As death has thus passed upon all men, so disease, more or less aggravated, at one time or other, has become the lot of all; for what are pain and disease and sickness but forerunners, remote it may be, of death, and for-feitures of sin? The original punitive sentence was not *Moth tumath,* "Thou shalt be put to death," that is, immediately or instantaneously; but *Moth tamuth*, "Thou shalt die," namely, by a process now commenced, and, though slow, yet sure; for sin has planted the germ of death in the system. It is as though, simultaneously with the breath of life, the process of decay and death began, part after part wasting away in consequence of disease or in the so-called course of nature, till the vital spark at last becomes extinct, and " the dust returns to the earth as it was." A heathen poet preserves the remnant of an old tradition, which, like many of the traditions of heathenism, is evidently a dispersed and distorted ray from the light of revelation. He tells us that a crowd of wasting diseases invaded this earth's inhabitants in consequence of crime; while a Christian poet speaks of that lazar-house which sin has erected on our earth, "wherein are laid numbers of all diseased, all maladies, . . . and where dire are the tossings, deep the groans." But for transgression manhood would have remained in all its original health and vigour and perfection, like "Adam, the goodliest man of men since born his sons;" and womanhood would have retained all the primitive grace and loveliness and beauty that bloomed in "the fairest of her daughters, Eve."

IV. TIME AND PLACE OF THE CURE. The time was the sabbath day; and this was one of the seven miracles which our Lord performed on the sabbath. Of these St. Mark records three—the cure of the demoniac at Capernaum, the cure of fever in the case of Peter's mother-in-law, and the cure of the withered hand; the former two recorded in the first chapter of this Gospel, and the last in the passage under consideration. Two more of the sabbath-day miracles are recorded by St. Luke—the cure of the woman afflicted with the spirit of infirmity, and also of the man who had the disease of dropsy; the former in the thirteenth and the latter in the fourteenth chapter of St. Luke's Gospel. Besides these, two more are recorded by St. John—the recovery of the impotent man at the pool of Bethesda, and the restoration of sight to the man born blind; the former in the fifth and the latter in the ninth chapter of St. John's Gospel. Our Lord had vindicated his disciples for plucking the ears of corn on the sabbath; he had now to vindicate himself for the miracle of healing, which he was about to perform also on the sabbath. The place where he was going to perform this miracle was the synagogue.

V. PERSONS PRESENT AT THE PERFORMANCE OF THE CURE. This is a most important item in the narrative, and a most important element in the transaction. There was a multitude present, and that multitude consisted of foes as well as friends. It could not, therefore, be said that the thing was done in a corner, or that it was done only in the presence of friends, with whom collusion or connivance might possibly be suspected. The persons, then, in whose presence this cure was effected were the worshippers on that sabbath day in the synagogue—a goodly number, no doubt, comprehending not only those who assembled ordinarily for the sabbath service, but many more drawn together by the rumours about the great Miracle-worker and in expectation of some manifestation of his wonder-working power. But besides these ordinary worshippers and these curiosity-mongers, as perhaps we may designate them, there were others—the scribes and Pharisees, as we learn from St. Luke—whose motive was malignancy, and whose business on that occasion was espionage. They kept watching our Lord closely and intently (παρετήρουν) to see if he should heal on the sabbath; not in admiration of his wondrous power, nor in gratitude for his marvellous goodness, but in order to find some ground of accusation against him.

VI. OBJECTION TO THE PERFORMANCE OF THE CURE ON THE SABBATH. In pursuance of their plan, they anticipated our Lord, as we learn from St. Matthew, with the question, "Is it lawful to heal on the sabbath day?" Our Lord, in reply, as we are informed in the same Gospel, appealed to their feelings of humanity and to the exercise of mercy which men usually extend even to a dumb animal—a sheep, which, if it fall into a pit on the sabbath, is laid hold of and lifted out. The superiority of a man to a sheep justifies a still greater exercise of mercy, even on the sabbath. But to their captious and ensnaring question he made further answer, replying, as was his wont, by a counter-question, "Is it lawful to do good on the sabbath day, or to do evil? to save life, or to kill?" The alternative here is between doing good and doing evil, or, putting an extreme case, between saving a life and destroying it (ἀπολέσαι in St. Luke). We may observe, in passing, that the received text, which reads τί in this passage of St. Luke's Gospel, admits one or other of the two following renderings, according to the punctuation: either (1) "I will ask you, further, *What is allowable on the sabbath*—to do good or to do evil?" or (2) "I will ask you, further, *a certain thing: Is it allowable on the sabbath to do good or to do evil?*" The first is favoured by being nearly the same as the Peshito-Syriac, which is to the effect, "I will ask you what is it allowable to do on the sabbath? What is good or what is bad?" But the critical editors, Lachmann, Tischendorf, and Tregelles, read εἰ, and the latter two have the present of the verb, viz. ἐπερωτῶ. Of course the translation of the text thus constituted is, "I ask you, *further, if* it is allowable on the sabbath to do good or to do evil—to save a life or to destroy?" With this the Vulgate coincides, as follows:—*Interrogo vos, si licet sabbatis benefacere an male: animam salvam facere, an perdere?* This was a home-thrust to these deceitful, wicked men who, while he was preparing to restore a human being to the full enjoyment of life in the unimpeded and unimpaired use of all his members, were murderously plotting the destruction of the great Physician's own life. No wonder they were silenced, as St. Mark tells us, for they must have been conscience-stricken, at least in some measure. At all events, they were confuted and confounded, but not converted, though they maintained a stolid, sullen silence. The question of our Lord left them in a dilemma. They could not deny that it was disallowable to do evil on any day, still more on the sabbath, for the holiness of the day aggravated the guilt; and yet they were seeking means of inflicting the greatest evil—even the destruction of life. They could not deny that it was allowable to do good on any day, especially on the sabbath; for the good deed, if not enhanced by, was fully in keeping with, the goodness of the day on which it was done. They found themselves shut up to the inevitable conclusion that it was not unlawful to do good on the sabbath day. And so our Lord turns to the performance of that good act on which he had determined, but which they in heart disallowed, notwithstanding their enforced silence or their seeming to give consent.

VII. MODE OF PREPARATION FOR THE CURE. He commanded the man who had his hand withered to stand forth. This was a somewhat trying ordeal for that poor disabled man. Standing forward, he became the gazing-stock of all eyes. He thereby made himself and his peculiar defect conspicuous. He thus practically confessed his helplessness and eagerness for relief. There he stood, an object of heartless curiosity to some, an object of contempt to others; the scrutinizing looks of some, the scowling glances of others, were fixed upon him. Few like to be thus looked out of countenance. Besides, in addition to all this, he was publicly expressing confidence in the ability of the Physician, and so exposing himself to like condemnation. And then there was the contingency of failure. What of that? The man must have had some, yea, much, moral courage to brave all this. Thus it is with all who will come to Christ with earnestness of spirit and manfully confess him. False shame must be laid aside. The scowl of enemies, perhaps the sneer of friends, the scorn of the world, may be calculated on and contemned; much must be done and dared in this direction. Yet the true confessor will not shrink from all this, and more. His spirit is—

> "I'm not ashamed to own my Lord
> Or to defend his cause,
> Maintain the glory of his cross,
> And honour all his laws."

VIII. OUR LORD'S LOOK WHEN PROCEEDING TO PERFORM THE CURE. The man was now standing forth in the midst, with the eyes of all present fastened on him. Our Lord, before actually speaking the word of healing power, looked round upon the persons present—upon *all* of them, as St. Luke informs us. There was deep meaning in that look. The expression of that look needed an interpreter, and so St. Mark tells us that the feelings which that intent and earnest look into every man's face gave expression to were twofold—there was anger and there was grief at the same time. This *anger* was righteous indignation; as the apostle says, "Be angry and sin not." This anger was incurred by the wicked malevolence which the Saviour, in his omniscience, read in the dark hearts of those dark-visaged men; for, as St. Luke reminds us, "he knew their thoughts," or rather their reasonings. But there was *grief* as well.
1. Though the compound verb συλλυπούμενος is interpreted by some as identical with the simple form, yet the prepositional element cannot be thus overlooked, but must add

somewhat to the meaning of the whole. 2. This additional significancy, however, may be variously understood. The preposition σύν may mean (1) that he grieved with and so within himself—in his own spirit; or (2) that his grief was simultaneous with his anger and accompanied it; or (3) that, angry though he was, he grieved nevertheless or sympathized with them. The ground of this complex feeling was the hardness of their hearts. The root-word denotes a kind of stone, then a chalkstone, also a *callus*, or substance exuding from fractured bones and joining their extremities; and the derivative noun, which occurs here, is the process of reuniting by a *callus*, then hardening, hardness, callousness; while the verb signifies to petrify, harden, or make callous. This hard-heartedness is thus a gradual, not an instantaneous, formation. It is a process which may commence with some small omission or trifling commission; but in either case it continues unless checked by grace—the once soft becoming hard, and the hard yet harder, till it is consummated in fearful obduracy of heart or complete callousness of the moral nature.

IX. THE CURE PERFORMED. "Stretch forth thy hand!" is the command; and as the aorist imperative, used here, generally denotes a speedy execution of the order given, like o҆ phrase, "Have it done!" the command amounted to "Stretch forth thy hand *at once!*" How unreasonable this command, at the first blush of the matter, appears! Many a time the attempt had been made, but in vain; many a time before he had tried to stretch it out, but that withered hand had refused obedience to the volitions of the will. Was not the Saviour's command, then, strange and unnatural in bidding him extend a hand that had long lost the proper power of motion; a hand crippled and contracted in every joint, shrunken and shrivelled in every part—in a word, completely lifeless and motionless? And yet this man did not cavil nor question; he did not doubt nor delay. Soon as the mandate came he made the effort; soon as the command was uttered, hard as it must have seemed, he essayed compliance; and no sooner is compliance attempted than the cure is effected, Divine power accompanying the command, or rather both acting with simultaneous effect. Thus his word was a word of power, as we read, "He sent his word and healed them." And now the tendons are unbound, the nerves act, the muscles are suppled, the vital fluid flows once more along the reopened channel. Thus it was brought back again to what it once was; in power, appearance, and use it was restored to its original condition, whole and sound.

X. CONSEQUENT ON THE CURE WAS AN UNNATURAL COALITION. The enemies were filled with folly, wicked and senseless folly (ἀνοίας), but not madness, as it is generally understood, for that would properly be μανίας. They felt humiliated in the presence of so many people. Their pride was humbled, for they were silenced; their logic was shown to be shallow, for with them "to do or not to do"—that was the question; but our Lord showed them that "to do good or not to do good, while not to do good was tantamount to doing evil," was in reality the 'question; and so they were put to shame. They were disappointed, moreover, for they were deprived of any ground whereon to found an accusation, because, in the mode of effecting the cure, there had been no touch, no contact of any kind, no external means used—nothing but a word, so that even the letter of the Law had been in no way infringed. In their desperation they communed one with another, held a council, or, as St. Mark informs us more explicitly, "took or made counsel with the Herodians." Misfortune, according to an old saw, brings men into acquaintance with strange associates, and never more so than on this occasion. In theology the Herodians, as far as they held any theological opinions, fraternized with the Sadducees, the latitudinarians of that day ; in politics they were adherents of Herod Antipas, and so advocates of the Roman domination. To both these the Pharisees were diametrically opposed. Yet now they enter into an unholy alliance with those who were at once their political opponents and religious antagonists. Nor was this the only time that extremes met and leagued themselves against Christ and his cause. Herod and Pilate mutually sacrificed their feelings of hostility, and confederated against the Lord and his Anointed. It has been thought strange that Luke, who from his acquaintance with Manaen, the foster-brother of Herod the Tetrarch, had special facilities for knowledge of the Herods, their family relations, and friends, omits this alliance of the Herodians with the Pharisees ; while it has been surmised that, from that very acquaintance, sprang a delicacy of feeling that made the evangelist loth to record their hostility to Christ.

XI. LESSONS TO BE LEARNT FROM THIS SECTION. 1. The first lesson we learn here is the multitude of witnesses that are watching the movements of the disciples of Christ; for as it was with the Master so is it with ourselves. The eye of God is upon us, according to the language of ancient piety, "Thou God seest us;" the eyes of angels are upon us to aid us with their blessed and beneficent ministries; the eyes of good men are upon us to cheer us onward and help us forward; the eyes of bad men are upon us to mark our halting and take advantage of our errors; the eyes of Satan and his servants—evil angels as well as evil men—are upon us to entrap us by their machinations and gloat over our fall. How vigilant, then, must we be, watching and praying that we fall not into, nor succumb to, temptation! 2. In every case of spiritual withering we know the Physician to whom we must apply. Has our faith been withering, or has it lost aught of its freshness? we pray him to help our unbelief and increase our faith. Has our love been withering and languishing? we must seek from him a renewal of the love of our espousals, and meditate on him till in our hearts there is rekindled a flame of heavenly love to him who first loved us. Is our zeal for the Divine glory, or our activity in the Divine service, withering and decaying? then we must seek grace to repent and do our first works, stretching out at Christ's command the withered hand to Christian work, whether it be the resumption of neglected duty, or the rendering of needful help, or relieving the wants of the indigent, or wiping away the tears of the sorrowing, or usefulness of whatever kind in our day and generation, or honest endeavours to leave the world better than we found it. 3. It is well worthy of notice that if we are doing no good we are doing evil; nay, if we are doing nothing, we are doing evil; still more, if we are not engaged at least in helping to save, we are guilty of abetting, if not actually causing destruction. Let us, then, be "not slothful in business; fervent in spirit; serving the Lord." 4. The mercifulness of the Saviour is an encouragement to faith and obedience. With his anger against sin was mingled grief for sinners' hardness of heart. Many a tear he shed for perishing souls in the days of his flesh. He dropped a tear at the grave of a beloved friend—only dropped a silent tear (ἐδάκρυσεν); but over the impenitent inhabitants of a doomed city his eyes brimmed over with tears and he wept aloud, for we there read ἔκλαυσεν. In this restoration of the withered hand we have evidence of the Saviour's gracious disposition, a warrant to take him at his word, and a guarantee that when he gives a precept he will grant power for its performance. 5. Divine power was here displayed in human weakness. The sinner has a warrant to believe, and in responding to that warrant he realizes Divine help; in his willingness to obey he experiences Divine power; in his earnest entreating Christ for strength to believe, he is actually and already exercising a reliance on Christ for salvation. Divine power harmonized with the faith of this afflicted man, and the Saviour's strength made itself manifest in his obedience. And yet faith lays claim to no inherent power; it is, on the contrary, human weakness laying hold of Divine strength. Its potency is derived entirely from that on which it rests; believing the Word of God, trusting in the Son of God, relying on aid from the Spirit of God, it surmounts every obstacle, overcomes every difficulty, and triumphs over every enemy. It is a principle that develops most wonderful potencies for good; in its exercise we cross the borderland that lies between the humanly impossible and heavenly possibilities; for "what is the victory that overcometh the world? Even our faith."—J. J. G.

Vers. 7—12. Parallel passage: Matt. xii. 15—21.—*Popularity of Christ on the increase.* I. THE POPULARITY OF JESUS. It was ever increasing, as is proved by this passage. A great multitude followed him from Galilee in the north; from Judæa and its capital in a central position; and from Idumæa in the far south, situated as it was between Judæa, Arabia, and Egypt; then from Peræa, east of the Jordan; the people of Tyre and Sidon also in the north-west;—all these, attracted by the fame of what Jesus was doing, flocked unto him. So great were the multitude and pressure that he directed his disciples to procure a little boat to keep close to him in order to escape the crowding (διὰ τὸν ὄχλον) and consequent confusion.

II. HIS POWER TO HEAL. This appears to be as yet the main attraction. The miracles of healing were abundant, so much so that the afflicted sufferers actually fell against him (ἐπιπίπτειν), that by the contact their plagues might be removed. Unclean spirits also, wherever they saw him, kept falling down before him, crying out, "Thou art the Son of God."

III. PECULIARITY OF THE SYRIAC VERSION IN THIS PLACE. It strangely combines the two last classes in its rendering, namely, "Those that had plagues of unclean spirits, as often as they saw him, kept falling down before him." Our Lord, however, invariably reprobated and rejected their testimony, as if there were something insidious in it or injurious to his cause.

IV. THE PHYSICAL HEALTH RESTORED TO SO MANY AFFLICTED BODIES WAS A GUARANTEE OF SPIRITUAL HEALTH FOR THE SOUL. In all the ages, and in all the annals of medical science, and in all the countries of the world, we have account of one Physician, and only one, who was able to lay his hand on the aching head and diseased heart of suffering humanity, bringing immediate cure and effectual relief. No malady could resist his healing power, no sickness withstand his touch, and no illness remain incurable once he but spoke the word. No disease, however deep-seated in the system, or deadly in its nature, or inveterate from long duration, could baffle his skill or defy his power. Whether it was palsy, or dropsy, or asthma, or convulsions, or ulceration, or bloody issue, or fever, or even consumption, or, what was still worse, leprosy itself,—whatever the form of disease might be, he cured it. Persons labouring under organic defects— the deaf, the dumb, the blind, the lame—were brought to him, and he removed all those defects. Mental ailments also, as lunacy and demoniacal possession, all were relieved by him. Sometimes it was a word, sometimes a touch, again some external appliance, not as a remedy but to act as a conductor, or to show a connection instituted between the operator and the patient, but, whatever was the plan adopted, the power never failed to produce the desired effect. Now, whatever he did in this way to the body is proof positive of his ability and willingness to do the same and more for the soul. We may be diseased with sin so as to be loathsome in our own eyes and morally infectious to our neighbours and acquaintances; we may be leprous with sin so as to be cut off from the fellowship of the saints and the communion of the holy; we may be under the ban of man and the curse of heaven; yet if we approach this great Physician of soul as well as body, confiding in his power and trusting in his mercy, we shall obtain, and that without fail, healing and health for our diseased spirits and sin-sick souls. Thousands alive this day can testify from actual happy experience to the healing power of Jesus' word, the cleansing efficacy of his blood, and the renewing, purifying, and sanctifying influences of his Spirit. Millions this day in the realms of bliss above are enjoying the health and the happiness, the brightness and the beauty, the purity and perfection of that upper sanctuary, though on earth the diseases of their souls had been of the most desperate character—utterly incurable had it not been for the mercy and grace of this great Physician. And he is still the same—"the same, yesterday, to-day, and for ever," and able as ever to "save to the uttermost all that come unto God by him."

V. A RECONCILIATION. It is thought by some that a discrepancy exists between the fourth verse of the fifty-third chapter of Isaiah and the seventeenth verse of the eighth chapter of St. Matthew. But if we take the first clause of each verse as referring to bodily diseases, and the second clause to the diseases of the mind or soul, we shall have an instructive harmony in place of an insuperable difficulty or seeming discrepancy. The verbs will then be most suitable and appropriate: the *nasa* of the Hebrew, being general in its meaning, to take up in any way, or to take up in order to take away, will correspond in its generality of signification to ἔλαβε, to take in any way; while *saval*, for which ἐβάστασε of St. Matthew is an exact equivalent, is to bear as a burden. "Thus," says Archbishop Magee, in his invaluable work on the Atonement, "are Isaiah and Matthew perfectly reconciled; the first clause in each relating to *diseases removed*, and the second to *sufferings endured.*" Thus too there is a close correlation between the removal of the diseases of the body and the expiation of the sins of our souls.—J. J. G.

Vers. 13—19. Parallel passages: Matt. x. 2—4; Luke vi. 12—19.—*The choosing of the twelve.* 1. THE CHOICE AND ITS OBJECT. The Saviour ascends the mountain that was near at hand, probably *Karun Hattin*, "and calls to him whom he wished." At once they went off away (ἀπό), leaving other things, and turning to him as their sole object. Of these he appointed, or ordained—though the original word is more simple, viz. "he made"—twelve for a threefold purpose: (1) to "be with him," to keep him company, assisting him and sympathizing with him; (2) to be his messengers to men, heralding the good news of salvation; and (3) to alleviate miraculously human misery—curing diseases and expelling demons.

II. THE LIST OF NAMES. The order and meaning of the names require only a few remarks. The twelve are distributed into three classes. Simon, the Hearer, whom our Lord surnamed the Rock-man, heads the first class; next to him were James, the son of Zebedee, and John his brother, both of whom were surnamed Boanerges, "Sons of Thunder," that is, *bene* (*oa* equivalent to *e*) *regesh;* and Andrew. The second class is headed by Philip; then comes Bartholomew, which means the son of Tolmai, the word being a patronymic—in all probability the person meant was Nathanael, the proper name of the same; also Matthew and Thomas. The third class begins with James the son of Alphæus; then Judas, surnamed Thaddæus, or Lebbæus, the Courageous; and Simon the Kananite, that is, the Zealot, not a Canaanite; while Judas Iscariot, that is, the man of Kerioth, the traitor, is the last in every list.—J. J. G.

Vers. 20—30. Parallel passages: Matt. xii. 22—37; Luke xi. 14—23.—*Mistaken friends and malignant foes.* I. MISTAKEN FRIENDS. 1. *The connection.* Between the appointment of the apostles and the transactions here narrated several important matters intervened. There was the sermon on the mount, recorded in the Gospel of St. Matthew, chs. v.—vii.; and an abridgment or modification of the same repeated in the Gospel of St. Luke, ch. vi. 17—49. Next followed the events recorded throughout the seventh chapter of St. Luke, and which were as follows :—The cure of the centurion's servant; the restoration to life of the widow's son of Nain; the message sent by John the Baptist; the dinner in the house of Simon, with the anointing by a woman who had been a sinner. Previously to this last had been the doom pronounced on the impenitent cities, narrated by St. Matthew in ch. xi. towards the end; the second circuit through Galilee, of which we read in Luke viii., at the beginning; while immediately before, and indeed leading to, the circumstances mentioned in this section was the healing of a blind and dumb demoniac. 2. *The concourse.* Our Lord had just returned, not into the house of some believer, as Euthymius thinks; nor into the house in which he made his abode while at Capernaum, as this meaning would require the article; but more generally, "to home," as in ch. ii. 1. And no sooner is his return reported than he is followed by a great concourse of people. Again a crowd, as on several previous occasions, especially that mentioned in ch. ii. 2, when "there was no room to receive them, no, not so much as about the door," pressed after him. Such was the curiosity of the crowd, and so great their eagerness, that no opportunity was allowed our Lord and his apostles to enjoy their ordinary repasts; "they could not so much as eat bread." This rendering corresponds to that of the Peshito, which omits the second and strengthening negative, for, while in Greek a negative is neutralized by a subsequent *simple* negative of the same kind, it is continued and intensified by a following *compound* negative of the same kind. The meaning, therefore, is stronger, whether we read μήτε or μηδὲ; thus, "They were able, no, not (μήτε) to eat bread;" or, stronger still, "They could not even (μηδὲ) eat bread," much less find leisure to attend to anything else : though, it may be observed in passing, if μήτε were the right reading, the meaning would rather be that they were neither able nor did eat bread. In fact, the crowd was so great, so continuous, so obtrusive, that no time was allowed our Lord and his apostles for their ordinary and necessary meals. From this we learn that our Lord's popularity was steadily as well as rapidly increasing, and that the excitement, instead of diminishing, was daily, nay, hourly, intensifying. 3. *The concern of our Lord's kinsfolk.* Hearing of this wonderful excitement which the presence of Jesus was everywhere occasioning, his friends or kinsmen were alarmed by the circumstance; and, dreading the effect of such excitement upon his physical constitution—fearing, no doubt, that he might be carried away by his enthusiasm and zeal beyond the measure of his bodily strength, and even to the detriment of his mental powers—our Lord's relations went forth to check his excessive efforts and repress his superabundant ardour. The statement is either general, that is to say, "they went forth," or it may be understood in the stricter sense of their coming out of their place of abode, probably Nazareth, or possibly Capernaum. The expression, οἱ παρ' αὐτοῦ, according to ordinary usage, would mean persons sent by him or away from him, as οἱ παρὰ τοῦ Νικίου, in Thucydides, is "the messengers of Nicias." But the expression cannot mean (1) his *apostles*, who though sent out by him and selected for this purpose, as we read in ver. 14, were now with him in the house; nor can it mean (2) his *disciples*, or those about him, for this would confound the expression with οἱ περὶ αὐτόν. It must, it appears, be taken to signify his kinsmen—the sense assigned to it by most commentators, ancient and modern. And, though this is a rare use of the expression, it is not quite without parallels, as for example in Susanna, ver. 33, ἔκλαιον δὲ οἱ παρ᾽ αὐτῆς, "but her friends wept;" and in this Gospel, ch. v. 26, τὰ παρ᾽ αὐτῆς πάντα is "all the things from with her," that is, all her resources—"all her living," as we read in the parallel passage of St. Luke. 4. *Their course of action.* We have now to consider their course of action or mode of procedure, and the object which they had in view. They went out to lay hold of him, and so (1) to put him under salutary restraint, if the literal meaning of supposed derangement be adhered to. It may indeed mean (2) to hold him back from such superhuman efforts, in consequence of their believing him to be in an unnatural and abnormal state of mind or body, or both. But, though the word rendered "he is beside himself" is often used in that sense, sometimes elliptically as here and in 2 Cor. v. 13, but mostly in conjunction with νοῦ, or γνωμῆς, or φρενῶν, and so equivalent to παραφρονεῖν, still it may be employed figuratively, and merely import that he was transported too far. What with the watchings of the preceding night, and the fastings of that morning, and his unceasing labours in addressing his newly chosen apostles, preaching to the people, and working miracles, all of which we learn, by a comparison with the sixth chapter of St. Luke, both mind and body must have been taxed to the utmost, the strain was excessive, they thought, and far too great to be long borne; and so an earnest but friendly interference was deemed by them to be necessary. There is, however, (3) another view of the matter, which some prefer. They understand the word ἐξέστη as equivalent to ἐλειποθύμησε or ἐλειποψύχησε, and to denote fainting from bodily exhaustion, and consequently the object of his kinsfolk was to support and sustain him (κρατῆσαι). But some resort to the still more questionable expedient of changing the object of the verb just mentioned, and so understanding (4) that his disciples went out to repress the crowd, for they (*i.e.* the disciples) said, "It [the crowd] is mad." This last (4) view is untenable; the preceding one (3) is not well supported; the one going before it (2) is plausible, but rather specious than sound; while the first (1) alone, notwithstanding the difficulty it presents in connection with our Lord's relatives, is the plain and natural meaning of the expression. 5. *Their confined notions of religion.* It is painfully manifest that the kinsfolk of our Lord entertained very contracted and very commonplace, or rather indeed low, ideas of religion. They were very imperfectly acquainted with the great object of Jesus' mission; their notions of his work were of the crudest kind; their faith, if at this period it existed at all, must have been in a very incipient state. Their anxiety at the same time for his safety, and their alarm at the public agitation and the probable upshot of that agitation, all combined to force on them the conclusion that he was on the border between fanaticism and frenzy, or that he had actually made the transition into the region of the latter. 6. *A common experience.* We find in this mistake no new or very strange experience. The Rev. Rowland Hill, on one occasion, strained his voice, raising it to the highest pitch, in order to warn some persons of impending danger, and so rescued them from peril. For this he was warmly applauded, as he deserved. But when he elevated his voice to a similar pitch in warning sinners of the error and evil of their ways, and in order to save their souls from a still greater peril, the same friends who before had praised him now pronounced him fool and fanatic.

II. MALIGNANT FOES. 1. *The charge of the scribes.* The evangelist never suppresses truth; he keeps nothing back, however harsh or unnatural it may at first sight appear. Having shown the effect of the Saviour's ministry on his friends, he proceeds to exhibit the impression it made on his foes. A notable miracle had been performed, as we learn from St. Matthew's Gospel, ch. xii. 22, a blind and dumb demoniac—sad complication—had been cured. Now, there are two ways in which men diminish the merit of a good quality, and destroy the credit of a noble action—denial is the one, and depreciation is the other. The scribes, or theologians, of the Pharisaic sect, had come down as emissaries from the metropolis, to dog our Saviour's steps and destroy, if they could, his influence. Had denial of the miracle been possible, it is plain they would have adopted that course; but facts are stubborn things, and denial in the face of facts is impossible. The miracle was too plain, too palpable, and too public to admit denial. The next best thing for their nefarious purpose was depreciation or detraction. "He casteth out devils," they say—they could not deny this; "but he hath Beelzebub, and in union (ἐν) with him, or by the prince of the devils casteth he out devils," or rather "demons," as we have already seen. Beelzebub was the god of Ekron, and got this name from the supposed power which he possessed to ward off flies, like the Latin *averrunci* or the Greek ἀποτρόπαιοι, who were named *averters*, which those words signify, as though they possessed the power of averting disease or pestilence from their worshippers. But the name Beelzebub was changed, contemptuously and insultingly no doubt, into Beelzebul, the god of dung; nor is the affinity between the god of flies and the god of the dunghill difficult to discover, while the filth of idolatry is not obscurely implied. Now, this name was given to the evil one, whose proper name is either Satan the adversary, in Hebrew, or Diabolos the accuser, in Greek. Other names he also bears, such as "prince of darkness," "prince of the power of the air," "the tempter," "the God of this world," "the old serpent," "the dragon," and Belial. All of these, more or less indicate his hostility to God and man, his opposition to all good, and instigation to all evil. 2. *Confutation.* The Saviour refutes this charge by four different arguments. The first argument is an appeal to common sense, the second is *ad absurdum*, the third is *ad hominem*, and the fourth from human experience. The first (1) points out the fact that the stability of a kingdom, or the success of a family depends on unity and peace; as the proverb has it, "Concordia res parvæ crescunt, discordia maximæ dilabuntur." So the kingdom or family of demons would perish by dissensions. Again (2), "if Satan cast out Satan"—not "if one Satan cast out another Satan," which is the rendering of some, but, "if Satan cast himself out," his policy is suicidal. He had by his demons taken possession of men's bodies, and thereby exercised his power over his victims; but if he countenanced or combined with the Saviour in casting out these demons, he was destroying his own subjects and diminishing his own power. Thus his kingdom, like many another and many a better, "could not stand," or rather "could not be made to stand" (σταθῆναι), or, as the other synoptists express it, "it is brought to desolation" (ἐρημοῦται); and, in that case, "house falleth against house," according to Meyer's rendering of the parallel expression in St. Luke, or, as it stands in the Authorized Version, "a house *divided* against a house falleth." The conditional proposition in reference to kingdom and house is of that kind which denotes probable contingency, not a mere supposition; but that applied to Satan rising up against himself implies possibility without any expression of uncertainty. Why is this? How can we account for this somewhat striking difference? Because in the former case civil commotions may distract a kingdom, and an unhappy feud may divide a family or household. Such things have occurred; and it is likely enough that they may occur again, and so their occurrence comes within the limits of probability. But, according to the supposition or imputation of the scribes, the thing has already actually occurred, and Satan has risen up against himself, and is divided. Such suicidal policy it would be utterly absurd to attribute to a power so subtle as Satan, unless, indeed, he be supposed to be possessed of less than ordinary worldly prudence. He now turns (3) to another line of argument which comes home to them more closely. This argument, though omitted by St. Mark, is found in both St. Matthew and St. Luke, and is the following:—"And if I by Beelzebub cast out devils, by whom do your children ['sons,' in St. Luke] cast them out?" This they assumed to do, as we learn from Acts xix. 13, 14, "Then certain of the vagabond Jews, exorcists, took upon them to call over them which had evil spirits the name of the Lord Jesus, saying, We adjure you by Jesus whom Paul preacheth. And there were seven sons of one Sceva, a Jew, and chief of the priests, which did so." Our Lord, in his reasoning and for the purpose of his argument, employs the fact of the assumption which they made, without necessarily admitting the reality of their accomplishing what they pretended. If they were asked by what power or whose aid their sons cast out or took upon them to cast out devils? by Beelzebub or by the Spirit? he knew well what their answer would be, and that they would not acknowledge their children to be leagued with Satan in casting out devils, but that they would contend for the co-operation of Divine power. If, then, our Lord would say, you impute that power which I exert to Beelzebub, and that same power of which they claim the exercise to God, they will be your judges, and condemn you of hostility to me, while you are guilty of such partiality to themselves. There was no escaping from this argument. But he urges (4) yet another argument —one from human experience: How can I rob Satan of his subjects until I have conquered him? And how can I, besides, distribute the spoils of victory unless that conquest be complete? His enemies had accused him of being in alliance with Satan; he argues on the contrary that, instead of being an ally of Satan, he has made open war on him and bound him, invaded his dominions, subdued his subjects, having first overpowered their prince.

III. PICTURE OF SATAN. 1. *His power.* He is the strong man. He is strong in his princedom. He is "prince of the power of the air;" that is, chieftain of those powerful spirits that have their residence in the air. He is strong in his power to destroy, and hence he is called Apollyon, or Abaddon, the destroyer. By his powerful temptations he destroyed the happiness of our first parents and ruined their race. He is strong in the power of cunning. Oh, how subtle, how insidious, how cunning, in his work of destruction! "We are not ignorant," says the apostle, "of his devices." He is strong in the power of calumny, and consequently he is called "the accuser of the brethren," while his accusations are founded on falsehood. He maligned the patriarch of Uz, upright and perfect though he was, misrepresenting that good man's principles and practice and patience. He is strong in the sovereignty which he exercises over his subjects, and strong in the multitude of those subjects, leading thousands, yea, millions, of men and women captive at his will, and enslaving them with his hellish yoke. He is strong in the fearfully despotic power with which he controls the souls and bodies of his slaves; and every sinner is his slave, and, what is worse, a willing slave, so that, though we urge them by the tenderest motives, address to them the most solemn warnings, allure them by the most precious promises, and appeal to them by the most valuable interests, thousands reject all our overtures, preferring to go on and continue, to live and die, in slavish subjection to the complete control and terrible power of Satan—this strong man. 2. *His palace and property.* St. Luke is fuller in his description here. He speaks of his complete armour, his panoply; he speaks of his palace, the other synoptists speak of his house; he speaks of his goods and of those goods as spoils, the other two speak of his vessels. They all tell us of one stronger than the strong one. St. Luke again tells us that, though the strong man is armed *cap-à-pie*, and stands warder of his own palace, and keeps his goods in security, yet that he who is stronger than the strong one, having effected an entrance, overcomes him, strips him of his armour in which he reposed such confidence, and distributes his spoils; while the other two Evangelists tell us that, having entered the strong man's dwelling, he binds the strong man, and plunders, taking as a prey both his house and his vessels —the container and the contained. The groundwork of the description is to be found, perhaps, in Isa. xlix. 24, 25, " Shall the prey be taken from the mighty, or the lawful captive delivered? But thus saith the Lord, Even the captives of the mighty shall be taken away, and the prey of the terrible shall be delivered: for I will contend with him that contendeth with thee, and I will save thy children." But what are we to understand by these particulars? The strong man is Satan, the stronger than the strong man is our blessed Saviour; this world is his palace or house; his goods in general and vessels in particular which are made spoils of are inferior demons according to some, or men according to others, rather both, as Chrysostom explains the meaning when he says, "Not only are demons vessels of the devil, but men also who do his work." In a still narrower sense, man or man's heart is the palace, and its powers and affections are the goods. The heart of man was once a palace, a princely dwelling, worthy of and intended for the habitation of God. But that palace is now in ruins. We have gazed on a ruined palace; and oh, how sad the sight! Its chambers are dismantled, its columns are prostrate, its arches are broken; fragments of the once stately fabric are scattered about. Ivy twines round its ruined walls, grass grows in its halls, weeds and nettles cover the courtyard. Owls look out of the apertures that once were windows, or hoot in melancholy mood to their fellows. Mounds of earth or heaps of rubbish occupy the apartments once grand and gorgeous. The whole is a sad though striking picture of decay, desolation, and death. Just such a place is the heart of man. It was a palace once; it is a palace still, but the palace is now in ruins, and over these ruins

Satan rules and reigns. But what are the *goods*, or *vessels*, or *spoils*? If the unrenewed
heart itself be the palace where Satan resides, and which he has made his dwelling,
then the powers of that heart—for the Hebrews referred to the heart what we attribute
to the head—its faculties so noble, its feelings so tender, its affections so precious, are
Satan's goods, for he uses them for his own purposes; they are his vessels, for he
employs them in his work and service; they are his spoils, for he has usurped authority
over them. His, no doubt, they are by right of conquest, if might ever makes right. He
is not only a possessor, but wields over them the power of a sovereign. He is enthroned
in the sinner's heart, and exalted to a chief place in his affections. Accordingly, he
receives the homage of his intellect, he claims and gets the ready service of his will, he
controls the actions of the life; and thus over head and heart and life he sways his
sceptre, exercising unlimited and incessant control. To one faculty or feeling he says,
"Come," and it cometh; to another power or principle of action he says, "Go," and it
goeth. 3. *His possession, and how he keeps it.* In the heart of man there are what
Ezekiel calls "chambers of imagery." These chambers of imagery in the human heart
are of themselves dark enough and dreary enough; but Satan, if we yield to him and
resist him not, for he cannot control us without our consent or coerce us against our
consent, will curtain those chambers with *darkness*—spiritual darkness. As long as
he can keep us in the darkness of ignorance—ignorance of God, of Christ, of the way
of salvation, of ourselves, of our responsibility, of our slavery, of our danger, and of our
duty—he is secure in his possession. "The god of this world hath blinded the minds
of them that believe not, lest the light of the glorious gospel of Christ, who is the
image of God, should shine unto them." By subtlety and stratagem, by wiles and
wickedness, he holds possession of those chambers, actually furnishing them with his
own hand, while the furniture thus supplied consists of *delusions*—strong delusions,
sinful delusions. Even the pictures on the walls are painted by him; scenes base and
bad, wicked and abominable, are there portrayed to pervert the judgment and incline
it to what is perverse, to debase the imagination with visions foul and filthy, to inflame
the affections with objects indelicate and impure. Another effectual way in which
Satan holds possession of the palace of man's heart is by keeping it under the influence
of *sense*. He occupies men with the things of sense and sight, to the neglect of things
spiritual and eternal; he employs them with material objects and worldly interests; he
amuses them with the trifles of the present time, to the neglect of the interests of the
never-ending future; he engrosses our attention with worldliness, vanity, and pride—
things sensual, earthly, and perishable; thoughts about the body and its wants are
pressed on men, to the neglect of the soul and its necessities. Such questions as,
"What shall I eat, or what shall I drink, or wherewithal shall I be clothed?" are
ever present, while the vastly more important question, "What must I do to be
saved?" is lost sight of or left in abeyance. Present profits and worldly pursuits
absorb attention, to the neglect of present responsibilities and future realities; the
pleasures of sin, short-lived and unsatisfactory as they are sure to prove, divert men's
thoughts from those "pleasures which are at God's right hand for evermore." But, as
the Word of God warns us of Satan's devices that we may be on our guard against
them, it may not be amiss to pay the more particular attention to them. Another
way by which he holds possession of the palace of what Bunyan calls Mansoul is
delay. This is a favourite method, and one specially successful with the young.
"Time enough yet," Satan whispers into the young ear, and the inexperienced heart
of youth is too ready to believe the falsehood. He persuades them into the belief that
it is too soon for such grave subjects, too early to engage in such solemn reflections.
Many other and even better opportunities, they are induced to think, will be afforded;
they are yet young and strong, and with a keen zest for youthful pleasures, and the
world is all before them. Every year the delay becomes more difficult to break away
from, and the delusion the more dangerous; and while the difficulty as well as the
danger increases, the strength of the sinner, or his power to overcome the suggestions of
Satan, decreases. A more convenient season is expected, and thus procrastination becomes,
as usual, "the thief of time; year after year it steals till all is past, and to the mercies
of a moment leaves the vast concerns of an eternal scene." But to delay succeeds at
length another means by which he keeps possession, and that other means, in one respect
the opposite, is *despair*. Thus extremes meet. Satan had long flattered them with the

delusive fancy that it was too soon ; now he drives them to the desperate notion that it is too late. Once he flattered them with the false hope of a long and happy future, with death in the remote distance, and with means of grace not only ample but abundant, and power at pleasure to turn to God ; now he tortures them with the thought that the day of grace is gone, irrevocably gone. Once he made them believe that the time to break up their fallow ground and sow to themselves in righteousness had not yet come ; now, on the contrary, he induces the belief that "the harvest is past, the summer ended, and their souls not saved. Once he deluded them with the thought that sin was only a trifle, and they were willing to lay to their soul the false unction that sin was too small a matter to incur the wrath of Heaven ; now he prompts the despairing thought that their sin is too great to be forgiven, and their guilt too heinous to be ever blotted out. 4. *The peace he produces.* All the while he produces a sort of peace ; all the while " his goods are in peace ; " all the while sinners are promising themselves " peace, peace ; but there is no peace," saith God, " to the wicked." Satan may promise, and even produce, a kind of peace ; but that peace is perilous—it is a false peace. He may lead them into a sort of calm, but it is the lull before the storm ; he may amuse them with a species of quietude, but it is the sure forerunner of the fast-approaching hurricane. The only true peace is that which the Spirit bestows—a " peace that passeth all understanding," a peace which the world with all its wealth cannot give, and with all its wickedness cannot take away. This peace is compared to a river : " Then shall thy peace be as a river "—a river broad and beautiful, glancing in the bright sunshine of the heaven above, and reflecting the varied beauties along its banks ; a river deepening and widening at every reach, bearing health and fertility throughout its course, broadening out and expanding at last into the boundless, shoreless ocean of everlasting bliss. 5. *Satan's defeat and dispossession.* Though Satan be strong, there is One stronger than he—One "mighty to save," even from his grasp, and "lead captivity captive." That stronger One is the mighty Saviour, whose mission of mercy was meant to take the prey from the mighty, to bruise his head and destroy his works, and so rescue man from the thraldom of Satan and the dominion of sin. Himself mightier than the mighty, he is "able to save to the uttermost all that come unto God by him." St. Luke informs us of the manner in which he effects the great emancipation. He comes upon him (ἐπελθὼν) both suddenly and by way of hostile attack. He comes upon him suddenly, and so takes him by *surprise.* Satan's goods are meantime in peace, and he fancies he has it all his own way, and that for ever. The Saviour comes upon the heart enslaved by Satan with the sword of the Spirit, which is the word and *truth* of God, and immediately the chains are burst asunder and the shackles fall off. Henceforth it enjoys that freedom with which Christ makes his people free. He comes upon the sinner's soul with the *power* of the Spirit, convincing of sin, of righteousness, and of judgment. The Spirit takes of the things of Christ and shows them to the sinner, and so the truth is brought home to the heart and conscience ; not in word only, " but also in power, and in the Holy Ghost, and in much assurance." He comes upon the sinner, whose powers lay dormant, or rather " dead in trespasses and sins," and he awakens the powers that thus lay dormant, and quickens the soul, it may be long dead, into new spiritual *life,* and makes it "alive unto God through Christ Jesus." But with life comes *light.* Soon as the life-giving Spirit operates upon the mass erewhile chaotic and dead, living forces are developed, and light springs up ; the light of the glorious gospel of the grace of God shines through all that heart, however dead and dark it had been before. Every soul thus awakened, enlightened, quickened, and truly converted to God, is a victory of the Saviour over Satan—a trophy snatched from the strong one by him who thus proves himself stronger than the strong man. Every such one is evidence of Satan's defeat, and proves the destruction of his power, as also his expulsion from his usurped dominion—a thorough and blessed dispossession of the spirit of evil. 6. *Satan's armour.* His offensive weapons are his snares, his devices, his wiles, his lies, his lusts ; of all these we read in Scripture. But he has other armour ; and, as panoply has its root in ὅπλον, or " thing moved about," as the shield, from ἕπω, according to Donaldson, the reference may rather be to defensive armour. The parts of this armour may be regarded as consisting of our ignorance of God and hatred of him, our unbelief and ungodliness, hardness of heart and unrighteousness. Theophylact explains Satan's armour to be made of our sins in general; his words are Πάντα τὰ εἴδη τῆς ἁμαρτίας, αὕτη γαρ ὅπλα τοῦ Διαβόλου, equivalent to "All forms of sin, for this is the arms of the devil." By such armour he defends his possessions and maintains his interest in them; by such armour he repels all attacks on his goods, opposing the impressions of the Divine Word, the influences of the Holy Spirit, and the leadings of God's providence. Christ captures his arms when he enables us to guard against his devices and wiles, to avoid his snares, to discredit his lies, shun his lusts, and resist his temptations. Further, he takes from Satan the armour in which he places such confidence when he breaks the power of sin in the soul, opens men's eyes to the perils that surround them, regenerates the heart, and renews the life, humbles their spirit, rectifies their errors, checks their corruption, and, in a word, bruises Satan under their feet. 7. *Division of the spoils.* This is usually the consequence of conquest. When Satan led the sinner captive and made him his prey, he took him with all he is and all he has for his spoil, employing all his endowments of mind and energies of body, his time, his talents, his health, his influence, his estate, small or great, in his service. But again, in the day of the sinner's conversion to God, not only is Satan defeated and dispossessed, Christ recovers the long-lost possession—all of it for himself. He regains those energies and endowments, that time, those talents, that influence; he restores all to their right use and to the great end for which they were intended. The whole man—body, soul, and spirit—is brought back to the service of his Maker, and every thought becomes subject to the law of Jesus Christ. Further, the Saviour not only regains those spoils and recovers them for himself, but also, like a great and good Captain, he divides them among his followers. In every case when he defeats, disarms, and dispossesses Satan, Christ shares with his soldiers—his servants—the spoils consequent on victory. The sinner thus rescued is blessed "with all spiritual blessings in heavenly things in Christ Jesus;" but he is not only blessed in his own soul, he is made a blessing to all around. He becomes a blessing to friend and fellow-man. In this way the spoil is divided and the blessing distributed. He becomes a proof of Divine power and a pattern of purity to an ungodly world; while his talents, be they many or few—ten, or five, or one—are employed for the good of Christ's Church, "for the perfecting of the saints, for the edification of the body of Christ." To sinners he serves as a beacon-light to warn them of the sunken rocks or breakers ahead, and to direct their course into the haven of heavenly rest. A curious and not uninteresting exposition by Theophylact of the distribution of the spoils is to this effect, that men, being the spoils first taken by Satan, and then retaken by Christ, the Saviour distributes them, giving one to one angel and another to another angel as a faithful guardian, that, instead of the demon that lorded it over him, an angel may now have him in safe keeping—of course, in order to be his guide and guard him. 8. *Practical lessons.* (1) The sinner still in the power of the strong man should cry mightily to Christ to rescue him from such base servitude, and deliver him from such dreadful drudgery. He, and he alone, can free him from enslavement, because he is stronger than the strong man. (2) The saint already delivered, while still to be on his guard against Satan, has nothing to fear from his assaults. He can never again regain possession, for he is vanquished, and the means of retrieving his lost possessions and forfeited power are for ever wrested from him. If he goes out of himself without being dislodged, he is sure to return and resume possession with increased forces and power, as the parable which follows in St. Luke teaches. (3) The believer is bound to bless his deliverer, which he may suitably do in the words—

> "Thou hast, O Lord most glorious,
>   Ascended up on high;
> And in triumph victorious led
>   Captive captivity. . . .
> Bless'd be the Lord, who is to us
>   Of our salvation God;
> Who daily with his benefits
>   Us plenteously doth load."

(4) Neutrality in this cause is criminal. If we are not on Christ's side, contending against Satan, we evince our unwillingness that his kingdom should be destroyed; and if not engaged in seeking to bring subjects into Christ's kingdom, as a shepherd

collects his flock and pens them in the fold, we are scattering the sheep away from and leaving them without the place of safety.

IV. THE BLASPHEMY AGAINST THE HOLY GHOST.   1. *Patristic explanations of this sin.* Some have understood it of *apostasy* in time of persecution. This was the opinion of Cyprian (A.D. 248), who says, in 'Epist.' xvi., that "It was a very great crime which persecution compelled men to commit, as they themselves know who have committed it, inasmuch as our Lord and Judge has said, 'Whosoever shall confess me before men, him will I confess before my Father who is in heaven. But he that denieth me, him will I also deny.' And again, 'All sins and blasphemies shall be forgiven to the sons of men: but he that blasphemeth against the Holy Ghost, shall not have forgiveness, but is guilty of eternal sin' (*reus est æterni peccati*)." Some understand it of the *denial of the divinity* of our Lord, as Athanasius (A.D. 326), who says that "the Pharisees in the Saviour's time, and the Arians in our days, running into the same madness, denied the real Word to be incarnate, and ascribed the works of the Godhead to the devil and his angels, and therefore justly undergo the punishment which is due to this impiety, without remission. For they put the devil in the place of God, and imagined the works of the living and true God to be nothing more than the works of the devil." And elsewhere the same Father says, "They who spake against Christ, considering him only as the Son of man, were pardonable, because in the beginning of the gospel the world looked upon him only as a prophet, not as God, but as the Son of man: but they who blasphemed his divinity after his works had demonstrated him to be God, had no forgiveness, so long as they continued in this blasphemy; but if they repented they might obtain pardon: for there is no sin unpardonable with God to them who truly and worthily repent." Others again have understood it to consist in the denial of *the divinity of the Holy Ghost.* Thus Epiphanius (A.D. 368) charged with this sin the Macedonian heretics, because they opposed the Godhead of the Holy Spirit, making him a mere creature. In like manner Ambrose (A.D. 374) accused these same heretics of blasphemy against the Holy Ghost, because they denied his divinity.

2. *The two most important patristic authorities on this subject.* These are Chrysostom (A.D. 388) among the Greek Fathers, and Augustine (A.D. 396) of the Latin Fathers; both near the close of the fourth century. The former on the *nature* of the sin itself says, "For though you say that you know me not, you are surely not ignorant of that also, that to expel demons and cure diseases are the work of the Holy Spirit. Not only, then, do you insult me, but the Holy Spirit also. Therefore your punishment is inevitable both here and hereafter." Again, in reference to the *unpardonableness* of this sin, he says, "'Ye have said many things against me—that I am a deceiver, that I am an opponent of God. These things I forgive you on your repentance, and I do not exact punishment of you; but the blasphemy of the Holy Spirit shall not be forgiven even to the penitent.' And how could this have reason, for truly even this sin was forgiven to persons repenting? Many, then, of those who said these things believed afterwards, and all was forgiven them. What, then, does he mean? That this sin above all is least capable of pardon. Why at all? Because they were ignorant who Christ was; but of the Holy Spirit they had had sufficient proof. For truly the prophets spake by him what they did speak, and all in the old dispensation had had abundant knowledge of him. What he means then is this: 'Grant it, you stumble at me because of the garb of flesh I have assumed; can you also say about the Holy Spirit that you are ignorant of him? Therefore this blasphemy shall not be forgiven you; both here and there you shall suffer punishment.'" Further on he proceeds to say, "For truly some men are punished both here and there; others only here; others only there; while others neither here nor there. *Here and there,* as these very persons (*i.e.* the Pharisees), for truly both here they suffered punishment when they endured those irremediable sufferings at the capture of their city; and there they shall undergo the most severe punishment, as the inhabitants of Sodom, and as many others. But *there only,* as that rich man when tortured in flames was not master of even a drop of water. Some *only here,* as the person who had committed fornication among the Corinthians. Others again, *neither here nor there,* as the apostles, as the prophets, and as the blessed Job; for what they suffered did not belong to punishment, but was exercises and conflicts." The blasphemy against the Holy Spirit is, according to Chrysostom, greater than the sin against the Son of man, and, though not absolutely irremissible to such as repent, yet in

the absence of such timely repentance it will be punished both here and hereafter. Augustine has several references to this sin, but his opinion of the matter may be briefly summed up in continued resistance to the influences of the Holy Spirit by insuperable hardness of heart, and in perseverance in obduracy and impenitence to the last. Thus in his Commentary on Romans he says, "That man sins against the Holy Spirit who, despairing or deriding and despising the preaching of grace by which sins are washed away, and of peace by which we are reconciled to God, refuses to repent of his sins, and resolves that he must go on hardening himself in a certain impious and fatal sweetness of them, and persists therein to the end." He further insists that neither pagans, nor Jews, nor heretics, nor schismatics, however they may have opposed the Holy Spirit before baptism, were shut out by the Church from that sacrament in case they truly repented; nor after baptism in case of falling into sin, or resisting the Spirit of God, were they debarred from restoration to pardon and peace on repentance, and that even those whom our Lord charged with this blasphemy might repent and betake themselves to the Divine mercy. "What else remains," he asks, "but that the sin against the Holy Spirit, which our Lord says is neither forgiven in this world nor in that which is to come, must be understood to be no other than perseverance in malignity and wickedness with despair of the indulgence and mercy of God? For this is to resist the grace and peace of the Spirit of which we speak."

3. *Modern expositions of this sin.* Some of these reproduce or nearly so the interpretations of the ancients. They may in the main be divided into three classes. The *first* class consists of those who, like Hammond, Tillotson, Wetstein, understand the sin in question to be the diabolical calumny of the Pharisees, in ascribing to the power of Satan the miracles which the Saviour by the Spirit given him without measure performed. Here was evidently the mighty power of God, but these men, maliciously, wantonly, and wickedly, as also presumptuously and blasphemously, pronounced the miracle just wrought before their eyes and in their presence to be an effect produced by the evil one. The connection instituted between the twenty-ninth and thirtieth verses of this third chapter of St. Mark by the word ὅτι, corresponding to the parallel διὰ τοῦτο of St. Matthew, and the imperfect ἔλεγον, equivalent to "they kept saying," are both in favour of this interpretation. Under this first class are several modifications, such as that which proceeds on the supposed distinction between "Son of man" and "Son of God," as though he said that whosoever spake a word against Jesus as the Son of man, having his divinity shrouded and veiled in his humanity, might obtain forgiveness; but blasphemy against him as the Son of God, evidencing his divinity by miracles, could not obtain forgiveness. Another modification understands our Lord's warning the Pharisees that they were fast approaching an unpardonable sin by wickedly rejecting the Son of man as a Saviour; that one step further—one other blasphemy, that of the Spirit who, if not then, might hereafter reveal this, or a coming, Saviour unto them, would deprive them of the means and agent and so of the hope of salvation, and consequently of pardon. Yet another modification is that of Grotius, following in the steps of Chrysostom, to the effect that it is easier for any or all sins to obtain forgiveness than that this calumny should be pardoned; and that it will be severely punished both in the present and coming age. The *second* class, to which Whitby, Doddridge, and Macknight belong, holds that the Pharisees, by their conduct on this particular occasion or at the time then present, were not guilty of the sin referred to, and in fact that the sin against the Holy Ghost could not be committed while Christ still abode on earth, and before his ascension; because the Spirit was not yet given. They hold, therefore, that after our Lord's resurrection and ascension, when he would send down the Holy Ghost to attest his mission, and when his supernatural gifts and miraculous operations would furnish incontestable proofs of almighty power, any such calumny or blasphemy uttered against the Spirit then would be unpardonable. The reason was plain, because the Son of man, while he was clothed in human flesh, and his divinity shrouded from human sight, and while his work on earth was not yet finished, might be slandered by persons unwittingly, or, according to the Scripture phrase, "ignorantly in unbelief;" but once the Holy Spirit had come down, and shed the light of heaven over the events of the Saviour's life from the cradle to the cross, and had illumined with glory unspeakable the scenes of Gethsemane and Calvary and Olivet, making plain to every willing mind the momentous import of all those marvellous transactions, the blasphemy of the

Spirit could not then be in ignorance or for lack of sufficient demonstration; but presumptuous against light and against knowledge, from sheer malevolence and unaccountable malignity. The Pharisees were preparing for this—they were approaching the brink of this fearful abyss, and our Lord warns them back before it was possible for them to take the fatal plunge, and involve themselves in ruin without remedy. A *third* class of interpreters generalizes the sin in question in much the same way as we have seen Augustine do, and resolves it into continued resistance and obstinate opposition to the grace of the gospel, impenitently and unbelievingly persisted in till the end. This is the view which Dr. Chalmers elaborates with great eloquence and power in his sermon on "Sin against the Holy Ghost." In that sermon we read as follows:—" A man may shut against himself all the avenues of reconciliation. There is nothing mysterious in the kind of sin by which the Holy Spirit is tempted to abandon him to that state in which there can be no forgiveness and no return unto God. It is by a movement of conscience within him, that the man is made sensible of sin, that he is visited with the desire of reformation, that he is given to feel his need both of mercy to pardon, and of grace to help him; in a word, that he is drawn unto the Saviour, and brought into that intimate alliance with him by faith which brings down upon him both acceptance with the Father and all the power of a new and constraining impulse to the way of obedience. But this movement is a suggestion of the Spirit of God, and, if it be resisted by any man, the Spirit is resisted. The God who offers to draw him unto Christ is resisted. The man refuses to believe because his deeds are evil; and by every day of perseverance in these deeds, the voice which tells him of their guilt and urges him to abandon them is resisted; and thus the Spirit ceases to suggest, and the Father, from whom the Spirit proceedeth, ceases to draw, and the inward voice ceases to remonstrate—and all this because their authority has been so often put forth and so often turned away. This is the deadly offence which has reared an impassable wall against the return of the obstinately impenitent. This is the blasphemy to which no forgiveness can be granted, because, in its very nature, the man who has come this length feels no movement of conscience towards that ground on which alone forgiveness can be awarded to him, and where it is never refused even to the very worst and most malignant of human iniquities. This is the sin against the Holy Ghost. It is not peculiar to any one age. It does not lie in any one unfathomable mystery. It may be seen at this day in thousands and thousands more, who, by that most familiar and most frequently exemplified of all habits, a habit of resistance to a sense of duty, have at length stifled it altogether, and driven their inward monitor away from them, and have sunk into a profound moral lethargy, and so will never obtain forgiveness—not because forgiveness is ever refused to any who repent and believe the gospel, but because they have made their faith and their repentance impracticable. . . . The whole mysteriousness of this sin against the Holy Ghost is thus done away. Grant him the office with which he is invested in the Word of God, even the office of instigating the conscience to all its reprovals of sin, and to all its admonitions of repentance; and then, if ever you witnessed the case of a man whose conscience had fallen into a profound and irrecoverable sleep, or, at least, had lost to such a degree its power of control over him, that he stood out against every engine which was set up to bring him to the faith and repentance of the New Testament,—behold in such a man a sinner against conscience to such a woeful extent that conscience had given up its direction of him; or, in other words, a sinner against the Holy Ghost to such an extent that he had let down the office of warning him away from that ground of danger and of guilt on which he stood so immovably posted." There are some modifications of this view which it may be well to notice. One is that which makes the sin against the Holy Ghost to be resistance to conscience as the voice of God in the soul—the voice which the Holy Spirit employs in testifying to truth and goodness, and in reprobating sin and recommending the Saviour. Another modification is that which makes blasphemy against the Holy Ghost to consist in the expression of malignant unbelief of, and wilful apostasy from, the truth of God, and that, because it is the Holy Ghost which illumines the understanding and applies the truth to the heart of believers.

4. *Remarks on the foregoing theories.* In our observations on the foregoing theories we do not deem it prudent dogmatically to determine which of them is the correct one. In a case where such diversities of opinion have prevailed, even among the ablest

scholars and the most eloquent theologians, it is better that every one should be persuaded in his own mind. We may, however, be permitted to state that view which
has recommended itself most to our mind, and some grounds for the preference to which
we think it entitled. The view held by the first class above mentioned appears to us
on the whole the most tenable, for (1) it is most in harmony with the context, as it
stands both in this Gospel and that of St. Matthew. The Pharisees had witnessed an
undeniable miracle in the cure of a blind and dumb demoniac ; but, instead of acknowledging the finger of God in the miraculous cure, they ascribed it to complicity or
collusion with the power of darkness. This was a gratuitous and malicious calumny ;
it was a sin of speech as well as of thought—a blasphemy, in fact, in the literal sense.
The form which the sin is represented as taking is that of *speech*, as appears plainly
from the contrast between speaking a word against the Son of man and speaking
against the Holy Ghost. Again, (2) the allegation of the second class, that the Holy
Ghost was not given till after the Ascension, though quite true in reference to the
disciples, does not apply to the Master, to whom the Spirit was given without measure
from the first. Further, (3) the view of the third class, so ably advocated by Dr.
Chalmers and many others, and which in substance was that held by Augustine,
appears too wide in extent and too general in its character; whereas the blasphemy
against the Holy Spirit is something peculiar and special, and of rare occurrence.
Besides, if the sin in question consisted in obstinate resistance to the gospel, continued
till that resistance culminated in final unbelief, it would be little, if anything, different
from sin in general which, by obstinate continuance therein, becomes unpardonable,
and that, not from lack of cleansing power in the blood of Christ, nor from any peculiar
aggravation, but solely on account of continued persistence therein.

5. *Perilous approximations to this sin.* That many have been unduly exercised and
harassed by fancied guiltiness of this sin, is certain ; that some have despaired or become
melancholy on this account, is credible ; that many have been driven to insanity by it
we can scarcely believe. To any who are troubled with anxious thoughts about the matter
we may say that, according to the theories of the first and second classes, they could
not have committed the same sin in *kind*—as they did not, like the Pharisees, see the
miracles wrought by our Lord, nor did they witness the supernatural operations of the
Spirit after his descent at Pentecost—whatever the *degree* of their sin may have been ;
while, with respect to the third, the sin being that of continued resistance, they have only
to abandon their dogged opposition, the abandonment of which their very anxiety proves
to have become already an accomplished fact. To all, of whatever class of opinion,
who are apprehensive—earnestly apprehensive and afraid of having committed this sin
—their very uneasiness on that score is proof of their guiltlessness of the fancied crime,
for these very upbraidings of conscience prove incompatibility with commission of this
sin. At the same time, there are approximations to this sin which we should most
carefully guard against. A rejection of the truth of Scripture wilfully persisted in ; or
trifling with the operations of the Holy Spirit in the heart ; or ridicule of religion and
opposition to its ordinances in general ; or hostility to Christianity in particular ; or
contempt, malevolence, and slander directed against God and the things of God, or
against the Church and people of God ; or mockery of sacred things ; or blasphemous
suggestions harboured and indulged in—each of these involves an awfulness of criminality and a fearfulness of guilt that betoken a considerable similarity or close approximation to the heinousness of the unpardonable sin. We do not affirm that any of these
is actually that sin, but only such an approach to the verge of the precipice as is
sufficient to startle men to a sense of danger, and drive them back before they venture
a step further. Alford, who makes the blasphemy against the Holy Ghost to be a state
of wilful, determined opposition to the present power of the Holy Ghost, in which state
or at least approaching very near to which the act of the Pharisees proved them to be,
compares, among other Scriptures, Heb. vi. 4—8 and x. 26, 27. But the purport of
the last-cited Scripture is that, in case the sacrifice of Christ is rejected, there is no
other sacrifice available, all others having been done away, and consequently no other
means of escape from the wrath of God ; while the former passage refers to apostasy
so aggravated as to render restoration impossible, because the persons guilty of it fell
away in spite of the clearest possible evidence to the truth of the Christian faith.
Another Scripture frequently compared with that before us is 1 John v, 16. The sin

there mentioned as tending unto (εἰς) death is regarded by some to be the act of denying Jesus to be the Christ, the Son of God, or the state of apostasy indicated by that act; others hold it to be apostasy from Christianity, combined with diabolical enmity, and that in the face of extraordinary evidence; but it appears to be a specific act of sin, of the commission of which the evidence is clear and convincing, distinct and precise— such an act of apostasy as blasphemes the Holy Ghost by ascribing his operations to Satanic power. This sin unto death is certainly the nearest approach to the unpardonable sin, if it be not, as many hold it to be, identical with it. Of the three different readings, κρίσεως, κολάσεως, and ἁμαρτήματος, the last is the best supported; while the expression "an eternal sin" signifies either a sin that is not pardoned or a sin of which the punishment is not remitted. The connection of the aphoristic expression which immediately follows in St. Matthew, viz. "Either make the tree good, and his fruit good; or else make the tree corrupt, and his fruit corrupt: for the tree is known by his fruit," is briefly but correctly pointed out in the remark of Chrysostom, "Since they did not reprove the works, but calumniated him that did them, he shows that this accusation was contrary to the natural sequence of affairs."—J. J. G.

Vers. 31—35. Parallel passages: Matt. xii. 46—50; Luke viii. 19—21.—*The real relationship.* I. No SLIGHT INTENDED. The crowd that sat around prevented his relatives reaching him; they therefore sent a message, to which his reply cannot with any propriety be twisted into an expression of contempt. His obedience to his parents in the humble home at Nazareth during the years of youth, and his tender solicitude for his apparently widowed mother when, as he hung on the cross, he commended her to the care of the beloved disciple, preclude the possibility of such a meaning.

II. HEAVENLY KINSHIP. He looked round in a *circle;* this expression of the look, like that of the sitting posture of the multitude, implies the report of an eye-witness. Looking round about him and directly into the face of every faithful follower sitting there, he announced a higher and holier relationship than that formed by an earthly tie; he acquainted them with the existence of kinship near and dear as that which unites the nearest and dearest of human kindred. The Church is Christ's family, and to every true member of that family he is bound by the tenderest bonds of love. What a privilege to be thus closely united to and tenderly loved by Christ!

III. CONDITION OF THIS RELATIONSHIP. It is not the possession of varied knowledge of God's will and works and ways, though that is important; nor is it the possession of faith, though that is the root; nor is it the acceptance of Christ in the exercise of faith, though that is indispensable to salvation; but it is a more practical condition, and one more easily known and more readily discernible;—it is doing the will of God.

IV. THE MEASURE OF ENDEARMENT BELONGING TO THIS KINSHIP. The Saviour makes his natural affections the measure of his spiritual friendship. When we are enjoined to love our neighbour as ourselves, it does not mean that we should love ourselves less, but our neighbour more; so here, he does not love his mother and brothers and sisters less, but his true disciples more. The poorest and meanest as well as the richest may attain to this honour and share this love. We may obtain in this way a name better than that of sons and daughters; we may be honoured with that new, best name of love.

> "Behold th' amazing gift of love
> The Father hath bestow'd
> On us, the sinful sons of men,
> To call us sons of God."

J. J. G.

EXPOSITION.

CHAPTER IV.

Ver. 1.—**And again he began to teach by the seaside.** This return to the seaside is mentioned by St. Mark only. From this time our Lord's teaching began to be more public. The room and the little courtyard no longer sufficed for the multitudes that came to him. The Authorized Version says that "a great multitude was gathered unto him." The Greek adjective, according to the most approved reading, is πλεῖστος, the superlative of πολὺς, and should be rendered "a very great" multitude. They had probably been waiting for him in the neighbourhood of Capernaum. **He entered into a boat**—probably the boat mentioned at ch. iii. 9—**and sat in the sea,** *i.e.* in the boat afloat on the water, so as to be relieved of the pressure of the vast multitude (πλεῖστος ὄχλος) gathered on the shore.

Ver. 2.—**He taught them many things in parables.** This was a new system of teaching. For some months he had taught directly. But as he found that this direct teaching was met in some quarters with unbelief and scorn, he abandoned it for the less direct method of the parable. The parable (παραβολή) is etymologically the setting forth of one thing by the side of another, so that the one may be compared with the other. The parable is the truth presented by a similitude. It differs from the proverb inasmuch as it is necessarily figurative. The proverb *may* be figurative, but it need not of necessity be figurative. The parable is often an expanded proverb, and the proverb a condensed parable. There is but one Hebrew word for the two English words "parable" and "proverb," which may account for their being frequently interchanged. The proverb (Latin) is a common sentiment generally accepted. The parable (Greek) is something put by the side of something else. Theologically, it is something in the world of nature which finds its counterpart in the world of spirit. The parable attracts attention, and so becomes valuable as a test of character. It reveals the seekers after truth, those who love the light. It withdraws the light from those who love darkness. **And said unto them in his doctrine** (ἐν τῇ διδαχῇ αὐτοῦ); literally, *in his teaching,* namely, that particular mode of teaching which he had just introduced; "he taught them" (ἐδίδασκεν). He said, "in his teaching" (ἐν τῇ διδαχῇ αὐτοῦ).

Vers. 3—8.—**Hearken** ('Ακούετε). This word is introduced in St. Mark's narrative only; and it is very suitable to the warning at ver. 9, "Who hath ears to hear, let him hear. **The sower went forth to sow.** The scope of this beautiful parable is this: Christ teaches us that he is the Sower, that is, the great Preacher of the gospel among men. 1. But not all who hear the gospel believe it and receive it; just as some of the seed sown fell by the wayside, on the hard footpath, where it could not penetrate the ground, but lay upon the surface, and so was picked up by the birds. 2. Again, not all who hear and believe persevere in the faith; some fall away; like the seed sown on rocky ground, which springs up indeed,

but for want of depth of soil puts forth no root, and is soon scorched by the rising sun, and, being without root, withers away. 3. But further, not all who show faith bring forth the fruit of good works; like the seed sown among the thorns, which, growing up together with it, choked it (συνέπνιξαν αὐτὸ); such is the meaning. St. Luke has the words (συμφυεῖσαι αἱ ἄκανθαι ἀπέπνιξαν), "the thorns grew up with it and choked it." 4. But, lastly, there are those who receive the gospel in the love of it, and bring forth fruit, not, however, in equal measures, but some thirtyfold, some sixty, some a hundred; and this on account of the greater influences of grace, or on account of the more ready co-operation of the free-will of man with the sovereign grace of God. The whole parable marks a gradation. In the first case the seed produces nothing; in the second it produces only the blade; in the third it is near the point of producing fruit, but fails to bring forth to perfection; in the fourth it yields fruit, but in different measures.

Ver. 9.—**And he said, Who hath ears to hear, let him hear.** St. Luke (viii. 8) has a stronger word than (ἔλεγεν) "he said." He (viii. 8) has (ἐφώνει) "he cried." Our Lord uses this expression, "he that hath ears to hear," etc., when the subject-matter is figurative or obscure, as though to rouse the attention of his hearers. He has "ears to hear" who diligently attends to the words of Christ, that he may ponder and obey them. Many heard him out of curiosity, that they might hear something new, or learned, or brilliant; not that they might lay to heart the things which they heard, and endeavour to practise them in their lives. And so it is with those who go to hear sermons on account of the fame of the preacher, and not that they may learn to amend their lives; and thus the words of Jehovah to Ezekiel (xxxiii. 32) are fulfilled, "And, lo, thou art unto them as a very lovely song of one that hath a pleasant voice, and can play well on an instrument: for they hear thy words, but they do them not."

Ver. 10.—**When he was alone.** These words do not appear in St. Matthew's account. He simply says that "the disciples came and said unto him." This must have been upon some other occasion. It could not have been when he was preaching from the boat; for St. Mark says, **they that were about him with the twelve.** He is the only evangelist who notices this. We must not forget that, besides the twelve, there were seventy other disciples. They **asked of him the parables** (τὰς παραβολάς), according to the best reading. The inquiry was a general one, although St. Mark here gives the explanation of one only.

Vers. 11, 12.—To know the mystery. The Greek verb γνῶναι, to know, is not found in the best manuscripts, in which the words are (ὑμῖν τὸ μυστήριον δέδοται), *unto you is given the mystery of the kingdom of God.* Our Lord here explains why he spake to the mixed multitude in parables; namely, because most of them were as yet incapable of receiving the gospel: some would not believe it, others reviled it. Therefore our Lord here encourages his own disciples to search out his words spoken in parables, and humbly to inquire into their full meaning, that so they might become able ministers and efficient preachers of the gospel. Moreover, by this he shows that this efficiency cannot be obtained by our own strength, but must be humbly sought for from God   For it is his own gift which he bestows on the disciples of Christ, and denies to others, whom he leaves to the blindness of their own hearts. It is as though he said, " To you, my disciples, my apostles, it is given, since you believe in me as the Messiah, to have continually more clear revelations from me of the mysteries of God and of heaven, by which you shall day by day increase in the knowledge and love of him. But from the scribes and others, because they will not believe in me as their own Messiah, God will take away even that small knowledge which they have of him and of his kingdom. Yea, he will deprive them of all the special privileges which they have hitherto possessed." But the words are not limited in their application to those who were living on the earth when Christ sojourned here. He says to all in every age who come within the reach of his gospel, " Those who come to me with a sincere heart and a simple desire to know the truth, as you, my apostles, are doing, to them I will reveal the mysteries of my kingdom, and I will help them onwards in the path of holiness, by which they may at length attain to the heavenly kingdom. But they who have not this pure desire of truth, but indulge their own lusts and errors, from them that little knowledge of God and of Divine things will by degrees be taken away, and they will become altogether blind." Observe the expression (ἐκείνοις δὲ τοῖς ἔξω), but **unto them that are without.** There were then, just as there are now, those who were outside the realm of spiritual things; not caring for, not understanding, not desirous of spiritual truth. **Lest at any time they should be converted** (μήποτε ἐπιστρέψωσι)—*lest haply they should turn again* (the verb is active)—and their **sins should be forgiven them.** According to the best reading, τὰ ἁμαρτήματα is omitted; so it runs, *and it should be forgiven them.* The use of the active verb brings out the sin-

ner's responsibility with respect to his own conversion.

Ver. 13.—Know ye not this parable? and how shall ye know all the parables? that is, " How, then, can you expect to understand all parables, as they ought to do who are instructed unto the kingdom of heaven ?" It is St. Mark alone who recalls and records these words. They are striking and vivid, as illustrating the condition of mind of the disciples at this time—slow of apprehension, and yet desirous to learn.

Ver. 14.—The sower soweth the word. St. Matthew (xiii. 19) calls it "the word of the kingdom"—an expression equivalent to "the gospel of the kingdom," not merely moral truth, but spiritual and eternal.

Ver. 15.—Straightway cometh Satan. St. Matthew (xiii. 19) says, "then cometh (ὁ πονηρὸς) the evil *one*;" the same expression which our Lord uses in the Lord's Prayer, and which helps to justify the English rendering in the Revised Version there. As the seed falling by the wayside is refused by the hard and well-trodden ground, and so is readily picked up by the birds; in like manner, the seed of God's Word, falling upon a heart rendered callous by the custom of sinning, is straightway snatched away by " the evil one," urging the heart again to its accustomed sins. Well may we pray to be delivered from this " evil one."

Vers. 16, 17.—And these are they likewise which are sown on stony ground. This sentence would be better rendered, *And these in like manner are they that are sown upon the rocky places,* where the words "likewise," or "in like manner," mean "by a similar mode of interpretation." This is the second condition of soil on which the seed is sown—a better condition than the former; for the former plainly refused the seed, but this, having some soil favourable to the germination of the seed, receives it, and the seed springs up, though but for a little while. So the rocky ground is like the heart of that hearer who hears the Word of God, and receives it with joy. He is delighted with its beauty, its justice, its purity; and he breaks forth with holy affections. But alas! he has more of the rock than of the good soil in his heart. Hence the Word of God cannot strike a deep root into his soul. He is not constant in the faith. He endures but for a time, and in the hour of temptation he falls away.

Ver. 18.—And these are they which are sown among thorns. According to the best authorities, the words are (καὶ ἄλλοι εἰσίν), *and others are they,* etc. This marks a considerable difference between the two classes. This is the third condition of soil; and it is so much better than the former, inasmuch as the thorns present less obstacles to the growth of the seed than the rocky ground does. This similitude indicates the heart of that hearer who is beset with the cares of this world and the deceitfulness of riches and the lusts of other things.

Ver. 19.—**The cares of the world** (τοῦ αἰῶνος); literally, *of the age;* that is, temporal and secular cares, incident to the age in which our lot is cast, and which are common to all. These, like thorns, distress and trouble, and often wound the soul; while, on the other hand, the care of the soul and the thought of heavenly things compose and establish the mind. **The deceitfulness of riches.** Riches are aptly compared to thorns, because, like thorns, they pierce the soul. St. Paul (1 Tim. vi. 10) speaks of some who, through the love of riches, "have pierced themselves through with many sorrows." Riches are deceitful, because they often seduce the soul from God and from salvation, and are the cause of many sins. "How hardly," says our Lord, "shall a rich man enter into the kingdom of God!" They have a tendency to choke the Word of God, and to weaken the power of religion. "Those are the only true riches," says St. Gregory, "which make us rich in virtue."

Ver. 20.—**Those are they that were sown upon the good ground.** The good ground represents the heart which receives the Word of God with joy and desire, and true devotion of spirit, and which steadfastly retains it, whether in prosperity or in adversity; and so yields fruit, "some thirty, some sixty, and some a hundredfold." St. Jerome remarks that, as of the bad ground there were three different kinds—the wayside, the rocky, and the thorny ground; so of the good ground there is a threefold gradation indicated in the amount of its productiveness. There are differences of conditions in the hearts both of those who believe and of those who do not believe.

Ver. 21.—**Is a candle brought to be put under a bushel,** etc.? The Greek is ὁ λύχνος, and is better rendered *the lamp.* The figure is recorded by St. Matthew (v. 15) as used by our Lord in his sermon on the mount. It is evident that he repeated his sayings, and used them sometimes in a different connection. The lamp is here the light of Divine truth, shining in the person of Christ. *Is the lamp brought to be put under the bushel?* It comes to us. The light in our souls is not of our own kindling; it comes to us from God, that we may manifest it for his glory. "The bushel" (μόδιος), from the Latin *modius,* a measure containing flour, was the flour-bin, a part of the furniture of every house, as was the tall lampstand with its single light. St. Luke (viii. 16) calls it "a vessel" (καλύπτει αὐτὸν

σκεύει). The light is to be set on "a lampstand," and in like manner the light which we have received is to shine before men. As Christians, we are Christ's light-bearers. By this illustration our Lord teaches that he was unwilling that the mysteries of this great parable of the sower and of other parables should be concealed, but that his disciples should unfold these things to others as he had to them, although at present they might not be able to receive them.

Ver. 22.—**For there is nothing hid which shall not be manifested.** The Greek of the latter part of this sentence, according to the best authorities, runs thus: ἐὰν μὴ ἵνα φανερωθῇ; so the true rendering of the words is, *there is nothing hid save that it should be manifested;* that is, there is nothing now hid, but in order that it may be made known. There is a great principle of the Divine operations here announced by our Lord. Much, very much, is now hidden from us, in nature, in providence, and in grace. But it will not always be hidden. In natural things more and more is revealed as science advances, and in providence and in grace the mysteries of the kingdom will one day, and at the fitting time, be laid open to all. "What I tell you in the darkness, speak ye in the light" (Matt. x. 27).

Ver. 24.—**Take heed what ye hear.** Attend, that is, to these words which ye hear from me, that ye may understand them, and commit them to memory, and so be able to communicate them effectually to others. Let none of my words escape you. Our Lord bids us to pay the greatest attention to his words, and so to digest them that we may be able to teach them to others. **With what measure ye mete it shall be measured unto you: and more shall be given unto you.** Our Lord's meaning is clearly this: If you freely and plentifully communicate and preach my doctrine to others, you shall receive a corresponding reward. Nay, you shall have a return in far more abundant measure. For thus the fountains, the more water they pour out below, so much the more do they receive from above. Here, then, is great encouragement to all faithful teachers of the Word, of whatever kind; that by how much they give to others in teaching them, by so much the more shall they receive of wisdom and grace from Christ; according to those words of the apostle, "He that soweth bountifully shall reap also bountifully" (2 Cor. ix. 6).

Ver. 25.—**For he that hath, to him shall be given.** He that uses his gifts, whether of intellect or of goodness, bestowed upon him by God, to him shall be granted an increase of those gifts. But from him who uses them not, God will gradually take them away. Christ here encourages his apostles and disciples to diligent and earnest preaching of his gospel, by promising them in return yet greater influxes of his wisdom and grace.

Vers. 26—28.—This parable is recorded by St. Mark alone. It differs greatly from the parable of the sower, although both of them are founded upon the imagery of the seed cast into the ground. In both cases the seed represents the doctrine of the gospel; the field represents the hearers; the harvest the end of the world, or perhaps the death of each individual hearer. So is the kingdom of God, in its progress from its establishment to its completion. The sower casts seed upon the earth, not without careful preparation of the soil, but without further sowing. And then he pursues his ordinary business. He sleeps by night; he rises by day; he has leisure for other employment; his work as a sower is finished. Meanwhile the seed germinates and grows by its own hidden virtues, assisted by the earth, the sun, and the air, the sower knowing nothing of the mysterious process. First comes the blade, then the ear, then the full corn in the ear. Such is the preaching of the gospel. Here, therefore, the sower represents human responsibility in the work. The vitality of the seed is independent of his labour. The earth develops the plant from the seed by those natural but mysterious processes through which the Creator is ever working. So in spiritual things, the sower commences the work, and the grace of God perfects it in the heart which receives these influences. The earth beareth fruit of herself. In like manner, by degrees, the faith of Christ increases through the preaching of the gospel; and the Church grows and expands. And what is true of the Church collectively is true also of each individual member of the Church. For the heart of each faithful Christian produces first the blade, when it conceives good desires and begins to put them into action; then the ear, when it brings them to good effect; and lastly the full corn in the ear, when it brings them to their full maturity and perfection. Hence our Lord in this parable intimates that they who labour for the conversion of souls ought, with much patience, to wait for the fruit of their labour, as the husbandman waits with much patience for the precious fruits of the earth.

Ver. 29.—But when the fruit is ripe (ὅταν δὲ παραδῷ ὁ καρπὸς). The verb here is active; it might be rendered *delivereth up*, or *alloweth*. It is a peculiar expression, though evidently meaning "when the fruit is ready." He putteth forth the sickle, because the harvest is come. As soon as Christ's work is completed, whether in the Church or in the individual, "immediately" the sickle is sent forth. As soon as a Christian is ready for heaven, God calls him away; and therefore we may infer that it is unwise, if not sinful, for a Christian, oppressed it may be with sickness or trouble, to be eager in wishing to leave this world. "It is one thing to be willing to go when God pleases; it is another thing to speak as though we wished to hasten our departure." "When the fruit is ripe, *immediately* he putteth forth the sickle." If, therefore, the sickle is not yet sent forth, it is because the fruit is not yet fully ripe. The afflictions of the faithful are God's means to ripen them for heaven. They are the dressing which the Lord of the vineyard employs to make the tree more fruitful, to make the Christian more fruitful in grace, and more ripe for glory.

Vers. 30—32.—Whereunto shall we liken the kingdom of God? or with what comparison shall we compare it? In the first clause of this verse the best authorities give πῶς for τίνι, *How shall we liken the kingdom of God?* and in the second clause, instead of the Greek of which the Authorized Version is the rendering, the best-approved reading is (τίνι αὐτὴν παραβολῇ θῶμεν), *in what parable shall we set it forth?* Our Lord thus stimulates the intellect of his hearers, by making them his associates, as it were, in the search for appropriate similitudes (see Dr. Morison, *in loc.*). The kingdom of God, that is, his Church on earth, is like a grain of mustard seed. By this image our Lord shows the great power, fertility, and extension of the Church; inasmuch as it started from a very small and apparently insignificant beginning, and spread itself over the whole world. It is not literally and absolutely true that the grain of mustard seed is less than all seeds. There are other seeds which are less than it. But the expression may readily be allowed when we compare the smallness of the seed with the greatness of the results produced by it. It is one of the least of all seeds. And so the preaching of the Gospel and the establishment of the Church was one of the smallest of beginnings. Perhaps the well-known pungency of the seed of the mustard plant may suggest the quickening, stimulating power of the Gospel when it takes root in the heart. The mustard plant shoots out large branches, which are used as fuel in some countries, quite large enough for shadow for the birds. A traveller in South America says that it grows to so large a tree upon the slopes of the mountains of Chili that he could ride under its branches.

Vers. 33, 34.—With many such parables; such, that is, as he had just been delivering —plain and simple illustrations which all might understand; not abstruse and difficult similitudes, but sufficiently plain for them to perceive that there was heavenly and Divine truth lying hidden beneath them, so that they might be drawn onwards through that which they did understand, to search into something hidden beneath it, which at present they did not know. **But privately to his own disciples he expounded** (ἐπέλυε) **all things.** This word (ἐπιλύω) occurs nowhere else in the Gospels. But it does occur in St. Peter's second Epistle (i. 20), "No Scripture is of any private (ἐπιλύσεως) exposition, or interpretation." This suggests a connection between St. Mark's Gospel and that Epistle, and may be accepted as an auxiliary evidence, however small, as to the genuineness of the Epistle.

Vers. 35, 36.—And on that day,—the day, that is, on which the parables were delivered, at least those recorded by St. Mark—**when even was come, he saith unto them, Let us go over unto the other side. And leaving the multitude, they take him with them, even as he was, in the boat.** It was the boat from which he had been preaching. They made no special preparation. They did not land first to obtain provisions. It would have been inconvenient to go ashore in the midst of the crowd. They made at once, as he told them to do, for the other side. **And other boats were with him.** This is another interesting circumstance. Probably those who were in these boats had availed themselves of them to get nearer to the great Prophet, the boatmen themselves having seen the vast crowd that was gathered on the shore, and so having been attracted thither. Thus he had a large audience on the sea as well as on the land. And now it was so ordered that he was surrounded by a fleet and by a multitude of witnesses when he stilled the tempest.

Ver. 37.—And there arose a great storm of wind; literally, *there ariseth* (γίνεται λαῖλαψ). St. Mark often uses the historical present, which gives vigour and point to his narrative. **And the waves beat into the boat, insomuch that the boat was now filling** (ἤδη γεμίζεσθαι). St. Matthew says (viii. 24), "the boat was covered with the waves." St. Luke (viii. 23), "they were filling with water, and were in jeopardy." Bede and others have thought that the boat in which Christ was was the only boat that was tossed by this storm; in order that Christ might show his power in limiting the area of the tempest. But it is far more probable that the other boats were subject to it; for they were very near to the boat in which Christ was. There must have been some

reason for the allusion to these boats; and the wider the reach of the tempest, the greater would appear the Divine power of Christ in stilling it, and the greater the amount of testimony to the reality of the miracle. The miracle was wrought to show his power over all creation, the sea as well as the dry land; and that they, his disciples, and all who were with him might believe in him as the Omnipotent God. But further, this tempest on the sea of Galilee was a type and symbol of the trials and temptations which should come on the Church. For the Church of God is as a ship in a storm, ever tossed upon "the waves of this troublesome world." And then, moreover, as the rude storm urges the ship onwards, so that it more quickly reaches the desired haven, so afflictions and temptations quicken Christ's disciples to the greater desire of holiness, by which they are borne onwards more speedily to "the haven where they would be."

Ver. 38.—And he was in the hinder part of the ship, asleep on a pillow; more literally, *he himself was in the stern* (ἦν αὐτὸς ἐπὶ τῇ πρύμνῃ) *asleep on the cushion* (ἐπὶ τὸ προσκεφάλαιον καθεύδων). He had changed his posture. He was weary with the labour of addressing the great multitude. He had sought the momentary rest which the crossing of the lake offered to him. He was resting his head upon the low bench which served both for a seat and for a pillow. But while he slept as man, he was watchful as God. "Behold, he that keepeth Israel neither slumbers nor sleeps." **Master, carest thou not that we perish?** This question savours of impatience, if not of irreverence. Who so likely to have put it as St. Peter? Nor would he be likely afterwards to forget that he had put it. Hence, probably, its appearance in St. Mark's Gospel.

Ver. 39.—And he arose—literally, *he awoke* (διεγερθεὶς)—**and rebuked the wind, and said unto the sea, Peace, be still** (Σιώπα, πεφίμωσο); literally, *Be silent! be muzzled!* The Greek perfect implies that before the word was uttered, the thing was done by the simple fiat of his will preceding the word. The combined descriptions of the synoptists show that the storm was very violent, such as no human power could have composed or stilled. So that these words indicate the supreme authority of Christ as God, ruling the sea with his mighty power. Thus Christ shows himself to be God. In like manner, Christ is able to overrule and control the persecutions of the Church and the temptations of the soul. St. Augustine says that "when we allow temptations to overcome us, Christ sleeps in us. We forget Christ at such times. Let us, then, remember him. Let us awake him.

He will speak. He will rebuke the tempest in the soul, and there will be a great calm." **There was a great calm.** For all creation perceives its Creator. He never speaks in vain. It is observable that, as in his miracles of healing, the subjects of them usually passed at once to perfect soundness, so here, there was no gradual subsiding of the storm, as in the ordinary operations of nature, but almost before the word had escaped his lips there was a perfect calm.

Ver. 40.—**And he said unto them, Why are ye fearful? have ye not yet faith?** Not πῶς οὐκ ἔχετε, but οὔπω ἔχετε. If they had faith, they would have known that, though asleep, he could preserve them.

Ver. 41.—**And they feared exceedingly, and said one to another, Who then is this, that even the wind and the sea obey him?** This would seem to have been said by the sailors, though it was doubtless assented to by all.

HOMILETICS.

Vers. 1—20.—*Spiritual sowing.* It is a picturesque and memorable sight. Multitudes of people, of all classes and from every part of the land, have assembled on the western shore of the Galilean lake, where Jesus is daily occupied in teaching and in healing. To protect himself from the pressure of the crowd, and the better to command his audience, Jesus steps into a boat, and pushes off a few yards from the beach. There, with the fair landscape before him, corn-fields covering the slopes, the birds of the air above, winging their flight over the still waters,—the great Teacher addresses the people. His language is figurative, drawn from the processes of nature and the employments of husbandry, probably at the very moment apparent to his eye. How natural that, at this moment and in this scene, our Lord should introduce a new style of teaching, should enter upon a new phase of ministry! The parable, as a vehicle for spiritual truth, had indeed been employed by Jewish teachers and prophets; but it was our Lord himself who carried this style of spiritual instruction to perfection.

I. THE SOWER. Every man, and especially every teacher, is a sower—intellectual, moral, or both. Christ is emphatically *the* Sower. He was such in his ministry on earth; in his death, when the corn of wheat fell into the ground and died, he was both the Sower and the Seed; in the gospel dispensation he continues to be the Divine Sower. His apostles and all his ministers have been sowing through the long centuries, or rather he has been sowing by their hands. How wise, liberal, diligent, unwearied, is Christ in this beneficent work!

II. THE SEED. This is the Word of God. All truth is spiritual seed; the truth relating to God—his will and grace—is "the seed of the kingdom." Like the seed, the gospel is comparatively small and insignificant; it has within it inherent vitality, a living germ; it is seemingly thrown away and hidden; its nature is to grow and to increase and multiply; it is tender and depends upon the treatment it meets with whether it lives or dies.

III. THE SOIL. The human heart is adapted to receive and to cherish the spiritual seed. But as on the surface of the earth some ground is fertile and some is barren, some ground is adapted to one crop and other ground to a crop of different kind, so it is in the spiritual husbandry. Whilst all hearts are created to receive the heavenly seed, and only fulfil their end when they bear spiritual fruit, we cannot but recognize the marvellous diversity of soil into which the gospel is deposited. Yet we must not so interpret the parable as to countenance the doctrine of fatalism.

IV. THE SOWING. Was the sower in the parable guided, in the manner and measure of his sowing, by the likelihood or otherwise that the land would prove fruitful? No; neither should the gospel sower reckon probabilities: his Master did not. The sower should be liberal and indiscriminate, should "sow beside all waters," should remember that he "knows not which shall prosper, this or that." It is for him to do his work diligently and faithfully, and leave results to God; *e.g.* the mother and the child, the teacher and the class, the master and the pupil or apprentice, the preacher and the congregation, the author and the reader.

V. THE GROWTH. This is not universal; for, as the parable reminds us, it comes to pass, both in the natural and the spiritual sowing, that in some cases the seed disappears and comes to nought. Yet the redemption of Christ proclaimed, and the grace of the

Holy Spirit vouchsafed, co-operate oftentimes to most blessed results, even as in nature seed and soil, showers and sunshine, produce a vigorous growth.

VI. THE HARVEST. What is the end of sowing and tilling, of culture and toil? It is fruit. And, in the spiritual kingdom, what is the aim and recompense of the Divine and of all human sowers? It is fruit—of holiness, obedience, love, joy, peace, eternal life. It shall not be wanting. "My word shall not return unto me void;" "They that sow in tears shall reap in joy;" "They shall bring their sheaves with them;" it may be "after many days." There is a harvest in time, and a richer, riper harvest in eternity.

PRACTICAL LESSONS. 1. One of encouragement for all gospel sowers; they are doing the Master's work, they are following the Master's example, they are assured of the Master's support. 2. One of admonition to all to whom the Word is preached. Take heed what and how you hear. The seed is heavenly; is the soil kindly, prepared, grateful, fruitful?

Vers. 4, 15.—*The Word stolen from the heart.* Young preachers, in the strength of their convictions and the ardour of their benevolence, are often inspired with enthusiastic expectations concerning the results of the preaching of the gospel. It seems to them that the Word has only to be addressed to men's minds in order to meet with an eager, grateful, and immediate acceptance. As their experience enlarges, and as they learn in how many cases reason and conscience are silenced by the clamour of passion and interest, or disregarded through the power of sinful habit or the influence of sinful society, they turn to this parable, and learn how just was the view and how tempered the expectations of the Divine Teacher and Saviour, as to the acceptance with which his gospel should meet.

I. THE HEART HARDENED BY WORLDLINESS AND SIN IS NOT RECEPTIVE OF THE WORD. 1. *Worldly thoughts and cares* preoccupy the mind, so that there is no response to the appeals of the gospel. When the attention is absorbed by things seen and temporal, spiritual realities appear imaginary and uninteresting. As there was no room for the babe Jesus at the inn, so the nature which welcomes every passing guest finds no place for the King and for his Word. 2. *Sin* shuts out the truth. There is no fellowship between light and darkness. The sinner's heart is closed against the heavenly rays. What preacher could not, from his own observation, offer many a living illustration of the saying, "Men love darkness rather than light, because their deeds are evil"? To revert to the figure of the text, sin loved and unrepented of treads down the heart into a hard, impenetrable pathway, where no glebe breaks up, in frost, in shower, or in sunshine, to give a welcome, a home, a cradle, to the germ of spiritual life. 3. *Familiarity with truth* unheeded hardens any nature against the gospel. Who are the least hopeful in our congregations? Surely they are those who have, from habit or through influence, been attending the "means of grace" for many years, to whom every statement, every appeal, every remonstrance, every warning, is an old familiar sound, "a twice-told tale." The nature becomes not only indifferent, but callous; there is no real heed, no living susceptibility, no response of faith and joy.

II. THE ENEMY OF SOULS SNATCHES THE WORD FROM THE HARDENED HEART. The condition of the sinner's soul is such as offers to Satan an occasion for frustrating the benevolent designs of the Divine Sower. Had the seed fallen into good ground and been covered over, there would have been no invitation or opportunity for the birds to snatch it away. So it is only the worldly, sensual, or unbelieving nature that, so to speak, tempts the tempter himself. By the birds it is usually understood that the great Teacher intends to represent evil thoughts and imaginations and desires, such as possess the unspiritual and unthinking. How true to the life is this account! How many careless and unbelieving hearers of the gospel no sooner leave the church in which they have listened to the Word, than common, foolish, selfish, sinful thoughts take possession of their mind, and the Word is snatched away—is as though it had not been! The necessary result is that there is no fruit. How can there be fruit when the Word has not been mixed with faith in the hearer's heart? "Do you take care that it falls not on, but in, your souls." "Break up your fallow ground; for it is time to seek the Lord."

Vers. 5, 6, 16, 17.—*The Word starved in the heart.* The Christian preacher has sometimes reason to exclaim, " Who hath believed our report? " But sometimes he has occasion to lament over those who apparently have believed but whose goodness proves, as time passes, "as the morning cloud and as the early dew, which goeth away." Our Lord warns us that we shall meet with such cases, which first excite hope and expectation, and then cloud the soul of the Christian labourer with disappointment and sorrow. Such are compared to the rocky soil, with just a scattering of earth upon the surface, where the seed may grow, but where it will never live to produce a crop.

I. GROWTH EXCITES HOPE. In the cases symbolized by this part of the parable there is much to please and encourage the inexperienced sower of the Divine Word. We observe : 1. *Sensibility and susceptibility.* How different from the wayside hearer is this! Here we behold the truth obtaining at once a lodgment and welcome in the heart. An impressible nature is affected by the glad tidings which Christ brings from heaven. The conscience is aroused, the judgment is convinced, the heart is captivated. The first contact of the truth with the soul is of the most hopeful character. 2. *Gladness* follows the reception of the Word; for this is an emotional nature, responsive to the joyful tidings. This is indeed what ought to be expected; yet its occurrence is so rare as to occasion surprise and enkindle the most glowing expectations. It is especially in times of "revival" that such instances abound. A general excitement heightens the emotion of joy which springs up in the heart of the impressible hearer; it is joy as of one who finds a great treasure. 3. *Precocity* of growth is the natural consequence. The soil is of a "forcing" character, and yields speedy and surprising, if temporary, results. Very different from the slow, steady, gradual growth, which is most, on the whole, to be desired, is the rapid development of the religious life in the superficial convert of the apparent "revival." Extreme views, extravagant expectations, thoughtless but ardent resolves,—all testify to the quick, unhealthy growth.

II. WITHERING BRINGS DISAPPOINTMENT. 1. After a while a *season of trial* comes. Time tries all, and affliction and persecution arise. This is the providential appointment; it is discipline which Divine wisdom deems necessary. In the early days of Christianity this was a common test, and in some form and in some measure it continues and will long continue to be so. 2. Before the scorching sun the feeble growth is *withered and destroyed.* The furnace which refines the gold consumes the straw. The effect at first produced was owing to novelty, excitement, company, enthusiasm. Only the surface was reached, below was nothing. The transitory joy is followed by depression, carelessness, stolidity, obduracy. Perhaps there is a hope of the renewal of excitement, which never comes. It is seen that belief is not faith, feeling is not principle, joy is not life. To endure that test there is needed an inward, hidden life, hidden with Christ in God. There is needed a soil watered continually by heavenly dews and showers. "Blessed is he that endureth!"

APPLICATION. 1. Let sanguine preachers and teachers take a sober and scriptural view of their work, and guard against being misled by enthusiasm and extravagant expectations. 2. Let hearers of the gospel seek grace that the truth may not only touch but may penetrate their heart; let them seek the Holy Spirit's aid that they may hear the Word of God, and *keep* it!

Vers. 7, 18, 19.—*The Word choked in the heart.* Thorns make a good hedge but a bad crop. The soil here described was in itself rich, good soil. But it could not grow both thorns and wheat, and, when occupied by the one, failed to yield the other.

I. WHAT ARE THE THORNS THAT OVERGROW THE SOIL? Thorns, thistles, brambles, briers, are signs of neglect. They are the emblems of the primeval curse, for the garden was by our first parents exchanged for the thorny wilderness. In our parable the thorns are explained to represent: 1. "*The cares of this world.*" Cares, whether of State or business, of letters or science, of family or calling, may occupy the mind which has received the truth of God, to such an extent as to hinder that truth from growing up.

> "Care, when it once hath entered in the breast,
>   Will have the whole possession ere it rest."

Cares are distractions, and, even when concerning lawful things, if unchecked, are detrimental and disastrous. This is the special temptation of the poor and hardworking. Well are we directed to be " careful for nothing," etc., and " to take no thought for the morrow," etc. 2. " *The deceitfulness of riches*" is depicted under the figure of the thorns. The possession of wealth may be a curse to the rich, and the search—the race—after riches may be a curse to the avaricious and worldly. The unwary are deceived ; for riches promise what they cannot give, and they sometimes draw away the heart from the treasure in heaven, which alone can truly enrich and satisfy for ever. How many, trusting in riches, have failed of the kingdom ! 3. " *The lusts of other things*" have much of mischief laid to their charge. Pleasure is a fair and fragrant flower, but it may hide a thorn. It may be manifestly sinful, it may be doubtful, it may be innocent but unduly absorbing,—and in any such case it may choke the Word. How many are the things which men put in the place of religion ! They are left unnamed, that we may supply them from our own knowledge of our own hearts and their mani- fold and varied snares. To desire aught earthly overmuch is to desire things heavenly too little.

II. How DO THESE THORNS CHOKE THE SEED? In two ways : 1. By *taking up the room* which the Word requires. They occupy the short and fleeting period of time allotted for our probation. The leisure for pondering and practically obeying the truth never comes. Time flies : the soul dies. They absorb attention and engage the heart. The words of the world must be listened to, and Christ must wait until " a more con- venient season"—which never comes. But if the world must have our ears, must claim our hands, Christ should have our heart. Alas ! men plan and toil, prosper and grow rich, respected, powerful, famous; and in doing so neglect the Word. Little know they of the mind of Paul, " To me to live is Christ." 2. By *counteracting the influence* of the truth. In the former case (the rocky ground) it was persecution ; in this case it is the allurements of the world which prove injurious to the soul. Cares and lusts are thorns which must be choked or they choke. So thorn and corn grow side by side with a fair show. But gradually the evil gains the victory, and goodness perishes. What experienced sower has not seen and mourned over the process ? Warnings are in vain. The thorns grow apace ; the soul becomes insensible to all the claims of Christ, to all the appeals of the gospel. So the Word is unfruitful as before.

> " Stones mar the root ;
> Thorns spoil the fruit."

What poor produce there is comes to no maturity, no perfection. Labour is wasted, promise is blasted, hope is clouded, all is lost !

APPLICATION. None who receive the Word of life are free from the danger here described. Search and find out the hindrances to vigour and fruitfulness in the spiritual life. Root them all up, that the Word may live and grow and yield abun- dance. Look for fruit ; God looks for it as the only proof of life. Else, when the Lord comes and finds no fruit, the thorns will indeed be burned, but the ground will be exposed as fruitless and worthless, and " nigh unto cursing."

Vers. 8, 20.— *The Word fruitful in the heart.* Most varied results attend the preaching of the gospel. Look at our Lord's own ministry. On the one hand, we are told, " He did there no mighty works because of their unbelief ; " " yet they believed not upon him ; " and we find him exclaiming, " Woe unto you, cities ! " etc. On the other hand, " the multitude heard him gladly ; " of the Samaritans, " many more believed because of his word," and sometimes, in their eagerness, " they pressed upon him to hear," etc. Nor was this fact peculiar to Christ's ministry ; the apostles confessed that they were to some a savour of life, to others of death ; and the historian records, as a matter of fact, that " some believed, and some believed not." So is it with Christian preachers in every age ; there are instances which rejoice and recompense them, and others which disappoint and depress them. The great Teacher foretells in this part of the parable that there shall ever be cases in which the Lord's Word " shall not return unto him void."

1. THE PREPARED SOIL. The good ground was in contrast with the several varieties of poor and bad soil. It was soft and yielding, as distinguished from the trodden earth of the wayside. It was deep, as distinguished from the shallow sprinkling of earth upon the rock beneath. It was clean, as distinguished from the foul, weedy, thorny land.

So with the honest and good heart, prepared by Divine influences and responsive to Divine culture and care. There is in this figurative language no countenance given to fatalism. We meet with good ground sometimes amongst those brought up in the Christian family and Church, as in Timothy; sometimes amongst those not specially privileged, but candid and guileless, as in Nathanael; sometimes even among the outwardly wicked, who yet may not be hardened, but may be ready to welcome deliverance from their evil ways, as in some of the publicans and sinners. Similar instances are recorded in the Acts of the Apostles.

II. THE VITAL PROCESS. In the other cases, the seed sooner or later perishes; in this case it lives. It is neither stolen, nor starved, nor choked. The reason is that the soil accepts and retains the seed. So with the heart that not only receives but holds fast the Word of life, that cherishes and matures it, that gives it a resting-place, and welcomes all heavenly influences which can quicken and strengthen and prosper it. That nature will develop into Divine life and immortal fruitfulness which ponders the truth of God, assimilates it, keeps for it the place of honour, pre-eminence, and power, gives it room and scope and play, watches over it and prays for its vitality, energy, and increase. In such a nature the seed germinates and lives and grows, for it finds there congenial soil and cordial welcome and sustenance. The power of this life is that of the Holy Spirit: "God giveth the increase."

III. THE FRUITFUL HARVEST. What is meant by "fruit"? Spiritual result for spiritual toil and agency and culture. In the case of the sinner, the first and most welcome fruit is that of conversion unto God. But the rich fruits expected are these: obedience, righteousness, holiness, Christlikeness, consecration, self-denial, usefulness. "The fruit of the Spirit is love, joy, peace," etc. Such fruit is the only proof of life and growth. "By their fruits ye shall know them;" i.e. by the quality, the flavour, and fragrance of the moral produce. "Herein is my Father glorified, that ye bear much fruit;" i.e. by abundance alone can the husbandman be satisfied and recompensed. The multiplication of the seed is one of the many points of resemblance between the physical and the spiritual life. Who has not seen a heart changed by one sermon, a life made anew by one utterance or by one lesson of Divine providence? Seemingly an insignificant seed, yet a crop of glorious ripeness and luxuriance. And as for variety, every congregation of Christians is a living witness to this. Either because the same opportunities have been, in some cases, more diligently used, or because different advantages have been employed with equal assiduity; it results that some yield fruit thirty, some sixty, and others a hundredfold.

PRACTICAL LESSONS. 1. The responsibility of hearing the Word. God provides the seed; but the preparation of the soil is largely in our hands. 2. The expectation of the Sower is great in proportion to the greatness of our advantages. Nothing less than much fruit can satisfy him from you.

Vers. 10—13, 21—25.—*The lamp of parabolic teaching.* Probably the opposition, malignity, and misrepresentation of the scribes and Pharisees were the occasion of the commencement by our Lord of a new style of public teaching. He did not wish at present to excite so much turmoil and violence as should lead to the interruption of his ministry. His design was to introduce into men's minds new ideas of the spiritual reign of God—ideas altogether in contradiction to their own carnal notions and hopes. He knew, however, the importance of considering the character and the mental position of the learner, in order that the mature might be thoroughly enlightened and instructed, in order that the immature might be encouraged to inquiry and to thought, in order that, for a season, the doctrine might remain concealed from the unspiritual and the unsympathetic.

I. THE LAMP OF DIVINE TEACHING IS INTENDED TO GIVE LIGHT. The Galilean cottage had its lampstand, its bed, its corn-measure; and every peasant could see the absurdity of first kindling the lamp and then hiding it under the meal-box or the couch. Let it be put upon the lofty stand, and it will give light to all. So when Christ came, the great Teacher, the great Saviour, he came a light into the world, to be the light of men. His words, his character, his deeds, his whole life, were an illumination from heaven. When he taught he taught for all humanity and for all time.

II. THE PARABOLIC FORM OF TEACHING WAS NO EXCEPTION. The parable hid the truth, made a secret of it, enclosed it like a jewel in a casket. But it was never intended that the truth should remain concealed; the intention was that it should be manifested, that it should come to light (ver. 22). And, as a matter of fact, the figurative and pictorial form has served to display and illumine rather than to hide the great truths of Christianity. To how many simple, childlike minds have the parables of our Lord Jesus brought home lessons of wisdom, grace, hope, and consolation! And what materials for reflection, what profound spiritual help and illumination, have they afforded to the thoughtful student of the Word! And what themes for the teacher, the preacher, the expositor, have these parables ever been found! They are "a mystery;" but a mystery is a truth once hidden but now made clear and published abroad.

III. IN FACT, PARABOLIC TEACHING IS DARKNESS TO THE UNSPIRITUAL AND LIGHT TO THE SPIRITUAL. Like all good things, it may be used and it may be abused. When Christ speaks, there are those who do not perceive, who do not understand. Is this the fault of the Word? No, it is the fault of their own inattentive, unreceptive, unsympathizing nature. It is they, the hearers, who are to blame; not the truth which they will not appreciate (ver. 12). Yet are there those "who have ears to hear;" and these hear. To them the Word is as music, satisfying their souls, bringing to them the thoughts of the Divine mind, the love of the Divine heart, the secret of the Divine purposes. To them it is said, "Happy are your ears, for they hear!"

IV. CHRISTIANS LEARN THE MYSTERY THAT THEY MAY PUBLISH IT. Speaking especially to his apostles, but through them to all who receive the gospel, our Lord bids those who welcome and value the truth to proclaim it far and wide. It is light intended for the world's illumination; let it be set up on high, that all in this great dark house of humanity may see their way to God. It is meal for the hungering multitude; let it be dealt forth to every applicant with no sparing hand, no grudging heart. There is light enough for all who are in darkness; bread enough for all who are in danger of starving. It is the office of the members of Christ's Church to hold forth the light of life, to take of the food and, as it multiplies in their hands, to give to the vast multitude in the barren wilderness.

V. WE ARE ACCOUNTABLE BOTH FOR THE WAY IN WHICH WE RECEIVE AND FOR THE WAY IN WHICH WE IMPART DIVINE TRUTH. 1. "Take heed what and how ye hear." It is unprofitable and wrong to offer a willing ear to every teacher, to all tidings. On the other hand, it is folly and sin to turn away from him who speaketh from heaven, or to listen to him with inattention, with unconcern, with unsympathizing, unbelieving hearts. 2. "With what measure ye mete it shall be measured unto you." Be faithful, be diligent, fulfil your trust with zeal and wisdom, display benevolence towards the untaught and the unblessed, and you shall receive more—more of truth and more of spiritual enrichment and joy. On the other hand, the selfish, the unpitying, the unfaithful, shall gain nothing by spiritual niggardliness; from them shall be taken away even that which they have.

Vers. 26—29.—*Spiritual growth.* There are common truths and a common interpretation underlying this and several other parables. In all this group the seed is the Word of God, the soil is the heart of man, the life is the spiritual history and development, the fruit is Christian character, and the harvest is eternal result and retribution. But the peculiar lesson of this parable is the nature of spiritual growth. It this case it is presumed that the seed is sown in good soil.

I. IT IS HIDDEN, AND CANNOT BE TRACED AND WATCHED. Until it is deposited in the ground, seed may be beheld and examined by the eye. But then it is covered up and concealed, and germinates and begins to grow beneath the surface. In like manner you may see the truth as written, you may hear it as spoken; but when once it gets into the heart, germinates, and goes to its work, the preacher and teacher fail to follow it, and altogether lose sight of it. In the silent soul the Divine seed works in secret, lives, strives, moves, grows. Probably those reared in Christian homes cannot recollect when the truth, quickened by the Spirit, first began to live in them. Certainly you can only very dimly follow the process of growth in others. Years pass; the youth grows into the man, goes about daily duty, takes nightly rest, and all the while the hidden seed is living and developing slowly or swiftly, but unperceived even by those who planted it. How little, in some instances, preachers and teachers and parents can follow the Word, as it does its work within the hearts of those for whom they care! Yet "the kingdom of God comes without observation." Convictions of their own spiritual nature and immortal destiny, of the character and government of God, of the love and reign of Christ, are all forming within, becoming part of the spiritual being. And the vital growth, though unperceived, is giving signs of its reality.

II. IT IS MYSTERIOUS AND NOT TO BE UNDERSTOOD. The husbandman, the gardener, "knoweth not how." Even the scientific observer cannot explain the mystery of life and growth. There is no caprice; all is reason and law, yet the process baffles our understanding. So in the working of God's kingdom within, there is much that is mysterious. How can Divine truth, naturally so unpalatable, gain a hold upon the heart? How can it overmaster other principles so that it shall flourish as they fade? And, looking to the external, how can we account for it, that the kingdom of God, so unworldly, can advance to universal victory? The power of life must be that of the Holy Spirit, acting like the sunlight and the genial warmth, the frequent showers and the morning dew. It is the Lord's doing, invisible, incomprehensible, admirable, adorable, Divine!

III. IT IS ACCORDING TO ITS OWN LAWS, NOT OURS. In dealing with vegetation, there is much which we can do if we work *with* nature. We can till the soil, expose the seed to moisture and warmth, protect it from unfavourable conditions. But we cannot work *against* laws of nature; we cannot make pebbles grow, acorns produce elm trees, or barley yield a crop of wheat; we cannot grow the produce of the tropics at the poles. Providence has imposed laws upon nature, and with regard to life some things are possible, and others impossible. So spiritual life follows laws which we cannot change, and much of our interference has no influence or but little. The seed grows "of itself," *i.e.* as God appoints for it. The truth of God is not trammelled by our notions or fancies; the Spirit of God is not hampered by our rules. Men prove their own pettiness when they attempt to prescribe how the Divine seed shall grow. The Giver of the seed and Lord of the harvest does his work in his own way and time. He carries on a heavenly process in the conscience and the heart, in the bosom of human society. Vain is our fancy that we can rule the life. "Paul plants, Apollos waters, and God gives the increase."

IV. THE PROCESS IS USUALLY GRADUAL AND PROGRESSIVE. There is a regular law of development, "first the blade," etc. We never get the fruit first, the blade last. Everything in its season. So in the spiritual kingdom of God. In the child or the young convert, we look first for signs of life—the blade which proves that the seed has germinated. By Christian nurture, scriptural instruction, and Divine discipline, gradual and sure progress is made. The promise is partly realized when the ear is formed; it is the time of vigour and manifest growth. Then with the long and profitable years comes the full corn—the ripeness of Christian knowledge, experience, and service. A few favourable years bring the seedling to the sapling, and the sapling to the stalwart tree; a few months cover the broad brown tilth with the golden shocks. So in the Church of Christ we see the gradual unfolding of character, the gentle ripening of experience, one stage of growth left behind in making way for that which succeeds.

V. THE HARVEST IS THE END AND THE RECOMPENSE OF ALL. If the growth is unobtrusive, the harvest is conspicuous. The secret working has prepared for the open result. Life ends in fruit. It is so in the spiritual field. When there is ripeness, then the time has come for the sickle to be put in. The harvest is gathered, and the garner of God is filled with golden grain. Fruit is yielded upon earth; and the richest crop is reaped hereafter.

APPLICATION. 1. The Christian sower and labourer may learn to think humbly of himself, highly of his work. 2. There is encouragement for the "babes in Christ;" their stage of experience is the necessary preparation for the more complete fulfilment of the high purposes of God. 3. The glory must be given to God when life is vigorous and when fruit is ripe.

Vers. 30—32.—*The mustard seed.* The kingdom of God has its intension and its extension, its rule over the individual soul, and its sway over human society, its invisible work within and its manifest and mighty achievement without; it transforms character and it renews the world.   Perhaps it is fair to regard the preceding parable of " the seed growing secretly " as a parable of the history of the Word in the *heart*; and this of the mustard seed as a parable of the fortunes and destiny of the Word in the *world*.   Our attention is here directed to—

I. THE SMALL AND INSIGNIFICANT BEGINNINGS OF CHRIST'S KINGDOM.   The suggestions of nature here are many and striking.   Not only does the tree begin with a seed, the eagle comes from an egg, the river is first a little rill, the fire is ignited by a spark, and every day, however gorgeous, begins with a faint and glimmering dawn.   1. The *Lord Jesus himself*, in his simplicity and humiliation, seemed most unlikely to be the Founder of the greatest of all kingdoms.   " Despised and rejected of men," cast out, calumniated, and crucified, Jesus was as the grain of mustard seed.   2. The *apostles* of the Saviour were termed " ignorant and unlearned men," and were apparently little adapted to revolutionize the world.   But in them God chose " the weak things of the world to confound the mighty."   3. The *early Church* may well have seemed to an observer to have had a poor prospect of growing into a world-embracing community.   In many a thoughtful mind, only doubt and perplexity could arise as to " whereunto this thing should grow."   Few, feeble, contemned, these little societies were, however, the earnest of a universal Church.   It was then " the day of small things."   4. The very characteristics of Christianity gave little promise of the diffusion of this religion throughout the world. Its defiance of worldly principles and powers, its spirituality, its dependence upon unseen might, its warfare with prevailing error and sin,—all seemed prejudicial to its prospects of progress and victory.

II. THE SECRET OF THE PROGRESS OF CHRIST'S KINGDOM.   The figurative language of the parable suggests what this is.   It is the supernatural *life* which inspires it.   Life comes from life; and the Divine vitality and growth of the Christian Church is owing to the indwelling of a heavenly principle and force.   A Divine Saviour, a Divine Spirit, a Divine Word,—these account for the fact that Christianity lives and grows, expands and conquers, day by day and year by year.   These alone explain its resistance alike of force and of corruption, its endurance amidst all changes of civilization, its permanence when all things else fleet, vanish, disappear.

III. THE DESTINED MAJESTIC GROWTH OF CHRIST'S KINGDOM.   The Oriental mustard tree, with its large, strong branches, where the birds settle and eat the pungent seeds, beneath the shadow of which men rest, serves as an emblem of the vastness and capacious hospitality and ample provision of Christianity in its ultimate perfection.   The records of our religion tell of noble character, of sublime heroism, of saintly devotion, of marvellous patience, of mature wisdom, of boundless benevolence.   And all have sprung from that seed which fell into the ground and died eighteen centuries ago in Judæa.   The progress of Christianity during the first centuries of persecution, its conquest of the barbarian conquerors, its purification under the Reformers, its modern missions to the East and to the South,—all prove its inherent vitality, and predict its ultimate universality of dominion.   The predictions alike of the Old and New Testaments are glowing and inspiriting, yet, in our own days, even calm calculation will not deem their fulfilment improbable, whilst faith beholds them already realized.   The " kingdoms of this world shall become the kingdoms of our Lord and of his Christ."

APPLICATION.   1. The discouraged may learn here a lesson of patience.   The growth of knowledge, virtue, and piety, may be slow, but it is sure.   " The husbandman waiteth for the precious fruit."   2. All labourers in Christ's cause may be of good cheer; for what has been beheld of progress is enough to inspire with confidence and animate to toil : " Your labour will not be in vain in the Lord."

Vers. 35—41.—*The storm : the two questions.*   The scene here depicted by the evangelist is an emblem of the condition, of the needs, of the fears, of the Church of Christ; and of the perpetual presence, the brotherly care, the Divine dignity, of the Lord.   The disciples were on the Sea of Gennesaret; and we are upon the sea of life— of this uncertain world.   They took Christ with them in the boat; and we have him with us alway.   A storm arose and threatened their safety ; and we, as long as we are here, are exposed to the tempests of trial, doubt, and danger.   Jesus slept; and to us it sometimes seems as though he had forgotten and abandoned us.   At the disciples' cry, Jesus arose and stilled the storm ; and never can we call upon him without experiencing his friendly and effectual interposition. He reproached the faithless; and for us too he has often a word of expostulation. His authority impressed the disciples' minds with reverence; and never can we contemplate his character and his saving might without renewing our faith and adoration. There are two questions in the record which represent the two movements of the narrative.

I. THE QUESTION OF THE DISCIPLES, "HAST THOU NO CARE?" It was the cry of impulse, and a cry which has often sprung from the heart of the Lord's people in their griefs and dangers. 1. A cry of *fear.* Christians have the same natural passions as other men. In times of bodily danger, in scenes of public commotion and disaster, in circumstances of threatening and suffering to the Church, the fears of Christ's people have often been awakened. "We perish!" "Carest thou not?" "Save us!" Such are the exclamations uttered by imperilled, anxious, and terrified souls. 2. A cry, evincing some *faith.* If the disciples had been altogether without faith, they would not have appealed to Jesus, they would not have called him "Master!" they would not have entreated him to save them. So, when in our distress we call upon the Lord that he will deliver us, we prove that we have some faith in him whose help we seek. 3. A cry, however, evincing *defect of faith.* If the disciples' faith in their Master had been perfect, they would not have given way to panic, and they would not have been rebuked. Our attitude of spirit often proves the deficiency and imperfection of our confidence in our Lord. There was want of faith in his *knowledge.* Did he not, though sleeping, understand their danger and their need? A want of faith in his *interest and care.* He did care; and they ought, even in such circumstances, to have felt assured of this. A want of faith in his habitual *rule.* Though slumbering, he was nature's Lord. And how often are we, Christ's people, guilty of overlooking, in our distresses, the acquaintance of Jesus with our case, the power of Jesus over our foes, the love of Jesus for our souls!

II. THE QUESTION OF THE CHRIST, "HAVE YE NO FAITH?" Well might Jesus appeal thus to his disciples. Often had they experienced his power. Always had he justified their confidence. Never had he forgotten or forsaken them. How justly may our Lord address a similar expostulation to us when we are ready to abandon ourselves to sorrow and to despair! 1. *No faith,* when there is such an *Object* of faith? Christ has shown himself, by his character and his work, to be deserving of all faith; and when we have least confidence in ourselves or our fellow-men we may well have all confidence in him. 2. *No faith* when in human life there is so much *need of faith?* From danger, temptation, sorrow, sin, there is no exemption. If we throw up faith in Christ, we throw up all. 3. *No faith,* when we have *so many examples* and instances to justify faith? Refer to Old Testament history in the light of Heb. xi.; refer to the Gospel narratives of the centurion, of the Canaanite woman, etc.; refer to the instances of our Lord's gracious reply to the appeal and prayer of faith;— and ask if there is any excuse for withholding faith. 4. *No faith,* when *absence of faith must leave the heart desolate and helpless?* What do you lose and forfeit if you are without confidence in Christ? Peace of mind, strength for life's conflicts, hope in suffering and in age and in death. Can we forego all these? 5. *No faith,* when there is such express *encouragement* to trust in Christ? He himself invites our confidence: "Believe in me;" "Be not faithless, but believing;" "Have ye not *yet* faith?"

APPLICATION. 1. Let the unbelieving repent of their unbelief, and look unto and call upon Jesus; that henceforth, knowing his grace, they may surely trust in him. 2. Let the doubting Christian be encouraged to put away his fears, and to pray, "Lord, increase our faith!" 3. Let the believing Christian remember that Christ's people can never perish.

> "With Christ in the vessel,
> I smile at the storm."

4. Let all who experience the Saviour's delivering power and grace unite in adoring him and witnessing to him: "What manner of man is this?"

HOMILIES BY VARIOUS AUTHORS.

Vers. 1, 2.—*The nature-preaching of Christ.* I. CIRCUMSTANCES OCCASIONING IT. The order of Matthew and Mark preferable and explanatory. Various considerations led him to adopt this method of teaching. 1. *A reasonable prudence.* His enemies were busy, and scarcely suffered a single opportunity to pass without spying or planning means by which to destroy him. Out of doors he would be able to keep the crowd at a greater remove, and so hostile listeners would be under better observation. 2. *Sympathy for those who were "without."* In the small country cottages, where for the most part he resided, there was no accommodation for the numbers that thronged to his ministry. Stifling heat and inconvenient jostling would ill accord with the dignity of his message. Multitudes were unable to hear or see him, and he had compassion on their souls. A different class of people, too, might be reached by this new method. 3. *The charm of nature.* There are abundant evidences of Christ's poetic and artistic sense of nature. He would be drawn forth from the heat and squalor of the small cottage to the spaciousness, grandeur, and ever-varying phenomena of the outside world. It was his own world. He was present when "the morning stars sang together" at its birth, "and without him was not anything made that was made."
    II. ADVANTAGES OF THIS MODE OF TEACHING. 1. *It linked the ideas of the spiritual world with the real world of every-day experience.* 2. *By its associating the common life of men with the Divine and eternal, the former was refined and elevated.* The many were thus addressed, and a certain general benefit received by them. 3. *The inner meaning of such teaching could only be discerned by the spiritual and devout, and thus his safety was secured.* His enemies were baffled and kept in ignorance. 4. *This teaching was attractive to all.*
    III. WHAT IT SUGGESTED AS TO THE SPHERE AND FUNCTION OF THE "KINGDOM OF GOD." 1. *That it was coextensive with the universe.* 2. *That the heavenly element is to penetrate and include the earthly element in God's world.* 3. *That the senses, if rightly used, are aids to the spirit.*—M.

Vers. 3—9; 18—23.—*The parable of the sower.* The kingdom of God as—
    I. A PRINCIPLE OF LIFE. Outwardly insignificant; exposed to the uncertainties of human agency and the vicissitudes of circumstance; yet embodying vital force, and capable under suitable conditions of producing its kind. Ever commencing anew, in germ and vital unit. A result as well as a cause, even as the seed is a fruit in the first instance. Requiring everything external of itself that is necessary to its being deposited in the minds of men to be done for it; yet containing an independent, original power of its own, viz. reproduction.
    II. A PROCESS OF GROWTH. *Dependent upon:* 1. *Manner of its reception;* 2. *Character of the hearer, i.e.* whether deep or shallow, thorough or otherwise, like the soil; 3. *Place which it holds in human regard*—whether considered as the chief or only as a subordinate interest in life; 4. *Time,*—this in all cases.
    III. A CONDITION OF FRUITFULNESS. The soul, just like the ground, if left alone, will be barren or overgrown with weeds. It must be tilled, sown, and tended. Sometimes these duties are divided, sometimes combined, but all are necessary. 1. *All true believers are not alike fruitful.* This is analogous to material and mental culture. 2. *It is enough if each brings forth according to capacity and ability.* 3. *In all cases there is compensating power of increase in the Word, beyond the natural qualities and powers of the believer, although a certain relation is always observed to the proportion of faith and diligence.* The blessing of God is especially manifest in the fruits of the Word.—M.

Vers. 3—9; 18—23.—*The parable of the sower.* As illustrating the purpose of God in his Word.
    I. TRUTH IS MEANT FOR ALL MEN.
    II. TRUTH IS OFFERED TO ALL.
    III. IT IS RECEIVED BY MANY DIFFERENT SORTS OF PEOPLE, AND IN DIFFERENT WAYS.
    IV. IT IS FRUITFUL ONLY WITH A FEW.—M.

Vers. 3—9; 18—23.—*The parable of the sower.* As exhibiting the kingdom of God—

I. IN ITS BEGINNINGS.

II. ITS PROCESSES.

III. ITS RESULTS.—M.

Vers. 3, 9.—*Christ's claim upon the attention of men.* "Hearken!" "Who hath ears to hear, let him hear!" A frequent peculiarity in Christ's speech. It is well to note when he uses it. It is the whisper of Christ. John seems to have caught and represented this manner of the Master most closely.

I. THE VALUE OF THE STATEMENTS OF THE GOSPEL. 1. *Affecting the personal interest of every one.* Happiness or misery, life or death. 2. *Determining the character of every one.* 3. *The condescension and compassion of infinite love.*

II. THE DIFFICULTY OF GIVING THEM THE ATTENTION AND CONSIDERATION THEY DESERVE. 1. *They appeal to the least-developed side of human nature.* 2. *They have little or no immediate earthly interest to commend them.* 3. *They have commoner and more latent meanings, and the latter may not be apprehended.* 4. *They have many counterfeits.* "Lo here! Lo there!" 5. *The earthly life of men is full of distractions.*

III. THE RESPONSIBILITY ATTACHING TO THEM. This remains with the hearer, and he cannot free himself. The language of Scripture and the deepest experiences of human nature alike assure us of this. 1. *God has given all men power to understand and receive his gospel.* That is, of course, provided they have not lost their reason. 2. *Personal moral effort is required with respect to them.* (1) To cease delaying. (2) To use what faculty and opportunity we have. (3) To suppress prejudice, aversion, sin, etc.—M.

Ver. 11.—*The reward of discipleship.* The sense of the word "mystery." Eleusinian and other heathen mysteries. Something previously hidden, but revealed in the gospel; or rather, something hidden from certain conditions of the moral nature of man, but revealed to other conditions.

I. IT AGREES WITH THE MANIFEST END OF DISCIPLESHIP. The learner seeks for knowledge. The disciple of any master desires to receive his special doctrine or discovery. It is the highest, the esoteric, teaching that is here promised. There are to be no secrets or reserves between the Master and his disciples. Revelation not the mere anticipation of experience, but its determining influence and its consummation.

II. IT IS BEYOND THE COMPASS OF UNAIDED HUMAN FACULTY. Christ said, "*To you it is given.*" They were not to discover it of themselves. 1. *The noblest saints who had preceded them were not able to understand* (1 Pet. i. 10—12). 2. *The wisdom of man could not discover them.* "Eye hath not seen," etc. (1 Cor. ii. 8—10; cf. Eph. i. 15—23; Col. i. 9, *seq.*).

III. IT IS A DIVINE GRACE FOR MORAL PURPOSES. This appears from the negatives of ver. 12. To produce: 1. *Repentance and faith.* 2. *Sympathy with Christ in his aims, works, and sufferings.* 3. *Triumphant superiority to the evil circumstance of the world.*—M.

Ver. 13.—*From one learn all.* I. THIS IS A PRINCIPLE NOT TO BE UNIVERSALLY ACTED UPON IN EARTHLY THINGS. Because of: 1. *Limitation of human powers.* 2. *Obscurity, complexity, and occasional discontinuity and non-uniformity of nature and human life.*

II. TO THOSE WHO ARE ILLUMINATED IT IS ABSOLUTELY VALID IN DIVINE THINGS. 1. *Not because the forms and successive stages of the truth are mere repetitions of one another.* 2. *But they are all centred and interpreted in one Person.* 3. *They all require the exercise of the same spiritual faculty.*—M.

Vers. 21, 22.—*Revelation and not concealment the final purpose of the truth.* I. THIS APPEARS FROM: 1. *Its very nature.* That which reveals (*e.g.* light) is not to be itself hidden. Its whole tendency is and has been towards greater manifestation. Each revelation of God has been grander than that which preceded. 2. *Its central signifi-*

cance in the Divine economy. It has evidently a practical relation to the whole, just as " *the* lamp " had to the peasant's room, as the general means of illumination. Everything in the world, in human lives, and in the constitution of the human soul answers to its interpreting light, which is the only true light by which they can be understood. 3. *The existence in man of a faculty for its discernment.* This may have been overlaid or perverted; but it really exists, and will answer to the believing effort to exercise it. It is Satan, not God, who has blinded the minds of those who are lost.

II. HOW STRONG MUST HAVE BEEN THE REASONS FOR TEMPORARY CONCEALMENT ! 1. *The fearful wickedness of the contemporaries of Jesus.* A *last* time with reference to many preceding stages of darkening spiritual consciousness. 2. *The revelation of that wickedness in convicting it of ignorance of Divine things.* 3. *The preservation of the Personal Truth in human form until his manifestation should be complete.*—M.

Vers. 24, 25.—" *Measure for measure ; " or, the law of equity in its relation to Divine knowledge.* A wider law (Matt. vii. 2) with special application to spiritual learning. One of the phases of the exactitude of relation between God and man, which yet admits of grace and blessing.

I. THE WORD OF GOD MUST BE RIGHTLY ATTENDED TO IN ORDER TO ITS BEING UNDERSTOOD. There is no process of mere mechanical transfer of truth into the nature of man. Experience and progress in truth are subject to the conditions of all intellectual inquiry, and also to special moral ones.

II. ACCORDING TO THE PROPORTION OF HEARING WILL BE THE SPIRITUAL BENEFIT. 1. *It is to the use of faculties, and not to their mere possession, the reward attaches.* 2. *The communication of truth is therefore a spiritual discipline.* " Quicquid recipitur, recipitur ad modum recipientis." Obedience is the gateway of knowledge. "Holding the truth in unrighteousness," we shall sooner or later lose it; holding it "in a pure conscience" and a willing spirit, we shall advance to the fulness of truth.—M.

Vers. 26—29.—*The seed cast upon the earth ; or, the self-development of truth in the heart of man.* I. THERE IS A PRE-ESTABLISHED HARMONY BETWEEN THE TRUTH AND HUMAN NATURE. The seed left in the soil germinates because of the mutual adaptation; so the Word of God.

II. THE WORD OF THE KINGDOM HAS AN INNATE POWER OF DEVELOPMENT. Under the appointed conditions it is bound to grow.

III. GOD DOES NOT INTERFERE WITH IT OR REMOVE IT UNTIL IT HAS PRODUCED ITS FRUIT. 1. *It is left to the law of gradualness.* First " the blade," etc. 2. *It is taken account of and judged in its final result.*—M.

Vers. 26—29.—*Man used and then dispensed with.* I. WHAT GOD DOES BY AND THROUGH HIS SERVANTS. *The mere sowing of the seed.* 1. Receiving the seed for one's self. 2. Imparting it vitally to other minds.

II. WHAT GOD DOES WITHOUT HIS SERVANTS. The pre-existence and independent growth of the seed a great mystery. Its hidden processes provocative of spiritual discipline to the sower. In God's hand and the womb of time (Ps. lxv.). Committing it thereto, and leaving it there, a proof and exercise of faith.

III. RESULTANT RESPONSIBILITIES. 1. *The harvest* a living growth, not a dead, mechanical effect ; manifold in its producing, modifying, and enriching causes, one in result. 2. *Judgment* on sower and sown alike. It is in the final product that the evidence as to faithfulness, obedience, and diligence is found.—M.

Vers. 30, 31.—" *Whereunto shall we liken it ?* " An invitation to mutual effort of spiritual thought and imagination. An instance of sympathetic condescension.

I. THERE ARE MANY SIMILITUDES OF THE KINGDOM OF GOD.

II. SOME ARE BETTER THAN OTHERS. Either absolutely or relatively to present circumstances.

III. WE ARE NOT TO BE ONLY PASSIVE RECIPIENTS OF CHRIST'S TEACHING.

IV. SAINTS ENJOY FELLOWSHIP WITH CHRIST IN THE DISCOVERY OF TRUTH AND IN SPIRITUAL REALIZATION.—M.

Ver. 34.—" *Without a parable spake he not unto them.*" To be understood of Christ's general habit or manner of teaching. It was specially characteristic of him after it became evident that the Pharisees were seeking an occasion for his destruction. This practice proved—

I. THE VASTNESS OF HIS SPIRITUAL RESOURCES. 1. *When prevented from using direct statements, he adopted an indirect mode of expression.* The truth was not stifled, it only assumed another form. There was not the least sign of labour or effort in making this transition. He played upon the varying moods and appearances of nature as a skilled musician upon his instrument, so as not only to discourse sweet sounds, but to suggest Divine ideas and principles. His supplies of spiritual truth must have been as inexhaustible as nature itself. He must have had many modes and degrees of expression in which to clothe the same truth. Restriction of speech in one direction only developed a larger liberty in another. 2. *In order to this his perception of truth must have been of a very deep and vital nature.* His parables were not only facile, they were felicitous. In them truth lived and breathed. It is not as more or less distant analogies one reads them, but as one might look at the naked truth itself. How instinctively must he have discerned the Divine side of things! And there is in his figurative teaching an unassuming originality, a vigour and vividness that could spring from nothing less than inward understanding of spiritual principles—a practical, sympathetic familiarity with them in their root and essence. The author of such similitudes cannot be conceived of as standing apart from Divine truth, but as one with it ; therefore the conclusion, " I am the Truth," is inevitable.

II. HIS DIDACTIC SKILL. The parables are beautiful, but it is not as creations of artistic genius that they chiefly impress us. Jesus was not the slave of his imagination. A careful adaptation of means to ends is perceptible in all his utterances. You feel that he did not want to paint a beautiful picture, but simply to tell the truth. The latter was thus rendered : (1) *self-demonstrative ;* (2) *familiar and forcible ;* and (3) *memorable.*

III. HIS PRACTICAL MORAL PURPOSE. By his parables our Lord : 1. *Demonstrated the unity of creation.* The words and works of God were one in their meaning and message. A multitude of phenomena so varied and different, yet so mutually suggestive and harmoniously concurrent in testimony, could not be a soulless medley or a resultant of blind forces ; it must be a system throughout, informed and controlled by one governing mind, and moving onward to a worthy if at present inadequately apprehended end. 2. *Redeemed nature and human life from base associations.* " In everything there was discernible the idea ; " the humblest thing was suggestive, if rightly interrogated, of the Divine. Henceforth nothing was to be considered " common or unclean." 3. *Rendered human experience a Divine discipline.* Every-day events and circumstances were charged with spiritual lessons, and revealed as " working together for good to them that love God."—M.

Vers. 30—32.—*The grain of mustard seed ; or, the growth of the kingdom of God relatively to its beginnings.* I. THE BEGINNINGS OF THE KINGDOM OF GOD, AS COMPARED WITH THOSE OF OTHER INFLUENCES AFFECTING THE WORLD'S LIFE, ARE VERY SMALL AND INSIGNIFICANT. A parable and a prophecy. Two plants, either of which might have been referred to by Christ—*Sinapis Orientalis,* a garden herb, bushy in habit, with black or white seeds, from four to six in a pod ; or the *Salvadora Persica,* commonly known as the tree mustard ; the latter the most likely. The comparison expressed in the phrase, " the least of all seeds," is a free one, and not to be understood absolutely. How minute and obscure have been the first origins of Christianity ! The Incarnation ; the upper room at Jerusalem. The first throb of repentance ; the dawning power to resist temptation ; the first acts of faith and charity ; the first words of invitation and appeal. As a *seed,* it has been for the most part hidden ; as a *plant,* it has seemed in its first upspringing like the herbs. This is true of (1) the understanding of the kingdom of God ; (2) of interest in spiritual things ; (3) of spiritual influence. 1. *It contrasts in this respect with powers founded on force, material advantages, prestige, or accidental circumstances.* Political empire ; military aggrandizement ; advance of mechanical arts and material improvements. 2. *In this respect it resembles but far exceeds the moral and intellectual movements that have marked the progress of the world :* philosophies, civilization, the sentiment of humanity, growth of science, etc.

II. Its ULTIMATE DIMENSIONS WILL BE DISPROPORTIONATELY VAST. 1. *It grows according to its own law, yet imperceptibly.* As the bud into the rose, the village into the city. 2. *It becomes comprehensive.* Other forces and vital principles are revealed as in relation to it and ultimately included. 3. *Its increase is in the direction of beneficence and universal blessing.* The truth of the epithet, "Mother Church." All the best interests of humanity are included and protected. It saves and ennobles whatever it affiliates. 4. *This is due to its own inherent genius;* not an accident. Circumstances have *not* favoured Christianity, but it has grown in spite of opposition, and converted obstacles into auxiliaries, enemies into friends. It is an absolutely *central*, and therefore the only truly *universal*, principle.—M.

Vers. 33, 34.—*The parable an instrument of mercy and judgment.* I. AN INSTRUMENT OF JUDGMENT. 1. *As concealing more than it revealed to the popular mind.* 2. *As convicting men of sinful ignorance and spiritual incapacity.* II. AN INSTRUMENT OF MERCY. 1. *The Word of God was not wholly withdrawn.* 2. *This, the only practicable form of teaching that remained to Christ, was used with constant regard to the benefit of the hearers.* 3. *The desire for Divine knowledge was thereby stimulated.* 4. *Further instruction was ever attainable by sincere inquirers.*—M.

Vers. 35—41.—*Christ and his disciples in the storm.* The service of Christ—
I. CONSISTING IN OBEDIENCE, SYMPATHY, AND CO-OPERATION.
II. INVOLVING HARDSHIP AND APPARENT RISK.
III. A TRIAL AND DISCIPLINE OF FAITH. 1. *Left to the realization of imminent destruction.* 2. *Discovering the weakness of the carnal nature.* 3. *Affording opportunity for the moral teaching of the Master.*
IV. A REVELATION OF THE DIGNITY AND POWER OF CHRIST. "This is the first of a second group of miracles. Those before mentioned are cures of bodily disease. These are deliverances from other adverse influences—the elements of nature, evil spirits, and the sins of men. Christ has authority also over these" (Godwin, on Matt. viii. 23). "Who then is this, that even the wind and the sea obey him?" The great inference: Although indefinite, yet practically a complete demonstration of Christ's Godhood.—M.

Vers. 35—41.—*The Church in the world.* Communion with Christ in—
I. SEPARATION.
II. TRIAL AND APPARENT DANGER.
III. MUTUAL SYMPATHIES AND CARES.
IV. FINAL VICTORY AND ATTAINMENT.—M.

Vers. 37—39.—*The Christian's extremity Christ's opportunity.* I. THE CHRISTIAN FREQUENTLY SUFFERED TO ENTER INTO APPARENT PERIL. 1. *Outward losses and troubles.* Persecution in its various phases and degrees. The major calamities of life. Everything seems against him, and he is continually disappointed; yet the objects sought are reasonable and proper. 2. *Inward griefs and fears.* Self-questionings as to being in a state of grace; as to whether or not God's favour has been turned away; doubts; prevailing sins.
II. IN THESE CIRCUMSTANCES ORDINARY MEANS OF DELIVERANCE ARE OF NO AVAIL. The ordinances of the Church fail to comfort or strengthen. Work for Christ becomes distasteful and mechanical. Prayer itself appears to be unanswered, etc.
III. THE REASONS FOR THIS. 1. *To correct and strengthen character.* Besetting weakness is discovered; defective principles of belief are exposed; the backward graces of the Spirit are stimulated; the whole nature is roused to keener sensitiveness, and awakened to the solemn responsibility and greatness of the Divine life. 2. *A more signal and immediate manifestation of God is vouchsafed.* (1) To create a closer and higher communion, and a more vivid sense of the supernatural, and to deepen and correct the creed of the believer. A conscious dependence upon his heavenly Father takes the place of the former distance and semi-legalism. Self and self-dependence are subdued, and practical faith made the daily experience. *One* such great and signal providence may do more than anything else to elevate and confirm the spiritual life. (2) To be a sign to them that are without. For a "means of grace," or simply as a

warning and an undeniable demonstration, which may make them, with the devils, "believe and tremble" even in their rebellion.—M.

Vers. 38, 40.—*Human and Divine remonstrances.* Christ and his disciples chide one another, yet gently and affectionately. Representative positions—

I. As suggesting the opposite standpoints from which practical difficulties of the religious life may be regarded.

II. As furnishing their solution.—M.

Ver. 1.—*Divine teaching from the fisherman's boat.* Matthew gives us, in the thirteenth chapter of his Gospel, a series of seven parables, which correspond with the three which Mark records here. They all illustrate the nature and the progress of the kingdom of God which Christ sought to establish. The parable of the sower describes the founding of the kingdom, and the various difficulties with which it would meet; the parable of the seed growing secretly teaches us that its progress would be natural, unostentatious, and certain; while the parable of the mustard seed declares that in its final consummation it would have wide-reaching influence. The second of these is peculiar to Mark. We propose to consider, not the parables themselves, but the circumstances under which they were uttered, which also suggest and illustrate truths concerning the kingdom. Our Lord's teaching from the fisherman's boat suggests the following thoughts :—

I. That hostility may change our method, but must not be allowed to prevent our work. The Pharisees had become openly antagonistic to our Lord. Their spies followed him everywhere. Their controversial champions argued with him and misrepresented him in the synagogues. This hostility drove the Lord from the sanctuaries of his people. He would not suffer his Father's house to be desecrated by such tactics. Accordingly, he no longer, as a rule, was found in the synagogues, but in the fields and streets, in the homes of the people, or in the fishing-boats that rocked on the Sea of Galilee. He thus acted on the principle he laid down for his disciples when he said to them, "If they persecute you in one city, flee to another." And that principle still holds good, and may have the widest application. St. Paul acted on it when he adapted himself, under varying circumstances, to the conditions of his hearers. If he addressed the people of Lystra, he did not argue from the Old Testament, of which they knew nothing, but pointed to the mountains and fields, and spoke of the God who gave them "fruitful seasons." If he was surrounded by Athenians in their beautiful city, he referred to the temples which crowned the Acropolis, and to the statues which adorned the Agora. If he was in the synagogue at Antioch, in Pisidia, he argued from the sacred Scriptures, the authority of which his hearers acknowledged. He became "all things to all men, if by any means he might win some;" and in this he followed in the footsteps of the great Teacher, who, when refused a fair hearing in the synagogue, preached beside the open sea. Thus, with the utmost flexibility and freedom, Christian workers should alter their methods to meet the changing circumstances in which they find themselves; never for a moment losing sight of the object they have set before themselves, but seeking to attain that by the most suitable means. This may be applied to those who preach or teach, whether amongst the sceptical or the indifferent, among the children or the cultured.

II. That there is no place where God's work may not be done. The change in method, indicated by the text, did not trouble our Lord as it would have troubled any one to whom place and mode seem everything in worship. All the earth was holy in his eyes. The heavenly Father was near him everywhere. The rippling of the sea or the rustling of the corn would be more grateful to him than the murmured repetitions of formal prayers by the mechanical and unspiritual worshippers in the synagogue. Apart from persecution, he would often have chosen, from preference, such a sphere of work as this, as indeed he did when he preached the sermon on the mount. Read his teaching to the woman of Samaria (John iv. 20, 21), and see how acceptable to God is spiritual worship wherever it may be offered. Study the parable that immediately follows our text, and you will notice that the sower threw out his seed broadcast upon all kinds of soil. Our Lord would preach in a Pharisee's house, or on a mountain, or from a boat, as readily as in a synagogue or in the temple; for "Holiness to the Lord"

(Zech. xiv. 20) was written everywhere, and he accounted "nothing common or unclean" (Acts x. 15). Too often Christian workers select their little sphere for service, and strictly confine themselves to it, contented that multitudes should be left untouched who might easily be brought under their influence. The true sower is willing to scatter his seed broadcast.

III. That the mode of our Lord's teaching made his utterances more widely acceptable. This was not only true of his own day, but of ours. Publicans, lepers, and outcasts, excluded from the synagogue, could hear him on the beach; and all "the common people heard him gladly," for he spake "as one having authority, and not as the scribes." It is well for us also that it was so. There is wonderfully little local colouring about his words; a marvellous freedom from such theological technicalities as the rabbis were wont to use; and his teaching, therefore, comes home to us as it never would have done if couched in the phraseology currently used for the interpretation of the Law. His utterances are fragrant with the fresh air, and they ring with a pleasant freedom, for which we cannot be too thankful; for what might have been Jewish is human, and the words of him who called himself, not "the Son of David," but the "Son of man," are so simple and natural, that there is not a fisherman on our coasts, not a merchant in our streets, not a housewife in our homes, not a sower in our fields, who may not know something of the meaning and beauty of the doctrine of the great Teacher who has come from God.

IV. That our Lord's position in the fishing-boat is a sign of the transient nature of abused privileges. Christ in the boat has often been regarded as an emblem of Christ in his Church. From both he preaches to the world. The Church, in comparison with the world it seeks to influence, is small, as the boat with the few in it was small compared with the crowds listening upon the beach; and her comparative poverty may be represented by that fisherman's barque, which had about it, we may be sure, no costly adornment. But small and poor as the Church may seem, and the Christ who is in it, she is *free* as the Master was, who could in a moment leave those who were hostile or unreceptive, and pass over to the other side (Luke viii. 37). There are yet to be found amongst us the impenitent and foolhardy, to whom he will have to say, " Because I have called, and ye refused; I have stretched out my hand, and no man regarded; but ye have set at nought all my counsel, and would none of my reproof: I will also laugh at your calamity; I will mock when your fear cometh."—A. R.

Vers. 4—8.—*Human hearts tested by truth.* "The seed is the Word." Such is the interpretation given by the Lord himself, in his exposition of the parable of the sower. In other words, the seed represents the truth uttered by Christ and embodied in Christ, who is himself declared to be the everlasting Word (John i. 1). This heavenly seed is the gift of God. It has life in itself (John v. 26); it is the germ of life to the world; and, when it is received, it brings forth those "fruits of the Spirit" of which St. Paul speaks. The mode in which that seed is received is a test of character, and this is illustrated in the words before us. The four kinds of soil upon which the sower cast his seed represent four conditions of heart, which we propose to consider.

I. The hardened heart. Our Lord speaks of some seed falling by the *wayside*; that is, on the trodden pathway running through the field, which is impervious to anything which falls gently, as seed falls. Finding a lodgment there, either the birds carry it away or else it is crushed by the foot of the wayfarer. Just as the once soft soil becomes hard, so do our moral sensibilities become blunted by the frequent passing over them of ordinary duties, and still more of evil words and deeds. We often read in Scripture of the hardening of the heart. Pharaoh is said to have "hardened his heart" because, after being stirred to some thought by the earlier plagues in Egypt, he conquered feeling until he became past feeling. Hence, after the most terrible of the plagues, he pursued God's chosen people to his own destruction. The Israelites, too, hardened their hearts in the wilderness. All the issues of this sin recorded in sacred history give a significant answer to the question of Job, "Who hath hardened himself against God, and prospered?" This process still goes on, not least amongst regular attendants on the means of grace. Address a gathering of outcasts, and though you may hear a mocking laugh, you will more probably see the penitential tear as you speak of the Saviour's death and of the Father's love; but speak of this to those who have often heard the truth, and their calm impassivity will drive you to despair, if it does not drive you to God. He who knows all but feels nothing is represented by the wayside; for the truth preached to him is gone as swiftly from his thoughts as though evil birds had carried it away.

II. THE SUPERFICIAL HEART is also graphically portrayed. The stony ground is not ground besprinkled with stones, but rocky soil covered with a thin layer of earth, such as might often be seen in the rocky abutments which ended the terraces of cultivated soil on a hillside in Palestine. Seed falling there would take root and grow, but would soon strike rock, and then withering would begin. This represents those who "receive the Word with gladness." They are interested, instructed, impressed; but they have no understanding of its spiritual meaning or of Christ's requirements. They have no sense of sin, and no conflict with it. Their knowledge and experience alike are shallow, and they have "no root," because they have no depth of nature. Very significant is the phrase, "They have no root *in themselves;*" for there is a want of individuality about them. Their faith depends upon surrounding excitement and enthusiasm, and they are wanting in the perseverance which can only arise from personal conviction. Let temptation come to them, and they give up at once their poor shreds of faith; let them go among sceptics, and soon their mockery will be the loudest; let persecution arise, and straightway they stumble to their fall.

III. THE CROWDED HEART. "Some fell among thorns;" that is, in soil in which thorns were springing up. The soil possibly was good, and therefore unlike the last, but it was already *full.* Soon the thorns springing up choke the seed, crowding it down, and so depriving it of air and sunshine that the withering stalk can produce no fruit. Every one knows the meaning of this who has pondered the words, "Ye cannot serve God and mammon," or who understands the warning against "the cares of the world, the deceitfulness of riches," and inordinate desires after other earthly things. Here is such a one. He was once earnest in work for God; he made time for the study of his Word; he was eager for the quiet hour when he could speak to his Father in secret. But this is only a memory to him now. And how came the woeful change? There has been no hour when he has deliberately cut himself adrift from holy influence, nor can he recall any special crisis in his history. But the cares of life, the plans he felt called upon to make, thoughts concerning money and the best way to make it or to keep it, obtruded themselves more and more, even on sacred times, till holy thoughts were fairly crowded out. Thorns have sprung up, and they have choked the seed, so that it has become unfruitful.

IV. THE HONEST HEART. The seed which fell into "good ground" not only sprang up into strong stalk, but brought forth fruit in the golden harvest-time, and over it the sower rejoiced. Our Lord often spoke of the conditions which are essential to the fulfilment of this in the spiritual realm. For example, he said, "He that is of the truth heareth my voice;" and he bade his disciples become as little children, that they might rejoice in him. Nathanael was a beautiful example of what Jesus meant. When the truth is thus received, in the love of it, it guides the thoughts, rules the affections, checks and controls the plans, and sanctifies the whole being of the man. "Christ is formed" in his heart "the hope of glory." Abiding in prayer, under the influence of the Holy Spirit, he experiences a quickening and a refreshment like that which the growing corn has when enriched and blessed by showers and sunshine, and "the fruits of the Spirit" appear in him, to the glory of God the Father. "Herein is my Father glorified, that ye bear much fruit."—A. R.

Vers. 15—20.—*The perils and the prospects of the good seed of the kingdom.* The importance of the parable of the sower is shown by the prominence given to it by the evangelists, and by the question of our Lord in the thirteenth verse, "Know ye not this parable? and how then will ye know all parables?" In some respects it was the basis of similar teaching, while the key to its interpretation, given by the Lord himself, opens the door of other mysteries. The illustration is an analogy, going deeper than many suppose. Husbandry was the appointment of God when man dwelt in the bliss of paradise, before the Divine order had been interfered with by human sin and self-will. Even in man's unfallen state, seed had to be sown and cared for, while the blessing of heaven was always essential to its productiveness. He who made the first

Adam a sower in things natural, made the second Adam a Sower in what was spiritual. Our Lord referred to himself and to all who follow him in his work when he said, " Behold, the sower went forth to sow." Now, soil and seed are essential to each other. Many a man has the " honest and good heart ; " but he must not be content with that, for, as the richest soil will remain empty unless seed be in it, so even such a heart will be unproductive of spiritual results without Christ, the true and living Word. While the soil is thus useless without the seed, the seed is unproductive without the soil. Hence Christ urged men to receive him, and hence he said of his teaching, " He that hath ears to hear, let him hear." Christian truth may be intellectually known and propagated, but the world is only the richer for it as it becomes the inspiration of human hearts. Christ's words must be translated into men's lives, that they may be read as " living epistles." In a sense, the Lord himself must become incarnate in each of his followers (Col. i. 27). For the world's sake, as well as our own, may we receive the seed of the kingdom ! This parable speaks of—

I. THE PERILS WHICH THREATEN THE GOOD SEED. Let us seek to recognize them in the various thoughts which contend for the mastery with Christ's truth. 1. *Evil thoughts*. They come through companions, from books, etc., but find their source in Satan (ver. 15). Often we find that they are most intrusive just after or during our holiest hours. They are like the birds of prey which swooped down on Abraham's sacrifice when he was making his covenant with God (Gen. xv.). Like him, we must seek by constant watching and effort to drive them away. 2. *Vacant thoughts*. The foolish habit of letting thoughts wander as they list, settling nowhere on what is definite or dignified, is a characteristic of the shallow characters represented by the rocky soil. Earnest conviction and the abiding stability which follows it cannot belong to these. Well is it when each can say, " I hate vain thoughts, but thy Law do I love." 3. *Anxious thoughts*. " The cares of this world " (ver. 19) are destructive of the serenity and rest which Christ's true disciples should always rejoice in. Therefore our Lord so urgently warns us against them (Matt. vi. 25—34). St. Paul says, " Be careful for nothing ; but in everything by prayer and supplication with thanksgiving let your requests be made known unto God," and then " the peace of God . . . shall keep your hearts." 4. *Adverse thoughts*. " The lusts of other things " so absorb some that their minds are like a soil full of growing thorns. " If any man love the world, the love of the Father is not in him." Judas Iscariot was a terrible example of this. It would be useless to point out such perils as these if it were not that our hearts are not like the soil, which is destitute of will, of effort, and of a voice to cry to Heaven. Our condition largely depends upon our choice, or rather on the prayer which is the outcome of it ; so that it is not in vain that we have guarded ourselves against the perils which beset the seed. From them let us turn to consider—

II. THE PROGRESS WHICH AWAITS THE SEED in various hearts. 1. *Swiftly gone*, devoured by the birds, *i.e.* dissipated or destroyed by other thoughts. Warn against the flippancy and worldliness of much conversation in Christian homes on the Lord's day, and point out the injury which young people may thus receive. 2. *Springing soon, withering soon*. This is specially seen in sentimental natures. There is a shallowness in thought and experience from which we should earnestly pray for deliverance. It is well when such underlying rock is broken up by the plough of affliction. 3. *Growing, not fruit-bearing*. This is the condition of many professed Christians, whose homes witness to unconquered tempers and whose Churches mourn unattempted service. 4. *Producing fruit and increase*. All do not bring forth the same fruit, either in kind or in degree. Still we see the "thirtyfold," the "sixtyfold," and the "hundredfold," according to the gift and capacity of each. God only expects of us according to that which we have, and not according to that which we have not. The different talents entrusted to the servants (Matt. xxv.) remind us of this ; yet that every one of them could win the reward of him who had been "good and faithful." Allude to various examples of fruit-bearing among Christians, *e.g.* the quiet ministrations in the home, of which no one outside it hears ; the steadfast adherence to Christian principle when slight swerving from it would bring an advantage, which as a keen man he is quick to see, but as a devout man is swift to spurn ; the privilege of writing words which go forth to unseen multitudes, stirring in them loftier thoughts of God and of his Word and works ; the pleasantness of the gentle girl who at school or at home thinks of every one before herself; the influence of the brave lad whose "wholesome tongue is a tree of life," etc.   Each of these bears fruit, and that fruit is the new seed from which future harvests spring.—A. R.

Vers. 26—29.—*The progress of Divine life in the soul.*   Mark alone records this parable.   It occupies the position of the parable of the tares in Matt. xiii., following "the sower," preceding "the mustard seed," but is not to be identified with it.   It teaches us that Divine life, like ordinary seed, requires time for its development, that its growth is unnoticed and but little dependent upon human interference, and that it will have a glorious consummation.

I. THE GROWTH OF THE DIVINE LIFE.   1. *It is secret* (ver. 27).   Man "knoweth not how" the seed springs.   Our "natural laws" are little more than generalizations of observed facts, and afford no adequate explanation of the nature of life and growth. While we are busy or are resting the seed is quietly growing up under the care of God. We know but little more of the Divine life, even in ourselves.   We know that we have it and that it produces certain effects, but of its essential nature our keenest analysis discovers but little.   Still less do we know of the Divine life in others; and, as Christian teachers or parents, we must neither intrude upon it, as a child will do on growing seed, nor be over-anxious about it, as a foolish husbandman may be.   With faith in God, leave it prayerfully to him, and "in due season we shall reap, if we faint not."   2. *It is independent* (ver. 28).   The meaning of the phrase, "The earth bringeth forth fruit of herself," is this, that she has powers of developing life which exclude our agency, though they include God's agency.   After sowing his seed, man may sleep or rise, leaving it to natural influences.   We are not taught to be idle, but are reminded that we can do but little after sowing.   In religious work we must never try to force growth by unnatural methods.   First religious feelings are too sacred and delicate to be treated as they sometimes are.   Intrusive and over-anxious teachers may sometimes do harm, not least in the confessional.   The principle applies to our own life also.   A morbid brooding over our own spiritual condition, a petty and constant measurement of our own feelings, is injurious.   "He that observeth the wind shall not sow, and he that regardeth the clouds shall not reap."

II. THE MANIFESTATION OF THE DIVINE LIFE.   True seed, under favourable conditions, cannot keep hidden beneath the soil.   It must grow, and, if it grows, it must ultimately be seen.   Nor can we keep our spiritual life a secret from others if it be true; for in holy influence and loving deeds and devout life it must appear.   This parable describes its gradual progress, representing it in three stages, which correspond with those represented by St. John (1 John ii.) in his references to "children," "young men," and "fathers."   1. *The blade* represents the "little children" in grace, "whose sins are forgiven for his Name's sake."   A wise husbandman never despises the blades of corn.   He knows their value, their tenderness, their possibilities.   God has provided for their safety.   When the wind sweeps over the fields they bend before it and are uninjured, though much that is stronger is swept away.   So young Christians, though in some respects weak, give promise of the future, have a special grace and beauty of their own, and, amidst temptations under which those older fall, abide and appear more fresh and fair.   2. *The ear* represents the "young men," who have "overcome the wicked one."   Here there is a loss of freshness, but a gain in strength.   There is less enthusiasm, but more principle.   The showers of adversity as well as the sunlight of prosperity are necessary to this.   Speak of some who in special circumstances of temptation have proved the power of the grace of God.   3. *The full corn in the ear.* The "fathers," who have "known him that is from the beginning," are like the full-grown wheat, bending its head under the weight of the rich grain it bears, ready to be cut down and carried home.   Such a one has a fulfilment of the promise, "Thou shalt come to thy grave in a good old age, like as a shock of corn cometh in in his season."

III. THE CONSUMMATION OF THE DIVINE LIFE.   (Ver. 29.)   Here the reference is to its earthly consummation only, for when the ripe corn is carried home, though it no longer adorns the field in which it grew, it is only beginning to fulfil its true destiny.   The moment of death is the time when the reaper puts in the sickle, because the harvest is come; and the same sickle which destroys one life gives new energy to another and higher life. Mortality is swallowed up of life. The outcome of time shall be the seed of eternity.—A. R.

Vers. 30—32.—*Great issues from small beginnings.* The lesson which our Lord intended to teach by the parable of the mustard seed is stated in the announcement of our subject. If he had wished to set forth the splendour of his kingdom, he would have chosen as an illustration the stately cedar or the fruitful vine. The mustard in its greatest growth is by no means majestic; but it is large in proportion to its seed, and although it was not literally "the smallest of seeds," it was the smallest of those used in ordinary husbandry, and was proverbially used to denote what was little and despicable. All references to the supposed qualities of the seed, *e.g.* to its corrective power in disease, to its efficacy against venom, to its fiery vigour, to its giving out of virtue after being bruised, and so forth, appear to us beside the main purpose of the parable, which was to set forth the great issues which, in the kingdom of our Lord, would spring from small beginnings. This principle we propose now to illustrate.

I. IT IS EXEMPLIFIED IN THE EARTHLY HISTORY OF OUR LORD. In his history we see, as in a microcosm, the history of his Church. With limitless powers of choice, he selected for himself the most humble and obscure modes of ministry. His ways are not as our ways. Man makes a pretentious beginning, and often comes to a disastrous ending. The building of the Tower of Babel is a typical instance of this. Our Lord, who came to effect the stupendous work of redeeming the world, began by spending thirty years in comparative seclusion as a dependent infant, as an obedient child, as the son of a village carpenter. During his two or three years of public ministry his converts were few, and for the most part poor and ignorant. At last he died in agony and shame, amidst the hooting of a rabble and the hatred of the reputable; and his body was laid to rest in a borrowed grave. As we consider his life on earth, we see that it may be represented by a seed less in appearance than many others. But there was a fulfilment of his own words about himself, "Except a corn of wheat fall into the ground and die, it abideth alone; but if it die, it bringeth forth much fruit."

II. IT IS EXEMPLIFIED IN THE SPECIAL DOCTRINES OF CHRISTIANITY. They were not truths which would commend themselves to sensuous imaginations or to worldly hearts. They did not appear in such form and phrase as at once to win popular applause. Notice some of our Lord's special doctrines as laid down in the sermon on the mount and elsewhere: *e.g.* happiness is to be found in the sacrifice of self; sin is to be hated, not because its results are painful, but because it is sin; outward obedience and large gifts and sacrifices are valueless in themselves, etc. After his crucifixion, this fact was still more prominent. Paul said, "We preach Christ crucified, unto the Jews a stumbling-block, and unto the Greeks foolishness; but unto them which are called, both Jews and Greeks, Christ the power of God, and the wisdom of God." Indicate some of the reasons for the non-reception of Christian truth.

III. IT IS EXEMPLIFIED IN THE HISTORY OF THE CHRISTIAN CHURCH. Christianity at the time of our Lord's crucifixion appeared to be buried in the hearts of a few disciples and forgotten by the world. But on the spring day of Pentecost it appeared in a vigour and beauty which amazed all onlookers. It was like the bursting forth of forgotten seeds where you have been busily employed planting something else. Christianity rapidly spread. Give evidences of this from early Christians and from Suetonius, Pliny's letter to Trajan, etc. This, humanly speaking, was the work of poor and illiterate men. Manifestly the result was due, not to the sower, but to the seed. Describe the condition and influence of the Christian Church now: the most powerful and civilized nations largely ruled by its authority; the indirect work it is doing through just laws, wholesome literature, philanthropic agencies, etc. Draw a contrast between the social and religious condition of the peoples now and at the time of Christ's coming. The seed has become a tree, "so that the fowls of the air may lodge under the shadow of it."

IV. IT IS EXEMPLIFIED IN THE EXPERIENCE OF EACH CHRISTIAN. "The kingdom of God" is not to be a something outside ourselves. We are not among its subjects because we can say, "This nation in which we dwell is Christian." "The kingdom of heaven is *within* you," said our Lord to his disciples. It is within us when we welcome Christ, its King, with all that he represents, to our own hearts to love and obey for evermore. That being so, a new life is ours, the test of whose vitality is to be found in growth until every thought and affection and purpose (like the birds spoken of in this parable) dwell under its influence. If there has been no growth, let us examine ourselves.   When a flower or plant is fading, drooping, and likely to die, we try to discover the cause. Perhaps it wants water, perhaps it is shut off from sunshine, perhaps it has been too long coddled under artificial heat and is therefore weakly, or perhaps a worm is gnawing at the root. If our spiritual life has no growth, let us ask why this is.   We want showers of blessing, the sunshine of God's favour, independence of artificial stimulants, and above all, freedom from the sin which doth so easily beset us, and then we shall grow like plants of God's right hand planting.—A. R.

Vers. 1—25.—*The duty of faithfully hearing the Word.* He who taught by every act of his life, and who had already given many most important lessons with his lips, now, after the interruptions just recorded, "began to teach" more formally. It was "by the seaside," the multitude standing "by the sea on the land," and he "entered into a boat, and sat in the sea." "He taught them many things in parables." The first of these and one of the chief of the parables and the chiefest of all on the subject of "the Word," is, with its explanation, the key to many others. The lesson of the whole is summed up in the words of ver. 24, "Heed what ye hear." It was not without purpose that he spoke of hearing. All depends upon it. Noah, Moses, Paul, Jesus himself, will preach in vain if men hear not with care. The parable teaches—

I. THE ESPECIAL EVILS AGAINST WHICH MEN MUST GUARD IN HEARING THE WORD. 1. The first evil is losing the Word before faith has made it fruitful. "The parable is this: the seed is the Word of God." The kingdom of heaven grows from this seed only. By it alone is conviction of sin wrought; by it is faith begotten; by it Christ is revealed; by it regeneration is effected; by it the way of life is defined; by it are men sanctified; by it hope, and patience, and charity, and all graces are strengthened. This great lesson is, by both preachers and hearers, to be pondered. But the Word, by whomsoever sown, may be lost before it is fruitful. It may be taken out of the heart, out of the memory, from the understanding. "When they have heard, straightway cometh Satan, and taketh away the Word which hath been sown in them." 2. A second danger is from a mere temporary faith. There is "no deepness of earth," "no root in themselves." They "endure for a while." A little thing turns them away from that which they received "straightway with joy," but without counting the cost. 3. A third evil is the fruitlessness of the Word through the "cares of the world, and the deceitfulness of riches, and the lusts of other things," especially "the pleasures of this life." The ground is good; the seed is good; it is well received and kept in the heart; yet is it choked. Yea, even God's good Word sown in the heart by Christ's own hand may be choked. This is a danger to which every believer is exposed. It is allowing other growths to sap this, other things to take up the time and attention, to absorb the interest, to steal the affections. The poor are in danger from "the cares of the world;" the rich from "the deceitfulness of riches." The parable teaches—

II. THE REWARD OF FAITHFUL HEARING. "He that hath, to him shall be given." To him that hath as the fruit of his diligence, not simply what was given to him—all had this—to him shall be added the Lord's increase, over and above the natural consequences of his carefulness. He who so uses Divine truth as to be the better for it is in more favourable circumstances to receive and understand. Such know the truth, for "the mystery of the kingdom of God is given" to them. Every step in the ascent makes the next step possible. Truth grows to its perfection (that is to say, the character which is the product of truth) when it is "heard" and held fast in "an honest and good heart;" a heart inwardly good and outwardly honest; a heart honestly desiring the Word and acting honestly by it. To such there is "fruit, thirtyfold, and sixtyfold, and a hundredfold." This is the truly prepared ground—ploughed, as could not be said of "the wayside" or the "stony ground." The parable further teaches—

III. THE CONDEMNATION OF HIM WHO HEARETH NOT TO PROFIT. 1. "He that hath not," *i.e.* hath not any fruit of his careful hearing, hath nothing more than was first given to him; "even that which he hath"—that which was given to him—"shall be taken away." Disregarded truth becomes disliked truth, and by him who does not use his understanding about it, it is naturally forgotten. So the condemnation takes the form of a removal of the truth. 2. In carelessness he puts the truth away from him. His measure is small, so he metes it to himself. 3. To hear is a duty; to neglect brings God's condemnation. 4. He who does not so receive God's truth as to become a true subject of the kingdom of heaven, is in the kingdom of evil, and continued disobedience leaves the man further and further from God. 5. So truth assumes the form of a parable to him. His eye is dimmed. He sees only the outward word; of the inward meaning, which is experimental, he knows nothing. Even Christ, his work and his gospel, may be to men a mere parable. They know not " the things " which are spoken. Thus is to be seen : (1) The terrible and to-be-dreaded consequence of not heeding the Word. It becomes a parable, a dark saying, a riddle. " If they hear not Moses," etc. (2) The mercifulness of him who would hide truth in a beautiful parable, to tempt the careless to inquire that they may be roused to effort and be saved. (3) The great lesson, " to hear the Word," " to read, mark, learn, and inwardly digest the same, that by patience and comfort of the Scriptures we may embrace and ever hold fast the blessed hope of ever-lasting life, which is given to us in our Saviour Jesus Christ."—G.

Vers. 26—34.—*The kingdom of God further illustrated by parables.* No single parable holds the entire truth in itself; therefore, by "many such parables " Jesus " spake the Word unto " the multitude. Of those spoken at this time, St. Mark selects only two others besides that of the sower, and both of them, as was the first, are drawn from seeds. How suitable a simile of that kingdom, whose inherent, vital, self-expanding force is one of its most distinguishing features ! These two parables stand related : the one leading us to think of the part " the earth " plays in bearing " fruit "—the power, as before we saw the duty, of the human heart to receive and to nourish the seed, to yield its due results; the other teaching the history of the little seed when received into suitable soil. This parable, the only one peculiar to St. Mark, is simple and very beautiful, and full of rich teaching. It embraces all the history of the seed in the heart, from its sowing, through its stages of growth, to its ripeness and ingathering. It may be summarized as—

THE LAW OF THE DEVELOPMENT OF THE CHRISTIAN LIFE. 1. The human heart is the suitable " earth " for the heavenly seed. But one kind of seed, " the Word," is named. From this alone the kingdom grows. Yet the seed is not always sufficiently winnowed. The same hand sometimes scatters darnel with the wheat, or the gaudy, bright, but useless poppy. But seeds, bad and good, will grow together in the same field. What will not grow in the human heart ! He who made the warm soil suitable for the growth of the useful herb for the service of man, and adapted the seed to the earth, has made the heart so that the best and highest truths will grow therein. There, what would otherwise be a dead truth—a hard seed—may find the suitable conditions for its nourish-ment and growth. There it is quickened. Every holy truth may find a home in the heart of man ; the richest, ripest, most wholesome, most abundant fruit may be gathered in that Eden. 2. The needful committal of the seed to the earth has its parallel in Christ's committal of his kingdom to the fruit-bearing heart. There it grows, " we know not how," though we know so much. There is but one true Sower to whom the field belongs, and who provided the one basket of seed. But many sow in his Name and by his direction—preachers, parents, teachers, writers, friends. But the truth once sown in the heart must be left to Heaven's own influence. Days and nights follow. Patient waiting is needed, for the growth of good principles is slow and the perfect fruitfulness not immediate. And the lesson of patience is silently hidden in the words of the parable. He who causes the seeds of the earth to swell and burst and die, and out of the hidden germ a new life to spring up, brings the truth to the remembrance, awakens dormant thought, stirs the indolent conscience, carries conviction deep within, whence springs faith, to be followed by all holiness. The growth retains its own distinctive character, being nevertheless affected by the nature of the soil—" the earth which beareth fruit of herself." 3. The progression of the spiritual life is as the growth of the field. The truth quickly works its way. The first signs are found in a slightly changed manner of life, as it submits to the restraining and guiding truth; the tint on the face of the field is slightly altered ; a delicate tinge of spring green blades mingles with the russet-brown of the soil. All is immature and feeble, but beautiful, as the field in the first days of spring; and it is full of promise. A longer space follows ere the ear appears. It is the time of growth. The responsibility of the sower is transferred to the earth, save that he may guard it from being trampled by the rude, rough hoof of stray cattle, or from being ploughed up wrongfully by careless hands.   Now the sower must "sleep and rise night and day." He cannot hurry the growth.   This is the time of trial, exposure, and danger.   It is the needful time for Christian culture, for the gradual acquisition of strength and wisdom, and the slow building up of character.   And what is true of the individual growth is true also of the great wide field which is the world, where all good, and alas! all evil, may grow, and whose prolonged history goes on slowly towards the great harvest. "The full corn in the ear" points to the matured Christian character, the trained, subdued, chastened spirit.   Sunshine and shadow, calm and storm, darkness and light, have all passed over the field; all helpful, each in its own way, in promoting the growth, strength, and fruitfulness, alike in the less or the greater field; and all tending towards that moment "when the fruit is ripe."   Then, and not until then, "he putteth forth the sickle, because the harvest is come."   So is it with every believer—every varied growth in the wide field; so is it with the entire history which tends towards that "harvest" which "is the end of the world."

Hence from this parable, which is one long teaching, we learn the wisdom and duty: 1. Of thankfully receiving the Word into our hearts.   2. Of faithfully cherishing it. 3. Of patiently waiting for its full fruits.—G.

Vers. 30—32.—*The parable of the mustard seed.*   This parable stands related to the former.   That pointed to the history of the growth of the seed; this points to the inherent vitality of the seed.   That laid the emphasis on the field; this lays it on the seed.   The simile is so exact that we are in danger of transgressing a needful canon in the interpretation of parables, and to treat it as a realism.   *The parable illustrates the history of the kingdom of heaven in its outward manifestation,* especially the smallness of its beginning contrasted with the greatness of its results.

I. The kingdom of God finds its appropriate symbol in a seed with its inherent, vital, self-expanding force.   This is true, whether we interpret the kingdom of God to refer to its essential principle—the dominion of the Divine Spirit over the human spirit; or to its outward manifestation in the visible Church of God—the gospel developing itself in the heart and life of mankind; or even to its instrument—the Divine Word.   Gathering these together as all comprised in the idea of the kingdom of God, we must see it to be truly represented by a seed—a living, inherently vital power.   This parable leads us to think more particularly of the outward manifestation of the kingdom of God; and wherever we see it planted we sooner or later see signs of growth and extension.   One of the first sentiments stirred in the breast of the newly converted is a desire for the conversion of others; and the first activities evoked from the new life are found in efforts to lead others to like blessing.   Each believer becomes the germ of a Church; each is a self-propagating seed.   From one may spring a thousand, nay, as many as the stars of heaven for multitude.   So was it with the Church in the beginning—the little quickened seed in Jerusalem.   So has it been in every age.   To-day we joyfully witness the signs of this vitality on every hand.

II. A second feature of the kingdom of God is the extreme smallness of its origin.   Still thought of as an outward manifestation, how small was its beginning! How little a seed!   Judging Christ's work by the greatness of its aims, how small were his means!   What books did he write?   What organization did he frame?   What cities did he build?   What armies did he raise?   What did he?   Estimated by outward signs—a mere nothing.   A few women and fewer men gathered; no multitude, no Church, no forms of worship, no writings.   No; no; nothing.   What then?   Just a living seed dropped into the warm heart.   Not more than a human heart could treasure—not more than Matthew could remember.   The record of a brief life, with its few words; its few noble deeds of sincerity, love, and self-denial; and its sad death and marvellous resurrection.   All the kingdom of God in that one life, all the heavenly treasure in that one earthen vessel; all in a "mustard seed, . . . less than all the seeds that are upon earth."   But it grew to be "a tree."

III. This the third feature of the parable: The ultimate extension of the kingdom of God.   And the point of interest seems to be it grows beyond its probable limits, "greater than all the herbs;" yea, it "putteth out great branches, becometh a tree, so that the birds of the heaven" not only "lodge under the shadow" of it, but "in the branches thereof." Its growth is beyond, far beyond, what might have been reasonably expected. So we see to-day; so will it be more and more seen. These parables Jesus spake unto the multitude "as they were able to hear;" and privately then, as he now does to them who care to know, "he expounded all things."—G.

Vers. 35—41.—*The stilling of the storm: the deliverance of the Church.* The miracles so far recorded were miracles of healing, and demonstrate the dominion of Christ in the realm of the human life—he is Lord of the human body. Now he declares his equal dominion in the realm of disturbed nature, "even the wind and the sea obey him." The Church has found two uses in the miracles of our Lord. 1. In an earlier age they were a sign to unbelievers, evidences of the authority of the Teacher, attestations to the truth of his message. Christ appealed to them : "The works that the Father hath given me to accomplish, the very works that I do, bear witness of me, that the Father hath sent me. Though ye believe not me, believe the works." 2. In later times they have been found to be a treasure of spiritual teaching, a word of revelation and power to believers. Thus they form a part of the Church's inestimable possessions. The instruction divides itself into two branches : the positive knowledge which they convey—as in this, the lordship of the world's Redeemer over external nature ; and the typical and more hidden spiritual lessons. The Church has ever seen herself represented in that ship. "The ark of Christ's Church" is a consecrated term, and in the sea she has beheld the wild, raging, unfriendly world. So the incident becomes typical : (1) of the Church's exposure in the world, as a bark on a stormy sea ; (2) of the Church's true safety in the presence of Christ ; (3) of the ever-present and final stilling of the rage of the world and the perfect deliverance of his own from all surrounding peril.

I. THE HISTORY OF THE CHURCH OF THE LORD JESUS IS A HISTORY OF EXPOSURE TO DANGER. What perils have threatened the holy writings—that ark in which all the truth is held! At first but a few scattered recollections of men ; Heaven's high treasures held in earthen vessels. Then written on a few flying leaves of parchment by tremulous human hands in uncertain human letters. Afterwards followed dangers from the errors of dim-sighted transcribers, from injudicious interpolators, from the destructive ravages of fire. Yet after the long ages it is probable we possess a more accurate transcript of the original documents than the Church ever possessed since the very early transcripts were penned. To what perils has the true Society of Jesus—the holy Catholic Church—been exposed in her very varying history ! Scarcely had this barque left the shores ere the strong surf of Judaism threatened to overturn it. Then fitful winds of human wisdom—"the profane babblings and oppositions of the knowledge which is falsely so called." Dangers have arisen from internal contentions—a mutinous crew ; from unsteady hands at the helm, and clouded eyes upon the watch ; from overlading with worldly goods, gold, raiment, precious stones ; from sunken rocks of pride and worldly glory. False lights have threatened to wreck the vessel upon rugged and uncertain coasts, while black darkness has overcast the heavens, when "for many days neither sun nor stars have shone and no small tempest lay" on the exposed craft. Truly this Galilean boat, this "ark of Christ's Church," has been often in perilous seas. But with all she has not sunk. Christ has said, "Let us go over unto the other side." A wider view would lead us to think of the exposure of the whole spiritual interests of men. Though these have been exposed to dire destruction, they still survive, and faith, and hope, and love, and truth, and righteousness abound.

II. THE CHURCH'S SAFETY HAS EVER BEEN, IS NOW, AND EVER WILL BE, IN CHRIST. This no believer will doubt. To all human appearance *asleep*, he hastily responds to the cry of prayer, of fear, and desire. The Church to-day is as truly safe in the midst of her many dangers as in that night when the whole Church and the Lord thereof were in that one fishing-boat, when all seemed to be risked, and men accustomed to the sea cried, being fearful, "We perish." Up out of the evils of this stormy life will he lift his own by the miracles of his supremacy. His sweet, calm voice will yet be heard above "the raging of the sea and the tumult of the people," above strife and war and cruel hate, above ignorance, and sin, and sorrow, and pain. Even to evil he will say, "Peace, be still." So that unto him whom winds and seas obey shall be glory and honour from the quiet spirits of his whole Church for evermore.—G.

Vers. 1—20.—*The process of truth in the soul.* "Word" in the parable stands for truth in general. It is the Greek *logos,* which contains everything relating to ideas and the reception of them.

I. THE RELATION OF TRUTH TO THE SOUL. It is mysterious, because in it the secret of life lies. We know certain things about the seed; we know certain things about the soil; we know that their contact is necessary that germination and growth may take place. Sight, experience, teach us this. But the relation itself is unseen and defies the grasp of thought. Well may the poet say of the "flower in the crannied wall" that he has plucked and holds in his hand, could he know its mystery, he should know "man and God and all things." Piety lacks root without reverence; and reverence is begotten of mystery, *i.e.* of the sense that God is present in every fact of life, in every act of thought.

II. THE RECEPTION OF TRUTH IN THE SOUL. The parable clearly teaches that the whole intelligence and will are closely concerned in this. 1. There must be *attention.* The frivolous listener lets the sound of instruction "go in at one ear and out at the other." Pictures of life and duty, which need to be seized and fixed in conduct so soon as they arise in the inner chambers of imagery, melt away like dissolving views. 2. There must be *retention.* Memory depends on attention : "Therefore we ought to give earnest heed to the things we have heard, lest at any time they should slip by us." Memory is a talent of which some have more, some less ; but in every case it may be increased. Truth does not strike all minds in the same way; the important thing is to seize the truth which *does* strike us, and which we know to be truth by the way in which it strikes us. If conscious of the frailty of our memory, let a few things be constantly brought before our thoughts. *Non multa, sed multum.* 3. There must be *simplicity of choice.* Truth is jealous, and admits no rival. We must be true to her, for she alone gives freedom. Passions, cares, excitements of the imagination—these cannot be avoided in our active life in the world. For a time they may overcloud our ideal, cause us to lose sight of our goal. But the cloud will lift again, and directness of purpose will dispel these mists and cause the weight of the μέριμναι βιωτικαί (see ' Ecce Homo !' p. 221) to fall. Christ sympathizes with our life-difficulties, but implies that we may overcome them.

III. THE PROGRESS OF TRUTH IN THE SOUL. 1. *It follows the analogy of plant-growth.* We can hardly think of spiritual growth under any other image. Herein the need of some knowledge of natural science to the theologian. There lie some of his best instructions and illustrations. It is the Divine counterpart in nature of the ideal truth of spirit. 2. *There is diversity in spiritual as in natural growth.* Here the corn only is used as an analogy. But we may generalize. The differences in *kind* as well as degree of produce are not less numerous than in the immense plant-world. The world of souls is as varied as a garden—as a tropical forest. 'Tis a universe of variety. God spiritually unfolding himself in endless forms of beauty and of strength, delicacy and vigour. "He that hath ears to hear, let him hear." For the parable is in fact a sketch-picture of the ideal world—of God's kingdom of the invisible and eternal. We are in this world to be acted upon by him, that we may react upon him in all the devout activities of a fruitful life.—J.

Vers. 21—25.—*The use of the spirit.* I. THE FACULTIES OF THE HUMAN SPIRIT COMPARED TO LIGHT. We may take any division of them we please: intellectual, emotional, volitional; head, heart, hand ;—the comparison holds good. 1. Light is cheering, so is intellect ; sound reasoning, bright fancy, lambent wit, genial humour, sound knowledge. 2. With light goes heat. The sound head is generally associated with the large heart. Carlyle said that a great heart was the foundation of talent. 3. Light promotes morality, purity, progress ; dispels the thoughts and deeds of darkness. Great is the blessing of the presence and action of the man of high principle in the home, the Church, the court, the senate, the judgment seat. 4. It is revealing. The beauties of nature exist not for us in the darkness. Nor can we see the wonders of God in the spiritual or ideal world without the light shed by the genius of the scientific man, the moralist, the philosopher, and the poet.

II. FACULTIES GIVEN TO BE USED. 1. If not *used* they are hardly *possessed.* They dwindle and become enfeebled in disuse. "To him that hath shall be given," etc. In this lies the important differences between man and man.   The seeming stupid becomes bright by patient friction with difficulty, while the idle clever man rusts and blunts his edge.

> " If our virtues go not forth from us, 'tis all
> As one as though we had them not."

2. God is an exact creditor.   He starts us in life with a certain fixed capital of energy; just such and such a sum or number of talents.   The rest is our part.   The increase may be indefinite, in this world and worlds to come.   He " lends not the smallest scruple of his excellence, but, like a thrifty creditor, demands both thanks and use." Let life be the grateful repayment of the spiritual loan.   If we do not " pay our way " we shall suffer for it.

> " Wouldst thou seal up the avenues of ill?
> Pay every debt as if God wrote the bill."

3. In the long run, success or failure, prosperity or ruin, is the reaction of our own deeds.   We reap as we sow.   A Nemesis presides over all our works.   " If you serve, or fancy you serve, an ungrateful master, serve him the more.   Put God in your debt. Every stroke shall be repaid.   The longer the payment is withholden, the better for you; for compound interest on compound interest is the rate and usage of this exchequer."   " The benefit we receive must be rendered again, line for line, deed for deed, penny for penny, to somebody.   Beware of too much good staying in your hand. It will fast corrupt and breed worms.   Pay it away quickly in some sort."—J.

Vers. 26—29.—*The beauty of growth.*   I. The small beginning.   What smaller or more seemingly feeble than the seed—the thought—the word—the volition?   Yet in the beginning lies the end, in the acorn the oak.

II. The immense Divine power.   We lie on the bosom of nature as the seed lies in the earth.   For as winds blow and waters move and earth rests, God in his might and love bears up and onward the living soul.   All things are ours to work our good.

III. The secrecy and slowness of the process.   God does the best for us while we sleep.   The Greek artist represented Fortune driving cities into the net of the sleeping conqueror Timotheus.   Cultivate a wise patience.   Know the power of the word *Wait!*

> Think you of all the mighty sum
> Of things for ever speaking,
> That nothing of itself will come,
> But we must still be seeking?"

"Ripeness is all."   'Tis worth waiting a lifetime for the fruition of an hour.   Each hour is a fruition of eternity to him who lives in God.   And we may be reaping when we seem only to be sowing.—J.

Vers. 30—34.—*The power of ideas.*   I. The kingdom of God is the kingdom of ideas.   All forms of the true, holy, and good are included in this kingdom.   Life would be intolerable, amidst the greatest physical comfort, without ideas.   Our spirit is born to love and live among them.   Novelty of ideas is the condition of change for the better in every life-department.

II. Ideas are self-multiplying.   Start a beautiful pattern in trade; it gives birth to a whole creation of beauty.   Cast in a golden hour a seed of truth or love into the general mind; up springs a flower, whose seed will presently be in all gardens (see Tennyson's poem).   Do a noble deed, speak a word from the full voice of the heart; an infinity of echoes will awake; a thousand imitators will arise.   Let us speak in these parables of nature to the many; and for the few let us analyze and elicit their wider meaning.   For the truths of the seen are less than those of the unseen.   Illustrations light up a truth not understood; but their value is transient.   The truth escapes from this or that clothing into other forms.—J.

Vers. 35—41.—*Storm and calm.*   I. Storms break unexpectedly upon us.   The Lake of Galilee was peculiarly exposed to them from the north; the wind rushed as through a funnel down those gulleys and ravines.   This was known to the sailors, yet the storm was unexpected.   Life is the lake; change may come at any moment, we know; and yet it is the "unexpected which always happens."

II. Presence of mind is needed.   To know that the mind is our real place, and all that happens elsewhere is not our affair,—this makes us independent of change, calm amidst scenes of terror.   Nature is for mind.   Divine reason subdues the wild forces of nature.   Faith in that reason is what we need.   It is the true and deepest source of "presence of mind."

III. The absence of confidence and courage is blameworthy.   "*Why* are you so fearful?"   You may know at any time the worst.   Fear is the reflection in our mind of some image of overwhelming power, threatening our existence.   With Christ on board, our spiritual existence is safe.   Perfect abandonment to duty, truth, and God alone, lifts above this anxiety.

"If my bark sinks,
'Tis to another sea."

J.

Vers. 1—20.   Parallel passages: Matt. xiii. 1—23; Luke viii. 4—18.—*Parabolic teaching*.   I. The parable of the sower.   1. *Benefit of acquaintance with Scripture topography*.   To the right comprehension of Scripture acquaintance with Scripture topography is indispensable.   This is easily obtainable at the present day from several books of travels now accessible to all.   Much may be gained in this way even by those who have not had any opportunity of visiting Bible lands.   2. *Peculiarities in this parable*.   Here several things are peculiar, and only such as are to be met with in the East.   First, the sower went forth (ἐξῆλθεν) from his homestead, for his fields evidently lay at a considerable distance from his dwelling.   In the next place, the different kinds of soil are represented in close proximity.   Further, the seed is scattered on the highway as well as on the ordinary and proper ground.   The produce likewise in one case appears unusually large. Now, on turning to Stanley's book on 'Palestine,' or to Thomson's 'The Land and the Book,' we get a glimpse at the state of things in the East, which proves all this to be clear, correct, and consistent.   From those interesting records of Eastern travel, with their graphic sketches of Eastern scenes, we learn that the sower has to *go forth* frequently a distance of some miles from his home in order to deposit his seed in the ground.   On reaching the corn-land, he finds it devoid of fences, a *pathway* passing through it, *thorn bushes* growing in clumps together, with *rocks* here and there peering through the surface of sparse and scanty soil, while not far off are patches of exceeding *fertility ;* the produce at the same time amounting to the high figure of a *hundredfold*, but reckoned in the following peculiar fashion :—Of three bushels sown one is lost by the birds, particularly the crows; another third is destroyed by mice and insects, but out of the one remaining bushel one hundred bushels are reaped.   3. *Confirmatory facts*.   Speaking of the verification of the parable with respect to the different kinds of ground, Thomson, in his enter aining manner, proceeds thus : "Now, here we have the whole four within a dozen rods of us.   Our horses are actually trampling down some seeds which have fallen by the wayside, and larks and sparrows are busy picking them up.   That man, with his mattock, is digging about places where the rock is too near the surface for the plough; and much that is sown there will wither away, because it has no deepness of earth. And not a few seeds have fallen among the *bellan*, and will be effectually choked by this most tangled of thorn bushes.   But a large portion, after all, falls into really good ground, and four months hence will exhibit every variety of crop, up to the richest and heaviest."   Stanley's account, though quite independent, is remarkably similar and confirmatory of the foregoing in all the main particulars.   The following extract contains the substance of it :—Referring to the plain of Gennesaret, he says, "There was the undulating corn-field descending to the water's edge.   There was the trodden pathway running through the midst of it, with no fence or hedge to prevent the seed from falling here and there on either side of it or upon it; itself hard with the constant tramp of horse and mule and human feet.   There was the 'good,' rich soil, which distinguishes the whole of that plain and its neighbourhood. . . . There was the rocky ground of the hillside protruding here and there through the corn-fields. . . . There were the large bushes of thorn, the 'nabk,' that kind of which tradition says that the crown of thorns was woven, springing up in the very midst of the waving wheat ; " while in a note he adds, "I observed that the same mixture of corn-field, pathway, rock, and thorn extended through the whole of this part of the shores of the lake." 4. *Naturalness of our Lord's imagery.* The comparisons employed by our Lord are every way appropriate, not only suitable to the comprehension and habitudes of the persons addressed, but springing naturally out of the circumstances in which he and they find themselves placed, or the scenery by which they are surrounded. His eye rests on a rich pasture-ground of Southern Palestine, where a flock of many sheep is grazing amid green herbage or reposing by still waters ; or perhaps he sees them following the shepherd, with whose kindly voice they are so familiar, as he goes before them, in Oriental fashion, and gently leads them along the hillside or down in the deep valley ; or they are returning to the shelter of the fold on the sunny slope, and passing through the wicket gate under the friendly shepherd's care ;—immediately and naturally the scene suggests the illustration, "He that entereth in by the door is the shepherd of the sheep. . . . I am the door : by me if any man enter in, he shall be saved, and shall go in and out, and find pasture. . . . I am the good shepherd : the good shepherd giveth his life for the sheep. And other sheep I have, which are not of this fold : them also I must bring, and they shall hear my voice ; and there shall be one flock, and one shepherd." Again, among the many once vine-clad hills of Judah, he stands beside the steep side of the terraced hill that bears the vine ; or he is passing along the street of one of its towns or cities, and he sees the vine climbing up the wall or spreading its branches along the trellis-work beside the door of a dwelling, or standing by itself alone at the house-side ;—at once the thought is present to his mind and finds utterance by his lips, "I am the true vine, and my Father is the husbandman. Every branch in me that beareth not fruit he taketh away : and every branch that beareth fruit, he purgeth it, that it may bring forth more fruit." Again, in Northern Palestine he gazes on the fertile plain of Gennesaret, with its luxuriant vegetation, its rich corn-ground carefully tilled if not highly cultivated, and waving in harvest-time with its heavy masses of ripened grain ;—and thence he draws his parables of the sower going forth to sow his precious seed and again returning laden, bearing his sheaves and rejoicing by the way ; of the tares ; and the secret growth of the seed ; perhaps also that of the mustard tree. When he surveyed the blue waters of the Sea of Galilee and contemplated its calm expanse, while its waves came gently rippling to the beach or slumbered in silence at his feet ; or when the hum of its busy industry sounded in his ears, and his attention was turned to the variety of vessels that ploughed its surface, and its numerous fishing craft ;—he thence derived the illustration, which is found embodied in the parable of the draw-net with its great length and extensive reach, gathering within its folds of every kind both bad and good—the valuable and the vile alike. Once more, when he gazed on the city of Capernaum, "his own city," so highly exalted in religious privilege, and the riches of its merchandise, and the resources of its commerce ;—the merchantman with his goodly pearls or with his carefully hoarded and cautiously hidden treasures was naturally suggested to his mind. 5. *Variety in the independent records.* In that chapter of parables, the thirteenth of St. Matthew's Gospel, no fewer than seven parables are recorded ; in the parallel passage of St. Mark four are recorded ; and by St. Luke in the corresponding section only two. Of the seven parables in St. Matthew's record, two are also recorded by St. Mark, with two additional ; of the four in St. Mark's record, two are recorded by St. Luke. But all three relate the parable of the sower contained in this chapter. Accordingly, the seven parables of the chapter of St. Matthew's Gospel referred to are—the sower, the tares, the mustard seed, the leaven, the hidden treasure, the pearl, and the draw-net ; of these parables, the first teaches the production or founding of the kingdom ; the second and seventh, the persons commingling in it or its mixture ; the third and fourth, its progress ; and the fifth and sixth, its preciousness. In the corresponding section of St. Mark are the four parables—the sower, the mustard seed, the secret growth of the seed, and the candle set on a candlestick, if we may properly call it a parable ; in the corresponding portion of St. Luke we find the parable of the sower and that of the candle on a candlestick.

II. COLLATION OF THE THREE RECORDS. 1. *A complete whole.* By comparing the three gospel narratives and piecing them together, as it were, we obtain a complete whole. It is often of much importance and always of great interest thus to consolidate the narrative by a comparison, if not a combination, of the text. 2. *The seed by the wayside.* In the narrative of the seed sown by the wayside, St. Matthew and St. Mark both tell us of the fowls, or winged creatures, of the heaven devouring it ; while St. Luke states in addition the fact that it was *trodden down.* In the interpretation which our Lord gives of this same portion of the parable, all three agree in informing us that the Word that was sown in the hearers' hearts is taken away by the devil, or Satan, or the wicked one, as they severally designate him ; while St. Matthew gives us the additional information that this occurs in the case of persons hearing the Word and *not understand-ing* it, and that he *snatcheth* it away ; and St. Luke subjoins the object for which it is thus taken away, " lest they should *believe* and be *saved.*" 3. *The seed on stony ground.* In the narrative of the seed sown on stony ground, or on the *rock* according to St. Luke, all three tell us that it withered away ; but St. Matthew and St. Mark add that, before withering, it was *scorched,* after the sun had risen, from *want of root,* and that owing to *lack of soil* ; while St. Luke states simply that the withering was due to *lack of moisture.* In the explanation, again, all three tell us that those sown on stony ground receive the word with joy, but that they have no root, and that they endure or believe for a while ; St. Matthew and St. Mark further state that when " affliction or persecution ariseth because of the Word, immediately they are *offended,*" or stumble ; but St. Luke speaks of such a season more generally as a *time of trial,* and intimates that they then stand aloof, or *apostatize* altogether. 4. *The seed among thorns.* In the narrative of that sown among thorns, all three inform us that the thorns choked it ; but St. Luke further informs us that the thorns grew up *simultaneously* with it ; and St. Mark adds, what in these circumstances might be expected, that it yielded no fruit. In the explana-tion, all three acquaint us with the fact that it is choked and becomes unfruitful ; they trace the unfruitfulness to its being choked ; St. Luke says, by cares and riches and the *pleasures of this life,* as men go on their way in it ; St. Mark uses a more comprehensive expression than the " pleasures of this life," which St. Matthew altogether *omits,* namely, " the *lusts of other things* ; " while both St. Matthew and St. Mark qualify riches by an expressive term, adding " the *deceitfulness* of riches." 5. *The seed sown on good ground.* In the narrative of the seed sown on good ground, we are informed by all three that it bore fruit, but on a graduated scale—a hundredfold, sixtyfold, and thirtyfold, according to St. Matthew ; but in *reverse order* according to St. Mark ; while St. Luke merely specifies the *maximum* at a hundredfold, as if he had in view Gen. xxvi. 12, " Then Isaac sowed in that land, and received in the same year an hundredfold, and the Lord blessed him." Here again, in the explanation, all three coincide in the matter of fruitfulness. St. Matthew tells that " they *understand* the Word," St. Mark that " they *receive* it," St. Luke that " having heard it in an *honest and good heart,* they *keep* it, and bring forth fruit with *perseverance.*" 6. *A gradation.* Thus the seed by the wayside did not even spring up at all ; that on the rock did indeed spring up, but withered ; that among thorns sprang up and grew, but being choked yielded no fruit ; only that on good ground sprang up, grew, and brought forth fruit to perfection.

III. INTERPRETATION OF THE SEED. 1. *The seed is the Word of God.* The seed is that Word of which, as has been well said, " Truth is the substance, salvation the end, and God the author." The seed is that Scripture all of which " is given by inspiration of God, and is profitable for doctrine, for reproof, for correction, for instruction in righteousness ; that the man of God may be perfect, thoroughly furnished unto all good works." The signature to a will or other document does not need to be rewritten or repeated from time to time ; nor does the seal to such an instrument need to be restamped once and again ; so with those *miracles* which were the sign manual of God to the truth of his Word, and the seal affixed to it in attestation of its Divine author-ship. Once wrought, as those miracles were, according to the record of the most authen-tic history in the world—and no facts of history were ever more fully or more clearly testified, or more carefully and critically scrutinized—they remain to the present hour the signature of the Divine Author ; and not only that, but his seal to the reality of the Divine origin of Scripture. Thus Heaven has stamped approval on the document with its own seal and signature ; while these proofs, authenticated by the most unex-ceptionable witnesses, remain permanent and powerful as ever. 2. *Proof from prophecy.* But view Scripture again in the light of prophecy. The Messianic prophecies, for example, were delivered by different persons, in different places, at differ-ent times, under different circumstances, and on different occasions ; yet these prophecies, when carefully and correctly put together, portray unmistakably Jesus of Nazareth as the Messiah—the Christ of God. Suppose a painting executed in a somewhat similar way—the head painted in Berlin, the hands in Boston, the arms in Paris, the trunk in St. Petersburg, the legs in Vienna, and the feet in Rome; suppose these different parts all brought to London and placed together, each in its proper position, and that, when thus put together, they present the exact picture of Christ which is seen in the famous " Descent from the Cross " as painted by Rembrandt, or by Rubens, or even by Jouvenet : what conclusion would we, or should we, come to from such a phenomenon? Would it not be that some great master painter had presided over and prepared the whole, guiding in some way every hand, directing every brush, and inspiring every head so that one of the finest specimens of pictorial art was thus wondrously brought into existence? In like manner, let the Old Testament prophets who foresaw and foretold the sufferings of Christ as well as the glory that should follow—let Moses and Malachi, David and Daniel, Isaiah and Micah, Jeremiah and Zechariah, be brought together round the cross of Calvary, and let their pictures and prophecies meet together there, and they will unite in perfect harmony, and present the exact picture of him whose hands and whose feet were pierced with nails, who " was wounded for our transgressions, and bruised for our iniquities," and on whom " the chastisement of our peace was laid," and in whose riven side was opened that cleansing " fountain for sin and for uncleanness." Though the portions contributed, the prophets themselves, the periods at which they lived, the plans they pursued, the predictions they delivered, were all different, yet one Spirit testified in them, one God inspired them, one unseen but almighty hand superintended them all; and the picture, brought together from so many different quarters and composed of so many different parts, is one. 3. *Practical proof.* But let us take a still plainer and more practical test. See yon venerable patriarch whose locks are silvered with years; he resides in a remote hamlet, he dwells in a humble cottage. Observe with what reverence he takes down the ancestral Bible, and with what grace he reads its sacred page at the hour of morning or evening worship. He has never read, perhaps never heard of, any of the great writers on the evidences—Butler, or Paley, or Lardner, or Leslie, or Leland, or Watson ; and yet, if you ask him how he knows that volume, which he reads so dutifully and devoutly, to be the Word of God, he will at once and unhesitatingly reply that he knows it must be the Word of God, for he has felt its power to be Divine, bringing, as it has done, pardon to his soul, peace to his conscience, light to his feet and a lamp to his path, joy to his heart, and the " sure and certain hope " of eternal life and immortal glory to his never-dying spirit. Wherever we find a man of that stamp, whether he lives in town or country, in city or village ; whether he is the peer that owns a castle or the peasant that is only a tenant in a cottage ; whether he be a native of merry England, or broad Scotland, or green Ireland, or gay France, or proud Spain, or the German Fatherland, or classic Italy ; whatever be his caste, or calling, or country, or clime, that man, having God's truth in his heart, the grace of God in his soul, and the Spirit of God to guide his feet in the path of peace—that man, whoever he is, or in whatever rank he is found, is a living witness that the seed, of which the Saviour speaks in this parable, is the Word of God and the abiding seed of holiness, for " being born of God he doth not commit sin ; for his seed remaineth in him : and he cannot sin, because he is born of God." 4. *The seed is the Word of the kingdom.* The seed is also called, and so explained to be, the Word of the kingdom. The King of the country to which we travel has issued this Word as a Guide-book to every pilgrim who is travelling to the kingdom of glory. It is the Law of him who is anointed to be a King for ever— who is enthroned as King upon the holy hill of Zion, yea, who is seated at the right hand of the Majesty on high. It is the Word of that kingdom which at its first beginnings is as a little stone hewn out of the mountain without hands, but which afterwards becomes a great mountain and fills the whole earth. It is the Law of that King whose kingdom is to be without bounds, and whose reign is to be without end. Of his kingdom it is the Statute-book. From that kingdom it comes and to that kingdom it conducts, translating the sinner out of the kingdom of darkness into the kingdom of light, out of the kingdom of sin into the kingdom of grace, out of the kingdom of Satan into the kingdom of God. And no sooner has any traveller set his face and turned his feet from the City of Destruction towards the city of the great King, than, like Bunyan's pilgrim, he is observed with this Book in his hand, and at every progressive step in his pilgrimage his eye is on the Book, and thus he reads and walks, and walks and reads, ever reading as he goes.   Like David, "his delight is in the Law of the Lord, and in that Law he meditates day and night."   In reference to this Law it was said of Israel, " What nation is there so great that hath statutes and judgments so righteous as all this Law which I have set before you this day ? "   We, with Law and Gospel in our hands, are surely bound to be grateful, and to feel—

"How greatly blessed the people are
The joyful sound that know ! "

5. *Our duty in relation to the Word of the kingdom.*   The statutes of an earthly kingdom are carefully studied as well as frequently perused.   How much more ought the Word of the kingdom, that is, the statutes of the kingdom of heaven, to be daily and diligently read and consulted !   If the King of heaven condescends to be at pains to teach us his statutes and his judgments, surely the least that we, who are "of the earth, earthy"—creatures of a day, worms of the dust, should do, is to be at pains to learn those statutes of the Lord that are right, "rejoicing the heart."   Again, where the word of a king is there is power, consequently the Word of him who is King of kings and Lord of lords should come home to our hearts, not in word only, " but in power, and in the Holy Ghost, and in much assurance."   When the word or law of an earthly king is transgressed, such transgression is usually visited with pains and penalties proportionate to the transgression.   Can we reasonably expect, then, that the transgressors of Heaven's Law shall escape with impunity ?   The King who rules in Zion will, we are assured, rule also in the midst of his enemies.   If we refuse to touch the sceptre of his mercy, or if we reject the Word of his grace, then assuredly we shall be broken with a rod of iron and dashed in pieces like a potter's vessel.   The Word of the kingdom is the Word of the King of glory ; if we follow its directions they will conduct us on the way to glory.   It is the Word of him whose kingdom is not of this world ; if we walk according to its instructions, then shall our conversation, or citizenship, even now be in heaven.   6. *This seed is absolutely necessary for salvation.*   It is, as we have seen, the Word of God and the Word of the kingdom, but it is still the seed ; and what the seed is in the natural world, the Word of God, or of the kingdom, is in the spiritual world.   Without seed there can be no vegetation—neither root nor fruit, neither bud nor blossom, neither leaf nor flower, neither stalk nor plant.   The *soil* may be as rich as that of the primeval forest when it is cleared, or as that of the virgin prairie when it is for the first time opened by the ploughshare ; there may be gentle showers and genial sunshine, reviving heat and refreshing dews.   The *seasons* may be most propitious ; they may follow each other with successive and suitable blessings— the purifying winds of winter, the freshness of spring, the sultriness of summer, the maturity of autumn ; but notwithstanding all this, if the seed be wanting, there cannot be a single stalk of grain nor plant of any kind—neither " grass for the cattle nor herb for the service of man."   So spiritually, the Word of God is seed of regenerating power ; for are we born again?   Then it is "not of corruptible seed, but of incorruptible, by the Word of God, which liveth and abideth for ever."   Thus the Word of God is seed—the seed of grace in this world, and of glory in the next ; the seed of holiness in time, and of heaven through eternity.   7. *The seed needs quickening.*   We have seen that without the seed of God's Word there is neither grace nor glory, neither holiness nor heaven ; and therefore as much as justifies the inference that all that is good and gracious, all that is really noble and truly Christian, every grace and every good work,—all spring from the seed of the Word.   In the economy of nature, the vigorous stem, and green leafage, and lovely blossom, and abundant fruit are all owing to the seed, and could not possibly exist without it; so in the economy of grace, strong faith, lively hope, and ever-advancing holiness,—all spring out of the seed which is the Word of God.   But granting all this, the seed only contains the material of life—it is the means of life ; but it is dependent on the quickening, vivifying, life-giving Spirit of God.   By his Spirit he fructifies the seed ; by his Spirit he vivifies his Word.   The Word of God, the Son of God, and the Spirit of God must all go together in the salvation of every human soul.   The Son of God brings salvation, the Word of God reveals it, and the Spirit of God applies it.   8. *There is vitality in every verse as well as in the whole volume.*   Even where the Bible

is not found collectively and in all its component parts, fragments of it may exist in the shape of single books, or chapters, or verses. And wherever it is thus met with even in dispersed portions, there is seed, there is the germ of life, and, by the blessing of God and the operation of his Spirit, there will in due time be the full development of life and fruitfulness. While it is a blessed privilege to possess the whole of God's Word, and sufficient means of understanding it, and abundant material for its enforcement ; still persons not so privileged, but having in possession some small portion of God's Word, are not without the means of safety and salvation. Paragraphs of the Bible, verses of the Bible, sentiments of the Bible, are often blended with the religious compositions of human authors ; yet still they retain their vitality, and only want the Spirit of God to quicken them into living power.

IV. THE WAYSIDE HEARERS. 1. *Nature of the wayside.* By this we may understand a highway, or byway, or bridle-way, or ordinary footpath ; but whether the way be broad or narrow, whether it be a well-constructed road or merely a beaten pad, whether it be a public road or pathway, two notions attach to it. We connect with it, first, the idea of a *passage,* along which people walk, or ride, or drive, or along which traffic is conveyed. But a second idea attached to it, and one which is the consequence of the first, is that of *hardness,* because of the constant resort along it. Both ideas characterize the hearts of wayside hearers. Just as the highway is that along which people travel on foot, or horseback, or in vehicles of whatever kind, and that too along which their goods are conveyed and their commerce carried on—along which, in fact, their merchandise is transported ; so the heart of the wayside hearer is a highway for the *passage of worldly thoughts.* Such thoughts are constantly passing to and fro along it. Temporal things make it their thoroughfare ; unchecked, unhindered, unimpeded, and uninterrupted, they pass and repass. Earthly, or sensual and sinful, objects are constantly found on the highway of that carnal heart. Passion and pride, avarice and ambition, luxury and lust are ever traversing that highway or the byways that diverge from it. Memories of the past, anticipations of the future, present reflections on worldly things, earthly joys or sorrows, worldly cares and anxieties, schemes of wealth and thoughts of indulgence, or hopes of worldly aggrandizement,—all find free passage along the wayside hearer's heart. No foot, however unhallowed, is forbidden to enter there. Now, these hearers come to the house of God and seem to hear his Word: "They come unto thee as the people cometh, and they sit before thee as my people, and they hear thy words, but they will not do them. . . . And, lo, thou art unto them as a very lovely song of one that hath a pleasant voice, and can play well on an instrument: for they hear thy words, but they do them not." With this free and constant passage of thousands of earthly, temporal, worldly, and sinful thoughts along the open thoroughfare of the wayside hearer's heart there is small space for thoughts of God. They come " to hear of heaven and learn the way," but their heart is preoccupied, and their thoughts engaged with other objects. Besides, from this constant traffic along it, the heart becomes *hard* as the wayside, and like the common highway. When thoughts of what is good or gracious do enter, they pass over it, going out as they came in. They never settle on it or sink into it. Any good impressions or gracious influences are merely transient. 2. *The wayside hearers understand it not.* They hear the Word, but they understand it not. How could they ? Understanding requires attention, but worldly thoughts engross the attention that should be given to thoughts of God. Not only so, the heart has become so hard by the constant traffic upon it that such thoughts, when they do enter, cannot penetrate the surface so as to find lodgment in the understanding. What with the crowding together and crushing along of worldly thoughts, and the consequent hardness of heart, the understanding remains untouched. Instead of minds enlightened by the Spirit of God, such hearers come with hearts hardened by the deceitfulness of sin and like a common highway ; and so any serious notions that do force an entrance are lost amid the host of other thoughts, and lie on the hard surface. Any truths or facts not duly attended to cannot be properly understood ; when only partially, or imperfectly, or perhaps not at all understood, they cannot be retained in the memory. So the wayside hearer neither takes heed to the Word nor keeps hold of it, and therefore gets no benefit from it. But another circumstance increases the culpability of the hearer and claims our notice. 3. *It is trodden down.* Many a precious seed of gospel truth has been thus treated. Many a time have the truths of God's Word been trodden down. Many an assurance of Christ's ability and readiness "to save to the uttermost" has been trodden down. Many an offer of grace and salvation has been trodden down. Many an "exceeding great and precious promise" by which the hearer might be made partaker of a Divine nature has been trodden down. Many a Scripture picturing the joys of heaven, inviting and even urging us to make those joys our own, has been trodden down. Many a faithful warning of the sinner to forsake his ways and flee from present wrath and eternal ruin has been trodden down. Thus the Word of God has been despised and despite done to the Spirit of grace. The pure precepts of that Word as well as its precious promises, its earnest entreaties as well as its solemn exhortations, its faithful reproofs as well as its friendly remonstrances, its gracious invitations as well as its many warnings, have all been trodden down, and so treated with carelessness, indifference, and even contempt. 4. *Satan snatches it away.* "The fowls of the air came and devoured it up." Here again we should notice the verisimilitude of our Lord's representation. "In the countless birds of all kinds—aquatic fowls by the lake-side, partridges and pigeons hovering, as on the Nile-bank, over the rich plain of Gennesaret, we may still see," says Stanley, "the 'birds of the air' which 'came and devoured the seed by the wayside,' or which took refuge in the spreading branches of the mustard tree." Again he observes, "The flocks of birds in the neighbourhood of Gennesaret have been already observed. Their number, their beauty, their contrast with the busy stir of sowing and reaping and putting into barns visible in the plains below (whether of Hattin or Gennesaret), must have always courted observation." Never did a bird of the air rush with greater swiftness on its prey than Satan rushes to take away the Word of God as it lies unheeded and despised—trodden down, in fact, on the sinner's heart. Never did the birds that in such multitudes frequent the lake and plain of Gennesaret, whether pigeons, or partridges, or aquatic fowls, hasten with greater eagerness to pick up the seeds let fall by the sower on the pathway running through the corn-land in the plain of Gennesaret, than Satan hurries to take away the seed of truth out of the wayside hearer's heart. The wayside was not meant for cultivation nor intended to be sown; so there are hearers who come to hear the Word from custom, or fashion, or from conformity to a respectable observance, or for sake of appearance, or perhaps from a slight twitching of conscience, but not out of a sense of duty, or feeling of privilege, or any earnest desire to get good from it or profit by it. When they do come, their minds detach themselves, as it were, from their bodies and wander miles away; their thoughts wander on the mountains of vanity, or are absorbed in their worldly plans, or prospects, or purposes. Thus the seed lies on the beaten pathway, and is trodden down. Satan is "the prince of the power of the air," and multiplies himself in his emissaries, here represented by fowls, or winged creatures (πετεινὰ), of the air. He turns away their thoughts from the truth that is being proclaimed and engrosses them with some worldly object; he amuses them, it may be, with some peculiarity of the preacher, or engages their attention with some article of a neighbour's dress; he prejudices their minds against the truth, or preoccupies them with thoughts widely different from those that should be suggested by the subject in hand; he may rob them of the seed by an after-sermon critic, or by the sarcasm of some worthless witling, or the sneer of a sceptically inclined friend. He has thousands of little birds of the air to carry away any thoughts of God, of the soul, of sin, of salvation, of heaven, of hell, of death, of judgment, of eternity, that might lie as seeds of truth on the heart. 5. *The immediateness of his arrival.* St. Mark draws attention to this point by the word εὐθέως, which occurs so often in his Gospel; but much the same thing is implied by the word which St. Matthew employs to represent Satan's method of taking away the seed. It is not αἴρει, equivalent to "taketh it away," used by both the other evangelists who record the parable; but ἁρπάζει, equivalent to "snatcheth it away" in hot haste, and in the eagerness of his desire to prevent any possibility, however remote, of its growth. This is a very remarkable feature in the narrative. Was it not enough that, from the continuous stream of other thoughts passing through the mind, and the myriad multitude of such, the seed had been neglected? Was it not enough that it was let lie on the surface of a heart that had contracted a sort of highway hardness? Was it not enough at least that it was trodden underfoot, trampled on, and despised? Strange that all this was not sufficient for Satan's purpose! But Satan knows too well the living energy of the

Divine Word; and, however neglected or jostled aside, however trodden down or trampled on it may be, however hard and impervious that wayside hearer's heart may be,—Satan, fully alive to the vitality of the seed of Divine truth, apprehends danger from its presence to his own sovereignty over his subjects. If he allowed the seed some time to lie on the heart it might, after all, recover from the trampling and root itself downward, and in the end bear fruit upward. He therefore comes immediately. And though he came immediately, still the seed had been already trodden down; and we therefore infer that the seed had no sooner fallen on the heart than it was instantly trodden down. 6. *Satan's object in all this.* This object is plainly stated in the words, " lest they should believe and be saved," or, as the Revised Version renders them, " that they may not believe and be saved." Here we have the whole plan of salvation in the briefest form; here we have the system of Divine grace for saving the souls of men. Here, too, we have the subject, the object, the instrument, and the result. The subject is every one on whose heart the seed of Divine truth is sown; the object to be accepted by faith is that truth; that faith, again, is the instrument; while salvation is the grand result. The object offered for our belief is the Word of God; the means by which we embrace that Word is faith; and the final and blessed end is salvation. Reader, this Word is now presented to you, and even pressed on your acceptance; if you prefer remaining in ignorance of it, or refuse to believe it, or neglect to apply it, and so fail to feel its saving efficacy, and obey, and enjoy it; then do you judge yourself unworthy of everlasting life, reject the offer of mercy, and put away from you the means—the only means of salvation. If when the truth of God, with its sanctifying and saving influences, is sown on your heart, you allow Satan to snatch it away, or, what amounts to the same thing, to occupy your mind with other topics, or divert your attention from it, or perhaps provoke your hostility against it, then will the end which should be the salvation of your soul remain unattained!

V. PRACTICAL LESSONS. 1. We learn from all this the great sin of carelessness, heedlessness, and thoughtlessness, or rather thinking of other things, when the Word of God is being read or preached. 2. We learn the necessity of careful preparation for Divine ordinances. If we would hear the Word of God with profit, we must supplicate the Spirit of God to prepare our hearts to receive the Word, and to enlighten our minds to understand it, and to bring it home to our souls in demonstration and power. 3. We learn the importance of withdrawment from worldly thoughts as well as worldly business, of spending the morning of the sabbath in religious exercises and hallowed engagements, of avoiding idle gossip and all trifling conversation, and also of watchfulness against vain thoughts and wandering thoughts and sinful thoughts when in the house of God, so that Satan may neither hinder the work of God in, nor snatch the Word of God out of, our hearts. 4. Three processes are thus indispensable— breaking up the fallow ground by previous preparation, covering the seed sown by subsequent meditation and faithful pleading for the dews of Divine grace to water the seed sown, as well as taking earnest heed that we do not let it slip.

VI. THE STONY-GROUND HEARERS. 1. *Their shallowness.* The first characteristic of such is their shallowness. This is better expressed by *rocky* ($\pi\epsilon\tau\rho\tilde{\omega}\delta\epsilon\varsigma$), than stony ground. The first class of hearers had no receptivity in consequence of their heart being so hard, and the traffic along its thoroughfare so continuous. The seed falling on its surface lay there, was instantly trodden down, and immediately taken away by the evil one himself or some of his numerous emissaries. Now, this second class of hearers is so far superior to the former that they possess receptivity, but only to a limited extent. The surface of this soil is soft, it is true, but shallow. A soil may be stony in the proper sense; the stones may be small and loose; they may be tolerably close together or considerably apart. In either case the plant makes way in the inter-spaces, and roots itself where there is sufficient depth of earth. The present case is different. The ground is in the strict sense rocky; the rock—the limestone rock which prevails so extensively in Palestine—reaches the surface and comes fully into view, or is only covered and concealed from the eye by a sparse and shallow sprinkling of earth. Seed sown on such soil soon springs up, quickened into vegetation and warmed into life by the heat of an Eastern clime; and all the more so as the plant, when impeded in its development downward, would, by curious plant-instinct, the more rapidly propagate itself upward. But the very heat that helps the rapid springing of the seed upward out of that thin, shallow soil, soon becomes hurtful because of that very shallowness of soil, where the root has no room for healthy development, and finds no moisture to invigorate its growth and counteract the excess of heat. Soon as the plant has sprung up and the sun has risen upon it, it is scorched. The sun's heat, so beneficial to a strongly rooted plant, is thus most prejudicial to that of which the root is not sufficiently developed. The whole is a correct representation of those shallow, impulsive creatures who at once fall in with any current excitement, or are carried away by some shallow sensationalism. 2. *Immediate and joyful reception of the Word.* This is the first particular which our Lord, in his exposition of this portion of the parable, specifies. Those who hear the Word in this way are in advance of that large portion of the population, sometimes called the lapsed masses, who never enter the house of God, nor wait at the posts of wisdom's doors to hear what God the Lord will say to their souls. They are also in advance of those who do indeed frequent the house of God, but who, like the wayside hearers, from carelessness, heedlessness, indifference, inattention, and the indulgence of vain, wandering, and sinful thoughts, are entirely irreceptive, never admitting the Word into their understanding or minds at all. They are in advance of those too who, though they attend the public worship of God, do so only as a matter of form, and regard it as a piece of decent drudgery, to which the force of public opinion, or compliance with the wishes of friends, or a notion of respectability, obliges them to submit. The persons referred to hear the Word with a large amount of satisfaction, and so far they are considerably ahead of multitudes of mankind and of many of their neighbours; yet they fail miserably at the end, and fall short of heaven. They receive it *anon*, at once, and without hesitancy or delay; but they are somewhat precipitate in their reception of it; they do not take time to "mark, learn, and inwardly digest" it. They receive it readily, neither "proving all things" nor "holding fast that which is good." They receive it with pleasure, but without profit. They receive it as an intellectual treat or literary enjoyment, but there its influence is at an end. They receive it with mental approbation, but, though gratified with it, they are neither guided nor governed by it. They receive it with eagerness as the good Word of God, and it is sweet to their taste; but it does not check their beloved lusts and besetting sins, nor change their evil habits and ungodly lives. Or, if it do produce any change, that change is merely transient. Their goodness is like the morning cloud, now careering it in the vault of heaven, and for a short time visible as a rain-cloud, then vanishing without the promised shower—a moment seen, then gone for ever; or like the early dew-drops scattered as pearls upon the grass, and sparkling in the morning sun, but brushed away by the foot of the passing traveller before it reaches the earth to moisten its surface or fructify its soil. But how or why is this? How is it possible that persons may receive the Word with gravity and solemnity, with frequency and apparent fervour, with eagerness and gladness, and yet without any beneficial effect or abiding result? Because they do not receive it with faith, and therefore "the Word does not profit, not being mixed with faith in them that hear it." 3. *They want root.* The secret of unsuccess here is want of root; "they have no root in themselves," and so they "endure but for a time," or last only for a season (πρόσκαιροι). The seed falling on the surface soon penetrates the thin layer of soil, but when it has pierced through that shallow covering, it comes upon the hard, impenetrable rock. It can go no further; it can neither go round that stratum of rock nor enter it. So with the seed of the Divine Word when sown on rocky hearts. It has no real root in them, and so it dies away and is soon gone; it has no root in the judgment, and so there can be no fixed principles of life or action; it has no root in the understanding, and so there are no clear conceptions of truth nor correct apprehensions of duty; it has no root in the will, and so the will remains without proper restraint and right direction; it has no root in the affections, and so no habits of goodness are properly formed or of permanent continuance; it has no root in the conscience, and so no regulative force is exercised over that vicegerent of God in the heart of man; it has no root in the memory, and, as a matter of course, it is either consigned to oblivion or is only remembered as the sound of a pleasant song. The tender plant cannot penetrate the hard rock nor root itself in the unyielding limestone; it is no wonder, then, that the rootless plant cannot in any case exist for long, much less resist for any considerable time the scorching rays of the midday sun. There is (1) no *fixity* in the root and no firmness in the stem.   See the languishing aspect of that lovely floweret which has been uprooted from the genial soil of its parent earth; how soon it droops and dies! Compare it with the plant, or shrub, or tree fast rooted in the earth.   Look at yon old oak tree deep moored in the rifted rock; it is subjected to every blast; it is assailed by every storm, fretted by every gust of heaven, and exposed to every wind that blows. The wind has bent it, but never broken it; the storm has shaken it, but could never uproot it; the tempest assailed it, but it has withstood the shock.   Centuries have rolled over its aged top and widespread branches, but time has only left it sturdier than ever—deeper rooted than before.   "Woodman, spare that tree," for the strength of wind and the stress of weather have proved its deep-rooted stability—firm as the rock in which it is rooted, and immovable as the everlasting hill of which that rock is a part. May the Word of the eternal God take root in our hearts, and, when so rooted, may it gradually attain a greater depth of soil; and may the Spirit of the living God enable us, by meditation, prayer, self-examination, and closer communion with Father, Son, and Holy Spirit, to maintain to the end such deep-rooted strength and Christian stability!   But the root serves another purpose, for not only does it give fixity and firmness to the plant, it is (2) the means of conveying *nourishment* to the plant; it is the channel of communication between the seed and the soil.   Plants need nourishment as well as animals, and accordingly they are furnished with the apparatus necessary for receiving such nourishment.   At the extremity of each fibre of a root there is a spongiole, or small sponge, to suck up nutriment from the soil.   The substances required for the nourishment of plants must be in a state of solution—dissolved in many times their own bulk of water; otherwise they could not pass through the exceedingly minute apertures or pores of the spongioles.   Now, it is obvious that there are two ways in which we may make a plant to perish—either by withdrawing the moisture from the soil, and the inorganic substances by which the plant is fed cannot be made available; or by destroying the root and those vessels through which the small particles of matter in solution are absorbed by the plant.   In the former case the nourishment designed to sustain life is altogether withheld, or, if present, cannot be utilized; in the latter case that very nourishment tends to accelerate disorganization, for when moisture remains stagnant in the sponges they are soon saturated, and disease and putrefaction ensue.   Now, in the case which the parable supposes, both the nourishment is wanting, and the means of receiving it are absent—both moisture and root are deficient, or rather entirely lacking.   Where then, or how, can the plant draw the supply of nourishment which it requires?   Now, the channel of communication, as well as the means of connection, between the spiritual seed and the spiritual soil— the Divine Word and the human heart—is faith.   When, therefore, that which is the medium of communication and means of life is absent, how or whence can spiritual life, not to speak of growth or health, be maintained?   The seed and the soil have no means of contact; the root of faith that should bring them into vital union is deficient; and so there is no nourishment, no development of vitality—in a word, no spiritual life. 4. *A temporary semblance of life.*   "For a while they believe," or for a *season* they endure.   We have seen a young twig sprout seemingly verdant and vigorous from the lifeless trunk; and so for a while a plant may appear to have life, while it is virtually dead.   For a while it may seem even to flourish, where the root is dying or already dead, and where the source of life and vigour, as well as the means of communicating it, are wanting.   Just so is it in things spiritual: men may for a while have a name to live, while yet they are dead; the blade of profession may be green, while the root of grace may be withered or wanting; men may profess much and seem to practise what they profess, while that profession is hollow and that practice heartless; there may be a beautiful blossom and a fair flower, and yet no fruit ever come to maturity or even come forth at all.   Without the power of life in the root there is no vital principle, no genuine practice, and therefore no final perseverance.   But to put the case more practically, there may be both conviction and confession of sin, and yet no conversion. Felix trembled when St. Paul "reasoned of righteousness, temperance, and judgment to come;" but yet to St. Paul, after his powerful sowing of the heavenly seed, the answer was, "Go thy way for this time; when I have a convenient season, I will call for thee." There may be a commendable disposition to hear God's Word and so receive the seed; there may be many good resolutions formed, and yet the result may be the same as in the case of Agrippa, when he said to St. Paul, "Almost thou persuadest me to be a Christian ;" still the almost Christian, as the old divines used quaintly yet truly to say, is only almost saved.   Men may not only wait on the ordinances of religion with satisfaction, listen to the gospel with pleasure, and receive the preached Word with gratification and gladness, but also reform much in life and conduct, just as it is written of Herod, that he "feared John, knowing that he was a just man and an holy, and observed him; and when he heard him he did many things, and heard him gladly ;" and yet the end may be no better than that of that wicked and unhappy monarch.   5. *The testing-time.*   A time of temptation or trial cometh—"tribulation or persecution ariseth because of the Word."   Here we have the genus and the species very clearly set before us ; the trial in general and its specific kinds.   The *trial* is of a hostile kind ($\pi\epsilon\iota\rho\alpha\sigma\mu o\tilde{\nu}$), and the two sorts of it are distinctly stated, namely, personal affliction within, and persecution without.   The affliction or painful *pressure* is such as comes upon us in connection with our own individual circumstances, and may affect us in soul, body, or estate. The *persecution* is that which assails us from without.   But why is this?   Why does this persecution arise?   "Because of the Word."   The world hates God's Word, because the holy doctrines of that Word are opposed to and condemn the unholy principles of the world, and because the pure precepts of that Word are contrary to and rebuke the unrighteous practices of the world.   The carnal mind hates the Word, for that Word exposes and reprobates its sinful and shocking enmity to God.   The flesh hates the Word, because that Word denounces "those fleshly lusts that war against the soul," and commands men to "crucify the flesh with its affections and lusts."   The sinner hates the Word, for the principles of that Word are the means which the Spirit employs to reprove him, as well as "convince him of sin, of righteousness, and of judgment."   Every unrenewed heart and every unregenerate soul hates the Word, because the Law of God, which it contains, is holy and just and good—exceeding "spiritual," and its "commandments are exceeding broad."   Satan hates the Word, because it is "the sword of the Spirit" by which he is vanquished, by which souls are rescued from his grasp, and the destroyer deprived of his prey.   Hell hates the Word, for where that Word is unknown, or unread, or unpractised, hell enlarges itself beyond measure.   Hence it is that tribulation and persecution arise because of the Word.   6. *Their failure in the day of trial.*   "Immediately they are offended"—scandalized; that is to say, a stumbling-block is laid in their way, and they fall over it.   After a season of special privileges and gracious influences, a time of trial may be expected to come, in order to prove the sincerity of professors and the genuineness of their religion.   After such a period a testing-time may be looked for, and then it is seen who in reality have the root of the matter in them.   Persecution is like the heat of the sun's rays, and this indeed is the figure which our Lord himself employs in this parable.   If the plant be well rooted, the heat of the sun exercises a genial influence on it, promoting its growth and bringing it to maturity.   Once the Word of God has struck deep root and become firmly rooted in our hearts, the clouds of adversity may roll over us, the tempest of persecution rage around us, and the storms of temptation beat at our feet ; yet the firmness of our attitude shall defy the storm, and the fixity of our root shall be strengthened instead of shaken.   The tree rooted in the rock may be uptorn, the grey rock of centuries may itself be upheaved by the earthquake ; the oaks of Bashan may be uprooted, and the cedars of Lebanon may be rent and riven by the lightning of heaven ; the mountains may shake with the swelling of the waters, and the solid earth itself be removed from its deep foundations ; yet, with the seed of truth fast rooted in the heart, and the heart itself grounded in love, the believer stands unmoved, unterrified, and unhurt.   He stands like the spectator on the high summit of a lofty mountain that seems to pierce the clouds ; he hears the hoarse and dreadful roarings of the storm far below him ; he sees the broad and vivid flashes of the lightning glare beneath him ; and listens to the "live thunder as it leaps far along from peak to peak among the rattling crags."   The eminence he occupies elevates him above the storm ; the firmness of his position secures him against its fury ; the storms of an angry world may rage, but he is rooted.   How different it is with plants where there is no deepness or depth of earth, where there is lack of moisture, and where the root is deficient or defective !   The sun's heat scorches them, and they wither.   Thus it ever is: the Word of God is either "the savour of life unto life," or "of death unto death ;"   Christ crucified is to " the Jews a stumbing-block, and unto the Greeks foolishness; but unto them which are called, both Jews and Greeks, Christ the power of God, and the wisdom of God." So is it with trial, whether tribulation or persecution; while it only confirms the faithful and leaves them more firmly rooted, it becomes an occasion of stumbling and even of final apostasy to the unfaithful who have no root in themselves. The trials, that help the believer onward to an " exceeding and eternal weight of glory," are such a hindrance in the way of the barren professor that he is offended and falls away. " The same fire," says Augustine, " turns straw into ashes, and takes away the dross from gold." 7. *Final apostasy.* "They fall away." How sad this statement! "They fall away," that is finally. Such is the closing scene! Many a one runs well for a time, but something hinders him, and then he stumbles and finally falls! Many a one, who bade fair to be the Lord's in the great " day when he maketh up his jewels," thus falls away and sinks into apostasy! Many a one, who appeared to be so running that he might obtain the incorruptible crown in company with the pure and holy, falls away from these high hopes and glorious prospects, and perishes for ever! Alas! how dreadful the thought of having a reward so rich in prospect, a diadem so bright in anticipation, an inheritance so incorruptible to look forward to, and yet of finally and for ever falling away and forfeiting all!

VII. PRACTICAL LESSONS.   1. Warned by all this, we are surely called on solemnly to consider *how* we hear, and carefully examine our motives as well as our manner of hearing.   2. We should ever have in recollection the Scripture admonition in reference to such matters, which says, "Therefore we ought to give the more earnest heed to the things that we have heard, lest at any time we should let them slip." 3. We must not be content with a certain change of conduct and conversation; this may last for a time, but, unless the heart be changed, there is no permanence in the change. Unless there is the root of faith, there can never be the real fruit of righteousness. 4. We are warned to expect trial. "All who will live godly in Christ Jesus" must be prepared for it. But, instead of being discouraged thereby or deterred from the path of duty, we must rather rejoice as the apostle directs, saying, "Count it all joy when ye fall into divers temptations [or trials];" and again, "Blessed is the man that endureth temptation: for when he is tried, he shall receive the crown of life, which the Lord hath promised to them that love him." 5. We must beware of being turned aside from the path of duty, or from the study of God's Word, or from prayer, or from the worship of the sanctuary, or from religious service of any kind, either by sneers or taunts, or by unkindness or even persecution on the part of the ungodly. By doing so we prove ourselves of those here represented by the rocky ground. 6. What need we have earnestly to seek the aid of the Holy Spirit to preserve us from an evil and hard heart of unbelief, in which the seed of God's Word can neither take root nor grow!

VIII. THE THORNY GROUND. 1. *Superiority to the two preceding.* "Some fell among thorns." Now, we have, in the descriptions of the several kinds of ground, an ascending climax. In the first the seed lies on the surface, and never enters the soil at all, and by such are understood the *unenlightened* or unintelligent hearers. In the next the seed finds its way into the soil, but that soil is so shallow and so sparse—a mere thin coating on a rock—that the progress of the root downward is soon prevented by the hard, opposing, impenetrable rock: by these conditions are represented the *superficial* hearers or readers of God's Word. We now enter on a third stage upward. The seed, instead of lying on the surface, or remaining rootless in the layer of mould thinly spread upon a rock, has good soil to sustain it, and takes root therein; but the soil, though of itself good enough and deep enough, suffers from preoccupation; thorns, or roots of thorns, have found a place in it: by this description *worldly* hearers are meant. 2. *The growth of the thorns.* We are not to understand full-grown thorns, but thorn roots that had been left in the ground through defective tillage. Proper culture would have completely eradicated them. On the contrary, these thorns grew up along with the sprouting seed (συμφυεῖσαι), and quite choked it. The thorns overtopped the young plant that sprang from the good seed; in this way they overshadowed it, shutting out at the same time both light and air; while a still worse consequence ensued from their roots absorbing the nourishment furnished by the soil, and withdrawing it from the tender plant. The inevitable result was, by robbing it of the strengthening nutriment afforded by the richness of the soil and moisture, to reduce it to a thing of sickly, stunted growth. 3. *The signification of the thorns.* Our Lord, in his interpretation of this part of the parable, shows us that by the thorns we are to understand cares and riches, according to the first Gospel; while a third element is added by St. Luke, namely, "the *pleasures of life*;" and by St. Mark under the still more general expression of "the *lusts of other things.*" All classes of society are comprehended here; all sides of human life are here exhibited. The poor and rich here, as elsewhere, meet together. The third class, embracing such as are devoted to the pleasures of life, or who are concerned about lustings after other things, may be regarded either as a distinct class, or may be reckoned as a sub-class under either the poor or rich; especially the latter, inasmuch as the poor have often as keen a desire for pleasure, and as much zest in pleasure, as the rich, but without equal means of gratification. 4. *How thorny cares choke the seed of God's Word.* The cares referred to are distracting cares—anxieties pulling a man like so many cords in different directions. When such harassing cares come into conflict with thoughts about the things of God, the man in whose breast such a struggle is going on must needs be a double-minded man, in the sense of his heart being divided between God and the world. The cares here mentioned are more particularly such as distress the poor. With many the struggle for daily bread is a severe one—the battle a hard one. To provide food and raiment, a suitable place of abode, and proper education for the members of a household, with requisite preparation for their business in life or special life-work, whatever it is to be, demands a certain amount of careful attention. Nor is this anywhere forbidden in the Word of God; nay, it is commanded. We are required to "provide things honest in the sight of all men;" to be "not slothful in business, but fervent in spirit, serving the Lord;" while it is added that "if any provide not for his own, and especially for those of his own house, he hath denied the faith, and is worse than an infidel." Besides such domestic duties, there are social duties, and personal individual duties, which we are bound to discharge as individuals and as members of society, as well as those which belong to us in our family relations. For the faithful and efficient discharge of such duties care and thought must be employed, time and pains expended. 5. *Two extremes to be avoided.* But, while carelessness about duties of the kind specified is sinful, there is another and opposite extreme, which our Lord deemed it necessary to rebuke by two most beautiful comparisons—the fowls of the air and the flowers of the field; the birds which in such multitudes frequented the lake and plain of Gennesaret, and the flowers which in such variety and surpassing loveliness clothed with spring beauty the hillsides of Galilee. It is our heavenly Father who clothes the one and feeds the other, thus caring for both. How much more will he take care of his children by redemption and adoption as well as by creation! "If," says an old divine, in his own plain and pithy way, "our heavenly Father feeds his birds, he will never starve his babes." God will have us cast our care upon him; he will have us feel convinced that he careth for us; he will have us to be "careful"—that is, anxiously careful—"for nothing, but in everything"—little as well as great, momentous or minute—"by prayer and supplication . . . make our requests known unto God." In this way, avoiding either extreme—that of criminal carelessness on the one hand, and that of corroding carefulness or over-anxiety on the other, and ever by prayer rolling our burden over on the Lord, we get rid of those thorny cares that choke and strangle the growth of the good seed in our hearts. Worldly objects do claim a due share of attention, worldly duties must not be neglected; but heavenly subjects are of paramount importance, and heavenly interests bear the same ratio to earthly that heaven itself does to earth, or eternity to time. Thorns served for fences, and in some places separated the fields in Palestine, as we infer from Micah (vii. 4), where the prophet uses the comparison of "a thorn hedge." They were useful, therefore, in their own way and in their own place for fences in fields, but most baneful when left to grow up in fields of corn, or grain, or other crops. So with worldly cares; they have their place. Of course, by worldly cares we do not mean those anxieties which are strictly forbidden under all circumstances, but only that amount of attention that is required for the right discharge of the worldly duties that devolve upon us. Anything beyond this is injurious to our best and highest interests. Uneasy, anxious cares, like the thorns among the growing grain, choke the Divine Word and strangle the springing plant of grace. Such cares, when yielded to or indulged in, interfere unduly with those thoughts and feelings and affections that are claimed, and justly claimed, by the lessons of God's Word. Things present take the place of things everlasting; anxieties about our worldly affairs crush out altogether, or leave little room for, spiritual concerns. The thorns of this parable are represented as encroaching on the good seed, and usurping the place which of right belongs to the useful plant; so these cares of the present world, if allowed, are sure to usurp the place that belongs to the world to come. The thorns took away from the seed-root, and drew to themselves the nourishment of the rich soil; so the concernments of a passing and perishing world take away our thoughts from God and heaven and eternity. The things that are seen and temporal withdraw our attention from things unseen and eternal. The body and its wants take the place of the soul and its necessities. Exertions and energies that should be devoted to higher and spiritual objects are squandered on the trifles of earth and sense. Under such conditions and in such circumstances the seed of the Word sown in the heart necessarily becomes unfruitful. The soil may be excellent, the seed may be carefully sown, the Word faithfully ministered, it may, moreover, take root and grow; but the thorns deprive it of its proper nourishment, its growth is obstructed, the plant becomes weak and sickly; without strength or vigour it can yield no fruit. It may have stem, and leaf, and bud, and blossom, and growth to a certain extent, but it brings no fruit to perfection or maturity (οὐ τελεσφοροῦσι). In such hearers of the Word there is no fruit of the Spirit, no Christian grace, no works of faith, or deeds of charity, or labour of love in any direction; "it becometh unfruitful." 6. *Another class of these mental thorns.* With the cares of this world our Lord classes riches, as another division of the thorns of this parable. There is nothing sinful in riches when honestly acquired or justly inherited, and when at the same time they are rightly used. We read of the father of the faithful himself that he was "rich in cattle, in silver, and in gold." Two circumstances make the possession of riches to be perilous. The circumstances referred to are the love of riches and the abuse of riches. "The love of money," we read, "is the root of all evil: which while some coveted after, they have erred from the faith, and pierced themselves through with many sorrows;" or, according to the Revised Version, "The love of money is a root of all kinds of evil: which some reaching after have been led astray from the faith, and have pierced themselves through with many sorrows;" and hence it is that they occupy the thoughts and engross the affections to the exclusion of the lessons of inspired truth— the precepts of the Law and the promises of the gospel. They pierce and pain, moreover, like the pricking of thorns. What sorrow as well as solicitude they occasion! Men set their minds to work, and perplex themselves with plans to obtain them, and minds thus preoccupied have no room left for better objects and holier pursuits; men torture themselves most unwarrantably in order to increase them and augment their store; men are distressed with restless schemes in order to retain secure possession of them; men, again, are so in love with them that they cannot bear to part with them, or share them with others for the noblest purposes—religious, educational, or charitable, nor even for the means of profiting their own souls. When the love of riches thus dominates the heart, and when such plans and projects regulate its thoughts and rule its affections, no wonder that such bushy and prickly thorns choke *out* (ἀπεπνίξαν), or crushing *together* suffocate (συμπνίγουσι) and stifle the seeds or plants in their growth. 7. "*The deceitfulness of riches.*" Both St. Matthew and St. Mark mention this characteristic of riches. How often does it occur that men rise up early, sit up late, and eat the bread of carefulness with the hope of becoming rich; but the wealth they are in quest of, like some phantom form, eludes their grasp. Wealth, just as the meteor of the marsh, leads them till it leaves them in the quagmire, deluded, deceived, disappointed. They die neither rich in worldly goods, nor rich toward God. Again, men struggle long and hard for many years, and at length succeed in amassing wealth (πλοῦτος, from the root πλε entering into the verb "to fill," the noun "multitude," and the word "wealth," in Greek), and in scraping together *much* of this world's goods; but scarce has their object been attained, their hopes realized, when, lo! through some untoward event, such as a conflagration, the breaking of a bank, or a robbery, their riches "make to themselves wings and fly away;" and thus they are deceived by a fluctuating, vanishing possession, for the attainment of which they have strained every power of mind and body, to the entire neglect of the soul and spiritual things. Once more, we can well suppose the case of men succeeding in the race for riches, and retaining in security the fruits of their labour. But by this time they are no longer young ; desire has failed, the power of enjoyment has ceased ; the advance of age, with its accompanying decay and decrepitude, kept pace with the accumulation of wealth ; and now in the end, after years of toil, they have no relish for the enjoyments they had anticipated ; they have experienced "the deceitfulness of riches," and, what is worse, their heart is now hard, their conscience seared, the seed of truth has been so long stifled, and its instructions so long suffocated by the crowding thoughts of wealth. Further, riches deceive by their promises. They promise happiness, but instead of happiness they often bring miserable apprehensions; they promise peace of mind, but they often prove the chief disturbers of that peace; they promise contentment, but the craving for more produces restlessness and dissatisfaction ; they promise to lighten the burdens of life, but they frequently superadd a crushing load of care to all its other burdens; they promise relief from care, but it is as true now as in the poet's day, that "black care mounts behind the knight." The seed of the Word may be sown on the rich soil of a young, warm heart, it may strike root deeply downward, it may develop a tender stem and green leaf upward, it may struggle for light and air, but in vain! These thorns rob the root of nourishment, and shut out the genial sunlight and healthy atmosphere from the top; and though there may be foliage, there is no fruitage. If, then, poverty distresses with its cares and distracts by its anxieties, riches may divert the mind by their abundance and deceive by their promises ; in either case, the Word may be unfruitful, the life barren, heaven missed, salvation lost, and the soul ruined. 8. *Other perils to profitable hearing.* When we reflect on the dangers to our spiritual life and growth attending both poverty and riches, we may well say with the wise man, "Give me neither poverty nor riches," or give me grace to bear myself discreetly and devoutly in either. But if the poor man is in danger from his poverty, and the rich man in danger because of his wealth, what of the man of pleasure ? The word βίος differs from ζωή both in the classics and in the Scriptures; but the difference thus existing is reversed, so that in Scripture the latter denotes the higher kind of life, and is the word of moral meaning involving moral distinction, while the former is more closely connected with natural life, or that life which we have in common with other animals. Accordingly, we read of "the pride of life" (βίου), "the affairs of life," and here "the pleasures of life," with the same word in each. "The pleasures of life," or of *this* life—our versions supplying the pronoun—may be the pleasures of sense and sin, such as the apostle enumerates under works of the flesh, when he says, in his Epistle to the Galatians (v. 19), "Now the works of the flesh are manifest, which are these ; Adultery, fornication, uncleanness, lasciviousness, . . . drunkenness, revellings, and such like." Or the pleasures here referred to may be the less gross and more fashionable pleasures which minister to pride, to pomp, to luxury, and to ambition. These desires about the remaining or other things may refer to gay clothing, costly furniture, rich equipages, stately mansions, works of art, broad acres, wide domains, popular applause, worldly advancement, and whatever else may be comprehended under "the lust of the eye and the pride of life." Even lawful desires inordinately pursued, proper objects too eagerly sought after, right employments and occupations too keenly followed, even natural affections carried to excess,—all these, when they are allowed to interfere with or draw away the attention from everlasting verities, the lessons of Scripture, and the concerns of the soul, and are not restrained by the grace of God, become spiritual thorns. They choke the seed, distract and distress the mind, and in the end "make a death-bed difficult." We have read somewhere that when the famous French cardinal Mazarin drew near his end, he caused himself to be dressed, shaved, rouged, and enamelled. Then he had himself rolled in an easy-chair through his picture-gallery, exclaiming at times as he went along, "See that Correggio, this Venus of Titian, that incomparable Caracci ! Must I quit them all? Farewell, beloved ones! None can know how my heart bleeds to leave you." He was next wheeled into the promenade, where the feeble hands of the old sinner were actually held up while he joined in a game of cards! And so, it is added, he continued till the papal nuncio came to give him plenary indulgence.

IX. PRACTICAL LESSONS. 1. The first lesson here that presents itself to our attention may be expressed in that exhortation of the Apostle John, "Love not the world, neither the things that are in the world. If any man love the world, the love of the Father is not in him." 2. We are warned so as to beware of the cruel disappointment of going on successfully for a time, and then coming short at the last; of being, in other words, an almost Christian, and so only coming in view of but not reaching salvation. Here the surface was not hard, as in the case of the wayside, nor was the soil shallow, as in the case of the stony ground; on the contrary, there was a soft surface to admit the seed, there was soil neither shallow nor stony to retain it; and yet the seed, though well and deeply rooted, was stifled at the top and suffocated at the root, so that it never reached maturity.   3. With seeming progress there may be real retrogression.   In the case of the wayside it is trodden down at once, never penetrating even the surface before Satan snatches it away; in the stony ground the seed finds lodgment in the soil, springs up speedily, but for want of root or depth of earth to maintain the root, it is scorched and withers away; in the thorny ground it enters the surface, roots itself in the soil, springs up and grows, but after all it remains barren and fruitless.   The last state, in one point of view, is worse than the preceding, and that, again, than the first; because more progress has been made by the seed among the thorns than by that on the rocky ground, and more by that, again, than by the seed cast on the wayside; and thus to go so far as to take root and grow, and then fall short at last, is more disappointing than the case of the seed which, though it enters the soil, never takes root, and only endures for a time; and still more than that which never penetrates the surface at all.   4. It has been remarked, that the first corresponds to the carelessness of childhood, the second to the shallowness of youth, and the third to the worldliness of age; the first also implying inattention, the second impulsiveness or ardour, and the third indulgent selfishness.

X. THE GOOD GROUND. 1. *Its character*. The chief characteristic of the good ground is its *productiveness;* while our Lord, in his explanation, indicates several other interesting particulars. The good ground represents an honest and good heart. Absolute goodness is out of the question, for " the heart is deceitful above all things, and desperately wicked;" and so the question comes to be—Is it the comparative goodness of the natural heart, or is it the heart of the believer, in reference to whom we read, that " the preparations of the heart in man are from the Lord"?   That there are differences in unregenerate men and in the condition of their hearts is, we think, unquestionable. It is so with individuals: as Nathanael, of whom, when coming to Jesus according to Philip's direction, the Saviour himself said, " Behold an Israelite indeed, in whom is no guile; " or as Cornelius, " a devout man, and one that feared God, with all his house ; " or as the Ethiopian eunuch, who, while he was returning in his chariot, read carefully and pondered closely " the prophet Esaias."   It was so with the members of the Berœan community, who were " more noble than they of Thessalonica, in that they received the Word with all readiness of mind."   Thus even by nature some are more candid, honest, and upright than others; more earnest and desirous of knowing, as well as more ready to receive, the truth.   Such natural differences, as well as those made by grace, are due to God, who alone makes men to differ.   If the reference is to believers, the meaning is perfectly plain.   The heart of such becomes " honest and good " in the highest human sense, when God, by his Holy Spirit, renews the heart and sanctifies the life, having united the soul by faith to the Saviour.   Hearts thus quickened and purified are in a condition to receive, and do receive, the Word in simplicity and godly sincerity.   Thus receiving it they grow thereby, being nourished and strengthened, and built up in their most holy faith. 2. *The reception of the Word by such*. Three terms are employed in this regard. St. Mark says, παραδέχονται, they *receive* it, with a feeling of inward satisfaction, it may be, or even delight. The stony-ground hearers are represented by the same evangelist and by St. Matthew as receiving it (λαμβάνουσι), and by St. Luke (δέχονται), with joy. The joy with which such hearers received it was a sudden impulse, which soon ceased— a quick, joyous emotion, which played on the surface without stirring to any great extent the depths of the heart. But the reception accorded to it by those having an honest and good heart is accompanied by a deep, steady, abiding interest. The usage of this word in the LXX. seems to imply a *cordial* reception; thus, in Isa. xlii. 1 we read, " Israel is my chosen, my soul has accepted (προσεδέξατο) him;" and in Prov. iii. 12 it is written, " For whom the Lord loves he rebukes, and scourges every son whom he receives (παραδέχεται)." But whether this shade of meaning be attributable to the context or inherent in the word, certain it is that such hearers receive the Word not wearily nor listlessly, nor as a formal duty, but as a matter of privilege, and in order to be instructed and edified thereby, and that their souls may be satisfied as with marrow and fatness. But, secondly, such hearers *understand* (συνιών) the Word. The interest we feel in any truth or fact helps us greatly in its right comprehension; once our interest is fully awakened our attention will be excited; we shall examine its bearings more thoughtfully. It is thus especially with the Word of God: we shall study it more carefully, as well as more prayerfully; while the Holy Spirit, promised to them that ask him, will guide us into all truth, even "the truth as it is in Jesus." A third element in this reception of the Word is the retention of it (κατέχουσι, used by St. Luke): they *keep* it. Having received the truth in the love of it, and having mingled it with faith, it becomes the ingrafted Word—ingrafted as a fruitful shoot in the wild unfruitful stock, or implanted in them, at all events, incorporated with their very being. As a natural and necessary consequence, they hold it fast, so that Satan cannot snatch it away, nor vain thoughts crush it down, nor worldly concerns stifle it, nor any evil influence destroy it. It becomes the subject of regular, constant, daily meditation; and so it gets linked with the thoughts and feelings and affections, while it is reduced to practice in the life. The individual so receiving it is "not a forgetful hearer, but a doer of the Word," and so blessed in the deed. This corresponds exactly with the apostle's statement (1 Cor. xv. 2), "By which also ye are saved, if ye keep in memory [κατέχετε, literally, *hold fast*, as here] what I preached unto you." 3. *Fruitfulness.* Fruit is borne in varying proportion, according to the talents bestowed and the surrounding circumstances. This fruit is borne *in patience*, that is, enduringly and perseveringly, and to the end; and not only the seed itself, but the fruit—each grain in every ear in turn becoming seed multiplies itself.

XI. PRACTICAL LESSONS. 1. *Right way of receiving the Word.* There must be the exercise of attention, understanding, and memory; as far as possible the attention must be lively and earnest, the understanding active and practical, and the memory retentive. 2. *The fruitfulness.* The fruit, though it varies in quantity, is a uniform product, evidencing the root of the matter, and ministering at once glory to God and grace to man.—J. J. G.

Vers. 21—25. Parallel passage: Luke viii. 16—18.—*Light and illumination.* I. TEMPORARY OBSCURATION. The heathens in their mysteries had esoteric doctrines only made known to the initiated, and not designed to be revealed at any time to the uninitiated. The obscuration in their case was permanent. Our Lord, at a particular period of his ministry and for a special purpose, veiled his teaching in parable. But this obscuration was only meant to continue for a time. Our Lord guards against the notion that the doctrines thus propounded were designed for perpetual concealment, or for revelation only to a select few. Accordingly he asks *whether at all* (μήτι) a lamp (λύχνος) is brought into an apartment in order to be secreted or to be set on a lampstand. The lamp is not brought, is it, to be put under a bushel (rather, a peck-measure, equivalent to the Roman *modius*) or under a bed, and not to be set on a lamp-stand? The light in a dwelling may be concealed for some necessary purpose and for some short time, but this is contrary to its regular and proper use. So our Lord here implies that the light of his teaching may be partially concealed by parable, and confined for a time to a few immediate followers, but shall be manifested, and is meant to be manifested, all the more afterwards. The matter is expressed in two **ways**—first as a prediction, and secondly as a purpose. As a prediction, "There is nothing hid, that shall not be manifested;" or, more literally, *There is not anything hid, that* (or *whatsoever*) *may not be revealed.* As a purpose, " Neither was anything kept secret, but that it should come abroad;" rather, *Neither did anything become secret, but that it might come into open view.* Like a lamp placed under some piece of domestic furniture for a short space and for some sufficient reason, the light of our Lord's doctrine was placed under the veil of parable or other obscuring medium for a time. But this position was never meant to be permanent—nay, the purpose was the very opposite; that is, to promote rather than prevent the future splendour and the further outshining of that bright and beautiful light.

II. RELATION OF LEARNING TO TEACHING. Our Lord's maxims never undergo a change of meaning, but their application necessarily varies with the context. After enunciating one of these maxims, viz. "If any man have ears to ear, let him hear," as a safeguard against possible error, and to prevent a not unlikely misconception, he proceeds to state another principle of his teaching, and another purpose to be accomplished. This principle was that the measure of attention given by the disciple to his Master would be rewarded with a proportionate measure of improvement; that in proportion to the desire of instruction and the use made of it by the disciple would be the benefit bestowed by the teacher. Again, the purpose was that the instructions thus received should be utilized for the advantage of others, so that the more the disciples profited as learners, so much the more they themselves would be able to impart to others, as preachers of the gospel and as teachers of the truth. Further, ulterior and higher attainments are promised to him who makes a right use of present attainments ; while he " who has not," that is to say, who has not for ready use, and who does not make available his present or previous attainments, shall forfeit even what he has, or fancies he has. We thus learn that spiritual attainments and spiritual knowledge are never exactly at a standstill. They are either increasing by proper application and improvement, or decreasing by misuse and diminishing by neglect.—J. J. G.

Vers. 26—29.—*Spiritual vegetation or secret growth.* I. RELATION TO THE IMMEDIATELY PRECEDING PARABLE. This parable, which may very appropriately be called "the secret growth," is recorded by St. Mark alone. It is peculiar to his Gospel. Its relation to the parable of the sower, which precedes it, is somewhat of the following kind :—The former parable describes the *soil*, this one, the *seed ;* the former the *quality* of the soil, and this the *vitality* of the seed. II. THE KINGDOM OF HEAVEN. "The kingdom of heaven" is an expression of frequent occurrence in Scripture. Thus we read, "The kingdom of heaven cometh not with observation," that is, "outward show," as the margin expresses it; also, "The kingdom of heaven is within you," or "among you," as the margin again has it. The meaning of this important expression is sufficiently plain to every reader of the New Testament, and does not, at least in its present connection, require any lengthened explanation. It denotes the reign of Heaven's principles in the heart of man, the spread of Heaven's principles among the families of man, and the glory of Heaven's principles as exhibited in all their plenitude and in all their power in that new heaven and new earth in which dwelleth righteousness. It may be more briefly summed up as the kingdom of grace in the heart, of peace in the family, and of glory through all the world. In Luther's 'Smaller Catechism,' on that petition of the Lord's Prayer, "Thy kingdom come," it is asked, "How does this take place?" and the answer is, "When our heavenly Father gives us his Holy Spirit, that through his grace we believe his Holy Word, and live a godly life, here in time and yonder in eternity." III. QUALITY OF THE SEED. The seed here, as in the former parable, is the Word of God ; thus we read, at the fourteenth verse of this chapter, "The sower soweth the Word :" so also in that other Scripture, "Being born again, not of corruptible seed, but of incorruptible, by the Word of God, which liveth and abideth for ever." Husbandmen are particularly careful about the quality of the seed which they cast into the furrows of the field, and very properly so, for the prospect of the harvest depends so much thereon. They reject the seed that is mixed, or unhealthy, or dead; otherwise the result would be most disastrous. Exactly so should it be with the Word of God. Here is a duty incumbent both on those that speak and on those that hear that Word ; it behoves them both to see well to it that it is in truth the Word of God which they speak and hear. It must be the Word of God—nothing less, and nothing else; the Word of God in its purity, the Word of God without any mixture, whether of human error or human passion, or doubtful disputation, or unsettling speculation, or tradition of men, or doctrines of men, or philosophy and vain deceit. That Word, too, must be faithfully spoken, not handled deceitfully; for we are not to speak as pleasing men, but God, which trieth our hearts ; the whole counsel of God must be declared, and no part kept back ; its force, too, must not be weakened, or its meaning explained away. Thus, "the truth as it is in Jesus" must be exhibited faithfully and fully, plainly and openly, just as the apostle says, "But as of sincerity, but as of God, in the sight of God speak we in Christ." The danger of the contrary course is very forcibly pointed out in a remarkable Scripture (1 Cor. iii. 12), where the apostle, after stating the true and only foundation to be Jesus

Christ, proceeds to say, "Now if any man build upon this foundation gold, silver, precious stones, wood, hay, stubble," that is, either doctrines more or less sound, or practice more or less consistent with profession, "the fire shall try every man's work of what sort it is. . . . If any man's work shall be burned, he shall suffer loss: but he himself shall be saved; yet so as by fire."

IV. ADAPTATION OF THE SEED TO THE SOIL. In natural husbandry men are at pains to get seed suited to the soil. Every kind of seed does not suit every kind of soil; seed suitable for one kind may not be suitable for another. There is need, therefore, of selection and adaptation. There must be proper discrimination and judicious distribution. So with the seed of the Word; there is enough for all, and something for each, but it must be duly and discreetly apportioned. This is the direction of Scripture itself, for we are told therein that there are little children, young men, and fathers in Christ, and each is to get his portion of meat in due season; and, again, milk is intended for babes, and strong meat for them that are of mature age. Accordingly, the careless are to be aroused, the unawakened are to be stirred up, the indifferent to be alarmed; the ignorant, again, are to be instructed, the timid to be encouraged, and the presumptuous to be rebuked; the tempted are to be fortified against temptation, the weak are to be strengthened, and the sorrowful to be consoled in their time of trouble; such as have backslidden, or have been overtaken in a fault, are to be restored in the spirit of meekness; saints are to be edified, believers built up in their holy faith; the lukewarm are to be brought back to their first love, and the graces of all quickened. For these various purposes there is enough in the treasury of God's Word, and out of that treasury are to be brought forth things both new and old.

V. THE PART WHICH BELONGS TO HUMAN AGENCY. Man's part is to sow the seed. This is his plain duty, this is his palpable concern, and his practical part of the business. He has not to make the seed, or manufacture the seed, or meddle in any way with the production of the seed; this were a task far above his ability and beyond his power. The seed is ready to his hand, and provided for his use. All he has to do, and all that is required of him, is to put the seed into the soil, and deposit it properly in the furrows—suiting, of course, as far as may be, the seed to the soil and to the sort of previous preparation made for it. We insist on the indispensable necessity of casting the seed into the furrow of the field, and likewise of sowing the seed of truth in the human heart; we affirm, moreover, the need of diligence in accomplishing this part of the operation, which is man's work and man's duty; we assert the absolute requirement of human instrumentality in this part either of natural or spiritual husbandry. The passage we are considering sets this duty clearly before us in the words, "As if a man should cast seed into the ground."

VI. THE NECESSITY FOR DIVINE INFLUENCE. There must be Divine influence as well as human agency; for in ver. 27 we read that the husbandman, after sowing the seed, may sleep by night and rise by day, while the seed springs up and grows he knows not how. Here, in the first place, we must take note of the vitality of the seed: it buds and lengthens ($\beta\lambda\alpha\sigma\tau\acute{a}\nu\eta$ $\kappa\alpha\grave{i}$ $\mu\eta\kappa\acute{v}\nu\eta\tau\alpha\iota$). God gave it this vital energy at the first, and so wonderfully powerful is this energy, that the seed which had lain three thousand years in the hand of the mummy will, when deposited in the earth under the ordinary conditions, sprout, spring up, and grow. We have seen that the deposition of the seed in the ground is necessary for any produce, but it must be added that for the development of the seed itself another distinct and indeed a Divine influence is required. Man can only go a certain length either in the department of nature or the sphere of grace. "Paul may plant, and Apollos water, but it is God that giveth the increase." When the seed has been committed to the earth in the most careful and skilful manner, the husbandman must wait for the fertilizing shower to make the seed grow and fructify. So in the spiritual sphere; not only has the seed of truth to be sown in the heart, and the lessons of God's Word to be deposited in the soul—and all this may be effected by human agency—but the influence of the Holy Spirit of God must be added. If the Word of God be the seed, as we are assured it is, then the Spirit of God is the rain-shower, the descent of which on the heart, or rather on the seed sown therein, is indispensably required for germination and fructification, or whatever else may be included under spiritual growth. Thus two distinct agencies must come together, unite, and blend in this great and important as well as mysterious process of spiritual vegetation. There must be the Word of God—that is the seed; there must be the Spirit of God—that is the shower. Without the seed and the shower, without the Word and the Spirit, there can be no spiritual vegetation. The soil may be good, the seed both good and suitable; but the dews of heavenly grace—the influences of the Divine Spirit—cannot be dispensed with. Again, the influences of the Spirit may be vouchsafed at the proper season, and in sufficient abundance; but if the seed of truth, if the lessons of the Divine Word, have not been sown in the heart, there is no germination, no quickening. However favourable the conditions of growth may otherwise be, there can be no growth, for the material is wanting. There is no seed, and so no germ of life, and consequently no life. The presence of both is absolutely and indispensably necessary. There are two elements of growth in the natural world—the seed and the shower; the deposition of the former in the soil belongs to man's department of work, the descent of the latter is God's good gift. The one acts upon the other, while the united operation results in healthy vegetation. The seed supplies the material, the shower is the fructifying agency; the shower gives efficacy to the seed, the seed expands by the combined action of the sun and shower. In spiritual husbandry the seed is the Word, the shower represents the Spirit; the Word has life, but the Spirit is required to develop it. Without the Spirit the Word would remain inert, by the Spirit it is made productive; the Word is the germ of spiritual life, the Spirit unfolds and quickens it; their mutual action issues in the happiest results.

VII. THE BOND OF UNION BETWEEN THE TWO AGENCIES, DIVINE AND HUMAN. The absence of either agency would end in disaster. Nothing can supply the place of the seed, neither the soil itself nor the stones imbedded in it. Where there are no seeds the showers of heaven may fall in abundance, the sunshine of heaven may be bright and beautiful, but neither, in the absence of the seed, would be of any avail. Contemplate in the season of harvest a field of golden grain; the stalks are strong and vigorous; the ear is filled with kindly fruit, and bending under the weight; the whole is white unto the harvest. Let this be the case not in one field, but in all; not in one district, but in many; not in one part of the country, but in every part where the land is arable and under cultivation; and yet not one particle of the plenty thus supposed sprang up without seed having been previously put into the earth. Among all the multitudinous stems that constitute that rich, luxuriant crop that waves in the autumn wind, and covers with such abundance the face of the earth in the time of harvest, not one is found that grew without a root, and not a root that grew without a seed. And just so it is with the seed of truth rooted in the heart, and producing the harvest of grace in the life of man. But, as we have already intimated, the fructifying energy of the Divine Spirit, whether it acts by the dew, or shower, or sunshine, or all combined, is equally important, and indeed absolutely necessary in producing the manifold blessings of the spiritual harvest. What, then, is the link that brings these two agencies together —the seed which man sows in the soil, and the shower or other influence which God sends down from the sky? What means must be used to procure for the seed, when sown in the human heart, the quickening and refreshing power of the Divine Spirit? The only means available to man is the power of prayer, and prayer is a power as well in the domain of the temporal as of the spiritual. No doubt man has done his all when he has properly deposited suitable seed in fertile soil; but, though he cannot actually and of himself go further or do more, there remains a duty, the proper performance of which may carry the work much further, and set other and mightier energies in operation; for " prayer moves the hand that moves the world." Once upon a time, long ago, in the land of Israel, drought and dearth prevailed; " the prophet prayed, . . . and the heaven gave rain, and the earth brought forth her fruit." So when, in answer to believing prayer, God bestows his Spirit, the seed of truth germinates in the heart, and yields the fruits of the Spirit in the life.

VIII. THE FRUITFUL EARTH AND THE FAITHFUL HUSBANDMAN. " The earth bringeth forth fruit of herself." God, in his wise and powerful organization of our earth, gave it this power. In obedience to his original command, and in virtue of power originally imparted, the earth brings forth grass, and herb yielding seed after his kind, and the tree yielding fruit after his kind—the three great divisions of the vegetable kingdom. The productive earth still retains the power which God at first impressed on it, and to God it is still indebted for its productiveness, as we read, " He watereth the hills from his chambers : the earth is satisfied with the fruit of thy works.   He causeth the grass to grow for the cattle, and herb for the service of man, that he may bring forth food out of the earth."   We can only follow the process of vegetation a very short way.   We know, indeed, that the seed dies, and is decomposed, for it is not quickened except it die ; and then it germinates, and new life succeeds.   But the entire process is mysterious as it is invisible ; it is hidden from man's scrutiny, and high above man's comprehension ; while in those secret processes in the sky above and in the earth below we trace the handiwork of God, without which the earth would be barren as the granite and unfruitful as the sea.   The faith of the husbandman rests securely on the established law of the earth's fertility, produced and promoted as it is by the mighty power of God ; while his patience is justified by the uniformity of such natural law. " Behold," says James, " the husbandman waiteth for the precious fruit of the earth, and hath long patience for it, until he receive the early and the latter rain."   This parable affords great encouragement to both faith and patience, and the encourage- ment thus afforded forms a main feature of the parable.   When, therefore, like the husbandman, we prepare the soil of the heart diligently and dutifully, and when we sow thereon the seed with carefulness and caution, and duly supplicate the blessing of heaven on our spiritual handiwork, looking up and expecting an answer, we have no more that we can do, and no more that we need to do.   We may then safely leave the result to God ; we may commit it quietly and confidingly to his hand, assured that he will give the increase in due time and in due measure.   This principle is embodied in the husbandman sleeping and rising night and day, while the seed springs and grows up, he knows not how.   There is much comfort in this assurance, much also to strengthen faith and brighten hope.   Though all our care will not cause the seed to grow, though we cannot give power to the Word, though God alone can make it effectual, though we must wait patiently for his influence, though the process is mysterious in itself and hidden from the eye of man ; yet we may forbear all hurtful anxiety, and forego all unseemly impatience, leaving the issue entirely to God.   We must beware of enacting the part of those silly children who pull up their plants or flowers from time to time in order to examine the roots and inspect the process of growth.   Though we cannot unveil the inward processes of grace any more than of nature, yet we need not dread any failure in those processes.   What is required of us is to use aright the means, and instrumentalities and agencies within our reach, without meddling with what is too high above us or too deep below us ; and we may feel fully persuaded that, if we labour in the Lord, our labour will not be in vain.

IX. The gradual growth.   By the earth of herself according to the course of nature, and by the concurring power of the God of nature, fruit is brought forth ; " first the blade, then the ear, after that the full corn in the ear."   In like manner, the Word of truth received by faith into the heart becomes the work of grace.   This the Spirit carries on while the preacher sleeps and can do no work, or is engaged in other business, or has entered into rest ; for the Word preached not unfrequently does its work even after the preacher has been gathered to his fathers.   When men sow their seed, they sow "not that body that shall be, . . . but God giveth it a body as it pleases him."   The old dies, but the new blade shoots up ; in this we have an emblem of the new nature, for "if any man be in Christ, he is a new creature."   Next comes the ear, and in this we find the promise of, and preparation for, fruitfulness.   At length we have the full corn in the ear ; this is the fruit of righteousness to the praise and glory of God, and this includes all the graces of the Christian character, and all the virtues of the Christian life.   Thus Divine truth, under the teaching of the Holy Spirit, first enlightens the mind, then convinces the understanding, gradually quickens the conscience, and converts the heart, while, last of all and best of all, it saves the soul.

X. The harvest.   Now the great end is attained.   The faithful recipient of the Divine Word has grown in grace ; he has added to his "faith virtue ; and to virtue knowledge ; and to knowledge temperance ; and to temperance patience ; and to patience godliness, and to godliness brotherly kindness, and to brotherly kindness charity ;" he has attained to deadness to the world, spirituality of mind, heavenly dispositions, resigna- tion to the Divine will, conformity to the Divine image, and assimilation to the Divine character.   When, moreover, the Christian has thus borne the fruits of godliness, made himself useful in the Church and in the world, having served his generation in both ;

and when the good purposes of his heavenly Father have been fulfilled in him and by him; at length the harvest comes, the sickle is put in; meetened for heaven, ripened for the garner of the skies, he is taken home like a shock of corn in his season. Thus to the child of God "to die is gain"—the gain of heaven for earth, of rest for labour, of glory everlasting instead of the varied sorrows of this present time.—J. J. G.

Vers. 30—34. Parallel passage: Matt. xiii. 31, 32.—*The mustard seed.* I. DIFFERENCE BETWEEN THE PARABLE OF THE MUSTARD SEED AND THE LEAVEN. The latter parable refers rather to the growth of grace in the heart, the former to the extension of the Church in the world; the latter to the assimilating power of Divine grace in the human heart, the former to progressive development and final establishment of the Church on earth.

II. THE SMALLNESS OF THE MUSTARD SEED. The smallness of the mustard seed, if the expression be not proverbial, furnishes at least a striking and frequent subject of comparison. Thus, our Lord uses the illustration in reference to faith, "If ye have faith as a grain of mustard seed;" and the present comparison, both here and in the parallel passage of St. Matthew, presents the same figure.

III. THE PROGRESS OF THE CHURCH. While this parable may possibly refer to the progress of religion in the heart, its best exemplification is found in the constantly and rapidly progressive extension of the Church of Christ since apostolic times. When all its members met in that upper room in Jerusalem, they numbered only a hundred and twenty. Other believers, no doubt, were to be found in the holy city at that early day of the Church's history; but, be that as it may, the number above given included the entire membership of those who publicly met together and professed themselves disciples of the Nazarene. Ten days after—the interval between the Ascension and Pentecost—there took place a signal outpouring of the Holy Spirit, and in connection with St. Peter's sermon there were added to the Church about three thousand souls. Some short time after this, as we read in Acts iv., "the number of the men" who publicly avowed their faith in Christ "was about five thousand." The next notice of the numerical progress of the gospel is contained in Acts v., where we are informed that "believers were the more added to the Lord, *multitudes* both of men and women." In the beginning of the very next chapter we have an incidental notice to the effect that "the number of the disciples was multiplied." A further and still fuller notice is found in the seventh verse of the same chapter (Acts vi.), where it is stated that "the Word of God increased; and the number of the disciples multiplied in Jerusalem greatly; and a great number of the priests were obedient to the faith." And all this occurred within a period of less than two years, and in the very place where the Founder of our holy religion had been put to death as a malefactor. Thus the mustard seed, comparatively, if not absolutely, the smallest of seeds, becomes a plant, and the plant becomes a tree, and the tree spreads out its branches, and the branches shelter with their shadow, and lodge the fowls of the air beneath their umbrageous foliage. So with the Church of Christ: it has spread from country to country; it has extended from continent to island, and from island to continent; it has enlarged its borders and multiplied its members. It has powerfully influenced all civilized nations, and all barbarous nations to which it has extended have become civilized. And now kingdoms many and mighty repose in safety and rest in security under this widespread gospel tree, like the birds of the air taking refuge under and nestling among the branches of the magnificent mustard tree of this parable.—J. J. G.

Vers. 35—51.—(See on ch. vi. 45—56.)—J. J. G.

EXPOSITION.

CHAPTER V.

Ver. 1.—**And they came to the other side of the sea.** The other side of the sea would be the south-east side of the sea. **Into the country of the Gadarenes,** or rather, *Gerasenes,* which is now generally admitted to

be the true reading, from Gerasa, Gersa, or Kersa. There was another Gerasa, situated at some distance from the sea, on the borders of Arabia Petræa. The ruins of the Gerasa, here referred to, have been recently discovered by Dr. Thomson, 'The Land and the Book'). Immediately over this spot is a lofty mountain, in which are ancient tombs; and from this mountain there is an almost perpendicular declivity, literally (κρημνός) corresponding accurately to what is required by the description in the narrative of the miracle. Dr. Farrar ('Life of Christ') says that in the days of Eusebius and Jerome, tradition pointed to a "steep place" near "Gerasa" as the scene of the miracle. The foot of this steep is washed by the waters of the lake, which are at once very deep.

Vers. 2—5.—**There met him out of the tombs a man with an unclean spirit.** St. Matthew says that there were two. St. Luke, like St. Mark, mentions only one, and him "possessed with devils." The one mentioned by St. Mark was no doubt the more prominent and fierce of the two. This does not mean merely a person with a disordered intellect. No doubt, in this case, as in that of insanity, physical causes may have helped to lay the victim open to such an incursion; and this may account for cases of possession being enumerated with various sicknesses, though distinguished from them. But our Lord evidently deals with these persons, not as persons suffering from insanity, but as the subjects of an alien spiritual power, external to themselves. He addresses the unclean spirit through the man that was possessed, and says, " Come forth, thou unclean spirit" (ver. 8). *There met him out of the tombs.* The Jews did not have their burial-places in their cities, lest they should be defiled; therefore they buried their dead without the gates in the fields or mountains. Their sepulchres were frequently hewn out of the rock in the sides of the limestone hills, and they were lofty and capacious; so that the living could enter them, as into a vault. So this demoniac dwelt in the tombs, because the unclean spirit drove him thither, where the associations of the place would accord with his malady and aggravate its symptoms. St. Matthew, speaking of the two, says that they were "exceeding fierce, so that no man might pass that way." The demoniac particularly mentioned by St. Mark is described as having been possessed of that extraordinary muscular strength which maniacs so often put forth; so that all efforts to bind and restrain him had proved ineffectual. **No man could any more bind him, no, not with a chain** (οὐδὲ ἁλύσειν). Chains and fetters had often been tried, but in vain. Frequently too, in the paroxysms of his malady, he would turn his violence against himself, **crying out, and cutting himself with stones.**

Ver. 6.—**And when he saw Jesus from afar.** These words, "from afar," explain the fact of our Lord being immediately met by the man as soon as he left the boat. Vers. 3—5 inclusive must be regarded as parenthetical. They describe the ordinary condition of the demoniac, and his sad wild life from day to day. From the high ground which he frequented he had seen the boat, in which Jesus was, nearing the shore. He had seen the other boats. Perhaps he had seen the sudden rise of the storm and its equally sudden suppression; and he, like others who witnessed it, was affected by it. So he hastened to the shore; he ran and worshipped him. He felt the power of his presence, and so he was constrained through fear to do him reverence, for "the devils also believe and shudder (φρίσσουσι)" (Jas. ii. 19).

Ver. 7.—**He cried with a loud voice**; that is, the evil spirit cried out, using the organs of the man whom he possessed. **What have I to do with thee, Jesus, thou Son of the Most High God?** From hence it appears that, although at the great temptation of our Lord in the wilderness, Satan had but an imperfect knowledge of him; yet now, after the evidence of these great miracles, and more especially of his power over the evil spirits, there was a general belief amongst the hosts of evil that he was indeed the Son of God, the Messiah. **I adjure thee by God, torment me not.** The torment which he dreaded was that which he might suffer after expulsion. So St. Luke says that they entreated him that he would not command them to depart into the abyss. Great as this mystery of evil is, we may believe that the evil spirits, although while they roam about upon this earth they are in misery, still it is some alleviation that they are not yet shut up in the prison-house of hell, but are suffered to wander about and find their depraved pleasure in tempting men; so that, if possible, they may at last drag them down with them into the abyss. For they are full of hatred of God and envy of man; and they find a miserable satisfaction in endeavouring to keep men out of those heavenly mansions from which, through pride, they are themselves now for ever excluded.

Vers. 8, 9.—**For he said unto him, Come forth, thou unclean spirit, out of the man;** literally, *for he was saying* (ἔλεγε). The unclean spirit endeavoured to arrest, before it was spoken, that word of power which he knew he must obey. So in what follows, **He was asking him** (ἐπηρώτα), **What is thy name?** Why does our Lord ask this question? Clearly to elicit from him an answer that would reveal the multitude of the evil spirits, and so make his own power over them to be fully known. **And he saith unto him, My name is Legion; for we are many.** The Roman legion consisted of six thousand soldiers. But the word is here used indefinitely for a large number. St. Luke so explains it where he says (viii. 30), "And he said, Legion : for many devils were entered into him." This revelation is doubtless designed to teach us how great is the number as well as the malignity of the evil spirits. If one human being can be possessed by so many, how vast must be the host of those who are permitted to have access to the souls of men, and if possible lead them to destruction! Satan here imitates him who is "The Lord of hosts." He too marshals his hosts, that he may fight against God and his people. But "for this purpose was the Son of God manifested, that he might destroy the works of the devil."

Ver. 10.—**And he besought him much that he would not send them away out of the country.** It would appear as though this evil spirit felt (speaking in the name of the other evil spirits) that if they were driven out from their present dwelling-places, their condition would be changed for the worse; and that until the time should come when they were to be cast into the abyss, their best relief was to possess some materialism, to occupy flesh and blood, and that flesh and blood tenanted by a spiritual being, through whom they might torment others. They could find no rest, no relief, but in this. "The unclean spirit, when he is gone out of the man, passeth through waterless places, seeking rest, and findeth it not" (Matt. xii. 43). Even the swine were better than nothing; but that dwelling did not serve the evil spirits long.

Ver. 11.—**Now there was there nigh unto the mountains**—literally, *on the mountain side* (πρὸς τὰ ὄρη)—**a great herd of swine feeding.** St. Matthew says (viii. 30), "There was a good way off from them : " our Lord's interview with the demoniac was on the seashore. "The herd of swine," two thousand in number (as St. Mark tells us, with his usual attention to details), were at a distance, feeding on the slopes of the mountain. The Jews were not allowed to eat swine's flesh. But Jews were not the only inhabitants of that district. It had been colonized, at least in part, by the Romans immediately after the conquest of Syria, some sixty years before Christ. It was in this district that ten cities are said to have been rebuilt by the Romans, whence the territory acquired the name of "the Decapolis." And though the Jews were forbidden by their Law to eat this kind of food, yet they were not forbidden to breed swine for other uses, such as provisioning the Roman army.

Ver. 12.—**Send us into the swine, that we may enter into them. And he gave them leave.** They could not enter even into the swine without Christ's permission; how much less into "the sheep of his pasture"!

Ver. 13.—**The unclean spirits came out, and entered into the swine : and the herd ran violently down a steep place** (κατὰ τοῦ κρημνοῦ)—literally, *down the steep*—**into the sea, . . . and were choked in the sea.** By this Christ shows of how little worth are earthly possessions when set in the balance with the souls of men. The recovery of this demoniac was worth far more than the value of the two thousand swine.

Ver. 14.—**And they that fed them fled, and told it in the city, and in the country.** St. Matthew mentions only the city. St. Mark's narrative is more full. No doubt many of these swineherds lived in the country districts; and so the fame of the miracle was spread far and wide. The swineherds would take care that the owners should understand that it was through no fault or carelessness on their part that the swine had perished; but that the destruction was caused by a power over which they had no control. **And they**—*i.e.* the owners—**came to see what it was that had come to pass.** Their first care was to see the extent of their loss; and this was soon revealed to them. They must have seen the carcases of the swine floating hither and thither in the now calm and tranquil sea; and when they had thus satisfied themselves as to the facts, "they came to Jesus." St. Mark here uses the historic present, "they come to Jesus," that they might behold him of whom these great things were told, as well as the man out of whom the evil spirits had gone when they entered into the swine. They were, of course, concerned to know the magnitude of their loss, and the mode in which it had happened, that they might see whether there were any means by which it might be made up to them.

Ver. 15.—**And they come to Jesus, and behold him that was possessed with devils sitting, clothed and in his right mind, even him that had the legion; and they were afraid.** St. Luke adds that they found him sitting at the feet of Jesus. It is likely enough that the man, as soon as he found himself dispossessed, had cast himself at the feet of Jesus, and was worshipping him; but that, when bidden by Christ to sit, he chose to place himself at his feet. "He was clothed, and in his right mind." What a contrast to the previous description! "And they were afraid." They dreaded Christ's power. They saw that he was almighty; but they did not seek to know his love, and so to attain to that love which "casteth out fear."

Vers. 16, 17.—**How it befell him that was possessed with devils, and concerning the swine.** The loss of the swine. They could not get over that. They thought far more of the worldly loss than of the spiritual gain; and they began to beseech him to depart from their borders. St. Luke (viii. 37) says that "they were taken (συνείχοντο) [literally, *were holden*] with great fear." This was the dominant feeling. They did not entreat him to depart out of humility, as though they felt themselves unworthy of his presence; but out of servile, slavish fear, lest his continued presence among them might bring upon them still greater losses. They saw that Jesus, a Jew according to the flesh, was holy, powerful, Divine. But they knew that they were Gentiles, aliens from the commonwealth of Israel. Wherefore they feared lest he should punish them more grievously, both on account of their being Gentiles and on account of their past sins. It was not, therefore, so much on account of hatred, as out of a timorous fear, that they besought Jesus that he would depart out of their borders.

Vers. 18—20.—**And as he was entering into the boat, he that had been possessed with devils besought him that he might be with him.** It was natural that he should desire this. It would be grateful and soothing to him to be near to Christ, from whom he had received so great a benefit and yet hoped for more. **And he suffered him not, but saith unto him, Go to thy house unto thy friends, and tell them how great things the Lord hath done for thee.** Our Lord here takes a different course from what he so often took. He saw, no doubt, that this restored demoniac was fitted for missionary work; and there was no reason to apprehend any inconvenience to himself in consequence from a people who wished to get rid of him. **And he went his way, and began to publish in Decapolis**—in Decapolis, *i.e.* through the whole district of the ten cities—**how great things Jesus had done for him.** This would bring him into contact alike with Gentiles and with Jews; and so this dispossessed demoniac became a missionary to both Jew and Gentile. Here he planted the standard of the cross.

Ver. 21.—Jesus now crosses over the sea again, and apparently in the same boat, to the other side, the opposite shore, near to Capernaum. St. Matthew (iv. 13) distinctly tells us that he had left Nazareth, and was now dwelling at Capernaum, thus fulfilling the ancient prophecy with regard to Zebulun and Nephthalim. The circumstances under which he quitted Nazareth are given by St. Luke (iv. 16—31). St. Matthew (ix. 1) calls Capernaum his own city. Thus as Christ ennobled Bethlehem by his birth, Nazareth by his education, and Jerusalem by his death, so he honoured Capernaum by making it his ordinary residence, and

the focus, so to speak, of his preaching and miracles. When Jesus returned, **a great multitude was gathered unto him; and he was by the sea.** St. Luke says that the people welcomed him, for they were all waiting for him. Again he placed himself by the sea, probably for the convenience of addressing a multitude, and of relieving himself of the pressure, as before, by taking refuge in a boat.

Vers. 22, 23.—**One of the rulers of the synagogue, Jairus by name.** He appears to have been one of the "college of elders," who administered the affairs of the synagogue. The name Jairus, or "Ya-eiros," is probably the Greek form of the Hebrew *Jair*, "he will illuminate." **He fell at his feet, and besought him greatly;** it is literally (πίπτει καὶ παρεκάλει), *he falleth at his feet, and beseecheth him.* We picture him to ourselves, making his way through the crowd, and as he approached Jesus, kneeling down, and then bending his head towards him, until his forehead touched the ground. **My little daughter is at the point of death.** St. Matthew says, "is even now dead;" St. Luke says, "she lay a dying." The broken sentences of the father are very true to nature. All the expressions point to the same conclusion, that she was *in articulo mortis.* In each narrative the ruler is represented as asking that Christ would hasten to his house. He had not reached the higher faith of the Gentile centurion, "Speak the word only."

Ver. 24.—**And he went** (καὶ ἀπῆλθε μετ' αὐτοῦ)—literally, *and he went away with him* —**and a great multitude followed him, and they thronged him** (συνέθλιβον αὐτόν); literally, *pressed close upon him, compressed him.* This is mentioned purposely by St. Mark, on account of what follows. St. Matthew says (ix. 19), "And Jesus arose, and so did his disciples." Observe here the promptitude of Christ to assist the afflicted. St. Chrysostom suggests that our Lord purposely interposed some delay, by healing, as he went, the woman with the issue of blood, in order that the actual death of Jairus's daughter might take place; and that so there might be full demonstration of his resurrection power.

Vers. 25, 26.—**A woman, which had an issue of blood twelve years.** All the synoptic Gospels mention the length of time during which she had been suffering. Eusebius records a tradition that she was a Gentile, a native of Cæsarea Philippi. This disease was a chronic hœmorrhage, for which she had found no relief from the physicians. Lightfoot, in his 'Horæ Hebraicæ,' gives a list of the remedies applied in such cases, which seem quite sufficient to account for St. Mark's statement that she **was nothing bettered, but rather grew worse.** St. Luke, himself a physician, says that she "had spent all her living upon physicians, and could not be healed of any."

Vers. 27, 28.—This woman, **having heard of Jesus**—literally (τὰ περὶ τοῦ Ἰησοῦ), *the things concerning Jesus*—**came in the crowd behind, and touched his garment.** St. Matthew and St Luke say "the border (τοῦ κρασπέδου) of his garment." St. Matthew tells us that "she said within herself, If I may but touch his garment, I shall be whole." From this it appears that, though she had faith, it was an imperfect faith. She seems to have imagined that a certain magical influence was within Christ and around him. And the touching of the border of his garment (the blue fringe which the Jews were required to wear, to remind them that they were God's people) was supposed by her to convey a special virtue. Yet her faith, though imperfect, was true in its essence, and therefore was not disappointed.

Ver. 29.—**And straightway**—St. Mark's favourite word—**the fountain of her blood was dried up; and she felt** (ἔγνω)—literally, *she knew*—**in her body that she was healed of her plague** (ὅτι ἴαται ἀπὸ τῆς μάστιγος); literally, *that she hath been healed of her scourge.* The cure was instantaneous.

Ver. 30.—The words in the Greek are ἐπιγνοὺς ἐν ἑαυτῷ τὴν ἐξ αὐτοῦ δύναμιν ἐξελθοῦσαν: **Jesus, perceiving in himself that the power** emanating **from him had gone forth, turned him about in the crowd, and said, Who touched my garments?** Christ sees the invisible grace in its hidden operations; man only sees its effects, and not always these.

Ver. 31.—St. Luke (viii. 45) adds here, "When all denied, Peter said, and they that were with him, Master, the multitudes press thee and crush *thee*. But Jesus said, Some one did touch me; for I perceived that power had gone forth from me." This incident shows the mysterious connection between the spiritual and the physical. The miraculous virtue or power which went forth from the Saviour was spiritual in its source and in the conditions on which it was imparted, but it was physical in its operation; and that which brought the two together was faith. Multitudes thronged the Saviour, but only one of the crowd *touched* him.

Ver. 32.—**He looked round about** (περιεβλέπετο)—another favourite word of St. Mark.

Ver. 33.—**The woman fearing and trembling, etc.** Every word in this verse is expressive. It was her own act. She seemed to herself as though without permission she had stolen a blessing from Christ; and so she could hardly venture to hope that the

faith which had prompted her would be accepted. Hence her fear and terror, and her free and full confession. We thus see the gentleness of Christ in his dealings with us. Perhaps the woman had intended to escape, satisfied with a temporal benefit, which would hardly have been a blessing at all, if she had been suffered to carry it away without acknowledgment. But this her loving Saviour would not permit her to do. It was the crisis of her spiritual life. It was necessary that all around should know of the gift which she had endeavoured to snatch in secret. Our Lord might have demanded from her this public confession of her faith beforehand. But, in his mercy, he made the way easy to her. The lesson, however, must not be forgotten, that it is not enough to believe with the heart. The lips must do their part, and "with the mouth confession must be made unto salvation."

Ver. 34.—Our Lord here reassures this trembling woman, who feared, it may be, lest, because she had abstracted the blessing secretly, he might punish her with a return of her malady. On the contrary, he confirms the benefit, and bids her be whole of her plague. The Greek expression here is stronger than that which is given as the rendering of what she had used when we read that she said within herself, "I shall be saved (σωθήσομαι)." Here our Lord says, **Go in peace, and be whole** (ἴσθι ὑγιὴς). It is as though he said, " It is not the mere fringe of my garment, which you have touched with great faith, and with some hope of obtaining a cure—it is not this that has cured you. You owe your healing to my omnipotence and your faith. Your faith (itself my gift) has delivered you from your issue of blood ; and this deliverance I now confirm and ratify. 'Go in peace.'" The original Greek here (ὕπαγε εἰς εἰρήνην) implies more than this. It means " Go for peace." Pass into the realm, the element of peace, in which henceforth thy life shall move. It is here obvious to remark that this malady represents to us the ever-flowing bitter fountain of sin, for which no styptic treatment can be found in human philosophy. The remedy is only to be found in Christ. To touch Christ's garment is to believe in his **incarnation**, whereby he has touched us, and so has enabled us by faith to touch him, and to receive his blessing of peace.

Ver. 35.—Our Lord had lingered on the way to the house of Jairus, perhaps, as has already been suggested, that the crisis might first come, and that so there might be full evidence of his resurrection power. The ruler must have been agonized with the thought that, while our Lord lingered, the life of his dying child was fast ebbing away.

And now comes the fatal message to him. **Thy daughter is dead** (ἀπέθανε); the aorist expresses that her death was now a past event. **Why troublest thou the Master any further?** (τί ἔτι σκύλλεις τὸν διδάσκαλον;). The Greek word here is very strong. It is to vex or weary; literally, *to flay*. The messengers from the ruler's house had evidently abandoned all hope, and so probably would Jairus, but for the cheering words of our Lord, "Fear not, only believe."

Ver. 36.—The words of the narrative, as they stand in the Authorized Version, are: **As soon as Jesus heard the word that was spoken, he saith unto the ruler of the synagogue, Be not afraid, only believe.** But there is good authority for the reading παρακούσας instead of εὐθέως ἀκούσας, which requires the rendering, *but Jesus, not heeding*, or *overhearing*. This word (παρακούω) occurs in one other place in the Gospels, namely, in Matt. xviii. 17, "And if he refuse to hear them (ἐὰν δὲ παρακούσῃ αὐτῶν)." Here the word can only have the meaning of "not heeding," or "refusing to hear." This seems to be a strong reason for giving the word a somewhat similar meaning in this passage. And therefore, on the whole, "not heeding" seems to be the best rendering. Indeed, it seems to cover both meanings. Our Lord would overhear, and yet not heed, the word spoken.

Ver. 37.—Here we have the first occasion of the selection of three of the apostles to be witnesses of things not permitted to be seen by the rest. The other two occasions are those of the transfiguration, and of the agony in the garden. We now follow our Lord and these three favoured disciples, Peter and James and John, to the house of death. They are about to witness the first earnest of the resurrection.

Ver. 38.—St. Matthew here says (ix. 23) that when Jesus came into the ruler's house, he "saw the minstrels (τοὺς αὐλητὰς)," *i.e.* the flute-players, "and the people making a noise." This was the custom both with Jews and with Gentiles, to quicken the sorrow of the mourners by funeral dirges. The record of these attendant circumstances is important as evidence of the fact of death having actually taken place.

Ver. 39.—Some have regarded the words of our Lord, **the child is not dead, but sleepeth**, as really meaning that she was only in a swoon. But although she was actually dead in the ordinary sense of that word, namely, that her spirit had left the body, yet Christ was pleased to speak of death as a sleep; because all live to him, and because all will rise at the last day. Hence in the Holy Scriptures the dead are constantly described as sleeping, in order that the terror of death might be mitigated, and im-

moderate grief for the dead be assuaged under the name of sleep, which manifestly includes the hope of the resurrection. Hence the expression with regard to a departed Christian, that "he sleeps in Jesus." Then, further, this child was not absolutely and irrecoverably dead, as the crowd supposed, as though she could not be recalled to life; since in fact our Lord, who is the Lord of life, was going at once to call her back by his almighty power from the realms of death into which she had entered. So that she did not appear to him to be dead so much as to sleep for a little while. He says elsewhere, "Our friend Lazarus sleepeth; but I go that I may awake him out of sleep." Christ, by the use of such language as this, meant to show that it is as easy with him to raise the dead from death as sleepers from their slumbers.

Ver. 40.—**They laughed him to scorn.** He suffered this, in order that the actual death might be the more manifest, and that so they might the more wonder at her resurrection, and thus pass from wonder and amazement to a true faith in him who thus showed himself to be the Resurrection and the Life. He now put them all forth; and then, with his three apostles, Peter, James, and John, and the father and the mother of the child, he went in where the child was. The common crowd were not worthy to see that in which they would not believe. They were unworthy to witness the great reality of the resurrection; for they had been deriding him who wields this power. It is remarked by Archbishop Trench that in the same manner Elisha (2 Kings iv. 33) cleared the room before he raised the son of the Shunammite.

Ver. 41.—The house was now set free from the perfunctory and noisy crowd; and he goes up to the dead child, and takes her by the hand and says, **Talitha cumi**; literally *Little maid, arise.* The evangelist gives the words in the very language used by our Lord—the *ipsissima verba*, remembered no doubt and recorded by St. Peter; just as he gives "Ephphatha" in another miracle.

Vers. 42, 43.—Here, as in other miracles, the restoration was immediate and complete: **straightway the damsel rose up, and walked.** Well might the father and the mother of the maiden and the three chosen apostles be **amazed with a great amazement** (ἐξέστησαν ἐκστάσει μεγάλῃ). And then, for the purpose of strengthening that life which he rescued from the jaws of the grave, our Lord **commanded that** something **should be given her to eat.** It has often been observed that in the examples of his resurrection power given by Christ there is a gradation: 1. The daughter of Jairus just dead. 2. The widow's son from his bier. 3. Lazarus from his grave. The more stupendous miracle is yet to come, of which our Lord's own resurrection is at once the example and the pledge, when "all that are in their graves shall hear his voice, and shall come forth."

HOMILETICS.

Vers. 1—20.—*The Lord of spirits.* There was for Christ, during his earthly ministry, no escape from personal toil—from the claims made upon his benevolence by human misery, or from man's ingratitude. He crossed the lake to seek repose, but at once, on landing, was met by a case of the utmost wretchedness and need, demanding the exercise of his compassionate authority. His stay was brief, yet long enough to earn the thanks and the devotion of one poor liberated captive, and long enough to qualify and to commission one for a sacred ministry of benevolence.

I. We have here a representation of THE WRETCHED STATE OF THE SINNER. 1. That state is attributable to *possession by an evil power.* This does not, indeed, affect man's responsibility, but it affirms the action of supernatural agency. Sinners "have fallen into the snare of the devil." 2. The *signs* of that state are many and distressing. Like the demoniac, the sinner is injurious to himself, is harmful to others, and consequently is unfit for society. 3. A picture is here painted of the sinner's *hopeless condition.* As the demoniac's possession was manifold ("we are legion"), was prolonged, and was so severe that all human efforts had failed to bring relief, so was the condition of the heathen world when the Saviour came to earth—a condition so debased and so confirmed in its misery that to the human eye no dawn-streak of hope was visible. And the heart, abandoned to the control of evil, is in a state for which no human relief or help is available.

II. We have here a representation of THE SINNER'S MIGHTY SAVIOUR. A greater contrast than that between the wretched and raving maniac and the calm and holy Jesus it would not be possible to imagine. Yet the two came together. Divine authority and compassion encountered human sin, foulness, and degradation, and the demon was exorcised and the sufferer made whole. 1. Observe the *Divine authority of the Lord is acknowledged.* It is certainly remarkable that from the mouth of the demoniac should come the confession that Jesus is "the Son of the Most High God." This Christ is; and, were he not this, his approach would bring no comfort to the sinner's heart. 2. In addition to this verbal acknowledgment, we observe *an actual submission* to and experience of Christ's power. "The unclean spirit came out." Jesus is "mighty to save." As during his ministry, so wherever the gospel is preached, the power of Christ is proved in actual experience. However formidable the foe may be, Jesus is the Conqueror.

III. We have here a representation of THE SINNER'S SALVATION. 1. There is *complete deliverance* from the tyranny of former enemies. "Taken captive by the Lord's servant unto the will of God"—such is the description given by an apostle of the great and spiritual emancipation which nevertheless brings souls into a new and better bondage. 2. *Sanity* is a consequence of our Lord's interposition. "When he came to himself" is the description of the change which took place in the repenting prodigal. Only he who turns to God can be truly said to be "in his right mind." 3. *Tranquillity* is a natural sign of a spiritual restoration. The Saviour is the Prince of peace, and the gospel is a gospel of peace, and peace is a fruit of the Spirit. True religion calms agitation, stills the tempests of the soul, and brings harmony to human life.

IV. We have an example of the WITNESS OF THE SAVED SINNER TO THE SAVIOUR. The conduct of the healed demoniac is an emblem of the consecrated testimony of the ransomed soul to the great Deliverer. 1. It is prompted by grateful affection—affection that would fain abide in the valued society of the Redeemer. 2. It is appointed and authorized by the Lord himself: "Go to thy house," etc. 3. It is borne especially to those nearest and dearest: "thy friends." 4. It consists of personal experience: "how great things the Lord hath done for *thee.*" 5. It excites interest and wonder. Such testimony from such a witness cannot be without effect.

The saved lead others to the same Saviour whose virtue they have themselves experienced.

Vers. 21—24, 35—43.—*The maiden's spirit recalled.* This narrative is a striking example of intercession, and of its appreciation and reward by the Lord Jesus. The suppliant, Jairus, pleaded for his daughter, and he did not plead in vain. Jesus wrought upon his behalf one of the three miracles of raising from the dead which have been recorded by the evangelists.

I. MAN IS TROUBLED, AND JESUS IS COMPASSIONATE. The distress of a father's heart, when his child lies at the point of death, is intense indeed. Jesus comprehended and entered mentally into all relations and all experiences of humanity, for he was himself the Son of man. How touching in its simplicity is the record of our Lord's response to the ruler's appeal: "He went with him"! He is ever the same, "touched with a feeling of our infirmities." He will go with us to the house of mourning, to the chamber of sickness, to the bed of death; and his presence will lighten the sufferer's load and soothe the sufferer's heart.

II. MAN IS IN HASTE, AND JESUS LINGERS. The entreaty of the father and the concern of the thronging multitude are vividly portrayed. How natural that, in so critical a case, there should be a general anxiety to reach the abode where the dying maiden lay! Yet the great Physician pauses to entertain another application for relief, to speak words of grace to another—to a timid, downcast spirit. There is no haste in Christ's methods. It often seems to those who seek him that he delays his succour. In their impatience they may think themselves unheeded. But it is not so; the Divine leisure with which the Lord of grace is wont to act should awaken our admiration and our confidence.

III. MAN DESPAIRS, AND JESUS REASSURES. There was a limit to the faith which was cherished towards Christ. It was thought that he could heal the sick, but it was not dreamt that he could raise the dead. When the little maiden had breathed her last, the household was abandoned to hopeless grief. But this was the moment when the Divine Friend displayed the deepest tenderness of his nature. "Fear not, only believe." Such were his words of comfort, fitted to soothe and to inspire desponding hearts with heavenly hope. Let us learn the lesson that, where Jesus is, there is no place for despair. These words of his come to us when downcast, cheerless, and oppressed beneath the cares and woes of life.

IV. MAN IS AGITATED, AND JESUS IS CALM. There is a sublime contrast between the demeanour of the friends of Jairus and the demeanour of Jesus. A tumult of weeping and wailing is quite in accordance with Eastern manners, and it is in accordance with human nature that the same persons who bewailed the maiden's death should, when another turn was given to their excited dispositions, have laughed the Lord to scorn. How noble and dignified in such a scene appears the demeanour and the language of Christ! He rebukes the noisy crowd and puts them forth, and with tranquil and authoritative mien leads the parents, with the three favoured apostles, into the sad chamber of death. "The world is for excitement, the gospel for soothing." There is but One whose presence can banish alarm and disquietude, and can shed a sweet calm over the dwelling agitated by fear and anguish.

V. MAN IS POWERLESS, AND JESUS IS MIGHTY TO HELP AND SAVE. The anxiety of the parents, the lamentations of the mourners, were vain and powerless to save the child from death or to recall her to life; but the touch and the call of Christ summoned back the spirit that had fled. In the deepest woe the grace and might of Jesus are most conspicuous. He is able to quicken such as are dead in trespasses and sins, to breathe upon them the breath of life. The soul that hears his word, "Arise!" awakens from the long, deep lethargy of sin and lives anew.

VI. MAN IS AMAZED, AND JESUS IS COLLECTED AND CONSIDERATE. No wonder that the parents of the girl were overwhelmed with astonishment. And how like the Lord, to display an interest so tender in the reanimated damsel as to direct that she should be supplied with food! And how like him, too, instead of seeking to increase his fame and favour with the people, to arrange that the miracle should for the present, as far as possible, be concealed! Wisdom, consideration for others, were apparent in his whole demeanour.

PRACTICAL LESSONS. 1. The incident gives us a beautiful representation of the power and the love of a Divine Saviour. 2. And an example of the necessity and the advantage of faith in Jesus, in order to spiritual life and blessing. 3. And a striking instance of the efficacy of intercessory prayer. We may well be encouraged to imitate the believing and urgent entreaties of Jairus.

Vers. 25—34.—*Faith conquering timidity*. Far from withdrawing from scenes of distress and woe, our Lord Jesus was found wherever human sin or misery invited his compassion and invoked his aid. On this occasion he was passing towards the house of mourning, the chamber of death, and on his way paused to pity and to heal a helpless, timid, trembling sufferer.

I. A PICTURE THIS OF HUMAN NEED AND SUFFERING. Amidst the thronging multitude were persons of various circumstances, character, and wants. In all companies there are those who have spiritual ills which only Christ can heal, spiritual desires which only Christ can satisfy. Sin and doubt, weakness, sorrow, and fear, helplessness and despondency,—these are to be found on every side. The case of this poor woman deserves special attention. 1. Her need was *conscious and pitiable*. 2. It was of *long continuance :* for twelve years had she suffered and had obtained no relief. 3. Her case was *beyond human skill* and power. She had gone to many physicians, had endured much in undergoing treatment, had expended all her means, and yet, instead of being better, was worse than before. And now apparently hope was taking flight, and the end seemed near. An emblem this of many a sinner's case—conscious of sin and of a tyranny long endured, yet helpless and despairing of deliverance.

II. A PICTURE THIS OF THE APPROACH AND CONTACT OF TREMBLING FAITH. The graphic narrative of the evangelist is very suggestive as well as very impressive. 1. There was *faith* in the woman's coming to Christ at all. She might have questioned the possibility of his curing her. She might have fancied that, lost in the crowd, she should not gain his notice and help. 2. The faith, however, seems to have been *imperfect*. Something of superstition probably impelled her to seize the hem or sacred fringe of his garment, as though there were magic virtue in the bodily presence of the Saviour. 3. Yet the venture of faith *overcame the natural shrinking* and timidity she experienced. Doubt and diffidence would have kept her away; faith drew her near, and she stole to him. It was the last resource; as it were, the dying grasp.

> "I have tried, and tried in vain,
> Many ways to ease my pain;
> Now all other hope is past,
> Only this is left at last:
> Here before thy cross I lie;
> Here I live or here I die."

4. Faith led to *personal contact*, to the laying hold of the Redeemer. Jesus often healed with a touch, by the laying on of his hand; and here he acknowledged the grasp of trembling confidence. They that come to Jesus must come confessing their faults and needs, applying for his mercy, and laying hold upon him with cordial faith.

III. A PICTURE THIS OF CHRIST'S TREATMENT OF A BELIEVING APPLICANT. The conduct of Christ has been recorded in detail, for the instruction and encouragement of all to whom the gospel comes. 1. Remark his recognition of the individual. This woman was one of a multitude, yet she was not unobserved by the all-seeing and affectionate Saviour. He never overlooks the one among the many; his heart can enter into every case, and succour every needy soul. 2. Remark the immediate and efficacious exercise of his healing power. What others could not accomplish in long years, the Divine Healer effected in a moment. Thus Jesus ever acts. His grace brings pardon to the penitent, justification to the guilty, cleansing to the impure. Immediate grace is the earnest of grace unfailing. 3. We see our Lord accepting grateful acknowledgments. Pleasing to him was the courage that, spite of timidity, "told him all the truth." He ever delights in the thankful tribute of his people's praise and devotion. 4. We hear our Lord's gracious benediction. The language is very rich and full. There is an authoritative assurance of blessing; there is the adoption of the healed one into the spiritual family, conveyed in the one word, "Daughter;" there is the recognition of her saving faith; there is the dismissal in peace; and there is the assurance that the healing is complete and permanent.

APPLICATION. 1. Let this representation of the Saviour induce every hearer of the gospel to bring his case to Jesus. 2. Let every applicant to Christ be encouraged by the assurance of the Lord's individual regard and interest. 3. Let faith lay firm hold of Christ, and that at once without delay.

HOMILIES BY VARIOUS AUTHORS.

Vers. 1—20.—*Legion.* General question of demon-possession. An aggravated form of Satanic influence. Intelligible enough on the principle of provocation and desperation: light and darkness are strongest side by side. The advent of Christ roused to intense activity and excitement the whole demoniacal realm. In this scene there is exemplified—

I. MORAL ANTAGONISM. (Vers. 2, 6.) 1. *Instinctive.* Spontaneous; prescient; yet furnishing no intelligible reason. "An intensified spiritual presentiment" (Lange). 2. *Weakness of the demoniac shown* by: (1) Excitement. (2) Self-contradiction. Attraction and repulsion alternating. (3) Use of borrowed weapons. The exorcism, doubtless so often uttered over him by magicians and ecclesiastics, is all the lore he seems to possess in the way of religion. 3. *Strength of Christ proved by calmness and self-possession, and resolute pursuit of his object.* 4. *Utter and absolute.* "What have I to do with thee? . . . Torment me not."

II. MORAL ASCENDANCY. (Vers. 9—13.) 1. *Instant exercise of authority.* Calm, self-possessed, and fearless. He had already discerned and measured his opponent, and decided as to how he would deal with him. 2. *Spiritual insight and skill.* The great Physician had made diagnosis of his case. Mental surgery was needed, based upon the most profound truths of psychology. The man had to be discriminated and freed from the indwelling demon. The former had little or no sense of his own personal identity. A Roman legion had probably been quartered near, and when he saw their number and power he felt that they somewhat resembled that which had quartered itself within his own nature. With maniacal vanity he readily adopted the title, "Legion." Pride and wretchedness were probably both involved in the retention of the name; it represented the dominant principle in his confused consciousness. Christ asked him, "What is thy name?" that he might rouse him to a sense of personal identity: a wise measure. 3. *Rectoral discipline.* "He gave them leave:" apparently their own suggestion, but granted (1) on principle of highest curative psychology—objective disenchantment; the character and distinctness of the unclean occupants of the man's nature being thus outwardly and visibly set forth, his better self, enfranchised, would be the more likely to assert itself; (2) in pursuance of rectoral discipline. The unclean, unprincipled habits of the people in violating the Law being thus avenged.

III. MORAL DECISION. (Vers. 14—20.) The Gadarenes had to make up their minds with respect to the great Stranger. 1 *The data.* (Vers. 14—16.) Material and moral stood forth in opposition, as in so many other instances. How was their relative importance to be estimated? 2. *The decision.* A unanimous petition for him to depart. How could such men be expected to judge otherwise? They had grand ideas of Christ, but of the wrong sort. 3. *The response.* Instant departure. He took them at their word. "They believed not on him," and acting upon their unbelief urged their request. The conflict of anger and fear, fawning and obstinacy. *A word was enough;* nay, a wish, even unexpressed, has often secured the same result. Not the storm, not the evil repute of the people, not even the horror of the demoniac, could deter him from coming; but a word sent him away! How careful should men be in their attitude to the heavenly Visitant! He went, but not without leaving, in the person of the restored maniac, a monument of his saving power and grace. Every region and every heart has its witness to the same.—M.

Vers. 9, 10.—*Satanic possession a destruction of personal identity.* I. INSTANCES AND ILLUSTRATIONS.

II. Importance of personality for true religious and moral life.

III. The restoration of this the great work of Christ.—M.

Vers. 10; 12, 13; 17—19.—*Prayers granted and denied.* No caprice visible in our Lord's decisions. On the contrary, great moral principles are revealed. The whole conduct of Christ on this occasion, therefore, is of importance for the practical guidance of Christians.

I. The petition of the demoniac. (Ver. 10.) "He besought him much that he would not send them away out of the country." No heed is paid to this request, notwithstanding its passionate earnestness. Why? 1. *The man himself was not praying.* He was depersonalized and besotted by the possession of the devils, and not responsible for his words or actions. It was to free him from this thraldom Christ had undertaken his case. 2. *It would have neutralized the intended mercy to the man to inflict the evil upon others.* 3. *There was no real submission in the real petitioners.* They were still devils, unchanged in their character, and desirous of working further mischief. Powerless, they still desired to do evil.

II. The request of the devils. (Vers. 12, 13.) This was granted, notwithstanding the character of those who made it. A marvel, truly; devils heard and answered by Christ! Is he in league with them? 1. *It was a choice of a lesser of two evils.* It seemed necessary that some visible form should receive the dispossessed spirits, that all, especially the man himself (cf. on the probable principle of cure, the preceding sketch), might be able to realize that the dispossession had actually taken place. As simply dispossessed, they might have taken up their abode in some other soul; but by giving direction to them after dispossession, they were confined to brutes; and the catastrophe that resulted was probably foreseen by Christ. In the destruction of the swine the demons were dismissed speedily right out of the terrestrial sphere. 2. And *in that destruction a punishment was inflicted upon the Gadarenes*, who as yet were sordid, neglectful of the Law (forbidding the rearing of swine), and unspiritual.

III. The entreaty of the Gadarenes. (Vers. 17, 18.) It was at once answered, Because: 1. *It involved a deliberate and intelligent rejection of the Saviour.* They had seen his wondrous moral triumph and the destruction of the swine; but in their estimate the material loss far outweighed the spiritual gain. 2. *There were others elsewhere who were "waiting for him."* 3. *The healed demoniac might be even more effectual as a preacher than himself.* He was a lasting monument of his power and grace. Time might be needed to let the miracle sink into the popular conscience.

IV. The prayer of the restored man. (Vers. 18, 19.) A natural desire under the circumstances. Fear lest the devils should return if he were left to himself, and gratitude and love for his Benefactor, doubtless actuated him. But he is denied! This must have wounded his feelings, and disappointed him. But: 1. *It was not prudent for Christ at that time to have one so closely identified with devils in his company and occupied in his service.* The charge had been made (ch. iii. 22) that he was in league with Satan. 2. *It was not the best life for him to lead in his present condition.* Privation and excitement were not suited to one who had been emaciated and weakened by the devils. 3. *A work of greater use and personal obligation awaited him where he was.* He was the only disciple of Christ in that benighted land. Those who had been scandalized by his previous life, and had suffered from it, were to be first considered. The home that had been desolated was to be revisited, and cheered by the kindly presence and saving influence of the redeemed one.

General lessons. 1. *Prayers may be granted in anger, and denied in love.* 2. *Lesser evils may be allowed to prevent greater ones.* 3. *Duties are to be considered before privileges.*—M.

Ver. 14.—*Unfriendly heralds of Christ.* I. Difficulty of getting the gospel truly and faithfully preached.

II. Contrast this with the rapid spread of false notions about Christ, heresies, unsettling alarms, etc.

III. Compensations. 1. *The existence of Christ is made known.* By-and-by his character will vindicate itself. 2. *Curiosity is aroused and feeling excited.* Almost anything is better than indifference. And the witnesses of his truth and grace are everywhere. 3. *The disciples of Christ are compelled to vindicate their Master.*—M.

Ver. 15.—*Monumental miracles.* The tableau—Christ, and the demoniac sitting at his feet. More impressive and sublime than even the rebuking of the storm. Such trophies are better than sermons, because—

I. THEY ARE AN ABIDING REMINDER AND EXAMPLE.

II. THEY ARE PATENT TO ALL, AND CAN BE UNDERSTOOD BY ALL. " Living epistles, known and read of all men."

III. THEY DEFY REFUTATION, AND DEMAND TO BE EXPLAINED.—M.

Vers. 21—34.—*Ministries broken in upon.* Seldom do we find Christ going straight through with a course of teaching or work. Interruptions constantly occurring ; many ministries making up the one great ministry. The more intimate connection of ver. 21 is given in Matt. ix. 18 (" while he yet spake these things "). Not that Matthew means that Christ was still at table, nor that Mark's order is wrong. The feast of Matthew (ch. ii. 15) is not stated by Mark to have taken place in immediate succession to the conversion, but is narrated in the second instead of the fifth chapter, because of the obvious connection of the two events. Accepting, therefore, the order of the first Gospel, we see—

I. CHRIST INTERRUPTED. 1. *In his teaching.* (Ver. 21; Matt. ix. 18.) Yet how full of interest the subjects—eating with publicans, and fasting ! How significant these breaks ! How natural, in a world so full of disturbing and changing influences as this ! 2. *In his intended mercy.* As he goes to the ruler's house the incident of the woman in the crowd takes place (vers. 25—34), and he is delayed. Yet the prayer of Jairus was urgent, and broken with apprehensive emotion. Only this was still more pressing, for it was (1) actual, present, long-endured suffering and shame ; (2) a demand of faith on behalf of its own possessor (not, as in Jairus's case, for another).

II. FRAGMENTS THAT MAKE A GRANDER WHOLE. We have no time to lament the breaking off—the seeming incompleteness—ere we are astonished at the commentary which is furnished in the incidents that follow. He is the great Physician—to the ruler's daughter, the woman with the issue, and the two blind men alike ; the Bringer of joy, too, to many by his healing mercies and gracious words. All need him, if they only knew it ; and, participating in the blessings of his presence, they cannot mourn or fast, but must needs rejoice. And so in the case of the ruler ; the delay really rewarded his faith by an actual illustration of Christ's power, and so sustained him in the higher exercise of faith. " My daughter is even now dead : but come and lay thy hand upon her, and she shall live " (Matt. ix. 18). This is a picture of many lives. We cannot escape interruptions. Yet are we not therefore to abandon *unity of purpose.* We may fail to finish all we seek to do, or to do it as we would ; but *God holds the connecting harmony,* and will reveal it at last—or even sooner. The sermon broken off, the merciful intention delayed or frustrated, may prove greater blessings in the event than if suffered uninterruptedly to proceed to a visible or immediate completeness within themselves. The life or work divinely interrupted, but pursued with unity of faith and purpose to the end, will be a grander, more Divine thing than otherwise it could possibly have been.

LESSONS. 1. *How infinite the resources of the Saviour !* 2. *His teaching is inseparable from action and life.*—M.

Vers. 21—43.—*Jairus's daughter ; or, the uses of bereavement.* I. DISCOVERING THE NEED OF A SAVIOUR.

II. PERFECTING THE SPIRITUAL LIFE OF THE BEREAVED.

III. REVEALING THE INFINITE MERCY, SYMPATHY, AND POWER OF CHRIST.—M.

Vers. 21—43.—*Jairus's daughter ; or, the course of a true faith.* I. ORIGINATED BY MANY CIRCUMSTANCES EVIDENT AND OBSCURE. The general ministry of Christ. Perhaps Jairus had been a witness of the centurion's faith.

II. CALLED INTO EXERCISE BY GREAT AFFLICTION AND NEED.

III. TRIUMPHING OVER DIFFICULTIES.

IV. REWARDED BY INEFFABLE ANSWERS AND CONFIRMATIONS.—M.

Vers. 25—34.—*The healing of the issue of blood. The magnifying power of faith.* 'Twas but a touch, humanly speaking; yet was it a means of salvation to the believing soul.

I. TRANSFORMING LITTLE THINGS INTO MEANS OF GRACE. 1. *Many touches, but only one touch of faith.* This alone was effectual and saving. It is not human effort that saves, but the spirit of faith that lays hold of Christ. 2. *Only the hem of his garment.* Yet as effectual as if she had touched the body of Christ. How so? Because she touched him spiritually. All ordinances and outward means of grace are in themselves little—no better than the hem of the garment of Christ. It is the Saviour who is great when appealed to by a great faith. 3. *Making use of what was within reach.* Not perhaps the best means possible. But enough when accompanied by faith.

II. IN IMMEDIATE EARTHLY ENDS SECURING ULTERIOR SPIRITUAL ONES. The trembling and fearing woman not only secured the physical boon; the Saviour said, "Thy faith hath saved thee,"—a word that had a larger meaning than could be exhausted by a merely temporal relief or physical wholeness.—M.

Vers. 25—34.—*Salvation without money and without price.* A figure of the spiritual experience of man.

I. CONTRASTED WITH EARTHLY EXPEDIENTS OF SALVATION. These are expensive because: 1. *They waste the spiritual nature of man.* 2. *They increase rather than diminish the evil.* How forlorn the poor woman! How great the contrast with the "sleeping" child! Death in life is far worse than the natural death. It is not mourned for as the latter, and has all the added sorrow of disappointment and despair. 3. *They keep away from the true Saviour.*

II. YET IT MUST BE LEGITIMATELY SOUGHT. The grace of God cannot be stolen. The Saviour knows when a sinner receives his "virtue." There is only one way—the way of faith. The salvation of God is given, not taken by force or stealth; graciously given, with a benediction and a confirming assurance.

III. IT COSTS THE SINNER NOTHING, BUT THE SAVIOUR EVERYTHING.—M.

Vers. 25—34.—*The little of things of Christ great things for men.* How great an idea this woman had of Christ! If there was any fault, it was that she believed in the power, but did not trust the love of Christ. Yet her humility, which was as manifest as her faith, and her shame may account in great part for the stealth and surreptitiousness of her action.

I. MEANS OF GRACE ARE NOT TO BE DESPISED BECAUSE THEY APPEAR OUTWARDLY INSIGNIFICANT. Superstition, ritualism, etc., deprecated; yet an error incident to the opposite extreme. We are not saved by works, neither (literally) are we saved by faith. It is *Christ* that saves. This woman was touching Christ. God's sufficiency so different from man's.

II. NOT THE OUTWARD CHARACTER OF ANY ACT, BUT THE SPIRIT IN WHICH IT IS DONE, IS TO BE CONSIDERED CHIEFLY. The great end of religious acts is to bring us into communion with Christ. This of the woman was a mere touch, scarcely perceptible in the pressure of the crowd. The disciples had not observed it. But Christ felt that it had taken place, and had been effectual. There are manifold ways in which he reaches souls and is reached by them. The common experiences of life may be channels of greater blessing than the ordinances of the Church, when they are regarded in a believing, pious spirit.

III. PIETY IS OFTEN APPARENTLY OUT OF PROPORTION TO ADVANTAGES AND OPPORTUNITIES. 1. *Small things may often bring people to Christ, or keep them away from him.* 2. *Faith may often discover itself in the midst of ignorance and the absence of conventional religion.* 3. *Spiritual privileges may hinder instead of helping religious progress if they be not spiritually used.* This poor woman will rise in judgment against many who have made great show of religious observance, and condemn them. We may hear too often, if we do not lay to heart and obey. We require "grace for grace."—M.

Vers. 30—33.—"*Who touched me?*" I. CHRIST'S SAVING GRACE IS ALWAYS CONSCIOUSLY EXERCISED.

II. It is faith which makes effectual and peculiar the sinner's touch of the Saviour.

III. The secret believer is summoned to an open testimony. For the sake of: (1) *honour*; (2) *spiritual health*; and (3) *the advantage of others.*—M.

Ver. 35.—" *Why troublest thou the Master any further?* " A complaint that gives a glimpse of the harassing nature of Christ's work; drawn hither and thither by human distress and want, he was ever on the march, as men discovered their need of him.

I. The apparent reasonableness of the question. A complaint very rarely occasioned, still more rarely justified. On the present occasion, however, it seemed reasonable enough. For: 1. *Would not further urgency be useless?* "Thy daughter is dead;" and there was an end of the matter. Nothing more could be done. The sufferer had been taken out of the power of man. Surely it could not be expected that death would yield up its prey? Circumstances like this are constantly occurring in human experience. A distinction is made, often must be made, between things in which help may be looked and prayed for, and those in which it is inadmissible to pray. Are there not desperate cases of unbelief and sin for which we have given over praying? 2. *There were others requiring his attention and help.* It seemed wrong to monopolize Christ, especially when nothing could be done. Our grief may become a form of selfishness if it makes us inconsiderate of those who have perhaps suffered more than ourselves. If religion does anything for us, it should take us out of ourselves, and make us sympathetic with others. 3. *Christ was probably weary.* It had been an exciting day. The multitude thronged and pressed him. One poor sufferer had ventured to touch his garment, and at once he detected the action. Was it because he had to husband his force that he had taken such notice of it? Perhaps there were signs of weariness in his features and gait. It was thoughtfulness and respect for him that dictated the words. " *The Master* : there were, therefore, disciples of Jesus in the family of Jairus" (Bengel).

II. The fallacies it involved. It is obvious that a great portion of the previous considerations apply only to the human state of Christ, the days of his flesh and feebleness. But there are many objections to importunate and unceasing prayer that depend for their validity upon very human and limited conceptions of God the Son. It will be evident, therefore, that if the conduct of Jairus can be defended in "troubling the Master" when he was on earth, and subject to the conditions and infirmities of our nature, much more the urgency of those who besiege the throne of grace night and day with their requests. Doubtless Christ was often troubled by suitors for his aid and sympathy; but: 1. *It troubled him more when men did not care to seek him.* He reproved the unbelieving Jews : " Ye will not come to me, that ye may have life " (John v. 40). Indifference is more hateful to him than the greatest importunity. It is better to have a superstitious faith than no faith at all. Let us bless the weakness or the sorrow that brings us to him, making us feel our need of him. For, whether we think it or not, we cannot do without him. 2. *He himself encouraged men to "trouble" him.* What bold promises were his!—" I am the bread of life : he that cometh to me shall not hunger, and he that believeth on me shall never thirst " (John vi. 35) ; " I am the resurrection, and the life : he that believeth on me, though he die, yet shall he live " (John xi. 25) ; "He that believeth on me, the works that I do shall he do also; and greater works than these shall he do " (John xiv. 12); " All things are possible to him that believeth " (ch. ix. 23); and how often as here, " Only believe "! How universal his invitations!—" If any man thirst, let him come unto me, and drink " (John vii. 37) ; " Come unto me, all ye that labour and are heavy laden, and I will give you rest " (Matt. xi. 28). " Ask, and it shall be given you," etc. (Matt. vii. 7). 3. *There is no case too desperate to bring to Christ.* No disease could baffle him whilst he was amongst men ; even the grave gave up its dead at his potent word. And now " all power in heaven and earth " is his. Let us "trouble" him, therefore, with our sorrows and difficulties until he gives us relief. The care or desire which is not brought to him will sever us from him. We need not fear offending him; he is the Saviour, and it was that he might comfort and save men he came. Even whilst we think our case desperate, or say within ourselves, " It is no use ; it is not seemly to trouble him," we grieve his Spirit and resist his grace. The sinner who has sinned above measure, and is altogether vile, may come. How is that promise fulfilled in him, "Come now, and let us reason together, saith the Lord : though your sins be as scarlet, they shall be as white as snow ; though they be red like crimson, they shall be as wool!" (Isa. i. 18.)—M.

Vers. 2—6.—*The demoniac of Gadara.* This is the most detailed and important account given in the Gospels of demoniacal possession. Some are content to identify this phenomenon with lunacy or epilepsy, and suppose that our Lord used current phraseology upon the subject, although it expressed a popular delusion. We are slow to accept an explanation which would seem to credit him, who was always true, and himself "the Truth," with thus sanctioning error; especially as he used the same language when he was alone with his disciples, to whom he said it was "given to know the mysteries of the kingdom" (ch. ix. 28, 29). On the other hand, "possession" was not identical with moral degradation. The idea that Mary Magdalene was one of peculiarly evil life, because "out of her the Lord cast seven demons," is untenable; and there is little doubt that Caiaphas, who was shrewd, callous, and self-controlled to the last, was morally worse than such sufferers. Yet a weak yielding to animal passions was possibly the primary cause of possession by evil spirits, in whose existence we cannot but believe. Good was incarnate in those days, and evil also appeared as in a special sense incarnate. Buckle shows that there have been ebb and flow in the currents of national history; and so there have been in moral history, and in the days of our Lord spiritual forces were at the flood. The more we study the works and the Word of God, the more we are convinced that the inexplicable is not to reverently thoughtful men incredible or absurd. We enter on the study of this scene not with the hope of elucidating all mystery, but with the prayer that we may gain from it some spiritual help. Depicted as it is in strong, dark colours, it may enable us to understand the nature of Christ's work in the soul. We see here—

I. A MAN UNDER BONDAGE TO EVIL. The expression an "unclean" spirit, and the strange willingness to enter "the swine," denote the nature of the man. By the indulgence of appetite habit had conquered will, and he had no mastery over himself. That is the essence of "possession." Modern forms of it are not difficult to find. Describe the drunkard in his downward progress. At last, although he knows that ruin is before him, if temptation is in his way, his resolutions go to the winds. He is fascinated, or "possessed." So with the gambler and others. The condition of the demoniac resembled theirs. Domestic comfort was gone ; the respect of others was lost; life was laid waste. He could see fingers pointing at him, eyes glaring on him, hell yawning for him, and his foes seemed coming on him resistlessly as the advance of the dreaded Roman "legion." Notice also the *deranging* effects of evil. He was "dwelling in the tombs"—a dreary, fearsome place, in harmony with his melancholy state. "All they that hate me, love death." The prodigal must "come to himself" before he returns to the Father. As this demoniac cut himself with stones, caring nothing for pain, so some destroy their moral sensibility; as he was a cause of misery or of terror, so is it with them; as he dreaded the near approach of a Judge he could not deceive, of a King he could not escape, so do they. Beware of tampering with sin.

II. A MAN CASTING OFF HUMAN RESTRAINTS. He was not without those who loved him. They had done their best to restrain or cure him. As they saw the growth of the evil, his parents would try to make the home attractive, inviting companions who would divert his thought; sisters would give up their innocent pleasure to fall in with his wishes; and when the outburst came, he was "bound with fetters and chains," lest he should harm himself or others. All in vain. Human restraint will never conquer moral evil. It represses it or alters its form, but does not root it out. The disorder and restlessness now seen in society portend serious issues, and indicate a breaking down of much in our boasted civilization. Education only changes Bill Sykes, the burglar, into Carker, the smooth, lying villain. We may restrain dishonesty, drunkenness, swearing, etc., so that they are no longer in respectable homes ; but though we shut our eyes to the fact, the demoniac has only slipped his chains, and is there in "the tombs" and dens of our land. Parental restraint does much, but a time comes when independence and self-assertion make themselves felt, and the father or mother can only pray. Speak to those who still remember the old home in which they were so different from what they are now.

III. A MAN MEETING HIS SAVIOUR. With his morbidly quickened sensibility he knew who Jesus was, and had a presentiment of what was coming. His abject prostration, coupled with his daring misuse of the sacred name, indicate the distraction and disorder characterizing him. Christ dealt with him wisely, firmly, lovingly. He asked, "What is thy name?" He tried to summon the man's better self, to bring about a severance in his thought between himself and the evil; he gave him time to think what need he had of help, and what hope and possibility there was of it. Then to the demons came the decisive word, "Go!" and in a short time he was to be seen "sitting at the feet of Jesus, clothed, and in his right mind." In each of us the dominion of sin must be broken, and Christ only can break it. Appeal to those who have long been under the dominion of sin, not to despair of themselves, on the ground that Christ does not despair of them. It was when his friends had given up this demoniac as hopeless that his redemption came. So, when self-reform has proved useless, and benefactors fail, and friends lose heart, he proves "able to save to the uttermost." Dealing pitifully with the sinner, he deals ruthlessly with his sin, and will hurl it into the depths of the sea.—A. R.

Vers. 17, 21.—*The rejection and the reception of Jesus.* Our text presents us with a striking contrast. Only a few miles of sea separated these people physically, but morally what a gulf was between them! On both sides of the lake Christ's words had been heard, and his works of power had been seen, but how different were the results! If he had been like us, variable in temper and disposition—at one time moody, at another genial—we might more easily account for this. For the dispositions of sinful men are like the Lake of Galilee—now raging in a storm, and now calm and still under the smiling heavens. But there was no such variableness in the Perfect Man. He was not cheery when the palm branches were waved on Olivet, and angry when his disciples forsook him and fled. He was not one thing in Gadara, and another in Capernaum. "He is the same yesterday, to-day, and for ever." We must look elsewhere to account for this phenomenon, and we shall find its causes to be those which sever so widely in character and destiny, two hearers who sit in the same church, or two children who kneel beside the same mother's knee. I. THE VARIOUS ASPECTS IN WHICH CHRIST PRESENTED HIMSELF. His relations to those around him were not simple, but complex. We may be great in *one* aspect of our character, but he was great in every aspect. 1. *He appeared as a Teacher.* In the synagogue, on the beach, amidst the crowd, he uttered Divine truth, and expected on the part of his hearers humble and obedient minds. He assumed that he knew what they did not know, respecting the nature of God, the meaning of the old dispensation, the phenomena of life, the coming future, etc. He adduced no arguments, but demanded (as he still demands), on the ground of what he was and is, the acceptation, or the rejection of his words. "He spake as one having authority." "This is my beloved Son; *hear* him." The acceptance of Christ as a Teacher implied much, because he taught no abstract theories, but enunciated principles which would revolutionize the views held about the Jewish economy, and would banish popular sins. Show what Christ demands of disciples now, and the spirit in which we should receive his revelation. 2. *He appeared as a Saviour.* Thought and action were blended harmoniously in Christ, and should be blended in every Christian. The Teacher of the people was the Healer of their bodies and the Purifier of their souls. This complex work is entrusted to the Church. Christ cured the demoniac, and restored sight to the blind, and health to the leper, as signs of what he had come to effect for men. 3. *He appeared as a Friend.* He entered the homes of the people at Capernaum and elsewhere, to cure illness in Peter's house, to bless children in another home, to share festivity in Cana, to weep with mourners in Bethany. This friendship the disciples rejoiced in. The presence of that Friend had delivered them in the storm. As such he presents himself at each heart, saying, "Behold, I stand at the door and knock," etc. II. THE DIFFERENT EFFECTS OF SUCH PRESENTATION ON THE PEOPLE. This may be illustrated not only by the conduct of the disciples and of the cured demoniac, but by contrasting the condition of the people of Gadara with that of the people in Capernaum. This exemplifies: 1. *The rejection of Christ.* The most astounding miracle will not produce faith in those who care more for their possessions than for purity and love, such as Christ had imparted to the man who had the unclean spirit. The loss of the swine first awakened terror, but shortly afterwards indignation, amongst the people, who with mingled fawning and obstinacy " began to pray him to depart out of their coasts." He yielded to their wish, and, so far as we know, never returned again. Similarly he was rejected at Nazareth (Luke iv. 29) and in Jerusalem (Matt. xxiii. 37). In the instance before us the people feared the Holy One more than they had feared the demoniac. Their greed was up in arms against the destroyer of their swine ; they cared more for them than for the rescue of a brother-man. Even now sometimes property is more jealously defended than personal rights. Christ laid down the principle that a man is better than a sheep, and he expressed that principle in his action at Gadara. Show how possessions and position are preferred to simple obedience to our Lord's will, so that from love to the world he is still rejected. 2. *The reception of Christ.* A right royal welcome was awaiting him on the other side of the lake. There the people had seen changes wrought in their homes by his power, and they had listened eagerly to his words of wisdom and love. They could not go back to their work as if there were no Christ who had come to save and comfort them. When he was gone, they prayed that the little boat might again come over the sea ; and when the first glimpse of its sail was seen, the news spread swiftly far and wide. Fishers left their nets, and ran to call their mates, saying, " Jesus is coming ! " old people tottered down to the sea because Jesus was coming ; women who were mourning over their dear ones thought with thankfulness and love of his sympathy ; and little children left their games in the market-place in order to be made glad by his smile. And still he comes amongst us in earnest words, in sacred song, in holy thought, in solemn memories. Then fling open the door of your heart, pour out the treasures of your love, wake up the songs of praise, as you say, " Even so, come, Lord Jesus ! "—A. R.

Vers. 18—20.—*Desire and duty.* There was wonderful variety in the methods of treatment adopted by our Lord in dealing with those who surrounded him. He touched the eyes of the blind; he gave his hand to those prostrate by illness or stricken with death ; he sometimes spoke the word of healing first, and sometimes the word of pardon, always suiting himself to the special condition of each, according to his perfect knowledge of his deepest need. The same completeness of knowledge and of consideration reveals itself in his intercourse with those who had been blessed, and were now among his followers. Some were urged to follow him, others were discouraged by a presentation of difficulties. A beautiful example of this is given by Luke (ix. 57—62), in his account of those who spoke to our Lord just before he crossed the lake. The same gracious consideration of what was really best for one of his followers is seen here. And his disciples now do not all require the same treatment, nor have they all the same work to do or the same sphere to fill.

I. THE CONVERT'S DESIRE. (Ver. 18.) "When Jesus was come into the ship," or, more correctly (Revised Version), "as he was entering into the boat," the delivered demoniac prayed that he might be with him. It was a natural desire, and a right one, although all the motives which prompted it were possibly not worthy. As in us, so in him, there was a mingling of the noble with the ignoble. Let us see what actuated him. 1. *Admiration.* No wonder that he sat at the feet of this Mighty One, and gazed upon him with adoring love. Angels bow before him; the redeemed cast their crowns at his feet. Reverence and awe are too rarely felt now. Proud self-sufficiency characterizes the civilized world, and even the professedly Christian Church. It is well to know, but it is better to adore. Consciousness of ignorance and weakness, in the presence of God, leads to worship. Let reverence characterize our search into the Divine Word, our utterances in God's name, our approaches to his throne. 2. *Gratitude.* Having received salvation, this man longed to prove his thankfulness, and he naturally thought that an opportunity would be found, while following Jesus, to defend his reputation or to do him some lowly service. Under the old economy many thank-offerings were presented. The firstfruits of the fields and flocks were offered to the Lord, and any special blessing received from him called forth special acknowledgment. Show how thank-offerings have died out of the Church, and how they might be profitably revived. Point out various modes of showing thankfulness to God. 3. *Self-distrust.* Near the Deliverer he was safe, but might there not be some relapse when he was gone? A right feeling on his part and on ours. See the teaching of our Lord in John xv. on the necessity of the branch *abiding* in the vine. 4. *Fear*. The people were greatly excited. They had begged Christ to go out of their coasts, lest he should destroy more of their possessions. It was not improbable that they would wreak their vengeance on a man whose deliverance had been the cause of their loss. They did not believe, as Christ did, that it was better that any lower creatures should perish if only one human soul was rescued. But this is in harmony with all God's works, in which the less is being constantly destroyed for the preservation and sustenance of the greater. The luxuriant growth of the fields is cut down that the cattle may live; myriads of creatures in the air and in the sea are devoured by those higher in the scale of creation than themselves; living creatures are slain that we may be fed and clothed. In harmony with all this, the destruction of the swine was the accompaniment of, or the shadow cast by, the redemption of the man. And high above all these mysteries rises the cross of Calvary, on which the highest life was given as a sacrifice for the sins of the world. In this event we can see glimpses of Divine righteousness and pity; but these people of Gadara shut their eyes to them, and were angry at their loss. Amongst them this man must "endure hardness as a good soldier of Jesus Christ."

II. THE CONVERT'S DUTY. (Ver. 19.) 1. *His work was to begin at home*. "Go home to thy friends." His presence there would be a constant sermon. In the truest sense he was " a living epistle." Sane instead of mad, holy instead of unclean, gentle instead of raving; he was "a new creation." All true work for God should commence in the home. Self-control and self-sacrifice, gentleness and patience, purity and truth, in the domestic circle—will make the home a temple of God. 2. *His work was to be found among old acquaintances*. Some had scorned him, others had hated and perhaps ill-treated him. But resentment was to be conquered in him by God's grace, and to those who knew him at his worst he was now to speak for Christ. Such witness-bearing is the most difficult, but the most effective. John the Baptist told the penitents around him, whether publicans or soldiers, to go back to their old spheres, and prove repentance by changed life and spirit amid the old temptations. 3. *His work was to be quiet and unostentatious*. Perhaps Christ saw that publicity would injure him spiritually, for it does injure some; or it may be that the excitement involved in following the Lord would be unsafe for him so soon after his restoration. For some reason he had assigned to him a quiet work, which was not the less true and effective. Luke says that he was to *show* "how great things God had done for him," as if the witness-bearing was to be in living rather than in talking. Speak of the quiet spheres in which many can still serve God. 4. *His work was to spread and grow*. The home was too small a sphere for such gratitude as his. He published the fame of the Lord in "all Decapolis." This was not wrong, or forbidden, for there were not the reasons for restraint of testimony in Peræa which existed in Galilee. It was a natural and legitimate enlargement of commission. Similarly the apostles were to preach to all nations, but to begin in Jerusalem. He who is faithful with a few things is made ruler over many things, sometimes on earth, and invariably in heaven.—A. R.

Ver. 22.—*The faith of Jairus*. Faith was the one thing which Christ demanded of every suppliant who came to him. He asked the blind man the question, "Believest thou that I am able to do this?" He said to the father of the lunatic child, "All things are possible to him that believeth." Here he assured the woman in the crowd who had been healed, "Thy faith hath saved thee;" and to Jairus he said, "Be not afraid, only believe." All these are exemplifications of the words, "Without faith it is impossible to please God." Faith is the hand which the soul stretches out to receive the blessings of pardon, salvation, and peace. If two men have sinned, and are both conscious of guilt, one may walk at liberty, while the other is burdened ; because, though he is grieved about his sin, and hates it, and therefore has truly repented, the latter fails to believe the assurance, "Thy sins are forgiven thee." Similarly, in trouble a Christian may exhibit a serenity which fills onlookers with wonder, not because his trouble is lighter or his sensibility less, but because he has faith to believe that God is doing good through the trouble, or that he will ultimately bring good out of it. This faith in Christ Jairus had, though imperfectly, and his peace was in proportion to his trust.

I. JAIRUS'S FAITH WAS UNEXPECTED. He was "the ruler of the synagogue;" in other words, he was the president of one of the synagogues in Capernaum. It was his duty to superintend and direct its services, and to preside over its college of elders. As a pastor and professor—to use modern terms—he would have strong prejudices against a heretical teacher, such as our Lord was esteemed to be. We all know how difficult it is to go out of the usual course in any professional work; but although those who were associated with Jairus were hostile to our Lord, he dared to fall humbly at his feet. Sometimes the least hopeful, in human opinion, are the most richly blessed by Divine favour. Those who have often been taught and prayed for in our congregations may remain untouched, while some poor waif who has drifted in from the sea of life may find rest in Christ. Many shall come from the east and from the west, to sit down in the kingdom, while those who are favoured by circumstances and birth will be shut out.

II. JAIRUS'S FAITH GERMINATED IN GRIEF. He had been shut up with his little daughter who was ill, and for a time had been cut off from ordinary duties and associations. We can picture him to ourselves sitting beside her, with her little hand in his, while her eyes would often seek his with filial love. She had heard of Christ (what child in Capernaum had not?); possibly she had seen him, and loved him, as most of the children did. And while she spoke to her father, when his heart was specially tender, he could not but drink in thoughts of the love and power of Jesus, until, daring the worst that his friends could say of him, he fell at Jesus' feet. Sometimes those who have been associated with Churches or Sunday schools remain untouched by holy influence, until, having left their old connections, they fall into sin and shame, and then, knowing not whither in the world to turn, they look to Jesus. Sometimes professing Christians feel that they are far from God, and that even in their prayers he appears vague and unreal; till trouble comes—illness assails one whose life is precious, and then they pray in an agony of earnestness, as Jairus did, when "he besought Jesus greatly, saying, My little daughter lieth at the point of death." Faith often springs up in the soil of trouble.

III. JAIRUS'S FAITH WAS SEVERELY TRIED. His hope was quickened when he saw Jesus rise up at once to follow him; but the crowd would not let our Lord hasten, and the poor woman meanwhile stole her blessing, and Christ delayed to speak with her and with others. Looking towards his home with ever-growing anxiety, at last Jairus saw what he dreaded seeing—a messenger, who said, "Thy daughter is dead: why troublest thou the Master any further?" But he had to learn that no one in earnest was ever a "trouble" to the Lord; that when he seemed to be caring for another he was really thinking of him, and preparing him to receive a far greater blessing than any he had come to seek. Christ delayed that "the trial of this man's faith, being much more precious than that of gold that perisheth, though it be tried with fire, might be found to God's glory." We often find that there is delay in the coming of answers to prayer. We cry for light, and yet our way is dark, and we see not even the next step. We ask for deliverance, but the disaster comes which overwhelms us with distress. We entreat the Lord to spare some cherished life, but the dear one is taken away. Nevertheless, "let patience have her perfect work, that ye may be perfect and entire, wanting nothing."

IV. JAIRUS'S FAITH WAS LOVINGLY ENCOURAGED. The storm tested this tree till its roots struck deeper; but when there appeared some risk of its falling, Christ said to the tempest, "Peace, be still." When the messengers said, "Thy daughter is dead," at once Jesus spoke; and "as soon as Jesus heard the word that was spoken, he saith, . . . Be not afraid, only believe." Again, when Jairus entered his house, you can imagine how the father's heart sank as he saw the mourners for the dead already there. Till then he had been hoping against hope, as sometimes we do till we actually enter the darkened house where the dead one lies. Again Jesus interposed, saying, "The damsel is not dead, but sleepeth;" for so would he keep alive trust and hope till the blessing came, for which they were the preparation. "He will not break the bruised reed, nor quench the smoking flax."—A. R.

Ver. 24.—*The Lord amongst the needy.* The two miracles recorded in this passage were blended both in fact and in narrative, and together they illustrate some of the beauties of our Lord's character and work. Of these we select the following:—

I. HIS DISINTERESTED KINDNESS. No doubt his miracles were attestations of Divine power, but none of them were wrought with the idea of gaining personal fame. On the contrary, he endeavoured to silence the demands of gaping curiosity, and rebuked those who sought for signs and wonders. He refused the worldly homage which the people proffered when they wished to make him a king. He checked the spread of his own fame, lest men should care too much for material blessings, or should offer him the adulation a wonder-worker would have sought. If he had willed it, all the riches of the world would have been poured at his feet; but he had not where to lay his head; and although Jairus and others would have given all their possessions as the price of the benefits they sought, Christ bestowed the blessing "without money and without price." Herein he appeared as the true Representative—"the express Image" of him who delights in mercy for mercy's own sake. God gives air and sunshine without any effort, or solicitation, or thanksgiving on the part of man. He makes the garden of the cottager as fruitful as the fields of the rich, who can do so much more in return for his gifts. Ferns grow in shady hollows, and flowers adorn lonely cliffs, and even heaps of refuse. With a lavish hand the Creator bestows his gifts. "He is good to all, and his tender mercies are over all his works."

II. HIS PERSONAL CONSIDERATION FOR EACH SUPPLIANT. If we are acquainted with many subjects, our knowledge of each is often proportionately inaccurate; if we know many persons, our acquaintance with them is but casual. If we concentrate our thought upon a person or a thing, that concentration is often exclusive of other persons and things. It was never thus with our Lord. Though he rules the worlds, there is not a single prayer unheard, or a feeble touch of faith unfelt. One who has been left alone to battle with his griefs may still say to himself, "But the Lord cares for *me.*" He will no more hurry over a case than over that of the poor woman in the crowd, nor will he allow any delay to prevent the full coming of a blessing such as that which Jairus had at last.

III. HIS CONSTANT DESIRE FOR SPIRITUAL RESULTS. The temporal was to be the channel of the eternal. Healing of the soul often accompanied his healing of the body, and for the former he chiefly cared. On this occasion every moment was precious. The result of delay would be death and mourning in Jairus's home; yet he stayed not only to cure the woman, but to get her acknowledgment, and to give her and others fuller instruction. Had it been only her physical cure he sought, she could have waited a few hours; but the delay was largely for the spiritual good of Jairus. This ruler had not the faith of the centurion, who believed that Christ need not touch his servant, or even enter his house. Jairus's faith needed strengthening, and it was with this end in view that he saw what he did—a woman shut out from the synagogue of which he was ruler, who was saved by her simple faith, and this with the greatest possible ease on the part of the Lord. Hence it was that when the news came, "Thy daughter is dead," Jairus was not utterly dismayed, and under the influence of the cheering words of our Lord his faith revived in purer form. It is still true that delay in answer to prayer, during which grief and loss comes, is meant to work in us the peaceable fruit of righteousness.

IV. HIS BROAD SYMPATHIES AND ACTIVITIES. The love of Christ was not like some little stream which is confined between its two banks, and must be so confined if it is to be a blessing; but it was like the sea, which, when the tide rises, floods the whole shore, and fills every tiny creek as well as every yawning bay. He was never so absorbed in one mission as to neglect the side opportunities of life. Some of us have a tendency to absorption in one single duty, and the temptation is strong in proportion to the intensity and earnestness of our nature. But intenseness must not be allowed to make us narrow. To set before ourselves a special end is good, but this may lead to a neglect of other duties which is unnecessary and sometimes sinful. For example, some concentrate their interests in business or in pleasure, and declare that they have no time for devout thought; and at last they will find that they have grasped shadows and lost the substance. Christians fall into a similar error. Some do public service, and their names are widely known in the Church, but they have scarcely exercised any good influence at home. The Church benefits, but the children are neglected. And often the opposite is true; for to many the home is everything, and the Church is nothing. Others, again, are so absorbed in one special work (that of the Sunday school, or temperance reform, for example), that they have little sympathy for their brethren who are engaged in other spheres of the manifold life of the Church. And there are others more guilty by far than these, who are absorbed in future work. They are always "going to do" this or that; but meanwhile their neighbours are uninfluenced and their own children are neglected. As they are not faithful with the few things, it would be contrary to God's law if they became rulers over many things. If our Lord had been animated by the spirit displayed by any of these, he would have said to the woman, "My errand is one of life and death; there must be no touching even the skirts of my garment now. All else must wait till I have discharged this mission." But, by the course he took, he taught us this lesson. There is nothing within the range of our power that is beyond the range of our responsibility. In all these respects Christ has left us an example, that we should follow his steps.—A. R.

Ver. 31.—*The touch of faith.* We may see in this poor woman what our Lord expects to see in all who would receive his blessing.
I. THE TREMBLING SUPPLIANT. There are many legends respecting her: that her name was Veronica; that she maintained the innocency of our Lord before Pilate; that she wiped his face on the road to Calvary with a napkin, which received the sacred impress of his features; that she erected a memorial to him at Paneas, her native town; etc. Improbable as much of this may be, it indicates that her faith was highly esteemed by the early Christians. The evangelists describe her as a certain woman who was worn by suffering, haggard from poverty (ver. 26), and ceremonially unclean, so as to be excluded from the consolations of public worship. She stole into the crowd, and by her touch of faith won the blessing she sought. 1. *Illness brought her to Jesus.* Most of those who came to him were afflicted—the blind, the leprous, the bereaved, the hungry, etc. Every sorrow is a summons to us to go to him. 2. *Faith prepared her for a blessing.* Even material gifts are received by the hand of faith. We all act in daily faith that the laws of God will continue—the farmer, the tradesman, etc. When Christ wrought a miracle (which was an epitome of one of God's works) he demanded faith. "He could not do many mighty works" where there was unbelief. He demanded trust in himself, both of Jairus (ver. 36), of this woman (ver. 34), and of us (Acts xvi. 31). If faith was truly exercised, erroneous views, such as this woman had, did not prevent a blessing.
II. THE EFFECTUAL TOUCH. "The border of the garment," to which Luke with more definiteness refers, was a sign of belonging to the chosen people (Numb. xv. 38), and Christ blamed the Pharisees for making it specially broad, as if they would assert their peculiar sanctity. The woman touched it, not only as the most convenient, but as the most sacred, part of the robe, and her superstition required to be cleansed away. 1. *There may be close outward contact with Christ without the effectual touch* (ver. 31). The crowd represents many who are in Christian lands and congregations. 2. *There cannot be living contact between us and him without his knowledge* (ver. 30). Though there was only one in the crowd who so touched him as to win salvation, that one was not unrecognized. So, if in the large congregation one earnest prayer, one praiseful song, is offered, it is accepted of him. The garment may represent to us our Lord's humanity, which is most within the reach of our understanding and love. St. Paul speaks of his "flesh" as a "veil," through which we pass into God's presence. Our Lord himself says, in another figure which sets forth the same truth, "Hereafter ye shall see heaven open, and the angels of God ascending and descending upon the Son of man." He was the true ladder between heaven and earth, between God and man, of which Jacob once dreamed.
III. THE REQUIRED CONFESSION. To acknowledge the change wrought in us by Divine grace is for God's glory, for the development of our own faith, and for the encouragement of others. We have responsibilities to the Church as well as to the Lord, which even shame and modesty must not lead us to ignore. Our Lord called for acknowledgment on this occasion, and it led to fuller instruction and to a deeper peace. He did not ask his question because he was ignorant, any more than Elisha

did after his heart had gone with Gehazi, or Jehovah did when he asked of Adam, "Where art thou?" If we know which of our children has done a certain act, we may nevertheless ask, "Which of you did this?" and whether it has been a right act or a wrong, the confession on such occasions is for the child's own good. With truer wisdom than we ever display Christ Jesus asked, "Who touched my clothes?" although he knew perfectly the life of her whose faith in him had made her whole; "For with the heart man believeth unto righteousness, and with the mouth *confession* is made unto salvation."—A. R.

Ver. 41.—*The dead maiden.* There are three instances of Christ's raising the dead recorded by the evangelists. In them a suggestive progression may be observed. On this occasion, a child had but recently died, and was laid upon the bed in her own home, amongst those who could still see the dear face, which was now void and irresponsive. On another occasion a young man had been dead long enough for his funeral to have begun, and he was being carried forth on a bier through the village in which he had lived. On the third occasion we read that when Jesus came to Bethany he found that Lazarus "had been dead three days already," and that the grave had closed on him. In all these he gave evidences of his life-giving power, and this with ever-growing intensity until that glorious day when he himself, in spite of the Sanhedrim's seal and the Roman guard, appeared as being in his own person the Conqueror of death and the grave. In answer to the prayer of Jairus, and perhaps to the prayer of his child before she died, Jesus came into the ruler's house. He found it filled with hired mourners, and heard the music of their flutes, the droning of liturgical chants, the wails and cries by which they sought, not only to express grief, but further to excite it. There was something stern about his utterance—"Give place!" Such an exhibition could not be other than offensive to One so sincere and true and natural as he was. And they who have his Spirit would rather be lamented by the few whose hearts are really touched with sadness, than by a multitude who offer ceremonial lamentation. Christ Jesus "put them all out." And we must get rid of all that is artificial and false if we would feel that Jesus is near, and we must be out of the company of the mockers who "laugh him to scorn" if we would hear his voice. It is in the quiet hour that he speaks, and we then can say—

"In secret silence of the mind,
My God and there my heaven I find."

We may look upon that dead maiden—
I. As AN EXAMPLE OF PHYSICAL DEATH. When Jesus said, "She is not dead," he did not mean, as some suppose, that she was in a trance. He spoke metaphorically, just as he did when he said, "Our friend Lazarus sleepeth," though immediately afterwards he said "plainly, Lazarus is dead." A boaster would have laid stress on the fact of her death in order to exalt his own power in restoring her, but Christ spoke of it as a sleep, because he wished, not to magnify himself, but lovingly to prepare her friends for the overwhelming joy that awaited them. Sleep is a true image of death. Like it, death follows weariness when the work of life has been hard and its sorrows many; it gives quietude of which the stillness of the body is but an outward sign; and it will be followed by a glorious awakening on the morning of the eternal day. Christ is "the resurrection and the life." He who gave this child back to her parents, and the lad at Nain back to his widowed mother, and Lazarus back to his sisters, will restore to us all those dear ones who now "through faith and patience inherit the promises."
II. A SYMBOL OF SPIRITUAL DEATH. The child lay there, unconscious that her friends were weeping for her, and that Jesus Christ was near. But suddenly she felt the touch of his hand. She heard his voice in language such as her mother and nurse used—the language of the children—saying, "Talitha cumi!"—"Dear child, arise!" and she opened her eyes and saw Jesus, and from that moment her heart was his. As truly he speaks now, in the stirring of sacred feeling, in the revival of old memories, in the loving influence of Christian friends; and they who obey his voice begin from that moment a happier life than they ever knew before. Very significant is the command of Christ "that something should be given her to eat." It was a reminder that she

really lived, that she had natural appetite, that he lovingly thought of the little things his dear ones needed, and that she was back again in the old life and home, though with a new love in her heart. So, many now who are dead to the old life and alive unto righteousness are called upon by their Lord to go back to their former work and companionship, but to serve him by shedding on these the light of holiness and love. From some he demands the public confession that they are on his side which he asked of the woman who had been secretly cured; but there are others to whom publicity is painful, whose experience is not to be blazed abroad, lest the beauty of childlike trust and the bloom of early piety be destroyed.—A. R.

Vers. 1—20.—*A man with an unclean spirit.* It is no part of the office of the homilist to enter upon the field of apologetics or exegesis. Criticism and inter- pretation provide the words with their definite meanings. Homiletics unfold and apply practical lessons. The difficulties of this narrative must, therefore, be discussed elsewhere.

I. Our attention is first arrested by the physical derangement exhibited in this case of possession by "an unclean spirit." The sadness of this spectacle is amply exhibited in the words of vers. 2—5. The overpowering of the entire personality of the victim by "an unclean spirit" points to a fearful possibility of the human life. Does sin open the door to the spirit of evil? The man was under the power of an unclean spirit, was led to do unclean acts. He dwelt remote from his fellows, "in the tombs." He was possessed of unusual physical strength; he could not be bound, "no, not with a chain." "No man had strength to tame him." This unusual power was exercised in "crying out and cutting himself with stones." Whatever the precise nature of this affliction, the scene exhibits the human life in *its uttermost derangement.*

II. On the moral side the attitude of the unclean spirit towards Jesus is expressed as one of utter repudiation: "What have I to do with thee, Jesus, the Son of the Most High God?" They had nothing in common. What can the spirit of evil have to do with Jesus? They mutually recede; they are mutually opposed. These appear before us as representing two kingdoms, wholly diverse in character. The one is a kingdom of evil and uncleanness; the other a kingdom of peace and righteousness. In the one the human life is disorganized; in the other it attains its true dignity, har- mony, and blessedness. The one is for it a kingdom of darkness; the other a kingdom of light. In the one is death; life is found in the other. They have nothing in common; they are mutually exclusive, mutually destructive.

III. The supreme authority of Jesus, "Son of the Most High God," in the sphere of the human life is again illustrated, as also his attitude towards all human suffering. "With authority he commands," "Come forth, thou unclean spirit, out of the man," and in pitifulness he releases the oppressed. Thus is fulfilled that "which was spoken by Isaiah the prophet, saying, Himself took our infirmities, and bare our diseases." Else- where is this more amply illustrated.

IV. The changed condition of the life when Jesus has exerted upon it his power, and evicted the spirit of uncleanness, is simply and beautifully portrayed in the picture pre- sented to the eyes of the multitude who "came to see what it was that had come to pass," and beheld "him that was possessed with devils sitting, clothed, and in his right mind." With affectionate gratitude he now cleaves to Jesus, beseeching "him that he might be with him." The refusal was not in harsh judgment against the redeemed one, but for the instruction and profit of all others—that he may go and "publish how great things Jesus had done for him." Out of this incident let the central words, "What have I to do with thee?" be chosen as a test by which each may prove his nearness to Jesus or his recession from him. At one extreme lies this word of utter rejection—the word of Satanic repudiation; at the other, words which express the most complete absorption of the life in devotion to him—"To me to live is Christ." This declares the perfect identification of the individual life with the person, the mission, the spirit of Jesus. The one affirms, "I know no life within the sphere of Christ's kingdom;" the other, "I know no life beyond it. His name defines the boundary of my aims, my activities, my hopes. I am lost, buried, absorbed in him; to all things else I die."

How many are the gradations between these extremes! Let each test himself as to the attitude he assumes towards Jesus. 1. As to a supreme submission to his authority as "the Son of the Most High God." 2. As to a calm and loving reliance upon him as "Jesus," the "Saviour, which is Christ the Lord." 3. As to a sincere alliance with him in the work of raising men from the dominion of evil—casting out the spirit of all foulness from the human life. 4. As to a perfect fellowship with Christ in the communion of sympathy and love.—G.

Vers. 21—43.—*Avowed and hidden faith.* The two incidents here grouped together show that in the neighbourhood of Capernaum faith in Jesus' power to heal has been established; nor is it to be wondered at, seeing the many instances of healing with which the people must be acquainted. The picture is striking. The "Teacher" has returned from his sail across the lake, where truly "the power proceeding from him had gone forth," even the stormy wind yielding to it. A crowd gathers around him. He is standing by the sea speaking, when "one of the rulers of the synagogue, Jairus by name," who had come seeking him, "and seeing him, he falleth at his feet," making supplication for his "little daughter," who is "at the point of death." Yet does he believe that if the hands of the Healer be laid upon her she shall "be made whole and live." Therefore his earnest entreaty, "Come thou." He who would that children should come to him refused not to go to them—a single child's life is precious in his sight. Presently the sad tidings are brought, "Thy daughter is dead." Why, therefore, should the Master be troubled any further? The faith of the father might well fail since now all hope of recovery is cut off. Is this man mighty enough "in hope" to believe "against hope"? Perhaps not without the strengthening word, "Fear not, only believe, and" (as St. Luke caught) "she shall be made whole." Truly "belief cometh of hearing, and hearing by the word of Christ." Then, as on another occasion (cf. Luke vii. 11—17), the word of command—"Arise"—is uttered to the dead by the "Lord of both the dead and the living," and another handful of the firstfruits of his resurrection power is plucked by his hand. Thus is the resurrection presented to us as the awaking of a little child, for in his view the dead "but sleepeth." Who can wonder that "they were amazed straightway with great amazement"? But this instance of open and avowed faith is for ever intertwined with an example of hidden faith of equal strength, though less obtrusive. The faith of the woman was hidden "within herself," its ingenuity only was showed, in that she came "in the crowd behind, and touched his garment." Surely this was not faith in the touch which was the supposed appropriate medium, the contact judged to be needful by the many that "pressed upon him that they might touch him." This, if a suitable sign, was not a necessary one, as the faith at least of one declared; "but say the word, and my servant shall be healed." All faith in the nostrums of physicians had died out from this woman's heart, for she had "suffered many things" of them, and was "nothing bettered, but rather grew worse." But in this Healer she did believe, and her faith, which the Lord detected as truly as he "perceived in himself" that the healing power which could proceed from him alone "had gone forth," he amply rewarded. "Who," of the many thronging me, "touched me" with that touch of faith? Faith was united with humility and truth; and "trembling and fearing, she fell down and confessed all." Once more, and for the instruction of the needy in all time, Jesus points to the "faith" thus honoured: it "hath made thee whole." Yes, the faith instrumentally, as our fathers have said, the touch mediately; but in reality, "I have healed thee in response to thy faith—I, who only can say, 'Go in peace, and be whole of thy plague.'" Hence are we to learn: 1. The power of Christ to raise the dead and to heal the sick, so that we may sleep calmly in death till he bid us arise. 2. His pitiful consideration towards even struggling faith, whether assailed by the rude doubt, "It is too late," or is too timid to declare itself openly. So that they of little faith need not doubt. 3. The true attitude of suffering in its confident approach to Christ for healing and help; even patient trustfulness, fearing not, and though persistent, yet humble. 4. The real support of all faith, the word of Christ, with such patient consideration of his works as leads to an apprehension of his Divine ability. May we not now stretch out our hand and touch him?—G.

Vers. 1—20.—*Christ, the Redeemer of the intellect.* I. THE EXTREME OF HUMAN

DEGRADATION AND MISERY. Bondage, impotent violence, suicidal mania. We cannot make out a theory of the facts; the facts are certain, and sad enough in this as in that age. There may be a *duplicity* in the consciousness of man, so that the being is threatened with a rending asunder. There is a certain reflection of this duplicity in all of us.

II. VIOLENT CONFLICT PRECEDES HAPPY CHANGE. There are crises when we dread the presence of the power of good; it means a sharp struggle at hand in the depths of the soul for our very life. Men will sometimes endure the present misery rather than undergo the pain which is to cure it. But the surgeon is no cruel tormentor; nor is the faithful teacher of the truth to be feared, but loved.

III. THE BLESSING OF A SOUND MIND. It may be lost; thank God it may be recovered. As there are parasites which prey upon the lower forms of animal and vegetable life, so there are ideas which may possess the imagination and confound the whole conscious life of the soul. Nowhere do we find the hope of *salvation* in all its senses, from physical and moral maladies, and those inscrutable to science, so clearly held out as in the gospel.

IV. THE DIVINE POWER AND PITY. "Tell thy friends how much the Lord has done for thee, and that he pitied thee." Power and pity fused in love: this is the soul of the world, the principle of its redemption. It has infused its strong enchantment into nature, and healing is ever open to us if we will yield to its influence on our being.—J.

Vers. 25—34.—*The magic of faith.* I. THE CURE OF THE SICK WOMAN RESEMBLES A MAGICAL CURE. Magical belief universally prevailed. The principle of it was, an operation on the nervous system through the wishes and the imagination. A representation in the mind of a cure is assumed, and acted on as a reality. So mysterious and great is the power of imagination over the mechanism of life, that cures might occasionally occur without any real cause external to the sufferer's mind.

II. BUT HERE THERE WAS A REAL CAUSE AT WORK. Coincident with the touch of the woman was the knowledge of curing virtue going forth from him, in the mind of Christ. Here is something impossible to explain—a connection that defies thought; but a real connection. And the great general lesson remains. Every change in the mind from sickness to health implies the correspondence of a thought on the sufferer with a reality without him. Whenever and however the energy of God is reflected as a thought of reality or a faith in us, a change for the better must and will occur.—J.

Vers. 35—43.—*Life victorious.* I. LIFE IN ITS FULNESS KNOWS NO FEAR. Cruel anxieties for the life of those we love are hushed by the voice of Jesus. He ignores death, being the resurrection and the life. We are under a deception of the senses, which Christ saw through. "The child did not die, but is sleeping." From another point of view our saddest facts may be lustrous with the significance of joy.

II. LIFE IS COMMANDING. "I say, Arise!" And the words are instantly obeyed. Richer as a parable than as a mere story. The fact is soon exhausted; the allegory is infinite. The voice is ever speaking, and resurrections are ever taking place. Lost joys are being recovered, dead forms reanimated. Who knows, as the Greek asked, whether what we call dying be not living, and living dying? But where Christ is, there is no death, no loss; only change from less life to more.—J.

Vers. 1—20. Parallel passages: Matt. viii. 28—34; Luke viii. 26—40.—*Gadarene or Gergesene demoniacs.* I. CURE OF THE GADARENE DEMONIAC. 1. *The district.* The country called Gilead in the Old Testament, at a later period and in the New Testament goes by the name of Peræa. It was south of Bashan, and formed a sort of peninsula, bounded by the Yarmuck (anciently Hieromax) on the north, Arnon (now Wady el Mojeb) on the south, and Jordan on the east. The part of Gilead between the Yarmuck and Jabbok at present Wady Zurka, is now *Jebel Ajlun*; while the section south of the Jabbok is the Belka. In this region was a district called Decapolis, from the fact of its being studded over with ten cities, all, except Scythopolis, east of the Jordan. Of these cities one was Gadara, identified with the ruins of *Um Keis*, the capital of Peræa;

while Gergesa was the name of a little town, identified with the present Kerza, on the Wady Semakh, opposite Magdala. Either the territory adjacent was named after one or other of these towns, or St. Mark and St. Luke give a general indication of the district that was the scene of the miracle, when they call it the country of the Gadarenes; while St. Matthew gives the exact name, when he places it in the country of the Gergesenes. Dr. Thomson, in 'The Land and the Book,' says, "The city itself where it was wrought was evidently on the shore. . . . And in this Gersa, or Chersa, we have a position which fulfils every requirement of the narratives, and with a name so near that in Matthew as to be in itself a strong corroboration of the truth of this identification. It is within a few rods of the shore, and an immense mountain rises directly above it, in which are ancient tombs, out of some of which the two men possessed of the devils may have issued to meet Jesus. The lake is so near the base of the mountain, that the swine, rushing madly down it, could not stop, but would be hurried on into the water and drowned. . . . Take your stand a little south of this Chersa. A great herd of swine, we will suppose, is feeding on this mountain that towers above it. They are seized with a sudden panic, rush madly down the almost perpendicular declivity, those behind tumbling over and thrusting forward those before; and, as there is neither time nor space to recover on the narrow shelf between the base and the lake, they are crowded headlong into the water and perish." The name Gergesa has led to the supposition that the Girgashites, one of the seven Canaanitish nations, originally occupied this territory. Be this as it may, the district was pleasantly situated east and southeast of the Sea of Galilee, and the towns of Gadara and Gergesa were flourishing. The former was much the larger, and, according to Josephus, was rich—he says, "Many of the citizens of Gadara were rich men"—while that of Gergesa was of considerable importance. 2. *A sad contrast.* We cannot forbear noticing, as we pass, how much wretchedness may exist at the same time and in the same place with material wealth and mercantile prosperity, and amid all the beauties of natural scenery. This world itself all through is a strange mixture of mercy and of wrath; of the beautiful and the terrible; of plenty and of poverty; of sorrow and of joy; of sunshine and of shower. No April day was ever more variable. Here, in the country of the Gadarenes, with its well-to-do and wealthy inhabitants, and their profitable herds of swine, were two wretched creatures in extreme misery, both mental and bodily. While others bought and sold and got gain, these creatures were a terror to themselves and all around. While others occupied comfortable dwellings, these unfortunates tenanted sepulchral caverns which abounded in the district, and of which, as we have seen, some remain to the present day. While others were decently clad, or even gorgeously attired, these miserable individuals refused the decency of raiment. While others went at large, enjoying the sweets of life and that liberty which makes life sweet, these demoniacs had to be bound with chains and fetters (πέδαις, equivalent to shackles for the feet, and ἁλύσεσι, equivalent to chains in general). 3. *The number accounted for.* St. Matthew mentions two; St. Mark and St. Luke speak of one. How are we to explain this? The one mentioned by two of the evangelists was fiercer than his fellow; he was wilder and worse than the other. Or perhaps he had belonged to a higher class in society, and had moved in a better rank of life; or perhaps his position had been in some respect more prominent, whether owing to wealth, or profession, or education; and so the calamity that had befallen him was more conspicuous, and he himself better known. Something of this sort seems hinted at by St. Luke, when he speaks of the demoniac who met Jesus, as "a certain man *out of the city.*" At all events, from any or all these causes St. Luke separates his case from the other, and singles him out from his comrade in affliction. 4. *A distinct feature added by each evangelist.* St. Matthew tells us that they made the way impassable for travellers; St. Luke, that he was without clothing; and St. Mark, in the passage specially under consideration, that he cried night and day, and cut himself with stones. St. Matthew's narrative of this case is somewhat meagre, St. Luke's fuller, and St. Mark's more circumstantial than either. 5. *The period in particular of demoniac possession.* That demoniac possession was distinct from disease, or lunacy, or epilepsy, is sufficiently evident from a single Scripture, namely, Matt. iv. 24, where we read that they " brought unto him all sick people that were taken with divers diseases and torments, and those which were possessed with devils, and those which were lunatic, and those that had the palsy; and he healed them." If asked why demoniac possession so manifested itself at the time of our Lord's appearance on earth, and not before, nor at least in the same way since? we must simply reply, in addition to what we have formerly said on this subject, that we can no more tell this than we can tell why small-pox manifested itself as a terrible scourge to our race at a certain time, and not sooner; or why cholera ravaged Europe at a certain period since the beginning of this century, and not before; or why that fearful plague, which the Greek historian has described with such graphic power and thrilling effect, never visited them till the time of the Peloponnesian war, and has never returned again, as far as history informs us, to renew its work of desolation there. But, though Scripture does not explicitly specify the cause, we can readily suppose a reason which has the appearance at least of probability. That reason we have already alluded to as found in Satan's well-authenticated powers of imitation, and we shall only subjoin in this place a few additional circumstances to confirm its probability. In early times, when the Lord afflicted Egypt with his plagues, and his servants, Moses and Aaron, wrought miracles in the field of Zoan, Satan had his servants there also, and Jannes and Jambres either possessed or pretended the power to work miracles too, counterfeiting or counteracting to the utmost of their capacity those of Moses and Aaron. From time to time, in the subsequent history of Israel, the Lord raised up prophets to instruct and forewarn the people; but who can be ignorant of the fact that Satan at times employed his prophets—false prophets to beguile and mislead? When our Saviour was on earth he warned his disciples that false Christs would arise and deceive many. Satan raised them up, and so history confirmed the statement. In like manner, when the Lord Jesus Christ had taken to himself a true body and a reasonable soul—when the Word was made flesh, and dwelt among men—Satan, by himself or by his servants, took possession of the bodies of men, cruelly torturing their flesh and agonizing their spirit. Nor are we prepared to say that demoniac possession has altogether ceased. We have seen men so act, and heard men so speak, and have been informed of such fiendish atrocity on their part, that we could account for their violent and outrageous conduct, or for their mischievous and diabolical acts, or for their horrid and blasphemous expressions, in no other way than that some demon, or the devil himself, had been permitted to take temporary possession of them.

II. THE PAST HISTORY OR PREVIOUS STATE OF THIS DEMONIAC. 1. *His madness.* When we compare and combine the account given of this poor demoniac by St. Mark and St. Luke, as also the brief notice of both demoniacs by St. Matthew, we have a most affecting picture. He had lost his senses and become exceeding fierce, so that no man could tame him, and no man could in safety pass that way. To the folly of the lunatic he had added the furiousness of the madman. Reason had reeled and left the helm; the once goodly ship had lost compass and chart and helmsman; it was drifting along, the sport of furious winds and stormy waves. 2. *His wretchedness.* This wretched man had not lost life, it is true, but all that could make *life desirable,* or render it happy. Unclothed, uncared for, he had fallen back into the condition of savage life, and to some extent had sunk lower than the brute. Houseless and homeless, he led a vagrant life—now a dweller in the mountains, now a tenant of the tombs. His *agony of mind* was fearful. When not attacking others he acted the part of a self-tormentor. His cries waked the echoes of the mountains, or made the gloom of the sepulchre more dreadful. But cries were insufficient to vent the deep anguish of his spirit. He cut himself with stones, and, by making gashes in his body, sought to transfer his suffering from the mind to the body, or at least divide it between them. All this had *lasted for years,* as it would appear from the statement, "he had devils long time." Neither had he known much of respite or aught of relaxation; "always night and day" this sorrowful and suffering condition continued; no lucid interval that we read of; no pleasant period of relief, however short, that we know of. At times, moreover, he was deprived of his *liberty.* This had frequently occurred. "He had often been bound with fetters and chains," until, by a sort of superhuman power, he plucked them asunder or broke them in pieces. 3. *The lessons to be learnt from all this.* There are two lessons to be learnt from this part of the subject. The *first* lesson we may learn from it is the condition of the sinner, and the *second* is the hostility of Satan. Confining attention to the first, while we have examined the condition of the demoniac as a fact—a stern fact, and a sad one—we cannot help thinking that it furnishes us at the same time with a figure of what the sinner more or less is. He may, indeed, have the use of all his faculties, both of mind and body; nevertheless, he is a fool. "The fool hath said in his heart, There is no God." He is beside himself; for we read of the prodigal, on his repentance and return to his father's house, that " he came to himself." Was ever folly greater than that of the man who prefers the trifles of time to the realities of eternity; who day by day barters the salvation of the soul for some gratification of sense; who, amid all the uncertainty of life, braves the danger of delay; who, notwithstanding the shortness of time, neglects from one season of opportunity to another, from one period of existence to another, the things that belong to his peace? What madness can equal his who treats all these things as though they were cunningly devised fables; who turns his back on God and his Word, on the sabbath and the sanctuary, on prayer and praise; who trifles with the great things of God until death stares him in the face, entertaining the vain fancy that a few tears, or prayers, or sighs on the bed of death will reverse all the past, make amends for a life of sin, and serve as a passport to heaven? That man is a demoniac in very fact, whom Satan so possesses, so leads captive at his will, and whose eyes he so blinds, that, though Providence is speaking with many a solemn voice; though his own frailty is pleading with him in the silence of his chamber, and during the night-watches; though mortality in sundry ways forces itself on his attention; though conscience is upbraiding, until it becomes so seared that it upbraids no longer; though the Spirit of grace is striving, as he has been striving long; though the Saviour with outstretched arms is saying, "Come, come and welcome," "Come unto me, all ye that labour and are heavy laden, and I will give you rest;" though the eternal Father is waiting to embrace the returning penitent, and swearing, "As I live, I have no pleasure in the death of the wicked;"—yet that sinner, in spite of all, keeps running along the downward way to hell, plunging deeper and deeper into wretchedness, rushing upon ruin, and rushing at the same time against the thick bosses of Jehovah's buckler. If you exhort him, he is sullen; if you remonstrate with him, he is offended; if you reprove him, he is outrageous; if you speak plainly, yet affectionately, it may be he returns a surly answer, proving himself to be what Scripture describes, as "such a son of Belial, that a man cannot speak to him." What though he is neither naked, nor houseless, nor dwelling among the tombs, nor bound with fetters! Are not the fetters of sin the worst that ever bound any man? "What fruit had ye then in those things whereof ye are now ashamed? for the end of those things is death." Has not a course of iniquity clothed thousands in rags, yea, left them without anything like decent clothes at all? Has not drunkenness, or lewdness, or idleness left hundreds without either house or home? Does not wilful waste make woeful want? Who can ever forget the story of the prodigal, when " he would fain have filled his belly with the husks which the swine did eat," when "no man gave unto him," and when he said, "I perish with hunger"? Has not the devil's service brought many a man to his tomb, humanly speaking, before his time? for the wicked do not live half their days. We need not speak of the misery which the sinner feels when the iron enters into his soul, the bitter regret, the unavailing remorse, the terrors of conscience, the second death, and the smoke of their torment ascending up for ever and ever.

III. THE PRESENT CONDITION OF THE CURED DEMONIAC. 1. *The great change.* "The unclean spirits went out;" or, as St. Luke expresses it, "Then went the devils out of the man." Here was a practical exemplification of the Saviour entering into the strong man's house and spoiling his goods. The strong man was expelled by One stronger than himself. His terrible hold was loosened, his power paralyzed, captivity led captive, and the prey taken from the mighty. It is thus with every one who has been rescued from the grasp of Satan, who has been "snatched as a brand out of the burning," who has been convinced of sin and its attendant miseries and everlasting wretchedness, who has been enlightened with the knowledge of the grace and mercy of the Saviour, whose will has been renewed by the Spirit of God, and who has thus been made willing in the day of Divine power. Oh that the time may soon come, when in every land, and through all parts of the habitable globe, God in his great mercy shall open the blind eyes, and smite the fetters off the gyved limbs, and emancipate the oppressed of Satan, setting the captives for ever free! 2. *Evidences of the change.* People were curious to see the mighty miracle that had been wrought, and came to Jesus to see the strange sight about which, no doubt, they had heard much. And, arriving at the place, they "see him that was possessed with the devil, and had the legion, *sitting*." Ah! there is a change, and clear evidence of it. What a subject for a painting! The madman is come to his right mind; the maniac is tamed; reason, that godlike faculty, is restored; his fierceness is subdued. The anguish of his spirit has subsided; his wild cries have ceased; his self-inflicted bodily pains—those shocking wounds—are healed. People talk of the man who could tame the most savage horses, and hold them for a time as if spell-bound; they speak of menagerie-men who can tame lions and conquer bears; they laud the poet's comic humour in his piece entitled 'The Taming of the Shrew;' but the taming of shrew, or lion, or bear, or horse is nothing compared with the taming of this demoniac man, or of any other man whose fierce passions have been let loose, whose soul and body have been subjected to Satan's sway, and whose wicked and wayward career has been marked with as bad, if not worse, than demoniac madness. There he sits! as though the lion had become a lamb; as though the tiger had forgotten his fury, and laid aside his fierceness; as though the bear had changed its nature, and become a mild domestic creature—an emblem of that better day when all men shall become such, and a foreshadow of that coming time which the prophet describes so beautifully, when "the wolf also shall dwell with the lamb, and the leopard shall lie down with the kid; and the calf and the young lion and the fatling together." 3. *His posture a proof of docility.* There he sits, *with the docility* of the child and the guileless simplicity of the Christian. There he sits, as Saul did in the days of his youth, an apt scholar at the feet of Gamaliel. Rather, there he sits, as Mary, at the feet of the same Saviour who bestowed on her the high encomium, "One thing is needful: and Mary hath chosen the good part, that shall not be taken away from her." There he sits, with thoughtful countenance and attentive mind, and listening ear, to drink in every word that falls from the Saviour's lips. There he sits, humbly at the Saviour's feet, while his eye rests placidly on that Saviour's face, as though he said, "Lord, how I love thee for all thy grace to me! Lord, what wilt thou have me to do, that I may express that warm love which glows in my breast, and exhibit the effects of that wondrous grace?" It is thus with every converted sinner. We sit at Jesus' feet, and whether he speaks himself to us in his Word, or by his servants who preach to us from that Word, or by his Spirit who applies that Word, it is all the same. Willingly we will lose no lesson, we will miss no opportunity, we will neglect no means of grace, where we expect that Jesus will manifest himself to our souls and talk to us by the way, opening to us the Scriptures. The whole of the hundred and nineteenth psalm is a commentary on this teachableness of spirit, and willingness to sit at the Master's feet; vers. 33—40 inclusive may be specially read in this connection. Down to old age we will sit at the Saviour's feet, in order to learn of him. Like Simeon, like Anna, like the picture of the righteous set before us in the ninety-second psalm, "The righteous shall flourish like the palm tree: he shall grow like a cedar in Lebanon." Now, who are they, and where are they, that flourish so? "Those that be planted in the house of the Lord shall flourish in the courts of our God." And when and why do they flourish so? "They shall still bring forth fruit in old age," and "to show that the Lord is upright." We are bound to make all due allowance for the decay of nature and such weakness as is incident to the decline of life; but it is distressing to find at times the aged magnifying their infirmities as an excuse for absenting themselves from the house of God; worse still, perhaps, when they stay away without pretending any excuse. It is one of the worst signs; for none that ever truly followed the Lord in youth or in maturity ever forsook him in old age. We remember well seeing a very old man, much above ninety years of age, helped into his pew in church every sabbath; and there was the patriarchal man leaning on his staff, as he sat at Jesus' feet, a devout and venerable and earnest worshipper. Even when age may have blunted the faculties and dulled the hearing, it is still our duty to forsake not the assembling of ourselves with the people of God. We knew the case of a deaf man who, though he could not hear a word preached, came regularly to church, because, as he said, he could see to read the psalms and lessons and other parts of the service, and in any case could help the attendance by his presence and example. 4. *His place of safety was there.* This demoniac sat at Jesus' feet *for safety*. May we suppose that he had heard of the man, of whom we read in the parallel passage of another Gospel (Luke xi.), from whom the unclean spirit, having gone out, came back again with seven other spirits more wicked than himself, and entered in and dwelt there, so that "the last state of that man was worse than the first"? At all events, he felt that there was no safety but in nearness to Christ; and this is the proper sentiment for every follower and friend of Jesus to entertain. When Peter followed Christ afar off, Peter fell. Nearness to Christ is safety, separation or distance from him is insecurity and danger. We need his grace, for by it we stand; his strength, for by it we are fortified against temptation; his blood, for by it we are cleansed, and we need a fresh application of it daily; his sacrifice, it is the ground of our acceptance, and we must look to it always; his example, it must be our daily pattern; his faith, "the life which we now live in the flesh we must live by the faith of the Son of God, who loved us and gave himself for us;" his person, "Christ in you, the hope of glory;" his presence, it is our comfort, for he has said, "I will never leave thee nor forsake thee;" his protection, that, where Satan would sift us as wheat, he may intercede for us, that our faith fail not; his love, to keep up the flame, that would otherwise burn low or go out altogether. 5. *His clothing evidence of restored sanity.* He was sitting as a scholar at Jesus' feet, as also for safety, as we have seen; he was *clothed*, and in his right mind, the former being, as well as his sitting, evidence of the latter. We dislike and disapprove of those naked figures which we see in books and paintings and statues; of whatever use they may be to the anatomist or painter or statuary, they are, we think, unsuitable to Christian refinement and inconsistent with Christian purity. Their usefulness to people in general is questionable. The passions of fallen humanity are bad enough of themselves, and in their own nature, without exciting them. The demoniac cured by our Lord is clothed; the sinner converted to Christ is clothed likewise. When brought to the foot of the cross, and seated at the feet of Jesus, he is clothed. He has on the "fine linen, clean and white," which is "the righteousness of saints." He is "found in Christ, not having on his own righteousness, which is of the Law, but that which is by the faith of Christ, the righteousness of God by faith." He has obeyed the precept, accepted the advice, feeling the benefit of the counsel, "I counsel thee to buy of me gold tried in the fire, that thou mayest be rich; and white raiment, that thou mayest be clothed, and that the shame of thy nakedness do not appear; and anoint thine eyes with eyesalve, that thou mayest see." A practical question is here suggested. Do you, reader, possess that robe? It is put on by the hand of faith. Have you that precious faith? If not—if you have not already "good hope through grace," pray for that faith. Do not be ashamed or afraid to do so. Do not neglect or delay to ask it. Ask the Holy Spirit to work faith in your heart, and so unite you to Christ, for "if any man be in Christ, he is a new creature;" and God gives his Holy Spirit to them that ask him. 6. *Restoration to reason.* His mind is right about sin, as "that abominable thing which God hates," and hurtful to man as hateful to God; right about Satan, "as a roaring lion, seeking whom he may devour"—"a murderer from the beginning;" right about the Saviour, as "the chief among ten thousand, and altogether lovely;" and right about holiness, as the way of happiness and the way to heaven.

IV. THE POWER THAT RESCUED THE DEMONIAC FROM WRETCHEDNESS AND RUIN. 1. *The greatness of that power.* The possession of this demoniac was something singularly shocking. It was not one demon, but many, that had made him their prey. "My name," he said, "is Legion: for we are many." The name is a Latin name, and denotes a levying or enlisting, then, a body of troops so levied. The full complement of a Roman legion was six thousand infantry, and a squadron of three hundred cavalry. Each legion was divided into ten cohorts; each cohort into three maniples; and each maniple into two centuries. Then again, when arrayed in order of battle, there were three lines—Principes, Hastati, and Triarii. What a formidable host! How powerful, and how numerous! The host and the hostility, the multitude and the enmity, the strength and the skill thus conveyed by the name here applied to the demons which had had possession of this man, are fearful to contemplate. Yet the power of Christ expelled them, mighty, multitudinous, and malicious though they were. It was the power of Christ did it all. Demons owned that power. They had faith in him, but not of the right sort; "they believed and trembled." So here they feared he was coming to judge them and consign them to torment before the time. Jesus has the self-same power still; "he is able to save to the uttermost all that come unto God by him." 2. *The miserable home of those demons.* They would rather go anywhere than

go home. They trembled at the power of Christ, while they dreaded the torments he
will one day inflict. They would rather enter into swine, rather go into the sea, rather
go into the worst and filthiest spot of earth, than go back into the deep abyss of hell.
It was not the abyss of earth or the abyss of ocean, but the abysmal depth of that
unfathomed pit of hell, which they so much dreaded. And oh! are sinners not afraid
of rushing with eyes open into that dreadful, deep abyss? 3. *Their fiendish malice.*
Now that they are cast out, and can no longer destroy their victim, they are actuated
by demon-like malevolence, and try to keep others from the Saviour by causing the loss
of their swine. In this way they seek to prejudice and even enrage them against the
Saviour. They seem to have succeeded, for the Gadarenes "began to pray him to depart
out of their coasts." 4. *The sufferings of the brute creation.* Why, it may naturally
enough be asked, are poor dumb animals subjected to sufferings? Or how is it possible
that the demons could exert any influence of the kind stated upon them? In reply
to the latter question, it may be sufficient to mention the influence which man exerts
upon animals such as the dog, the horse, the elephant, in the way of training and
teaching. If animals are thus receptive of human influence, why should they not be
receptive of other and, in some respects, more powerful influence? Why should they
not be accessible to, and receptive of, demoniac influence, as well as that of men? The
other question stands on different ground. The lower animals, placed under man's
control at the first, and granted to man for useful service, share to some extent in man's
varying fortunes, and are entitled to humane and kind treatment at the hands of man;
but that they suffered in consequence of man's fall and sin is, we think, unquestionable.
Their position now is abnormal just as man's own position is abnormal, for does not "the
whole creation groan and travail in pain together until now"? Besides, they often suffer,
in common with man, in special disasters—such as conflagrations, shipwrecks, and
catastrophes of similar kinds. 5. *A mixture of mercy and judgment.* While mercy
was shown to the demoniac in his miraculous cure, judgment was inflicted on the
owners of the swine for their sin. Jesus performed the act of mercy, and permitted the
exercise of the other. The demons could not have moved an inch without his permission.
This side of the miracle was judgment, and well deserved. Who were these Gadarenes
or Gergesenes? Were they Gentiles or were they Jews? If the former—if Gentiles,
they were tempting their Jewish neighbours, and they had no right to do that. If they
were Jews, they were breaking the Law of God, and they could not long expect to
prosper, and to continue doing that. If they were Jewish proprietors, who employed
Gentile swineherds for the purpose of tending and herding their swine, they were both
sinning themselves and tempting others to sin; and so both partook of the result and
shared the consequences of their crime. Here, too, we must notice the hardening effect
of sin long persevered in. These Gadarenes, whatever their nationality, whether Jew
or Gentile, had become like swine themselves—swinish in spirit and disposition. They
actually preferred their swine to the Saviour, and "besought him to depart out of their
coasts!"—J. J. G.

Vers. 21—43. Parallel passages: Matt. ix. 18—26; Luke viii. 41—56.—*Touching in the throng.* I. THE WOMAN WITH AN ISSUE OF BLOOD. 1. *A painful disease.*
The woman mentioned in this section had been a sorely afflicted sufferer. For
twelve long and weary years she had suffered from a painful and weakening malady
(ἐν ῥύσει, the preposition ἐν here resembles the *beth essentiæ* of Hebrew, denoting
in the capacity, character, or *condition* of, *i.e.* in the condition of an issue). During
that time, we may well suppose, she had sought every means of cure; and found
none. During that time she had applied to various physicians; but obtained no
relief. During that time she had, no doubt, taken many a bitter draught and many
a nauseous drug; but all to no purpose. During that time she had, doubtless, submitted to many severe experiments or even some harsh operations; but all in vain.
During that time she had expended much, yea, all her means; she "had spent,"
we are told, "all her living upon physicians," and that *in addition* to her sufferings,
as is implied by the prepositional element in the word (προσαναλώσασα) employed
by St. Luke; while St. Mark tells us plainly in this passage that she "had suffered
many things of many physicians, and had spent all that she had." And now she
remains poor and destitute, diseased and weak, and miserable as ever; for she "was

nothing bettered, but rather *grew worse;*" "neither could be healed of any." What is she now to do? Where is she to seek relief? To whom can she further go? Is there any application she can yet make? Or is there any remedy still remaining to be tried? 2. *One resource yet remains.* She has tried all the physicians; she has tried all means of cure that have been prescribed, or suggested, or that she has ever heard of; she has, besides, spent her all in quest of health. Still one, and only one, remains to be tried. She has heard of a wondrous Man who goes about continually, doing good; she has been told of most wonderful cures he has effected; of diseases, previously deemed incurable, which he has healed; of sufferers whom, when all else failed, he has relieved. She has never seen him, it is true—she has only heard of him; but what of that? Though she has not seen him, she has no reason to doubt the reports she has heard of him; she has no reason to doubt the greatness of his power and the might of his mercy, in accordance with these reports; she believes the accuracy of these reports, she has somehow confidence in their correctness. She has schooled herself into faith in his power to effect her cure and heal her disease. 3. *Obstacles to be overcome.* A difficulty here presents itself. Her disease is peculiar— such a one as she is loth to name in public. She cannot bring herself to talk of it in presence of so many people; womanly delicacy forbids her. Besides, it was such a disease as caused ceremonial uncleanness, so that her contact was polluting. People would, not without reason, upbraid her for coming among them, or thrust her away from them, as impure and contaminating. 4. *A happy thought.* A happy thought occurred to her in her difficult position—a thought which we may regard at once as the outcome of strong faith, and the suggestion of deep affliction. It flashed on her mind as a bright idea. She had heard that the great Physician, to whom her thoughts now turned, often accomplished his cures and conferred health by a touch. She naturally infers that if she could but touch him even stealthily, her cure would be effected. Accordingly she conceived the thought of stealing a cure; she thought within herself, "If I may touch but his clothes," or his garment, or even the border of it, "I shall be whole." 5. *Pressure of the crowd.* Our Lord at this time was on his way to the house of Jairus, the ruler of the synagogue, in order to cure his daughter. The crowd that followed him on the occasion was unusually large. It was drawn together by respect for the distinguished official whose daughter was so ill, as also by the remembrance of past miracles, and the prospect of seeing the performance of another. Dense as the crowd was, she kept to her purpose, pressing onward through it, and elbowing her way till she had got up to his very side. 6. *The cure effected, but concealment impossible.* She attains her object; she touches the hem of his garment, and all at once—strange circumstance! blessed relief!—the malady of many years' standing is healed, the issue is staunched, the pain and grief have ceased. But a disquieting circumstance still remains; a matter of some uneasiness has now to be got over. She is cured, it is true, but she is struck with terror at her own temerity; she is filled with alarm when she sees Jesus looking round inquisitively (περιεβλέπετο, imperfect, equivalent to "he kept looking all round"), and hears him earnestly asking those about him, "Who touched me?" She knew that her touch was polluting; she was well aware that it conveyed ceremonial defilement. She had, indeed, only touched the hem —the extreme border of his garment, as if in hope that so slight a touch would defile him but little, while it might benefit her so much. 7. *Astonishment of the bystanders.* The persons next our Lord in the crowd were amazed at the question; some would be disposed to say in reply, "All touched thee," and others, again, would be inclined to think and to say, when they gave expression to their thought, "None touched thee." At length, after all had denied, Peter as usual, acting as spokesman of the disciples, said, "Master, the multitude throng thee and press thee [συνθλίβοντα, equivalent to 'pressing greatly, or pressing upon on every side'], and sayest thou, Who touched me?" "Not so," says our Lord; "all the persons in this large crowd do indeed throng and press around me, and yet but one touched me—'somebody touched me.'" 8. *Surprising graciousness of the Saviour.* Our Lord looked round to discover the one individual in all that crowd who had touched him. At last his eye rested on the abashed, affrighted woman; when, lo! instead of a rebuke for her temerity, instead of a sharp reproof for her audacity, instead of a harsh reprimand for her polluting touch, instead of blaming her for her presumption, instead of a single unkind expression of any sort, he commends her faith, confirms her cure, ratifies her desire, and gladdens her heart by these most gracious words, " Daughter, be of good comfort: thy faith hath made thee whole; go in peace."

II. THE PECULIARITY OF THIS WOMAN'S TOUCH. 1. *There must be contact.* The first thing we are taught by it is that, in coming to Christ and in seeking cure from him, there must be not merely *contiguity* but actual contact, and that of a peculiar kind. All the persons in the great crowd that followed our Lord on this occasion were near him comparatively, some were quite close to him; yet only one derived benefit from him. There were, moreover, several, we can scarcely doubt, in that multitude who needed some temporal boon or spiritual blessing; yet only one obtained such a blessing. There were numbers of persons all around and on every side of him; yet virtue proceeded from him only in one direction. Not only so; *mere contact itself* is not sufficient. Intelligent connection—special and spiritual contact—is needed. There were many crowding on and crushing our Saviour, yet only one touched him in the true and proper sense. The motives that moved that multitude were various. Some were borne thoughtlessly along with the mass of persons that formed the procession; they went with the crowd. Others, and perhaps the major part, were attracted by curiosity—they were desirous of seeing some miracle; or they had itching ears, and hoped to hear some startling statement. Others, again, were, no doubt, drawn into the crowd by feelings of admiration for the Saviour. While various motives thus actuated the individuals that composed that crowd—the units that made up that multitude; only one, it would seem, was influenced by the right motive; only one approached the Saviour in the right way; only one at that time was healed. 2. *Her feelings and her faith.* That one individual felt the misery of her condition, the iron had entered deeply into her soul; that one felt intensely her need of health. That one, besides, had resolved to overcome every obstacle in order to obtain relief. That one, also, was fully persuaded that Christ could confer health and cure. Nay, she felt assured that, as he frequently touched the persons cured by him, a touch of his person, or even of his clothes, or if it were but of the border of his garment or of the fringe of his robe, would make her whole. Now, here was *faith*—true faith, strong faith; and this faith it was that made the difference between her touch and that of the crowd that pressed upon him—between the multitude that *thronged* him and the woman that *touched* him. Others touched him, but their touch was incidental; hers was intentional. Others touched him, but it was owing to the pressure around; hers was from a deliberate purpose within. Others touched him, not feeling any need of help at his hand, or, if they felt any need, yet not expecting any relief in that way; she touched him, conscious of her malady and convinced of his power to effect her cure. Others touched him, but then it was curiosity, chance as the world calls it, the crowd, the multitude, the pressure that brought them into such close proximity to Christ; she touched him, but it was the result of deliberation on her part, design, earnest purpose, strong desire, anxious hope of cure, and confident expectation of deliverance. There was thus all the difference in the world between the thronging of that multitude and the touching of that invalid. Faith is thus seen to be the means of union with Christ, and union not mechanical and physical, but union rational and spiritual. We may approach him by ceremonies, by profession, by lifeless prayers, by dead works; but in none of these cases do we really touch him: and not coming into living contact with him, we cannot expect to be recognized by him. 3. *An example worth imitation.* We may profit by the example of this poor invalided woman as contrasted with that great crowd. We cannot agree with those who disapprove of thronging the Saviour, while they approve of touching him. We approve of both. It is good to be in the throng that crowds round Christ, if only one should be healed at a time, for you yourself may be that one, while all that are far from him shall perish. It is good to be near the pool of Bethesda, for some one is sure to be cured every time the angel troubles the waters, and you yourself may be the happy individual. It is good to wait at the posts of wisdom's door, for that is the way of duty, and the way of duty is the way of safety. But while it is good to be in the crowd that throngs Christ, it is better—far better to touch Christ. There must be real union—complete connection with Christ. The electric telegraph, one of the greatest wonders of a marvellous age—those wonderful wires that pass over lands and under seas, connecting Ireland with Britain, and Britain with the Continent, and one continent with another; that link the Old World with the New, flashing its messages over more than half the globe, thus facilitating the intercommunion of nations, and expediting the exchange of intelligence from East to West and from West to East;—if those electric wires stretched from one place on the earth's surface to another hundreds of miles remote, and if they reached very near to that other place, just within a yard, or a foot, or an inch, and yet stopped short by that small interval; no communion could be carried on, and no intelligence conveyed. Its hundreds of miles of extent would be unavailing; that yard, or foot, or inch would render the whole useless, and cause all the labour to be lost. It might as well stretch only three-fourths of the way, or one-half the way, or one quarter of the way, or no part of the way at all. Nothing short of a close and complete uniting of the two places, and that without any interval, will do. Alas'! how many come close up to Christ, but never close with him. How many are in the throng that never touch him! How many there are like the young man in the Gospel—that amiable young man whom our Lord loved, who did so much, and went so far, and yet after all came short! They seem to be very close to Christ, and very near his cross; but there is one link wanting —"One thing thou lackest." How many are at the very threshold of the kingdom of heaven, and ready to say with Agrippa, "Almost thou persuadest me to be a Christian;" and yet they never cross the threshold, nor enter the kingdom, nor become Christians, in the true and proper sense, at all! How many are on the spot at the very time when Christ is passing by, without ever touching so much as the fringe of his garment! How many frequent the place where his presence is promised and his blessing bestowed; and yet they never feel the one nor enjoy the other! There is nourishment in food, but you must partake of it; or the most wholesome food will do you no good and give you no strength. There is sweetness in music, but you must have an ear for it and give ear to it; else the sweetest music will be but mere noise—an empty sound. There is fragrance in the rose, but your olfactory nerves must be sound and sufficiently near the odoriferous flower; or its fragrance will be wasted on desert air! The electric current is a potent agency, as we have seen, but it must needs have the electric wire to pass along; or it loses its practical utility. In view of such facts and considerations, our duty as well as interest is, by grace, to realize union with Christ; we should give no sleep to our eyes, nor slumber to our eyelids, until by grace, through faith, we are united to Christ, and one with him—Christ in us and we in Christ, Christ our life, and our life devoted to Christ. For while Christ is able to save, and waiting and willing to save, and while God sent his Son to seek and save that which was lost; yet there must be faith, or we cannot be saved. Let us, therefore, seek the aid of God's Holy Spirit, that he may form the link of faith between our soul and the Saviour; or, if it already exist, that he may strengthen and brighten it. 4. *How healing virtue is obtainable from Christ.* There was healing power in the Saviour—inherent in him, in him alone, and in none besides. This poor invalid drew it forth by the touch of faith. The virtue to heal that proceeded from Christ may be compared to the electric current, while the faith of the woman may be likened to the wires along which it passed. Now, if faith be the gift of God, as it is, and the operation of his Spirit, as we know from his Word, it may be asked, "Why blame any for the want of it?" We do not, and cannot with fairness, blame for want of it; but we may blame persons for not asking it, for not wishing for it, for not seeking it, or for not accepting it. If God gave his Son before you asked him, and without your asking him, "will he not with him also freely give you all things;" in other words, will he not give you faith in him for the asking? If he have given the greater gift, will he withhold or refuse the less? If he has promised his Spirit to them that ask him, and if he invites us and presses us to ask him, do we not tempt God when we refuse to ask him, seeing it is the Spirit that works faith in the heart of man? We are far, very far, from ignoring or over-looking the sovereign grace of God, whereby he takes one out of a city, and two out of a family, and brings them to Zion: but if we refuse the course that God has prescribed to us; if we reject the conditions on which he offers grace and every mercy; if we neglect the ordinances where he has appointed to meet and bless us, or if, attending them, we forget the object for which we are urged to attend them, or if we use the means without thinking of the great end we should have in view, or if we are not at pains to examine our motives, or if we have no care to meet Christ in his ordinances, no longing for his presence, no thirsting for his grace, no hungering for his righteousness, no earnest inquiry, " What must we do to be saved? " and no seeking of the fulfilment of the promises ;—in all such, or any such cases, are we not thronging Christ instead of touching him? If custom, or curiosity, or the crowd, or habit, or respectability, or worldly advantage, or early training, brings us near to Christ, and if we have no higher object and no holier end in view, are we not thronging Christ, and yet not touching Christ? " Many," we know from the declaration of God's own Word, " will say, Lord, Lord, have we not prophesied in thy name? and in thy name have cast out devils? and in thy name done many wonderful works? And then," adds the Saviour, " will I profess unto them, I never knew you." What was all this more or better than thronging Christ without touching him? 5. *Confession consequent on cure.* She sought Christ privately, but was obliged to confess publicly. So with ourselves; we must confess his name before men, and tell of the gracious Saviour we have found ; just as the psalmist says, " Come and hear, all ye that fear God, and I will declare what he hath done for my soul." " With the heart men believe unto righteousness, and with the mouth make confession unto salvation." 6. *Character of the cure.* The cure was immediate; "from that hour." It was complete; the fountain was staunched. It was perpetual; " Be thou whole." This our Lord probably added lest she should think the cure too sudden to continue, too speedy to last, too good news to be true. Not so; it was no transient remedy, no mere temporary relief. All that God does is well done ; he does not leave any part of his work unfinished. Having " begun a good work in us, he will perform [rather, *perfect*] it till the day of Jesus Christ." The testimony to the Saviour's work on earth was that " he hath done all things well." 7. *Peculiarity of expression.* The words εἰς εἰρήνην are properly " into peace," which refer more to the future than to the present. Peace is not only the present element in which she finds herself, but the future sphere in which her life is to move. Brought into peace by the great Peacemaker, she is ever after to continue therein. The addition of the words ἴσθι ὑγιὴς was not superfluous, but most reassuring, in order to ratify the stolen cure and to convince her of its durability and permanence. Further, we may notice the relation of the πίστις of the woman to the δύναμις of the Saviour. The former saved her *mediately*, or instrumentally, that is, as the connecting link between herself and Christ; the latter was the healing power of Christ, which, working along the line of that faith, saved her as the *energetic* and efficient cause.

III. THE RESTORATION TO LIFE OF JAIRUS'S DAUGHTER. 1. *Position of Jairus.* The official position of Jairus was highly respectable. He was ruler of the synagogue. Though there is some difference of opinion on the subject, yet the officers of the synagogue appear to have been the following :—(1) The ruler or president of the synagogue, on whom devolved the right ordering and regulation of the service, and with whom were conjoined the elders ; (2) the *sheliach tsibbor*, the angel or messenger of the congregation, who offered up the public prayers, and who acted as secretary to conduct the correspondence, or to serve as deputy, when required, between one synagogue and another ; (3) the *chazzan* (ὑπηρέτης), or ordinary reader, who read the appointed portions, or who handed the book to an occasional reader ; he also had charge of the sacred books ; (4) the διάκονος, or sexton. 2. *The substantial harmony of the narratives.* The ruler of the synagogue, according to St. Mark, tells our Lord that his daughter (ἐσχάτως ἔχει) is extremely ill, " at the point of death "—in fact, *in extremis* ; according to St. Matthew, that (ἄρτι ἐτελεύτησεν) she is dead by this time—" even now dead ; " she was so ill when he left that he did not now expect to see her again alive when he returned ; according to St. Luke, that (ἀπέθνησκεν) she was dying, or " lay a dying ; "—all perfectly consistent. 3. *The special tenderness of the parent.* Though St. Mark very frequently employs diminutives with little, if any, difference from the simpler form, yet we see good reason for his use of the diminutive θυγάτριον here. It becomes a term of special endearment and affectionate tenderness in this place, from the circumstance, of which another evangelist, St. Luke, apprises us, namely, that this little girl was an *only* daughter (θυγάτηρ μονογενής), perhaps, indeed most probably, an only child. We can easily imagine the terrible uneasiness of the father, when our Lord had been delayed by the unwelcome incident of the cure of the woman with the bloody issue. Jairus must have looked on this as a most provoking and unpleasant interruption ; and now that the messengers bring word that his daughter is dead, and so his worst fears realized, he and they evidently give up all for lost. The great Healer might have restored her to health, however ill, or however far gone she might have been ; but how can he restore her to life now that she is dead? 4. *Jesus' power over death*. He had heard, or, if we read a compound of the same word, though slightly supported (παρακούσας), he had overheard the conversation between the messengers and Jairus ; he had heard them dissuade the ruler from fatiguing with the length of the journey, or in any other way worrying the Physician (σκύλλεις, root σκῦλον, spoils, means " to spoil, despoil, flay, trouble, harass, or worry "), as it was only bootless labour—quite useless work—for the child was dead. Our Lord tried to revive the father's hopes, encourage his fainting heart, and strengthen his weak faith, saying, " Do not be afraid, only believe." The mourners, especially the hired mourners, who were making so much ado, and beating themselves (ἐκόπτοντο), in grief more seeming than sincere, began to deride our Lord, or laugh him down (κατεγέλων). In fact, they did not wish her restored, lest perhaps their occupation would be gone. Taking the maiden by the hand, he addressed her, in the vernacular Aramaic of the district, saying, " *Talitha cumi*, Maid, arise." Straightway she arose and *walked* ; her motion proved strength, and strength and motion belong to life ; and so death, after all, is a sleep, from which the Saviour brings awakening. His power over every stage of death appears by the restoration of one just departed as this maiden ; of one being carried out to burial, as the son of the widow of Nain; of one already in the grave four days, as Lazarus. 5. *Practical character of our Lord*. When Simon's mother-in-law was cured, she turned to her domestic duties ; when this young girl of twelve years of age was restored, she walked about (περιεπάτει)—how natural! When others wondered, Jesus thought of the keen appetite of the young girl, and ordered her *food*.—J. J. G.

EXPOSITION.

CHAPTER VI.

Ver. 1.—Our Lord now left the neighbourhood of Capernaum, and came into his own country, the district of Nazareth, where he had been, not born indeed, but brought up, and where his kinsfolk after the flesh still lived. Nazareth would be about a day's journey from Capernaum. This was not the first public exercise of his ministry at Nazareth. Of that and its results St. Luke gives us the account (iv. 16). It would seem reasonable to suppose that, after the fame which he had now acquired, he should again visit the place where he had been brought up. His sisters were still living there. St. Mark here again uses the historical present ἔρχεται, "he cometh," for which there is better authority than for ἦλθεν. His disciples follow him. Only the chosen three had been with him in the house of Jairus. The presence of the whole body of the disciples would be valuable at Nazareth.

Ver. 2.—As usual, he made the sabbath the special time for his teaching. And many hearing him were astonished. They were astonished at the ability, the sublimity, the holiness of his teaching, as well as at the signs and wonders by which he confirmed it. "Many" hearing him; not all. Some listened with faith ; but "the many" (there is some authority for οἱ πολλοί) were envious of him. Whence hath this man these things? The expression, "this man," is repeated, according to the best authorities, in the next clause, What is the wisdom that is given (not "unto him," but) unto this man? There is a contemptuous tone about the expression.

Ver. 3.—Is not this the carpenter? St. Matthew (xiii. 55) says, "the carpenter's son." We infer from this that our Lord actually worked at the trade of a carpenter, and probably continued to do so until he entered upon his public ministry. We may also infer that Joseph was now no longer living, otherwise it would have been natural for his name to have been mentioned here. According to St. Chrysostom, our Lord made ploughs and yokes for oxen. Certainly, he often drew his similitudes from these things. "No man putting his hand to the *plough*, and looking back, is fit for the kingdom of God" (Luke ix. 62). "Take my *yoke* upon you, and learn of me" (Matt. xi. 29). Christ was the son of a carpenter. Yes; but he was also the Son of him who made the world at his will. Yea, he himself made the world. "All things were made by him," the Eternal Word. And he made them for us, that we might judge of the Maker by the greatness of his work. He chose to be the son of a carpenter. If he had chosen to be the son of an emperor, then men might have ascribed his influence to the circumstances of his birth. But he chose a humble and obscure condition, for this, among other reasons, that it might be acknowledged that it was his divinity that transformed the world. Is not this the carpenter, the son of Mary, and brother of James, and Joses, and Judas, and Simon? Some have thought that these were literally brethren of our Lord, sons of Joseph and Mary. Others have considered that they were his legal half-brothers, sons of Joseph by a former marriage. This view is held by many of the Greek Fathers, and has something to recommend it. But, on the whole, the most probable opinion is that they were cousins of our Lord—sons of a sister of the Virgin Mary, also called Mary, the wife of Cleophas, Clopas, or Alphæus. There is evidence that there were four sons of Clopas and Mary, whose names were James, and Joses, and Simon (or Symeon), and Judas. Mary the wife of Clopas is mentioned by St. Matthew (xxvii. 56) as the mother of James the Less and of Joses. Jude describes himself (Jude 5) as the brother of James; and Simon, or Symeon, is mentioned in Eusebius as the son of Clopas. It must be remembered also that the word ἀδελφός, like the Hebrew word which it expresses, means not only "a brother," but generally "a near kinsman." In the same way the "sisters" would be cousins of our Lord. According to a tradition recorded by Nicephorus (ii. 3), the names of these sisters or cousins were Esther and Tamar. **And they were offended in him.** They took it ill that one brought up amongst them as a carpenter should set himself up as a prophet and a teacher; just as there are those in every age who are apt to take it amiss if they see any one spring from a trade into the doctor's chair. But these Nazarenes knew not that Jesus was the Son of God, who of his great love for man vouchsafed to take a low estate, that he might redeem us, and teach us humility by his example. And thus this humility and love of Christ, which ought to have excited their admiration and respect, was a stumbling-block to them, because they could not receive it, or believe that God was willing thus to humble himself.

Ver. 4.—**A prophet is not without honour, save in his own country,** etc. One reason for this is that it is almost natural for persons to hold of less account than they ought, those with whom they have been brought up and have lived on familiar terms. Prophets are commonly least regarded, and often most envied, in their own country. However unworthy may be the feeling, the inhabitants of a district, or members of a community, do not like to see one of themselves put above them, more especially a junior over a senior, or a man of humble origin over a man well born. But it should be remembered that God abhors the envious, and will withhold the wonders of his grace from those who grudge his gifts to others. The men of Nazareth, when they saw Christ

eating, and drinking, and sleeping, and working at his trade, like others, despised him when he claimed respect and reverence as a Prophet, and especially because his relations according to the flesh were of humble condition; and Joseph more particularly, whom they supposed to be his real father, for they could not imagine or believe that he was born of a virgin, and had God alone for his Father.

Vers. 5, 6.—**And he could there do no mighty work.** This is a remarkable expression. *He could do no mighty work there.* The words imply want of power—that in some sense or other he was unable to do it. He did indeed perform some miracles. **He laid his hands upon a few sick folk, and healed them;** but he wrought none of his greater miracles there. Of course, even these less striking miracles ought to have sufficed. In a miracle there must be the suspension of some known law of nature; and one clear instance of such suspension ought to be as conclusive as a hundred. Then it must be remembered that it is not God's method in his dealings with his creatures to force conviction upon them when the ordinary means prove insufficient. For men's actions must be free if they are to be made the test of judgment, and they would not be free if God constrained men to obey his will. The men of Nazareth had sufficient evidence had they not chosen to be blinded, and a greater amount of evidence would only have increased their condemnation. So their unbelief thwarted his purposes of mercy, and he went in and out amongst them like one hampered and disabled, marvelling at their unbelief, or rather **marvelling because of their unbelief** (διὰ τὴν ἀπιστίαν αὐτῶν). The condition of mind of these Nazarenes was what caused amazement to the Saviour. At length he turned away from Nazareth, never, so far as we know, to visit it again; for this was their second opportunity, and the second occasion on which they deliberately rejected him. What, however, they refused he immediately offered to others. He was not discouraged. **He went round about the villages teaching.**

Ver. 7.—At ch. iii. 7 we had the account of our Lord's selection of the twelve. Here we find the notice of their being first sent forth. Their names have already been recorded. **He gave them authority**—mark the imperfect (ἐδίδου)—**over unclean spirits.** St. Matthew (x. 1) adds, "and to heal all manner of sickness and all manner of disease." But St. Mark here fixes the attention upon the great central object of Christ's mission—to contend against evil in every form, and especially to grapple with Satan in his stronghold in the hearts of men.

Ver. 8.—**They should take nothing for their journey, save a staff only.** St. Matthew says (x. 10), according to the best authorities (μηδὲ ῥάβδον), they were not to take a staff. St. Luke says the same as St. Matthew. The meaning is that they were not to make any special provision for their journey, but to go forth just as they were, depending upon God. Those who had a staff might use it; those who had not one were not to trouble themselves to procure one. The scrip (πήρα) was the wallet for food. They were to take **no money in their purse** (μὴ εἰς τὴν ζώνην χαλκόν); literally, *brass in their girdle.* St. Mark, writing for Romans, uses this word for money. St. Luke, writing for Greeks, uses the term (ἀργύριον) "silver." St. Matthew (x. 9) says, "provide neither gold, nor silver, nor brass."

Ver. 9.—**But be shod with sandals.** This is quite consistent with what St. Matthew says (x. 9), that they were not to provide themselves with shoes (μηδὲ ὑποδήματα). According to St. Matthew, shoes are forbidden directly; according to St. Mark, they are forbidden by implication, where he says that they were to be shod with sandals. Shoes are here forbidden which cover the whole foot, not sandals which only protect the soles of the feet lest they should be injured by the rocky ground. The soil of Judæa was rocky and rough, and the climate hot. The sandals therefore protected the soles of the feet, and yet, being open above, kept the feet more cool, and therefore fit for the journey. It is worthy of our notice that, after our Lord's ascension, we find St. Peter using sandals when the angel, who delivered him out of prison, said to him (Acts xii. 8), "Gird thyself, and bind on thy sandals."

Ver. 10.—**There abide, till ye depart thence.** They were not to change their lodgings in any place. This direction was given to them, lest, if they did, they might appear to be fickle and restless; or lest they might hurt the feelings of those with whom they had first lodged. And they were not to stay too long anywhere, lest they should be burdensome to any.

Ver. 11.—**Shake off the dust** (τὸν χοῦν)— literally, *the soil*—**that is under your feet.** St. Matthew and St. Luke use the word (κονιορτὸν) "dust." A very significant action. The dust was shaken off as an evidence of the toil and labour of the apostles in journeying to them. It witnessed that they had entered the city and had delivered message, and that their message had been refused. The very dust, therefore, of the place was a defilement to them. "It shall be more tolerable," etc. This clause is omitted by the best authorities; it was probably copied from St. Matthew.

Ver. 12.—**They preached that men should repent.** This was their great work, to which the miracles were subordinate.

Ver. 13.—**And anointed with oil many that were sick, and healed them.** It is hardly possible to separate this from the reference to the use of oil for the sick, in Jas. v. 14. Unction was employed extensively in ancient times for medicinal purposes. It is recorded of Herod the Great by Josephus ('Antiq.,' xvii. 6, 5) that in one of his sicknesses he was "immersed in a bath full of oil," from which he is said to have derived much benefit. The apostles used it, no doubt not only on account of its supposed remedial virtues, but also as an outward and visible sign that the healing was effected by their instrumentality in the name of Christ, and perhaps also because the oil itself was significant of God's mercy, of spiritual comfort and joy— "the oil of gladness." Neither this passage nor that in St. James can properly be adduced to support the ceremony of "extreme unction;" for in both these cases the result was that the sick were restored to health. The so-called sacrament of "extreme unction" is administered immediately before death, when the sick person is *in articulo mortis.*

Ver. 14.—This Herod is called by St. Matthew (xiv. 1) "the tetrarch;" and so also by St. Luke (ix. 7); though it should be noticed that St. Matthew, in the same context, at ver. 9, calls him "king." The word "tetrarch" properly means the sovereign or ruler of the fourth part of a territory. He is known as Herod Antipas, son of Herod the Great, who had appointed him "tetrarch" of Galilee and Peræa. Herod Antipas had married the daughter of Aretas, King of Arabia, but deserted her for the sake of Herodias, his brother Philip's wife. **John the Baptist is risen from the dead;** that is, "is risen in the person of Jesus Christ." St. Luke (ix. 7) says that at first Herod was "much perplexed (διηπόρει)" about him. At length, however, as he heard more and more of the fame of Christ's miracles, he came to the conclusion that our Lord was none other than John the Baptist risen again. Such is the opinion of St. Chrysostom, St. Augustine, and others. At that time the views of Pythagoras respecting the transmigration of souls were generally current, and probably influenced the troubled mind of Herod. He had put to death an innocent and holy man; and it is a high testimony to the worth of the Baptist that, under the reproaches of a guilty conscience, Herod should have come to the conclusion that he had risen from the dead, thus probably giving the lie to his own opinions as a Sadducee; and terrified lest the Baptist should now avenge his own murder. "What a great thing," exclaims St. Chrysostom, "is virtue ! for Herod fears him, even though dead." It should not be forgotten that this is the same Herod who set Jesus at nought and mocked him, when Pilate sent him to him, in the hope of relieving himself of the terrible responsibility of condemning one whom he knew to be innocent.

Ver. 17.—**In prison.** Josephus ('Antiq.,' xviii. 5, 2) informs us that this prison was the fort of Machærus, on the confines of Galilee and Arabia, and that there John was beheaded. Herod's father had built a magnificent palace within that fort ; and so he may have been keeping the anniversary of his birthday there.

Vers. 18, 19.—**For John said unto Herod.** The Greek tense (ἔλεγε) implies more than the simple expression, "he said ; " it implies a repeated warning. We learn from St. Matthew (xiv. 5) that Herod would have killed John before, but he feared the people. Here St. Mark says that **Herodias set herself against him, and desired to kill him ; and she could not ; for Herod feared John.** There is no contradiction between the two evangelists. The case appears to have been this : that at first Herod desired to put John to death, because John had reproved him on account of Herodias. But by degrees John gained an influence over Herod by the force of his character, and by his holy life and teaching.

Ver. 20.—The words in the Authorized Version are, **When he heard him, he did many things** (πολλὰ ἐποίει), **and heard him gladly.** But according to the best authorities the reading should be (πολλὰ ἠπόρει), *he was much perplexed.* In St. Luke, as stated above, we have (διηπόρει), "he was much perplexed." Nor is there any inconsistency in the next clause in St. Mark, if we accept this reading. Herod was not utterly depraved. There was to him a charm, not only in the character, but in the discourses of John the Baptist. But he was an inconsistent man, and was continually the victim of a conflict between the good and the evil within him, in which evil, alas ! triumphed. Herodias, on the other hand, had always wished to get rid of John, as the stern and uncompromising reprover of her adultery and incest ; and so at length she persuaded Herod to give way. "For," says Bede, "she feared lest Herod should at length repent, and yield to the exhortations of John, and dissolve this unreal marriage, and restore Herodias to her lawful husband."

Ver. 22.—The words should run thus : **And when the daughter of Herodias herself came in** (καὶ εἰσελθούσης τῆς θυγατρὸς αὐτῆς τῆς Ἡρωδιάδος). The intention of the evangelist is to point out that it was Herodias's own daughter who danced, and not a mere professional dancing-girl. Josephus mentions that dancing-women were admitted to feasts by the Jews ; and Xenophon testifies to the same custom amongst the Greeks.

Ver. 24.—**And she went out, and said unto her mother, What shall I ask ?** (τί αἰτήσομαι ;) —according to the best authorities (τί αἰτήσωμαι ;), *What should I ask ?*

Ver. 25.—**I will that thou forthwith give me in a charger** (ἐπὶ πίνακι) **the head of John the Baptist.** John the Baptist seems to have had a presentiment of his speedy end when he said, "He must increase, but I must decrease."

Ver. 26.—**And the king was exceeding sorry.** We cannot suppose that this was a pretended grief. The true reason is doubtless to be found in the relentless animosity of Herodias. Herod must have known well that he could not be bound by his oath in reference to a petition so unreasonable and so iniquitous. Nevertheless he thought that "the words of a king were law." St. Augustine says, "The girl dances ; the mother rages. A rash oath is made amidst the excitement and the voluptuous indulgence of the feast ; and the savage desires of Herodias are fulfilled." **For the sake of his oaths** (διὰ τοὺς ὅρκους) ; the plural shows that he repeated the rash promise once and again.

Ver. 27.—**He sent forth an executioner** (σπεκουλάτωρα) ; literally, *a soldier of his guard ;* one of his body-guard, in constant attendance as messenger or executioner. It is a Roman word from *speculari,* to watch. St. Jerome relates that when the head of the Baptist was brought, Herodias barbarously thrust the tongue through with a bodkin, as Fulvia is said to have done over and over again, the tongue of Cicero ; thus verifying what Cicero had once said while living, that "nothing is more revengeful than a woman." Because they could not bear to hear the truth, therefore they bored through with a bodkin the tongue that had spoken the truth.

Ver. 29.—The taking up of the corpse by the disciples would seem to intimate that it lay uncared for and unburied until the disciples showed their respect for it. Josephus says that after the beheading, the mutilated remains were cast out of the prison and left neglected. God's judgments at length found out Herod. For not long after this he was defeated by Aretas in a great battle, and put to an ignominious flight. Herodias herself and Herod were banished by a decree of the Roman Senate to Lyons, where they both perished miserably ; and Nicephorus relates that Salome, the daughter of Herodias, died by a remarkable visitation. She fell through some treacherous ice over which she was passing, and fell through it in such a manner that her head was caught while the rest of her body sank into the water, and thus it came to pass that in her efforts to save herself her head was nearly severed by the sharp edges of the broken ice.

Ver. 30.—The narrative, which had been interrupted by this parenthesis relating to John the Baptist, is now taken up again. **The apostles.** This is the only place where St. Mark calls them apostles. In the parallel passage, St. Luke (ix. 10) says that they told him all that they had done. St. Mark adds, with more detail, **and whatsoever** (ὅσα) **they had taught.** They gave him a full account of their mission.

Ver. 31.—Our Lord cared for his disciples. They required rest after the labour and excitement of their ministry; and it was impossible to find the needful refreshment and repose where they were so thronged by the multitude.

Ver. 32.—**And they went away in the boat** (τῷ πλοίῳ) **to a desert place apart**—the boat, no doubt, which our Lord had ordered to be always in attendance upon him. We learn from St. Luke (ix. 10) that this desert place was near to "a city called Bethsaida." It seems that there were two places called Bethsaida—one in Galilee proper, and the other to the north-east of the Sea of Galilee. It was to the neighbourhood of this latter place that our Lord here directs the boat to take him. The other Bethsaida is mentioned lower down at ver. 45. The word Bethsaida means the "fish village."

Ver. 33.—This is very graphic. The Greek in the first part of this verse runs thus, according to the best authorities: Καὶ εἶδον αὐτοὺς ὑπάγοντας, καὶ ἐπέγνωσαν αὐτὸν πολλοί: **And they**—*i.e.* the people—**saw them going, and many knew** them. They saw them departing, and observed what direction the boat took, and then hastened thither on foot, and outwent them; and so were ready to meet them again on the opposite shore when they landed. The distance by land from the place where they started would be about twenty miles.

Ver. 34.—Our Lord had gone to this desert place for retirement and rest; but finding the multitude waiting for him, his compassions were stirred, **and he began to teach them many things.** He was moved with compassion, **because they were as sheep not having a shepherd.** No animal is more helpless, more stupid, more in need of a shepherd, than the sheep. St. Chrysostom observes that the scribes were not so much pastors as wolves, because, by teaching errors both by word and by example, they perverted the minds of the simple.

Ver. 35.—**And when the day was now far spent.** The English, like the Greek, is here very idiomatic (καὶ ἤδη ὥρας πολλῆς γενομένης). The English is retained in the Revised Version as it came through the Authorized Version from Tyndale. The present participle γενομένης appears in the Sinaitic Manuscript and in the Cambridge Codex. **His disciples came unto him, and said.** The best reading is (καὶ ἔλεγον), *and were saying.* St. Matthew (xiv. 16) says, "They need not depart; give ye them to eat." Thus our Lord prepared the way for his miracle. He detained the multitude till the day was far spent, so that the disciples might be induced to pray him to dismiss them. This would open the way for him to direct the disciples to feed them. And thus the miracle would appear all the more evident in proportion as they found themselves in a strait, and utterly destitute of the needful supplies of food for such a multitude in the desert. St. John's account here is much more full. He tells us (vi. 5) that Jesus, addressing Philip, said, "Whence are we to buy bread, that these may eat?" And he adds, "This he said to prove him: for he himself knew what he would do." Our Lord, it would seem, asked Philip rather than the others, because Philip was simple-minded, sincere, and teachable, rather than clever, and so was accustomed to ask things which appeared plain to others. We have an instance of this simplicity of mind in the question which he asks (John xiv. 8), "Lord show us the Father, and it sufficeth us."

Ver. 37.—**Two hundred pennyworth of bread.** The penny, or "denarius," was the chief Roman silver coin, worth about eightpence halfpenny. Upon the breaking up of the Roman empire, the states which arose upon its ruins imitated the coinage of the old imperial mints, and in general called their principal silver coin the "denarius." Thus the denarius found its way into this country through the Anglo-Saxons, and it was for a long period the only coin. Hence the introduction of the word into the Authorized Version. Two hundred pennyworth would be of the value of nearly seven pounds. But considering the constant fluctuation in the relation between money and the commodities purchased by money, it is in vain to inquire what number of loaves the same two hundred denarii would purchase at that time, although it was evidently the representation of a large supply of bread.

Ver. 38.—**Five (loaves), and two fishes.** St. John tells us (vi. 9) that the loaves were of barley, and that the fishes were small (ὀψάρια); St. Mark says δύο ἰχθύας. Barley bread was considered an inferior and homely kind of food, very inferior to bread made of wheat flour. The comparative value of the two kinds of bread is given in Rev. vi. 6. "A measure of wheat for a penny, and three measures of barley for a penny." The psalmist alludes to the greater excellence of wheat flour: "He would have fed them also with the finest wheat flour" (Ps. lxxxi. 16).

Ver. 39.—All were to sit down by companies (συμπόσια συμπόσια)—St. Luke (ix. 14) says that the companies were about fifty each (ἀνὰ πεντήκοντα)—upon the green grass. St. John says (vi. 10) that "there was much grass in the place." This indicates the time of the year. The grass was growing, and it was green. It would not be green in that district after April. Thus St. Mark's account of the state of the grass at that time (an account evidently repeated from an eye-witness) coincides with the account of St. John, who says that "the Passover, a feast of the Jews, was at hand" (vi. 4).

Ver. 40.—And they sat down in ranks (ἀνέπεσον πρασιαὶ πρασιαί); literally, they reclined. The Greek word πρασια means "a garden plot" or "bed," literally, a bed of leeks. They were disposed symmetrically. Probably the English word "ranks" expresses the meaning as clearly as any could do. This arrangement was probably made, partly that the numbers might be better known, partly that all things might be done in an orderly manner, and that each might have his portion. St. Matthew's account (xiv. 21) seems to imply that the "men" were separated from the "women and children."

Ver. 41.—All the synoptists give our Lord's acts in the same words. The taking of the food into the hands would seem to have been a formal act before the "blessing," or "giving of thanks," for it. Probably our Lord used the ordinary form of benediction. This is one amongst other instances showing the fitness and propriety of "grace before meat." In considering the miraculous action which followed the benediction, our reason is baffled. It eludes our grasp. It is best simply to behold in this multiplying of the food, both the bread and the fishes, an act of Divine omnipotence; not indeed now, as at the beginning, a creation out of nothing, for here there was the nucleus of the five loaves and the two fishes, but an act of creative development of the food in its best kind; for all the works of God are perfect. He gave (ἐδίδου) would be better rendered, he was giving. It was in his hands that the miracle was wrought, and the food continually multiplied.

Vers. 42, 43.—They did all eat, and were filled (ἐχορτάσθησαν). It might be rendered, were fulfilled, according to the old meaning of "fulfil." It is probable that the women and children were a considerable number;

for they would be, if possible, even more eager then the men to see the great Prophet. When all had eaten and were satisfied, they took up broken pieces, twelve basketfuls, and also of the fishes. St. John tells us that this was done by the express command of Christ (vi. 12); and the existence of these fragments, far more in quantity than the original supply, was a striking testimony to the reality of the miracle, and that there was enough and more than enough for all. It does not become us to pry too curiously into the method of our Lord's working; but the number of these baskets (κοφίνους), namely, twelve, seems to suggest that he first broke the loaves, and in breaking multiplied them, and distributed them into these baskets, one for each apostle, and that the food, as it was distributed by the disciples, was more and more multiplied, as needed, so that at length they brought back to Christ as many basketfuls of fragments as they had first received from him, and much more than the original supply. It is obvious here to remark that by this stupendous miracle our Lord showed himself to be the true Bread of life, by which the spiritual wants of all hungering souls may be supplied. "For," says St. Augustine, "he was the Word of God, and all the acts of the Word are themselves words for us. They are not as pictures, merely, to look at and admire; but as letters which we must seek to read and understand."

Ver. 45.—The other side. It would seem, as has already been stated, that there were two Bethsaidas (or "places of fish"—fish-villages)—one to the north-east of the Sea of Galilee, not far from where the Jordan enters it, called Bethsaida Julias; and the other on the western side of the sea itself, near to Capernaum. Again and again our Lord crossed this sea to escape the crowds who followed him about, and now wished "to take him by force and make him a king." He desired for a time to be in retirement, in order that he might pray with the greater earnestness, and freedom from interruption. He also wished to make occasion for the miracle which was to follow, namely, the stilling of the tempest.

Vers. 46, 47.—St. Mark is careful, like St. Matthew, to tell us that when the even was come he was alone on the land. Both the evangelists desire to call attention to the fact that, when night came on, the disciples were alone in their boat and Jesus alone on the land. It was nightfall; and St. John informs us that "the sea was rising by reason of a great wind that blew." Then it was that the Lord left his place of prayer on the mountain, and walked upon the sea, that he might succour his disciples now distressed by the storm. It would appear that our Lord had been obliged to use a little pressure to induce his disciples to leave him: "He constrained them (ἠνάγκασε τοὺς μαθητὰς αὐτοῦ).

Ver. 46.—And when he had sent them away (ἀποταξάμενος)—more literally, *had taken leave of them*, that is, the multitude— **he departed into a mountain** (εἰς τὸ ὄρος); literally, *into the mountain;* that is, the high table-land at the foot of which the multitude had been fed. Towards the north-east of the Sea of Galilee the land rises rapidly from the shore. **To pray** (προσεύξασθαι). This is a very full word, implying the outpouring of the heart to God. Our Lord did this that he might teach us in our prayers to shun the crowd, and to pray in silence and in secret, with collected mind. There is here, too, a special example for the clergy, namely, this: that when they have preached they should go apart and pray that God would make effectual that which they have delivered; that he would himself give the increase where they have planted and watered, and renew their spiritual strength, that they may return again to their labour refreshed by communion with him.

Ver. 47.—And when even was come. It was now advancing onwards into night; the wind was rising and blowing against them. Then it was that the Lord left his place of prayer on the mountain, that he might succour his disciples in their difficulties.

Vers. 48—50.—And he saw them toiling in rowing. The Greek is, according to the best readings, καὶ ἰδὼν (not εἶδεν) αὐτοὺς βασανιζομένους ἐν τῷ ἐλαύνειν. The word βασανιζομένους means more than "toiling;" it means literally, *tormented*. It is well rendered in the Revised Version by *distressed*. It was only by painful effort that they could make head against the driving storm blowing upon them from the west, that is, from the Mediterranean Sea. **About the fourth watch of the night he cometh unto them, walking on the sea.** The Jews formerly divided the night into three watches; but when Judæa became a Roman province they adopted the Roman division. The Romans changed the watches every three hours, lest through too long watches the guards might slumber at their posts. These periods were called "watches." If the night was short, they divided it into three watches; if long, into four. Therefore the fourth watch began at the tenth hour of the night, that is, at three o'clock in the morning, and continued to the twelfth, that is, to six o'clock. It would seem, therefore, that this storm lasted for nine hours. During that time the disciples had rowed about twenty-five or thirty furlongs, that is, about three Roman miles—eight furlongs

making a mile. The Sea of Galilee is not more than six miles broad at its widest part. They were therefore now (ἐν μέσῳ τῆς θαλάσσης) "in the midst of the sea," as St. Mark expresses it; so that, after rowing for nine hours, they had hardly crossed more than half over the sea. The Sea of Galilee is, speaking roughly, about twelve miles from north to south and six from east to west. It may be asked why our Lord suffered them to be tempest-tossed so long; and the answer is: 1. It was a trial of their faith, so as to urge them to seek more earnestly the help of God. 2. It was a lesson to accustom them to endure hardness. 3. It made the stilling of so tedious and dangerous a storm all the more grateful and welcome to them at last. The Fathers find a fine spiritual meaning in this. Jerome says, "The fourth watch is the *last*." So, too, St. Augustine, who adds that "he who has watched the ship of his Church will come at length at the fourth watch, at the end of the world, when the night of sin and evil is ended, to judge the quick and the dead." Theophylact says, "He allows his disciples to be tried by dangers, that they may be taught patience, and does not come to them till morning, that they may learn perseverance and faith." Hilary says, "The *first* watch was the age of the Law, the *second* of the prophets, the *third* of the gospel, the *fourth* of his glorious advent, when he will find her buffeted by the spirit of antichrist and by the storms of the world. And by his reception into the ship and the consequent calm is prefigured the eternal peace of the Church after his second coming" (see Wordsworth's 'New Testament:' St. Matt. xiv.). *He walked on the sea.* This he did by his Divine power, which he possessed as God, and which, when he pleased, he could assume as man. Infidelity is at fault here. Paulus, the rationalist, revived the ridiculous idea that Christ walking on the sea merely meant Christ walking on the shore, elevated above the sea; but the interpretation was rightly denounced by Lavater as "a laughable insult on logic, hermeneutics, good sense, and honesty." Was it because our Lord simply walked on the shore that the disciples "cried out and were troubled"? Was it merely for this that they were "sore amazed at themselves beyond measure and wondered"? Yet such are the shifts to which unbelief is reduced when it ventures to measure itself against the acts of Omnipotence. **He would have passed by them.** An expression something like that in St. Luke (xxiv. 28), "He made as though he would go further," although there the Greek in St. Luke is different (προσεποιεῖτο πορρωτέρω πορεύεσθαι). Here it is ἤθελε παρελθεῖν: literally, *he wished to pass by them;*

so at least it appeared to the disciples. It has been suggested that our Lord did this that the disciples might more clearly see how the wind was stilled in his presence. They supposed that it was an apparition (ἔδοξαν ὅτι φάντασμα εἶναι); literally, *a phantom.* Why did they suppose this? Partly from the idea that spectres appear in the night and in the darkness to terrify men, and partly because in the darkness they could not so readily recognize that it was Jesus. Then the fact that our Lord " would have passed by them," flitting past them as though he cared nothing for them and had nothing to do with them, but was going elsewhere; this must have increased their terror. But now came the moment for him to calm their fears. Straightway he talked with them soothingly. **Be of good cheer: it is I; be not afraid.** Now, Christ did this that he might teach his disciples to conquer fear and temptation, even when they are very great, and that so the deliverance and the consolation might impress them all the more powerfully and sweetly in proportion to their former terror. " ' It is I '—I, your Lord and Master, whom you know so well, and of whose goodness and omnipotence you have already had so much experience; I, your Master, who do not come to mock you as a phantom, but to deliver you both from fear and from storm." It will be observed that St. Mark omits all mention of Peter's act of faith " in going down from the boat, and walking upon the waters to come to Jesus," as recorded by St. Matthew (xiv. 28). Throughout this Gospel, as already noticed, St. Peter is kept in the background.

Vers. 51, 52.—The amazement of the disciples was very great. Nor was the impression confined to them alone. St. Matthew (xiv. 33) tells us that they who were in the boat came and worshipped him. They felt, at least for the moment, that they were brought into awful nearness to One whose " way is in the sea," and whose " path is in the great waters," and whose

" footsteps are not known." They needed not, however, to have been so amazed, for they had just witnessed his power in the miracle of the loaves; but **they understood not** (ἐπὶ τοῖς ἄρτοις) **concerning the loaves, but their heart was** (πεπωρωμένη) **hardened ;** literally, *stupefied and blinded.*

Ver. 53.—**They came into the land of Gennesaret ;** literally (ἐπὶ τὴν γῆν ἦλθον εἰς Γεννησαρέτ), *they came to the land unto Gennesaret.* This was the plain on the western side of the sea sometimes called " the Lake of Gennesaret." The name Gennesaret (says Cornelius à Lapide) means " a fertile garden." There was a city originally called " Chinnereth" or " Cinneroth," mentioned in Josh. xix. 25, which probably gave one of its names to this lake.

Vers. 54—56.—**Straightway** the people **knew him.** Some, no doubt, had known him before. He was now the general object of interest and attraction wherever he went. They **began to carry about on their beds** (ἐπὶ τοῖς κραββάτοις) **those that were sick, where they heard he was.** The original is very expressive (ὅπου ἤκουον ὅτι ἐκεῖ ἐστι), *where they heard, He is there.* But the best authorities omit ἐκεῖ. **Villages, or cities, or fields** (Greek, ἀγρούς) ; literally, *country,* where the pursuits of agriculture would be going on. **They laid the sick in the streets** (Greek, ἐν ταῖς ἀγοραῖς)—literally, *in the market-places ;* the proper rendering—that **they might touch if it were but the border of his garment.** The border (κράσπεδον) means the " fringe " or " hem ; " the garment was the outer robe worn over the tunic. **And as many as touched him were made whole** (ὅσοι ἂν ἥψαντο αὐτοῦ ἐσώζοντο) ; αὐτοῦ might mean either " him " or " it," that is, " the border of his garment." But the difference is of little importance ; for it was faith in those who touched which brought the healing virtue to the sick, whether they touched the Saviour himself or only his clothes.

HOMILETICS.

Vers. 1—6.—*Unbelief.* Our Lord may have had two reasons for leaving Capernaum and for visiting Nazareth. One, a *personal* reason—to see his mother and his sisters, who seem to have been married there. The other, a *ministerial* reason—to escape from the busy throngs who resorted to him by the lake, and to take a new centre for evangelistic labours on the part of himself and his disciples. It is singular and instructive that Nazareth should have perhaps twice furnished a striking instance of human unbelief and offence with " the Nazarene."

I. THE UNREASONABLENESS AND INEXCUSABLENESS OF UNBELIEF IN CHRIST. There were several facts, which took away all excuse from the conduct of the inhabitants of Nazareth. 1. He was well known to them. They had been acquainted with him for many years, and they had seen in him nothing but truth and integrity. His claims, therefore, should have been fairly and candidly considered. 2. He brought with him a great and acknowledged reputation. In the most populous parts of Galilee he had fulfilled a ministry which had excited the deepest interest. His miracles were undeniable and undenied. He was the object of general attention and of widespread faith. 3. He came to Nazareth and taught publicly, thus giving his townsmen an opportnnity of judging for themselves of his wisdom and moral authority. They confessed with astonishment the extraordinary character of his teaching. Yet they did not believe. And how many among us, who have even greater opportunity of forming a just judgment concerning Jesus, are found judging falsely, and consequently rejecting the Lord of life and of salvation! They judge against the evidence, and their conclusion—in no way damaging to him—is condemnation to themselves.

II. THE GROUNDS OF UNBELIEF IN CHRIST. It was unreasonable, but not inexplicable or arbitrary. 1. The Nazarenes were prejudiced against Jesus, because of *his origin and circumstances.* The son of so lowly a mother, the brother of sisters in so obscure a position, how could Jesus be regarded by his worldly townsmen with reverence? A craftsman himself, and one of an humble family, he was little likely to be received at Nazareth as he had been received elsewhere, even in the metropolis itself. 2. The other ground of prejudice was *educational deficiency* on the part of Jesus. He was the Prophet of Nazareth, and had not been trained in the rabbinical schools of learning. Whence had he his qualifications? What had been the source of his knowledge, the inspiration of his wisdom, the secret of his power? It was all a mystery to them— something at variance with their beliefs, and in contradiction to their prejudices. Very similar are the objections which men still make to Christ. Had he come a king, a conqueror, a philosopher, a scholar, then men might have honoured and welcomed him. But he came from God; and to the unspiritual there could be no more serious and fatal ground of offence than this.

III. THE REBUKE OF UNBELIEF. "A prophet is not without honour," etc. There was sadness in Christ's language and tones. Yet what a reproach was hereby conveyed to the unbelieving! They might be offended; there were those who would believe, who would evince gratitude and render honour. When we think how clearly our Lord must have foreseen the stupendous and eternal results of his ministry, we may appreciate the nobility and self-restraint of his attitude and language, and at the same time we may recognize the severity of his rebuke.

IV. THE CONSEQUENCES OF UNBELIEF. 1. The impression upon the Saviour's mind is briefly described: "He marvelled." An expression this, which gives us an insight into his humanity, and which reveals to us the depths of moral obliquity into which the cavillers had fallen. 2. The results to the people of the town were lamentable. The Prophet had come with power to bless, and prepared to heal and help. But he required the co-operation of faith; and, when this was withheld, "he could do no mighty work." A few sick folk were healed, but many forfeited a blessing within their reach. 3. Yet the rejection of Jesus by his fellow-townsmen was the occasion of benefit to others. Finding no congenial soil at Nazareth, Jesus proceeded elsewhere, to labour where labour might be more appreciated. "He went round about the villages teaching." The indifference or contempt of the unspiritual and self-sufficient may be the occasion of enlightenment and consolation to the lowly, the receptive, the needy.

APPLICATION. 1. The coming of Christ to a soul, to a community, is a moral probation, involving the most serious responsibility. 2. It is the most fatal guilt and folly, in considering the claims of Christ, to overlook the wisdom and the grace of his character and ministry, and to regard circumstances at which the superficial and the carnal may take offence.

Vers. 7—13.—*The mission of the twelve.* The twelve disciples now first became apostles. This sending forth was a prelude to their life-long mission, to be fulfilled after their Lord's ascension. They had now been long enough with the Master not only to have imbibed much of his spirit, but to have learned the nature of his ministry and to have entered into its methods. Their evangelistic journey would be disciplinary to themselves and profitable to the population of Galilee, and it would increase and extend the interest of the people in the ministry of the Lord.

I. THE PREPARATION FOR THE MISSION. Wisdom and simplicity are here alike apparent. 1. The twelve were *grouped into pairs.* This was for the sake of companionship, and to secure that none should be unfriended and unsupported; as well as, in all likelihood, to bring about that one should supply the other's lack. 2. They were sent *as pilgrims.* Two things only they were to take with them—their sandals and their staves, which were part of their natural equipment as travellers afoot. 3. Yet they were *forbidden to provide* for their journey. Luxuries and superfluities they must not take with them, neither must they provide for their subsistence, but must act upon the expectation that the labourer would be deemed worthy of his hire. In all these respects the instructions given to the twelve were significant of the method in which our Lord desires his people to undertake their spiritual mission to mankind. The work is to be done in fellowship and with mutual sympathy and support; it is to be done in the spirit of those who are in the world but are not of the world, who are not entangled in its snares, and who mind heavenly things.

II. The nature and purpose of the mission. Like their Lord, the apostles were enjoined to have compassion upon the varied needs of their fellow-men, to address themselves to the supply of both spiritual and temporal wants. 1. They were to summon men to repentance, the indispensable and universal condition of pardon and life to sinful, guilty men. A change of mind and heart alone could prepare men for the blessings of the Messianic kingdom. 2. At the same time they were to confront the power of evil in its most malignant manifestations, and to cast out demons in the name of that stronger One who was binding the spiritual tyrant of mankind. 3. And they were to heal the sick, both as a symbolic act, and as a proof and exercise of true and practical benevolence. All this they did efficiently and successfully, in the authority of their Divine Lord. The nature of this commission is parallel with that given by our Saviour to his whole Church; for he has put his people in charge with the welfare of mankind, both socially and temporally, and also spiritually.

III. The spirit of the mission. The directions given by the Master as to the apostles' bearing with regard to those to whom they ministered were worthy of himself. There is a beautiful combination of meekness and dignity in these instructions, very like the Lord who gave them. Wherever received with cordiality, the apostles were directed to abide with their hosts, grateful for kindness and content with their entertainment. Wherever their message was rejected and they were disregarded, the twelve were commanded to "shake off the dust under their feet" for a testimony against the unbelieving and impenitent. The servants of the Lord Jesus cannot too carefully study these counsels, in considering in what spirit they shall fulfil the commission entrusted to them in human society. On the one hand, all selfish desires, all pride and restlessness, must be repressed; on the other hand, the high vocation must be esteemed, the office must be magnified, the authority of the Redeemer must be upheld, and the responsibility of rejecting the gospel must solemnly, and with appropriate dignity, be cast upon the unbelieving and unspiritual.

Practical lessons. 1. All Christians may be reminded of their position in this world as the representatives and ministers of Christ. 2. All hearers of the gospel may be admonished as to the serious responsibility they incur when a message from heaven is brought before their minds.

Vers. 14—29.—*Sin-hating righteousness.* The growing fame of Jesus reached all parts of the land and all classes of society. Not only the poor and diseased, the neglected and the despised, heard of the compassionate heart and the mighty deeds of the Son of man; the learned were jealous of his influence with the people, and powerful rulers wondered what was the secret of his power. Many were the explanations given of the new Teacher's authority. Whilst some traced a resemblance between him and the olden Hebrew prophets, others even deemed him the greatest of the order—Elijah himself, returning to the land of his ministry, in accordance with what was deemed the inspired prediction. But the most singular of all conjectures was that of Herod—that John the Baptist, whom he had beheaded in circumstances of atrocious dishonour to himself, had arisen from the dead. Mentioning this conjecture, the evangelist is naturally led to relate the incident of the forerunner's violent death—one of the most awful, tragic incidents in all history. Simply tracing the narrative, we meet with successive embodiments of moral fact and law.

I. The apprehensions of a guilty conscience. There seems to have been but little in the ministry of Jesus to recall that of John. John did no miracle; the fame of Jesus was largely owing to the miracles by which his ministry was continuously signalized. The power to attract multitudes was the one point obviously in common. But any association was sufficient to revive within Herod's breast the memory of his weakness and his crime, and to reproach him with the destruction of a blameless and heroic, prophetic man. "Thus conscience doth make cowards of us all!"

II. THE RESENTMENT OF THE VICIOUS UNDER REBUKE. Antipas was guilty of a double incest and a double adultery; he married his niece, who was also his brother's wife, that brother being still alive; and drove his own spouse from him by contracting this sinful union. Herodias was probably influenced by ambition in accepting a position so disgraceful. Amidst the silence or the applause of the courtiers, one voice arose to condemn this shameless conduct. It was the voice of the upright and dauntless John, whose rebuke was, "It is not lawful!" No wonder that the wretched woman set herself against the stern prophet; his presence, his life, must have been to her an incessant reproach. Fain would she have killed him, fearing this influence with the king, and trembling for her own precarious position. There is no hatred so virulent and awful as the hatred of sinners against faithful and righteous rebuke.

III. THE CONFLICT BETWEEN CONSCIENCE AND PASSION. The unhappy Herod was torn by two conflicting forces. On the one hand, the malice of Herodias urged him to put the fearless John to death, and thus to silence his rebukes; on the other hand, he respected and feared the holy and dauntless prophet, and he was impelled to listen to his words, hearing him eagerly, yet with unsolved perplexity of mind. He kept his prisoner safely, even from the malice of his paramour, whom he would gladly have gratified had not his conscience barred the way.

IV. YOUTH AND BEAUTY THE INSTRUMENT OF VINDICTIVENESS. There is a strange contrast between the frivolous and fascinating performances of youth and loveliness, and the dark designs in the background. Herodias watched and delighted to see the passions of her sensual husband moved at sight of her daughter's charms, to hear the rash promise from those unrighteous lips. Base were the means, and baser still the end. When woman's charms are used not only to provoke lust, but to induce to cruelty, can there be a more awful instance of the misuse of the fair gifts of the Creator? Yet history tells of many a tale like this, though perhaps of none so utterly and so irredeemably mournful.

V. FALSE HONOUR AND WICKED PRIDE PREFERRED TO JUSTICE. Vengeance and malice in Herodias are fitly matched with weakness and unrighteousness in her paramour. There can be no question that it is right to break a promise when the promise involves in its fulfilment the commission of a crime. Such a promise it is wrong to make, but to fulfil it makes one wrong two. The motives of Antipas were vile and mean; he wished to gratify the malice of a woman, and to vindicate his arbitrary authority in the presence of his guests. And for such motives he was ready to sacrifice a good man's life.

VI. MALICE TRIUMPHANT. The foolish word was kept; the wicked woman was gratified; the infamous deed was done. As the Lord expressed it, "Elijah came, and they did unto him whatsoever they listed." Although the world is ruled by a just Providence, righteousness does not always prosper; vice and crime are not always restrained, or even immediately and manifestly punished. The voice of just rebuke is often silenced; the head of innocence is often laid in the dust; "the godly man faileth;" the vilest men are exalted. All this is permitted that there may be scope for the exercise of faith; that virtue may be tried as in the furnace; that men may learn to look forward to a future state, in which grievances shall be redressed, and retribution shall be made, and the righteousness of the Divine Judge shall be fully vindicated.

VII. THE GOOD MOURN WHOM THE BAD DESTROY. During his brief ministry John had made many disciples, had attached to him many friends. During his captivity, his admirers had been severed from him. Now came the last opportunity for manifesting their reverential affection. When the company of the Baptist's disciples, hearing of their master's violent death, gathered themselves together, and carried the mutilated body to the tomb, what a contrast they afforded to the company of carousers, in whose presence Herod's foolish oath had doomed a brave, pure man to death! It is well, even if "evil entreated" by the frivolous, sensual, and malicious, to have a place in good men's hearts, and after death to live in the remembrance of the righteous.

Vers. 30—44.—*No rest for Jesus.* The twelve have fulfilled their brief mission of evangelization, have returned to their Master, and tell him of the incidents and results of their mission. Jesus takes occasion to rest, and to give them rest, and with this intent withdraws to a desert place. This passage shows us with what result.

I. THE PURPOSES FOR WHICH THE LORD SEEKS RETIREMENT. 1. Perhaps to escape from the notice of Herod, who, having heard of his fame, may seek to get him within his power, even as before he had imprisoned John. 2. To secure a brief period of bodily repose for himself and for the twelve. Their time and attention have been so occupied, that they have had no leisure even for their meals. It is bad economy in Christian workers to neglect the claims of the body, which needs to be kept, by food, exercise, and repose, in a sound and healthy state, that work for Christ may be done vigorously and cheerfully. 3. To enjoy leisure for spiritual intercourse. The twelve need to be taught that they may teach others; and this is a kind of work which needs leisure and quiet, and uninterrupted hours. The wise and experienced may spend their time to advantage in equipping the young and active among Christ's disciples for spiritual campaigns.

II. THE MULTITUDE INVADE THE LORD'S RETIREMENT. 1. It is a sign of their eager interest to see and hear the great Teacher and Physician. The tidings spread; the people anticipate their Benefactor; they outrun him, and are ready to meet him when he disembarks. 2. They find him willing to sacrifice his ease for the sake of his ministry. Having perhaps taken a few hours' repose and slumber as the boat has rocked at anchor near the shore, Jesus lands, only to find the people awaiting him upon the beach. Instead of pushing off again and seeking a remoter seclusion, Jesus readily addresses himself to his work. A lesson this in diligence and zeal! 3. The sad condition of the people awakens Christ's commiseration. Others might have said, "The people are comfortable and cared for." But Jesus sees that spiritually they are as sheep without a shepherd, and his heart is touched at the spectacle. It needs the Spirit of Jesus to look thus upon the spiritually destitute and famishing, to penetrate through their outward guise to their souls' needs.

III. JESUS PROVIDES FOR THEIR SPIRITUAL WANTS. 1. He teaches them; he, the Source of wisdom, imparts from his abundance to their necessities. 2. He teaches them at length and with variety. What the "many things" were in which he instructed them we know not, but may judge from the record of his discourses. So the swift hours pass on. He speaks as never man spake, and the people hear him gladly.

IV. JESUS SUPPLIES THEIR TEMPORAL NEEDS. 1. In this his action is in contrast with the spirit of his disciples, who would first have him dismiss the multitude, and who then put obstacles in the way of supplying their wants. We have no reason to blame the disciples, but we have reason to admire the Master. 2. Jesus uses the provision which is at hand. The bread is obviously and utterly insufficient, yet the Lord makes use of it, and chooses rather to multiply than to create. Our Divine Master here gives us a needed lesson—to turn all things to good account— to employ the circumstances, the opportunities, the gifts Providence appoints for us, rather than to grieve that we have not other means of usefulness. 3. He acts in an orderly method. His directions as to the seemly and convenient arrangement of the multitude are in consonance with Divine wisdom, and are an example and admonition for us. God is not the author of confusion in any Churches; confusion is the devil's work. "Order is Heaven's first law." 4. Jesus sets an example of gratitude. "Looking up to heaven, he blessed." A rebuke to such as take their daily food without giving of thanks; an admonition to remember whence the most common and customary of our mercies come. 5. He makes use of his disciples. Observe the honour which the Divine Lord puts upon human agency and instrumentality. The disciples could not provide; that was no reason why they should not distribute. The feeblest can offer, to his hungering neighbours, the bread of life eternal. 6. He satisfies the need of all. It is a vast crowd; yet not one is left unfed. There is in Christ "enough for all, enough for each, enough for evermore." It is a symbol of the sufficiency of the Divine provision for all the spiritual necessities of mankind. The bread of heaven came down, and "giveth life unto *the world.*" 7. The provision is even superabundant; it is more than enough. How royally and munificently the Lord of all provides for his dependent creatures! There is yet room at his table, and bread in his store, bounty in his heart, and blessing in his hands. "Come, for all things are ready!"

Vers. 45—52.—"*It is I.*" How picturesque and impressive is the scene! Jesus has dismissed the multitude, and has sent his disciples away in the boat to the western shore. He himself has retired to a mountain, by prayer to calm his spirit and to strengthen himself for his ministry. Night comes on; the wind rises from the west, and the waters of the lake are lashed into a storm. By the fitful light of the moon, breaking now and again through the drifting clouds, Jesus, as he stands upon the hill-top, observes the boat tossed upon the waves. Her sails are down, and the disciples are rowing, toiling, but are making no way against the gale. Jesus descends the hill, and, in the exercise of his supernatural power, walks upon the water. The superstitious fishermen, naturally enough, take the figure approaching them for a spectre—some foreboding spirit of the deep—and they cry aloud in terror. Then come the words, so authoritative and so gentle, "Be of good cheer: it is I; be not afraid!" The hearts of the disciples and the waves of the lake alike are calmed. Amazement fills every breast, and as they approach the land, the rescued mariners adore with fresh admiration their Deliverer and Lord.

I. CHRIST'S PEOPLE HAVE SOMETIMES TO PASS THROUGH A SEA OF TROUBLE. 1. Circumstances without may conspire with fears within. Christians are in trouble as other men, and they sometimes dread lest they should be overwhelmed. 2. Christians may encounter trouble in the very act of obeying Christ. Just as the twelve met the storm in fulfilling their Lord's directions to return to Gennesaret, so we may meet with trials and dangers in the path of obedience. If so, let us not count it strange.

II. CHRIST OBSERVES AND SYMPATHIZES WITH HIS PEOPLE IN THEIR TROUBLE. They may be unconscious and forgetful of this. Little did the twelve, as they toiled in rowing, imagine that the eye of their Master was upon them; but it was. From the hill-top he witnessed their struggles; he, the Lord of the waves, suffered their violence; he, his disciples' Friend, allowed them to come into extremity, and did not prevent their fears. So he may, for good reasons, allow his people to experience distress. Yet he is not unmindful and not unmoved. He thinks of them, watches over them, sympathizes with them. He may seem absent, but he is not.

III. CHRIST'S PRESENCE AND VOICE BRING COMFORT AND PEACE TO THE HEARTS OF THE TROUBLED. Faith discerns that presence, though unseen; that voice, though unheard. "'It is I!'—I, who love you; I, who died for you; I, who provide for your wants, and watch over your souls; I, who sent you on life's voyage; it is I, who am with you always, who now come to seek and save you!" When Jesus says, "Be of good cheer; be not afraid!" his are no empty words; they are words fitted to banish fear, to instil confidence, to inspire courage, to awaken hope.

IV. CHRIST'S POWER AND GRACE BRING DELIVERANCE TO HIS TROUBLED ONES. We are indebted to him for more than sympathy. His tender kindness, his strong promises, his unfailing faithfulness, all issue in practical aid, in gracious interposition. He is the Lord of all hearts, and can assuage the tempests of the soul. He controls all circumstances, and compels all to co-operate for his people's good. "He maketh the storm a calm;" "So he bringeth them to the desired haven." Who, upon the troubled sea of time, would be without a Comforter so gracious, a Helper so mighty?

V. CHRIST'S INTERPOSITIONS AWAKEN THE AMAZEMENT, REVERENCE, AND GRATITUDE OF HIS PEOPLE. Like the twelve, we have often too much reason, when we experience the compassionate interference of our Lord upon our behalf, to blame ourselves because our hardness of heart has made Divine deliverance seem strange to us. This is just what we ought to have looked for, to have expected with assurance. Oh for grace, that when the voice from heaven addresses us, "It is I," we may respond, "It is Thou, indeed, O Lord, whom we honour, upon whom we call, in whom we trust! It is thou, whose presence is ever dear, whose voice is ever welcome, whose heart is never cold, and whose help is never far!"

APPLICATION. 1. An encouragement to obedience. 2. A rebuke to fear. 3. An assurance of Divine sympathy and aid. 4. A call to grateful adoration.

Vers. 53—56.—*The popularity of the Divine Physician.* At this time the tide of

Christ's popularity was at the flood. In a few verses, the evangelist strikingly depicts the general excitement which the presence of the Prophet of Nazareth awakened amidst the thronging and busy population.

I. THE PRESENCE OF THE DIVINE PHYSICIAN AMONG THE PEOPLE. Jesus sometimes retired to desert solitudes; but, for the most part, he chose to live among the people, and to be accessible to all classes and to all characters. This might well be his motive for spending so much of his life in the thickly peopled district on the western shores of the Lake of Gennesaret. As the Son of man, Jesus mingled freely with the race he came to save and bless.

II. THE SPREAD AMONG THE PEOPLE OF THE GOOD TIDINGS. If Jesus was willing to live and work amongst the inhabitants of this district, they, for their part, were eager to embrace every opportunity of intercourse with him. Not that they were generally influenced by high motives that they resorted to him as to a spiritual teacher. It is evident that the interest felt in Jesus was very largely owing to his power and willingness to heal the sick and suffering. But, from whatever motive, it is of the highest importance that the children of men should be led to interest themselves in Christ. The tidings that Jesus is the Saviour of the world deserve to be published far and wide, as the best news for all mankind.

III. THE AGENCY EMPLOYED TO BRING THE NEEDY INTO THE PRESENCE OF THE SAVIOUR. As we read the vigorous language of the evangelist, we seem to see the eager, kind-hearted people, the peasantry and the fishermen, hurrying throughout the district, seeking out all the diseased and infirm, carrying them on their couches to the places where Jesus is expected, and laying them in the open spaces, that they may be brought under the notice of the mighty and benevolent physician.

IV. THE CONTACT OF THE PATIENTS WITH THE PHYSICIAN. The healing looked for was effected, not by means and instruments, but by the great Healer himself. Accordingly, what the sufferers desired was, to lay hold upon Jesus, or even upon the hem or fringe of his garment. An indication this of the method of the sinner's salvation. To come to Christ, and spiritually to lay hold upon him,—such is the condition of securing all the blessings which Jesus brings to man.

V. THE EXPERIENCE OF HEALING. It mattered not how many came, by whom they were brought, in what place they encountered Jesus, from what disease they suffered; "as many as touched him were made whole." There is no limitation to the healing power or to the healing grace of Immanuel. He is "mighty to save;" he saves "to the uttermost;" and his salvation is perfect and eternal.

APPLICATION. 1. This narrative reminds the sinner where to look for deliverance—to Christ, and Christ alone. 2. This narrative sets before us the office of the Church; it is to bring sinful souls to the one Divine, almighty Saviour.

HOMILIES BY VARIOUS AUTHORS.

Vers. 1—6.—*Jesus visiting his own country.* By going thither—
I. HE GRATIFIED A HUMAN YEARNING. In a previous chapter he is reported to have asked, "Who is my mother and my brethren?" He now shows that those broad human relations he had claimed did not imply the neglect of nearer ones, or indifference to them. He sought to benefit his own people in the highest way, even whilst he would not suffer the narrow claims of his home to interfere with the wider claims of his kingdom. Have we so interpreted home relations, patriotism, local attachment, social ties?
II. HE ILLUSTRATED AFRESH AN OLD AND FAMILIAR EXPERIENCE. 1. *He was one of many, yet by himself even in this.* 2. *One of the greatest of griefs to a pious spirit, to be hindered from doing good and conferring benefit.* 3. *A greater humiliation than his human birth, because a moral one consciously experienced.*
III. HE EXHIBITED DIVINE MERCY. 1. *Past offences were forgiven.* 2. *Although conscious of restriction because of their unbelief and indifference, he still persisted in his works of mercy.*—M.

Vers. 2, 6.—*The twofold wonder awakened by the gospel.* I. IN MEN. 1. *Because of contrast between the apparent origin and the Divine pretensions of Christ.* 2. *Because of the seeming disproportion between the results actually produced and the instruments.* A curious phase this of human incredulity, as if the works did not speak for themselves! Failing the discovery of an evidently great cause, the results themselves are not credited with being what they seem to be. This is characteristic of human nature in all ages.

II. IN CHRIST. The unbelief itself, of which the human astonishment at his words and works was but the sign, was a still greater marvel to our Saviour. The believing, ingenuous soul cannot understand unbelief. And truly there is something unnatural and not to be looked for in the incredulity exhibited by men towards truth and goodness, and the proffered mercy of God.—M.

Vers. 2, 3.—*Detracting from the Divine greatness of Christ.* I. HOW THIS IS DONE. 1. *By attributing to secondary causes Divine effects.* 2. *Absence of faith and spiritual sympathy.* 3. *By being offended at the mystery of his humiliation, either in himself or his followers.* II. WHAT IT PRODUCES. 1. *Unsatisfied indecision.* Perpetual questioning. 2. *Hardening of heart.* 3. *The doubter's own loss.* Not only the works of mercy he might have wrought, but the Merciful One himself, are thus forfeited.—M.

Ver. 6.—*Christ ministering to the villages.* I. REJECTED IN ONE DIRECTION, THE SAVIOUR BEGINS AFRESH ELSEWHERE. 1. *Indomitable zeal, and inextinguishable love for souls.* 2. *Divine wisdom.* The sinning city or individual not altogether abandoned even when left alone. When the Redeemer cannot work within a heart, he will work about it. Where faith is not at once forthcoming, evidence is accumulated, and the unbelieving are approached from new directions and points of vantage. Every sinner is besieged by Christ. The country sends up fresh elements to the growing population of the cities; how important that it should send godliness and righteousness with these! II. IT IS THE SPIRIT OF CHRISTIANITY TO CARE FOR THOSE WHO ARE AT A DISADVANTAGE. 1. *They were out of the way and apt to be overlooked.* 2. *They were unfavourably situated for the rapid spread of new ideas.* 3. *They were for the most part humble.* "To the poor the gospel is preached" was one of the characteristics of Christianity, of which John was to be informed; and it might have been added, "by Christ himself." The moral influence of this example. How ought all ministers of the gospel and Christian labourers to eschew self and the love of fame! The grandest work of the ministry may be performed in the humblest sphere. Men are to be evangelized for their own sakes.—M.

Vers. 7—13.—*The mission of the twelve.* Already the Master had called them more than once. He had "many things to say" unto them, and was ever drawing them into closer sympathy with himself, and a higher sense of individual responsibility. St. Mark is not so full as St. Matthew, but from what he does tell us we are able to understand the nature of the work and its reason. The disciples are now to become apostles. I. CHRIST PREPARES AND AUTHORIZES HIS OWN MINISTERS. There was need for this. Many whom he had cured were proclaiming him, not only without permission, but against his express command; and the devils were continually confessing him. This was inconvenient on account of danger to his person, because of the fact that he had been charged with being in collusion with Beelzebub, and the misrepresentation that took place as to the nature and aims of his kingdom. Christ first says, "Come, follow me," ere he says, "Go." He *began* to send them forth by two and two," *i.e.* tentatively, as they were ready, and as his purpose demanded. "Great is the *authority of conferring authority*" (Bengel). 1. *The representatives of the Christian ministry were qualified for their task by the personal instruction of the Master, and communion with him in suffering.* 2. *Those most highly qualified to proclaim the gospel waited until he authorized them.* 3. *Their appointment had relation to their personal fitness and the exigencies of Christ's work.* *All* the disciples do not seem ever to have been away from Christ at one time. II. WHEN CHRIST HAS PREPARED HIS DISCIPLES HE HAS WORK FOR THEM TO DO. 1. *Their office was not to be a sinecure.* The state of society, its rampant evils, its transitional character, and the attitude of expectancy exhibited by many, were so many reasons for their being sent forth. 2. *There is never a time when earnest Christian effort is not needed.* 3. *The adaptation of men is to be considered in determining the ministry they have to perform.*

III. THE APOSTLESHIP INVOLVED TESTIMONY, MORAL APPEAL, AND SUPERNATURAL POWER. (Vers. 7, 11—13.) The particular duties of the Christian ministry are determined by the demands of the age, etc., in which it is carried on, but in essence they are always the same.

IV. IT INVOLVED A DIVINE COMMUNION AND A HUMAN FELLOWSHIP. 1. *He sent them forth, but his spiritual presence went with them.* It was only of what he had given that they could communicate to others, and as he accompanied their efforts with his power. 2. *He sent them " by two and two."* For mutual comfort, help, and co-operation. The deficiencies of one would be made up in the gifts of the other.

V. THE EQUIPMENT FOR IT WAS SPIRITUAL, NOT MATERIAL; DIVINE, NOT HUMAN. What they were to take with them is suggested only by the directions as to what they were *not* to take. It was in their message and its spiritual accompaniment their influence was to consist. The Master who sent them would provide for them. Christianity, which subsidizes all honourable means and influences, is independent of all. " Silver and gold have I none, but what I have give I thee " (Acts iii. 6).—M.

Vers. 14—16.—*Accounting for Christ.* Interesting as a photograph of contemporary opinion. Abrupt, picturesque, graphic. " He said " (" they said," in some ancient authorities, as in Luke) is to be understood impersonally or of Herod. If the latter, the very repetition of Herod's statement, in ver. 16 (which in both Authorized and New Versions is worded similarly to the order and style of ver. 14, but which ought to have its inverted, twisted character represented in the English, viz. " whom I beheaded—John : he is risen "), gives us fresh insight into the workings of Herod's mind.

I. THERE IS EVER A VARIETY OF OPINION IN THE WORLD ABOUT CHRIST. Whenever he is heard of human thought is exercised about him. The element of the extraordinary is always recognized as attaching to his personality and action. " However great be that variety, yet often the truth lies outside of it " (Bengel).

II. CHRIST HAS TO BE ACCOUNTED FOR. Very little was as yet known about him in Galilee, yet the question as to who he was at once arose. The reason of this is that *the character of Christ is a challenge to the spiritual nature of man.* 1. *It appeals to the spiritual hopes of men.* Even with the most debased and degraded, it is from the unseen that help and salvation are looked for. The common Jewish notion, that Elijah should come again, and the more general one, that the prophets were not dead, but reappeared at different times to repeat their messages, were but phases of the inextinguishable hope that characterizes the popular mind in all ages. They both start into life again at the appearance of Christ. He cannot be thought of by them but religiously or spiritually, the religious nature of his work is so pronounced. " The thoughts of many hearts shall be revealed." 2. *Conscience is addressed.* It is the king who fancies he detects the ghostly association. The guilty past started up in all its horror. John's faithful teachings and lofty example could not be forgotten. Was it the long-slumbering national conscience of the Jews that identified Christ with the prophets, whom their fathers had killed? It is the guilty conscience that fears him; the believer hails him with rapture and delight. So the Son of man judges the secrets of men all through time, and at the judgment day.

III. ANY BUT THE HIGHEST ESTIMATE OF CHRIST WILL PROVE UNSATISFACTORY. Popular opinion was at variance within itself; it falls below the true dignity of Christ. 1. *There was, of course, an element of truth in their guesses.* All true spiritual workers are represented by Christ, and their work is identified in greater or less degree with his. The kingdom of God is one in all its manifestations through all time. The higher personality and office of Christ is inclusive of all lesser ones. He was a Prophet, and more. 2. *It was an inversion of the true order of reference which they perpetrated.* Those prophets were but dependents of Christ, owing all their power and illumination to his indwelling Spirit. 3. *Their error was due to moral causes.* Had their fathers received the prophet's message instead of killing him, the generation of Christ's day might better have understood his gospel. The laws of heredity and traditional mental attitude had much to do with their blunders, but most of all their own rejection of John, or supine allowance of his death. It seemed as if the spiritual consciousness of the Jews was condemned to stationariness at the very point of Divine revelation where John had failed to reform them. And so all men's lack of faith and their unworthy conceptions of Christ have a moral root also. It is only as Christ himself, by his Spirit and teaching, enables us that we can truly say, "Our Lord, and our God."—M.

Vers. 17—29.—*A soul's tragedy.* I. FALSE STEPS. (Ver. 17.) 1. *Unlawful relations.* 2. *Resisting the messenger of God.* II. CONFLICTING INFLUENCES. (Vers. 19, 20.) The fearless court-preacher and the woman he denounced. The messenger of Truth and the associate in pleasure and vice. Representative of the way in which evil and good incarnate themselves, and work upon the heart of every man. The temptation to which Herod was subject was great; but he was not left without moral witness and aid. III. SATAN'S INSTRUMENT AND OPPORTUNITY. (Vers. 21—25.) 1. *The instrument is in a sense self-prepared,* coming as it does out of the very heart of moral complication and love of unhallowed pleasure. 2. Yet is it *also chosen and armed by the evil one.* 3. *It is an instrument calculated to work insidiously, unsuspectedly, and yet surely and irrevocably.* Who would imagine that a damsel would wield such tremendous destinies? The weakness of every man is thoroughly understood by the enemy of souls, and unscrupulously appealed to. The works of Satan are rather hidden than manifest. 4. *The attack is made when the moral sense is drowned in sensual pleasure and excitement.* Company, wine, the fascination of the dance, and the flattering of pride by the presence of the Galilean nobles. What importunity cannot secure, a skilful manœuvre may attain by surprise. The end is gained, provisionally, in the royal offer to the maid; a concealed, implicit pledge of what is not at the moment realized. Indefinite promises like this are full of danger; they cover so many unthought-of possibilities, and carry with them the illegitimate show of obligation even with respect to things not contemplated when the promise is given. The moral sense which is insensible to real duties avenges its perversion by manufacturing fictitious obligations, and attributing chief importance to them. "Honour" is the counterfeit of morality in many minds. A promise made as Herod made his is foolish and wrong, yet it cannot bind its maker to the performance of a further wrong. If men were only a tithe as attentive to their vows to God as to their vain and boastful promises and challenges to one another, they need fear no consequences. We bind ourselves with our own ropes. It was a *birthday* on which Herod committed spiritual suicide. Many a parallel to this may be found in the lives of men. IV. THE CATASTROPHE. The career of sin has been likened to playing the devil with his own loaded dice. The thoughtless word of Herod committed him according to his perverted sense of honour, and the sequel was already predetermined and inevitable. 1. In sanctioning John's death, Herod *violated the deepest instincts of his nature, and rejected the voice of God.* 2. *Crowned a life of sin by a heinous and irrevocable crime.* 3. (Humanly speaking) *Destroyed his own hopes of salvation.* His history henceforth is one of steady degeneration and ever darker crime. In many lives there are determining circumstances like this of Herod; they put mountains and abysses between the sinner and the God he has dishonoured. "John the Baptist is risen from the dead;" "Whom I beheaded—John: he is risen," are discoveries which lighten not one whit the burden of his guilt, and bring no hope to his despair. They are the wails of a remorse from which has departed the grace and power of repentance. Yet is Christ greater than John, and able to save from even greater crimes than the murder of John, if he be but recognized and believed.—M.

Vers. 30, 31.—*Telling Jesus.* (Cf. Matt. xiv. 12, 13.) Christ the central Figure all through the evangelic narrative. His personal importance is never obscured. It is from him apostles go forth; it is to him they return. Kings note his presence and works, and the people crowd to his ministry. I. WHAT THE APOSTLES TOLD JESUS. "All things whatsoever they had done, and whatsoever they had taught." 1. *They narrated their experience.* Most of them had to speak of their work and its results. It had exceeded their most sanguine expectations. The people had received them everywhere with joy, and they had nothing but success to relate. A few, however (Matt. xiv. 12), had a tale of personal sorrow to pour into his ears. They had been disciples of John the Baptist, whom Herod had just beheaded. Their hopes had been dashed to the ground, and they scarcely knew what else to do than "tell him." More disquieting still was their story, for they informed him that the tetrarch was anxious to see him, as he fancied he was John, whom he had beheaded, risen from the dead. So varied is the history of the Christian life! 2. *It was but imperfectly understood by themselves.* What they had *done* (*i.e.* miracles and exorcisms) was in their estimation most important, and is naturally enough mentioned first by the evangelist. By-and-by they were to learn that it was only for the sake of the teaching accompanying them that the "signs" were of any value. And so it was with the sorrow and fear of the disciples of John; they knew not their real consequence. Both were probably exaggerated. Still they did not feel they had to wait until everything was clearly and fully understood. All alike are drawn towards him. We, too, spontaneously pour forth our sorrow and joy, our fear and our confidence, into his ear, sure of sympathy and help.

II. WHY DID THEY TELL JESUS? 1. *A sense of responsibility.* It was he who commissioned them at the first, and they felt bound to carry back their report. He was the subject of their preaching, and of chief importance. And it was only as his power was imparted and continued to them that they were able to proceed. 2. *A feeling of interest.* The very enthusiasm and excitement brought them back to Jesus—the pleasure of telling him all the wonders and successes of their mission. Points, too, that specially struck their attention were referred to him for explanation. 3. *A yearning for sympathy.* They felt that he would most heartily respond to their mood, whether of elation or despondency. No one ever came with a genuine human feeling to Christ, and received a rebuff.

III. HOW DID HE RECEIVE THEM? He had evidently listened to their whole story. Now they met with: 1. *Kindly appreciation.* 2. *Gracious provision for their needs.* 3. *Precautions for their mutual safety.*—M.

Ver. 31.—*Christ's offer of rest.* I. THE PECULIAR GIFT OF JESUS TO HIS SERVANTS. "Into a desert place;" only Christ to speak with them, to comfort and to advise.

II. A MANIFOLD PROVISION FOR HIS SERVANTS' NEEDS. Calm after excitement; repose after labour; meditation upon Divine marvels and experiences. Security from threatening dangers.

III. A PREPARATION FOR FUTURE SERVICE. "Rest *a while.*"—M.

Ver. 31.—*The Christian worker's rest.* I. IN A WORLD WHERE THERE IS NO TRUE REST.

II. PROCEEDING FROM THE LORD. 1. *Divinely commanded.* 2. *Divinely prepared.* 3. *Divinely shared.*

III. TO FIT FOR FURTHER SERVICE.—M.

Ver. 31.—"*Coming and going.*" I. A PICTURE OF THE WORLD'S LIFE.

II. INDICATIVE OF THE WORLD'S SPIRITUAL STATE.

III. AN OCCASION OF DIFFICULTY TO THE CHURCH.—M.

Vers. 32—34.—*Christ's sympathy for men.* I. HOW IT WAS CALLED FORTH. 1. *The physical exhaustion and hunger of the people.* 2. *Their restlessness.* 3. *Their inarticulate longing for some higher truth and life.*

II. THE CHARACTER IT ASSUMED. Shepherdly anxiety and care. 1. *An intense compassion and solicitude.* 2. *A deep religious sense of the Divine ideal from which they had departed.* The spirit, the very words of prophecy, occur to him in the connection (Numb. xxvii. 17; Zech. x. 2). 3. *A practical undertaking of their care.*

III. HOW IT EXPRESSED ITSELF. He taught them many things. By word and act he strove to lift their hearts to God, and to suggest the ineffable mysteries of his kingdom. The miracle that followed.—M.

Ver. 34.—*The shepherdly emotion of Christ.* I. NATURALLY ELICITED.

II. A DIVINE INTERPRETATION OF HUMAN DISTRESS.

III. A FULFILMENT OF THE WORLD'S HOPE.
IV. AN UNCONSCIOUS PROOF OF HIS BEING THE SAVIOUR OF MANKIND.—M.

Vers. 35—44.—*Feeding the five thousand : a miracle.* One of the most signally demonstrative and masterly of Christ's miracles, whether we consider the circumstances in which it was wrought, the details of its carrying out, or the dimensions and absoluteness of the result. How carefully the evidence was accumulated by Christ of the truly miraculous nature of this work ! It was a grand display of—
I. WISDOM. 1. *A practical (and symbolical) discipline of the Church in its great function towards the world.* 2. *A demonstration to the world of the principles and order of the kingdom of God.*
II. POWER. 1. *Creative.* 2. *Multiplying human resources.*
III. MERCY. Wisdom and power co-operative towards the accomplishing of the highest blessing. Mercy the chief work of God as of man. 1. *Bodily,* in the relief of the hunger, consideration for the weariness of the multitude. 2. *Spiritual,* in giving spiritual bread, in teaching dependence upon God, and in enjoining economy of Divine gifts.—M.

Vers. 35—44.—*Feeding the five thousand : a parable.* It is no less remarkable in this aspect; perhaps it was its suggestion of spiritual things which was its chief aim. It sets forth the physical and spiritual dependence of men upon God, and the Divine Father's willingness and power to provide for his children; or, the sufficiency of the kingdom of God for the sustenance of its subjects. The nature and principles of Divine mercy to mankind are also suggested.
I. THE POVERTY OF THE CHURCH. Both discovered and concealed; discovered to itself, concealed from the world. How delicate the consideration and tact of Christ! 1. *In position.* In the desert. For its needs no dependence upon the world is suffered, whose gold and silver and bread are "not convenient." 2. *In material supplies.* Only five loaves and two fishes, and these, as it were, adventitious. 3. *In spiritual resource.* (1) *In evangelical sentiment.* How callous the suggestion—"Send them away"! There is no sense of responsibility for the well-being of the multitude, physically or spiritually. The question as to the "two hundred pennyworth of bread" is full of selfish dismay; the sacrifice is contemplated as not only great, but not to be entertained. "Give ye them to eat" conveys rebuke as well as command. (2) *In administrative expedients.* They had everything to learn. No spiritual imagination is forthcoming to conceive of Divine aid in a grave exigency of the kingdom of God, to plan for the supply of those who have been led, by eagerness for the bread of life, to imperil their command of material necessities. Had the true feeling been there, the ideas and inspirations required to give effect to it would not have been wanting. Has the Church of to-day yet risen to its high vocation? Our missionary enterprise and inward institutional development have not been proportionate to our light and privilege. Surely the day is at hand when all these half-hearted and disappointing efforts shall be left behind and forgotten in more vigorous, comprehensive, and statesmanlike undertakings.
II. THE RICHES OF CHRIST. 1. *A satisfying, saving fulness, administered through the appointed means of grace already existent in his Church.* The material resources of his people can never be of primary consequence; for: 2. *Means rightly used in his name will be indefinitely multiplied to satisfy all the demands made upon it.* One man, with the Spirit of the Lord in him, will be more powerful than Synods and Churches without it. And the means used thus must ever appear disproportionately insignificant as compared with the result. "What is little becomes an abundance through the blessing of God" (Godwin).
III. CONDITIONS OF DIVINE COMMUNICATION TO MEN. There was an antecedent ground for Christ's consideration, viz. that the people had exposed themselves to inconvenience and danger through desire for his doctrine; corresponding to the principle, "Seek ye first the kingdom of God and his righteousness, and all these things shall be added unto you." "He provideth the lower good for those who were seeking the higher" (Godwin). But the immediately declared conditions were: 1. *Obedience.* The disciples were to do as he bade them, and so through them, in turn, the crowd.

The resources at hand—loaves and fishes—were to be sought for, calculated, and brought forth. The people are bidden to place themselves in a position most fittingly and impressively to receive the benefit to be conferred. 2. *Order.* There is something very impressive in the symmetrical arrangement, " by hundreds and by fifties." It was manifestly a measure of the highest importance from the point of view of " supply." " Order is Heaven's first law." In the kingdom of God all things must " be done decently and in order." A settled government, properly appointed officers, and, in general, method, system. So in the economy there must be no waste. The saving from one season is to be the supply of another. 3. *Divinely commissioned service.* Some have supposed that the multiplication of the bread was effected in the hands of Christ; some, in the hands of the disciples; some, in the hands of the multitude; others, in all three stages of its administration. Yet are the apostles—the called and commissioned servants of Christ—the true " stewards of the mysteries." The qualification, however, is not mechanical, but spiritual. It is the Spirit of Christ in them that fits them for their task, and ensures their efficiency. 4. *Prayer.* The meal is a communion with God. His blessing must be asked. It is sacramental. Only as God blesses the provision can it be sufficient. It is obvious that the grand condition of all these requirements is *faith.* It is the calling forth and exercising of this which crowns the miracle as a consummate grace.—M.

Ver. 43.—*Spiritual economy.* From other accounts we learn that this measure was ordered by Christ. The power and the restraint of Christ are about equally demonstrative of his divinity. A strict and immediate economy is demanded in his kingdom. We are to appreciate the grace received; its very fragments are to be precious. The life and work of the Christian have to exhibit a wise and careful stewardship. This direction—
I. IS A SOLUTION TO ONE OF THE GREATEST DIFFICULTIES IN CONNECTION WITH PRAYER. 1. *Answers are apparently withheld because they have already been granted and we do not realize it.* 2. *Further blessing is denied because that actually received has been wasted or despised.*
II. DISCOVERS A COMMON SOURCE OF WEAKNESS AND WANT IN SPIRITUAL LIFE. 1. *We have not enough because there has been carelessness and waste.* 2. *We have not enough (or abundance) because we have been selfish.* There has been no desire to keep what has been received for others.
III. TEACHES US GREAT HUMILITY AND GRATITUDE IN THE USE OF SPIRITUAL SUPPLIES.—M.

Vers. 45—52.—*Jesus walking on the sea.* I. THE SERVANTS OF THE LORD ARE EXPOSED TO OPPOSITION AND DANGER IN CARRYING OUT HIS COMMANDS.
II. WITHOUT THE CONSCIOUSNESS OF HIS PRESENCE DIFFICULTY APPEARS INSURMOUNTABLE.
III. HE IS EVER AT HAND TO BLESS THOSE WHO ARE STRIVING TO OBEY HIS WORD.
IV. WHEN HIS SERVANTS ARE READY TO RECEIVE HIM HE WILL COME TO THEIR RESCUE, AND EVERY OBSTACLE WILL BE OVERCOME.
V. SUCH TEMPTATIONS ARE INTENDED TO DISCOVER THEIR NEED OF HIM, AND TO CONFIRM THEIR FAITH IN HIM.—M.

Vers. 45—52.—*Jesus walking on the sea : interpreted of the Church.* I. EVANGELICAL TYPES. The vessel and crew represent the Church of Christ; the sea, the variable circumstance of world-life; the voyage, the commission of the Church from her Lord; the storm, the adverse spirit of the world; the apparition, the spiritual advent of our Lord into the heart and mind of his Church; Capernaum—Christ's " own city "—the city of God, to which the Church brings all true believers.
II. SPIRITUAL LESSONS. 1. *The Church of Christ, in discharge of her great mission, must be separate from the spirit of worldliness.* The crowd left upon the darkening shore was animated by the unconverted, carnal mind that cannot understand the things of God; but it must nevertheless be ministered to. This mind is full of unspiritual interpretations of the mission and person of Christ (cf. John vi. 14,

15). But Christ himself, from whom the disciples were parted, was not yet manifested to themselves as the Son of God and Saviour of the world. He was as yet, so far as their conceptions of him were concerned, the "Christ after the flesh" of whom Paul spoke, and therefore but an element or phase of that world-spirit with which he had been associated in the miracle of the loaves and fishes. These together represent, then, the forms the world-spirit assumes, and through which it endeavours to work. 2. *The Church's distress arises from various causes, external and internal, but chiefly the latter.* (1) *The opposition of the world-spirit,* increasing as the direction of the vessel becomes more determinate, and developing bitterness, fury, and persecution. Against these the Church strives. (2) *Inward sources of disquietude and weakness.* The conception of Christ carried away by the disciples was in large measure a fleshly one, and a worldliness struggles within the heart of believers. The first stages of Christian life in the individual and in the historic Church are marked by low ideas of the person and work of Christ, producing estrangement from him, fear, and weakness. 3. *The deliverance of the Church consists in receiving Christ "after the spirit," in faith and communion.* This advent is supernatural. It is out of the eternal calm, spiritual elevation, and moral stability of the mountain of Divine communion. Advancing to and with his people through the turmoil of world-life, he is at hand to bless according to the measure of reception accorded him, ready to reveal himself to them that look for him and cry to him, and proving himself the One who "overcometh the world." This spiritual Christ (not an apparition, though appearing to the superstitious fear and ignorance of the Church as such) is the true, substantial, and eternal Christ, who will work out an instant and complete salvation for his people, perfecting their spiritual life, and leading them to their journey's end.—M.

Vers. 45—52.—*Christ's retirement.* There are three essential elements discernible—withdrawal from man, approach to God, and return to man.

I. Seasons of privacy and retirement are essential to the spiritual welfare of those who have much public life and work.

II. A great ministry must be sustained by constant, profound devotions.

III. The prayer of the saint is as helpful and necessary to the welfare of others as his practical work.

Or—

I. Difficult of attainment. Much publicity jarred and fretted his nature. Yet he could not be rude or unkind. The multitude must be sent home; the disciples required to be removed from the dangerous excitement of the scene. "Constrained"—"sendeth the multitude away." Only Christ could do this, and at what cost! His rest must be legitimately won, and therefore no duty or kindness is neglected.

II. A necessity of his spiritual nature.

III. Utilized in the highest occupations.

IV. Broken in upon by human sympathies and solicitudes.—M.

Vers. 53—56.—*Secondary benefits of the gospel.* I. These are generally its first recommendation.

II. The end they are meant to serve. 1. *To draw men to Christ.* 2. *To demonstrate that the gospel—the Christ—blesses the whole man and the whole life.*

III. Their snare and danger.—M.

Vers. 2, 3.—*Jesus, the rejected Teacher.* When the evangelist states, in the preceding verse, that Jesus "went out from thence," he is referring not so much to the house of Jairus as to the town of Capernaum. Thence he went forth to the village of Nazareth, in whose fields he had often played as a child, and in whose houses and streets he had laboured as a man. In the world, yet not of it. On a certain sabbath day he preached in the synagogue (for Nazareth possessed but one), where he had worshipped in his childhood with Mary, and which he had afterwards attended as a village artisan. St. Luke records the address he delivered, in which he proclaimed himself to be the Messenger of comfort of whom Isaiah had spoken. This only led to his rejection and to a brutal attempt upon his life, so that the Nazarenes unconsciously justified Nathanael's question, "Can any good thing come out of Nazareth?" In a true and lofty sense, the Lord was the Representative of his brethren, the Ideal to which they are to be conformed. From what he was and from what he experienced, we may constantly learn something respecting ourselves. We are reminded by this scene of the following truths :—

I. THAT WE DO NOT ALWAYS FIND ENCOURAGEMENT WHERE WE MOST NATURALLY LOOK FOR IT. If there was a place in Palestine where the Lord might have fairly anticipated a welcome, it was Nazareth. Other cities might suspect him, when he came to them as a stranger, but in Nazareth he had been known for years. There had never been an act of unkindness done by him, or a word of evil uttered by his stainless lips. With gentleness greater than a woman's, with bravery loftier than a hero's, he had walked uprightly and lovingly amongst this people. Cast out elsewhere, he ought to find shelter and be surrounded by love and loyalty here. He came as King Alfred came among his Saxons : when overwhelmed by superior forces, he yet refused to bate one jot of heart and hope. He came, as we come sometimes from places where we have been suspected or wronged, to the home where we believe the best will be made of us. But even Nazareth cast him out. Truly, he was "despised and rejected of men." It is enough for the servant that he be as his Master. Sometimes, like him, we may suffer from want of sympathy where we confidently expected it. Possibly, for example, you are brought to serious thought ; you feel that the world passes away, and the lust thereof ; you are conscious that there is around you a spiritual world, for which you are utterly unprepared. Filled with anxiety and distress, you venture to open your heart to those at home ; but, although it is nominally a Christian home, you are laughed at for your pains, or are recommended change and cheerful society. But you feel that it is not this you want, when your "heart and flesh cry out for the living God." Whenever, under such circumstances, you are tempted to anger or discouragement, lift up your thoughts to him who was tempted even as you are, and yet was without sin.

II. THAT MAN IS NOT THE MERE CREATURE OF CIRCUMSTANCES. The Son of God was in one sense infinitely removed from us, yet in his human relations he was "made like unto his brethren." And he, in all his purity and devoutness, came forth from a town notorious for its ignorance and degradation. He grew up there as a sweet flower does upon a heap of refuse, drawing nourishment to itself from the reeking soil, and transmuting it into beauty and fragrance by the power of its own life. So has it been with many of his followers. No man is absolutely dependent upon the place in which he is born or educated for what he is. He has a God-given individuality. Besides the external training, there is also an inward education, which is more productive of result. Examples of this are seen in social life. There are some who are envied now for their circumstances of abundance, who were not born in them. They have had many an effort and many a failure, but have been faithful and hopeful throughout. They started with few advantages, were sent early to business, had but slight education ; yet, with a sense of independence of man, linked with a consciousness of dependence upon God, they have risen above their former mean surroundings. Thus is it in the moral and religious sphere. You must not suppose that, because you have not a Christian home, you are "committed to do" some abominations ; or that, because you live out of sight of the worse forms of degradation and irreligion, you are discharged of all responsibility in regard to these. Circumstances are not to mould you, but you are to rule and triumph over them ; and, by the grace of God, may come forth from a despised and degraded condition as one of the kingly sons of God.

III. THAT NO MAN IS DEGRADED BY COMMON WORK. "Is not this the carpenter?" What right has he to assume the position of a teacher? Yet these Jews were for the most part more sensible in their views of manual work than many Englishmen. It was the custom amongst them even for rabbis to learn some handicraft. But then, as now, it was one thing to be a learned man with power to turn to manual occupations for amusement, and quite another thing to earn bread by it, and in the intervals of labour to teach others. This is what Jesus did.' Whether, as Justin Martyr reports, he made ploughs for the husbandmen or not, at least it is certain that the Builder of the heavens and the earth humbled himself to so lowly a condition that his neighbours could say of him, "Is not this the carpenter?" or, as Matthew puts it, "Is not this the carpenter's son?" He had fallen in with Joseph's condition, and had recognized his own as being marked out for him by his reputed father's choice. Often our work is so settled for us, and our plans and preferences are thus altered by others, or rather through them by him who appoints for every man the bounds of his habitation. Sometimes, for example, a young fellow has entered on the study of the law; but his father dies, and leaves a business on the continuance of which the livelihood of the widow and younger children depends. All the cherished prospects of life are then rightly sacrificed upon the altar of love and duty. It would not be right to dissipate the work of another's life, especially if it were that of one's own father; and if the business be one in which you could serve others and serve God, let it be undertaken heartily and gladly. Let there be no department of life-work in which you would be unwilling to bend your back for the heaviest burden. All such occupations Christ has touched and sanctified and honoured, so that in them "whatsoever you do, you may do it heartily, as unto the Lord."—A. R.

Vers. 3—5.—" *They were offended in him.*" Whether the narratives of the three synoptic evangelists refer to one visit to Nazareth or to two visits, is a question which has been eagerly discussed. Give suggestions for the settlement of the dispute. Possibly such discrepancies were allowed to exist that we might care less for the material, and more for the spiritual element in the Gospels; that we might concern ourselves less with external incidents in the life of Jesus, and more with the Christ who liveth for evermore. Those who rejected our Lord at Nazareth have their followers in the present day, who are influenced by similar motives. Let us discover the reasons and the results of their conduct.

I. INDIFFERENCE TO CHRIST SOMETIMES ARISES FROM FAMILIARITY WITH HIS SURROUNDINGS. The inhabitants of an Alpine village live for years under the shadow of a snow-clad mountain, or within hearing of a splendid fall which comes foaming down its rocky bed; but they do not turn aside for a moment to glance at that which we have come many miles to see. This indifference, bred of familiarity, characterized the Nazarenes. They had known the great Teacher as a child, and had watched his growth to manhood. He did not come upon them out of obscurity, as a startling phenomenon demanding attention; but they knew the education he had received, the teachers at whose feet he had been sitting, the ordinary work he had done, etc. Jesus himself acknowledged the influence of this, when he said, " A prophet is not without honour, save in his own country, and among his own kin, and in his own house." We warn our hearers against similar peril; for there are many who have known their Bibles from childhood, who remember the old pictures which at first aroused some interest in it, who have attended public worship for years, and yet their lives are prayerless, and it may be said of them, " God is not in all their thoughts." Beware of that familiarity with sacred things which will deaden spiritual sensibility. Most of all, let us who think and speak and work for Christ pray that our hearts may ever be filled with light and love, and may be kept strong in spiritual power.

II. CONTEMPT FOR CHRIST SOMETIMES SPRINGS FROM ASSOCIATION WITH HIS FRIENDS. "Is not this . . . the brother of James, and Joses, and of Juda, and Simon? and are not his sisters here with us?" Possibly there was nothing known about them which was in antagonism to the truth and purity Jesus proclaimed, but as there was nothing wonderful about them, it was the more difficult to believe there was anything Divine about him. Far more reasonably, however, does the world misjudge our Lord because of what is seen in us. Earthly, ordinary, and spiritually feeble as we are, we nevertheless represent him. He speaks of truth, and is " the Truth," yet sometimes the world asks concerning his disciples, "Where is their sincerity and transparency?" We profess to uphold righteousness, yet in business, and politics, and home-life we sometimes swerve from our integrity. Let there be but living witnesses in the world such as by God's grace we might become, and through whom there should be the outgoings of spiritual power, and then society would be shaken to its very foundations. When the rulers saw the boldness of Peter and John—the moral change wrought in these Galilean peasants—"they took knowledge of them, that they had been with Jesus;" and "seeing the man who had been cured" standing beside them, as the result of their work, "they could say nothing against it."

III. THE REJECTION OF CHRIST BRINGS ABOUT A WITHDRAWAL OF HIS INFLUENCE. "He could there do no mighty work." He *could* not. His power was omnipotent, but it conditioned itself, as infinite power always does in this world; and by this limitation it was not lessened, but was glorified as moral and spiritual power. In Nazareth there was an absence of the ethical condition, on the existence of which miracles depended—an absence, namely, of that faith which has its root in sincerity. If we have that, all else is simplified; if we have it not, we bind the hands of the Redeemer, who *cannot* do his mighty work, of giving us pardon and peace, because of our unbelief. Christ marvels at it. He does not wish to leave us, but he must; and old impressions become feebler, the once sensitive heart becomes duller, and we become " hardened through the deceitfulness of sin." "To-day, if ye will hear his voice, harden not your hearts." Nevertheless, he leaves not himself without a witness. If he must quit Nazareth, he will go " round about the villages teaching," encircling the town with the revelations of power which it will not receive into its midst. And though he "can do no mighty work" such as Capernaum had seen, he will lovingly "lay his hands upon a few sick folk," who in an unbelieving city have faith to be healed. "Thou despisest not the sighing of a contrite heart, nor the desire of such as be sorrowful."—A. R.

Vers. 7—12.—*Preparations for preaching.* From amongst his disciples our Lord selected a few who were to be in a peculiar sense his representatives and ambassadors, and they have had their successors in all the ages of Christendom. Mark significantly says, "Then Jesus *began* to send them forth;" for ever since that day he has been giving similar work, and qualifying similar representatives. A study of their characteristics and of their instructions may be profitable to us.

I. THEY WERE TO GO FORTH FROM THE PRESENCE OF JESUS. All the apostles had companied with him, and so had heard his instructions and been witnesses of his work. This qualified them for their mission. They were not to teach dogmas which might be read up as for an examination, but they were to tell of a life, of a person, of a death, of a man through whom they had known God. Hence Jesus "called them to be with him," and then sent them forth. This principle has always prevailed in the Church. Moses would never have proclaimed God's Law, or known it, unless he had gone into his presence on Sinai. Elijah would never have dared to attempt what he did, had he not been able to realize the truth of his often-uttered declaration, "The Lord God of Israel, before whom I stand!" These disciples could not have spoken as they did, unless they had been with Jesus. So, if we merely get up certain facts or theories, and rehearse them in the audience of the people, without ever having a sense of our Lord's nearness, our work will be a spiritual failure. First let us come and see the Lord in the temple, as Isaiah did, and when we hear his voice, and have our tongue touched with a live coal from off the altar, we shall be ready to say, " Here am I; Lord, send me."

II. THEY WERE TO BE WILLING TO WORK TOGETHER. "He began to send them forth by two and two," for their mutual encouragement and help. Show the advantage of Christian friendship and fellowship. We lose spiritual culture by the isolated condition of Christian life. United work does not always bring pleasure, but it always brings discipline, often through the trials which come from incompatibility of temperament. Picture to yourself the experience of the disciple who was appointed by our Lord to have Judas Iscariot as his companion. Simon the Cananaian would see and lament his growing selfishness and avarice; he would fear to weaken his influence or damage his reputation among strangers, and yet would feel he must be loyal both to Judas, and his Lord. What self-control this would beget! what charity, which would shut its eyes to evil to the very last! what discipline of self! what earnestness of prayer for guidance! And if an unpleasant companionship may be thus fruitful, much more may the companionship that is pleasant become so, if it be the appointment of the Lord. When two young people agree to link their destinies for weal or woe, to bear with each other's failings, and to strengthen one another's hands, it is a happy thing when they can say and feel, that " the Lord Jesus sent them forth by two and two."

III. THEY WERE TO BE CONTENT WITH THE USE OF MORAL INFLUENCE. On entering a town, they were not to demand accommodation from strangers by some display of miraculous power, but they were to inquire who in the town was worthy, *i.e.* who was receptive, being numbered amongst the devout ones who were " waiting for the consolation of Israel." The home of such a one was to be the centre from which the apostles worked. If their message was rejected, on leaving the place they were to "shake off the dust under their feet for a testimony against them"—an act symbolic of renunciation of influence and responsibility, and of the announcement of coming judgment. They were not to attempt to *force* men to listen and obey. Spiritual work is slow, but sure. We are not to endeavour, by the establishment of a great organization, to embrace all in a nominal Christianity, nor are we to conquer men by physical force, as Mahomet did; but are to seek lovingly and prayerfully to turn one soul from darkness to light, that it may become the source of illumination to others.

IV. THEY WERE TO EXERCISE SELF-DENIAL AND CHEERFUL TRUST IN GOD. This was the meaning of the instructions given in vers. 8, 9. They were to make no special provision for their journey, but were to go forth prepared to deny themselves; ready to live in the spirit of pilgrims; burdened with the fewest possible earthly things; free from all care, because the Father cared for them. When the Church has their spirit, she will win their results.—A. R.

Vers. 21—28.—*The murderers of John the Baptist.* The name of Herod Antipas is associated with that of our Lord on three occasions. The first is mentioned in this chapter. On the second he sends a threatening message through the Pharisees (Luke xiii. 31); and on the third, with his men of war, he mocked the world's Redeemer (Luke xxiii. 8—12). These together afford an example of the progressive nature of sin. Herod passed from superstitious fear to anger, and from anger to mockery and scorn. He "walked in the counsel of the ungodly," and "stood in the way of sinners," and at last "sat in the seat of the scornful" (Ps. i.). It appears to have been the extension of our Lord's influence, doubtless through the work of his newly appointed apostles, which aroused the interest and fear of Herod. The miracles which were wrought vividly brought before his guilty conscience the terrible crime which he had recently committed, in the murder of John the Baptist, of which Mark gives us the most graphic and detailed narrative we have. The feast described could hardly have taken place in Tiberias, but probably in some other palace close by the castle of Machærus, in which John was a prisoner. In the scene which is here portrayed we see three types of character, represented by the three chief actors in this tragedy, which are worthy of our study.

I. CONSIDER HEROD AS AN EXAMPLE OF MORAL WEAKNESS. He was the son of Herod the Great, by Malthace, a Samaritan woman, and inherited his father's vices without his vigour. Profligate and luxurious, he had no vestige of moral greatness. His language was that of a braggart, as we can see in his promise that he would give "the half of his kingdom;" as if he were a mighty Ahasuerus, whereas he was but the subordinate ruler of the small districts of Galilee and Peræa. In the scene before us we notice in him the following faults:—1. *He was disloyal to his convictions.* Impressed by John's words, he did not forsake his sins. Like Pilate, he acknowledged the innocence and dignity of his victim, yet he had not the moral courage to set him free. To know the right, and yet to fail in following it, is the germ of grosser sins. 2. *He was easily influenced by circumstances.* "A convenient day" came at last for Herodias's purpose, a time when the weak king would be inflamed by wine and lust. The tempter ever waits and watches for such occasions to effect the moral ruin of those who do not resolutely resist him. The opinion of the civil and military officials around him also prevented Herod's refusal of Salome's request. Like all moral cowards, he had more fear of the scorn of men than of the wrath of God. 3. *He was led gradually to the worst crime.* There had been a time when he would have shrunk from the murder of John; but he had been gradually prepared for it. His sinful connection with Herodias blunted any sensibility to good, as sensuality always does. His unwillingness to put her away led him to silence the bold preacher who denounced his crime. And when licentiousness had led to persecution, it was not long before persecution led to murder. 4. *He was moulded by the stronger will of his companion in guilt.* The weakness of a vacillating man is easily overcome by one who is resolutely bad. Give examples from Scripture, and illustrations from daily life, of the perils besetting those who have no moral firmness and strength.

II. CONSIDER SALOME AS AN EXAMPLE OF ABUSED GIFTS. Physical beauty is as much God's gift as wealth, or position, or mental talent. Too often it has been used for the sake of display, for the gratification of vanity, or for the excitement of evil passions.

Many have hereby been led into moral ruin. Salome degraded herself unspeakably by coming forward in this shameless dance. Forgetting all decency and decorum, she danced " in the midst," that is, in a circle of half-intoxicated admirers. 1. *Her regal dignity was forgotten.* With amazement the historian records that it was the " daughter of Herodias herself" (not "of the said Herodias")—a princess of royal blood. Even social position and family repute may be fairly regarded as defences against sin. 2. *Her maiden modesty was sacrificed.* In modern social life Christians should set themselves against all that seems to have the slightest tendency to this. 3. *Her feminine tenderness was repudiated.* The twenty-fifth verse indicates that she eagerly shared her mother's hatred against John. But her womanly pity should have pleaded for the life of a helpless prisoner, and this God-given characteristic of her sex being trampled underfoot, made her crime the more revolting when she accepted the bleeding head of the murdered prophet.

III. CONSIDER HERODIAS AS AN EXAMPLE OF UNSCRUPULOUS WICKEDNESS. She was to Herod what Jezebel was to Ahab, or what Lady Macbeth was to her husband. 1. *Her vices were great.* Abandoned licentiousness and malignant cruelty. 2. *Her influence was disastrous* over both Herod and her own daughter Salome. She ruined herself and others too. For all such there will come a terrible awakening and retribution. " Who hath hardened himself against God, and prospered?"—A. R.

Ver. 31.—*Recreative rest.* The disciples had been teaching the people, and meeting their objections; they had been curing the sick, and had seen effects startling even to themselves. Exultant over the work they had done, they were in some danger of forgetting its spiritual issues, and needed a reminder that it was more important to have one's name in the book of life than to have power to cast out devils. Agitated, restless, and weary, they returned to their Lord, and he, understanding their deepest wants, bade them follow him into a quiet retreat, that they might rest a while. Each sabbath day should bring us also to Jesus, that he may lead us into rest.

I. RECREATIVE REST IS RECOGNIZED BY GOD AS A NECESSITY FOR MAN. We are so constituted that a constant strain on the same powers will either degrade or destroy them. The absence of physical rest would produce madness or death. But if we had only physical recreation, if there were no provision for the cultivation of the mind and of the affections, if we knew nothing of the quietude of home and the rest of the Lord's day, we should soon become little better than the beasts which perish. This revelation shows that our " Father knoweth that we have need of these things." The Holy Book is not out of the sphere of our human necessities. It is wet with the tears of the sorrowful, and thumbed by the horny hands of the toiler, and through it the Son of man still cries, " Come unto me, all ye that labour and are heavy laden, and I will give you rest." The second chapter in the Book of Genesis speaks of rest as well as of work. One of the fundamental laws given on Sinai ordained that on six days we should work, but that on the seventh we should do no manner of work. Prophecy points on to a distant future, and declares " there remaineth a rest for the people of God." There is, indeed, no true want which God has not met. If the feeblest of his creatures requires food of a certain kind, it is placed beside it from the first. The butterfly, for example, which we sometimes use as a type of carelessness, deposits her eggs by unerring instinct where the young caterpillars may find their proper food. And the God who giveth to each his food sees that we want rest, and provides for it. When our day's work is done, and we are tired, weariness provides and fits for repose, and " the sleep of the labouring man is sweet." When we are in danger of becoming hard and worldly amid the cares of business, God places around us at home restful endearments and softening influences. And often on the sabbath day he says with effectual power, " Oh, rest in the Lord, and wait patiently for him."

II. RECREATIVE REST SHOULD HAVE A JUST RELATION TO EARNEST WORK. Everything of value has its own standard. Art, for example, is of value in proportion to taste. Rest finds its value in proportion to work. The mere pleasure-seeker loses the very thing he seeks because he seeks it; for pleasure is the complement of effort, toil, and sacrifice. Rest is the shadow thrown by the substance work, and you reach the shadow when you have passed by the substance that throws it. Nothing is more pitiable than the sight of a *blasé*, self-indulgent epicure, who has never done any genuine work.

and who saunters through life voting everything to be a weariness. How vivid is the contrast between his enjoyment and that of the schoolboy who comes home after passing his examination; or the man of business who rejoices to get free and renew the joys of his boyhood! The same principle applies to things spiritual. Those who have known no struggle with doubt or temptation, who have made no sacrifice for the Master, know little or nothing of the rapture which comes to others when, as they pray, there comes a burst of sunshine through the darkness. There would be more enjoyment of God's rest if only there were a more thorough doing of God's work. The converse of all this is true. Legitimate rest prepares for work. If an indulgence or recreation makes duty distasteful, so that we go back to it with surly discontent, then either the pleasure has been of the wrong kind, or it has been indulged in in a wrong spirit. The disciples who went into the desert to rest "a while" were soon at work again, and their retirement with Christ had increased their knowledge and power. Such should be the effect of each sabbath day. Its morrow should find us endued with more courage, patience, and hope, in our daily toil. The rest at Elim was as important for Israel as the march from the Red Sea.

III. RECREATIVE REST IS INTENDED TO EXERCISE A WHOLESOME INFLUENCE ON CHARACTER. Many questions are asked concerning various forms of recreation, whether for Christians they are legitimate or not. Incidentally some tests have already been suggested. What is their effect upon the work of life? Do they fit us for doing it better, or do they lead us to turn from it with loathing? And what is their effect on Christian work? Is that more, or is it less hearty, devout, and spiritual, because of our pleasure-taking? But, besides these, there is a more subtle test to be found in the effect of recreation on character. Rightly chosen and enjoyed, it may do much to supply our personal deficiencies. We are seeking to become men in Christ Jesus—to have all the possibilities of manhood, so far as they are innocent, developed and strengthened, and not to have a few characteristics abnormally strong. If we are becoming stern in our fight with difficulties, the relaxations of home-life should make us considerate and gentle. It is well that there is a time to laugh, as well as a time to weep; and that God sends us that which will lift us out of the narrow groove in which the uniformity of life would keep us. If recreation is to have the effect on character which is highest and best, it must be enjoyed in conscious fellowship with Christ. The final test about any doubtful recreation would be—Would Christ share this? Is it he who has said, "Come ye apart with me, and rest a while"? We rejoice in the belief that he does share in our recreations. He is with us under the whispering trees, and beside the sea as it rolls in upon the shore. He walks with us, as of old, across the corn-fields, and beside the hedgerows, with their marvellous wealth of life and beauty; and as we commune together he bids us think of the minuteness and tenderness of our Father's care. To many weary disciples he still is saying, "Come ye yourselves apart into a desert place, and rest a while."—A. R.

Ver. 41.—*Christian care for the needy.* Observe the contrast between this feast on the mountain and the festival just alluded to in the palace of Herod. There self-indulgence, folly, and guilt prevailed; here the necessities of the body were generously met, and hungry souls were satisfied and gladdened. Describe the scene. Let us learn some of the lessons here inculcated by him who on all occasions was an example to his disciples.

I. WE SHOULD DEVOUTLY RECOGNIZE GOD IN THE SUPPLY OF EARTHLY WANTS. When our Lord came here he found religion divorced from common things. It had become a matter of ceremonies, of place and time, of ecclesiastical fast and feast, and therefore one of the main purposes of his teaching and miracles was to associate God with everything in men's thoughts. He worked as a carpenter, and so toil was sanctified; he cured diseases, and the work of the physician and of the nurse was ennobled; he went to a wedding feast, and hallowed marriage; he blessed little children, and directed their joys heavenward; he spoke of lilies in the field, of corn white unto the harvest, of birds nestling in the trees, and so made nature vocal with God's teaching; and here, when he took into his hands the bread and fish with which he would provide a labourer's meal for the hungry people, he looked up to heaven as the source whence it came, and blessed it, so that to the disciples the common meal became a sacrament.

Too often we are unmindful of this teaching, and attribute our successes to our own skill and strength. Therefore God allows some disaster to come, so that in the recognition of human helplessness Divine goodness may begin to be considered. " Lord, we cannot satisfy this great necessity," said the disciples; and as they looked despondently on the handful, he looked hopefully and thankfully to heaven, leading them to think of him who satisfies the desire of every living thing.

II. WE SHOULD ALWAYS CULTIVATE THOUGHTFUL CONSIDERATION FOR OTHERS. These people, on their way to the Passover at Jerusalem, had turned aside to hear the Prophet of Nazareth. They did not profess to be his followers, although they were sufficiently interested in what they heard to remain till all their provisions were exhausted. Then the disciples thought it was time that they should depart, and were unprepared for the command, "Give ye them to eat." Our Lord was not like those Christians who withhold their sympathy from all but their fellow-believers, nor did he argue that the hungry people ought to have foreseen the difficulty, and made reasonable provision to meet it. He was the "express Image" of him who is kind to the unthankful and to the unworthy. God never withholds his beneficence till his creatures deserve it. He watches the supplanter leaving his father's house after a shameful sin, and even to him, in his merited loneliness, the heavens are opened. He hears the murmuring of the people of Israel, yet causes the manna to fall round about their camp. And when he sees no sign of the world turning to him, he sends for its redemption his only begotten Son; and "while we were yet sinners, Christ died for the ungodly." The goodness of the Lord, as well his chastisement, should lead us to repentance. Through us that goodness should reveal itself to others. Jesus said of this undeserving crowd, " I have compassion on the multitude;" and so he sought to inspire his disciples with pitifulness towards all who are in need.

III. WE OUGHT WILLINGLY TO MAKE SACRIFICES FOR OTHERS EVEN WHEN OUR GIFTS SEEM INADEQUATE TO THEIR WANTS. The disciples themselves were hungry, and all that was to be had was this bread and fish which a boy in the crowd was carrying; but of it Jesus said, "Bring them hither to me." At once it was given up, though it was evident that what might have sufficed for the twelve disciples was ridiculously insufficient if divided between five thousand men, besides women and children. Yet even this, which was very small as a gift, but very great as a sacrifice, was by the Lord's blessing made enough for all. It is the sacrifice in it which constitutes the value of every offering presented to God. We might have supposed that one with infinite power would have despised so trivial a supply as this; but God always uses what man has, as far as it will go. Even under the wing of the cherubim the hand of a man must be. When man can do nothing, God does all; but when man can do anything, God requires he should do it to the utmost. The manna will cease directly it is possible to revert to the old law of sowing and reaping. It is thus with Christian enterprise. The world shall be won for Christ—not independently of human effort, but as a result of God's work through it. Concerning all that we can offer of wealth and talent and work, though it is inadequate to the world's necessity, Christ says, "Bring it hither to me."—A. R.

Vers. 45—51.—*Christ walking on the sea.* This miracle was no unmeaning portent, but was full of spiritual significance. In Scripture the people are often spoken of under the figure of the sea and its waves (Dan. vii. 3; Rev. xiii. 1). Christ had just assuaged popular passion, and now he calmed the troubled sea, which was symbolic of it. Here, then, we may see a sign of the coming dominion of the spirit of Christianity over the sea of nations. We content ourselves, however, now with learning a few truths respecting our Lord and his disciples which are exemplified here.

I. WE LEARN RESPECTING OUR LORD: 1. *Christ's disciples would send away the people who were hungry, but Christ himself sends them away when they are too well satisfied.* (Compare vers. 36, 45.) The reason for dismissing the crowd is given in John vi. 15. They were greatly excited by a miracle, repetitions of which would ensure the provisioning of armies, and the success of a revolution. Hence Christ sent them away. "He hath filled the hungry with good things, but the rich he hath sent empty away." The prodigal is welcomed when he comes home starving and helpless. We must go to him acknowledging sin and weakness, and not confident in ourselves. 2. *Christ withdrew himself from earthly honours, whereas too often his disciples greedily seek them.* Our Lord "constrained" his disciples to go away, for they were evidently loth to do so. It was for their good. They were in danger of becoming infected (if they were not already infected) with the spirit of the people. To them it seemed that the longed-for kingship of their Lord was within reach. But for the second time he resisted the temptation—"All this will I give thee, if thou wilt fall down and worship me." And for them he answered in a most unexpected way the prayer, "Lead us not into temptation, but deliver us from evil." 3. *Christ left us an example of secret and earnest prayer.* He was alone with God at the close of that exciting day. The quiet of even-tide calls us also to secret prayer. Our Lord hereby renewed his strength, and from it he came forth to conflict and victory. "Pray to thy Father, which is in secret." 4. *Christ is often out of our sight, but we are never out of his.* Lost to the sight of his disciples, he nevertheless "saw them toiling in rowing."

II. WE LEARN RESPECTING HIS DISCIPLES : 1. *We are sometimes left to toil on in dark-ness, without Christ's realized presence.* He leaves us alone for a time that we may feel our need of him. Though the wind may be "contrary" to us, it is a good wind if at last it brings our Saviour near. 2. *Our extremity is his opportunity.* It was about "the fourth watch of the night"—between three and six in the morning—that Jesus came ; and the hours had been so long and weary since they started upon their voyage, that they must have been fast losing hope and courage. The darkest hour is just before the dawn. 3. *If our strength is insufficient to bring us to him, his strength is sufficient to bring him to us.* It was so when he redeemed the world. He came to earth because we could not climb to heaven. It is so in our special occasions of necessity. He sometimes comes for our deliverance in unexpected ways—"walking on the sea." 4. *In all our troubles Jesus says, "It is I; be not afraid."*—A. R.

Vers. 1—6.—*The carpenter ; or, the dignity of honest labour.* "In his own country," "in the synagogue" where he had learned in his youth, he now "began to teach." There were "many" who knew him, who had seen him pass in and out amongst them, talking to them, perhaps like, yet unlike, the other growing youths and the young men working for them, an artisan—one of many. These "hearing him were astonished ; " and though "the wisdom" of his teaching they could not deny, nor the "mighty works" wrought by his hands, yet, as they knew him and his relatives full well, they were "offended in him," and believed not. So easily is the poor frail heart led away from blessing by prejudice. How great was the loss of these needy Nazarenes ! "He could there do no mighty work, save" (oh, wonderful reserve!) "that he laid his hands on a few sick folk, and healed them." Let us leave this unbelief for the present—it will arrest our attention again and again—and let us see the high tribute paid to the honourableness of lowly labour by this Doer of "mighty works"—this "Prophet" robbed of his "honour among his own kin, and in his own house." If labour was first imposed as a curse, it is turned truly into a bless-ing by this example of him who thus helped to cultivate the fields around. Here pride is truly shamed if it looks upon labour as beneath it: it was not beneath him who is above us all. Let every son of toil see in this "carpenter" the highest evidence that all handicraft is exalted to a true dignity, and that hard industry, so far from being a degradation, is honourable and honoured. Now, since the "prophet is not without honour," let not "the carpenter" be ; for in this instance they are one. The occupancy of a sphere of lowly industry by Christ henceforth consecrates it as—

I. A SUITABLE OCCUPATION OF TIME. The responsibility of rightly occupying our time cannot be evaded. Of it, as of all other talents, an account must be rendered. 1. Diligent, honest labour is a profitable employment of time. 2. It is healthful. 3. It saves from the degenerating influence of indolence. 4. It is a source of pure and bene-ficent enjoyment.

II. AS AN HONOURABLE MEANS OF MAINTENANCE. 1. There is nothing degrading in honest toil. 2. It has its essential value in the world's great market. It deserves its fair remuneration ; and, inasmuch as it is in a high degree necessary for the well-being of society, its claims are everywhere, if not always justly, recognized. 3. In a man's employment of his strength and skill in procuring what is needful for his own life and for those dependent upon him, his independence of character is preserved and his best affections stirred.

III. AS A WORTHY SERVICE TO OTHERS. By the constitution of human society, it is the plain duty of each to promote to the utmost of his ability the well-being of all others. The products of industrial toil, especially of handicraft, are useful in the highest degree. Without them the comfort of large communities must be greatly impaired. He, therefore, who is called to labour, "working with his hands" the thing that is good, is a useful and honourable servant of his race. 1. In the lowliest spheres, the loftiest powers are not necessarily degraded. The "Christ of God" was a "carpenter." 2. In those spheres the holiest sentiments may be cherished, and the holiest character remain untarnished. 3. Whilst in them the humblest labourer may know that his toil is honoured, for it was shared by his Lord.—G.

Vers. 7—13.—*The apostolic commission.* "The harvest truly is plenteous" and "the labourers are few," therefore "the Lord of the harvest" would "send forth labourers into his harvest." To this end "he called unto him the twelve," and gave them the grandest commission ever entrusted to man. Let us consider that commission in—

I. ITS IMPOSED CONDITIONS. 1. In company: "by two and two." Thus for mutual encouragement and help. For the heart of the strongest may fail in presence of danger, difficulties, and threatened death. 2. In poverty: "He charged them that they should take nothing for their journey, save a staff only; no bread, no wallet, no money in their purse." The source of their power and influence with men was thus shown to be not of earth, while no false motives were present to draw men to them. And they, the teachers of faith in God, would be the highest examples of that faith. So in simple wisdom were they to go forth, and in every city seeking the man that was worthy, abide with him, honouring with their prayer of peace the house that judged them worthy to enter. 3. In danger: "As sheep in the midst of wolves" shall ye be. They whom ye go to bless will become your foes. "Up to councils" shall ye be delivered; "in their synagogues they will scourge you;" "before governors and kings shall ye be brought;" "hated of all men," ye shall be persecuted from city to city. 4. Yet in safety the life exposed for truth and righteousness is not wholly undefended. "The Spirit" of the "Father speaketh in" them in the hour of need; the patiently enduring "shall be saved." Even if men "kill the body," they "are not able to kill the soul;" and the Father, without whom not a sparrow shall fall on the ground, watches the minutest incident of the imperilled life—"the very hairs of your head are all numbered;" while at length the confessor of Christ among men will he also confess before his "Father which is in heaven." Moreover, in all this "the disciple" is but "as his Master"—that Master and Lord who will reward the least service done to himself, and punish their foes as his own—that Master and Lord who declared that the life lost in his cause should be most truly found.

II. ITS TRUST; or, the terms of the commission. How grand, how honourable, how precious to the world—the world of ignorant, suffering, sinful men! "He gave them authority over the unclean spirits." "As ye go," he said (Matt. x. 7, 8), "preach, heal the sick, raise the dead, cleanse the lepers, cast out devils." So the great mission has for its object the removal of the evils of human life. Its foulness, its suffering, its error, its subjugation to evil, are all to be combated. Truly this was "to preach the kingdom of God" (Luke ix. 2). Happy are the subjects of so good a King!

III. ITS LIMITATION. "Not into any way of the Gentiles, not into any city of the Samaritans," but solely "to the lost sheep of the house of Israel," may they go. So the promises to the fathers are fulfilled. Truly "God did not cast off his people which he foreknew." Truly "all the day long" did he "spread out" his "hands" even to them who "as touching the election are beloved for the fathers' sake." Yet "the time is at hand" when "even to the Gentiles also God will grant repentance unto life;" and out of them will he take "a people for his name." But, according to his will; the order must be observed: to "the Jew first," and, seeing he is the God of Gentiles, "also to the Gentile." Yet, "let the children first be filled."

IV. ITS SUCCESS. "And they went out, and preached that men should repent," and they preached the gospel, and cast out devils, and healed the sick. Few and simple are these words; yet do they declare conquests greater than armies could gain, and works of service to men that lift these labourers to a pitch of unapproachable honour. When the world is won to true wisdom, these men and their works shall be magnified above every other; and when the Church awakes to her true wisdom, she will see that herein is the pattern for all time of the chief principles by which the kingdom of God is to be extended in the earth.—G.

Vers. 14—29.—*Herod : the disordered conscience.* The fame of the disciples reaches the ears of Herod, and has the effect of recalling to him a shameful deed of blood with which his memory is charged, and leads him, in contradiction to his Sadducean professions, to declare, "John, whom I beheaded; he is risen." Thus two diverse characters are brought near together. There are others in view, but they are not prominent. There is the royal dancer, with her skilfulness and obedience, sacrificing her high prospects —"unto the half of my kingdom"—to the foul wish of her mother. We see her visage of corrupt loveliness, over which a cloud gathers, settling on her heated brow, as she finds that her whole reward is to be a gory dish; and we see the half-exposed coarseness of her unmaidenly spirit, which could receive and carry the bleeding head and lay it at her mother's feet. That mother—no. Alas, to what depths can poor human nature descend! Few words are needed to describe the two principal figures. The peace, the serenity, and the brightness of a heavenly life in the one, standing beside the darkness— the pitchy black darkness—of evil in the other. One a rough man from the wilderness, but the chosen herald of the great King, of whom it was declared that of all born of women a greater than he had not been. A great man, yet humble and meek; not worthy to loose the sandals of his Master's shoes, yet brave enough to reprove a wicked prince to his face. This was one. The other is that prince, the representative of a licentious court in a licentious age, big with the pride of conquest, yet trembling from fear of the people. A mixture of coarse animal courage with the weakness and vacillation which indulgence brings. But a man with a conscience. His heart a dungeon, across whose dark gloom shoots one ray of light. Little is said of John—very few words; a mere profile. "It is not lawful for thee to have thy brother's wife." What faithfulness! What brave fearlessness! Good men and brave always bear testimony to the authority of law. "It is not lawful" is a prickly hedge on either side of the path of life. Once more of John, bringing Herod more into view. "Herod feared John, knowing that he was a righteous man and a holy, and kept him safe. And when he heard him, he was much perplexed; and he heard him gladly." So the silent power of a holy life is declared by the example of its influence over this reprobate. Into the darkest chambers of that dark heart this ray penetrates. And the words of warning and teaching alternately please and pain—"he was much perplexed." Herod is evidently a weak man. He is impressible, but he lacks firmness of character—the hardness of texture that retains the impression of the hand laid upon it. He yields to good, but it is not lasting; he yields equally to evil. He is sufficiently alive to the claims of holiness to pay them tribute, but not sufficiently so to prevent the rage of passion. He is open to the appeals of a holy life; not less to the demands of a dancing-girl. He fears John, and he fears public opinion. He is weak—that weakness which is wickedness. He would give half his kingdom to a girl whose dance delighted him, and he would give the head of the man whom in his heart he honours to satisfy her demands. True, he was sorry—"exceeding sorry;" "but for the sake of his oaths, and of them that sat at meat, he would not reject her." Oh, what noble fidelity! Oh, what honour! Yet has he not sufficient fidelity to truth to say, "Over that man's life I have no power;" nor honour enough to say, "That head is not mine to give." What an unbalanced spirit! what a turbulent sea! This character reveals—

I. THE NECESSITY FOR A RULING PRINCIPLE IN LIFE; "the single eye," which, while it gives unity to the whole character, preserves by its simplicity from the entanglements of temptation.

II. THE NECESSITY FOR PROMPT DECISION, BASED UPON PRINCIPLES ACKNOWLEDGED BY CONSCIENCE.

III. THE DUTY OF AN UNQUESTIONING SUBMISSION TO THE LAW OF RIGHT.

IV. And it teaches the terrible lesson that THE HABITUAL INDULGENCE IN ONE SIN WILL UNDERMINE THE WHOLE STRENGTH OF MORAL CONVICTION AND SENSE OF RIGHT.—G.

Vers. 30—44.—*The miracle of the loaves.* The apostles, having returned to Jesus after their first tour of healing and preaching, relate to him "all things whatsoever they had done, and whatsoever they had taught." Touched with consideration for them,

Jesus withdraws them "apart into a desert place, to rest a while." But they could not be hid. The people saw them departing, and gathered, "from all the cities, a great multitude." To the eye of the Merciful they were " as sheep not having a shepherd," and his deepest sympathies were touched. " He had compassion on them," and he "healed their sick," and he became the Shepherd of their souls, and " began to teach them many things." So the day passes and the evening draws nigh, and the disciples in their fear desire him to send the people away to "buy themselves something to eat," little knowing that the source of all was near at hand. Jesus' demand to the disciples to "give them to eat" quickly evoked the demand, "Shall we go and buy?" for little recked they that " five loaves" and " two fishes" could feed so great a multitude. But he, "looking up to heaven, blessed," and that for which he blessed was blessed; and he brake, and still he brake, for probably the increase was in his hands. " And they did all eat, and were filled." So the insufficiency of our poor human resources is shown to be no hindrance to the accomplishment of the great Divine purposes; and the folly of having regard to our means alone is strikingly shown. Five loaves, with his blessing who gives bread daily, are ample to meet the wants of a multitude. In those five loaves were the apostles—so small a band—represented. How could they meet the needs of the world? But he would meet that need, and with but a little Church, a few apostles, and a few writings; and this he foreshadowed. The ground of the world's hope lies in his compassion and his means of help. But the miracle stands for ever to condemn the fear of those who think that the time must come when the fields will be insufficient to feed the nations of men. The " compassion" which then saw the multitudes will still be awake, and the power which could feed that multitude on a few cakes will in all time give daily bread for the asking. To fear in the presence of God for our life, what we shall eat, is as grave a fault as to fear him is a lofty virtue. The miracle is a doing in an unusual way what at all other times is done by well-known and ordinary methods—methods that are so regular in their orderly succession we are led to depend upon them as unfailing; and we call them "laws of nature."

I. It teaches us (if we did not otherwise know it) that all feeding is from the Divine hand.

II. It declares that God feeds men in tenderness and compassion. The bread comes to the thoughtful, made savoury with the Divine goodness.

III. It points us to those many processes of nature which are (like the disciples in this account) the hands of the servants of his will to bear to us God's gifts.

IV. It shows to us that, in all God's good gifts to us, the littleness of the human means and of natural resources is no hindrance to the fullest satisfaction of our wants.

V. It illustrates to us that in God's house economy reigns, and that with all plentifulness there is to be no waste—nothing lost. His gifts are precious in his own sight at least.

VI. And it quietly teaches the duty of a thankful reception of all he bestows— a blessing God for his gifts, which speedily returns as a blessing upon the gift.

But though this miracle met the bodily wants, and though it teaches its good lessons concerning the care that in compassion gives daily bread to the needy, yet it has its lofty spiritual aspect. It leads our wondering and admiring thoughts up to him who is the Bread of life to the world, and the very Life itself. And it demands from disciples that they catch the spirit of their Master, and in compassion care for every multitude in every place that " is desert."—G.

Vers. 1—6.—*Christ at home.* I. THE WONDROUS IN EVERY-DAY LIFE. When they heard him in the synagogue they were "much struck," Mark says. Where did all this wisdom come from? So does the parent wonder at the sayings of the child. "Where did he get such thoughts?" The boy goes from the village, and soon comes back to astonish the gossip, with his broad views of life and his easy and confident manners. Experience is full of these surprises. Nothing is more astonishing now than the empire which the Child of Nazareth sways in the world of thought and conduct.

II. THE JEALOUSY OF HOME-GROWN GREATNESS. The people of Nazareth stumbled at Jesus. So are our thoughts under the tyranny of custom. If one should tell us that our little son or brother was great, we should find it hard to believe. 'Tis want of faith in the living God, who works wherever, whenever, howsoever he wills. Beware of that narrow egotism which even now may be shutting us out from light and beauty, divinity and blessedness.

III. THE MOST INVINCIBLE OF OBSTACLES IS THE WILL OF MAN. How deep was the truth of the saying, that against stupidity even the gods fight in vain! There was sarcasm in the saying of Jesus (ver. 4). Often has it been repeated. He " wondered at their want of faith." Full of faith and love himself, 'twas hard to understand the want of response to it. " He was not able to do any work of power there." Ask, when the business of the kingdom does not seem to be going forward (except on a small scale, ver. 5), whether the cause may not be want of wish, want of will, want of prayer.—J.

Vers. 7—13.—*Missionaries.* I. MISSIONARIES MUST NOT BE, AS A RULE, SOLITARY MEN. For counsel, defence, cheerfulness, "two are better than one." Without artificially imitating this example, in natural and quiet ways it will be found good to follow.

II. MISSIONARIES, AS A RULE, MUST BE FRUGAL MEN. No luxuries; bare necessaries compose their outfit. It is like the soldier in "marching order," or the exploring traveller. Luxury is a relative term, but the Christian minister will always put it in a secondary place.

III. MISSIONARIES, AS A RULE, MUST NOT BE SEDENTARY MEN. They are sent with a witness. They must deliver a few clear statements, sound a blast upon the trumpet that calls to repentance, and then forward again. The rule for the pastor is very different. We must try to understand our call.

IV. MISSIONARIES, AS A RULE, MUST ACT DIRECTLY UPON THE CONSCIENCE OF MEN. This is a great canon, and a mark of distinction between the missionary and the pastor. "They, departing, proclaimed that men should repent." A fresh voice, delivering this word, "Repent!" with intensity and power, will awaken echoes. But, repeated in the same place by the same person, the effect must wear off. Solid and continuous instruction then is needed. The teacher must sow where the exhorter has broken uʳ the fallow ground.—J.

Vers. 14—16.—*Wonder and fancy.* Incidentally how much light on human nature do we gain from the Gospels!

I. PERSONAL FORCE ALWAYS ATTRACTS ATTENTION. The man cannot be hidden. Even the "lion" of the hour merely is an expression of spiritual force. Who is he? Whence came he?

II. THE POPULAR CONSCIENCE RECOGNIZES THE FORCE OF CHARACTER. They *felt* that something new had come into the world of thought and feeling. It is always worth while taking note of the direction of popular interest. Herod learned much from the people. However wide of the mark their conjectures as to the personality of Jesus might be, their instinctive recognition of his greatness was unerring.

III. THE SUPERSTITION OF THE BAD MAN. It is often seen that unbelief and superstition, as in the expressive language of the Germans, *Unglaube* and *Aberglaube*, are generally found together, springing from one root. The truth is, that in an idle, voluptuous mind any sort of thought springs up, rife as weeds in warmth and rain. The only way to think truly is to feel purely and act rightly.—J.

Vers. 17—29.—*The hero's death.* I. THE HERO OF CONSCIENCE CONTRASTED WITH THE VOLUPTUARY. The former chooses to be true and loyal to the right rather than to live; the latter postpones everything to "life," in the lowest and most sensual acceptation of the word. Yet the wicked man involuntarily respects the good man.

II. THE SLAVE OF SPURIOUS HONOUR CONTRASTED WITH THE SERVANT OF THE TRUTH. Herod excuses his violent deed; nay, he pretends that it is required in order to satisfy his word as a man of honour. Such a one as his victim would never have given his word in such a case.

III. THE TRUE PARTS OF MEN IN LIFE OFTEN SEEM TO BE REVERSED. John loses his head at the order of Herod. The sublime hero bows before the weak tyrant. So is it in the "whirligig of time." Unless we keep our eye firmly fixed on the unseen and spiritual, it may appear that all things are turned upside down. But there is only one relation of things, and that is God's. Herod is really to be pitied. Over John is extended the shield of omnipotence, and in the very moment of his violence Herod is most weak. (Compare R. Browning's poem, 'Instans Tyrannus.')—J.

Vers. 30—34.—*Rest and work.* I. THERE IS NO TRUE REST WHICH HAS NOT BEEN EARNED BY WORK.
II. THE DUTY OF RESTING HAS THE SAME REASONS AS THE DUTY OF WORKING.
III. SOLITUDE IS THE PROPER REFRESHMENT AFTER PUBLIC WORK, AND PREPARATION FOR IT.
IV. THE SPIRIT CAN NEVER BE AT LEISURE FROM COMPASSION, SYMPATHY, AND LOVE.—J.

Vers. 35—44.—*The multitude fed.* I. THE COMPASSION OF CHRIST. It is for the body as well as the soul. The foundation of work upon the soul is cure for the body. It is contrasted with the disciples' carelessness. Their spirit is that which leads men to get rid of irksome duty. "Send them away!" Let them shift for themselves. Christ's example teaches that where a want is seen, those who see it should be the first to seek to supply it.
II. LOVE IS RICH IN RESOURCES. It seemed a physical impossibility to feed those thousands without bread, without money. This beautiful story, like that of Elijah and the widow of Zarephath in the old time, teaches that "a little may go a long way." If the best use is made of existing means, they will be found insensibly to multiply; not always by what we term a "miracle," *i.e.* some process out of the ordinary operation of law, but in accordance with law, which may be better.
III. METHOD IN BENEFICENCE. The multitude is broken up and distributed in parties, as if in preparation for a grand banquet. The spirit of love and goodness works by method. When we introduce order into our works, we reflect the law of Heaven and imitate the thought of God. Waste of material and waste of labour is generally for want of this.
IV. IN GOD'S FEASTS THERE IS EVER ENOUGH AND TO SPARE. The people were not only satisfied, but there was enough left to furnish forth a future repast. The whole is a parable of the truths and laws of the Spirit. Love is the deepest root of social and political economy. It teaches the value of means, in view of the greatness of the ends. It stimulates prudence and calculation. For the individual, the complaint is generally not sound, that he has "not enough to live on." To reduce wants is the same as to increase means, and is a sure secret of wealth. For the community, the far-reaching and benevolent wisdom of the legislature may avail more than mere abundance of harvests. With order, religious principle, liberality and frugality, the tables of the people will be furnished with bread. To cheapen the means of living and oppose war is the duty of the Christian politician.—J.

Vers. 45—52.—*The vision on the lake.* I. THE FRAILTY OF FAITH. 1. In loneliness. Jesus had gone away. The disciples were in the middle of the lake, amidst a stormy sea. It is a picture of a life-experience. In loneliness we sink into weakness and cowardice, having been brave in the fellowship and under the contagious influence of superiors. 2. In the withdrawal of its Object from the field of vision. They could not *see* Christ. We want to see, when the whole need is that we should trust. We want to unite incompatible things; willing to trust so soon as we see a good prospect of safety; cast down with apprehension when the inner sight, kept clear, would open its vista of cheering hope. Those men were yet to learn, in the language of one of them, to "believe in the Saviour, though now we see him not."
II. TERROR AT THE SUPERNATURAL. They saw Jesus passing, and were terrified, for they thought it was a ghost. Involuntary fear in the presence of the supernatural is the symptom of our weak and dependent nature. When Jesus appeared as Jesus, he drove all fear away; when he passed into the *chiaro-oscuro* of perception, standing as it were in a region intermediate between earth and heaven, as here on the lake, as on the Mount of Transfiguration, terror fell upon their souls. Fear in the mind reflects the

presence of God. Modified by intelligence, purified from superstition, fear passes into that reverence which is the ground-tone of religious feeling.

III. THE TERRORS OF GOD CONCEAL HIS LOVE. Behind the tempest is his "smiling face." The voice of the Comforter and Saviour of man speaks from the dread apparition of the lake. So from out the mystic scenes of nature, the Alpine tempest and avalanche, the mountainous swelling of the sea, and all human changes and turbulences of history, speaks a voice, clear, calm, and still, if we will but hearken, like that which greeted Elijah: "Have courage; it is I. Child of man, I love thee; rest on me and be at peace." It is when we realize that we are members of the kingdom of spirit and under the protection of its Head, that we can defy the "wild deluge of cares." It is not because God is not near to us, or that help is not available, that we tremble and feel forlorn; it is because, like the disciples, our "minds have become dull."—J.

Vers. 53—56.—*Commotion in Gennesaret.* I. A STIR AMONG THE SICK AND THEIR FRIENDS. We read of "fashionable events" and "arrivals in the fashionable world." This was not such. The quality of a movement teaches much as to its origin. The poor and sick know their friends, and their thronging is a testimonial to worth.

II. THE PROGRESS OF HEALING AND PITY. Contrast with the progress of the conqueror or the cold pomp of royalty. Wherever Christ goes, and men come into contact with him, they are made well. Worth much is the testimony of any suffering one to the private Christian: "I am the better for seeing you; you do me more good than the doctor." There is a contagion of health as well as of disease.—J.

Vers. 1—6. Parallel passage: Matt. xiii. 54—58.—*The rejection at Nazareth.* I. OUR LORD'S VISIT TO NAZARETH. This chapter commences with our Lord's removal from the house of Jairus, the ruler of the synagogue, where he had performed the miracle recorded at the close of the last chapter; or rather from Capernaum, where the synagogue appears to have been situated. In either case he proceeded to visit his fatherland—not in the wide sense of that term, but in the narrower meaning of the township where his parents' home had been, and where his own childhood, youth, and early manhood had been spent. It is scarcely necessary to remind our readers that, while Bethlehem was the place of our Lord's nativity, and while Capernaum is called his own city, as the place of his frequent resort and the scene of so many of his mighty works, Nazareth was the place where he had been brought up. In a beautiful, basin-like valley, enclosed by some fifteen hills, was situated this place of world-wide renown. The town or village of Nazareth seems to sleep among the hills. The hills around this happy valley, as it has been called, have been compared to the petals of a rose, or the edge of a shell, with the little town on the lower slope of the western hill which rises high above, and which, from its elevation of nearly six hundred feet, commands one of the finest prospects in Palestine, with the Great Sea and Carmel on the west, the great plain of Esdraelon two miles to the south, Tabor six miles to the south-east, and Hermon's snowy summit away to the northward.

II. CAUSE OF HIS REJECTION. A previous rejection, if we mistake not, had taken place at Nazareth, and with greater violence than at this time, according to the record of St. Luke. On the previous occasion passion had impelled them; now prejudice blinds them. He had begun to address the congregation; his eloquence and oratory amazed them. He had not gone far, however, without interruption. They admit his superiority; they acknowledge his wisdom; but, in a sinister manner, they question its source and character, asking, "Whence is it? From above or below? What is it? Is it supernal or infernal? And then such mighty works are wrought by his hands! He is the instrument of some superior power—not the originating cause or author of them." Such seems to be the insinuation. Envy and jealousy were at the root of this prejudice. They canvassed the humble position of his family, and the lowly occupation of its members. "Is he not," they said, "a carpenter—a common carpenter, and the son of a carpenter—the village carpenter? Is he not a carpenter himself?" They were ignorant of the dignity of labour, and the nobility of honest toil. They overlooked the fact that Jews were wont to learn a trade, and that, according to Jewish ideas, a parent who did not have his son taught a trade was regarded as guilty of training him to dishonesty. Justin Martyr preserves the tradition of our Lord having made ploughs and

yokes and other agricultural implements. But they knew his family and friends—
knew them so well that familiarity begat contempt. They knew who Mary was,
Joseph having in all probability died before this time. They knew his brethren:
sons of Joseph and Mary ; or possibly his half-brothers—sons of Joseph by a previous
marriage; if not his cousins, children of Clopas and Mary. They knew his sisters.
They could not brook his great and manifest superiority. Verily envy is a green-eyed
monster ; and so "they were offended in him." Our Lord, no doubt, felt all this acutely,
but accounted for it by the principle embodied in the proverb, that a prophet is without
honour in three circles—his neighbours, relatives, and members of his household. No
wonder he could not do mighty works there; not that there was any physical
inability in the Saviour himself, but the forth-putting of his power was conditioned
by the faithful disposition or otherwise of his hearers. Thus Theophylact makes this
want of ability relative and owing to the want of faith in the recipients. "Not," he
says, "because he was weak, but because they were faithless." Here there was a
want of receptivity to such an extent that he marvelled—not at their unbelief, but on
account of it. It was not the object, but the cause (διὰ), of his astonishment. He
wondered, as we read, at the faith of some no less than at the unbelief of others.—J. J. G.

Vers. 7—13. Parallel passages : Matt. ix. 35—38; x. 5—42; Luke ix. 1—6.—*The
mission of the twelve.* I. THEIR FIRST MISSIONARY ENTERPRISE. Our Lord had
already, as recorded in ch. iii., made choice of his twelve disciples, to accompany
himself during their time of training, and subsequently to go forth on their apostolic
mission and with indubitable credentials of their commission. The time had now
come for their first brief and tentative effort in that direction. They go "forth by
two and two"—in pairs (δύο δύο, a Hebraism for κατὰ δύο, or ἀνα δύο). The wisdom of
this method is obvious for many reasons. It was the condition of true testimony
according to the statement of the Old Testament, that "at the mouth of two or three
witnesses every word should be established" or confirmed. Two are better than one
for counsel and encouragement. Two would numerically warrant the expectation
of the Divine presence in prayer, for "where two or three are met" together in
God's name, his presence is promised. In many ways two would be mutually helpful,
and abundantly justify the prudence of the arrangement. Endued with miraculous
power, they had no need of human recommendation; the powers they possessed were
amply sufficient to certify the Divine origin of their mission; while the works of
heavenly beneficence to suffering humanity were well adapted to gain them acceptance.
With such abundant spiritual equipment, they received the Master's word of command
(παρήγγειλεν) to set out on their first expedition.
II. THEIR PHYSICAL EQUIPMENT. Their physical equipment, however, was of the
scantiest kind. In fact, they were to make no special provision for themselves whatever; such provision might delay them when setting out, and impede them on their
journey. Consequently they proceeded at once to their sphere of labour, without
delay and encumbrance of any kind. Without staff, except the one in common or
daily use—they were even expressly forbidden to acquire or *provide* for themselves
(μὴ κτήσησθε) another in addition, or for the particular purpose of their present
mission ; without shoes, save the sandals they every day wore (ὑποδεδεμένους) ; without
bread for immediate use; without scrip for provisions by the way, or copper in their
purse to procure such; without two tunics, or under-garments,—they set out on their
first mission, pensioners on the providence of God and the pious hospitality of his
people.
III. THE ARRANGEMENT FOR THEIR LODGING. They were not at liberty to lodge
in any or every house that might open its door to them. They were to act circum-
spectly in this matter, and carefully inquire, on entering a city or village, who in it
was worthy. By acting without due discrimination in this particular, and lodging in
disreputable quarters, they might imperil their own reputation or bring discredit on
their mission. Once they had obtained a suitable stopping-place, they were not to
change for another, even if the offer of a better place of sojourn or superior accommodation should tempt them to such a step. Their wants were few, their mode of life
simple, and with the humblest hospitality it behoved them to be content. In case such
Oriental and usual hospitality was denied them, or in the event of their being refused

admittance, they were, by a significant symbolic act, to express their renunciation of all intercourse with persons guilty of such churlish rudeness or barbarous want of hospitality. They had rejected them, though they went in their Master's name; and, rejecting them, they rejected the Master who sent them, and thus cut themselves off from future opportunities of blessing.

IV. THE DOCTRINE THEY PREACHED. Above all was the great doctrine which they preached. That doctrine was repentance—the doctrine which our Lord's forerunner had proclaimed before; the doctrine which our Lord himself reiterated; the doctrine which, joined to faith, became afterwards one of the elements in that twofold apostolic testimony, when, after their Lord's resurrection and ascension, the apostles went forth, declaring "repentance toward God, and faith toward the Lord Jesus Christ." While thus busied in seeking the salvation of men's souls, they did not neglect the sufferings of the body; but cast out devils and healed the sick, using oil, if not medicinally, at least symbolically, to establish a point of contact or connection between them and their patients.—J. J. G.

Vers. 14—29. Parallel passages: Matt. xiv. 1, 2; 6—12; Luke ix. 7—9.—*The murder of the Baptist.* I. CONJECTURES ABOUT CHRIST. The name of Jesus had now attained great celebrity; it was fast becoming a household word; the cures he had effected, the demons he had ejected from human bodies, the dead he had raised—his wonderful works were on every tongue. Some detracted, others wondered, but most applauded. The missionary tour of the apostles, brief as it was, had given fresh currency and wider diffusion to reports already circulated far and near. His fame had made its way into the court of the tetrarch, and thus reached the ears of royalty itself. The personality of the great Wonder-worker was keenly canvassed; conjectures were rife on the subject. Some affirmed he was Elias, who had come as the forerunner of Messiah; others, not seeing their way to go so far as to accept him for *the* Prophet long expected, or even the precursor of that great Prophet, simply asserted he was a prophet; while some fancied that, after a long and dreary interval, a new era of prophetic activity was commencing, and so that a person like one of the old prophets had appeared.

II. CONSCIENCE STRONGER THAN CREED. Such were the conjectures afloat, and such the conflicting opinions of the people. Not so Herod; other thoughts stirred within him; something more than mere curiosity was at work in his case; he was startled— thoroughly perplexed, and quite at a loss (διηπόρει, St. Luke) to know what to think of the matter. In his extreme perplexity and agitation he expressed his opinion in a very surprising manner, and in the following very striking and abrupt words :—"Whom I myself beheaded—John : he is risen from the dead ; " adding, " And on this account mighty powers operate in him." What a wonderful evidence of the power of conscience we have here ! Herod, we have good reason to believe, was a Sadducee, for " the leaven of Herod," mentioned by St. Mark (viii. 15), is identified with " the leaven of the Sadducees " spoken of in the Gospel of St. Matthew (xvi. 6). The Sadducees denied the existence of angel or spirit, and also the resurrection of the dead; and yet this loose-living, unbelieving Sadducee fell back at once on an article of belief which he had all his life denied. The power of conscience had overmastered his creed. His guilty conscience had conjured up before him the murdered man as restored to life, and returning, as it were, with power from the spirit-world.

III. A PARALLEL CASE. A somewhat similar instance of the mighty power of that monitor within occurs in an instructive narrative in the forty-second chapter of the Book of Genesis. When Joseph, before making himself known to his brethren, had put them in ward three days, and subsequently released them on condition of retaining one as a hostage till the rest returned with their youngest brother, in proof of their good faith and of their being true men and no spies, " they said one to another, We are verily guilty concerning our brother, in that we saw the anguish of his soul, when he besought us, and we would not hear ; therefore is this distress come upon us." There was nothing apparently in the circumstances of the case, unpleasant as those circumstances were, nor in the condition imposed on them, hard as it seemed, to remind them of their cruel treatment of their long-lost brother—nothing to recall his memory, absolutely nothing, save the still, small voice within ; in other words, the power of a guilty conscience.

IV. THE CIRCUMSTANCES THAT OCCASIONED THE BAPTIST'S DEATH. The evangelist now turns aside to narrate the circumstances that led up to the death of John the Baptist. Herod Antipas, ethnarch of Galilee and Peræa, called "tetrarch" by St. Matthew, as inheriting only a fourth part of the dominions of his father, Herod the Great, and styled "king" by St. Mark, had seduced his brother Philip's wife, with whom he was now living in an adulterous connection. The Baptist boldly but faithfully lifted up his voice against this sin, addressing earnest and repeated remonstrances to Herod; for, as we read, he kept saying (ἔλεγε being imperfect), "It is not lawful for thee to have her." The vindictive spirit of Herodias was roused in consequence; she resolved to have her revenge, but was unable to prevail on her husband to gratify her fully in this particular. He arrested the Baptist and imprisoned him, putting him in chains. He still, however, retained some respect for him, as a good and holy man whom he had heard often, and by whom he had been influenced to do many things; though συνετήρει rather means that Herod kept him in safety, or preserved him from Herodias's machinations, than that he esteemed him highly. Besides, state policy stood in the way of further violence. Herod shrank from the unpopularity which he was certain to incur by such a course; perhaps even worse consequences might ensue. To deprive the people of their favourite might lead to insurrection. Josephus, however, attributes the murder of John by Herod to Herod's "fear lest the great influence John had over the people might put it into his power and inclination to raise a rebellion." This wicked woman bided her time, harbouring her secret grudge and ill-concealed resentment (ἐνεῖχεν, equivalent to "she held fast within or cherished inward wrath," or "set herself against," Revised Version); while ἤθελεν implies "she had a settled desire"); but the favourable opportunity at last arrived. The king was celebrating his birthday festival by an entertainment to the magnates of his realm—high officers of the army, military tribunes, or chiliarchs, and other functionaries, civil or ecclesiastical, of distinguished rank. But besides this great assemblage of Galilean nobles and the splendour of the feast itself, a new feature was added to the entertainment. Salome, daughter of Herodias, in forgetfulness of the due decorum of her rank and the natural modesty of her sex, volunteered to play a part little better than that of ballet-girl before the assembled grandees of Galilee, and thus to heighten the enjoyment of the king's guests. The king looked on in rapture, immensely pleased by the easy condescension, and charmed with the agility and graceful movements of the fair *danseuse*. He was sensible of the sacrifice she had made in compliment to his majesty; for a Persian queen once lost her crown, and was willing to submit to the loss, rather than, at the sacrifice of her queenly or womanly modesty, to appear, even by the king's express command, in the presence of his banqueters. Being, in consequence, in a grateful, generous mood, he determined not to be outdone in magnanimity. There and then, of his own motion, he promised Salome whatever she asked, if it should amount to half his kingdom; he backed his promise by an oath, yea, by more than one, for we read of oaths (ὅρκους), as confirmatory of that promise. The girl was somewhat nonplussed by the largeness of the king's bounteous offer. She hesitated; but a prompter was not far to seek. She repaired to her mother, no doubt expecting direction in the matter of gold, or jewels, or diamonds, or girlish ornaments of some sort. But no; that wicked woman had set her heart on what no gold could purchase, and no gems procure. It was no less than the Baptist's head.

V. REFLECTIONS ON ALL THIS. 1. Surely the maiden, bold as she was, must have been shocked at the proposal; surely she must have recoiled from such a cruelty; surely she must have required strong and powerful urgency to bring herself to present such a bloody petition. And this we think is implied in the word προβιβασθεῖσα, employed by St. Matthew, and signifying "made to go forward," and so instigated. She soon, however, recovered her sprightliness. Once her scruples were overcome, she returned in haste, and with eagerness preferred the ghastly request for John the Baptist's head to be given her immediately—lest time might cool the royal ardour—and in a charger, one of the platters used in the feast, and thus one of those just at hand, to make sure of the execution on the spot. The terms are expressive of the utmost eagerness and haste: "Give me here—immediately in a charger," is the demand after she had "come in straightway with haste." 2. The king at once repented, but too late; he was excessively sorry (περίλυπος). This word is only used twice again in the New Testament—of the Saviour in his agony, and of the rich ruler in parting, perhaps for ever, from the Saviour. But then there was the false shame consequent on repeated oaths, and because of the presence of so many persons of quality. How could he break the former? How could he insult, by withdrawal of his kingly promise or breach of faith, the latter? How could he set aside (ἀθετῆσαι) a promise made before so many, and confirmed by so many oaths? 3. At once a guardsman (σπεκουλάτωρ, either equal to δορυφόρος, a satellite or body-guard, or equal to κατάσκοπος, a spy, or scout; at all events, a guardsman of Herod now at war with Aretas) is despatched. The head is brought, dripping with blood. Oh, horrid sight! It is handed on a platter to the maiden; and she, maiden though she was, received it, and, maiden though she was, bore it away to her mother. The word "maiden" (κοράσιον, equivalent to little or young maiden) is repeated, as if to stigmatize the untender, unfeeling, and beyond expression unmaidenly, conduct of this princess. 4. So ended the last act of this bloody tragedy. It now remained for the sorrowing disciples of the Baptist tearfully and tenderly to take up the corpse (πτῶμα, equivalent to *cadaver*) of their beloved master, and consign it to its last resting-place in the tomb.

VI. ADDITIONAL REMARKS. 1. A nearly parallel case, or a crime somewhat similar to that of Herod, is referred to in strongest terms of condemnation by Cicero, in the twelfth chapter of his ' Treatise on Old Age,' as follows :—" I indeed acted unwillingly in banishing from the senate L. Flaminius, brother of that eminently brave man, T. Flaminius, seven years after he had been consul ; but I thought that his licentiousness should be stigmatized. For when he was consul in Gaul, he was prevailed on by a courtesan, at an entertainment, to behead one of those who were in confinement on a capital accusation ; . . . but lewdness so abandoned and so desperate, which was combining with private infamy the disgrace of the empire, could by no means be visited with approbation by myself and Flaccus." 2. It was in a gloomy dungeon, in the strong old castle of Machærus, that the Baptist was imprisoned and beheaded. That place was in Peræa, nine miles east of the Dead Sea, and on the borders between the dominion of Herod and of Aretas. It is thus described by Josephus in relation to its strength : " The nature of the place was very capable of affording the surest hopes of safety to those that possessed this citadel, as well as delay and fear to those that should attack it ; for what was walled in was itself a very rocky hill, elevated to a very great height; which circumstance alone made it very hard to be subdued. It was also so contrived by nature that it could not be easily ascended; for it is, as it were, ditched about with such valleys on all sides, and to such a depth that the eye cannot reach their bottoms, and such as are not easily passed over, and even such as it is impossible to fill up with earth."—J. J. G.

Vers. 30—44. Parallel passages : Matt. xiv. 13—21; Luke ix. 10—17; John vi. 1—14.—*Miraculous provision.* I. THE FEEDING OF THE FIVE THOUSAND. 1. *The vivid description of St. Mark.* In connection with this miracle, St. Mark describes the recognition of our Lord by the multitude, their running together on foot, their outspeeding the Saviour, their arrival at the place of disembarkation before him, the compassion that moved him, the instruction he gave them. He describes, moreover, the green grass on which the multitudes sat down, their divisions into hundreds and fifties, their reclining company after company (literally, a convivial party, and συμπόσια συμπόσια, a Hebraism, like δύο δύο of ver. 7) or as though in military order, the resemblance of the multitudes thus seated to the plots of a garden (πρασιαὶ πρασιαὶ, equivalent to "beds of leeks," from πράσον, a leek, and the structure another Hebraism)—the whole exhibiting a stirring and life-like scene. The importance of this miracle may be inferred from all four evangelists recording it. 2. *The time of year.* From the fresh greenness of the grass we infer the season of the year, and can better account for the great multitudes that crowded the grassy space near Bethsaida. It was spring—March or April—and so the season of the Passover, as we are expressly informed by St. John ; the pilgrim companies were on the move in that direction, and hence the greatness of the crowds that followed the Saviour. Another miracle of feeding the multitudes is recorded by St. Matthew, in the fifteenth chapter of that Gospel towards its close, and also by St. Mark (viii. 1—9). That the two miracles are quite distinct, is shown by the following circumstances :—(1) In the miracle of feeding the four thousand just referred to, our Lord himself introduces the matter of supply. (2) The provision for the smaller number of four thousand was greater, being *seven* loaves and a few small fishes ; while here for the five thousand there are only *five* loaves and two fishes. (3) The baskets in this first miracle are called by the four evangelists κοφίνοι, small wicker-baskets ; on the second occasion they are called both by St. Matthew and St. Mark σπυρίδες, rope-baskets, so large that in one of them Paul was let down the wall of Damascus ; and from σπεῖρα, as if woven work, or rather from πυρός, wheat, as if a vessel for wheat. Our Lord also, when making reference to the two miracles, makes the same distinction ; thus, " When I brake the five loaves among five thousand, how many baskets (κοφίνους) full of fragments took ye up ? They say unto him, Twelve. And when the seven among the four thousand, how many baskets (σπυρίδων) full of fragments took ye up ? And they said, Seven."

II. Some salient points of the miracle, and the lessons taught. 1. *The way of duty the way of safety.* The first lesson here taught us is that the way of duty is the way of safety. We see on the surface of the narrative the satisfaction of the multitudes on recognizing our Lord, their eager haste in coming up with him, their earnest desire for his teaching, their prolonged attention to his utterances. Long without a right guide, long wanting a true leader, long panting for the green pastures and still waters, long athirst for " the sincere milk of the Word " they have found at last the Good Shepherd ; they know his voice, and follow him. They had much to learn, and our Lord taught truths he taught them, they had almost forgotten the claims of the body till the cravings of nature forced themselves upon them ; at all events, they had laid aside their usual forethought for the supply of those wants. And now the day is far spent, the shades of evening are closing round them ; they find themselves in a place distant from any human habitation, and destitute of the articles of human food. How are they to meet the emergency ? Whence are they to obtain the refreshment they so much need ? How were they to get " two hundred pennyworth of bread," which, if we reckon the denarius at eightpence halfpenny, would cost upwards of £7 ? No doubt they thought of different expedients. The disciples proposed one course, our Lord pursued another. The Lord is a rich provider ; he never falsifies the promise, " Seek ye first the kingdom of God and his righteousness, and all these things shall be added unto you." Here, then, we are bidden to " stand still, and see the salvation of God." The result is recorded in the words, " They did all eat, and were filled." 2. *The compassion of the Saviour.* His compassionate heart embraces all his people's wants, and those wants at all times. In the exercise of that compassion he remembers the body as well as the soul. He remembered it in creation ; he remembered it in redemption : "We wait for the adoption, to wit, the redemption of the body." He remembers it in his providential care over it, and provision for it from day to day. With his own lips he taught this cheering lesson when on earth, " Your heavenly Father knoweth ye have need of all these things." And he that gave us so much unasked, will not refuse us what we need when he is asked. " He that spared not his own Son, but delivered him up for us all, shall he not with him also freely give us all things ? " 3. *Nature of this miracle by which he supplied their wants.* Our Lord on this occasion exhibited his compassion in supplying the people's wants by an act of creative power. Some of his miracles are restorative, as when he restores sight to the blind, speech to the dumb, motion to the lame, hearing to the deaf, and power to the palsied limb. Some are redemptive, as when he rescues the poor demoniac from the foul fiends that had usurped such power over him. Some are punitive, as when he blasted the barren tree, as a symbolic lesson to all cumberers of the ground, and swept away the ill-got gains of the swinish Gadarenes. One is transforma-tory, as when he turned the water in the waterpots of Cana into wine. The miracle before us is an act of creative power ; for in what other light can we regard the multiplica-tion of five loaves and two fishes into a supply of food sufficient for such a multitude, so that " they did all eat, and were filled " ? He lays all nature under contribution to supply his people's wants. Even an act of creation will not be withholden, if their necessities require it. 4. *The Saviour's love of order.* " Order," says the poet, " is Heaven's first law ; " " Let everything be done decently, and in order," is the apostle's command. Our Lord confirms both by his example, in the orderly arrangement and disposition into rank and file, as it were, which he here directs. Whether we are in the Church or in the world—that is, whether we are engaged in the arrangements of the one or in the affairs of the other—we shall do well to observe this law of order. "A place for everything," says the old maxim, " and everything in its proper place; a time for everything, and everything at its right time." Such orderly regulation of all our matters would save time; it would save trouble; it would facilitate work; it would further largely the success of our pursuits and plans. Here all saw the miracle, all were fed, all were satisfied; no one was neglected, no one passed over or passed by. 5. *His devotion.* Never did our Lord lose sight of the glory of God. This was the object ever prominently kept in view. Before he brake he looked up to heaven and blessed, and brake at once (κατέκλασε, aorist) the loaves, and was giving (ἐδίδου, imperfect) bit by bit, as it were, to the disciples for distribution by them among the multitude. As Creator, he multiplied the loaves; as creature, he looked up for Heaven's blessing on them. From every gift we are to look up to the Giver; in every gift we are to recognize the Author; for every gift we are to record our grateful acknowledgments; in every bounty we are to own the grace and goodness and greatness of the heavenly Benefactor. To see God in all his works, to trace him in all his ways, to obey him in all his will, to adore him in all the outgoings of his loving-kindness towards us, and to see him in every blessing he bestows, is the lesson taught us by the example of Christ in this passage, and by the exhortation of his apostle in that other passage, " Whether therefore ye eat or drink, or whatever ye do, do all to the glory of God." 6. *The duty of frugality.* Mighty and magnificent as the works of nature are, there is no needless expenditure of force. Many of the great agencies employed serve a variety of ends. Many results often proceed from one single cause. So in the domain of miracle. He never resorts to miracle when ordinary means will suffice. Amid all that vast abundance which our Lord created on this occasion, he suffers nothing to go to loss. Here we see the same attention to the great things and the little things. He allows nothing to go to waste. " Gather up the fragments," he said. Surely this teaches us economy, surely this enjoins thrift, surely this enforces the old proverb, " Waste not, want not." Surely this is condemnatory of all extravagance in every department, whether of food, or raiment, or place of abode, or manner of life, or course of conduct.

III. DAILY BREAD AND ITS PROVISION. 1. *The wonderful is not necessarily miraculous.* Some hold that the daily bread which God gives us, which we eat, and by which we are sustained, is a miracle as great, or greater, because a standing miracle, than the feeding of five thousand with five loaves and two fishes, or the feeding of four thousand with seven loaves and a few small fishes. They refer to the fact that the seed covered in the earth dies and lives again, growing up under the rains of the spring and the suns of the summer, and in due season ripening into the golden grain of the harvest, then made into bread, and becoming wholesome food; and allege that in all this we have a miracle great as the multiplying by our Lord of the loaves and the fishes; that omnipotence is as much required in the one case as in the other; but that what is rare we call miraculous, while what is common and usual we call a law or process of nature; though both alike are manifestations of the mighty power of God. This reasoning appears plausible, and has an element of truth in it, but it mistakes the real nature of miracle. It is, in fact, pretty much the view of Augustine, who, besides confounding the wonderful with the miraculous, regards miracle as simply an acceleration of a natural process; for he says of the miracle at Cana that " he made wine in a wedding feast, who makes it every year in the vines; but the former we do not wonder at, because it occurs every year: by its constant recurrence it has lost, or ceased to command, admiration." The chief element of miracle is hereby overlooked. We admit that nature is an effect whose cause is God, and that omnipotence is at work in the processes of nature as well as in the really miraculous result; yet not in the same way. That which differentiates the one from the other is, that God in the one case produces the result by immediate efficiency, in the other by means of secondary or subordinate causes; in the one by a direct act of volition, in the other by the processes of nature. To attribute a miracle to the operation of a higher but unknown law is a gratuitous assumption, and is as unnecessary as it is unsatisfactory. To regard it as the result of an accelerated law of nature, is overlooking the fact that the really miraculous element in such a case is this very quickening into rapid result, or hastening in a forcible and extraordinary manner the ordinary process. It has been said, somewhat rhetorically, "We breathe miracles, we live by miracles, we are upheld every day miraculously, and that individual has a blind mind or a hard heart (or both) who does not see, or seeing does not recognize, the hand of our heavenly Father in all those gifts of his providence and bestowments of his bounty, by which we are sustained and surrounded." Now, to convert the rhetorical into the real, we must substitute for "miracles," each time the word occurs in the cited paragraph, "marvels" or "wonders," that is, processes that are wonderful—indeed, quite marvellous, but in no strict sense miraculous; and then, with this alteration, the devoutness of the sentiments expressed commends itself to our admiration. 2. *Daily bread, though not a miracle, is God's gift.* It may be objected, that our daily bread is not so much God's gift as the fruit of man's labour. Who then, O man, we may well ask, has given you the hand to labour, the strength to use it, the health to employ it? Who, moreover, has given you the fruitful field to till, the former and the latter rain to refresh and ripen the growing grain? Or, going further back, who has imparted to the seed, sown or planted, the power of growth or development? Still further, who counteracts the hurtful effects of too much drought, or neutralizes the baneful consequences of excessive moisture, or tempers the scorching heat, or checks the pinching cold? Who protects the root from the worm that would injure it, or saves the ear from the blight that would taint it? Who prevents the mildew that would damage the maturing grain, or the disease that would quite destroy it? Or who rebukes the curse of barrenness that would render all efforts useless? Who watches over the various stages of the crop—first the blade, then the ear, afterwards the ripe corn in the ear, till, having weathered all the storms that endangered it, and escaped all the perils to which it was exposed, the golden grain is safely gathered at length into the garner? Who has thus blessed the labour of your hands, establishing your handiworks each one? Who but God? Who, then, is the Giver of your daily bread? Who but God? Thus Moses said to Israel: "When thou hast eaten and art full, then thou shalt bless the Lord thy God. . . . Beware . . . lest when thou hast eaten and art full, and hast built goodly houses, and dwelt therein ; and when thy herds and thy flocks multiply, and thy silver and thy gold is multiplied, and all that thou hast is multiplied ; then thine heart be lifted up, and thou forget the Lord thy God, . . . and thou say in thine heart, My power and the might of mine hand hath gotten me this wealth. But thou shalt remember the Lord thy God: for it is he that giveth thee power to get wealth." Who has not admired and fallen in with the sentiments of the beautiful hymn ?—

> O God of Bethel, by whose hand
> Thy people still are fed ;
> Who through this weary pilgrimage
> Hast all our fathers led ;
>
> "Our vows, our prayers, we now present
> Before thy throne of grace ;
> God of our fathers, be the God
> Of their succeeding race."

IV. SPIRITUAL FOOD : ITS NATURE AND NECESSITY. 1. *The necessity of spiritual food.* From this miracle of feeding the multitude with bodily food, our Lord, as was his wont, took occasion, as we learn from the parallel passage of St. John, to call attention to spiritual food. From the bread wherewith he had fed their bodies, he passed naturally to that which is equally necessary and equally indispensable to support and sustain the soul. He showed them that, as bread is the staff of life for the body, there is something equally essential to the life of the soul. It matters not by what name we call it— whether manna, or bread, or flesh—the thing remains the same. 2. *The nature of this spiritual food.* He proposes himself to them for the purpose specified, telling them plainly and positively that he himself was that spiritual nutriment. "I," he says, "am the Bread of life." Nor does he stop with this; he proceeds to explain in some sort, or at least to extend, the sentiment to which he had given utterance, by the additional statement, "My flesh is meat indeed, and my blood is drink indeed." By this, as it appears to us, he hinted at his coming in the flesh and shedding his blood upon the cross; for how else could his blood be separated from his flesh but by being shed?

He thus intimated, under the thin veil of an almost transparent figure, his incarnation and atonement—his life as an example, and his death as an expiation, in other words, the benefits procured by his manifestation in the flesh, and the blessings purchased by his sacrificial blood-shedding on the cross. 3. *This food partaken of by faith.* He enforces all this by urging their acceptance of these benefits and blessings. They have been secured, but, in order to be fully enjoyed, they must be partaken of; and they cannot be partaken of without faith—they cannot be made our own without faith; in a word, great as they are and precious as they are, they can in no way benefit or profit us without the exercise of faith. Accordingly, he sets forth faith under the suitable symbol of eating and drinking, and graciously invites to its exercise. He encourages them to the performance of this duty by several considerations of the most cheering kind. He holds forth to them the prospect of a living and lively union that would thence ensue, and ever after exist, between him and them; he promises them nourishment, life, and comfort as the consequences of that union; and he comforts them with the assurance of fellowship and friendship in time, and unspeakable felicity through all eternity; for he says, "He that eateth my flesh, and drinketh my blood, dwelleth in me, and I in him;" again he says, "My flesh is meat indeed, and my blood is drink indeed;" while he further adds, to crown all, "Whoso eateth my flesh, and drinketh my blood, hath eternal life." 4. *Want of food, natural and spiritual: its effects.* There is no difficulty in forming a correct idea of the condition of body that would result from want of daily bread. It would stunt an individual's growth, make him a starveling in appearance, and leave him without strength for work of any kind. Similar, but still worse, is the condition of soul resulting from the want of spiritual bread. Without Jesus, who is the living Bread that came down from heaven, there is neither life nor growth, neither grace nor strength, nor spiritual power of any description in the soul. On the other hand, by union with Christ we live. So it was with the apostle: "Nevertheless I live; yet not I, but Christ liveth in me: and the life which I now live in the flesh I live by the faith of the Son of God, who loved me, and gave himself for me." By virtue of that union we are strengthened. So with the same apostle: "I can do all things through Christ which strengtheneth me." By means of this union we receive spiritual food daily, and thus "grow in grace, and in the knowledge of our Lord and Saviour Jesus Christ." By this heavenly food we are qualified for spiritual work and warfare. Hence our Lord's direction, "Labour not for the meat which perisheth, but for that meat which endureth unto everlasting life." Hence the blessing pronounced on those "who hunger and thirst after righteousness;" hence, too, we can cordially join in the well-known words—

"Good is the Lord! He gives us bread;
He gives his people more;
By him their souls with grace are fed,
A rich, a boundless store."

Three practical duties we learn from the whole: (1) cordiality in accepting the provisions of the gospel by living faith on our living and loving Lord; (2) contentment with our lot, and thankfulness for daily bread, as also for the spiritual food of the soul; and (3) entire consecration to that God in whom "we live, and move, and have our being," "who satisfieth our mouth with good things," and "filleth our soul as with marrow and fatness."—J. J. G.

Vers. 45—56. Parallel passages: Matt. xiv. 22—36; John vi. 15—21.—*Miraculous protection.* I. WALKING ON THE WATER. 1. *Almighty power.* Every one who has glanced over the early pages of English history is familiar with the story of Canute the Dane. That king wished to reprove the fulsome flattery of his courtiers when they spoke of his power as unlimited. He ordered his chair to be set by the sea-side as the tide was coming in. He peremptorily commanded the waves to withdraw, and waited a while as if for their compliance. He seemed to expect prompt obedience, and watched to see them retire; but onward, onward came the surging sea; its waves kept steadily advancing, till the monarch fled before it, and left his chair to be washed away in its waters. He then turned to his courtiers, and solemnly reminded them that that Sovereign alone was absolute whom the winds and waves obeyed—who controlled the former, and set bounds to the latter, saying, "Hitherto shall ye come, but no further." The sacred writers claim it as the peculiar preroga-tive of God to gather the wind in his fists and bind the waters in a garment. Job, in celebrating the attributes of the Almighty, applies to him the sublime and striking sentence, " Which alone spreadeth out the heavens, and treadeth upon the waves of the sea." 2. *Comparison of two similar miracles.* There are two miracles of our Lord which have a close resemblance to each other, and at the same time considerable dissimilarity. One of these is that recorded in this passage, and called his " walking on the waters;" the other is distinguished by the name of his "stilling the storm" (ch. iv. 35—41). By comparing these together, we find that the circumstances of the disciples were much worse, and their distress much greater, at the time referred to in this passage than on the former occasion. We may glance (1) at the stilling of the storm, which we purposely passed over at its proper place in the fourth chapter. Combining the words of the three evangelists who describe that former miracle, we cannot fail to be struck with the exceedingly graphic nature of that description, and that in so few words. We are, in fact, made to see it as though the whole were transpiring before our eyes, so truly pictorial is the recital. There is first the sudden squall (λαῖλαψ, St. Mark and St. Luke), its severity (μεγάλη, St. Mark), its rapid descent upon the lake (κατέβη, St. Luke), the agitation that ensued (σεισμὸς, St. Matthew), the waves as they kept sweeping over the deck of the small craft (ἐπέβαλλεν, imperfect, St. Mark), their beginning to fill with water (συνεπληροῦντο, St. Luke, and γεμίζεσθαι, St. Mark, but καλύπτεσθαι, St. Matthew), the peril in which the passengers found themselves (ἐκινδύνευον, St. Luke); while Jesus remained all the time fast asleep in the hinder part of the ship on a pillow (προσκεφάλαιον, St. Mark). Then follow the alarm of the disciples, the twice-repeated appeal of " Master, master" (ἐπιστάτα, ἐπιστάτα, St. Luke) evidencing their trepidation and terror, their eager cry for *instant* help (σῶσον, aorist imperative, St. Matthew) in their present perishing condition (ἀπολλύμεθα, SS. Mark, Matthew, and Luke), the quiet dignity and self-possession of the Saviour, his rebuke to the spirit of the storm (σιώπα, πεφίμωσο, only re-corded by St. Mark); or perhaps we may regard the former word as a command to the sea and the latter to the wind, as if he commanded the roar of the water to be silent, and the howling of the wind to be still, the spirit thereof being muzzled, as the word literally imports; while the imperative of the perfect implies that the work was instantaneous—completed soon as the word was uttered. Then we have the storm falling as suddenly as it rose—at once spending its force, wearing itself out and ceasing from very weariness (ἐκόπασεν, St. Mark). The calm that ensued was as great in proportion as had been the storm, with the milky whiteness of the foam that now alone remained from the storm, on the tranquil waters (γαλήνη), if we derive the word from γάλα, milk ; or with the "smile that dimpled " the face of the deep, if we derive the word from γελάω. All these incidents are not so much narrated as exhibited. It may be added, as an interesting circumstance in the respective descriptions of the evangelists St. Mark and St. Matthew, that while the former, in his usual graphic and pictorial style of description, represents the waves as pitching or beating, or actually throwing themselves on the vessel so that it was filling (γεμίζεσθαι), the latter describes the boat as covered (καλύπτεσθαι) with the waves. Hence it has been inferred, with good reason, that St. Matthew's point of view was plainly from one of the other vessels that, we are told, accompanied, and from which he saw the waves hiding out of sight, the boat in which the Saviour was ; while St. Mark, or rather St. Peter, from whose lips he had the description, was evidently in the same boat with our Lord, and from inside the vessel observed the waves rushing up against her sides, and filling her. Besides, the word πεφίμωσο reminds us of the use of φιμοῦν, to put to silence, literally *muzzle,* used by St. Peter in 1 Epist. ii. 15. But (2) though the storm may have been equally great in the case of the miracle just described as in that of the passage before us, yet there were several modifying circumstances in the former that are not found in this latter case. On that occasion we read that " there were also with him other little ships;" at the time specified in this passage the ship in which the disciples sailed was alone. On the former occasion the Saviour was with them and in the boat; on this he was both absent and distant. On the former occasion they had the advantages, no inconsiderable ones, of day and light about them ; on this they were surrounded by the darkness and dead of night. On the former occasion they were not, it would seem, far from land—they had just launched forth (ἀνήχθησαν), as St. Luke informs us; on this they were in the midst of the sea (μέσον). On the former occasion the storm had come down on the lake, and, for aught we know, was bearing them rapidly forward towards their destination; on this, we are expressly told, it was against them—"the wind was contrary (ἐναντίος) unto them." These points of comparison prove the extreme peril in which the disciples were at this time. Great as had been their danger before, it is greater now. 3. *Cause of these dangerous storms.* Such sudden dangerous storms are still of frequent occurrence on that small inland lake. The best comment on all this physical commotion, and the best explanation of the nature and cause as well as scene of this miracle, may be found in Thomson's 'The Land and the Book.' There, after his notice of a storm which he had witnessed on the lake, we find the following account :— " To understand the causes of these sudden and violent tempests, we must remember the lake lies low—six hundred feet lower than the ocean ; that the vast naked plateaus of Jaulan rise to a great height, spreading backward to the wilds of the Hauran and upward to snowy Hermon; that the water-courses have cut out profound ravines and wild gorges, converging to the head of this lake, and that these act like gigantic funnels to draw down the cold winds from the mountains. On the occasion referred to we suddenly pitched our tents at the shore, and remained for three days and nights exposed to this tremendous wind." 4. *The difficulty of the disciples.* Their difficulty was equal to their danger. They were *toiling* (βασανιζομένους, literally, *tortured, baffled,* tested as metals by the touchstone) in rowing, and we cannot but commend them for their conduct. They were using the proper means, and that is ever right to do ; but the means did not avail. They were employing every energy ; but it was to no purpose. They were putting forth all their strength ; but it was utterly fruitless, and without result. The wind was still against them. Whether it was blowing a gale, as it does when it travels at the rate of sixteen miles an hour, or whether it was blowing a high gale, when it goes with the rapidity of thirty-six miles an hour, or whether it was blowing a storm, which it does when it sweeps with the speed of sixty miles an hour, or proceeding with hurricane fury at ninety miles an hour,—whatever may have been the velocity of that wild wind, it was rude and boisterous; and, what made matters worse, it was directly opposite—right ahead. There they were struggling, toiling, tugging; but all in vain. There they were working with all their might ; but still their frail barque was the plaything of wind and water—tossed by the waves and the sport of the storm. They themselves were every moment expecting to find a watery grave in that tempestuous sea. 5. *Another source of distress.* There was another source of distress, and one which aggravated their difficulty and added to their danger. That was the continued absence of the Master. When he had sent them away—in fact, " constrained " (ἠνάγκασε) them, as though reluctant to go without him—he remained alone on the land. But why leave them at all? Or why leave them so long? Or why especially leave them at such a critical juncture? Or why, at least, delay his coming in their great emergency? They would naturally think of the storm that once before had befallen them on that self-same sea. They would think of the glorious Personage that then sailed with them in the self-same boat. They would think of the sound slumber he enjoyed, as he lay on the cushion in the stern. They would think of his calm composure when he awoke. They would think of the short but stern command he uttered, when he rebuked so effectually the tempest, and hushed it into a calm. They would think of that gracious presence that curbed the winds and calmed the waves and checked even the swell of the waters. They would think, " Were he with us now, he would still the storm, and we should soon be safe on shore." They would think of the petition they presented to him, the prayer they prayed, the fervency of spirit that inspired it, the faith that dictated it, the frailty that cleaved to it when they said, "Lord, save us ! "—there was faith ; " we perish ! "—there their faith was weak. Ever and anon, as they regarded the war of elements that raged around, they would sigh for their absent Lord, and long for land. No wonder, for had Christ been in the boat all would have been well. 6. *The Saviour's presence is safety.* Nearly half a century before Christ, a great conqueror attempted to cross the stormy Sea of Adria in a small boat. The waves rolled mountains high. The courage of the sailors failed them. They refused to venture further. It was a sea in which no boat could live. Soon, however, they were reanimated and encouraged to renew their toil, when the conqueror discovered himself, and told them who and what he was, in the characteristic words, "You carry Cæsar and his fortunes." With Christ in the boat, the disciples might have flung their fears to the winds, for One infinitely greater than Cæsar would have been there—One who could have stirred their hearts and raised their courage with the emboldening words, "You carry Christ and his Church."

II. THE EYE OF CHRIST IS ON THE BOAT THAT CARRIES HIS DISCIPLES. 1. *His omniscience.* He saw it all—their difficulty and danger and distress. His eyes were upturned to heaven in prayer, yet he saw all that was transpiring. The night was pitchy dark, yet he saw that small speck tossed like a cork upon the waters of that stormy sea. He had constrained them to embark, but he kept his eye upon them. He saw their fears, but he meant to teach them a new lesson of faith and confidence. He saw them from the distant mountain to which he had retired apart to pray. It is positively stated that he saw them. He saw them, though he was on the mountain-side and they were on the sea; he saw them from a distance which the ken of no mortal eye could reach; he saw them through the darkness of the night; he saw them in their panic terror; he saw them and all their embarrassments; he saw them when they did not, and when they could not, see him. "Be of good cheer!" he said. I did not forget you; I did not forsake you; I had you on my heart; I had you in my eye all the time. I did not fail to look on you, though you failed to look to me; I did not shut up my compassions, though you restrained prayer. You were neither out of sight nor out of mind. I was resolved you should not perish, nor a hair of your head fall. Boisterous as the wind was, I had charged it not to presume to harm you; rough as the sea was, I had commanded it not to dare to destroy your frail craft or damage one of the crew. Absence does not limit my power; distance does not separate you from my presence; danger and difficulty and distress only make you dearer, and call forth my more tender care. 2. *His love is unchanging.* Jesus is the same Saviour still, "the same yesterday, to-day, and for ever." "Be of good cheer!" he said. These words, though addressed to the first disciples, have sent their echo down along the centuries, and bring comfort to disciples still. In them Christ addresses you, reader, and myself. By them he says to every faithful follower, "Mine eye is on thee; it has been on thee hitherto; it will be on thee to the end. You may rest assured I will never fail thee—no, never forsake thee." Again, the words of the Saviour, "Be of good cheer!" are backed by another fact which presents itself to us in this passage, and that fact is the purpose for which our Lord had retired to the lone mountain-side. He was passing the night in *prayer,* not specially for himself but for his disciples—his disciples then and now; yes, for his disciples in that slight ship and on that stormy sea. They toiled and rowed; he prayed. They were suffering; he was supplicating. They were struggling; he was interceding. They were buffeting the waters; he was bearing them, as High Priest, on his heart before God in the holy of holies of that mountain solitude. They were ready to faint; he was praying for them that they might not faint, and that their faith might not fail. They were longing for the Master; he was exercising his love on their behalf. 3. *A true picture of the Christian's life.* It is so still—as it was it is, and ever shall be, on the part of our dear Redeemer and his redeemed ones. We have before us a true picture of life—of human life, of the Christian's life. We are toiling in this world below; the Saviour is employed on our behalf in the world above. We are in circumstances of peril and pain; the Saviour bids us "be of good cheer!" and look up to him; "he has overcome the world." We are afloat on the sea of life; our barque is fragile, the wind is high, the storm scaresome, the sea raging, and we are tossed upon its waters; but Jesus is over all, and looks down on all, and will save through all, for "he is able to save to the uttermost all that come unto God by him." 4. *The suitable season for succour.* Once more he says, with yet another meaning, "Be of good cheer!" I did not come, it is true, when the storm began, nor when the first night-watch set in. I knew you would have wished me then, that you would have been glad to see me coming then, that you would have hailed my arrival then. But you knew little of the difficulties that beset you then, little of your own inability to cope with them then, little of the impotence of your own efforts then. You knew not, at least not sufficiently then, that the power of man is weakness, and the wisdom of man is folly. You knew comparatively little of your need of a higher hand and a stronger arm to save you then, and little also of the great mercy of deliverance. For the like reason I came not in the second watch, nor even in the third. The fourth watch had commenced, and still I saw reason to delay my coming. It was half run and more before the proper moment arrived. I did not postpone nor defer an instant longer than was meet. Soon as the minute-hand pointed to the right moment on the dial-plate of time, I came, and came at once, without further or any unnecessary delay. 5. *God's time is the right time.* God's time is not only the right time, but the best time. By his coming the time he did, the Saviour said in effect to the disciples, and through them to us, when we, like them, are tossed by the down-rushing winds and the upheaving waves of a troublesome world, Had I come sooner, it would have been premature on my part, and not expedient for you. Had I come sooner, it would have been pleasanter, but not so profitable for you. Had I come sooner, I should have consulted your feelings more than your interests. This fourth watch, and this last part of it in particular, is the season of your extremity and the time of my opportunity. Thus it is still. When you, reader, were saying, "Hath God forgotten to be gracious? Is his mercy clean gone for evermore?" his grace and mercy were drawing very near. When you were ready to give up all for lost, and about sinking into despair, then the Saviour said, I have come to give you confidence, to impart to you consolation, and inspire you with hope; in a word, to impress on your heart these words of comfort that now fall upon your ears. I come, therefore, as is my custom, at the moment best for the Creator's glory and the creature's good. Further, by the words, "Be of good cheer!" he reminds us of the fact that we never enjoy rest so much as after long hours of labour, we never enjoy safety so much as after a time of danger, we never enjoy sleep so much as after a day of toil, and we never enjoy a calm so much as after a time of storm. Some of us can attest this by personal experience. We have often been to sea, but only once in a storm. And never did we so thoroughly enjoy the land, or rest so sweetly on the shore, as after that terrible storm. 6. *Application to ourselves.* Thus will it be with all the dear children of God. After the tempests of earth, we shall enjoy the tranquillity of heaven all the more. After weary wanderings and a sorrowful sojourn in this vale of tears below, we shall relish far more keenly the rest and home above. Not only so, there is no common measure by which we can gauge the true relative proportions of these storms of earth and that sunshine of the skies. The great apostle of the Gentiles felt this when he said, "Our light affliction, which is but for a moment, worketh for us a far more exceeding and eternal weight of glory."

III. The announcement of our Lord's presence. 1. *A mistake.* The announcement of the Saviour's presence is contained in the words, "It is I." When he did come the disciples mistook him. First they see through the gloom of night the dark object at some distance, then they discern the outline of a human figure standing out amid the darkness of the night and against the lowering sky. They never for one moment supposed it was the Saviour. "What can that phantom form be?" they thought within themselves. They had doubtless many conjectures, but sin gave its gloomy interpretation to the scene. It is a phantom—a spirit! they said; a spirit of evil, a spirit of woe, to take vengeance on the guilty! So it was with Herod; and so it was with Joseph's brethren, as we have seen; so it was with Belshazzar. So, too, with ourselves many a time. Not unfrequently we mistake our own best blessings; we think them distant when they are close at hand. Nay, we often mistake them altogether; we regard as a curse the very thing that God meant to prove a blessing. The dark cloud of his providence "we so much dread," even when it is "big with mercy," and ready to burst with "blessings on our head." We continue our mistake, until God becomes "his own Interpreter, and makes his meaning plain." It was thus with the disciples here, until Jesus revealed himself in a manner not to be mistaken, and said, "*It is I.*" Often and often in time of trouble, of trial, of toil, of difficulty or danger or distress, of adversity or affliction, we have said individually, "All these things are against me;" all these things are tokens of Divine displeasure; all these things are messengers of wrath. Jesus draws near and whispers to the soul, Not so; that trial, that cross, that bereavement, that sickness, that distress of whatever kind, came from me; it was my doing; it was I sent it; I was the Author of it; I sought by it your good; it is I, and you are to recognize me in it; it is I. "Let not your heart be troubled: ye believe in God, believe also in me." 2. *A calm succeeds the storm.* When all is storm around, when all is dark within, when of all human sources of consolation we are constrained to say with the patriarch of Uz, "Miserable comforters are ye all;" just then, it may be, a happy thought occurs to us, a ray of heavenly light shines down upon us, a gleam of comfort comes to cheer us. We fear we are imposing on ourselves. Not so. Jesus comes in a way not to be misapprehended, and says to us, "It is I;' you need not be afraid. The winds have fallen and the waters subsided. It was I, says Jesus; they did it at my bidding. 3. *The real source of succour.* Relief comes. We are rescued from danger; from sickness we are restored to health; out of a situation of discomfort and unrest we are relieved. At such times we are apt to speak of the immediate instrumentalities in the case, and to attribute the change to second causes. This passage corrects that error. In it Jesus says, "It is I;" in other words, that medicine that proved so effectual derived its efficacy from me; it was I directed to it. Those friends that were so kind in the day of your trouble were moved to sympathy by me. It was I prompted them; it was I put it into their heart; it was I placed it in their power. "While some trust in horses, and some in chariots, we will make mention of the Name of the Lord." Thus, in all that betides the Christian, Jesus takes a part; in all the variety of change, and scene, and condition, and circumstance—that wonderful co-operation of all things for our good—we trace the presence of the Saviour. In the painful things and the pleasant, in the heights and depths, in the ups and downs, in the joys and sorrows, we are assured of the Saviour's power and presence; he is conducting us through all to the goodly land afar off.

> "When the shore is won at last,
> Who will count the billows past?"

4. *Jesus with us all the way.* (1) When the hour of our departure is at hand, when the last conflict approaches, when the darkness of death is beginning to envelop us, when we are passing through the dark valley of death-shade, the same Friend is at our side, the same friendly hand is on our shoulder, and the same fond voice sounds in our ears. It is the voice of Jesus, saying, "It is I;" death is my minister, my messenger; he can do you no harm; I have removed his sting. My rod and staff will comfort you; through me you will be more than conqueror, and will be able to challenge Death himself, and say, "O Death, where is thy sting? O Grave, where is thy victory?" "This God is our God for ever and ever: he will be our guide even unto [rather, *over*] death." (2) Again, on the resurrection morning, when all that are in their graves shall hear the voice of the Son of God and come forth, the same voice will reverberate through the graves of the poor and the tombs of the rich with the words, "It is I;" "I am the resurrection and the life;" "My dead men shall live; together with my dead body shall they come;" or, more literally and more correctly, "my dead body shall they come." There is not merely conjunction, not only union—all this is true, and all this is much; but more is meant, for the words "*together with*" are in italics, and so we are notified that they are not in the original. Thus there is identity; our Lord identifies himself with the dead in Christ. He is the Head, they are the members; and thus, one in life, one in death, they shall be one in the resurrection, and one through all eternity; therefore it is, "My dead body shall they come." (3) Also in the day of judgment, when "we shall all stand before the judgment-seat of Christ," the same loving tones will cheer us. The Judge on the throne will stoop down and say to his people, "It is I." The same Saviour that shed his blood for you—in whom you believed, whom you obeyed, whom you followed, loved, and served—is now your Judge. It is I that said to you on earth, "Come unto me, all ye that labour and are heavy laden, and I will give you rest." It is I, your Elder Brother, who say to you now in heaven, "Come, ye blessed of my Father, inherit the kingdom prepared for you before the foundation of the world." 5. *Words of courage as well as comfort.* Words of courage are also spoken by him. He adds, "Be *not afraid.*" Be not afraid of temptation, for with every temptation he will prepare a way of escape. Be not afraid of trials; they enlarge your experience: "the trial of your faith worketh patience; and patience, experience; and experience, hope." Be not afraid of tears; they will soon be wiped away: even now the tears you shed cleanse the eyes, so that you see spiritual things more clearly. Be not afraid of toils; they will soon be past, and then "there remaineth a rest for the people of God." Be not afraid of troubles, for "through much tribulation we must enter the kingdom of God." Be not afraid of the perplexities of the wilderness; he will "guide

you by his counsel" all the way. Be not afraid of the dark night of storm; for the dark clouds will scatter, and the feet of Omnipotence will come walking on the water. Be not afraid of the storms of persecution; "blessed are ye when all shall persecute you for the Saviour's sake." Only make sure you are his, and all the blessings of the covenant will be your portion. 6. *The feeling of danger a precursor of safety.* "He would have passed by them." Why was this? Just that they might fully feel their need of his help, and earnestly apply for it. Salvation is the response of heaven to man when, in his misery, he cries for it. We have read of a young prince who toiled much and travelled much, who was often in danger, many times in perplexity, frequently in difficulties. But he was never left alone; a faithful friend called Mentor was ever at his side—his counsellor, caretaker, guide, and guardian. How much greater is our privilege, to whom Jesus says, "It is I;" I will be with you all the way; I will be with you at every turn of the way; I will be with you in every time of need; I will be with you in every place of peril; I will be with you in the darkness of the night and amid the terrors of the storm! In calm majesty he will come, walking on the surface of the foam-crested wave; nor will he pass you by, but provoke your confidence, and prove your faith, and pour into your ears the inspiriting words, "Be of good cheer: it is I; be not afraid."

> "Thus soon the lowering sky grew dark
>   O'er Bashan's rocky brow;
> The storm rushed down upon the bark,
>   And waves dashed o'er the prow.

> "The pale disciples trembling spake,
>   While yawned the watery grave,
> 'We perish, Master—Master, wake!
>   Carest thou not to save?'

> "Calmly he rose with sovereign will,
>   And hushed the storm to rest.
> 'Ye waves,' he whispered, ' Peace! be still!'
>   They calmed like a pardoned breast."

J. J. G.

EXPOSITION.

CHAPTER VII.

Vers. 1, 2.—These verses, according to the Greek construction, should run thus: **And there are gathered together unto him the Pharisees, and certain of the scribes, which had come from Jerusalem, and had seen that some of his disciples ate their bread with defiled, that is, unwashen, hands.** The word (ἐμέμψαντο) translated in the Authorized Version, "they found fault," does not appear in the best authorities. It seems to have been interpolated to help the construction. St. Mark explains the meaning of the word κοιναῖς (literally, *common*), by the word (ἀνίπτοις) "unwashen." The disciples, doubtless, washed their hands, but they abstained from the multiplied ceremonial washings of the Pharisees, which they had received by tradition and punctiliously observed. The scribes and Pharisees, who had come from Jerusalem, were doubtless sent as spies, to watch and to report in no friendly spirit the proceedings of the great Prophet of Nazareth.

Ver. 3.—**Except they wash their hands oft.**

The Greek word here rendered "oft" is πυγμῇ: literally, *with the fist,* i.e. with the closed hand, rubbing one against the other. This word has caused a vast amount of criticism; and the difficulty of explaining it seems to have led to the adoption of a conjectural reading (πυκνῷς or πυκνῇ) rendered "oft;" *crebro* in the Vulgate. But the Syriac Peshito Version renders the Greek word by a word which means "diligently," and it is interesting and helpful, as a matter of exegesis, to know that it also renders the Greek word (ἐπιμελῶς) in Luke xv. 8 by the same Syriac synonym, "diligently." The "clenched fist" implies vigour and resolution, and points to "diligence," and there are very high authorities in favour of this rendering, as, Epiphanius, Isaac Casaubon, and Cornelius à Lapide, to say nothing of our best modern expositors. It is also adopted in the Revised Version. **Holding the tradition of the elders.** The Pharisees pretended that this tradition had been orally delivered by God to Moses on Mount Sinai, and then transmitted orally down to their time. These oral precepts were afterwards embodied in the Talmud.

Ver. 4.—**And when they come from the market** (ἀπὸ ἀγορᾶς); literally, *and from the market-place;* there is no verb in the principal manuscripts, although the Cambridge Codex has ὅταν ἔλθωσιν, and the old Latin gives *redeuntes.* In the market-place there would be every kind of men and things, clean and unclean, by contact with which they feared that they might be polluted; and so they considered that they had need to cleanse themselves from this impurity by a more careful and complete ablution. Another Greek word is used here, namely, βαπτίσωνται. In the former verse the word is νίψωνται, a more partial and superficial kind of washing than that implied in βαπτίζω. It should, however, be added that two of the great uncials, Vatican and Sinaitic, have ῥαντίσωνται, "sprinkle themselves," instead of βαπτίσωνται—an authority sufficient to justify the Revisers of 1881 in putting it into the margin. **The washing of cups, and pots, and brasen vessels, and of tables.** The words (καὶ κλινῶν) wrongly rendered, "and of tables"—because they could only mean "couches"—have not sufficient authority to be retained in the text. "Cups" (ποτηρίων) mean "drinking vessels." The "pot" (ξεστῆς) is a Roman word, *sextarius,* a small liquid measure, the sixth part of a *congius,* corresponding nearly to the English gallon, so that ξεστῆς would be rather more than a pint measure. *Brasen vessels.* These would probably be copper vessels, such as are still used in Syria for cooking purposes. These are particularly mentioned. Earthenware vessels would be broken. **Which they have received to hold** (ἃ παρέλαβον κρατεῖν); literally, *which they received to hold:* observe the aorist.

Ver. 5.—The Law of Moses prohibited contact with many things deemed to be unclean; and if any one had touched them he was counted unclean, so that he might not approach the temple until he had cleansed himself by the washing prescribed in the Law; the design being that by means of these ceremonial and bodily washings the Jews might be awakened to the necessity of spiritual cleansing. Hence the Jews, and especially the Pharisees, who wished to be esteemed more righteous than others, placing their whole religion in these external ceremonies, frequently washed themselves before their meals, and even at their meals. At the marriage feast in Cana of Galilee we read that there were placed "six waterpots of stone (λίθιναι ὑδρίαι)" for these purifying purposes; so that if any Jew had by accident come into contact with any unclean thing, and so had contracted any ceremonial impurity, he might remove

it. This, however, was only a custom, and not a thing of legal obligation until it was exalted into a law by the Pharisees. Now, this punctilious observance of traditions by the Pharisees and other Jews yielded little or no religious profit; for it occupied their time with external purifications, and so drew away their attention from the duty of far greater moment—the cleansing of the soul from sin. They made clean "the outside of the cup and platter," but neglected the inward cleansing of the heart. Therefore our blessed Lord, who came to put an end to the old ceremonial law, and to these vain and frivolous traditions which now overlaid it, and who wished to direct all the care of his disciples to the making of the heart clean, cared not to enforce these external washings upon his disciples, although he did not say this in so many words to the Pharisees, lest he should provoke their envy and their malice. He therefore meets their question in another way.

Vers. 6, 7.—Our Lord qoutes against them a prophecy of Isaiah (xxix. 13), **This people honoureth me with their lips, but their heart is far from me. But in vain do they worship me, teaching** as their doctrines **the precepts of men.** The prophet here gives the cause of the blindness of the Jews, because they honoured God with their lips, while their heart was far from him; and their worship of him (for that is the meaning of "their fear") was the commandment of men, which they had been taught; that is, they worshipped God, not according to that spiritual worship which he had commanded, but after the traditions of men and of their own scribes, partly futile, partly perverse, and contrary to God's Law. So he says, **Well did Isaiah prophesy of you.** The word is καλῶς, "excellently—beautifully—did he prophesy concerning you (τῶν ὑποκριτῶν), *the* hypocrites." Not that the prophet had the hypocrites of our Saviour's time in his mind when he uttered these words, but that the Spirit of God which was within him enabled him to describe accurately the character of those who seven centuries afterwards would be doing the same things as their forefathers. And observe how they were punished. For as they gave a lip-service only to God, praising him with their mouth indeed, but giving their heart to vanity and the world; so God on his part would give them the words only —the shell, so to speak, the letter which killeth; but take away from them the kernel—the spirit and the life, so that they might not lay hold of it nor taste it.

Ver. 9.—Here the word καλῶς is repeated. **Full well** (καλῶς) **do ye reject the commandment of God, that ye may keep your** tradition. It is as though our Lord said, "Your traditions are not instituted by God, or by his servants the prophets, but they are modern inventions, which you desire to defend, not out of love or reverence for them, but because you are the successors of those who invented them, and arrogate to yourselves the power of adding to them and making similar new traditions.

Ver. 10.—Our Lord now gives an example of one of these human traditions. **Moses said, Honour thy father and thy mother;**—that is, obey and love them, and succour them, if they need it; for here "honour" means not only reverence and love, but support, as is clear from ver. 12—**and, He that speaketh evil of father or mother, let him die the death;** that is, let him "surely die," without any hope of pardon. Our Lord means this: "That if he who by words only speaks evil of his father or his mother is, by law, guilty of death, how much more is he guilty of death who wrongs them by deed, and deprives them of that support which he owes them by the law of nature; and not only so, but teaches others so from Moses' seat, as you scribes and Pharisees do when you say, 'It is Corban.'"

Vers. 11—13.—**But ye say, If a man shall say to his father or his mother, That wherewith thou mightest have been profited by me is Corban, that is to say, Given to God** —these words, "that is to say, Given to God," are St. Mark's explanation of "corban" —**ye no longer suffer him to do aught for his father or his mother; making void the word of God by your tradition, which ye have delivered.** Now, this the scribes and Pharisees did for their own covetous ends. For most of them were priests, who received offerings made to God as his ministers, and then converted them to their own uses. In this they greatly erred; because the obligation of piety by which children are bound to support their parents when they need it, is a part of the law of nature, to which every vow, every oblation, ought to yield. Thus, if any one had devoted his goods to God, and his father or his mother became needy, those goods ought to be given to his parents and not to the temple. The word "corban" is a Hebrew word, meaning "that which is brought near," "a gift or offering to God." Hence, figuratively, the place where these offerings were deposited was called the "corbanas," or, "sacred treasury" (see Matt. xxvii. 6, κορβανᾶν). Hence to say of anything, "It is Corban," was to say that it had a prior and more sacred destination. And when it was something that a parent might need, to say, "It is Corban," i.e. it is already appropriated to another purpose, was simply to refuse his request and to deny him assistance, and so to break one of the first of the Divine commandments. Thus the son, by crying "Corban" to his needy parents, shut their mouths, by opposing to them a scruple of conscience, and suggesting to them a superstitious fear. It was as much as to say, "That which you ask of me is a sacred thing which I have devoted to God. Beware, therefore, lest you, by asking this of me, commit sacrilege by converting it to your own uses." Thus the parents would be silenced and alarmed, choosing rather to perish of hunger than to rob God. To such extremities did these covetous scribes and Pharisees drive their victims, compelling a son to abstain from any kind offices for his father or his mother. St. Ambrose says, "God does not seek a gift wrung out of the necessities of parents." *Making void* (ἀκυροῦντες); literally, *depriving it of its authority, annulling.* In Gal. iii. 17 the same word is rendered "disannul." *By your traditions;* the traditions, that is, by which they taught children to say "Corban" to their parents. Observe the words, "*your* tradition" (τῇ παρδόσει ὑμῶν); your tradition, as opposed to those Divine traditions which God has sanctified, and his Church has handed down from the beginning. **And many such like things ye do.** This is added by St. Mark to fill up the outline, and to show that this was only a sample of the many ways in which the commandment of God was twisted, distorted, and annulled by these rabbinical traditions.

Vers. 14, 15.—In the Authorized Version the beginning of this verse runs thus: "And when he had called all the people unto him, he said." But according to the best authorities, the adverb πάλιν should be inserted, and the words will run as follows:—**And he called to him the multitude again.** It is probable that he had waved them from him while he held this discourse with the scribes from Jerusalem. But now he calls the people near to him again, that all might hear that which concerned all alike. It is probable, indeed, that this discussion with the scribes may have taken place in the house, into which he again returned after having made this authoritative declaration to the multitude. The words are given with more emphasis here than as recorded by St. Matthew. Every one was solemnly invited to hearken and understand, while he announced a principle of the highest importance. Our Lord did not intend to disparage the difference between clean and unclean meats as it had been laid down in the Levitical Law. His object rather was to clear that teaching from the obscurities in which it had been involved by the scribes and Pharisees, who laid stress only on external acts. His object was to show that all impurity springs from the heart; and that, unless the heart is cleansed, all external washings are in vain. It is as though he said, "The scribes teach you that it is not lawful to eat with unwashen hands, because unwashen hands make the food unclean, and unclean food defiles the soul. But in this they err; because not that which enters from without into the mouth, but that which proceeds from within through the mouth, and so from the heart, if it be impure,—this defiles the man;" as he more fully explains at ver. 21.

Ver. 16.—This verse has some good authority, but not sufficient to be retained in the text. The Revisers of 1881 have placed it in the margin.

Ver. 17.—Our Lord, having proclaimed this great principle to the multitude in the presence of their teachers, the scribes and Pharisees, returned into the house (the true reading is here εἰς οἶκον, without the article). It means, of course, the house where he was lodging. And then **his disciples asked of him the parable.** St. Matthew (xv. 15) says that the question was put to him by St. Peter, speaking in the name of the other disciples —another instance of the reserve maintained in this Gospel with reference to this apostle.

Vers. 18, 19.—Our Lord had already, in his sermon on the mount, taught his disciples fully wherein purity or impurity of heart consists, and he might, therefore, with good reason, ask them how it was that they, even they who had been so favoured by being constantly with him, had forgotten or misunderstood him. Our Lord's illustration is physically accurate. The portion carried off is that which by its removal purifies what remains. The part which is available for nourishment is, in its passage through the system, converted into chyle, the matter from which the blood is formed. What is not available for nourishment passes away into the ἀφεδρών, or **draught. Purging all meats.** The most approved reading here is undoubtedly the masculine (καθαρίζων), and not the neuter (καθαρίζον). This change of reading compels a somewhat different construction. Accepting, therefore, the masculine as the true reading, the only possible rendering is that which makes this last clause a comment by the evangelist upon our Lord's previous words, in which he indicates to the reader that our Lord intended by this illustration to show that no food, of whatever kind, when received with thanksgiving, can make a man unclean. The clause must, therefore, be connected with the preceding words, by the introduction of the words, in italics, "*This he said*, making all meats clean." The passage, thus rendered, becomes a very significant exposition of what has gone before. It is well worthy of notice that this explanation is to be found

in St. Chrysostom (Homily on St. Matthew xv.): Ὁ δὲ Μάρκος φησὶν, ὅτι καθαρίζων τὰ βρώματα, ταῦτα ἔλεγεν: "But Mark affirms that he said these things, making the meats clean." It may be added that this explanation agrees finely with the words in Acts x. 15, "What God hath cleansed, that call not thou common."

Vers. 20—23.—**From within, out of the heart of men;** that is, from the reason and the will, of which the heart is the symbol and the laboratory. For the heart ministers the vital force to the intellect to enable it to understand, and to the will to enable it to live, although the seat of the intellect is in the brain. St. Mark's enumeration of evil things is in a somewhat different order from that of St. Matthew; and he adds to St. Matthew's list (ἀφροσύνη), **foolishness,** showing how all evil terminates in the loss of all moral and intellectual illumination. **All these evil things proceed from within, and defile the man.** Dr. Morison, in his admirable commentary on St. Mark, well observes here that "these things have an inward origin, and are vomited forth from the crater of the heart or soul;" and further on he says, "In a little sphere of things, and as regards *acts*, though not as regards *substances* or *essences*, men may be spoken of as creators. Men, that is to say, are the efficient causes of their own choices. If they were not, they would not be really free. If it was not so, there would be no real responsibility." St. Matthew (xv. 20) adds here, "But to eat with unwashen hands defileth not the man." This is the end and scope of the parable, which is to show that unwashen hands and unclean meats defile not a man, but only an impure and depraved will. It seems almost needless to observe that our Lord does not condemn the washing of the hands before meals as a thing in itself in any way wrong. All nations approve of ablutions as tending to cleanliness and health.

"Dant famuli manibus lymphas, Cere-
    remque canistris
  Expediunt, tonsisque ferunt mantelia
    villis."

(Virgil, 'Æneid,' i. 701, 702.)

"It was thought sordid and mean to sit down to meals with unwashen hands. Whence not the clergy only, but the people, washed their hands before prayer." The moral of all is this, how carefully is the heart to be guarded, instructed, and adorned, seeing that it is the instrument and laboratory of all evil and all good, of all vice and all virtue! "Keep thy heart with all diligence," so that nothing may enter therein and nothing go out therefrom and you not be conscious of it, and your reason may not approve; "for out of it are the issues of life."

Ver. 24.—Our Lord now passes out of Galilee into a heathen country, Syrophœnicia, **into the borders of Tyre and Sidon, that** he might begin to impart his miracles and his doctrine, which the scribes and Pharisees had rejected, to the Gentiles. There is not sufficient authority for omitting "Sidon" from the text. Both these cities were renowned for their extensive commerce and for their wealth. It is probable that the true reading in ver. 31, which will be noticed presently, may have led to the omission by some authorities of "Sidon" here. But there is really no inconsistency in retaining the words "and Sidon" here ; and accepting the reading "through Sidon" there. Tyre, which was the capital of Phœnicia, lay to the south, bordering on Judæa ; Sidon to the north : and multitudes flocked to Christ from these parts. **He entered into a house, and would have no man know it : and he could not be hid.** He would have no man know it, partly for the sake of quiet, and partly lest he should rouse the Jews more bitterly against him, and give them occasion to cavil that he was not the Messiah promised to the Jews, because, having left them, he had turned to the Gentiles. St. Mark (iii. 8) has already informed us that his fame had spread to those about Tyre and Sidon.

Vers. 25—27.—The construction of this verse is Hebraistic (see Acts xv. 17). Instead of ἀκούσασα γὰρ, the approved reading is ἀλλ' εὐθὺς ἀκούσασα : **But straightway a woman, whose young daughter** (θυγάτριον)— literally, *little daughter ;* St. Mark is fond of diminutives—**had an unclean spirit.** All ages were liable to this incursion of unclean spirits. The woman seems to have come from a distance. She was **a Greek**—that is, a Gentile—**a Syro-phœnician by race,** as distinguished from the Libyan Phœnicians, of Carthage. She was a descendant from those seven nations of Canaan which had been driven out by God's command. They were called in their own language "Canaanites." **And she besought him** (ἠρώτα); literally, *asked him.* St. Matthew (xv. 22) says that "she cried (ἐκραύγασεν), Have mercy on me, O Lord, thou Son of David." Aristotle says that "parents love their children more than their children love them ; because love descends, and because parents desire that their children should survive them, that they may live on in their children, as it were, after death ; that they become, so to speak, immortal through their children, and possess that eternity, which they cannot have in themselves, in their children and their children's children." St. Matthew (xv. 23) tells us that at first "he answered her not a word," and he does not record the remarkable saying, **Let the children first be filled,**

which in St. Mark precedes the words, **it is not meet to take the children's bread and cast it to the dogs.** Dogs abound in Palestine and the surrounding districts, but they are not cared for. They go about in packs, with no particular masters and no particular homes. They seem to be chiefly useful as scavengers. Nevertheless, the dog of the East is amenable to kindness shown him by man, and there, as in England, children and young dogs soon become friendly. It is of (κυνάρια) "little dogs" that our Lord here speaks. Our Lord here speaks after the manner of the Jews, who called the Gentiles dogs, as distinguished from themselves, the children of the kingdom. *Let the children first be filled.* Suffer me first to heal all the Jews who need my help. Our Lord makes at first as though he would refuse her request ; and yet it is not an absolute denial. There might be hope for her when the children were filled. Thus Christ oftentimes deals with holy souls, namely, by humbling and mortifying them when they desire anything at his hands, in order that with yet greater importunity and humility they may seek and obtain it. St. Chrysostom says, " Whether we obtain that which we seek for, or whether we obtain it not, let us ever persevere in prayer. And let us give thanks, not only if we obtain, but even if we fail to obtain. For when God denies us anything, it is no less a favour than if he had granted it ; for we know not as he does what is most expedient for us."

Ver. 28.—In this verse there is a slight change of reading, causing a change of rendering ; namely, thus : **Yea, Lord : even**—καὶ instead of καὶ γὰρ—**the dogs**—τὰ κυνάρια, *the little dogs*—**under the table eat of the children's crumbs.** Observe the antithesis : "the children" (the little daughter) sitting *at* the table ; the "little dogs" *under* the table. It is as though she said, " Give me, most gracious Lord, only a crumb (a small mercy compared with thy greater mercies), the healing of my little daughter, which may fall as it were *obiter* from thee upon us Canaanites and Gentiles, and be gratefully picked up as one of the lesser benefits." Cornelius à Lapide enlarges beautifully upon this : " Feed me, then, as a little dog. To me, a poor Gentile, let a crumb of thy grace and mercy be vouchsafed ; but let the full board, the plentiful bread of grace and righteousness, be reserved for the Jewish children. I cannot leave the table of my Lord, whose little dog I am. No ; if you spurn me away with your foot, or with a blow, I will go away ; but I will come back again, like a little dog, through another door. I will not be driven away by blows. I will not let thee go until thou hast given me what I ask of thee.' For this Canaanite constrains Christ, arguing her case from his own words, prudently, modestly, forcibly, and with a humble faith which perceives that he is not unwilling to be overcome by petition and by reason. Indeed, she entangles him in the meshes of his own words. So great is the plenteousness of his table, that it shall abundantly suffice for her if she may but partake of the crumbs which fall from the table of his children."

Ver. 29.—St. Matthew says here (xv. 28), "O woman, great is thy faith: be it done unto thee even as thou wilt. And her daughter was healed from that hour." If we suppose St. Mark's words to come in after St. Matthew's words "be it done unto thee even as thou wilt," the two narratives are perfectly consistent. Our Lord could no longer restrain himself, or resist these wonderful appeals of faith. Overcome by the skilful reasoning and importunity of the Canaanite, he gives her that which she asks, and more. He heals her daughter, and he sets a crown of gold upon her head. It is here obvious to remark that this child vexed by the unclean spirit represents the soul tempted by Satan and polluted by sin. In such a condition we must distrust our own strength, and rely only on Christ, and call upon him with humility and repentance; acknowledging ourselves to be but as dogs in his sight; that is, miserable sinners; yet not such as that we should despair of pardon, but rather that we should hope for the mercy of Christ the greater we feel our misery to be. For it is worthy of a great Saviour to cleanse and save great sinners. Again, this Gentile daughter represents the Church of the Gentiles, which, shut out from salvation by the justice of God, enters the kingdom of heaven through the door of mercy. Here was a great conversion indeed; for now the Jews through their unbelief change places with the Gentiles, and, like them, can only be admitted through the same gate of Divine mercy.

Ver. 30.—There is an inversion in the order of the clauses in this verse, according to the best authorities. The words should run thus: **And she went away unto her house, and found the child** (τὸ παιδίον) **laid upon the bed, and the devil gone out.** She found her little daughter set free from the possession, but exhausted by the convulsions which he caused in departing from her; weary with the violence of the struggle, but restful and composed. So the sinful soul, set free from sin by the absolution of Christ, rests upon the couch of a conscience pacified by the blood of Christ, and at peace with God.

Ver. 31.—According to the most approved authorities this verse should be read thus: **And again he went out from the borders of Tyre, and came through Sidon unto the sea of Galilee, through the midst of the borders of Decapolis.** St. Matthew (xv. 29) simply says that he "departed thence, and came nigh unto the sea of Galilee." But from the more full statement of St. Mark we learn that he made a circuit, going first northwards through Phœnicia, with Galilee on his right, as far as Sidon; and thence probably over the spurs of Libanus to Damascus, mentioned by Pliny as one of the cities of the Decapolis. This would bring him probably through Cæsarea Philippi to the eastern coast of the Sea of Galilee. Here, according to St. Matthew, he remained for a time in the mountainous district above the plain; choosing this position apparently for the sake of quiet and retirement, as also that, being conspicuous to all from the mountain, he might there await the multitude coming to him, whether for instruction or for healing.

Ver. 32.—**They bring unto him one that was deaf, and had an impediment in his speech** (πωφὸν καὶ μογιλάλον). The radical sense of κωφός (from κόπτω) is "blunt" or "dull;" and so it is used to represent both deafness and dumbness. But in St. Mark it means deafness as distinguished from dumbness (see ch. ix. 25). This patient, however, was not ἄλαλος absolutely, but μογιλάλος, i.e. he spoke with difficulty. Long-continued deafness is apt to produce imperfect utterance.

Ver. 33.—**And he took him aside from the multitude privately.** This was done, no doubt, to fix the attention of the afflicted man upon himself, and upon the fact that he was about to act upon his ears and his tongue. **And he put** (ἔβαλε)—literally, *cast or thrust*—**his fingers into his ears.** The action was very significant. It was as though he said, "I am about to open a passage for hearing through these ears." **And he spat, and touched his tongue;** that is, he touched his tongue with saliva from his own sacred lips. These symbolical actions must have had a great meaning for the afflicted man. They were a *tableau vivant*, an acted metaphor, teaching him what he might expect from the mercy of Christ. The analogy of the miracle recorded in St. John (ix. 6) should be noticed here. It is an interesting circumstance (noticed in the 'Speaker's Commentary') that, in the Latin Church, the officiating priest touches the nostrils and ears of those who are to be baptized, with saliva from his own mouth. We may be assured that, in the case before us, these signs used by our Lord were intended to awaken the afflicted man's faith, and to stir up in him the lively expectation of a blessing.

Vers. 34, 35.—**And looking up to heaven,**

he sighed, and saith unto him, **Ephphatha, that is, Be opened.** He looked up to heaven, because from thence come all good things—words for the dumb, hearing for the deaf, healing for all infirmities; and thus he would teach the infirm man by a manifest sign to what quarter he was to look for the true source of his cure. *He sighed* (ἐστέναξε); literally, *he groaned*. Why did our Lord sigh at such a moment? We know indeed that he was "a man of sorrows, and acquainted with grief;" but now we might almost have expected a momentary smile of loving joy when he was about to give back to this afflicted man the use of these valuable instruments of thought and action. But he sighed even then; for he was touched with the feeling of human infirmity, and no doubt his comprehensive eye would take in the vast amount of misery, both bodily and spiritual, which has come upon the world through sin; and this, too, immediately after having looked up to heaven, and thought of the realm of bliss which for a time he had left "for us men, and for our salvation." *Ephphatha, that is, Be opened.* This word is, of course, addressed to the man himself; and the evangelist has retained the original Syro-Chaldaic word, as he has retained "Talitha cumi" elsewhere; so that the actual word which passed through the Saviour's lips, and restored speech and hearing to the afflicted, might be handed on, as doubtless it will be, to the end of time.

The word applies of course, primarily, though not exclusively, to the ear; for not only were his ears opened; but the bond of his tongue was loosed, and he spake plain. Vers. 36, 37.—**He charged them** (διεστέλλετο). The word is a strong one: "he gave them clear and positive orders." The injunction seems to have been given, both to the deaf and dumb man, and to those who brought him. And it was given partly, no doubt, for his own sake, and for reasons connected with his gradual manifestation of himself to the world, and partly for the instruction of his disciples, and to show that he did not desire by his miracles to win the vain applause of men. St. Augustine says that "our Lord desired, by putting this restraint upon them, to teach how much more fervently they ought to preach him, whom he commissions to preach, when they who were forbidden could not be silent." **He hath done all things well.** He did nothing that the Pharisees, captious and envious as they were, could reasonably find fault with. St. Matthew (xv. 30, 31) intimates that at this time our Lord exhibited a vast number of miracles, a bright galaxy of wonders, amongst which this shone out conspicuously, as a very prominent and instructive one. But, indeed, "he went about doing good." His whole life on earth was one connected, continued manifestation of loving kindness.

HOMILETICS.

Vers. 1—23.—*Ceremonialism and spirituality.* The teaching of our Lord Jesus was often in opposition to that of the religious leaders of his age and nation. The Pharisees and scribes were most religious, but their religion was of a bad type. They themselves practised, and they inculcated upon the people, the observance of religious forms and ceremonies; whilst, generally speaking, they were negligent of the weightier matters of the Law. They laid great stress upon the outward, but they were careless of the spiritual. Our Lord's teaching, on the contrary, exalted the spiritual, and insisted upon the supreme importance of a true, a pure, a reverent heart. The contrast between ceremonialism and spirituality is exhibited in this passage in several particulars.

I. CEREMONIALISM SUBSTITUTES WASHING WITH WATER FOR PURITY OF HEART. Ablutions occupied an important place in the system of ritual. In addition to the washings and sprinklings required by the Law, many others were invented by the superstitious. It was a religious duty to wash the hands before eating and upon returning from market; to sprinkle and cleanse ceremonially cups and pots, vessels and furniture. In contradistinction from all these ritual purifications, our Lord laid stress upon the true baptism, the washing and purifying of the thoughts and intents of the heart.

II. CEREMONIALISM SUBSTITUTES THE TRADITIONS OF THE ELDERS FOR THE COMMANDS OF GOD. The Jews were a nation highly conservative in character and habit. They cherished their history, they revered the memory of their heroes, they treasured and superstitiously honoured their sacred books, and any doctrines or practices which came down from antiquity were, by that fact, commended to their respect. Their fault here was in magnifying the precepts of men rather than the commands of God. Human interpretations, human additions, human corruptions of the Word, were put in the place of the Word itself. The Lord Jesus came not to destroy, but to fulfil the Law; yet with mere tradition he would have no truce.

III. CEREMONIALISM SUBSTITUTES THE WORSHIP OF THE LIPS FOR THE WORSHIP OF THE HEART. This was an old error and fault. The prophet Isaiah had seen reason to complain of its prevalence among the Hebrews of his time; and, as it is the product of sinful human nature, it need not surprise us if we meet with instances of the working of the principle of formality in any nation and in any age. Our Lord Jesus had frequent occasion to censure the vain repetitions, the prayers in the market-places, which he knew were in many cases the proof, not of a devout but of a hypocritical nature. " God is a Spirit : and they that worship him must worship in spirit and truth."

IV. CEREMONIALISM SUBSTITUTES A SUBTLE EVASION FOR FILIAL DUTY. Natural piety concurs with the revealed commandment, in requiring of children honour and reverence towards their parents. To support them when in old age and poverty has ever been deemed a plain duty and, indeed, a true privilege. The way in which the unrighteous but religious Jews evaded this obligation is characteristic. Whatever a parent needed, the son declared to be dedicated to God, and therefore not applicable to the relief of the parent's wants. Such a device was hateful in the eyes of the holy and affectionate Saviour, who not only condemned unfilial conduct, but still more the mean hypocrisy which could use religion for its cloak.

V. CEREMONIALISM SUBSTITUTES AVOIDANCE OF UNCLEAN FOOD FOR AVOIDANCE OF IMPURE AND MALICIOUS THOUGHTS. Even Christ's disciples found it difficult to understand their Master's position with regard to clean and unclean food. The distinction was in itself recognized by the Law, but additions were made by human ingenuity, and the distinction itself was exaggerated, so as to imply more than was divinely intended. In the exercise of his authority, he " made all meats clean." He taught that sin works not from without inwardly, but from within outwardly ; that the heart of man needs to be guarded against sinful thoughts and desires, in order that the life may be just, peaceful, and pure.

APPLICATION. It is possible to be, in a sense, religious, and yet, in a deeper sense, sinful, and out of harmony with the mind and will of God. It is a temptation from which none is wholly free, to substitute the external, the formal, the apparent, for what God requires—the faith, love, and loyalty of the heart. Hence the need of a good heart, which must be a new heart—the gift and the creation of God by his Spirit. The religion of the New Testament both enjoins this and provides for its acquirement. He who is "in Christ" is a new creation ; and having the fountain cleansed, sends forth pure and purifying streams.

Vers. 24—30.—*The alien's faith.* In quest of repose and retirement, the Lord Jesus often, even during the busiest periods of his ministry, withdrew from crowded cities and busy shores to some accessible seclusion. On this occasion he travelled to the borders of Phœnicia, but though so far from his accustomed resorts, he was known and sought and followed. From Tyre and Sidon people had already, attracted by his fame, found their way to the neighbourhood of Capernaum, to hear his discourses and to behold his works. No wonder that now, even in these distant regions, though desiring retirement, the Divine Prophet "could not be hid." Hence the application recorded in this touching and encouraging narrative. We observe here—

I. FAITH ARISING IN UNFAVOURABLE CIRCUMSTANCES. A woman—described as a Canaanite, a Gentile—appealed to Jesus for help. Probably a heathen, she yet had confidence in the power of the Hebrew Rabbi and Prophet to bring her some relief. It is singular that two conspicuous instances of faith in Christ during his ministry—this, and that of the centurion—should be displayed by Gentiles. And this when many of our Lord's own countrymen despised and rejected the Son of David! Yet every preacher of the gospel has met with cases which show us that faith springs up where it is least expected, and in circumstances the least favourable. An inducement this for the Christian sower to " sow beside all waters."

II. FAITH PROMPTING TO INTERCESSION. Personal faith will lead to pleading prayer. This was the faith of a mother, concerned for her afflicted daughter, possessed by an unclean spirit. Maternal love incited to the appeal, and sustained under discouragement and rebuffs. True faith will ever lead to action, and will impel the anxious soul to lay its anxieties before a mighty and compassionate Lord. We cannot be satisfied to come to Christ for ourselves alone; for those dear to our hearts some true request will be preferred, some petition will be urged. The heart's compassionate impulse the Lord of the heart will not despise.

III. FAITH REPULSED AND SORELY TRIED. The language addressed by Jesus to this woman was certainly unlike what he was wont to address to suppliants. His mission was to Israel; the bread he brought for Israel's sons; Canaanites and all Gentiles were but as dogs, having no claim upon the provision made for the household of the favoured. It is mysterious, yet it is unquestionable, that it seems good to God to "try" the faith of men. So Jehovah had tried Abraham, and so Jesus now tried this poor, pitiable woman. He will try your faith; but misunderstand not his treatment of you.

"Ye fearful saints, fresh courage take;
The clouds ye so much dread
Are big with mercy, and shall break
In blessings on your head."

IV. FAITH TRIUMPHANT. The woman neither resented the Lord's comparison nor did she, disheartened by the reception she met with, turn away without a blessing. She took the Lord at his word, and followed out his figure. "Be it so; let the bread, the loaf, be for the children; let the dogs keep their proper place; yet, even there, surely there is some provision even for them. There are crumbs, and with these the dogs may be content; for these the dogs may be grateful." This is the way to plead with Heaven. God will have earnestness and persistency and perseverance in prayer. Christ's grace is ever for those who seek, and who seek not fitfully, but resolutely and enduringly.

V. FAITH RECOGNIZED AND REWARDED. Christ was pleased because the applicant cast herself upon his compassion, because she was willing to receive the boon desired upon his own terms. "For this saying go thy way." It was a saying expressing so much humility, so much earnestness, so much faith, that the heart from which it came might not remain unsatisfied, unblest. The evangelist tells, in a way very picturesque and affecting, how, upon her return to her house, the poor woman found that the power had been exercised, that the demon had departed, and that her daughter was healed.

APPLICATION. The narrative (1) affords encouragement to offer intercessory prayer; (2) shows the value of humility in our approach to Jesus; and (3) assures us that persevering faith shall not be unrewarded.

Vers. 31—37.—*The deaf hears; the dumb speaks.* In this incident is much of the dramatic. It could not well be otherwise. Our Lord's teaching was usually by speech, but this was a case in which oral language was needless and useless. Christ accordingly employed the language of gesture and action. He thus adapted himself and his ministry to the necessities of this poor man, who was doubly afflicted with privation of hearing and of speech. The condition of the sufferer and the conduct of the Healer are alike symbolical of spiritual facts and suggestive of spiritual lessons.

I. A PICTURE OF THE SINNER'S STATE. 1. Here is an insight into the *nature of human depravity.* It is a distortion of, a departure from, the proper, the higher, and original nature. Man, in his true bodily constitution, possesses hearing and speech, and in his true spiritual constitution he has faculties which bring him into communion with the Divine. The privation of such capacity by sin is pictured by the state of this sufferer. 2. Here is *insensibility to Divine realities.* Voices, music, thunder, are all to the deaf as though they were not. So with the sinner; he hears not the tones of the Divine voice; the Word of God is nothing to him—has neither authority nor charm. The dumb cannot speak or sing; whatever the occasion for utterance, the occasion appeals to him in vain. So with the sinner; he has no witness to offer to the God of creation, providence, and grace. 3. Here is *deprivation of the highest joys.* How much of happiness is inaccessible to those who are afflicted with deafness! Nature, art, and friendly voices have no message for their ears. And, similarly, sin closes the approaches of highest spiritual joys to the spiritual nature of the children of sinful men. 4. Here is helplessness and hopelessness. It is not a pleasant or a flattering picture; but is it not true?

II. A VIEW OF THE SAVIOUR AND OF THE PROCESS OF SALVATION. Remark: 1. The *individual character* of salvation. As Jesus took this deaf man apart from the crowd, that he might deal with him privately and by himself, so the Lord ever singles out each individual whom he saves. Sometimes he lays such a one aside by affliction, quietly to converse with him and work upon his nature. 2. Salvation is *through Christ's personal contact* with the soul. When Jesus put his fingers into the man's ears and anointed his tongue with spittle, this was a striking and effective lesson to one who could not be reached by the usual channel of articulate speech. It was the touch of Christ, and the communication of his virtue, that healed. A lesson to us that restoration to spiritual capacity and health is the effect of an immediate contact of the soul with Christ, the soul's Saviour. 3. A profoundly *compassionate Saviour.* "He sighed;" not simply because of this instance which he encountered of human misery and need, but doubtless also because of all the world's sin and misery. His was a heart moved at the spectacle of the wretchedness of this fallen race. His work of redemption was inspired by pity and by love. 4. An *authoritative Saviour.* The word of Jesus, "Be opened!" reminds us of the original and authoritative utterance of the Creator, "Let there be light!" It is thus that the Lord of light and vision ever speaks: he utters his royal command as one who is certain to be obeyed.

III. A REPRESENTATION OF THE RESULTS OF SALVATION. Simple as is the record of the mandate and summons of Immanuel, equally simple is the record of the success which attended his word. The response to the command was immediate. Similarly with the release which it is the prerogative of our Redeemer to effect for the soul of man. The nature which Christ renews becomes sensitive to those heavenly voices to which it has so long been deaf, and finds delight in holy and grateful utterances to which it has before been utterly strange.

IV. AN ILLUSTRATION OF THE IMPRESSION PRODUCED BY THE EXERCISE OF CHRIST'S POWER. 1. Astonishment; for who but he can work such marvels? 2. Publication; for the healed, and the beholders of the spiritual change, are unable to restrain themselves—are impelled to tell the story of redemption and deliverance. 3. Witness and praise; for such must needs be offered to him of whom it is said, "He hath done all things well."

HOMILIES BY VARIOUS AUTHORS.

Vers. 1—23.—*Externalism versus righteousness.* In vers. 3, 4 of this chapter we are furnished with an interesting piece of antiquarianism. The daily life of the devout Jew is set before us in its ceremonial aspect; not as Moses had originally ordered it, but as custom and human casuistry had gradually transformed it. The light thrown upon several questions is very searching and full of revelation, viz. the various senses in which *baptism* seems to have been understood by the contemporaries of Christ, and the punctilio, vigour, and detail with which ceremonial purifications were carried out. It is only as we realize the background of daily Jewish life, against which the life to which Jesus called his disciples stood out so prominently, that we are in a position to appreciate the current force of the objections raised by Pharisee and scribe. We have here—

I. CHRISTIANITY CRITICIZED FROM THE POINT OF VIEW OF RELIGIOUS TRADITION. (Vers. 1—5.) The exaggerated form the latter assumed brought out the more strikingly the peculiarity and essential character of Christ's teaching. 1. *It was an age in which Jewish ceremonialism had reached its highest.* The doctrine of Pharisaism had penetrated the common life of the people. They might be said to have fallen in love with it. The distinctions are artificial and super-refined, *e.g.* between " common," "profane," or "defiled" hands, and hands ceremonially clean. They washed "diligently" (a paraphrase of the original substituted by our revisers for "oft" of the Authorized Version, and apparently the best rendering of the difficult word in the original), "carefully," or "thoroughly;" and no detail or minute application was forgotten of the "many other things" "which they have received to hold" (*i.e.* to hold fast, retain). Amongst the respectable Jews ceremonial strictness and nicety held a place very similar to what "good manners," or polite behaviour and refinement, occupy with ourselves, having, of course, an additional supernatural sanction from association with the Law. Thus to-day the customs and observances of nations amongst whom civilization has long existed might equally serve as a foil for the Christian moralist; and all *casuistries* or secondary, *customary moralities*. 2. *The objectors were the leaders and representatives of the religious life of the time.* " Pharisees, and certain of the scribes, which had come from Jerusalem." They were the leaders and teachers of metropolitan fanatical ritualism. It is well when Christianity is judged that such men appear on the bench; there can then be no question as to the representative and authoritative character of the criticism. It would be a splendid thing if the representatives of modern political, social, and ecclesiastical life could be convened for such a purpose. 3. *What, then, is the objection thus raised?   It concerned an observance of daily life.* Christians are now judged on the same arena. In small things as in large the difference will reveal itself. *It depended upon an abstract distinction:* the hand might be *actually* clean when it was not *ceremonially* so. It was, in the eyes of those who made it, *the worst accusation they had it in their power to make.* The moral life of the disciples was irreproachable; they " had wronged no man, corrupted no man, taken advantage of no man." The Christians of to-day ought to emulate this blamelessness; infidels can then fire only blank cartridge.

II. THE TABLES TURNED. (Vers. 6—23.) The critics are themselves reviewed. Trifling captiousness must be summarily dealt with, especially when it wears the garb of authority. The *character* of the objectors is of the first consequence in judging of Christ's tone. Grave issues were at stake. The *ground* of the fault-finding was superficial and untrustworthy, and a truer criterion must be discovered. " Deceivers may be denounced, that the deceived may be delivered" (Godwin). The essential nature of rectitude—the grand moral foundations must be laid bare. 1. *Christ begins with an appeal to Scripture.* He is careful to show that the distinction between righteousness and ritualism is a scriptural one, and not of his own invention. At the same time, he gives the reference a satirical or ironical turn by making a *prophetic identification!* We don't know how much is lost in ignoring the written Word of God. It is " profitable for doctrine, for reproof, for correction, and for instruction in righteousness." 2. *He next pointed out the opposition that existed between their traditions and the Law.* The instance selected is a crucial one, viz. that of the fifth commandment—" the first commandment with promise." Others might have been given, but that would be sufficient. Family obligations are the inner circle in which religion most intensely operates; if a man is wrong there, he is not likely to be very righteous elsewhere. To prove their opposition to the Law was to strip them of all pretence to religion. 3. *Lastly, common sense and conscience were appealed to as regarded rites and ceremonies.* The " multitude " is here addressed; it is a point which the common man is supposed able to decide. There are many weapons that may thus be supplied to the evangelical armoury. If philosophy was rescued from barrenness by this method in the hands of a Socrates or a Reid, may we not hope for greater things with regard to a common-sense religion ? The great foundation of all religious definitions and obligations is the *true nature of man.* The essential being of man is spiritual; the body is only the garment or case in which he dwells. Purity or its opposite must therefore be judged of from that standpoint. If the soul, will, spirit, inner thought of a man is pure, he is wholly pure. Spiritual and ceremonial cleanness must not be confounded. Religion is not a matter of forms, ceremonies, or anything merely outside; but of the heart. Yet the thought and will must influence the outward action, habit, and life. The spiritual is the only eternal religion (John iv. 23, 24). The private question of the disciples is worthy of notice. A " parable " seems to have been their common name for a difficult saying of Christ's. Their incapacity was not intellectual but spiritual. Professed Christians themselves often require to be more fully instructed. The progressive life of the true Christian will itself solve many problems. " Had our Saviour been speaking as a physiologist, he would have admitted and contended that *many things from without,* if allowed to enter within, will corrupt the functions of physical life, and carry disorder and detriment into the whole fabric of the frame. But he was speaking as a moralist, and hence the antithetic statement of the next clause (cf. ver. 15) " (Morison).—M.

Vers. 24—30.—*The prayer of the Syro-phœnician woman.* An atmosphere of publicity about Christ: crowds follow him wherever they hear of his presence, and even in strange regions his fame anticipates him. The many who took advantage of his power to heal are forgotten in the special case which now presented itself. This may have been the spiritual result of many unsatisfactory cases in which the cure only affected the body; the rumour of them awoke at least one heart to a new sense of spiritual power. Speaking about Jesus and his work in this place or that, to one soul or another, may be a blessing in unthought-of quarters. Jesus "could not be hid" for other reasons; his disciples were with him, and, more than all, he carried about in himself a revelation of love and pity that spoke to every heart. Spiritual influence is a mysterious thing, and yet there are some conditions of its exercise which are only too plainly declared. Matthew has a fuller account, but our evangelist gives us the chief details. The Saviour was touching the great world outside of Judaism, the scene of his greater ministry in the future through the Holy Spirit. The incident is remarkable, as suggesting this universal relation of him who as yet was but a Jewish Rabbi. It tells us the nature of the limitation which hemmed in his work, and how that limitation was to be removed, when he "should open the door of faith to the Gentiles."

I. AT THE DOOR OF MERCY. (Vers. 25, 26.) 1. *The motive.* It was not for herself, but her child, whose distress she sought to relieve. The nature of this "unclean spirit." Moral parallels. A mother's instinct: how near the human affections and family obligations bring us to the gospel! The instinct is a natural one, but tending to the spiritual. She was in the school of sorrow, noble and unselfish sorrow, which searches the heart and awakens the latent forces of the spiritual nature. How many have been brought by such sentiments and experiences to the cross! 2. *The attraction.* She had heard of him and his merciful works. We all stand in need of mercy, and are insensibly affected as we hear of its exercise upon others. Make known the Saviour, and proclaim his saving grace! *The most unlooked-for will come.* "Faith cometh by hearing, and hearing by the Word of God." But now she saw and heard himself. Her great yearning, grieving heart read the lineaments of his countenance, and the character they expressed. "He will not turn me away." Christ, by his spiritual presence in the Word, ever touches human hearts thus, awaking by what he is the deepest longings and most instinctive trust.

II. THE DOOR AJAR. (Ver. 27.) 1. *It sounds like a rebuff.* What claims has she upon him? But: 2. *Is really a trial of her faith.* It sounds logically conclusive, yet is it intended to call forth the inmost spiritual nature. Delays and adverse experiences in prayer should not all at once be accepted as final. Prayer is not a mere asking; it is a discipline. Remember Abraham's importunity. 3. *Encouragement is given even under the appearance of refusal.* Matthew tells us of a *silence* that preceded this; for Christ to speak was itself an omen not to be despised. "First" is a word that hints at postponement, not ultimate rejection. And the picture he sketches is not to be taken literally, but is for the spiritual imagination. As the reasoner, in making an induction, introduces an element into his reasoning that is not in the facts in themselves, so the petitioner at Heaven's throne must learn to interpret his experiences, and to sift the rejections that he may discover the elements of hope. Here the petitioner answers the objection by *completing the picture in which it is couched.* True, it would be wrong to cast the children's "loaf" to the dogs; but that is not the only conceivable way in which the dogs may be fed. Her *Greek* experience comes to her assistance. Whilst the Jews hated dogs as "unclean," and could not tolerate them in their houses, the Greeks had a peculiar affection for them, and tamed and trained them to feed from the hand. In many a Greek home the dog had its place beside the table or beneath it. And the "crumbs" found their way there in various ways, either by intention or accident. The term she uses is a diminutive of endearment. The twenty-eighth verse is full of diminutives—"little dogs," "little children's," and "little crumbs"—which are full of subtle, tender appeal. This is her argument, then. It is a self-humiliating one, for she is willing to take the dogs' place. She is not a Jewess—a "child;" she is only a Gentile, and her daughter is "a little dog." And here is the children's loaf—the Bread of life—at the very edge of the table. May not some "little crumbs" fall over? To such humility, such faith, there can be no refusal; and *there was never intended to be one.* This is how we must *all* come to Heaven's door—vile, miserable sinners, with no claim save upon the mercy of God!

III. THE DOOR OPENED. (Vers. 29, 30.) 1. *It is opened to faith.* "For this saying." It was an inspiration of faith. She had found the master-key for all time, and as she used it the door flew open. If we but "ask in faith, nothing wavering," all our petitions will be granted. 2. *It is opened by Divine grace.* We are not to suppose the request granted because the feeling of Christ was wrought upon. The yielding has only a superficial appearance of being due to constraint. In reality the delay was but interpolated that the faith of the woman might be developed in her own soul and manifested to the Jewish spectators; and so the final answer would **be** justified on every hand, and prove a blessing to others beside the recipient. The cure is already effected when she returns home. 3. *It stands open for ever to such petitioners.* The ground of assent to her appeal having been "evidently set forth," she becomes a precedent for all believers to plead. She is the pioneer of all who, not being Jews according to the flesh, are nevertheless children of faithful Abraham according to the spirit. To all who thus believe the invitation is given, "Ask, and ye shall receive; seek, and ye shall find; knock, and it shall be opened unto you."—M.

Vers. 31—37.—*"Ephphatha."* A rest, then a fresh journey ("again"). How long the interval we cannot determine. To free him from embarrassment, perhaps danger, and allow time for spiritual meditation. "Tyre *and* Sidon." The best manuscripts have "*through* Sidon," which was north of Tyre. "Decapolis:" ten cities, east and south-east of Sea of Galilee; named by the Romans B.C. 65. A favourite scene of our Lord's labours (cf. Matt. iv. 25). In Matt. xv. 29—31 a multitude of cases is mentioned. Here one is singled out as an illustration.
I. THE CASE. Familiar and ordinary; comparatively helpless; difficult to educate, mentally and spiritually.
II. THE CURE. 1. *The manner of the great Physician.* "They beseech him *to lay his hand upon him*"—a grand expression. (1) With respect to the people. He does not like the publicity, etc., and so he withdraws the poor man from the excited crowd. (2) With respect to the patient. This step was full of consideration and delicacy. He sought to gain the confidence of the man. How deliberate and thoughtful was his mercy! 2. *The means employed.* (1) Of what kinds. Physical—touch, saliva. Devotional—a heavenward look, a heavenward sigh. Authoritative—a word, "Ephphatha!" Not used as a charm, but plainly intended to be otherwise understood; a word of the vernacular. (2) He spoke to the man through signs, as he could not understand words. The means were only *morally* necessary; that the man might have some basis for confidence, intelligence, and faith. He ever desired to be understood.
III. THAT WHICH IS SYMBOLIZED. The shut heart of the world, dead to spiritual things. Which is worse? Only the compassion of Christ can save us.—M.

Ver. 24 (first part).—*The seclusion of Jesus.* Our Lord, during his ministry, frequently sought retirement, and the text mentions one of these occasions. Seclusion is sometimes coveted by his disciples from improper motives, but these found no lodgment in the heart of the sinless One. We sometimes withdraw from active service for God because a feeling of indolence creeps over us, but he constantly found it to be his meat and drink to do the will of his Father in heaven. We sometimes shrink back from suspicions and reproaches in a spirit of cowardice, whereas in Christ there was no trace of the fear of man, that brings a snare. Nor did he ever exhibit the slightest indication of the selfishness which leads us to shut ourselves up in the narrow circle of our petty personal interests. On the contrary, his whole life, the fact of his living here at all, the death which he could easily have averted, conclusively showed that he "came not to be ministered unto, but to minister, and to give his life a ransom for many." We may at once and confidently set aside any explanation of Christ's withdrawal from a place or people which is drawn from some supposed imperfection in him who was absolutely sinless. At the same time, we must remember that we cannot always discover with certainty the reasons for our Lord's actions, not only because these are not mentioned by the evangelists, who never try to explain or justify what may be open to misrepresentation, but also because his nature transcended ours, and his acts had issues not only here but in an unseen world. So that whenever we suggest explanations of his conduct, we must say to ourselves, "Lo, these are parts of his ways: but how little a portion is heard of him!"

I. OCCASIONAL SECLUSION WAS GOOD FOR THE LORD HIMSELF. He was as truly the Son of man as the Son of God. His life would not have been complete, it would not have touched ours at so many points, if he had always worked and never waited. Hence, though he had to do a work so stupendous that it would affect the destinies of the world, and of the unseen universe of God, there are no signs in his life of bustle or impatience. He waited thirty years before he preached the gospel; and although he allowed himself only three short years for public ministry, he broke off from it again and again; and when at work he was so unhurried that he could stop in his progress to Jerusalem to heal a blind beggar, or halt on his way to save a dying child in order to heal and teach a poor woman in the crowd that thronged him. What a lesson to us in this fast-living age! What a rebuke to our feverish anxiety and excitement! Doubtless we should have to sacrifice something to break off from work as our Master did; indeed, this is one modern form of taking up our cross to follow him. It will be a fatal mistake to let business hustle prayer out of our life. The busy Christ could sometimes be alone, and he could not have been all he is to us if he had not been so. In the wilderness of temptation he was alone, and the real struggle of every human life is fought out and won in the presence of him who sees in secret. The greatest agony of Christ was endured in solitude; and in our Gethsemane friends fail us, but our God is near. It is good to be alone, if only we are alone with God, as Jesus was.

II. THE OCCASIONAL SECLUSION OF OUR LORD WAS GOOD FOR OTHERS. It was well for the disciples that they should be sometimes withdrawn, with their Master, from circumstances in which they would be harmed by men's applause or overwrought by nervous excitement; but besides this, Christ's withdrawal would benefit some who were not his disciples. 1. *It was a possible means of grace to his foes.* When the rage of the Pharisees was intensely aroused (and no anger is more unreasoning and devilish than that which professedly bases itself on religious conviction), it was well for them that the object of their wrath should disappear for a time. Christ's withdrawal saved them again and again from the awful crime which they committed at last on Calvary; it allowed for the subsidence of hasty excitement, which prejudiced them, and gave them time and opportunity for recovering better and wiser thoughts about the Lord. The loving Saviour would fain have helped even those who hated him. 2. *It was for the advantage of the mass of his hearers.* They saw his miracles, marvelled at them, discussed them, crowded to see more—without the least perception of their spiritual significance; so that if the series of miracles had been unbroken they would have failed of their purpose. 3. *It was for the good of those who needed him that he should be sought.* This is clearly exemplified in the experience of this woman of Syro-phœnicia. The disciples tried to drive her away. But Jesus meant her to come, had gone thither partly that she might come, gave her rebuffs which aroused yet more her apprehension of want; and so tested and developed her faith as to make her ready to receive the great blessing he longed to give. If Christ does not reveal himself so unmistakably to us as we wish, it is because he sees that we may win a higher benediction when we obey his command, "Seek, and ye shall find."—A. R.

Ver. 24 (latter part).—*He could not be hid.* On several occasions when Jesus sought retirement it was denied him, either by the enthusiastic zeal of his followers or by the pressing need of those who had heard of his fame. Still he seems to hide himself, and yet from no earnest seeker can he be hidden. In respect to many things besides the saving knowledge of Christ, it may be said they can only be discovered by diligent search. Our present knowledge of the physical world has come to us through those who would not be denied in their eager exploration. The forces of nature, too, have not obtruded themselves in their various uses, but have been won to our service by costly experiments and diligent thought. Speaking broadly, all life is an experiment— a discovery. A child learns to judge distances by trying to grasp what is within reach; he discovers the limit of strength by falls and hurts; he prattles before he talks. Very little of what we know has come intuitively. It sought to hide itself, but because we could not do without it we strove after it, and from us it "could not be hid." If in regard to other good things these words are true, it is not unreasonable that they should be true of him who is the highest good our souls can have or eternity can reveal. Our text implies, what other verses explicitly assert, that Christ, in the full plenitude of his salvation, does not come to us when we are spiritually inert, but that when the Holy Spirit has shown us that we need him, and when we seek him, he must be found of us. But if we spurn him he will hide himself, till he will have to say of us, concerning the things that would give us peace, "But now they *are* hid from thine eyes." The truth on which we wish to lay stress is this—that even in the days of his earthly ministry, whether Jesus was found as a Saviour or not depended on the condition of those who sought him. It was not a question of place, but of purpose. Contrast this story with the incident narrated in the first part of the preceding chapter. There we read of his visit to Nazareth, his own city, where we should expect he would be most eagerly sought after and most rich in blessings; but he could not reveal himself there as he wished to do, "because of their unbelief." Now, on the borders of a heathen district, the inhabitants of which had been shut out from the blessings of the covenant, there was a certain woman, a Gentile by birth, a heathen by religion, who wanted to find him, and from her "he could not be hid." Character may be, but circumstances cannot be, a barrier between the soul and Christ.

I. CHRIST CANNOT BE HID, BECAUSE GREAT NEED WILL SEEK HIM OUT. It was so with her who, poor and ill, crept into the crowd and touched the hem of his garment; with the sisters of Bethany, who sent the message, "He whom thou lovest is sick;" with the woman who was a sinner, who ventured into the Pharisee's house to find him; and with this Canaanite, who made her way to the Jewish Teacher, who, so far as she knew, had never before blessed one outside the house of Israel. It is God's design in our bodily illnesses, in our bereavements, in our grief about children going wrong, to lead us to the feet of him who never has said, "Seek ye my face in vain."

II. CHRIST CANNOT BE HID, BECAUSE TRUE LOVE WILL SURELY FIND HIM. True love in a parent or lover will give persistence and hope in the search for one who is lost. So will love to him who is worthy of the highest affection lead us to his presence.

III. CHRIST CANNOT BE HID, BECAUSE EARNEST FAITH WILL EVER LEAD TO HIM. The shepherds of Bethlehem who heard the angels' song believed its message, and found the holy Child. The wise men from the East, being faithful to the light they had, at last bowed at the feet of the Light of the world. Let us not suffer our doubts to prevent the outgoings of our soul to the Lord.

IV. CHRIST CANNOT BE HID, BECAUSE HIS OWN HEART WILL BETRAY HIM. Recall the pathetic story of Joseph. When he was the lord of Egypt, and his brethren came as suppliants to him, his heart could scarce contain itself, and at last the strength of his love forced him to avow himself and to welcome them to his heart. But that is only a faint emblem of the nobler love which filled the heart of the Son of God. Heaven could not hold it; the cross could not check it; the grave could not keep it back from his people. All through his life you see the outgoings of that mighty love. If his disciples are toiling in rowing, he will walk right over the raging waves to comfort them. If after his resurrection he stands as a stranger beside Mary, it can only be for a moment, for, like the good shepherd, he will soon call her by name, that she may be glad in his love. Still he stands among his disciples, and there his heart bewrays itself.

V. CHRIST CANNOT BE HID, BECAUSE HIS DISCIPLES WILL MAKE HIM KNOWN. In spite of the unfaithfulness of many, he has never been without his witnesses. The healed demoniac went back to his home to tell what Jesus had done for him; Andrew no sooner found the Messiah than he went to tell his own brother Simon. So the witness-bearing is to continue till the whole earth is filled with his glory.—A. R.

Ver. 32.—*Deaf and dumb.* Christ's acts of healing were very often performed while he was passing from place to place. This occurred on his way from the borders of Tyre and Sidon to the eastern side of the Lake of Galilee. His life was like a river, which not only, when it reaches the sea, bears mighty fleets on its bosom, but carries blessings all along its course through secluded pastures and quiet corn-fields. The case of this man was one of physical infirmity and not of demoniac possession. He was deaf, and had an infirmity in his speech. In considering the spiritual significance of a miracle, we must not overlook or underrate the physical blessing. Such an act of healing as this is the germ whence innumerable good works have come. Institutions for the deaf, hospitals for the sick, homes for the crippled, are the smiling harvest arising from this seed-sowing; and the signs by which the deaf and dumb are now taught find their principle in the signs which our Lord, in loving condescension, used in dealing with this afflicted man. The spirit of Christ reigns over and blesses the bodies of men still. If we have the use of all our faculties, and know nothing of the irritability of the deaf, the loneliness of the blind, and the agony of the dumb, let us not only be thankful, but let us remember our responsibility for their use, lest we fall into condemnation because we close our ears against the truth and refuse to move our lips in prayer. Let us also learn to cultivate pity for those who are not so richly endowed, allowing for the irritability of those who can only partly hear, and the cynicism to which the dumb and blind are tempted, and seeking to become eyes to the blind and ears to the deaf. " Be merciful, as your Father in heaven is merciful." Be pitiful and gentle, as he who sighed over and then blessed the sufferer. The spiritual significance of this act of healing is the more important, because deafness to God's voice and dumbness in his praise are more general, and less manifest to others than the physical privations which are their counterparts. In this light regard the sufferer and observe—

I. THAT HE WAS DESTITUTE OF TWO OF OUR NOBLEST FACULTIES. In those days there existed none of the mitigations of such distress with which we are familiar, and which are the products of patient and skilful training. He could not hear his children's voices, nor the cry of warning, nor the whisper of love. All that transpired in the synagogue was but dumb-show to him. He could not take refuge from loneliness in reading, as we can do. His wants he could not articulately express. When we see a child as yet unable to talk we are glad that his wants are limited, simple, well known, and easily supplied. But this sufferer had the thoughts and feelings of a man, yet could not utter them. In our congregations, and outside them, multitudes fail to hear God's voice. The preacher speaks of sin, but there is no consciousness of it stirred in their hearts; he proclaims free pardon, yet there is no sense of grateful acceptance. Voices around are eloquent of the Father's love to a Christian, but by these they are unheard. Meanwhile their voices are inarticulate on God's side. If a word of warning ought to be spoken, if the cause of Christ is to be defended, if there are vices which a God of sobriety and purity would destroy, these are dumb, or are as men who have an impediment in their speech.

II. THAT THESE FACULTIES WERE MUTUALLY DEPENDENT. He was not absolutely dumb, but was inarticulate in utterance; therefore, after his cure, it is said "he spake plain." It is true he had some physical defect, for we read, "the string of his tongue was loosed;" but it is evident that he could not speak aright, partly because he could not hear—perversion of speech being a general accompaniment of total deafness, for a deaf person cannot detect and alter his malpronunciations. There is a connection in spiritual life between the similar faculties of the soul. If we try to teach others, we must be taught of God. The ears must be opened before the mouth speaks plainly, and unless they be, the fluent talker is but a poor stammerer in spiritual utterance. Right speaking is conditioned by right hearing. If, therefore, the habit of evil or foolish talk has been acquired, it is not enough to vow that it shall be broken off, for it is " out of the abundance of the heart that the mouth speaketh." The fountain wants change, not the channel. Such a one must give up light reading for a time of earnest reflection, must keep clear of vain and idle companionships, and, above all, cultivate fellowship with God, the Source of all wise and holy thought.

III. THAT HE WAS BROUGHT TO THE TRUE PHYSICIAN. Satan is the great destroyer and damager, and Christ is the great Repairer and Redeemer. Let us bring our friends to him by counsel, by sympathy, and by prayer.

IV. THAT HE LEFT HIMSELF IN THE LORD'S HANDS. Friends asked the Lord to lay his hands on the sufferer, probably because they had seen him do this before. But Christ was divinely free, was far broader in method than their expectations, and he took him by the hand—not to cure him by that touch, but to lead him apart; and with this Stranger the helpless man was satisfied trustfully to go. Let us leave our Lord to do with us and with our dear ones as seems good to him. Though he may deal with us differently from his dealing with others, his choice is wisest and best.—A. R.

Vers. 33—35.—*A typical cure.* In our Lord's different acts of healing there were remarkable variations of method. We should expect this of the Son of the *Creator*, whose variety in nature is infinite. No two leaves in the forest are alike—no two faces in a flock of sheep; and even the same sea changes in its aspect from hour to hour. This variety is greater as we go higher in the scale of creation, and is most conspicuous in man, whether considered individually or collectively. And Christ Jesus was the Image of the invisible God, who is *omniscient*. He knew the avenue to every heart, and how best to win affection or arouse praise. If there was one string in the harp which could be made tuneful, he could touch it. Hence the variety in his method of dealing with those who came to him. One was called upon for public avowal, and another was charged to tell no man; one was cured by a word, another by a touch; the servant of the centurion was healed at a distance, but of the lunatic boy Jesus said, "Bring him hither unto me." Bartimæus was suddenly restored, but this man was gradually given his speech and hearing. This change in mode was not from outward hindrance to the Lord's power, nor because that power was intermittent, but because he put restraint on himself for the sake of the sufferer or of the observers. Mark appears to have taken special interest in cases of gradual restoration. It is not because he would minimize the miraculous element, as some suggest, but possibly because, seeing in all miracles types of what was spiritual, he saw his own experience more clearly in these. He had been brought up under holy influences. As a lad he had heard the Word in the house of his mother Mary, and had been gradually enlightened, like the blind man at Bethsaida; or like this man, without abrupt suddenness, had his ears opened and his tongue loosed to glorify the God of Israel. The method of this sufferer's cure is given in detail, and deserves consideration.

I. JESUS LED HIM APART FROM OTHERS, dealing with him as with the blind man, whom he also took by the hand and led out of the town. This, we think, was not "to avoid ostentation," nor to prevent distraction in his own prayer, but for the man's good. Christ would be with him alone, and so concentrate attention on himself. He took him into solitude that he might receive deeper spiritual impressions, and that the first voice he heard might be the voice of his Lord. It is always good for men to be alone with God, as was Moses in Midian, David watching his flock at Bethlehem, Elijah in the cave at Horeb, and others. Our quietest times are often spiritually our most growing times—illness, bereavement, etc.

II. JESUS BROUGHT HIM INTO VITAL CONTACT WITH HIMSELF. "He put his fingers," etc. We must remember that the man could not speak nor hear, but he could feel and see, and therefore what was done met the necessities of his affliction. With his finger Jesus touched his ear, as if to say, "I am going to cure that;" then, with finger moistened with saliva, he touched his tongue, to show that it was a going out of himself which would restore him. The man was brought into vital contact with Christ, as the child was brought close to the prophet who stretched himself upon him. Our Lord seeks that personal contact of our spirit with his, because the first necessity of redemption is to stir faith in himself. The man yielded to all the Saviour did—watched his signs and expected his word of power; and it is for that expectant faith he so often waits.

III. JESUS RAISED HIS THOUGHTS TO HEAVEN. He looked up to heaven. Watching that loving face, the sufferer saw the Lord look up with ineffable earnestness, love, and trust; and the effect of this would be that he would say to himself, "Then *I* also should pray, 'O God of my fathers, hear me!'" We are called upon, in the light of Christ's example, to look above the means we use for discipline or instruction, and away from ourselves and outward influences to the heavenly Father, who is neither fitful nor indifferent to our deepest needs.

IV. JESUS MADE HIM CONSCIOUS OF PERSONAL SYMPATHY. "He sighed." It was not a groan in prayer, but a sigh of pity, that escaped him when he gazed on this sufferer, and realized, as we cannot do, the devastation and death wrought by sin, of which this was a sign. Even with us it is the one concrete case of suffering which makes all suffering vivid. With that feeling we must undertake Christian work. Sometimes we are busy, but our hands are cold and hard; and when our heads are keen to devise, our hearts too often are slow to feel. But when we, followers of Christ, look on those deaf and indifferent to God, who never repent or pray, and who are sinking into irreligion and pollution, we should yearn over them and pray for them with sighs and tears. If our hearts are heavy with pity, God will make our hands heavy with blessings. After the sighing and prayer came the word of power, "Ephphatha!"—"Be opened!"

and the sealed ear opened to his voice and the stammering tongue proclaimed his praise. See Keble's lines—

> " As thou hast touched our ears, and taught
> Our tongues to speak thy praises plain,
> Quell thou each thankless, godless thought
> That would make fast our bonds again," etc.

CONCLUSION. Henceforth this man would be a living witness to Christ's power. Though it was expressly forbidden to blaze abroad his cure, all who saw him at home or at work would say, " That is the man whom Jesus healed." So let us go forth to live for Jesus, resolving that our words shall utter his praise and that our lives shall witness to his holiness, till at last another " Ephphatha ! " shall be heard, and we pass through the golden gates, into the land where no ears are deaf and no tongues are mute.—A. R.

Vers. 1—23.—*The ritual and the reality of purification.* I. THE MOST NATURAL ACT MAY BE PERVERTED INTO A RITUAL SIN. The disciples were seen eating with unholy hands, that is, unwashed! How this came about we are not told ; probably it was a case of necessity : there was no water to be had. Probably it was a choice between going without food and being ritually correct, or being ritually incorrect and supplying the wants of nature.

II. THE MEANING AND USE OF RITUAL IS CONSTANTLY LOST SIGHT OF BY SMALL MINDS. " The Pharisees and all the Judæans, unless for a pygmy's length they wash the hands and arms, do not eat." The Talmud (Lightfoot) directs that the hands be washed to the elbow—a rule like that here hinted at ; " pygmy " denoting the arm and hand. The custom went beyond what the original ritual required. And so the associations of the market-place were thought peculiarly profane. They carried the rule out in application to cups, jugs, copper vessels, and couches ; things which cannot feel, which are not spiritual, and which therefore are no subjects of " baptism." The root of the error was : 1. Blind respect for custom. Custom commands our respect ; but a blind respect defeats its end and meaning. 2. The reversal of the spiritual order. That order is : first the spiritual, then the material ; the body for the soul. The Pharisaic order was : first the material, and the spiritual through the material. 3. The postponement of the present to the past. What tradition of the fathers can make it a duty to neglect the welfare of the sons ? The rules of the past conserved the privileges of the present ; if they block the way and tend to hurt human life, they must give way. We must study the *perspective* of duties if we do not desire to become narrow in intelligence, and defeat the spirit of law.

III. ATTACHMENT TO RITUAL MAY ACTUALLY OBSCURE THE VIEW OF RELIGIOUS DUTY. Religion begins in the heart. Unless we love our God and our fellow-man, we shall miserably blunder in our construction of duties. Great teachers have always placed us at this moral centre ; face to face with God, in immediate relation to his universal imperative. 1. Isaiah (xxix. 13). He taught that the lips might readily be made to do duty for the heart ; and that invented obediences might distract from the genuine, natural obedience of the right and loving heart. 2. Moses. To go back further in the stream of sacred tradition : no name more honoured than that of the great lawgiver of the desert. He distinctly enunciated the duty of filial reverence, founded on the instincts of the heart. How were the Pharisees carrying this out ? The way in which Christ refers to this is keenly ironical. 3. Christ himself. The Pharisees can and do actually evade the great command of filial piety under the show of obedience to the ceremonial Law. " By a *general* consecration to the temple of whatever might be useful to parents, it was made sacrilege to give anything to them, because whatever was given to them was included in the vow." A miserable trickery, cheating God of his due while seeming to obey him ! Tradition may be so followed as to subvert its very essence ; for there is no tradition respectable which does not enshrine Divine commands.

IV. THE TRUE VIEW OF PURITY RESTORED. 1. *Impurity is not from without but from within.* The external defilement may be cleansed away. It is not *part of the man.* The moral impurity *is.* It is only what the imagination conceives and the will

affirms that is real for us. "In morals and in religion the conscious mind is everything" (Godwin). 2. *This true view may require an effort to attain.* Strange! the disciples "could not quite see it!" "And he said to them, Are you also so inconsiderate?"
And Christ must explain to them the lesson as to a class of tyros. Want of thoughtfulness in the mind is like want of stirring and raking to the garden-ground. The weeds
and mosses soon creep. The man's thought is soon overrun by the trash of opinion
and empty practice, if he will not think for himself. 3. *The human source of evil.* It
lies in the thought, the fancy, or imagination. Lust "conceives" a thought of pleasure,
clashing with the thought of right. The conception germinates, and brings forth a
deed. But a splash of mud that we receive on our garments in crossing the street
has no effect on our conscience. And generally, what we do not *adopt* as part of
ourselves, cannot be imputed to us as sin. "What does not affect the moral character,
cannot affect the relation of man to God" (Godwin).—J.

Vers. 24—30.—*The heathen mother.* I. THE HEATHEN AND THE JEW. 1. In
general, *no relation could be more bitter;* no estrangement more wide. No modern
analogy can well enable us to realize this. They were "wide as the poles asunder."
2. *Jesus the Reconciler.* In him there is neither Jew nor heathen. This sublime truth
was first to be made clear by his own conduct. All truths must be represented in
practice if the world is to receive them. Christ did not deal in the *sentiment* of unity.
He did not propound a theory of humanity, nor of enthusiasm for humanity; he took
the hand of the sufferer; he healed the sickness; he made reconciliation a *fact.* "Go
thou and do likewise!"
II. THE IRONY OF CHRIST. We have all heard of the irony of Socrates. It was the
jesting way the great master had of hinting the truth to the mind, which was concealed in words. Irony is often the disguise of sensitive and keenly truth-loving
minds. Here he conceals tenderest compassion for the poor woman under the mask of
sarcasm. It has the effect of eliciting her deep feeling—profound humility and trust.
All methods of the teacher are good which love prompts, and which subserve the ends
of love. "Faith always finds encouragement and obtains reward" with Christ. To
take the remark of Jesus in ver. 27 as seriously meant, would be contrary to his spirit.
It is the echo of the harsh feeling of the bigoted Jew, and really illustrates by implicit
contrast the tenderness and benignity of Christ.—J.

Vers. 31—37.—*The deaf and dumb.* I. THE GREAT PRIVATION OF SUCH A
SUFFERER. Deafness cuts the person off from society more than blindness. He is not
blessed by that music which expresses the soul of things. He cannot hear that sound
of the human voice, which is the most delicious of all music. One sense needs the
sisterly help of another. Sight tantalizes without hearing. To be full of thought and
feeling, yet not to be able to speak,—than this sense of restraint upon the noblest part
of our nature, nothing may seem more hard.
II. THE CURE IS SYMBOLIC OF THE NATURE OF CHRIST'S MISSION. 1. *The mode
of the cure.* The symbolic action was appropriate. Ordinary language could not be
understood by the sufferer. Jesus employs gesture instead. There are special institutions for teaching the deaf and dumb. Consider how holy a work it is, and how
consecrated by his example. The up-looking denoted internal prayer. So let prayer
be the soul of all our action on others and for others (ch. vi. 41; John xi. 41; xvii. 1).
2. *The cure itself as symbolic.* Christ's love entering the heart enlarges the intelligence,
opens the world of music and harmony. As love opens the gate into a sphere of
unearthly beauty to the lover, so to the soul captivated by the love of God all things
have become new. There is a "sacred silence, offspring of the deeper heart;" and
dumbness has its sanctity, for here is "the finger of God." But sacred is the eloquence
of the tongue, set free by the larger life of mind and heart. God made us for utterance,
as he made the streams to flow.—J.

Vers. 1—23.—*The tradition of men in competition with the commandments of God.*
Pharisees and scribes of Jerusalem had detected some of the disciples of Jesus eating
bread "with defiled, that is, with unwashen, hands." "Holding the tradition of the
elders" with great tenacity themselves, they demand of the new Teacher a reason for

his disciples' departure from the old paths. It was a favourable opportunity for exposing the error of substituting human for Divine precepts, and for placing the external in its right relation to the internal and spiritual. Christ here appears as the authoritative Interpreter of the Divine commands; and, as a true Teacher, discriminating between the "commandment of God" and "the tradition of men." Of old time it was well said, "Man looketh on the outward appearance, but God looketh on the heart." Here the men who "sit on Moses' seat," alike in what they "bid" and in what they "do," lay great stress on the "washings of cups, and pots, and brasen vessels," and of hands. Truly great matters! But the searching eye Divine discerns the hidden "heart" that is "far from" God, and whose many evils send forth a thick stream of pollution in unholy practices, defiling not merely the hands but the whole life. Jesus rebuts their accusation against his disciples, first by a justly merited rebuke, and then by readjusting the relative authority of the commandment of God and the tradition of men, which, in the practice of these accusers, through their selfish, grasping covetousness, had been so greatly distorted. He teaches once and for ever that no commandment of men, no tradition of elders, must be allowed to make "void the Word of God." Thus Jesus, who is so often erroneously spoken of as despising "mere commands," redeems the very "word," and pays his utmost tribute to the letter of the command. In the conflict between the Church and the sacred relationships of common life, to the latter must be assigned the pre-eminence. The necessities of the temple, of its services or its servants, must not be met at the expense of filial faithfulness. The sin of the Pharisees and scribes was—

I. A GROSS PERVERSION OF THE RELATIVE CLAIMS OF THE PARENT AND THE CHURCH.

II. A WICKED INTERFERENCE WITH THE FIRST COMMANDMENT WITH PROMISE.

III. A CRUEL UNDERMINING OF FILIAL AFFECTION AND FIDELITY, AND AS CRUEL AN EXPOSURE OF THE AGED AND ENFEEBLED PARENTS TO A FALSELY JUSTIFIED NEGLECT. And it was—

IV. AN UNWARRANTED USURPATION OF AUTHORITY TO WEAKEN THE OBLIGATION OF A DIVINE LAW.

Christ's words, whilst correcting these errors, (1) traced the tradition to its true source—"your tradition, which ye have delivered;" (2) reduced it to its proper place of inferiority ; and (3) exalted the Divine command, "Honour thy father and thy mother," to its unassailable supremacy. So he prepares the way for a correction of the "many such like things" which were done by these "hypocrites," who taught "as their doctrines the precepts of men."—G.

Vers. 14—23.—*The real and the imaginary defilement.* The question of "the Pharisees, and certain of the scribes which had come from Jerusalem," yet remains to be answered, Jesus having turned aside to weaken the force of "the tradition of men." The answer is given in the ears of "the multitude." It is simple. "There is nothing from without the man that can defile him :" defilement is of that which proceeds "from within out of the heart of man." The man's heart is the fountain of evil; it is his heart, not his hands, that needs washing. No wonder that "the Pharisees were offended, when they heard this saying." Then, having "entered into the house from the multitude," the disciples "asked of him" what is to them as yet "the parable ; " for so are they "without understanding also." In few words he distinguishes the true nature and source of defilement from the untrue, leaving for all time these lessons hidden in his words—

I. ALL POLLUTION IS MORAL POLLUTION. From this all mere ceremonial defilement must be distinguished. Such uncleanness is not moral impurity, nor is ceremonial correctness to be regarded as the testimony of moral purity. The stainless externalist may harbour "within" all "evil things." The perversion of a wise teaching on the necessity for personal cleanliness and of instructive ceremonials had led to the foolish supposition that a touch of the dead, or the diseased, or the decaying matter, conveyed moral impurity. This is once for all contradicted. Whatsoever is "without the man" conveys not the defilement. It is a moral condition. The heart can defile all things. As that which is from without the man cannot defile, so let it be known "there is nothing from without the man that going into him can" cleanse "him."

II. The source of all impurity is not in God's works, but in man's heart. "All these evil things proceed from within." Thus Jesus, with his just judgment, traces evil to its hidden source. The heart, not the flesh, is the seat of defilement. This is the fountain which can corrupt God's good and pure gifts. How marked a contrast does he make between a possible ceremonial uncleanness—a very trifle at most (as to moral uncleanness it is *nil*)—and the greatness, the multiplicity, and the foulness of the "evil things which proceed from within"! Material things cannot in themselves convey moral impurity. Even the excess in the use of the food, which destroys life, comes from within. That the good things of God may be turned into occasions of evil all know, but it is only the heart that can so turn them. Whatsoever is "without the man cannot defile him, because it goeth merely into his body, not into his heart;" and the heart, not the body, is "the man," the true man, the very man.

III. From the thraldom of a false ceremonialism Christ redeems his disciples, "making all meats clean." How needful not only to say what is sin, but to say also what is not sin! From many a yoke which the fathers were not able to bear Christ sets his people free! From child's play to serious work he calls them. From a mere adjustment of articles of dress and of furniture; from punctilios of ritual observance having in themselves no moral significance, and liable to withdraw men from great works and great truths, he turns them aside. He exposes the true evilness in the long catalogue of "evil things" of which the heart, not the flesh, is capable; and he, without many words of exhortation, directs men to seek the cleansing of their unholy hearts, that their lives, their whole man, may be clean also.—G.

Vers. 24—30.—*The Syro-phœnician woman.* Now, in prudence, not in fear, Jesus withdraws from the districts under Herod's jurisdiction, where he had created sufficient excitement to expose him to hindrance both by friends and foes. He fain would hide himself in secret. "He entered into a house, and would have no man know it;" but it was unavailing—"he could not be hid." One at least sought him out with an eager intrusiveness which was only justified by the greatness and pressing nature of her need —"a little daughter grievously vexed with a devil"—and the brilliancy of her faith, which, while it wrought so great good for her home, secured so high commendation from her Lord. On that faith our eye must be fixed.

I. The demand for faith on the part of the stranger was very great. Not one of "the children," but one of "the dogs," she had not been trained in the hope of Israel; though, living in neighbourly relation with the Jews, she was not wholly uninformed. Yet the very name given to the "Lord," of whom "mercy" is sought—"thou Son of David"—was an excluding term for her who could claim no relationship to the sacred family. She belonged not to the house; she was a village dog. Truly it needed great faith on her part to burst through the barriers and ask for "the children's bread." But she shared the common humanity; she had heard of the many healings—even "as many as touched but the border of his garment," though no appeal were made; and the keen eye of need and maternal anxiety saw the largeness of the compassion of him who had not yet denied any.

II. Strangely, however, that faith is tested by absolute silence, by apparent indifference. "He answered her not a word." The disregarded prayer, even though she "besought him" to help her, returned to chill the heart of hope and faith. Her continued appeal, "she crieth after us," engages the intercession of the disciples, who, evidently for their own relief, add their beseeching to hers. Still the appeal is unavailing, and on high and unassailable grounds, with which no personal consideration mingles. "I was not sent" to the heathen. But the struggling faith braves difficulties, and casts this mountain into the sea. Prostrate at his feet she falls with the plea, soon to be effectual, "Lord, help me." Yet even this appeal fails to conquer. He who always acts according to what is right and just declares, "It is not meet"—it is contrary to all propriety and right—"to take the children's bread and cast it to dogs."

III. The parabolic or figurative argument has its weak place, which quick-sighted faith, untiring and unfainting, detects and thereby secures its triumph. "'Yea, Lord.' Yea, it is true; they are the children; yea, I am but a dog; truly it is not right to give the children's bread to dogs; yet in every house the dog is not wholly forgotten." The argument has its (intended) flaw, for God cares for dogs; and from every well-supplied

table something goes to them. Give me that—" the crumbs that fall." Give me " the
children's crumbs ; " what they need not, what they despise, what I may have without
robbing them.

IV. It is enough; the patient, triumphant faith at length finds its REWARD. It shall
be written for future generations of needy ones to learn how to succeed in presence of
difficulties and hindrances and impossibilities. The Lord's honour is upon thee.
" Great is thy faith." And more, thy suit is gained, thy word is mighty. For "this
saying go thy way ; the devil is gone out of thy daughter." It was even so. Let
every suffering one, even though outcast from the holy, happy community, and every
one within that community, learn from this little story that if men have faith as a grain
of mustard seed, it shall be even as they will. And let every timid, unbelieving child
bend lowly before this " dog," and learn the power of living, hopeful, resolute faith.—G.

Vers. 31—37.—*The healing of the deaf and dumb man.* Another case of healing, the
record of which is peculiar to St. Mark, throws into prominence both the pitifulness of
men and the power of the Lord. It is that of one unable to speak for himself, and unable
to hear of the many wonderful works which are being done around. " They bring unto
him one that was deaf, and had an impediment in his speech ; and they beseech him
to lay his hand upon him." Ah, they have gained faith in the power of that hand.
Jesus " took him aside from the multitude privately." Thus the man, at least, would
know the work was the work of Jesus only. Then, for reasons that are not assigned,
possibly as signs to him who could not hear, he "put his fingers into his ears, . . .
spat, . . . touched his tongue," and looked "up to heaven," and "sighed" and spake,
and "saith"—saith " to him" the first word he should hear, "Ephphatha!" Then
" his ears were opened, and the bond of his tongue was loosed, and he spake plain."
Thus is presented to us *a typical example of the redemption of the disorganized life.*

I. One of the disorganizing effects of evil is that it closes the ear. It stops the
avenues to the soul by which the word of truth and love may enter. The wicked man
is deaf to the appeals of righteousness. Its gentle, winning tones fall unheeded on the
inattentive, unmoved heart, which is as insensible to them as is a stone. How great is
the injury thus inflicted! The man is shut out from the elevating, ennobling, the
satisfying, sanctifying influence of truth. The words which minister grace to the
hearers can convey none of their treasures to his heart ; the way is not open. The
human or Divine voice, so rich in its ministries to the ignorant, to the inquirer, to the
hungry, is powerless here. The corrections of wisdom, the lofty motive, the noble aim,
the calming, comforting voice of truth, guiding and blessing wherever it is heard, has
no power here. All is lost. Not more is he to be pitied who, by physical infirmity,
hears not the voice of friends, the songs of birds, the harmonies of sweet sounds. Sin
robs the life of its truest, its highest enrichment. Christ's greatest ministries to the
world were by his lips. Though the words were of earth, they were vessels holding
heavenly treasure. But the deaf hear them not. So truly is a state of sinfulness
typified in deafness.

II. But sin equally impedes the free and profitable service of the life of its victim.
It closes his mouth. The mouth, which may be a fountain of wisdom, if unsealed. The
life, which might be a spring of blessing to many, is as a dry and parched land, or as a
well having no water. That beneficent ordination by which one life—even every life—
is designed to be a source of blessing to every other, is, by evil, frustrated; and it
becomes, instead, a cause of injury.

III. It is here Christ appears to bless the race by opening the eyes of the blind, by
unstopping the ears of the deaf, by loosing the tongue of the dumb. His holy work
stands over against the evil of sin. He unstops the deaf ear. Awaking the attention
of the sleeper, he gives to the receiving soul the words of eternal life. His heavenly
teaching renews, exalts, ennobles. The ignorant one becomes wise in his school. His
truth raises the beggar from the dunghill. Righteousness puts the soul *en rapport* with
all that is good, and beautiful, and wise, and holy. It makes a man to be at one with
all the kingdom of God, with all truth and all life.

IV. But the redeemed life becomes a source of blessing to others—a fountain of living
waters. The unsealed lips speak forth the heavenly wisdom. The psalm of praise, the
song of thanksgiving, the word of truth, of peace, and of blessing, and the activities of

the good life, are all serviceable. The life now becomes an active power for good.
Each, when he has " turned again," is able to strengthen his brethren. The first effect
of the eviction of evil from the life is that the eyes are opened, that all that surrounds
may enter to enrich the life. The second effect is, the lips are opened, the life becomes
a centre of useful influence. It is a new acquisition to the world, a new joy. So from
without flows into the redeemed life all that is calculated to minister to it, to nourish,
to purify, to exalt, to gladden and perfect it; while back again from the nourished,
purified, and gladdened life, new sentiments, new emotions, new aims, and new efforts
proceed. The effect of which reciprocal influence is that each becomes a point of light,
a form of loveliness; each a stream of holy, useful influence, refreshing this weary
desert and making it glad. Truly, of him who " maketh even the deaf to hear, and the
dumb to speak," it may be said, " He hath done all things well." It is no less well
said, " And they glorified the God of Israel."—G.

Vers. 1—23. Parallel passage: Matt. xv. 1—20.—*Exposure of Pharisaism : its
errors and evils.* I. DOCTRINE OF DEFILEMENT. 1. *Contents of this chapter.* This
chapter contains three principal sections. The first section treats of *defilement* ; the
second gives an account of a *demon* being expelled from the daughter of a Syro-
phœnician woman; and the third narrates the cure of a *deaf* mute. The first section,
again, contains the following:—The charge of defilement which the Pharisees preferred against the disciples; the evangelist's digression for the purpose of explaining
to his Gentile readers the Jewish notions and usages in this matter ; Christ's applying to the Jews of his day a description of their fathers by Isaiah ; the reason of this
application in the displacement by them of God's Law to make room for the traditionary teachings of man; a much graver delinquency in nullifying the Law of God
not merely with respect to ceremonial washings, but in regard to moral duties; a specific
example of this in a glaring and most culpable neglect of filial obligation ; our
Lord's exposition, publicly in the presence of the assembled people and privately to the
disciples, of the true nature of real, that is, moral defilement ; and a reference to the
distinction of clean and unclean in the matter of meats, which formed a main partition between Jews and Gentiles. The way was thus prepared for, and an easy
transition made to, the subject of the second section, which narrates our Lord's only
recorded visit to the Gentile world, and the miracle there wrought in the case of the
Gentile maiden who was dispossessed under singularly interesting circumstances. The
third section records a miracle which is only mentioned by St. Mark, and so peculiar to
his Gospel. Our Lord, having just returned from the cities of Phœnicia, was making
his way through the midst of the region of the Ten Cities, when he cured the deaf
mute or dumb man of Decapolis in a very remarkable manner, and by a method of
external application not employed hitherto in the miracles wrought by our Lord.

2. *Linguistic peculiarities in the first section.* (1) The first peculiarity of the kind
indicated is the use of the Greek word πυγμῇ, which is a *hapax legomenon*, and qualifies
the verb " wash." In our English version it is translated (*a*) *oft*, and in the margin (*b*)
diligently, which is adopted in the Revised Version. The former is supported by the
Vulgate, which has *crebro*, and depends on the analogy of similar but not really
related words, such as πυκνῇ or πυκνῶς ; while the marginal rendering has the support of
the Peshito Syriac *b'tiloith*. Some of the older interpreters understand it as (*c*) a
measure of length, and so Euthymius has μέχρι τοῦ ἀγκῶνος, " as far as the elbow ; " and
Theophylact similarly, adding that it is the space from the elbow to the knuckles ; the
water poured out into the hollow of the hand would thus, by the elevation of the same,
flow down to the elbow. The more natural explanation seems to be that which takes
it (*d*) in the primary signification of the word, which is clenched hand or fist; not in the
sense of the closed hand being raised so as to allow the water to flow down to the
elbow; nor yet in the sense of rubbing the closed hand or fist with the hollow of
the other hand, which, as Fritzsche suggests, would require the words to be τῇ παλαμῇ
νίψωνται τὴν πυγμήν; but in the sense of washing the hand with the fist, that is, by
rubbing one hand with the other closed or clenched or with the fist, in the sense of
vigorously. This explanation, which corresponds with that of Beza, amounts to the
idea of diligence conveyed by the Syriac. This verb νίπτω, it may be observed in passing,
generally refers to "washing the hands or feet," as πλύνω signifies to "wash clothes," and

λούω to "wash," usually the body, and therefore in the middle voice "to bathe." (2) Again, in ver. 4, a different kind of washing must be meant by βαπτίσωνται. Olshausen and others refer the washing which it implies, not to the Pharisees themselves, but to the articles of food bought in, and brought from, market; and explain the middle voice consistently with its usual meaning, that is to say, in the signification of washing for themselves. This rendering scarcely deserves the serious consideration given to it, and is to be rejected unhesitatingly. It must, as we think, refer to the men themselves. The washing of ver. 3 is partial, only including the hands; it was the ordinary custom with the Jews of that day before partaking of food; but in case they had been to the market or bazaar, and had come into contact with the crowd that resorted thither, it was scarcely possible to escape defilement of some kind in mixing with that motley multitude, and therefore a more general washing, extending to the whole body, became a ceremonial necessity. The other reading (ῥαντίσωνται), denoting "to sprinkle" or "cleanse by sprinkling," is properly regarded as a gloss; the word βαπτίσωνται, in the absence of regimen, is quite unrestricted as to mode, signifying "wash themselves," as it is rendered in the Revised Version. There is (3) a slight diversity about the connection of the words ἀπὸ ἀγορᾶς, which are joined by Krebs and Kuinoel to ἐσθίουσι, in the sense of eating of things bought in the market, like the construction which occurs in ver. 28 of this same chapter, where the dogs are said to eat of the crumbs (ἐσθίει ἀπὸ τῶν ψιχίων); while ἀγορὰ is admitted to have in the classics the signification of provisions bought in the market, as in the phrase ἀγορὰν παρεῖχον. This, however, appears a straining both of the sense and construction, the plain rendering being "after market," or, as the English has it, "when they came from the market;" thus ἀπὸ δείπνου means "after supper."

3. *Additional baptisms.* These washings, which the Pharisees and indeed all the Jews practised, were not confined to their hands or whole persons; but, besides such personal ablutions, there were baptisms of cups and pots, of brazen vessels, and of couches. Of these domestic utensils the first are named from the *use* to which they are applied, namely, for drinking, as is expressed by its root; the second, corresponding to the Roman *sextarius,* from which, and not from ξέω, to polish, is the word derived, are named from their *size,* and contain a pint, or sixth part of a congius (somewhere about a gallon); the third are called from the *material* copper of which they are made; the fourth get their name like the first, from their *use,* to wit, of reclining on, either for the purpose of sleep or at meals.

4. *The origin of these washings.* Several chapters of Leviticus (xii.—xv.) contain a tolerably full account of the ablutions enjoined in the Law, and employed for Levitical purifications. These purifications were resorted to for the purpose of ceremonial cleansing. They had generally respect to certain states or conditions of the body, symbolical of the defiling nature of sin. In some of these cases we read that the person to be cleansed "shall wash his clothes, bathe his flesh in running water, and shall be clean." But Pharisaism extended these washings far beyond the limits of the Law—applied them to cases neither contemplated by, nor comprehended in, the Law, and multiplied them to an absurd amount. Persons, before engaging in the commonest acts of domestic or social life, were compelled to a strict observance of such washings; nay, the very articles of household furniture, including those here enumerated, had to be subjected to them. God had, for good and wise purposes, instituted certain temporary means of ceremonial cleansing; but man perverts and pollutes, or, when he does not pollute, he perverts the wisest means to the worst ends. The perversions in the case before us, besides being excessively burdensome and extremely inconvenient from their multiplicity, were perfectly contemptible from their very puerility and triviality, and positively sinful from the seemingly magical efficacy with which they invested mere mechanical operations.

5. *Ceremonialism.* Ceremonies of human invention, especially when multiplied and perverted from their legitimate or appointed use, like the ablutions referred to, instead of being helps, become hindrances to devotion. They promote irreligion at the same time that they foster pride. Their tendency is to put outward purifying in the place of inward purity, to substitute external cleansing for internal cleanness, to prefer clean hands to a clean heart, and to rest in "the righteousness which is of the Law" instead of "the righteousness which is of God by faith." True religion, under whatever

dispensation, begins with the heart. Thus the psalmist prays so beautifully, "Create in me a clean heart, O God; and renew a right spirit within me." The promise here is limited to such, as when it is said, "Truly God is good to Israel, even to such as are of a clean heart;" the prospect hereafter is for them, and for them alone; for it is only "the pure in heart" that shall "see God." No amount of outward observances or ceremonial ablutions could constitute real religion or supply its place, nor entitle the person that performed them to the privileges of a true child of God. The apostle insists on this when he says, "He is not a Jew, which is one outwardly; neither is that circumcision, which is outward in the flesh: but he is a Jew, which is one inwardly; and circumcision is that of the heart, in the spirit, and not in the letter; whose praise is not of men, but of God."

6. *Tradition*. Tradition in general is that which is handed down from father to son, or from one generation to another. The word is sometimes used in a good sense, and signifies instructions, whether relating to doctrine or duty, faith or practice, and whether the delivery be oral or written; but, and this is the main thing, consisting of truths immediately delivered by inspired men. Such is its signification in 1 Cor. xi. 2, where the apostle commands or exhorts the Corinthians to "hold fast the *traditions*, even as I delivered them to you;" also in 2 Thess. ii. 15, "Therefore, brethren, stand fast, and hold the *traditions* which ye have been taught, whether by word, or our epistle;" and again in the same Epistle (iii. 6), "Withdraw yourselves from every brother that walketh disorderly, and not after the *tradition* which he received of us." But it has another sense also in Scripture, and is employed to denote what is merely human and untrustworthy, as when St. Paul speaks of himself as he was in his original sinful, unconverted state, and says, "I profited in the Jews' religion above many my equals in mine own nation, being more exceedingly zealous of the *traditions* of my fathers;" and again, when he warns the Colossians, saying, "Beware lest any man spoil you through philosophy and vain deceit, after the *tradition* of men, after the rudiments of the world, and not after Christ." It is in this latter sense that it is used in ver. 6 of the present chapter, when "the Pharisees and scribes asked him, Why walk not thy disciples according to the tradition of the elders?" The Jewish theory of tradition was that, along with the written Law, Moses received at Sinai a second or oral law, and that this latter law was handed down through succeeding generations. This law, consisting of traditional interpretations and gradual additions, was at length embodied in the text of the Talmud, called "Mishna," or "second law." This oral law held a higher rank, and was more highly esteemed than the written Law. It not only supplemented the written Law by large additions, but was employed as the key to its interpretation. Thus in the end it was used in instances innumerable to supplant, or supersede, or set aside, the written Law at pleasure. We do not despise tradition in the proper and legitimate sense which, as we have seen, the word sometimes has, nor in its present ordinary sense of something handed down—ordinance or ceremony—provided it be agreeable to the Divine Word; but we must not set up tradition side by side with the written Word of God, nor bring God's Word into conformity with tradition; on the contrary, whenever God's Word and human tradition clash, the latter must be corrected by the former. One example of this kind we have in relation to the Apostle John, about whom the saying went abroad that he should not die. Jesus had said, "If I will that he tarry till I come, what is that to thee?" This was in the first instance misinterpreted, then the misinterpretation spread from mouth to mouth as a regular tradition, till the apostle himself felt called upon to correct it by the specific statement, "Yet Jesus said not unto him, He shall not die; but, If I will that he tarry till I come, what is that to thee? follow thou me."

7. *Isaiah's prediction as applicable to the Pharisees as to their fathers.* The statement of Is   , though not in the strict and specific sense a prediction concerning our Lord's contemporaries, was a description so all-embracing and so pregnant with meaning, that it exhibited with striking exactness the chief features of their religious life, or rather of their irreligious, soulless formality. Isaiah foretold it (προεφήτευσεν, aorist) in the past, but it stands written from then till now, and so our Lord, in this case, uses the perfect (γέγραπται.) What was said then, so long before, was equally true in the Saviour's day; it was as true of the children, or remote descendants, as of their ancestors, as though the traits of character referred to had become stereotyped.

(1) He charged them with hypocritical lip-service, saying, as though with withering scorn, "Ye hypocrites, ye honour me with lip-service, but without sincere heart-worship!" (2) with vanity or empty form in worshipping according to the commandments which human tradition taught; and (3) our Lord, in stating the ground of the application which he makes of the prophet's words, brings home the charge, asserting that by those human precepts they displaced the commandments of God; and then (4) he backs his assertion by an example of most glaring and flagrant criminality as the natural result of such Pharisaic teaching.

8. *Practical remarks on the preceding.* We cannot fail to notice (1) the depth of meaning in the Divine Word; of this characteristic of Scripture we have here a notable illustration. What Isaiah spoke in his moral portraiture of his contemporaries, applied to their children's children many centuries after, as accurately and as exactly as if he had had the latter solely in view, or rather as if the distant ancestors and the remote posterity both sat together before this great spiritual limner. Such apt and felicitous delineation was not the result of human intuition or prophetical sagacity, but of Divine inspiration; it was the Spirit that gave the prophet such foresight, and thus testified the truth beforehand. The word "hypocrite" (2) originally meant one who answered in a dramatic dialogue, and thus an actor; and further, one who wore a mask as actors did. It denotes one who assumes a character which does not really belong to him, or acts a part that is unreal, or feigns virtues not possessed. The persons to whom the word is here applied approached God with their lips, while their heart was far distant from (πόρρω ἀπέχει, "holds far aloof from") him. They were acting the part of true worshippers, but were not so in reality; they were wearing a mask of profession, which they put on to conceal their real character. They pretended to be honouring God, but the honour which they gave him did not proceed from the heart; it was only in outward seeming, or for external show. This worship (3) was confined to the utterances of their lips as the main instrument employed in such worship; but the understanding and its faculties, the heart and its affections, were not engaged, and took no part in it. It was hollow-hearted and false-hearted; it was vain (μάτην, in vain, a word which may come from μάω, to seek but without finding). It was meant as worship, no doubt, but it was fruitless, being worship that God could not accept. The vanity (4) of this worship, however, did not arise so much from the *manner* of it—heartless as that was, and spiritless as it was—but from the *matter* of it. All worship presumes certain doctrines and duties, and proceeds in accordance with these. Every time we open our lips in praise or prayer, or other act of worship, doctrines or duties of some sort are involved, implied, or referred to. But the doctrines which these Pharisaic formalists taught were the commandments of men; they had no higher source and no better origin. If we would worship God aright, we must worship according to the way and means which God himself has prescribed; if we teach acceptably, we must teach the doctrines which God directs. Not so the Pharisees: their doctrines were human commandments; their teaching, therefore, was often false, always fallible, often puerile, and not unfrequently pernicious. But worse still, their teachings were not merely negative, in so far as they did not teach what God commanded, but only what men invented; they were positively subversive of the commandment of God in *any given case*, and hence the word here is singular (ἐντολὴν); as our Lord himself affirms, when in ver. 8 he states the ground on which he applies to the Pharisees of his time the words spoken by Isaiah in relation to their ancestors. Ye give up or *let go* the commandment of God, but *hold fast* the tradition of men in the matter of ceremonial washings, and of many other things of like kind. Not only so; ye *set aside* the commandment of God (not *by*, as in the Authorized Version, but) *for the sake of* your tradition (διὰ τὴν παράδοσιν ὑμῶν, St. Matthew), or, as St. Mark more fully expresses it, "in order that ye may keep your own tradition." Thus there is a climax; for, first, they *let go* or *dismiss* the commandment of God, while they hold with obstinate tenacity human tradition; then, secondly, they *set aside* or *displace*, putting something else in its room, or reject with something akin to contempt, the commandment of God; from omission they proceeded to commission as usual, and all this in order to *guard*, observe, or maintain their own tradition. Isaiah had finely (καλῶς) described them beforehand, and now they finely (καλῶς, the same word, but used ironically in this second instance, and not with the meaning of "entirely") act up to that description.

9. *Moral obligation set aside through Pharisaism.* Our Lord proceeds to expose the practical and pernicious effect of Pharisaic traditionalism in the domain of ethics. He had shown the hollowness of its teaching in cases of ceremonial cleansings; but he now advances from the ceremonial to the moral. For this purpose he selects the fifth commandment, and proves that the antagonism between the written Law, or Law of God, and the oral, or human law, in respect to this commandment, is complete. He quotes the prescriptive part of the commandment, and omits the promissory as not required by the object he has in view; instead of the promissory clause attached to obedience, he substitutes the punitive sentence pronounced on the person guilty of a breach of the commandment in question. " Moses said "—and here it will be observed that the commandment of God, who spake by Moses, is identified with the commandment of his inspired servant, so that what was really said by God is here attributed by our Lord to his servant Moses—"Honour thy father and thy mother." These words were graven by the finger of the Almighty on the stone tablet at Sinai, and the precept thus solemnly delivered at first was enforced by the awfully severe sanction which follows:— " Whoso curseth "—that is, speaketh ill of or revileth—" father or mother, let him die the death." (1) In the " precept " the possessive pronoun and article are used with both words, " father " and " mother," as if to individualize, and point out specifically to every reader or hearer of the Law, the duty as individual and personal; but, in the penalty clause, the pronoun and article, though expressed both in the original Hebrew and Septuagint Version, are omitted in the record of both evangelists, as if to generalize or treat as a class, and present the duty in the abstract, thus denoting unfaithfulness to *such* a relationship—*such a sacred* object of affection as a father and a mother. The omission of the article by itself draws attention to the quality, character, or nature, rather than the substance, of the thing thus spoken of. (2) The original Hebrew expression is a peculiar idiom of that language, implying intensity by means of an infinitive mood joined to the finite verb of the same signification, and denoting, " Let him be surely put to death "—literally, " dying, let him be put to death." The Septuagint Version has two ways of expressing this Hebrew idiom, either by the verb and cognate noun in the dative, or by the verb and its participle; the former is the mode not exactly adopted, but only approximated in this instance, with merely an insignificant variation, by the evangelist, namely, " Let him end with death." But (3) the words " he shall be free " of the common version are supplied in order to make out the sense. If the reading of the received text, which begins the next verse with καὶ, be retained, the verse before us may be regarded (*a*) as an instance of the figure aposiopesis, by which our Lord, as if with inexpressible indignation at the thought of conduct so unnatural and reprehensible, breaks off without completing the sentence; while the supplied words of the English version express the acquittal conceded in the case by Pharisaic casuistry. Another way (*b*) of evading the difficulty was suggested by Fritzsche, who supplies here the closing words of ver. 10 with a negative—that is, μὴ θανάτῳ τελευτάτω—so that this verse would read as follows:—" But ye say, If a man shall say to his father or mother, It is Corban, that is to say, a gift, by whatseover thou mightest be profited by me, *let him not die the death.*" The Revised Version, (*c*) however, cuts the knot by adopting the reading which excludes καὶ from the beginning of ver. 12; thus, " But ye say, If a man shall say to his father or his mother, That wherewith thou mightest have been profited by me is Corban, that is to say, Given to God; ye no longer suffer him to do aught for his father or his mother."

10. *Further development of our Lord's retort.* The word " corban " meant anything brought near to the altar or to the God of the altar for presentation, and applied, like the cognate verb *hikrib*, to bring near, to any offerings, whether bloody or unbloody, animal or vegetable. The evangelist, as is his custom, explains it by a Greek word denoting a gift in general, but more particularly, according both to Homeric and Hellenistic usage, a gift to God, or a votive offering. It is thus a correct equivalent of the word which the evangelist explains by it. When, then, a Jewish child wished to discard, and entirely free himself from, filial obligation, he had only to pronounce this mystic word of potent meaning, and the traditional law of Pharisaism gave him a full release. Whenever a man said of any part of his property or of his whole possessions, " It is Corban," that is, " given to God," he was bound by his vow, and the property was devoted to the service or support of the altar or temple or national religion; it was

made over for religious purposes, though the time of fulfilling such vow was left to his own option, and so its fulfilment became discretionary, or was evaded. To revile or curse father or mother was surely bad enough and wicked enough; but to refuse to supply the wants of a parent when reduced to poverty, or to support a parent in old age and when needing such support, or to withhold from an indigent parent the necessaries of life, on the plea that the means or resources out of which such could be supplied were devoted to religious uses, was a refinement of unnatural and inhuman wickedness almost incapable of being expressed in words. And thus, as the next verse informs us, they suffered him no longer to do anything for his parents, even if he would; or, if he would not, they suffered him to have his way, conniving at his sin and overlooking his shame, nay, putting words into his mouth to enable him to perpetrate in the name of religion such abominable villainy. If, from a spirit of greedy avarice, or miserable meanness, or detestable stinginess; or in a fit of spiteful passion; or under the influence of superstition, a wicked Jew pleased to say to either parent suffering from disease, or labouring under age and poverty, " That whereby I might have helped, or relieved, or in any way benefited you, is devoted to the service of God and religion, and cannot now be withdrawn," the oral law of the Pharisee granted full liberty to do so, taught him its formula for that very purpose, and salved his conscience that he might withal feel at ease. Now, to those censorious Pharisees who watched our Lord and his disciples with such lynx-eyed vigilance and malign intent, and who had seen, not all the disciples, but some of them, partaking, not of a regular repast, but eating a morsel of bread with hands common, that is, in the ordinary or general state—clean, it may be, but not ritually cleansed—our Lord may be supposed to say, Ye blame my hungry disciples for snatching the fragment of a hurried meal without ceremonial ablution, and censure them for neglecting a silly ceremony enjoined no doubt, by your traditional law, which is only of human origin, and, in such a case as that just referred to, of most nefarious tendency; but ye teach your disciples to violate, not a trivial ceremonial observance for which only human authority can be pleaded, and from which no benefit can be derived, but a moral duty, based on closest human relationship, written by God's own finger, recorded in his written law, and enforced by the most solemn sanction! Is not this to establish man's law and set aside God's Law; to adhere punctiliously to the miserable tradition of miserable or wicked men, but to invalidate and even abrogate the Law of an infinitely pure and holy God—a Law, too, like its Author, holy and just and good! To wash the hands before a regular meal, or any meal, may be proper enough as a custom, or for cleanliness, or as a matter of delicacy, yet can never be exalted into a religious act or rite; but to trifle with or trample underfoot the law of natural affection, of filial piety, of common humanity—a law specially honoured with a most gracious promise, and sternly hedged in with the severest sanction—must bring down the vengeance of Heaven on the guilty head of its transgressor. Thus our Lord left them to look at this picture and on that.

II. DISTINCTION BETWEEN CLEAN AND UNCLEAN. 1. *Statement of a principle.* After our Lord had put to silence and covered with confusion these intermeddling, faultfinding, censorious, and cavilling Pharisees, he proceeds to state a great and fundamental principle, which covered the whole ground and went to the very root of the matter. Before doing so, he requests the particular attention of the multitude. Whether they had withdrawn to a respectful distance during our Lord's interview with the Pharisees and triumphant answer to their objection, or whether, from indifference to their obtrusive questionings the malevolent intention of which was obvious, they had sunk into a state of listless inattention, does not appear. They required, from whatever cause, to have their attention stimulated. For this purpose he calls on all and each, not only to listen attentively, but to reflect, with intelligence wide awake and active, on the great principle he is about to enunciate. Having thus gained their intelligent attention and roused their powers of reflection, he states the important distinction that "there is nothing from without a man, that entering into him can defile him: but the things which come out of him, those are they that defile the man." After making this statement, he again appeals to them to give it their careful consideration.

2. *Important distinction.* Our Lord, in the principle stated, distinguishes between the physical and spiritual natures of man, as also between ceremonial and moral defilements; between positive regulations and moral requirements; and thus between pre-

cepts given for a particular purpose and obligations for a limited time, and those laws that were unvarying in their nature and perpetual in their obligation. The principle in question our Lord propounds in the form of an antithetic paradox. The first part of it seemed to collide with the distinction between meats clean and unclean, which God himself had appointed and minutely specified; and, if taken in a ceremonial sense, so it did; but understood morally, as our Lord had intended, it pointed not obscurely to the purpose for which such distinctions had been instituted. That purpose was temporary in its duration, and for the segregation of the chosen people from the mass of mankind, as well as for the symbolic intimation of the difference that should exist between the holiness to which the people of God were called, and the heathenism that prevailed around. Our Lord meant to correct an injurious error under which the people of the Jews in general then laboured. He had rebuked their superstitious punctiliousness about certain ceremonial washings, and their sinful regardlessness of moral obligations. This naturally leads him to expose the grave mistake they made when they foolishly supposed that meats of themselves exercised any moral efficacy or possessed any moral potency. That they defiled ceremonially, and exposed to disabilities of a ceremonial kind and entailing purification, was not doubted; but that they had any power of themselves either to cleanse or purify is here most positively denied. The cause of defilement was man's fallen nature; the source of it was within; the seat of it was the heart; the stagnant pool from which such polluted waters issued was deep down in the very depths of his being. Thence proceeded defilements of speech through the mouth, defilements of work in the conduct, defilements of thoughts in the character and conversation. The disciples had shared the errors and prejudices of their race to a very large extent, and not understanding the strange paradoxical statement, sought an explanation in private. After a gentle reprimand for their dulness of apprehension, they were favoured by their Master with a full explanation.

3. *Moral impurity.* The belly is the stomach and viscera, or organs of digestion generally; the heart is used for both the intellect and affections—the whole soul. These are totally distinct; what enters the former does not and cannot reach the latter. There is no connection between these parts of man's nature, and no compatibility between the objects that affect them. Meats only enter the stomach and intestines, and minister to man's life and strength; even the exclusion of their refuse tends to purification rather than defilement. But the things that do defile proceed out of the heart; and they are *sins* against God's Law, or *dispositions* that incline to those sins, and *incentives* that prompt to them. Those *sins* are against the commandments in the so-called second table of the Law. According to a rough classification that has been made, some are sins against the sixth commandment, as murders, wickedness, and an evil eye; some against the seventh, as fornication, adultery, and lasciviousness; some against the eighth, as theft and deceit; some against the ninth, as blasphemies, or evil-speaking, and false witness (in St. Matthew's enumeration); and some against the tenth, as covetousness, or, literally, "reachings after more." But of the evil dispositions that lead to overt acts of sins, the chief place is occupied by evil thoughts, whether the reference is to evil thoughts in general, or to such vicious reasonings (διαλογισμοὶ) as those in which the Pharisees were accustomed to indulge. While such inward thoughts or reasonings are the *seminal principles* from which sinful actions proceed— the bitter roots from which they shoot up and grow—a *leading motive* to sin is specified: it is pride (ὑπερηφανία, a desire to appear above others), the wish for conspicuous elevation. In pride itself the predominant element is selfishness—that selfishness that prompts men to seek the pre-eminence in all things, and to prefer self to all other persons or interests, in contrariety to the scriptural precept which directs us "in honour to prefer one another." Pride implies that overbearing demeanour and haughtiness of carriage that make men look down on others, supposing themselves so much superior. Pride centres all in self, disregarding others' interests whenever they seem to stand in the way; at the same time proud persons, male or female, "sacrifice to their own net, and burn incense to their own drag." Pride is thus a most powerful motive to sin, to selfish indulgence, to self-aggrandizement, to supercilious speech in regard to others, and to self-interest, whatever form it may assume, and however much detriment may be done to the rights of others. Further, one *characteristic* of all sin, and a name frequently used in Scripture as synonymous with "sin," is "folly" (ἀφροσύνη). This

senselessness denies God the glory that pertains to him, for "the fool has said in his heart, There is no God." While it thus robs God, it refuses to man his due. In the end it ruins the individual himself. "This their way is their folly." Oh, the folly of sin! The enumeration of the things which defile a man, as given here by St. Mark, is fuller than that given by St. Matthew. The latter mentions only seven; while St. Mark specifies thirteen. The cause of this additional number by the latter may be found in the vices that commonly prevailed among the Romans, for whom in the first instance St. Mark wrote, as compared with those to which the Jews, whom St. Matthew more especially kept in view in his Gospel, were addicted. A comparison also of the catalogue of crimes, which St. Paul, in writing to the Romans, gives at the close of his first chapter, will probably confirm the same conclusion, that the cause of the difference in the enumeration is connected with the different classes of sins to which persons belonging to these different nationalities were respectively addicted. Judaism at its worst, if this theory be correct, had greatly the advantage of paganism; so the lowest type of Christianity is superior to heathenism.—J. J. G.

Vers. 24—30. Parallel passage: Matt. xv. 21—28.—*Daughter of a Syro-phœnician woman healed.* I. OUR LORD'S WITHDRAWAL INTO THE REGION OF TYRE AND SIDON. Our Lord's retirement at this time into the region indicated was probably occasioned by a desire to avoid the further attention and inquiries of Herod, and perhaps his presence also there in his tetrarchy, which comprised Galilee and Peræa; while it may have been a symbolic intimation of the mercy in store for, and ere long to be extended to, Gentile lands; or it may have been simply for the purpose of seclusion and rest after a time of toil, and to escape from the cavils of scribes and Pharisees. The territory here described as "the borders of Tyre and Sidon" was not a district interjacent between Tyre and Sidon, as Erasmus understood it; nor yet the territory proper of Tyre and Sidon, as Fritzsche explained it; or the neighbourhood of the former city, as Alford took its meaning to be; but originally a tract of border-land or neutral ground which separated Palestine from Phœnicia, subsequently ceded by Solomon to the King of Tyre and incorporated with Phœnicia, yet still retaining its ancient name of borderland.

II. THE APPLICANT, AND HER WRETCHEDNESS. This applicant is called by St. Matthew a Canaanitish woman, and by St. Mark a Syro-phœnician. Phœnicia, in which the old and famous commercial cities of Tyre (from Tzor, "a rock," now *Sur*) and Sidon (from Tsidon, "fishery," now *Saida*, twenty miles further north) were situated, was part of ancient Canaan, and so inhabited by a remnant of that doomed race. But, as the Phœnicians were the great seafarers and colonizers of ancient times, they had sent out and founded many settlements. One of these was in Africa, and the colonists were distinguished by the appropriate name of Liby-phœnicians, from the parent stock which went by the name of Syro-phœnicians. Horace has the expression, "Uterque Pœnus serviat uni," and Juvenal twice employs the word "Syro-phœnix." It is probable that, while the coast-line retained the name Phœnicia, the more inland parts, where Syrian and Phœnician intermingled, got the name of Syro-phœnicia. But, while this woman was a Syro-phœnician by race, she was a Greek, that is, a Gentile; for the name Greek was used generally for all Gentiles, as distinguished from Jews, just as Frank is employed in the East for all Europeans; thus, we read in Rom. i. 16, "To the Jew first, and also to the Greek." Thus Greek was the same as Gentile, and the inhabitants of the world were distributed into Greeks and Jews. The applicant, then, in the narrative under consideration, belonged to a different nationality from the Jews, for she was a Syrophœnician, and to a different religion, for she was a heathen. This poor woman, born and bred amid the darkness of heathenism, with little to sustain and comfort her in this world, and without hope for a better, had her full share of the miseries of mortal life. She appears from the narrative to have been a widow, as there is no mention or notice of her husband. If so—and we have no reason to doubt it—she had to bear the hardships and fight the battle of life alone, without the head of her little household, without the bread-winner of her family, and without a partner to share and so divide the current of her grief. She had a daughter, probably an only daughter, mayhap an only child; but that one daughter, that only child, instead of being a source of comfort or support to the widowed mother, was the cause of the great grief that pressed upon and crushed her heart.   That beloved child—that dear daughter, round whom alone, in the absence of other objects, the mother's affections were now all entwined—was an invalid, and an invalid whom no medical skill and no human power could relieve.   It was not merely disease under which she laboured; if that had been all, however bad the case or severe the distemper, it might, even after medical appliances had proved unavailing, have exhausted itself, as is sometimes known to happen, or even the *vis medicatrix naturæ* might have effected a cure.   But no, it was something worse, much worse, than any ordinary disease, however virulent; it was demoniac power—diabolical possession.   The girl had "an unclean spirit," and was "grievously vexed with a devil," so that the case was taken out of the common category of diseases, and entirely hopeless. The poignancy of the mother's grief, the bitterness of her sorrow for a daughter so dear to her, and yet so hopelessly, helplessly afflicted, we can well imagine.   Indeed, we seem to hear the echo of her wail in the pathetic cry for mercy : " Have mercy upon me, O Lord, thou Son of David ! "

III. HER APPLICATION.   What led her to think of Jesus at all ?   In the first instance, no doubt, it was her *misery* on account of her daughter's distressed condition.   She had, we are persuaded, tried many means before this; she had left nothing undone, we are very sure; but all was in vain!   Her wretchedness had found no relief; her misery remains without alleviation.   She is now ready to do or to dare anything that may hold forth the slightest hope of relief.   But while it was the feeling of misery in the first instance, and that strong maternal affection which the sufferings of her daughter roused into such active exercise, there was, besides, a *rumour* that had somehow reached her ears of the great Jewish Teacher, who was Prophet and Physician both in one.   His fame had reached that distant heathen land.   He wished, indeed, that no man should know of his journey thither or of his being there; he meant to travel *incognito*.   But that he soon found to be impossible, for, as the evangelist expresses it, " he could not be hid;" there was that about him, conceal it as he might, which revealed his majesty and bespoke the greatness and dignity of his person.   This Canaanitish woman has heard, moreover, that this powerful Healer has quitted the holy city, and left the Galilean hills, the flowery slopes, the glancing waters of the lovely lake; and that he is at present travelling in that remote north-west.   Now she feels that her opportunity is come, that the time for trying another remedy has arrived, and that a Physician, greater than any she had ever applied to or heard of before, is now accessible.   A load is lifted off her heart; her hopes are raised, and with buoyant spirit she sets out to where she heard he was.   But she has not been long on the road till hope and fear begin to alternate.   Had she not been buoyed up with similar hopes before, and yet those hopes had ended in disappointment?   May it not be so again? May it not be so now?   Still she feels that the object of all this solicitude can scarcely be worse, and may perhaps be better.   At all events, she is determined to make the trial, if it should be the last.   She has heard of multitudes of cures he has performed, of wonderful cures—cures of demoniacs as well as those afflicted with diseases; and so she plucks up heart anew, and again resumes her journey.   Here were two strong motives impelling her to take the course she was doing—her sense of misery, and the reports about Jesus.   And yet there was, we think, a third impelling power; for what suggested the resolution she came to in view of the wretchedness of her own and her daughter's condition, and on the ground of the reports that had reached her ?   What or who empowered her to make up her mind at once and form the resolution ?   What it was we are not told in so many words; it is not expressly stated, perhaps not even clearly implied; and yet such an impulse must have been given to her will.   We speak of God putting this or that thought into the heart; and so we believe that it was God that opened her eyes to see her real condition, that opened her ears to hear the report— the good news about One who was mighty to heal and cure; that quickened the seed of thought thus sown in her soul, making it fructify, blossom, and bear fruit; in other words, that produced the resolution and prompted to action in carrying it out.   It is exactly thus with the sinner; his eyes are opened to see his sin and consequent misery; his ears are opened to hear, and his heart to believe, the report of a Saviour ; and he is persuaded and enabled to form the right resolution of applying at once to Jesus for pardon and peace—made willing, in fact, in the day of God's power.

IV. HER RESPECTFUL ADDRESS.   The respectful mode of her address, and the earnest petition which she prefers, are calculated to surprise and even astonish us. We must presuppose some knowledge of the Saviour, from whatever source it came. She had obtained in some way, and to some extent, knowledge of Jesus—how or whence we have not sufficient information to enable us to say. The terms of her address, when we consider her heathen antecedents and surroundings, are truly wonderful. "O Lord, thou Son of David"—these are marvellous words to come from heathen lips; "have mercy on me!" are words easily read between the lines of her misery, and easily accounted for by the sympathetic chord which her daughter's affliction had touched in her heart. The former words are not so readily accounted for. "O Lord," she said, and thus she acknowledged his power and his providence. She confesses her faith in his power as almighty, and in his providence as universal; she owns a providence which extends to, and is employed about, all the affairs of the world and men, and a power that regulates and controls all events. Nor are we sure that this term, as it was uttered by the lips of this woman, did not embrace more than matters of mundane interest. But whether or not it comprehended authority over things in heaven as well as things on earth—celestial as well as terrestrial concerns—one thing is certain, that the expression immediately following clearly embraced Messianic hopes and prospects. "Son of David" is a name or title of Messiah in Old Testament Scripture. He was to be the Son of David according to the flesh, as well as "the Son of God with power;" David's Son as well as David's Lord, according to the Saviour's own words. She thus acknowledged him as Lord, and so possessed of unlimited power over all beings, human, angelic, and demoniac; over all agencies of every order; and over all ailments, whether diseases proper or diabolic possession. She acknowledged him also as the Christ of God, whose very mission was to impart prophetic instruction, to make priestly satisfaction, and to exercise kingly authority in, over, and on behalf of his people. There was thus a whole creed, at least in germ, contained in the words of this woman's address to the Saviour. How had she attained such knowledge? Had the Spirit of God enlightened her? Had the Saviour been made known to her, as afterwards to Saul, by direct and special revelation? We believe that there was the agency of the Spirit in making application, but that there had been human instrumentality in conveying instruction. We read in the third chapter of this Gospel, at the eighth verse, that, in addition to the great multitude that followed Jesus from Galilee, Judæa, Jerusalem, Idumæa, and beyond Jordan, also "they about Tyre and Sidon, a great multitude, when they had heard what great things he did, came unto him." Was it not most likely that from some of these, on their return home, this woman had heard something about the Saviour—who he was, what he was, as well as about the great things he was doing? The Spirit's agency was needed to make application to her heart of the fragmentary truths she may have gleaned in the way indicated. Here, again, the sinner's case is similar. He hears about Christ, he reads about him, he is taught many facts in relation to his life, death, resurrection, ascension, saving power, and second coming to judgment; but yet "no man can call Jesus Lord, but by the Holy Ghost." We need the instruction, it is true, but we require also the illumination of the Spirit. That we may derive real benefit from Scripture truth, and spiritual profit from the facts of Christ's history, the Spirit must "guide us into all truth," even the "truth as it is in Jesus."

V. HER EARNEST PLEADING. In her earnestness she makes her daughter's case her own; she regards the affliction of so near a relative as personal; in her daughter's affliction she was afflicted. "Have mercy on me!" she said—on me, who feel myself so identified with my daughter, who suffer in her suffering, who am distressed in her distress, whose life is bound up in her life. Again, "Have mercy on me!"—a wretched woman, a sorely tried and almost broken-hearted mother. Then she repeats the petition with a slight variation, saying, "Lord, help me!" How touching this repeated request! how pathetic! How eloquent as well as earnest! It is, indeed, this earnestness that forms the chief element of its eloquence.

VI. THE TRIAL OF HER FAITH. She had been sorely afflicted, and now her faith is sorely tried. In the Gospel of St. Matthew the recital is fuller, and these trials stand out more conspicuously. The first trial of her faith is our Lord's *silence*. "He answered her not a word." What can this strange silence mean? Is it indifference or neglect? Is it want of sympathy with her own distress and her daughter's affliction?

Or is it dislike and contempt for a descendant of a sinful and accursed race? And yet she must have heard of his compassionate kindness and tender pity, as also of the ready relief he was in the habit of granting to every son and daughter of affliction. She must have heard, from all who told her of him, that no applicant had ever met with repulse or refusal at his hand. Is she to be an exception? Will he not condescend to take the slightest notice of her? Another sore discouragement arose from the inconsiderate and unsympathetic conduct of the disciples, who came forward and actually besought him to dismiss her. "Send her away," they said, "for she crieth after us"—send her away at once (ἀπόλυσον, aorist imperative), and get rid of her annoyance; it is troublesome and even indecorous to have her following us, and painful to have to listen to her crying after us in this fashion. Either dismiss her summarily or grant her request, that, one way or other, we may get rid of her. Even if we understand the disciples in this latter sense, as asking their Master to give her what she wanted and let her go, it was a cold selfishness that prompted it, and an ungracious spirit that thus wished to be done with her importunity as speedily as possible. Their interference, however, had only the effect of drawing forth in reply a reason for *refusal*. When our Lord did break silence, it was only to indicate the circumscribed sphere of his present mission, and thus to imply her exclusion: "I am not sent but unto the lost sheep of the house of Israel." It appears to some that even in this refusal there was a faint gleam of hope, and that this despised woman of Canaan might have replied,—Though not of the house of Israel, yet I am a lost sheep, and greatly need the Good Shepherd's care; and though he has not come specially on an errand of mercy to my race or me, yet I am come in quest of him and to seek his favour. But another obstacle, seemingly more formidable, bars the way. There had been silence and seeming indifference; there had been a refusal, and that backed by a reason—a strong reason, and one that did not admit of any questioning; and now there is *reproach*—apparent reproach. This sorrowful woman, in this her direst extremity and the darkest hour of her misery, summoned up all her strength of resolution to make one final effort; and coming closer to the Saviour, and with still greater reverence as well as earnestness, she "worshipped him, saying, Lord, help me." And yet, the reply to all this profound respect and unflagging importunity appeared at least to be of the most discouraging character, and in fact the unkindest cut of all: "It is not meet to take the children's bread, and cast it to dogs."

VII. Her perseverance and humility. Her perseverance was truly wonderful, and her humility was equal to her perseverance. She turns the seeming slight into an argument. Our Lord, in the similitude he employs, does not refer to the wild, ferocious, gregarious dogs of the East, that are owned by no master, but prowl about for food, and that supply, in some sort, the place of street-scavengers. He refers to young or little dogs (κυνάρια), and to children, or little children (παιδίων), and the friendly relations that are well known to exist between them, denying the propriety of defrauding the children of food in order to feed even their canine pets—to take their bread and cast it to dogs (where observe the paronomasia in λαβεῖν and βαλεῖν). "Yes, Lord: for indeed the little dogs under the table eat of the children's crumbs." The proverbial expression implied (1) the impatience of dogs desirous of food; and (2) the impropriety of taking the bread intended for children and giving it to dogs before the children had got their portion; consequently (3) the injury of conferring benefits on one to the detriment of others, and prematurely before the claims of those others had been properly met and fully satisfied. Such might be the feeling of the Jews, if the Gentile stranger should step into some privilege before they had received their proper place and promised share. The opinion of Theophylact, and of many besides, that the Gentiles are meant by the dogs, because they are looked upon as unclean by the Jews, or the narrower notion of Chrysostom, that this woman herself is stigmatized by the name of dog from her persistence and blandness of entreaty, are unnecessary, if not unwarranted. The appropriateness of the proverb, and of the mode of treatment it implied, is admitted by this woman who gives it a most felicitous turn and favourable interpretation on her own behalf. She frankly and fully admits the reasonableness of supplying food to the children first, but insists at the same time on the humane principle and considerate practice of allowing the little dogs to eat the crumbs that fell accidentally, or were let fall on purpose, beneath the table. She accepted the situation thus indicated; she was content to take the place of dogs under the table; she was satisfied with the crumbs that remained after the children had got their full share. It was as if she said,—I own my inferiority; I am not a descendant of Abraham, nor a daughter of Israel; I do not claim equal privileges or equal dignity with one of that highly favoured race. I only ask the position which a kind master allows his dog that is under the table, and the friendly treatment which such a master is in the habit of granting to his canine favourite; and that is to be fed from the children's crumbs, as the source (ἀπὸ) of their nourishment. A crumb is all I crave. One crumb from my Master's table will comfort me and cure my child.

VIII. The reward of her perseverance as an example and encouragement. We have seen how, in the face of what seemed contemptuous silence, of positive refusal —a refusal made more positive by the strong reason alleged in its support—of apparent reproach and depreciation, this woman kept to her purpose, converting a slight into a sound argument. By firmness of purpose, by strength of will, by great humility, by astonishing earnestness, above all by vigorous faith, she held on, and, like Jacob with the angel, she did not let the Saviour go until she obtained the blessing which she sought. What a pattern of faith and patience combined this woman exhibits! She had made probably a long journey, undergone much fatigue, spared no pains, shrunk from no toil, till she reached Jesus; and, after going so far and doing so much to reach him, she seems doomed to disappointment; and is treated with silence, with sternness, and with something like scorn; and yet by a quick instinct she makes that scorn helpful to her suit. And now at last she has her reward. Not only does she gain the object about which she was so earnestly solicitous, but she receives the cordial commendation of our Lord. "For this saying go thy way; the devil is gone out of thy daughter;" or, as St. Matthew has it, "O woman, great is thy faith: be it unto thee even as thou wilt. And her daughter was made whole from that very hour."

IX. Practical lessons. 1. We learn from this most interesting and encouraging narrative the *power of faith* and its prevalence. If "all things are possible with God"— and we are sure they are—"all things are possible to him that believeth." It was faith brought her to Christ; it was faith kept her close to Christ, in spite of so many and so great discouragements; it was faith obtained the blessing from Christ; it was faith called forth the commendation of Christ, for in that faith he recognized the gracious principle he had himself implanted in her soul. Accordingly, it was her faith he so commended. He did not say, "Great is thy humility," and yet she displayed the grace of humility in an eminent degree; nor "Great is thy fervency," and yet she was uncommonly fervent in her petitions; nor "Great is the love thou bearest thy child," and yet she was a model at once of womanly tenderness and motherly affection; nor "Great is thy patience," and yet her patience had few parallels; nor "Great is thy perseverance," and yet her perseverance commands our admiration, even across the centuries. No; but "Great is thy faith." It was the mother grace and parent of all the rest. Lord, grant each of us like precious faith! 2. Our *duty to our children*, and to the young in general, is strikingly taught us here. Taking this woman for a pattern, we should plead with God frequently, fervently, and faithfully on behalf of our children, until Christ be formed in their heart. And oh, if any of them should be a victim of the evil one, and possessed by some evil passion, some sinful propensity, some destructive lust— in case any should be thus "grievously vexed with a devil"—how anxious, how laborious, how perseveringly prayerful we should be on their behalf! and how we should imitate this woman's importunity, and, like her, make their case our own until we obtain for them the blessing! 3. A further lesson is to go to Christ in every *season of distress*, nor despair, however long he is pleased to keep us waiting. Here are two lessons put together, for they properly go together. Whatever be our distress—whether personal affliction or domestic trial, whether the undutifulness of children or the godlessness of their lives, whether it be hostility of foes or the coldness of friends, whether it be worldly loss or sore bereavement—we should go and tell Jesus, acknowledging his all-sufficiency, spreading the whole case before him, confessing our great unworthiness, and pleading earnestly with him for mercy and help. And here another and a kindred lesson suggests itself, and that is firmness and *freedom from despondency* in trial. It pleased the Saviour to try the woman of Canaan severely and long; but it was for her good, for the glory of his grace in her, and for a pattern to ourselves. He proved her faith, but his object was to improve and strengthen it; he meant to exhibit its sterling qualities as a pattern to his disciples. Many a one, tried as this woman was, would have sunk down into sullen silence, or hurried off in a fit of passion, and given up her suit. It might have been so with some of ourselves; but he will humble us before he exalts us; he will have us trust in him, though he slay us. Some token will be vouchsafed for our encouragement, even in the sorest testing-time. It was probably so with this woman. She may have discerned a tenderness in the tone of the Saviour's voice, or a gentleness in his look, that encouraged her to persevere. But, even in the absence of such, we must impress on ourselves the conviction that there "may be love in Christ's heart while there are frowns on his face," as it is quaintly expressed by an old divine. Further, we may be kept long waiting, but we shall not wait in vain, any more than this poor woman. Our prayers may not be favoured with an immediate answer; but, though not answered at once, they will be accepted at once, and answered at the time most expedient for us, as well as most conducive to the Divine glory.

> "For though he prove our patience,
> And to the utmost prove,
> Yet all his dispensations
> Are faithfulness and love."

J. J. G.

Vers. 31—37.—*A miracle of restoration.* I. THE DEAF MUTE HEALED. 1. *A difference of reading.* According to the common text we learn that our Lord, "departing from the coasts [borders] of Tyre and Sidon, came unto the Sea of Galilee, through the midst of the coasts [borders] of Decapolis;" but according to the best critical authorities "through Sidon" must be substituted for "and Sidon;" and then the sentence reads as it stands in the Revised Version: "Again he went out from the borders of Tyre, and came through Sidon unto the Sea of Galilee, through the midst of the borders of Decapolis." This reading is unquestionably the more difficult, but exceedingly interesting, as it shows the extent of our Lord's tour through those Gentile lands. Proceeding twenty miles northward from Tyre, he came to Sidon, the great seat of Phœnician worship and of the idols Baal and Astarte; and then passing along the foot of Lebanon, and crossing the Leontes or Litany, the largest river of Syria, he came to the sources of the Jordan, whence he descended along the eastern bank into the region of Decapolis. The probable object of this *détour* was to gain privacy, instruct more thoroughly his disciples, escape his enemies, and visit the many towns and villages dotting this route. 2. *An interesting though practically unimportant question.* Was the subject of this miracle deaf, with an impediment in his speech, or both deaf and dumb; in other words, a deaf mute? If he was deaf and had (1) only an impediment in his speech, he had not been born deaf, for in that case he would have been destitute of speech altogether. He may have become deaf in early childhood, before the organs of speech attained their full development; or he may have been deaf for such a length of time that, through long disuse, his tongue had lost its power; or disease may have supervened, and inflammation or ulceration tied the lingual nerve. Whatever the cause of this impediment was—whether it was occasioned by rigidity of the membrane arising from long desuetude, or whether it was produced by the diseased state of the muscles, or whether it was the result of early deafness—the impediment was so great that it differed little from the entire absence of the power of articulation. This poor man was thus little, if at all, better than a deaf mute. But (2) several reasons induce the belief that this man was actually dumb as well as deaf. Among these we may mention the statement at ver. 37, where the Jews, who witnessed this miracle, said, "He maketh both the deaf to hear, and the dumb (ἀλάλους) to speak;" and the word μογιλάλος is used in the LXX. Version of Isa. xxxv. 6 in the signification of dumb; also, in a reference by St. Matthew to this same journey of our Lord, and to the miracles performed at that time, the evangelist mentions the dumb speaking, (κωφοὺς λαλοῦντας). It may be observed that, while κωφὸς, meaning "dull" or "blunt," may be applied to either hearing or speech, the meaning of the word in St. Mark is always "deaf," though the usual meaning of it is "dumb," being synonymous with ἄφωνος in the classics. 3. *Nature of this privation.* This affliction was twofold. Two

organs were virtually wanting, two senses were sealed, two channels of communication with the external world were closed. The case of this person, if not actually
identical with that of a man deaf and dumb, is illustrative of it. And oh, how great this
double privation! How difficult for those, whom God has blessed with the free use of
all their bodily organs, to appreciate the privation of one who is deaf and dumb! These
twin calamities are, it is true, physiologically reducible to one. They stand related as
cause and effect. Deafness at birth, or loss of hearing soon after, usually involves
dumbness. Deafness is the radical defect, dumbness is its natural result. This man is
said to be κωφὸς, which expresses the primitive want; while μογιλάλος (the root is μογ,
equivalent to μεγ, as in μόχ-θος, labour, equivalent to something great laid (θε) on one)
expresses the natural and necessary consequence—the great obstacle to speech. This
latter word, therefore, is wrongly rendered "stammering," and rather denotes one unable
to utter articulate words. *Hearing*, like *sight*, and as much as sight, is an inborn faculty;
but *speaking* is a learnt art. Man of himself can utter sounds, and that is all, but not
speak words. The latter he learns by hearing; but how can he learn without hearing,
and how can he hear if he is born deaf? Further, in deafness the organ is wanting or
defective; in dumbness the organ is present, but it might as well be absent, as it is
disabled and incapable of use. When the ear is stopped, silence seals the tongue.
But, though the cause may thus be one, the calamity affects two senses, and debars
the use of both. 4. *Extent of this privation.* On due consideration, it will be found
that these "children of silence," as they have been called, are doomed to as severe
deprivations as any to be found in the whole catalogue of human woes. By nature
they are excluded from all those pleasures which the ear drinks in and the tongue gives
out. Nor do we refer merely or mainly to the melody of sweet sounds—to the thrilling
tones of harmony, to the witching spell of minstrelsy, to the rapturous delights of
music, as it is heard from the birds that make the woodland vocal with their notes, or
from the itinerant musicians that stay for a few moments' space the step of the man of
business, or cheer the spirit of the downcast; or as it swells in the concert, or sweeps so
grandly in the oratorio, or is wafted aloft from a thousand voices on the open air of
heaven. The deaf are excluded from other joys more homely, but not less hearty.
They are shut out from the pleasant voice of childish prattle, from domestic or friendly
converse, from intellectual interchange of thought, from literary amusement, scientific
research, or political intelligence. From all these sources of information, instruction,
and enjoyment they are by nature shut out. And here we come to the worst phase of
their condition—the blank it leaves the mind. When sound is shut out, a chief
entrance of knowledge is barred. The exclusion of sound is the exclusion of all
that knowledge and of all that multitude of ideas that sounds convey or suggest to
the mind. 5. *Contrast between the respective privations of the deaf and blind.* We
deeply commiserate the condition of the blind, from whom the fair face of nature is
shrouded in darkness, whose eyes are never gladdened by the light of the sun by day
or of the moon and stars by night, from whom the beauty of the human countenance
and the loveliness of the landscape scenery are alike hidden, while "the shadow of
death" rests "upon their eyelids." And yet the deaf mute is in a worse condition
than even they. You can talk with that blind man, and tell him many things. He
has an ear to hear, and learns much from your lips. You can read to him, and he
listens to the lessons of heavenly wisdom, or human philosophy, or every-day experience, which you thus communicate. He is entertained at the same time that he
lays up a store of useful knowledge. Not so the deaf mute; he is unimproved by all
you say or read. Your speech does not instruct him, for he cannot hear. Books are
useless to him, for he cannot read because he is ignorant of sounds made visible. He
learns not, for thus the key of knowledge is taken away. Deaf mutes are, therefore,
shrouded in deeper than midnight gloom; they grope in a "darkness that may be felt."
Thus one of the great inlets of knowledge is taken away; one of the main sources of
enjoyment is hermetically sealed; one of the chief links that bind men in social
intercourse is snapped; one of the silken bands that unite men in intercommunion is
severed. Thus the deaf mute stands apart, and in lonely isolation from his fellow-men;
thus one of the sweetest streams of human happiness is frozen up. We have thus
looked at the condition of the deaf mute of our own day, as closely resembling, if not
quite the same with, that of the man that was brought to our Lord, as it is here

written, "They bring unto him one that was deaf, and had an impediment in his speech."

II. THE SIGNS WHICH THE SAVIOUR USED. 1. *What these signs were.* After taking him aside, he "put his fingers into his ears, and he spit, and touched his tongue." These signs which he employed did in no way contribute to the cure he effected, and yet they were significant of what he was about to do. They were far from meaningless manœuvres or purposeless displays of power. They were no empty make-believes. Our Lord meant to arrest the man's attention and excite his expectations. He did so with the impotent man when he said, "Wilt thou be made whole?" He did so with the blind men when he asked them, "What will ye that I should do unto you?" and when he added, "Believe ye that I am able to do this?" He does the same in the case before us. But as this man knew nothing of the language of sounds, our Lord addressed him in the language of signs. He touched the parts affected to apprise him of his intention to reach the seats of the infirmities and remove the maladies. He put his fingers into the ears to signify that he would take away the obstructions that were therein, and open up the way for sound to enter—that he would penetrate every opposing barrier, and bestow a new acoustic power. He touched the tongue with moisture from his own mouth to lubricate the stiffened member, to loosen whatever impediment confined it, and restore its agility of motion. Thus by signs he gave the man some indication of what he meant to do. But by these signs he taught him another lesson. The second lesson was one of faith in our Lord himself as the Author of his recovery, as the Source from which healing power flowed, and as able to do all and accomplish all fully and perfectly which he had signified. A third thing, perhaps, he meant to convey was that he sanctions the use of those means which he himself appoints. Here the means are all his own. His own fingers he inserted into the deaf man's ears; with his own saliva he moistened his tongue. The power of healing is all his own. He can work without means, or against means, or by means; he here directs to the use of means, but only such means as he himself devises. These he sanctions, these he consecrates, sanctifies, and crowns with success. Further, our Lord adapts his signs to the source of the ailment, and accomplishes a perfect cure. It might seem sufficient to insert his finger into the deaf ear without touching the tongue with saliva; and likewise, in the account of the cure, it might be thought enough to say "his ears were opened," without adding that "the string of his tongue was loosed, and he spake plain." The touching and consequent opening of the ear would undoubtedly have reached the origin of the ailment, and cured the defect at its source; but there would not have been a complete cure. The sufferer would only have been put into the condition of one *learning* to speak; but the cure, in the very mode of it, was meant to save him this trouble, and to secure to him the *ability* to speak at once. Hence it is not only said of him ἐλάλει, "he spake," that is, had now the power of speaking, but the term ὀρθῶς is subjoined, from which we learn that, without any loss of time, and without any process of educating the ear, he spake correctly and normally, as if he had been accustomed to do so from his youth, and not as one exercising a power just bestowed. The distinction between the sense of hearing and the organ of hearing in this passage is noticeable: the former is ακοὴ, and the latter ὦτα. 2. *Symbolic actions.* Another and a different symbolic action follows the signs we have been considering. The Saviour turned his eyes to heaven. By this time the Saviour had familiarized the sufferer to the use of signs, and accustomed him to the language which they conveyed. He guards him against any misinterpretation of the fore-mentioned signs. He turns his mind from those signs, as though by themselves they were in any way conducive to his cure. He raises his thoughts to heaven, to remind him that all relief was to be looked for from thence; that the blessing which made the means effectual came from above; that "every good gift and every perfect boon is from above, coming down from the Father of lights;" that the power to cure in this case was Divine; and that, as the Lord from heaven, he himself had brought that power down to earth. While, on the one hand, he showed that the power emanated from himself, he, on the other hand, acknowledged the Father who had sent him to put forth such power. While he was manifesting by certain signs or one kind of symbolic action that power proceeded from his own person, he was proving by another kind that in that person divinity was shrined; that "it pleased the Father that in him"—the Son—

" should all fulness dwell ; " that " all power in heaven and on earth " was entrusted to his hands. He was indicating, moreover, the unity of purpose and of plan that subsisted between the Father and the Son ; that he was doing the will of the Father, and accomplishing the work with which he had been commissioned. "The Father," he said, " worketh hitherto, and I work ; " " It is my meat and my drink to do the will of him that sent me." He sought thereby the Father's glory, as he himself said, " Now is the Son of man glorified, and God is glorified in him ; " and again he says, " I have glorified thee on earth : I have finished the work that thou gavest me to do." Thus here and now, as always, he sets forth his mediatorial dependence on the Father, and the eye he had to his praise : " My doctrine is not mine, but his that sent me ; " " He that speaketh of himself seeketh his own glory ; but he that seeketh his glory that sent him, the same is true, and no unrighteousness is in him." 3. *Duty of imitating the Master.* As it was with the Master, so in measure is it with the disciple still. Ever and anon we must turn our eyes to heaven. While our hands are duly employed in the daily occupations of our calling upon earth, our hearts must mount upward on the wings of faith, in praise for mercies received and in prayer for the blessing to be bestowed : " I will lift up mine eyes unto the hills, from whence cometh my help. My help cometh from the Lord, which made heaven and earth." Otherwise our most strenuous efforts will be frustrated, our most fondly cherished hopes blasted, and our highest aspirations doomed to disappointment ; for " except the Lord build the house, they labour in vain that build it : except the Lord keep the city, the watchman waketh but in vain." While we thus lean on an Almighty arm, and depend for everything on God, we must have a single eye to his praise, ever keeping his glory as our chief end in view, and ever seeking from himself grace and strength and steady purpose to do his will.

> " To do thy will I take delight,
>   O thou my God that art ;
> Yea, that most holy Law of thine
>   I have within my heart."

4. *The significance of the Saviour's sigh.* " He sighed ; " and no wonder, when he thought of the *ruin* that sin had wrought, and of the wreck which man had in consequence become. The Saviour sighed when he looked abroad on suffering humanity, when he reflected on the miseries of a fallen race, and when especially he contemplated the living example of that misery that then stood before him. He sighed in sympathy with our sufferings, " for we have not an High Priest that cannot be touched with the feeling of our infirmities." Blessed be God for such " a merciful and faithful High Priest in things pertaining to God." He sighed in sorrow for our *sins.* In them he saw the cause of all ; in them he saw the bad and bitter fountain-head ; in them he saw the fruitful source of so much woe ; in them he saw that fearful thing that darkened heaven above us, opened hell beneath us, and cursed the earth on which we tread ; in them he saw that fell infection that has disordered, in a certain sense and to a certain extent, all the members of the body and all the faculties of the soul, so that " the whole head is sick, and the whole heart faint ; " in them he saw the prolific germ of all those "ills that flesh is heir to," and of all those pangs that make the heart of humanity ache : for " by one man sin entered into the world, and death by sin," and not only death, but with it all our woe ; in them he saw, too, the grievous load he was himself one day to bear, when he " bare our sins in his own body on the tree," so that it has been truly as tersely said—

> " With pitying eyes, the Prince of peace
>   Beheld our helpless grief ;
> He saw, and oh ! amazing love !
>   He came to our relief."

He sighed when he thought of the works of the *devil* and his malice against man, and how human weakness had given him power to deform the body by disease, and deface the image of the Creator in the soul of his creature. Perhaps, too, he sighed when, as has been shrewdly suggested by an old divine, he saw the new *temptation* to sin that the man's renewed powers would expose him to—the evil things the ear would hear, the idle things the tongue would speak, the wicked things in which both organs might be made instrumental. "Therefore," said the psalmist, "I will take heed to my ways, that I sin not with my tongue: I will keep my mouth with a bridle, while the wicked are before me." The explanation of the Saviour's sigh by a German writer on the miracles, though ingenious, is not sufficiently comprehensive, when he traces its cause to "the closed ear of the world" of which the deaf man was the symbol, "which does not perceive his Word, and therefore does not receive it;" and thinks his view commended, if not confirmed, by St. Mark's numerous exhortations to spiritual hearing by maxim, parable, and symbol. The maxim is, "If any man have ears to hear, let him hear;" and connected with it is the parable of the earth's producing fruit after the reception of the seed, or salvation attained by right hearing of the word, while the present symbol corroborates the same truth.

> "The deaf may hear the Saviour's voice,
>   The fettered tongue its chain may break;
> But the deaf heart, the dumb by choice,
>   The laggard soul, that will not wake,
> The guilt that scorns to be forgiven—
> These baffle e'en the spells of Heaven:
> In thought of these, his brows benign
> Not e'en in healing cloudless shine.

The correct explanation, while not exclusive of this view, is inclusive of much more. 5. *The single word spoken by the Saviour.* "Ephphatha," that is, "Be opened," was the single utterance after the heavenward look and inward sigh. The root of this word is the Hebrew *pathach*, to open; from a similar Syriac root comes *ethpatach*, the imperative of the passive conjugation Ethpael; then, by assimilation of *theta* and aspiration, we get *ephphatha*. And no sooner had he spoken that word than its omnific power appeared. The dull ear was endowed with a power it had never known before, or to which it had been long a stranger. The hindrance that prevented the free passage of the air, or deadened its undulations, was removed; the defect in its organism was remedied. The pleasure of drinking in sweet sounds and of listening to the music of human speech came with all the freshness of a new faculty. The man felt as though he had found himself in a new world, or had entered on a new and improved existence, or had risen many steps higher in the scale of being. And so, in truth, he had. But this was not all; the tongue was freed completely and at once from whatever it was that had fettered it, the impediment was quite gone, and the articulation was, notwithstanding the long disease, immediately perfect. He could now tell to all around the happy change he had undergone—the perfect nature of the cure, the pleasure that filled his soul, the gratitude that glowed in his heart and which then flowed from his lips. 6. *The cure a cause of adoring wonder.* Here we must admire, and, while we admire, adore, the power of Christ, for it is the power of God. Nothing short of Almighty power could have accomplished this wonder-work of mercy, for "Who hath made man's mouth? or who maketh the dumb, or deaf, or the seeing, or the blind? have not I the Lord?" And none, surely, save the Lord could thus unmake what sin and Satan had marred, removing all deficiencies, and renewing the afflicted with more than original powers. Here, too, we trace distinct proofs of his Messiahship. Blind as the multitude so frequently were, they could not shut their eyes on this fact; they were so astonished that they could not help admitting it. They said, "He maketh both the deaf to hear, and the dumb to speak;" they evidently had an eye to the words of the prophet, and the works he predicted the Messiah would do, when he said, "Then the eyes of the blind shall be opened, and the ears of the deaf shall be unstopped. Then shall the lame man leap as an hart, and the tongue of the dumb sing."

III. PRACTICAL INSTRUCTION. 1. *Inferences.* This miracle, like others of our Lord's miracles, warrants three inferences: (1) his superhuman power, and by consequence his Divine commission; (2) a glorious coming day foreshadowed, when all physical disabilities shall be finally and for ever removed; and (3), what is of personal and practical importance, the inference of the Saviour's ability to do for the soul what he so often and so effectually did for the body. The impediments of the body are but dim shadows of the worse impediments of the soul. By nature the ear is deaf to the Divine commands, the tongue dumb when it should celebrate his praise; while the heart is hard, the affections frozen, the mind shrouded in darkness—the man in a state of isolation, without fellowship with God or communion with the saints. Christ says, "Ephphatha," and oh, what a change ensues! The ear is opened to hear God's Word, the heart, like Lydia's, to receive his grace, the tongue untied to praise his name and call upon him in prayer. 2. *His due meed of praise.* In view of all this we must join with the multitude and say, "He hath done all things well." It was well for the man that was healed, because in his case it was next to life from the dead; it was well for his relations, for their trouble was all but over; it was well for his friends, because their enjoyment of him and pleasure with him were unspeakably increased; it was well for mankind, that the Son of man had authority to exercise such power upon earth; it was well for each of us, because herein we have an earnest of what he will do for the soul, a pledge of the renovation of soul and body, an assurance of the future and final perfection of both. He did all things well, for he "did no iniquity, neither was guile found in his mouth;" he did all things well, for he went about continually, doing good. More particularly, he did all things well, for whatever he did he did largely and liberally, modestly and humbly, generously, graciously, gratuitously, and yet gloriously. Like the first creation, when God saw everything that he had made, "behold, it was very good;" so, when the works of Christ are contemplated, the concurrent testimony of heaven and earth will be, that "he hath done all things well." Saints on earth will say it, for they are the trophies of his mercy, the triumphs of his grace, the memorials of his goodness, and the monuments of his power; saints in heaven will say it, adding, He opened our ears by his power, our hearts by his spirit, our tongues by his grace; he washed us from our sins in his blood, making us kings and priests unto God. Multitudes when he was on earth said it; multitudes yet unborn will say it. We ourselves are entitled to say it, for his healing power has reached us; he has removed our maladies, renewed our souls, made us to delight in his Word and rejoice in his love.

> " He speaks, and, listening to his voice,
>   New life the dead receive;
>   The mournful, broken hearts rejoice,
>   The humble poor believe.

> " Hear him, ye deaf; his praise, ye dumb,
>   Your loosened tongues employ;
>   Ye blind, behold your Saviour come;
>   And leap, ye lame, for joy."

                                                    J. J. G.

EXPOSITION.

CHAPTER VIII.

Vers. 1, 2.—The opening words of the first verse seem to imply that our Lord remained for some time on this, the north-east, side of the Sea of Galilee. **The multitude being very great.** The word here rendered " very great " is παμπόλλου, a word not to be found anywhere else in the New Testament. But according to the best authorities, the true reading is πάλιν πόλλου; so that the words would run, *when there was again a great multitude.* It has been supposed with some reason that, as an old ecclesiastical Lection began with this chapter, this may have led to the substitution of παμπόλλου for πάλιν πόλλου, in order to make the Lection more complete in itself, avoiding this reference to

the context. In the original Greek construction the word ὄχλος, in the singular, is disintegrated in the next clause by a passage into the plural (καὶ μὴ ἐχόντων τί φάγουσι). This is properly marked in the Revised Version by the words, a great multitude, and they had nothing to eat. Our Lord has compassion on them. He desires not only to heal the sick, but to feed the hungry. We may here notice the burning zeal of the multitude. They were so intent upon hearing Christ, that they forgot to provide themselves with the necessaries of life. They continued with him for three days and had nothing to eat. Whatever small supplies they might have brought with them at first were now exhausted; and still they remained, "esteeming his words to be more than their necessary food." Our Lord on his part was so full of zeal for their good, that during all that time, with little interval, he had been preaching to them, denying himself rest, refreshment, and sleep. So true were those words of his, " My meat is to do the will of him that sent me, and to finish his work."

Ver. 3.—**For divers of them came from far.** These words, as they stand in the Authorized Version, might be supposed to be an observation thrown in by the evangelist himself. But the correct rendering of ἥκασι is not " came," but *have come*, or rather, *are come ;* and instead of τινὲς γὰρ at the beginning of the clause, the more correct reading is καὶ τινὲς. This change makes the clause almost of necessity to be a part of our Lord's own words going before. It was not until the third day that our Lord interposed with a miracle, when the people were absolutely without food, and would therefore feel more sensibly the blessing as well as the greatness of the miracle. Their extremity was his opportunity.

Ver. 4.—**Whence shall one be able to fill these men with bread here in a desert place ?** St. Matthew (xv. 33) gives the question thus: " Whence should we have so many loaves in a desert place, as to fill so great a multitude ?" The disciples, measuring the difficulty by human reason, thought that it was impossible to find so many loaves in the desert. But Christ in this necessity, when human resources fail, supplies Divine; and meanwhile the disciples' estimate of the impossibility illustrates the grandeur of the miracle.

Ver. 5.—The seven loaves and the few small fishes appear to have been the modest provision for our Lord and his disciples. As he often retired into the desert, they were no doubt accustomed to carry small supplies about with them, though poor and scanty. In the former miracle of the multiplying of the loaves (ch. vi. 35), we find that their stock consisted of five loaves and two fishes. It was, of course, just as easy for our Lord to multiply the smaller quantity as the larger. But he chose so to order it that the original quantity of food, as well as the number requiring to be fed, should in each case be different, in order that it might be evident that they were different occasions, although the miracles were of the same kind.

Ver. 6.—**And he commandeth the multitude to sit down** (ἀναπεσεῖν)—literally, *to recline*—on the ground (ἐπὶ τῆς γῆς); not the green grass, as before. It was a different season of the year. " He gave thanks." In this expression is included the recognition of the Divine power to enable him to work the miracle. Christ indeed, as God, was able of his own will and by his own power to

multiply the loaves. But as man he gave thanks. And yet, as Dr. Westcott excellently remarks, " The thanksgiving was not for any uncertain or unexpected gift. It was rather a proclamation of his fellowship with God. So that the true nature of prayer in the case of our blessed Lord was the conscious realization of the Divine will, and not a petition for that which was contingent." And having given thanks, he brake, and gave to his disciples (ἔκλασε, καὶ ἐδίδου). Observe the aorist and the imperfect. The giving was a continual act, till all were filled.

Ver. 8.—**And they did eat, and were filled** (ἐχορτάσθησαν). Wycliffe renders it, " were fulfild ; " according to the original meaning of " to fulfil," namely, " to fill full." **And they took up, of broken pieces that remained over, seven baskets**—as many as there were loaves. In the record of the other similar miracle, the number of baskets corresponded to the number of the disciples. Here, as in the former miracle, far more food remained after all were fed than the original supply on which our Lord exercised his miraculous power ; for each basket would contain much more than one loaf. The Greek word here rendered " basket" (σπυρίς) is a different word from that used for " basket" in the record of the other miracle (ch. vi. 43). There it is κόφινος. The κόφινος was a hand-basket of stout wicker-work. The σπυρίς was a much larger basket, made of a more flexible material, perhaps " rushes," like our " frail." It was by means of such a basket, called in Acts ix. 25 σπυρίς, but σαργάνη in 2 Cor. xi. 33, that St. Paul was let down through a window at Damascus. This supplies another evidence, if it were needed, that these two recorded miracles took place on different occasions. Cornelius à Lapide mentions an opinion that the σπυρίς was double the size of the κόφινος, a large basket carried by two.

Ver. 10.—**He entered into a ship** (εἰς τὸ πλοῖον)—literally, *into the boat ;* probably the same boat which he had ordered to be in attendance upon him (ch. iii. 9)—**and came into the parts of Dalmanutha.** St. Matthew (xv. 39) has " the coasts of Magdala ; " more properly, " the borders of Magaden." This place was in all probability about the middle of the western shore of the Sea of Galilee, where now stand the ruins of the village of El-Mejdel.

Ver. 11.—**And the Pharisees came forth**—St. Matthew (xvi. 1) says that the Sadducees came with them—**and began to question with him, seeking of him a sign from heaven, tempting him.** They had already asked for a sign from heaven (Matt. xii. 38); but now this miracle gives them occasion to ask again. For when they saw how greatly it was extolled by the multitudes who had benefited by it, it was easy for them to urge that it was an earthly sign, and might have been wrought by him who is called "the god of this world;" and so they insinuated that he had wrought this miracle as well as his other miracles by the power of Satan. Therefore they seek a sign from heaven, that he who dwells in heaven might thus bear witness that he came from God, and that his doctrine was Divine; the Pharisees probably meant that if he did this they would believe in him as the Messiah, and lead the people to the same faith. The Sadducees, who were practically atheists, thought that no sign could be given from heaven by God, seeing that in their opinion it was doubtful whether there was any God to give it.

Ver. 12.—**He sighed deeply in his spirit** (ἀναστενάξας). Another graphic touch of this evangelist; such as he had learnt in all probability from St. Peter. The word occurs nowhere but here. It is the outcome of grief and indignation, in which, however, grief predominates. **There shall no sign be given unto this generation** (εἰ δοθήσεται σημεῖον). This is a Hebrew idiom, based upon a form of taking an oath which prevailed amongst the Jews. The full form would be, "God do so and so to me, if so and so." Hence the hypothetical part of the clause came to be used alone, expressing a very strong form of denial or refusal.

Ver. 13.—**And he left them, and again embarking**—ἐμβὰς for ἐμβὰς εἰς τὸ πλοῖον—**departed to the other side.** Again and again our Lord crossed this sea, that he might instruct the Galileans dwelling on either side; in fulfilment of Isa. ix. 1, "The land of Zebulun and the land of Naphtali, . . . by the way of the sea, beyond Jordan, in Galilee of the nations. The people that walked in darkness have seen a great light."

Ver. 14.—**And they had forgotten** (ἐπελά-θοντο)—literally, *they forgot*—**to take bread** (ἄρτους); *loaves.* The conversation which follows took place on the boat while they were crossing. The passage would take perhaps six hours. And it was during that time that they would want food; for when they reached the port, they would find it in abundance.

Ver. 15.—**Beware of the leaven of the Pharisees and the leaven of Herod.** St. Matthew (xv. 6) says, "Beware of the leaven of the Pharisees and Sadducees;" thus St. Mark identifies the leaven of the Sadducees with that of Herod. "Leaven" here means "doctrine." They were not to beware of this, so far as the Pharisees rightly taught and explained the Law of Moses; but only so far as they corrupted that Law by their own vain traditions, contrary to the Law of

God, St. Luke (xii. 11) calls this leaven "hypocrisy;" because the Pharisees only regarded outward ceremonies, and neglected the inward sanctification of the Spirit. St. Jerome says, "This is the leaven of which the Apostle speaks where he says, 'A little leaven leaveneth the whole lump.' Marcion and Valentinus and all heretics have had this kind of leaven, which is on every account to be avoided. Leaven has this property, that, however small it may be in quantity, it spreads its influence rapidly through the mass. And so if only a little spark of heretical doctrine be admitted into the soul, speedily a great flame arises, and envelopes the whole man."

Ver. 16.—According to the most approved readings, this verse should be read thus: **And they reasoned one with another, saying, We have no bread.** There is something very artless and simple in this narrative. Our Lord speaks of "leaven;" and the mention of this word reminds the disciples that they had forgotten to bring bread with them in the boat; and fearing lest Christ should direct them, according to his wont, to land on some desert shore, they were in some anxiety how they might obtain what they would need; and so they disputed among themselves; one, it may be, throwing the blame upon another.

Ver. 17.—**And when Jesus knew it** (καὶ γνοὺς ὁ Ἰησοῦς)—literally and far more correctly, *and Jesus perceiving it*—**he saith unto them, Why reason ye, because ye have no bread?** Jesus perceived the direction in which their thoughts were moving, by the power of his divinity. It is as though he said, "Why reason ye because ye have no bread, as though I was referring to natural things, and speaking concerning bread for the body, and wishing you to be anxious about that; as though I could not provide that for you, if necessary, just as easily here on the sea as I did just now in the desert?" Dr. John Lightfoot ('Hebrew Exercitations on St. Matthew,' vol. ii. p. 204) says, "The rule of the Jews was very strict as to the kind of leaven that was to be used; and the disciples supposed that our Lord was alluding to this when he cautioned them to beware of the leaven of the Pharisees." Perhaps they also thought that our Lord was conveying a silent reproof to them for not having brought a sufficient supply of bread with them. The whole incident, while it shows their transparent simplicity of character, exhibits also their dulness of apprehension.

Vers. 19, 20.—Here St. Mark is as careful as St. Matthew to mention the details of the two miracles, even to the reference to the two kinds of baskets in which the fragments were gathered up. They had a distinct recollection of the facts, but they had failed to catch their spiritual import.

Ver. 21.—**How is it that ye do not understand?** A better reading here is οὔπω instead of πῶς οὐ. Therefore the words should run, *Do ye not yet understand?* It is as though our Lord said, "You ought to have perceived, both from my words and from my actions, that I was not speaking concerning earthly leaven or earthly bread, but concerning spiritual doctrine." St. Matthew here (xvi. 12) is careful to tell us that this reproof of Christ quickened their intellects, and forced them to understand.

Ver. 22.—This miracle is recorded by St. Mark alone. **And he cometh to Bethsaida.** A better reading is ἔρχονται for ἔρχεται, *they come unto Bethsaida.* Which Bethsaida? It seems most probable that it was Bethsaida Julias. This Bethsaida was in the tetrarchy of Philip, who improved and adorned it, and named it Julias, in honour of the emperor's daughter Julia. A reference to ver. 27 seems to make it quite clear that it must have been this Bethsaida, and not the Galilean Bethsaida on the other side of the lake. It is not surprising that there should have been, adjoining this great lake, more than one place called Bethsaida, *i.e.* the "place of fish." **And they bring a blind man unto him, and besought** (παρακαλοῦσιν)—literally, *beseech*—him to touch him. St. Mark is fond of the graphic present. There is here, as at ch. vii. 32, something almost like dictating the mode of cure. They seem to have imagined that the healing virtue could not go forth from Christ except by actual contact.

Ver. 23.—**And he took** (ἐπιλαβόμενος)—literally, *took hold of*—**the blind man by the hand, and led him**—this is the rendering of ἐξήγαγεν; but a great weight of manuscript authority points to ἐξήνεγκεν as the better reading, *brought him*—**out of the village** (ἔξω τῆς κώμης). This Bethsaida was a village; but Philip had raised it to the rank of a city (πόλις), though it still seems to have retained its old appellation. Our Lord "led" or "brought" the blind man out of Bethsaida, for the same reason that he led the deaf and dumb man (ch. vii. 33) away from the multitude: (1) for the sake of prayer, that he might collect his mind, and unite himself more closely to God, and pray more intently and earnestly; (2) that he might shun vain-glory and human praise, and teach us to shun it also. **And when he had spit on his eyes**—this act had a mystical meaning; it was the instrument by which his Deity operated—**and laid his hands upon him, he asked him, Seest thou aught?** Here were three acts—(1) the spitting, (2) the laying of the hands on him, (3) the questioning of him. We gather from ver. 25 that our

Lord's hands were applied to the blind man's eyes. From the analogy of the miracle in the last chapter (vii. 33), we may perhaps infer that our Lord touched the man's eyes with saliva on his finger, and that the hands were withdrawn before he asked him if he saw aught.

Ver. 24.—**And he looked up, and said, I see men as trees, walking.** He looked up—a natural action. He instinctively looked in the direction of the source of light. The words in the Greek of the next clause are as follows:—βλέπω τοὺς ἀνθρώπους, ὅτι ὡς δένδρα ὁρῶ περιπατοῦντας: *I see men; for I behold them as trees, walking;* that is, "I see something confusedly and obscurely, not clearly; for I see what I think must be men, and yet so dimly that they look to me like trees, only that I know that men move from their places, whereas trees do not." The word "walking" refers to the men, and not to the trees, as is evident from the Greek. This man, as yet partially blind, saw men as in shadow, magnified by the mist, looking much larger than they really were.

Ver. 25.—**Then again he laid his hands upon his eyes, and made him look up**—this is the Authorized Version rendering of ἐποίησεν αὐτὸν ἀναβλέψαι: but the better authenticated reading is simply καὶ διέβλεψε, *and he looked steadfastly*—**and was restored, and saw all things clearly.** Now, here it pleased our Lord, not suddenly, but by degrees, to give perfect sight to this blind man. And this he did (1) that he might give examples of different kinds of miracles, showing that "there are differences of operations," and that he, as sovereign Lord, was not absolutely tied to any one particular method of working; and (2) that he might administer his power in increasing measures, as the faith of the recipient waxed stronger; that so he might gradually kindle greater hope and desire in him. It may be that the spiritual condition of this blind man was one which specially needed this gradual method of treatment. Our Lord was a wise and skilful Physician. At first he healed him in part, as one who imperfectly believed; that he who as yet saw little with a little sight, might believe more perfectly, and so be healed at last more perfectly; and thus by this miracle Christ teaches us that for the most part the unbeliever and the sinner is by degrees illuminated by God, so as to advance step by step in the knowledge and worship of God. "By this miracle," says Bede, "Christ teaches us how great is the spiritual blindness of man, which only by degrees, and by successive stages, can come to the light of Divine knowledge." The experiences of this blind man in gradually recovering his eyesight show as in a parable the stages of the spiritual change from absolute darkness to glimmering light, and thence to bright and clear vision. Cornelius à Lapide says, "We see an example of this in children and scholars, who must be taught and instructed by degrees. Otherwise, if the master, impatient of delay and labour, seeks to deliver all things to them at once, he will overwhelm their mind and their memory, so that they will take in nothing; as wine, when it is poured into a narrow-necked vessel, if you attempt to pour in the whole at once, scarcely any will enter, but almost all is wasted." À Lapide adds the well-known Italian proverb, "Piano, piano, si va lontano."

Ver. 26.—This verse, according to the best reading, runs thus : And he sent him away to his home, saying, Do not even enter into the village. It thus appears that Bethsaida was not the home of this blind man. He might naturally have wished to exhibit himself in Bethsaida, where many must have known him, and to have sung the praises of his great Benefactor. But this was far from what Christ wished. He wished to be in seclusion. He had no desire to excite more than could be helped the idle curiosity of the multitude. His miracles were for the sake of his doctrine, and not his doctrine for the sake of his miracles. The whole character of his administration was retiring and gentle. "My doctrine shall distil as the dew." "He shall not strive, nor cry; neither shall any hear his voice in the streets."

Vers. 27, 28.—And Jesus went forth, and his disciples, into the villages of Cæsarea Philippi. This verse seems to corroborate the view that the Bethsaida just referred to was Bethsaida Julias. Cæsarea Philippi lies at the roots of Libanus. Cornelius à Lapide says that it was originally called Dan, the place where two little streams united, namely, Jeor and Dan. These two streamlets so united make the Jordan, whence the name Jeor-Dan, or Jordan. But since Pan, the god of shepherds, was better known to the Gentiles than Dan, a Hebrew tribe, it was hence called by them "Paneas." It is called Banias at the present day. It lay at the extreme north, as Beersheba lay at the extreme south. Hence the phrase, "from Dan even to Beersheba." On this account many neighbouring Gentiles, especially the Phœnicians, flocked to this city, as is frequently the case with border towns. And so Christ visited this neighbourhood, not only because it presented favourable opportunities to him for teaching Jews and Gentiles alike, but also that he might speak more freely than he could have done in Judæa concerning a Messiah, whom the Jews expected as their king. In Judæa itself, and especially in the neighbourhood of

Jerusalem, it would have been perilous to speak on such a subject ; for the scribes would at once have accused him to the Roman power that he was seeking the kingdom. The student who wishes for further information respecting the site of Cæsarea Philippi may consult with advantage Stanley's 'Sinai and Palestine' (ch. xi., "The Lake of Merom and the sources of the Jordan"). A more familiar derivation of the Jordan than that given by À Lapide is that of the "descender," from Jarad, "to descend." Our Lord went from Bethsaida Julias directly northwards towards Paneas, named by Philip the Tetrarch Cæsarea Philippi, to distinguish it from the other Cæsarea in Samaria on the Mediterranean coast. It will be observed that he went into the villages of Cæsarea Philippi, avoiding the city itself. In the way thither he asked his disciples, . . . Who do men say that I am? This incident is mentioned also by St. Matthew and St. Luke. St. Luke (ix. 18) says that he was alone praying, his disciples being doubtless not far off. According to this evangelist, our Lord says, "Who do the multitudes say that I am?" thus distinguishing them more particularly from his own disciples. The common people among the Jews knew that not long after the Babylonish Captivity the gift of prophecy had ceased amongst their nation. So they thought that Christ was not a new Prophet, but one of the old. They could not but see in him the renewal of the powers of the old prophets, their miracles and their teaching ; but there were very few of them who believed that he was the Messiah. The great body of them were offended at his poverty and humility; for they thought that Messiah would appear amongst them with royal state as a temporal king. So that when some said, moved it might be by the sight of his miracles, "This is that Prophet that should come into the world," they did but give utterance to a momentary and fugitive feeling, and not a firm or abiding conviction. The mass of mankind are fickle, easily led to change their opinions. Perhaps some of the Jewish multitude thought that the soul of one of the ancient prophets had entered into Christ, according to the Pythagorean notion of the transmigration of souls ; or perhaps they thought that one of the old prophets had risen again in the person of Jesus. For though the Sadducees denied a resurrection, the great body of the Jews believed in it. Some thought that Christ was John the Baptist, because he resembled the Baptist in age (there was only six months difference in age between them), as he also resembled him in holiness and in fervour of preaching. It was but a short time before, that John the Baptist had been put to death by Herod.

His character and actions were fresh in their memories; and Herod himself had given currency to the idea that the Baptist had risen again in the person of our Lord. Then there was Elijah. Some thought that our Lord was Elijah, because it was known that Elijah had not died, and because there was an expectation, founded on Malachi's prophecy (iv. 5), that he would return. They thought, therefore, that Elijah had returned, and that our Lord was Elijah.

Ver. 29.—By this second putting of the question, our Lord warned his disciples that they who had been better instructed ought to think greater things of him than these. It was necessary that he should show them that these current opinions and floating notions were far below his real claims. Therefore he says with emphasis, **But who say ye that I am?**—ye, my disciples, who, being always with me, have seen me do far greater things than they; ye, who have listened to my teaching, confirmed as it has been by those miracles; ye, who yourselves also have been enabled to work many miracles in my name; —who say ye that I am? **Peter answereth and saith unto him, Thou art the Christ.** St. Peter here spoke as the mouthpiece of the rest. The suddenness and terseness of the answer is eminently characteristic of St. Peter. In St. Matthew's narrative it is given a little more in full, "Thou art the Christ, the Son of the living God." But the strength of the answer really lies in St. Mark's words, "Thou art the Christ," that is, the promised Messiah. What, however, St. Mark does omit here—a circumstance not to be passed without notice—is the great blessing pronounced by our Lord upon St. Peter (Matt. xvi. 17—19) as the reward of his confession. The explanation of this omission is to be found in the fact that this Gospel is really for the most part St. Peter's Gospel, recorded by St. Mark. It has already been observed, that, as far as it is possible to do so, considering Peter's prominent position amongst the other apostles, he retires into the background. It was necessary that it should be recorded that he made the good confession of our Lord as the Messiah; but beyond this the evangelist suppresses all mention of the distinction subsequently conferred upon him, although the rebuke which he afterwards received is recorded in full. It is, moreover, a significant circumstance (noticed in the 'Speaker's Commentary') that this Gospel was written at Rome, and in the first instance for Roman readers.

Ver. 30.—**And he charged them** (ἐπετίμησεν)—a strong word, implying almost rebuke, *he strictly charged them*—**that they should tell no man of him.** Why was this? There were many reasons for this reticence. The state of parties in Palestine was most inexpedient for such a disclosure at that time. Those who were favourable to his cause would have wanted at once to take him by force and make him a king. In fact, some of them made no secret of their intentions (John vi. 15). Those, on the other hand, who were opposed to him were only watching their opportunity to destroy him. Moreover, his own disciples had yet many things to learn; and besides all this, faith in his Godhead would be easier when his death should have been followed by his glorious resurrection and ascension.

Ver. 31.—**And he began to teach them, that the Son of man must suffer many things,** etc. In St. Matthew's narrative he says (xvi. 21), "From that time began Jesus to show unto his disciples," etc.—from the time, that is, of this great confession; from the time when he had openly acknowledged to his disciples the truth of his essential Divinity; from that time he began to instruct them as to his passion and his death. There are two great principles of faith, namely, (1) the Divinity and the humanity of Christ, and (2) his cross and passion, whereby he has redeemed the world. And it was necessary that the disciples should be thus instructed in his amazing dignity as the Son of God, lest, when they saw him put to death, they might doubt as to his Godhead. **And after three days rise again.** St. Matthew and St. Luke say, "on the third day"—the day of his death counting for one, and the day of his resurrection for another, with one clear day intervening.

Ver. 32.—**And he spake the saying openly** (παρρησίᾳ); literally, *without reserve.* This sudden announcement excited St. Peter. It was a new and startling communication. **Peter took him, and began to rebuke him.** The word προσλαβόμενος indicates that he "took hold of him," to lead him apart, as though to have the opportunity of warning him with the greater familiarity and secrecy. So say St. Chrysostom and others. Peter would not have his own confession of Christ thus evacuated, as it were; nor does he think it possible that the Son of God could be slain. So he takes him apart, lest he should seem to reprove him in the presence of the other disciples; and then he says (Matt. xvi. 22), "Mercy on thee, Lord (ἵλεώς σοι, Κύριε): this shall never be unto thee."

Ver. 33.—**But he turning about, and seeing his disciples, rebuked Peter.** The words indicate a sudden movement (ὁ δὲ ἐπιστραφεὶς), accompanied by a keen searching look at his disciples. Then he singles out Peter, and addresses to him, in their presence, the severe rebuke, **Get thee behind me, Satan: for thou savourest not** (οὐ φρονεῖς)—literally, *thou mindest not*—**the things of God, but the**

things of men. The form of words is the same
as that used by our Lord to Satan himself,
when he was tempted by him in the wilderness. It reminded him of that great conflict. The visions of worldly glory again
floated before him. The crown without the
cross was again held out to him. This
explains his language. Peter was indeed
rebuked; but the rebuke was aimed through
him at the arch adversary who was addressing him through Peter. Here is the
striking significance of his "turning about."
Peter was for the moment doing the
tempter's work, and in "turning about"
our Lord was again putting Satan behind
him.

Ver. 34.—**He called unto him the multitude with his disciples.** This shows that
there was an interval between what had
just taken place and what is now recorded.
Our Lord now, without any further special
reference to St. Peter, delivers a lesson of
universal application; although, no doubt,
he had Peter in his mind. **If any man
would** (εἴ τις θέλει) **come after me, let him
deny himself, and take up his cross, and
follow me.** This self-denial ought to
extend to everything, even to life itself,
which we ought to be willing to resign, if
need be, for the sake of Christ. *Take up
his cross.* It is as though he said, "Let him
take up his cross, as I have borne my cross,
that I might be the standard-bearer and
Leader of all cross-bearers—I, who carried
the cross on which I was to be crucified to
the mount of Calvary." St. Luke (ix. 23)
adds the words (καθ' ἡμέραν), "daily:" "let
him take up his cross daily;" thus showing
that "every day," and often "at every
hour," something occurs which it becomes
us to bear patiently and bravely, and so on
continually through our whole life. He
takes up his cross who is crucified to the
world. But he to whom the world is
crucified follows his crucified Lord. This
cross assumes various forms; such as persecution and martyrdom, affliction and sorrow of whatever kind, appointed by God;
temptations of Satan, permitted by God for
our trial, to increase our humility and
virtue, and to make brighter our crown.

Ver. 35.—**Because the cross is sharp and
afflicting,** our Lord animates his followers
to bear it by the thought of its great and
everlasting rewards. The meaning of the
verse is this: He who by trying to shun
the cross and to escape self-denial would
save his life here, will lose it hereafter.

But he who loses his life here for the sake
of Christ, either by dying in his cause or by
denying and mortifying his lusts out of
love for him, he in the life to come shall
find his life in the bosom of Christ and in
eternal joy.

Ver. 36.—**What doth it profit a man, to
gain the whole world, and lose his own
soul?** (ζημιωθῆναι); literally, *forfeit his life*
(ψυχή). The word ψυχή in the Greek,
originally meaning simply "breath," as the
sign of life, is of very comprehensive import,
embracing not merely "the breath of life,"
but also the "soul," or immortal part of
man, as distinguished from his mortal body,
also the mind or understanding, as the organ
of thought. "Life" seems here to be the
best English synonym, as being, like the
Greek ψυχή, the more comprehensive term.

Ver. 37.—**In exchange** (ἀντάλλαγμα) **for
his life.** The Greek term here means an
"equivalent," "a compensation." The "life,"
in its largest sense and meaning, defies all
comparison, surpasses all value. It has
been bought and redeemed with the precious
blood of Christ; therefore the whole world
would be a poor price for the soul of one
man.

Ver. 38.—Our Lord here looks onward to
the day of judgment. **Whosoever shall be
ashamed of me.** "Whosoever:" the word
includes all, whatever their position or circumstances may be. "Shall be ashamed of
me;" that is, shall deny my faith, or blush
to confess me here. **Of him shall the Son of
man be ashamed;** that is, Christ will
despise him, when he shall appear with
power and great glory, in that sublime
majesty which he gained by his death upon
the cross. **In this adulterous and sinful
generation.** It adds to the disgrace of being
ashamed of Christ that the shame is manifested in the presence of the base and the
worthless; and therefore our Lord exhibits
the contrast between the mean and contemptible people in the presence of whom
men are ashamed of him here, and the
magnificent assemblage in whose presence
he will be ashamed of them hereafter. The
cross of Christ appeared to the great body of
mankind to be shameful and contemptible.
To the Jews it was a stumbling-block, and
to the Greeks foolishness. Hence vast
numbers, whether through shame or fear,
did not dare to confess it, and still less to
preach it. And therefore it is that St.
Paul says (Rom. i. 16), "I am not ashamed
of the gospel of Christ."

HOMILETICS.

Vers. 1—10.—*The Giver of bread.* That the miracle of feeding the multitude
should be repeated, and that two evangelists should record both events, is a testimony

to the generous and considerate kindness of the Saviour, and to the instructive nature of the sign. We discern in this narrative an illustration of—

I. CHRIST'S ATTRACTIVE MINISTRY. A great multitude followed him to listen to his teaching, and were so absorbed in his words as to neglect attention to their bodily wants. Far from home, and without a supply of food, they hungered. Eating of the spiritual bread, they were satisfied in their souls. But they had bodily wants also.

II. CHRIST'S CONSIDERATE COMPASSION. A man himself, Jesus was touched with a feeling of human infirmities. He had known hunger. The people had come from far; they had remained in the neighbourhood where he was for three days; their little stock of provisions was exhausted, and, should he send them away fasting, many might faint upon the road. All this Jesus thought of, and his sympathy was aroused. He had compassion, not only upon their souls, but upon their bodies.

III. CHRIST'S USE OF ORDINARY HUMAN RESOURCES AND MEANS. Jesus might doubtless have created bread of stones, as the tempter had once challenged him to do. But he chose to use what provisions were at hand, and to make the few loaves and fishes which the disciples held as a reserve of food, the basis, so to speak, of his miraculous action. The Lord does not despise, or dispense with, human means or human agencies. As on this occasion he directed his disciples to distribute the bread they had, so ever does he use his people and their powers and possessions as means of good to their fellow-men.

IV. CHRIST'S DEVOUTNESS IN THANKSGIVING. Being himself the Son of the Father, he yet, in the name of the dependent children, acknowledged the bounty and beneficence of the Giver of all.

V. CHRIST'S MIRACULOUS POWER. We are not told how it came to pass, but it is recorded that the four thousand found the slender provision sufficient for all their wants. When the Saviour provides, there is always enough and more than enough for all.

VI. CHRIST'S FRUGALITY AND ECONOMY. The Lord was liberal, but not lavish. There was no waste in his arrangements. The broken pieces that remained were gathered, and doubtless saved and used. Because he miraculously supplied what was needed, it did not follow that he would suffer anything to be wasted and lost.

Ver. 4.—*Whence shall man's soul be fed?* God's creatures are altogether and for ever dependent upon him. It is not now and then only that our Creator and Lord interposes upon our behalf, to supply our wants and to relieve our distresses. There are times when we specially recognize, and occasions when we specially feel, his care. But his bounty and watchfulness are, in fact, unceasing. "In him we live, and move, and have our being;" "He openeth his hand, and satisfieth the desires of every living thing." *Bread for the body, and bread for the soul, alike are from him.* Our daily bread is his daily gift, and our daily remembrancer of him the Giver. In most cases the provision is so regular, by reason of fruitful seasons, by which he fills us with joy and gladness, that men take the gifts of his providence as a matter of course, and are (in instances) only now and then reminded of their dependence when he withholds his bounties. Our souls equally wait upon him, and to them he also giveth "their portion in due season." The sinless beings above doubtless receive from him abundant spiritual good, in an unceasing stream. If our human spirits are not constantly and of course enriched by his Spirit, it is not that his loving-kindness is little or intermittent; it is because our sin prevents us from receiving what is, to believing, lowly, and obedient natures, ever accessible. There is, accordingly, something altogether special in the supply provided for the deep and everlasting needs of human spirits. The unfallen angels, by reason of their purity, have constant fellowship with God, and doubtless are daily fed from his presence, and drink of the stream of his life. But we—poor, sinful children of men—need to be dealt with in a way Divine wisdom alone can devise, to suit the emergency of our position. The plenty of the Divine granary must be brought to our perishing souls by a heavenly interposition and grace. It is in Christ Jesus, the Son of the Eternal Father, that the bread of God becomes the bread of man. Needy, and therefore longing for spiritual food; sinful, and therefore unable to obtain and partake of such food, except in the way Infinite wisdom and grace may open up to us,—we are in a pitiable case until the beneficent Father sends unto us a heavenly and all-

sufficient supply.   No fellow-creature can give what our circumstances demand and
our nature craves; no fellow-creature can satisfy the necessities of one suppliant, far less
those of the unnumbered race of humanity.   "From whence can a man satisfy these
men with bread here in the wilderness?"

I. This language suggests THE CRY OF THE SPIRITUALLY HUNGRY FOR BREAD.   Man
cannot "live by bread alone."   Unless he change his nature, or blunt its urgencies, and
stifle its voice, it calls aloud for God.

> "Far and wide, though all unknowing,
>   Pants for thee each mortal breast;
> Human tears for thee are flowing,
>   Human hearts in thee would rest."

Oftentimes do men try to misinterpret this utterance, to persuade themselves that it is
not God they want; that they are as the brutes, to which due fodder and litter and
shelter suffice for satisfaction and enjoyment.   When one looks upon the vain endeavours of misguided, self-deluded men, one cannot help crying aloud, in the memorable
language of the Hebrew prophet, "Wherefore do ye spend money for that which is
not bread, and your labour for that which satisfieth not?"   There is a deep-seated
longing, a recurring appetite, which prompts all men in whom is any spiritual vitality
at all to look for more than earth, than man, can give.   We ask for truth, for without
truth—and especially truth concerning God—is no satisfaction possible to the created
soul.   "Oh that I knew where I might find him!"—him, my Maker, Lord, and Judge;
that I might know why he has made me, why he has stationed me here on earth, what
is the purpose of his wisdom concerning me!   Mock me not with dust and stones, but
give me bread indeed, even the true knowledge of God!   And as conscience assures
each child of man that, if this God whom he fain would know take any interest in him,
he cannot but remark his disobedience and his errors, the heart within calls aloud for
the favour and acceptance of the great King.   "How shall a man be just with God?"
"Wherewithal shall I come into his presence?"   Will he "lift the light of his countenance" upon me, and be gracious to me?   Must my sins be a barrier between me and
my God; or can he, will he, overturn and cast them away, and admit me to his grace
and fellowship and peace?   Turning his regard inward upon himself, and perceiving
his own helplessness in the struggle which is not to be avoided, the poor and feeble
child of man asks for strength.   How shall I gain strength for duty in times of weakness and temptation?   How realize the intention of the Creator concerning me, that I
shall enter into the conflict, sustain its toils, brave its dangers, and come forth victorious?   And when the day of suffering and the night of sorrow come, can the human
soul find comfort in the lessons of human philosophy, in the balm of human sympathy?
Alas! these cannot suffice.   Nor can aught truly soothe and effectually succour the
weak and weary, the sad and lonely, the bereaved and dying, save the hand which
fashioned the soul and made it susceptible to anguish—the heart that, by a Divine sympathy and consolation, heals the wounds that it permits.   And when "heart and flesh
fail," who but the Creator and Saviour can prove "the Strength of the heart, and its
Portion for evermore"?   No human plummet can fathom the river all must cross, no
human hand uphold the feeble, trembling feet amidst the dark, cold waters.   Be sure
of this: as long as man retains a nature higher than that of brutes that perish, so long
as his heart is subject to grief, his life is surrounded by trouble, his nature prone to sin;
so long he will ever and anon cry out for supernatural succour and comfort, and call
upon his God.   Spiritual hunger is no fancy of the sentimental, no artificial demand
of the leisurely and cultivated.   It is a fact—a fact which (however it may be regarded)
is not to be denied, and without considering which, our view of our human nature and
our knowledge of ourselves must needs be incomplete and delusive.   Bread for his soul
man will ask for, and, unless he have it, he will hunger, pine, and perish!

II. This language suggests THE SILENCE OF THE WILDERNESS TO THIS APPEAL.   Out
beyond the Lake of Tiberias, away from towns and villages, in the solitudes of the green
hillsides, how was the want of the multitude to be supplied?   Blades of grass were
not ears of corn, stones were not bread.   "Here in the wilderness" was no answer to
the demand of the hungering—none!   The wilderness could only leave those to perish
who trusted to its tender mercies.   An emblem of the world's powerlessness to meet

the case of our spiritually dependent and hungering race! The world is the scene of our trial and proving, the occasion of our manifold temptations. Of what use is it to look to it for sympathy, succour, strength, and salvation? It cannot satisfy you, search and prove it how you may. Is that rich and luscious fruit that hangs from yonder bough? Alas! it is the apple of the Dead Sea, dust and ashes between the teeth. Is that a lake of sweet, pellucid waters which gleams in the glowing sun in yonder hollow? Alas! it is the mirage of the desert, which mocks the thirsty travellers, offering them sand for water. So with the pretences of the world to satisfy the hungering soul. These pretences are vanity and delusion. Equally vain to help, though more honest, is the world, when its response is otherwise. It sometimes acknowledges its utter powerlessness: none to help, none to pity, none to deliver and to save! Whilst some who reject and despise the message of religion abandon themselves to selfish and worldly aims, and seek to still the voice of conscience and to repress the aspirations of the soul in the pursuits of pleasure, pelf, or power, there are others in whose breasts is no peace and no hope. They cry aloud in the wilderness; but no answer comes to them, save the mocking echoes from the hard, dead rock. No truth, no law, no grace, no hope, no heaven, no God! Such is their interpretation of the echoes of the desert. And we cannot wonder that, incredulous of every higher, better message, they abandon themselves to doubt, despondency, despair. From this cheerless and desolate prospect, let us turn to facts fitted to gladden every depressed and anxious heart.

III. The language suggests to us THE DIVINE PROVISION OF THE BREAD OF LIFE. When the disciples of Jesus asked him this question, "Whence shall one be able to satisfy these men with bread here in the wilderness?" they must have been thinking of their own inability. For they could not have forgotten how, not far from this very spot and not long since, their Master had fed five thousand men with five loaves and two fishes. If they had been there without him, they might have been as helpless as they were when the father of the lunatic boy brought his son into their presence, and entreated their compassion and aid. But the Lord Jesus was himself the answer to this inquiry. He had but to bless the bread, and distribute it by the hands of the disciples, and, for even so vast a multitude, there was "bread enough and to spare." Thousands were fed when Jesus was the Master of the feast. No miracles were more evidently and decisively than these of feeding the thousands, parables concerning Christ himself. St. John has recorded the discourse which our Saviour uttered in Capernaum, in which Jesus asserted his own mission and office and power. "My Father," said he, "giveth you the true Bread from heaven. For the Bread of God is he which cometh down from heaven, and giveth life unto the world. . . . I am the Bread of life: he that cometh to me shall never hunger; and he that believeth on me shall never thirst." In this language our Divine Lord evidently referred to that marvellous incident in the history of Israel when the wants of the people were supplied by daily provision of manna in the wilderness. More especially he brought before the minds of his hearers the great fact that the supply of human wants is due to the grace and interposition of God himself. Bread does not come to us *from* the wilderness, but it comes to us *in* the wilderness; and it is the Father above who sends it—none but he! Obviously, the figurative language in which Christ describes himself appeals to our best, purest, most sacred feelings. God is the Father, who will not leave his children without bread. He cares for his spiritual family, considers their wants, hears their cry, and in his wisdom and love secures for them all that he sees to be for their good. Our Lord Jesus Christ is himself the Divine provision for the needs of men. "He that eateth the flesh, and drinketh the blood of Christ, has life eternal." For it must be borne in mind that the heavenly Father who has given us his Son, has in him virtually given us all the resources of his boundless compassion and grace. "He who spared not his own Son, but delivered him up for us all, how shall he not with him also freely give us all things?" Do our hearts cry aloud for spiritual truth? God gives us this in Christ, who is himself the Truth—the revelation of the Father's mind and will. The heart that finds "Immanuel—God with us," finds God himself—for Christ is "the brightness of the Father's glory"—reads the writing of God's own hand, hears the utterances of Truth Divine. "He that hath seen me," says Christ, "hath seen the Father." Is our heart restless until assured of the forgiveness and the favour of our God? Hungry for the smile of Heaven, does it turn heavenward a wistful gaze? God in Christ gives us this first great necessity of the sinful soul. Jesus came to call sinners to repentance, but he came at the same time to assure the penitent of pardon—the purchase of his precious blood. What bread is to the hungry, that is pardon to the contrite, humbled, suppliant transgressor. And this is the gift of Christ, who came with " power on earth to forgive sins." Do we feel an inner craving for a strength which we do not find within ourselves— for a power which shall uphold us in the labour and the conflict of this earthly life? Not only to know the will of God but to do it—this is the want of man's soul. Power to do this is bread to his hungering nature. Do you not, indeed, when you best know yourselves, feel that truly to live you must have strength to live to God? And who but God himself can impart this strength? It is given in Jesus. Eat of this bread, and labour shall be sweet and work welcome. His meat and drink was to do the will of him who sent him, and to finish his work. And in his people is " the mind of Christ." Does not the sorrowful and tempted soul—the soul oppressed by the infirmities of the flesh and the ills of life—hunger for a consolation not to be found from the wilderness? Who of us has not felt this, in seasons of grief and anxiety? Surely, God knows the heart which he has fashioned; he reads its laments, he witnesses its struggles, he comprehends its fears. It was to allay our anxiety, to assuage our griefs, that Jesus dwelt on earth, wept our tears, tasted the bitterness of our death; that he might be a " High Priest touched with the feeling of our infirmities." As long as " man is born to sorrow," so long shall the " Man of sorrows, acquainted with grief," be the dearest Friend the heart can know. Jesus is a " brother born for adversity."

> " But what to those who find? Ah! this
> Nor tongue nor pen can show;
> The love of Jesus, what it is
> None but his loved ones know."

IV. This language suggests THE SATISFACTION FOUND BY THOSE WHO PARTAKE OF THIS SPIRITUAL FOOD. We read in the Gospel that, when the great Lord of nature and of men miraculously supplied the wants of the hungering crowds, " they did all eat, and were filled." In this they prefigured all who, in every land and age, should feed by faith upon the Son of God. Of him it may truly be said, " He filleth the hungry soul with goodness." Three remarks may be made upon the power of the Lord Jesus to appease the spiritual hunger and to supply the spiritual wants of men. He is sufficient for each, sufficient for all, sufficient for evermore. Each soul, however drawn or driven to Christ—driven by the desperation of want, or drawn by the excellence and abun- dance of the Divine supply—finds in him all that he himself has promised. To believe, to trust, to love, to follow Christ,—this is to appropriate him, to prove and learn his Divine sufficiency. " He that cometh to me," says Jesus, " shall never hunger; and he that believeth on me shall never thirst." The same faith which first reveals Christ to the soul, and stays its hunger, is the means of attaching the soul to Christ and the means by which the soul finds in him all the fulness of God. For he of God is made unto his people " wisdom and righteousness, sanctification and redemption." The bounty of the Lord Jesus is unrestricted. As the vast multitude of his auditors were fed by his beneficence—as men, women, and children all ate and had enough, so that basketsful of fragments were taken up—so throughout this wide world its teeming and varied populations are all destined to find in him the Saviour of mankind. " I," said he, " if I be lifted up from the earth, will draw all men unto me." Untold myriads have feasted at the table of Christ, and none have risen hungry and dis- satisfied. Still have the ministers of his grace the privilege of announcing to the starving children of men, " ' Yet there is room.' Come ye in, that the guests may be many and the tables filled. ' Eat ye that which is good, and let your soul delight itself in fatness.' " Still further to enhance the conception of the preciousness of the great salvation, let it be remembered that it is an unfailing, an everlasting, an imperishable satisfaction which is to be found in Jesus Christ. He that eats of earthly bread and drinks of earthly streams hungers and thirsts again; but he who, by Divine mercy, feeds on heavenly food and drinks of the living water hungers and thirsts no more. For him is provided a perpetual feast, an immortal satisfaction and content. Generation succeeds generation, and age follows age. The experience of humanity is prolonged from century to century. Opportunity is given to every system, to every creed, to every philosophy, to deal with the deep and spiritual necessities of mankind. As one attempt of human wisdom succeeds another, and as each fails in its turn, we hear in our soul within us the cry arise, suggested by human effort and by human powerlessness, "From whence can a man satisfy these men with bread here in the wilderness?" There is no answer. None has been given; none can be given. Happy are we who hear a voice, Divine alike in sweetness and authority, rising above the plaint of the hungry, or breaking the silence of the baffled and the helpless, and uttering forth the welcome declaration of pity and of love, "I am the Bread of life"! And happier still if, convinced of the sincerity and the power of this Divine and compassionate Benefactor, prompted by our human need, and guided by the Spirit of God, we respond, in faith and gratitude and hope, "Lord, evermore give us this Bread"!

Vers. 11—13.—*Signs.* This was not an isolated case of the demands on the part of the Jewish leaders that Jesus should work some miracle which they might receive as a sign from heaven. And it was not only during our Saviour's ministry that they preferred such a request. For Paul had occasion long afterwards to complain of the Jews that they "required a sign," and were dissatisfied with the doctrines and with the evidences of Christianity.

I. THE REQUEST OF THE PHARISEES. These men made a point of seeing Jesus, and seem, on this as on other occasions, to have come as a deputation from his adversaries. 1. *What* was it they asked? Not an ordinary miracle, for such Jesus had already repeatedly and publicly performed. It was a sign, not from himself, but from heaven. Any wonder he might work they would attribute to magic or to Beelzebub. But, such was their profession, if he would furnish them with some splendid celestial portent—if he would give bread from heaven or stay the sun in its course—then they would be convinced of his Messiahship. 2. *Why* did they ask such a sign? They were tempting, testing him—putting him to the proof. Had he complied with their wish, they would have seen in him the Messiah they wanted—one prepared probably to wield supernatural power for personal aggrandizement and for political dominion. Should he refuse, they would be confirmed in their rejection of his claims.

II. THE REFUSAL OF CHRIST. Observe: 1. The *feeling* with which he refused. "He sighed deeply in his spirit." Had they come asking for healing, relief, assistance, he would have joyfully complied; but it grieved him to the heart that they should come thus. And he read in their conduct the sign of a widespread carnality, unspirituality, and unbelief. 2. He *disapproved of the spirit* in which the request had been made. He was not only pained by it, he censured and condemned it. They who came, came to carp and criticize, and confirm themselves in their unbelief. 3. He had *already given evidence enough* to justify the faith of such as were candid and open to conviction. He had wrought miracles so many and of such a kind as might assure the thoughtful and spiritually susceptible that he was from God. 4. He knew that *what they asked for, if granted, would not convince them.* The deficiency was not in him; it was in themselves. The principle was applicable, "If they hear not Moses and the prophets," etc. 5. There was *one great sign yet to be given,* in God's time—a sign that should surpass all granted in the olden days; a sign that should leave all unbelievers without excuse—his resurrection from the dead.

Vers. 14—21.—*Misunderstanding.* The evangelists have left untold much which we would fain know, and they have recorded some things which our unwisdom would have dispensed with. The incident here recorded seems trivial, and the conversation arising upon it commonplace. Yet it was not without a purpose that two evangelists were directed to preserve this passage in our Lord's ordinary life.

I. THE WARNING WHICH THE DISCIPLES MISUNDERSTOOD. Christ's ministry of teaching seems to have been one long protest against the current doctrines and practices of the religious leaders of the time. The Pharisees were very generally formalists, and the Herodians secularists, and against both tendencies our Divine Lord's opposition was unceasing and uncompromising. Using figurative language, Jesus cautioned his disciples against the leaven, *i.e.* the influence, of such errors as were characteristic of these religious schools. Although they were so much in his society and so attached to his ministry, they were not deemed by the Master beyond the need of this wise and faithful admonition.

II. THE CONSTRUCTION WHICH THEY PUT UPON HIS WORDS. The word "leaven" reminded them of bread, and the thought of bread reminded them of their negligence in not having made proper provision for their journey. But their misunderstanding was scarcely due to their oversight; it was rather the consequence of their own slowness of mind to take in their Master's manner of speech. We do not trace impatience, but we do trace a certain dissatisfaction and reproachfulness, in the Lord's language: "Do ye not yet perceive, neither understand?" How often has Christ occasion thus to expostulate with his too unspiritual and inappreciative disciples! We often take Christ's words too literally, without that discernment and sympathy which a wise and gracious Master expects from his scholars.

III. THE CONSIDERATIONS BY WHICH CHRIST REPROVED THEIR MISUNDERSTANDING. 1. They should have known him better than so to misapprehend him. Where were their eyes, their ears, their heart? Had they been susceptible and active, surely a truer, a loftier judgment would have been formed of the Christ, the Son of God. In this case they would not have supposed that he was troubling himself or them with such a trifle as now excited their concern. 2. They should have better remembered the past, especially the occasions upon which the Lord had supplied the wants of multitudes in the exercise of his omnipotence. Such a recollection would have saved them from the misapprehension into which they had fallen.

APPLICATION. Christ's words are to be understood in the light of his nature and his works. To understand what Christ says we must think of him aright, and we must study his teaching in the light of the wonderful deeds which he has performed for the relief and the salvation of mankind. It is want of sympathy and of remembrance which often leads to misunderstanding. He that will do the Divine will shall know of the doctrine.

Vers. 22—26.—*Sight for the blind.* Every form of human privation, suffering, and infirmity which came under the notice of Christ elicited his compassion and his healing mercy, and every such disorder was treated by him as a symptom of the moral malady which afflicts mankind. The diversity of his miracles of healing may serve to represent his power and willingness to restore our sinful humanity, afflicted with many and various ills, to spiritual soundness and health. In this miracle we observe—

I. A SYMBOL OF THE SPIRITUAL BLINDNESS OF HUMANITY. The blind man of Bethsaida may not have been born blind; but his sightless state was well known, and excited the commiseration of his neighbours and acquaintances, who led him to the great Healer and Enlightener of men, that he might touch and cure him. He is an emblem of this humanity, darkened in understanding, incapable of discerning truth, blind to moral beauty, to heavenly glory.

II. A SYMBOL OF SALVATION BY DIVINE CONTACT. Jesus treated this man in a way appropriate to his condition and infirmity. He appealed to the sense of touch, for there was no sense of sight to which to appeal. He led the blind man by the hand, took him apart, spat on his eyes, laid his hands upon him. All this was to make the patient feel that the Divine Physician was there, was interested in him, was working for his cure. It was to reveal his own presence and to call forth the sufferer's faith. And there is no salvation for any by merely hearing or reading about Jesus Christ. The spiritually blind cannot experience his illuminating power except by coming to him in faith. If he enter the heart, reveal his truth and love and power, come into immediate contact with the springs of the spiritual nature and life, then the mind, before insensible to the light of Heaven, begins to appreciate the great realities of being —the nature, the character, the will, of a holy God and Father.

III. A SYMBOL OF THE PROGRESSIVE CHARACTER OF SPIRITUAL ENLIGHTENMENT. The most noticeable feature of this miracle is the way in which the cure was wrought—gradually and progressively. Why Jesus did not effect the result at once does not appear. It may have been to teach us how difficult and slow is the process of human illumination, even by the gospel and the Spirit of God. As at first the man saw human figures, which appeared like trees, but moved, so that even his half-recovered vision judged them men; so those to whom the light of the gospel first comes often discern but dimly those spiritual facts and relations which time and experience and Divine teaching will render more vivid and distinct. It is not to be expected that young Christians or recent converts shall understand all such truth as is comparatively clear to the mature and instructed. God's ways herein are like his ways in other departments of his government; order and progression are characteristics of his reign.

IV. A SYMBOL OF THE POWER OF CHRIST TO EFFECT COMPLETE ILLUMINATION. After the further application of the wonder-working hands of Jesus, it is recorded that the blind man "was restored, and saw all things clearly." So in God's light we shall see light. He hath "shined into our hearts." We shall "see God." The vision shall brighten here; and it shall be more than bright—it shall be glorious—hereafter.

HOMILIES BY VARIOUS AUTHORS.

Vers. 1—15.—(Cf. on ch. vi. 32—41.)—M.

Vers. 11—13.—*Seeking for a sign.* Christ knew at once what this meant. He "knew what was in man," and refused to commit himself to the pretended inquirers. We have a more difficult course to pursue.

I. THE CHARACTER OF THE DEMAND DEPENDS UPON CIRCUMSTANCES. It may be made in an honest, inquiring spirit, or in order to injure religion. In the former case too much consideration can hardly be given to it, as it is the indispensable preliminary to rational conviction, and the gospel offers evidence for its claims. The spirit in which the inquiry is made may be determined by: 1. *The character of those who inquire.* Bad men *may* be genuine inquirers, but it is well to know their antecedents. Christ could read the underlying design of the Jews. It may reasonably be expected that inquirers should give some proof of their sincerity, especially if already furnished with many evidences. 2. *The kind of sign asked for.* Here it was "a sign from heaven," *i.e.* differing from the miracles and previous manifestations of Christ. This implied that they were insufficient, and indirectly pronounced judgment upon the previous words and works of Christ. A question may sometimes reveal a more thorough scepticism than a dogmatic denial. Whilst apparent liberty is given as to what particular sign might be produced, there is really a tone of dictation and unseemly assumption.

II. SUCH A DEMAND EXPOSES THE REPRESENTATIVES OF CHRISTIANITY TO STRONG TEMPTATION. They are invited to criticize God's methods of revelation, and to despise the "means of grace." A position full of unbelief and presumption may insensibly be assumed, such as that of Moses at the rock: "Must *we* fetch you water out of this rock?" (Numb. xx. 10). They may be induced to attempt to "force the hand" of God. The crime of such a proceeding could only be equalled by its folly. As if those who are insensible to the cross of Christ could be converted by a thunderbolt or a merely supernatural spectacle! It is for Christ's servants in times of popular excitement to preach the old truths, and to appeal to every man's *conscience* in the sight of God. The improbability of sensationalism producing belief is a *growing* one. "If they hear not Moses and the prophets, neither will they be persuaded, if one rise from the dead" (Luke xvi. 31). So we may now add, "If they believe not One who has risen from the dead, neither will they believe, though he were to be manifested to them in heaven itself."

III. EVEN WERE IT DESIRED IT WOULD BE REFUSED. "This generation" represents all who ask in a similar spirit. 1. *Because the evidence for Christianity is spiritual, not carnal; moral, and not material.* 2. *Because the patent, outstanding facts of the gospel are sufficient:* (1) For the conversion of sinners; and (2) for the confirmation and edifying of saints. 3. *Because it is part of the punishment appointed to such inquirers that they shall ask and not receive, and seek and not find.* 4. *Because it may become a means of turning attention back to the evidence that has been despised or ignored.* It is high time our philosophical inquirers began to inquire why their researches have produced no fruits in evidence or conviction as yet. Why is it that whilst the evidence for the gospel is at least equal to that for any other matters of history, it is yet disbelieved when they are accepted? Is not the reason a moral rather than an intellectual one?—M.

Vers. 14—21.—*The leaven of the Pharisees and of Herod.* The parabolic habit of mind of Christ was essential to the setting forth of Divine truth to the comprehension of men; but as yet the persons who might have been expected to understand his teaching most thoroughly, were continually mistaking it. Whilst their Master discoursed of heavenly things, the thoughts of the disciples were upon the earth. There is nothing so reveals the moral and spiritual distance of persons from one another as the difference in their habits of mind.

I. HOW TOO GREAT A REGARD FOR OUTWARD THINGS BETRAYS ITSELF. 1. *In over-anxiety.* The disciples had by inadvertency omitted to take in a supply of bread ere leaving the shore, and their minds were full of trouble. They began to forecast the inconvenience to which it might expose them. Over-carefulness is a common feature of worldly character. It arises from too great self-dependence and too little faith in God. A certain, moderate attention to earthly wants is a duty, and will be bestowed by every well-regulated mind; but there are limits to be observed. "Be not anxious for your life," etc. (Matt. vi. 25). It is a great aim of the spiritual life to be free from this bondage to minute worries and cares. 2. *In failure to attend to or understand Divine things.* The disciples were so taken up with this little matter that they utterly failed to perceive Christ's meaning, when he warned them against the Pharisees and Herodians. That they should be so was also a proof that they had forgotten the teaching of the two miracles of the loaves and fishes. For this Christ reproved them. His cross-questioning elicited the fact that the *details* of these miracles were still recollected; but the spiritual lessons had been completely lost. So to speak, these spiritual *tours de force* had been thrown away upon them. How hard a race has the Divine life with earthly concern and anxiety in the soul! There is a littleness in such habits of thought that effectually prevents the great ideas of the Divine kingdom from entering the mind. Herein is to be found the explanation of the failure of many services and sermons, which in themselves may have been faithful and devout enough : the hearers are occupied with worldly cares. "The cares of the world, and the deceitfulness of riches, and the lusts of other things entering in, choke the Word, and it becometh unfruitful" (ch. iv. 19).

II. THE DANGER TO WHICH IT EXPOSES. 1. Christ, referring to the doctrine of the Pharisees and Herodians, warned against *that conception of the Messiah, as one who was to be an earthly king, establishing a temporal dominion, which the leaders of Judaism held.* The state of mind of the disciples was eminently favourable to such a view. In them it was only a tendency, in the Pharisees a fixed point of view; and thus the latter wholly missed the spiritual element in the Saviour's teaching. They were filled with visions of national restoration and individual aggrandizement; and failing to receive encouragement from Christ in these, "they were offended in him," and began to seek his destruction. The same danger still haunts the Church of Christ, the absolutely spiritual nature of the Divine kingdom having been one of the most slowly developed of Christian doctrines. 2. *The power and the insidiousness of this point of view are suggested by the figure of "leaven."* Leaven works slowly, but a very little affects a large amount. "A little leaven leaveneth the whole lump." To minds already prepared by habit and tendency in that direction, it would be a comparatively easy thing to adopt the worldly interpretation of prophecy given forth by the Pharisees. Indeed, if they were only let alone, the "leaven" was already within them, and would assuredly develop into the same fundamental heresy. To think thus of Christ and his kingdom is "to come short of it," to our own hurt and ruin ; "for the kingdom of God is not eating and drinking, but righteousness and peace and joy in the Holy Ghost" (Rom. xiv. 17).—M.

Ver. 21.—"*Do ye not understand ?*" The last of a series of surprised, sorrowful, and indignant questions on the part of Christ.

I. SPIRITUAL UNDERSTANDING WAS A RESULT TO BE LOOKED FOR FROM CHRISTIAN EXPERIENCE. 1. *From the teaching of Scripture.* It unfolds the will of God, and reveals his mind and character. It is the record of the spiritual history of man in the past. The lives of the Old Testament saints and the history of God's chosen people were intended to acquaint us with the principles of the Divine kingdom, and the purpose of God's dealings with men. "Now these things happened unto them by way of example; and they were written for our admonition, upon whom the ends of the ages are come" (1 Cor. x. 11). "These are written, that ye may believe that Jesus is the Christ, the Son of God" (John xx. 31). 2. *From personal experience.* In the case of the disciples, the teaching, example, and miracles of Christ were intended to reveal the merciful and loving purpose of God to redeem the world. This was to be (1) the basis of a personal faith; (2) a principle for interpreting the circumstances of life; (3) an influence for delivering and elevating the human spirit. The consistent lesson of Christ's works—especially of his crowning miracle of the loaves—was that men were to seek first the kingdom of God and his righteousness, and all needful things of the earthly life would be added. Instead of being lost in anxious deliberations and "reasonings" about ways and means, the true disciple was to look steadfastly to the great end.

II. THE LACK OF IT IN HIS DISCIPLES DISAPPOINTED CHRIST. He was astonished and pained at their hardness of heart. The works specially intended to produce faith and understanding had hitherto failed of their legitimate result. We seem to detect in his tone: 1. *Wounded feeling.* He had yearned for spiritual companionship and co-operation. It was ever his desire to draw his disciples into a closer fellowship; but they were discovered to be unfit and unworthy of the privilege. It is as if, too, he was indignant that the honour and love of his Father should be suspected. 2. *Apprehension.* They were in a dangerous spiritual condition, ready to be the prey of every passing temptation. It was as if the foreboding, "When the Son of man cometh, shall he find faith on the earth?" (Luke xviii. 8), had already flitted across his spirit.

III. IT IS AN ACQUIREMENT TO BE DILIGENTLY CULTIVATED. 1. *How?* By remembrance. The dealings of God with others are plainly set forth in Scripture; but every Christian has a special history of his own in which God has revealed himself. None of the incidents of that personal history should be forgotten. Let him remember all the way by which the Father has led him, the gracious interpositions and revelations that have marked it, etc. By meditation. These circumstances are to be pondered and studied, that their inward meaning may be discovered. Above all, we ought to consider "what manner of love the Father hath bestowed on us" (1 John iii. 1). 2. *Why?* Because (1) it is essential to the usefulness and happiness of the Christian; (2) it may be increased. In some it can hardly be said to exist at all. Yet if there be faith as a grain of mustard seed it will grow, where diligence and prayerfulness are exercised. Of even those very men Christ at last declared, "No longer do I call you servants; for the servant knoweth not what his lord doeth: but I have called you friends; for all things that I heard from my Father I have made known unto you" (John xv. 15). "He that doeth the will shall know of the doctrine, whether it be of God."—M.

Vers. 22—26.—*Restoring the blind to sight.* Illustration of Christ's—

I. WISDOM. He rebuked a vulgar curiosity, and perhaps baffled a Pharisaic intrigue. His privacy, so needful for bodily rest and spiritual preparation for the great conflict he felt to be impending, was thus preserved; and the course of teaching and working upon which he had entered was not seriously disturbed. The subject of the miracle was himself preserved from undue excitement with its attendant dangers. And shall we not suppose that a deeper and more spiritual understanding may have arisen between the Saviour and the recipient of his mercy during those solemn and deeply moving experiences which preceded his recovery? His deep, unbroken attention was secured as he felt the Saviour's touch and listened to his voice. By *leading* him away he tested and exercised his faith. By emphasizing the stages of recovery he made it clear to the man himself that it was no accidental occurrence, but a deliberate cure. And in the means used—so evidently inadequate to produce such a result—he showed how supernatural the power that was being exercised. The questions asked encouraged the man to put forth his own power as he received it, and thus to co-operate in the curative process. The final injunction to silence and home-going present the incident as a deep personal experience in the mind of the man, and as an evangelic message to those who were most likely to receive it in simplicity and gratitude.

II. MERCY. *Although the shadow of death was falling upon the soul of Jesus, he was full of the instinct and will to save.* There is scarcely any appreciable pause in his work; and retirement is not inactivity, but quieter, deeper, and more continuous, because more naturally prompted, action. Each case of distress as it arises receives his deliberate and careful attention. His diagnosis of the blind man's state must have been perfect. It was impaired original power that had to be restored, and the treatment corresponded to this fact. The *interest* of the Saviour in the case is as great as that of the saved. The sinister ends of those who brought the blind man, or watched to see what would be done, did not prevent him showing the mercy required. When the bodily cure had been completed, the spiritual welfare of the recovered one was carefully provided for. The aim is complete salvation in every sense of the word. What Christ does he will do perfectly.

III. JUDGMENT. Unworthy men were debarred from seeing the wonders of his saving power. They might have perverted the privilege to an evil end, and so injured themselves and the cause of Christ; so they were shut out. It is a fearful sentence against a place or a person when the spectacle of the Lord's saving grace is denied, and the things that make for peace are hidden from view.—M.

Vers. 22—26.—*The Saviour's method in dealing with individual souls.* I. HE ISOLATES FROM DISTURBING INFLUENCES. The gossips and scheming politicians of the town of Bethsaida. Notoriety. The sense of importance. By his dealings with the sinner in conviction and repentance, he spiritually removes him to his own retirement. He is first brought to be *with* Christ, that by-and-by he may be *in* him.

II. HE ENCOURAGES AND CONFIRMS FAITH. By leading the blind man away, although as yet a stranger to him. By personal contact and operation, and by kindly words, the inner free-will and power of the patient were evoked. The means and the gradual working out of the cure were a demonstration of the Power by whom the miracle was wrought. The gradual realization of spiritual power in those being saved is a crucial evidence of Divine grace, and encourages belief in the ultimate accomplishment of a complete salvation.

III. HE EXACTS IMPLICIT OBEDIENCE. This was the highest exercise of a spiritual kind he had demanded. It was but a phase of the faith already called forth—"the obedience of faith." Having won the trust and confidence of his people, he proves and perfects that by directing the fulfilment of duties the reason for which may not be apparent. It is sufficient that he has commanded. The first use of the restored vision is to avoid those upon whom he had formerly depended—a hard task! The life Christ's people are bidden to lead may not commend itself to their judgment or desire, but it is best for their spiritual interests; and if Christ is to be a complete Saviour, he must be an absolute and unquestioned Lord.—M.

Vers. 22—26.—*Curing spiritual blindness.* I. DELIVERANCE FROM BLIND GUIDES.
II. TRANSFER OF CONFIDENCE TO THE TRUE GUIDE.
III. REVELATION OF THE INVISIBLE POWER OF GOD.
IV. EXERCISING THE SOUL'S NEWLY ACQUIRED POWERS OF SPIRITUAL VISION.
V. GIVING SPIRITUAL DIRECTION FOR THE FUTURE.—M.

Vers. 27—30.—*Peter's good confession.* The scene of this is worth notice. It lay to the northward of Bethsaida, amongst the villages in the neighbourhood of Cæsarea Philippi. This town, on the site of the ancient Paneas (now Banias), was built by the tetrarch Philip in honour of Tiberius Cæsar, and is to be distinguished from the Cæsarea of the southern Mediterranean seaboard of Palestine. The country was magnificent (Tristram, 'Land of Israel,' p. 586); wild, wooded, and mountainous, and dominated by the royal castle of Subeibeh. Here, too, was the chief fountain-head of the Jordan (ibid., p. 585). It was a region where the utmost seclusion could be enjoyed, pending the great things which were to take place in the near future. Immediately behind the disciples were the great works which had occasioned such universal wonder and speculation concerning their Master; and they were in a position of comparative leisure and quietude duly to recall and meditate upon them. No better opportunity had hitherto presented itself for the crowning question of Jesus, "*Whom say ye that I am?*"

I. THE IDENTIFICATION WAS DISTINGUISHED FROM SEVERAL ALREADY CURRENT. So marvellous was the career of Jesus, that all ideas of explaining on ordinary grounds had to be abandoned. In the popular mind the only personages corresponding to Jesus, save John the Baptist, were those of ancient Jewish history, the heroic ages of the theocracy. All were agreed that in him there was a revival or reappearance of the religious spirit of the best days of Israel. 1. *The knowledge of these opinions rendered the judgment of the disciples highly conscious and deliberate, and therefore of great critical importance.* Each of them, as it came to their ears, would doubtlessly be considered and weighed. The popular guesses would be compared with the full and complete experience of Jesus and his work, which they alone possessed, and one by one rejected. But they would serve to awaken their critical attention and their spiritual discernment—constitute, in fact, a sort of ascending scale according to which to adjust their own thoughts. 2. *The certainty to which they had arrived, notwithstanding the variety of opinions of which they were aware, proves how overwhelming the evidence must have been upon which they based their conclusion.* There is no hesitation in Peter's answer. And as spokesman of the twelve he utters their unanimous conviction. How much previous examination and interchange of views does that imply?

II. HOW WAS THIS CONCLUSION ARRIVED AT? 1. *Not from unscientific guessing.* From their peculiar circumstances this was impossible. 2. *Not from information furnished by Jesus himself.* There is no trace of hinting or suggesting on the part of the Master. His withdrawal from that course of policy which might have enabled him to take advantage of popular influence was against the idea of his being the Messiah of the people's dreams. It was in spite of his mysterious behaviour, therefore, and in complete absence of any information furnished by himself, that they formed their opinion. 3. *It was by a twofold process, viz.:* (1) *Induction from their experience of his character and works.* For this they were peculiarly fitted; and the searching training of the Master led them gradually but surely to make it. And they were well versed in Scripture. (2) *Inspiration of God.* Elsewhere (Matt. xvi. 17) we read the declaration, "Flesh and blood hath not revealed it unto thee, but my Father which is in heaven." These two sources of information were not mutually exclusive, but mutually supplementary and confirmatory, as in every Christian mind to-day. Indeed, in a larger view of evidence the spiritual intuition—the most truly *moral* evidence of the conscience—is but an element of the general moral evidence upon which the induction is based. It is the conscience which is the ultimate judge of all spiritual questions the ordinary understanding cannot completely or satisfactorily settle.

III. THE SIGNIFICANCE OF ITS ATTAINMENT. 1. *It was but a recognition of certain correspondences between Jesus and the Messiah spoken of in Scripture.* There was certainty and intelligent perception, so far as their knowledge went. But the full conception of his personality and work was reserved for the future. They knew *that* it was he of whom the prophets spoke, but about himself in his deeper nature and the spirituality, etc., of his work—in short, of *what* he was—they were not fully aware. 2. *What they did arrive at altered their entire relation to him.* A new, vague authority attached henceforth to him, and the future was full of a keen expectancy and interest. It gave a new meaning to every word and action proceeding from him, and prepared them for the special training and teaching which they had to receive as his apostles; just as the principle attained by induction of many facts, when its light is turned back upon them interprets them, and we see them as we could not before.—M.

Vers. 29, 32, 33.—*Peter's self-contradiction.* I. WHEREIN IT CONSISTED. 1. *In identifying Jesus with the Messiah and yet deprecating his sufferings.* That Messiah should suffer was abundantly declared by the prophets. His death was the greatest testimony he could give to the righteousness of God. A comfortable, earthly, prosperous king could never occupy the spiritual position of the Christ; moral influence, the essential feature of the latter's reign, would be entirely wanting. To the thorough student of prophecy and contemporary life, Messiahship "connoted" suffering, not as an accidental but necessary qualification. 2. *In identifying Jesus with the Messiah and yet assuming such an attitude and tone towards him.* The utmost reverence and submission were not only due to his Lord, but would have been voluntarily rendered had he understood what was meant by his own declaration. In such a case he would never have presumed to dictate or chide.

II. TO WHAT IT WAS DUE. 1. *Insufficient realization of what he knew.* He had divined the true dignity of his Master, but what it involved was not yet felt. The doctrine is often correct when the sense of obligation it ought to produce is not awakened. A great spiritual truth may be perceived and adopted long ere its relations to practical life are recognized ; just as a principle in mechanics or a law of nature. Deeper spiritual experience and more sympathetic agreement with Christ in his desire to abolish sin were needed ere this could take place. 2. *Impulse and thoughtlessness.* This was his temperament. He was a man of impulse and affection, rather than of calm, spiritual intuition, or careful, painstaking reflection. It was due to his forward and impulsive temperament that he generally spoke for the others, and was so confident respecting himself in the future. Christianity owes much to such spirits, but they have to be kept in check by more sober thinkers, and disciplined by the lessons of providence. 3. *Worldly conceptions of the kingdom of God.* Had he entertained purer and more spiritual hopes respecting his Master's work, the mischief of his impulsiveness might have been minimized, although it would still have been a source of danger. But with such habitual materialism of aim and desire (common to him with the others) he was constantly committing mistakes, and ready to compromise the cause of Christ. "This world has many Peters, who wish to be wiser than Christ, and to prescribe to him what it is needful to do" (Hofmeister). We ought not to be too severe with Peter whilst we ourselves lean so much for the guidance of the Church to merely human wisdom, and set our own affections for particular persons, or for ourselves, above the well-being of the race; and estimate that well-being not from a spiritual but from a material standpoint.—M.

Vers. 31—33.—*The Christ foretelling his own career.* I. How UNIQUE AND MARVELLOUS THE PREDICTION ! It is a clear, consistent, even symmetrical scheme; as exquisitely balanced and progressively developed as any tragedy of Æschylus or Euripides. A person who could ideally mark out such a future for himself could not have been mere man. The gospel challenges investigation because of the originality and Divine moral elevation of its conception. And by such statements as this it proves how closely the Old and New Testaments are interwoven, and sympathetically and ideally correspondent.

II. IT DEMONSTRATED THAT HIS SUFFERING AND DEATH MUST HAVE BEEN IN THE HIGHEST SENSE VOLUNTARY. He was still at a point where the future was in great degree within his own power. That he clearly knew what lay before him in the event of his continuing steadfast proved that his will was absolutely, divinely free. There were several alternatives within easy reach: these, comprehensively, he put from him in spurning Peter's interference. It is no fate that is blindly shaping out the destiny of a powerless victim; the necessity is a moral and spiritual one, consequent upon motives and aim deliberately preferred.

III. ONLY THE HIGHEST MORAL END COULD JUSTIFY SUCH CONDUCT. To suppose that earthly aims or selfish objects could have determined such a career is a palpable absurdity. Christ is, therefore, through all time, the type of noble self-sacrifice. But it is only spiritual motives and principles that can so inspire. And conscience justifies the sacrifice upon such grounds alone. Whilst we may be incapable of it ourselves, we feel, nevertheless, that it is not madness, but the fulfilment of the great end of our being, and its highest blessedness. If it be but fairly and fully regarded, it furnishes its own justification, and constitutes a judgment bar before which all so-called religious acts and schemes must stand or fall.

IV. BY MAKING THIS ANNOUNCEMENT CHRIST: 1. *Tested the loyalty of his disciples.* 2. *Vindicated and revealed his own pure, unalterable spiritual resolution.* 3. *Furnished them with a support for faith and enthusiastic sympathy.*—M.

Vers. 32, 33.—*Covert temptation.* This scene has, of course, certain features connected with it which cannot be imitated by ordinary persons, or by mere men. Christ exercised a Divine insight and authority. But there are certain *principles* illustrated. We see—

I. How IT PRESENTS ITSELF. 1. *Under the guise of friendship.* The love may be real in the individuals who are the instruments of temptation, but their knowledge is not sufficient, or their moral character not so high as it should be. Many of the most terrible moral trials of life owe their power to this circumstance. 2. *With great assumption of reasonableness.* In Peter there was a domineering, "superior" tone. He spoke as one who knew the world, and the impracticableness of his Master's ideas. But even where this is absent there may be a latent contempt for religious aims, and an unconscious appeal to the utilitarian standards of conduct. With many persons the test of reasonableness in moral action is the immediate advantage of those immediately concerned, or the most directly pleasant course of procedure, or the attainment of some recognized worldly object.

II. How IT IS TO BE DETECTED. 1. *By the aid of the Divine Spirit.* There are necessarily many occasions for moral decision in which it would be impossible to assign reasons for the steps taken, because these are not clearly discerned ; yet there may be moral certainty. It is the Spirit of God that is to guide us in such cases. 2. *By comparing spiritual things with spiritual,* e.g. : (1) In moral questions we should distrust proposals which too readily fall in with our own desire for ease, or a pleasant life, or worldly advantage. It is not usual for great duties so to approve themselves. (2) Suggestions are to be rejected which stand in the way of personal consecration, or interfere with moral duties and Divine impulses.

III. How IT IS TO BE OVERCOME. 1. *By distinguishing between the agent or instrument and the inspirer.* It was a painful thing for Christ to do, but he did not shrink from denouncing the spirit to which the suggestion was due, and the evil one who had used Peter as his tool. This detection, whether it be declared or not, is a great part of the victory. 2. *With promptitude and decision.* Christ turned his back upon the tempter. There must be no dallying or temporizing. Upon every moment that follows discovery of evil an eternity hangs. 3. *By casting one's self upon the Spirit of God.* In prayer : "Deliver us from the evil one." In abiding union and voluntary submission : "Not my will, but thine, be done." "Minding" the things of God, and having the whole attention and affection absorbed by them.—M.

Ver. 34—ch. ix. 1.—*The Master's summons to his disciples.* Like a commander addressing his soldiers. Full of clear vision and resolve.

I. THE AIM. (Ver. 38, ch. ix. 1.) It is the overcoming of spiritual error and Satanic influence, and the establishment of the kingdom of God.

II. THE CONDITIONS OF ITS ATTAINMENT. (Ver. 34.) These are open to all. The multitude is addressed equally with the disciples. There appears to have been a disposition in many to join themselves to his fortunes. He therefore lays down the terms of his service, so that none may enter it without knowledge of its nature. 1. *Self-denial.* 2. *Cross-bearing.* Not quite identical with the preceding, although involving it. " A *Christian,*" says Luther, "is a *Crucian* " (Morison). " *His* cross," each having some personal and peculiar grief, sorrow, death, through which he has to pass. This cross he is to take up voluntarily, and to carry, long ere it shall have to bear him. 3. *Obedience and imitation.* There can be no self-assertion or private end to be sought by individual believers. "The footsteps of Jesus." It is a cross even as the Master has to be crucified. The same spirit and plan of moral life must be shown. He is our law and our example.

II. INCENTIVES. (Ver. 35—ch. ix. 1.) 1. *Christ's example and inspiration.* He says not "Go," but "Come." He goes before, and shows the way. 2. *The endeavour to save the lower " self " will expose to certain destruction the higher " self ; " and the sacrifice of the lower " self " and its earthly conditions of satisfaction will be the salvation of the higher " self."* " Life," or " soul," is used here ambiguously. A moral truism ; a paradox to the worldly mind. "It is in self-denial that we first gain our true selves, recovering our personality again " (Lange). 3. *The value of this higher life cannot be computed.* All objective property is useless without that which is the subjective condition of its possession. Righteousness is that which makes individuality and the spiritual nature precious, and imparts the highest value to existence. Every man has to weigh the " world " against his " soul." 4. *Recognition of Christ on earth is the condition of his recognition of us hereafter.* It is not merely that we are " not to be ashamed ; " we are to " glory " in him. The recognitions, the " well done " of Heaven, the highest reward. Even here the great triumphs of truth confer honour upon those who have striven for them. 5. *The triumphs of the kingdom of God are not long deferred.* Some of Christ's hearers lived to see the overthrow of Jerusalem and the universal diffusion of the gospel. The spiritual vision is purified to discern the progress of truth in the world. Those victories which Christian morals and spirituality have already won within the experience of living Christians are an ample and abundant reward.—M.

Ver. 38.—*Ashamed of Jesus and his words.* This warning is evidently called forth by the unholy presumption of Peter, and the wavering of the disciples divined by the penetrating spirit of Christ. He rebukes the spirit of false shame as a heinous offence against himself and his cause.

1. JESUS AND HIS WORDS AN OCCASION OF FALSE SHAME. The penalty attaching to unreal or unjustifiable feelings is that, sooner or later, they commit their subject to some egregious folly or inexcusable sin. This is a result of natural law. 1. *Why should men be ashamed of Jesus?* That they can ever be justified in such shame is, of course, impossible. But there are reasons that, human nature being what it is, explain the phenomenon. (1) Their opposition to the spirit and conduct of the world. Fashion, custom, perverted and corrupted religion, the general principles upon which worldly men conduct their affairs, are alike condemned by the gospel. The wisdom, authority, and influence of the world are therefore arrayed against its teachings. The methods of the Divine life are in contradiction to those of the ordinary life of men. It involves humiliation and self-sacrifice. Christ, as the embodiment and central principle of this, is therefore "rejected and despised." (2) The objects and aims of Christ's teaching seemed so remote, and so unsupported by the external evidences to which men are wont to appeal. What sign was there of a coming "kingdom," other than those with which they were already familiar? Never had wickedness appeared so secure and influential, or religion at such a discount. The same causes are at work in all ages; and to-day there are many evidences of the same spirit. 2. *How does this shame manifest itself?* In shrinking from open discipleship. Bringing an eclectic spirit to the teachings of the gospel. Making compromises with fashion, selfish principles, or demoralizing amusements and pursuits, etc. 3. *What renders such conduct peculiarly heinous?* The weakness of the cause of Christ, and the power and reputation of its enemies. Sin had never so lifted itself up against God. It was "a wicked and adulterous generation," and was to crown its apostasy by crucifying the Son of man. At such a critical time every individual had an influence that might affect the issue of the conflict, and gratitude and honour urged him to exercise it. Unbelief was at the root of the shame which many felt.

II. JESUS AND HIS WORDS JUDGING FALSE SHAME. 1. *By the fulfilments of prediction.* The destruction of Jerusalem, the sign of the inauguration of the kingdom of God, was at hand. Some of those addressed were to live to see it. And as in major historic events, so in minor ones. Every success attending Christian effort, every verification of Christian doctrine in experience, is a judgment of the unbelief which is ashamed of the gospel. 2. *By exclusion from the blessedness and glory of Christ's advent.* Just when such men have begun to see how unfounded their suspicions and doubts, and how real are the promises of Christ, they are unable to partake of them. They have no fellowships with the redeemed and glorified, are out of place and covered with confusion because of their guilt and folly. A personal element adds poignancy to their shame; they are openly repudiated by him whom all adore and glorify. A simple but terrible and inevitable retaliation, due not to vengeance, but to spiritual laws. The exposure will be overwhelming and absolute.—M.

Ver. 8.—*Christ's beneficence and economy.* I. CHRIST'S BENEFICENCE. 1. *It embraces all human wants.* He came to save from sin, but he also delivered men from its manifold effects. The dead were raised, the sick were cured, the hungry were fed. Herein signs were shown of the coming of that heavenly state in which the redeemed hunger no more, and wherein there shall be no more pain. The Church should seek to deal with human necessities as broadly as her Lord did — overlooking neither the temporal nor the spiritual. 2. *It was not exercised as we should have expected.* John the Baptist, "the friend of the Bridegroom," was not delivered from death, yet this crowd of men and women, who were so undeserving, were relieved from the pangs of hunger. He is kind to the unthankful and to the unworthy. 3. *It was free from ostentation and from pride.* A plainer, cheaper meal could scarcely have been given than this, of barley loaves and fish. The absence of luxury on this and on other occasions during our Lord's ministry is a rebuke to our self-indulgence. "Feed me with food convenient for me." As ostentation was avoided, so also was *pride.* Our Lord did not look down with contempt upon the pitifully small provision offered by the disciples—"seven loaves" and "a few small fishes." He did not put these aside and create afresh, as he might have done; but although he needed not to take the loaves, he did take them. Use to the utmost what God has already given you. Do the best you can with what you have. As you use any gift, it will increase as the loaves did which the disciples carried to the multitude. 4. *It was accompanied by devout acknowledgment of God.* Jesus "gave thanks" over this labourer's dinner. God's presence will make the eating of common loaves a sacrament to us. Let us thankfully receive his gifts, and in his name distribute them, that our beneficence may be a humble copy of our Lord's.

II. CHRIST'S ECONOMY. On this occasion, as on that near Bethsaida, the evangelists tell us that the apostles gathered up the remnants of the feast; and, judging from John vi. 12, we may be sure that on both occasions they were obeying their Lord's command. In God's gifts to man there is no waste, except where our ignorance and carelessness misuse them. The leaves of a tree are not mere ornaments, as was once imagined, but are means of nourishment; and when they fall and are driven by the wind into secret resting-places, they still enrich the soil. Not a drop of rain is wasted, fall where it may. Every year we are learning more and more that what was squandered as refuse from factories and sewers was meant by God for use. Science is following in the footsteps of these disciples of Christ. 1. *Economy is needed in regard to the use of our daily food.* This wealthy nation is peculiarly wasteful. Servants use extravagantly anything of which there seems plenty. Artisans are prodigal in expenditure when wages are good. The middle classes and the upper classes are increasingly luxurious. All this was rebuked when Jesus taught his disciples that, although he could multiply food so easily, they were humbly and patiently to take up the fragments. 2. *Economy is called for in the use of all God's gifts. Physical strength* we should husband, and not squander. In seeking wealth or honour, many a man lives to repent his disobedience to this law. The whole life is God's. We have no right to force into a few years what he meant to occupy its whole length, but are called upon to work thoughtfully and lawfully. There is a great waste of *mental strength* also going on amongst us. Some books and papers occupy the mind only to debase it. In education we ought to seek for ourselves and others well-trained and well-developed powers, so that nothing may be wanting to our complete manhood when we lay ourselves as living sacrifices on God's altar. *Spiritual sensibility,* also, is wasted when it evaporates in temporary excitement. The engines which make most noise are those which are doing nothing. When steam is up it must be used. So when feeling is aroused it must be turned into activity. 3. *Economy is the more requisite when gifts are diminishing.* At the end of an abundant feast little was left, yet even about it the Lord Jesus was concerned. Gather up what is left *of former religious teaching,* which is too often lost; *of good resolutions,* which have been broken again and again; *of old beliefs,* which have been shattered, and must be rearranged; *of good reputation,* although so little is left; *of opportunities for Christian service,* which may appear slight and casual, but fairly used will multiply and grow.—A. R.

Vers. 22—25.—*The blind man of Bethsaida.* The variety of method adopted by our Lord in his acts of healing finds a striking illustration in the contrast presented between the cure of this blind man and that of Bartimæus. The sight of the latter was instantaneously and perfectly restored, but it was otherwise with the former. If, as we believe, Christ's miracles were symbols of spiritual experiences, we must expect variety in these also; and we see them in the contrast existing between the sudden transformation of a profligate, and the religious life of one who from a child has known the Scriptures, and loved the things that are excellent. For the further elucidation of such truth, consider—

I. THE SUBJECT OF THIS MIRACULOUS CURE. 1. *He was a blind man.* Although light blazed around him, to him it was as darkness, and objects which appeared to others real and near were unperceived by him. Hence we often, and properly, speak of "moral blindness" or "spiritual blindness," by which we mean, that he who suffers that privation is incapable of discerning the moral or spiritual truths which are obvious to others. And the faculty which he lacks is something distinct from, although not independent of, mental perception. In other words, a man must have brains to understand spiritual truth; but he needs something more—a faculty of soul, to which St. Paul alludes when he says, "Spiritual things are spiritually discerned;" "The god of this world hath blinded the eyes of them that believe not." 2. *He was brought by his friends to the Lord.* Unlike him, they could see. They knew better than he did what he lost by his blindness. They could find their way to the place where Jesus was, and see his face. Another blind man could not have led him thither. It becomes parents, teachers, and friends, who are rejoicing in God's light, to bring others by pleading and by prayer to Jesus' feet. 3. *He was willing to confide in the unseen Saviour.* When Jesus took him by the hand, he did not withdraw it. In this wonderful Stranger, of whom he had heard so much, he had implicit confidence. His touch meant a blessing. How often, by our wilfulness and unbelief, we lose what by trustful waiting we might receive!

II. THE METHOD OF THIS MIRACULOUS CURE. 1. *Jesus led him apart.* He wished to have him alone. Separation, secrecy, solitude, often precede the reception of blessing from Christ. He takes us away from the multitude by illness, in worship, etc. 2. *Jesus gave him glimmerings of light* (see ver. 24). He saw slightly and indistinctly. His companions, who had been left at a little distance, appeared to him to be moving, but seemed vague, large, formless, like trees waving in the wind. Perhaps this cure was gradually wrought because the man's faith was weak, and the slight change already experienced would strengthen his expectation, and make him ready for a fuller blessing. It is at least a beautiful type of the gradual illumination of the soul with light. Lydia was an example of this. 3. *Jesus by repeated touch gave him perfect sight* (ver. 25). He leaves nothing incomplete. He is "the Author and the Finisher of faith." The imperfect vision of earth will be followed by the perfect vision of heaven.—A. R.

Vers. 34—38.—*The worldling and the Christian : a contrast.* Our Lord had just foretold his own sufferings, and now he goes on to speak of his requirement—that his disciples should be willing to follow him in the way of the cross. Soon they would be involved in persecution and trials, which they would be unprepared to meet unless they had wholly surrendered themselves to him. He never hid from his disciples what it would cost them to follow him. Again and again, when there were signs of defection on the part of the people, he gave the twelve an opportunity of leaving him if they wished to do so (John vi. 67). Only whole-hearted service is acceptable to our Lord. It seems strange that his definite announcements of his sufferings, death, and resurrection should have been so imperfectly understood by his disciples. This can only be accounted for by the fact that they often took figurative language literally (Matt. xvi. 1; John iv. 33; xi. 12), and literal language figuratively (Matt. xv. 15—17; John vi. 70). In this passage some of the distinguishing points between a worldling and a Christian are suggested, and by them we may test ourselves.

I. THE ONE FOLLOWS THE WORLD, THE OTHER FOLLOWS CHRIST. Our Lord speaks here of following him, *i.e.* doing what he did, going where he went, etc. In any doubtful sphere let us fairly and frankly ask ourselves—Would the Lord be here? He did not confine himself to the synagogue or to the temple, but dwelt in the home at Nazareth, worked at the carpenter's bench, sat at the wedding feast, went out on the lake with the fishermen, etc. In our innocent enjoyments and ordinary work we may still be following him. Suggest occasions on which there is a distinct choice between the worldly and the Christ-like.

II. THE ONE INDULGES HIMSELF, THE OTHER DENIES HIMSELF. A complete surrender of will is called for if we would truly serve Christ. Whenever his will points in one way and our inclination points in another, we must deny ourselves. This is an indispensable condition of following. The true denier of self is the true confessor of Christ. Wishes, tastes, and appetites must be restrained and (where obedience to the Lord requires it) denied by a Christian.

III. The one cares for what is outward, the other for what is inward. Many desire to "gain the world," and in the attempt use selfish and sinful means, such as the Lord spurned when they were offered to him (Matt. iv. 9). But what seems to us to be "gain" we must learn to "count loss for Christ" (Phil. iii. 7, 8). His disciples cannot be content with the outward show of happiness. Character to them is far more important than circumstances. If the world be gained, nothing is gained; if the soul be lost, everything is lost.

IV. The one seeks ease, the other risks the loss of it. We want a test of the different courses which are sometimes presented for our choice. Speaking broadly, two are possible to us, and our use of the one as of the other proclaims what manner of men we are. The worldling asks, "Which is the pleasantest and easiest thing to do?" the Christian asks, "Which is the right thing?" and will choose that, whatever its issues.

V. The one finds death a loss, the other a gain. Our life reaches far beyond things seen. Death is the grave of earthly pleasures, but it is the gateway of heavenly joys.

VI. The one will be ashamed, and the other exalted, in the day of judgment. Christ speaks here of his coming again, "in the glory of his Father," as his Representative in judgment and as the Founder of a new heaven and earth, in which righteousness will dwell. Around him will be "the holy angels"—those servants of God who rejoice over the penitent (Luke xv. 10), who minister to the saints (Heb. i. 14), and who will finally execute the judgments of the Lord (Matt. xiii. 41). Then he who knows us altogether will separate us, according to his unerring judgment of our characters. All will awake, "some to everlasting life, and some to shame and everlasting contempt." (See also ver. 38.)—A. R.

Vers. 1—21.—*A sign from heaven.* "There was again a great multitude, and they had nothing to eat." Again Jesus had "compassion." Again are the disciples perplexed. "Whence shall one be able to fill these men with bread here in a desert place?" Speedily, of "seven loaves" and "a few small fishes" "about four thousand men, beside women and children, did eat and were filled," and "broken pieces remained over" to the extent of "seven baskets." Jesus left the miracle to give its own teachings —the great work to sink down into their hearts, while that he sought relief and rest, entering into the boat and coming "into the borders of Magadan." Perversely, the Pharisees, now joined by the Sadducees, came tempting him, putting him to the proof, "seeking of him a sign from heaven." They knew not that he had already put them to the proof by the signs already wrought, which, had they had eyes to see, would have led them to believe. He had, without words, proved that the veil was on their hearts. Had they been children of truth, how soon would they have acknowledged the truth! But now, with words, he would carry home to their hearts a conviction of their blindness in presence of spiritual things. "A sign from heaven," would ye? Quick are ye to discern the signs in the reddened sky of the morning or evening. See ye no red "signs of the times"? Do the passing clouds of heaven foretoken storm or calm? and do not the passing incidents of earth in the political or the social sphere, or the sphere of the individual life? Look around. Was it ever so seen in Israel as it is now seen? Your fathers did eat manna in the desert—is it not so now? Are not the words of the prophets finding their exact fulfilment in these hours? Are not "signs" abundant in the healed ones and in the wonderful words? Would ye have "blood, and fire, and pillars of smoke"? Would ye have the sun "turned into darkness . . . the moon into blood"? Verily the sun shall be darkened; verily the sign of blood shall be in the heavens and upon you. Alas! having eyes they saw not, and having ears they heard not. Then "deeply" from the heart of compassion and sorrow a sigh arose mingling with his words of astonishment and inquiry, "Why doth this generation seek a sign?" followed by the stern condemnation, "There shall no sign" such as they desire "be given;" though God's own sign—"the sign"—will not be wanting, nor be unseen by the watchers. Why will men "seek a sign"? Why "cannot" men "discern the signs"—even those which are always the peculiar and appropriate "signs of the times"? The questions admit of one reply, for that age and this, and for every age. The answer is found—

I. In the prevalent spirit of unbelief. The strange closing of the eyes and shutting of the ears and hardening of the heart. And if the light abound the closed eye cannot see, and if the air be filled with angel-songs, or the voice of the Teacher lade the air with heavenly truth, the closed ear admits it not. And though the hand of the Lord be present, the hardened heart receives not its impress. It is unmoved, untouched.

II. But why do not men believe? Is it that they cannot or that they will not believe? Alas! both. Some cannot because they have not been solely or sufficiently attentive to the Word, from the hearing of which cometh faith, or for a time they labour under the soul-hindering perplexity which some unresolved sceptical difficulty has involved them in. But these, being seekers of the faith, "shall find." They must be patient; for with our partial views of things we cannot suddenly quadrate all our truth with every suggested opinion, or point out the fallacy of that opinion. But some will not believe. In a foolish, even stupid—yea, wicked—resistance of evidence, they shut out the force of conviction; while others are hindered, being "slow of heart to believe," and therefore "foolish men."

III. Moral conditions affect the power of faith. Jesus showed this when he said, "How can ye believe which receive glory one of another, and the glory that cometh from the only God ye seek not?" And the self-seeking and world-loving, the evil and the sensual, the disobedient, and all who have "refused to have God in their knowledge," must gain both an indisposition and an inaptitude of mind to receive God's testimony in that spirit of faith which implies faithfulness to the truth when known. These are the "wicked and adulterous" to whom "no" special "sign shall be given;" for, refusing the many signs that are around, they will not be "persuaded, if one rise from the dead." But to all one "sign" shall "be given"—"a sign which is spoken against," but which remains ever the one "sign" in heaven and in earth and in all "times," "the sign of Jonah the prophet."—G.

Vers. 14—21.—*Leaven.* After the great miracle of the feeding of the four thousand, Jesus "entered into a boat with his disciples, and came"—for rest, probably—"into the parts of Dalmanutha. And they forgot to take bread." Had not emphasis been laid on their forgetfulness, we might have supposed they had been led to think "one loaf" enough; for if the Master could feed four thousand with seven loaves, surely he could feed twelve men with one! These men were yet but children in understanding, and Jesus, their watchful Guardian, therefore warns them against the spirit of the men who had recently made the strange demand from him for signs—"the leaven of the Pharisees and the leaven of Herod," "the leaven of the Pharisees and of the Sadducees." Strangely enough, they think the reference is to "leaven of bread," which must find an explanation in the engrossment of their minds by the astounding miracle they had witnessed. And yet they see not the thing signified. Jesus, by a brief teaching on the two bread-miracles, draws them away from the "leaven of bread" to "the teaching of the Pharisees and Sadducees." Is this a lesson for all time? Was the leaven of Herod wholly put out of the house with his name? Do Sadduceeism and Pharisaism still linger amongst men; and are the disciples of Jesus still exposed to their corrupting influence? It is but too true that these questions must be answered by one affirmative. Herod is described as "a frivolous, voluptuous, unprincipled man." His name symbolizes a morally vile life. Readers of the Gospels know well what the word "Pharisee" stands for—"the leaven of the Pharisees, which is hypocrisy." The Sadducees, though less prominent, are not wholly unknown. Their rejection of great truths on no higher authority than their own opinion points at once to the dangerous tampering with revealed truths. These two rivals as schools were one in the evilness of their teaching so aptly alliterated as "unbelieving hypocrisy and hypocritical unbelief." They stood in united opposition to the Lord's Christ. Thus is the Church for all ages warned against evils that threaten the entire strength and the very existence of the life of the Spirit. Those evils are—

I. HEATHENISH SELF-INDULGENCE. Faith grows not in a heart given over to self-indulgence. "The Author and Perfecter of our faith" has made demand, in unmistakable terms, of all who would be his disciples: "Let him deny himself, and take up his cross, and follow me." Evil self-indulgence saps the strength of all faith. The highest evidence of the truth and authority of Christ's teaching is given to the obedient. "If any man willeth to do his will, he shall know of the teaching, whether it be of

God, or whether I speak from myself." Evilness of life puts men out of harmony with the truth; and as all disobedience is a denial of authority, it disposes men to desire that its authority may be questioned : while the continuous acknowledgment of the authority of the truth makes disobedience the more guilty. These "hold down the truth in unrighteousness." This spirit will support the second evil, namely—

II. SADDUCEAN SCEPTICISM. If scepticism were a true spirit of inquiry, or even that sensibility of faith that longs to know, and is eager to defend itself from deceit, it were a healthy guard against childish credulity. But if it become a proud self-sufficiency, a resolute resistance and despisal of truths that are apprehended only by faith —truths which by their very nature do not admit of scientific demonstration, or of truths that do not harmonize with preconceived notions—it then stands in the way of all holy and healthy influence from the highest truths that could reach the heart. It is the opposite of the hearing ear, of the childlike teachableness. There is a faith which is wrought in the heart by the truth's own testimony—the belief that "cometh of hearing," the hearing that is hearkening. But yet another danger lies in the path of the followers of Christ. It is—

III. HYPOCRITICAL PRETENTIOUSNESS. Here the truth is acknowledged, but neither the heart nor the life is true to it. It is unfaithfulness, deceit, hypocrisy. It is the vice against which the severest words that escaped the lips of Christ were directed. A "double-minded man is unstable," but a double-faced man is utterly unworthy. He is open to all seductions; he may become the tool of all evil, and all the time hiding the filthiness of his evil heart in a show of righteousness whose deceitfulness reduces it to the lowest grade of evil. Of this leaven all disciples from the earliest hour have been in danger. Even a little may be "hid" in the heart "till all is leavened." To how many of the disciples may it be said to-day, "Do ye not understand?"!—G.

Vers. 22—26.—*The gradual healing of the blind man.* In each of the many cases of healing there were, doubtless, peculiarities of incident of great interest to the healed, if not to us. But of only a few have we the details. Perhaps where we have them they have their more important relation to us than to the subjects of the healing themselves. In this case, as in others, the compassion of friends is called into play. "They bring to him a blind man, and beseech him to touch him." Not without service to us all is this little feature preserved. How may we who have proved his power to heal learn here the duty, the propriety, the encouragement to bring to Jesus, by kindly, leading hands, those who see not their way to him. Gently Jesus took the hand of the blind man in his, and led him away from the crowd, "out of the village"— itself a judgment to this Bethsaida. But oh, how beauteous a picture—Jesus leading the blind ! This is itself a homily. Singular to us appear the actions of Christ, both here and elsewhere. But why did he "spit on his eyes"? That he should work gradually and through the medium of outward signs was very becoming, if only to identify himself with the miracle. But who shall tell the thoughts they stirred in the hearts of the healed, for every one of whom Jesus cared ! There was no need of spittle even to loosen the gummed eyelids, though such loosening may have been necessary, and needed no wasting of power by the doing it miraculously. Nor was there any absolute need of the touch of the hand; no, nor even at any time of the word. His will was enough. But he who chose to use his word or his touch or his breath here identifies himself with the miracle by the spittle. The progressive character of the work stands in contrast to the somewhat hasty "touch him." As there is no mention of faith (so generally commended where found) on the part of the blind man, it may have been but small, if there were any. Perhaps this may afford some reason why the healing was not instantaneous. It may have responded to the growing faith of the recipient—a seeing far more important even than beholding men and trees. Would no virtue come from the touch of that leading hand? Were no words spoken to awaken faith? Was there a Lydian spirit in the man "whose" eyes "the Lord" so gently "opened"? We may not know. But to us the miracle is a type of many healings in our suffering, blind world, where faith and hope have need to be roused into activity by some measure of healing—some sign. And it may be that here the full trust of that half-hoping heart was gained by the very lingering of the light on the threshold of those half-opened eyes.

> " For thou wouldst have us linger still
> Upon the verge of good or ill,
> That on thy guiding hand unseen
> Our undivided hearts may lean."

Certainly we may learn, in the midst of the variety of the Lord's ways of working:
1. That it may please him to use many means to accomplish that which by a word, a
touch, a look—or without—he could instantly effect. 2. That it may equally please him
to detain hope till it is made strong by tried faith—the faith that is as severely tried
by time as by fire. 3. That it may as truly please him to draw out the heart's love by
its sense of dependence upon him. So is it by all those slow but beautiful processes of
nature, which are the Lord's hands for ministering to us bread and wine. 4. And most
assuredly may we learn not to despise the Lord's work while it is in process. For what
seems to us to be but imperfectness of work or tardiness of method, may be his kind
and gentle and instructive way of leading us to see things in their perfectness—even
" all things clearly."—G.

Vers. 27—30.—*The confession of Peter.* The brief record of St. Mark leads us to
turn to the fuller statements of St. Matthew. Jesus tests the faith of his disciples
" as they were able" to bear it. First, " in the way he . . . asked, Who do men say
that I am ?" What is the general opinion ? Then, more closely, " But who say ye that
I am ?" It was a day of testing. There had been a general blindness. Immediately
before he had occasion to say, "O ye of little faith, why reason ye among yourselves,
because ye have no bread ? Do ye not yet perceive?" But there was amongst them
one discerning spirit; and he who "knew all men" saw the elevation of character, the
quick perception, the sympathetic, sensitive soul. "Who say ye?" "Simon"—of
whom it had been early said, " Thou shalt be called Cephas (which is by interpretation,
Peter)," which is by interpretation, " Rock," or " Stone "—" Simon Peter answered and
said, Thou art the Christ, the Son of the living God." It is enough. Here is one
who, seeing, can see the true character of the Sent of God; not a mere teacher, or
rabbi, but the Hope of Israel—the long looked-for Christ, "the Son of the Blessed."
The wise Master-builder stood ready to lay the firm foundation-stones of his enduring
Church—" a spiritual house," built up of " living stones;" and in this first confessor,
the first to acknowledge his exalted person and high office, in this man who is a rock,
Jesus discerns the suitable stone to lay first on the prepared earth. " Thou," of whom
it was once said, " Thou shalt be," now " art, Peter: and upon this rock I will build
my Church." Not upon Peter's mere confession; not upon Peter apart from his
confession; nor, indeed, upon Peter alone. For the Church of Jesus is not a column,
a pillar, of stones. But of those " twelve foundations," of what afterwards was seen
by one of them to be a city, and on which are the " twelve names of the twelve
apostles of the Lamb," this was the first to be laid. Or of that " household of God,"
which is " built upon the foundation of the apostles and prophets, Christ Jesus himself
being the chief Corner-stone," this stone gained the honourable position of being laid
immediately next to the corner. The house is spiritual, the stones are spiritual, the
total idea is spiritual—every stone is a " living stone." Here is no dead body of
rubbish; but spiritually discerning men, who, like Peter, can discern and confess the
Lord's Christ. There need be no hesitation in acknowledging the high position
assigned to Peter—the prince, the very primate of the apostles—by his Lord and ours.
An immeasurable gulf lies between this and the assumption of the exclusive authority
of Peter by Rome. Yea, though the improbability of Peter's ever having visited Rome
were exchanged for a certainty that he both visited the city and founded its Church,
yet would that claim be baseless. Nor does the putting into his hands " the keys of
the kingdom of heaven," with which, by God's good grace, he opened the gates of the
kingdom to Jews and Gentiles, which work, done on earth, was truly confirmed in
heaven, give Rome the slightest warrant for her assumption.

I. The first great lesson for every Peter obviously is—TO SEEK A PENETRATIVE
DISCERNMENT OF JESUS AS THE CHRIST, THE SON OF THE LIVING GOD. The beholding
Jesus, the Son of Mary, as the common eye may, is a primary step. A life so pure, so
beneficent, so exalted, justly claims the attention of all. It stands pre-eminently above
all. It is out of the common category. But this is not the perfect view. There is

more hidden in the word "Christ;" and this demands a fuller insight. Some, like Nicodemus, acknowledge him to be "a Teacher come from God." But in their view he is only one of many; with whom Homer, and Shakespeare, and Dante, and a thousand others rank as sent of God, and filled with the spirit of wisdom and understanding and all knowledge, like a Bezaleel of old, to work in all manner of work for the building up of an outer temple of God. But he stands alone in Peter's judgment, and in that of all who are "blessed" like Peter, in that the truth is revealed to them not by "flesh and blood," but by the "Father which is in heaven." But even this falls short of the final term: "Thou art . . . the Son of the living God." "God of God, . . . very God of very God, begotten, not made, being of one substance with the Father;" he "being the Effulgence of his glory, and the very Image of his substance." Yet let every discerning one acknowledge, "no one knoweth the Son save the Father."

II. A second lesson is for every one who seeth the Son as he is revealed of the Father, TO CONFESS HIM IN PRESENCE OF THE WORLD'S ERROR, SELF-SEEKING, CONFUSION, AND SIN. This each, who having seen Jesus has seen the Father in him, is called to do. And thus shall the kingdom of heaven be opened more and more. Thus shall the great Church be extended, whose inviolable security is pledged to every one who, in the spirit of Peter, can hear and receive the assuring words, "The gates of Hades shall not prevail against it."—G.

Ver. 31—ch. ix. 1.—*Discipleship*. Having elicited Peter's noble confession, Jesus puts the disciples to further proof by declaring that "the Son of man"—his own lowly title, contrasting so strangely with Peter's word—must "suffer," "and be rejected," "and be killed," "and after three days rise again." And this was said in no enigmatical or hidden way, but "openly." Whereupon the weaker side of Peter's character obtruded itself: he "took him and began to rebuke him." The Messianic hopes which had been expressed by the confession, and confirmed by the Lord's testimony to that confession, were contradicted, if not dashed to the ground, by the suggestion of a suffering and conquered Christ. "This shall never be unto thee." Now does Peter need correction. The strong word of which shows how good and bad may mingle in our present imperfectness. The great proto-confessor denies his Lord by denying the true spirit to Christ, and by opposing his earthly to the heavenly method of conquest—"the things of men" to "the things of God." In the yet imperfect heart, though, indeed, taught of God, this would be a prevailing of the "gates of Hades." Therefore we must say, "Be it far from thee, Lord." In presence of the disciples, for their instruction, as for Peter's correction, the Lord utters his displeasure in the strongest terms—terms quite sufficient to prevent any boasting on account of the previous honourable distinction. "Get thee behind me, Satan." So near the words spoken "to the evil one," "Get thee hence, Satan." One only word is needed to add to this by way of explication, "Thou art a stumbling-block to me;" and another word by way of application, "For thou mindest not the things of God, but the things of men." Is it so, then, that "the things of men" stand in direct contradiction to "the things of God"? That which is purely "of men" do; and all that is not "of God" is of the adversary, "Satan," and must be silenced. That silencing is effected by words which have ever since appeared as in letters of fire over the gate of entrance to discipleship. And "the multitude" is "called" together to hear them. "If any man would come after me, let him deny himself, and take up his cross, and follow me." How simple, yet how comprehensive! how easy, and yet how difficult, is this tri-unity of duty! In its simplest presentation it is: 1. *A thorough, complete, continuous, self-denial.* 2. *A patient endurance.* 3. *A diligent obedience.* "With men this is impossible, but not with God; for all things are possible with God."

I. It was not only during the early struggles of the Church of Christ, or merely in its conflict with the anti-Christian world, that the disciple must needs "deny himself." It is the groundwork of all discipleship, and finds its necessity in the natural revulsion from the duties, the restraints, and the discipline of the gospel. That it should be more needful to urge the necessity for a total self-abnegation in the midst of an unfriendly, antagonistic worldly power, is obvious. But a spirit of self-indulgence is wholly removed from the idea of the disciple of Jesus. The habitual refusal to hearken to the appeals of the sinful self when those appeals contradict the voice of conscience, the inward echo of Christ's outward voice, is a rule allowing of no relaxation, even under the most favourable religious influences. The true idea of the disciple suggests the absolute, unconditional self-surrender—the whole life laid at the feet of the Master.

II. The subsequent words point to a buying of the life at the expense of the life. A paradox designed to awaken thought, and that finds its solution in the dual character of life. The outward and visible, the inward and spiritual; the life temporal, and the life eternal. In Jesus' view a man might suffer, be rejected of men, be killed, and yet truly "save his life" and "find it;" while, on the other hand, a man might save his life from the toils, the sacrifices, the self-inflictions and self-denials which discipleship would require, from the cruelties of men, from the death which human hands could inflict, and yet "lose his life"—lose life in the truest, highest, best, and therefore only real sense. Jesus saw that, so far from losing all, a man might gain all—all the world could give him—the "whole world" itself; yet all this might be at the forfeiture of the life. And if he forfeit his life, "what shall a man give in exchange for" it again? Once forfeited, it is forfeited for ever. There is no possibility of returning to regain it. Well were it, therefore, for his disciples to carry a cross daily, a symbol of dying to self, to sin, and the world, and in the patient endurance of that self-inflicted death to find the true life—the life in Christ, the life in the region of righteousness, and the pledge of a being "raised up" to life everlasting. Before the words were formulated, the disciples of Jesus attained the high estate, "I have been crucified with Christ; yet I live; and yet no longer I, but Christ liveth in me: and," with a reaching far and forward, "that life which I now live in the flesh, I live in faith."

III. It was in this spirit of unflagging obedience—even to a hard, self-restraining, self-denying, and self-crucifying rule—that the disciple was, with his far-reaching and fore-reaching vision, to "live in faith," anticipating the time when "the Son of man shall come in the glory of his Father with his angels, and render unto every man according to his deeds." After these hard sayings with which Jesus had shaken the hearts of the disciples, and proclaimed to the "great multitude" the severity of his rule, he comfortingly assures them of the nearness of his kingdom, by declaring "some of them" should "in no wise taste of death" till they had seen it "come with power."—G.

Vers. 1—10.—*Compassion for the many.* I. CHRIST'S COMPASSION FOR THE MANY CONTRASTED WITH THE NARROW HEARTS OF THE DISCIPLES. 1. Narrow hearts often are caused by narrow means. Alas! grinding poverty makes even naturally kind hearts indifferent to others' sufferings. Where there is "little to earn and many to keep," this will be so. There are circumstances in which the whole kindly current of the man's being is frozen, and he becomes utterly egotistic. 2. The Divine heart is of boundless compassion. All those ancient pictures of God as unwearied and unworn after all his creative activity, may be used of his redemptive activity. There is no exhausting the Divine intelligence, no draining the resources of the Divine heart.

II. CHRIST'S ACTION ON THIS OCCASION A PARABLE OF THE CALL OF THE GENTILES. The present feeding of the multitude differs from the former; the numbers given are different. Again, the present work was done after a long journey in heathen lands. "The one miracle was chiefly, if not entirely, for Jews; the other chiefly, if not entirely, for Gentiles. The feeding of the five thousand was an exceptional miracle, which Jesus had refused to repeat on behalf of Jews. It was therefore quite natural that the apostles should not at once receive the intimation of Jesus respecting what he was willing to do for the multitude. They spoke only of their own inability to supply the wants of the people; but they did not forget what he had done a few weeks before. There were only a few miraculous cures for the Gentiles, while those for the Jews were innumerable; and it might therefore be doubted if Jesus would now do for Gentiles what he had only once done for Jews" (J. H. Godwin). The Divine compassion and love exceed our noblest and largest thoughts, and are extended alike to all peoples.—J.

Vers. 11—21.—*Craving for signs.* I. WHENCE THE CRAVING SPRINGS. "The Jews seek after a sign." It is the spirit we nowadays term "sensationalism." It is a natural desire for a certain pleasure of the mind. Fixed ideas, a sameness of mental representations, wearies and saddens the mind. Hence the craving for amusement, which gives change to the perpetual march past of the same old thoughts. The feeling is natural enough. The Jews, who had no science in our sense, and did not live in an interesting age like ours, wanted signs and wonders to amuse. We can understand the feeling, and allow it to be natural, but at the same time not religious.

II. CHRIST REFUSES TO FOSTER SENSATIONALISM. 1. *The form of denial and refusal is very strong and emphatic indeed.* (Ver. 12.) Signs will be given to those who are ready to profit by them, not to gratify idle curiosity. How severely does Christ discountenance "sensationalism" in connection with his religion! He will have as little noise, as little rumour, finger-pointing, gaping of vacant crowd, as possible. "The kingdom of God cometh not with observation." 2. *Besides, an express warning is given :* against "the leaven of the Pharisees and of Herod." This means much the same as the Pharisees and Sadducees, apparently. The political Herodians were many of them Sadducees. Again, the Pharisees and Sadducees had a certain common basis of teaching. Both were at once in opposition to Jesus and the aims of his kingdom. The Pharisees, strongly conservative of Judaism, would disparage Jesus and his works. The other party would object to any "kingdom of heaven," acknowledging only the Roman empire. The "leaven" means both the teaching and the spirit of it (cf. Matt. xvi. 12; Luke xii. 1).

III. THE UNSPIRITUAL MIND CONSTANTLY MISUNDERSTOOD HIM. The disciples stuck at the word "leaven"—leaven-loaves. "We forgot to bring provisions with us!" The error was double. They caught at the sound instead of the sense. And they showed forgetfulness of the miracle they had so recently witnessed. "How is it that you do not consider?" Christ is just as much misunderstood to-day as he was then. We forget the spirit of Christianity; we blunder over its meaning. He says to us to-day, "How is it that you do not consider?" "Moral evidence is most profitable and proper for religious truth. Lower proof is desired when higher is disregarded and despised. Forgetfulness of the past occasions needless anxiety for the future" (J. H. Godwin).—J.

Vers. 22—26.—*The blind man.* I. "THE KNOWLEDGE OF CHRIST AWAKENS FAITH IN THOSE WHO ARE BROUGHT TO HIM BY THE FAITH OF OTHERS."
II. "BENEFITS ARE RECEIVED ACCORDING TO THE MEASURE OF FAITH IN HIM" (J. H. Godwin).—J.

Vers. 27—30.—*Jesus the Messiah.* I. SOME MISTAKEN IDENTIFICATIONS OF JESUS. John Baptist; Elijah; a prophet; Jeremiah, according to Matthew. There was some truth here. They recognized the prophetic inspiration and power of Jesus. Truth in feeling, error in thought; Jesus was the greatest of the prophets, not reproducing his predecessors, but going beyond them. God hath spoken by his Son (Heb. i.).
II. A TRUE IDENTIFICATION. Peter's, "Thou art the Messiah," *i.e.* the Anointed of God (cf. Matt. xvi. 13—20). The Messiah includes Prophet, Priest, and King within his person and functions.
III. THE ACCEPTANCE OF THE IDENTIFICATION BY JESUS. 1. It is implicitly accepted here, as explicitly in Matt. xvi. Jesus claims to be Prince and Saviour of his people and mankind. 2. Yet it must not be made known. Probably the statement, "The Prophet Jesus is the Messiah," noised abroad, would have produced a false impression. When by his death all hopes of an earthly kingdom had been destroyed, it would not be so. "Only with a knowledge of his character would the statement at any time be beneficial; and from this it would receive the best and surest confirmation" (J. H. Godwin).—J.

Vers. 31—38.—*Unwelcome prophecies.* I. PLAIN TRUTHS SELDOM WELCOME. He now spoke of suffering, rejection, even murder, at the hands of a conspiracy. The veil was drawn aside; at last it was seen what the Messiahship of Jesus meant. The same thing had before been expressed parabolically (John ii. 19; iii. 14; vi. 51).
II. THE FLATTERY OF FRIENDSHIP. The honest-hearted Peter is endeared to us. He is so human; his feelings always on the right side, his intelligence often confused. How true his heart here! how wrong his thought! Suffering and death seem an evil

to him, as to most of us. Not so to Christ. The mere suggestion that the real is to
be preferred to the ideal, mere life to duty, self-interest to the kingdom of God, he
spurns from him as the suggestion of a dark spirit.

III. SELF-RENUNCIATION. " Let him renounce himself ! " says Christ to the recruit
for his army, the would-be citizen of his kingdom. Deep words: the meaning behind
them it requires a life to learn. 1. The resolve of egotism *must* end in failure. To
determine to save one's life is to cast it away ; to cast away one's life for the sake of the
ideal is to save it. Christianity is the kingdom of the ideal. 2. In the spiritual
sphere there is no real loss. Life is one, and is *not* " in the abundance of the things
possessed." It cannot be " priced," nor bartered away. It is the man's very *self*.
3. To disavow our ideal is to incur eternal shame. There are the ideals of comfort,
of luxury ; the ideals of society ; the ideals of God, of the spirit. We must take our
choice. We *may* make a choice of the lower which shall exclude the higher, or of the
higher which shall *include* all of worth in the lower. There is no other rule than
" Seek first the kingdom of God ! " If we are ashamed to be true to our ideal, the time
will come when we shall be put to shame in the presence of it. To disavow greatness
when it comes to us under the guise of obscurity, this is to ensure our being disavowed
of greatness when it appears in its true and heavenly glory.—J.

Vers. 1—21. Parallel passage : Matt. xv. 30—xvi. 12.—1. *The feeding of the four
thousand.* 2. *The sign sought by the Pharisees.* 3. *The leaven of the Pharisees.* I.
OMISSION. Having pretty fully considered the feeding of the five thousand recorded in
the sixth chapter, and its relation to the feeding of the four thousand narrated in the
above section of this eighth chapter, we waive further notice of this subject, as the two
miracles are in fact twin miracles, having much in common, and many circumstances so
similar that, as we saw, some erroneously identified them. We may add, however, that
on the former occasion the northern villagers would have made Jesus a king ; the dwellers
on the eastern shores make no demonstration. Further, the five thousand were fed
after the return of the twelve ; the four thousand after our Lord's return from the
borders of Tyre and Sidon. In the former case, the disciples went away by sea and
Christ retired to the mountain, but met them again at the fourth watch, as he walked
upon the waters. On the present occasion the multitude had been with Jesus three
days, and afterwards he departed with the disciples in the ship.

II. THE PHARISEES. At this juncture they had made common cause with their
bitter opponents, the Sadducees ; both together made a combined and desperate attack
on our Lord. He seems to have avoided Bethsaida and Capernaum, which were further
north, and to have landed near Magdala, now *El-Mejdel*, in the neighbourhood and about
three miles to the north of which was Dalmanutha, on purpose, it would seem, to
escape from those inveterate enemies who appear to have made Capernaum or Bethsaida
their head-quarters. Consequently they were under the necessity of coming in quest
of him ; for they " came forth, and began to question with him." Their ostensible
object on this occasion was to seek of him a sign from heaven, but their real design
was, in all likelihood, to entrap him. They were insincere as well as sceptical ; and, had
the sought-for sign been granted, it would not have overcome their deeply rooted prejudices and hypocritical pretences. The conduct of these wretched men was suicidal.
Their curiosity craved a sign ; their unbelief unfitted them for its performance, as also
for its proper perception had it been performed. Besides, had there not been many
signs ? Had not a multitude of the angelic host celebrated Christ's birth on the plains
of Bethlehem ? Had there not been the reception by Simeon, and the response of Anna
at his presentation in the temple ? Had not the star appeared in the East ? Had not
the Magi followed its guidance to worship the infant Saviour and to present their gifts ?
Had not an audible voice from heaven acknowledged him at his baptism, it did as on
two subsequent occasions ? Had not the Spirit, in visible, dove-like form, descended
upon him ? Thus in the temple two pious Jews expressed their grateful acknowledgments and recorded their joy, confessing their Lord. Soon after, Gentile Magi, men of
scientific knowledge and literary pursuits, came from a far-off Eastern land to pay their
homage. Here we have at once Hebrew piety and Gentile philosophy uniting to do
honour to the infant Saviour, and bow in humility at his feet. Here, too, we have male
and female—that godly old man Simeon and that holy, aged woman Anna repre-

senting their respective sexes in owning his Messiahship. So afterwards, on his triumphal entry into Jerusalem, when the crowd that went before and the crowd that followed after had cried, "Hosanna to the Son of David : Blessed is he that cometh in the Name of the Lord; Hosanna in the highest!" the children in the temple responded, saying in the selfsame strain, "Hosanna to the Son of David!" Old and young, male and female, Gentile and Jew, thus unite their tribute to that Saviour whose mercy they need, whose grace they share, by whose work they are benefited, and in whose salvation they participate. But not so these captious, sceptical, false-hearted, and malignant Pharisees. On three other occasions we read of a sign being demanded—after the cleansing of the temple, the journey through the corn-fields, the feeding of the five thousand; so also on the occasion mentioned here. What was the nature of the sign for which they clamoured? The signs they sought were marvels of a garish kind—appearances in the sky, such as manna coming down from heaven, as they themselves intimated in John vi.; or the standing still of the sun and moon, or the sudden descent of thunder and hail, or some change of the atmosphere, as Theophylact suggests; or the calling down of fire and rain, or the receding of the sun's shadow on the dial, or some great, overmastering, and stupendous miracle. "They thought," says Theophylact, "he could not perform a sign from heaven, as one who in league with Beelzebub could only perform signs on earth." But had they not seen even greater signs than these? And, had they been favoured with the signs of their own choosing, would they have been satisfied? There is no reason to believe they would. Our Lord, however, never gratified an idle curiosity, nor wrought a miracle to create wonder, but usually to supply some want or relieve some necessity.

III. THE DISCIPLES' WANT OF SPIRITUAL DISCERNMENT. Our Lord, as we have seen, had to contend with the hostility of the Pharisees, their stubborn disbelief and ensnaring captiousness. In view of these, and of the subtilty of the temptation which claimed a miracle to prove his Messiahship, as also perhaps of the crisis that was hurrying on, there welled up from the depths of his heart that sigh of mingled patience and pity. But he had more to contend with than Pharisaic opposition and disbelief; he had the perverseness of his own disciples. If he had the stolid stubbornness of the Pharisees to encounter on the one hand, he had the stupidity of his own disciples to oppose on the other. On the one side there was sullen scepticism, on the other sad slowness of heart; on the one malignant frowardness, on the other wayward misconception. How often is the disciple of Christ similarly situated! He meets with open enmity on the part of godless, Christless men, while unaccountably he finds obstacles thrown in his way by the professed friends of truth. If foes are bitter in their opposition, friends sometimes fail to render the expected and much-needed support—often, however, more from want of thought than want of will. But when distressed and depressed, what by fightings without and fears within, we have the example of our Lord to encourage us and keep us from desponding. If such things were done in a green tree, what may we not expect to be done in a dry?

IV. MEANING OF THE WARNING AGAINST THE LEAVEN. Our Lord broke off his interview with these hypocritical Pharisees abruptly, and re-embarked rather hurriedly. He abandoned them in their unbelief, renouncing and rejecting them as impracticable malignants. The disciples, whose duty it was to provide for their own and Master's wants, had somehow overlooked or neglected the duty that thus devolved on them. Either, owing to their hasty re-embarkation, they had forgotten (ἐπελάθοντο being used in a pluperfect sense) to provide bread before starting—a strange oversight after having collected seven large baskets (σπυρίδας) full of fragments; or, after landing, and when they had come to the other side, they forgot (ἐπελάθοντο having the ordinary past signification of the aorist) to take bread for their land-journey further, though they had had only one loaf with them in the ship. Our Lord, as usual, improving the occasion, and intending to guard his disciples from the subtle, insinuating errors and example of the Pharisees, warned them against their plausible but pernicious teaching, and in doing so he employed terms, as was his custom, suggested by recent occurrences. "Take heed, beware," he said, "of the leaven of the Pharisees, and of the leaven of Herod;" or, as Meyer understands the word (βλέπετε), "Take heed, turn your eyes away from the leaven of the Pharisees, and from the leaven of Herod;" or, as St. Matthew has it, from "the leaven of the Pharisees and of the Sadducees," so that Herod, from his Sadduceeism, may here, by way of eminence, represent that sect. Leaven, with the single exception of the parable of the leaven, is always used for evil of some sort, especially evil secretly working and silently diffusing itself; and hence, in preparation for the Passover, leaven was to be purged out of all the households of the Hebrews. Accordingly the leaven of the Pharisees, if used here in a specific and not in a generic sense, may be taken to denote *hypocrisy*, while the leaven of the Sadducees may signify *misbelief*, and that of Herod *worldliness*; and as the Sadducean creed allows full scope to worldly pleasures and pursuits, and because of their many points of contact, the two latter may coincide or change places; while the whole three are animated by one and the same spirit of opposition to God and true religion. Our Lord here warned his disciples against all doctrine, practice, or teaching of like character under the name of leaven. His disciples, in their low, grovelling notions, and through their slowness of spiritual apprehension, understood him to speak of bread in the literal sense, and of bread baked with leaven got from the Pharisees on landing. They supposed that the Saviour was warning them against anything of that kind that might corrupt them. How different the Master and the disciples! The latter allowed their thoughts to be too much engrossed with the bread that perisheth; the former had his mind occupied with the bread that endureth unto eternal life, and warned them against any teaching or any practice that might interfere with their possessing it. No wonder our Lord was some-what sharp in his rebuke of their spiritual dulness, for, having eyes for the physical part of the miracles, they failed to see their spiritual import. They had eyesight only for the outward shell, but did not perceive the kernel. Hence it is that he inquires, "Having ears, hear ye not?" and again, "How is it that ye do not understand?"

V. Exegetical note on certain words and phrases in the preceding sections. 1. The clause, "They have now been with me three days," is literally, *There are now three days to them remaining with me*. To the original expression thus exactly rendered has been cited the following parallel from the 'Philoctetes' of Sophocles:— Ἦν δ' ἦμαρ ἤδη δεύτερον πλέοντί μοι: "It was now the second day to me sailing." 2. Instead of ἐν ἐρημία of St. Matthew, we have here in St. Mark ἐπ' ἐρημίας, which is slightly different in sense, meaning, "In circumstances consequent on or connected with being in a desert." 3. In ver. 12 the received text reads ἐπιζητεῖ, which yields a very suitable sense, namely, seeks a sign *in addition* to those already given. The critical editors, Lachmann, Tischendorf, and Tregelles, however, read the simpler verb ζητεῖ. 4. In this same verse there is a Hebraistic form of strong abjuration. The clause in our English Version is, "There shall no sign be given;" so also the Syriac has simply "*not;*" but the strict rendering is, "If a sign shall be given," which, resolved according to the idiom of the original, is, "May I not live if a sign shall be given," or "God do so to me and more if a sign shall be given." 5. So also in the same verse, "he brake," that is, at once, because the verb is the aorist tense; and "kept giving," as the verb is imperfect. 6. The two participles meaning respectively "having given thanks" and "blessed" amount to nearly the same thing, and set us an example suitable, seemly, and seasonable of thanking God and asking his blessing when we partake of our daily food; in other words, of conforming to the time-honoured practice of saying "grace," as it is called, before meals, by which we thankfully acknowledge the Giver, and ask his blessing on and with the gift.—J. J. G.

Vers. 22—26.—*The healing of a blind man at Bethsaida.* I. Several miracles of a similar kind. The miracle here recorded was performed at Bethsaida Julias, or the northern Bethsaida, on the route from the north-east shore of the lake to Cæsarea Philippi. It is related by St. Mark alone. The peculiarity of this miracle of restoring sight to the blind is the circumstance of its being wrought at twice; that is to say, the cure was progressive or gradual. In the ninth chapter of St. John's Gospel we have the account of a like miracle of opening the eyes of a blind man; but one peculiarity of the miracle there recorded consists in the fact that the man on whom the miracle was performed had been born blind. There is again the opening of the eyes of two blind men near Jericho, recorded in St. Matthew (xx.), one of whom only is mentioned by St. Mark (x.) and by St. Luke (xviii.), and called by the patronymic Bartimæus, or the son of Timæus. There is also the record of another similar miracle in the ninth chapter of St. Matthew, when our Lord, after putting their faith to the test, cured two blind men in the house whither they had followed him. Besides these specially recorded cases, we have several references of a general kind to our Lord's healing of the blind. The great number of instances of this kind is accounted for by the fact that blindness is a disease much more common in the East than in the lands of the West, while several causes have been assigned for that prevalence, such as the small particles of dust and sand impinging on the eye, and persons sleeping in the open air at night.

II. The condition of this man. This man was blind, but, as we shall see, he had not been born blind—he was not blind from birth. He had become blind from accident or disease. At all events, he was destitute of that most valuable sense, the sense of sight. He had been long a stranger to the beauties of nature. "The light is sweet, and a pleasant thing it is for the eyes to see the sun;" but that sun, that light, those beauties, those bright colours, those lovely forms that appear in the heaven above, in the earth beneath, in the waters round the earth—all, all had long been to him a blank. He was in that state which Milton, in the days of his blindness, so poetically and pathetically deplores—

> "Thus with the year
> Seasons return; but not to me returns
> Day, or the sweet approach of ev'n or morn,
> Or sight of vernal bloom, or summer's rose,
> Or flocks, or herds, or human face divine;
> But cloud instead and ever-during dark
> Surrounds me, from the cheerful ways of men
> Cut off! and, for the book of knowledge fair,
> Presented with a universal blank
> Of nature's works, to me expunged and rased,
> And wisdom at one entrance quite shut out."

We know not whether this blind man had wife or child. It is probable he had; and, if so, when he rose in the morning his wife ministered unto him, his children clung to his knees and kissed him while he blessed them. They led him forth to the street or elsewhere out of doors. He could feel them, but could not behold them. Their smiles, their tears, their bright eyes, and sweet faces were to him unknown and by him unseen. All the region round Bethsaida was charming—the glancing waters of the lake, the lovely flowers of the Galilean hills, were a sight worth seeing; but what were all these to this blind man? The district might as well have been dark and dismal, bleak and black; at any rate, a blank, a night without moon or star, midnight with its darkness visible, even "darkness that might be felt."

III. Peculiarity in the mode of cure. Here the peculiarity is twofold: 1. Jesus took him by the hand and led him out of the town. 2. The cure was effected progressively, or at twice. What reason can we assign for the *former* peculiarity? Why did he conduct him outside the town? Several reasons have been assigned. Some say that our Lord thereby meant to intimate the unworthiness, through unbelief, of the inhabitants of this town, or rather village (κώμη), and his consequent dissatisfaction with them; this, of course, is a mere conjecture. Others suppose, with more apparent reason, that, as the process of cure in this case was more than usually protracted, our Lord led the man out of the town in order to be free from interruption or any obstruction on the part of the crowd, just as in the preceding chapter he is said to have taken the deaf mute aside from the multitude. Bengel, with his usual ingenuity, conjectures the cause to be the Saviour's intention that, when the blind recovered sight, his eyes might rest on the more cheerful aspect of the sky and of the works of God in nature—that is, in the country—than of the works of man in the town. The thought is a beautiful one, but only the product of a fertile imagination. Of two remaining reasons, which have been suggested with considerable plausibility, one is the avoidance of witnesses on account of the somewhat disagreeable application of spittle, or saliva, to the person of the invalid, exactly as in the case of the deaf mute already referred to; and the other is that our Lord, by varying the mode of cure, "sometimes doing more, sometimes less, and sometimes nothing," signified his freedom from any fixed form of gesture or manipulation. Some, again, reject with regard to the saliva all these, holding that our Lord meant to graft the supernatural on the natural, the saliva being an ordinary medical application in such cases.   We are rather inclined to adopt the view of variation, for the purpose of proving independence of any specific or stereotyped mode in such miraculous performance.   With respect to the *progressiveness* of the cure a similar diversity of opinion prevails.   Theophylact attributes it to the imperfect faith of the blind man himself, and of those who brought him to the Saviour; others imagine that on a sudden recovery of sight the man would have been unable to distinguish objects from each other.   But to this latter, which proceeds on the assumption of his being born blind, it is sufficient to reply (1) that this man had not been born blind, as is implied in the word ἀποκατεστάθη—he was restored to or reinstated in his once normal condition; and (2) he was able to discriminate trees from men, so that he must have seen both before this blindness supervened.   Before Berkeley's time visual distance was traced to an original law of our constitution, and considered an original perception; but the bishop proved, as is very generally admitted, that our information on this subject of the distance of objects is acquired by experience and association; while, if we judge of the distance of objects solely from the visible impressions on the retina, we fall into great mistakes.   The case, too, of Cheselden, who had been born blind, appeared to confirm the theory of Berkeley, for when couched he at first had no correct notions of distances, but supposed all objects to touch and to be in close contact with the eye.   It was gradually he corrected his visible by his tangible impressions, and gained a correct understanding of the situation of the objects that surrounded him, as well as of their shape and size.   Had the blind man in this passage been thus born blind, we could readily concede the necessity of a gradual operation—first to get his eyes opened, and secondly to gain correct notions of the objects about him.   No gradual miracle of this sort was required in the case of this man, because he had originally possessed the sense of sight and lost it.   The true cause appears to be either an evidence on the part of the Saviour that he is not tied down to any particular mode of operation, but manifests his mercy in divers manners, according to his sovereign good pleasure; or, if this theory be not accepted, the cause may be assigned to the symbolic nature of the miracle, as exhibiting the gradual recovery of spiritual eyesight, the removal of spiritual blindness being, for the most part and with some rare exceptions, gradual and progressive.

IV. EXPLANATION OF TERMS WITH DIFFERENCES OF READING.   1. Our Lord led the blind man out, having taken him by the hand, which is a very expressive action, for it is a guide which the blind, whether physically or spiritually, so much need; and this is just the kind of guide here mentioned—a Divine and therefore infallible Guide.   This guidance is expressed in the received text by ἐξήγαγεν, though some critical editors prefer ἐξήνεγκεν, equivalent to "conveyed out;" while in both the phrase "out of" is strongly expressed by the preposition in composition with the verb and the separate ἔξω.   2. The reading of the common text is properly rendered, "I see men as trees, walking;" that is to say, he saw men, but so indistinctly and at first apparently motionless, that they seemed more like trees; but then he saw them walking, and so discriminated them from trees.   The expression is rather abrupt, but most accurate in describing the three stages indicated.   The reading of the critical editions is different, and is rightly represented by the following rendering:—"I behold men, because as trees I see [them] walking."   Even according to this reading the expression is abrupt, as significant of sudden and joyful surprise; as if he said, "I see men not much differing in shape and form from trees; but I know they are men, and not trees, for I see them in motion."   3. Succeeding this is the expression, he "made him look up," not "see again"—a signification of the word quite admissible, yet not in accord with the sense here; but for this whole phrase Tischendorf Tregelles and Alford read διέβλεψεν, "he saw clearly," that very instant (aorist); then, after restoration, he saw all things or all persons plainly—rather, continued looking on (ἐνέβλεπεν, imperfect, instead of ἐνέβλεψε, aorist) all things with clear vision.   4. The word τηλαυγῶς, from τῆλε, at a distance, and αὐγή, equivalent to "bright light," "radiance," and in the plural "beams of the sun," signifies generally "far-shining" or "far-seen;" but here, from shining in the distance, "far-sightedly," "clearly," "plainly."   5. An important distinction is made between ὄμμα and ὀφθαλμὸς in this passage, the latter being the organ of sight, and as such used by prose-writers, the former or more poetic word being here the sense or inner power of seeing; and so the latter is the instrument employed by the former.

V. The spitting and the application of the hands denote, according to Theophylact, word and work; they rather denote—the former the virtue proceeding from the Saviour, which restored the extinct sense of sight, the latter the rectification of the organ. Just as in the case of the person born blind, who was couched for blindness, the recovery here also was gradual; so with the spiritually blind we proceed gradually from one degree of light to another, from grace to grace, and from strength to strength. When the spiritually blind recover sight, they discern many things before shrouded in darkness, but not all things, nor even those many things with perfect clearness, or in their correct relations or relative proportions. We need the hand of Jesus to touch our eyes many a time before our spiritual eyesight is perfected; that sight, by the gentle touch of our loving, living Saviour, goes on improving till our dying day. We are in the hand of our Saviour just as this blind man; and as he led him forth, fully restored his sight, and sent him away from his old associations, so we must give ourselves up to his guidance, depend on him entirely for full restoration of sight and other spiritual powers, turn our back on old sinful courses or companions, and go with our Lord whithersoever he leads us. The following context exemplifies the gradual recovery of spiritual sight in those who identified Jesus with John, or Elias, or a prophet, and in the disciples who acknowledged him to be the Christ. The former had a glimmering of the truth; the latter saw its full-orbed clearness. The former only saw "men like trees, walking;" the latter saw it in this particular with perfect plainness.—J. J. G.

Vers. 27—34. Parallel passages: Matt. xvi. 13—24; Luke ix. 18—23.—*Christ's prediction of his death and rebuke of Peter.* This section will be considered in connection with a like prediction in the following (ninth) chapter of this Gospel.—J. J. G.

Vers. 35—38. Parallel passages: Matt. xvi. 25—27; Luke ix. 24—26.—*Secular profit and spiritual loss.* 1. A CURIOUS CALCULATION. These verses present themselves in the light of an arithmetical calculation regarding profit and loss—a calculation as important as it is curious. In this calculation the soul is on one side, and the world on the other; secular matters on the one hand, spiritual concerns on the other. A calculation of this sort involves a difficulty, for there is no common standard to which we can bring things so different in their nature. There is no common measure by which we can simplify their comparison, and so better gauge their real relative proportions. They have no common factor; they stand prime to each other. But perhaps it were better to regard these verses as an allusion, not so much to a bare arithmetical calculation, as to a practical mercantile reckoning. It is customary with merchants and others, at some particular period of the year, to look into their books and see how they stand with the world, and how the world stands with them—to balance their accounts, ascertaining their profits and determining their losses. Now, the course thus pursued in secular may with still greater advantage be adopted in spiritual concerns, while the adoption of some such course seems suggested by the inquiry, "What shall it profit a man?"

II. SUPPOSED PROFIT. The supposed profit is here set forth to the greatest advantage. The supposed gain is the very maximum—the greatest possible. It is, in fact, much greater than any man has ever reached. That any one individual should gain the whole world is quite improbable—nay, it is almost, if not altogether, impossible. No man has ever gained so much, no man is ever likely to do so; no man nowadays ever dreams of such a thing. We read, indeed, of one in ancient times that made an approximation to it. We are informed that Alexander the Great subjected the surrounding hostile tribes to the arms of Macedon; conquered the provinces of Asia Minor, deciding the empire of all Asia in three great battles at Granicus, Issus, and Arbela; received the submission of Italian, Scythian, Kelt, and Iberian ambassadors; penetrated to the furthest limit northward, and overthrew the Scythians on the banks of the Jaxartis; pushed his victories far eastward, even to the Hyphasis or Sutlej; founded cities and planted colonies in the Punjab. And when at that point his progress was checked by the murmuring of his troops, and he was obliged to retreat to the Hydaspes or Jhelum, he built a fleet, sailed down the Indus to its mouth, and there, standing in view of the Indian Ocean, and feeling he had arrived at the limit of his career, tears filled his eyes, and he wept because his victories were at an end, and there was no more for him to subdue—"no other world," say the old historians, "for him to conquer." But, if we examine the matter with any degree of accuracy, we shall find that this bold adventurer overran only a few countries of the then known world, and but a very inconsiderable portion of those immense continents and many islands which modern geographical discovery has added to the present huge dimensions of the globe. We have all heard of another in modern times who grasped at the sceptre of universal empire, who rose rapidly from a lieutenant of artillery to captain, and from captain to colonel, and from colonel to general of division. Soon he became first consul for ten years, then for life, and afterwards ascended the imperial throne. The empire of France he increased by one-third; but what was that to the high-vaulting ambition of Napoleon? He must needs reign supreme and without a rival in Europe, and in prosecution of that gigantic scheme of conquest he actually added to his empire Italy, Switzerland, the Netherlands, Hanover, the Hanse towns. He seized on Spain and Portugal, and set his kinsmen on foreign thrones. He sought Russia, but above all he sighed for England. He pounced on Egypt; thence, as the most potent point of attack, he fixed his eye on India. India once gained, the world, he thought, would be laid subject at his feet, and he its one and sole possessor. This, doubtless, would have been the result of its successful invasion. But the tide of fortune ceased to flow. To his failure in Spain succeeded his retreat from Moscow, next his defeat at Leipzig, then his banishment to Elba, and, last of all, his final and fearful overthrow on the plains of Waterloo. No one individual has ever yet attained to the possession of the world; no one has advanced beyond a distant approximation to it. But let us for a moment fancy the supposition to have become an accomplished fact. Let us suppose the wide empire of earth in the hands of one man; let us take for granted that the possession of the world—the whole world—is realized by a single individual; let us imagine all the benefits of that vast dominion—its conveniences and comforts, its riches and honours, its pleasures, praises, and profits, all at the command of one man.

III. THE DURATION OF SUCH PROFIT BRIEF. What then would be the continuance of such? Why, he would find it impossible to retain it for any considerable length of time. We cannot calculate with certainty on the continuance of any worldly possession during the whole of life; we cannot reckon on its lasting for even a few years of that life in advance; and, even if we could, we are not sure of life itself for a single moment. "Life is even a vapour, that appeareth for a little time, and then vanisheth away;" "There is but a step between us and death;" "This night the soul may be required." There is no permanence of possession upon earth; there is no fixity of tenure here below. The heirloom handed down from father to son, and again from son to father, shall pass into strangers' hands. The hereditary estate, secure it as you may by deeds and settlements, will soon, notwithstanding all your caution, change proprietorship. The baronial residence will in time become a ruin grey, round which the ivy twines. Truly as well as eloquently has the poet said—

> "The cloud-capp'd towers, the gorgeous palaces,
> The solemn temples, the great globe itself,
> Yea, all which it inherit, shall dissolve."

Our most cherished possessions must soon revert to others. It matters not how firmly we hold them; force, or fraud, or casualty, or imprudence, or disease, or death—one or other of these will wrench them from our reluctant grasp; and the question may be asked of us, as of the fool in the Gospel, "Then whose shall these things be?" If, then, we possessed the whole world, every instant we lived in it we should run the risk of losing it or leaving it, of being taken from it or having it snatched from us, of being compelled to give up the possession either by the open violence of enemies or the treacherous avarice of friends, by folly on our part or dishonesty on that of others, by some sudden reverse of fortune or by some sad dispensation of providence.

IV. THE ENJOYMENT OF IT IMPOSSIBLE. Further, if we had the whole world in actual possession, and were able to retain it in inalienable and never-failing proprietorship, still we could not enjoy it all. With all the progress of modern times, with all the advances of science, with all the forward strides of this nineteenth century, with all that geological research and chemical analysis and botanical skill have discovered, there are still many plants and many substances of which we know not the nature, or at least have not yet learned the use. So long as the properties of any object remain unknown, it is manifest that that object itself cannot be enjoyed. And even if we knew all the qualities of every fowl of heaven, of every fish of the sea, of every plant that grows on the surface and of every mineral that is buried in the bowels of the earth, yet what use could any one individual make of them all? What a small portion of them would meet all the real necessities of life! How few of them would suffice for man's limited powers of enjoyment! How few of them would supply a substantial answer to that wide question, "What shall I eat, or what shall I drink, or wherewithal shall I be clothed?" If the cattle on a thousand hills were ours, if all the mineral wealth of the world were our own, if earth and all its store of gold and silver and precious stones were at our feet, if earth with all its fruits and flowers, its animal and vegetable productions, were at our disposal, what could one individual, possessing limited powers and capacities, do with them all? How could he enjoy them? Where would he store them that they might be safe? What, in a word, would they really profit him? Ah! how forcibly is the whole expressed in the simple lines!—

> " Man needs but little here below,
> Nor needs that little long."

V. THE UNSATISFACTORY NATURE OF IT. The world, if we possessed it all, and could retain it always, and enjoy it fully, would not satisfy us. We all know the possibility of being as much or more disappointed in a thing, as inconvenienced by being disappointed of it. Hope has its pleasures, and they are frequently as great, sometimes far greater than those of enjoyment. The poet, when he wrote of " the pleasures of hope," knew well that hope was one main source of human enjoyment. But in the supposed possession of the whole world that source of enjoyment would be cut off, as in that case man would have nothing to hope for. The distance, that lent its enchantment to the view, would be annihilated; desire would still be unsatisfied, and yet hope would be at an end. Besides, where is the rich man who is perfectly satisfied with his wealth, and who feels that it is a sufficient source of happiness? Where is the man of pleasure who can truly say that his pleasures have been without alloy? Where the ambitious aspirant who is not in feverish dread of the fickleness of popular favour? Where the heart that has not yearned for more than earth can furnish? Who has not felt that " aching void" which " the world can never fill"? It is not in the increase of riches, nor in the accession of honours, nor in any augmentation of creature enjoyments, that true satisfaction is to be found: the wealth of this world cannot purchase it; the pleasures of sense and sin cannot procure it; honours bestowed by fellow-creatures cannot confer it. Nor yet do we mean to decry the importance of temporal things. We know that they can minister much to man; they can add to our convenience and comfort; they can furnish their quota to our enjoyment; they can supply enlarged means of usefulness; they can contribute to the decency and dignity of life; they can shield us from the distresses, and difficulties, and discomforts of poverty. But we deny altogether that they can prevent or remove the vanity and vexation of spirit that are inseparably associated with all worldly things. In the midst of all that this world can furnish men have been heard to cry out, if not in words, at least in the sentiments of the patriarch, " I would not live alway." When this is the way with the prosperous worldling, often too has the child of God, amid the perplexities of life, cause to repeat the saying—

> " I would not live alway; I ask not to stay
> Where storm after storm rises dark o'er the way.
> The few fleeting mornings that dawn on us here
> Are enough for life's sorrows, enough for its cheer.

> " Who—who would live alway, away from his God;
> Away from yon heaven, that blissful abode,
> Where rivers of pleasure flow o'er the bright plains,
> And the noontide of glory eternally reigns?"

VI. SPIRITUAL LOSS. 1. *Practical bearing of all this.* What, it may be asked, is the practical lesson from all this? It is to lead us to God as the end, and to Christ as the way to the Father; to show us the value of salvation, the importance of eternal

things; to make us alive to the things of God; and, above all, to impress on us the worth
of the soul and spiritual life. We have seen that if a man could possess the whole
world he might still be unhappy—ay, perfectly miserable; fears harassing him,
conscience tormenting him, afflictions overwhelming him, death overtaking him, and
his worldly all departing from him amid " the swellings of Jordan." But in general men
stop far short of what has been thus supposed. They are willing to lose the soul for
infinitely less than the world : at all events, a small thing takes the place of all the
world to the sinner, and is made the means of his losing the soul. Thus, to the
drunkard, the indulgence of his passion for strong drink is the horizon that bounds the
world of his happiness and of his hopes; while to gain his object he submits to the loss
of his soul. So with the licentious; the gratification of their low lust is all the world to
them, and to it they sacrifice the soul. "Avoid," says the apostle, "youthful lusts,
that war against the soul." So with the ambitious; the attainment of the object on
which their heart is set is their world of gratification, and, for the sake of it, they will
not only run the risk of losing the soul, but rush upon sure destruction. We might
enumerate many and various classes of sinners—the horse-racer, the gamester, the
blasphemer, the liar, the murderer—all ruining their own soul for the sake of questionable pleasures; at all events, pleasures that last but for a season, and that perish in the
using. With sinners of every grade the indulgence of sin is their world of gratification,
their all of wretched happiness, for which they are every day throwing away their
chances of salvation and deliberately damning their own soul. Oh, what fearful folly !
What unspeakable madness! Oh, may we not with propriety appeal to that sinful
man, to whatever category or class his sin belongs, and with all the earnestness of our
nature plead with him to spare his own soul? Should we not urge him, with all the
powers of persuasion we can possibly command, to part with his vice at once and for
ever, rather than plunge his soul into a hell of eternal misery ? 2. *Exegetical note.* (1)
The word θέλῃ is not " will " of future time, but " will " connected with choice or purpose.
It is correctly rendered " would " in the Revised Version. The word is also distinguished from βούλομαι, which expresses a wish—mere willingness or inclination.
Homer employs the latter for the former in the case of the gods, for with them *wish* is
will. Thus the meaning is, " Whosoever may will [or choose] to save his life; " while in
the next clause it is taken for granted that no one, of his own free will and choice, would
desire to lose it, and therefore the expression is different, being literally, *Whosoever
shall (as a matter of fact) destroy* (ἀπολέσει) *his life.* (2) The word ψυχὴ is the bond
of union between the body and the spirit in the triple trichotomy of "body, soul,
and spirit " (1 Thess. v. 23). Viewed in connection with the body, it is the natural or
animal life, but in its relation to the spirit it is the spiritual or higher life. Thus in
one sense it is less than what we understand by soul, and in another sense it is more,
comprehending not only the immortal life of the soul, but the never-ending life of soul
and body when reunited. (3) Zημιωθῇ denotes forfeiture, and so it is correctly rendered
in the Revised Version "forfeit; " while ἀντάλλαγμα (from the roots ἀντί, instead of, and
ἄλλος, another) denotes one thing given in exchange for another, and so an equivalent or
ransom, the idea being that if a man have lost, by way of mulct or forfeiture, his life
or soul, what ransom will he be able to give in order to buy it back or redeem it ? The
expression in St. Luke is, " What is a man advantaged, if he gain the whole world, and
destroy himself " or " suffer forfeit ? " 3. *A celebrated choice.* The fabled choice of Hercules has at least a useful moral. Two ladies of gigantic stature—one graceful and
modest, with raiment white as snow, the other florid and affected ; the former called
Virtue, the latter Pleasure, though self-named Happiness, approached the youthful hero.
The latter promised him the possession of all pleasures, and that his path in life would
be strewed with flowers, if he chose to follow her, reminding him at the same time that
the path of virtue was tedious and thorny ; the former promised to make his name
glorious to posterity, and introduce him at death into the society of the gods, reminding him that the pleasures of the senses are the enjoyments of the brute, and that
true pleasure springs from virtuous conduct. The hero, as the fable goes, did not
long hesitate, but, giving his hand to Virtue, bade her be his guide, saying, " Lead on,
and I will follow you."

VII. THE VALUE OF THE SOUL, OR EVERLASTING LIFE. 1. *Value of the soul variously
estimated.* We may estimate the value of the soul in several ways ; we may enumerate

four of these as the most obvious. We may estimate it by the infinite price paid for it, by the immensity of its capacities, by its intrinsic worth, and by the immortality of its being. 2. *The price paid.* The price paid for the soul was a precious ransom price, " for the redemption of the soul is precious." That price was not " corruptible things, as silver and gold," but " the precious blood of Christ, as of a lamb without blemish and without spot." In him we have " redemption through his blood, the forgiveness of sins, according to the riches of his grace." On account of the soul Christ died ; on account of the soul the Holy Spirit, the Sanctifier, is at work ; on account of the soul the Word of God is given, the gospel is preached, and " the arm of the Lord revealed." Thus, from the pains God takes to save the soul, from the power the Spirit exerts to sanctify the soul, from the efforts Satan makes to destroy the soul, as well as from the blood which Christ shed to redeem the soul, we may infer the value of the human soul, and consequently infer the exceeding greatness of its loss. 3. *Its intrinsic worth.* Again, we think of its intrinsic worth. It is a scintillation of Deity ; it is the breath of the Almighty ; it is the candle of the Lord in man. " God breathed into his nostrils the breath of life, and man became a living soul." It was at its creation the image of its Maker as well as the masterpiece of his workmanship ; it was stamped with the likeness of the Eternal. And though the superscription is sadly defaced by sin, it is an infinite spirit still, and the direct offspring of the Father of spirits. 4. *Its immense capacities.* When we reflect on its great capacities, we bethink ourselves of its capability of suffering, which is immense. No pain of body is to be compared with the unspeakable anguish of the soul. There is, on the other hand, no pleasure of bodily organization to be compared with the intensely thrilling joyousness of the soul, when it delights itself in God, or meditates on his Word and works, or soars aloft in high and holy contemplation. Even a worldly poet, speaking of the happiness of thought, says, " I have oft been happy thinking." Besides, there is its wonderful power of development. The little that the lower animals possess is soon perfected ; instinct flows in at once. The mind of man contains in itself the elements of almost unlimited improvement. As long as life lasts, accessions may be made to our knowledge, additions made to our attainments, new discoveries made in science, fresh advances in art. Better still, it is the very prerogative of the soul, as it is the very purpose for which its powers were bestowed, to glorify God on earth and be glorified with him in heaven, to enjoy him both here and hereafter, to see him and serve him, to hold converse with angels and glorified spirits, to have fellowship with Father, Son, and Spirit, to drink deep of the fountain of grace and love that wells up beside the throne of the Eternal. 5. *The immortality of its being.* Add to all this the immortality of its being. It is an immortal spirit ; it is a flame that can never be extinguished ; it is a light that can never be put out ; it is unseen, but eternal. The babe that is only a span long has a soul that will outlive this world. In the bosom of that babe, as it sleeps in the cradle, or hangs on the breast, is a soul that will last longer than sun and moon endure. When the elements shall melt with fervent heat, when the earth shall be burnt up, and the heavens rolled together like a crumpled scroll, that soul shall survive, and remain unhurt amid " the wreck of matter and the crush of worlds." Not so the body. 6. *The shroud of Saladin.* Who has not heard, or rather read, of that famous Asiatic warrior, Saladin? After subjugating Egypt, establishing himself as Sultan of Egypt and Syria, taking towns without number, and retaking Jerusalem itself from the hands of the Crusaders, this Moslem hero of the Third Crusade, and beau-ideal of mediæval chivalry, had at length to yield to a still mightier conqueror. A few moments before he breathed his last, he ordered a herald to suspend on the point of a lance the shroud in which he was to be buried, and to cry as he raised it, " Look, here is all that Saladin the Great, the conqueror, the emperor, bears away with him of all his glory." Thus all the honours and riches of this world, all bodily pleasures and gratifications, all earthly greatness, are reduced by death to the shroud and the winding-sheet ; but the soul, immortal in its nature, and secure in its existence, " smiles at the drawn dagger " or other implement of death. From all these considerations may be inferred the immeasurable loss of the soul ; for—

> " What is the thing of greatest price,
> The whole creation round?
> That which was lost in Paradise,
> That which in Christ is found.

> " The soul of man, Jehovah's breath,
>   It keeps two worlds in strife;
> Hell works beneath its work of death,
>   Heaven stoops to give it life."

7. *The full force of the question.* What, then, we may repeat, shall it profit a man, if he shall gain the whole world—and yet all the gain any man can expect is infinitely less than that—and lose his own soul or higher heavenly life? What shall it profit him, if he shall make a little sordid gain, but lose his soul? What shall it profit him, if he shall indulge some degrading passion, and thereby lose his soul? What shall it profit him, if he gratify some vile lust, and by it lose his soul? What shall it profit him, if he swallow a few more intoxicating draughts, and in the end lose his soul? What shall it profit him, if he gratify a few more lusts of the flesh, and lose his own soul? What shall it profit him, if he enjoy a little longer the society of evil companions, or even the smile and favour of the great ones of the earth, and lose his soul? What will it profit him, if he have a few more pleasures of any kind—pleasures that last so short a space, and satisfy so very little while they do last—and in lieu of them lose his own soul? Who is not, on due reflection, prepared to answer any such questions with the strongest negative? The angels in heaven, and the spirits of the just made perfect that are already there, if asked the same question, would declare, in tones of loudest earnestness and solemn emphasis, " Nothing, nothing!" Lost souls in hell, if malice prevented not, would assert the same. God the Father, who sent his Son to save the soul; God the Son, who suffered on the cross to redeem it; God the Spirit, who came to sanctify it; the Almighty undivided Three in One, would answer their own question in this passage by a negative that neither man nor angel, fallen nor unfallen, would gainsay, and that would wake an echo both in heaven above and in earth or hell beneath.

VIII. EXTENT OF THE LOSS. 1. *This is an entire loss.* The loss in question is an entire and unqualified loss. When Francis I. lost the important battle of Pavia, he described it by saying, " We have lost all but honour." And thus, though the disaster was overwhelming and the loss exceeding great, yet there was one qualifying circumstance—the preservation of honour intact and unsullied. Not so with the loss of the soul : there is nothing to qualify it, nothing to mitigate it. It is the loss of losses, the death of deaths—a catastrophe unequalled in extent, and unparalleled in its amount through all the universe of God. 2. *A loss without compensation.* The loss of the soul is a loss for which there is no compensation. The great fire of London consumed six hundred streets, thirteen thousand dwellings, and ninety churches, and destroyed property to the amount of seven and a half millions of pounds sterling. Yet that calamity was in some sort changed into a blessing; for the rebuilding of the city, in a superior style of architecture, and with more regard to sanitary arrangements, banished for ever the fearful plague which had previously made such havoc in that populous place. There is, besides, a well-known compensatory principle in the providence of God, so that, when a man loses his sight, the sense of hearing becomes more acute, and the perception of sounds more exact and accurate. The deaf mute, again, is said to have the sense of sight quickened; while the man both blind and dumb gains a more exquisite sense of touch. But the loss of the soul is a calamity for which there is nothing to compensate, and which nothing can countervail so as to make amends for it. 3. *The loss is irreparable.* Other losses may be repaired. The friend you love as your own soul may take an umbrage; he may misunderstand you, or you may be misrepresented to him ;—

> " Angry words will soon step in,
>   To spread the breach that words begin."

But let a proper explanation be given, and his friendship may be regained; or, if he continue obstinate, other and even better friends may supply his place. You may lose your health; you may be like the poor woman who had suffered so much from, and expended so much on, physicians without any improvement; but, under the blessing of Providence on the skill of yet another physician and the use of proper medicines, or by the intervention of the great Physician apart from any means, or when all means have failed, you may regain that inestimable blessing. You may lose your property, like Job when his cattle were lost, and when his children had perished, and want had come in like an armed man; yet, by years of patient industry and steady perseverance, under the Divine blessing, you may, like that same patriarch, gain double of all you lost. But oh! there is no reparation for the loss of the soul; that loss can never be retrieved, and can never be recalled. When Sir Isaac Newton had lost some most important and complicated calculations, the result of years of patient thought and investigation, by the burning of his papers, the loss to him was immense; and yet, with patience equal to his genius, he could say to the favourite animal that caused it, " Diamond, Diamond, thou little knowest the labour thou hast cost me!" But what is the loss even of years of patient philosophic investigation and profound mathematical research compared with the loss of a human soul, capable of conducting, in some degree, similar investigations, and of repeating and repairing, in case of loss, those investigations? 4. " *Cast away.*" This is the expression in the parallel passage of St. Luke. Though it may serve in exposition, it is not quite exact. The word ζημιωθείς has rather the signification of having *incurred a forfeiture;* but, in sooth, a fearful forfeiture—a forfeiture that involves the fate of being cast away into that " blackness of darkness," unrelieved by any starlight of hope or sunshine of promise, and where no rainbow of mercy ever spans the sky. The heathen, without any proper notion of a future state, shrank from the death of the body, because they were then deprived for ever of the light of day. "There is a magnificent fulness of life," says Bulwer, " in those children of the beautiful Hellas. They ever bid a last lingering and half-reluctant farewell to the sun. The orb which animated their temperate sky, which ripened their fertile fields, in which they saw the type of eternal youth, of surpassing beauty and incarnate poetry—human in its associations, yet divine in its nature—is equally beloved and equally to be mourned by the maiden tenderness of the heroine or the sullen majesty of the hero. The sun was to them a familiar friend. The terror of the nether world lay in the thought that its fields are sunless." Oh, what shall we, to whom futurity has been revealed, then say of the second death, when the lost soul is cast away, through a fatal forfeiture of the light of heaven, into that sunless region where the "blackness of darkness" ever reigns, where it is consigned to the companionship of devils and the damned, where it sinks deeper and deeper into the bottomless abyss of misery, "where their worm dieth not, and the fire is not quenched"?—J. J. G.

END OF VOL. 1.

THE
GOSPEL ACCORDING TO ST. MARK

VOL. II.

EXPOSITION

CHAPTER IX.

Ver. 1.—Till they see the kingdom of God come with power. In St. Matthew (xvi. 28) the words run thus: "Till they see the Son of man coming in his kingdom." In St. Luke (ix. 27), "Till they see the kingdom of God." All these evangelists connect their record of the Transfiguration with these predictive words—a circumstance which must not be lost sight of in their interpretation. The question, therefore, is whether or how far the Transfiguration is to be regarded as a fulfilment of these words. One thing seems plain, that the Transfiguration, if a fulfilment at all, was not an exhaustive fulfilment of the words. The solemnity of their introduction forbids us to limit them to an event which would happen within eight days of their utterance. But there was an event impending, namely, the destruction of Jerusalem, involving the overthrow of the Jewish polity, which, coming as it did within forty or fifty years of the time when our Lord uttered these words, might reasonably have been expected to take place within the lifetime of some of those then standing there. And that great catastrophe was frequently alluded to by our Lord as a type and earnest of the great judgment at the end of the world. What relation, then, did the Transfiguration hold to these two events and to the prediction contained in this verse? It was surely a prelude and pledge of what should be hereafter, specially designed to brace and strengthen the apostles for the sight of the sufferings of their Master, and to animate them to endure the toil and the trials of the Christian life. So that the Transfiguration was an event, so to speak, parenthetic to this prediction—a preliminary manifestation, for the special advantage of those who witnessed it; though given also "for our admonition, upon whom the ends of the world are come." Such were the views of St. Hilary, St. Chrysostom, St. Ambrose, and others. "When our Lord was transfigured," says St. Jerome, "he did not lose his form and aspect, but he appeared to his apostles as he will appear at the day of judgment." And elsewhere he says, "Go forth a little out of your prison, and place before your eyes the reward of your present labour, which 'the eye hath not seen, nor the ear heard, neither hath it entered into the heart of man.'"

Vers. 2, 3.—After six days. St. Luke (ix. 28) says, "About eight days after these sayings." There is no real discrepancy here. There were six whole days that intervened between our Lord's words and the Transfiguration itself. **Jesus taketh with him Peter, and James, and John.** He chose these three, as the leaders amongst the disciples, and he showed to them his glory, because he intended also to show them afterwards his bitter agony in the garden. This magnificent splendour—this "excellent glory," as St. Peter (2 Epist. i. 17) describes it—this, together with the voice of the Father, "This is my beloved Son," would assure them that Christ was truly God, but that his essential Deity was hidden by the veil of the flesh; and that, although he was about to be crucified and slain, yet his Godhead could not suffer or die. It was an evidence beforehand, a prospective evidence, that he underwent death, even the death of the cross, not constrained by infirmity or necessity, but of his own will, for the redemption of man. It was plain that, since he could thus invest his body with this Divine glory, he could have saved himself from death if he had so willed. *He taketh with him Peter, and James,* *and John.* St. Peter's reference to the transfiguration (just alluded to) shows what a deep and abiding impression it made on his mind. St. James, too, was there, as one who was to be amongst the first to die for his sake. St. John also was with them, who, having seen the glory of the Son of God, which is subject to no limits of time, might be bold to send forth his grand testimony, "In the beginning was the Word, and the Word was with God, and the Word was God." **And bringeth them up into a high mountain apart by themselves.** "It is necessary for all," says Remigius, "who desire to contemplate God, that they should not grovel amidst low thoughts and desires, but ever be lifted up to heavenly things. And thus our Lord was teaching his disciples that they must not look for the brightness of the Divine glory in the depths of this world, but in the kingdom of heavenly blessedness. And he leads them *apart*, because holy men are in intention and desire separated from evil, as they will be altogether separated from it in the world to come. For they who look for the glories of the resurrection ought now in heart and mind to dwell on high, and to seek these glories by continual prayer." *Into a high mountain.* A tradition of the time of Jerome identifies this mountain with Tabor, in Galilee. But there are two weighty objections to this view: (1) that our Lord was at this time in the neighbourhood of Cæsarea Philippi, a considerable distance from Tabor, and (2) that there is strong reason for believing that Tabor had at this time a fortress on its summit. It must be remembered that Cæsarea Philippi was at the foot of Libanus; and the spurs of Libanus would present several eminences answering to the description, "a high mountain (ὄρος ὑψηλὸν)." The Mount of Transfiguration was in all probability Hermon, a position of extreme grandeur and beauty, its snowy peaks overlooking the whole extent of Palestine. "High up," says Dean Stanley, "on its southern slopes there must be many a point where the disciples could be taken 'apart by themselves.' Even the transient comparison of the celestial splendour with the snow, where alone it could be seen in Palestine, should not, perhaps, be wholly overlooked. At any rate, the remote heights above the sources of the Jordan witnessed the moment when, his work in his own peculiar sphere being ended, he set his face for the last time to go up to Jerusalem." Although compelled to dismiss from our minds the old tradition of Tabor as the scene of the Transfiguration, we still think of that mountain as near to Nazareth, where our Lord was brought up; and of Hermon, where he was transfigured, as we rejoice in the fulfilment of the old prophecy, "Tabor and Her-

mon shall rejoice in thy Name." **And he was transfigured** (μετεμορφώθη) **before them.** The fashion of his appearance was changed. It was no illusion, no imaginary appearance, but a real transformation. It was the Divine glory within him manifesting itself through his humanity; and yet not that glory of Deity which no man hath seen or can see; but such a manifestation that the disciples might in some degree behold the glory and majesty of Deity through the veil of his flesh. Nor, we may believe, did our Lord in his transfiguration change the essence or form of his countenance. But he assumed a mighty splendour, so that, as St. Matthew (xvii. 2) tells us, "his face did shine as the sun." This splendour was not in the air, nor in the eyes of the disciples, but in the person of the Son of God—a splendour which communicated itself to his raiment, so that **his garments became glistering** (στίλβοντα), **exceeding white; so as no fuller on earth can whiten them.** This figure is taken from natural things. The first idea of "fuller" from the Latin *fullo*, is that of one who cleanses by "stamping with the feet." His business is to restore the soiled cloth to its natural whiteness. The evangelist uses an earthly thing to represent the heavenly. The heavenly Fuller gives a purity and a brightness infinitely exceeding the power of any "fuller on earth." It would almost seem as if the figure was one specially supplied by St. Peter.

Ver. 4.—**And there appeared unto them Elijah with Moses.** Moses and Elijah were there because Moses was the lawgiver of the old covenant, and Elijah was conspicuous among the prophets; so that they were the representatives, the one of the Law, and the other of the "goodly fellowship of the prophets." They appear together to bear witness to Christ as the true Messiah, the Saviour of the world, prefigured in the Law, and foretold by the prophets. They appear to bear witness to him, and then to resign their offices to the great Lawgiver and Prophet whom they foreshadowed. Then, further, Moses died, but Elijah was translated. Moses, therefore, represents the dead saints who shall rise from their graves and come forth at his coming, while Elijah represents those who shall be found alive at his advent. Our Lord brought with him, at his transfiguration, Moses who had died, and Elijah who had been translated, that he might show his power over both "the quick and the dead." St. Luke (ix. 31) says that Moses and Elijah "appeared in glory, and spake of his decease (τὴν ἔξοδον αὐτοῦ) which he should accomplish at Jerusalem." They appeared in glory; the Divine splendour irradiated them. They "spake of his decease," literally, *his departure*—his departure not only out of Jerusalem, but out of this life, by his death upon the cross. The death of Christ was thus shown to be the ultimate end to which the Law and the prophets pointed. Even in that hour of his glory, on the Mount of Transfiguration, this was their theme; and thus the disciples were nerved to look with hope and faith to that which they had contemplated with dismay.

Ver. 5.—**Peter answereth, and saith to Jesus.** We learn from St. Luke (ix. 33) that this happened just as Moses and Elijah were departing. Peter was excited, and there was fear mingled with his excitement. He was bewildered. His first idea was to seek that they might remain, for he saw that they were just preparing to depart. Theophylact says upon this, "Do not say with Peter, 'It is good for us to be here;' for it behoves us ever, whilst in the flesh, to be advancing, and not to remain in one stage of virtue and contemplation, but to pass on to other degrees." It is, perhaps, too curious a question to ask how the three disciples knew them to be Moses and Elijah. The same Divine power which presented them with a vision of the other world gave them an intuitive knowledge on the subject. And we may, perhaps, infer from hence that in that world to come there will be not only recognition, but knowledge, at once imparted, of those whose faces we have not seen "in the flesh." St. Luke (ix. 32) says that Peter and his companions "were heavy with sleep (βεβαρημένοι ὕπνῳ)." It is probable that the Transfiguration took place at night. The whole manifestation would be rendered more conspicuous and striking amidst the darkness and stillness of night. But St. Luke is careful to add, "when they were fully awake (διαγρηγορήσαντες)." This word might be rendered, "having remained awake." But whichever translation be adopted, the intention of the evangelist is evidently to show that it was not in a dream or a vision of the night that they saw this. It was a great reality, on which they looked with open eyes.

Ver. 6.—**They became sore afraid.** There is a slight change of reading here. Instead of ἦσαν γὰρ ἔκφοβοι, the best authorities give ἔκφοβοι γὰρ ἐγένοντο. A sense of great awe and terror overpowered the bliss and brightness of the scene. All the revelations of the other world strike terror, even though abated as this manifestation was by the presence of their dear Lord and Saviour.

Ver. 7.—**There came a cloud overshadowing them.** The cloud enfolded them all, so that they could not be seen, it was so ample and dense, and yet so bright and shining. St. Matthew (xvii. 5) says it was "a bright cloud." The cloud was a symbol of

the grandeur and unapproachable glory of God. The disciples were admitted within this cloud that they might have a foretaste of future glory, and that they might be witnesses of what took place under the cloud, and especially that they might be able to give evidence throughout all ages of the voice which they heard come out of the cloud from "the excellent glory" (the expression is equivalent to the Hebrew "Shechinah," and St. Peter says (2 Epist. i. 18), it came from heaven), **This is my beloved Son: hear ye him.** But at the same time that this cloud was the symbol, it was also the veil of Deity, of the glory of Deity. "He maketh the clouds his chariot," says the psalmist (Ps. civ. 3). Moreover, the cloud abated and subdued the splendour of Christ's appearance, which otherwise the mortal eyes of the disciples could not have borne. It will be observed that St. Mark omits the words, found in St. Matthew (xvii. 5), "in whom I am well pleased." So does St. Luke. But it is remarkable that they are found in St. Peter (2 Epist. i. 17); from whence we might have expected to find them here. In St. Luke (ix. 35) the most approved readings give, "This is my Son, my chosen (ἐκλελεγμένος)." The words, "my beloved Son," are impressed upon us in order that epithets so sweet and endearing might kindle our love and devotion. "Hear ye him"—not Moses, who has now departed, but Christ himself, the new Author of a new Law. "Hear ye him" was not said when our Lord was baptized, because he was then only just proclaimed to the world. But now these words signify the abolition of the old dispensation, and the establishment of the new covenant in Christ.

Ver. 8.—**And suddenly looking round about, they saw no one any more, save Jesus only with themselves.** St. Matthew here says (xvii. 6), "When the disciples heard it, they fell on their face, and were sore afraid. And Jesus came and touched them, and said, Arise, and be not afraid." St. Mark omits this; but in his characteristic manner states that which implies what St. Matthew has recorded. It was the "touch" of Jesus that caused them to look round about; and then in a moment they perceived that they were alone with Jesus, as they were before this manifestation began. The order of incidents in the Transfiguration appears to have been this: Our Lord is praying. The disciples, fatigued with the ascent of the mountain, are heavy with sleep; and Christ is transfigured. Then appear Moses and Elijah; and they are talking with Jesus about his exodus—his decease to be accomplished at Jerusalem. The disciples roused from their sleep by the supernatural brightness, and by the conversation, and now, fully awake, behold the glory of Jesus, and Moses and Elijah talking with him. As Moses and Elijah are preparing for their departure, Peter, excited, enchanted, bewildered, and yet grieved to see that they were going, seeks to detain them by the proposal to make some temporary resting-place for them. Then comes the bright overshadowing cloud, and a voice out of the cloud, " This is my beloved Son : hear ye him." At the sound of this voice the disciples fall terrified to the earth. But they are soon comforted by Christ, and, looking up, they see him alone with themselves.

Ver. 9.—**He charged them that they should tell no man what things they had seen, save when the Son of man should have risen again from the dead.** They were not even to tell their fellow-disciples, lest it might cause vexation or envy that they had not been thus favoured. The time of our Lord's resurrection would be a fitting opportunity for revealing this mystery ; and then the disciples would understand and believe it, when, after his passion and death, which were an offence to them, they should see him rising in glory, of which event the Transfiguration was a type. For, by the Resurrection they would certainly know that Christ underwent the death of the cross, not by constraint, but of his own accord, and out of his great love for us.

Vers. 10, 11.—**Questioning among themselves what the rising again from the dead should mean ;** that is, his own rising from the dead, of which our Lord had just been speaking. No doubt the general resurrection at the end of the world was an article of faith with which the disciples were familiar. But they could not understand, when he spake of his own immediate rising from the dead. So their perplexities led them at last to ask him the question ; or rather to make the remark to him, **The scribes say that Elijah must first come ;** with a view to obtaining some clearer understanding. They had just seen Elijah in the Transfiguration, and they had seen him disappear. They wondered why he should have departed. They thought, it may be, that he ought to have remained, that he might be the forerunner of Christ and of his kingdom and glory, according to the prophecy of Malachi (iv. 6). This the scribes taught ; but they erred in the confusion of times, for they did not distinguish the first coming of Christ in the flesh from his second advent to judgment. The thought upon the mind of the disciples appears to have been this : They heard Christ speak of his own resurrection as close at hand, and they had seen the type of it in his transfiguration ; and they thought that immediately after that, Christ's kingdom would come, and he would

reign gloriously. Why, then, had not Elijah remained, that he might be his precursor ? St. Matthew (xvii. 13) tells us that our Lord's words which follow showed the disciples that when he said that Elijah was to come first and restore all things, he meant them to understand " that he spake unto them of John the Baptist." Upon the question of a future coming of Elijah, it seems safest to confess our ignorance. The prophecy of Malachi was no doubt in part fulfilled in the coming of John the Baptist ; but it would be rash to affirm that it may not receive another and more literal fulfilment before the second advent. A host of ancient Christian expositors have held that Elijah will appear in person before the second advent of Christ. St. Augustine, in his 'City of God' (xx. 29), says, "Not without reason do we hope that before the coming of our Judge and Saviour Elias will come, because we have good reason to believe that he is now alive ; for, as Holy Scripture distinctly informs us, he was taken up from this life in a chariot of fire. When, therefore, he is come he shall give a spiritual explanation of the Law which the Jews at present understand carnally, and will turn the hearts of the fathers to the children, and the children to the fathers ; that is, the Jews who are the children will understand the Law in the same sense as their fathers the prophets understood it." Indeed, this is one of the principal reasons assigned by the Fathers for this appearance of Elijah, that he may convert the Jews.

Ver. 14.—**And when he came to his disciples, he saw a great crowd around them.** High authorities support the reading adopted by the Revisers, *when they came to the disciples, they saw a great multitude about them.* "They" would thus mean our Lord and the three chosen disciples who had been with him on the Mount of Transfiguration. "They" came to the other disciples who had been left below. St. Luke (ix. 37) adds " On the next day, when they were come down from the mountain." This would seem to confirm the supposition that the transfiguration took place in the night. All the synoptists agree in placing the following miracle immediately after the transfiguration. Scribes were questioning with the disciples who had been left behind. As usual, they had assembled in the neighbourhood where Jesus was, for the purpose of watching him. Their object in questioning with the disciples was doubtless to throw discredit upon Jesus, because they, his disciples, had failed to work the miracle.

Ver. 15.—The multitude were favourably disposed towards Jesus, and were glad that he had returned at an opportune moment to defend his disciples against the scribes,

But why were they greatly amazed? The word in the Greek is ἐξεθαμβήθη. It seems most probable that they saw in his countenance, always heavenly and majestic, something even yet more Divine, retaining some traces of the glory of his transfiguration, even as the face of Moses shone when he came down from the mount (Exod. xxxiv. 29). It hardly seems likely that the amazement of the people was simply caused by our Lord having arrived at an opportune time to relieve his disciples of their difficulty. The Greek word expresses something more than would be satisfied by the fact of our Lord having come upon the scene just when he was wanted. Even if there were no remains of the transfiguration glory upon his countenance, the vivid recollection of the scene, of the conversation with Moses and Elijah, and the subject of it, and the voice of the Father, must have invested his countenance with a peculiar majesty and dignity. The same word, though without its compound (ἐθαμβοῦντο), is used further on in ch. x. 32 to express the amazement of the disciples, as he pressed eagerly onwards before them on his way to Jerusalem and to his cross. There was no doubt something then in his countenance which astonished them. The multitude **running to him, saluted him.** The scribes had not been able to shake their faith. In their view he was still "that Prophet that should come into the world."

Ver. 16.—**And he asked them;** that is, the multitude. The context shows this. The reading here is αὐτούς, not τοὺς] γραμματεῖς.

Ver. 17.—**One of the multitude answered him, Master I brought**—the Greek is ἤνεγκα—**unto thee my son.** He brought his son, expecting to find Jesus; but failing in this, he applied to our Lord's disciples to cast out the evil spirit, but they could not. St. Matthew (xvii. 14) says that the man came kneeling to Christ, "and saying, Lord, have mercy on my son: for he is lunatic." The word in the Greek there is σεληνιάζεται. Etymologically, no doubt, "lunatic" conveys the meaning of the word most nearly. But the graphic description here of St. Mark corresponds exactly to epilepsy, and to epilepsy acted upon by an unclean spirit, who in this instance deprived the sufferer of his speech. Lunatics were so called from the prevailing impression, not without foundation, that the light and the changes of the moon have an influence upon the body, and so act through the body upon the mind. This influence seems to be recognized in Ps. cxxi. 6, "The sun shall not smite thee by day, nor the moon by night."

Ver. 18.—**Wheresoever it taketh him** (καταλάβη); literally, *it seizeth hold of him.*

This is the Greek word from which comes our "catalepsy," the active form of "epilepsy." It teareth him (ῥήσσει). This is doubtless the literal meaning. But there is much evidence to show that it means here "it striketh or throweth him down." This is the rendering of the Peshito Syriac, and of the Vulgate. The same interpretation is also given by Hesychius as one of the meanings of the word. St. Luke (ix. 39) describes the symptoms thus: "A spirit taketh him, and he suddenly crieth out, and it teareth him (σπαράσσει αὐτὸν) that he foameth (μετὰ ἀφροῦ), and it hardly departeth from him, bruising him sorely." This it will be remembered is the record of one who was himself a physician. **He grindeth his teeth, and pineth away** (ξηραίνεται), as though the springs of his life were dried up. The father of the boy is here minutely describing the symptoms when the fit was upon him. He seems here to express the stiffness and rigidity of the body in the approaches of the malady. **And I spake to thy disciples that they should cast it out; and they were not able.** They had tried and failed. This failure is attributed by our Lord (see Matt. xvii. 20) to their want of faith; or rather to their "little faith (διὰ τὴν ὀλιγοπιστίαν ὑμῶν)."

Ver. 19.—**O faithless generation.** These words were no doubt intended primarily as a rebuke to the Jews and their scribes; though not without a glance at the weakness of faith of his own disciples. The words are the complaint of one weary of the unbelief of the masses and of the weakness of faith in even his own. **Bring him unto me** (φέρετε); literally, *Bring ye him to me.*

Ver. 20.—**And they brought him unto him.** The father, it would seem, was not able of himself to bring him, so fierce and violent were the paroxysms of the disorder. **And when he saw him, straightway the spirit tare him** (συνεσπάραξεν)—it might be rendered, *convulsed him*—**grievously.** Observe the Greek construction (καὶ ἰδὼν αὐτὸν τὸ πνεῦμα), masculine participle with neuter noun. The sight of Christ stirred the evil spirit dwelling in the child. He was irritated by the presence of Christ; for he knew his power, and feared lest he should be cast out. Then came the last and most violent convulsion. **He wallowed foaming.** The word "to wallow" is probably from the Latin *volvo.* He rolled about in his agony. St. Gregory, quoted by Trench ('Miracles,' p. 397), shows how true all this is to nature; and that "the expulsion of a deadly evil from our spiritual being is not accomplished without a terrible struggle, followed in some cases by extreme prostration."

Vers. 21, 22.—Our Lord asks the father, not the sufferer, which in this case would have been useless—he was but a lad, and he was dumb. Our Lord's question, **How long time is it since this hath come unto him?** was intended, not of course for his own information, but to inspire the father with hope and confidence. The father briefly answers, **From a child**; and then returns to a description of the perils to which his child was continually exposed through these paroxysms. And then, half doubting, half in despair, he says, **If thou canst do anything, have compassion on us, and help us.** It is as though he said, "Thy disciples have failed, perhaps thy power may be greater."

Vers. 23, 24.—The most approved reading here is, not Εἰ δύνασαι, πιστεῦσαι, but simply Εἰ δύνασαι. So that the English rendering is, **If thou canst!** All things are possible to him that believeth. Our Lord takes up the father's words. It is as though he said, "Thou sayest to me, 'If thou canst do anything!' Ah, that 'If thou canst!' All things are possible to him that believeth." In other words, our Lord said to him, "Believe in me, and your child shall be healed." It was right that Christ should demand faith in himself; for it was not fitting that he should confer his special benefits on those who disbelieved or doubted about him—that he should thrust his blessings on those who were unworthy of them. The answer of the father is touching and beautiful. Greatly agitated, he cried out and said (we might well suppose (μετὰ δακρύων), "with tears," although the weight of evidence is against this addition being retained in the text), **I believe; help thou mine unbelief.** It is as though he said, "I do believe; but my faith is weak. Do thou, therefore, increase and strengthen it; so that whatever there is in me of doubt or remaining unbelief may be taken away, and I may be counted worthy to obtain from thee this blessing for my son." Nor can we doubt that Christ heard a prayer so humble and so fervent, and took away from him the last remains of doubt and unbelief.

Vers. 25—29.—The multitude had been much excited by the dispute between the scribes and our Lord's disciples. And now, when they noticed that he had taken the father apart, as no doubt he had done, to question him, **they came running together** (the word is ἐπισυντρέχει, an unusual word, meaning "they ran together to the place") where he was, crowding upon him. Then he came forward, and with a voice of sublime authority he said, **Thou dumb and deaf spirit, I command thee, come out of him, and enter no more into him.** The rest of the narrative shows how malignant and powerful this evil spirit was, who dared so to resist and defy Christ that, in his departure

out of the afflicted boy, he almost robbed him of life. "Most unwillingly," says Archbishop Trench, "does the evil spirit depart, seeking to destroy that which he can no longer retain." And he quotes Fuller, who says that he is "like an outgoing tenant, that cares not what mischief he does to the house that he is quitting." Some have supposed that this was an evil spirit possessed of more than ordinary power as well as malignity, and that this was the reason why our Lord's disciples could not cast him out: so that this expulsion needed the mighty arm of One stronger than the strong. The words in the Greek are powerful, severe, and authoritative: "He rebuked (ἐπετίμησε) the unclean spirit, . . . Thou dumb and deaf spirit (τὸ πνεῦμα τὸ ἄλαλον καὶ κωφὸν), I command thee (ἐγώ σοι ἐπιτάσσω), come out of him, and enter no more into him." This explains our Lord's words when the disciples remarked afterwards, **We could not cast it out.** . . . **This kind can come out by nothing, save by prayer**; that is, this particular kind of malicious spirit. For there are different degrees of malice and energy in evil spirits as in evil men. The words "and fasting" are added in many ancient authorities.

Ver. 30.—This verse informs us that our Lord and his disciples now left the neighbourhood of Cæsarea Philippi. Their route would be across the Jordan above the Sea of Galilee, and so by the usual track through Galilee down to Capernaum. Our Lord now wished for privacy, that he might further instruct his disciples with regard to his sufferings and death.

Ver. 31.—**For he taught his disciples** (ἐδίδασκε γὰρ τοὺς μαθητὰς αὐτοῦ); literally, for he was teaching (imperfect) his disciples. **The Son of man is delivered** (παραδίδοται). The whole is present to his mind, as though it were now taking place. **And they shall kill him** (ἀποκτενοῦσιν). This is a stronger form of κτείνω. **And when he is killed, after three days he shall rise again** (ἀναστήσεται); literally, he shall rise up. Our Lord repeats this prediction, in order that, when these events actually took place, his disciples might not be alarmed or offended, or abandon their faith in him, as though he could not be the Messiah because he underwent so terrible a death. It will be remembered that, notwithstanding these repeated warnings from their Lord, when these events actually took place, "they all forsook him and fled." It was therefore necessary that this coming event of his crucifixion should be repeatedly impressed upon them, that they might thus be assured that he was willing to undergo this bitter death; that he was not going to his cross by constraint, but as a willing Sacrifice, that he might do the will of his Father, and so redeem mankind. Therefore he repeated all this in Galilee, when he returned from his transfiguration, and after he had cast out the evil spirit from the epileptic child, and so had gained to himself great renown. He would thus restrain the excited feelings of his disciples, and impress upon them the reasons for his journey to Jerusalem, and prepare them for the dread realities which were awaiting him there.

Ver. 32.—**But they understood not the saying, and were afraid** (ἐφοβοῦντο) **to ask him.** St. Matthew (xvii. 23) says, "They were exceeding sorry." They saw that something very dreadful was about to happen. Their Master's words and looks showed them this. But it was a mystery to them. All his words staggered them, but especially those which spoke of his rising again. They did not understand whether it was an entrance into a higher state or a restoration to a common life. They did not understand why he was to die, and how these words of his about his death could agree with those in which he had told them that his kingdom was at hand. Perhaps, on the whole, they inclined to the view most pleasing to them, that Christ would not die; for this was what they wished and most desired. And so they tried to persuade themselves that his words respecting his sufferings and death had some other hidden meaning; and were to be understood in a figurative sense and not a literal. But anyhow, they dreaded to ask him.

Vers. 33, 34.—They have now reached Capernaum. **And when he was in the house** —the house, that is, which he frequented when staying in Capernaum—**he asked them, What were ye reasoning in the way?** The words "among yourselves," of the Authorized Version, are not found in the best authorities. St. Matthew (xviii. 1) does not record this question of our Lord, which brings to light the fact that they had been disputing by the way which of them should be the greatest. The Greek is (τίς μείζων) **who was greater,** that is, than the rest. It has been well noticed that this passage, given in substance in all the synoptic Gospels, is a striking evidence of the truthfulness and impartiality of the disciples. This dispute of theirs might easily have been suppressed as scarcely creditable to them. But in writing the Gospels the evangelists thought more of what exalted the Saviour than what abased themselves. This dispute of the disciples shows how thoroughly they realized the nearness of his kingdom, and at the same time how much they had yet to learn as to the qualifications necessary for admission to it. It is not unlikely that the preference given by our Lord to Peter, James, and John may have given occasion for this contention.

Ver. 35.—**And he sat down, and called the twelve.** He sat down, with the authority of the great Teacher, to inculcate solemnly a fundamental principle of the Christian life. **If any man would be first, he shall be last of all, and minister of all.** These words are capable of two interpretations. They might be regarded as analogous to our Lord's words elsewhere, "He that exalteth himself shall be abased;" as though they indicated the penalty which attaches to unworthy ambition. But it is surely far more natural to regard them as pointing out the way to real greatness, namely, by humble service for Christ's sake.

Ver. 36.—**And he took a little child** (παιδίον), **and set him in the midst of them.** St. Mark adds, what is not recorded by the other synoptists, that he took him in his arms. **And taking him in his arms** (ἐναγκαλισάμενος); literally, *folding him in his arms; embracing him.* It is probable that the house where he was was the house of Simon Peter; and it is possible that this little child might have been Simon's. A tradition not earlier than the ninth century says that this child was Ignatius.

Ver. 37.—**Whosoever shall receive one of such little children in my name, receiveth me.** Whosoever shall "receive;" that is, show him offices of kindness and charity. *One of such little children;* that is, such in simplicity, in innocence and humility, such as this little child is in age and stature. *In my Name,* that is, with special regard to my Name. He thus seems to link all that is good and beautiful with his Name; as all that is really good and excellent in man is a reflection of his goodness. St. Luke (ix. 48) says, 'Whosoever shall receive *this little child* in my Name receiveth me." Our Lord, therefore, speaks first, literally, of a little child, and secondly, in a mystical sense, of those who are like little children; making that little child in his arms the figure and type of all those who are like little children. The sense, therefore, of his words is this: "Humility, which is the foundation and the measure of spiritual perfection, so pleases me that I delight in little children. And all who would be my disciples must become as little children, and so will they deserve to be received by all; for men will think that they receive me in them, because they receive them for my sake."

Ver. 38.—This verse, according to the best authorities, should begin simply, **John said unto him**—although in St. Luke (ix. 49) they stand, "And John answered and said"—**Master, we saw one casting out devils in thy name: and we forbade him, because he followed not us.** The casting out of evil spirits was one of the foremost signs of apostleship; and what surprised St. John was that one who followed not Christ should have been able to work this miracle —a miracle in which, it will be remembered, the disciples had recently failed. It thus appears that our Lord's teaching had been so influential, that some, not reckoned amongst his disciples, had shown this proof of a strong and overpowering faith. We know that there were those in our Saviour's time, of Jewish race, who cast out devils (Matt. xii. 27). And Justin Martyr, in his 'Dialogue with Trypho the Jew,' states that while exorcism, as practised by the Jews, often failed when it was attempted to be exercised "by the God of Abraham, Isaac, and Jacob," was eminently successful when administered "by the name of the Son of God, who was born of a virgin and crucified under Pontius Pilate" (c. 85). That spirit has power over spirit in many mysterious ways is one of those truths which science has not yet been able to explain (see Dr. Morison on St. Mark, in loc.). To return, however, to the instance here alluded to by St. John, it should be observed that they who acted thus had faith in Christ; and that by thus acting with him and for him, though not amongst his recognized followers, they contributed towards his honour who, by means of these imperfect instruments, carried out the great purpose of his manifestation, namely, "to destroy the works of the devil." Then further, the disciples forbade them not out of envy or hatred, but out of zeal for Christ, as though they were thus serving his cause and upholding his honour. But this was "a zeal, not according to knowledge." They had forbidden them, without having first taken counsel of their Master.

Ver. 39.—**But Jesus said, Forbid him not.** It is as though our Lord said, "Do not forbid him; do not hinder him from a good work—a work which does honour to me and to my cause; because, although he does not actually follow me as you do, he is nevertheless engaged in the same cause; he is celebrating my Name by the casting out of evil spirits. Therefore he is not opposing my Name; on the contrary, he is publishing and recommending it." Here is a warning against that exclusive spirit, which is eager for its own ends rather than for Christ's glory, and would limit the exercise of his gifts and graces to its own system or school, instead of inquiring whether those whom it condemns are not working in Christ's name and for the promotion of his glory, although it may be allowable to think that in some instances they might find a more excellent way.

Ver. 40.—**For he that is not against us is for us.** In St. Matthew (xii. 30) we find our Lord using a somewhat similar expres-

sion, only in an inverted order. He there says, "He that is not with me is against me." The lesson which both these apothegms teach is the same, that there is no such thing as neutrality in reference to Christ and his cause. We must be either with him or against him. Dr. Morison on St. Mark in this place says, "When in applied morals we sit in judgment on ourselves, we should in ordinary circumstances apply the law obversely and stringently, 'he who is not with Christ is against him.' But when we are sitting in judgment on others, into whose hearts we cannot look directly, we should in ordinary circumstances apply the law reversely and generously, 'He that is not against Christ is with him.'"

Ver. 41.—**In my name, because ye belong to Christ.** The reading adopted in the Revised Version is, ἐν ὀνόματι ὅτι χριστοῦ ἐστε: literally, in name, that ye are Christ's; or, because ye are Christ's. The force of this observation seems to be this: "If he who gives you a cup of water to drink in my Name, and out of regard for me, does well, and shall be rewarded of God, much more shall he be rewarded who casts out devils in my Name." The disciples are thus taught that it is contrary to the whole spirit of Christianity to disparage works of beneficence, or to suggest unworthy motives for them (see 'Speaker's Commentary,' in loc.).

Ver. 42.—This verse stands out as the severe antithesis to what has gone before. As he who receives and encourages Christ's little ones and those who are like little children and believe in him, receives him, and so shall receive from him the glorious rewards of Heaven; so, on the contrary, whosoever shall offend one of these little ones that believe in Christ is guilty of deadly sin; and **it were better for him if a great millstone** (μύλος ὀνικός)—literally, a millstone so large as to require to be turned by an ass—**were hanged about his neck, and he were cast into the sea.**

Ver. 43.—The hand, or the foot, or the eye represents any instrument by which sin may be committed; and it applies to those who may be the means of drawing us into sin. If your relative or your friend, who is useful or dear to you as your hand, your foot, or your eye, is drawing you into sin, cut him off from you, lest he should draw you into hell, into the **unquenchable Gehenna.** Gehenna, or the Valley of Hinnom, lay to the south of Jerusalem. Originally a pleasant suburb of the city, it became in later times the scene of the worship of Molech, "the abomination of the children of Ammon." On this account the valley was polluted by King Josiah. It thus became the receptacle of everything that was vile and filthy.

These noisome accumulations were from time to time consumed by fire; and the things which were not consumed by fire were the prey of worms. Hence "Gehenna" became the image of the place of eternal punishment, where "the worm dieth not and the fire is not quenched." These terrible images are conclusive as to the eternity of future punishment, so far as our nature is concerned and our knowledge reaches. They are the symbols of certain dreadful realities; too dreadful for human language to describe or human thought to conceive.

Ver. 44.—**Where their worm dieth not, and the fire is not quenched.** These words are a quotation from Isa. lxvi. 24, and they are repeated three times in the Authorized Version. But the best ancient authorities omit them in the two first places, retaining them at ver. 48. The metaphor is very striking as well as awful. Ordinarily the worm feeds upon the disorganized body, and then dies. The fire consumes the fuel, and then itself expires. But here the worm never dies; the fire never goes out. The words of Cornelius à Lapide on the original passage in Isaiah are well worth recording here: "I beseech you, O reader, by the mercies of our God, by your own salvation, by that one little life entrusted to you and committed to your care, that you will ever keep before your eyes the living memory, as of eternity and of eternal torments, so also of the eternal joys on the other side offered to you by God, and concerning which you here cast the die, and that irrevocable. Let these two things never depart from your mind. In this world, 'Vanity of vanities, and all is vanity.' Oh, what a void there is in earthly things! Oh, how vain is all our life without Christ! In the world to come, truth of truths, and all is truth; stability of stabilities, and all is stability; eternity of eternities, and all is eternity. An eternity in heaven most happy, in hell most miserable, 'Where their worm dies not, and the fire is not quenched.'" St. Bernard says "the worm that never dies is the memory of the past, which never ceases to gnaw the conscience of the impenitent."

Ver. 49.—**For every one shall be salted with fire; and every sacrifice shall be salted with salt.** According to the most approved authorities, the second clause of this verse should be omitted, although it is evident that our Lord had in his mind the words in Lev. ii. 13, "Every oblation of thy meat offering shalt thou season with salt." *Every one shall be salted with fire.* "Every one." The statement is general in its application. There is no limitation. The good and the evil alike shall be "salted with fire." There is an apparent incongruity here. But it must be remembered that both the salt and

the fire are here used in a metaphorical sense; and there is a fire which is *penal*, and there is a fire which *purifies*. In the case of the wicked the fire is penal; and the salting with fire in their case can only mean the anguish of a tormented conscience, which must be commensurate with its existence in the same moral condition. But there is a fire which purifies. St. Peter, addressing the Christians of the Dispersion (1 Epist. iv. 12), bids them not to think it strange concerning the "fiery trial" which was among them. This was their "salting with fire." Those persecutions which they suffered were their discipline of affliction, through which God was purifying and preserving them. This discipline is necessary for all Christians. They must arm themselves with the same mind, even though they may not live in a time of outward persecution. He who parts with the hand, or the foot, or the eye; that is, he who surrenders what is dear to him—he who parts with what, if he was only to confer with flesh and blood, he would rather keep, for the sake of Christ, is going through the discipline of self-sacrifice, which is often painful and severe, but nevertheless purifying. He is salted with fire; but he is preserved by the power of God through faith unto salvation.

Ver. 50.—**Salt is good;** that is, it is useful and beneficial. This is true of the literal salt. Its wholesome antiseptic properties are universally recognized. But our Lord has before his mind in this whole passage the spiritual meaning. He is thinking of the salt of Divine grace, of the salt of a spirit informed and influenced by the Holy Spirit. He had already told his disciples that they were "the salt of the earth." Not, indeed, that they could deliver the earth from corruption —that was beyond their power. But when Christ had delivered it by his mighty sacrifice and the gift of his Spirit, it was their business, as it is the duty of all Christians, to keep it in a healthy state; so that by their wisdom and purity, their holy lives and holy teaching, they might season the whole world. But **if the salt have lost its saltness** (ἐὰν τὸ ἅλας ἄναλον γένηται), **wherewith will ye season it?** This insipid, tasteless condition of salt is familiar to travellers in the East. Examples are to be found of large masses of salt which "has lost its savour." Our Lord here applies this in a spiritual sense to his disciples. "If ye, my disciples, who are the salt of the earth,—if ye lose the true properties of salt; if your Christianity loses its heart, its quickening, stimulating influence; so that on account of the love of the world, or the fear of man, or through lust or ambition, you fall away from the heavenly doctrine and life;—who shall restore you to your former spiritual health and vigour? With what can salt itself be seasoned when its own chemical energies are lost?" Our Lord plays upon this figure of salt, and cautions his disciples, lest by any means they should lose the qualities of this mystic salt. **Have salt in yourselves, and be at peace one with another.** This sentence fitly winds up the whole. Have the salt of wisdom and purity, and of a Christian life, namely, humility, charity, contempt of the world, and especially peace. Do not be idly contending about place or position, as not long ago you were dis-puting (ver. 33). Our Lord foresaw that this kind of contention, these rivalries, and these ambitious aims, would prove a great scandal and a great hindrance to the pro-gress of his Church in the future ages of the world. But he also knew that if his disciples in every age would endeavour to "keep the unity of the Spirit in the bond of peace," their influence would be irresistible, and they would draw all men to them and to himself, the great Centre of attraction, and "the confidence of all the ends of the earth" (Ps. lxv. 5).

HOMILETICS.

Vers. 2—13.—*Transfiguration*. Observe the crisis of our Lord's ministry at which this marvellous and memorable incident took place. The period of novelty, of popu-larity, of prosperity, was past and gone; the period of hostility, of persecution, of endurance, was commencing. Already Jesus had forewarned his disciples of the speedy approach of his death at the hands of his enemies. And it seems as though this unique and impressive display of his proper majesty, and of the affection and confidence of his Father, came exactly at the needed conjuncture. It was for his own sake, that a vivid consciousness of Divine favour might go with him to the scenes of ignominy and of suffering which awaited him. It was for the sake of the nearest and dearest among his friends, that they might carry with them, especially in those trials of their faith and attachment which were coming upon them, a conviction concerning their master's nature and mission which might support them and preserve them, if not from weak defection, still from shameful apostasy. The close connection between the glories of the Transfiguration and the shame and woe of Calvary, is evident both from the narrative itself and from the central and critical position it occupies. Regarding the Mount of Transfiguration as a mount of witness, we observe—

I. THE WITNESS CHRIST HERE BEARS TO HIMSELF. The sun in heaven is his own witness, shines by his own light, tells of his own nature and power. So with the Lord Christ. When, amidst the darkness of the night, upon the slopes of Hermon, his garments glistened, and his face shone with a dazzling radiance, his proper glory shone through the disguise of his human weakness and humiliation. For once he appeared to be what he really was—the Son of the Father, and the Lord of the world. It was testimony very powerful and very effective, and produced its impression upon those who were privileged to behold that "great sight."

II. THE WITNESS HERE BORNE TO CHRIST BY THE LAWGIVER AND THE PROPHET. After Abraham, no personages in their history were more honoured and venerated by the Jews than Moses and Elijah: Moses the giver of their Law, and Elijah the head and leader of their prophets. These two had not only in life fulfilled the will of God, they had at the close of their life-service been taken to himself by their Lord in very remarkable and singular circumstances. From the seats of the blessed, and in their vesture of immortality, these illustrious and glorified saints came to converse with the Son of God regarding the decease which he was about to accomplish at Jerusalem. They had foretold him, they had prefigured him, they now gave place to him; and what more appropriate than that they should thus tender to him their homage and their admiration? 1. They manifested interest in his mission, for this gave the meaning to their own—explained in the old economy much which would otherwise have been inexplicable. 2. They acknowledged his authority, for they had already testified to a Greater than themselves who should come, and their appearance on this occasion was an evidence of the reverential honour in which they held the Divine Lawgiver, the Divine Prophet. 3. They anticipated his decease; the event which he had so recently foretold, and for which he was now so deliberately, so sacredly pre-paring—an event of stupendous magnitude in the history of our sinful humanity.

III. THE WITNESS BORNE TO CHRIST BY HIS FRIENDS AND APOSTLES. 1. It may be asked—Why was it appointed that the Transfiguration should be witnessed by so small and select a group, and in so secluded a spot? Why were not multitudes permitted to behold a spectacle so amazing in itself, and so fitted to bring conviction to the minds of all beholders? Surely, it might be urged, no unbeliever, no caviller, could have withstood the evidence of our Lord's authority which such a scene afforded! It is recorded that the leaders of the Jews, the Pharisees, asked from Jesus a sign from heaven. This he refused them. But he allowed three favoured friends to behold his glory, when the customary veil was in some measure withdrawn. What is the explanation of this? It may be replied that it was not in harmony with the plans of our Lord Jesus to overpower the senses of the people with some irresistible display of supernatural power and glory. This would not have been to secure a moral result by moral means. Jesus would not have valued the admiration which was withheld from his moral character and his benevolent life, but which was accorded to the effulgence of celestial glory, striking all eyes with amazement. But there was another reason for the limitation of the witnesses of our Lord's transfiguration. The highest revelations of God's wisdom and holiness and love are for those only who are prepared to receive them. You may walk round the outside of a vast domain, a splendid palace; you may make the circuit of the walls, you may see the tree-tops shaken by the wind, you may catch glimpses of the lofty roofs and towers of the lordly edifice. But how little do you know of the imposing palace and its enchanting environments! If, however, you are permitted to enter the gates, to tread the stately gardens, to explore the mansion, to look through the library, to admire the sculptures and paintings, and, above all, to spend hours and days in converse with the choice spirits who make the abode their home,—then you can form a judgment, and cherish an appreciation which, so long as you were on the outside, you would never have been able to do. So with the knowledge of every high and pure and noble soul. Such a one is only to be known by those who have sympathy with him, and opportunities of fellowship with him. It cannot be otherwise than that the ignorant, the vulgar, the selfish, should misunderstand him. In like manner, but in the highest degree, it needed some sympathy with the Lord Christ in order to judge aright of him. It seems likely that when Jesus took with him only his three most intimate and congenial friends to behold his glory upon the holy mount, he did so because none others were sufficiently advanced in spiritual knowledge and appreciation to be capable of partaking and profiting by the privilege. Even the bulk of his own twelve disciples would have been, at that time, out of place upon the Mount of Transfiguration. As for the scribes and Pharisees, and all the vulgar formalists who desired a sign, they had no spiritual eyes with which to see the vision which was then and there vouchsafed to three lowly fishermen, whose hearts the Lord had touched, and whose sight the Lord had cleansed and quickened. 2. The emotions with which the favoured three were affected, when they beheld Christ's glory, deserve attention. There was *awe*: and this was honourable to them, that they experienced the feeling of trembling reverence in a presence so august, and before evidence so majestic and convincing. There was *delight*: hence the exclamation and the proposal of Peter. They felt it "good" to be in such a scene and in such society, and they would fain have prolonged the precious opportunity, and dwelt for a season upon the mount. 3. The convictions which they formed may be known from the language of Peter in his Second Epistle, from which it is apparent that the Transfiguration produced upon the minds of the witnesses a profound and ineffaceable impression concerning their Master's dignity and authority.

IV. THE WITNESS BORNE TO CHRIST BY THE FATHER HIMSELF. In the voice which came from the Father we observe: 1. A *declaration* to be believed: "This is my beloved Son." Jesus was beloved: (1) For the relation he sustained to the Father; for he was "the only begotten," and was by nature what no other human being can be affirmed to have been. (2) For his congenial character; for he pleased the Father alway; his character embodied every moral excellence. (3) For his willing obedience; for, as he had undertaken his mission in the spirit of the prophetic language, "Lo, I come . . . to do thy will, O my God," so he acted throughout his ministry in a manner conformable to the just and holy will of God the Father. (4) For his perfect submission; for he "learned obedience by the things which he suffered," and shrank not from any sufferings appointed, and refused not the cup which the Father gave. As God's beloved Son, he was "obedient unto death, even the death of the cross." 2. An *appeal* to be obeyed: "Hear ye him!" As in the former clause the address is to the intelligent nature, so in this clause it is to the practical nature, of men. It is a Divine imperative. The appeal is to the sense of human obligation. Hear his teachings as your Master! Hear his promises as your Friend and Saviour! Hear his commands as your Leader and Lord! Hear to rejoice, to respond, to obey!

APPLICATION. 1. Receive this witness concerning Christ. It is the witness of the most trustworthy of men, the most competent of observers; it is the witness of the Eternal Father, of him who cannot lie. 2. Repeat this witness concerning Christ. It is the vocation of the disciple to give testimony to the master. The Church is Christ's witness to the world. It is ours to tell who Jesus is and what he has done; it is ours to invite the faith, to require the allegiance of all mankind to him who is the Son of God.

Vers. 14—29.—*The lunatic boy.* In Raphael's picture of the Transfiguration, which has often been called the greatest of all paintings, the foreground is occupied by a vivid representation of this marvellous miracle wrought by our Lord upon his descent from the mountain. The conjunction of the two incidents, which are in such striking contrast with each other, seems suggestive. The native glory of the Redeemer shone forth in the presence of the three favoured disciples upon the holy mount. But the redemptive work of the Son of God is brought out most prominently by his mighty work of healing, in which he shows himself able to deliver a human sufferer from the agonies of a terrible disease, and from the clutches of a cruel foe. The one incident serves to bring out the other into a bolder relief; and the two must be taken together, in order that we may obtain a fair and complete view of the nature, and especially of the ministry, of Jesus.

I. OBSERVE THE DISTRESSING CASE OF HUMAN MISERY HERE PORTRAYED. St. Mark has depicted this whole incident with a graphic minuteness that cannot fail to impress itself upon the reader's mind. 1. The case itself is unique in the wretchedness of its symptoms. An epileptic boy, speechless, often convulsed and sometimes flung into the fire and the water, a sufferer in this way from childhood, and now wasting away from long-continued disease,—can a more affecting picture of human misery be painted than this? Add to all the particulars related the possession by an evil spirit; and the hopelessness of the case, the powerlessness of all human endeavours, becomes apparent. 2. The anguish of the father's heart is beyond description; his attitude, his language, declare his distress and his dejection. 3. The interest of the multitude is evident; a spectacle such as this could not fail to excite the commiseration and compassion of every feeling heart. Observe in this case a striking figure of the condition of the sinner as a captive of Satan, and of the state of this ungodly and sin-accursed humanity!

II. REMARK THE INABILITY OF ALL HUMAN MEANS AND AGENCIES TO RELIEVE THIS CASE OF WRETCHEDNESS. All that a father's watchfulness and care could effect had long been tried. Doubtless the best known and most skilful physicians had exhausted the resources of their art. But all had been in vain. And now the disciples of our Lord had been appealed to with earnest entreaties. In the absence of their Master upon the mountain they had put forth their endeavours, had exercised their authority. But all was in vain. It was the assertion of the father; it was the confession of the disciples themselves: "They could not cast out" the demon. And there is no power on earth that can deal effectually with the sinner's case—that can expel from this humanity the spirit of evil that has so long ruled, afflicted, and defiled it.

III. CONSIDER THE APPLICATION WHICH WAS MADE TO JESUS AS TO THE DIVINE HEALER. How spiritually significant and instructive is the approach of the suppliant father to the Christ! The importance attached to *faith* comes out in this narrative perhaps more prominently than in any other part of the Gospel. We recognize: 1. *The demand for faith.* The father states his case, describes the sufferings of his son, implores compassion, and entreats help. His qualification, "If thou canst do anything," calls forth Christ's marvellous and memorable utterance: "If thou canst! All things are possible to him that believeth." This is, indeed, a repetition of the teaching of Scripture in every page. Faith is the posture of the heart which God approves, and which renders those who assume it capable of being blessed. Faith is the cry of the heart which God will never disregard or reject. And this condition comes out in a very impressive manner in this dialogue. 2. *The assertion of faith.* The poor father was driven to faith by need and suffering, by sympathy and despondency, by his repeated failures to obtain relief. He was drawn to Christ by his gracious and majestic presence as he came down from the Mount of Transfiguration. The leper had doubted the will of Christ to save; this father seems to have had confidence in the disposition and readiness of the Divine Teacher and Healer, and upon the suggestion and requirement of the Redeemer he exclaims, with fervour and with earnestness, "Lord, I believe." 3. *The confession of unbelief.* He doubts, or until now has doubted, Christ's power to save, as appears from his "If thou canst," and as he himself acknowledges in his cry, "Help thou mine unbelief." If he had not believed at all, he would not have come to Jesus; if he had believed firmly, he would have come with other words and in another spirit. This combination is very true to nature. There are degrees of faith even in the faithful. Where is perfect faith in Jesus? Who has not had reason to cry, "Help thou mine unbelief;" "Increase my faith"? 4. *The cry for help.* The earnest applicant did not wait until his faith was stronger—until more assurances and encouragements were given. He pleads as for his life, for he pleads for his child. Hating his unbelief, he struggles against it. His appeal is the utterance of his heart, which has no hope and no resource save in Immanuel, the Son of God. An example this to all hearers of the gospel, and especially to the penitent, the doubting, the timid, and the tempted.

IV. REMARK THE HEALING GRACE AND POWER OF JESUS. 1. His compassion was excited. He might pause to call forth the father's faith; but he would not withhold his sympathy from the suffering. 2. His authority was exercised over the evil spirit; for he rebuked and bade the demon to come out, and this with a commanding voice, which even so potent an agent of evil could not resist. 3. His healing, gracious aid was extended to the boy. When the sufferer seemed as if dead, by reason of the exhausting convulsions in which the departing demon displayed his malicious power, the Lord of life took him by the hand and raised him up, and he arose. How beautiful and encouraging an illustration of our Lord's personal interest in, and spiritual contact with, those whom he commiserates, relieves, and saves!

APPLICATION. 1. There is no case of need, sin, and wretchedness beyond the power of Christ to aid. 2. There is no faith, however feeble, which will not justify an approach to Christ, and elicit his compassion and his willingness to help. 3. By spiritual discipline Christ's people may train themselves for grappling with every form, however extreme, of human misery and helplessness.

Vers. 30—32.—*Death foretold.* The evangelists have recorded that on several distinct occasions our Lord foretold, in the hearing of his disciples, what would be the close of his earthly career. It is evident, accordingly, that these predictions, though only partially comprehended at the time, nevertheless made a deep impression on the minds of those who listened to them. After all that Jesus had foretold had been fulfilled, his apostles naturally enough recalled his sayings, and pondered them in the light of actual events, and published among their fellow-disciples the communications which have been recorded in the Gospels.

I. THE OCCASION OF THESE REVELATIONS. This *second* declaration by the Son of man of his approaching death and resurrection was made not long after the first. 1. It was in the course of the journey from Cæsarea Philippi through Galilee to the most ordinary scenes of his ministry that Jesus thus spoke to his disciples. They were apart from the multitude and the busy towns, where the great Healer was continually beset by applicants for relief and healing. There was quiet leisure, of which opportunity was taken by the Master to unfold anew to his disciples facts of tremendous import. 2. It was soon after the Transfiguration upon the mount—a display of his glory which must have enlightened the minds of his friends with regard to his nature, and must have disposed them to receive with deeper reflectiveness declarations concerning himself. That a Being so glorious and so remarkably in correspondence with celestial intelligences, and so intimately in the fellowship and the favour of the Eternal, should look forward to a fate so dread—this was indeed likely to provoke them to profound inquiry and meditation.

II. THE SUBSTANCE OF THESE REVELATIONS. The matter of these very remarkable and repeated communications was threefold. 1. He foretold his apprehension by his enemies. That there were among the ruling classes at Jerusalem many who were violently opposed to his teaching and to his claims, must have been known to his disciples as well as to himself. But hitherto Jesus had eluded the efforts of his foes, and had always proved himself able both to refute them in argument and to defy their efforts to seize and kill him. But the Lord's express words assured them that the time was at hand when the foes, whose enmity and malice had hitherto been defeated, should prevail against the Holy One and the Just. 2. He foretold the violent death which his enemies should inflict upon him. He had saved many from death, and had raised some from the dead; strange it must have seemed to them that he himself should submit to be put to death by the violence of men! Why should he submit to power which he was evidently capable of defying? Why should he endure treatment from which he could certainly save himself? Why should he endure a fate which he might easily avert? 3. He foretold his resurrection after three days' submission to death. This must have perplexed them still more. To what purpose need he die if he intended so soon to revive? Why not rather avoid death than, first submitting to it, then prove himself superior to its power? Yet such a prediction was fitted to enhance their conceptions of his majesty and authority.

III. THE EFFECT OF THESE REVELATIONS UPON THE MINDS OF THE DISCIPLES. Very simply are we informed that: 1. They understood not the saying. The words which the Lord had used were simple and unmistakable; the events he had foretold were such as were familiar to their observation, or such as they were acquainted with from the Old Testament narrative. What was it that they failed to understand? Probably the consistency between such a prospect and the view they were forming of Jesus' Messianic character and glory, and the expectations they were cherishing of his speedily approaching kingdom. Their minds were utterly confused by declarations which accorded neither with their primitive nor their more mature apprehensions of their Master's nature and ministry. 2. They were afraid to ask him. There seem to have been times when the disciples stood in awe of their Master. It could not well be otherwise. Sometimes his grace and friendliness drew them to him, and the intimacy was as that subsisting among brothers; at other times the superiority of Jesus seemed to cleave a chasm of separation which they had not confidence or courage to bridge over by their approaches. They could not then even question him concerning the import of his own language.

IV. THE REASON OF THESE REVELATIONS. 1. Jesus intended thus to open the eyes of his companions to his own character. Such sayings as these must have awakened their renewed inquiry, "What manner of man is this?" Thus Jesus would impress upon them the fact that his nature and character, his kingdom and mission, were altogether unique. 2. Jesus intended, in some measure, to prepare them for the events which were about to happen. This was effected but partially; yet it would be a mistake to suppose that such teaching was lost upon the twelve. The events of the Passion did indeed amaze and dismay Christ's disciples, yet not to that extent which would have been the case had no such communications been vouchsafed. 3. Jesus designed to open their minds to the spiritual nature of his kingdom. What he foretold could not happen without dispelling, or at least weakening, many preconceived notions and expectations; and even before these things came to pass, some light regarding the unworldly and spiritual kingdom must have streamed into their dim minds. 4. Jesus purposed that, after he should have arisen from the dead, they should call to memory the sayings they had heard from him, and that their faith should thus be confirmed in his superior knowledge, and in the divinity of his purposes, so clearly conceived and so gloriously accomplished. Thus was provision made for their thinking aright of him who laid down his life for the sheep, and in due time and of his own accord took to him that life again.

Vers. 33—37.—*True greatness.* Our Lord's ministry was not only to the people generally, but to his own disciples and friends; and even to these he had occasion sometimes to address language, not only of instruction, but of rebuke and expostulation. On the occasion here referred to, a serious fault was displayed among the chosen circle, which called for the Lord's interference and reprimand. At the same time the great Teacher pointed out to the erring a more excellent way. Ambition was the fault, and its appearance among the twelve occasioned our Lord's lesson in true greatness.

I. AMBITION AMONG THE FOLLOWERS OF CHRIST. 1. Notice its occasion. It seems as if recent events gave rise to the desire for pre-eminence among the friends and disciples of Jesus. The special commendation of Peter which the Master had recently pronounced, and the selection of the same apostle, with James and John, to witness the Transfiguration, probably prompted the aspiration and the discussion here recorded. 2. The exact form this disposition assumed. The twelve looked forward to the Messianic kingdom, of which they had come to regard Jesus as the divinely appointed Head, and in which they all expected to occupy posts of dignity and power. But who should be greatest? Who should be the chief minister under the Messianic King? Such was the matter in dispute, and that it should be so shows us how much the apostles had yet to learn. 3. The evil fruits of this ambition. It is quite in accordance with human nature that such a disposition should lead to disagreement and to contention. The twelve not only reasoned, they disputed; rivalry took the place of brotherhood. It is ever so; when the desire for pre-eminence and supremacy takes possession of men's hearts, farewell to contentment, harmony, and peace!

II. CHRIST'S REBUKE AND REMEDY FOR AMBITION. The observant eye of Jesus had remarked the wrangling which had gone on among his disciples, and his heart was pained. When he inquired into what had happened, they were ashamed and silenced; and he proceeded to unfold a principle which should operate, not in this company only, but throughout all periods of his Church. 1. Christ reveals the new and Christian law of greatness. Only those who are willing to be last of all, and ministers of all, shall be foremost in his kingdom. This was *paradoxical*, altogether in contradiction to the prevalent plan and principle among men in all grades of society, and in all communities, civil and ecclesiastical. It was *exemplified most illustriously in the Lord Jesus himself*. "Though he was rich, he became poor;" "He took on him the form of a servant;" "The Son of man came not to be ministered unto, but to minister." In his own person—in his incarnation, his humiliation, his obedience unto death, even the death of the cross—our Lord furnished the one incomparable example of humility and self-denial, and laid the axe to the root of the tree of self-seeking and pride. It was *a law containing within it its own sanction and power*. The humiliation and self-sacrifice of the Lord Jesus were more than an example; they introduced a new motive of spiritual persuasiveness and constraint into human society. The cross of Christ has been the great moral power which has changed human society, and is now the one hope of human regeneration. 2. Christ enforces his new law of greatness by a striking symbol. Our Lord often taught by act, thus enforcing the lessons embodied in his words. On this occasion he took a little child, and preached an ever-memorable sermon from this beautiful and touching text. The infant was in himself a living and evident illustration of submissiveness, teachableness, and humility. And not only so; the infant furnished the great Teacher with the lesson he needed: "Whosoever shall receive one of such," etc. Instead of seeking to be preferred above their brethren, Christians are here taught to seek out, and to minister to, the lowliest and the feeblest; and the inspiriting assurance is added, that those who in the Master's spirit receive and aid the least of his disciples—the lambs of his flock, the babes of his household— shall be regarded as having rendered a service to the Christ himself; nay, as having "received" the Creator and Lord of all, even him who sent and gave his Son for the salvation of mankind!

APPLICATION. 1. Dispositions which we are ashamed to bring into the presence and under the notice of Christ, are by that very fact condemned, and must be at once repressed and checked. 2. Towards one another it behoves the disciples of Jesus to cherish sentiments of esteem and honour. 3. Towards the feeble and the obscure they should display the tenderest consideration, remembering that those who serve Christ's lowliest people serve Christ himself.

Vers. 38—41.—*The judgment of charity.* It is clear, from this passage, that the influence of our Lord Jesus was wider than was known by his own immediate friends, and that his work was, even during his lifetime, advancing in directions of which they were not aware. Accidentally, as it were, we gain an insight into the progress of the kingdom of Christ outside the immediate circle of his acknowledged and professed disciples; and the incident which affords us this insight, at the same time presents to us truths and lessons of vast practical importance.

I. BIGOTRY IS HUMAN, AND CHARITY IS DIVINE. If any one of the twelve might have been deemed free from all suspicion of bigotry, surely it would have been John, often called " The Apostle of Love." Yet from this incident, and from his wishing upon another occasion to call down fire from heaven upon unbelievers, it is plain that, at all events during the Lord's ministry, he was wont to give way to an ardent, impetuous, violent spirit. In the view of a bigot, one who does not work in his own way is censured and condemned as unfit to work for God at all. The Lord Jesus proved his superiority to human infirmity by permitting and encouraging service which his followers would have forbidden.

II. OUTWARD UNITY AND CONFORMITY ARE NO SUFFICIENT TEST OF CHRISTIAN DISCIPLESHIP. Men are naturally prone to lay great stress upon this. The complaint, " He followeth not with us," has not been confined to the first followers of Jesus. The "following," in such cases, means outward association and agreement in language, usages, forms of policy and of worship. But two considerations should check that narrowness which would limit discipleship to those who conform to established custom : 1. Some conform, who prove themselves to be lacking in the mind and spirit of Jesus Christ. 2. Some refuse, or neglect to conform, who display such spirit, and whose actions show them to be Christ's.

III. ONE TEST OF DISCIPLESHIP IS THE SPIRIT IN WHICH MEN WORK FOR CHRIST. The stranger, to whom reference is made, is said to have done what he did *in Christ's Name*, and the Lord declares that the presumption is markedly in the favour of one whose practice may be so denoted. What are we to understand by the expression, " in Christ's Name"? It is an idiom which involves more than lies upon the surface. The Name of Christ implies his nature, his character, his claims, his mission. What is done truly in his Name, is done from reverence towards him, from faith in him, from love to him, in reliance upon his grace, and with a view to his honour and his approval. Now, our Lord teaches us that they whose life is animated and governed, controlled and guided, by a constant reference to himself, are to be honoured and encouraged. Such may have an imperfect acquaintance with the Lord Jesus, an insufficient apprehension of his nature or his work, an indisposition to consort with his professed followers. In all this it is possible they may be inferior to ourselves, though it is not certain. But this must not rouse us to bigotry, to conceit, and opinionated self-complacency. Let us recognize and admire the spirit which such "outsiders" may display, and wish them God-speed, and rejoice in their witness and in their work !

IV. ANOTHER TEST OF DISCIPLESHIP IS THE WORK WHICH MEN DO FOR CHRIST. This passage reminds us that: 1. It may be a mighty work or a power. This is not necessarily miraculous; it may be moral. The mark of God's finger may be upon the work. In our own state of society this "note" of true Christianity may sometimes be recognized among those who are unassociated with our Churches, and even among the "unorthodox." 2. It may be the casting out of demons. In the Gospel narrative this was literally the case. And in modern life there are many demons of ignorance, impurity, sloth, and selfishness, which need expulsion. And those who devote their time and energies to combating these ills, are doing the work of our Master, and will not be able quickly to speak evil of him. Let us rejoice, not only in their work, but in themselves. 3. It may be the giving of a cup of cold water to Christ's people in Christ's Name. Not the magnitude, but the moral tendency, the inner motive of the act, is of importance in the sight of our Lord. If the act itself be kind and beneficent, that is sufficient to recommend it to us, and to make it acceptable to the Lord. There is an obvious harmony between a good work and the good spirit in which the work is performed.

V. A CANON OF JUDGMENT. It may be determined that the rule of ver. 40, "He that is not against us is for us," refers to our judgment of others and of their actions. It is a wise as well as a charitable principle. It is a preservative against bigotry, and it is fitted to ensure equitable and considerate treatment of our neighbours. The rule elsewhere recorded, " He that is not for us is against us," applies to ourselves, and warns us against lukewarmness in our piety and negligence in our service. Let us be stricter with ourselves, and more charitable with others, and we shall the better please our righteous and gracious Lord.

Vers. 42—50.—*Warnings.* With these solemn words our Lord closed his arduous and faithful ministry in Galilee. Christ's language was usually language of grace and encouragement; but there were occasions, like the present, when he spoke words of faithful warning in tones almost of severity. Yet it should be noted that these admonitions were addressed to his own disciples, and were intended to quicken their spiritual sensibility, and to induce them to use with diligence the privileges with which they were favoured, especially through their association with himself.

I. POWERS AND MEANS OF USEFULNESS MAY BECOME OCCASIONS OF SPIRITUAL OFFENCE. This is a very serious consideration. Increased privilege brings increased responsibility, and none can possess powers of body or of mind without being exposed by such possession to liability to unfaithfulness and to consequent deprivation. 1. *Social intercourse and influence* come under this general principle. Our Lord speaks of his disciples, and especially of the inexperienced and immature, as "his little ones who believe on him." We cannot be associated with such without affecting them for good or for evil. To cause them to stumble, to betray them into errors or into sin, is an offence against our Lord, and it would be better for a man to be flung with a millstone about his neck into the deep water, than so to offend against the Lord of the little ones. 2. Our *active powers* may become occasions of offence. The hand and the foot may be taken as emblematical of these powers, the proper and intended purpose of which is undoubtedly their employment in works of justice and of charity and helpfulness. Yet these good faculties may cause their possessors to offend. The hands may work deeds of violence, the feet may lead into the way of sinners; and in such a case the purpose of the Creator is frustrated, and condemnation is incurred. 3. *Sense and intelligence may be productive of harm as well as of good.* The eye may fairly be taken as representing sense generally, and the apprehensive faculty. When the eyes wander where they should not, are closed when they should be open, or are open when they should be closed, they are an offence. When the intellect is directed to the wrong topics, or to the right topics in the wrong temper, its glory is dimmed, for its intention is thwarted, and it becomes a curse instead of a blessing.

II. THE ABUSE OF POWERS AND MEANS OF USEFULNESS WILL INVOLVE PUNITIVE SUFFERING AND RUIN. Under the rule of a righteous God, it cannot be that faithfulness and unfaithfulness, watchfulness and remissness, obedience and rebellion, will be treated alike. From the lips of the Lamb of God, the "meek and lowly in heart," language such as that which our Lord here employs is doubly impressive. Nevertheless, it is in mercy that the fruits of sin are shown to be apples of Sodom, that the wages of sin are expressly declared to be death. The figurative representations of the doom of the sinful are indeed terrific. This doom is worse than the vengeful overwhelming in the Lake of Galilee; it is compared to the casting out of corpses into Gehenna, below the walls of Jerusalem, where the fire consumed or the worms gnawed the unburied bodies of the dead. Such teaching leaves us in no doubt as to the view which the omniscient and most gracious Saviour takes of the future and eternal prospects of those who desecrate their powers and misuse their opportunities in the service of sin.

III. On the other hand, WATCHFULNESS AND SEVERITY WITH SELF WILL ENSURE THE BLESSING OF THE ETERNAL LIFE, AND THE HONOURS OF THE HEAVENLY KINGDOM. Even supposing that self is denied and crucified, that pleasures are foregone, that privations are incurred,—is all this worth thinking of with regret when the recompense of the faithful is borne in mind? What is this recompense? The Giver of life himself promises "entrance into life;" the Sovereign of the spiritual kingdom promises "entrance into the kingdom of God." If in some sense the saved are, in the process, exposed to a thousand ills and sorrows, still, though they enter lame and maimed and half-sightless into the kingdom of life, of God, they *do* enter, and entering are for ever glorious and for ever blessed. It is promised that through much tribulation Christ's followers shall enter into the kingdom of heaven.

HOMILIES BY VARIOUS AUTHORS.

Vers. 2—8.—*The Transfiguration.* I. THE CIRCUMSTANCES. At an interval of six or eight (Luke) days from Peter's confession and the teaching of the cross. "Into a high mountain," *i.e.* into some glen or secluded spot in the mountain. As there is no mention of any movement southward, and distinct assurance that they did not at this time go into Galilee (ch. ix. 30), the notion of Tabor being the mountain is unfounded. The slightness of its elevation, and the circumstance that its summit has been a fortified spot from the earliest times, render it almost certain that it was not the scene of the Transfiguration. All the evidence is in favour of Hermon, the snow-clad, sentinel-like peak in which the Anti-Libanus range culminates. Its name means "the mountain," and it is spoken of in the Old Testament as "holy." Its cool slopes and upland solitudes would afford congenial retirement to the weary Christ. It was mental trouble he had to overcome, and this he sought to do in prayer and Divine communion. For this reason, and the signs afforded by the rest of the chapter of the day having well begun as they descended, it has been supposed it was a night scene. He was wont to pray during the night, and the disciples were "heavy with sleep." It gives a peculiar character to the occurrence to suppose this to have been the case. But that they were fully awake when the vision appeared, Luke again assures us. The duration of the vision is not suggested; probably, as in dreams, time was an inappreciable element.

II. THE INCIDENTS. 1. *Transformation.* "He was transfigured before them," etc. The change described by the Greek word is literally one of *form*, but this must not be pressed. "It was a change in the externality of the person," says Morison; "a kind of temporary glorification, effected no doubt from within outward, rather than from without inward. It would reveal the essential glory of the spirit that 'tabernacled' within, its glory at once in that lower sphere that was human, and in that higher sphere that was Divine" ('Practical Commentary,' *in loc.*). The general brightness of his appearance is noted by the three evangelists, Matthew comparing his face to the sun, and his garments to the light. Mark speaks of the fuller's white in his description of it. The face is referred to by Matthew and Luke, and all three refer to the garments. Luke tells us it occurred "as he was praying." 2. *Association with Moses and Elias.* They *were seen* by the apostles, but did not purposely present themselves. They were talking with him, and Luke tells us the subject of their converse: "his decease which he was about to accomplish at Jerusalem." They were representatives of the righteous spirits in Hades, the world of the unseen, of disembodied spirits; representatives, too, of the Law and the prophets. They had laid the foundations of the kingdom of righteousness which he perfected. They spoke of his death as the grand means of the fulfilment of the hopes of immortality, they themselves having in the manner of their own "exodus" afforded the shadow and prophetic type of which his was the substance. He is in essential, spiritual oneness with them. 3. *Peter's suggestion.* Outcome of zeal, but not according to knowledge. It is seemingly enough for him to see his Master on terms of *equality* with those great spirits of the past. There is an undiscriminating comprehension in his proposal; a desire also to extend the duration of the ecstasy in which he and his companions were. It breaks the grand harmony of the evolution of the scene, and yet is full of instruction. 4. *Divine attestation.* The three accounts agree in the words, "This is my Son: hear ye him." Matthew and Mark have also "beloved," for which Luke substitutes "my chosen;" and Matthew alone adds, "in whom I am well pleased." The words are but human renderings of the unspeakable "voice." They prove that the great Centre of attention and attraction for the Church is Jesus, not Moses or Elias. 5. *Restoration of Christ to his usual appearance.* The distinguished associates of his glory vanish. The vision was no "baseless fabric," but it was over, and now the spectators must return to common life and mundane duties. Jesus "was found alone;" "Jesus only."

III. THE LESSONS. These are innumerable, and we must content ourselves with a few of the more prominent. There was revelation for both Christ and his disciples. A new light was thrown upon past and future, and the fear of death was broken. But the whole scene is best understood as a *revelation and glorification of Christ*. 1. *The Divine Father has glorified his Son, and thereby attested him to himself and to the confidence of believers.* This was the "sign from heaven" vainly asked by the unbelieving Pharisees, and now granted to the three leaders of the apostles. And a corresponding revelation will take place in the experience of every true child of God, whereby his faith shall be confirmed, and he shall be "sealed unto the day of redemption." The yearning, praying, aspiring spirit of the Son at last, in foretaste, attains; and he and his followers are strengthened. The personal glory, the sublime association with the precursors of the kingdom in the past, and the transcendant commendation, leave no room for doubt in the heart of the true believer. The evidence is intuitive, but it is spiritually complete. 2. *The loftiest tendencies and aspirations of the Law and the prophets are fulfilled in the* "*obedience unto death*" *of the Divine Son.* "They spake with him of his decease;" it was evidently central to their thoughts. The religious hopes of the past were to be satisfied in that way alone; by that alone was the righteousness of God to be satisfied. Self-sacrifice is the spirit of both Law and prophecy. To them the profound mystery of the hereafter was solved in the spirit of his death and in his resurrection; "life and immortality were brought to light" in him. It is as associated with them and representative of them that he looked forward to his dying. The manifestation of the Divine Son is therefore of universal significance, and relates itself to all that was highest and most spiritual in ancient religious movements. 3. *What God did for his Son on this occasion he will do for all who vitally belong to his* "*Body.*" Even as the bodily frame of Christ was transfigured, and partook of the inward glory of his spirit, so shall all in whose nature his grace is found appear with him in the glory of the resurrection. The spiritual law is manifest and certain, and it is evidently the same in the believer as in his Lord. Glory of spirit must sooner or later appear in glory of external appearance, and the body shall partake in the blessedness of the spirit.—M.

Ver. 8.—"*Jesus only.*" The transition from the glory and the spiritual vision to the sober light of common day—from the Christ uplifted in the radiance of heaven, and waited upon by the greatest spirits of ancient Hebrew religion, to the humiliated form of the man Jesus—was a perilous one for ordinary mortals to pass through. But it was necessary. It is for faith to penetrate the spiritual significance of ordinary forms and appearances, and grasp the Divine. It is to faith, and faith alone, that God is manifest in the flesh.

I. JESUS OUTLIVES HIS RECOMMENDATIONS. He is ever more, far more, than he appears to be. Some things and persons have nothing remaining when you strip the pretence and tinsel away. The radiance subsides into damp mist, and the glorious brightness proves but bottle-glass. It is this overmastering intrinsic worth and power of Jesus which explains his enduring influence. Eloquent advocacy has been engaged in his cause, great ideas have been associated with him, his claims have been attested by miraculous powers and signs, and ever and again the background of the Divine mystery from which he emerged has revealed itself, and a multitude of external proofs etc., are forthcoming when required; but he himself is greater than them all, and contains their latent possibilities within himself. When excitement, etc., are over, there still remains the power to elicit faith and constrain personal attachment. He himself is the ultimate verification of the faith of his disciples.

II. NOT THE SIGN OR MARVEL, BUT CHRIST IT IS THAT SAVES. The former only provisional, the latter permanent. The familiar, continuing, sympathizing Christ. The crucified One; the risen again; and in spiritual presence the Dweller in the heart of faith. It is this Christ whose power is felt within, a vital energy and a moral impulse; an Interpreter of the mysteries of life and death.

III. HE ALONE IS SUFFICIENT FOR OUR NEED. There is an unhealthy longing for dainties in things spiritual as in bodily satisfactions. His teaching, his example, his sympathy, his perfect sacrifice, are ours if we but believe. God hás testified his approval and acceptance, and commends him to us. Our own experience will seal and confirm the prophecies and attestations of others: "Now we believe, not because of thy saying: for *we have heard him ourselves,* and know that this is indeed the Christ, the Saviour of the world" (John iv. 42).—M.

Vers. 9—13.—*The saying that was kept.* The disciples did not understand their

Master—a common experience. Why was this saying so difficult? It seems plain
enough to us. But then we look at it after its accomplishment; they before that.
And their rabbinic training taught them to look for something very different from
what Christ seemed to be referring to. He spoke as if he alone was to rise again. They
had been taught to think of the resurrection as universal, and altogether; not an
experience of one here and another there. Moreover, their teachers had told them that
Elias must first come. In fact, their habits of thought were all going in one direction,
and this saying of Christ's in another. Yet, like fair and candid men, they did not
dismiss the words as impossible of accomplishment or interpretation; but they " kept
the saying."

I. How ARE WE TO EXPLAIN THE HOLD WHICH THE HARD SAYINGS OF CHRIST HAVE
UPON THE DEVOUT MIND? Their "keeping" the saying was doubtless for the most
part a voluntary thing, yet there was also a sense in which it was involuntary. The
subject it concerned awed and interested them, and they could not, if they had
wished to do it, throw off its fascination. And so it is with the other hard sayings;
that which is to be said of this may be said of them. 1. *Because of relation with
similar experiences.* Many a time had the actions of Christ, or their own spiritual
history, presented enigmas that refused to be summarily explained. They were continually stumbling upon some new, strange thing. They had just come out of a scene
of which the wisest and soberest of them might well wonder whether it was fairyland
or fact. And they were conscious of deep yearnings and aspirations to which the
Saviour's words seemed to answer as the key to the lock. These had evidently something in common. The doctrines of Christianity may be difficult for the carnal mind
to construe, but they appeal to a deep, universal, albeit depraved, human consciousness,
which forbids their being at once dismissed from the thought. 2. *And the sense of
mystery is itself an element of fascination.* The mind goes forth freely after the
infinite and eternal in speculation and fancy, if not in serious moral interest. If there
be but a substratum of apparent fact upon which thought can build, the sense of a
mystery lying beyond is congenial to man; and he *will* continually return to it in
efforts to penetrate it. This is why—at least, one reason why—the world around us
never palls upon our senses. Its commonest things are steeped in wonder of the
unknowable, if we but take one or two steps onward in the study of them. 3. *In
addition to this, the disciples knew that no mystery was uttered by their Master without
some gracious meaning in it, which would sooner or later be made known.* The hardest
doctrine was, they felt, closely connected with their welfare, and would be seen to be
so by-and-by. And Christians have experienced the same ever since. Our daily life
is, if we be thoughtful, the best expositor of the deep things of grace, and keeps hovering within our horizon many an angel of revelation ready to deliver his message in
due time.

II. How SHOULD THESE BE DEALT WITH? The disciples "kept," *i.e.* held fast, the
saying; thus affording an example to all true Christians. 1. *We should continually
endeavour to understand or learn their meaning.* Sometimes simple communion with
one's own heart will be enough; or, again, it may be necessary to discuss them with
others of a kindred spirit. Many of the happiest hours of life are so spent. Not that
we shall always succeed; very often there will remain an element of the infinite or the
unknown that will trouble us. 2. *But when human wisdom fails, Divine wisdom
may be invoked.* "They asked him," and he cleared away the difficulty to the extent
to which they made it known. To the praying soul the light will come in ever-
increasing fulness. More light will break forth from the book of earthly experience,
and from the written Word of comfort and revelation. And when the mystery still
remains insoluble, the Spirit of Jesus will give us faith and patience until "the day
dawn, and the day-star arise in our hearts," and we know even as we are known.—M.

Vers. 14—29.—*The cure of the demoniac child.* This stands out in striking contrast
with the halcyon hour on the mountain with which the three had been favoured.
Their brethren were experiencing a greater difficulty than they had ever yet known.
But the discussion of the saying they had kept, formed for the three an intermediate
step down into actual life, and daily events and troubles. Christ, on the other hand,
appears to have received a greater fulness of Messianic consciousness and power

through his transfiguration, as was his wont after similar retirements into spiritual seclusion. This incident affords a view of *Christ's manner of dealing with exceptional difficulties in spiritual service.*

I. ACCREDITED SERVANTS OF CHRIST WERE BEING DESPISED AND DISCOURAGED. (Vers. 14—18.) 1. *Their spirit was being daunted.* The people ceased to respect them, and the scribes began to turn the failure to account as an argument against their Lord. What could they say or do? Their Master was absent, and they were at their wits' end. A situation with its parallels in every age of the Church. Moral phases of individual, social, and national life which seem to defy remedy or even amelioration. Difficulties and failures in mission work, etc. 2. *Their usefulness was at a standstill.* The enemies of their cause had now the upper hand, and they were pressing them with objections and sneers. Perhaps they were even asking why their Master had gone away so mysteriously, and left them to cope with difficulties for which they were unequal. It was high time Jesus should come to their rescue. And lo! as the thought arose within them almost despairingly, he appeared! "The multitude, when they saw him, were greatly amazed." He had come just at the right moment, as if he divined the need for his presence.

II. THEIR MASTER MADE THE DIFFICULTY AN OCCASION FOR SPIRITUAL REBUKE AND INSTRUCTION. 1. *To the people,* or generally. He laments their want of faith, and slowness to receive the things of God. They had the highest reasons for faith— his works and himself—in their midst, and yet would not believe. He gives vent to the feeling of weariness and moral disgust which overcame him, and in the face of which he still laboured and forbore. The want of faith, only immediately manifested towards the disciples, was in reality towards himself. That was the root and spring of their readiness to cavil, and their questionings and arguments. 2. *To the father.* His conversation with Christ is made by the latter a perfect spiritual discipline. Already the dealings of God had been experienced in his home and heart, and that which has been begun is carried to a successful issue. It is amongst the compensations of great sorrows that, if they do not themselves induce a high spirituality of mind, they, at all events, help us to feel our need of the Saviour. There was a preparatory work already done, and Christ wastes no advantage thus gained. Having signified his willingness to undertake the cure, he begins to question the father, partly as an expression of sympathy, partly to show the true character of the case. In this he succeeds in eliciting an expression of the sceptical spirit of the man: "If thou canst do anything, have compassion on us, and help us." Here there is room for a commencement, and the Saviour repeats in grieved astonishment, *"If thou canst!"* It was a qualification that had no business in such a request, and it showed how poor was the spiritual life or power of the man. He then declares the grand condition of all his cures, "All things are possible to him that believeth;" which in this connection meant that all the blessings Christ conferred were given only in response to faith, but where that was there was no limit with regard to their bestowal. He did not mean that any request, of whatever kind it might be, would be granted if it were only *accompanied* by faith, but that all requests that were the outcome of a Divine faith, and consequently subject to its conditions—as, for instance, their being agreeable to God's will—would be granted, however hard they might appear to man. This remark awoke the slumbering spiritual nature of the father, whose love for his son was also at work to quicken his susceptibilities, and he cried out, "I believe; help thou mine unbelief." There is great difference of opinion as to the true meaning of these words, and no certainty would seem to be attainable. Yet that they reveal a low, self-contradictory spiritual state is evident. Still, progress is perceptible. He at least knows his shortcoming, and has asked for its removal. That was probably effected by the cure of his son, which took place, not because of satisfaction with the father's confession—a very faulty one at best—but through desire to prevent tumult, etc.; for when *" he saw that a multitude came running together,"* he quickly completed the miracle. But even in his expedition there is no hurry. The whole scene is solemn and expressive, and must have had a strong influence on all who looked on. 3. *To the disciples.* A call to a more intense and elevated communion with God. Prayer (and fasting) was a means to that. Faith is thus seen to be a condition both of getting good and doing good. It is because Christians live habitually on such a worldly plane that they lack power.

Oneness in heart and life with God would remove "mountains." This power should be sought by all.

III. He made it also an occasion for more signal display of his glory. The delay, failure of disciples, gradual extraction of all the circumstances of the case from the father, etc., all tended to increase the moral effect of the final exercise of power. His *authority* as the moral Governor of the universe, and Destroyer of the works of the devil, is also vindicated in addressing the demon. Not less, but far more, awful are the effects of sin upon the soul. Its expulsion is a work of Divine power and grace, and exhaustive of the nature in which it has dwelt. It is for Christ to raise up and revivify the poor wreck, the spiritual impotency that survives. So are the failures of weak disciples retrieved, and where disgrace is, humanly speaking, inevitable, the glory of God is revealed. The servants of Christ may despair of themselves, but never of him.—M.

Ver. 23.—*The omnipotence of faith.* This is a case in which the revisers have introduced a dramatic play of expression into what has seemed a merely conditional statement; and apparently with the authority of the best manuscripts. The words of Christ are seen to be those of surprise and expostulation. He sends back the qualification which the man had uttered, and asserts the virtual omnipotence of faith, and, at the same time, the dauntlessness of its spirit.

I. The spirit which characterizes the believer. 1. *Confidence and fearlessness.* The true believer will never say, "If thou canst." The greatest difficulties will not seem insuperable, and the testimony of sight and ordinary experience will be distrusted. Inward weakness and uncertainty will be conquered. The one thing of consequence will be, "Is this promised?" "Though he slay me, yet will I trust in him" (Job xiii. 15; cf. Hab. iii. 17). 2. *It is to be distinguished from self-confidence.* There is no immediate reference to self in such a conviction; it bases itself upon the unseen and eternal, the laws and promises of God. Hence we may speak of the *humility* of faith. 3. *It is exceptional and divinely produced.* Most men are guided by their ordinary experience. When that experience is deliberately set aside or ignored, it must be because of some fact or truth not visible to the natural mind. But such a discovery would be equivalent to a Divine communication. The faith which proceeds upon this must, therefore, be supernaturally inspired. It cannot exist save in one conscious of God, and of a peculiar relation to him.

II. The possibilities of faith. If not wholly dependent upon the actual experience of the power of faith, the confidence of the believer is nevertheless greatly sustained and strengthened by it. Resting in the first instance upon the consciousness of One mighty to save, whose help is promised and assured, and concerning whom it may be said, "If God be for us, who can be against us?" the man of faith will also prize every indication that God has been with man. For he is assured from within and from without that the possibilities of faith are: 1. *Unlimited—because it identifies itself with the power of God.* Faith is the union of the spirit of the believer with him in whom he trusts. It ensures nothing less than his interest and help. The weakest child of God can secure his aid. "If God be for us, who can be against us?" 2. *Unlimited—save that it subjects itself to the will of God.* Just as God is omnipotent and yet incapable of unrighteousness, so the faith of the believer will only avail for things pleasing to his heavenly Father. But, then, it never desires any other. The promises of God, however, declare the direction in which Divine help may be certainly expected; and there are countless instances in which the believer can plainly discern the lawfulness and propriety of the objects for which he pleads. (1) The work of faith is ever blessed. (2) The prayer of faith is never denied; for if the answer do not assume the form expected, it will nevertheless prove to be substantially, and under the best form, the blessing that is required. And fervent, earnest, repeated prayer is unmistakably encouraged by the teaching of Christ. It is for Christians not to pray less, but more and more importunately, only leaving the particular mode in which the answer is to come to the wisdom and love of God. 3. *Unlimited—as illustrated in Scripture and the biographies of godly men.* The eleventh chapter of Hebrews is a magnificent confirmation of the promises of the Lord; and there can be no better exercise than the study of the answers to prayer recorded in the Word of God and the lives of saints.—M.

Ver. 29.—"*And he said unto them, This kind can come out by nothing, save by prayer.*" The work of the Christian Church essentially the same from age to age, although the external phase of it may change and pass away. " Casting out devils " sounds strangely on modern ears; its associations, whilst they are weird and picturesque, are too far away to seriously engage our attention. We are in the habit of dismissing it in an offhand fashion, as a form of religious activity necessarily confined to a transitional period of the development of Christianity, and having no relation to our own or any other age. But that is only a superficial view of the work of the gospel which will lead to such a judgment. "Casting out devils" is a task which belongs as much to the servant of Christ to-day as in the apostolic'age. The particular form assumed by the "possession" may not be the same, but the fact of "possession" still continues; and the mission of the Son of God to "destroy the works of the devil" must be fulfilled, until human souls are freed from the thraldom to which Satan subjects them. In every sinful wish or thought Satan gains a foothold; in every sinful habit formed he may be said to "possess" the nature in which it exists. Until we regard sinful habits as not mere habits, but as involving the presence and power of the evil one, we need not expect to grasp or deal with the problem of evil in our world. In the work of converting human souls, we are contending not merely with those who are the immediate objects of our solicitude, but with a supernatural antagonist, holding them in subjection, and deeply skilled in the arts requisite for the maintenance of his influence. " For our wrestling is not against flesh and blood, but against principalities, against the powers, against the world-rulers of this darkness, against the spiritual *hosts* of wickedness in the heavenly *places*" (Eph. vi. 12). It is due to this permanent characteristic of evil in human nature that such difficulties are met with as the text explains.

I. EXCEPTIONAL DIFFICULTIES IN SPIRITUAL WORK. 1. *Occasioned by* (1) a peculiar intensity of indwelling evil. We cannot explain it, but it is full of stubbornness, subtlety, and power of resistance. There is a mysterious sympathy, it may be, between the sinner and the special sin that besets him, or prevents his yielding himself to Divine grace. And this may go the length of (2) total enslavement of the nature. Like the epileptic of the story, not only the body but the spirit may be enthralled. The will is so weak that it is practically powerless. The external ministries of the Church are insufficient to deliver, unaccompanied as they are by any strong desire for salvation on the part of the sinner. It sometimes happens, too, in more general work, that a spirit of opposition displays itself, or circumstances are persistently unfavourable. The Christian toils on, but his efforts are like the dashing of himself against a rock, or the ploughing of the sand. There are none of God's people who are strangers to such experiences, which are: 2. *From their very nature unexpected.* The spiritual worker goes on with comparative or even brilliant success for a time, and then encounters sudden breakdown. The reason of this in most instances is, that a great proportion of Christian work is all but mechanical. It consists in a routine of duties; its results represent a sum total of indirect and sometimes unconscious agencies; religious institutions are originated perhaps in an impulse once imparted but not repeated, and are carried on thus far by "their own momentum." There occurs all at once a check, and a sense of helplessness and humiliation ensues, involving the baffled worker in spiritual perplexity. Such difficulties are: 3. *Not an unmitigated calamity.* They have their uses in the Divine economy. When searching of heart is induced, and hidden sins are revealed, or absence of direct communion with God is made manifest, or pride and self-sufficiency are brought low, they have accomplished a good and necessary work.

II. HOW ARE THEY TO BE OVERCOME? 1. *The means.* "Prayer," or, in the Authorized Version, "prayer and fasting." There is a singularity about such a specific. A particular case of failure occurs, in apparently exceptional circumstances, and the remedy is not new or peculiar, but general. Could devils, then, come out by anything else than prayer, when man was the exerciser? It would almost seem as if the disciples had done their work hitherto by virtue of an external commission, using the name of Christ as a sort of talisman. This was sufficient for ordinary cases, but whenever one out of the usual occurred they were at a loss. 2. *The reason for its necessity.* The immediate occasion for the Master's admonition probably was the increasing laxity of the disciples in personal prayer, their outwardness, and their failure to grasp the essential principles of his kingdom. But there was a more profound reason for the advice. The servant of

God should be in complete sympathy and oneness with his Master, and that can only be cultivated by frequent acts of devotion and the exercise of a constant faith. It is not in his own strength that difficulties are to be met, but in Christ's. But that can only be imparted through fellowship with his spirit, which depends for its efficiency and depth upon repeated acts of the spiritual nature. The disciple by this rule is called into conscious personal fellowship with God, whose power will only then be granted. Oneness with God is the secret of spiritual power. 3. *The same principle applies to the whole life of the Christian.* True success depends upon vital spiritual effort, upon conscious co-operation with God, and consequent fasting from self. If we would not be taken at unawares we must be watchful, in constant actual exercise of faith, and uninterrupted personal communion with God. We are in danger of making too much of the external and accidental element in religion; we can never make too much of him who "worketh in" and through "us to will and to do of his good pleasure" (Phil. ii. 13).—M.

Vers. 30—32.—*The gospel a source of sorrow and perplexity.* Something very grand and pathetic in those rehearsals of the drama of redemption. The great heart of Christ yearning for sympathy, and yet shrinking from the kind that was evoked; wondering, meanwhile, at the "hardness of heart" of his disciples, who "understood not the saying." How inexplicable this failure to affect their moral nature! So far as *words* are concerned, it was the same gospel as that which woke the nations at Pentecost; yet it was as if still-born; an abstraction; a mystery past finding out. It is a sad monologue; a recitative upon a minor key. Reasons for this failure and ineffectiveness—

I. IT WAS NOT UNDERSTOOD. From human standpoint all but incomprehensible; as it certainly could not have been originally conceived by man. A mood and sentiment too elevated for ordinary moral natures. An important consideration in determining the question as to who founded Christianity—Christ or his disciples. The "prophet" must not discourse in an unknown tongue.

II. IT COULD NOT BE UNDERSTOOD UNTIL IT WAS ACCOMPLISHED. Intelligence, moral perception, and spiritual illumination waited upon the finished work. It was, so to speak, a moral creation, which beforehand only the Author could comprehend, and afterwards still he alone perfectly. Each step in the evolution of it, up to a certain point, only deepened the mystery. When Christ *realized* his work of salvation in act, his people began to realize it in thought and experience.

III. AND THEN ONLY COULD IT BE UNDERSTOOD THROUGH THE SPIRITUAL LIFE IT CALLED FORTH. Christ had to evoke the very faculty by which the plan and spirit of his work were to be discerned. It is "unto Jews a stumbling-block, and unto Gentiles foolishness; but unto them that are called, both Jews and Greeks, Christ the power of God, and the wisdom of God" (1 Cor. i. 23, 24). The world by wisdom knew it not, "but we received, not the spirit of the world, but the spirit which is of God; that we might know the things that are freely given to us by God. . . . Now the natural man receiveth not the things of the Spirit of God, for they are foolishness unto him; and he cannot know them, because they are spiritually judged" (1 Cor. ii. 12—14). It is not until we learn the true character of God, and, in the light of that, the nature of sin, that we can from the heart approve of the career of Jesus as "the way of salvation."—M.

Vers. 33—37.—*Who shall be greatest?* The selection of Peter, James, and John for exceptional association with Christ; the primacy of Peter suggested by the words of their Master on a certain occasion; and the spirit of the sons of Zebedee, shown in the request made by their mother, a little later, on their behalf (ch. x. 35—41), were circumstances that soon attracted the attention of the others, and gave rise to discussion as to relative superiority. In dealing with this unseemly dispute, our Saviour showed—

I. THAT IT WAS A QUESTION THAT OUGHT NOT TO BE ASKED AMONGST CHRIST'S FOLLOWERS. (Vers. 33, 34.) 1. His question elicited no reply. They were ashamed that he should have detected them. It was evidently contrary to his spirit, as they felt, although they might be unable to explain. 2. That it is foreign to the genius of Christianity is further shown by the evils it has created within the Church. A vast percentage of the failures and scandals of Christians has arisen from this contention, whether carried on in silence or expressed. Nevertheless that it is deeply seated in human nature is shown by its persistency from age to age. A motive of action we are ashamed to confess when a sense of Christ's presence is upon us cannot be a right one. And in proportion as the presence of the Master's spirit is felt, it is suppressed or destroyed.

II. THE PRINCIPLE BY WHICH IT SHOULD BE SETTLED WHEN IT ARISES. (Ver. 35.) "If any man would be first, he shall be last of all, and minister of all." This is, and probably was meant to be, slightly enigmatical. Without altering the future of the sentence ("he shall be") into the imperative ("let him be"), as some, without sufficient warrant, have done, it is still possible to read in it several distinct meanings. It might mean that that was to be the penalty of such presumption; that God would so regard presumptuous men; that this was a discipline to which they should subject themselves; that the avenue to official pre-eminence was the greatest serviceableness and humility; or, lastly, that *the highest excellence in the kingdom of God is his who abases and forgets himself altogether in the benefit and advancement of others*. It is in the last sense that Christ should be understood, if we are to take the general spirit of his teaching for our guide. In the Christian the virtue and usefulness are ends in themselves, and not stepping-stones to external, official pre-eminence. At the same time, there is a colourable suggestion, supported by experience, in the first three interpretations. The second last is the spirit of the Roman curia, which in literal expression looks so like the precept it contradicts. The sitting down of Christ, and his summons to all, prove the importance of the lesson.

III. AN ILLUSTRATION OF THE PRINCIPLE. (Vers. 36, 37.) "A little child," perhaps one of Peter's family. He gives an example in his own behaviour, simply and ingenuously, by embracing the child. 1. *The lowliest in the kingdom of God should receive the purest sympathy and consideration*. This is the most disinterested and unselfish service. The noblest deeds in God's world are of this kind: "Pure religion and undefiled before our God and Father is this, to visit the fatherless and widows in their affliction, and to keep himself unspotted from the world" (Jas. i. 27). We can "receive" to the heart when we cannot to the home; to kindness and love when we cannot to great earthly advantage. 2. *The motive which distinguishes this conduct from ordinary human tenderness and affection*. It is to be "in my Name," *i.e.* "on account of me," impelled by my example and spirit, and for the sake of my cause. It is only a "grace" or quality of the regenerate nature as he inspires it. 3. *So regarded, the object of our love and compassion is really the representative of Jesus and of God*. Christ has thus commended the children and the poor to the care of his people. And their sympathies thus awakened and directed are to be looked upon not as supplementing the deficient provisions of the Divine love, but only, in our own degree and measure, expressing and executing the infinite, loving will of "our Father in heaven." Herein, therefore, the lowliest service and the highest coincide. "See that ye despise not one of these little ones; for I say unto you, that in heaven their angels do always behold the face of my Father which is in heaven" (Matt. xviii. 10).—M.

Vers. 38—42.—*The comprehensiveness of Christ's service*. The connection with what preceded is to be sought in John's keen sense of having transgressed the spirit of the beautiful words just uttered. Christ would acknowledge all who professed his name; John had to confess that he had forbidden such a one from working. This leads to Christ's indicating—

I. MARKS OF HIS TRUE SERVANTS. The general link between the several classes is his "Name," *i.e.* conscious oneness and sympathy with him as the Son of God and Saviour of the world. Accepting that as the test, he lays down: 1. *A general principle of comprehension*. (Ver. 40.) It is negative. If a man does not oppose him, he is to be considered as an ally and a friend. There is no neutrality in man's relations to Christ. This was especially the case in that age: the devil was too active in human nature to suffer any opposition to be undeveloped. The powers of darkness and of light were in deadly antagonism, and all who were aware of the conflict were certain to have their sympathies engaged for the one side or the other. This seems a dangerous principle, and apt to lead to entanglement or disaster. "Divinely dangerous." Yet is it the teaching of the Spirit of God, and beautifully harmonious with it. 2. *That those are his servants who do mighty works in his Name*. This mere statement suggests how profoundly the work of Christ was leavening the community.   There were many besides his professed followers who were influenced by his spirit.   (1) That they should be able to do these works (which were of a miraculous nature) showed that they must already be in communion with his spirit.   To cast forth devils could not be to further the cause of their prince, or to be aided by him.   And so of the complementary work of awaking spiritual life in conversion, etc.   Such work is manifestly of God, and these results prove his presence and approval.   (2) The honour and cause of Christ will be dear to such, even as to those more openly and professedly connected with him. Christ's servants do not work magically, by the mechanical force of dark formulas, but by sympathy and moral oneness with him.   3. *That sympathy and help towards a disciple, as such, is itself a proof of discipleship.*   (1) The slightest sign of this spirit is to be welcomed in faith and hope, as a firstfruits of greater things to come.   (2) But in itself it is already truly a great service, and as such will be certainly rewarded.   It seems almost more precious, in its connection, than the "mighty works;" for these may sometimes incommode, and be mingled with much error and evil, but the merciful kindness is ever serviceable, and flows from no other fountain than the heart of God.

II. THE SPIRIT IN WHICH THESE ARE TO BE REGARDED.   The child of grace is to be trustfully [disposed, and ready to put a charitable construction upon the merely negative behaviour of men.   And, moreover, it is to be recollected that the principle is not one of judgment, but of policy.   "Jesus would impress it upon his disciples that they must honour and protect the isolated beginnings or germs of faith to be found in the world" (Lange).   Towards all who do not oppose Christ there is to be an attitude of hopeful and trustful encouragement (cf. Matt. xi. 42).   1. *Christian acknowledgment.* "Forbid them not."   Involving (1) brotherly recognition—not mere toleration; (2) fostering and protecting care; (3) devout thankfulness and humility.   2. *Remembering their relation to the same Master.*   (1) He acknowledges them; (2) he will afterwards reward them; (3) we shall be sternly and awfully judged if we "cause them to stumble."   "The word for millstone indicates the larger stone-mill, in working which an ass was generally employed, as distinguished from the smaller hand-mill of Luke xvii. 35.   The punishment was not recognized in the Jewish Law, but it was in occasional use among the Greeks (Diod. Sic., xvi. 35), and had been inflicted by Augustus (Sueton., 'Aug.,' lxvii.) in cases of special infamy.   Jerome states (in a note on this passage) that it was practised in Galilee, and it is not improbable that the Romans had inflicted it upon some of the ringleaders of the insurrection headed by Judas of Galilee.   The infamy of offending one of the 'little ones' was as great as that of those whose crimes brought upon them this exceptional punishment.   It was obviously a form of death less cruel in itself than many others, and its chief horror, both for Jews and heathen, was probably that it deprived the dead of all rites of burial" (Plumptre, in 'New Test. Com.').   This punishment, such as it was, was but a shadow of the more terrible penalties of the spiritual state.—M.

Vers. 43—49.—*The value of deliverance from spiritual snares.*   I. ILLUSTRATED BY: 1. *Relative importance of that which is sacrificed and that which is saved.*   They are as parts to the whole: as external limbs or members compared with the entire nature, or central *ego*.   "Our Saviour of course specifies hand and foot only for rhetorical purposes. It is a fine, bold, graphic way of bringing home to the imagination and the bosom the idea of *what is near and dear to our natural feelings.*   He speaks in hieroglyphics" (Morison). They represent also our natural lust, tendencies, and carnalized faculties.   2. *Terrible consequences to the wicked in the world to come.*   "Gehenna;" "the Gehenna of fire." "Originally it was the Greek form of Ge-hinnom (the Valley of Hinnom, sometimes of the "son" or the "children" of Hinnom), and was applied to a narrow gorge on the south of Jerusalem (Josh. xv. 8)" (Plumptre).   It became the common cesspool and place for consuming filth.   Dead bodies of great criminals were probably cast forth without burial into it; and fires were continually burning for the destruction of the offal.   It is, of course, only a type of the punishment of the lost.   "There is a commingled reference to two modes of destruction—vermicular putrefaction and fire.   When men's bodies are destroyed, it is generally either by the one agency or by the other. Both are here combined for cumulative rhetorical effect.   And the dread climax of the whole representation is found in the ceaselessness of the twofold operation"

(Morison). There are two elements in this destruction, viz.: (1) internal corruptions—"their worm;" and (2) external consuming forces—"fire." Both of these are to be understood of their spiritual analogues.

II. MORALLY STIMULATIVE BECAUSE OF APPEAL TO FREE-WILL AND SPIRITUAL AGENCY OF MAN. These considerations would have no weight but for this. Just as one *can* cut off a hand or a foot, and pluck out an eye, so one can restrain erring desires and affections, and curb unruly appetites. This is the *sin* of the ruined one, viz. he is *self*-ruined. And all corrupting influence one exerts, returns upon himself to his own destruction. *Self-sacrifice is, therefore, the only way of salvation.* The power to do this is given by Christ. " It is better to make any sacrifice than to retain any sin " (Godwin). "The meaning is not that any man is in such a case that he hath no better way to avoid sin and hell [than being maimed]; but if he had no better, he should choose this. Nor doth it mean that maimed persons are maimed in heaven; but if it were so, it were a less evil " (Richard Baxter).—M.

Vers. 49, 50.—*Christian purity—its origin and influence.* These verses have been the subject of much controversy. They are obscure and difficult; but the context is of great assistance, and a uniform interpretation of the term "salted" in the first and second clauses of ver. 50 will do much to remove the hindrances in the way of construing them together. Manuscript authority is not strong enough to compel the rejection of either clause, although our revisers have omitted the latter. Everything turns upon the sense given to "salted." It is evidently " purified," " preserved from corruption," in the second clause. So ought it to be understood in the first. " Consumed " is a sense implied in the sense " purified," and secondary to it. The whole emphasis of the passage is thus in favour of Christian purification. Again, the second clause of ver. 50 does not appear to have been quoted merely in confirmatory or illustrative allusion, but as a statement of the consequence which will flow from the first; the conjunction having a slightly illative force.

I. How SPIRITUAL PURITY IS PRODUCED AND SUSTAINED. 1. " *With fire:* " a figurative term, relating itself to the fire that is not quenched of the preceding passage, and the description of the baptism of the Holy Ghost (Matt. iii. 11, 12). " Even when manifested in its most awful forms, it is still true that they who ' walk righteously and speak uprightly ' may dwell with ' everlasting burnings' " (Plumptre). " Thy God is a consuming fire " (Deut. iv. 24); and that to the evil *in* his people, as well as that out of which they are taken. This may refer (1) to the general spiritual experience of the child of God as subject to the influences of the Holy Spirit; (2) to Divine chastisement; (3) to " the spirit to which our Saviour refers in vers. 43—48, *the spirit that parts, for righteousness' sake, with a hand, a foot, an eye* " (Morison). It is " an alternative fire," " which indeed scorches the sensibility to agony, but which in the end consumes only what is bad, and leaves the soul freed from those moral combustibles on which the penal fire of Gehenna could feed." " He is *preserved from corruption, and consequent everlasting destruction, by the fire of unsparing self-sacrifice* " (ibid.). 2. *This is the universal experience of true Christians.* Because it is essential to the Divine life in the soul, if indeed it be not rather identical with it. Have we endured this " scourging," without which no son is received by our Father? Is this our spirit? Herein we can examine ourselves.

II. ITS INFLUENCE. It affects: 1. *Christians* (1) individually; (2) collectively. " Have salt in yourselves, and *be at peace* one with another." Purity of aim and spirit will obviate misunderstandings, and allay bitternesses between true believers. 2. *Their sacrifices.* It is in a sense the spirit of Christ's sacrifice communicated to theirs. As it was a law of the Levitical code that " every sacrifice should be salted with salt," so it is a law of the spiritual life, fulfilled through the spirit of self-sacrifice communicated to the particular act and object of sacrifice. This applies to the whole outcome and expression of the spiritual life of the children of God, their thought, word, action, as well as to their gifts to the cause of Christ. 3. *The general life of the world.* " Ye are the salt of the earth." An indirect and incomplete, but still a positive blessing to the world of the unconverted. For this constant renewals of grace are required, from a source independent of ourselves. Watchfulness, prayer, ceaseless self-sacrifice in the spirit of Christ.—M.

VER. 36.—*Christ and the child: a sermon to children.* The disciples of Jesus had been disputing amongst themselves which of them should be the greatest in his kingdom. Though they were ashamed to confess this, Jesus knew all about it; for he overhears even whispered and secret conversations. He rebuked their ambition by calling a little child to him, who was glad enough to come to One so loving; and taking him up in his arms, he bade his disciples become childlike, not caring for money and high positions, but being glad in the love of the Lord. Probably the child never saw Jesus again; but he would never forget him. Legend reports that his name was Ignatius, and that he grew up to be an earnest and devout man, who at last bravely died for the faith. But the treatment of this child by Jesus is only an example of his treatment of children now. He loves them, and they should love him.

I. WHY DID JESUS CALL THE CHILD TO HIM? 1. *Because there was something in the child which Jesus liked.* We do not call to us and take into our arms those we hate and avoid. It was not sinlessness that Jesus saw in the child, but *simplicity*. He was something like what Jesus himself had been in the home at Nazareth, when he was subject to his parents, and so sweet, humble, and gentle that every one loved him. Children are not perfectly innocent; they do many things that are wrong, and need to be forgiven. Jesus did not say to the child, " You can do without me," but, " Come to me." So, when he saw the young man who said he had kept the commandments, Jesus " loved him ; " yet he did not leave him as he was, but bade him go and sell all that he had. 2. *Because there was in the child something he wanted.* He wanted the child's *love*. " My son, give me thine heart." The way to be loved is to love; and Jesus loves us, not as crowds, but as individuals. Each can say with Paul, " He loved *me*, and gave himself for me." The child knew this from the look and tone of the Lord. 3. *Because there was something he hoped to do for the child.* He meant to *save* him. To be saved from sin involves something more than being forgiven. If bad temper asserts itself, you may be forgiven for an outburst; but it rises again and again. Jesus would conquer that temper so that it should never trouble you any more.

II. WHY DID THE CHILD GO TO JESUS? He might have hesitated and said, " He does not mean it ; " or, " The disciples are rough, and will push me back, or laugh at me ; " or, " Perhaps I had better wait a little, till I am older." Instead of this, he went at once, and went as he was. There are reasons why you, as children, should go to him. 1. *Because conscience says you need him.* Conscience is more sensitive, and speaks more clearly in childhood than in age; and this is an evidence that childhood is the appointed and the best time to hear God's voice. 2. *Because affection says you need him.* Some children feel much secret grief because they have an impression that no one cares much for them. Their brothers and sisters are more popular than they are, so they are always supposing that they are being slighted. Or perhaps they are at school, and are thoroughly homesick among strangers. How pleasant it is to feel that One who is always near loves you personally, intensely, fervently! and how naturally should your love flow forth responsively to him! 3. *Because energy says you need him.* A child is naturally active. The fingers itch to touch what is forbidden, to try what is unknown; and mischief often results from no evil intention. All that pent-up energy is from God; stored up for the doing of life's work, and the bearing of its burdens. And the Lord wants in his kingdom these vigorous frames and powerful minds, that he may sanctify and bless them—that the children may lead off the hosannas in which the world will join in the New Jerusalem. 4. *Because hope says you want him.* Every child has some hope of becoming better and greater. It is a sign that Paradise is lost, but that heaven is possible, else we might be satisfied. Many boys and girls have quiet times, little spoken of to others, when they say, " I wish I could be better; that I could get over this evil habit; that I was steadfast, pure, and true; that I loved God, and was glad he loved me." That is the time when Jesus is near, when he stretches out his arms and says, " Come unto me ; " and in answer to the secret prayer he will take the little one in his arms, put his hands on him, and bless him.—A. R.

VER. 41.—*Christian beneficence.* Loving consideration for others and generous kindness to them are among the fruits of the Spirit and the signs of true discipleship. Their effects it would not be easy to exaggerate. The law of kindness for Jesus' sake is of all things the most likely to remove prejudices against Christianity, and to bring together those whose interests are separate, so as to ensure the salvation of society. Even on lower grounds, therefore, this law demands our obedience, for there is much in our social condition to cause anxiety to the Church. Questions once carefully ignored are being boldly discussed; classes of men whose ignorance and poverty made them political nonentities are now powers in the State. Capitalists and producers are discussing anew their respective rights; owners of land are being openly asked whether the proportion they have received of its value is not greater than their due. And in all these movements agitators are exaggerating claims, some of which have in them germs of right. Meanwhile it is to be feared that religion, as a factor in the settlement of such disputes, is being disregarded, and debate is rife whether indeed the Christian faith is longer credible. Anything which would suddenly change the relations of various classes, any outburst of the communistic or nihilistic spirit, would bring about far more evil than good. Evils must be abolished now as they were in the early days of the Christian faith. When slaves were held in cruel bondage, and profligacy assumed hideous forms, and accumulated wealth appeared side by side with abject want, Christ and the teachers who followed him aroused no servile war, but by word and life showed a more excellent way. They taught that the highest bliss was not in abundance of possessions, but in abundance of spiritual life; that the loftiest dignity was to be found not in the indulgence, but in the denial, of self; that all a man possessed he held as a responsible steward; and that those removed from others in social position were brothers and sisters to be cared for. All this was exhibited in the life of One who went about doing good, and was seen in its ultimate victory on the cross where Christ died for us, that we henceforth might live no more to ourselves. One phase of this law of kindness is brought before us in our text, where its manifestation is recognized as a germ of discipleship.

I. The duty of Christian beneficence is asserted throughout Scripture. Under the old dispensation, the blessedness of him who considers the poor was exemplified in the experience of Job, and of the widow of Sarepta, and of multitudes besides. The duty was made still more clear in the New Testament; and this is noteworthy, because the disciples of our Lord were themselves poor, so that no one of them could give out of his superabundance; and even of our Lord himself this was true, though he so often showed that it was more blessed to give than to receive. On this principle the Church acted. Spontaneously Barnabas sold his estates to aid those who were in special difficulties because they were cast out of trade and home, and his example was contagious. There was no law passed that Christians should do this; but though as a compulsory law it would have been an unsound dictum for all times, it was right and good when Christians, moved by pity for their poor persecuted brethren, distributed as every man had need. Spontaneity gives worth to such acts. He who thus gives, though it be but a cup of cold water, shall not lose his reward.

II. The objects of Christian beneficence. All less favoured than ourselves have a claim, not necessarily on our money, but on our help and sympathy, in some form, when an opportunity comes for service in Christ's Name. 1. *Human relationship* has its claims on us, and he who does not "provide for his own," even though he benefits some religious organization, fails in his duty to his Lord. 2. *Neighbourhood* has claims on us. No follower of Christ can be like the rich man, who would give alms to be seen of man, but would let poor Lazarus die at his gate, fighting for crumbs with the dogs. 3. *Fellowship in the same Church* has claims on us, though those needing our aid may be least in knowledge, least in capacity, least in attractiveness, or least in desert. 4. *But we are to do good unto all men*, though especially to such as are of the household of faith. Christ died for all, and in his Name, for his sake, in his spirit, we must seek to aid them, even though it only be by a cup of cold water.

III. The reasons for Christian beneficence are numerous, but we may mention one or two. 1. *All we have is from God.* His providence has made us to differ. Our birth, our inheritance, our education, our natural capacities,—these are in no sense the results of our own creation or choice. He who gave us these, demands that we should use them in part to promote the peace and the comfort of those for whom his Son died. "Freely ye have received, freely give." 2. *Our superabundance is for others.* When our cup runs over, the droppings are not for ourselves but for others. When our harvest is gathered, room must be made for gleaners as well as for reapers. Waste

is against God's law. The breath we throw off from our lungs is wanted by nature.
The rain poured down so lavishly is not lost. The refuse flung on the soil is to reappear
in new forms. All nature rebukes the waste and extravagance of which we are often
guilty; and Ambrose has well said, "It is no greater sin to take from him that rightly
possesseth than being able not to give to him that wanteth."—A. R.

Vers. 43, 45, 47.—*Causes of stumbling.* "If thy hand . . . if thy foot . . . if thine
eye offend thee." The passage from which these few words are chosen is stern and
severe; yet it was uttered by the gentle Teacher who would not break the bruised reed.
Christ Jesus was not like the Pharisees, punctilious over little things, so he would not
have uttered these words needlessly. He was not ignorant of human temptations and
weaknesses, but had the most perfect knowledge of our nature. He was not one of
those scribes who would bind heavy burdens on others, and yet not touch them with
one of their fingers, but was tempted as we are, and by a life and death of sacrifice
endeavoured to put away the sin of the world. Words stern as these, coming from One
who had generous views of sinners and unerring views of sin in its nature and effect,
deserve our serious consideration. Our Lord thought them so important that he now
repeated them, although none who had heard them previously in his sermon on the
mount would be likely to forget them. The general lesson taught is this—that it is
better to die than to sin, and so to wrong ourselves and others; but we confine ourselves now to the causes or incitements to sin here suggested by the "hand," the
"foot," and the "eye."

I. OF WHAT IS THE HAND AN EMBLEM? 1. *Companionship.* We shake hands with
those to whom we are introduced or with whom we are friendly, not with those who
are unknown or hostile. If we have quarrelled, and reconciliation has been effected, the
outstretched hand is a sign that we are reconciled. It is often said that a man is known
by his friends, and it is perhaps equally true that he is made by his friends, especially
in the time of youth, when character is plastic and habits are readily formed. Some
communication with others is a necessity of school and business life; but friends may
be chosen; and it is of the last importance that they be chosen well. Yet Christians
will sometimes form a lifelong companionship with those whose worldliness will
inevitably lead them astray from the ways of God. "If thy hand" in such a companionship "cause thee to stumble, cut it off, and cast it from thee." 2. *Work.* The
hand is the medium through which we put forth our skill and strength. Daily work
may have "holiness to the Lord" written on it, or may be the means of spiritual
injury. There are shops in which dishonesty is a necessity; there are positions young
girls are called upon to fill which cannot but injure their modesty and purity; there are
undertakings which can only succeed by a sacrifice of truth. Whatever their external
and material advantages, these are amongst the causes of offence which our Lord calls
on us to sacrifice.

II. OF WHAT IS THE FOOT AN EMBLEM? By it we make progress. It may be taken,
therefore, as a figure for getting on in the world. Parents are sometimes too eager for
this on their children's behalf. They are like Lot, who sought the place of prosperity
and was regardless of its temptations. It were far better to be less swift to attain
wealth and position than to have the terrible awakening that will come to many at last.
"What shall it profit a man, if he shall gain the whole world, and lose his own
soul?"

III. OF WHAT IS THE EYE AN EMBLEM? Through it most offences to the soul's
purity come. Fatal has been the issue with many of "seeing life." David saw, lusted,
and fell into adultery and murder. Eve saw, longed, and put forth her hand and took
the forbidden fruit, and so came death into the world, and all our woe. Achan saw the
garment and the gold, and covetousness led him to disobedience. Better to have been
blind than to have seen that. How many now fall into evil ways who assure any one
remonstrating with them that they are only going to that place of temptation because
they wish for once "to see what it is like"! There are books, too, which, from the
doubts they insinuate or from the morality they implicitly commend, should be
abjured. It may be sometimes an intellectual loss, but it results in larger gain; and
the law of the gospel is that which is here, and which St. Paul repeats in the words,
"Mortify therefore your members which are upon earth."—A. R.

Vers. 43, 44.—*Better die than sin.* Christ is speaking here of injuries which we may do ourselves or others. Most men guard themselves carefully against physical injury. They insure against accidents, avoid miasma, and attend to the first appearance of the germs of disease. Yet sometimes they are like a commander who is on the alert against external assault, but is unsuspicious of treachery within. In a moral sense, it may often be said, "A man's foes are they of his own household." The allusion to the hand, the foot, and the eye indicate that the causes of sin are found in our own nature; that evil is natural to us as the use of these members. Sins spring from within: "Out of the heart proceed evil thoughts." When acts are repeated, habits are formed which become part of ourselves. Then these habits are allowed for and excused by others, so that we no longer get our attention directed to them as otherwise we might do. A notoriously selfish man is not asked to help others; a passionate or suspicious temper becomes regarded as a personal peculiarity. Yet, though it seems a part of ourselves, God says, "Cut it off, and cast it from thee."

I. GOD'S TREATMENT OF SIN IS RADICAL. We naturally shrink from the severe method indicated here. Who has not suffered an agony of pain rather than apply to the surgeon or dentist, although it must come to that at last? Nothing short of amputation of evil habit will save the life of the soul. Some are satisfied that they have confessed, received absolution, and done penance at the bidding of a human priest. Others are told to exercise discretion even when the taste and smell of intoxicants are sources of peril, and their only hope is to cut them off. Many excuse the young in their follies, and say, "They must sow their wild oats." Ay, but they will never plough them up, and no subsequent sowing will alter the effects of the first. "Whatsoever a man sows, that shall he also reap." Now, if we see deformity in a child which will mar its beauty for life, the pain he would immediately suffer would not prevent our cutting it off; and if there be a moral weakness or an evil habit that deforms spiritual beauty, the treatment must be as radical. When the moth is in a garment, the careful housewife does not leave a few and run the risk. When a man is bitten by a mad dog, the hot iron will sear the flesh, though it causes agony. When a child dies of diphtheria, the clothes are burnt and the little toys, which the mother would gladly keep, lest the other children should take the infection. The house is purged so as by fire. The treatment is severe, no doubt; but Christ did not come to lead us in the path of ease, but of self-denial. He knew that it was not painless to cut off the hand or the foot and to pluck out the eye, but he declared it was better to suffer what was represented by this than that the man with all his powers should be cast into hell. If this word comes as the sword of the Spirit to cut your heart in twain—

> "Oh, throw away the worser part of it,
> And live the purer with the other half."

Christ "died to put away sin by the sacrifice of himself," and in his Name we are called upon to "crucify the world with its affections and lusts."

II. GOD'S CALL TO OBEDIENCE IS URGENT. 1. *We are urged to this for the sake of others.* What anxiety would be relieved and what joy would be imparted to Christian friends if, by the transforming power of God's Spirit, you were delivered from evil! Besides this, by delaying repentance you may be causing others to stumble. There is a word in this passage about children—little ones, young people who may be influenced by you for evil. If you laugh at serious impressions, jeer at another as a saint, discourage earnestness, and lead to folly or guilt,—take heed, for it were better that a millstone were hanged about your neck than that such a crime should curse you. Parents especially can hold back their children from evil, and encourage them to good, if they prayerfully seek to do so. By allowing sceptical or immoral literature, by encouraging worldly companionships, they may foster a life of sin, and check the life of God in the soul. Still more power have they by example and personal influence. 2. *We are urged to this for our own sakes.* Christ was the King of Truth. He never deceived, misrepresented, or exaggerated. Ponder, therefore, his solemn words, "It is better for thee to enter life maimed," etc. This is not a literal description of hell. It is an allusion to Isa. lxvi. 24, where the prophet describes apostates from Jehovah lying outside the holy city in the valley of Hinnom, where refuse was cast, and the worm of corruption died not, and the fires of destruction were not extinguished. This

was used as an emblem of "everlasting destruction from the presence of the Lord."
Figurative as the language is, it is ominous, and warns us against the untold terrors
which await the impenitent—the retribution which follows unrepented sin. A man
may escape the consequences of sin here, but the punishment must ultimately come.
True, "God is merciful." But when a man on the sea-shore disregards warning, and
the tide comes in, his cries and prayers are of no avail, and soon his dead body is flung
up as a useless waif. He has defied the merciless law of a merciful God. Put yourself
in harmony with that law and it brings benediction, but oppose it and it brings
destruction. The amazing sacrifice of Christ is only explicable on the theory that sin
has effects beyond those which are visible here. "How shall we escape, if we neglect
so great salvation?"—A. R.

Vers. 1—8.—*The Transfiguration.* A brief interval of six days occurs, "days of
the Son of man," of which no record remains. How much of even this brief ministry
to men seems to be lost! Yet is the account of each day to be given when, to every
man favoured with his presence and teaching, it is said, "Render the account of thy
stewardship." The silence of the record is an appropriate prelude to the sublime event
which follows. "He went up into a mountain to pray." "Peter, James, and John"
—"the flower and crown of the apostolic band"—were the privileged three who alone
witnessed the scene, though the few graphic words of the historian, "kept and told to no
man until after the Son of man had risen from the dead," have presented to the eye of
the Church in all ages a clearly defined picture of it. And yet in viewing it we are
dazzled by excess of light. Few and simple must be our words. "He was transfigured," a word which is afterwards explained to apply to "the fashion of his countenance." It was "altered;" so St. Luke. St. Matthew adds, "his face did shine as the
sun;" while "his garment became glistering, exceeding white," "white as the light,"
"so as no fuller on earth can whiten them." Beautiful addition—so naïve, so simple!
That Divine nature, which in the incarnate body was always transfigured before the
eyes of men, now burst forth to view, radiating from within; the hidden divinity
shining through the veil of the flesh until its veil of raiment became radiant with
light.

I. In the history and development of the incarnate Son this event must have had
its high import. What is personal to himself, however, is almost entirely hidden. Of
the "talking" we hear only one word. The two men, "which were Moses and Elijah,"
"the founder and the great defender of the old dispensation," "spake of his *decease.*"
Very soon after "the days were well-nigh come that he should be received up," and
"he steadfastly set his face to go to Jerusalem." Henceforth his steps tend to the
cross.

II. But, whatever purpose was answered in respect of Jesus himself, the revelation
most assuredly was, in the highest degree, important to the disciples, and through them
to the Church at large. 1. Here is beheld the harmony, the unity, of the Law and the
prophets and the Christ. 2. Here, within the "bright cloud" which "overshadowed
them," though "they feared as they entered into it," they were made "eye-witnesses
of his majesty;" they witnessed the "honour and glory" which "he received from
God the Father." 3. They heard the "voice," and heard it "come out of heaven,"
which bore testimony for all to receive: "This is my beloved Son." In this lay the
"honour and glory" which "he received." So thought that one of the three who
declared, "It is good to be here," and who would fain have built tabernacles on this
"holy mount." This testimony had already been borne when, at the baptism, "a
voice out of the" same "heaven" declared *to* him, "*Thou art* my beloved Son." Here
the witness is *of* him to others: "*This is* my beloved Son;" and with the additional
word of command, "Hear ye him." Once again afterwards, when the Father glorified
his Name, there came "a voice out of heaven" directly speaking to him; though, as he
declared, "this voice hath not come for my sake, but for your sakes." How truly
might he say of all that he received, "not for my sake, but for your sakes"! Now,
not to Peter only, but also to James and John, is it revealed, "Thou art the Christ, the
Son of the living God." Now they with him share this blessedness which "flesh and
blood" could not impart; now we, and with us all the Church, rejoice in the knowledge of this primary truth. How our hearts long to see his glory and hear the

heavenly voice, and dwell on "the holy mount" of vision! And yet, how "good" soever it might be, it is better for the cultivation of our hearts in righteousness, and far better for the suffering, sinful world, that we go down into the valley to struggle with the evil spirit, and by faith and love and obedience glorify our living Head, and seek a meetness for those "tabernacles" which are not made by human hands.—G.

Vers. 14—28.—*The healing of the lunatic youth.* Descending from "the holy mount," where he had "received honour and glory from God the Father," a scene presented itself in direct contrast to "the majesty" of which the favoured three had then been "eye-witnesses." Around the disciples "they saw a great multitude, and scribes questioning with them." They had suffered a painful defeat. One of the multitude had brought to them his son, having "a dumb spirit;" and he spake to the "disciples that they should cast him out; and they were not able"! A more pitiable object could scarcely be imagined. "From a child" he was "epileptic," and suffered "grievously;" "the spirit ofttimes" casting "him both into the fire and into the waters" as if "to destroy him;" and so dire was its influence over him that, as the father said, "wheresoever it taketh him, it dasheth him down: and he foameth, and grindeth his teeth, and pineth away;" "it teareth him that he foameth, and it hardly departeth from him, bruising him sorely;" and when it "taketh him" he, in inarticulate tones, "suddenly crieth out." To add to the sadness of the case, the spirit was "unclean," compelling its victim to acts of filthiness. The poor boy, too, suffered the grievous aggravation of being "dumb," so that he could not tell out his sorrows; and he was "deaf," so that no word of strengthening consolation could be spoken to him. It was almost a misfortune to him not to be blind, for he could contrast his sad state with that of other youths around him. The father, wearied and disappointed with long and daily watching—for it seized him "suddenly"—and unable to find relief, brought him to the disciples, and met the sad rebuke of their inability. "They could not" cast him out. As a last resource, with timid, wearied heart, and with a hesitancy that surely found its justification in the failure of all efforts to obtain relief, he brought him to Jesus, uttering the word so descriptive of timid doubt, "If thou canst do anything, have compassion on us, and help us." It is now that he who bears alike our sins and sorrows, who "bears with" our weakness and our ignorance, who, even in his greatest works, strives so to work as to teach, corrects the imperfect view of the father, and makes his demand even upon his faulty faith, gently rebuking his pardonable insinuation. "It is not, 'If I can,' but, 'If thou canst!'" And he adds for all ages the all-inclusive teaching, "All things are possible to him that believeth." Christ's words, even of correction, rouse faith. The assurance that "all things" were "possible" to faith drew forth from the tremulous lips the profession of faith, "I believe;" while the tearful eyes (margin) bore witness to the genuineness of the confession hidden in the lowly prayer, "Help," and therein forgive, "thou mine unbelief." It is enough. With his word, in presence of a "multitude" that "came running together," he cast out the dumb and deaf spirit, and commanded him to "enter no more into him." The scene is full of teaching:

I. ON THE SAD CAPACITY OF THE HUMAN LIFE FOR SUFFERING AND DEGRADATION.

II. ON THE GLORIOUS POWER OF CHRIST TO HEAL AND RESTORE THE UTMOST DISORGANIZATION AND DEGENERATION OF THE HUMAN LIFE. It is an instance of his "power over all the power of the enemy." With such a picture before their eyes, who need hesitate to come to Jesus, in any need whatsoever? But the greatest teaching lies in the words spoken to the disciples in reply to their demand as to the reason why they "could not cast it out,"—"because of your little faith."

III. For us and for all, a third teaching, ON THE POWER OF PRAYER AND FAITH, lies openly on the face of the Lord's words to the distressed father. It is impossible to read the Gospels without learning that in Christ's view the exercise of Divine power over the suffering human life is often suspended on the attainment of certain conditions on the part of the sufferers. There is a fitness of things. Suffering and need seem to come of departures from the Divine order. The voluntary return to that order is most aptly, perhaps most easily, expressed by "faith." It indicates the lowly submissiveness of the spirit. It is the plasticity of the clay which truly prepares it for the hand of the potter. It is the least, and yet the best, self-fitting work that can be done by any who

would experience "the power of the Lord to heal." It is at once the acknowledgment
of the human impotence, need, and receptivity; it is the symbol of departure from all
other and competing helpers; it is an acceptance of the Lord himself, and in and with
him the germ of all healing, whether of body or soul.—G.

Vers. 28, 29.—*The conditions of success in spiritual work.* As might have been
expected, "when he was come into the house, the disciples asked him privately,"
"How is it that we could not cast it out?" The reply is simple: "This kind can
come out by nothing, save prayer." St. Matthew helps us to gain a clearer insight into
the cause: "Because of your little faith." "Many ancient authorities add *and fasting*"
(margin). The "little faith" must have approached closely to "unbelief," or to no
faith, for the Lord adds, "If ye have faith as a grain of mustard seed . . . nothing shall
be impossible to you." A little thought will compel us to learn much concerning the
influence of faith and of prayer, if not also of fasting, in the work assigned to the
disciples and in the general and ceaseless conflict with evil. That there was some
hindering cause palsying the strength of the disciples is obvious. But recently Jesus
had "given them power and authority over all devils," "and to cure diseases," and
they are suddenly powerless in the use of that authority. That they may have been
cherishing feelings which were inconsistent with so sacred a trust, the subsequent record
plainly declares. But our attention is riveted on the words of our Lord in his demand
for prayer and faith; and we learn at once, that the bestowment of great authority,
even with high endowments, does not set aside the necessity for cherishing suitable
conditions of mind in order to the effective discharge of the duties which that authority
imposes. The calling to be apostles, the investiture with power to cast out devils and
to cure diseases, does not release from the necessity to be clothed with humility—to
live in that spirit of withdrawment from the world, and communion with the Father,
which "prayer," even if not joined with "fasting," implies. The mere symbols of
office are useless in the spiritual realm. Rank in these hierarchies conveys no might.
Yea, though the very "power" be given, and given by Christ himself, no presumption
of personal freedom from the need of the lowliest spirit may be entertained. As
Christ's own power was arrested by the "unbelief" of those amongst whom he would
do "many mighty works," so the "power" entrusted to apostles is defied by "the
unclean spirit" if the minds of those apostles are not freed from unbelief, and not
raised to an alliance with heavenly powers by prayer. Entangled in nets that beset
even their feet, exposed to temptations that rudely assail even them, they, though
armed by the great power and authority of the kingdom, become weak, and are as other
men. Hence we learn that in the spiritual kingdom—
I. THE MERE AUTHORITY OF OFFICE IS INSUFFICIENT FOR DOING GREAT WORKS IN
THE KINGDOM OF HEAVEN. Apostles, prophets, preachers, teachers, rulers, are all taught
that there is a condition of heart needed as well as an investiture of office.
II. NO ENDOWMENT OF POWER OR GIFTS SETS ASIDE THE NECESSITY FOR LOWLY
SPIRITUAL EXERCISES. For while these acknowledge and minister to lowliness of heart,
they bring their possessor into a true and living sympathy with the heavenly kingdom,
and make him a meet channel for the conveyance of its healing grace. No mere
talent suffices.
III. FAITH AND PRAYERFULNESS DESCRIBE THE TRUE CONDITION OF THE SOUL OF HIM
OF WHOM IT IS TO BE SAID, "THOU HAST POWER WITH GOD AND WITH MAN, AND HAST
PREVAILED." The spiritual, who wield spiritual weapons, must maintain a spiritual
sensibility. This cannot be maintained without that true fasting which is a withdrawment from the spirit of the world, or without that prayerfulness which is a true
communion with the Father, or without that faith which is the real might of the soul.
These are steps in the spiritual progress; the final attainment being, not the feeble
word on the lip, "Come out of him," but that perfect oneness with the Divine which,
while it acknowledges the human impotence, makes the feeble man a true and fit
instrument of the Divine power. For by that power alone, after all, is the devil
cast out.—G.

Vers. 33—37.—*Honour.* By slow steps Jesus had brought the chosen band of the
disciples onward in that course of instruction which prepared them to ascend "the holy

mount" and behold "his glory," "glory as of the only begotten from the Father." He had also begun to show unto them that "he must suffer many things," and " be killed," making them "exceeding sorry." And he had spoken to them of the time "when the Son of man should have risen again from the dead; " but "what the rising again from the dead should mean" they understood not. Now by silent and hidden byways, secretly, for "he would not that any man should know it," they passed through Galilee and came to Capernaum. Jesus, taking advantage of this quiet, "taught his disciples" concerning the dark future that loomed upon him. But their minds seem to have been preoccupied, and "they understood not the saying." Scarcely had they entered the house when he demanded of them, "What were ye reasoning in the way?" Shame covered their face, the searching question revealing the power of him before whom all hearts be open. They were dumb before him, for "they had disputed one with another in the way who was the greatest." The distinction conferred upon the three, or the signal honour paid to Peter, may have been the occasion for this dispute, fanned perhaps by the anticipation of the decease at Jerusalem. Possibly there may have been an assumption of superiority on the part of one in that little republic. But such a spirit must be instantly crushed; and on the dark human background must the principles of the true heavenly kingdom be thrown forward. In calmness "he sat down," and solemnly "called the twelve" to him, and laid down as a principle to be then and for ever remembered, that in his house, or kingdom, or brotherhood, things are different from what they are in ordinary communities of men. And strange as the paradox may seem, the lowest is the highest, the most laborious servant is the true lord, the least is the greatest. "If any would be first, he shall be last of all, and minister of all." Further to impress this truth upon the hearts of the men who were contending for the highest room, the chief seat, the father's place in the house, "he took a little child"—the least in the house, and the furthest removed from the head; lower even than the servants, for they command the little children—"and set him in the midst." The Lord's sermon from this visible text is elsewhere recorded at length. The lesson for us to ponder, and often to ponder, for we are in great danger of forgetting it, is—He is the chief, the greatest, the first, in the kingdom of heaven who does most service in it. The honour is not to him who sits at the head of the table—any feeble one can do that; but to him who, girt with a towel, waits on the rest—to him who sees the true greatness of the kingdom; who so discerns its lofty, spiritual, and heavenly character, as to learn his own littleness in presence of it; who perceives that its highest end and aim is reached in rendering the utmost service to men. He who has seen the "Lord and Master" of all girded with a towel, stooping to wash and wipe the feet of his servants; he who has most of this his Master's spirit, who follows most closely in his Master's steps of toilsome, self-sacrificing service; he who, like his Master, does the most and the hardest work in the house;—yea, he is really and indeed the chief, the greatest, the first, in the house. And so, in truth, is it in all houses and in all kingdoms; the truly great are the labourers, the men who always see the kingdom to be greater than they, and, seeing the aim of the kingdom to be greater than the kingdom itself, are lowly enough and great enough to serve that aim, and have their greatness and most honourable place, not in medals, and decorations, and plaudits, and rewards, but in the deep if hidden fact, that the kingdom's welfare has been most advanced by them, that they have saved it from ruin or advanced it in honour, prosperity, and blessing. Then let every one seek eagerly the first, the highest place; but let every toilsome servant know that, in Christ's view, that is most prized which is furthest from self-adulation, from empty vanity, from indolent glorying in place; that he who most obeys, who hardest works, who lowliest walks—he, even he, is chief. This is the highest tribute paid (1) to all lowliness of mind, (2) to all diligent industry, (3) to all willing, self-sacrificing service to the common good.—G.

Vers. 38—50.—*Stumbling-blocks.* The same spirit which had led to the disputing as to "who was the greatest," had prompted the forbidding of one who, in Jesus' Name, was "casting out devils." The only reason assigned for the authoritative prohibition was, "He followed not us." If to pride envy succeeds, and if hatred lurks near to envy, malice is not afar off. The simple correction, "Forbid him not," is supported by the assurance that such a one cannot quickly become an enemy—"speak evil of me;" and "he that is not against us is for us." This admonition is urged by a teaching which branches out in three directions, relating to—

I. THE FAITHFUL ACKNOWLEDGMENT AND REWARD OF THE LEAST SERVICE RENDERED TO THE DISCIPLES IN THE NAME OF CHRIST—even "a cup of water to drink." Very wide apart are the two works, the "casting out devils" and the giving "a cup of water to drink." The one act may be performed by a mere child in age or in grace; but the other is the work of the man in grace and years. That the disciples were in the wrong in forbidding him who did the greater work, is shown by the assurance that he who does the less is acknowledged and rewarded by the Lord of all. Did not the disciples know that the casting out of devils was service done to them? Were they as ignorant as so many to-day are, not knowing that in the conquest of evil every one's best interests are advanced? Intimately is the well-being of one bound up in the well-being of all. The human body is not more closely knit and compacted together than is human society. To do good to any part is to do good to the whole. And each part suffers in the suffering, or loss, or injury of any other. Then by whomsoever or howsoever devils are cast out, let every true lover of his race and every wise lover of himself rejoice. Such a worker is not "against us," but "for us."

II. THE EQUALLY FAITHFUL PUNISHMENT OF ANY WHO SHALL CAUSE ONE OF THE LOWLIEST—one "of the least of these little ones that believe on me"—TO STUMBLE. But a rude interference with any worker of good is an offence against that good Lord, from whom alone men have power to do good. Here not only were devils cast out, but they were cast out in the Name of Christ. Plainly this was a servant of Christ, and a disciple, acknowledged as "one of these little ones that believe on me," to whom the Lord had given "power and authority." And that power was being used obediently. How serious a stumbling-block was thrown in the way of his obedience by the authoritative prohibition of the (possibly jealous) disciples! But how great the penalty—worse than to have "a great millstone hanged about his neck," and to be "drowned in the depth of the sea"! So jealously does the Lord of all guard the interests even of "little ones." It were better for a man to lose his own life in time than to lead another astray, so that he should lose the life eternal; better for them both. But what was the greater evil to which the layer of stumbling-blocks was exposed? Was it not the certainty that the Lord would do with his own body what he taught the disciples to do with theirs?—"cut off" the "hand" or "foot," "cast out" the "eye" that caused the body to stumble, whomsoever that foot or eye or hand might be? Was the foot cut off when Judas was severed from the body, and cut off to save the body, so that through all ages, of the twelve chosen, one must be wanting? Sad was the possibility, severe the warning; but how merciful and gracious! Men act on the principle, and sever a limb to save a life. So in spirituals should it be.

III. THE WISDOM OF EVERY DISCIPLE UTTERLY RENOUNCING WHATEVER MIGHT CAUSE HIM TO STUMBLE, OR BE A STUMBLING-BLOCK TO OTHERS. For every disciple the principle holds good. It is wise to forego anything that threatens the true life rather than lose that life. To retain all and be "cast into hell"—not into the mere hiding, or hidden place, but into "the unquenchable fire," the fire into which the spirit will be cast; worse than that, into which the body may be thrown, the real Gehenna, not the symbolical one—is to lose all. "To enter into the kingdom of God," having suffered the loss of that which was dear as an eye, a hand, or a foot, "is good" indeed in comparison with being "cast into" that "hell." There is a final fire, a fire that "is not quenched," which is punishment. And there is a present temporary fire, a salting fire, which is corrective and disciplinary. To this the cutting off of the hand corresponds. It is a pain-giving, fiery ordeal, with which every one in God's good way is "salted." And there is a salt of self-denial, which leads men to be "at peace one with another." It is held in the thought, which the "many ancient authorities" teach, that if any one would be a true sacrifice to God he must faithfully apply the fiery salt to the green, cankerous wound and burn out the evil, lest the evil burn out and burn up the life.—G.

Vers. 2—18.—*Glimpses of the glory of Jesus.* I. SPECIAL FAVOURS FOR SPECIAL SERVICES. The three disciples had given up all to follow Christ, had submitted themselves entirely to the Divine will. Only to such consecration is the deeper vision of truth granted, and ascent to the loftiest heights of spiritual enjoyment.

II. DIFFERENT ASPECTS OF CHRIST'S APPEARANCE. 1. He wore one appearance for the multitude, another for the circle of disciples. In the multitude he was the Prophet and the Wonder-worker; to the disciples the Friend and familiar Teacher. The multitude felt that he must be a great Man; the disciples knew him to be the Anointed One and Divine. 2. Among the disciples themselves: there was the familiar and ordinary, the extraordinary and unusual aspect of Christ. Here he passes out of the earthly medium of vision into one of celestial and supernatural glory.

"How nigh is grandeur to our dust!
How near is God to man!"

3. The manifestation of Christ is one in which extremes meet. The Man of sorrows, the beloved Son, delighted in of God. The lowly Teacher and Missionary of the kingdom of God; the enthroned Messiah. The Man, the God, and "both together mixed." 4. We cannot always enjoy the higher views in their clearness and brilliancy. After the vision and the voice, they look round and see "Jesus only!" Well for those who can ever see and find in Jesus of Nazareth the highest revelation they need of the Divine majesty and the Divine love.—J.

Vers. 9—13.—*Dark sayings.* I. RESERVE AND DELAY IN THE UTTERANCES OF TRUTH. There is an economy and an order in the kingdom of God. It is constantly observed by Christ. Certain truths there are always and everywhere to be made known; others must wait their time. As we are not to pry into the secrets of God, so neither are we hastily to blab them. Peculiar personal revelations should be treated with delicacy, not made an affair of the news-room or the market-place. The hour will come when our holiest memories, our deepest convictions, will be extracted from us by the need of the time.

II. ILLUSIONS OF RELIGIOUS THOUGHT. The prophecy concerning Elijah (Mal. iv. 5) was misunderstood, being taken literally. It was fulfilled in the person of the Baptist (John i. 21; Luke i. 17). John came to restore the Jewish people from the wrong teaching and preachers of later times, to the earlier and better lessons of the Law and the prophets. Another illusion was that the Messiah was to be a glorious earthly sovereign, and exempt from suffering. The scribes overlooked the predictions concerning the sufferings of Christ. So has every age its illusions; and God in every age fulfils himself unexpectedly. Even out of the humble and the lowly, the base things of the world, he causes his purpose to unfold, his power to be made manifest. The spirit of prophecy teaches that suffering belongs to the present service of God.—J.

Vers. 14—29.—*The demoniac.* I. WANT OF SPIRITUAL POWER IS CAUSED BY WANT OF FAITH. Faith is a mighty word in the gospel. It really includes all the energies of knowing, feeling, and willing; it is the entire affirmation of the man in favour of truth, goodness, and love. It is life in the power of God. In a sense it is unnatural to be without faith, for it is the pulse of the world. If we have not this we are weak, we cannot move a step beyond the bounds of actual knowledge—can take nothing for granted.

II. FAITH, WHEN WEAK, BECOMES DIMINISHED BY ASSOCIATION WITH THOSE WHO HAVE NONE. We become cowards or braver in company: pessimists or optimists. We trust in the good order of the world as God's, or give up everything for lost to the devil. "God desires from all eternity cheerful and brave sons," says Luther. Let us keep company with cheerful and trustful souls.

III. ON THE OTHER HAND, STRONG FAITH IS COMMUNICATIVE AND INSPIRING (J. H. Godwin). Tell an invalid he is looking ill, and you make him feel worse. Tell him he is improving, and his faith in his physical future will revive at the brighter picture. We are governed by imagination, and faith is a kind of imagination. It is exposed to the most contagious influences for health or disease. Whenever a strong deed is done, or mighty word spoken—

"Our hearts, in glad surprise,
To higher levels rise."

IV. FAITH IS THE CONDITION BOTH OF DOING AND RECEIVING THE HIGHEST GOOD. Faith gives a mental picture, distinguished from other mental pictures in that it is as *good as a reality* to him who views it. Now, we must have the distinct idea of a good to be received before we can place ourselves in the attitude to receive it; or of the good to be done and the possibility of doing it, before we can set about attempting it. The question then arises—Can faith be commanded by the will? The answer is—Not directly. "Paint a fire, it will not therefore burn." But the rebuke of Jesus implies that the disciples ought to have had faith. And the lesson is that faith may indirectly be obtained, be promoted, fostered, and preserved by communion with God.—J.

Vers. 30—32.—*Renewed prediction of death.* I. UNWELCOME OUTLOOKS SHOULD BE FIRMLY FACED. 'Tis not well to hide the head in the sand, like the ostrich, and try to fancy danger absent because not seen. For, if faced, the worst prospect loses at once half, and presently all, its terrors.

II. THE WILL OF GOD IS TO BE RECOGNIZED, EVEN IN THE WICKEDNESS OF MEN. It is by conflict that his will is wrought out. Outbursts of crime represent only one side of great living forces, and onward moving facts.

III. UNWELCOME TRUTHS NEED TO BE REPEATED, BUT NOT FOR ALL. There is an esoteric and an exoteric in Christianity. We do not tell children all we know of life. But there is an age, and there are persons, to whom all should be told that we know. Let truth be economized and wisely administered.—J.

Vers. 33—37.—*The symbolic child.* I. THE EXAMPLE OF CHILDREN. They are humble [and trustful in the presence of superior wisdom. Man not always so, but ought always to be so.

II. THE SECRET OF POWER LIES IN SERVICE. Command others by being useful to them. Rise in a community by working your way through all the grades of service, from the lowest to the highest.

III. TO STOOP IN LOVE IS TO RISE IN HONOUR. Jesus puts his arms around the little ones and around the weak, and is enthroned in the dependent heart of mankind.

IV. THE SCALE OF SERVICE, AND THE INCLUSION OF THE LOWER IN THE HIGHER. The order of duty is not to begin with the high and the remote, but with the lowly and the mean. "God is served by obedience to Christ, and Christ by kindness to the least and lowest who belong to him" (Godwin).—J.

Vers. 38—50.—*Marked sins.* There are some sins which are singled out for peculiar denunciation by the Spirit and Word of Christ. They are *extremely* opposed to the ends and purport of the kingdom.

I. INTOLERANCE. That is, the hindering of good, because the good is not done in our way. Christianity says the good deed justifies itself. Coming from a good source, it is not likely to be associated with evil opinions or teaching. Any one who does good nowadays may be said *virtually* to do it in the Name of Christ. To do good one need not, cannot, pass out of the Christian atmosphere. And experience of history confirms the statement of Christ. Good men really love him, whatever difference there may be in their mode of conception of him and statements about him. All that is done for love's sake is virtually and really done in his Name.

II. CAUSING SIN IN OTHERS. Involuntarily people may take offence, "stumble" at what we do or say. We cannot help false inferences being drawn, nor turn bad reasoners or conduct into good, nor weak brethren into strong. But we can avoid doing what we know will hurt others. If we are reckless in this respect, the will and the intelligence are involved in guilt.

III. DELIBERATE PREFERENCE OF PLEASURE TO RIGHT. The old story of the man who defended his dishonesty by the plea, "One must live," has its meaning for us. The judge replied to the culprit, "I do not see the necessity." So with the Christian: luxury is not a necessity; pleasure is not a necessity; even life in the lower sense is not a necessity; but only life in the higher sense—a good conscience, a soul in purity and integrity. It is ever a good bargain to part with a sin, and a losing business to compromise with a lust.

IV. SIN CAN ONLY BE CURED BY SUFFERING. Sin is in the intelligence want of principle; in the will want of energy for true self-realization. Our mistakes and troubles throw us upon the true principles of conduct, on the moral law of God. The fallacy of expecting blessedness by false methods leads us back to the true. Stern but kind is the discipline by which God uproots our follies and trains us for himself.—J.

Vers. 1—13.   Parallel passages: Matt. xvii. 1—13; Luke ix. 28—36.—*A glimpse of glory.*   I. THE TRANSFIGURATION.   1. *Allusions to the Transfiguration.*   The scene described in the above parallel passages is as singular as solemn. There are, however, two allusions to it in other books of the New Testament. One is in St. John's Gospel (i. 14), "And the Word was made flesh, and dwelt among us, (and *we beheld his glory, the glory as of the only begotten of the Father,*) full of grace and truth." The other occurs in 2 Pet. i. 16—18, "For we have not followed cunningly devised fables, when we made known unto you the power and coming of our Lord Jesus Christ, but were *eye-witnesses of his majesty.* For he received from God the Father honour and glory, when there came such a voice to him from the excellent glory, This is my beloved Son, in whom I am well pleased. And this voice which came from heaven we heard, when *we were with him in the holy mount."* There is, moreover, an intimation of the same in the three preceding verses, where the apostle, speaking of his "decease," uses the same word (ἔξοδος) which is found in this passage and nowhere else in the same sense in the New Testament, and where he speaks once and again of his σκήνωμα, "tabernacle," saying, "As long as I am in this tabernacle," and "Shortly I must put off this tabernacle." As undesigned coincidences are acknowledged to be strongly corroborative of the truth of a narrative, so such allusive references as those just quoted are in the highest degree confirmatory of the reality of the awful event referred to.   2. *Persons present.*   The persons permitted to witness this event were truly privileged individuals—of the chosen the more select, and of the loved the more beloved. This inner circle of the disciples consisted of Peter and James and John. They alone were present with the Saviour in the death-chamber of the daughter of Jairus, they alone were eye-witnesses of the Transfiguration, and they alone accompanied him in his agony.   3. *Place of the occurrence.*   The place where the Transfiguration occurred was long believed to be Tabor, that solitary hill rising abruptly from the great plain of Esdraelon, the ancient Jezreel. This tradition, prevalent since the sixth century, has been set aside in more recent times. The locality last named as visited by our Lord was Cæsarea Philippi, too far distant from Tabor and necessitating too great a change of place. It is certain that the summit of Tabor was occupied at the time in question by a Roman fortress, and did not afford the solitude which the event referred to presupposes. Besides, that town of Cæsarea Philippi lay under the range of Hermon, so that one of the heights of that snow-capped mountain was the most likely place. Hermon is the most conspicuous mountain in Palestine; hence its present name of *Jebel esh Sheikh,* the chief mountain. There is, moreover, an expression of comparison in one of the narratives, which points in this same direction, for the graphic touch of St. Mark, "white as snow," might well be suggested by the snowy cone of Hermon. It must, however, be admitted that the words of comparison (ὡς χιών) are omitted in ℵ, B, C, L, Δ, 1, in several versions, and by most of the critical editors, though found in A, D, E, F, G, and eight other uncials; in the Syriac, Coptic, Gothic, and most of the Latin versions.   4. *The time of the event.*   The time is specified by each of the three evangelists. Two of them, reckoning exclusively, specify a period of six days, and one of them, adopting the inclusive method, speaks of it as "about an eight days." This note of time, thus given in all the three narratives, has in it something surely special and significant. Nor is it to be passed over slightly, for the element of time in this instance is helpful, not only in tracing the sequence of events in the life of our Lord, but also in indicating in some measure the significance of the particular event here recorded. Peter had made his famous confession of the Christ, and had been commended for the words of truth he spoke. Our Lord had followed this up by foretelling his own death and passion. But now, instead of words of praise, he had to use the language of sharp rebuke, when Peter deprecated our Lord's sufferings, and, tempter-like, sought to divert his thoughts to an earthly kingdom, like those very kingdoms of the world and their glory which Satan had proffered in one of his great assaults. After these and other conversations about Messiah's work and the nature of his kingdom, a week or thereabouts had elapsed when the Transfiguration scene took place—a scene having an important bearing on the disciples at that crisis, on the Master in the near prospect of his passion, and on the Church at all periods and in all places.

II. CONCOMITANTS OF THE TRANSFIGURATION. 1. *Mountain scenery.* In the scenery of Scripture, as in the natural landscape, mountains form a conspicuous object. They are the spots so often selected for Divine manifestations, and so frequently signalized by solemn service or severe sacrifice. Why they have been chosen for such purposes we may be unable to explain. Whether it is that their sublime grandeur tends to elevate the thoughts from earth to heaven; or that their separation from the plains and valleys around promotes meditative seclusion, helping to shut out the world and leave the soul alone with God; or whether the fresh free air that surrounds their summits has a bracing effect upon the human spirit;—whatever be the cause, the fact of their selection remains the same. When Abraham, the father of the faithful, was summoned to surrender his son, his only son Isaac, whom he loved, the sacrifice was to take place on Mount Moriah. When God was pleased to appear to Moses in the bush that burned with fire and yet was not consumed, it was on Mount Horeb. When he came down in awful majesty at the giving of the Law, it was on the top of Sinai he descended. It was on bleak and barren Ebal the curses were pronounced; it was on fair and fertile Gerizim that the blessings were uttered; while at each curse and blessing the living voice of the mighty multitude rolled up the hillsides, pronouncing the long "Amen." On Carmel Elijah denounced the prophets of Baal, and destroyed the worship of that idol. It was on Mount Zion that the ark and tabernacle found a resting-place in David's day, and there in consequence was the centre of Jewish religious service; though it was on Mount Moriah that the temple was subsequently built. From Pisgah Moses looked across the flood and gazed on the land of promise. On Nebo God took his servant home to heaven. So also our blessed Lord himself chose mountains as the scenes of his discourses, doings, and devotions. On the Mountain of the Beatitudes he delivered those blessed utterances contained in that wondrous sermon on the mount. On a mountain in Galilee he manifested himself after his passion; and from Olivet he ascended. And now he leads his disciples to that mountain apart; and so retirement, it would seem, was one ground of the selection of a mountain on this occasion. 2. *The preparation.* But more important than the place of transfiguration was the Saviour's preparation for it. That preparation, we learn, was *prayer.* In every crisis of his history, and at every great event of his life, we find the Saviour engaged in prayer. One main feature of his life on earth was prayer. When he was inaugurated by baptism, and when he formally entered on his own ministry, he prayed; for it is written, "It came to pass, that Jesus also being baptized, and praying, the heaven opened." Before he set apart his twelve apostles to found his Church and propagate his doctrine, he spent a whole night in prayer. When he wrought his greatest miracle, "he lifted up his eyes in prayer and said, Father, I thank thee that thou hast heard me. And I knew that thou hearest me always." During his agony in the garden of Gethsemane he prayed once and again, and a third time, with still-increasing earnestness. When he hung upon the cross he prayed, and prayed even for his murderers. As he ascended to heaven his hands were uplifted in holy prayer and heavenly benediction. And now that he is seated at the right hand of the Majesty on high he prays on behalf of his people; for he is our Advocate with the Father, and ever lives to intercede. In like manner, the purpose for which he ascended the Mount of Transfiguration was prayer: "He took Peter, and James, and John, and went up into a mountain to pray." 3. *Peculiarity of the Saviour's prayer.* We must mark the peculiarity and purport of his prayer. It had this *peculiarity*, that one element of prayer was wanting—indeed, it must have been wanting. There were thanksgiving and petition, we know, but there could be no confession. He had no sin to confess, no contrition to feel for personal sin, no sorrow on that head to express, and so repentance in his case was impossible. Yet in his humanity, sinless though it was, he needed prayer. The *purport* of such prayer we are at no loss to discover. It included petition for himself and intercession for his people; while this spirit of prayer served as a pattern for all his followers. Not only was he an Expiation, but an Example; for he left us an example, that we should follow in his steps. The character of his intercession may be learned from his prayer for Peter, and his great intercession (John xvii.)

for all his followers in all times and in all lands. His petition for the cup to pass away from him had its answer in the power that sustained him in his agony, in the submission of his human will to the Divine, and in the angel strengthening him.

III. CHARACTERS CONCERNED.   1. *Representative characters.*   In addition to the three favourite apostles, who were merely spectators but not actors, properly speaking, in this scene, we have Moses, Elijah, and Jesus, all of them in a representative character. Here were the Law-giver, the Law-restorer, and the Law-fulfiller. The Law was given by Moses; it was restored, after a time of sad defection, by Elijah; it was fulfilled in all its requirements by Jesus, who came expressly not to destroy the Law or abrogate the prophets, but to fulfil them both. They represented still more. Moses represented the Law and Elijah the prophets; both doing homage to Jesus, who represented the gospel, or rather Law and prophets merged in the gospel dispensation. Here, again, is one that never tasted death, but was transferred in a fiery chariot from earth to heaven. No doubt that very translation effected some change analogous to death. At all events, he may fitly represent those that are alive and remain till the coming of the Lord, who shall not sleep as others sleep, but who shall be changed; "for," saith the apostle, "we shall not all sleep, but we shall all be changed." Here, too, is one that died as mortals die, but how or where his body was laid to rest no one knoweth till this day; the only record is that "God buried him." Here, also, is One that died a violent death and by wicked hands; he died and was buried, his grave being made with the rich in his death. Thus we get a hint that it matters little how we die—whether by the decay of nature, or fell disease, or dread catastrophe, or the hand of violence; neither does it matter where or how we are buried—whether in the country churchyard, or city cemetery, or the desert sands, or the depths of ocean; whether in the grave of the poor or mausoleum of the rich, whether in obscure privacy or with funereal pomp; in any case, if servants of God, we shall be compeers of Moses and Elijah, and shall appear with Christ in glory.   2. *A foreshadow of heavenly fellowship.*   Once more, though the apostles were mainly present as witnesses, still they were representative men. They were publishers and preachers of the new economy, and thus representatives of the Christian dispensation. Here, last of all and greatest of all, was Jesus, the Mediator of the new covenant and the Representative of all times. So in that heavenly state, of which the Transfiguration was merely a foreshadow, saints of all times and of all dispensations shall be found. Believers during the legal age, believers in the times of the prophets, believers in the days of the apostles, believers from then till now, and onward till the consummation of all things, shall be there; "They shall come from the east, and from the west, and from the north, and from the south, and shall sit down in the kingdom of God." Even a philosophic heathen could exult in the prospect of meeting the shades of departed worthies in a future state. "What bounds," he exclaims, "can you set to the value of conversing with Orpheus and Musæus and Homer and Hesiod? What delight must it be to meet with Palamedes and Ajax, and others like to them! Then we should experience the wisdom of that great king who led his troops to Troy, and the prudence of Ulysses and Sisyphus." Oh, how infinitely greater and holier is the joy with which the Christian can anticipate that grand gathering of all the faithful in Christ Jesus—patriarchs, prophets, apostles, martyrs, and confessors, all who purely lived and nobly died; not only the one hundred and forty-four thousand sealed ones of all the tribes of the children of Israel, but "a great multitude, that no man can number," in that day when we shall "come unto Mount Zion, and unto the city of the living God, the heavenly Jerusalem, and to an innumerable company of angels, to the general assembly and Church of the Firstborn, which are written in heaven!"   3. *Recognition.*   Here it must be observed, in passing, that the apostles at once recognize Moses and Elijah, in what manner or by what means we cannot tell; whether from their discourse, or by information from Christ, or by some spiritual intuition, we do not know. At all events, we may fairly infer from this fact that in heaven there shall be distinct recognition; otherwise the crowded ranks of the celestial inhabitants would only present one vast collection of unknown and so less interesting faces. Other Scriptures confirm this. Thus Abraham seems acquainted with all the circumstances of Lazarus' life, and Dives knows the state of his brothers on earth. Paul gives us to understand that our mental faculties shall be enlarged and expanded. Can we imagine, then, that memory alone shall be impaired and diminished? Oh, what zest such recognition will give to the joys of heaven! Who is not alive to the pleasures of social intercourse on earth? With what satisfaction does a happy family surround the domestic hearth, or meet round the festive board! With what delight of family and friends is the wanderer, after long years of absence, welcomed to his native land! And oh, how great shall be the joy in heaven when the faithful minister meets those to whom he had preached the gospel, telling of heaven and leading the way! Or when the man of prayer meets those for whom he had offered supplication in seasons of danger, or difficulty, or distress, or disease, or at the hour of death! Or when the spiritual teacher, whether in sabbath school, or Bible class, or cottage meeting, meets those who had been once his pupils, but are now his companions in glory!

IV. CHANGE DESCRIBED. 1. *The glory of his person.* Here we are to notice, in the first place, the glory of his person. From eternity he had been in the form ($\mu o \rho \phi \hat{\eta}$) of God. This had been his original form, but in the fulness of time he took upon him the form of a servant. Now for a while he resumes the form which he had laid aside. The form of a servant is changed back ($\mu \epsilon \tau \epsilon \mu o \rho \phi \omega \theta \eta$) into that of Deity. He "was transfigured before them" is the statement of St. Matthew and St. Mark. The veil of mortal flesh became transparent. The glory of the Godhead broke through tne concealment. Like a sudden sunburst from behind the murky clouds on a dark and wintry day, there was a glorious outburst of Divine effulgence. It irradiated his body, it diffused itself over his whole person, it surrounded him with an atmosphere of brightness and beauty. Beams of heavenly light flashed from head to foot. The whole man presented an unearthly splendour. His appearance was a reflection of that glory which he had had with the Father before all worlds, and in which he appears among the inhabitants of heaven. 2. *The change of his countenance.* "The fashion of his countenance was altered" is the statement of St. Luke, who, writing for Gentiles, avoids the word transformed, or *metamorphosed,* on account of its association with heathenism; while St. Matthew explains the nature of that alteration by saying, "His face did shine as the sun." After Moses' interview with God on Mount Sinai, the skin of his face shone so that he was obliged to cover it with a veil as soon as his public official duty had been discharged. Similarly, when Stephen, the proto-martyr, was brought before the council, "all that sat in the council, looking steadfastly on him, saw his face as it had been the face of an angel." But in the case of Stephen and of Moses it was a borrowed brightness, whereas the Saviour's face shone with native irradiation. It was no reflected lustre, like that of the moon in the heavens, deriving all her light from the sun. The light and loveliness were all his own. The face soon to be marred more than any man, and his countenance more than the sons of men, possessed a brilliancy that was dazzling and that outrivalled the radiance of the sun at noon. That face, soon to be smitten and spit upon, and from which men hid in scorn and sorrow, now displayed a glory indescribable. The veil of humanity became too thin to hide the outshining of the divinity within. Like a magnificent temple grandly lighted up on every side and throughout its entire extent, from nave to porch and from dome to pavement, the Saviour's face and entire person—the whole temple of his body—was brightened up and beautified with celestial glory. 3. *The glistening of his garments.* Even his garments shared this heavenly transformation. They brightened, they glistened, they dazzled. The sacred penmen seem at a loss for similitudes to give us a correct notion of a change so marvellous and glorious. "White as the light," says St. Matthew; "shining, exceeding white as snow," says St. Mark; "white and glistering"—white and flashing forth as lightning ($\dot{\epsilon} \xi \alpha \sigma \tau \rho \dot{\alpha} \pi \tau \omega \nu$)—says St. Luke. They lay both natnre and art under contribution for the purpose of describing it. They became "white as snow," says one— white as the snowy peak of the neighbouring hill with the sunbeams resting on it; "exceeding white," he says again, "so as no fuller on earth can white them." When St. John saw him in apocalyptic vision, his head and hair were white as wool. Ages before, when Daniel saw him in prophetic vision as the Ancient of days, his garments were white as snow. On the Mount of Transfiguration his human nature was closely assimilated to his Divine nature, in which he clothes himself with light as with a garment. Such was Christ on Hermon; what must he be in heaven? Such was he in his transfigured humanity; what must be his divinity revealed? What shall he be when, with face unveiled, we shall see him as he is? But, better and more blessed still, in that day we shall be like him. If, under a former portion of this subject, we caught a glimpse of our companionship in heaven, here we get a glance at our condition in the heavenly state.

V. CONSEQUENCES. 1. *One consequence common.* Some of the consequences of the Transfiguration scene are general, and some special. There is one common to the saints of all times and of all climes. That transfigured body of Christ is the model and pattern of all the glorified. He is the Head, they are the members. "As we have borne the image of the earthly, we shall also bear the image of the heavenly." Here and now our bodies, though fearfully and wonderfully made, are bodies of humiliation. They are subject to many infirmities, liable to painful and even loathsome diseases, doomed to dissolution in a few years at most, while, worst of all, they contain the seed of sin, and their members too often are instruments of unrighteousness; "for I know," says the apostle, "that in me (that is, in my flesh) dwelleth no good thing." But these bodies of humiliation shall be fashioned like unto Christ's glorious body; these bodies, now "of the earth, earthy," shall be elevated to the condition of the heavenly; these bodies, now so frail, shall be endued with immortal health and vigour. Here and now the beauty of the fairest face soon fades; then the plainest face shall become beautiful, and that beauty shall be truly amaranthine. The features now saddened by sorrow, or marred by disease, or disfigured by age, shall become "bright as the sun when he goeth forth in his strength," bright as the Saviour's on the Mount of Transfiguration, bright as the face of our Lord was seen by Peter and James and John at that time, bright as it always appears to the saints in glory. Every blemish shall be blotted out, every wrinkle shall be smoothed, every disease expelled, and all decrepitude for ever removed. Then, too, on the sightless eyeballs of the blind shall flash the light of an eternal day, the ear of the deaf shall be unstopped, the tongue of the dumb sing, and the lame man for ever lay aside his lameness. Moreover, the richest raiment of earth will be but rags when compared with those robes of brightness which the ransomed in heaven wear. In view of all this may we not exclaim?—

"Oh for the robes of whiteness!
Oh for the tearless eyes!
Oh for the glorious brightness
Of the unclouded skies!
Oh for the no more weeping
Within the land of love,
The endless joy of keeping
The bridal feast above!"

2. *An immediate consequence.* Another and immediate consequence was to reconcile the disciples to the sufferings of their Master, and sustain them amid their own. Then, as now, the Jews overlooked the first appearance of Messiah in weakness, through haste for his glorious second advent. Then, as now, their pride rebelled against the idea of a suffering Saviour, in their anticipation of his glory. Then, as afterwards, they looked for a great temporal potentate, to whom all thrones would be subject and whom all sovereigns would obey. They antedated the glory of his reign. But this experience of heaven upon earth, of glory so surpassing was surely enough to make amends for those disappointed hopes. It was meant also to prepare them for the approaching crisis, to comfort them when it came, and to confirm their faith in his Divine majesty, even when, as a malefactor, he was nailed to the cross. 3. *An additional consequence.* Again, it not only helped to reconcile the disciples to the death of their Master, but doubtless went far to comfort Immanuel himself in the near prospect of his agony and bloody sweat, and of his cross and passion. Elsewhere we are informed that, "for the joy that was set before him, he endured the cross, despising the shame." This short space of heavenly enjoyment, coming in as a parenthesis amid the wearisome struggles and strivings of earthly life, would cheer him onward towards the end. The foretaste thus afforded of the coming glory that would crown everlastingly the brief sorrows of the present would sustain him in the approaching sufferings. The cloud of witnesses that surrounds the Christian in his pilgrimage serves as a motive to urge him on, so that, laying aside every weight, he runs with patience the race set before him; so these witnesses, representative of t n thousand times ten thousand, intensely interested in the

Redeemer's work and intently looking on, would encourage the human spirit of the Saviour, so that, braced with new alacrity, he would hold on the course appointed and pass through the baptism of blood. As his baptism was the commencement of his ministry, his transfiguration was his consecration to suffering.

VI. THE CONVERSATION HELD. 1. *The persons engaged in converse.* Here were two *prophetic* men, of whom one died and was buried by mystic hands, no one knew how or where.

> " By Nebo's lonely mountain,
>   On this side Jordan's wave,
> In a vale in the land of Moab,
>   There lies a lonely grave.
> And no man knows that sepulchre,
>   And no man saw it e'er;
> For the angels of God upturned the sod,
>   And laid the dead man there.
>
> .   .   .
>
> " And had he not high honour?—
>   The hillside for a pall;
> To lie in state while angels wait,
>   With stars for tapers tall;
> And the dark rock-pines, like tossing plumes,
>   Over his bier to wave;
> And God's own hand, in that lonely land,
>   To lay him in the grave!"

The other never died, was never buried; but went straight from earth to heaven–

> " All undrest
> From his mortal vest,
> He stept on the car of heavenly fire;
> To prove how bright
> Are the realms of light,
> Bursting at once upon the sight."

And now these two visitants from the heavenly world have taken their place together on that lone mountain apart. Here also were three *apostolic* men—the foremost of the apostolic band: John, with his heart of love; James, with his high standard of law—both of them sons of thunder with outspoken courage; and Peter, honoured with the keys that opened the door of faith to Jew and Gentile. " And why these?" asks the devout Bishop Hall, in his 'Contemplations on the Holy Scriptures.' " We may be too curious: Peter because the eldest; John because the dearest; James because, next Peter, the zealousest: Peter because he loved Christ most; John because Christ most loved him; James because, next to both, he loved and was loved most. I had rather," he adds, " to have no reason, but because it so pleased him. Why may we not as well ask why he chose these twelve from others, as why he chose three out of the twelve?" But with prophets and apostles, the foundation of the future Church, was Jesus Christ the *God-man* and the Church's chief Corner-stone. The converse, however, was confined to Moses and Elias and Jesus; the apostles were only listeners. One is naturally curious to know the subject that engaged the attention of that small but wonderfully select company. The subject must have been worthy of such an august assembly. 2. *The subject of conversation.* What, then, was the subject that occupied them? Was it political, embracing the fate of kingdoms, or the fall of dynasties, or fast-coming times of calamity and change? Was it the extent and power and future breaking up of the great Roman empire? Was it the subjection of Palestine to Roman rule, or the relation of the Tetrarch of Galilee to the Procurator of Judæa? Nothing of all this. But if the subject was not political, was it one of Jewish casuistry, such as divided the schools of Hillel and Shammai, about binding or loosing? Was it in reference to the primary or derivative prohibitions of sabbath work—the *avoth* or the *toldoth?* Was it about the *Halakoth* or *Hagadoth*—the rules of jurisprudence or the legends illustrative of them, and both afterwards embodied in the Gemara? None of these, or such as these, was of sufficient importance to command their attention. We might, however, reasonably enough expect that it would be the beauties of heaven, with its gates of pearl, and streets of gold, and jasper wall, and foundations of precious stones; or the grandeur of its minstrelsy and melody of its songs; or the blessedness of the heavenly state and the ecstasies of its joys, or all the untold glories of the beatific vision; or the unspeakable magnificence of the heavenly hierarchy, with its thrones and dominions and principalities and powers. And yet it was none of these. It might have been the atmosphere of heaven brought down by Christ to earth, the perfection of his life when here below, the power of his miracles, the purity of his precepts, the preciousness of his promises, his words and works of benevolence. And yet it was none of these. It was perhaps a less inviting, but certainly not less important, theme. Over and above what is common to all the evangelists, each contributes a part peculiar to himself. As St. Mark omits mention of the change that passed over the countenance of the Saviour, and fixes attention on the garments so white and glistening; so St. Luke alone records the *subject* about which they discoursed. Our curiosity is thus gratified at least in part. True it is that, while we are made acquainted with the topic of conversation, the evangelist gives no hint of the conversation itself. And yet perhaps we have an echo of that conversation in the writings of those favourite apostles who were privileged to form the audience on that remarkable occasion. 3. *A peculiar term.* That most interesting subject was the *decease* he was to accomplish at Jerusalem. The expression is so remarkable, it is no way strange that attention has often been directed to it. Elsewhere in Scripture death is literally spoken of, or it is represented from its physical effect as "giving up the ghost," or it is euphemistically expressed as "sleep." This latter expression, however, is never applied to the death of Christ, for that death was no babe-like slumber—no gentle falling asleep. It was death in all its hideousness, in all its bitterness, with cruelly aggravated horrors and fearfully augmented terrors. In consequence of these sufferings the believer's death is now changed into sleep, and so we read that "them who sleep *by* ($\delta\iota\grave{a}$) Jesus will God bring with him." The death of the Saviour is here set forth as an $\xi o \delta o s$, exodus or departure, so that the term would cover all that was peculiar in the exit of Moses, or Elijah, or Christ himself; while it is the result of his own voluntary act, and an event, too, in which he was more active than passive; and so the ordinary verb $\xi\theta a\nu\epsilon\nu$ is not used in his case. Likewise in the narrative of his death the evangelists use a similar expression, namely, $\xi\xi\epsilon\pi\nu\epsilon\nu\sigma\epsilon$, "he breathed forth," St. Luke and St. Mark; "he delivered up the ghost" ($\pi a\rho\epsilon\delta\omega\kappa\epsilon$), St. John; or "dismissed," sent away his spirit ($\grave{a}\phi\eta\kappa\epsilon$), St. Matthew. The decease he was about to accomplish at Jerusalem was thus lifted up out of the rank of ordinary deaths, and raised by a whole heaven above them. It was a *voluntary* surrender: "No man taketh my life;" "I have power to lay it down," he said, "and power to take it again." It was *vicarious* as well as voluntary; for he suffered, "the just for the unjust, to bring us to God." It was *valid* for every expectant soul; because "to them that look for him he will appear a second time without sin unto salvation." It realized the types of the old economy, for it was the great antitype that finished all. It crowned the sacrifices under the Law; for "by one sacrifice he hath perfected for ever them that are sanctified." It fulfilled the promises of the past and guaranteed the bestowal of them all; for "he that spared not his own Son, but delivered him up for us all, shall he not with him also freely give us all things?" It put new meaning into many otherwise dark and obscure statements of Old Testament Scripture. It was the death of deaths. It was the gateway to eternal life; it "opened the door of heaven to all believers." It was an offering; for he gave himself an offering and a sacrifice of sweet-smelling savour. It was a propitiation; for "we have an Advocate with the Father, Jesus Christ the righteous; and he is the Propitiation for our sins." It was a ransom; for "he came not to be ministered unto, but to minister, and give his life a ransom for many." Confessors took joyfully the spoiling of their goods, but that spoiling was the test of their own sincerity. Martyrs shed their blood unmurmuringly and even triumphantly, but the martyr's death was the preparation for the martyr's crown. Yet martyrs and confessors stood each in his own lot, suffering for themselves and by themselves. Not so Jesus; for others, not for himself, he drained the bitter cup; for others, not himself, he underwent the bloody baptism; for sins, but not his own, he endured the cross, despising all the pain and shame. 4. *Character of their conversation.* The subject, then, as we have just seen, was that death—a death which patriarchs, and priests, and prophets, and pious persons under the old dispensation looked and longed for; a death which not only fulfilled the predictions, but realised the typical institutions of the old economy; that death which was the complement of the legal economy and the consummation of the Jewish Church, and which, at the same time, formed the commencement of a new epoch and of a higher order of events. What a glorious subject! More glorious far than the fate of kingdoms or the fall of kings; more glorious than all the discoveries of science, or applications of art, or improvements of society. In their *conversation* on this high theme they spake, no doubt, of the nature of the decease to be accomplished: of its necessity, to realise types and fulfil prophecies; to "magnify the Law and make it honourable;" to save miserable man and glorify Almighty God, restoring peace between heaven and earth, and "by one sacrifice perfecting for ever the sanctified;" to overthrow the kingdom of Satan, and diffuse light and life and love through all the world; to extract the sting of death, "destroying him that had the power of it, that is, the devil," and throwing the radiance of heavenly glory over the darkness of the tomb. They conversed, no doubt, of the travail of the Redeemer's soul, and of his mediatorial reward in the eternal approbation of the Father, the salvation of the lost, and the praises of the redeemed for ever. Of all subjects this was the most important to men, the most interesting to Christ, and the most glorifying to God. This subject is still the great theme of the Church militant on earth, and the glorious song of the Church triumphant in heaven. 5. *Apparently out of place.* But glorious as the subject of conversation was, and edifying as the manner of that conversation was, it might in one sense seem inopportune. Hence says an old divine already cited (Hall, in his 'Contemplations'), "A strange opportunity! in his highest exaltation to speak of his sufferings; to talk of Calvary on Tabor; when his head shone with glory, to tell him how it must bleed with thorns; when his face shone like the sun, to tell him it must be blubbered and spit upon; when his garments glistered with that celestial brightness, to tell him they must be stripped off and divided; when he was adored by the saints of heaven, to tell him how he must be scorned by the basest of men; when he was seen between two saints, to tell him how he must be seen between two malefactors: in a word, in the midst of his Divine majesty, to tell him of his shame; and, while he was transfigured on the mount, to tell him how he must be disfigured upon the cross." So thought good Bishop Hall. But this subject is never out of place, it is never out of time. It is the theme of our praises both here and hereafter, and should be the subject of our prayerful meditations till we feel its transforming power, and are "changed into the same image from glory to glory, even by the Spirit of the Lord."

VII. CONCLUSION. 1. *St. Peter's proposal.* "Let us make three tabernacles," said Peter, "one for thee, and one for Moses, and one for Elias." Chrysostom thinks that Peter's object was to remain away from the holy city, and thus, by remaining on the mount and remote from Jerusalem, prevent the Saviour's sufferings. God had tabernacled in *Shechinah* glory, why should not the Saviour embody the same? But the expression of Peter was rather the expression of an ecstasy of delight—a plenitude of joy which words could not express. So great was his rapture that he wist not what he said. A little of the joy of heaven would be too much for flesh and blood—it would overwhelm us. Besides, Peter was overlooking the fact that the wilderness work and warfare must needs be resumed. The journey of life was not ended. Some droppings of heavenly blessedness had transported him into rapture, but the full wealth of its downpour was not yet at hand. He antedated the bliss of heaven, forgetting for the moment that he was still on earth. More sacrifice, more suffering, more sorrow, more self-denial, more days of toil and nights of trouble, must intervene before he crossed the Jordan and entered the promised land. 2. *The effect of emotion.* Peter's exclamation partook more of the emotional than of the rational. It was rather the offspring of ardent desire than of deliberate judgment. It proceeded more from the heart than from the head. But head as well as heart must be influenced by religion. If it were confined to the head, it would tend to formality; if to the heart, it might issue in fanaticism. On one hand, Peter's exclamation was quite excusable. "It is good for us to be here," a fine thing, a pleasant thing; not good in a moral sense, which is differently expressed ($\dot{\alpha}\gamma\alpha\theta\grave{o}\nu$), but good physically ($\kappa\alpha\lambda\grave{o}\nu$), which is the expression here. If there were a place on earth of which this might be said, it was that Mount of Transfiguration. It was, perhaps, the spot on earth nearest and likest heaven. There was a *hill*, an emblem of heaven, which is the hill of God's holiness. There were two *saints*, an epitome of heaven, representing as they did the quick and the dead—those alive on earth, and the dead raised up at the day of judgment. There was the *Saviour* himself, in uncreated light and unveiled glory, at once the Source and Centre of heavenly blessedness. There was *conversation* such as may be presumed to be held among the redeemed in heaven, for the burden of their song is, " Worthy is the Lamb that was slain." There, moreover, was temporary seclusion from the toil and turmoil of earth, from the business and bustle of the world, from the sorrows and sufferings of this mortal life and strife. There, too, was enjoyment of the unclouded sunshine and untroubled rest of heaven. There was a ravishing foretaste of the joys of heaven. No wonder, then, that Peter proposed to perpetuate the happiness, continue the enjoyment, and carry on the fellowship, erecting tabernacles and dwelling on the mount. But, on the other hand, there was something selfish, if not exclusive, in the proposal, for he was leaving behind his friends and fellow-worshippers on the plain below ; he was speaking in forgetfulness of the bodies of the saints that slept ; he was acting unreasonably in requiring Moses to forsake the Divine presence, after the uninterrupted enjoyment thereof during fifteen centuries, for a tent-like dwelling, and Elijah to forget the car of fire in which he had gone up, and now abide below ; he was strangely overlooking the recent subject of discourse with which Moses and Elijah had been so occupied—the decease that was to be accomplished, the death to be endured, the redemption to be effected, the sacrifice to be offered, and the salvation to be procured. In entire obliviousness of, or indifference to, all this, his proposal was to forestall the future and have a present heaven upon earth. In momentary rapture he forgot he was still in a scene of pilgrimage and in a state of sojourn ; he forgot he was a stranger in a strange land, which was neither his rest nor his home, and where no abiding city is to be found. He forgot that the Christian's life is a journey ; and what traveller can reach his destination without the toil of travelling? He forgot life is a race ; and where is the racer who is rewarded without a struggle, and who, without running, yet obtains the prize? He forgot that life is a warfare, in which a fight, a hard fight, is to be fought before the combat is ended and the conqueror crowned. It is only when we shall have fought the good fight, and finished our course, and kept the faith, that we may say with Paul, " Henceforth is laid up for me a crown of glory, which God, the righteous Judge, will give me at that day." But Peter wist not what ($\lambda a\lambda \acute{\eta} \sigma \eta$) he should speak ; he wist not even what he ($\lambda \acute{\epsilon} \gamma \epsilon \iota$) actually does say ; so enraptured was he with delight, so carried out of himself by the extraordinary occurrence, and so bewildered with terror at the same time. 3. *Due in part to sleep.* Further, and finally, they had been " heavy with sleep," but either kept awake throughout it, or awoke after an interval, or rather started all at once into perfect wakefulness, now wide awake and fully alive to all that was seen or said. They had been asleep, wrapped perhaps in their *abbas*, according to Oriental fashion, on the ground, when the celestial light, bursting upon them, roused them thoroughly so as to witness all that transpired. 4. *Miscellaneous remarks.* (1) The disciples thought this was the predicted coming of Elijah, but our Lord corrects their mistake, and tells them he had already come in the person of John the Baptist ; and as the prediction relating to John has been fulfilled, *a fortiori* will the prediction of Messiah's sufferings be fulfilled. Thus the seemingly awkward clause, " and how it is written of the Son of man," is best explained (*a*) as a parenthetic exposition of the preceding clause, and an *a fortiori* confirmation of the succeeding one. There is, however, (*b*) another explanation which takes " how " as directly interrogatory ; thus, " But how is it written of the Son of man ? that he must suffer many things, and be set at nought ; " so that, after the coming of Elijah had been stated, the object of Messiah's coming is specified by way of question and answer : " For what purpose is it written that Messiah cometh?" In order that he may come to suffer as a malefactor, not to conquer as a warrior. (2) The apostles were sorely puzzled about "the rising from the dead." This does not refer to the general doctrine of the resurrection of the dead, which must have been known to them and believed by them ; but they regarded that resurrection as far off, and understood, and rightly understood, our Lord to speak of a resurrection near at hand, affecting himself in some mysterious way which they did not then comprehend, and which they were only convinced of by that wondrous event itself when it actually occurred. (3) The conversation before and the miracle after the Transfiguration are equally recorded by all three synoptists. In the narrative the *prostration through fear* is peculiar to St. Matthew; the *subject of conversation* to St. Luke, as we have seen; while the *sudden departure* of the heavenly visitants, and the perplexed *questioning* about the rising from the dead, are only related by St. Mark. (4) His teaching henceforth turned towards the cross; while his miracles between this and his passion were confined to five.—J. J. G.

Vers. 14—29. Parallel passages: Matt. xvii. 14—21; Luke ix. 37—43.—*Healing of a demoniac youth, after the disciples' failure.* I. STRIKING CONTRAST. We can scarcely imagine a greater contrast than that which is here presented between the scene on the mountain and that in the plain below—the tranquillity of the one, the tumult of the other; the calm repose of the one, the unrest of the other; the blessedness of the one, the distress of the other; the gladness of the one, the sadness of the other; the glory of the one, the gloominess of the other; the heavenly quietude of the one, the unseemly wrangling of the other; the happiness of the one, the misery of the other; the ecstatic rapture of the one, the excruciating pain of the other; the confidence and comfort of the one, the disputatious unbelief of the other. The contrast was just that which we can conceive to exist between the holiness of heaven and the sinfulness of earth. The contrast is transferred to the canvas and made visible and palpable in the great picture of "The Transfiguration," by Raphael.

II. DESCRIPTION OF THE ILLNESS. This illness may be distributed into three elements—the supernatural, the natural so called, and the periodical. By the supernatural we understand the demoniac possession. This poor boy was under the influence of a foul and fiendish spirit that made him deaf and dumb. The natural element, if natural may be applied in any sense to a state that is abnormal and unnatural because the result of sin, consists in the fearful manifestations, consisting of epileptic fits, madness, convulsions, grinding the teeth, foaming at the mouth, and pining away. The periodical element is the fitful paroxysms, the crises of which were synchronous with the changes of the moon, so that "demoniac" and "lunatic" were both applied, and properly applied, to this peculiar case.

III. A DOUBLE PERSONALITY. The change of subject with respect to the verbs used in this description brings into view a startling fact and exhibits a strange complication. Two personalities, or two personal agencies, are here combined, and the union between them is so close and complete that the transition from the one to the other is as singular as sudden. Thus the first two verbs descriptive of the sad condition of this wretched sufferer have for their subject, though not directly expressed, yet distinctly implied, the *demon.* He it is of whom the poor father of the unhappy boy says, "Wheresoever it taketh him"—or, more literally, *wheresoever it seizeth* (καταλάβῃ) *him*—"it teareth, or dasheth down, or *breaketh* (ῥήσσει) him." This is very graphic, and as terrible as graphic. The demon so convulsed the lad as if he would dislocate the entire frame or dismember his whole body, breaking limb from limb. But the remaining verbs in the description, as it passes rapidly from the agent to the sufferer, require a different subject; for it is only the boy of whom it can be said, "He foameth," "grindeth his teeth," "becomes parched" (ξηραίνεται), or "pines away." The same curious commingling of terms—some applicable to the demon, and others to the possessed, occurs in describing the paroxysm which came on when the lad was brought into our Lord's presence. In the expression, "when he saw him," the participle is used, and is in the masculine gender, so that it appears to refer to the boy, and if so, it must be used absolutely; but if it apply to the unclean spirit, the word πνεῦμα, spirit, is neuter, and thus it must be constructed *ad sensum*, and indicate the personality of that spirit; in either case, there is an irregularity of construction arising from this unusual blending of personal agencies. Further, when the demoniac or the demon saw Jesus, the demon or unclean spirit *grievously tore* (ἐσπάραξεν, from σπάω, whence *spasm*, and signifying "to pull to pieces," not the same verb as that used in ver. 18) or convulsed the poor demoniac; while he fell on the earth and wallowed (akin to the Latin *volvo*), that is, rolled himself (κυλίω, equivalent to κυλίνδω, used of rolling in the dust, in token of grief), foaming.

IV. The arrival of Jesus on the scene. Soon as the crowd saw him, they were quite amazed—perfectly astounded, the prepositional element in the compound verb implying the greatness of their astonishment. But what caused their excessive amazement? It might be (1) the suddenness of the appearance of one whom they had been looking for in vain; but now that they had ceased to expect him, all at once, to their surprise, he is seen approaching; or (2) it is concluded by some, on rather slender grounds, that the term used does not denote mere surprise, much less joyful surprise, at the sudden and unexpected appearance of the Saviour, but rather a degree of alarm or perplexity on account of expressions to which utterance had been given in the dispute between the disciples and the scribes in our Lord's absence, and in reference to his power of casting out devils. There is much more probability (3) in the opinion that the astonishment was occasioned by some remnant of the heavenly radiance still beaming on and brightening his countenance. This view is strongly supported by the analogous case of Moses, of whom we read that, on his descent from Mount Sinai, "the skin of his face shone," so that Aaron and the children of Israel "were afraid to come nigh him." If this explanation be accepted, there is in the two cases a similarity and a dissimilarity: the brightness of Moses' face made the onlookers afraid, and deterred them from approaching him; the heavenly splendour that still lingered on the countenance of the Saviour affected the spectators in the very opposite way, attracting them to him. Accordingly, while some waited for his approach, as appears from St. Matthew's account, which speaks of his *coming to the multitude*, others, detaching themselves from the crowd, sallied forth to meet him, *running to him*, as we learn here from St. Mark; while St. Luke informs us that on his coming down from the hill much people *met him*. The accounts of St. Matthew and St. Luke are thus harmonized by St. Mark's statement, from which we rightly conclude that part of the crowd went to meet him, and part waited where they were for his approach. Their salutation, including, as we think, welcome and friendly greeting, if not from the scribes, at least from the rest of the crowd, is opposed to the notion of perplexity or alarm referred to in (2). Our Lord's popularity with the multitude had not yet suffered any diminution, nor begun to wane. He finds on his arrival that a somewhat keen discussion had been going on between two parties very unequally matched—the scribes, with their general learning and special Biblical lore, on the one hand, and his disciples, illiterate and imperfectly enlightened, on the other. The surrounding crowd, divided, most likely, in sentiment, and acting as partisans—some favouring the disciples and some the scribes—expressed approbation and disapprobation accordingly. The subject of disputation may be readily inferred from the sequel. Meantime our Lord asks the scribes with authority, "*What* question ye with [rather *at*, or *against* (πρὸς)] *them?*" or, better perhaps, "*Why* question ye with them?" What proper ground is there for such acrimonious questioning? What sufficient reason can be shown for it? But another reading, having the reflexive pronoun, is represented by the margin—"among yourselves," or "with one another;" in which case both scribes and disciples are addressed in common.

V. Application of the demoniac's father. To our Lord's interrogatory, one of the multitude, or rather one *out of* (ἐκ) the multitude, stepping forward, volunteers an answer. He felt that his child's misfortune had given occasion to the altercation, in which the disputants had waxed warm, if not angry, and that it devolved of right on him to make the requisite explanation. Another and a more urgent reason calling for his interference was his paternal solicitude. "I brought [ἤνεγκα, aorist] some short time ago my son to thee;" such had been his intention, as he had not been aware of the Saviour's absence. "I spake to thy disciples, in thy absence [ἵνα, denoting here the purport of what he said, as also the purpose for which it was said], *that* they should drive the demon from my son; but they *could not*;" while it must be observed that this verb is not an auxiliary, nor even a part of δύναμαι, but a stronger term (ἴσχυσαν), which, preceded by the negative, means that they had not *strength* enough for such a difficult operation. After stating, in reply to a question of our Lord about the length of time the suffering had lasted, that his son had been afflicted in this shocking manner from childhood, he went on to enumerate other aggravating circumstances of the affliction, to the effect that the demon often cast him into the fire and into the waters to destroy him. He then concluded with the remarkably earnest appeal, "If thou canst do anything, have compassion on us, and help us." The expression βοήθησον (from βοή, cry, and θέω, to run) is very significant, being equivalent to "hasten to our cry for help;" it is more than *succour* (from *sub* and *curro*, to run), which means to run to one's aid; it is "run to our aid at our earnest, urgent cry for help." The compassion is taken for granted, being expressed by a participle; and it also is a very expressive word, denoting the yearning of the bowels or heart in tenderness and pity.

VI. THE SAVIOUR'S ANSWER. Our Lord utters a reproof on the ground of their want of faith. In that reproof he includes his own disciples, the scribes who had been in conflict with them, and the father of the afflicted boy—one and all comprehended in the "faithless generation" of that time. The failure of the apostles to drive out the demon had been a matter of humiliation to themselves, and of exultation to those hostile scribes, who had, no doubt, made the most of this case of unsuccess; and that failure had been owing in part to weakness, if not want, of faith. The scribes all along had acted the part of obstinately incredulous sceptics. The distressed father, earnest as he was, and eloquent as he was in his appeal, betrayed much weakness of faith, saying, "If at all thou canst—if in any way thou canst," or "if thou canst do anything." This refers the matter of cure to the *power* of Christ; the leper resolved the cure in his case into the *will* of Christ, "If thou wilt, thou canst." How prone we are to circumscribe the Saviour by our own narrow conditions! and yet he shows us demonstratively that he is above and independent of all such limitations. He proved to the leper his possession of the will, and to the demoniac's father his possession of the power; and to us, through both, his ability as well as willingness to do to us and in us and for us "exceeding abundantly above all we can ask or think." The limitations are all on one side—all on our side, and are owing to the weakness of our frail and naturally faithless humanity. The possession in the present instance had been from childhood. The distress was thus of comparatively long standing; it had become chronic; it was an apparently hopeless case. It had defied the power of the disciples, and baffled their utmost skill and strength. While this failure had lowered them in the estimation of the crowd, and left them at the mercy of the biting taunts of the sarcastic scribes, it at the same time lessened still more the faith of the unhappy parent. The cure, therefore, which our Lord effected in this seemingly hopeless, certainly desperate case, holds forth encouragement to the weakest and the worst—those morally so—to apply to him.

VII. HIS APPLIANCE. The *first* direction is, "Bring him unto *me :* " you have tried the power of my disciples; I now invite you to try mine. You have been disappointed by their failure; but I will remedy that failure by my favour to thee and thine. You have been disheartened—too much disheartened; I now bid you take heart of hope. His *next* step was to secure the confidence and strengthen the faith of the father; and for this purpose he employs his own words and (1) according to the common reading he said to him the (τὸ) *saying*, "*If thou canst believe*, all things are possible to [or possible to be done for] him that believeth." But (2) the word πιστεῦσαι is omitted in three or more of the oldest uncials, in several versions, by the critical editors Tregelles and Tischendorf, and by Meyer and some commentators; and with this omission the sentence reads, "*Jesus said unto him, As for thy If thou canst*, all things are possible to him that believeth." And (3) some, putting the acute on the antepenult πίστευσαι, take it to be imperative aorist middle, and translate, "*Believe what you expressed by your If thou canst*, all things are possible to him that believeth." Again, (4) others take it interrogatively, "*The If thou canst ?* or *What ? If thou canst ?* " so that the sense is as if he asked, "Is this what you say?" or, "Do you really mean this?" The man's own words were thus thrown back on him, and by this judicious retort he is brought to understand that faith in the Saviour's power and propitiousness is a prerequisite for the bestowal of the boon he sought; he is also brought to feel that the hand of faith must likewise be outstretched for the reception of spiritual benefits and blessings; at the same time he is made conscious of the great deficiency—the entire inadequacy of his faith for the attainment of the favour he is so anxious to obtain. Suspending his petition on behalf of his son, but resuming his request with the same term and now in his own interest, he called aloud, with eyes brimful of tears—if this reading (μετὰ δακρύων) is accepted, at all events—affectingly and touchingly, "Lord, I believe; help thou mine unbelief." He affirms the possession of belief, but that belief is so weak as to be scarcely worthy of the name; that he has some faith, but that faith is small, exceeding small, like a grain of mustard seed. Persuaded that his faith is too insignificant to satisfy the condition, he prays (1) for its increase; in other words, he seeks to be helped against his unbelief. Another interpretation, though advocated by some good and great men, to the effect, (2) " Help me, notwithstanding the weakness of my faith," has but little, we think, to commend it to favour and acceptance. Now at length all is ready for the beneficent operation; the people are running together to the place, or running together yet more (ἐπί, denoting intensity or addition), when our Lord addressed the unclean spirit in terms of stern rebuke, and words of unmistakable authority, saying, "I" [ἐγώ expressed, and so emphatic and distinctive]—I, thy Master; I, whose authority you cannot evade; I, whose word of command you dare not disobey; I, not my disciples, who were non-plussed by the strange and sudden outburst of thy fiendish malignity; I order thee to come out of him at once, and never again to enter into him.

VIII. THE COMPLETENESS OF THE CURE. The command to " enter no more into him " may be attributed to the weakness of the father's faith—to assure him there would be no relapse, to convince him there would be no return of the paroxysm; it may also be owing in part to the malignant obstinacy of the foul fiend, who now, after crying aloud, and after convulsing the poor boy's whole frame with a horrible spasm, came out of him, leaving him all but dead, so that the many said he was dead. The great primary act of expelling the demon had been accomplished, but the effect of his long dominion over the lad, and the shock to his system at departure, left him so thoroughly exhausted and prostrate that a second miracle was required to supplement the first. In conse-quence, our Lord seized him by the hand, or seized his hand, and lifted him up, so that he stood upon his feet well and sound and strong, as though the whole had been but the memory of a troubled dream. An explanation was subsequently given to the disciples touching their inability in the present case, and their want of success in the exercise of a gift which had been bestowed, and which had been most probably effectual in other instances. The explanation appears to have respect to the character of the demon, and the conduct of the apostles themselves. First, there is mention of " this kind," by which some understand (1) the race of demons in general—"the race of all demons," according to Euthymius; others limit the expression to (2) a special kind of spirits, peculiarly obstinate and stiffnecked, and consequently more difficult to be driven out; while a recent authority on the subject suggests that the reference is to (3) a class of demons which manifested their presence by unexpectedly sudden and frightfully severe outbreaks, and for the expulsion of which the exorcist or physician operating required uncommon presence of mind and strength of nerve, as well as vigorous exercise of faith. But, waiving a discussion of this doubtful kind, and merely expressing our preference for the second of the opinions stated, we may notice briefly a strange term employed here, namely, go out (ἐξελθεῖν). If the statement in which this word is used is to be interpreted literally, the meaning appears to be that demons of this kind could not go out, even if they would, of the persons possessed by any other means or in any other way than in the use or by the exercise of prayer and fasting. If this be the real, as it is the literal meaning, it is a circumstance of a strange, inscrutable kind; and, among matters more or less mysterious, it is not the least so. We may, however, give to the words a freer interpretation and take them in the more ordinary sense, that this kind can be expelled by nothing but by prayer and fasting. The conduct of the apostles themselves had most to do with their powerlessness to cast out the demon in this instance. They had received the requisite power, as we read in ch. vi. 7 that, in sending them forth by two and two, he " gave them power over unclean spirits ; " but they had neglected the discipline indispensable to the efficient and successful employment of that power. Two circumstances in close connection with this neglect are assigned as the cause of failure—weakness of faith is mentioned by St. Matthew, and neglect of prayer is hinted by St. Mark. We may regard them as standing together in the relation of two joint causes, or rather as cause and effect in relation to this matter—neglect of prayer being the former, and debility of faith the latter.

PRACTICAL LESSONS. 1. We learn the important duty of parental solicitude for the spiritual as well as, or rather more than, for the bodily, well-being of their offspring. In the case of the Syro-phœnician woman we saw how she identified herself with her afflicted daughter, saying, " Lord, help me ! " Here likewise the father of the demoniac makes common cause with his child, in the words, " Have compassion on us, and help us!" Especially should we travail, as in birth, till Christ is formed in their heart, and till by grace they are enabled to renounce the devil and all his works. 2. Great importance attaches to the element of time. The demon got possession early of this sorely distressed boy, and the demoniac power seems to have grown with the child's growth, and to have strengthened with his strength, so that dispossession had become next to an impossibility. The apostles were not competent to the task, and when our Lord, in the exercise of his almighty power, expelled him, it was only after he had made horrid havoc of the lad's system, frightfully convulsing him and leaving him half-dead. So, if Satan unhappily gain the ascendant in a young heart, he will do his best to blight the whole life; he will hold his dominion with tenacity, and, if possible, to the end; he will seat himself firmly on the throne of the affections, and exercise a despot's sway; his dethronement will be attended with the greatest difficulty; and if, by Divine mercy, his power is at last overthrown, it will cost pain of body, distress of mind, and grief of heart. Oh, how careful young persons should be to guard against the solicitations of the evil one, and to resist his power! How determined not to yield to his temptations, and to vanquish youthful lusts that war against the soul! How resolved, by the aid of Divine strength, to keep him out, remembering how difficult it is to get him out once he has gained an entrance, and especially if he has gained it early! 3. Every gift that God bestows should be diligently cultivated, and husbanded with care. The power bestowed on the apostles was, as we have seen, lost through their own remissness. Faith required to be kept in healthy exercise and active vigour; devotion and self-denial were required for its maintenance. The neglect or undue performance of these left them weak before the power of the evil one, and caused them to be humiliated in the presence of their enemies. Thus it was with the apostles and miraculous gifts. How much more is such likely to be the case with ordinary persons in the exercise of ordinary gifts! We greatly need to use all the means that tend to strengthen faith; above all, we must pray earnestly, in the beautiful words suggested by this passage "Lord, increase our faith;" avoiding at the same time any and every indulgence that might weaken faith or slacken prayer.

> "Restraining prayer we cease to fight;
> Prayer keeps the Christian's armour bright;
> And Satan trembles when he sees
> The weakest saint upon his knees."

4. This passage cannot legitimately apply to any attempt at working miracles in the present day. The age of miracles is past. The power thus possessed by the apostles was not to continue, and needed not to continue, after the great purpose for which miracles had been bestowed had been attained. Faith and prayer and fasting cannot of themselves confer the power; they were needed to sustain it only where it had been bestowed; they were required for its successful exercise where it did exist. 5. The greatness of the believer's privilege is immense, yet not without certain well-defined limits. "All things are possible to him that believeth:" this appears to comprise at once omnipotence in action and universality in possession. To the former we have the parallel statement of St. Paul, "I can do all things through Christ which strengtheneth me;" or rather, "in (ἐν) Christ that giveth me inward strength (ἐνδυναμοῦντι);" and thus the strength as to its source is obtainable by virtue of living and lively union with Christ, while as to its nature it is spiritual. But the reference is rather to what it is possible for us to get than to do; and so all things are ours, for "we are Christ's, and Christ is God's." There are here two limitations which, though not expressed, must be implied: (1) The first limitation restricts the "all things" to things truly beneficial —beneficial spiritually as well as temporally, beneficial for eternity rather than for the brief relations of time; they are such things as are thus of real benefit, when regard is had to the believer's condition and present position. (2) The second limitation has respect to the circumstances of others, that is to say, of those with whom we come into close contact, or with whom we have to do and deal in the affairs of life. All things are thus possible to be attained by the believer, as far as they are consistent with his real benefit, and compatible at the same time with his relations in the widest sense— relations to his Father in heaven and to his fellow-man on earth. Such is the potentiality of faith—it extends to all things; such, too, is its practicability, excepting only such things as, at the present or in the long run, do not comport with his own personal

good, as also with his relation to God, whose glory is paramount, and to his fellow-man, whose good, as well as our own, we are in duty bound to seek.—J. J. G.

Vers. 30—32. Parallel passages: Matt. xvii. 22, 23; Luke ix. 43—45.—*Prediction of his passion.* I. SECRECY. "To everything there is a season, and a time to every purpose under heaven." Every man has a work to do, and a time allowed him to do it in. Every man, moreover, is immortal till that work is done, and God's will with him accomplished. In like manner there was a time allotted for our Lord's mission on earth. There was a time fixed for his ministry of mercy to man. When the fulness of the time was come, he made his descent into our world; when the work he came to do was done, and when the proper period again arrived, he took his departure from our world. The appointed interval of his sojourn on earth no enemy could shorten by one day, no power could abridge it by a single hour; nothing could interfere with it, so long as "his hour was not yet come." Yet, notwithstanding this, our Lord never neglected the use of such means as were proper for the prolongation of his stay on earth till his great work should be performed, and the destined period completed. Accordingly, we find him at one time returning to Galilee, and "walking no more in Jewry, because the Jews sought to kill him." Afterward, when Herod's attention had been directed to him, and his abode even in Galilee had thus become somewhat insecure, we find him withdrawing to the more remote and less populous districts of that province. We are, moreover, informed that subsequently he had gone yet further from contact with his enemies, passing beyond Galilee into the Phœnician territory. This he did in order, it would seem, to escape observation, for while there he "entered into an house, and would have no man know it: but he could not be hid." This course our Lord pursued for various reasons. While each particular occasion on which he courted privacy had its own specific reason, we can state in general the motives that seem to have influenced him in this direction. As already intimated, he avoided such publicity as would bring him into hostile conflict with his enemies, so as to precipitate the crisis, and hasten his death, before the proper and purposed period. Again he sought seclusion, now for required rest, oftener for more time and better opportunity of instructing his apostles for their future work and important mission. But while our Lord thus sought seclusion to prevent any interference either with the space of his ministry or with the plan of instructing his apostles, there was another eventuality which he carefully avoided, namely, any attempt on the part of the people to make him a king; as, after the miracle of feeding the five thousand, we read that, "when Jesus perceived that they would come and take him by force, to make him a king, he departed again into a mountain himself alone." This was no very improbable contingency. In a moment of excitement, under the influence of enthusiasm, yielding to the impulse of popular feeling, they might attempt to place him at the head of a rebellion, if not a revolution, against existing authorities, and try to restore to Israel the temporal kingdom which Israel so ardently, though mistakenly, sought. This would have been a result greatly to be deprecated. It would have left a stigma on the Saviour's name, and caused a suspicion about his design, both of which would have been most detrimental to the interests of that spiritual kingdom—the kingdom "not of this world," which he came to set up. Accordingly, we find that when he had restored the deaf mute, he charged them that "they should tell no man." Again, when he cured the blind man at Bethsaida, he sent him away to his house, saying, "Neither go into the town, nor tell it to any in the town"—any townsmen he might chance to meet on his way home. Also, after the Transfiguration, "he charged them that they should tell no man what things they had seen, till the Son of man were risen from the dead." And now that they passed along (παρεπορεύοντο) through Galilee, "he would not that any man should know it." Even an apparent exception is easily accounted for: nor is there any real discrepancy between the injunction he laid on them after the restoration of the deaf mute (ch. vii.), to "tell no man," and the direction he gave the demoniac (ch. v.), to "go home to thy friends, and tell them how great things the Lord hath done for thee, and hath had compassion on thee." No doubt it was the same district of Decapolis where both commands were given: but on the latter occasion our Lord was about to leave the district in question, so that there was no risk of his ministry being obstructed by the matter being blazoned abroad; on the former occasion he was going to tarry for a time in the same region, and hence he resorts to the precaution necessary under circumstances which were thus quite different.

II. HE FORETELLS HIS DEATH.   There were three great epochs in our Lord's ministry. The first was that of miracles, by which he attested the divinity of his mission ; the second was that of parables, by which he developed the nature of his kingdom ; and the third was that of suffering, by which he made satisfaction for the sins of his people. The miracles began with that at Cana ; the parables, properly so called, began somewhere about the commencement of the last year of the Saviour's work and ministry. Though his parabolic teaching began at this period to assume a more formal shape, he had all along employed on certain occasions parabolic utterances of a briefer sort. Thus, for example, in the sermon on the mount the agreement with one's adversary there recommended is of the nature of parable ; the similitude of the wise and foolish builders, with which that sermon closes, is still more distinctly parabolic ; while subsequently, and before the beginning of his regular method of strictly parabolic instruction, we find such proverbial or brief parabolic representations as that of the new patch and the old garment, and that of the new wine and the old bottles, besides that of the creditor and the two debtors. Still, from the period indicated, his teaching by parables became more frequent and methodical. The reasons of our Lord's adopting this method are such as the following :—1. The harmony existing between the kingdom of nature and that of grace, and the similarity in their laws of development.   2. The adaptation to our nature of the historical element, real or ideal, contained in them.   3. The amount of truth communicable in this way to the dull apprehension of the disciples.   4. Their helpfulness to memory by linking the spiritual truth to some familiar natural object, the frequent occurrence of the latter always suggesting the former ; and : 5. A judicial veiling of the truth because of past dulness and indifference. The constant theme of his teaching henceforth consists of his sufferings and death, as is implied in the imperfect tense (ἐδίδασκε, "he kept teaching") here used.

III. PREVIOUS INTIMATIONS ON THE SUBJECT. The previous intimations had been obscure. There had been the intimation of the Baptist when he pointed the Saviour out as "the Lamb of God, which taketh away the sin of the world" (John i. 29), and in the repetition of part of the same at ver. 36. He had himself given several figurative intimations of it, as when he spake of his death by violence, and his resurrection in three days under the similitude of the demolition and rebuilding of a temple. "Destroy," he said, "this temple, and in three days I will raise it up." This had occurred at the celebration of the first Passover after the commencement of his public ministry. Again, in his discourse with Nicodemus, he represented his crucifixion as an uplifting, and its beneficial effects by a comparison with Moses' lifting up the serpent in the wilderness, when the bitten Israelite looked and lived. Another intimation of his death, and the first allusion to that event recorded in this Gospel (St. Mark's), is the removal of the bridegroom, of which he said, "The days will come, when the bridegroom shall be taken away from them" (ch. ii. 20 ; Matt. ix. 15). Also, after the feeding of the five thousand, in the synagogue of Capernaum he made a reference to it in the words, "The bread that I will give is my flesh, which I will give for the life of the world." But the first clear and *distinct* declaration is that of the preceding chapter (ch. viii.), when "he began to teach them, that the Son of man must suffer many things, and be rejected of the elders, and of the chief priests, and scribes, and be killed, and after three days rise again."

IV. SIMILAR DECLARATIONS IN THE PRESENT AND SUBSEQUENT CHAPTERS. The first public, or at least the first direct and unreserved announcement of his sufferings, death, and resurrection, was made, as recorded in the preceding chapter, after the disciples had been convinced of, and Peter had confessed, his Messiahship, saying, "Thou art the Christ." On that occasion we learn from the fuller report of St. Matthew that our Lord warmly commended Peter's confession, but soon after, as both St. Matthew and St. Mark inform us, found cause to condemn his indiscreet and unwelcome rebuke. The commendation is contained in the words, "I say also unto thee, That thou art Peter, and upon this rock I will build my Church." The latter clause of the promise, just cited has, as is well known, excited no little controversy, and called forth a variety of interpretations. 1. Augustine will have it that the rock on which the Church is built, according to the Saviour's promise, is *Christ himself.*

2. Chrysostom maintains that the *confession of faith in Christ*, that Peter had just given utterance to, is the rock on which the Church is based. We admit the show of reason and the plausibility with which both opinions have been expressed and enforced ; still we cannot concur in either. Chrysostom's explanation is chargeable with over-looking the context. So to some extent, though less so, is that of Augustine ; but the latter rests, besides, on a very doubtful distinction between two words which are frequently used in classical writers as interchangeable. According to this interpreter its import would be, " Thou art Peter (πέτρος), a small stone ; but I am Christ, a strong Rock (πέτρα), and on this Rock, that is, myself, I will build my Church." In the Aramaic there is one word (*Kipho*) for *Peter* and for *rock*, just as in French there is one word for both—*Pierre*, Peter, a man's name, and *pierre*, a stone or rock. But in Greek there are the two words already mentioned, viz. πέτρος and πέτρα, so that in this play upon the word there is a slight variation in the Greek, without, how-ever, real difference of meaning. Even admitting the distinction between the two words, which has been questioned, if not entirely disproved, the explanation is evidently forced. We require to look more closely at the context as furnished by the eighteenth verse itself, and by the sixteenth. As recorded in the latter, Peter's answer was, " Thou art the Christ, the Son of the living God." Our Lord, after expressing approval of Peter's reply, and assuring him that the truth contained in it was the outcome, not of human discovery, but of Divine revelation, takes occasion to state another and no less important truth, and that in a form accommodated to the statement of Peter, " And I say also unto thee, That thou art Peter [πέτρος, a rock], and upon this rock (πέτρα) I will build my Church ; " that is to say,—You have made a good and true confession in acknowledging my Messiahship and divinity ; I also, in my turn, will confess what I have in store for you in connection with my Church. 3. Your name is significant—it means a rock ; and *according to your name will be the nature of your work*. With the foundation of the Church you will have much to do. On your preaching of the faith which you have just professed its foundation shall be laid. Similarly, elsewhere we read that the Church is "built on the foundation of apostles and prophets, Jesus Christ himself being the chief Corner-stone ; " whereas apostles and prophets are only the foundation in so far as they themselves, *knit together with and cemented to Christ, lay the foundation by their exhibition of Christ and declaration of the truth concerning Christ*. It is as though our Lord had said to Peter, Among Jews and Gentiles your work is appointed you. Among the Jews on the day of Pentecost your proclamation of the selfsame faith, which you have just confessed, will lay the foundation of the Christian Church ; while to Cornelius the same gospel preached by you will inaugurate a similar blessed result among the Gentiles, introducing the first-fruits of the Gentile world into the Church. Still more, to the united Church of the believing Jew and converted Gentile I shall promise and provide security from all the devices of the most wily, and all the assaults of the most Satanic, foes.

V. WHY IS THIS COMMENDATION OMITTED BY ST. MARK? It has often been remarked that many things redounding solely to the honour of St. Peter are omitted by St. Mark ; while at the same time his infirmities are fully and faithfully recorded by the same evangelist, extenuating circumstances being less noticed by this evangelist than by the other synoptists. An example of this is furnished in the case before us. The blessing pronounced on him because of this noble and brave confession of the Christ, the Divine origin of his knowledge and faith, the promise just considered, and the further promise of the keys of the kingdom of heaven, are all omitted by St. Mark. But the rebuke to which he soon after subjected himself is carefully recorded. Many instances of both kinds occur. This is one of those incidental circumstances that go far to confirm the voice of history in regard to the relation in which St. Peter stood to St. Mark and his Gospel, namely, that the latter penned his Gospel, as disciple and by the dictation, to some extent, of the former. If so, and we think it extremely probable, we have proof herein of the veracity of the one and the humility of the other.

VI. REPETITION OF THE PREDICTION. Reverting to the subject of the Saviour's sufferings, so plainly announced in the eighth chapter, we have a repetition of a similar announcement in this ninth chapter, and another, again, in nearly the same terms in the tenth chapter. These repeated as well as direct and unreserved declarations on this subject—a subject so distasteful and saddening to his disciples—show their unwillingness to associate the idea of death with the Messiah, their tenacity in clinging to a temporal king and worldly kingdom, their slowness and lothness to apprehend or accept the notion of a spiritual, unworldly kingdom. The idea of a suffering Messiah has, therefore, to be dinned into their ears and impressed on their hearts by frequent and earnest reiterations. Nor has this subject lost aught of its importance or interest even for ourselves and at the present day; while the faithful inculcation of it is as much a duty and a necessity now as when our Lord in person urged it so solemnly and so often on the mind and heart of his sorrowing disciples. Though the cross was a stumbling-block to the Jews, and foolishness to the Greeks, it is still the power of God, and the wisdom of God, to the salvation of every believer. The way to the crown is still by, and only by, the cross; humiliation precedes glorification. The preacher of the gospel cannot dwell too frequently or too earnestly on a theme that bulked so largely in the sight of the Saviour himself. The doctrine of Christ's suffering for us to put away our sins—suffering, "the just for the unjust, to bring us to God"—cannot be too much insisted on; neither can we be too often instructed in the duty of giving ourselves fully, freely, and for ever to him "who loved us and gave himself for us." If, moreover, Christ was "obedient unto death, even the death of the cross," in all its shame and with all its pain, it surely behoves us, in daily, holy obedience, to take up our cross, deny ourselves, and follow him.—J. J. G.

Ver. 33. Parallel passage: Matt. xvii. 24—27.—*The tribute money.* I. ANOTHER OMISSION. In the first line of the thirty-third verse we approach the subject of the tribute money; but in St. Mark's narrative we only approach it, and that in the statement, "he came to Capernaum;" but in the parallel section of St. Matthew we read of the demand for the tribute money, of Peter being commissioned to procure it from "the fish that first cometh up," of the exemption Jesus might have claimed but waived, and the reason of his doing so. Here, again, St. Mark omits the part of the narrative which relates to the honour conferred on Peter by our Lord, when he commissioned him to work the miracle by which the tribute money was procured from the fish's mouth. But, though St. Mark omits this portion of the recital, the preceding and succeeding portions are coincident with those of St. Matthew. The peculiar relation of the apostle to the evangelist, already considered, can alone account for the omission.

II. GROUND OF LEGITIMATE EXEMPTION. In Matt. xvii. 24, 25, we read, "When they were come to Capernaum, they that received *tribute money* came to Peter, and said, Doth not your Master pay tribute?" Then at the last clause of the twenty-fifth verse, our Lord asked Peter, "What thinkest thou, Simon? of whom do the kings of the earth take *custom* or *tribute*? of their own children, or of strangers?" A slight amount of archæological knowledge makes this plain. The word "tribute" in the twenty-fourth verse is τὰ δίδραχμα; the word "tribute" in the twenty-fifth is κῆνσον; while "custom," a word of kindred meaning, is τέλη. Also in the twenty-seventh verse, the word στατὴρ, or "shekel," rendered "piece of money" in the English version, occurs. The stater, or shekel, equivalent to two shillings and sixpence of our currency, was the exact amount of tax payable by two. Now, there is a very wide and important distinction between these terms, and a distinction necessary to be kept in view for the right understanding of the passage. For (1) the δίδραχμα were equal in value to the Jewish half-shekel, or some fifteenpence of our money, and may be called a sacred tribute or annual contribution paid by every male among the Jews, from twenty years of age and upwards, for the support of the temple at Jerusalem—to defray the general expenses, to provide the sacrifices and other things required for the service. The persons who collected it were not the civil tax-gatherers, called *publicani*, or rather *portitores*; nor, indeed, was the tax a civil one at all, but a sacred one. From overlooking this fact, the point of the argument is liable to be missed, as it actually has been by several of the Fathers. It is briefly, though correctly, developed by Alford, in the following sentence:—"If the sons are free, then on me, being the Son of God, has this tax no claim." It requires, however, to be somewhat more fully and plainly exhibited. In order to set the matter in a clear light, we premise (2) that the κῆνσος, for which St. Luke employs the classical Greek term φόρος, was a poll or capitation tax, like the Roman *tributum*; while by τέλη are to be understood the *toll* or *customs' duties,* which are identical with the *vectigal* of the Romans. Further, let it be borne in mind that Peter's confession of faith that Jesus was "the Christ, the Son of the living God," had been made, being recorded in the sixteenth chapter, and so had preceded the present conversation. Our Lord now argues from analogy that he was entitled to, and might fairly claim, exemption. In doing so, he asks Peter this question, "What thinkest thou, Simon? of whom do the kings of the earth take custom or tribute? of their own sons, or of strangers?" It is here admitted by implication that civil rulers have a right to impose taxes for the support of civil government, but that, in exercising this right, they impose taxes on the other members of the state, not on the members of their own household. When kings levy taxes, or have them levied in the ordinary constitutional way, they impose them on their subjects, not on their sons. Peter had confessed Jesus to be the Son of God; the tax demanded was for the support of God's house; according to the principle of action among earthly kings, God, the great King of heaven and of earth, while requiring contributions for the maintenance of his service from his subjects, would exempt his own Son, for, from his position of Sonship, which the apostle had recently acknowledged, and from the principle of taxation in which he had just acquiesced, it was necessarily inferred, "then are the sons free." Not as a mere member of the Hebrew race, or as an ordinary Jew, but from his dignity as the Son of God, in the highest and most exalted sense, our Lord might have claimed exemption from the tax in question. This was the gist of his reasoning: but he waived his right; and proceeds to explain to Peter the ground on which he foregoes his privilege, saying, "Lest we should offend them," or more plainly in the Revised Version, "Lest we cause them to stumble;" in other words, lest he and his disciples should be regarded as indifferent to, or be charged with, neglect of the house of God and the maintenance of its service.—J. J. G.

Vers. 33—37. Parallel passages: Matt. xviii. 1—5; Luke ix. 46—48.—*The lesson of humility.* The exquisite lesson of humility taught in the remainder of this section (the first clause of the thirty-third verse, as it stands in St. Mark, having been already considered) may be appropriately taken up in connection with the section of next chapter, where the lovely comparison of childhood is again employed.—J. J. G.

Vers. 38—41. Parallel passage: Luke ix. 49, 50.—*Rebuke of sectarian narrowness.*
I. THE KEY-NOTE OF THE PASSAGE. The sentence which appears to furnish the key to the understanding of this instructive and interesting passage is contained in the following short sentence:—"He that is not against us is on our part," or, as it stands yet more concisely in St. Luke, "He that is not against us is for us."
II. A SEEMING CONTRADICTION. The statement just quoted from the Gospel of St. Luke (ix. 50) appears to be at variance with another statement further on in the same Gospel, where, at the eleventh chapter and twenty-third verse, it is written, "He that is not with me is against me." The discrepancy, however, is only apparent. In order to perceive this, we must consider the occasions on which the words recorded were respectively spoken; for, as our Lord and his apostles usually adapted their language to the occasion, we shall thus best learn the design with which each of those sentiments was uttered. Accordingly, we learn that some one not consorting with Christ or his apostles was, nevertheless, casting out devils in the Saviour's name, and that John forbade him. Our Lord sets John right in the matter by saying, "Forbid him not;" that is, do not interfere with any who may be attempting anything good in my name. And then he assigns the reason; for "he that is not against us is for us;" he who is not directly opposed to us is rather to be regarded as on our side; he who is not preventing our progress may be looked upon, at least negatively, as promoting it. Just as is intimated by the Apostle Paul on a certain occasion, even though envy and strife should be the impelling motive, if Christ is preached his cause is advanced, and "I therein do rejoice." So here we may fairly understand the words of the Master to mean —Whosoever this man may be, or whatever may be his object, he is weakening Satan's kingdom by casting out devils, and therefore, so far from being against me, he must be looked upon as an auxiliary in the great war against the great enemy of man. Besides, by such forbearance as I thus counsel, he may be drawn into closer and more effective co-operation against the common adversary. Such is the plain meaning of the passage

before us. On the other hand, in the second passage, our Lord had been charged by the hostile, cavilling Pharisees with casting out devils by Beelzebub the prince of devils. This charge had called forth the rejoinder of our Lord, that "every kingdom divided against itself is brought to desolation." Such would be the case if Satan cast out Satan. The only reasonable alternative was that the Saviour was casting out devils by the Spirit of God, and so the kingdom of God had come unto them. He follows up this reply by a warning against lukewarmness and an exhortation to decision, that the crisis had come when men must choose sides, that they must elect to take part with God or with Satan. Neutrality was impossible. In view of two kingdoms so opposed, there was no possibility of belonging to both; nay, there was no middle ground between loyalty and rebellion. If not on the side of the Saviour, he must be on the side of Satan; if not a subject of the former, he must be a slave of the latter, and so an enemy to the cause of Christ: "He that is not with me is against me."

III. THE SAME SUBJECT VIEWED FROM A PRACTICAL STANDPOINT. The one text implies that men may take different roads to the same place, or reach the same point by different routes. This is true morally as well as geographically. It condemns the narrowness that refuses to tolerate want of uniformity, and commends forbearance towards all who in reality serve the same Master and seek the same object, viz. the glory of God, though their forms may be diverse, their modes of worship different, and even their creeds divergent in expression. The other text affirms that, in the natural and increasing conflict between good and evil, our hesitation to unite with the good is tantamount with adhesion to the evil. The one text does not insist on uniformity, the other inculcates unity. Again, conformity to the same standards is not an indispensable condition of Christianity, as we infer from the one text; but cordiality in embracing Christ and espousing his cause is of its very essence. We are taught by the one that there may be many folds, though there is but one flock; but by the other that, as there is but one Shepherd, union to him is indispensable to membership in his flock. Further, the one makes charity to others imperative, provided they have the same great end in view, however divergent the means adopted for its attainment; the other requires of us decision for ourselves in seeking that end.—J. J. G.

Vers. 42—50. Parallel passage: Matt. xviii. 6—9.—*Christ's love to his little ones, and offences*. I. LOVE TO THE LITTLE ONES. Christ's little ones are either young believers or weak believers. A kindness shown them is accepted by Christ as done to himself. Even a cup of cold water will be rewarded. However much they may be despised by men or neglected in the world, they are dear to God and near to the Saviour's heart; while angels of highest rank are commissioned to guard them—even angels who are privileged to stand in the immediate presence of the great King; for "in heaven their angels do always behold the face of my Father which is in heaven." Angels of all grades have a twofold function—they worship and they minister; they worship in the heavenly sanctuary the Father everlasting ($\lambda\epsilon\iota\tau o\nu\rho\gamma\iota\kappa\grave{\alpha}$), they wait for ministry ($\epsilon\grave{\iota}s\ \delta\iota\alpha\kappa o\nu\acute{\iota}\alpha\nu$) to man on earth. But those of most exalted dignity are the guardians of Christ's little ones.

II. CONSEQUENCES OF OFFENCES. The sin of offending one of these little ones is great in proportion to Christ's love to them. How careful men should be, and how cautious, not to put a stumbling-block in the way of these little ones! The sin of turning weak believers or young Christians aside from the truth, or from the faith, or from the path of purity, or a career of virtue, by evil advice or bad example, or by casting doubt on the Word of God, or by insinuating sceptical notions, or by mockery of Divine things, is a sin so great that a preferable alternative would be for the person guilty of it to have a millstone of large size, turned by an ass ($\grave{o}\nu\iota\kappa\grave{o}s$), lying around his neck, and himself cast into the sea. Such is the fearfully emphatic declaration of the guilt and danger of scandalizing or offending the youngest child that believes, or the weakest Christian.

III. OTHER OFFENCES. Our Lord passes by a common law of suggestion to speak of offences by ourselves and against ourselves. The hand may offend by doing wrong, the foot may offend by going on what is wrong. But if the most serviceable member, as the hand, do amiss, or the most useful member, as the foot, walk astray, or the most precious member, as the eye, look with delight on objects sinful and forbidden, then there must be no hesitation in divesting ourselves of such rather than risk the fearful fate of those who are tormented in the Gehenna of fire, "where their worm dieth not, and the fire is not quenched."

IV. SALTED WITH FIRE. This difficult expression is taken by some as a promise and by others as a punishment. In the former sense, fire is taken in the signification of purifying and preserving, and this twofold property it shares with salt. Salt preserves from putrefaction, fire purifies from corruption. The sacrifice of old required to be offered with salt. According to the Law in Lev. ii. 13, the meat offering was to be seasoned with salt, and salt was to be offered with all offerings. So, when we present ourselves living sacrifices to God, we may be purified by fiery trials; we may be called to pass through the fire of affliction, perhaps of persecution, certainly of self-denial. But thus purified by fire, like the sacrifice on the altar, salted with salt, we shall be saved. This gives a good sense, but does not suit the context. In the second sense, fire is taken to mean punishing and preserving. Six times does the evangelist represent unceasing torments by unquenchable fire; and as the salt applied to the sacrifice was the symbol of preservation, so fire here is symbolical of preservation, not, alas! from punishment, but for punishment, so that the undying worm and the unquenchable fire, instead of annihilating, preserve while they punish. Here is a fearful figure, and a terrible warning!

V. PEACE. They are exhorted to keep the salt of moral purity and covenant concord rather than have the salt of fiery punishment, and, as the effect and evidence thereof, to be at peace among themselves, and so avoid the strife for pre-eminence and the discord of ambition.—J. J. G.

EXPOSITION.

CHAPTER X.

Ver. 1.—Instead of the words, into the coasts of Judæa by the farther side of Jordan, the passage, by a change of reading from διὰ τοῦ to καὶ, will run thus: *into the coasts (borders) of Judæa and beyond Jordan.* Our Lord was now on his last progress towards Jerusalem. It would appear from St. Luke (ix. 51) that in the earlier part of his journey he touched the frontier of Samaria. Putting the accounts together, we conclude that, being refused by the Samaritans, he passed eastwards along their frontier, having Galilee on his left, and Samaria on his right; and then crossed the Jordan, perhaps at Scythopolis, where was a bridge, and so entered Peræa. As Judæa and Galilee both lay west of the Jordan, this route above described would be literally coming "to the borders of Judæa and beyond Jordan." Again multitudes flocked together to him, and again he taught them. St. Matthew (xix. 1) says that "he healed them." His miracles of healing and his teaching went hand in hand.

Ver. 2.—And there came unto him Pharisees—the article should be omitted—and asked him—they came forward before the people, and publicly questioned him—Is it lawful for a man to put away his wife? St. Matthew (xix. 3) adds to the question the words, "for every cause." There were causes for which it was lawful. They put this question to our Lord, tempting him; of course with an evil intent. This question

about divorce was one which was much agitated in the time of our Lord. In the century before Christ, a learned rabbi, named Hillel, a native of Babylon, who afterwards came to Jerusalem, studied the Law with great success, and became the head of the chief school in that city. One of his disciples, named Shammai, separated from his master, and set up another school; so that in the time of our Lord the scribes and doctors of the Law were ranged in two parties, namely, the followers of Hillel, the most influential; and the followers of Shammai. These two schools differed widely on the subject of divorce. The followers of Shammai only permitted divorce in the case of moral defilement, while the followers of Hillel placed the matter entirely in the power of the husband. The object, therefore, of this artful question was to entrap our Lord, and to bring him into collision with one or other of these two opposing parties. For if he had said that it was not lawful for a man to put away his wife, he would have exposed himself to the hostility of many of the wealthy classes, who put away their wives for any cause. But if he had allowed the lawfulness of divorce at all, they would have found fault with his doctrine as imperfect and carnal, although he professed to be a spiritual Teacher of a perfect system, sent down from heaven.

Vers. 3, 4.—And he answered and said unto them, What did Moses command you? They professed much reverence for Moses;

he therefore appeals to their great law-giver. And they said, Moses suffered to write a bill of divorcement, and to put her away. If we now turn to St. Matthew (xix. 4, 5), we shall find that our Lord then appeals to the original institution of marriage. " Have ye not read, that he which made them from the beginning, made them male and female, and said, For this cause shall a man leave his father and mother, and shall cleave to his wife; and the twain shall become one flesh? So that they are no more twain, but one flesh. What therefore God hath joined together, let not man put asunder." He thus reminds them that marriage is a Divine institution; that as Adam and Eve were united by him in a union which was indissoluble, therefore he intended that the marriage bond should remain ever, so that the wife ought never to be separated from her husband, since she becomes by marriage a very part of her husband. To this purpose St. Augustine says (' City of God,' bk. xiv. 22), "It was not of the spirit which commands and the body which obeys, nor of the rational soul which rules and the irrational desire which is ruled, nor of the contemplative virtue which is supreme, and the active which is subject, nor of the understanding of the mind and the sense of the body; but plainly of the matrimonial union, by which the sexes are mutually bound together, that our Lord, when asked whether it were lawful for any cause to put away one's wife, answered as in St. Matthew (xix. 4, 5). It is certain, then, that from the first men were created as we see and know them to be now, of two sexes—male and female—and that they are called one, either on account of the matrimonial union, or on account of the origin of the woman, who was created from out of the side of the man."

Ver. 5.—St. Matthew appears to give the more full account, of which St. Mark's is an abbreviation. If we suppose the scribes here to interpose their question, "Why then did Moses permit a bill of divorcement?" the two narratives fit exactly. Our Lord here answers their question, For your hardness of heart he wrote you this commandment. He permitted (not commanded) them to put away their wives, lest dislike might turn to hatred. From the beginning God joined them in one indissoluble bond; but man's nature having become corrupt through sin, that sin changed and corrupted the institution, and so was the occasion of bills of divorcement, and polygamy. The Law of Moses put some restraint upon the freedom with which men had till then put away their wives; for thenceforth, a divorce could not take place until some legal steps had been taken, and a regular instrument had been drawn up; and this delay might often be

the means of preventing a divorce which might otherwise have been effected in a moment of passion. Thus this legislation was adapted to the imperfect moral condition of the people, who were as yet quite unprepared for a higher moral code.

Ver. 10.—The discussion with the Pharisees, related in the previous verses, had taken place in public. But now in the house, and in private, the disciples asked him again of this matter; so that what follows seems here to have been said to them privately. But it would appear from St. Matthew (xix. 8) that our Lord had already said this in public; so that here he proclaims a new law, or rather affirms the sanctions of the primitive institution, abrogating the " bill of divorcement " excepting in the one case of fornication, and restoring the rite of marriage to its primæval and indissoluble character.

Ver. 11.—Committeth adultery against her (μοιχᾶται ἐπ' αὐτήν). This must surely mean the wife that has been put away. The adultery is against her, against her rights and interests.

Ver. 12.—This verse should be read thus: And if she herself shall put away her husband, and marry another, she committeth adultery (καὶ ἐὰν αὐτὴ ἀπολύσασα τὸν ἄνδρα αὐτῆς, γαμήσῃ ἄλλον, μοιχᾶται). This reading is well supported. These words indicate that, according to our blessed Lord's teaching, wives and husbands have equal rights in reference to divorce; and so the Greek, according to the best authorities, is (γαμήσῃ) "shall marry," not (γαμηθῇ) "shall be married." Josephus, however, makes it evident that in his time husband and wife had by no means equal rights in these matters (' Antiq.,' xv. 7, 10).

Ver. 13.—It is worthy of notice that this touching incident follows here, as well as in the parallel passage in St. Matthew (xix. 13), immediately after the discourse about the marriage bond. And they brought unto him (προσέφερον)—literally, were bringing—little children (παιδία)—St. Luke (xviii. 15) calls them "babes" (βρέφη)—that he should touch them (ἵνα ἅψηται αὐτῶν). St. Luke has the same word (ἵνα ἅπτηται); but St. Matthew (xix. 13) says "that he should lay his hands on them and pray." The imposition of hands implies a formal benediction; the invoking of Divine grace upon them, that they might grow up into wise and holy men and women. Why did the disciples rebuke them? Perhaps because they thought it unworthy of so great a Prophet, whose business was rather that of instructing those of full age, to be spending his time upon little children.

Ver. 14.—But when Jesus saw it (ἰδὼν δὲ ὁ 'Ιησοῦς). The Greek shows that there was no interval between the acts of the parents and the disciples, and our Lord's seeing it. The parents were bringing the children, the disciples were rebuking them, Jesus was perceiving. **He was much displeased** ($ἠγανάκτησε$); literally, *he was moved with indignation.* His words imply eagerness and earnestness: **Suffer the little children to come unto me; forbid them not.** The copulative $καὶ$ is not to be found in the best authorities. The omission adds force and vividness to the words. The simplicity, candour, and innocence of little children are very attractive. This narrative shows with what care children should be educated. **For of such is the kingdom of God**; that is, of such little children as these. The kingdom of heaven belongs in a peculiar manner to little children. We know for certain that little children who have been brought to Christ in Holy Baptism, if they die before they are old enough for moral accountableness, are undoubtedly saved. They pass at once into a nearer position to the throne. "They are without fault before the throne of God."

Ver. 15.—**Verily I say unto you, Whosoever shall not receive the kingdom of God as a little child, he shall in no wise enter therein.** Observe the "verily" with which our Lord introduces these words. He here adds something which extends what he has just said to those who are, not literally, but figuratively, little children. We must first receive the kingdom into our affections before we can really enter into it. It is as though Christ said, "It is not unworthy of my dignity to take little children into my arms and bless them, because by my benediction they become fit for the kingdom of heaven. And if you full-grown men would become fit for my kingdom, you must give up your ambitious aims and earthly contests, and imitate the simple unworldly ways of little children. The simplicity of the little child is the model and the rule for every one who desires, by the grace of Christ, to obtain the kingdom of heaven. Our Lord's whole action here is a great encouragement to the receiving of little children by Holy Baptism into covenant with him.

Ver. 16.—**And he took them in his arms, and blessed them, laying his hands upon them.** This is considered the true order of the words, according to the best authorities. The word rendered "taking in the arms" ($ἐναγκαλισάμενος$) has already occurred in this Gospel at ch. ix. 36 (where see the note). The description here is very graphic. Our Saviour would first embrace the little child, folding it in his arms; then he would lay his right hand upon the child's head, and bless it.

Ver. 17.—This verse should be rendered, **And as he was going forth** ($ἐκπορευομένου$

$αὐτοῦ$)—that is, just as he was leaving the house—**there ran one to him, and kneeled to him, and asked him.** St. Matthew (xix. 20) says that he was "a young man." St. Luke (xviii. 18) that he was "a ruler." He had apparently been waiting for our Lord, waylaying him, though with a good intention. He showed zeal—as soon as he saw Jesus he ran to him; and he showed reverence, for he kneeled down to him. He wanted advice from one whom he must have heard of as a celebrated Teacher; and he wanted this counsel as a matter of great interest to himself. **Good Master.** This would be the ordinary and courteous mode of accosting a person professing to be a teacher, so as to conciliate his attention and interest. **What shall I do that I may inherit eternal life?** It is as though he said, "Rabbi, I know thee to be good, both as a man and as a teacher, and a prophet, well able to teach me perfectly those things which are really good, and which lead to blessedness hereafter. Tell me, therefore, What shall I do?" St. Matthew (xix. 17) says, "What good thing ($τί$ $ἀγαθὸν$ $ποιήσω$) shall I do that I may inherit eternal life?"

Ver. 18.—**Why callest thou me good?** According to the best authorities, the words in St. Matthew (xix. 17) run thus: "Why askest thou me concerning that which is good? One there is who is good." The word "good" is the pivot on which our Lord's answer turns, both in St. Matthew and here. The question is doubtless put to test the young ruler's faith. If, as may be supposed, the young man used the term, "good Master," as a mere conventional expression, it was not the proper epithet to apply to our Lord, who at once transfers the praise and the goodness to God, that he might teach us to do the same. This ruler, by his mode of accosting our Lord, showed that he had not as yet a right faith in him —that he did not believe in his Godhead. Our Lord, therefore, desired to rouse him and lift him up to a higher faith. He seems to say to him, "If you call me good, believe that I am God; for no one is good, intrinsically good, but God. God alone is essentially good, and wise, and powerful, and holy. It is from him that angels and men derive a few drops, or rather some faint adumbration, of his goodness. There is none essentially, entirely, absolutely good but one, that is, God. Therefore seek after him, love him, imitate him. He alone can satisfy your longing desires, as in this life with his grace, so in the life to come with his glory; yea, with himself. For in heaven he manifests himself as the supreme good, to be tasted and enjoyed by the blessed for ever."

Ver. 19.—In St. Matthew (xix. 17, etc.) the record of our Lord's conversation with the young ruler is more full; and it should be read side by side with the more condensed narrative of St. Mark. It will be observed that it is upon the commandments of the second table that our Lord here lays stress. For the love of God produces the love of our neighbour; and he who loveth not his brother whom he hath seen, how can he love God whom he hath not seen?

Ver. 20.—**Master, all those things have I observed from my youth** (ἐφυλαξάμην); literally, *I kept, I guarded.* St. Matthew adds here (xix. 20), "What lack I yet?"— "What is still wanting in me, that I may inherit the life to come in its fulness of glory and bliss? You seem, good Master, as a heavenly Teacher, to set forth a higher and more excellent way than that pointed out by our scribes and Pharisees. Tell me what that way is. Tell me what I still lack; for I earnestly desire to go forward in the right way that leadeth to everlasting life."

Ver. 21.—**And Jesus looking upon him loved him** (ἐμβλέψας αὐτῷ, ἠγάπησεν αὐτόν). This is another of St. Mark's graphic touches —an exquisite piece of word-painting, probably supplied to him by St. Peter. The words express most vividly an earnest, tender, searching look. They seem, if it may be said reverently, to combine the Divine penetration with human sympathy and compassion. The counsel of our Lord which follows was not a general command, but a particular precept, which the young ruler specially needed. **One thing thou lackest.** In St. Matthew (xix. 21) the words are, "If thou wouldest be perfect." But our Lord's words here, "One thing thou lackest," fit in excellently with the young ruler's question given just before in St. Matthew, "What lack I yet?" showing a substantial unity in the narrative, with just that variety which we should expect in the account of the same incident given by two independent but equally trustworthy witnesses. The "one thing thou lackest" of St. Mark, and "if thou wilt be perfect" of St. Matthew, both point to the same conclusion—that our Lord's object was to reveal this young man to himself. His stumbling-block was his wealth; and so our Saviour at once pierces his besetting sin of covetousness. The precept was a special counsel to him; it directed him to do something which, as our Lord saw, was in his case necessary to his salvation. He could not follow Christ without parting with this sin, and with that which ministered to it. This was his particular spiritual difficulty.

Ver. 22.—**But his countenance fell at the saying** (ὁ δὲ, στυγνάσας ἐπὶ τῳ λόγῳ). The same word is used in St. Matthew (xvi. 3) for a "lowering," "frowning sky" (οὐρανὸς στυγνάζων). **And he went away sorrowful** (ἀπῆλθε λυπούμενος); for he had (ἦν γὰρ ἔχων) —literally, *for he was one that had*—**great possessions.**

Ver. 23.—**And Jesus looked round about, and saith unto his disciples** (καὶ περιβλεψάμενος ὁ Ἰησοῦς λέγει). St. Mark frequently uses this word περιβλέπω. Our Lord turned from the young man, who was now going away, and looked round about, no doubt with a sad and disappointed look, and said to his disciples, **How hardly shall they that have riches enter into the kingdom of God!** Why is this? Partly because the love of riches tempts men to heap them up, whether lawfully or unlawfully. Partly because the love of riches binds the soul to earth, so that it is less likely to think of heaven. Partly because riches are an incentive to pride and luxury and other sins. The heathen poet Ovid could speak of riches as "irritamenta malorum." Poverty and contempt of riches often open that heaven which wealth and covetousness close.

Ver. 24.—**And the disciples were astonished** (ἐθαμβοῦντο)—literally, *were amazed*—**at his words.** The Greek word here implies bewilderment. It is used again below at ver. 32. We find it also at ch. i. 27. This doctrine of our Lord was so new and strange to them. They had been accustomed to think little of the dangers, and much of the advantages of wealth. But Jesus answereth again, and saith unto them, **Children, how hard is it for them that trust in riches to enter into the kingdom of God!** He uses the endearing expression of "children" (τέκνα), and takes off somewhat of the edge of the severity of the expression, by changing the form of it into the words, "how hard is it for them that trust in riches to enter into the kingdom of God!" There is some authority for omitting the words, "for them that trust in riches;" so to reduce the sentence to the simple form, "How hard is it to enter into the kingdom of God!" Such is the reading in the two great uncial manuscripts, the Sinaitic and the Vatican. But on the whole the balance of evidence is in favour of that which was adopted in the Authorized Version, and has been retained by the Revisers of 1881; and it is reasonable to believe that our Lord qualified the former expression, in order to relieve the minds of his amazed disciples.

Ver. 25.—**It is easier for a camel to go through a needle's eye,** etc. This is a strong hyperbolic proverbial expression to represent anything that is very difficult to do. Dr. John Lightfoot, in his Hebrew exercitations upon St. Matthew's Gospel (vol. ii. p. 219), quotes instances from the rabbinical writings of a very similar phrase intended to represent something that is im possible. For example, he quotes one rabbi disputing with another, who says, "Perhaps thou art one of those who can make an elephant pass through the eye of a needle;" that is, "who speak things that are impossible." St. Jerome says, "It is not the absolute impossibility of the thing which is set forth, but the infrequency of it."

Ver. 26.—**And they were astonished exceedingly** (περισσῶς ἐξεπλήσσοντο), **saying among themselves**—according to the best reading the words are, *saying unto him* (πρὸς αὐτόν)—**Then who can be saved?**

Ver. 27.—**Jesus looking upon them** (ἐμβλέψας δὲ αὐτοῖς). The Greek verb implies an earnest, intense looking upon them; evidently narrated by one who, like Peter, had watched his countenance. St. Chrysostom says that he looked on them in this way that he might mitigate and soothe the timid and anxious minds of his disciples. It is as though our Lord said, "It is impossible for a rich man, embarrassed and entangled with his wealth, by his own natural strength to obtain salvation; because this is a supernatural blessing, which we cannot obtain without the like supernatural aids of grace. But with God all things are possible, because God is the Author and Source, as of nature, so of grace and glory. And he enables us, by his grace, to triumph over all the difficulties and hindrances of nature; so that rich men shall not be hindered by their riches; but, by being faithful in the unrighteous mammon, shall make it the means of their being received unto 'the eternal tabernacle.'"

Ver. 28.—**Peter began to say unto him, Lo, we have left all, and have followed thee.** Peter *began* to say unto him. He had been thinking of himself and his companions, the other disciples, in reference to these last words of our Lord. It is probable that the sacrifice which Peter and the rest of the disciples had made when they became his followers, was small, compared with the sacrifice which our Lord demanded of the rich young ruler. Nevertheless they forsook their all, whatever it was. They had forsaken their boats and their nets. They had forsaken their means of subsistence. They had forsaken things which, though they were not much in themselves, were nevertheless such things as they would have desired to keep. Cornelius à Lapide says, "Such things are forsaken by those who follow Christ, as are capable of being desired by those who do not follow him." St. Augustine says, "St. Peter not only forsook what he had, but also what he desired to have. But who does not desire daily to increase what he has? That desire is cut off. Peter forsook the whole world, and he received in return the whole world

They were as those who had nothing, and yet were possessing all things."

Ver. 29.—St. Matthew (xix. 28) here introduces the great promise, to be fulfilled in the regeneration, that is, at the second coming of Christ—at the second birth of the world to a new and glorious state. It may be that St. Matthew was guided to record it, inasmuch as his Gospel was written for Jews. Its omission by St. Mark and St. Luke may be explained by the fact that they were writing, the one to Romans, and the other to Gentiles generally. Omitting further notice here of this great promise recorded only by St. Matthew, St. Mark's words seem general, common to all faithful Christians. This leaving of house, or brethren, or sisters, etc., might be rendered necessary from various causes. But they are all covered by that one expression, **for my sake, and for the gospel's.**

Ver. 30.—**But he shall receive a hundredfold now in this time** (ἑκατονταπλασίονα). St. Luke (xviii. 30) says (πολλαπλασίονα), "manifold more"—an indefinite increase, to show the greatness and multitude of the recompense. He who forsakes his own for the sake of Christ will find others, many in number, who will give him the love of brethren and sisters, with even greater affection; so that he will seem not to have lost or forsaken his own, but to have received them again with interest. For spiritual affections are far deeper than natural; and his love is stronger who burns with heavenly love which God has kindled, than he who is influenced by earthly love only, which only nature has planted. But in the fullest sense, he who forsakes these earthly things for the sake of Christ, receives instead, God himself. For to those who forsake all for him, he is himself father, brother, sister, and all things. So that he will have possessions far richer than what earth can supply; only **with persecutions** (μετὰ διωγμῶν). This is a very striking addition. Our Lord here includes "persecutions" in the number of the Christian's blessings. And no doubt there is a noble sense in which persecutions are really amongst the blessings of the believer. "If ye be reproached for the Name of Christ, happy are ye; for the spirit of glory and of God resteth upon you" (1 Pet. iv. 14). St. Peter, who must have had in his mind the "with persecutions" of our Lord when he wrote these words, here shows that the blessedness of the Christian when suffering persecution is this, that he has a special sense of the abiding presence of the Spirit of God, bringing with it the assurance of future glory. "Rejoice, and be exceeding glad: for great is your reward in heaven." The words are also, of course, a warning to the disciples as to the persecutions that awaited them. **And in the world to come eternal life.** This is that splendid inheritance in which the blessed shall be heirs of God and joint-heirs with Christ; and so shall possess not only the heaven and the earth, and all things that are in them, but even God himself, and all honour, all glory, all joy, not merely as occupiers, but as heirs for ever; as long as God himself shall be, who is himself "the eternal God."

Ver. 31.—**But many that are first shall be last; and the last first.** Most fitly does our Lord add this weighty sentence to what has just gone before. For thus he places himself, his grace, and his gospel in direct opposition to the corrupt teaching of the scribes and Pharisees. Perhaps the disciples thought within themselves, "How can it come to pass that we, the poor, the unlearned, the despised, are to sit upon thrones judging the twelve tribes of Israel, amongst whom are men far our superiors in station, in learning, and in authority, such as are the scribes and Pharisees, and that rich young ruler just mentioned." Our Lord here teaches them that the future will reveal great changes—that some who are first here will be last there, and some who seem last here will be first there. The disciples, and others like them, who, having forsaken all and followed Christ, seemed to be last in this world, will be first in the world to come—most dear to Christ, the King of Heaven, in their lives; most like to him in their zeal for his cause.

Ver. 32.—They were now going up from Jericho to Jerusalem, going up with Christ to his cross and his death. He went before them, eagerly leading the way for his timid disciples, who were now beginning to realize what was about to happen, and that he would be condemned and crucified. Therefore the evangelist adds, **they were amazed** (Greek, ἐθαμβοῦντο); the same word which is used at ver. 24. The words in the original, according to the best reading, make a distinction between the utter amazement of the disciples and the fear of the others who followed (οἱ δὲ ἀκολουθοῦντες ἐφοβοῦντο). St. Mark draws a distinction between the disciples, who would be following him, though at a little distance, and the mixed company, who were also following him, though at a greater distance. The whole scene is before us. Our blessed Lord, with an awful majesty on his countenance, and eager resolution in his manner, is pressing forwards to his cross. "How am I straitened until it be accomplished!" His disciples follow him, amazed and bewildered; and even the miscellaneous crowd, who no doubt gazed upon him with keen interest as the

great "Prophet that should come into the world," felt that something was going to happen, though they knew not what—something very dreadful; and they too were afraid. In the case of the disciples, Bede says that the chief cause of their amazement was their own imminent fear of death. They were amazed that their Master should hasten forward with such alacrity to his cross, and they feared lest they too should have to suffer with him. **He took again the twelve;** and once more impressed upon them the dread realities which were awaiting him. They were still slow of apprehension; they required to be told again and again.

Ver. 35.—**And there come near unto him James and John, the sons of Zebedee, saying unto him, Master, we would that thou shouldest do for us whatsoever we shall ask of thee.** St. Matthew (xx. 20) informs us that this request was made by Salome, "the mother of Zebedee's children." The two accounts are readily reconciled if we consider that the request was made by Salome and her sons, and by her in their behalf. This request was made by them not long after they had heard our Lord's great promise that his apostles "in the regeneration" should "sit upon thrones," judging the twelve tribes of Israel" (Matt. xix. 28), and very soon after they had heard his repeated announcement of his sufferings and death. But the thought of the glory which was to follow swallowed up the thought of the suffering that was to precede it; and so these two disciples were emboldened at once to ask for prominent positions amongst the thrones. St. Chrysostom finds an excuse for the imperfection of their faith. He says, "The mystery of the cross was not yet accomplished; nor yet was the grace of the Holy Spirit poured into their hearts. Wherefore, if you desire to know the strength of their faith, consider what they became after they had been endued with power from on high."

Ver. 38.—It will be observed that in St. Matthew (xx. 20), while Salome is represented as the person who makes the request, the answer is given, not to her, but to her sons. **Ye know not what ye ask.** Our Lord knew that the sons had spoken in the mother and by the mother. They knew not what they asked (1) because his kingdom was spiritual and heavenly, not carnal and earthly, as they supposed; (2) because they sought the glory before they had gained the victory; (3) because perhaps they thought that this kingdom was given in right of natural relationship (they were his cousins); whereas it is not given save to those who deserve it and take it by force. **Are ye able to drink the cup that I drink? or to be baptized with the baptism** that I am baptized with? It is as though he said, "It is by my cross and passion that I am to attain to the kingdom; therefore the same way must be trodden by you who seek the same end." Our Lord here describes his passion as his cup. The "cup" everywhere in Holy Scripture, as well as in profane writers, signifies a man's portion, which is determined for him by God, and sent to him. The figure is derived from the ancient custom at feasts, by which the ruler of the feast tempered the wine according to his own will, and appointed to each guest his own portion, which it was his duty to drink. Our Lord then proceeds to describe his passion, which he had already spoken of as his cup, as his baptism. He uses this image because he would be totally buried, immersed, so to speak, in his passion. But it seems probable that the idea of *purification* entered into this image. It was a baptism of fire into which he was plunged, and out of which he came forth victorious. The fire of his bitter passion and death tried him. It was his "salting with fire." It pleased God thus to "make the Captain of our salvation perfect through sufferings." Our Lord asks these ambitious disciples whether they could drink his cup of suffering, and be baptized with his fiery baptism.

Ver. 39.—James and John seem to have understood the meaning of the cup; and perhaps also of the baptism. They both of them drank the cup, though in different ways. St. James, preaching Christ more boldly and fervently, became an early martyr, having been slain by the sword of Herod (Acts xii. 2). St. John also drank of this cup, and was baptized with this baptism, when, if we may trust the authority of Tertullian ('De Præscript.' c. xxxvi.), he was cast by order of Domitian into a caldron of boiling oil, before the Porta Latina at Rome, although the oil had no power to hurt him. Another legend states that he drank a cup of poison, and took no harm. On this account he is frequently represented with a cup in his hand.

Ver. 40.—But to sit on my right hand or on my left hand is not mine to give; but it is for them for whom it hath been prepared. The Arians gathered from this that our Lord was not of one substance with the Father. But this arose from a misunderstanding of the words. For the antithesis is not here between Christ and the Father; but between James and John on the one side ambitiously seeking the pre-eminence, and those on the other side to whom it ought of right to be given. St. Jerome wisely says, "Our Lord does not say, ' Ye shall not sit,' lest he should put to shame these two. Neither does he say, ' Ye shall sit,' lest the others

should be envious. But by holding out the prize to all, he animates all to contend for it." Our Lord is also careful to point out that he who humbles himself shall be exalted. But Christ is the Giver, not indeed by way of favour to any one who asks, but according to the eternal and unalterable principles laid down by the Father. That Christ is the Giver is plain from St. Luke (xxii. 29), "I appoint unto you a kingdom, even as my Father appointed unto me."

Ver. 41.—And when the ten heard it, they began to be moved with indignation concerning James and John. How did they hear it? It is most likely that Salome and her two sons sought this favour secretly from Christ, lest they should excite the envy of the others. But they, the ten, must have noticed the approach of James and John with their mother to our Lord. They came in a formal manner, worshipping him first, and then making their request (see Matt. xx. 20). The ten would naturally be desirous to know the nature of this interview; and when it was explained to them, they began to show indignation. Our Lord perceived that they were disputing; and he then called them and addressed the whole body. For he saw that they were all labouring under this disease of ambition; and he wished to apply the remedy at once to all, as we see in the words which follow.

Ver. 42.—In these words our Lord does not find fault with that power or authority, whether civil or ecclesiastical, which is exercised by princes or bishops; for this is necessary in every state, and so is sanctioned by Divine and human law. What he condemns is the arbitrary and tyrannical exercise of such power, which the princes of the Gentiles were accustomed to.

Vers. 43, 44.—In these words our Lord enjoins him who is raised above others to conduct himself modestly and humbly; so as not to lord it over those beneath him, but to consider for them and to consult their security and happiness, and so to conduct himself that he may appear to be rather their minister and servant than their lord; ever remembering the golden rule, "All things whatsoever ye would that men should do to you, even so do to them." At the same time, our Lord here teaches all alike, whether superiors or inferiors, by what way we should strive to reach heaven, so as to sit at the right or left hand of Christ in his kingdom, namely, by the way of humility. For those who are the lowliest and most humble here will be the greatest and most exalted there.

Ver. 45.—A ransom for many (λύτρον ἀντὶ πολλῶν; from λύω, to loose, or set free). Not that Christ died only for the elect. For Christ died for all; and has obtained for all the means necessary and sufficient for their salvation. Yet the fruit of his death and his full salvation comes only to those who persevere to the end. When our Lord says that he came "to give his life a ransom for many," he regards the vast multitude of those who are included within his purposes of mercy. He "is the Saviour of all men, specially of them that believe."

Ver. 46.—**And they come to Jericho.** Jericho, situated in the midst of a fertile, well-watered country, celebrated for its palm trees, was situated about seventeen English miles east-north-east of Jerusalem, and about six miles from the nearest bend of the river Jordan. In the time of our Lord it was one of the most important cities next to Jerusalem. It is now known by the name of Richa or Ericha, and is almost deserted. The journey from the Jordan to Jericho is through a flat country; but that from Jericho to Jerusalem is very hilly. It is supposed that it was upon the rocky heights overhanging this city that our Lord's temptation took place. Jericho derives its name, either from "the moon," or from the fragrant odours of the "balsam" plant, which was extensively cultivated in the neighbourhood. Its palm groves and balsam gardens were bestowed by Anthony upon Cleopatra, from whom Herod the Great purchased them. It was here that Herod the Great died. It is now one of the most filthy and neglected places in Palestine. To this place our Lord came; and St. Luke (xviii. and xix.) gives a full account of his reception there. St. Matthew speaks of two blind men; but he agrees with St. Mark in saying that the cure took place as he went out from Jericho. St. Luke mentions only one; but he places the cure at the time of our Lord's entrance into Jericho. How do we reconcile St. Mark's account of one only, specially named, Bartimæus, the son of Timæus? St. Augustine says that there were two blind men; but that the one, better known, overshadowed the other. He also says that Bartimæus was a well-known character, and that he was accustomed to sit by the wayside, not only blind, but as a beggar. It is of course possible that St. Luke may refer to another case altogether. But on the other hand, with the exception that he mentions only one, and that he places the cure at the time of the entrance into Jericho, and not at the time of the departure, all the other circumstances are identical. May not this latter discrepancy be reconciled thus?—the blind man may have sought a cure from Christ at his first entrance into the city; but he may not have been able to be heard on account

of the crowd. Or our Lord may have passed him by at first, in order to stimulate his faith and hope. So the day after, he may have placed himself at the gate of the city, close by where Christ would pass through; and there again he may have urged his request, and so obtained healing. Dr. John Lightfoot (p. 348) says that the careful description of Bartimæus would seem to imply that his father may have been a person of some note. Dr. Lightfoot adds that it is possible that Timæus, or "Thimai," may be the same with *Simais*, blind, from the use of the letter *thau* from *samech*, common amongst the Chaldæans; so that Bartimæus might mean nothing more than "blind son of a blind father."

Ver. 48.—**Many rebuked him, that he should hold his peace.** They rebuked him, perhaps, out of reverence and regard for Christ, who might perhaps at that moment have been preaching to the people, and so might be disturbed by the blind man's loud and noisy appeal. But the rebuke of the crowd gave additional energy to his entreaties; and **he cried out the more a great deal,** that his voice might be heard above them all. He was in good earnest, and would not be restrained. A useful lesson is here suggested to all. He who desires to serve God must overcome all earthly shame and fear; for, indeed, this unworthy feeling keeps back many from Christ.

Ver. 49.—**And Jesus stood still** (στὰς ὁ Ἰησοῦς)—literally, *Jesus stood*—and said, **Call ye him.** St. Jerome says that our Lord stood still on account of the man's infirmity. There were many walls in Jericho; there were rough places; there were rocks and precipices over which he might stumble. Therefore the Lord stood, where there was a plain path by which the blind man might approach him. The crowd show their sympathy. There is something very genuine as well as touching in their words, **Be of good cheer: rise, he calleth thee.**

Ver. 50.—**And he, casting away his garment, rose**—the word in the Greek is ἀναπηδήσας, literally, *sprang to his feet*—**and came to Jesus.** He cast away his "garment," that is, the loose outer robe which covered his tunic. He was in haste, and desired to disengage himself from every impediment, in his eagerness to approach Jesus. We seem here to have the description of a keen eye-witness, such as St. Peter would be.

Vers. 51, 52.—Our Lord well knew what he wanted; but it was necessary that he and those around him should hear from the lips of the blind man the confession of his need, and of his faith in the power that was present to heal him. **And the blind man said** unto him, **Rabboni, that I may receive my sight.** "Rabboni," or "Rabbuni," means literally, *my Master.* It was a more respectful mode of address than the more simple form "Rabbi." This expression shows that Bartimæus had yet much to learn as to the Divine character of our Lord. But his faith is accepted; and he showed that it was genuine as far as it went, by forthwith

following Jesus in the way. There were six occasions on which our Lord is recorded to have healed the blind: St. Matthew (ix. 27; xii. 22; xxi. 14); St. Mark (viii. 24; x. 46); St. John (ix. 1). St. Chrysostom says of Bartimæus, that as before this gift of healing he showed perseverance, so after it he showed gratitude.

HOMILETICS.

Vers. 1—12.—*Marriage and divorce.* Our Lord Jesus is the great moral Legislator of humanity. His authoritative teaching applies to all classes and to all relationships of mankind. And it is to be noticed that he bases his commands and counsels both upon grounds of natural right and reason, and also upon the revealed Mosaic Law. With regard to the latter, it is observable that he professes not to destroy it, but to fulfil it—to inspire it with a new motive, and to give it a wider range; whilst he allows no authority to mere traditions and usages, but treats them simply upon their own merits.

I. Upon what our Lord bases the sanctity of marriage. It is to be observed that Jesus goes back behind the old Mosaic Law, which was universally accepted among the Jews as the authoritative standard of conduct. 1. There is reference to what we should call *natural adaptation.* If there is design in any arrangement or provision of nature, there is certainly design in the division of mankind (as, indeed, of other races of living beings) into two corresponding and complementary sexes. Man was made for woman, and woman for man; and the equality in numbers of male and female is evidently a natural reason both for marriage and for monogamy. 2. There is reference to the *creative, historical basis* of marriage. The record of Genesis is adduced, and Jesus reminds the Pharisees that marriage dated, as a matter of fact, from the beginning of the creation—that our first parents lived together in this relationship from their first introduction to each other until the close of life. 3. Jesus asserts marriage to be *a Divine ordinance.* "God hath joined together" husband and wife. The Law of Moses came in with its additional provisions and sanctions; but it presumed the existence of the marriage state. God, who orders all things well, had seen that it would not be good for the man to be alone; accordingly he instituted wedded life, and hallowed it.

II. What our Lord deduces from the sanctity of marriage. 1. A condemnation of the custom of facile divorce. It was a common practice for the Jews, when dissatisfied with their wives, to put them away for very trivial reasons—even because they were not pleased with them, without any offence having been committed. They were wont to appeal to a permissive provision in their law as a warrant for acting thus. In our own times, in many countries even professedly Christian, it is too common for regulations of great laxity to be made regarding divorce. In some countries even incompatibility of temper is a sufficient ground for permanent separation. Such practices are condemned by Jesus as contrary to the Divine intention regarding marriage, and as subversive of all sound morality. As the family is the unit and the basis of all communities, and of all moral unity and welfare, it is of the highest importance that the sacredness of this Divine institution should be upheld, and that all practices and sentiments which undermine it should be discountenanced and opposed. Lax views upon divorce are to be repressed, as inimical to all social welfare as well as to domestic concord. 2. A declaration that such divorce is conducive to adultery. Our Lord does not say that the remarriage of divorced persons is in all cases adulterous; but, speaking of those who are separated for trivial offences, and for any offence short of the most serious, he declares that for such persons to marry again is nothing less than adultery. They are not really and in God's sight released from one another, and a second union is therefore unlawful. "What therefore God hath joined together, let not man put asunder."

Application. 1. Learn our Lord's independence as an ethical and spiritual Teacher, and his superiority to traditional and even Mosaic authority. 2. Learn his interest in all our human relationships; he consecrates them by the regard of his grace and by the imposition of his Law. 3. Let Christians discountenance lax opinions and practices upon a question so vital to social and national well-being as the ordinance of marriage.

Vers. 13—16.—*Christ and the children.* That three of the evangelists should have recorded this incident is proof of the impression it made upon the early Christians, and of the importance they attached to it. The Son of man interested himself in all classes and conditions of humanity; and it is not strange that he should have come into direct and tender relations with the very young.

I. THE CHILDREN who were brought to Jesus. They were very young, for they are called "little children," and they were so small as to be taken up in the arms. Jesus had himself been a child, and had passed through the stages of infancy and boyhood, so that from his own experience he could sympathize with this age and condition of human life. These children may have been children of the house where Jesus had been staying, and of the neighbours. It should be remembered that, not long before, Jesus had taken a little child and used him as an example of simplicity and humility. We may certainly learn from this incident that no child, however young or feeble, is disregarded by our Lord Jesus. In every one he sees an immortal, God-given nature, capable of fellowship with the Creator's mind, and of obedience to his commands.

II. THE PARENTS OF THE CHILDREN. 1. They revered and honoured Jesus themselves, or they would not have acted thus. They would not have treated another rabbi thus. There must have been something in our Lord which attracted them and induced them to believe that he would not repel them should they ask a favour on behalf of their little ones. 2. They brought their children to Jesus. The babes had neither knowledge nor strength to come of themselves; but their parents acted for them. Parents should regard it as their duty and privilege to bring their offspring to the Saviour. This they may do by instructing them as to who and what Jesus is, by leading them into the society of Christ's people. 3. They had a definite purpose in bringing the children to Jesus, viz. that he should touch them and should pray for them. To tell our children of Christ is, or should be, with a view to their personal spiritual contact with him, and with a view to their enjoying both the regard of his friendship and the benefit of his intercession.

III. THE TWELVE, AND THEIR TREATMENT OF THE CHILDREN. It is instructive to observe that the very persons whose office it was to make Jesus known to men, and to introduce all the needy to his notice, and to commend them to his aid, should have on this occasion interfered with the approach of those whom Jesus would have welcomed. The twelve rebuked the parents, and forbade the children to be brought to Jesus, probably from a mistaken idea that the Lord would not care to be troubled with those so young and so helpless. How important that Christians should not interpose to prevent children from seeking Christ and the fellowship of his people!

IV. JESUS, AND HIS TREATMENT OF THE CHILDREN. The narrative gives us a delightful view of the Saviour's character, as the children's Friend. 1. What he *felt.* A very strong expression is used to denote our Lord's disapproval of his disciples' conduct. He was "moved with indignation" by their demeanour. They were both misrepresenting him and inflicting a wrong upon the applicants for blessing. 2. What he *said.* His language includes a special reference to the occasion, and a general statement of a Divine principle. "Suffer the children to come!" "Forbid them not!" How gracious a revelation of the Saviour's mind and disposition, and how instructive a lesson for his people! The general principle he enunciates is even more valuable: "Of such is the kingdom of heaven." The reference is doubtless to the dependence and teachableness of little children. God's kingdom is composed of childlike natures. The proud, self-sufficient, and self-confident are out of harmony with a spiritual society which recognizes a Divine Head and is governed by Divine laws. 3. What he *did.* Doubtless, in these actions, Jesus was obeying the impulse of his affectionate nature. Yet he intended to teach the world how gracious is his heart, how compassionate are his purposes, how vast and widely extended are the arms of his love. He took them in his arms, verifying the prediction concerning him as the Good Shepherd. He laid his hands upon them, signifying his tender interest. He blessed them, praying for them, and pronouncing over them words of Divine benediction.

APPLICATION. 1. An encouragement to Christian parents to bring their children to the Saviour. 2. An inducement to the young to look to Jesus as the Giver of true blessing. 3. An example to the Church of Christ as to the spirit in which the Lord's people should deal with the young—with inexperienced and immature natures. No impatience or contempt, but rather gentleness and consideration, should distinguish the attitude of Christ's people towards the lambs of the flock.

Vers. 17—22.—*Loved, yet lacking.* An interesting character this, coming in the Gospel history like a meteor out of the darkness for a brief moment, and then vanishing again, to be no more seen. An interesting conversation this, casting valuable light upon the character and the demands of Christ, and upon the aspirations and virtues, the tests and the deficiencies, of human nature. Strange that Jesus should love one who came before him in this one short interview; stranger still that, in this loved one, he should find a lack so serious and even fatal, that such promise should issue in such disappointment! In this young ruler we have a type of a class of applicants to Christ.
I. HE POSSESSED MANY THINGS. How much was in this young man's favour! 1. His *worldly position.* Though young, he was a ruler, and the possessor of great riches. It was to his credit that, when his worldly condition and circumstances were such, he yet acted as he did, evincing a mind set upon higher blessings than this world can give. 2. His *character.* There is no reason to disbelieve his assertion that he had in his outward life kept the Law of the Decalogue. Christ did not charge him with hypocrisy in this profession; he rather admitted its truth in requiring more than compliance with the rules of morality. 3. His *reverence for Jesus.* This is apparent in his action and attitude: "he came kneeling down on the road before Jesus;" and in his address, "Good Master," as well as in the fact that he reverently asked the judgment of the prophet of Nazareth upon a most important question. 4. His *aspiration after eternal life.* This was a proof of a noble dissatisfaction and a noble desire; this question which the young ruler addressed to the one Being who was able to answer and resolve it.
II. HE WAS LOVED AND TESTED BY CHRIST. 1. Jesus *loved* him, doubtless seeing in him an ingenuous disposition, a thirst for truth, a reverence for goodness; doubtless looking back upon a pure and honourable life in the past, and forward to the bright possibilities of the future. What an insight we thus gain into the truly human nature of the Saviour! And are there not *now* those whom he looks upon and loves, beholding in them so much that is congenial to his heart? 2. Jesus *tested* him. He did this in love, yet in faithfulness. And in three ways. (1) His faith in Himself. Why call him "good"? The epithet was too honourable if he were man. Was his disciple prepared to apply it to him with the clear understanding that it involved his Deity? (2) His character. This test the young ruler stood; he had "a conscience void of offence." (3) His love and devotion. Was the young ruler prepared to give up all at the Master's bidding? This leads to the observation that—
III. HE LACKED ONE THING. Consider: 1. *Christ's demand.* (1) It was that he should part with his wealth, and bestow all upon the poor. Not that this is universally obligatory or desirable. It was the form of *complete surrender* which in this case was most appropriate. A hard test, a stern requirement; yet most necessary "to prove the sincerity of his love." (2) The promise. There was an inducement held out, of "treasure in heaven," which should more than compensate his loss. Our Lord shows his compassion upon our human nature in thus alluring to his side. (3) The call. It was to discipleship: "Follow me." What an opportunity was, in these words, opened up before this ardent, aspiring mind! Who can say what position he might have held in the circle of the apostles, in the memory of Christendom, had he responded to this heavenly summons? 2. *The young ruler's failure under trial.* The saying was too hard; the test was too severe; the world was too strong! His heart sank within him, and his countenance fell. And then he went away sorrowful, grieving to leave Christ, yet feeling that the grief would be greater of leaving the riches in which he delighted and trusted. Had he given, not his admiration, his respect, only, to Christ, but his very heart, then it would have been possible to him to have "left all, and followed him." But one thing he lacked—the surrender of self, of the spiritual nature, which would have involved the surrender of all.

APPLICATION. Christ will be satisfied with nothing less than our heart, our all. We may have many things, and yet lack the spirit of perfect surrender and consecration. The test is certain to be applied; how shall we endure it?

Vers. 23—31.—*Christ must be all.* Sometimes our Lord gave utterance to paradox. Certainly it was so on this occasion. Any ordinary observer would have pronounced the rich young ruler blessed, and would have pitied the poor fishermen who neglected their petty craft and followed the homeless and penniless Rabbi of Nazareth. But God's ways are not our ways. Jesus looked below the surface. To him the case of the favoured of fortune and the admired of society was a sad case, and the choice of the twelve was the choice of the good part, which none can take away.

I. THE SPIRITUAL DISADVANTAGES AND PERILS OF WEALTH. This is not a popular or acceptable lesson; and most people would be willing to accept, without a murmur, the position of danger and temptation occupied by the affluent. However, the warnings of the Master are fully borne out by the experience of those who have watched the working of human nature under the influence of riches. 1. To have wealth is to be in danger of trusting in wealth. 2. To trust in wealth is not conducive to humility, penitence, and faith—the dispositions peculiarly suitable to those who would be saved. 3. To lack these dispositions is to be disqualified for the kingdom of God. 4. Yet the grace of God, with whom all things are possible, is able to overcome difficulties and temptations great as these.

II. THE BLESSEDNESS OF GIVING UP ALL FOR CHRIST. 1. Really and truly *the Christian surrenders all he has to his Lord.* That Lord may give him back, as it were, of what was his own, but even when used for himself, it is consecrated, and is still the Lord's. (1) Christians may be called upon to give up earthly possessions. This the rich young ruler should have done, but did not; this Peter and the rest of the twelve actually did. It has often been remarked that the apostles did not give up much in order to become disciples of Jesus. But the answer is fair—What they had they gave up; it was their all. When plainly called upon to part with property, as, *e.g.*, in times of persecution, or for the sake of charity, Christ's people willingly make the sacrifice required. (2) Christians may have to renounce earthly aims and prospects. How often does this happen still! The convert feels constrained to break away from old associations, which might well be the stepping-stone to honour, station, emolument; and in sacrificing what the world would give, he reaps a rich reward in the approval of his conscience, the progress he makes in the Divine life, the increased opportunities of usefulness he enjoys. Such are foremost in inviting their fellow-men to the better path—

> "Come, learn, your follies quitting,
> That this world's gain is loss;
> To his mild rule submitting
> Who bare for you the cross."

(3) They renounce the pleasures and the applause of the world. The pleasures of sin it is their aim to relinquish; the praise of men they regard with indifference; for they "have left all." (4) All this renunciation is spiritually valuable just so far as it expresses the renunciation of self-will, and the acceptance of the will of Christ. "I count all things but loss for the excellency of the knowledge of Christ Jesus the Lord." 2. In so doing *the Christian reaps a rich reward.* This is twofold. (1) There is recompense in this life. To follow Jesus is in itself an honour and happiness. Who that loves him would not willingly share his lot? Surrender all you have to Christ, and Christ will bestow all he has on you. He not only confers upon his people the favour of his heart, he gives them to enjoy the approbation of a good conscience. And Jesus points out the provision made by God's goodness for many of his faithful followers. It happened, as he foretold, that many of the persecuted disciples experienced marvellous interpositions and unexpected relief; that their confession of Christ was the occasion of the attachment and affection, the ministrations and gifts, of those who witnessed and admired their fidelity. (2) There is a yet richer recompense hereafter. Simply and grandly does Jesus assure his people that they shall have "in the world to come eternal life." It was an assurance which was repeated by Christ's inspired

apostles, which was addressed from the throne of his glory by the triumphant Redeemer to his struggling soldiers upon earth. "Be thou faithful unto death, and I will give thee a crown of life." Many a faithful witness and warrior has been animated by the glorious prospect, and has learned joyfully to toil and patiently to endure, with the blessed hope of the future before his eyes. The light afflictions are light, because they introduce the exceeding and eternal weight of glory.

"When the shore is won at last,
Who will count the billows past?"

Vers. 32—34.—*The reiterated prediction.* This was the *third* occasion upon which Jesus expressly and formally intimated to his followers the approaching close of his ministry and life. The occasion was the last great journey up to Jerusalem. He wished the disciples to understand what their discipleship involved, into what scenes they were now about to follow him; that, forewarned, they might be forearmed. Observe—

I. THE PREPARATION FOR THIS COMMUNICATION. Mark, in a few words, graphically and vividly portrays the scene. An unusual state of excitement pervades the company. The attitude of the Master, and the expression of the disciples' countenances, display the prevalence of common emotion. Jesus goes before, absorbed in contemplation of his approaching sufferings; the group of disciples are amazed at the prospect opened up to them in the words of warning they have just heard; and the people around are silent with dread and awe!

II. JESUS PREDICTS THE PLACE OF HIS SUFFERINGS. They are going up to Jerusalem. The city, in which he has often preached and wrought his mighty works, is about to reject him. The metropolis is in this act to fulfil the counsels of the nation. "He came to his own, and his own received him not." "It cannot be that a prophet perish out of Jerusalem."

III. IT IS FORETOLD WHO SHALL BE THE INSTIGATORS OF THE MARTYRDOM. The chief priests and the scribes have opposed him at every point; have disputed with him, calumniated him, stirred up the people against him. And now it is into their hands that he is to be delivered, and they are to take the initiative in his destruction. The leaders of his own nation are to compass the violent end of him who is that nation's Glory and Redeemer.

IV. IT IS FORETOLD WHO SHALL BE THE AGENTS IN HIS MARTYRDOM. It is a proof of our Lord's prophetic foresight, that he predicts that the instrumentality by which the leaders of the Jews shall effect their purpose is not a native but a foreign agency. He came "a Light to lighten the Gentiles, and the Glory of God's people Israel;" and it was permitted that he should be "despised and rejected of men," and that both sections of the human race should conspire and concur in his martyrdom.

V. JESUS FORETELLS THE INSULTS AND INDIGNITIES WHICH SHALL PRECEDE HIS DEATH. The circumstantial manner in which the great Sufferer describes beforehand the cruel and inhuman treatment with which he shall meet, is pathetic and instructive. He reads the very hearts of his foes, and marks their malignity and baseness, their hostility to himself and to all that is good. Death is formidable, but the prospect of such a death as this awakens horror.

VI. THE RESURRECTION IS FORETOLD AS THE COMPLETION OF THE MARTYRDOM. Christ's death was not merely a martyrdom; it was a sacrifice. Its purpose would not have been answered had it not been shown that it was impossible that he should be holden of death. Thus was there given to the world an assurance from Heaven that this was indeed the Christ, declared to be the Son of God with power. And for the sake of the disciples themselves, the Lord Jesus foretells his approaching victory over the grave, that their hearts may be cheered and their hopes inspired, that they may learn the more truly to reverence him and the more ardently to trust him.

Vers. 35—45.—*True ministry is true dignity.* Some of the most sacred and precious lessons which the Lord Jesus has taught mankind were suggested by incidents which occurred in his own ministry. This is true, both of lessons regarding his own grace and of lessons regarding our duty and life. His hand turns all that he touches into gold. Who would have thought that the selfish and thoughtless request of a mother and her sons could have led to one of the profoundest statements concerning the Saviour's mission, and to the publication of one of the most novel and powerful laws that were to govern the subjects of the Saviour's kingdom? Yet so it is.

I. THE REQUEST OF AMBITION. There is scope in every position of human life for the display of this principle of human nature. The desire to be wiser and better and more influential for good than we are is to be commended; but the desire to have more power and honour than our fellow-men is bad, unless it be cherished with a view to their advantage. There is such a thing as religious ambition, as the history of the Church in all ages abundantly shows. And the passage in the Gospel history now before us exhibits the working of this principle in the breasts of some of our Lord's first followers and apostles. Observe: 1. *By whom* this request was preferred. Salome was the wife of Zebedee, the owner of fishing-boats upon the Galilean lake. As the sister of Mary, the mother of Jesus, she may naturally have thought she and hers had some claim upon the Founder of the new kingdom. Her sons, James and John, joined with her in this petition for pre-eminence, so that it was in all likelihood discussed and arranged beforehand. It is remarkable that these ambitious followers of Jesus, who herein showed so little of the Master's spirit, were, with Peter, his most intimate and trusted friends, who might have been supposed the most to resemble him in disposition and character. A warning which none should neglect, as to the possibility of even eminent Christians falling into this snare. 2. On *what occasion* was this petition presented? It is observable that, shortly before, Jesus had promised his disciples honour and dignities; in fact, thrones of dominion and judgment in the kingdom that was to be. Yet more recently, however, he had amazed his disciples by informing them of events which he plainly foresaw—his own approaching persecution, sufferings, and death. The end was indeed near, and Jesus seems to have foretold its accompaniments the more clearly the nearer the time approached. It is singular that the ambition of the brothers, instead of being subdued by the mournful prospect, was inflamed by the glorious promise. They thought of their thrones more than of his cross. 3. There was *some good* in this request. It recognized Christ's authority, for the petition was urged upon him as upon a King who was able to grant it. It evinced faith in his character and in his future; for unless the kingdom had been a real thing to them they would not have sought participation in its glories. Not only did they refer the appointment to him; they evidently desired above all things to rule, not only under him, but with him. 4. Yet there was still more manifestly what was *bad* in the request. Their great error was that they overlooked the sublime truth, that fellowship is spiritual and not circumstantial. To be Christ's, whether upon a throne, or in a hovel, or a dungeon—that is the aspiration of the true Christian's heart; the aspiration to share in his outward glory (as if that were the best) is mean and contemptible. What a carnal conception was theirs of the kingdom! They laid hold of the emblem, but the underlying truth and reality escaped them altogether. And yet, again, we discern in the request a selfish desire for personal aggrandizement. They were thinking of themselves when they should have been thinking of their Lord. They ought to have asked, "How, Lord, can we serve thee, or suffer with thee, and so please and glorify thee?" Instead of which they were scheming what they might get from Christ, and how a connection with him might be turned best to their own advantage.

II. THE REBUKE OF AMBITION. Our Lord had on several occasions to rebuke the pride, vain-glory, and strife for pre-eminence which broke forth now and again even in the chosen band of the twelve. This he did by symbolical acts, as when he set the little child in the midst and exhorted them to a childlike spirit; and again when he washed their feet, bidding them follow his example of condescension and humility. On the occasion before us our Lord censured the conduct of the brothers with a peculiar and memorable solemnity. 1. Remark *what he refused.* The places asked for he would not grant them. He gave them to understand that the bestowment of honours in Christ's kingdom is not a matter, so to speak, of favouritism, of private and personal feeling. It is governed by great moral laws. It is the result of their operation in the heart and in society. There is nothing arbitrary or capricious in it. It is the expression of the Father's wisdom. The future shall reveal what for the present lies hid from all. 2. Remark *what Jesus promised.* He first puts it to them in the form of a question;

but he very graciously passes from interrogation to assurance and promise. These two men who asked for thrones were promised—what? The cup of sorrow and the baptism of suffering. But it was to be *his* cup, *his* baptism. What Jesus meant we are at no loss to decide. The cup he drank in the garden of Gethsemane; the baptism all but overwhelmed him upon the cross of Calvary. Of all this they should know something by bitter, yet blessed, experience. They had some foretaste of their portion when they saw their Master in his humiliation and in his death. After years enlarged their experience. James fell a victim to the sword of the persecutor; John lived a long life of witness, both by work for Christ and by steadfastness in suffering for Christ. Both were faithful unto death. Both lost all taint of earthly ambition, and knew the fellowship of their Lord's cross and passion. 3. Consider how *contrary to their expectations* was this revelation of the mode in which Christ's disciples should share with him. The manner in which the Lord dealt with them showed alike his knowledge of human nature and his habitual power of spiritual sympathy. How fitted was his treatment of them to draw out and encourage their better feelings! How much higher and nobler a view of human nature and its possibilities and destinies was this which Jesus presented! And he did it in such a way as not to discourage those whom yet he felt it needful to rebuke; in such a way as to prepare his friends to give, in due time, the convincing proof that their friendship was genuine, sympathetic, and unselfish.

III. THE REMEDY FOR AMBITION. Here, as everywhere, Christianity is Christ. Jesus never merely tells us what he would have us be; he first shows us this in his own Person, and then he supplies us with the Divine and all-sufficient motive in his own ministry and sacrifice. "For verily the Son of man came not to be," etc. 1. Not that Jesus absolutely and always refused to be ministered unto. In his infancy his mother nurtured him; during his ministry his friends supplied his wants, and welcomed him to their homes. Gracefully and graciously he accepted their kind and affectionate service. 2. But that his chief purpose in his earthly life was to minister to men. He observed and pitied those whom he came to save and bless, for their wants were many and their woes were great. He supplied their bodily necessities, he relieved their bodily privations, he healed their bodily maladies; he sympathized with them in their griefs, and brought both health and consolation to their hearts. Their spiritual wants aroused his deepest commiseration. He taught the ignorant, aroused in the sinful the conscience of sin, brought pardon to the penitent, hope to the downcast, and salvation to all prepared to receive it. His career on earth was one long ministry of wisdom, faithfulness, love, and power. 3. And his death was voluntary sacrifice and service, in the highest form. The purpose of our Lord's coming was a purpose of "obedience unto death, even the death of the cross." There was nothing accidental or unforeseen in the close of our Lord's earthly career. He consciously and voluntarily *gave* his life. What others prized, he surrendered; what others strove to save, he was content to lose. A sublime spectacle of self-abnegation! But there was a purpose in this act of Jesus. It was that he might pay a ransom that he deigned to die. He is the Redeemer, and redemption was his great work. From the bondage and power, from the penalty and curse of sin, he died to set us free. And observe the expansive benevolence that characterized his redemptive work. It was to ransom *many* that he died. Not to exalt himself merely, as was the carnal aim of his half-trained followers. but to save multitudes, to redeem mankind.

IV. THE CURE OF AMBITION. We must not lose sight of the close connection between our Saviour's statement regarding himself, his ministry, and death, and his language to the twelve, especially to the ambitious brothers. Observe: 1. *How the remedy works.* Difficult as it is to explain the bearing of our Saviour's redemption upon the Divine character and government, there is little difficulty in explaining its bearing upon human character and life. The soul that by faith lays hold upon the Redeemer, and accepts the redemption as the provision of God's free grace, comes under a new impulse and motive. Gratitude and love towards him who gave himself for us lead, both naturally and of purpose, to devotion, obedience, and assimilation of character. Such motives the Holy Spirit applies to the nature, and thus overcomes the native tendency to selfishness and sinful pride. The Christian feels that Jesus lived and died to redeem from all evil, and certainly from this prevailing fault and folly. Our Saviour is both the *Model* and the *Motive* of our new service. Himself the highest example of humility and benevolence, he furnishes in his cross the power which inspires us to conflict with sin, and encourages us to hope for victory. It is Divine wisdom which has devised the plan, and Divine grace which has executed it, and the results are worthy of him to whom we owe them. 2. *By what signs* the efficacy of the remedy is made apparent. Our Lord clearly saw how contrary is the law of his kingdom to that which prevails in earthly society. He observed how men aim at pre-eminence and dominion; and, instead of qualifying this practice, he condemns it; instead of lopping the boughs, he strikes at the root of the tree. "It is not so among you." On the contrary, he unfolds the new law: "Foremost in service, foremost in kingdom, in honour." Accordingly, if you would know whether an individual, a community, is truly Christ's, apply this test. Do not ask—Is the creed orthodox? Are the devotions splendid or fervent? Is profession loud and ample? But ask—Is the Spirit of Jesus manifest? Is the law of Jesus observed? For "if a man have not the Spirit of Christ, he is none of his." They are truly Christians who, instead of asking—How can we enjoy ourselves? how can we raise ourselves? ask, on the contrary—How can we live as ministers of one another, and as servants of all? In the family, in the Church, in the world, we have ever-widening circles within which our influence may extend. To promote the bodily, the social, the educational, the moral, and spiritual welfare of our fellow-creatures—this is an aim worthy of all adoption, and an aim which will supply a sufficient and conclusive answer to the somewhat foolish question of the day, "Is life worth living?" To work for others and to work for Christ,—this is what the Lord expects from his people. And this is the manner of moral life which leads to his approval; this is the pathway to the stars.

APPLICATION. 1. Adore the compassion and humility of the Redeemer. 2. Accept the deliverance which he has wrought in the payment of your ransom. 3. Check the rising spirit of self-seeking and ambition. 4. Live as ministers of blessing to those around you. "Freely ye have received, freely give."

Vers. 46—52.—*Blind Bartimæus.* It is not without a purpose that the evangelists have put upon record so many of our Lord's miracles wrought on behalf of the blind. In all such miracles the "sign" is prominent, the moral lesson is instructive, impressive, and encouraging.

I. We recognize, in the privation of Bartimæus, AN EMBLEM OF THE SINNER'S STATE. For: 1. The sinner is without spiritual knowledge. The blind are necessarily, by their deprivation of the highest of the senses, cut off from much knowledge of the outer world, and of the properties of matter, and consequently of the appeals of the Creator to the mind and heart of man. 2. The sinner is a stranger to many pure and elevating pleasures. The enjoyments of the sightless are grievously curtailed. The votary of sin has indeed his pleasures, but they are impure, debasing, and unsatisfying. 3. The sinner lacks true guidance. Just as the blind man depends upon others to lead him, and unless so assisted goes astray, so the unenlightened are doomed to wander in the mazes of error and of sin. 4. The sinner has no assurance, for he has no means of safety. As the blind fall into dangers for want of sight, so those whose minds are dark know nothing of true spiritual security, and have no well-founded hope.

II. Here we have AN EXAMPLE OF THE CRY OF DAWNING FAITH. 1. There is presumed a sense of privation, of misery, of need. This expresses itself when opportunity invites the expression. 2. We observe a recognition of Christ's power and willingness to help and save. When Bartimæus heard that it was Jesus who drew near, he cried aloud for help, having no doubt heard from some credible quarter of the customary compassion and the miraculous powers of the Prophet of Nazareth. 3. This shapes itself into a definite appeal for mercy. 4. And this appeal is distinguished by perseverance and persistency. Hindrances and dissuasions are of no avail; they only incite the applicant to more earnest supplications. The soul that truly feels its need, and has caught a true glimpse of Jesus, is not to be deterred from entreaties for grace and help. Obstacles may hinder the indifferent; they quicken the zeal of those who are earnest.

III. AN INSTANCE OF CHRIST'S COMPASSIONATE INTEREST. When the blind beggar cries aloud, Jesus hears; he pauses to allow an interview; he bids that the suppliant be brought to him. It is ever so. Nothing is so welcome to the Saviour as the entreaty and appeal of the penitent and believing sinner. No voice is unheard, no wretchedness unfelt, no applicant rejected, by him. The sinner's need is his concern: the sinner's cry prompts his interposition.

IV. AN INDICATION OF THE CHURCH'S PROPER MISSION. The people, attentive to Christ and friendly to the sufferer, call the blind man, raise his hopes, encourage his approach. This conduct is exactly that of our Lord's faithful ministers and of all his true disciples. The Church cannot save, but its privilege and its duty is to point to him who can save. The vocation of the Church is to tell of Jesus, to point to Jesus, to lead to Jesus. This is the true ministry, at once humbling and ennobling; for whilst it presumes the spiritual powerlessness of man, it affords to human benevolence an abundant scope, and assimilates it to the pity of the Saviour's gracious heart.

V. AN ILLUSTRATION OF EARNESTNESS RESPONDING TO THE INVITATION OF CHRIST. How picturesquely does Mark tell us that this blind man, casting away his garment, "sprang up, and came to Christ"! A suggestion that he who hears the gospel should fling from him all his doubts, should abandon his evil companions and the sin that doth so easily beset him, should forsake his evil ways and thoughts, and so should draw near to Christ.

VI. THE CHARACTERISTIC MANNER IN WHICH CHRIST IMPARTED THE BLESSING SOUGHT. The dialogue between Jesus and Bartimæus was brief, and it was "to the point." Question, answer, and final assurance were all satisfactory. The point upon which stress is chiefly laid is the *faith* which makes whole. It is the one condition. When this is complied with, all things are possible; the blind see, the prayer is granted, the soul is saved.

VII. THE GRATEFUL RECOGNITION OF THE BOON CONFERRED IS A LESSON TO ALL WHO ARE BLESSED BY CHRIST. As Bartimæus followed Jesus in the way, doubtless to testify to the pity and the power of the Redeemer, to glorify his Deliverer, and to invite others to extol and praise him; so does it become all those whose eyes Christ has opened to witness to the Divine Healer, and to say fearlessly in the presence of all men, "He hath opened mine eyes;" "Whereas I was blind, now I see."

HOMILIES BY VARIOUS AUTHORS.

Vers. 1—12.—*Christ's statement of the Divine law of marriage.* It is well to note his locality at this time. He was approaching the centre of the Judæan party, out-lying members of which encountered him as he was entering Judæa from beyond Jordan. Nevertheless he no longer observes "counsels of prudence." He freely addresses the crowds that throng to his ministry, and confronts the attempts of his enemies to catch him in his words. This Divine abandonment is very noble and beautiful, and argues that he now clearly foresaw all that was to take place. There are two intentions in the reply of Jesus which it is necessary to distinguish, viz. that of defence, and that of teaching. His words are to be studied, therefore, as—

I. A MEASURE OF DEFENCE. That his questioners meant him mischief there can be no doubt. The word "tempting" is used for "trying," "proving," and that in an evil sense. 1. *What, then, was the danger that lay in such a question?* According to his reply they hoped: (1) To discredit him with the respectable classes, and to found a charge against him of overturning the social and religious institutions of the land. It is the reproach and shame of nearly all "heresies" in religion that they sooner or later attempt to abolish the safeguards of society, and the time-honoured customs of the social order. Marriage is a touchstone that betrays the inherent unrighteousness and impracticability of a large proportion of them. His enemies hoped on this point to array him against Moses. (2) To discredit him with the common people. It was a vexed question at the time in the rival schools of Hillel and Shammai, the latter being stricter, the former laxer, in their view of the lawfulness of divorce. Probably convinced of their own view of the case, they relied upon easily confuting his arguments, and thereby "showing him up" as a pretender and impostor. 2. *But in this twofold scheme they were defeated,* Jesus making his interrogators themselves the declarers of the Law which he accepted and simply interpreted. He appeared, therefore, as a defender and not an assailant of the Law. And then he showed how deep the basis of obligation really was, and how much less strict the "precept" of Moses was than it might have been, and the cause of this.

II. A PERMANENT DOCTRINE OF RIGHTEOUSNESS. The historical circumstances of the time when the precept was formulated were probably considered at greater length than could be represented in Mark's account, and the position justified that it was a compromise or provisional measure necessitated by "the hardness of heart" of the Jews, the drawing up of a formal document being a check upon hasty and passionate ruptures of the marriage tie. He thus proved that *moral obligation is deeper and more permanent than convention or external law*. He next considered marriage as a law of nature anterior to the social sanction, which does not therefore create the institution, but ought only to recognize and enforce it. To this end *he traces it to the original purpose of God in creation*, quoting Gen. i. 27; and strengthening the inference from this by the positive command of Gen. ii. 24, long anterior to the time of Moses. It is not for man to interfere with or modify an arrangement so manifestly Divine. *The only ground upon which marriage can be set aside is therefore that of one or other party to the marriage bond having already broken it by sinful action, and thus destroyed it as an actual thing.* The Law then simply steps in to defend the rights of the party who has been injured, setting that party free from further possibility of like injury. This transgression of the marriage bond which amounts to its annulment is not stated, but is clearly implied, viz. adultery. The Saviour thereby proves his teaching in harmony with the teaching of nature and previous revelation. But the gospel which is proclaimed in his Name does more than this. It seeks to fit man for the highest social and religious duties, by purifying and strengthening his moral being.—M.

Vers. 13—16.—*Jesus blessing the little children: a children's sermon.* One of the scenes in the life of the Saviour which illustrate most strongly and beautifully the genius of the gospel. The imagination loves to dwell upon it, and the heart is its best interpreter. There is, so to speak, a climax in the action.

I. LITTLE CHILDREN ARE ATTRACTED TO JESUS. There must have been something in the aspect, etc., of the Saviour which drew the little ones and their mothers to his side. Christianity differs from the systems of idolatry in presenting us with One whom we instinctively can love. A little girl, when asked why she thought Jesus must have smiled, said, "He must have smiled when he said, 'Suffer little children,' etc., else they would never have come!" A chief object of preaching and living the gospel is to exhibit this charm.

II. LITTLE CHILDREN ARE INVITED TO JESUS. How many people won't come to a place unless they think they are welcome, and therefore they expect an invitation. Now, when the disciples thought that their Master was too engrossed with high thoughts and important affairs to attend to the children, they took it upon themselves to send them away. This was not done through unkindness, but simply through a mistake. Christ corrected the mistake, and deliberately invited the little children. That proves—does it not?—in the strongest way that he intends them to come to him. But Jesus does more than invite.

III. LITTLE CHILDREN ARE CLAIMED BY JESUS. "For of such is the kingdom of heaven." That means that little children are very near to him already. They are really *in* his kingdom, and he is their King. He has a greater right, therefore, to their obedience and service and society, than father or mother, or brother or sister. When little children are good and loving they *are with* Jesus, and it is only when they do or think what is wrong that they go away from him. And all who come into his kingdom have to come in as little children, *i.e.* they are to be childlike—simple, loving, trustful, and obedient.

IV. LITTLE CHILDREN ARE BLESSED BY JESUS. He took them in his arms and embraced them. But he also put his hands on them, and gave them his Father's blessing. How great a thing did the Jews think a blessing was! Let us try and live so that we shall at last get the blessing Christ has in store for us. Do you love to be with Jesus? Do you do whatever he commands you? Then you are a subject of his kingdom, and a child of grace; and hereafter you will share his glory.—M.

Vers. 17—22.—*The great inquiry.* This seems a better title for the subject than "The Great Decision," as we have no reason to believe that the decision come to was a final one. But the reference to "eternal life" proves how momentous the occasion was to him who inquired. Such a time comes but seldom, yet it comes to every man, when he feels that everything else dwindles into insignificance in comparison with "life." As to this inquiry, notice—

I. How IT WAS MADE. 1. *Earnestly.* The manner of the man is vividly portrayed by St. Mark: "running, and kneeled to him." This spirit is a primary requisite. "*Seek first* the kingdom of God, and his righteousness." He seized the passing opportunity and despised the judgment of onlookers. 2. *Intelligently.* What he was seeking was definitely before his mind. His previous training had prepared him to think of the object he sought more or less correctly. He used the word "inherit," which implied something different from "have," or "possess" (Matthew). 3. *With real but defectively justified acknowledgment of Christ's character.* This vague instinct which he expressed in the title "Good," had to be grounded in some true apprehension of the nature and character of Jesus ere it could be accepted as satisfactory. How radical this misconception was appears as he answers the question regarding the commandments.

II. How IT WAS ANSWERED. 1. *With the needful correction to the question.* It is of the utmost importance that we clearly perceive what real "goodness" is, and to whom alone it can belong, ere we seek it. 2. *With a provisional test.* The commandments; perhaps those emphasized which bore most directly upon his position and circumstances. *Self-restraint* is a first requisite, and that is witnessed to by the Law. But he still stands outside the true conception of "goodness," for he answers from the conventional and not from the absolute and spiritual standpoint. "The Law is our schoolmaster to bring us to Christ," by showing us our imperfection and need of a Saviour. 3. *With a final test.* "One thing thou lackest: go, sell whatsoever thou hast," etc. Self-restraint being insufficient, *self-denial*, and that specially corresponding with his circumstances, is invited. This was the *crucial* test. It has to be varied according to the difference in individual tastes, ideals, circumstances, etc., of different people. 4. *By a look of love.* It was spontaneous, full of attraction, and, up to a certain degree, of approval; then of yearning sorrow and concern. Such questions and such a disposition can never be received by Christ with indifference.

III. IN WHAT IT RESULTED. "His countenance fell," etc. There was grief, disappointment, perhaps even a little resentment, and also inward shame. Not decision; rather indecision. Tested by highest test and found wanting. Drawn by tenderest love of the Son of God, yet unwilling to yield. The grieved heart may yet return: its sad disconsolateness is its most hopeful attribute.—M.

Vers. 23—27.—*Riches a spiritual drawback.* Valuable to the moral as to the scientific or artistic teacher to have a real instance—a study from the life. Yet it is not given to many to seize the salient points and analyze the character as Christ did. He did it, too, in a manner the most natural.

I. THE SAYING OF CHRIST. "How hardly shall they that have riches enter into the kingdom of God!" It is no proverb culled from the pages of the past, but evidently his own instinctive, penetrating "moral" from what they had just seen. It was self-evident to him "how hardly," *i.e.* with what difficulty, such a thing could take place. He knew by personal experience the price that was to be paid for the realization of that kingdom, and what its nature would be when realized; but he alone. As fruit of his own inward experience it was a distinct discovery in morals. The disciples, not so conversant with the inner nature of the kingdom, were amazed. It was the exact opposite of their own idea. They thought that it would be absolutely necessary to gain such disciples if the kingdom was ever to be realized. It was impossible for them to conceive of spiritual power apart from material means and influence. They could not get rid, moreover, of the dream that a political shape would sooner or later be assumed by this coming power. Their mistake was deeply rooted in the whole habit of thought of the ancient world. The well-to-do had not only the material advantage of their riches, but a certain reflected honour as enjoying the theocratic blessing upon the keeping of the commandments. And in the case of the ruler this moral excellence was not only an ancestral trait but a personal characteristic. The Greek who styled the rich and powerful of his nation οἱ ἀγαθοί, or καλοί, and the poor οἱ κακοί, was representative of his age; cf. the Latin *optimates*, the Saxon *good men* (opposed to *lewd people*, *base hinds*), the French *prudhommes*. And the modern mind has not yet got rid of the twist. There is a superficial gentleness of manners, refinement, and honour, identified, by long association, with the "better classes," that is easily mistaken for a deeper moral principle. Nor can we ignore the "minor moralities," the conventional proprieties and respectabilities which wealth generally brings in its train. It is only when the *emphasis* is laid on character that these are estimated at their proper worth. Therefore the necessity for—

II. The justification of the saying. It is done in a spirit of tender, condescending sympathy—"children." 1. *The general difficulty attending entrance into the kingdom is declared* (the clause, "for them that trust in riches," being probably not genuine). The reason for this difficulty is not, however, stated. It ought to have been remembered. "Taking up his cross" was the condition imposed upon every would-be "disciple." 2. *A figure of speech is employed in relation to the rich.* The tradition identifying the "needle's eye" with a certain gate of Jerusalem is hardly well enough supported to be reliable. It was probably but an impromptu hyperbole that flashed from the mind of Christ. But it would recall the teaching of the "strait gate." Κάμιλος, a rope, may, however, be the true reading. Everything that exaggerates and pampers "self" hinders from the better life. The disciples had learnt that lesson in part (ver. 28), but its absolute import and spiritual realization they were not to arrive at until their Master had gone away. Their astonishment is not, therefore, lessened, but rather increased, by the repeated statement; and they said, "*Then who can be saved?*" A question which seemed to imply, "If the rich cannot be saved without difficulty, the poor will have still less chance." The temptations of poverty were probably prominent in their minds. From the human point of view this would seem to be a just observation; therefore he qualified his statement, and under certain conditions declared—

III. The saying superseded. "*With men it is impossible, but not with God : for all things are possible with God.*" There is here a double hint, viz. as to the objective work which he himself was to do *for* men, and the spiritual aid which would be experienced *in* men by the advent of the Holy Ghost. The difficulty is wholly on the human side. Salvation is thus vindicated as a supernatural achievement—a Divine grace, and not a human virtue.—M.

Vers. 28—31.—*The hundredfold.* I. Is Christian self-sacrifice worth while? 1. *A question repeatedly asked*, by worldlings and by Christians themselves : by the former because they do not comprehend or perceive the things of God, and by the latter from an imperfect experience and an imperfectly matured spiritual consciousness. 2. *Reasonably enough.* The privation to which Christianity exposes men is sometimes extreme. They are called upon virtually or actually to renounce all things. Peter not to be accused of sordidness—of a desire to "make the best of both worlds." Life and the things of life are precious gifts with which we should not lightly or aimlessly part; and the neophyte in Christian life cannot be expected to have all his aims perfectly spiritual. Christianity is a means of raising men from the carnal to the spiritual, and it does so by gradually spiritualizing the desires and interests of the soul. It is an instinct of our being not to part with a real, tangible good unless in exchange for another of equal or higher value, although not necessarily estimated from a selfish or self-regarding point of view. 3. *It is only from the highest point of view and the most advanced experience that this question can be properly and adequately answered.* There is, therefore, a Divine fitness in Jesus, our Example, being the Answerer and Judge. Yet out of the most imperfect experience of the Divine life, if that experience be properly interpreted, the answer would still be satisfying and justifying.

II. The considerations by which this question is decided. 1. *The measure of recompense.* "A hundredfold :" an estimate not to be literally construed. It is intended to express "overwhelmingly more." "In the preceding verse the connective between the items is *or*; here it is *and*. There is great propriety in the exchange, for here the Saviour is giving, as it were, an *inventory of the Divine fulness of blessing*, so far as it is available for the most ample compensation of those who have suffered loss.

And there is, besides, in the spiritual sphere of things a kind of mutual involution of blessed relationships; the sum total of them all belongs to every true disciple" (Morison). 2. *The manner of it.* It is to be *correspondent to the things renounced*, although not necessarily similar in kind. *" With persecutions:"* an addition that seems strange, but is justified in the experience of the Christian; as that which is *lost* is *gain* (cf. Matt. v. 10; Phil. i. 29; 1 Pet. iii. 14), so that which is *endured* for Christ's sake is a new occasion and factor of blessedness. *Suited to the differing conditions of this life and that which is to come.* Here there is variety, objectiveness, material embodiment; there there is one grand reward, subjective, spiritual, viz. eternal life. *And the relative position of Christians will be very much altered from that which they occupy here.* The honour and blessedness conferred will depend, not upon accident of birth or fortune, but upon intrinsic worth and direct Divine appointment.—M.

Ver. 31.—*The kingdom of God a revolution of the world-order.* I. BECAUSE REWARD WILL BE ACCORDING TO CHARACTER AND WORK.
II. IT WILL NOT BE OF DESERT, BUT OF GRACE.
III. EVERY SAINT WILL RECEIVE WHAT IS ESSENTIAL TO HIS HAPPINESS, USEFULNESS, AND SPIRITUAL ADVANCEMENT.
IV. BUT THERE WILL BE DEGREES IN THE GLORY AND BLESSEDNESS OF THE REDEEMED. 1. *Reflecting the manifold glory of God.* 2. *Correcting and compensating the inequalities of time.* 3. *Stimulating to nobler attainment.*—M.

Vers. 32—34.—(Cf. ch. ix. 30—32.)—M.

Vers. 35—45.—(Cf. ch. ix. 33—37.)—M.

Ver. 45.—*The greatness of the Son of man.* I. HOW IT DISPLAYED ITSELF. In a quasi-concealment: reversal of order and method of worldly greatness. The great of this world exercise authority for the most part and generally to their own advantage, and the loss and degradation of others. This precedent is only mentioned that it may be condemned. The greatness of the Son of man showed itself in: 1. *Service.* Typically set forth in the washing of the disciples' feet (John xiii. 4). Realized: (1) In his position. Incarnate: born into the pain and shame of sinful humanity. In humble social circumstances; accustomed to labour and obedience to authority. (2) In his work. His whole life, in its example, teaching, and miracles, was a ministry. What men needed was help, and he rendered it. And that his doing so might not be regarded as accidental, he declares it as the purpose of his coming into the world. And in relation to God, in the demands of his Law, he was obedient, "fulfilling all righteousness." 2. *Sacrifice.* The culmination and seal of service. "To give his life" "indicates the *climax* of the service in which he was engaged (comp. Phil. ii. 6: obedient—obedient unto death on the cross). The term *ministering* expresses the spirit of the life of Christ. His sufferings and death illustrated and displayed the submission of his whole course; they shed the fullest light on the object of his life" (Lange).
II. WHAT IT WAS TO ACHIEVE. It was to be no barren spectacle, or merely personal glory, but was to exert a practical influence upon the condition of those amongst whom he came. The kind of work it had to do corresponded to the needs of man. It was for men the Son of man lived. And as they were in a state of wretchedness and danger, he undertook to save them. In respect of this purpose the death of Christ availed for: 1. *Redemption.* His life was given as the *ransom*. "It is the first distinct utterance, we may note, of the plan and method of his work. He had spoken before of 'saving' the lost (Matt. xviii. 11); now he declares that the work of 'salvation' was to be also one of 'redemption.' It could only be accomplished by the payment of a price, and that price was his own life" (Plumptre). The natural state of men is one of bondage to sin. A "ransom" is an equivalent for a man's life or service (cf. Exod. xxi. 30; Lev. xxv. 50; Prov. xiii. 8). This price our Saviour gave "instead of" ("for") men, as their Representative before God—in a certain sense as their Substitute (cf. Matt. xvii. 27; Heb. xii. 16; Rom. iii. 24; 1 Cor. vi. 20; 1 Pet. i. 19). 2. *The redemption of many.* "The expression 'many' is not intended to indicate an exclusive minority, or a smaller number as compared with *all*, for the latter expres-

sion occurs in Rom. v. 18; 1 Tim. ii. 4. The term is intended rather by way of antithesis to the *one* whose life was the ransom of the *many*" (Lange). Its efficacy was to be felt far beyond the personality in which it first took place. We are invited to take wide, comprehensive views of the work of Christ. And there is nothing in the language of Scripture to lead to the supposition that only some may be saved. That which avails for one will avail for all who choose to comply with the condition of salvation, viz. faith in the Lord Jesus Christ's death as an atoning sacrifice for sin. The sinlessness and perfect obedience of Christ are his qualification for this work.

III. IN WHAT WAY IT SHOULD BE ACKNOWLEDGED. The verse commences with "for"—a word connecting it with the previous verses, to which it is appended as a *reason* for what is there enjoined. Our duty, therefore, with respect to the service and sacrifice he has rendered is: 1. *To accept them for ourselves.* By believing in the redemptive work of Christ we honour him, and the Father by whom he was sent. 2. *To imitate his spirit.* His kingdom is based upon service, and its dignities and authorities are the result of the spontaneous affection thereby secured. Service and self-humiliation are not only means toward the attainment of future greatness; they are that greatness already. Offices in the Church are not thereby abolished; they are only interpreted as functions of love: all dignity and authority otherwise derived are discountenanced, and convicted as usurpations. 3. *To declare his work amongst men.* In so doing we shall truly glorify him, and extend his kingdom to the ends of the earth.—M.

Vers. 46—52.—*Blind Bartimæus.* I. THE BEHAVIOUR OF THOSE WHO ARE IN EARNEST ABOUT BEING SAVED. They will: 1. *Seize every opportunity that presents itself.* 2. *Make the most of it,* by (1) putting all their knowledge to the proof, and (2) exerting all their powers to attract attention and help. 3. *Not be easily discouraged.* 4. *Hasten to do what Jesus commands.*

II. THE SPIRIT THAT OUGHT TO BE SHOWN BY CHRIST'S SERVANTS TOWARDS THOSE SEEKING SALVATION. Two standards of conduct observed by them, viz. the dignity and glory of their Master, and the good of men. The mistake has been in overemphasizing the one or the other of these, or in divorcing them. They are really but the two sides of one thing. The glory of Christ is that of a Saviour, *i.e.* in saving from misery and sin. 1. *Christ corrects what is faulty in their attitude.* 2. *Employs them to further his purpose of mercy.* 3. *Infuses his own spirit of gentleness and love.* "Be of good cheer: rise, he calleth thee," is the expression of the spirit of the gospel as it ought to be proclaimed to the world.

III. CHRIST PROVING HIMSELF THE SAVIOUR OF MEN. 1. *By his sympathy for distress.* He heard the cry of the beggar notwithstanding the tumult, and the thoughts which agitated his mind. It was natural for him to postpone everything to attend to such a cry. 2. *By inspiring others with his own spirit, and employing them to further his purpose.* 3. *By calling forth and exercising the principle of faith in the subjects of his mercy.* 4. *By freely and completely delivering from distress, pain, and sin.*—M.

Ver. 52.—"*Saving faith.*" I. NOT ONE OF SEVERAL KINDS OF FAITH, BUT SIMPLY FAITH PROPERLY DIRECTED, AND PRACTICALLY TAKING ADVANTAGE OF CHRIST'S POWER. Much confusion on this subject. Theologians have spoken of different sorts of faith, as speculative, practical, historical, realizing, and saving. There is but one faith, a faculty of the soul. What is needed is not the faculty, which already exists, but the proper direction or destination of it. That is a *true faith* by which I see and appropriate the truth; that a *saving faith* by which salvation is seen and received.

II. FAITH DOES NOT SAVE THROUGH ITS OWN VIRTUE OR POWER, BUT BY BRINGING THE SOUL INTO CONTACT WITH THE VIRTUE AND POWER—THE SALVATION OF CHRIST. It is not the *cause* of salvation, but the *condition.* The only Saviour is Christ, but he saves us through our having faith towards him. By our having faith towards Christ what is his becomes ours; we enter into union and fellowship with him. His life, righteousness, spirit, become ours; and we are identified with him in his sacrifice for sin.

III. SO ALSO OUR FAITH IS THE MEASURE OF THE SAVING GRACE WE RECEIVE. St. Matthew puts it thus: "According to your faith be it unto you." Bartimæus's faith was strong and practical, and it saved him, by uniting him to the power and holiness of Christ. A weak faith will ever entail spiritual weakness. To be "made whole" we must believe with our whole heart.—M.

Vers. 17—21.—*The excellences of the young ruler.* Too often religious teachers have attempted to classify all who are mentioned in the Bible as being either definitely good or utterly bad. If the latter exhibit any excellency it is depreciated, or explained away; and if the former have faults, they are carefully concealed. But the Bible gives no such definite decision respecting them. It mentions the faults of the saints, and exhibits the excellences of those whose character and destiny are left doubtful. Here, for example, one is mentioned who was not what he ought to have been, of whom it is boldly said, "Jesus beholding him loved him." The feeling with which our Lord regarded him was *not the result of regard for his social position,* which led to a discreet hiding of his faults. Amongst us too often one of dubious character, because he has wealth or brilliant prospects, is admitted to circles from which he ought to be excluded; and a rich man is not told of his sins as a poorer man would be, so that it is the more hard for him to enter into the kingdom. But with our Lord esteem was won not by what a man had, but by what he was. Nor was our Lord influenced by *the young man's religious knowledge,* for he made small account of theological lore, such as was possessed by lawyers and Pharisees. And as knowledge would not win his love, neither did ignorance and error prevent it. There was evidently much in this young ruler that was commendable and lovable, all of which found its source in God; for even those who are not decided followers of Christ have in them gleams of heavenly light, and must beware of quenching the Spirit.

I. THE YOUNG RULER WAS GENUINE AND SIMPLE. Christ rebuked nothing so severely as unreality. He exposed the Pharisees mercilessly, because they pretended to be what they were not. He declared that if a man's eye was "single" his whole body would be full of light; that he who was of the truth (who was a true man) would hear his voice. Such was this man. He expressed his real want. He felt that he had obeyed the commandments, and frankly said so; and when told to go and sell all that he had, he made no fallacious promise to do so. We should cultivate the grace of truthfulness in all the relations of life. If we are engaged in a common occupation, we should be true enough not to be ashamed of it; if in Church relationships, we should never ignore them; if we have done a wrong, we should candidly confess it either to God or man. In proportion as we are true we are nearer to the kingdom of truth.

II. HE WAS SINGULARLY COURTEOUS. He kneeled before the peasant Teacher of Galilee, and addressed him reverently. Courtesy is a small thing if it be identical with outward mannerism, which observes a suitable deportment, and carefully discriminates between those in different social ranks. But true courtesy is consideration for others, thoughtfulness for their feelings, respect for their age and experience and character; and this was exhibited by the young ruler whom Jesus loved. There was no rudeness like that of the Sadducees and Herodians, nor any outburst of hot temper at the sacrifice demanded of him.

III. HE WAS OF IRREPROACHABLE LIFE. So far, at least, as human judgment could determine. A young man whose passions had not misled him; rich enough to indulge evil propensity, yet outwardly pure and without reproach. The morality of the noblest does not win heaven, but it is good in itself and in its source. The idea that a profligate is the happier after his conversion because of his sinful experience, is utterly false. His experience is more remarkable, but he is not so blessed, nor so strong for Christian service; for if evil thoughts stain the mind, and sinful habits are indulged, these have their effects.

IV. HE WAS NOT SELF-SATISFIED. Self-satisfaction is one of the greatest preventives of good: *e.g.* the lad who can do without his father's counsel; the girl who scorns her mother's advice; the children who drift away from Sunday schools, to live without God and without hope in the world. This is most perilous in spiritual things. No condemnation is more severe than that of the Church which says, "I have need of nothing;" no welcome is more loving than that given by our Lord to the children, who could give him nothing but love, or to the young ruler who wistfully asked, "What lack I yet?" "He fills the hungry with good things, but the rich he sends empty away." If your heart is hungry for the love of God, our heavenly Father is pleased, just as an earthly father is when he knows his child wants him. If your son had run away and been hidden for years, and at last was found abroad, what would you wish to hear? Not that he was doing well, and had lost all care for you; but that, although he had everything to make him happy, he was sad because he wished to see his father, and obtain the assurance of his forgiveness.

V. HE CAME TO CHRIST WITH AN EARNEST QUESTION. What shall I do, not to gain wealth or fame, but eternal life? In the New Testament life is not spoken of as equivalent to existence, but it means life coupled with conditions which make it blessed, and therefore desirable. Life and holiness are correlatives, as are death and sin. So a man may be dead in part, and alive in part. A person struck with paralysis may lie for months in a living death, unable to reason, to speak, or to move a limb. Sin does that to our moral being. It paralyzes sensitiveness to God's presence, the power of speaking to him with naturalness and the capacity for hearing his voice. It is an endless existence, with the full enjoyment of these attributes (the exercise of which constitute the joys of heaven), which is involved in the phrase "eternal life."

VI. HE BROUGHT HIS EARNEST QUESTION TO THE LORD JESUS. It was a great thing for a man in his position to do. He faced the scorn of his friends when he ran eagerly to Christ and humbly knelt before him, beseeching him to teach and guide him. "And Jesus beholding him loved him," as he loves all who in this spirit fall at his feet.—A. R.

Ver. 21.—"*One thing thou lackest.*" This incident occurred on a journey to Jerusalem, which our Lord undertook between the Feast of Dedication, at which the Jews sought to stone him, and the Passover, during which he was crucified. Hostility, therefore, was both before him and behind him, but his serenity was not ruffled, nor his willingness to bless impaired. There was never in him a sign of *the indiscriminate judgment* which leads us to condemn a whole nation or sect as being outside the bounds of Christian charity. He was, and still is, gracious to one seeker, even though he dwells among the heathen; and hears any prayer, though it rises from a godless home. We notice here also our Lord's freedom from the *pandering to popular passion*, which has often been the snare of statecraft, and sometimes of the Christian Church. We naturally bend before an adverse current of opinion, and count it good policy to withhold the advocacy of our opinions for a season. But here was a crisis in Christ's ministry which would lead to his reception or rejection, when the decision of each one would make a weight in the scale of popular judgment. Judicious hedging just then might avert hatred or win a convert. Here was a ruler of the synagogue—a man of wealth, position, and good repute—who was willing to become a disciple; but he was met with words of discouragement, and the great Teacher put his claims before him in the strongest form. The fact is, that he thought more of the suppliant than of himself. He would rather bring him to deep repentance than have his showy following. With all his estimable qualities, the young ruler had spiritual deficiencies, which were seen by the Searcher of hearts, and revealed to himself by the test applied to him. What were these?

I. HE WAS MISTAKEN AS TO THE NATURE OF "GOODNESS." "Good Master, what good thing shall I do?" asked he. Christ at once put him in the way of discovering his mistake by answering, "Why callest thou me good?" etc. He did not decline the appellation, but repelled it when used in this superficial sense. He wanted him to weigh his words, to know what they implied, to say exactly what he meant; and this he requires of us. He reminded him that God was the Source of all goodness, because he would not have him regard any good act or good person as isolated or independent, but in connection with the God of goodness. He was himself "good;" but why? Because he was one with God. The young man might do a "good thing;" but how? Not as an isolated act, but by loving God supremely, and living in him. He enumerated the commandments as declarations of the will and character of the good One, which could only be obeyed in fulness when supreme love to God was the master passion of the soul; the duties to his fellows being mentioned because these constituted the easiest test of obedience.

II. HIS GREAT DEFICIENCY WAS AN ABSENCE OF COMPLETE SELF-SURRENDER. When told to sell all that he had, this was not the special "good thing" which would gain eternal life; but the command was given because the attempt to obey it would reveal the fact that he did not love the Lord with all his heart and soul and strength. This is the one important thing so often lacking, short of which so many halt, but which is essential to the righting of life. If we set down a series of noughts we may say they only want one figure to make them millions; but that one figure is all-important. So is it with "the one thing" lacking to many a moral life, namely, the consecration to God, of which prayer is the natural expression.

III. HE BROKE DOWN UNDER THE TEST APPLIED. The command, "Sell whatsoever thou hast," was to be obeyed literally by him, but not by all. Christ came in contact with other rich men, and did not call upon them to do this. But it was the best thing to teach this man the special lesson he needed. The test our Lord applies to those who come to him varies greatly, but in some form it comes to all such. It may appear to be so *trifling* a thing as the giving up of an amusement or pursuit, or so *peculiar* a thing that no one has previously been asked to do it. But it is the test of character to that one, and the trifle is fraught with future destiny. That which is not a source of peril to some may be disastrous to others. A blessing in some circumstances may prove a curse in others. The lighted candle, which is useful in the home, may be a destroyer in a mine. Anything which seems a source of danger must be abjured for Christ's sake. The young ruler did not make the required sacrifice when it was called for. He went away sad; and if he went away for ever, it was to far deeper sadness, for he left the Saviour of the world—the King of heaven. Dante says that in his journey through hell he saw him "who with ignoble spirit made the great refusal." But was the refusal final? We hesitate to believe it. We hope that this inquirer, who was so sincere, earnest, and humble, only went away to consider the question, not in the excitement of the moment, but alone, on his knees, and that then and there he gave himself up, to be Christ's consecrated servant for evermore.—A. R.

Vers. 35—45.—*The request of the sons of Zebedee.* As we read the history of our Lord's dealings with his disciples, we are amazed at his unfaltering patience. They had preconceived theories about his kingdom which, in spite of his teaching, they held fast till after his death and resurrection. They constantly expected him to assume temporal power. Why he delayed they did not know; the reason for his present obscurity they could not conceive; but to all his allusions to suffering they gave, and were resolved to give, a figurative interpretation. With all this persistent misconception our Lord was patient. In this he has left us an example of the patience we should cherish towards those who, as we think, misunderstand the truth. James and John, the sons of Zebedee, were two of the favoured triumvirate, and their mother, Salome, was a near relation of the Virgin Mary. It was she who expressed the request of her sons, first asking for an unconditional promise—such as a Herod might give, but our Lord never. The Old Testament counterpart of this scene is the coming of Rebekah, with her son Jacob, to win the blessing of the firstborn.

I. THE REQUEST OF THE DISCIPLES. 1. *It was the offspring of ignorance.* They little knew what it would be to stand on the right hand and on the left of their Lord in the day when the word would be fulfilled, "I, if I be lifted up, will draw all men unto me." Well might he say, "Ye know not what ye ask." We often set our desires on some object which is vain or wrong. "We know not what we should pray for as we ought;" and sometimes we learn by a bitter experience that it is best to put ourselves trustfully in God's hands. Lot found it so. Of the Israelites, too, it is said, "God gave them their request, but sent leanness into their soul." 2. *It was the dictate of ambition.* Ambition is a wholesome stimulus, if only it is free from selfishness. A teacher can do little with a child who is always satisfied with the lowest position in the class. If your ambition be a lawful one it will not allow you to shirk difficulties, or to get over an obstacle by a doubtful expedient, but it will lead you to a patient and faithful doing of what your hand finds to do. You will go higher, as you faithfully fulfil the duties of the lower sphere. Ask yourself whether the object you are aiming at is worthy of a Christian man; whether the time spent in its pursuit could be better employed; whether God or self is supreme in the motives which are prompting effort, etc. Ambition can be and ought to be tested. Some people are like precious stones, glittering, but non-productive; others are like the plainer millstones, which, by steadfast work, minister food to the hungry and wealth to the nation. 3. *It was the outcome of selfishness.* One of the best tests we have of the lawfulness of ambition is this question— How does it affect my feelings towards others? There is reason to fear that the idea of these disciples was that the chief places in the kingdom should be allotted to them, regardless of the claims of their brethren. No wonder, then, that they were rebuked by their Lord, and that when the ten heard it they had great indignation. Self-seeking ever tends to separate friends, and to arouse discord in the Christian Church. Selfishness is the root of the indolence that dishonours the disciples of Christ; it is the cause of civil dissensions; it is the spring of the bloody wars that desolate the world; and when it asserts itself in sectarianism it checks the advance of Christ's kingdom, and brings upon the Church paralysis and death. Against it Christ Jesus declared ruthless war. He declared that men must deny themselves if they would follow him; he taught us to love our enemies, and still more our neighbours, and said that if a man would be really great, he must minister to others for his sake.

II. THE REPLY OF OUR LORD. He pointed out the distinction between real greatness and seeming greatness, and declared that dignity in his kingdom was bestowed according to a certain law—the law of moral fitness. A similar law asserts itself everywhere in God's economy. Each plant and animal have their own habitat, and for their well-being we are compelled to study those conditions which the Creator designed for them. The disciples supposed that honour was at the arbitrary disposal of the Lord on the ground of personal favour. It was so with the positions held under the Roman government. The favour of an emperor might appoint a Pontius Pilate Procurator of Judæa, in complete disregard of character and suitability. It was not to be so in Christ's Church, whether on earth or in heaven. There would be distinctions of rank and honour, but they would be given by God to those worthy of dignity, and fit for it. In the kingdom of righteousness nothing would be arbitrary, or dependent upon caprice. To some extent this is so in the attainment of knowledge. Knowledge cannot be given by a teacher because a pupil is a favourite, or because a pupil wishes to be first among competitors; but it is the reward of individual work and consequent fitness. And greatness in heaven will not consist in so many pleasures or dignities, but in the enjoyment of so much life, in the developments of power and in the possibilities of service. These, then, are some of the principles laid down in our Lord's reply : 1. *Prepared places are for prepared people.* (Ver. 40.) 2. *Humble ministry is the source of highest exaltation.* (Vers. 43, 44.) 3. *Christ's mission is the pattern of Christian service.* (Ver. 45.)—A. R.

Vers. 46—52.—*Blind Bartimæus: the publicity of Christ's miracles.* Our Lord stood face to face with men. He said with truth, "I spake openly to the world, and in secret have I said nothing." His life was spent in the glare of publicity. His miracles were not performed among chosen witnesses, who might be interested in the propagation of what was false; nor in the secrecy of some convent or retreat. They were wrought on the mountain-side, in full view of five thousand men, besides women and children; in a synagogue full of worshippers hostile to his claims; or on a public road, crowded with pilgrims going to the Passover. This not only strengthened the evidence of the supernatural, but it was a sign that the blessings signified by such wonders were not intended for a class but for a race. Therefore we must beware lest we, by act or word, should be saying to any earnest seeker, what the crowd said to Bartimæus, "Hold thy peace!" By our coldness we may tacitly rebuke enthusiasm, and by our inconsistencies we may destroy the desires of the contrite. Christ can save us from this. He can by a word transform us, as he transformed that crowd, so that those who had just been saying, "Hold thy peace," became ready to say, "Be of good comfort, rise; he calleth thee." Subject—*In this miracle we have reminders of some characteristics of our Lord.*

I. THE POWER OF JESUS. Its exemplification outside Jericho was appropriate both to the beauty of the city and to its memories. Jericho was an oasis in the desert. There palms flourished and roses grew. Whether approaching it from the robber-haunted road from Jerusalem, or from the Dead Sea valley, it was significant of the Paradise Christ came to restore, which would be beautiful with the flowers of his grace and fragrant with the sweetness of his love. And here Joshua, the Jesus of the Old Testament, had proved the power that was his because the Lord was with him. The angel of the covenant which appeared to him was a precursor of the mighty Conqueror who came now.   As the giant walls of the city had fallen by the simplest means, so now the darkness was conquered by light through a single word.   1. *This power is manifest if you consider the condition of the sufferer.*   Blindness then was common, unalleviated, incurable.   No wonder that it was used as an emblem of insensibility to spiritual facts and things.   There is a sphere of thought, hope, and desire which many never know.   Intelligent and active, they ask, "Are we blind also?" and the Lord says, "Because being blind you say, We see, therefore your sin remaineth."   Because there is no sense of want there is no cry for a blessing, and because there is no such cry the light is not given. "The god of this world hath blinded the minds of them which believe not."   Tests may be applied to the spiritual condition as to the physical malady which represents it.   An oculist is not satisfied with a casual question; he patiently and variously tests the organ, by presenting objects and asking respecting one after another, "Can you see this?"   So we may test ourselves by seeing what sin is, and what God is to us.   2. *This power appears greater as you contrast it with the weakness of men.*   Like those in the crowd, we can see the Lord and hear his voice, and as far as sympathy and prayer go may lead others to him.   But after all the main issue rests between each man and Christ.   If there is no spiritual contact he is left in darkness.   Sometimes the most unlikely are chosen.   A publican like Zacchæus is visited in a city of priests, and a blind beggar on the road is invited to join the festal procession.   3. *This power appears in the exercise of its Divine freedom.*   Bartimæus was not dealt with as were those of whom he had heard.   The man born blind had been told to wash in the pool of Siloam, and he of Bethsaida was led out of the town uncured.   Yet no one would question the reality of the change in the other.   Each could say, "Whereas I was blind, now I see." Let us not expect the same experiences, but only the same effects of Divine contact with Christ.   He is willing to lead us into light, but each one of us in his own way.

II. The pity of Jesus.   Describe the pitiable condition of Bartimæus.   It is sad enough for a rich man to be blind, but it is a terrible aggravation of the privation when he who endures it has to beg his daily bread.   Nor did Bartimæus know, as we do, God's love in Christ.   He had not the assurance that "all things work together for good." He had not seen the cross which sanctifies sadness to each believer.   In his darkness he cried to the Light of the world, and not in vain.   The pity of the Lord always surpassed infinitely that of those around him.   The disciples rebuked the children, but Jesus said, "Suffer them to come."   Simon the Pharisee condemned the sinful woman, but Jesus let her bathe his feet with her tears.   Judas blamed the waste of the ointment, but the Lord said, "She hath wrought a good work on me."   The crowd said, "Hold thy peace," but the Lord said, "What wilt thou that I should do unto thee?"

III. The presence of Jesus.   A crisis had come in the life of Bartimæus, when a single resolve would make all the difference to his future.   Jesus was "passing," and therefore was within reach; but he was "passing by," and therefore would soon be beyond reach.   Such crises appear unexpected to us; but he who knows the heart sees that they are not really so.   Bartimæus had heard of the words and works of Jesus before this, and, shut up to his own thoughts, he had pondered them in the dark; so he was ready now to salute Jesus as "the Son of David."   Similar preparation has been going on in your heart.   A trouble has solemnized your thoughts; a tender touch at home has aroused new sensibility; a word has startled you to consideration; and now you are nearer Christ than before.   "Jesus is passing by."   Unseen, as by Bartimæus, yet able to hear the believing prayer for mercy.   See to it that the world's "Hold thy peace!" does not stifle the cry for help.—A. R.

Vers. 1—12.—*Divorce.*   Again with low motives, "tempting him," the Pharisees propound a question as to whether it was "lawful for a man to put away his wife." Opinions were divided, and the Teacher was in danger of offending one or other party by his reply.   This was the trap "to involve him with the adulterous tetrarch, in whose territory he was."   But he wisely referred them to Moses, and their thought, which was for evil, he turned to good; for he took occasion by it to show the grounds of Moses' "commandment" to have been to their condemnation, their "hardness of heart;" and he further took occasion to lay down for all Christian times, for the blessedness of the Christian home and for the preservation of Christian morals, the true, the wise, the beneficial law of marriage, founded upon the conditions of the original creation; and he defined with authority and precision what constituted "adultery." These words remained to condemn the disobedient, and will remain to "judge him in the last day." The indissoluble bond of the marriage relation Jesus here affirms, and in the old words, spoken at "the beginning," "the twain shall become one flesh." To the propriety, the goodness, the blessedness of this law many Christian centuries bear their unequivocal testimony. The purest institution and the best, so hallowed, so beneficent, promoting in the highest degree individual happiness, the peace and sanctity of family life, the purity of public morals; preserving national health, stability, and greatness; guarding against wild lust, and a long train of envy, jealousy, revenge, and other passionate crimes; preserving the honour and dignity of women, the love and careful training of children; imposing responsibilities, but cherishing virtue and peace and joy. The family life is the symbol of the heavenly community; the marriage bond the type of the Redeemer's relation to his people, who are "the bride, the wife of the Lamb." It is God's ordination, and is very sacred; nor may it be set aside, but "for the kingdom of heaven's sake;" nor may its bond be broken, but for the one cause of fornication, from which it is the most efficient guard. Its rites were honoured by Jesus, and its "holy estate adorned and beautified with his presence and first miracle." The wisest legislation tends to the conservation of the family, whose multiplied relations, whose sweet fellowship, whose united interest, and whose common possessions give rise to the lofty idea of the *home*. Conjugal, parental, filial, fraternal affection are cherished. Obedience on the one hand, care and providence on the other; discipline and wise authority; the sense of dependence arising from want; responsibility arising from the power to meet that want; common interests and common aims, go to make each home a miniature kingdom. Teaching to those in authority the beneficence of rule, and to those under authority the lessons of submission, the home lays the foundation for stable national life; while mutual interests and obligations teach all to respect the rights and just claims of the entire community; whilst each learns his responsibility to the whole, and his deep interest in the general welfare. The nation that honours the home and the sanctities of family life is honoured of God. The Christian teaching, reverting to the condition of things as it was "from the beginning of the creation," shows how truly it is in harmony with natural law, which is the expression of the Divine will.—G.

Vers. 13—16.—*Little children.* Parental anxiety led thoughtful women to bring "unto him little children, that he should touch them," according to a custom which has its approval in the hearts of all races and all times, of presenting young children to persons of sanctity and age that they may invoke a blessing upon their young life. Such are brought to Jesus, "that he should lay his hands on them and pray." Touched, perchance, by a remembrance of the humiliating lessons which the presence of a child must now have suggested, "the disciples rebuked them." Why obtrude children on the attention of One who is so competent to deal with adult wisdom? But he who came to correct error and false views, who had redeemed and established the essential marriage laws, now raises child-life to its rightful place. "Moved with indignation" at the indiscretion of the disciples, he said, "Suffer the little children to come unto me; forbid them not: for of such is the kingdom of God"—words which (1) are inscribed as on a banner of defence, that has floated from that hour over the heads of "little children;" words which (2) have been an admonitory corrective of personal vanity and assumption; (3) have expounded the spirit of the heavenly kingdom; (4) have expressed the qualification needed by all who would enter within its gates; (5) have been seized upon as affording a justification for the admission of children into the visible community of the Church by the sacrament of baptism; and (6) have, especially in these later days, become the stimulus to diligent endeavour to bring the young under religious training and to give them the benefits of religious instruction. By so much did the Master's words of truth rebut the disciples' error, and found upon it a teaching of unlimited benefit. Thus did Christ pay his tribute to the preciousness of life, even in its infancy and imperfectness, and throw the shield of his protection around it. Thus did he compel the attention and effort of his Church in all ages to be paid to young life, knowing its susceptibility and the important bearing of its right treatment on the general condition of human society. "Forbid them not" transforms itself into a command to the heart of the Church, ever attentive to catch the

Lord's will, to remove every hindrance from the way of a child's participation in spiritual benefits. And "suffer them to come unto me" becomes an equally authoritative command to bring them unto him; to place them in close alliance with him, and, if with him, then with his kingdom. For if he, the Head of the house, receive them, they of the household may not reject them; and if he take them up in his arms, surely they may come within the embrace of his Church. If they lie in his bosom at the head of the table, they may not be denied a place in the house, or be denied a portion of its bread or a measure of its care; while their purity, helplessness, trustful dependence, and tractableness form the typical example of that spirit which he desires shall characterize all the subjects of his kingdom, all the members of his household, in every age.—G.

Vers. 17—22.—*The rich young ruler.* Never did a more becoming question escape from human lips than when "there ran one"—"a certain ruler"—"to him," and, kneeling at his feet, "asked him, Good Master, what [what good thing] shall I do that I may inherit eternal life?" With characteristic calmness Jesus drew him away from the thought of his ability to do any "good thing," and from his question concerning that which is good. Only the good can do good things, and "none is good save One, even God." Therefore thou art not good; therefore thou canst not do *any*—that is, every —good thing. But there is a way unto life, even that of the commandments. "If," therefore, "thou wouldest enter into life, keep the commandments." They lead unto eternal life. Along that path, he replied, I have ever walked. "All these things have I observed from my youth." And this was no vain boast, for "Jesus looking upon him loved him." But the thought of doing good things, and of establishing a claim to eternal life as to an inheritance, still fills the young ruler's thoughts, and the bold demand is pressed to the utmost—"What lack I yet?" Alas! "one thing thou"—even thou—"lackest." Then, hesitatingly, knowing so well "what was in man," Jesus offers to this loved one the highest attainment: "If thou wouldest be perfect," if thou wouldest lack nothing— *If!*—ah, *if!* Jesus was neither unkind nor severe in his demand. The young man pressed him for a reply, and the prize was within his reach. Whether he could pay the price, whether he really was prepared to do *any* good thing, as the "*what* good thing" implied, whether he valued the eternal life so highly as his words seemed to indicate, must be proved. "Go, sell whatsoever thou hast, and give to the poor, and thou shalt have treasure in heaven: and come, follow me." Alas! "his countenance fell, . . . and he went away sorrowful: for he was one that had great possessions." He was not the only sorrowful one. A lowering cloud must have passed over the brow of the Rabbi himself. It is not out of place to inquire—What did Jesus offer him for his riches; and what did he lose by retaining them? The offer embraced—

I. PERFECTNESS OF CHARACTER—that which can be gained only by great sacrifice and effort, by withdrawment from the world, by such apprehension of the spiritual as to lead to the surrender of the material; that faith in God which lifts the trusting heart from its confidence in the "possessions" which the eye can see and the hands handle, and which promise "much goods" for "many years," to that "treasure in heaven" which fadeth not. For imperfect man there is a perfectness, to which he shall be led if he forsake all and follow Jesus. From that path the young ruler at this time turns away, perhaps to reflect, to repent, to turn again to the Master who was patient, and finally, after earnest struggles, to join the company of those who made the sacrifice of all things for the kingdom of heaven's sake. Again be it said that he who forsakes all for Christ's "sake and the gospel's" sake enters upon a path that leads to perfection.

II. A second part of the offer made to the young man was "TREASURE IN HEAVEN"— "in the world to come eternal life." It was this the young man desired; but he knew not that the heart could find its "treasure in heaven" only by consenting to have it there alone. He who would really have "eternal life" must be content to be freed from anything and everything that withdraws the heart from that life. The living unto this present world does so withdraw the heart. Therefore the earthly possessions must be sacrificed. That many rich men enter, though "hardly," into the kingdom of heaven, and retain their place therein, is a sign of the prevalence of Christ's grace. Yet these cease to "trust in riches," or the "deceitfulness of riches" would choke in them the seeds of eternal life. For the present, at least, the rich, eager, honoured young ruler cannot say his whole treasure is in heaven.

III. But Jesus further offered him A PLACE AMONGST THE MOST HONOURED BAND OF MEN THE WORLD HAS KNOWN, AND A SHARE IN THE MOST HONOURABLE WORK. "Come, follow me." Who can tell what might have been the effect of his sacrifice? His example might have saved Judas. He might have enriched the world with a fifth Gospel. He might have drawn many of the rulers to believe. But for the time he lost his chance, and the world is the worse for his decision, as it is the worse for every error of men. What did he gain? His "great possessions." But only for a time—it may have been a very brief time. And, when enjoying the fruits of his wealth, would the thought ever spring unbidden to his mind, "I purchased this with the price of eternal life; for this I gave up the hope of being perfect; this I chose rather than follow the 'good Master'"? He who forsakes all for Christ finds all in Christ; but he who has any possession which he would not forego, even for eternal life, loses both the life and the possession. Well may the hope be cherished that this one on whom the loving look, if not the loving kiss, of Christ rested, turned again, and laid all at his feet, yea, "and his own life also," or joined those who "were possessors of lands or houses," and who "sold them, and brought the prices of the things that were sold, and laid them at the apostles' feet." Gently did Jesus thus teach the rich ruler that with all his wealth he lacked at least "one thing." He that would have eternal life as an inheritance must establish his claim, and that claim must be faultless. One flaw is sufficient to invalidate that claim. Further, the Lord taught that eternal life is ours, not by this title of inheritance, but is a gift of God.—G.

Vers. 23—31.—*The entry of the rich into the kingdom of heaven.* So impressive a scene as that which had just been witnessed needed some explanation, and was well suited to be the basis of important teaching. With much meaning, therefore, "Jesus looked round about," and, arresting the attention of his disciples, taught them further concerning the entry of the rich into the kingdom of God.

I. IT IS DIFFICULT. It is difficult for the rich to enter the kingdom! But that difficulty lies, not as the disciples thought, simply in the possession of riches, but in the proneness of men to love riches. And how short is the step from having riches to loving them! Only by exertion, only by the painfulness of self-denial, by giving up trust in riches and fondness for them, can the rich enter the kingdom of heaven. How hard is this to them who have abundance! How easy it seems to them who possess little! So difficult did this appear to him who knew all men, that the parabolic illustration has no extravagance, though to the disciples it shut out all hope, and rightly so from their point of view, as was confirmed by the Master's word, made the more impressive by his tender look—"With men it is impossible." Happily, however, there are springs of hope for men other than those which rise from among themselves. "The things which are impossible with men are possible with God." So it comes to pass that, concerning the entry of rich men into the kingdom of heaven, it may be proclaimed—

II. IT IS POSSIBLE. Yes, it is "possible with God," without whom, indeed, nothing is possible. The human inability to effect salvation stands in direct contrast to the efficiency of Divine grace. Many things hinder the salvation of men; but few have more power than "the deceitfulness of riches," which lure to self-security and self-indulgence, which lead men to think they are better than other men, and are not in the same danger or need. The voice of riches is a syren voice; the hold of riches on the heart is firm as a death-grip. Riches prevent the lowliness, the childlike feeling of utter nothingness, of trustful timidity, of tractable weakness. They inspire a false sense of strength, and security, and abundance, and superiority. Often are they the devil's counters with which he buys men's souls. But "with God" the mighty may be made to feel themselves feeble, the wealthy to be truly poor. Great is the trust reposed; great the difficulty of fidelity. But "with God" even this may be done. And in our days, as has been happily in all the days of Christ's Church, men have learned to forsake all—even when that all was much—to follow Christ in lowly humility, in the poverty of self-abasement. Let the poor know that if they lack the hindrance which riches throw in the way, they also need the help of God; if they will rise and accept it, that help shall be freely given. And let the rich know that help awaits them; if they will stoop lowly and ask, it shall not be withheld from them. Then shall "the brother of low degree glory in his high estate: and the rich in that he is made low." All of us are poor before God; all by him, and by him alone, may be made rich. In proportion as the rich become poor shall they be truly enriched; and it shall be proved that they who press through difficulties hard as the passing of a camel through a needle's eye, are not left unrequited. Of the entry of the rich into the kingdom of heaven it may further be said—

III. IT IS REWARDED. How gently did the Lord of all warn his disciples of days of poverty and loss which were coming upon them apace, when both voluntarily, in the fulness of their love, they would sell "their possessions and goods, and part them to all according as any had need," and when with ruthless hands all would be torn from them; when "houses" and "lands" would be confiscated; when from the fellowship of brethren and sisters, of mother and father, and even from their own children, they would be separated "for the gospel's sake"! But how graciously did he assure them of the "hundredfold" which should be repaid them "now in this time," though "with persecutions;" and the great reward which should be theirs in the hereafter—"in the world to come eternal life." Who of the many disciples of those early times of suffering and persecutions was not rich in "house, or brethren, or sisters, or mother, or father, or children, or lands"? And who that "left" these for his "sake and for the gospel's sake" did not—does not and will not ever—find, in the undying love and fellowship of the great spiritual community, and in the eternal riches of the heavenly inheritance, more than the "hundredfold"? Yet shall there be no pre-eminence, but a true equality; for the "first shall be last, and the last first."—G.

Vers. 35—45.—*The post of honour.* How soon are the Master's words misapprehended! James and John, concerning whom it is recorded that on the call of Jesus "they straightway left the boat and their father, and followed him," come now apparently to secure the promised reward. With cautious words, and by the aid of their mother, the demand is urged upon that good Master on whose lips are ever the gracious words, "What would ye that I should do for you?" We would fain "sit, one on thy right hand, and one on thy left hand, in thy glory." Ah! the old leaven is not yet wholly purged out. The self-seeking, the love of supremacy, place, and honour still lurk within. The chaff mingles with the pure grain. He who holds the winnowing fan is at hand; and with decisive though gentle words, heavily weighted with their sad import, corrects their error. He had but recently "in the way" told them "the things that were to happen unto him." Direful were the words, "The Son of man shall be delivered unto the chief priests and the scribes; and they shall condemn him to death, and shall deliver him unto the Gentiles: and they shall mock him, and shall spit upon him, and shall scourge him, and shall kill him; and after three days he shall rise again." But these words could have had little influence, for "they understood none of these things." Perchance then they understood not "the cup that I drink," or "the baptism that I am baptized with," or there had not been so ready a response, "We are able." With prophetic eyes the Master sees the future of these brethren, and declares, "The cup that I drink ye shall drink; and with the baptism that I am baptized withal shall ye be baptized. Doubtless "this saying" also "was hid from them" until the very hour when that cup touched their lips, or the waters of that baptism fell upon them. But even this could not entitle them to the high place they desired; certainly not on the grounds they desired it—that of arbitrary selection. It is given to them "for whom it hath been prepared." Out of all this the lesson arises—

I. THAT THE POSTS OF REAL HONOUR ARE NOT ATTAINED BY MERE FAVOUR OR BY ARBITRARY ALLOTMENT. All such endowment, either in the kingdom of heaven or among men, would instantly rob the distinction of all worthiness and make it a sham. The incident presents an example of that kind of false estimate of honour which supposes that it can be conferred without regard to the fitness of him who seeks it. It is true medals may be placed on the breast of him who has never fought, and the ribbon may adorn him who never did one deed of distinction; but such a decoration is a deceit or an empty title—a mere ribbon which a child might wear. No mere will of the ruler can make a life honourable and worthy. Signs of a sovereign beneficence may be heaped upon favourites, but they add no lustre to the character of him who is adorned or enriched. And the posts of honour in the highest of all kingdoms are not assigned arbitrarily to favoured ones. As the kingdom is open to all, so are its seats of honour. Each receives according to his deserts—" according as his work shall be."

II. So is learnt a second lesson like unto the first: ALL TRUE HONOUR LIES IN SERVICE AND MERIT, NOT IN ITS RECOGNITION. How often are men attracted by the reward! They esteem the honour which attaches to attainments, to position, to wealth, to learning, or brave deeds. The eye is on the medal. Such seldom do much that is worthy, or make themselves really great. The man who works for praise and prizes is selfish and little, and the world in its deep heart hates both. He has his reward. Others steadily do their duty, undiverted by anxiety respecting honour; these finally achieve true distinction. So is it in all kingdoms.

III. IN THE SPIRITUAL KINGDOM HONOUR COMES TO HIM WHO IS MEET FOR IT. Christ has no favourites to lift to emolument and dignity. He who would reach the highest place must climb up to it. But how many truly and wisely desire to stand well in the heavenly kingdom? They desire a happy freedom from evil, a lot among the sanctified! It is well. Yet the words of the great Lord come back to such, "Ye know not what ye ask." Would you be spiritually great? Would you make high attainments in spiritual knowledge? Would you do good works in the spiritual kingdom? How much of self-denial, of patient labour, of disciplinary correction— "the chastening of the Lord," which we should "regard not lightly"—how much of sacrificial endurance is needed! How many hours of quiet communion must be passed with the Redeemer if we would catch his spirit! How much of fasting and prayer, and diligent self-culture, and patient self-denial! How many strong acts of faith! What baptism of fire, what bitterness of the cup, is needed to make the disciple like his Master! But after all another spirit is to prevail. Christ's disciples are exhorted not to aim at superiority of position, at rank and order. Let the Gentiles "lord it over" one another. "It is not so among you." The greatest is the least truly. The minister, the servant of all, is chief and first. The true lesson being, "In my kingdom there is neither first nor last, highest nor lowest, near and afar off. Dismiss the thought of primacy. Look not for high places. Such there are not in my kingdom. Look for posts of service. Fix your eye on your ministering, and remember that the Lord of all came to give all—even ' his life a ransom for many.'"—G.

Vers. 46—52.—*Bartimœus.* On the roadside near Jericho sat a blind beggar, making his appeals to the pilgrims that passed up to Jerusalem to attend the feast. "A great multitude" accompanied Jesus on his leaving Jericho on his way to the holy city. The tramp of many feet and the hum of many voices caught the quick ear of the sufferer, and "he inquired what this meant." Learning it was "Jesus of Nazareth," he, having evidently some knowledge of the great Healer, cried aloud, "Jesus, thou Son of David, have mercy on me!" Thus did the blind sufferer of that day formulate a cry—a prayer for all sufferers and sinners in all subsequent ages; a cry which will ascend to heaven as long as suffering saddens the history of our race. The hindering, self-occupied crowd strove to silence the cry. But the very impediment to his earnestness only gave greater intensity to it, and "he cried out the more a great deal" the same pitiful words. As every earnest, fervent prayer, this entered the ears of the Lord of Sabaoth, without whom not one sparrow falleth, and who again and again had laid an emphasis of attention on individual sufferers and sinners. Standing still, for a cry of need arrests him, he silenced their rude, unfriendly words by, "Call ye him." Then the same selfish spirit veers round to the favourite, and they cheer him and bid him rise. Casting aside his loosely flowing garment, he sprang to his feet and came to Jesus." Brief and beautiful is the colloquy, in its sweet and simple haste. "What wilt thou?" "My sight." "Go . . . thy faith" hath brought it thee. Straightway he receives his sight, and follows in the way. Brief as this narrative is, it holds much teaching.

I. ON THE TRUE METHOD OF PRAYER.

II. ON THE SPIRIT OF HIM TO WHOM PRAYER IS ADDRESSED.

Prayer springs from a sense of need, and it must express the sincere desire of him who prays. Words thrown into the form of a petition do not of themselves constitute prayer; without the heart of him who utters them they are dead, being alone. He who asks with his lips only cannot expect him to hear who looketh on the heart. Prayer must needs be offered to One who it is believed is able to answer. Jesus laid down the clear and definite rule in his demand, " Believe ye that I am able to do this ? " " The prayer of faith " is the true prayer, though the patient Lord will " forgive " even the "unbelief" of timidity.   Nevertheless, the Lord declares the immediate cause of the answering cure in this case : " Thy faith hath made thee whole." Prayer must be prepared to push its way through surrounding discouragements and opposition ; nor will it exceed propriety if it the more fervently plead by how much it is hindered and impeded.   Prayer must, moreover, have respect to proper objects.   Here one imperfectness in the life called forth the one petition when the " What wilt thou that I should do ? " opened wide the permission to ask many things.   Surely to him who came to redeem life, it was a perfectly right subject of petition : " That I may receive my sight." Thus we learn that for the freeing of the life from its incumbent evils, and for whatever will lead that life on to perfectness, we may ask, and ask in the full assurance of faith, in the readiness and ability of the Lord of life to hear and to answer. Happy the man who has learned thus to pray.—G.

Vers. 1—12.—*The law of marriage.*   I. THE DIRECTIONS OF SCRIPTURE FOLLOW THE OLDER LAW OF NATURE.
II. THE SANCTITY OF MARRIAGE IS FOUNDED ON NATURE.
III. IN ITS IDEAL, MARRIAGE IS FOR LIFE, AND INDISSOLUBLE.
IV. YET THE ACTUAL CONDITION OF HUMAN NATURE COMPELS SOME RELAXATION.
V. BUT WHAT IS PERMITTED IS NOT, THEREFORE, TO BE APPROVED OR FOLLOWED PRACTICALLY.   Christianity is throughout ideal.   It makes appeal to our higher nature. At the same time, it admits the difficulty of carrying our ideals unexceptionably into practice.—J.

Vers. 13—16.—*The blessing of the children.*   I. THE CONTRAST: WHAT MEN THINK IMPORTANT, AND WHAT GOD RECOGNIZES AS OF WORTH.   Children are " only children." They are often "in the way." They are " out of place." They are to be "sent out of the way."   But Divine intelligence and love shed a bright light upon the little ones.   They are living parables of the Christian spirit.   Ever are they to be associated with Christ.   Learning, wealth, rank,—all draw away from our true attitude, nay, tend to falsify our spirit.   'Tis the sight of the children that must win us back.
II. CHRISTIANITY THE RELIGION OF REVERENCE FOR THOSE BELOW US.   In them God is found.   " The religion of reverence for what is above us is ethnic religion.   This delivers from degrading fear.   The religion of reverence for what is around us is the philosophical.   The philosopher stations himself in the middle, and must draw up to him all that is lower, and down to him all that is higher.   This is the religion of wisdom.   Reverence for what is under us,—this is Christian, and is the last step mankind was fitted and destined to attain " (Goethe).   The lowly, the hated, the despised, the contradictory, are glorified by the insight and the sympathy of Christ.—J.

Vers. 17—23.—*The rich man's temptation.*   I. THE RICH MAN FEELS THE NEED OF SALVATION.   "Money answereth all things," but only in a limited sphere after all. Riches bind as well as set free ; close certain doors to the spirit, as well as open them to others.   The poor man knows "straitness" of one kind, the wealthy man another. Could he but unite the advantages of wealth with freedom and joy of spirit !
II. SALVATION IS POSSIBLE TO THE RICH MAN.   But the practical conditions may be different from those in other cases.   It is some idea, some phantasy, a pride, or a dread, or a lust, that every man needs to expel from his mind in order to salvation. In some way the idea of his riches stood in the way of this man's bliss.   But the way to salvation was pointed out to him.   It would be wrong to generalize the direction of the Saviour.   All that can be said is that there doubtless are cases where entire renunciation may be indispensable to salvation.   The principle is : the false opinion of ourselves must be given up, and our being must be grounded on the truth, if we would "enter into life."
III. IT IS ONE OF THE HARDEST THINGS IN THE WORLD TO RENOUNCE RICHES.   How very rare are the cases where this is done !   For money represents our root in earth.

Let us, without affectation or hypocrisy, confess that it is so. Power, service, and estimation of others, a flattering self-representation,—this is what riches mean. To have grown into this circle of ideas, and to be asked suddenly to break them up, 'tis a wrench, like parting with life itself. But let us not exaggerate in any particular. Renunciation of any object with which the imagination in its dearest play is interwoven, is hard. It may be as hard for some to give up the retirement of a humble home for Christ's sake, as for others to renounce station and splendour.—J.

Vers. 24—27.—*Moral impossibilities.* I. "MORAL IMPOSSIBILITIES" IS A PHRASE OF HUMAN EXPERIENCE. Like all such phrases, saws, and proverbs, it represents the side of truth that is obvious and turned to general view. Men being what they are, certain changes in the character and conduct are not likely, are scarcely probable or possible. So we argue, and justly. So Jesus speaks, using a very strong figure of speech.

II. "MORAL IMPOSSIBILITIES" MAY NEVERTHELESS BE OVERCOME. As Napoleon, in the physical sphere, blotted the word "impossible" from his dictionary, so is the Christian taught to do in the moral sphere. In one light, it looks unlikely that anybody can be saved, considering the power of sin, the "weight," and the "besetment," and the apparent lack of moral energy. But nothing that is conceivable is impossible. Nothing that is morally desirable may not be expected to come to pass. 1. We are prone to a scepticism about our own nature, which we ought to overcome. It is not justifiable, in the light of the facts of history, of personal experience, of the might and love of God. 2. A deep faith in the possibilities of human nature is inspired by the love of God. Love is the spring of the human mechanism, the leaven that works in its lump, the struggling force contending against immense disadvantages, but destined to final victory. "All things are possible with God!"—J.

Vers. 28—31.—*Compensation.* I. TO EXPECT COMPENSATION FOR WORTHY LOSS IS NATURAL AND RIGHT. The gospel encourages this. Compensation is founded on the law of things. God hath set the one over against the other. The conservation of energy is a law that applies to the life of the soul. "It will be made good to us." We cannot help feeling that the integrity of our being has a worth which must be preserved.

II. CHRIST ENCOURAGES THIS EXPECTATION TO THE HIGHEST DEGREE. Self-abandonment to the good cause will bring its reward. God pays a high rate of interest.

> "Fear not, then, thou child infirm;
> There's no God that will wrong a worm.
> Laurel crowns cleave to deserts,
> And power to him who power exerts.
> Hast not thy share? On wingèd feet,
> Lo! it rushes thee to meet;
> And all that Nature made thy own,
> Floating in air, or pent in stone,
> Will rive the hills and swim the sea,
> And, like thy shadow, follow thee."

"Every stroke shall be repaid. The longer the payment is withholden, the better for you; for compound interest on compound interest is the rate and usage of this exchequer." "The martyr cannot be dishonoured. Every lash inflicted is a tongue of fame; every prison a more illustrious abode; every burned book enlightens the world; every suppressed or expunged word reverberates through the earth from side to side."

III. THIS PRINCIPLE HAS UNEXPECTED APPLICATIONS. Success is not always what it seems; nor apparent failure. There will be great "reversals of human judgment" (see Mozley's fine sermon on this). "Those who begin early and do much are not always preferred." Some show in the front early in life's race, but fail of the goal. Others lag at first, and come out first in the end. Gain in power may be loss in time; or self-extension involve loss of intensity. The great lesson is to live for the soul, for the inner and spiritual world. Everything gained then is gained for ever; and seeming loss and failure are converted into means of progress.—J.

Vers. 32—34.—*The coincidence of opposites.* Once more the forecast of shame and death.

I. MEN FLY IN THE FACE OF THEIR INTEREST, AND TREAT THEIR BENEFACTORS AS ENEMIES. Christ foresaw that the ruling party would be angry with him "because he told them the truth." And we partake of this guilt. We are blind to love in its disguise. We hate that which reproaches us. It is an error of the understanding and of the heart.

II. PROVIDENCE BRINGS GOOD OUT OF OUR EVIL, AND FURTHERS OUR SALVATION IN SPITE OF OURSELVES. So limited is the power of passion, it gains but a momentary end. The patriot or the traitor falls by the hand of the assassin or the judicial murderer; and his principle takes the deeper root, watered by his blood. Christ's resurrection is the eternal type of all moral victories.—J.

Vers. 35—45.—*Ambition.* It is ambition for place and power that is here illustrated.

I. IT IS NATURAL IN THE SENSE IN WHICH ALL HUMAN INSTINCTS ARE NATURAL. 1. To be without ambition of some kind is a defect of organization; a negative, not a positive; a weakness, not a virtue. Man is man because he aspires. He ceases from his worth when he becomes content to remain what he is. Milton speaks of the last "infirmity of noble minds." It is an infirmity of which a man will be ashamed to be ashamed, though he will try to conceal it under that name from others. Shakespeare makes one of his characters exclaim, "If it be a sin to covet honour, I am the most offending soul alive." 2. This passion reveals our social nature. We delight in the picture of others' respect, love, obedience, esteem. Such pictures goad us to our noblest actions. 3. Vice lies not in the passion itself, but in the wrong direction of the will, the mistake of our proper objects. We are ambitious to govern when we are only fit to serve; to teach when we should still be learning; to act when we have need to be acted upon; to be artists when we are only fit for clay, to be moulded by the Divine Artist; to be assessors of Christ when our initiation into the ways of the kingdom has only just begun.

II. CHRIST'S CORRECTION OF AMBITION. 1. By showing its ignorance of its proper objects. There is a condition attached to every distinction. The price must be paid. Have we counted the cost? One illusion is that we separate the pleasure from the means to it in our thought. Another is that we represent to ourselves incompatible things, *e.g.* a high place with a satisfaction only to be obtained by working up from a low place. Crabb Robinson said that having read, as a young man, Mrs. Barbauld's essay on the vanity of inconsistent expectations, it had cured him for life of idle wishes. 2. By showing its impossibility. Places are reserved in Providence for those fit to fill them. In the kingdom of God there is no putting of wrong men into wrong places. The principle of spiritual selection unerringly prevails in the kingdom, and "the fittest survive." The path of self-denial and suffering is open to all. It coincides at many points with that of duty for all; and it may be throughout coincident for some. It leads to blessing, but that blessing is internal. If we confound the inward blessing with the outward place, we deceive ourselves. If God gives us the higher, let us not envy those to whom he is pleased to allot the lower.

III. CHRIST'S EXPOSURE OF THE UNSOCIAL CHARACTER OF AMBITION. 1. The other disciples were indignant when the failings of the brethren were brought to light. Our secret vices never look so hideous as when we see them mirrored in another. For then the illusion of self-love has vanished, and we stand before the naked and ugly fact. 2. To desire to be above others is not Christian. To dominate and exact is the reverse of the Christian temper. It makes self the centre the world revolves around. To serve, to be useful, is the Christian temper; this makes human good the centre of every sphere of life—the family, the Church, the nation. 3. The example of Christ is the eternal light for conduct. His glory arises out of service, as in an immortal passage St. Paul teaches (Phil. ii.). Without method there is nothing sound. We need a method of thought and life—to put the first before the second. The whole is before the part, humanity more than the individual; there must be giving in order to receiving; and for the highest possible objects of our aspiration nothing less than the whole life must be paid.—J.

Vers. 46—52.—*Blind Bartimæus.* Viewed from the side of Christ, the incident
may teach—

I. The opening of the eyes of the blind is the mission of Christianity.
If the physical boon be great, let it express for us the far greater spiritual boon.
Ignorance is painfully felt by large numbers. Few who have not received a good
education but bitterly feel the lack at some period or other of their life. In spreading
knowledge freely we follow the example of Christ.

II. The mission of Christianity is peculiarly to the lowly and the mean.
It is easier to be kind to our inferiors than to avoid jealousy among our equals. The
gifts that bless both giver and receiver the most are worth much, though they cost little.
From the side of Bartimæus we may reflect—

III. Long sitting in darkness may prepare for the welcoming of the light.
Yet in the darkness the lamp of hope may be kept burning, as did Bartimæus. "In
our griefs we find reliefs." As every night gives place to morning, so the very constitution of nature prophesies the deliverance of mankind and of the individual. The
memories of the dark hours of life mingle with attained joys. Life would not have its
full significance without these mingled threads in the texture.

IV. Perseverance is ever rewarded. Faith proves itself by constancy, and is
in fact the perseverance of the whole man towards his hope, the realization of his life
in God. In the change of events, things will change for the better to him who endures.
"All things come round to him who waits." "Yet a little while, and he who is on the
way shall come." The tarrying of God is in our imagination. To gain one sight, to
see God and the world in God,—this compensates for an age of waiting and watching,
suffering and toil of the spirit.—J.

Vers. 2—12. Parallel passage : Matt. xix. 3—12.—*Doctrine of divorce.* I. Events
in the interval. There is a gap in the narrative of St. Mark between the events of
the preceding and present chapter. We need not do more than intimate them, and
that for the continuity of the history. They are the following :—1. His *journey* to
Jerusalem on the occasion of the Feast of Tabernacles. 2. Occurrences by the way :
(1) Inhospitality of certain Samaritan villages; (2) rebuke of the "Sons of Thunder"
by the Saviour; (3) journey continued through Samaria rather than Peræa; (4) cleansing
of the ten lepers as he passed through Samaria. 3. The sending out of the seventy,
and its similarity to the previous mission of the twelve. 4. *Presence and preaching* at
the Feast of Tabernacles. 5. Various discourses during that feast, as recorded in the
eighth chapter of St. John's Gospel, and escape from a murderous assault. 6. Ministrations in Judæa, recorded in part by St. Luke (x.—xiii.) and partly by St. John (ix.—xi.),
including the following :—(1) Instruction of a lawyer, explanation of "neighbourhood,"
and parable of the good Samaritan; (2) hospitality of the family of Bethany, disciples
taught to pray, and return of the seventy; (3) cure of a man born blind, our Lord's
comparison of himself to the Good Shepherd, celebration of the Feast of Dedication at
Jerusalem, retirement to Bethabara beyond Jordan, and subsequent raising of Lazarus
at Bethany; also his retirement to Ephraim. 7. His *tour through Peræa,* referred
to in Matt. xix. 1, 2, and Mark x. 1; his teaching during that tour, recorded by
St. Luke (xiii. 22—xviii. 10), including, among other things, (1) the multitudes
from all quarters in the kingdom of God, the great feast and generous invitation, also
true discipleship; (2) parables of the lost sheep, lost coin, and prodigal son; (3)
parables of the unjust steward, Dives and Lazarus, importunate widow, the Pharisee
and publican.

II. A new departure. The Pharisees now change their tactics, and adopt a new
mode of opposition. They, in fact, make a new departure. The old hostility remains
bitter as ever, or perhaps is increasing in intensity, but the manner of its manifestation
is new. Up till this period their method of attack consisted in fault-finding—objecting
to the conduct of our Lord and his apostles, or taxing them with violations of the Law;
henceforth it consists in questioning—captious questioning—for the purpose of eliciting
his opinion on doubtful or debatable matters in order to entangle him. The subjects
on which his views were sought were those keenly discussed by the Jews of that day,
and an answer could scarcely fail to give offence to some party or expose him to peril
on some side. The present question was eminently one of this class. It was likely

to entrap him into the charge of lax morality on the one hand, or of want of respect for the authority of Moses on the other; perhaps to embroil him with the tetrarch Herod Antipas, in whose dominions he now was.

III. THE ORIGINAL MARRIAGE LAW. In the days of our Lord one of the burning questions was the law of divorce. The school of Shammai limited the law of divorce, and allowed it only in the case of adultery; that of Hillel affirmed its legitimacy in case of dislike, or disobedience, or incompatibility in general, thus granting an arbitrary or discretionary power in the matter. The ground of the controversy is found in a difficult or obscure expression in Deut. xxiv. 1, 2, where we read, "When a man hath taken a wife, and married her, and it come to pass that she find no favour in his eyes, because he hath found *some uncleanness* in her: then let him write her a bill of divorcement, and give it in her hand, and send her out of his house. And when she is departed out of his house, she may go and be another man's wife." The difficulty or obscurity of this passage arises from the original words *ervath davar*, rendered "some uncleanness" in the text of our version, and in the margin, "matter of nakedness," or more exactly still, "nakedness of word or matter." The important point to be determined, and that which produced such diversity of opinion in its determination, was whether the expression referred to meant lewdness or merely something disagreeable.

IV. NATURE OF THE BILL OF DIVORCEMENT. The bill of divorcement was called "a writing of cutting off" (*sepher kerithuth*). This bill or writing of divorcement implied, not only a mere separation from bed and board, as some restrict it, but a complete severance of the marriage tie. It was a certificate of repudiation, and either stated or omitted the cause of such repudiation. If the cause was adultery or a suspicion of adultery, the husband might prove himself (δίκαιος) *just* (*vide* Matt. i. 19), that is, a strict observer of the Law in dismissing the guilty wife with a bill of divorcement; and yet, not wishing to expose her, he might send her away privately. If, however, the guilty person or the suspected person were brought openly to justice, and the crime proved, certain death was the penalty, as is distinctly stated in Lev. xx. 10, "The man that committeth adultery with another man's wife, even he that committeth adultery with his neighbour's wife, the adulterer and the adulteress shall surely be put to death." Most commonly, therefore, when a bill of divorcement was resorted to in accordance with the Mosaic permission, it was for some less cause or minor offence than conjugal infidelity; and in such cases it served the wife as a certificate of character.

V. REASON OF THIS WRITING. Our Lord, in his reply, proceeds to the original marriage law; first, however, accounting for the Mosaic regulation referred to. That regulation is regarded by many as a *relaxation* of the Law; but it can scarcely be viewed in that light, because it would thus appear to be a lowering of the standard in favour of wrong-doing. It was rather a *remedy* for harsh treatment of wives, resulting from violations of the Law; it was rather a relief bill for wives who suffered from the unkindness of cruel husbands acting in defiance of the Law. It was a remedial measure to check the bad effects of their hardness of heart; it was to (πρὸς) this the lawgiver had respect. It was, in fact, to minimize the evil results that proceeded from their transgression of the Law rather than any relaxation of the Law itself. Of two evils it was the less, and even the less owed its existence to their hardness of heart. Besides, it was not an express command, as the Pharisees appear to make it from the word ἐνετείλατο in Matthew, but a permissory injunction (ἐπέτρεψε), as subsequently acknowledged by the Pharisees themselves.

VI. ORIGINAL MARRIAGE LAW. The Saviour argues the indissoluble nature of the marriage law from the original unity of male and female, from the extreme closeness of the marriage bond taking precedence of every other union even parental and filial; above all, from its Divine origin. Marriage was thus an ordinance of God; it was instituted in Paradise in those bright and sunny bowers before sin had marred the freshness and the loveliness of the new-created world. Even then God saw that it was not good for man to be alone, and accordingly he gave him a help meet for him—one that was bone of his bone and flesh of his flesh. "Therefore shall a man leave his father and his mother, and shall cleave unto [literally, *be glued* unto] his wife: and they shall be one flesh." It was an ordinance of God himself, an ordinance nearly coeval with the creation, an ordinance made for man even in his unfallen state of innocence, an ordinance which our blessed Redeemer himself, when in sinless humanity he trod our earth and tabernacled among our race, honoured with his presence, and at the celebration of which he was graciously pleased to work his first miracle. In Cana of Galilee, at the marriage at which Jesus and his disciples and his mother were present, Jesus made the beginning of his miracles by turning water into wine, manifesting forth his glory, "and his disciples believed on him."

> "Living, he own'd no nuptial vow,
>   No bower to Fancy dear:
> Love's very self—for him no need
> To nurse, on earth, the heavenly seed:
> Yet comfort in his eye we read
>   For bridal joy and fear."

The conclusion at which he arrives is in keeping with all this—that an institution created by God at first, coeval with our race, and confirmed by so many sanctions, can neither be nullified nor modified by any human enactment, nor set aside by any authority other than his who created it. "What therefore God hath joined together, let not man put asunder."

VII. ONE EXCEPTION TAKEN FOR GRANTED. Conjugal infidelity, as it is a violation of the marriage vow, is a virtual dissolution of the marriage relation. This is implied or taken for granted in the passage before us, though it is expressly stated, in the parallel passage of St. Matthew, where it is written, "Whosoever shall put away his wife, except for fornication, and shall marry another, committeth adultery." With respect to marriage with the divorced wife, there is a great and important diversity of sentiment. This diversity is in a certain way and to some extent connected with the right rendering of the word ἀπολελυμένην in Matt. xix. 9. 1. Some translate it as if it were preceded by τὴν, and so equivalent to "her which is put away," or "the divorced woman." Thus it stands in the common English Version, and reference to the woman lawfully divorced, that is, for fornication, is presumed. 2. Others, more accurately, render it "her when she is put away," as it is translated in the Revised Version, the reference being thus to her who is unlawfully divorced, that is, divorced not on the ground of adultery. This view is maintained by Stier and Meyer, the latter confirming it by the fact that "under the Law the punishment of death was attached to adultery, . . . and consequently, under the Law, the marrying of a woman divorced for adultery could never happen." 3. There is, however, another rendering, namely, "a divorced woman," that is, any divorced woman. This is the rendering advocated by Wordsworth, who says, "In no case does our Lord permit a person to marry a woman who has been divorced." This is the view of the matter taken by the Latin Church, which declares marriage with a divorced woman under any circumstances unlawful. The Oriental and most Reformed Churches, on the contrary, hold that, in the excepted case, both husband and wife may contract a fresh marriage. These are the two extreme views; but what of the case of unlawful divorce, that is to say, where the wife has been divorced for some other and less offence than that of adultery, or πορνεία, which is of widest extent, comprehending ante-nuptial as well as post-nuptial unchastity (μοιχεία)? This is the case to which the guilt of subsequent marriage attaches, for it is that in which the marriage bond has not been really ruptured. The delay connected with getting a divorce or after its being granted might give time for better counsels to prevail; second thoughts might be found preferable; angry passion might in the mean time cool down, and reconciliation and reunion be effected.—J. J. G.

Vers. 13—16. Parallel passages: Matt. xix. 13—15; Luke xviii. 15—17.— I. CHILDREN BROUGHT AND BLESSED. 1. *Our Lord's love of children.* Our Lord, when on earth, had no greater favourites than children. He set them in the midst; he laid his hands on them; he blessed them; he invited them to his presence; he welcomed them to his person; he folded them lovingly in his arms. He calls them the lambs of his flock; he provides them suitable spiritual food, and with it he bids us feed them. He represents by them his faithful followers; he reproves his disciples when they would have prevented their access to him. He reminds us all that they are precious in our heavenly Father's sight, preserved by his providence and protected by his power. He assures us, as we have seen, that "their angels do always behold the face of my Father which is in heaven." 2. *Individual features of the three narratives.* The request of those who brought the little children, as reported by St. Matthew, is not only that the Saviour should touch them, as in St. Mark and St. Luke; but "put his hands on them, and *pray.*" In St. Mark, we are told that Jesus not only touched the little children, as requested, but "took them up in his arms." They thus got more than they asked. This is usually the way with Christ; he does more for us than we ask or think. An additional feature of the narrative, as supplied by St. Luke, is that some of these children were of very tender age—mere infants (βρέφη).

II. THE CHANGE BY WHICH WE BECOME AS LITTLE CHILDREN. 1. *A parallel passage.* In St. Matthew's Gospel (xviii. 3) we have a statement exactly corresponding to the fifteenth verse of this tenth chapter of St. Mark, with this difference, however, that the former passage goes further back, bringing us up to the turning-point at which we become as little children. The verse referred to reads thus, " Verily I say unto you, Except ye be converted, and become as little children, ye shall not enter into the kingdom of God;" the Revised Version has, "Except ye *turn,* and become as little children, *ye shall in no wise enter into* the kingdom of heaven." This rendering of οὐ μὴ εἰσέλθητε in the last clause brings out the meaning with due emphasis, and is thus more accurate than that of the common version; the substitution of *turn* for *be converted* in the first clause is intended to divest the term of the technical theological sense which some attach to it. The word στραφῆτε (second aorist passive) may be translated as a passive, or as a middle, since the aorists passive have often a middle meaning, equivalent to *turn yourselves,* or simply *turn* intransitively, as we have it in the Revised Version. In its application, as shown by the context, it urged those addressed to turn away from their ambitious notions, self-seeking eagerness, and fondness for precedence. The term is general, we readily acknowledge, and denotes a change such as that referred to; but before men are capable of turning from the courses indicated, and of exhibiting the characteristics of little children, they must have become the subjects of a special and greater change, of which that immediately referred to is a manifestation. We may read the statement of St. Mark, that "Whosoever shall not receive the kingdom of God as a little child, he shall not enter therein," or, as it is more accurately rendered in the Revised Version, "he shall in *no wise enter* therein," in the light which St. Matthew's statement sheds on it. 2. *Divine agency.* We have seen that the word in the closely corresponding text is limited by some, and may indeed be limited, to its literal sense, and understood of a turning away from such highmindedness as the disciples had displayed on that occasion—a turning away from such haughtiness of spirit as led to the question asked by them, " Who is the greatest in the kingdom of heaven?" Others may be disposed to take it in the sense of recovery from backsliding, of a return to the Lord after some wrong step, as a compound form of the same verb is employed (ἐπιστρέψας) in the words addressed to Peter, "When thou art converted, strengthen the brethren;" or, as we read it in the Revised Version, "And do thou, when once thou hast turned again, stablish thy brethren." Others may prefer the wider and more technical sense of conversion. But whatever sense be attached to the one particular term, a change effected by Divine agency must be presupposed; otherwise the changes implied in the lower sense cannot be rightly accomplished, nor the characteristics of childhood fully attained. "Whosoever shall not receive the kingdom of God as a little child, shall in no wise enter therein," is the statement of St. Mark, and suggests the inquiry—What is it to receive the kingdom of God? Now, to take the simplest and plainest view of this matter, to receive the kingdom of God is to receive the gospel of the kingdom; and to receive the gospel of the kingdom is to receive him who is the Subject of that gospel, and the Sovereign of that kingdom—the Christian's King and Head; and to receive him, again, is the turning-point in a man's spiritual history, the greatest and most important event of his whole life. This reception of the Saviour implies faith of the operation of God—faith, which is God's gift and the Spirit's work in the heart. Wherever faith exists, even as a grain of mustard seed, Christ is formed in the heart. It matters little what name is given to this change, whether we call it " the new birth," or " regeneration," or " conversion;" to be subjects of it is the great thing, for it is the principle of all right action, and the prolific source of all Christian graces and of all truly virtuous conduct. 3. *Statement of a difference.* We may notice a difference which will help to a clearer apprehension of the change in question. Conversion is akin to regeneration; it is most nearly similar, and cannot be separated from it, and yet it is not quite the same thing. Regeneration implants a new principle in the soul; conversion is the practical putting forth of that principle. Regeneration imparts new life to the soul; conversion is the exercise of that life. Regeneration bestows new power; conversion is the manifestation of that power. For sake of illustration, let us suppose a man dead and buried. Regeneration may be compared to life entering into the sepulchre, opening the eyes that death had sealed, giving back the healthy colour to the cheeks and causing the vital fluid once more to circulate through all the frame; conversion may be represented by the same man, after being thus reanimated, exerting the power of life which he has just received, rising up from among the dead, coming forth from the tomb, and entering on the various duties and activities of life. Conversion and regeneration are thus so closely linked together as cause and effect that they often stand for one another. 4. *Human instrumentality.* Here, too, the power of God and the work of man unite; Divine agency and human instrumentality combine. The hand of man may roll away the stone and remove the grave-clothes, as in the case of Lazarus; but nothing short of the power of God can resuscitate the buried corpse, or speak the dead to life. So, also, it is when the dead in trespasses and sins are quickened. By the instrumentality of man, the stone that stops the mouth of the sepulchre may be taken away and the grave-clothes unbound; but nothing less than " the working of God's mighty power which he wrought in Christ, when he raised him from the dead," can make any one of us alive through Christ Jesus. We may preach and pray, and it is our duty to combine both, and our privilege to engage in either; but the power that raises the dead to life is the power, and not only the power, but the mighty power of God. The prophet of old acknowledged this, for after he had prophesied to the dry bones in the valley of vision, he followed up his prophesying by prayer, saying, " Come from the four winds, O breath, and breathe upon these slain, that they may live." The psalmist felt the same when he said, " Create in me a clean heart, O God; and renew a right spirit within me." The apostle was of the same mind when he wrote, " But God, being rich in mercy, for his great love wherewith he loved us, even when we were dead through our trespasses, quickened us together with Christ (by grace have ye been saved)." 5. *The means employed, and the manner in which the change is effected.* God treats us as reasonable beings; he makes his appeal to the faculties with which he has endowed us. He addresses us as his intelligent creatures, and challenges us to inquiry, saying, " Judge ye what I say." He speaks to us in his Word and by his ambassadors, and even entreats us to be reconciled to God. He bestows his Spirit, for without the agency of that Spirit all the rest would be but as the rolling away of the stone and the unbinding of the grave-clothes already spoken of. 6. *The nature of the change.* After the creation of the heavens and the earth, the first work of God was light. God said, " Let there be light." In the change in question, which, for convenience' sake, we may call conversion, the first work is also *light;* he enlightens our understanding in the knowledge of Christ. God's Word, indeed, is light, " a light to our feet;" but while we are unconverted there are scales on our eyes, and if we see at all, it is only " men like trees, walking." The Spirit takes away the scales; and we see the suitability and sufficiency of the Saviour, the completeness of his work, the fulness of his offices, the freeness of his mercy, the riches of his grace, the length and breadth and depth and height of his love; we see also our sins in the light of his sufferings, and his sufferings endured for and expiating our sins. This is not all; it is not enough to have light in the head. There is often natural light, intellectual light, the light of science, even the light of theological speculation or doctrine or controversy; but such light by itself never brought any soul to the Saviour. Of such light we may say, it is the light of the moon shining on an iceberg away in a frozen sea; it is the nocturnal light of twinkling stars, as they sparkle in the firmament, and shed their flickering radiance on some far-off mountain capped with snow. In this gracious change there is an additional element. With light in the head it combines love in the heart. Like light and heat from the same fire, they go hand in hand. The heart follows the head, and they act and react upon each other. The will obeys the understanding, and the affections go along with both. The subject of this blessed change can say with one of old, " Whereas I was blind, now I see; " but he goes further, and can say with the apostle, " The love of God has been shed abroad in our hearts through the Holy Ghost which was given unto us." The regenerate soul can say, "I know whom I have believed;" but it stops not there; it adds, "Whom having not seen, I love." Conversion, if we may use the term in its popular sense, is the love of Christ constraining us; it is the Word of Christ instructing us; it is "the light of the knowledge of the glory of God in the face of Jesus Christ;" it is the work of Christ renewing us; it is the Spirit of Christ enlightening us; it is the life of Christ imparted to us—"because I live, ye shall live also;" it is the love of him "who first loved us, and gave himself for us." This love expels the enmity of the carnal mind, gives a new bent to the will and a new bias to the feelings; it lays hold of the affections, and influences all the energies of our being, operating at once on the faculties of the mind and the members of the body. It is God making us willing, as well as welcome, to be his people in the day of his power.

III. The characteristics of childhood. 1. *Infant salvation.* When it is said that "of such [that is, children] is the kingdom of God," it may mean children *literally;* and so many understand it, and refer kingdom to the state of future blessedness, maintaining that, as the majority of mankind die in infancy, and as they are redeemed, children will constitute the majority of the saved. But there is another interpretation, which understands children *spiritually,* that is, those who resemble children in character; thus St. Paul says, "Brethren, be not children in understanding: howbeit in malice be ye children, but in understanding be men." While we are fully persuaded that all children dying in infancy are saved because of the superabundant grace of God in Christ Jesus, we are far from supposing that regeneration is not necessary in case of children as well as of others. Indeed, the Word of God proves it indispensable; for thus says the psalmist, "I was shapen in iniquity, and in sin did my mother conceive me;" and again, "We go astray as soon as we be born, speaking lies;" and further, the Prophet Isaiah says, "All we like sheep have gone astray." It thus becomes our duty to seek, by all available means, to bring children to Christ the Good Shepherd, who carries the lambs in his bosom, that he may bless them and make them members of his flock. There are, however, several characteristics of children which serve well to illustrate the character and conduct of God's spiritual children. 2. *The first characteristic is humility.* When converted to God, we become like little children in humility. Pride is the ruin of our race; we trace it back to Paradise. Satan introduced it there. It was the great inducement with our first parents that they should be "as gods, knowing good and evil." We mark its dark waters along the stream of time from then till now. It was a fruitful source of disaster to King David. In the pride of his heart he numbered the people, and the dreadfully calamitous choice was allowed him to elect between seven years' famine, three months' war, or three days' pestilence. Another instance occurs in the case of Naaman, commander-in-chief of the host of Syria. Leprous as he was, and consequently miserable as he must have been, he felt his pride wounded when the prophet directed him to wash seven times in Jordan; he turned away in a rage, saying, "Are not Abana and Pharpar, rivers of Damascus, better than all the waters of Israel?" Come we to New Testament times, we have another still more awful instance of pride and its punishment. Herod sat upon his kingly throne; he made an oration—a king's speech, and more eloquent, no doubt, than royal speeches generally are; at all events, the people were in raptures with him and it, so that they shouted, "It is the voice of a god, and not of a man." He was arrayed in royal robes; he was proud of his pomp, of his power, and of his popularity. But the angel of the Lord smote him; "he was eaten of worms, and gave up the ghost." The same evil propensity of fallen humanity finds thousands and tens of thousands of living exemplifications in those whom the Scripture calls "proud boasters," "heady, high-minded," and classes with the vilest and the worst. On the contrary, the first evidence of conversion to God is humility. The child of a prince will, if permitted, amuse itself with the child of a peasant. As they sport together there is no distinction of riches or of rank; they meet together on the same common level; they stand on the same footing of equality. We are not universal levellers; we would not do away with the distinctions of rank that exist, and perhaps must exist. We find in the membership of the human body some members discharging honourable functions, others functions less so. We find in the heavenly hierarchy various grades—thrones, and dominions, and principalities, and powers. But we would willingly do away with, and

Christianity tends to do away with, that proud spirit that sets up castes and opposes class to class, preventing that cordial sympathy that should ever bind together all the many members in the great family of man. Why should we be proud? What are we proud of? Is it of our bodies? They are "fearfully and wonderfully made," yet dust they are, and unto dust they must return. Is it of our souls? God "breathed into man's nostrils the breath of life, and he became a living soul." Is it of what we are? We are only creatures of a day, and 'our foundation is in the dust. Is it of what we have? We have nothing, be it worldly wealth, or intellectual endowment, or physical superiority, or spiritual grace,—nothing that we have not received. We are pensioners on the Divine bounty, daily recipients of the Divine favour, almoners on the liberality of God. Most of us have read the Rev. Legh Richmond's little book entitled 'The Dairyman's Daughter,' and the text which by the blessing of God became the means of converting that once poor, proud girl. That text was, "Be ye clothed with humility " (ἐγκομβώσασθε : literally, "wrap tight round you your humility," in allusion to Christ girding himself with a towel to wash his disciples' feet), and by its application to her heart she was led to feel her own emptiness and Christ's fulness. Next to the robe of Christ's righteousness, and inseparably connected with it, is this garment of humility which distinguishes every converted soul, which every child of God puts on, and which every Christian wears. Of all the many promises of Scripture, not one is made to the proud. "God resisteth the proud, and giveth grace to the humble;" "The humble and the contrite heart the Lord will not despise." 3. *A second characteristic is teachableness.* Christ was "meek and lowly in heart." He invites us to learn of him. Most children are docile; at all events, childhood and youth are the seasons for learning. Though there is no age however advanced at which we should not be learners, and no stage of progress at which we shall not have still much to learn—for here " we only see through a glass, darkly "—yet there is truth in the trite old proverb, " Learn young, learn well." The Christian, by his very profession and by his practice, when truly converted to God, is a disciple; and what is that but a learner, a scholar in the school of Christ? There are three teachers in this school—the Word of God, the providence of God, and the Spirit of God. The entrance in of that *Word* giveth light; it makes "wise unto salvation." Every time we hear it preached, or peruse it prayerfully and thoughtfully, the light is brightened and increased. It is our privilege, and should be our pleasure, to study that Word daily and diligently, dutifully and devoutly. If it were only a single text meditated on each day, it would result in spiritual blessing. We are to search this Word. There is a treasure in it, and we are to dig for that treasure—a pearl of great price, and we are to seek for that pearl, and, if needs be, part with everything else rather than miss it. That treasure is Christ, "in whom are hid all the treasures of wisdom and knowledge." That pearl is Christ—a pearl of exceeding price. There are shallows in this Word where a child may wade, and depths which no human line can fathom. "Search the Scriptures," said our Lord; "for in them ye think ye have eternal life: and they are they which testify of me." The *providence* of God teaches us in many ways and furnishes many lessons. We need grace to mark those lessons and follow the leadings of that providence, and in this way the most afflictive dispensations are productive of good, so that there is occasion to say, "It is good for me that I have been afflicted." The *Spirit* of God is the great Teacher, he leads us into all truth, he takes of the things of Christ and shows them to us, he convinces us of sin, of righteousness, and of judgment. Let us pray for childlike docility of spirit; let us come to the three teachers we have named, and hear what God the Lord will say to our souls. 4. *A third characteristic is trustfulness.* Children are proverbially confiding. When we pass from the years of childhood we become wary—too wary; cautious—often far too cautious, though never too circumspect. Let a parent make a promise to his child; that child never questions his father's word, he never doubts his father's ability to perform his promise, he never suspects his father's willingness to make good what he has said. Would that we all acted thus towards our heavenly Father! Would that we all took him in this childlike manner and with this childlike trustfulness at his word! Would that we all sought the Spirit of adoption, by which we could look up and say, "Our Father in heaven," and inward and say, "Abba, Father," and outward and around saying, "All things work together for good to them that love God,"—the beautiful things of earth and sea and sky are mine, for my Father made them all. In the 'Life of Sir

Henry Havelock,' one is amused with a remarkable example of childlike confidence on the part of his son which is recorded therein. Sir Henry had had occasion to call at a public office on business. He left his son at the door to wait for him outside. The father, after despatching the business in hand, passed out of the office by another way, in total forgetfulness of his son and of the appointment made with him. The boy, however, had such perfect confidence in his father's promise and usual punctuality, that he waited, and waited, and continued waiting all the day long, till the shades of evening were gathering. By that time something had occurred to remind Sir Henry of his son, when, going immediately to the place, he found him on the spot where he had left him in the morning. God has given us his sure Word of prophecy and promise; he bids us wait, and that prophecy will be fulfilled and that promise performed. An earthly parent may fail or forget; God never forgets his promise, nor fails to perform it to his people. He is never slack concerning his promise; at the time appointed it shall come, and not tarry. It is ours to wait and watch and work, "for the day of redemption draweth nigh." It is ours to exercise filial trust and childlike confidence in our heavenly Father, who "is not a man, that he should lie; neither the son of man, that he should repent." 5. *A fourth characteristic.* Another characteristic is simplicity. We do not mean that a child of God must be a simpleton; quite the opposite. We are to be "wise as serpents, and harmless as doves." Now, by Christian simplicity we understand guilelessness and harmlessness. We take it to denote singleness of heart, of tongue, and of eye; it becomes the Christian, it glorifies God and impresses man. "Out of the mouth of babes and sucklings God hath ordained strength." The children in the temple proclaimed, "Hosanna in the highest!" Once in a stage-coach, as we have read, a little interesting girl five years old was sitting beside her mother. A gentleman was paying attention to the child. After a time, turning her full blue eyes upon him, with childlike lovingness and in her own simple accents, she said, "You love God?" The gentleman passed the child's question off as best he could. The coach reached the place of destination, the journey ended. But still the words of that child haunted him. The question she asked was new to him; he had never thought of it before. He never rested till, by the grace of God, he was able to answer it by felt experience. Time rolled on. A few years after, as he passed through the streets of a town, he saw the mother of that little child at a window, in weeds of mourning. He called to inquire for his favourite, but she was gone; God had taken her home to glory, and to be for ever with himself.

IV. CONSEQUENCES. 1. *Contrast.* Over the entrance to Plato's famous academy at Athens was written the sentence, "Let no one enter here who does not possess a knowledge of geometry." Over the gate of heaven is written, not the proud maxim of the philosopher, but this plain statement, "Whosoever shall not receive the kingdom of God as a little child, he shall in no wise enter therein." 2. *What is implied in exclusion.* Not to enter heaven, in other words, exclusion from heaven, implies the absence of holiness, of hope, and of happiness. It is never to see the King in his beauty, never to see the land that is afar off, never to enjoy peace, never to enter into rest, never to meet God in mercy, never to sit down with Abraham and Isaac and Jacob, and never to join the general assembly and Church of the Firstborn which are written in heaven. Still more, exclusion shuts out from wearing the crown and occupying the throne, from tenanting the mansion, and tuning the harp, and swelling the anthem of "Worthy is the Lamb that hath been slain to receive the power, and riches, and wisdom, and might, and honour, and glory, and blessing." Not to enter heaven is to be excluded from the holy presence, from the blessed fellowship of patriarchs and prophets and apostles and martyrs and confessors; to be shut out from the life and light and love of the upper sanctuary; to be shut up with the devil and the damned, with lost spirits, with devouring fire and everlasting burnings; to be doomed to "weeping, and wailing, and gnashing of teeth," and to dwell for ever in that prison-house of hell, "where their worm dieth not, and the fire is not quenched."—J. J. G.

Vers. 17—31. Parallel passages: Matt. xix. 16—30; Luke xviii. 18—30.—1. *The rich young ruler's great refusal.* I. HIS APPLICATION. 1. *The position of this man.* We have in this section a most interesting narrative. The subject of it was a *young* man, in the bright and beautiful prime of life, as St. Matthew tells us; a *ruler* of the synagogue, as St. Luke informs us; an exceedingly *rich* man, as all three synoptists relate; for St. Luke tells us he was *very rich*, and St. Matthew and St. Mark that he had *great* possessions. Besides this, he was an exceedingly interesting person—frank, sincere, amiable; he thus possessed many winning and endearing qualities. Nor was this all; he was outwardly moral, outwardly observant of God's Law, and so not far from the kingdom of heaven. 2. *His mode of approaching the Saviour.* His approach was all that could be desired. It was marked by thorough earnestness and sincerity. Our Lord was *going forth* into the way, or on his way—starting, it would seem, on his last journey from Peræa beyond Jordan to Bethany, the town of Mary and her sister Martha and Lazarus. This young ruler, in breathless haste, lest he should miss his opportunity before the Saviour departed, came running up and fell on his knees before him. The manner, too, in which he put his question was highly respectful, and even reverential, as appears from the words with which he addressed him. By the title "Good Master" he acknowledged his authority as a teacher, and his kindness of heart, having just witnessed the graciousness and benevolence with which he had received the little children and folded them in his arms. Our Lord appears to reprove him in a gentle way on the ground of this title, and especially to reject the term "good," thus applied to him; he apparently refuses to accept it as a mere conventional expression, flippantly and thoughtlessly applied. But, on examining the subject more closely, it will be evident that our Lord wished to elevate the young ruler's notion about himself as the Messiah, and raise his thoughts to God. He wished to give this young man a hint that he was more than an ordinary teacher in Israel, that he was more than a mere teacher possessing great excellence of character and goodness of heart; that he was a Teacher sent from God, and therefore invested with highest authority, and holding a Divine commission—yea, and himself Divine. To this end he requires the ruler to reflect on what ground he applied the term "good," reminding him that there was no one absolutely good save God, and implying the inconsistency of his position, and the unwarrantableness of his calling him "good" when he did not regard him as Divine. Our Lord intimates, obscurely indeed, that, while rejecting the term in the sense in which the ruler meant it, as a mere complimentary one paid to a rabbi of eminence, and regarding it as inapplicable from that standpoint, he can only accept it in conjunction with the One alone who is good, that is, God. But, as the ruler did not apply it in that sense, our Lord takes occasion to lift up his thoughts to the only One absolutely good; as though he said, "Why askest thou me concerning that which is good? One there is who is good;" and, "Why callest thou me good?" and, Why inquirest about the good from any mere human teacher whose goodness of head and heart, however great, is necessarily defective? Why not go at once to the One who is alone truly and absolutely good, and the Fountain-head of all goodness, and whose will is the rule and standard of what is good; while the revelation of his mind on the subject is made known in the commandments? 3. *His motive in coming.* With all this young man's advantages he felt his need of something better; he had cravings for something higher. His wealth, with all the facilities it afforded, and all the profits it implied, and all the pleasures it procured, did not satisfy his desires or supply his spiritual needs. His longings for something better than earth or sense could furnish remained unappeased; there was still a void within which the world could not fill; he felt irrepressible yearnings for immortality. He had heard the promise of a kingdom made to the little children who believed, or rather to all who possessed their childlike spirit. He had himself come recently into the inheritance of much wealth and great possessions, and thus he is prompted to ask the question very natural under the circumstances, "What shall I do that I may inherit eternal life?" He was alive to the worth of his soul; he felt the paramount importance of eternal life. His question, therefore, was not prompted by mere curiosity, neither was it a cold or careless inquiry; it was a downright earnest one; it was a matter of life or death with him.

II. HIS SELF-SUFFICIENT INQUIRY. 1. *Nature of the inquiry.* The inquiry is that recorded by St. Matthew, "What lack I yet?" to which the answer of our Lord is that recorded by St. Mark in the words, "One thing thou lackest." We must first consider the question itself. This was a second question; the first was, "What shall I do that I may inherit eternal life?" and contained the very essence of Pharisaism, which made religion consist in *doing*—scrupulously adhering to outward rules of conduct. This young man's error was that of the better part of his nation; for "Israel, which followed after the Law of righteousness, did not attain to the Law of righteousness. Wherefore? Because they sought it not by faith, but as it were by the works of the Law." 2. *His Pharisaism.* This young man's first inquiry shows that he expected to entitle himself to eternal life by doing many great things, or some special good thing, as the question in St. Matthew's Gospel is, "What good thing shall I do, that I may inherit eternal life?" To this our Lord replied, "If thou wilt enter into life, keep the commandments." By this reply he meant to convince him (1) that "by the deeds of the Law there shall no flesh be justified in his (God's) sight: for by the Law is the knowledge of sin;" and (2) to bring him to the conclusion that "the righteousness of God without the Law is manifested, being witnessed by the Law and the prophets; even the righteousness of God which is by faith of Jesus Christ unto all and upon all them that believe." 3. *His surprise.* The young ruler was somewhat surprised at the commonplace nature of the answer, and, lest he had misheard or misapprehended it, he proceeds to inquire further, "Which" or, more accurately, "What kind of commandments?" He evidently expected that some new commandment would be announced by the great Teacher, or that some recondite rule of the oral Law would be set forth, or that certain minute ceremonial regulations would be made known to him. But no; the plainest, simplest, broadest commandments of the Decalogue were repeated in his hearing. The thing appears at first sight so plain, the direction so very trite, and the answers so commonplace, that the ruler, half puzzled by this very plainness, and surprised at the simplicity of the instruction of One whom he regarded as a distinguished public teacher, if not something more, exclaims in amazement,—Of what kind? Which commandments do you mean? Is it those ten uttered in an audible voice on Sinai, amid thunderings and lightnings, and other circumstances of splendour and solemnity? Is it those ten that were delivered to our nation amid scenes of such unparalleled publicity as well as grandeur? Is it those ten *words,* as they are beautifully called in the original, which are now hoary with the antiquity of long years gone by, which claim the respect of the whole Hebrew commonwealth, and to which every respectable member of the community renders an outward obedience? Is it those ten commandments to which your direction refers—commandments with which compliance is enforced even by an earthly judge, and transgression of which is visited with penalties by the common law? 4. *Our Lord's repetition of the commandments.* In reply to this further inquiry of the young ruler, our Lord specifies the commandments of the second table in the following order, according to St. Mark:—the seventh, sixth, eighth, ninth, tenth, and fifth. The expression "Defraud not" is taken by some (1) as a repetition of the eighth; (2) by others as a summary of the four commandments that preceded, or of the fifth that succeeded and that by way of anticipation; or (3) it is a peculiar form of the tenth, which we regard as the most natural and correct opinion. These commandments he quoted from the second table as the most obvious; appending a general principle which embraced all these commandments, and summarily comprehended the whole of the second table of the Law. That principle was love—love to brother man, and a love required to be equal in intensity and extent to the love of self, as it is added, "Thou shalt love thy neighbour as thyself." 5. *Our Lord's object in this.* He saw that this in many respects estimable young man depended on his works for eternal life, and he reminded him that he must in that case keep the commandments, and keep them perfectly. The Saviour meant to show him that such had not been the case. He meant to show him that he was a sinner, and as such needed a Saviour; he meant to show him that, as far as the Law is concerned, every mouth must be stopped, and all the world become guilty before God. Even if a man from a certain point—an early period in life—kept all the requirements of God's Law at all times and in all ways, what would atone for previous sins or remove original guilt? 6. *The Law a schoolmaster.* He meant to show him that he had "sinned, and come short of the glory of God;" that, as a matter of fact, he had been very far from attaining to universal, perfect, and constant obedience; that, in the absence of such obedience, all were concluded under sin, and that there was no exception. In this manner usually the way is prepared: the filthy rags of self-righteousness are torn off; men are led to abandon their own righteousness as a ground of pardon and acceptance before God, and to rest upon a better righteousness, even that "everlasting righteousness," which Daniel and others of the prophets long years before had predicted as to be wrought out and brought in by Messiah. Such was probably the import of that instructive symbolic transaction, of which we read in the third chapter of Zechariah, when the filthy garments were taken away from Joshua the high priest; and when a fair mitre was set upon his head, and he was clothed with change of garments, as it is there written: "Behold, I have caused thine iniquity to pass from thee, and I will clothe thee with change of raiment." Such is the significance of the contrast between the righteousness of the Law and the righteousness of faith in the tenth chapter of the Epistle to the Romans: "For Moses describeth the righteousness which is of the Law, That the man which doeth those things shall live by them. . . . If thou shalt confess with thy mouth the Lord Jesus, and shalt believe in thine heart that God hath raised him from the dead, thou shalt be saved. For with the heart man believeth unto righteousness; and with the mouth confession is made unto salvation." 7. *True obedience inward and spiritual.* When the young man had heard our Lord's answer he looked upon the whole matter as a very simple thing, and possibly stood higher in his own estimation than he had done before, if that were possible. He seemed to say, If these be the commandments which you include in your direction, and if these be all, then have I obeyed them—every one of them—from my youth up, nay, from childhood till the present hour; they have been the rule of my life. Is there anything still wanting? Have you any new commandment to add? Is there anything needed to supplement those which I long since learnt from the Law, and to which I have duly conformed from the earliest dawn of reason? And though you have overlooked the traditions of the elders, I have neither forgotten them nor neglected them, but observed them most punctiliously. What then remains? What lack I yet? Ah, how little this young man knew of his own heart! how little of the spirituality of God's Law! how little of the exceeding broadness of the commandment! In the Law of God, as in the love of God, there are a length and breadth and depth and height to which this ruler was entirely a stranger. He had not, we are sure, been one of the audience when our Lord preached his sermon on the mount; or, if he had, he must have failed entirely to comprehend the explanation of the Law as contained in that sermon. At all events, he remained apparently ignorant that the Law in its requirements extends to the heart as well as to the life; to the principles as well as to the practice; to the feelings as well as to the facts; to the internal passions as well as to the external acts; to the inmost thoughts as well as the outward deeds. This young man had, we doubt not, maintained an unblemished character before the eyes of men; he had been guiltless of such sins as are public and common in the world, and free from all notorious vices; he had kept the Law in the letter and as prohibiting outward acts of sin; for the Saviour does not call his assertion in question. Besides, had he not been a young man of blameless conduct as well as of promising talents, he could not have attained, and at an early age, his honourable position as one of the rulers of a local synagogue, or perhaps a member of the Sanhedrin, or great council of the nation. 8. *The young man's deficiency in his own department of morals.* "What lack I yet?" may be taken as a boast rather than a question for information or an inquiry about future duty. He lacked much, we are sure, even on the low ground of morality; for taking the Law in its spiritual sense, and as Christ expounded it, he had no doubt offended at many times and in many ways; "for in many things we offend all." Instead of the self-righteous, self-sufficient assertion, "all these have I kept from my youth up," had he looked inward he might, nay, he would, have found reason to say, "All these have I broken;" for we have it on the authority of God's own Word, that "every imagination of the thoughts of man's heart is only evil continually." The first commandment which our Lord specified, according to the common order as given by St. Matthew, is, "Thou shalt do no murder." The young ruler judged himself guiltless of any breach of this commandment, because his hands had been free from blood. He forgot that blood-guiltiness attaches to the heart as well as to the hand, to the tongue as well as to the arm that wields the deadly weapon. The teeth, as we learn from the fifty-seventh psalm, may be murderous as "spears and arrows;" and the tongue may wound as mortally as "a sharp sword;" while "out of the heart," as our Lord himself has declared, "proceed murders." "All these have I kept from my youth up." And hast thou never, O young man, been angry with thy brother without a cause—when no real offence was offered and no insult intended? Hast thou never indulged the angry feeling till it formed itself in the contemptuous expression? Hast thou never said to thy brother, "Raca?" Hast thou never permitted thine anger to proceed still further, till it vented itself in terms of deepest guilt? Hast thou never said to thy brother, "Thou fool"? If so—if thy heart be thus pure, thy tongue innocent, and thy hand without stain of thy brother's blood—then in regard to this commandment thou mayest say, "What lack I yet?" But we may take one other example. "Thou shalt not commit adultery." This is another requirement of God's Law, and another branch of duty towards man. Here the young ruler again declares his innocence: "This also have I kept." Here again we must take him to task and catechize him. Is it, O young man, the external act merely of which you plead not guilty, or do you include what God's Law includes, the impure thought and the wanton imagination? Do you include the secret desire of the heart, the lascivious look of the eye, and the indelicate utterance of the lips? Or have you never read of "eyes full of adultery," of evil concupiscence, and of filthy communication proceeding out of the mouth? Have you never listened to or taken part in the lewd song, or the foul anecdote, or the equivocal innuendo, or the expression of double meaning? Have you ever regarded the vengeance of Heaven as due to every wanton affection, and every unchaste desire, and every roving glance, and every lustful look, and every lascivious gesture, and every impure word? Has your observance of this requirement always been thus severe, strict, and spiritual? If so, then mayest thou say with regard to this commandment also, "What lack I yet?" 9. *The Scripture standard of morality.* Oh, how exceeding broad and deep, pure and spiritual, are the commandments of an infinitely pure and holy God! In his sight the bright and beautiful sky above us is not pure, and in his presence the angels themselves—those pure spirits whose nature is like fiery flame, and who minister the high behests of the Eternal—are not unimpeachable with folly. Morality of outward action is highly commendable, and may pass current in sight of men like ourselves; but who can boast of his obedience, inward as well as outward, to all God's commandments, in the sight of that God whom the prophet in vision saw sitting on a throne high and lifted up, before whom holy seraphic intelligences veiled their faces in deepest homage and holiest reverence, while the burden of those seraphim's song was a just acknowledgment of his infinite holiness, saying, "Holy, holy, holy, is the Lord of hosts: the whole earth is full of his glory"? Who, in the sight of that God who "searcheth all hearts, and understandeth all the imaginations of the thoughts," can, like this young ruler, ask proudly, or even boastfully, "What lack I yet?"

III. HIS IMPERFECTION PROVED. 1. *The great defect.* "One thing thou lackest" was our Lord's declaration. But that one thing was the most important, the most needful, and the most indispensable of all. He was outwardly moral, but a stranger to spiritual religion; he had a form of godliness, but wanted the power. The one thing he lacked was love, and love which manifests itself in entire self-surrender to God and in self-denial for man. After our Lord had reminded him of the commandments and of the duties required by God's Law, he stated a general principle that included them all, saying, as St. Matthew records it, "Thou shalt love thy neighbour as thyself." In fact, the whole Law, including the commandments of both tables, is fulfilled in that one word "love"—love to God and love to man; for "love is the fulfilling of the Law." And now he brings the principle just stated to a practical test, and puts the young ruler to the proof. "One thing thou lackest"—one thing, without which no obedience can be really beautiful before men or truly acceptable to God; one thing, without which obedience is neither real nor reliable, neither permanent nor performed consistently and efficiently; one thing, without which obedience is merely mechanical, and nothing more than a whitening of the outside of the sepulchre, while the inside is dead men's bones and all uncleanness. That one thing was the principle of love, which is the moving spring of all gospel obedience. This principle of love is the great impulse to all genuine morality; it is the essential element in all holiness. By this principle our Lord tested the young ruler, and in this practical way,—You profess entire obedience to God's Law; now, the sum and substance of that law is love—love to God and love to man, and this love must be supreme. You must love the Lord your God with all your mind, and soul, and strength, and heart; and your fellow-man as yourself. Go, then, and act out that great principle by selling all that you have, and distributing it to relieve the necessities of your poorer brethren of mankind, and to maintain and promote the service of God. The test was found too severe for the young man's morality ; his love was more of outward observance than of spiritual obedience, more of profession than of practice, more of the lip than of the life. He was not prepared to subordinate all, to surrender all, to sacrifice all, and to suffer all, if necessary, in fulfilment of that Law, the whole of which is contained in that one word "love." This one thing he lacked ; weighed in the balance, he was found wanting. He needed another to fulfil the Law in his stead ; he required a better righteousness than his own.

IV. APPLICATION OF THE SUBJECT. 1. *In relation to the irreligious.* Men may have fame and fortune ; they may have intellectual endowments and worldly wealth ; they may have every earthly comfort and convenience ; they may have kind friends, happy homes, and pleasant family relations ; they may have all that heart can wish. But, if they want religion, then they lack the one thing that can make men truly prosperous—blessed in time and happy through eternity. 2. *With respect to the amiable, and persons possessing certain good qualities.* Persons may be amiable ; they may be frank and affable and obliging ; they may be generous and liberal, hospitable and kind-hearted ; they may be upright in their dealings, and honourable in all the business of life ; they may have strong natural affection in their various relationships, as sons or husbands or parents ;—they may be all this, and have all these good natural quali-ties, without either possessing or professing religion. We may admire and even love them for their amiability and other natural excellences, for men differ widely by nature as well as by grace ; but, wanting religion, one thing they lack, and that one thing is the one thing needful. 3. *In regard to professors of religion.* Men may pro-fess themselves to be on the Lord's side ; they may be hearers and readers and students of God's Word ; they may by study make themselves acquainted with its precious truths—its doctrines and duties, its precepts and promises, its entreaties and exhortations, its warnings and reproofs ; they may have respect for the Scriptures, for the sabbath, for the sanctuary, and its services ; they may unite with God's people in prayer, in praise, in the sacraments, and in other exercises of religion ;—and after all this, and notwithstanding all this, their heart may not be right toward God ; one thing they lack, and, continuing to lack it, they must perish in the end. Oh, how dreadful to think of such having their lot at last with the openly irreligious, the profligate, and the profane ! And how such will gloat over those professors of religion when they descend to the abode of the lost, and exultingly say, "Are you also become as we ? Are you become like unto us ? " You, who professed religion, who offered prayers, and sang praises, and piqued yourselves on your superiority to profligates like us ; you, who did so much and went so far,—are you become our comrades in misery, our companions in distress ? Oh, we may imagine the fiendish glee with which false or fallen professors shall be jeered, when they sink down into partnership with the utterly abandoned in the place of destruction and the region of despair ! 4. *With reference to ourselves, and to avoid self-deception.* The young ruler was practising self-deception, without know-ing it. He did not know his deficiency till the Saviour brought him to the severe practical proof before us. Here is a salutary lesson and a solemn warning to beware of deception in our estimate of ourselves. We too, even we, may be resting on a morality that is hollow and defective ; we may fancy ourselves religious, while our heart is not right toward God, and has no real love to man. We may mistake enthusiasm, or the excite-ment of the occasion, or the power of sympathy, especially in times of revival, for love to Christ and his cause. We may enrol our names among the followers of the Lamb, and profess our readiness to follow him whithersoever he leadeth, through evil report and good report ; we may worship with a degree of devoutness in the sanctuary, partake of the sacraments, wear the so-called "livery of religion," and practise strict outward morality. All this is right and proper, all this we should do ; and yet, notwithstand-ing all this, we may not possess supreme love of the Saviour ; and so this one thing we lack, and thus are destitute of the chief thing, the main thing, the one thing most essentially needful, and absolutely indispensable to our present and everlasting well-being. 5. *How we are undeceived.* We may be ignorant of our deficiency till the Saviour calls us to self-renunciation in some form or other ; till he summons us to surrender some besetting sin or mortify some beloved lust—to cut off a right hand or a right foot or pluck out a right eye; to take up our cross in some way and follow him. He may require us to contribute more liberally to the claims of his religion, to give more largely to his cause, to work more vigorously as well as pray more earnestly for the extension of his kingdom; or, it may be, he demands a more unreserved consecration of our time, or talents, or influence, or example, or eloquence, or wealth, or whatever else we have to give and can give. Our refusal or reluctance to comply in any of the cases supposed, proves that one thing we lack, and the lack of it proves the entire absence or imperfection of that love which is the basis of duty and the principle of religion. 6. *Evidence of our possessing that love which works by faith.* If we have true love to the Lord Jesus, our surrender to his service will be complete; we shall give on all proper occasions and in due proportion to his cause; we shall, in a word, do and dare, and even die, if needs be, for his sake. We shall put in practice that principle of self-sacrificing love which our Lord requires, and which is ready to give all and do all and suffer all for him who loved us and gave himself for us. Wherever there is real affection, whether it be to friend or fellow-man or fatherland, that affection may be modified by national character or natural temperament, but it will be sure to manifest itself in some shape and develop itself in some way; it will unfetter the feet, it will untie the hands and set them to work, it will give utterance to the tongue, and impart activity to the life. We find an illustration of this in that remarkable military enterprise, "The Retreat of the Ten Thousand Greeks" out of the heart of the Persian empire. They had crossed deep rivers and climbed high mountains; they had overcome difficulties almost incredible, and encountered dangers of every kind; they made good their retreat in the face and in spite of all the artifice and arms of Persia. At length they reached the summit of a hill called Thēchēs (now Tekeh), between Erzeroum and Trebisond; and when, from the top of that high hill, those gallant Greeks, many of whom were islanders and all of them accustomed to the sea, descried in the distance the dark waters of the Euxine, they raised a loud and long-continued cheer. "The sea! the sea!" was the shout of every tongue. The sea reminded them of their native waters, and of their island homes; and the tide of affection rose in their bosoms, high as the laughing tides that "lave those Edens of the Eastern wave." So, wherever true affection exists, it needs but the occasion to call it forth—something to move the memory, and it vents itself spontaneously with overflowing fulness.—J. J. G.

Vers. 22—31. Parallel passages: Matt. xix. 22—30; Luke xviii. 23—30.—2. *Riches and their relation to the kingdom.* REFLECTIONS TO WHICH THE INCIDENT GAVE RISE. 1. *Effect on the young ruler.* He went away grieved. He is now brought to see that he cannot obey two masters; he cannot serve God and mammon. "He was sad at that saying." The word στυγνάσας here used is peculiar. In one other place it is applied to the appearance of the sky, and translated *lowering*; and so a cloud came over the young man's brow. Our Lord esteemed him (ἠγάπησεν), for he undoubtedly manifested several endearing traits of character—he was sincere, ardent, and evidently aspiring to something heroical in religion. For the present, however, he went away. 2. *Question about his return.* Whether this young man was Lazarus, as some have conjectured from a certain similarity of incidents, such as "One thing is needful," compared with "One thing thou lackest," is of course uncertain, as is also the probability of his afterwards returning to the Saviour. "He *was having* (ἦν ἔχων) great possessions," is a somewhat striking phrase, and denotes habitual as well as actual possession. His preference was given to worldly things for the present, and was called by Dante "the great refusal." One thing is certain, that those possessions soon reverted to others; and whether it was force, or fraud, or casuality, or death that at last deprived him of them, they were taken away; and if he continued to cling to them, and to prefer them to the heavenly inheritance, then he could reckon on no reversion in the skies—no portion of which it could be said, "it shall not be taken away from" him. 3. *The rich man's difficulty.* "It is easier for a camel to go through the eye of a needle, than for a rich man to enter into the kingdom of God." The difficulty of his entrance into the kingdom of heaven is stated (1) *proverbially.* This proverb is quite in keeping with the Oriental style of exaggeration, or hyperbolical expression. Some have read (2) κάμιλον, a *rope*, instead of κάμηλον, a camel, but without adequate authority. Some, again, understand it to mean (3) the narrow *side-gate* for foot-passengers beside the large gates of Eastern cities. This, however, is rather a modern conception to explain an ancient idea. The difficulty is connected with *trusting* in riches, and arises from the temptations to which riches expose their possessors. The love of riches is the root of the evil. A rich man may sit loose to the riches he possesses, while a poor man may set his heart upon the wealth to which he aspires. The astonishment of the apostles was occasioned partly by the extreme difficulties placed in the way of the rich by the temptations inseparably connected with riches; and partly by temptations of other kinds which they felt as placing difficulties in the way of salvation, specially, perhaps, among these the need of that inward subjective righteousness which is to be wrought out, and which, though it is not the title to, is the meetness for, the heavenly inheritance. The universal desire for wealth, and their own secret expectations of the rich rewards of an earthly kingdom, all of which were reprobated by the words of our Lord, increased the anticipated difficulty and intensified their amazement. 4. *The claim preferred by Peter on behalf of himself and fellow-disciples.* The refusal of the ruler to take up his cross and follow Christ suggests a comparison. Peter is the mouthpiece, as usual, and gives utterance to his own and the unspoken thoughts of his fellow-apostles. "Lo," he says, "we have left all, and have followed thee;" he draws special attention to the fact by a "Lo," or "Behold." Others soon after did the same, and literally acted out the requirement which our Lord proposed to the ruler as the practical test of that principle of self-denying, self-sacrificing love which is the spring of true obedience; for in Acts iv. 34, 35, we read, "As many as were possessed of lands or houses sold them, and brought the prices of the things that were sold, and laid them down at the apostles' feet: and distribution was made unto every man according as he had need." Peter, however, supplements his statement of fact by the inquiry, "What shall we have therefore?" as St. Matthew informs us. Peter reckons on a reward—he calculates on a *quid pro quo*; and so far forth he shows that he has failed in the spirit of the requirement, though he has fulfilled it in the letter. An earthly kingdom with its attractive rewards was still looming before the eyes of these partially enlightened men. 5. *The promised compensation.* In the compensatory reward the equivalents for "father" and "wife" are omitted. The reason is not far to seek; we have not many fathers in Christ. As the apostle writes to the Corinthians, "Though ye have ten thousand instructers in Christ, yet have ye not many fathers;" but contrariwise we may have many spiritual mothers, as well as brothers and sisters. Thus Paul reckons among his spiritual mothers the mother of Rufus, when he says (Rom. xvi. 13), "his mother and mine." The jeer of Julian, with respect to a multiplicity of wives, is referred to by Theophylact in the following terms:—"Shall he then also have a hundred wives? Yes. Though the cursed Julian mocked this." Theophylact then proceeds to explain it of the ministry of holy women supplying food and raiment, and relieving the disciples of care about all such things. The compensation of a hundredfold for all we abandon or lose for Christ's sake must be understood figuratively and spiritually— figuratiwise as to the quantitative proportion, spiritually with regard to quality or kind. The apostles enjoyed the fulfilment of this promise to the utmost in the presence and companionship of their Lord and Master, his instructions, his guidance, and his grace. There is no one who will make a similar sacrifice for his *name's* sake, according to St. Matthew—that is, as read in the light of the other evangelists, for sake of Christ and his cause, or Christ and his kingdom, not by reason of a calculation of reward—that will not gain what is a hundred times more valuable than all they sacrifice: Divine favour, pardon of sin, purity of heart, peace of conscience, spiritual consolations, friends in Jesus; and all these not only in the present dispensation, but at the present season (καιρῷ); while in the coming dispensation we shall have eternal life; that is to say, every blessing we need in this world, and eternal blessedness in the world to come. One of the items here enumerated is generally understood as a limitation; but μετὰ διωγμῶν does not denote (1) *after* persecutions, which would require the accusative, nor (2) *amidst* persecutions, but (3) *with* persecutions, implying that persecutions have a place among the enumerated blessings, just as in the sermon on the mount we read, "Blessed are they that have been persecuted for righteousness' sake: for theirs is the kingdom of heaven." We should also compare with this promise of the Saviour the inventory of the Christian's possessions, as reckoned up by the apostle in 1 Cor. iii. 22, 23. Further, strictly temporal blessings are not excluded, but either directly or indirectly included. Godliness enables us in a certain sense to make the best of both worlds, being profitable for all things, and "having the promise of the life that now is, as well as of that which is to come." The blessing of the Lord maketh rich ; for with his blessing and the enjoyment of his favour men cultivate those virtues and habits that tend to temporal as well as spiritual well-being, such as industry, thrift, temperance, health, purity, prudent management, proper economy, and consequent credit, all of which bear directly on worldly wealth and present happiness.—J. J. G.

Vers. 32—34. Parallel passages : Matt. xx. 17—19; Luke xviii. 31—34.—*A third prediction by our Lord of his passion and resurrection.* I. REPEATED PREDICTIONS ON THESE SUBJECTS. The disciples required line upon line on this subject; they were so slow to grasp it and so loth to entertain it. It appeared to them inconceivable and incredible. When it was first directly and definitely announced, Peter deprecated it in the strongest terms, and so far forgot himself that he presumed to rebuke his Master, which drew down on him in turn that severe and sharp reproof, "Get thee behind me, Satan," as though Satan had employed Peter as his emissary, and to do his work on that occasion by tempting our Lord to shrink from the sufferings he foretold. Instead of affording our Lord that support and sympathy, that strength and encouragement which, in view of the approaching ordeal, his human nature craved, his servants whom he loved and who loved him so well, though not always wisely, fell in with Satan's own suggestion at the temptation to the Saviour, to seek the crown without the cross. Why not prove his Messiahship and assume his Kingship over the nations without such suffering and sorrow, without the sharpness of death and shade of the sepulchre?

II. PREVIOUS PREPARATION. The previous training which the disciples had received from the Lord would, one might think, be sufficient to have disabused their minds of the prejudices of their race and nation to which they were so prone. Even after they had been convinced of his Messiahship, and after Peter's notable and noble confession of it, they needed to be repeatedly reminded of the necessity of his suffering and death to the completion of his work, and to be instructed once and again about the needfulness of his resurrection to demonstrate the divinity of his mission, and that he had power to lay down his life and power to take it again, as also that, delivered for our offences, he was to be raised for our justification. The notion of a temporal kingdom was so firmly fixed in their minds, and intertwined with all their Messianic hopes and expectations, that it was next to impossible to eradicate it. And yet, at an early period of his ministry, and almost immediately after his proclaiming the near approach of the kingdom of heaven, he expounded the principles, laws, and spiritual nature of that kingdom. Thus, in the sermon on the mount, he explained the object and elucidated the *rules* of that kingdom in the fifth chapter of St. Matthew ; he then interpreted, according to the rules of the kingdom, those *religious exercises* in which the subjects of the kingdom engage, in the sixth chapter of the same Gospel ; while in the seventh he lays down the *mutual duties* of the members, with other duties of a more general but practical kind. In his seaside parables, again, as recorded in the thirteenth chapter of the same Gospel, he traces the gradual progress, steady development in spite of all obstacles, and ultimate success of that kingdom. When thus prepared for it, he proclaimed to them once and again, and now the third time, in distinct, definite, and decided terms, his passion, death, and resurrection.

III. AN ADDITIONAL FEATURE IN THIS PREDICTION. In this third direct prediction a new element is introduced, the Gentiles are mentioned for the first time in connection with our Lord's death. "The Son of man shall be delivered unto the chief priests, and unto the scribes ; and they shall condemn him to death, and shall deliver him to the *Gentiles.*" And yet, strange, yea, passing strange, "they understood," as St. Luke tells us, "none of these things." It is probable that they understood his language as figurative, and expressive of the great difficulties to be overcome, and the formidable obstacles he would have to encounter in making his way to his Messianic throne. Hence it was that they were amazed at his alacrity, as he went before them and led the way as they were going up to the capital. This much, at the least, they must have known, that he was soon to face his bitterest foes ; they must have had some gloomy foreboding of the risk he was about to run, and the perils to which he was going to expose himself. Consequently they were amazed at the more than wonted energy with which he pressed forward to the place of danger and the scene of suffering; and though, like a dauntless leader, and fearless but faithful general, he marched at their head, preceding them and leading them forward, they fell timorously behind, afraid to follow him in the perilous path he was pursuing. We may here recall to mind that the first direct prediction of his death was in the neighbourhood of Cæsarea Philippi, soon after Peter's confession; the second shortly after, as they were returning to Capernaum; and now, on their way up to Jerusalem, he states the particulars more fully and clearly than ever before. The "spitting" is here mentioned by both St. Mark and St. Luke, the condemnation of the Jewish Sanhedrim is referred to by St. Matthew and St. Mark; the execution by the Gentiles is recorded by all three synoptists; while the mode of death by crucifixion is mentioned by St. Matthew alone.—J. J. G.

Vers. 35—45. Parallel passage: Matt. xx. 20—28.—*The ambition of the apostles: the sons of Zebedee.* I. PROBABLE ORIGIN. Peter and James and John certainly enjoyed a sort of precedence over the other apostles; they were *primi inter pares* at least, and constituted an inner circle among the members of the apostolic office. They were not only the first called to follow Christ, and to undertake special service in his cause; they had been privileged with his closest confidence; and they were admitted as his sole attendants, as we have already seen, on three most remarkable occasions. It was soon after one of these occasions, that of the Transfiguration, that the dispute about precedence occurred, on their journey to Capernaum. The natural inference seems to be that the prominence assigned to these three favourite apostles excited the jealousy of the rest, and occasioned the dispute referred to. And now again two of these aspiring men, having their heart still fixed on an earthly and secular kingdom, had their ambition fired by our Lord's mention of twelve thrones, as recorded by St. Matthew, and the apostles seated on them, in the regeneration, that second birthday of our world, in which the present sufferings and sorrows of earth's travail-throes shall at length issue. Accordingly, ashamed perhaps to present the petition themselves, they induce their mother Salome, according to St. Matthew's record, to present it for them, "desiring a certain thing of him;" and according to the principle, *Quod facit per alterum facit per se.* They thus try by a sort of trick, if we may so say, to make sure of our Lord's consent before specifying the nature of this unreasonable petition.

II. THE CUP AND THE BAPTISM. By "cup" is meant one's lot or destiny, be it good or bad, especially the latter. Thus, "Thou makest my cup run over," where the lot is plenty; and the words, divested of the figure, are nearly equivalent to, Thou givest me a plentiful supply as my lot. Again, it stands for vengeance allotted to the wicked, as is said of Jerusalem, "Thou hast drunk at the hand of the Lord the cup of his fury; thou hast drunken the dregs of the cup of trembling, and wrung them out;" and in Ps. lxxv. 8, it is the cup of wrath, or the portion of Divine and deserved indignation apportioned to the wicked, for it is there written, "In the hand of the Lord there is a cup, and the wine is red; it is full of mixture; and he poureth out of the same: but the dregs thereof, all the wicked of the earth shall wring them out, and drink them." Baptism, again, has three different meanings, or rather applications, in Scripture. There is baptism with water, a Christian sacrament; there is baptism by the Holy Spirit, or regeneration, which is that change by which we become truly Christians; and there is baptism in the sense of suffering, which is its meaning here.

III. A MISRENDERING. "But to sit on my right hand, and on my left, is not mine to give, but *it shall be given to them* for whom it is prepared of my Father." This verse, as it stands in our version, seems to limit the power of the Saviour, and to be at variance with his own statement in Luke xxii. 29, where he says, "I appoint unto you a kingdom, as my Father hath appointed unto me; that ye may eat and drink at my table in my kingdom, and sit on thrones judging the twelve tribes of Israel." It also appears flatly to contradict that promise of our Lord recorded in Rev. iii. 21, "To him that overcometh will I grant to sit with me in my throne." Various methods of rectification have been resorted to. The Latin Vulgate cuts the knot by inserting *vobis*, to you, and so rendering the clause in question, "It is not mine to give *to you*, but to them for whom it is prepared of my Father." But as this addition is not supported by any manuscript authority, it must be rejected as arbitrary.

Still more unwarrantable is the explanation of some, who understand the answer of our Lord as having reference only to the time previous to his sufferings, as though it meant, "It is not mine to give till after I shall have suffered; then all power will be vested in my hands." Now, the difficulty is in a great measure created by the words supplied in our version, and therefore marked in italics as above. The ellipsis thus indicated is either too little or too large. It must either be extended or eliminated altogether. We might enlarge the ellipsis, and take the clause to signify, "It is not mine to give (as a matter of favouritism), but it is mine to give (on the ground of fitness) to them for whom it is prepared of my Father." It is much better, however, to omit entirely the words supplied. This at once does away with the difficulty, and removes the seeming contradiction, while the sense of the original thus becomes plain and clear. Accordingly, we would read the last part of the verse thus, "Is not mine to give, but [save] to them for whom it is prepared." The preparedness of the recipients, not the power of the Saviour, is the only limitation of the bestowment in question. This power, again, is exercised in accordance with the Divine purpose, while in Rom. viii. 29, 30 we have a full declaration of such purpose: "Whom he did foreknow, he also did predestinate to be conformed to the image of his Son. . . . Moreover whom he did predestinate, them he also called: and whom he called, them he also justified; and whom he justified, them he also glorified." The view which we thus adopt corresponds with the rendering of the old Syriac, which translates the portion of the verse before us without supplying any words. It is confirmed by Luther's German translation. It has the sanction of several other important versions, both ancient and modern. The only objection to this, namely, that ἀλλά has thereby the sense of εἰ μὴ, is set aside by comparing Matt. xvii. 8 with Mark ix. 8, where, in recording the same fact, in nearly the same words, St. Matthew uses εἰ μὴ, while St. Mark expresses the same sense by ἀλλά. Even in the chapter immediately foregoing (Matt. xix.), ἀλλά is employed in nearly the same signification at the eleventh verse: "All men cannot receive this saying, save (ἀλλά) they to whom it is given." Though not identical, they closely approximate, for "res eodem recidit sive oppositione sive exceptione." If an ellipsis be at all admissible in the verse we are considering, then the words suggested by Alford, "Is not mine to give, but *it shall be given by me*," or those supplied by De Wette, "Sondern denen wird es verliehen," or even those supplied in the Revised Version, "Is not mine to give: but *it is for them* for whom it hath been prepared," are undoubtedly preferable to those supplied in our common version, and express the sense much better. Still, even the words thus introduced to eke out the meaning of the original seem awkward and unnecessary.—J. J. G.

Vers. 46—52. Parallel passages: Matt. xx. 29—34; Luke xviii. 35—43.—*The cure of two blind men at Jericho.* I. BLIND BARTIMÆUS. 1. *His condition.* He was *blind*; he was deprived of that most valuable sense of sight. He was a stranger to the beauties of nature. "The light is sweet, and a pleasant thing it is for the eyes to see the sun;" but that sun, that light, those beauties, those bright colours of sky or earth or sea; those lovely forms that appear in the heaven above, the earth beneath, and the waters round the earth—all, all were to him a blank. We know nothing of this blind man's family or friends, but from the patronymic, "Son of Timæus," we may infer that his father or family had been of some note; but the former had gone the way of all the earth and the latter had fallen into decay. That morning, however, whether by relative or friend or neighbourly hand, he was led forth to his accustomed seat by the wayside. He could hear the sound of the voices round him, but he could not see the persons who spoke; he could feel them if they came in contact with him, but could not behold them. Of all that passed by that way he could only judge by the voice or sound. The expression of their countenance, their form or figure, their smiles or tears, their bright eyes or sad looks, their faces sweet or sullen, were to him unknown and by him unseen. Our Lord, having continued his journey through Peræa, crossed the Jordan opposite Jericho, and arrived at that once famous city, upwards of five or six miles to the west of the river, and fifteen miles in a direct line eastward of Jerusalem. This ancient place, round which so many associations gather—such as its conquest by Joshua, its rebuilding by Hiel the Bethelite in the reign of Ahab, notwithstanding the curse; its mention in the history of the prophets Elijah and Elisha, its close connection at an early period with our Lord's own ancestry—was celebrated for its palms and balsams. Its fertilizing spring contributed to its wealth and importance. It was beautified by Herod the Great; subsequently destroyed, but rebuilt by Archelaus; celebrated by the historian Josephus as a populous and prosperous place in his day. But its glory long ago passed away. It is now a miserable hamlet called *Riha*. At the time of our Lord's visit, however, it was a flourishing town, and entitled to its ancient designation of the "city of palm trees," or "city of fragrance," as the name derived from the verb *ruach* imports. Fragrant flowers and aromatic shrubs perfumed the air; the scenery around was fresh and lovely; while every prospect was pleasing, and "man alone was vile." On the morning of the day that our Lord arrived at Jericho the gardens round the town bloomed in beauty, as usual, and charmed the eye of the beholder; the feathery palm lifted high its head in air or waved in the morning breeze; the Jordan valley stretched away into the distance. It was springtime, moreover, for multitudes were on their way to the great spring festival of the Passover at Jerusalem, and spring had clothed the landscape with vernal beauties. Over all the loveliness of earth was spread the clear blue of a Judæan sky, while down on all the glorious sun was shedding his bright beams, lighting up the whole with brilliancy and beauty. But what were all these beautiful sights and bright scenes to the blind Bartimæus? As far as he was concerned, they might as well have been dark and dismal, blank and black, like a moonless, starless night, with its darkness thick as in the land of Egypt, even "darkness that might be felt." 2. *His circumstances.* He was poor. Incapable of any worldly calling, he was a dependant on the charity of others; he was reduced to solicit alms of the passing traveller. Thus he was not only blind, but a beggar. Troubles love a train: one trouble seldom comes alone. The blindness of Bartimæus was aggravated by his poverty, and his poverty had no relief nor remedy but begging. His blindness had been the visitation of God; his poverty and beggary were misfortunes consequent thereon. For both he was to be pitied, for neither to be blamed. There was no special sin in his blindness, and therefore none in his begging. What a complication of misery had fallen to this poor man's lot in life! One almost fancies he sees Bartimæus as he sat that day by the wayside, with face pale, his head bare, perhaps bald from age; while those placid features—as the features of the blind always are—and those sightless eyes might well move the hardest heart to pity. The blind man hears the footsteps of travellers going on their way; he hears the earnest conversation of passers-by, eagerly bent on business or pleasure. Many a time the proud priest has gone that way, but ever passed by on the other side; or the haughty Levite has only cast a glance of curiosity at the blind man; sanctimonious Pharisees, with broad phylacteries, have looked with scorn on the poor mendicant. Many a time the cheerful voices of men and women have sounded in his ears, and many a time he has listened to the sound of childhood's fun and frolic. Day by day, as such sounds were repeated in his hearing and close at hand, all must have seemed to him lively, all cheerful, and all happy save himself, the poor blind beggar, doomed to melancholy darkness. This day, however, he hears the rush of many feet, the tread as of a numerous crowd, the shouts as of a mighty multitude. He wonders what the sound of those many footsteps means, what the swell of those voices can be. He listens till the crowd comes nearer, and he hears them speak in praise, a few, perhaps, in blame, of the Prophet of Nazareth. 3. *The corresponding state of the unconverted.* Many in the state of their soul resemble that poor blind beggar. The Scriptures speak of *blind* people that have eyes—"they have eyes, but see not;" their understanding is darkened, being alienated from the life of God through the ignorance that is in them because of the blindness of their heart. Satan, the prince of darkness, blinds the minds of them that believe not. His followers are of the night and of darkness, and at last, if they follow him to the end, they shall be cast into outer darkness. By nature men are spiritually blind. They are face to face with great realities—God and heaven and eternity—but they do not see them. They are on the brink of a great precipice, they are close to great peril, but they do not see it. Like a blind man on the edge of a frightful abyss, and yet seemingly secure just because he is blind to the danger. They are side by side with great truths, but, not seeing them, they deny their existence, as if a blind man denied the existence of mountains and rivers, the great sea and the bright sun, because he does not see them. There are great beauties just beside them—beauties of holiness, of grace, of glory, of Christ, and God; but they are as blind to spiritual beauties as a blind man to all the multiform beauties of this lovely world—a world so lovely notwithstanding the blight of sin. The spiritually blind see no comeliness in Christ that they should desire him, no glory in the gospel that they should embrace it, no preciousness in salvation that they should seek it, no beauty in holiness that they should practise it. Neither do they see any terror in the threatenings of God, nor much, if any, sinfulness in sin; nothing to attract in the promises of the gospel, and nothing to terrify in the curses of a broken Law. Sinner, you are blind, though you know it not! The sinner is *poor* as well as blind. He has no peace in this world, no prospect for the next; he has no real satisfaction on earth, and no sure hope of heaven. He has no shelter from the storm of Divine wrath, and no refuge in the day of danger. He has neither part nor lot with the people of God, no interest in the covenant of promise, no title to the heavenly inheritance, and no meetness for it. He is without the only blood that can cleanse from sin, the only righteousness that can justify a sinner, the only Spirit that can sanctify the soul. In a word, he is without Christ, and without God, and without hope. This surely is poverty—spiritual poverty, the deepest and the worst. This is the sad state of all unregenerate persons. They are, in the words of Scripture, "wretched, and miserable, and poor, and blind, and naked." They are blind in soul as Bartimæus in body, poor in spiritual things as he was in temporal. And yet to such the advice is addressed, "I counsel thee to buy of me gold tried in the fire, that thou mayest be rich; and white raiment, that thou mayest be clothed, and that the shame of thy nakedness do not appear; and anoint thine eyes with eyesalve, that thou mayest see."

II. THE APPLICATION OF BARTIMÆUS TO JESUS. 1. *His inquiry.* The first step here was inquiry. Hearing the noise of the on-coming crowd and the voices of the multitude passing by, he asked what it meant, and the answer returned to his inquiry was "that Jesus of Nazareth passeth by." This was good news for the poor blind beggar. Bartimæus had no doubt heard of Jesus, of his works of wonder and miracles of mercy. Some report may, nay, must, have reached him about the lepers cleansed, the demoniacs cured, the sick restored to health, the deaf whose ears were opened, the dumb whose tongues were loosed, even the dead raised to life, and, what came more closely home to himself, the blind whose eyes were opened. Bartimæus might, most probably did, hear all this; but how was he to reach the Prophet? Where could he find him? How could he, a poor, blind beggar, make such a long and weary way? Unless Jesus came into the neighbourhood of Jericho, he could not expect to be blessed and benefited. Now, however, what he never expected has come to pass. Jesus is at his side—he is passing by; and now Bartimæus feels that it is his opportunity, a most precious opportunity, far too precious to be lost. When his condition had rendered it impossible for him to go to the Saviour, the Saviour has come to him. Instantly and energetically he avails himself of this blessed opportunity. Now or never, he thinks with himself. He does not lose a moment; he cannot afford it, for he knows not but that the chance may be lost for ever. Bartimæus bethinks himself of all this, reasoning thus:—He is come to me; I could not go to him; and it is do or die now. If I lose this opportunity I may never have another. The tide will soon ebb; I must take it at the flow. The steamer will soon start; I must enter it or it will go without me. The bell is ringing and the train will soon be off; if I do not take my place at once I am left behind, and perhaps for ever. Somehow thus reasoned the poor, blind beggar—if we may be permitted to translate his words, or rather express his thoughts, in modern parlance. 2. *His earnest appeal.* And so "he began to cry out, and say, Jesus, thou Son of David, have mercy on me." Previous occurrences had prepared for this : Christ was passing by that way; Bartimæus was informed of his approach; he felt his need, and the Friend of sinners was near. Thus the various stages were inquiry, information, felt necessity, and the Saviour's presence. His appeal was earnest as well as instant. He cried out, and it was a strong and loud cry. Many things might have prevented his appeal, but they did not; many impediments lay in the way, but he did not allow them to keep him back. The crowd did not deter him, for he was in earnest, and cared not what the crowd either said or thought. The fact of so many strangers being round him did not stop him, for their presence was nothing to him, and he was too anxious for relief to feel false shame. The circumstance of his poverty did not prevent him; on the contrary, it prompted him all the more. True, he had no introduction to the Prophet from Galilee—no one to make known his situation or explain his unhappy circumstances, and bespeak the Saviour's favour on his behalf. Still he hoped his earnest appeal would find an echo in the bosom of the illustrious Stranger. He had no merit, he knew, to recommend him, and no particular claim on that Stranger's clemency; yet he was resolved to try whether his misfortune might not awaken his sympathy. 3. *A lesson for ourselves.* Jesus passeth by; he is near to us, and his presence is close at hand. In this sense he passeth by every time a sabbath dawns upon us, and every time we see the light of the sabbath sun. He passeth by, that is, is present, every time we enter the sanctuary and assemble ourselves with the people of God. He passeth by, and we are apprised of his presence, every time we are privileged to listen to a gospel sermon. He passeth by us every time we read his Word, or sing his praise, or call on God's name in prayer. He passeth by us every time we partake of the sacrament of the Supper, and he maketh himself known to us in the breaking of bread. Oh, how often on such occasions has " our heart burned within us as he talked to us by the way, and opened to us the Scriptures"! He passeth by us every time his Holy Spirit strives with us or exercises his gracious influences upon us. He passeth by and makes us feel his presence times and ways past specifying or reckoning. He assures us of this; for has he not said, " Behold, I stand at the door, and knock : if any man hear my voice, and open the door, I will come in to him, and will sup with him, and he with me"? Jesus has come near and close to each of us. He assumed our nature and became our Kinsman. He saw us in our blood, cast out into the open field on the day in which we were born; he pitied us and passed us by, and his time was a time of love. He has come to us, or we should never have gone to him; he has sought us, or we should never have sought him. He has passed us by and made his mercy known to us. He has made good his word, "I bring near my righteousness; it shall not be far off, and my salvation shall not tarry." Nor is it a mere hasty and passing visit he pays us. He has stood at the door of our heart until his head has become wet with dew and his locks with the drops of the night. But he will not stand always. He passeth by; and while we understand this statement of his presence, and of that presence manifested to our souls, of his gracious presence in his ordinances, and of his Holy Spirit stirring in our hearts, yet we must not make the fatal mistake of supposing that this will last always. In the very nature of things it cannot continue. Life itself is uncertain, and time is short. Besides, the day of grace will not always tarry; like the Saviour himself, it passeth by. Jesus never visited Jericho again, nor did he ever pass by that way again. So with ourselves. He has visited us often; who can say when or which shall be his last visit? Oh, then, for such earnestness and eagerness as Bartimæus showed, on the part of all that hear the gospel! Jesus has passed near us many a time, and yet some of us, up to the present moment, care for none of these things. We have never cried for help as we ought, or sued for mercy as we should; we have never eagerly sought his grace, or earnestly supplicated forgiveness. We have been lukewarm, and neither cold nor hot. If so, let us beware lest, like the Laodiceans, we are spued out of his mouth. We may have been at ease in Zion, and like wine settled on the lees, forgetful of the woes pronounced on such. How little of the earnestness of this blind beggar do we show in the things of God! And yet, if like him we felt our need, we could not but be earnest and energetic. The hungry man will beg for bread; the thirsty man will repair to the clear cool spring; the starving babe, by the very instinct of its nature, will cry for nurture; even the dumb animals have ways of making known their wants and of seeking a supply : and shall we be so indifferent to spiritual necessities and eternal interests? 4. *Characteristics of discipleship.* Bartimæus exhibited several characteristics of true discipleship—characteristics which all should seek to possess. He was *prompt.* There is need for promptness, for God's long-suffering has its limits. He may wait long, but will not wait always. He passeth by, vouchsafing his presence for a time, but withdrawing it when he sees fit so to do. He was *humble,* for his plea was for mercy: " Have mercy on me." He was conscious of the entire absence of all merit. He came at once, and came as he was—in his blindness, in his poverty, and in his beggary. So should it be with ourselves. We must come according to the spirit of the simple lines—

"Just as I am—without one plea
But that thy blood was shed for me,
And that thou bidd'st me come to thee,
O Lamb of God, I come!

"Just as I am—poor, wretched, blind—
Sight, riches, healing of the mind,
Yea, all I need, in thee to find,
O Lamb of God, I come!"

His *faith* was remarkable; he was fully abreast of his times in theological knowledge; he was fairly ahead of the crowd in his knowledge of the Saviour. They informed him that it was *Jesus of Nazareth* that was passing by. They represented him correctly, as far as they went; but their representation was sadly imperfect and shamefully incomplete. They regarded him as a prophet, but a prophet of a despised place and of a despised province. His native town and native province were both of little, or rather of ill, repute. "Can any good thing," asked Nathanael, "come out of Nazareth?" The Pharisees said scornfully to Nicodemus, "Search and look: for out of Galilee ariseth no prophet." Bartimæus knew better. Blind as he was, and so shut out from books as the source of knowledge; poor as he was, and so deprived of the means of acquiring information, he had made himself in some way or by some means acquainted with the descent and dignity of Messiah. Hence he accosted him, not as Jesus of Nazareth, but addressed him, "Jesus, thou Son of David." In any case the Spirit of God had been his instructor. Thus, too, we must come to Jesus with a proper apprehension of his character and claims, of his mercy and his might, as well as of our own worthlessness and helplessness. Feeling ourselves sinners, our individual inquiry must be, "What must I do to be saved?" Accepting the answer furnished by God's Word, we must "believe in the Lord Jesus Christ, and we shall be saved." Feeling ourselves lost, we are encouraged by the Saviour's own gracious assurance, that He "came to seek and save that which was lost." Feeling ourselves deep down in the pit of sin, in this low and lost condition, we are cheered by the declaration that his errand into our world was to save sinners, even the chief. However blind the eyes, Christ can open them; however hard the heart, he can soften it; however dark the stain of our sin, his blood can wash it out; however desperate our case, his grace can meet it; however sorrowful and forlorn our spirits, he can soothe and comfort them. His *perseverance* was also remarkable. His ardour was not to be repressed, his earnestness was not to be checked. Having found the long-expected Deliverer, he was determined not to be parted from him; having attained a conviction—a rapidly growing and speedily maturing conviction—that he was now within reach of One who could convert the soul as well as cure the body, he continued to cry to him, and ceased not till his cry was heard and answered. The crowd wished to impose silence on him, yet he persevered; the multitude rebuked him, that he should hold his peace, yet he "cried the more," says St. Matthew; "the more a great deal," says St. Mark; "so much the more," says St. Luke. They protested against his appeal, and many—not one, or two, or three, but many of them—charged him to hold his peace. His outcry appeared to them, no doubt, so loud, so boisterous, so rude, that they did their best to suppress it; but he refused to desist. Some thought him too contemptible to deserve notice, or to delay the procession; others, perhaps, felt or feigned concern for the Master, as having too many objects of solicitude on his spirit, and too many and too heavy burdens on his shoulders already; but in spite of all these obstacles, and in face of all this opposition, Bartimæus persisted, and in the end succeeded. Such was this poor beggar—this brave, blind man! When sinners set about seeking God, they may expect similar obstruction, and rebukes equally heartless and cruel. Satan will be sure to rouse opposition from some quarter. The world will flatter them or force them to desist; friends will speak words of pity or persuade them to abandon their self-imposed task; formalists may shake the head and speak of fanaticism, enthusiasm, or unwisdom. But earnest souls, like Bartimæus, will not, must not, give up or give over. Once they have put their hand to the plough, they may not turn back; once they have set their face Zionward, they must not turn away or turn aside. The language of the twenty-seventh Psalm will be on their lips, and acted out in their life, as the psalmist says, "Though an host should encamp against me, my heart shall not fear : though war should rise against me, in this will I be confident. One thing have I desired of the Lord, that will I seek after. . . . Hear, O Lord, when I cry with my voice : have mercy also upon me, and answer me." Thus waiting on the Lord, they shall be enabled to hold on their way; waiting on the Lord, they shall be strengthened ; waiting on the Lord, they shall experience that merciful support, of which mention is interjected six and twenty times in the psalm which records Israel's trials and triumphs —" for his mercy endureth for ever."

III. THE SUCCESS WHICH CROWNED THE APPLICATION. 1. "*Jesus stood still.*" So says St. Matthew, so says St. Mark, so says St. Luke; all three evangelists agree in record- ing this fact. He was on his last journey to Jerusalem; he was hurrying on to drink and drain the cup of bitterness, and be baptized with the baptism of blood; he was hastening forward with eager steps to bear his people's sins in his own body on the tree, to satisfy Divine justice by the sacrifice of himself, to vindicate God's truth, express God's love, and magnify God's Law, to maintain the glory of the Divine attributes, and secure the salvation of countless human souls. Never was there a journey so important, never was errand so deeply interesting, and never was there another embassy involving such weighty consequences and vast concernments. Heaven and earth and hell were all affected by that journey; the glory of God was connected with it; and the redemption of man depended on it. And yet, notwithstanding all the urgencies of that journey, and all the ardour, even bordering on impatience, with which our Lord was speeding forward on that journey, the cry of distress arrested him; the prayer of a blind beggar stopped him ! And so it is still, for the prayer of the penitent has a potency that Divine mercy never resists, and will not repel. The waves of the sea stood still, and the waters of the river stood still, in the interests of God's people, and in order that they might pass over; the sun and moon stood still at the cry of Joshua, and that the hosts of Israel might prolong their victory ; the shadow stood still, or rather went back, on the dial-plate of time at the prayers of good King Hezekiah, and to assure him of an addition of fifteen years to his limit of life. But what are the waters of the sea, or the luminaries of the sky, or the element of time to him who furrowed the channel for the one and fixed the place of the other, and who himself fills all space with his presence and all time with his fulness ? And yet he stood still when that crisis, the greatest in all this world's history, was fast approaching—for Messiah to be cut off, sin to be made an end of, and everlasting righteous- ness brought in ; and all this in answer to Bartimæus's earnest entreaties, and to restore sight to his blind eyes and impart life to his dead soul. 2. *What he did on standing still.* We have three accounts of this also, but, while identical in the main, they exhibit the same thing under different aspects. "He called" is the statement of St. Matthew ; " he commanded him to be called" is the version of St. Mark ; "he commanded him to be brought " is the addition of St. Luke. In the first we have the sovereignty of God, who calls us by his grace—calls us out of darkness into marvellous light. In the second we have the ministry of man. "The Lord gave the Word," we read : "great was the com- pany of those that published it." In the third we have the agency of the Holy Spirit. God, of his sovereign grace and mere good pleasure, calls us—calls us, as St. Peter assures us, "unto his eternal glory by Christ Jesus ; " and so, as stated in other Scriptures, it is a "high calling," a "holy calling," and a "heavenly calling." To men, as his ambassadors, is committed the ministry of reconciliation ; they are employed to explain the Divine call, to enforce it and repeat it. The Holy Spirit's agency must accompany the minister's message, to bring it home in power and demonstration and assurance, convincing of sin, of righteousness, and of judgment. Thus we are made willing in the day of his power ; and thus at his own command we are brought unto him. The lessons of his Word, the dispensations of his providence, the ordinances of religion, the movements of his Holy Spirit on our hearts, are all employed in drawing us to Christ for the salvation of our souls. 3. *A strange question.* We almost see the blind man rise in haste at the word of command, which is now repeated to him by the crowd, with the encouraging "Be of good comfort," and, in obedience to the Saviour's call, rush forward, " casting aside his garment," in his eager, earnest haste. We almost hear the Saviour answer the unspoken thought of the blind man's heart, as he said unto him, " What wilt thou that I should do unto thee ? " There was little need for such an inquiry, one would think, on the part of our Lord. There was not one in all that crowd that could not guess, and guess correctly, the answer ; the Saviour knew the thought that was uppermost in the blind man's heart, for he knew what was in man. Why, then, does he ask the question? Just in order to give him an opportunity of presenting his petition and making known his wants in his own words. (1) So in our own case we come to Jesus by his command and gracious invitation; that command is expressed in many forms, such as "Come unto me, all ye that labour and are heavy laden;" "Come, buy wine and milk without money and without price." His invitations are multiplied. (2) In coming we must lay aside every weight, and the sin that would most easily beset us, just as Bartimæus cast aside his outer garment, to be free from every entanglement that might retard or altogether prevent our reaching him. The young ruler, as we have seen, came to Jesus; he longed for Jesus, and Jesus esteemed him; he panted for life eternal, but could not bring himself to part with the things of this present life; he did not cast aside his garment. (3) We are to come with prayer. Once the gracious desire is formed in our heart by the Spirit of grace, it will soon shape itself in prayer, for the spirit of grace is also the spirit of supplication. Though he knows our wants better than we ourselves, and before we ask him, and even our ignorance in asking; yet he will have us express them in prayer, so that "Behold, he prayeth!" indicates the first outgoing of spiritual life. God grants to our feeblest petitions what he will not give without them. Prayer fits us for receiving the blessing; it puts us into the proper position—that of humble dependence; it exalts the Giver without in any way degrading the receiver; it brings us into conformity with God's own plan. Fixed, as the alternation of day and night, or as the succession of the seasons, or as the order of the universe itself, is God's purpose that we must ask in order to receive, seek in order to find, and knock in order that it may be opened. When our necessity is greatest, let us go to him by prayer, and he will supply it; when the trial is sorest, let us go to him in prayer, and he will alleviate it or entirely remove it; when the burden is heaviest, let us go to him in prayer, and he will lift it entirely off our shoulders or at least enable us to bear it. (4) Another reason for the question was to suggest the large liberality and great generosity of the Saviour; there is a glorious fulness in the inquiry, "What wilt thou?" There is a gracious freeness in it at the same time. There is a royal ring in the question; there is a kingly munificence. It reminds us of, though it surpasses, both in reality and richness, the question of King Ahasuerus to his queen, "What is thy petition? and it shall be granted thee: and what is thy request? even to the half of the kingdom it shall be performed." So to Bartimæus the Saviour said, What wilt thou that I should do unto thee?" and it shall be done; you have only to make your choice; you have only to mention what you want. I do not limit you; if straitened, it is in and through yourself. So to the suppliant still Christ says, "What wilt thou that I should do unto thee?"—The wealth of worlds is mine; the power of omnipotence is mine; the treasures of wisdom and knowledge are mine; ask, and you shall receive what you want, as much as you want, yea, all you want, provided it be really expedient for you, conducive to the Divine glory, and consistent with the welfare of your fellow-man. 4. *The blind man's direct reply.* Bartimæus, we are sure from all the known circumstances of the case, wanted many things—better clothing, more wholesome food, a more comfortable place of abode, more of the necessaries of life in general; some even of its simple comforts would not be likely to spoil this poor mendicant, who had suffered so long from privation, pining in poverty and pinched with want. Bartimæus refers to none of these things, or such things as these; he comes directly to the point; he names at once the thing which he needs most; he mentions the one thing needful for the relief of his direst necessity. "Lord," he said, "that I might receive my sight." In like manner, whether we engage in public supplication, or family worship, or private devotions, we should have before our mind our most urgent necessities, rightly discriminate them, really feel them, and with pointed earnestness and plain directness of speech express them; we should have some felt want, some real necessity, an actual petition to present or hearty thanksgiving to render. 5. *The cure.* It was immediate: "immediately he received his sight." It was a wonderful change for this poor, blind man; it was a new and blessed experience; it was like a transference into a new and beautiful world; in fact, we cannot realize, and words fail to express it. Equally new, and gracious, and wonderful, and blessed is the translation out of the kingdom of darkness into the kingdom of light, out of the kingdom of Satan into the kingdom of God, which takes place in regeneration, when the eyes of the understanding are opened and the light of the knowledge of the glory of God flashes in upon the soul. 6. *The means employed.* The gentle touch of Jesus' hand was the *outward* instrumentality. Lovingly, tenderly, he passed his hand over the sightless eyeballs. What a thrilling touch that was! What condescension withal! How it helped the sufferer to hope for the best, and to have faith in the Saviour's power! The inward means was *faith*: "Thy faith hath saved thee." Nor is it said, "Thy promptness hath saved thee," though his promptness was laudable; nor "Thy humility," though that was most becoming; nor "Thy perseverance," though that was commendable; nor "Thy Scriptural knowledge in relation to the Messianic hopes of the nation," though that was of a superior kind; but "Thy faith." Faith and salvation go hand in hand together; God has joined them, let not man separate them; God has wed them, and let not man divorce them. 7. *How faith saves.* It saves, not by any merit in itself, not by any virtue of its own; it saves by bringing us into contact with Christ. It is the instrument that extracts virtue from the grace of Christ; it is the link of gold that unites with and binds us to Christ; it is the arm that puts on the robe of Christ's righteousness, and that is the robe of salvation; it is the hand stretched out to receive the gifts that grace bestows. "He that believeth shall be saved, he that believeth not shall be damned."

IV. How BARTIMÆUS PROVED HIS GRATITUDE. 1. *He followed Christ.* His faith, as usual, wrought by love; and love keeps near, and delights in, the presence of the beloved object. So with all who love the Lord; they follow him. Soon as the eyes are enlightened to see his beauty and his excellence, we follow him; soon as the heart begins to burn within us by his teaching, we follow him; if true disciples, we follow him; if sheep of the Good Shepherd, we follow him. "My sheep hear my voice, and I know them, and they follow me." In Old Testament as well as in New Testament times, it was so with all who loved the Lord. Thus it is recorded to the honour, and redounded to the salvation, of Caleb and Joshua that they "wholly followed the Lord." The psalmist speaks his personal experience in the words, "My soul followeth hard after thee." The children of God in both Testaments followed the Lord as monuments of his mercy, as trophies of his grace, as living witnesses of the power of his love, and as witness-bearers to his truth. Bartimæus followed him "in the way." We read of the Israelites, in their journeyings, being on one occasion sorely "discouraged because of the way." It may be so with ourselves, yet we must follow the Saviour whithersoever he leads; whether it be up the hill of difficulty, or down the hill into the valley of humiliation; whether it be a way of toil and trial, of danger and distress, or in green pastures and by still waters; taking up our cross, we shall, by his gracious help, follow him; through evil report and good report we shall follow him. Even when his way, as often, is in the sea, and his path in the great waters, and his footsteps are not known, we will follow him. But how do we make sure that it is the way—the right way? He has himself marked out the way in his Word, and said to us, "This is the way, walk ye in it;" his providence has erected signposts along the way, so that a "wayfaring man, though a fool, need not err therein" or wander therefrom; his Spirit guides us in the way and comforts us by the way. Thus instructed in his Word, led by his providence, and guided by his Spirit, we shall follow him in the way which, rough though it be at times, and painful, and even distressing, leads in the end to glory, honour, and immortality. 2. *He glorified God.* "Glorifying God," says St. Luke. So, too, shall we. We have always admired that opening statement in one of the Westminster standards, which says, "Man's chief end is to glorify God and enjoy him for ever;" it contains at once the whole duty of man, and the chief blessedness of man. We glorify God by deep and heartfelt gratitude; we glorify him when we praise his name and defend his cause; we glorify him by the devotedness of our life and our consecration to his service. Thus by the homage of the heart, by the fruit of the lips, and by the sinlessness and faithfulness of the life, we glorify him. We have good cause to glorify God for his unspeakable gift—the Son of his love and our beloved Saviour. We glorify God for raising up "a horn of salvation for us in the house of his servant David;" for the perfection of his person, the purity of his life, the suitability of his offices, the efficacy of his death, the prevalence of his intercession; for "his agony and bloody sweat, for his cross and passion, for his precious death and burial, for his glorious resurrection and ascension, and for the coming of the Holy Ghost;" for all he has done for us, for all he is doing, and for all he has promised to do. 3. *The happy influence exerted on others.* "All the people," says St. Luke, "when they saw it, gave praise unto

God." There is a holy contagiousness in this work. When one gets good for his own soul, he cannot keep it to himself, he cannot hide it; the gratitude is so deep, the joy is so great, that he must declare it aloud and to all around, just as the psalmist, saying—

> "All that fear God, come, hear; I'll tell
> What he did for my soul."

Or again—

> "God will I bless all times; his praise
> My mouth shall still express.
>
> .   .   .
>
> Extol the Lord with me, let us
> Exalt his name together."

4. *Conclusion.* We would sum up our study of the case of this poor, blind beggar in the now somewhat trite, but still touching and tender verses of a poet lately departed—

> "Blind Bartimæus at the gates
> Of Jericho in darkness waits;
> He hears the crowd;—he hears a breath
> Say, 'It is Christ of Nazareth!'
> And calls, in tones of agony,
> 'Ιησοῦ, ἐλέησόν με!

> "The thronging multitudes increase;
> 'Blind Bartimæus, hold thy peace!'
> But still, above the noisy crowd,
> The beggar's cry is shrill and loud;
> Until they say, 'He calleth thee!'
> Θάρσει, ἔγειραι, φωνεῖ σε!

> "Then saith the Christ, as silent stands
> The crowd, 'What wilt thou at my hands?'
> And he replies, 'Oh, give me light!
> Rabbi, restore the blind man's sight!'
> And Jesus answers, Ὕπαγε·
> 'Η πίστις σοῦ σέσωκέ σε!

> "Ye that have eyes, yet cannot see,
> In darkness and in misery,
> Recall those mighty voices three,
> 'Ιησοῦ, ἐλέησόν με!
> Θάρσει, ἔγειραι, ὕπαγε!
> 'Η πίστις σοῦ σέσωκέ σε!"

We may here add, in a very few words, the common solution of two seeming discrepancies of the evangelists' narrative: viz. our Lord cured *two* blind men together on this occasion; but Bartimæus was better known, either previously, as already hinted, in reference to the patronymic, or subsequently as a "monument of the Lord's miracle;" while in reference to the *place* or *time* of cure, one of the two had made his application to our Lord as he approached or entered Jericho, yet was not cured at that time, but in company with the second, as our Lord left the city.—J. J. G.

EXPOSITION.

CHAPTER XI.

Ver. 1.—**And when they drew nigh unto Jerusalem, unto Bethphage and Bethany, at the mount of Olives.** St. Matthew (xxi. 1) says, "When they drew nigh unto Jerusalem, and came unto Bethphage." St. Mark mentions the three places together, because Bethphage and Bethany, being near together, were also both of them close to Jerusalem.

The distance from Jericho to Jerusalem (about seventeen miles) would involve a journey of about seven hours. The country between Jerusalem and Jericho is hilly, rugged, and desolate. It is from the height overhanging Bethany that the finest view of Jerusalem is gained. It appears from St. John (xii. 1) that our Lord on the preceding sabbath had supped, and probably passed the night, at Bethany; and that on the following day (answering to our Palm Sunday) he had come still nearer to Jerusalem, namely, to Bethphage; and from thence he sent two of his disciples for the ass and the colt. So his way to Jerusalem was from Bethany by Bethphage, the Mount of Olives, and the Valley of Jehoshaphat. The Valley of Jehoshaphat, through which flows the brook Kedron, lies close to Jerusalem. Bethphage literally means "the house of green figs," as Bethany, lying a short distance west of it, means "the house of dates." The date palm growing in the neighbourhood would furnish the branches with which the multitude strewed the way on the occasion of our Lord's triumphal entry. **He sendeth two of his disciples.** Who were they? Bede thinks that they were Peter and Philip. Jansenius, with greater probability, thinks that they were Peter and John, because a little after this Christ sent these two to prepare for the Passover. But we know nothing certain on this point.

Ver. 2.—**Go your way into the village that is over against you.** The village over against them would most likely be Bethphage, towards which they were then approaching. **Straightway as ye enter into it, ye shall find a colt tied, whereon no man ever yet sat.** St. Mark mentions only the colt; St. Matthew mentions the ass and the colt. But St. Mark singles out the colt as that which our Lord specially needed; the mother of the animal accompanying it as a sumpter. Animals which had never before been used were alone admissible for sacred purposes. We read in Numbers (xix. 2) of "the heifer on which never came yoke." Our Lord here beholds things absent and out of sight, as though they were present. So that he revealed this to his disciples by the gift of prophecy which his divinity added to his humanity. Here, therefore, is a manifest proof of his divinity. It was by the same Divine power that he revealed to Nathanael what had taken place under the fig tree.

Ver. 3.—**And if any one say unto you, Why do ye this? say ye, The Lord hath need of him; and streightway he will send him back hither.** The Greek, according to the best authorities here, is εὐθέως αὐτὸν ἀποστέλλει πάλιν ὧδε: literally, *straightway he sendeth it back hither again.* The verb here in the present may represent the verb in the future, "he will send it back." But the word "again" (πάλιν) is not quite so easily explained. There is strong authority for the insertion of this word, which necessarily changes the meaning of the sentence. Without the πάλιν, the sentence would actually mean that our Lord, by his Divine prescience, here tells his disciples that when the colt was

demanded by them the owner would at once permit them to take it. But if the word πάλιν be inserted, it can only mean that this was a part of the message which our Lord directed his disciples to deliver as from himself, "The Lord hath need of him; and he, the Lord, will forthwith send him back again." The passage is so interpreted by Origen, who twice introduces the adverb in his commentary on St. Matthew. The evidence of the oldest uncials is strongly in favour of this insertion. Our Lord was unwilling that the disciples should take away the colt if the owner objected. He might have taken the animals away in his own supreme right, but he chose to accomplish his will by his providence, powerfully and yet gently; and, if the reading here be allowed, he further influenced them by the promise that their property should be returned to them. It was the will and purpose of Christ, who for these three years had gone about on foot, and travelled over the whole of Palestine in this way, to show himself at length the King of Judah, that is, the Messiah and Heir of David; and so he resolves to enter Jerusalem, the metropolis, the city of the great King, with royal dignity. But he will not be surrounded with the "pomp and circumstance" of an earthly monarch. He rides on an ass's colt, that he might show his kingdom to be of another kind, that is, spiritual and heavenly. And so he assumes a humble equipage, riding upon a colt, his only housings being the clothes of his disciples. And yet there was dignity as well as humility in his equipage. The ass of the East was, and is, a superior animal to that known amongst us. The judges and princes of Israel rode on " white asses," and their sons on asses' colts. So our Lord rode upon an ass's colt; and there were no gleaming swords in his procession, or other signs of strife and bloodshed. But there were palm branches and garments spread all along his path—the evidences of devotion to him. So he came in gentleness, not that he might be feared on account of his power, but that he might be loved on account of his goodness.

Ver. 4.—**By the door without, in a place where two ways met** (ἐπὶ τοῦ ἀμφόδου); literally, *in the open street.*

Ver. 8.—**Others cut down branches off the trees,** etc. According to the best authorities, the words should be rendered, *and others branches* (or, *leaves for strewing*), *which they had cut from the fields* (ἄλλοι δὲ στοιβάδας κόψαντες ἐκ τῶν ἀγρῶν). The branches were cut in the fields; and the smaller, leafy portions of them, suitable for their purpose, were carried out.

Ver. 9.—The word **Hosanna** literally means "Oh, save!" It may have been originally the cry of captives or rebels for mercy; and thus have passed into a general acclamation, expressive of joy and deliverance.

Ver. 10.—This verse should be read thus: **Blessed be the kingdom that cometh, the kingdom of our father David**—that is, the kingdom of Messiah, now coming, and about to be established—**Hosanna in the highest;**—that is, Hosanna in the highest realms of glory and blessedness, where salvation is perfected.

Ver. 11.—This visit to the temple is not mentioned by St. Matthew. It is an important addition to his narrative. The moment of our Lord's triumphant entry into Jerusalem was not the moment for the display of his indignation against the profaners of the temple. He was then surrounded by an enthusiastic and admiring multitude; so he contented himself on this occasion with **looking round about upon all things** (περιβλεψάμενος πάντα). His keen and searching eye saw at a glance all that was going on, and penetrated everything. But without any comment or action at that time, **he went out unto Bethany** (it was now eventide) **with the twelve.** No doubt the disciples, and especially Peter, saw what was involved in this visit of inspection, which prepared them for what took place on the morrow.

Ver. 12.—**And on the morrow, when they were come out from Bethany, he hungered.** This was, therefore, the day after Palm Sunday (as we call it)—on the Monday, the 11th day of the month Nisan, which, according to our computation, would be March 21. *He hungered.* This showed his humanity, which he was ever wont to do when he was about to display his Divine power. The fact that he hungered would lead us to the conclusion that he had not been spending the night in the house of Martha and Mary. It is far more likely that he had been in the open air during the previous night, fasting and praying.

Ver. 13.—**And seeing a fig tree afar off having leaves, he came, if haply he might find anything thereon.** St. Matthew (xxi. 19) says he saw "*one* fig tree" (μίαν συκῆν), and therefore more conspicuous. Fig trees were no doubt plentiful in the neighbourhood of Bethphage, "the house of figs." Dean Stanley ('Sinai and Palestine,' p. 418) says that "Mount Olivet is still sprinkled with fig trees." This fig tree had leaves, but no fruit; **for it was not the season of figs** (ὁ γὰρ καιρὸς οὐκ ἦν σύκων). Other trees would all be bare at this early season, but the fig trees would be putting forth their broad green leaves. It is possible that this tree, standing by itself as it would seem, was more forward than the

other fig trees around. It was seen "from afar," and therefore it must have had the full benefit of the sun. Our Lord says (St. Luke xxi. 29), "Behold the fig tree, and all the trees: when they now shoot forth, ye see it, and know of your own selves that the summer is now nigh." He puts the fig tree first, as being of its own nature the most forward to put forth its buds. But then it is peculiar to the fig tree that its fruit begins to appear before its leaves. It was, therefore, a natural supposition that on this tree, with its leaves fully developed, there might be found at least some ripened fruit. Our Lord, therefore, approaches the tree in his hunger, with the expectation of finding fruit. But as he draws near to it, and realizes the fact that the tree, though full of leaf, is absolutely fruitless, he forgets his natural hunger in the thought of the spiritual figure which this tree began to present to his mind. The accident of his hunger as a man, brought him into contact with a great parable of spiritual things, presented to him as God; and as he approached this fig tree full of leaf, but destitute of fruit, there stood before him the striking but awful image of the Jewish nation, having indeed the leaves of a great profession, but yielding no fruit. The leaves of this fig tree deceived the passerby, who, from seeing them, would naturally expect the fruit. And so the fig tree was cursed, not for being barren, but for being false. When our Lord, being hungry, sought figs on the fig tree, he signified that he hungered after something which he did not find. The Jews were this unprofitable fig tree, full of the leaves of profession, but fruitless. Our Lord never did anything without reason; and, therefore, when he seemed to do anything without reason, he was setting forth in a figure some great reality. Nothing but his Divine yearning after the Jewish people, his spiritual hunger for their salvation, can explain this typical action with regard to the fig tree, and indeed the whole mystery of his life and death.

Ver. 14.—**No man eat fruit from thee henceforward for ever** (εἰς τὸν αἰῶνα). These words, in their application to the Jewish nation, have a merciful limitation—a limitation which lies in the original words rendered "for ever," which literally mean *for the age.* "No man eat fruit of thee henceforward, for the age;" until the times of the Gentiles be fulfilled. A day will doubtless come when Israel, which now says, "I am a dry tree," shall accept the words of its true Lord, "From me is thy fruit found," and shall be clothed with the richest fruits of all trees. (See Trench on the Miracles). St. Matthew (xxi. 19) tells us that "immediately the fig tree withered away." "Straightway a shivering fear and trembling passed through its leaves, as though it was at once struck to the heart by the malediction of its Creator." Our Lord's disciples heard his words; but they appear not to have noticed the immediate effect of them upon the tree. It was not until the next day that they observed what had happened. This miracle would show his disciples how soon he could have withered his enemies, who were about to crucify him; but he waited with long-suffering for their salvation, by repentance and faith in him.

Ver. 15.—**And they come to Jerusalem: and he entered into the temple.** Not the holy place, nor the holy of holies (into which the high priest might alone enter), but into the temple court; for into that the people went to pray, and to witness the sacrifices which were being offered before the holy place; for this court was, so to speak, the temple of the people. Our Lord was not a Levitical priest, because he was not sprung of Levi and Aaron. Therefore he could not enter the holy place, but only the outer court of the temple. **And began to cast out** (ἐκβάλλειν)—it was a forcible expulsion—**them that sold and them that bought in the temple.** There were two occasions on which our Lord thus purged the temple—one at the beginning of his public ministry, and the other at the end of it, four days before his death. There was a regular market in the outer court,¦ the court of the Gentiles, belonging to the family of the high priest. The booths of this market are mentioned in the rabbinical writings as the booths of the son of Hanan, or Annas. But this market is never mentioned in the Old Testament. It seems to have sprung up after the Captivity. Our Lord adopted these strong measures (1) because the temple courts were not the proper places for merchandise, and (2) because these transactions were often dishonest, on account of the avarice and covetousness of the priests. The priests, either themselves or by their families, sold oxen and sheep and doves to those who had need to offer them in the temple. These animals were, of course, needed for sacrifices; and there was good reason why they should be ready at hand for those who came up to worship. But the sin of the priests lay in permitting this buying and selling to go on *within* the sacred precincts, and in trading dishonestly. There were other things needed for the sacrifices, such as wine, and salt, and oil. Then there were also the **money-changers** (κολλυβιστής, from κόλλυβος, a small coin)—those who exchanged large coins for smaller, or foreign money for the half-shekel. Every Israelite, whether rich or poor, was required to give the half-shekel, neither less nor more. So when money had

to be exchanged, an allowance or premium was required by the money-changer. Doves or pigeons were required on various occasions for offerings, chiefly by the poor, who could not afford more costly offerings. From these also the priests had their gain. **The seats of them that sold the doves.** These birds were often sold by women, who were provided with seats.

Ver. 16.—**And he would not suffer that any man should carry a vessel through the temple.** It was a great temptation to make the temple, at least the great court of the Gentiles, a thoroughfare. It was so extensive that a long and tedious circuit would be avoided, in going from one part of the city to another, by passing through it. To those, for example, who were passing from the sheep market, Bethesda, into the upper part of the city, the shortest cut was through this court and by Solomon's Porch. The distance would be greatly increased if they went round it. So the priests permitted servants and labourers, laden with anything, to take this shorter way through the great court of the temple. But our Lord hindered them, forbidding them with the voice of one that had authority, and restraining them with his hand, and compelling them to go back. He would have the whole of his Father's House regarded as sacred.

Ver. 17.—**My house shall be called a house of prayer for all the nations** (πᾶσι τοῖς ἔθνεσιν). St. Mark, writing for Gentiles, assures them that the God of the Jews is the God of all the nations; and that the court of the Gentiles, which was then so profaned, was a constituent part of his house of prayer. St. Jerome notes Christ's action in driving out the profaners of the temple as a great proof of his Divine power, that he alone should have been able to cast out so great a multitude. He says, "A fiery splendour flashed from his eyes, and the majesty of Deity shone in his countenance." The words, "My house shall be called the house of prayer," are a quotation from Isa. lvi. 7; and it is a remarkable coincidence that in ver. 11 of that chapter the rulers of the people are described as looking "every one for his gain from his quarter." **A den of thieves** (σπήλαιον ληστῶν); this should be rendered, *a den of robbers.* The Greek word for "thief" is κλέπτης, not ληστής. The two terms are carefully distinguished in St. John (x. 1), "the same is a thief (κλέπτης) and a robber (ληστής)." These priests, wholly intent upon gain, by various fraudulent acts plundered strangers and the poor, who came to purchase offerings for the worship of God. Observe that the temple is called the house of God, not because he dwells in it in any corporeal sense, for " he dwelleth not in temples made with hands," but because the temple is the place set apart for the worship of God, in which he specially gives ear to the prayers of his people, and in which he specially promises his spiritual presence. Hence we learn what reverence is due to the houses of God; so that, as the master of a house resents any insult offered to his house as an insult to himself, so Christ reckons any wilful dishonour done to his house as a wrong and insult to him.

Ver. 18.—**And the chief priests and the scribes** — this is the right order of the words — **heard it** (ἤκουσαν), **and sought** (ἐζήτουν)—*began to seek*, or *were seeking* (imperfect)— **how they might destroy him** (ἀπολέσουσιν). ‍ They were seeking how they might, not only put him to death, but " utterly destroy him," stamp out his name and influence as a great spiritual energy in the world. This action of his raised them to the highest pitch of fury and indignation. Their authority and their interests were attacked. But the people still acknowledged his power; and the scribes and Pharisees feared the people.

Ver. 19.—**And when even was come;** literally, *and whenever* (ὅταν) *evening came;* that is, *every evening.* During these last days before his crucifixion, he remained in Jerusalem during the day, and went back to Bethany at night. St. Matthew says (xxi. 17), speaking of one of these days, " And he left them, and went forth out of the city to Bethany, and lodged there." So true it was that "he came unto his own, and his own received him not." No one in that city, which he loved so well, offered to receive him. The end was drawing near. But the intercourse with Martha and Mary must have been soothing to him; and Bethany was less than two miles from Jerusalem.

Vers. 20, 21.—**And as they passed by in the morning, they saw the fig tree withered away from the roots.** They had returned the evening before, probably after sunset, to Bethany; and so, in the twilight, had not noticed the withered tree. St. Matthew gathers the whole account of the fig tree into one notice. St. Mark disposes of the facts in their chronological order. It was on the Monday morning, the day after the triumphant entry, and when they were on their way to Jerusalem, that our Lord cursed the fig tree. Thence he passed on at once into Jerusalem, and drove out the profaners of the temple, and taught the people. In the evening he returned to Bethany; and then on the next morning, as they were on their way into the city, they saw what had happened to the fig tree. And then **Peter calling to remembrance**

saith unto him, Rabbi, behold, the fig tree which thou cursedst is withered away (ἐξήρανται), the same Greek word as in the preceding verse. Some have thought that the fig tree was the tree forbidden to Adam and Eve in the garden of Eden. (See Cornelius à Lapide on Gen. ii. 9).

Vers. 22, 23.—**Have faith in God;** literally, *have the faith of God*—full, perfect, effectual faith in him; faith like a grain of mustard seed. You may be staggered and perplexed at what you will see shortly; but " have faith in God." The Jews may seem for a time to flourish like that green fig tree; but they will "soon be cut down as the grass, and be withered as the green herb." What seems difficult to you is easy with God. Trust in the Divine omnipotence. The things which are impossible with men are possible with him. Our Lord then uses a metaphor frequently employed to indicate the accomplishment of things so difficult as to be apparently impossible. He employs a bold and vivid hyperbole; and, pointing probably to the Mount of Olives overhanging them, and on the shoulders of which they were then standing, he says, "With this faith you might say to this mountain, Be thou taken up and cast into the sea, and it shall come to pass."

Ver. 24.—**All things whatsoever ye pray and ask for, believe that ye have received them; and ye shall have them.** But you must "ask in faith, nothing wavering."

Ver. 25.—**And wheresoever ye stand praying** (στήκητε προσευχόμενοι). The ordinary attitude of Eastern nations in prayer is here indicated, namely, "standing," with the head, doubtless, bowed in reverence. The promise of this text is that requests offered in prayer by a faithful heart will be granted—granted as God knows best. The connection of these verses with the former is close. One great hindrance to the faith without which there can be no spiritual power, is the presence of angry and uncharitable feelings. These must all be put away if we would hope for a favourable answer from God.

Ver. 26.—There appears to be sufficient evidence to justify the Revisers in their omission of this verse; although its omission or retention does not affect the general exegesis of the passage.

Vers. 27, 28.—**By what authority doest thou these things?** We learn from ver. 18 that the chief priests and scribes had already been seeking how they might destroy him, and they wanted to establish some definite charge, whether of blasphemy or of sedition, against him. They now approach him as he walked in the temple, and demand by what authority he was doing these things, such as casting out the profaners of the temple, teaching and instructing the people, accepting their Hosannas, etc. **And who gave thee this authority to do these things?** According to the best reading, this sentence should run, *or* (ἤ instead of καί) *who gave thee,* etc., instead of "and who gave thee," etc. So that the questions are directed to two things—was his authority inherent? or, was it derived?

Ver. 29.—**I will ask of you one question** (ἐπερωτήσω ὑμᾶς ἕνα λόγον). The verb justifies the translation, *one question,* for "one word." The question which our Lord put to them was one on which hung the solution of that proposed by the scribes. It is as though he said, "You do not believe me when I say that I have received power from God. Believe then John the Baptist, who bare witness of me that I was sent from God to do these things."

Ver. 30.—**The baptism of John, was it from heaven, or from men?** By the "baptism of John" our Lord means his testimony concerning himself, his doctrine, and all his preaching. It is a synecdoche—the part put for the whole. The argument is incontrovertible. It is this: "You ask from whence I derive my authority—from God or from men? I in my turn ask you from whom did John the Baptist derive his authority to baptize and to teach? from heaven or from men? If he had it from God, as all will confess, then I too have the same from God; for John testified of me, saying that he was but a servant, the friend of the Bridegroom; but that I was the Messiah, the Son of God: and this too when you sent messengers to him for his special purpose, that you might know from him whether he was the Messias." (See John i. 20; x. 41.) **Answer me.** This is characteristic of St.

Mark's style, and of our Lord's dignified earnestness.

Vers. 31, 32.—**They reasoned with themselves,** like men anxious and perplexed. If **we shall say, From heaven; he will say, Why then did ye not believe him?** For he told you I was the promised Messias, and bade you prepare yourselves by repentance to receive my grace and salvation. But should we say, **From men—they feared the people:** for all verily held John to be a prophet. This is a broken sentence, but very expressive. The evangelist leaves his reader to supply what they meant. They deemed it prudent not to finish the sentence; and probably cut it short with some significant gesture. They did not like to confess that they feared the people; although this was the true reason why they hesitated to say that John's baptism was of men. They knew that all the people held John to be a prophet. They were thus thrown on one or other horn of a dilemma.

Ver. 33.—**We know not.** They had seen the life of John. They had heard his holy and Divine teaching. They were witnesses to his death for the truth; and yet they lie. They might have said, "We think it imprudent or inexpedient to say;" but for this they had not sufficient moral courage. **Neither tell I you by what authority I do these things.** You will not answer my question; neither will I therefore answer yours; because your answer to mine is the answer to your own. "He thus shows," says St. Jerome, "that they knew, but would not answer; and that he knew, but did not speak, because they were silent as to what they knew." Our Lord did thus but mete out to them the measure which they meted to him.

HOMILETICS.

Vers. 1—11.—*The triumphal entry.* Christ was a King, but his royalty was misunderstood during his ministry upon earth. The devil had offered him the kingdoms of this world, and he had refused them. The people would have taken him by force and have made him a king, but he had hidden himself from them. Yet it was right and meet that he should in some way assume a kingly state and accept royal honours. The triumphal entry interests us, because it was the acknowledgment and reception of Jesus with the joyful homage due to him as King of Israel and King of men.

I. THE OCCASION OF THIS HOMAGE. Our Lord Jesus knew well what was to be the issue of this his last visit to the metropolis. He foresaw, and he had foretold in the hearing of his disciples, that he was about to be put to a violent death. Notwithstanding his clear perception of this his approaching sacrifice, he had come cheerfully to the city where he was to share the fate of the prophets. It is absurd to draw from this narrative the inference that Jesus was now looking for popular and national acceptance; he was not so misled. But it is remarkable that he should choose to receive the homage of the multitude almost upon the eve of his betrayal and condemnation. In his apprehension, the Priesthood and the Kingship of the Messiah were most closely connected. And to our minds there is no discordance between the sorrows

Jesus was about to endure and the honours he now consented to accept. The occasion was well chosen, and brings before us our Lord's independence of all human standards and preconceptions. Ours was a King whose royalty suffered no tarnishing of its splendour when he rode in majesty, although he rode to death.

II. THE SCENE OF THIS HOMAGE. 1. It was the scene of his ministry. In and near Jerusalem many of Christ's mighty works had been wrought, many of his discourses had been delivered, many of his disciples had been made. It was becoming that for once, in this scene of his labours, his claims should be publicly recognized and his honour publicly displayed. 2. It was to be the scene of his martyrdom and sacrifice. It has often been noted, as a witness to human fickleness, that the same roads and public places should within a few days resound with the incongruous shouts, "Hosanna!" and "Crucify him!" How true was the language of Pilate—they crucified their King! On the one hand, it could not be that a prophet should perish ou? of Jerusalem; on the other hand, it was fitting that the city of David should openly welcome and acknowledge David's Son and David's Lord, and the establishment of the predicted kingdom.

III. THE OFFERERS OF THIS HOMAGE. There were, amongst those who welcomed Jesus, his own attendants and disciples, the villagers from Bethany, the citizens of Jerusalem, and the Galilean pilgrims who had come up to the feast. The multitude was a very varied and representative crowd, including Israelites of many classes, and doubtless differing from one another in the measure of their knowledge of Jesus and their appreciation of his character and his claims. As is often the case when Christ is extolled and praised, some were drawn into the general enthusiasm and rejoicing by the force of example and under the inspiration of feeling. The general welcome was an anticipation of the honour which shall be rendered to Jesus, when "every tongue shall acknowledge him to be Lord, to the glory of God the Father."

IV. BY WHAT ACTIONS THIS HOMAGE WAS EXPRESSED. The simple circumstances of this entry, so natural and almost childlike, are all significant of our Saviour's dignity and majesty. In the bringing of the ass's colt for him to ride, there was a fulfilment of an ancient prediction; and the act itself, according to the usage of the East, was becoming to royalty. In the spreading of their garments upon the foal's back, the strewing the road with their clothes and with the branches of trees, there was a picturesque, if very simple, expression of their admiring reverence and loyalty.

V. THE LANGUAGE IN WHICH THIS HOMAGE WAS UTTERED. The unpremeditated shouts and exclamations with which Jesus was greeted were an expression of fervid, popular sentiment. Yet they were also to some extent a confession of Jesus' Messiahship and an acknowledgment of his royalty. 1. Notice the character in which they hailed him: he came "in the Name of the Lord;" he brought in "the kingdom of David." Drawn from Hebrew prophecy, these appellations could not be used without a very special significance. 2. Notice the joyous language in which they hailed him. They called him "Blessed!" they greeted him with the cry, "Hosanna in the highest!" It was enthusiastic and lofty language; but meaner terms would have been inappropriate, unworthy, and unjust.

Vers. 12—14, 19—25.—*The fruit of the fruitless fig tree.* This action of our Lord Jesus is one of the very few he is recorded to have performed to which exception has been taken. It has been objected that the "cursing" of the fig tree was a vindictive act, and unlike and unworthy of the gracious and beneficent Redeemer. In answer to this objection, a distinction must be drawn between a vindictive and a judicial proceeding; the latter having no element of personal irritation or ill feeling. It must not be forgotten that the Lord Jesus was and is the Judge, and this symbolical action was a picture of his judicial function in exercise. It has also been objected that the doom pronounced and carried into effect was unjust, inasmuch as the season for figs had not yet come, and Jesus looked for what, in the nature of things, it was not reasonable to expect. In answer to this, it must be remembered that trees have no consciousness, and no capacity for sentient suffering; and that, in the analogous case of the barren professor of religion, no sentence of condemnation is pronounced except as the consequence of moral culpability. This passage has two distinct movements, each containing its own spiritual lesson impressively conveyed.

I. Here is a symbol of "judgment in the house of God." 1. The fruitless fig tree is an emblem of the immoral or useless professor of Christianity. Leaves are beautiful in themselves, are indicative of life and vital vigour, and seem to promise fruit; yet, in the case of such trees as that here spoken of, it is the fruit which is the end for which the tree is allowed to occupy ground, to absorb nourishment, to engage the toil of the husbandman or gardener. So in the moral domain. The foliage corresponds to outward position, to visible standing, and audible confession. These are excellent and admirable where they are not deceptive. But where there is "nothing but leaves" to meet the eye of the husbandman, where there is the "name to live" without the life, where there is the language of belief and of devotion with no corresponding principles and conduct,—all this is disappointing to the Divine Husbandman and Vine-dresser. 2. The withering of the fig tree is symbolical of the moral doom and destruction of the unfruitful professor of religion. The tree may live, although it bear no fruit. But the fruitless Christian carries his own condemnation within him. The Lord who came to earth to save, lives in heaven to reign, and finally will return to judge. It would not be just to found an argument upon what is but an illustration. Nevertheless, there is very much express teaching from our Lord's lips as to the doom of the hypocrite. The fruitless scribes and Pharisees incurred his anger and his condemnation; and there is no reason to suppose that those more privileged, and equally false and spiritually worthless, can escape their doom. To be fruitless is to "wither away." For the barren there is no place in the vineyard of God.

II. Here is instruction as to the power of faith and prayer. It is a lesson we should scarcely have expected to find attached to this miracle. The amazement of Peter and the other disciples was excited by this exercise of power on the part of the Master. In reply to their expressions of wonder, Jesus, who was ever ready to give to the conversation a practical and profitable turn, discoursed upon the power of faith and prayer. 1. Faith gives efficacy to *effort*. It removes mountains. But such is not the work of the doubter or of the vacillating. All moral miracles and spiritual triumphs are due to the faith which is placed, not in human skill or power, but in God himself. 2. Faith gives efficacy to *prayer*. There are those who are mighty in prayer. This is because they believe in God, to whom "all things are possible." Hesitating, half-hearted prayer is dishonouring to God. We are directed to believe that we have received, at the very moment when we offer our entreaties; which is certainly only possible to strong faith. Yet what encouragement is there so to pray! 3. The works which may in this manner be accomplished, the blessings which may thus be obtained, are described in remarkable language. Trees may be withered, mountains may be removed, *all things* may be had, by those who have faith. No wonder that the poet says of faith, it—

> "Laughs at impossibilities,
> And cries, 'It shall be done!'"

4. Yet there is a condition of a moral kind laid down by Christ. A sincere and forgiving disposition is indispensable. If we appeal to a gracious and benignant Father, if we ask of him needed forgiveness, we must approach him with a mind unstained by wrath, by malice, by any lack of charity.

Vers. 15—18.—*The holy house.* It is significant that our Lord should have performed the authoritative and symbolical act of cleansing the temple *twice*—at the commencement, and again at the close, of his ministry. We learn that no real reformation had taken place in the religious habits of the chief priests and the people who frequented the holy place; they continued to practise the abuses which had been already so justly and so sternly rebuked. And we learn also that Jesus, although hated and despised by the rulers, had abated none of his claims to authority and jurisdiction.

I. The occasion of Christ's authoritative interference. 1. This was the *abuse* of the temple. The holy house had been erected for the manifestation of the Divine glory, the celebration of Divine worship, the realization of Divine communion. No other material structure has ever possessed the sanctity which attached to this. There were grades of sanctity, culminating in the holy of holies; yet all the precincts and courts were consecrated to the God of Israel. To turn such a building to any

secular purpose was an unjustifiable abuse.   2. The *profanation* of the temple.
Three stages of profanation were referred to: vessels used for common purposes were
carried through the courts; money was exchanged—foreign money, with the images,
the superscription, the symbols, which denoted heathenism, for the shekels of the
sanctuary; and doves and other victims, used for sacrifice and offerings, were openly
bought and sold.   Turning the sacred precincts to purposes of gain was a heinous
offence against the majesty of the Lord of the temple.   3. But even this was not
the worst, for there is implied the *violation* of the temple.   The traffic which took
place was distinguished by injustice and fraud: "Ye have made it a den of robbers."
The family of the high priest are known to have made this merchandise a source of
unlawful gain.   In the exchange of money there was unfairness, in the sale of animals
there was extortion.   It was bad enough that in the Lord's house there should be
trading, it was far worse that there should be rapacity and fraud.

II. THE MANNER OF CHRIST'S AUTHORITATIVE INTERFERENCE.   **1.** This was
independent.   Jesus took counsel of no one, but acted of his own accord, as One who
had no superior to whom to refer.   He acted in his own Name and in that of his
Father.   2. It was *peremptory.*   We feel that it was but seldom that the meek and
lowly Jesus acted as on this occasion.   There was an unsparing severity in his action
and in his language, when rescuing the holy house from the profane intruders.   He
did well to be angry.   3. It was *impressive.*   The priests, who profited by the robbery,
were enraged; the scribes, who resented the exercise of authority by the Nazarene,
were incensed; and the people, who witnessed this remarkable act, were astonished.

III. THE JUSTIFICATION BY CHRIST OF HIS AUTHORITATIVE INTERFERENCE.   Our
Lord not only acted; he taught and explained the meaning of his action.   We cannot
suppose that he was animated by any superstitious feelings in so acting, and the record
shows us what were his motives.   1. He regarded the temple as the *house of his
Father, God.*   2. It was in his view the *house of prayer,* and was to be reserved for
communion between human spirits and him who is the Father of spirits.   3. And it
was intended for the service of all nations, which gave it a peculiar dignity and sacredness in his eyes.   These considerations show why a Teacher, whose whole teaching
was peculiarly spiritual, should display a zeal for the sanctity of a local and material
representation of a Divine presence.

IV. THE RESULTS OF CHRIST'S AUTHORITATIVE INTERFERENCE.   **1.** Its immediate
effect was to provoke the dread, the malice, and the plots of the scribes and priests.
The incident occurred but a few days before our Lord's crucifixion, and it appears to
have led to that awful event.   In their own interests, the religious leaders of the Jews
felt themselves constrained to crush the power of One whose conduct and teaching
were so inconsistent with their own.   Thus one of the highest exercises of our Lord's
righteous authority was the occasion of his most cruel humiliation and shameful
death.   2. Its more remote effect has been to enhance the conception entertained of
Christ's character and official dignity and power.   Humanity is God's true temple, too
long defiled by the occupation of the spiritual foe, and desecrated to the service of sin.
Christ is the Divine Purifier, who dispossesses the enemy, and restores the sanctuary to
its destined ends, the indwelling, the worship, and the glory of the Eternal!

Vers. 27—33.—*Authority vindicated.*   The conflict between the Divine Prophet and
the leaders of the Jewish people was now at its height.   Jesus knew that his hour
was at hand, and no longer either concealed himself, or restrained his tongue from
words of merited indignation, rebuke, and almost defiance.   Thus the enmity of his
foes was provoked, and his condemnation was assured.

I. CHRIST'S AUTHORITY WAS PUBLICLY ASSERTED AND EXERCISED.   In three respects
this was now made most plain.   1. The teaching of Jesus at this time was characterized by the assumption of a superiority of knowledge and insight which must have
been galling to the pride of his questioners, and which they may have deemed
altogether arrogant.   2. His public entry into Jerusalem in a kind of kingly state
must have aroused their hostility; for, without courting their favour or support, he
took to himself the homage due to the King of Israel.   3. His cleansing of the temple
was an authoritative act, which was felt all the more acutely by his enemies as an
attack upon themselves, because their own practices were rebuked and their own

credit was threatened, not to say that the base gains of some of them were imperilled. In these respects Christ claimed and exercised a special and vast authority.

II. CHRIST'S AUTHORITY WAS PUBLICLY QUESTIONED AND IMPUGNED. It is evident that it was a formal deputation which surrounded him in the temple, and sought to overawe and silence him by the question which they put: "By what authority doest thou these things? and who gave it thee?" There was on their part the assumption of their own judicial right to inquire, to silence, to condemn. They had acted in a very similar manner with respect to John the Baptist. To us this deputation, and its inquisitorial proceedings, are interesting, because they conclusively establish the fact that the Lord Jesus *did* claim to act as none other acted, and thus aroused the hostility of his unsympathizing and unspiritual foes.

III. CHRIST'S AUTHORITY WAS PUBLICLY VINDICATED BY HIMSELF. The way in which he did this is remarkable. 1. Why did not Jesus directly account for his actions to the priests, scribes, and elders? *Because* he had done no wrong ; in the acts he had publicly performed there was nothing for which they dared expressly to impugn him. *Because* they themselves had corruptly suffered and justified one of the evils which he had redressed. To this their conscience testified. *Because*, being unable to defend their own position, they could not be allowed to attack his. *Because*, above all, being what he was, he was not accountable, either to them or to others, for his actions. 2. Why did Jesus vindicate himself by retorting upon his assailants? by reducing them to helpless silence? *Because* he thus made evident the agreement between John's ministry and his own. It was well known that John had confessed Jesus to be the One who should come, the Messiah. Jesus appealed to John's witness, at the same time claiming to have greater witness than that of John. *Because* he thus exhibited the utter incompetency of his enemies to judge his claims. They were not prepared publicly either to avow or to disavow sympathy with, confidence in, the ministry of the great forerunner. How, then, could any stress be laid upon their judgment with respect to him to whom John had witnessed? 3. What was the effect of this method of dealing with his assailants? It is evident that the leaders of the Jews were discredited and put to shame. It is equally evident that the minds of the people were influenced in Christ's favour. But, above all, the true, proper, underived, and incomparable authority of Christ shines forth in unrivalled brightness and beauty. The surf beats upon the rock, but it falls off, powerless and defeated; whilst the rock stands out in its rugged and impressive grandeur, its stability appearing all the more manifestly immovable because of the feebleness and vanity of the repeated and furious assaults of the tempestuous sea.

HOMILIES BY VARIOUS AUTHORS.

Vers. 1—11.—*The triumphal entry into Jerusalem.* "To Jerusalem, to Bethphage and Bethany," the order of mention being determined by reckoning *from the place whither* the movement was being made. They began, therefore, with Bethany. It was familiar ground, fragrant with tender associations with both the human and the Divine.

I. PREPARATIONS. The triumph was foreseen by Christ, and he made arrangements for its being celebrated with becoming order and dignity. 1. *The unforeseen and unexpected was foreseen and prepared for by Christ.* If Divine advents are delayed, or Divine celebrations fail of their loftiest end, it is not because of failure or unreadiness in him. He was willing to have made this triumph a real, permanent, and universal one. He is ever in advance of the event, whether it be a triumph or a crucifixion. Above all, he was ready in himself. 2. *It was to his own disciples he looked for the supply of what was required for his triumph.* He appealed to their recognition of his authority—"the Lord." The claim was allowed by the stranger who owned the colt. It was freely given when asked. Christians are to make ready for their Lord's triumph. They have all that he needs, if it be but freely rendered. He will throne himself amidst their gifts if they have him enthroned in their hearts. Nothing but what is freely rendered is acceptable to him or desired by him. It should be enough for a disciple to know what the Lord will have him do and of what the Lord has need.

II. THE TRIUMPH. It was a simple procession, gradually increasing in volume and excitement as it approached the city. 1. *The movement was natural and spontaneous.* No signs of getting it up. The enthusiasm it expressed already existed. Direction and order were imparted, but the motive was self-developed. 2. *It was of a predominantly spiritual character.* The attraction did not lie in the accessories, but in the central Figure. Never had the native glory of the Messiah been so manifest. The Jews, had they only known, were on the verge of an apocalypse, which only depended upon their spiritual preparedness. " Meekness is nobler and mightier than force, goodness than grandeur " (Godwin). 3. *It was a manifest fulfilment of prophecy.* The people were conscious of it as they shouted. Their words are a quotation from Ps. cxviii. "(1) 'Hosanna!' The word was a Hebrew imperative, ' Save us, we beseech thee,' and had come into liturgical use from Ps. cxviii. That psalm belonged specially to the Feast of Tabernacles, and as such was naturally associated with the palm branches; the verses from it now chanted by the people are said to have been those with which the inhabitants of Jerusalem were wont to welcome the pilgrims who came up to keep the feast. The addition of ' Hosanna to the Son of David' made it a direct recognition of the claims of Jesus to be the Christ; that of ' Hosanna in the highest ' (comp. Luke ii. 14) claimed heaven as in accord with earth in this recognition. (2) 'Blessed be ['the King,' in St. Luke] he that cometh in the Name of the Lord.' These words, too, received a special, personal application. The welcome was now given, not to the crowd of pilgrims, but to the King. (3) As in St. Luke, one of the cries was an echo of the angels' hymn at the Nativity, ' Peace on earth, and glory in the highest' (Luke ii. 14). (4) As in St. Mark, ' Blessed be the kingdom of our father David.' We have to think of these shouts as filling the air as he rides slowly on in silence. He will not check them at the bidding of the Pharisees (Luke xix. 39), but his own spirit is filled with quite other thoughts than theirs" (Plumptre). Yet, because of the unpreparedness of the people, the fulfilment was only provisional, not ultimate; typical, not actual. In its spiritual idea, its universal influence ("all the city was moved "), its spontaneous acclaim, it spoke of that which is to come; in its outwardness, its question, " Who is this? " and answer, " This is Jesus, the Prophet of Nazareth of Galilee," its readiness to pass from praise to execration, it showed how distant the people were from the true realization.

III. CULMINATING SOVEREIGNTY. 1. *Seen in the destination to which he came. "He entered the temple."* He is Priest as well as King. " Yet have I set my King upon my holy hill of Zion " (Ps. ii. 6). It is from the holy place that his rule extends; and there it begins, and is most intensely and specially exercised. He is Key to all the mysteries there; Centre of all the symbols and rites. This suggests that his reign is primarily and essentially a spiritual one. As King of saints he reigns in the earth. 2. *Expressed and exercised in a "look." " He looked round about upon all things."* " Not simply as one might gaze who had never been there before: an arbitrary and wanton idea; but as one who had a right to inspect the condition of the place, and who was determined to assert and exercise that right" (Morison). So is he Lord of that temple not made with hands—the *body* in which he dwelt, and the *spirit* in which he offered the eternal sacrifice; and so will he take account of the secrets of human nature in the great day, for is he not "the Son of man"?—M.

Ver. 3.—" *The Lord hath need of him.*" How singular the conjunction! Need of a *colt!* In what sense was such a creature necessary for the Lord of all? In what sense is anything created necessary to the Creator? As showing forth his glory, and fulfilling his purposes.

I. THE LOWLIEST THINGS HAVE SOME HIGH PURPOSE, OR CAPACITY OF GLORIFYING GOD.

II. IN SOME CIRCUMSTANCES THE LOWLIEST THINGS MAY EXCLUSIVELY OR MORE FITTINGLY EXPRESS A CERTAIN PHASE OF THE DIVINE GLORY. What else could so set forth the meekness, the lowliness, of the Son of man? or the privilege and freedom of the young Church, of which he was the only burden and law? In that colt the brute world had its most honoured representative. So in human poverty, simplicity, weakness, and ignorance, the glory of God may be shown forth the more conspicuously.

III. LET US LOOK FOR AND GIVE EFFECT TO THE GLORY OF CHRIST, *i.e.* OF GOD, IN ALL THINGS.

IV. A FORTIORI LET US OFFER OUR OWN SELVES, SO GLORIOUSLY ENDOWED, IN PER-
SONAL CONSECRATION AND EFFORT FOR THE GLORY OF GOD. If he had need for a
colt, we cannot say he has no need for us.—M.

Ver. 11.—*Jesus surveying the temple.* I. A SIGN OF AUTHORITY. Supreme, absolute, spiritual.

II. AN EXERCISE OF JUDGMENT. Inward, unerring, and from the highest standpoint.

III. AN EXPRESSION OF GRIEF AND DISAPPOINTMENT. There is nothing upon which
the look can rest with approval and satisfaction. It goes round, but returns not. It
goes through and beyond. The temple in its condition was symbolical of the people.

IV. A TOKEN OF FORBEARING MERCY. Only a look, for the present. He has it not
in his heart to inflict the final stroke at once. He will wait. A day of grace is still
left. Is this our case—as a Church? as individuals?—M.

Vers. 12—14, 20—25.—*The destruction of the fig tree.* I. THE SUFFICIENT
REASON FOR THE ACT. 1. *Not an outcome of petulance or disappointment.* The idea
of Christ being "in a temper" is preposterous! The difficulty as to the phrases, "if
haply he might find anything thereon," and "he found nothing but leaves; for it was
not the season of figs," is for the most part factitious and artificial. Our Lord was not
mistaken—first expectant and then disappointed. "He came to the tree, not for the
sake of eating, but for the sake of performing an adumbrative action (sed aliquid
præfigurandi causa)" (Zuingli). "His hunger, too, was the occasion that gave shape
to his adumbrative action, when he went to the leafy tree to see if there was fruit
on it" (Morison). 2. But neither was it *an action symbolizing the penalty of spiritual
barrenness.* Its proximity in spirit and time to the cleansing of the temple inclines
the mind to a parabolic meaning in that direction; so also Peter's strong word
"cursedst," which seems at first to convey an impression of moral displeasure. As a
merely natural incident, it is hard to reduce the disproportion it exhibits between the
apparently judicial sentence and its occasion. On the other hand, it is harder still to
explain Christ's total silence as to the reference to spiritual barrenness and its penalty,
if such a reference had ever been intended. The circumstance that a day intervened
between the sentence of Christ and Peter's noting the result, would seem to demand
that the Master should have "pointed the moral" in some more manifest way. Again,
what he did teach concerning the occurrence, so far as it has been preserved, suggests
that the action was "adumbrative" in a simpler and more direct sense, of that,
namely, of which he spoke—*the power of God commanded through faith.* "The significance of this event is different from that of the parable given by St. Luke (xiii. 6),
to show the doom of impenitence. In that, the fig tree was planted in a vineyard;
everything was done for its culture that could be done; and not till after years of
barrenness was it cut down. Here the fig tree was growing by the road; it belonged
to no one, and nothing had been done for its improvement; and it was destroyed when
its uselessness was made manifest. It was fruitless, because the fruit season had not
come, and no old fruit remained on the branches. It was, therefore, not a fit emblem
of the impenitent Jews. But the destruction of a senseless and worthless thing made
known the power of Christ, as sufficient to destroy, though used only to restore" (Godwin, 'Matthew'). As illustrative of Divine power it was splendidly significant. To
wither was within the power of any one, but to *wither by a word* was a supernatural
act only possible to one in closest fellowship with God.

II. CHRIST'S OWN APPLICATION OF THE INCIDENT. "Have faith in God." 1. *Greater
results than it are attained by his servants if they will but believe.* (1) In doing. The
words "shall say unto this mountain," etc., are figurative. A magnificent promise! Not
only such an act as the withering of the fig tree, but one comparable to the uprooting
of the Mount of Olives on which it grew (against which, by the way, there could surely
be no "judicial resentment" even in the most metaphorical sense). It is spoken of
moral and spiritual difficulties met with in fulfilling the great commission, or in
individual spiritual growth. (2) In receiving. Here the whole doctrine of prayer
came up again for review. The answer was not to be merely looked forward to as
coming, or even imminent, but was to be realized as already fulfilling itself in present

experience. A secret of intense and successful devotion. 2. *The ground of all such power is moral and spiritual oneness with God.* The general conditions of prayer being answered, viz. agreeableness to the Divine will, advantage of the kingdom of God, etc., are all supposed. But, in addition, the boon of forgiveness is chiefly referred to as of greatest moment; and, in connection with it, the necessity of a forgiving disposition in the petitioner, as a condition of his being answered. This is one of the highest phases of spiritual or moral power, and is only possible through partaking of the Divine Spirit, in other words, through oneness with God.—M.

Vers. 15—19.—*Jesus cleansing the temple.* A second occasion; the first occurring at the beginning of his ministry (John ii. 13—17). A fulfilment of Mal. iii. 1, 2.

I. THERE IS A TENDENCY IN THE MOST SACRED INSTITUTIONS TO DECAY AND ABUSE. Most of the abominations swept away by Christ had their origin in immemorial custom, and the demands of the worshippers themselves. Traffic came to assume a religious character, and gain was excused on account of ceremonial exigencies and conveniences. This tendency recurs and culminates. How suggestive the contrast—"a house of prayer," "a den of thieves"!

II. THIS IS DUE TO LOSING SIGHT OF THE ORIGINAL SPIRIT AND PURPOSE. The essence of the old worship was simple, personal devotion, of which rites and sacrifices were only of use as the expression. Through the intrusion of the business spirit, the latter came to be regarded as important for their own sake.

III. JESUS CHRIST IS THE CHIEF AUTHOR AND RESTORER OF PURE WORSHIP. This act of Christ is in perfect accord with his whole character and life. It but expresses his spirit and influence. Every reform or advance of the Church is due to his agency.

IV. HE EFFECTS THIS THROUGH HIS SPIRIT, AND THE REVELATION HE MAKES OF THE CHARACTER OF GOD AND THE SIGNIFICANCE OF SACRED THINGS. The original purpose of the temple is restated, and he emphasizes the spiritual side of worship. It is to pray, to commune with our Father, we go up into the temple. Everything which interferes with or corrupts that simple motive, is an abuse and an evil. The gospel, in recalling men to a sense of righteousness and the love of God, creates the prayer-spirit. And the Holy Ghost sustains the communion thus established. From time to time the Spirit takes of the things of God and reveals them afresh, making fresh advents to the heart, and kindling the flame of zeal and love.

V. REFORMING ZEAL, IN PROPORTION TO ITS SPIRITUALITY AND ENLIGHTENMENT, WILL PROVOKE HATRED AND OPPOSITION IN THOSE WHOSE INTERESTS ARE THREATENED; BUT THERE WILL EVER BE OTHERS BY WHOM IT WILL BE WELCOMED. Those who are interested in the *status quo* will resent interference with it. Priestly importance and the spirit of selfishness are potent antagonists to true worship. But the "multitude" has within it ever some who yearn after better things. The human longing after the Divine is enshrined in the common heart of man.—M.

Ver. 17.—*The Church—ideal and actual.* I. THE CHURCH IN ITS IDEAL. As viewed under this aspect it has: 1. *A twofold character.* (Isa. lvi. 7.) (1) A house of prayer. This recognition of a spiritual end to be secured by the institution of the temple is most remarkable, as having taken place in an era of ceremonialism. It is not a priestly but a prophetic point of view, in which details are lost sight of in the inward and eternal. The temple was to be "called a house of *prayer*" as indicative not of a special but rather of an exclusive purpose; any other being a transgression and an offence. It was to be set apart for the most sacred occupations of the soul—intercourse and communion with God. An emphasis was thereby given to the Divine side of life. Men were to seek the presence of God that they might receive his grace and truth. A space was marked off from the business and secularities of life, so that, undisturbed from without, and aided by all the circumstances of devotion, the higher nature might be called forth and educated. Instead of worldly cares and competitions distracting the worshippers, they were to be engrossed for a while with their Father's business. How important is this witness of the Church to the claims of the unseen and eternal! It is the sphere within which the highest exercise of human faculties may take place, and the noblest life may be laid hold of. There may be no immediate demand for what it provides, yet does it minister to the deepest and most lasting human needs. (2) The spiritual home of mankind. The defect of Judaism was that it was too national and exclusive: all that was to cease. From the earliest times the universality of the Divine grace was declared by the prophets. Even from within a principle of expansion began to discover itself. The presence of the "stranger" within the camp led to the recognition of the "proselytes of the gate," and by-and-by to the institution of the "court of the Gentiles" in the temple itself. The fundamental doctrine of Jehovah itself implied such an intention as ultimate if not immediate, for before him there was no respect of persons, and he was the Father of all. The promises, too, were all couched in terms that precluded a merely local or temporary enjoyment of their blessings. Even as taught in the Old Testament the doctrine of election is declared to be a temporary provision for the benefit of others besides the elect. The chief end of the temple, or the Church which it represented, could not be secured save by the conversion of the world to the knowledge of Jehovah, and the spiritual coming of mankind to Zion. It is therefore the great mission of Christianity, as the spiritual successor of Judaism, to give effect to this. The Church is a witness to the oneness of the race in its origin and destiny, and the great foster-mother of mankind. Through her charity, and not by mechanical necessities or material interests, is the unity of the world to be realized. 2. *This twofold intention of the Church is certain to be fulfilled.* As we have seen, it is (1) the Divine purpose: everything God wills will be ; and (2) the genius of Christianity. If Judaism declared a universal brotherhood, Christianity *is* that brotherhood. It teaches us to say, "Our Father," and realizes itself in the communion of saints. The Church is not an end in itself, but is *for* the world. Christianity is nothing if it is not evangelistic and aggressive.

II. THE CHURCH IN ITS CORRUPTION. In the mean time what God intended has been frustrated by the worldliness of men. The consequence has been: 1. *A complete contradiction to its original purpose.* Even in Jeremiah's day the epithet, "a den of thieves," could be applied to it (Jer. vii. 11); so soon does spiritual decay run to its term! That which was meant to be a universal good became a universal curse. The abuse of sacred things is ever the most mischievous of all abuses. Instead of Divine charity, human selfishness: the wrangling and violence of robbers where the peace of God was to be looked for. The contrast is utter, but the transition is easy and natural. The very extension of Judaism, outstripping as it did the expansion of affection in its members, sufficed to ensure its corruption. Worshippers came from distant places to offer sacrifice, and being unable to bring animals with them for the purpose, they sought for them on the spot. Gradually, therefore, the courts of the temple were invaded by cattle-dealers and their herds. Another inconvenience was felt in the difficulty of exchanging foreign money for the sacred coin which could alone be accepted in the treasury. Here the money-changer stepped in. The whole process was gradual and easily explained; but the result was none the less an evil, which required to be sternly corrected. Nor can Christians plead innocence of this sin. "The history of Christian Churches," says Plumptre, "has not been altogether without parallels that may help us to understand how such a desecration came to be permitted. Those who remember the state of the great cathedral of London, as painted in the literature of Elizabeth and James, when mules and horses, laden with market produce, were led through St. Paul's as a matter of every-day occurrence, and bargains were struck there, and burglaries planned, and servants hired, and profligate assignations made and kept, will feel that even Christian and Protestant England has hardly the right to cast a stone at the priests and people of Jerusalem." It is a great deal, however, when it is recognized that this is not the purpose for which the sanctuary has been hallowed, and the lesson of the past is surely that of a constant watchfulness against insidious abuses, and above all of the need of a deeper and more continuous consecration of the worshippers themselves. 2. *Divine anger and rejection.* The wrath of the Lord of the temple was typical for all time. As the temple, so the Church or the soul which defiles itself will be visited by penal consequences. Sacred names and ceremonies will not consecrate vile ends. There is nothing more abhorrent to God than the travesty of religion, the seeking of gain under the mask of godliness.—M.

Vers. 27—33.—*Christ's authority challenged and defended.* This was a necessary consequence of his action in the cleansing of the temple. By so doing he claimed to be the Judge of things religious and sacred, and to direct the conscience of man.

I. THE ULTIMATE QUESTION BETWEEN CHRIST AND THE RELIGIOUS SYSTEMS AND INSTITUTIONS OF MEN IS ONE OF AUTHORITY. Only direct Divine sanction, or a higher truth vindicating itself at the bar of reason and conscience, or in the field of experience, can justify the attitude of Christ and his religion towards the religions and superstitions of men. Arbitrary assumption will soon betray itself, and the spiritual nature of man must be satisfied. This question of authority is sure to be raised sooner or later by the upholders of the systems and beliefs Christianity impugns. And Christians are counselled to " give a reason of the hope that is in " them.

II. TO ALL GENUINE INQUIRERS CHRISTIANITY PRESENTS A SUFFICIENCY OF EVIDENCE. 1. *The life and works of Christ are his justification.* They prove him "sent from God." The evidence upon which our belief in these is based is as strong, at least, as for any other historic matter. 2. *The experience of the operation of Christian doctrine and practice in the ages subsequent to the Cross.* 3. *The immediate witness of the conscience and the heart.* With the first and the third of these the temple authorities were already conversant.

III. HYPOCRITICAL AND ILLEGITIMATE INQUIRIES INTO THE AUTHORITY OF CHRIST OR HIS SERVANTS MAY BE RESISTED AND EXPOSED. 1. *Christ knew the motives of his inquisitors.* 2. *He placed them in a false position in order to expose these to themselves and others.* 3. *All Divine revelations have similar evidence, and stand or fall together.* Had they believed John, they would have believed Jesus. As they believed neither, it must have been because they hated the truth. It was for the interests of true religion that this fact should be made evident. He proceeded to prove the traditional unrighteousness of the Jewish people and their leaders in a series of " parables " or similitudes, which were at the same time so many appeals to conscience. (It would be well for the preacher to remark upon the unbroken consecution of ch. xi. and xii. in the spoken discourse of Christ.)—M.

Vers. 1—3.—*Jesus the King.* On the occasion described in these verses Jesus assumed kingly authority. Loved as a Friend, revered as a Teacher, and followed as a Worker of miracles, he now declared his kingliness, and demanded obedience and homage. Therein he taught us, his subjects, some lessons.

I. AS A KING, JESUS REQUIRES ABSOLUTE OBEDIENCE. To the two disciples this command must have appeared strange. After finding the animal denoted, they were not to ask for it, but to take it; and if their action was questioned they were merely to say, "The Lord hath need of him." If it belonged to a foe, some might arrest or assail them for robbery. It was not the first occasion, however, on which they simply obeyed. Christ had a right to their absolute obedience, and their faith was tested by this demand upon it. Unquestioning obedience to truth and to duty is far too rare. We want to see the reasons for a command, the probable issues of it, and when we see neither too often we withhold obedience. Peril from this is now more frequent, because authority as such is weakened on all sides. Children in the home, which is the true sphere for the cultivation of obedience, are too often allowed to question when they ought to be told to obey. If we are sure of duty as followers of Jesus Christ, we must be regardless of consequences. He anticipates our difficulties, as he foresaw the question of the owner of the colt. He asks us to take one step, and to take it boldly, although we do not see what the next will be, nor whither it may lead us. If we go on to the Red Sea, it will afford us a path of safety and cut off our foes from following us. If an angel rouses us from sleep, and we arise and follow him, the great iron gate we cannot stir will open to us of its own accord.

II. AS A KING, JESUS CLAIMS THE USE OF ALL THAT HE REQUIRES. We forget that we are not the absolute owners of anything. All we have is held in trust; but our seeming possession tests our disposition, and helps to develop character. If we wish to prove the honesty of a servant, and let his skill in management grow, we do not give him a small sum each day, and check and watch him till the evening, and then expect a strict account. No; we put a large sum at his disposal, and "after a long time" reckon with him, with the result, that if he has been faithful he has increased his capital and his fitness. So God puts at our disposal wealth, talents, etc., in the hope that for our own sake we will use all loyally for him. Christ Jesus, during his ministry, was as one "having nothing, and yet possessing all things." No colt was his, but one was there, and when its owner heard "The Lord hath need of him," it was ready for the Lord's use. The message sent to that man, when it comes home to our hearts, should silence all objections to the making of effort or sacrifice. If we have to give up some luxury so as to help the poor, if we have to sacrifice leisure that is hardly earned to teach the ignorant, if we have to part with one who is dear to us, our anger and defiance will be quieted when we say to ourselves, "The *Lord* hath need of them." The owner was perhaps a secret disciple. The Lord knew him, although the apostles did not. Now, after loving Jesus quietly, the opportunity for showing his love was suddenly proffered, and he gladly gave what he could. Christ asks of us, as he asked of him, what is possible and reasonable ; and instead of waiting to do something great, let us do what we can, and that which is mean in itself will be hallowed and glorified when used by our Lord.

III. As a King, Jesus exercises a spiritual rule. Until now his kingliness had been concealed except from the nearest and dearest disciples. On this occasion it was declared. Yet the spiritual nature of that kingliness was so evident in his dress, in the animal he bestrode, and in his attendants, that when a few days afterwards he was charged with calling himself a King, no reference was made to this incident before Herod or Pilate. Such is the nature of his kingdom still. His sovereignty is not advanced by material force or by worldly cunning. To him, as a spiritual Ruler, gifts do not take the place of earnest prayer ; nor is attendance on the means of grace a substitute for fellowship of soul with God. His kingdom was inaugurated by death ; it was founded on a grave ; it was built up by the Spirit, "that the excellency of the power may be of God, and not of us." Hence he approached Jerusalem, not on the war-horse of the conqueror, but on an ass, on which rode messengers of peace ; as if he were determined that he would not come in judgment till to the last love had been tried. Thus he comes to us, in quiet suggestions, in holy desires, in tears, and prayers ; but hereafter he will come in power and great glory, fulfilling the vision St. John saw of One upon the white horse, going forth conquering, and to conquer.—A. R.

Vers. 8—10.—*Palm Sunday.* We sometimes wonder that the greatest Teacher, the divinest Master the world ever saw, was so little recognized during his ministry. Our surprise would be lessened if we fairly put ourselves in the position of his contemporaries. Suppose news came to our metropolis that in a distant hamlet, among working people, a child had been born, and that rumours of portents accompanying his birth found favour in that country-side. Suppose that, as years rolled on, it was reported that this child, now a man, had done some marvellous works ; and that, after several visits to the city, he came into it accompanied by his followers, chiefly peasants, neither learned nor wealthy. The probabilities are that although some might know him to be a great teacher, a man of unquestioned holiness and of astonishing pretensions, the hum of business would not be hushed for a moment, and few would turn aside to see his festal procession.

I. The welcome given to Jesus. 1. *His welcome would have been more speedy and general had he come differently.* All through his ministry we find evidence of that. There was eagerness for a Messiah of a certain type. A promise to restore the theocracy, and overthrow the Roman tyranny, would have been hailed with a unanimous shout of delight. But our Lord would not be content, and never is, with a worldly homage, such as a Christian nation, for example, offers when it calls itself by his Name, and violates his principles. Unless he rules human hearts, he has no joy and the ruled no bliss. Even an earthly king desires real loyalty ; but he cannot read men's thoughts nor see how in heart his flatterers despise him. If he could, how thankfully would he turn from the adulation of courtiers to the unsophisticated love of his children ! So our Lord turned from priests and Pharisees to the humble peasants of Galilee and the loving children in Jerusalem. In order to avoid false homage, Christ came, and still comes, quietly. He comes not with peals of thunder and visions of angels, nor even as a national leader appealing to popular passion and armed force ; but, in quiet thoughts and in happy Christian homes, he reveals himself to those seeking the truth, or burdened with sin. 2. *Even such a welcome as this given on Palm Sunday was unusual.*

His motto seemed to be, "He shall not strive, nor cry, nor cause his voice to be heard in the streets." Popular applause was suppressed, and even natural enthusiasm was cooled. If people would take him by force to make him a king, he departed and did hide himself from them. If the disciples saw a glimpse of his glory on the Mount of Transfiguration, he said, "See that ye tell no man." His miracles were quietly wrought, generally with but few witnesses, and those blessed were often told not to publish it. But on this first day of the last week he wished to have an unwonted procession. In the crowds who had come together for the Passover all the elements of it were ready, if he only gave a sign of his willingness to receive it. And this he did. He arranged for it. He sent to the village for the young colt, and when it was brought he sat upon it, and allowed a simple procession to be formed, which increased in numbers and enthusiasm as they drew nearer to Jerusalem. 3. *This exceptional scene was wisely ordered.* (1) The memory of it would help the disciples in the dark days which ended that eventful week; for they would reflect that it was not want of power, but want of will, which did not allow him to rouse the people in his defence. "The Good Shepherd *giveth* his life for the sheep." (2) Besides, it would give an opportunity to the people to see him as the King he claimed to be, and it was possible that some who had resisted other influences might yield to this, and pay him homage now, He had come as a babe to Jerusalem, and few had loved him; he had come as a child, only to be wondered at when he sat among the doctors; he had come to the feasts, and scarcely any had recognized him. He had come "unto his own, and his own received him not." Once more, in a new way, he would draw near. He would try one more avenue to the closed heart before uttering the pathetic lament, "O Jerusalem, Jerusalem, how often would I have gathered thy children . . . and ye would not!" (3) Further, there was something prophetic and typical in this procession. The triumphal entry was a symbol of the resurrection on that day week, and of his later ascension to heaven amidst the hosannas of the angels. It was a prophecy also of his kingly progress through history, and of his second coming in glory, when all in heaven and all on earth will cry, "Blessed is he that cometh in the Name of the Lord!"

II. THE CROWD SURROUNDING JESUS. In some of those there we may see, perhaps, representatives of ourselves. 1. *Enthusiasts were there.* They had seen his miracles, and with loud hosannas spread their garments in his way. He foresaw with sadness the change that would come over them. They appplauded on Olivet, but they were absent from Calvary. Beware of spasmodic enthusiasm, and ask for grace to stand by Christ's cause in times of trouble as well as in times of triumph. 2. *Foes were there.* They kept quiet while the crowd of his followers surrounded them; but soon they would raise the cry, "Crucify him! crucify him!" It is possible to "crucify the Son of God afresh, and put him to an open shame." 3. *Disciples were there.* The blind who had been restored, demoniacs who had been delivered, learners who had sat reverently at his feet. In the procession which still is following the Lord, may we find our place!—A. R.

Ver. 15.—*"And Jesus went into the temple."* "Jesus went into the temple." The act was characteristic and suggestive.

I. IT EXEMPLIFIED THE DISTINCTION BETWEEN HIS WORK AND THAT OF JOHN. From the beginning to the end of his ministry the Baptist, so far as we know, was a stranger to the temple courts. John was in the wilderness, and the people from Jerusalem and Judæa "went out" to hear him. Christ was never apart from his people. He was not a "voice crying in the wilderness," but the Good Shepherd, who, instead of expecting his strayed sheep to seek him, came after them, to seek and to save that which was lost. In accordance with this, Jesus entered into the temple, or taught in the synagogues, or went into the homes of the people, to teach the ignorant and to bless the needy. Here is a distinguishing mark of the great Redeemer as contrasted with the great reformer; and it is also distinctive of their work. A reformer points the way of righteousness to those willing to walk in it. A Redeemer, by the power of his love and life, touches and turns the hearts of the children of men. John said in effect, "Do what you can in the way of moral reform." Christ in effect said, "I have come to do for you what you cannot do for yourselves." These ministries are still maintained. Morality is uplifted to her lofty pedestal; but, conscious of her beauty and of his failures, the sinner can only say, "It is high, I cannot attain unto it." Christ Jesus comes down amongst us from the lofty heavens, as One meek and lowly, and says, "Behold, I stand at the door, and knock : if any man will open the door, I will come in to him."

II. IT ILLUSTRATED OUR LORD'S RELATION TO THE OLD DISPENSATION. He was often accused of setting himself against the Law. This act was one of many proofs he gave of the truth of his words, "I came not to destroy, but to fulfil." He knew, as others did not, that the work of the temple was almost done, and that it would shortly perish in the flames ; he knew that, though it had such marvellous material stability, it was one of " the things that could be shaken," and would be removed, so that " the things which could not be shaken might remain." But so long as the temple remained as the house of God he honoured it, and encouraged his disciples to do so. He kept its feasts ; he taught and healed its worshippers ; he led his followers to join in its praises and prayers and he showed the people, by this act of cleansing, that they were guilty if they desecrated God's appointed house of prayer.

III. IT INCULCATED FOR ALL AGES LESSONS OF FORBEARANCE AND PATIENCE. As followers of Christ we should learn to put up with, and to use to the utmost, what we know is imperfect and transient. If we see an organization which aims at what we approve, but which in our judgment is imperfect, and resolve to withhold our sympathy and support till it perfectly accords with our views, we are not following our Lord in this. If we recognize the faults of our fellow-Christians, and are so vexed at their folly that we determine to have no more fellowship or co-operation with them, we are not following our Lord in this. If we have attempted to reform society or to rescue a sinner, and have apparently failed, so that we give up all further effort in despair, we are not following our Lord. For once before, at the beginning of his ministry, he had cleansed this temple and driven forth the buyers and sellers, but the evil had reasserted itself, so that it was defiled as much as formerly. Still patiently and hopefully he cleansed it again, and made the place ring with his words of truth, and beautified it by his works of mercy.

IV. IT UTTERED A SIGNIFICANT REBUKE TO ALL THAT WAS FALSE AND EVIL. He went to the temple to worship, although in the crowds he saw there so few that were spiritually in sympathy with him. But he would not allow any mistake to be made about his association with evil. He was not like those who are so silent about wrong-doing or false teaching that all around suppose that they sympathize with it. Such silence is guilty. If Christ saw evil he looked upon it with pain and shame, and therefore once more before he left the temple, which was the scene of it, he made a bold protest and uttered a final rebuke. He associated with the good, but he cast out the evil.—A. R.

Vers. 15—17.—*Christ cleansing the temple.* The acts of our Lord were not merely intended to accomplish an immediate result. Had they been, they were sadly ineffectual. If, for example, he had simply set before himself the design of clearing the temple of intruders, he could have secured that end more permanently than he did. But he recognized that the noblest thing is not to cut off a public abuse, but to dry up the spring whence it flows, which often lies deep in the human heart. Remedial measures are better than repressive legislation. When our Lord for a second time cleansed the temple, his main object was not to put down the abuse immediately by force, but to rebuke the sin, and so to lead the people to think about it, confess, and forsake it. He wished to establish the principle that the temple of God should be free from worldliness, a principle which is capable of world-wide application. As the material temple rises before our vision through the mists of past years, we hail it as an image of the invisible temple in which the Eternal God is praised and served by his people. Two truths appear prominently in this incident.

I. THE TEMPLE OF GOD IS OFTEN DESECRATED. In considering the sins of other people and of other times, we are : 1. *Apt to forget how naturally and imperceptibly they obtained place and power.* The Jews easily lapsed into this desecration. The Mosaic code ordained sacrifices of oxen, goats, and sheep in great numbers. In process of time the habits of the nation changed, so that it was no longer possible, as it had been in the pastoral period, to take a victim from a flock or herd close at hand. Jerusalem was now a large and crowded city. Space was costly, and a large area seemed to be necessary where worshippers could obtain victims. In the vast temple area a large space was available. It was close by the sacrificial altar, and not set apart for the actual worship of the chosen people. If it were used for stalls and pens, a good rental would be secured which would pay for the repair and decoration of the building, and so the glory of the sanctuary would be maintained and devout worshippers accommodated. So the abuse grew up, amid the protests of the few and the silence of the many, and all were tolerating an evil which they could not openly defend. Evils have generally sprung up in the Church insidiously. If they had come in their hideous maturity they would have been repelled with horror, but they were welcomed when they came like the tiny child a legendary saint took on his shoulders, to find him grow so heavy as to crush him with his weight. Examples of this may be found in ecclesiastical history: *e.g.* papal pretensions, simony, erastianism; all of which in their germ seemed to have about them something reasonable and right. 2. *The root of the special evil here denounced was covetousness.* Probably that was the besetting sin of the nation in our Lord's day. Publicans sold themselves to the tyrants of their country, because wealth was more to them than patriotism. Priests and Sadducees let out sites to the temple traders, because they would make gain of godliness, and cared more for the temple income than for spiritual worship. This spirit pervaded the entire nation. There was no sign of the splendid generosity of David, and no need, as in Moses' days, to restrain the people from giving. The sin appeared among the apostles. We see it in all its hideousness in Judas Iscariot, who betrayed his Lord for thirty pieces of silver, and then flung the money at the feet of the priests as they sat in the temple of God. The love of money is declared to be "the root of all evil," and the statement is in harmony with the words of our Lord about the difficulty a rich man would find in entering his kingdom. Show how generally such teaching is forgotten among different classes of our population. See the effects of this in the floating of unsound speculations in which the fortunes of the unwary are wrecked; in the unfairness of men to each other in the common relations of life; in the unjust wars of aggression which the nation has sometimes waged. The Christian Church is called upon to set an example of the opposite of all this, in her princely generosity and in her Christ-like self-sacrifice. 3. *There are other ways besides covetousness by which desecration may enter God's temple.* There is unbelief, which silences the voice of prayer in professed believers; worldliness, which puts material organization in the place of spiritual power; pride, which prevents hearty fellowship amongst God's people; expediency, which usurps the throne of truth; and self-indulgence, which expels self-devotion. So the temple is defiled; for "know ye not that ye are the temple of God?" Jesus Christ felt burning indignation when he saw the sanctuary of his Father transformed into a place of worldly traffic, and he feels it still as he beholds a Christian community desecrated by the power of sin.

II. THE DESECRATED TEMPLE NEEDS CHRIST AS ITS PURIFIER. We too soon get accustomed to evils, and tolerate them, until One mightier than ourselves alone can expel them. What priests and Levites failed to do, Jesus did, and none resisted him. 1. *His coming was an act of sublime condescension.* It would have been far pleasanter to him to go into the fields, where the sower cast his seed; or to sail over the lake, in which fishermen plied their nets; or to walk over the hillsides, on which the flowers whispered of his Father's love. He knew what the temple was, yet he did not forsake it; but came again and again, in spite of the unreality and sin that prevailed in it. As willingly he will enter the heart or the Church, which is unworthy of his presence. 2. *His coming was not such as might have been expected.* The Jews had often read the words, "The Lord, whom ye seek, shall suddenly come to his temple," etc., but as they were looking heavenward the prophecy was fulfilled by the coming of this young Galilean Peasant. As they waited in vain for a startling advent, so some now wait for a special manifestation of his presence, and ignore the fact that he is already with them in the holy thoughts which they refuse to welcome. "Behold, there standeth one among you, whom ye know not." It is the realized presence of the living Christ which will purge the heart or the Church of evil thought and habit, and transform it into the temple of the Most High. May he, who is the source of spiritual power and heavenly purity, come amongst us and abide with us for ever!—A. R.

Vers. 1—10.—*The royal entry into the royal city.* Simple indeed are the preparations for the entry of Zion's King into his own city. "Go your way into the village that is over against you: and straightway as ye enter into it, ye shall find a colt tied, whereon no man ever yet sat; loose him, and bring him." The long-waiting prophecy is now to be fulfilled—

> "Rejoice greatly, O daughter of Zion;
> Shout, O daughter of Jerusalem:
> Behold, thy King cometh unto thee:
> He is just, and having salvation;
> Lowly, and riding upon an ass,
> And upon a colt the foal of an ass."

And the daughter of Zion did rejoice greatly. What a scene of gladness! What a shout of triumph! They bring the colt covered with their garments, while the way is prepared by the soft branches of palms scattered and loose robes cast upon the ground. And the lowly, mighty King enters, and the cries rend the still air.

> "Hosanna;
> Blessed is he that cometh
> In the Name of the Lord:
> Blessed is the kingdom that cometh,
> The kingdom of our father David:
> Hosanna in the highest."

There are times when truth bursts through all that hides it, and declares itself as the sun through a rent cloud. So is it here. Without restraint the children of Israel proclaim their King as did Pilate when he wrote, "The King of the Jews." True, Pilate did not believe, nor did the shouting crowd at the gates of the city for long together. The same walls soon heard the cry, "Crucify him! crucify him!" But for the time the truth prevails. It is uppermost. As in the Transfiguration, the hidden glory is revealed. Perhaps unconsciously, these voices bear witness to the truth. It is a scene to carry in the eye, to be engraven on the heart. Let us learn—

I. THAT TRUE ROYALTY NEEDS NOT THE SYMBOLS OF AUTHORITY. It is not constituted or upheld by them; it is not destroyed by their absence. Christianity is independent of external support.

II. THAT IMMUTABLE TRUTH WILL SOONER OR LATER ASSERT ITSELF. Yea, though it may be rejected, it will leave its testimony for following ages of faith and unbelief to ponder according to their respective needs.

III. THAT THE REAL AND PERMANENT RULER IS HE WHO COMETH IN THE NAME OF THE LORD. Other kings and other kingdoms will rise in a temporary prevalence of power, and fall into dark oblivion and disgrace. But the true will quietly assume its rightful place, whether men accept or reject. Jesus is a King. "To this end have I been born." Jesus is "King of the Jews," though their priests cry aloud, "We have no king but Cæsar." Jesus is the King of kings. But the kingdom is "not of this world," nor will it pass away as the kingdoms of this world. It abideth for ever. And happy is the man who is a true and faithful subject under this heavenly reign.—G.

Vers. 11—25.—*The barren fig tree.* How changed is the scene! The great King entered into the royal city, and the great High Priest into the holy temple. Then—O significant words!—" he looked round about upon all things." Alas, what scenes caught those calm eyes! In the eventide he left Jerusalem, accompanied only by the twelve. On the morrow, returning again to Jerusalem from Bethany, where he had spent the night, " he hungered." A mere touch of the pen discloses a link of connection between him and every one who in hunger seeks and has not his daily bread. But a " fig tree having leaves " from " afar " attracts his keen sight, and " he came, if haply he might find anything thereon," as the leaves which usually appear after the fruit promised. Alas, his hope is mocked! " He found nothing but leaves." Then he, who giveth nature its greenness, who maketh the fig tree to blossom, and hangeth the fruit on the vine and the olive, uttered his "curse" in prohibiting it to minister any more to the wants of man. The morrow finds it "withered away." There were watching disciples for whose use this and the other trees grew in the great garden, and this must be used for their highest good. By it he will impress upon their hearts a solemn truth. It is a parable enacted. But the parable goes unexpounded, while a great lesson on faith in God is given. By common consent, this withered tree conveys a deep teaching on immature professions. Following so immediately after the jubilant cry of yesterday, it seems to speak in condemnation of that all too hasty and untrustworthy demonstration, those shouts of welcome to the King of Jerusalem which would be so soon exchanged for the cry of repudiation, "We have no king but Cæsar." The strength of the tree is exhausted in the immature foliage. This seems to point to the immature haste of profession made by them who cried "Hosanna!" and who would show how vain the hopes would be that relied upon that cry, for in a few days it would be exchanged for "Crucify him!" It was the one visible curse of him who in reality curses everything that is false and pretentious. Significantly it is related, "and his disciples heard it." The morrow declares that the Lord's word is a word of power, as the drooping leaves and dried-up branches and trunk, even "from the roots," declare. Peter's exclamation draws forth from the Master a profound reply, which seems designed to lead the thoughts of the disciples away from all that is false, unreal, and untrue, on which they may not place their hope, to him who is worthy of their faith, and who never disappoints them that trust in him. Henceforth this fig tree stands before us as—

I. A SYMBOL OF INSINCERITY, or of that uncultured strength which is presumption.

II. A SIGN OF THE DELUSION AND DISAPPOINTMENT WHICH MUST FOLLOW FROM TRUST IN EMPTY, UNNATURAL BOASTS AND PROMISES. Many are dependent upon, or at least influenced by, the professions of others. There are weak souls that lean upon stronger ones for support, who are comforted and strengthened by their fidelity, or led astray by their dejection.

III. Therefore this must be A SOLEMN WARNING AND ADMONITION TO ALL TO TRUST IN THE TRUSTWORTHY. And in this case, perhaps, not to commit themselves to the frail, unworthy cry of an excited multitude, but to have calm faith in God, who can sweep away the false and delusive, the weak and fruitless fig tree, and with equal ease the firmly rooted mountain from its place. The "mountain" may have found its antitype in the firmly fixed power that waged its opposition to the world's Redeemer, and would soon hang him on a tree. That which could not satisfy the hunger, and that which could crush and overwhelm the King, were equally amenable, as is every mountain and every deceitful thing to the mighty power of God, invoked by a faith held in a true spirit.—G.

Vers. 15—18.—*The cleansing of the temple.* Jesus came to "bear witness unto the truth." One truth was the sanctity of that "house of prayer" which was opened for "all the nations." But have the rightful guardians of that house preserved for it this sacredness, that the feet of the wearied and the heart of the sorrowful of all nations might be allured within its hallowed walls, where in humble penitence and prayer, and with strong cries to the God of heaven and earth, they might find rest and peace and shelter? Nay, verily. Cruel covetousness has let out the sacred enclosure for gainful purposes. The love of money, the root of this evil, has led men to sell God's house to purposes of merchandise; and, if worse could be, to trickery and thieving. Ah, they robbed God of his rightful honour; and they robbed the poor, and the sorrowful, and the homeless, and the heart-sick, and the sin-sick, of the one place of refuge where they might find peace and healing and rest! They turned the "house of prayer" into "a den of robbers." In the place where men might seek heavenly blessing, they filched earthly pelf. Sin is great in proportion to its nearness to the restraints of righteousness. How great, then, was this! Their cry was, "This is the place for money-changers and barterers, for pilferers and thieves." So great a lie must be contradicted by "the Truth;" even if he lose his life in doing it. The true fire burns in his breast: he cannot be silent. The zeal of the Lord consumes him. He takes advantage of the popular enthusiasm which now for a time runs in his favour. The astonished multitude "hung upon him, listening." And though he needs not their help, yet he disappoints not their hope. He put forth his own regal authority, and with his word and holy hands "cast out" the traders, "overthrew" the tables of "the money-changers," and refused to allow men to desecrate the holy 'pavement by carrying burdens over it. Nor would he "suffer that any man should carry a vessel through the temple." It might be asked—How could he do this single-handed?

Apart from that Divine power which now and again he restrained not, "the chief priests and the scribes feared him," and the multitude stood "astonished at his teaching." Cowardice and guilt are always staggered at religious enthusiasm. In this incident we may learn—

I. Christ's DEFENCE OF THE SACREDNESS OF PLACES DEDICATED TO PURPOSES OF WORSHIP. It is his high testimony to the efficacy of prayer, that the very place where it is offered is holy ground. If all places are holy in his view, all are not to be used indiscriminately. There is an appropriate place for each work. And sacred places are devoted to sacred acts. This is here declared to be according to Christ's will.

II. Christ's DECLARATION THAT THE INTRUSION OF EARTHLY AFFAIRS INTO THE HOUSE OF THE LORD IS A WICKED AND UNWARRANTABLE DESECRATION. How strongly this speaks against intruding worldly thoughts into acts of Divine worship, and worldly motives into holy service! He who "set a bound for the waters that they may not pass over," has forbidden the trespass upon the threshold of his house of anything that is "of the earth, earthy."

III. With a view to the encouragement of prayer among all the nations, THE HOUSE OF THE LORD IS CONSECRATED FOR THEM TO THIS PURPOSE. It cannot, however, be that only one house should be opened. It is, therefore, the house in every nation that is so opened is consecrated and sacred whither the tribes of men may go up to offer worship and service, to present the sacrifice of song, to seek help and rest and mercy.

IV. But through all the teaching there runs a deeper truth: THE CLEANSED AND CONSECRATED TEMPLE OF THE HEART WHERE THE LORD IS TRULY WORSHIPPED MUST BE PRESERVED FREE FROM CORRUPT DESECRATION. The hidden place, the quiet solitudes of the soul where prayer is to be truly made, may not be polluted by trickery and deceit. And the very consecration of it as a temple where God may be approached declares that it need not be a place of burdens; for he will speak the word of faith and peace, will ease and comfort the troubled, will give rest to the weary, and solace and salvation to the tempted and tried. Happy the man whose heart is a pure temple of God!—G.

Vers. 1—11.—*The symbolic triumph.* I. THE ASSUMPTION OF AUTHORITY BY CHRIST. He issues his mandate, as having a pre-emption or right to be served before all others. The act was the more impressive because standing out in rare contrast to the ordinary tenor of Christ's conduct.

II. THE MILD POMP OF HIS ENTRY. He is acknowledged with loyal shouts as King and Lord. Hosanna is "Save now!" The words of acclamation are cited from a "Hallelujah" psalm (cxviii. 25, 26), which both celebrates and foretells deliverance. His kingdom prevails by truth, meekness, and love. May "his unsuffering kingdom" come!

III. THE ACCEPTANCE OF THE POSITION ASSIGNED HIM IN PROPHECY. He is the predicted King and Saviour, the Representative of God upon earth. Thus in this cheerful, humble scene of instructive, popular gladness, and rejoicing, we have an emblem of the progress of Christianity through the world.—J.

Vers. 12—19.—*God's house vindicated.* THE TEMPLE WAS DESIGNED AS A RELIGIOUS CENTRE FOR THE NATIONS. It contains the idea of the Divine house, and therefore of the home for all men.

II. THE ASSOCIATIONS SHOULD BE SUCH AS BECOME THE PLACE. "Peace and purity should be maintained in the service of God." The Church should be like the home. The associates of traffic and the passions it excites should be shut out.

"Let vain and busy thoughts have there no part;
     Bring not thy plough, thy plots, thy pleasures thither.
Christ purged his temple; so must thou thy heart.
     All worldly thoughts are but thieves met together
To cozen thee. Look to thy actions well;
For churches either are our heaven or hell."   (George Herbert.)

III. IN THE RELIGIOUS CALLING MEN ENJOY GREAT ADVANTAGES, AND ARE EXPOSED

TO GREAT TEMPTATIONS. Religion intensifies all it touches. "We become better or worse in dealing with sacred things" (Godwin).—J.

Vers. 20—26.—*The withered tree.* I. DESTRUCTION MAY SERVE THE PURPOSES OF LIFE. Here the fig tree is destroyed for the sake of a lesson to the spirit. Much lower life is destroyed from day to day that the higher may be preserved.

II. THE INCIDENT ILLUSTRATES THE RESERVE OF CHRIST'S MIRACULOUS POWER. He could destroy; that was evident. But he came not to destroy, but to save. And while he lavished his power upon the sick and suffering, to heal, cheer, and deliver, he economized the dread power of destruction. Compare what is said on this subject in 'Ecce Homo!'

III. FAITH THE ONE SECRET OF POWER. Our Lord here employs, as often, a bold figure of speech. To the undivided thought and will nothing is ideally impossible. Actually our power is limited, as is our thought. But we are born for the ideal, and to overcome our limitations. Prayer is essentially part of faith; it is the exercise of the will, the entire going-forth of the man in that direction in which he is called endlessly to exert himself.

IV. LOVE IS AN ESSENTIAL CONDITION OF TRUE FAITH. Faith works by love. How mistaken is it to limit faith to intellectual assent! Devils believe, but love not, and are weak. Faith and love are other words for the might of God in the soul. "Oh, my brothers, God exists! Believing love will relieve us of a load of care!"—will lift mountains' weight from the spirit, and make our ideals a present reality. But the unloving, unforgiving soul remains fettered in itself, unreleased, unfree, and weak.—J.

Vers. 27—33.—*Critics criticized.* I. THE SPIRIT OF FAULT-FINDING NEVER LACKS FOOD. The action is wrong; or, if it is right, it is done from a wrong motive, or done by the wrong person. "Ill will never said well."

II. IT ASKS FOR REASONS, BUT REFUSES TO GIVE THEM. It will call others to account, and refuse to give account of itself. The arbitrary temper is directly opposed to the "sweet reasonableness of Christ."

III. THE UNTRUE MAN THINKS ONLY OF POLICY IN HIS ANSWERS. The true man thinks of the fact, and tries to get at it and state it. The other, of how much he can afford to tell; how much 'twere well to keep back. "Truth should be the first question with men, not consequences."

IV. THERE IS A USE IN SILENT CONTEMPT. Christ, so ready to discuss with candid inquirers and give instruction, here holds his peace. Sometimes the rule is, "Answer a fool according to his folly;" sometimes, "Answer him not according to his folly." Truth and the good of souls must be our guide. "Incompetency may be exposed and assumption resisted for the sake of truth."—J.

Vers. 1—11. Parallel passages: Matt. xxi. 1—11; 14—17; Luke xix. 29—44; John xii. 12—19.—*Our Lord's public entry into Jerusalem.* I. JOURNEY FROM JERICHO. Jerusalem is at an elevation of three thousand six hundred feet above Jericho in the Jordan valley. The distance between the two cities is upwards of fifteen miles. Travel-stained and weary with this uphill journey, gradually ascending all the way, our Lord stayed over sabbath with the family of Bethany, where he got rested and refreshed. Bethany, which St. John calls "the town of Mary and her sister Martha," is fifteen furlongs, or nearly two miles, from Jerusalem, and gets its name from the fruit of the palm trees that once flourished there, signifying "house of dates." It is now called *El-Azariyeh*, from the name of Lazarus, and in memory of the miracle wrought in raising him from the dead. Next day, being the 10th of Nisan, or 1st of April—the day on which the Paschal lamb was set apart—was the day chosen by him, who is our true Paschal Lamb, for his public entry into Jerusalem, there to be sacrificed for us. Of the caravan of pilgrims that accompanied our Lord and his disciples in the journey from Jericho, some had proceeded onward direct to the holy city; others had pitched their tents in the wooded vale of Bethany; and others, again, on the western slopes of Olivet, opposite to and in full view of the city. Those who had advanced to Jerusalem had, it is probable, brought word thither of the approach of the Prophet of Nazareth.

II. PUBLIC PROCESSION. The life and ministry of our Lord were fast drawing to a close. The time of his departure was at hand. There is no longer need of enjoining secrecy with regard to his miracles, or of concealment in respect of his office, lest public excitement might ensue, or lest his work might be interfered with or interrupted by the opposition of enemies, before the seed of truth, which he had sown by his discourses and parables, should get time to take root in the public mind. Publicity rather than secrecy is now needed. The great Passover Lamb is to be sacrificed, and so the Priest is on his way to the place of sacrifice; the Prophet is going up to the house of God to renew the work of reformation, to rectify abuses, to restore, or at least exhibit, the purity befitting the service of the sanctuary, and to teach daily, as he did, in the temple. Above all, the King is going up to his capital; the daughter of Zion is to receive her King with rejoicing. Hitherto he had indeed gone about continually, doing good, yet with little or no outward show; save by the crowds that followed for healing or hearing, and on some rare occasions and with some signal exceptions, he had been little recognised, being rather "despised and rejected of men." Now the time has come for him to announce his kingdom and claim the honour of a King. The public avowal of his dignity, the official declaration of his Messiahship, and the formal proclamation of his kingdom, now behoved to be made. He was now going to assert his right to reign. Now, for the first and only time, he assumes somewhat of royal state in entering his metropolis. Nor yet was there anything very great or very garish in this exhibition of royalty; the whole was carried out in lowly guise. Christ was indeed a King, but King of the realm of truth; and his entrance into Jerusalem was a royal procession—a right royal one, though in a spiritual sense. He was King, but not such a King as the multitude, and even his disciples, expected. He was not a King coming with chariots and horses, with battle-bow or weapons of war, as earthly rulers and worldly conquerors; but "just, and bringing salvation." He was the spiritual King of an unworldly, but universal and unending kingdom.

III. OMNISCIENCE APPARENT IN HIS ORDERS. In the directions which our Lord gives his disciples, probably Peter and John, to go to the village over against them—perhaps Bethphage, which means "house of figs"—there are several particulars so precise, minute, and striking, that they imply superhuman knowledge. How else could he tell them beforehand (1) that immediately on entering the village they would find an ass and her colt; (2) that they were not loose, but tied, and so ready to be employed by their owner; (3) that that colt had never been tamed, or broken in, and that no man had ever sat on its back; (4) the exact position in which the colt would be found—not in the courtyard, but outside; at the door, yet not in the public street, but on a road that ran round (ἀμφόδου) the rear of the house or village; (5) that in case of any demur on the part of persons standing by, they should inform them for whose use it was required; and (6) that the ready consent of the owner would be obtained—"and straightway he will send them"? Another reading of this latter clause has the future, and adds πάλιν, so that the sense is, "He [Christ] will send it back again."

IV. THE HUMBLE YET HEARTY PAGEANT. All was done as had been directed. The colt was brought and led quietly along, its mother by its side, accompanying it. Then the disciples cast their *abbas*, or outer garments, on them, and set Jesus upon them —ἐπάνω αὐτῶν being either on the garments, or on one of the animals. The former view is that of Theophylact, who refers the pronoun to the garments, saying, "Not the two beasts of burden, but the garments;" so also Euthymius, Beza, and many others. Many explain the pronoun of the beasts of burden, but understand it variously—some supposing our Lord to have mounted them alternately; others supplying τινός, as Krebs and Kuinoel; and others, again, having recourse to an enallage of number; while some copyists have ventured to substitute αὐτοῦ or αὐτῆς. The intention of the disciples was to do their Master royal honour in the true Eastern style of improvising, and just as in Old Testament times, a throne had been extemporised for Jehu, as we read in 2 Kings ix. 13, "Then they hasted, and took every man his garment, and put it under him [Jehu] on the top of the stairs, and blew with trumpets, saying, Jehu is king." Scarcely had the disciples prepared the housing and got their Master mounted on the colt thus caparisoned, when the very great multitude, or rather the most part of the multitude, not to be outdone in devotion and loyalty, strewed some their garments, while others cut down branches off the trees or out of the fields (ἀγρῶν, read by Tischendorf and Tregelles), and spread them in the way. Thus the streaming multitude from

Galilee, from Bethany—some before, some behind the central figure of the Saviour—tapestried the line of march with their garments, or strewed it with fronds (στοιβάδας, a rare word, as if στειβάδας, from στείβω, to tread; and thus, that which is trodden on, a litter of leaves or bed of small leafy branches, then the material of such, viz. young branches). It may perhaps be worthy of note, that in the former case the aorist (ἔστρωσαν) is used to denote the throwing down of their garments as a thing done readily and at once; while the cutting of the branches and the spreading of them in the way, as requiring more time, are expressed in the imperfect; that is, they kept cutting them and continued strewing them as they proceeded. Many similar tokens of honour and respect are on record, and practised even to the present day. Thus, when Mordecai issued from the palace of Ahasuerus, the streets (Targum on Esther) were strewn with myrtle; like honour was shown to Xerxes by his army before crossing the Hellespont; so also, as we are informed by Robinson, in his 'Biblical Researches,' the Bethlehemites threw their garments under the feet of the English consul's horses at Damascus, when they had come to implore his aid. In the 'Agamemnon' of Æschylus, too, we read that the doomed monarch, when entering the palace on his return to Mycenæ, was, in imitation of the barbaric pomp of Eastern kings, tempted to walk on costly carpets.

V. A PEACEFUL THOUGH TRIUMPHAL PROCESSION. The lowliness of the animal was in keeping with the character of the procession. It was humble, yet right royal. The ass in the East is stately, sprightly, sleek, and shiny; it is highly esteemed, and employed alike for work and riding. Persons of *rank* used it commonly for the latter purpose. Thus we read of Balaam, of Caleb's daughter, and of Abigail riding on asses. Moses' wife rode on an ass, as she went down with her husband from Midian into Egypt. At a still earlier period it was the same animal that Abraham rode on that eventful day, when, rising early in the morning, he saddled his ass and went to offer his son Isaac in sacrifice. It was, moreover, the animal on which the judges of Israel rode, as we learn from such passages as the following:—" Speak, ye that ride on white asses, ye that sit in judgment; " so also Jair the Gileadite, who judged Israel two and twenty years, " had," as we read, " thirty sons that rode on thirty ass colts, and they had thirty cities." We have evidence of the same in Jacob's blessing of his sons, when he says of Issachar that he is " a strong ass, couching down between two burdens." Animals unyoked or unused were employed for *sacred* purposes; thus, in Num. xix. 2, it is written, " Speak unto the children of Israel, that they bring thee a red heifer without spot, wherein is no blemish, and upon which never came yoke; " again, in 1 Sam. vi. 7, " Now therefore make a new cart, and take two milch kine, on which there hath come no yoke." Thus it was every way suited to the procession, sacred and solemn, peaceful and royal, that advanced on this occasion towards Jerusalem. The horse, on the other hand, would have been unbecoming in such a procession, since the horse was the emblem of war from an early to a late period in Hebrew history; thus, in Exod. xv. we read, " Sing ye to the Lord, for he hath triumphed gloriously: the horse and his rider hath he thrown into the sea; " and also in Jer. viii. 6, " Every one turned to his course, as the horse rusheth into the battle."

VI. THE PROCESSION FROM THE CITY. Another crowd of persons, passing out of the city gates, crossed the Kedron, and advanced in one long continuous line up the opposite side of Olivet till it met the procession that accompanied our Lord. The persons that composed this crowd had been attracted by the miracle of the raising of Lazarus, and they bore their willing testimony to that stupendous fact, as St. John informs us (xii. 17), where we read ὅτι, *that*, instead of ὅτε, *when*, " The people therefore that was with him bare record *that* he called Lazarus out of his grave, and raised him from the dead." The people from the city bore in their hands palm branches, the emblems of victory. In the ancient games the crowns were various—olive, laurel, pine, or parsley; but in every game the victor bore in his hand the palm branch of victory. Accordingly, with these palm branches in their hands, they welcomed him as victorious over death and the Conqueror of the king of terrors. Soon the crowd from Jerusalem and the multitude from Bethany met and mingled; and now all united formed one grand triumphal procession, the like of which had never climbed or crossed that hill before.

VII. THE ENTHUSIASM. The enthusiasm had reached its height. Hitherto the acknowledgment of the Saviour's kingly power was confined to actions—those of himself and his disciples; now the multitudinous voices of the united crowd made the welkin ring with shouts of triumph. The proclamation, no longer limited to action, now found utterance in words—words in which the men of Bethany and the people from Jerusalem all took part, saying, " Hosanna to the Son of David ! " as we have it in the Gospel by St. Matthew. This term "Hosanna!" was originally a supplication, signifying " Save now!" and thus some understand it here, " Grant salvation to the Son of David ! " as the Hebrew verb from which it comes is sometimes followed by a dative. It would in this way be nearly equivalent to " God save the king ! " It may, however, be better understood as a joyful acclamation of welcome to the Saviour-King long promised, but now present, like the *Io triumphe* of the Romans or the pæan of the Greeks. " Blessed is he that cometh in the Name of the Lord ! " Here we have one of the designations of Messiah, who was spoken of as *the Coming One*; ages had passed, but still his arrival was a matter of expectation; centuries had rolled away, but his advent was still future. And now that he has come, it is in the name, invested with the authority and bearing the commission, of the great Jehovah. He came as the Vicegerent of God on earth, and as the Mediator for man with heaven. On the occasion here referred to, the crowd accorded him a most cordial welcome and received him with truly regal honours. So enthusiastic were they in the reception of their Messiah, that they did not confine themselves, in expressing their gratulation, to the well-known words of the familiar psalm; carried away with the outburst of general joy, they expressed in their own spontaneous utterances their fond anticipation of his Messianic reign, saying, " Blessed is the *kingdom* that cometh, the kingdom of our father David ! " for David was the great theocratic king, and eminently typical of Messiah's kingly power. "Hosanna in the *highest* ! " that is, the highest places or the highest strains. So difficult did they find it to express their exuberant joy, and to vent their feelings of jubilation, that they appealed to Heaven itself to give its sanction, and called as it were on the heavenly hosts to join them and take part in their exultation, heaven and earth being presumed of one accord and in perfect unison on the subject. Another explanation makes the words mean "in the highest degree," in order to convey still greater intensity of feeling; while a third regards it as an address to the Most High, equivalent to " O thou that dwellest in the heavens, save, we pray ; for all salvation owns thee as its Source ! "

VIII. FULFILMENT OF OLD TESTAMENT SCRIPTURE. The fulfilment of Zechariah's prophecy is here noticed by St. Matthew. "Tell ye the daughter of Sion, Behold, thy King cometh unto thee, meek, and sitting upon an ass, and a colt the foal of an ass," is the prediction in Zech. ix. 9; or the exact rendering of the last clause may rather be, " and sitting upon an ass (*chamar*), *even* a colt (*air*), son of she-asses (*athonoth*)," the *ve* being exegetical. The evangelist, in quoting the prophet's words, informs us that the purpose of what now transpired was their fulfilment. The meaning of ἵνα here, as in other similar passages, is either *telic*, or final, " in order that ; " or *ecbatic*, that is, eventual or consecutive, " so that." If the word be taken in the former sense, it marks the Divine purpose, and with God purpose and result are coincident; if in the latter sense, it is a consequence, or the evangelist's reflection on the circumstance of what had been foretold being duly fulfilled. That ἵνα had acquired in later Greek a weakened or modified meaning, so as to stand midway between purpose and result, or even to denote the latter, is pretty generally admitted.

IX. PRACTICAL REMARKS. 1. *A cause of circumspection*. This is one practical effect of Christ's omniscience. He had perfect knowledge of the state of matters in and round the village whither he sent his two disciples on the errand we here read of. He told them beforehand where the animal he wanted would be found and how it would be found—the how and where; the inquiry that would be made of them and the answer they were to return, and the readiness with which the desired permission would be granted them. It is a natural and indeed necessary inference that he is equally acquainted with ourselves—our persons, situations, and circumstances. He knows perfectly the great things and the little things of our histories; our condition and conduct in matters the most minute, as well as in those we deem of most importance. From all this we learn the necessity of circumspection. The old Roman wished his house so constructed that all that transpired inside might be seen outside—that to the eye of every passer-by the interior of his dwelling and all that was done in it might be visible. The Saviour's eye penetrates not our houses merely, but our hearts. All we think, as well as all we say and all we do, is every moment uncovered to his inspection and open to his cognizance. How circumspect, then, we should be! Who would not shrink from having exposed to the view of neighbour or friend or kinsman every thought that lies deep down in the recesses of his heart? Who would care to have every word he utters in the secret chamber made known to his fellow-man? And who would feel quite at ease if he knew that the eyes of some great man or nobleman or prince rested on all his actions throughout an entire day? How careful we are to have things presented in the best possible light, when we expect the presence of some person of consequence or superior rank for the space of a few hours! Oh, then, how we should feel chastened and subdued by the thought that One greater than even the greatest of the kings of the earth knows all we do, hears all we say, and is cognizant of all we think; and that, not for a few hours of a single day, but every hour of every day! Surely this reflection, if duly realized, would be a powerful help to make us circumspect in thought and word and work, guarding our hearts, "for out of them are the issues of life," "keeping the door of our lips that we offend not with our tongue," and using circumspection in all our works and ways. 2. *A source of consolation.* The presence of a friend is often most encouraging. The consciousness that a friendly eye is upon us in time of difficulty, or emergency, or at some critical juncture, is a source of strength, inspiring with courage and stimulating to energy. In sorrow or suffering, also, a sympathetic eye goes a long way to give relief, or, where that is out of the question, to sustain us in our sufferings. But to know that from behind the silent blue of the arching heaven a friendly eye is ever on us, a friendly heart ever beats in sympathy with us, a friendly hand is ever stretched forth to wipe away the tear of sorrow, is a source of comfort unfailing as unspeakable. The little things that vex us, the heavy griefs that crush us, our afflictions, whether physical, or mental and more inward, are known alike to that Friend who never changes, and who never fails nor forsakes us. 3. *A ground of confidence.* The fulfilment of God's Word in the past and at the present is one of the surest grounds of confidence in time to come. St. Matthew, writing in the first instance for Hebrew Christians who had the prophecies in their hand, and were thus in a position to compare prediction with performance, and having, besides, a special propensity in that direction, is careful to note the fulfilment of prophecy, and to draw the attention of his countrymen to the fact. The prediction referred to in this passage had preceded its fulfilment by five centuries and a half; but it did not fail. God's words are "pure words: as silver tried in a furnace of earth, purified seven times;" not one of them shall ever fail or be falsified.

> "How firm a foundation, ye saints of the Lord,
> Is laid for your faith in his excellent Word!"

4. *Human inconstancy.* A heathen moralizes on the fickleness of popular favour; it is changeable as the breeze. The psalmist no doubt had experience of it, when he hastily concluded and hurriedly said that all men are liars; but though his generalization was, as subsequent experience taught him, too sweeping, yet he had had sufficient ground for his statement just then. Hence we have the salutary caution in another psalm, "Trust not in princes, nor man's son." Paul upbraids the Galatians with their change-ableness, when he says, "I bear you record, that, if possible, ye would have plucked out your own eyes, and have given them to me. Am I therefore become your enemy, because I tell you the truth?" A great and good man, now with God, having had a bitter experience on one occasion of the variableness of human favour, wrote down in his diary the cool but cutting words, "Is it strange that men and the moon should change?" Yet never were the fickleness and consequent worthlessness of human popularity so strikingly exemplified as in the case of the crowd that shouted long and lustily, "Hosanna! Hosanna in the highest!" but just four days after, and before the week was out, cried long and loudly, "Crucify him! crucify him!" What a lesson is thus taught the follower of Jesus! What a warning to set little store by human favour and popular applause!

X. THE TEARS JESUS SHED OVER JERUSALEM. 1. *The sight of the city.* Of the three roads that led over the Mount of Olives—one between the two northern crests, a second right over the summit,—the third, or southern, then as now the main road, and the one most frequented from Bethany, was that by which the procession was approaching the city. At a spot where it winds round the southern ridge of the hill, the city, by a turn of the road, is at once brought full in view. At the descent from this shoulder of Olivet, "when he was come near, he beheld the city," looking across the Valley of Jehoshaphat. Its temple, its buildings, its dwellings, rising full before him, were all seen in the clear air of a Judæan sky; at the same time, its guilty inhabitants and their future fate were equally open to his eyes. 2. *Jesus weeps.* He paused and pondered. The sight of that splendid capital, the knowledge of its crimes, the remembrance of God's mercies, the thought that it might have been spared if, like Nineveh, it had known the day of its visitation and the things that belonged to its peace,—all these considerations awoke the sorrow and called forth the sympathy of the Saviour. "Jesus wept over it," as St. Luke informs us. He dropped a tear in silence (ἐδάκρυσεν) at the grave of Lazarus, a departed friend; but in view of the doomed city of Jerusalem he shed a flood of tears, weeping aloud (ἔκλαυσεν). But while his tears testified his love and showed his tenderness, his lips pronounced the city's fearful doom. 3. *His affecting apostrophe.* "If thou hadst known, even thou, at least in this thy day, the things which belong unto thy peace!" Jerusalem had its day, and in vain was that day protracted. "If thou hadst known, even thou," O ill-fated city; even thou, with all thy guilt; even thou, who hast so long abused the forbearance of a long-suffering God; even thou, who hast been so often reproved, and yet ever hardened thyself against reproof; even thou, who hast had so many warnings from the prophets of God and apostolic men; even thou, whose children I would have gathered as a hen gathereth her chickens under her wings; if thou, even thou, after so many days of mercy and of privilege have been misspent, after so many days of grace have been lost and for ever; if thou, even thou, hadst known, at least in this thy day, in this thy last day of privilege and of promise, in this thy last day of heavenly ministration, in this day of merciful visitation still thine, though the eleventh hour of thy existence and the eve of thy destruction! Never was apostrophe to place or person so tender, and never was aposiopesis so terrible; for the sentence is suddenly broken off and left unfinished; the clause which should state the consequence is omitted. After this omission the Saviour pauses, and then adds, "But now they are hid from thine eyes." The sentence might be taken as the expression of a wish: "Oh that thou hadst known the things that belong to thy peace!" and the sense would have remained the same and the sentiment equally solemn. 4. *Application to ourselves.* Our Lord's address on this occasion is as practical as it is pathetic. Personally applied, what an appeal it makes to each one of us! Jerusalem had its day, patriarchs and prophets had their day, evangelists and apostles had their day, ancient Jews and early Christians had their day, the apostolic and other Church Fathers had their day, the schoolmen and the reformers had their day, our forefathers and the men of preceding generations had their day; but "our fathers, where are they? and the prophets, do they live for ever?" Now, the present is our day. God says to each of us—This, the present, is thy day! Let conscience re-echo the solemn truth, for the past is gone, and gone for ever; the future is to come, and may never come to us; the present is all we can call our own. This, then, is our day; for "now is the accepted time, and now is the day of salvation." 5. *The purpose for which it is vouchsafed.* Day is not merely a measure of time, or portion of duration, or period of light, or a unit of a month or of a year, or a fragment of existence, made up of so many hours; it is that season for getting good and doing good which God has given us, and which he has assigned us for accomplishing the work for which he sent us into the world. It is thy day, reader; for God has given it to thee for a great purpose, and that purpose is the securing of thine own eternal well-being and the welfare of thy fellow-creature, and in both the glory of the great Creator. It is thy day; for it is thy property as long as Heaven is pleased to continue the boon. It is thy day; but not thine to waste or misspend; it is not thine to while away, or trifle away, or sin away, at thy option. It is thine; for it is a talent lent, a treasure given you by God, and for which thou shalt have to render an account. It is thy day for imitating the Saviour in working the work of him that sent thee: and "This is the work of God, that ye believe in him whom he hath sent;" "This is his commandment, that we should believe on the Name of his Son Jesus Christ;" this is thy day for attending to the conditions of peace, the things that tend to and make for peace, such as the righteousness of Christ received by faith, repentance of sin, and reformation of life. It is thy day for cultivating personal and practical religion in thine own soul; thy day, moreover, for the discharge of the duties of relative religion, because, in a certain sense, every man should be his brother's keeper, and no man is to live wholly to himself, or to seek entirely and selfishly, and therefore sinfully, his own things only, but to look also upon the things of others. It is thy day to do something for God, something for the Church, something for the world, endeavouring to leave it better than you found it —something useful in thy day and generation.—J. J. G.

Vers. 12—26.   Parallel passages: Matt. xxi. 12—22; Luke xix. 45—48.—*The blighting of the barren fig tree.* I. SYMBOLISM. 1. *Miracles of mercy.* Mercy has been called God's darling attribute; judgment is his strange work. The only-begotten Son, who has declared the Father unto us, has manifested the selfsame character. His miracles are miracles of mercy—all save two. Of these two, one was permissive and punitive, when our Lord allowed the devils to enter into the swine of the Gadarenes; the other, which is recorded in this passage, is a sort of symbol such as the old prophets used when they inculcated any solemn utterance, or wished specially to impress any predicted event. This custom was common in New as well as in Old Testament times. Thus Jesus washed his disciples' feet. Thus also Agabus, when he foretold Paul's imprisonment at Jerusalem, symbolized the fact by taking the apostle's girdle and therewith binding his own hands and feet, saying, "So shall the Jews at Jerusalem bind the man that owneth this girdle." In like manner our Lord, by this miracle of the blasted fig tree, most symbolically and significantly sets forth the blight of barrenness which so justly fell upon the Jewish people, and which is sure to fall upon any people or any person who has only the leaves of an outside profession, but who wants the fruits of a genuine faith or a heartfelt piety. To pronounce a curse on a senseless tree might appear meaningless—it might even seem vindictive. Not so, however, when the Saviour, in order to express the hopes which the appearance of the tree excited, and the disappointment which its want of fruit occasioned, devoted that tree by a striking figure to future and for ever fruitlessness. He thereby converts that tree into a symbol of the hypocrite or false professor, be he Gentile or be he Jew; and makes it a danger-signal, at once to warn us of the danger and ward off the doom. 2. *Judgment succeeds the abuse of mercy.* Another lesson which our Lord teaches us by this tree is the consequence of abused mercy. When mercy has been abused, judgment must succeed. The day of grace does not always last; and when that day has passed, and its privileges have been misused, the axe is then laid to the root of the tree, that it may be hewn down and cast into the fire. Such was the case with the body of the Jewish nation at the very time this miracle was wrought. Their day of grace was expiring. Their heart had remained untouched by that most pathetic appeal, "If thou hadst known, even thou, at least in this thy day, the things which belong unto thy peace!" Now, however, they were hid from their eyes. A woe similar to that pronounced on Chorazin and Bethsaida and Capernaum had gone forth against all that people, notwithstanding the fact that they had once been the people of God, and notwithstanding the many and great privileges which they had enjoyed, as well as the loud and leafy professions they had made. 3. *The relation of the miracle of the fig tree to the parable of the fig tree.* The fact of this relationship should be kept in view. The miracle narrated in this passage and the parable recorded by St. Luke are in a great measure the converse of each other. The parable of the fig tree long spared through the intercession of the vine-dresser, and this miracle of the fig tree suddenly withered to the very roots, are to a large extent the right opposite of each other. The one represents mercy pleading, the other judgment suddenly and surely overtaking the guilty; the one the long-suffering kindness of God, the other the swift vengeance of Heaven; the one mercy prevailing over judgment, the other judgment without mercy; the one a tree spared in hope of fruitfulness, the other a tree suddenly scathed to the very earth because of its barrenness. There is, however, one point, and only one point, in common; and that is, the end of continued unfruitfulness is cursing, the end of barrenness is burning, and the end of all leaf and no fruit is the speedy execution of the sentence, "Bind them in bundles, and burn them." 4. *A comparison and a contrast.* In the sixth chapter of the Epistle to the Hebrews, we find a beautiful comparison and an awful contrast; by the former the lesson of the parable is enforced, and by the latter the warning of this miracle receives a solemn sanction. "The earth," we there read, "which drinketh in the rain that cometh oft upon it, and bringeth forth herbs meet for them *for* whom it is dressed, receiveth blessing from God: but that which beareth thorns and briers is rejected, and is nigh unto cursing; whose end is to be burned."

II. OUR LORD'S DISAPPOINTMENT. 1. *He hungered.* The Saviour was on his way from Bethany to Jerusalem. It was in the morning, and he was hungry. This may appear strange. What had been the matter with the friendly family of Bethany, under whose roof our Lord had been so often and so hospitably entertained? Had they forfeited the high character for hospitality which they had so well earned? Had they forgotten its rights and become inconsiderate towards their Guest—a Guest whom they so highly honoured, and who had such claims upon them? Had they forgotten his wants, or neglected to supply them? Had Martha ceased her thrift, and given up her housewifery? Be this as it may, it could be no intentional neglect, much less a studied slight; it must have been some strange oversight. Or, as our Lord's time on earth was soon to terminate, and as much was to be done that day, perhaps he left Bethany at an earlier hour than usual; and, doing so, he could not wait till the customary hour for breakfast, and would not allow the household arrangements to be broken through for his convenience. Or perhaps he wished to reach the temple in time for the morning sacrifice at nine o'clock, before which time a devout Jew seldom broke his fast. Or perhaps he was so intent on his Father's business, and so intensely absorbed in his own great work, and so rapt in contemplation of its grand results, that he neglected the food provided for him. Or, in the absence of any direct statement, and where we are left to conjecture, we may suppose that it is just possible that he had shunned the shelter of any roof, and spent the previous night in prayer on some lone hillside or other sequestered spot. At all events, the broad fact stands out that he, by whom all things were made, became hungry; that he, who had fed thousands in a wilderness with a few loaves and fishes, would fain have satisfied the cravings of appetite with a few unripe figs. 2. *Leafage without fruitage, or all leaf and no fruit.* The district through which our Lord passed on his way, as he went from Bethany to Jerusalem, was a fig region. A village by the way had its name from this very circumstance; that village was Bethphage, which, as we have already seen, means "house of figs." Journeying through this district, he would, as might be expected, see many fig trees. His eye, however, rested on one at some distance. From St. Matthew's special mention of this *one* fig tree we conclude that there must have been something peculiar in its appearance. Our Lord singled it out from all or any in the district. It was rich in leaves, and so, full of promise. We must have in recollection the well-known fact in reference to the fig tree, that it puts forth its fruit before its leaves. The leaves of the fig tree, when they appeared, warranted the expectation of the figs. The leaves of this tree, visible to a distance, must have been large and numerous, and thus they held out the hope of abundant figs. The leafy honours of the tree bespoke its abundant fruitfulness. On the other hand, we are informed that "the time of figs was not yet," by which some (1) understand that the fig harvest had not yet come—the time of gathering the figs had not yet arrived. According to this understanding, in which Wakefield, Wetstein, Newcome, Campbell, Bloomfield, and others coincide, while the leaves indicated the existence of figs on the tree, the season of the year intimated with equal certainty that they had not been gathered off the tree; whatever fruit, therefore, the tree had, it retained. Figs there should have been, and if the tree had been true to its promise, figs there would have been. Figs there should have been still on the tree, for they had had time to grow, but not yet time to be gathered. There was every reason to expect figs on that fig tree, still green they might be, still immature, and not yet fully ripened. And yet this forwardness of the foliage implied the forwardness of its fruit. The advanced state of the one naturally induced the hope of a proportionately advanced state in the other. But not so. Our Lord approaches this goodly tree, but no fruit is there—not one fig among all its branches, not one fig among all its leaves. We must notice another explanation of the supposed difficulty in the words "for the time of figs was not [yet]." We put aside at once such attempted explanations as that of Heinsius, who, by accenting and changing the breathing, read οὖ instead of οὐ the negative, and rendered accordingly, "for where he was, it was the season of figs," that is, fruits ripened in Judæa considerably earlier than in the less mild climate of Galilee; also the still more forced interpretation of those who read the clause interrogatively, viz. " for was it not the time of figs ? " and the no less objectionable explanation of καιρὸς in the sense of a favourable season, for in that case the season, not the tree, would have deserved the malediction; or in the signification of favourable weather, as Olshausen. All these, however ingenious they may appear, are evasive shifts and no more. But, discounting them, we find an interpretation other than that first given and simpler, which, (2) understanding the reference to be to a *precocious* or *premature foliation,* takes the words in their plain and natural sense. It was not the time or season of figs—"denn es war nicht Feigenzeit," as Fritzsche properly renders it ; but this tree antedated the season by putting forth its leaves prematurely. The appearance of the leaves was unseasonably early; still, as their appearance implied the prior existence of fruit, the passer-by was thus invited to approach the tree, and induced to expect and hope for fruit. The show of leaves, though not the season of the year, favoured this expectation; accordingly he came, if therefore (ἄρα), as it was reasonable to expect from the tree having leaves, he shall find anything in it (ἐν αὐτῇ) within the compass of this umbrageous tree, among its leaves and branches. But though he came (ἐπ' αὐτὴν) close upon it, right up to it, yet, notwithstanding his nearness to it, and the narrowness with which he inspected it, he found nothing but leaves. 3. *Symbol of profession without performance.* According to either of the explanations above given, either (1) or (2), especially perhaps the latter, that large fig tree, with its fine foliage and luxuriant leaves, occupying, as it did, a prominent position near the wayside, and visible far off by reason of its grand proportions and magnificent appearance, was nothing better than a huge practical lie, an embodied falsehood, a palpable untruth. That tree made a promise, but it broke it; it held out a hope, but it disappointed it; it professed much, but performed nothing. Never was there a more striking symbol of any people than that fig tree was of the Jews. They had enjoyed covenant promises and covenant privileges and covenant hopes, and their professions corresponded therewith. These were their leaves, but they had no real fruitfulness. They occupied a high and prominent position ; theirs were a very fruitful hillside—the horn of the son of oil—an exceedingly fertile soil, glorious fostering sunshine, and rich refreshing dews; " they were Israelites; to whom pertained the adoption, and the glory, and the covenants, and the giving of the Law, and the service of God, and the promises ; " but they proved themselves unworthy, shamefully unworthy, of these favours. They had commandments and ordinances ; they made loud professions and long prayers ; they were strict in certain religious observances, and scrupulous in their ritual. In some things they went beyond the letter of the Law, for they tithed rue and anise and cummin ; but, in matters of much greater magnitude and really enjoined by the Law, they fell short, and were in fact woefully deficient. God " looked for judgment, but behold oppression ; for righteousness, but behold a cry." They called themselves children of Abraham, but they had none of that precious faith that so distinguished Abraham. They were proud of Moses, their great lawgiver, but they attended not to the Prophet to whom Moses pointed as greater than himself, and to whom he commanded them to hearken. They professed themselves expectants of Messiah, but when he came to them they received him not. They were no better than the dark world around—" a world that knew not when he came, even God's eternal Son." We need not trace further the application of this symbolic fig tree to the Jews; let us see its application to Gentiles also. 4. *Adumbrative of Gentile as well as Jew.* There may be the leaves of profession without any corresponding fruitfulness in the case of Gentiles as well as Jews. This symbolic fig tree may have a personal application to ourselves. We may profess Christ to please men, to keep up appearances, to maintain a respectable position, or advance in some way our worldly prospects. We may rest in a mere form ; we may have a form of godliness without the power ; we may have a name to live, and yet be spiritually dead; we may be content with the outward visible sign, and care nothing for the inward spiritual grace. This was the complaint of God against his professing people in the days of Ezekiel: " They come unto thee as the people cometh, and they sit before thee as my people, and they hear thy words, but they will not do them : for with their mouth they show much love, but their heart goeth after their covetousness. And, lo, thou art unto them as a very lovely song of one that hath a pleasant voice, and can play well on an instrument : for they hear thy words, but they do them not." Here is the too common defect of profession without practice, naming the name of Christ and not departing from iniquity. Others, again, it is to be feared, are downrightly insincere; they put religion on like a cloak, and lay it aside when it suits them ; like their Sunday clothes, they wear it on the sabbath, but lay it past throughout the week. They impose on their fellow-men, they trifle with the Almighty, and deceive their own souls. 5. *The Saviour's dissatisfaction with barren professors.* Many a time Christ comes to professors, and when he finds no fruit, no figs, no real goodness, nothing but leaves, oh, how he is disappointed! Many a time he is wounded in the house of his friends; many a time he has reason to be indignant with the false professor; many a time religion is scandalized by the leaf of profession and the life of sin. We can conceive Christ coming to such professors and saying—Was it for this you trod my courts? for this you joined yourself to my people? for this you sat at my table? for this you took the cup of salvation in your hand? for this you avouched yourself to be the Lord's in solemn sacramental action? 6. *His remonstrance.* Besides the expression of just indignation, there is tender remonstrance on his part. That remonstrance may be supposed couched in some such terms as the following :—After all my care for you, and love to you, and provision for your salvation ; after all my goodness and grace to your soul; after all my sufferings, both in life and death; after all my agony of soul and anguish of body; after the many precepts I have given you, the exhortations I have addressed to you, the warnings I have sent you ; after all the checks of conscience, and after all the strivings of my Spirit,—is this the return you make me? Have you so soon forgotten your covenant engagements; so soon forgotten all your vows; so soon belied the profession you made, saying by act, if not by word, "O Lord, I am thy servant: thou hast loosed my bonds"? Have you so soon and so sadly violated your pledged allegiance expressed in the words, "I am not my own; I am bought with a price ; and bound therefore to serve the Lord with body and spirit, which are the Lord's"? God forbid that this should be the case with any of us! May better things be hoped, and reasonably hoped, of us all, and "things that accompany salvation"! Let our motto be, "Now being made free from sin, and become servants of God, we have our fruit unto holiness, and the end everlasting life." Let our conduct be in accordance with the statement, "I have put off my coat; how shall I put it on? I have washed my feet; how shall I defile them?" Let our meditation be on "whatsoever things are true, whatsoever things are honest, whatsoever things are just, whatsoever things are pure, whatsoever things are lovely, whatsoever things are of good report;" and "if there be any virtue, and if there be any praise," let us "think on these things."

III. DOOM PRONOUNCED ON THE FIG TREE. 1. *He stereotypes its state.* Christ does not make this fig tree barren, he only stereotypes its barrenness; he found it in that state, and, as far as its condition of barrenness was concerned, he left it pretty much as he found it. It bare no fruit before, it should bear no fruit afterwards, and so no fruit for ever. As far, however, as his own action was concerned, he did more; for he withered its leaves, he scathed its trunk, he blighted it both root and branch. It was cursed, and so devoted to barrenness; it was dried up from the roots, and so inevitably destined to decay; it was completely withered, and so doomed to entire destruction. To the present hour the Jew has an unmistakable resemblance to this symbolic fig tree. Nationally, he is barked and peeled; he is a tree of which the branches are withered; he is one of a nation on which the blight of Heaven rests; the curse has come upon them to the uttermost. He has [neither Church, as in days of old, nor State, nor proper nationality. He has neither temple, nor priest, nor sacrifice. He is still doomed to the "wandering foot and weary breast"—one of a people resembling this withered fig tree to which the curse of Heaven clings. 2. *Applicability of the symbol to our own case.* What is the conclusion from all this, and what is its connection with ourselves? Just that of which the apostle, in writing to the Romans (xi. 21, 22) speaks: "For if God spared not the natural branches, take heed lest he also spare not thee. Behold therefore the goodness and severity of God: on them which fell, severity; but toward thee, goodness, if thou continue in his goodness : otherwise thou also shalt be cut off." 3. *Responsibility pertaining to the Church of God.* It is no light matter to have the Church of God in our midst, its ordinances dispensed to us, its sacraments enjoyed by us, its doctrines proclaimed to us, its duties declared to us. What weighty responsibilities does all this impose? "Unto whomsoever much is given, of them shall much be required." What a blessing, if we improve these privileges, and know the time of our merciful visitation! What a millstone weight of condemnation is hung about our neck, when, in the full enjoyment of ordinances, we prove ourselves at once unfaithful and ungrateful? We see here what Christ expects of us, and what he has every right to expect. He sees on us the leaves of profession; he requires the living power of religion in our souls. He beholds the leaves of confession; he demands correspondence of character, conduct, and conversation. He has heard your proclamation with the lips to the effect, "Henceforth shall the Lord be my God;" he looks, therefore, for piety of heart and purity of life. He observes with you the show of godliness; he will not be satisfied unless you diffuse the savour of it all around. Truth binds you to this; you have sworn, and must not go back; you have vowed, and must fulfil your vow; you have avouched the Lord to be your God, and the covenant entered into may not be broken, except at terrible risk. Gratitude binds to this. What shall we render unto the Lord for all his gracious benefits and gifts to us?

> " Love so amazing, so Divine,
> Demands my heart, my life, my all."

Consistency binds to this. What can be thought of any one who enters into the most solemn engagements and then practically repudiates them? Our welfare, both for time and eternity, binds to this; for "blessed is every one that feareth the Lord; that walketh in his ways. For thou shalt eat the labour of thine hands: happy shalt thou be, and it shall be well with thee."

IV. APPLICATION OF THE WHOLE. 1. Think for a moment of the awful doom of this withered fig tree. It is the doom of every hypocrite and of every false professor. The first blessing pronounced on man was fruitfulness; one of the severest curses is barrenness. The leaf of the merely nominal Christian will soon wither; it will soon decay and die. There is no root, and so even the leaf of profession will not last long; no faith, and so no fruitfulness; no principle, and so no practical godliness. The sparks of his own kindling make but a flickering light at best; and that light, bad as it is, soon goes out altogether in utter darkness. "The wicked is driven away in his wickedness, but the righteous hath hope in his death." 2. As it fared with the Jews, so will it fare with every individual who abuses God's mercies by continued unfruitfulness. God's ancient people has been unchurched, and, if we may so say, unpeopled; and if this was done in a green tree, what shall not be done in a dry? The seven Churches of Asia had been unfaithful, and the candlestick was removed out of its place. So with the African Churches—Alexandria, Hippo, and Carthage. 3. God looks for fruit, and claims it as his due. The more fruitful you are, the more is he glorified. " Herein," said the Saviour, " is my Father glorified, that ye bear much fruit;" the more, also, is your own soul benefited and blessed. Often, when men become unfruitful, and prove false to their vows, neglecting God's ordinances, and abusing his mercies, he gives them over to judicial blindness of mind, hardness of heart, searedness of conscience, or to strong delusion, or to a famine not of bread but of hearing the Word of the Lord. Sickness, or age, or poverty, or removal of their habitation, deprives them of the once possessed, but little esteemed and much abused, mercies. So with Ephraim; he is "joined to his idols: let him alone." 4. During our walks in summer or early autumn we used to see a tree withered and decayed; its leaves were gone, its bark peeled off, and its branches quite bare. Near to it on every side were trees green and leafy, healthy and vigorous, beautiful and flourishing. How ghastly looked that naked skeleton tree beside them! We often said as we passed it by—What a true type of a barren professor, "twice dead, plucked up by the roots"! 5. From this miracle our Lord took occasion to speak of the wonders which faith works, and to urge the necessity of faith to the success of prayer.—J. J. G.

Vers. 27—33. Parallel passages: Matt. xxi. 23—32; Luke xx. 1—8.—*Christ's authority questioned*. I. CAUSE OF CHRIST'S AUTHORITY BEING CALLED IN QUESTION. The ostensible cause was the events of the preceding day; the real cause Satan's opposition to the work of Christ. On the day before he had displayed his zeal for the sanctity of God's house and the purity of its worship. He is now called to account because of the extraordinary efforts he had made to put a stop to the public profanation of the house of God, and because of the no less extraordinary authority which he had exercised. Such appears to be the right reference of the ταῦτα in the question, though along with the purging of the temple may be included the miracles of healing that had been performed on the blind and lame who, as St. Matthew informs us, had resorted to him in the temple. Others, with less probability, refer the word to his teaching; for "he taught daily in the temple," as we read in St. Luke. All these, together with our Lord's triumphal entry, had sorely displeased and greatly discomfited the Jewish rulers, who now proceeded to call his authority in question. But the prime mover of this cavilling opposition was Satan. He was pursuing his usual tactics. Good is often done in an informal way, or by voluntary agencies, or by very humble instrumentalities; and Satan, when the fact of the good done is undeniable, stirs up men to impugn the authority or assail the commission of those Christian workers by whom the good is done, thus endeavouring to raise a false issue and stay its progress.

II. GREED OF GAIN VERSUS GODLINESS. The Church has its counterfeits as well as the world; there is no class altogether free from false disguises. Some, perhaps many, of those unholy traffickers who were desecrating the temple so that a second cleansing of it within the short period of three years had become a necessity, fancied they were doing God service and accommodating his worshippers; while their own sordid and selfish interests—their own love of gain and usurious greed—were their real and actuating motives. Was it strange that our Lord was roused to indignation, and resorted to the most active measures to expel from the sacred precincts those dealers in sheep and oxen, with their droves of cattle, those dove-sellers and money-changers, who, under the pretext of supplying the requisites for sacrifices to such as came from a distance, and the temple half-shekels to foreign Jews for their larger coins or coins with heathenish images and inscriptions, had their heart set on driving a profitable trade in this matter of the sacrifices, and their eye fixed on the κόλλυβος, or twelfth of a shekel, as the agio of exchange; while the noisy bargainings, unseemly wranglings, and general hubbub made the house of God resemble one of those caves where robbers quarrelled over their ill-got gains?

III. OUR LORD'S ANSWER TO THE QUESTION ABOUT AUTHORITY. The twofold question about our Lord's authority and its source was put by a deputation from the Sanhedrim—a deputation representative of the three chief sections of that body: namely, chief priests or heads of the twenty-four classes; scribes, the theologians or authorized interpreters of Scripture; and the elders or heads of the principal families. The question of this formidable deputation called forth a counter-question on the part of our Lord; nor was there any evasion in this. By asking them whether John's baptism was of heavenly or human origin, he effectually answered their question, and put them into a dilemma from which there was no escaping. If they admitted John's mission to have been from God, the matter was settled at once and decisively; for John had testified most positively and repeatedly to the Divine mission and consequent Divine authority of Jesus, saying, "Behold the Lamb of God, which taketh away the sin of the world;" and declaring that he would "baptize with the Holy Ghost." The alternative of John's mission being derived from a human source was what they dared not face, for it would bring them into collision with the crowd, and they were too cowardly for that.

IV. THE UNFAIRNESS OF THE QUESTION OF THE SANHEDRIM. Had they not had evidence of Jesus' authority in his exceptionally sinless life in the midst of all the temptations of a sinful world? Had they not evidence of his Divine authority in his teaching?—"for he taught as One having authority, and not as the scribes;" in "the gracious words that proceeded out of his mouth"?—for the universal testimony was that "never man spake like this Man." Had they not proof in the miracles which he wrought—not prodigally, but properly and appropriately?

> "But who so blind as those who will not see?
> And who so deaf as those who will not hear?"

J. J. G.

EXPOSITION.

CHAPTER XII.

Ver. 1.—**And he began to speak unto them in parables.** This particular parable which follows was specially directed against the scribes and Pharisees; but it was uttered in the presence of a multitude of the people. "He *began* to speak ... in parables." He had not used this form of instruction till now in Jerusalem. **A man planted a vineyard.** The imagery of the parable would be familiar to them from Isaiah (v. 1). But Palestine was eminently a land of "vineyards," as well as of "oil olives." The man who planted the vineyard is no other than God himself. "Thou hast brought a vine' out of Egypt; thou hast cast out the heathen, and planted it." The imagery is specially appropriate. No property was considered to yield so rich a return as the vineyard, and none required such unceasing care and attention. The vine represents the kingdom of God in its idea and conception; not the Jewish Church in particular. The owner of this vineyard had himself made it. [He had "planted it." This planting took place in the establishment of the Jewish polity in the land of Canaan, when the heathen were cast out. He **set a hedge about it.** This and the following descriptions are not mere ornaments of the parable. The "hedge" was an important protection to the vineyard. It might be a wall or a "quick hedge," a living fence. The vineyards in the East may now be seen often with a strong hedge planted round them. Such hedges, made of the prickly cactus, are to be seen at this day in the neighbourhood of Joppa. Figuratively, this hedge would represent the middle wall of partition which then existed between the Jew and the Gentile; and in this, their separation from the idolatrous nations around them, lay the security of the Jews that they should enjoy the continued protection of God. It is well remarked by Archbishop Trench that the geographical position of Judæa was figurative of this, the spiritual separation of the people—guarded as Judæa was eastward by the river Jordan and its chain of lakes, northward by Anti-libanus, southward by the desert and Idumæa, and westward by the Mediterranean Sea. **Digged a place for the winepress** (ληνός, *torcular*); the words are literally, *digged a pit for the winepress* (ὤρυξεν ὑπολήνιον); the digging could only apply to the pit, a place hollowed out and then fitted with masonry. Sometimes these pits were formed out of the solid rock. Examples of these are frequent in Palestine. There were usually two pits hollowed out of the rock, one sloping to the

other, and with openings between them. The grapes were placed in the upper pit; and the juice, crushed out by the feet of men, flowed into the lower pit, from whence it was taken out and put into wine-skins. "I have trodden the winepress alone." **And built a tower.** The tower (πύργον) was probably the watch-tower, where a watchman was placed to guard the vineyard from plunderers. Particular directions are given in the rabbinical writings (see Lightfoot) for the dimensions both of the winepress and of the tower. The tower was to be ten cubits high and four cubits square. It is described as "a high place, where the vine-dresser stands to overlook the vineyard." Such towers are still to be' seen in Palestine, especially in the neighbourhood of Bethlehem, of Hebron, and in the vine-growing districts of Lebanon. **And let it out to husbandmen.** The husbandmen would be the ordinary stated teachers of the people, though not excluding the people themselves. The Jewish nation in fact, both the teachers and the taught, represented the husbandmen, each member of the Church, then as now, being required to seek the welfare of the whole body. **And went into a far country** (καὶ ἀπεδήμησε); literally, *and went into another country.* St. Luke (xx. 9) adds (χρόνους ἱκανούς), "for a long time."

Vers. 2—5.—**And at the season he sent to the husbandmen a servant, that he might receive from the husbandmen of the fruits of the vineyard.** St. Matthew (xxi. 34) says he sent "his servants." St. Mark mentions them in detail. These servants were the prophets, as Isaiah, Jeremiah, and others, whom the Jews persecuted and slew in different ways, as the reprovers of their vices. But the mercy of God was long-suffering, and still triumphed over their wickedness. In his account of this parable St. Mark is very minute. The first servant that was sent received no fruit, and was beaten. The second received much worse usage. According to the Authorized Version the words are, **At him they cast stones, and wounded him in the head, and sent him away shamefully handled** (κἀκεῖνον λιθοβολήσαντες ἐκεφαλαίωσαν, καὶ ἀπέστειλαν ἠτιμωμένον). The word λιθοβολήσαντες is, however, not to be found in the best authorities; and the right reading of the next word is apparently ἐκεφαλίωσαν, a very unusual word; but the context makes it plain that it expresses some injury done to the head. The other form of the word is usual enough; but it ordinarily signifies "a summing up," "a gathering up into a head." *And handled shamefully* (ἠτιμωμένον); literally, *dishonoured.* The third messenger they killed outright. The words run, **And him they killed; and many others; beating some, and killing some.** The construction here is incomplete, although the meaning is plain. The complete sentence would be, " And him they killed; and *they did violence to* many others, beating some and killing some."

Vers. 6—8.—**Having yet therefore one son, his well-beloved.** There is strong evidence in favour of a different reading here, namely (ἔτι ἕνα εἶχεν, υἱὸν ἀγαπητὸν), *he had yet one, a beloved son.* There is something very touching in this form of expression. Many messages had been sent; many means had been tried. But one other resource remained. " There is one, a beloved Son. I will send him; they will surely reverence him (ἐντραπήσονται τὸν υἱόν μου). They will reflect, and reflection will bring shame and submission and reverence." This was the last effort of Divine mercy—the sending of the Incarnate God, whom the Jews put to death without the city. St. Mark's words seem rather to imply that they killed him within the vineyard, and cast out the dead body. But it is possible that in his narrative he mentions the climax first—they killed him, and ,then returns to a detail of the dreadful ,tragedy; they cast him out of the vineyard, and there slew him. (See Matt. xxi. 39.)

Ver. 9.—**What therefore will the lord of the vineyard do?** In St. Matthew's narrative the scribes answer this question. St. Luke, as St. Mark here, assigns the answer to our Lord. It would seem probable that the scribes first answered him, and that then he himself repeated their answer, and confirmed it by his looks and gesture; so that from thence, as well as from what followed, they might sufficiently understand that he spake these things of them. Then, according to St. Luke (xx. 16), they subjoined the words, " God forbid!" an expression wrung from their consciences, which accused them and told them that the parable applied to them. Here, then, we have a distinct prediction of the rejection of the Jews and the call of the Gentiles.

Vers. 10, 11.—This quotation is from Ps. cxviii. 22, where David prophesies of Christ. The meaning is plainly this, that the chief priests and scribes, as the builders of the Jewish Church, rejected Christ from the building as a useless stone; yea, more—they condemned and crucified him. They rejected him (ἀπεδοκίμασαν). The verb in the Greek implies that the stone was first examined and then deliberately refused. But this stone, thus disallowed and set at nought by the builders, was made **the head of the corner.** The image here is different from that used in the Epistles, where Christ

is spoken of as the chief Corner-stone in the foundation. Here he is represented as the Corner-stone in the cornice. In real truth he is both. He is the tried Foundation-stone. But he is also the Head of the corner. In the great spiritual building he is "all and in all," uniting and binding together all in one. **This was the Lord's doing** (παρὰ Κυρίου ἐγένετο αὕτη); literally, *this was from the Lord.* The feminine (αὕτη) refers apparently to κεφαλή. This lifting up of the despised and rejected stone to be the Corner-stone of the cornice was God's work; and was a fitting object for wonder and praise.

Ver. 12.—The scribes and Pharisees knew, partly from the words of this psalm, and partly from the looks of Christ, that they were spoken against them. So **they sought** in their rage and malice **to lay hold on him**; but **they feared the people,** with whom he was still popular. Thus, however, by his rebuke of the scribes and Pharisees, he prepared the way for that death which, within three days, they brought upon him. And the counsel of God was fulfilled for the redemption of men by the blood of Christ.

Vers. 13, 14.—St. Matthew (xxii. 15) tells us that " the Pharisees took counsel how they might ensnare him (ὅπως αὐτὸν παγιδεύσωσιν) in his talk;" namely, by proposing to him captious and insidious questions, which, in whatever way he might answer them, might expose him to danger. On this occasion they enlisted the Herodians to join them in their attack upon him. These Herodians were a sect of the Jews who supported the house of Herod, and were in favour of giving tribute to the Roman Cæsar. They were so called at first from Herod the Great, who was a great supporter of Cæsar. Tertullian, St. Jerome, and others say that these Herodians thought that Herod was the promised Messiah, because they saw that in him the sceptre had departed from Judah (Gen. xlix. 10). Herod encouraged these flatterers, and so put to death the infants at Bethlehem, that he might thus get rid of Christ, lest any other than himself might be regarded as Christ. They said that it was on this account that he rebuilt the temple with so much magnificence. The Pharisees took, of course, altogether the other side, and stood forward as the supporters of the Law of Moses and of their national freedom. So, in order that they might ensnare him, they sent to him their disciples with the Herodians, and in the most artful manner proposed to him, apparently in good faith, a question which answer it how he might, would, as they hoped, throw him upon the horns of a dilemma. If he said that tribute ought to be given to Cæsar, he would expose himself to the malice of the Jewish people, who prided themselves upon their freedom. If, on the other hand, he said that tribute ought not to be given to Cæsar, he would incur the wrath of Cæsar and of the Roman power.

Vers. 15, 16.—St. Matthew (xxii. 18) says, "But Jesus perceived their wickedness, and said, Why tempt ye me, ye hypocrites?" You pretend that you are approaching me with a good conscience, sincerely desirous to know how you ought to act in this matter; when at the same time you are enemies alike of me and of God, and are thirsting for my blood, and are doing all in your power to torment me, and to entangle me by fraud. "The first virtue," says St. Jerome, "of the respondent is to know the mind of the questioner, and to adapt his answer accordingly." These Pharisees and Herodians flatter Christ that they may destroy him; but he rebukes them, that, if possible, he might save them. **Bring me a penny, that I may see it.** The Roman *denarius* was equal to about eightpence halfpenny. This was the coin in which the tribute money was to be paid. It had stamped upon it the image of Tiberius Cæsar, the then reigning Roman emperor. The cognomen of Cæsar was first given to Julius Cæsar, from whom it was devolved to his successors. The current coin of the country proved the subjection of the country to him whose image was upon it. Maimonides, quoted by Dr. John Lightfoot (vol. ii. p. 230), says, "Wheresoever the money of any king is current, there the inhabitants acknowledge that king for their lord."

Ver. 17.—**Render unto Cæsar the things that are Cæsar's, and unto God the things that are God's.** It is as though our Lord said, "Since you Jews are now subject to Cæsar—and there is here this evidence of it, that his coin is current amongst you; you would not use it were you not obliged, because all Gentile rites and symbols are an abhorrence to you;—but since Cæsar demands nothing of you but his tribute—the coin stamped with his own image and name —it is your duty to render to him his own *denarius* for tribute. But spiritual things, such as worship and obedience, give these to God; for these he demands from you as his right, and by so doing you will offend neither God nor yet Cæsar." Our Lord, in his infinite wisdom, avoids the question altogether whether the Jews were rightly in subjection to the Romans. This was a doubtful question. But there could be no doubt as to the fact that they were tributary. This was made plain by the evidence of the current coin. Now, this being so, it was manifestly the duty of the

Jewish people to give to Cæsar the tribute money which he demanded of them for the expenses of government, and especially of supporting an army to defend them from their enemies. And it was no less their duty to give their tribute to God, which he in his own right demanded of them as his creatures and faithful subjects. The rights of Cæsar are one thing, and those of God are another; and there is nothing that need clash between them. State polity is not opposed to religion, nor religion to state. Tertullian says, "'Render to Cæsar the things that are Cæsar's, and to God the things that are God's;' that is, give to Cæsar his image stamped upon his coin, and give to God his own image stamped upon you; so that while you render to Cæsar the coin which is his due, you may render your own self to God." This wonderful answer of our Lord teaches us that we ought to try to speak so wisely, and so to moderate our speech amongst those who are captious, that we may, if possible, offend neither side, but steer safely between Scylla and Charybdis. **And they marvelled at him.** The true Greek reading of the verb here is not ἐθαύμασαν, but ἐξεθαύμαζον, *they marvelled greatly at him; they stood marvelling greatly at him.* They marvelled at his wisdom and skill in extricating himself so readily out of this net in which they had hoped to entangle him. Indeed, the words of the psalmist (Ps. ix. 15) were verified in them: "The wicked is snared in the work of his own hands." He vaulted over the trap set for him, leaving them entangled in it. He lifted up the question far above the petty controversy of the hour, and affirmed a great principle of natural and religious obligation which belongs alike to all times and persons and places.

Vers. 18—23.—**And there come unto him Sadducees, which say that there is no resurrection.** Josephus states that in the time of Judas Maccabæus there were three sects of the Jews, differing amongst themselves, namely, the Pharisees, the Sadducees, and the Essenes. The Hebrew word *Zadoc*, from which the Sadducees derive their name, means "just," or "righteous." These Sadducees accepted the Pentateuch, and probably more than the Pentateuch; but they rejected any oral tradition. They were known in the time of our Lord as denying those doctrines which connect us more immediately with another world, such as the existence of spirits and of angels, and the resurrection of the body. They altogether denied fate, affirming that all things are in our own power. They heard Christ preach the resurrection, and by means of it persuade men to repentance and a holy life. They therefore proposed to him a question which appeared to them to be fatal to the doctrine of a future state and a resurrection. The case supposed is that of seven brethren, who, in compliance with the Law of Moses, one after another, as each died in succession, took the same woman to wife. It is probable that such a case may actually have occurred; at any rate, it was a possible case. And the question founded upon it by the Sadducees was this—Whose wife would she be of them in the resurrection? Here, then, they hoped to entangle him, and to show that the doctrine of the resurrection was absurd. For if our Lord should say that in the resurrection she would be the wife of one only, the other brethren would have been excited to envy and continual strife. Nor could he have said that she would be common to the seven brothers. Such were the absurdities which, as they intimated, would flow out of his doctrine of the resurrection, if it could be proved. But our Lord scatters to the winds all this foolish reasoning, by adding one clause omitted by them, and overlooked by men of mere earthly minds, namely, that in the world to come this widow would be the wife of none of the seven brethren.

Ver. 24.—These Sadducees erred in two ways: (1) They did not know or remember the Scriptures, such as that in Job (xix. 25), "I know that my Redeemer liveth," etc., or in Isaiah (xxvi. 19), "Thy dead men shall live, together with my dead body shall they arise;" or in Daniel (xii. 2), "Many of them that sleep in the dust of the earth shall awake," etc. (2) They did not know the power of God, namely, that he can raise the bodies of the dead again to life, even as at first he created them out of nothing; for a greater power is required to make that to be which was not, than to make that again to be which once was. But then the resurrection life will be a new life, spiritual, glorious, eternal, like that of the angels. So in these words our Lord struck at the double root of the error of the Sadducees: (1) ignorance of the Scriptures, which plainly teach the resurrection; and (2) ignorance of the power of God, which led them to interpret these Scriptures, which speak of the resurrection, to mean only a mystical resurrection from vice to virtue.

Ver. 25.—But are as angels in heaven—not "the angels;" the οἱ is omitted. The blessed, after the resurrection, will be like angels as to purity, as to a spiritual life, as to immortality, as to happiness and glory. There will be no necessity for marriages in heaven. Here, on earth, the father dies, but he lives on in his children after death. In heaven there is no death, but every one will live and be blessed for ever; and therefore it is that St. Luke adds here, "Neither

can they die any more." St. Augustine says, "Marriages are on account of children; children on account of succession; succession on account of death. But in heaven, as there is no death, neither is there any marriage."

Ver. 26.—St. Mark is here careful to state that what St. Matthew describes as "the word spoken by God" was to be found in the book of Moses (Exod. iii. 5), in the place concerning the Bush (ἐπὶ τῆς βάτου), as it is correctly rendered in the Revised Version. Our Lord might have brought yet clearer proofs out of Job, Daniel, Ezekiel, etc.; but in his wisdom he preferred to allege this out of Moses and the Pentateuch, because, whatever the views of the Sadducees may have been as to other parts of the Old Testament, these books of Moses they readily acknowledged. I am the God of Abraham, and the God of Isaac, and the God of Jacob. The force of the argument is this, that "God is not the God of the dead, but of the living." Their souls are still alive; and if these patriarchs are still alive, there will be a resurrection. If men are to live for ever, they will, sooner or later, live again in the completeness of their being, namely, of body and soul and spirit. Our Lord would, therefore, say this: "In a few days you will put me to death; but in three days I shall rise again from the dead. And after that, in due time I shall raise them from the dead at the last day, and bring them in triumph with me into heaven." The Sadducees and the Epicureans denied the resurrection, because they denied the immortality of the soul; for these two doctrines hang together. For if the soul is immortal, then, since it naturally depends upon the body, it is necessary that the body should rise. Otherwise the soul would continue to exist in a dislocated state, and would only obtain a divided life and an imperfect existence. Hence our Lord here distinctly proves the resurrection of the body from the immortality of the soul. When he speaks of Abraham, Isaac, and Jacob, he does not speak of their souls only, but of their whole being. Therefore, though they are for a time dead to us, yet they live to God, and sleep, as it were, because ere long God will raise them from death, as from a sleep, to a blessed and endless life. For all, though they have passed out of our sight, still live to him.

Ver. 27.—Ye therefore do greatly err. The Greek is, omitting the οὖν, simply ὑμεῖς πολὺ πλανᾶσθε, Ye greatly err. The omission is more consistent with St. Mark's usual style. The Sadducees entirely misunderstood the meaning of their own Scriptures.

Ver. 28.—St. Matthew (xxii. 34) says here

that the Pharisees, when they heard that he had put the Sadducees to silence, gathered themselves together, and that then one of them, who was a lawyer (νομίνος), that is, "a scribe," asked him this question, **What commandment is the first of all?** It appears here from St. Mark that this scribe had been present at the discussion with the Sadducees, and he had probably informed the others of what had taken place, and of the wisdom and power of our Lord's answer; so he was naturally put forward to try our Lord with another crucial question. It does not necessarily appear that he had an evil intention in putting this question. He may, in his own mind (seeing the wisdom and skill of our Lord), have desired to hear what Christ had to say to a very difficult question on a matter deeply interesting to all true Hebrews. The question was one much mooted amongst the Jews in the time of our Lord. "For many," says Bede, "thought that the first commandment in the Law related to offerings and sacrifices, with regard to which so much is said in Leviticus, and that the right worship of God consisted in the due offering of these." On this account the Pharisees encouraged children to say "Corban" to their parents; and hence this candid and truth-loving scribe, when he heard our Lord's answer about the love of God and of our neighbour, said that such obedience was worth "more than all whole burnt offerings and sacrifices." With regard to the love of God, St. Bernard says, "The measure of our love to God is to love him without measure; for the immense goodness of God deserves all the love that we can possibly give to him."

Ver. 31.—**Thou shalt love thy neighbour as thyself.** God is to be loved above everything—above all angels, or men, or any created thing. But after God, amongst created things, our neighbour is above all to be loved. And we are to extend to our neighbour that kind of love with which we love ourselves. Our love of ourselves is not a frigid love, but a sincere and ardent love. In like manner we should love our neighbour, and desire for him all those good things both for the body and for the soul that we desire for ourselves. This is what our Lord himself teaches us. "All things whatsoever ye would that men should do to you, even so do unto them." **There is none other commandment greater than these.** St. Matthew (xxii. 40) says, "On these two commandments hang the whole Law and the prophets." There is no commandment greater than these, because all the precepts of the Divine Law are included in them. So that our Lord here teaches us that we ought continually to have these two precepts in our minds and before our eyes, and

direct all our thoughts and words and actions by them, and regulate our whole life according to them.

Ver. 32.—The first words of this verse should be rendered thus: **Of a truth, Master, thou hast well said that he is one.** In the remainder of the scribe's answer we find a different word used in the Greek for "mind," or "understanding," from that just used by our Lord. In our Lord's answer the word is διάνοια. Here it is σύνεσις. Both words are well rendered by "understanding." It is an act of understanding. It is the thought associating itself with the object, and "standing under" it so as to support it. (See Dr. Morison on St. Mark.)

Ver. 33.—**Is more** (περισσότερόν)—according to the most approved reading, *much more*—**than all whole burnt offerings and sacrifices.** This scribe was evidently emerging out of the bondage of ceremonial things, and perceiving the supremacy of the moral law.

Ver. 34.—**And when Jesus saw that he answered discreetly** (νουνεχῶς), **he said unto him, Thou art not far from the kingdom of God.** It would appear from this answer that our Lord regarded him as one who approached him with the sincere desire to know the truth, and so he encouraged him. This shows how powerful an influence our Lord's teaching had already exercised amongst all classes of the Jews. This scribe, notwithstanding the prejudices of his class, had reached the border-land of the kingdom. He had learnt that the true way to the kingdom was by the love of God and of our neighbour. He was not far from the kingdom—not far from "the Church militant here on earth," by which is the way to the Church triumphant in heaven. He was not far from the kingdom, but still he wanted that which is the true pathway to the kingdom—faith in Christ as the Saviour of the world. **And no man after that durst ask him any question.** St. Matthew (xxii. 46) places these words after the next occurrence. But there is no inconsistency in the two narratives, because in this next incident our Lord puts the question to them; and this silenced both their questioning and their answering. All felt that there was such a vast reach of wisdom and knowledge in all that he said, that it was in vain to contend with him.

Ver. 35.—Our Lord was now in the temple, and he took the opportunity for instructing the scribes and Pharisees concerning his person and his dignity. Thus, as ever, he returned good for evil. He here taught them that the Messiah was not a mere man, as they supposed, but that he was both God and man, and that therefore they ought not to wonder or to be offended because he called himself the Son of God. St. Matthew (xxii. 42) more fully gives their answer first, namely, that "Christ is the Son of David." They should have said that, as God, he was the Son of God, according to those words, "Thou art my Son; this day have I begotten thee;" but that, as man, he was the Son of David. Their answer was very different from that of Peter: "Thou art the Christ, the Son of the living God." But they wanted the Divine knowledge which the disciples had gained.

Ver. 36.—**The Lord said unto my Lord.** From this verse (Ps. cx.) our Lord shows that the Messiah, such as he was, was not a mere man, as the Pharisees thought, but that he was God, and therefore David's Lord. The meaning, therefore, is this, "The Lord God said to my Lord," that is, Christ, "Sit thou at my right hand," that is, when, after his cross, his death, and his resurrection, he will exalt him far above all principality and power, and place him next to him in heaven, that he may reign with supreme happiness and power and glory over all creatures. These words show that this is a Divine decree, fixed and irrevocable. **Till I make thine enemies thy footstool** (ὑποπόδιον τῶν ποδῶν σου); literally, *the footstool of thy feet;* that is, reign with me in glory until the day of judgment, when I will make the wicked, all opposing powers, subject to thee. The word "till" does not imply that Christ will then cease to reign. "Of his kingdom there shall be no end." But he will then formally deliver up the kingdom to God, even the Father, only that he may receive it again as the second Person of the Godhead.

Vers. 38, 39.—These verses are a condensation of the woes recorded at length by St. Matthew (xxiii.). **And he said unto them in his doctrine** (ἐν τῇ διδαχῇ αὐτοῦ)—literally, *in his teaching*—**Beware of the scribes which desire** (τῶν θελόντων) **to walk in long robes** (ἐν στολαῖς). The στολή was a rich robe which reached down to the ankles, and was adorned with fringes. The scribes took pleasure in this kind of display. The salient points in their character were ostentation, avarice, and religious hypocrisy.

Ver. 40.—There is a change in the construction here, which is not marked in the Authorized Version. The sentence in this fortieth verse should stand alone, and be read thus: **They which devour** (οἱ κατεσθίοντες) **widows' houses, and for a pretence make long prayers; these shall receive greater condemnation.** The sentence thus read is far more graphic. The statement thus becomes indeed more general, but the reference is still to the scribes who through their avarice swallowed up the property of help-

less widows, and through their hypocrisy, in the hope of thus more effectually imposing upon their victims, lengthened out their prayers. *Greater condemnation.* The word in the Greek is κρίμα, that is, "judgment." A severer sentence would fall upon them in the day of judgment and a heavier condemnation, because, under the semblance of piety, they practised iniquity, and indulged their avarice under the mask of religion.

Ver. 41.—**He sat down over against the treasury** (γαζοφυλάκιον, from γάζα, a Persian word meaning "treasure," and φυλάττειν, to guard). This was the receptacle into which the offerings of the people were cast, for the uses of the temple and for the benefit of the priests and of the poor. Hence that part of the temple in which these gifts were kept was called the treasury. **He beheld** (ἐθεώρει)—literally, *he was beholding; he was observing*—**how the multitude** (πῶς ὁ ὄχλος)—that is, in what manner, with what motives (for he was the heart-searcher) the crowd of givers—**cast money** (βάλλει χαλκόν); literally, *is casting.* St. Luke uses the term (τὰ δῶρα) "their gifts." Many that were rich cast in much (πολλά), that is, "many pieces." There were several apertures in the treasury, which from their shape were called trumpets. Some of these had special inscriptions, marking the destination of the offerings.

Ver. 42.—**A poor widow** (μία χήρα πτωχή); literally, *one poor widow;* one specially singled out for notice. St. Luke says, εἶδε δὲ καί τινα χήραν πενιχρὰν: literally, *a widow who supported herself by her own little labour.* **And she cast in two mites** (λεπτὰ), **which make a farthing.** The farthing was the fourth part of an *as*, and ten of these made a *denarius.* The Greek word (λεπτὰ) means literally "thin pieces."

Vers. 43, 44.—**This poor widow hath cast in more.** The right reading of the verb here is ἔβαλε, not βέβληκε; this aoristic rendering has very good authority—*this poor widow cast in more.* Her act is completed, and has gone up for a memorial before God. She "gave" more than all the others who are **casting** (τῶν βαλλόντων), not "have cast in (τῶν βαλόντων)." She gave more, when she threw in those two mites, than all the others were giving—more, that is, in the estimation of him who sees not as man sees. God does not weigh the gift so much as the mind of the giver. That gift is really the greater in his sight, not which is actually of greater value, but which is greater in respect of the giver. Therefore this poor widow, when she gave her farthing, gave more than they all, because she gave all her living—all, that is, that she had beforehand for that day, trusting that the Lord would give her her bread for that day. And so she carried off the palm for liberality, Christ himself being the Judge. St. Ambrose says, " That which God esteems is not that which you proudly present, but what you offer with humility and devotion."

HOMILETICS.

Vers. 1—12.—*Rebel vine-dressers.* By this time there was no further prospect or possibility that the fate of Jesus might be averted. His entry into Jerusalem in state, and his cleansing of the temple, were acts that the priests, scribes, and Pharisees could not pardon, for they were a claim to authority altogether incompatible with their own. And the words of Jesus were as bold as his acts; their justice and severity enraged the rulers beyond all degree. The enemies of truth and righteousness were by this time fully resolved to strike down him whose character and ministry were the living embodiment of what they most hated. It was only a question of time and manner and instrumentalities. All this Jesus knew, and he knew that "his hour was come." There was no occasion now for reticence, and there was no longer any end to be subserved by it. His speech was always plain and faithful, but now his denunciations were unsparing, and his warnings terrible. On this Tuesday morning of his last week, our Lord summed up in this parable of "the wicked husbandmen," "the rebel vine-dressers," the rebellious history of Israel in the past, and the approaching doom of Israel in the future. It was in the temple precincts, and in the presence both of the people and of the chief priests, that the great Teacher so boldly aserted his own special mission and authority, and so emphatically foretold his own fate and the judgment which should overtake the guilty nation. The immediate application of the parable is clear enough. Israel was the vineyard planted in the election of Abraham, and hedged about and provided with all things needful, in the giving of the Law by Moses and in the settlement in Canaan under Joshua. The Eternal, who had so favoured the chosen people, had sent prophets in three periods—that of Samuel, that of Elijah and Elisha, and that of Isaiah and Jeremiah—to summon Israel to a life of spirituality and obedience corresponding with their privileges. The Jews had not fulfilled the Law of God, or rendered to Heaven the fruits meet for repentance. And now he, the Son of God, was among them, the final Embassy from the throne of the great King. It was but too plain to all eyes that the unfruitfulness and rebellion of Israel reached the most awful height just when their advantages were the greatest, and the mercy of the Eternal was most conspicuous. They, who had rejected and slain the prophets, were now plotting against the very Son of God. They were about to put him to death, because he told them the truth and urged the rightful claims and demands of his Father. They might think, and did think, that this would be the end; but such an expectation was delusive: it was incompatible with the righteous government of God. And the Lord plainly foretold them that, as surely as God reigned in heaven and on earth, so surely should the rebellion of Israel be awfully and signally chastised, their special privileges come to a perpetual end, and the blessings which they were rejecting be conferred by God's sovereign favour upon others, who should render the fruits in their seasons. Forty years afterwards Jerusalem was destroyed, the Jews were scattered, and their national life came to an end; and the kingdom of God was established among the Gentiles. The parable has lessons, not only for Israel, but for us; it embodies truth spiritual, practical, and impressive.

I. Our EARTHLY OCCUPATION: TO TILL THE VINEYARD OF GOD. The figure sets forth our vocation and responsibility. It represents our life as one of *privilege.* It is not a wilderness, but a vineyard, which we are called to cultivate. God has done much for us, in appointing for us the circumstances and opportunities of our existence. Our life is one of *work.* The most favourable situation and the most fruitful soil avail little if the plot be neglected; only faithful and diligent labour on our part can secure that the purposes of the Divine Lord shall be fulfilled. It is for us to "give diligence to make our calling and election sure." The greater our privileges, the more need that we should be diligent, laborious, and prayerful. Opportunities must be used, and not neglected or abused.

II. God's RIGHTEOUS EXPECTATION: THAT WE SHALL YIELD HIM FRUIT. *What* is the crop, the produce, he desires to see ? Holiness and obedience, love and praise, as far as he is concerned; and, as far as regards our fellow-men, justice and gentleness, benevolence and helpfulness. He looks for repentance from the sinner, for faith from the hearer of the gospel, for improvement in character and for usefulness in service from the Christian. *Why* he does this is obvious enough. He has given us the means of knowledge and the opportunities of devotion, and looks for a return. " What more," he says, " could I have done than I have done?" And this expectation is for our sake as well as for his own. Our fruitfulness is our welfare and our happiness; it brings its own reward.

III. GOD'S REQUIREMENT AND DEMAND UPON MEN, BY HIS MESSENGERS AND BY HIS SON. Our Lord appeals to us both by the Law and by the gospel. The teaching of his Word brings before us his rightful claims, and shows us how much it is for our highest advantage that we should not be unmindful of them. He summons us by the lessons of his providence, and by the counsels of our Christian friends, to a religious life. Yet there is no appeal so powerful, so persuasive, as that which God makes to us by his own " dear Son." Christ comes to us with authority; he comes to us with grace. He comes from the Father, and he comes with the deepest interest in our condition, anxious to overcome our rebelliousness, and to lead us to a holy and grateful obedience. The gospel of Jesus Christ is the one great, Divine appeal to the hearts of men. It is the method which infinite Wisdom and Mercy have devised of winning our confidence and love, and securing our ready obedience and loyal service. Those who have rejected other messengers of Heaven may justly be enjoined to receive with reverence the Son of God.

IV. THE PENALTIES OF FRUITLESSNESS AND REBELLION. These are described in this passage in the most affecting terms. Privileges are removed from the unfaithful. The negligent and rebellious are punished and cast out. The advantages which they have spurned are transferred to others.

V. THE REWARD OF FRUITFULNESS AND LOYALTY. 1. Christ is glorified, even though there may be those who reject and contemn him. Christ himself quotes a passage of Scripture, in which this great truth is set forth, though by a change of figure. " The stone which the builders rejected is become the Head of the corner." The purposes of God are accomplished, and cannot be frustrated by the guilt of man. 2. Other husbandmen are found who will deal more faithfully with the sacred trust. These shall offer the fruits of obedience, which shall be acceptable to the Lord of the vineyard. They shall be confirmed in their occupation, shall be blessed in their work, shall enjoy the Master's favour, and shall live in the light of their Master's glory.

Vers. 13—17.—*Cæsar's due.* There could not have been a more decisive proof of the duplicity and hypocrisy of the Jewish leaders than that furnished by this incident. It is certain that they were opposed to the Roman sway, that they nursed in their hearts hopes of Jewish independence, that they would have eagerly welcomed such a Messiah as they looked for—one who should deliver them from the yoke of foreign bondage. Yet, in their malignity, they were ready to denounce Jesus to the Roman governor should he express an opinion adverse to the paying of tribute, just as they were ready to deliver him up to the fury of the populace should he formally approve and sanction the rights of the empire over the Jewish people. Thus—

I. A JUST BUT INSINCERE COMPLIMENT VEILS A MALIGNANT DESIGN. It is an astounding instance of duplicity, this method of approaching the Lord Jesus. These Pharisees and Herodians make admissions which they would never have made except as the means to an evil end. They address the Master with the acknowledgment that he is " true "—in this a striking contrast to themselves; that he is impartial, caring not for any one, nor regarding the person of men; that he taught the way of God. This was not empty, complimentary language; it was just. Whether in their hearts they believed it to be so, we cannot say; but Christ's enemies were often unintentional witnesses, both to his virtues and to his Divine authority and mission. Their only aim was to conciliate him, so that, in an unguarded moment, he might, with natural frankness, commit himself to some judgment which they might use to his harm.

II. A CRAFTY ALTERNATIVE, AN INSIDIOUS SNARE, IS WISELY ELUDED. " Is it lawful to give tribute unto Cæsar, or not?" A categorical answer either way would have been immediately and effectively used to his injury; he could not, after so answering, both stand well with his countrymen and remain free from the imputation of disloyalty to the then supreme power of Rome. The alternative was fairly evaded, and the snare was escaped, by the method in which Jesus dealt with the question propounded. There was something picturesque and impressive to the popular mind in his asking for the *denarius*, and pointing to the emperor's image and superscription. There was manifest reasonableness in yielding to Cæsar what was so obviously his own ; yet it was pointed out that this might be loyally done without detriment to the higher obligations of religion.

III. A PRINCIPLE OF ACTION IN THE SEVERAL DEPARTMENTS OF HUMAN LIFE IS ONCE FOR ALL ASSERTED. 1. We have here a recognition that civil government is of Divine authority. It does not follow from this that every government deserves approval, or even that under no circumstances is it lawful to resist constituted authority. But our Lord teaches, and his apostles teach, as a general principle, that civil governors are to be obeyed, that "the powers that be are ordained of God." 2. An implication that there is a province into which civil governors may not intrude, that there are obligations which take precedence even of the duties we owe to the earthly sovereign. There are claims which the Divine Lord himself prefers, and which he regards as supreme. The apostles clearly grasped this principle, and put it into practice when the rulers interfered with their discharge of what they held to be their religious duties. When a conflict occurs between the allegiance due to the civil ruler and that due to the supreme King, our Lord's words warrant the preference of the Divine to the human law. In times of persecution especially, the principle of our Lord's words has often guided the wavering and sustained the feeble. " Whether it be right to obey God rather than man, judge ye ! " We may say that the modern privilege of religious liberty has grown out of this incident in our Lord's ministry, these words from our Lord's lips. And to the same source we may attribute the growing tendency on the part of secular powers to withdraw from the province of religion, and to allow free scope to the action of conscience and full liberty for the profession and for the rites of religion. There is a province into which no earthly authority may intrude, and where the Creator reigns supreme and alone.

Vers. 18—27.—*Sadducees confuted.* Of all the subjects which awaken the speculative curiosity and inquiry of men, none approaches, in dignity and importance, the future life. The nobler spirits, in every civilized and cultured community, have either held as an article of faith, or have cherished with fondest hope, the prospect of immortality. Annihilation is a prospect which none but the degraded and sinful can consent to accept without shuddering horror. It has often been observed as very remarkable, though not inexplicable, that the Pentateuch contains no express, explicit statement regarding a future life. It appears that the revelation of immortality was progressive ; for expectations regarding a conscious existence of happiness after death are certainly found with growing frequency in the later books of the Old Testament. The psalmists and prophets rejoiced in the hope of a heavenly rest and an imperishable fellowship with the Father of spirits. At the time of our Lord's ministry there was a division among the religious authorities of the Jewish people upon this all-important subject; the Pharisees holding to the doctrines of immortality and resurrection, and the Sadducees denying and apparently ridiculing both. Amongst the Sadducees were many of the most intellectual of the upper classes of society. They also retained in their own leading families the office of high priest. Both our Lord Christ and his apostle Paul took a very decided stand against the Sadducaic doctrine and party. During the last week of our Lord's ministry, when the conflict with his enemies was reaching its height, many assaults were made from various quarters against Jesus and his claims and teaching. This passage records the attack of the rationalistic party upon the Divine Master, and his original and conclusive repulse of that attack.

I. THE REASONING OF THE SADDUCEES AGAINST THE TEACHING OF OUR LORD UPON IMMORTALITY AND RESURRECTION. 1. It was indirect reasoning. Instead of attacking the doctrine, they simply attacked a supposed inference from it, viz. the continuance of physical human relations in another life. 2. It was frivolous reasoning. They must have found it hard to state with serious faces a case so absurd. It would have been childish had they supposed the woman to have married twice ; the supposition that she should confront in the resurrection life the rival claims of seven husbands was ridiculous. This is not the temper in which great problems regarding human destiny should be discussed.   3. It was inconclusive; for no one of the alternative solutions of the difficulty proposed would have been incompatible with a future life.

II. THE GENERAL REPLY OF THE LORD JESUS TO THIS REASONING. 1. He refutes the argument, if it can be so called, which they had adduced. Marriage is an earthly institution, and is especially adapted to a mortal race, providing that generation shall succeed generation. Love is indeed imperishable, and shall be perfected in heaven; but marriage shall no longer be necessary when men shall be equal to the angels, and shall sin and die no more. Therefore no reasoning founded upon the continuance of this physical relationship has place with reference to the life beyond the grave. 2. He bases the doctrine of the future life upon the power of God, which they strangely overlooked. It is the reasoning which was repeated by St. Paul, "Why should it be thought a thing impossible with you that God should raise the dead?" The omnipotence which first called human nature into being is surely able to revive the spirit and perpetuate its consciousness and activity. This is an unanswerable argument still against all dogmatic denial of the future life. It does not in itself establish the doctrine, but it is conclusive against those who deny it. It removes the presumption from the opponents to the upholders of immortality. 3. He refers to the Scriptures for grounds for belief in a future life. Those who admitted their authority would find it hard to reconcile such admission with disbelief in the resurrection.

III. THE SPECIAL ARGUMENT BY WHICH THE LORD JESUS ESTABLISHES FAITH IN IMMORTALITY AND A FUTURE LIFE. 1. Jesus refers to an authority which the Sadducees professed emphatically to revere—the Pentateuch. "The Law" was their especial pride, and they may have justified their scepticism by the absence of explicit teaching upon this great doctrine from the books of Moses. 2. Jesus quotes a familiar passage, in which he reads, or from which he deduces, a new and striking and convincing argument. It is upon record that God declared himself to Moses as "the God of Abraham, of Isaac, and of Jacob." Now, what did this imply? That God *had been* their God, but that, they having ceased to exist, he was no longer? Or, that he was the God of their mouldering or dispersed dust, which, upon the theory of annihilation, was all that remained of them? Either those who had been wont to read this passage must have passed it over without reflection, or they must have been satisfied with an interpretation crude and empty. Or else they must have drawn the inference which the great Master now drew: "God is not the God of the dead, but of the living." Once he declares himself his people's God, he remains such for ever; and they remain his,—conscious recipients of his favour, and responsive partakers of his Divine and Fatherly love. He is a covenant God; his promises are never broken, and his declarations never fail. An immortal God involves the immortality of those whom he has created in his image, redeemed by his grace, renewed by his Spirit. If he is what he has revealed himself as being, if his people are what he has declared them to be, then death has no power over them; they are destined to "glory, honour, and immortality." For "all live in him."

Vers. 28—34.—*The great commandments.* This passage of the Gospel affords common ground, upon which those who lay the greatest stress upon Christian doctrine may meet with conciliation and harmony those who are wont to insist most upon Christian morality. Here is a statement, upon the highest authority, as to what God requires of man, as to what man owes to God and to his fellow-men. "Do this, and thou shalt live!" It is a sublime view of the great purposes of our spiritual being. Beyond this religion cannot go; for this is the end for which our nature was framed, for which revelation was vouchsafed. Yet who can read these requirements of a holy and benevolent Creator and Ruler without feeling that by himself they have not been fulfilled? The man must be besotted by self-conceit, or must have silenced conscience, who claims to have loved God with all his powers, or to have uniformly loved his neighbour as himself. The purer, the more stringent the Law, the deeper the humiliation and contrition of the transgressor. What, then, more fitted to induce sinners to receive the gospel with faith and gratitude than these words of Jesus? What can make so welcome the tidings of Divine forgiveness secured through the redemption wrought by the Saviour on the cross? And, further, as we meditate upon this ideal of a beautiful and acceptable moral life, how profoundly are we impressed with a sense of our own weakness! And surely this must lead us to seek and to accept the aid of the Spirit of God, who is the Spirit at once of power and of love! Thus the inculcation of Christian morality naturally suggests the doctrines upon which we build our hopes for time and for eternity. On the other hand, in the presence of these inspiriting words of the Master, how is it possible for the candid and the faithful to rest in that view of the gospel which represents religion as merely securing the forgiveness of sin, and immunity from wrath and punishment? Here is a summons to a spiritual, a self-denying, and a benevolent life.

I. THE QUESTION PROPOSED TO JESUS. 1. In itself it was a worthy, a noble question. Unlike the trifling and ridiculous riddle propounded by the Pharisees, it was an inquiry becoming on the part of the scribe who urged it, and fit for the consideration and judgment of the holy Master himself. It respected commandments, and thus acknowledged the rule of a just God, and the duty of man's obedience and submission. It concerned morality—the highest of all human interests. It evinced an evident desire to do what was right, and to give precedence to what should be acknowledged best. There can be no nobler inquiry than this—What is the will of God? What is the duty of man? What shall I do? 2. In its spirit and purport, the question was commendable. The questioner observed that Jesus had answered well; that he had solved with marvellous wisdom the difficult question of the Pharisees; that he had dealt skilfully and conclusively with the cavilling of the Sadducees. The limits of civil submission are an interesting branch of study; the future life is of all speculative questions the most engrossing to the thoughtful; but of even wider interest are the foundation, the character, the means, of human goodness. The inquiry as to the first of commandments was put as a testing question, but in no captious spirit; it was the expression of a desire to learn—to learn from the highest authority, to learn the most sacred principles of moral life. And not to learn only, but doubtless to practise the lesson acquired.

II. THE ANSWER OF JESUS TO THE SCRIBE. There was no hesitation in the Master's reply to the question proposed; the challenge was at once taken up. And consummate wisdom was shown in the reference to the Mosaic Law, the very words of which were quoted. Thus the right-minded were conciliated, yet at no expense, but rather by the manifestation, of truth. And the hostile were silenced; for who of the Jewish rabbis could call in question the authority of their own sacred books? When we look into the substance of the response, several remarkable facts become apparent. 1. Love is represented as the sum of the Divine commandments. The Pentateuch contained the injunctions our Lord repeated, but they were included in a vast body of precepts and prohibitions. It could scarcely be said with justice that love was the most prominent of the Mosaic commandments. Christ's independence, discernment, and legislative authority were shown in his fixing upon the two requirements which occur in different books and in different connections, and in bringing them out into the light of day, and exhibiting them as in his view of surpassing importance, and so promulgating them as the laws of his spiritual kingdom through all time. God himself is love; Christ is the expression and proof of the Divine love; and it is therefore natural and reasonable that love should be the law of the Divine kingdom, the badge of the spiritual family. 2. The Object of supreme love is God himself. The *personality* of God is assumed, for we cannot love an abstraction, a power; only a living being, who thinks, feels, and purposes. The *unity* of God is asserted; for although, when Jesus lived on earth, the Jews were no longer subject to the temptation to idolatry, such temptation had beset them when the Law was originally given, and for a long period subsequently. The *relationship* between God and man is presumed—"thy God;" for he is ours and we are his. The *claims* of God are implied; his character, his treatment of men, his redeeming love in Christ. "We love him, because he first loved us." 3. The description and degree of love demanded are very fully stated in the text. The expression is a very strong one: "With all thy heart, soul, mind, and strength." Attempts have been made accurately to discriminate among these. But it seems sufficient to say that the love required in such language is cordial and fervent; cordial, as distinguished from mere profession, and fervent, as distinguished from lukewarmness and indifference. The whole of our nature is expected to combine, so to speak, in this exercise. Not only so, but God is to be regarded as the supreme Object of affection and devotion. He demands the first place in our heart; and those who see his grace in Christ cannot find it hard to offer what he demands. 4. Love to man follows upon love to God. It may, indeed, in order of time, in some measure precede and prepare for it. But in the moral order, in the order of obligation, love to God comes first, and, indeed, furnishes the one sound and safe basis for human love. The *designation* of the objects of this love deserves notice; they are our "neighbours." We must interpret this term in the light of our Lord's answer to an earlier question put to him by a certain lawyer: "Who is my neighbour?" In the parable of the good Samaritan Jesus then laid a broad foundation for human charity. Not our own family, or Church, or nation, but all mankind, are to be regarded with good will, and treated, not only with justice, but with kindness. Practically, those have a claim upon our kindly feeling and good offices whom Providence brings into any contact with us in human society. Remark the *measure* of this love: "As thyself." It is, then, right to love self; but in subordination to Divine love, and in accordance with love to neighbours. The test is an effective one, and can always be applied; the Law is parallel with the golden rule, "Do unto others as ye would they should do unto you." The *dependence* of this law upon the preceding is obvious. Christianity bases morality upon religion; we love our fellow-men as the children of God, because he loves them and for his sake. 5. Love, to be acceptable, must display itself in practical forms. The love we cherish toward God should lead to worship and to obedience—in a word, to a religious life. The love we entertain to our fellow-men will reveal itself in the demeanour, the language, and still more in the conduct. Helpfulness, self-denial, liberality, forbearance, are all fruits of love; which is destructive of discord, malice, and envy, of jealousy, hatred, and persecution. Here is the power to banish the vices, and the remedy to heal the spiritual maladies which afflict mankind!

III. THE SCRIBE'S APPROVING CONSENT TO CHRIST'S REPLY. 1. He thus proved his independence of judgment. Others, when answered and silenced by Jesus, retired discomfited, but unconvinced. This rabbi, with a mind candid and open to the truth, receives the Lord's saying as sufficient and decisive, and renders his own consent and approbation in the words, "Thou hast well said." 2. He shows his pleasure in the grand utterances of inspiration by repeating the language which Jesus had quoted—language evidently both familiar to him and congenial to his character. 3. His boldness and spirituality are apparent in his stating, what Jesus had implied, the superiority of the heart's affection to all service of the hands.

IV. THE COMMENDATION EXPRESSED BY JESUS. 1. The position of the lawyer was very different from that of others. There were many who were "far" from God's kingdom. The Pharisees for the most part by their formality, the Sadducees by their scepticism and arrogance, the publicans and sinners by their vices, the multitude by their ignorance,—these were far from the kingdom. Amongst those who may justly be so described are always some who are outwardly numbered among the religious, as well as multitudes who are without God, and manifestly have no hope. 2. There were several respects in which this scribe approached the spiritual kingdom of the Saviour. (1) He was acquainted with God's Word, and was interested in it; he explored and studied it. He appreciated the grandeur and beauty of the Divine Law, and he was bold and earnest in speaking of it. In all this he displayed sympathy with him who came to magnify and to fulfil the Law, and who bade the people search the Scriptures. (2) He thoroughly agreed with the dictum of the great Master, with regard to the first and most binding and comprehensive ordinances of the inspired Word. Whether or not he was prepared with this answer to the question he proposed, it is evident that the answer commended itself to his judgment and conscience, and that the Divine Respondent was regarded by him with reverential admiration. It is well to find the truth; but it is also well, when others have found it, to recognize and to accept it. (3) Grand indeed was this scribe's confession, that love "is much more than whole burnt offerings and sacrifices." All religions—the true as well as the false—are corrupted by a tendency in human nature to substitute the sacrificial, the ceremonial, the verbal, for the real, the spiritual. Men think that to comply with directions, instructive and profitable in themselves, but having reference only to symbolical actions, is all important, and they give diligent attention to these, and neglect the weightier matters of the Law. It is presumed that bodily service is sufficient, in forgetfulness of the fact that God is the Searcher of hearts, and that he will be worshipped in spirit and in truth. This is a lesson which still needs to be inculcated, even in days of Christian light and evangelical fervour. Never be it forgotten that character and conduct are of supreme importance, and that the only sufficient, conclusive evidence that a man has received the benefits of redemption, and has felt the renewing power of the Spirit of God, is to be found in the reign of love within his soul, and the manifestation of love in his whole character and life.

V. The reservation and qualification in our Lord's approval. If there was so much that was admirable in the spirit and the language of this student and expositor of the Law, what was lacking? If he was near the kingdom, what separated him from it, and prevented him from entering in? This question we cannot answer with certainty; we can only surmise. There may have been an inadequate sense of sin; his admiration of Jesus may have come short of true faith in him; and he may have been unready to make a complete surrender of himself to the Lord Jesus. At all events, we have no difficulty in enumerating various hindrances which, as a matter of fact, do keep outside of the kingdom those who are very near its confines. Christ's dominion is one which cannot be entered except through the door of repentance and of faith. True subjects come in sincere and childlike humility, and receive the welcome promised; by the new birth they enter the new life of the kingdom. The laws of the kingdom are spiritual, and demand spiritual conformity. And the King is enthroned in the heart as well as in society. You must become as little children in order that you may enter the kingdom of God.

Application. 1. Let faith work by love in Christian natures; and let those who love Christ prove by their spirit and their actions the sincerity of their love. 2. Let those who are near the kingdom, instead of resting in their nearness, regard this as a reason why they should, without delay, enter the gates before which they stand.

Ver. 34.—"Not far from the kingdom." That this scribe should have shown so deep an admiration for the Divine Law, so clear a perception of the superiority of the spiritual to the ceremonial, so discerning an appreciation of the Divine Master,—all this was to his credit, and awakened the approval and elicited the commendation of our Lord. In the language Jesus addressed to him, a description is given of not a few hearers of the gospel, who present in their character much that is admirable, but who come short of true consecration to Christ, who are "not far from the kingdom of God." Of this class we may ask—

I. How near have they come to the kingdom? 1. They have been, in many cases, brought near by the action of others. A Christian education and Christian influence have moulded their habits and improved a naturally well-inclined disposition. 2. They are well acquainted with the truths of religion, have studied the Scriptures, and have mastered the doctrines as well as the facts they contain. 3. They assent to the revelation contained in the Bible, either unreflectingly or after inquiry and doubt. 4. They admire Christ's moral character and beneficent life, his pure teaching, and his purposes of compassion towards mankind. 5. They conform to the practices of Christian worship, and even make use of the language of praise and prayer. 6. They obey many of the laws of Christ, either from habit or from a conviction of their justice and expediency. 7. They have had many desires, and may even have formed resolutions, to go further than this—to yield all to the Saviour. Of such it may indeed be said, they are "not far from the kingdom of God."

II. How far are they still from the kingdom? Men may travel a long distance in the right direction, and yet may leave untraversed the last and most important stage of the journey. So is it with many hearers of the gospel. 1. They may yet have to receive the gospel of Christ with their whole nature. The assent of the understanding must be followed by the consent of the will. 2. They may yet have to surrender themselves and their all to Jesus. Men may give much, but withhold more. The test which our Lord proposes is a readiness to offer the heart, and with it all powers and possessions, unto himself. Less is not acceptable to him who claims, and has a right to, all. 3. They may need to overcome much self-righteousness, self-confidence, self-seeking, before their state of mind is such as to enable them to accept the terms of Heaven : " Except ye become as little children," etc.

III. How should those so situated now act ? 1. They should reflect how vain is past progress except it lead to future consecration. 2. They should rejoice at the thought that their approach to the kingdom makes it easier for them to enter in. All their knowledge, good feelings, and partial obedience are so many steps upon the road, leaving the fewer to be taken in order to salvation. 3. They should remind themselves how unwise and dangerous and sinful it is to pause where they are. " It is the first step which costs ; " and it is the last step which pays ! Why should not that last step be taken at once ? True repentance, sincere faith, cordial surrender, the new birth,— such are the descriptions given of the change yet to pass over those who are not far from the kingdom, in order that they may enter it. Illustrations : The builder rears the arch of a bridge ; the keystone has yet to be placed ; if that be left undone a storm may rise, the river may swell, his work may be swept away, and all that has been done may count for nothing. The traveller exploring a continent may endure many hardships and perils, may come within a day's march of the vast lake of which he hopes to be the discoverer : shall he turn back ? The manslayer, pursued by the avenger of blood, may be within sight of the city of refuge : to pause is to be slain ; to summon up all his strength and to bound forward is to find himself safely within the protecting walls. The captain, the adventurous explorer, after a long voyage over unknown seas, sights the land of which he has dreamed : shall he give orders to put about the ship, and abandon the glorious discovery within its reach, and all the honour, wealth, and fame which now at length await him ?

Vers. 34, 37.—*Various effects of Christ's ministry.* There was a vigour and directness, an unsparing boldness and fidelity, peculiar to the ministry of our Lord in Jerusalem during the last week of his life. This no doubt precipitated the crisis, enraging his enemies at the same time that it silenced their reasonings. Two remarks are made by the evangelist which show us what was the effect of Christ's discourses and conversations both upon his foes and upon the multitude.

I. His enemies were silenced. These included most of the members of the more prominent classes, who occupied positions of influence and authority in Jerusalem. 1. Their varied efforts to entrap Christ in his speech are recorded at length. The Pharisees, the Herodians, the Sadducees, and the scribes, all questioned Jesus and reasoned with him, largely with the hope of either weakening his influence or taking some advantage of his replies. There was much craft in the way in which they sought thus to injure him and his work. 2. Their uniform confutation by his wisdom and moral authority. All their efforts, from whatever quarter, and however conducted, proved in vain. None were able to withstand him. He either put them to shame, or convinced them by the wisdom of his answers. The evangelist sums up the impression produced by our Lord's demeanour and language in these several interviews in the words, " And no man after that durst ask him any question." Christ's wisdom is flawless ; Christ's authority is irresistible. Now, as then, it is true that none can dispute with him except to be discomfited. " Why do the heathen rage, and the people imagine a vain thing ? "

II. The multitude were attracted and delighted. Whilst the self-confident and the self-righteous were put to shame and confusion, the common people, or rather the multitude, " the people " (as we say), heard him gladly. There were several sufficient reasons for this. 1. He spoke to them as one of themselves. Not from a height of official distance and superiority, but in their own language, with illustrations drawn from their own daily life, and as one who knew them and their ways. 2. His personal interest and sympathy were very marked. He did not break the bruised reed. Often brought into contact with the suffering, he pitied and healed them. Often meeting with sinners contrite and penitent, he pardoned and cheered them. 3. His fearless exposure and denunciation of the wickedness of the religious leaders of the Jews. The selfishness and hypocrisy of Pharisees and lawyers were well known ; but such was the mental bondage of the people, that they dared not speak of the iniquities of the rulers save with bated breath. Jesus, however, who regarded not the person of any man, boldly upbraided the iniquitous rulers for their misdeeds. And those who suffered from the extortion and oppression which they endured, rejoiced in the Lord Jesus as in a Champion of the down-trodden, and an Upholder of the right. 4. His direct appeal to the conscience and heart of the people. It is thus, indeed, that masses of men are ever to be moved. Whilst in the preaching of Jesus statement of Divine truth and exhibitions of Divine love formed the substance of his addresses, he so spoke as to reach the moral nature of his hearers. No raving, no exaggeration, no vulgarity; but simplicity, vigour, earnestness, moral authority, were manifest in all his utterances. 5. He brought the fatherly grace of God home to the erring and helpless. This was what the religious leaders of the time did *not*. The hearts of men responded to the revelation of the heart of God. How could the people do otherwise than hear him gladly, when he said, "Come unto me, all ye that labour and are heavy laden, and I will give you rest"?

Vers. 35—40.—*The scribes.* The profession of scribes, which had existed among the Jews ever since the Captivity, was in itself an honourable and useful profession. And there were members of this learned body who came into contact with the Lord Jesus who showed a candid disposition, a love of the truth, and who evinced respect and admiration for the great Rabbi. Yet some of the most bitter and virulent of our Lord's enemies were of this class. Their superiority to the people was a snare as well as an advantage. Many of them hid beneath the cloak of learning an evil heart, selfishness, arrogance, and unspirituality. In the discourse of Jesus here recorded, we find a protest against the general teaching, and a protest against the too common character, of these adversaries of his ministry and doctrine.

I. CHRIST'S CORRECTION OF THE SCRIBES' TEACHING REGARDING THE MESSIAH. 1. What was this teaching? It was the simple statement, that the Messiah should be a descendant of David. This was Scriptural truth, and the Gospels exhibit its application to Jesus. But it was only part of the truth. 2. In what respects did Jesus add to this conception of the Messiah? He quoted from the Scriptures, and he attributed their declarations to the inspiration of the Holy Spirit. And thus he transmuted the bald doctrine of the scribes into a doctrine full of spiritual significance and dignity. These points especially are brought out: (1) Pre-eminence is assigned to the Messiah over even his illustrious ancestor, David. (2) The Messiah is represented as the Assessor of the Most High himself. (3) The Messiah is depicted as the Conqueror of his foes. In all these respects the truly Scriptural representation of the Christ is an immense advance upon the customary teaching of the Jewish scribes. Thus Christ teaches concerning himself.

II. CHRIST'S DENUNCIATION OF THE CHARACTER AND CONDUCT OF THE SCRIBES. 1. Their loud professions of sanctity, and their ostentatious devotions, are censured. Long prayers may sometimes be the outcome of deep feeling and many needs; they may, as in the case of these scribes, be a cloak for sin. Long robes, like long prayers, may be a profession with which nothing spiritual corresponds. Hypocrisy was a crying evil of the times. There is no vice that is more hateful to God; and it may be questioned whether it often imposes upon men. 2. Their love of pre-eminence is blamed. Both in "Church and State" they loved to be supreme, and in all social relations they sought the honour which cometh from man. In the synagogues, in the market-places, and at festive gatherings the scribes would fain be first. 3. Their cruel rapacity is held up to obloquy. The bereaved and the defenceless were their victims. On some pretext or other they gained possession or management of the property of widows, and were not satisfied until they appropriated the whole. There are those in our own days, and in Christian lands, who grow rich by similar practices, and who incur by such infamous cruelty "the wrath of the Lamb." 4. Christ predicts the condemnation of such sinners, and at the same time puts the people on their guard against them. His threat of condemnation was authoritative; and his warning was one which was needed and timely. Against the wrongs and cruelties, the assumptions and the errors of such pretenders, the Good Shepherd would fain protect his feeble and defenceless sheep.

Vers. 41—44.—*The widow's mite.* The presence of this poor widow, among unspiritual and ostentatious worshippers and offerers, is as a sunbeam amidst the gloom, a rose in the wilderness. It is a touching picture, this of the lonely woman, who had lost her husband, and whose heart was sad, whose means were scanty, and whose life was obscure and cheerless. But she had found strength and consolation in waiting upon God. And the temple, the appointed place for worship, with its services, so helpful to devotion, and associated with holy gatherings, and with opportunities for Divine communion, was dear to her heart. She could not be absent when the sacred services were proceeding, nor could she withhold her little gift in passing the treasury, as she left the scene of worship and of fellowship. And thus she was noticed by the Master, and her memory was immortalized, and her action has become a model and an inspiration to Christ's people through all time. We may learn from this incident—

I. WHAT IN GIFTS AND ALMS IS, IN GOD'S SIGHT, INCONSIDERABLE. The view taken by men is different. But we are, as Christians, bound by the judgment of our Lord, who here teaches us that: 1. The actual amount is in itself of little moment. With reference to the material ends to be obtained by money, this is of course not the case. When a spacious, durable, and handsome church is to be built, when an expensive missionary expedition to some distant land is to be undertaken, there is need of large pecuniary contributions; and it is only where there is large wealth that such enterprises are possible. But as far as the spiritual value and acceptableness of alms and benefactions are concerned, the mere pecuniary amount is unimportant. The mite of the widow is as much approved by God as the gold of the wealthy. 2. The comparative amount which is contributed is in this regard unimportant. The offering which is less than that presented by a neighbour is not, therefore, necessarily bad; nor is the offering which exceeds that of a neighbour, therefore, necessarily good. It is too common among givers to ask—What is customary? What is the amount contributed by others? The relative sum is disregarded by the Observer of all donations and the Searcher of all hearts. If one gives largely from his superfluity, he may nevertheless give less than his neighbour, who out of his poverty gives what seems a trifling sum.

II. WHAT IN GIFTS AND ALMS IS VALUABLE IN GOD'S SIGHT. 1. The relation they bear to the giver's means. This is brought out very effectively in this narrative. The poor widow "of her want" gave "all that she had," even "all her living," i.e. perhaps what she had in hand for that day's sustenance. It has often been remarked that God has regard, not merely to what a man gives, but to what he keeps. The gifts of the opulent are acceptable, but "dearer to God are the gifts of the poor." 2. The purpose and intent for which they are given. Money, which is bestowed merely with a view to secure the good opinion of men, to attain a certain position socially or in the religious community, is not regarded by the Omniscient as given to his cause. If the motive be the relief of human suffering, the enlightenment of human ignorance, the diffusion of religious knowledge and privileges, then doubtless gifts are acceptable, even though there may be some deficiency in the worldly wisdom according to which the means are directed to the ends in view. 3. The spirit in which they are given. An unostentatious act of charity, an ungrudging devotion of property, a disposition to forego some luxury, some personal comfort or pleasure, in order to do good, a pious reference of the act of giving to him who gives alike the means and the inclination for liberality,—these are qualities which render beneficence acceptable to the Lord and Judge of all. "The Lord loveth a cheerful giver." He who thus bestows his charity shall indeed receive again from him who acknowledges all true service. A gift is accepted according to what a man hath, and not according to what he hath not.

HOMILIES BY VARIOUS AUTHORS.

Vers. 1—12.—*The parable of the vineyard.* The imagery adopted would at once address itself to the understanding of the hearers. Palestine pre-eminently a land of the grape. The prophetic writings are full of symbols and figures from the vine. This was spoken in continuation of his dispute with the Sanhedrim, and in the presence of all the people in the temple. The historical allusions to the prophets and the personal one to himself must have been only too clear. It was a detailed and crescent indictment of the most solemn and awful character.

I. God's LOVING PROVISION FOR THE SPIRITUAL INTERESTS OF HIS PEOPLE INVOLVED CORRESPONDING OBLIGATION.

II. INSTEAD OF SERVING God, THE RELIGIOUS LEADERS OF ISRAEL SOUGHT THEIR OWN ADVANTAGE.

III. SELFISHNESS AND UNBELIEF LED TO THE REJECTION OF THE PROPHETS, AND EVEN OF THE SON OF God HIMSELF.

IV. SUCH CONDUCT ENTAILS A JUDGMENT, WHICH, ALTHOUGH DELAYED, IS NEVERTHELESS SURE AND TERRIBLE.

V. THE LOVING PURPOSE OF God, ALTHOUGH HINDERED BY SUCH MEANS, WILL BE ULTIMATELY AND GLORIOUSLY FULFILLED.—M.

Vers. 13—17.—*The politics of Christianity.* Christ, in his visits to the temple, met with the various representatives of religious, ecclesiastical, and political opinion in Palestine. He is the centre and touchstone of all. Their very attacks and dishonest questions were so many confessions of his moral and intellectual supremacy. To Christ do the different schools of thought and life amongst men still come, and the problems they raise can never be satisfactorily settled until he solves them.

I. A TRAP LAID FOR CHRIST. 1. *By whom?* Ultimately and originally by the Pharisees, the leaders of ultra-Judaism and advocates of a restored theocracy and national independence. But that this view, having its root at first in profound spirituality of aim and motive, had been subsidized by baser considerations, is only too evident. Their hatred for Christ on the present occasion led them to throw away all scruples they might have felt, and to assume a disingenuous position of inquiry. But they could do this the more effectively in concert with others, with whom, although somewhat disagreeing on the solution to be accepted of the theory of national independence, they yet agreed upon the general question itself. The Herodians were a recent party, attached to the fortunes and politics of the Herods, and accepting their rule as a satisfactory compromise of the difficulty arising from the theocratic views of the Jews and the actual supremacy of the Roman empire. They are supposed to have originated with the Pharisees, with whom they still retained general relations, and with whom they for the most part co-operated. Menahem the Essene, who was a Pharisee, being captivated, it is said, by the predicted ascendency of the house of Herod, attached himself to Herod the Great, and brought over many of his co-religionists. They believed that in the monarchy of Herod the national aspirations of the Jews were reasonably met, and at the same time the demands of Rome, whose creature he was. They were as a party, as might be expected, less scrupulous than the original Pharisees. The latter imagined, as many like them have done since, that by suborning others to do a dishonourable action they avoided the disgrace of it themselves. 2. *In what did the snare consist?* In an attempt to get Christ to commit himself to the tenets of one or other of the political parties of the day. This was not with the view of strengthening the influence of either, but simply to compromise him, according to his answer, either with the Roman government on the one hand, or with the national party of Judaism on the other. 3. *How was it baited?* With flattery : yet flattery which unwillingly witnessed to the "openness" and uprightness of Christ's character, his Divine impartiality, his fearless truthfulness.

II. THE TRAP EVADED. The simplicity of Christ, upon which they had calculated for the success of their scheme, was the very cause of its failure. "Wise as serpents, but harmless as doves," is a principle which has its root in the nature of the Divine life. The inquiry is answered : 1. *By an appeal to matter of fact.* "Show me a penny," etc. The existence of such a coin (the *denarius,* which was the standard silver coin of the Romans, value about eightpence or ninepence), with its "image and superscription," proved beyond question the subject condition of Palestine. The actual situation being, therefore, what it was, and, so far as they could do anything, irreversible, it was not right for them to ignore it. If the privileges attending it were freely made use of, the duties involved should also be discharged. 2. *By enunciating a deeper and wider principle than they recognized.* As things were, the practice of their own religion was freely permitted to the Jews, toleration being a principle of imperial policy. There was, therefore, no really spiritual difficulty involved. The political nostrums of Pharisee and Herodian alike were, therefore, party cries and nothing more. They were thus convicted of unreality, of hypocrisy, or acting a part.   It was not religion they cared for, but their own personal or party ends.   Yet at the same time, for such as then or at any future time might have their religious scruples affected by political conditions, Christ laid down a general principle of action.   When human government is not opposed to Divine, submission may be conscientiously made to both.   Only where they differ is there any room for doubt ; but even such a doubt will be satisfactorily dealt with by beginning from the Divine side of obligation.   This principle, which stands good for all times, is essentially a spiritual one.   Under all circumstances, therefore, the *duty of the Christian,* or conscientious religionist, *is shown to be fundamentally a moral one.*   Actually existent authority imposes obligations which have to be recognized in the spirit of submission and piety, when not conflicting with Divine prerogatives.   *Christianity has only indirectly a bearing on politics ; its direct and immediate concern is with morals.*—M.

Ver. 15.—*"Bring me a penny."*   I. CHRIST WILL HAVE ACCOUNT OF THE SMALLEST THINGS.   The *denarius* was a small coin in common use.   The spirit of Christ, sunlike, discovers even the "motes."   In all things there is duty.   Christ's attitude to the Law not only general but particular.   "Not one jot or tittle" was to pass away unfulfilled because of the influence of Christianity.   "Ye are my disciples, if ye do *whatsoever* I have commanded you."   We shall have to give account of smallest things *at last*—idle words, false shame, "the cup of cold water," etc.   The parable of the pounds has for its moral, "He that is faithful in that which is least," etc.   There is no slurring over of little things because of a general disposition and amiable intention.

II. SMALL THINGS OFTEN REPRESENT GREAT PRINCIPLES, AND BECOME THE VEHICLES OF GREAT DUTIES.   Coins are often of value, apart from their intrinsic worth, in witnessing to conquests, political influences, the progress of civilization, etc. ; and numismatists have made many important contributions to history through their testimony.   In this case the witness was even more pregnant and precious.   It proved what actually existed, and represented the claim of earthly powers.   The duty to God was shown thereby to be something quite distinct, and the general relation of the human and the Divine in human obligations was thereby permanently settled and set forth.   It is equally so in regard to other things.   "A straw will show which way the wind blows, or the water flows."   Illustrated in such instances as the Massacre of St. Bartholomew ; watchwords and flags of truce in time of war; the petty dealings of common life ; the "minor moralities" of the Christian, etc.

III. WE ARE ENCOURAGED AND COMMANDED TO BRING SMALL THINGS TO CHRIST   Do not say he has no interest in them.   See how he looks at that widow with her two mites.   Hear how he calls the little children.   We need a *more thorough* Christianity, and if we follow this rule of bringing our daily concerns, our griefs, our moral difficulties, our sins, to the throne of grace, we shall become "Israelites indeed, in whom is no guile."   He will interpret the minutest uncertainty or perplexity, and show us the great in the little.   Erasmus Darwin wrote (April 13, 1789) : "I have just heard that there are muzzles or gags made at Birmingham for the slaves in our islands.   If this be true, and such an instrument could be exhibited by a speaker in the House of Commons, it might have a great effect.   Could not one of their long whips or wiretails be also procured and exhibited ?   But an instrument of torture of our own manufacture would have a greater effect, I dare say " ('Life,' p. 46).—M.

Vers. 18—27.—*The puzzle of the Sadducees.*   I. THE CASE STATED.   An extreme one ; and probably a *locus classicus* in the works of the rabbins.   It was supposed to be a *reductio ad absurdum* of all theories of resurrection or immortality.   "In the resurrection" is used apparently in a pregnant sense, as including the judgment, when all questions would be decided, and the conditions of the future state settled.   The case as stated referred only to legal and external conditions, questions of sentiment or spiritual attachment being ignored.   The only case in Scripture of Christ coming into direct collision with the Sadducees.   That the questioners were not maliciously disposed in presenting these difficulties may be inferred from the manner in which they are answered : not indignantly, or with an epithet expressing moral condemnation ; but in a straightforward, matter-of-fact way, although censure is also expressed—a kind of censure peculiarly distasteful to such men, who generally pretend to great originality and critical acumen. They are accused of ignorance and spiritual inexperience.

II. How CHRIST DISPOSED OF IT. 1. *By reference to the possibilities of Divine power.* "In the resurrection state there will not be a repetition, pure and simple, of present conditions; there will be advance of inward and outward development. Love will continue; but in the case of the holy it will be sublimed. 'The power of God' is adequate, not only to the re-formative, but also to the transformative changes that may be requisite; and his wisdom will see to it that they be in harmony with the perfectibility of individual personality and the general procession of the ages. Even on earth there are loftier loves than those that are merely marital" (Morison). "They neither marry, nor are given in marriage." "His words teach absolutely the absence from the resurrection life of the definite relations on which marriage rests in this, and they suggest an answer to the yearning questions which rise up in our minds as we ponder the things behind the veil. . . . The old relations may subsist under new conditions. Things that are incompatible here may there be found to coexist. The saintly wife of two saintly husbands may love both with an angelic, and therefore a pure and unimpaired, affection. The contrast between our Lord's teaching and the sensual paradise of Mahomet, or Swedenborg's dream of the marriage state perpetuated under its earthly conditions, is so obvious as hardly to call for notice" (Plumptre). "The present life is but a partial revelation of the Divine power. All the relations of earthly families do not continue in heaven" (Godwin). 2. *By interpretation of Scripture.* Not the letter of Scripture is appealed to, but the underlying truth involved in the statement of Scripture, "I am the God of Abraham, and the God of Isaac, and the God of Jacob. *He is not the God of the dead, but of the living.*" The copula connecting the first clause of the quotation is not in the original, so that no argument can be founded upon it. Professor Plumptre's explanation—" The 'principle implied in the reasoning is, that the union of the Divine Name with that of a man, as in 'I am the God of Abraham,' involved a relation existing, not in the past only, but when the words were uttered. They meant something more than 'I am the God whom Abraham worshipped in the past'—is, therefore, manifestly inadequate. That of Dr. Morison is more explicit and profound: "It amounted to this: *If there was at all a patriarchal dispensation, embracing a Messianic or redemptive scheme, and thus involving a Divinely commissioned Messiah or Redeemer, who was to be in due time incarnated, then there must be a life to come. But there was such a dispensation, if it be the case that God became 'the God of Abraham, and the God of Isaac, and the God of Jacob,' in any distinctive sense whatever.* And then, moreover, as Abraham, Isaac, and Jacob took personal advantage of the Messianic covenant into which God entered with them, they 'live.' They have 'life,' 'everlasting life,' in the intense acceptation of the term" (*in loc.*). Cf. Heb. xi. 13, 14, 16. A more direct proof might have been obtained in other portions of the Old Testament, but the skill of this argument lay in the reference to a book received by the Sadducees, and in the unexpected interpretation of familiar words. Thus their literalism and narrowness were rebuked, and the popular longing of the Jews confirmed. The line of evidence led by Christ not only meets the objection to resurrection, but includes the proof of that of which resurrection is only a portion, viz. immortality. If such depth of meaning lay in the words of an old pre-Christian revelation, what may not the gospel itself unfold, when spiritually interpreted in the light of new conditions and experiences?—M.

Ver. 24.—*Sources of heresy.* I. PRINCIPAL CAUSES OF RELIGIOUS ERROR. 1. *Ignorance of Holy Scripture.* (1) Unaided human nature is prone to error. Rather might it be said that of itself human nature cannot possibly know the truth. We have but to remember the *idola* of which philosophy warns us, to perceive how much there is in the circumstances and very constitution of the human mind to interfere with the attainment of intellectual truth. Difficulties of this nature, however, may be practically overcome by diligence, candour, and careful study; and the phenomena of the senses will yield up the secret of their working to the educated thinker. But there are things beyond sense concerning which the methods of intellectual research can give us no information. The agnosticism of science concerning these things is therefore, as a

whole, to be accepted as real. Were it not that there are moral as well as purely intellectual and constitutional causes for this ignorance, no fault need be found with it. But
any view of mental error which omitted consideration of the fact of human depravity
could not be considered adequate. The natural mind "loves darkness rather than
light." (2) Scripture is intended to correct human error. "The entrance of thy words
giveth light" (Ps. cxix. 130). They reveal the existence, works, character, and purpose
of God. By so doing they solve the mysteries attaching to human life and duty. They
are the Word of God, anticipating and transcending the findings of the world's experience.
This is done, not only by communicating what is above sensible perception, but by
affording a discipline to the spiritual nature. "For the Word of God is quick, and
powerful, and sharper than any two-edged sword, piercing even to the dividing asunder
of soul and spirit, and of the joints and marrow, and is a discerner of the thoughts and
intents of the heart" (Heb. iv. 12). "Every Scripture inspired of God is also profitable
for teaching, for reproof, for correction, for instruction which is in righteousness : that
the man of God may be complete, furnished completely unto every good work" (2 Tim.
iii. 16). "Ye search the Scriptures, because ye think that in them ye have eternal life ;
and these are they which bear witness of me" (John v. 39). 2. *Lack of spiritual
experience.* "Nor the power of God." This ignorance may consist partly in ignorance
of the facts of the Divine history of mankind as recorded in Scripture; but it is chiefly
due to absence of personal, experimental consciousness of God in the spiritual nature.
It is the "darkness of the heart" which exaggerates and intensifies the effects of
general ignorance. "The power of God" works its miracles in the inward as well as
the outward life; in conversion, sanctification, communion, and providential grace.
II. IN WHOM THESE MAY EXIST. The Sadducees were, according to the standards of
their day, educated men. With the letter of the books of Moses they were familiar
(ver. 26); and they were most careful to preserve them from addition or intermixture.
1. *Highly educated men may err in Divine things.* "Thou didst hide these things from
the wise and understanding, and didst reveal them unto babes" (Matt. xi. 25). Secular
culture has not furnished an atom of the transcendental knowledge upon which religion
is based; the Bible is not its product, nor can it be interpreted by it. Yet is not
literature, art, or science to be discarded as a secondary aid to the interpretation of
Scripture. If God does not require our knowledge, neither does he, as it has been
finely said, require our ignorance. 2. *There are many who know the letter of God's
Word without knowing its spirit.* Religious training may bestow an acquaintance with
Scriptural history and doctrine and the chief outlines of moral duty, but it cannot
ensure the inward knowledge of the heart. The interpretation of Scripture is only
possible to those who are spiritually enlightened. Knowing the Bible externally may
actually prove a hindrance to an inward knowledge of it, if it be made too much of, or
imagined sufficient in itself. Superficial acquaintance with Biblical literature, doctrine,
etc., "puffeth up;" and it requires the sternest and most frequent assaults ere its true
character is exposed to itself.
III. HOW THEY ARE TO BE REMOVED. 1. *The teaching of Christ;* awakening a sense
of inward need and repentance, and revealing the correspondence of the Word of God to the
expanding and maturing spiritual consciousness. 2. *The gift of the Holy Spirit;* which
takes of the things of God and reveals them to us. "Things which eye saw not, and
ear heard not, and which entered not into the heart of man, whatsoever things God
prepared for them that love him. But unto us God revealed them through the Spirit :
for the Spirit searcheth all things, yea, the deep things of God" (1 Cor. ii. 9). Not
least of the enlightening influence of the Holy Ghost is due to the purification of the
heart.—M.

Vers. 28—34.—*The Law akin to the gospel, but inferior to it.* I. TRUE RELIGIOUS
INQUIRY IS ENCOURAGED BY CANDOUR AND SPIRITUAL INSIGHT ON THE PART OF RELIGIOUS
TEACHERS. Matthew tells us that the Pharisees "came together to the same place,"
when they saw the discomfiture of the Sadducees; and "then one of them, a lawyer,
asked him a question, tempting him, and saying." Mark introduces him as one of the
scribes. In the one Gospel the motive and encouragement are represented as experienced
by the Pharisaic party in general; in the other they are represented as individually felt
and acted upon. There were, therefore, elements of earnestness and spirituality amongst

the Pharisees, and these were called forth by our Saviour's teaching. They were now in a more favourable attitude for receiving the truth than they had ever been before. As to the idea expressed by "tempting," it need not be understood in a sinister sense, but generally as proving, testing, etc. Our Lord did not crush the spirit of inquiry, but courted it. They felt that there was more in him than they could explain, and that his knowledge of Scripture was spiritual and profound, and therefore *they wished to discover what he could possibly have to tell them that was not already taught by Moses or his prophetic exponents.* He had all but converted his enemies and critics into his disciples. He had infected them with his own spirit of religious earnestness. Of this mood the "lawyer" was the mouthpiece. He pushes inquiry to its highest point, and desires to know the chief duties of religion.

II. The best mode of answering such inquiry is that which presents the spirit and substance of duty, or true religion in its unity and universality. "Deut. vi. 4. This is not given as a part of the Law of Moses, but as the principle of all service. Lev. xix. 18 contains a similar principle for all social duties" (Godwin). Passing over all matters of mere ceremonial, and questions of less or more, he lays hold of the spirit of the Law and presents it to his inquirer. It is out of the very heart of the book of ceremonies (Leviticus) that the duty to neighbours is extracted. He declares "the three unities of religion : (1) the one God ; (2) the one faith ; (3) the one commandment" (Lange) ; and compels the agreement and admiration of his questioner. "Note also the real reverence shown in the form of address, ' Master,' *i.e.* ' Teacher, Rabbi.' He recognized the speaker as one of his own order" (Plumptre). All religion is summed up by him in a "great commandment," viz. the *love of God,* and that is shown in its earthward aspect to involve *loving our neighbour as ourselves.* That true religion is not ceremonial but spiritual is thus demonstrated ; and in quoting the highest utterances of the prophets, the scribe but endorses and restates the same doctrine. Teacher and inquirer are therefore theoretically one. But more is needed ; and towards the attainment of this the stimulus is given, "Thou art *not far from the kingdom of God.*" This meant that—

III. Such inquiry can only be satisfied and crowned by acting upon its highest spiritual convictions. "The words are significant as showing the unity of our Lord's teaching. Now, as when he spoke the sermon on the mount, the righteousness which fulfils the Law is the condition of the entrance into the kingdom of God (Matt. v. 19, 20). Even the recognition of that righteousness as consisting in the fulfilment of the two commandments that were exceeding broad, brought a man as to the very threshold of the kingdom. It is instructive to compare our Lord's different method of dealing, in Luke x. 25—37, with one who had the same theoretical knowledge, but who obviously, consciously or unconsciously, minimized the force of the commandments by his narrowing definitions" (Plumptre). "The kingdom of heaven is, for the moment, pictorially represented as *localized,* like the ordinary kingdoms of the world. The scribe, walking in the way of conscientious inquiry, and thus making religious pilgrimage, had nearly reached its borderland. He was bordering on the great reality of true religion, *subjection of spirit to the sovereign will of God*" (Morison). This state can only be attained to by conversion, the identification of the sinner through faith with the righteousness of the Saviour, and the indwelling of the Spirit of God. It is thus scientific conviction becomes moral, and we are able to carry into effect what we know to be true and right.—M.

Ver. 34.—"*Not far from the kingdom of God.*" I. The highest interpretation of human duty approaches the gospel, but falls short of it.

II. The conditions of entrance into Christ's kingdom are moral, and not merely intellectual. Faith ; obedience ; love. The heart, or central being.

III. No man ought to be satisfied with merely being "not far" from the kingdom. 1. *To stop there is to stultify our highest spiritual instincts and tendencies.* 2. *To stop there is to fail of salvation.* 3. *To stop there is to aggravate our misery and sin.*—M.

Vers. 35—37.—*Great David's greater Son.* I. Unspiritual interpreters of Scripture are involved in inconsistency and self-contradiction. 1. *In the present instance they proved to be so with respect to the most important truths.* It is only the spiritual mind that can harmonize the apparent discrepancies of revelation (1 Cor. ii. 14; cf. Heb. v. 12, *seq.*).   2. *This results in their own loss and injury* (1 Pet. iii. 16).   They failed to recognize the Messiah when he did come, because of their false conceptions of what he was.

II. The glory of the Messiah is seen from prophetic Scripture to be more than royal—to be, in fact, Divine.   The hundred and tenth psalm is rightly called "a psalm of David."   Merely to apply it to David is to destroy its Messianic character. "The psalm is not only quoted by our Lord as Messianic in the passages already referred to (viz. this and Matt. xxii. 41—46); it is more frequently cited by the New Testament writers than any other single portion of the ancient Scriptures. (Comp., besides these passages in the Gospels, Acts ii. 34, 35; 1 Cor. xv. 25; Heb. i. 13; v. 6; vii. 17, 21; x. 13.)   In later Jewish writings, in the Talmud and the rabbis, nearly every verse of the psalm is quoted as referring to the Messiah" (Perowne).   "The majority of ancient Jewish interpreters apply the psalm to the Messiah" (Strauss, 'Leben Jesu,' ii. 6, 79).   If, then, it is David's own composition, and is Messianic, the language used with respect to the Royal One who is to come is only to be explained as involving divinity: "Jehovah said to *my Lord.*"

III. In applying the psalm to himself, Christ suggested the true solution of the apparent contradiction.   The psalm is deliberately and by implication adopted by Christ.   He testifies to the Divine inspiration of its author.   His own person and work are the key to its meaning.   As he was Son of David on the human side, so was he David's Lord by virtue of his Divine Sonship.—M.

Ver. 37.—" *The common people heard him gladly.*"   I. The persons thus affected. The reference of the words " common people " misunderstood.   Literally the expression is, " the great multitude."   It was in the temple, and must have comprehended all classes, especially the middle and upper; the very lowest being but sparsely represented.   It was also nationally homogeneous—Jewish.

II. Reasons for their being so.   Not on account of eloquence, or so-called " popularity " of address.   That the highest qualities were exhibited "goes without saying." The full splendour and majesty of Messianic teaching were exhibited.   The Man himself was more, and felt to be more, than his words.   Two circumstances lent a passing interest to his teaching: he exposed and defeated the religious pretenders of the day, Pharisees, Sadducees, lawyers, whose true character the people's instinct felt had been revealed; and he appealed to the national religious spirit, in setting forth the true doctrine of the Messiah.

III. The moral value of this reception of Christ.   1. It showed that the deepest instincts of humanity are on the side of religion and Divine truth.   2. But it did not involve discipleship.   Admiration, intellectual assent, even some wonder at what was truly Divine; but no moral conviction.   There are many to whom the gospel is a thing gladly heard, but soon dismissed from the thoughts.   It is in obedience and faith that the "glad tidings" are practically and permanently experienced by the human heart.—M.

Vers. 41—44.—*The widow's two mites.*   The treasury, "in front of the sanctuary," consisted of thirteen brazen chests, called "trumpets" from their peculiar shape, " swelling out beneath, and tapering upward into a narrow mouth or opening, into which the contributions were put."   The contributions given were towards the sacrifice fund, and they were voluntary.   This incident has a deep, permanent interest for all Christians.

I. Christ's observation of religious giving.   He " sat over against the treasury, and beheld how the people cast money into the treasury."   This has been felt to be typical of his eternal attitude: he still sits "over against the treasury" of his Church.   1. *It was deliberate.*   He did it as one who had purposed to do it; and he was not in any hurry.   The position was chosen, and was well suited to carry out his intention.   2. *It was careful and discriminating.*   The different classes of people were noted—rich and poor, ostentatious and retiring, mean and generous.   He beheld *how* the people cast in.   3. *It was comprehensive.*   No individual seems to have escaped his attention. Even the poor widow is observed. 4. *It was his last act ere quitting the temple for ever.*

II. HIS KNOWLEDGE OF ITS MOTIVES AND CIRCUMSTANCES. 1. *How penetrating!* The outward actions and bearing of the donors would doubtless reveal to his eye, who "knew what was in man," their real characters. Now he looks directly upon our secret thoughts and feelings, and is acquainted with all the conditions of mind and heart through which we pass. He knows the *history* of the gift, as well as its actual bestowal. 2. *How complete!* The domestic circumstances of the widow were well known to him. No tax-surveyor could have reckoned the income of the people more accurately. 3. *How minute!* The exact nature and number of the widow's coins are noted.

III. HIS JUDGMENT AS TO ITS WORTH. His attitude now, as on the day when "he looked round about upon all things," was authoritative and judicial. He sat as one who had a right to be there. It is from a supreme elevation of moral sentiment that he looks, for already clearly visible to his spirit is his own great gift—of himself. 1. *Given from a spiritual point of view.* Not the objective amount, but the motives and feelings of the givers. The spirit of sacrifice, the religious enthusiasm of each, is measured and declared. 2. *The standard indicated is not how much is given, but from how much it is given.* They all cast in "of their abundance." What they gave was, therefore, a mere superfluity. Their comforts were not decreased, their luxuries still abounded. The need—the absolute poverty—of the widow rendered her gift a sacrifice, and a heroic act of faith. It was prophetic of the Divine charities that were to be awakened in the breasts of regenerate men, when his own great sacrifice should have borne its fruit. The Macedonian Churches (and many a one since) gave not only to their power, but beyond it, their deep poverty abounding to the riches of their liberality (2 Cor. viii. 1, 2). "Now, many would have been ready to censure this *poor widow*, and to think she did ill. Why should she give to others when she had little enough for herself? . . . It is so rare a thing to find any that would not blame this widow, that we cannot expect to find any that will imitate her! And yet our Saviour commends her, and therefore we are sure that she did very well and wisely " (Matthew Henry).—M.

Ver. 41.—*Jesus lingering in the temple.* This is one of the best-known incidents in the life of our Lord. It is strange that it should be so. If we consider the greatness of his work, we should hardly expect that room would be found in a brief record of it for so trivial an event. It was an every-day occurrence for the worshippers who entered the temple to cast their offerings into the treasury, and not a few widows would be found among them. Yet an evangelist, who was inspired of God to select or reject any of the multitudinous facts of Christ's ministry, did not leave untold the story of the widow's mite; and it is repeated with equal emphasis by Luke. Evidently God judges not as man does. We think much of a philanthropic scheme which loudly asserts itself; but he probably estimates more highly the scheme of some obscure Christian worker, who gathers together the poor and wretched, telling them of a nobler, purer life, and lifting them up towards the light of God's love. In trivial incidents great principles are found, and we should dig in them as for hid treasure. Our Lord Jesus Christ is naturally the Centre of this scene, and we will see what we may of his characteristics as exhibited in it.

I. THE GENTLENESS OF CHRIST. For the last time our Lord had appeared in the temple as a public Teacher. Before crowds of people he had once more strongly denounced the hypocrisy of the scribes and Pharisees. They were convicted by their own consciences, and incapable of reply, so " they answered not a word ; " but, in their desperation and malignity, they resolved the more speedily to put him to death. He knew it perfectly well. Yet, after speaking as the righteous Rebuker of sin, he gladly turns aside to discover and commend a hidden act of goodness. Indeed, he seemed eager to see something which would redeem his Father's house from the wickedness which dishonoured it. Hence " he sat over against the treasury," and watched till he saw one worshipper whose sacrifice he could rejoice over—that of a poor widow, who cast in all the living that she had. That act of hers came to him like a streak of sunshine through the clouds. How tenderly and patiently does he still watch for any glimmer of faith and love in human hearts!

II. THE SERENITY OF CHRIST. His calmness was like the blue of the heavens, unruffled and unchanged by storms that stir the lower atmosphere. An ordinary man, after uttering a rebuke which enraged his foes to madness, would put himself out of reach. He would not linger in their stronghold, which was full of perils to him. But in patience Jesus Christ possessed his soul. He knew his hour had not yet come. He would not hasten away. It might be that some of his hearers would repent, and come to him, confessing and forsaking their sins. So, while many passed him whose beetling brows were black with hatred, he in the court of the women quietly sat and waited. Such serenity was habitual with him. When there was haste and agony and terror in Bethany, Jesus abode three days in the same place where he was. When the warning came, "Depart hence, for Herod will kill thee," he calmly continued his works of mercy. When the armed band followed him into Gethsemane, he confronted them with a calmness that paralyzed them. When he conquered death and rose from the grave, there was no sign of haste—the linen clothes were laid orderly, and the napkin was folded in a place by itself. Too often our hearts are perturbed. We are fussy, anxious, fretful ; but, if we will but receive it, this is his legacy : "Peace I leave with you, *my* peace I give unto you : not as the world giveth, give I unto you. Let not your heart be troubled, neither let it be afraid."

III. THE CONDESCENSION OF CHRIST. Our Lord was full of great thoughts, not only respecting this world, but that other world from which he came, with its vivid realities and awful mysteries. He looked on to the future of the work he had begun, and which in a few days would be consummated on the cross—a work which would not only stir Jerusalem, but shake the Roman empire, and go onward through distant ages with growing force, till all nations would call him blessed. Yet here he was, watching a few Jewish worshippers go into their temple ; and he notices each one. He sees even this poor widow, whom others brush past with haste or contempt. He knows her struggle and sacrifice and single-heartedness, as she brings that tiny offering, with a blush of shame that it is so little, and secretly lets it fall into the treasury of her God. His condescension is still displayed to the meanest and the humblest worshippers, and broken words, paltry gifts, and feeble efforts will not be without his notice and recompense. May he see, in all Christian assemblies, not the outward formalism which he must rebuke, but prayer and praise, gift and work, which loyal hearts are offering to the Lord their God !—A. R.

Vers. 42—44.—*The widow's mite.* If we get a single ray of light, decompose and analyze it, we may argue from it to all the light that floods the world; to its nature, its source, and its effects. So this act of generosity and devotion, simple and slight though it is in itself, contains in it elements of truth which are world-wide in application. Amongst the many lessons it teaches, we select the following :—

I. THAT GOD'S PEOPLE ARE EXPECTED TO BE GIVERS. Many have a singular objection to insistence upon that. They willingly listen to words of solace; they rejoice in descriptions of heaven; they are not reluctant to hear the errors of their theological antagonists exposed and rebuked : but the duty of Christian giving is scarcely so popular with them. However, "it is enough for the servant that he be as his Master ;" and we find that he who taught in the temple also "beheld how the people cast money into the treasury." That treasury was a Divine institution. In spite of abuses, it was for many generations a witness of what God expects; as a recognition of his claims, and of the claims of others, on the part of rich and poor. If God is our Creator and Preserver, if every day we live and every power we have is his gift, we must honour him "with our substance, and with the firstfruits of all our increase." If he has redeemed us by his Son, if "we are not our own, but bought with a price," any sacrifice we make in gift or work should be a source of joy. If we be members of one brotherhood, we are bound to have the same care one for another. We are to do this, not in the way which is easiest to ourselves, most accordant with our tastes, or most likely to bring us credit; but as those who are seeking to become like him, who is kind to the unthankful and to the unworthy.

II. THAT SOME KINDS OF GIVING ARE OF HIGHER WORTH THAN OTHERS. Our Lord did not blame or despise the gifts which the rich made when they cast in much. They were doing what was right. Whether their offerings went to support the temple, or as a substitute for sacrifices, or for distribution to the poor, they were given towards what was regarded as the work of God. But there was nothing in the offering of the rich which called for the *special* praise bestowed on the widow. 1. *It is to be observed here that Christ commended what most people would blame.* You would probably argue thus : " Two mites were of little importance to the treasury, but of great importance to her. If she had given one and kept the other, she would have showed not only piety, but good sense. As it was her gift was insignificant, and at the same time it was rash and needless." Yet, in the eyes of our Lord, the gift was right; and it was commended for this very reason—that she had cast in all the living that she had. We cannot but be reminded here of an incident in the house of Simon. When Mary broke the alabaster box, and poured the spikenard on her Saviour's head, the disciples said that it was a foolish impulse—that if sold for three hundred pence, and given to the poor, it would have been of real utility ; now a waste of the ointment had been made. In reply, Jesus taught them that nothing given to God was wasted; that the aroma of such an offering went beyond the world of sense. On both occasions our Lord commended what others blamed. 2. *Further, the reason for his commendation was not what many would expect.* It was not the value of the gift ; for two mites was a smaller sum than we could give if we tried to find our smallest coin. Nor was it the object to which the money was given which Christ approved. He knew how much there was of what was false under the glitter of the ceremonial worship of the temple. He had just rebuked the very men who would manipulate these funds. He looked on to the day when the temple would perish, and a nobler Church would arise on its ruins. Hence, in commending the widow's gift, which supported this ritual, he condemned those who withhold their help till an organization is exactly what they wish—who refuse to support what does not accord precisely with their tastes and views. Those who habitually do this crush in their hearts the germ from which gift and sacrifice spring. 3. *The widow's gift was approved because it was the offering of a simple heart, full of love to God.* She wished to show gratitude, and to give a deliberate expression of her confidence in God ; and therefore she gave up her living, and threw herself on him who feeds the birds, and never forgets his children. 4. *Most of all the gift was valued because it represented self-sacrifice.* They gave of their abundance—she gave all her living; in other words, herself. Too often we lose the highest blessedness because we do not cross the border-line which lies between self-indulgence and Christ-likeness. When we begin to feel that some service is a burden, and demands a strain, we give it up to some one else to whom the effort would be less! Let us seek the spirit of the poor widow, who knew that God could do without her gift, but felt that her love could not be satisfied without her sacrifice.

III. THAT OUR LORD QUIETLY WATCHES OUR GIFTS AND SERVICES. We may put into the treasury wealth, talents, prayers, tears, etc. None are unnoticed by him. And he looks in order to approve, not to condemn. His disciples might have said, " She is imprudent to give her all ; she is priest-ridden ; she is supporting a formal worship which is a barrier to the kingdom of Christ." But the Lord looked beneath the surface. He saw the pious intention, the pure purpose, and out of all the chaff on that threshing-floor he found one grain of purity and reality, and rejoiced over it as one finding great spoil.

IV. THAT OUR LORD APPROVES ALL THAT IS DONE IN A RIGHT SPIRIT. He did not praise her to her face, nor in her hearing. When the delicate flower of devotion is taken in the hot hand of popular applause, it withers; but, left in the cool shadow of secrecy, it lives. Hence the widow heard no flattery or approval, though she went home with inward satisfaction because she had done what she could. It is a pleasure to make a sacrifice for one we love. The young girl gives up her money, her position, her future, herself, to the man she loves, and rejoices in doing it. The father will not begrudge it when he looks at his children's faces, though for their sakes he goes off in a shabby coat to his daily duty. Love longs for sacrifice, and glories in making it. Now, it is a sacrifice so inspired which our God approves and commends. In the day when the secrets of all hearts shall be disclosed, when nothing will be overlooked, services which the doer had forgotten, which the Church thought trivial and the world laughs to scorn, will be recompensed, and even " a cup of cold water, given in the name of a disciple, will not lose its reward."—A. R.

Vers. 1—12.—*The parable of the vineyard; or, unfaithfulness and its reward.* A rude demand upon Jesus for his authority led him to ask in reply "one question" which awakened the consciences of his interrogators and threw them into confusion and difficulty. They were hurrying him on to his final hour, and he must needs take advantage of every opportunity of finishing the work given him to do. Therefore "in parables" he spake both "unto them" and "against them," which but roused their ire, and sent them away to plot and plan for his destruction. No word was needed to declare who was represented by the vineyard. "For the vineyard of the Lord of hosts is the house of Israel." And the details of the parable were minutely historic. How often had "a servant" been sent "that he might receive of the fruits of the vineyard"! How often had he been "handled shamefully"! Now a last chance is offered. "He had yet one, a beloved son: he sent him last unto them." The rest is prophecy ready to be fulfilled, and so soon to become history also. But the appeal, "What therefore will the lord of the vineyard do?" he does not leave them to answer, but supplies it in simple words and in such manner as to make the reply an admonitory warning. Alas! our eyes behold the precise fulfilment. And the rejected stone is now the Foundation-stone, "the Head of the corner." The parable reveals—

I. A GRACIOUS EXAMPLE OF THE DIVINE GOODNESS AND PATIENCE. It was a direct dealing with Israel, but it was an indirect dealing with all men. The comment is found in the historic development of the history of Israel.

II. A PAINFUL INSTANCE OF HUMAN UNFAITHFULNESS. This, as in all instances of a want of fidelity to important trusts, was sadly disastrous. But not only to them to whom the trust was committed, for all men expiate the sins of every unfaithful one. The condition of society is lowered; good fruits are blighted and cannot be gathered; pains and penalties are incurred which fall heavily upon all. Had every man been faithful to his trust, what a paradise this hard earth would have presented! But the world walks on a lower plane for every unholy life passed upon it. Had that vineyard brought forth its due fruits, all nations would have been made partakers. Of the few small patches which bore, the world has the fruit in those holy records which are as the salt of the earth. But how much of the corn and the oil and the wine is wanting! On this account is presented—

III. A SAD ILLUSTRATION OF THE DIVINE JUDGMENT. Israel is deposed. The sacred trust is withdrawn. The vineyard is in other hands. The unfaithful husbandmen, as such, are destroyed. Alas for Israel! Her crown is in the dust, her harps upon the willows. She does not with her voice sing the pleasant songs of Zion. She is not the great spiritual power in the earth for which she was designed. Her calling and election she did not make sure. True, for the fathers' sakes she remains a testimony in the earth. But it is as a broken-off branch. The world gains nothing by Israel's rejection. The Gentiles are wise to weep and mourn on her behalf; and, knowing that "God is able to graft them in again," they are wise to pray earnestly for their recovery. "The receiving of them" would be "life from the dead." So let every Gentile believer pitifully behold the nation sitting in the dust, having become the uncircumcision in the spirit: and at this time, alas! "separate from Christ" and really "alienated from the commonwealth of" the true "Israel, strangers from the covenants of promise, having no hope." Nor can it be otherwise till they who now are "far off are made nigh in the blood of Christ."—G.

Vers. 13—17.—*The tribute money.* Unable to take him with their wicked hands, because they dared not, they send selected men from the Pharisees and the Herodians. They have instructions to lay a trap with a view "to catch him in talk." "In vain is the net spread in the sight of any bird." But these blind catchers thought him to be blind also. In specious words they ply him with a question relating to an oppressive tax. "If he held that payment should be refused, he would compromise himself with the Romans; if he sanctioned it, he would embitter himself both with the Herodians and the ultra-national party." But he who "knew what was in man" knew "their hypocrisy," and in a word, and doubtless with a look, exposed it. "Why tempt ye me?" Then with the coin before their eyes, which was at once the symbol of their unfaithfulness to God and their subjection to man, he threw back upon them the onus of answering themselves in their own conscience and by their own deeds.

Ah! "in the net which they hid is their own foot taken." But Jesus does not only evade the dilemma on which they had cast him; nor does he merely utter a word of condemnation to them who had failed to "render unto God the things that are God's," and who would be only too glad to escape rendering "to Cæsar the things that" were "Cæsar's." But he, in high wisdom, teaches the great truth for all time, that fidelity to the demands of God and fidelity to the constituted powers of earth need not clash. The loyalty of the subject and the obedience of the saint are on the same plane. So a just distribution is made of things pertaining to Cæsar and of things pertaining to God, and yet the true unity of the service rendered to both is declared; and, moreover, as God is above all, the duty to him includes the duty to Cæsar. For our learning we may see—

I. THAT CHRIST BEARS HIS TESTIMONY TO THE RIGHTEOUSNESS OF THE CLAIMS OF EARTHLY AUTHORITY. The Christian need be under no apprehension of following this principle out to its extremest limits. For if the earthly government be oppressive and unjust, he knows full well that the King of kings has his own methods of deposing; for he believes that "he putteth down one and setteth up another." He has learned to submit even to oppression for conscience' sake. But these questions respect the extreme, the occasional, the exceptional conditions of political life. Fidelity to the constituted head of authority would, according to Christian principles, secure the divinely appointed Head.

II. CHRIST UTTERS HIS EVER-REITERATED DEMAND FOR FIDELITY TO THE INALIENABLE CLAIMS OF GOD. "Render unto God the things that are God's." Is anything not God's? If in truth all is first rendered to him in an honest consecration to his will, then may that which he ordains for the neighbour be given to the neighbour; that which is for the poor to the poor; or that for the family, or for self even, so given; and therefore that which is for "the king, as supreme," to the king may be rendered.

III. LET THE MAN HIMSELF, WHO TRULY IS GOD'S, BE RENDERED UNTO GOD. One has beautifully taught thus: "That which bears Cæsar's image is, as belonging to Cæsar, to be given to him; but that which has God's image belongs to God." Had Israel been faithful to "render" themselves "to God" they would not in those late days have been given up to the Romans, as in earlier days fidelity to God would have kept back the armies of Nebuchadnezzar. The great principle to guide nations and individuals alike is truly to be the Lord's. Then, when he is the God of the nation, all other service and all other obligations fall into their proper order and degree of importance. And he who serves his God in humility will serve his king in fidelity. He who is obedient to the Lord's claims will know how to render the claims of masters, and lords, and rulers, and sovereigns. Not more truly is the Law one, "Thou shalt love the Lord thy God," and "Thou shalt love thy neighbour," than is "Render unto Cæsar the things that are Cæsar's, and to God the things that are God's."—G.

Vers. 18—27.—*The resurrection from the dead.* A new class of antagonists now assail the great "Master" with a case of casuistry, designed evidently to bring the doctrine of the resurrection into contempt. "In the resurrection whose wife shall she be of them?" Was this one of the flimsy difficulties on which they relied for a defence of their position, as so often men screen their scepticism behind a mere veil of difficulty? And did they depend in any real degree upon an imaginary inconsistency to warrant them in denying the grandest hopes of the human heart? Be it so or not, they gave opportunity for the most precious defence of the common faith. The Church to-day is rich in an inheritance of defensive writing drawn from the pens of holy apostles and righteous men. But though it is of unspeakable value to her to read the inestimable words of the great Apostle to the Gentiles, yet to them who have wholly committed themselves to Jesus, who truly own him as "Master," and no other, it is most comforting to find him entering the lists against all Sadducean unbelief for all ages. It is enough: Jesus is the defender of the faith. We want no more. In one sentence we read both an answer to the difficulty and a confirmation of the truth: "For when they shall rise from the dead, they neither marry, nor are given in marriage; but are as angels in heaven." Thus is clearly revealed—(1) *The fact of the resurrection;* and (2) *the conditions of the resurrection life.*

I. The first clear teaching is, THE DEAD LIVE. "That the dead are raised even Moses showed;" so little had these sons of Moses understood his words. And now Jesus shows it more clearly, and points to the life as an immortal life: " Neither can they die any more: for they are equal unto the angels; and are sons of God, being sons of the resurrection." True, this is affirmed of them "that are accounted worthy to attain to that world, and the resurrection from the dead." But that "the dead"—that is, all the dead—"are raised Moses showed, as touching the dead that they are raised." Oh, precious words! Thanks be to God, life does not end in a tomb! Abraham and Isaac and Jacob live; yea, "all live unto him," if unto us they die. Jesus points to the source of all error on this as on so many subjects: "Ye know not the Scriptures, nor the power of God." On these two hang all the true faith of men. No one can read "the Scriptures" and deny the resurrection. In Jesus' view the old Scriptures sufficiently affirmed the great truth. And he who in these days would defend himself against the assaults of unbelief must sit at the feet of Jesus. No one can doubt his belief in the resurrection. "And why is it judged incredible?" All difficulties vanish in presence of "the power of God." If the question of the "foolish one" be urged, "How?—How are the dead raised?" the only answer faith should vouchsafe is, "The power of God." And if the further demand is pressed, but "with what manner of body do they come?" it must still be replied, "God giveth it a body." Let the true believer stand by the Word of God. The resurrection rests not for its certainty on a foundation of human ratiocination or scientific deduction, neither is it by them to be overturned. The one impregnable wall of defence for this most precious article of human faith and this most precious condition of human life is in the combined words, "The Scriptures: the power of God."

II. As to the CONDITION OF THE RESURRECTION LIFE. We wait to know this. One only truth is enough to carry with us, an earnest of all—"as angels in heaven." The truths are almost antiphonal: "Neither can they die any more; as angels in heaven."—G.

Vers. 28—34.—*The great command.* One more question ere it could be said, "No man after that durst ask him any question." Alas! on the human side it, like the others, is a mere quibble, or based on one. But though man asks in his folly Jesus never answers according to it, but always according to his supreme wisdom, in a manner so high, so far-reaching, so seriously. He trifled not with the perplexities of men. He knew nations and tribes of men would feed on his words to the end of time, and he gladly bore witness to all those truths against which the human errors in that erring age stood out in humiliating contrast. The Christian teaching grows up out of the Mosaic. The later development of the one system does not set aside a single moral principle of the earlier. The solution of the difficulty which beset a few amidst the many commandments for which priority was urged laid down a permanent principle for all time, and took up into Christianity the essential teaching of Mosaism. We read—

I. THE SIMPLICITY OF THE CHRISTIAN TEACHING. One word embodies it—the word "love." To this Christ gave the utmost prominence and the most beautiful illustration. This simple rule engages the devotion of the central energy of the entire life. It describes the first effort of feeble infancy and the ripest experience of the mature Christian age. It is at once the point from which all pure and active obedience takes its departure, and it is the end towards which all spiritual growth and culture tends. It is the alpha and the omega of the Christian spirit. To love, to love God first and supremely, and in that love to love the neighbour, is so complete a dedication of the entire inner man to the service of the Most High, that all commands requiring the details of that service are anticipated. From these branches hang all the rich, ripe clusters of fruitful obedience.

II. THE ELEVATING TENDENCY OF THAT TEACHING, WHICH SETS FORTH THE LOVE OF THE INFINITE EXCELLENCE AS THE HIGHEST AND MOST OBLIGATORY OF ALL ITS REQUIRE-MENTS. That holy system of spiritual morality first called Mosaism, or Judaism, and now called Christianity, is for ever raised to the highest pitch of excellence and worthiness by making this its central, its almost solitary, command. All that is good in morals, all that is pure in aspiration, all that is beneficent in action, flows from this fountain. The perpetual aim to reach to the most entire love of the most exalted Object of human thought must insensibly raise the moral and spiritual character of every one who is controlled by so worthy an endeavour. It ensures the recognition of the soul's subjection to the authority of God; it makes the Divine excellences objects of ceaseless contemplation; it subordinates all the aims and activities of life to the holiest purposes; and, while withdrawing the life from the degradations of low and unworthy motives and pursuits, it regulates the whole by an ever-present, powerful, and satisfying principle of life, at the same time preserving the simplicity and moral cohesion—the unity—of the character. Never was a holier law uttered; never were the feet of men directed to a purer, safer path; never was a firmer, truer basis laid on which to found a kingdom of truth, of peace, and of well-being.

III. THE PRACTICAL CHARACTER OF THE CHRISTIAN TEACHING—"Thou shalt love thy neighbour." To present rules for the government of every hour and the regulation of every transaction of life would be far less effective than to seize upon a principle like this, which underlies all conduct. It may be entrusted with the guidance of the life in the absence of controlling regulations and minute details of obligatory observance. It leaves the spirit free to act according to its own generous impulses or prudent caution. Such a rule prevents the necessity for "Thou shalt not steal;" "Thou shalt not kill." Love embraces all virtues; it fulfils all righteousness. The regulating principle, "as thyself," points to the due estimate of one's own life; such a love for it as would prevent its exposure to evil, and such a discernment of the true interests of life, and the common participation in those interests, as would lead to right adjustment of the relative claims of self and the apparently conflicting claims of others. Truly, "there is none other commandment greater than these." This, indeed, is "much more than all whole burnt offerings and sacrifices." And he who has come to appreciate the truth and beauty of this is "not far from the kingdom of God;" while he who keeps this commandment already dwells within the security and shares the blessedness of that kingdom.—G.

Vers. 41—44.—*The widow's gift.* How many lessons cluster around this unique incident! The watchful eye which is ever over the treasury of the Lord's temple; the discernment between the gifts that come of "superfluity," large perhaps in themselves, but small in comparison with the abundance left untouched; and the gifts that betoken the penury of the giver, but at the same time declare the entireness with which all his living is devoted to the service of God; and the great Master's principle of judgment. "Many that were rich cast in much;" one that was "poor" cast in little; yet the one "cast in more than all." Let not our thoughts leave the Lord's treasury, and let that treasury denote to us whatever is employed for the right ordering of the Lord's worship in his own holy house; all that is expended in charitable works for the benefit of men, whether in ministering to their spiritual or temporal necessities. The good Lord has himself chosen to represent works of benevolence shown to the suffering and poor to be works done unto himself. All that is thrown into their treasury is thrown into his. "Inasmuch as ye did it unto one of these my brethren, even these least, ye did it unto me." So it comes to pass that both the Lord and the poor—the Lord in heaven and the suffering and needy on earth—make their appeal to our charity for such help as we may be able to render. In responding to this double appeal let us measure our gifts: 1. *By the claims of our Lord upon us.* 2. *By the necessities of our neighbour.* 3. *By the measure of our sympathy with him and them.*

I. If THE CLAIMS OF OUR LORD guide us, what limit shall we put upon our "gifts"? To him we owe more than our all. To him we are indebted for life and breath, and all things; for the bright light of the morn and the cooling shades of eventide; for reason and affection and friendship. The good and perfect gifts of righteousness, of holy hope, of calm faith, of heavenly love, come down from him. All that is beauteous and bright in life; all that raises us from degradation and need. Ah! the sands on the sea-shore are as little likely to be numbered as the gifts of the Lord's bounty, which lay us under tribute from sheer thankfulness to him.

II. But OUR NEIGHBOUR'S NEED presents little less impressive claims upon us. How multiplied! How various! How imperative! Christian charity needs little labour to find out the suitable channels of its activity. How greatly has that charity grown and multiplied since the Lord cast the first handful of seed into the warm heart of man! Many ages have been characterized by large gifts for the comfort, the physical need, the spiritual help of man. This present age is not a whit behind the chief in the largeness and variety of its gifts and efforts. To the Lord be praise!

III. But the true spring of all charity and the true quality of it is to be found in a PERFECT UNITY OF INTEREST WITH MEN, AND A PERFECT SYMPATHY WITH THE LORD. True charity is the outflow of the love of God and love of man. It is one of the highest reaches of wisdom to discern the perfect community of interest which every man has with every other. This the Lord saw: this, alas! is but little seen by us. He who can once become possessed of the belief that he has no true and permanent interest which is not identical with the highest interests of his race, has taken the first step towards the attainment of a pure, a boundless, a Divine charity. And he who would sustain this lofty sentiment must learn to see that all he has he holds by the will and for the good pleasure of the Lord on high. He will learn that concerning himself his utmost wisdom is, with St. Bernard, to say, "Lord, I have but two mites, a body and a soul; I give them both to thee."—G.

Vers. 1—12.—*The evil husbandmen.* I. FAITHLESS TO GOD; UNJUST TO MEN. If men do not know God, neither can they know those who are sent of him. The Pharisees were set against Jesus because he was the only living presentment of their own neglected duties to God.

II. VIOLENCE FALLACIOUS TO THOSE WHO EMPLOY IT. The wicked husbandmen blindly slay the emissary. It is of no avail. The Erinys, the fury, the avenging spirit of the dead man, will come back. The violence against Jesus brought about the removal of his murderers from their place.

III. ABUSE OF GOOD MEANS ITS LOSS. "The vineyard given to others." So do great inheritances melt away from their possessors; and the industrious servant comes to the seat of the dissipated lord. The very intelligence that is misused decays; and the loss of influence means loss of moral life.

IV. THE SCALES OF DIVINE AND OF HUMAN ESTIMATION OFTEN DIFFER. A lesson often suggested by Christ. "Men are not what they seem." In science, in literature, in politics, the greatest men often rise up, untrained in the schools, to confute the conventional judgment of the time about education. So in religion. It is difficult to realize that the Saviour was once scoffed at as a rustic, illiterate teacher from Nazareth. Yet so it was. There is a profound wonder in the turns of human life; and so long as we have eyes for the hand and working of God, miracles in the truest sense will never cease.—J.

Vers. 13—17.—*The dialectic of Jesus.* 1. DISHONEST SUBTLETY MATCHED BY CLEAR-SIGHTED WISDOM. We must be, if possible, "wise as serpents," but, above all, honest in purpose. It is the false tongue that stammers, and the fox-like cunning that entraps itself.

II. VERBAL TRUTH MAY CONCEAL HEART FALSEHOOD. They spoke most truly to Jesus about himself, and yet most untruly. So of all words designed to flatter and deceive. There may be a divorce between the tongue and the heart.

III. CONDENSED ARGUMENT. In the use he made of the coin, Jesus suggested a whole train of argument. The coin with its image was a symbol of earthly rule. The kingdom of Jesus is ideal, and independent of the forms of this world (John xviii. 36). The loyalty of the Christian to the kingdom which is righteousness, peace, and joy in the Holy Ghost, teaches him how to act in relation to worldly governments. But Christianity is not to be confounded with politics. "No earthly governments can prevent the spiritual service of God. That should not be rendered to them which is due to God only" (Godwin).—J.

Vers. 18—27.—*Sadducean error.* I. DIFFICULTIES OF BELIEF ARE OFTEN IDLE LUXURIES OF THE MIND. One cannot suppose that these men were really troubled by such a question as they raised. It was sheer idleness, bred of useless school life. And so with many theoretical questions pretended to be of serious importance: pressing into what is inaccessible and kept in reserve by God. They are "solved by walking." Act—act rightly here and now, and the question will solve itself, or cease to interest.

II. Disingenuous reasoning falls into stupidity.   What else but childish is
this confusion of earthly relations with the spiritual kingdom?   Marriage, birth, and
death are time-changes; belong to the idea of earth and time, not to eternity.   And
the least instructed mind *feels* that this is so.   There are enough mysteries in the
present life to engage our attention without prying into those beyond.

III. The ray of truth.   The one great historic Word, the basis of the national
consciousness, sheds its sufficient light upon the question.   God does not claim dead
objects for his own.   Souls that he calls his, "do of his own dear life partake," and
"never will he them forsake."   It was a mystical interpretation of the ancient Word ;
and often there are times when we may take refuge in the mystical interpretation, and
feel that it is the deepest and the best.   "Those who are now dead to men still live in
God."—J.

Vers. 28—34.—*The essence of religion.*   I. The leading idea for the intelligence.
The unity of God, his personality, his supreme lovableness.   "All love is lost save
upon God alone."

II. The leading maxim for the will.   To love one's neighbour as one's self.
Kant said, trying to translate the gospel into his own dialect, "Act so that the maxim
of thy will may be the principle of an universal legislation."

III. The moral surpasses the ritual in religion.   Surpasses it by including it
with itself.   Nothing can be offered to God dearer than a just and a loving life.   Love,
in fact, is the measure of life's worth.   And he who believes and acts upon these
principles is recognized by Christ as being a Christian.—J.

Vers. 35—37.—*David's Son.*   I. David's prophetic spirit.   "He was moved by the
spirit of truth when he foretold that his son would rule over all, and when he owned
him as Lord."   The psalm had originally another bearing.   But as all true poesy
"smacks of something greater than it seems," and has deeper meanings than meet the
eye, so did the words of the psalmist reach forth into remoter times and higher
relations.

II. Christ's identification.   "He declared that he was the Son of David, and that
his priesthood and kingdom were universal and everlasting."—J.

Vers. 38—40.—*Traits of the scribe.*   I. The seeming good often thrive and are
honoured.   Insight into character is rare; men are judged by the outside, and are
taken largely at their own valuation.

II. Pretension ever hides emptiness, and often guilt.   Fixed for ever for our
repugnance, hatred, and contempt is the character of the religious pretender in the
Gospel.   Men need to be warned that there is more danger to the soul in pretending to
a piety we have not got, than in merely having none at all.—J.

Vers. 41—44.—*The gift of poverty.*   I. The motive makes the action spiritual.
It is mechanical, conventional, without relation to the spiritual sphere, otherwise.

II. Love magnifies the value of the smallest gift.   The flower to the sick
person, the penny in the plate, may be worth much.   The condition of the world would
be intolerable without the multitude of such little deeds.

III. The true standard of worth in life should be clearly kept in mind.
We confuse mere giving and doing with that which springs from love too much.
Let us not despise little things: seeds of love which become great in their result of
blessing.—J.

Vers. 1—12.   Parallel passages: Matt. xxi. 33—46; Luke xx. 9—19.—*Parable of
the vineyard.*   I. The Lord's vineyard.   A vineyard is often used in Scripture as an
object of comparison.   The heart is probably represented under this pleasing and
beautiful image in the Song of Solomon, where it is written, "My mother's children
were angry with me ; they made me the keeper of the vineyards; but mine own vineyard have I not kept."   God's ancient people are set forth under the same figure in the
eightieth psalm, to denote his care for and kindness to them: "Thou hast brought a
vine out of Egypt: thou hast cast out the heathen, and planted it."   And a few verses

afterward we have the touching prayer, "Return, we beseech thee, O God of Hosts: look down from heaven, and behold, and visit this vine, and the vineyard which thy right hand hath planted, and the branch which thou madest strong for thyself." In the fifth chapter of Isaiah we have the parable of a vineyard and its explanation, where we are expressly told that the house of Israel is God's vineyard; the men of Judah his pleasant plants; the grapes which he looked for, judgment and righteousness; the wild grapes produced, wickedness and oppression ; so that instead of honesty in the dealings of the people there was the cruelty of the oppressor, and instead of the strict administration of justice on the part of the magistrates there was the cry of the oppressed. Every reader of the New Testament is familiar with our Lord's representation of himself as the true Vine, of disciples as the branches, of his Father as the Husbandman, and union with himself as the secret of fruitfulness. The parable in the passage before us is recorded, with slight variation, by St. Matthew and St. Luke. This threefold occurrence of the same parable proves its importance, shows its instructiveness, claims our attention to it, and commands our interest in it.

II. God's CARE OF HIS CHURCH. 1. *The culture of the vine laborious.* The care necessary for the proper culture of a vineyard is surprising, and to those unacquainted with it almost incredible. It is so in the vineyards of the Rhine, for example, at the present day. As you pass along the "wide and winding" river, many a vine-clad hill presents itself to view. Vineyard rises above vineyard, and terrace above terrace, from the bottom to the top of the hill, in some instances to the height of a thousand feet. How beautiful they look! How pleasant to work among them and keep them! you are apt to suppose. If, however, you visit them and talk with the vine-dressers, you will find your supposition a grave mistake. The duty of the vine-dresser is no sinecure. His work is never over. It is continued throughout the year. Every season brings something for him to do. Planting, propping, pruning, plucking the useless leaves, weeding, hoeing, and gathering the vintage occupy all his time. From year in till year out he knows little or no relaxation; his care ceases not all the year round. How beautifully this illustrates God's care of and attention to his people! It was so also in ancient times. There is a fine didactic poem on husbandry by an old poet who flourished nearly two thousand years ago, and whose works are read at school and college still. He has left us a glowing and life-like description of the continuous toil and laborious industry of the Italian vine-dressers in his day. He there tells us that it was indispensable to plough the soil three or four times a year, to break the clods daily, to unload the branches, and thin the leaves. Even in winter the vine, after being bared of its leaves and fruit, has to be subjected to the pruning-knife, the ground to be dug, the lopped branches burnt, and the props brought into the house. Besides, twice in the year the luxuriant leaves, and twice the weeds and brambles, were to be removed. Further, it remained to cut the reeds and willows that grew on the river's bank, and prickly shrubs in the woods, to bind the vines withal and fence them. In addition to all this, the ripening grapes must needs be protected from hail, and rain, and rust, and accidents of the weather. No wonder, then, he adds, that the husbandman's care ran in a circle, nor ending with the closing year, extended to the coming season. So great is the attention in *general* needed by vineyards, whether in ancient or modern times; such and so great God's care for the vineyard of the Church. But particular instances are here enumerated. 2. *The planting.* He planted it. The vineyard *soil* needed to be the choicest and the best. Soil that would do very well for pasturage, or soil that might be quite suitable for tillage, would not answer for a vineyard. Nothing but soil of rich and generous mould would suit the planting of the vine. The *situation* required to be carefully selected. A good deal depended on the aspect, and it needed to be sheltered from the wintry wind, screened from the ungenial cold, and exposed as far as possible to the bright beams of a warm Southern sun, like the sunny slopes of Zion, the sides of Lebanon, or the vale of Eshcol. Hence the prophet says, "My well-beloved hath a vineyard on a very fruitful hill." It naturally followed that vineyards were the most valuable of all property, at least in land. So the Church of God is very precious in his sight. It is very costly, too, for he bought it with his blood; and hence the injunction, "to feed the Church of God, which he hath purchased with his own blood." It is a place distinguished for fruitfulness and enriched with blessings; a place of precious privileges, of numerous ordinances, of heavenly light, where the Sun of Righteousness sheds his brightest beams, and spiritual life is cherished; a place where the Word of truth is possessed, perused, and faithfully preached; where the gospel of his grace is proclaimed; where his Spirit is poured down; where gracious influences are at work and Divine power felt; where the Divine presence is promised and enjoyed; and where every promised blessing is sure to be bestowed and fully realized. The *plants,* moreover, are the most precious—even the best of their kind. Man, in his original state, was made but a little lower than the angels. God made man upright, and thus, when he proceeded from his hands, he was stamped with the Creator's image, possessed of uprightness, and invested with dominion. And man, even in his fallen state, possesses noble endowments and distinguished faculties. He has understanding capable of studying the works and ways of God, affections to love and prize him, a will that can be moved by motives, tender emotions, and far-reaching sympathies—high powers of head and heart. These powers, it is true, are all weakened and misdirected in consequence of sin. But oh! when they are quickened by the Spirit of God and influenced by his grace; in other words, when the sinner is united to the Saviour, when by faith he is engrafted into him and become a living branch of the living Vine, a fruitful branch of the true Vine, he is then a plant of the choicest kind, qualified for yielding spiritual fruit, and capable of showing forth the praises of the Creator. Then does he correspond and come up in some measure to his original condition as God himself describes it: "Yet I had planted thee a noble vine, wholly a right seed: how then art thou turned into the degenerate plant of a strange vine unto me?" 3. *The fencing.* He set an hedge about it. The people of Israel were hedged in, both politically and physically. The position of Palestine contributed to this separation of its inhabitants. On the north were the slopes of Lebanon, on the south the Idumæan desert, on the west the Great Sea, on the east the Jordan with its lakes, and Peræa beyond. But God's spiritual vineyard was his Church, as existing first among the Jewish people and then in Gentile lands. The direct reference is to the Jewish Church as established under Moses, Joshua, the judges, and the theocracy; the great fence that hedged it in was the Law. But we may go back yet further; for God set an hedge about his Church in Old Testament times, from the call of Abraham, by the covenant of circumcision made with that patriarch, and by the whole written Law, moral as well as ceremonial, given to his descendants. In this way he separated the vineyard of the Church from the wide and wild common of the world. The Law was "the middle wall of partition" between Jew and Gentile. But in Christian times, and among Gentile peoples also, the Church is fenced around. There is still a hedge between the communion of saints and the world of the ungodly. Profession of the doctrines which Christ and his apostles taught, and the practice of the duties they enjoined, compose that hedge. Faith in his promises and obedience to his precepts draw the line of demarcation broad and wide between them. The exercise of wholesome discipline keeps the hedge in order. And a Church that does not or cannot exercise this salutary check on its members, saying who are and who are not worthy of its membership, is so far forth powerless for good, or like salt that has lost its savour. The vineyard of which the Prophet Isaiah (v. 5) speaks had a double fence—both a hedge and a wall—as it is written, "I will take away the hedge thereof, . . . and break down the wall thereof." We have frequently seen two hedges round a garden—the outer one of thorn, the inner one of beech. Thus it is with the vineyard of the Lord. A visible profession of Church membership is the outer hedge; an interest in Christ is the inner one—and, it must be added, the essential one. All who have embraced the mercy of God in Christ Jesus are within the enclosure of the Church in the true sense; all who have not are aliens to the commonwealth of Israel. "As many as received him, to them gave he power to become the sons of God, even to them that believed on his name." These are safe within the hedge. "He that believeth not shall not see life, but the wrath of God abideth on him." All such are outside the hedge. 4. *Important practical question.* Inside this hedge or outside it? This is the question—the great question. What, then, is our position individually? Out of Christ, we are without God, for "no man cometh to the Father but by him;" and without hope, for the hope of the hypocrite will perish; and without happiness, the secret and source of which is to "delight one's self in God, and he gives thee thy heart's desire;" without life, for "this is life eternal, to know thee the only true God, and Jesus Christ, whom thou hast sent;" and without heaven, for Christ is the way thither, as well as the door of entrance. In Christ we are sheltered from the storm of coming wrath. The sunshine of the Divine favour rests on us; the fruit of the Spirit is borne by us. We can then say, "There is now no condemnation to them who are in Christ Jesus, who walk not after the flesh, but after the Spirit." There is the hedge of Divine providence about the Church, as we read, "In that day sing ye unto her, A vineyard of red wine. I the Lord do keep it; I will water it every moment: lest any hurt it, I will keep it night and day." We are invited to walk about Zion and consider her strong fortifications, counting her towers, contemplating her bulwarks, and considering her palaces, so as to convince ourselves that those defences, unscathed by the assaults of enemies in the past, will remain as impregnable for the future.

> "On the Rock of Ages founded,
>   What can shake thy sure repose?
> With salvation's walls surrounded,
>   Thou may'st smile at all thy foes."

5. *Gospel ordinances.* The wine-fat, or vat, was a large stone trough deposited in the ground, to receive the juice of the grape squeezed out in the winepress placed over it. The winepress thus consisted of two parts—a receiver for the grapes, and beneath that a receptacle for the expressed juice. The press above, or upper trough, in which the grapes were placed to be trodden out by human feet, amid songs and shouts of joy, was called by the Latins *torcular*; by the Greeks ληνός, the word used by St. Matthew; and by the Hebrews *gath*. Through a hole in the bottom of this the expressed juice flowed into the vat beneath, or lower trough, which the Romans called *lacus*; the Greeks ὑπολήνιον, the word used by St. Mark in the passage before us; and the Hebrews *yekev*, from a root meaning "to hollow out" or "deepen;" while both words occur together in the Prophet Joel (iii. 13), "The press (*gath*) is full, the vats (*yekavim*) overflow." The winepress and wine-vat were sometimes made out of one block, and communicated by an aperture; sometimes they were distinct stones connected by a tube. If, then, we are to follow out the allegory explaining its particular parts, we may understand by the winepress the ordinances of the gospel, namely, prayer, praise, the Word, and sacraments; though others understand thereby gospel fruits or graces, as charity, thanksgiving, and devotion flowing like wine through it. If, then, we understand by the winepress gospel ordinances, by the wine-vat we may understand the place where the grace conveyed through these ordinances is received and enjoyed. God has appointed certain means for the communication of wisdom, strength, consolation, and every needful gift and grace. These means are the winepress; and the place where these spiritual supplies are obtained and preserved is the wine-vat. Let us take as an example, and in order to illustrate our meaning, the sacrament of the Supper. The Saviour, when he made himself a sacrifice for sin, trod the winepress of God's wrath alone, while "of the people there was none with him." The sacrament of the Supper is a feast after and upon that sacrifice; the place where this feast is dispensed, and its benefits to our spiritual nourishment and growth in grace partaken of, is the wine-vat. The bread is a lively emblem of Christ's body, and a striking symbol of the hidden manna; the wine is a true token of his blood, and a sweet foretaste of that wine which we shall drink new in the kingdom of our Father; the table of the Lord, round which the faithful meet and share the feast, is symbolized by the wine-vat. In any case, even if we may not attach a specific meaning to each particular detail, these details imply generally God's care of and provision for his Church. 6. *Practical remarks.* Mark, then, the connection of the press and vat; they go together. So is it with the ordinances, and the place of their administration; the ordinances, and the benefits they convey; the ordinances, and the blessings God gives us to enjoy through them. If we would glorify God, it must be in the manner he has appointed; if we would enjoy him, it must be in the use of the means he has provided; if we would enjoy not only the communion of saints, but also the communications of Divine grace, we must not forsake the assembling of ourselves with the people of God; if we would promote at once the glory of God and the growth of grace in our own hearts, we must "remember the sabbath day to keep it holy," and the sanctuary to frequent it duly and devoutly. In a word, if we would be truly wise for both worlds, we shall ask wisdom of God, who "giveth to all men liberally, and upbraideth not," waiting at the posts of wisdom's

doors to hear what God the Lord will say to our souls. 7. *The tower*. This was a place of safety and strength for the watching and guarding of the vineyard, and for the protection of its fruits. The temple in the old economy was the tower, and the priests that lodged around might be regarded as acting the part of the watchmen. More usually, however, the prophets are spoken of as the watchmen. "I will stand upon my watch, and set me upon the tower, and will watch to see what he will say unto me, and what I shall answer when I am reproved." The faithful preachers of the gospel and pastors of the Christian Church are watchmen now, who watch as those who must give account; while to both teachers and taught, pastors and people, preachers and hearers, the words of the Lord, as addressed to the Prophet Ezekiel, while he sat by the river of Chebar, are applicable still. In that instructive passage we read, "Son of man, I have made thee a watchman unto the house of Israel: therefore hear the word at my mouth, and give them warning from me. When I say unto the wicked, Thou shalt surely die; and thou givest him not warning, nor speakest to warn the wicked from his wicked way, to save his life; the same wicked man shall die in his iniquity; but his blood will I require at thine hand. Yet if thou warn the wicked, and he turn not from his wickedness, nor from his wicked way, he shall die in his iniquity; but thou hast delivered thy soul." In consideration of all these careful arrangements, surely God might well say, as he did by the Prophet Isaiah, "What could have been done more to my vineyard, that I have not done in it?"

III. GOD'S EXPECTATIONS FROM THE VINEYARD OF THE CHURCH. 1. *He sends his servants to claim a portion of the fruit*. The parable shows in its immediate application the privileges of the Jews, their perversion and abuse of those privileges, and the consequent punishment. If, then, by the husbandmen we understand the ordinary ministers of the Jews' religion, as the priests and Levites; the servants sent were the extraordinary messengers, the prophets raised up on special occasions and for special purposes, and other eminent preachers of righteousness. The householder or owner claimed a portion of the produce. The rent was thus payed in part of the fruit; it was to be in kind, on the well-known *metayer* principle, long so prevalent and still practised in parts of Europe; it was to consist of grapes, not gold. The occupiers acknowledged the claim, but failed, or rather refused, to meet it, and were ruined in consequence. God expects fruit; why should he not? Who ever planted a vineyard that did not expect to eat of the fruit of it? Who, then, will venture to gainsay the justness of God's claims? He is no hard Master; he is no rack-rent Proprietor; he does not "reap where he has not sown, nor gather where he has not strawn;" he never requires impossibilities. 2. *Correspondence between the fruit of the vineyard and the owner's expectations*. The fruit of the spiritual vineyard should correspond with the expectations of the great proprietor in three respects. (1) In *quality* this correspondence should exist. He looks for grapes—good grapes off every vine which he has planted in his spiritual vineyard. There is heart-fruit, consisting of faith, hope, charity, purity, the thoughts being purified by the inspiration of the Spirit; there is the lip-fruit of prayer, praise, holy conversation, edifying discourse, and speech seasoned with salt; life-fruit follows, and is manifested in works of faith, labours of love, patience of hope, devotion of spirit, all holy living, and the necessary sequel in holy dying at the last. In a word, God looks for holiness in all his people. He looks for those blessed and beautiful fruits of which St. Paul writes to the Philippians, when, summing up the Christian graces, he says, "Finally, brethren, whatsoever things are true, whatsoever things are honourable, whatsoever things are just, whatsoever things are pure, whatsoever things are lovely, whatsoever things are of good report; if there be any virtue, and if there be any praise, think on [or take account of] these things." He looks for those excellences of character, conduct, and conversation which St. Peter recommends to the strangers scattered abroad, saying, "Giving all diligence, add to your faith virtue; and to virtue knowledge; and to knowledge temperance; and to temperance patience; and to patience godliness; and to godliness brotherly kindness; and to brotherly kindness charity. For if these things be in you, and abound, they make you that ye shall neither be barren nor unfruitful in the knowledge of our Lord Jesus Christ." God the Father had these fruits in view when he planted the vineyard, for he "predestinated us to be conformed to the image of his Son;" God the Son prepared for them when he gave up the ghost, for it was to "redeem us

from all iniquity, and purify unto himself a peculiar people, zealous of good works;"
God the Holy Spirit provided for them when he renewed us in the spirit of our
minds, making us new creatures in Christ Jesus, and so commenced our sanctification. He is waiting and willing to produce them; for "the fruit of the Spirit
is love, joy, peace, long-suffering, gentleness, goodness, faith, meekness, temperance." The gospel calls us to holiness, and when embraced in sincerity and truth,
produces it in increasing measure from day to day, leading us to the higher Christian
life; for "the grace of God that bringeth salvation hath appeared to all men, teaching
us that, denying ungodliness and worldly lusts, we should live soberly, righteously,
and godly, in this present world." (2) But the *quantity* of the fruit borne must be
directly proportionate to the grace bestowed. It must be in exact correspondence with
the talents God has given us, and the time those talents have been lent us; with the
mercies great and manifold which he has conferred upon us; with the privileges with
which we have been favoured, and the period of their possession; in a word, with all
the opportunities of whatever kind and advantages of whatever sort, which we have
been permitted to enjoy. With every talent God is pleased to give us he says,
"Occupy till I come." Every one of the blessings bestowed—and oh, how great the
number!—lays us under an additional obligation; every mercy imposes increased
responsibility. Is it health or wealth? is it influence or example? or any other
means of receiving good for ourselves, or imparting it to others? Whatever it is, it
adds to our accountability, and, if abused, it will be sure to augment our guilt, and in
the end aggravate our condemnation. 3. We are reminded, further, that the fruit must
be in *season*; for "at the season," that is, when the season for the fruit arrived, the
proprietor sent his servants for the stipulated portion. "When the time of the fruit
drew near," says St. Matthew; when sufficient time for growth and for reaching
maturity has been allowed, the time of fruit draws nigh. After opportunities of usefulness have been enjoyed, God comes to see how we have employed them. The
righteous man yieldeth the right fruit in right quantity, and at the right time. This
is his characteristic, as stated in the words of Scripture: "He shall be like a tree
planted by the rivers of water, that bringeth forth his fruit in his season." In the
natural world, every season of the year has fruit peculiar to itself. Spring has its
flowers, in addition to its buds and blossoms; summer has its plants, and tubers, and
waving fields of corn; autumn has its own abundant fruitfulness in golden grain,
matured fruits, and ripened grapes. So in the spiritual world and in the vineyard of
the Church; in a season of prosperity God expects gratitude as well as gladness; in a
season of adversity he expects patient resignation to his will; in a season of depression
and consequent privation, he expects dependence on his providence; in provocation he
expects meekness; in temptation, resistance by the help of God; in wintry days of
darkness, contentment with the Divine allotments; in seasons of sunshine, humility;
and in all seasons diligent seeking and faithful serving of God.

IV. GOD'S PUNISHMENT OF UNFAITHFULNESS. 1. *Shameful treatment of God's servants.* These wicked husbandmen went from bad to worse. They were determined
that God should get no fruit from his vineyard; and accordingly they maltreated, in
the most scandalous and barbarous manner, the servants sent by the proprietor to
demand his due portion of the produce. Their conduct shows a gradation of wickedness—they beat, they wound, they kill. The word ἐκεφαλαίωσαν, rendered "wounded in
the head," is peculiar, and for this, which appears to be its primary sense, there is no
classical parallel. Where it occurs, it is generally used in the secondary sense of bringing under one head or sum: hence it has been variously rendered in accordance with
this signification, some explaining it to reckon with one in a summary manner, paying
with blows instead of fruit; others to deal with one summarily; and others, again, to
complete and bring to a head their maltreatment; but the ordinary rendering of "wounding in the head" is confirmed by the Syriac and Vulgate, and is commonly accepted.
More important for us is the historical evidence which the Scriptures of the Old
Testament afford of this shameful treatment of God's servants. They were threatened
with death, thrown into dungeons, actually slain, stoned, sawn asunder, as passages
that readily suggest themselves to any careful reader of God's Word abundantly prove.
The special honour reserved for the Son marks his superior rank, and distinguishes him
from all others, whether designated servants or dignified with the name of sons of God.

He is the one Son—the well-beloved—claiming and entitled to peculiar reverence; the rightful Heir, too, of the inheritance. Thus, as we read in the beginning of the Epistle to the Hebrews, "God, having of old time spoken unto the fathers in the prophets by divers portions and in divers manners, hath at the end of these days spoken unto us in his Son, whom he appointed Heir of all things." The Son took upon him "the form of a servant" while sojourning in our world. 2. *A supplementary parable.* The parable of the vineyard and the wicked husbandmen, with all its fulness of details, omitted— necessarily omitted—one or rather two points, which are supplemented by a parabolic statement from the hundred and eighteenth psalm. Whereas the son and heir is left dead outside the vineyard, as Christ suffered, "without the gate," while the lord of the vineyard himself avenges his death, and punishes the husbandmen for their dia- bolical conduct; it was necessary to complete the picture by his revival and return to the place of dignity and power, as the Foundation and chief Corner-stone, upbearing and binding together the two walls of the sacred edifice. And not only so; it behoved to represent him as revenging in person his wrongs on those who slew him, according to the one parable, or who rejected him according to the other; while this feature is more fully exhibited by the first and third evangelists, who tell us that "whosoever shall fall on this stone"—that is, stumble and fall over this stumbling-stone of his humiliation—"shall be broken"—sorely bruised (συνθλασθήσεται)—and so receive great hurt and grief: "but on whomsoever it shall fall"—in wrath, because of their final impenitence—"it shall grind him to powder;" literally, *winnow* (λικμήσει) him, just as the stone cut out of the mountains without hands was seen in prophetic vision to smite and shatter the great world-image, and scatter its fragments like chaff before the winds of the winter. 3. *Improvement of the subject.* The primary reference is to the Jews as a Church and people. Their own conscience made application of it to them- selves; hence their indignation, but not their improvement. The transference of the vineyard was not exactly from the Jews to the Gentiles, but to the faithful who should be collected together out of both, and connected by the chief Corner-stone into one. (1) The first lesson taught us here is of a national character. The Jews had great privileges, but their misuse or abuse of those privileges subjected them at last to fear- ful retribution. God had shown much forbearance, sending servant after servant to call them to repentance and reformation, and last of all and greatest of all, his own Son; but in vain. They refused to return and repent, crowning their wickedness by crucifying the Son of God. At length the cup of their iniquity was full and overflowing; and, forty years after this climax of their enormities, Jerusalem was laid in ruins, the beautiful house in which their fathers worshipped reduced to ashes, and themselves scattered throughout the world. (2) We learn God's mode of dealing with Churches or nations that, like the Jews, are highly privileged, and have long enjoyed instructions and ordinances and spiritual benefits. As he continues blessing after blessing, so he sends call after call, and by his servants summons them to the improvement of those blessings. If they refuse compliance—if they neglect to use those blessings in his service and to his glory—ruin, and that without remedy, shall be, must be, the sad but sure result. The destiny of the Jewish Church was repeated to some extent in that of the Oriental Churches, and in that of the African Churches; and by all these cases the Churches of our own land and of every Christian people are solemnly warned against the misuse of mercies, and the abuse of privileges, and the just judgments of God with which apostate Churches and sinful nations are visited. (3) Individual units make up the aggregate of a nation or the membership of a Church, so in our individual capacity we add our quota to the general guilt on the one hand, or to the purity of a Church and the righteousness of a nation on the other. Therefore are we bound individually to serve God "in holiness and righteousness before him all the days of our life," and to intercede for the practice and prevalence of that righteousness in all others, which exalts a nation or a people, so that the mercies of God may be improved and his judg- ments averted. 4. *A practical and personal question.* Are those fruits which God, as we have seen, expects from us, ours? Are we duly meeting his claims upon us? Are we responding to them gratefully and faithfully? Have we, by the constraining mercies of God, and by the constraining love of Christ, and for the love of the Spirit, presented ourselves, body, soul, and spirit, "a living sacrifice, holy, acceptable unto God, which is our reasonable service"? Do we appreciate as we ought all God's care and kindness, our privileges and means of instruction and improvement? Or, like certain vines in the land of Palestine, which, as we read in Scripture, produced poisonous berries, are we bearing fruit of similar poisonous quality? It may be that, instead of grapes, good grapes and proper fruit, we may be bearing grapes—wild grapes, not only inferior in quality, but poisonous in their nature. Our lips, instead of being instruments of righteousness, may be polluted and polluting with falsehood and deceit and evil-speaking; with corrupt communication, levity, and profanity. Our life, instead of a living epistle, seen and legible to all, may be an exhibition of bitterness and wrath and anger; of envy, pride, injustice, and uncharitableness; of sensuality and sinfulness. Our heart, which is the fountain-head and source of all, may, by remaining unrenewed and unpurified, continue the wellspring of evil thoughts, vile affections, and corrupt desires. If this be the case with any of us—which may Heaven forfend!—how great must be the disappointment of the Lord of the vineyard! how base our ingratitude! how awful the doom! how swiftly and suddenly destruction may come! 5. *Fatal error.* Delay is not deliverance. Many flatter themselves, as Agag, that the bitterness of death is past, at the very moment that vengeance is on the road and ready to overtake them. Some regard warnings as words of course, and consequently worthless. Others, like the Jews of old, treat shamefully the messengers of Divine mercy; and neglect, or despise and make light of, or speak evil of, the ministers of religion, forgetting the fact that whoso despiseth the messenger despiseth the Master that sent him. Thank God but few reach this bad eminence in their enmity to God, and the things of God, and the servants of God! We may neglect ordinances and abuse privileges, but, in doing so, we treasure up for ourselves "wrath against the day of wrath and revelation of the righteous judgment of God;" we may despise the terrors of the Lord, and turn a deaf ear to the voice of warning; we may disappoint the reasonable expectations of ministers and members of the Church; we may defraud the great Proprietor of the fruits which his grace was calculated to produce, and which he had every reason to expect; and God may not take vengeance on our evil works speedily; yet that vengeance will be aggravated by delay, and more fearful when it comes. Those guilty of such sinful neglect and abuse of privileges shall in the day of Divine vengeance be swept as with the besom of destruction, or thrown as into a furnace seven times heated, and that for ever and ever. Let us beware of the progressive nature of sin; for if we forget instruction, that forgetfulness will cause us to neglect it; that neglect, again, will lead us to despise it; that contempt for instruction will beget dislike of our spiritual teachers who impart it; and this dislike will engender hatred of the truth in general; and the end, the fearful end, will be destruction irremediable and terrible from the presence of the Lord and the glory of his power. "And thou, Capernaum, which art exalted unto heaven, shalt be brought down to hell."—J. J. G.

Vers. 13—17. Parallel passages: Matt. xxii. 15—22; Luke xx. 20—36.—*Question of the tribute money.* I. A SNARE LAID. This tribute money (κῆνσος) was the poll or capitation tax payable to the Roman Government, from the time Judæa became subject to the Roman power. Judas of Galilee headed a revolt against this tax, but perished with his followers. If our Lord allowed the lawfulness of paying tribute to Cæsar, it would have compromised him with the Jewish nationalists, who would not have been slow to charge him with contempt of the Law of Moses for the words of Deut. xvii. 15, "Thou mayest not set a stranger over thee," were explained by them as forbidding the payment of tribute to a foreign power. If he acknowledged the unlawfulness of such payment, he came into direct collision with the Roman authorities. In the one case, he offended the Judæan patriots and his own Galilean followers; in the other, he incensed the Herodian royalists who acquiesced in Roman rule. On the one side, it was treachery to national and patriotic aspirations and Messianic prospects; on the other, it was treason against the Roman Cæsar and Pilate his governor. Such was the snare laid for him; such was the trap they set in order to catch him. Thus they thought to entangle him, rather, *ensnare* (παγιδεύσωσιν) him, in his talk, as a fowler ensnares a bird.

II. THE SUBTLETY WITH WHICH THE SNARE IS LAID. 1. They put the question in such a categorical form as seemed to them to necessitate a simple "yea" or "nay;" thus,

"Is it lawful to give tribute, or not? Shall we give, or shall we not give?" The double question is to emphasize their earnestness, and to invite a prompt reply, affirmative or negative; though the first question may refer to the lawfulness of the payment, and the second to its expediency or advisability. 2. The *motive* which actuated them to interrogate our Lord so peremptorily was most sinister and insidious. The evangelists, viewing their conduct from different standpoints, characterize it differently. This difference, which we discover by comparing the parallel passages, is most instructive. Their *conduct* in propounding this ensnaring interrogatory was wickedness (πονηρίαν), according to the first evangelist; it was craftiness (πανουργίαν), according to the third; while, according to the second, it was hypocrisy (ὑπόκρισιν). Their question had a close connection with and combined all these three elements; it was conceived in wickedness, cradled in craftiness, and cloaked by hypocrisy. Thus the interrogators acted as spies, or "liers in wait" (ἐγκαθέτους), as St. Luke calls them, while they feigned themselves just men. Our Lord tore off their mask, exposing them in their true colours, and addressing them in their real character, when, according to St. Matthew, he says, "Why tempt ye me, ye hypocrites?" 3. The *object* they had in view was to embroil the Saviour with the royalists, and so compass his destruction. For this purpose it is plain they desired a negative answer, as appears suggested by the words, "Thou regardest not the person of men," implying such fearlessness as would enable him to reject foreign authority as inconsistent with acknowledging God as their King. Their ulterior object, as stated by St. Luke, was "that they might take hold of his speech, so as to deliver him up to the power and to the authority of the governor;" in other words, to deliver him to the Roman power, rule, or magistracy (ἀρχῇ), and to the lawful authority or jurisdiction (ἐξουσία) of Pilate, the Roman procurator. 4. Necessity brings together strange companions. The Pharisees were as mean as they were unprincipled, and as untruthful as they were unprincipled and mean. They proved their want of principle by the unnatural coalition which they formed with the Herodians—the patriots so called who opposed foreign dominion with the elastic politicians who owned the Roman power; the foes with the friends of Cæsar; sticklers for the Law with the supporters of an authority deemed inimical to the Law. Their meanness was manifest in the fulsome flattery with which they addressed our Lord; while in their base untruthfulness they pretended to approach him with a quasi-case of conscience, though in reality they were carrying out the counsel for his destruction.

III. The Saviour's reply. Had he replied in the affirmative, he would have forfeited his popularity; had he answered in the negative, he would have forfeited his life. The latter was the consummation wished for by the members of this unholy alliance of superstition with political expediency. To give vividness to the transaction, our Lord ordered the production of a Roman penny, or *denarius,* a small silver coin of the value of sevenpence halfpenny, or eightpence halfpenny at most. On that coin was an image, the head of the then reigning sovereign, Tiberius, while round it ran the usual superscription or inscription, consisting of the name and titles of the emperor. Our Lord, as if in surprise, asks, half in irony and half in indignation, what all this meant, and whose it was? Their unavoidable answer was, "Cæsar's;" and this very answer broke the snare, and the bird escaped out of the net of the fowler. Then said our Lord—Give back (ἀπόδοτε) to Cæsar what belongs to him; pay back to Cæsar what you acknowledge to be his. The coinage proves the king, the currency affords evidence of his property; while, on the other hand, you render to God the things that are his.

IV. Important principle. This principle, so important and far-reaching, though plain enough in its general bearing, has been differently understood. Some have regarded the two parts of the answer as entirely distinct, as though belonging to different spheres, or placed on different planes, and so incapable of clashing or even coming in contact; as though he said, "Pay your taxes, and perform your religious duties, but keep the two things apart." More usually they are understood as two separate departments of human duty, coexisting and compatible; or as standing to each other in the relation of the part to the whole. According to the second of these three views, the payment of civil dues and the observance of religious duties stand side by side together, and as equally obligatory; that is, render to Cæsar, as civil ruler, the obedience that belongs to him, and to God, as spiritual Sovereign, the homage of the soul stamped with the Divine image, and therefore his due; or, in a more literal and narrow sense, according to some, pay the civil taxes to the government of Cæsar, and the *didrachma*, or temple-tribute, for the support of the sanctuary and service of God. We understand it in the larger sense of obedience to our earthly sovereign and duty to our heavenly King, as co-ordinate and coexistent, perfectly compatible but not competitive; or, according to the third view, the former may be regarded as part of the latter. This great principle, properly understood and acted on, would have prevented many an unseemly collision of Church and State, and many a sinful encroachment of one on the domain of the other. It would have prevented the papal power from trampling the crown of kings in the dust, as in the reign of John, and it would have prevented, on the other hand, the persecution of the Church by the State, as in the days of the Puritans. Our Lord intimated by his reply, that so long as the Jews were allowed to worship God according to his own appointment, and enjoyed the protection of the Roman power therein, they were under obligations to contribute to the taxes that supported that power. But these obligations to civil government were not to suspend, or set aside, or in any way interfere with the higher and holier obligations which they owed to God. Duty to God must be the regulating principle of duty to civil rulers; the latter is then part of, or rather part and parcel with, the former. Thus our Lord clearly indicated the respective provinces of civil rulers and of religious teachers—the relative positions of secular authority and spiritual power. Thus he solved the problem of two kings and two kingdoms in one realm; thus he taught obedience to civil governors in temporal things, while in spiritual their duty to God was paramount. No doubt many nice points may present themselves, and many delicate questions may arise in practically carrying out the principle stated; but we are not without light from other parts of Scripture to guide us in the application of this principle, even in cases of greatest difficulty.—J. J. G.

Vers. 18—27. Parallel passages: Matt. xxii. 23—33; Luke xx. 27—40.—*Question of the Sadducees touching the resurrection.* I. IMPORTANCE OF THE QUESTION. Though the question propounded in this section was proposed for a captious purpose, and in order to entangle, yet, divested of its technicalities, it is a most important one. There is no subject more closely connected with the immortal hopes of man than that to which the above section refers. The doctrine of the resurrection is implied, or directly inculcated, in several passages of the Old Testament. In the New, in which life and immortality are so clearly brought to light, we find many plain statements in regard to it. The whole subject is discussed at large, and fully elaborated in that magnificent chapter, the fifteenth of the First Epistle to the Corinthians, while our Lord, in the Scripture under consideration, puts the argument pithily and pointedly in reply to a question from the Sadducees.

II. AN ASSUMPTION. In clearing away the rubbish, with which they overlaid the difficulty whereby they thought to ensnare him, the Saviour charges them with ignoring the mighty power of God, who quickeneth the dead and calleth the things which be not as though they were. He taxes them with resting their reasoning on an unwarrantable assumption, to the effect that the condition of life in heaven would be the same as here on earth, while, on the contrary, the occupants of that spirit-world are as the angels of God. Having, moreover, affirmed their ignorance of those Scriptures which they themselves acknowledged, he proceeds to the proof of the doctrine impugned.

III. IMMORTALITY OF THE SOUL. By his quotation from the third chapter of Exodus, he establishes the immortality of the soul. God is the God of the living, for the relationship thus indicated is connected with the bestowal of benefits and blessings, while the dead are beyond the reach of these: but the passage quoted affirms God to be the God of Abraham, Isaac, and Jacob; therefore these patriarchal men, whose earthly tabernacles, long dissolved, had mouldered and mingled with kindred dust, still lived in some sense and state and place. Their souls lived in God's sight and in God's presence and to God's praise. The immortality of the soul is thus a clear enough conclusion, but the proof is not so plain with regard to the resurrection of the body; and yet this is the very point in dispute. It is a well-known fact that several of the heathen philosophers who believed in the immortality of the soul, seem never to have dreamt of the resurrection of the body. How, then does our Lord's plain proof of the former doctrine serve the purpose of establishing the latter? This is the difficulty of the passage. The following considerations will resolve it :—

IV. GROUND OF SADDUCEES' DENIAL OF THE RESURRECTION. The chief reason of the Sadducees denying the resurrection of the body was their disbelief in the immortality of the soul. They repudiated the last-named doctrine, and on this very ground rejected the former. They said the soul does not exist apart from, or after, the dissolution of the body. "They gainsay the duration of the soul" is the testimony of Josephus to their opinion on this point. From this they inferred that there is no likelihood of, nor need for, the body to be raised up, as, according to this erroneous opinion of theirs, there was no soul to reanimate, or reinhabit, or be reunited therewith. Our Lord meets inference with inference. Having proved, as we have seen, the immortality of the soul, he thus prepares the way for the corollary, that the body would be raised from the dust of death, and that soul and body would be then and for ever reunited. They insisted on the extinction of the soul at the death of the body, or its non-existence as distinct from that body, and so wished it to be inferred therefrom that the body would not be raised, and no reunion ever take place. The Saviour proves the distinct and undying existence of the soul, and leaves the Sadducees to infer the resurrection of the body and its reunion with that soul from which death had for a time separated it. In this way he opposed the inferential part of his argument to the inferential part of their doctrine, inasmuch as they did not, it would seem, employ expanded argument or developed reasoning. Having demolished the main pillar of their system, he left the frail fabric erected thereon to fall of itself. Our Lord's reasoning, though concise, was nevertheless conclusive.

V. CONFIRMATION. This view of the subject derives some confirmation from a custom of the ancient Egyptians. They embalmed the bodies of their dead, and so preserved them for centuries. Their object, as is with strong probability supposed, was that the mummy corpse might be prepared for the reception of the returning soul, and for reoccupancy by that former inhabitant. If such were their belief, it was doubtless a ray of light derived from revelation, but distorted as usual in such cases. While they anticipated the glorious fact of a reunion of soul and body, they added thereto the fancy that the same body, unaltered and unimproved, would be its receptacle. Revelation, however, confirms the one, but corrects the other; for these vile bodies shall be raised spiritual bodies, and fashioned like unto Christ's glorious body.

VI. OTHER EXPLANATIONS. Some, we are aware, understand by resurrection in this passage merely a renewal of life, restricting that life to the soul. In this way they remove to some extent the difficulty involved in the reasoning, but destroy at the same time the proper meaning of the word, as might easily be shown from other Scriptures. Paul, for example, speaks of the resurrection in the ordinary and usual sense when he asks, "How are the dead raised up? and with what *body* do they come?" Besides, it is to be observed that, in our Lord's quotation, God is not called the God of the souls of the patriarchs, but of their compound being, consisting of both soul and body. The reference to marriage in the verses preceding also points to the resurrection of the body as well as to the life of the soul. Life is thus implied in relation to both the constituent parts of man—present life for the soul, future life for the body. Others there are who, understanding the argument to relate exclusively to those who die the death of the righteous, elucidate it in this manner. The Scripture cited by our Lord, in which God declares himself the God of Abraham, Isaac, and Jacob, involves the Fathership of God and the sonship of believers, as appears from such Scripture statements as "I will be to him a God, and he shall be to me a son;" also, "I will be to you a Father, and ye shall be to me sons and daughters." Again, our adoption as children of God includes the redemption of the body, and consequent recovery from the power of the grave, as may be gathered from Rom. viii. 23, "We wait for the adoption, to wit, the redemption of the body." Now, though this explanation, it must be admitted, is plausible, yet it appears too restricted, and not quite in harmony with our Lord's own words in John v. 28, 29, "The hour is coming, in the which all that are in the graves shall hear his voice, and shall come forth; they that have done good, unto the resurrection of life; and they that have done evil, unto the resurrection of damnation."

VII. PRACTICAL OBSERVATIONS. 1. A few practical thoughts connect themselves with this subject. We learn hence the value of an accurate acquaintance with the

Scriptures of the Old as well as of the New Testament. Our Lord refuted his adversaries as he repelled Satan, by an appeal to the Law and to the testimony. He took every opportunity of putting honour on, and claiming respect for, the Divine Word. It is our safeguard against error. His quotation is from a portion of that Pentateuch which has in recent times been the object of repeated and insidious attacks. 2. We see how our Master meets his opponents on their own chosen ground, and reasons with them after their own favourite mode. They put their objections inferentially; our Lord, who always adapted his discourse, whether sermon, or parable, or argument, to his audience, adopts the selfsame method. The Sadducees believed, at least, the five books of Moses; he quotes from an early portion of those books. He denounced their error with mildness, and demonstrated it from the very Scriptures to the authority of which they themselves deferred. He took the ground from under their feet by hard arguments, not by hard words. Persuasiveness, not abusiveness, characterizes his reasoning. 8. Let us seek grace that we may appreciate as we ought the *comfort* of this doctrine. Our very dust is dear to God. The visible sky above us may pass away, but no particle of this dust shall perish. Let us realize the duty of seeking a part in the resurrection of the just. Let the doctrine have a practical effect upon our lives. With this prospect in view, "what manner of persons ought we to be in all holy conversation and godliness"?

> "Those bodies that corrupted fall
> Shall incorrupted rise,
> And mortal forms shall spring to life,
> Immortal in the skies."

Having this hope within us, let us purify ourselves, and by grace keep the bodily temple undefiled.—J. J. G.

Vers. 28—34. Parallel passage: Matt. xxii. 34—40.—*Question about the greatest commandment.* I. PUERILITIES OF THE PHARISEES. The Pharisees busied themselves about the letter of the Law, but had little practical acquaintance with its true spirit. The Jews generally divided the commandments of the Law into the preceptive and prohibitory—the "Do" and the "Do not;" nor was there anything amiss in this. But the Pharisees, we are told, counted the affirmative precepts, and found them as many as the members of the body; they counted the negative, and reckoned them equal in number to the days of the year, viz. three hundred and sixty-five; they then added them together, and found that the total made up the exact number of letters in the Decalogue. They also divided the commandments into great and small—the more important and the less important, or the heavy and the light; those of greater weight being such commandments as related to the sabbath, circumcision, sacrifice, fringes, and phylacteries. They did not stop with puerilities of this sort, but descended to trifling minutiæ, which we have neither time nor wish to record. Some of their distinctions were of a more mischievous kind, such as preferring the ceremonial to the moral Law, the oral to the written Law, and the trifles of the scribes to the teachings of the prophets. They also taught that obedience to certain commandments atoned for the neglect of others; in some measure like persons in much more recent times, who

> "Compound for sins they are inclined to.
> By damning those they have no mind to."

II. THE WHOLE DUTY OF MAN. Our Lord rebuked by his answer those miserable trivialities of the Pharisees, who seemed disposed to bring him into conflict with one or other of the contending parties, headed respectively by Hillel and Shammai. The subject of the question was one about which the schools of these great Jewish schoolmen differed. If he decided in favour of the one, he necessarily offended and lost in reputation as a public religious Teacher with the other; or perhaps they hoped to bring him into contradiction with an answer to the same question which he had sanctioned with his approval. Our Lord shoved aside their rabbinical quibbles, and passed by their hair-splittings and contendings about such petty trifles, to the neglect at once of the spirit and the really weightier matters of the Law. And as "whosoever shall keep the whole Law, and stumble in one point, he is become guilty of all," our Lord, instead of singling out or specifying any particular commandment of the Law, states two comprehensive precepts which embrace the whole Law; and not only so—he not only reduces the ten commandments of the Decalogue to these two precepts, but under- lying these two precepts is one single principle into which they are both capable of being resolved. He thus simplifies the statement of moral duty into a single principle, and that principle itself expressed in the one word "love;" for "love is the fulfilling of the Law."

III. THE SUPREMACY OF LOVE. It has been conjectured that our Lord, when quoting in reply the passage from Deut. vi. 4—9, one of the four Scriptures usually inscribed on the parchment slips of the *tephillin*, or phylacteries, and called *Shema*, "Hear," from beginning with this word, pointed to the lawyer's *tephillin*. This would add to the pictorial or graphic nature of the reply; but nothing could be added to the beauty of the words quoted. He cites the preface, teaching the unity of God in oppo- sition to polytheism, and then proclaims the love of God as the source, and love to man as similar and only second thereto. But *whence* comes this love? Not by nature, for by nature we are "hateful, and hating one another;" only, therefore, by the new birth, when we partake of a new nature; for "if any man be in Christ, he is a new creature, old things having passed away, and all things having become new." Once we love him who first loved us, we are in the proper position for loving our Father in heaven and our fellow-man on earth. The *manifestation* of this love to man is doing to others as we wish others to do to us, and this exercise of the so-called, and properly so-called, golden rule, is loving our fellow-man as a brother, and son of the same heavenly Father; while our love to that Father is supreme, influencing the affections of the heart, the faculties of the mind, the spiritual powers of the soul or life, and employing the whole strength of all and each of these. God is worthy of all this—worthy of our best affections, worthy of our earliest and strongest love. The practice of this principle would make this earth a paradise, restoring it to all the freshness and happiness of its first and early dawn; rather, would it make a heaven upon earth.—J. J. G.

Vers. 35—37. Parallel passages: Matt. xxii. 41—46; Luke xx. 41—44.—*The counter- question of our Lord.* I. QUESTION OF OUR LORD IN TURN. Our Lord had by this time been asked, and had triumphantly answered, the most perplexing, difficult, and delicate questions that the ingenuity of man could devise. His adversaries had been signally confuted, and covered with shame. These questions were five in all. One concerned his authority; another was political, about the tribute money; the third was doctrinal, about the resurrection; the fourth speculative, about the greatest commandment; and the fifth disciplinary, about the adulteress. By his more than masterly reply to the first, he defeated the Sanhedrim: by his reply to the second, he surprised and silenced the Phari- sees and Herodians; by his answer to the third, he confuted, if he did not convince, the sceptical Sadducees; by his reply to the fourth, he satisfied the Pharisaic scribe, learned in the Law; by his answer to the fifth, he settled, if not to the satisfaction of scribes and Pharisees, at least to their shame, the question of discipline. It is now time that, having passed this ordeal, he should retaliate.

II. OBJECT OF HIS COUNTER-QUESTION. Our Lord's design was not so much to show them their ignorance, and overwhelm them with confusion, as to instruct them with respect to the true character and person of the Christ. Their low views were to be elevated, their carnal notions were to be spiritualized, their blind eyes were to be enlightened. Their idea of the person of Messiah was that he would be just a man like themselves; of his position, that he would be a powerful temporal king; and of his reign, that it would extend over a great earthly kingdom. By his question he let light in upon their dark minds in reference to all these subjects. With the Scriptures in their hands, and all their trifling about the minute things concerning the letter, they had no right spiritual apprehension of their long-desired and much-respected Messiah. His question proves to them that Messiah was not only human, but Divine; not only David's Son, but David's Lord; that before his exaltation he must suffer humiliation. They expected a triumphant Messiah, but were not prepared for his lowly condition as a sufferer; they overleaped the cross, expecting all at once and from the first the crown. Crucifixion before glorification was what they could not understand; a spiritual kingdom of righteousness and peace and joy they would not understand, "their wish being father to their thoughts."

III. PRACTICAL USE OF THE QUESTION. "What think ye of Christ?" was his question, as recorded by St. Matthew. We repeat to ourselves and others the same question —What think we—"What think ye of Christ?" What think ye of his life—that sinless life, that surprising life, that life which believer and unbeliever alike so much admire, and even rival each other in lauding and extolling? What think ye of the events of that life—its purity and yet its suffering, its power and yet its sorrows? What think ye of his death—so wonderful in many ways, so singular in all its aspects, and so efficacious in all respects? What think ye of his resurrection? Are ye risen with him, to seek the things above? Do ye look to him as the firstfruits of a glorious harvest? and are ye seeking a part in the resurrection of the just? What think ye of his ascension? Are ye satisfied that he has ascended up on high, leading captivity captive, and having received gifts, even for rebellious men? And have ye shared in these gifts? What think ye of his intercession? Do ye feel that he is interceding for you, and are ye glad—right glad—of having an Advocate with the Father, even Jesus Christ the righteous? By your answers to such questions ye may judge your state, and entertain, we trust, "good hope through grace."—J. J. G.

Vers. 38—40. Parallel passages: Matt. xxiii. 13—39; Luke xx. 45—47.—*Warning against the scribes and Pharisees.* He warns his disciples against (1) their ambition, (2) against their avaricious greed, and (3) against their hypocrisy. We need daily to pray for preservation from all these.—J. J. G.

Vers. 41—44. Parallel passage: Luke xxi. 1—4.—*The widow's mite.* I. THE VALUE INDICATED. A mite (λεπτόν) was something very small; our word to represent it being from *minute*, through the French *mite*. The value of the two was three-fourths of an English farthing. But it was her all, and showed her singular self-denial. Accordingly, our Lord measured the merit of her liberality not by the amount she gave, but by the self-denial which the gift involved.

II. CHRIST SEES ALL THINGS. He saw this poor widow—what she gave and why she gave. He sees all we do and all we think, for he knows what is in man. He sees us to restrain the evil that we do, overrule it, and punish it; he sees us to approve of the good we do, encourage in the present time and recompense it in the time to come.

III. TRUE STANDARD OF LIBERALITY. Christ on this occasion did not overlook the large gifts of the rich; but they could spare these out of their abundance, without stinting themselves or really pitying the poor. He fixed attention on the widow's mite, for it was her all; and so she could ill spare it, and could only be considered as giving it from sympathy with and compassion on the poor. Three things are to be taken into account in our estimate of Christian liberality: (1) the *motive* of giving—it must be the glory of God and the good of man; (2) the *manner* of giving—not by constraint, but of a ready mind, and so God loves the cheerful giver; and (3) the *measure*, which should be just in proportion as God has prospered us.—J. J. G.

EXPOSITION.

CHAPTER XIII.

Ver. 1.—And as he went forth out of the temple, one of his disciples saith unto him, Master, behold, what manner of stones and what manner of buildings! This would be in the evening. According to St. Luke (xxi. 37), our Lord, during the early part of this week, passed his nights upon the Mount of Olives, taking his food at Bethany with Martha and Mary, and spending his days in the temple at Jerusalem, teaching the people. It is most probable that he left the temple by the golden gate on the east, from whence the view of the temple would be particularly striking. We learn from St. Matthew (xxiv.) that our Lord had just been predicting the fall of Jerusalem. It was, therefore, natural for the disciples to call his attention at that moment to the grandeur and beauty of the building and its surroundings. The temple at Jerusalem was one of the wonders of the world. Josephus says that it wanted nothing that the eye and the mind could admire. It shone with a fiery splendour; so that when the eye gazed upon it, it turned away as from the rays of the sun. The size of the foundation-stones was enormous. Josephus speaks of some of the stones as forty-five cubits in length, five in height, and six in breadth. One of the foundation-stones, measured in recent times, proved to be nearly twenty-four feet in length, by four feet in depth. But all this magnificence had no effect upon our Lord, who only repeated the sentence of its downfall.

Ver. 2.—**There shall not be left here one stone upon another, which shall not be thrown down.** The word (ὧδε) "here" is rightly inserted; and the prophecy is justified by scientific investigation. The expression is not hyperbolic. Modern investigation shows that the present wall has been rebuilt, probably on the foundation of the older one.

Ver. 3.—**And as he sat on the mount of Olives over against the temple, Peter and James and John and Andrew asked him privately, Tell us, when shall these things be?** St. Matthew and St. Luke only mention his disciples generally. St. Mark, going more into detail, gives the names of those who thus asked him; namely, Peter and James and John, already distinguished, and Andrew, who enjoyed the distinction of having been the first called. These men appear to have been our Lord's inner council; and they asked him (κατ' ἰδίαν) *privately*, or *separately*, not only from the multitude, but from the rest of the disciples. It was a dangerous thing to speak of the destruction of the temple, or even to inquire about such an event, for fear of the scribes and Pharisees. It was this accusation that led to the stoning of Stephen. It is evident from St. Matthew (xxiv. 3) that the disciples closely associated together the destruction of the temple and his final coming at the end of the world. They knew from our Lord's words that the destruction of Jerusalem was near at hand, and therefore they thought that the destruction of the world itself, and the day of judgment, were also near at hand. Hence their questions.

Vers. 5, 6.—**Take heed that no man lead you astray.** The Greek word is πλανήσῃ. Their first temptation would be of this kind—that many would come in Christ's name, saying, "I am he;" claiming, that is, the title which belonged to him alone. Such were Theudas (Acts v. 36) and Simon Magus (Acts viii. 10), who, according to Jerome, said, "Ego sum Sermo Dei, ego speciosus, ego Paracletus, ego omnipotens, ego omnia." Such were Menander and the Gnostics.

Ver. 7.—**Wars and rumours of wars.** "Rumours of wars" are mentioned, because they are often worse and more distressing than wars themselves; according to the saying, "Pejor est bello timor ipse belli." **Be not troubled**; be not troubled, that is, so as to let go your faith in me, through fear of the enemy, or through despair of any fruit of your apostolic labours; but persevere steadfastly to preach faith in me and in my gospel. **These things must needs come to pass; but the end is not yet.** There would be a succession of calamities, one leading on to another. But they must take courage, and prepare themselves for greater evils, not hoping for lasting peace on earth, but by patient endurance of evils here, reach onwards to a blessed and eternal rest in heaven. Our Lord, when his disciples asked him, as in one breath, about the destruction of their city, replied obscurely and ambiguously; mingling together the two events, in order that his disciples and the faithful through all times might be prepared, and never taken by surprise. Some of our Lord's predictions, however, clearly refer to the generation then living on the earth.

Ver. 10.—**And the gospel must first be preached unto all the nations.** St. Matthew (xxiv. 14) says it shall be preached "in the whole world, for a testimony unto all the nations" (ἐν ὅλῃ τῇ οἰκουμένῃ, εἰς μαρτύριον). This literally took place, as far as the inhabited world was concerned at that time, before the destruction of Jerusalem. St. Paul (Rom. x. 18) reminds us that "their sound is gone out into all lands, and their words unto the ends of the world;" and he tells the Colossians (i. 6) that the gospel was come unto them, and was bearing fruit and increasing in all the world. But even if we regard these expressions as somewhat hyperbolic, it is unquestionable that before the armies of Titus entered Jerusalem, the gospel had been published through the principal parts and provinces of the then inhabited world (οἰκουμένη). And it is certainly a wonderful fact that within fifty years after the death of Christ, Christian Churches had been planted in almost every district of the earth as then known to the Romans. But if we extend these prophetical sayings so as to reach onwards to the end of all things, we must then understand the expression, "all the nations," in its most unrestricted sense; so that the prophecy announces the universal proclamation of the gospel over the whole inhabited earth as an event which is to precede the time of the end. It is interesting to observe the difference in the amount of knowledge possessed by us of this earth and its population at the present time, as compared with the knowledge which men had of it at the time when our Lord delivered this prediction. It was not until the beginning of the sixteenth century, nearly fifteen hundred years after Christ, that Christopher Columbus and Amerigo Vespucci laid open that other hemisphere which takes its name from Amerigo; and there are few facts more interesting to a philosophic mind than the discovery of this new continent, now so important to us in England as the chief receptacle, together with Australia, of our redundant population. But this new world, as we call it, although there are material evidences that portions of it at least were occupied in very remote times by men of high civilization, was present to the mind of our Lord when he said that "the gospel must first be preached unto all the nations." So that the prophecy expands, as the ages roll onwards and the population of this earth increases; and it still demands its fulfilment, embracing the vast multitudes now dwelling on the face of the earth to the number of about 1,450,000,000. Such a consideration may well lead us to the inference that we are now approaching sensibly nearer to the end of the world. There are no other new worlds like America or Australia now to be discovered. The whole face of the earth is now laid open to us; and there is now hardly any part of the world which has not at some time or other received the message of salvation.

Ver. 11.—**And when they lead you to judgment, and deliver you up, be not anxious beforehand what ye shall speak.** Our Lord does not mean by this that they were not to premeditate a prudent and wise answer. But he means that they were not to be too anxious about it. In St. Luke (xxi. 15) he says, " I will give you a mouth and wisdom, which all your adversaries shall not be able to withstand or to gainsay." So here, **it is not ye that speak, but the Holy Ghost** who shall inspire you with wisdom and courage. The words "neither do ye premeditate" (μηδὲ μελετᾶτε) are omitted in the Revised Version, as not having sufficient authority.

Ver. 12.—Our Lord further warns his disciples that they would have to suffer persecution even from their own relations, their brethren, and their fathers, who, forgetful of natural affection, would persecute the faithful even unto death. It is related of Woodman, a martyr in Sussex, in Queen Mary's time, that he was betrayed and taken by his father and his brother, and that he comforted himself with the thought that this very text of Scripture was verified in him. Bede says that our Lord predicted these evils, in order that his disciples, by a knowledge of them beforehand, might be the better able to bear them when they came.

Ver. 13.—**And ye shall be hated of all men for my name's sake** (ὑπο πάντων). The faith

and preaching of a crucified Saviour was a new thing. Hence everywhere, the Jews, accustomed to their own Law, and the Gentiles, to their own idols, set themselves against the preachers of the gospel, and against those who were converted to it. "All men " means great numbers, perhaps the greater number. Just as, when we say, " The majority are doing anything," we say, in popular language, " Everybody does it." **But he that endureth to the end, the same shall be saved** (ὁ δὲ ὑπομείνας εἰς τέλος). What is "the end " here referred to? Not, I imagine, the end of the age, but the end of the moral probation of the individual. The Greek word for "endureth " is very significant; it implies "a bearing up, and persevering under great trials." It is not enough once and again or a third time to have overcome, but, in order to obtain the crown, it is necessary to endure and to conquer, even to the end. "Be thou faithful unto death, and I will give thee a crown of life." The crown of patience is perseverance.

Ver. 14.—**But when ye see the abomination of desolation standing where he ought not.** In the Authorized Version, after the word "desolation," the words "spoken of by Daniel the prophet," are introduced, but without sufficient authority. They were probably interpolated from St. Matthew, where there is abundant authority for them; and thus their omission by St. Mark does not affect the argument drawn from them in favour of the genuineness of the Book of Daniel, against those, whether in earlier or in later times, who reject this book, or ascribe it to some mere recent authorship. The "abomination of desolation " is a Hebrew idiom, meaning "the abomination that maketh desolate." St. Luke (xxi. 20) does not use the expression; it would have sounded strange to his Gentile readers. He says, "When ye see Jerusalem compassed with armies, then know that her desolation is at hand." This reference to the Roman armies by St. Luke has led some commentators to suppose that "the abomination of desolation " meant the Roman eagles. But this was a sign from without; whereas "the abomination of desolation " was a sign from within, connected with the ceasing of the daily sacrifice of the temple. It is alluded to by the Prophet Daniel in three places, namely, Dan. ix. 27; xi. 31; xii. 11. We must seek for its explanation in something within the temple, "standing in the holy place" (Matt. xxiv. 15)—some profanation of the temple, on account of which God's judgments would fall on Jerusalem. Now, Daniel's prophecy had already received one fulfilment (B.C. 168), when we read (1 Macc. i. 54) that they set up "the abomination of desolation upon the altar." This was when Antiochus Epiphanes set up the statue of Jupiter on the great altar of burnt sacrifice. But that "abomination of desolation" was the forerunner of another and a worse profanation yet to come, which our Lord, no doubt, had in his mind when he called the attention of his disciples to these predictions by Daniel. There is a remarkable passage in Josephus ('Wars of the Jews,' iv. 6), in which he refers to an ancient saying then current, that "Jerusalem would be taken, and the temple be destroyed, when it had been defiled by the hands of Jews themselves." Now, this literally took place. For while the Roman armies were investing Jerusalem, the Jews within the city were in fierce conflict amongst themselves. And it would seem most probable that our Lord had in his mind, in connection with Daniel's prophecy, more especially that at ix. 27, the irruption of the army of Zealots and Assassins into the temple, filling the holy place with the dead bodies of their own fellow-citizens. The Jews had invited these marauders to defend them against the army of the Romans; and they, by their outrages against God, were the special cause of the desolation of Jerusalem. Thus, while St. Luke points to the sign from without, namely, the Roman forces surrounding the city, St. Matthew and St. Mark refer to the more terrible sign from within, the "abomination of desolation"—the abomination that would fill up the measure of their iniquities, and cause the avenging power of Rome to come down upon them and crush them. It was after these two signs—the sign from within and the sign from without—that Jerusalem was laid prostrate. Therefore our Lord proceeds to warn both Jews and Christians alike, that when they saw these signs they should flee unto the mountains—not to the mountains of Judæa, for these were already occupied by the Roman army (Josephus; lib. iii. cap. xii.), but those further off, beyond Judæa. We know from Eusebius (iii. 15) that the Christians fled to Pella, on the other side of the Jordan. The Jews, on the other hand, as they saw the Roman army approaching nearer, betook themselves to Jerusalem, as to an asylum, thinking that there they would be under the special protection of Jehovah; but there, alas, they were imprisoned and slain.

Ver. 15.—Let him that is on the house-top (ἐπὶ τοῦ δώματος) not go down, nor enter in, to take anything out of his house. The roofs of the houses were flat, with frequently a little "dome" (δῶμα) in the centre. The people lived very much upon them; and the stairs were outside, so that a person wishing to enter the house must first descend by these outer stairs. The words, therefore, mean that he must flee suddenly, if he would save his life, even though he might lose his goods. He must escape, perhaps by crossing over the parapet of his own house-top, and so from house-top to house-top, until he could find a convenient point for flight into the hill country.

Ver. 16.—And let him that is in the field not return back to take his cloke (τὸ ἱμάτιον αὐτοῦ). This was the outer garment or pallium. They who worked in the field were accustomed to leave their cloak and their tunic at home; so that, half-stripped, they might be more free to labour. Therefore our Lord warns them that in this impending destruction, so suddenly would it come, they must be ready to fly just as they were. It was the direction given to Lot, "Escape for thy life; look not behind thee."

Ver. 17.—But woe unto them that are with child and to them that give suck in those days! Women in this condition would be specially objects of pity, for they would be more exposed to danger. The words, "Woe to them (οὐαὶ)!" are an exclamation of pity, as though it was said, "Alas! for them." Josephus (vii. 8) mentions that some mothers, constrained by hunger during the siege, devoured their own infants!

Ver. 18.—And pray ye that it be not in the winter. According to the best authorities, "your flight" (ἡ φυγὴ ὑμῶν) is omitted, but the meaning remains very much the same. St. Matthew (xxiv. 20) adds, "neither on a sabbath." But this would be comparatively of little interest to those to whom St. Mark was writing. Our Lord thus specifies the winter, because at that season, on account of the cold and snow, flight would be attended with special difficulty and hardship, and would be almost impossible for the aged and infirm.

Ver. 19.—For those days shall be tribulation, such as there hath not been the like from the beginning of the creation. These expressions are very remarkable. To begin with, the tribulation would be so unexampled and so severe that the days themselves would be called "tribulation." They would be known ever after as "the tribulation." There never had been anything like them, and there never would be again. Neither the Deluge, nor the destruction of the cities of the plain, nor the drowning of Pharaoh and his host in the Red Sea, nor the slaughter of the Canaanites, nor the destruction of Nineveh, or of Babylon, or of other great cities and nations, would be so violent and dreadful as the overthrow of Jerusalem by Titus. All this is confirmed by Josephus, who says, speaking of this overthrow, "I do not think that any state ever suffered such things, or any nation within the memory of man." St. Chrysostom assigns the cause of all this to the base and cruel treatment of the Son of God by the Jews. The destruction of their city and their temple, and their continued desolation afterwards, were the lessons by which the Jews were to be taught that the Christ had indeed come, and that this was the Christ whom they had crucified and slain.

Ver. 20.—**And except the Lord had shortened the days, no flesh would have been saved: but for the elect's sake, whom he chose, he shortened the days.** St. Matthew's record (xxiv. 22) differs from that of St. Mark in the omission of the words "the Lord," and the clause "whom he chose." If the time of the siege of Jerusalem had lasted much longer, not one of the nation could have survived; all would have perished by war, or famine, or pestilence. The Romans raged against the Jews as an obstinate and rebellious nation, and would have exterminated them. But "the Lord" shortened the time of this frightful catastrophe, for the elect's sake, that is, partly for the sake of the Christians who could not escape from Jerusalem, and partly for that of the Jews, who, subdued by this awful visitation, were converted to Christ or would hereafter be converted to him. We learn from hence how great is the love of God towards his elect, and his care for them. For their sakes he spared many Jews. For their sakes he created and preserves the whole world. Yea, for their sakes, Christ the eternal Son was made man, and became obedient unto death. "All things are yours, and ye are Christ's, and Christ is God's." It may be added that a number of providential circumstances combined to shorten these days of terror. Titus was himself disposed to clemency, and friendly towards Josephus. Moreover, he was attached to Bernice, a Jewess, the sister of Agrippa. All these and other circumstances conspired in the providence of God to "shorten the days."

Vers. 21, 22.—**And then if any man shall say unto you, Lo, here is the Christ; or, Lo, there, believe it not; for there shall arise false Christs and false prophets.** Josephus mentions one Simon of Gerasa, who, pretending to be a deliverer of the people from the Romans, gathered around him a crowd of followers, and gained admission into Jerusalem, and harassed the Jews. In like manner, Eleazar and John, leaders of the Zealots, gained admission into the holy place, under pretence of defending the city, but really that they might plunder it. But it seems as though our Lord here looked beyond the siege of Jerusalem to the end of the world; and he warns us that as the time of his second advent approaches,

deceivers will arise, to seduce, if it were possible, even the elect. The word "to seduce" (ἀποπλανᾶν) is more properly rendered, as in the Revised Version, to **lead astray.** Every age has produced its crop of such deceivers; and it may be expected that, as the time of the end draws nearer and nearer, their number will increase. Sometimes those idiosyncrasies in them which show themselves in lying wonders, are the result of self-delusion; but still oftener they are deliberate attempts made for the purpose of imposing on the unwary. Sometimes they are a combination of both. In the cases to which our Lord refers there is evidently an intention to lead astray, although it may have had its origin in self-deceit. In our day there is a sad tendency to lead men astray with regard to the great fundamental verities of Christianity. And the words of St. Jerome may well be remembered here: "If any would persuade you that Christ is to be found in the wilderness of unbelief or sceptical philosophy, or in the secret chambers of heresy, believe them not."

Ver. 23.—**But take ye heed** (ὑμεῖς δὲ βλέπετε). The "ye" is here emphatic. The disciples were around him, hanging upon his lips. But his admonition is meant for Christians everywhere, even to the end of the world.

Ver. 24.—**But in those days, after that tribulation, the sun shall be darkened, and the moon shall not give her light.** St. Matthew (xxiv. 29) has the word "immediately," before the words "after that tribulation." If this word "immediately" is to be understood literally, then the things spoken of subsequently must be understood in a figurative and spiritual sense. But it would seem more natural to understand "immediately" according to the reckoning of him with whom "a thousand years are as one day." Our Lord now passes away from the events connected with the overthrow of the Jewish polity, and proceeds to speak of things connected with the new dispensation. His mind is now turned to "the last time"—to the whole period between his first and his second advent. The things towards which he was now looking belonged, not to the end of the Jewish dispensation, but to the end of the present age and the present dispensation. Eighteen centuries have passed since the destruction of Jerusalem; and more years, it may be, will come and go before the end. Nevertheless, all this time, although it may seem long to us who are confined within the narrow limits of a short life, is nevertheless, when compared with the eternity of God, but as a moment. "The sun shall be darkened." The signs here enumerated are mentioned elsewhere as the signs that would appear before the second coming of Christ. (See Joel ii. 31 and Luke xxi. 25, 26.) St. Augustine (Ep. 80, ' Ad Hesychium') says, " The light of truth shall be obscured; because in the great tribulation that shall come on the world, many will fall from the faith, who had seemed to be bright and firm, like the sun and the stars." " And the moon," that is, the Church, " shall not give her light."

Ver. 25.—And the stars shall be falling from heaven (ἔσονται ἐκ τοῦ οὐρανοῦ πίπτοντες), and the powers that are in the heavens shall be shaken. In the great events of the creation recorded in Gen. i. the sun and the moon and the stars did not show their light until that period which is called the fourth day. So in the end of the world, the sun and the moon and the stars are represented as withdrawing their light, perhaps figuratively, but perhaps also literally, in the course of some of the unknown physical changes which shall accompany the winding up of the present dispensation. To this agree the next words, " the powers that are in the heavens shall be shaken." The powers may here mean those great unseen forces of nature by which the universe is now held in equipoise. When the Creator wills it, these powers shall be shaken. (See Job xxvi. 11, " The pillars of heaven tremble and are astonished at his reproof;" see also Isa. xxxiv. 4, " And all the host of heaven shall be dissolved, and the heavens shall be rolled together as a scroll.") As the end of the world approaches, the elements will quiver and tremble.

Ver. 26.—And then shall they see the Son of man coming in clouds with great power and glory. St. Matthew (xxiv. 30) introduces here the words, " And then shall appear the sign of the Son of man in heaven." Many of the Fathers, as St. Chrysostom, Jerome, Bede, and others, think that this sign will be the cross. Josephus (v. 3) says that shortly before the destruction of Jerusalem, a portent like a sword, glittering as a star, appeared in the heavens. But surely the sign of the Son of man at the end of the world will be the Son of man himself coming in clouds. The clouds, covering the troubled heaven and now illuminated by the brightness of his coming, will constitute " the sublime drapery of his presence " (Dr. Morison).

Ver. 27.—And then shall he send forth the angels. This represents the great harvest at the end of the world, when the angel-reapers shall be sent forth to separate the wicked from the just. The elect will be gathered from the four winds (ἐκ τῶν τεσσάρων ἀνέμων); literally, out of the four winds—the winds representing figuratively

every corner of the world; or, from the uttermost part of the earth to the uttermost part of heaven. At its extremities, in the horizon, there appears to be the end alike of earth and of heaven, as though earth and heaven joined, and the heaven terminated by melting into the earth and becoming one with it. The expression simply means, " from horizon to horizon," or from every part of the earth.

Vers. 28, 29.—Now from the fig tree learn her parable; that is, her own particular teaching. Our Lord makes frequent mention and use of the fig tree, as we have seen already. It is probable that a fig tree may have been near to them. When her branch is now become tender, and putteth forth its leaves, ye know that the summer is nigh. The branch (κλάδος) would be the young shoot, now become tender under the quickening influences of the spring; and this was an evident sign that the summer was at hand. The Asiatic fig tree requires a considerable amount of warmth to enable it to put forth leaves and fruit. Its rich flavour requires a summer heat to mature it. Aristotle says that the fig is the choice food of bees, from which they make their richest honey. Then the fig tree does not flower after the ordinary manner; but produces flower and fruit at once from the tree, and rapidly matures the fruit. The lesson, therefore, from the fig tree is this—the speed with which she ripens her fruit when she feels the warmth of summer. In like manner, as soon as the disciples perceived the signs of Christ's coming, they were to learn that he was close at hand, as certainly as the ripening fruit of the fig tree showed that summer was at hand.

Ver. 30.—This generation shall not pass away, until all these things be accomplished. This is one of those prophecies which admit of a growing fulfilment. If the word " generation " (γενεὰ) be understood (as it may undoubtedly be understood) to mean the sum total of those living at any time on the earth, the prediction would hold true as far as the destruction of Jerusalem was concerned. The destruction of Jerusalem took place within the limits of the generation living in our Lord's time; and there might be some of those whom he was then addressing who would live to see the event. His prediction amounted, in fact, to this, that the destruction of Jerusalem would take place within forty years of the time when he was speaking. But it may have a wider meaning. It may mean the Jewish people. Their city would be destroyed—their power overthrown. They would be " peeled and scattered." But they would still remain a distinct and separate nation to the end of the world. And there are other prophecies which show that with their national conversion to Christianity will be associated all that is most glorious in the future Church of God.

Ver. 31.—**Heaven and earth shall pass away: but my words shall not pass away.** Here is a distinct prediction that the present structure of the universe will pass away; that is, that it will be changed, that it will perish, as far as its present state and condition are concerned; but only that it may be refashioned in a more beautiful form. "We look for new heavens and a new earth, wherein dwelleth righteousness" (2 Pet. iii. 13). With this declaration of our blessed Lord all the discoveries of science coincide. Astronomy and geology alike concur in the conclusion that the whole system of the universe is moving onwards to its change. Our blessed Lord did but affirm that which is demonstrated by science. *But my words shall not pass away*; not merely the words which with his full self-consciousness he had just uttered respecting Jerusalem, but all his other words—all the revelation of God, all the words of him who is the Truth.

Ver. 32.—**But of that day or that hour knoweth no one, not even the angels in heaven, neither the Son, but the Father.** He who from all eternity has decreed the time when this day is to come, is pleased to hide it in the hidden depths of his own counsels. But the eternal Son, and the Holy Spirit, both alike one with the Father, are of his counsels. They are not excluded from this knowledge; they, equally with the Father, know the day and the hour of the end, since they are of the same substance, power, and majesty. Why, then, does St. Mark here add, "neither the Son"? The answer is surely to be found in the great truth of the hypostatic union. The eternal Son, as God, by his omniscience, and as man, by knowledge imparted to him, knows perfectly the day and the hour of the future judgment. But Christ as man, and as the Messenger from God to men, did not so know it as to be able to reveal it to men. The ambassador, if he is asked concerning the secret counsels of his sovereign, may truly answer that he knows them not so as to communicate them to others. For as an ambassador he only communicates those things which are committed to him by his sovereign to deliver, and not those things which he is bidden to keep secret.

Vers. 33—37.—These exhortations, which gather up in a succinct form the practical bearing of the parallel passages and parables in St. Matthew, must not be understood as implying that our Lord's coming in judgment would be during the lifetime of his disciples. The preceding words would teach them plainly enough that the actual time of this coming was hidden from them. But the intention was that, while by the certainty of the event their faith and hope would be quickened, by the uncertainty of the time they might be left in a continual state of watchfulness and prayer. According to the Jewish reckoning, there were only three watches—namely, the first watch, from sunset to 10 p.m.; the second watch, from 10 p.m. to 2 a.m.; and the third watch, from 2 a.m. to sunrise. But after the establishment of the Roman power in Judæa, these watches were divided into four; and were either described as the first, second, third, and fourth respectively; or, as here, by the terms **even**, beginning at six and ending at nine; **midnight**, ending at twelve; **cockcrowing**, ending at three; and **morning**, ending at six.

HOMILETICS.

Vers. 1, 2.—*The downfall of the temple.* Our Lord's ministry in the temple was now over. Within those precincts he had taught the teachable, he had rebuked the selfish and profane, he had received the homage of the children, he had healed the afflicted, and he had denounced and warned the unfaithful and the hypocritical. How strange the contrast between the early days, when Jesus had taken his place in the midst of the rabbis, "both hearing them, and asking them questions," and these later days, when the same edifice witnessed his keen and truceless conflicts with the leaders of the nation, whose errors he exposed and whose vengeance he incurred! It was as Jesus left the gorgeous and consecrated building that his disciples, with national pride and affection, pointed out to his eyes the magnificence of the temple, the stupendous stones of which it was composed, and the costly gifts with which it was adorned. Upon this suggestion, Jesus uttered the prediction, which he could not have uttered without emotions of disappointment and distress, "Seest thou these great buildings? there shall not be left here one stone upon another, which shall not be thrown down."

I. Nothing earthly and human, however stately and sacred, is imperishable.

It was, no doubt, a splendid spectacle to which his disciples directed the gaze of Jesus. "They stopped to cast upon it one last lingering gaze, and one of them was eager to call his attention to its goodly stones and splendid offerings—those nine gates overlaid with gold and silver, and the one of solid Corinthian brass yet more precious; those graceful and towering porches; those bevelled blocks of marble, forty cubits long and ten cubits high, testifying to the toil and munificence of so many generations; those double cloisters and stately pillars; that lavish adornment of sculpture and arabesque; those alternate blocks of red and white marble, recalling the crest and hollow of the sea-waves; those vast clusters of golden grapes, each cluster as large as a man, which twined their splendid luxuriance over the golden doors. They would have him gaze with them on the rising terraces of courts—the court of the Gentiles, with its monolithic columns and rich mosaic; above this, the flight of fourteen steps which led to the court of the women; then the flight of fifteen steps which led up to the court of the priests; then, once more, the twelve steps which led to the final platform, crowned by the actual holy, and holy of holies, which the rabbis fondly compared for its shape to a couchant lion, and which, with its marble whiteness and gilded roofs, looked like a glorious mountain whose snowy summit was gilded by the sun" (Farrar). Majestic, however, as was the edifice, sacred as were its purposes, ennobling as were its associations, the temple at Jerusalem was not indestructible. All things finding their foundation upon this changing earth, all things reared and fashioned by human hands, are transitory and perishing. Nothing continueth in one stay. "The solemn temples," like "the great globe itself," are destined to decay and destruction. The material perishes, and that which is spiritual alone abides.

II. AN UNFAITHFUL NATION'S GLORY IS, IN THE PROVIDENCE OF GOD, MADE THE SYMBOL OF ITS SHAME. There was nothing which the Jews so valued and reverenced as their temple and all the paraphernalia of the temple-worship. The national life seemed to flow from that sacred spot as from a beating heart. Not only was it, in its situation, its structure, its services, priesthoods, and sacrifices, itself most majestic and imposing; but to the Hebrew mind it was the expression of the peculiar interest and favour of the Supreme. How could the Israelite think, without a shudder of horror and dismay, of the time when the noble building should be laid in the dust; when the chants should be silenced, the altars be overturned, the priests be slain, and the services and offerings be no more? Yet this was the doom which the last and greatest Prophet now foretold—a doom which they might have averted by timely repentance and by cordial faith, but which their rejection of the Christ of God made certain and irrevocable. Thus was Israel smitten in the most vulnerable, the most sensitive point; thus was the rule of the righteous Lord awfully and sublimely vindicated; thus was a lesson of Divine government and human subjection thereto published for the benefit of all generations to come.

III. ALL THAT IS MATERIAL IN RELIGION IS DESTINED TO VANISH AND DISAPPEAR. The temple at Jerusalem was the temple of the Lord; yet it served a temporary purpose, and when this purpose was accomplished it was superseded by the temple of the Lord's Body, and by the imperishable temple constituted by consecrated spiritual natures, and inhabited by the Holy Spirit of God. Human nature is such that men are prone to lay stress upon the outward, the visible, the tangible, the material. Even the truly religious are in danger of regarding the vestment of religion rather than the form it clothes, of hallowing places, observances, offices, and institutions. But Christ's whole teaching is a protest against this natural error and folly. The temple of Jerusalem disappeared; but its disappearance, so far from ruining the prospects and crippling the power of religion, was, in reality, the occasion of placing religion upon a sounder basis, and giving to religion a world-wide and an everlasting sway. Let not men cling too closely to the form; it is the spirit which quickeneth; it is the spirit which endures.

IV. SPIRITUAL TEMPLES ALONE ENDURE FOR EVER. Even the destruction of Jerusalem and its sacred buildings did not involve a universal ruin. What was good in Judaism, what was vital and hopeful in Israel, still survived. There were truths which outlasted the forms in which they had been embodied. There were pure and faithful souls which outlived the institutions amidst which and by means of which they had been called to virtue, to piety, to God. A new Israel arose, as it were, out of the ashes of the old. A temple statelier and sublimer, based upon a more enduring foundation, and rising to loftier spiritual heights, sprang into glorious being, as the armies of Titus levelled the glory of Moriah with the ground. The living stones of which this heaven-born fabric is composed can never crumble, and the services of this sanctuary shall never cease. Time and space are spurned; earthly forces are powerless; this temple groweth "an holy temple unto the Lord." It is imperishable, because it is spiritual; it is eternal, because it is Divine.

Vers. 3—13.—*The witness of the persecuted.* It was natural enough that the disciples, when the Lord foretold the destruction of the temple, should wish to know *when* an event so stupendous and awful should occur. On their way to Bethany at eventide, the little party, composed of Jesus and his four most intimate friends, paused upon the crown of Olivet, and looked back upon the glorious but guilty city, and upon that edifice which was its proudest ornament and boast. The anxious, awed disciples took this opportunity of asking at what time the disaster foretold by the Lord should take place, and by what signs they might be led to expect its approach. Jesus did not state the exact date of the impending catastrophe, but he did mention certain signs by which his disciples might be forewarned; and he took occasion to forearm them against the troubles which were at hand. His words may not have gratified their curiosity, but they must have established their confidence in their Master, and they must have prepared them for the tribulation and the trial now so near. The great lesson is that Jesus would have his people prepared, especially in times and amid circumstances of affliction and probation, to bear a firm and faithful witness to himself. Our Lord, in this language, enjoins upon his disciples—

I. FIDELITY AMID TEMPTATION AND APOSTASY. Days of trial were at hand; impostors should appear, professing that the Messiah had only now arrived; and by such deceits and pretences many should be led astray from their allegiance to Jesus. Then should the faithfulness of the disciples be tested. It is always so. Rivals come forward at all periods in history, asserting claims which they cannot substantiate, but by which they impose upon the excitable and unstable. Teachers, leaders, systems, philosophies, are ever seeking to displace the Divine Christ from the throne of the human heart, of human society. Let every Christian, when exposed to such assaults, when staggered by the success with which these are too often directed against the professed followers of Jesus, be upon his guard, and listen to the voice of the rightful and authoritative Lord sounding across the ages, "Let no man lead *you* astray!"

II. PEACE OF MIND AMID WARS AND CALAMITIES. The troubles and conflicts which befell the nations during the period which elapsed between the crucifixion of Christ and the fall of Jerusalem, are well known from the records of history. It could have been no easy thing for the Christians to have preserved a quiet mind amidst such constant alarms; nor can we suppose that our Lord intended to forbid or blame the natural and proper sympathy and solicitude which such circumstances must have induced. But he warned them that these events must precede the end, and must not be allowed to fill the mind with dismay, to weaken faith in Divine providence, or to deter from the fulfilment of an appointed ministry. In every age there occur events which, taken and considered alone, might appal the stoutest, bravest heart. But it is for the follower of Christ to bear in mind that light and darkness will contend until the victory of the Redeemer is complete, that the Lord reigneth, and that the convulsions of the nations are the birth-throes of the kingdom of the Christ. It is he who admonishes us, "Be not troubled!"

III. STEADFASTNESS AMID THE HOSTILITY OF FOES. The first followers of Christ were forewarned that they should incur the enmity of authorities, both civil and ecclesiastical. Before councils and in synagogues, at the bar of governors and in the presence of kings, they should be arraigned upon charges true or false, but always with a temper of enmity and with purposes of malice. How were they to demean themselves in circumstances of peril? They were to remember that they were but treated as their Master had been treated before them, that they were honoured by being summoned to act as his *witnesses*, that they were the spokesmen, so to speak, of the very Spirit of God. Amidst trials so severe, they were directed to take heed how they comported themselves—never to yield to fear, to dismiss all anxiety, and to trust to a heavenly inspiration for their defence. And there is no age in which servants of Christ are not exposed to some of the attacks of the foe, and in which there is not need for watchfulness, fortitude, and courage. Let the persecuted remember that the eye of the Divine Lord is upon them; and let them bear themselves as those who would honour their Leader and maintain his cause—quit them like men, and be strong.

IV. ENDURANCE AMID THE TREACHERY AND DESERTION OF FRIENDS. The great Prophet foretold that discords should reveal themselves among families and social communities; that one should rise up against another. In this way was fulfilled his saying, "I am not come to send peace, but a sword." To most hearts, treason within the camp is more painful and more trying than hostility without. Yet even against this our Lord would have us proof. It is a trial to which most faithful and consistent servants of the Lord Jesus are at some time exposed; it is a trial which shakes the faith and damps the zeal of not a few. Christ calls his people, when so tried, to exercise the grace of perseverance. Whoever forsake Jesus, let their desertion only drive us closer to him we love!

V. NOTWITHSTANDING OPPOSITION, THE GOSPEL MUST BE PREACHED. It is not enough to be steadfast ourselves; we have to think of and to care for others. The glad tidings the followers of Jesus have themselves freely received, it is for them freely to communicate to their neighbours. How devotedly and valiantly the first disciples fulfilled this trust we well know. Not only the twelve, but even more notably others who were raised up in the first age, preached the gospel to all nations whom they were able by any toil and hardship to reach. The light streamed upon many a dark, benighted land, and brought hope and peace, joy and life, to many a wretched heart. The labour of the apostles and their companions was not in vain in the Lord. Far from being deterred by opposition, this seemed to act as a stimulus to new exertions and to new daring. Nor is this function of the Church peculiar to the first age. So long as there are nations unvisited by the news of salvation, so long is there a summons to engage in missionary enterprise. If this can only be done in certain cases at the risk of safety, liberty, and life, so much the more do present circumstances correspond with the predictions of our Lord. "The more danger, the more honour." There is a crown to be gained by following Christ and his apostles in the perils of the holy war.

VI. PATIENCE UNTO SALVATION. It is well known that, whilst multitudes of Jews perished in the siege and the destruction of Jerusalem, the Christians escaped. Faithful to the instructions of their Lord, they were delivered from the ruin and the death which were the fate of their fellow-countrymen. Enduring in constancy and obedience to the end, they were saved. And their exemption from disaster and death was a symbol of the salvation of all those who retain their faith and allegiance amidst the temptations and the trials of this earthly life. Endure! endure unto the end! and the unfailing promise of your Divine Lord shall be fulfilled in your experience. You shall be *saved!*

Vers. 14—23.—*Warnings.* Very clearly did our Lord foresee, and very plainly did he foretell, the consequences which the Jews were bringing upon themselves by their rejection of God's Messiah. The language here recorded is in itself sufficient to convince a candid mind of the justice of the claims of the Lord Jesus to be the Prophet and the Son of the Most High. He sets us an example here of the propriety of uttering truthful warnings, even though they may be painful to the speaker and unwelcome to the hearer.

I. AFFLICTIONS ARE FORETOLD. The severity and variety of these afflictions render this prediction one of the most awful to be met with in the whole compass of Scripture. 1. *National disaster.* It was upon the whole nation, and especially upon the inhabitants of Jerusalem, the upper and ruling classes, that the retribution fell. 2. *Temple desecration.* This is probably what is designated "the abomination of desolation." The fanatical pollution of the temple by the Zealots was doubtless one of the most distressing accompaniments of the awful siege. 3. *Religious imposture.* In times of general excitement, enthusiastic pretenders are sure to make their appearance. It was so during the uttermost calamity of Israel. And there is no age when the warnings of vers. 21, 22, are not timely and appropriate. 4. *Individual sufferings.* Several circumstances here predicted, especially the distress in which miserable mothers should be involved (ver. 17), serve to deepen and darken the tone of this picture of calamity.

II. COUNSELS ARE IMPARTED. Christ was not a mere Prophet of evil. He exhibited the approaching dangers, but he provided for the safety and deliverance of those who, amidst general unfaithfulness, should be faithful to him. 1. He directed flight from the scene of distress. As Noah had been sent into the ark, as Lot had been hurried out of Sodom, so the primitive Christians were directed, when Jerusalem should be besieged, to forsake the guilty city and to take refuge in the mountains. There are times when flight is prudence, when life may be preserved for future service. 2. He advised disregard of impostors. To hold to Christ is a sufficient motive for rejecting antichrist. It is condemnation enough of any pretender that he professes to be what we know the Son of God alone can be. 3. He counselled general preparation and watchfulness. "Take ye heed!" Christians are to use their own powers of observation, to exercise vigilance, to meet all circumstances with preparation and discretion. No piety, no attachment to the Saviour, can absolve us from the duty of using our own faculties, of being upon the alert. "Watch and pray!" These are admonitions which are never obsolete; for the need of them is never, whilst we are upon earth, left behind.

Vers. 24—32.—*The second coming.* It is very difficult exactly to discriminate between some words of Christ which refer to the destruction of Jerusalem, and others which refer to our Lord's coming to judge all mankind. There seems to be a designed blending of the references to these events. We are thus taught to remember that we are called to be as men that wait for their Lord.

I. THE CERTAINTY OF CHRIST'S COMING. If his words are to be accepted, this great event of the future is not to be denied or questioned. In the fulfilment of the special prediction regarding the downfall of Jerusalem in the lifetime of the generation then living, we have the pledge of the ultimate accomplishment of the larger prophecy. At his trial Jesus repeated the assurance; and his inspired apostles have foretold that he shall come again the " second time without sin unto salvation."

II. THE UNCERTAINTY OF THE TIME OF CHRIST'S COMING. The words in ver. 32 are very distinct. The date of our Lord's return is known only to the Father. If neither the angels nor the Son himself could communicate this knowledge, how ridiculous and presumptuous is the conduct of those who, treating the Scriptures as a riddle, profess to have discovered the secret, and put forth their own fancies and follies as the declarations of the oracles of God! It is wisely hidden from us, and we show our wisdom by contented acquiescence in ignorance.

III. THE SIGNS OF CHRIST'S COMING. Changes on earth and in heaven are indications of the approaching day. As the leaves of the fig tree tell that summer is nigh, so events will occur which to the understanding mind will herald the Lord's return. Yet even these events do not tell us *when* our Saviour shall appear; but, since they remind us that he is at hand, they answer the purpose, for they put us upon our guard, and admonish us to be prepared.

IV. THE PREPARATION FOR CHRIST'S COMING. 1. Heedfulness and observation. 2. Watchfulness. 3. Prayer.

Vers. 33—37.—" *Watch!*" There can be no doubt as to the impression made by these and similar instructions and admonitions, uttered by the Lord Jesus towards the close of his ministry. It was understood by all his disciples that the Master, in leaving the world, retained his hold upon the world's heart and conscience. It was currently believed in the early Church, as it has been believed ever since by all Christians, that the Lord will come again, and will take account of his servants, and especially will inquire into the way in which they have acted as his representatives and ministers among men. Hence the stress which has always been laid upon the duty to *watch.* The apostles not only obeyed, they repeated the commandment of their Lord. Peter admonished his readers, " Be ye therefore sober, and *watch* unto prayer;" John said, " Blessed is he that *watcheth* ;" and Paul exhorted thus, " *Watch* ye, stand fast in your faith, be strong!" The very names which the early Christians gave to themselves and their children may be taken as an indication of the prevailing tone of feeling.

Gregory among the Greeks, and Vigilantius among the Latins, both signify simply "The Watcher."

I. WATCH! FOR THIS IS THE CHARGE OF CHRIST IN THE PAST. 1. We are to consider *from whom* this charge proceeds. It is the word of the All-wise, and of One of unique authority. Coming from Christ, this is not counsel, it is command. The general has the right to station a guard, a sentry, and to expect vigilance and fidelity. 2. The *occasion* of the charge gives it a peculiar power and sacredness. It was when the Lord Jesus was leaving his house—to use the figurative language of the text—to sojourn in another country. "While I was with them," were his words in prayer, "I kept them in Thy Name. . . . Now come I to Thee." How can we do otherwise than attach an especial force of obligation to what our Master said when he was about to leave this world, for the salvation of whose inhabitants he had lived, and was about to die? 3. Look into the *charge itself*. He gives to each one his *work*. All his people are his servants; all have a task to accomplish, a service to render, an office to fill. And every one has his own work, for which he is individually qualified, and which is committed to him and to no other. It is a practical, an elevating view of the Christian life, this which is here unfolded to us. All whom Jesus saves and redeems, he commissions and consecrates. And so long as we live here we have a trust to fulfil, a work to do. He invests each one with *authority*. There must be in every community a source of power, a ruling mind; the father in a family, the magistrate or the king in a state. In the Church of the Lord Jesus, he himself is the Head, the Lawgiver, the Fountain of honour, the Judge. Yet he gives authority; not making an order of men lords over his heritage, but authorizing every servant to fulfil his own special duties. The bishop rules, the teacher teaches, the evangelist preaches the gospel, nay, every member of every congregation fulfils his duties, at the bidding and by the authority of the Lord. This conviction should give dignity and devotedness to our daily toil. We are where the Lord has placed us; we are doing what he commands. And he requires each one to *watch*. Working and watching go together; for Christians are like the Jews in the time of Nehemiah, who built the walls of Jerusalem, whilst they were armed and on their guard against the foe. Our Master has left us in the midst of dangers, not to depress our courage, but to quicken our vigilance. This duty devolves especially upon the porter, the janitor. The house contains precious treasures, and it must not be allowed to every stranger to enter, lest the Master's property should be stolen, and the careless keepers dispossessed, and the house occupied by foes. All must watch, that at the Lord's return it may appear that his charge has been kept, and his possessions have been faithfully guarded.

II. WATCH! FOR THERE IS A PROSPECT OF CHRIST'S REVELATION IN THE FUTURE. Whilst we look back to the Lord's departure, and his solemn injunctions and his sacred trust, we look forward to his return, according to his promise. 1. This is an *assured* fact. Our Lord's second coming has been declared by him under many figures, each having its own shade of spiritual meaning and practical profit. He is a Householder, who will come to take account of his servants; a Proprietor, who will come to learn how his agents have traded and what they have gained; a King, who will come to make inquiry into the conduct of his citizens and great officers of state; a Judge, who will come to summon the people before his tribunal. 2. At the same time, the period of the Lord's return is *hidden* from us, and we are informed that to the unprepared it will be sudden and unexpected. Men have been presumptuous enough to foretell, with foolish confidence, what neither the angels nor the very Son of God would communicate. And again and again, in the course of history, there have been outbreaks of millennial fanaticism. But it is easy to see why the close of the age should be reserved as a secret in the Father's mind. Had the Church been told that the advent was near, Christians would have been unfitted for the sober discharge of the duties of life; had the Church been assured that it was remote, such an assurance would have prompted sloth and negligence. 3. Yet we may all live under a sense of the nearness of the Lord's return. The personal interest to us of that return lies in the glory of Christ's kingdom, and in the acknowledgment of our own faithfulness. This life we know is short, and the day of our account is not far off. And Christ would have us live as though he had but gone from us for a season, and were about again to come to us.

> "And well I know
> That unto him who works, and feels he works,
> This same grand year is ever at the doors."

III. WATCH! FOR THIS IS THE PLAIN DUTY OF THE PRESENT. We have spoken of the past and of the future; of the charge given by our Lord whilst yet on earth, and of the prospect of our Lord's return from heaven. But both these aspects of our religion bear upon the life and duty of to-day.

> "Trust no future, howe'er pleasant;
> Let the dead past bury its dead:
> Think, act, in the living present—
> Heart within, and God o'erhead!"

1. *Work!* "Whatsoever thy hand findeth to do, do it with thy might." Now, whilst strength of body and mind are continued, labour for the Lord who lived and died for you. Now, whilst you have control of your property, use it as stewards for God. Now, whilst you have influence over your domestic and social circle, use that influence for Christ. Ministers of the gospel, parents and teachers of youth, officers of congregations, followers of Jesus in every position of life,—be it yours to work for the Lord you love and honour! To-day is yours; to-morrow may be too late. 2. *Pray!* This you will do, if you realize your dependence for spiritual impulse and power upon the great Source of spiritual grace and blessing. So far from there being any inconsistency between work and prayer, the two blend in perfect harmony. Prayer without work is mockery, and work without prayer is mechanical and powerless. 3. *Watch!* That is, keep guard over yourself and your trust; cherish an attitude of expectation and a feeling of responsibility. Oh for grace to live "as ever in the great Taskmaster's eye"! "Ye know not when the time is." Watch! "lest coming suddenly he find you sleeping!"

> "Watch, for the night is long;
> Watch, for the foe is strong;
> Watch, for the treasure's dear;
> Watch, for the Lord is near!"

"Happy is that servant, whom his Lord when he cometh shall find so doing!"

HOMILIES BY VARIOUS AUTHORS.

Vers. 1, 2.—*Temple admiration.* In the case of the Jews a natural and venial fault, if not carried to excess. Esteemed the type and pattern of architectural excellence, and one of the wonders of the world. Herod's rebuilding was on a scale of magnificence unknown to their ancestors. The essential features of the temple of Solomon were restored, but these were "surrounded by an inner enclosure of great strength and magnificence, measuring, as nearly as can be made out, one hundred and eighty cubits by two hundred and forty, and adorned by porches and ten gateways of great magnificence; and beyond this, again, was an outer enclosure, measuring externally four hundred cubits each way, which was adorned with porticoes of greater splendour than any we know of attached to any temple of the ancient world; all showing how strongly Roman influence was at work in enveloping with heathen magnificence the simple templar arrangements of a Shemitic people" (Smith's 'Dictionary of the Bible'). Josephus, in his 'Antiquities,' xv. 11, 3, speaks of stones "each in length twenty-five cubits, in height eight, in breadth about twelve;" and in the 'Wars,' v. 5, 6, of "some of the stones as forty-five cubits in length, five in height, and six in breadth." Many of these were of sculptured marble. The reply of Jesus may be read either affirmatively or interrogatively, or with a mixture of both assertion and question. The apodosis is, "*There shall not be left here stone upon stone,*" etc. Thus their lingering gaze is quietly but grandly rebuked, and their thoughts directed with solemn, practical earnestness to the Divine future in which all that pomp of masonry and decoration was to have no place.

I. THE NATURAL MIND IS MOST IMPRESSED BY WHAT IS GREAT AND BEAUTIFUL IN OUTWARD APPEARANCE. The simple Galilean peasants were carried away with enthusiastic admiration of the princely buildings, so unparalleled in their experience. To such an extent was this the case that they were in danger of being ensnared. 1. *Sensuous admiration is easily confounded with spiritual attachment.* The mind, in order to correct this error, must dwell on the spiritual truths of which external objects are but the symbols, and realize that, whilst the latter shall pass away, the former must endure for ever. 2. *The world, in its sensuous totality, is similarly pregnant with temptation to the soul that has not learnt to look through the visible into the invisible and eternal.*

II. THAT WHICH FAILS OF ITS DIVINE IDEA, OR OPPOSES THE DIVINE PURPOSE, SHALL BE DESTROYED. The splendid building upon which they were gazing had ceased to minister to the higher spiritual life of the people, and had, through its officers and representatives, rejected the Son of God. It had thereby sealed the warrant of its own extinction: not one stone should stand upon another. So is it with the individual, institution, or nation which fails to realize its chief end. 1. *This is penal.* There was no process of natural decay, no growing beautiful with age—the sensuous slowly merging into the spiritual; no succession of normal changes ensuring expansion, adaptation, and continuity; but sudden, awful destruction, accompanied by unheard-of misery. God must witness to his righteousness even in judgment. The soul that sins shall die. 2. *It is in order to give place to a worthier realization of the Divine will.* The "house not made with hands" was nearer when this external sanctuary, which had been defiled, was removed. "The hour cometh, when neither in this mountain, nor in Jerusalem, shall ye worship the Father. . . . God is a Spirit: and they that worship him must worship in spirit and truth" (John iv. 21—24). Not until the temple had been destroyed would the temple's Lord make advent to the world. Judgment must begin at the house of God (1 Pet. iv. 17). "But on all these points the first and great question is not what is to be done, but who is to do it. Is the reform of the Church to be consigned entirely to politicians and economists, *who only look at the goodly stones and gifts of the temple,* some with an anxious, others with a greedy eye, and care nothing about the service of the sanctuary nor the edification of the worshippers? Or will any part of the work be put into the hands of sincere and zealous and enlightened lovers of the Church? In the latter case we may securely hope for the best. In the other, it is to be feared that, if beneficial changes ever take place, they will have been purchased by great losses and a disastrous experience" (Thirlwall, 'Letters,' vol. i. p. 107).—M.

Vers. 3—5 (and the rest of the chapter generally).—*The signs of the coming of the Son of man.* I. THERE IS A CURIOSITY CONCERNING THE FUTURE WHICH IS NATURAL AND LEGITIMATE. The disciples were not rebuked when they came with their inquiry. It was not so when Peter asked, "Lord, and what shall this man do?" (John xxi. 21). Some inquiries concerning the future are therefore lawful, others not. How are we to distinguish between them? We may ask *concerning things the knowledge of which is necessary to the rational direction of spiritual aims and efforts.* God has chosen to make known *the general scheme of redemption in its evolution in the world's history.* The prophecies of Scripture ought, therefore, to be studied in the light of contemporary events. The teaching of Christ on this occasion was manifestly the germ of the Apocalypse.

II. THIS CURIOSITY IS GRATIFIED BY OUR SAVIOUR FOR MORAL AND SPIRITUAL ENDS. (Vers. 5, 7, 9, 13, 23, 34—37.) The great discipline of the disciples was to take place after their Master's death, and before the general inauguration of his kingdom. The three general directions of Christ are: (1) *Take heed unto yourselves;* (2) *beware;* (3) *watch.* "It does not behove us to know time and hour, but to observe the signs antecedent to the judgment of God" (Starke). The Holy Spirit is promised, amid all trials and difficulties, to them who truly believe. The gospel itself was to receive universal proclamation, notwithstanding the perils and evils that were to take place. So that the disciples were assured, whatever might occur in the external life of the world, of ultimate glorious realization of all the spiritual ends of God's kingdom.

III. MANY TEMPORARY EVILS WERE TO FORESHADOW, AND TO PREPARE FOR, A PERMANENT DIVINE GOOD. 1. *The catalogue of woes is long, detailed, and specific:* spiritual delusions; wars, earthquakes, and famines; persecutions; pollution and destruction of the temple; political and cosmical revolutions. 2. *These are all to pass,* in their process tempered and modified by Divine mercy and guidance. 3. And *they were to result in the advent of the Divine kingdom.* The gospel was to be proclaimed and the universal communion of saints to be realized. The political and natural troubles were to be justified by their being made instrumental of moral and spiritual benefits. So in the general experience of Christians "all things work together for good."—M.

Vers. 30, 31.—*The fulfilments of the kingdom of God an evidence of the truth of Christianity.* I. THE WHOLE SOCIAL, POLITICAL, AND NATURAL CONSTITUTION OF THINGS WAS INFLUENCED BY, AND MADE SUBSERVIENT TO, ITS ACCOMPLISHMENT. Compare the history of the world from the death of Christ to A.D. 70. A period of destruction, calamity, and revolution. Judaism deposed from its spiritual leadership, robbed of its prestige, discredited, stunted, and stultified by the very circumstance which awakened and intensified the spirit of Christianity, and (in the Roman empire) led to its world-wide diffusion. The suffering, uncertainty, and newly discovered solidarity of the race tended to prepare mankind for a more spiritual and universal religion. Through the Spirit of Christ the Jewish Christians conquered their conquerors and overcame the world. Witness the testimony of Tertullian as to the number of Christians in the Roman empire in his time.
II. THIS WAS FORETOLD BY JESUS CHRIST. It was a marvellous insight and foresight which could look through such a series of evils and destructions to the ultimate success of his kingdom. And it had not a little to do with the bringing about of the effect anticipated. The period can only be adequately explained from the standpoint of universal history or the philosophy of history, as one of spiritual evolution conditioned and determined by the peculiar doctrines of Christianity.
III. THE VERIFICATION WAS COMPRISED WITHIN THE LIMITS OF INDIVIDUAL EXPERIENCE. "*This generation shall not pass away, until all these things be accomplished.*" If the destruction of Jerusalem be the terminal point of the various series of events foretold in this chapter, then "this generation" must be literally understood as referring to the persons alive at the time Christ spoke. And, allowing for poetic hyperbole (as in the figurative expressions, "heaven and earth," "sun," "moon," and "stars," "earthquakes," etc.) and the general style of prophetic imagery, the careful student must believe that in the destruction of Jerusalem the great, imminent coming of the Son of man was actually effected, as history proves that circumstances that might fittingly be described by the words of Christ took place and in the order he announced.—M.

Ver. 31.—*The words of Christ and the world-revolution with which they were associated.* I. A PREDICTION OF IT. The date of these utterances and their authorship beyond all reasonable question. A daring forecast, identifying the fortunes of Christianity with vast cosmical movements. Insight such as this more than human; dependent upon perception of unseen principles and absolute faith in God. The immediate effect of the changes predicted is acknowledged to be adverse to the outward circumstances of his followers; yet inwardly and ultimately the result is regarded as beyond question, and declared with unfaltering authority. This predictive element in the gospel not accidental, but essential; its entire credibility as a word of God to man being made to depend upon its fulfilment as a prophecy.
II. A SUSTAINING PRINCIPLE THROUGH IT. The faith of Christians is fostered: 1. *By the fact that all things were foretold*: "I have told you all things beforehand." 2. *By their intelligent perception of the signs, the method, and the outline of God's working.* 3. *By their experience of special Divine grace*—(1) in guidance and indwelling of the Holy Ghost; (2) in experience of special Divine favours, *e.g.* the shortening of the days of tribulation; and (3) in the inward spiritual comfort and edification of the precepts and promises of the gospel.
III. A CAUSE OF IT. As representing the eternal moral principles which underlie and determine the historic evolution of the race. An exciting cause of the hatred to Divine things which was the motive of so much that was done. A directive influence in shaping the destinies of the new institutions and movements which were evolved from the chaos of the old world.

IV. A SURVIVAL FROM IT. Not one has passed away. The great doctrines of Christendom have slowly but surely formulated themselves in sympathetic relation to the experience and progress with which they have been associated. As a *system* of truth, they can be more comprehensively grasped now than at any previous time. The fulfilment of its predictions did not exhaust the moral fulness and depth of Christian truth, or its applicability to the extant problems of future ages. The gospel is thus seen to be, not only for a time, but for all time, the central principle of progress and destiny for the human race.—M.

Vers. 32—37.—*The element of uncertainty in the Christian revelation.* I. To WHAT IT RELATES. "That day or that hour." Proximately and very evidently these words refer to the precise date of the inauguration of Christ's kingdom, through the destruction of Jerusalem (A.D. 70), about forty years subsequent to their utterance. Through that period it was possible for any of those addressed to continue alive, and consequently they were all admonished with respect to it. But, secondarily, the absolute, final coming of the Son of man is referred to adumbratively, and so also all intermediate advents connective of these two terms of the progress of his coming. That the attention of the hearers was specially or particularly addressed to this secondary coming does not appear. There were other words which more clearly indicated it.

II. WHOM IT AFFECTED. That it should affect *believers* could be understood, although at first to them it must have been an occasion of perplexity; that *angels* should not know might be explicable on the ground that it was an earthly evolution of events, and that although in a state of blessedness and spiritual illumination their nature is finite; but that the "Son" should be ignorant is a great mystery. Yet there are considerations which throw some light even upon this. "The Father's absolute omniscience, and his consequent absolute prescience, is assumed by the Saviour, even although the object of the prescience is chronologically conditional on millions of intervening free acts on the part of millions of free agents. When absolute prescience, however, is denied by the Son on the part of himself, he is, of course, referring to himself *as Son, begotten on a certain day* (Ps. ii. 7; Acts xiii. 33) in the Virgin's womb (Luke i. 35). He is, in other words, referring to himself, as he was self-realized in his finite nature, to be for ever distinguished from that infinite essence in which he made the worlds (John i. 3), sustains them (Col. i. 17), sees the end from the beginning (John vi. 64), and 'knows all things' (John xxi. 17). . . . It is only when we proceed on a 'monophysist' hypothesis, and assume that our Saviour's divinity was his only mind, and the soul of his humanity, that overwhelming difficulty is encountered" (Morison). Apart from this, although intimately connected with it, there were *moral* reasons for Christ's remaining ignorant. As "Christ's not knowing rests upon his knowing rightly (in a natural manner), or upon the holy *extension* of his range of vision" (Lange), it follows that this ignorance, referring to a subject of such transcendent consequence in relation to his own work amongst men, must have formed an important element and condition of his moral and spiritual subjection to the Father. He rose through weakness, limitation of knowledge of Divine counsels (although not of Divine *principles*), and finitude of nature, to the full comprehension of the mind of God, and realization of the perfection of the Divine-human personality, beyond the cross. To the spiritual and perfect Christ, therefore, belongs *all power*; for he was *made perfect* through suffering and subjection. His obedience was perfect, and his gradual moral development in act and consciousness because of this limitation of knowledge.

III. How IT IS TO BE REGARDED BY BELIEVERS. The parabolic form of Christ's teaching here is very beautiful and striking. Vers. 34, 35 should be translated thus: "As a man away from home, having (or, who has) left his house, and given the authority to his servants, and to each his work, also commanded the porter to watch— 'Watch, therefore' (*i.e. so say I*, 'Watch,' etc.), 'for ye know not when the Master of the house cometh,'" etc. (1) With *watchfulness*; that is, sleepless vigilance, which comprehends and leads to (2) *prayer* and (3) *diligence*. And these duties are of universal obligation (ver. 37).—M.

Ver. 34.—"*To every man his work.*" The circumstances under which these words were uttered imparted to them peculiar solemnity. Our Lord had left the temple for the last time, and in the waning light was walking home to Bethany, when he sat himself down to gaze with lingering love on Jerusalem. The evening sun was still glorifying her palaces; but the light was fading, darkness was coming; and he talked with his disciples of darker shadows about to fall, which would leave her bereft of the light of God. But he looked beyond that—to the time when he would return from the "far country," and, gathering his servants around him, would give each one recompense according as his work should be. During his absence he has given "to every man his work." This clause suggests several thoughts concerning *Christian service.*

I. THE UNIVERSALITY OF CHRISTIAN SERVICE. It is appointed for "every man" who is in the Lord's household. God works in us in order that we may will and do of his good pleasure. He gives us love to others, and understanding of his Word, an experience of his faithfulness, mental and spiritual faculties, in order to fit us for serving him. Science teaches us that natural agents are so closely related that they are mutually convertible. Motion passes into heat, heat into electricity, electricity into magnetism, magnetism into animal force, and so on in an endless circle. In the sphere of nature God arouses no force which does not arouse another; and though the primal energy passes on into many manifestations, it does not return to him void. So is it in the spiritual realm. He excites in your heart love to Christ, and that arouses thought about him, speech concerning him, activity for him; and these go forth like advancing waves of influence into the lives of others, and none can foresee the end. The Church is not meant to be like the phantom ship of which the poet sings, manned by a dead crew; but is likened to a living "household," in which all the servants are eager, watchful, and diligent; for their Lord has given "to every man his work." (Show the variety of capacities distributed amongst the old and young, the rich and poor, and the diverse forms of Christian service to which these point.)

II. QUALIFICATIONS FOR CHRISTIAN SERVICE. 1. *Earnestness.* Too often this is fitful. It passes from us uselessly when in contact with the worldly, just as electricity passes off when insulation has been neglected. We want insulation of spiritual force. A modern Christian, surrounded by symbols of idolatry, would not always have "his spirit stirred" within him as Paul did at Athens. The present age is enlightened rather than enthusiastic; self-complacent rather than self-sacrificing. 2. *Love* to Christ and love to souls is the true inspiration of successful Christian service. It is gained at the foot of the cross.

> "A life of self-renouncing love
> Is a life of liberty."

3. *Constancy.* Such as Paul had, who, amid temptations to indolence, and amid persecutions which might have made him falter, pressed forward steadfastly. "This one thing I do" was the motto of his life. Is it ours? 4. *Watchfulness.* A special exhortation to this lies in the passage before us. Let us watch (1) for opportunities of service, (2) for results of work, and (3) for the coming of the Lord.

III. THE RECOMPENSE OF CHRISTIAN SERVICE. 1. *There is blessing to be found in doing it.* On the inactive mind and irresolute will doubts will gather, as limpets do on a motionless rock. Powers fairly exercised, whether they be physical, mental, or spiritual, develop by use. 2. *There is blessing awaiting us when we have done it.* It was not without reason that our Lord spoke (ver. 28) of the signs of his coming as being like the indications that "summer is nigh." His advent will be to his people not a winter, but a summer, from which gloom and death will be banished, and in which there will be fruit-gathering after toil, and manifestation of beauty and glory arising from the discipline of the past. That summer is nigh! The world is ripening for it. Our work is preparing for it. Then shall the faithful reap fruit unto life eternal.—A. R.

Vers. 1—37.—*Watching.* This chapter relates almost exclusively to the inhabitants of Jerusalem. Yet in its testimony to the Divine power of foretelling future events, it has its evidential value to all students of the person of our Lord; while its central and simple lesson, "Watch! the day of your Lord's coming ye know not," may be profitably reiterated with frequency in the ears of all. One of the disciples, on passing out of the temple, drew the attention of the Master to the massiveness and grandeur of its building. How great! how stable! how wondrous! In this, as in so many instances, he saw what they saw not; and his thoughts were not as theirs. It must have been to their great surprise that he declared, "There shall not be left one stone upon another, that shall not be thrown down." Sad and doleful words follow, as strikingly in contrast to the expectations of his questioners as were the former. The eager desire to know " when shall these things be," was met by threats of deception, war, earthquakes, and famines, the mere presages of trouble, to be followed by personal afflictions, persecutions, hatreds, and deaths, mingled with the uttermost national and religious confusion. The dire symbols were, "the sun shall be darkened," "the moon shall not give her light," "the stars shall be falling from heaven." We who read these words with the picture of Jerusalem's destruction before us, and in the light of modern Jewish history, see a depth of meaning in them which, the words being words of prophecy, the disciples failed to see. Pitifully do our hearts move towards Israel according to the flesh, and pray for the lifting up of the veil that is upon their eyes, that they in a true sense may " see and believe." The lesson is founded upon this prediction of judgment. In interpreting it in its application to ourselves we must see that it teaches—

I. THE EXTREME PERILOUSNESS OF HINDERING THE DEVELOPMENT OF THE KINGDOM OF HEAVEN BY UNFAITHFULNESS. The Jew was favoured as was no other nation under heaven. Fidelity to the great trust reposed in that people would have been attended with unmeasured Divine blessing; while unfaithfulness resulted in the direst calamity and judgment. Who shall describe the bitterness to Israel of those dread days? A free and wider diffusion of the spiritual kingdom followed. But Israel, in giving birth to a gospel of blessing to the nations, suffered throes of travail " such as there hath not been the like from the beginning of the creation which God created until now, and," happily, " never shall be."

II. IN OUR IGNORANCE OF THE TIMES OF GREAT AND SUDDEN CHANGES IN THE DEVELOPMENT OF THE KINGDOM OF HEAVEN, OUR HIGHEST WISDOM IS A DILIGENT ATTENTION TO THE DUTY OF THE HOUR. The hour is always uncertain when the Lord cometh to judgment. The indolent spirit that is deluded into neglect because there is no sign of his coming, will be inevitably found " sleeping." How often has the Church been lulled thus to slumber! How often have the most responsible trusts been unfaithfully held! Times of judgment awake the sleepers often to find their work neglected or undone. The watching spirit that momentarily devotes itself to the doing of the Lord's will is the only safe spirit. Such a spirit is never surprised, never taken unawares. It matters not when " the lord of the house cometh," whether " at even, or at midnight, or at cockcrowing, or in the morning." The watching servant hails and rejoices in his lord's approach.

III. THE CERTAINTY OF THE FINAL RECOGNITION OF HUMBLE, FAITHFUL, CONTINUOUS SERVICE. 1. The gracious words of warning stimulate to effort. 2. The help of the Divine Spirit is comfortingly promised to the suffering. " It is not ye that speak, but the Holy Ghost." 3. The perseveringly patient one shall reap in due time. " He that endureth to the end, the same shall be saved." 4. The scattered ones whom cruel persecution has driven into all lands shall finally be restored, and the felicities of the heavenly life compensate for the sufferings of earth. " He shall gather together his elect from the four winds, from the uttermost part of the earth to the uttermost part of heaven." The Lord's one command, holding all within itself, is " Watch!" " Blessed is that servant, whom his lord when he cometh shall find so doing."—G.

Vers. 1—13.—*Prophetic adumbrations.* I. "MATERIAL TEMPLES, POLLUTED BY MEN'S SINS, MUST PERISH."

II. "THE TEMPLE OF HUMAN MINDS, PURIFIED BY THE DIVINE SPIRIT, WILL ABIDE FOR EVER " (Godwin).

III. THE EDUCATION OF ILLUSIONS. (See F. W. Robertson's sermon on 'The Illusiveness of Life!') God in history is God in disguise. To detect his presence is not always easy. Surface and show are constantly taken for truth and reality.

IV. VAGUE TROUBLES PRECEDE GREAT CHANGES. We live in restless times. " Something is in the air." We know not what is meant; but something is meant. The beginning of a process must not be mistaken for the end.

V. A MORAL PRINCIPLE AND PURPOSE LIES IN ALL CHANGE. This is the secret leaven which occasions all the ferment. Deep was the truth expressed by the philosopher when he said, "War is the father of all things." Or in the myth, *conflict* and *love* are close companions. In convulsed times, be sure Divine love is profoundly working. Persecution represents the expiring struggles of error and its fellow, passion.

VI. THE CONSTANT HEART NEED FEAR NO EVIL. Nothing can bring us peace but loyalty to principle. Nothing can exempt us from unmanning fears but the sense that truth is on our side. The only secret of eloquence lies here. There is no salvation for the coward, the untrue, and the disloyal. For the true heart there is salvation from every possible danger.—J.

Vers. 14—31.—*Dark sayings.* I. SACRED LITERATURE, LIKE NATURE, IS FULL OF HINTED TRUTH. "Truths in nature darkly join." So in Scripture. The mystic element in Daniel and Scripture generally was fully recognized by Christ.

II. PRUDENCE IN MEN IS THE REFLECTION OF PROVIDENCE IN GOD. It is the light within us. In unsettled times we must be more than usually on our guard. Keen love of truth will make the mind critical and sceptical of the talk that goes on. Let us not have to say, surprised by calamity, "We might have known this before."

III. THERE IS A METHOD AND A SELECTION IN THE WAYS OF PROVIDENCE. When the observer of physical nature finds a principle of "natural selection," he finds only the visible counterpart of a law in the kingdom of God. God, through all changes, "gathers his chosen" from the end of the land to the end of the sky.

IV. CHANGES IN THE SPIRITUAL KINGDOM ARE NATURAL, AND THOSE THAT ARE NATURAL HAVE A SPIRITUAL SIGNIFICANCE. Changes in plants visibly show forth changes in institutions. Below both is truth, is life. And as Christ is one with life and truth, his words abide. There is a moral conservation of force through all evolutions.—J.

Vers. 32—37.—*Indefinable truth.* I. AN ELEMENT OF UNCERTAINTY MINGLES WITH ALL THAT IS MOST CERTAIN. We know that certain things must happen, certain forces exert themselves, certain laws be executed in the course of things. But where, when, how? "The rest is silence." And this is spiritually profitable. Imagination and faith live and thrive in the clear-obscure of thought.

II. THERE WERE THINGS UNKNOWABLE EVEN TO JESUS. It is but a small portion of truth that can be rendered into definite conceptions and expressed in words. "Truth in closest words must fail." But Jesus "received from the Father all desirable knowledge" (Godwin).

III. THE MOOD AND HABIT OF MIND IS MORE IMPORTANT THAN DEFINITE KNOWLEDGE. Living is better than any theory of life. Being ready for any emergency is better than being certain about when this or that emergency will arise. "We should be ready every day for what may come any day."

IV. A BRIGHT AND QUICK INTELLIGENCE IS ABOVE ALL NECESSARY FOR THE CONDUCT OF LIFE. We must not dare to "fall behind the times." We must be punctual. It was said of one that he was always "a day too late." Sleepy men and institutions will certainly be shocked out of their lethargy. Christ's warning has been unheeded. Ecclesiastical Christianity has always been a day too late; has risen later than science, than business energy, than private zeal. We lean on one another too much. It is as if each sentinel should go to sleep, trusting to the vigilance of his comrade. Every Christian worker and watcher should act as if the fate of the host depended on him alone.—J.

Vers. 1—13. Parallel passages: Matt. xxiv. 1—14; Luke xxi. 5—19.—*Unexpected events.* I. PROPHECIES. 1. *Distribution of prophetic intimations.* Great diversity of opinion prevails in regard to the predictions contained in this chapter. About one part of it, however, there is unanimity; the early portion contains, as all admit, a prophecy about the destruction of the temple which was literally and actually fulfilled within forty years after it had been uttered. The remainder of the chapter is understood by the majority of interpreters to refer to the destruction of Jerusalem, and the end of the world or present dispensation. In relation to this second part there are many divergent theories, but these in the main are reducible to two: (1) that which regards these two subjects as separately and successively exhibited; and (2) that which maintains their coexistence throughout, and according to which they are so blended and intermingled that separation is all but impossible. 2. *Practical observations.* There is (1) the duty of diligently studying prophecy, as a very important and deeply interesting portion of the Divine Word; thus St. Peter says, " We have the Word of prophecy made more sure; whereunto ye do well that ye take heed, as unto a lamp shining in a dark place " (Revised Version). But while the study of prophecy is a pleasing duty, we may not forget that it is attended with special difficulties arising from the very nature of the subject. It is evident that the design of prophecy would be frustrated if it were fully understood beforehand ; in such a case men would be found desirous, some of antedating, others of defeating, the predicted events. (2) In the study of prophecy we must not strive to be wise above what is written, nor lean too much to our own understanding. We are to have in recollection that " the secret things belong unto the Lord : but those things which are revealed belong unto us and our children for ever." In our attempts at the interpretation of unfulfilled prophecy, in addition to diligent comparison of Scripture under the teaching of the Holy Spirit, we are to pursue the study as far as possible along the lines of prophecies already fulfilled. (3) Two uses of fulfilled prophecy are obvious. One is the corroboration of the truth of God's Word, and so a strong confirmation of our faith in that Word; the second is a guarantee for the future from the past. The predictions which have been already and actually fulfilled warrant the expectation that such as still wait for fulfilment shall one day be most certainly accomplished; and then shall the light shed by Divine providence shine so brightly on those portions of the Divine Word now mysterious, that they shall appear plain and clear as noonday. 3. *Character of the disciples' observation.* The object which the disciples had in view, when they called the attention of their Master to the great stones of the temple, is not quite clear. We may consider their remark a casual one, called forth by the sight of such huge structures—such immense stones, measuring, according to Josephus, some of them twenty-five cubits in length, eight in height, and twelve in breadth ; others forty-five cubits in length, five in height, and six in breadth. Or perhaps the numerals in case of the cubits, in both the passages of Josephus, should be the same, namely, twenty-five. The sight of stones of such vast dimensions, of enormous marble blocks, of the gorgeousness and grandeur of the buildings, would justify their remark ; still the sight of all these would not vindicate it from being somewhat superficial and commonplace, natural enough to Galilean peasants, and such as might be made by very unsophisticated persons. We may perhaps be warranted, therefore, in reading a deeper meaning into their observation. Might it not be that the thought occurred to them that an edifice of such splendour and magnificence would be no way unsuitable to, nor unworthy of, Messiah's reign and of the temporal kingdom which they still clung to? 4. *The point of time at which the observation was made.* Jesus was leaving the temple, and leaving it for the last time. What solemn thoughts must have occupied his mind as he bade farewell to that beautiful sanctuary ! How different they must have been from those of his disciples, in whatever way their words are to be understood ! He is now turning his back for ever on the national temple, long the centre of Jewish worship, with its august shrine, where the Shechinah glory had appeared above the cherubim, where the Divine presence in visible symbol had been manifested, where the most solemn acts of religious service had been performed, and where the one living and true God had been worshipped, while polytheism had prevailed in the nations all around. Now, however, the spirit of the theocracy was gone, Judaism had fallen into decrepitude, the national temple still stood in all its splendour; but the great Inhabitant was about to take his departure. The Messenger of the covenant had come suddenly to his temple ; but with his rejection and death already determined on, life and light and liberty were on the eve of departing for ever, and the kingdom about to pass into other and more worthy hands. The disciples, who, like other Jews, still indulged the daydream of a worldly kingdom and political independence in connection with Messiah, must have been more than surprised by our Lord's reply. Their pleasant fancies are dispelled ; to their fondest aspirations a rude shock is given. They are startled, stunned, and silenced. Stone not left upon stone that shall not be loosened from its place and thrown to the ground! and all this affirmed with the utmost positiveness of assertion! What can it mean? They roll the matter over in their thoughts; they reflect, but cannot persuade themselves that the words are to be understood in their strict, unfigurative sense. The statement is past their comprehension. 5. *Their inquiry*. And now they have left the temple courts, descended the side of Moriah, crossed the Kedron, and are seated on a slope of Olivet. What a lovely prospect is there presented to their gaze! Right opposite and full in view was the temple, with its white marble, its roof and pinnacles overlaid with gold, the prodigious stone substructures already the objects of such admiration, all sparkling in the clear light of an Eastern sky. Here was a sight of such surpassing splendour that it was esteemed equal to one of the wonders of the world; a spectacle of such beauty that once seen it remained ever after a part of sight. Here was a prospect corresponding to the eloquent and withal exact words of Milman, when he says, "At a distance the whole temple looked literally like a mount of snow, fretted with golden pinnacles." And was the glory of all this, like ordinary mundane things, to pass so soon away! The disciples naturally desire more information on this stupendous subject; they have by this time recovered somewhat from their surprise. They break silence by trying to ascertain with certainty and preciseness some particulars in regard to the wonderful event predicted, and its consequences, immediate and remote, implied in the expression, "these things" —an expression erroneously referred by some to the world itself, and by others to the buildings of the temple. They are at once curious and anxious to be informed of the *time* when what was foretold would be fulfilled; of the *sign* of the Saviour's coming for the performance of what he had thus predicted; and further, as we are informed by St. Matthew, of the *end* of the world. 6. *Minuteness in details*. As usual, St. Mark is most minute in his record of particulars, such as an eye-witness, or one writing the words of an eye-witness, would be most likely to take note of. He tells us here the exact *position* of our Lord and his disciples—on a knoll of Olivet, *right* over against (κατέναντι, the κατὰ being intensive) the temple. He also informs us that the disciples who were closest to our Saviour on the occasion, or who were most earnest and urgent in their inquiries which they probably repeated (ἐπηρώτων, imperfect), were Peter and James and John and Andrew. These were the *persons* who spoke in their own name and that of their brethren—acting at once for themselves and the other disciples. There was in this an evident appropriateness. These four disciples, consisting of two pairs of brothers, were the first who had enrolled themselves in the list of discipleship; they were the first of the apostolic band. They had been longest with our Lord, and, it would seem, on the most familiar terms with him; and now they are nearest to him in position, and, on the ground of their close intimacy, venture to put questions from which perhaps the others shrank. Three of these, moreover, had been specially privileged—already on two, as subsequently on another and third occasion—to accompany our Lord. Long attendance on the Master, as the consequence of early and faithful discipleship, would thus appear to have peculiar advantages, and to elevate, not by merit but by grace, to higher privileges. How important, then, for the young to join themselves early to the ranks of Christ's disciples, remembering their Creator in the days of their youth, and coming in early childhood to the Saviour! 7. *Peculiarity in and fulfilment of the prophecy*. We may not overlook, or lose sight of, the prediction that led to the inquiries of the disciples, and of these special favourites who represented the wishes of their brethren, as well as their own, on this occasion. The prediction in question is one of the most remarkable on record, if we consider all the circumstances. There was scarcely anything more unlikely at that time than the overthrow of such a stable fabric, where the buildings and substructures were so massive that Titus himself attributed his triumph to the hand of God. The original temple had been built by Solomon, and having stood for four centuries, was destroyed, after the lapse of that period, by Nebuzaradan, commander-in-chief of the forces of Nebuchadnezzar, King of Babylon. It was rebuilt by Zerubbabel, at the head of the restored Jews, somewhat more than five centuries before Christ. This was the second temple; and though it was renewed by Herod the Great, and had several magnificent additions made to it by that king, such as a porch with white marble slabs, towers, and so on, it was still known, not as the third, but second temple. The work of renovation commenced by Herod had continued six and forty years, as we learn from the Fourth Gospel (ii. 20), where we read, "Then said the Jews, Forty and six years was this temple in building." It was still much more improbable even if, contrary to all expectation and all reasonable calculation of chances, it should be destroyed, that that destruction would be carried to such an extreme of demolition that no ruins should be left—no, not so much as one stone upon another. Other temples have been destroyed by hostile attack, or fallen into decay and yielded to the corroding tooth of time ; but their ruins at least remain, while the magnificence of those ruins attracts the visitor, and excites his admiration or astonishment. Witness the far-famed Parthenon or temple of Minerva at Athens, or the temple of Baalbek, or Karnak, or Luxor. But though the Roman general did his utmost to save the temple, it was destroyed by fire ; and subsequently the work of demolition was carried out so thoroughly by the tenth legion, under Terentius Rufus, that the temple area and precincts were dug up. The great peculiarity of the prophecy was its uncommon clearness, distinctness, and definiteness at a time when all the probabilities were against it ; while the exactness of its fulfilment has so puzzled infidels, that they have tried to make themselves and others believe that the prediction was *post eventum ;* and, finding that impossible and incredible, others have resorted to such miserable shifts as coincidences, lucky guesses, or skilful prognostications. All in vain ; for it remains, and must remain, an irrefragable testimony to the truth of God. There was, besides, the fulfilment of an older prophecy by Micah : " Zion shall be ploughed like a field, and Jerusalem shall become heaps." 8. *The perspective of prophecy.* There is a very general agreement that in the predictions contained in this chapter of St. Mark and the corresponding chapters of the other synoptists, the two events of Christ's coming at the fall of Jerusalem, and of his coming at the end of the world or present dispensation, are combined. While some explain this according to the theory of two applications, one primary and another secondary ; and others by the typical theory, one event being typical of another, so that the one description covers both ; others again prefer that theory of prophecy according to which it exhibits events without regard to the periods of time or portions of space that intervene between them and separate them from each other ; just as in the landscape hill rises above hill, while to the spectator at a distance the valleys that lie between, or the interspaces that separate them, are not seen nor observed, and it is only when the summit of each hill is reached that the interval between it and the next is discernible. So we may conceive it to be with respect to the close of the αἰὼν which was marked by the fall of Jerusalem, and the completion, or τέλος, of the present dispensation or current age.

II. THE SIGNS SPECIFIED. 1. *Enumeration.* There is some slight difference in the enumeration of the signs ; they are also divided by some into negative and positive. We prefer dividing them into the immediate and more remote, and enumerate them as follows :—(1) False prophets or pretended Messiahs ; (2) wars and rumours of wars, that is, wars actually declared or commenced, and wars threatened or reported as imminent. St. Luke employs, instead of "rumours," the somewhat different expression of "commotions," or "unsettlements" (ἀποκαταστασίας) ; these are the more remote premonitions, for it is added by St. Matthew and St. Mark, " The end is not yet," while St. Luke has, " The end is not immediately." (3) Wars on a larger scale, implied in nation rising against nation and kingdom against kingdom. After these political agitations come physical, as (4) earthquakes ; then other providential events, as (5) famines, and troubles, the latter word being omitted in some manuscripts and in the Revised Version ; also (6) pestilences. That all these signs preceded the fall of Jerusalem at a greater or less distance from that event, and that, on a still wider area and a still grander scale, they shall precede the winding up of the present dispensation, appears to be the teaching of this portion of Scripture. The intermingling of the predictions relating to the two great events may in some measure be accounted for by the circumstance that the Jews would regard the overthrow of the Jewish state as the signal of, and coincident with, the end of all present things. Other signs of a less general and more personal kind are subjoined, so that we have (7) persecutions befalling the disciples both in and outside of Judæa ; and (8) sad apostasies and the evils consequent on such defections, as we learn from the first evangelist ; also (9) the proclamation of the gospel proceeding from Jerusalem and Judæa, and its diffusion among all nations, as a witness everywhere to Christ and his salvation. 2. *Verification.* Scripture itself bears witness to the fulfilment of the *first* sign ; for St. John says, " Even now are there many antichrists, whereby we know that it is the last time ; " while Josephus acquaints us with the fact that " the land was overrun with magicians, seducers, and impostors, who drew the

people after them in multitudes into solitudes and deserts, to see the signs and
miracles which they promised to show by the power of God." Several names, moreover, are expressly mentioned, of such persons as Dositheus, Simon Magus, Theudas,
Barchochab; but it is objected that some of these were too early, and others too late,
in point of time. In like manner it may be objected to the statement of the Apostle
John, that, while it is so distinct in relation to the fact, it is indefinite with respect to
the element of time. But if some were too early and others too late, it is not likely
that the intervening period had the good fortune of being freed from their presence;
while, from the statements of St. John on the one hand and Josephus on the other, we
may rightly conclude a succession of pretenders, and quite a number of them all along,
as true coin is seldom for long without its counterfeits. The *second* sign had its
verification in the violent deaths of no less than four Roman emperors—Nero, Galba,
Otho, and Vitellius—within a year and a half, and the scenes of tumult and bloodshed
consequent thereon; while the Jews were assailed with three threats of wars by Cali-
gula, Claudius, and Nero respectively. There were other rumours of wars, in consequence
of Bardanes, and subsequently Volageses, declaring, but not carrying out, war against
the Jews; as also by Vitellius, Governor of Syria, declaring war against the Arabian
king, Aretas. These two signs were among the more remote, for, as we have seen, it
is added, "The end is not yet;" that is, the end of the Jewish polity at the destruction
of Jerusalem was not to follow immediately. This caution was subjoined to prevent
that state of excitement and alarm which the Apostle Paul, at a subsequent period,
found it necessary to allay among the Thessalonians. The *third* sign may be illustrated
by the general character of the period, which the Roman historian Tacitus describes as
"rich in calamities, horrible with battles, rent with seditions, savage even in peace
itself;" as also by particular catastrophes, as the conflict between the Syrians and Jews
at Cæsarea, in which twenty thousand of the latter perished; another at Seleucia, in which
fifty thousand Jews lost their lives; with others similar at Joppa, Scythopolis, Ascalon,
and Tyre, recorded by Josephus in his 'Wars of the Jews,' a title of itself significant
of the state of the times; while Philo makes mention of a serious outbreak between
Jews and Greeks in Alexandria, though at a much earlier period. The *fourth* sign
consisted of tremors of the earth, by which towns and cities were often shaken and
ruined. These earthquakes were to occur in divers places. Never perhaps, in an equal
period of time in the history of our earth, did so many of these fearful convulsions occur,
as in the interval between the Crucifixion and fall of Jerusalem. Seneca, in a somewhat rhetorical passage in one of his Epistles, mentions a surprising number of such
casualties having occurred in many different quarters, and with the usual disastrous
results; in his list of places where earthquakes had taken place are proconsular Asia,
Achaia, Syria, Macedonia, Cyprus, and Paphus. Tacitus makes mention of several in
different localities—in Crete; in Italy, one at Rome and another in Campania; in
Phrygia, at Apamea, and Laodicea. Josephus speaks of one in Judæa; and several
others are recorded about the same time. Of the *fifth* sign, or famines, we have the
record in the Acts (xi. 28), where Agabus foretold "that there should be great dearth
throughout all the world: which came to pass in the days of Claudius Cæsar;" and
the testimony of Tacitus, Suetonius, and Josephus to similar effect. The whole time
of the reign of Claudius appears to have been one of scarcity; that in the ninth year of
his reign appears to have been particularly severe. Three other famines occurred in
his reign. During this period, Rome, Syria, and Greece suffered most painfully. From
the famines we might naturally infer the existence of the *sixth* sign, or pestilences, even
if we had no historical record of their occurrence, according to the old proverb, that
"after famine comes pestilence," so neatly expressed in the Greek μετὰ λιμὸν λοιμός.
And yet disasters of this kind are recorded—one in Babylonia, by Josephus; one in
Rome, which swept away thirty thousand persons in one autumn, by Tacitus and
Suetonius. The New Testament itself furnishes proof enough, and more than enough,
of the persecutions which were the *seventh* sign. In Acts iv. 3—7 we read of the
Apostles Peter and John being arrested, thrown into prison, and brought before the
Sanhedrim; in Acts v. 18 we read that they "laid their hands on the apostles, and put
them in the common prison," and at the twenty-seventh verse of the same chapter that
they "brought them and set them before the council;" in Acts xvi. 23, 24, that they
"laid many stripes upon them [Paul and Silas], and cast them into prison," where the

jailor "thrust them into the inner prison, and made their feet fast in the stocks;" in Acts xviii. 12 of Paul being brought to the judgment, and in xxiii. 1 of his appearing before the council and being smitten on the mouth, by command of the high priest Ananias. One of the duties of the *Chazzan*, a minister of the synagogue, was to exercise discipline, and of this Paul had his share, when, as he tells us, "Of the Jews five times received I forty stripes save one;" and again, "Thrice was I beaten with rods." The εἰς before "synagogues" is pregnant, implying that they were previously brought into the synagogues and then beaten therein. The distinction that makes εἰς refer to the persons present before whose eyes the punishment was inflicted, while ἐν only indicates the place, is more than doubtful. Again, St. Paul affords an exemplification of the succeeding statement that they should "be brought before rulers and kings," having appeared before Felix, Festus, and Agrippa in succession, as recorded in Acts xxiv.—xxvi.; also before Nero, as we may infer from 2 Tim. iv. 16, 17, where he speaks of his first answer, and of being delivered out of the mouth of the lion. Of apostasies, the *eighth* sign, we have both direct and indirect evidence. The latter is found in the many and earnest warnings which the Epistle to the Hebrews contains against such, while evidence of the former kind is supplied by the heathen historian Tacitus. The rapid progress which the preaching of the gospel had made, notwithstanding all the opposition and hindrances, and cruel persecutions, and sad apostasies, is perhaps the most surprising fact of all; while of this we have such incidental notices as the following :—" Your faith is spoken of throughout the whole world," writes St. Paul to the Romans; to the Galatians he writes of his own circuit to Arabia, back to Damascus, and then to the head-quarters in Jerusalem; to the Colossians he says of "the Word of the truth of the gospel, which is come unto you, as it is in all the world; and bringeth forth fruit, as it doth also in you;" and again, in the same chapter (Col. i. 23), he speaks of the hope of the gospel, and adds, "which ye have heard, and which was preached to every creature which is under heaven." Thus was verified the *ninth* sign.

III. THE MORAL LESSONS INTERSPERSED. 1. *Practical directions.* With the important predictions of this section, and indeed of the whole chapter, practical directions of greatest consequence are blended. Similarly, in the writings of the apostles, we usually find along with exposition of doctrine the enforcement of duty. The principal practical directions of our Lord in this portion of Scripture are mostly of the nature of moral lessons, and are the following :—*Heedfulness,* which is several times repeated in the course of the chapter; *needfulness of perseverance; prayerfulness;* and *watchfulness.* Other lessons of great practical importance, though expressed rather as categorical statements or predictions than in the form of directions, like those enumerated, are contained in it. 2. *The first of these great moral lessons.* The *first* of these lessons occurs in the fifth verse, in the words, "Take heed lest any man deceive you." The same, though slightly altered, and in a somewhat different connection, occurs in the ninth verse, in the words, "But take heed to yourselves;" again, in the twenty-third verse, we read, "But take ye heed;" and once more, in the thirty-third verse, it is set as a preface or introduction to other duties: "Take ye heed, watch and pray." In its first occurrence, it warns the disciples against being deceived by others; in the second, it cautions them in reference to their own deportment; in its third occurrence, it calls on them to do their duty, as the Saviour had done his by them in full predictions and directions; while, in its last occurrence in the chapter, its repetition seems designed to add emphasis to the injunctions immediately coming after. This first lesson is as elastic in its application as practical in its nature, which is manifest from the varying context with which it is connected. In its first context in this chapter, it puts us on our guard against deception. As originally applied, it warned the disciples against pretenders to Messiahship—competitive claimants to that dignity, or rather personators of Christ himself, alleging they were himself returned again, according to the promise of his second advent. But in principle and spirit it applies to ourselves, and is needed by Christians at all times. In a world like this, where so many things are not what they seem, we are required to be upon our guard. Satan is watching to impose on us with his lies, and deceive us to our destruction; we must beware of him. Sinners are waiting to deceive us by their enticement; we must beware of them, and when they entice us not yield consent. Sin itself contains the very essence of deception. It promises pleasures; but the pleasures of sin last only for a season, and that season is a short one, while during that season, short as it is, they do not satisfy. Often instead of pleasure it brings us pain; and it is always pain in the end. In the second of its occurrences, as above specified, the warning related to the deportment of the disciples themselves, in the extremely trying circumstances in which they would often find themselves placed. Other perils and other unsettling circumstances were of a general nature; their attention is now claimed for those more imminent and more immediately affecting themselves. When arraigned before councils or shamefully maltreated in synagogues, when scourged or scorned, amid indignities and insults and injuries, it behoved them, after their Master's example, to bear themselves bravely; when they suffered, to forbear threatening; when evil entreated, to bear up with patience and meekness as well as fortitude. When brought before rulers and kings, magistrates of the lowest and highest rank, they are reminded of the duty then especially incumbent on them—to be valiant for the truth. They were to take heed to themselves, that no unfaithfulness on their part should mar their message which they had for men, high or low, rich or poor, foes or friends, or induce them to keep back aught of the testimony they had to bear. Nay, more, they were to take heed to themselves lest they should esteem Christ's yoke a weariness, or duty to him a drudgery; but, on the contrary, to consider it a privilege to have an opportunity to testify to his cause and claims, however perilous or painful the position. In like manner, whenever opportunity is fairly afforded us to present Christ's claims, or plead his cause, or testify to the truth of his religion, it is incumbent on us joyfully to avail ourselves of it, faithfully to declare the whole counsel of God, to stand up bravely for the truth, and to "contend earnestly for the faith once delivered to the saints." 3. *The second great moral lesson.* The *second* of these lessons is, as already intimated, the necessity of *perseverance.* "He that shall endure unto the end, the same shall be saved." This, in the first instance, was applicable to the apostles, and peculiarly appropriate in their case; but it has a wider scope and more general bearing. It warns against that *fickleness* which enters on the path of duty with eagerness and seeming earnestness, it may be, but speedily turns aside, as did the Galatians, of whom the apostle had reason to complain, "Ye did run well, but something hindered you." It cautions us against putting our hand to the plough and then turning back, as many do when they realize the arduous nature of the work, or when some discouragement comes in their way, or some formidable obstacle has to be encountered. It urges us to *endurance* amid the toils, the trials, the troubles, the many perplexities, the sore sufferings, and manifold afflictions which the Christian has to endure during this mortal life and strife. It exhorts us to *patience,* withal; we are to endure patiently, that is to say, unmurmuringly. Some endure, indeed, but their endurance loses half its virtue through the complaining and frettings that accompany it. Further, it encourages us to *perseverance* —a manful holding out to the last, and to a brave persistence in the way and work of God, however arduous our task may be, and however difficult or dangerous the path we have to travel. In a word, we are to "stand fast in the faith, quit us like men, and be strong." The path of duty here, as elsewhere and often, shall prove the way of safety. If we suffer with him, we shall reign with him; if we bear the cross, we shall wear the crown.

> "Then steadfast let us still remain,
>   Though dangers rise around,
>   And in the work prescribed by God
>   Yet more and more abound;
> Assured that, though we labour now,
>   We labour not in vain;
> But, through the grace of heaven's great Lord,
>   Th' eternal crown shall gain."

J. J. G.

Vers. 14—23. Parallel passages: Matt. xxiv. 15—28; Luke xxi. 20—24.—*The end imminent.* I. IMMEDIATELY PROXIMATE SIGNS. Hitherto we have had the signs, more or less remote, of Christ's coming at the fall of Jerusalem, and so an answer to the second part of the question contained in ver. 4. Here, however, we have the immediately proximate sign, or rather an answer to the first part of the question of that same verse, namely, "When shall these things be?" Along with the sign here intimated, we have instructions about the ways and means of escape. But with respect to the immediately proximate sign or time of the destruction of Jerusalem, we read that it is "the abomination of desolation" foretold by Daniel. The expression is regarded as relating to the Roman army, that brought desolation on the holy city; but whether the actual reference be to the besieging host itself, or to their standards, the eagles, as objects of idolatry, or to the outrages of the Zealots in the sacred courts, is not so certain. The parallel expression in Luke xxi. 20, "When ye shall see Jerusalem compassed with armies, then know that the desolation thereof is nigh," is deemed by some conclusive for the reference being to the Roman armies; most commentators understand the expression of the Roman eagles planted in *a holy place*, that is, round Jerusalem, first by Cestius Gallus A.D. 66, then by Vespasian two years after, and two years later still by Titus; while a third explanation refers the sign to the atrocities of the Zealots at this time. In this way the sign was twofold—internal and external; the latter consisting of the Roman legions now drawn round the city, the former of the abominations of the Zealots, causing the cup of Jewish iniquity to overflow, and thus directly leading to the desolation that immediately ensued. Two circumstances seem to favour this last view of the matter: the holy place is properly referable to the temple, and the sign of the Roman eagles would be rather indefinite, as they had been seen in Palestine for a considerable period previously. Inward desecration caused by sin in some way issued in outward desolation.

II. PRECAUTIONS SUGGESTED. It is not the duty of Christians more than of non-Christians to rush unnecessarily into peril any more than into temptation; we are not to endanger life and limb recklessly and negligently. Our first duty is self-preservation when no principle is compromised and no matter of spiritual moment is at stake; we are required to use all legitimate means for the preservation of our own lives and the lives of others. Confessors, indeed, have taken joyfully the spoiling of their goods, and martyrs have cheerfully shed their blood, rather than surrender a jot of truth or renounce their allegiance to the Saviour; but there are special occasions and particular circumstances when our duty is to escape from, not court, danger. The disciples, when persecuted in one city, were to flee to another. Our Lord himself, passing through the midst of the wicked Nazarenes, went his way, when they had led him to the brow of the hill whereon their city was built, and would have cast him down headlong. And now he gives directions beforehand for his followers not to imperil their lives needlessly and uselessly, when, by signs of which he forewarns them, they should know that the ruin of Jerusalem was imminent and inevitable, and when the wrath of God was about to be poured out on their unbelieving countrymen. The methods of escape were various. Those who found themselves in Judæa were to flee to the mountains. These, with caves and rocky fastnesses, were favourite places of refuge in time of danger in the land of Palestine; thus, Lot was urgently pressed by the angel to flee to the mountain: "Escape for thy life; look not behind thee, neither stay thou in all the plain; escape to the mountain, lest thou be consumed;" David was hunted by Saul as "a partridge in the mountains." Such as were already on the house-top, or could readily reach it by the steps outside, were not to return into the house to carry off with them any article of property, however prized or valuable, but to hasten their flight with all speed along the flat roofs of the houses till they reached the city walls, and thence make good their escape. Persons engaged in field labour, at which the outer garment (ἱμάτιον) was usually stripped off and laid aside, were not to act so indiscreetly as to run the risk of life itself by returning for the sake of saving an article of raiment probably of no great value.

III. THE THIRD GREAT MORAL LESSON. This, as we have already stated, is *prayerfulness*. Our Lord, after the particular directions enumerated, bethought himself of other cases to which those directions were inapplicable owing to the inability of the persons concerned to comply with them. With tender females in such circumstances of delicacy as precluded the possibility of flight, and with nursing mothers whose womanly affections forbade the thought of abandoning their offspring—with persons thus unfitted for flight, so encumbered as to retard it except through an impossible sacrifice—our Lord expresses the deepest sympathy and tenderest compassion. If, however, we may trace the sequence of thought in the mind of the Saviour as in the human mind in general, the thought of weakness by the law of contrast suggests a power which the weakest can wield and the strongest cannot dispense with, and which in the most untoward circumstances commands success. "And pray ye," says our blessed Lord, " that your flight be not in the winter. " St. Matthew adds, " neither on the sabbath day." The same God who has appointed the end has appointed the means that conduce to that end. One great means is *prayer*. The end and means are connected as links of the same chain. Other means of escape had been prescribed, and even urged on such as could employ those means; some there would be who, from circumstances already indicated, would be precluded from availing themselves of those means; besides, both these classes must, in the dark outlook into the future, anticipate circumstances over which they could have no possible control, such as the season of the year, or the day of the week when the predicted calamities might suddenly burst over them. What, then, was the course to be pursued? Where means were available, prayer was a leverage which imparted to the means a potency multiplied manifold; where the means were not available, prayer was the only element of power that could be employed; while in both cases there were certain obstacles which human power could not overcome, and certain circumstances with which it was incompetent to grapple. It was only by prayer that difficulties of this sort could be vanquished. The *subject-matter* of the prayers our Lord graciously condescends to suggest. They were to pray for the avoidance of the winter, when its cold and inclemency would greatly aggravate the general distress, or when its heavy rains, swollen streams, and winter torrents might render flight or escape impossible. They were to pray that they might not be necessitated to infringe the sanctity of the sabbath, on which a lawful journey did not exceed a mile; and when, the city gates being closed, would either shut them in or shut them out, and in either case cut them off from a place of safety; or when they might expose themselves to punishment from the cruelty of fanatics for a breach of the sabbath law. Our Lord suggested to them such topics of supplication, putting desires into their hearts and words on their lips.

IV. GOD'S GOODNESS TO HIS CHOSEN. "For the elect's sake, whom he hath chosen, he hath shortened the days." His elect are his chosen—chosen to salvation through sanctification of the Spirit and belief of the truth, chosen in Christ before the foundation of the world, chosen of God and precious, a chosen generation, called, chosen, and faithful. The privileges of God's people are very many and very great. God avenges his own elect; nothing shall be laid to the charge of God's elect; he will gather them at last from the four winds; while here we learn that those days of direst disasters and unspeakable horrors were shortened for their sake. How great the blessedness of being children of God! The psalmist had affirmed the blessedness of such centuries before; he had affirmed it on the highest authority and for the best of reasons. "Blessed," he said, "is the man whom thou choosest, and causest to approach unto thee, that he may dwell in thy courts. . . . By terrible things in righteousness wilt thou answer us, O God of our salvation."

V. GOD'S PROVIDENTIAL DEALINGS WITH HIS PEOPLE. The dispensations of God's providence prove, while they illustrate, his goodness to his people. In the present instance the Saviour *warned* his followers; this was the first link in the chain of his love. Acting on this warning, they fled; and God, in his mercy, favoured their flight and facilitated it. In *answer* to the petitions previously taught them and presented, we may be sure, by them, their flight was not in winter, or at least needed not to be so, for the siege commenced in the October of 66 A.D.; the final siege began in the April or May of the year of our Lord 70. Thus they had the opportunity of flight before or at the beginning of the siege, and consequently before the rigours of winter had set in; or, if perchance any delayed their flight and lingered on till near the concluding catastrophe, they in like manner avoided the winter. The consequence was that the Christian Jews effected their escape to Pella, now *Tabathat Fakkil*, near the northern border of Peræa, among the hills of Gilead, on the other side of Jordan, and a hundred miles from the besieged city. The merciful dealings of Divine providence were also manifested by the *curtailment* (ἐκολόβωσε) of the period of distress. In the midst of wrath he remembered mercy, and for his elect's sake he so overruled matters that the siege was brought to a speedy termination. So terrible was the time that, in the words of the evangelist, "except the Lord had shortened the days, no flesh would have been saved." The Scripture statement is fully confirmed by the historical details of Josephus, who makes it abundantly evident that the wretchedness of men and the wickedness of men had then culminated. Unprecedented before, they have remained without parallel since. It was Passover time, and multitudes thronged the city. What from this state of matters inside the city and the siege outside, famine ensued; its usual attendant, pestilence, followed. Men and women seemed to have divested themselves of the instincts of humanity; nameless barbarities were perpetrated. The city was torn by sedition within—three factions being in constant conflict with each other; war raged without, hundreds of Jewish prisoners being crucified in sight of their friends. More than a million Jews perished in the siege, and ninety-seven thousand were taken captive—some of them sold into slavery, some sent to Egyptian mines, and others reserved for the gladiatorial games. "Those days shall be affliction," according to the correct rendering; and never was prediction fulfilled with more terrible literality. But two circumstances, under Providence, abridged this reign of terrors : one was the terrible energy of the besieger, who pressed the siege and at last stormed the city; and the other was the fearful infatuation of the besieged. The city, which had withstood Nebuchadnezzar more than a year and a quarter, fell before the power of the Roman general in less than five months. Had things continued much longer, Judæa itself would have been desolated, and its inhabitants, including, no doubt, many sincere Christians, would have perished. But God, for his people's sake, shortened those days of shocking suffering and unspeakable sadness. The Saviour again, and for the third time, repeats his exhortation to heedfulness against those who at such a crisis deceived, either consciously or unconsciously, themselves, and who should deceive others by holding forth hopes of deliverance by the coming of the Christ.—J. J. G.

Vers. 24—31. Parallel passages : Matt. xxiv. 29—35; Luke xxi. 25—33.—*The second advent.* I. THE GREATNESS OF THE EVENT. Whether our Lord's coming shall be pre-millennial or post-millennial we stay not to inquire. The great importance attaches to the fact of the second coming of the Son of man, which this section describes and which all Christians believe. The future coming of the Son of man naturally leads us back in thought to his first coming. The world had waited long for that blessed day. Patriarchs had looked forward to it, but it was in faith; prophets saw it, but it was in vision; saints sighed for its approach, but it was still a great way off—they hoped for its arrival, but they died before the promise was fulfilled; servants of God longed for its coming, and when it at length arrived they felt so satisfied that there seemed nothing further for them to desire—the language of Simeon expressed their thoughts, "Now, Lord, lettest thou thy servant depart in peace, according to thy word: for mine eyes have seen thy salvation." Angels celebrated it on the plains of Bethlehem, and sang in heavenly carol, "Glory to God in the highest, peace on earth, and good will to men." The people of God look forward with equal longing and equal eagerness to the day of Christ's second coming. They look and long for it as the period of complete redemption; they expect it as the time of home-gathering of all their brethren in the Lord; in anticipation of that great deliverance and of that blessed reunion they cry, "Even so, Lord Jesus, come quickly."

II. THE GLORY OF HIS COMING. He will come, we are taught to believe, personally, visibly, and gloriously. He will come "in the *clouds.*" The clouds of heaven serve many important purposes; they screen from the heat of the sun by day, and moderate the radiation of the earth by night. Sometimes they supply from their contents moisture to plants, and bring gladness to the thirsty ground; sometimes they pour down the water that originates springs or swells rivers; sometimes they cover with snow the polar regions. Those cloud-masses, as they float in the atmosphere, now approach within a mile of the earth, again ascend to the distance of five or six miles above its surface. Sometimes they curl in thin, parallel, silvery streaks; sometimes they form dense conical or convex heaps; sometimes, at the approach of night, they spread out in wide low-lying horizontal sheets; sometimes, fraught with storm, they move like a dark canopy overhead; again they unite and form various combinations. At all times they claim our attention, and commend themselves to our admiration by their fantastic forms, their changing colours, their varying density, and their strange combinations. The views of a kaleidoscope are nothing compared with the manifold aspects of the clouds. The clouds of heaven, then, are objects of great beauty, grandeur, and glory. The ancient heathens had a just appreciation of the magnificence of the clouds, and accordingly associated them with their highest conceptions of *majesty.* They represented their deities as clothed with clouds, or seated on clouds, or surrounded with clouds, as if to hide from mortal gaze their excessive splendour. In Scripture, also, the true God is represented as making the clouds his chariot, and walking upon the wings of the wind; and, again, we read that "his pavilion round about him were dark waters, and thick clouds of the skies." When Isaiah predicts the destruction of Egypt and the confusion of its idols from the hand of the Lord, he uses the sublime representation, "Behold, the Lord rideth upon a swift cloud, and shall come into Egypt." Daniel employs similar language in relation to the Son of man: "Behold, one like the Son of man came with the clouds of heaven, and came to the Ancient of days, and they brought him near before him. And there was given him dominion, and glory, and a kingdom, that all people, nations, and languages, should serve him." The representation before us here is in accordance also with our Lord's reply, when, in answer to his question about his Messiahship, he directed their attention from the humility of his first to the honour of his second coming, saying, "Ye shall see the Son of man sitting on the right hand of power, and coming in the clouds of heaven." So also, when he was going to part from his disciples, when he was going to leave our world, when his feet last stood on Olivet, when he was about to ascend to his Father and our Father, to his God and our God, the cloud became his vehicle, and coming *under* him received (ὑπέλαβεν) him out of the disciples' sight; and in that car of cloud he rose onward, and mounted upward to the right hand of the Father everlasting. Thence he shall come again with glorious majesty, according to the promise, "This same Jesus, which is taken up from you into heaven, shall so come in like manner as ye have seen him go into heaven." Further, in the Apocalypse, the Apostle John's representation of Christ's coming with clouds is designed and calculated to signify the grandeur and the glory, the solemnity and the sublimity of his second advent: "Behold, he cometh with clouds; and every eye shall see him, and they also which pierced him: and all kindreds of the earth shall wail because of him. Even so, Amen."

III. THE GLORY AND POWER WITH WHICH HE COMES. Every manifestation of glory shall attend him; every symbol of unspeakable splendour shall accompany him; every token of dignity shall signalize him; every adjunct of might and magnificence shall mark his advent. The Son of man shall come with great power and glory; all the holy angels shall swell his train. The dead in Christ shall rise first, and swell that assemblage; they that are still alive, and remain till that dread day, shall be caught up together with them in the clouds to meet the Lord in the air. Can anything be grander than this? Can anything be more august? Can anything be more solemn? Can anything be more awe-inspiring? Is there anything more calculated to overwhelm with consternation the wicked? Is there anything more fitted to create deep and universal alarm among the ungodly? What, on the other hand, can be more inspiriting to the believer? What more encouraging and comforting to the child of God? What more suitable to nerve to high effort and holy purpose than the prospect of being presented faultless in that day, and amid that assembly, and before the presence of his glory, with exceeding joy?

> "A hope so great and so Divine
> May trials well endure,
> And purge the soul from sense and sin,
> As Christ himself is pure."

IV. THE OBJECT OF HIS COMING. We may now reflect for a moment on the great purposes for which Christ shall come the second time. At first he came in weakness, but at his next coming he will take to him his great power and reign. At first he came in dishonour, born in a stable, cradled in a manger, being "despised and rejected of men;" but then he shall come in dignity, and so that "every eye shall see him," every tongue confess him, and every knee bow before him. At first he came in a servile, suffering state; but then in awful majesty and glory everlasting—in his own glory, and in the glory of his Father. At first he came to call sinners to repentance; but then to summon each to his reward, be it recompense or retribution, and "to give every man according as his work shall be." It is true that the coming of the Son of man described in the verses immediately before us has for its specific object the grand

assemblage of his saints to meet him; the accessories of the resurrection, the transformation of the living, and the general judgment are left out of sight. From the
tribulation connected with the fall of Jerusalem the Saviour had looked far forward into
other days, when great changes, whether literal and cosmical, or figurative and political,
shall precede and serve as precursors of the second coming of the Son of man. If the
language is understood figuratively, the darkening of the sun may denote the eclipse of
ecclesiastical authority; that of the moon, the collapse of civil polity; while the stars
or potentates shall be falling or waning (the form of the future made up of substantive
verb and participle, implying a more durable effect than the simple future). In the
parable of the fig tree, however, he reverts to the precursors of the dissolution of the
Jewish state and the destruction of its capital; and affirms that, as the tender leaf-buds
of the fig tree signified the near approach of harvest-time (θέρος), so the signs already
specified in an early part of this chapter indicated the fast-approaching destruction of
the sanctuary and city of Jerusalem. If, then, the statement of ver. 30, "that this
generation shall not pass, till all these things be done," be referred to the end of the
Jewish state, the word γενεὰ retains its ordinary sense of generation or contemporary
race, which some insist on. If, on the other hand, the end of the age or world be
referred to, whether the coming of the Son of man be for the purpose of ushering in the
millennium, that is, pre-millennial, or for the final winding up of all things, the word
γενεὰ must be understood as equivalent to γένος, race, that is, the people or nation of
the Jews, or, according to some, the race of men in general, more especially the
generation of the faithful.

V. THE DIFFERENT FEELINGS WITH WHICH HIS COMING IS REGARDED. The visit of
some distinguished person to our neighbourhood or to our habitation may, according
to circumstances, awaken emotions of a very different or even diverse character. Our
feelings in view of the expected visit will be either pleasant or painful, according to
the character of the visitor or the object of his coming. If he comes as a friend to
further our interests, to favour our fondly cherished hopes, and to confer on us certain
benefits, we naturally hail his coming with delight and rejoice at the prospect of his
speedy advent. If, on the contrary, we have reason to believe that his intentions are
hostile, that he means to oppose our plans, that he has some unpleasant measure to
enforce or some punishment to inflict, we just as naturally dread his arrival and recoil
from his approach. With similarly opposite views and feelings, saints and sinners,
believers and unbelievers, look forward to the coming of him to whom this passage
refers.—J. J. G.

Vers. 32—37. Parallel passages: Matt. xxiv. 36—51; Luke xxi. 34—36.—*Preparation for Christ's coming.* I. TRANSITIÓN FROM THE DESTRUCTION OF JERUSALEM
TO THE DAY OF JUDGMENT. Again our Lord passes from the typical event to the antitypical consummation of all things—from the destruction of the holy city to the
dissolution of things visible. The limitation of our Lord's knowledge with respect to
" that day and that hour " must be understood of his human nature as the Son of man,
in which he was subject to such other sinless conditions of humanity as increasing in
wisdom, growing in stature, feeling hunger, thirst, lassitude, and the like; or it did
not come within the sphere of his prophetic office to reveal it, as it belonged to "the
times or the seasons which the Father hath set within his own authority." Our Lord,
according to Meyer, knew this κατὰ κτῆσιν, *i.e.* with respect to possession, of which,
however, in his humiliation he had divested himself; not κατὰ χρῆσιν, in regard to
use, viz. for revelation.

II. THE GREAT EVENTS CONSEQUENT ON HIS COMING. One of these events shall be
the *resurrection* of the dead. " Now," says the apostle, "is Christ risen from the
dead, and become the firstfruits of them that slept;" but then shall be this world's
great harvest-day. Then shall a shout be heard, so loud, so piercing, that it will reach
the dull, cold ear of death; the voice of the archangel shall re-echo through the dismal
recesses of the tomb, and call to life the buried dead; the trump of God shall resound
through the caverns of earth and the caves of ocean, till earth and sea shall give up
the dead that are in them. Then shall be fulfilled the saying of our Lord elsewhere
recorded, that " the hour is coming, in the which all that are in their graves shall
hear the voice of the Son of God, and come forth; they that have done good, to the

resurrection of life; and they that have done evil, to the resurrection of condemnation."
Further, on his coming at the day or hour here spoken of, the Son of man shall *judge*
the world in righteousness. The dead, small and great, shall stand before him; the
judgment shall be set, and the books opened. All nations, and kindreds, and tongues,
and peoples shall be assembled at that bar of God; "we must all appear before that
judgment-seat of Christ, to give an account of the deeds done in the body, whether
they be good or evil." The decisions of that day shall be final, allowing no alteration,
no appeal, and no reversal. Not only so; based on the unvarying principles of justice
and equity, righteousness and truth, they shall commend themselves to the consciences
of all concerned. The condemned and justified alike shall acquiesce in them; sinners
shall assent to them as just; saints shall approve of them as gracious; angels shall
applaud them as worthy of the Judge; and all intelligences shall acknowledge them
to be as impartial as irreversible.

III. The FOURTH PRACTICAL DIRECTION. The fourth great moral lesson of the
chapter is *watchfulness*. This lesson our Lord insists on, repeating it with great
earnestness, and conjoining with it the duty of prayerfulness: "Take ye heed,
watch and pray;" "Watch ye therefore;" and again, "Watch:" The two duties of
watchfulness and prayerfulness are frequently associated; thus, "Watch and pray, lest
ye enter into temptation." Both together represent Divine and human strength in
co-operation with each other. If we watch without prayer, we depend on human strength,
and dispense with Divine aid; if we pray without watching, we depend on Divine
strength alone, and despise the human means of help which God himself has commanded
us to employ. They are the two strong arms of defence against the evil one; and we
may not, we cannot, without serious dereliction of duty and gravest danger, part with
either of them. This duty of watchfulness is enforced by a beautiful parabolic illustration; though it is not a formal parable, as the words supplied in the Common Version
make it. Those words, "For the Son of man is," should be struck out; equally
unnatural is it to supply the words, "The kingdom of heaven is;" neither is Kuinoel's
mode of supplying the ellipsis by ποιῶ any better; while Euthymius, who seems to refer
the words to Christ and to understand the future of the substantive verb, as though it
were, "I shall be as a man setting out on a far journey," is even less satisfactory. In
addition to this, ἀπόδημος, said of one "already abroad, or an absentee from his people,"
is confounded with ἀποδημῶν, which signifies "going abroad." Fritzsche rightly explains
as follows:—"Res ita habet ut—die Sache verhält sich so wie," and compares therewith
the Horatian use of *ut si* in the words, "Ut tibi si sit opus liquidi non amplius urna."
So also the Revised Version, correcting both the errors of the Common Version, renders
correctly: "*It is* as *when* a man, sojourning in another country, having left his house,
and given authority to his servants, to each one his work, commanded also the porter to
watch." This translation helps us much in the right understanding of the illustration.
The man is already abroad; but before he went abroad, he, as a matter of course, left his
house, having previously to leaving given authority to his servants in general to manage
matters for him in his absence, and having appointed to each in particular his special
work; and when on the threshold, as it were, he gave a charge to the porter *also* to
watch, and so be prepared for his return.

IV. REASONS FOR THE WATCHFULNESS ENJOINED. Though there is no express application of the illustration, a circumstance which adds much to the ease and grace of
the narrative, we are at no loss for, and find no difficulty in making, that application.
The Master of the house is our Lord; his disciples, in the first place, are the domestics
whom he entrusted with the management of the household when he himself took his
departure to the goodly land afar off, appointing each believer his own sphere of
labour and the special duty he was bound to perform, and leaving a strict charge of
watchfulness with the porter who kept the door; that is, either the ministry in general,
who are watchmen on the walls of Zion, or Peter in particular, to whom had been
entrusted the power of the keys in opening the door of faith to Jew and Gentile. Nor
do we thereby concede anything to the Romanist in reference to Peter's supremacy—
a rank which the apostle himself never claimed. Be this as it may, however, the duty
of watchfulness is enjoined on all, (1) because the time of the Master's coming back is
unknown. We know neither the day nor the hour of our Lord's return. No fellow-
creature can tell us; no minister nor man can inform us; no angel can give us any

intimation ; no messenger from either world can bring us word. "Of that day and of that hour knoweth no man, no, not the angels of God." Now, though the coming of the Son of man is not to be confounded with death—for the two events are quite distinct—yet for all practical purposes, and as far as our personal interests are concerned, death is the coming of the Son of man to us individually ; for whether he come to us or he call us to him, it is virtually the same thing for us, as then our destiny is finally and for ever fixed.   We are urged to watchfulness (2) because this event, which, though not the coming of the Son of man to the Church in its universality, is tantamount to his coming to the Christian in his individuality, is *uncertain* as to time.   This great event may be near at hand while we least expect it.   This day may be our last, on earth, and our first in the spirit-world; on this very night the soul may be required.   This very day our lamp may lose its oil and go out in darkness; this very day our taber-nacle may totter and tumble into dust; this very day our wondrous harp, with its thousand strings, may go out of tune and lose its melody.   "What is your life? It is even a vapour, that appeareth for a little time, and then vanisheth away."   What is your lease of life?   It is the breath in your nostrils, and at any moment that breath may be withdrawn.   In any case—

> "Determined are the days that fly
> Successive o'er thy head;
> The number'd hour is on the wing
> That lays thee with the dead."

Further, watchfulness is indispensable, because (3) at his coming he will deal with us *separately and singly*.   We shall be assembled in the aggregate, but dealt with in detail.   The great fact is as prominently stated, as it is positively sure, that we must each stand in his lot at the end of the days.   You, reader, and I and all must soon give an account of our stewardship—must soon be reckoned with for the talents, whether ten, or five, or one, that God gave us; whether we have buried them in the ear.h, or brought them forth employed, improved, and augmented; whether we have wasted our Lord's goods, or used them in his service and for his glory; whether we have occupied till the time of his coming, or loitered out our day of life.   We are required to be watchful, for (4) in the last great day each and all—the one and the many—shall stand *face to face* with the Judge of all the earth.   If we pause and ponder the vastness of that crowd, we are almost overwhelmed by the thought.   Let us think of all the people of a single nation being brought together; what a crowd they would make!   Let us think of all the subjects of a great empire being assembled at one place and at one time; what an assembly that would be!   Let us then think of all the inhabitants of one of the quarters of the globe being congregated; what an immense mass-meeting would be thus formed!   Yet the thought of the great congregation at the coming of the Son of man far outgoes all that.   The assemblage which it implies, and which shall one day take place, shall consist, not only of the inhabitants of a province, or a nation, or an empire, or even a quarter of the globe, but shall comprehend the inhabitants of all provinces, nations, empires, and quarters of the globe, down along the ages and throughout all the centuries of time.   And yet not one in all that crowd shall be hidden from the eye of him that cometh in that day; not one shall be able to evade his presence, not one escape his sentence, not one shall be so remote as to be unable to catch a glance of him, not one on whom his eye shall not rest.   "Every eye shall see him!"—the eye that con-templated his goodness and his grace; the eye that "beheld his glory, as of the only begotten of the Father, full of grace and truth;" the eye that looked and longed for his appearing; the eye, on the contrary, that looked only on the objects of sense and sin, the pomps and vanities of the world, and the follies of life; the eye that never gazed upon the cross, or never cast more than a passing glance thereat, and then turned away in coldness or carelessness, or perhaps contempt; the eye of friend and follower; the eye of foe and false professor.   Oh, what a sight to the unpardoned sinner, to the god-less transgressor, to the swearer, to the sabbath-breaker, to the slanderer, to the adulterer, to the murderer, to the drunkard, to the liar, to the lewd and licentious, to the unholy and the unjust, to the impure and impenitent!   Gladly would the wicked shut their eyes on that sight; gladly would they sink into the bowels of the earth or the depths of ocean to escape the glance of that searching eye!   Earnestly will they pray, who never prayed before, for the mountains and rocks to fall on them and hide them from the face of the Judge. But no, that cannot be; for it is added in another Scripture, "They also that pierced him." We all, whether ministers or members of the Church of Christ, are bound to watchfulness—"What I say unto you I say unto all, Watch!"—and that lest (5) we should be found among those that *pierced* him. This refers to his actual murderers in the first instance—the Jews that condemned him, the Romans that crucified him, the scribes and Pharisees that plotted against him, the priests and people that persecuted him, the passers-by that wagged the head, the men that scoffed him, and those that scourged him, and they that spat upon him; the fierce mob that cried, "Away with him! away with him!" the judge that condemned him, the disciple that betrayed him—all that imbrued their hands in his precious blood or had aught to do with his death. But we may not stop here. Others have pierced him, too; for we read of those who "crucify Christ afresh, and put him to an open shame." Ah! is there any of ourselves included in that number? Is there any of us who have pierced his heart by our sin, by our disobedience, by our ingratitude, by our backsliding, by our coldness, and by our carelessness? Ah! is there none of us to whom he can say, "See, here are the wounds with which I was wounded in the house of my friends"? "Watch ye therefore!" is repeated once and again and a third time. While one of the terms used signifies to keep awake and remain sleepless, the other means to awake or arouse from sleepiness; and thus the sense seems to be, if the distinction is admitted, to guard against sleep overtaking us at the post of duty; or, if unhappily we have been overtaken by drowsiness, to rouse ourselves at once from our slumber and repent of our sinful somnolence. And all the more as we are left in such entire uncertainty and ignorance of the hour when the Master shall come and reckon with us in our individual capacity, and, if we are found culpable, condemn us with the wicked. That hour may be at any of the four watches of the night—nine o'clock, or twelve, or three, or six in the morning. So important is this lesson that our Lord, in St. Matthew's Gospel, enforces it by two parables—that of the virgins and that of the talents; the former inculcating watchfulness over the spirit, and probably implied in ver. 36 of the present chapter; the latter quickening faithfulness in duty, and seemingly epitomized in the two preceding verses of this same chapter.

V. OTHER LESSONS OF THE CHAPTER. 1. *The truth of Scripture.* Besides the lessons already noticed, there are others to which we can only advert. The lessons scattered through this chapter are like flowers in a summer field. Another of these is the truth of Scripture. "Heaven and earth shall pass away." The frame of nature, stable as it now seems, has in it the elements of change. There are changes in the geological strata of the earth beneath us, in the sky above us, in the natural world around us. Great changes have already taken place in earth and sea and sky; great physical changes are daily going on; still greater changes may be expected to occur in time to come. The surest inductions of science point to such changes and collapses. "But my words," said our Lord, "shall not pass away." His words have passed into the spiritual fibre of his people, living in their lives, exhibited in their conduct, illustrated by their character, and consoling them in the hour of dissolution. Statesmen have been guided by them, lawgivers have framed laws by them, philosophers have made more use of them in building up their systems than they have been willing to acknowledge to others, or have even been conscious of, themselves. The words of Christ have for eighteen hundred years or more blended with the inspirations of the poet; they have almost moved in the marble of the statuary, and spoken from the canvas of the painter. Time has not exhausted their fulness; no taint has touched their freshness, nor has aught of their fragrance decayed. Further, the inspiration of Scripture is safely inferred from the statement in ver. 11, "It is not ye that speak, but the Holy Ghost," compared with St. Luke's parallel statement, "I will give you a mouth," the expression, "and wisdom," the matter to be expressed. 2. *The publication of the gospel among all nations.* The gospel must first be published. Here was the great end to be attained. We have seen how this was virtually accomplished before the fall of Jerusalem; but the world has widened its boundaries since then. Continents and islands have been added to it; navigation and travel have enlarged geography, and geography has added to the dimensions of the globe, or at least has revealed those before unknown. And still the gospel is preached, and shall be.

> "Jesus shall reign where'er the sun
> Doth his successive journeys run;
> His kingdom stretch from shore to shore,
> Till moons shall wax and wane no more."

3. *Watchfulness the lesson of the ages.* Scenes similar to those that preceded Christ's coming at the fall of Jerusalem may be repeated, and repeated over a wider area and on a grander scale. Then, as before, there may be wars—some actual, others rumoured—great international conflicts, and fatal internecine strife; then, as before, there may be physical catastrophes, providential visitations, as the travail-throes of greater events—the travail-pangs in the genesis of the new order of things; then, as before, there may be persecutions, prolonged and repeated, and the severance of the nearest ties of kinship, with universal hatred for the Saviour's sake. Yet, through all, men must possess their souls in patience, or rather, according to the correcter reading, gain their souls, their real life, by patience—patient endurance, not violent resistance. Men may be worn with watching, pining for peace, and aweary for rest; still the same lesson has to be repeated, the same duty practised: "What I say unto you I say unto all, Watch!" Watchfulness is still the duty of the Church and of the Christian.

> "Yet saints their watch are keeping;
> Their cry goes up, 'How long?'
> And soon the night of weeping
> Shall be the morn of song."

J. J. G.

EXPOSITION.

CHAPTER XIV.

Ver. 1.—Now after two days was the feast of the passover and the unleavened bread; literally, *the passover and the unleavened* (τό πάσχα καὶ τὰ ἄζυμα). It was one and the same festival. The killing of the Paschal lamb took place on the first of the seven days during which the festival lasted, and during the whole of which they used unleavened bread. Josephus describes it as "the festival of the unleavened, called *Phaska* by the Jews." **The chief priests and the scribes.** St. Matthew (xxvi. 3) says, "The chief priests and the elders of the people." The two classes in the Sanhedrim who actually combined to put our Lord to death were those here mentioned by St. Mark. **They sought how they might take him with subtlety** (ἐν δόλῳ), **and kill him.** It is, literally, *they were seeking* (ἐζήτουν). The verb with its tense implies continuous and eager desire. They used subtlety, because they feared lest he should escape out of their hands. Moreover they feared the people, lest they should fight for him, and not suffer him to be taken.

Ver. 2.—For they said (ἔλεγον γὰρ)—literally, *for they were saying*—**Not during the feast, lest haply there shall be a tumult of the people.** The same cause induced them to avoid the time of the feast. The feast brought a great multitude of Jews to Jerusalem, amongst whom would be many who had received bodily or spiritual benefits from Christ, and who therefore, at least,

worshipped him as a Prophet; and the rulers of the people feared lest these should rise in his defence. Their first intention, therefore, was not to destroy him until after the close of the Paschal feast; but they were overruled by the course of events, all ordered by God's never-failing providence. The sudden betrayal of our Lord by Judas led them to change their minds. For when they found that he was actually in their hands, they resolved to crucify him forthwith. And thus the Divine purpose was fulfilled that Christ should suffer at that particular time, and so the type be satisfied. For the lamb slain at the Passover was a type of the very Paschal Lamb to be sacrificed at that particular time, in the predetermined purpose of God; and to be lifted up upon the cross for the redemption of the world. St. Matthew (xxvi. 3) tells us that they were gathered together "unto the court of the high priest, who was called Caiaphas." It was necessary to state his name, because the high priests were now frequently changed by the Roman power.

Ver. 3.—And while he was in Bethany, in the house of Simon the leper, as he sat at meat, there came a woman having an alabaster cruse (ἀλάβαστρον)—literally, *an alabaster;* as we say, "a glass," of a vessel made of glass—**of ointment of spikenard very costly** (μύρου νάρδου πιστικῆς πολυτελοῦς); **and she brake the cruse, and poured it over his head.** This anointing of our Lord appears to have taken place on the Saturday before Palm Sunday (see John

xii. 1). The anointing mentioned by St. Luke (vii. 36) evidently has reference to some previous occasion. The narrative here and in St. Matthew and St. John would lead us to the conclusion that this was a feast given by Simon—perhaps in grateful acknowledgment of the miracle which had been wrought upon Lazarus. He is called "Simon the leper," probably because he had been a leper, and had been healed by Christ, although he still retained the name of "leper," to distinguish him from others named Simon, or Simeon, a common name amongst the Jews. *There came a woman.* This woman, we learn from St. John (xii. 2, 3), was Mary, the sister of Martha and Lazarus. The vessel, or cruse, which she had with her was made of alabaster, a kind of soft, smooth marble, which could easily be scooped out so as to form a receptacle for ointment, which, according to Pliny ('Nat. Hist.,' xiii. 3), was best preserved in vessels made of alabaster. The vessel would probably be formed with a long narrow neck, which could easily be broken, or crushed (the word in the original is συντρίψασα) so as to allow of a free escape for the unguent. The ointment was made of spikenard (νάρδου πιστικῆς). The Vulgate has *nardi spicati.* If this is the true interpretation of the word πιστικῆς, it would mean that this ointment was made from a bearded plant mentioned by Pliny ('Nat. Hist.,' xii. 12), who says that the ointment made from this plant was most precious. The plant was called by Galen "nardi spica." Hence πιστικὴν would mean "genuine" ointment—ointment made from the flowers of the choicest kind of plant. Pliny ('Nat. Hist.,' xii. 26) says that there was an inferior article in circulation, which he calls "pseudo-nard." The Syriac Peshito Version uses an expression which means the principal, or best kind of ointment. The anointing of the head would be the more usual mark of honour. It would seem most probable that Mary first wiped the feet of Jesus, wetting them with her tears, and then wiping off the dust, and then anointing them; and that she then proceeded to break the neck of the cruse, and to pour its whole contents on his head.

Ver. 4.—**But there were some that had indignation**—the word in the original is ἀγανακτοῦντες, *ached with vexation*—**among themselves.** St. Mark says, "there were some;" avoiding any more particular mention of them. St. Matthew (xxvi. 8) says that the disciples generally had indignation. The murmuring seems to have been general. At length it found a definite expression in Judas Iscariot (see John xii. 4).

Ver. 5.—**For this ointment might have been sold for above three hundred pence, and given to the poor.** Three hundred pence would amount to about £10 12s. 6d. of English money. It appears from St. John (xiii. 29) that the wants of the poor were carefully attended to by our Lord and his disciples. **And they murmured against her** (ἐνεβριμῶντο αὐτῇ); another very expressive verb in the original, *they growled at her; rebuked her vehemently.*

Ver. 6.—It appears from St. John (xii. 7) that our Lord here addressed himself pointedly to Judas in the words, **Let her alone;** . . . **she hath wrought a good work on me,** a work worthy of all praise and honour. "What," says Cornelius à Lapide, "what more noble, than to anoint the feet of him who is both God and man? Who would not count himself happy, if it were permitted to him to touch the feet of Jesus and to kiss them?"

Ver. 7.—**For ye have the poor always with you, and whensoever ye will ye can** (δύνασθε) **do them good: but me ye have not always.** The little clause, "whensoever ye will ye can do them good," occurs only in St. Mark. It is as though our Lord said, "The world always abounds with poor; therefore you always have it in your power to help them; but within a week I shall have gone from you, after which you will be unable to perform any service like this for me; yea, no more to see, to hear, to touch me. Suffer, then, this woman to perform this ministry now for me, which after six days she will have no other opportunity of doing."

Ver. 8.—**She hath done what she could.** She seized the opportunity, which might not occur again, of doing honour to her Lord by anointing him with her very best. Our Lord might have excused this action, and have praised it as a practical evidence of her gratitude, her humility, and her love for him. But instead of dwelling on these things, he said, **She hath anointed my body aforehand for the burying.** Our Lord here, of course, alludes to the spices and ointments with which the Jews wrapped up the bodies of their dead before their burial. Not that this was what Mary intended. She could hardly have dreamed of his death and burial so near at hand. But she was moved by the Holy Spirit to do this, at this particular time, as though in anticipation of his death and burial.

Ver. 9.—**Wheresoever the gospel shall be preached throughout the whole world, that also which this woman hath done shall be spoken of for a memorial of her** (εἰς μνημόσυνον αὐτῆς). "Mnemosyné was the mother of the Muses, and so called because, before the invention of writing, a retentive memory was of the utmost value in every effort of literary genius" (Dr. Morison on St. Mark). When our Lord delivered this prediction, none of the Gospels had been written; nor had the gospel been preached at this time throughout the then known world. Now it has been published for more than eighteen centuries; and wherever it is proclaimed, this deed of Mary's is published with it, in continual memory of her, and to her lasting honour.

Ver. 10.—**And Judas Iscariot, he that was one of the twelve** (ὁ εἷς τῶν δώδεκα), **went away unto the chief priests, that he might deliver him unto them.** The betrayal follows immediately after the anointing by Mary. We may suppose that the other disciples who had murmured on account of this waste of the ointment, were brought to their senses by our Lord's rebuke, and felt its force. But with Judas the case was very different. The rebuke, which had a salutary effect on them, only served to harden him. He had lost one opportunity of gain; he would seek another. In his cupidity and wickedness he resolves to betray his Master, and sell him to the Jews. So while the chief priests were plotting how they might destroy him, they found an apt and unexpected instrument for their purpose in one of his own disciples. Judas came to them, and the vile and hateful bargain was concluded. It marks the tremendous iniquity of the transaction that it was "one of the twelve" who betrayed him—not one of the seventy, but one of those who were in the closest intimacy and nearness to him.

Ver. 11.—**And they, when they heard it, were glad, and promised to give him money. And he sought** (ἐζήτει)—*he was seeking;* he made it his business to arrange how the infamous plot might be managed—**how he might conveniently deliver him unto them** (πῶς εὐκαίρως αὐτὸν παραδῷ); literally, *how at a convenient season he might betray him. And they, when they heard it, were glad;* glad, because they saw the prospect of the accomplishment of their wishes; glad, because it was "one of the twelve" who covenanted to betray him. *They promised to give him money.* St. Matthew (xxvi. 15) tells us the amount, namely, thirty pieces of silver, according to the prophecy of Zechariah (xi. 12), to which St. Matthew evidently refers. These pieces of silver were shekels of the sanctuary, worth about three shillings each. This would make the whole amount about £4 10s. of our money; less than half the value of the precious ointment with which Mary had anointed him. Some commentators, however, think that this was only an instalment of what they promised him if he completed his treasonable design. *How he might conveniently deliver him unto them.* St. Luke (xxii. 6) explains this by saying, "in the absence of the multitude;" that is, when the people were not about him, and when he was in private with his dis-

ciples. And so he betrayed him at night, when he was alone with his disciples in the Garden of Gethsemane.

Ver. 12.—**And on the first day of unleavened bread, when they sacrificed the passover, his disciples said unto him, Where wilt thou that we go and make ready that thou mayest eat the passover?** The first day of unleavened bread would begin on the evening of the Thursday (the 14th day of the month Nisan). *Where wilt thou that we prepare?* They do not inquire in what city or town. The Passover could not be sacrificed anywhere but in Jerusalem. The question was in what *house* it was to be prepared.

Ver. 13.—**And he sendeth two of his disciples.** St. Luke (xxii. 8) informs us that these two were Peter and John. It is characteristic of St. Mark's Gospel throughout that Peter is never mentioned oftener than is necessary. **Go into the city, and there shall meet you a man bearing a pitcher of water.** The bearing of the pitcher of water was not without its meaning. It was a solemn religious act preparatory to the Passover. This man bearing a pitcher of water was not the master or owner of the house. The owner is distinguished afterwards by the name οἰκοδέσποτης, or "goodman of the house." The owner must, therefore, have been a man of some substance, and probably a friend if not a disciple of our Lord. Tradition says that this was the house of John whose surname was Mark; and that it was in this house that the disciples were assembled on the evening of our Lord's resurrection, and where, also, they received the miraculous gifts of the Holy Spirit, on the day of Pentecost. It was to this house that Peter betook himself when he was delivered by the angel out of prison. Hence it was known, as one of the earliest places of Christian worship, by the name of "Cœnaculum Sion;" and here was built a church, called the Church of Sion. It was the oldest church in Jerusalem, and was called by St. Cyril, "the upper church of the apostles." (See Joseph Mede, p. 322.)

Ver. 14.—**The Master saith, Where is my guest-chamber** (κατάλυμα μοῦ); literally, *my lodging.*

Ver. 15.—**And he will himself show you a large upper room furnished and ready.** He himself, that is, the goodman of the house; perhaps John Mark. This upper room was furnished and ready (ἐστρωμένον ἕτοιμον); furnished, that is, with table and couches and tapestry, and in all respects ready for the purpose.

Ver. 16.—**And they made ready the passover.** This would consist in obtaining the Paschal lamb, and taking it to the temple to be sacrificed by the priests. It would then be brought to the house to be cooked ; and the unleavened bread, the bitter herbs, and the wine would have to be provided, and the water for purification. After all these preparations had been made, the two disciples would return to their Master.

Ver. 17.—**And when it was evening he cometh with the twelve.** It was in the evening that the lamb was to be eaten. Peter and John having returned from their preparation, the twelve (including Judas Iscariot) all went back with their Master to Jerusalem.

Ver. 18.—**Verily I say unto you, One of you shall betray me,** even **he that eateth with me** (ὁ ἐσθίων μετ᾽ ἐμοῦ). Much had doubtless happened before our Lord said this; but St. Mark only records the important circumstances. These words of our Lord were uttered with great solemnity. The presence of the traitor was a burden upon his spirit, and cast a gloom over this usually joyous festival. A question here arises whether Judas remained to partake of the Holy Communion when our Lord instituted it. The greater number of the Fathers, and amongst them Origen, St. Cyril, St. Chrysostom, St. Augustine, and Bede, consider that he was present; and Dionysius says that our Lord's words to him, "That thou doest, do quickly," were intended to separate him from the rest of the twelve as one who had partaken unworthily; and that then it was that Satan entered into him, and impelled him onwards to this terrible sin.

Ver. 19.—**They began to be sorrowful, and to say unto him one by one, Is it I?** The disciples were naturally disposed to be joyful at this great festival. But their Master's sorrow and his words, and the solemnity with which they were uttered, cast a shadow over the whole company; and the disciples began to be sorrowful. The words, "And another said, Is it I?" are omitted by the best authorities.

Ver. 20.—**And he said unto them, It is one of the twelve, he that dippeth with me in the dish.** St. Mark here uses the present participle (ὁ ἐμβαπτόμενος), bringing the action close to the time when he was speaking. St. Matthew (xxvi. 23) has (ὁ ἐμβάψας) "he that dipped his hand," using the aorist form. St. Mark's form is the more graphic. The dish probably contained a sauce called *charoseth*, into which they dipped their food before eating it. The following appears to have been the order of the events :—First, our Lord, before he instituted the Holy Sacrament of the Eucharist, foretold that he would be betrayed by one of his disciples ; but only in general terms. Then came the eager question from them, "Is it I?" Then Christ answered that the traitor was he who

should dip his hand together with him in the dish. But this did not bring it home to the individual, because several who sat near to him were able to dip with him in the dish. So that our Lord had as yet only obscurely and indefinitely pointed out the traitor. Then he proceeded to institute "the Lord's Supper;" after which he again intimated (Luke xxii. 21) that "the hand of him that betrayed him was with him on the table." Upon this, St. Peter hinted to St. John, who was "reclining in Jesus' bosom," that he should ask him to say definitely and by name who it was that should betray him. Our Lord then said to St. John, "He it is, for whom I shall dip the sop, and give it him" (John xiii. 26). Our Lord then dipped the sop, and gave it to Judas Iscariot. Then it was that our Lord said to Judas, "That thou doest, do quickly" (ὃ ποιεῖς, ποίησον τάχιον) (John xiii. 27). Then Judas went straightway to the house of Caiaphas, and procured the band of men and officers for the completion of his horrible design.

Ver. 21.—**For the Son of man goeth** (ὑπάγει)—goeth, departeth from this mortal scene : the reference is, of course, to his death—**even as it is written of him** ; as, for example, in Ps. xxii. and Isa. xli. It was foreordained by God that he was to suffer as a victim for the sins of the whole world. But this predestined purpose of God did not make the guilt any the less of those who brought the Saviour to his cross. **Good were it for that man if he had not been born.** The Greek is καλὸν ἦν αὐτῷ, εἰ οὐκ ἐγεννήθη ὁ ἄνθρωπος ἐκεῖνος : literally, *good were it for him, if that man had not been born.* Better not to have lived at all than to have lived and died ill. Existence is no blessing, but a curse, to him who consciously and wilfully defeats the purpose of his existence. St. Matthew (xxvi. 25) here introduces Judas as asking the question, "Is it I, Rabbi?" And our Lord answers him affirmatively, "Thou hast said." This was probably said in a low voice. Had it been said so as to be heard by others, such as Peter and John, they might have risen at once to inflict summary vengeance upon the apostate traitor.

Ver. 22.—The last clause of this verse should be read thus : **Take ye: this is my body** (Λάβετε· τοῦτό ἐστι τὸ σῶμά μου). The institution of this Holy Sacrament took place at the close of the Paschal supper, but while they were yet at the table. The bread which our Lord took would most likely be unleavened. But this does not surely constitute a reason why unleavened bread should be used ordinarily in the celebration of the Holy Communion. The direction of the Prayer-book of the English Church is wise and practical, "It shall suffice that the

Bread be such as is usual to be eaten." *This is my body* ; that is, sacramentally. St. Augustine ('Sermo.,' 272) says, "How is the bread his body? and the cup, or that which the cup contains, how is that his blood? These are, therefore, called sacraments, because in them one thing is seen while another thing is understood" (quoted by Dr. Morison, p. 392).

Ver. 23.—**And he took a cup.** There is no definite article either here or in St. Matthew.

Ver. 24.—**This is my blood of the covenant.** There is not sufficient authority for the retaining of the word "new" (καινῆς) in the text.

Ver. 25.—**I will no more drink** (οὐκέτι οὐ μὴ πίω) **of the fruit of the vine, until that day when I drink it new in the kingdom of God.** It is observable that our Lord here calls the wine "the fruit (γέννημα) of the vine," after he has spoken of it as sacramentally his blood. Our Lord here refers to the time of the regeneration of all things, when the heavenly kingdom shall appear in the fulness of its glory; and when his disciples, who now feed upon him sacramentally and by faith, shall then eat at his table in his kingdom, and drink of the river of his pleasures for ever.

Ver. 26.—**And when they had sung a hymn, they went out unto the mount of Olives.** Some suppose that this was one particular hymn out of the Jewish service-books appointed for use at the close of the Paschal supper. The word in the Greek is simply ὑμνήσαντες. What they sang was more probably the Hallel, consisting of six psalms, from Ps. cxiii. to Ps. cxviii. inclusive. *They went out unto the Mount of Olives.* It was our Lord's custom, in these last days of his earthly life, to go daily to Jerusalem, and teach in the temple, and in the evening to return to Bethany and sup; and then after supper to retire to the Mount of Olives, and there to spend the night in prayer (Luke xxi. 37). But on this occasion he did not return to Bethany. He had supped in Jerusalem. Besides, he knew that his hour was come. So he voluntarily put himself into the way of the traitor (John xviii. 2).

Ver. 27.—**All ye shall be offended.** The words which follow in the Authorized Version, "because of me this night," are not to be found in the best manuscripts and versions. They appear to have been imported from St. Matthew. *Shall be offended* (σκανδαλισθήσεσθε); literally, *shall be caused to stumble.* Our Lord was to prove "a stone of stumbling" to many, not excluding his own disciples. Even they, under the influence of terror, would for a time lose confidence and hope in him. For it is written,

I will smite the shepherd, and the sheep shall be scattered abroad. This is a quotation from Zechariah (xiii. 7), "Awake, O sword, against my Shepherd, and against the man that is my Fellow, saith the Lord of hosts: smite the Shepherd." This passage brings out in a remarkable manner the Divine agency in the death of Christ. *The sheep shall be scattered abroad.* The disciples all forsook him and fled, when they saw him actually in the hands of his enemies. They felt doubtful for the moment whether he was indeed the Son of God. "They trusted that it was he who should redeem Israel;" but now their hopes gave way to fear and doubt. They fled hither and thither like frightened sheep. But God gathered them together again, so that when our Lord rose from the dead, he found them all in the same place; and then he revived their faith and courage. Our Lord and his disciples had no settled home or friends in Jerusalem; so they had no other place to flee to than that upper chamber, where, not long before, Christ had kept the Passover with them. The owner of that house was a friend; so thither they went, and there Christ appeared to them after his resurrection.

Ver. 28.—**Howbeit, after I am raised up, I will go before you into Galilee.** This our Lord said to reassure them. Galilee was more like home to them than Jerusalem, and they would there be less afraid of the unbelieving Jews.

Ver. 29.—**But Peter said unto him, Although all shall be offended, yet will not I.** Our Lord had just distinctly stated that they would all be offended, and therefore these words of St. Peter were very presumptuous. Conscious of his own infirmities, he ought to have said, "I know that through my own infirmity this may easily happen. Nevertheless, I trust to thy mercy and goodness to save me." Just such is the Christian's daily experience. We often think that we are strong in the faith, strong in purity, strong in patience. But when temptation arises, we falter and fall. The true remedy against temptation is the consciousness of our own weakness, and supplication for Divine strength.

Ver. 30.—**Verily I say unto thee, that thou to-day, even this night, before the cock crow twice, shalt deny me thrice.** The day had begun. It began at six in the evening. It was already advanced. This second crowing of the cock is mentioned by St. Mark only; and it forms an additional aggravation of Peter's sin. The "cockcrowing" was a term used for one of the divisions of the night (see ch. xiii. 35). But it appears that there were three times at which the cockcrowing might be expected—namely, (1) early in the night, between eleven and twelve; (2) between one and two; and (3) between five and six. The two cockcrowings here referred to would be the two last of the three here mentioned. It would probably be about 2 a.m., when the first trial of our Lord took place in the house of Caiaphas.

Ver. 31.—**But he spake exceeding vehemently** (ἐκπερισσῶς ἐλάλει), **If I must die with thee** (ἐάν με δέῃ), **I will not deny thee.** The right reading (ἐλάλει, imperfect) implies that he kept asserting over and over again. He was, no doubt, sincere in all this, but he had yet to learn his own weakness. St. Hilary says on this, "Peter was so carried away by the fervour of his zeal and love for Christ, that he regarded neither the weakness of his own flesh nor the truth of his Master's word."

Ver. 32.—**And they come** (ἔρχονται)—here again St. Mark's present gives force to the narrative—**unto a place which was named Gethsemane.** A *place* (χωρίον) is, literally, *an enclosed piece of ground*, generally with a cottage upon it. Josephus tells us that these gardens were numerous in the suburbs of Jerusalem. St. Jerome says that "Gethsemane was at the foot of the Mount of Olives." St. John (xviii. 1) calls it a garden, or orchard (κῆπος). The word "Gethsemane" means literally "the place of the *olive-press*," whither the olives which abounded on the slopes of the mountain were brought, in order that the oil contained in them might be pressed out. The exact position of Gethsemane is not known; although there is an enclosed spot at the foot of the western slope of the Mount of Olives which is called to this day *El Jesmániye*. The real Gethsemane cannot be far from this spot. Our Lord resorted to this place for retirement and prayer, not as desiring to escape the death that awaited him. It was well known to be his favourite resort; so that he went there, as though to put himself in the way of Judas, who would naturally seek him there. **Sit ye here, while I pray.** St. Matthew (xxvi. 36) says, "While I go yonder and pray."

Ver. 33.—It appears that our Lord separated himself from all the disciples except Peter and James and John, and then the bitter agony began. He **began to be greatly amazed, and sore troubled** (ἐκθαμβεῖσθαι καὶ ἀδημονεῖν). These two Greek verbs are as adequately expressed above as seems possible. The first implies "utter, extreme amazement;" if the second has for its root ἄδημος, "not at home," it implies the anguish of the soul struggling to free itself from the body under the pressure of intense mental distress. The three chosen disciples were allowed to be witnesses of this awful

anguish. They had been fortified to endure the sight by the glories of the transfiguration. It would have been too much for the faith of the rest. But these three witnessed it, that they might learn themselves, and be able to teach others, that the way to glory is by suffering.

Ver. 34.—**None** but he who bore those sorrows can know what they were. It was not the apprehension of the bodily torments and the bitter death that awaited him, all foreknown by him. It was the inconceivable agony of the weight of the sins of men. The Lord was thus laying "upon him the iniquity of us all." This, and this alone, can explain it. **My soul is exceeding sorrowful even unto death.** Every word carries the emphasis of an overwhelming grief. It was then that "the deep waters came in," even unto his soul. "What,' says Cornelius à Lapide, "must have been the voice, the countenance, the expression, as he uttered those awful words!"

Ver. 35.—Our Lord now separated himself, though apparently, as St. Luke (xxii. 41) says, only "about a stone's cast" from the three disciples, and threw himself on the ground in mortal agony, and prayed that this hour of his supreme mental anguish might, if possible, pass from him.

Ver. 36.—**And he said, Abba, Father.** Some commentators suppose that our Lord only used the Hebrew or Aramaic word "Abba," and that St. Mark adds the Greek and Latin synonym (πατήρ) for the benefit of those to whom he was writing. But it is far more natural to conclude that St. Mark is here taking his narrative from an eye and ear witness, St. Peter; and that both the words were uttered by him; so that he thus, in his agony, cried to God in the name of the whole human family, the Jew first, and also the Gentile. We can quite understand why St. Matthew, writing to Jews, gives only the Hebrew word. **All things are possible unto thee.** Speaking absolutely, with God nothing is impossible. But the Deity is himself bound by his own laws; and hence this was impossible, consistently with his purposes of mercy for the redemption of the world. The Lord himself knew this. Therefore he does not ask for anything contrary to the will of his Father. But it was the natural craving of his humanity, which, subject to the supreme will of God, desired to be delivered from this terrible load. **Remove this cup from me.** The "cup," both in Holy Scripture and in profane writers, is taken to signify that lot or portion, whether good or evil, which is appointed for us by God. Hence St. John is frequently represented as holding a cup. **Howbeit, not what I will, but what thou wilt.** Our Lord has no sooner offered his conditional prayer than he subordinates it to the will of God. St. Luke (xxii. 42) here says, " Nevertheless not my will, but thine, be done." Hence it appears that there was not, as the Monothelites taught, one will, partly human and partly Divine, in Christ; but there were two distinct wills, one human and the other Divine, both residing in the one Christ; and it was by the subjecting of his human will to the Divine that he wrought out our redemption.

Ver. 37.—**And he cometh, and findeth them sleeping, and saith unto Peter, Simon, sleepest thou? Couldest thou not watch one hour?** St. Luke says (xxii. 45) that they were "sleeping for sorrow." So on the Mount of Transfiguration he says (ix. 32) that they were "heavy with sleep." This rebuke, which St. Mark tells us here was pointedly addressed to Peter, seems to glance at his earnest protestations of fidelity made not long before. And our Lord calls him by his old name of Simon. In St. Matthew (xxvi. 40) it is less pointed; for there, while our Lord looks at Peter, he addresses them all. " He saith unto *Peter*, What, could not *ye* watch with me one hour?" This is just one of those graphic little incidents which we may suppose St. Mark to have received directly from St. Peter.

Ver. 38.—**Watch and pray, that ye enter not into temptation.** The great temptation of the disciples at that moment was to deny Christ under the influence of fear. And so our Lord gives here the true remedy against temptation of every kind; namely, watchfulness and prayer—watchfulness, against the craft and subtlety of the devil or man; and prayer, for the Divine help to overcome. **The spirit indeed is willing, but the flesh is weak.** Here our Lord graciously finds excuses for them. It is as though he said, " I know that in heart and mind you are ready to cleave to me, even though the Jews should threaten you with death. But I know also that your flesh is weak. Pray, then, that the weakness of the flesh may not overcome the strength of the spirit." St. Jerome says, " In whatever degree we trust to the ardour of the spirit, in the same degree ought we to fear because of the infirmity of the flesh."

Ver. 39.—**Saying the same words.** The repetition of the same words shows his fixed determination to submit to the will of his heavenly Father. Although the human nature at first asserted itself in the prayer that the cup might pass from him; yet ultimately the human will yielded to the Divine. He desired to drink this cup of bitterness appointed for him by the will of God; for his supreme desire was that the will of God might be done.

Ver. 40.—**And again he came, and found** them sleeping, for their eyes were very heavy (καταβαρυνόμενοι); literally, *weighed down.* They had not deliberately yielded themselves to sleep; but an oppressive languor, the effect of great sorrow, had come over them, so that they could not watch as they desired to do; but by an involuntary action they ever and anon slumbered. **They wist not what to answer him.** They had no excuse, save that which he himself had found for them.

Ver. 41.—**And he cometh the third time, and saith unto them, Sleep on now, and take your rest: it is enough** (ἀπέχει); **the hour is come.** Some have thought that our Lord here uses the language of irony. But it is far more consistent with his usual considerate words to suppose that, sympathizing with the infirmity of his disciples, he simply advised them, now that his bitter agony was over, to take some rest during the brief interval that remained. *It is enough.* Some commentators have thought that the somewhat difficult Greek verb (ἀπέχει) would be better rendered, *he is at a distance;* as though our Lord meant to say, " There is yet time for you to take some rest. The betrayer is some distance off." Such an interpretation would require a full stop between the clause now rendered, " it is enough," and the clause, " the hour is come; " so that the passage would read, "Sleep on now, and take your rest; he (that is, Judas) is yet a good way off." Then there would be an interval; and then our Lord would rouse them up with the words, " The hour is come; behold, the Son of man is betrayed into the hands of sinners." This interpretation all hangs upon the true rendering of the word ἀπέχει, which, although it might be taken to mean " he," or " it is distant," is nevertheless quite capable of the ordinary interpretation, " it sufficeth." According to the high authority of Hesychius, who explains it by the words ἀπόχρη and ἐξαρκεῖ, it seems safer on the whole to accept the ordinary meaning, " It is enough."

Ver. 43.—**And straightway, while he yet spake, cometh Judas, one of the twelve.** How the stupendous crime is here marked! It was so startling a fact that "one of the twelve" should be the betrayer of our Lord, that this designation of Judas became linked with his name: "Judas, one of the twelve." He comes not only as a thief and a robber, but also as a traitor; the leader of those who were thirsting for Christ's blood. St. Luke (xxii. 47) says that Judas "went before them," in his eagerness to accomplish his hateful errand. **And with him a multitude** (not a great multitude; the word πολὺς has not sufficient authority). But though not a great multitude, they would be a con-

siderable number. There would be a band
of soldiers; and there would be civil officers
sent by the Sanhedrim. Thus Gentiles and
Jews were united in the daring act of
arresting the Son of God. St. John (xviii.
3) says that they had "lanterns and
torches;" although the moon was at the
full.

Ver. 44.—**Now he that betrayed him had
given them a token, saying, Whomsoever I
shall kiss, that is he; take him, and lead him
away safely.** Why was Judas so anxious
that Christ should be secured? Perhaps
because he feared a rescue, or because he
feared lest our Lord should hide himself
by an exercise of his miraculous power;
and so Judas might lose the thirty pieces
of silver.

Ver. 45.—**And when he was come,
straightway he came to him, and saith,
Rabbi; and kissed him** (κατεφίλησεν αὐτόν);
literally, *kissed him much.* The kiss was
an ancient mode of salutation amongst the
Jews, the Romans, and other nations. It is
possible that this was the usual mode with
which the disciples greeted Christ when
they returned to him after any absence.
But Judas abused this token of friendship,
using it for a base and treacherous purpose.
St. Chrysostom says that he felt assured by
the gentleness of Christ that he would not
repel him, or that, if he did, the treacherous
action would have answered its purpose.

Ver. 47.—**But a certain one of them that
stood by drew his sword, and smote the servant of the high priest, and struck off his
ear** (ἀφεῖλεν αὐτοῦ τὸ ὠτίον). We learn from
St. John (xviii. 10) that this was Peter.
St. John also is the only evangelist who
mentions the name (Malchus) of the high
priest's servant. Malchus would probably
be prominent amongst them. St. Luke
(xxii. 51) is the only evangelist who mentions the healing of the wound by our Lord.

Ver. 48.—We learn from St. Matthew
(xxvi. 52) that our Lord rebuked his disciples for their resistance; after which he
proceeded to rebuke those who were bent
upon apprehending him. **Are ye come out,
as against a robber** (ὡς ἐπὶ λῃστὴν), **with
swords and staves to seize me?** The order
of events in the betrayal appears to have
been this: First, the kiss of the traitor
Judas, by which he indicated to those who
were with him which was Jesus. Then
follows that remarkable incident mentioned
only by St. John (xviii. 4—6), "Jesus . . .
went forth, and saith unto them, Whom seek
ye? They answered him, Jesus of Nazareth.
Jesus saith unto them, I am he. And
Judas also, which betrayed him, was standing with them. When therefore he said
unto them, I am he, they went backward,
and fell to the ground." The presence of

Christ in his serene majesty overpowered
them. There was something in his looks and
manner, as he repeated these words, "I am
he," words often used before by him, that
caused them to retreat backwards, and to
prostrate themselves. It was no external
force that produced this result. The Divine
majesty flashed from his countenance and
overawed them, at least for the moment.
At all events, it was an emphatic evidence,
both to his own disciples and to this crowd,
that it was by his own will that he yielded
himself up to them. Perhaps this incident
fired the courage of St. Peter; and so, as
they approached to take our Lord, he drew
his sword and struck off the ear of Malchus.
Then our Lord healed him. And then he
turned to the multitude and said, "Are ye
come out as against a robber, with swords
and staves, to seize me?"

Ver. 49.—**But this is done that the Scriptures might be fulfilled.** This, as it stands
in the original, is an incomplete sentence;
in St. Matthew (xxvi. 56) the sentence occurs
in its complete form. In both cases it has
been questioned whether the words are those
of our Lord, or whether they are the comment of the evangelist. On the whole, it
would seem more probable that they are our
Lord's words, which seem almost required
to conclude what he had said before.

Ver. 50.—**And they all left him, and fled.**
But soon afterwards two of them, Peter and
John, took courage, and followed him to
the house of the high priest.

Ver. 51.—**And a certain young man followed with him, having a linen cloth cast
about him, over** his **naked** body: **and they lay
hold on him.** St. Mark is the only evangelist
who mentions this incident; and there seems
good reason for supposing that he here describes what happened to himself. Such is
the mode in which St. John refers to himself
in his Gospel, and where there can be no
doubt that he is speaking of himself. If
the conclusion in an earlier part of this commentary be correct, that it was at the house
to which John Mark belonged that our Lord
celebrated the Passover, and from whence
he went out to the Mount of Olives; what
more probable than that Mark had been with
him on that occasion, and had perhaps a
presentiment that something was about to
happen to him? What more likely than that
the crowd who took Jesus may have passed
by this house, and that Mark may have been
roused from his bed (it was now a late hour)
by the tumult. *Having a linen cloth* (σινδόνα)
cast about his naked body. The *sindon* was
a fine linen cloth, indicating that he belonged
to a family in good circumstances. It is an
unusual word. In every other place of the
New Testament where it is used it refers
to the garment or shroud used to cover the

bodies of the dead. The *sindon* is supposed to take its name from Sidon, where the particular kind of linen was manufactured of which the garment was made. It was a kind of light cloak frequently worn in hot weather.

Ver. 52.—**But he left the linen cloth, and fled naked.** This somewhat ignominious flight is characteristic of what we know of St. Mark. It shows how great was the panic in reference to Christ, and how great was the hatred of the Jews against him, that they endeavoured to seize a young man who was merely following with him. It shows also how readily our Lord's enemies would have seized his own disciples if they had not taken refuge in flight.

Ver. 53.—**And they led Jesus away to the high priest.** This high priest was Caiaphas. But we learn from St. John (xviii. 13) that our Lord was first brought before Annas, the father-in-law of Caiaphas. Annas and his five sons held the high priesthood in succession, Caiaphas, his son-in-law, stepping in between the first and the second son, and holding the office for twelve years. It is supposed that it was in the house of Annas that the price of the betrayal was paid to Judas. Annas, though not then high priest, must have had considerable influence in the counsels of the Sanhedrim; and this will probably explain the fact of our Lord having been first taken to him.

Ver. 54.—**And Peter had followed him afar off, even within, into the court** (εἰς τὴν αὐλὴν) **of the high priest.** This court was the place where the guards and servants of the high priest were assembled. Our Lord was within, in a large room, being arraigned before the council. St. John informs us (xviii. 15) that he himself, being known to the high priest, had gone in with Jesus into the court of the high priest; and that he had been the means of bringing in Peter, who had been standing outside at the door leading into the court. We now see Peter among the servants, crouching over the fire. The weather was cold, for it was early spring-time; and it was now after midnight. Peter was **warming himself in the light** of the fire (πρὸς τὸ φῶς), and so his features were clearly seen in the glow of the brightly burning charcoal.

Ver. 55.—**Now the chief priests and the whole council sought witness against Jesus to put him to death, and found it not.** Their supreme object was to put him to death; but they wished to accomplish their object in a manner consistent with their own honour, so as not to appear to have put him to death without reason. So they sought for false witnesses against him, that they might deliver the Author of life and the Saviour of the world to death. For in real truth,

although they knew it not, and were the instruments in his hands, he had determined by the death of Christ to bestow on us both present and eternal life.

Ver. 56.—**For many bare false witness against him, and their witness agreed not together.** Whatever things these witnesses brought forward were either false, or self-contradictory, or beside the purpose.

Vers. 57, 58.—**And there stood up certain, and bare false witness against him, saying, We heard him say, I will destroy this temple that is made with hands, and in three days I will build another made without hands.** St. Matthew (xxvi. 60) says that they were two. What our Lord had really said was this—we read it in St. John (ii. 19)—"Destroy this temple; and in three days I will raise it up." These words the false witnesses perverted; for they assigned to Jesus the work of destruction which he left to the Jews. He did not say, " I will destroy;" but " Do ye destroy, and I will rebuild." Nor did he say, "I will build another;" but "I will raise it up," that is, from the dead; for St. John tells us that "he spake of the temple of his body," in which, as in a temple, there dwelt the fulness of the Godhead. He might have said plainly, "I will rise from the dead;" but he chose to speak as in a parable. According to their witness, however, our Lord's words would appear as little more than an empty boast, certainly not as anything on account of which such a charge as they desired could be brought against him.

Vers. 60, 61.—**And the high priest stood up in the midst, and asked Jesus, saying, Answerest thou nothing? . . . But he held his peace, and answered nothing.** The high priest would naturally be seated at the top of the semicircle, with the members of the Sanhedrim on either side of him, and the Accused in front of him. Now he rises from his seat, and comes forward into the midst (εἰς τὸ μέσον), and demands an answer. But Jesus answered nothing. It would have been a long and tedious business to answer such a charge, which involved a garbled and inaccurate statement of what he had said. It would have answered no good purpose to reply to an accusation so vague and inaccurate. Our Lord knew that, whatever his answer was, it would be twisted so as to make against him. Silence was therefore the most dignified treatment of such an accusation. Besides, he knew that his hour was come. The high priest now asks him plainly, **Art thou the Christ, the son of the Blessed?** Here he touches the point of the whole matter. Christ had frequently declared himself to be such. Caiaphas, therefore, now asks the question, not because he needed the information, but that he might condemn him.

Ver. 62.—To this question our Lord returns a plain and candid answer, out of reverence for the Divine Name which, as St. Matthew and St. Luke tell us, had been invoked by the high priest, and also out of respect for the office of the high priest, by whom he had been put upon his oath. St. Chrysostom says that our Lord answered thus that he might leave without excuse all those who listened to him, who would not hereafter be able to plead in the day of judgment that, when our Lord was solemnly asked in the council whether he was the Son of God, he had either refused to answer, or had answered evasively. This answer of our Lord is full of majesty and sublimity. He is arraigned as a criminal, standing in the midst of the chief priests and scribes, his bitter enemies ; and it is as though he said, "You, O Caiaphas, and you the chief priests and elders of the Jews, are now unjustly condemning me as a false prophet and a false Christ ; but the day is at hand when I, who am now a prisoner at your judgment seat, shall sit on the throne of glory as the Judge of you and of all mankind. You are now about to condemn me to the death of the cross ; but I shall then sit in judgment upon you, and condemn you for this terrible guilt of slaying me, who am the true God and the Judge of the world."

Ver. 63.—**And the high priest rent his clothes** (διαρρήξας τοὺς χιτῶνας); literally, *his tunics* ; St. Matthew (xxvi. 65) has τὰ ἱμάτια, literally, *his garments*. None but people of rank wore two tunics. The Greek verb here rendered "rent" implies violent dramatic action. The Jewish tunic was open under the chin, and large enough to receive the head, so that it could easily be placed over the shoulders, by inserting the head. When the wearer wished to give this sign of indignation or grief, he would seize the garment at this opening with both hands, and violently tear it asunder down to the waist. But it was unlawful for the high priest to do this in a private grief (Lev. x. 6). Some of the Fathers think that by this action Caiaphas involuntarily typified the rending of the priesthood from himself and from the Jewish nation.

Ver. 64.—**They all condemned him to be worthy of death** (ἔνοχον θανάτου). There were, therefore, none there but those who were known to be opposed to our Lord. It will be remembered that all these proceedings were illegal.

Ver. 65.—**And some began to spit on him.** St. Matthew (xxvi. 67) says, "Then did they spit in his face." That Divine face, to be reverenced and adored by every creature,

was exposed to this vile contumely ; and he bore it patiently. "I hid not my face from shame and spitting" (Isa. l. 61). **And the officers received him with blows of their hands** (οἱ ὑπηρέται ῥαπίσμασιν αὐτὸν ἔλαβον).

Ver. 66.—**And as Peter was beneath in the court.** The room in which the Sanhedrim were assembled was an upper chamber.

Ver. 67.—**And seeing** (ἰδοῦσα) **Peter warming himself, she looked upon him** (ἐμβλέψασα αὐτῷ). She looked upon him, in the light of the fire, so as to see his features distinctly. This was one of the menial servants who attended to the outer door of the court, and perhaps had been the one to let in Peter ; so that she could say with some confidence, **Thou wast also with the Nazarene, even Jesus.**

Ver. 68.—**But he denied, saying, I neither know, nor understand what thou sayest.** "This shows the great terror of Peter," says St. Chrysostom, "who, intimidated by the question of a poor servant-girl, denied his Lord ; and who yet afterwards, when he had received the Holy Spirit, could say, 'We ought to obey God rather than man.'" *I neither know, nor understand what thou sayest.* Every word here is emphatic. It amounts to this : "So little do I know who this Jesus is, that I know not what you say or what you ask concerning him. I know not who or what he is or anything about him. A question has been raised as to the number of times that Peter denied our Lord. The narratives are best explained by the consideration that all the denials took place in the house of Caiaphas. Furthermore, the accounts of the evangelists may be reconciled thus : First, Peter denied the Lord in the court of the high priest, when he was first asked by the maidservant, as he sat over the fire (Matt. xxiv. 69) ; secondly, he denied him with an oath ; thirdly, when urged still more, he denied him with many oaths and execrations. The cock crew the first time after the first denial, when we read (Matt. xxvi. 71) that he went out into the porch (προαύλιον). This crowing would be about one or two in the morning. The second crowing would not be until five or six. This shows us the length of time that the proceedings lasted. It was doubtless as Jesus passed through the court that he gave Peter that look of unutterable pain and grief which moved him at once to repentance.

Ver. 72.—**And when he thought thereon, he wept** (καὶ ἐπιβαλὼν, ἔκλαιε, not ἔκλαυσε). The word implies a long and continued weeping.

This concludes the preliminary trial, the whole proceedings of which were illegal.

HOMILETICS.

Vers. 1, 2.—*The plot.* The apprehension and death of Jesus were brought about by a combination between his foes and a professed friend. The avowed enemies employed the necessary force, and secured the authority of the Roman governor for his crucifixion ; and the disciple suggested the occasion, the place and time of the capture, and delivered his Master into the hands of the malignant persecutors. The events of the first three days of this Passion week had been such as to enrage the Pharisees and scribes beyond all bounds. The only way in which it seemed possible for them to retain their threatened influence, necessarily diminished and discredited by their repeated public confutation, seemed to be this—to strike an immediate and decisive blow at the Prophet whom they were unable to withstand upon the ground of argument and reason.

I. The enemies who plotted against Christ. These seem to have included all classes among the higher orders of society in Jerusalem, who, whatever their distinctions, rivalries, and enmities, concurred in hatred of the Holy One and the Just. The chief priests, who were largely Sadducees, the scribes, and the Pharisees, who were the most honoured leaders of the people in religion, all joined in plotting against him who attacked their various errors with equal impartiality, and whose success with the people was undermining the power of them all.

II. The craft and caution of Christ's enemies. It was in accordance with the nature of such men that they should have recourse to stratagem. Open violence was scarcely after their manner, and was out of the question in this case ; for many of the people honoured the Prophet of Nazareth, and would probably have interfered to protect or to rescue him from the onset of his enemies. Upon days of great popular festivals the people thronged every public place, where Jesus might be found teaching those who resorted to him ; and those who delighted to listen to Jesus would certainly resist his capture. The opposition of Christ's enemies to his teaching had been captious, and it is not surprising to find that their plot for his destruction was cunning and secret.

III. The purpose of Christ's enemies—his destruction. This had, indeed, been foreseen and foretold by himself; but this does not lessen the crime of those who compassed his death. The resolution to slay Jesus seems to have been taken because of the popular impression produced by the raising of Lazarus, and because of the discussions which had only just now taken place between him and the Jewish leaders, whom he had overcome in argument and put to silence. Thus, he had come up to the metropolis with the intention of so conducting his ministry as he was well aware would bring down upon him the wrath of his bitter foes.

IV. The season and occasion of this plot. It was at the time of the Passover assemblies and solemnities that these deliberations took place. In this there was a coincidence which was not unintended, and which did not escape the observation of the Church. "Christ our Passover"—our Paschal Lamb and Sacrifice—"was slain for us." The Lamb of God came to take away the sin of the world. His death has become the life of humanity ; his sacrifice has wrought the emancipation of a sinful race.

Vers. 3—9.—*Tribute of grateful love.* A singular interest attaches to this simple incident in Christ's private life. Proud and foolish men have tried to turn it into ridicule, as unworthy of the memory of a great prophet. But they have not succeeded. Our Lord's own estimate of Mary's conduct is accepted, and the world-wide and lasting renown promised by Jesus has been secured. The record of the graceful act of the friend of Jesus is instructive, touching, and beautiful. And the commendation which the Master pronounced is an evidence of his human and sympathizing appreciation of devotion and of love.

I. The acceptable motive to Christian service is here revealed. Mary was prompted, not by vanity and ostentation, but by grateful love. This had been awakened both by his friendship and teaching, and by his compassionate kindness in raising her brother from the dead. What Jesus appreciated was Mary's love. Services and gifts are valuable in Christ's view, not for themselves, for he needs them not, but as an expression of his people's deepest feelings. Let Christians consider what they owe to their Saviour—salvation, life eternal. They may well exclaim, " We love him, because he first loved us." Acceptable obedience does not come first, for in such case it would be a form only ; but if love prompts our deeds and services, they become valuable even before Heaven.

II. THE NATURAL MODES OF CHRISTIAN SERVICE. These are severally exemplified in this incident. 1. *Personal ministry.* Mary did not send a servant ; she came herself to minister to Jesus. There is some work for Christ which most Christians must do by deputy ; but there is much work which may and should be done personally. In the home, in the school, in the Church, in the hospital, we may individually, according to opportunity and ability, serve the Lord Christ. What is done for his " little ones " he takes as done for himself. 2. *Substance.* Mary gave costly perfume, estimated to have cost upwards of ten pounds of our money. She had property, and therefore gave. All we have is his, who, when he purchased us with his blood, purchased all our powers and possessions. It is a precious privilege to offer him his own. "It is accepted according to what a man hath." 3. *Public witness.* Mary anointed the Master's feet in the presence of the company, and thus declared before all those assembled her devotion to him. It is good for ourselves that we should witness to our Saviour, and it is good for others who may receive our testimony. It is a disgrace to professing Christians when they are ashamed of the Lord who redeemed them.

III. THE TRUE MEASURE OF CHRISTIAN SERVICE. She did, it is recorded, what she could ; she gave what she had to give. This is an example worthy of universal imitation. We are reminded, as it were paradoxically, of two apparently opposed characteristics of Christian action and liberality. 1. *How much* devoted friends of Christ may do! Men may do much for harm and evil ; and, on the other hand, what good even one person has sometimes accomplished in private life ! What *can* be done *should* be done. 2. Yet, *how limited* are men's powers ! If Christians could do more than they do, how vast a field of labour stretches around them ! We are limited in our powers for usefulness. Our means may be small, our circle of influence restricted. Our powers of body and of mind are often a restraint upon us ; our life is brief, even at the longest. The sister of Bethany could not do what others might ; nevertheless, what she could do she did. And we are never to rest in inactivity and indolence, because the claims are so many, and our powers are so small, and our opportunities so few.

IV. THE APPROVAL AND ACCEPTANCE OF CHRISTIAN SERVICE. 1. The Lord accepts what his friends bring to him, as the expression of their love, in proportion to their means and powers. He is not influenced by men's regards. Good men as well as bad men often disapprove wise and benevolent actions. He judgeth not as man judgeth. 2. The Lord rewards the grateful and devoted friends who minister unto him. He enlarges their opportunities of usefulness and service here. "To him that hath shall be given." And he will hereafter recompense them in the resurrection of the just, when he shall say, " Enter thou into the joy of thy Lord."

APPLICATION. 1. Let Christians give love its way, and follow where it leads. There is no danger of our loving our Saviour too ardently, or of our serving him too zealously. 2. If your means of showing devotion be but few, fret not ; only let it be said, " They have done what they could."

Vers. 10, 11.—*The traitor.* That there should be a traitor in the camp of our Lord's followers and professed friends, may be regarded as an instance of the Divine forbearance, which tolerated one so unworthy, and also as a fulfilment of the predictions of Scripture. The fact is, however, one which is fraught with instruction and warning to every disciple of the Lord.

I. THE AGGRAVATIONS OF THE TRAITOR'S GUILT. These are to be recognized in two circumstances which have been recorded regarding Judas Iscariot. 1. He was not only a disciple and follower of Jesus ; he was actually *one of the twelve.* These were admitted to an especial intimacy with Jesus ; they knew his movements, they shared his privacy, they heard his language of friendship and partook his counsels. All this made the treachery of one of this select band the more guilty and reprehensible. 2. He was entrusted with office in the little society to which he belonged. The treasurer of the twelve—although, doubtless, their means were always small—Judas bare the bag, and made the purchases necessary for the wants of the companions, and even gave from the general poverty for the relief of those poorer than they. He was accordingly a trusted official, who abused the confidence reposed in him.

II. THE MOTIVES TO THE TRAITOR'S GUILT. These were probably two. 1. Judas was dissatisfied with his Master's methods. Doubtless his expectations were of a carnal character; he wished Jesus to declare himself a King, and to assign to his twelve friends posts honourable and lucrative in this new kingdom. It may have been to hasten on this catastrophe that the Iscariot acted as he did. 2. Judas was covetous, and was prompted in his treason by the love of money. He secured from the chief priests the thirty shekels which formed the customary price of a slave—"the price of him that was valued!" Surely it is a warning against avarice and covetousness, to find a professed friend of Jesus misled by these degrading vices!

III. THE OUTCOME OF THE TRAITOR'S GUILT. 1. It might have been difficult for our Lord's enemies to have seized him had they not been in the confidence of one of his companions. There were obvious reasons why the arrest could not have taken place at Bethany or in Jerusalem. It was the duplicity and treachery of Judas that suggested the garden of prayer as the scene of this disgraceful apprehension. 2. To Judas the consequences were terrific. In remorse and despair he afterwards took his life. 3. Yet how was all this overruled for wise and gracious ends! The treachery of the Iscariot was the occasion of the crucifixion of Jesus, and this was the means of the salvation of the world!

Vers. 12—26.—*The Paschal supper.* The Lord's Supper is a distinctively Christian ordinance. Yet this record shows us that it was our Lord's design that it should be linked on to an observance with which his disciples were already familiar. He thus took advantage of a principle in human nature, and connected the associations and recollections which to the Hebrew mind were most sacred, with what was to be one of the holiest and most pathetic engagements of his people throughout all time.

I. THE OCCASION AND CIRCUMSTANCES OF THE INSTITUTION OF THE LORD'S SUPPER. 1. The *place* in which this festival was first celebrated was provided by willing friendship. The circumstantial narrative points to the high probability that some wealthy friend of the Lord Jesus placed the guest-chamber of his house at Jerusalem at the disposal of the Master whom he honoured. There was something very appropriate in the consecration in this manner of the offices of human love. 2. The *time* is very instructive and pathetic. It was evening; it was the last evening of rest and peace our Lord should enjoy; it was the evening which preceded the day of his sacrifice. 3. The *company* consisted of the twelve favoured companions of Jesus. Judas was at the meal, but retired before the institution of the Eucharist. How sacred and congenial a gathering! How sweet and touching this calm which came before the bursting of the storm! 4. The *occasion* was the observance of the Paschal meal. Thus the light of the Hebrew Passover was shed upon the Christian sacrament and Eucharist. Thus it was suggested to the apostle that "Christ our Passover was slain for us."

II. THE TROUBLE WHICH SADDENED THE SUPPER. Evidently this made a deep impression upon all who took part in the meal. They saw that their Master was distressed, and they felt with him the touching sorrow. The treachery of Judas was known to him who needed not to be told what was in man. The grief which weighed down the heart of the Lord was communicated by him to all the sympathizing members of the group. The sin which was bringing Jesus to the cross was gathered up and made visible and palpable in the conduct of the traitor. And the sensitive nature of our High Priest was affected and oppressed by it.

III. THE SPIRITUAL IMPORT OF THE SUPPER. 1. It was a *commemoration* of the Lord's sufferings and death. The broken bread was intended to keep in perpetual memory the body which was broken; the wine poured out to recall to Christian hearts throughout all time the blood which was shed. 2. It was a *symbol.* Here is the explanation of the Lord's own words concerning eating the flesh and drinking the blood of the Son of man. Thus are we taught and helped to feed on him by faith who is the Bread of life.

IV. THE PROPHECY AND PROMISE OF THE SUPPER. It had a first chief bearing upon the past, yet it pointed on to the future; it prefigured the marriage supper of the Lamb. In the kingdom of God the heavenly wine should be quaffed; in the upper temple the plaintive hymn of the sacrament should be exchanged for the triumphal anthem of the glorified, immortal host and choir.

APPLICATION. 1. The blood was shed for many; have we shown our consciousness that it was shed for us? 2. Let every communicant tremble lest he betray the Lord, and ask with concern and contrition, "Lord, is it I?"

Vers. 27—31.—*Anticipation.* Long before had our Lord clearly realized what would be the end of his ministry of benevolence and self-denial. The prospect of ungrateful violence leading to a cruel death had not deterred him from efforts for the good of those whom he loved and pitied. And now that the blow was just about to fall upon him, his mind was no less steadfast, although his heart was saddened.

I. JESUS ANTICIPATES HIS OWN SUFFERINGS, AND THE RESURRECTION WHICH SHOULD FOLLOW HIS DEATH. 1. He foresaw that, as the Good Shepherd, he should be smitten. He was to lay down his life for the sheep, that they might be saved and live. 2. He foretold that he should rise, and should be found in Galilee in an appointed place. This assurance gives us an insight into the considerate kindness of the Redeemer, who not only resolved to triumph for mankind, but took care for his own friends that their solicitude might be relieved, and that his intimacy with them might be renewed.

II. JESUS ANTICIPATES THE CONFUSION AND UNFAITHFULNESS OF HIS DISCIPLES. Sorely as this prospect must have distressed his heart, he was not by it to be deterred from his purpose. He foretold to his friends how they were about to act, that they might learn a lesson of their own frailty and dependence upon unseen aid. 1. Offence and scattering were foretold concerning all. This, as the record informs us, came to pass; for in the hour of his apprehension "they all forsook him, and fled." 2. The denial of the foremost and the boldest of the twelve was also foretold. Peter loved Christ, had displayed a remarkable insight into Christ's nature, and now professed, in the ardour of his attachment, a readiness to die for his Lord. It was as though nothing that could distress the Divine Saviour should be wanting to his sufferings and sacrifice; he consented even to be denied by the foremost of the select and beloved band. 3. Jesus knew the hearts of his disciples better than they knew their own. They vehemently asserted their attachment, their devotedness, their unswerving fidelity. But he knew the underlying nature which afforded at present no foundation for their resolutions and protestations. And he was evidently prepared for what actually happened; it did not take him by surprise. Only after his ascension, and the baptism with the Spirit, could the apostles withstand the onset of the foe, the rage of the persecutor.

PRACTICAL LESSONS. 1. Learn the frailty and feebleness of human nature. 2. Learn the steadfastness and the love of the Saviour. 3. Learn the necessity of dependence upon Divine grace to keep from falling.

Vers. 32—42.—*Gethsemane.* How pathetic is this scene! Here we are in the presence of the sorrow of the Son of man; and there is no sorrow like this sorrow. Here we see Christ bearing our griefs, carrying our sorrows—a load beneath which even he almost sinks! It is not to us a spectacle merely of human anguish; we are deeply and personally interested in the agony of the Son of God. It was for our sake that the Father spared not his own Son. It was for our sake that Jesus, our High Priest, offered up prayers and supplications with strong crying and tears unto God, and learned obedience by the things which he suffered. The last quiet evening of fellowship has been passed in the upper room at Jerusalem by Jesus and the twelve. The last discourse—how full of encouragement and consolation!—has been delivered. The last, the most wonderful and precious, prayer has been offered by the Master for his disciples. Instead of returning, as on the earlier evenings of the week, to the seclusion of hospitable Bethany, the little company proceed to a spot where Jesus was wont to retire, from the excitement of the city ministry, for meditation and for prayer. By the light of the Paschal moon they pass through the open gate, and, leaving the city walls behind them, descend into the valley of the Kedron. Every heart is full of the sacred words which have just been spoken, and silence falls upon the pensive group. On the slope of Olivet they halt at an enclosure, where aged olive trees cast a sombre shade, and the rocks offer in their recesses a meet scene for lonely prayers. It is the garden of the olive-press, well known to every member of the band. Leaving the rest behind him, Jesus takes with him the favoured three, who are witnesses to the awe and deadly sorrow that come upon him. He entreats their sympathy and watchfulness, and then withdraws to a spot where in solitude he pours out all his soul in prayer. The hour indeed has come. The ministry of toil is over, and the ministry of suffering and of sacrifice only now remains. He is straitened until the last baptism be accomplished. The shadow of the cross has often before darkened his holy path; the cross itself is just upon him now. Hitherto his soul has been almost cloudlessly serene; in this hour the tempest of sorrow and of fear sweeps over him and lays him low. There is no resource save in prayer. Earth rejects him, man despises him. So he turns to heaven; he cries to the Father. He is feeling the pressure of the world's sin; he is facing the death which that sin, not his, has merited. It is too much, even for Christ, in his humanity, and he implores relief. "Oh that this cup may pass untasted!" Yet, even with this utterance of natural feeling, there is blended a purpose of submission: "Not my will, O my Father, but thine, be done!" It is the crisis of agony, unexampled, never to be repeated! An agony of grief, an agony of prayer, an agony that finds its vent in every pore. Angelic succour strengthens the fainting and exhausted frame. Is there human sympathy with the Sufferer? Surely the dear friends and scholars—they are praying with and for him! His craving heart draws him to the spot, to find them neither watching nor praying, but asleep! He treads the winepress alone! It is an added drop of bitterness in the bitter cup. "What, could ye not—not even Peter—watch with me—not for one short hour?" Alas! how feeble is the flesh, even though the spirit be alert and active! The prayer of Jesus, repeated with intensest fervour, gains in perfectness of submission. Thrice he retires to renew his supplication, with a growing acquiescence in the Father's will; thrice he approaches his chosen friends, each time to be disappointed by their apathy. But now the victory has been won. Jesus has wrestled in the garden that he may conquer on the cross. He leaves his tears and cries behind. For the eleven there is no further opportunity for sympathy; for the Master there is no more hesitation, no more outpouring of personal distress. He loses himself in his work. With the cross before him, a former exclamation seems to arise from the depths of his spirit: "For this cause came I unto this hour." He goes forward to meet the betrayer and his band. "Rise up, let us go; behold, he is near who betrays me!"

I. Our Saviour's sufferings in his own soul. It is noticeable that, up to this point in his earthly career, Jesus had maintained singular tranquillity of soul and composure of demeanour. He had been tempted by the devil; he had been calumniated by his enemies; he had been disappointed in professed friends; but his calm seems to have been unruffled. And it is also noticeable that, after his agony in the garden, he recovered his equanimity; and both in the presence of the high priest and of the governor, and (generally speaking) when enduring the agonies of crucifixion, showed the self-possession, the dignity, the uncomplaining resignation, which have been the occasion of world-wide and enduring admiration. But this hour in Gethsemane was the hour of our Lord's bitter grief and anguish, when his true humanity revealed itself in cries and tears, in prayers and prostration, in agony and bloody sweat. How is this to be accounted for? That his nature was pre-eminently sensitive we cannot doubt. Never was a heart so susceptible to profound emotion as the heart of the High Priest who is touched with the feeling of our infirmities, because he had been in all points tried and tempted even as we are, though without sin. But what occasioned, in this hour, feeling so deep, anguish so poignant? To a certain extent we can clearly understand his sorrows, but there is a point here at which our finite understanding and our imperfect human sympathies necessarily fail us. It is clear that Jesus foresaw what was approaching. He was not ignorant of the hostility of the Jewish leaders, of the treachery of Judas, of the fickleness of the populace, of the timidity of his own disciples. And, by his Divine foresight, he knew what the next few, awful hours were to bring him. There awaited him bodily pain, scourging, and crucifixion; mental distress in the endurance of the insults of his foes, the desertion of his friends, the ingratitude of the people for whom he had laboured and whom he had benefited. All this we can understand; but what careful reader of the narrative can deem even all this a sufficient explanation for woe unparalleled? It is, indeed, true that the sufferings and death of Jesus were undeserved; but this fact, and his own consciousness of innocence, might rather relieve than aggravate his distress. The fact is that, when we read of his being amazed and appalled—"exceeding sorrowful unto death," and asking that if possible he might be spared the approaching experience of shame and anguish—we are compelled to regard our Saviour in the light of our Representative and Substitute. His mind was, in a way we cannot understand, burdened with the world's sin, and his body was about to endure death which he did not deserve, but which he consented to pass through that he might be made perfect through sufferings, and that he might give his life a ransom for many. In the garden of the olive-press the Redeemer endured the unprecedented pressure of human sin and human woe!

II. OUR SAVIOUR'S PRAYER TO THE FATHER. The words of Jesus are reported somewhat differently by the several evangelists, from which we may learn that it is not so much the language as the meaning which is important for us. 1. Observe the *address*: "Abba, Father!" It is clear that our Lord was conscious of the personal favour and approval of him to whom he was rendering obedience, never so acceptable as in the closing scenes of the earthly ministry. 2. The *petition* is very remarkable: it was that the hour might pass, and that the cup might be taken away untasted. We are admitted here to witness the workings of Christ's human nature. He shrank, as we should do, from pain and insult, from slander and cruelty. Although he had forewarned his disciples that there was a baptism for him to endure, a bitter cup for him to drink, now that the time approached, the trial was so severe, the experience so distressing, that had he been guided by his individual feelings he would fain have avoided a doom so unjust and so overwhelming. 3. The *qualification* added explains what would otherwise be inexplicable. Jesus did not absolutely ask for release; his condition was, "If it be possible," and his conclusion, "Not my will, but thine, be done!" There was no resistance to the Father's appointment; on the contrary, there was perfect submission. Not that the Father took pleasure in the Son's sufferings, but the Father appointed that the ransom should be paid, that the sacrifice should be offered.

III. OUR SAVIOUR'S CLINGING TO HIS DISCIPLES. Very touching is our Lord's attachment to the eleven; "he loved them unto the end;" he took them with him to the garden. And very touching is his craving for human sympathy. Although his anguish could be best endured alone, he would have the little band not far off, and the favoured three he would have close by him. If they would watch with him one hour, the one only, the one last remaining hour of fellowship—if they would pray for themselves, perhaps for him—it would be a solace to his tender soul; to be assured of their sympathy, to be assured that, even on earth, he was not alone; that there was, even now, some gratitude, some love, some sympathizing sorrow, left on earth. Why Jesus should have gone thrice to see whether his three nearest friends were watching with him in the hour of his bitter woe, seems only to be explained by considering his true humanity, his heart yearning for sympathy. Even his prayers, fervent though they were, were interrupted for this purpose! There is a tone of reproach in his final permission, "Sleep on now!"—now that the glimmering of the torches is seen through the olive boughs as their bearers cross the deep ravine, now that the step of the traitor falls upon the ear of the betrayed. A sad reminder of "the irreparable past;" an everlasting expostulation, again and again in coming years to ring in the ear of each slumberous, unsympathizing disciple, and rouse to diligence, to watchfulness, to prayer.

IV. OUR SAVIOUR'S RESIGNATION AND ACCEPTANCE OF THE FUTURE BEFORE HIM. His bodily weakness was supported by angelic succour. His spirit was calmed by prayer, and by the final assurance that from the cross there was no release, except at the cost of the abandonment of his work of redemption. From the moment that the conflict was over, and his mind was fully and finally made up to accept the Divine appointment—from that moment his demeanour was changed. Instead of seeking sympathy from his disciples, he spoke words of authority and encouragement to them, in their weakness and their panic. Instead of falling upon his knees or upon his face, in agony and tears, he went forward to meet his betrayers. Instead of seeking release from the impending fate, he offered himself to his foes. He put forth his hand to take the cup from which he had so lately shrunk. He boldly met the hour which, in the prospect, had seemed almost too awful to encounter. He had now no will but his Father's, no aim but our salvation. Even now he saw "of the travail of his soul, and was satisfied." "For the joy that was set before him, he endured the cross, despising the shame!" The unity of the Saviour's sacrifice is thus apparent. He was obedient unto death; and the triumph of the spirit in Gethsemane was part of his filial and perfect obedience. Indeed, it would seem that the price of our redemption was paid, spiritually, in the garden; and, in the body, upon the cross!

APPLICATION. 1. This representation of our Saviour's character is peculiarly fitted to awaken our reverence, gratitude, and faith. As we trace our Saviour's career of active benevolence, our minds are constantly impressed with his unselfishness and pity, his willingness and power to relieve the wants, heal the disorders, pardon the sins, of men. But when we behold him in suffering and anguish, and remember that he consented to this experience for our sake, for our salvation, how can our hearts remain untouched? The innocent suffers in the place, and for the benefit of, the guilty. If we are the persons benefited, how sincere should be our thanksgiving, how lowly our adoration, how ardent our faith, how complete our devotion! 2. In the demeanour of our Saviour in the garden there is much which we shall do well to imitate. His patient endurance of grief and trouble encountered in the path divinely appointed, the absence of any hatred or vindictiveness towards his foes, his forbearance with his unsympathizing friends, and, above all, his submissive prayer offered to the Father,—all these are an example which all his followers should ponder and copy. Whilst we cannot suffer as he did for the benefit of the whole human race, our patience under trouble, our perseverance in resignation, and consecration to the will of God, are qualities which will not only prove serviceable to ourselves, but helpful and advantageous to some at least over whom our influence may extend. 3. Nothing is more fitted to deepen our sense of the enormity of human sin, nothing is more fitted to bring our sinful hearts to penitence, than the contemplation of the dread scenes of Gethsemane. Jesus was oppressed by a burden of sin—the sin of others, which we may take as an example of the sins of mankind, and ourselves—all of which he then bore. The coldness and callousness of the eleven, the treachery of Judas, the cowardice of Peter, the malice of the priests, the fickleness of the multitude, the injustice of the Roman governor, the unspiritual and unfeeling insolence of the rulers,—all these in this awful hour pressed heavily upon the soul of Jesus. But these were only samples of the sins of humanity at large, of the sins of each individual in particular. He took all upon his own great heart, and bore them, and suffered for them, and on the cross submitted to that death which was their due penalty. In what spirit should we contemplate these sufferings of our Redeemer? Surely, if anything is adapted to bring us in lowly contrition before the feet of God, this scene is pre-eminently so adapted. Not indeed in abject, hopeless, terror, but with humble repentance and confidence. For the same scene that reminds us of our sins, reminds us of Divine mercy, and of the Being through whose sacrifice that mercy is freely extended to every contrite and believing suppliant. This is the language of every Christian who is a spectator of these unparalleled woes: "He loved me, and gave himself for me!" 4. And what more fitted to awaken within the breast of every hearer of the gospel a conviction of the greatness and sufficiency of the salvation which is by Christ unto all who believe? There is no extenuation of the seriousness, the almost desperateness, of the sinner's case; for sin evidently needed, if this record be true, a great Saviour and a great salvation. The means used were not trivial to bring sinners to a sense of their sin and need, to make it consistent with the Divine character to pardon and accept the contrite sinner. "Ye were redeemed . . . with the precious blood of Christ!" Therefore, without hesitation or misgiving, receive Jesus as your Redeemer; "be ye reconciled to God!"

Vers. 43—52.—*Betrayal and arrest.* The agony and the betrayal are most closely related. Neither can be understood apart from the other. Why did Jesus so suffer in the garden, and endure sorrow such that there was none like it? Doubtless it was because he was anticipating the approaching apprehension, and all the awful events which it involved. His soul was darkened by the knowledge that the Son of man was about to be betrayed into the hands of sinners. And how came Jesus, when the crisis arrived, to meet his foes so fearlessly, and to bear his pain and ignominy with patience so inimitable, so Divine? It was because he had prepared himself in solitude, by meditation, prayer, and resolution; so that, upon the approach of his foes, his attitude was one of meekness and of fortitude. We observe here—

I. An exhibition of human sin. It seems as if the iniquity of mankind reached its height at the very time when the Saviour bore it in his own body, in his own soul. As the awful and sacred hour approached when the Good Shepherd should lay down his life, sin appeared almost omnipotent; the Lord confessed as much when, upon his apprehension, he said to his captors, " This is your hour, and the power of darkness." Observe the combination of the various forms of sin manifested on this occasion. 1. *The malignity of the conspirators* is almost incredible. The chief priests, scribes, and elders had long been plotting the death of the Prophet of Nazareth. It had all along been the case that his truthful and dignified assertion of his just and lofty claims, and the performance of his best deeds, excited their worst feelings. They had especially been angered by his miracles of healing and help ; both because they led the people to regard him with favour, and because they were a rebuke to their own indifference to the people's welfare. And it was probably the raising of Lazarus which determined them, at all hazards, to attempt the destruction of the Holy One and Just. Their own deeds were evil, and they hated the light. Hence their hateful and cruel conspiracy. 2. *The baseness of the authorities.* The Sanhedrim leagued itself with the Roman governor. With the temple servitors and officers were conjoined the band from Antonia. Discreditable to the Roman authorities, and disgraceful to the Jewish, was this leaguing together for a purpose so unjustifiable. Ecclesiastical and civil authorities concurred in reversing the true canon : they were a praise to evil-doers, and a terror to those who did well. 3. *The treachery of the betrayer.* Whatever may have been the motive of Judas, his action was traitorous and flagitious. Pretending still to be Jesus' friend, he conspired with his enemies against him, took their money to betray him, and even used to his disadvantage the knowledge his intimacy gave him of his Master's habits of devotion. Unparalleled was the baseness with which the traitor betrayed the Son of man with the kiss of the seeming friend. In suffering all this, our Lord showed his readiness to submit for our sake to the uttermost humiliation, to the keenest anguish of soul. 4. *The cowardice apparent in the time, place, and manner of the Lord's apprehension.* His indignation with these circumstances the Lord did not conceal. Why did not his enemies seize him in the temple, instead of in the garden ? when teaching in public, instead of when praying in private ? by day, instead of in the partial darkness of the night? Why did they come armed as against a robber, when they knew him to be peaceable and unresisting ? If all this shows some consciousness of our Lord's majesty and authority, it certainly reveals the depth and degradation of the iniquity which could work deeds at once so foul and so cowardly. 5. *The timidity and desertion of the disciples.* Shall we call this excusable weakness ? If so, it is because we feel that we might have acted as they acted had we been in their place. But, in truth, it was sin. They could not watch with him when he prayed, and they could not stand by him when he was in danger and encompassed by his foes. There is something infinitely pathetic in the simple statement, " They all left him, and fled." Even Peter, who had protested so lately his readiness to die with him; even John, who had so lately reclined upon Jesus' breast; even the young man (was it Mark himself?) whose affectionate curiosity led him to join the sad procession, as it passed through the still streets of Jerusalem !

II. A revelation of Christ's divinely perfect character. Circumstances of trial prove what is in men. When the sea is smooth and the wind is still, the unsound vessel seems as stout and as safe as that which is seaworthy ; the tempest soon makes the difference manifest. Even our sinless, holy Lord shines out more gloriously in his adversity, when the storm breaks upon his head. 1. We recognize in him a calm and dignified demeanour. He had been disturbed and distressed in his solitude, and his feelings had then found vent in strong crying and tears. But his agitation has passed away, and his spirit is untroubled. He meets his enemies with unquailing boldness of heart and serenity of mien. 2. We are impressed with *his ready, uncomplaining submission to his fate.* He acknowledges himself to be the One whom the high priests' myrmidons are seeking ; he offers no resistance, and forbids resistance on the part of his followers ; he acts as One who knows that his hour has come. There is a marked contrast between the action of our Lord on this and on previous occasions. Before, he had eluded his foes, and escaped from their hands; now, he yields himself up. His conduct is an illustration of his own word : " No one taketh my life away from me ; but I lay it down of myself." 3. We remark *his compassion exercised towards one of his captors.* The impetuous Peter aims a blow at one of the attendant and armed bonds-men; but Jesus rebukes his friend, and mercifully heals his foe. How like himself, and how unlike all beside ! 4. We admire *his willingness to fulfil the Scriptures and the will of God.* It was a moment when, in the case of an ordinary man, self would have asserted its claims, and the purposes of Heaven would probably have been lost sight of. It was not so with Jesus. The word of the Father, the will of the Father,—these were pre-eminent in their authority.

III. A STEP TOWARDS CHRIST'S SACRIFICE AND MAN'S REDEMPTION. If the whole of our Saviour's career was part of his mediatorial work, the closing stages were emphati-cally *the* sacrifice. And it was in Gethsemane that the last scene opened ; now was the beginning of the end. 1. We discern here *conspicuous self-devotion.* Jesus appears as One baring his breast for the blow. From this moment he has to suffer, and of this he is evidently clearly conscious, and for this prepared. 2. His action is evidently in *obedience to the Father* ; he treads the path the Father marks out, and drinks the cup the Father presents to his lips. 3. He already *stands in our place.* The innocent and holy One submits to be treated as a guilty offender; the most benevolent and self-denying of all beings allows himself to share the contumely and the doom of the criminal. He is "numbered with the transgressors." Unmerited sufferings and insults are endured for our sake by the very Son of God. 4. *Thus he prepares for death.* "He is led as a lamb to the slaughter." He is bound as a victim, to be laid upon the altar. His sensitive nature tastes, in anticipation, the agonies of the cross. Already he is taking to himself, that he may bear it and bear it away, the sin of the world.

APPLICATION. How deserving is such a Saviour as this narrative portrays of the faith of every sinner, and of the love and devotion of every believer ! His forbearance, patience, and compassion show the tenderness of his heart, and the firmness of his purpose to save. This may well justify the confidence of every poor, sinful, helpless heart. His love, his sacrifice, demand our grateful trust. And to such a Saviour what adequate offering can be presented by those who know his power and feel his grace ?

Vers. 53—65.—*The trial before Caiaphas.* Surely this is the most amazing scene in the long history of humanity ! The Redeemer of mankind upon his trial ; the Saviour at the bar of those he came to save ;—there is in this something monstrous and almost incredible. But the case is even worse than this. The Lord and Judge of man stands at the tribunal of those who must one day appear before his judgment-seat. They judge him in time whom he must judge in eternity. It is a spectacle the most affect-ing and the most awful this earth has ever witnessed.

I. THE TRIBUNAL. Jesus has already been led before the crafty and unrighteous Annas. He is now led into the presence of the high priest, the Caiaphas (son-in-law to Annas) who has declared that it was good that one man should perish for the people; which meant, that it was better that the innocent Jesus should die, rather than that the ruler's influence with the people should be imperilled by the prevalence of the spiritual teaching of the Prophet of Nazareth. With Caiaphas are associated, first informally, and then in something like legal fashion, the chief priests, elders, and scribes. It appears that these are mainly of the Sadducees, of the party who aimed at political power. The tribunal before which Jesus is arraigned is composed of the Sanhedrim, so far as it may be said to exist at this time. It is observable, accordingly, that the accusers of Jesus are his judges. These are the men who sent down spies into Galilee, to lay in wait and tempt Jesus, and catch him in his speech. These are the men who instigated the cavillers who, in the public places of Jerusalem, opposed the teaching of the Lord with foolish questions, uncandid criticisms, unfounded calumnies. These are the men who, after the raising of Lazarus, plotted against the mighty One, and resolved that they would have his life. These are the men who themselves sent out the band that apprehended Jesus in the garden. He appears, therefore, at the bar of those who have watched and pursued him with eager malice, who have persecuted him with unscrupulous hatred, and who have now got him within their toils. Such was the court before which Jesus appeared. From a tribunal like this there was no prospect, no expectation, no possibility, of justice. This Jesus had long foreseen, and for the consequences Jesus was perfectly prepared.

II. THE EVIDENCE. When the judges condescend to become the accusers, it is no wonder that they *seek* evidence against the accused. In such circumstances Jesus must be obviously, undeniably innocent, if no charge can be substantiated against him. False witnesses appear; but so flagrantly inconsistent are their unfounded accusations, that even such a court, so prejudiced, cannot condemn upon testimony so mutually destructive. At length, however, false witnesses stand up, who distort a memorable saying of Christ into what may be construed as a disparagement of the national temple which all Jews regard with pride. Jesus, speaking of the temple of his body, had said, " Destroy this temple, and in three days I will rear it again." This saying is misrepresented, and made to appear the utterance of an intention to destroy the sacred and noble edifice. Even so, however, the witnesses agree not. If this is the worst charge that can be brought against Jesus, and if even this cannot be substantiated; if no remembered words can be twisted so as to give some colour for condemnation before a tribunal so constituted and so prejudiced; then this is certain, that the ministry of Jesus must have been discharged with amazing wisdom and discretion. At the same time, the sin of the Lord's enemies appears the more enormous and the more inexcusable. Jesus was not condemned upon any evidence, any testimony, against him.

III. THE APPEAL AND ADJURATION. 1. The president of the court, stung with disappointment, springs from his seat, indignant at the silence and calmness of the accused; and, with most unjudicial unfairness, interposes, and endeavours to provoke Jesus into language which may inculpate himself. But he is met with a dignified demeanour and with continued silence. 2. This effort being in vain, the high priest *adjures* the accused, and requires him to say whether or not he persists in the claims which he has made in the course of his ministry to be the Messiah, and the Son of the Blessed. Let him say " No," and he is for ever discredited and powerless; let him say " Yes," and then his admission may be construed into a claim which may be represented to the Roman procurator as a treasonable assumption of royal power. The intention of the judge in this proceeding was evil; but an opportunity was thus given for the great Accused publicly to put himself right with the court and with the world.

IV. THE ACKNOWLEDGMENT AND DECLARATION. Our Lord does not think it worth while to refute witnesses who have refuted themselves and one another. But now that the ruler of the people puts him upon his oath, and requires of him a plain answer to a plain question, Jesus breaks his silence. 1. He acknowledges what he has often asserted before, that no claim can be too high for him to make with truth. If he is to die— and upon that he has resolved—Jesus will die, witnessing to the truth and for the truth. He is the foretold Deliverer, the anointed King, the only Son of the Blessed and Eternal. This he will not conceal; from this avowal nought shall make him shrink. 2. He adds that his high position and glorious office shall be one day witnessed by his persecutors and judges, as well as by all mankind. There is true sublimity in such an avowal, made in such circumstances and before such an assembly. To the view of man Jesus is the culprit, powerless before the malice and the injustice of the mighty, and in danger of a cruel and violent death. But in truth the case is otherwise. He is the Divine King, the Divine Judge. His glory is concealed now, but it shall shine forth in due time and ere long. Men on earth shall bow in his Name, receive his laws, and place themselves beneath his protecting care. The world shall witness his majesty, and all nations shall be summoned to his bar, and heaven shall crown him " Lord of all." What striking harmony there is between this profession and expectation of Christ on the one hand, and on the other that wonderful statement of an apostle, " For the joy that was set before him, he endured the cross, despising the shame "

V. THE SENTENCE. 1. The avowal is treated as a confession. No witnesses are now needed. From his own mouth he is judged. The charge, which Jesus' own language is held to justify and substantiate, is one of blasphemy. And, if Christ were a mere man, this charge was just. 2. The whole court concurs in the judgment. The president is eager to condemn, but not more eager than his assessors. One mind moves them all— a mind of malice and hatred, a mind rejoicing in iniquity, grasping at the fulfilment of base hopes. 3. The sentence is death. It was a foregone conclusion. The destruction of Jesus had been resolved upon long since. Death for the Lord of life; death for the Benefactor of mankind; death for the innocent but willing Victim of human ferocity and human sin!

VI. THE INSULTS. Again and again, in the course of that awful night, that awful morning, was the Lord of glory treated with derision, ignominy, and contempt. The record is almost too distressing to be read. We can read of the agony in the garden, of the anguish of the cross, but we scarcely know how to read of the treatment our Saviour met with from our fellow-men, from those he came to save and bless. The spitting, the buffeting, the mockery, the blows,—those will not bear to be thought upon. We may believe, we cannot realize, the record!

APPLICATION. 1. Here we behold sin at its height, raging and seemingly triumphant. Whether we look at the witnesses who maligned Jesus, the court which condemned him, or the officers who abused him, we are confronted with appalling proofs of the flagitiousness of human sin. 2. Here we behold innocence in its peerless perfection. No fault is found in Jesus. Even his demeanour, amidst all this injustice, is consummate moral beauty. His unruffled calm, his Divine dignity, his immovable patience,—all command the profoundest reverence of our heart. 3. Here we behold a willing Sacrifice. Jesus is "obedient unto death, even the death of the cross." With these stripes we are healed. These are a part of the suffering Jesus bore for us. That we may be freed from condemnation, he is condemned; that we may live, he is delivered unto death. 4. A glorious example is here presented for our imitation. "Christ also suffered for you, leaving you an example, that ye should follow in his steps . . . who, when he was reviled, reviled not again; when he suffered, threatened not; but committed himself to him that *judgeth righteously.*"

Vers. 66—72.—*Peter's denial.* The story of our Saviour's humiliation and suffering is a story not only of the malice and the injustice of his enemies, but of the frailty and unfaithfulness of his professed friends. It is true that the priests and elders apprehended him with violence and condemned him with unrighteousness; and that the Roman governor, against his own convictions, and influenced by his weakness and his selfish interests, condemned him to a cruel death. But it is also true, that of the twelve chosen and intimate associates one betrayed him and another denied him.

I. THIS CONDUCT WAS AT VARIANCE WITH PETER'S USUAL PRINCIPLES AND HABITS. No candid reader of the Gospel narrative can doubt either the faith or the love of this leader among the twelve. His confidence in the Master and his attachment to him were thoroughly appreciated by Christ himself. Had not Jesus named him the Rock? Had he not, upon the occasion of his memorable confession that Jesus was the Son of God, warmly exclaimed, "Blessed art thou," etc.? A warm and eager nature had found a Being deserving of all trust, affection, and devotion; and the Lord knew that in Peter he had a friend, ardent, attached, and true. He admitted the son of Jonas into the inner circle of three; he was one of the elect among the elect.

II. THIS CONDUCT WAS AT VARIANCE WITH PETER'S PREVIOUS INTENTION AND PROFESSION. When the seizure and capture were approaching, the Lord warned his servant that he would be found unfaithful. Peter's declaration had been, "I am ready to go with thee, both into prison, and to death;" "If I must die with thee, I will not deny thee." And he was no doubt sincere in this bold and confident declaration. But sincerity is not enough; there must be stability as well. The professions of the ardent, experience teaches, must not always be taken with implicit trust. Time tries all; and endurance in trial is the true test of character. Peter's fall is a lesson of caution to the confident and the ardent.

III. THIS CONDUCT WAS FORESEEN AND FORETOLD BY THE LORD JESUS. The Master knew his servant better than he knew himself. In warning him of his impending fall, Christ had assured Peter that only his prayers should secure him from moral destruction.

IV. THIS CONDUCT MUST BE EXPLAINED BY THE COMBINATION IN PETER'S MIND OF LOVE AND FEAR. It was his affection for Jesus which led this apostle to enter the court, and to remain in the neighbourhood of the Lord during his mock-trial. The others had forsaken their Master, and had fled; John only, being known, and Peter, being introduced by his friend, clung thus to the scene of their Master's woe. Peter, like John, felt unable to desert his Lord. Strange that he should feel able to deny him. He felt for his Master, but he feared for himself. Cowardice for the time overpowered the courage which first brought him to the spot and then deserted him.

V. THIS CONDUCT IS AN INSTANCE OF THE TENDENCY OF SIN TO REPEAT ITSELF. A single falsehood often brings on others in its train. To get it believed, the liar lies again, and confirms his falsehood with oaths. Peter found himself in a position in which he must either repeatedly deny his Lord, or else expose his own falseness, and run into the very danger which he had sinned to escape. Ah! how slippery are the paths of sin! How easy it is to go wrong, and how difficult to recover the right way! Who knows, when once he lies, or cheats, or sins in any way, where, if ever, he shall stop? How needful the prayer, "Hold up my goings in thy paths, that my footsteps slip not"!

VI. THIS CONDUCT COULD NOT ENDURE THE REBUKE OF CONSCIENCE AND THE REPROACH OF CHRIST. There was inconsistency between what Peter felt in his inmost heart, between the prayers which he was wont to offer, and what in this night he did and said. The falsehood and the fear were on the outside of his nature; below, there was a sensitive conscience and a loving heart. It was the look of the Master, as he was led through the open court, and met his faithless servant's eye, which melted Peter's heart, recalling in a moment the warning which had been disregarded and the profession which had been belied. If there had not been a heart, a conscience, responsive to the appeal and the reproach conveyed in that look, those eyes would have met in vain. All Christ's servants are liable to temptation, and it is possible that any one among them may be betrayed into faithlessness towards Christ; but it is only where there is true love that there is susceptibility to the Saviour's tender expostulation and affectionate rebuke. It is thus that the Lord makes manifest who are his; he shames them because of their own weakness and cowardice, and awakens what is best within them to a sense of personal unworthiness, and to a desire of reconciliation and renewal.

VII. THIS CONDUCT WAS THE OCCASION OF SHAME AND CONTRITION. "When he thought thereon, he wept." Thought, reflection, especially upon the words of Jesus, are fitted to bring the misguided soul to itself. It is the haste and hurry of men's lives which often hinder true repentance and reformation. "They that lack time to mourn lack time to mend." These tears were the turning-point, and the earnest and the beginning of better things. Another evangelist relates to us at length the restoration of Peter to favour, and his new commission of service. But the simple words with which this narrative closes furnish the key to what follows, to the rest of Peter's life. Judas's sin led him to remorse; Peter's sin led him to repentance. The root of the difference lay in the two men's distinct and opposed characters. Judas's principle was love of self; Peter's was love of Christ. The recovery, which was possible for the one, was therefore morally impossible for the other.

APPLICATION. 1. A warning against self-confidence. 2. A suggestion as to the spirit in which to encounter temptation: Watch and pray; look to Jesus! 3. An encouragement to true penitents.

HOMILIES BY VARIOUS AUTHORS.

Vers. 3—9.—*The precious spikenard; or, the impulse of the absolute.* The house of Simon the leper was a familiar resort to Jesus. It is Mary the sister of Lazarus who now approaches him as he reclines at meat. Let us look at—

I. HER ACT OF DEVOTION. The nard or spikenard was an unguent of the East. It was "genuine" and costly. Probably it had been kept against that day. She now entered, probably at first unperceived, and, breaking the neck of the alabaster cruse, poured the precious nard upon the Saviour's person (John says his feet; Matthew and Mark, his head; probably both received the anointing). John adds, "And wiped his feet with her hair; and the house was filled with the odour of the ointment." The offering was: 1. *Sudden.* It was given ere any one could interfere. The *breaking* of the cruse may also have pointed to the quick, spontaneous impulse which prompted. The woman who had come forward so unexpectedly, at once retired again before the tumult and anger her act had occasioned. 2. *It sprang from secret sources of reverence und love.* The disciples could not comprehend it. They were not consulted. It expressed her own feeling unshared with any other. 3. *It was oblivious of cost.* The price put upon it by the disciples—three hundred *denarii*—was about ten pounds of our money, but of greater actual value at that time. Mary belonged to a respectable family, and could probably afford the gift, although its purchase would tax her personal means. Of that she does not think. It is freely given, poured out without care or stint upon him for whom it had been designed.

II. The criticism to which it exposed. The disciples "had indignation among themselves." It presently broke forth in reproaches and murmurs. The action was stigmatized as purposeless "waste." Another use it might have served, viz. the relief of the poor, was mentioned. This judgment was partly honest, partly knavish; wholly ignorant and wrong. "What is not outwardly useful may be highly proper;" and men ought to be very careful in pronouncing upon religious offerings. A higher platform of principle is often affected by those who are really less spiritual.

III. Christ's vindication. "Why trouble ye her?" They had no business to interfere. 1. *The act was commended.* "A good [noble, beautiful] work." He saw the inward character of it. In his sight alone was it justified. 2. *It was defended as more opportune and urgent than almsgiving.* "Ye have the poor always with you, . . . but me ye have not always. She hath done what she could: she hath anointed my body aforehand for the burying." Many and mingled feelings prompted the offering—gratitude for the restoration of Lazarus, adoration of the character of Jesus, recognition of him as "the Way, the Truth, and the Life," as the Lord of life and death, etc.; but may not the foremost motive have been the reverent one which sought to do honour to One about to die? She who sat at the feet of Jesus divined his teaching more deeply than his professed followers. How are we to characterize this emotion which overcame her? It was deep, pure, unselfish, overwhelming. May it not fitly be termed "the impulse of the absolute"? It is the essence of religion. Thus the devout soul responds to the infinite sacrifice. Martyrs, apostles, missionaries, have felt its power. It obeyed a higher reason than the rudimentary religious experience of the apostles could comprehend. When the "length, and breadth, and depth, and height" of the passion of Jesus are perceived, no gift can fully express the sense of worship and obligation that arises. The highest sentiments of human nature are appealed to, and all the resources of our life are at his service, at the same time that we are profoundly conscious how far short they fall of his deserts or the claim he has upon us. It is a transaction, when it takes place, which others cannot judge; it is between the soul and its Lord.—M.

Vers. 4, 5.—*The spirit that betrays.* I. Selfishness. An exaggeration of the natural principle of self-love. Judas, as chief representative of this spirit, shows the virtues of his great vice, and naturally enough becomes keeper of the bag, containing the earthward dependence of the band. He looks at everything from this point of view. Already his thrift or prudence has degenerated into avarice, the more quickly owing to the grace which he resisted. The money value of the offering is at once appraised, the spiritual worth being wholly discounted.

II. This is represented (by St. Matthew and St. Mark) as not confined to one individual. In truth, every disciple had a share of it, although in a few it was more strongly manifest, and in one it may be said to have become incarnate. St. John, who is more given to this personalization of principles, speaks only of Judas. This, then, is a general danger to which the Church is liable, and requires the most careful self-examination. It can only be washed out of the soul by frequent and copious baptisms of Divine purity; it can only be consumed by the constant fire of the Divine love.

III. Here it is called into greater strength by the presence of the spirit of sacrifice. It is provoked by the display of self-forgetful affection. Why so? 1. *Because it fails to discern the imminence and significance of the Divine event spiritually revealed to the soul of Mary.* 2. *Because, in resisting that spirit, its own evil is exaggerated and confirmed.* It seeks, therefore, to discredit the special manifestation of the spirit of devotion taking place. The indirect form of Divine charity, viz. alms, is declared preferable to the direct, viz. self-sacrificing devotion to God in Christ. How often is this exchange actually made in the history of the Church; almsgiving (with all its attendant corruptions) taking the place of the soul's immediate allegiance to Jehovah! But on this occasion it is only a cloak for a deeper depth of selfishness, perhaps hardly confessed to himself by the chief culprit. He would by-and-by have stolen the worth of the gift, diverting it thus wholly from its rightful destination. Soon this self-seeking will declare itself in selling the Christ himself for money; a lesser sum (thirty pieces of silver, the price of a slave) being temptation enough.—M.

Vers. 10, 11.—*Volunteering to betray.* The "and" connects this with the preceding paragraph, not only historically but psychologically. His present action was (immediately) determined by the gift of Mary and the mild rebuke of the Master.

I. THE CRIME CONTEMPLATED. To deliver up Christ to his enemies. Whether he fully realized how much was involved as a result of this step is uncertain. He might imagine that not death, but the checking of his Master upon the career he had marked out, would ensue. But there is recklessness as to any consequences, provided he himself should be no loser. In robbing the alms from the bag, he was guilty of a breach of trust; in this new development of his master passion the unfaithfulness culminated. It is manifest that the spiritual side of Christ's ministry had for him no value. It was only the earthly rewards that might attend on discipleship that made it attractive to him. Was it to force the hand of the ideal, unpractical Christ that he sought to deliver him up? A miracle of deliverance might then result in a realization greater than his most brilliant hopes could depict, and thus his (passing) act of villainy be condoned. Or was it in sheer disgust and desperation respecting the course affairs seemed to be taking that he conceived of his deed? We cannot tell. In a mind like that of Judas there are depths beyond depths.

II. THE MOTIVE. That *selfishness* was at the root we may be sure. *Avarice* is the direction it took. He proposed money, and asked how much (Matt. xxvi. 15). Thirty pieces of silver a small sum? Yes, but he might be at that moment in real or fancied need, or the amount might be looked upon as a mere instalment of further reward, when he might have made himself useful, perhaps necessary, to the rulers. *Fear of consequences,* if he followed Christ further in the direction in which he was moving, may also have influenced his mind. And there can be no question as to the immediate impulse of *wounded feeling,* through baffled dishonesty and the sense that Christ saw through him. Falling short of the higher illumination and power of the Spirit, he was at the mercy of his own base, earthly nature.

III. CONSPIRING CIRCUMSTANCES. The background to all this mental and spiritual movement on the part of Judas is the attitude of the chief priests and scribes, "seeking how they might take" Christ. But for opportunity afforded the treachery of Judas might have remained an aimless mood or a latent disposition, instead of becoming a definite purpose. In this consists the danger of unspiritual states of mind: they subject those in whom they are indulged to the tyranny of passing influences and circumstances.—M.

Vers. 12—16.—*Preparing for the Passover.* The festival of "unleavened cakes," or "unleavened bread," commenced on the night of the 14th of Abib or Nisan (Exod. xii. 16) after sunset; that day, corresponding to our 16th of March, was therefore popularly called the first of the festival, because it was the preparation day for it. This preparation of the Passover, *i.e.* the killing of the lamb, etc., had to take place between three and six o'clock, the ninth and twelfth hours of the solar day. "Sacrificed," or "killed," has the force of "accustomed to sacrifice or kill." The room was to be "furnished," literally "strewn," *i.e.* the tables and couches were to be laid; and it was to be ready, *i.e.* cleansed, etc., in conformity with ceremonial purifications. A considerable amount of work had to be carefully gone through ere all things would be ready. The lamb, unleavened bread, bitter herbs, wine, and "conserve of sweet fruits," had to be purchased; the lamb had to be slain by the officiating priest in the temple; and then it had to be roasted with the herbs. From the circumstances connected with this preparation in the case of Christ and his disciples we see—

I. THE REPRESENTATIVE HEADSHIP OF CHRIST. The disciples looked to him for direction. They spoke of *him,* and not themselves severally, as being about to observe the Passover, which indicated, not that they themselves were not going to observe it, but that they ranged themselves under him as constituting, so to speak, his household. That they should have to seek his direction at the last was no proof of carelessness, but only of habitual dependence upon him; and it pathetically suggested how closely their circumstances corresponded with the typical character of the first celebrants, who as strangers and sojourners partook of the hasty feast. Fittingly enough, he who sought at birth the shelter of an inn, goes to such a place to observe the Passover with his disciples, in a separate and distinct capacity from that of any other household in Israel. They were to ask, "Where is *my guest-chamber?*" it was he who was to entertain.

II. HIS REGARD FOR THE OBSERVANCES AND INSTITUTIONS OF THE LAW. This is shown in the careful attention he gave to the details of the feast. Whether the arrangements made were due to the exercise of supernatural foresight, or merely to the natural forethought and human care of Christ, it is impossible to determine. In the former case, the "man bearing a pitcher of water," who was to meet them, would be indicated as a Divine token; in the latter, the man would be simply arranged for with the master or "goodman" of the hostelry. Either way, the feast was really prepared for by Christ, and no regulation was neglected. When the poverty, homelessness, and personal danger of the Saviour are remembered, his observance of the Passover will be seen to possess an emphasis and intention quite special.

III. THE CONTINUITY IN WHICH THE "LORD'S SUPPER" STANDS. It was a "moment" or stage of the Paschal feast, and therefore a portion of the same celebration. Doubtless the feast would be protracted, or at any rate the actual eating of the lamb would be distinguished in time from the partaking of the bread and wine, which came a little later, as a new commencement after Judas had withdrawn at the bidding of the Master. In this way the retrospective character of the eating and drinking is quite natural. The two great feasts of Judaism and Christianity are thus vitally connected, the new celebration being a survival of the old one, and a perpetuation of its spiritual meaning. In such instances do we see the continuity of essential ideas, observances, and institutions throughout the varying phases and progressive stages of religious development.

IV. THE SPIRITUAL PREPARATION OF CHRIST FOR THAT WHICH THE PASSOVER SYMBOLIZED. It is just in the attention to these minute details, paid by One to whom in general the "spirit" was ever of so much more consequence than the "letter," that the inward preparedness of the Saviour is suggested for his great sacrifice. The whole typology of the sacred festival had been spiritually realized by him, and its connection with his own death. In Matthew's Gospel this foreboding consciousness of doom, elevated into a higher mood by spiritual willinghood, is expressed: "The Master saith, *My time is at hand*," etc.—M.

Vers. 17—21.— *The betrayer denounced.* I. THE SHADOW AT THE FEAST. Not *fear*, as of a criminal under sting of conscience; nor *over-anxiety*, the spectre that sits with the worldling at his board; but *moral repugnance expressing itself in sympathetic sorrow.* An inward sense of interrupted sympathy and fellowship.

II. THE BETRAYER INDICATED. It is necessary to declare what it is which prevents the full communion of the household of Christ. This is done in order: 1. *To awaken the spirit of self-examination and self-distrust.* "Is it I?" Therefore the indication given is general and anonymous. 2. *To characterize and accentuate the moral hideousness of the crime.* It was shown to be an evil foretold from afar. The betrayal is to take place, "that the Scripture [Ps. xli. 9] may be fulfilled, *He that eateth my bread* [or *his bread with me*] *lifted up his heel against me*" (John xiii. 18). And so, anticipatively, a new evidence is furnished by which to identify Jesus as the Messiah (John xiii. 19). As done by one enjoying the benefits of the Christian household, and reclining in pretended communion with the Lord, it is declared to be an act of the basest treachery and ingratitude. 3. *As a personal discovery determining the further action of the guilty one.* The special sign given was perceived by Judas alone, although explicitly mentioned. In answer to John's inquiry (the question of spiritual love), the partaking, which is here spoken of as a general thing, is specialized in a definite way with respect to the individual meant (John xiii. 26). The further command is given, not to do the deed, but, as he is determined even then to do it, to do it quickly

(John xiii. 27, 30). Thus the foulest crime against the Son of God is determined and accelerated amidst communion and sacred celebration—a psychological truth. 4. *As an occasion for solemn lamentation over the miserable destiny of Judas.* The " woe " is not spoken so much as a denunciation, but rather in commiseration. All the good of life is spoken of as forfeited—and more than forfeited. " The apophthegm is rather remarkable when microscopically examined, for, strictly speaking, nothing would be *good* to a man who never existed. But our Saviour's meaning is not microscopic, but obvious, and most solemn. *A man's existence is turned into a curse to him when he inverts the grand moral purpose contemplated in its Divine origination* " (Morison). At the feast of love there is ever a sense of mingled reprobation and sympathy with respect to sinners.

III. The principle of the interdependence of good and evil stated. " The Son of man goeth," etc. *Evil is overruled and made the occasion of good.* Not that it is thereby necessitated : it is still the product of the free-will of the creature. Yet is it foreseen, and the operation of good is modified so as to produce the greater good. That Christ should die was foreordained ; it was the expression of an eternal determination of the Divine nature ; but the particular circumstances affecting the external character of his death were not foreordained. And, therefore, as freely committed, *evil is not altered in its moral character by the result flowing from its being divinely overruled.* Judas was a criminal awfully and uniquely wicked, and his " woe " is wailed forth by Infinite Love himself !—M.

Vers. 22—25.—*The Lord's Supper.* A good title, as it was an evening meal; and it was appropriated to a new and special purpose by our Lord, in connection with whom its significance is received. He is the Host, while his disciples are the guests. Consider it—

I. In relation to the Passover. The general meaning of the Passover was perpetuated in a spiritual sense. There was: 1. *A transfer.* Not of the whole Passover, but of a portion. It was during the progress of that meal, " as they were eating," that this particular occurrence took place. " He took bread [or *a loaf*]," thus adopting that, and the cup which was passing round, as something distinct from the main portion of the Passover meal, viz. the eating of the lamb itself. The cup was usually passed round three times, the bread frequently. We can conceive Christ's manner unusually solemn and impressive, as he raised these otherwise subordinate elements of the Paschal feast into prominent distinctness. 2. *An interpretation.* He took the brittle cake of unleavened bread and broke it, saying, " This is my body ; " and the cup, saying, " This is my blood." The doctrines of transubstantiation and consubstantiation are philosophical refinements upon the simple meaning of the phrases, and lead inevitably to contradiction and absurdity. Christ was alive before them, and using his body, as he spoke. It must, therefore, have been distinct from the bread. " When our Lord said that the bread which he took in his hands was his body, and that the wine which he held in the cup was his blood, he used a simple figure of speech, such as he often employed. He called himself bread, a door, a vine ; meaning that these objects resembled and so represented him. The words are understood figuratively by all, and must be so. Controversies merely concern the nature of the figure. . . . The Romanist interpretation is figurative. It supposes a figure without a precedent, a miracle without a parallel ; and it attributes the salvation of men, not to the actual death of Christ, but to what he did with the bread and wine. As the Passover was simply a symbolical service, the addition to it would be regarded as similar " (Godwin). " Note that, according to our Saviour himself, the liquid contained in the cup was not literal blood, but *the fruit of the vine* " (Morison).

II. In itself. 1. *A covenant or testament.* It was " a disposition of things," by virtue of which the good to be obtained through the obedience and sacrifice of Christ is secured to those who believingly partake. It is a " testament," inasmuch as it was to have effect after Christ's death, and through the fact and manner of that death believers were to become heirs of the blessings it secured. This " agreement," which is contained in the covenant-idea, is a mutual affair, and involves mutual obligations. It also, after the precedent of ancient Israel, constitutes the true recipients God's people and him their God. The thing handed over is not the body and blood, but that life and grace which they represented. 2. *A communion.* "Take ye." "He gave to them: and they all drank of it." It is only as a communion that the covenant has effect. To those who have received the life and spirit of Christ there is forgiveness and peace. Their sins are blotted out, and they are *passed over* in the mercy of God. And so the act of communion is a spiritual one, and involves fresh realization of the meaning of the great facts of atonement, and the duties of the reconciled children of God. 3. *An anticipation.* There is to be another feast, when the Saviour comes to his people, and his people enter with him into the scene of the "marriage supper of the Lamb." It was Christ's last earthly Passover: he looked thence confidently forth to the final victory over sin and death, and the consummation of all things. 4. *A thanksgiving.* "Eucharist." In view of all the blessings to be conferred through Christ's death, and as acknowledging the mercy and love of God in common viands and (as symbolized by them) in the benefits of salvation.—M.

Vers. 22—25.—*The Lord's Supper a celebration of death.* It is elsewhere spoken of as a "memorial," *i.e.* a funeral feast for the Saviour. Not merely a vain regret, an indulgence of disconsolate affection, but—

I. A CELEBRATION OF DEATH AS COMPLETED SELF-SACRIFICE. 1. *Therefore all that was most precious in the life was secured, in the highest degree and the best way, as a blessing for others.* The early disciples were not handling mangled, useless remains, but touching a living spirit, pregnant with grace and power and inspiration. The "body" and "blood" of Christ, kept from moral corruption and death, were a spiritual fruit "rich and rare." 2. *And believers are made partakers of the spiritual fulness of Christ's perfected nature, in receiving the "elements" of his "body" and "blood."*

II. A CELEBRATION OF DEATH AS THE REVELATION AND AVENUE OF IMMORTALITY. This "funeral feast" is full of hopeful, confident anticipation, because in the death that is celebrated: 1. *The higher spiritual life is seen as the result of the sacrifice of the earthly nature.* It is in the voluntary and obedient laying down of this earthly life that Christ set free his Spirit as an influence to savingly affect mankind, and satisfied and commended that perfect righteousness which is the ground of acceptance and union with God, the true life of the Spirit. 2. *A foretaste is given of the final victory of righteousness over sin and death.* The Captain of salvation, about to enter into final conflict with the powers of darkness, confidently looks forward, and invites his followers to look forward with him, "to glory, and honour, and immortality." In prospect of the final feast of victory and joy that was set before him, he was ready to go down into the gloom and shadow of death.—M.

Vers. 27—31.—*Peter's denial foretold.* Christ's thoughts dwelt constantly upon the prophecies that foretold the sufferings and death of the Son of man. They were passing through his spiritual consciousness, voluntarily adopted as the expression of his own inward life, and consequently wrought out in external actions. He now quotes Zech. xiii. 7. It taught him how absolutely solitary his position would be in judgment and death, as other passages had done; and suggested to him the reason for it.

I. THE UNIVERSAL DEFECTION OF THE DISCIPLES BEFORE CHRIST'S DEATH WAS A SPIRITUAL NECESSITY. They could not understand or allow it. It seemed so unnatural and unlikely. But their Master felt, by gauging his own spirit, how much would be required to enable them to be steadfast, and how wanting they were in the higher principles of spiritual life. He accepted the situation, and sought beforehand to prepare his disciples for the revelation of their own weakness, that when it took place it might not destroy all hope or desire to return to their fidelity. It was, then, at once in expression of his own inward Messianic consciousness, and in order to their warning and instruction, that he quoted the prophecy. How was this desertion of their Master a necessary experience? Because the realization of absolute oneness with Christ in the spirit of self-denial, or rather of love, would only be possible after his own sacrifice, as its ground or condition. They were, meanwhile, still in a state of pupilage or infancy. They could not understand the reason of his strange path, so unlike what they had anticipated. Had they been able to stand by the Lord when he was delivered up, they might have been their own saviours, and his work would not have been requisite.

II. SELF-CONFIDENCE IN ASSERTING ITS SUPERIORITY TO THIS LAW WOULD ONLY THE MORE SIGNALLY ILLUSTRATE IT. Peter, the representative of theoretic faith, was strong in his contradiction to this statement. It was he who had said, "Lord to whom can we go?" etc., and who had heard the approving response, "Blessed art thou, Simon Bar-Jona: for flesh and blood hath not revealed *it* unto thee, but my Father which is in heaven" (Matt. xvi. 17); and who had been called the *rock*. He therefore goes forward in the strength of his own convictions, and courts the disaster he sought to avoid, and that in an exaggerated form. (The seeming discrepancy between the evangelists as to the crowing and crowing twice is easily explained.) That very day, nay, that night, ere the dawning, he should deny his Lord thrice, *i.e.* absolutely and utterly; and, that he might test his Master's faithfulness and his own failure, the sign was given—"before the cock crow twice." His bold self-confidence and resolute endeavour to be with Christ were shown in his penetrating the hall of justice, and mingling in the very crowd amidst which the Saviour stood. But this only provoked the challenge before which all his manhood quailed. The others did not orally deny Christ, because they had fled beforehand.

III. BUT WITH THE WARNING A WORD OF HOPE AND COMFORT WAS UTTERED. The Shepherd would reassemble his scattered flock, when he went before them into Galilee. But they could not receive the saying upon which that depended—"after I am raised up." It was to be lodged in their consciousness, nevertheless, to be recalled again when its fulfilment took place, and to be put on record as another evidence of the faith. Then they would no longer be told, "Whither I go ye cannot come," as he would give his Spirit to them.—M.

Vers. 32—42.—*The agony in the garden.* I. ITS SORROW. 1. *The manner in which it was experienced.* There were premonitions. All through life there ran a thread of similar emotions, which were now gathering themselves into one overwhelming sense of grief, fear, and desolation: it was crescent and cumulative. He did not artificially create or stimulate the emotion, but entered into it naturally and gradually. Gethsemane was sought, not from a sense of æsthetic or dramatic fitness, but through charm of long association with his midnight prayer, or simply as his wonted place of retirement in the days of his insecurity. As a good Israelite observing the Passover, he may not leave the limits of the sacred city, yet will he choose the spot best adapted for security and retirement. 2. *At first awakening conflicting impulses.* He craved at once for sympathy and for solitude. The general company of disciples were brought to the verge of the garden, and informed of his purpose; the three nearest to him in spiritual sympathies and susceptibilities were taken into the recesses of the garden, into nearer proximity and communion. And yet ultimately he must needs be alone. All this is perfectly natural, and, considering the nature of his emotion, explicable upon deep human principles: "Sympathy and solitude are both desirable in severe trials" (Godwin). There was a sort of oscillation between these two poles. 3. *To be attributed to the influence of supernatural insight upon his human sympathy and feeling.* What it was he saw and felt cannot be adequately conceived by us, but that it was not emotion occasioned by ordinary earthly interests or attachments we may assure ourselves. The exegesis which sees in "exceeding sorrowful to die" a reason for concluding that it was the idea of dying which so overwhelmed our Saviour, may be safely left to its own reflections. The "cup" he felt he had to drink to its dregs he had already alluded to (ch. x. 38). It had "in it ingredients which were never mingled by the hand of his Father, such as the treachery of Judas, the desertion of his disciples, denial on the part of Peter, the trial in the Sanhedrim, the trial before Pilate, the scourging, the mockery of the soldiery, the crucifixion, etc." (Morison). "He began to be sore amazed [dismayed, sorrowful], and to be very heavy [oppressed, distressed]," are terms which are left purposely vague. He saw the depths of iniquity, he felt the overwhelming burden of human sinfulness. 4. *He betook himself to prayer as the only relief for his surcharged feeling.* The safest and highest way of recovering spiritual equilibrium. Well will it be for a man when his grief drives him to God! There is no sorrow we cannot take to him, whether it be great or small.

II. THE SOLITUDE. 1. *Symbolized by his physical apartness from the three disciples.*

" Is there any sorrow like unto my sorrow?" We may not intrude. God only can fathom its depths and appreciate its purity and intensity. 2. *Suggested by their failure to " watch."*

III. THE CONFLICT. The physical effects of this are given by St. Luke. His prayer was a "wrestling," not so much with his Father as with himself. But the struggle gradually subsides to submission and rest. This shows itself in his detachment from his own emotions and attention to the condition of his disciples, and soon in his movement towards the approaching band of the betrayer. There is a complete "grammar" of emotion gone through, however, ere that spiritual result is attained. Uncertainty, dread, the weakness of human nature, are overcome by the resolute contemplation of the Divine will. His own will is deliberately and solemnly submitted to his Father's, and the latter calmly and profoundly acquiesced in as best and most blessed for all it concerns.—M.

Vers. 43—50.—*The betrayal.* It involved in its very conception a rude, profane intrusion upon our Lord's devotions. At the head of the band was Judas, and with him the Roman soldiers with their swords, and the servants of the chief priests with staves (cudgels, thick sticks). Having met the temptations of the soul in the solitude of prayer, the Lord is now the better able to meet the external trials of which the garden is also the scene.

I. THE PRETENDED FRIENDS OF CHRIST ARE HIS WORST ENEMIES. Only a disciple can betray as Judas did. The kiss and salutation of respect, "Rabbi!" have become classical.

II. NOT THE SKILL OR FORCE OF HIS CAPTORS, BUT HIS OWN MEEKNESS AND MERCIFUL PURPOSE, RENDERED THEIR SCHEME EFFECTUAL. There was no surprise, for the Victim of the treachery was fully aware of it, and, indeed, warned his disciples of the approach of the band (ver. 42). As a stratagem, the midnight expedition was therefore a failure. And there is something unspeakably ludicrous in the portentous weapons which were thought necessary, and the large number of men. This is the sting of many a carefully hatched villainy, viz. that eventually it loses even the merit of originality or cleverness. The wisdom of this world is in any case no match for the wisdom of God.

III. THE INTERESTS OF CHRISTIANITY ARE NOT SERVED BY FORCE OR VIOLENCE. It was Peter whose impulsiveness had betrayed him into the thoughtless act. Hidden probably by the darkness, he was not detected, save by the eye of the Master. Had it even been expedient to oppose force with force in the general conflict of Christ with the world-power, on that occasion the odds were tremendous (cf. Matt. xxvi. 52).

IV. THE SON OF MAN HAD TO MEET THE ONSET OF EVIL ALONE. His prediction was fulfilled (ver. 27).—M.

Vers. 43—50.—*The betrayal.* I. A TRANSCENDENT CRIME. Because of: 1. *The character of Jesus.* 2. *The betrayer's relations to him.* Ingratitude. Callous selfishness. Breach of trust. 3. *Circumstances of the act.* Intrusion upon holy retirement. Simulation of highest regard and purest sentiment. The spiritual interests of humanity trifled with.

II. A SUPREME FOLLY AND FAILURE. Overdone. Foreseen. Ending in contempt and misery.—M.

Vers. 53—65.—*Jesus at the bar of Judaism.* I. THE CHARACTER OF THE EVIDENCE AGAINST HIM. 1. *Not in support of any clear and definite indictment.* 2. *Encouraged by a desire on the part of the judges to incriminate.* "They sought witness." The death of the Prisoner a foregone conclusion. 3. *The accusations unreliable and conflicting.*

II. HIS REPLY TO HIS ACCUSERS. *Silence:* (1) Because of their character, and (2) his own. The impressive dignity of this attitude. He would not justify himself before an earthly tribunal.

III. HIS ANSWER TO THE HIGH PRIEST'S QUESTION. *He declared himself the Messiah and the Judge of all the earth.* This was done out of respect to the representative character of the high priest, and in order to assure and inform faithful Jews.

IV. How THIS WAS CONSTRUED. *As blasphemy:* either (1) on the ground of imaginary, or feloniously represented, resemblance of the words, "I am," to Jehovah's Name; or (2) because the claim was *a priori* assumed to be false.

V. HE WAS REJECTED AND DISHONOURED BY THOSE HE CAME TO SAVE, OUT OF SHEER WANTONNESS AND UNBELIEF.—M.

Vers. 54, 66—72.—*Peter denying Christ.* The seeming discrepancies of the accounts by the evangelists of Peter's threefold denial are explained on the ground of their independency of one another, and their making prominent various portions of a lengthened and complex series of actions. "Three denials are mentioned by all the evangelists, and three occasions are distinguished; but on some of these there was more than one speaker, and probably more than one answer." This circumstance was—

I. AN EVIDENCE OF THE POWER OF EVIL IN GOOD MEN. This is the great lesson of the sins of the saints. There ought to be continual watchfulness, and living and walking in the Spirit. 1. *It is not well to expose one's self to temptation unless from the highest motives.* Curiosity seems to have been the ruling principle in Peter's mind. He was following the highest good, but not as perceiving it to be so, or truly desiring it—a perilous state of things. There are many unworthy followings of Christ, which have the "greater condemnation." Duty and self-sacrifice will, on the other hand, carry men safely through the most terrible trials. 2. *Low views of Christ's character and office tend to unworthy conduct.* The whole spiritual state of Peter was such as to expose him to the perpetration of the worst actions, and this arose from prevalence of false conceptions of Christ's person and work. His attitude and occupation immediately beforehand ("afar off;" "warming himself") have been regarded by many as symbolical of his spiritual position with regard to his Master. Scepticism and mental confusion on religious subjects, if not corrected or neutralized by close fellowship with Christ, or loyalty to the highest truth one knows, have sad moral results. Peter was still clinging against hope to his idea of a worldly Messiah. 3. *Evil words and actions, if once indulged in, are the more easily repeated and aggravated.* He proceeds from an equivocation—"I neither know nor understand what thou sayest"—to a stronger and more direct negative, and then to oaths and profanities.

II. AN EVIDENCE OF THE NECESSITY AND POWER OF CHRIST'S ATONEMENT. Even good men like Peter, if left to themselves, will grievously err and sin. How are men in such a position to be recovered? 1. *There must therefore be a saving principle outside, and independent of, ourselves.* It is by virtue of his completed sacrifice in spirit that Christ by a look recalls his fallen disciple, and thus shows: 2. *The power of his Spirit to redeem.* In connection with such a power over spirit and conscience the greatest sins may be made the turning-points of repentance. Memory was appealed to, and the outward signs predicted by the Saviour served as a spiritual index or clock of conscience. The cockcrowing has also an element of hope in it; it marked the dawning of a new day of penitence and enlightenment.—M.

Ver. 6.—*"She hath wrought a good work on me."* Describe the feast in the house of Simon the leper, and distinguish the incident from that which is recorded in Luke vii. Indicate Mary's reasons for loving the Lord, with all her heart and soul and strength, and show that this act of exquisite self-abandonment was the natural expression of her love. Learn from the subject the following lessons :—

I. THAT AN ACT WHICH IS PLEASING TO OUR LORD MAY BE MISCONSTRUED AND CONDEMNED BY HIS DISCIPLES. All the disciples were guilty of murmuring against Mary, but John points out that Judas Iscariot began it. Entrusted with the bag in which the common fund was kept, he had carried on for some time past a system of petty thievery. It has been suggested that, as our Lord knew his besetting sin of avarice, it would have been kinder not to have put this temptation in his way. There is, however, another aspect of this question. Evil habits are sometimes conquered by a tacit appeal to honour and generosity. An outward habit may be got rid of by removal of temptation, but absence of temptation does not root out the sin. In effect our Lord said to Judas, "I know your sin, but yet I put this money in your charge; for surely you would not rob the poor, defraud your brethren, and dishonour me!" This appeal might have saved Judas; but he yielded to his sin till it damned him. Such a man would be likely to feel aggrieved at this generous act of Mary's.   He felt as if he had been personally defrauded.   He knew that if this spikenard, which had vanished in a few minutes of refreshing fragrance, had been sold he would have had the manipulation of the proceeds.   Therefore he was angry with Mary, and angry with the Lord, who had not rejected her offering.   We can easily understand the feeling of Judas.   But how was it the disciples re-echoed his complaint?   They sided with him, although they certainly were not actuated by his base motive.   Well, we all know that if a word of censure be uttered in the Church it swiftly spreads, and is like leaven, which soon leavens the whole lump.   Suspicion and slander find easier access to men's hearts than stories of heroism and generosity.   Weeds seed themselves more rapidly than flowers.   The disciples had more to justify their fault-finding than we sometimes have.   They were plain peasants, who had never known the profusion of modern life, and they were aghast at the idea of such a prodigality of luxury as this.   From all they knew of their Lord they supposed that he would have preferred the relief of the poor to any indulgence for himself, and that he himself would have been disposed to say, "To what purpose is this waste?"   Many now imagine that they can infallibly decide what will please or displease their Lord, yet in their condemnation of others they are often mistaken.   Mary, no doubt, was discouraged and disappointed.   Her gift had been the subject of thought and prayer, and now that her opportunity had come for presenting it she eagerly seized it.   She was prepared for the sneers of the Pharisees; but surely the disciples would be glad to see their Lord honoured.   At their rebuke her heart was troubled; her eyes filled with tears as she thought, "Perhaps they are right.   I ought to have sold it."   Then Jesus looked on her with loving approval, and threw over her the shield of his defence.

II. That any service which is the offspring of love to the Lord is acceptable to him.   He perfectly understood and approved her motive, and therefore was pleased with her offering.   Whether it came in the fragrance of this ointment, or in the form of three hundred pence, was of comparatively little consequence.   It meant, "I love thee supremely," and therefore he was glad.   Naturally so.   When a child brings you the relic of some feast which you would rather not have, yet because it has been saved from love to you, you eat it with as much gusto as if it were nectar from Olympus.   Why?   Because you judge of the gift from the love it expresses; and this, in an infinitely higher sphere, our Lord also does.   Unlike us, he always knows what the motive is, and about many an act condemned by his disciples he says, "She hath wrought a good work on me."   Καλόν, translated "good," means something beautiful, noble, or lovely.   Mary's act was not ordered by the Law, nor dictated by precedent, nor suitable to everybody; but for her, as an expression of her love, it was the most beautiful thing possible.   She poured her heart's love on Jesus when she poured the spikenard from the broken cruse.

III. That a gift or act prompted by love to the Lord may have far more effect than we design.   "She is come aforehand to anoint my body to the burying."   Some argue from this that Mary knew Jesus was about to be crucified, and would rise again from the dead, so that this would be the only time for such anointing.   I doubt that.   Probably she had no distinct, ulterior design when she simply did what her love prompted.   But in commending her Jesus in effect said, "In this act she has done more than you think—more than she herself imagines; for she is anointing me for my burial."   In God's Word we find that we are credited for the good or for the evil latent in our actions, by Divine justice or in Divine generosity.   We read of some standing before the Judge of quick and dead who are amazed at the issues of their half-forgotten acts for or against the Saviour.   "When saw we thee an hungred or athirst?" etc.   This was the principle on which Christ attributed to Mary's act a result she could not have foreseen.

Conclusion.   This is true of evil as of good.   There is not a sin you commit but it may beget other sins, and in effect as well as in memory the words are true, "The evil that men do lives after them."   For the far-reaching effects of sinful words and deeds, of which he may know nothing till the day of judgment, the sinner is responsible to God.   What an encouragement is here to steadfast continuance in well-doing!   That which has the smallest immediate result may have the greatest ultimately.   The story of Mary's inexpressible love has had far greater effect in blessing the world than the distribution of three hundred pence among the poor, which human judgment might have preferred.—A. R.

Ver. 12.—*The Passover.* The Passover was by far the most important of the Jewish feasts. The disciples of 'our Lord were sure that he, who ever fulfilled the righteousness of the Law, would not fail to observe it. Their reminder of what they supposed he had forgotten, but which really was the subject of far profounder thought with him than they could fathom, immediately led to the remarkable incidents which are here recorded—the strange provision of the feast by a secret disciple, and the spiritual institution which Christ founded on the ancient rite. There were truths set forth by the Mosaic festival of which the Jews were never to lose sight, and which are full of significance to us. A few of these we will recall.

I. THE PASSOVER REQUIRED A SPOTLESS VICTIM. In this, as in many other Jewish ordinances, the spiritual was represented by the visible. The victim might be chosen from the goats or from the sheep. (Kids were offered as late as Josiah's reign (2 Chron. xxxv. 7), although in our Lord's time only lambs were sacrificed.) This was of less consequence than the rule that the victim chosen should be "without blemish." Not deformed, sickly, or injured. 1. *Doubtless this taught the worshippers to offer their best,* and do so cheerfully, with humble acknowledgment of the Divine right. The Jews learnt the lesson. Their religion cost them something, and they nobly responded to its claims, as we see when the tabernacle was erected and when the temple was built. Christians, in their gifts and in services, too often act as the Israelites would have done had they chosen their blemished and sickly lambs for sacrifice. 2. *Besides, this provision was significant of the sacred purpose to which the victim was devoted,* and symbolical of the moral integrity of the person it represented. The male of the first year, in the fulness of its life, stood for the firstborn sons of Israel, who were spared, while it died. 3. *Nor does this exhaust the meaning. The spotless lamb points to him of whom John Baptist said, " Behold the Lamb of God ! "* to him who "offered up himself; " to him of whom we read, " Ye are not redeemed with corruptible things . . . but with the precious blood of Christ, as of a lamb without blemish, and without spot."

II. THE PASSOVER REQUIRED PERSONAL PARTICIPATION. It might have seemed to human wisdom hardly reasonable that deliverance from a pestilence should be the result of sprinkling the blood of a slaughtered lamb on the two side posts and lintel of the door; but he would have suffered the penalty of his rashness who had run the risk of his incredulity. Every saved household had its own lamb, and every saved one in that household was compelled to remain, for his safety, in the blood-sprinkled house. This arrangement, on the basis of family relationship, was not made so much for convenience as it was to sanction and sanctify home life, and to teach all who were united by earthly love to find their centre in the Paschal lamb. The Israelites were not saved because they were descended from Abraham, but because of the blood sprinkled in faith and obedience.

III. THE PASSOVER WAS TO BE ACCOMPANIED BY PENITENCE AND SINCERITY. 1. *The use of unleavened bread was ordained.* Leaven, the presence of which was strictly forbidden, was a symbol of moral corruption, which the people were to put away from their hearts. Christ Jesus warned his disciples against "the leaven of the Pharisees, which is hypocrisy." St. Paul (1 Cor. v. 7, 8), referring to evil in the Church, said, "Christ our Passover is sacrificed for us : therefore let us keep the feast, not with old leaven, neither with the leaven of malice and wickedness, but with the unleavened bread of sincerity and truth." More than anything else our Lord rebuked insincerity. As the King of truth he still says, "He that is of the truth heareth my voice." 2. *Bitter herbs were also to be eaten at the Passover.* Not because ahey would give flavour to sweeter food, nor as a mere accompaniment to it, but as an essential part of the feast. The bitter bondage of Egypt was thereby represented, which was overpowered by the sweetness of the lamb. It may symbolize the bitter sorrow with which we should mourn our guilt.

IV. THE PASSOVER WAS A SOURCE OF PEACE, AND A PLEDGE OF PROGRESS. 1. The Israelites in Egypt knew that judgment was falling around them, and in that ominous dreadful night the peace of each one was proportioned to his trust in the appointed means of deliverance. 2. Those who partook of the feast were prepared for the march through the Red Sea and the wilderness, until Canaan was reached and won.—A. R.

Vers. 22—24.—*The Lord's Supper.* The Lord's Supper was the natural outgrowth of the Passover. The broken bread, which was made a symbol of our Lord's broken body, had been seen and partaken of for generations by the Jews, who had regarded it as "the bread of affliction" which their fathers once ate in Egypt. "The cup of blessing," transformed into "the communion of the blood of Christ," was the third cup in the feast, which followed on the distribution of the Paschal lamb, and preceded the singing of the Hallel. The whole Passover was a symbolical festival of remembrance, and this we believe the Lord's Supper was intended to be. It was not to be a repeated sacrifice, as Gregory the Great was the first to suggest, but was a feast to be eaten in remembrance of the Saviour. No symbols could be more appropriate. The bread represented the Bread of life; the broken bread that it was broken for us. The wine was "the blood of the grape" (Gen. xlix. 11), poured out from the true Vine (John xv. 1), which was its Source. The expression, "This *is* my body," surely could not have been taken in any literal sense by the disciples, who had their Lord in his physical presence visible amongst them when he spoke. It was equivalent to "This represents my body;" just as elsewhere we read, "The field *is* the world;" "I am the true Vine;" "Leaven . . . which is hypocrisy" (see also Gal. iv. 24; Heb. x. 20). What, then, are some of the advantages of this commemorative feast?

I. IT REPRESENTS THE PROPITIATORY CHARACTER OF CHRIST'S DEATH. His blood was shed for many, for the remission of sins. His death was not merely a martyrdom; it was an atonement. He gave his life for the sheep. The prophets foretold this (Isa. liii.); the apostles declared it (Rom. v.); the redeemed praise the Lamb who was slain, because he washed them from their sins in his own blood.

II. IT REMINDS US OF THE NECESSITY FOR PERSONALLY PARTAKING OF CHRIST. "Take, eat: this is my body." What we eat and drink becomes a part of ourselves. Once our Lord said, "Except ye eat the flesh of the Son of man, and drink his blood, ye have no life in you." Food is useless unless we partake of it. Christ came to us in vain unless we trust him as our own Saviour and Lord.

III. IT IS IN ITSELF A MEANS OF GRACE. This is to be proved in experience rather than by Scripture. Just as a word which we can see or hear conveys a thought which we cannot see or hear, so the bread and the wine convey thoughts of Christ, of his sacrifice, of his claims, of his love, which refresh and strengthen our inmost life.

IV. IT IS A PROCLAMATION OF FELLOWSHIP. 1 Cor. x. 16, etc., "For we being many are one bread, and one body: for we are all partakers of that one bread." A "communion" is that of which we are common partakers, and St. Paul argues that by eating and drinking together thus we proclaim our unity; just as the Israelites in Egypt, on the night of the Exodus, met in families, each finding its centre of thought and safety in the Paschal lamb. It is the idea of the family, and not of the priesthood, that God makes the germ of the Christian Church. Those in it are to "bear one another's burdens, and so fulfil the Law of Christ." By the extension of the Church will come about the true brotherhood, for which the world still sighs.

V. IT IS A PLEDGE OF FIDELITY. The "sacramentum" was the oath taken by the Roman soldier that he would never desert the standard, never turn his back on the foe, and never be disloyal to his commander. By our presence at the sacrament we pledge each other, before God, that with his help we will be true men, more courageous, more pure, more victorious, than before.

VI. IT IS A SIGN OF SEPARATION. The Egyptians had no part in the Passover. The scribes and Pharisees were not invited to the upper room. Judas, so far as we can judge, left before the new rite was instituted. St. Paul spoke of the duty devolving on the Church at Corinth to remove the immoral from fellowship. Yet all true disciples, though they may doubt as Thomas did, or deny their Lord like Peter, are invited to eat and drink with each other, and with their Lord.—A. R.

Vers. 32—35.—*Gethsemane.* The Mediator between God and man experienced all the vicissitudes of human life. From the loftiest height of joy he plunged into the deepest depths of distress. Because of the fulness of his nature he surpassed us in these experiences, alike in the glory of the Transfiguration and in the agony of Gethsemane. Therefore we are never beyond the range of his sympathy. We are all familiar with the outward circumstances of this incident, but the wisest of us knows but little of the depths of its mystery. Indeed, although our interest in the scene is intense, although we feel it is fraught with the destiny of our race, we shrink with hesitation from speaking much of it. A sense of intrusiveness overpowers those who are conscious of ignorance and sin, when they would gaze on that sinless agony of grief. It seems as if our Lord still said to his disciples, " Sit ye *here*, while I shall pray." The place whereon we stand is holy ground.

I. THE SUFFERING SAVIOUR. 1. *There is mystery about his agony.* Our recognition of the proper deity and humanity of our Lord leads us to expect seeming contradictions in him. They appear in his intercessory prayer. In one breath he speaks as the Son of God, in another he wrestles as a weak man might do. Sometimes he pleads as a Mediator, and sometimes he expresses himself with Divine majesty and authority. It is so with our Lord's agony, which must ever be a stone of stumbling to all who refuse to recognize that they only know in part and prophesy in part. Thus some assert that this experience contradicts the composure and resolution with which our Lord had previously announced his sufferings; and that his prayer is in antagonism with his omniscience as the Son of God. Here is the Prince of peace seemingly destitute of peace; the world's Redeemer wanting deliverance; the Comforter himself needing consolation. As the old myth reminds us, we sometimes come across a fact which appears like a glittering ring which a child could lift when we walk around it and talk about it ; but, when we try to lift it, we find it is no isolated ring, but a link in a chain which we can hardly stir, for it girdles the earth and reaches heaven and hell! " Behold, God is great, and we know him not; and darkness is under his feet." 2. *There is a meaning in this agony.* We gain some little insight into it when we remember the vicarious nature of Christ's sufferings; that " the Lord hath laid upon him the iniquities of us all." If Jesus Christ were only a great Prophet, who came to enlighten the world, he might now seem to have lost his courage. If he were only an Exemplar of unconditional resignation or heroic endurance, he was surpassed by others. All points to the conclusion that his sufferings were not like those of Job, or Jeremiah, or Paul, or Stephen, but were unique in the world's history. He, the sinless One, was the Representative and Substitute of the sinful world.

II. THE TROUBLED BELIEVER may find instruction and comfort in this experience of his Lord, especially in the consciousness of his sympathy. 1. *Sympathy was longed for even by our Lord.* He wanted to have near him those who could best understand him, so that in the thought of their affection and prayer he might find comfort. It failed him. They were overpowered by sleep, and when aroused, they fell back into the old drowsiness. It was another pang in his anguish. He trod the winepress *alone.* How tenderly he feels for lonely sufferers ! 2. *Absence of sympathy intensified prayer.* When our trouble is very heavy it has a tendency to paralyze prayer, and makes the heart stony ; but we should rather follow him who, being in an agony, prayed the more earnestly. If, in answer to prayer, the cup is not taken away, still the prayer is not useless. Paul thrice besought the Lord in vain to remove the thorn in the flesh; but he had an answer, " My grace is sufficient for thee." And our Lord came forth from the place of prayer as one who had already gained the victory. 3. *Earnestness in prayer led to absolute submission.* When we pray we realize with growing intensity that there is another will besides ours and above ours firm and wise and good. If God sees further than we see; if he knows what would harm and what would bless us, when we do not; if he looks not only to this little life, but to the eternity to which it leads ; let us seek in prayer to know what his will is, and then say, even though it be with tears, " Nevertheless not what I will, but what thou wilt."—A. R.

Ver. 36.—*The cup of experience.* The mystery of our Lord's suffering is beyond our power of accurate analysis. We cannot fathom the depths of sin and grief which he experienced. We must not suppose that, because we are so familiar with this narrative, we know all its significance. At the most we have only felt one wave of the sea of sorrow which sobbed and swelled in his infinite heart. Only one phase of this many-sided subject will engage our attention. Leaving the atoning nature of the sufferings of our Lord, we will now regard him as the Representative of his people, their Forerunner in this as in all things. The "cup" is a figure familiar enough to all students of Scripture.

I. THE CUP OF EXPERIENCE may be represented by the cup which was the symbol of the mockery and shame and grief the Saviour suffered. 1. *The phrase reminds us that our joys and griefs are measured.* A cup is not illimitable. Full to the brim, it can only hold its own measure. (1) *Our joys are limited by what is in us, and by what is in them.* If a man prospers in the world, his wealth brings him not only comfort, but care, anxiety, and responsibility, so that he may occasionally wish himself back in his former lowlier lot. And family joys bring their anxieties to every home which has them. No one drinks here of an ocean of bliss but he thanks God for a "cup" of it, measured by One who knows what will be best for character. This is true even of spiritual joys. The time of ecstasy is followed by a season of depression. The Valley of Humiliation is passed, as well as the Delectable Mountains, by Christian in his pilgrimage. Nowhere on earth can we say, "I *am* satisfied;" but many, like the psalmist, can exclaim, "I *shall be* satisfied." (2) *Our griefs are limited also.* They are proportioned to our strength, adapted for our improvement. Even in the saddest bereavement there is much to moderate our grief if we will but receive it: gratitude for all our dear one was and did; gladness over all the testimonies of love and esteem in which he was held; hope that by-and-by there shall be the reunion, where there shall be no more sorrow and sighing, and where "God shall wipe away all tears from our eyes." God does not let an ocean of sadness surge up and overwhelm us, but gives us a cup, which we may drink in fellowship with Christ in his sufferings. 2. *The phrase in our text suggests not only measurement, but loving control.* Our Lord recognized, as we may humbly do, that the cup was filled and proffered by him whom he addressed as "Abba, Father." In one sense the events in Gethsemane and on Calvary were the results of natural causes. Integrity and sinlessness called forth the antagonism of those whose sins were thereby rebuked. Plain-spoken denunciations of the ecclesiastical leaders aroused their undying hate, and no hatred is more malignant than that of irreligious theologians. Judas, disappointed and abashed, was a ready instrument for evil work. Yet, behind all this, One unseen was carrying out his eternal purpose, fulfilling his promise, "The seed of the woman shall bruise the serpent's head." Hence Jesus speaks not of the plot accomplished by his foes, but of the cup given him by the Father. We are at an infinite remove from him, yet, as the same law which controls worlds controls insects, so the truth which held good with the Son of man holds good also with us. We may recognize God's overruling in man's working, and accept every measure of experience as provided and proffered by our Father's hand.

II. THE PURPOSE OF ITS APPOINTMENT. That it comes from our "Father" shows that it has a purpose, and that it is one of love, not of cruelty. It is not like the cup of hemlock Socrates received from his foes, but like that potion you give your child that he may be refreshed, or strengthened, or cured. 1. *Sometimes the purpose respects ourselves.* Even of Jesus Christ, the sinless One, it is said he was "made perfect through sufferings;" that as our Brother he might feel for us, and as our High Priest might sympathize, being "touched with the feeling of our infirmities." Much more is the experience of life a blessing to us who are imperfect and sinful; correcting our worldliness, and destroying our self-confidence. 2. *Sometimes the purpose respects others.* It was so with our Lord pre-eminently. He "came not to be ministered unto, but to minister, and to give his life a ransom for many." "None of us liveth unto himself." If our cup of blessing runs over, its overflowings, whether of wealth, or strength, or spiritual joy, are for the good of those around us. If our lot be one of suffering, we may in it witness for our Lord, and from it learn to console others with the comfort wherewith we ourselves have been comforted of God.—A. R.

Vers. 39—43.—*Sorrow, sleep, and sin.* When a dear friend is in trouble our footfall is quiet and our voice hushed. Even children are awed to silence when they see the face they love stained with tears and pale with anguish. How much more does stillness of soul become us when we enter into the Garden of Gethsemane and see the Lord we love in his agony! Christ completed the cycle of human temptations in Gethsemane. In the wilderness he had been tempted to desire what was forbidden, to obtain provision in a wrong way, to manifest Divine power in an act of presumption, to gain the kingdom by force and fraud. Now he was tempted to avoid what was ordained. And to do what we ought not, not to do what we ought, sums up all temptations. He " was in all points tempted like as we are, yet without sin." In this mysterious scene we discern a concentration of human history.

I. THE SIN-FORGETTING CHURCH is represented by the disciples who failed their Lord. 1. *They did not understand the necessity and dreadfulness of Christ's struggle with the powers of darkness.* They allowed natural weariness to overcome them, so that they had no share in the conflict endured near them and for them. As little does the Church share the purpose of Christ in the redemption of the world from sin; nor does she see the need for being in an "agony" about it. Is there the feeling about sin, even about our own sin, that there should be? Are we not too often like those who, under the shadow of Christ's sorrow, slept, though he himself had said, "Tarry ye here, and watch"? 2. *Nor did these disciples reach the source of power that night.* It was impossible to find victory through human passion, as Peter discovered after he had drawn and used his sword. Indiscriminate zeal, which will attack heretics and sceptics with bitter words and penalties, is sure to fail. Power to overcome is found in obedience to the command, "Watch and *pray*." To watch without praying is presumption; to pray without watching is fanaticism. The difference between our Lord and his disciples was this : they refreshed themselves by natural means, and he by spiritual ; they fell back on sleep, and he on prayer—just as too often we rely on human agencies, and not on Divine. 3. *Their confusion and indecision increased as they diverged from their Lord.* He became more calm, and more sure of victory. They became more heavy with sleep, more cowardly and unprepared, till they all forsook him and fled. Only when they assembled again in his Name to pray in the upper room were they endued with power from on high. "Let us not sleep as do others, but let us watch and be sober," lest again he should say, "Sleep on now, and take your rest. . . . Behold, the Son of man is betrayed."

II. THE SIN-COMMITTING WORLD. (Ver. 43.) 1. While the disciples slept, the hostile world was alert. This vigilance was a rebuke to their sloth. Still it is so. Frequenters of haunts of pleasure are often more eager than members of Christ's Church to invite their companions to join them. 2. Those who assail the cause of Christ are animated by different motives. Some are malignant, as the priests were; others join in the popular cry, though it be " Crucify him!" The mob in Jerusalem had little idea what they were doing—casting out of the world the Son of God, who had come to be their Saviour and Friend. Men's acts have more in them than appears ; and some who are simply careless will be amazed to find themselves reckoned amongst his foes! The world had no power over Christ except through the traitor Judas. The weakness of the Church, the inconsistency or apostasy of Christians, ever lead to the most successful attacks. Judas knew where Jesus resorted, and betrayed him by a kiss. The fall of one sentinel may prove the destruction of the camp.

III. THE SIN-BEARING SAVIOUR. It is no figment of theological imagination that he himself took our infirmities, that " he was wounded for our transgressions, and bruised for our iniquities." He made atonement for us, as well as learnt sympathy with us. He took the cup of bitterness that we might receive the cup of blessing.—A. R.

Ver. 54.—*Following afar off.* The story of Peter's denial is not omitted by any of the evangelists. They were more anxious for truth than for reputation. They set before us the strongest disciple at his weakest moment without a word of wonder, of blame, or of excuse. Our text indicates the state of mind which led to his fall. He was just beginning his descent to the depths of shame. Because he " followed afar off " he found the door of the house shut against him, cutting him off from John and from his Lord. Outside, alone, in the dark, he became more despondent as he reflected that Jesus was in the power of his foes, and that any attempt at rescue had been rebuked by himself; so by the time John came out he had given up hope, and still stood afar off from his Lord, amidst his foes. Then and there occurred this moral tragedy in Church history. Let us consider—

I. SOME MOTIVES WHICH SHOULD HAVE INDUCED PETER TO FOLLOW CLOSELY. 1. *The remembrance of his own professions.* When Jesus had asked, " Will ye also go away?"

Peter had made a noble response; and when an earnest warning had been uttered a few hours before this, he had exclaimed, "Though all shall be offended, yet will not I." He meant his promises, and to abide by them; but though the spirit was willing, the flesh was weak. The world is fair in expecting more from those who are professed followers of Christ. Flight is more disgraceful to a soldier in uniform than to a camp-follower. 2. *Peter's recognized leadership of his brethren* was another reason for close following. The Lord indicated that Peter would be their leader from the first, and the disciples acquiesced in this, always making way for him to speak and act on their behalf. His responsibility was the heavier. If he had continued to watch, they would have done so; if he had followed closely, they might have rallied. The failure of one was the failure of all. Each one is responsible to God for the talent, position, or force of character which constitutes him a leader of men. To whom much is given, from him much is required. 3. *The loneliness of the Lord ought to have appealed to Peter's heroism and generosity.* We can hardly understand how, with his noble impulses, he could have left Jesus alone amongst his foes. Yet how often do Christians now fail to stand forth like men to rebuke wrong-doing at any risk! The fact that they alone represent their Lord amid evil companions, is an appeal to all that is chivalrous in them to speak. 4. *The remembrance of Christ's personal love to him might have drawn him nearer.* Jesus had dealt gently and generously with Peter. He had chosen him, with two of his brethren, to see his glory on the Mount of Transfiguration, and to see something of his dire agony in the garden. He had been faithfully warned of danger, and assured of the intercession of his Lord. Yet all seemed forgotten, and he only "followed afar off." It is when we realize the words, "He loved *me*, and gave himself for *me*," that we can say, "My soul followeth hard after God."

II. SOME EXCUSES WHICH PETER MIGHT HAVE URGED FOR HIS CONDUCT. 1. *It seemed as if he could do no good to his Lord.* He had tried in his own way to defend him, but had been rebuked, and no other way seemed open. He forgot that, though his Master had refused the use of physical force, he would have gladly welcomed human sympathy. John had deeper insight. Amid the sea of hatred which surged around him, our Lord saw at least one face which expressed love and sympathy. Utilitarianism sometimes keeps us from beautiful and graceful acts, because we do not see immediate, practical good in them. We should probably not have poured out the spikenard as Mary did, but should have joined with those who asked, "To what purpose is this waste?" Let us never follow afar off because we do not see the practical advantage of walking closely with our Lord. Heaven's best blessings are too subtle to be tabulated. 2. *It seemed as if evil would befall himself if he stood close beside his Master.* On entering the palace amongst this excited rabble, he might fear personal violence, especially if he were recognized as the assailant of Malchus. He wished, therefore, to conduct himself as one of the miscellaneous crowd. In doing so he put his soul in danger, instead of his body. "He that saveth his life shall lose it," his Lord had said, and Peter learnt the meaning soon. This mingling of courage and cowardice puts many a man in danger. May God give us the whole-hearted fidelity which even Peter failed that night to show!—A. R.

Ver. 70.—*A detected disciple.* This chapter is crowded with contrasts. 1. The unmeasured love of Mary of Bethany shines radiantly beside the unexampled treachery of Judas Iscariot. 2. Contrasts occur also in the experience of our Lord. He passes from the fellowship of the upper room to the solitude of Gethsemane; from the secrecy of prayer to the publicity of a mock-trial before his foes. 3. There are also great changes visible in the spiritual condition of certain disciples. Judas appears amongst the chosen disciples, listening to the Master's words and eating at the same table with him; and a few hours after he is seen at the head of a band of ruffians, betraying his Lord with a traitorous kiss. Peter, in the garden, starts forth as a hero in defence of his Master; but in the palace of the high priest, with trembling heart, denies all knowledge of him. To this last scene our text points us. (Describe it.)

I. THAT THERE ARE CIRCUMSTANCES IN WHICH THE CAUSE OF CHRIST AROUSES UNCOMPROMISING HOSTILITY. Peter was experiencing this in the palace of Caiaphas. 1. *Paganism was instinctively hostile to Christ's teaching.* Far-seeing men amongst the Gentiles soon saw its drift. They spoke of the apostles, not inaptly, as men who would turn the world upside down. Christ's doctrine of brotherhood would be the destroyer of slavery. His inculcation of purity and righteousness threatened licentious pleasures and tyrannous exactions. Men who could win high positions by force or fraud, and immoral people, who loved brutal or sensual amusements, would unite in antagonism to the Christian faith. Some would hate it the more intensely because their worldly interests were associated with the continuance of paganism. Many a Demetrius saw that his craft was in danger, and priests, with their crowds of attendants, would contend zealously for the idolatry which gave them their living. They would have granted Christ Jesus a niche in their Pantheon; but his followers claimed that he should reign supreme and alone. 2. *The Jews, however, were the first instigators of opposition.* Christianity threatened to destroy their national supremacy by inviting the Gentiles to all the privileges of the kingdom of God. They hated a Messiah who came not to deliver them from political bondage, but from their own prejudices and sins. 3. *Heathenism in our own day, whether at home or abroad, is at enmity with Christ.* The vicious, who live to gratify their passions, the worldly, who would make this life their all, as well as the idolaters in distant lands, hate the teachings of our Lord. 4. *Even in nominally Christian society there is sometimes seen an ill-suppressed dislike to earnest fidelity to Christ's cause.*

II. THAT A DISCIPLE OF CHRIST, IN THESE CIRCUMSTANCES, MEETS WITH A TEST OF HIS MORAL COURAGE. We all appreciate the heroism of the apostles, who, with their lives in their hands, witnessed for their Lord before Jews and pagans, rejoicing that they were counted worthy to suffer for his sake. Equal courage is occasionally exhibited in lives which are unromantic and prosaic, which endure each day the bitterness of scorn and shame. 1. *Sometimes a Christian shows heroism by speech.* Profanity is thus rebuked, slander is silenced, impurity is indignantly reproved, and the cause of Christ defended against mockery. It is well when this can be done without any sign of a Pharisaic spirit or of a censorious temper; so that from the tone of the defence the godless are compelled to say, "These men have been with Jesus, and have learnt of him." 2. *Silence may also be on occasion the display of courage.* If one, by reason of youth or sex, cannot speak, witness may be borne by quitting the scene where Christ is dishonoured. The responsibility for witness-bearing is the heavier in proportion to the weight of our influence. The effect of Peter's denial was the greater because he was like a standard-bearer in the army of Christ. Even although his testimony might not have changed the opinion of one in the crowd around him, he was none the less bound to give it; and our Lord was grieved because he withheld it.

III. THAT VERY TRIVIAL THINGS MAY SOMETIMES REVEAL ASSOCIATION WITH JESUS CHRIST. Peter had no expectation of being discovered. He was a stranger; the crowd was large, and the excitement great; it was dark, and attention seemed centred in Christ Jesus, to the exclusion of all beside. A question unexpectedly put necessitated an answer, and his rough Galilean brogue increased the suspicion to a certainty that he was a peasant who had come up with Jesus from Galilee, and was intimate enough with him to know of his secret and sudden arrest. 1. Even the nominal connection with Christ which we all have as Englishmen is betrayed by speech in foreign parts; and how often is the work of our missionaries hindered there by dishonest traders, or profligate sailors and soldiers, who are supposed to be "Christians," but who by word and act deny the Lord! 2. Others, who have been under direct Christian influences in their homes, are sometimes tempted, at school or in business, to keep that fact secret, as if it were something to be ashamed of. But when some small phrase or act unexpectedly betrays the truth, and one of those standing by says, "Surely thou art one of them, . . . thy speech agreeth thereto," then comes the crisis, the turning-point, on which the whole future will hinge. Happy is it if then they are saved from Peter's fall! 3. Occasionally those who are devout disciples wish, like Nicodemus, to remain secretly so. They wish to avoid all responsibility, and therefore make no profession of their love. Little do they suspect how many are discouraged by their failure to avow their loyalty to their Lord. Let all our influence everywhere be consecrated to him.

CONCLUSION. *The hall of judgment is still standing.* Christ Jesus is being examined and questioned now by men who resent his claims. Still we hear the cry, "Prophesy! who is it that smote thee? Tell us something new. Work some miracle now, that we may believe thee." And to it all Jesus answers nothing. His Church is keeping close beside him, as John did, and is glad to share his reproach. But many are like Peter; they have followed afar off, so that the world should not notice them. They would not be so near as they are, but that others have led them, as John led his brother apostle. Yet, after all their friends have done, they are still outside, in the courtyard, among the foes of their Lord. They hope that all will end well; they dare not help in the conflict, so they keep far enough away to retain their popularity, and yet to see the end. As the light of the fire revealed Peter, as his speech further betrayed him, so something has called attention to these, and companions begin to say, "Surely thou art one of them." What shall the answer be? Shall it be, "I know him not;" or shall it be, "Lord, thou knowest all things; thou knowest that I love thee"?—A. R.

Vers. 1—9.—*The alabaster cruse.* A scene of great interest and beauty is described in these words and in the supplement supplied by St. Matthew and St. John. On the last sabbath eve before his crucifixion, Jesus came to Bethany. In the house of Simon the leper a feast was made in his honour. The disciples were there, and, of necessity, Martha and her sister Mary, and Lazarus. What a representative group! Simon, the type of suffering, healed, and restored human nature. Lazarus, a living testimony to the Lord's power over life and death—a blossom from the tree of life plucked in that early spring-time, promising a final fruitfulness in richness and beauty. Martha, who in her true character served, type of all faithful, diligent, practical, hardworking disciples. Mary, who also served in her way, with her heart full of meditative love; the incarnation of pure, rapt, fervent devotion, and the sanctity of deep thought. And the disciples were there. Those wonderful men, who have led and will continue to lead the world, as the pillar of cloud of old time led the hosts of God through the desert. And the Master was there, sanctifying all life, as he was the Spring of all. Jesus was there, about whom we cannot say too much. They had met in his honour, for he received honour and hospitality from lowly men. They were met in his Name, and he was "in the midst." Around, outside, were the assailants, the Pharisees and the multitude, the powers of the world, surrounding as with a black drapery; while all within was pure and white and heavenly, save the stream of hot breath from one earthly spirit, himself set on fire of hell. Judas was there. Our thoughts must fix themselves, first, *on the silent deed of Mary*; then *on the open word of Judas*; then *we must hear the words of Jesus*, who, on this occasion at least, made himself a Judge and a Divider over them.

I. THE DEED OF MARY. (Ver. 3.) No reason for the act is assigned. Is one needed? Was it the offering of gratitude, or duty, or love? Was there goodness enough in that heart to lead it to do a kind action spontaneously, without respect to any previous personal obligation? Was there a sufficiently clear discernment of the true character of the distinguished Guest to compel her to offer her best gifts? We know not. One thing we know—Lazarus was there, "whom Jesus raised from the dead." Then upon that head so hot, and upon those feet so weary, she pours her costly perfume; pours it freely, so "that the house was filled with the odour."

II. Could any one have suspected a spot could be found in this almost heavenly feast? Alas! so is it with all things and all times of earth. Though all the college of the apostles was there; though there was one who had been raised from the dead, and one whose body had been purified and made anew; though all had seen the miracles which he did; though there were renewed and chastened spirits present, types of perfect love and faithful service; and though the Master himself was in the midst, on that sweet last sabbath eve;—yet even in this Eden of blessing was the trail of the serpent to be seen. Hearken (vers. 4—6), poor human nature! Though Heaven itself come down to us, we tarnish it with some earthly foul breath.

III. Jesus, by his words, passes judgment on Mary's deed and on Judas's pronouncement upon it. He appears for her defence. "Why trouble ye her?" (vers. 6, 8, 9). He may have been troubled, but in self-forgetfulness he thinks of her as she did of him. The work was a good one. "She hath anointed my body aforehand for the burying." Did she really know the meaning of her act? Did she really know that he would so soon be taken away? Then, to her quick apprehensive grief, he was dead already. Did she unconsciously predict his burial, or was love quick-witted here? We know not; but who can tell what she learnt at his feet? Probably she knew not on this quiet sabbath evening that on the next he would be in the tomb, or her heart would have been broken as well as her alabaster box. But if her gift of grateful love meant more than she supposed, it was only as all gifts of love do. They go beyond the discernments of intellect and judgment; they reach further; they mean more. So is it with all works done to Jesus. When we comfort the sorrowful, or minister to the sick or destitute, or do any "good work" in him and for him, he makes them symbolize himself. They show forth his praise. They reveal his spirit. As to the poor and our help of them, who, to our disgrace, are always with us. Let us see how Jesus honours even their lot by placing himself in the position of a receiver of doles of charity and human kindness. And let us, undeterred by the misuse which some make of our gifts, still break our alabaster boxes. Let us pour over the world the fragrance of a godly life, the sweetness of our Christian temper, the labour of our Christian zeal, the gifts of our Christian love.— G.

Vers. 10, 11, 17—21, 43—52.—*Betrayal.* We now approach the darkest of all the dark hours through which our Redeemer passed in this world, so overcast with clouds. "The Son of man is betrayed into the hands of men." It was by "one of the twelve," and "unto the chief priests," and for "money"!

I. What lessons on THE FRAILTY OF THE POOR HUMAN HEART! The hand that received "the sop," that dipped into the same dish with Jesus, received into its hardened palm the miserable pittance—a slave's price. Ah! even in the presence of the holy One could he plot and scheme for his delivery. Let us, when we decry the deed, bow our heads lowly, remembering that we share the same frail nature. How barefaced the lie—walking, reclining, talking with the little band, carrying their common purse, and so trusted by them all, yet stealing away in the darkness to meet his enemies and plot with them how, "in the absence of the multitude," he could deliver him unto them! And going so far as to choose the symbol of brotherly affection—a kiss—to be the sign by which in the darkness they should distinguish him! "Woe unto that man through whom the Son of man is betrayed! good were it for that man if he had not been born." Truly so; for what theory or process of restoration could prevent the name Judas from being for ever the symbol of treachery and base desertion and sordid misery. "Woe," indeed! "And he went away and hanged himself." It is impossible to contemplate the heights from which men have fallen into deep abysses, without a feeling of shame and humiliation. But it would be wrong to think of them without being warned by them of the sad possibilities to which we are all exposed.

II. THE INSUFFICIENCY OF OFFICE TO SECURE ITS RIGHTFUL SPIRIT. The parallel of Judas's infamy is found in the men who stood as the head and representatives of the very religion it was Jesus' high mission to fulfil and perfect. How deplorable is the contrast between the sanctity of the position held by these officials and the spirit in which they held it! It was theirs to be the leaders of religious thought, and the embodiment of the religious spirit. But the sad testimony is borne to the insufficiency of official relationship to secure the true spirit of office. Truly may the Shepherd say, "I was wounded in the house of my friends;" and the poor one, "yea, mine own familiar friend, in whom I trusted, which did eat of my bread, hath lifted up his heel against me."

III. THE POWER OF COVETOUSNESS. And this was all for money! Well might it be written, "For the love of money is a root of all kinds of evil." But it is needful to return to the preceding incident to find the hidden clue to such a deed of darkness. St. John has left the sad record, "He was a thief, and having the bag took away what was put therein." So, yielding little by little to the love of pelf, this chosen one, who harboured the demon of covetousness within the folds of his dress, had lost all strength of virtue, and being overcome of evil, and under the influence of a master-passion, sold his Master for thirty pieces of silver—"the price of him that was priced, whom certain of the children of Israel did price." But our thoughts should rest less upon the faithless disciple or the more faithless priests than upon the patient, submissive One who drank so deeply of our cup. He who descended to that lowest condition of human shame was found, like the slaves in the market, "priced" and sold. Revolting from that unfaithfulness which could sell a friend for gain, from that love of pelf which could crush all the fine and noble and generous feelings of the heart, even closing it to the sweet, winning voice of him who spake as never man spake—revolting equally from that deceitfulness which could occupy holy office without the slightest apprehension of the sanctity of demeanour, or the slightest possession of the purity of spirit due to such a position—let us mark and imitate the lowly, patient, self-possessed, forgiving, trustful spirit of him who endured all that the Scriptures of the prophets might be fulfilled, that the will of the Father might be done, that the redemption of the lost might be effected.—G.

Vers. 12—16, 22—26.—*The Lord's Supper.* During the process of the betrayal, the "first day of unleavened bread" came round, and "the Master," with "his disciples" in "a large upper room furnished and ready," sat and together partook of the Passover. It was the last time. The long series of observances begun in Egypt had now come to an end. Before the next year should bring round the time of the Passover, it would be "fulfilled in the kingdom of God." A deeper and wider meaning would be given to it. Another Lamb would be slain, whose blood, sprinkled by faith, would cleanse the "conscience from dead works." New symbols would supplant the old, by means of which the Lord's death should be showed forth until his coming again. The simplicity of the newly appointed ordinance stands in marked contrast to all the elaborate rites of the earlier service, and to the scarcely less elaborate forms of the extreme schools of the Christian Church.

I. THE ELEMENTS. Taking up the common articles of their daily food, he made them symbolize himself. The "bread" his "body;" the "wine" his "blood." Anything more simple could not have been conceived, anything more ready-at-hand, more truly universal. At the same time, he glorified that food by making it to represent, to memorialize, himself—his body given and his blood shed, through which spiritual life and nourishment were secured for them. Thus materials and spirituals are united; and a portion of our daily food may be taken in remembrance of him who gives life to the world, and "feeds the strength of every saint."

II. THE REPRESENTATION. To the simple "This is my body" of St. Mark, St. Luke adds, "which is given for you"—given up unto death on your behalf. He who "gave himself"—his entire personality—for our sins, gave his body "unto death, yea, the death of the cross." This is the sacrifice offered "once for all," "when he offered up himself." The blood represents, he says, "my blood of the covenant;" or, in St. Luke's words, "This cup is the new covenant in my blood, even that which is poured out for you." It is "shed for many unto remission of sins." Both are to be taken with the impressive and tenderly touching words, "This do in remembrance of me."

III. THE COMMAND. "Take ye;" "Take, eat;" "Drink ye all of it;" "This do in remembrance of me;" "This do, as oft as ye drink it, in remembrance of me." With these words our Lord enjoins on his disciples the observance of this simple, central Christian rite; and they form the warrant for the observance of *the Lord's Supper.* Gathering together the several words of direct and indirect reference to this Christian service, we see how it is the centre from which radiate many lines of relation to the entire circle of the Christian life. 1. It is *an affectionate memorial service,* bringing to remembrance the entire self-devotion of the Redeemer—"in remembrance of *me.*" It calls up all that the one word *me* represents, with an especial allusion to the supreme act of self-immolation, "I lay down my life." 2. It is *a covenant service.* He who drinks of the cup places himself under the bonds of the new covenant, and receives at the same time the seal of the certain inheritance of all covenant blessings (see Heb. viii. 6—12). 3. It is *a service of communion.* It symbolizes our joint participation with the whole body of Christ (1 Cor. x. 14—17). It declares the perfect oneness of the Church of Christ: "We, who are many are one bread, one body;" and it affirms our perfect community of interest: *we* "all eat the same spiritual meat;" *we* "all drink the same spiritual drink." 4. It is at once a service of lowly confession and humble faith, of exulting hope—"As often as ye eat this bread, and drink the cup, ye proclaim the Lord's death till he come"—of brotherly love. It is to the believer the pledge of all blessing and help; while from him it is the pledge of all obedience. And the Eucharistic song speaks of the life, the fellowship, and the joy of heaven.—G.

Vers. 27—31, 66—72.—*Peter's fall.*   The painful declaration that the words of
the prophet, "I will smite the shepherd, and the sheep shall be scattered abroad,"
would find their fulfilment in them, and in "All ye shall be offended," roused Peter's
spirit, and with a bold but mistaken estimate of his own courage and devotion, he
fearlessly, even presumptuously, affirmed, "Although all shall be offended, yet will not
I." St. Luke has preserved for us words which throw much light upon the incident of
Peter's fall, and upon the position which Peter held amongst the disciples : " Simon,
Simon, behold, Satan asked to have you, that he might sift you as wheat : but I made
supplication for thee, that thy faith fail not : and do thou, when once thou hast turned
again, stablish thy brethren." So Satan, the enemy of man, the agent for testing his
religious character, has made demand to put all the disciples into his sieve. Men sift
wheat to reveal and separate the useless from among the valuable—the bad from the
good. Such is the good end of temptation. Brought to bear upon the great Master
himself, it was powerless. He could say, "The prince of the world cometh : and he
hath nothing in me." There was no chaff mingled with that pure grain. Assailing
Judas—alas! how little of any thing but husk! In Peter how strange a mixture! In
each of us? Peter, warned by the first prophetic admonition, by the parabolic words
of Jesus, and by the yet more definite assurance that ere "the cock crow twice thou
shalt deny me thrice," repeats his boast of fidelity with an emphasis, "If I must die
with thee, I will not deny thee." The sieve is ready. Peter is accosted by a woman,
"one of the maids of the high priest." "Thou also wast with the Nazarene, even
Jesus." The story is well known, and needs not to be repeated. The word of Jesus
found its exact fulfilment. "Thrice" did he deny, "and straightway the second time
the cock crew." "And the Lord turned, and looked upon Peter." It was enough;
with broken heart he "went out, and wept bitterly."

Let us learn : 1. Our constant liability to be tempted to evil. Go where we will,
temptation assails us. Amidst the blessedness of Eden or the sanctities of the temple,
the tempter hides. The felicities of home, the marts of trade, the seclusions of contemplation, are all as open to the evil presence as to the air of heaven. Our steps are
dogged, our life assailed. Surely for this—for such an exposure of the precious life—
a sufficient justification can be adduced. 2. One end of temptation is to search out
existing evil for its exposure and destruction. On the elevated plateau, over the
hardened and smooth floor, the wheat is shaken from the sieve. The gentle winds blow
aside the chaff, for which the consuming fire is prepared, and the pure grain falls to the
ground. Peter little knew that cowardice and fear lay lurking beneath the folds of his
dress; but temptation revealed them. As men pass the magnet through the metal
dust to discover and separate the particles of iron from more precious metals, and those
particles respond, leaping up to the attractive force ; and as men test the strength of
iron beams by means of heavy weights or blows ; so the wily temptation tests the
purity of our hearts and the strength of our principles, and draws forth the lurking
evil, that, being exposed, it may be separated ere it ruins the whole life. 3. If by
temptation a weakness or flaw is discovered, our wisdom is, by penitence and contrition,
to return for recovery and healing. We may be sadder and humbler, but we shall be
wiser. Happy for us if we have strength so to do, and not, Judas-like, in blank self-
despair and self-disgust, sink to rise no more. 4. But a further lesson is to guard against
those evils which are the especial cause of danger to our spiritual life. Each has his
own especial liability. Peter's was not covetousness ; Judas was not in danger from
pride of power. Our danger is always as the amount of alloy in our character—the
amount of chaff amongst the wheat. 5. Again, let us seek the removal of our own
peculiar faults by the winnowing fan and purging fire of the Spirit, that we may not
be exposed to the destructive surprises of sudden temptation. 6. An additional lesson
is so to guard our spiritual life that the current of our thoughts be pure. How often a
coloured stream, or one holding earthy salts in solution, gives its own tint to the banks,
or determines the growths on either side ! Well also is it for us to separate from those
habits of life which are condemned by any conviction of right. 7. The great lesson, on
the surface of this incident, is the necessity for humility—that we boast not of our
religion, that we presume not on our power; but, in lowly dependence on the strength
of Divine grace, walk warily, watching lest we enter into temptation.—G.

Vers. 32—42.—*Gethsemane.* With reverent steps and bent head must we approach this scene. It would be improper to intrude upon the privacy of the Saviour's suffering had not the Spirit of truth seen fit to "declare" this also unto us. The disciples, with the three exceptions, were excluded by the words, " Sit ye here, while I pray." And even from the favoured three " he went forward a little," " about a stone's cast." Then, "sore troubled," and with a " soul exceeding sorrowful even unto death," he " fell on the ground," kneeling, with his face to the earth. Then, from that spirit so sorely wrung, the cry escaped, which has ever been the cry from the uttermost suffering, " If it be possible, let this cup pass from me." Thrice the holy cry was heard, and in so great " an agony " that " his sweat became as it were great drops of blood falling down upon the ground," though strengthened by " an angel from heaven." Thrice the words of uttermost submission, " Thy will be done!" completed his act of entire surrender and self-devotion. " The will of the Father," which had been his law through life, was no less his one law in death. For all ages and for all sufferers Gethsemane is the symbol of the uttermost suffering, and of the supremest act of devotion to the will of the Father on high. Its depth of suffering is hidden in its own darkness. The bearing of this hour upon the great work of redemption, as well as the precise references of the Redeemer in his words, and many other solemn questions that this scene suggests, deserve the most careful thought. But we turn, as in duty bound, to consider its instruction to us. By him, who taught us to pray, we have been led to desire the accomplishment of the Divine will. By him, who is ever for us the Example of righteous obedience, we have been constrained to seek to bring our life into conformity with that will. And by him, from whom our richest consolations have descended, we have been led to submission and lowly trust in the times of our deepest sufferings. We would that his example should gently lead us to keep the sacred words upon our lips, " Thy will be done !" If we would use them in the supreme exigencies of our life, we must learn to use them as the habitual law of our life. Therefore, let us so use them that they may express: 1. *The abiding desire of our heart.* 2. *The habit of our life.* 3. *The uppermost sentiment in the hour of our trial and suffering.* The former steps lead to the latter. We cannot desire the will of the Lord to be done by our suffering unless we have first learnt to submit to it as the law of our activity.

I. " THY WILL BE DONE!" IS TO BE THE ABIDING DESIRE OF OUR HEARTS. The habitual contemplation of the Divine will is likely to lead us to desire its fulfilment. We shall see, if faintly, the wisdom, the goodness, the pure purpose, which that will expresses. It is a desire for the Divine Father to do and carry out his own will in his own house on earth, " as it is in heaven." Seeing God in all things, and having entire confidence in the unsullied wisdom and unfailing goodness of the Father on high, it desires both that he should do his own will in all things, and that by all that will should be sought as the supreme law. It knows no good outside of the operation of that will. Within its sphere all is life, and health, and truth, and goodness ; without is darkness and the region of the shadow of death.

II. As our prayer becomes the true expression of our desire, we shall seek to embody it in our daily conduct. It will then become THE HABIT OF OUR LIFE. Our great Exemplar said, " My meat is to do the will of him that sent me ; " " I seek not mine own will, but the will of him that sent me ; " " I am come down from heaven, not to do mine own will, but the will of him that sent me." And the spirit of his obedience is uttered in one word: " I delight to do thy will, O my God : yea, thy Law is within my heart." How blessed to have a " will of the Lord " to turn to for our guidance ! How holy a Law is it ! The truest greatness of life is to hold it in subjection to a great principle. There can be no higher one than " the will of the Lord." Devotion to a great principle transfigures the whole life ; it makes the very raiment white and glistering.

III. But there are exigencies in life when the crush of sorrow comes upon us. He who has habitually sought to know and observe the will of the Lord in his daily activity will easily recognize the Divine will in his sufferings ; and to bow to that will in health will prepare him to acquiesce in it in sickness. To say, "Thy will be done!" when health and friends and possessions all are gone, needs the training of days in which all the desires of the heart have been brought into subjection. Many things transpire which are contrary to the Divine will ; but obedient faith will rest in the

Divine purpose, which can work itself out by the least promising means. Though held in "the hands of wicked men," it will cry, "If it be possible, let this cup pass from me : nevertheless not my will, but thine, be done."—G.

Vers. 53—65; ch. xv. 1—5.—*Heaven's righteous King at earth's unrighteous judg-ment-seat.* "They led Jesus away to the high priest." So he appears before that ecclesiastical tribunal, whose duty it was to see that his own laws were obeyed. He who is the true Judge is arraigned before one who will prove himself to be the real culprit. But an accusation must be brought, even though the court is an unjust one. To this end "the chief priests and the whole council sought witness against Jesus." Their efforts were vain, for though "many bare false witness against him," yet "their witness agreed not together." Then, with directness, the high priest questioned him, asking the all-important question, "Art thou the Christ, the Son of the Blessed?" Jesus, who knew how to maintain a dignified silence when suborned men bare false witness, and who knew equally how to reply with withering and confusing words when foolish men presented quibbling questions, boldly and promptly replied to the demands with an authoritative "I am." And then, in lowly humility, he bore further witness to the truth, saying, "Hereafter ye shall see the Son of man sitting on the right hand of power, and coming in the clouds of heaven." With rage and indignation the high priest tears his clothes, and declares his words to be "blasphemy," which could only be true on the supposition that he was bearing false witness. He appeals for judgment, and the universal testimony is, "He is worthy of death." The ecclesiastical court has condemned him. "Straightway in the morning," after due consultation on the part of "the whole council," they "bound Jesus, and carried him away, and delivered him up to Pilate." He is now arraigned before the civil tribunal. Pilate's direct inquiry, "Art thou the King of the Jews?" The reply, "Thou sayest," is an affirmative. Pilate has no idea of a spiritual kingship. In each court Jesus is tried, and found guilty. Pilate could have no fear that the calm Prisoner before him, who confessed his kingdom to be "not of this world," would be able to establish his claim, and having his interest in him excited by various circumstances, is disposed to release him. But the instant assertion, "If thou let this man go, thou art not Cæsar's friend," and his desire "to content the multitude," and lest there should be an uproar, "delivered Jesus, when he had scourged him, to be crucified." Underneath all this show of human judgment we must see other forces at work. In "the determinate counsel and foreknowledge of God" we must find the roots of this delivering up. The Lamb was slain from the foundation of the world. Nor must we lose sight of that voluntary consecration of himself to the will of the Father which guided Jesus when he laid down his life that he might take it again. Other aspects of this remarkable incident come into our view, when we hear Jesus refusing to make the appeal which could bring to his help "more than twelve legions of angels," and that because he would that "the Scriptures of the prophets might be fulfilled." It is needful to group together the various details given by the several writers, each throwing into promi-nence one or other important feature of the scene, and it is equally needful to read the records in the light of various portions of the epistolary writings of Paul and others, especially that to the Hebrews. There we see the end it was designed should be answered by his appearing "as a lamb before her shearers—dumb." But the judgment of Jesus is really the judgment of his accusers; of them at whose bar he is arraigned, and by whom his sentence is pronounced. We see in it the most humiliating condem-nation of itself by its unwarranted condemnation passed by the Jewish nation upon its innocent Victim. Even Pilate declared he found no fault in him; nor would he have delivered him up had he not been hounded on by zealots, whose sensibilities he feared in his weakness to excite, and whose tool he lent himself to be. This repudia-tion of the truth, this despisal of holiness—holiness as exhibited in the life of One who has become the world's type of righteousness—and this revolt from the will of the Father as declared in the writings of the acknowledged prophets, condemns them as children of error, of unholiness, and of wicked disobedience.—G.

Vers. 1, 2.—*Approach of the end.* I. "A TIME OF SILENCE AND SOLITUDE PROPERLY PRECEDES THE DAY OF DEATH."

II. "WITH THE HIGHEST ECCLESIASTICAL AUTHORITY, AND MUCH WORLDLY PRU-
DENCE, THERE MAY BE GREAT WICKEDNESS" (Godwin).—J.

Vers. 3—9.—*Anointing for martyrdom.* I. PURE LOVE RISES ABOVE THE CON-
SIDERATIONS OF THRIFT. Logic must give place to love. The full heart disdains the
question of money expense. Habitual extravagance is one thing, the redundancy of
grateful affection is another. We are never safe, in conduct or in thought, except
when we follow the heart's lead.
II. SYMPATHY PRESERVES THE JUDGMENT FROM ERROR. The disciples did not
understand the woman's act. Christ lifted it into the light of truth. There is a
narrow scale of judgment—of those who stand too close to the act, and see only its
immediate bearings. To see truly we must see far. There is a *perspective* of acts.
This Christ points out. The acts of instinctive faith and love, of obedience and
loyalty, are worth more than those based upon prudence and calculation.
III. THE DEATH OF CHRIST MEASURES THE WORTH OF ACTS. This act will go
down in history inseparable from his death. It was a forecast and a memento. The
loving self-devotion of the Saviour attracts the like from those who surround him and
who know him.
IV. THE TRUEST REWARD OF GOODNESS IS TO BE HELD IN THE LOVING RECOLLECTION
OF OTHERS. "The righteous shall be had in everlasting remembrance." One great
man prays, "Lord, keep my memory green!" A poet turns the wish into song, that
he may be "only remembered by what he has done."—J.

Vers. 10, 11.—*Black conspiracy.* I. "THE BEST INFLUENCES FOR GOOD MAY BE
RESISTED AND BECOME VAIN."
II. "HYPOCRISY PREPARES FOR DISHONESTY AND ALL WICKEDNESS" (Godwin).—J.

Vers. 12—21.—*The Paschal supper.* I. THE DUTIFUL MIND IS THE CLEAR-SEEING
AND THE PREPARED MIND. What struck the evangelists was the calm foresight and
method of Jesus. It was like the strategy of a general; the presence of mind of one
who holds the clue to events, because he knows the moral sequence. On another
occasion "Jesus himself knew what he would do." Here the disciples "found even
as he told them." So generally, "everything will be found as Jesus has declared."
II. THE PUREST SOCIETY IS NOT FREE FROM AN IMPURE LEAVEN. A Judas among
the twelve; and an incipient Judas in the conscience of the rest. Better for us, instead
of looking round for *the* Judas, to look into the heart to discover how much of Judas
is there.
III. THERE MAY BE A COINCIDENCE OF DIVINE APPOINTMENT AND HUMAN GUILT IN
THE SAME ACT. It is in the law of things that the good should suffer from human
violence. But it is not in the law of things that any man should take part in that
violence. We may not be able to seize the secret unity of principle behind the
seeming contradiction of the knowledge of God and the responsibility of man. But
the latter is our *fact,* clear and definite. The former is of the "secret things that
belong to the Lord our God."—J.

Vers. 22—25.—*Eucharistic service.* I. THE SYMBOLIC BREAD AND WINE. Eating
and drinking are the most significant physical acts of life. For they are the foundation
of life. Hence the act is appropriate as a symbol of the foundation of spiritual life. The
appropriation of Christ by the intelligence and will is analogous to the appropriation
of food in the process of digestion.
II. THE SERVICE IS THE VISIBLE SEAL OF A NEW COVENANT. Which is a continuation, an enlargement or evolution of the old; founded on better promises.
Objectively, the grace of God is more clearly revealed and abundantly poured forth in
the New Testament than in the Old. Subjectively, the conditions of blessing are purer
and simpler. The spiritual act of faith includes them all, including the man as a whole.
III. IT IS DESIGNED AS MEMORIAL. The form, the words, the spirit of the loving
and suffering Saviour, appear and reappear at each celebration. It is the memorial of
devotion for our sakes, and the reminder to us of the duty to live not for ourselves,
but for the spiritual ideal contained in him.

IV. It is designed to be prophetic. "Until that day!" Our purest earthly joys are the buds of celestial flowers. The reunion of the family on feast-days speaks of the reunion in heaven. All our best earthly joys are promises of better joys in heaven. The scene of the Lord's Supper lifts us out of the commonplace associations of life. We realize in it prophetically the truth of our personal and social existence.—J.

Vers. 26—31.—*Warnings.* I. Human nature is not to be depended on. The most loyal hearts are not fear-proof. Men act much like sheep; are gregarious both in good and in evil. Often they will follow a leader through the greatest dangers; remove the leader, and throw them upon themselves, and courage vanishes, and we know how frail a thing our nature is. Jesus foreknew all this.

II. Yet Divine love trusts our nature. Jesus knew that he should return and again gather these scattered sheep. If our salvation depended on ourselves, all were lost. It is the power and the wisdom greater than ourselves which deliver us from ourselves; and there is no worse enemy to be found than the treacherous heart within our breast.

III. Idle resolves. "Sincere purposes are not sufficient to ensure steadfastness." Good men have said that the more resolves they make, the more sins they find they commit. This may not be strictly so. Still, to add to the original fault the fault of a broken resolve, does hurt to the soul. All experience teaches us our frailty. And the practical lesson is—not to indulge in offensive protestations of humility before our fellow-men, but to see ourselves as we are, and seek strength, not in self-dependence, but in God-dependence.—J.

Vers. 32—42.—*Gethsemane.* I. The spirit's need of occasional solitude. We need to collect and concentrate ourselves. "We must go alone. We must put ourselves in communication with the internal ocean, not go abroad to beg a cup of water of the urns of other men. I like the silent church before the service begins better than any preaching. How far-off, how cool, how chaste the persons look, begirt each one with a precinct or sanctuary! So let us always sit" (Emerson).

II. Its need to throw itself on God. We ask advice of others too much, and depend on human sympathy when we ought only to depend on God. But God does not speak his deepest messages to men amidst a mob, but in the desert, when they are alone with him. Amidst the confusion of opinion and conjecture, his will becomes clear to us. In solitude it shines, the pole-star of our night. His will is ever wisest and best. It is ever possible to follow:—

> "When duty whispers low, 'Thou must,'
>   The soul replies, 'I can!'"

It is ever safest:—

> "'Tis man's perdition to be safe
>   When for the truth he ought to die."

III. The need of watchfulness and prayer. Porphyry says, in his affecting life of the great philosopher Plotinus, that the latter, though full of suffering, never relaxed his attention to the inner life; and that this constant watchfulness over his spirit lessened his hours of sleep. And he was rewarded by an intimate union with, or absorption in, the Divinity. He was ever interrogating his soul, lest it should be yielding to fallacy and error. This was the great man of whom his disciple again says, that he was ashamed of having a body. Even in ascetic extremes, there are lessons for us. "The spirit indeed is forward, but the body is feeble."—J.

Vers. 43—52.—*Violence and meekness.* I. The influence of self-command. How majestic does the Saviour appear in this refusal to employ force against force! Moral grandeur is illustrated against the background of brute violence. It is but the show of violence that can ever be opposed to the majesty of truth. The Divine and the spiritual is conscious that it cannot be hurt. Evil, having no real substance nor personality, flees from it.

II. In the providence of God is our sure refuge amidst the prevalence of

EVIL. "Thus it is, and thus it must be." Chance is an unmeaning word, when the soul is bound up in God's will.

> " This is he men miscall Fate,
> Threading dark ways, arriving late;
> But ever coming in time to crown
> The truth, and hurl wrong-doers down."
>
> J.

Vers. 53—65.—*First trial of Jesus.* I. JUDICIAL INJUSTICE. *Optimi corruptio pessima.* The judge who should represent on earth the equal dealing of God, may turn the name of justice into a mockery. Names will not influence men to right if the heart be not right. Under the name and garb of judge, men have sometimes concealed the worst passions, the most arbitrary instincts. So do extremes meet in human life. Only in God do names and realities perfectly correspond.

II. TRUTH ITSELF MAY BE REPRESENTED AS IMPOSTURE. The Saviour is here made to appear an impostor. It is the triumph of party-spirit. Misrepresentation within every one's power. Insight into character is rare. We ought to take no second-hand estimate of character. The wrong we do to others by false construction is great; still greater may be the wrong we do ourselves.

III. YET IN THE END TRUTH IS ELICITED BY OPPOSITION. The majesty of the Saviour is enhanced in proportion as he is assailed. God is revealed in him and upon him, and his glory is reflected from human falsehood and villainy.

> "Though rolling clouds around his breast are spread,
> Eternal sunshine settles on his head."

IV. THE TEMPORARY SUCCESS AND ETERNAL FAILURE OF CONSPIRACIES. Here the noble and mean combined to dishonour the Christ of God, to treat him as if he had been the offscouring of the earth. So later were his disciples treated. But where are those conspiracies and conspirators now? For a small moment they triumphed; everlastingly they are branded with shame and defeat. What feeble folly were those blows aimed at the head of the meek and unsuffering kingdom!

> " This is he who, fell'd by foes,
> Sprung harmless up, repulsed by blows;
> He to captivity was sold,
> But him no prison-bars would hold;
> Though they seal'd him in a rock,
> Mountain chains he did unlock."
>
> J.

Vers. 66—72.—*Extremes meet in character.* I. SELF-CONFIDENCE AND WEAKNESS. What is a man without self-reliance? Yet it seems to fail, and offers no security in temptation. In a true self-reliance is contained dependence and trust. Confidence in our thought is right, if we recognize that our true views are revealed to us; that it is not we who think, but God who thinks in us. Separated from our root in God, whether in thought or will, we become mere individuals. Once isolate the picture of yourself and your powers and activities from the Divine whole to which it belongs, and it will soon be found that you are in a false position.

II. IMPETUOSITY AND DELIBERATION. We admire the generous eagerness of Peter, but it topples over into precipitous haste. And the hasty falsehood is followed by the deliberate persistence in it. Brazening it out one moment, the next he breaks into a flood of remorseful tears. " Who can understand his errors?" Easy to criticize Peter, not easy to act better. Let us humbly own that he represents us all, in greater or less degree. Our life oscillates between extremes. God can make profitable to us the experience of our sins and errors. The chemistry of his love can bring our tragic scenes to a happy ending.—J.

Vers. 1—11, 18—21, 43—50. Parallel passages: Matt. xxvi. 1—16, 21—25, 47—56; Luke xxii. 1—6, 21—23, 47—53; John xviii. 2—12; xiii. 21—35.—*The betrayal by Judas.* I. INTRODUCTION TO JUDAS. The individuality of Judas comes prominently before us in this chapter. We make his acquaintance in the house of Simon the leper in Bethany. We are introduced to him in connection with the alabaster box of ointment of spikenard very precious; for though not mentioned here by name, we know from the other evangelists that he was among those who felt indignant at the supposed waste of the ointment, and who expressed that indignation by murmuring against the worthy woman who had poured it on the Saviour's head. Either Judas had muttered dissatisfaction, and others of the disciples, in their simplicity, concurred, or Judas was spokesman of others who, accustomed to scant ways and means, were surprised at what naturally enough appeared to such men extravagant expenditure. "When his *disciples* saw it, they had indignation," according to St. Matthew's narrative; "There were *some* that had indignation within themselves," is the record of St. Mark; "Then saith one of his disciples, *Judas Iscariot*, Simon's son, which should betray him, Why was not this ointment sold for three hundred pence, and given to the poor?" is the explicit account furnished by St. John. There was only the one single point of contact between Judas and those of the other disciples who agreed with him about the matter of waste. Their motive differed from his; their thoughts were not his thoughts. The large-hearted liberality of this loving woman was, however, rightly comprehended by the Master himself, and justly commended by him. Our curiosity is not gratified by any particulars of information about Simon. Whether he was a brother of Lazarus, or a brother-in-law, being Mary's husband, or some other relative, or only a friend, we neither know nor need to know. The meaning of the epithet πιστικῆς is also little more than a matter of conjecture. Some of the Greek and Latin interpreters understand it to mean *genuine* or pure, and connect it with πιστός, faithful; others hold the meaning to be potable or *liquid*, from πίνω; while Augustine derives it from the name of the place whence it came, that is, Pistic nard. The Vulgate and Latin versions render it *spicati*; and similar, too, is our English spikenard, as the name of a fragrant oil extracted from the spike-shaped blossoms of the Indian *nardus*, or nard-grass. The costliness of this unguent was well known among the ancients; hence Horace promised Virgil a nine-gallon cask of wine for a small onyx box of this nard; while the evangelist informs us that the value of Mary's alabaster box of ointment was upwards of three hundred pence, that is, of Roman coinage, each *denarius* being equivalent to sevenpence halfpenny or eightpence halfpenny of English currency. The amount would thus be about ten guineas.

II. MARY'S LIBERALITY. This liberality of Mary had its origin in deep devotedness to our Lord, but her devotedness was the outcome of enlightened faith. She had a correct understanding of his character and claims. A believer in his Divine commission and in his kingly authority, she did not stumble as many at the prospect of his death. She knew he was to die, and hence she anticipated that sad event by the exceedingly expensive preparation in question. The custom of employing perfumes on such an occasion has an illustration in the record of King Asa in the sixteenth chapter of the Second Book of Chronicles, where we read, "They laid him in the bed which was filled with sweet odours and divers kinds of spices prepared by the apothecaries' art." The disciples of Christ surpassed the generality of their nation in the knowledge of, and belief in, his person as Messiah; but though they had full faith in his Messiahship, they still clung to the notion of a temporal kingdom, with all its high honours and earthly distinctions. From this arose the difficulty which they had in reconciling themselves to his death, or rather the stumbling-block which his death placed in the way of their faith, as the two disciples to whom Jesus joined himself on the way to Emmaus, after speaking of his death and crucifixion, added, "But we trusted that it had been he which should have redeemed Israel." Mary's faith excelled theirs as much as theirs excelled that of the Jews in general. Her faith did not fail in prospect of Messiah being cut off, her love was not chilled by the coming coldness of his death, nor did her hope go out like a taper in the darkness of his sepulchre. She believed that as Messiah Jesus would die and revive and rise and reign. She believed, and her faith worked by love. She believed, and therefore she poured the precious ointment ungrudgingly on her Saviour's person.

III. THE BESETTING SIN OF THE TRAITOR. Judas is usually held up as a monster of iniquity, and his sin regarded as something diabolical. While we would not diminish by one iota the heinousness of his sin, nor say one word in extenuation or mitigation of his guilt, we feel that, owing to certain exaggerated representations of his criminality, the lessons to be learnt from his character and conduct are to a large extent lost. On the contrary, if we carefully analyze his character and examine his career, we shall find much to learn, at least by way of warning, from the sad lesson of his life. Of course, by placing him outside the pale of humanity altogether, and regarding him more as a fiend than a man, we leave ourselves without any common measure whereby it is possible to compare his career with that of ordinary mortals. Now, we hold that he was just in roll with common men, though by his sin in its results he rose at last to such an exceptionally bad eminence. He was, as is admitted on all hands, a bad man, a wicked man, and a man as wretched as he was wicked. All the elements of evil in his character, however, may be resolved into one besetting sin, and that sin was *avarice.* His greed of gain was insatiable, and he loved gold much more than God. This inordinate love of money was the root of the evil in his nature. This love of money is a growing sin, for, as the old proverb has it, the love of money increases as much as the money itself increases—nay, it usually increases much faster. He was naturally avaricious, and he gave full swing to his natural disposition. Here we learn a lesson of the greatest utility and of very general application. In the Epistle to the Hebrews we read of "the sin which doth so easily beset us." The case of Judas exemplifies the baneful tendency and the fatal result of such a single besetting sin. Most people have some propensity in excess, some strong passion, some evil principle in their nature more likely to overpower them than any other. It is of vital importance to ascertain what the weak point is, in what direction it lies, and where the risk of entanglement is greatest. A physician is careful in the very first instance to discover the seat of the patient's disease, and its nature. So we should look carefully into our heart and out upon our life till we find out the source of weakness; and once it is discovered—nor can the discovery be a matter of any difficulty to the honest inquirer—we must be ever on our guard against it, and use every available means to fortify ourselves in that particular quarter. However strong our character may be otherwise and in other respects, one besetting sin, unless resisted and shunned, will ruin all. One weak link will spoil the strongest chain, and no chain is stronger than its weakest link; one small opening in a dam will flood a district, or even a province.

IV. OFFICIAL DIGNITY, OFFICIAL DANGER. It often happens that a man is placed exactly in that situation in life which, owing to his peculiar disposition, is fraught with greatest danger to him. Thus, for good and wise ends, God in his providence is pleased to try us, as gold is tried, that we may be proved and purified and strengthened. When so situated we need to seek daily increase of faith that we may be kept from falling, and constant supplies of grace that it may be sufficient for us. Judas had been clever at finance, and in consequence became bursar of the little society. This situation of purse-bearer was one of extreme danger to a man like Judas; his hand was too often in the purse, his fingers were too frequently on the coins it contained. With such an opportunity without and such a disposition within, what, in the absence of restraining grace, could be expected? His greedy disposition, combined with the temptation of his office, was too much for him; his covetousness developed into thievishness. He failed to check the evil propensity; he did not resist the strong temptation. The first act of pilfering was committed. The Rubicon was crossed; the line of demarcation between honesty and dishonesty became fainter and fainter, and was gradually effaced. Other acts of petty pilfering succeeded; and though we have little reason to suppose that the disciples' purse had ever been a deep or heavy one, or that it ever contained more than supplied the bare necessaries of daily life, yet we have much reason to believe that the paltry peculations of the purse-bearer were a constant drain upon it. "He was a thief," our Lord tells us plainly, "and carried the bag." Here we have a second lesson, which is the absolute necessity of resisting the first temptation to evil; for as the habit grows by indulgence, the power of temptation diminishes by resistance.

V. DISAPPOINTED AMBITION. The chief attraction to Judas had probably been the prospect of a temporal king and earthly kingdom; and thus of some lucrative position or highly remunerative office in the service of that king and in the affairs of that kingdom. Others of his fellow-disciples had been looking forward to posts of honour—to sit on thrones in the future Messianic kingdom. Judas cared less for honour than for profit, and however he may have esteemed such honour, it was mainly as the way to wealth. But now our Lord had referred in terms unmistakable, once and again, to his death and burial, this gave a rude shock to the hopes of the traitor, and seemed to cut off at once and for ever the prospect of worldly gain. This was a bitter disappointment to the greedy spirit of Judas; the cup of plenty was rudely dashed away as he was about to raise it to his lips; the time of discipleship he looked upon as a dead loss; his profits had been small at best, but the prospect of improving his circumstances is now blighted; and his occupation is gone. Tantalizing, and even torturing, as all this must have been to *him*, another disappointment, though of a minor sort, is added. A sum of three hundred *denarii*, or more, that is to say, upwards of ten guineas, had been profusely lavished in a way and for an object with which he had not the least possible sympathy, nay, in a manner as he thought highly reprehensible. It was sheer waste, and worse, for no one gained anything; the poor were not benefited—"not that he cared for the poor," except as a matter of hypocritical pretence; he himself missed the disbursement of a sum from which he could have appropriated a percentage that might have been a crumb of comfort in present disastrous times and during the dull days he must now look forward to. But there was even more than this; he must have felt himself by this time an object of suspicion; conscience must have made him aware of this; he must have known that the Master, at all events, saw through the thin disguises that concealed his real character from ordinary eyes. He did not feel at home with the brotherhood; and, his occupation being gone, a spirit of recklessness was creeping over him. Besides, he was stung into hostility by the severe but well-deserved reproof which our Lord now saw right to administer to him. "The poor always ye have with you," said our Lord; and it was thus hinted that it was his duty—part of his office— to look after them, and that opportunity was never wanting for that purpose. Thus wrought on, Judas bethought himself that it was high time to look to his own interests; and, having failed in one direction, to try the opposite.

VI. WARNINGS WASTED. It is truly astonishing what effect the continued indulgence of a single sin has in hardening the heart, searing the conscience as with a hot iron, blinding the mind, and banishing for a time at least all feelings of shame and even of common humanity. The black crime soon to be committed had cast its shadow before. More than one hint had been given, more than one warning note had been sounded; but all to no purpose. The first intimation appears to have been after our Lord had washed the disciples' feet, impressing by that expressive symbolic action the great lesson of humility on all his followers. On that occasion he said, "Now ye are clean, but not all" (John xiii. 10). In the second section of this chapter, where the traitor is again referred to, words of warning still more distinct are uttered: "One of you which eateth with me shall betray me;" and while all of them, "one by one," as St. Mark particularly mentions, deprecated with surprise and sorrow such an impeachment, asking, "Is it I?" or literally, "It is not I, is it?" Judas had the amazing effrontery to pretend innocence, and ask with the rest, "Is it I?" The intimation about the betrayer being "one of the twelve, he that dippeth with me in the dish," and the individual who should receive the sop, may have been whispered into the ear of the beloved John, and through him to Peter; but the final fearful warning was uttered aloud and in the hearing of all. And yet that terrible sentence, "Woe to that man by whom the Son of man is betrayed! good were it for that man if he had never been born," had no effect on him; at all events, it failed to shake his diabolical purpose. It is possible that during the first shower of questions—each asking, "Is it I?"—Judas had sat silent, either sullenly through contempt, or conscious-stricken; that subsequently, with an air of careless coldness, and in order to conceal the confusion of the moment, he asked not, "Lord, is it I?" but "Rabbi, is it I?" when he received the answer, "Thou hast said," in the affirmative, unheard perhaps except by the disciples John and Peter, who sat close by. The expression, too, which our Lord added, namely, "What thou doest, do quickly," though heard by all, was misunderstood, and referred by them to directions about the purchase of requisites for to-morrow's feast, or making distribution to the poor; but it must have been perfectly comprehended by the traitor himself. At all events, on receiving the sop, he went out immediately, and, in spite of all, pursued his foul and fiendish purpose. All these checks, all these warnings, were utterly ineffectual. His besetting sin, growing like the mountain snowball, and gathering within its compass other elements, as disappointment, resentment, ingratitude, and envy, had now become too powerful to be overcome. The sin that might have been checked effectually at the first had now become uncontrollable; the evil one, who might have been successfully resisted at the commencement, had now gained complete mastery over this wretched man. To such a fearful extent was this the case, that the evangelist informs us that "Satan entered into him." In no other way, as it seems, could the enormity of his crime be accounted for. No wonder it is added, "And it was night." It was night with earth and sky—night with all its darkness, night with that dark heart of the traitor, night in every sense with that unhappy man! How all this inculcates, as another and a third lesson, the importance of cultivating prayerfulness of spirit, and enforces the necessity of praying frequently and praying fervently, "Lead us not into temptation, but deliver us from the evil one"!

VII. ANOTHER SCENE IN THE TRAITOR'S LIFE. We now open another chapter in his history. The bargain is struck, the sum weighed and delivered, and in the paltry sum thus realized we have another proof of the grovelling spirit of this unspeakably mean and mercenary man. He has secured the thirty pieces of silver, or thirty shekels—some £3 15s. of British money. Both parties seem satisfied with the bargain. The chief priests are glad of the promised opportunity of arresting in private him whom the dread of popular tumult or probable rescue prevented them arresting in public. Public opinion was still so favourable to the Prophet from Galilee, and had such force, that, hostile as the Jewish authorities were, they dreaded, and with good reason, the risk of a public apprehension. Judas, too, is content with his pieces of silver. We almost fancy we see him, like Milton's picture of Mammon in the nether world, eyeing with furtive, downcast glance the proceeds of his bargain. But the satisfaction of the wicked seldom lasts long. We scarcely think that Judas at first realized the consequences of his wickedness; we cannot believe that he at all anticipated the sequel of his crime. Perhaps he thought that he who had wrought so many miracles would work one in self-defence, and not allow himself to be apprehended; or perhaps he thought that, if arrested, he would escape out of the hands of those who came to apprehend him; or it may be he thought Jesus would now be forced to set up the expected kingdom. All his calculations are at fault.

VIII. THE ACTUAL BETRAYAL AND APPREHENSION. Some two hours have elapsed from the revelation of the traitor and his departure from that upper room, when a motley multitude of men, armed with swords and staves—some of them Levitical guards from the temple, others Roman soldiers from the tower of Antonia, together with priests and elders—is marching down the hillside from Jerusalem to the valley of the Kidron. Already they have crossed the brook and reached the garden. But what mean those lanterns, for the Paschal moon is at the full? Perhaps the moon was obscured by clouds, or shining dimly that night; or the deep shadows of the hills and rocks and trees made the light of the lanterns necessary. The concerted signal was not really needed, owing to our Lord's forwardness to meet his fate. Had he pleased, he might have frustrated the attempt, as by a word he felled them to the earth (John xviii. 6); he might have ordered to his help twelve legions of angels, had he been unwilling to suffer. And yet, willing as he was to suffer, he is equally willing to save; his sufferings were in our stead, and for our sake. His ready willinghood to undertake for us and die for us assures us of equal willinghood to have the benefit of those sufferings transferred to us. The traitor's kiss, which was a *fervent* one (κατεφίλησεν), was the signal for arrest. From this we learn the terms of familiarity and friendship that existed between Christ and his disciples. Nor is he changed, or become colder in his friendship for his true followers; he is as cordial as ever, and still bends on earth a Brother's eye. His address to Judas, however, is too strongly expressed in the Common Version. The term "friends" (φίλοι) he reserves for his true disciples; the word addressed to Judas is ἑταῖρε, which signifies "companion" or "acquaintance," and does not necessarily imply either respect or affection.

IX. THE COWARDICE OF SIN. Cowardice is generally associated with sin, so true it is that "sinful heart makes feeble hand." Our first parents, after their sin against God, hid themselves among the trees of the garden. The chief priests and elders, with the captains, are here charged by our Lord with cowardice. "Be ye come out," he asks, "as against a brigand or bandit (λῃστήν), with swords and staves?" Had he been an evil-doer, why did they not apprehend him publicly in the broad light of day as he taught in the temple? Poor, sinful souls! their cowardly spirits shrank from this; the power of public opinion, or the dread of a rescue, or the danger of a riot, they could not brave; but now skulkingly, secretly, stealthily, at the dead hour of night, they came upon the Saviour by surprise, with a strong posse of men well armed. Their sin was seen in their cowardice. Our Lord is now in the hands of his enemies. He had healed the servant's ear—the right ear (St. Luke and St. John)—having asked freedom to stretch forth his arm to touch and heal the wounded ear, saying, "Suffer ye thus far;" if the words do not mean—Excuse resistance to this extent. Judas has betrayed him; all the disciples—even John the beloved and Peter the brave—have forsaken him and fled!—J. J. G.

Vers. 12—17, 22—25. Parallel passages: Matt. xxvi. 17—19, 26—29; Luke xxii. 7—13, 19, 20; 1 Cor. xi. 23—34.—*The old dispensation merging in the new.*—I. THE PASSOVER AND THE INSTITUTION OF THE SUPPER. 1. *Comparison of the records.* The memorial Passover differed from the Egyptian or original Passover in several points. A still greater change is now made. The substance now takes the place of the symbol. The antitype supersedes the type. The true Paschal Lamb—Christ our Passover, about to be sacrificed for us—being come, the Jewish Paschal lamb disappears. The unleavened cakes and wine, formerly only secondary and subordinate, now become the primary and principal elements of the feast, as representing the body and blood of the Lamb to be slain. The idea of Christ's sacrificial death, previously intimated with more or less clearness, is now fully exhibited. In the fact of the particulars being foretold there is a close resemblance to that prediction which preceded the triumphal entry. The record of the Lord's Supper is fourfold. It is recorded by three evangelists and by one apostle. These are the evangelists Matthew, Mark, and Luke; with Paul, the apostle of the Gentiles. Some points are brought out more fully or distinctly in one, and some in another, of these; accordingly, a brief comparison of their respective records with each other helps to a better understanding of the whole. (1) Instead of "blessed," used by St. Matthew and St. Mark, St. Luke and St. Paul employ the expression, "gave thanks." (2) In addition to the statement of "This is my body," found in St. Matthew and St. Mark, St. Luke and St. Paul give an explanation, the former adding, "which is given for you;" the latter, "which is broken for you;" while both enforce it by the suitable exhortation, "This do in remembrance of me." (3) St. Luke and St. Paul append a note of time—"after supper," or "when he had supped." (4) Whereas (*a*) St. Matthew and St. Mark say simply, "This is my blood of the new testament, St. Luke and St. Paul introduce the word "cup," and alter the arrangement of the sentence, in this way rendering the whole clause clearer and more explicit; thus, "This cup is the new testament [more correctly 'covenant,' Revised Version] in my blood." Mark alone (*b*) supplements the accounts of the other evangelists by stating the fact, "They all drank of it." (5) St. Matthew and St. Mark have, "shed *for* many," using the preposition περὶ equivalent to *in behalf of*, or *for the benefit of*; but St. Luke has "shed for you," employing ὑπὲρ which, from the idea of superposition, covering, defence, or protection, may mean *in the stead*, or *place*, or *room of*, and so conveying the idea of substitution, though not so distinctly and definitely as ἀντί. (6) St. Matthew alone points out the purpose in the expressive words "for the remission of sins." (7) It is also to be noted that the original word for "shed" is ἐκχυνόμενον, a present participle passive, and so signifying literally *being shed*, as though the sufferings were already begun, the passion entered on, and the sacrifice commenced. These four records of the inspired penmen, each writing from his own standpoint, but all under the direction of the Holy Spirit, furnish a full exhibition of this ordinance in its different aspects; while they impress us with its solemnity and sacredness, deepening the interest we should take in it and the importance to be attached to it. Besides, there is usually this difference between the record of the same fact or truth when presented in a Gospel and then in an Epistle, that the record of the former is historical, that of the latter doctrinal; the former contains the plain narrative, the latter its practical application; the concise enunciation of the former finds its complete development in the latter; the direct statement of the Gospel is commented on or treated somewhat controversially in the Epistle. 2. *The Author of this ordinance.* The Lord

Jesus Christ is the Author of this solemn institution; both evangelist and apostle refer its appointment to him. He is sole King and Head of his Church. His kingship is the result of a Divine decree. "I have set my King," says Jehovah, "on my holy hill of Zion." The government, both legislative and executive, is in his hand, as the prophet had foretold, "and the government shall be upon his shoulders." He is also "Head over all things to the Church." Not only so; this ordinance in particular is his special appointment, for it is the memorial of his death, and keeps the memory of his dying love green in the Christian's soul. To him, therefore, we owe its institution, the manner of its observance, the time of its continuance, and the persons admissible to its enjoyment. Nor is there any ordinance more closely identified with the Saviour than this ordinance of the Supper. He is its "all in all," its Alpha and Omega. The words are his, and speak of him; the symbols are his, and point to him; the blessings embodied are his, being the purchase of his blood; the praise is his, for "unto him that loved us, and washed us from our sins in his own blood, . . . to him be glory and dominion for ever and ever." The new covenant, with all its benefits, present and prospective, is his, for he ratified it. 3. *Abuses.* Little more than a quarter of a century had elapsed when human abuses were beginning to overlay this holy ordinance in the Church of Corinth, so common is it for man to leave an impure print on all his hand doth touch. A reformation of the holy rite had become necessary, and a republication followed. The abuses removed, and the ordinance restored to its original simplicity and sanctity, St. Paul received it by revelation, and republished it in his First Epistle to the Corinthian Church, as he says, "For I have received of the Lord that which also I delivered unto you." With this fresh publication of it, we have a fuller exposition of its nature, and increased obligation for its observance; while it is restamped, as it were, with the seal, and resanctioned by the signature of the Church's Head. 4. *The time of its appointment.* The time of its appointment was "the same night in which he was betrayed." This of itself, apart from all other evidence, is proof positive that Jesus was more than man. It was the night when the Jewish Sanhedrim concerted measures for his apprehension; when chief priests and scribes and rulers were planning his condemnation and plotting his death; the night when one of his own disciples played the part of traitor and betrayed him into the hands of his deadliest foes; when another disciple denied him, and all forsook him; the night when he was to be delivered to his persecutors—to their malice and mockery and the worst tortures that their malevolence could devise.

> " 'Twas on that night, when doom'd to know
> The eager rage of every foe,
> That night in which he was betray'd,
> The Saviour of the world took bread."

It was the *eve* of his crucifixion; nor were the events of the coming morrow unknown to him. From the unrelenting hatred of his enemies, and the steady purpose of their persecuting fury, he might have anticipated them; he might, without much risk of error, have forecast them. But with him it was no forecasting of probabilities; he clearly foresaw all, and consequently in a measure foretasted all. Had he been a weak mortal and nothing more, the certainly approaching danger and disaster must have occupied his thoughts and oppressed him with grief. In this case he would have been insensible to the wants, and incapable of administering to the comforts, of others; he would have been too much occupied with himself and his own position to spare any thought for the concerns, or make any provision for the consolation, of his friends. On the contrary, instead of concentrating his thoughts on himself and the crisis just at hand, his thoughts were engrossed with his followers then, thenceforth, and onward for ages yet to come. All his thoughts, all his feelings, all his sympathies, were enlisted on the side of his disciples, and exercised for their benefit. The self-abnegation that had characterized the whole course of his life became yet more conspicuous, if that were possible, at the period when he came within measurable distance of death and dissolution. Self was absolutely lost sight of, the interests of his people bulked so largely that they occupied the whole field of vision. 5. *A comparison.* A comparison has frequently been instituted between the life and teaching of the Saviour and Socrates—between the Prince of peace and the prince of pagan philosophers. Their respective sentiments on the eve of execution may for a moment be compared, or rather contrasted, here. On the part of Socrates we find a sort of posthumous ambition, present doubt, and practical indifference. There was posthumous ambition; for he allowed his vanity to be flattered by reckoning on the praises of posterity, and referred, with a feeling half of self-gratulation and half akin to revenge, to the false position in which his death would be sure to place his enemies, and especially his accusers. There was present doubt; for beautifully as he reasoned on the subject of immortality and a future state on previous occasions, now, in the presence of the great change, he doubted whether he himself or his friend Crito, who was to survive him, were likely to fare better. There was practical indifference; for the interests of his family and the upbringing of his children appear to have cost him little or no concern. With our Lord, on the other hand, there was no borrowing of comfort from the praises of posterity; his chief concern was for the well-being of posterity. There was no shadow of a cloud upon futurity; all was bright and blissful there. There was, instead of indifference, the deepest and most absorbing concern for the spiritual well-being and everlasting welfare of his friends and followers through all coming time. Far be it from us to undervalue the sage of Athens—he was one of the lights of heathendom; but we find him to the last human, intensely human; while Jesus was both Divine and human—unmistakably Divine, and yet truly human. 6. *Use of monuments.* Monuments draw attention to the facts of history and to the incidents of biography. How many thousands there are who would never have heard of Nelson, or Wilberforce, or Wellington; or who would have remained ignorant of their great achievements, and of the stirring times in which they lived, were it not for the monuments erected to their memory! How many have had their minds directed by some monument or other memorial to the life and times of men of whom otherwise they would never have heard even the names, or studied the history, or reflected on the lives however eventful! Thus it is, in a higher sense, with the institution of the Supper; it is a monument to Christ, and helps to keep up the remembrance of him, which would else have been more or less forgotten. It reminds men of his death, and shall continue to do so till he come again; it reminds us of the debt of obedience we owe to his dying command, "Do this in remembrance of me;" it reminds us, too, of a day when he will come "to be glorified in his saints, and admired in all them that believe."

II. The NATURE OF THE ORDINANCE. *A sacrament, not a sacrifice.* The Lord's Supper is a sacrament, not a sacrifice. We reject and reprobate the teaching of those who regard the bread and wine in the Lord's Supper as a sacrifice—the so-called sacrifice of the Mass or the offering up of the bread and wine converted into the flesh and blood of Christ; and who represent it as a bloodless, yet true, proper, and propitiatory sacrifice for both the living and the dead. Nothing could be more contrary to or contradictory of the Word of God. In forming a correct notion of this ordinance, of which the passage before us contains the institution, it may be helpful to clear away the rubbish which, in the course of time, accumulated round it. In doing so it may be well to state what *it is not,* and then what *it is*—to exhibit the *negative* side of this sacrament, and then the *positive.* 1. In the first place, then, we reject the doctrine of transubstantiation held by the Latin Church. This doctrine, first formulated by the Abbot of Corbey, Paschasius Radbert, in the beginning of the ninth century, first denominated *transubstantiation* by Hildebert of Tours in the beginning of the twelfth century, and made an article of faith by the Lateran Council in the beginning of the thirteenth century, means the conversion or change of the elements of bread and wine into the real body and blood of our Lord. We repudiate this dogma (1) as opposed to *Scripture*; for St. Paul calls the elements after blessing by the same name as before, saying, "For as often as ye eat this bread, and drink this cup;" thus they are still bread and wine as much and the same as ever. It is (2) contradicted by the evidence of the *senses*; for handle them, and they remain the same; taste them, they are the same; smell them, they are the same; they are still bread and wine, with all their sensible qualities or accidents, as they are called, unchanged. Now, the testimony of the senses ranks the highest—the testimony of the most credible witnesses cannot overthrow it, and to refuse the information of the senses overturns the certainty of all knowledge; while one of the acknowledged tests of Scripture miracles is an appeal to the senses. It may fairly be admitted that one single sense may, under certain circumstances, err, but it can be corrected by the others; whereas all the senses together cannot and do not err. It is (3) repugnant to *reason*, which convinces us that the material body of Christ cannot possibly be in heaven and on earth at the same moment; that is, at the right hand of the Majesty on high and on thousands of earthly altars at the same time. In this case the flesh and blood of Christ would be present, while their sensible qualities are absent; on the contrary, the sensible qualities of bread and wine would be present, while those substances themselves are absent. Thus we should have the subject without the accidents in the one case, and the accidents without the substance in the other. But this is palpably absurd, for substances are known by their qualities, and qualities do not exist apart from their substances. Once more, (4) this dogma is derogatory to the *sacrifice* of Christ—that great sacrifice offered once for all and for ever, because it represents it as needing continuous repetition in the so-called sacrifice of the altar. Moreover, (5) it destroys the very nature of a sacrament, for every sacrament necessarily consists of two parts, a sign and a thing signified—"an outward and visible sign of an inward and spiritual grace;" in other words, a sensible object and certain spiritual blessings set forth and sealed by that object. But transubstantiation does away with the sign altogether, and puts the thing signified in its place. We reject the doctrine of transubstantiation, then, because of the absurdities it involves, as also because of the superstitions connected with it, and the idolatrous practices engrafted on it. 2. In the second place, we reject the Lutheran doctrine of consubstantiation, which teaches that though the substance of the elements is not changed, yet the body and blood of Christ are mysteriously but really and corporeally present *in, with*, and *under* the elements, and are received corporeally with the mouth by communicants along with the symbols. Though this opinion is rather speculative than otherwise, though it does not convert the sacrament into a sacrifice, though it does not lead to the adoration of the elements, and though it does not impart to the sacrament a physical virtue apart from the dispositions of the recipient, yet it involves several grave difficulties. It necessitates a literal interpretation of the words of institution, and so a substantial presence of the body and blood of Christ in this sacrament. The Lutherans are at pains to define this presence. It was not a change of one substance into another (μετουσία), nor the mixing of one substance with another (συνουσία), nor the inclusion of one substance in another (ἐνουσία), nor the absence of substance (ἀπουσία); but the real coexistence or presence (παρουσία) of the one substance with the other, that is, the earthly with the heavenly. For this purpose, however, a communication of properties is requisite, so that the humanity of Christ shares the omnipresence of his divinity. The Lutheran doctrine, it is true, makes the ubiquitous presence of the body of Christ unique and peculiar to the Lord's Supper. It is further alleged that the humanity of Christ is at the right hand of God, and that the right hand of God is everywhere; therefore Christ, as to his humanity, is everywhere present. It is plain, however, that this omnipresence of the flesh and blood of Christ in the sacrament of the Supper is contrary to the nature of a body, and thus self-contradictory. Besides, this omnipresence of the body and blood of our Lord would imply their presence in every ordinary meal as well as in the Lord's Supper. Neither is it a sufficient or at all satisfactory answer to this to say, as Lutherans do, that omnipresence in this case means no more than accessibility, that is, the fact of being everywhere given, for the body and blood, if thus given and received everywhere, would be everywhere operative. 3. In the third place, we do not agree with the Zwinglians, including Zwingle himself, Carlstadt, Myconius, Bucer, Bullinger, and the reformers of Zurich, who went to the opposite extreme from the Lutherans. They regarded the elements as signs or symbols, and nothing else and nothing more; these they held to be memorials of the absent body of our Lord. The tendency of the Zwinglian doctrine was to lessen the efficacy and lower the character of this sacrament. Looking upon the elements as mere signs, viewing them as memorials and not means of grace, denying the special presence of the Saviour, they made the sacrament of the Supper little, if anything, more than a bare act of commemoration or a mere badge of profession. And so it happens that the doctrine of the Supper, as set forth by Zwingle himself, is that still held by Remonstrants and Socinians to the present day. Here we are reminded of the memorable conference that once took place on this subject. For a full account of the discussion, the district where it was held, and the disputants on the occasion, we must refer the reader to the description by D'Aubigne, which, as usual, is at once picturesque

and instructive. We can only notice the fact in its bearing on the subject of the Supper.
On an eminence overlooking the city of Marburg stands an ancient castle. Away in the
distance sweeps the lovely valley of the Lahn. Further still, the mountain-tops rise
one above another till they are lost in the clouds or disappear in the remote horizon.
In that old castle was an antique chamber, with vaulted roof and Gothic arches. It
was called the Knight's Hall. There, more than three centuries and a half ago, a conflict took place, not with carnal weapons, but intellectual and spiritual. Princes,
nobles, deputies, and theologians were there. The combatants were the mighty Luther
and the mild Melancthon on the one side, with the magnanimous Zwingle and the meek
Œcolampadius on the other. It was this very subject that formed the ground of debate.
Luther held by the literal sense, dogmatically repeating "This is my body," while his
opponents urged the necessity of taking the words figuratively. And here, in passing, it
may be observed that much as both Romanists and Lutherans insist on the literal sense
of the words, they are figurative even according to their interpretation. As used by
the Romanists they are an instance of the figure synechdoche, as used by Lutherans
they are a metonymy, while as used by Protestants in general they are admitted to be
metaphorical. 4. Now, in the fourth place, and in opposition to all these, we give in
our adhesion to the creed of the great majority of the Reformed Churches on this
doctrine. Here it is necessary to bear in mind that, among the Reformed themselves,
Zwingle occupied one pole, Calvin held the opposite, while the form of the doctrine
ultimately agreed on and acquiesced in by the great body of Reformed communions was
intermediate. Zwingle's view, as already seen, made the sacrament of the Supper
symbolical and commemorative, reducing it to a mere sign; Calvin, on the other hand,
held that believers receive an emanation or supernatural influence from the glorified
body of Christ in heaven. The illustration he employed made his meaning plain : it
was to this effect, that the sun is absent and distant from us in the heavens, but his
light and heat are present with us and enjoyed by us on earth. The Reformed, however, maintained that believers received the sacrificial virtue of Christ's atoning death.
Eventually the *Consensus Ligurinus* (1549 A.D.) was drawn up by Calvin. The immediate object was to harmonise the Zwinglians and Calvinists; but it accomplished
much more than this. It embodies the doctrine of the Supper which is held by all the
Reformed Churches. The various Reformed Confessions are in harmony with it. The
second Helvetic Confession and the Heidelberg Catechism, which constitute the
doctrinal standards of the Reformed Churches of the Continent; the Thirty-nine
Articles of the Church of England; the Westminster Confession of Faith and Catechisms,
are in full accord with it. The doctrine of these Churches and Confessions may be
expressed in, or rather compressed into, the following brief statement, slightly modified
from the Westminster Confession :—" The body and blood of Christ are as really but
spiritually present to the faith of believers in this ordinance as the elements themselves
are to their outward senses." Hence it comes to pass that while we outwardly and
visibly partake of the sensible signs, which are bread and wine, we inwardly and faithfully receive Christ and him crucified with all the benefits of his death. The real
presence of Christ is enjoyed by his people in this sacrament; but that presence is not
bodily, it is spiritual. His body broken and blood shed are present, not materially, but
virtually; by this we mean that the beneficial effects of his sacrificial death upon the
cross are conveyed to the faithful recipient. These benefits are received, not by the
mouth, but by faith. The whole is made effectual by the Holy Spirit to our spiritual
nourishment and growth in grace.

III. The doctrines made visible by the Supper. *Nature of a sermon.* A
sermon is intended to explain some doctrine, or enforce some duty, or both. The great
object to be attained is the glory of God in Christ and the Christian's good. The sacrament of the Supper has often been compared to a sermon; but it is a sermon to the eye
—a visible sermon, if the expression be allowed. It is a sermon, too, that thus visibly
sets forth several of the leading doctrines of our holy religion. 1. The first doctrine
visibly exhibited in the Lord's Supper is the *Incarnation.* The Incarnation, or Christ's
coming in the flesh, was the great event of the ages; for " when the fulness of the time
was come, God sent forth his Son, made of a woman." " The everlasting Son of the
Father," when he took upon him to deliver man, " did not abhor the Virgin's womb; "
and so, in the language of one of the Church's creeds, he " was incarnate by the Holy

Ghost of the Virgin Mary." Now, the *bread* symbolizing the body, and the *wine* the blood, both together set forth the body of flesh with the living fluid that circulates through it; and thus the elements of bread and wine teach the doctrine of the Incarnation, speaking to us the same language as the Evangelist John, when, in the first chapter of his Gospel, he tells us, at the first verse, that "In the beginning was the Word, and the Word was with God, and the Word was God;" and then adds, at the fourteenth verse, "And the Word was made flesh, and dwelt among us." The bread and wine, therefore, inculcate the same sacred truth as the inspired writer of the Epistle to the Hebrews, when he says, "Forasmuch then as the children are partakers of flesh and blood, he also himself likewise took part of the same." 2. The second doctrine visibly taught in the Supper is that of the *Atonement*, or the setting-at-one of persons alienated. The parties in this case are God and men, the latter alienated, and enemies in their minds by wicked works, the carnal mind being enmity against God; while "the wrath of God is revealed from heaven against all ungodliness and unrighteousness of men." This setting-at-one is the work of reconciliation, from which, however, atonement only differs as being the more comprehensive term, and including not only the reconciliation itself, but the means by which reconciliation is effected. The atonement, then, or those sufferings of the Saviour by which reconciliation is accomplished, in other words, the bruising and breaking of Christ's body and the shedding of his blood, are set forth visibly by *breaking* the bread and *pouring out* the wine in the Lord's Supper.

> "Bread of the world, in mercy broken,
> Wine of the soul, in mercy shed,
> By whom the words of life were spoken,
> And in whose death our sins are dead;

> "Look on the heart by sorrow broken,
> Look on the tears by sinners shed;
> And be thy feast to us the token
> That by thy grace our souls are fed."

3. The third doctrine presented to the eye in the sacrament of the Supper is that of *Faith*, by which we feed on Christ to our spiritual nourishment and growth in grace. The exercise of faith on the Son of God is symbolized by our *eating* the bread and *drinking* the wine. These same acts of eating and drinking are employed by our Lord in the sixth chapter of John to symbolize and signify the exercise of faith. Thus he says in the chapter cited, "Except ye eat the flesh of the Son of man, and drink his blood, ye have no life in you;" and again, "Whoso eateth my flesh, and drinketh my blood, hath eternal life; and I will raise him up at the last day;" still further it is added, "He that eateth my flesh, and drinketh my blood, dwelleth in me, and I in him." Thus the most intimate fellowship with Christ, the closest union and communion with him, life spiritual here and everlasting hereafter, together with part in the resurrection of the just, are conditioned by and connected with that faith of which eating and drinking are the symbols.

> "Sweet feast of love Divine;
> 'Tis grace that makes us free
> To feed upon this bread and wine,
> In memory, Lord, of thee.

> "Here conscience ends its strife,
> And faith delights to prove
> The sweetness of the bread of life,
> The fulness of thy love."

4. The fourth doctrine thus visibly taught in the Lord's Supper is the *Communion* of saints. The word "communion" implies our discharging some duty together (*munus*)— doing something in common. At the Lord's table we partake of bread in common and of wine in common—the same bread and the same cup; and this *common participation* is a visible manifestation of the doctrine of the communion of saints. Hence the apostle says, "The cup of blessing which we bless, is it not the communion of the blood of Christ? The bread which we break, is it not the communion of the body of

Christ? For we being many are one bread, and one body: for we are all partakers of that one bread." This communion of saints is based on union to Christ. As branches, we are grafted into the living Vine, and thence draw life and strength and nourishment; as living stones, we are built up into a spiritual temple, the foundation being apostles and prophets, with Jesus Christ as the chief Corner-stone; as members of his mystical body, we are knit by joints and bands to him as the living Head. By virtue of this union of all true Christians with Christ, they have communion each with the other. We have common privileges, common benefits, common blessings, and common duties. We have hopes and fears in common, joys and sorrows in common, trials and triumphs in common; and all these not merely in connection with the same congregation or the same Christian communion, but to some extent "with all that in every place call upon the name of Jesus Christ our Lord, both theirs and ours." Oh that Christians realized this more in their own souls, and exhibited it more in their lives, and manifested it more to the ungodly world around! Oh, when shall the great inter-cessory prayer be fulfilled: "That they all may be one; as thou, Father, art in me, and I in thee, that they also may be one in us: that the world may believe that thou hast sent me"! Oh, when will that proof of the divinity of our Lord's mission be given to an unbelieving world and a misbelieving age! Oh, when shall the holy Church cease to be rent asunder by schisms, distressed by heresies, and oppressed by the scornful!

> "Elect from every nation,
>   Yet one o'er all the earth,
> Her charter of salvation
>   One Lord, one faith, one birth;
> One holy Name she blesses,
>   Partakes one holy food,
> And to one hope she presses
>   With every grace endued."

5. The fifth doctrine is that of the glorious second *Advent*—that advent which the Church is looking for and hasting to. But this doctrine is presented in the communion, not visibly, but orally; not to the eye, but to the ear, in the words, "Ye do show the Lord's death *till he come.*"

IV. THE SACRAMENTAL SIGNS; THEIR SIGNIFICANCE. 1. *The sacramental elements.* These are two in number—bread for nourishment and wine for refreshment. One of these might serve the purpose; then why are two employed? Two are employed instead of one (1) for *assurance.* Thus we read in relation to Pharaoh's dream, "The dream is doubled to Pharaoh twice, because the thing is established by God, and God will shortly bring it to pass." In like manner the two signs show the certainty of the covenant and strengthen our faith in its provisions. Like the everlasting covenant made with David, well ordered in all things and sure, the promised blessings of the New Testament are firmly established, being "Yea and Amen in Christ Jesus." Their bestowal on the specified conditions is sure, soon, and certainly coming to pass. Again, they are (2) for *apprehension;* that is, in order that they may be rightly and more readily apprehended. Thus two signs were granted to Moses, as it is written, "If they will not believe nor hearken to the voice of the first sign, they will believe the voice of the latter sign;" the reason assigned being the character of the Israelites, stiffnecked and hardhearted as they were. So God, because of our slowness of apprehension and hardness of heart, has added sign unto sign, mercifully accommodating himself to us, the frail and fallen children of men. But (3) they imply *abundance.* While they quicken our faith and help us to a clearer view of Christ, they exhibit the plenitude of his resources, for "it pleased the Father that in him should all fulness dwell," and "in him are hid all the treasures of wisdom and knowledge," the ample supplies he has in store for our necessities, the full forgiveness and plenteous redemption that are found in him, the rich abundance of all needful gifts and necessary graces, as also the sufficient nourishment he bestows on us. 2. *The sacramental actions.* Some of these are performed by the administrator, others by the recipient. On the part of the former they are *taking, blessing, breaking,* and *giving.* The *taking* symbolizes the assumption of our nature, "the mystery of the holy incarnation." The *blessing* signifies separation from a common to a special purpose, from an ordinary to a sacred use, as also thanksgiving to God for the unspeakable gift of his Son, for the means of salvation thus made available, and for this solemn ordinance itself as a sign and seal of the benefits bestowed —in a word, for all the mercies of his covenant, for all his love to our souls, for all his faithfulness to his promises, for all he has done, is doing, and has promised to do. The *breaking* is expressive of the breaking and bruising of his body; that is, the painful death on the cross, the pouring out of his life unto death, the making of his soul an offering for sin to satisfy Divine justice, to pacify Divine wrath, and purchase salvation for us. The *giving* denotes the gift of the Father, who "so loved the world, that he gave his only begotten Son, that whosoever believeth in him should not perish, but have everlasting life;" the gift of the Son, of whom the believer can say, "He loved me, and gave himself for me;" every needful gift, for "he that spared not his own Son, but delivered him up for us all, shall he not with him also freely give us all things?"— the gift of all things, for "all things are yours, because ye are Christ's, and Christ is God's." The Christian's inventory is as follows :—" Paul, or Apollos, or Cephas, or the world, or life, or death, or things present, or things to come;" all are yours, because Christ is yours—Christ, in the glory of his Godhead, in the dignity of his person, in the suitability of his offices, in the perfection of his work, in the sufficiency of his atonement, in the power of his resurrection, in the prevalency of his intercession, in the preciousness of his promises, in all the blessedness of his benefits; no benefit kept back, no blessing withheld, and no promise excepted. Thus he is "made of God to us wisdom, and righteousness, and sanctification, and redemption;" and thus we are "complete in him." There are also sacramental actions on the part of the recipients— *taking, eating and drinking, dividing.* These also are significant. Our *taking* implies intelligent acceptance of Christ and cordial reception of him. We embrace him fully as he is offered freely. We take him in all the capacities pertaining to his person or identified with his work. We take him as our Teacher, to be taught to know and believe and do the truth; as our Sin-bearer, who bore our sins in his own body, suffering, the just for the unjust, to bring us to God; as our King, to rule in us and over us and for us. We take him as our Saviour and Redeemer, the mighty One of Jacob, that we may be saved from the guilt and filth of sin, from the pollution and power of sin, from the defilement and dominion of sin; we take him as "the Lord our Righteousness" and Strength; as the Beloved of our soul—the chief among ten thousand in our esteem. We take his laws for our direction, his love for our consolation, his precepts to guide us, his promises to gladden us; his cross in time, his crown in eternity; for if we bear the cross now, we shall wear the crown hereafter. Thus St. Paul says, "God forbid that I should glory, save in the cross of our Lord Jesus Christ;" and again, "Henceforth is laid up for me a crown of glory, which the Lord, the righteous Judge, will give me at that day." By *eating and drinking* we understand the necessary application. Bread must be eaten in order to nourish, and wine drunk that it may refresh. The elements thus entering our bodies incorporate with our system and become part of our frame. As the application of Christ by faith unites us with Christ, so by this symbolic application of his body and blood that union becomes still closer. By such sacramental action, too, we profess publicly our union with Christ, and proclaim to the Church and to the world that Christ is one with us and we with him—Christ formed in our heart the hope of glory, and our life hid with Christ in God. By eating and drinking we say in action what Thomas said in words, " My Lord and my God;" we claim sacramentally that mutual relationship which the Spouse in Canticles claims verbally when she says, " My Beloved is mine, and I am his." The *dividing,* according to the direction in St. Luke, "Take this and divide it among yourselves," is expressive of practical communion with each other in the charities and amenities of life; consequently of hallowed fellowship, Christian affection, and brotherly love; of the widest, yet tenderest, sympathies with all followers of our common Lord, with all fellow-travellers to the heavenly home, and with all fellow-heirs of the future glory in our Father's house above. 3. *The sacramental words.* These comprise an *injunction,* an *explanation,* and an *obligation.* The *injunction* or command is comprehended in the following terms :—"Take, eat;" "This do in remembrance of me;" "Drink ye all of it;" "This do ye, as oft as ye drink it, in remembrance of me." The *explanation* consists of the two following sentences :—"This is my body, which is broken for you;" "This cup is the new covenant in my blood, which is shed for many for the remission of sins." Here there is an obvious reference to the words of Moses, "Behold the blood of the covenant, which the Lord hath made with you" (Exod. xxiv. 8). The *obligation* or enforcement applies to the whole, and is contained in the single sentence, "For as often as ye eat this bread, and drink this cup, ye do show [' ye proclaim,' Revised Version] the Lord's death till he come." 4. *Concluding observations.* The Lord's Supper is thus not a sacrifice, but a feast after a sacrifice, and a feast upon a sacrifice. It is a wellspring in the wilderness, a green spot in the desert, a feast to refresh us on our pilgrimage, and a foreshadowing of that feast above, where "many shall come from the east, and west, and north, and south, and sit down [recline] with Abraham, Isaac, and Jacob in the kingdom of heaven." We are constrained, somewhat reluctantly, to pass over several interesting topics in this connection—the *reasons* for partaking of this sacrament, the *uses* to be made of it, the *benefits* to be derived from it, as also the *qualifications* for worthily observing it. Here we may just notice in regard to the latter (1) that a man must prove himself, and so partake; (2) discern or discriminate the Lord's body by faithful apprehension and spiritual appreciation; and (3) discern or discriminate himself and his relation to his Lord. Failing these he incurs judgment, viz. judicial visitation. Yet mercy mingles with such judgment, for it is the chastening of our heavenly Father for our good, and to prevent our final condemnation with the ungodly world.—J. J. G.

Vers. 26—42. Parallel passages: Matt. xxvi. 30—46; Luke xxii. 39—46; John xviii. 1.—*The agony in Gethsemane.* I. SCENE AND SEVERAL CIRCUMSTANCES CONNECTED WITH THE AGONY. 1. *Anticipation.* From the entrance of our Saviour upon his public ministry his life was one of continued trial. All along symptoms of the approaching crisis appeared, all along the bitter cup was steadily filling, all along the clouds were gradually gathering. At length, towards the close of his career, the storm-clouds in all their fury burst upon him. After his last entrance into Jerusalem the bitter cup became brimful, and he was now to drink and even drain it to its very dregs. The anticipation of those sufferings he was to undergo had made a deep impression on his mind; forebodings of them had frequently disturbed his repose, dread of them overwhelmed his spirit. He foresaw all, he anticipated all, he in a measure foretasted all; accordingly, several days before his passion, he cried out, "Now am I troubled; and what shall I say? Father, save me from this hour: but for this cause came I to this hour;" or, as some erroneously read it, "What shall I say? Shall I say *this*, Father, save me from this hour?" 2. *Preceding circumstances.* On examining the circumstances that precede the agony, we find that the Wednesday and the Thursday before the Passover our Lord himself spent at Bethany, while on the latter day his disciples went to Jerusalem to engage an apartment and prepare a lamb for the coming solemnity. When the evening of the day was come, Jesus also repaired to Jerusalem. Having there joined the disciples, he sat down with them to the sacred feast which had been prepared, and which he purposed to render still more sacred by engrafting thereon (as we have seen) the new festival to be observed in remembrance of himself, as a memorial of his death, and in exhibition of his body broken and blood shed for many for the remission of sins. Such were the order and connection of events. The Passover had been observed—that Passover which he had desired so earnestly to eat with his disciples. The sacrament of the Supper had been instituted by our Lord, and kept for the first time in company with his faithful followers. Subsequently he had delivered that touching and pathetic, yet most consolatory and truly sublime discourse recorded in the fourteenth, fifteenth, and sixteenth chapters of the Gospel of St. John. He had poured forth, out of the fulness of his heart, that fervent and beautiful prayer contained in the seventeenth chapter of the same Gospel. He had warned the disciples against deserting him in the hour of temptation. He had selected three of them specially to attend him in his sorrows. Then, late at night, after delivering the discourse and praying the prayer and making the arrangements referred to, he left the city for the scene of his agony. 3. *The scene.* The place where this occurred was a spot often frequented by our Lord and his disciples. On this account St. Luke does not designate the place by name; he merely says, "When he was at the place." St. John accounts for the traitor's knowledge of the place from its being a frequent resort of the Saviour: "Judas also," he says, "knew the place: for Jesus ofttimes resorted thither with his disciples." The place was a garden, little more than half a mile from the city of Jerusalem, and only a stone's throw from the brook Kidron, situated on the western slope and near the foot of the Mount of Olives. That garden had not been laid out for the production of herbs, but as an olive plantation. The name of that garden, as given by St. Matthew and St. Mark, was Gethsemane, so called from two words meaning "oil-press." As just intimated, it appears to have been a frequent and favourite resort of our Lord and his disciples. To that spot he often went as a meeting-place with his disciples scattered through the city during the day, according to the meaning assigned by some to the term συνῆχθη, rendezvoused. Thither the Saviour often retired from the world, and to be alone with God. Thither he often repaired for prayer and meditation. There he often spent the night in intercourse with Heaven. There, amid the deep gloom of that solitary plantation, was the place of the memorable and most affecting scene to which this section refers. That garden, if tradition has rightly marked the site, remains to the present day. That enclosure still stands, surrounded by a wall formerly of loose stones but now plastered and whitened, and contains eight large and venerable olive trees. Up to the present time it is a gloomy and forsaken place, yet from its associations it must ever be to the Christian a sweet and sacred spot. To this day it is a peculiarly sombre as well as solitary place, with that rude stone wall enclosure and those grey old olive trees. It was here an event took place the full purport of which eternity perhaps can alone reveal. At all events, for suffering and sorrow it ranks next to the Crucifixion itself. But sad and sorrowful as are the memories associated with Gethsemane, it is invested with a sacredness that makes it unspeakably dear to every Christian heart.

> " Gethsemane can I forget,
> And there thine anguish see,
> Thine agony and bloody sweat,
> And not remember thee ? "

Let us imagine ourselves, then, in that sombre and solemn enclosure on the eve of man's redemption, in company with our Lord and along with Peter and James and John. The same three had been spectators of the Transfiguration. The same three had stood by while their Master restored to life the ruler of the synagogue's daughter. The same three are now privileged to be witnesses of that fearful struggle of the Redeemer's soul, called in this passage his agony. And as we stand in that society and on that spot, eastward rises high above us the lofty summit of Olivet. Westward we are overshadowed, or at least our view is shut in, by the gigantic walls of the holy city. Below us lies the valley of the Kidron, with the little freshet from which it takes its name. Yonder at a distance, amid the gloom of the overhanging olive trees, is seen the Saviour's person dimly revealed by the pale light of the silvery moon. It is a chilly night, but chilly as is the night-air, the warm perspiration bursts forth from every pore, moistens every limb, and falls like big drops of blood down to the ground.

II. The struggle and its severity. 1. *Meaning of the term.* The word " agony " is due to St. Luke, and employed by him only in the record of this transaction ; while the use of this word helps considerably to the right understanding of the whole. The idea of pain so usually associated with agony is not the exact sense of the word. It rather means *conflict* or struggle. It was a word which the Greeks applied to their games. Thus the runner in the race, the pugilist in the combat, and the wrestler in the contest, were properly said to agonize. *Pain* connected itself with the word only as a secondary and subordinate notion. But what was the nature of this struggle? It could not be with sin, for he had no sin; he was " holy, harmless, undefiled, and separate from sinners." It was not with the development of any unholy tendency or the uprising of any evil passion; from all such his humanity was exempt. Nor yet are we without a hint respecting the *source* whence the struggle proceeded. If we compare an expression at the close of the temptation with another in the narrative of the agony we may arrive at a tolerably safe conclusion. In the first-named passage Satan is said to have left our Lord for a season, or rather *until a convenient season ;* while in this passage the subject of prayer, which he suggests to his disciples, was the avoidance of temptation. Putting these two things together, we have good ground to believe that the suitable season for another onslaught of the evil one had arrived; that the attack was renewed; that Satan had returned; that the tempter, though foiled once and again before, had resumed with increased facilities, or from a vantage-ground, or at a more favourable opportunity, the terrific trial. A passage in the Epistle to the Colossians favours this view. It is there (Col. ii. 15) said that he stripped off or put away from himself the hostile principalities or powers that clung to him like a deadly Nessus-robe. The thrice-repeated assaults of Satan in the wilderness had been repelled, and the tempter defeated, but only for a time. The attack was renewed in Peter's effort to dissuade the Saviour from suffering; and unconscious as the apostle was of the source whence the suggestion sprang, it was none the less a device of the great enemy, as we may infer from the sternness of our Lord's rebuke when he said, " Get thee behind me, Satan." But the tempter was again baffled and beaten. Once more, however, the prince of this world mustered all his forces for the last and fiercest onslaught. This was the hour and power of darkness, beginning with the agony and ending with the Crucifixion. And now Satan and the powers in league with him are not only vanquished, but Jesus "made a show of them openly, triumphing over them," as we read in that passage of Colossians; that is, they were boldly exhibited as trophies by the Victor, and led in triumph as captives bound to the Conqueror's car. 2. *Point of attack.* Still curiosity would desire information with respect to the particulars of the present trial, or the character of the struggle in which the Saviour is now engaged. What was its turning-point? Was he pressed to repudiate the responsibility he had assumed for sinners, and did the struggle consist in resisting such pressure? Was he tempted to renounce the great work of man's redemption? Was there a shrinking of the flesh from the terrible ordeal that was fast approaching, while the spirit drew in the opposite direction? It can be no matter of surprise that the pure humanity of our Lord should recoil from what was coming in the near future, for he foresaw it all—the sneer, the scorn, the spitting, and smiting; the robe of mockery, and the thorn crown, together with the scourging and suspension on the cursed tree. We cannot wonder that the anticipation of all this, and vastly more, should produce a struggle of no ordinary kind in the breast of the Son of God. But whatever the exact nature of the struggle was, from whatever cause he agonized, one thing is perfectly plain, and that is the extreme intensity of the agony. 3. *Evidence of its intensity.* So unspeakably intense was its severity, that he sweat as it were great drops or clots (θρόμβοι) of blood which ran down to the ground. With reference to this proof of its severity, several similar instances of sweating blood have been adduced. Ancient authors and modern writers alike record cases of it. Diodorus of Sicily mentions bloody sweat as resulting from the bite of Indian serpents. Aristotle speaks of it as caused by a diseased state of the blood. Some recent medical authorities reckon it among the consequences of excessive terror or extreme exhaustion. But by far the most striking case of all is one narrated by the infidel Voltaire. In his essay on the civil wars of France, he says that the king, Charles IX., soon after the Bartholomew Massacre, was attacked by a strange malady, which carried him off at the end of two years. His blood was always oozing out, forcing its way through the pores of the skin—an incomprehensible malady, against which the art and skill of the physicians were unavailing. This, he adds, was regarded as an effect of the Divine vengeance; but elsewhere he attributes it to excessive fear or violent agitation, or to a feverish and melancholy temperament, admitting that other cases of the same have occurred.

III. THE SAVIOUR'S SORROW AND ITS SOURCE. 1. *The description of his sorrow.* There is a climax in this description. He began to be sorrowful; his *soul* was sorrowful, *exceeding* sorrowful, even unto *death.* He was *amazed*, and very *heavy.* One of the words here employed is peculiar. It denotes, according to one derivation, *satiety*, but according to another a state and consequent feeling of *strangership*—a sort of home-sickness. How applicable to the Saviour's sorrow! He must have been more than satiated with earth, and homesick, if we may use the expression, for heaven. But, looking deeper down, we find three words descriptive of the Redeemer's sorrow, which require closer and more careful consideration. The original word for being *sorrowful* (λυπεῖσθαι) is in this narrative peculiar to St. Matthew; that for being sore *amazed* or stunned (ἐκθαμβεῖσθαι) is only used by St. Mark; while those equivalent to *very heavy* (ἀδημονεῖν), and to the soul being *exceeding sorrowful* (περίλυπος) even unto death, are common to both. The first expression is one of frequent occurrence, but is here intensified by a subsequent compound and several adjuncts. Further, while the seat of this sorrow is the soul, the sorrow itself is exceeding and overwhelming, and enwraps the soul, the soul being distressed all round—grieved on every side (περί). Nor is that all; it is so excessive that soul and body seem ready to part, or actually to part, under the pressure and the death-pang to be anticipated. If it be not the fulfilment of, it is at least in correspondence with, the words of the psalmist—

> "The pains of hell took hold on me,
> I grief and trouble found."

The next term, that peculiar to Mark, imports a complex state of feeling made up of *horror* and *amazement*, or extreme alarm and consternation, approaching to stupefaction or being stunned, while here, again, an augmenting particle increases the notion to the highest degree. Once more, the former of the two words employed by St. Matthew and St. Mark in common, whatever origin is assigned to it, is used to denote a state of distress that combines at once *dejection* of mind and *disquietude* of spirit, or anxiety and anguish. 2. *The cause of this sorrow.* Now, those words and phrases employed in describing the Saviour's sorrow, weighty as they are in themselves separately, when taken together represent an extreme of sorrow and a weight of woe which no utterances of human speech appear adequate fully to express. To this sorrow may be applied the words of the prophet, " Is it nothing to you, all ye that pass by? behold, and see if there be any sorrow like unto my sorrow, which is done unto me, wherewith Jehovah hath afflicted me in the day of his fierce anger." It is now time to inquire into the cause or causes from which such sorrow sprang. To what must we attribute this sorrowfulness, this sore amazement, this extreme heaviness and exceeding sorrowfulness of soul even unto death? We may answer (1) *negatively.* To attribute it to fear of death would be a glaring outrage on all probability, and the gravest libel on the Son of God. Who has not heard of that Athenian sage who philosophized so calmly and conversed so pleasantly with his friends till the poison-cup did its work? Many a soldier, both in ancient days and modern times, has faced death fearlessly and unshrinkingly. Many a soldier of the cross has displayed equal, and in cases not a few still greater, heroism. Not only men, but delicate matrons and tender maidens, have heroically braved the persecutor's rage, and bidden him do his worst. In the days of the martyrs, many courageously and cheerfully encountered death in its most ghastly form. Some endured the most cruel tortures without complaint. Some were torn to pieces by wild beasts. Some were left to look at the ocean's tide as it approached nearer and nearer, rising higher and higher till they sank in the gurgling wave. Some were sawn asunder. Some were crucified with the head downwards. Some went upward from the stake in a chariot of fiery flame. And is it possible that the Founder of our faith had less fortitude in the near prospect of death than many of his weakest followers? Many, supported by a good cause and a good conscience, have despised death, and surrendered life unhesitatingly and unfalteringly. Many, of different ranks and different ages and of both sexes, have submitted to a death of cruellest torture, undaunted and undismayed. Hundreds have in their last moments illustrated the words of the poet—

> " Resting in the glorious hope
> To be at last restored,
> Yield we now our bodies up
> To earthquake, fire, and sword."

Is it, then, for a moment supposable that the servant should so far surpass his Master, and the disciple his Lord, that what caused the latter such agony and anguish was matter of exultation and triumph to the former? We answer (2) *affirmatively.* What, then, was the cause of the Saviour's sorrow? Was his case different from any or all of those referred to? Yes, most certainly; they were wide as the poles apart. Those illustrious heathens, those great and good men, those noble martyrs, those death-defying followers of the Saviour, stood each in his own lot in the end of the days. Not so the Saviour: his was a *representative* capacity ; he was the second Adam—his people's federal Head. He came to give his life a ransom for many, to bear the sin of many, and to be numbered with the transgressors. He came to take the place of the guilty, and to stand

in the stead of millions. Then the sword of justice was to be unsheathed against the
Shepherd, the man that was God's Fellow. The Shepherd must lay down his life for the
sheep, else they must perish, and perish entirely, and perish everlastingly; "for the wages
of sin is death," and "all have sinned, and come short of the glory of God."

> "Die man, or justice must
> Except some other as able and as willing pay
> The rigid satisfaction—death for death."

The exact relation of the Saviour's sufferings to the penalty incurred we need not dwell
on here. Whether it is a relation of *diversity* (aliud pro quo), as Grotius maintained ;
or of *equivalence* (tantundem), according to others; or of *identity* (idem), in accordance
with the view of a third class, we shall not attempt to determine further than to reject
the first, and express our preference for the second rather than for the third. Further,
as his life had been stainless, his death must be *sinless*. Holy and harmless as that
life had been, his death must be equally free from sin and separate from sinners. But
now came the severest test and sorest trial. If the awful sufferings in near prospect
should weaken his purpose; if, foreseeing the shame and pain and torture, his resolution should give way; or if, what would equally defeat his undertaking, his heart
should conceive or cherish any feeling of revenge; or if the burning sense of wrong
should provoke complaint, or any word of impatient murmuring should escape his
lips; if, in a word, any sin were to mingle with thought or feeling, or find utterance
in speech, his life-work would miscarry and the whole would end in irreparable
failure. No wonder, then, that, in view of all this mighty burden which he bore—
in view of the dread responsibility laid upon him, in view of that mountain-load of sin
he was to transfer to himself and bear away, in view of that great sacrifice which he
was to offer, in view of the great satisfaction he was to make, in view of that great
salvation he was to effect, the Saviour's humanity began to shrink. If we turn to the
fifty-third chapter of Isaiah, a passage written more than seven hundred years before
the time of our Lord's agony, we find at once a comment on that agony and a key to its
cause: "The Lord hath laid on him the iniquity of us all," or, more literally rendered,
"The Lord hath made the iniquities of us all to meet or fall on him," or, more
strictly still, "The Lord hath made the iniquities of us all to rush on him." In those
words thus understood our sins are figuratively represented as beasts of prey, and Jesus
is their Victim; or as cruel enemies, and Jesus is the Object on which their vengeance
vents itself. Like bulls of Bashan, they beset him round. Like ravening and roaring
lions, they gaped upon him with their mouths. Other adversaries, less powerful but
more vexing, compassed him like dogs. It was as though fiercest foes of every kind and
on every hand assailed him.

IV. THE SUPPLICATION AND THE STRENGTH THEREBY SECURED. 1. *The meaning of
this cup.* No wonder he prayed, "Let this cup pass from me." The meaning of "cup"
here is obviously suffering and sorrow—a bitter mixture to be drunk. Thus Isaiah (li. 17)
says, "O Jerusalem, which hast drunk at the hand of the Lord the cup of his fury;
thou hast drunken the dregs of the cup of trembling, and wrung them out;" while in
the seventy-fifth Psalm we read that "in the hand of the Lord there is a cup, and the
wine is red; it is full of mixture; and he poureth out of the same: but the dregs
thereof, all the wicked of the earth shall wring them out, and drink them." A similar
figure is found in Homeric poetry ('Iliad,' xxiv. 528)—

> "Two urns by Jove's high throne have ever stood;
> The source of evil one, and one of good.
> From thence the cup of mortal man he fills;
> Blessings to these, to those distributes ills.
> To most he mingles both: the wretch decreed
> To taste the bad unmix'd, is cursed indeed."

But while the figure itself is clear, the fact underlying it is not so clearly or easily
understood. 2. *The mixture in this cup.* What elements mingled in this cup? What
were the bitter ingredients in the mixture it contained ? It was not, as already seen,
the mere shrinking of our Lord's humanity from death, however painful and shameful,
though we do not by any means exclude this element. Neither was it an apparition of

the evil one in some form specially dreadful and terrible, as some have conjectured. There was something worse than all this—something more and bitterer still. There can be little doubt, though some seem to think otherwise, that the assaults of the Prince of darkness were peculiarly powerful at this juncture, and went to make up part of the bitterness of this cup. Of this we are not without some intimation from our Lord himself, for before entering Gethsemane he says, "The prince of this world cometh," and before leaving the scene of the agony he adds, "This is your hour, and power of darkness." From all this, and from the circumstance already adverted to, that Satan had relinquished his attempt only until another and more suitable season arrived, we have reason to conclude that Satan was again at work during the agony, that he was renewing with redoubled energy his fiery darts, deterring from the work that was being done, and at the same time in every way depreciating its worth. The conflict foretold in the garden of Eden was to be fought out in Gethsemane; the heel of the Seed of the woman was to be bruised, and the head of the old serpent to be crushed. It was not strange, then, that the serpent should hiss most horridly, while his head was thus being crushed. It were strange indeed if, when the spoiler was to be spoiled, the captor deprived of his prey, and captivity led captive, Satan should not rouse himself to one fearful, final effort to retain at once his power and his prey. His temptation then mingled in and embittered the draught which the Saviour was to drink and drain to its dregs. Whatever the nature of Satan's suggestion may have been, whether resistance to the Divine will, or refusal of the destined draught, or desertion of the post assigned, or something yet more shocking, it is needless to inquire. It is enough to know that when our Lord tasted the cup he turned aside, so exceeding bitter was that mixture; a dark cloud passed over the serene spirit of the Son of God; his inward vision was obscured; the Father's will became invested in mystery, and the cross in blackness. 3. *Other ingredients in the cup.* Another ingredient in that cup was the withdrawal of the Divine presence—the hiding of his heavenly Father's face. Sin shut man out of Paradise; sin excludes man from the favour of God. The Saviour took our sin upon him; he became our Substitute; he acted as our Surety; he stood in our stead, and eventually offered himself a Sacrifice for us. He thus exposed himself to the temporary withdrawment of the light of the Divine countenance. Nor can anything be more trying or more painful to a child of God than the loss of the Divine fellowship for a season. When deprived of the sensible enjoyment of Divine communion, he is comfortless. It was thus with Job (xxiii.): "Behold, I go forward, but he is not there; and backward, but I cannot perceive him: on the left hand, where he doth work, but I cannot behold him: he hideth himself on the right hand, that I cannot see him." Similar is the complaint of the psalmist in the eighty-eighth psalm: "Lord, why castest thou off my soul? why hidest thou thy face from me? I am afflicted and ready to die from my youth up: while I suffer thy terrors I am distracted. Thy fierce wrath goeth over me; thy terrors have cut me off." If a child of God, a sinner saved by grace, feel so acutely the hiding of God's countenance, how unspeakably more the sinless Son of God! This withdrawal of God's presence—favourable presence—is one element, perhaps a main element, in the misery of the world of woe, and forms no small part in the punishment of the lost. But this part of the Saviour's distress had a positive as well as a negative side. Not only was there deprivation of the joys of Divine favour and fellowship, the overclouding of his heavenly Father's face; there was in all probability some actual infliction of chastisement, as may fairly be inferred from the strong language of the prophet, when he says, "It pleased the Lord to bruise him; he hath put him to grief." But of all the bitter ingredients in the cup of the Saviour's suffering, nothing would pain him more than the sense of our sins being laid upon him, that he might be made sin for us; and the sight of that accursed thing, so abhorrent to his pure nature, as the burden he was to bear; together with the consciousness of the close connection of sin and death and hell. It was then that sorrow arose on every side; sufferings, with concentrated bitterness, overwhelmed him. The hatefulness of sin, God's indignation against it, that loathsome load of human guilt he was to bear, the work he was to go through in order to remove it, the wrath of Heaven manifested against it,—all these ingredients mixed together in that bitter cup. 4. *His supplication.* It was then he prayed, "O my Father, if it be possible, let this cup pass from me: nevertheless not as I will, but as thou wilt." Here we find, side by side with the deepest suffering, the meekest submission. The prayer is conditioned by possibilities. If justice can be satisfied, if redemption can be effected, if the government of God can be upheld, if, consistently with all this, sinners can be saved without such excess of sorrow, so let it be! The prayer was prayed three times. He went away and prayed; he kneeled down and prayed; he fell on his face or on the ground and prayed. Thus he offered up prayers and supplications, with strong crying and tears. His prayer was heard and answered, and yet the cup did not pass away. He was "heard in that he feared" ("for his godly fear," Revised Version); or, according to another rendering of the words, "he was heard, and delivered from the fear of death." Though the cup was not removed, the dread of death was thus taken away; at all events, strength was imparted. 5. *The strength secured by his supplication.* "There appeared an angel unto him, strengthening him;" literally, *infusing* strength (ἐνισχύων αὐτόν). The immediate consequence of this increased or renewed strength was more earnest and energized supplication: "He prayed more earnestly (ἐκτενέστερον)." Strictly speaking, he continued praying (προσηύχετο), and that more intensely; the tense (imperfect) of the verb and the qualifying adverb imply prayer sustained and intensified. But intensely earnest as his supplication for the removal of the cup had been, it was equalled by the entire surrender of his own will to that of his heavenly Father. He had said, "O my Father, if it be possible, let this cup pass from me: nevertheless not as I will, but as thou wilt" (so St. Matthew); he had said, "Father, if thou be willing, remove this cup from me: nevertheless not my will, but thine, be done" (so St. Luke); while here, according to the record of St. Mark, he says, "Abba, Father, all things are possible unto thee; take away this cup from me: nevertheless not what I will, but what thou wilt." And once more, as we read in the Gospel of St. Matthew, he said, "O my Father, if this cup may not pass away from me, except I drink it, thy will be done." As though he had said,—I feel it may not be; I know I must drink it; and as I must I will. Not as I will, but as thou wilt. Thy will be done. 6. *His example.* He was in all things an Example for us. We may pray, and with perfect propriety, for deliverance from danger, or disease, or difficulty, or distress of any kind. If the answer come directly and as desired, it is well; if not, succour of some sort will be brought us, strength suitable and grace sufficient will be given us; in either case, our duty is submission to a will that is wiser than our own, and a full surrender of ourselves into the hands of our heavenly Father, who, in disposing all things to his own glory, disposes them at the same time for our good. The address, as reported by St. Mark, repeats the word for "Father;" thus "Abba" is the Aramaic for "Father," and to it is added the Greek word of the same signification. It may be that (1) St. Mark, as frequently, explains the vernacular Syriac of Palestine in our Lord's day by the equivalent Greek word; or (2) the repetition may imply intensity of feeling and strong emotion, just as the thrice-prayed prayer imports intense earnestness of spirit; or (3) it may be that by this conjunction of two terms, Oriental and Occidental—the one used by the Jew, the other by the Greek— our Lord meant to express his interest on behalf of both Jew and Greek. Further, it has been questioned whether the shrinking of our Lord's humanity on this occasion was in view of all the sufferings as a whole which, in the capacity of our Surety, he was to endure, or only of those apparently incidental and possibly unessential sufferings, occasioned, for example, by the treachery of one disciple, the denial by another, the desertion of them all, the Jewish trial and the Roman trial, the scourging, spitting, scoffing, and such like. We can hardly thus separate the essential from the unessential, the indispensable from the incidental, in our Lord's sufferings. As a man, he shrank from the wrath of God; but his ultimate submission to that sorest of all trials showed triumphantly his obedience to his heavenly Father's will. Thus, in order to save his people, his endurance was complete and his example perfect.

V. THE SLEEPINESS OF THE DISCIPLES AND THE SADNESS THAT CAUSED IT. 1. *Object of the disciples' watching.* The Saviour had selected three disciples, as already seen, to be with him. No doubt one object, perhaps the primary object, in view was that they might be eye-witnesses of his agony, and bear testimony thereof to his Church. But another object, and one little if at all less in importance, was that they might be near him for sympathy and support. It was with this view, no doubt, he had said, "Tarry ye here, and watch with me." But even of this human succour he was deprived, for ever as he came to them—once and again and a third time in the interval of prayer—he found them asleep; so Jesus was left alone in his agony. 2. *Nature and cause of their sleepiness.* And yet it was not a sleep of stupidity, or insensibility, or want of sympathy, in any sense. The cause was the very opposite. And here it is noteworthy that while the other evangelists record the *fact*, Luke, the beloved physician, alone assigns the *cause*. How characteristic of his profession! From his skill in physiology he here tells us that "he found them sleeping for sorrow;" just as afterwards, from his knowledge of psychology, he accounts for disbelief from joy where he says, "While they yet believed not for joy." And so it was from very sorrow that they slept. It is not an unusual experience that sorrow acts the part of a narcotic, and sadness causes sleep; thus the psalmist says, "Reproach hath broken my heart, and I am full of heaviness." And a merciful arrangement it is that men under such circumstances can sleep for a season and forget their sorrows. 3. *Different explanations.* The words which Jesus addresses to his drowsy disciples have been variously understood. Some take them (1) interrogatively,—Do ye sleep now and take your rest? This seems favoured by the parallel in St. Luke, "Why sleep ye?" As though he said,—Is it a time for indifference or indulgence of this sort? Is a time of present distress and approaching danger a suitable season for sleep? Others take them (2) as a sort of sorrowful irony, as if he said,—Sleep on now if ye can, and if that be possible, in such perilous circumstances. But (3) many prefer taking them as a permission slightly tempered with reproof, viz.,—Sleep for the interval that remains. I can now calmly watch and wait alone; the season of needful sympathy is past. He thus implies, moreover, according to Chrysostom, that he has no need of their help, and that he must by all means be betrayed. We may suppose that between this and the following verse some interval of time elapsed, and that then Judas and the band approached when Jesus roused the disciples with the words, "Rise, let us be going." The whole is thus, no doubt, perfectly consistent and clearly intelligible. Intermediately, however, occurs another difficult expression, ἀπέχει, which in the active voice refers sometimes to local distance, and sometimes signifies to have back, or get again, or receive in full, and so to be satisfied. According to the first signification, the word is here rendered by some personally and with reference to Judas—(*a*) *he is far off*, or (*b*) in relation to the crisis of the agony—*it is past*; while (*c*) the great majority of interpreters, in accordance with the second meaning of the word, translate it impersonally—*it is sufficient*, or enough. Thus understood, if taken in close connection with what precedes, the sense is,—Sleep on now and take your rest: it is enough; your *watching* is no longer required; but, if connected with what succeeds, it signifies,—It is enough: you have had sufficient *sleep*; the hour is come. By combining (3) and (c) we get what on the whole is most in agreement with both text and context; that is to say,— Sleep during the rest of the interval that may be allowed you, and take your rest; I require you to watch no longer. Then, after the lapse of a short interval, or even as an after-thought occasioned by the sight or sound of the enemy's approach, he checks himself in the additional words, "The hour is come . . . rise up, let us go."

VI. THE CHIEF OBJECT OF THE AGONY. 1. *Preparation.* One great object of the agony was, as we conceive, preparation for the final, fearful struggle near at hand. The Saviour was to brace himself for the conflict. Hence the difference between the agony and crucifixion was this: The agony was, if we may so say, the prelude, the crucifixion the performance; the one was—with reverence be it spoken—the rehearsal, the other the reality; the one was the anticipation, the other the accomplishment; the one was the *will*, the other the *work*. The language of the one is,—I am willing—I am going to suffer, and so put an end to sin; that of the other is,—I have already and actually suffered, and so put away sin for ever. The grand issue of Gethsemane was preparedness for future and final suffering, and, if put in words, it would be,—I am ready, and in no way reluctant to suffer; while from Calvary proceeds a shout of triumph over suffering endured to the uttermost and attainment of finality as expressed in the words, "It is finished." In the agony we see the sinless human nature of our Lord shuddering in sight of sin, and on the brink of fearful suffering because of sin, though not his own; in the crucifixion we see the same nature sustaining the load of human sin, and succumbing under the consequent suffering and sorrow, yet victorious even when vanquished, and conquering by being slain. The agony was a forecasting of the final struggle; it was going over all beforehand—going over all in mind, in spirit, and in body too; the crucifixion was the successful realization of the same. Once the agony was over, the bitterness of death was to some extent past. 2. *The loneliness of our Lord in his sufferings.* In all this the Saviour was alone—as much alone in the garden as on the cross, in his agony as in his crucifixion. Sleep on now, he said; you have let the opportunity of sympathizing with and sustaining me pass by. Such, at least, is one not unnatural interpretation of the words. Miserable comforters ye have been, yet I blame you not; the spirit was willing, but the flesh was weak. Sleep on now—it matters not; for the struggle is over, and over without your co-operation; of the people there was none with me. I have trodden the winepress alone, from first to last. They had been saddened by the prospect of losing their Lord and Master, by his pathetic discourses, by his touching intercession, and by his present supplication, and in consequence they slept. 3. *Summary.* In summing up the lessons to be learnt from this subject, we are taught (1) the terrible nature and fearful evil of sin. It was the cause of our Lord's agony—of the intense struggle, the overwhelming sorrow, the bloody sweat. The three chief ingredients in that bitter cup were, first, the unspeakable and indescribable load of human guilt; for though guilt in its moral demerit is not transferable, yet in liability to punishment it is. On the Lamb of God was laid the sin of the world, and he took it away; on our great High Priest were laid the iniquities of us all; the pressure of our transgressions rested on his head, as the sins of Israel on the head of the scapegoat. But another element entering into the cause of his agony was the temptation of Satan. The hour of darkness had come, the powers of darkness were doing their worst, the hosts of darkness rushed to the conflict. What fiendish power they exerted, what fiery trial they occasioned, what foul temptations they suggested, what fearful struggle they engaged in, we cannot even conjecture. A third element, and the worst of all probably, was the hiding of his heavenly Father's face; it commenced in the agony, continued during the crucifixion, and culminated in those words of awful import, " My God, my God, why hast thou forsaken me ? " But (2) the next great lesson is connected with prayer. And here we find several important particulars suggested by the prayer of our Lord in his agony—the matter of prayer, the manner of it, the posture in it, the spirit of it, the intensity of it, and the success of it. From the *matter* of the Saviour's prayer we learn the allowableness of supplicating relief from circumstances of distress or disaster, as far as is consistent with God's will and expedient for us. The *manner* sanctions not vain repetition, but only such repetition as great earnestness frequently employs. The *posture* was kneeling, then prostration even on the cold and clammy ground. The *spirit* was that of perfect submission to the Divine will, with devout and holy resignation to his Father in heaven : " If it be possible, let this cup pass from me." The *intensity* included increasing earnestness; it was the outpouring of the heart with continued importunity and augmented fervour. The *success* consisted not in the removal of the cup but of the fear, and in communicated strength and encouragement fortifying for the coming ordeal. Again, (3) there is an affecting contrast. While all within was storm, all without was calm. Nature all around was tranquil; the moon was shedding her mild radiance over the top of Olivet, the Garden of Gethsemane, and the valley of the Kidron ; no wind was blowing, no leaf was stirring, and no ripple moving. All was hushed in silent awe and wrapt in profound astonishment at the bloody baptism with which Jesus was baptized that night.—J. J. G.

Vers. 53—72. Parallel passages: Matt. xxvi. 57—75; Luke xxii. 54—62; John xviii. 13—27.—*The denial by Peter.* I. THE CAUSES THAT LED TO PETER'S SIN. 1. *The first cause of Peter's sin.* The first cause, as we may infer from this very chapter, was *self-confidence.* Our Lord foretold the smiting of the Shepherd, as predicted long before in ancient prophecy—of himself the good Shepherd, appropriating the title; and along with the smiting of the Shepherd, he foretold, as a consequence, the scattering of the sheep. Peter, yielding to the impulses of his own ardent and impetuous nature, repudiated the notion of desertion thus implied. He did so in a manner that involved an invidious comparison of himself with others, and an overweening opinion of his own strength of will and purpose of fidelity. " Although " (καὶ εἰ, equivalent to " even if," viz. a supposed case not likely to exist; εἰ καὶ read by Tregelles, equivalent to "although," viz. a case really existing) " all shall be offended, yet will not I," were his somewhat boastful or egotistical words. The smiting of the Shepherd may be a stumbling-block to others—to all of them, but not to me; the others may fall over it, yet will not I ;

the rest may act the cowardly, unmanly part indicated, breaking and scattering like feeble sheep soon as the wolf is seen to approach, but not I. I will prove myself the rock-man, and stand my ground in face of all danger, and in spite of all enemies. Thus Peter exalted himself at the expense of others; he also presumed too much on his own strength, and took too much credit for his own courage. Peter possessed physical courage, we have good reason to believe, but he lacked moral courage; nor do these two qualities always go hand in hand. There may be great physical courage with but little moral courage, and much moral courage where physical courage is defective. Peter was courageous enough—or rash enough, some might be disposed to say—to cut off the ear of a manservant of the high priest; but he was cowardly enough to quail before the glance of one of the maids of the high priest. He had physical courage enough to do the deed of violence, but not moral courage enough to tell the truth to an inquisitive, intermeddling, though perhaps light-hearted, thoughtless girl. If we *contrast* the conduct and character of two comrade apostles, John and Peter, we shall find a confirmation of our view. As compared with Peter, John had less physical courage, for on a subsequent occasion, as we read, " Peter therefore went forth, and that other disciple, and came to the sepulchre. So they ran both together: and the other disciple did outrun Peter, and came first to the sepulchre. . . . Yet went he not in. Then cometh Simon Peter following him, and went into the sepulchre." This is a very interesting and instructive statement. They both ran, in their eagerness and expectancy, to the rifled sepulchre; but John, being the younger and therefore swifter man, outran Peter, and reached the sepulchre before him. But there he paused; he had not the physical courage to enter that gloomy abode; a sudden awe arrested him. At length Peter came up, and as soon as he arrived at the place, without fear, or dread, or hesitancy, without stop, or stay, or a moment's pause, he dashed in. "Then went in also that other disciple which came first to the sepulchre." On this occasion Peter proved himself the physically bold, courageous man; while John, though younger and stronger probably, was the physically timid and hesitating. The scene shifts to the palace of the high priest; and these two apostolic men change places. John is now the bold, courageous man—morally so, for he "went in with Jesus into the palace of the high priest; but Peter stood at the door without." John was known to the high priest, and known to him as a disciple of Jesus, and yet he went boldly into the palace, neither ashamed nor afraid to acknowledge his discipleship. Not only so, he spoke to the portress, and got Peter admitted. But now came Peter's turn and time of weakness. Though John, a man of much less physical courage, had gone in boldly, and then gained admission for his companion, yet Peter, with far less moral courage, is frightened into sinful denial of his discipleship in the first instance by the brusque boldness of a somewhat pert maid. And yet, notwithstanding all this, a certain cause, or at least somewhat of an excuse, may be found for Peter's moral cowardice, as compared with the moral courage of John at this juncture. Peter was conscious of a crime with which John had no complicity or connection—a crime that might shape itself into a constructive charge of an attempt at rescue. He had cut off the ear of Malchus, and so he may have dreaded the consequence of that act, or the more serious charge of interfering with the officers in [the discharge of their appointed duty, in order to prevent the capture of his Master. These considerations may have increased the apprehensions of Peter, and added to the supposed danger of his position. The fact of discipleship of itself did not involve peril of any kind, and so John breathed more freely and moved about at large in the palace of the high priest without dread of danger. 2. *A second cause leading to Peter's sin.* A second cause leading to Peter's sin was *unwatchfulness* and neglect of prayer. When our Lord, in the Garden of Gethsemane, found the three disciples sleeping, he addressed himself specially to Peter, with the words, " Simon, sleepest thou? couldest not thou watch one hour?" and then he spake words of warning to all: " Watch ye and pray, lest ye enter into temptation." A curious incident, in a certain respect the converse of this, though generally overlooked, deserves well, we think, to be noticed in this connection. In the warning just referred to, our Lord passed from the particular to the general, from the singular to the plural—from Simon to the associated apostles. In the warning recorded by St. Luke (xxii. 31, 32), and which introduces the passage of that Gospel parallel to ch. xiv. 37, 38, of the Gospel before us, our Lord passes in reverse order from the plural to the singular—from the whole of the apostles to Peter; thus: "The Lord said, Simon, Simon, behold, Satan asked [or 'demanded'] to have *you*, that he might sift you as wheat : but I made supplication for *thee*, that thy faith fail not," where it is remarkable that Satan's demand comprehended all the apostles—the rest as well as Peter, as seems clearly implied in the plural ὑμᾶς, while our Lord's supplication embraced him in particular, as must be inferred from the singular σοῦ.   Just as Satan had demanded all the apostles, including Peter, so our Lord prayed for all the apostles, but for Peter in particular.   It was not without reason that our Lord thus individualized in his supplication for Peter, for he it was that stood in greatest peril.   The most confident of them all was the most imperilled of them all.   Some, like Judas, were soon to be blown away, or had already been blown away, as chaff, and had been separated from the good grain; but the word "wheat" applied to the remainder had in it both comfort and encouragement, while the Saviour's great intercessory prayer was a guarantee of safety.   The fact, moreover, that he prayed for Peter specially and individually, affords strong consolation to all the children of God in every age and clime.   Not one of all is forgotten by him who ever lives to intercede ; not one of all is forsaken by the all-prevailing Intercessor.   No doubt some may be disposed to object, and say that after all, and notwithstanding all, Peter fell.   How is this reconcilable with the prevalence of the Saviour's prayer?   He fell, but he rose again; he fell, and fell far, but did not fall away; he fell sadly for a time, but he did not fall finally and for ever. And this is the very thing implied in the form of the word rendered "fail;" for it is not the simple verb, but ἐκλείπῃ, or, according to the critical editors, ἐκλίπῃ, which signifies to fail *out and out, utterly*, or *finally*.   Thus this utter and final failure was exactly the thing prevented by the Saviour's intercession.   But, reverting to Peter's want of watchfulness, we can find no hint nor indication of any kind in all this chapter, or in the parallel sections of the other Gospels, that would lead us to believe that Peter paid proper, or indeed any, attention to the warning of our Lord. We search in vain for proof that he watched against going into the place of tempta- tion, or that he watched against the company where he might expect to be assailed with temptation.   There is no evidence whatever that he either watched against the approach of temptation, or that he prayed for grace to resist the tempter or strength to overcome his temptations.   He seems, in fact, to have had no idea whatever of the danger that was drawing near him so stealthily and so suddenly, and no suspicion of the snares which Satan was so subtly drawing round him; neither does he seem to have used the means which his Master had urged on him as necessary for safety and defence.   He appears to have let the warning entirely slip, or for a time to have let it sink into oblivion.   Accordingly, we find that, when years afterwards he called to mind his fearful neglect and its well-nigh fatal consequences, he addresses to others a most solemn warning, in words that echo his own mistakes, and the means he should have taken to avoid it; for in his First Epistle (v. 8) he writes, "Be sober, be watchful: your adversary the devil, as a roaring lion, walketh about, seeking whom he may devour." 3. *A third cause of Peter's sin.*   A third cause of Peter's sin was his following Christ *afar off*.   This, of course, refers literally to the fact that Peter followed our Lord at a distance, keeping considerably aloof.   He followed him, but at a long interval between ; he followed him, but not close or near at hand.   Instead of walking side by side, or close behind him, he kept away and afar off.   It was, doubtless, the fear of man that kept Peter at this distance; it was the fear of man that thus unnerved him; it was the fear of man that prevented him coming immediately after his Master, as he should have done.   He wished to be near his Master, but his heart failed him.   He wished, we are sure, to be with his Master, but he lacked moral courage to share the reproach of Jesus of Galilee.   It was not the personal risk so much as the ridicule he shrank from.   This physical distance was a sign of moral distance, and a symbol of the condition of others as well as Peter, when they follow Christ afar off.   Peter's duty was to have been at his Lord's side, or close behind him, or in some way near at hand. So with ourselves.   Instead of following Christ afar off, we are bound by privilege as well as duty to follow him closely; instead of following him afar off, we must follow him faithfully; instead of following him fitfully, we are to follow him fully ; instead of following him sneakingly, we are to follow him fearlessly; instead of following him by constraint, we are to follow him freely and of a ready mind; instead of following him for a short space of time, we are to follow him all our life, and so always. From Peter's disastrous fall and foul denial of his Master, we learn the important lesson of following Christ freely, fully, fearlessly, faithfully, and for ever. Distance from Christ is real danger, nearness to him is true safety. Distance from the Sun of Righteousness is coldness, darkness, and spiritual death; nearness to him is love, light, and life. In Canticles the question is asked, " Who is this that cometh up from the wilderness, leaning upon her Beloved?" If this refer to the Church, as we are of opinion it does, it is a picture of her true attitude. The world is the wilderness through which the Christian is passing, and from which he is ascending to a better and promised land; while it is on the arm of Christ that he leans. Thus leaning on Christ, looking to Christ, and living by the faith of Christ, we journey safely from the wilderness of earth to the promised land of heaven. Away from his presence, away from his power, we are every moment in greatest peril; away from the range of his protection and the guidance of his providence, we expose ourselves to the temptations of the evil one, and speedily become his easy prey. 4. *The fourth cause of Peter's sin.* The fourth cause of Peter's sin was bad company. " He sat," we read, " with the servants " of the high priest, " and warmed himself at the fire." What was this but going into the company of his Master's enemies? This was mixing, and without necessity, with the enemies of the Saviour. He thus went with his eyes open into the place of peril, among the attendants of the high priest and the adversaries of his Lord and Master. Here there is every reason to believe he would hear little good of any kind spoken; while he would be sure to hear his Master's name vilified, his character slandered, and his cause reproached. In all this contempt and reproach there is too much cause to believe Peter must for the time have concurred. Possibly he not only agreed with them, but acted as they did, the better to conceal his real connection with Christ. It is shocking even for a moment to suppose that Peter was so weak and so wicked, during the short space he consorted with such company, as to join them in reviling his Master. Suspecting him, as they did, of being Christ's disciple, and finding him thus readily uniting with them in heaping scorn upon his Master, what must they have thought of that Master? What estimate could they form of either disciple or Teacher? Must they not have concluded that Christ's discipleship was neither happy nor honourable? Must they not have inferred, and inferred with reason, that the disciple of such a Master was knave, or fool, or villain? When, on the other hand, we consider what Peter should have done and what he might have done at the time of his Master's difficulty and danger, we almost blush for the name of disciple so degraded and disgraced! Had he been true to his confession of the Christ, had he been staunch in his adherence to his Master, he would either have kept out of the company which he knew consisted of his Master's bitter enemies, or, if he found it necessary to stand by or sit among them, he would have defended him at whatever risk.

II. THE AGGRAVATIONS OF PETER'S SIN. 1. *Ingratitude.* Peter had been on the most familiar terms with his Master, and had been highly favoured by him. Of the chosen, he was one of the choicest; of the elected, he was one of the *élite*. With James and John he shared the Saviour's closest intimacy. Like them, he was with him on the Mount of Transfiguration, and was privileged to witness that wondrous scene and see that glorious sight. Like them, he was admitted to the solemnities of the death-chamber, and was present at the restoration to life of the daughter of Jairus. Like them, he had been invited to accompany his Lord in the Garden of Gethsemane, and to watch with him during the agony and bloody sweat. Still more, our Lord had commended his good confession of the Christ the Son of God, and traced it to heavenly revelation; he had bestowed on him the honourable surname of "Rock-man," in acknowledgment of his firmness and the foundation he should help to lay; besides, he had promised him a high position and also distinguished privileges in his kingdom. Peter had walked to him on the water, and been kept from sinking by his Master's hand. Yet now, for all these special marks of friendship and favour that had been lavished on him, he shows himself utterly and basely ungrateful. He turned his back on his best and kindest Friend, denying all knowledge of him. Now, when a return of friendship was most needed, he not only failed to act the part of a friend in need, and reciprocate the kindness he had received, but actually consorted with his bitterest enemies. 2. *False-*

hood. When our Lord stood in most need of sympathy, Peter, as we have seen, stood aloof or ranged himself on the side of his enemies. When he might have given valuable testimony in favour of his Master, silence sealed his lips, and he refused to acknowledge him. Nor was this all; he falsified to the most fearful extent and in the foulest manner. He denied all or any knowledge of Jesus ; he repeated the denial in the most positive way; he backed his repeated falsehood with an oath. When challenged the third time, he "began to curse and swear, saying, I know not the man." Surely one falsehood of the kind indicated would have been bad enough and wicked enough, but its repetition once, again, a third time, greatly aggravated the sin and augmented Peter's guilt. The violence of language which was prompted by, and which gave expression to, his virulence of feeling is difficult to account for. There was fear of detection and imagined danger, but there must have been rage as well, to explain his violent and passionate language. Several of the bystanders recognize him; a kinsman of Malchus is there who had seen him in the garden; his Galilean dialect bewrays him; accusations crowd upon him; proofs multiply against him. Peter gets irritated, and completely loses his temper and self-control. At the supposed discrepancy, or at least difficulty, in Peter's denial of his Master we can only glance. The *place* of the first denial was by the fire in the high priest's hall, or quadrangular court under the open air (αὐλή), while that of the third is not specified. The place of the second was in the προαύλιον according to St. Mark, and the πυλῶνα according to St. Matthew; while St. John tells us that he was standing and warming himself. Now, the fire was in the open court (αὐλή), the passage from this to the street was προαύλιον, and the portal or entrance door of this passage was πυλών. He had removed to a short distance from the fire, but not so far as to lose the influence of its heat or warmth. With respect to the *persons*, the first question that called forth his denial was put by the portress. On the occasion of the second denial the same maid addressed the bystanders, who echoed her words, so that several persons (male ἕτερος) and (female ἄλλη) another maid different from the portress—all (εἶπον, plural) assailed Peter with their inconvenient and unwelcome questions. In replying to or repelling these, Peter kept denying (ἠρνεῖτο, imperfect). At the third denial more of the bystanders (οἱ ἑστῶτες of St. Matthew, and οἱ παρεστῶτες of St. Mark), with some other different person (ἄλλος τις of St. Luke) as ringleader, drew attention to his being a Galilean; while the relative of Malchus confirmed this by alleging that he had seen him in the garden. There is thus neither real difficulty nor discrepancy of any kind. 3. *Profanity and perjury.* By this time Peter is excited and enraged. Goaded to madness, he breaks out into language of shocking profaneness. The falsehood already repeated he backs by an imprecation. He also swears the lie, invoking the name of Jehovah and calling the omniscient One to witness his reiterated untruth, and thus lays foul perjury on his soul. He began, we read, to anathematize, that is to say, he used a formula of imprecation such as "God do so to me and more also," thus cursing himself if what he said was untrue ; but, besides this, he employed the customary formula of an oath, invoking God as witness of his words, false as he knew them to be. Naturally impetuous and passionate, and in youth, or before his discipleship, perhaps addicted to profane swearing, he relapsed into his old sin in order to corroborate his statements and to force credence on the incredulous. One sin leads to another ; one lie especially needs another to support it. The bystanders must have known little of Jesus' character and teaching, or Peter's profanity of itself would have convinced them that he knew not that Teacher—nothing, at least, of his spirit and doctrine. Could it be possible that Peter, in the madness of his rage and fear, meant by his profanity to leave this impression on his questioners, and that there was thus a method in his madness? At all events, he spoke as one who was a stranger to the fear of God and the ordinary dictates of religion, not to speak of discipleship to a Teacher who said, "Swear not at all . . . but let your communication be, Yea, yea; Nay, nay." 4. *Other aggravating circumstances.* There were several other circumstances of aggravation which we can only indicate, and may not dwell on, among them the following :—The faithful and frequent warnings he had received, and had received so recently ; his own vehement protestations of loyalty and fidelity to his Master—that if all others should be offended he would not, that if he should die with him he would not deny him in any wise. There were also other considerations connected with the denial that greatly added to the sin : there were the circumstances and time—

our Lord being now deserted, delivered into the hands of cruel enemies, and dragged before inexorable judges; there were the persons to whom the denial was addressed, namely, servants and other humble officials, with little influence and less power, not magistrates or functionaries invested with authority; there were the flagrant breaches of Peter's own positive and repeated promises. All are forgotten or falsified! Alas, what is man! At the strongest but weakness, and at the best but imperfection!

III. PETER'S REPENTANCE. 1. *Extenuating circumstances.* We may just notice, very briefly, in connection with Peter's repentance, certain extenuations of his sin. His sin, largely the outcome of his own impulsive nature, came on him with the suddenness and strength of an unexpected impulse. There had been no premeditation, no *deliberate plan*, and no deceitful design, as in the case of Judas. His plans and purposes had all been of the very opposite character; his determination and resolutions had all tended in the very contrary direction. He did *not remain* in his sin, *nor* ever afterwards *repeat* it. The sin was exceeding great and the guilt enormous, but it would have been still more so had he continued it, or persevered in it, or subsequently returned to it. Satan took him by surprise, as though asleep or off his guard; but once roused from the lethargy into which he had fallen, or brought back to the post which he had abandoned, he never again wandered from the path of duty or sank in sin. 2. *How he was recalled to duty.* Two circumstances were the means externally, or the occasions of reminding Peter of his sin and recalling him to duty. But, while all the evangelists record Peter's sin, St. Mark alone records the second crowing of the cock, which was one of the two circumstances referred to; and St. Luke alone records our Lord's look at Peter, saying, "And the Lord turned, and looked upon Peter." The first crowing of the cock had passed unheeded. St. Mark, who gives us such an exact transcript of Peter's fall and feelings, probably from Peter's own lips, informs us that it was not till the second or regular morning cockcrow that Peter was brought to the recollection of his Lord's warning and his own sin. It was then he awoke as from a troubled dream or terrible nightmare; while much about the same time our Lord, either from the open front of the chamber in which the trial had been proceeding, or as he passed across the courtyard from the apartments of Annas to the palace of Caiaphas, turned towards Peter and looked him into repentance. 3. *His repentance.* The same evidence of repentance is found in the words, "He went out, and wept bitterly" (ἔκλαιε, he continued weeping aloud; not ἐδάκρυε, he shed tears). The participle (ἐπιβαλὼν) attached to this verb is variously rendered. The most usual and probable meaning assigned to it is that of our version, "When he thought thereon," that is, cast (his mind) on it. Some explain it, "He began to weep," as in the margin of the Revised Version, as well as of the Authorized Version; others, "He flung his mantle over his head;" others, again, "He flung himself forth [*i.e.* on the ground] and wept." Further, it is understood by others in the sense of *abundantly*, that is, "He wept abundantly," also in the margin of Authorized Version; while a more interesting explanation, if well founded, is, "He cast his eyes on him and wept," as if Peter reciprocated his Lord's look, and consequent compunction of soul vented itself, not in a transient outburst, but in a long-continued, copious flood of tears. Thus, while the Evangelist Luke records the look of Christ on Peter, the Evangelist Mark, if this rendering be at all tenable, records the corresponding look of Peter on Christ; so that, when eye met eye, Peter was overpowered by strong emotion, and gave way to his deep grief by bitter (πικρῶς, St. Matthew and St. Luke) weeping. 4. *Real repentance distinguished from remorse.* It is very important to distinguish true repentance from mere regret or remorse; while a contrast of the case of Judas with that of Peter will materially help us to see and clearly comprehend the difference. Certain elements are common to both, and these we must eliminate before we can rightly distinguish them. On the part of Judas there was sorrow of the intensest kind—remorse of the most distressing nature; there was the fullest and most ingenuously candid confession; there was also the strongest possible desire to make any and all the reparation that was possible. All these elements are found in true repentance; but as they are found also in the remorse of Judas, they are common alike to genuine repentance and mere remorse. The first material point of difference is that the sorrow of the true penitent is caused by the sight of sin in *itself*, apart altogether from its consequences; the sorrow of remorse is occasioned chiefly, if not entirely, by those *consequences*. Judas did not foresee the terrible consequences of his sin; he little dreamt, perhaps, that it would lead to Jesus being evil entreated, condemned, and crucified.   When he pocketed the reward of iniquity, he felt satisfied with the bargain and sure that the Master would find some way of escape.   Had this been the case; had no ill consequences resulted from his treachery; had nothing beyond the arrest of Jesus taken place, and no worse results followed;—Judas, there is reason to believe, would have felt neither sorrow nor shame at what he had done; nay, he would have had a feeling of satisfaction rather than a sense of sin.   He would scarcely have shrunk from the society of the apostles; he would have been able to find some pretext or frame some excuse for all that had happened.   But the consequences of his treachery— the terrible consequences—made all the difference.   Greedy as Judas was, and mean as he was, and treacherous as he was, he was by no means a cruel man or a man of blood. When, however, contrary to his expectation, the most appalling consequences were certain to ensue; when a judicial murder and a cruel death awaited the Master whom he had betrayed; then Judas for the first time saw his sin in its consequences, and was overwhelmed with the sight.   It was quite different with Peter.   His sin, heinous as it was, did not produce any such fearful effects as the sin of Judas.   His denial of his Master did not lead to his apprehension; it had nothing to do with his condemnation; it did not cause his death.   Peter saw it not in any such consequences, but in its own baseness and sinfulness.   He saw the iniquity of his sin as committed against his loving Lord, as a sin against truth and righteousness, as a sin against goodness and justice, as a sin by which he wronged conscience and hurt his own soul.   The sight filled his heart with sorrow and shame, while his eyes brimmed over again and again with salt and bitter tears.   The next point of difference is that the true penitent seeks *mercy*, but the subject of remorse sinks in despair.   Of this also we have a striking illustration in Judas and Peter respectively.   The former confessed his guilt, acknowledged the innocence of his Master and the injury he had done him; not only so, in self-abhorrence and loathing he flung back the price of blood.   But all this sorrow and remorse fell short of repentance; true penitence was as far off as ever.   He had no heart to pray; no heart to seek God's face and favour free; no heart to sue for mercy.   His heart was hardened, not softened, by sin; the blackness of despair enveloped him; blank ruin stared him in the face.   Not so Peter: he sorrowed, but after a godly sort; instead of giving himself up to despair, he sought mercy.   He was humbled, not hardened; the tears he shed washed his eyes, and his spiritual vision became clearer; he saw the blackness of his sin, but he saw also the benignity of the Saviour.   That look of his Master had pierced his heart with a feeling of his guilt, but brought withal a sense of Divine grace; he was fully alive to the misery of sin, as also to the mercy of the Saviour. After the terrible storm which had swept across the horizon of his soul, the rainbow of hope remained upon the cloud, reflecting the sunshine of heaven on the tears of sorrow shed by the penitent.   He saw his iniquity to be very great, yet he sued for pardon. He looked not away from, but to, the Saviour whose heart his sin had pierced, and mourned in bitterness.

   IV. PRACTICAL LESSONS.   1. *A picture.*   Our Lord and his apostles are often seen grouped together in a picture; the Gospels exhibit a moral picture of the group.   In this picture there is much dark shading; but this dark shading helps to bring out more clearly the bright and brilliant colours of the picture and to enhance its beauty.   If there were no dark shading in it, it would represent angelic life in heaven rather than human life on earth; in that case, the very perfection of the figures would diminish its fitness for our warning or comfort.   2. *Good educed from evil.*   Peter, when restored (ἐπιστρέψας), was better fitted to help others.   His own weakness became by grace a source of strength to others.   When he had turned again, and been restored (as those referred to in ἐπεστράφητε, 1 Pet. ii. 25) to the Shepherd and Bishop of souls, he was better able from his own experience to keep other sheep from straying, or restore them from their wanderings.   3. *A lesson never forgotten.*   The circumstances connected with Peter's sin were so engraven on the tablet of his memory as never to be forgotten, as is evident from several passages of his Epistles and his speech as recorded in Acts.   When he would warn men against one of those mistakes which caused his sin, he says (1 Pet. v. 8), "Be vigilant," or "*watchful*" (Revised Version).   When he charged the Jews with the foulest crime, he expresses that charge in words that echo his own dark deed : "**Ye** *denied* the Holy One and the Just;" "Ye denied him in the presence of

Pilate," as we read in Peter's speech (Acts iii. 13, 14). When he pictured the highest state of spiritual prosperity, he describes it as freedom from *falling* : "If ye do these things, ye shall never fall" (2 Pet. i. 10). His most solemn warning is, "Beware lest ye also . . . fall from your own steadfastness" (2 Pet. iii. 17). The change that was effected in Peter after the descent of the Holy Spirit is wonderful, for in the early part of Acts we find him possessed of moral courage equal to his natural physical courage, and on all occasions acting a bold, manly, and courageous as well as prominent part. Whatever grace we need, we are thus encouraged to seek the Spirit to supply.

V. THE OMITTED PORTIONS OF THIS CHAPTER. 1. For section vers. 51, 52, peculiar to St. Mark, see Introduction. 2. For section vers. 55–65, containing the account in part of the Jewish trial, see beginning of next chapter, where that trial is concluded.—J. J. G.

EXPOSITION.

CHAPTER XV.

Ver. 1.—**And straightway in the morning the chief priests with the elders and scribes, and the whole council, held a consultation, and bound Jesus, and carried him away, and delivered him up to Pilate.** *Straightway in the morning* (εὐθέως πρωί). The proceedings recorded in the last chapter terminated probably between five and six ; the cock-crowing helps to fix the time. Now came the more formal trial. The whole Sanhedrim united in consultation. All the proceedings hitherto had been irregular and illegal. Now, for form's sake, they tried him afresh. But there was another law which was also violated. It was now Friday. In capital cases, sentence of condemnation might not legally be pronounced on the day of the trial. Yet our Lord was tried, condemned, and crucified on the same day. They " bound him," that he might be impeded in any attempt to escape. They " carried him away " (ἀπήνεγκαν), with the semblance of force ; although we know that he went "as a lamb to the slaughter." How truly might it be said of these chief priests and elders, " Their feet are swift to shed blood !" *And delivered him up to Pilate.* Judæa now was added to the province of Syria, and governed by procurators, of whom Pontius Pilate was the fifth. It was necessary for the Jews to deliver Christ over to the Roman power ; because the power of life and death had been taken from them since they became subject to the Romans. " It is not lawful for us," they say (John xviii. 31) " to put any man to death ; " that is to say, they could not put to death without the authority of the governor. Our Lord predicted of himself, " They shall deliver him to the Gentiles."

Ver. 2.—**Art thou the King of the Jews ?** It appears from St. Luke (xxiii. 1—5) that when Pilate demanded particularly what the charges against Jesus were, on account of which the Jews urged that he should be crucified, they alleged these three things :

(1) that he perverted the nation ; (2) that he forbade to give tribute to Cæsar ; (3) that he said that he was Christ, a King. Whereupon Pilate, who had heard by many of the blameless life, the pure doctrine, and the famous miracles of Jesus, goes at once to the point, and asks him, " Art thou the King of the Jews ? "—a question which, of course, affected the position of Cæsar. Our Lord's answer, **Thou sayest** (σὺ λέγεις), was in the affirmative, amounting to this— " Thou sayest that which is true."

Ver. 3.—**And the chief priests accused him of many things.** The words in the Authorized Version, " but he answered nothing," are not to be found here in any of the best manuscripts or versions. But they are to be found in St. Matthew (xxvii. 12) ; and Pilate's question in the next verse confirms St. Matthew's statement, and makes the sentence unnecessary here. Our Lord answered nothing, because all that they had to say against him was manifestly false or frivolous, and unworthy of any reply. St. Augustine says on this, " The Saviour, who is the Wisdom of God, knew how to overcome by keeping silence."

Ver. 4.—It would seem that Pilate had led Jesus out of his palace, into which the Jewish priests could not enter (John xviii. 28), lest they should be defiled by entering a house from which all leaven had not been scrupulously removed. This would have been a violation of their religious scruples ; and therefore he went out into the open court, and there heard the accusations of the chief priests. It is supposed that the building occupied by Pilate was the palace built or rebuilt by Herod near the gate of Jaffa, north-west of Mount Zion. It was doubtless occasionally occupied by Pilate, and it was conveniently situated, being near to Herod's palace—the old palace of the Asmoneans, between it and the temple.

Ver. 5.—**Pilate marvelled.** He marvelled that the innocent Saviour, wise and eloquent, standing before him in peril of his life, should remain silent when thus vehemently accused by the leading men of the Jews. Pilate marvelled at his forbearance, his calmness, his contempt of death; from all of which he argued his absolute innocence and holiness, and resolved to do everything in his power to deliver him. The silence of a blameless life pleads more powerfully than any defence, however elaborate.

Ver. 6.—St. Mark omits here what took place next in the order of events, namely, the sending of our Lord by Pilate to Herod (Luke xxiii. 5). This was Herod Antipas, ruler of Galilee; and Pilate, apparently convinced of our Lord's innocence, hoped to escape the responsibility of condemning an innocent man, by handing him over to Herod; for Pilate had heard that our Lord was a Galilean. Moreover, he hoped to accomplish another good result, namely, to recover the favour of Herod, which was desirable on political grounds. The first intention failed; for Herod sent our Lord back to Pilate in mockery, "arraying him in gorgeous apparel" (περιβαλὼν ἐσθῆτα λαμπρὰν). But the second succeeded: "Herod and Pilate became friends with each other that very day" (Luke xxiii. 12). There was now, however, another resource. At the feast (κατα ἑορτὴν)—literally, at feast-time—he used to release unto them one prisoner, whom they asked of him (ὄνπερ ἠτοῦντο). In St. John (xviii. 39) we read that Pilate said, "Ye have a custom, that I should release unto you one at the Passover."

Ver. 7.—And there was one called Barabbas, lying bound with them that had made insurrection, men who in the insurrection had committed murder. Pilate appears to have thought of Barabbas, not doubting but that, by limiting their choice between him and Jesus, he would secure the liberation of our Lord. But Pilate little knew the temper of the chief priests and scribes, and their bitter hostility to Christ. The word "Barabbas," better written "Bar-Abbas," means "son of father."

Ver. 8.—And the multitude went up and began to ask him to do as he was wont to do unto them. Went up (ἀναβὰs). This is the reading to be preferred to the old reading, "crying aloud" (ἀναβοήσας). The reading ἀναβὰs is supported by the Sinaitic, the Vatican, and the Cambridge manuscripts; also by the Old Italic, the Gothic, and other versions. The Æthiopic Version combines the two, "going up and crying aloud." The geographical position of Pilate's residence quite justifies the use of the term ἀναβὰs.

Ver. 9.—Pilate doubtless hoped that they would ask for Jesus. He knew that the chief priests had delivered our Lord for envy. That he could not help observing, as a shrewd Roman judge, from their gestures and manner. And then he knew also, at least by report, of the purity of Jesus, and of the holy freedom with which he rebuked their vices. So he thought, reasonably enough, that if the chief priests wished to destroy him for envy, the people, who had experienced so many kindnesses from him, would desire that he should live.

Ver. 10.—Envy was the low passion that influenced the chief priests. They saw that Jesus was gaining a great and increasing influence over the people by the sublime beauty of his character, by the fame of his miracles, and the constraining power of his words. And hence they concluded that, unless he was arrested in his course, and put out of the way, their own influence would soon be gone. The whole world was going after him. Therefore he must be destroyed.

Ver. 11.—But the chief priests stirred up the multitude (ἀνέσεισαν τὸν ὄχλον), that he should rather release Barabbas unto them. St. Matthew (xxvii. 20) says, "They persuaded the multitudes" (ἔπεισαν τοὺς ὄχλους). St. Mark's word (ἀνέσεισαν) implies a rousing of their bad passions; agitating them to a blind zeal for his crucifixion.

Ver. 12.—And Pilate again answered and said unto them, What then shall I do unto him whom ye call the King of the Jews? The word "again" has the support of three great uncials, and the best of the cursives. Pilate did not give way without many an inward struggle. And now at last he puts the matter, so to speak, in their own power; so that it might be an act of their clemency, and that they might have the honour of saving our Lord's life. But it was all in vain. For the chief priests had resolved to press for his crucifixion, little dreaming that they were doing what "God's hand and God's counsel had before determined to be done." Pilate puts the question before them with much shrewdness and tact. He speaks of our Lord as one whom "they called the King of the Jews." He appeals to their national pride and their national hopes. Would they degrade themselves, and extinguish their hopes, by giving up to the most ignominious of deaths one who had established such claims upon their reverence and their love?

Ver. 13.—And they cried out again, Crucify him. These words might seem at first to justify the old reading in ver. 8, adopted in the Authorized Version, "crying aloud." But there the word was ἀναβοήσας, here it is ἔκραξαν. Moreover, in ver. 14, it is not (περισσοτέρως) "the more exceedingly," but (περισσῶς) "they cried exceedingly."

Ver. 15.—**And Pilate, wishing** (βουλόμενος) **to content the multitude, released unto them Barabbas, and delivered Jesus, when he had scourged him, to be crucified.** St. Luke and St. John are more full in details here. From their narratives it appears that when Pilate found that his attempt to rescue our Lord, by putting Barabbas in contrast with him, had failed, he next hoped to move the multitude to pity by the terrible punishment of scourging, after which he trusted that they would relent. Scourging was a vile punishment, inflicted on slaves. But it was also inflicted upon those who were condemned to death, even though freemen. This scourging, which was a part of the punishment of crucifixion, was of frightful severity. Horace ('Sat.' i. 3, 119) speaks of it as "horribile flagellum." But it appears from St. John (xix. 1) that the scourging of Jesus took place before his formal condemnation to be crucified; we may therefore suppose that it was not a part of the ordinary punishment of crucifixion. At all events, there is nothing, upon a careful comparison of the narratives, to lead us to the conclusion that our blessed Lord was scourged twice. In fact, Pilate anticipated the time of the scourging, in the vain hope that he might by this means save our Lord from the capital punishment. A comparison of the narratives of St. Matthew and St. Mark with that of St. John will make this clear; for they all three refer to one and the same scourging. Recent investigations at Jerusalem have disclosed what may probably have been the place of the punishment. In a subterranean chamber, discovered by Captain Warren, on what Mr. Fergusson holds to be the site of Antonia, Pilate's prætorium, stands a truncated column, no part of the structure itself, but just such a dwarf pillar as criminals would be tied to to be scourged. The chamber cannot be later than the time of Herod (see Professor Westcott on St. John xix.).

Ver. 16.—**And the soldiers led him away within the court, which is the Prætorium; and they call together the whole band.** This was the principal court of the palace, where a large number of soldiers were always quartered. "The whole band" would be the "cohors prætoria" of Cicero; Pilate's body-guard.

Vers. 17, 18.—**And they clothe him with purple, and plaiting a crown of thorns, they put it on him; and they began to salute him, Hail, King of the Jews!** *They clothe him with purple* (ἐνδύουσιν αὐτὸν πορφύραν). So also says St. John (xix. 2, ἱμάτιον πορφυροῦν). St. Matthew says (xxvii. 28), "They put on him a scarlet robe (περιέθηκαν αὐτῷ χλαμύδα κοκκίνην)." Purple and scarlet are not such very dissimilar colours. Purple is a royal

colour; and the *chlamys* of St. Matthew was a short military cloak of scarlet, intended to be a kind of royal livery. St. Cyril says that the purple cloak symbolized the kingdom of the whole world, which Christ was about to receive, and which he was to obtain by the shedding of his most precious blood. It was designed in mockery of his claim to be a King, and it probably had a reference to his supposed insurrection against Cæsar. All this was permitted by Pilate, in order that he might the more easily, after this ignominious treatment, deliver Christ from the extreme sentence. *And plaiting a crown of thorns, they put it on him.* The crown of thorns was in all probability woven from the *Zizyphus spina Christi* (the *nábk* of the Arabs), which grows abundantly in Palestine, fringing the banks of the Jordan. This plant would be very suitable for the purpose, having flexible branches, with leaves very much resembling the ivy leaf in their colour, and with many sharp thorns. The pain arising from the pressure of these sharp thorns upon the head must have been excruciating. *And they began to salute him, Hail, King of the Jews!* (Χαῖρε, βασιλεῦ τῶν Ἰουδαίων). This word, χαῖρε, was an ancient form of salutation; here used by the soldiers in bitter mockery of his claim to be a king.

Ver. 19.—**And they smote his head with a reed**—the same reed, according to St. Matthew (xxvii. 29, 30), which they had first put into his right hand as a sceptre, to complete the mocking symbolism—**and did spit upon him** (ἐνέπτυον αὐτῷ). The verb is in the imperfect; they did it again and again.

Ver. 20.—**And when they had mocked him, they took off from him the purple, and put on him his garments.** The silence of our blessed Lord during these wanton and aggravated insults is very remarkable, and also the total absence of any legal grounds for his condemnation. **And they lead him out to crucify him.** Assuming the palace of Pilate to have been near the gate of Jaffa, north-west of Mount Zion, and the place of crucifixion that now assigned to it, within the Church of the Holy Sepulchre,—the distance would be about one-third of a mile.

Ver. 21.—**And they compel one passing by, Simon of Cyrene, coming from the country, the father of Alexander and Rufus, to go with them, that he might bear his cross.** It seems from St. Matthew (xxvii. 32) that our Saviour bore his own cross from the palace to the gate of the city. The tablet, with the inscription afterwards attached to the cross, would be carried before him; and a certain number of soldiers would be appointed to go with him to the place of execution, and to see the sentence carried out. Having passed out through the gate of the city, they met one Simon of Cyrene, coming from the country, and they compel him (ἀγγαρεύουσι); literally, *they impress him*. The Cyrenians had a synagogue in Jerusalem (Acts vi. 9), and this Simon may probably have been one of those who had come up to keep the Passover. He must have been a Hellenistic Jew, a native of Cyrene, on the north coast of Africa. Alexander and Rufus, his sons, were no doubt, at the time when St. Mark wrote his Gospel, well-known disciples of our Lord. St. Paul, writing to the Romans (xvi. 13), sends a special salutation to Rufus, "chosen in the Lord, and his mother, and mine;" a delicate recognition by St. Paul of something like maternal care bestowed upon him by the mother of Rufus. It is probable that his father Simon, and perhaps his brother Alexander, may have been dead by this time. Rufus is also honourably mentioned by Polycarp in his Epistle to the Philippians. There is a tradition, mentioned by Cornelius à Lapide, that Rufus became a bishop in Spain, and that Alexander suffered martyrdom. *To go with them, that he might bear his cross.* St. Luke (xxiii. 26) adds the touching words, "to bear it after Jesus (φέρειν ὄπισθεν τοῦ 'Ιησοῦ)."

Ver. 22.—**And they bring him** (φέρουσιν αὐτὸν); literally, *they bear him*. At ver. 20 another word has been used (ἐξάγουσιν), "they lead him out." It seems as though, when they had reached the gate of the city, they saw symptoms that our Lord was fainting under his burden; and so they pressed Simon into the service, that he might be ready to assist. At first our Lord carried his own cross. Tradition says (Cornelius à Lapide) that the cross was fifteen feet long, the transverse limb being eight feet; and that he so carried it that the upper portion rested on his shoulder, while the foot of the cross trailed on the ground. When they saw that he was breaking down under the weight of the cross, they laid it on Simon, that they might the more quickly reach the place of crucifixion. **The place Golgotha, which is, being interpreted, The place of a skull.** "Golgotha" is a Hebrew, or rather Chaldaic, word, applied to the skull on account of its roundness, that being the idea which lies in the root of the word. The Greek equivalent to the word is Κρανίον; and this is rendered in the Vulgate, *Calvaria*, a skull, from *calva*, bald. St. Luke is the only evangelist in whose Gospel (xxiii. 33) this word (Κρανίον) is rendered "Calvary." In the Revised Version it is rendered "the skull." The place was so called, either from its having been the spot where executions ordinarily took place (though in this case we might have expected to find it called τόπος κρανίων

rather than κρανίον); or, more probably, it was derived from the configuration of the place itself, perhaps a round-like mound, or knoll, sufficiently elevated to be seen at a little distance and by a large number. As to the actual site of Golgotha, recent researches seem to have done much to confirm the ancient tradition. The Bordeaux pilgrim, A.D. 333, says, "On the left side of the original Church of the Holy Sepulchre is the hillock (*monticulus*) Golgotha, where the Lord was crucified. Hence, about a stone's throw distant, is the crypt where his body was deposited." St. Cyril of Jerusalem alludes to the spot frequently, and there was no doubt about it in the time of Eusebius, A.D. 315. Professor Willis says that the rock of Calvary still stands up, some fifteen feet above the pavement. "It appears likely," he says, "that in its original state this rock was part of a little swell of the ground that jutted out from the slope of Sepulchre Street, and probably always formed a somewhat abrupt view on the west and south sides" (see 'Speaker's Commentary' on St. Matthew). Captain Conder (*Palestine Exploration Fund, Quarterly Statement* July, 1882) thinks that he shall be able to show that the traditional Golgotha is the site of the original temple of Ashtoreth, and that this temple was the Jebusite sanctuary before David took Jerusalem, and round which the sepulchres of the kings were hewn after the worship of Jehovah had consecrated the temple hill.

Ver. 23.—**And they offered him wine mingled with myrrh: but he received it not.** There were two occasions on which drink was offered to our Lord during the agonies of his crucifixion. The first occasion is that mentioned by St. Matthew (xxvii. 34), when they offered him wine mingled with gall. This was a kind of stupefying liquor, a strong narcotic, made of the sour wine of the country, mingled with bitter herbs, and mercifully administered to dull the sense of pain. This was offered before the actual crucifixion took place. It is to this first occasion that St. Mark here refers. The words in the original are (καὶ ἐδίδουν αὐτῷ ἐσμυρνισμένον οἶνον), "they were giving, they offered him." *But he received it not.* He would not seek alleviation of the agonies of the crucifixion by any drugged potion which might render him insensible. He would bear the full burden consciously. The second occasion on which drink was offered to him was after he had been some hours on his cross, and when the end was drawing near; and it was then given in answer to his exclamation, "I thirst." This drink does not appear to have been mingled with any stupefying drug; and we do not read that he refused it. St. Mark does not record this second occasion.

Ver. 24.—**And they crucify him** (καὶ σταυροῦσιν αὐτὸν). Such is the most approved reading. The evangelist states the fact without staying to dwell on the painful circumstances connected with the act of nailing him to the cross; and passes on to the mention of other things. They **part his garments among them, casting lots upon them, what each should take.** The outer robe and the tunic would have been removed previously to the crucifixion. St. John (xix. 23) here goes into details. " They took his garments, and made four parts, to every soldier a part; and also the coat: now the coat was without seam, woven from the top throughout." *His garments* (τὰ ἱμάτια). This would be the loose, flowing outer dress with girdle. The tunic (χιτών) was a close-fitting dress, worn underneath the ἱμάτιον. There were four soldiers employed for each crucifixion. St. Cyril refers to the clothes of criminals as the perquisite of the executioners. Here was another ingredient of bitterness in our Lord's cup, that he saw before his eyes his garments torn by the soldiery, and his tunic divided to them by lot. But he divested himself of these garments of mortality, that he might clothe us with life and immortality.

Ver. 25.—**And it was the third hour, and they crucified him.** The third hour would literally be nine o'clock. But we gather from ver. 33 that our Lord was on his cross, and still alive, at the sixth hour, that is, at twelve o'clock. The simplest mode of solving the chronological difficulty seems to be this: The Jews divided their day into four parts, which they called hours, namely, the first, from six to nine; the third, from nine to twelve; the sixth, from twelve to three; and the ninth, from three to six. It was, then, within the third hour, that is, between nine and twelve, that they crucified him; and it was from the sixth to the ninth hour that he was actually upon his cross. St. John employs the Asiatic mode of computing time.

Ver. 26.—**And the superscription of his accusation was written over, THE KING OF THE JEWS.** This would probably be the shortest form of inscription, and in Latin, " Rex Judæorum." All the evangelists mention the inscription; but no two of them in precisely the same words. It appears by a comparison of them that the whole title was, "This is Jesus of Nazareth, the King of the Jews." In the case of remarkable prisoners the accusation was written on a white tablet, and carried before them as they went to the place of execution. It was then placed over their heads when the cross was erected. St. John tells us that our Lord's title was

written in three languages—Hebrew, Latin, and Greek. Such appears to be the proper order of the words, namely, the national, the official, and the common dialect. St. Mark, writing at Rome, would naturally mention the Latin title. It is quite possible that the superscription may have varied in the different renderings in which it was given. It is evident from St. John (xix. 19—22) that the title was much canvassed by the Jews and the chief priests. Bede says that this title was fitly placed over his head, because, although he was crucified in weakness for us, yet he shone with the majesty of a King above his cross. The title proclaimed that he was after all a King; and that from henceforth he began to reign from his cross over the Jews. And therefore Pilate was divinely restrained from making any alteration in the title, so that it should mean anything less than this.

Ver. 27.—**And with him they crucify two robbers** (λῃσταί)—not "thieves" (κλέπται); St. Luke (xxiii. 32) shows that these two robbers formed a part of the procession to Calvary; but they were crucified after our Lord—**one on his right hand, and one on his left.** We know from St. Luke (xxiii. 40) that one of these malefactors was saved; while it would appear that the other died in his sins. And thus Christ upon his cross, between these two men, and with the title of King over his head, presented a striking and awful picture of the final judgment. Such is the view of St. Ambrose on St. Luke xxiii., and of St. Augustine, who says, " This cross, if you mark it well, was a judgment-seat. For the Judge being placed in the midst, the one who believed was set free; the other who reviled him was condemned; and thus he signified what he will do with the quick and the dead. Some he will place on his right hand, and some on his left " (Augustine, Tract. 31 in S. Johan.).

Ver. 28.—This verse is omitted in the oldest manuscripts. It is supposed to have been taken from St. Luke (xxii. 37).

Vers. 29, 30.—**And they that passed by railed on him, wagging their heads.** Here was another fulfilment of prophecy, and another aggravation of the misery of Christ. " All they that see me laugh me to scorn : they shoot out the lip, they shake the head, saying, He trusted on the Lord that he would deliver him; let him deliver him, seeing he delighteth in him " (Ps. xxii. 7, 8). The torment of crucifixion itself was terrible; but it was a still greater torment to the Crucified to be insulted in his agony. Our Lord may well have had these words in his mind, "They persecute him whom thou hast smitten, and they tell of the sorrow of those whom thou hast wounded " (Ps. lxix. 26). *They that passed by.* Calvary was probably near to one of the thoroughfares leading to the city; so that there would be a continual stream of persons passing to and fro; more especially at this time, when Jerusalem was thronged with visitors. And no doubt the words of the accusation against him in its incorrect form would pass freely from mouth to mouth, **Ha! thou that destroyest the temple, and buildest it in three days, save thyself.** If you could make such a boast as this, show your power by coming down from the cross.

Ver. 31.—The chief priests and the scribes are more bitter than the people. In fact, they had all along endeavoured to rouse the bad passions of the people against our Lord. And now they take advantage of this his present degraded condition to renew the old charge that his miracles of healing had been wrought by Beelzebub, because, if they had been wrought by God, God would have interposed in this his sore extremity and have set him free. **He saved others.** They cannot deny this fact. But they now try to turn this fact against him, by alleging that he who pretended to work miracles upon others, wrought them, not by the finger of God, but by Beelzebub, seeing that, if they had been wrought by a Divine power, the same power would now be exercised for his deliverance. They desired to take advantage of this public opportunity of exposing him as an impostor, and so they hoped to get rid of him, and at the same time to blot the very name of Christianity from out of the earth.

Ver. 32.—Christ might have come down from the cross; but he would not, because it was his Father's will that he should die upon the cross to redeem us from death. So he despised the taunts of the wicked, that he might teach us by his example to do the same. If he had chosen to descend from the cross, he would not have ascended. He knew that the death upon the cross was necessary for the salvation of men; and therefore he would go through the whole. He withheld the exercise of his power. His omnipotence restrained the natural longings of his suffering humanity to escape from these unutterable torments. So he would not come down from the cross, although within three days he would rise from the grave. And yet there was no word of indignation against his tormentors. On the contrary, he proclaimed mercy; for as he hung on his cross he said, "Father, forgive them; for they know not what they do."

Ver. 33.—**And when the sixth hour was come.** This would be midday, twelve o'clock; and the darkness continued until the ninth hour, that is, three o'clock. This supernatural darkness came when the day is wont to be at its brightest. The moon was now at the full, so that it could not have

been caused by what we call an eclipse, for when it is full moon the moon cannot intervene between the earth and the sun. This darkness was doubtless produced by the immediate interference of God. An account of it is given by Phlegon of Tralles, a freedman of the Emperor Adrian. Eusebius, in his records of the year A.D. 33, quotes at length from Phlegon, who says that, in the fourth year of the 202nd Olympiad, there was a great and remarkable eclipse of the sun, above any that had happened before. At the sixth hour the day was turned into the darkness of night, so that stars were seen in the heaven; and there was a great earthquake in Bithynia, which overthrew many houses in the city of Nicæa. Phlegon attributes the darkness which he describes to an eclipse, which was natural enough for him to do. The knowledge of astronomy was then very imperfect. Phlegon also mentions an earthquake. This brings his account into very close correspondence with the sacred narrative. **There was darkness over the whole land** (ἐφ᾽ ὅλην τὴν γῆν). "Land" is a better rendering than "earth." We are not informed precisely how far the darkness extended. Dionysius says that he saw this phenomenon at Heliopolis, in Egypt, and he is reported to have exclaimed, "Either the God of nature, the Creator, is suffering, or the universe is dissolving." St. Cyprian says, "The sun was constrained to withdraw his rays, and close his eyes, that he might not be compelled to look upon this crime of the Jews." To the same purpose St. Chrysostom, "The creature could not bear the wrong done to its Creator. Therefore the sun withdrew his rays, that he might not behold the deeds of the wicked."

Ver. 34.—**Eloi, Eloi, lama sabacthani?** St. Mark here uses the Aramaic form Ελωΐ. St. Matthew refers to the original Hebrew. St. Mark in all probability took his form from St. Peter. It seems from hence that our Lord was in the habit of using the vernacular speech. **Why hast thou forsaken me?** (εἰς τί με ἐγκατέλιπες;). This might be rendered, *Why didst thou forsake me?* It is generally supposed that our blessed Lord, continually praying upon his cross, and offering himself a sacrifice for the sins of the whole world, recited the whole of the psalm (xxii.) of which these are the first words, that he might show himself to be the very Being to whom the words refer; so that the Jewish scribes and people might examine and see the cause why he would not descend from the cross; namely, because this very psalm showed that it was appointed that he should suffer these things.

Ver. 35.—Notwithstanding the supernatural darkness, there were those who lingered about the cross. Indeed, the darkness would add greatly to the awfulness of the place. It was out of that darkness that the voice of Jesus was heard; and inasmuch as Elias, or Elijah, was believed to hold some relation to the Messiah, it was natural for some of those who stood by to understand the words to mean that our Lord was actually calling for Elias.

Ver. 36.—There is a slight difference here in the narratives. St. Matthew (xxvii. 49) says, "And the rest said, Let be; let us see whether Elijah cometh to save him." Here in St. Mark the words are recorded as having been spoken by him alone who offered our Lord the vinegar. According to St. John (xix. 28), the offering of the vinegar followed immediately upon the words of our Lord, "I thirst." This drink was not the stupefying potion given to criminals before their crucifixion, to lull the sense of pain, but the sour wine, the ordinary drink of the soldiers, called *posca*. The reed was most probably the long stalk of the hyssop plant. Dr. J. Forbes Royle, in an elaborate article on the subject, quoted in Smith's 'Dictionary of the Bible' (vol. i. p. 846), arrives at the conclusion that the hyssop is none other than the caper plant, the Arabic name of which, *asuf*, bears a strong resemblance to the Hebrew. The plant is the *Capparis spinosa* of Linnæus. The apparent difference between the narratives of St. Matthew and St. Mark may be reconciled by weaving in the narrative of St. John with those of the synoptists—the "Let be" of the soldiers in the one case being intended to restrain the individual from offering the wine; and the "Let be" of the individual, corresponding to our "Wait a moment," while he answered our Saviour's cry, "I thirst."

Ver. 37.—**And Jesus uttered a loud voice, and gave up the ghost.** The three synoptists all mention this cry, which appears to have been something different from the words which he uttered at or about the time of his death. It was evidently something supernatural, and was so regarded by the centurion who stood by; and who had no doubt been accustomed to scenes like these. Usually the voice fails the dying, more especially when the natural forces have been weakened by long agony, as in the case of our Lord. It seems, therefore, the right conclusion that he cried out, just before he expired, by that supernatural power which his Godhead supplied to him; and thus he showed that, although he had gone through all the pains which were sufficient in ordinary cases to produce death, yet that at length he did not die of necessity, but voluntarily, in accordance with what he had himself said, "No one taketh my life from me. . . . I have power to lay

it down, and I have power to take it again" (John x. 18). Victor Antiochanus, in commenting upon this chapter, says, "By this action the Lord Jesus proved that he had his whole life, and his death, in his own free power."

Ver. 38.—**And the veil of the temple was rent in twain from the top to the bottom.** There were two veils—one before the holy place, and the other before the holy of holies. The holy place would correspond to what we call the nave of the church, in which the priests were continually present; the holy of holies would correspond to our chancel choir —the holiest part of the building. This was always kept closed; nor might any one enter it but the high priest, and that only once in the year, on the day of expiation. The veil which was rent at our Lord's death was that which was placed before the holy of holies; it was called the καταπέτασμα. The outer veil was called κάλυμμα. It was the duty of the officiating priest, on the evening of the day of preparation, at the hour of evening prayer, which would correspond to the time of our Lord's death, to enter into the holy place, where he would of course be between the two curtains, or veils, the outer veil, or κάλυμμα, and the inner veil, or καταπέτασμα. It would then be his business to roll back the κάλυμμα, or outer veil, thus exposing the holy place to the people, who would be in the outer court. And then and there they would see, to their amazement, the καταπέτασμα, the inner veil, rent asunder from the top to the bottom. These veils or curtains, according to Josephus, were each forty cubits in height and ten in breadth, of great substance, very massive, and richly embroidered with gold and purple. Now, this rending of the veil signified (1) that the whole of the Jewish dispensation, with its rites and ceremonies, was now unfolded by Christ; and that thenceforth the middle wall of partition was broken down, so that now, not the Jews only, but the Gentiles also might draw nigh by the blood of Christ. But (2) it further signified that the way to heaven was laid open by our Lord's death. "When thou hadst overcome the sharpness of death, thou didst open the kingdom of heaven to all believers." The veil signified that heaven was closed to all, until Christ by his death rent this veil in twain, and laid open the way.

Ver. 39.—**And when the centurion, which stood by over against him** (ὁ παρεστηκὼς ἐξ ἐναντίας αὐτοῦ) **saw that he so gave up the ghost.** The words, "so cried out," are not in the most important authorities. It was the business of the centurion to watch all that took place, and to see that the sentence was executed. He must have been standing close under the cross; and there was that in the whole demeanour of the dying Sufferer, so different from anything that he had ever witnessed before, that it drew from him the involuntary exclamation, **Truly this man was the Son of God.** He had observed him through those weary hours; he had noticed the meekness and the dignity of the Sufferer; he had heard those words, so deeply impressed upon the faith and reverence of Christians, which fell from him from time to time as he hung there; and then at last he heard the piercing cry, so startling, so unexpected, which escaped him just before he yielded up his spirit; and he could come to no other conclusion than this, that he was in very deed God's Son. It has been supposed by some that this centurion was Longinus, who was led by the miracles which accompanied the death of Christ, to acknowledge him to be the Son of God, and to be a herald of his resurrection, and was ultimately himself put to death for the sake of Christ in Cappadocia. St. Chrysostom repeats the common report, that on account of his faith he was at last crowned with martyrdom.

Ver. 40.—**And there were also women beholding from afar** (ἀπὸ μακρόθεν θεωροῦσαι). St. Matthew (xxvii. 55) says that there were many. Amongst them were **Mary Magdalene, and Mary** the wife of Clopas, or Alphæus, **and mother of James the less and of Joses,** called brethren of our Lord, and the mother of Zebedee's children, that is, **Salome.** The mother of our Lord had been there until the time when, having with St. John crept as near the cross of Jesus as she might venture, she was consigned by our Lord to St. John's care, and taken away by him. St. Mark mentions this to show the faith and love of these holy women, because in the very presence of the enemies of Christ they dared to stand by his cross, and shrank not from testifying their piety and devotion. St. John says that they stood near. He must have known; for at one time at least he was standing near. St. Matthew and St. Mark speak of them as at a distance. They were at a distance, no doubt, for the most part, as compared with the soldiers, whose duty it was to be in close attendance and to keep the people off. But these devoted women came as near as they could, so as to see and hear their Lord. Perhaps they were sometimes further off and sometimes nearer, as they saw opportunity, or as the humour of the officials suffered them.

Ver. 41.—From this verse we learn that these women **followed him, and ministered unto him when he was in Galilee;** and that many other women came up with him unto Jerusalem. The sublime beauty of his character, and the spiritual influence which he wielded, attracted them; and they were able to minister to the various needs of his humanity.

Ver. 42.—**And when even was now come.** The sabbath commenced on the Friday evening at six o'clock. The evening commenced at three o'clock. Our Lord must be buried before six o'clock.

Ver. 43. — **Joseph of Arimathæa.** St. Jerome says that this city was called Ramathaim-Zophim (the lofty place), where dwelt Elkanah and Hannah of old, and where Samuel was born. Joseph was most probably a native of Arimathæa; but he was now a citizen and counsellor of Jerusalem. He was **an honourable counsellor** (εὐσχήμων βουλευτής), *a councillor of honourable estate* (Revised Version). St. Matthew says he was a rich man. It is evident that he regarded himself as a settled inhabitant of Jerusalem, since he had thus provided himself with a place of sepulture. He was **waiting for** (προσδεχόμενος)—literally, *looking for*—**the kingdom of God.** St. Matthew (xxvii. 57) says that he was a disciple of Jesus. These circumstances explain his desire to bury our Lord. **He boldly went in** (τολμήσας εἰσῆλθε)—literally, *he took courage and went in*—**unto Pilate, and asked for the body of Jesus.** A poor man would not have dared to approach Pilate for such a purpose as this. St. Chrysostom says, "The courage of Joseph is greatly to be admired, in that, for the love of Christ, he exposed himself to the danger of death." The fact that he was "looking for the kingdom of God" explains his conduct. It shows that he believed in Christ, and through his grace hoped for everlasting salvation; and in this hope he thought little of showing his reverence for Christ, and so "boldly went in unto Pilate, and asked for the body of Jesus."

Ver. 44.—**And Pilate marvelled if he were already dead: and calling unto him the centurion, he asked him whether he had been any while dead.** It must have been somewhat early in the afternoon, probably not long after three o'clock, when Joseph went. The day being the Preparation, the Jews were anxious to satisfy the letter of the Law (Deut. xxi. 13), and that, more especially, because the coming sabbath was a "high day." So they had gone early to Pilate to obtain permission to accelerate the deaths of the sufferers by the terrible additional punishment called σκελοκοπία. This violence was not inflicted upon our Lord, because he was already dead; and so another Scripture was fulfilled, "A bone of him shall not be broken." But it was necessary that Pilate should be assured of the fact that death had taken place before he gave up the body; and thus, in the providence of God, another evidence was given of the reality of Christ's death. Joseph asked for the body (σῶμα). Then Pilate asked the centurion "whether he had been any while dead." The verb here is in the aorist, and the adverb means "formerly" (εἰ πάλαι ἀπέθανε); literally, *if he died some time ago.*

Ver. 45.—**And when he learned it of the centurion, he granted** (ἐδωρήσατο) **the corpse** (τὸ πτῶμα) **to Joseph.**

Ver. 46.—**And he bought a linen cloth** (σινδόνα). This was a fine linen garment, or shroud, something like that in which the young man fled the night before (ch. xiv. 51, 52). **And taking him down** (καθελὼν αὐτὸν). It appears from these words that Joseph himself, assisted probably by Nicodemus and others, actually took the body of our Lord down from the cross, wrapped the *sindon* round him, and laid him in his own new tomb, which had been hewn out of the rock. The word rendered "tomb" is μνημεῖον, as being intended to be a memorial of the departed. **And he rolled a stone against the door of the tomb.** The door here means "the opening," or "entrance." Thus, while our Lord died with the wicked, he was with the rich in his death (Isa. liii. 9).

Ver. 47.—**And Mary Magdalene and Mary the mother of Joses beheld where he was laid** (ἐθεώρουν ποῦ τίθεται); literally, *were beholding where he was laid.* These women were two of the group mentioned at ver. 40. They remained, after the body of our Lord had been deposited, in sad and silent contemplation. The women appear to have broken up into two groups. One group went alone to purchase spices and ointments, which it was necessary for them to do before six o'clock, when the sabbath commenced; in readiness for the embalming. Mary Magdalene and Mary the mother of Joses and Salome appear to have bought them after six o'clock on the Saturday night.

HOMILETICS.

Vers. 1—15.—*The trial before Pilate.* How true it is that "God spared not his own Son, but delivered him up for us all"! Jesus was first examined by Annas, then tried before Caiaphas, the high priest, then formally condemned by the Sanhedrim. But these mock-trials, with all their injustice and their indignities, were not enough to exhaust the appointed humiliation and suffering. Christ must needs be brought before the Roman governor, who had come up from Cæsarea to Jerusalem to attend the Feast of the Passover. In order that he might endure the curse attaching to every one that hangeth on a tree, in order that he might fulfil his own prediction that he should die by crucifixion, he must needs be sentenced, not merely by a Hebrew, but also by a Roman tribunal. The passage before us exhibits the several agencies by which the condemnation of Christ was brought about.

I. THE MALICE AND ENVY OF THE PRIESTS. Pilate "perceived that for envy the chief priests had delivered him up." They both hated the spiritual teaching of the Prophet of Nazareth, so much at variance with their own; and they were jealous of the influence which he had acquired over the people, not only in Galilee, but in Judæa. The hatred and envy of the priests, Pharisees, Sadducees, and scribes, had been abundantly shown by their treatment of Jesus for some time past, but was made more apparent by the events of the past night. Their apprehension of him in the garden, their treatment of him before the high priest, had been flagitiously malicious and unjust. And now their charge against him at the bar of Pilate—a charge virtually of political treason against the authority of the Roman empire—was a proof of the length to which their hatred and hypocrisy could proceed. They brought this charge, simply because they thought that this would tell most against him in the estimation of the procurator.

II. THE FICKLENESS AND THE UNPRINCIPLED CHOICE OF THE MULTITUDE. But a few days ago the crowds in the streets of Jerusalem had welcomed the Prophet of Nazareth with the cry, "Hosanna to the Son of David; blessed is he that cometh in the name of the Lord." Of those who thus hailed the triumphal entry of the Nazarene, probably the greater part were Galileans. And the apprehension of Jesus had been effected at night; the trial of Jesus had been hurried on before the day, probably with this intent, that the pilgrims from the north of Palestine, who were so largely adherents of Jesus, might be prevented from taking any steps to rescue the Prisoner, or at all events from making a demonstration on his behalf. Yet the populace inhabiting and sojourning in the city cannot be acquitted of proverbial fickleness. The minions of the priesthood, no doubt, led the way, and raised the first shouts of popular outcry against Jesus. The multitude were instigated by the sacerdotal party and their adherents to this position of hostility, this ferocious howl for the blood of the Innocent. The infamous choice of the populace, who preferred Barabbas to Jesus, is one of the most distressing incidents of the awful martydom. A rioter and murderer was apparently represented as a champion of national independence, whilst " the Holy One and the Just" was charged with being the enemy of the temple and its services and solemnities. In this way the people were wrought upon to demand the death of the precious and the liberation of the vile.

III. THE WEAKNESS, SELFISHNESS, AND FEAR OF THE ROMAN GOVERNOR. After all, the responsibility of capital punishment lay with Pilate. Had he stood firm for justice and right against lawlessness and violence, Jesus would have been saved. But so it was not to be. The governor's own conviction of the innocence and excellence of the accused are evident, both from his language, " Why, what evil hath he done?" "I find no fault in him," and also from his repeated though unsuccessful, because irresolute, efforts to save his life. It is clear that Pilate admired and respected the Prisoner, whilst he despised the accusers and the mob. Yet he yielded to the savage outcry, from a desire to content the Jews, with whom it was his interest to stand well, and from fear lest, if he acquitted the Prisoner, his conduct might be misrepresented to the emperor to his disadvantage, and so might prove the occasion of his ruin. Desire of popularity, fear of the tyrant's frown,—these were the two motives which, in the mind of the cynical and selfish procurator, outweighed all considerations of righteousness and humanity. So it came to pass that Jesus " suffered under Pontius Pilate."

IV. THE CONFESSION AND THE DEMEANOUR OF CHRIST HIMSELF. The demeanour of Jesus was dignified and honourable, but far from fitted to procure his release. Silence, when false witnesses testified against him, only infuriated his foes. Before the Jewish tribunal he acknowledged that he was the Messiah and the Son of God. Before Pilate he confessed himself a King—a confession which, however explained as a claim to spiritual dominion, was an embarrassment to his well-wisher and judge. And his reminder that there was a higher, because a Divine, authority, to which all earthly authority is subordinate, was itself irritating to a proud and absolute ruler. There was a marvellous mingling of boldness and meekness in the conduct of the innocent and holy Prisoner. Morally, this demeanour exculpated him ; but legally it was to his disadvantage. And his confession of royalty became his sentence of condemnation ; written upon his cross for the apparent vindication, but for the real and eternal censure, of those who accused and of him who sentenced him. Thus did Jesus " witness a good confession before Pontius Pilate."

APPLICATION. 1. Observe the force and virulence of sin taking possession of human nature, and corrupting and degrading it. The malice, bigotry, and falsehood of the priests, the fickleness and unreasoning fury of the mob, the selfishness and cowardice of the governor,—all illustrate the length to which sin can go. The innocence and benevolence of the Victim render more conspicuous the enormity of his foes. 2. Observe the faultless and beautiful spirit displayed by the Sufferer, the absence of all resentment or complaint, the meek submission to all that he needs must suffer. A Being so morally perfect demands our admiration and our worship, invites our confidence and our love. 3. Consider the price of our redemption. Jesus bore all this injustice, these insults, for man. He was condemned that we might be acquitted; he was slain that we might live.

Vers. 16—20.—*Christ mocked.* During this awful night and morning our Lord thrice underwent the suffering and indignity of public and vulgar derision. First before the high priest, at the hands of the officers and servants of Caiaphas ; then again when he was set at nought and mocked by the brutal soldiery of Herod Antipas ; and now yet once more, when Pilate delivered him into the keeping of the Roman soldiers, a company of whom were about to lead him forth to crucifixion. Insult was added to insult, and his bitter cup ran over.

I. THE MOCKERS. The whole band or cohort are said to have joined in the ribald sport in the Prætorium. What they did, it must be remembered, they did largely in ignorance. These Roman legionaries knew nothing of a Messiah, and were probably utterly unacquainted with the character and career of him whom Pilate had delivered over to them. Their insensibility to human suffering was equal to their indifference to human innocence and virtue. All they knew was that their master, though professedly convinced of Jesus' blamelessness, was yet content to give him up into their hands to ill treat and to put to a shameful death. We cannot, therefore, wonder at their insolence and cruelty. Yet we cannot read the sad story without feelings of shame and of sorrow, as we remember that persons belonging to our race, and sharing our nature, should have inflicted such indignities upon " the Holy One and the Just," upon the world's Friend and Saviour.

II. The mockeries. These were many, base, and repeated. 1. Jesus was invested with a purple robe. Probably this was a military cloak, whose crimson hue might render it an emblem of the imperial purple. 2. He was crowned with a circlet of thorns, another symbol of royalty, doubtless roughly woven from the stem of a prickly shrub. 3. He was addressed as " King." Utterly incapable of understanding a moral sovereignty, a spiritual sway, these coarse soldiers, to whom force was all, insulted the meek and unresisting Sufferer by the use of a title which from their lips could be only derisive. 4. He was saluted with the semblance of honour and homage; they " bowed the knee, and worshipped him." 5. They smote his sacred head with the sceptre-reed. How affecting this treatment! The very fact which should have been Christ's claim to respect, confidence, and adoration—his royal authority over the conscience and heart of humanity— was turned into a ground of reproach and a matter of reviling. Thus men treated their Divine and rightful King.

III. The stern reality to which the mockery was a prelude and a contrast. Knowing what was before the Condemned, decency and humanity should have led them to spare him these insults. But when they were over, there was worse to come. The purple was stripped from his form; his own garments were placed on him; the beam of the cross was laid upon his shoulders; he was thrust into his place in the rude procession; and then was led away to crucifixion.

Application. 1. Admire the meekness of him "who, when reviled, reviled not again; when he suffered, threatened not." Never was sorrow like his sorrow, and never patience like his patience. 2. Recognize the true royalty which a spiritual judgment may discern underlying the mockery and derision here recorded. See in Jesus a King, though crowned with thorns. 3. Learn to confide in a Saviour whose purpose to save was so resolute and so benevolent, as is apparent here. A salvation procured at such a cost is a salvation of which none should hear unmoved, and which none who needs it should hesitate or delay to accept.

Vers. 21—32.—*The crucifixion.* The bigots and the mob have gained their end, and now have their own way with "the Holy One and the Just." The power of Rome is brought into the service of Jewish fanaticism and malice. All evil influences have conspired together. Now is their hour and the power of darkness. The world's sin has culminated in the rejection of the world's Saviour. All happens as has been foreseen in the counsels of God, and foretold by inspired prophets and by the Son of man himself. The Christ of God is crucified.

I. The preparations for the crucifixion. The story is very simply told; there is no endeavour to excite feeling by any other means than by the clear and artless relation of the facts. But this is enough to awaken the sympathy of every mind capable of realizing the injustice of Christ's enemies, and the meekness, compassion, and fortitude of the Sufferer. 1. *The bearing of the cross.* That Jesus, exhausted by the events of the past night and of this morning, by the wakeful hours, the scourging and the insults he had endured, should now be incapable of carrying the instrument of his final sufferings, is natural enough. The soldiers, indisposed themselves to bear the burden, beneath which they see the Sufferer sinking, impress into the service a Cyrenian Israelite, who has come to the Passover now celebrating at Jerusalem, and who has been sleeping in one of the villages near the city, but is on his way to the scene of the sacred solemnities. What seems to the soldiers and to the mob a degradation, is to become an honourable and happy memory to Simon, whose family is destined in after years to hold a high place in the regard of the Christian community, and whose name is henceforth to be linked with that of the Redeemer by this sacred and touching association. 2. *The approach to Golgotha.* Imagination has filled the void wisely left by the evangelists; and the *via dolorosa* has been marked by " stations," each of which has been signalized by some episode of suffering, mercy, or sympathy. The spot where the execution of the iniquitous sentence took place may have been to the north-west of the city, and the name—"the place of a skull"—may have been derived from its form, rounded and bare. It needs no fanciful legends to endear a spot so memorable to the heart of Christendom; the pathos of the plain fact is enough. Calvary—"lovely, mournful Calvary"—was the scene of Immanuel's passion. 3. *The offering of myrrh-mingled wine.* The compassion of the ladies of Jerusalem is said to have provided a soporific, stupefying, narcotic draught, to be administered in humanity to the criminals who were condemned to die a painful and lingering death. It seems to have been in conformity with custom and from motives of sympathy that the draught was offered to Jesus.

> "Fill high the bowl, and spice it well, and pour
> The dews oblivious: for the cross is sharp;
> The cross is sharp, and he
> Is tenderer than a lamb."

His refusal was owing to his determination to accept to the full the lot of unde-served pain and anguish appointed for him. "Thou wilt feel all, that thou may'st pity all." He had already exclaimed, "The cup which my Father hath given me, shall I not drink it?" and it would seem that this cup of woe could not be drunk except by the retention of his faculties to the very last. 4. *The parting of his garments.* These were the perquisite of the executioners, who divided amongst themselves some of his raiment, and who cast lots for the seamless robe. This was not only the fulfil-ment of a prediction, but it was an element in the humiliation and self-sacrifice of the Son of man.

II. THE CRUCIFIXION AND ITS ACCOMPANYING CIRCUMSTANCES. "They crucified him;" such is the brief notification of the most stupendous crime committed in the history of mankind. Every circumstance recorded in such a connection is worthy of attention. 1. There is *a note of time.* It was the third hour, *i.e.* nine o'clock in the forenoon. From this we infer how hurried had been the proceedings since the break of day, and how prolonged were those sufferings, which did not close until three in the afternoon. 2. There is *a memorandum of the superscription.* This was the accusation, upon which, unproved and misrepresented, Pilate had been induced to sanction this legal murder. A King crucified, and crucified by his subjects; no wonder that such a crime should be disowned, or rather such a stigma resented, by the priests and elders. When Pilate persisted that the inscription should remain, he bore witness uncon-sciously alike to the spiritual royalty of Jesus and to the flagitious rebellion of the leaders of the Jewish nation. The cross was in truth Christ's earthly throne, the symbol of a world-wide empire. He had said, "I, if I be lifted up from the earth, will draw all men unto me." 3. There is an account of *his companions upon the cross.* If anything could possibly add to the ignominy of our Saviour's death, it was the society in which he suffered. Barabbas had, indeed, been released; but there were two robbers condemned to death, and awaiting the execution of their sentence. Accordingly, advantage was taken of the opportunity to carry out the sentence against the Christ and the criminals upon the same occasion. Thus was he "numbered with the transgressors," and an additional stigma attached to him by his association with the vilest of the vile. No wonder that the ignorant and unspiritual made this a ground of reviling against Jesus, and of reproach against his followers.

III. THE MOCKERY THAT FOLLOWED THE CRUCIFIXION. To add to the insults, the jeering, the scoffing, which Jesus had endured during his trials, it was permitted that his dying hours should be disturbed, and his dying agonies intensified, by the mockery of various classes of his foes. 1. The *passers-by* railed on him. With the customary contempt for the fallen and deserted, those passing in and out of the city insulted the Crucified, with gestures of derision and tones of contempt, recalling the language in which he had asserted his authority, and contrasting it with his pitiable condition, terrible sufferings, and apparent helplessness. 2. The *chief priests and scribes*, who had been foremost in effecting his downfall, were prominent in glorying over the work of their hands, and in scoffing at him upon whom they had wreaked their vengeance. From their lips came the language which, intended to be a reproach, was really, and has ever been deemed, one of the most glorious tributes ever paid to the Redeemer: "He saved others; himself he cannot save!" When they asked that he should come down from the cross upon which their malice had raised him, and professed their willingness upon such evidence to believe in him, we cannot doubt that their words were hollow, vulgar mockery. 3. That no element of misery might be wanting in the Saviour's anguish, it was permitted that the very thieves should join in the raillery with which Jesus was encompassed and tortured. This, indeed, only gives an additional touch of pathos to the story of the penitent thief which St. Luke tells so exquisitely, and shows, in the brighter colours of contrast, the powerful gentleness and unselfish pity of the dying Saviour.

APPLICATION. 1. Admire the submission and meekness of Christ's demeanour. 2. Consider with gratitude the redemptive purpose which animated and sustained the Sufferer. 3. Learn to glory in that cross, which, from an emblem of shame, has by Christ been transformed into a symbol of salvation.

Vers. 33—41.—*The death of Jesus.* Jesus had, in the course of his ministry, raised the dead to life. Three such instances are recorded in the Gospels; and it is intimated that there were other cases which have not been circumstantially related. And now the time came for himself to die, to accomplish at Jerusalem the decease he had foreseen and foretold. That he might have avoided this fate is obvious; and he had himself declared that no man took his life from him. The time, however, had arrived for him to lay down that life of himself, in submitting to be, "by wicked hands, crucified and slain."

I. The evangelist relates CIRCUMSTANCES PRECEDING CHRIST'S DEATH. 1. The darkness which brooded over the city, and over the whole land, for the space of three hours (from 12 until 3 p.m.), was apparently supernatural, and has usually been regarded as a manifest token of Nature's sympathy with her Lord. It was an appropriate accompaniment to the sad and awful event that was transpiring. 2. The utterance of desertion and of woe. The dying Saviour's cry has ever been regarded as affording a glance into the innermost, the sacred, the unfathomable mysteries of his soul. Explain it we cannot; disregard it we dare not. Surely, this cannot be regarded as a mere exclamation of distress! Surely, it cannot have been wrung from the Redeemer by the severity of bodily pain and anguish! It has been well said that the sufferings of his soul were the soul of his sufferings. The only explanation of the cry, "My God, why hast thou forsaken me?" is that furnished by the mental agonies which the world's Redeemer was enduring, which clouded his sense of the Father's favour. On the one hand, we cannot suppose this language to have been a mere cry of distress; on the other hand, we cannot conceive that the Father had withdrawn his favour from his well-beloved Son, who was now proving himself to be obedient unto death, even the death of the cross. The fact is that the burden of the world's sins and sorrows pressed like a dense cloud upon his soul, and obscured from his view the shining of the Father's face. 3. The ministry of pity. Although at the commencement of the crucifixion Jesus had refused the stupefying draught which had been offered him, now that he had hung six hours upon the cross he was consumed with an intolerable thirst. The expression of his distressing sensation seems to have followed upon the cry of desertion. A bystander, doubtless in pity, offered him a sponge filled with the sour wine which was the soldiers' ordinary drink, and it would seem that he did not now refuse the alleviation offered. It is not easy to understand who could have so misapprehended his cry as to suppose the dying Sufferer to invoke the ministry of Elijah; though it is easy to believe that some would jeeringly propose to wait for the prophetic intervention. 4. The dying cry. Mark gives no words; but from the other Gospels we learn that, immediately before his expiring, Jesus uttered aloud two ever-memorable sayings: viz. "It is finished!" and "Father, into thy hands I commend my spirit!" It is clear, therefore, that the cry was not an inarticulate utterance of pain. There was an expression of his conviction that his ministry of humiliation was ended, that the purpose of his incarnation was completed, that nothing more remained for him to do on earth. And in addition to this utterance, which was ministerial, was another, which was personal. As he had said "*My* God," so now he says "*Father*," an address which proved his possession of the assurance of his Father's undiminished and undimmed approval. The hour of agony and dissolution was thus **an** hour of triumph: Christ's work was completed, his obedience was perfected, his acceptance was assured, his victory was achieved.

II. The evangelist records THE FACT OF CHRIST'S DEATH. How simply is it related!—"He gave up his spirit." In one word is recorded, without exaggeration, without a word to heighten the effect, without a comment of any kind, the most stupendous, pathetic, and momentous event which this world has witnessed. The Being who was "the Life" bowed his head in death. He who, whilst his hour was not yet come, had eluded his foes, now submitted to the felon's doom. The Lord of immortality, who was to hold the keys of death and of the unseen world, saw and tasted dissolution, though not corruption. He knew, though the spectators, friends and foes alike, were ignorant of the fact, that his death was destined to be the life of the world. He had foretold that, when lifted up from the earth, he should draw all men unto himself; that the grain of wheat should fall into the earth and die, and should bring forth much fruit. And the events which have followed have verified the Saviour's words. Even those who have no disposition to regard Christ's character and work as supernatural cannot be blind to the fact that the cross has proved a tree whose fruits have been for the satisfaction, and whose leaves have been for the healing, of the nations. But, to us Christians, the death of Christ was the redemption of our souls.

> "Oh, never, never canst thou know
>   What then for thee the Saviour bore,
> The pangs of that mysterious woe
>   Which wrung his bosom's inmost core.

> "Yes, man for man perchance may brave
> The horrors of the yawning grave;
> And friend for friend, or son for sire,
> Undaunted and unmoved expire,
> From love, or piety, or pride;
> But who can die as Jesus died?"

III. The evangelist puts upon record CERTAIN CIRCUMSTANCES FOLLOWING UPON CHRIST'S DEATH. 1. One incident occurs which is typical of the influence of our Saviour's death upon the elder, the Jewish, dispensation: the rending of the temple veil. This curtain screened off the holiest place, which was representative of the Divine indwelling, and at the same time of the necessity of a mediatorial scheme by which God can admit men to his fellowship and favour. And when this veil was rent, it was signified that by the death of Jesus, the true High Priest, the way was made open into the presence of a holy God. The distinction between Jews and Gentiles was abolished, and a Divine mediation was declared available for all mankind. 2. The witness of the centurion was an earnest of the world's witness to the crucified Redeemer. It was the manner of Jesus' death—the demeanour and the language of the innocent, uncomplaining, forgiving Sufferer, the darkness and the general awe—which together produced upon the mind of this Roman officer the impression that this was, not merely no criminal, but no ordinary mortal; that he had been superintending the crucifixion of a Son—*the* Son—of God. It is significant that, in his death, our Lord effected the conversion of a sinful fellow-sufferer, and the enlightenment, to say the least, of one so little likely to be prepossessed in his favour as this Roman officer. 3. Mention is made of the gaze of some of those who had been, and still were, the faithful friends of Jesus. The mother of the Lord had been led away from the painful scene by the disciple to whose care she had been entrusted by her dying Son. But Mary of Magdala, Mary the mother of James and Joses, and Salome the wife of Zebedee, are mentioned as, with others, lingering at some distance from the cross, and yet within sight of it, to behold the end. Whilst their services could be of use to him, they had attended his steps and supplied his wants; and now that they could do no more for their beloved and revered Master, they remained near his dying form, to watch with him, to sympathize with him to the last, to hear his dying words, to keep him in sight until the lifeless body should be disposed of, and hidden from them in the earth. Sweet **is** the thought that, when his disciples forsook Jesus and fled, when he had to endure the anguish caused by the treachery of one, the denial of a second, and the desertion of others, there were devout and attached women who would not leave the sacred spot, or take their eyes from off the hallowed form.   Even by human devotion and love Jesus was not utterly forsaken, was not left utterly alone.   Some there were who had proved his kindness, tested his wisdom, profited by his authority during his ministry, whose hearts changed not towards him in the hour of his darkness, anguish, and woe. Memorable is the ministry of those holy and affectionate women, who are recorded to have been " last at the cross, and earliest at the tomb."

APPLICATION.   Christ's death is: 1. To sinners the means of salvation.   The Lord paid on the cross the ransom-price of the souls of sinful men; he bore our sins; he redeemed us with his precious blood.   Here is pardon, healing, and life, for those who receive the good tidings with sincere faith.   2. To suppliants the assurance of the gracious answer of Heaven to their prayers.   "If God spared not his own Son, but delivered him up for us all, will he not with him also freely give us all things?"   3. To struggling souls the inspiration of resistance and endurance, the earnest and pledge of victory.   "Our old nature is crucified with him;" "Reckon ye yourselves dead unto sin."   4. To Christian teachers and preachers the theme of their ministry.   In this Paul is an example to us all, who exclaimed, "We preach Christ crucified;" "God forbid that I should glory, save in the cross of our Lord Jesus Christ."

Vers. 42—47.—*The burial of Christ.*   The reality of the death of our Lord Jesus has been questioned, at various times and upon various grounds.   Some have denied the possibility of a resurrection from the dead, and have absurdly supposed that Jesus only fainted or swooned, and that his recovery from a swoon was reputed among his followers to be a resurrection.   Against all such unreasonable and incredible assumptions the record of the evangelists, who relate his burial, and that in the most minute and circumstantial manner, ought to be regarded as definitely and certainly conclusive.

I. THE APPLICANT.   Of Joseph of Arimathæa we know only what is recorded in connection with Christ's interment.   In circumstances he was rich.   His rank was that of a member of the Sanhedrim; his character is described in the words, "a good man and a just;" his religious position may be inferred from the two facts, that he waited for the kingdom of God and that he was a disciple of Jesus, though secretly, from fear of the Jews, whilst his view of what had taken place with respect to Jesus is expressly put upon record in the statement that he had not consented to the counsel and deed of the priests and elders.   His coming forward on this occasion is an instance of the way in which circumstances may bring out virtues, such as courage and fidelity to conviction, which have long been latent.

II. THE APPLICATION.   The boldness with which Joseph asked for the body is mentioned as something to his credit, for such a step would certainly not commend him to his fellow-citizens and fellow-councillors.   As the Jews approved of the burial of the dead in every case, and as it was not considered decent that the bodies of the crucified should be exposed upon the coming sabbath of Paschal solemnities, there was the more obvious ground for this appeal.   And it was seemly and honourable in Joseph to wish to rescue his Master's corpse from the indignity of a criminal's interment.   The procurator had no ill will to Jesus, and perhaps took a pleasure in what would offend the priests.   At all events, he was amenable to bribery.   His surprise was excited by the tidings that Jesus had already expired, concerning which he required to be satisfied by an official report.   Whether or not he received money from Joseph, he readily gave permission to him to take possession of the body.   In the case of Joseph, who begged the body of Jesus, and of Nicodemus, who purchased the spices and aided in the interment, we see a remarkable instance of the power of the cross—of the death and love of Jesus—to overcome the fears excited by a regard to the world's opinion, and by a wish to stand well with the world.   The cross brings out latent love and undeveloped courage, and leads to boldness and confession.

III. THE ENTOMBMENT.   In preparation for this the body was taken down from the cross, was wound in linen bought for the purpose, being enfolded in fragrant myrrh and aloes.   Joseph was the owner of a garden near to Calvary, where in the solid rock was hewn a tomb, destined probably for the reception of his own remains—what we might term a family vault.   In this suitable and peaceful sepulchre Joseph, aided (as John tells us) by Nicodemus, laid the sacred form in which the Lord of life and glory had laboured and suffered for mankind. Against the entrance of the grave a huge stone was rolled, to secure the resting-place from intrusion. Thus, as in a garden Christ had endured his agony, in a garden he rested in the repose of death. How cherished in the memory and heart of Christendom were and are these sad and sacred scenes, none can be ignorant. Christ's "precious death and burial" have been celebrated in Christian hymns, commemorated in Christian ordinances, embalmed in Christian liturgies of prayer and intercession. The crucifixion, the descent from the cross, the mourning of the faithful women (the *pieta*), the entombment of the Saviour,—all these have been favourite and congenial themes with Christian painters. And of all subjects of Christian preaching, none are so pathetic, so melting, so fitted to awaken contrition for sin, so fitted to produce contempt for the world, as the topics suggested by these mournful incidents. It is solemnly affecting to think of this earth as being, during those sacred hours, the sepulchre of the Son of God.

IV. THE WITNESSES OF CHRIST'S BURIAL. It is observable that the holy and faithful women, who had ministered to Jesus in his public career, who had stood in the neighbourhood of the cross, and who had seen him die—they who were to be the first witnesses of his resurrection,—these were present at the entombment, as loth to part from the Lord whom they honoured and loved, as lingering for the last look upon the form of him to whose words they had so often listened with joy, and at whose hands they had received blessings priceless and immortal.

APPLICATION. 1. The moment when sin seems triumphant is the moment when Divine Providence is preparing for its confusion and destruction. To Christ's enemies his death appeared simply the end of his holy ministry, and when his lifeless form was committed to the grave they deemed his influence for ever at an end. Yet, in truth, now was about to commence the reign of him who tasted death for every man, but was about to ascend to the throne of spiritual empire. 2. The burial of our Saviour is to us the token of his love and of the completeness of his mediatorial work. That he did not shrink from even the ignominy and the weakness of the grave should be to us an assurance of his perfect humanity, his complete sympathy, and a pledge that the salvation which he did and suffered so much to secure shall be thorough and complete, shall be sure and everlasting. 3. The burial of Christ is to be, in a spiritual sense, shared by all his believing and renewed people. We are one with Christ, in his death and in his resurrection. And, as if to show how thoroughly we participate in our Saviour's death unto sin, we are represented as even buried with him. By baptism or consecration unto his death we are said to enter, as it were, his tomb; that, dying unto sin, we may rise again and live unto righteousness, holiness, and God. 4. The interment of our Lord seems to cast most precious and consolatory light upon our own and our friends' mortality. That there is naturally a repulsiveness in the grave and in dissolution is not denied. Yet to know that our gracious Lord deigned to taste death for every man, and to be laid to rest in a cave of the earth, is to be fortified against the unpleasing and distressing associations which are all that unbelievers connect with dissolution. When the lifeless form of a good man is borne to the grave, let us think of such an event in close connection with the burial of him who was and is the Lord of life. 5. Secret disciples should take encouragement from the conduct of Joseph and Nicodemus. Remember this, that whilst you have less excuse than they had for concealing your faith and disguising your attachment to Jesus, you have more reasons and stronger inducements to open confession. The Lord Jesus has not hidden his love for you; he has expressed it in words, and proved it by sufferings as well as actions. And he expects that you should boldly avow yourselves his, that you should confess him before men. Then he will not be ashamed of you before his Father and the holy angels.

HOMILIES BY VARIOUS AUTHORS.

Vers. 1—5.—*Jesus at the bar of the Roman power.* In its officers and agents representative of the whole Gentile world; so that the whole human race is involved in his condemnation and death.

I. THE PURPOSE OF THE FURTHER REFERENCE. To obtain authority for carrying out the death-sentence. This would not be allowed to a simple Jewish tribunal. The step taken was, therefore, a practical abdication of their theocratic pretensions. Hatred drives men into inconsistency and hypocrisy.

II. THE CHARGE MADE. Not the same as that upon which they themselves condemned him, but such an interpretation of it as would most readily render him liable to the judgment of the Roman government.

III. HIS REPLY TO PILATE. An idiomatic equivalent for "Yes," "I am so." The question is understood as an assertion put interrogatively, "Thou art the King of the Jews?" "The rationale of the idiom is that *when the interrogative form is withdrawn from the class of interrogations referred to, the saying that remains is the reality*" (Morison). A similar purpose to that which animated the reply to the high priest is here apparent. The Roman world was certified as to the dignity of Christ. In John's Gospel (xviii. 36—38) the true interpretation of this title as a moral and spiritual one is recorded as having been given by Christ to Pilate. It involved no treason, therefore, against the Roman power.

IV. THE GENERAL DEMEANOUR OF CHRIST TOWARDS HIS ACCUSERS. *Silence.* 1. *A marvel.* The calmness of the Prisoner was unlike the behaviour of prisoners generally, and appeared supernatural. 2. *It was equivalent to an appeal to a higher tribunal.* 3. *An impressive moral victory.*—M.

Vers. 6—15.—*Christ or Barabbas.* I. A REVELATION OF THE HATRED OF THE NATURAL MIND FOR TRUTH AND GOODNESS. Several ancient authorities are in favour of readings here and elsewhere which would give us, "Jesus Barabbas" (*i.e.* son of a father or rabbi), as the full name of the "robber" who was here the favourite of the populace. If this be so, there would be two of the name Jesus, and the choice would thus be strikingly emphasized. The character of Barabbas as a rioter and murderer is glossed over by the semblance of patriotism, as he is said to have been engaged in the insurrection caused by Pilate's appropriation of the corban of the temple for building an aqueduct. In any case the personal character is utterly subordinated, and motives of policy prevail. The season of the Passover recalled the historic sparing of Israel's firstborn and the destruction of Egypt's. The positions seemed now to be reversed, or Israel deliberately assumed the character of Egypt, preferring that the guilty should be set free. We have here the self-conviction of: 1. *Perverted religious instincts.* In the case of the chief priests and people of the Jews. Their whole religious training ought to have prepared them to receive Christ. 2. *Popular opinion unguided by the Spirit of God.* A prey to unscrupulous influences, to false sentiment, and to passing excitements. 3. *Spiritual indifference.* In the person of Pilate, in whom it lent itself readily to unprincipled diplomacy and the surrender of innocence.

II. A PARABLE OF THE CHOICE EVERY MAN IS CALLED UPON TO MAKE. 1. *In daily life.* Minute occurrences in which the contrasts may not seem so striking, or the choice so final. Their ultimate influence in the determination of character and destiny. 2. *In the great crises of religious decision.* It is well at such times to consider carefully the respective ends of the courses of conduct that present themselves.

III. A SYMBOL OF THE CENTRAL MYSTERY OF REDEMPTION. In the gospel the method of salvation is that the innocent shall suffer for the guilty. Jesus the Christ thus became the substitute of Barabbas the robber. The latter only gained the prolongation of his earthly life thereby ; a questionable benefit. But those who believe in Christ as the vicarious Sacrifice and voluntary Self-sacrificer for sinners will receive eternal salvation.—M.

Vers. 16—20, 29—32.—*The mockery of Jesus.* The scene, the courtyard of the governor's residence ; the actors, the Roman soldiery and the Son of God ; and the awful fate that awaited the Sufferer, render this mockery one of the most impressive incidents in human history. It was deliberate, brutal, and inhuman.

I. WHAT IT WAS IN HIM THAT WAS MOCKED. The crown and the purple and the sham homage are interpreted by the cry, "Hail, King of the Jews!" 1. *It was his kingly pretensions they ridiculed.* So the Jews had laughed to scorn his prophetic office. To those Roman soldiers, impressed with the grandeur of the power they themselves represented, the claim to be king of a small and subject land like Palestine was very petty. They could afford, so they thought, to laugh at it; even as Pilate was not afraid to have released him who preferred it. 2. But even more *did they despise his title as a theocratic King.* How far these citizens of the empire of law were from realizing the true character of the kingdom of righteousness! Had he even been recognized by the Jews themselves as their ruler, the nation was too small, too insignificant in a political or military point of view, to be of any consequence. There was no suspicion in their minds of danger to the Roman empire, or of the influence which his moral and spiritual character was to wield in the new ages of the world. It is, although they knew it not then, by virtue of this same moral majesty and power that he, in turn, has become the Conqueror of mankind, and is maintaining and extending his sway in regions where mouldering ruins and obsolete statutes are all that remain to witness to Rome's vanished greatness. It is the mockers themselves that are now ridiculous.

II. How MEN MAY MOCK HIM STILL. There is a feeling of human tenderness that is outraged as we imagine the meek Sufferer amidst the brutal throng. But the true sentiment that ought to be awakened is that which concerns the principles of righteousness and truth, of which he was the embodiment and representative. It is for them he would have us solicitous even to jealousy. Men still wound and mock Christ: 1. *When they render to him a merely nominal homage.* "When we pervert the truth of the Word for our own evil ends, we scourge the Son of man; when to justify our evils we fabricate a system of ingenious error, and thus exalt our own wisdom above the wisdom of Jesus, we plait a crown of thorns and put it on his head; when we substitute our own righteousness for the righteousness of Christ, we clothe him with a purple robe; when we are inwardly worshippers of self and outwardly worshippers of the Lord, our worship of him is a mocking salutation of 'Hail, King of the Jews!' while every presumptuous sin we commit is a stroke inflicted on the Son of man" (W. Bruce). 2. *When they ignore the moral nature of his power,* relying on material and external means instead of spiritual. When they use the methods of business in a business spirit, or even the arts of diplomacy, to advance his kingdom. So men clothe Christ in the insignia of Herod. "The kingliest King was crowned with thorns!" 3. *When they would accept the advantages of his kingdom without observing its conditions.* As when persons profess to enjoy the preaching and ordinances of the gospel, but do not carry its doctrines into practice; or when they are "straightway offended" at the tribulations and privations which true discipleship involves.—M.

Vers. 31, 32.—*The Saviour's helplessness.* A paradox. The situation as regarded by those who surrounded the cross was manifestly in contradiction with the pretensions of Jesus. This *primâ facie* impression was not accidentally produced, but belonged, so to speak, to the very essence of the gospel as a "mystery;" and it had its ends to serve in the inscrutable wisdom of God. That it tended at first to conceal the true character of the Saviour's sufferings there can be no doubt; but as certainly it prepared the way for subsequent spiritual revelation. It served—

I. To EXCITE ATTENTION. This apparent self-contradiction in the career of Jesus was a matter of public notoriety. Had it been overlooked by any, the enemies of the truth were eager to point it out. There is something piquant to the curiosity and speculation of men in a matter which wears such an aspect.

II. AS A MEANS OF AVENGING THE TRUTH UPON ITS ADVERSARIES. How quick they were to seize upon it and turn it to the best advantage! For a little while they had it all their own way. So infatuated were they, that they put the seeming contradiction in the strongest possible form; the antithesis is all but perfect. Not quite so, however. They had to confess that he *had* "saved others." The monuments of his work remained, and facts are hard to discredit. There was something in the very sound which would recall histories of gracious sympathy and help; miracles of saving power. It was precisely this element of stubborn matter of fact which could not be accounted for on the theory of mere pretension, and which in turn vitiated their argument. A thousand presumptions will not disprove, but must yield to, a single fact. Now, the fact of Christ's miraculous works is certified to us by those who sought to discredit and disprove them. Out of their own mouths are they condemned. They are self-sentenced to a vicious mill-round of mere logic. The natural man cannot understand the heavenly mystery.

III. As a means of disciplining and rewarding faith. 1. That the disciples themselves did not comprehend it at first is evident from the Gospel narrative. It must have been hard for them to see what appeared the falsification of their hopes; harder still to be taunted by those who had so cruelly slain their Master. What part may it not have had in the "cup" the Saviour himself had to drink? 2. But by this very discipline it prepared them for the inner and spiritual "discerning of the Lord's body." Their spiritual susceptibilities were awakened, and they began to realize the meaning of the mystery. Gradually they were to emerge from the bewilderment and perplexity. Peter and the rest of the disciples travelled far ere they reached Pentecost, but each step in the journey of their faith was a revelation of the secret of Jesus. It was not to human force he had submitted, but to his Father's will. The necessity that bound him to the cross was a spiritual one. It was because he wished to save others absolutely that he would and could not save himself.—M.

Vers. 40, 41.—*Women watching the cross.* The prominence of women in the Gospel narrative suggests the fact that Christianity has done more to awaken the spiritual nature of women, and to furnish them with a sphere for the exercise of their special gifts and graces, than any other religion. For the first time the gospel gave to woman dignity and recognized position in spiritual things. In the gospel, the feminine as well as the masculine aspects and phases of morality are represented. Why were they at the cross?

I. A proof of their attachment to Christ. 1. *They had already shown this.* They were, some of them, of good social standing, and had command of considerable means. This advantage they had employed in the interests of Christ and his work— "they ministered unto him" when he was in Galilee. And the service they rendered involved a certain inconvenience and trouble, for they had to follow him almost as much as his apostles. 2. *Now they gave even more signal evidence.* Modestly retiring to the outskirts of the rabble, they persistently watched him. They might have been excused by ordinary scruples from witnessing the horrible scene, but they could not allow themselves to go away. He still represented their highest spiritual interest, and they were willing to brave anything for his sake.

II. A trial of their love. It rose into heroic resolution and sacrifice. 1. *How typical their experience was of that which their sisters have had to go through in all ages!* They stood by helpless, unable to render any further service. It was not for them to attempt a rescue when brave men had forsaken him and fled. But they could show the virtue of passive endurance. They could prove to the Sufferer that their love was unabated, their faith forlorn, but not dead. So many a noble wife, sister, or mother has had to stand by when loved ones have been done to death, or ruined by great concerns in which they might not interfere. They have been able only to trust and wait and pray, to comfort when they could not deliver. One consolation remained to them—they *had* done what they could. 2. *To so try it was the grandest recognition of its genuineness.* They were accounted worthy to suffer with Christ. Their affection was to pass through the fires seven times refined. Peter might be faithless, and the rest of the disciples sadly fail, but *they* could watch with the Saviour as his spirit sank beneath its accumulated woe.—M.

Vers. 42—47.—*The burial of the Crucified.* I. Provided for by God. There are several striking proofs of providential arrangement in the burying of the Saviour. He never stipulated as to where or how he should be buried; his mind was too much occupied as to how he should die. Yet were great things to turn upon the manner, the time, and the place of his burial. He whose angels hid the grave of Moses, was equally careful to make known the place where his Son lay. The sepulchre was new, and in the midst of a garden, therefore isolated from other graves. The identity of the risen One is thus secured against all possibility of mistake. In inspiring the agents through whom the burial was effected, God fulfilled his own eternal appointment. The death, hastened by the unusual delicacy of the Sufferer, and the intervention of the sabbath, secured on the one hand that "not a bone should be broken," and, on the other, that he should be buried on the day before the sabbath, his rest in the grave coinciding with the sabbatic rest of the Creator, fulfilling the week, so to speak, of the old economy, and ending with the beginning of the first day of the next week, thus ushering in a new economy, a new creation. The garden-tomb of Joseph a fit resting-place for him who was to be the Firstfruits of the resurrection. If the cross was shameful, the tomb was honourable. "They had appointed him a grave with the despised ; and among the honoured (did he obtain it) in his death " (Isa. liii. 9, Lange's translation).

II. VOLUNTARILY EFFECTED BY MEN. 1. *A victory of faith.* A "councillor of honourable estate " is moved by an inward impulse to make this his own special concern. The tragic circumstances of the last few hours had touched his heart and kindled his enthusiasm ; and he and his friend Nicodemus—" the same who came to Jesus by night "—casting off all secrecy or fear of man, vied with one another in paying the last tribute of respect to the illustrious Dead. His simple request was an act of faith; the boldness which rendered it so effectual was a victory of faith. Already the power of the cross was being felt. The centurion, the governor, Joseph, and Nicodemus alike confess to its influence. 2. *A tribute of love.* How careful are the two in their preparations! The linen cloth and the spices are the offering of affection, which follows its object even to the tomb. As in Mary's spikenard, the question of expense is put wholly out of sight. The richest and best that they may offer are brought forth for the occasion. 3. *In token of undying hope.* The spices arrested the process of corruption, and witnessed to the expectation of the resurrection.—M.

Vers. 11, 12.—*The foes of Jesus.* It is remarkable that the evangelists speak of their Lord's enemies with such unruffled calmness. If our dearest friend had been subjected to inhuman treatment, ending in his death, we should have held up the names of his oppressors to the execration of the world. But in the Gospels we look in vain for a strong epithet, or a burst of indignant declamation. This was not because the evangelists were deficient in love to their Lord, but because they had caught something of the spirit of him "who, when he was reviled, reviled not again," and because they had learnt that amid these strange, sad scenes the Divine purpose was being fulfilled, and that he who was the Victim of sinners was the Sacrifice for sin. Hostility to the Lord Jesus Christ is the irrefragable proof of man's antagonism to goodness and truth. The cross of Calvary, stained by his blood, is a witness at once to the depravity of man and the infinite love of God. Hatred to goodness was never more pronounced and desperate, for goodness was now both incarnate and aggressive. It was no longer an abstraction, but a Person ; no longer inert, but active. The Jews were generally left unmolested, because they were content to dwell as a peculiar and separate people, without assailing idolatry in others. But our Lord and his disciples endeavoured to make the truth known and felt. Moses said in effect, " Keep yourselves from surrounding peoples, lest ye be defiled." Christ said, " Go ye into all the world, and preach the gospel to every creature." The old economy was represented by the temple, which was compact, perfect, kept free from the defiling tread of the heathen ; the new was represented by the mustard seed, which would grow under the open sky till it became a tree, and many nations found rest under its shadow. It was partly because Jesus Christ was aggressive in his work that the world rose in arms against him. Let us study the characteristics of some of his foes, and discover their motives, that we may be on our guard against becoming their modern representatives. In the two verses we have chosen we have glimpses of the priests, of the people, and of Pontius Pilate.

I. THE PRIESTS WERE HOSTILE TO OUR LORD FROM PRIDE. They should have been the first to welcome him. As Jews they were familiar with the utterances of the prophets, and as priests they should have known the meaning of the sacrifices they offered. They had heard the preaching of John when he announced Messiah, and they had again and again had evidence respecting the work and teaching of Jesus. But pride summoned prejudice to build up an obstacle impervious to all assaults. Their social dignity refused to recognize this peasant Teacher; their intellectual culture spurned the utterances of the Prophet of Nazareth; and their ecclesiastical prestige held it to be incredible that a carpenter's Son should be " the Light of the world." In our day, too, pride has such disastrous influence. Many admit that Jesus Christ was a pattern of benevolence and of moral purity; but when he declares himself to be an infallible Teacher of Divine truth, when he claims superhuman power, when he demands submission to his will, they rise against him, as those did who once exclaimed,

"For good works we stone thee not, but for blasphemy; because thou, being a man, makest thyself God."

II. PILATE WAS HOSTILE TO OUR LORD FROM POLICY. He saw at a glance the vindictiveness of the priests, and the innocence of him they accused; and, after a few minutes' conversation, frankly said, "I find in him no fault at all." But this was followed by a pitiful struggle and fall. He tried to rid himself of responsibility by sending the Galilean to Herod; he offered to release him, not on the ground of innocence, but as an act of grace, usual at the Passover; he cruelly scourged him, in the hope that this would satisfy the bloodthirsty mob. But when these devices failed, and the people threatened Pilate himself, as a traitor to the emperor, he delivered Jesus to be crucified. He fell through moral cowardice, brought about by former crimes, fearing lest he should lose office and honour unless he fell in with the demands of this brutal crowd. Things seen rule the man who has no faith in things unseen. Personal interests seemed more to him than the life or death of one poor Prisoner. He yielded to clamour; and though at the time he knew it not, he crucified the Christ.

III. THE PEOPLE WERE HOSTILE TO OUR LORD FROM PASSION. "The chief priests moved the people." They would urge that Jesus had been condemned by their own orthodox court, and that it was the duty of every patriot to induce the Romans to support its decisions; and they would further urge that Barabbas, the leader of an insurrection, was a friend of the people and a champion of their liberties, so that he was to be preferred to Jesus of Nazareth. The mass of the people were not intelligently hostile to our Lord. Some knew little of him, and thought that the Sanhedrim was best able to judge of such questions; and others went with the popular current, whether it led them to shout "Hosanna!" or "Crucify him!" Hence they were included with the soldiers in the prayer of our Lord, "Father, forgive them; for they know not what they do."—A. R.

Ver. 33.—*Darkness around the cross.* When we remember who he was who was dying amidst the mockery of the world he came to save, we are no longer incredulous about this statement. The "Light of the world" was in darkness, the Saviour was refusing to save himself, the King of glory was wearing thorns as his crown, and had ascended the cross as his throne. The event referred to in our text is one of many examples of the deep and secret connection existing between the kingdoms of nature and of grace. We believe that the Invisible created the visible, and still acts upon it, producing now and again transmutations of its energies, though never making a break in their continuity, and that when Christ Jesus came forth from the invisible world there was manifested in him a peculiar communication between these two realms. In him was seen the connection which had so often been indicated in the Divine economy, *e.g.* a curse had accompanied man's spiritual fall. Promises of temporal good were associated with moral worth. Images drawn from the "desert" and the "trees" and "rivers" by the prophets found their justification in the truth uttered afterwards by St. Paul, "The whole creation groaneth and travaileth in pain together until now," etc. The darkening of the sun was the testimony of Nature to her dying Lord; a hint that creation is dependent on him, that Nature is supported by unseen spiritual powers, and that the fate of the earth is involved in the kingdom of God. It is no meaningless portent described here, but an event which had its teaching both immediate and remote. Consider—

I. THE EFFECTS OF THIS DARKNESS ON THOSE AROUND THE CROSS. 1. *This supernatural gloom would increase the solemnity of the event.* As the darkness grew denser, silence would fall on the gibing tongues and every noisy laugh would be stilled; and as the gloom deepened into unearthly night over the busy streets, the open fields, and the sacred temple, many would ask themselves, "What meaneth this?" Carelessness and flippant scepticism are always out of place in view of the cross. If the narrative be mythical, it should at least be rejected intelligently and seriously; for, if it be true, it involves stupendous issues to us all. 2. *It hid his agony from the onlookers.* Faithful friends and, above all, the loving mother stood there till they could bear no more; and God would not suffer them to be tried above bearing, so darkness shrouded the Sufferer. And the foes of our Lord were shut out from a scene too sacred for them to witness. Beyond what was necessary, the well-beloved Son should not be exposed to their brutal jeers. 3. *It was an admonition to our Lord's foes.* They were readers of Old Testament Scriptures, and knew well how their fathers had been dealt with. They remembered that in the day of their national deliverance darkness had fallen on Jehovah's foes, and had proved the precursor of heavier plagues, and therefore we do not wonder that some went home " beating their breasts," and saying, " What next?" Would that they had turned even then!

II. THE SUGGESTIONS OF THIS DARKNESS TO THE WORLD. 1. *It indicated the going out of the world's Light.* Jesus had plainly declared, " I am the Light of the world;" " Walk while ye have the light, lest darkness come upon you." To some, at least, such words would come back with new meaning and power. To reject Christ is to shut off light from the soul, and become ready for the outer darkness. A Christless world was set forth when the sun was darkened. 2. *It suggested the ignorance of the Gentiles and the malignity of the Jews.* The soldiers were brutal, yet knew not what they did. Pilate, in political scheming, had lost all sense of righteousness and truth, and so in ignorance delivered Jesus to be crucified. " Darkness covered the earth, and gross darkness the people." On the other hand, the Jews had in themselves the fulfil- ment of the words, " The god of this world hath blinded the minds of them that believe not." 3. *It reminded the Church of the mystery of the Atonement.* The death of the Lord Jesus had a Godward as well as a worldward aspect. It was to attract human love, but at the same time to reveal Divine love. When the darkness passed away, and the sun shone upon the cross, the returning light was like the bow of promise after the Flood—a sign of peace between man and God, and a pledge of " the rainbow round about the throne," in the land where all give thanks to God and to the Lamb that was slain.—A. R.

Ver. 43.—*Joseph of Arimathæa.* In comparison with the leading apostles of our Lord Joseph of Arimathæa was not distinguished. He had not the spirituality of St. John, nor the prominence of St. Peter, nor the world-wide influence of St. Paul. We are consciously turning from the generals of Christ's army to contemplate one of the ordinary soldiers; but it was he who, when his natural leaders had fallen, stepped to the front and proved himself a hero. We know but little of Joseph beyond such facts as these: he was a rich man, respected by his countrymen as one who was " good and just;" a member of the Sanhedrim, who refused his consent to the resolution passed that Jesus should be put to death; and a resident in Jerusalem, who, having prepared for himself a new grave, dedicated it to his crucified Lord. We may learn valuable lessons from his courage and fidelity, the more so if we blend together all the references made to him by the evangelists.

I. THAT WE OUGHT TO REFUSE OUR CONSENT TO A WRONG, EVEN THOUGH OUR REFUSAL WILL NOT PREVENT ITS ACCOMPLISHMENT. Except for Nicodemus, Joseph stood alone in protesting against the action resolved on by the council against Jesus. He was, no doubt, strongly urged to yield to the majority, so that the council might appear united in the endeavour to put down One who had disregarded its authority. But although his protest was seemingly powerless, he resolutely persisted in it, and to the last he " did not consent to the counsel and deed of them." He was an example in this to all who conscientiously object to habits and practices which obtain in their own sphere of activity, be they politicians, men of business, or boys and girls at school. But let all such be sure that a real principle is at stake, not a prejudice, and that they are not moved by self-assertion, obstinacy, or pride.

II. THAT BY BRAVELY DOING WHAT WE BELIEVE TO BE RIGHT WE EMBOLDEN AND HELP OTHERS. Joseph required courage on the council, and still more now when he went in to Pilate to beg the body of Jesus. So terrible was the hatred felt against Jesus by the chief priests that the procurator himself had trembled before it, and Peter, with his fellow-disciples, had forsaken the Lord. Yet Joseph stepped to the front as a friend of the crucified One, and Nicodemus followed him. All men of decided convic- tions thus influence others. Thousands thanked God secretly for the stand which Elijah made on Carmel. Multitudes wait to be led aright by those whose character and ability bring responsibility.

III. THAT IF WE GO RIGHT ONWARD IN THE PATH OF DUTY WE SHALL SUCCEED BETTER THAN WE EXPECT. When Joseph undertook his mission he knew that he might risk his life, or at least his reputation; that he might be called on to pay a heavy and prohibitory ransom as a bribe to the governor; or that he might be refused with scorn and insult. Yet, when he went in boldly to Pilate, to his own amazement, his request was freely granted! Many have had a similar experience: *e.g.* the Israelites when they obeyed the command, "Go forward," and saw the sea divide before their advancing footsteps; and Peter, who followed the angel and found the great gate of the prison open of its own accord. Apply this to typical experiences in a Christian's life.

IV. THAT A CRISIS COMES IN THE HISTORY OF MEN WHICH DETERMINES THEIR WHOLE FUTURE. The crucifixion of Jesus constituted a crisis to Joseph. Under the influence of sorrow and indignation he was prompted to this step, and the future destiny of this secret disciple depended upon his taking it. Such times come to us all. Our spiritual life has not always the same even flow. Occasionally we are strangely, strongly moved to resolve, to speak, or to act, and tremendous issues depend upon our obedience to God-given impulse. If the vessel aground on the harbour bar is not set free when the tide is highest, she will be wrecked in the coming storm.

V. THAT THE MOVING CAUSE OF DECISION FOR GOD IS THE CROSS OF THE LORD JESUS CHRIST. Joseph had listened to the teaching of Jesus, and witnessed his superhuman works, but till now had been a disciple "secretly," for fear of the Jews. That position was a false one, and so long as he was in it he was deficient in gratitude and courage. But when he saw Jesus on the cross he felt as the centurion did when he cried, "Truly this was the Son of God;" and henceforth he was known as the Lord's disciple and servant. Christ's death has been to millions the beginning of new life.

VI. THAT GOD WILL FULFIL HIS PURPOSES WHETHER HIS AVOWED SERVANTS ARE LOYAL TO HIM OR NOT. The twelve were scattered and the Church seemed destroyed, when suddenly there came forth from their former obscurity two secret disciples, who took upon themselves the work which others had left. And in all ages God has his faithful ones who are sometimes unrecognized by the Church; yet, filled with his Spirit, they shall aid in establishing the kingdom of the crucified, and now risen, Christ. —A. R.

Vers. 6—15.—*Barabbas; or, the evil choice.* A strange custom prevailed. To appease the anger of the rabble, and to curry favour with them, Pilate was wont, on the recurrence of certain feasts, to release a prisoner, giving the mob permission to choose who should be the favoured one. At this feast "the multitude went up and began to ask him to do as he was wont to do unto them." Knowing that "for envy the chief priests had delivered him up," he tested the feeling of the multitude by asking them if he should release "the King of the Jews," thus giving them the opportunity of repudiating the deed of the priests. The question hangs as in a balance. The voice of a rabble is called upon to decide the fate of "the Son of man. On that voice hinges (apparently) the course of the work of the world's redemption. The die is cast. The multitude make their election. The choice is proclaimed in a wild, uproarious cry, "Not this man, but Barabbas." So the besotted rabble declare their spirit, their low moral condition, their attitude towards truth and righteousness. Barabbas, we learn, was "a robber," and he was cast into prison "for a certain insurrection made in the city, and for murder." Thus they "denied the holy and righteous One, and asked for a murderer to be granted unto" them. Nothing could more clearly declare the spirit they were of. Sadly and in silence many pure hearts mourned while the rabble gave vent to their evilness, pouring forth the uttermost malignity as a flood to sweep away "the Prince of life." The insensate tools of a corrupt, self-condemned priesthood, they, by yielding all too readily to them who should have guided them into the right way, become identified with "the chief priests" in a choice which for ever brands them with the utmost vileness. The spirit of the people must be judged by their attitude towards Jesus on the one hand, and towards Barabbas on the other; and a word is sufficient to declare it. In the one we behold the Teacher of righteousness, who had endeavoured to enforce the laws of God. He represented truth. To it he bore witness. He denounced evil in thought, in word, in deed. He opened to the feet of the people the path of virtue; he pointed to the gates of the eternal city, and gave men assurance of immortality. Never had the world looked upon so perfect an embodiment of pure goodness; never will it look upon his like until he himself appear again and every eye beholds him. The other is the embodiment of evil. His name is the synonym of it. The one name men dare not assume from its loftiness; the other they would not from its lowness. But this rabble-host chooses the evil one, and so declares its spirit is in accord with his. It is self-condemned. How painfully we read: 1. The perilous influence which unscrupulous leaders may exert over an undisciplined, untutored mob. 2. How possible it is for the human heart so to deceive itself that the highest representatives of the purest system of truth and morals may be debased into an alliance with the most corrupt and degraded, and may prostitute the holiest functions to the most evil ends. High priests of God may lead men to the service of the devil. 3. The sad consequences of (1) a blinded intelligence, (2) an undisciplined moral nature, (3) a corrupt prejudice. High priests and people have their way. "Their voices prevailed." And Pilate, moved with fear, and evidently against his convictions of right, "to content the multitude," "released him . . . whom they asked for; but Jesus he delivered up to their will." Thus the world to-day demands its Barabbas and rejects Jesus. Truth, goodness, charity, patience, heavenly mindedness—all that is pure and good—is sacrificed, and by "the multitude" still evil is preferred, and they, alas! are "content."—G.

Vers. 16—32.—*The crucifixion: the human deed.* To the contemplation of that supreme fact in history, around which the thoughts, the hearts, of men gather more and more, we are directed by the few sad, solemn words, "Pilate . . . delivered Jesus, when he had scourged him, to be crucified." The preliminary incidents are minutely related. They describe the most solemn mockery ever perpetrated. The scourging first. He is stripped to the waist, his hands tied behind him; his bent back is beaten with leathern thongs weighted at the ends with bits of lead or sharpened bone. Bleeding, he is led within the court, "the Prætorium," where the whole cohort of soldiers vent their ingenuity in exposing their Victim to ridicule. They cast a purple-dyed military cloak over him; with their hard hands they twist twigs of *nâbk*, with its long, hard, sharp spikes or thorns, into a mock-crown, and press it down upon his fever-heated brow. In his yielding hand they thrust a reed, and bow their knees in mock submission and homage, and with coarse gibes hail him "King of the Jews." Snatching the reed from his hand, they beat him with it on his bleeding head; they strike him with their fists or with rods; and in the direst indignity spit upon him. Then, "wearing the crown of thorns and the purple robe," he is led out. To this uncomplaining Sufferer—this smitten and forsaken One—Pilate calls the attention of the multitude with words which, like those he wrote, float on through the ages, bearing their different message as the listening ears differed—"Ecce homo!" The echoing cry from the mingled voices of "the chief priests and the officers" arose above all others, "Crucify, crucify!" A miserable squabble between Pilate and the Jews ends in his "Behold your King!" and their reply, "Away with him, away with him, crucify him! . . . We have no king but Cæsar." In the temple Judas is casting down "the thirty pieces of silver," making confession, in a repentance all too late, "I have sinned in that I betrayed innocent blood," and his agonized spirit seeks a vain relief in a hasty destruction of a life he cannot support. Jesus, "bearing the cross," is led away to be crucified, when, sinking, exhausted with suffering, beneath its weight, he is relieved by its being laid on "one Simon of Cyrene"—the first in a long line of lowly cross-bearers who endure the shame for Jesus' sake. "And they bring him unto the place Golgotha." One only spark of humanity is left. "They offered him wine mingled with myrrh." Then upon a cross—symbol of the uttermost degradation and shame, and more than a symbol of the uttermost suffering—they stretched his sacred, quivering limbs, piercing his hands and his feet with rough nails. Thus "*they crucified him.*" Then from out of the most indescribable agony of body broke forth the gentle murmur of a loving heart in modest prayer, "Father, forgive them; for they know not what they do." Ah! they crushed, they broke that heart; but it sent forth only the sweet fragrance of its love, as a crushed flower its perfume. But he is not alone. "With him they crucify two robbers, one on his right hand and one on his left." Thus is he "numbered with the transgressors." "Racked by the extremest pain, and covered with every shame which men were wont to heap on the greatest criminals; forsaken and denied by his disciples; no sigh escaped his lips, no cry of agony, no bitter or faltering word; only a prayer for the forgiveness of his enemies. They had acted in blindness, under the influence of religious and political fanaticism; for, to use St. Paul's words, had they known it they would not have crucified the Lord of glory." Surely they could not know, or it would not have to be recorded in one sentence: "And they crucify him, *and part his garments among them, casting lots upon them, what each should take.*" So hard, so insensible! In presence of the central fact in the world's history, men gamble!

Here we must find our lessons, in the contrasted intensity of interest in human salvation which is shown from above, and that careless, blind indifference which marks men "before whose eyes Jesus Christ [is] openly set forth crucified." The world must see itself represented in the actors on that dread evening; and each of us may see himself in one or other of the many surrounding "*the Man*" on that day of darkness, doom, and death. Let each bring himself into presence of that cross—the true judgment-seat—of Christ, and there test his heart, and try and prove his life. And further, let each one learn how his hand is not wanting among those rude hands that smote that tender flesh; nor his words from those that fell on that quick ear; nor his sins from those that burdened that too heavy-weighted heart.

> " Our sins of spite were part of those that day,
>   Whose cruel whips and thorns did make him smart;
>   Our lusts were those that tired him in the way;
>   Our want of love was that which pierced his heart:
>   And still when we forget or slight his pain,
>   We crucify and torture him again."
>
>   G.

Vers. 33—41.—*The crucifixion: the Divine words.* Seven words are counted by them who now treasure his sayings, as spoken by Jesus on the cross. Each evangelist contributes his portion towards the little perfect stock.

I. The first was A WORD OF PRAYER FOR FORGIVENESS, itself a forgiveness. "I forgive them: do thou, O Father, forgive." It was a word of excuse for them who did it ignorantly and in unbelief. "They see only a malefactor: open their eyes that they may see and know." If the prayer may be offered for them who, with wicked hands, crucified the Lord of glory, because they did it ignorantly, learn we that such a prayer may be offered, and surely will be heard, for all ignorant, blinded ones who, in sinning against the Lord, are sinners against their own souls. In proportion as we sin wilfully, having knowledge of the truth and of what we do, we put ourselves further and further away from the possibility of forgiveness. How true is it that men to-day sin, not knowing what they do! This prayer covers all sin, for no one knows truly and fully what he does when he sins against Christ.

II. The second word is A WORD OF PROMISE IN RESPONSE TO PRAYER AND CONFESSION. The time was brief; the last moments of the twelfth hour were hurrying past. In the heart of one of the malefactors some early teaching remained to quicken the conscience into life; and the punishment of crime was working its right effect. "We indeed justly . . . we receive the due reward of our deeds." The word which passed the sacred lips, unmoistened with the stupefying wine, were words of life and healing and promise in response to the prayer, "Jesus, remember me when thou comest in thy kingdom." What faith is here! Faith in the kingdom, in the coming, in the readiness to hear! "Jesus" may not have had the same meaning to him it has to us. The reply to a dying, penitent thief has been a fountain of life to many. "Verily I say unto thee, To-day shalt thou be with me in Paradise."

III. A third word was A WORD OF TENDER, FILIAL LOVE. The languid, bloodshot, half-closed eyes turned, and "Jesus . . . saw his mother, and the disciple standing by, whom he loved." The fountain of love was not stayed; the holy heart was well-nigh breaking, yet it beat truly in all filial affection. From out of his great suffering he thinks of her, and thinks with fervent love. "Hail, thou that art highly favoured!" He is still her Son, henceforth to be represented in the "son" who is now to regard her as "mother." But he makes provision for her future. Ere those lips which spoke so often to the disciple "whom he loved" were closed, he uttered one last word to him, revealing the deep thought of the Sufferer's heart, and committing to him a sacred charge he would entrust only to one "whom he loved"—"Behold thy mother." It is all beautifully human ; but as all human deeds, when they are true and beautiful, approach the Divine, so was this beautifully Divine. It was enough. A wish from that heart and those dried lips was sacred. "From that hour the disciple took her unto his own home"—took her with the sword piercing through her soul.

IV. A fourth word is FROM THE VERY ABYSS OF SUFFERING—perhaps from a greater depth than any word arose that ever escaped from the lips of man. Darkness was over the land ; darkness was over the pure Sufferer's soul. The words present the deepest of mysteries ; we cannot open it. Was it, as has been suggested, the effect of the combination of profound mental anguish with the well-nigh intolerable pangs of dissolution, rendered all the more natural and inevitable in the case of One whose feelings were so deep, tender, and real ; whose moral consciousness was so pure, and whose love was so intense ? Had his abiding conviction of fellowship with God for the moment given way under the pressure of [extreme bodily and mental suffering ? Was it a mere passing feeling, *as though* he were no longer sustained by the power of the Divine life ? Surely more than this. Ah! who can know ? It is only as we descend to these depths that we can understand how dark, how cold, how sad they are. Mere words can never convey an idea of suffering. The bitterness of this cup he only knows who drinks it. *What* is the forsaking by the God to whom he still clings—"My God, my God"—and "why" is he forsaken, remain for us depths into whose darkness we may peer but cannot fathom.

V. A fifth word is FROM THE POOR FEVERED FRAME. Fainting from loss of blood, from acute pain, from unrelieved suffering. "I thirst." Truly he may say, "My strength is dried up like a potsherd, and my tongue cleaveth to my jaws." The former cry ascended to heaven; this sinks upon the earth. A moistened sponge on a hyssop rod brought him temporary relief, and brought him strength sufficient to utter—

VI. A sixth word, uttered with "a loud" (was it a triumphant?) "voice," declaring, "It is finished." Yea, all is finished, notwithstanding the efforts of wicked men to prevent it. They unconsciously wrought out that which the Divine "hand and counsel foreordained to come to pass." "It is finished;" yea, Jesus' work is finished. The great end is reached. The last supreme act, or consummation of the continuous act of that life which was "one offering of himself," is now in process of completion. So far as relates to the toil, and service, and sacrifice, and suffering of earth, all is finished; and the last act of the conscious life, the last breath of the living frame, the last word of the lips of truth, seal the whole past.

VII. And in a seventh word, with one supreme effort to that Father from whom he seemed momentarily separated, he yields up himself—"gave up his spirit." Now are the words fulfilled, "I lay down my life, that I may take it again. No one taketh it away from me, but I lay it down of myself. I have power to lay it down, and I have power to take it again. This commandment have I received from my Father."—G.

Vers. 42—47.—*The entombment.* The sabbath hurried on—the day of rest. Joseph of Arimathæa, "a councillor of honourable estate, who also himself was looking for the kingdom of God," begged permission of Pilate to have the body of Jesus for interment. Pilate, being satisfied of the death of Jesus, "granted the corpse to Joseph." Then with tender hands he wrapped the body in a linen cloth and laid it in a tomb; "and he rolled a stone against the door of the tomb." Now the work is complete. The human rage is satisfied. The voice of the accuser is silent. The Divine condescension is perfect. It could descend no lower. The grave is the goal of human weakness. It is the lowest step ; then begins the upward ascent. The humiliation being complete, the exaltation begins. The grave is really the pathway to glory and honour. Jesus, who has sanctified every path of life, now sanctifies the grave. He has withdrawn the sting from death ; he dissipates the darkness from the tomb. And though we cannot desire the grave, yet it is no longer the repulsive, loathsome place it had ever been. Christ in the tomb of earth plainly speaks to us many lessons.

I. Concerning him, it teaches us that NO DESCENT WAS TOO GREAT FOR HIM TO MAKE IN HIS LOVING SERVICE TO THE CHILDREN OF MEN. He who stooped so low as to be born in a manger, sharing his first bed with lowing oxen, stoops lower still in making ready for the children of men their last sleeping-place. He who washed the feet of his disciples shared the grave with guilty men. Forasmuch as they whom he was not ashamed to call brethren must needs die and be buried, "he also himself in like manner partook of the same;" as "it behoved him in all things to be made like unto his brethren," he refused not this.

II. Concerning the grave, it is A SANCTIFICATION OF IT. We need not be ashamed to descend into this valley of humiliation, for our "Head" has gone before. If we can endure the sufferings of our cross, we can despise the shame of our tomb. We need not fear to die, for he hath brought "to nought him that had the power of death, that is the devil;" nor need we fear to lie down in the tomb, for Jesus lay there.

> "'Tis now a cell, where angels use
> To come and go with heavenly news,
> And in the ears of mourners say,
> 'Come, see the place where Jesus lay.'"

It is not the final goal of the human feet, as we shall soon learn. Its bolts can be withdrawn; its seal can be broken; its stone can be rolled away. The grave may be the pathway to the throne.

III. But it brings home to our hearts CHRIST'S CLAIM UPON US FOR OUR UNDYING GRATITUDE. Never shall we repay that debt. Even the bitterest cup he will drink for us; the most laborious service he will undertake for us; the uttermost humiliation he will endure for us. We owe all to him in the constitution of our life and its surrounding conditions; we owe no less the entire redemption of our life from all evils; we owe the smoothing of the rough places of life, our uplifting above the pains of life, and we owe the sanctification and perfecting of life. Truly we owe all. Only by reverent faith, by lowly service, by growing love, can we acknowledge our deep-abiding debt. This we may perfect by a calm and trustful yielding up our life to our Father on high, both in the daily dying to self and in a final committal of all to him, breathing out our life into his hands.

> "So, buried with our Lord, we'll close our eyes
> To the decaying world, till angels bid us rise."

G.

Vers. 1—20.—*The second trial*. I. IT ELICITED THE INNOCENCE OF JESUS. Charges were made that he had excited sedition through the country, had prohibited the Roman tribute, and had claimed royalty. The last only had any show of plausibility in it. Jesus admitted his kingship, but declared it in immortal words to be the sovereignty of truth over the consciences of men. Reading the narratives of the other evangelists, we gain a clear impression of the innocence of Jesus, as it was exhibited to all who looked on, and defied the inventions of malice. Especially is that innocence reflected from the bearing of Pilate. To him our Lord replied when he asked for information; but met the accusations of the priests with a silence equally significant. And Pilate was struck dumb with conviction. Character is self-sufficiency. It is "centrality; the impossibility of being displaced or overset." Words will not prove innocence; it speaks louder in silence. Passion and unreason illustrate it. We are generally more anxious to avoid misconstruction than to act as we think right. Jesus teaches us to be servants of the truth, and to be indifferent to the constructions of our enemies. God and the angels are the true spectators of our actions; and the judgment of posterity will reflect the judgment of God.

II. IT ELICITED HIS PERFECT LOYALTY. There must come a time when the truths we have professed will demand to be sealed by our action. Christ had taught men to "seek first the kingdom of God;" to postpone everything to duty; to take heed to the light within; to esteem the soul of greater worth than the whole world. His conduct now falls into harmony with his words; and perfect music flows through the world from both. He preferred the fulfilment of duty to the preservation of life.

III. IT ELICITED HUMAN INJUSTICE AND VICE. Socrates told his judges at Athens that it was they who were really on their trial. So it was the Sanhedrim, and also Pilate, who were on this occasion tried and condemned. The ages have since been reverberating their damnation. Expediency and worldly favour were in one scale; right, innocence, truth, in the other. The former dipped. Worldly authority was opposed to spiritual majesty; the former struck a blow at the latter, which recoiled with Divine effect. The condemnation of Christ was an outrage upon the conscience of the world, both Jewish and pagan. Pilate's illustrious countryman, Cicero, had taught with enthusiasm that the useful and the right form a unity; that the useful can never be put before the right without defeating the social good ('De Officiis,' iii.). An action can never be useful unless it is first right. Here was a great reversal of that order. That Jesus should die is expedient, said the Sanhedrim; but not right, said their conscience. On other grounds, Pilate took the same position; while his wife, like a second conscience, would have restrained him. In similar crises of personal experience, let us remember that to subordinate right to expediency is to condemn the Lord of life afresh.

IV. IT ILLUSTRATES THE METHODS OF PROVIDENCE. When innocence suffers and violence prevails, the foundations of moral order seem to be shaken, and the righteous exclaim, "What shall we do?" The face of Providence seems obscured. But God is One who hideth himself. What we call the evil in nature may be the disguise of his wisdom; and not less does he conceal himself behind the evil of men. Here the greatest evil on their part gave occasion for the greatest good.

V. IT ILLUSTRATES THE ILLUSIVENESS OF APPEARANCES. Jesus is insulted by Roman soldiers; himself the spiritual Emperor of mankind. He is mocked with a semblance of royalty; the mocking expresses an eternal fact. "Ridicule is the test of truth." Beware of mockery and insolence; we may be defying the Spirit of God. Seek below the praise and the blame of men, their applause and their abuse, for the eternal fact. Judge not of Christianity by what men say of it, but by itself. Estimate not its divinity by the worldly honour that attaches to it; but rather by the dishonour of the many, and the loyalty and life of the few. Truth and meekness, truth and spiritual force,—these are mightier than all falsehood and scorn.—J.

Vers. 21—32.—*The Crucifixion.* I. THERE MAY BE A BLESSING IN ENFORCED SERVICE. Simon the Cyrenian is raised into the light of history; perhaps to teach us this. No nobler honour for the Christian than to reflect, "I have been called to bear the cross." And for some to reflect, "I was forced into carrying the cross I would have refused, or left on the ground." So with that other Simon, surnamed Peter.

II. PAIN IS RATHER TO BE STRUGGLED WITH THAN ARTIFICIALLY SUPPRESSED. We seek anodynes for our troubles. Jesus teaches us to react against them by the force of faith. In the hour of duty we are to seek presence, not absence, of mind; to collect our faculties, not to distract them.

III. WHAT IS PHYSICALLY POSSIBLE MAY BE MORALLY IMPOSSIBLE. Christ could have come down from the cross in the former sense, *could not* in the latter. He presents the ideal of suffering service for us, and the revelation of God's ways. There may be things which God cannot do, in our way of speaking, because he knows they are not well to be done. We, at least, cannot save ourselves at the expense of duty, and must be content to appear foolish or impotent to many. Suffering and salvation are facts eternally wedded and at one.—J.

Vers. 33—39.—*Death of Jesus.* I. THERE MAY FOR A TIME BE AN ECLIPSE FOR THE FAITHFUL. "No light!" There is an extremity of trial in these words. No hope! The very sun of life seems extinguished, and all worth of existence vanished. Reason can find no foothold in this darkness.

II. YET THERE IS NO ABSOLUTE DARKNESS. Out of it comes the cry of faith. The first words of a long-remembered psalm break from the lips of Jesus; a psalm that rises out of the minor into the major key, from the darkness into the blaze of prophetic vision. Doubtless in that moment the soul of Jesus passed swiftly through the whole scale of that psalmist's experience, and rose into joy upon the wings of thanksgiving.

III. MAY THE TERMINUS OF LIFE AND OF SERVICE BE IDENTICAL! We may breathe this prayer before the cross of Christ. Our work finished, what need have we to tarry? Pericles, in his oration over those who fell for Athens' good, says that, devoting their lives which had been usefully passed in peace on the field, their happiness and their life ended at the same moment. As Christians, our ideal is service, terminable only with life. "Too busy with the crowded hour to fear to live or die." May we

> " Obey the voice at eve obey'd at prime ;
> Lowly faithful, banish fear,
> Right onward drive unarm'd ;
> The port, well worth the cruise, is near,
> And every wave is charm'd."

IV. Finis coronat opus. " Many signs showed that he who died upon the cross was the Son of God." " Regard the end." It reflects its light upon the whole course from its beginning. What deep conviction of sin, of righteousness, of judgment ; of the frailty of man, the power and wisdom and the love of God, roots itself in the cross of Jesus ! It is an end which is a beginning.—J.

Vers. 40—47.—*The burial.* I. Faith thrives in sorrow. Remoter disciples draw near, and secret disciples come forth, in the hour of humiliation and defeat. The sun sets, but not their hope ; and the stars rise, but their faith is earlier up.

II. Love survives all loss. Its burning ray, like that of a hidden gem, flashes out in the gloom. The nobleness of Christ had taught them to master selfishness and despair. His form was enshrined in the " amber of memory." They who had been all eye when he was present, were all recollection now that he was gone.

III. Griefs are certain, joys come by surprise. It was certain that Jesus was dead ; and none expected his resurrection. There is change, not loss, in the kingdom of the spirit. God takes away a good to restore it in a new form. Disappointment vacates the heart for higher blessings. His revelation is in light and shadow.—J.

Vers. 1—15. Parallel passages : Matt. xxvii. 1, 2, 11—26 ; Luke xxiii. 1—7, 13—24 ; John xviii. 28 ; xix. 16.—*Judicial processes.* I. Jesus sent from the Sanhedrim to Pilate—from the Jewish trial to the Roman trial. 1. *The first stage of the Jewish trial.* After the arrest at Gethsemane, our Lord was conducted back to the city, across the Kidron to the palace of the ex-high priest Annas, the father-in-law of Caiaphas, the actual high priest that same year. The influence of this functionary was very great ; his age, astuteness, riches, power, perhaps presidency of the Sanhedrim—all contributed to it. In answer to the inquiries of Annas about our Lord's disciples and doctrine, the Saviour appealed to his teaching in the synagogue, in the temple, always in public ; and referred him to his auditors on these occasions. This reply was construed into disrespect towards the ex-high priest, and resulted in the first act of violence, apart from the arrest itself ; for one of the officers struck Jesus with the palm of his hand or with a rod (ῥάπισμα), as rendered in the margin. This was the *first* of the *three* stages of the Jewish trial. Here we remark (1) that both Jews and Gentiles took part in arresting Jesus and conducting him to the high priest. " The band and the captain," or *chiliarch,* that is, tribune, formed the Roman or Gentile element ; while the " officers of the Jews " composed the Jewish element. Thus from first to last " the Gentiles and the people of Israel " combined against the Lord and his Anointed. The mention (2) of both Annas and Caiaphas as high priests by St. Luke (iii. 2) tallies with the fact that, owing to the arbitrary interference of the Romans, there might be several high priests alive at the same time ; that is, those who had held the office and been deposed, and the person actually exercising the office. Of course, according to the Law of Moses, there could only be one high priest at a time, and that rightful high priest was the hereditary representative of Aaron. Even in the Roman period the high priesthood had not become a yearly office, though the frequent depositions and displacements occasioned many changes and much confusion. Thus Annas had been deposed in the twelfth year of our era by Valerius Gratus, the immediate predecessor of Pilate in the procuratorship of Judæa ; yet, so great was his influence, that he had his own son Eleazar, his son-in-law Caiaphas, and four other sons subsequently appointed to the high priesthood. (3) The preliminary inquiry before Annas might elicit information with regard to the extent of discipleship, and so of sympathy among the rulers, as in the case of Nicodemus, that might be calculated on ; not only so, it would result in a prejudgment of the case through the shrewdness and influence of the ex-high priest. Further, a higher object—an object most probably not dreamt of by either Annas or Caiaphas—was antitypical. We read in Lev. xvi. that on the great day of Atonement, Aaron laid both his hands upon the head of the live, or scape, goat, and

confessed over him all the iniquities of the children of Israel, and all their transgressions
in all their sins, putting them upon the head of the goat; and sent him away by the
hand of a fit man into the wilderness; and the goat bore upon him all their iniquities
into a land not inhabited.   Similarly, the high priests concerned in this trial were, in
the exercise of an analogous function, pronouncing sin to be upon the head of the Victim
before he was led forth to crucifixion.   2. *The second stage of the Jewish trial.*   The
second stage of the Jewish trial consisted of an informal investigation before Caiaphas,
and a committee or commission of the Sanhedrim.   In order that a conviction might be
obtained, it was necessary to secure two witnesses at least to depose to some definite
charge.   But while the testimony of some was irrelevant, that of others was self-contradictory.   At length two volunteered to testify in the case.   For this testimony, such as it was,
they were obliged to travel back over a period of some three years.   Then, fixing on
certain words of our Lord at the first Passover after entering on his public ministry, in
reference to the temple, they either misunderstood them, or misinterpreted and consequently misrepresented them.   The words in question were constructed into contempt
of the temple ; this contempt, if fully proved, would have constituted a capital charge,
just as, in the case of the protomartyr Stephen, the charge was that he ceased not to speak
" blasphemous words against this holy place and the Law."   But this charge was not substantiated ; the evidence broke down in consequence of the disagreement of the witnesses.
Our Lord had said, " *Destroy* (λύσατε) this temple, and in three days I will raise it up "
(ἐγερῶ, a word quite suitable to resurrection, but no way appropriate to rebuilding);
" but he spake of the temple of his body."   One of the witnesses perverted this into, " I
will destroy (καταλύσω) this temple that is made with hands, and within three days I
will build (οἰκοδομήσω) another made without hands " (ch. xiv. 58); the other testified,
" I *can* destroy (δύναμαι καταλῦσαι) the temple of God, and build (οἰκοδομῆσαι) it in three
days" (Matt. xxvi. 61).   Accordingly, St. Mark adds, " Neither so did their witness
agree."   What our Lord had spoken in a figurative sense they applied literally; for
upraising they substituted *building* ; what was really a promise they twisted into a
threat; if they themselves destroyed their temple, he promised replacement.   The temple
had long been distinguished by the Shechinah glory or visible presence of Jehovah, yet
was doomed to destruction ; the human body of Jesus, in which dwelt the fulness
of the Godhead bodily, when raised up would supersede the inhabitation of God in the
literal temple.   3. *Pretence of legality.*   What now can the members of the Sanhedrim
present on this occasion do ?   They wish to keep up the semblance of law and justice, but
the evidence has signally failed.   The condemnation of Jesus is a foregone conclusion,
in whatever way it is to be effected, and still the appearance of legality must be maintained.   A clever thought occurs to the mind of the high priest, and in default of
evidence he resorts to the desperate expedient of causing Jesus to criminate himself.
Accordingly, standing up into the midst (εἰς μέσον), and thus passing from his seat to
some conspicuous position, as St. Mark graphically describes it, he adjured Jesus most
solemnly to declare if he were indeed the Messiah, that is, " the Christ, the son of the
Blessed," viz. if he claimed to be not only the expected Messiah, but also to be a Divine
person—the Son and equal of God.   Whereupon followed the avowal by which he criminated
himself, and gave ground of condemnation.   Though he had acknowledged the confession
of Peter to the same effect, and even commended it ; though he had accepted the same
or an equivalent title on the occasion of his public entry into Jerusalem, he had not as
yet publicly claimed it.   Now, however, he avowed it in the most public manner, in
the presence of the high priest and members of council.   According to St. Mark, this
avowal was expressed by " I am ;" according to St. Matthew by " Thou hast said ; "
while in St. Luke's report of the third Jewish trial, the two are combined with a trifling
variation, namely, " Ye say that I am."   4. *Hypocrisy in high places.*   If our Lord had
remained silent, they would have probably charged him with imposture; now that he
confessed his Messiahship and future exaltation, they proceeded to condemn him for blasphemy.   The council sought nothing further ; they wanted only evidence against him
—something to inculpate, not to exculpate, him.   They did not wish to hear the grounds
of his claim ; they wanted no explanation.   With the Jews the setting up of a claim to
any Divine attribute was regarded as blasphemy ; the claim of Christ, according to their
opinion of him, came under the Mosaic law of blasphemy.   And now the hypocrisy of
the high priest is something shocking.   As the highest ecclesiastical functionary of the

nation, and the principal officer of its great council, his duty surely was to investigate the confession and claim of one who professed to embody the hopes of the nation, and to scrutinize the true nature of that claim, the real meaning of it, the grounds on which it rested, the reasons of it, and the evidence for it. On the contrary, he grasped with avidity at the prospect of a condemnation. His sense of justice was no higher than his sense of religion; on anything that might tend to explain, or extenuate, or exculpate, he shut his eyes and closed his ears. But what is still more disgusting in the conduct of this ecclesiastic was his abominable hypocrisy. He feigned abhorrence at the crime which he was so anxious to establish. Glad as he was to have this constructive crime of blasphemy to allege, he pretended the most extreme horror by tearing his garments from the neck to the waist. Here, indeed, was "spiritual wickedness in high places." 5. *The third stage of the Jewish trial.* This was the more formal trial; it was held at dawn of day, and in the presence of the whole Sanhedrim (ὅλον τὸ συνέδριον). The previous trial, being held at night, was invalid; besides, it had been conducted only by a representation—an influential representation or committee of the Sanhedrim, consisting, it is probable, mainly of the priests. At the present stage the whole council was present, with its three constituent parts—elders, chief priests, and scribes. This is the meeting of council mentioned in the first verse of the present chapter, and in the parallel verses of St. Matthew and St. Luke, viz. xxvii. 1 of the former, and xxii. 66 of the latter. The object was to ratify a predetermined decree. They also found it necessary for their purpose to change the charge, and consequently also the venue. It was more, perhaps, with the object of consummating than of ratifying their sentence that this meeting was hastily summoned. The judicial murder which they had decided on was not in their power to carry out. Had it been so, stoning would have been the death-penalty. A deputation of an influential and imposing kind waited upon Pilate, to whom the Prisoner is now transferred, either hoping, through the facile condescension of the procurator, to get the case remitted to themselves for execution, or to devolve it on the Roman governor.

II. THE ROMAN TRIAL, OR TRIAL BEFORE PILATE. 1. *Incidents leading to crucifixion.* Crucifixion was a mode of death unknown to Jewish law, and unpractised by the Jewish people. It was fearfully familiar as a mode of execution among the Romans—this we learn from their writings; as, "Thou shalt not feed the crows on the cross," of Horace; "It makes no difference to Theodore whether he rots on the ground or aloft, *i.e.* on the cross," of Cicero; also from such expressions as the following:— "Go, soldier, get ready the cross;" "Thou shalt go to the cross." It was not, however, till the Roman period that it was introduced into Judæa. It was only after Jew and Roman had come into collision, and had taken respectively the position of conqueror and conquered, of sovereign and subject, that this cruel mode of death found its way into the Holy Land. And yet, strange to say, long years before the Romans had risen to pre-eminence and power, and centuries before Judæa had been catalogued as a province of their vast empire, it had been foretold that Messiah's death would be by crucifixion. We refer to the well-known prediction in the twenty-second psalm, where we read, "They pierced my hands and my feet" ("piercing my hands and my feet," according to Perowne; "geknebelt ['fastened,' as the extremities were in crucifixion] meine Hände und Füsse," according to Ewald). Before that prophecy was fulfilled a long series of events had to be evolved; dynasties had to rise and fall; a kingdom had to pass through the hands of many successive rulers and become extinct; an empire, the greatest of ancient times, had to rise to unprecedented power; that kingdom had to be absorbed, and become a province of that empire. In a word, Judæa had to become tributary and Rome triumphant before the event could take place. The facts referred to changed the complexion of our Lord's trial. Of the many charges they might have manufactured, such as violation of the sabbath law, contempt of oral tradition, purification of the temple, heretical teaching, or esoteric doctrines of a dangerous kind, they elected that of blasphemy, grounded on his own confession of divinity, or of being "the Son of God;" while he strengthens the admission by foretelling that, *besides* (πλὴν) the verbal avowal, they would have ocular proof when they should see him—the Son of man as well as Son of God—"sitting at the right hand of power, and coming on the clouds of heaven." This admission was, as we have seen, extorted after the suborned witnesses had entirely broken down, and the two best of them had shamefully perverted and prevaricated; but, notwithstanding, it was seized by the high priest from his false notions of Messiah as an acknowledgment of the charge preferred. Stoning was the mode of death which the Law appointed for that crime; but though the Jews could pass sentence, they could not execute it. One of the signs of Messiah's advent thus stared them in the face; "the sceptre had [thus] departed from Judah, and a lawgiver from between his feet." Accordingly, they were obliged to have recourse to the Roman procurator, Pilate; but then they knew that he would not interfere with their religious controversies. What now is to be done? They take new ground; they change the accusation from blasphemy to treason, in order to subject their Prisoner to the secular power. 2. *Charges preferred.* The charge was really constructive treason, but their indictment as first advanced consisted of three articles. They charged him (1) with perverting the nation; (2) with forbidding to give tribute to Cæsar; and (3) with affirming that he himself was Christ, a King. Pilate pays no attention to the first and second, and only notices the third. His mode of procedure was in accordance with the Roman respect for law and sense of justice. He refused to confirm the sentence of the Sanhedrim, and proceeded to hold a private and preliminary examination (ἀνακρίσις: as we read in Luke xxiii. 14, ἀνακρίνας), having removed Jesus into the Prætorium, or governor's palace. This examination Pilate conducted in person, as he had no *quæstor*; and was satisfied of the harmlessness of the title of King by the Saviour's explanation that his kingdom was not of this world. Pilate was convinced of our Lord's innocence, but hearing Galilee mentioned, he at once caught at the idea of shifting the responsibility, or at least sharing it with Herod Antipas, and at the same time of conciliating the tetrarch by an act of courtesy; and in consequence remitted (ἀνέπεμψεν) the accused to Herod's as the higher court, or technically from the court *apprehensionis* to the court *originis*. Herod, having been disappointed by seeing no miracle performed by the reputed miracle-worker, and dissatisfied by his dignified silence, sent him back to Pilate, arrayed in a white or gorgeous (λαμπρὰν, from λάω, to see) robe, thus caricaturing his candidateship or claim to royalty, and thereby hinting to Pilate that instead of a punishable offence, it was rather a matter of contempt and ridicule. Pilate is perplexed, and no wonder; his vacillation now begins to take effect. He sins against his sense of justice as a Roman magistrate; he sins against conscience; he proposes a most unjust and unlawful compromise, namely, the chastisement (παιδεύσας) of an innocent person. But this concession, unrighteous as it was, did not satisfy; and again he tried to avail himself of the custom of releasing one at the feast in compliance with the clamour of the multitude; but the cry of the populace, instigated by the agents of the priests, was, "Not this man, but Barabbas." By a symbolic act, this weak judge seeks to transfer the guilt to the infuriate mob, and still clinging to the hope that the multitude would be content with a compromise, he delivered Jesus to be scourged, and that, not with the rods of the lictors, but with the horrible scourge tipped with bone and lead (φραγελλώσας). 3. *Retrospect at the indignities.* The first act of insult and violence was, as we have seen, during the inquisition by Annas, who sought to entangle him by insidious interrogatories, when one of the officers struck Jesus with his hand or with a rod (ῥάπισμα), as St. John informs us. The next was in the course of the second Jewish trial, which was conducted by Caiaphas, and by which the confession of being "the Christ, the Son of God," was extorted. In describing this sad scene, no less than five forms of beating are mentioned by the Evangelists Matthew and Mark and Luke. The latter has (1) δέροντες, properly to skin or flay, and then beat severely; (2) ἔτυπτον, imperfect, they kept smiting him; (3) παίσας, to inflict blows or strike with violence; St. Matthew has (4) ἐκολάφισαν, they buffeted with clenched fist; and (5) ἐρράπισαν, they struck with open palms or rods; while St. Mark has ῥαπίσμασιν . . . ἔβαλλον, they received him with blows of the hands or strokes of rods. It was on this occasion they did spit in his face and blindfold him, derisively bidding him "prophesy, who is it that smote thee?" with many other vilifications, in some or all of which the members of the council, as well as the menials of the court, took part. We now hasten from such a disgraceful scene—from the scornful spitting, the shameful scoffing, the savage smiting, the ribald revilings, the shocking cruelties, and the savage barbarities of the miscreants of the Sanhedrim—and pass on to his treatment by Herod. He joins with his men of war in setting him at nought and mocking him, and arrays him in a gorgeous robe, as if to caricature his pretensions, or, as some think, a bright or white robe, as though in mimicry of his candidature for royal honours.   Thus sent back to Pilate, he is scourged by the procurator's command.   The very thought of that scourging makes the blood run cold and the heart sick.   All that preceded, cruel as it was and devilish as it was, caused but little of bodily pain as compared with the scourging.   He had indeed suffered dreadfully, in both body and mind.   He had been betrayed by one disciple, denied by another; three slept when they should have sympathized; at length all forsook him and fled.   He has been hurried from one tribunal to another—from the Sanhedrim to the Roman governor, from the Roman governor to the Tetrarch of Galilee, and from Herod back to Pilate.   See him the night preceding in the Garden of Gethsemane, in the midst of his agony, when perspiration bathed his body, and that bloody sweat trickled in big drops down to the ground.   See him now in the place where he is scourged, cruelly scourged, his face marred, his body mangled, the quivering flesh fearfully torn with the bits of lead and bone plaited into the leathern thongs, while he is still barbarously smitten, and savage stripes inflicted on him.   See him again, surrounded by a band of ruffian soldiers—provincial or rather Roman soldiers, to their disgrace be it recorded—who plait a crown of *nâbk* thorns, and press it down so that the sharp and prickly points more painfully pierce his temples and lacerate his bleeding brows.   While his body is still smarting from the wounds made by the scourging, while the blood is still running down on every side from the thorn-crown, while insult is being heaped on insult and added to injury, they smite his sacred head with a reed as if to gash that head more brutally, and leave the thorns yet deeper in the skin.   One other act in that bloody tragedy precedes and prepares for the crucifixion itself.   Instead of the gorgeous or white robe with which Herod and his men of war had, in their bitter mockery, clothed him, the Roman soldiers of the governor arrayed him with the military scarlet or purple war-cloak, mimicking the imperial purple.   He is stripped a second time—the mock-garments are pulled off him, and his own put on; and thus all his wounds are opened afresh and their pain renewed.   During the mock-coronation, in which the leaves of thorn burlesqued the imperial wreath of laurel, the reed the royal sceptre, and the soldier's cloak the emperor's purple, they spat upon him, they smote him on the head, they bowed the knee in mockery, and they scoffed him, saying, "Hail, King of the Jews!"   4. *Pilate's last effort to release him.*   Once more Pilate makes another effort to prevent the crucifixion of Christ.   Though scourging was usually the frightful preparation for crucifixion, yet Pilate is most anxious to proceed no further.   He seeks to have it regarded, perhaps, in the light of trial by torture without anything worthy of death being elicited, or perhaps he wishes to have it accepted as a sufficient substitute for crucifixion.   With some such purpose—a purpose, as it is generally and properly understood, of commiseration—he exhibits the Saviour in that unspeakably sad and sorrowful plight—worn, wan, and wasted; his features here befouled with spitting, there besmeared with blood; his face disfigured by blows—marred more than any man's and his countenance more than the sons of men; while blood-drops trickle from many a wound down on the tesselated pavement.   He calls their attention to this woe-begone and most pitiable spectacle, saying, in words that have thrilled many a heart, and shall thrill thousands in the generations that may be yet to come, "Behold the Man!"   But in vain.   The only response was a louder, sterner, fiercer cry: "Crucify him! crucify him!"   He deserves to die, "because he made himself the Son of God."   Moved to the inmost depths of his being, Pilate struggles on for his release; but, amid the loud clamour for the Victim's blood, there are ominous growls that boded a possible impeachment on the charge of treason against the governor himself.   "If thou let this man go, thou art not Cæsar's friend;" "We have no king but Cæsar."   Shame upon those bloodthirsty hypocrites who could say so; though they hated Cæsar and all his belongings, and were real rebels at heart!   And shame upon that cowardly judge, who, as a Roman magistrate, quailed before such cruel clamour, and had not the courage of his own certain convictions!   5. *Agencies co-operating to compass the crucifixion.*   If we glance for a moment at the various influences that were at work to compass our Lord's death upon the cross, we find in the foreground the envy and malice of chief priests and rulers; the mean-spirited avarice of the wretched traitor Judas; the want of firmness and thorough conscientiousness on the part of Pilate; the fury of a fickle mob misled by designing demagogues; the submission of the soldiers to the orders of their superiors;—all obeying the propensities of their own nature, though ignorant of the reason or the results; all fulfilling the predictions of Scripture, though not knowing it; and all accomplishing the purposes of God, though not intending it. But in the background, as we shall see in connection with the crucifixion itself, it was sin on the part of man, and substitution on the part of the Saviour. "He bore our sins," says the apostle, "in his own body on the tree." It was determinate counsel and foreknowledge on the part of God. In accordance with that counsel and foreknowledge, and in consequence of our sin and the Saviour's substitutionary self-sacrifice, "ought not Christ to suffer these things?" Was it not necessary for him to become "obedient unto death, even the death of the cross"?—J. J. G.

Vers. 16—41. Parallel passages: Matt. xxvii. 27—56; Luke xxiii. 26—49; John xix. 17—37.—*The closing scene.* I. THE CRUCIFIXION AND ACCOMPANYING EVENTS. 1. *The words of the Creed.* The words of the Creed, "crucified under Pontius Pilate," are familiar to almost every young person who has been trained in the Christian religion. All down the centuries the name of this Roman knight, who was Procurator of Judæa under the Proprætor of Syria, has been associated with the greatest crime that has blotted and blackened the page of history since the beginning of the world. He was a descendant of the great Samnite general, C. Pontius Telesinus, and so belonged to the Pontian *gens.* His surname, Pilatus, is usually derived from *pilum*, a javelin, and so means "armed with a javelin;" though others connect it with *pileatus*, from *pileus*, a cap worn by manumitted slaves, implying that he had been a freedman, or the son of one. His head-quarters were at Cæsarea, on the sea, but during the Jewish feasts, when such crowds assembled in Jerusalem, in discharge of his duty he came up to Jerusalem to keep order. In like manner Herod, whose usual residence was at Tiberias, had come up to Jerusalem to keep the feast, ostensibly in conformity to the Jews' religion, but more especially to conciliate the favour of the Jewish people. It thus happened that the tetrarch and Roman governor were both at Jerusalem at the same time—the former occupying the old Asmonean palace, and the latter Herod's Prætorium a palace of Herod the Great, or perhaps a part of Fort Antonia. 2. *Pilate's embarrassment and earnestness to secure the Saviour's acquittal.* He had offended the Jews by bringing the Roman standards to Jerusalem, and had been obliged to retrace this step; he had quarrelled with them about secularizing the corban, or sacred treasury money, to provide a suitable water-supply for Jerusalem; he had been engaged in a deadly feud with the Samaritans; and had mingled the blood of the Galilæans with their own sacrifices. He was thus on bad terms with the people of every province in the land, and could not, therefore, afford further to provoke their wrath. On the other hand, he had had three warnings—the voice of his own conscience, the dream of his wife, Claudia Procula, and the announcement of Jesus' mysterious title of "Son of God." On the one side was the fear of the Jews whom he had so deeply offended, and fear also of compromising himself with the emperor, now that his patron Sejanus had fallen; on the other were his remaining sense of justice, his respect for Jesus as an innocent man, perhaps as something more—so that Tertullian says of him, "Jam pro conscientia Christianus"—and the threefold warning already mentioned. In consequence he does his best, in his perplexing circumstances, to have Jesus released; for he sent him to Herod, then offered to release him as a favour, according to an established custom. Next he thought to substitute scourging for crucifixion; and when that had failed, he appealed to their pity. But all to no purpose. What was he to do? Why, assert, as he was bound to do, the power of the Roman law, maintain the cause of justice, and obey the voice of conscience at all hazards. But instead of this he vacillated at the beginning, temporized afterwards, and yielded to his fears in the end. Unhappily, he allowed fear for his personal safety to stifle the voice of conscience. 3. *The crucifixion.* Crosses were of different sorts and shapes. There was the *crux simplex*, or simple cross, which was rather a stake on which the body was impaled; there was the *crux decussator*, or St. Andrew's cross, in the form of the letter X; there was the *crux immissa*, or Latin cross, in the form of a dagger with point downward †; there was the *crux commissa*, in the form of the letter T. On account of the inscription the form of the cross on which our Lord suffered is generally supposed to have been that of the third sort.   And now we are arrived at the last sad scene in that shocking drama.   Criminals usually carried their cross, or the cross-beams of it, as they went to execution ; hence the term *furcifer,* or cross-bearer.   Jesus, exhausted by all he had previously endured, and crushed beneath that heavy cross, sank by the way.   Simon, an African Jew, is impressed into the service (ἀγγαρεύουσι, send out a mounted courier, from the mounted couriers ready to carry the royal despatches in Persia ; then force to do service, compel) and compelled to carry the Saviour's cross.   Jesus is fastened to that cross ; his hands and his feet are pierced with nails ; the cross is hoisted, and with a rude and sudden dash it is sunk deep into the earth.   There the bleeding Victim hangs, his bones disjointed, his veins broken, his wounds freshened, his skin livid, his face wan, his strength exhausted ; blood flows from his head, blood from his hands, blood from his feet, blood from his opened side.   There he hangs, wounded, tortured, fainting, bleeding, dying.   There he hangs upon that cursed tree, the passers-by reviling him and wagging their heads, soldiers mocking him, rulers deriding him, malefactors railing on him,—a fearful fourfold mockery.   He is offered vinegar and gall (or wine and myrrh, *i.e.* wine myrrhed, or made acid), but, in the first instance, will not drink, lest it should blunt the pain of dying or cloud his faculties ; " The cup that my Father gave me, shall I not drink it ? "   He suffers the withdrawment of his heavenly Father's countenance, and in consequence exclaims, " Eloi, Eloi, lama sabachthani ? "—" My God, my God, why hast thou forsaken me ? "   At length, with a loud voice, he cries out, " It is finished ! " and bows his head in death.   We do not marvel at the accompanying circumstances, strange and marvellous as they were.   No wonder the sun drew back from the spectacle, and shrouded his glorious rays in darkness, rather than gaze on such a scene.   No wonder that dense darkness settled on the land for three long hours.   No wonder earth trembled and quaked in horror at the foul deed that had been done.   No wonder that rocks rent and graves opened, and the tenants of the tomb came forth as though in consternation, shocked at human sinfulness, and in sympathy with the heavenly Sufferer.   No wonder the veil of the temple, strong and thick, is torn in twain from top to bottom, for the humanity of the Saviour is torn with thorns, and smitings, and nails, and spear-thrust ; while he is pouring out his life unto death.   4. *The inscription.*   The *main* part of the superscription, viz. " The King of the Jews," is found in the record of each evangelist—the same in all and correct in each. In one it is completed by the name, " Jesus," which a Roman, proud of the purity of his speech, and jealous of preserving it, naturally enough left out of the Latin title ; in another it is supplemented by the name of the place, " Nazareth ; " while the words " This is " are only introductory.   Otherwise the inscription was trilingual, and exactly recorded as written in the three languages by three of the evangelists respectively, while St. Mark records the actual charge—the superscription of his *accusation* (αἰτίας) common to them all ; and this was the assumption of royalty.   5. *The time of the crucifixion.*   The crucifixion really commenced at 9 a.m.   The darkness began at noon ; death took place at 3 p.m.   The apparent discrepancy between the synoptists and John xix. 14 is not to be removed by the similarity of the Greek numerals for six and three (ς′ and γ′) respectively, and the supposed substitution or rather misreading of the former for the latter in the Johannean Gospel.   The reconciliation is more probably effected by a difference of time-reckoning—the synoptists adopting the Jewish and St. John the Roman method.   Thus the delivery and preparations began at 6 a.m. according to the latter.

II. THE DESIGN OF THE CRUCIFIXION.   1. *Not for personal chastisement.*   The design could not in any sense be for *personal* chastisement, for Jesus had been " holy, harmless, undefiled, and separate from sinners ; " it is expressly stated, too, that he was " cut off, but not for himself."   Neither could it be as an *example,* for the example of One perfectly innocent suffering so severely would only discourage the guilty, and might well drive them to despair ; for if this were done to a green tree, what would be done to a dry—if the guiltless suffered so fearfully, what might the guilty expect ?   Besides, if Christ suffered as an example, what possible good could his example do to those that lived before his day ?   Neither was it for *confirmation* of his teaching—to confirm the doctrines which he taught and seal them with his blood ; for some of the prophets had done this before him, several of the apostles did so after him, and the martyrs all down the ages have suffered in like manner.   And yet, though thus entitled, according to the theory in question, to stand on the same platform with Jesus, of none of them could it ever be asked, with the expectation of an affirmative answer, " Was he crucified for you ?" Of no one in all the glorious company of the apostles, or in all the goodly fellowship of the prophets, or in all the noble army of martyrs, or in all the holy Church throughout all the world, could it be said, " He was crucified for you." How, then, are we to account for the unparalleled sufferings of the Son of God ; for the indescribable distress that overwhelmed him during those sufferings ? What reason can we render for the transcendent value ascribed to the gift of God's Son—that unspeakable gift ; for the incomparable worth of the boon, so that all other benefits sink into insignificance when placed beside it ? How are we to explain the fact that, amid the utmost chariness of human eulogy, we find the highest praises everywhere throughout this Book lavished on the Son of God ? How comes it to pass that while we are instructed to " cease from man, for wherein is he to be accounted of ? " we are invited to look up with greatest reverence to the Man Christ Jesus, as placed far above the proudest pinnacle of earthly grandeur, and his name raised high above every name, so that in honour of that name " every knee should bow and every tongue confess that Jesus Christ is Lord, to the glory of God the Father " ? Even in heaven the Lamb, in the midst of the throne, as he had been slain, is still the marvel of the universe ; while the key-note of the song sung by the redeemed in glory, and ever sounding along the arches of the sky, is, " Worthy is the Lamb that was slain to receive power, and riches, and wisdom, and strength, and honour, and glory, and blessing." What is the solution of all this ? We have no doubt, and feel no difficulty in giving a decided and definite answer to all questions of the sort proposed, for Scripture itself supplies that answer. It is because he " came not to be ministered unto, but to minister, and to give his life a ransom for many ; " it is because he " hath loved us, and hath given himself for us an offering and a sacrifice to God for a sweet-smelling savour ; " it is because he " bare our sins in his own body on the tree," suffering, " the just for the unjust, to bring us to God ; " it is because " he was made sin for us, though he knew no sin, that we might be made the righteousness of God in him ; " it is because in him " we have redemption through his blood, the forgiveness of sins, according to the riches of his grace." Why, again, are there so many Scriptures all bearing on this same subject ? Just to exhibit it under its various aspects and from sundry standpoints ; just to explain it more clearly and enforce it more fully ; and, still more, to awaken our liveliest interest in it, and impress us with a due sense of its supreme and paramount importance. 2. *The sufferings of the cross vicarious.* Objections have been urged against the fairness of the holy suffering in the stead of the unholy, and the objectors strive to explain away the fact of such substitution. - To such objectors we reply—If you object to the fairness of the holy suffering in the room of the unholy, and seek to explain it away, we object to the fairness of what you can never explain away—of what you must admit, however reluctant, and cannot deny, however desirous. If you object to the holy suffering in place of the unholy, we object to the holy suffering at all ; and yet you are bound to acknowledge that the Holy One has suffered, and cannot venture, so long at least as you credit the Gospel narrative, to gainsay the historic fact. But perfect holiness is justly entitled to happiness, and by the law of Heaven is (as it should be) entirely exempt from suffering ; and therefore, unless the Holy One suffered in the room and stead of the unholy, his sufferings would not only be most unjust, but at the same time altogether meaningless. 3. *The doctrine of substitution in both secular and sacred history.* Of the very many instances of this doctrine of substitution met with in the pages of both sacred and secular history, a few examples may be here adduced. Judah intreated Joseph that he might be kept instead of Benjamin—a bondman in his room. After an address of most pathetic and powerful pleading, he says, " Now therefore, I pray thee, let thy servant abide instead of the lad a bondman to my lord ; and let the lad go up with his brethren. For how shall I go up to my father, and the lad be not with me ? lest peradventure I see the evil that shall come on my father." In the days of King David an unnatural war broke out. Rebels banded themselves against their sovereign ; his son became their leader. A disastrous battle was fought in the wood of Ephraim, and the young man Absalom was slain. One messenger follows on the heels of another, saying, " Tidings, my lord the king ; " while his question is once and again the same, " Is the young man Absalom safe ? " The king, it is plain, would rather have lost the battle than his son ; he would have parted with his kingdom rather than his son; nay, he would have given life itself for his son's life. For now, when he has learnt at length that that fair and favourite son had fallen by the hand of the martial but merciless Joab, "the king," we read, " was much moved, and went up to the chamber over the gate, and wept : and as he went, thus he said, O my son Absalom, my son, my son Absalom! would God I had died for thee, O Absalom, my son, my son !" Even Caiaphas enunciated the doctrine, though ignorant of its true bearing and unconscious of the great truth it involved, when he "gave counsel to the Jews, that it was expedient that one man should die for the people." The sins of the whole people laid on the head of the scapegoat, the sins of the individual person transferred to the head of the sin offering,—such acts as these symbolically teach the same. When we turn to the secular classics, we find that one of the sublimest poems and simplest tragedies of antiquity is based on the doctrine of substitution ; it represents a deity suffering in the cause of humanity and on account of favours bestowed on man. Another instance, and one containing the most genuine example of conjugal affection in the old Greek drama, represents a wife giving her life a substitute for that of her husband. So familiar was this doctrine to the ancients. The great Theban poet, with wonted power, sketches in a few stirring sentences the loyalty and love of the brave Antilochus in defence of his aged parent Nestor, the renowned knight of Pylos. Enfeebled by years and endangered by younger warriors, his horse wounded by the archery of Paris, his chariot impeded, and himself fiercely assailed by the Ethiop Memnon, the old man, in trepidation of spirit, called loudly on his son for succour; nor did he call in vain. Promptly was his call heard and heeded. The faithful son proved his devotion to his sire; he hastened to his side ; he defended him from the strong spear of the assailant ; he saved that sire's life, but not without the sacrifice of his own ; he rescued his parent from ruin, but received his own death-blow; he averted the fate that impended over his father, but at the expense of his own heart's blood. Hundreds of years have rolled away since that deed of daring and devotedness was done, and still it is enshrined in the immortal verse of the Pindaric muse, and the hero's memory embalmed among the younger men of ancient days as first in affection to his father. Again, we admire the Roman poet's graphic delineation of the battle-scene in which the gallant son of Mezentius fell. We admire still more the filial affection of that son who, when the deadly blow had been aimed at his father, interposed himself in his father's stead, received the blow, lost his own life, but saved his father's. "By thy death I live, my son; by thy wounds I am saved!" the veteran warrior exclaimed. In like manner the Son of God took the sinner's place, and stood in the sinner's room; and in the words of inspiration, the sinner who trusts in him can say, "He was wounded for my transgressions, he was bruised for my iniquities : the chastisement of my peace was upon him ; and with his stripes I am healed." For us the Saviour hung upon that cross ; for us that frame writhed in agony; for us those limbs quivered in torture; for us that ghastly paleness overspread his face; for us those eye-strings broke in death; for us that side was pierced with the rude soldier's spear ; for us he suffered and for us he died. 4. *The power of the cross in conversion.* The first convert of the Greenland mission was a robber-chief, called Kajarnak. That mission had long been unsuccessful; the missionaries had been sorely tried. At last, disheartened, they were about to leave the country, when one day the bandit, with his followers, came to rob the mission tent. On entering, he saw the missionary writing, and wondered what it meant; the missionary explained to him that, by the marks he was making on the paper, he could tell the thoughts that had passed through the mind of a man called John hundreds of years before. "Impossible!" exclaimed the savage chief. The missionary, who was finishing his translation of the Gospel of St. John, read to these heathen Greenlanders the record of the crucifixion as contained in the nineteenth chapter of that Gospel, on which he was then employed. The chieftain and his men were strangely interested in the narrative. At length Kajarnak, with much emotion, cried out, "What had the man done that they treated him so?" The missionary addressed him in reply, "That man did nothing amiss, but Kajarnak has done much wrong ; Kajarnak murdered his wife; Kajarnak has robbed as well as murdered ; Kajarnak has filled the land with violence ; and that man was bearing the punishment of Kajarnak's sins that Kajarnak might be saved." Tears rolled down the cheek of the rude robber-chief, and he besought the missionary to read him all that over again, "for," he added, "I too would like to be saved." We do not wonder that the story of the cross had such a powerful effect on the first convert in Greenland. *5. Christ's death on the cross a satisfaction.* The death of Christ did not cause God to love us, but, on the contrary, was the expression of that love; it did not originate God's love to man, but, contrariwise, was the effect and evidence of that love; and in accordance with this we read that " God so loved the world, that he gave his only begotten Son, that whosoever believeth in him should not perish, but have everlasting life." A mighty debt was due to the government, law, and justice of God, as well as to his truth and holiness and purity; that debt was sin. This huge hindrance barred the way of access to communion and fellowship with God; but God himself appointed, accepted, and applied the means for the removal of that hindrance and the reopening of the way. Again, the sun is always shining, though we do not always see it; either clouds overspread the sky and cover the fair face of day, or earth rolls round upon its axis, and so during the hours of night we are turned away from the sun. Notwithstanding this, the sun is ever sending out his rays; and when the clouds scatter, or the earth rolls round again, his full-orbed brightness beams upon us, we see him in the splendour of his shining; and "a pleasant thing it is for the eyes to behold the sun." So the face of God is ever shining, but the clouds of sin darken the sky above us and separate between us and our God; by the death of Christ those clouds are driven away, and that severance ceases; we are brought back into the clear light of unclouded day, and bask in the bright effulgence of our heavenly Father's face. The death of Christ on the cross thus bridged the chasm that sin had made; it spanned the gulf that iniquity had fixed; it opened the new and living way to yon bright world above. By the cross is the way of safety and salvation; for by that cross our sins were expiated, by that cross propitiation was effected, by that cross atonement was made. By that cross, moreover, the Creator and his fallen creature were brought together; by that cross man and his Maker were reconciled; by that cross the offended Sovereign and the rebel sinner were set at one again. In that cross we see the vicarious suffering of one for many, the wondrous substitution of the just for the unjust, the punishment of the sinner inflicted on the Saviour. Through that cross we see the Law magnified, justice satisfied, truth vindicated, government established, sin punished, God glorified, our debt cancelled, the handwriting against us blotted out, and the believing sinner saved.

> "Thus from the Saviour on the cross
> A healing virtue flows;
> Who looks to him with lively faith
> Is saved from endless woes."

6. Double aspect of Christ's death on the cross. The death of Christ on the cross is a purification as well as a propitiation; it is the source of sanctification and the ground of satisfaction. In reply to the question of the elder in Revelation, saying, " What are these which are arrayed in white robes? and whence came they?" the answer is returned, "These are they which came out of great tribulation, and have washed their robes, and made them white in the blood of the Lamb." So, also, in Heb. ix. 14," How much more shall the blood of Christ, who through the eternal Spirit offered himself without spot to God, purge your conscience from dead works to serve the living God?" There is a seeming incongruity in blood purifying. We speak of being defiled with blood or stained with blood, but Scripture speaks of blood cleansing, which is the opposite. We may to some extent illustrate this by certain ceremonies that had to be gone through in olden times by a person who had committed homicide. Among the ancient Greeks the person in question forfeited life. The soul of the slain was supposed to demand life for life, but that life might be redeemed or bought off by the vicarious substitution of a victim. This victim was usually a ram, the slaying of which symbolically denoted the surrender of the guilty man's own life. This was the ceremony of atonement to appease the soul of the slain, and was called *hilasmoi.* But another ceremony was needed—a ceremony of purification to fit the man, whose guilt had been atoned by the propitiatory sacrifice just mentioned, for intercourse with his fellow-men. He then stood on the fleece of the ram of atonement or propitiation, in order to come into the closest possible contact and most intimate connection with the victim which had, as we have seen, vicariously represented him, when an animal of another kind was slaughtered as a victim of purification, and slaughtered in such a way that the blood which spurted from the wound fell upon the hands of the homicide, and thus the human blood which still cleaved to his hands was conceived to be washed away by the blood of this second victim.   This process was called *katharmoi,* and thus was he purified.   The custom to which we have alluded, borrowed, like so many other heathen customs, from scattered and distorted fragments of Divine truth, shows, among other things, that the idea of cleansing by means of blood was familiar to the ancients.   At the same time that we use this illustration we do not understand the blood of the cross in the gross literal sense, but understand by it the death of Christ upon the cross, and, as that was a bloody one, we are not surprised that it should be called in several Scriptures his blood.   The death of Christ (1) as a *propitiation* turns away the wrath of God, due to sin, from man : this is its propitiatory efficacy.   It turns away man from sin : this is its purificatory effect.   God loved us with an everlasting love, but sin he hates with an infinite and everlasting hatred.   As a Friend God loves us, but as a Lawgiver he denounces our sin, as a Judge he condemns it, and as a King he must root it out of his dominions altogether.   The love of God is like a mighty river.   It has flowed from eternity in the majesty of its strength and in the glorious fulness of its stream ; but sin rose as a vast obstruction to the current—it lay like a formidable boom across the stream.   At length, in the fulness of time, the cross of Christ broke through the boom, forced aside the obstruction, and opened up the channel ; and now the sinner, sheltered beneath the shadow of that cross, can say, " Though thou wast angry with me, thine anger is turned away, and thou hast comforted me."   " God was in Christ, reconciling the world unto himself."   How?   " Not imputing unto men their trespasses;" not charging us with those offences by which we justly incurred his displeasure and merited his wrath ; forgiving them, forgetting them, and so reconciled to us, and reconciling us to him, through the blood of the cross.   But the death of Christ (2) is a *purification.*   It purifies the whole man ; its purifying influence goes on, and is needed, till death.   "The blood of Jesus Christ," we read, "cleanseth us from all sin."   No doubt it cleanseth as a propitiation from the guilt of sin, but more especially it cleanseth as a purification from the filth of sin.   It cleanseth the soul from the love of sin and the body from the practice of it; the faculties from thoughts of sin, the members of the body from works of sin.   The hands are purified from deeds of darkness ; they are fitted for and filled with works of faith and labours of love on earth, and thus prepared for sweeping the harps of gold and swelling the symphonies of heaven.   The eyes are purified ; they are cleared of scales, and opened to see the wondrous things of God's Law, and the gracious things of both Law and gospel.   Thus, too, are they prepared for gazing on the radiant splendour of the eternal throne and the glories of the upper sanctuary.   The ears are opened to hear what God the Lord says to his servants, and are thus prepared at length for drinking in the music of the skies and for being charmed with the melodies of heaven.   The feet are kept back from every false step and every wrong way, and furnished as though with wings to move readily and rapidly in the way of God's commandments ; and thus they are prepared at last to stand upon the glassy sea and tread the golden streets.   The head is freed from every iniquitous scheme, and enlightened to comprehend the Divine counsels of mercy ; and thus it is prepared to wear a crown, fair in its form, fresh in its colouring, brilliant in its lustre, unfading in its beauty, and amaranthine in its bloom.   The heart is purified from every propensity to evil ; it overflows with the love of God on earth, and waits to have that love still more intensified amid the raptures and ecstasies of heaven.

III. LESSONS TAUGHT US BY THE CROSS.   1. *God's hatred of sin* is seen in the cross. We trace the wrath of God in the waters of the flood that swept away the antediluvians ; in the sin-ruined cities of which few fragments remain to tell where once they were ; in the dreary waters that roll over the desolated plain where Sodom and Gomorrah once stood ; in the peeled and scattered and sifted race whose fathers' awful imprecation, "His blood be upon us, and our children," called down the withering curse of Heaven ; in that dark abode where the angels that kept not their first estate are reserved in everlasting chains under darkness unto the judgment of the great day ; in that region of despair where the finally impenitent are doomed to weeping and wailing and gnashing of teeth, and where the smoke of their torment ascendeth up for ever and ever.   And yet the wrath of God, we think, is revealed in clearer light and blazoned in more glaring characters in the sacrifice of the cross, because "God spared not his own Son," when that Son undertook the penalty of our sin, " but delivered him up for us all." 2. *The highest morality comes from the cross.* No theory of morals is so persuasive, no precepts so powerful, as the picture of dying love exhibited in the cross. "The love of Christ constraineth us," says the apostle; "because we thus judge, that one died for all, therefore all died; and he died for all, that they which live should no longer live unto themselves, but unto him who for their sakes died and rose again" (Revised Version); and also, "He gave himself for us, to redeem us from all iniquity, and to purify unto himself a peculiar people, zealous of good works;" and once more, "The life which I now live in the flesh I live by the faith of the Son of God, who loved me, and gave himself for me." Oh, how can we go on in sin if we reflect, as we ought, that sin crucified the Lord of life and glory; if we reflect that it was sin inflicted those wounds upon him; if we remember that sin caused him that agony of soul as well as anguish of body, when, in the language of the prophet, he might well say, "Is it nothing to you, all ye that pass by? behold, and see if there be any sorrow like unto my sorrow, which is done unto me, wherewith Jehovah hath afflicted me in the day of his fierce anger;" if we consider that our sin was laid upon him and borne by him when "he became obedient unto death, even the death of the cross," and when "he put away sin by the sacrifice of himself"? The way to purify our fallen humanity and elevate the standard of morality is not by moral lessons, however proper and useful in their own place, but by leading sinners to the foot of the cross, and by pointing to that cross as embodying three arguments, than which there is nothing more potent or more powerfully persuasive in all the universe besides. The first argument which the blood that flowed on that cross embodies is the mercy of God the Father, in reopening the channel of his love which sin had dammed up and closed. The second argument is the love of God the Son, in assuming our nature, in agonizing and sweating, in being smitten and scourged and spit upon and scorned, in being cruelly crowned and crucified; and all to "finish transgression, and to make an end of sins, and to make reconciliation for iniquity, and to bring in everlasting righteousness." The third argument is the grace of God the Holy Spirit, in sprinkling the blood thus shed on the conscience, when he brings home the death of Christ, in the power and demonstration of faith, to the sinner's heart. How is it possible to resist this triple argument? How is it possible to go on in sin, which caused our Lord such suffering, and when such love—the love of the Trinity—is constraining us to abandon it for ever? 3. *The innocence of the Sufferer.* Heaven and earth attested his innocence. Friend and foe bore witness to it. A noble Roman lady, wife of the governor, warned her lord, saying, "Have thou nothing to do with that just man." Pilate himself, the judge, informed chief priests and people, "I find no fault in this man." Again a second time, having assembled chief priests and rulers and people, he affirmed publicly and positively Jesus' innocence in the following strong terms:—"Behold, I, having examined him before you, found no fault in this man touching those things whereof ye accuse him : no, nor yet Herod : for he sent him back unto us; and behold, nothing worthy of death hath been done by him" (Revised Version). Once more, for the third time, he asserted his innocence, saying, "Why, what evil hath he done? I have found no cause of death in him." Judas, the traitor, admitted the same thing, saying, "I have betrayed innocent blood." The Roman centurion, who superintended the execution, cried out, "Certainly this was a righteous man;" and again, after he had seen the earthquake and those things that were done, "Truly this was the Son of God." One of the malefactors, his companion in suffering, frankly acknowledged, "This man hath done nothing amiss." The whole record of his trial furnishes the plainest and most positive evidence of his innocence. Satan had tried him, and found nothing in him. God the Father had owned him three times by an audible voice from heaven. He had committed no offence against the religion of the land, no crime against the laws of his country, no sin against God. He went about continually doing good; he was acknowledged to have done all things well; he was "holy, harmless, undefiled, and separate from sinners."

> "We held him as condemn'd by Heaven,
>   An outcast from his God,
> While for our sins he groan'd, he bled,
>   Beneath his Father's rod.

" His sacred blood hath wash'd our souls
    From sin's polluted stain;
His stripes have heal'd us, and his death
    Revived our souls again."

4. *His seven sayings on the cross.* Of these three are recorded by St. Luke, other three by St. John, and the remaining one by both St. Matthew and St. Mark. The first of those seven sayings, or seven words, is a *prayer* for his murderers: " Father, forgive them; for they know not what they do." There is no doubt that they were acting in ignorance and unbelief; yet they were not excusable on that account, for men are accountable for their belief, and especially so when they have abundant means of recti- fying their misbelief or removing their unbelief. The spirit of forgiveness which this prayer breathes is truly wonderful. There is an entire absence of revenge and of all vindictiveness, and yet this was only the negative side; there was the positive feeling of love to his enemies, pity for his murderers, and prayer for those who used him so despitefully. Thus he practised what he preached, and exemplified what he taught in the condition of the petition, " Forgive us our trespasses, as we forgive them that tres- pass against us." The second of those words is a *promise* to the penitent sufferer beside him: " To-day shalt thou be with me in Paradise." At first it would appear that both malefactors had railed upon him, or the plural is used idiomatically for the singular. One became penitent, rebuking the railing of his fellow-sufferer. By faith he looked to the pierced One at his side, and mourned. His faith became marvellously strong in an incredibly short space. The right rendering of his prayer in the Revised Version makes this more manifest: " Jesus, remember me when thou comest in thy kingdom." The common rendering of *into*, as if it were εἰς with the accusative, would imply that Jesus passed into his kingdom at the hour of his dissolution, so that faith would not have long to wait; but the expression " in thy kingdom " (ἐν with the dative) points not to the immediate future like the former, but to the more distant future when Jesus would come again in his kingdom; and still the faith that prompted the petition patiently looked forward to that far-off day. Thus there is no sinner beyond the reach of mercy; no time too late to seek salvation; and no prayers of faith rejected. The soul united to Jesus is safe in his arms, and admitted to glory soon as separated from the body. The third saying is a *provision* for his widowed mother in her sore bereave- ment: " Woman, behold thy son!" and to the disciple he said, " Behold thy mother!" It was to the beloved John the intimation was given to treat the Virgin mother as his own mother, while Mary was to regard and depend on John as her son. The hint was understood by both; the new relationship was accepted, John under- took the responsibility, and Mary confided herself to his care. Jesus, as he hung in agony, was thus mindful of his mother, making careful provision for her. What a lesson of filial love is taught us here! What a lesson of dutifulness to a parent, especially when that parent is bereaved and desolate! The fourth saying is a *position* of spiritual loneliness: " My God, my God, why hast thou forsaken me?" Here there is faith, but faith wanting the assurance of sense. There is faith in Jesus acknow- ledging God as his God; but a sense of the Divine presence is absent. The complaint of Divine abandonment is caused by that absence, and the deserted soul is in agony. The condition of the Christian is sometimes similar—when, like Job, he goes forward, but God is not there; backward, but he cannot perceive him; and when he turns himself to every side, but cannot find him. But oh, how great the difference! Such a season of darkness is for the most part occasioned by sin; so in our Saviour's case it was indeed for sin, but not his own! The fifth is the *pain* of bodily suffering: " I thirst." The pain of thirst is worse to bear than that of hunger; when long continued it is distressing in the extreme. Men who have travelled in a desert district or under a tropical sun can realize the severity of this condition. In the case of our Lord there was a peculiar aggravation. Near the cross had been placed a vessel of sour wine (*posca*) for the use of the soldiers, the sight of which would increase the feeling of thirst and pain on the part of the Sufferer. Nor was that all; among the cruel mocking of our Lord in the earlier stage of the crucifixion was the circumstance that the soldiers tantalized him by raising to his lips their jar or sponge of vinegar, and then suddenly withdrawing it, for we read, " The soldiers also mocked him . . . offering him vinegar." The sixth is the *perfection* of his work: " It is finished." As has been beautifully said, " Finished

was his holy life; with his life his struggle, with his struggle his work, with his work the redemption, with the redemption the foundation of the new world."

> " ' 'Tis finished!' was his latest voice :
> These sacred accents o'er,
> He bow'd his head, gave up the ghost,
> And suffer'd pain no more.

> " ' 'Tis finish'd!'   The Messiah dies
> For sins, but not his own ;
> The great redemption is complete,
> And Satan's power o'erthrown.

> " ' 'Tis finish'd!'   All his groans are past ;
> His blood, his pain, and toils,
> Have fully vanquishèd our foes,
> And crown'd him with their spoils.

> " ' 'Tis finished!'   Legal worship ends,
> And gospel ages run ;
> All old things now are pass'd away,
> And a new world begun."

The seventh is *presentation* of his spirit to his Father : " Father, into thy hands I commend my spirit." Many a time have these words waked a corresponding sentiment in the dying Christian's breast; many a time have they been used by the dying Christian to express his soul's surrender to God. Similarly the protomartyr's " Lord Jesus, receive my spirit." Likewise in the language of ancient piety, " Into thine hand I commit my spirit : thou hast redeemed me, O Lord God of truth." Hence too we infer the immateriality of the soul, and its independence of the body. Here also we learn how to die, yielding our soul into the hand of our heavenly Father.—J. J. G.

Vers. 42—47. Parallel passages: Matt. xxvii. 57—61; Luke xxiii. 50—56.—*The burial.*
I. SECRET DISCIPLES. Among secret disciples of our Lord were Joseph of Arimathæa and Nicodemus. The residence of the former was Ramah, or Ramathaim, the name signifying a hill ; while some identify it with Ramleh in Dan, others with Ramathaim in Ephraim, and others, again, with Ramah in Benjamin. But the character of the man is of much more importance to us than his place of abode. Accordingly, one evangelist describes him, as has been ingeniously pointed out, according to the Jewish ideal, as a *rich* man,—so St. Matthew ; a second according to the Roman ideal, as an honourable (εὐσχήμων) councillor, or councillor of honourable estate (Revised Version),—so St. Mark; while a third according to the Greek ideal, as good and just, somewhat similar to the Greek καλὸς καὶ ἀγαθός, implying a person of good social position and respectable culture, and thus presumably of correct morals,—so St. Luke. In any case, the third Gospel represents him as a moral man and a religious man—two characteristics that should never be dissociated. We are further informed that Joseph, being one of the seventy Sanhedrists, protested against the conduct of the Sanhedrim in their condemnation of our Lord. Though it is not expressly stated, we may be sure that Nicodemus, the same who is characterized as coming to our Lord by night, if present, joined him in the protest ; but they were a small minority, and so the majority of that body accomplished their counsel and crime. Of Joseph's discipleship St. Matthew says, " Who *also* himself was Jesus' disciple ; " and St. Luke, " Who *also* himself waited for the kingdom of God." The *also* in both cases implies that he was a faithful follower of Christ, though in secret, as well as the more open disciples ; while St. John tells us the reason of the secrecy in the words, " secretly for fear of the Jews." He now laid aside his timidity, and proved himself no longer deficient in Christian courage; for he went in boldly (τολμήσας) to Pilate and craved the body of his Lord. Though "not many mighty according to the flesh, not many noble," are called ; yet, thank God ! there are still some such. Among these, Nicodemus, a ruler of the Jews, a master in Israel, a Sanhedrist, or member of the great national council, who had absented himself, or at all events refused consent to the condemnation, " brought a mixture of myrrh and aloes, about a hundred pound weight," for his burial. On mention of Nicodemus, it is remarkable we are still reminded

of his night interview with our Lord. " He that came to Jesus by night," says St. John, and again, " which at first came to Jesus by night," as is added by the same evangelist. Now he too has been emboldened by the cross. Joseph, on obtaining the body, laid it in his own new tomb, so that the prediction was fulfilled to the effect that, though his grave was made with the wicked intentionally, that is, according to the intention of his enemies, yet was actually with the rich in his death. Crucified with male-factors, it was intended and expected that he would share their fate in burial. Not so, however ; for though he died as a criminal, he was not buried as one.

II. THE SURPRISE OF PILATE. The usual time for death to supervene in the case of persons crucified was some three days, the very shortest a day and a half. Consequently Pilate expresses his astonishment, and requires the evidence of the centurion to satisfy him of Jesus' death. He first asks in surprise if he were already dead (τέθνηκε), and then, calling the centurion, inquires if he had been any while dead (ἀπέθανε). Here the accurate use of the Greek tenses is worthy of attention, and brings out the governor's amazement more clearly. His first inquiry is expressed by the perfect, and refers to the *state*—if he was already in the state of death ; satisfied of that, and not a little sur-prised, he asks an *additional* question (ἐπηρώτησεν) of the centurion, and in this second inquiry he employs the aorist in relation to the *occurrence*—if death had occurred any length of time previously, or how long, in any case to make sure it was not a swoon. It has been stated and maintained, on respectable medical authority, that the direct cause of Christ's death was rupture of the heart. In that case the blood passed from the interior of the heart out into the heart-sac, and, like all extravasated blood, separated into the red clot and watery element. This would agree well with the suddenness of the Saviour's death, after only some six hours on the cross—a circumstance which, as we have just seen, took Pilate himself so much by surprise ; whereas crucifixion usually caused death by exhaustion, and after many hours' lingering. This would also agree well with the *loud* voice of that cry which the Saviour uttered when he yielded up the ghost. This would agree well with the quantity of blood shed to fill that fountain, of which the prophet speaks, saying, " In that day there shall be a *fountain* opened to the house of David, and to the inhabitants of Jerusalem, for sin and for uncleanness ; " for in crucifixion the loss of blood is diminished by the nails choking up the wounds they make. This would agree well with such Scriptures as the following :—" Reproach hath broken my heart ; " " My heart is like wax ; it is melted in the midst of my bowels." This would, moreover, agree well with the fact that when he poured out his soul unto death, his bodily sufferings, bitter as they were, had less effect than his mental agony in producing that death. This would still further agree well with what occurred when the soldier pierced the Saviour's side with his broad-headed spear. That rude Roman had no command to inflict such a wound ; it was mere bootless barbarity on his part. The body was dead ; why gash it so, except perhaps to make sure it was death and not syncope ? Nevertheless, he fulfilled prophecy without thinking it ; he realized the opening of the prophet's fountain without knowing aught about it. He made a passage for the blood and water already escaped from that broken heart ; he helped to open the fountain that cleanseth from all sin.

III. SIGNIFICANCE OF THE BLOOD AND WATER. The blood and water that flowed from the fountain thus opened in the Saviour's side are significant of the two great blessings which believers partake through Christ. There was blood for redemption, water for regeneration ; blood for remission, water for renewal ; blood for pardon, water for purity ; blood to put away the guilt of sin, water to purge away its filth ; blood for justification, water for sanctification ; blood for atonement (and this is the special work of the Son of God), water for purification (and this is the province of the Spirit of God) ; blood and the sacramental wine is a symbol of it, water and the baptismal element is a sign of it. Thus the two great agents in salvation—the Son of God and the Spirit of God ; the two great works they accomplish—redemption and regeneration ; the two great doctrines of a standing and spiritual Church—justification and sanctifica-tion—are kept fresh in the memory and visible to the eye by the sacramental seals of the covenant. In allusion, probably, to this St. John (1 Epist. v. 6) says, " This is he that came by water and blood, even Jesus Christ ; not with water only, but with the water and with the blood " (Revised Version). These two must always go together ; these two flowed forth together from the pierced side of the Saviour ; these two the apostle has joined together. These two form the streams of the prophetic fountain ; and by means of the twofold stream of this fountain " ye are washed, ye are sanctified, ye are justified in the Name of the Lord Jesus, and by the Spirit of our God."

> " Rock of ages, cleft for me,
> Let me hide myself in thee ;
> Let the water and the blood,
> From thy riven side which flow'd,
> Be of sin the double cure,
> Cleanse me from its guilt and power."

IV. THE FUNERAL. The funeral consisted, as far as we can learn, of few persons. There are only four persons named by name as present on the occasion—two men and two women ; though it is probable that a few females besides, who had accompanied him from Galilee, were also at least spectators, as St. Luke tells us that " the women also, which came with him from Galilee, followed after, and beheld the sepulchre, and how his body was laid." Joseph wrapped the body in the fine linen he had purchased, and sprinkled the myrrh and aloes among the folds, then laid the body in the rock-hewn tomb, and rolled a stone of large size to close therewith the entrance of the sepulchre. In these several operations, but especially in that of rolling the huge stone, Joseph was assisted, we may be certain, by Nicodemus, and both by their servants or attendants; while Mary of Magdala, and Mary the mother of Joses, and the other women from Galilee, were looking on. They beheld (ἐθεώρουν), carefully observing the place and manner of the sepulchre.—J. J. G.

EXPOSITION.

CHAPTER XVI.

Ver. 1.—**And when the sabbath was past, Mary Magdalene, and Mary the** mother of **James, and Salome, bought spices** (ἠγόρασαν ἀρώματα) **that they might come and anoint him.** A hasty but lavish embalming of our Lord's sacred body had been begun on Friday evening by Joseph and Nicodemus. They had "brought a mixture of myrrh and aloes, about a hundred pound weight" (John xix. 39). This would be a compound—the gum of the myrrh tree, and a powder of the fragrant aloe wood mixed together, with which they would completely cover the body, which was then swathed with linen cloths (ὀθόνια), also steeped in the aromatic preparation. Then the *sindon* would be placed over all. Compare the ἐνετύλιξεν of St. Luke (xxiii. 53), as applying to the *sindon*, with the ἔδησαν of St. John (xix. 40) as applying to the ὀθόνια. This verse records a further stage in the embalming. What had been done on the Friday evening had been done in haste, and yet sufficiently for the preservation of the sacred body, if that had been needful, from decay. The remaining work could be done more carefully and tenderly at the tomb. Observe the aorist in this verse (ἠγόρασαν), "they bought ;" not "they had bought."

Ver. 2.—**And very early on the first day of the week** (λίαν πρωΐ τῇ μιᾷ τῶν σαββάτων), **they come** (ἔρχονται) — not "they came," St. Mark is fond of the graphic present—

to the tomb when the sun was risen. They bought the spices that they needed on the Saturday evening, after the sabbath was past; and then set out early the next morning, reaching the tomb when the sun was risen.

Ver. 3.—**And they were saying** (ἔλεγον) **among themselves, Who shall roll us away the stone from the door of the tomb?** The usual form of tombs in Palestine was the following :—There was generally an approach to the tomb open to the sky; then a low entrance on the side of the rock, leading into a square chamber, on one side of which was a recess for the body, about three feet deep, with a low arch over it. The stone here referred to by the women would be the stone which covered the actual entrance into the vault. It would probably be not less than six feet in breadth and three in height. This great stone had been rolled by Joseph to the mouth of the tomb ; and then he had departed. Now, as the women approached, "they were saying (ἔλεγον) among themselves, Who shall roll us away (ἀποκυλίσει) the stone?" They had seen the arrangements, and had observed the size of the stone on the Friday evening. (ch. xv. 47).

Ver. 4.—**And looking up** (ἀναβλέψασαι), **they see** (θεωροῦσιν) **that the stone is rolled back** (ἀποκεκύλισται): **for it was exceeding great** (μέγας σφόδρα). At this point we learn from St. John that Mary Magdalene ran away to tell Peter and John (John xx. 2).

Ver. 5.—**And entering into the tomb, they saw a young man sitting on the right side, arrayed in a white robe; and they were amazed.** They enter the tomb, the expression "tomb" including the ante-chamber. They see that the stone has been rolled back, so as to expose the entrance into the place where Jesus had lain. On that stone a young man was sitting. The angel appeared in the form of a young man, because youth indicates the vigour, the beauty, and the strength of angels. The good angels always appear in beauty and comeliness of form. There will be no deformity in heaven. The angel appeared as arrayed in a white robe. This white robe, or *talar*, indicated a heavenly spiritual being. St. Matthew (xxviii. 3) says that "his countenance was like lightning," flashing with splendour, and his raiment was as white as snow. It may be that he appeared more terrible to the keepers (Matt. xxviii. 4), and that he abated something of his dazzling brightness when he appeared to the women; but "they were affrighted" (ἐξεθαμβήθησαν); literally, *they were amazed*. Amazement was the dominant feeling, though probably not unmingled with fear.

Ver. 6.—**And he saith unto them, Be not amazed**—μὴ ἐκθαμβεῖσθε, the same word—**ye seek Jesus, the Nazarene, which hath been crucified: he is risen; he is not here: behold, the place where they laid him**; that is, *behold, here is the place where they laid him* (ἴδε, ὁ τόπος). St. Matthew (xxviii. 6) says, "Come, see the place where the Lord lay" (Δεῦτε, ἴδετε τὸν τόπον). This seems to imply that the women actually entered the inner chamber, and saw the very place where the Lord lay. Who does not see here how irrefragable is the evidence of his resurrection?

Ver. 7.—**But go, tell his disciples and Peter, He goeth before you into Galilee: there shall ye see him, as he said unto you.** St. Gregory ('Hom. in Evan.') says, "If the angel had not named Peter, he would not have dared to come amongst the disciples. Therefore he is specially named, lest he should despair on account of his denial." It was evidently intended as a special message of comfort to Peter. St. Luke (xxiv. 34) records the personal appearance of our Lord first to Peter. Here St. Mark, with characteristic modesty, keeps Peter in the background. In ch. xiv. 28 our Lord is recorded to have said, "After I am raised up, I will go before you into Galilee." He would go before them as their Shepherd, and lead them to that part of the Holy Land which, as he had honoured it before his resurrection, so he would honour it again now.

Ver. 8.—**And they went out**—the word (ταχὺ) "quickly" is omitted—**and fled from**

the tomb; for trembling and astonishment had come upon them (τρόμος καὶ ἔκστασις)—*agitation and ecstasy*; they were in a state of the utmost excitement. **And they said nothing to any one; for they were afraid.** The vision of angels had terrified them. They were probably afraid to say anything to any one, on account of the Jews, lest it should be said that they had stolen the body of Jesus. It has been well remarked that independent accounts of events occurring in a time of supreme excitement, and related by trustworthy witnesses, but from different points of view, naturally present difficulties which cannot be cleared up without a full knowledge of all the particulars. (See 'Speaker's Commentary' in Matt. xxviii. 9.)

Ver. 9.—**Now when he was risen early on the first day of the week, he appeared first to Mary Magdalene, from whom he had cast out seven devils.** St. Luke (viii. 2) mentions that "seven devils had gone out of her;" and St. Mark repeats it here, to show the power of love and penitence, that she was the first to be permitted to see the risen Saviour. The vision of the angel had scared her, and she said nothing; but the actual sight of her risen Lord gave her confidence, and she went immediately, in obedience to his command, and told the disciples (see John xx. 11—18). She had lingered about his tomb; her strong affection riveted her to the spot.

Ver. 10.—**She went and told** ἐκείνη πορευθεῖσα ἀπήγγειλε **them that had been with him, as they mourned and wept.** The aorist here indicates immediate action. This word πορεύεσθαι occurs again in vers. 12 and 15, but nowhere else in St. Mark's Gospel. It is to be noticed, however, that it occurs twice in the First Epistle of St. Peter, and once in his Second Epistle. This seems to connect St. Peter with the writer of these verses.

Ver. 11.—**And they, when they heard that he was alive, and had been seen of her, disbelieved** (ἠπίστησαν). They refused to believe on the bare statement of Mary Magdalene, although M. Renan says, "Sa grande affirmation de femme, 'Il est ressuscité!' a été la base de la foi de l'humanité." They did not believe her until the risen Lord stood before them. (See 'Speaker's Commentary' (St. Mark), p. 297.)

Ver. 12.—**And after these things he was manifested in another form unto two of them, as they walked** (πορευομένοις) **on their way into the country.** This appearance is doubtless the same as that which is related fully by St. Luke (xxiv. 13).

Ver. 13.—**And they went away and told it unto the rest: neither believed they them.** This want of faith happened by the per-

mission and providence of God. "This
their unbelief," says St. Gregory, "was not
so much *their* infirmity as *our* future constancy on the faith."

Ver. 14.—**And afterward** (ὕστερον δὲ) **he
was manifested** (ἐφανερώθη) **unto the eleven
themselves** (αὐτοῖς τοῖς ἕνδεκα) **as they sat at
meat.** There is an emphasis here on the
word "themselves." The former appearances had been to persons not having any
official character. But now he appears to
the eleven apostles, when they were all
gathered together at the close of that
memorable day. "Unto the *eleven*." If, as
seems evident, this appearance refers to the
day of our Lord's resurrection, there would
be only *ten* present; for Thomas was not
then with them. Still, they might be called
the eleven, because the apostolic college
was reduced to eleven after the betrayal by
Judas; so that they might still be called
the eleven, although Thomas was absent.
St. Bernard says on this, "If Christ comes
and is present when we sit at meat, how
much more when we kneel in prayer!"
He upbraided them (ὠνείδισε). This is a
strong word of rebuke. They ought to have
received the testimony of competent witnesses. But their doubts were only removed
by the evidence of their senses; just as
afterwards in the case of Thomas. St.
Mark is always careful to record the rebukes
administered by our Lord to his apostles.

Vers. 15, 16.—**And he said unto them, Go
ye into all the world, and preach the gospel
to the whole creation** (πάσῃ τῇ κτίσει). **He
that believeth and is baptized shall be saved;
but he that disbelieveth shall be condemned.**
Here is a considerable interval of time, not
noticed in any way by the evangelist. *And
he saith unto them*; not on the day of his
resurrection. It would seem that this
charge was delivered to them in Galilee,
and that it is the same as that recorded in
St. Matthew (xxviii. 19), which was again
repeated immediately before his ascension
from Bethany. *Go ye into all the world;* not
into Judæa only, but everywhere. This
command has expanded with the discovery
in later times of new portions of the inhabited earth; and must ever be coextensive with geographic discovery. *Preach
the gospel to the whole creation;* that is,
"among all nations." Man is the noblest
work of God. All the creation is gathered
up in him, created after the image of the
Creator. *He that believeth and is baptized
shall be saved; but he that disbelieveth shall
be condemned.* These words are very important. The first clause opposes the
notion that faith alone is sufficient for salvation, without those works which are the
fruit of faith. *He that believeth and is
baptized shall be saved;* that is, he that

believeth, and as an evidence of his faith
accepts Christ's baptism, and fulfils the
promises and vows which he then took upon
himself, working out his own salvation with
fear and trembling, shall be saved. *But he
that disbelieveth shall be condemned* (ὁ δὲ
ἀπιστήσας, κατακριθήσεται). The condemnation anticipates the doom which will be
incurred by continual unbelief.

Vers. 17, 18.—**And these signs shall
follow them that believe.** Such evidences
were necessary in the first dawn of Christianity, to attract attention to the doctrine;
but our Lord's words do not mean that they
were to be in perpetuity, as a continually recurring evidence of the truth of Christianity.
St. Gregory (on 1 Cor. xiv. 22) says, "These
signs were necessary in the beginning of
Christianity. In order that faith might
take root and increase, it must be nourished
by miracle; for so even we, when we plant
shrubs, only water them until we see that
they are taking root, and when we see that
they have rooted themselves, we cease to
water them. And this is what St. Paul
means where he says 'Tongues are for a sign,
not to those who believe, but to the unbelieving' (1 Cor. xiv. 22)." **In my name
shall they cast out devils.** St. Mark, of all
the evangelists, dwells most perhaps on this,
as characteristic of our Lord's work, and as
the evidence of his supreme dominion over
the spiritual world. **They shall speak with
new tongues.** This was the first intimation
of the great miracle to be inaugurated on
the day of Pentecost. The gift was continued but for a very limited time. **They
shall take up serpents.** The instance of St.
Paul at Melita (Acts xxviii. 3—5) would be
familiar to St. Mark's readers. **And if they
drink any deadly thing, it shall in no wise
hurt them.** There are some few traditionary
notices of the fulfilment of this promise;
as in the case of "Justus Barsabas,"
mentioned by Eusebius ('H.E.,' iii. 19),
and of St. John, mentioned by St. Augustine. It may be observed of this passage,
that no one could have interpolated it after
the cessation of the signs to which it refers,
which took place very early.

Ver. 19.—**So then the Lord Jesus, after he
had spoken unto them, was received up into
heaven.** Here is another interval. The
evangelist has gathered up some few of the
most important words and sayings of Christ;
and now he takes his reader to Bethany, the
scene of our Lord's ascension. It has been
well observed (see Bishop Wordsworth, *in
loc.*) that the fact of the Ascension is gradually revealed in the Gospels. St. Matthew
does not mention it at all. St. Mark refers to
it in this brief and very simple manner. But
St. Luke describes it with great fulness, both
in his Gospel and in the Acts of the

Apostles, throughout which book he leads his readers to contemplate Christ as ascended into heaven, and as sitting at God's right hand, and as ruling the Church and the world from the throne of his glory.

Ver. 20.—**And they went forth, and preached everywhere, the Lord working with them, and confirming the word by the signs that followed. Amen.** These words are alluded to in several passages by Justin Martyr (about A.D. 160), and, for the reasons given above, could not have been written later than the time of miracles being wrought. They form a fitting introduction to the Acts of the Apostles. Cornelius à Lapide concludes his Commentary upon St. Mark with the following beautiful apostrophe of St. Augustine:—"O kingdom of everlasting blessedness, where youth never grows old, where beauty never fades, where love never waxes cold, where health never fails, where joy never decreases, where life never ends!"

HOMILETICS.

Vers. 1—8.—*The empty sepulchre.* In this passage there is no direct narrative of the Saviour's resurrection. The evangelist probably tells what, and only what, he had heard from credible and well-known witnesses. There were no such witnesses to the act of the Lord's emergence from the tomb. But the Marys and Salome had stated what they had seen and heard. They declared that, although they went early to the sepulchre, they found it both open and empty. They related their interview with the young man, the angel, who informed them that Jesus had risen. And it is upon their testimony that the evangelist bases in the first instance his gospel of the resurrection.

I. LOVE WILL FIND OCCASIONS AND WAYS OF EXPRESSING ITSELF. In our Lord's ministry, devout and attached women had often provided for his wants. When the end of that ministry arrived, these affectionate friends were found faithful to their Master; they were amongst the witnesses of his crucifixion and his death. Nor did they then withdraw, but lingered by the lifeless body until it was deposited in the new-hewn tomb. Even then their love was not satisfied; it remained for them to finish the rites which had been so hastily performed by Nicodemus and Joseph, and so abruptly suspended by the sunset which was the commencement of the Jewish sabbath. Behold them, accordingly, in the garden immediately after sunrise. On the past evening they have purchased spices; and they have now, at early morning, come, laden with the fragrant preparations, to perform the last offices to the body of him they have long honoured and loved. The incident reminds us of the grateful and most graceful tribute offered to Jesus by the sister of Lazarus, who poured the costly perfume over the sacred feet of her Lord, her Benefactor. In both cases the value and the charm of the services are owing to the love by which they were inspired. Love followed Jesus, not only in the way, and into the dwelling, but to the cross and to the grave. They who truly love the Lord Christ will find opportunities in abundance of proving their affection.

II. WE IMAGINE DIFFICULTIES WHICH GOD HAS ALREADY SOLVED FOR US. No wonder that these feeble women questioned one with another, "Who shall roll us away the stone?" Strong men had closed the entrance to the tomb by placing this huge stone against it; how should this barrier to the carrying out of their intentions be removed? They looked up, and lo! the stone was rolled away. This had been done at daybreak by the celestial messenger. Very similar is much of Christian experience. We perplex ourselves, it may be, with speculative difficulties. Nature and revelation teem with mysteries. To our finite and untrained, inexperienced intelligence it must be so. Our penetration is too dull, our wisdom is too short-sighted; our powers, knowledge, and opportunities are all unequal to the task. But all is clear to that Being who is infinitely wise; and when we lift up our eyes we shall in due time see the resolution of our doubts. We perplex ourselves, it may be, with practical difficulties. How shall we do our work—that work being so vast, and we so helpless? How shall we train our family, conduct our business, discharge our responsibilities? We cannot tell. But, looking unto him, we shall be lightened. He shall bring our way to pass. We perplex ourselves, it may be, with difficulties as to the Church and kingdom of Christ. How shall the Lord's people be awakened to zeal, or reconciled in unity, or qualified for the work assigned them in a dark and sinful world? Our mind is baffled by the problem, which we have no means of solving. Let us go on our way. When we come to our difficulty, we may perhaps find that it is gone. Let us leave the problems of the future to be solved by him with whom all is one eternal "now." Let us commit the distant in space and in time to him to whom belong alike the far-off and the near. There is no stone so exceeding great that he cannot roll it away; none that he will suffer to hinder or delay the execution of his own purposes.

III. CHRIST MAY BE SOUGHT IN THE GRAVE, BUT HE IS FOUND IN THE RISEN LIFE, THE SPIRITUAL REALM. Notwithstanding that Jesus had foretold both his death and his resurrection, the disciples were overwhelmed with astonishment at his crucifixion, and were amazed and incredulous at the tidings of his triumph over the grave. The men do not seem to have come to the tomb until they were summoned; the women came, but they came to embalm the dead, not to welcome the living—the risen. It needed that they should be assured "He is risen; he is not here!" in order that the current of their mournful thoughts should be arrested and reversed. In the tomb they did not find him, but they met him in his glorious resurrection-body. There are many who still commit the same mistake regarding our Saviour. They think of his bodily and earthly life, of its outward incidents and of its tragic close. They think of him as if his ministry and his mediation came to an end on Calvary. They do not think of him as risen, as living in human society, as working in human hearts, as governing and blessing human lives. Yet, for us, what is the significance of the Redeemer's rising from the dead? Is it not just this—that the Saviour's resurrection-life is his moral and spiritual sway over humanity? It is not in his body that his presence consists. It is in the penetration of the world's moral nature by his ever-present, all-pervading Spirit; it is in the transformation of the world's moral life by the power of his sacrifice, his obedience, his self-denial, his benevolence. Many a king and conqueror has died, after a life of ambition, a career of slaughter and of oppression. The death of such has been welcome, for it has put an end to a power for mischief which has cursed the world. But every teacher, every discoverer of truth, has implanted in the soul of humanity a seed which has outlived himself. How much more does the Divine Light and Life of men continue to illumine and to inspire the world, which first rejected him, and then found out his inestimable worth, his incalculable power!

IV. THE MOST WELCOME AND GLORIOUS REVELATION IS RECEIVED AT FIRST WITH FEAR, ASTONISHMENT, AND SILENCE. Of the women we read, "They were amazed;" "trembling and astonishment came upon them;" "they were afraid;" "they said nothing to any one." It is a strange effect to follow from such a cause. Nothing could be so welcome and so joyful as the news which greeted them. But it was too startling, too surprising, too unexpected. They "departed with fear and great joy," just as the eleven afterwards "disbelieved for joy." There is news which seems too good to be true. Even so now there are doubting souls, who fain would believe in a Divine Saviour, and who withhold their faith, not from unspirituality of nature and habit, but from the intensity of their appreciation of the blessing needed—the revelation of Divine favour, and the prospect of a glorious immortality. Let such raise their minds to the height of the Divine benevolence. "Why should it be thought a thing incredible with you that God should raise the dead?" Such an interposition is surely worthy even of the Supreme! "That our faith and hope might be in God." Surely such an end may be believed to justify the most unexampled revelation and the most stupendous display of power. It is well that the tidings should be received with some sense of their amazing importance and their unique bearing upon the state and prospects of mankind.

V. THE NEWS OF THE RESURRECTION IS GOOD TIDINGS TO BE PUBLISHED ABROAD. The faithful women were directed to act as messengers. They have been called "the apostles of the apostles." They were to find Peter and the other disciples, to tell them that Jesus had risen, and to direct them where they should meet him. This they did, and in so doing they set an example to Christians in all coming time. Whatever else may be said of the resurrection of Jesus, this must be said of it first and fore-most: It is good news, worthy of all acceptation. As such the apostles received it, and as such they published it. In the record of their ministry, nothing is so promi-nently put forward as their preaching Jesus and the Resurrection. A risen and glorified Saviour was the Saviour they preached—a Saviour who had died, but who liveth evermore. Glad tidings to be proclaimed in every language and to all mankind!

APPLICATION. 1. Let us learn to live a life of faith in a risen, exalted, reigning Saviour and Lord. Our religious life should receive its impulse and its motive from looking upwards to the Lord of life. 2. Let us regard it as our sacred ministry to publish as good tidings the truth that Christ is risen. This is the office and privilege of the Church of him who was dead and is alive again, and lives for evermore.

Vers. 9—14.—*Disbelief convinced.* The day of Christ's resurrection was a day which opened in gloom and closed with gladness. In the morning our Lord's disciples and friends were mourning their Master's death, were grieving at what they deemed their forsaken and friendless lot; in the evening the same persons were rejoicing in a risen and triumphant Redeemer. They had found the key to their perplexities; they had received a new impulse and aim, the power and the promise of a new life. To what was it all due? Simply to this: they exchanged unreasonable disbelief for reasonable faith.

I. THE EVIDENCE DISBELIEVED. In some cases we are justified in refusing our assent to testimony; in others we are justified in withholding that assent until the testimony is confirmed. Such was not the case on the occasion under consideration. The evidence was that of credible persons, and of persons whom the eleven knew to be credible. Mary of Magdala, and Cleopas, and his companion were well known to the company of our Lord's friends and disciples. They were persons of unquestionable veracity. They had been themselves convinced against their own persuasions and prejudices. Mary had gone to the grave to complete the rites of burial—a proof that she was not expecting the resurrection. The two who walked to Emmaus regarded the death of Jesus as the destruction of their hopes; they were sad of countenance and slow of heart. If the testimony of Mary were rejected as that of an enthusiast, how could the testimony of the two companions be disputed? Besides, from the other Gospels we know that the other women had also borne witness to having seen Jesus, and that the Lord had appeared to Simon, who had announced the good news to the others. Testimony so varied, repeated, and credible as this deserved a better reception than was accorded to it. But whatever was said of the rising of the Lord Jesus, the disciples during that day disbelieved.

II. THE EXPLANATION OF THIS DISBELIEF. There must have been and there were reasons, or rather motives, for the attitude of the unbelieving disciples. According to this passage, grief was one explanation. The sorrow which possessed the hearts of Christ's friends, when they saw him insulted, tortured, and slain, was deep and poignant. Time had not elapsed for that grief to be allayed. They were still prostrate beneath the anguish which had crushed their hearts. They would hear of nothing that might alleviate and soothe them. And with grief was mingled disappointment. Their mounting hopes were smitten as with a bolt, and fell lifeless to the earth. They had looked for conquest, and they thought they saw defeat. They had looked for a kingdom, and lo! their King was slain. Doubtless, the sentiments of all were expressed in the pathetic lament, "We trusted this had been he who should have redeemed Israel." Such hopes, so crushed, could not easily arise again. Minds so amazed, staggered, utterly perplexed, were all unready to welcome tidings of encouragement. The storm-blast had passed over the tree and snapped the trunk in twain; the calm and the sunshine could not rear the prostrate head.

III. THE BLAMABLENESS OF THIS DISBELIEF. When the Lord himself appeared unto them he doubtless made allowance for their feelings. Yet it is here recorded, "He upbraided them with their unbelief and hardness of heart, because they believed not them which had seen him after he was risen." This implies that they ought to have felt and acted otherwise. 1. And they would have done so had they cherished a juster view of the nature of the Lord himself. Had they remembered the witness borne to him by the Father, had they recalled his own lofty claims, had they pondered his wonderful works, and especially his miracles of raising the dead to life, then the tidings that he had risen would not have fallen upon unreceptive minds. 2. Further, the disciples should have remembered the Lord's promises, some of which had been given in figurative language, but some of which had been couched in the plainest

terms. He had said that, after being put to death, he would rise on the third day.
How is it that they had so utterly forgotten a promise so express and so surprising?
3. And they should have borne in mind the predictions of the Old Testament regarding
the Messianic kingdom, which should be based upon humiliation and suffering, but
should be built up in glory. Jesus himself reproached them for having missed the
purport of the Messianic prophecies: "Ought not Christ to have," etc.?

IV. DISBELIEF VANQUISHED. What Christ's messengers could not do, he did himself.
What could not be wrought by testimony, was wrought by evidence of eyesight and
hearing. The change which came over the disciples demands attention. Their conversion from disbelief to faith was: 1. Instantaneous. For long hours they had resisted
the witness of those who had seen the risen Lord; but, upon themselves seeing him,
they yielded an immediate assent. 2. It was complete and joyful. There was no
further questioning, and no further sadness. For a moment "they believed not for joy;
but "then were the disciples glad when they saw the Lord." Their minds went quite
round; from doubt they passed to confidence, from depression to exhilaration. 3. And
this conversion was enduring. Never did they hesitate in their own testimony. They
thenceforth regarded themselves as witnesses of the resurrection, and spake boldly of
what their eyes had seen, their ears had heard, their hands had handled, of the Word
of life.

V. THE LESSONS OF THEIR DISBELIEF. 1. It makes the testimony of the disciples
the more valuable. Clearly, those men were not credulous, were not disposed or
prepared to believe. It must have been conclusive evidence indeed which convinced
them. There can be no danger in accepting the testimony of such men as these.
2. It is a rebuke to those who, through hardness of heart, believe not in a risen
Saviour. With the clear, full evidence which we possess, we shall indeed be blamable
if we withhold our cordial faith from him who for us died and rose again. "Blessed,"
says the Lord, "are they who, not having seen, yet believe."

Vers. 15—18.—*The great commission.* Whether these words were spoken at once
upon one occasion, or whether they are the summing up of many words uttered by
our Lord between his resurrection and ascension, one thing is clear—they are the
unburdening of his great heart of what was the load chiefly pressing upon it. Why
had he condescended to live upon earth, to fulfil a ministry of humiliation, to endure
unequalled woes, to die a death of ignominy and of shame? Surely not that after his
departure from earth all things might be as before. But rather and only that, as the
great foreseen result of his earthly advent and ministry, a new and heavenly power
might be introduced into humanity, a new spiritual kingdom might be set up in the
world, and a new day might dawn upon the long, dark night of time. Hence the
gospel which he caused to be proclaimed, the commission which he entrusted to his
disciples and especially his apostles. Hence the authority Jesus entrusted to his
servants, and the vast sphere he contemplated for their labours of witness and of work.
I. THE COMMISSION ENTRUSTED TO THE CHURCH. 1. What they were to take. "The
gospel," glad tidings of salvation and eternal life through a Divine Redeemer, who
died for the world's sins, and lives for the world's eternal life. 2. To whom they were
to take it. "To the whole creation," *i.e.* to all mankind, of every race and every
language, as what is intended for all and is adapted to all. 3. Who were to take it?
The eleven first received the sacred charge, but all Christ's disciples who should believe
through them on his Name were entrusted with this great commission. "Freely," said
Christ, "ye have received; freely give." No order of men, but the whole Church,
receives this sacred trust.

II. THE RESPONSIBILITY LAID UPON THE WORLD TO WHICH THE GOSPEL COMES. A
great alternative is propounded. There is no middle course supposed. Belief and
baptism are the condition of salvation; disbelief ensures condemnation. We may well
admire the wisdom and the condescending compassion which determined such a
condition as faith as the condition upon which the highest spiritual blessings may be
enjoyed. It is possible to the youngest, to the least learned, to the feeblest of men.
Yet it is a mighty principle; being able, when directed towards a Divine Saviour, to
secure all good which man can need and God can give, both for time and for eternity.

III. THE CREDENTIALS ACCOMPANYING THE PUBLICATION OF THE GOSPEL. 1. What they were. There are enumerated: power to exorcise demons, power to speak with tongues, immunity from harm by poison or by serpent-bite, the ministry of supernatural healing. 2. Why they were given. It was to authenticate the message and the messengers. As in Christ's ministry spiritual authority was indicated by miraculous works, so was it in the ministry of Christ's followers and apostles. As a matter of fact, attention was thus drawn to the Word of life. 3. Why they were withdrawn. *When* this exactly was we cannot perhaps decide; but as the purpose of their bestowal was temporary, it is evident that when this purpose was answered, and Christianity was launched upon the waters of the world, it was in accordance with Divine wisdom that miracles should cease.

Vers. 19, 20.—*Ascension.* Christ ascended on high. How could it be otherwise? He came into this world in a manner and with accompaniments so remarkable, he lived in this world a life so singular and unique, that it was but appropriate that he should quit this world as none other has ever done. What is meant by his being "received up"—where "heaven" is,—this we do not know; our knowledge is limited, and our power of conceiving the eternity and infinity around us is feeble. One thing we do see, and that is, that Jesus finished his work on earth and then departed; and one other thing we see, almost as clearly, viz. that the moral, spiritual work which was the object of his mission, so far from coming to an end with his bodily departure, really then commenced, and has been proceeding ever since. *How* he interests himself in it and carries it on, we can only tell in general and scriptural language; *that* he does so, is plain to every spiritually enlightened man. St. Mark, who plunged at the outset so boldly into his task of relating "the gospel of the Son of God," here, with characteristic brevity, clearness, and vigour, tells the last portion of his narrative—the ascension of the Saviour into heaven, and the consequent continuation of his work on earth.

I. THE ASCENSION IS THE COMPLETION OF OUR SAVIOUR'S EARTHLY MINISTRY. To those who believe that the Lord Jesus arose from the dead, the narrative of the Ascension can present little difficulty. It is impossible to believe that he who consented to die, and who conquered death, could again enter the grave. It remained for him to quit the earth without dying; and what we read of his resurrection-body leads us to believe that this was not only possible, but natural and easy. In fact, the Ascension may be regarded, not as the consequence so much as the completion of the Resurrection; and, in apostolic language, the two events are sometimes referred to in one and the same expression. How explicitly had Jesus foretold this great event! Early in his ministry he had declared, "No man hath ascended into heaven, save he that descended out of heaven, even the Son of man, who is in heaven." Expostulating with the cavillers at Capernaum at a later period, he had asked them, "What then if ye should behold the Son of man ascending where he was before?" And on the day of his resurrection he had directed Mary to take to his disciples this message: "I ascend unto my Father and your Father, and my God and your God." The foresight and authority of our Saviour were proved by the correspondence between his words and the event which exactly fulfilled them. The Ascension implied that all the purposes of the incarnation and advent of the Redeemer were accomplished. What he came to do, to suffer, and to say, he had already done, suffered, and said. He did not leave the earth until on earth there was no more for him to do. In his recorded intercessory prayer, addressing his Father, he said, "I have glorified thee on the earth: I have finished the work which thou gavest me to do."

II. THE ASCENSION IS THE COMMENCEMENT OF OUR SAVIOUR'S REIGN. We are too prone to think of human life as if it closes when the last breath is drawn and the heart beats no more. We forget that this is but the birth to the higher, the proper, the eternal life. Similarly with our view of the Redeemer's ministry of service, his tenure of priestly, royal office. We are too prone to regard his life as closing with the conclusion of our Gospel narratives. We follow him in thought until the cloud, descending upon Olivet, receives him out of our sight, and then we say, "It is all over! His course is run, his work is finished!" But it is not so. The very contrary of this is the case. That Christ's ascension draws a sharp line of demarcation, is true; but the one side is finite, the other is infinite. We can comprehend the one; the other baffles all our powers of penetration. The steps of Jesus through this earthly pilgrimage are steps which we can trace; but we lose sight of them, and faith alone can follow, when he ascends on high. This, however, is certain to us, that, with the ascension of Jesus, the second, the more spiritual, the more beneficent, the more enduring stage of this Divine ministry, commenced. He did much in his humiliation; he is doing more in his glory. He came to found a kingdom; he went to administer it; and he must reign until his foes become his footstool. Contemplate the Son of man as he is here represented, no longer wearing the disguise of feebleness and submitting to the insults and the hatred of the wicked. His days of toil, of hunger, and of weariness, his nights of exposure and of mental conflict, are over. No more is he to endure the misrepresentations of the hypocritical and the malicious; no more to baffle the insidious snares of the crafty and the unscrupulous; no more to be patient under the cold mockery of the unspiritual and ungrateful. His deeds of mercy shall never again be attributed to the powers of evil; never again shall those he fain would benefit seek to cast him headlong from the precipice; nor shall he sigh because of the hardness of heart and insensibility of his foes. It is well that he has gone through it all; that he has been despised and rejected of men, that he has been overwhelmed with the baptism of suffering, that he has drunk to the dregs earth's bitter cup of woe. All this is well. But it is better that it is past and over; that he takes with him into the unseen state the memory of his humiliation, his obedience, his death; that he enters upon his purchased possession; that he sees "of the travail of his soul, and is satisfied;" that he is "received up into heaven, and sits down on the right hand of God." What are we to understand when told that Christ "sat down" in heaven, and by the Father's side? The evangelist speaks here in such a way as to convey to us important religious truth. Christ's earthly ministry had been one of unrest and homelessness; from the commencement of his public labours until those labours ended on the cross, few had been the intervals of repose. With the Ascension began the period of rest. The seat upon the throne is becoming to royalty: the monarch sits whilst the courtiers, guards, and attendants stand. So the expression implies the kingly dignity of Immanuel. He has exchanged the crown of thorns for the diadem of empire. "On his head are many crowns." Further, a judge sits upon the judgment-seat, whilst the criminal stands at his bar. Jesus not long before had stood, as the vilest culprit might have done, before the malignant Caiaphas, before the vacillating, unrighteous Pilate. Now, no longer the accused, he is the just, majestic, and almighty Judge, ordained by God to be the Judge of quick and dead. How bold and plain, although metaphorical, is Mark's language here! "The Lord Jesus sat down at the right hand of God." "The right hand of God" is one of those expressions, so frequent in Scripture, which are used, in condescension to our infirmities, to convey to us, in a striking and effective manner, truth otherwise not easily communicated. A courtier, when at the right hand of his sovereign, is near him, is readily addressed; is in a position either to give information or to receive instructions; can easily obtain a signature, or an authority or warrant under the sign-manual; is in a position to introduce to the king any applicant or petitioner; in brief, occupies a post of privilege, trust, influence, honour, and authority. And when our Saviour is pictured as at the right hand of God, we are to understand that he is the Mediator, through whom the Divine power and guidance, favour and blessing, are bestowed upon those in whom he has shown himself interested by undergoing on their behalf the labours and the sacrifices of the earthly humiliation. No wonder, then, that the position occupied by Christians is described in language so rich, full, and inspiriting—that all things are declared to be theirs, for they are Christ's, and Christ is God's.

III. THE ASCENSION WAS THE PREPARATION FOR A NEW AND SPIRITUAL ECONOMY. The bodily absence of the Redeemer was the condition of a new dispensation of spiritual power and of world-wide extent. Hitherto the evangelizing journeys of the twelve had been restricted in scope and local in range; they had gone only to the lost sheep of the house of Israel, and they had directed attention to the speedy approach of the kingdom. But the aim of Jesus was one of universal benevolence; other sheep, not of the Israelitish fold, were to be brought in; he was to draw all men unto himself. This was to be done by spiritual agencies, which were dependent upon the removal of the Lord to heaven. In fact, the ascension of the Lord Jesus was, in the Divine counsels, the condition and the occasion of the bestowal of the Holy Spirit, in the manner and measure distinctive of the new, the Christian dispensation. He himself had put this with great plainness before his disciples' minds : " If I go not away, the Comforter will not come unto you; but if I go, I will send him unto you." This was a doctrinal statement of the nature of a revelation. What was the intelligible and manifest fact corresponding to it? Surely this—that the earthly mission of the Saviour being complete, the gospel was to be preached, and should be made, by a spiritual force acting on human natures, the means of awakening men to a new conscience of sin, a new yearning for holiness, a new purpose of an unselfish and unworldly life. It is no more unreasonable to attribute the fruits of the gospel to the Spirit of God, than it is to attribute human purposes to the spirit of man. It is a spiritual universe, and things material and outward actions are nothing but the garb and utterance of what is spiritual. If there be truth declared, revealed, and if there be a nature capable of receiving, feeling, responding to truth, there is one all-sufficient explanation of this wonderful and beneficent correspondence, and that is, the presence and the action of the Holy Spirit of God. The ascension of Christ changed the life of the apostles, and through them, the history of the world. 1. Now and henceforth there was an express *theme for them to publish*. This was the gospel, the good tidings, which only now was complete, and so divinely perfected by all that Jesus had done and suffered, that it was adapted to fulfil the purposes of Divine wisdom. Before, the disciples had directed attention to what was to come ; now, to what had occurred actually and really. Christ had died for men's sins, according to the Scriptures; he had arisen from the dead for their justification and salvation. Around the great central facts of Christ's birth, crucifixion, and resurrection gathered all the Divine truths which constituted the gospel. Accordingly, in the first place, the facts were related as facts abundantly attested, and as facts of interest and precious moment to all mankind. And, when these facts were believed, then they were explained, and (under the guidance of the Holy Spirit given from above) the inspired apostles taught their bearing upon the position and prospects of the sinful race of man. It should never be forgotten that our religion consists in something more than laws of life, sentiments of virtue, promises of help, hopes of immortality. In accordance with the constitution of things, all these depend upon and flow from the great central facts relating to the Lord Jesus Christ. 2. Besides having a theme, the apostles of our Lord now had *a commission which authorized them*. They did not go unbidden, without instructions, without authority, upon this errand of mercy and blessing to mankind. He who had all power in heaven and in earth had given them their commission. He had said " Go ! " and they went; not in their own strength and wisdom, but in his. The same warrant and authentication abides with the Church of Christ throughout all the ages. The apostles were, as the name implies, those who were *sent ;* in this respect, as distinguished from personal endowment and equipment, an apostolic mission is entrusted to the whole body of Christ's followers to the end of time. 3. *The sphere* within which this commission was to be executed was world-wide. " Go ye into all the world," Jesus had .said, " and preach the gospel to the whole creation." " Make disciples of all nations." A grand and noble design, worthy of the source whence it emanated, in the heart of him who is " the Saviour of all men, specially of them that believe." The habitable globe is the field in which the Christian missionary is called to work; for the human race is the object of Divine compassion, the destined participant in the bounty of the Divine beneficence. None, however large-hearted and compassionate, can complain that the operations of mercy and benevolence are restricted and restrained. 4. In fulfilling this commission, the heralds of Christ's gospel were assured that they should enjoy, not only personal assistance, but the assistance involved in undoubted *credentials,* by which they and their message should be commended to the attention of men. (1) The Lord wrought with them. They were workers, but they were fellow-workers with him. What was to be done in the renewal of human hearts, and the transformation of human character, was not to be done by the exercise of merely human power. A Divine energy and operation were alone adequate to secure results so difficult, so glorious. (2) Signs followed. Signs, *i.e.* of a Divine presence and energy. There were such in abundance, as is evident from the record in the Acts of the Apostles. Signs outward, manifest, obvious to every eye, as in the case of those miracles of healing which accompanied the ministrations of the first Christian preachers. Signs of a less obtrusive, but of an even more convincing character, as in the case of those Jews who were delivered from formalism, those Gentiles who were emancipated from idolatry, those flagrant transgressors of the moral law who were turned from darkness unto light, and from the service of Satan unto God. (3) Thus the Word was confirmed. Miracles, preaching, all were means to an end, and that end the establishment and extension of a spiritual kingdom. For the Word of God was no mere instrument of music to charm the ear and captivate the imagination; it was and is "the sword of the Spirit." Its work is to conquer, to subdue, to govern; and this work it does with incomparable keenness of edge, with incomparable force and efficiency. It has been promised, "My Word shall not return unto me void." It has proved itself a Word of power, a Word of salvation, a Word of life.

APPLICATION. 1. In heart, let Christ's people ascend with their ascended Lord and Leader. "Risen with Christ," "set your affection upon things above." 2. In life, let Christians seek to execute their Master's parting commission. He has left them a trust to fulfil, a work to do; let them not be found slothful, but diligent and watchful. 3. In hope, let all who "love his appearing," look forward to his return. For in like manner shall he come again, to receive his people to himself. "Even so, come, Lord Jesus!"

HOMILIES BY VARIOUS AUTHORS.

Vers. 1—14.—*Resurrection proofs.* The last days of the manifestation of God in Christ were signalized by a great deprivation and a great recovery. A life beyond the dread confines of the grave completed the cycle of wonders associated with the earth-life of Jesus. This, although not sufficiently realized ere it actually occurred, is a part of a continuative development. It is no awkward and hasty fragment joined on to another and more legitimate narrative. To intelligent students of the life, it appears the sublimely consistent outcome of all that preceded the death. The evangelists, from the very beginning of their histories, prepare one almost unconsciously for such a *dénouement.* It is in a sense the necessary conclusion towards which they move, and it throws into new relations and proportions all the preceding events. The earthly actions and experiences of Christ are sufficiently verified, but *in describing them the evangelists do not seem to think of having to furnish proof.* It is only *when they begin to tell us of the resurrection* that all is alertness, and *that conscious collation of evidence takes place.* This is the arcanum of the faith which must be preserved from all uncertainty; this fact must be certified that all else may be made intelligible and morally effectual. And *the moral significance of the Resurrection is even more insisted on than its physical wonder.* It is the defeat of evil machinations, and a triumph over every precaution of his enemies.

I. SOME IMPORTANT ELEMENTS OF EVIDENCE FOR THE RESURRECTION. The number and variety of Christ's appearances have been noted by the evangelists. The spiritual nature perceives the supplementary effect and educative efficiency of his resurrection fellowship. There is also a marked absence of all appearance of collusion. 1. Conspirators would have striven to keep the grave sealed until its emptiness should be discovered. 2. The Roman watch was all but inviolable. 3. Those who might be expected to conspire remained at a distance, and were informed of the event. 4. Many of them at first refused to believe the news. 5. From the Emmaus and embalming incidents, we see that most of the disciples did not look for his (at all events immediate) reappearance.

II. THE NATURE OF THE RESURRECTION. The question of those who deny the physical, yet emphasize the ideal and spiritual resurrection—"What can a few pounds more or less of dust and ashes matter?"—is shallow and impertinent. 1. *The senses were appealed to:* sight, hearing, touch; physical results were produced; fellowship was realized with him under physical conditions (the fish and honeycomb). 2. *He was not recognized at first.* A great change had, therefore, been produced. And *such a thing might be looked for.* Mary, Emmaus, Thomas and the stigmata. 3. *The manner of disappearance as described is suggestive of a real body* (Acts i. 9; Luke xxiv. 50, 51).

III. THE BEARINGS OF THIS FACT UPON CHRISTIAN FAITH AND LIFE. In considering these, we see how the foregoing question betrays an incapacity for discussing the highest practical problems. 1. *Christ came to save the entire nature*—body, soul, and spirit. He is, therefore, himself the Firstfruits and the Type. There is, in his resurrection state, a hint as to the possibilities of our material nature when completely purified and redeemed. 2. *The bodily resurrection of Christ is a more signal marvel than the spiritual alone would have been, and was at the same time more susceptible of sensible demonstration.* 3. *It was in harmony with the method of his miracles, and the grand key to them.* How the moral element in this life grew and expanded into ever more powerful effects and general relations! At last, when earnestly and carefully regarded, doubt is overwhelmed by it. How it appeals to our sense of the highest fitness, and answers the unconscious longings of the spiritual life!—M.

Vers. 3, 4.—" *Who shall roll us away the stone?* " Two things occurred together in attempting the last service to the buried Christ—weak, though willing and loving instruments, and a practically insurmountable difficulty. They themselves were unable to roll away the stone which closed the sepulchre, "for it was exceeding great." This experience has often been repeated.

I. HOW FOREBODINGS OF DIFFICULTY IN CHRISTIAN SERVICE OFTEN ARISE. 1. *By discounting the help of Christ.* They thought him dead and helpless. 2. *By calculating only one's own resources.* Looking inward. The healthy outward and upward look at the indications of Providence and experience.

II. HOW THE GOOD INTENTION OF LOVING HEARTS IS REWARDED BY THE SAVIOUR. 1. *By finding the difficulty which had been anticipated already removed.* 2. *By finding the intended service rendered unnecessary.* The empty grave at first a disappointment, but afterwards a source of joy.—M.

Ver. 6.—" *He is not here.*" I. THE PLACE WHERE CHRIST HAS BEEN IS NOT ALWAYS THE PLACE WHERE CHRIST IS.

II. IT IS A LIVING AND NOT A DEAD CHRIST THAT CHRISTIANS ARE TO SEEK.

III. THEY THAT TRULY SEEK CHRIST WILL, EVEN THROUGH DISAPPOINTMENT, LEARN WHERE TO FIND HIM.

IV. THE DUTIES OF SORROWING LOVE ARE DISPLACED BY THE DUTIES OF REJOICING FAITH.—M.

Vers. 19, 20.—*The gospel the Word of the ascended Lord.* These words, at the end of Mark's account, give the great sequence of our Lord's manifestation. The Ascension was the divinely necessary result of the Resurrection; the gospel is the necessary fruit on the human side of the experience produced in the hearts of the disciples by his life and work. Such a series of events could not end in silence. As in life, so in death, resurrection, and exaltation, Jesus Christ "could not be hid." The preaching of the gospel is a result, therefore, of an express command and an inward impulse. The two verses are in sequence to the preceding account, and the one to the other, logically, spiritually, and potentially. Notice in this connection—

I. THE POINT AT WHICH THE PREACHING OF THE GOSPEL BEGINS. At the final withdrawal and exaltation of Jesus. 1. *Its subject is a completed one.* 2. *The various portions of it are self-evidently connected, and mutually interpret one another.* The final transcendent issues of the contest of Christ with sin and death are each representative and interpretative of what preceded and led up to them. The life and its relation to the Divine purpose, prophetic anticipation, and human yearning, would be incomprehensible without this glorious trinity of consummations: death, resurrection, and ascension.

II. THE POWER IT REPRESENTS. The power of a finished work of atonement, a victory over death and hell, and an exalted, glorified humanity. 1. *The highest exaltation has been reached by him of whom it speaks.* He is invested with Divine power, and executive authority in the universe of God. Whether there be any such *place* as the "right hand of God" may be a curious question; that there is a *state* which such a phrase describes is a matter of spiritual revelation and experience. "*All power* is given," etc. 2. *Its tone is therefore authoritative in the highest degree.* The gospel is a throne-word. Preachers are ambassadors. The dignities and pretensions of earth are nothing to them. The Lord through them "*commands* all men everywhere to repent." Herod is a sad illustration of what occurs when even a king attempts to patronize the gospel. 3. *This pretension is confirmed by practical proofs.* The works accompanying it and resulting from it are "signs." You cannot explain them unless on the highest ground. Although physical miracles have ceased, spiritual results are still more demonstrative and glorious. In changing the heart, renewing the nature, purifying the affections, the "Word of his power" achieves what nothing else can. And such signs are to be looked for whenever and wherever it is proclaimed. "The Lord working with them"—*everywhere*, because *ascended* and *glorified*.

III. THE PEOPLE IT CONCERNS. "And they went forth, and preached *everywhere*." This was no accident or caprice of choice: *he commanded it* (ver. 15). But it is also divinely fitting that this should be so. 1. *The gospel is intended for all men.* 2. *It is adapted to all men.* 3. *The work of Christ's servants is to seek the salvation of all men.* Until all have had an opportunity we must continue to preach: *that is our responsibility.* It is not said that all will believe or be saved: *that is the responsibility of those who hear.* Only of this are we certain: "The Lord is not slack concerning his promise, as some count slackness; but is longsuffering to you-ward, *not wishing that any should perish, but that all should come to repentance*" (2 Pet. iii. 9).—M.

Vers. 3, 4.—*The stone rolled away.* Day was dawning on Jerusalem when the women saw this strange sight. Day was dawning in their hearts too, for slowly and surely the darkness of doubt and grief was stealing away. And day was dawning on the whole world, and on all future ages of history, for the Sun of Righteousness had risen, bringing life and immortality to light. No three days in human history were so momentous as these of which the context speaks; for it was on them that the great conflict between death and life was fought out, and for ever won, by the Captain of our salvation. (Describe the varied feelings which swayed the minds of Christ's foes and friends after the Crucifixion, as they thought of his quiet grave in the garden.) The resurrection of Jesus Christ was put boldly in the forefront of apostolic teaching. Of all the miracles, this was the chief; of all evidences of the supernatural, this was the most important. In almost every recorded address and extant letter, this is insisted on as the cardinal fact of the Christian faith; indeed, Paul says, "If Christ be not risen, your faith is vain."

I. WE RECOGNIZE THE STONE ROLLED AWAY FROM THE SEPULCHRE AS BEING TO US A SIGN OF CHRIST'S VICTORY. 1. Accepting the fact of our Lord's resurrection, not only as proved by the credible, concurrent, and cumulative evidence of trustworthy men, but on the ground that this fact alone will rationally account for the victory of the Christian faith over men of all nations and conditions, we do not wonder at its prominence in New Testament teaching. Because Christ has risen, his death becomes more than a martyrdom for the truth; it appears as the voluntary offering of himself on the part of One who said of his life, "I have power to lay it down, and I have power to take it again." It is the sign that God was still well pleased with the beloved Son, for it was the Divine reversal of the world's judgment upon him. It is a proof that the same Jesus who once walked this weary world still lives, with the old sympathy and power to help, fulfilling his promise, "I am with you alway, even unto the end of the world." It is the pledge to us, the only pledge we have in history, that the splendid utterances of St. Paul about the resurrection of the saints will have their fulfilment. For the redeemed, as well as for their Lord, heavenly hands have rolled away the stone that once sealed the grave. 2. The victory of Christ on the Resurrection morning was dramatically complete in its details, and in this we see a suggestion of the absoluteness of his triumph over his foes. The Gentiles had mocked and crucified him; he passed by their strong guard without an effort. The Jews had accomplished their purpose against him; the seal of the Sanhedrim was broken. Death had seized upon him, and some had cried, "Himself he cannot save;" but, the Son of God, it was not possible that he should be holden of death. The grave had closed over him; but he passed through its portals resistlessly, as Samson came forth from Gaza, bearing on his shoulders its gates of brass and bars of iron. "He must reign till he hath put all enemies under his feet"—the pride that will not let us become as little children; the self-will that declares, "We will not have this man to reign over us;" the lusts which, like the horses of the sun, would drag their victims to destruction; the death that strikes down all our defences, and tears away our dear ones from our embrace. Victory over these will be his, not ours. To the eye of faith the rolling away of the stone appears to be the loosening of the keystone in the great fortress of sin and death, of which at last there shall not be left one stone upon another.

II. The stone rolled away may also be regarded by us as a reminder of expected difficulties unexpectedly removed. It was natural enough that these feeble women should say among themselves, "Who shall roll us away the stone from the door of the sepulchre?" For a moment it appeared as if all their labour of love, in the preparation of spices, would be thrown away—that the last tender ministry must be given up. But as they went forward, trembling yet hoping, they discovered that the difficulty they had dreaded was gone. God had done for them what they could not have done for themselves. Too often we discourage ourselves by thinking of future difficulties, until they loom so large in our imagination that we turn back from the path of duty. 1. It is so with our *anxieties about temporal things*. But whatever lies in the future, let us go on steadfastly and trustfully, and by-and-by we shall make the conquered difficulty an Ebenezer, which shall witness to others of the fact, "Hitherto hath the Lord helped me." 2. Similarly we must deal with *some difficulties respecting Christian doctrine*. "Whosoever shall *do* the will of God shall know the doctrine." 3. So let us go on also to *attempt our appointed work for God*; and the difficulties which are insurmountable by us will be removed by hands mightier than our own.—A. R.

Vers. 1—18.—*The Resurrection.* In the early dawn—"at the rising of the sun"—on the morning after the sabbath—that one most wondrous sabbath, the last of the old series—hasty feet were hurrying to the sepulchre. They were those of Mary Magdalene and Mary the mother of James, and Salome. Love drew them thus early to the sacred tomb. But they were bringing "spices that they might come and anoint him," so far were they from expecting what had taken place. It does not appear that any of the disciples were looking for the Resurrection. As they neared the place a difficulty suggested itself to them: "Who shall roll us away the stone from the door of the tomb?" To their astonishment, it was rolled away. "Entering into the tomb," they found not the body as they expected; but "they saw a young man [an angel] sitting at the right side, arrayed in a white robe." Calming their affrighted spirits, he declared for the first time, "He is risen; he is not here." The few details of the excited doings of that first morning of the week—that first Lord's day—have a deep interest, which their meagreness cannot destroy, if indeed it abates it. Again and again Jesus appears to the disciples, now in smaller, now in larger companies, and gives them as true and deeply settled an assurance of his resurrection as was before given of his death. To that resurrection we turn as to the signal incident in the life of the world's Redeemer—the central fact in all human history. Nothing abates the significance of the Incarnation; but the raising up of the dead body into life is supreme in its bearing on the history of the human race.

I. The resurrection of Christ is the crucial test of the world's redemption. "If Christ hath not been raised, your faith is vain." Then the whole structure of Christianity is shaken to its foundations. It has no longer its present significance. It has wrought only imaginary changes. "Ye are yet in your sins." It has deluded its most devoted adherents. Itself aiming at truth, exalting, glorifying it, it has deceived and disappointed the hopes of its faithful ones. "They also which have fallen asleep in Christ have perished." The Christian Church has never shrunk from the alternative, exulting in its jubilant assurance, "But now hath Christ been raised from the dead." Herein the completeness of the atoning work of Christ is demonstrated, the warrant of faith in that atonement is presented, and the end of all is attained in the righteousness of men. With a divinely attested atonement, of which, to avail themselves, men are warranted in appropriating by faith the justification—the righteousness which they need. He "was delivered up for our offences, and was raised for our justification."

II. The resurrection of Christ is THE FIRM GROUND OF HUMAN HOPE. "As in Adam all die, so also in Christ shall all be made alive." Back to this event the eye of the believer has turned to see the assuring sign. Our friends lie still in the grave; but the Church has never since that early morning looked to a Christ in a tomb. It is easy to see how the horizon of the human life would be overclouded had we to think of the Redeemer as still in the grave.

III. THE BRIGHTEST ASPECT OF HUMAN LIFE is seen in the resurrection of Christ. Life with or without a future suggests the two utmost extremes. The barest glimmer of a possibility of a future life beyond the grave would be the greatest enrichment of that life had there not been a previous assurance of it. This fact added to human life transforms it at once. It is an inestimable possession. What possibilities does it not open before our eyes! What an encouragement to patience! "The sufferings of this present time are not worthy to be compared with the glory which shall be revealed to us-ward." The resurrection of Christ throws an altogether new light upon all human history; but its brightest light is thrown upon the gloom of the future.

IV. The resurrection of Christ is THE ILLUSTRIOUS EXAMPLE OF THE UNIVERSAL RESURRECTION. "Christ the Firstfruits." The ingathering and presentation of the first-fruits must be taken as the pledge of the ingathering and presentation of the entire harvest. The inspired teaching on this lofty subject is such as to give the utmost assurance and comfort. The "weakness," the "dishonour," the "corruption," with which we are made familiar by death, stand in contrast with the "incorruption," the "glory," the "power," which we learn shall characterize the resurrection. While the casting off the "natural body," to be clothed with "a spiritual body," the exchange of "the earthy" for "the heavenly," is exemplified in the one Example which is for every believer the most comfortable assurance.

V. The resurrection of Christ is THE COMPLETE DEMONSTRATION OF TRIUMPH. "Destroy this temple, and in three days I will raise it up." It has ever been held that the Resurrection was the Divine seal of testimony to the perfectness and acceptability of the work of Christ. The rage of wicked men, the antagonism of error, the whole power of the enemy, triumphed in crushing the truth; but the Resurrection is a demonstration of complete superiority to all, and casts its illuminating comment upon the words, "I lay down my life, that I may take it again. . . . I have power to lay it down, and I have power to take it again." These and many other teachings cluster around this most precious incident in the history of this typical life. He who would derive the utmost advantage therefrom must needs share the experience of the holy apostle: "I count all things to be loss for the excellency of the knowledge of Christ Jesus my Lord: for whom I suffered the loss of all things, and do count them but dung, that I may gain Christ, and be found in him, not having a righteousness of mine own, even that which is of the Law, but that which is through faith in Christ, the righteousness which is of God by faith: that I may know him, and the power of his resurrection, and the fellow-ship of his sufferings, becoming conformed unto his death; if by any means I may attain unto the resurrection from the dead" (Phil. iii. 8—11).—G.

Vers. 19, 20.—*The Ascension.* And now after "he was manifested" many times, showing "himself alive after his passion by many proofs, appearing unto them by the space of forty days," and having taught to his disciples, in the new light of his resurrec-tion, "the things concerning the kingdom of God," he—"the Lord Jesus"—"was received up into heaven, and sat down at the right hand of God," "the heaven" receiving him "until the times of restoration of all things." Now the holy, earthly life of Jesus is terminated. He has "ascended on high;" now the luminous pathway to heaven is open; now the eyes of the disciples of the Lord Jesus are ever turned upward, and their steps tend to heaven. Now the great truth is exemplified; life ends not in a grave, nor even in a resurrection from the dead, but in an ascension into heaven. This is the true goal. This the final hope. The regained Paradise is not on earth, but on high. The home of the weary is in "my Father's house." The world's rest is in heaven. Now life is a pilgrimage; men "seek a country," "a better country, that is, a heavenly;" and "God hath prepared for them a city." The typical life is a perfect one; the cycle is complete. He "came down from heaven." He has ascended up "where he was before." So is it with the revelations of Holy Scripture. They begin in an earthly paradise; they end in a heavenly one. Such is the cherished hope of all believers. We must consider the ascension of Jesus in its bearing upon his own life, and upon the life and hope of his disciples, and upon the aspect of human life generally.

I. The Ascension into heaven is THE JUST VINDICATION OF THE LIFE AND CLAIMS OF JESUS. The position which he assumed amongst men as the Son of God, as the Saviour of the world, as the Judge of human actions; the call which he addressed to men to believe in him, to accept his teachings as of supreme authority, to trust in him for salvation and eternal life; and the great promises which he held out to men;—all needed a demonstration of their validity. To the patient reader of the Gospels this demonstration is afforded again and again "by divers portions and in divers manners." But all would lack their crowning affirmation had Jesus remained enchained by death, or had he not ascended up on high. It were impossible to believe in such a Mediator as still in the grave. The Ascension, which is the necessary consequence of the Resurrection, is the complement of the Incarnation. Such a life and such a death as Jesus' demanded a triumph and a vindication. It was, in the absence of the Resurrection, the failure of the truth. Sin, error, the world, conquered the truth and righteousness of heaven. So for the one brief sabbath—the dead lull in the world's active history—it seemed to be; but the Resurrection, completed in the Ascension, is the effectual vindication of truth and of righteousness, as it is the vindication of the righteous One.

II. Not less is the Ascension THE VINDICATION OF THE WORLD'S FAITH IN JESUS. They who accept a teacher as authoritative, who commit great interests into his hands, who have so great faith in him as to entrust their reconciliation with God into his hands, who accept him as a mediator between themselves and God, who depend upon him for eternal life, who concentrate all their hopes of the future upon his word, must be prepared to justify their conduct. That justification is found in the Ascension. Too great a confidence cannot be placed in One concerning whom it may be said, "The third day he was raised again from the dead; he ascended into heaven, and sitteth on the right hand of God." Jesus, who vindicated himself in every step of his progress, vindicates also the daily, humble, entire faith of "them that put their trust in him."

III. There is a step further. THE CONDUCT OF THOSE WHO REJECT CHRIST AWAITS VINDICATION. Where shall it be found? Given the facts of Jesus' life, his death, his resurrection, and ascension on high, where can any justify their repudiation of him? Precisely as faith and obedience are vindicated, so is unbelief and neglect condemned. The bearing of Christ's ascension on the universal life is of so great significance, that its rejection imposes the heaviest penalties on the disobedient. Not only is their own life debarred the beneficent influences of so great a fact, and the long train of facts of which it is the completion, but the life of others surrounding is proportionately injured. He who has faith in a great truth throws the influence of his encouragement over the faith of all amongst whom he moves, while he who abides in unbelief tends to wither the confidence of those around him. His example is contagious, and his life is impaired in its character. It cannot, therefore, exert the same beneficial influence upon others that it might do if under the control of great truths. Men must sooner or later vindicate to their fellows their conduct towards them. If it be good, the world's testimony will be joined to the Divine testimony. If evil, the world's condemnation must be added to that of the eternal Judge. Man's highest wisdom is to place himself near to great truths, that he may feel their power and elevation; and, by a thorough sympathy with them, be prepared to extend their influence far and wide. How greatly the world to-day needs men having faith! Such only can move the mountains which stand in the way of human progress and blessing. No truths have equal power for the uplifting, the ennobling, the appeasement, the satisfaction, the glorification of the human life, as have those which, beginning with the Incarnation, end with the ascension into heaven of the Lord Jesus Christ; "to whom be glory and dominion for ever and ever. Amen."—G.

Vers. 1—8.—*The sepulchre.* I. SELF-REWARDING LOVE. The women obey the longing to serve, though they know not how. Of love it is said, "All other pleasures are not worth its pains." In lavishing care upon the remains of one beloved, we show that the

proper objects of love are persons. It is not to the love of an abstraction, but to the love
of himself, that Christ calls us. The suffering in this world are to us as the body of
Jesus.

II. ANGELIC MINISTRY. " Angels minister to the followers of Christ, and share their
joy." The chain of sympathy is electric between earth and heaven; and all that we
know in sorrow and joy has its immediate reflection and response above.

III. THE EMPTY TOMB. The contents have escaped, as some ethereal vapour eludes
its bonds. He could not be holden of the tomb. It bore witness to his resurrection;
and earth is no more a sepulchre, but a portico to heaven.—J.

Vers. 9—14.—*Appearances of the risen One.* I. THEY WERE REPEATED AND VARIED.
So in the history of the Church and the world; there are epochs of the manifestation of
Christ and of apparent concealment. Though history in one sense repeats itself, in
another it does not. Christianity is the exhibition of the new in the old, the old in
the new. And so in the individual.

II. THEY WERE MET BY PREJUDICE. New truth finds in us something ever to overcome. The victory over a prejudice gives us cause for thanks; what we really possess
of truth we possess because we have resisted it. We do not understand it till we have
contended against it. " We may believe more surely in the Resurrection, because they
were so slow to believe."

III. THE SPIRITUAL EVIDENCE OF CHRISTIANITY IS THE REAL EVIDENCE. Unless we
see that Christ's resurrection coincides with spiritual truth and needs, we shall not see it
at all. Mediate knowledge can never be free from doubt; certainty lies in that which is
immediate.—J.

Vers. 15—18.—*Final utterances.* I. CHRISTIANITY IS A GOOD MESSAGE FOR ALL
MANKIND.

II. ALL WHO HAVE AFFIANCE IN CHRIST ARE MEN CONSECRATED AND SAVED.

III. IF FAITH BE POSSESSED, ALL NECESSARY CONFIRMATIONS OF FAITH WILL BE
GRANTED.

IV. IN THE KINGDOM OF CHRIST, THE OUTWARD IS ONLY OF VALUE AS SIGNIFICANT
OF THE INWARD AND SPIRITUAL.—**J.**

Vers. 19, 20.—*The Ascension.* I. THE ASCENT OF CHRIST FOLLOWS FROM HIS
DESCENT. His glory was conditioned and prepared for by his self-humiliation for our
sakes.

II. HE IS NOW IN THE SEAT OF SPIRITUAL POWER AND GLORY. The right hand of
God is a figure of omnipotence. This power is felt in and through all the thought and
development of the world.

III. THIS POWER IS FELT IN HUMAN WORKS OF LOVE. Good signs ever are following
the course of the good message. Faith working by love in us corresponds to power
working by love in God. For us there is Divine encouragement to work for humanity
in this last page—

> " In dens of passion and pits of woe,
> To see God's love still struggling through,
> To sun the dark and solve the curse,
> And beam to the bounds of the universe."

Vers. 1—18. Parallel passages: Matt. xxviii. 1—15; Luke xxiv. 1—49; John xx.
1—23.—*An eventful day.* I. THE RESURRECTION OF CHRIST. 1. *The morning of our
Lord's resurrection.* The first day of the week on which the events recorded in
this section of the chapter took place was an eventful one. On the morning of
that day we are placed side by side with some weeping women. They are Mary
Magdalene, Mary the mother of James, and Salome the wife of Zebedee. They had
loved their Lord in life; they had stood by him in death; they had cleaved to him
on the cross; and now his lifeless corpse is to them an object of affectionate concern.
In the grey dawn of the morning twilight they quit their couch, they leave their
cottage, and, setting out, come to the tomb (ἔρχονται, present, " come," so St. Mark,

graphically) with the spices and perfumes they had carefully prepared, the sun by this time having begun to rise. But lo! in their confusion and haste and sorrow they have overlooked an important fact; they have not known, or forgotten, the efforts of his enemies to make sure the sepulchre, already secured with a great stone, sealing it with the imperial signet and setting a guard. In their hurry they have forgotten all this— the stone, the seal, the sentry. Soon as the thought occurs to them they look anxiously at each other and sorrowfully inquire, "Who shall roll us away the stone from the door of the sepulchre?" Of the stone, at least, they were well aware. 2. *The rolling away of the stone.* Not pausing for an answer, they press forward to the sepulchre. On reaching the spot their fears are disappointed and their expectations exceeded. An earthquake had shaken the place, an angel had descended; and when they looked up (ἀναβλέψασαι, another graphic trait) they see that the stone is rolled away. So is it with many another stone of huge dimensions—with many a stone of difficulty and doubt and danger. So with the stone that barred the entrance of the heavenly world against the sinner; so with the stone that closes the grave's mouth where the dear dead dust of loved ones lies; so with the stone that may be laid on the spot where our own ashes shall one day repose. The rolling away of this stone from the sepulchre of the Saviour involves the rolling away of all these stones. 3. *The evening of the same day.* In the evening of the same day two lone pilgrims are traversing the pathway between the vineyards. They are journeying to a little village embosomed in vine-clad hills, and seven miles distant from Jerusalem. They are glad to escape from town; for a heavy heart seeks solitude. Their Master had been crucified, their hopes had been dashed, and their fond anticipations disappointed. They were returning home in sadness, for what was there in the capital to interest them now? All that had been dear to them there was now gone, and to all appearance gone for ever, for their Lord and Master was no more. The lovely scene around, the bright sky above, the cheerfulness of the season, but little harmonized with their sadness of heart and sorrow of spirit.

> "The spring in its beauty on Carmel was seen,
> And Hermon was dress'd in its mantle of green;
> While the pathway which led to Emmaus was made
> All fragrant and cool by the olive trees' shade;
> The dove in Jehoshaphat's valley was wailing,
> The eagle round Olivet proudly was sailing:
> But all was unheeded, for doubt and dismay
> Were distracting those two lonely men on their way."

They walked and talked, and talked and walked, beguiling the difficulties of the way, and forgetting the lapse of time. They commune and reason together; they balance probabilities. They comment on the early visit of the women to the sepulchre, on the stone being rolled away, and the vision of the angels, and so for a moment they entertain a faint hope that their Master might have risen, and would now restore the kingdom to Israel. But that hope is like a brief glimpse of sunshine which the dark clouds soon blot again from the sky. Immediately it occurs to them that the words of the women had been treated as an idle tale. Their wish might have been father to the thought, while hope and love are proverbially quick-sighted. Why had Peter not seen the vision? Why had John not been privileged with the sight? A third traveller overtakes them. He joins their company. He asks the cause of the sadness pictured on their countenance; he inquires the subject of their communings; he converses with them cordially and confidentially; their heart was burning within them while he spake to them by the way and while he opened to them the Scriptures. These two scenes— one in the morning, the other in the evening of the same day; the former described by St. Mark and St. Matthew, the latter by St. Mark, but more fully by St. Luke (xxiv. 13—35)—occurred on the day of our Lord's resurrection from the dead.

II. A VISIT TO THE SAVIOUR'S TOMB. 1. *The place where they laid him.* "The place where they laid him," as St. Mark terms it, or the place where the Lord lay, was the tomb of Joseph of Arimathæa. We visit the tomb of an earthly friend; we venerate the place of our fathers' sepulchres; we gaze pensively on the green hillock that overlays the mortal remains of one we love; with willing hand we plant the shrub—the myrtle or the cypress—which marks the place where the heart's treasure is enshrined;

we snatch the early flowers of the spring and strew them on the grave of some dear one gone; carefully we wreathe the garland and place it on the spot or hang it on the shrub that points it out.   Many a time have we stood in cemeteries more like a flower-garden than a garden of the dead, and admired the care, the tenderness, and the affection of surviving relatives, as evinced in the plants and wreaths and flowers which ornamented the last resting-place of the departed. "Come, see the place where the Lord lay," was the invitation of the angel to the women in the parallel record of St. Matthew. The passage of the Gospel before us is thus a visit to a tomb—to the tomb of Joseph of Arimathæa, the tomb where Jesus lay, the tomb of the dearest Friend we ever had, the tomb of the most loving One that ever lived, the tomb of him who "came not to be ministered unto, but to minister," of the good Shepherd that laid down his life for the sheep, of him in regard to whom the believer can say, "He loved me, and gave himself for me." 2. *Object of our visit to the Saviour's sepulchre.* The followers of the false prophet Mahomet make their weary pilgrimages from year to year to that impostor's tomb. We pity their delusion, we pray for their deliverance; but we admire their devotedness. The mighty military enterprises that roused the martial spirit of European peoples during the Middle Ages, and employed the hands and hearts of bravest warriors, had for their object the rescue of the holy sepulchre from the possession of the infidel, and the protection from injury and insult of all Christian pilgrims who might please to visit that shrine. The conception was a grand one, but somewhat gross—gigantic in one sense, and yet grovelling in another. The subject of our section leads us in the same direction; but our visit is spiritual, not literal; it is not to the mere geographical position, but to the glorious Person who made a brief repose there, and accomplished a triumphant resurrection therefrom. 3. *The lessons to be learnt from this visit.* When we visit in this sense the place where they laid him, the first lesson we are taught by it is (1) the *lowliness* of our Lord. It was wondrous condescension on his part to visit earth at all. For the Holy One to come into this sin-blighted world, for the eternal Word to be made flesh and dwell among us, for the Son of God to be made of a woman, made under the Law, for the King of saints to endure the contradiction of sinners, for the King of glory to make himself of no reputation,—in a word, for him who was in the form of God, and thought it no robbery to be equal with God, to take upon him the form of a servant, was surely most astonishing humiliation. But for that high and holy One, not only to empty himself and become obedient to death, and a death so painful and so shameful as that of the cross, but to enter the region of the dead, to be laid in the tomb, and to lie as a corpse in the cold grave where they laid him,—this may well challenge the surprise of man, as it commands the study of angels. We admire that patriot king who quitted for a time his throne and left his kingdom and travelled through the nations of Europe, visiting their dockyards, their workshops, and their manufactories, and actually working as a mechanic, in order that when he returned home and resumed the reins of government he might benefit his kingdom and improve his subjects. Still more are we astonished at Charles V., who had done daring deeds of chivalry, gained brilliant victories, achieved great successes, exhibited strokes of skilful diplomacy, and wielded a mighty power among the potentates of Europe, at length, as though wearied with royalty and fatigued with dominion and surfeited with splendour, giving up and resigning all, retiring into private life, and spending the remainder of his days in a cloister. But what was the temporary resignation of the Czar of all the Russias, or the final abdication of him who wore the imperial crown of Germany and swayed the proud sceptre of Spain, compared with the King of kings and Lord of lords resigning the sovereignty of the universe for the stable of Bethlehem, the crown of glory for the cross of Calvary, the sceptre of heaven for the garden sepulchre? "Though he was rich, yet for our sakes he became poor, that we through his poverty might be rich." (2) "Come, see the place where the Lord lay," and consider the lesson of his *love*, for it was his love that laid him there. It was love that made him submit to the indignities which, as we have seen, were heaped upon him— the scoffing, and scourging, and spitting, and smiting. It was love that subjected him to the insults of priests and people, to the sentence of an unjust judge, the torture of a most cruel death, and the disgrace of an ignominious execution. It was love that thus nailed him to the cross and suspended him on that cursed tree, as the gazing-stock of earth and heaven. So was it love that bound him in the habiliments of death, wrapped him in the cerements, and laid him in the coldness of the tomb. Was it strange, then, that the sun suffered an obscuration when the Saviour expired, that the sky put on mourning when the Lord of glory gave up the ghost, or that the frame of nature shook when the Divine Upholder of its system died? Was it strange that rocks rent as if in commiseration of what might rend even a heart of stone? Was it strange that graves opened and their ghastly occupants came forth, and with bloodless face and skeleton form entered the holy city, and moved through the streets in grand and solemn silence, or flitted as strange and fearful apparitions among the living population that passed along the thoroughfares, when he who was the living One, having all life in himself, entered the abode of death and was laid in the grave? Long before, a dead man had started into life, when he was laid in a prophet's grave and touched a prophet's bones. Was it strange if the dove cooed plaintively in the valley of the Kidron, if the vine drooped mournfully on the hillside, if the brook murmured dolefully as it rolled over its pebble bed that night? Was it strange that the disciples hung their heads in sorrow, in sadness, and in silence, when their Master was entombed? "Come, see the place where they laid him," and "where the Lord lay;" and will not love beget love? Will you not love him who thus loved you, or rather can you forbear loving him who thus loved you first of all and best of all? Who ever heard of love like this before? "Greater love hath no man than this, that a man lay down his life for his friends;" but while we were yet sinners, and therefore enemies, "Christ died for us." (3) "Come, see the place where the Lord lay," and reflect on a third lesson which is taught us there. This lesson respects the *light* that is thus shed into the gloom of the grave, and into the dreariness of that dark and narrow house. Darkness had reigned in all deathland before, but then life and immortality were brought to light. In some places, where railways run beneath high hills, all at once you pass out of the light of day into a dark subterranean passage. In a moment or two you find that tunnel not so dark as at first you thought it; the lamps on either side relieve the gloom and interrupt the darkness. By-and-by you quit the tunnel and emerge into the light of day, brighter and more beautiful, you think, than before because of the very contrast. The grave was a dark subterranean passage once; no light entered it, no ray brightened it; but now lamp after lamp is hung up in it, and on the other side the Christian finds himself in the everlasting light and unclouded brightness of heaven.

III. THE GRAVE WHENCE THE LORD ROSE: THE RESURRECTION OF CHRIST. 1. *Honour shown Christ in death.* "Ye seek Jesus of Nazareth, which was crucified: he is risen; he is not here: behold the place where they laid him;" and mark the honour paid him there. Even in death he was not unhonoured. A few faithful females, a few devoted though dejected disciples, refused to believe that the past was only a delusion, the present merely a dream, and the future altogether darkness. They entertained an undefined expectation, and that expectation now glimmered before their mind's eye like the meteor of a moment, anon disappeared, leaving the gloom still denser. It was a dark hour with the disciples of our Lord, but it was the hour before the daybreak. These few faithful followers, however, ceased not in their attention to the body and attendance at the grave. They watched and waited, and visited the spot. The Jewish ruler Nicodemus, and Joseph of Arimathæa, a rich and honourable counsellor, as we saw in the preceding chapter, failed not in tender devotedness and affectionate dutifulness to the lifeless corpse. 2. *Honour of a higher kind.* Greater glory awaits that body. The resurrection work of wonder takes place. Scarce had the morning of the third day arrived, scarce had the morning-star announced its early dawn, when the mediatorial reward began to be bestowed, and the faithfulness of the eternal covenant became manifest. Come once more, and see the place where the Lord lay, and as it can never be seen again. There—O wondrous sight!—lies the Prince of life; he is sleeping the sleep of death—silent and still as the grave where they laid him. Satan exults, the hosts of darkness hold jubilee, all pandemonium triumphs, hell cannot contain its satisfaction, if aught like satisfaction ever enters there. But hark! a voice from heaven echoes through that sealed sepulchre; it is the voice of God. The words "Awake, arise!" resound. In an instant the grave-clothes drop from off the body; without the help of human hand they are wrapped together and carefully laid aside; the napkin falls from the face; the stream of vital fluid circulates through the veins; the limbs that a moment before had been stiff and stark in death are in motion. The form of sinful flesh—of a servant and a sufferer—is laid aside for ever. The Saviour rises; he rises in glory indescribable; he rises by his own and his Father's power; he rises triumphant over death, and the Conqueror of the grave. The angels of God come down to do him honour; one of them rolls away the stone and opens the sepulchre; the keepers shake and become as dead men; earth becomes tremulous for joy under the feet of its risen King; all nature puts on its fairest spring attire and joins in celebrating the Redeemer's triumph. Thus on all sides are re-echoed the words, "He is not here: for he is risen, as he said. Come, see the place where the Lord lay." 3. *Positive proof of his resurrection.* If you have any doubt of this, you need not go further for proof, and proof to demonstration, than the lie of the adversaries. "His disciples," say they, "came by night, and stole him away while we slept." What! eleven disciples overpower a company of Roman soldiers armed to the teeth, or roll away the huge stone in silence, or enter the tomb in secrecy, or range things so securely there? Or, granting this, how could they carry the body unnoticed through the streets of Jerusalem, while thousands bivouacked in or patrolled those streets and thoroughfares at that Passover season, and while the full-orbed moon shone down upon the scene? Or, allowing this, is it likely that Roman soldiers would sleep on guard while death was the penalty, or that a whole detachment of them should all fall asleep at the same time? Or, conceding even this, suppose they slept, how could they see the purloiners of the body, or how could they say whether disciples did it or not? We need not stay to answer these questions; they sufficiently show the truth of the statement, "He is not here: for he is risen."

IV. REASONS FOR THE RESURRECTION OF OUR LORD. 1. *It was necessary for justification.* We have visited the empty tomb, and now we may inquire *why* he lay there and rose thence. It was in the first place for our justification. "He was delivered for our offences, and raised again for our justification." "By his death," says one, "he paid our debt, in his resurrection he received our acquittance." Another says, "Had no man been a sinner Jesus had not died, had he been a sinner he had never risen again." In other words, his death shows his sufferings for sin, his resurrection proves full satisfaction made by those sufferings. The meaning of his death is summed up in the words, "God sending his own Son in the likeness of sinful flesh, and for sin, condemned sin in the flesh;" the meaning of his resurrection runs thus: "Who shall lay anything to the charge of God's elect? It is God that justifieth. Who is he that condemneth? It is Christ that died, yea rather, that is risen again, who is even at the right hand of God, who also maketh intercession for us." His resurrection was thus his acquittal from the obligations he had come under, and our absolution through him from the debt we owed, so that, once united to him by faith, our persons are justified, our sins remitted, and our services accepted. Thus we see the meaning of that empty tomb. It is as though the voice of the Eternal proclaimed in thundertones through all the universe, "This is my beloved Son," in whose person and work, in whose life and death, "I am well pleased." His resurrection is the full recognition of the Redeemer's work. It is the protest of Heaven against the accusations with which he was loaded. It is the vindication of him whom Jew and Gentile condemned as deserving of death. It is the authoritative announcement that the work was finished, the debt paid, justice satisfied, the Law fulfilled, obedience rendered, punishment endured, wrath exhausted, sin put away, righteousness brought in, Satan vanquished, and God glorified. It is the consent of Heaven to the cancelling of the handwriting that testified against us. Therefore "all power is given unto him in heaven and in earth." And had he not all power, as Jehovah's Fellow, from everlasting? Yes, but now he has it as our Mediator; he holds it on our behalf, and exercises it for our benefit. Therefore "he received gifts." And why needed he gifts in whom all fulness dwelt, and who shared the Father's glory? As Head over all things he received them for his people's use, "even for the rebellious, that the Lord God might dwell among them." "Therefore doth my Father love me, because I lay down my life, that I might take it again." And did not God love him when he was in his bosom, before all worlds? Yes, but now he loves him as our Representative, and us in him; and consequently the apostle prays so earnestly to "be found in Christ." He is "crowned with glory and honour." And why? That he might communicate to us that glory which, as God, he had laid aside, and as Mediator resumed, and thus make his own peculiar privilege the common property of all believers. 2. *It was necessary also for our sanctification.* "Planted together in the likeness of his death, we shall be also in the likeness of his resurrection;" "As Christ was raised from the dead by the glory of the Father, even so should we also walk in newness of life." To live habitually in any known sin is to deny practically that sin is death; to indulge presumptuously in sin is to ignore the fact that Christ has risen from the dead; to persevere in sin is to resist the influence of Christ's resurrection, and shut our ears to the loud call that comes from the empty tomb, saying, "Awake, thou that sleepest, and arise from the dead, and Christ shall give thee light." We turn to some practical illustrations of the subject of sanctification. What is a saint? He is one that is risen with Christ, and acts accordingly, seeking the things that are above. Though in this world, he is not of it; he is above it. His conversation, treasure, heart, hope, home,—all are in heaven, whence he looks for the Saviour. Among the currents in the Atlantic Ocean is the great Gulf Stream; it has been called a river in the ocean. The water of this stream is on the average twenty degrees higher than the surrounding ocean; it preserves its waters distinct from those of the sea on either side, so that the eye can trace the line of contact. It retains its physical identity for thousands of miles, casting branches and fruits of tropical trees on the coast of the Hebrides and Norway. It greatly influences the Atlantic, keeping one-fourth of its waters in constant motion. The sanctified person— that is, the saint—is like that Gulf Stream; he is in the ocean of this world, but he has no affinity with it; he is not conformed to it; he has a higher temperature, for "the love of God is shed abroad in his heart by the Holy Ghost which is given unto him." Nevertheless, his influence is great and always for good; he keeps the dead waters from stagnation and in healthy movement.

> " With Christ the Lord we died to sin,
>   With him to life we rise;
> To life which, now begun on earth,
>   Is perfect in the skies."

3. *The resurrection of Christ is necessary for our resurrection.* "Now is Christ risen from the dead, and become the Firstfruits of them that slept;" "He has destroyed the last enemy, and that is death." During the reign of Augustus Cæsar a reverse befell the Roman army in the densely wooded valley of the Lippe. It was led by Varus to quell an insurrection of the Germans. The legions got embarrassed amid the entanglements of the forest; they fell into disorder; a violent tempest coming on at the same time aggravated their difficulties; four and twenty thousand of them were cut to pieces, and the general fell upon his sword. Six years after succeeding legions reached the plain, where lay the bleaching bones of former comrades, strewn in disorder or piled in heaps as they had fought and fallen. Fragments of weapons, limbs of horses, heads of men stuck on trunks of trees, were to be seen on every hand. In groves hard by were the savage altars where tribunes and centurions had been victimized; while those who survived that fatal field pointed out the place where lieutenants were butchered, standards taken, Varus wounded, crosses erected for the captives, and the eagles trampled underfoot. In addition to all, in a night-vision the ill-fated Varus, smeared with blood and emerging from the fens, seemed present to the imagination of his successor, and beckoning him to a like defeat. The description of the whole scene by Tacitus, the Roman historian, is vivid and terrible in the extreme. Ever after throughout his reign the Emperor Augustus was heard at times to exclaim, "Varus, Varus, give me back my legions!" So, when we reflect on the ruins of frail humanity—the wreck of generation after generation—we may well imagine Mother Earth appealing to Death in pitiful accents, and exclaiming, "Death, Death, give me back my sons and daughters; restore to me my children thou hast slain." That appeal shall be heeded one day, not by Death, but by him who was swallowed of Death—swallowed as a poison, and so destroyed the destroyer. Christ, by his resurrection, says to Earth, widowed and weeping over the graves of her children, "Weep not! I will ransom them from the power of the grave; I will redeem them from death." To Death he says at the same time, "O Death, I will be thy plagues! O Grave, I will be thy destruction!" Further, he will not only raise us up, he will fashion the body of our humiliation and make it like his own glorious body. Plants and animals have their proper habitats; different

species demand different situations; different vegetable tribes are allotted to different latitudes and different elevations. The palms of the torrid zone will dwindle and die in the temperate; the trees of the temperate, again, shrink into shrubs in the frigid. Such is the difference of latitude. That of elevation has a similar effect. A French traveller tells us that, in ascending Mount Ararat, he found at the foot the plants of Asia, further up those of Italy, at a higher elevation those of France, then those of Sweden, and at the top those of Lapland and the northern regions. Just so we shall be adapted to our future dwelling-place. "Flesh and blood cannot inherit the kingdom of God;" therefore the living shall be changed, the dead quickened, and all God's people, quick and dead, glorified together; "for this corruptible must put on incorruption, and this mortal must put on immortality."

V. PRACTICAL LESSONS. 1. Come, "behold the place where they laid him," and there see the fruits of Christ's death and the benefits of his resurrection; come, seek the pardon and peace which the justified possess; come, secure the holiness and happiness of the sanctified; come, entertain the "sure and certain hope of the resurrection to eternal life." 2. We have considered the lowliness of Christ, and dwelt on his love, and now we may rejoice in the light he has shed on the tomb. We are hastening to that "bourn whence no traveller returns." As we advance, desire fails; a little longer, and the grasshopper will be a burden. Once we reach the summit we soon go down the hill, and it is well and wisely so arranged.

> " Heaven gives our years of failing strength
> Indemnifying fleetness,
> And those of youth a seeming length
> Proportion'd to their sweetness."

3. " Ye seek Jesus of Nazareth, which was crucified." So, too, we seek Jesus, though condemned as a Nazarene in the spirit of the contemptuous question, "can any good thing come out of Nazareth?" We seek Christ crucified, though to the Jew a stumbling-block, and to the Greek foolishness. We are not ashamed of the offence of the cross. Nay, like Paul, we glory in that cross. The day was when Paul gloried in his pedigree, for he was an Hebrew of the Hebrews; in his sect, for he belonged to the straitest sect of the Jews' religion, being a Pharisee; in his morality, as touching the Law blameless; in his learning, brought up at the feet of Gamaliel; in the seal of the Abrahamic covenant, being circumcised on the eighth day; in his Roman franchise, born free; in his citizenship, a citizen of no mean city—his native Tarsus, beautifully situated in the plain and on the banks of the Cydnus; in his persecuting zeal, haling men and women to prison. But once his eyes were opened, once his heart was renewed, once he obtained mercy, then his ground of glorying was altogether changed. "God forbid that I should glory, save in the cross of our Lord Jesus Christ, by whom the world is crucified unto me, and I unto the world." 4. We shall not see his face until either we stand on the sea of glass, or his feet stand again on Olivet; we cannot hold him as those who "met him by the way . . . and held him by the feet, and worshipped him;" we cannot minister to him as certain women in the days of his flesh; we cannot serve him at food like Martha, nor pour oil on his head like Mary. What, then, remains for us to do? How are we to express our love to him? We are to think of him, believe on him, pray to him, accept him for our King and submit to his laws, call on his name, take the cup of salvation and keep his memory green in our souls, show forth his death, glory in his resurrection, partake of the sacrament of the Supper—it is the memorial of his death; and delight in the sabbath—it is the monument of his resurrection. 5. " Come, see the place where the Lord lay," and let the sight encourage you. Dread not death; you believe in him that conquered it. Dread not the grave; you love him who lay in it. Dread not hell; you believe in him who rescued you from it. But dread sin and depart from it; "go and sin no more."—J. J. G.

Vers. 19, 20.   Parallel passages: Luke xxiv. 50—53; Acts i. 9—12.—*The Ascension.* I. CIRCUMSTANCES IMMEDIATELY PRECEDING.   Our Lord led the apostles out " as far as to Bethany," on the eastern slope of the mount of Olives, a mile, or somewhat more than a mile, below the summit of the ridge, whence they afterwards returned by the way across the mount to Jerusalem. The middle summit of Olivet, Jebel-et-Tur, is, however, the traditional place of ascent. He has led ourselves further than to Bethany, for he has led us all our life till now; while all the way by which he has led us has been strewn with blessings—blessings temporal and spiritual. When he had led them as far as to Bethany (ἔως εἰς, or ἔως πρὸς, as far as towards Bethany, or the descent that led down to the village, or over against it), he lifted up his hands and blessed them. The high priest of the Aaronic order had three things to do—offer sacrifice, make intercessions, and bless the people in the name of the Lord. What a beautiful benediction was put into his lips and pronounced upon the people, "The Lord bless thee, and keep thee: the Lord make his face shine upon thee, and be gracious unto thee: the Lord lift up his countenance upon thee, and give thee peace"! Better and more beautiful, if that be possible, are the blessings which our great High Priest invokes on our behalf and commands upon us. Of these we have a specimen in his intercessory prayer, as contained in the seventeenth chapter of St. John.

II. THE PARTING. "He was parted from them," or "stood apart from them (διέστη)," as it is expressed by St. Luke. Amid certain cheerful tones one sorrowful note is struck, one sad word occurs, one painful sentiment is expressed. Some find the motto of this world in the words, "Man weeps;" others write it in the words, "We part;" a yet higher and better authority has expressed it in the words, "Vanity of vanities, all is vanity." This last combines the other two, for this world is a vale of weeping and a place of parting. What tongue could tell the painful partings that from time to time take place? Who could count the bitter tears that are shed? Those partings ofttimes wring the stoutest heart and wet the manliest cheek. At the railway station, or before going on board the emigrant ship, many a sorrowful separation we have all seen. The separation caused by death usually lasts the longest, and is, therefore, in proportion sorrowful. Yet it is not all pain in the parting of a Christian; this passage suggests an element of pleasure. When our Lord was parted from his disciples, he was carried up to heaven; when the Christian is parted by death from friends, loving and beloved, he sleeps *by* Jesus, and them that so sleep the Lord will bring with him. The day, moreover, is coming when Christian friends, parted by death, shall be caught up to meet the Lord in the air, and so shall we ever be with one another, and with our Lord.

III. THE ASCENSION ITSELF. The expressions employed to describe our Lord's ascension are, "He was received up into heaven," St. Mark; "Carried up into heaven," St. Luke; while in Acts we read (1) that "he was taken up," an expression similar to that of either Gospel; and again, (2) that "he went up" or "he went" (Revised Version). Here, then, we have the power of the Father and the Son. As he rose by his own and his Father's power, he ascended by the same. Further, it may be implied that he went up with joyfulness to those realms of glory whence he had descended while the Father welcomed him home, and took him to that paternal bosom where he had been before all worlds. It must have been a splendid sight to witness. Some time ago we stood where many thousands were assembled to see an aeronaut ascend. With gradual ascent the aerial machine rose; upward and upward it glided; higher and higher still it mounted, while majestically and magnificently it moved. At length a silvery cloud received it, and screened it from the view; again, on emerging from the cloud, it pursued its way along the sky till it dwindled to a dark spot in the distance, and then passed out of sight. How grand, we thought, must have been the sight, apart from every other consideration, of our Lord's ascent from that spot where his feet last stood on Olivet! If, when our Lord was transfigured, his face did shine as the sun, and his raiment became white as the light—if on that occasion his face and figure assumed somewhat of heavenly splendour—equally or more resplendent and heavenly, we may well suppose, was his appearance as he rose from earth in his journey through the sky. The glory of heaven was round about him; that glorified body shot upward with wondrous buoyancy. Enoch was translated—we are not told how; Elijah was borne up amid a whirlwind by a chariot, of fire and horses of fire; Jesus, who had walked upon the waves, now mounts upon the winds, making the cloud his chariot and upborne on the wings of the wind. Glorious in his appearance, glorious in his motion, glorious in all the indescribable grandeur of his heavenward ascent, he proceeded on his way till a cloud—a bright cloud, a cloud silver-lined and beautiful—coming *underneath* received (ὑπέλαβεν) him as in a chariot, and hid him from their eyes.

IV. His ATTENDANTS. Neither went he alone; thousands of invisible beings formed his escort and carried him aloft. To this perhaps the psalmist, foreseeing it in prophetic vision, may allude when, in the sixty-eighth psalm, he says, " The chariots of God are twenty thousand, even thousands of angels." No conqueror ever enjoyed such a triumph, no monarch ever had such a train. At length they reach the high battlements of heaven; the accompanying angels demand admittance; standing without the portals, they raise the voice like the sound of many waters as they say or sing, " Lift up your heads, O ye gates; and be ye lifted up, ye everlasting doors; and the King of glory shall come in." The angels within respond, making inquiry, " Who is this King of glory?" Then both, uniting in full chorus together, sing, " The Lord of hosts, he is the King of glory." The Father everlasting takes him by the hand, and sets him at his side, and there he sits for ever at the right hand of the Majesty on high.

> " Who is this King of glory—who?
>   The Lord, for strength renown'd;
> In battle mighty, o'er his foes
>   Eternal Victor crown'd.

> " Who is this King of glory—who?
>   The Lord of hosts renown'd,
> Of glory he alone is King,
>   Who is with glory crown'd."

V. THE WITNESSES OF THE SCENE. The witnesses of the scene were men on earth and angels from the sky—the one to testify that he rose from earth, the other to bear witness that he entered heaven. The former fact may perhaps be expressed by ἐπήρθη, the other by ἀνελήφθη; while his intermediate progress and journey between may be expressed by ἀνεφέρετο, imperfect, and πορευομένου, participle—both marking his gradual ascent. The human spectators, struck with the grandeur of the scene, stood as if riveted to the spot, and continued gazing up into heaven as though they would never be satisfied with seeing such a sight; or perhaps the surprise it occasioned was blended with sorrow, as if their Lord and Master had gone from them never to return. But two angels, apparelled in white, comforted them with the assurance that "this same Jesus, which is taken up from them into heaven," shall come again in like manner through the riven sky visibly and gloriously. The human witnesses of the Ascension felt personally interested in the result, the angelic looked pryingly into the things connected therewith. The sorrow of the disciples was succeeded by great joy, for though they had lost his bodily presence, his spiritual presence—nearer, closer, in every place, and at all times—is promised them instead.

VI. THE PLACE WHENCE HE ASCENDED. The place of the Ascension suggests a lesson of instruction and comfort. A garden on the western slope of Olivet had been the place of his sorest trial and the scene of his deepest tribulation prior to the Crucifixion; an upland on the eastern side, or near the summit of the same hill, was the place of his triumph. On one side was the dark enclosure, still noted for its sombre aspect and gloomy olives, where the Saviour agonized, sweating great drops of blood, and praying for the bitter cup, if possible, to pass; on the other side was the spot whence he ascended. There, too, men and angels met—men asleep from sorrow and oblivious of sympathy, an angel ministering strength and succour to the suffering Son of God; here men are rapt spectators, and angels swell his train. On one side of the mount were sorrow and suffering, on the other glory and triumph. May it not to some extent be the same with ourselves? The valley of Achor, which means " trouble," has often proved the door of hope. " We glory in tribulation also: knowing that tribulation worketh patience; and patience, experience; and experience, hope." Humiliation goes before exaltation; the cross precedes the crown: " If we suffer with him, we shall also be glorified together;" while our trials here shall enhance our triumph hereafter.

VII. THE PURPOSES SERVED BY THE ASCENSION. One purpose was *triumph* over his and our enemies. Having spoiled principalities, or reft them from him, he made a show of them openly. It was a custom of antiquity for a conqueror on the day of his triumph to have captives bound to his chariot and dragged along at his chariot-wheels. So with Christ. When he led captivity captive, he bound to his chariot-wheels sin, Satan, death, and hell. Sin he buried in his own grave, having borne its penalty. As for

Satan, the old serpent, he has bruised his head, destroying his works. Death he overcame by dying, and through death he has destroyed him that had the power of it; while in him and by him we can adopt the tone of triumph and say, "O Death, where is thy sting? O Grave, where is thy victory?" Of the grave he has said, "I will be thy destruction;" and the day is hastening on apace when the earth shall cast forth her dead. Another purpose of the Ascension is the *bestowal of gifts*. On the day of a triumph the conqueror distributed many and costly gifts, sometimes dealing them out deliberately, and sometimes throwing them broadcast among the multitude. We read of Julius Cæsar, on the occasion of a great triumph, bestowing munificent donations on his soldiery, and distributing many gifts of grain and gold to the people as they crowded around. A greater than Cæsar or Solomon is here. Jesus, on the day of his triumph, having receiving gifts for triumphal distribution, "gave gifts unto men . . . he gave some, apostles; and some, prophets; and some, evangelists; and some, pastors and teachers; for the perfecting of the saints, for the work of the ministry, for the edifying of the body of Christ." Even on the rebellious he has conferred his favours, "that the Lord God might dwell among them." From the day of his ascension until now he has lavished on his people, with unstinted generosity and most bountiful hand, the benefits of salvation and the results of his redemptive work.

VIII. PREPARATION ABOVE. Having made provision for us when he was here below, he is gone to prepare a place above. He ascended to provide a place for us; and, having prepared it for us, he is now preparing us for it. In his Father's house are many mansions; he is gone to prepare one of those mansions for each of his followers. A mansion! Here is a word that denotes stability and implies duration. The most solid structure that ever man reared shall yield to the tooth of time. The pyramids of Egypt shall one day, we doubt not, be levelled with the sands of the desert that blow around them. The Roman Colosseum shall perish. The Parthenon of Athens shall be left without one pillar standing. St. Peter's and St. Paul's shall become heaps of rubbish. The castles of kings, that seem to defy decay, shall moulder. Earth itself shall be removed, and its everlasting hills shaken. But all the many mansions in glory shall be durable as the throne of God himself, and stable as the pillars of the universe.

> "O Lord, thy love's unbounded—
> So full, so vast, so free!
> Our thoughts are all confounded
> Whene'er we think on thee:
> For us thou cam'st from heaven,
> For us to bleed and die,
> That, purchased and forgiven,
> We might ascend on high."

J. J. G.

HOMILETICAL INDEX

TO

THE GOSPEL ACCORDING TO ST. MARK

—◆◆—

CHAPTER IV.

CHAPTER V.

VOLUME II.

ST. LUKE

EXPOSITION BY

H. D. M. SPENCE

HOMILETICS BY

J. MARSHALL LANG

HOMILIES BY VARIOUS AUTHORS

W. CLARKSON   R. M. EDGAR

THE
GOSPEL ACCORDING TO ST. LUKE

VOL. I.

INTRODUCTION

—◦—

I. St. Luke's Gospel received as an Authoritative Writing in the First Age of Christianity.

In the last quarter of the second century—that is to say, in less than a hundred years after the death of St. John—the canon of the New Testament, as we have it now, was generally[1] accepted in all the Churches of the East and West.

How widespread was the religion of Jesus Christ before the close of the second century we have abundant testimony. Justin Martyr,[2] for instance, before the middle of the century, wrote how " there existed not a people, whether Greek or barbarian, whether they dwelt in tents or wandered about in covered waggons, among whom prayers were not offered up in the name of a crucified Jesus, to the Father and Creator of all things." Tertullian, a few years later, living in quite another part of the Roman world, told the heathens that his brethren were to be found filling the camp, the assemblies, the palace, the senate." [3]

Before the year 200 the well-known and voluminous writings of Irenæus in Gaul, Clement in Alexandria, and Tertullian in Carthage, the capital of wealthy Proconsular Africa, testify to the wide and general acceptance of the books composing the New Testament canon. These writings clearly tell us what was the judgment of the Catholic Church at that early period

---

[1] The books which at that early date had only received a *partial* acceptance were the Epistle to the Hebrews, the two shorter Epistles of St. John, the Second Epistle of St. Peter, the Epistles of St. James and St. Jude, and the Apocalypse.

[2] Justin Martyr, ' Dial. cum Trypho,' 117.

[3] Tertullian, 'Apol.,' 37.

in the matter of the sacred Christian books. They were the holy treasure-house whither men resorted for authoritative statement on doctrine and on practice. Here men sought for and found their Master's words, and the teaching of his chosen followers. In the weekly services of the Church, as early as the middle of the century, we learn from Justin Martyr, the memoirs of the apostles (by which term he designated the Gospels) were read on the same footing as the writings of the prophets of the Old Testament.

Among these books, which in the last years of the second century were among Christians so universally received as authoritative and honoured as Holy Scripture, was *the Gospel according to St. Luke.*

We will now see how far it is possible to trace the *existence* of the Third Gospel from the close of the second century upwards towards the source.

There is no question that it was generally known and received in the last quarter of the second century: *was it referred to as a sacred writing before this date?*

From A.D. 120 *to* 175. *Irenæus,* Bishop of Lyons, in Gaul, succeeded Pothinus in the episcopate about A.D. 177. He tells us how, in his youth, he had been acquainted with Polycarp in Smyrna, who had known St. John. The date of his birth was about A.D. 130. In the writings we possess of Irenæus we find no reference by name to any book of the New Testament; but we meet with such striking coincidences of language and thought with many of those books, that it is perfectly certain he was intimately acquainted with them. St. Luke's Gospel was one of these.

The Canon of Muratori was discovered in the Ambrosian Library at Milan in a manuscript of great antiquity, containing some of the works of Chrysostom. It is but a fragment, yet it gives us, with fair completeness, the judgment of the Western Church on the canon of the New Testament about the year of our Lord 170. The date is clearly ascertained by internal evidence. Among the other sacred books it writes thus of the Third Gospel: "The Gospel of St. Luke stands third in order, having been written by St. Luke the physician, the companion of St. Paul, who, not being himself an eye-witness, based his narrative on such information as he could obtain, beginning from the birth of John."

Justin Martyr, of whose writings we possess several important pieces,[1] was born at the close of the first century, and died about A.D. 165. His works that are preserved may be dated roughly A.D. 130 to 150-160. They contain a mass of references to the Gospel narratives, embracing the chief facts of our Lord's life, and many details of his teaching—never, save in one or two very unimportant details, travelling out of the track of the story of the four evangelists, his many references being free from legendary admixture. These circumstances connected with our Lord's life were

[1] Of the writings which bear now the name of Justin Martyr, two 'Apologies' and the 'Dialogue with Trypho' are genuine beyond a doubt (cf. Westcott on the Canon, 'The Age of the Greek Apologists,' ch. ii.).

derived for the most part, he tells us, from certain written records which, he said, rested on apostolic authority, and were used and read in the public assemblies of Christians. He never quotes these records by name, but refers to them simply as "memoirs of the apostles" (ἀπομνημονεύματα τῶν ἀποστόλων); two of these, he says, were written by apostles, two by their followers.

His references are for the most part connected with the *teaching* rather than with the *works* of Jesus. He weaves into the tapestry of his story the narratives especially of SS. Matthew and Luke, quoting often the very words of the evangelists. In his 'Apology' Westcott reckons nearly fifty allusions to the gospel history. In the 'Dialogue' about seventy facts peculiar to St. Luke's narrative are introduced by Justin; for instance, the account of the sweat which dropped as blood from the Redeemer in Gethsemane, and the Master's prayer for the passing of "this cup." These "memoirs" which Justin uses so freely, and which he is careful to state were read in the weekly services of the Christians, were, in the estimation of the Church of his time (which was roughly the middle years of the second century), evidently ranked with the Holy Scriptures of the Old Testament; and these memoirs of the apostles, it is perfectly certain, were the Gospels we know severally as the Gospels of SS. Matthew, *Luke*, and Mark.

As Justin wrote before and after the year of our Lord 150, we have traced St. Luke's Gospel as an authoritative sacred document a considerable way upwards towards the source.

The testimony of the early heretical schools is very useful to us here, and puts us a further step backwards. About A.D. 140 Marcion, the son of a Bishop of Sinope, claimed to reproduce in its original simplicity the Gospel of St. Paul. He took for his purpose *the Gospel of St. Luke* (which evidently, when Marcion taught, was a universally acknowledged book of Holy Scripture) and ten Epistles of St. Paul. The text of the Gospel and Epistles Marcion altered to suit his own peculiar views.[1]

Valentinus, the author of the famous heresy which bears his name, came to Rome, Irenæus tells us, in the episcopate of Hyginus, and taught there from about A.D. 139 to 160. In the fragments of his writings which are preserved, he cites, among other New Testament books, *the Gospel of St. Luke* as Scripture.[2]

Heracleon, the familiar friend of the heresiarch just alluded to, himself the great Valentinian commentator, has left commentaries on *St. Luke* and St. John, and fragments of these are still in existence. Clement of Alexandria refers to this *commentary on St. Luke*, which must have been put out *before* the middle of the second century.[3]

Cerdo, an heretical teacher who lived still nearer the beginning of the

---

[1] Cf. Westcott on the Canon, 'The Early Heretics,' ch. iv.; Tertullian, 'Adv. Marc.,' v.; 'Epiph. Hær.,' xlii.

[2] Cf. Westcott on the Canon, ch. iv.; Tertullian, 'De Præscr. Hær.'

[3] Cf. Westcott on the Canon, ch. iv; Clem. Alex., 'Stromata,' iv. 9, § 73.

second century, according to Theodoret, used the Gospels, *especially that of St. Luke,* in his system of theology.[1]

Basilides was one of the earliest Gnostics, who taught at Alexandria about A.D. 120. He thus lived on the verge of the apostolic times. His testimony to the acknowledged books in the canon of the New Testament Scriptures is clear and valuable. We have now but a few pages of his writings still remaining with us, but in these few are certain references to several of St. Paul's Epistles to the Gospel of St. Matthew, St. John, and *St. Luke.*[2]

Tatian, a pupil of Justin Martyr, according to the testimony of Epiphanius, Theodoret, and Eusebius, shortly after the middle of the century, composed what may be called the first *harmony* of the four Gospels—the 'Diatessarôn.' Although Tatian appears to have on some subjects adopted strange and heretical opinions, in general form his harmony or 'Diatessarôn' was so orthodox and helpful that it enjoyed a wide ecclesiastical popularity.[3]

It will materially add to the strength of our argument that the Gospel of St. Luke was generally received by the Churches as authoritative, because divinely inspired, throughout the second century, if it can be shown that the Gospel was publicly acknowledged at the same early date by *national Churches* as well as by individual scholars and teachers.

Two versions belong to this first period of the Church's history—the Peschito-Syriac and the Old Latin (used in North or Proconsular Africa).

The first, the Peschito-Syriac, represents the vernacular dialect of Palestine and the adjacent Syriac in the age of our Lord. Competent scholars consider[4] that the formation of this most ancient version is to be fixed within the first half of the first century. It contains the Gospel of St. Luke and all the books of the received canon of the New Testament save 2 and 3 John, 2 Peter, St. Jude, and the Apocalypse, and may be regarded as the first monument of Catholic Christianity.[5]

The second version, the Old Latin, was made in the great and wealthy province of Proconsular Africa, of which Carthage was the chief city, at a very early period.

Tertullian, writing in the latter part of the second century, describes the widespread influence of Christianity in his time. His own important province, no doubt, was before his eyes, when he wrote how "Christians were filling the palace, the senate, the forum, and the camp, leaving their temples only to the heathen." [6] To persecute the Christians in North Africa at the close of the second century would be to decimate Carthage.[7] Tertullian, in his voluminous writings, shows that he recognized a current Latin version (the Old Latin). For the North African Church to have

---

[1] Cf. Godet, 'St. Luke,' Introd., 6; Pseudo-Tertullian, 'De Præscr. Hær.,' 51. (Westcott doubts the independent authority of this quotation).

[2] St. Hyppolyti, 'Refutatio Omn. Hær.,' bk. vii., § 20, 25, 26, etc.

[3] Eusebius, 'Hist. Eccl.,' iv. 29; Westcott on the Canon, ch. iv.

[4] Westcott on the Canon, ch. iii., "The Early Versions."

[5] Professor Westcott.   [6] 'Apol.,' ii. 37.   [7] 'Ad Scap.,' c. 5.

attained the proportions described by Tertullian at the close of the second century, we must presuppose that Christianity was at a very early period planted in that province, and that its growth was exceedingly rapid. This would necessarily indicate an early date in the second century for the formation of that version in the dialect used in the province, and which Tertullian found evidently in common use.

St. Luke and most of the other books of the canon are found in this Old Latin version quoted by Tertullian; the only omitted writings were the Epistle of St. James and the Second Epistle of St. Peter. The Epistle to the Hebrews did not *originally* exist in this most ancient version; it was added subsequently, *but before* Tertullian's days, *i.e.* before A.D. 200.

Professor Westcott, after an elaborate discussion, concludes positively that the Old Latin version must have been made *before* A.D. 170. *How much more ancient* it really is cannot yet be discovered. This great scholar conjectures that it was, however, coeval with the introduction of Christianity into Africa, and that it was the result of the spontaneous efforts of the African Christians.

The absence of the few canonical books above mentioned in these most ancient versions indirectly are an evidence of their great antiquity. It was not that the first translators had examined the proofs of their authenticity and found them wanting, and in consequence had excluded them; but the truth, no doubt, was that these particular books had never reached the countries in question at the early date when the versions were made.

The omitted Epistles were, from their brevity, as in the case of the Epistle of St. Jude, 2 and 3 John, 2 Peter, or from the contents being more especially addressed to Jewish Christians rather than to the great Gentile world, as in the case of the Epistle to the Hebrews and the Epistle of St. James, less likely to be rapidly circulated. The Apocalypse, from its mystic nature, would naturally be less read, and consequently it would require a longer period to become generally known and accepted.

As might have been expected, *the Gospels of St. Luke* and St. Matthew have left more ample traces in the scattered fragments of early Christian literature which have come down to us than any other of the writings included in the New Testament canon.

We now come to the early years of the second century and the closing years of the first century—roughly speaking, the twenty or twenty-five years which followed the death of St. John. Here, as might be expected from the comparatively few remains of Christian writings of this very early period which we possess, the evidences of the existence and recognition of *St. Luke* and the other books of the New Testament are more rare. Yet even in the scanty fragments still remaining to us of this very early period, we find traces of the inspired writings of the followers of Jesus of Nazareth.

In that curious religious romance entitled the 'Testaments of the Twelve Patriarchs,' a writing which Bishop Lightfoot speaks of as " coming near the apostolic age," and which the best modern scholars generally conceive to have been put out some time between A.D. 100 and A.D. 120, it is evident that much of the New Testament canon was known to the writer, who weaves into the tapestry of his work many of the New Testament thoughts and expressions, and occasionally quotes whole passages more or less accurately. Especially the Gospels of St. Matthew and *St. Luke* are made use of. What is very noticeable in this ancient and curious treatise, written evidently by a Jewish Christian to his own people, is the influence which the books written by or under the influence of *St. Paul* evidently exercised upon the author.

From St. Luke's Gospel twenty-two rare (Greek) words are used by the writer of the 'Testaments of the Twelve Patriarchs,' of which rare words nineteen are found in no contemporary writer. From the Acts, which may be looked upon as a second part of St. Luke's Gospel, twenty-four rare words are taken, of which twenty are alone found in this book of the New Testament. The anonymous author of the 'Testaments' borrowed from the vocabulary of most of the New Testament books, though from none so largely as from those written by or under the influence of St. Paul.

This most ancient and singular treatise has received in the last few years considerable attention at the hands of scholars. Some consider it honeycombed by interpolations of a later date, but as yet this theory of later interpolation is supported mainly by ingenious conjecture.

Very lately the scholarly Archbishop Bryennios, Metropolitan of Nicomedia, discovered and published the known but long-lost 'Teaching of the Apostles' (Διδαχὴ τῶν δώδεκα 'Αποστόλων). This most ancient treatise probably belongs to the last decade of the first century, possibly to an earlier date. It is largely based on sayings of Jesus Christ reported in the Gospels, especially in that of St. Matthew; but St. Luke's Gospel was distinctly known and used by the writer. One clear reference to the Acts occurs in ch. iv. of the 'Teaching.' The words rather than the acts and miracles of the Lord are dwelt upon. No Gospel is quoted by name.

We have now traced the Third Gospel back to days when probably St. John was still living, certainly to a time when men who had listened to John and Peter, to Paul and Luke, were still living and teaching. The testimony of one of the most famous of these pupils or disciples of the apostles will close our long chain of evidence.

Clement of Rome was the disciple of St. Paul; the oldest traditions, too, couple his name with St. Peter. At a very early period, undoubtedly, in the lifetime of St. John he presided over the Church of the Christians at Rome. It is certain that in the Church of the first century he exercised a powerful and lasting influence. Various ancient writings have been preserved bearing his honoured name. Of these only the first Greek epistle can be confidently pronounced authentic; it has been variously dated, A.D. 68, 70, 95. Whichever of these dates be accepted, its testimony will be the witness of the belief in the years immediately succeeding the martyrdom of Paul, when certainly many of the pupils and disciples of the twelve still lived and worked among men. We will confine ourselves to this first Greek epistle of unquestioned authenticity.

Clement [1] was evidently a diligent student of the wrtings of Paul, Peter, and John. He occasionally uses words found only in St. Paul; still more frequently those common to SS. Paul and Peter; while the influence of their inspired writings is plainly visible throughout this first epistle. In two passages the Gospels are evidently expressly quoted. The first (cap. xiii.) begins thus: "Remembering the words of the Lord Jesus, which he spoke to teach goodness and long-suffering." Then follows a passage in which the writer seems to unite St. Matthew's and St. Luke's accounts of the sermon on the mount; but where, in the opinion of Volkmar, the text of St. Luke predominates (see Luke vi. 31, 36—38). The second is in the forty-sixth chapter, and contains the spirit and indeed the very words of the Lord as reported in Matt. xxvi. 24; xviii. 6; Mark ix. 42; Luke xvii. 2.

Archbishop Thomson sums up generally the evidence for the early reception of the Gospels among the Christian Churches of the first days as inspired authoritative writings, as follows: "In the last quarter of the second century the four Gospels were established and recognized, and held a place that was refused to all other memoirs of the Lord. At the end of the second quarter they were quoted largely, though not very exactly, but the authors' names were not made prominent; they were 'memoirs,' they were 'the Gospels,' and the like. At the opening of the second century the words of the Lord were quoted with unmistakable resemblance to passages of our Gospels, which, however, are quoted loosely without any reference to names of authors, and with a throwing together of passages from all three (synoptical) Gospels" (Introduction to Gospel of St. Luke, by the Archbishop of York, in the 'Speaker's Commentary ').

In the last decade, then, of the first century we find that the three first Gospels had been written, and were used as the authoritative basis of Christian teaching. Now, what is the probable story of *the composition* of these Divine memoirs?

To answer this question, let us go back to Pentecost (A.D. 33), and the months and first years succeeding that memorable day.

With startling rapidity the few *hundreds* who before the Ascension, with more or less earnestness, *believed* in Jesus of Nazareth, and accepted him as Messiah, became, after the first Pentecost, *thousands*, and these numbers kept growing in Palestine and the adjacent countries, with an ever-widening tendency. It was necessary at once to teach these "thousands" something beyond the great fact that the Son of God had died for them. The apostles of the Son of God felt at once that they must tell these "thousands" what was the *life* which the Son of God would have those who believed in him *live*. To do this they repeated to the listening crowds their Master's *teaching*; they rehearsed again and again the memorable

---

[1] Cf. Westcott on the Canon, 'Age of the Apostolic Fathers' ch. i.

discourses which they had listened to by the lake, in the synagogues of Capernaum, in the temple courts; some spoken to them alone in comparative solitude, some addressed to curious and even hostile crowds in the days of the public ministry.

At first, for many months, possibly for years, there was little, or even nothing, written. The apostles and their first disciples were Jews, we must remember—men trained more or less in the rabbinical schools, whose great rule was, *commit nothing to writing.* The training, we must be careful to remember, in the Jewish schools of Palestine in the time of our Lord was almost exclusively *oral.*

Now, the great teachers of the *first* days had all, perhaps, with rare exceptions, been with Christ. Out of their abundant memories of their loved Master's sayings, aided, we may reverently assume, by the Holy Ghost, they reproduced, after taking mutual counsel, just those words, sayings, discourses, which they considered would best paint the picture of the life. He wished "his own" to live. The acts which were done, the miracles which he worked, the incidents which happened, were gradually added in their proper places to complete the picture of "the life to be led," which they painted. Special doctrinal teaching at first was very simple—a few great truths, apparently, and no more, were taught.

Together the first great teachers "remained in Jerusalem, in close communion, long enough to shape a common narrative, and to fix it with requisite consistency. The place of instruction was the synagogue and market-place, not the student's chamber." [1] Provision for the *student's chamber* was made later by one of them, still acting under the Holy Spirit's influence, when John the beloved put forth his Gospel, which dealt rather with doctrine than with life. But in the first days—possibly for many years—the gospel preached by the great teachers was the gospel much as we find it in Mark, or Luke, or Matthew.

An original oral gospel, generally arranged by the apostles in the days immediately succeeding the first Pentecost, with one great general outline repeated over and over again, was, doubtless, the foundation of the three synoptical Gospels. This accounts for the identity of so many of the details, and also for the similarity in the language. It is highly probable that, in the first years, this oral gospel existed in Aramaic, as well as in Greek, to suit the various classes of hearers to whom it was presented.

St. Mark's, on the whole, was probably the first form in which the oral gospel was committed to writing. It is the shortest and the simplest recension of the preaching of the first days reduced to a consecutive history. "The Gospel of St. Mark, conspicuous for its vivid simplicity, seems to be the most direct representation of the first evangelic tradition, the common foundation on which the others were reared. In essence, if not in composition, it is the oldest, and the absence of the history of the infancy brings its contents within the limits laid down by St. Peter for the extent

---

[1] Professor Westcott, 'Introduction to Gospels,' ch. iii.

of the apostolic testimony."[1]   After the writing of St. Mark, it is probable that a considerable period elapsed before St. Matthew and St. Luke were composed. These two longer and more detailed memoirs of the Lord's earthly life represent "the two great types of recension to which it may be supposed that the simple narrative was subjected. St. Luke presents the Hellenic, and St. Matthew (Greek) the later Hebraic form of the tradition."[2]

The three first Gospels, in their present form, were, we believe, put out somewhere between the years A.D. 55 and A.D. 70, the year of the fall of Jerusalem. Some would, however, place the date of *St. Luke* shortly after than before the great catastrophe to the city and temple.

Ancient tradition and modern criticism, however, generally accept this date—A.D. 55 to A.D. 70. The hypothesis which places the publication of any one of the three after the fall of Jerusalem would only give a very few years later as the date.

Of any writings or memoirs upon which the Gospels were founded we have only vague and uncertain traces.

Papias, who lived very near the time of the apostles, and whom Irenæus calls " a hearer of John and a companion of Polycarp "—Papias, in a work termed Λογίων Κυριακῶν Ἐξήγησις, " An Exposition of the Oracles of the Lord," of which a few fragments are preserved by Irenæus and others, writes as follows : " Matthew wrote the oracles in Hebrew, and every one interpreted them as he was able."[3]   The word in the original for " the oracles " is τὰ λόγια. It is now impossible to be certain what exactly τὰ λόγια includes. Westcott paraphrases τὰ λόγια by " the gospel "—" the sum of the words and works of the Lord." Schleiermacher and others explain τὰ λόγια as " discourses " only. It is likely enough that this was not the same as the Gospel of St. Matthew as we now possess it, but simply a body of the Lord's discourses[4] committed to writing by St. Matthew at a very early period in the Hebrew or Aramaic dialect.

The one other reference to writings on the subject of the Lord's life put out anterior to the synoptical Gospels, is that statement of St. Luke himself in the prologue to his Gospel : " Forasmuch as many have taken in hand to draw up a narrative concerning those matters which have been fulfilled [or, 'fully established'] among us " (ch. i. 1). Here St. Luke, *without disapproval*, simply mentions others who had already written portions of the gospel story. The statement of the evangelist is studiedly brief, and seems to assume that, in his judgment, none of the " many " who had taken the " story " in hand had been completely successful. He by no means condemns these as inaccurate, and does not imply that he will not make use of them ; indeed, by his words, " it seemed good to me also," he

---

[1] Acts i. 21, 22.   [2] Westcott, ' Introduction to Gospels,' ch. iii.
[3] Routh, ' Reliq. Sac.,' i. vi. p. 14 ; Eusebius, ' Hist. Eccl.,' iii. 39.
[4] It is noticeable that the bases of the ' Teaching of the Apostles,' recently brought to light, are the Lord's *discourses* and words rather than his *acts*.

ranges himself on the same platform with these earlier students and writers
of the Divine story.   The truth probably was that these writings to which
he refers were incomplete portions rather than a whole.

To sum up, when St. Luke undertook his great work there was probably
current, in the Churches in which he lived and worked, a general oral
authoritative gospel, which had grown up in the apostolic circle in very
early days, in the months and years which followed the first Pentecost, much
in the way we have sketched out above.   In different Churches, we may
with all reverence assume, existed separate and distinct memoirs and
faithful oral traditions—memoirs and traditions written and preserved by
men and women, eye-witnesses of the scenes and hearers of the words so
preserved; such a memoir, for instance, as that evidently Aramaic fragment which treats of the birth and infancy and childhood of the Redeemer
woven into the tapestry of the first two chapters of St. Luke.   It is of such
pieces as these that St. Luke, no doubt, was thinking when he wrote the first
verse of his Gospel.

Of the three synoptical Gospels, the first and third are clearly compila-
tions, arranged with a definite aim, constructed out of materials before the
writer.   The second, as we have already affirmed, is the simplest, as it is
the shortest.   It probably represents, if not the very first, at least a very
early presentment of the story of the gospel of Jesus Christ.   With the
first and second we are not just now concerned.

The third, the Gospel of St. Luke, is the most carefully composed of the
three divinely inspired stories of the Redeemer.   It is the reply to questionings which would naturally present themselves to a thoughtful, cultured
man who had heard, and after hearing had been impressed with the
strange beauty and the intense reality of, the story of the cross.   There
were, to such a man, many things, apart from the simple narrative which
formed the groundwork of the preaching of the first days, which called for
explanation.   *Who* was this strange, marvellous Being, whose love for men
—a love passing understanding—had led him to die for men who only repaid
his love with the bitterest hate?

> " The very God! think, Abib; dost thou think?
> So the All-great were the All-loving too;
> So through the thunder comes a human voice,
> Saying, ' O heart I made, a heart beats here!
> Face my hands fashioned, see it in myself!
> Thou hast no power, nor mayest conceive of mine;
> But love I gave thee, with myself to love;
> And thou must love me, who have died for thee!'
> The madman saith, *He said so;* it is strange!"
>   (R. Browning, 'An Epistle of Karshish, the Arab Physician.')

Whence came he?   *How* and *when* and in *what guise* did he first appear
among men?   *Where* did he spend the first thirty years of his life?   What
was his *earthly home?*   Who was that honoured and mighty forerunner,

that John, whom Herod had foully murdered? What was the meaning of *the exclusion of Israel,* the chosen people, from his Church?

All these questionings would naturally occur to a cultured listener, who longed to embrace the promises of Jesus, about A.D. 60–70, when the Church was growing into a great and widespread company, and the "story" was being repeated at second and third hand in many a city far away from the Holy Land.

"No one could understand better than St. Paul the need of an exhaustive reply to such questionings, the need of an authoritative history, where an account of the rise and progress of the gospel of Jesus Christ was related with accurate and careful detail. And if Paul, among the helpers who surrounded him, had an evangelist distinguished for his gifts and culture—and we know from 2 Cor. viii. 18, 19 that there was really one of this description—how could he help casting his eyes upon him, and encouraging him to undertake so excellent a work? Such is the task which Luke has discharged" (Godet).

We have said this Third Gospel was *most carefully composed,* with the view of satisfying the requirements of a thoughtful, cultured man, such as was probably that "most excellent Theophilus" to whom the Gospel was addressed.

First, it contained, with its sequel the Acts, not a few historical notices, such as the census of Quirinius, under the decree of Augustus (ch. ii. 1—3); the contemporary Roman and Jewish rulers in the fifteenth year of Tiberius Cæsar (ch. iii. 1, 2); Pilate's and Herod's jurisdictions (ch. xxiii. 1, 12); with allusions by name to public persons, such as Cornelius, centurion of the Italian band (Acts x. 1); Herod (Acts xii. 1, etc.; xiii. 1); Sergius Paulus (Acts xiii. 7); the Emperor Claudius's decree (Acts xviii. 2); Gallio the deputy of Achaia (Acts xviii. 12—16); Claudius Lysias, Felix the Roman governor (Acts xxiii. 26); Porcius Festus (Acts xxiv. 27); King Agrippa and Bernice (Acts xxv.); the appeal to Cæsar (Acts xxvi. 32).

Secondly, it embodied in its narrative that beautiful and interesting account of the nativity and the events which preceded it and immediately succeeded it, with a few notices of the boyhood of the Lord. These details, as we have suggested in the Exposition, were evidently procured from information communicated to St. Luke (or St. Paul) by eye-witnesses, many of the details probably by the virgin-mother herself. These two first chapters would answer many a question which would naturally suggest itself to reverent inquirers who had listened to the simple gospel message as first delivered, and had enrolled themselves among the followers of Jesus Christ.

Thirdly, the picture of the gradual development of the Church of Jesus Christ is drawn with extraordinary skill and care by St. Luke—its development from Bethlehem and Nazareth to Jerusalem and Rome. On the morning of the nativity, in the opening chapters of St. Luke, the Church is confined to Joseph, Mary, and the holy Babe. To these, just the few shepherds of

Bethlehem are added. The close of the Acts shows us the foundation of the Church at Rome; but Rome was but a branch, an offshoot, of the great Churches of Antioch and Jerusalem. St. Luke traces the various stages in this development—from Bethlehem to Nazareth, from Nazareth to Capernaum, from Capernaum to the Galilæan and Peræan villages, then to Jerusalem. The Acts takes up the wondrous story, and shows how the Church, advanced from Jerusalem to the Syrian Antioch, from Antioch to the cities of Asia Minor, from great Asian centres like Ephesus across the seas to the old world-renowned cities of Greece, and then from Greece to Italy, and the story closes with the beginning of the Church at Rome.

Nor does St. Luke alone depict with his great skill the *geographical* development of the Church of Jesus Christ. He describes, too, how the *work* of the Divine Master and his chosen instruments developed. First, we have the story of the birth and growth of the pioneer, John the Baptist; then the birth and childhood of Jesus himself. He paints the beginning of his organized Church, when he summons the twelve out of the number of believers who gathered round him soon after he began his public ministry among men.

The wants of the growing organization soon called for more workers. In the Third Gospel the solemn summons of the seventy is related. For a moment the advancing work seems arrested by a fatal blow, and the death of the Master on the cross puts, as it seems, a final stop to the new Church and its work; but the Resurrection, which St. Luke describes as quickly following, gives a new and irresistible impulse to the Church and the Church's work among men. The same men are at work, and the same Master is guiding their labours. But the homeless Master is no longer guiding them as they walked together among the fields of Galilee and the streets of Jerusalem, but from his glory-throne in heaven; and the men, the same men, are quite changed: it is as though they had drunk of the waters of another and stronger life.

Luke describes in the Acts, the sequel to his Gospel, the rapid progress and the swift though orderly development of the now great and numerous Church. Deacons are chosen to assist the apostles; then we read of prophets and teachers and elders, of the foundation-stories of a great and powerful organization.

II. SOME OF THE SPECIAL FEATURES OF ST. LUKE'S GOSPEL.

We have dwelt upon the position of St. Luke's Gospel as a great Christian writing in the earliest days of Christianity, its teaching being considered as absolutely authoritative, as containing the mind, even the very words, of the Divine Founder. We have shown how it was received before four score years had been counted from the Ascension Day, not only by all the Churches, but by the principal heretical sects which sprang up so soon in the Christian story; and our data for this general very early acceptance of the Third Gospel were drawn, not merely from the scanty fragments which remain to us of individual scholars and teachers, but from versions which were the public work of whole Churches. Its author and his peculiar school of thought will be presently discussed. We will now proceed to a more detailed consideration of some of the contents of the Gospel named after St. Luke.

Of the three synoptical Gospels, St. Luke, though not the longest, is the fullest, that is, it contains the most details of the Saviour's life on earth. And some of these details peculiar to St. Luke are of very high importance in their practical teaching, as also in their bearing on the blessed life.

Among the more striking of these are—the raising of the son of the widow of Nain; the episode of the woman who was a sinner kneeling at the feet of Jesus when he was at the banquet given in the house of Simon the Pharisee; the tears which the Master wept over Jerusalem; the famous parables of the good Samaritan, with its broad, universal teaching; the parable showing how and why Jesus loved the lost—the lost *drachma*, the lost *sheep*, and the lost *son*; the parables of Lazarus and Dives, of the unjust steward, the unjust judge, the Pharisee and the publican, etc.; the prayer on the cross for those who were doing him to death; the promise to the dying thief hanging on the cross. by his side; the walk to Emmaus, and the conversation during the walk after the Resurrection.

We must not omit here to mention two considerable sections of this Gospel which contain many peculiar details touching the life or the teaching of Jesus, which alone are told by St. Luke. (1) The first two chapters treating of the infancy and boyhood of the Saviour. (2) The account of that prolonged journey, or perhaps four distinct journeys, toward Jerusalem related in ch. ix. 51—xix. 27. Some of the events related in this important section, and some of the words spoken by Jesus on these journeyings, are repeated in one or other of the evangelists, notably in St. John; but much in this great section is peculiar to St. Luke.

III. THE ESPECIAL TEACHING OF ST. LUKE.

St. Luke's Gospel has been charged by some critics with teaching certain doctrines alien to the teaching of primitive Christianity, in some respects differing from the teaching in St. Matthew or in St. John.

These critics complain that St. Luke, different to the older apostles, teaches in the Third Gospel "a universalism"—a breaking-down of all legal privileges and class distinctions, a free admission of all sinners alike to the mercy of God upon their repentance, a universality in Christ's promises, which jars upon some minds peculiarly constituted and specially trained, in the nineteenth century equally with the first.

There is no doubt that this Divine picture of the Lord's life and teaching that we call St. Luke's was mainly the work of that great servant of Jesus Christ whom men call Paul, only we maintain that there is no real difference between the fundamental doctrines taught in this Gospel and those laid down in the first, the second, and the fourth. We believe simply that in St. Luke—and the Epistles of St. Paul repeat the teaching —the universality of Christ's promises are more distinctly marked; the invitations to the careless, to the wanderer, to the forsaken of man—"les reprouvés" of this world—are more marked, more definite, more urgent. The doctrines of the four Gospels are the same, only in St. Luke this special feature of the Blessed One's teaching is more accentuated.

See how St. Luke alone, in his short *résumé* of the Baptist's preaching, dwells upon that peculiar feature of Isaiah upon which that great fore-runner evidently laid great stress, "All flesh shall see the salvation of God." Luke ignores all privilege of race, or caste, or training, by tracing back the ancestry of the Redeemer to *Adam*. Abraham is ignored here. In several cases faith alone wins forgiveness. The story of the good Samaritan reads a sharp, stern lesson, and suggests a grave warning to the self-styled orthodox of every age, from the first century to the nine-teenth. The reasons why Jesus loved the "seeming lost" of the world are strangely but beautifully shown in the parables of the lost coin, the lost sheep, and the lost son. The parable of the marriage supper accentu-ates the same teaching. The ingratitude of the nine Jewish lepers, painted in the strongest colours, sharply contrasts with the gratitude of the despised alien *Samaritan;* and the Lord's blessing in the latter case anticipates a possible tremendous reversal of human judgments at the last great day.

In these and such-like teachings in the Third Gospel, although there is a danger of their being pressed by expositors too far, many grave and anxious thoughts, however, are suggested, and warn us against hasty and imperfect estimates of others, on whom, perhaps, in our short-sighted judgment we look down.

This Gospel certainly dwells with peculiar emphasis on the infinite love and compassion of Jesus, which induced him, in his endless pity, to seek, yes, and to save, souls among all sorts and conditions of men.

It is especially the Gospel of hope and love, of pity and of faith. Very beautifully are these thoughts exemplified by the sayings of Jesus on the cross, reported by St. Luke. It is the Gospel of *hope.* The Divine Victim prayed for his murderers. There was *hope* still, even for them. Of whom shall *we*, then, despair? It is the Gospel of *love.* He so loved the men doing him to death that he could, in his great agony, *pray* for them. It is the Gospel of *pity.* He was so sorry for the poor ignorant but repentant thief dying by his side that he could promise him *paradise.* It is the Gospel of *faith.* With his last breath he could commend his departing spirit to his Father and ours.

"This is the Gospel from which shines most brightly the light of redemption, forgiveness, restoration, for all the human race; the two earlier Gospels are illuminated by the same light, for it is the light of the Spirit of Christ; but if differences are to be noticed at all, this is one of the most distinctly marked. . . . Many of the Lord's parables and words reported only by St. Luke lead the mind of his readers to understand the infinite love and pity of Jesus which led him to seek and save in every region and class. Before this love all questions of class break down. The door of redemption is opened wide; the Pharisee fails of forgiveness, and the penitent publican secures it. The priest and Levite pass on the other side, but the good Samaritan tends the wounded man. Simon the Pharisee, the host of Jesus, learns a new lesson from our Lord when the sinful woman is allowed to draw near and to wash the feet of Jesus. All this points to a breaking-down of all legal privileges and distinctions of class, and to the admission of all sinners alike to the mercy of the Lord upon their repentance. *God hath put down the mighty from their seat, and hath exalted them of low degree*" (Archbishop Thomson).

Some critics, too, have found fault with what they term Luke's heresy in regard to his bold assertion of the rights of the poor against the rich, alleging that, in St. Luke's presentment of the teaching of Jesus Christ, only the poor *as such* appear to be saved, the rich, on the other hand, seem condemned *as such*.

There was, we know, a tendency in the early days of Christianity to exaggerate the so-called blessings of poverty, and to depreciate the so-called curse of wealth or comparative wealth. We see it in the mistaken attempt in the primitive Church of Jerusalem, where, at all events, the greater number of members parted with their possessions and attempted to live a life of Christian communism. The disastrous result is told in the New Testament story, where the deep poverty of the Church of Jerusalem, the consequence of their mistaken interpretation of their Master's words, is frequently and pointedly alluded to. Later a distinct sect arose, the Ebionites, when this teaching concerning the evil of riches was pressed home in an exaggerated form.

But it is a strange mistake to see in St. Luke's Gospel any encouragement to this curious misunderstanding of the Lord's words and parables. Our Master saw and pointed out that there was a special compensation for poverty. Less tempted, less wedded to this life, the faithful poor man stood often fairer for the kingdom of God than his seemingly more fortunate, wealthier brother. But we see very clearly from St. Luke's teaching that it is never poverty which saves, or wealth which condemns. It was the Samaritan's righteous *use* of his substance which won the Lord's smile of approval.

IV. The Author of the Third Gospel.

The earliest traditions of the Church, and the writings which we possess of her teachers—of men who lived in the century following the death of St. John—the "remains," too, of the great heretical teachers who taught for the most part in the first half of the second century, all bear witness that the author of the Third Gospel was identical with the writer of the Acts, and that this person was the St. Luke well known in the days of the beginnings of Christianity as the companion and friend of St. Paul. Most of these early references in some form or other connect St. Luke's work with St. Paul.

Among the more interesting and important of these, *Irenæus*, writing in Southern Gaul *circa* A.D. 180, says, "Luke, the companion of Paul, put down in a book the gospel preached by him (Paul)" ('Adv. Hæres.,' iii. 1); and again, "That Luke was inseparable from Paul, his fellow-worker in the gospel, is shown by himself. . . . Thus the apostles, simply and without envying any one, handed down to all these things which they themselves had learned from the Lord ; thus, therefore, Luke also . . . has handed down to us the things which he had learned from them, as he witnesses when he says, 'Even as they delivered them to us which from the beginning were eye-witnesses and ministers of the Word'" ('Adv. Hæres.,' iii. 14).

Tertullian, who lived and wrote in Proconsular Africa in the last years of the second century, tells us how "Luke's digest was usually ascribed to Paul" ('Adv. Marcion,' iv. 5; see too 'Adv. Marcion,' iv. 2).

Eusebius, the Church historian, writing a little more than a century later, and who spent much of his life in collecting and editing the records of the first beginnings of Christianity, relates that "Luke, who was a native of Antioch, and by profession a physician, for the most part a companion of Paul, and who was not slightly acquainted with the rest of the apostles, has left us two books divinely inspired. . . . One of these is the Gospel. . . . And it is said that Paul was accustomed to mention the Gospel according to him, whenever in his Epistles speaking, as it were, of some Gospel of his own, he says *according to my gospel*" ('Hist. Eccl.,' vi. 25; see also St. Jerome, 'De Vir. Illustr.,' c. 7). And this apparently generally received tradition, which at all events very closely connects the Third Gospel with St. Paul, receives additional confirmation when the teaching and occasionally the very expressions of St. Luke's Gospel are compared with the teaching of the Epistles of St. Paul. The very important section of St. Luke's Gospel which describes the institution of the Lord's Supper, closely even in verbal coincidences, resembles St. Paul's account of the same blessed sacrament (comp. too 1 Cor. xv. 3 with ch. xxiv. 26, 27).

Then in the teaching. It is universally agreed that there is a general affinity between St. Paul and St. Luke. It is in the Third Gospel that especially those doctrines which are commonly termed Pauline are pressed with peculiar force. Both Paul and Luke, in their teaching, bring into special prominence the promise of redemption made to the whole human race, without distinction of nation or family, ignoring in the gracious offer *all* privilege whatsoever. "All flesh shall see the salvation of God." Many of the parables told only by St. Luke, notably that of the good Samaritan; in the parable-stories of the lost sheep, the lost coin, the lost son, illustrating the love of Jesus shown in seeking the lost—read as examples of the teaching pressed home in the Pauline Epistles, homely, vivid illustrations taken from the everyday life of Syria and Palestine. The appearances of the risen Jesus after the Resurrection almost exactly correspond with those related by St. Paul (1 Cor. xv.).

That a close connection existed between Paul and Luke we know from several allusions to Luke in the Epistles of Paul: "Luke, the beloved physician, and Demas, greet you" (Col. iv. 14); "There salute thee, Epaphras, my fellow-prisoner in Christ Jesus. . . . Lucas, my fellow-labourer" (Philem. 24); "Only Luke is with me" (2 Tim. iv. 11).

Some expositors have thought that this friendship of Paul and Luke only began at Rome, a city in which Luke was residing as a physician, and that he met the great apostle during his first imprisonment there, and was converted to Christianity during Paul's captivity, in which we know that many persons had access to him. This supposition would not be contradicted by the three special notices of Luke in the Pauline Epistles, two of them—that to the Colossians and the letter to Philemon—having been written from Rome during that imprisonment, and the third notice, in the Second Epistle to Timothy, occurring in a letter written some years later, when the apostle was confined a second time in Rome.

But the intimacy between Paul and Luke, we confidently believe, began much earlier. A very general and absolutely uncontradicted tradition, which dates from the early days of Christianity, ascribes the authorship of the Acts to St. Luke. Now, in this very writing, in three passages, two of considerable length, the author of the Acts passes abruptly from the third person to the first person plural. Thus the narrative changes from " and as *they* went through the cities," etc. (Acts xvi. 4), to "loosing from Troas, *we* came with a straight course to Samothracia," etc. (Acts xvi. 11), as though *the writer*—universally, as we have seen, acknowledged to be *St. Luke*—had joined the little band of missionaries who accompanied St. Paul at Troas (Acts xvi. 10). If this be, as is most probable, the case, then he must—having at some *previous* (unknown) date become acquainted with St. Paul—as early certainly as A.D. 53, have joined himself to St. Paul's company when the apostle was at Troas. With Paul, still following the Acts narrative, St. Luke journeyed as far as Philippi. Then, in Acts xvii. 1, when the apostle leaves Philippi, the third person is again used in the narrative, as though St. Luke was left behind at Philippi. After some six or seven years, again at Philippi, where we lost sight of him, in the course of what is termed the third missionary journey, the use of the first person plural—"These going before tarried for *us* at Troas, and *we* sailed away from Philippi"—indicates that the writer, St. Luke, had again joined St. Paul (Acts xx. 5). With the apostle he passed through Miletus, Tyre, and Cæsarea to Jerusalem (Acts xx. 5; xxi. 18). During the two years or more of St. Paul's imprisonment at Cæsarea (whither he was sent from Jerusalem after his arrival at that city with St. Luke), St. Luke was probably with or near him, for when the apostle was sent under guard as a prisoner of state from Cæsarea to Rome, St. Luke again evidently was with him; for throughout the voyage which ended in the memorable shipwreck and the subsequent stay at Melita, and on the voyage from Melita in the ship of Alexandria, we find the forms "we" and "us" used : "Then when *we* came to Rome;" "when the brethren heard of *us*." During that long period of imprisonment at Cæsarea, it is highly probable that St. Luke, acting under the immediate direction of his master Paul, made that personal investigation, searched out eye-witnesses of the events of the life of love, conversed with survivors—less than thirty years had elapsed from the Resurrection morning, it must be remembered, when Paul lay in his Cæsarean prison— procured memoranda in the possession of the holy women and others, and with the help and guidance of his great master, aided by the Holy Spirit (A.D. 60–62), we even think compiled much of what is known now as "the Gospel according to St. Luke." During the Roman imprisonment, which immediately followed A.D. 63–64, the work, and not improbably its sequel the Acts, was finally revised and put out.

We thus possess traces of an intimate friendship between the older and the younger man for a period of some twelve years—A.D. 53 to 64; for how long previous to A.D. 53 and the meeting at Troas (Acts xvi. 10) the friendship had existed we have no data even for conjecture.

V. "LUKE, THE BELOVED PHYSICIAN" (Col. iv. 14).

"And Luke, who was a native of Antioch, and by *profession a physician*, for the most part a companion (τὰ πλεῖστα συγγεγονώς) of Paul, and who was not slightly acquainted with the rest of the apostles, has left us two books divinely inspired, proofs of the *art of healing souls*, which he won from them " (Eusebius, 'Hist. Eccl.,' iii. 4).

"Luke, *a physician* of Antioch, not unskilled in the Hebrew language, as his works show, was a follower (*sectator*) of the Apostle Paul, and the companion of all his wanderings. He wrote a Gospel of which the same Paul makes mention," etc. (St. Jerome, 'De Vir. Illustr.,' c. 7).

"The Gospel according to Luke was dictated by the Apostle Paul, but written and put out (*editum*) by Luke, the blessed apostle and *physician*" (Synopsis Pseudo-Athanasii, in Athanasii 'Opp.').

The above-quoted references from Eusebius, Jerome, and the pseudo-Athanasius, tell us that the words of St. Paul (Col. iv. 14), when he referred to his friend Luke as "the beloved physician," very generally coloured all tradition in the early Church respecting the writer of the Third Gospel.

The profession of physician in the early days of the empire was filled almost exclusively by freedmen or the sons of freedmen (*libertini*). This calling implied a considerable amount of scientific knowledge, and shows that Luke the physician certainly belonged to the class of educated men. Dean Plumptre, of Wells, calls attention to the well-known list of the members of the household of the Empress Livia, the consort of Augustus Cæsar, compiled from the *Columbarium*, a sepulchre which was opened at

Rome in 1726. This "list" gives many examples of names with the word "medicus" attached to them.

It is remarkable that, with the exception of Hippocrates, all the extant medical writers were *Asiatic Greeks*—such as Galen of Pergamus, in Mysia; Dioscorides of Anazarba, in Cilicia; Aretæus the Cappadocian. Hippocrates, though not an Asiatic Greek, was born and lived in close proximity to the coast of Asia, being a native of Cos, an island off the coast of Caria.

In the first century of the Christian era no medical school stood higher, and few so high, as that of Tarsus, in Cilicia. There was a great temple of Æsculapius at Ægæ, only a few miles from Tarsus, which was resorted to by sick persons from all countries, who came to consult the priests or brotherhood of the Asclepiadæ.

A modern scholar, Dr. Hobart, of Trinity College, Dublin, has lately written an exhaustive treatise[1] of considerable length to show that the language of St. Luke, both in the Gospel and Acts, is very largely impregnated with technical medical words—words which none but a trained physician would have thought of using; words, too, employed in the general story in the course of relation of events not connected with healing a disease or any medical subject; the very words, in fact, which were common in the phraseology of the Greek medical schools, and which a physician, from his medical training and habits, would be likely to employ.

1. In the general narrative in the *Third Gospel* and the *Acts*, there are a number of words which were either distinctly medical terms or commonly employed in medical language, such as ἴασις, θεραπεία, συνδρομή, etc.

2. There are, again, certain classes of words which were used in medical language in some special relation.[2] St. Luke alone uses the special terms for the distribution of nourishment, blood, nerves, etc., through the body, such as διανέμειν, διασπείρειν, ἀναδιδόναι; and the terms to denote an intermittent or a failing pulse, such as διαλείπειν, ἐκλείπειν, etc.

3. The same combination of words are used by St. Luke as we find in medical writers, as for instance, τρῆμα βελόνης, δακτύλῳ προσψαύειν, θρόμβοι αἵματος, etc.

4. Other words are found, too, in this Gospel used very rarely save by medical writers in the sense which they bear in St. Luke's writings, as ἀνακάθιζεν, to sit up, ἐκψύχειν, to expose, etc.

5. Several curious indications of the writer of the Third Gospel and the Acts being a medical man are discoverable in the words made use of for marking time, such as ἑσπέρα, μεσημβρία, μεσονύκτιον, ὄρθρος; the first two of which are peculiar to him, and the last two almost so, as μεσονύκτιον is used but once outside his writings (Mark xiii. 35), and ὄρθρος, too, but once (John viii. 2). These latter were the usual times and the usual terms to denote them, for the accession or abatement of disease, visiting patients,

---

[1] 'The Medical Language of St. Luke,' by the Rev. W. K. Hobart, LL.D., printed in the Dublin University Press series, 1882.

[2] Ibid., Introd., p. xxxiv.

applying remedies, etc.   Dr. Hobart quotes Galen, ' Meth. Med.,' ix. 4, and
other well-known Greek medical writers in support of this.

As we should expect from the physician-evangelist, in the accounts of
the miracles of healing medical language is carefully employed.

In many parallel passages St. Luke will be found to use a term strictly
medical, the other evangelists one less precise, the terms chosen by St. Luke
being words all of which were in common use with the Greek physicians.

In such important sections, for instance, as in the account of the agony
in the garden, described by all the three synoptists, St. Luke's relation,
different from the other two, possesses all the characteristics of medical
writing, detailing carefully, in medical language, the prostration of strength,
and the outward and visible effect on his human frame of the inner anguish
of our Lord.[1]

It is a very probable hypothesis to ascribe the connection of the two
friends, Paul and Luke, in the first instance, to help given to the great
apostle in one of those many and grave illnesses to which, from many
casual references in his writings, we know the apostle was subject.

VI. Conclusion.

With the exception of (1) the direct but casual notices in the Epistles
of St. Paul, and the indirect allusions to himself in the later chapters of
the Acts above referred to, where in the narrative the third person is
changed for the first; (2) the universal tradition of the early Church that
Luke, the companion of Paul, was the author of the Third Gospel; (3)
the internal evidence contained in the Gospel and in the Acts, which
plainly shows that the writer was a physician;—with these exceptions
nothing further definite or trustworthy is known respecting Luke.
Epiphanius and others mention that he was one of the seventy disciples;
Theophylact believes that he was one of the two disciples who met with
the risen Jesus on their walk to Emmaus. These suppositions *may* be true,
but they are uncertain. The well-known tradition that Luke was also
a painter, and painted portraits of the blessed Virgin and of the chief
apostles, and even of the Lord himself, rests only on the statement of
Nicephorus, of the menology of the Emperor Basil, drawn up in A.D. 980,
and of other late writers, but none of them are of historical authority.[2]

After St. Paul's martyrdom (A.D. 67–68) our knowledge of St. Luke
is only vague, and rests on uncertain tradition. Epiphanius ('.Contr.
Hæres.,' lib. ii. vol. ii. 464, edit. Dindorf) tells us that, after the death
of his master, he preached in Dalmatia, Italy, Macedonia, and Gallia.
Gregory Nazianzen mentions that St. Luke was among the martyrs.
Nicephorus relates the manner of his martyrdom—how that, whilst working for the cause in Greece, he was hanged upon an olive-tree.

[1] Hobart, 'The Medical Language of St. Luke,' pt. ii. sect. lvi. p. 80.
[2] Archbishop Thomson, 'Introduction to St. Luke,' p. xli.

THE
GOSPEL ACCORDING TO ST. LUKE

—◆—

EXPOSITION

CHAPTER I.

THE origin of the Gospels—the four histories which relate in detail the circumstances of the foundation of Christianity—will ever be an interesting study. *Here* we shall never know the exact truth of the compilation of these writings, the foundation-stones of all our hopes and fears; a reverent, scholarly speculation is all that can be offered to the student of the Divine memoirs. The speculation, however, probably in this case comes very near the truth.

After the Ascension and the events of the first Pentecost, which quickly followed their Master's return to heaven, the twelve and a few others who had walked in the company which followed Jesus during the years of his public ministry no doubt often met together and talked over the teaching and the acts of their risen and now glorified Master. As time passed on, a certain number of these acts, a certain number of the public and private discourses in the apostolic company, became adopted as the usual texts or subjects of the teaching and preaching in the assemblies large and small gathered together by the followers of Jesus in Jerusalem and the neighbouring towns and villages, subsequently in other parts of the Holy Land, in Syria, and in more distant countries—in Africa and Italy. We may assume that the Holy Spirit aided the composition of these apostolic summaries by bringing to the memory of these holy men the more important of the words and acts of the Lord Jesus, spoken and done when in their midst.

That some such early authoritative summary existed among the first preachers of the faith we may positively assume, (1) from the *general* harmony of the facts and teaching of the first three Gospels; (2) from the almost total absence of any other traditional sayings and doings of the great Master besides those contained in the four Gospels.

Some twelve traditional sayings besides those related by the four, and those of no great importance, are all that we possess; no record of other miracles of any description have come down to us.

Years passed on. The precious treasure of the apostolic records, the simple memories of his words and acts preserved, and no doubt arranged in some order, were enough for the first preachers and teachers of the faith of Jesus of Nazareth.

There were, no doubt, many rough attempts to write these down on the part of apostles and their pupils. These are most probably the writings to which St. Luke alludes, without disparaging them, in his preface to his Gospel, in the words, "Forasmuch as many have taken in hand to set forth in order a declaration of those things which are most surely believed among us."

But something more accurate in the way of written memoirs was necessary for the Church, as the number of believers multiplied, and the original friends of the Master were one by one taken from their midst—the men who had seen the presence and heard the voice. When the first fervour of enthusiasm had passed away, or rather when the Church had so multiplied that, in the case of the great majority of its members who had only *heard* of Jesus, this fervour of enthusiasm had never been experienced at all, something of a critical spirit of inquiry sprang up in the various congregations. Who, for instance, was this Jesus of Nazareth, whom the apostles and their pupils preached? Whence came he? Who was that strange teacher John, who baptized him, and, so to speak, introduced him to Israel? Such natural questions necessitated the putting forth, on the part of the leaders of the new faith, documents at once comprehensive as well as authoritative.

Each of the four Gospels supplied an evident want of the early Church; each was the answer, on the part of responsible men, to the natural inquiry of some great section of believers.

The preface to the Gospel of St. Luke, with which we are at present concerned, with great clearness relates how its compiler, having availed himself of all the written and oral apostolic traditions then current in the Church, had personally, with careful and continuous research, traced up these various traditions to their very source, and, having arranged his many facts, presented the whole continuous story to a man of high rank in the Christian congregations, one Theophilus, a noble Greek or Roman, who may be taken as an example of a large class of inquiring earnest Christians of the years 70—90 A.D.

Vers. 1—4.—AN INTRODUCTION.

Ver. 1.—**Forasmuch as many have taken in hand.** The Greek in which St. Luke's Gospel is written is generally pure and classical, but the language of the little introduction (vers. 1—4) is especially studied and polished, and contrasts singularly with the Hebrew character of the story of the nativity, which immediately follows. St. Luke here, in this studied introduction, follows the example of many of the great classical writers, Latin as well as Greek. Thucydides, Herodotus, Livy, for instance, paid special attention to the opening sentences of their histories. The many early efforts to produce a connected history of the life and work of the great Master

Christ are not, as some have supposed, alluded to here with anything like *censure*, but are simply referred to as being *incomplete*, as written without order or arrangement. They most probably formed the basis of much of St. Luke's own Gospel. These primitive Gospels quickly disappeared from sight, as they evidently contained nothing more than what was embodied in the fuller and more systematic narratives of the "four." **Of those things which are most surely believed among us.** There was evidently no questioning in the Church of the first days about the truth of the story of the teaching and the mighty works of Jesus of Nazareth. It was the incompleteness of these first evangelists, rather than their inaccuracy, which induced St. Luke to take in hand a new Gospel.

Ver. 2.—**Even as they delivered them unto us, which from the beginning were eye-witnesses, and ministers of the Word.** The general accuracy of the recitals contained in those early Gospels is here conceded, as the source of these primitive writings was the tradition delivered by the eye-witnesses of the acts of Jesus; among these eye-witnesses the apostles would, of course, hold the foremost place. The whole statement may be roughly paraphrased thus: "The narrative of the memorable events which have been accomplished in our midst many have undertaken to compose. These different narratives are in strict conformity with the apostles' tradition, which men who were themselves eye-witnesses of the great events, and subsequently ministers of the Word, handed down to us. Now, I have traced up all these traditions anew to their very sources, and propose rewriting them in consecutive order, that you, my lord Theophilus, may be fully convinced of the positive certainty of those great truths in which you have been instructed." *Eye-witnesses, and ministers of the Word;* witnesses of the events of the public ministry of Jesus, from the baptism to the Ascension. These men, in great numbers, after Pentecost, became ministers and preachers of the Word.

Ver. 3.—**Having had perfect understanding of all things from the very first;** more accurately rendered, *having followed up* (or, *investigated*) *step by step all things from their source.* St. Luke, without depreciating the accounts of the life and work of Jesus then current in the Church, here sets out his reasons for undertaking a fresh compilation. His Gospel would differ from the early Gospels: (1) By going back much further than they did. It is doubtful if these primitive Gospels began earlier than with the ministry of John and the baptism of Jesus. St. Mark's Gospel—which, perhaps, represents one of the earliest forms of the apostles' preaching and teaching, —does not go further back than those events. St. Luke gave Theophilus, among other early details, a history of the incarnation and the infancy of the Blessed One. (2) By presenting the whole story in a consecutive form. Hitherto, apparently, "apostolic tradition probably had a more or less fragmentary character; the apostles not relating every time the whole of the facts, but only those which best answered to the circumstances in which they were preaching. This is expressly said of St. Peter, on the testimony of Papias, or of the old presbyter on whom he relied: Πρὸς τὰς χρείας ἐποιεῖτο τὰς διδασκαλίας ('He chose each time the facts appropriate to the needs of his hearers'). Important omissions would easily result from this mode of telling the great story" (Godet). **Most excellent Theophilus.** The term rendered "most excellent" (κράτιστε) denotes that the friend of Luke for whom nominally his Gospel was written was a man of high rank in the Roman world of that day. Nothing is known of his history. He was most likely, from Luke's connection with Antioch, a noble of that great and wealthy city, and may fairly be taken as a representative of that cultured thoughtful class for whom in a measure St. Luke especially wrote. The title κράτιστε, by which the Theophilus is here addressed, we find several times applied to high Roman officials, such as Felix and Festus (Acts xxiii. 26; xxiv. 3; xxvi. 25).

Ver. 5—ch. ii. 52.—THE GOSPEL OF THE INFANCY. The critical reader of the Gospel in the original Greek is here startled by the abrupt change in the style of writing. The first four verses, which constitute the introduction, are written in pure classical language; the sentences are balanced, almost with a rhythmical accuracy. They are the words evidently of a highly cultured mind, well versed in Greek thought. But in the fifth verse, where the history of the eventful period really begins, all is changed. The narrative flows on clearly with a certain picturesqueness of imagery; the style is simple, easy, vivid; but at once the reader is sensible that he has passed out of the region of Greek and Western thought. The language is evidently a close translation from some Hebrew original; the imagery is exclusively Jewish, and the thoughts belong to the story of the chosen people. It is clear that this section of St. Luke's writing, which ends, however, with ch. ii., is not derived from apostolic tradition, but is the result of his own investigation into the origin of the faith of Christ, gathered probably from the lips of the virgin mother herself, or from one of the holy women belonging to her kinsfolk who had been with her from the beginning of the wondrous events. St. Luke reproduced, as faithfully as he could in a strange tongue, the revelations—some perhaps written, some no doubt oral, communicated to him, we reverently believe, by the blessed mother of Jesus herself. The story of these two chapters is what St. Luke evidently alludes to when, in his short preface (ver. 3), he writes of his "perfect understanding in all things from the very first (ἄνωθεν)."

Vers. 5—25.—*The vision of Zacharias in the temple.*

Ver. 5.—**There was in the days of Herod, the King of Judæa.** The Herod here alluded to was the one surnamed "the Great." The event here related took place towards the end of his reign. His dominions, besides Judæa, included Samaria, Galilee, and a large district of Peræa. This prince played a conspicuous part in the politics of his day. He was no Hebrew by birth, but an Idumæan, and he owed his position entirely to the favour of Rome, whose vassal he really was during his whole reign. The Roman senate had, on the recommendation of Antony and Octavius, granted to this prince the title of "King of Judæa." It was a strange, sad state of things. The land of promise was ruled over by an Idumæan adventurer, a creature of the great Italian Republic; the holy and beautiful house on Mount Zion was in the custody of an Edomite usurper; the high priest of the Mighty One of Jacob was raised up or deposed as the officials of Rome thought good. Truly the sceptre had departed from Judah. **A certain priest named Zacharias;** usually spelt among the Hebrews, *Zechariah;* it means "Remembered of Jehovah," and was a favourite name among the chosen people. **Of the course of Abia.** Ἐφημερία (course) signified originally "a daily service." It was subsequently used for a group of priests who exercised their priestly functions in the temple for a week, and then gave place to another group. From Eleazar and Ithamar, the two surviving sons of the first high priest Aaron, had descended twenty-four families. Among these King David distributed by lot the various tabernacle (subsequently temple) services, each family group, or course, officiating for eight days—from sabbath to sabbath. From the Babylonish exile, of these twenty-four families only four returned. With the idea of reproducing as nearly as possible the old state of things, these four were subdivided into twenty-four, the twenty-four bearing the original family names, and this succession of courses continued in force until the fall of Jerusalem and the burning of the temple, A.D. 70. According to Josephus, Zacharias was especially distinguished by belonging to the first of the twenty-four courses, or families. **Of the daughters of Aaron, and her name was Elisabeth;** identical with *Elisheba,* "One whose oath is to God." Both the husband and wife traced their lineage back to the first high priest—a coveted distinction in Israel.

Ver. 6.—**And they were both righteous before God.** "One of the oldest terms of high praise among the Jews (Gen. vi. 9; vii. 1; xviii. 23—28; Ezek. xviii. 5—9, etc.). It is used also of Joseph (Matt. i. 19), and is defined in the following words in the most technical sense of strict legal observance, which it had acquired since the days of Maccabees. The true Jashar (upright man) was the ideal Jew. Thus Rashi calls the Book of Genesis 'The book of the upright, Abraham, Isaac, and Jacob'" (Farrar).

Ver. 7.—**And they had no child.** This, as is well known, was a heavy calamity in a Hebrew home. In the childless house there was no hope of the long looked-for Messiah being born in it. It was not unfrequently looked on as a mark of the Divine displeasure, possibly as the punishment of some grave sin.

Ver. 9.—**His lot was to burn incense;** more accurately, *he obtained by lot the duty of entering and offering incense.* The office of burning incense gave the priest to whom this important lot fell the right of entering the holy place. It was the most coveted of all the priestly duties. The Talmud says the priest who obtained the right to perform this high duty was not permitted to draw the lot a second time in the same week, and as the whole number of priests at this time was very large—some say even as many as twenty thousand—Farrar conjectures that it would never happen to the same priest twice in his lifetime to enter that sacred spot.

Ver. 10.—**And the whole multitude of the people were praying without at the time of incense.** This would indicate that the day in question was a sabbath or some high day. Dean Plumptre suggests that, lost among that praying crowd, were, "we may well believe, the aged Simeon (ch. ii. 25) and Anna the prophetess (ch. ii. 36), and many others who waited for redemption in Jerusalem."

Ver. 11.—**And there appeared unto him an angel of the Lord.** Critics have especially found grave fault with this "Hebrew" portion of our Gospel, complaining that it needlessly introduces the marvellous, and brings uselessly into everyday life beings from another sphere. Godet well answers these criticisms by observing "that as Christianity was an entirely new beginning in history, the second and final creation of man, it was natural that an interposition on so grand a scale should be accompanied by a series of particular interpositions. It was even necessary; for how were the representatives of the ancient order of things, who had to co-operate in the new work, to be initiated into it, and their attachment won to it, except by this means? According to Scripture, we are surrounded by angels (2 Kings vi. 17; Ps. xxxiv. 7), whom God employs to watch over us; but in our ordinary condition we want the sense necessary to perceive their presence—for that condition a peculiar receptivity is required. This condition was given to Zacharias. Origen ('Contra Celsum') writes how, "in a church there are two assemblies—one of angels, the other of men, . . . angels are present at our prayers, and they pray with us and for us." **Standing on the right side of the altar of incense.** The angel stood between the altar and the shew-bread table. On entering the holy place, the officiating priest would have on his right the table with the shew-bread, on his left the great candlestick, and before him would be the golden altar, which stood at the end of the holy place, in front of the veil which separated this chamber and the dim, silent holy of holies.

Ver. 12.—**He was troubled.** This was ever the first effect produced by the sight of a spirit-visitant.

Ver. 13.—**Thy prayer is heard.** What was the nature of this prayer? The Greek word (δέησις) used here implies that some *special* supplication had been offered, and which the angel tells had been listened to at the throne of grace. The righteous old man had not, as some have thought, been praying for a son,—he had long resigned himself in this private sorrow to the will of his God; but we may well suppose that on that solemn occasion he prayed the unselfish patriotic prayer that the long looked-for Messiah would hasten his coming. **His name John;** the shortened form for *Jehochanan,* "the grace of Jehovah." Under various diminutives, such as Jonah, it was a favourite Hebrew name.

Ver. 14.—**Many shall rejoice at his birth.** The gladness which his boy's birth was to bring with it was to be no mere private family rejoicing. The child of his old age, who was to be born, would be the occasion of a true national joy.

Ver. 15.—Great in the sight of the Lord.
To the pious old Jewish priest the strange
visitant's words would bear a deep signification. Zacharias would quickly catch the
angel's thoughts. His son was not to be the
Messiah of the people's hope, but was to be
like one of those great ones loved of God,
of whom the women of Israel sang on their
solemn feast-days—one like Samson, only
purer, or Samuel, or the yet greater Elijah.
Could all this deep joy be true? **Shall
drink neither wine.** The old curse then as
now. God's heroes must be free from even
the semblance of temptation. They must
stamp their high lives, from the beginning,
by the solemn vow of self-denial and abstinence. It is remarkable how many of the
great deliverers and teachers of the chosen
people were commanded from childhood to
enrol themselves among the abstainers from
all strong drink. **Nor strong drink.** The
word σίκερα includes all kinds of fermented
drink except that made from the grape; it
was especially applied to *palm* wine.

**Ver. 16.—And many of the children of
Israel shall he turn to the Lord their God.**
The state of the people at this period was
indeed unhappy. The dominant Italian
power had introduced into Syria and Palestine the vices and profligate life of Italy
and Greece. The great Syrian city Antioch,
for instance, in vice and sensuality, had gone
far beyond her conqueror, and was perhaps
at that time the most wicked city in the
world. In the court of Herod, patriotism
and true nobility were dead. The priests
and scribes were for the most part deeply
corrupted, and the poor shepherdless common folk only too readily followed the
example of the rich and great. The boy
who was to be born was to be a great
preacher of righteousness; his glorious mission would be to turn many of these poor
wanderers to the Lord their God.

Ver. 17.—In the spirit and power of Elias.
There was a confident hope among the Jews,
dating from the days of the prophecy of
Malachi, some four hundred years before
the vision of Zacharias, that the days of
Messiah would be heralded by an appearance of the Prophet Elijah. The selfsame
expectation is still cherished by every pious
Jew. **To turn the hearts of the fathers to
the children, and the disobedient to the
wisdom of the just.** The usual explanation
of these words of the angel, who uses here
the language of Malachi (iv. 5, 6), is that
the result of the preaching of this new
prophet, who is about to be raised up, will
be to restore harmony to the broken and
disturbed family life of Israel, whereas now
the home life of the chosen race was split
up—the fathers, perhaps, siding with the
foreign or Roman faction, as represented by

Herod and his friends; the sons, on the other
hand, being Zealots attached to the national
party, bitterly hostile to the Herodians.
So also in one house some would belong to
the Pharisee, others to the Sadducee, sect.
These fatal divisions would, in many cases,
be healed by the influence of the coming
one. There is, however, another interpretation far deeper and more satisfactory; for
nothing in the preaching of the Baptist, as
far as we are aware, bore specially on the
domestic dissensions of the people; it had
a much wider range. The true sense of the
angel's words here should be gathered from
prophetic passages such as Isa. xxix. 22, 23,
"Jacob shall no more be ashamed, neither
shall his face wax pale, when he seeth (כִּ
בִרְאֹתוֹ) his children become the work of my
hands;" Isa. lxiii. 16, "Doubtless thou art
our Father, though Abraham be ignorant of
us, and Israel acknowledge us not: thou,
O Lord, art our Father, our Redeemer!"—
The patriarchs, the fathers of Israel, beholding from their abodes of rest the works and
days of their degenerate children, mourned
over their fall, and, to use earthly language,
"were ashamed" of the conduct of their
unworthy descendants. *These* would be
glad and rejoice over the result of the
preaching of the coming prophet. Godet
well sums up the angel's words: "It will be
John's mission then to reconstitute the
moral unity of the people by restoring the
broken relation between the patriarchs and
their degenerate descendants."

**Ver. 18.—Whereby shall I know this?
for I am an old man.** There was something
evidently blamable in this hesitation on
the part of Zacharias to receive the angel's
promise. It seems as though the radiant
glory of the messenger, as he stood before
the curtain of the silent sanctuary in his
awful beauty, ought to have convinced the
doubting old man of the truth of the strange
message. The words of the angel, which
follow, seem to imply this. What! do you
doubt my message? "I am Gabriel, who
stand in the presence of the Eternal."
Others in Old Testament story before—for
instance, Abraham (Gen. xv.) and Gideon
(Judg. vi.)—had seen and listened to an
angel, had at first doubted, but had received
in consequence no rebuke, no punishment,
for their want of faith. Zacharias was,
however, condemned, we learn, to a long
period of dumbness.

Ver. 19.—I am Gabriel. The meaning of
the name *Gabriel* is "Hero of God," or
"Mighty One of God." In the canonical
books only two of the heavenly ones are
mentioned by *name*. Gabriel (here and
Dan. viii. 16 and ix. 21) and *Michael*,
which signifies "Who is like God" (Jude
9; Rev. xii. 7; and in Dan. x. 13, 21;

xii. 1). Of these two blessed spirits whose names are revealed to us in the Word of God, their appointed work seems to be in connection with the human race and its enemies. *Gabriel* is the special messenger of good news. He comes to Daniel, and tells him of the restoration of Jerusalem; to Zacharias, and announces the birth of his son, and declares what his glorious office would consist in; to Mary of Nazareth, and foretells the nativity. *Michael*, on the other hand, appears as the warrior of God. In the Book of Daniel he wars with the enemies of the people of the Lord; in Jude and in the Revelation of St. John he is the victorious antagonist of Satan the enemy of the Eternal. The Jews have a striking saying that Gabriel flies with two wings, but Michael with only one; so God is swift in sending angels of peace and of joy, of which blessed company the archangel Gabriel is the representative, while the messengers of his wrath and punishment, among whom Michael holds a chief place, come slowly. **That stand in the presence of God.**

"One of the seven
Who in God's presence, nearest to his throne,
Stand ready at command, and are his eyes
That run through all the heavens, and down
    to the earth
Bear his swift commands, over moist and dry,
O'er sea and land."
('Paradise Lost,' iii. 650.)

Milton derived his knowledge of the *seven* from the apocryphal Book of Tobit, where in ch. xii. 15 we read, "I am Raphael, one of the *seven* holy angels, which present the prayers of the saints, and which go in and out before the glory of the Holy One." In the very ancient Book of Enoch we read of the names of the four great archangels, Michael, Gabriel, Uriel, and Raphael.

Ver. 21.—And the people waited for Zacharias, and marvelled that he tarried so long in the temple. The Talmud tells us that even the high priest did not tarry long in the holy of holies on the Day of Atonement. The same feeling of holy awe would induce the ministering priest of the day to perform his functions with no unnecessary delay, and to leave as soon as possible the holy place. The people praying in the court without were in the habit of waiting until the priest on duty came out of the sacred inner chamber, after which they were dismissed with the blessing. The unusual delay in the appearance of Zacharias puzzled and disturbed the worshippers.

Ver. 22.—When he came out, he could not speak unto them; and they perceived that he had seen a vision in the temple. Something in the face of the old man, as, unable to speak, he made signs to the con-gregation, told the awestruck people that the long delay and the loss of speech were owing to no sudden illness which had seized Zacharias. We know that, in the old days of the desert wanderings, the children of Israel could not bear to look on the face of Moses when he came down from the mount after dwelling for a brief space in the light of the glory of the Eternal. Zacharias had been face to face with one whose blessed lot it was to stand for ever in the presence of God. We may well suppose that there lingered on the old man's face, as he left the sanctuary, *something* which told the beholder of the presence just left.

Ver. 24.—And after those days his wife Elisabeth conceived, and hid herself five months. Various reasons have been suggested for this retirement. It seems most probable that, amazed at the angelic announcement, the saintly woman went into perfect retirement and isolation for a considerable period, to prove well the words of the angel, and to consider how she best could do *her* part in the training of the expected child, who was to play so mighty a part in the history of her people.

Vers. 26—38.—*The annunciation of the Virgin Mary.* The recital contained in this little section is peculiar to this Gospel of St. Luke. It lay outside what may be termed the apostolic tradition. It neither helps nor mars the moral or dogmatic teaching of the men trained in the school of Jesus of Nazareth. It simply answers a question that probably few of the converts of the first quarter of a century which succeeded the Resurrection morning cared to ask.

We do not suppose that the true story of the birth of Jesus Christ was any secret, any precious *mystery* in the Church of the first days. It was known doubtless to the leading teachers, known to many of their hearers, but it was evidently unused as a popular text for preaching. It probably was not among those "memoirs" of the apostles which were read and expounded in the first forty years in the public synagogues and in the quiet upper rooms of so many of the cities of Syria, and in not a few of the towns of Egypt, Greece, and Italy. Nor is the reason of this doubtful; the wondrous story of the child Jesus' birth would add little to the simple faith of the first believers in the Crucified.

Of miracles and works of wonder they had heard enough to convince them that, if these were true, surely never man had worked like this Man. They had heard, too, of the crowning sign of the Resurrection. There were men in those first days, scattered abroad in all lands, who had *seen* these things, who knew that the Master had died on the cross, and who had seen him, touched him, and spoken to him *after* his resurrection. The mysterious miracle of the incarnation was not needed for the preaching of the first days.

But time went on, and naturally enough many of the thoughtful cultured men who had accepted the doctrine of the cross began to say—We ought to have the true story of the beginnings of these marvellous events authoritatively written down. Here and there we have heard something of the birth and childhood, why have we not the details authenticated? Men like Paul and Luke felt that such natural questionings should be answered. And hence it came to pass that, moved by the Holy Spirit—under, we believe, the direction of Paul—Luke went to the fountainhead, to the blessed mother herself, to those holy women some of whom we believe had borne her company from the beginning, and from her lips and their lips wrote down what she (or they) dictated, partly from memory, partly perhaps from memoranda which she and others had kept of that strange sweet time; and so these two chapters of the Third Gospel, of which the incarnation is the central narrative, were written down much in the original form in which Luke received it, the Greek simply translating the original Hebrew story. Around the words of the Gospel soon gathered a host of miraculous legends glorifying the blessed mother of the Lord. These are utterly unknown to Scripture, and should be quietly put aside. Strange speculations respecting her and the manner of the wondrous birth have been in all times, nay, still are favourite subjects of dispute among theologians. It is a pity to try and be wise beyond what is written. The believer will content himself with just receiving the quiet story of the holy maid as Mary the mother gave it to Luke or Paul, feeling assured that the same power of the Highest by which the crucified Jesus was raised from the tomb where he had lain for three days, was able to overshadow the virgin of Naza-

reth, was able to cause to be born of her that holy thing which was called the Son of God.

Ver. 26.—**And in the sixth month;** that is, after the vision of Zacharias in the temple. **Unto a city of Galilee, named Nazareth.** These explanatory notes make it clear that St. Luke was writing for those who were strangers to Palestine. Such details were no doubt added by St. Luke to the oral or written Hebrew narrative upon which this section is entirely based. Under the Roman domination the land of promise was divided into Judæa, Samaria, Peræa, and Galilee. Galilee was the northern department, and comprised the old territory of the tribes of Zebulun, Naphtali, and Asher. From Josephus we learn that at this period the northern division was rich and populous, and covered with flourishing towns. Nazareth, which still exists as a large village of some three thousand inhabitants, under the name of *En-Nazirah*, is about twenty-four miles to the east of the Lake of Tiberias. It is well situate in a valley among the hills which rise to the north of the Esdraelon plain. From one of the grassy slopes which rise behind Nazareth, one of the noblest views is obtained. The snowy summits of Lebanon and Hermon close the prospect on the north; on the south the broad Esdraelon plain, with the mountains of Ephraim; Gilead and Tabor lie on the east; on the other side, the green uplands of Carmel are bathed by the blue waves of the Mediterranean Sea. The meaning of the name *Nazareth* has been the subject of much learned controversy. The more usually adopted derivation, however, refers the word to נצר, "a shoot or branch," which conveys, as Dean Plumptre remarks, something of the same meaning as our *hurst* or *holm* in English topography. Burckhardt, the traveller, believes the name was originally used on account of the numerous shrubs which cover the ground in this locality.

Ver. 27.—**To a virgin espoused to a man whose name was Joseph, of the house of David;** more accurately, *betrothed.* The formal ceremony of betrothal took place among the Jews in most cases a year prior to the marriage. The question has arisen whether the words, "of the house of David," refer to Joseph or to Mary. *Grammatically,* they would seem to belong to Joseph; but the fact of the Gospel being here so closely translated from a Hebrew (Aramaic) original, prevents us from laying down any strict linguistic rules which belong to the Greek language. "Who was Mary the virgin?" has been often asked. Vers. 32 and 69 would lose their point altogether unless we regard Luke as being persuaded that the young

Hebrew girl was a descendant of David. In respect to the virgin's family, we read that she was a cousin or kinswoman of Elisabeth. This would at least ally her closely to the priestly race. Dean Plumptre quotes one out of the many ancient apocryphal legends current respecting Mary of Nazareth, deeming it worthy of mention as having left its impress on Christian art. " The name of the virgin's mother was Anne. Mary surpassed the maidens of her own age in wisdom. There were many who early sought her in marriage. The suitors agreed to decide their claims by laying their rods before the holy place, and seeing which budded. It was thus that Joseph became betrothed to her." The same scholar adds, " The absence of any mention of her parents in the Gospels suggests the thought that she was an orphan, and the whole narrative of the nativity presupposes poverty! The name Mary is the same as *Miriam* or *Marah*." (On the question of the genealogy recorded by St. Luke, see note on ch. iii. 23.)

Ver. 28.—**Hail, thou that art highly favoured.** The *plena gratiâ* of the Vulgate, said and sung so often in the virgin's famous hymn, is an inaccurate rendering. Rather, "gratiâ *cumulata*," as it has been well rendered. "Having been much graced (by God)" is the literal translation of the Greek word. **Blessed art thou among women.** These words must be struck out; they do not exist in the older authorities.

Ver. 29.—**She was troubled;** more accurately, *she was greatly troubled.* Different to Zacharias, who evidently doubted in the mission of the angel, and who required some sign before he could believe, Mary simply wondered at the strangeness of what was about to happen. Her terror at the sudden appearance of the angel, who probably appeared to her as a young man clad in garments of a strange dazzling whiteness, is most natural.

Ver. 31.—**JESUS;** the ordinary Greek form, the well-known Hebrew *Jehoshua*, the shortened *Joshua*, "The Salvation of Jehovah."

Ver. 32.—**The Son of the Highest.** It is singular that this title, given by the angel to the yet unborn child, was the one given to the Redeemer by the evil spirit in the case of the poor possessed (see Mark v. 7). Is this the title, or one of the titles, by which our Master is known in that greater world beyond our knowledge? **The throne of his father David;** clearly indicating that Mary herself was of royal lineage, although this is nowhere definitely stated (see Ps. cxxxii. 11). These words of the angel are as yet unfulfilled. They clearly speak of a restoration of Israel, still, as far as we can see, very distant. Nearly nineteen centuries have passed since Gabriel spoke of a restored

throne of David, of a kingdom in Jacob to which should come no end. The people, through all the changing fortune of empires, have been indeed strangely kept distinct and separate, ready for the mighty change; but the eventful hour still tarries. It has been well observed how St. Luke's report of the angel's words here could never have been a forgery—as one school of critics asserts—of the second century. Would any writer in the second century, after the failure of Jesus among the Jews was well known, when the fall of Jerusalem had already taken place, have made an angel prophesy what is expressed here?

Ver. 35.—**The Holy Ghost shall come upon thee, and the power of the Highest shall overshadow thee.** Again the angel makes use of the term "Highest" when alluding to the eternal Father. The expression of Gabriel, "the power of the Highest shall overshadow thee," reminds us of the opening words of Genesis, where the writer describes the dawn of life in creation in the words, "The Spirit of God moved [or, 'brooded'] over the face of the deep." "The Word was conceived in the womb of a woman, not after the manner of men, but by the singular, powerful, invisible, immediate operation of the Holy Ghost, whereby a virgin was, beyond the law of nature, enabled to conceive, and that which was conceived in her was originally and completely sanctified" (art. iii., Bishop Pearson on the Creed).

Ver. 38.—**Behold the handmaid of the Lord; be it unto me according to thy word.** "God's message," writes Godet, " by the mouth of the angel was not a command. The part Mary had to fulfil made no demands on her. It only remained, therefore, for Mary to consent to the consequences of the Divine offer. She gives this consent in a word at once simple and sublime, which involved the most extraordinary act of faith that a woman ever consented to accomplish. Mary accepts the sacrifice of that which is dearer to a young maiden than her very life, and thereby becomes pre-eminently the heroine of Israel, the ideal daughter of Zion." Nor was the *immediate* trouble and sorrow which she foresaw would soon compass her round by any means the whole burden which submission to the angel's message would bring upon the shrinking Nazareth maiden. The lot proposed to her would bring probably in its wake unknown sufferings as well as untold blessedness. We may with all reverence think Mary already feeling the first piercings in her heart of that sharp sword which was one day to wound so deeply the mother of sorrows; yet in spite of all this, in full view of the present woe, which submission to the Divine will would forthwith bring upon her, with an unknown future of sorrow in the background, Mary submitted herself of her own free will to what she felt was the will and wish of her God.

Ver. 39.—**Mary arose in those days, and went into the hill country with haste.** Between the annunciation and this journey of Mary to visit her cousin Elisabeth, we must interpose the events narrated in St. Matthew's Gospel, viz. the natural suspicion of her betrothed future husband, Joseph; his action in the matter; and then the dream of Joseph, in which her innocence was vindicated. As we believe that St. Luke's story here was derived from Mary's own narrative, we can understand well that these details, related by St. Matthew, were scarcely touched upon, and the mother would hurry on to the real points of interest in that eventful past of hers. The hill country here alluded to is the elevated district of Judah, Benjamin, and Mount Ephraim, in contradistinction to the low maritime plain on the east—the old Philistia. **Into a city of Juda.** There is no such city known as "Juda." Some have supposed that the text is corrupt here, and that for "Yuda" we should read "Jutta," which, according to Josh. xv. 55, was a priestly city in the hill country. There is a rabbinical tradition in the Talmud which places the residence of Zacharias at Hebron. It is very probable that Hebron, the great priestly city, is here signified.

Ver. 41.—**Elisabeth was filled with the Holy Ghost.** The Holy Spirit—that Spirit of prophecy, so often mentioned in the Old Testament—seizes her, and she salutes her young kinswoman, Mary, as the mother of the coming Messiah.

Ver. 42.—**And she spake out with a loud voice, and said, Blessed art thou among women** (see Judg. v. 24). The words which clothed the thoughts in these ecstatic expressions of intense joy and thankfulness on the part of the two favoured women, Mary and Elisabeth, are in great measure drawn from hymn and song contained in the Old Testament Scriptures. The song of Hannah, the hymn of Deborah, many of the psalms, the songs of the Canticles, the more glorious of the prophetic utterances, had been ever familiar to both these true women of the people; and they could find no language so fitting as the words of these loved national songs to express the intense joy, the deep awe and gratitude of their hearts. Think what must have been the feeling of the two— the one finding herself the chosen out of all the thousands of Israel, after so many centuries of weary waiting, to be the mother of the Messiah; the other, long after any reasonable hope of any offspring at all had faded away, to be the mother of Messiah's chosen friend, his herald, and his preacher,

the mighty forerunner of the King of whom the prophets had written!

Ver. 43.—**And whence is this to me, that the mother of my Lord should come to me?** But the Holy Ghost (ver. 41) raised Elisabeth's thoughts yet higher. Not only did she bless the mother of the coming Messiah, but the Spirit opened her eyes to see who that coming Messiah really was. Very vague indeed was the conception of the coming Messiah in Israel. The truth was, perhaps, revealed, and in rapt moments received by men like Isaiah and Ezekiel; and now and again men like David; Daniel wrote down visions and revelations respecting the Coming One, the true purport of which vision they scarcely grasped. Generally the Messianic idea among the people pictured a hero greater than Saul, a conqueror more successful than David, a sovereign more magnificent than Solomon. They pictured ever the glorious arm sustaining the coming Hero-King; but few, if any, dreamed of the "glorious arm" belonging to their future Deliverer. But here the Spirit in a moment revealed to the happy wife of the priest Zacharias that the Babe to be born of her young kinswoman was not only the promised Messiah, but was the awful Son of the Highest! Think, reader, what these simple words we are considering signify! Why am I so favoured "that the mother of my Lord should come to me"? "The contrast leaves no room for doubt," well argues Dean Plumptre, "that she used the word 'Lord' in its highest sense. 'Great' as her own son was to be (ver. 15) in the sight of the Lord, here was the mother of One yet greater, even of the Lord himself."

Vers. 46—56.—*The hymn of Mary, commonly called the Magnificat.*

Ver. 46a.—**And Mary said.** There is a great contrast between the behaviour of the two women when they met in Elisabeth's house. The elder was full of a new strange ecstatic joy. "She was filled with the Holy Ghost" (ver. 41), and spoke her words of lofty congratulation with "a loud voice" (ver. 42). *Mary*, on the other hand, was not conscious evidently, on this occasion, of any *special* presence of the Holy Spirit. Since the hour of the annunciation and her own meek faithful acceptance of the Lord's purpose, she had been dwelling, so to speak, under the immediate influence of the Spirit of the Lord. *Her cousin's* inspiration seems to have been *momentary and transitory,* while *hers*, during that strange blessed season which immediately preceded the Incarnation, was *enduring.* Hence the quiet introduction to her hymn, "And Mary said." It is, of course, *possible* that she had committed the beautiful thoughts to writing; but perhaps, in giving them to Luke or

Paul, she needed no parchment scroll, but softly repeated to the chronicler of the Divine story the old song in which she had first told her deep imaginings to Elisabeth, and afterwards often had murmured the same bright words of joy and faith over the holy Babe as he lay in his cradle at Bethlehem, in Egypt, or in Nazareth. The "Virgin's Hymn" for nearly fourteen centuries has been used in the public liturgies of Christendom. We find it first in the office of Lauds in the Rule of St. Cæsarius of Arles (A.D. 507).

Vers. 46b—48.—**My soul doth magnify the Lord, and my spirit hath rejoiced in God my Saviour. For he hath regarded the low estate of his handmaiden: for, behold, from henceforth all generations shall call me blessed.** This is the first of the four divisions of the Magnificat. In it she speaks of *herself*, and her deep feelings of adoration and of holy joy, and of intense glad surprise. It is a prayer, but the highest kind of prayer, for it asks for nothing—it simply breathes adoration and thankfulness. We may imagine the angels praying thus. They have all that created beings, however exalted, can desire in the beatific vision which they perpetually enjoy; and yet they pray continually, but only after *this* manner. The joy of her spirit, notice, is based on the fact of the revelation that he, *God*, was, too, *her* Saviour; and, of course, not *hers only*: her great joy was in the thought of the salvation of the suffering, sinning world around her. Then she passes into simple wonderment that she should have been chosen as the instrument of the boundless goodness of God. She had nothing to recommend her only her low estate. Though royally descended, she only occupied a position among the humblest Hebrew maidens, and yet, owing to God's favour, she will be deemed blessed by countless unborn generations.

Vers. 49, 50.—**For he that is mighty hath done to me great things; and holy is his Name. And his mercy is on them that fear him from generation to generation.** In this strophe, the second division of the hymn of praise, she glorifies three of the principal Divine attributes—God's power, his holiness, and his mercy. His *power* or might, alluding to the words of the angel (ver. 35), "The power of the Highest shall overshadow thee." Surely in all the records of the Lord's works since the world's creation, his might had been never shown as it was now about to be manifest in her. His *holiness* had been displayed to her in the way in which the mighty acts of ineffable love had been carried out. His *mercy*: this attribute of God came home with intense power to the heart of the Jewish girl, into which God's protecting Spirit was shining with so clear a light. She saw something of the great redemption mystery which was then in so strange a way developing itself.

Vers. 51—53.—**He hath showed strength with his arm; he hath scattered the proud in the imagination of their hearts. He hath put down the mighty from their seats, and exalted them of low degree. He hath filled the hungry with good things; and the rich he hath sent empty away.** From adoration, Mary's hymn proceeds to celebrate the mighty results effected by the Divine pity. As so often in these prophetic strains, the speaker or writer speaks or writes as though the future had become the past; so Mary here describes the Messianic reversal of man's conception of what is great and little, as though the unborn Babe had already lived and done his strange mighty work in the world. The "glorious arm" which, in old days, had wrought such mighty things for Israel, she recognized as belonging to the coming Deliverer (ver. 51). His chosen instruments would be those of whom the world thought little, like herself. The proud and mighty would be put down; the men of low degree, and poor and humble, would be exalted. The hungry would be filled; and they who were rich only in this world's goods would have no share in the new kingdom—they would be sent empty away. How strangely had the virgin of Nazareth caught the thought, almost the very words, of the famous sermon her Divine Son, some thirty years later, preached on the mountain-side near Gennesaret!

Vers. 54, 55.—**He hath holpen his servant Israel, in remembrance of his mercy; as he spake to our fathers, to Abraham, and to his seed for ever.** Her hymn dies down into a strain of gratitude for the eternal faithfulness to the cause of the chosen people. Had not God in very truth remembered his ancient promise? From one of their daughters, still speaking of the future as of the past, Messiah had been born—a greater Deliverer, too, than the most sanguine Hebrew patriot had ever dreamed of.

Vers. 57—80.—*John, afterwards called the Baptist, the son of Zacharias and Elisabeth, is born. The Benedictus.*

Ver. 58.—**How the Lord had showed great mercy upon her.** No doubt the vision of Zacharias in the temple, and his subsequent dumbness, had excited no little inquiry. That the reproach of Elisabeth should be taken away, no doubt few really believed. The birth of her son, however, set a seal upon the reality of the priest's vision. The rejoicings of her family were due to more than the birth of her boy. The story of the angel's message, coupled with the unusual birth, set men thinking and asking what then would be the destiny of this child. Could it be that he was the promised Messiah?

Ver. 59.—On the eighth day they came to circumcise the child. This was always, among the Hebrew people, a solemn day of rejoicing; it resembled in some particulars our baptismal gatherings. Relatives were invited to be present, as witnesses that the child had been formally incorporated into the covenant. It was, too, the time when the name which the newly born was to bear through life was given him.

Ver. 60.—Not so; but he shall be called John. It is clear (from ver. 62) that the old priest was afflicted with deafness as well as with dumbness. At the naming ceremony, the stricken Zacharias, who was patiently awaiting the hour when his God should restore to him his lost powers, made no effort to express his will. He had already in the past months, no doubt, written down for Elisabeth the name of the boy that was to be born. She interrupts the ceremony with her wishes. The guests are surprised, and make signs to the father. He at once writes on his tablets, "His name is John." The name had been already given. The word "John" signifies "the grace of Jehovah."

Ver. 63.—A writing-table; better, *a writing-tablet.* The tablets in use generally at the time were usually made of wood, covered with a thin coating of wax; on the soft layer of wax the words were written with an iron stylus.

Ver. 64.—And his mouth was opened immediately, and his tongue loosed, and he spake, and praised God. This, the first hour of his recovered power, was without doubt the occasion of his giving utterance to the inspired hymn (the Benedictus) which is recorded at length a few verses further on (vers. 68—79). It was the outcome, no doubt, of his silent communing with the Spirit during the long months of his affliction.

Ver. 65.—And fear came on all that dwelt round about them: and all these sayings were noised abroad throughout all the hill country of Judæa. The inspired utterance of the old priest, so long dumb, in his beautiful hymn of praise, completed as it were the strange cycle of strange events which had happened in the priestly family.

Ver. 66.—And the hand of the Lord was with him. This kind of pause in the history is one of the peculiarities of St. Luke's style. We meet with it several times in the gospel story and in the history of the Acts. They are vivid pictures in a few words of what happened to an individual, to a family, or to a cause, during often a long course of years. Here the story of the childhood of the

great pioneer of Christ is briefly sketched out; in it all, and through it all, there was one guiding hand—the Lord's. The expression, "hand of the Lord," was peculiarly a Hebrew thought—one of the vivid anthropomorphic idioms which, as has been aptly remarked, they could use more boldly than other nations, because they had clearer thoughts of God as not made after the similitude of men (Deut. iv. 12). Maimonides, the great Jewish writer of the twelfth century, in his 'Yad Hachazakah,' says, "*And there was under his feet* (Exod. xxiv. 10); *written with the finger of God* (Exod. xxxi. 18); *the hand of the Lord* (Exod. ix. 3); *the eyes of the Lord* (Deut. xi. 12); *the ears of the Lord* (Numb. xi. 18). All these are used with reference to the intellectual capacity of the sons of men, who can comprehend only corporeal beings; so that the Law spoke in the language of the sons of men, and all these are expressions merely, just as, *If I whet my glittering sword* (Deut. xxxii. 41); for has he, then, a sword? or does he slay with a sword? Certainly not: this is only a figure; and thus all are figures" ('Yad,' ch. i. 8).

Ver. 67.—His father Zacharias was filled with the Holy Ghost, and prophesied, saying. The inspired hymn which follows—thought out, no doubt, with the Holy Spirit's help in the course of the long enforced seclusion which his first want of faith had brought upon him—holds a prominent place in all Western liturgies. Like the Magnificat, it is believed to have been first introduced into the public worship of the Church about the middle of the sixth century by St. Cæsarius of Arles. It may be briefly summarized as a thanksgiving for the arrival of the times of Messiah.

Vers. 68, 69.—He hath visited and redeemed, . . . and hath raised up. The tenses of the verbs used in these expressions show that in Zacharias's mind, when he uttered the words of his hymn, the Incarnation, and the glorious deliverance commenced in that stupendous act of mercy, belonged to the past. *He hath visited;* that is, after some four hundred years of silence and absence, the Holy One of Israel had again come to his people. About four centuries had passed since the voice of Malachi, the last of the prophets, had been heard. **An horn of salvation.** A metaphor not unknown in classical writings (see Ovid, 'Art. Am.,' i. 239; Hor., 'Od.,' iii. xxi. 18), and a much-used figure in Hebrew literature (see, among other passages, Ezek. xxix. 21; Lam. ii. 3; Ps. cxxxii. 17; 1 Sam. ii. 10). The reference is not to the horns of the altar, on which criminals seeking sanctuary used to lay hold; nor to the horns with which warriors used to adorn their helmets; but to the horns of a bull—in which the chief power of this animal resides. This was a figure especially familiar among an agricultural folk like the Israelites. "A rabbinic writer says that there are ten horns—those of Abraham, Isaac, Jacob, Joseph, Moses, the horn of the Law, of the priesthood, of the temple, and of Israel, and some add of the Messiah. They were all placed on the heads of the Israelites till they sinned, and then they were cut off and given to the Gentiles" (Schöttgen, 'Hor. Hebr.,' quoted by Dr. Farrar). **In the house of his servant David.** Clearly Zacharias looked on Mary, as the angel had done (ver. 32), as belonging to the royal house of David.

Ver. 70.—**By the mouth of his holy prophets.** Zacharias looked on all that was then happening as clearly foretold in those sacred prophetic writings preserved in the nation with so much care and reverence. **Which have been since the world began.** He considered Messianic prophecy as dating from the first intimation after the fall in Eden (Gen. iii. 15), and continuing in an intermittent but yet unbroken line from Genesis to Malachi.

Ver. 71.—**That we should be saved from our enemies, and from the hand of all that hate us.** When Zacharias spoke these words, his mind, no doubt, was on Rome and its creatures, Herod and his party, whom Rome had set up. The deliverance of Israel, in every Hebrew heart, was the first and great work of the coming Deliverer; but the inspired words had a far broader reference than to Rome, and the enemies of Israelitic prosperity. The expression includes those spiritual evil agencies which war their ceaseless warfare against the soul of man. It was from *these* that the coming Deliverer would free his people. It was only after the fall of Jerusalem, and the total extinction of the national existence of the people, that, to use Dean Plumptre's language, "what was transitory in the hymn vanished, and the words gained the brighter permanent sense which they have had for centuries in the worship of the Church of Christ."

Vers. 74, 75.—**Might serve him without fear, in holiness and righteousness before him, all the days of our life.** What Zacharias looked on to was a glorious theocracy based upon national holiness. Israel, freed from foreign oppression and internal dissensions, would serve God with a worship at once uninterrupted and undefiled.

Ver. 76.—**And thou, child;** literally, *little child.* Here the father breaks forth into an expression of gladness at the thought of the great part his baby-son was to bear in this great national deliverance. His son, too—

oh, joy undreamed of!—is to be ranked among the glorious company of the prophets of the Highest.

Ver. 77.—**To give knowledge of salvation unto his people by the remission of their sins.** Zacharias goes on to celebrate the splendid part his son was to play in the great Messianic drama. He was to be Messiah's pioneer in order to give men the true information respecting the Deliverer's work. Israel was mistaken altogether in its conception of the salvation which they really needed. Godet puts it with great force. "Why," he asks, "was the ministry of the Messiah preceded by that of another Divine messenger? Because the very notion of salvation was falsified in Israel, and had to be corrected before salvation could be realized. A carnal and malignant patriotism had taken possession of the people and their rulers, and the idea of a political deliverance had been substituted for that of a moral salvation. There was need, then, of another person, divinely authorized, to remind the people that perdition consisted not in subjection to the Romans, but in Divine condemnation; and that salvation, therefore, was not temporal emancipation, but forgiveness of sins."

Ver. 78.—**Through the tender mercy of our God.** And, goes on Zacharias in his noble hymn, all this tender care for Israel (but really for mankind, though perhaps the speaker of the hymn scarcely guessed it) is owing to the deep love of God. **Whereby the Dayspring from on high hath visited us.** The beautiful imagery here is derived from the magnificence of an Eastern sunrise. In his temple service at Jerusalem the priest must have seen the ruddy dawn rise grandly over the dark chain of the distant mountains, and lighting up with a blaze of golden glory the everlasting hills as they stood round about Jerusalem. The thought which pictured the advent of Messiah as a sunrise was a favourite one with the prophets. We see it in such prophecies of Isaiah and Malachi as, "Arise, shine; for thy light is come, and the glory of the Lord is risen upon thee. For behold . . . Gentiles shall come to thy light, and kings to the brightness of thy rising" (Isa. lx. 1—3). "Unto you that fear my Name shall the Sun of Righteousness arise with healing in his wings" (Mal. iv. 2).

Ver. 79.—**To give light to them that sit in darkness and in the shadow of death.** It would *seem* that for a moment the Hebrew priest saw beyond the narrow horizon of Israel, and that here, in the close of his glorious song, he caught sight of the distant far-reaching isles of the Gentiles, over which so deep a darkness brooded for ages.

Ver. 80.—**And the child grew, and waxed**

strong in spirit. We have here another of St. Luke's solemn pauses in his narrative —one of those little passages in which, in a few words, he sets before us a picture clear and vivid of the events of long years. "The description," writes Dr. Farrar, "resembles that of the childhood of Samuel (1 Sam. ii. 26) and of our Lord (ch. ii. 40—52). Nothing, however, is said of 'favour with men.' In the case of the Baptist, as of others, 'the boy was father to the man;' and he probably showed from the first that rugged sternness which is wholly unlike the winning grace of the child Christ. '*The Baptist was no lamb of God. He was a wrestler with life, one to whom peace does not come easily, but only after a long struggle. His restlessness had driven him into the desert, where he had contended for years with thoughts he could not master, and from whence he uttered his startling alarms to the nation. He was among the dogs rather than among the lambs of the Shepherd*' ('Ecce Homo')." **And was in the deserts till the day of his showing unto Israel.** "The deserts" here alluded to were that desolate waste country south of Jericho and along the shores of the Dead Sea. We know nothing of the details of the life of the boy, the wonderful circumstances of whose birth are related so circumstantially in this opening chapter of St. Luke's Gospel. Mary, whose "memories," we believe, are recounted almost in her own words, was herself a witness of some of the circumstances narrated; from her friend and cousin Elisabeth she doubtless received the true history of the rest. But Zacharias and Elisabeth, we know, were aged persons when John was born. They probably lived only a short time after his birth. Hence his solitary desert life. Of it we know nothing. In those wild regions at that time dwelt many grave ascetics and hermit teachers, like the Pharisee Banus, the master of Josephus. From some of these the orphan boy probably received his training. It is clear, from such passages as John i. 31—33 and ch. iii. 2, that some direct communication from the Highest put an end to the ascetic desert life and study. Some theophany, perhaps, like the appearance of the burning bush which called Moses to his great post, summoned the pioneer of Christ to his dangerous and difficult work. But we possess no account of what took place on this occasion when God *spoke* to his servant John, the evangelist simply recording the fact, "The word of God came unto the son of Zacharias in the wilderness" (ch. iii. 2).

HOMILETICS.

Vers. 1—4.—*Preface to the Gospel.* Observe—

I. THE AUTHOR'S APOLOGY. How conspicuous in it are the elements of candour, simplicity, and earnestness! The first authorities as to the things related were "the eye-witnesses and ministers of the Word." He is careful to intimate that he is not one of them; not an apostle; not even one of the seventy, as some have supposed he was. The position which he assumes is simply this: Many had taken in hand to draw up "a narrative concerning those matters which had been fulfilled among them;" and he too felt constrained to place on record all the information which he possessed. And his claim to be heard is the painstaking which he has brought to the task, the desire to trace the course of the wonderful history with perfect accuracy. Can we fail to note the absence of all self-assertion? Pretentiousness of all kinds is abhorrent to the mind which is "of the truth." Especially when it contemplates the "holy glory" of Jesus, it is like the friend of the bridegroom, who rejoices greatly to hear, not his own, but the bridegroom's voice.

II. THE AUTHOR'S AIM. It is to give the sequence of events "accurately from the first." He had enjoyed exceptional advantages, on account of which he was able to relate the things connected with "the beginning" of the life of Christ. And his purpose is to unfold that life in the completeness and beauty of its development. Now, is not this the work of the Christian teacher still? Christianity is Christ. It is not a mere system of doctrines to be believed and of duties to be done; the root and strength of all doctrines and of all duties is the Person of Jesus. And the noblest function of the "minister of the Word" is to show the eternal life which was with the Father, and is manifested in the Son, who for us was incarnate.

III. THE DESIGNATION OF THE ONE WHOM THE AUTHOR ADDRESSES. "Most excellent Theophilus." Probably he had in view a man bearing this name—a man of high station or rank. The superlative employed is the same as that applied in the Book of the Acts to the Roman procurator, and once by Paul himself, when he replied, "I am not mad, most noble Felix." This Theophilus, therefore, may have been distinguished by position. "Not many mighty, not many noble, are called," but some mighty and noble are; and he may have been drawn through the teaching of St. Paul, and may have wished a full account of those things in which he had been catechized. But be this as it may, note the meaning of the name. "To thee, O lover of God, O soul, teachable, humble, desirous to find in Jesus the Way to the Father ; to thee, O hungerer and thirster after righteousness, seeking with pure heart God's gift of the living water ; to thee, O man, O woman, who knowest thyself to be the sinner who needs salvation, and wouldst see the Saviour who receives sinners and eats with them ; to thee, O Israelite indeed, in whom is no guile, this declaration of the gospel of the grace of God is sent! May he who opened the heart of Lydia open thine heart; and through the demonstration of the Spirit, making effectual the exposition of the message, mavest thou have that witness in thyself which is ' the certainty of those things wherein thou hast been instructed '!"

Vers. 5—23.—*Zacharias and his vision.* Notice some features in the sketch that is given of the priest and of that which happened at the altar of incense.

I. IT IS A PICTURE OF THE SOUL WAITING FOR GOD. That waiting which is emphasized in the Old Testament Scriptures as one of the essentials of piety. How beautifully are the words—"More than they that watch for the morning, my soul waiteth for the Lord;" "It is good that a man should both hope and quietly wait for the salvation of the Lord"—illustrated in the life and attitude of Zacharias and Elisabeth! Year on year they had waited in their hillside home, asking the blessing of a son. Apparently the hope had set in heavens that were only brass. But one thing was ever bright and real—their faith in the living God; and they walked in all his commandments and ordinances blameless. "Our wills are ours to make them thine." It is easier to consent to God's will when the demand is to act, than to consent when the demand is simply to wait, to direct our prayer to the Eternal, and look up. One of the lessons which we are slow to learn is, "Walk *humbly* with thy God."

II. THE PASSAGE BEFORE US REVEALS THE HEARER OF PRAYER. (Ver. 13.) "Thy prayer is heard." Was this the prayer for the son? Or was it the priestly prayer, offered at the altar and through the incense, for the hope and salvation of Israel? Both, it may be, are included. For it is noteworthy that in the two scriptural instances of intense longing for a son—that of Hannah and that of Zacharias—the blessing to the individual is associated with blessing to the whole Church of God. The prayer of faith has interconnections with the purpose of God far beyond our power to estimate, and the doing is " exceeding abundantly above all that we ask or think." "Thy prayer is heard;" the answer often looks a great way back. Matthew Henry quaintly says, "Prayers are filed in heaven, and are not forgotten though the thing prayed for is not presently given us. The time as well as the thing is in the answer; and God's gift always transcends the measure of the promise."

III. Again, LET THE FORM OF THE ANSWER RETURNED SPEAK TO US OF THE REALITY OF THE SPIRITUAL WORLD. (Ver. 19.) "The angel answering said unto him, I am Gabriel, that stand in the presence of God : and I was sent to speak unto thee, and to bring thee these good tidings." The same presence as that we meet in the Book of Daniel. Gabriel is the angel for the greatly beloved, the angel with the glad tidings; he who afterwards bore the most wonderful of messages to the Hebrew maiden. Our ideas are very confused as to the holy angels. There can be no doubt that the tendency of thought in our day is to narrow the sphere of the supernatural. Formerly, it dominated over thought and action; the influence of spirits and occult spiritual forces was brought in to account for much that is referable to laws and powers in nature. Nowadays men are occupied in tracing "natural law in the spiritual world." But who can accept the truth of this first chapter of St. Luke's Gospel and doubt as to the reality of a spiritual universe encompassing the material? And if there be such a universe, why should it seem incredible that spiritual presences should, at sundry times, be declared to men—that Gabriels and Michaels should " at God's bidding speed and post o'er land and ocean without rest; " " ministering spirits, sent forth to minister for them who shall be heirs of salvation "? The spiritual mind can have no difficulty as to this. It will recognize in the vision of Zacharias a truth for all. Where there is the praying heart there is " the angel on the right side of the altar of incense."

IV. Finally, THE PUNISHMENT RECORDED IS ONE OF MANY WARNINGS IN SCRIPTURE AGAINST THE UNBELIEF WHICH WOULD LIMIT THE HOLY ONE OF ISRAEL. "How can these things be?" "Whereby I shall know this?" are questions ever rising in the heart. The good priest had waited long. When expectation failed, he bowed his head to God's will. No doubt, one to another, he and his wife, now "well stricken in years," had often recalled the word to Abraham concerning Sarah's laughter, "Is anything too hard for the Lord?" But when the trial actually comes, the faith falters. Cannot we understand this? We limp when we should walk and not be weary. "Thou shalt be silent . . . because thou believedst not." Is not the constant result of unbelief spiritual silence? And the closed heart is followed by the closed lips—"silent . . . and not able to speak." "Lord, increase our faith."

Vers. 26—38.—*The announcement to the Virgin.* Gabriel, "the mighty one of God," or "the man of God," again sent with glad tidings. The work for the great-hearts, for the strongest and best, is the work of preaching the gospel of his grace. The God-sent preacher is he who, like Gabriel, "stands in the presence of God." "He that is now called a prophet was aforetime called a seer." But the true prophet is always a seer. "Sent to a virgin . . . and the virgin's name was Mary." It is significant that so little is said in Holy Scripture as to this one "blessed among women." Nothing is related as to her birth and parentage, as to her gifts of mind and person; it is not even directly asserted that she belonged to the royal stock of David—that is to be implied only from such a verse as the thirty-second. After the Lord, on the cross, solemnly gave her to the care of the beloved disciple, there is only one allusion to her —an allusion in Acts i. There is no reference to her in the Epistles of Paul; none in that of James, certainly nearly related to her; none in those of John, with whom she had lived. St. Luke, speaking of her in connection with the birth, says only, "A virgin espoused to a man whose name was Joseph." "Blessed," cried a woman one day to Jesus, "is she that bare thee!" He did not deny it; but that there might be no distraction of soul, he added, "Yea rather, blessed are they that hear the Word of God, and keep it." This Mary, or Miriam, is blessed among women. The word of the Lord's angel we need not hesitate to utter, "Hail, thou that art highly favoured!" But what is the real beauty of Mary? Is it not that she is in the foremost rank of those on whom the Lord's "yea rather, blessed" rested—that she is pre-eminently the hearer and keeper of the Word of God? The few touches of character which are presented suggest the picture of a rarely lovely nature. (1) Observe the *manner of the faith* which is evoked by Gabriel's message. First, there is the "casting in the mind." The sight is marvellous; the salutation is strange. She is troubled; but instead of any display of excitement or of alarm, there is only the quiet self-possessed casting in the mind. "What could this be? Was it from above? Was it a voice of God or a snare of the devil?" (2) When the birth is announced, there is no such reply as that which fell from Zacharias—no word of scepticism, no demand for a sign. She does not doubt that it shall be; she only inquires how it shall be. (3) And, lastly, when the angel's answer is given, concluded by the assertion, "With God nothing shall be impossible," or "No word shall be void of power," how complete is the response of the heart! Difficulty, trial, sorrow, for herself was certain. "Wherefores" and "hows" were no doubt beating against the bars of their cage; but there comes forth the submissive and quiescent, "Behold the handmaiden of the Lord; be it unto me according to thy Word." The portrait bears the marks of Divine wisdom. The reticence of Scripture might suggest that the inspiring Spirit of God, foreseeing the danger which so soon appeared, of an admiration scarcely separated from and insensibly sliding into grave error, moved the evangelist to abstain from any magnifying of the Virgin. But the mistaken honour paid to Mary should not withdraw the mind from what is truly honourable and exemplary in her conduct. She is a type of the believer for all times, in that quietness and confidence which are the believer's strength, in that receptiveness of soul which is his life, in that entire self-yielding to God which is his reasonable service. "Blessed is she that believeth." What is the angel's message? Do not attempt to expound the words in vers. 30—35. Be content reverently to receive a mystery so deep and dread. But two things may be noted as to ver. 35. (1) The force of the "therefore" or "wherefore," at the beginning of the last clause, bidding us see in the statement which precedes the reason of the assertion which follows. The statement is that the Holy Ghost should encloud the mother—therefore the holiness of the Lord. Mark, the difference between Christ's holiness and ours is not in kind; it is in this, that his generation was that which is denoted in our regeneration. Of course, in the human nature of Christ we must recognize an altogether exceptional work of Divine power. But the efficient cause in his birth is the efficient cause in all spiritual birth. Holiness, we see, is not a mere attainment, the result of adherence to a moral regimen, of obedience to a moral law; it is a new supernatural being—" born of the Spirit." What took place, in a marvellous way, even before the actual birth of the Son of Mary, takes place in the case of every one born from above. He is " born not of blood, nor of the will of the flesh, nor of the will of man, but of God." And *therefore* that which is born, being holy, is the Son of God. (2) The word, " that holy thing," or " that which is to be born," that sacred, separated entity, may suggest a hint as to the Person of Jesus. Body and soul are one thing, each having its own properties and qualities which cannot be transferred to the other, yet the two making one. It is not possible to tell where body ends and soul begins. Now, in the Son of Mary we have the humanity and the Divinity, each perfect and complete. Whatever can be said of man can be said of him; what can be said of God can also be said of him. Very man and very God. He is one Person. The one entity born of the Virgin is the Son of God. More than this let us not try to say.

> " Faith through the veil of flesh can see
> The face of thy Divinity,
> My Lord, my God, my Saviour."

" This is the doing of the Lord, and it is marvellous in our eyes."

Vers. 39—56.—*The two expectant mothers.* I. THE RETIREMENT. Elisabeth (ver. 24) had hidden herself when she knew that the promise of the angel would be fulfilled. Why she did so we are not told, but the language of ver. 26 suggests a religious motive. She was filled with gratitude, and she desired, perhaps, a season of holy rest and communion with God. " In silence and solitude," says Thomas à Kempis, "the soul advantageth herself, and learneth the mysteries of Holy Scripture." The same reason may partly have influenced Mary. But, besides this, there is no doubt that she wished to enjoy fellowship with her who alone could share her feeling, and with whom (ver. 36) her own prospect of motherhood was so intimately associated. Who can speak of the welcome, the salutations, the conferences, of the two cousins?

> " O days of heaven and nights of equal praise,
> Serene and peaceful as these heavenly days,
> When souls, drawn upward in communion sweet,
> Enjoy the stillness of some close retreat,
> Discourse, as if released and safe at home,
> Of evils past and danger yet to come,
> And spread the sacred treasure of the breast
> Upon the lap of covenanted rest!"

II. THE SONG OF MARY. Elisabeth, receiving Mary, speaks by the Holy Ghost. Mary had been told of her cousin's condition, but Elisabeth had received no intimation of Mary's. The arrival of the latter is the moment of special revelation. Elisabeth (ver. 42) lifts up her voice with a loud cry. The sound of Mary's voice (ver. 44) had occasioned the prophetic impulse. She declares the Virgin the mother of her Lord, and in beautiful humility asks, " Whence is this to me, that the mother of my Lord should come to me? " And, it may be, feeling the contrast between the faith of the Virgin and the unbelief of her husband, she pronounces a blessing on her who had believed. Then, in response from Mary, comes the song which the Christian Church has incorporated into its liturgies, which it has regarded as the opening of that fountain of praise, that wonderful hymnology, which has made glad the city of God. With regard to this hymn—" the Magnificat," as it is usually designated : 1. Compare it with the song of Hannah (1 Sam. ii.). In both there is the same blending of personal gladness with the emotion and experience of the Church; the same losing of self in the sense of an unspeakable loving-kindness; the same boasting in the Lord as he who "fills the hungry with good things, and sends the rich empty away." Mary was familiar with this song. Her thought would naturally take shape in utterance charged with its spirit and imagery, even as it represents the purest forms of Hebrew piety. Yet who can fail to see that her utterance is lifted to a higher plane, and is thrilled by a higher inspiration? 2. The song of Mary marks the transition from Old Testament to New Testament praise. The Old Testament is present, not only in the language employed throughout, but also (vers. 54, 55) in the earnest laying hold of the singular providence of God towards Israel, and the covenant made with Israel's fathers—"with Abraham and his seed for ever." But the germ of the New Testament is manifest in the special thanksgiving (vers. 48, 49). God the Saviour has appeared, and his might is to be declared in the Son because of whose birth all generations shall call her blessed. Thus the two covenants are united in all true Christian praise. The Old Testament is not a thing past; it is completed, and therefore more than ever one possession in Christ. "All the promises of God in him are yea."

> "Both theirs and ours thou art,
>   As we and they are thine;
> Kings, prophets, patriarchs, all have part
>   Along the sacred line."

3. Finally, the song of Mary illustrates Ps. xl. 1—8: whoso waits patiently for the Lord will, like Mary, know that he inclines to and hears the cry of the soul; and a new song will be given to the lips, even praise to our God. The new song of the redeemed soul has its prototype in that which arose. from the hillside dwelling in the uplands of Judah.

Vers. 59—80.—*The name-giving, and what followed it.* There is a quiet, gentle beauty in the picture of the home life given in ver. 58. The touches of nature in it make us feel our kinship with all the ages. We are told of the flood of congratulations and kind messages which surges towards the happy mother; how the cousins of the priestly families in and around Hebron, and the neighbours scattered over that part of northern Judæa, hastened to express their gladness to Zacharias and Elisabeth. The birth of a son of the old age is the talk of the whole country-side. Our attention is more particularly drawn to the ceremonial connected with the circumcision. Observe—

I. THE IMPORTANCE ATTACHED TO THE NAME IN THE BIBLE. Both in his word to Zacharias and his annunciation to the Virgin the angel is explicit as to the name. So, backwards in all the Hebrew records, the name is regarded as full of significance—*e.g.* Cain, Abel, Seth, Noah. Changes in character and destiny are marked by changes of name—*e.g.* Abram changed into Abraham; Jacob into Israel; Oshea into Jehoshua; Saul into Paul. The force of the names given to individuals should always be noticed —*e.g.* Isaac, Ishmael, Jehoshaphat. It is a sign of the deep religious feeling of the Hebrew nation that, in the name, there is so often a part of the ever-adorable name of God—*e.g.* Elijah, Elisha, Jehoshua. The name is the witness for personal responsibility and personal immortality, a reminder that each of us stands fully out, and alone, before God; that he deals with us separately. Moreover, as the Roman no less than the Hebrew understood, there is a capacity of acting on the imagination and, through the imagination, on the will, in the name. Note, with regard to the name, an interesting conjunction between Christian and Jewish habits. It was the Jewish custom to declare the name on the day of circumcision; it is a Christian custom to declare the name on the day of baptism. As the Hebrew word was the covenant name—that by which the child was to be recognized and individualized in midst of the covenant people—so, theoretically, the name which the parent bestows (not the surname) is that by which the child is individualized in the blood-bought Church of Christ.

II. THE DEPARTURE FROM "USE AND WONT" AT THE CIRCUMCISION OF ZACHARIAS'S BABE. A practice which had its root in a healthy instinct had come to be an accepted institution—the naming of the child after one of "the kindred." What should be the name of the babe? Surely that of the honoured father. "Not so," interposes the mother, who had been instructed by her husband, now dumb and deaf; "he shall be called *John.*" "John? No relative is called by this name! What shall the father decide?" Then, to the amazement of all, the writing on the slate, "His name is John." It was the angel name; it was the Divine name. Note: God the Father in heaven has his special name-giving (see Rev. ii. 17). Blessed—oh, how blessed!—to have this name—the name written in the Lamb's book of life, in which there is recorded "all that goes on in the depths of the heart between the inmost self and God"!

III. How THE PRIEST BECOMES THE PROPHET. The word is no sooner written than the mouth which for months had been closed is opened, and the long pent-up tides of feeling burst forth. When God brings back the soul's captivity, the soul's lost capacities are found. The tongue is loosed which unbelief always ties—tongue and ear as well. "Mine ears hast thou opened; then said I, Lo, I come;" "When I speak with thee, I will open thy mouth;" "We believe, and therefore speak." It is a song of exalted praise, in some of its features resembling Mary's, which flows from the opened lips. See how, towards the end, borne along by the ever-rising inspirations of the Spirit, the song swells into a grand missionary hymn. The Dayspring from on high, that shall visit Israel, will pour a light into the darkness that enwraps the earth, giving light to all that sit in it and in the shadow of death, and guiding their feet into the way of peace. Thus the father prophesied that the child should go before the face of the Lord.

IV. WHAT IS SAID AS TO THE CHILD WHOSE BIRTH AND MISSION HAVE BEEN THUS CELEBRATED. Is not the question discussed in the hill-country (ver. 66) one suggested by a birth, by looking at the tiny infant? How wonderful a birth is! What shall be the manner, type of mind, life-story, of the child? A being begun! A journey on and on for ever; but whither? O child!

> "God fill thee with his heavenly light
> To steer thy Christian course aright;
> Make thee a tree of blessed root,
> That ever bends with heavenly fruit."

"The child grew, and waxed strong in spirit." Blessed growth! High-spirited in the better sense of the word—the human guided by the Divine! The home far from the world, in the breezy uplands, where he could meditate in the Law of the Lord day and night, and realize the preparation for the work of the prophet of the Highest! Here we leave him for a little. For another Child has been born—he who is called "Wonderful, Counsellor."

HOMILIES BY VARIOUS AUTHORS.

Vers. 1—4.—*Certainties concerning Christ.* There are many things in connection with the gospel of Christ about which there is difference of view and some measure of uncertainty. But it is "those things which are most surely believed" that constitute the rock on which we rest, on which we build our hopes. We cannot live spiritually on uncertainties; they may serve the purpose of speculation or discussion, but they do not bring peace to the soul; they do not minister to life. We may thank God most heartily that there are some certainties concerning Jesus Christ, on which we can construct our life as it now is, and on which we can rely for that which is to come. There is no doubt at all respecting—

I. THE CIRCUMSTANCES OF OUR LORD'S CAREER. We have the testimony of "eye-witnesses," of men who could not have been mistaken, and who gave the very strongest assurances that they were not deceiving and misleading; we therefore *know* what were the scenes through which Jesus passed, what were the particulars of his life. We know: 1. His character—how pure, how perfect, it was. 2. His thoughts—how profound, how practical, how original, they were. 3. His works—how mighty and how beneficent they were. 4. His sufferings and sorrows—with what sublime patience they were endured. 5. His death—under what awful solemnities it was undergone. 6. The great and supreme fact of his resurrection. Of all these things we are thoroughly assured.

II. THE OFFER HE MAKES OF HIMSELF AS OUR DIVINE REDEEMER. It is perfectly clear that Jesus Christ regarded himself as One that was here on the highest mission, as One that was very far removed above ordinary manhood. He felt that he stood in a relation to the human race that was not only unusual, but unique. Otherwise he could not have spoken of "giving his flesh for the life of the world," of being "the Light of the world," of "drawing all men unto him;" he could not have invited all heavy-laden souls to come to him that they might find rest in him. It is abundantly clear that Jesus Christ offered himself, and still offers himself: 1. As the Divine Teacher, at whose feet we may all sit and learn the living truth of God. 2. As the Divine Saviour, in whom we may all trust for the forgiveness of our sins and our reconciliation to God. 3. As the Divine Friend, to whom we may trust our heart, and in whom we may find a Refuge. 4. As the Divine Lord, who claims the obedience and service of our lives.

III. The sufficiency of Christ for all that he undertakes. Can he, of whom his critics spoke so slightingly as "the carpenter's Son," *do* all this? Is he equal to such offices as these? There is the experience of eighteen centuries to which this appeal may be made. And from the first to the last; from the experience of the little child and of the man in middle life and of extreme old age; from that of health and of sickness; from that of adversity and of prosperity; from that of ignorance and of culture; from that of human souls of every conceivable variety of constitution and of human lives of every imaginable variety of condition;—the answer is one strong, unhesitating, enthusiastic "Yes!" Many things are disputable, but this is certain; many things are to be discredited, but these are to be "most surely believed;" and on them we do well to build our present heritage and our eternal hope.—C.

Vers. 5, 6.—*Life in its completeness.* A very beautiful picture, though on a very small canvas, is here painted; it is a picture of domestic piety. As we think of Zacharias and Elisabeth spending their long life together in the service of Jehovah, attached to one another and held in honour by all their kindred and friends, we feel that we have before our eyes a view of human life which has in it all the elements of an excellent completeness.

I. The domestic bond. Here we have conjugal relationship in its true form; established in mutual respect; justified and beautified by mutual affection; made permanently happy by common affinities and common aims; elevated and consecrated by the presence of another and still nobler bond—that of a strong and immovable attachment to God. A human life is quite incomplete without such tender ties of God's own binding, and these ties are immeasurably short of what they were meant to be if they are not enlarged and ennobled by the sanctities of religion.

II. Human and Divine estimation. These two godly souls enjoyed the favour of their Divine Father and of their human friends and neighbours: "They were both righteous before God," and they were "blameless" in the sight of men. God accepted them, and man approved them. He to whom they were responsible for all they were and did saw in them, as he sees in all his children, the imperfections which belong to our erring and struggling humanity; but he accepted their reverence and their endeavour to please and to obey him, forgiving their shortcomings. And their kindred and their friends recognized in them those who were regulating their life by God's holy will, and they yielded to them their fullest measure of esteem. No human life is complete without the possession of these two things: (1) the favour of the living God; and (2) the esteem of those amongst whom we live. To walk in the shadow of conscious estrangement from God, to miss the sweet sunshine of his heavenly favour,—this is to darken our life with a continual curse, this is to bereave ourselves of our purest joy and most desirable heritage. And while some of the very noblest of our race, following thus in the footsteps of the Master himself, have borne, in calm and heroic patience, the obloquy of the ignorant and the malice of the evil-minded, yet it is our duty, and it should be our desire and aspiration, so to walk in rectitude and in kindness that men will bless us in their hearts, will esteem us for our integrity, will hold us in their affection. The man who "wears the white flower of a *blameless* life" is the man who will be a power for good in the circles in which he moves.

III. Sacred service. It may be questionable whether any distinction is intended between "ordinances" and "commandments;" but there can be no question at all that both together cover religious observances and moral obligations. The Law which these two faithful souls obeyed enjoined the one as well as the other. And no human life is complete which does not include both these elements of piety. 1. *The worship of God*, in private prayer, in family devotion, in public exercises, is a serious and important part of a good man's experience. 2. And certainly not less so is the *regulating of conduct by the revealed will of God*; the walking, day by day, in uprightness and integrity, in sobriety and purity, in truth and in love. Beautifully complete, fashioned in spiritual symmetry, attractive and influential, is that human life which is spent in the home of hallowed love, which is bright with the favour of God and man, and which is crowned with the sovereign excellences of piety and virtue.—C.

Vers. 13—17.—*Parental ambition.* "What would we give to our beloved?" asks one of our poets. What would we ask for our children if we might have our hearts' desire? When the young father or mother looks down on the little child, and then looks on to the future, what is the parental hope concerning him? What is that which, if it could only be assured, would give "joy and gladness"? The history of our race, the chronicles of our own time, even the observation of our own eyes, give abundant proof that the child may rise to the highest distinction, may wield great power, may secure large wealth, may enjoy many and varied pleasures, and yet be a source of sorrow and disappointment. On the other hand, these same authorities abundantly prove that, if the parent is only true to his convictions and avails himself of the resources that are open to him, there is every reason to expect that his child will be such an one as to yield to him a pride that is not unholy, a joy that nothing can surpass. Not on the same scale, but after the same manner, every man's child may become what Gabriel told Zacharias his son should be—

I. ONE TAKING HIGH RANK WITH GOD. "Great in the sight of the Lord." By faith in Jesus Christ our child may become a "*son* of God" in a sense not only true but high (see John i. 12). "And if children, then *heirs*, heirs of God" (Rom. viii. 17). Obedience will ensure the *friendship* of God (see John xiv. 23; xv. 14). Earnestness will make him a *fellow-labourer* with God (1 Cor. ii. 9; 2 Cor. vi. 1). The acceptance of all Christian privilege will make him a "*king and priest* unto God" (Rev. i. 6). Who can compute how much better it is to be thus "great in the sight of the Lord" than to be honoured and even idolized by men?

II. ONE IN WHOM GOD HIMSELF DWELLS. "He shall be filled with the Holy Ghost." God desires to dwell with and in every one of his human children; and if there be purity of heart and prayerfulness of spirit, he will dwell in them continually (ch. xi. 13; John xiv. 17; 1 Cor. iii. 16; vi. 19; Rev. iii. 20).

III. ONE THAT IS MASTER OF HIMSELF. "He shall drink neither wine," etc. By right example and wise discipline any man's child may be trained to control his own appetites, to regulate his tastes, to form temperate and pure habits, to wield the worthiest of all sceptres—mastery of himself.

IV. ONE IN WHOM THE BEST AND NOBLEST LIVES AGAIN. "He shall go in the spirit and power of Elijah." In John the Baptist there lived again the great Prophet Elijah—a man of self-denying habit; of dauntless courage, that feared the face of no man, and that rebuked kings without flinching; of strong and scathing utterance; of devoted and heroic life. In any one of our children there may live again that One who "in all things in which John was great and noble, was greater and nobler than he." In the little child who is trained in the truth and led into the love of Christ there may dwell the mind and spirit of the Son of God himself (Rom. viii. 9; Phil. ii. 5).

V. ONE THAT LIVES A LIFE OF HOLY USEFULNESS. What nobler ambition can we cherish for our children than that, in their sphere, they should do as John did in his —spend their life in the service of their kind? Like him, they may: 1. Make many a home holier and happier than it would have been. 2. Prepare the way for others to follow with their higher wisdom and larger influence. 3. Be instrumental in turning disobedient hearts from the way of folly to the path of wisdom. 4. Earn the benediction of "many" whom they have blessed (ver. 14).

To ensure all this, there must be: 1. Parental example in righteousness and wisdom. 2. Parental training as well as teaching. 3. Parental intercession.—C.

Vers. 31—33.—*The greatness of Jesus Christ.* To Mary, as to Elisabeth, it was foretold by the celestial messenger that her Son should be "great." There can be no doubt that, after all that was then said, Mary expected unusually great things of the Child that should be born of her. But how very far short of the fact her highest hopes have proved to be! For to whatever exalted point they reached, the Jewish maiden could not possibly have attached to the angel's words such meaning as we know them to have contained. The greatness of that promised Child was threefold; it related to—

I. HIS DIVINE ORIGIN. He was not only to be her offspring, but he should "be called the Son of the Most High." And there was to come upon her and overshadow her the Holy Ghost, the Power of the Most High. He was to be not only *a* son of God, but *the* Son of God, related to the Eternal Father as no other of the children of men had ever been or should ever be. He was to be One that would in the *fullest* sense partake of the Divine nature, be one in thought and in aim and in action with the Father (John v. 19, 23; viii. 28; x. 30; xiv. 10, 11). He was to be "God manifest in the flesh."

II. THE WORK HE SHOULD ACCOMPLISH. "Thou shalt call his name Jesus;" and he was to be so called because he would "save his people from their sins" (Matt. i. 25). There have been "saviours of society" from whom this poor wounded world might well have prayed to be delivered, men who tried to cover their own hideous selfishness under a fair and striking name. What they have claimed to be, Jesus the Saviour was and is. He saves from sin. And to do that is to render us the very greatest conceivable service, both in its negative and positive aspects. 1. *Negatively* considered. To destroy sin is to take away evil by the root. For sin is not only, *in itself*, the worst and most shameful of all evils by which we can be afflicted, but it is the *one fruitful source* of all other evils—poverty, estrangement, strife, weariness and aching of heart, death. 2. *Positively* considered. Saving from sin means restoring to God; it includes reinstatement in the condition from which sin removed us. Jesus Christ, in the very act in which he redeems us from the penalty and power of sin, restores us to God—to his Divine favour, his likeness, his service. Accepting and abiding in the Saviour, we dwell in the sunshine of God's everlasting friendship; we grow up into his perfect image; we spend our days and our powers under his direction. It is not only that Jesus Christ delivers us from the darkest curse; it is that he raises us to the loftiest heritage, by the salvation which he offers to our hearts.

III. THE DIGNITY AND POWER HE SHOULD ATTAIN. He was to reign upon a throne, "over the house of Jacob for ever;" and "of his kingdom there should be no end." Great and large as Mary's expectations for her promised Child may have very justly been, they can have been nothing to the fulfilment of the angel's words. For the kingdom of Christ (as it is or as it shall be) is one that surpasses in every way that of the greatest Hebrew sovereign. It does so: 1. In its main characteristics. It is *spiritual*. The only homage which is acceptable to its King is the homage of the heart, the only tribute the tribute of affection, the only obedience the obedience of love. It is *beneficent*. Every subject in this realm is sacredly bound to seek his brother's well-being rather than his own. It is *righteous*. Every citizen, because he is such, is pledged to depart from all iniquity, to pursue and practise all righteousness. 2. In its extent. It has "no end" in its spacial dimensions. No river bounds it; no mountain, no sea; it reaches the whole world round. 3. In its duration. He shall reign "for ever;" his rule will go down to remotest times; it will touch and include the last generation that shall dwell upon the earth. Let us rejoice in his greatness; but let us see to it that (1) we have a part in the heritage of those whom he is blessing, and that (2) we take our share in the furtherance of his mission of mercy.—C.

Vers. 46—48.—*The voice of praise.* This "improvisation of a happy faith" is not more musical to the ear than it is beautiful to our spiritual discernment. It presents to us the mother of our Lord in a most pleasing light. We will look at these words of devout gratitude as—

I. MARY'S RESPONSE to God's distinguishing goodness to her. She received from God a kindness that was: 1. *Necessarily unique.* Only to one of the daughters of men could be granted the peculiar honour conferred on her. We are naturally and properly affected by mercies which speak of God's distinguishing goodness to us. 2. Fitted to fill her heart *with abounding joy.* She was to become a mother, and the mother of One who should render to his people services of surpassing value; no wonder that her "spirit rejoiced" in such a prospect. 3. *Calculated to call forth all that was highest and worthiest in her nature.* She would have to cherish and to rear, to teach and to train, that illustrious Son who should call her "mother." 4. *Certain to confer, upon her an honourable immortality.* All generations would call her blessed. 5. *Rendered to one who could not have expected it.* God had stooped low to bless, even to the low estate of "his bondmaiden." And, impressed with this wonderful and unanticipated goodness, she poured forth her gladness in a song of holy gratitude, of lofty praise. Such should be—

II. OUR APPRECIATION of God's abounding kindness to ourselves. 1. *The indebtedness* under which our heavenly Father has laid us. It is, indeed, as different as possible from that which inspired this sacred lyric. Yet may we most reverently and most becomingly take the words of Mary into our lips—both the utterance of felt obligation and the language of praise. For: (1) How *low* is the *condition* on which, in our case, God has mercifully looked! from what depth of error, of folly, of wrong, has he raised us!—a depth with which the lowly estate of Mary is not to be compared. (2) With what a *great salvation* has he delivered us!—a salvation with which even the national deliverance Mary would be expecting of her Son is of very small account. (3) And what a *lasting good* he confers upon us who have received God *our* Saviour! The blessing of an immortality of undying fame is very precious to these thirsting human spirits of ours: but is it comparable with that of an actual immortality of conscious, eternal life with God and with the good in the heavenly kingdom? Distant generations will not hear our name, but in remotest times we shall be dwelling and serving in unimaginable joy. 2. *The response* we should make to our Father. (1) Great gladness of heart. We should rejoice in God our Saviour; welcoming him, trusting and resting in him, finding our refuge and our strength in his faithfulness and his love. (2) Honouring him before all men. "Magnifying the Lord" with the utterance of the lip, with the obedience of the life, with active service in his vineyard.—C.

Vers. 49—55.—*God revealed in Jesus Christ.* We see much more in Mary's words than the thoughts which were present to her mind at the time of utterance; for we stand well within that kingdom of God of which she stood on the threshold. To the holy confidence she entertained in God's goodness to all Israel, and especially to herself up to that hour, there was added a reverent wonder as to this new manifestation of Divine mercy. So she sang of the power and the holiness, the mercy and the faithfulness, of Jehovah. Through bitterest experiences (ch. ii. 35) she passed into the light of truth and the rest of God, and now she sees how much greater occasion she had than she knew at the moment to sing in such strains of the character of God. We look at these Divine attributes as expressed in the coming of the Saviour.

I. HIS DIVINE POWER. "He that is mighty hath done . . . great things" (ver. 49); "He hath showed strength with his arm" (ver. 51). God's power is very gloriously manifested in the formation and furniture of this earthly home, in the creation of successive generations of mankind, in the providential government of the world, including the mastery of all physical forces and the control of all human energies; but by far the most wonderful exhibition of Divine power is in the redemption of the world by Jesus Christ. To exert a transforming power on one intelligent, free, disloyal spirit; to conquer a rebellious, to win an estranged, soul; to raise a fallen nature, and uplift it to a height of holy excellence; to make that which had lowered itself to the basest fit for the society of the holiest in heaven; to do this not in one individual case but in the case of "ten thousand times ten thousand;" to introduce a power which can elevate and ennoble families, communities, nations; which is changing the character and condition of the entire race;—this is "*the* power of God," this is the doing of him "that is mighty."

II. HIS DIVINE HOLINESS. "Holy is his Name" (ver. 49); "He hath scattered the proud," etc. (vers. 51, 52). God's holiness is shown in his providential interpositions, in his humbling the haughty, in his scattering the cruel and the profane, in his raising the lowly and the pure and the true. Thus he has been revealing his righteousness in every nation and in every age. But nowhere does his holiness appear as it is seen in (1) the *mission* of his Son, who came to put away sin; in (2) the *life and language* of his Son, who illustrated all purity and condemned all iniquity; in (3) the *death* of his Son, who by the sacrifice of himself uttered God's thought and feeling about sin as nothing else could speak it, and struck it such a death-blow as nothing else could strike it.

III. HIS DIVINE MERCY. (Ver. 50.) Many are the testimonies borne by Old Testament saints to the pity, the patience, the mercy, of the Lord. But in Jesus Christ—in his spirit, in his example, and more particularly in his redeeming death and work—is *the* manifestation of the grace of God. "God commendeth his love toward us, in that, while we were yet sinners, Christ died for us." In the gospel of Christ the pity, the patience, the magnanimity, of God rise to their fullest height, reach to their noblest breadth.

IV. HIS DIVINE FAITHFULNESS. (Vers. 53—55.) God, who made us for himself and for truth and righteousness, who has made our hearts to hunger for the highest good, does not leave us to pine and perish; he fills us with the "rich provision" of his truth and grace in Jesus Christ. "As he spake unto our fathers," so he has done, granting not only such a One as they hoped for, but One that has been to the whole race of man a glorious Redeemer, in whom all nations are blessed with a blessing immeasurably transcending the most sanguine hopes of his ancient people.

1. Let our souls be so filled with the greatness and the goodness of God as thus revealed, that we shall break forth into grateful song, magnifying his Name. 2. Let us return at once to him, if we yet remain at a distance from him; for we have no right to hope, and no reason to expect, that he will ever manifest himself to us in more attractive features than as we see him in the Son that was born of the lowly Virgin.—C.

Vers. 58, 66, 67.—*Joy and awe at a human birth.* When John was born his mother's heart was filled with great joy, and her neighbours rejoiced with her. And when the little child, a week old, was introduced into the Jewish commonwealth, a feeling of awe filled the hearts of those present, and there was much wonderment concerning him. "Fear came on them all," and every one was asking, "What manner of child shall this be?" No doubt the exceptional character of the circumstances attending his birth and his circumcision accounted for the joy and also for the fear; but apart from all that was unusual, there was reason enough for both sentiments to be felt and shown. At any ordinary human birth there is—

I. OCCASION FOR HOPEFULNESS AND GLADNESS OF HEART. "The mother remembereth no more her anguish, for joy that a man is born into the world," said our Lord (John xvi. 21). And why rejoice on this occasion? Because of: 1. The love which the little child will cherish. Not, indeed, to be manifested in its very earliest days, but to be felt and shown before long—the beautiful, clinging, whole-hearted love of childhood; a love which it is fair to see and most precious to receive. 2. The love which the little child will call forth—the love which is parental, fraternal; the love of those who serve as well as that of kindred and friends,—this, too, is one of the most goodly sights on which the eye of purity and wisdom rests; it is one of the sweetest and most wholesome ingredients in the cup of earthly good. 3. The discipline which the coming of the child will involve. All parents have an invaluable privilege, from which they ought to derive the greatest benefit. They may be so slow to learn, so unimpressionable, so obdurate, that they are none the wiser or better for their parentage; and in that case they will be something or even much the worse. But if the "little child" does not "lead" us, it is our own fault and folly. The child's dependency on his parent, trustfulness in his parent, obedience to his parent,—do these not speak eloquently of our dependence upon, our trustfulness in, our obedience to our heavenly Father? The love we feel for our little child, the care we take of him, the profound regret we should feel if he went astray, the sacrifice we are ready to make for his recovery,—does not all this summon us, with touching and even thrilling voice, to realize the love God has for us his human children, the care he has taken of us day and night through all our years, the profound Divine regret with which he has seen us go astray from himself, the wonderful sacrifice he made for us when he spared not his own Son but delivered him up for us all, in order to restore us to himself and reinstate us in our heritage? And the labour we are necessitated to bestow, the patience to exercise, and the self-denial and sacrifice to show,—these are essential factors in the forming of our character. We should not choose them, but we may well be most thankful for them. 4. The excellency to which he may attain; it may be that (1) of physical beauty, or (2) of intellectual ability, or (3) of spiritual worth, or (4) of valuable service. Who can tell what lies latent in that helpless infant? what sources of power and blessing are in that little cradle?

II. Occasion for reverent awe. It may well be that "fear" comes on all those who hold their own children in their arms. For they who are entrusted with a little child receive therewith a most grave responsibility. It is true that nothing can remove the accountableness of each soul to its Creator for what it has become; but it is also true that parents are very seriously responsible for the character and career of their children. Our children will believe what we teach them, will form the habits in which we train them, will follow the example we set them, will imbibe the spirit which we are breathing in their presence. *What* shall this child be? That depends on ourselves. If we are only true and wise and kind, our children will almost certainly become what we ourselves are—what we long and pray that they may be. Joy and awe are therefore the two appropriate sentiments at every human birth. When a child is born into the home, there enters that which may be the source of the greatest gladness to the heart; there also enters that which should make life a far more serious and solemn thing.—C.

Vers. 74, 75.—*The course of the Christian life.* These words of Zacharias will very well indicate the course through which a Christian life passes from its commencement to its close.

I. It begins in spiritual emancipation. "We being delivered out of the hand of our enemies." In order to "walk in newness of life," we must be rescued from the thraldom of sin. And there is a twofold deliverance that we need. One is from the *condemnation of our guilt*; for we cannot rest and rejoice in the love of God while we are under a troubled sense of the Divine displeasure, while we feel and know that our "sin has separated between" ourselves and our heavenly Father. The other is from the *bondage of evil.* So long as we are "held in the cords of our sins," we are helplessly disobedient; it is only when we have learnt to hate sin, and, loathing it, to leave it behind us, that we are free to walk in the path of righteousness. This double emancipation is wrought for us by the Lord whose way the son of Zacharias was to prepare. By faith in him, the great Propitiation for our sins (1 John ii. 2), we have full and free forgiveness, so that all the guilty past may be removed from our sight; and in the presence of a crucified Redeemer "the flesh and its affections are crucified," we die to our old self and our old iniquities, the tolerance of sin is slain, we hate that which we loved and embraced before, we are "delivered out of the hand of our enemies."

II. It proceeds along the path of filial service. We "serve him without fear." Here are two elements—obedience and happiness. As soon as we unite ourselves to our Lord and Saviour, *we live to serve.* "None of us liveth to himself;" "We thus judge, . . . that we who live should not live unto ourselves, but unto him who died for us" (2 Cor. v. 14, 15). And this is the only true life of man. The animal may live for itself, though even the higher animals live rather for others than for themselves. But all whom we should care to emulate live to serve. It is not the *sentence passed*, it is the *heritage conferred* upon us, that in Christ Jesus we live to serve God—to serve him by direct worship and obedience, and also, indirectly, by serving the children of his love and the creatures of his care. And we *serve in love*; and therefore without fear—without that fear which means *bondage*; for "perfect love casteth out fear." It is with no hesitating and reluctant step that we walk in the ways of God; it is our joy to do his bidding; we "delight to do his will: yea, his Law is within our heart" (Ps. xl. 8). "We have not received the spirit of bondage again to fear;" our spirit is the spirit of happy childhood, which runs to fulfil its Father's word.

III. It moves towards perfect excellence of character. "In holiness and righteousness before him." Here are three elements of the Christian life. 1. *A holy hatred of evil*; leading us to condemn it in ourselves and in others, and prompting us to expel and extirpate it to the utmost of our power. 2. *The pursuit and practice of all that is equitable;* endeavouring to do and to promote that which is just in all the relations in which we stand to others, or they to one another. 3. *Piety;* doing every right thing *as unto Christ* our Lord; living consciously "before him;" so that all our rectitude of heart and excellency of behaviour is something more than a habit of life; it is a sacrifice unto our Saviour.

IV. It perseveres even to the end. "All our days." There is no break in our course. Our upward and onward path may be undulating, but it is continuous, and is ever making for the summit. We do not retire, or resign, or abdicate, in this noblest work, in this sacred office of being "servant of the Lord," "king and priest unto God." Having loved his own, our Master loved them unto the end (John xiii. 1); and loving him whom we have not seen, and rejoicing in him with unspeakable joy, we are faithful unto death, and we know that

> "To him that overcometh
> A crown of life shall be;
> He with the King of glory
> Shall reign eternally."

C.

Ver. 79.—*Christ our Light.* To whom and to what extent the Messiah should "give light" probably Zacharias did not know. He may have limited the blessing, in his mind, to the people of Israel; or, inspired and illumined of God, he may have had a larger and truer outlook. We, at any rate, are unable to confine our thoughts to Jewry; we see in the Sun of Righteousness, in the Dayspring from on high, a celestial luminary "whose going forth is from the end of the heaven, and his circuit unto the ends of it, and there is *nothing* hid from the heat thereof." To us it is "the Light which, coming into the world, enlighteneth every one."

I. The degrees of darkness in which the world was shrouded when the Dayspring rose. It was a dark hour when Jesus Christ was born. "Darkness covered the earth." But the shadows were deeper in some lands than in others; some minds were more lost and buried in the thick darkness than others were. 1. *The dim twilight of Judaism*—a twilight, not of the morning, but of the evening. For Judaism had passed out of its manhood into its dotage, out of its strength and spirituality into a dreary and lifeless formalism. It had, indeed, escaped from idolatry, and it was free from the worst excesses of the pagan world; but of a pure piety, a spiritual and acceptable service, it knew but little. Compared, however, with surrounding peoples, the Jews may be said to have stood in the twilight of truth. 2. *The darkness of philosophy.* For philosophy was groping in the darkness; it had felt or was feeling its way out of the absurdities of polytheism and idolatry; it touched—but only here and there—the grand truth of monotheism; but it was peering in the direction of pantheism and atheism. "The world by wisdom knew not God." And even where it did reach the idea of one living God, it could not tell how he was to be worshipped, how his favour was to be won, what were the relations he desired to sustain to mankind. 3. *The thick darkness of paganism.* If the philosophers "sat in darkness," the idolaters of uncivilized communities were "in the shadow of death." What a death in life is the existence of those who are buried in the most blighting superstitions and the most debasing habits! There indeed "the light is as darkness;" it moves us to a profound pity as we think of it. We are not surprised to read in the text of—

II. The compassion of the Father of men in view of it. "The tender mercy of our God" was called forth by the sad spectacle of a world in deep shadow, a race without the Light of life. At their *best,* men were far enough from truth, from righteousness, from the love of God; at their *worst,* they had utterly gone astray, "stumbling on the dark mountains" of error and of iniquity. Well might the God of all pity compassionate such a lost race as this.

III. The visit of the heavenly Dayspring. "The Dayspring from on high hath visited us, to give light." Jesus Christ came to be the "Light of the world;" and such he is. He has illumined all the way from the blackness of darkness of sin to the light and glory of heaven. What precious rays of light has the Divine Teacher shed on (1) the nature and the disposition of God, our Father; on (2) the character and the consequences of sin; on (3) the way back to God and righteousness; on (4) the transcendent value of the human soul; on (5) the beauty and blessedness of the life of consecration; on (6) the certainty of future glory to the good and faithful! Let us draw near to him who is the Light of the human world, let us walk in the light of his reviving truth, "that we may be the children of light," and dwell in immortal glory.—C.

Ver. 79.—*Christ our Peace.* "To guide our feet into the way of peace." And how far has the mission of the Dayspring succeeded? How far *has* he guided the feet of men into the way of peace? Judged by the outward appearance, the answer would be quite unsatisfactory. To-day, after eighteen centuries of Christianity, there are four millions of men under arms in Europe only; and if another great war does not break out, it is not from humane or Christian considerations that it is suppressed. How do we explain the fact? 1. Christianity has had no fair chance of showing what it is *in it to do.* It has been so wretchedly misrepresented through whole centuries of time. 2. It *has* done much to moderate and mitigate the severities of war; amongst other things, it has carried the "red cross" of succour right into the heart of the battle-field. 3. It is impregnating the minds of statesmen with the truth that an unnecessary war is a heinous crime against God and man. 4. It has been leading the souls of men into a profounder peace. For there is a spiritual sphere in which there is strife and unrest worse by far than any physical contests can be. It is there that peace has been most missed, and that its absence has wrought the saddest evil. This worst restlessness has resulted from two things—

I. FROM MAN SEEKING HIS SATISFACTION WHERE HE CANNOT FIND IT. 1. What a vain thing is it to seek satisfaction in a life of pleasure, in living to be amused, in hunting happiness over the field of enjoyment! 2. What an unsatisfying thing is life lived on any lower plane, whatever it may be! Alas for those millions to whom it is a dreary and monotonous round of toil! And to those who move in the higher social circles, is it so very much better? When the veil is lifted, as it is occasionally by some honest memoirs or frank autobiography, how often do we find it full of disappointment, of disillusion, of wretched rivalry, of hunger and heart-ache! There is no peace or rest there that is worthy of the name. Where, then, shall rest be found? We shall gain it from him and find it in him who "knew what was *in man*," and who alone knew what would satisfy the hunger of his soul; it was he who came to guide our feet into the way of peace. We shall find it in his *friendship*, in his *service*, in his *cause.* When we have come to ourselves, and have returned unto the Lord our God; when we have lost sight of ourselves, and have entered his holy and happy service; then have we left disquietude and unrest behind us, then have we entered into a true, deep, and enduring peace.

II. FROM OUR SENSE OF SIN AGAINST GOD. There is no peace for man without reconciliation to God. He has left the home of his Father, has become estranged from him, has come under his righteous condemnation, and he can find no peace until he has been forgiven and restored. Apathy, indifference, the unconcern of a stolid ignorance, there may be; but that is not peace. Peace is a *well-grounded assurance that all is well with us.* This we can only obtain by knowing the truth concerning ourselves, and by taking the path which leads us home to God. It is just this we have in Jesus Christ. He (1) makes plain to the understanding and makes grievous to the soul our own great unworthiness and guilt; and then he (2) offers himself to us as our all-sufficient Saviour. Then "being justified by faith [in him] we have peace with God through our Lord Jesus Christ." And abiding in him, we continue in the path of peace—a path which leads on to holy joy and up to heavenly glory.—C.

Ver. 80.—*The service of solitude.* "And was in the deserts till the day of his showing unto Israel." John the Baptist had a long period of retirement before he began the active work of life; and we may be sure that the time spent in the wilderness was not lost. The communion he had there with God, and his prolonged reflection on the worth and purpose of human life, must have had much to do with the character he formed and the work he afterwards accomplished. Then good seed was sown which bore much fruit in later years. We should do well to "be in the desert" more than we are—to seek the solitary place where we are alone with God and with ourselves more than we do. "The world *is* too much with us." We cannot hear the stiller and deeper voices that speak to us, for its perpetual sound is in our ear—the hum of its activity, the rattle of its pleasures, the wail of its distress. Solitude would render an essential service if we would but ensure it and employ it.

I. THE SERVICES SOLITUDE WOULD RENDER US. 1. It would bring God near to us. When man is quite removed from us, and his voice is completely hushed; when we are alone, whether it be in the folds of the hill, or in the depth of the valley, or in our own chamber;—we have a sense of God's nearness to us which we have not amid the crowd. And what an inestimable advantage it would be to us to let the conscious-ness of God's own presence often fill our soul, and then to hold sustained communion with him! 2. It would place our past in full view before our soul. It is not well to be *very often* looking back on that which has gone. There is deep wisdom in "forgetting those things which are behind," both past follies and past successes. Yet is it well some-times to review the way we have been taking—to consider how much there is that should humble us, and how much that should teach us our weakness and cast us on the mercy and the help of God. 3. It would confront us with the future. It would make us ask whither we are going, what there remains for us to do before we die, how well we are prepared for death and the great day of account. 4. It would lead us to estimate our present spiritual condition—how good a use we have made of our privi-leges, whether we have been progressing or receding in our course, whether we are what our Divine Lord would have us be, how we stand in the sight of perfect truth and purity.

II. THE OCCASIONS WHEN IT IS MOST APPROPRIATE. 1. Between the night and the morning; when the soul has to address itself to new duties, new difficulties, new oppor-tunities. 2. Between the evening and the night; before a man commits himself to the "great Guardian of his sleeping hours," his hours of utter helplessness and uncon-sciousness. 3. Before leaving the shelter of the home; when the young heart goes forth into deeper waters—who shall say how deep?—of temptation and trial; when all, and far more than all, its resources will be required for the stern struggle before it. 4. In the crises of our career; when in the innermost chamber of the soul it is deter-mined whether the heart and life shall be yielded to the holy Saviour and rightful Sovereign, or shall be withheld from him. 5. At the time of religious avowal; when a human being takes upon himself the vows of God, and makes open declaration of attachment to the Lord his Redeemer. 6. Before special services which demand the full strength of the soul to meet them bravely and to render them worthily. At such times as these does it most become us to shut our doors upon ourselves and be long alone with God.—C.

Vers. 1—4.—*The absolute certainty of the Christian religion.* In this prologue by Luke we have an insight into the conditions and purposes of his publication. In an age without the art of printing, it was useful to obtain the patronage of the wealthy, and thus secure the production of such a number of "copies" as would save the volume from oblivion. Hence in the classic world dedications to rich men were the rule with authors rather than the exception. Luke's Gospel, which is the "classic" Gospel in the series, is thus written for Theophilus, presumably a rich convert, with whom the writer has had most intimate relations. It is to the same patron he dedicates the second volume of the life of Christ, which is commonly, though inaccurately, called "The Acts of the Apostles," but which is really a second volume of the acts of the Lord, accomplished in and through his apostles. The Gospel, as Luke tells us in the prologue to the Acts, was an account of all that Jesus *began* to do and teach (Acts i. 1). Our Lord's earthly life was thus, in Luke's view, only a first stage in an everlasting history. But while Luke, like other authors in the classical world, may have had the interests of his book in view in dedicating it to Theophilus, he had at the same time a nobler purpose, even to confirm Theophilus in the Christian faith. He proposes con-sequently to display the basis on which this convert has been building, and how absolutely certain the Christian faith is. It is well to revise the foundations. We ought to "walk about Zion, and go round about her;" we ought to "tell the towers thereof, and mark well her bulwarks, and consider her palaces; that we may tell it to the generation following" (Ps. xlviii. 12, 13). What, then, does Luke present to Theophilus as an account of the Christian faith?

I. THE CHRISTIAN FAITH IS NOT A SPECULATIVE SYSTEM. Man, left to himself, evolves out of his consciousness a system more or less complete, and calls upon his fellows to accept of it as their religious faith. But such an evolution of *religion* has proved a failure. Into the interesting study of comparative religion we cannot here enter at any length, but two tendencies in speculation may be noticed in passing. The first is the *outward, or idealistic tendency,* which may be found developed in the Indian religions; the second is the *inward, or self-reliant tendency,* which may be seen carried to its issues in Hellenism and the speculations of the West. Thus the tendency of the Oriental mind was and is to contemplate Nature and to reverence her underlying forces; while the tendency of the Occidental mind was to contemplate man or human nature, and to find in his individuality, his freedom, and his power the true unit and substance of thought. The Oriental mind consequently lost itself in speculations on the *absolute,* which became to the dreamers of the East an abstraction without personality, intelligence, or limitation, just as he has become of late to certain of our dreamers in the West; and the climax of being is in the *Nirvâna,* the utter extinction of human personality through absorption into the universal Spirit. The Western, or Grecian mind, on the other hand, held to man and human nature, cultivated a boundless self-reliance, and a supreme confidence in human nature and its powers. His gods and goddesses were but deified men and women; Olympus only a Greece enjoying larger latitude and more abundant sunlight; and reason and self the ultimate objects of trust. The issue, as we might expect, was "intense worldliness of spirit, that dread of death, that doubt of immortality, that decay of the religious sentiment, which finally covered classical life with such deep gloom and despair."[1] The two tendencies, Oriental and Occidental—the one making man nothing, the other making man all in all—had, before Christ's time, ample opportunity to prove their insufficiency. They had in Buddhism and in Platonism checks, but they were unequal to the needful reformation. It remained for a better faith to furnish man with certainty. Hence we remark—

II. THE CHRISTIAN FAITH IS FOUNDED ON THE HISTORY OF A PERSON. The gospel, as Luke here indicates, consists in the history of a Person whose advent is essential to the salvation of the world. Hence the substance of the Christian faith is historical, not speculative. Whatever certainty attaches to historical evidence as superior to speculation attaches, therefore, to the Christian faith. And here we have to notice: 1. *That the history rests on the testimony of eye-witnesses.* This is asserted by Luke in ver. 2. *Facts* consequently appealing to the senses of the apostles constitute the foundation of the faith. And if it be insinuated that they were "interested witnesses," we reply with Luke: 2. *That the witnesses gained nothing in the worldly sense by their testimony.* As ministers of the Word, they were persecuted, in many cases killed; in all cases life was much less comfortable in consequence of their testimony than if they had said nothing about the Saviour who died and rose again. 3. *Luke sifted the facts as carefully as he could.* It is significant that he makes no claim to inspiration in his prologue. And this is the rule with the sacred writers. Some have supposed that because the writers do not each and all put in a categorical claim to inspiration, it is superfluous to suppose that they are all inspired.[2] But we reply that it is far better for writers to *show* that they are inspired than to *say* they are. Inspiration, like all other good gifts of God, is to be "known by its fruits." This prologue shows that many tried their hands at writing lives of Jesus; but there has been a "survival of the fittest" in this case at all events, to the great advantage of mankind. Instead of asserting his inspiration, Luke used his best endeavours to sift the material and produce a careful and "classic" work. Instead of the Spirit of God despising *means,* he owns them and blesses them.

III. THE HISTORY OF CHRIST HAS A PERSONAL BEARING UPON EACH ONE OF US. Theophilus had been taught this, just as we require to be taught it. Now, we may see the application of Christ's life to our individual need by the two tendencies already referred to. The human mind is *idealizing* in its character. It can be shown that we owe even our scientific progress to the idealists, the Pythagoreans in Greece and the Platonists in Alexandria being the only men in the old world who really advanced

[1] 'The Secret of Christianity,' by S. S. Hebberd, pp. 54, 55.
[2] Cf. 'Die Stellung des Christlichen Glaubens zur heiligen Schrift,' zwei apologetische Vorträge, von Professor Dr. Hermann Schultz, in Heidelberg (1876).

science.[1] Now, Jesus supplies us, in his own perfect and sinless Person, with the "ideal" we individually need to satisfy the cravings and longings of the heart. He is, in fact, "altogether lovely." So that by his realized Personality we are saved from occupation with a pure abstraction, called the "absolute," and the self-effacement to which the Indian dreamers and others are led, as the hope and consequence of their speculation. The definiteness of the historic Person is thus placed in antagonism to the dreamy indefiniteness of speculation about the absolute. Again, the human mind is *introspective* and *self-reliant* in its tendencies. Jesus Christ again applies the requisite check and antagonism to the dangerous tendency. His perfect life shows us by contrast how imperfect our lives are; his mission as Saviour demonstrates our spiritual need; and so we end by taking up self-suspicion in place of self-confidence, and we delight ourselves in the Lord alone. Thus it may be seen that the life of Jesus, especially when we remember his Divinity and omnipotence, becomes a personal interest and a reforming power.[2]

IV. THE HISTORY OF CHRISTIANITY IS THE RESULT OF THE PERSONAL CHRIST INFLUENCING AS THEY NEEDED IT THE WILLING SONS OF MEN. The Book of the Acts has to be taken as the development of the Gospel. In it we see *the Lord* adding to the Church of such as shall be saved, and accomplishing his sacred purposes through human instrumentalities. The people are made willing in the day of his Pentecostal power (Ps. cx. 3). The great Personality is thus seen to be moulding men. It has been said truly that Christianity has been a progress through *antagonism* (cf. Hebberd, *ut supra*). Paganism was a development; Christianity has been a history of restraint. It has curbed men's passions, and conducted them through antagonism to their goal. "The flesh lusteth against the Spirit, and the Spirit against the flesh: and these are contrary the one to the other: so that ye cannot do the things that ye would" (Gal. v. 17). This policy of restraint or antagonism may be traced through Church history. Only an outline can be here suggested. Mohammedanism was a providential restraint upon the growing superstitions of the early centuries. Catholicism again was a restraint upon the vandalism of the Germanic tribes, and by the establishment of feudalism it changed nomadic nations into settled and sympathizing patriots. Protestantism followed, to restrain the "spiritual despotism" which accompanied Catholicism, and secure freedom and the rights of the individual. Even the scientific spirit, as can easily be shown, is due to Protestantism, and if it threatens us, as it does, with unspiritual developments, Christianity will take a new start and antagonize that spirit with a wholesome assertion of the spiritual nature and rights of man (cf. Hebberd, *ut supra*). A great restraining Saviour is thus seen to be moving among men and using their freedom to serve his glorious designs. The Christian faith is simple trust in this historic yet immortal Person, who can consider and consult at once the majestic cycles of human progress and the minutest needs of those who trust him. We have certainty at the foundation of our faith, and a living Lord continually at our side.— R. M. E.

Vers. 5—25.—*The inauguration of the dispensation of grace.* From the prologue about the historic certainty of the Christian faith, we now proceed to the first stage of the wonderful history in the annunciation of the birth of the Baptist. In this we have Luke mounting higher than either Matthew or Mark. We can understand this since he was writing for a Gentile audience, and the speculative turn of Grecian minds would certainly lead to inquiries as to the *origin* of the leaders in the dispensation of grace. Luke satisfies all just demands, and with that exquisite taste which should regulate thought upon such themes. Let us notice the facts as presented to us.

I. THE LORD UTILIZED EXISTING ORGANIZATIONS. Just as we believe the New Testament eldership was based upon the Old Testament office of elder, so here we have the great reformer taken from the Aaronic priesthood. Once more is honour put upon the line of Aaron. The parents of the forerunner both belonged to the priestly tribe. They are, moreover, godly people, being "both righteous before God, walking in all the commandments and ordinances of the Lord blameless" (ver. 6). By which could

[1] Cf. Hebberd's 'Secret of Christianity,' pp. 173—208.
[2] Cf. Isaac Taylor's 'Lectures on Spiritual Christianity,' pp. 10—43.

not be meant that they were sinlessly perfect, especially since in such a case the ritual through which they regularly passed would have been strangely unmeaning. They were a pious, God-fearing pair, walking before the Lord, and striving to be perfect. And here we may draw attention to the advantage John thus had in pious parents. It is, we believe, a *physical* advantage to be the offspring of those who have learned by God's grace to subdue their passions, and who may otherwise be healthy. Other things being equal, their physical development must be superior to that of those whose parents may be addicted to any forms of sinful indulgence.

II. NOTICE THE TRIAL OF THEIR FAITH. This consisted in their having no child. With the Jews there was, added to the natural desire of husband and wife for children, the stimulus arising from the Messianic promises. A Deliverer is expected: why not in my family? Thus Jewish mothers were kept in an expectant attitude, not knowing but that the Messiah was to be their Son. We see in such psalms as cxxvii., cxxviii., etc., evidence how the Divine blessing was associated with fruitfulness. Zacharias and Elisabeth had hitherto been denied the blessing of any child, and, though they had continued to pray about it, they had ceased really to hope. Just like the people who prayed for the release of Peter, and then would not believe it was he when he came knocking at the door (Acts xii. 12—16), so the aged priest and his wife seem to have kept up the form of prayer for a son long after they had ceased to expect such a gift. God keeps us waiting till we are hopeless, and then he surprises us with his blessings.

III. NOTICE NEXT THE PRAYING MULTITUDE AND THE OFFICIATING PRIEST. Zacharias belonged to the eighth of the priestly courses, and had consequently to come up twice a year for eight days' attendance at the temple. Those belonging to the same course met and cast lots for the privilege of officiating at the golden altar. So soon as a priest secured the privilege once, he retired from the contest, as once during the sojourn at Jerusalem was deemed ample honour. Zacharias happened to be successful; the Lord's will was that he should officiate on a given day. The lot left the destiny of each absolutely in the hands of the Lord. It is quite a different matter when people make an appeal to him in games of chance and such like.[1] Into the sanctuary (ναὸν) of the Lord accordingly he went, to burn incense at the *morning* hour, as seems most probable. And while he burned the pure perfume within, the multitude of the people prayed without. It was an acknowledgment that their prayers required something to make them acceptable. They could not ascend alone. And was this not the idea of the arrangement? Man's prayers needed to be supplemented by a divinely arranged perfume, just as we now expect our prayers to be accepted only through the *merits of Jesus Christ*. Again, must we not suppose that the people were praying for deliverance and the advent of the Deliverer? Their prayers and the aged priest's were really one. There was unison and harmony, even though presented from different standpoints. The people without and the priest within were acting in "pre-established harmony."

IV. THE ANGEL OF JOY APPEARS IN THE SANCTUARY. It was upon the path of duty Zacharias met the angel, just as Jacob had done long before at Mahanaim (Gen. xxxii. 1). Gabriel's visit at first terrified the solitary priest. But as the angel of glad tidings and so, as he has been called, "of evangelization" (cf. Godet, *in loc.*), he soon reassures Zacharias. He tells him that his wife is to bear him a son, and his name is to be called "John." 1. This itself is significant. The word "John" is derived from יְהוָֹה and חָנַן, and means "Jehovah giveth grace." It thus signalized the dispensation. The Baptist was really the morning star of the gospel dispensation. 2. He was to be *morally great*. The gracious name would not belie his character. He would be "great in the sight of the Lord," who "looketh on the heart." 3. He was to be *separated from the world as a true Nazarite*. He was not to drink either wine or strong drink. 4. He was to be *inspired from the womb*. The inspiration from wine was needless, when he was to be borne upwards and constantly exhilarated by the Spirit of God (cf. Eph. v. 18). 5. He shall be *correspondingly successful*. "Many of the Jews shall he turn to the Lord their God." 6. His reformation is to *resemble that of Elias*. Elijah lived to turn the nation to the worship of the true God; his work was preparatory, like the wind, the earthquake, and the fire, before the still small voice. So was it to be with John. He was by stern and solitary moral grandeur to bring the people to a sense of

---

[1] Cf. Dr. J. M. Mason's 'Considerations on Lots,' Works, vol. iii. pp. 265—317.

sin, and thus prepare them for the advent of the Saviour. No father ever got a more magnificent future laid before his son. The angel sketched a destiny which was fitted to make the old priest glad.

V. UNBELIEF INSISTING ON A FURTHER SIGN. The appearance of Gabriel, the transparent honesty of his words, the holy place, the whole circumstance of the vision, ought to have assured Zacharias and rebuked his unbelief. Here, after four hundred years of silence, a message has come again from God; and surely it should have been believed. But no! Zacharias asks for a further sign. Has he forgotten Abraham and Sarah? Has he forgotten Isaac and Rebecca? Surely the priest, though aged and with an aged wife, had every reason to believe the angel-brought promise of his God? His unbelief was criminal. He deserves a chastisement. The demand for miracles at the present day is on the part of some just as unreasonable. Unless some additional sign is granted, then faith will be withheld. There is a scepticism which deserves chastisement instead of sympathy or encouragement. And Zacharias is struck dumb. He is doomed to speechlessness for the most of a year. His dumbness was to be a sign of his unbelief and a pure judgment from God. We may compare his case with that of the man born blind (John ix. 2, etc.). In this case the deprivation was to be the basis of Divine mercy; in the case of Zacharias it was a clear note of Divine displeasure. Yet with judgment there is mixed mercy. He is promised a release on the day of the birth of John. For God's "anger endureth but a moment; in his favour is life: weeping may endure for a night, but joy cometh in the morning" (Ps. xxx. 5).

VI. THE PATIENT WORSHIPPERS AND THE DUMB PRIEST. The burning of incense occupied usually a certain length of time. But Zacharias tarries long beyond this. The people wait, but marvel as they wait. They wish his benediction. But when he at length appears, he can only make signs to them, and dismiss them without a word. And yet a *sign* is there for them. They see that a vision has been vouchsafed in the temple. If the priest is silent, it is because God has spoken. Better that man should be dumb before God, than that Heaven should be silent for ever! Zacharias's judgment is to the people a merciful sign. The week of temple-work was no sooner over than he went home to his house in the hill-country of Judæa. His affliction must have been very painful and humiliating. He would be regarded by his friends as one "smitten of the Lord." But in due season the mercy and grace of God are realized in the Baptist's conception. If Zacharias mourned over his unbelief and its chastisement, Elisabeth was enabled to rejoice over her good fortune and the removal of her reproach.

We have thus gone over the announcement of a great man's advent. Are not the truly great the gracious gifts of God? They should be called "John," as indicating whence the true heroes come, and to whom we should ascribe the blessing of their lives. A recent writer says that society has progressed mainly through a succession of great men, and he adds, "Society makes only so much of the great man as goes to the composition of the average man, leaving an overplus which is not to be put to the credit of society or previous human acquisition, but which is a gift from nature—from the Unknown. It makes all of the great man except his special genius, which is afterwards to improve society." [1] If in this quotation we substitute for "nature," nature's *God*, we shall have the true idea. Great men are God's gifts, and though the world may, as in this case, misuse and murder them, they confer, through confession and martyrdom, incalculable blessing upon the race. It is only right for us to recognize in God the Source of great souls, and to use them for his glory.—R. M. E.

Vers. 26—38.—"*The Beginning of the creation of God.*" We now enter upon another announcement, more wonderful still than that about John. It is the announcement about the advent of him who is indeed "the Beginning of the creation of God" (Rev. iii. 14). A deeper interest should gather round it than attaches to the beginning of the material universe. Both begin in mystery, but happily we see the mystery by the eye of faith safely lodged in the hand of God. *Genesis* gives to us the mysterious origin of the ordinary creation, and *Luke* gives to us the mysterious origin of the extraordinary creation of which Jesus is the real Head.

I. WE SHALL NOTICE THE SCENE OF THIS ANGEL-VISIT. We saw Gabriel last in the temple, holding intercourse beyond the first veil with Zacharias as he offered the

---

[1] Graham's 'Creed of Science,' pp. 66, 67.

incense. He was in "the holy place," on the threshold of "the holy of holies." But
now, by way of contrast, he repairs to Nazareth, that city of Galilee so hidden in the
hills that all who for various reasons needed a hiding-place resorted thither. It was
a rendezvous for the worst of people, and became proverbial as the one place out of
which no good thing need be expected (John i. 46). It was here the angel of mercy
made his way to carry good tidings to one in whose veins was the blood of kings. The
house of David had fallen indeed on evil days when its lineal representative was to be
found in a virgin betrothed to the village carpenter. Meanwhile let us comfort ourselves
with the thought that angel-visits, though reputedly few and far between, are not
confined to temple-courts or palaces of earthly kings. The lowliest of situations and
the lowliest hearts may be honoured by a messenger from heaven.[1]

II. THE MESSAGE GABRIEL BROUGHT. Having sought and found the virgin who was
espoused to Joseph, he first addressed to her a remarkable salutation. He salutes her
as one who is (1) "highly favoured" (κεχαριτωμένη), that is, the object of special favour
from God; and (2) as one enjoying God's special presence—"The Lord is with thee."
The other clause, "Blessed art thou among women," seems to be transferred from the
subsequent salutation of Elisabeth (ver. 42; and cf. Revised Version). It was a very
gracious assurance Gabriel brought to Mary. She needed all the support it gave her
in her present trying position. The immediate effect upon her mind was *fear*. She
is troubled at the unexpected apparition. But it led her to deep thoughtfulness. It
has been well said that praise comes as a surprise to the meek, but as a right, or rather
less than a right, to the proud.[2] Mary was thrown by her fear into anxious thought
as to what particular good fortune could be hers. Her idea was that she deserved
nothing, and so she could the more thoroughly appreciate whatever came. What a
relish Divine favour would be if we had Mary's meekness! Gabriel now bids her no
longer to fear, since she has found favour with God, and her good fortune is to consist
in this—that she is to be the mother of an everlasting Monarch. But we must pause
over Gabriel's message. 1. The *name of her Son is to be Jesus*. That is, he is to
be a Saviour of men from sin (cf. Matt. i. 21). The world has had *Joshuas* in abundance, captains of invasion, but only one *Jesus* as a Saviour from the curse and power
of sin. 2. *He is to be great*. And assuredly, if moral influence and genius constitute
the highest greatness, Jesus has no equal among the sons of men. 3. He is to be
called *the Son of the Highest*. God is to be his Father in a special sense. This does not
refer to his "Eternal Sonship," but to his human sonship. He is to stand to God in the
relation of son to father, so far as his human nature is concerned. Mary is thus to be
the mother of God's Son. 4. He is to *succeed to the throne of his father David*. Now,
are we to understand this of a succession to a world-kingdom, and a "personal reign"
over the Jews? If this be the meaning, then this reign is still to come, for through
the rejection of Messiah this kingship was prevented. And so some interpret this (cf.
Godet, *in loc.*). But our Lord's own words about the unworldliness of his kingdom
seem to set this idea at rest. He came to be King over a spiritual kingdom. Now,
David, we should remember, was a great *ecclesiastical* reformer. He exercised commanding influence in the *Church* as well as *State* of his time; and he realized his vice-
gerency under God. Jesus succeeds David upon the spiritual lines which were the
chief lines of David's influence as king. 5. *His reign and kingdom are to be everlasting*.
His is to be no dying dynasty, but an everlasting rule. Emperors and kings have come
and gone, and left their glory behind them; but this Son of Mary commands more
influence every year, and knows no decline. The kingdoms of the world run a longer
or shorter course; but Christ's kingdom outlasts them all. Such a message was fitted
to overwhelm an ordinary mind. Mary is to be the mother of a new King, and he is
never to be uncrowned—an everlasting Monarch! Surely an ordinary head would be
turned by such tidings as these.

III. HOW MARY TAKES THE MESSAGE. She is so meek that her head is *not* turned.
She is in amazement certainly, but there is calm dignity and purity in her reply. 1.
She asks how such a birth is to come about since she is a virgin? This was not the
inquiry of a doubter, but of a believer. She wanted direction. Was she to go on with

[1] Cf. Gerok's 'Evangelien-Predigten,' s. 301, etc.
[2] Cf. Arndt's 'Leben Jesu,' erster band, s. 18.

her proposed marriage with Joseph? or was she to break with him? or was she to do nothing but wait? Gabriel directs her to wait passively in God's hands, and all he has promised will come supernaturally about. Just as the Spirit overshadowed the old chaotic world, and brought the *cosmos* out of it, so would he overshadow Mary, and give her a holy Son. Mary was to sit still and see the salvation of God. And here we must notice that it was a "holy Child" which the world required as a Saviour, one in whom the law of sin affecting the rest of the race should be broken, who would be "holy, harmless, undefiled, and separate from sinners." David may say, "In sin did my mother conceive me;" but no such language must be heard from the lips of Christ. This moral break, this exception to the general rule, is brought about by a supernatural conception and birth. Is there not here a lesson about leaving things sometimes in God's hands altogether? It is a great thing sometimes to sit still and do nothing; to cultivate passivity. Like the Virgin, let us simply wait. As a further direction, Gabriel suggests a visit to Elisabeth, that her faith in God's power may be confirmed. The intercourse with her aged relative will do her a world of good in present circumstances. There in the hill-country of Judæa she will find increasing reason for trusting in God. 2. *Mary accepts the situation with all its risks.* Her submission is an instance of the holiest courage. She cannot but become for a time an object of suspicion to Joseph, and to many more. Her reputation will be for a time at stake. It is a terrible ordeal to encounter. But she bows to the Divine will, and asks God to do with her as he pleases. Faith alone could sustain her in such circumstances. God would vindicate her character in due season. How much are we willing to risk for our Lord? Would we risk reputation, the most precious portion of our heritage, if God clearly asked us to do so? This was what Mary was ready to do. In other words, are we ready to put God before personal reputation? Is he worthy in our eyes even of such a sacrifice?[1]

IV. Notice that we have here an intimation how the new creation must begin within us. The angel-message comes to us, as to Mary, that "Christ" may be formed in us "the Hope of glory." What we have got to do is just to wait for the overshadowing as Mary did. It comes to the waiting and *expectant* souls. Not the waiting of indifference, but the waiting of expectancy, secures the great blessing. Let us cease from our own efforts, let us be still, and we shall indeed see the salvation of God![2]—R. M. E.

Vers. 39—56.—*Inspirations amid the hills of Judæa.* We already have seen the angel suggesting to Mary the propriety of visiting Elisabeth. We may reasonably believe that she had no mother at this time to whom she could communicate her mighty secret, and that Elisabeth is the most likely person from whom to get the sympathy she now required. For the four days' journey from Nazareth to the priest's city in the south she would need some preparation; but she made her arrangements promptly, going "with haste," and reached the home of the dumb priest without delay. If she had any fear and trembling on the way as to how she would be received, it was instantly dissipated through timely inspirations. And here let us notice—

I. The inspiration granted to Elisabeth. (Vers. 42—45.) And here we may mark the *directness* of the inspired address. There was no lengthened introduction, no conversation about health, or weather, or news, but an immediate mention of the all-important matter which concerned the Virgin.[3] 1. *Elisabeth assures Mary of her signal blessedness in being selected to be the mother of Messiah.* She was to be the blessed mother of a blessed Son. How delightful a balm this would be to Mary's anxious heart! Instead of suspicion, there is a salutation such as a princess might thankfully receive. 2. *Elisabeth beautifully depreciates herself.* It is the way the Spirit takes with those he indeed inspires. It is not boastfulness, but self-depreciation he implants within them. Elisabeth feels herself so unworthy, that she wonders the mother of Messiah deigns to visit her! A royal visit would not have been to the priest's wife such an honour. She is Mary's humble servant, because Mary is to be the mother of her Lord. In fact, had Mary been a queen, she could not have been more lovingly and reverentially treated. 3. *A holy joy thrills through her from Mary's advent.* It

---

[1] Cf. Arndt's 'Leben Jesu,' erster band, s. 24.
[2] Ibid., s. 36.   [3] Ibid., erster band, s. 29.

was the "chief joy" of human hearts asserting his marvellous power. The Holy Ghost conducts the humble woman to the most entrancing joy. 4. *Mary's faith is recognized and encouraged.* The contrast between Mary's faith and Zacharias's doubt must have been very marked. The poor priest is stealing about the house dumb, while Mary is in the enjoyment of all her faculties and powers. Elisabeth would rejoice that Mary, through unhesitating faith, had escaped such a judgment as her husband was enduring. The *blessedness* of faith in God cannot be too emphatically asserted. It is the secret of real happiness just to take him at his word. As the "faithful Promiser" he never disappoints any who put their faith in his promised aid. Not only do we who believe enter into rest (Heb. iv. 3), but we also enter into blessedness (cf. μακαρία of ver. 45).

II. THE INSPIRATION OF MARY. (Vers. 46—55.) We have in the Magnificat of Mary the noblest of Christian hymns. There are traces of such earlier efforts as Hannah's prayer; but this only brings out the continuity of the revelation, and in no way affects the originality of Mary's inspiration. And here let us notice: 1. *How God is the Source of Mary's joy.* It is not in herself she rejoices, but in God as her Saviour. This is the great fact we have all got to realize—that our Saviour, not our state, is the fountain of joy. And when we consider his power, and his revealed purposes, and the course of his redeeming love, we must acknowledge that there is in him abundant reason for our joy. Mary felt in body, soul, and spirit the joy of her Lord. 2. *Mary recognizes in her own selection the condescending love of God.* It is not those the world would select as instruments whom God chooses. The world selects the rich. God chooses "the poor of this world rich in faith, and heirs of the kingdom which he hath promised to them that love him" (Jas. ii. 5); so here Mary signalizes her "low estate" as magnifying her Lord's condescending love. How beautiful a spirit to cultivate! Instead of the honour done her unduly exalting her, it only leads her to adore the Divine condescension in stooping to such as she was. 3. *She believes in her everlasting fame.* She knows that the Incarnation will prove such a stupendous fact that all generations will call her blessed. As the mother of Messiah, she cannot but have the homage of all coming generations. She ought consequently to be with all of us "the blessed mother of the Christ of God." 4. *She feels herself the subject of great mercy from the Holy One.* And is this not the acknowledgment which all God's people may make? Hath he not done great things for all his people, whereof they are glad (Ps. cxxvi. 1)? 5. *She takes the widest views of God's dealings with others.* Thus she recognizes: (1) That *those who fear God receive his mercy in every generation.* (Ver. 50.) This is the law of mercy—it is given to those who fear God. It was never meant to encourage men in recklessness or presumption. (2) The *proud experience his dispersive power.* (Ver. 51.) This is brought out in history.[1] The Jewish captivities, their present dispersion, "the decline and fall of the Roman Empire," and many a judgment since, have been illustrations of this line of procedure on the part of the Most High. (3) *The deposition of rulers and the exaltation of the humble.* (Ver. 52.) Mary is here speaking of the usurpers in Palestine, and the exaltation of those they despised. The law was marvellously illustrated in the case of Mary's Son, whose exaltation above all dynasties is the greatest fact in civilization (cf. δυνάστας of ver. 52). (4) *The satisfaction of the needy, and the disappointment of the rich.* (Ver. 53.) Here is another aspect of the law of the Divine dealings. Those who feel their need, and hunger after satisfaction, receive it from God. Mary experienced this, and so do all who really hunger after God and righteousness. They have a beatitude always in store for them (Matt. v. 6). On the other hand, those who are rich, that is, who feel independent and will not look to the Lord for help, who have, in short, "received their consolation," are sent empty away. Disappointment sooner or later becomes their portion. This was the experience of Pharisee and Sadducee and all the well-to-do and self-righteous classes in our Lord's time. And undoubtedly the arrangement is just. (5) *The fidelity of God to his covenant with Israel.* (Vers. 54, 55.) In the Incarnation God was sending real help to his people. It was the crowning act of mercy, and the fulfilment of the promises made to Abraham and his seed. Mary thus began with God's *holiness*, and passed in review his *power*, his *mercy*, and finally his *faithfulness*. All these are illustrated pre-eminently in the Incarnation.

III. THESE INSPIRATIONS PRESENT TO US THE CHARACTER OF THE GOSPEL. For

[1] Cf. Liddon's 'University Sermons,' vol. ii. pp. 205—210.

we have before us two lowly women, deep in their self-abasement. The self-righteous spirit has been annihilated within them, and they are thus fitted to be God's instruments. Secondly, we find them maintaining this beautiful spirit after they have become the special objects of the Divine favour. Grace does not spoil them, but provokes within them gratitude. They abound in praise, not in pride. Thirdly, they enter into hopes for their people and the world, as well as for themselves. It is so with real Christians. They become of necessity large-hearted. The inspirations received lead to outbursts of joyful anticipation for all the world. The assertion of Luke that Mary returned home (ver. 56) does not necessarily imply that she did not wait for John's birth and circumcision. The probabilities are in favour of supposing that she did so wait, and received the additional consolations which the song of Zacharias was so fitted to bring. Strengthened by her long visit to Elisabeth, she would be the better able to go back to Nazareth and brave all suspicion there. God, by a special communication, made Joseph's suspicion altogether to cease, and Mary was taken by him as wife, instead of being privately divorced. The Virgin's trust in God smoothing her way was thus gloriously fulfilled (Matt. i. 18—25), and she found herself passing onwards upon a path of peace towards that signal influence and power which she has exercised among men.—R. M. E.

Vers. 57—80.—*The birth and development of the Baptist.* We now pass from the inspirations of the holy women to the birth of the Baptist. We have before us what one has well denominated "a pious family in their good fortune."[1] As this preacher observes, we have here "the mother in her joy, the father with his song of praise, and the little child and his development." We cannot do better than allow our thoughts to group themselves round these three persons in this order.

I. CONTEMPLATE THE MOTHER IN HER JOY. (Vers. 57—63.) A mother with a firstborn son embodies as much joy as we can well imagine in a world like this. All pain and anguish over and forgotten in the mighty fruition (cf. John xvi. 21). Next there would be messages sent to friends, "neighbours and cousins," who would be expected to call with congratulations. And they gave their congratulations without stint—"They rejoiced with her." Next came the circumcision and the naming of the child, and the idea of the neighbours was that they could not do better than call him "Zacharias," *i.e.* "one whom Jehovah remembers," after his priestly father. But the joyful mother has a new name to give her son, and, though none of her ancestors have borne it, he must be called "John," which, as already noticed, signifies "Jehovah giveth grace." The new name is to herald the nature of the dispensation. The friends are not satisfied, however, until they consult the dumb fathe.. They accordingly make signs to him how he would have him called, and he, with most serious deliberation, wrote on the tablet, "His name is John." It was a *revelation* to the neighbours, and they took it as such, and "marvelled all." The joyful mother had thus the satisfaction of seeing her firstborn son introduced to the Jewish Church by the rite of circumcision, and receiving a name which was itself a promise of great grace from God. What a joy it should be to parents to have their little children thus early introduced into the Church of God, and identified with its brightening prospects!

II. CONTEMPLATE THE FATHER PRAISING GOD. (Vers. 64, 67—79.) The dumb priest now regains his speech, and no sooner is his mouth opened than he bursts into praise. Doubtless he praised God for his *judgment* on himself and for his *mercy* in the gift of the goodly child. He was able then to sing of both (cf. Ps. ci. 1). Moreover, the Holy Spirit as a Spirit of prophecy filled him, so that his praise took the beautiful poetic form here given. And this song of Zacharias divides itself into two portions—first, the establishment of the theocracy under Messiah (vers. 67—75); and secondly, the apostrophe to the little child about his part in the work of reformation (vers. 75—79). To these let us devote a few thoughts. 1. *The establishment of the theocracy under Messiah.* As a priest, Zacharias naturally looked at the new movement from an ecclesiastical and patriotic point of view. Hence he praised God for the deliverance of his people through raising up a horn for them in the house of his servant David. This horn, the symbol of "might," is the Messiah who is to be born of Mary. But what salvation is it to be? In the usual Jewish spirit, he speaks of it as a salvation from

[1] Cf. Gerok's 'Evangelien-Predigten,' band i. s. 504.

enemies and all that hate the people of the Lord. In other words, the inspired priest looks and longs for a *national* deliverance. And the true patriot can long for nothing less. The blessing which he praises God for on his own account, he desires for all his race. At the same time, it is to be noticed that it is *pious parents* who are to realize the mercy—parents " who had hoped for the blessing of their seed, and had mourned over the misery of their posterity."[1] Such were hoping always on the covenant-promises, and now they were to have them fulfilled. But it is to be further noticed that the national deliverance expected is a means, not an end. It is only that the *theocratic idea* may be carried out by the emancipated people, and God served by them without fear in holiness and righteousness before him all their days. It is here that the great difference between worldly aspirations and spiritual ones is to be appreciated. If people hope for blessing that they may the better serve and please themselves, then they are simply worldly and selfish; but if they seek blessing to fit them to serve God, they are entering into the nobility of his kingdom. It is the reign of God within us and around us which we should always hope for and try to promote. 2. *The priest's apostrophe to his little child.* In the father's address to little John we see the spirituality which underlay his hope. His boy is to be a *prophet* of the Most High, something superadded to the priestly privileges which belonged to the family by right of birth. By word of mouth, therefore, is he to prepare his Lord's way. But his message is to be in the first instance about " remission of sins." In other words, the reformation hoped for is to be *moral.* Beginning in pardon and penitence, it will indeed be the dawn of a better day to many who have been sitting in darkness and the shadow of death, and the " guiding light " into the way of peace. John is thus to be the herald of the dawn. The Messiah is the "Sun of Righteousness," whose presence constitutes the day. He enables us to say, " The Lord is my Light and my Salvation; whom shall I fear ? " (Ps. xxvii. 1). John is to be the voice in the desert to apprise the wandering and stumbling " caravan " of the approach of dawn and its guidance into peaceful paths. And, as we shall see, the moral reformation under John became *national*, so that before Messiah's baptism " all the people were baptized " (ch. iii. 21).

III. CONTEMPLATE THE LITTLE CHILD'S DEVELOPMENT. (Vers. 66, 80.) The result of such prophecies connected with the circumcision of the child was the growth of a wholesome " fear" throughout all the hill-country of Judæa. The people began to hope for important changes. And their hopes were so far confirmed by the development of John. In the first place, "the hand of the Lord," *i.e.* Divine power and grace, " was with him." He grew up a spiritually minded boy. All who saw the priest's son concluded that God was with him in his grace and love. There are children who grow up with the stamp of heaven upon their whole lives. The Spirit of God is manifestly moving them along the true path. In the second place, he had *due physical development.* "He grew." A dedicated boy, a Nazarite from his youth, he grew up robustly on his plain fare, physically fit for the life of toil which was before him. In the third place, " *he waxed strong in spirit.*" His whole inward man more than kept pace with his outward growth. He was not only a good and growing lad, but also *heroic* in his mental progress. The inspired boy was getting strength to become one of God's heroes. In the last place, he *betook himself to the deserts* until such times as he was manifested to Israel. It was to be a development amid the solitude of the desert down towards the Dead Sea which John was to realize. God was his Teacher. Even the poor Essenes, who lived a life of asceticism in the neighbourhood, must have kept John at a distance, and so made his loneliness the more intense. And yet it may be safely said that no one has ever done much for God who has not been much *alone with him.* It is the communion of the lowly spirit with the Supreme which fits for high service. A desert, and not a garden of Eden, may often be the fittest environment for the consecrated soul, seeing that he is thereby thrown more completely upon God. Like Moses and Elijah, John has his long season of solitude with God, and then he comes forth radiant for the work he has to do in Israel. May such a development as John's be realized by many ! —R. M. E.

[1] Cf. Weiss's ' Leben Jesu,' erster band, s. 233.

EXPOSITION.

CHAPTER II.

Vers. 1—20.—*The Redeemer's birth.*

Ver. 1.—**There went out a decree from Cæsar Augustus, that all the world should be taxed;** more accurately, *that there should be a registration,* etc.; that is, with a view to the assessment of a tax. On the historical note of St. Luke in this passage much discussion has arisen, not, however, of much real practical interest to the ordinary devout reader. We will glance very briefly at the main criticism of this and the following verse. Respecting this general registration it is alleged (1) no historian of the time mentions such a decree of Augustus. (2) Supposing Augustus had issued such an edict, Herod, in his kingdom of Judæa, would not have been included in it, for Judæa was not formally annexed to the Roman province of Syria before the death of Archelaus, Herod's son; for some years after this time Herod occupied the position of a rex socius. In answer to (1), we possess scarcely any minute records of this particular time; and there are besides distinct traces in contemporary histories of such a general registration. In answer to (2), in the event of such an imperial registration being made, it was most unlikely that Herod would have claimed exemption for his only *nominally* independent states. It must be remembered that Herod was an attached dependent of the emperor, and in such a matter would never have opposed the imperial will of his great patron.

Ver. 2.—(**And this taxing was first made when Cyrenius was governor of Syria.**) Hostile criticism makes a still more direct attack upon the historical statement made by St. Luke here. Quirinius, it is well known, was governor (legatus or præses) of Syria ten years *later,* and during his office a census or registration—with a view to taxation—which led to a popular disturbance, was made in his province. These critics say that St. Luke mentions, as taking place *before* the birth of Jesus, an event which really happened *ten years after.* Much historical investigation has been made with a view to explain this difficulty. It has been now satisfactorily demonstrated that, strangely enough, this Quirinius—who ten years later was certainly governor (legatus) of Syria—at the time of the birth of the Saviour held high office in Syria, either as præses (governor) or quæstor (imperial commissioner). The Greek word rendered by the English "governor" would have been used for either of these important offices. On the whole question of these alleged historical inaccu-

racies of St. Luke, it may be observed: (1) Strangely enough,*none* of the early opponents of Christianity, such as Celsus or Porphyry, impugn the accuracy of our evangelist here. Surely, if there had been so marked an error on the threshold of his Gospel, these distinguished adversaries of our faith, living comparatively soon after the events in question, would have been the first to hit so conspicuous a blot in the story they hated so well. And (2) nothing is more improbable than that St. Luke, a man of education, and writing, too, evidently for people of thought and culture, would have ventured on a definite historical statement of this kind, which would, if wrong, have been so easily exposed, had he not previously thoroughly satisfied himself as to its complete accuracy. *Generally,* the above conclusions are now adopted, lately, amongst others, by Godet, Farrar, Plumptre, and Bishop Ellicott (in his Hulsean Lectures). Godet has an especially long and exhaustive note on this subject. The conclusions are mainly drawn from the researches of such scholars as Zumpt and Mommsen. **Cyrenius**; Latin, *Quirinus.* He is mentioned by the historians Tacitus and Suetonius. He appears to have been originally of humble birth, and, like so many of the soldiers of fortune of the empire, rose through his own merits to his great position. He was a gallant and true soldier, but withal self-seeking and harsh. For his Cilician victories the senate decreed him a triumph. He received the distinguished honour of a public funeral, A.D. 21 (Tac., 'Ann.,' ii. 30; iii. 22, 48; Suet., 'Tib.,' 49).

Ver. 4.—**The city of David, which is called Bethlehem.** After all the long ages which had passed, still the chief title to honour of the little upland village was that there the greatly loved king had been born. Bethlehem ("house of bread") was built on the site of the old Ephrath—the Ephrath where Rachel died. **Of the house and lineage of David.** The position in life of Joseph the royally descended, simply a village carpenter, the equally humble state of Mary, also one of the great king's posterity, need excite no surprise when the vicissitudes of that royal house, and of the people over whom they ruled, are remembered. The old kingdom of David had been dismembered, conquered, and devastated. The people had been led away into a captivity from which few, comparatively speaking, ever returned. All that the house of David had preserved were its bare family records. Hillel, the famous scribe, who was once a hired porter, claimed to belong to the old princely house.

Ver. 5.—**With Mary his espoused wife**

The older authorities here omit "wife." Translate, *with Mary who was betrothed to him.*

Ver. 6.—**The days were accomplished that she should be delivered.** The universal tradition of the Christian Church places the nativity in winter. The date "December 25" was generally received by the Fathers of the Greek and Latin Churches from the fourth century downwards.

Ver. 7.—**Her firstborn Son.** This expression has no real bearing on the question respecting the relationship of the so-called brethren of Jesus to Mary. The writer of this commentary, without hesitation, accepts the general tradition of the Catholic Church as expressed by the great majority of her teachers in all ages. This tradition pronounces these brethren to have been (1) either his half-brethren, sons of Joseph by a former marriage; or (2) his cousins. In the passage in Hebrews (i. 6), "when he bringeth in the *First Begotten* into the world," "First Begotten" signifies "Only Begotten." (On the whole question, see Bishop Lightfoot's exhaustive essay on the "Brethren of the Lord" in his 'Commentary on the Galatians.') **There was no room for them in the inn.** "The inn of Bethlehem, what in modern Eastern travel is known as a *khan* or *caravanserai*, as distinct from a hostelry (the 'inn' of ch. x. 34). Such an inn or khan offered to the traveller simply the shelter of its walls and roofs. This khan of Bethlehem had a memorable history of its own, being named in Jer. xli. 17 as the 'inn of Chimham,' the place of rendezvous from which travellers started on their journey to Egypt. It was so called after the son of Barzillai, whom David seems to have treated as an adopted son (2 Sam. xix. 37, 38), and was probably built by him in his patron's city as a testimony of his gratitude" (Dean Plumptre). The stable was not unfrequently a limestone cave, and there is a very ancient tradition that there was a cave of this description attached to the "inn," or caravanserai, of Bethlehem. This "inn" would, no doubt, be a large one, owing to its being in the neighbourhood of Jerusalem, and would often be crowded with the poorer class of pilgrims who went up to the temple at the seasons of the greater feasts. Bethlehem is only six miles from Jerusalem.

Vers. 8—20.—*The Bethlehem shepherds see the angels.*

Ver. 8.—**In the same country;** that is, in the upland pastures immediately in the neighbourhood of Bethlehem. **Shepherds abiding in the field, keeping watch over their flock by night.** Why were *shepherds* chosen as the first on earth to hear the strange glorious news of the birth of the Saviour of the world? It seems as though this very humble order was selected as a practical illustration of that which in the future history of Christianity was to be so often exemplified—"the exaltation of the humble and meek." Mary would learn from this, the first visit of adorers to her Babe, that the words of her song (the Magnificat) would in very truth be realized. The subsequent visit of the learned and wealthy travellers from the East (Matt. ii. 1—12) would tell her that the words of the Isaiah prophecy were all literally, in their due order, to be fulfilled, some of them even in the unconscious childhood of her Son (see Isa. lx. 3, 6; Ps. lxxii. 10). Now, among the Jews at that period *shepherds* were held in low estimation among the people. In the Talmud (treatise 'Sanhedrin') we read they were not to be allowed in the courts as witnesses. In the treatise 'Avodah-Zarah' no help must be given to the heathen or to shepherds. The Mishna (Talmud) tells us that the sheep intended for the daily sacrifices in the temple were fed in the Bethlehem pastures. This semi-sacred occupation no doubt influenced these poor toilers, and specially fitted them to be the recipients of the glad tidings. They would hear much of the loved Law in the solemn ritual of the great temple. They would know, too, that there was a rumour widely current in those days that the long-looked-for Messiah was soon to appear, and that their own Bethlehem was to witness his appearing.

Ver. 9.—**The angel of the Lord came upon them;** better, *an angel.* The Greek word rendered "came upon them"—a very favourite word with St. Luke—suggests a sudden appearance. **The glory of the Lord shone round about them: and they were sore afraid.** The white shining cloud of intolerable brightness, known among the Jews as the Shechinah, the visible token of the presence of the Eternal, in the bush, in the pillar of fire and cloud which guided the desert-wanderings, in the tabernacle and the temple. It shone round the Redeemer on the Mount of Transfiguration. It robed him when, risen, he appeared to the Pharisee Saul outside Damascus. The occasional presence of this visible glory was exceedingly precious to the chosen people. The terror felt by the shepherds was the natural awe ever felt by man when brought into visible communion with the dwellers in the so-called spirit-world.

Ver. 11.—**A Saviour.** Another favourite word with SS. Paul and Luke. The terms "Saviour" and "salvation" occur in their writings more than forty times. In the other New Testament books we seldom find either of these expressions.

Ver. 12.—**Lying in a manger.** This was to be the sign. On that night there would, perhaps, be no other children born in the Bethlehem village; certainly the shepherds would find no other newly born infant cradled in a manger.

Ver. 13.—**With the angel a multitude of the heavenly host.** "The troop of angels issues forth from the depths of that invisible world which surrounds us on every side" (Godet). One of the glorious titles by which the eternal King was known among the chosen people was "Lord of sabaoth," equivalent to "Lord of hosts." In several passages of the Scriptures is the enormous multitude of these heavenly beings noticed; for instance, Ps. lxviii. 17, where the Hebrew is much more expressive than the English rendering; Dan. vii. 10, "Ten thousand times ten thousand stood before him" (see, too, the Targum of Palestine on Deut. xxxiii., " And with him ten thousand times ten thousand holy angels;" and "The crown of the Law is his [Moses'], because he brought it from the heavens above, when there was revealed to him the glory of the Lord's Shechinah, with two thousand myriads of angels, and forty and two thousand chariots of fire," etc.).

Ver. 14.—**On earth peace.** At that juncture, strange to say, the Roman empire was at peace with all the world, and, as was ever the case in these brief rare moments of profound peace, the gates of the temple of Janus at Rome were closed, there being, as they supposed, no need for the presence of the god to guide and lead their conquering armies. Not a few have supposed that the angel choir in these words hymned this earthly peace. So Milton in his 'Ode to he Nativity'—

" No war or battle's sound
Was heard the world around ;
The idle spear and shield were high uphung :
The hookèd chariot stood
Unstained with hostile blood,
The trumpet spake not to the armèd throng ;
And kings sat still with awful eye
As if they surely knew their souvran Lord
was by."

But the angels sang of something more real and enduring than this temporary lull. The gates of Janus were only too quickly thrown open again. Some seventy years later, within sight of the spot where the shepherds beheld the multitude of the heavenly host, the awful conflagration which accompanied the sack of the holy city and temple could have been plainly seen, and the shrieks and cries of the countless victims of the closing scenes of one of the most terrible wars which disfigure the red pages of history could almost have been heard.

Good will toward men. A bare *majority* of the old authorities read here, " On earth peace among men of good will ; " in other words, among men who are the objects of God's good will and kindness. But the Greek text, from which our Authorized Version was made, has the support of so many of the older manuscripts and ancient versions, that it is among scholars an open question whether or not the text followed in the Authorized Version should not in this place be adhered to.

Ver. 17.—**And when they had seen** it, **they made known abroad the saying which was told them concerning this Child.** Thus these men, at the bottom of the social scale in Israel, were chosen as the first preachers of the new-born King. Gradually the strange story got noised abroad in the city. The vision of Zacharias, the story of Mary, the two strange births, the marvellous experience of the shepherds. Following upon all this was the arrival of the Magi, and their inquiries after a new-born Messiah, whom they had been directed by no earthly voices to seek after in the neighbourhood of Jerusalem. It was then that the jealous fears of Herod were in good earnest aroused, and the result was that he gave immediate directions for the massacre of the innocents in Bethlehem, of which St. Matthew writes.

Ver. 19.—**But Mary kept all these things, and pondered** them **in her heart.** Such a note as this could only have been made by Mary herself. *She* knew her Child was in some mysterious sense the Son of God. A glorious being not of earth had told her that her Boy would be the Saviour of Israel. The visit of the rough shepherds to her in the crowded caravanserai, and their strange but quiet and circumstantial story of the angel's visit to them, was only another link in the wondrous chain of events which was day by day influencing her young pure life. She could not as yet grasp it all, perhaps she never did in its mighty gracious fulness ; but, as at the first, when Gabriel the angel spoke to her, so at each new phase of her life, she bowed herself in quiet trustful faith, and waited and thought, writing down, we dare to believe, the record of all that was passing, and this record, we think, she showed to Luke or Paul.

Vers. 21—40.—*Circumcision and presentation of the Child Jesus.*

Ver. 21.—**For the circumcising of the Child.** These ancient rites—circumcision and purification—enjoined in the Mosaic Law were intended as perpetual witnesses to the deadly taint of imperfection and sin inherited by every child of man. In the cases of Mary and her Child these rites were not necessary ; but the mother devoutly submitted herself and her Babe to the ancient customs, willingly obedient to that Divine Law under which she was born and hitherto had lived.

Ver. 22.—**When the days of her purification according to the Law of Moses were accomplished.** This period lasted forty days from the birth. The forty days, according to the date of the nativity accepted universally by the Catholic Church, would bring the Feast of the Purification to February 2.

Ver. 24.—**A pair of turtle-doves, or two young pigeons.** The proper offering was a lamb for a burnt offering, and a pigeon or dove for a sin offering; but for the poor an alternative was allowed—instead of the more costly present of a lamb, a second pigeon or dove might be brought. The deep poverty of Mary and Joseph is shown in this offering. They would never have put the sanctuary off with the humbler had the richer gift been in their power.

Vers. 25—35.—*The episode of Simeon and his inspired hymn.*

Ver. 25.—**And, behold, there was a man in Jerusalem, whose name was Simeon; and the same man was just and devout, waiting for the consolation of Israel : and the Holy Ghost was upon him.** Many expositors have believed that this Simeon was identical with Simeon (Shimeon) the son of the famous Hillel, and the father of Gamaliel. This Simeon became president of the Sanhedrin in A.D. 13. Strangely enough, the Mishna, which preserves a record of the sayings and works of the great rabbis, passes by this Simeon. The curious silence of the Mishna here was, perhaps, owing to the hatred which this famous teacher incurred because of his belief in Jesus of Nazareth. Such an identification, although interesting, is, however, very precarious, the name Simeon being so very common among the people. *Waiting for the consolation of Israel.* There was a general feeling among the more earnest Jews at this time that the advent of Messiah would not be long delayed. Joseph of Arimathæa is especially mentioned as one who "waited for the kingdom of God" (Mark xv. 43). Dr. Farrar refers to the common Jewish prayer-formula then in use : "May I see the consolation of Israel!" A prayer for the advent of Messiah was in daily use.

Ver. 26.—**That he should not see death.** The idea of the *aged* Simeon comes from a notice in the apocryphal 'Gospel of the Nativity,' which speaks of him as a hundred and thirteen years old. These legendary "Gospels" are totally devoid of all authority; here and there possibly a true "memory" not preserved in any of the "four" may exist, but in general they are extravagant and improbable. The Arabic 'Gospel of the Infancy' here speaks of Simeon seeing

the Babe shining like a pillar of light in his mother's arms. There is an old and striking legend which speaks of this devout Jew being long puzzled and disturbed by the Messianic prophecy (Isa. vii. 14), "A virgin shall conceive;" at length he received a supernatural intimation that he should not see death until he had seen the fulfilment of the strange prophecy, the meaning of which he had so long failed to see.

Ver. 27.—**And when the parents brought in the Child Jesus.** This was evidently the usual expression which the Nazareth family adopted when they spoke of the Child Jesus (see, again, in ver. 48 of this chapter; and also in ver. 33, where the older authorities read "his father" instead of "and Joseph"). The true story, which they both knew so well, was not for the rough Galilæan peasant, still less for the hostile Herodian. The mother knew the truth, Joseph too, and the house of Zacharias the priest, and probably not a few besides among their devout friends and kinsfolk. The Nazareth family, resting quietly in their simple faith, left the rest to God, who, in his own season, would reveal the secret of the nativity.

Ver. 29.—**Lord, now lettest thou thy servant depart in peace.** The beautiful little hymn of Simeon was no doubt preserved by the Virgin Mary and given to St. Luke. The *Nunc dimittis* has been used constantly in the liturgies of Christian Churches for fourteen centuries. The thought which runs through the hymn has been well put by Godet : "Simeon represents himself under the image of a sentinel, whom his master has placed in an elevated position, and charged to look for the appearance of a star, and then to announce it to the world. He sees this long-desired star; he proclaims its rising, and asks to be relieved of the post on the watch-tower he has occupied so long. In the same way, at the opening of Æschylus's 'Agamemnon,' when the sentinel, set to watch for the appearing of the fire that is to announce the taking of Troy, beholds at last the signal so impatiently expected, he sings at once both the victory of Greece and his own release."

Vers. 31, 32.—**Before the face of all people ; a Light to lighten the Gentiles ;** more accurately rendered, *all peoples.* Men like Isaiah, who lived several centuries before the nativity, with their glorious far-reaching prophecies, such as Isa. lii. 10, were far in advance of the narrow, selfish Jewish schools of the age of Jesus Christ. It was, perhaps, the hardest lesson the apostles and first teachers of the faith had to master—this full, free admission of the vast Gentile world into the kingdom of their God. Simeon, in his song, however, distinctly repeats the broad, generous sayings of the older prophets.

Ver. 33.—**And Joseph and his mother marvelled.** It was not so much that Simeon foretold *new* things respecting the Child Jesus that they marvelled; their surprise was rather that a stranger, evidently of position and learning, should possess so deep an insight into the lofty destinies of an unknown Infant, brought by evidently poor parents into the temple court. Was their secret then known to others whom they suspected not?

Ver. 34.—**And Simeon blessed them, and said unto Mary his mother, Behold, this** Child. It is noticeable that, while Simeon blesses Mary and Joseph, he refrains from blessing the Child, of whom, however, he pointedly speaks. It was not for one like Simeon to speak words of blessing over "the Son of the Highest." The words which follow are expressly stated to have been addressed *only to Mary.* Simeon knew that she was related—but not Joseph—to the Babe in his arms; he saw, too, that *her* heart, not Joseph's, would be pierced with the sword of many sorrows for that Child's sake. **Behold, this** Child **is set for the fall and rising again of many in Israel; and for a sign which shall be spoken against.** For nearly three centuries, of course with varying intensity, the name of Jesus of Nazareth and his followers was a name of shame, hateful and despised. Not only among the Roman idolaters was "the Name" spoken against with intense bitterness (see the expressions used by men like Tacitus, Suetonius, and Pliny), but also among his own nation, the Jews, was Jesus known as "the Deceiver," "*that* Man," "the Hung." These were common expressions used in the great rabbinical schools which flourished in the early days of Christianity.

Ver. 35.—**Yea, a sword shall pierce through thy own soul also.** Christian art has well caught the spirit of *her* life who was, in spite of her untold suffering, "blessed among women," in depicting her so often and so touchingly as the mother of sorrows (*Mater Dolorosa*). The childhood in the Nazareth home, and the early manhood in the Nazareth carpentry, were no doubt her happiest days, though, in those quiet years, expectation, fears, dread, curiously interwoven, must have ever torn that mother's heart. The days of the public ministry for Mary must have been sad, and her heart full of anxious forebodings, as she watched the growing jealousies, the hatred, and the unbelief on the part of the leading men of her people. Then came the cross. We know she stood by it all the while. And, after the cross and the Resurrection, silence. Verily the words of Simeon were awfully

fulfilled. Bleek, quoted by Godet, makes an interesting suggestion on the subject of the sword piercing Mary's heart: "Thou shalt feel in thine own heart their contradiction in regard to thy Son, when thou thyself shalt be seized with doubt in regard to his mission."

Vers. 36—38.—*Greeting of Anna the prophetess.*

Ver. 36.—**There was one Anna, a prophetess.** The name of this holy woman is the same as that of the mother of Samuel. It is not necessary to assume that this Anna had the gift of foretelling future events. She was, at all events, a preacher. These saintly, gifted women, though never numerous, were not unknown in the story of the chosen people. We read of the doings—in some cases the very words are preserved—of Miriam, Hannah, Deborah, Huldah, and others. **Of the tribe of Aser.** It is true that at this period the ten tribes had been long lost, the "Jews" being made up of the two tribes of Judah and Benjamin; but yet certain families preserved their genealogies, tracing their descent to one or other of the lost divisions of the people. Thus Anna belonged to Asher.

Ver. 37.—**Which departed not from the temple, but served God with fastings and prayers night and day.** Probably, in virtue of her reputation as a prophetess, some small chamber in the temple was assigned to her. This seems to have been the case with Huldah (2 Chron. xxxiv. 22). It has also been suggested that she lovingly performed some work in or about the sacred building. Farrar suggests such as trimming the lamps (as is the rabbinic notion about Deborah), derived from the word *lapidoth*, splendour. Such sacred functions were regarded among all nations as a high honour. The great city of Ephesus boasted her name of νεωκόρος, temple-sweeper, as her proudest title to honour.

Ver. 39.—**And when they had performed all things according to the Law of the Lord.** Another note, which tells us of the rigid obedience which Mary and Joseph paid to the Law of Israel, under which they lived. Marcion, the famous Gnostic heretic (second century), who adopted this Gospel of St. Luke, to the exclusion of the other three, as the authoritative Gospel for his sect (the Marcionites), omitted, however, all these passages of St. Luke's narrative in which the old Mosaic Law was spoken of with reverence. **They returned into Galilee, to their own city Nazareth.** To complete the story of our Lord's early life, we must insert from St. Matthew, before this return to Nazareth, the visit of the Magi, and the flight to and return from Egypt. It is probable—even if the Gospel of St. Matthew, as we have it, was not then written—that these details, the visit of the Magi and the flight into Egypt, were facts already well known to those whom this Gospel was especially designed to instruct.

Ver. 40.—**And the Child grew, and waxed strong in spirit, filled with wisdom : and the grace of God was upon him.** Another of this evangelist's solemn pauses in his narrative. In this short statement the story of twelve quiet years is told. From these few words St. Luke evidently understands the humanity of Jesus as a reality. The statement that "he waxed strong, filled with wisdom" (the words, "in spirit," do not occur in the older authorities), tells us that, in the teaching of SS. Paul and Luke, the Boy learnt as others learnt, subject to the ordinary growth and development of human knowledge ; thus condemning, as it were, by anticipation, the strange heresy of Apollinarius, who taught that the Divine Word (the Logos) took, in our Lord's humanity, the place of the human mind or intellect. *And the grace of God was upon him.* The legendary apocryphal Gospels are rich in stories of the Child Jesus' doings during these many years. But the silence of the holy four, whose testimony has been received now since the last years of the first century by the whole Church, is our authority for assuming that no work of power was done, and probably that no word of teaching was spoken, until the public ministry commenced, when the Messiah had reached his thirtieth year. "Take notice here," wrote Bonaventura, quoted by Farrar, "that his doing nothing wonderful was itself a kind of wonder. . . . As there was power in his actions, so is there power in his silence, in his inactivity, in his retirement."

Vers. 41—52.—*The Child Jesus at Jerusalem.*

Ver. 41.—**Now his parents went to Jerusalem every year at the Feast of the Passover.** The Law required the attendance of all men at the three great Feasts of Passover, Pentecost, and Tabernacles (Deut. xvi. 16). The dispersion and subsequent residence of so many Jews in distant lands had much broken up the regular observance of these directions. Still, many devout Jews were constantly present at these feasts. This Mosaic ordinance was only binding upon men, but R. Hillel recommended women always to be present at the Passover. The constant yearly presence of Joseph the carpenter and Mary at this feast is another indication of the rigid obedience of the holy family of Nazareth to the ritual of the Law of Moses.

Ver. 42.—**And when he was twelve years old, they went up to Jerusalem after the** custom of the feast. When a Jewish boy was three years old he was given the tasselled garment directed by the Law (Numb. xv. 38—41; Deut. xxii. 12). At five he usually began to learn portions of the Law, under his mother's direction ; these were passages written on scrolls, such as the shema or creed of Deut. vi. 4, the Hallel Psalms (Ps. cxiv., cxviii., cxxxvi.). When the boy was thirteen years old he wore, for the first time, the phylacteries, which the Jew always put on at the recital of the daily prayer. In the well-known and most ancient 'Maxims of the Fathers' ('Pirke Avoth'), we read that, at the age of ten, a boy was to commence the study of the Mishna (the Mishna was a compilation of traditional interpretations of the Law); at eighteen he was to be instructed in the Gemara (the Gemara was a vast collection of interpretations of the Mishna. The Mishna and Gemara together make up the Talmud. The Mishna may roughly be termed the text, the Gemara the commentary, of the Talmud).

Ver. 43.—**And when they had fulfilled the days, as they returned, the Child Jesus tarried behind in Jerusalem.** The feast lasted seven days. Now, a boy in the East, twelve years old, is usually far more advanced than is ever the case in our Northern nations, where development is much slower. We may well suppose that the Boy was left much to himself during these days of the feast. It requires no stress of imagination to picture him absorbed in the temple and all that was to be seen and learned there. It was, doubtless, *his* first visit since infancy to the glorious house. Slowly, surely, had he been growing up into the consciousness of *what* he was and *whence* he came : may we not in all reverence assume that his self-recognition first really burst forth from the depths of his childhood's unconsciousness in that solemn week spent in the storied temple courts? When Joseph and Mary and their friends, as was usual after the seven days, commenced their return journey, the Boy, instead of joining this homeward-bound company of pilgrims, went as usual to the temple and the great teachers there, wholly absorbed in the new light which was breaking in upon him. *There* they found him. Strange that they should have for so long searched in other places. Had they only called to mind the sacred secret of the Child, surely they would have gone at once to the temple; was it not, after all, his earthly home, that holy house of his Father in Jerusalem?

Ver. 46.—**And it came to pass, that after three days they found him in the temple.** According to the common way of reckoning among the Hebrews, this expression, "after three days," probably means "on the third day." One day was consumed in the usual short pilgrim-journey. His absence at first would excite no attention; on the second, as they missed him still, they sought him in the various pilgrim-companies; and on the day following they found him in the temple courts, with the doctors of the Law. **Sitting in the midst of the doctors, both hearing them, and asking them questions.** In the temple enclosure, says the Talmud, there were three synagogues—one at the gate of the court of the Gentiles, another at the entrance of the court of the Israelites, a third in the south-east part of the inner court: it was in these that the rabbis expounded the Law. Among the famous doctors, or rabbis, then living and teaching in Jerusalem, were the famous Hillel, then very aged, verging, we are told, on his hundredth year; his almost equally illustrious rival, Shammai; Gamaliel, the master of Saul of Tarsus; Jonathan, the compiler of the Chaldee Paraphrase of the sacred books; Simeon, the son and successor of Hillel; Nicodemus, who, some years afterwards, came to Jesus by night, and, when the end was come, reverently assisted in laying the King's Son with all honour in his tomb in Joseph of Arimathæa's garden. We may, with great probability, assume that amongst those "doctors" whom the Boy questioned at that Passover Feast, some if not all of these well-known men were sitting. The apocryphal Gospels, as usual, profess to give us details where the true story is reverently silent. The 'Gospel of Thomas' (second century), for instance, tells us that Jesus, when on the road to Nazareth, returned of his own accord to Jerusalem, and amazed the rabbis of the temple by his solution of the hardest and most difficult questions of the Law and the prophets. In an Arabic Gospel of somewhat later date than that of Thomas, we find the Boy even teaching the astronomers the secrets of their own difficult study. Probably Stier's simple words approach the nearest to the truth here, when he suggests that his questions were "the pure questions of innocence and of truth, which keenly and deeply penetrated into the confused errors of the rabbinical teaching."

Ver. 48.—**Son, why hast thou thus dealt with us? behold, thy father and I have sought thee sorrowing.** Mary's words have in them something of reproach. Joseph, it is noticeable, stands evidently apart; but the mother, strangely as it would seem at first, associates him in "thy father and I have sought thee sorrowing." Had she, then, *forgotten* the past? Who but Mary could have repeated this sacred memory of her mistake, and of the Boy's far-

reaching answer? What forger could have *imagined* such a verse?

Ver. 49.—**How is it that ye sought me?** To the gently veiled reproach of Mary, Jesus replies, apparently with wonderment, with another question. It had come upon him so quietly and yet with such irresistible force that the temple of God was his real earthly home, that he marvelled at his mother's slowness of comprehension. Why should she have been surprised at his still lingering in the sacred courts? Did she not know who he was, and whence he came? Then he added, **Wist ye not that I must be about my Father's business?** There was an expression of Mary's which evidently distressed the Child Jesus. Godet even thinks that he discerns a kind of shudder in his quick reply to Mary's "thy father and I have sought thee sorrowing." "In my Father's house, where my Father's work is being done, there ought I to be busied. Didn't you know this?" But the twelve silent uneventful years of life at Nazareth, the poor home, the village carpentry, the natural development of the sacred Child, had gradually obscured for Mary and Joseph the memories of the infancy. They had not forgotten them, but time and circumstances had covered them with a veil. Now they were very gently reminded by the Boy's own quiet words of what had happened twelve years before. Scholars hesitate whether or not to adopt the rendering of the old Syriac Version, "in my Father's house," instead of the broader and vaguer "about my Father's business," as the Greek will allow either translation. It seems to us the best to retain the old rendering we love so well, "about my Father's business." The whole spirit of Jesus' after-teaching leads us irresistibly to this interpretation of the Master's *first recorded saying.*

Ver. 51.—**And he went down with them, and came to Nazareth.** The question of Mary, and the quiet grave answer of the Child Jesus, were all that seems to have taken place. It served, no doubt, to bring back to Mary's mind what had long passed, and the memory of which for her was beginning somewhat to fade. This was, no doubt, *one* of the uses of the temple scene, but it had other and deeper purposes to serve. It was then, perhaps, as we have already reverently surmised, in the gradual development and growth of the Redeemer, that consciousness who he really was first dawned upon "the *Child* Jesus." **And was subject unto them.** This recital of the temple scene, the meeting with the great rabbis there, the few words of surprise addressed by the Boy to Mary and Joseph when they sought him "sorrowing"—"as if it were possible," to use Stier's expression, for "him to be in wrong or in danger "— this recital alone breaks the deep silence which shrouds the first thirty years of "the Life." For some eighteen years after that visit to Jerusalem Jesus appears to have lived and toiled as a carpenter at Nazareth, with Joseph and Mary while they both lived, with Mary and his half-sisters and brothers when Joseph was dead. Justin Martyr, living a century and a half later, speaks of the ploughs and yokes the Master's own hands had fashioned during that long quiet pause in his life. Why, it is often asked, were not these years spent in Jerusalem and in the temple neighbourhood, in the centre of busy life and active Jewish thought? Godet suggests an answer which, if not exhaustive, is at least satisfactory: "If the spiritual atmosphere of Nazareth was heavy, it was at least calm; and the labours of the workshop, in the retirement of this peaceful valley, under the eye of the Father, was a more favourable sphere for the development of Jesus than the ritualism of the temple and the rabbinical discussions of Jerusalem." Joseph is never again mentioned in the gospel story; the probability is that he died some time in that period of eighteen years. **But his mother kept all these sayings in her heart.** As twelve years before, Mary—pondering in her heart—had treasured up the rough adoration of the shepherds and their strange story of what the angels said to them about her Child (ver. 19), as doubtless she had done too when the Magi laid their costly gifts before the Babe at Bethlehem, and when Simeon and Anna in the temple spoke their prophetic utterances over the Infant; so now the mother, in quiet humble faith, stored up again her Son's sayings in her heart, waiting with brave and constant patience for the hour when her God should grant her to see face to face the mysterious things she had hitherto seen only "in a glass darkly."

Ver. 52.—**And Jesus increased in wisdom and stature, and in favour with God and man.** Another of these little word-paintings of St. Luke in which the work and progress of long years is depicted. The purpose of this brief statement is clear. The evangelist would teach us that, with Jesus, *bodily* development proceeded in the same orderly fashion as it does with other men, while wisdom—deepening with the years—passed into his soul as it passes into the souls of other men, by the ordinary channels of instruction, study, and thought. On the last words, "in favour with God and man," Dean Plumptre very beautifully writes, "The Boy grew into youth, and the young Man into manhood, and his purity and lowliness and unselfish sympathy drew even then the hearts of all men. In that highest instance, as in all lower analogies, men admired holiness till it became aggressive, and then it roused them to an antagonism bitter in proportion to their previous admiration." The Greek word in this verse translated "increased" would be more literally rendered "kept advancing." The word is used for pioneers hewing down trees and brushwood which obstruct the path of an advancing army. The word in the original, Englished by "stature" some scholars translate by "age;" either rendering is permissible, but the word used in the English Version is better fitted for the context of the passage.

HOMILETICS.

Vers. 1—7.—*The birthplace and the birth.* Two travellers, coming up from Galilee, approach the city of David. The knowledge they possessed of the event in which the glories of David's house were to culminate must have invested every feature with a peculiar sacredness of interest. Note Dean Stanley's description of Bethlehem, on the crest of a ridge of black hills terraced with vineyards. As beheld by Joseph and Mary, what a stream of patriotic memories, mixed with the inspirations which spring from the sense of ancestry, must have flowed over their souls! There is the scene of the notable gleaning of the gentle Moabitess who had accompanied Naomi from those mighty hills which rear their pinnacles in the distance behind. There, Jesse with his seven stalwart sons had lived. In those fields and gorges the youngest of the seven had learned to sling his stones and sing his psalms—had been prepared for the future which lay before him. From that city had come the mightiest of David's warriors— Joab and Abishai and others. Lo! there, too, by the gate is the famous well of Bethlehem, of which David had longed to drink, but, faint as he was, would not, because the drawing of its water had been at the cost of life, strength, and blood. Manifold is the appeal to the heart of the pilgrims, who, lowly as their condition is, are scions of Israel's royal house. They are nearing the place of which prophecy had said (Micah v. 2), "Out of thee shall One come forth unto me that is to be Ruler in Israel; whose goings forth are from of old, from everlasting." They know that the fulfilment is at hand. Whither shall they go? High time that one should be at rest. Shall they go to the inn—the khan or caravanserai? (See Farrar's sketch of that strange shelter for man and beast.) But the inn is full. There is no place in it for such as they. The necessity is urgent. And their refuge—so a tradition mentioned by Justin Martyr says—is a grotto or cave in the limestone rock on which the village stands, used as a stable for horses and a pen for cattle. The horses' manger is the cradle for the King of kings. Born there and thus, the precise date of the birth is not apparently determinable.

Vers. 8—20.—*The shepherds and the herald angels.* From limestone cavern, we are taken by the evangelists to the long grassy slopes which stretch to the east of the Jewish city. Hidden in some nook of these slopes rest pious shepherds. Shepherds have always been a meditative class of men, accustomed to the sweet silences of nature, and, apart from the bustle and stir of cities, invited to quiet communion with their own hearts. It would seem that these shepherds were men of the spirit of Simeon. They quickly understand the message borne to them. Calmly and promptly, they respond at once, as if it were the intimation of that for which they had been waiting. "Let us go and see." There they lie, "nursed in devout and lonely thought," unaware of the myriad myriads of the shining that hover over them. It is the moment of a pause, of a hush through nature. Lo! the angel of the Lord comes on them; in an instant a presence, a glory, is around them; and first into their hearts is poured the gospel for all the ages. Of this gospel, note: (1) *Its substance.* (Ver. 11.) "Born *to you* this day"—God's gift to men, to sinners, especially to those who believe. "A Saviour, which is Christ"—the Anointed One—he of whom the prophets spoke, and whom David, the shepherd of Israel, prefigured; the Sent, not *by* but *from* God, from the depths of the Divine Personality; the Son from the bosom of the Father. "Christ, the Lord"—the Jehovah, to whom every knee shall bow; the Ruler who shall restore the lost, and unite the scattered, and fulfil the kingdom which is righteousness and peace and joy. (2) *The character of this gospel.* (Ver. 10.) "Good tidings of great joy;" the most blessed message ever proclaimed—one of unspeakable blessedness; a joy to which no bound can be set, which no geographical limit can measure, which no thought of class, or race, or sect can embitter; joy to all the world's peoples. (3) *The sign of the gospel.* (Ver. 12.) "A Babe wrapped in swaddling-clothes, and lying in a manger." The Babe is the sign of the kingdom, is the token of the King. "Except ye become as little children, ye shall in no wise enter into the kingdom of heaven" (Matt. xviii. 3). And now suddenly as the sign is given, "a blaze of song spreads o'er the expanse of heaven," and

> "Like circles widening round
> Upon a clear blue river,
> Orb after orb, the wondrous sound
> Is echoed on for ever:
> 'Glory to God on high, on earth be peace,
> And love towards men of love—salvation and release.'"

The *announcement of the birth is made to shepherds.* Why were they selected for this great honour? Points of fitness may be traced. Was not the first blood of sacrifice (Abel's) that of a keeper of sheep? Was not the chosen type and earthly root of the Christ a shepherd taken from the sheepfolds? Is not one of the favourite symbols of the world's Saviour the good shepherd? Is not the Saviour's work that of him who leaves the ninety and nine and goes after the sheep which is lost? Of all earthly things, are not the pastoral life and spirit the nearest correspondents to the life and spirit of the incarnate Son of God? And as to the gospel that was preached, is there not a truth in the quaint language of an old writer, "It fell not out amiss that shepherds they were; the news fitted them well. It well agreed to tell shepherds of the yearning of a strange Lamb, such a Lamb as might take away the sin of the world. Such a Lamb as they might send to the Ruler of the world for a present." Any way, it is not to supercilious Pharisee, not to Sadducee cold and dry as dust, not to Essene ascetic and separatist, not to Herodian worldly and crafty, not to the mighty or the noble that the first tidings of the great joy are brought. The first preacher is the heavenly angel, and the first congregation some lowly, simple men, who are doing their duty in the place which God has appointed to them. Thence comes the lesson to us. Heaven is always near the dutiful. They who watch faithfully what has been given to their charge, not seeking " some great thing to do," not hurried and restless in their work, but caring for the things, many or few, over which God has placed them, are close to that gate of the celestial kingdom through which there peals the music, " Blessed are the pure in heart: for they shall see God." Two points in this portion of the narrative may be touched upon. (1) *The conduct of the shepherds* when the tidings of the birth are borne to them. On the withdrawal of the heavenly vision, they say (ver. 15), " Let us now go even to Bethlehem, and see this thing which is come to pass." The flocks are somehow disposed of. This is a matter to be at once attended to. A word of God, a voice of the Holy Spirit in the heart, a command or duty pertaining to the heavenly life, claims precedence over all other claims. " Seek first the kingdom of God." Prompt obedience is the way of blessing. " They came with haste." Yes; " the King's business requireth haste." Never delay. St. Paul acted in the spirit of the shepherds when, God having been pleased to reveal his Son in him, " immediately he conferred not with flesh and blood" (Gal. i. 16). (2) *The conduct of Mary.* The shepherds eagerly told their wonderful tale. And all the people who heard, wondered. " But Mary (ver. 19) kept all these sayings and pondered them in her heart." The wonder of the people soon passed away; it was but "as the morning cloud and the early dew." Religious feelings are conserved and deepened through reflection and prayer. Blessed secret—the keeping and pondering in the heart !

Vers. 21—38.—*The circumcision and presentation in the temple.* I. THE CIRCUM- CISION. With regard to the circumcision, observe : 1. The Son of God is not only " made of a woman," he is *" made under the Law."* He is entered into all the requirements and circumstances of the covenant " with Abraham and his seed." The apostle tells us why—" to redeem them that were under the Law." Christ took the bond under which Israel was bound, and became Israel's Surety for it. Now it is ended. There is a new form of righteousness in which the wall of partition between Jew and Gentile is removed. The apostle adds (Gal. iv. 6), " To redeem them that were under the Law, that we "—*i.e.* as many as have been baptized into Christ, Jew or Greek, bond or free—" might receive the adoption of sons." This adoption is now the standing through grace. 2. The circumcision has its *special place in the making of Jesus by God to us Wisdom, Righteousness, Sanctification, Redemption.* It is an evidence that the Son of God was sent " in the likeness of sinful flesh." Circumcision supposed its subject to be a sinner. It supposed that a condemnation rested on him as such. The Lord Jesus, God's beloved Son, therefore took the sinner's place, and in the drops of blood shed on the eighth day after birth served himself, as it were, the heir to the condemna- tion of sin. Of this condemnation he spoke when he bowed his head on the cross and said, " It is finished ! " 3. The circumcision has *its special meaning with regard to the spiritual history of believers.* See in this connection Col. ii. 10, " You Christians "— thus we may paraphrase the sentence—" have, through your union with Christ, the reality of circumcision. When you gave yourselves to Christ, a work was done in you which was equal to the sharp and painful renunciation—the putting off—of the body of flesh, of that mind of the flesh with its affections and lusts which is enmity against God. It was through the repentance wrought in you that you became partakers of the remission of sins. When you were buried with Christ in baptism, your old, unbelieving self was circumcised to the Lord. You found the new position, the new life, that is complete in Christ. (For the manifold suggestiveness of the circumcision of the infant Jesus, read Keble's hymn in his ' Christian Year.')
II. THE PRESENTATION. The forty days of purification prescribed by the Law of Moses having been accomplished, Joseph and Mary bring the Babe to Jerusalem, to present him to the Lord. As Mary's Firstborn, he must be formally separated. And in the narrative of this separation we are reminded of the lowly condition of the parents. Not the lamb and the pigeon, but the two young pigeons allowed in cases of poverty, constitute the sacrifice, so low had he stooped whose place is the bosom of the Father. Look at the welcome prepared for Christ as he is borne in Mary's loving arms into his Father's temple. 1. Think first of *the man by whom the welcome is expressed.* He is called simply " a man in Jerusalem." Not the priests. In connection with the infancy we trace three acts of adoration—that of the shepherds, that of Simeon and Anna, and that of the heathen Magi. In all there is no representation of the circles of authority;

at least, there is no dwelling on the importance of those through whom the homage is shown. The tribute of the human heart is sufficient for the Son of man. Of this man we know nothing more than is told us by St. Luke. His name is Simeon. He is (ver. 25) "righteous and devout, one of those who looked for the consolation of Israel, and the Holy Spirit is upon him." The character—all that is memorable—is summed up in the title he himself takes (ver. 29), "Thy servant." For years he has been looking—a sharer in the expectation which had become earnest and eager among the pious. But he thinks and prays and hopes in a light that is peculiar to himself. Somehow—we are not told how—the intimation has been borne into his soul (ver. 26) that "he should not see death before he had seen the Lord's Christ." Is not the picture of this "watcher for the morning" a beautiful one? Do we not seem to see him, weary of the word-wranglings, the fightings over pin-points of ceremonial, which abounded, piercing through the hypocrisies with which the religious world was honeycombed; amid confusions becoming worse confounded, breathing the prayer, "O thou Hope of Israel, come quickly"? Is not this man an example to us? Is not this present time the watch-night to Christ's people? Are we watching as he watched—"not asleep in sin, but diligent in the Lord's service, and rejoicing in his praises"? 2. Regard next *the scene in which the welcome is given.* The watcher is in the temple—there in the spirit of David's psalm, "That I may dwell in the courts of the Lord, beholding the beauty of the Lord, and inquiring in his temple." He is there led by the Spirit. When "two unnoted worshippers" enter, his eye fixes on the two; faster beats the heart, "It is he; that child is he—the Lord's Christ." An incident that is indelibly photographed in the heart of Christendom is that in which the venerable seer takes the Babe in his arms, and lifts his eyes to heaven "in prayers that struggle with his tears." (1) Behold the sign of the Babe realized. To welcome the true child-nature, as Simeon welcomed Jesus; to see heaven in the Child, and open the soul to the impression, becoming child-like, and therefore Christ-like;—this is to receive the kingdom of heaven. (2) Note that in spiritual history there is a moment of discovery—the discerning of the hidden glory in Jesus. This moment is typified in the conjunction of the watcher and the watched for (ver. 27)—when the parents brought the Child Jesus, then he received him into his arms. We may not be able always to distinguish the very time and way; but there is the morning hour in the life, the awakening to the claim of God on the soul, to the fact "I am a sinner, and I need the Lord's Christ," and the answering fact, "He is the Saviour, and he wants me." Would that Simeon's joy were realized in all who read, "Mine eyes have seen thy Salvation"! 3. Observe *the song,* the familiar "Nunc dimittis." What sweetness, what beauty in this, the "swan-song" of the Christian Church as it has been called! (1) How tenderly the heart asks the supreme release! What more can be desired! The servant has seen the Master. And yet it is no prayer of longing initiated by the heart itself. Had it not been revealed to him that the hour of departure would follow the vision of the Lord? The human will touches the Divine. "Let me depart ... according to thy word." (2) How the song thrills with the sense of a love free and universal as the light of God (vers. 31, 32)! So it is when the Lord's Christ is really seen. The place of Christ is "a place of broad rivers and streams." Christian love is necessarily a missionary love. The word which it sows into the innermost desire is, "Let there be light." Christians may learn this, too, from Simeon—he, the Israelite, seeks the good of the Gentiles. The salvation in which he rejoices is one "for revelation to the Gentiles." Should not we Gentiles reciprocate by embracing in our prayer and effort God's people Israel?—seeking that the whole thought of the venerable watcher may be fulfilled—the Lord's Christ, the Light for the Gentiles and the Glory of Israel. (3) A soul thus filled out of the fulness of God's love is ready to depart. Death to it is only a departing, the dismissal of the servant from the scene of earthly toil, that he may enter more fully into the joy of the Lord. "Lord, now lettest thou thy servant depart in peace." The aged servant has still another word. He has his blessing for the parents. 4. Mark *the prediction addressed to Mary.* (1) The more general announcement, which seems at variance with the exalted strain of the song; but in this variance it harmonizes with the words of prophecy (*e.g.* Isaiah's forecasts), and interprets the experience of the ages. For "Christ is both a Corner-stone and a Stumbling-stone, and perhaps, in some sense, he is both the one and the other to us all." (2) The more special announcement. Ah! how often the love which is the source of the purest joy is the occasion of the most poignant sorrow! Many a mother can understand the word of the seer to the mother, "A sword shall pierce through thine own soul." Well when the wound is that only of a holy sorrow! Thus (3) the prophetic word is attached to the blessing, that, through the Lord's Christ, "the thoughts of many hearts should be revealed." It is true: the attitude of every heart to Christ is the revelation of that heart in the roots and springs of its thinking. 5. *The sketch of Anna the prophetess is the concluding and consummating feature of the day.* She, too, is an interesting person. A widow, after seven years of married life, and now "advanced in many days" (ver. 36), at least four score and four. Devout, almost an inmate of the temple, and recognized as a prophetess. She, too, has her thanksgiving, as she comes in "at that very hour." But the notable circumstance in regard to her is that she is the first preacher of Christ in the city of the great King. "She speaks of him to all them that are looking for redemption." She is the pioneer of the great host of women that publish the tidings (Ps. lxviii. 11, Revised Version). In this host may many who read or hear be included!

Vers. 39—52.—*The childhood and the waiting-time.* Before the age of twelve, nothing is told. In modern biographies, all kinds of traits, incidents, forecasts of the man in the child, are mentioned. The Apocryphal Gospels fall in with this custom. God's thoughts are not our thoughts. The child-life of "the Lord's Christ" is thoroughly simple. A bright-eyed boy, learning to read the Scriptures at his mother's knee, running out and in to shop and cottage, and joining sometimes in the innocent pastimes of the hillside, taking at night his little quilt from the ledge surrounding the wall of the house, and laying himself down in peace and sleeping,— such, we may conceive, was the life of the holy Child. Thoughtful, wise, gentle, yet full of a nameless "grace and truth;" for (ver. 40) "he grew and waxed strong, filled with wisdom, and the grace of God was on him." The incident which alone breaks the silence is connected with his twelfth year, the completion of which was an important hour in Jewish history—the hour of transference from pupilage to a certain measure of responsibility. At that age Jesus, "a son of the Law," is taken by Joseph and Mary to Jerusalem. The journey, the caravans of pilgrims, the incidents of the way, the three nights' halting, and then the sight of Jerusalem with its temple shining in the sun,—we can imagine what all this must have been to the exquisitely sensitive soul of the Child! And the week's stay in the capital—what bursting of thoughts! what tides of inspiration! Let us dwell on the first recorded word of Jesus—his reply to his mother (ver. 49), when she and Joseph found him among the doctors. Regard it as the word of sanctified boyhood—as the awakenment to the consciousness of (1) the supreme relation of the life; (2) the supreme interest of the life; (3) the supreme necessity of the life.

I. THE SUPREME RELATION. "My Father." We may infer, from the fiftieth verse, that now for the first time this word had passed from his lips. "*Thy* father and I," said Mary. Quietly but distinctly comes the intimation of the Fatherhood—an intimation in which we can trace the disengagement. "Nay, not he whom I have honoured, and honour, as earthly parent, but he to whom I am truly bound—he who is, who only is, *my* Father." And a great, solemn hour it is when the feeling of a personal, individual relation to the Eternal dawns on the consciousness. In earliest years the child-nature is enfolded in others. The first crisis of the life is when it begins to realize that it cannot merely be led; that it has a place and calling of its own; that it must think and will, instead of only reflecting the thought and volition of those who have shaped its path. Here there is a parting of the ways—one way being towards a self-will, which has "torment" in it for the youth as for others, and which, unless corrected and disciplined by sharp experience, will bear the soul into hurtful alliances, will prove "a hewing out of broken cisterns which hold no water;" the other way being that of Divine grace, the acceptance of a higher rule and guidance, the learning of the great name Duty in the greater, the supporting Name of God, the response of the heart to a love and righteousness which asks its yes, the witness of the eternal Spirit with the human that the Boy is the Son of God. Who will not anxiously endeavour so to direct the mind, in the period when it is most susceptible of all right influences, as that the transition from childhood to youth shall be marked by a new glance upward, a loving and earnest "My Father"!

II. Further, NOTE THE SUPREME INTEREST OF THE LIFE. It matters not whether we read "about my Father's business" or "in my Father's house;" the idea is the same —that the irresistible attraction of the Son is the affairs which connect him with the Father. At twelve years of age the business was "hearing and asking questions." There is nothing forced or forward in the holy childhood. The "understanding and answers" are pronounced wonderful. But the Boy is only the "son of the Law;" he is not yet the Doctor. By-and-by he will be. Later on, he will be called to drink the bitter cup—to suffer and die. But everything in its right order. The life will evolve out of the principle that, in all, the Father's will is to rule, the Father's mind is to be read, the Father's kingdom is to be promoted. Here, surely, there is a suggestion as to the idea which should dominate in the education of the young. At home and at school, all culture, all training, should be associated with a higher reference; the boy, the girl, should feel that the life is among the heavenly Father's things. The sense of responsibility to him for the nature, and the opportunity of improving the nature, should be laid deep in the character. More than this, the generous instincts of youth should be supplied with a fitting aliment. Too often they run to seed because the intelligence was not enlisted in objects which formed a definite interest to the mind. Let young people be taken to their Father's house; let Church services recognize their place and part; let them be invited to a share in the hopes and the activities of Christ's cause. Plant them in the courts of the Lord, "in their Father's things."

III. Once more, OBSERVE THE SUPREME NECESSITY OF THE SPIRIT OF THE LIFE IN THE BOY JESUS. "Why hast thou thus dealt with us?" asks his mother reproachfully. "How is it that ye sought me?" is the rejoinder; "wist ye not that I must be where and as you find me?" We note the surprise in the answer. It is the flashing forth of a something, a secret, in the childhood which the mother had not noticed, so simple, so obedient, had the Child been. To the Boy, so full of the glories and solemnities of the Father's house, it seemed strange that they had not recognized whose he was—that they had not understood the obligation inlaid in the life itself. And when the constraint of God's love is acknowledged, when the soul awakes to the vision of the Father and the Father's business,—the spell of Christ's "I must" is irresistible. We come on it again and again in the course of the ministry. It was the *law* of the spirit of the life. And the same law operates in every one who is of the truth. In that sweet bondage stands the soul's perfect freedom: "I must work the works of him that sent me;" "I *must* be about my Father's business." Then, in perfect naturalness, yet with marvellous boldness, comes forth the first self-revelation of the Lord. Joseph and Mary understood it not. How often is the young heart, aroused and astir in consequence of a higher call, misunderstood, misjudged! Mary did not comprehend, but she sympathized; she loved and prayed. Type of the true mother, "whose eyes are homes of silent prayer." The sense of the higher sonship only enforces the obligations of the lower. In the higher love all other loves endure. "This is love," says St. John, "that we walk after his commandments"—after "the first commandment with promise, Honour thy father and mother." There is nothing lovelier in the human life of Christ than the renewed acceptance of the restraints of home. "He went down with them, and came to Nazareth, and was subject unto them"—to them, with the narrow round of their daily care and concerns; and he with the great thoughts glowing in his breast, and the kingdom of his Father opening to his gaze. Mark: 1. *What self-repression belonged to the time in Nazareth!* We see the Son taking the place in the carpenter's house a few years later than the visit to the temple; Joseph apparently is removed by death from the headship of the house. Is it beyond the probabilities of the case that he performed the part—always a touching one—of the eldest son and brother supporting the mother to whom he is subject, and guiding the younger members of the family? Nothing is left undone, and he who thus learned obedience to duty leaves an example which serves as a beacon-light both to youth and age. 2. *How this time consecrates labour and poverty!* He wrought at the common things; in them he could see his Father's things, and do all as part of his Father's business. The truth receives a new radiance that "work is the girdle of manliness." Faber sings truly—

> " Labour is sweet, for thou hast toiled;
>   And care is light, for thou hast cared.
>   Let not our works with self be soiled,
>   Nor in unsimple ways ensnared."

3. *How emphatic is the lesson on the fruitfulness of silence suggested by this time!* Between twelve years of age and thirty the Son of God was content to wait. The public life lasted for three years; he waited for thirty years. A great disproportion, we might say; but God's ways are not our ways. All the while he was growing in wisdom. As his bodily strength was compacted and matured, so was his mental; for in all things he was made like to his brethren. He studied his Father's Word and his Father's works. Nature disclosed to him her hidden meanings and beauties; he thought, he prayed, he lived, by the Father. The results of the long silence were evidenced in the exquisite parables of later years, in the wisdom which none could resist, in the authority which separated his doctrine from that of the scribes. The accumulated capital was great; when he went forth in the power of the Spirit he only drew the interest. Are we not, in these days, in too great haste both to be wise and to be rich? Do we not speak too soon as well as speak too much? Carlyle only apprehends the significance of Nazareth when he reminds us that in silence all great thought and work are done. We need more than " flashes of silence." Think, think of Jesus silent so long. Stier exclaims, " Oh what gracious words may have issued from his lips during those eighteen years which are not recorded! But the words which, by the Father's ordination, he was to testify to the world were sealed up till his hour was come. Then, one after another, bursts forth each as it were a deeper stream from the long pent-up fountains of eternal wisdom and truth!"

HOMILIES BY VARIOUS AUTHORS.

Ver. 7.—*Christ excluded.* Little did the occupants of that inn at Bethlehem imagine who it was they were turning away when Joseph and Mary sought admission there. They did not realize, for they did not know, whom they were excluding. Practically they were declining to receive, not only the Messiah of their country, but the Saviour of the world. What they did in guiltless ignorance, men too often do in wilful and culpable rejection. Jesus Christ is sometimes excluded by men—

I. FROM THEIR THEORIES OF THE DIVINE GOVERNMENT. They have constructed such a perfect theory of government out of the operation of physical law, that there is no room at all for an interposing Saviour. The whole space of their kingdom of truth is occupied.

II. FROM THEIR ESTIMATE OF THEIR INTELLECTUAL NECESSITIES. They believe that, by applying their knowledge, their reasoning faculty, their intuitive powers, to nature and to mankind, they can reach all the conclusions there is any necessity to attain. All that is over and above this is redundant; there is no room in their sense of need for a Divine Teacher. Well did the Master say that to enter the kingdom of heaven we must become as a little child. The self-sufficiency of a complacent maturity thinks it has nothing to learn; it bars its doors; it sends the light of the world elsewhere; its little " inn " of knowledge and aspiration is occupied from floor to roof.

III. FROM THEIR ESTIMATE OF MAN'S SPIRITUAL WANTS. Very many are they who are not unwilling to welcome a Guide, but who have no room for a Saviour; for they have no sense of sin. They want to know which of the commandments they have broken. It does not occur to them that they have been owing to their great Creator, to their heavenly Father, to their Divine Friend, ten thousand talents of reverence, obedience, gratitude; and that they have been only offering to him a few poor pence, or that they have had nothing at all to pay. They are not conscious of a deep and wide gulf between their indebtedness and their discharge, and they go on their way not knowing that " the God in whose hand their breath is, and whose are all their ways, they have not glorified; " that they have sinned against the Lord, and need his abounding mercy. They, therefore, have no room for Christ, the Divine Propitiation, the great Reconciler of man to God.

IV. From the habit of their life. Of all those who exclude Jesus Christ, the most numerous and perhaps the guiltiest are they who, recognizing his claims and his powers, refuse to welcome him to their hearts. Their lives are so crowded with *cares*, with the business of the market or of the household; or they are so filled up with the *pleasures* and the *prizes* of this world; or they are so occupied with *pursuits* which, if intellectual, are unspiritual, that there is no room for that Divine One who comes to speak of sin and of mercy and of the life which is spiritual and eternal, who claims to be trusted and loved and served as the Saviour of the human soul and the Sovereign of the human life. So, while admitting his right to enter, they do not open the door. Alas! of what enlightening truth, of what blessed restfulness of heart, of what nobility of life, of what eternity of glory, do men bereave themselves by crowding out the Lord who loves them, by excluding the Redeemer from the home of their hearts!—C.

Vers. 8—11.—*Welcome news from heaven.* It is surely not without significance that this most gracious manifestation and announcement was made to these humble Hebrew shepherds "keeping watch over their flock by night." It suggests two truths which are of frequent and perpetual illustration. 1. That God chooses for his instruments the humble rather than the high. Our human notions would have pointed to the most illustrious in the land for such a communication as this. But God chose the lowly shepherd, the man of no account in the estimate of the world. So did he act in the beginning of the gospel (see 1 Cor. i. 26—29). And so has he acted ever since, choosing often for the agents of his power and grace those whom man would have passed by as unworthy of his choice. 2. That God grants his Divine favour to those who are conscientiously serving him in their own proper sphere. Not to the idle dreamer, not to the man who will do nothing because he cannot do everything of which he thinks himself capable, but to him who does his best in the position in which God's providence has placed him, will God come in gracious manifestation; and it is he whom he will select to render important service in his cause. But the main thoughts of this passage are these—
I. Welcome tidings from the spiritual world. "They were sore afraid." "Fear not . . . I bring you good tidings." Why have men always been so sore afraid in the presence of the supernatural? Why have they feared to receive communications from heaven? Something much more than a popular belief (see Judg. xiii. 22) is required to account for so universal a sentiment. It is surely that sinful men are profoundly conscious of ill desert, and fear that any message that comes from God, the Holy One, will be a message of condemnation and punishment. What would be the expectation with which a camp of rebellious subjects, who had taken up arms against their sovereign, would receive a messenger from the court of the king? Had that guilty age known that God was about to announce "a new departure" in his government of the world, what ample, what overwhelming reason would it have had to apprehend a message of Divine wrath and retribution! How welcome, then, the words, "Fear not . . . I bring you *good* tidings"! Of what depth of Divine patience, of what boundless breadths of Divine compassion, do these simple words assure us!
II. Tidings of surpassing value. Tidings "of great joy." The birth of the Babe in Bethlehem "that day"—what did it mean? It meant: 1. Deliverance from a deadly evil. To these shepherds, if they were patriotic children of Abraham, the promise of a Saviour would mean deliverance from the national degradation into which Israel had sunk—a spiritual as well as a political demoralization. To them, if they were earnest religious inquirers, it meant deliverance from the bondage and penalty of sin. This is the significance which the word has to us: in that day was born into the world a Saviour, a Divine Redeemer, One who should save the souls of men from that which is the one curse of our humanity—*sin*. 2. The fulfilment of a great hope. To those who then learnt that "the Christ" was born, it meant that the long-cherished hope of their nation was fulfilled, and that whatever the Messiah was to bring about was at length to be accomplished. A great national expectation has passed, with us, into a glorious hope for the human race—the hope that under Christ this poor sin-stricken world will rise from its ignorance, its superstition, its godlessness, its vice, and its crime, and walk in newness of life, in the love and the likeness of its heavenly Father. 3. Restoration to our true position. That Saviour is "Christ *the Lord*." We who

have sought to rule ourselves and to be the masters of our own lives, and who have suffered so much in so many ways by this guilty dethronement and usurpation, are now to find our true rest and joy by submitting ourselves to him who is "the Lord" of all hearts and lives; in his service is abiding peace and "great joy."

III. TIDINGS OF GENERAL AND OF PARTICULAR APPLICATION. These glad tidings are for "all the people," and they were for those startled and wondering shepherds. "To you is born." As we hear the angel's words, we know that they are for all the wide world, and, whoever we may be, *for us.*—C.

Vers. 13, 14.—*The human and the heavenly world.* The strange and elevating experience through which the shepherds of Bethlehem were passing prepared them for a scene which was fitted to awaken still greater surprise and spiritual excitement. For suddenly, all of them appearing together, a multitude of the heavenly host began to make angelic music; strains of sweetest song filled the air, and the words of that celestial chant, so exquisitely sweet, so full of comfort and of hope to our human race, were fixed in the shepherds' mind; they found a place in the sacred record; they make melody in our ear to-day. The scene and the song suggest to us—

I. THE INTEREST WHICH THE ANGELIC TAKES IN THE HUMAN WORLD. It is a striking and significant fact that the advent of Jesus Christ to our world should be preluded and accompanied by the ministry of angels (ch. i. 11, 26; ii. 9). It confirms the truth elsewhere indicated that the history of mankind is the subject of deep interest to the holy intelligences of heaven. They inquire with a pure and heavenly curiosity into the relations of God with man (1 Pet. i. 12). They reverently admire the wisdom of God in his dealings with his human children (Eph. iii. 10). They rejoice over the smallest accession to the kingdom of God (ch. xv. 10). They expend their powers in the accomplishment of God's will concerning us (text, and Heb. i. 14). Our Saviour is One in whom they also have profound interest, though they need not his redemption, and their worship of him is a large element in their celestial joy (Eph. i. 10; Rev. v. 11—13).

II. THE ADVENT OF CHRIST AN EPOCH IN THE KINGDOM OF GOD. Well might a multitude of the heavenly host chant those words of the text, "Glory to God in the highest;" well might they join in the high praises of the King of heaven. For when Jesus Christ came as he thus came, in lowliness of perfect humiliation (ver. 7), that the world into which he thus entered as a helpless babe might be redeemed and restored (ver. 10), two things were done. 1. The exceeding greatness of the Divine grace received its most wonderful illustration. Possibly—may we not say probably?—even the records of the kingdom of God contained no event illustrative of a more magnanimous pity and a more sacrificial love than this expression of "good will to men." 2. The foundation was laid on which a Divine kingdom of truth and righteousness should be reared. On the rock of the Divine incarnation rests the whole grand edifice of the restoration of the human race to the love and the likeness of God. Then indeed, when Jesus was born in Bethlehem, the glory of God was most fittingly celebrated; for then was the glory of his grace manifested, and then was the glory that should be rendered him by our humanity assured.

III. THE COMING OF CHRIST TO OUR WORLD THE INCOMING OF ITS PEACE. "Peace on earth." It has taken long for the work of Jesus Christ to bring about this result, even as things are to-day. And how much remains to be done! To some eyes it may seem as if only the elementary lesson had been learned. But if we look long enough and deep enough we shall see: 1. That the gospel of Jesus Christ has been, and is, offering to every burdened human heart a peace which is immeasurably profound and inestimably precious. 2. That the teaching and the Spirit of Jesus Christ are perfectly fitted to inculcate and to inspire peace, and even love, between man and man. 3. That under his benign government, and just so far as his will is consulted, man is leaving strife and discord below and behind him, and is moving on an upward path toward the sphere where peace and purity dwell together.—C.

Ver. 19.—*The wisdom of devout meditation.* Mary "kept" all those things which she had heard, treasured them in the secret chamber of her mind, dwelt upon them in her heart. Much she must have wondered what it could all mean and what would be the issue of it. Doubtless the hope that was in her purified her heart as so sacred a hope would do (1 John iii. 3), and made her life a life of reverence and prayer. It was good for her to think much of the purpose God was about to accomplish through her instrumentality ; she would be the better fitted for that holy motherhood by which she was to be so highly honoured, and by which she was to render so inestimable a service to her nation and her race. The fact that she did keep and dwell upon these solemn and sacred mysteries may remind us of—

I. THE THINGS THAT ARE MOST WORTH KEEPING. These are not moneys that may be kept in the bank, nor jewels that may be treasured in the cabinet, nor parchments that may be guarded in the strong box ; they are none other than *Divine thoughts which we can hold in our hearts*. And of these there are Divine *revelations*. They may be of his holy purpose, such as Mary's heart held ; or they may be of his own character or disposition toward us his children, such as we may learn and hold ; or they may be revelations of our own true selves, of our character and our necessities and our possibilities ; or they may be of the way by which we can approach and resemble God. There are also Divine *invitations*—to return from our estrangement, to draw near to his throne, to accept his mercy, to walk by his side, to sit down at his table. There are Divine *exhortations* to duty, to service, to self-sacrifice. And there are Divine *promises*, of provision and protection and inspiration here, of blessedness and enlargement hereafter.

II. THAT WHICH CONSTITUTES THEIR SUPREME VALUE. 1. They pertain to God himself, and therefore connect us with the Highest. 2. They affect *us, ourselves*—our character, our inner life, our essential being. 3. They bring us into harmony with all things ; for he that is right with God and true to himself is adjusted to all other beings, and is ready for all other things. 4. They render us fitted for life anywhere and in the distant future ; so that death will be a mere incident in our history, not concluding our career, but only opening the gate into other and brighter spheres.

III. THE DANGER WE ARE IN OF LOSING THEM. There is a plausible philosophical theory that a thought once received into the mind cannot ever be wholly lost ; once there it remains there, though it may be in the far background, unperceived, unemployed. But, as a matter of practical life, we know too well, both from testimony and experience, that the best and highest thoughts may escape our view ; they may be only too easily lost sight of and disregarded. Neglect, or an engrossing interest in lower or in more exciting subjects, will make them invisible, ineffective, useless. It is a most pitiable thing that in every generation there are multitudes of souls that once welcomed and cherished the loftiest conceptions and the noblest aspirations, to whom these thoughts and hopes are now nothing whatsoever ; they are gone from their mind ; they have not been wisely " kept," but foolishly and culpably lost. Therefore—

IV. THE WISDOM OF A REVERENT MEDITATION. We do ourselves the truest service when, by pondering on them, we keep sound and whole within our hearts the great thoughts of God. The power of continuous meditation is one of the faculties of our human nature ; but the rush and strain of modern life constitute a powerful temptation to let this faculty rust in disuse. But as we love ourselves truly and wisely we shall resist and overcome the temptation. All souls that would do their sacred duty to themselves must *think* well and much on the things they know. If they would truly and thoroughly understand that of which they speak, if they wish Divine truth to have its own purifying and transforming power over them, if they aspire to build up a strong and influential character, if they wish to be " no longer children," but men in Christ Jesus, they must *ponder in their hearts* the doctrines they count in their creed, the language they take into their lips. It is the truth we *dwell* upon that we *live* upon.—C.

Vers. 25—30.—*A satisfied human spirit.* There are few more exquisite pictures even in Holy Writ than the one which is here drawn for us. An aged and venerable man, who has lived a long life of piety and virtue, and who has been cherishing an ever-brightening hope that before he dies he should look upon the face of his country's Saviour, directed by the Spirit of God, recognizes in the infant Jesus that One for whose coming he has so long been hoping and praying. Taking him up into his arms, with the light of intense gratitude in his eyes, and the emotion of deepest happiness in his voice, he exclaims, "Lord, now lettest thou thy servant depart in peace, ... for mine eyes have seen thy Salvation." Life has now no ungranted good for him to await. The last and dearest wish of his heart has been fulfilled; willingly would he now close his eyes in the sleep of death; gladly would he now lie down to rest in the quiet of the grave.

I. THOSE WHO MUST BE UNSATISFIED IN SPIRIT. There is a vast multitude of men who seek for satisfaction in the things which are seen and temporal—in taking pleasure, in making money, in wielding power, in gaining honour, etc. But they do not find what they seek. It is as true in London as it was in Jerusalem, eighteen centuries after Christ as ten centuries before, that "the eye is not satisfied with seeing, nor the ear with hearing." All the rivers of earthly good may run into the great sea of an immortal spirit, but that sea is not filled. Earthly good is the salt water that only makes more athirst the soul that drinks it. It is not the very wealthy, nor the very mighty, nor the very honoured man who is ready to say, "I am satisfied; let me depart in peace."

II. THOSE WHO MAY BE SATISFIED IN SPIRIT. Simeon knew by special communication from God—"it was revealed unto him by the Holy Ghost"—that he should reach a certain point in the coming of the kingdom of God, that his heart's deep desire for "the Consolation of Israel" should be granted him. And waiting for this, and attaining it, his soul was filled with joy and holy satisfaction. It is right for those who are taking a very earnest interest in the cause of Christ to long to be allowed to accomplish a certain work for him. Again and again has the parent thus striven and prayed and longed to see the conversion of all his (her) children, or the teacher of his (her) class; the minister of Christ to see the attainment of some pastoral design; the missionary to win some tribe from barbarism and idolatry; the translator to render the Word of God into the native tongue; the national reformer to pass his measure for emancipation, or temperance, or virtue, or education, or the protection of the lives and morals of women or children. And this deep desire of the heart has been a constraining power, which has nerved the hand and energized the life, which has brought forth the fruit of sacred zeal and unwearied toil. God has given to these souls the desire of their hearts, and they have gone to their grave filled with a holy, satisfying peace. So may it be with us. And yet *it may not be so.* We may be called upon to quit the field of active labour before the harvest is gathered in. Others may enter into our labours. But if it should be so, there is a way in which we may belong to—

III. THOSE WHO CANNOT FAIL TO BE SATISFIED IN SPIRIT. For we may be of those who realize that it is in God's hand to fix the bounds of our present labour, and to determine the measure of the work we shall do on earth. We may work on diligently and devotedly as those who have much to do for God and man, yet clearly recognizing that God has for us a sphere in the spirit-world, and that he may at any hour remove us there, though we would fain finish what we have in hand below. If we have the spirit of Christ in our service, if we go whither we believe he sends us, and work on in the way which we believe to be according to his will, we may rest in the calm assurance that the hour of our cessation from holy labour is the hour of God's appointment, and a peace as calm as that of Simeon may fill our soul as we leave a *not-unfinished work* on earth to enter a nobler sphere in heaven.—C.

Vers. 34, 35.—*The touchstone of truth.* We do not suppose that Simeon saw the future course of the Saviour and of his gospel in clear outline; but, taught of God, he foresaw that that little Child he had been holding in his arms would be One who would prove a most powerful factor in his country's history; and he saw that relationship to him would be a source of the greatest blessing, or of weightiest trouble, or of most serious condemnation. Thus guided by this venerable saint, we will regard the gospel of Christ as—

I. A TOUCHSTONE. Our Lord himself was a touchstone by which the men of his day were tried. He came not to judge the world, but to save the world, as he said (John xii. 47); and yet it was also true that "for judgment he came into the world," as he also said (John ix. 39). His mission was not to *try*, but to *redeem*; yet it was a necessary incidental consequence of his coming that the character of the men who came in contact with him would be severely tested. When the Truth itself appeared and moved amongst men, then it became clear that those who were ignorantly supposed to be blind were the souls that were seeing God ("that they who see not might see"), and equally clear that those who claimed to know everything had eyes that were fastened against the light ("that they who see might be made blind"). As Jesus lived and wrought and spoke, the hearts of men were revealed—those who were children of wisdom heard his voice (John xviii. 37), while those who loved darkness rather than light turned away from the revealing Truth. And to-day the gospel is the touchstone of human character. They who are earnest seekers after God, after wisdom, after righteousness, gladly sit at the feet of the great Teacher to learn of him; but they who live for pleasure, for gain, for the honour that cometh from man only, for this passing world, pass him by, indifferent or hostile. They who are prepared to come as little children to learn of the heavenly Father, receive his Word and enter his kingdom (ch. xviii. 16); while they who consider themselves able to solve the great problems of life and destiny keep their minds closed against the truth.

II. A SWORD OF SORROW. It was not only Mary's heart that was pierced by reason of her affection for Jesus Christ. Loyalty to him proved to that generation, and has proved in every age since then, a sword that has wounded and slain. At many times and in many places it has meant violent persecution—stripes, imprisonment, death. In every land and in every age it has exposed men to hostility, to reproach, to temporal loss, to social disadvantage, to a lower station, to a struggling life, to a wounded spirit (ch. ix. 23; John xvii. 14; 2 Tim. iii. 12). Our Lord invites us to regard this inevitable accompaniment of spiritual integrity as an honour and a blessing rather than a stigma and a curse (Matt. v. 10—12).

III. A STUMBLING-STONE. That "Child was set for the fall ... of many." The truth which Jesus spoke, the great work of salvation he wrought out, has proved to many, not only in Israel, but in every land where it has been made known, a rock of offence (see ch. xx. 18; 1 Cor. i. 23).

IV. A STEPPING-STONE. Not only for the fall, but for the "rising again," was that Infant "set." By planting their feet on that safe, strong rock, the humiliated and even the degraded rise to honour and esteem, the humble to hopefulness, the weak to strength, the blemished to beauty, the useless to helpfulness, the children of earth to spheres of blessedness and joy in the heavenly world.—C.

Vers. 36—38.—*The testimony of womanhood.* From this interesting episode, without which the beautiful story of the infant Saviour in the temple would hardly be complete, we learn—

I. THAT THERE IS ROOM IN THE KINGDOM OF CHRIST FOR THE SERVICE OF WOMANHOOD. It was well that the aged Simeon should bear his testimony to the birth of the Saviour; it was also well that this aged and honourable prophetess should "likewise give thanks." Woman as well as man was to utter reverent joy on this supreme occasion. Woman, in the person of Anna, might well rejoice; for in the kingdom of Christ there is "neither male nor female;" all distinction of sex is unknown. Woman is as free to enter that kingdom as man; she may reach as high a position, by personal excellency, in it; she is as welcome to render holy service and fruitful testimony; is as certain to reap the reward of fidelity in the kingdom of heaven to which it leads. Women were the most faithful attendants on our Lord during his earthly ministry; they have been, since then, the most regular worshippers and the most devoted workers in his Church (see homily on ch. viii. 2, 3).

II. THAT LONG LONELINESS MAY WELL BRING US INTO CLOSE COMMUNION WITH GOD. Anna had a very long widowhood (ver. 36), and in her loss of human fellowship she waited much on God. She "departed not from the temple, but served God ... with prayers night and day." When denied one another's society, what can we do better than seek fellowship with our heavenly Father, with our Divine Friend? What, indeed, can we do so well? Communion with the Father of our spirits will bring healing to the wounded soul, will be companionship for the lonely hour, will promote sanctity and submissiveness of will, will remind us of those other children of his who need our sympathy and succour, and will send us forth blessing and blest on the errands of love.

III. THAT A VISION FROM GOD SHOULD RESULT IN PRAISE AND TESTIMONY. Anna "gave thanks unto the Lord, and spake of him [the infant Christ] to all," etc. Inspired of God, she recognized the long looked-for Messiah, and immediately she broke into praise, and forthwith began to communicate the joyful fact to *all* whom she could reach. This is the true order and the right procedure. When God reveals himself or his truth to us, we must first go to him in gratitude and praise, and must lose no time in passing on to others what he has entrusted to us.

IV. THAT AGE HAS ITS OFFERING TO BRING, as well as youth and prime. It is pleasant to think of the aged Anna, some way past four score, bent and feeble with the weight of years, speaking to "all them that looked," etc., and telling them that he whom they had waited for so long had come at last. A fair sight it is in the eyes of man, and surely in his also who estimates our service according to our ability (ch. xxi. 3), when those whose strength is well-nigh gone and who have earned their rest by long and faithful labour will not be persuaded to retire from the field, but labour on until the darkness of death arrests them.

V. THAT HOLY EXPECTATION WILL MEET WITH ITS FULFILMENT. There were many looking ("*all* of them," etc.) for redemption (ver. 38); and as they waited for God and upon him, their hearts' desires were granted. God may delay his answer for a while, even for a long while, but in *due time* it will come. The seeker *will* find; the worker *will* reap.—C.

Ver. 49.—*The dawn of sacred duty: a sermon to the young.* "Wist ye not that I must be about my Father's business?" There comes a time in our history—usually in the days of later youth or early manhood—when all things begin to wear a more serious aspect to us; when "the powers of the world to come" arrest us; when we ask ourselves very grave questions; when we have to confront a new future. It is the dawn of sacred duty in the human soul.

I. AS IT PRESENTED ITSELF TO JESUS CHRIST. His parents thought that his absence from their company was due to thoughtlessness or to absent-mindedness; they supposed it was to be explained by the fact that their Son was still a boy. On the contrary, the one thing that accounted for it was that he was beginning to be a man; that the burden of manhood's responsibilities was already resting on his shoulders; that the gravest solicitudes were already stirring in his soul. And the form which this sacred anxiety took was a holy and filial concern to be "about his Father's business." It had dawned upon his mind that his heavenly Father had sent him into the world to accomplish a special work, and that the hour had struck when he must address himself to this high and noble task. Therefore it behoved him to learn all that he could possibly acquire, to understand the things he had been taught, to receive from parents and teachers every truth he could discover and preserve. And the deep earnestness of his own spirit made it a matter of surprise that others, especially his elders and superiors, should not have perceived the same thing. "Wist ye not," he said wonderingly, "that I must be about my Father's business?"

II. AS IT APPEARS TO OUR MINDS NOW. There are various ways in which sacred duty may dawn on the human mind; the special form which this holy earnestness will take is affected by peculiarities of mental constitution, of parental training, of personal experience. It may be a deep sense of: 1. The value of the human soul, with its possibilities of nobility on the one hand and of degradation on the other. 2. The nearness and the greatness of the invisible and eternal world. 3. The seriousness of human life in view of the glorious and true success to which it sometimes attains, and also of the pitiable failure into which it sometimes sinks. 4. The strength and weight of filial and fraternal obligations. How much is due to the earthly father, and how wise it is to be guided by his ripe experience! how serious a thing it is to be setting an example to those who are younger! 5. The attractiveness of Jesus Christ—his purity and lovableness, his worthiness of the full affection and devotion of the human heart. 6. The claims of the heavenly Father, of him from whom we came, in whom we live, and by whom we are momently sustained; of him who has loved us with so patient and so ceaseless an affection. Must we not listen when he speaks, respond to his call, be found in his service, become the object of his Divine approval? When this solemn and sacred hour dawns upon the mind of the young, it is a time (1) for profound and prolonged consideration; (2) for earnest prayer; (3) for unreserved consecration; it will then prove to be a time for (4) true and lasting joy (Ps. cviii. 1).—C.

Vers. 51, 52.—*Growth, our Lord's and our own.* The growth of Jesus Christ and his subjection to his parents teach us some things respecting him, and they suggest some things for our own guidance.

I. THE GROWTH OF JESUS CHRIST. 1. The fulness of his condescension. We find this in his stooping so far as (1) to make it becoming that he should "be subject to" his parents, and (2) to make it possible that he should grow. How the Infinite One could so bereave himself of his infinitude as to be able to increase in wisdom, we cannot understand. But we cannot understand infinitude at all, and we act wisely when we do not draw hard-and-fast deductions from it. We stand on far firmer ground when we take the statement of the historian in its natural sense, and open our mind to the fact that Jesus Christ, "our Lord and our God," did stoop so far that it was possible for him to increase in knowledge and in favour with God and with man. We do not question the reality of his growth in body; why should we doubt, or receive with any reserve, the affirmation that he grew also in mind? 2. The harmoniousness of his growth. He grew (1) in bodily stature, and, of course, in all bodily strength and skill; (2) in mental equipment—in technical knowledge, or in the "education" of his time, in appreciation of nature, in knowledge of mankind, in apprehension of Divine truth, in general intellectual enlargement; (3) in spiritual beauty and nobility—"in favour with God and man." Not that he was at any time faulty or lacking in any excellency which it behoved him at that time to show, but that, as his faculties expanded and his opportunities of manifesting character were multiplied, he developed all that was admirable in the sight of man and of God. There is a far greater possibility of spiritual beauty and nobility in a young man with matured faculty and widening relationships than in the very little child, restricted, as he must be, in powers and in surroundings. So, as Jesus increased in years and grew in wisdom, there was in him an unfolding of moral and spiritual worth which attracted the eyes of men and which satisfied the Spirit of the Holy One himself.

II. OUR HUMAN GROWTH. 1. Unlike our Lord, there is no element of condescension implied in our growth. We did not *stoop* to infancy; our course had then its commencement; and in the youngest child, with all its helplessness, but with all its latent capacities, there is a great gift from the hand of God. Whatever it means, in its humiliations and in its practical illimitableness, it is so much more than we could claim. 2. As with our Lord, our growth should be harmonious. All the three elements in our compound nature should undergo simultaneous and proportionate development. This is at first a parental question, but subsequently it is one that affects every one capable of growth. (1) Training of the body; its nurture and culture, so that it shall be continually advancing in strength and skill and symmetry. (2) Discipline of the mind; its instruction and exercise, so that it will be ever increasing in knowledge and enlarging in faculty. (3) Culture of the character; its guidance and formation, so that there shall be (*a*) attractiveness in the sight of man, and (*b*) worthiness in the judgment of God. It is, indeed, true that we may not give pleasure to men in proportion as we grow in moral and spiritual worth, for, as with our Master, our purity and devotion may be an offence unto them. It is also to be remembered that we may gain God's distinct approval long before we have reached the point of irreproachableness; for that which he delights to see in his children is an earnest *effort after*, and a constant *growth towards*, that which is true and pure and generous.—C.

Vers. 1—20.—*The Saviour's birth and the angel's sermon.* We now pass from the person of the forerunner to that of his greater Successor. The priest's son was great, but the Virgin's Son was greater. John was a great gift to the world, as every true reformer must be; but a Saviour is God's supreme Gift to the children of men. Now, in this narrative before us we learn—

I. HOW THE WILL OF EVEN HEATHEN MONARCHS IS MADE TO FULFIL THE WILL OF GOD. The Divine will, expressed seven centuries before this time by Micah the prophet (v. 2), was that Jesus should be born in Bethlehem. But until a short time before his birth appearances seemed to show that he must be born in Nazareth.

When lo! Augustus, the heathen emperor at Rome, demands a census, and the Jewish families must enrol themselves at the tribal cities. This simple circumstance, whose purpose was the levy of men or the levy of money, brought Mary to Bethlehem in time to become, in the appointed place, the mother of the Lord. It surely shows the full command which God has over the wills even of those who are not his worshippers. He is the Sovereign of all men, whether they like it or know it or not. Cyrus was his shepherd, although he did not know God (Isa. xliv. 28; xlv. 4); and Augustus orders a census and "keeps books" in subservience to Divine purposes and fulfilment of Divine promises.

II. How LITTLE WELCOME DID THE WORLD GIVE ITS NEW-BORN SAVIOUR. The birth in Bethlehem was the most important birth which ever took place in our planet. Had the world appreciated the advent, it would have heralded it on every shore; but so little wisdom was there in the world that the precious Child had, so to speak, to steal into the world in a stable and among the cattle. It was humiliating to be born, even had palace halls received him; but how humiliating to be born in the common cattle-pen, because there was no room for Mary in the inn! And yet, in thus making his advent, he identified himself not only with the poorest, but also made common cause with the beasts. They, too, have benefited through Christ being born—there is less cruelty to animals in Christian than in other lands; and the religion of love he came to embody and proclaim will yet do more to ameliorate the condition of the beasts. Meanwhile let us notice how sad it is if men have no hospitality to show to Jesus, but still exclude him from their hearts and homes!

III. THE FIRST GOSPEL SERMON WAS PREACHED BY AN ANGEL. The importance of the birth at Bethlehem, if unrecognized by man, is realized by angels. Heavenly hosts cannot be silent about it. They must begin the telling of the glad tidings. If we suppose that the shades of night threw their mantle over Mary when the Babe was born, then it would seem that interested angels looked for an immediate *audience* to hear the wondrous story. Where shall one be found? The inn is full of sleepers or revellers; they are not fit to hear the message of peace and joy. But outside Bethlehem in the fields are *shepherds*—humble men, doubtless, and despised as in all ages. Still, they are kind to the sheep—"saviours," in some sense, of the dumb animals they tend and feed—and now in the night watches they are awake and watchful. Here, then, is the angel's *audience*. Does it not instruct preachers to be content with very humble hearers, and it may be sometimes very *few* hearers? An audience may be most important, even though few and despised. But we must next notice the *message* of the angel. Coming with dazzling light, perhaps the Shechinah-glory encircling him, he first scared the poor shepherds. They were "sore afraid." It was needful, there-fore, that he should first put to flight their fears, and then proclaim the glad tidings of a *Saviour's* birth, which gospel is intended for all people. The sign also which he gives is that the Babe shall be found in swaddling-clothes and lying in a manger. It is a message about a Saviour in apparent weakness but in real power. Such is the gospel. It is a message about a personal Saviour, who, in spite of all appearances, is "the Mighty God, the Father of Eternity, and the Prince of Peace" (Isa. ix. 6). We must "preach Christ" unto men if we know what it is to preach the gospel. Again, we must notice the *angelic choir*. The angel has arranged for a "service of praise" along with his preaching. There is the angel's sermon and then the angels' song. The sermon is short, but its contents are of priceless value.[1] The same may be said of the angels' song. It speaks simply of "glory to God in the highest, and on earth peace among men in whom he is well pleased" (Revised Version). It must have been a melodious service—such music as heavenly harmony secures; angelic choristers doing their best to interest and elevate a few poor shepherds. Another lesson, surely, to those who would "sing for Jesus." The preaching of the gospel should be backed up by the singing of the gospel. Praise has its part to play as well as preaching and prayer. It was at the praise part of the dedication service in Solomon's temple that the glory of the Lord appeared (2 Chron. v. 11—14).

IV. THE AUDIENCE PUT THE PREACHING TO AN IMMEDIATE TEST. The shepherds, as soon as the angels passed away, went at once to Bethlehem. They were resolved to see for themselves. There was a risk in this, for the sheep might be endangered in

[1] Cf. Arndt's 'Leben Jesu,' erster theil, s. 58.

their absence; but they resolve to run the risk if they can *see* the Saviour. "Never venture, never win." Hence they came with haste to Mary, and gaze with rapture on her Child. They see and believe. They are ready to accept this "little Child" as the Saviour of the world. A little Child was leading them ! Next we find them becoming his *witnesses*. They tell all who will listen to them what the angel said, and what they consequently had been led to Bethlehem to see. Having found a personal Saviour, they cannot but proclaim him to others. One who listened to their story and profited by it was Mary. She pondered their sayings in her heart. The shepherds have become important witnesses for the incarnate Saviour. So should all be who have really seen him by the eye of faith. But yet again, the shepherds, like the angels, burst into *praise*. "They returned, glorifying and praising God for all the things that they had heard and seen, as it was told them." This is the real end of gospel preaching when it leads the audience up to praise. Hence this is represented as the chief employment of the redeemed. Experience is only perfected when God is praised.

V. WE SEE HERE A HUMAN SUCCEEDING AN ANGELIC MINISTRY. It does seem strange that such a gospel should not be preached by angels. That they are anxious to do so appears from this narrative. We may be sure that they would esteem it highest honour to proclaim the message of salvation unto man. But after short visits and short sermons, the angels are withdrawn, and these poor shepherds spread the glad tidings, telling in a very humble way what they have seen and heard. It is God's plan, and must be best. It is those who need and have found a Saviour who are best adapted to proclaim him to others. A human ministry is more homely and sympathetic and effectual than perhaps any angelic ministry could be. Besides, a human ministry is less cavilled at and objected to than an angelic would be. We thus learn at Bethlehem important lessons about preaching to humble audiences, and out of them manufacturing preachers. The angels were doubtless satisfied as they looked down upon the shepherds who had listened so eagerly to their story, and saw them becoming preachers in their turn. To multiply Christ's witnesses is the great work of preachers whether angelic or human.—R. M. E.

Vers. 21—40.—*The circumcision and presentation of Jesus.* We pass now from the angel's sermon and the shepherds' faithful verification of it to the next notable events in the great life which embodies the gospel for mankind. And we have here—

I. THE CIRCUMCISION. (Ver. 21.) This was the admission of Jesus when only eight days old into the Old Testament Church. It was a painful, bloody process, and as such it was the beginning of that life of suffering upon which God's Son had determined to enter in the interests of men. There are not the same details about this circumcision that there were about John's. The outstanding fact was that he received the name *Jesus,* indicating that he was to be the Saviour of mankind. Into the Jewish covenant, consequently, there has entered by this circumcision a Saviour, One destined, like his namesake Joshua, to lead the Lord's people out of all bondage into glorious liberty. This was a practical identification of him with the people of God, before he could, at least humanly, decide for himself. And there is nothing better for little children than to be thus early associated with the cause of God.[1]

II. THE PRESENTATION IN THE TEMPLE. (Vers. 22—24.) The circumcision constituted Jesus a member of the old covenant, but his presentation in the temple was his formal dedication to the service of the Lord. The mother was directed, at the end of forty days from the child's birth, to appear before the Lord with two offerings—one for a sin offering, the other for a burnt offering. In Mary's case, because of her poverty, the offerings consisted of two doves or two young pigeons. The one sacrifice expressed a sense of *sin,* the other a sense of *consecration,* both beautiful in the mother of our Lord. The first was entirely out of place if she was "immaculate," as some represent her. In addition there would be paid for Jesus the redemption price of five shekels, that he might be excused from temple service, and might dedicate himself to the Lord in another capacity. When we consider all his Messiahship meant, it was really a payment that he might have the privilege of serving the Father as the Fulfiller of the ritual, and thus as the Abolisher of the ritualism of the temple. It would have altogether confused matters

[1] Cf. Arndt's 'Leben Jesu,' erster theil, s. 81; also Gerok's 'Evangelien-Predigten,' s. 102; also Weiss's 'Leben Jesu,' erster band, s. 247.

if he had undertaken any service about the temple as the Levites and priests did. In a word, the Messiah could not well have come, like the Baptist, from the tribe of Levi; but it was better he should belong to one which was not bound to the altar. And here we must notice as a practical point that the claim made on the firstborn by the Lord as being his peculiar possession, is a claim which we should all recognize as just. We are not our own, but bought with a price, and so bound to glorify God with our bodies (1 Cor. vi. 19, 20). This Jesus alone realized in fulness, but we ought to try to realize it in increasing measure.

III. THE TESTIMONY OF SIMEON. (Vers. 25—35.) While Jesus was being presented, an aged believer called Simeon comes, Spirit-impelled, into the temple. His character is clearly sketched for us. He was (1) just and devout; (2) waiting hopefully for the advent of him who was to be Israel's Consolation; (3) the subject of special revelation about seeing Messiah before death. And now he comes into the temple to recognize intuitively the Messiah in Mary's little Child. The result is his appropriation of the Child for an instant, that he might fondle him in his breast. Then does he pour forth his swan-song, the "Nunc Dimittis," which has been such a pathetic word in the experience of the Church. This prayer of Simeon suggests such thoughts as these: 1. *A peaceful departure is not only possible, but most desirable.* Manifestly Simeon could go to his last sleep as quietly as to his nightly rest. We may commit not only the folded hours of the night to God, but also the folded hours of eternity. 2. *The preliminary of such a departure is the sight of the Saviour.* The Child Jesus was the Divine Saviour provided for the aged Simeon, and in his tender care we may also rest. 3. *The peculiar joy of salvation is that it is intended for all people, Gentile as well as Jew.* After all the talk about selfishness, there is no system which embraces all the world as Christianity does.[1] But after thus speaking gratefully to God, Simeon speaks sympathetically to the wondering Joseph and Mary. He gives them an old man's benediction. They had a mighty charge and needed great grace to fulfil it. And then he speaks special words of warning as well as of encouragement to Mary about the Child. And here we notice: (1) That *the fate of multitudes often hangs on the destiny of an individual.* So was it with the Child Jesus. (2) His fate will be one of *determined opposition even unto death.* (3) It will *involve Mary in desperate distress*; but (4) by the tragedy *many hearts shall be revealed.* The crucifixion of Jesus is the touchstone by which our spiritual condition may be best determined. According as we are attached to or repelled by a crucified Saviour must be our spiritual or carnal state.[2]

IV. THE TESTIMONY OF ANNA. (Vers. 36—38.) Anna was another inspired person waiting for the advent of Messiah. An aged widow, she seems never to have left the temple, and to have risen as near the ideal of ceaseless service as one in this life could. She also gave thanks to God as with eager eye she gazed upon her Redeemer in the Person of the holy Child. And to all who, like herself, were looking for redemption, she spoke of Jesus as the Redeemer promised and now given. There is not the same melancholy tone about Anna as about Simeon. She speaks about redemption, and will wait for it, while Simeon seems inclined to reach it as speedily as possible by death (cf. Godet, *in loc.*).

V. THE EARLY DEVELOPMENT OF JESUS. (Vers. 39, 40.) Its sphere was Nazareth; not the place human wisdom would have selected for a holy development. A sinless life there was the greatest of all miracles. And here we are told of: 1. His development in *physical strength.* "The Child grew." If the Saviour had never been a child, but always full-grown like our first parent, he would not have commanded so much sympathy in the world. Little children take delight in the thought of him who was once like them a little child. 2. His development in *spirit and in wisdom.* The reference seems to be to energy of will and to intuitive insight, and the reflective form of the verbs seems to attribute the progress to his own effort. That is to say, his will grew in *force* while his soul grew in *insight.* As a Boy he lacked no decision of character, and his insight was remarkable for one of his years.[3] 3. He became, consequently, *the Object of Divine grace.* This favour of the Father was his by right. He won his

[1] Cf. Saurin's 'Sermons,' tome v. p. 42.
[2] Cf. Tholuck's 'Light from the Cross,' pp. 9, 84; also his 'Werke,' v. ss. 223, 272.
[3] Cf. Godet's 'Études Bibliques,' deuxième serie, pp. 102—104; also Robertson's 'Sermons,' second series, no. xv.

way to it, and it could not have been justly denied him.   The human race was no longer
in the Father's sight utterly depraved.   A redeeming feature had appeared in the person
of the holy Child Jesus in Nazareth.   God's attitude towards the world was thereby
altered, and justly so.   There are persons who give a halo of holy attraction to the
sphere in which they live.   Nazareth became redeemed from universal suspicion
because of one little Child who was living there.[1]   It is for us to rejoice in such a
Saviour as we have in Jesus, One who passed through the stages which we individually
experience, and was sinless in them all.   Childhood attains new interest for us, and its
innocency was once a perfect reality as the little feet of the Lord of life and glory trod
the streets of Nazareth.—R. M. E.

Vers. 41—52.—*The visit of Jesus to Jerusalem when a Boy.*   We now proceed to the
solitary circumstance in the Child-life of Jesus which is given in the Gospels.   He had
been growing for twelve years in strength and in spirit, and the Lord loved him.   The
Child in Nazareth redeemed in God's eyes all the world.   It was the one absorbing
interest in the Divine outlook upon our race.   And now he is taken by his pious parents
to the Passover Feast in Jerusalem.   It is his second visit to the temple; this time he
comes himself; the first time, as we have seen, he was presented.   The following points
deserve attention in this narrative.

I. THE PARENTAL CARE EXERCISED OVER JESUS.   The pious pair, Joseph and
Mary, went, as we are told, every year to Jerusalem to the Passover.   And they had
given the holy Child committed to their charge such advantages as Nazareth afforded.
The home school especially, not to speak of synagogue services, to which he was doubtless regularly taken, evidenced their interest in the welfare of the Child.   No sooner,
therefore, has he reached the age of twelve, at which time little ones were deemed able
to become " children of the Law," than he is taken up by them to see the Passover at
Jerusalem.   Their pious, consistent life was an excellent preparation for the solemnities
of the great feast.   Jesus came face to face with the ceremonies after experiencing most
tender home care.   And the history before us affords ample evidence of the parental
consideration.   If it was not *perfect* parental care, this is only to allow that neither
Joseph nor Mary was sinless.   Indeed, one of the German preachers bases an admirable
discourse on parental duty upon this history, finding in it six separate hints upon it.[2]
But let us pause a moment over the care with which they must have explained to him
all the ritual.   Doubtless he saw more in it than they did, but he must have received
gratefully their help in the circumstances.   To them the Passover spoke of a great
deliverance afforded to their fathers; to him it spoke of a great sacrifice yet to come.
His insight must have been a deeper thing than they could then appreciate.   And now
let us pass to the *oversight* of which the parents were guilty.   Their care was great,
but it was not absolutely perfect.   In the bustle of preparation for the home-going,
the parents started with the caravan under the impression that he must be in the company of the boys who were in considerable numbers attached to the procession.   They
should have made sure, and not left such a Child to the chances of travelling.   We
have no right to impute the separation of Jesus from his parents to any lack of dutifulness on *his* part, but solely to an oversight on theirs.   What were all their bits of baggage and their acquaintances in comparison with the safe custody of " the holy Child "?
And in consistency with this view, it has been suggested that underneath Mary's
apparent expostulation and reproof there is a latent confession of her fault, which she
and Joseph tried to atone for in their diligent search for the missing Boy.

II. THE LONELY BOY TURNED INSTINCTIVELY TO THE TEMPLE.   The seven days of
the Passover Feast had been a rare feast to Jesus.   The priests and ritual and all the
varied life which thronged the temple court must have been a revelation to him.   He
brought the consciousness of a Jew instructed in the Law to bear upon the temple and
its services.   We must look into his mind through the Old Testament.   We there find
the idea of God's Fatherhood in relation to his people several times referred to (Deut.
xiv. 1, 2; Hos. xi. 1; Jer. xxxi. 9, 20; Ps. ciii. 13, etc.).   To the little thoughtful
Boy, therefore, the temple was regarded as the home of him who was a Father to all

[1] Cf. Manning's 'Sermons,' vol. ii., on 'Holiness in Childhood.'
[2] Cf. Gerok's 'Pilgerbrod,' s. 196; see also his 'Aus Ernster Zeit,' s. 97, for another view
of the same passage.

who trusted in him.   And this general idea of fatherhood became specialized in his deep, reverential musings, and he could not but feel towards God as no Jew had ever felt before.[1]   Whether he had as a Child the further revelation yet made to him of his peculiar relation to God as the Only Begotten, or reached this in the progress of the years, is what we cannot be certain of.   At all events, the temple was the Father's house.   To it the lonely Lad turned.   He felt drawn to God irresistibly, now that his earthly guardians had gone away.   "When father and mother forsake me," he could say, "the Lord will take me up."   The orphan Child, so to speak, turned to the temple as to his real home.

III. He became a holy Learner there.   Not only was the temple the scene of the sacrifices; it was also the place of learning for those interested in the Law.   Schools were established within the sacred precincts where the scribes discoursed to such pupils as chose to sit at their feet.   The method seems to have been by dialogue—the question and answer which once were so prized.   Here the Boy believed he would get light about the will of the great Father who dwelt there, and who had given his people the Law.   As a faithful Son, he wished to get all possible light about his Father's business, and so he frequented the schools.   He was a "model catechumen," as a suggestive writer on this whole passage calls him.[2]   Although he must have seen through the shallowness of some of his teachers, and had doubtless deeper insight than any, he was content to sit at their feet and get all the good from them he could.   It was an instance, surely, of great diligence in embracing every opportunity of improvement which came his way.   He wanted to learn all he could while he had the chance.   And most naturally did his answers and questions astonish the doctors.   They had never had such an apt scholar before.   His insight led them along lines they never had travelled hitherto.   And as for the Father's business, it at least embraces such elements as these: 1. The *understanding of the terms of access to his presence*.   The significance of the ritual which was celebrated in the temple, the meaning of sacrifice, of bloodshedding, of incense, and of approach by the appointed priests into the Divine presence,—all this belonged to the Father's business.   2. The *understanding of the meaning of his commandments*.   The Law as the expression of the Father's will, and read consequently in the light of love.   3. How *far the knowledge of the Father was to be extended*.   The kingdom of God in its universal range, as distinct from a narrow nationality,—this was part of the Father's business.   Hence the lingering of the holy Learner about the temple schools.   His apt answers would procure him lodging and food during the season of separation from his parents.   Having put God first, all these things were added unto him (Matt. vi. 33).

IV. His recovery by the anxious mother.   Joseph and Mary, on discovering at the end of the first day's march the absence of the Child, set out for Jerusalem to find him.   They doubtless inquire all the way back, and then they go hither and thither through the city, and at last think of the temple.   There, in the midst of the doctors, he is found and recovered by Mary.   Her words are apparent rebuke, but really confession upon her part of the oversight.   She had never before had any reason for fault-finding; it comes all the more surprisingly upon her now.   Jesus defends himself on the ground that he was looking after his Father's business.   In other words, he insists on putting God first, before Mary or Joseph.   We get an insight into what godliness is.   It means making God's business supreme.   God claims first place, and this is what the Boy Jesus gave him.   The Revised Version translates the words, "Wist ye not that I must be in my Father's house?"   This would simply refer to their folly in not first seeking him there.   The Authorized Version is as near the Greek, and of wider import.   But Mary and Joseph did not understand his meaning.   These are the first recorded words of Jesus; and how they harmonize with the last, when on the cross he said, "Father, into thy hands I commend my spirit"![3]

V. His obedience and development.   He has got all the doctors can meanwhile give to him.   It would not have been profitable for him to have remained longer in their schools, and to have merely witnessed their powers of disputation.   He is to have collision with them soon enough.   Besides, he will be safer out of their reach in the

---

[1] Cf. Weiss's 'Leben Jesu,' erster band, s. 268.

[2] See Glover's 'Finding of the Saviour in the Temple,' pp. 37—88.

[3] Cf. Gerok's 'Aus Ernster Zeit,' s. 104.

quiet of the northern home. And so he recognizes in his mother's call the voice of his Father in heaven, and in the privacy of Nazareth his Father's business. He has to wait as well as work. Hence without a murmur he goes away with them and is subject unto them. But this subjection and reverence did not hinder, but really helped, his development. "He increased in wisdom and in stature, and in favour with God and man." As a person under parental authority, he found his reward in wisdom, and became beloved of all around him as well as of the Lord above. It was a beautiful example to set us of being subject under God to parents and superiors. His growth in wisdom was also so considerate. He would take wisdom as others have to get it, *gradually*, and pass from the known to the knowledge of the unknown.[1] And God's favour will rest as well as man's favour upon all who follow in the footsteps of his Divine Son in this beautiful subjection.[2] There is no truth more important at the present time than this of realizing our development in due subjection.—R. M. E.

EXPOSITION.

CHAPTER III.

Vers. 1—22.—The Baptism of John.

Ver. 1.—**Now in the fifteenth year of the reign of Tiberius Cæsar.** St. Luke's Gospel is framed after the model of approved histories. He commenced with an elaborate rhetorical preface, most carefully worded, stating, in a few well-chosen sentences, the reasons which had induced him to undertake the work. He then (ch. i. 5—ii. 52) skilfully wove into the text of his narrative one or more original documents; these he translated, preserving, with great art, as closely as possible, the spirit, and oftentimes the very words, of his original authority. Now, in this chapter he comes to a period more generally known. Here he has a vast number of sources for his story, written and oral; these he shapes into a regular history, beginning, as was the ordinary custom with works of this description, with the names of the chief rulers of the countries in which the events, which he proposed to relate, took place. He first speaks generally of the great Roman Empire under whose shadow the Holy Land at that time cowered. Then he proceeds to describe more fully the political divisions of Palestine; and, lastly, he writes of the great Jewish ecclesiastical governors of the day. Tiberius was the stepson of the Emperor Augustus, whom he succeeded. It was about this time that this monarch retired to the island of Capreæ, where his life was disfigured with the grossest crimes. The government of his ministers, who ruled absolutely in his name, has become a by-word for evil and tyrannical government. The influence of the Roman emperors at this time in Palestine appears from the attempts at adulation on the part of the local rulers, who, among many other localities, renamed the Lake of Galilee, where so many of the scenes narrated in our story took place, "the Sea of Tiberius." The city of Tiberius, on the shores of this inland sea, was named after the emperor. **Pontius Pilate being governor of Judæa.** His proper title was ἐπίτροπος, procurator. In Judæa this civil functionary was also military commander. This double office gave the procurator of Judæa a higher rank and title; his official superior was the Roman Governor of Syria. Pilate became procurator in A.D. 26, and held the appointment for ten years. **Herod being tetrarch of Galilee.** This Herod is usually known as "Antipas" (properly, *Antipater*). He was a son of Herod the Great, and reigned for more than forty years; he was eventually deposed by the Roman authorities and banished to Gaul. Galilee at this period was the most flourishing and densely populated portion of the land of promise. Roughly speaking, it occupied all the centre of Palestine, the rich plain of Esdraelon (Jezreel) and the surrounding districts. **His brother Philip tetrarch of Ituræa and of the region of Trachonitis.** Herod Philip, another of the great Herod's sons, is well spoken of as a fair and judicious ruler. Cæsarea Philippi was built by him. His tetrarchate included the ancient Bashan and the Hauran, and the country lying round the base of Hermon. **Lysanias the tetrarch of Abilene.** This district lay to the east of the mountain range of Anti-Libanus, the river Barada flowing through it.

Ver. 2.—**Annas and Caiaphas being the high priests.** The older authorities read, "in the high priesthood of Annas and Caiaphas." The mention of two high priests arises from the fact of the legitimate high

---

[1] Upon the growth in wisdom of our Lord, see Moorhouse's 'Hulsean Lectures,' *passim*.
[2] Cf. Woolsey's 'Religion of the Present and the Future,' Scribner's edit., pp. 9—23.

priest, Annas, having been deposed some fifteen years previously by the action of the then Roman procurator, Valerius Gratus. In spite of this official deposition, he still apparently continued to be regarded as the legitimate high priest by the great majority of his countrymen. His great position and claim to the pontifical office, as we shall see, was markedly recognized at the time of the state trial of our Lord. Since his deposition by the Roman government, four high priests had been promoted in succession to the office of chief pontiff. It appears that at this time and for a long series of years, this great and powerful man, although not daring publicly to defy the Roman authority by assuming the insignia of the high priest, filled the office of Nasi, or president of the Sanhedrin. **The word of God came unto John the son of Zacharias in the wilderness.** In the days of the above-mentioned rulers—pagan and Jewish, civil and ecclesiastical—came the summons to the son of Zacharias in his solitude in the wilderness. From childhood he had been designated for some great work, and he knew it; his whole early life had been a training for it; and at last the summons came. We are not told of its special form; it was doubtless a theophany, or a vision somewhat similar to that which revealed to Moses and Isaiah, to Jeremiah and Ezekiel, their special work, and the way in which that special work was to be done.

Ver. 3.—**And he came into all the country about Jordan.** The reputation of John probably preceded the Divine summons. His family—the son of a well-known priestly family—the marvellous circumstances attendant on his birth, his ascetic manner of life from the beginning,—all this had contributed to make him a marked personage; so, when he left his solitude, we read in the other evangelists how multitudes came forth to hear the strange burning words, the Divine eloquence of one long looked upon by the people as set apart for a great work. He seems to have principally preached and taught in the Jordan valley—no doubt for the convenience of his candidates for baptism. But he evidently did not confine his preaching to one spot or even to one neighbourhood. The district here alluded to was about a hundred and fifty miles in length. The expectation of Messiah for centuries had been the root of all true life in Israel; gradually, as the clouds of evil fortune gathered thick over the people, the figure of the coming Messiah assumed a different aspect. At first *a holier Monarch* than their loved David, *a grander Sovereign* and a mightier than the Solomon of whom they were so proud, *a King* whose dominions should be broader far than even the wide

realm ruled over by the son of Jesse and his greater son, was the ideal dreamed of by the Hebrew. In the long period of misfortune which succeeded the golden days of the monarchy, the people at first longed for *a deliverer*, and then—as never a ray of sunlight pierced the clouds which surrounded them—*an avenger* took the place of a deliverer. The Messiah of the future must be One who should restore his people certainly, but in the restoration must exact a sharp and severe reckoning from those who had so long oppressed his Israel. They had no conception of their true state,—their hypocrisy, their formalism, their total ignorance of all true spiritual religion. Their higher and cultured classes were selfish, grasping, impure, untrue. The mass of the people were ignorant and degraded, cruel fanatics, excited and untutored zealots. From this mistaken notion of Messiah and his work it was necessary that a prophet, eminent and gifted like those mighty men who had wrought great things in times past among the people, should arise among them, and with strong, powerful, inspired words convince them of their fatal error—one who, in the language of the greatest of the order, should *prepare the way of the Lord.* How imperatively necessary, for the work of the Redeemer, this work of the pioneer was, is seen from the extreme difficulty which Jesus Christ himself found in persuading even his own little faithful band to realize anything of the nature of his work; in good truth they *never*, not even the noblest spirits among them, really grasped the secret of their Master's mission till the cross and the Passion belonged to history, and the Crucified had become the Risen, and the Risen the ascended God. **The baptism of repentance.** What, first, did John mean by *repentance?* The word translates the Greek μετάνοια, which signifies " change of mind." In the Gospel of St. Matthew, where John's work is told in slightly different language, he is represented as saying, " Repent ye" (μετανοεῖτε). There his words might be paraphrased, "Turn ye from your old thoughts, from your state of self-content, self-satisfaction; mend your ways; reform." Here, then, the baptism (what that signified we shall discuss presently) which he preached and summoned men to, must be accompanied with a change of mind; the baptized must be no longer content with their present state or conduct; they must change their ways and reform their lives. Let them, those who were convinced that he was indeed a man of God, that his words were right and true,—let them come to him, determined to change their conduct in life, and receive from his hands a baptism, a washing—*the symbol of the means of purifi-*

cation; for John's baptism was nothing more. Now, baptism, it is clear, was not at this time practised among the Jews. It was not, as far as we can trace, even used in the case of pagan proselytes to Judaism. This apparently only became a national custom *after* the fall of Jerusalem, A.D. 70, forty years later. His very title, "the Baptist," in some way shows us that he practised an unusual, if not a novel, rite in the course of his preaching and teaching. John's baptism (to use Dr. Morrison's vivid expressions, Commentary on Matt. iii. 6) was just the embodiment, in significant *optical* symbolism, of the significant audible symbolism of the Old Testament prophets, when they cried aloud and said, "Wash you, make you clean; put away the evil of your doings from before mine eyes" (Isa. i. 16); "In that day there shall be a fountain opened to the house of David, and to the inhabitants of Jerusalem, for sin and for uncleanness" (Zech. xiii. 1); "Then will I sprinkle clean water upon you, and ye shall be clean: from all your filthiness, and from all your idols, will I cleanse you. A new heart also will I give you, and a new spirit will I put within you" (Ezek. xxxvi. 25, 26). This view of John's baptism, viz. that it was a symbol, and nothing more, was suggested by Josephus writing for the Jews. "John," he says, "enjoined upon the Jews first to cultivate virtue and to put in practice righteousness toward one another, and piety toward God, and then to come to his baptism, for thus only would the baptism be acceptable to God" ('Ant.,' xviii. 5. 2).

Ver. 4.—**As it is written in the book of the words of Esaias the prophet, saying, The voice of one crying in the wilderness.** The prophet quoted (Isa. xl. 3) had been writing in his solitude, or more probably in some great popular assembly preaching to the people. There was doubtless at that time much national trouble threatening Israel; the future of the chosen race looked very dark and gloomy, within and without. We can hear the man of God speaking with intense earnestness, and looking on to brighter times. "Comfort ye, comfort ye my people, saith your God. Speak ye comfortably to Jerusalem, and cry unto her, that her warfare is accomplished, that her iniquity is pardoned," etc.; and then a sudden burst when the prophet, bending forward and straining his ears to hear some sound none other caught but he, goes on in his rapt utterance—I hear a voice, "The voice of him that crieth in the wilderness, Prepare ye the way of the Lord." **Prepare ye the way of the Lord, make his paths straight.** The image is a simple one, and in the East one well knows, where the roads are comparatively few, and where they do

exist are often in a bad state, when a sovereign is about to visit any part of his dominions, or still more if the march of an army has to be arranged for, the roads require considerable preparation. Josephus ('Bell. Jud.,' iii. 6) describes the advance of the Emperor Vespasian's army, and specially mentions how the pioneers and the vanguard had to make the road even and straight, and, if it were anywhere rough and hard to be passed over, *to plane it.* There was a Jewish legend that this special pioneering work in the desert was done by the pillar of cloud and fire, which brought low the mountains and filled the valleys before the Israelitic march. John's special work was to prepare the way for the advent of a Messiah very different to the one the people looked for—to prepare his way by a spiritual reformation in the heart, the mind, and the character.

Ver. 5.—**Every valley shall be filled, and every mountain and hill shall be brought low; and the crooked shall be made straight, and the rough ways** shall be **made smooth.** Godet and other commentators suggest, though they do not press, a particular application to each of the details of the picture. "For instance, the mountains that must be levelled may be referred to the pride of the Pharisees; the valleys to be filled up, to the moral and religious indifference of such as the Sadducees; the crooked places to be made straight, to the frauds and lying excuses of the publicans; and lastly, the rough places, to the sinful habits found in all, even the best.'

Ver. 6.—**And all flesh shall see the salvation of God.** And when this preparation is complete, then shall Messiah publicly appear. And the Baptist faithfully performed his work as pioneer of the Christ. He awoke men's slumbering consciences; his note of alarm aroused through Palestine multitudes of men and women who afterwards, no doubt, formed the nucleus at least of the crowds who thronged round Jesus as he preached in the cities washed by the Lake of Galilee, or in the streets and temple courts of Jerusalem.

Ver. 7.—**Then said he to the multitude that came forth to be baptized of him.** The following grave cutting rebukes, the burning reminders, must not be read as an extract from any one particular sermon of the Baptist, or even as a report of any of his discourses, but rather as a general sketch of the line of argument the great prophet adopted in his teaching. **O generation of vipers, who hath warned you to flee from the wrath to come?** In St. Matthew's account of John's work such scathing words as these were addressed to members of the Pharisee and Sadducee sects, who evidently flocked in great numbers to his baptism. They were alarmed and disturbed at his preaching; they feared that that drear time of awful suffering, generally known as the "woes of Messiah," a period which their great rabbis had told them would precede Messiah's advent, was at hand; they would provide themselves with some talisman against this time of sore calamity. The inspired predictor of these "woes"—men evidently looked on John as such—bade them come to *his baptism;* this baptism would be surely a safeguard, an easy bit of ritual, thought they, and one that readily approved itself to men trained in the rabbis' schools of that age, so they came to him in numbers. But John read their hearts; hence his stern fiery rebukes. "Let it be borne in mind that only teachers of transcendent holiness, and immediately inspired by God with fervency and insight, may dare to use such language" (Farrar).

Ver. 8.—**Bring forth therefore fruits worthy of repentance.** In other words, "Since you profess to have taken flight from the wrath to come, show at once, by your change of life, that your repentance is worth something, has some meaning in it." **Begin not to say within yourselves, We have Abraham to our father.** These words show that John had the splendid courage to strike boldly at the very root of Jewish pride. Gradually Jewish belief in the especial favour of God, which they were to enjoy through all eternity, had grown up till it resulted in such extravagant expressions as these: "Abraham would sit at the gates of hell, and would not permit any circumcised Israelite of decent moral character to enter it;" "A single Israelite is worth more in God's sight than all the nations of the world;" "The world was made for their (Israel's) sake." This incredible arrogancy grew as their earthly fortunes became darker and darker. Only an eternity of bliss, of which they alone were to be partakers, could make up for the woes they were made to suffer here, while an eternity of anguish for the Gentile world outside Israel was a necessary vengeance for the indignities this Gentile world had inflicted upon the chosen people. Long ago the great Hebrew prophets had warned the deluded race that their election would profit them nothing if they failed in their duties to their God and their neighbour. **For I say unto you, That God is able of these stones to raise up children unto Abraham;** pointing, no doubt, to the rough shingle lying on the river Jordan's banks. John's thought was the same which Paul afterwards expressed to the Galatians in his own nervous language, "Know ye therefore that they which are of faith, the same are the children of

Abraham;" "And if ye *be* Christ's, then are ye Abraham's seed, and heirs according to the promise" (Gal. iii. 7, 29).

Ver. 9.—**And now also the axe is laid unto the root of the trees: every tree therefore which bringeth not forth good fruit is hewn down, and cast into the fire.** This intensifies the statement respecting the power of God to raise up, out of the very river shingle at their feet, children who should inherit the glorious promises made to Abraham. Nay, more, the Divine Woodman had already laid the axe at the root of the tree of Israel; its hours, as the peculiar people, were indeed numbered. Let *these,* who said they were willing to wash and be clean, be ready and bring forth fruit worthy of their high calling and the lofty prerogative of which they boasted. The last of the prophets, from his lonely watch-tower of unerring insight into the future, saw the awful coming doom of the loved city, the scattering and captivity of the remnant of the chosen people. Within forty years of that time would the fatal axe, now lying at the root of the tree, be lifted. In uttering this stern prophetic saying, we believe John was gazing at the storm gathering round Jerusalem, which in A.D. 70 swept away city and temple, and destroyed the existence of Israel as a nation. When he preached it was about A.D. 30—32.

Ver. 10.—**And the people asked him, saying, What shall we do then?** Dean Plumptre's note here is interesting and suggestive: "The questions that follow are peculiar to St. Luke. They are interesting as showing that the work of the Baptist was not that of a mere preacher of repentance. Confession of sins followed naturally on the part of the penitents; that was followed, as naturally, by guidance for the conscience. St. Luke, as a physician of the soul, may well have delighted to place on record this example of true spiritual therapeutics." The same train of thought is followed out by Godet in his remark on the question contained in this verse: "It is the confessional after preaching." This little section (vers. 10—14), containing an epitome of questions placed before John by different classes of hearers touched by his soul-stirring preaching, is peculiar to our evangelist. It is clear that here, in the story of the ministry of the Baptist, Luke derived his knowledge of the details from an independent authority not used either by Matthew or Mark.

Ver. 11.—**He that hath two coats, let him impart to him that hath none; and he that hath meat, let him do likewise.** This advice is simple and practical. No difficult counsels of perfection are recommended, no useless penance. The great confessor simply presses home to his penitents the duty of unselfishness, the beauty of quiet generosity in the sight of God. The whole teaching of this eminent man of God was thoroughly practical. His predecessor, Micah, centuries before had given the luxurious and selfish Israel of his time the same Divine lesson: "He hath showed thee, O man, what is good; and what doth the Lord require of thee, but to do justly, and to love mercy, and to walk humbly with thy God?" (Micah vi. 8).

Ver. 12.—**Then came also publicans to be baptized, and said unto him, Master, what shall we do?** This is the first time this class of men, who on several occasions come before us in the gospel story, is mentioned. The English rendering is most unhappy, for to many of our people it either suggests nothing, or else supplies a wrong chain of reasoning. The τελῶναι, the Latin *publicani* (whence our rendering), were men who collected the Roman taxes or imposts. These imperial taxes, the most painful and ever-present reminder to the Jew of his subject and dependent position, were in the first instance leased out to jobbers and speculators of the equestrian order; these were properly the publicani. Beneath them and in their employ were a numerous staff who performed for these farmers of the imperial revenue the various disagreeable duties connected with the collection of the taxes. Then, as now in the East, bribery, corruption, oppression, and unfair dealing, were too common among all ranks of officials First, then, the duty itself, the being concerned in the collection of a tribute—for that is what these taxes really were—for Gentile Rome, and, secondly, the various iniquities connected with the gathering of this tribute, made the tax or tribute collectors of all ranks odious among the Jews dwelling in Palestine. Many of the posts, especially the subordinate ones, in this department of tribute and taxes, were held by Jews, in all ages singularly gifted in matters which have to do with finance. The Jew, however, in the days of John the Baptist, who could stoop to such an employment, lucrative though it might be, was looked upon by his stricter fellow-countrymen with feelings of intense scorn. Yet even *these* men are not bidden by this inspired prophet of the Highest to change their way of life, but only its manner. "Would you," he says to these men who belonged to the hated calling, "indeed wash and be clean in the eyes of the All-Seeing? then in that profession of yours, remember, be scrupulous, be honest."

Ver. 14.—**And the soldiers likewise demanded of him, saying, And what shall we do?** Commentators generally discuss here who these soldiers were. The question is of little moment whether they were legionaries of Rome, or mercenaries in the pay of one of the tetrarchs or neighbouring princes. The lesson is clear. As above to the publicans, so here to the soldiers, John says, "Remain in that profession of arms; you may, if you will, serve God in it, for it is never the *work* which ennobles, but the *way* in which the work is done."

Ver. 15.—**All men mused in their hearts of John, whether he were the Christ, or not.** There was general expectation at that time among the Jews that Messiah's coming was at hand. This strange feeling that something momentous was about to happen to mankind was not confined to the Jews of Palestine, it strongly influenced the Jews who were dispersed in foreign countries—Egypt, Greece, Italy, etc., and through them it had even reached many of the Gentiles who were brought into contact with the chosen people. This idea among the Jews, that John was probably the looked-for deliverer, is only mentioned by St. Luke—another proof that the source of his information was quite distinct from that used by Matthew and Mark.

Ver. 16.—**I indeed baptize you with water; but One mightier than I cometh.** To refute this growing conviction that he was the Messiah, John tells the people plainly that Another far greater than he was coming. He, John, certainly washed (baptized) those who came to him, but his washing was merely symbolical—*it* could not purify them; his work had been to stir them up to repentance, to arouse them to change their lives. But the One who was coming, before whom he (John) was unworthy to stand and perform the humblest menial office, that great One should baptize too, but his baptism would be a very different thing. **He shall baptize you with the Holy Ghost.** There was, indeed, a difference between John's baptism and the baptism of the Messiah who was to come after him. John could do no more with his words and symbol baptism than rouse the people to struggle after repentance and a change of heart and life, while Messiah would furnish to men the influence from above, that was really needed in order to purity of heart and life. He would procure and pour out the influence of the Divine Spirit (see Dr. Morrison, on Mark i. 8). **And with fire.** Not with *punitive* fire, which interpretation would be quite alien from the context here. Those expositors who have adopted this meaning of the fire here have been most likely influenced by the mention of the unquenchable fire in the next sentence. The fire which was to enter into Messiah's baptism was rather *the flame of purification.* So we read of the coal of fire taken from off the altar and laid on the mouth of Isaiah the prophet (Isa. vi. 6, 7). "With fire," writes Bishop Wordsworth, "to purify, illumine, transform, inflame with holy fervour and zeal, and carry upward, as Elijah was carried up to heaven in a chariot of fire."

Ver. 17.—**Whose fan is in his hand, and he will throughly purge his floor, and will gather the wheat into his garner.** But not only, taught John, was Messiah's work to consist in baptizing those who sought his face with the mighty baptism of the Holy Ghost and fire, there was another terrible aspect of his mission. The useless, the selfish, the oppressor, and the false-hearted, —these were to be separated and then destroyed. When will this separation and subsequent destruction take place? The separation will begin in this life. The effect of the revelation of a Saviour would be to intensify at once the antagonism between good and evil. Between the followers of Christ and the enemies of Christ would a sharp line of demarcation be speedily drawn even *here;* but the real separation would only take place on the great day when Messiah should judge the world; *then* would the two classes, the righteous and the unrighteous, be gathered into two bands; condemnation, sweeping, irresistible, would hurry the hapless evil-doers into destruction, while the righteous would be welcomed in his own blessed city. The imagery used is rough, but striking. It was taken, as is so much of Oriental teaching, from scenes from the everyday life of the working world around them. The *theatre* is one of those rough Eastern threshing-floors on the top or side of a hill, so chosen for the purpose of having the benefit of the wind. The *actor*, a peasant employed in winnowing. "Not far from the site of ancient Corinth," writes a modern traveller in Greece, "where the peasants in many of their customs approach near to Oriental nations, I passed a heap of grain which some labourers were employed in winnowing; they used, for throwing up the mingled wheat and chaff, a three-pronged wooden fork, having a handle three or four feet long. Like this, no doubt, was the *fan*, or *winnowing-shovel*, which John the Baptist represents Christ as bearing" (Dr. Hackett, quoted by Dr. Morrison, on Matt. iii. 12). The fan thus described would throw up against the breeze the mingled wheat and chaff; the light particles would be wafted to the side, while the grain would fall and remain on the threshing floor. **With fire unquenchable.** This image in itself is a terrible one; still, it must not be used in the question of eternity of punishment. The fire is here termed "unquenchable" because, when once the dry chaff was set on fire,

nothing the peasants could do would arrest the swift work of the devouring flame. All that is here said of the condemned is that they will be destroyed from before the presence of the great Husbandman with a swift, certain destruction. If it points to anything, the imagery here would hint at the total annihilation of the wicked; for the flames, unquenchable while any chaff remained to be consumed, would, when the rubbish was burnt up, die quickly down, and a little heap of charred ashes would alone mark the place of its burning. But it is highly improbable that any deduction of this kind was intended to be drawn. The Baptist's lesson is severely simple.

Ver. 18.—**And many other things in his exhortation preached he unto the people.** These words tell us that the above was merely a "specimen" of John the Baptist's preaching, trenchant, fearless, practical, piercing the hearts of all classes and orders of the people who thronged to hear the earnest, fiery appeals of the great desert preacher. In this and in the next two verses St. Luke once more gives us a little picture of the events which were spread over a considerable area of time. It is here introduced out of its proper place to explain the abrupt termination of the popular career of John the Baptist.

Ver. 20.—**He shut up John in prison.** It did not enter into St. Luke's plan to write any detailed account of the circumstances which led to the death of the Baptist. The story (related at length by St. Matthew) was, no doubt, well known in all the Gentile Churches. He simply mentions the act which consigned the dauntless preacher to the dungeons of Herod's palace-fortress, close to the Dead Sea; it was termed Macha, or Machærus. In closing his little sketch of the work of his Master's great pioneer, St. Luke wishes to show that the fearless Baptist was no respecter of persons. The despised collector of Roman tribute, the rough free lance or mercenary, the nameless legionary of Rome, was attacked for his evil life and his wanton excesses, with no greater hardihood than the prince who sat on the throne of the mighty Herods. True servant of his brave and patient Master, he paid the penalty of his splendid courage, and, "like so many of earth's great ones, he passed through pain and agony to his rest."

Vers. 21, 22.—*The baptism of Jesus.*

Vers. 21, 22.—**Now when all the people were baptized.** This is the shortest account of the first three Gospels of this event. Two circumstances related are, however, peculiar to St Luke—the fact that he ascended "praying" from the water, and the opening words of this verse, which probably signify that on this day Jesus waited till the crowds who were in the habit of coming to John had been baptized. **Jesus also being baptized.** There is a curious addition to the Gospel narratives of the baptism of the Lord preserved by Jerome. He tells us he extracted it from the Hebrew Gospel used by the Nazarenes, a copy of which in his day was preserved at Cæsarea. *" Lo, the mother of the Lord and his brethren said to him, John the Baptist is baptizing for the remission of sins; let us go and be baptized by him. But he answered and said unto them, In what have I sinned, that I should go and be baptized by him? unless, indeed, it be in ignorance that I have said what I have just said."* It is, no doubt, a very ancient traditional saying, and is *perhaps* founded on some well-authenticated oral tradition. If St. Luke knew of it, he did not consider it of sufficient importance to incorporate it in his narrative. In St. Matthew's account of the "baptism," John at first resists when asked to perform the rite on his kinsman Jesus. His knowledge of Jesus at this time was evidently considerable. He was acquainted, of course, with all that had already happened in his "cousin's" life, and probably it had been revealed to him, or told him by his mother (ch. i. 43), that in the Nazareth Carpenter, the Son of Mary, he was to look for the promised Messiah, with whose life-story his was so closely bound up. The answers to the question, *What was the reason of Jesus' baptism?* have been many. In this, as in many things connected with the earthly life of our Lord, there is much that is mysterious, and we can never hope *here* to solve these difficulties with any completeness. The mystic comments of the Fathers, though not perfectly satisfactory, are, however, after all the best of the many notes that have been made on this difficult question. Bishop Wordsworth sums them up well in his words: "He came to baptize water, by being baptized in it." Ignatius ('Ad. Eph.,' 18, beginning of the second century) writes, "He was baptized that, by his submission to the rite, he might purify the water." Jerome, in the same strain, says, "He did not so much get cleansing from baptism, as impart cleansing to it." It would seem that Jesus, in submitting to the rite himself, did it with the intention of sanctifying the blessed sacrament in the future. **And praying.** Peculiar to St. Luke. This evangelist on eight other occasions mentions the praying of Jesus. **The heaven was opened, and the Holy Ghost descended . . . upon him.** While he was praying and gazing up into heaven, the deep blue vault was rent asunder, and the Sinless One gazed far into the realms of eternal light;

and as he gazed he saw descend a ray of glory, which, dove-like, brooded above his head, and then lighted upon him. This strange bright vision was seen, not only by him, but by the Baptist (John i. 32, 33). That the form of a *dove* absolutely descended and lighted upon Jesus seems unlikely; a radiant glorious *Something* both Jesus and the Baptist saw descending. John compares it to a dove—this cloud of glory sailing through the clear heaven, then, bird-like, sinking, hovering, or brooding, over the head of the Sinless One, then lighting, as it were, upon him. In likening the radiant vision to a *dove*, probably John had heard of the rabbinical comment (it is in the Talmud) on Gen. i. 2, that the Spirit of God moved on the face of the waters *like a dove*. Milton has reproduced the thought—

" And with mighty wings outspread
Dove-like sat'st brooding on the vast abyss."
('Paradise Lost,' i. 20.)

John, for want of a better simile, reproduced the image which he had doubtless heard from his teacher in the Law, when he desired to represent in earthly language the Divine Thing which in some bodily form he had seen. In the early Church there was a legend very commonly current—we find it in Justin Martyr ('Dialogue with Trypho,' 88), and also in the Apocryphal Gospels—that at the baptism of Jesus a fire was kindled in Jordan. This was doubtless another, though a more confused memory of the glory-appearance which John saw falling on the Messiah. **And a voice came from heaven;** better rendered, *out of heaven.* We read in the Talmud that "on the death of the last prophets—Haggai, Zechariah, and Malachi—the Holy Spirit departed from Israel; but they (*i.e.* Israel) were availing themselves of the daughter (echo) of a voice, Bath-Kol, for the reception of Divine communications" ('Treatise Yoma,' fol. 9, col. 2). In the Gospels there is a mention of the heavenly voice being again heard at the Transfiguration (Matt. xvii. 5), and during the last week of the earthly ministry (John xii. 28—30). In the story of Israel the Persons of the ever-blessed Trinity were pleased to manifest themselves on various occasions to mortal eye and mortal ear. *Very frequently to the eye,* in the visible glory of the pillar of cloud and fire in the desert journeys; in the glorious light which shone in the holy of holies, first in the tabernacle of the wanderings, then in the temple; in the flame as in the burning bush, and in the visions of Isaiah and Ezekiel; in appearances as in the meeting with Abraham and with Joshua. **To** *the ear* the word of the Lord spoke, amongst others, to Abraham, Moses, Samuel, and the later prophets. So in this, the transition period of Messiah, the visible glory of God and the audible voice of God were again seen and heard by mortal man. Jerome calls attention here to the distinctness of each of the Persons of the blessed Trinity, as shown in this baptism of the Messiah. "The mystery of the Trinity is shown in the baptism of Christ. The *Lord* is baptized, the *Spirit* descends in the likeness of a dove, the voice of the *Father* is heard bearing witness to his Son, and the dove settles on the head of Jesus, lest any one should imagine that the voice was for John and not for Christ." We may with all reverence conclude that, after the hearing of the voice from heaven, "the Messianic self-consciousness would undoubtedly expand with rapidity, both intensively and extensively, into complete maturity. That self-consciousness, it must be borne in mind, would necessarily, so far as this human side of his Being was concerned, be subject, in its development, to the condition of time" (Dr. Morrison, on Matt. iii. 17).

Ver. 23a.—**And Jesus himself began to be about thirty years of age.** This was the age at which the Levites entered upon their work ; the age, too, at which it was lawful for scribes to teach. Generally speaking, thirty among the Jews was looked upon as the time of life when manhood had reached its full development.

Vers. 23b—38.—THE EARTHLY GENEALOGY OF JESUS CHRIST. Although in every Hebrew family the hope seems to have been cherished that the promised Messiah would be born among them, yet generally the prophetic utterances were understood to point to the Deliverer springing from the royal house of David. To demonstrate that this was actually true in the case of the reputed Son of Mary and Joseph, both the genealogies contained in the Gospels of Matthew and Luke were compiled from private and public records. It is well known that these family trees were preserved with care in well-nigh every Jewish family. The sacred books compiled after the return from Babylon— 1 and 2 Chronicles, Ezra, and Nehemiah— with their long tables of descent, show us that these family records existed then. Josephus (second century) thus writes: "I relate my genealogy as I find it recorded in the public tables" ('Life,' ch. i.). In his work against Apion (i. 7) he says, "From all the countries in which our priests are scattered abroad, they send to Jerusalem [in order that their children may be placed on the official roll] papers with the names of their parents and their ancestors; these papers are formally witnessed."

It follows that, if such care were taken in the case of the numerous priestly houses, equal attention would be paid to their family records by the comparatively few families who boasted their descent from King David and the ancient royal house. R. Hillel, the renowned teacher, who lived in the days of Jesus Christ, belonged to the poor among the people, and yet he was able to prove, from existent records, that he was one of David's descendants. Some seventy years later, the grandchildren of Jude, the reputed brother of the Lord, a son of Joseph, were summoned to Rome, and appeared before the Emperor Domitian as *descendants of the old royal house of David.*

Now, no further comment would be necessary upon this elaborate "table" of St. Luke did there not exist in St. Matthew's Gospel another family tree, purporting to be the line of Messiah's ancestors. Between these two tables there are many important differences. How are these to be explained?. On this subject in different times many works have been written. In the present Commentary the writer does not propose to examine the details of the two tables of SS. Matthew and Luke; the question of the existence of the two records will alone be dealt with. The various smaller points of discrepancy in the registers of SS. Matthew and Luke, although curious and striking, are utterly barren of interest to the great majority of students of the Divine Word. The reader who may wish to examine these is referred—among modern scholars' works on this subject—to Bishop Harvey's exhaustive work on the genealogy of the Lord ; to Archdeacon Farrar's Excursus in his 'Commentary on St. Luke' in the 'Cambridge Bible for Schools ; ' and to Professor Godet's Commentary on this Gospel.

We will confine ourselves here to three points. (1) Why does St. Luke insert his table of Messiah's earthly descent in this place ? (2) For what reason does he trace up the long ancestral line to Adam ? (3) What is the broad outline of the explanation of St. Luke's divergency from the genealogical table of St. Matthew ?

(1) and (2) can be shortly answered.

(1) St. Luke felt that this was the most suitable place in his narrative for such a table. His work was evidently most carefully and skilfully arranged upon the lines of formal history. Up to this point the story was mainly concerned with other personages—with the parents of the great forerunner John, with Mary the Virgin and Joseph, with the angels, with the shepherds, with Simeon and with Anna, and especially with the work of John the Baptist. But from henceforth all the minor persons of the Divine story pass into the background. There is now one central figure upon whom the whole interest of the Divine drama centres—Jesus. This, the moment of his real introduction on the world's stage, was, as St. Luke rightly judged it, the time to give the formal table of his earthly ancestry.

(2) Different from the Hebrew evangelist St. Matthew, whose thoughts were centred on the chosen race, and whose horizon was bounded by Palestine, or at least by those cities where his countrymen of the dispersion lived and worked, and who only cared to show that his Messiah had sprung from the great patriarch, the father of the tribes of Israel, St. Luke, feeling that the scene of the work of *his* Messiah was bounded by no Jewish horizon, traces up his Lord's reputed line of earthly ancestors to the first father of the human race. The Jesus of Luke was the Saviour, not only of the children of Abraham, but of the children of Adam. The noble Isaiah-prophecy, which we feel was one of the great mainsprings of Paul's life and work, was the real reason of Luke, the disciple of Paul, tracing up Messiah's family line to Adam. "It is a light thing that thou shouldest be my servant to raise up the tribes of Jacob, and to restore the preserved of Israel : I will also give thee for a Light to the Gentiles" (Isa. xlix. 6). Luke alone records the incident and the words of Simeon in the temple.

(3) The genealogy given by St. Luke differs from that presented by St. Matthew, because St. Luke has extricated from family records the line of *Mary*, while St. Matthew has elected to chronicle the family of *Joseph*. This solution of the differences between the two lists was apparently first suggested by Annius of Viterbo, at the close of the fifteenth century. Among the many eminent modern scholars who accept it, I would instance Professor Godet and Dean Plumptre. The arguments in favour of this view—viz. that the genealogy is Mary's, not Joseph's—are the following.

The table begins as follows : "And Jesus . . . being (as was supposed) the son of Joseph, which was the son of Heli, which was the son of Matthat," etc. In the original Greek *all* the older authorities, before the name Joseph, omit the article τοῦ, of the. This article is found before all the names in the long list with this solitary exception. This absence of the article τοῦ certainly puts the name of Joseph in a special position in the series of names, and leads us to suppose that the genealogy is not that of Joseph, but of Heli. (Heli being the father of Mary, the omission of *her* name will be treated later on.) The twenty-third verse would then read thus: "And Jesus, . . . (being as was supposed the son of Joseph)," after which parenthesis the first link in the chain would be Jesus, the heir and grandson, and in that sense *the son of Heli*.

It is by no means unusual in the Old Testament to find the grandson termed the "son" of his grandfather (compare, for instance, 1 Chron. viii. 1 and 3 with Gen. xlvi. 21 ; Ezra v. 1 and vi. 14 with Zech. i. 1, 7). On the omission of Mary's name, Godet quotes from the Talmud ('Treatise Bava Bathra,' 110, *a*), and urges with great truth that not only among the Hebrews did ancient sentiment not accord with the mention of a mother as the genealogical link. The Talmud treatise most singularly comes to our help again by mentioning that *Mary the mother of Jesus was called the daughter of Heli.* We have before dwelt upon the fact that not only general ancient tradition, but the plain sense of the gospel story, ascribed to Mary a royal Davidic descent. 'Bava Bathra' (quoted by Godet), with great force, asks (though with a different design), what sensible man, after declaring at the commencement of the list that the relationship of Joseph and Jesus was destitute of all reality (ὡς ἐνομίζετο), could take pleasure in drawing up such a list of ancestors? This most pertinent question can only be answered by showing that the list is a list, not of Joseph's ancestors, but of Mary's, who was in very truth the mother of Jesus.

In coming to any conclusion respecting the real history of the drawing up the two distinct genealogical tables, the one of Joseph, the other of Mary, it will be ever well to bear in mind that the early chapters of the two narratives of SS. Matthew and Luke, where the events of the birth and infancy of the Lord are told, were most probably based on memories written and oral, *proceeding from two distinct centres* or circles of believers, eye-witnesses many of them of the things they related or of which they preserved a faithful memory in writing. The one circle—to use Godet's words—of which Joseph was the centre, and which we suppose consisted of Cleopas, his brothers James and Jude the sons of Joseph, of whom one was the first bishop of the flock in Jerusalem, included, too, Simeon a son of Cleopas, the first successor of James. The narratives preserved amongst these persons might easily reach the ears of the author of the First Gospel, who doubtless lived in the midst of this flock. But a cycle of narratives must also have formed itself round Mary. These doubtless are those which Luke has preserved.

The genealogy, then, of St. Matthew, which has *Joseph* in view, must have proceeded from his family. That given, on the other hand, by St. Luke, no doubt issued from the circle of which Mary was the centre.

The other differences in the two genealogies are minor and of far less interest; they are exhaustively discussed in the various monographs which have been written on this subject, and to which reference has been made above.

HOMILETICS.

Vers. 1—18.—*The forerunner, and his ministry.* Some thirty years have passed since the birth of a son of the old age had filled the house of the good priest Zacharias with the voice of rejoicing. The blameless priest and his blameless wife are dead. The son who, when an unconscious babe, was called "the prophet of the Highest," has lived the life of a recluse, receiving his inspirations wholly from the study of the Law of the Lord, from lonely communings with God and truth in the great temple of nature. There were many solitaries in that period. There were the Essenes, one of the sects of the Jewish nation. Eremites, too, dwelt in dens and caves, fleeing far from the world, with its strife and tumult. But this man was no mere Essene, no mere Eremite. There was a vocation before him; like the Master who was to come after him, he was being filled with the Holy Ghost for the work the striking of whose hour is related in the passage. A man sternly, austerely simple. No phylacteries and fringes about him; no soft clothing and signs of luxurious culture. For dress there is only the skin of a camel thrown around him and held together by a rough leather band. His sole nourishment is the honey which he gathers in the moorland, and locusts steeped in water and dried in the sun. He wants nothing which the world can give to him, and he fears nothing which the world can do to him. He can stand alone, for God is with him. To him, in the fifteenth year of Tiberius, comes the Word of the Lord.

I. Observe, at the outset, THE TIME AND THE PROPHETIC DESIGNATION OF THE MINISTRY. The date bids us back to one of those times of confusion and uncertainty which mark the passing away of the old and the preparation for a new day or period. Note the names in ver. 1. Tiberius, a low, dull, sottish despot; Pontius Pilate, indolent, overbearing, greedy; Herod, disgracing his tetrarchate by open licentiousness; Caiaphas and Annas disputing for the priesthood, and neither of them worthy of respect. Typical of the world on which from his Judæan retreat the son of Zacharias looked forth. "The godly man ceased, for the faithful were failing from the children of men." Then—reminding us of Elijah the Tishbite, who abruptly confronts Ahab in his purple, protesting, "as the Lord God of Israel liveth before whom I stand"—on a sudden the popular vision is arrested, the popular imagination is excited, by the figure and preaching of John. The evangelist sees in this preaching the fulfilment of the sublime prophecy of Isaiah (xl. 3—5). Looking at this prophecy, we are struck with the greatness of the announcement, and the apparent insignificance of the fulfilment. There is nothing incongruous in applying to John the description, "a voice crying in the wilderness." But the results declared—the filling of every valley, the bringing low of every mountain and hill, etc.—seem too vast as a representation of the effect of John's cry. Reading Isaiah's sentences we imagine a work with inspiring circumstances, with grand, striking evidences of its accomplishment; turning to the Gospel pages we are introduced only to a rough preacher of the desert, uttering sharp sentences, and aiming at a spiritual repentance for the remission of sins. Yet in this preacher and in his work the prediction was fulfilled—in *God's way.* Let no one despise the poverty of the instrument. "The excellency of the power is of God." The chapter reminds us of a wonderful blaze of popularity. On the effete religiousness of Judæa it came as a new sensation to hear that a man, recalling the image of Elijah, was speaking in sentences which fell like thunderbolts; and forth from priestly Hebron, from Pharisee-worshipping Jerusalem, from city and village, there poured a mighty throng, all hastening to the desert-sanctuary of John. Again the long-silent Spirit of God was speaking; the chain of prophecy, which seemed to have ended with Malachi, had again been formed. They gather trembling and awe-struck around that strange, uncouth-looking saint; he bids them submit to his baptism; they do so; and sanctimonious religionist and haughty soldier and corrupt publican demand, "What shall we do?" It was a great religious revival, raising the question, "Can this be the dawn of Messiah's day? Is this indeed the Messiah promised to our fathers?"

II. Regard THE PREACHER AND HIS MESSAGE. What is the force of the man? What is the relation of his word to Christ? 1. *The preacher.* (1) There is the force of *earnestness.* He has looked through all the appearances and shams of his age, and has seen how hollow they are. He has been communing with the unseen realities; and to him heaven and hell are no distant futures, but are states actually encompassing men. He is possessed by the word which has come to him, and therefore he is beyond the region of fear. What are either smiles or frowns to him? Therefore, too, his is the eloquence of action. A man in earnest will not trifle among the flowers of rhetoric; he has no time to hunt for metaphors and tropes. Is not life very short? He must get by the most direct road possible to the human conscience. Ah! that is the power of the God-sent preacher. When men feel that there is no second-hand repeating, that there is no mere playing at dialectics, that there is no part-acting, that the utterance proceeds from conviction, that it is the expression of truth which is swaying the soul, they cannot but listen; so far they will yield. Earnestness is not noisy rant; but, calm and quiet as it is, like the kingdom of heaven, it breaks in with violence. It must work, fight, win. (2) There is the force, too, of *plain, downright, practical teaching.* To the anxious inquirers he returns answers which prove his tact in dealing with human nature. See how he hits each class at the point of its special temptation and besetting sin, and how at once he insists on the application of Isaiah's rule (i. 16): "Wash you, make you clean; put away the evil of your doings from before mine eyes; cease to do evil; learn to do well." It was a solemn peremptory summons to yield to the Eternal Righteousness. There were no honeyed phrases. The preacher laid the axe at the root of the tree; for it was no time for clippings and loppings here and there. No mercy was shown for the piety of outside appearances. Privilege! what mattered that if it was only a bed on which to sleep? He who conferred the privilege can take it away; nay, he is able of these stones to raise up children to Abraham. Was it wonderful that the crowd listened with bated breath; that souls cowered beneath the eagle eye and the searching incisive teaching of the mighty prophet of the wilderness? (3) Add to this the *thorough honesty and humility of the teacher.* Every person knows that the ordinary ambitions of men have no charm for him; even the extraordinary ambitions—to be a leader of thought, to guide and direct spiritual movement, to stamp the impression of his own mind on others—have no power over him. He claims to be only the voice. "Art thou the Christ?" so deputations of the Pharisees ask; to this effect the people muse. "No" is the answer; "there is One behind me. I am only the witness, only the herald. Mine is only the poor baptism with water. His is the baptism with the Holy Ghost and with fire." Thoroughly honest, unselfish, noble, is this prophet of the desert. 2. Now consider *his message* as that is stated by St. Luke. (1) Its *great word,* "Repent!"—the word which in every time, and never more than in this nineteenth century, is apt to be softened. People applaud discourses about faith and love, and the search for truth, and so forth; but proclaim the need of repentance, bring persons individually face to face with that need, and one of two things follow—either the resistance of the heart to condemnation, or the conviction of the soul to salvation. Have we not far too little of the preaching of " repentance for the *remission of sins*"? Mark this: There can be no real sending away of sin from between the soul and God without a change of mind, caused by the sight of sin as sin, as darkness, as death. God will never bless a man in his sins. " Repent " is the burden of all preaching on which the Holy Spirit sets his seal. (2) The *sacrament which accompanies the word*. There is the baptism of repentance. Sinners must take their stand with God as to their sins, joining him in his condemnation. They must confess their sins. They are commanded to do this in expressive act—to go down, soiled with dust and weary with their journey, into the river; standing there, with eye uplifted to heaven, to say, " I acknowledge my transgressions; against thee, thee only, have I sinned. God be merciful to me a sinner!" And then, as they sink beneath the water, they seem to have sunk in it their old sinful life; they arise, white and clean, pledged to walk henceforth in newness of life. A type yet to be fulfilled! John distinctly protested, " This baptism is only an instalment; the laver of regeneration is not with me." But it was a symbol rich with meaning; it was the act which expressed the word that rang through the wilderness, " Repent!" (3) The *hand which pointed forward*. This man, with the true second sight, sees the measure of iniquity all but filled up. He sees the tokens of rapidly hastening judgment. The nation is only the carcase of a nation, and the eagles are swooping down on it. " Flee, flee from the wrath to come." How? " Repent!" Whither? " The kingdom of heaven is at hand." He is there to prepare them for it, to lead them to it. Note: The preacher knows that a new order, that of the Coming One, is close on them. But he knows no more. While he is preaching, that new order is moving towards him in the person of the Cousin on whom his eyes, for long years, had never rested—perhaps, indeed, he had never even seen him. " I knew him not," he could afterwards say. All that he then knew, he knew through an inner teaching which was no lie, " One mightier than I cometh, and with him cometh the kingdom of heaven."

Vers. 21, 22.—*The baptism of Jesus, and the descent of the Holy Ghost.* The narrative of the meeting between Jesus and John is given at greater length, and with more completeness of detail, by St. Matthew (see homiletics on Matt. iii. 13—17). But the account of St. Luke suggests some points of interest.

I. THE IDENTIFICATION OF JESUS WITH THE PEOPLE. " When all the people were baptized, Jesus also having been baptized." In this, as in other things, " he is made like to his brethren." But, specially observe, he is still, and he is as yet only, " under the Law." His righteousness has been hitherto that indicated in the book of the Law. He has submitted to every requirement. He has completely done whatsoever was commanded. Sharing this position in common with all the people, he offered himself for the baptism unto repentance and the hope of the kingdom. This baptism was the fitting conclusion of a perfect legal righteousness. The man needs to be washed. The Law cannot make the conscience perfect. That which signified the inadequacy of the Law, Jesus of Nazareth must appropriate. A righteousness which is in and of the flesh cannot be the ground of acceptance with God. Jesus condemned sin *in the flesh* when, with the forerunner, he went down into the water of baptism.

II. THE PRAYER WHICH SOLEMNIZED THE BAPTISM. St. Luke alone makes mention of this prayer. With all the people, Jesus was baptized; but who of the people were with him in this—" baptized and *praying*"? To him there is no confession of personal transgression; he is yielding himself to his Father in perfectly loving resignation. The baptism was an act of communion. " I come to do thy will." " Here am I; send me." Not without purpose, surely, is notice taken of the prayer. Connect it with what follows—in praying, the heavens were opened. Behold the law of spiritual blessing, " Ask, and ye shall receive"! Behold that which makes all ordinances effectual, without which they are forms, not means of grace! Behold the evidence of the power of prayer! God is ready still to open his heaven to the obedient, desiring heart. " We enter heaven by prayer."

III. THE DESCENT IN A BODILY SHAPE LIKE A DOVE. The evangelist inserts "the bodily form" to signify that it was not a mere imagination, but a real descent assuming this shape. What of the descent of the Holy Ghost? Observe it (1) as between Christ himself and the opened heavens, and (2) as a token of the grace and truth which have come by Christ. 1. What we have before us is not a coming of the Spirit for personal holiness, for in this sense the Holy Spirit had been with Christ during the preceding thirty years. It is *the coming of the Holy Spirit into a new form of admini-stration.* The new thing is what St. John expresses. "The Spirit abode upon him." He dwelt henceforth in the Man Christ Jesus, not as a mere *limitless* abundance, but as an *undivided* abundance. All offices, gifts, graces, were realized in the Lord himself. He was Apostle, Prophet, Evangelist, Pastor, and Teacher; he was all in all. The fountain was sealed in his own Person; after the Ascension the seal was broken, and the power in the glorified humanity was divided. Some he gave as apostles, some as prophets, some as evangelists, some as pastors and teachers. But that which is signified by the investiture of Jesus coming out of Jordan is that in him, consecrated the Messiah, is the fulness of grace and blessing; that his exclusively is the baptism with the Holy Ghost. "The same is he that baptizeth with the Holy Ghost." 2. And see *the token of this administration.* "Like a dove"—recalling the mission of the dove which Noah put forth from the ark, and which returned to him with the olive leaf in its mouth. "Like a dove"—suggesting love tender and brooding, noiseless and winning, the Spirit descends. Is not this the characteristic token of the new covenant? (See Keble's thirty-third hymn.) It is the dove-like Spirit that dwells in Jesus. There is a fire that goes before him. When he began the public ministry, he took a passage full of gracious words, yet one which concludes with the proclamation of a day of vengeance of our God. There are "woes" in Jesus' discourses very scathing and stern. There is "the wrath of the Lamb." But the characteristic action of Christ is that of the Dove. The Dove is visible even in his Divinity, even in the lambent tongues, the lightning flashes, the arrows of conviction. He is waiting to be gracious. O sinner, yield thyself to him. For thee are prepared dove-like blessings, influences

> "To nurse the soul to heavenly love,
> The struggling spark of good within
> Just smothered in the strife of sin
> To quicken to a timely glow,
> The pure flame spreading high and low."

HOMILIES BY VARIOUS AUTHORS.

Vers. 1, 2.—*Roman worldliness and Hebrew devotedness.* We have these historical personages brought into view in order to fix the year when John began his ministry. At the time when they lived they would have scorned the idea that their names were only to be valuable in proportion as they shed light on the life and the work of this rugged Jewish saint. But so it is. We only care to know about these Romans because their figures cross the stage of sacred history, and because they came into temporary relationship with John and with John's great Master. Their names, however, being brought into conjunction with his, let us notice the contrast which they present to us.

I. THEY WERE UNLIKE AS THEY COULD BE TO ONE ANOTHER IN THE CIRCUMSTANCES AND SURROUNDINGS OF THEIR LIFE. These Roman worldlings dwelt in palaces, lived in luxury, surrounded themselves with everything that could minister to comfort and enjoyment; they were gorgeously apparelled, and lived delicately in their kingly courts (ch. vii. 25). John was a man who despised delicacies, and deliberately chose that which was coarse in garment, unpalatable in food, rude in dwelling. His life was positively devoid of that which was refreshing, comforting, delightful, so far as the outward and the visible were concerned.

II. THEY WERE DIAMETRICALLY OPPOSED IN CHARACTER. If we except Philip, who left a reputation for justice and moderation, and Lysanias, of whom nothing or little is known, we may say of the others that they were men whose character was not only reprehensible, but even hideous. Of Tiberius Cæsar we read that, after he came to the throne, he entirely disappointed the promise of his earlier years, and that he " wallowed in the very kennel of the low and debasing." Of Pilate we know from the evangelists' story that he was a man, not indeed without some sense of justice and pity, not incapable of being moved at the sight of sublime patience and innocence, but yet sceptical, superstitious, entirely wanting in political principle, ready to sacrifice righteousness to save his own position. Of Herod Antipas we know from Scripture that he was cunning, licentious, superstitious. But of John, the Hebrew prophet, we know that he was utterly fearless and disregardful of his own interests when duty called him to speak freely (ver. 19); that he was a faithful preacher of Divine truth (vers. 7—14); that he was perfectly loyal to that One who was so much greater than himself (ver. 16); that he was capable of a most noble magnanimity (John iii. 29). He was a godly, upright, heroic soul.

III. They have left very different memories behind them. Of one of these Romans (Tiberius) we read that he "deserved the scorn and abhorrence of mankind." Perhaps this language, only a very little weakened, might be used of two others of them. But concerning John, after our Lord's own eulogium (ch. vii. 28), we feel that we can be in little danger of thinking of him too highly and of honouring him too much.

IV. They resembled one another only in that they both ran great risks of earthly ill. Devotedness in the person of John exposed itself to severe penalties, to the condemnation of man, to imprisonment and death. But worldliness in the person of these Roman dignitaries ran great risks also; it had to encounter human fickleness and human wrath. Tiberius is believed to have become insane. Pilate committed suicide. Herod died in exile. Worldly policy may succeed for a time, may stand in high places, may drink of very sweet cups, but it runs great risks, and very often it has to endure great calamities. Alas for it, that, when these come, it is wholly destitute of the more precious consolations!

V. At death they confronted a very different future. Well might the least guilty of them shrink from that judgment-seat at which all men must stand! how must the worst of them be covered with shame in that awful Presence! and how serious must be the penalty that will be attached to such flagitious abuse of position and opportunity! On the other hand, how high is the power, how bright and broad the sphere, how blessed the hope, into which the faithful forerunner has entered! He has "passed into that country where it matters little whether a man has been clothed in finest linen or in coarsest camel's hair, that still country where the struggle-storm of life is over, and such as John find their rest at last in the home of God, which is reserved for the true and brave."—C.

Vers. 3—6.—*John before Jesus; repentance before salvation.* We may view this subject—

I. Historically. Jesus, as his name indicated, came to be a Saviour; but he came to bring a very different salvation from that which was expected of him. His contemporaries were not aware that *they themselves* were in any need of salvation. They supposed it was their political condition which needed to undergo a change. They were full of a fatal self-sufficiency so far as their own character was concerned; they esteemed themselves the prime favourites of Heaven, and thought that, when the great Deliverer appeared, it would be entirely on their behalf, in order that they might be restored to their rightful place and assume the government they believed themselves so worthy to conduct. If they were to receive, with any cordiality of welcome, a Saviour who came to *save them*, to deliver them from guilt, it was necessary that a voice should be heard speaking in plainest tones breaking through the hard crust of complacency and delusion, working conviction of guilt within the soul; it behoved that he should come "preaching the baptism of repentance for the remission of sins." Thus did John "prepare the way" for Jesus—the apostle of repentance for the Saviour of mankind.

II. Experimentally. That which was the historical order is also the order in our heart's experience. We repent of sin before we know the Saviour so as to possess his full salvation. It is indeed true that the words of Jesus Christ, the view of his holy life, the consideration of his dying love—that this is a power working, and working mightily, for repentance on the soul; yet must there be repentance, as an existing condition of mind, for a true and full appreciation of the great service Jesus Christ offers to render to us.   We cannot rejoice in him as in our Divine Saviour, redeeming us from the penalty and the curse of sin, until we have known and felt our own unworthiness and wrong-doing.   1. This is the *scriptural doctrine*.   Our Lord, before he left his apostles, instructed them to preach "repentance and remission of sins in his Name among all nations" (ch. xxiv. 47).   Peter said, "Repent . . . for the remission of sins" (Acts ii. 38).   Paul testified to Jews and Greeks "repentance toward God, and faith toward our Lord Jesus Christ" (Acts xx. 21).   John wrote, as he doubtless preached, "If we say that we have no sin, we deceive ourselves . . . if we confess our sins, he is faithful and just to forgive us our sins, and to cleanse us from all unrighteousness" (1 John i. 8, 9).   2. This is the *obvious spiritual order*.   For how can we make our appeal to Christ, how can we put our trust in him as in our Divine Redeemer and the Propitiation for our sins, until we have recognized in ourselves the sinners that we are ?   For this there is necessary :   (1) The *idea of* sin—in many hearts, in many places, found to be wholly wanting, and having to be planted there.   (2) The *sense of* sin— absent from a great many more; absent, it may be, because it is forgotten that our guiltiness before God is not only nor chiefly found in doing what he has forbidden, but in withholding what he has desired and required of us, in the non-payment of the "ten thousand talents" of reverence and gratitude and service we owe him.   (3) *Shame for* sin, and a strong and deep desire to be cleansed from its evil stain.   This true penitence brings us in eagerness and hope to the feet and to the cross of the Divine Saviour.—C.

Ver. 7.—*The ministry of fear*.   We read that "Noah, moved with fear," built the ark which, in saving him and his family, saved the human race.   Fear, dread of impending danger, has its place in the heart of man, and its work in the service of mankind.   God made his appeal to it when he dealt with Israel ; there was much of it in the Law.   It was not absent from the ministry of Jesus Christ ; it was he who spoke to men of the "millstone about the neck," of the undying worm, of the doom less tolerable than that of Tyre and Sidon.   John's teaching seems to have been composed very largely of this element; he spoke freely of the "wrath to come."   We are bound to consider—

I. THE FUTURE WHICH WE HAVE TO FEAR.   We are not to imagine that because those terrible pictures of physical suffering which arose from mistaking the meaning of our Lord's figurative words have long ceased to haunt the minds of men, *there is therefore nothing to apprehend* in the future.   That would be a reaction from one extreme to another.   If we take the authority of Scripture as decisive, it is certain that the impenitent have everything to fear.   They have to face : 1. *Judgment* and, with judgment, *condemnation*.   "We must all appear before the judgment-seat of Christ."   "Every one shall give account of himself to God."   What reason here for keen apprehension on the part of the impenitent sensualist, oppressor, defrauder, scorner !   2. *The penalty* which is due to guilt.   This may be heavier or lighter, according as the light in which a man lived was clearer or less clear; but when we think how sin is branded and smitten *now*, what shame and suffering follow in its train in this world of probation, how seriously Divine wrath visits iniquity even in the day of grace, we may well shrink, with a fear that is not craven but simply wise, from enduring the penalty of unforgiven sin in the world of retribution (see Rom. ii. 5—9).   It is not the brave, but the blind and the infatuated, who are indifferent to "the wrath to come."

II. OUR COMMON INTEREST IN THIS SOLEMN THEME.   "Who hath warned *you*," said John, addressing himself (as we learn from Matthew) more particularly to the Pharisees and Sadducees, "to flee from the wrath to come ?   How comes it that you, who are so perfectly satisfied with yourselves and charge yourselves with no defects, are concerned about judgment?   And how is it that you Sadducees, who profess not to believe in any future at all, are trembling in view of another world?"   Why did the rigid formalist and the sceptic come to listen so attentively to his doctrine of repentance?   The truth was and is that the supposed sufficiency of Pharisaical proprieties, and the barrier of sceptical denials, break down in the hour when the faithful and fearless prophet speaks, when the stern but friendly truth of God finds its way to the human conscience.   Our carefully constructed defences may last for days, or even years, but they will not last for ever; the hour comes when some strong reality sweeps them away.   There is not one of us, into how many different classes or denominations we may be divided, who does not need to inquire earnestly of God's spokesman what is the way of escape from the penalty of sin. And we know what is—

III. THE SURE WAY OF ESCAPE. It is that of *penitence*, on which John so strongly insisted; and of *faith* in that "Lamb of God" whom he pointed out as "taking away the sins of the world."—C.

Vers. 8—14.—*The futile in religion, etc.* In these verses we have brought into view four aspects of religious truth.

I. THE FUTILE. The Pharisee, if he were charged with any evil course, consoled himself with the thought that he was a "son of Abraham;" to his mind it was everything with God that he was lineally descended from the father of the faithful, and had been admitted by the rite of circumcision into the "commonwealth of Israel." John, anticipating the doctrine of Jesus Christ, demolishes this delusion. *That*, he tells his audience on the banks of Jordan, is a matter of very small account with Heaven; that is not the criterion of character; that is not the passport to the kingdom of God. Let no man think to build on that poor foundation. Not genealogical connection with the best of men (see John i. 13), not admission by outward rite into any visible community, decides our state before God. If we appear before him, and have no better plea than this to offer, we must prepare for his dismissal. All that is fleshly, all that is circumstantial, all that is outward and unspiritual, falls short of the Divine requirement. It does not bring us *into* the kingdom of heaven.

II. THE DIFFICULT. "God is able of these stones," etc. Nothing could be easier than for Almighty power to raise up children unto Abraham—to bring into existence more children of privilege. He had but to "speak, and it would be done; to command, and it would come forth." But it was quite another thing to win the disobedient and the disloyal to filial love and holy service, to bring the hard of heart and the proud of spirit to penitence and confession of sin, to conduct the feet that had long been walking in paths of selfishness and guilt into the ways of wisdom and of worth. This is a work in the accomplishment of which even the Divine Spirit employs many means and expends great resources and exercises long patience. He teaches, he invites, he pleads, he warns, he chastens, he waits. And on this great, this most difficult work, this spiritual victory, on which the eternal Father spends so much of the Divine, we surely may be well content to put forth all our human, strength.

III. THE SEVERE. "Now also the axe is laid unto the root . . . is hewn down, and cast into the fire." John intimates that a new dispensation is arriving, and with its coming there will come also a more severe sentence against disobedience and unfruitfulness. The shining of the fuller light will necessarily throw far deeper shadows. They who will not learn of the great Teacher will fall under great condemnation. The useless trees in the garden of the Lord will now not only be disbranched, they will be cut down. It is a very solemn thing to live in the full daylight of revealed religion. With every added ray of privilege and opportunity comes increase of sacred responsibility and exposure to the Divine severity.

IV. THE PRACTICAL. (Vers. 10—14.) Real repentance will show itself in right behaviour, and every man, according to his vocation, will take his rightful part. The man of means will be pitiful and generous; the man in office will be just and upright; the soldier will be civil; the servant will be faithful and be satisfied with the receipt of what is due to him; the master and the mistress will be fair in their expectation of service; the father will be considerate of his children's weakness; the children will be regardful of their parents' will. And while the right thing will be done, it will be done reverently and religiously, not only as unto man, but as "unto Christ the Lord."—C.

Vers. 15—17.—*The wisdom of a true estimate.* Those who are far up the social heights are usually under a strong temptation to climb to the very summit. We do not know how strong the temptation may have been to John to assume or to attempt the part of the Messiah. Popularity is very exciting and ensnaring; it leads men to prefer claims and to adopt measures which, on lower ground and in calmer mood, they would not have entertained for a moment. But John's mind never lost its balance in the tumult of great professional success. Unlike most men, he seems to have stood prosperity better than adversity (see Matt. xi. 2, 3). He does not appear to have wavered for a moment in his fidelity to the Lord whose way he came to prepare; he always retained a true estimate of himself, his work, and his Master. In this respect he was as wise as he was true, and we cannot do better than emulate his wisdom.

I. A TRUE ESTIMATE OF OURSELVES. John knew that in personal worth and dignity he was not for a moment to be compared with Jesus. That great Prophet whom he was preceding was "One mightier than himself," One for whom he was not worthy to discharge the meanest office which the slave renders his master. In cherishing this thought he was both right and wise. There is the truest wisdom in humility. To mistake ourselves, to think ourselves greater or worthier than we are, is to do ourselves the greatest injury and wrong. 1. It is to offend God and to draw down some sign of his serious displeasure (Jas. iv. 6). 2. It is to incur the disapproval and hostility of our fellow-men; for there is nothing that our neighbours more thoroughly dislike on our part than an exaggerated notion of our own importance. 3. It is in itself an evil and perilous condition, in which we are open to the worst attacks of our spiritual enemies. On the other hand, humility is acceptable to God, approved of man, and safe.

II. A TRUE ESTIMATE OF OUR POSITION and of the work we have to do in the world. John clearly recognized, and very distinctly declared, that his mission in the world was one altogether and immeasurably inferior to that of Christ; to those who would not have been surprised to learn that he claimed to be the Messiah he made it known that he was doing that which was slight and small in comparison with the work of Christ. It is indeed a good and a wise thing for us to aspire to do all that God gives us the capacity and the opportunity to do. But let us take great care that we do not, from pride or vain-glory, go beyond that boundary-line. If we do we shall make a serious and possibly even a calamitous mistake. Many that have done excellent service and have had great joy in the doing it *when they have worked within the range of their powers*, have done grievous mischief and have suffered sad trouble when they have attempted that which was beyond them. Nothing but injury to others, damage to the cause of God, and sorrow for ourselves can arise from an over-estimate of the position we are able to fill.

III. A TRUE ESTIMATE OF OUR LORD. That Mighty One who was coming should do the very greatest things. He would: 1. Act with direct Divine energy upon the souls of men—"baptize with the Holy Ghost." 2. Utter truth which should have a great testing and cleansing power; his fan would "throughly purge his floor" (see homily on ch. ii. 34). 3. Make a final distinction between the true and the false: "He will gather the wheat into his garner," etc. No man who cares for his own spiritual and eternal interests can afford to disregard the words or the work of this great Prophet that was to come, that has come, that "is now exalted a Prince and a Saviour," giving redemption and eternal life to all who seek his grace and live in his service.—C.

Vers. 21, 22.—*God's good pleasure in us.* There are some preliminary lessons we do well to learn before we approach the main one; *e.g.*: 1. That piety will sometimes prompt us to do that which we are under no constraint to do. Jesus was not under any obligation to be baptized with the baptism of repentance. Moreover, he could not be said to be enrolling himself as a disciple of John. But he felt that "it became him" to do what he did (Matt. iii. 15); probably his abstention would have been far more likely to be misunderstood than his compliance: hence his action. If we are earnestly desirous of doing everything we can in the cause of truth and righteousness, we shall not stop at the line of positive commandment or of necessity; we shall consider what *it becomes us* to do and how we shall *best* serve the purposes of God's love. 2. That God will not fail to manifest himself to us in the hour of need. Again and again he appeared in strengthening grace unto his Son; on this occasion, when "the heaven was opened," etc.; and when "his soul was troubled" (John x. 28); and in the garden (ch. xxii. 43). So did he appear to Paul in the time of his necessity (Acts xviii. 9; xxiii. 11; 2 Tim. iv. 17). So will he appear in all-sustaining power unto us in the crises of our life. 3. That in proportion to our true devoutness of spirit may we look for the manifestations of God's kindness. "*Jesus . . . praying*, the heaven was opened."

The main lesson is that those who are God's true children may be assured of his good pleasure in them.

I. GOD'S GOOD PLEASURE IN HIS SON JESUS CHRIST. "Thou art my beloved Son; in thee I am well pleased." The sentiment of Divine complacency and gladness in Jesus Christ probably had regard to: 1. Our Lord's past earthly life, to the innocency of his childhood, to the integrity of all his life at home, to the preparation he had been making in solitary study and devotion for his life-work. 2. To his then spiritual condition, especially to his attitude toward his Divine Father, his submission to his holy will, his readiness to undertake whatever that holy will should appoint him, and, therefore: 3. To his sacred and sublime purpose, his intention to enter on that great work which should issue in the redemption of mankind. It must have been no slight access of holy strength to the Saviour to be so strikingly assured of his Father's love and good pleasure as he entered on that most arduous and lofty enterprise.

II. GOD'S GOOD PLEASURE IN US. We cannot hope to have for ourselves the measure of Divine complacency which was possible in the Person of our Lord. Yet in our measure may we hope to have and to enjoy the good pleasure of our heavenly Father. For us there may be: 1. *Full forgiveness of the faulty past.* Grieved with all that is guilty, and resting on the abounding mercy of God in Jesus Christ, we are freely and frankly forgiven; so truly and thoroughly forgiven that our past transgressions and shortcomings are buried from the sight of the Supreme; they do not come between our souls and his favour; they are to him as if they were not; they do not make us less dear to his parental heart. 2. *Positive Divine delight in our filial loyalty and love.* As God, searching our hearts with pure and benign regard, sees in us a true filial spirit, a spirit of grateful love and of cheerful submission and of glad consecration to himself, he is glad in us with a Divine, parental joy. 3. *Divine satisfaction with our purpose for the future*—our intention to dedicate our life to the service of God and to spend our powers in the service of our kind.—C.

Vers. 1—20.—*The ministry of the Baptist.* We left Jesus, when last we studied Luke's narrative, in Nazareth, subject to his parents and realizing a gracious development in subjection. We have now to pass over about eighteen years, of which we know only that during them he had become a carpenter (cf. Mark vi. 3), that we may contemplate the preparatory movement under John the Baptist. In these verses we find Luke entering upon the description with the hand of a true artist. He summarizes for us a whole life in fewer verses a great deal than it had years. And yet they are so deftly written that, had John Baptist no other memorial, they would secure for him undying fame. Let us take the facts as they are put before us by Luke, noting such lessons as they are well fitted to suggest. And—

I. THE BAPTIST APPEARED WHEN DECAY HAD SET IN BOTH IN CHURCH AND STATE. (Vers. 1, 2.) The Jewish kingdom, which had a unity until the death of Herod the Great, has now been parcelled into tetrarchies, each governor reigning by grace of the Roman emperor. The sceptre is assuredly departing from Judah. The ancient glory of the Israelitish monarchy only makes the present decline the more impressive. The kingdom needs resuscitation or to be supplanted by a better kingdom. A national leader was never more needful than now. The fulness of time has surely come. Again, decay has seized upon the Jewish Church. The singular number used here (ἀρχιερέως), while two names are associated with the high priesthood, shows to what a condition the affairs of the Church had come. Annas is not allowed his lifetime of the office, according to the Law of Moses, but Caiaphas, his son-in-law happily, has been appointed by the civil power in his room. Reformation is, therefore, sadly needed; the hour has struck, and happily the man is here.

II. THE BAPTIST CAME AS THE PIONEER OF THE LORD. (Vers. 3—6.) Luke here borrows imagery from the prophecy of Isaiah (xl. 3—5), and a careful study of the passage endorses the application of it to the preparatory work in view of the advent of Messiah. John, like a pioneer, is to make a smooth path for the Prince of Peace; but the valleys to be raised, the mountains to be laid low, the crooked to be made straight, and the rough ways to be made smooth, are not outward and physical obstacles. It is not by *force* they are to be overcome, but by a voice, by a cry. They represent consequently the *characters* of men. The valleys represent the depressed and despairing;

the mountains, the exalted and proud; the crooked, the tortuous in sin; the rough ways, the rugged and uncouth in nature. All these classes, through John's preaching, are to be prepared for a sight of God's salvation in the Person of Messiah. How, then, did John try to prepare his generation for Jesus? By "preaching the baptism of repentance for the remission of sins." Now, this new rite introduced by John (cf. Godet, *in loc.*) was a tremendous indictment, so to speak, against human nature. It was as much as to say to every man, "You need to be washed, entirely washed; you are so defiled, you are sinners against God to such a degree that you must be not only washed and purified, but also pardoned, before you can take your places in the kingdom of Messiah." It was the proclamation to all his contemporaries that the one reformation needed in order to better times was *self-reformation*—reformation beginning at home in one's own bosom by the grace of God, as the most important preliminary to the reformation of the world. Repentance has been well defined as a taking of God's side against ourselves;[1] and this was the spirit of John's reformation. It was a call to arms, but to arms against self, not against one's neighbours. And it is here that every true reformer must begin. We must reform ourselves first by the grace of God, or we shall be quite unequal to any large reformation in the world.

III. THE BAPTIST'S PREACHING WAS EXCEEDINGLY PLAIN AND PRACTICAL. (Vers. 7—9.) Luke here gives a *résumé* of John's discourses. They were not certainly very conciliatory. They did not mince matters. The vast multitude which came to hear him was, he knew, largely of the Pharisaic class. They were proud to be children of Abraham according to the flesh. They fancied this was sufficient to secure their acceptance with God. But in spite of their good pedigree they were venomous at heart, would sting a neighbour like a viper, and do the most unbrotherly things. Hence, as a faithful messenger from God, John tells his hearers what they are—but "a generation of vipers." He asks them further who has warned them to flee from "the wrath to come," that is, the judgments of Messiah? He exhorts them in such circumstances to put away their fancied merit as children of Abraham, and to bring forth fruits worthy of repentance, for in case they did not do so, they would be cut down and cast into the fire. The "fruits" demanded were not, of course, graces of the Spirit, which they could not of themselves produce; but acts of reparation, of justice, and such like, which were fitted to show the better view they were taking of their previous life, and the amends it demanded at their hands. If sorrow for sin is genuine with us, it will work a reformation immediately in our conduct; we shall not do the old hard-hearted things we once were guilty of. Now, John, in thus dealing with the question of *human nature* and its depravity, is an example to all our reformers. It is here that reformation is required,[2] and the philosophy that fails here has no pretensions to the leadership of the world. No wonder, therefore, that "pessimism" hangs like a nightmare on the boasted philosophy of the time, and men by philosophy alone cannot get rid of it.[3]

IV. THE PRACTICAL ADVICE GIVEN TO DIFFERENT CLASSES BY JOHN. (Vers. 10—14.) The real success of preaching is proved by inquirers. When people begin to ask what they must do, the message has begun to tell. Now, different classes became inquirers. They were from the lower ranks of the people. The Pharisees largely declined baptism, as ch. vii. 30 shows. And: 1. *The common people asked John's advice as to what they should do.* He tells them to be brotherly instead of grasping. He preached "fraternity." He that had a second coat, or some meat to spare, would do well to impart to a needy brother. Co-operation in the battle of life is our first duty. 2. *The tax-gatherers ask what they should do.* John tells them to avoid their easily besetting sin of extortion. In fact, here, as always, the gospel begins by antagonizing man's selfish impulses. 3. *The soldiers also ask his advice.* These are believed to have been soldiers on the march to a war in Arabia Petræa on behalf of Herod Antipas, and to have been caught at the fords of the Jordan by the wave of religious excitement which was surging there. The brave Baptist advises them to avoid (1) *violence,* (2) *perjury,* and (3) *grumbling* about better wages. He thus sets each class to fight against its easily besetting sins.

[1] Cf. Monsell's 'Religion of Redemption,' p. 44.
[2] Cf. Graham's 'Creed of Science,' pp. 227—293.
[3] Cf. the admissions in 'Natural Religion,' by the author of 'Ecce Homo;' also in Graham, *ut supra.*

V. THE BAPTIST'S MISSION WAS BUT A PROMISE OF A BETTER BAPTISM. (Vers. 15—18.) When John's preaching had proved so successful, the people began to wonder if he were not Messiah himself; and then it was that he declined leadership and spoke of a greater Leader and a far more important baptism. So great was his successor to be, that John was not worthy to unloose his shoe-latchet; and he was to have the grand prerogative of baptizing the people with the Holy Ghost and with fire, or, as it perhaps had better be, "*in* the Holy Ghost and fire (ἐν πνεύματι ἁγίῳ καὶ πυρί)." The Spirit is an Agent, not a means, as water is; and his agency has all the purifying and sublimating effect of fire, rendering those on whom he descends pure and ardent in the service of the Lord. This baptism of the Spirit is what characterizes the dispensation of Messiah.[1] But Messiah will exercise authority and execute judgment, as well as baptize with fire. He will separate by his doctrine, which is his fan, the wheat from the chaff; and those who demonstrate their worthlessness by rejecting the gospel, will be consigned by him to fire unquenchable. If we will not accept of fire as purification, we shall receive it in another form as fire of judgment (cf. Godet, *in loc.*). Hence the solemn alternative which Jesus sets before us in his gospel.

VI. THE REWARD THE WORLD GIVES ITS SPIRITUAL HEROES. (Vers. 19, 20.) It has been supposed that John accepted a crafty invitation from Herod Antipas to come to his court. The last act in the tragedy of his life is when he appears before us as a courageous "court-preacher."[2] Here the Baptist would not take things easily, as courtiers do, but denounced the infamy of the monarch. His reward is a dungeon. The finale is his murder. So has the world rewarded its spiritual heroes. It has nothing better for the noblest than a castle-dungeon and a headsman's sword. This shadow is inserted in Luke's history by anticipation. But there is artistic power in so inserting it. It completes the picture of a great ministry. The forerunner of Messiah has not a much better fate than Messiah himself. The age of heroes is beginning in the person of John, the heroes who had heart to die for truth. Their blood is truth's most precious seed, and the gospel which can command "the noble army of martyrs" is destined to endure![3]—R. M. E.

Vers. 21—38.—*The baptism and genealogy of Jesus.* From the general features of the remarkable ministry of the Baptist, summed up as it is for us in the preceding verses, we now pass to the most notable instance of baptism performed by him. This was the baptism of Jesus. We are expressly told that it was when the movement under John had become *national*, when all the people (ἅπαντα τὸν λαόν) had submitted to the rite, with, of course, the Pharisaic exceptions already noticed (ch. vii. 30), that Jesus appeared at the Jordan to claim the rite too. We learn also from Matthew that John at first objected, feeling an incongruity in the case. Had he been allowed, he would have changed places with Jesus, and been the baptized rather than the baptizer. But Jesus never descended to the administration of water-baptism; he always maintained his high prerogative as the Baptizer of men with the Holy Ghost and fire. Hence, while he insisted on receiving water-baptism, he left it to others to administer it (cf. John iv. 2). Let us, then, proceed to the following inquiries:—

I. WHAT WERE CHRIST'S REASONS FOR SUBMITTING TO THIS BAPTISM UNTO REPENTANCE? We must reject at once the insinuation of Strauss and others, that it implied some sense of sin. Jesus never was conscious of sin, as his whole life and his express testimony show (cf. John viii. 46; see also Ullman's 'Sinlessness of Jesus,' *passim*). Why, then, should he come under even the suspicion through a baptism unto repentance? The national character of the movement will help to explain our Lord's act. The multitudes who submitted to baptism did so in hope of a place in Messiah's kingdom. But as a "kingdom of God" the impenitent and unpardoned could have no place in it. A way must be found for the pardon and purification and penitence of sinners. Christ's identification of himself, therefore, in baptism with the expectant people was his surrender of himself so far as needful for the accomplishment of this

---

[1] On this baptism of the Spirit, *die Geistestaufe*, cf. Weiss's 'Leben Jesu,' erster band, s. 307, etc.

[2] Cf. Bersier's noble sermon on 'Un Predicateur de Cour,' Sermons, tome ii. p. 3.

[3] Robertson's last volume has two sermons on 'The Character and Mission of the Baptist;' see also Gerok's 'Pilgerbrod,' s. 36.

great work.[1] It was not only a response to the Father's call to enter upon his peculiar Messianic work, as Weiss in his 'Leben Jesu' has very properly suggested, but also a deliberate assumption of the responsibilities of sinners.   Hence it has been supposed that, as the ordinary candidates for baptism confessed their personal sins (Matt. iii. 6), so Jesus most probably confessed the sins of the nation and people who were looking hopefully for his advent.   This dedication, moreover, implied self-sacrifice in due season.   The Messiah hereby became voluntarily "the Lamb of God" to take away the sins of the world, and John seems to have realized this himself (John i. 29).   It was consequently the most sublime dedication which history records.   It was not a mere entrance of the "valley of death," like a soldier in a battle-charge, with a few moments' agony and then all is over; but it was a dedication of himself, three years and more before he suffered, to a policy which could end only in his crucifixion.

II. In what way did the Father respond to this sublime dedication of the Son?   We are told that Jesus was "praying" during the administration of the rite.   As Arndt observes, "Instead of John urging Jesus to bring forth fruits meet for repentance, as he had done with others, it is here simply said by Luke, 'And Jesus prayed.'"   He prayed with uplifted eye, and for those gifts and graces which his great work needed.   His prayer was for his *rights* in the emergency of his sacrificial life. *We* seek grace from God as a matter of free favour, and for the Saviour's sake. *He* sought grace and gift as a matter of simple justice, seeing he was undertaking to perform the Father's good pleasure in the salvation of sinners.   And now we have to notice how the Father responded to his appeal.   1. The Father granted him *the gift of the opened heaven.*   When it is said "the heaven was opened," we are not to understand by it merely that a rent took place among the clouds to allow the Divine Dove to come fluttering down, but rather that the right of Jesus to access to the heavenly light and secrets is recognized.   As Godet puts it, it was the guarantee of a *perfect revelation* of the Father's will in this great work of saving men.   Any clouds which sin may have interposed between man and God were in Christ's case cleared away; and, as a sinless Representative, he is enabled in unclouded light to realize his duty in the matter of man's redemption.   It was a splendid assurance that Jesus, at all events, would not want light in the midst of duty.   And if we follow the Lord fully, we too shall have such opening of the heavens, and such revelation of duty, as will enable us to see the proper path, and to tread it for the benefit of mankind.   2. The Father granted him *the Holy Spirit in the organic form of a descending dove.*   This symbol is only used in Gen. i. 2, where the Spirit is represented as "brooding dove-like o'er the vast abyss," to use the Miltonic paraphrase; and here in connection with Christ's baptism.   The soul of Christ, upon which the Holy Spirit on this second occasion descended, was the scene of a mightier work than the chaotic abyss at first.   The new creation is greater than the old; and the sinless material upon which the Divine Dove had to brood guaranteed a more magnificent result than the sensible world affords.   The "supernatural evolution" hereby secured has been mightier and more magnificent than the evolution in nature.[2]   Now, regarding the significance of the symbol, we are taught that (1) the Holy Spirit came down in his *entirety* upon Jesus.   Other men receive the Spirit in measure, and hence as oil, as fire, as water, as wind,—these minor symbols sufficing to represent our tiny inspirations; but Jesus receives the Spirit as a dove, an organic whole—the Spirit without measure (John iii. 34).   We are also taught (2) that the *dove-like graces* were imparted in all fulness to Jesus.   "As the dove is the symbol of innocence, of purity, of noble simplicity, of gentleness and meekness, of inoffensiveness and humility, so Jesus stood there in possession of the Holy Ghost, as the complete embodiment of all these perfections."[3]   And it is out of his fulness we must all receive, and grace for grace.   His is the perfect inspiration, ours is the mediated inspiration, so far as we can receive the Spirit.   Let us look prayerfully for the descent of the Dove, and he will come to abide even with us!   But yet again (3) the Father granted to Jesus *the assurance of Sonship.*   From the account in Matthew we should suppose the words were spoken to John; from this in Luke we should infer that they were spoken only

[1] Godet, *in loc.*; also his 'Études Bibliques,' tome ii. p. 104; and his 'Explications en réponse aux quelques Remarques de M. Darby,' pp. 32—35.
[2] Cf. Dr. Newman Smyth's 'Old Faiths in New Light,' American edit., pp. 185—288.
[3] Cf. Arndt's 'Leben Jesu,' erster theil, ss. 181, 182.

and directly to Jesus. Both hearers were doubtless regarded in the paternal communication. Now, when we consider all that Jesus had undertaken in accepting baptism, he surely had a right to this assurance, that as a Son he was well-pleasing in all his consecrated life to the Father. It was upon this he fell back in the lonely crisis of his history (John xvi. 32). It was the only consolation left to him. And a similar assurance may be looked for by us if we are trying to follow in the footsteps of our Lord. It will in our case be a matter of free grace, and not of strict right; but it will in consequence be all the more precious. Most likely we shall have lonely hours when we shall be deserted by supposed friends, and be put upon our mettle as to our faith in the ever-present Father; but at such times the assurance that our conduct has been pleasing in some measure to the Father, and that he sympathizes with us in our work, will be the greatest earthly consolation. If, in studying to show ourselves approved unto God, we are denied every other approval, we can feel the Divine to be all-sufficient!

III. WHAT ARE WE TO LEARN FROM THE INTERPOSED GENEALOGY? Jesus had just been assured of his Sonship, according to St. Luke's history, and now the evangelist interposes between the baptism and the temptation the genealogy of his *human* nature, carrying it upwards, step by step, to God. The course taken is the reverse of Matthew's. Writing for Jews, Matthew simply starts with Abraham and descends to Joseph, the reputed father of Christ, and so fulfils all Jewish demands. But Luke, writing for a wider Greek-speaking audience, begins with Jesus, the all-important Person, passes to Heli, Mary's father, and then upwards, step by step, past Abraham to Adam, and from Adam to God. Is it not to make out, in the first place, a wider relation for Jesus than Jewish prejudice would afford; to show, in fact, that he is related by blood to the whole human family, and contemplates in the broadest spirit its salvation? In the second place, does the genealogy not clearly imply a direct relation between human nature and God? Man was made at first in the Divine image. This fact affords the basis and the key to the Incarnation. The Divine can unite with the human, since the human was originally the image of the Divine. This relation to God, this spark of Divinity within human nature, constitutes even still man's chief glory. "According to the gospel of the Spirit, Adam is the son of God; according to the gospel of the senses, man is the son of an atom. . . . If the former prove to be the true descent of man, then we are capable of religion, and we live in some personal relationship to a Being higher than ourselves, from whom we came." [1] We accept, with Luke, as truth the *Divine* "descent of man," whatever analogies may be made out between man and the beasts. It is surely evidence of our degradation that this Divine descent should be called in question, and its demonstrations disregarded. In the third place, we have to notice that some of Christ's ancestors were not very creditable—the "bar sinister" enters once or twice, as in the case of Thamar and of Rahab; yet this only shows that he owed nothing to his pedigree, but was willing to be related to all kinds of people that he might become their Saviour.[2] Let us, then, rejoice in the relation thus established between the eternal Son of God and the human race; and may that Divine image, implanted in the race at first, have its glorious renewal in our individual experience!—R. M. E.

EXPOSITION.

CHAPTER IV.

Vers. 1—13.—THE TEMPTATION.

The consecration of our Lord in his baptism was immediately followed by what is known as his temptation. It is, perhaps, the most mysterious and least understood of

any of the scenes of the public ministry related by the evangelists.

It is related at some length by SS. Matthew and Luke, with very slight difference of detail, the principal one being the order in which the three great temptations occurred. In St. Mark the notice of this

---

[1] 'The Religious Feeling,' by Dr. Newman Smyth, p. 9.
[2] Cf. Arndt's 'Leben Jesu,' erster theil, ss, 9, 10.

strange episode in the life is very short, but harmonizes perfectly with the longer accounts of SS. Matthew and Luke. St. John omits it altogether; first, because, with the earlier written Gospels before him, he was aware that the Church of his Master already possessed ample details of the occurrence; and secondly, the story and lessons of the temptation did not enter into the plan which St. John had before him when he composed his history of his Lord's teaching.

What, now, was the temptation? Did the evil one appear to Jesus actually in a *bodily* form? Did his feet really press some elevation, such as the summit of snowy Hermon, or the still more inaccessible peak of Ararat? and did the far-reaching prospect of sea and land, mountain and valley, bathed in the noonday glory of an Eastern sun, represent to him the kingdoms of the world, and the glory of them? Did he in very truth stand on the summit of the great temple-roof, and from that dizzy height gaze on the crowds below, crawling like ants across the sacred court, or toiling along the Jerusalem streets?

So *generally* thought the ancients, and so it would appear, on first thoughts, from St. Matthew's account, where we read (iv. 3), "The tempter *came* to him;" and the vivid realistic imagery of St. Mark (i. 12, 13) would rather help us to the same conclusion. Some expositors and students of the Word have imagined—for it comes to little more —that the devil manifested himself to Jesus under the guise of an angel of light; others have supposed the tempter came to him as a wayfaring man; others, as a priest, as one of the Sanhedrin council.

But on further consideration all this seems highly improbable. No appearance of the devil, or of any evil angel, is ever related in the Bible records. The mountain whence the view of the world's kingdoms was obtained after all is fanciful, and any realistic interpretation is thoroughly unsatisfactory and improbable. The greater of the modern scholars of different countries—the Germans Olshausen and Neander, the Dutch Van Oosterzee, the Frenchman Pressensé, the Swiss Godet, Farrar and Plumptre in our own land—reject altogether the idea of a presence of the tempter visible to the eye of sense. The whole transaction lay in the spiritual region of the life of Christ, but on

that account it was not the less real and true.

Nor is it by any means a solitary experience, this living, beholding, listening, and even speaking in the Spirit, narrated by the evangelist in this place as a circumstance in the Lord's life. Centuries before, Ezekiel, when in his exile by the banks of Chebar in Chaldea, was lifted up and borne by the Spirit to far-distant Jerusalem, that he might see the secret sins done in the temple of the Lord (Ezek. viii. 3). Isaiah again, in the year that King Uzziah died, saw the Lord on his throne, surrounded by seraphim; in this vision the prophet *speaks*, and *hears* the Lord speak, and a burning coal from off the altar is laid on his mouth (Isa. vi. 1—11). To pass over the several visions of Isaiah, Ezekiel, Daniel, and others, in which the transactions lay altogether in the spiritual region of their lives, we would instance from the New Testament St. Paul's account of himself caught up into paradise, " whether in the body or out of the body " he could not tell (2 Cor. xii. 1—4). And still more to the point, St. John's words prefacing his Revelation, how he was " in the Spirit on the Lord's day," when he *heard* the voice behind him, and *saw* his glorified Master. On that day and in that hour he heard and saw what he relates in his twenty-two chapters of the Revelation.

In language very slightly different, the temptation of the blessed Son of God is related by the evangelists, when they preface the history of the event with the words, " Jesus being full of the Holy Ghost . . . was led by the Spirit into the wilderness " (see, too, Matt. iv. 1).

We conclude, then, with some confidence, that the devil did not appear to Jesus in a bodily form, but that, in a higher sphere than that of matter, the Redeemer met and encountered—with the result we know so well—that spiritual being of superhuman but yet of limited power, who tempts men to evil, and accuses them before the throne of God when they have yielded to the temptation. " We believe "—to use Godet's words here—" that had he been observed by any spectator whilst the temptation was going on, he would have appeared all through it motionless upon the soil of the desert. But though the conflict did not pass out of the spiritual sphere, it was none the less real, and the value of the victory was none the less incalculable and decisive."

Ver. 1.—**And Jesus being full of the Holy Ghost returned from Jordan, and was led by the Spirit into the wilderness;** more accurately translated, *in the Spirit.* The question of the nature of the temptation has been discussed in the above note. The words, "full of the Holy Ghost," and "was led by the Spirit," lead us irresistibly to the conclusion that the Lord, during this strange solemn time—like Ezekiel, Daniel, Isaiah, and, later, Paul and John the beloved apostle—was especially under the influence of the Holy Spirit; that his eyes were open to see visions and sights not usually visible to mortal eye; and that his ears were unlocked to hear voices not audible to ordinary mortal ears. Tradition has fixed upon a hill district bordering on the road which leads up from Jericho to Jerusalem, as the scene of the temptation. The hill itself, from being the supposed spot where the Lord spent these forty days, is named Quarantania. The rocks in this neighbourhood contain many caves.

Ver. 2.—**Being forty days tempted of the devil** For some reason unknown to us, the number forty seems to possess some mystic significance. Moses was forty days alone with the Divine Presence on Horeb. Elijah fasted forty days in the wilderness before the vision and the voice came to him. Forty years was the period, too, of the wanderings of the chosen people. The existence of an evil power has been a favourite subject of discussion in those schools of thought who more or less question the authoritative teaching of the canonical books of the two Testaments. Keim, quoted by Godet, well and fairly sums up the present state of opinion of the more moderate and thoughtful schools of free-thought: "We regard the question of an existence of an evil power as altogether an open question for science." Those, however, who recognize the Gospel narratives as the faithful expression of Jesus Christ's teaching, must accept the repeated declarations of the Master that an evil being of superhuman power does exist, and has a great, though a limited, influence over the thoughts and works of men. Whatever men may feel with regard to the famous clause in the Lord's Prayer, which the Revisers of the Authorized Version render, "deliver us from the evil one," they must agree at least with the conclusion of the Revisers, that, in the Christian Church, a large majority of the ancients understood the Master's words in his great prayer as asking deliverance, not from "evil" in the abstract, as the English Authorized Version seems to prefer, but deliverance from the power of some mighty evil being. **And in those days he did eat nothing.** In this state of ecstasy, when the body was completely subordinate to the Spirit, the ordinary bodily wants seem to have been suspended. There is no difficulty in accepting this supposition, if the signification of the words, "in the Spirit," above suggested, be adopted. The whole transaction belongs to the miraculous. We, who receive as God's Word these Gospel narratives, find no difficulty in recognizing God's power to suspend, when he pleases, what men regard as fixed natural laws. We believe, too, that on certain occasions in the world's history it has pleased him to put this power into operation. **He afterward hungered.** Although still in the Spirit, in order to provide a field for the exercise of the peculiar typical temptation about to be dwelt upon, some of the bodily functions, which during the trance or the ecstasy had been temporarily suspended, were allowed again to play their usual part in the life, as in the case of Isaiah, Ezekiel, Daniel, Paul, and John.

Ver. 3.—**And the devil said unto him, If thou be the Son of God, command this stone that it be made bread.** It has been quaintly said of the tempter "that he had sped so successfully to his own mind by a temptation about a matter of eating with the first Adam, that he practised the old manner of his trading with the second." These diabolical promptings have been spoken of already in this Commentary as "typical." They represent, indeed, some of the principal temptations to which different classes of men and women in all ages are subject; the hard task of bread-winning, after all, suggests very many of the evil thoughts and imaginings to which men are subject, though, perhaps, they suspect it not. Weakened and exhausted by long abstinence from food, the temptation to supply his wants by this easy means at once was great. Still, had he consented to the tempter's suggestion, Jesus was aware that he would have broken the conditions of that human existence to which, in his deep love for us fallen beings, he had voluntarily consented and submitted himself. Should he, then, use his miraculous power for his own advantage? Then, remembering his own late experience, the long fast from all human food, and yet life enduring through it all; calling to mind the miraculous supply of manna in the old desert days, the preservation of Elijah's life through a similar fast,—Jesus, all faint and weary, exclaims in reply, "Man shall not live by bread alone."

Ver. 5.—**And the devil, taking him up into an high mountain, showed unto him all** the kingdoms of the world in a moment of time. This temptation was something more than "offering to One who had lived as a village carpenter the throne of the world." It appealed to his ambition certainly, but in Jesus' case it was a high, pure, sinless ambition. This much he certainly knew already, that he was destined to rule over men from pole to pole. It was for him a righteous longing, this desire to have the heathen for his inheritance, and the uttermost parts of the earth as his possession. No false ambition was this in Jesus, this desire to realize the glorious Messianic hope. Again, how typical a temptation! All ranks and orders are often soon tempted here. A noble end as they think, and in the beauty of the goal they forget that the road leading to it is paved with evil and wrong.

Ver. 7.—**If thou therefore wilt worship me, all shall be thine.** Dr. Morrison, on Matt. iv. 9, has well caught the thought here. The arch-tempter "as it were said to Jesus, 'I am indeed the prince and god of this world. Its kingdoms and their glory are at my disposal. I could at once open up thy way to the highest honours that a universal conqueror and a universal sovereign could desire. I could gather at once around thee a host of devoted Jewish troops; I could pave their way for victory after victory, until at no distant period the whole Roman empire, and indeed the whole world, should be subject to thy sway. Only abandon the wild chimera of putting down sin and making all men fanatical and holy; fall in with my way of things; let the morals of the world alone, more especially its morals in reference to God; work with me and under me, and all will go well. But if thou refuse this offer, look out for determined opposition, for incessant persecution, for the most miserable poverty, and for every species of woe.'"

Ver. 8.—**Get thee behind me, Satan; for it is written, Thou shalt worship the Lord thy God, and him only shalt thou serve.** Jesus repelled the offer with stern indignation. He would receive the splendid inheritance which he felt was his at no other hands than his Father's; he would win all and more than the tempter offered him, but it would be by a slow and painful process—by self-denial, self-sacrifice, self-surrender; the glorious consummation would only be attained at the end of a long vista of centuries. The words, "Get thee behind me, Satan," do not occur in the older manuscripts containing St. Luke's Gospel. These are evidently a later addition from the parallel passage in St. Matthew.

Ver. 9.—**And he brought him to Jerusalem, and set him on a pinnacle of the temple.** In St. Matthew Jerusalem is here called "the holy city," a name still preserved in the East, where it is still termed El-Khuds, *the holy. Pinnacle;* literally, "wing" of the temple. "Pinnacle" comes from the Vulgate translation, *pinnaculum.* The part of the great building evidently referred to here was that magnificent southern wing of the Lord's house constructed by Herod the Great, which was known as the royal portico. Josephus calls it *the most remarkable building under the sun* ('Ant.,' xv. 11. 5). One who stood on the roof of this portion of the temple would look from a dizzy height into the Valley of the Kidron. Such a spectator, writes Josephus ('Ant.,' ii. 5), "would be giddy while his sight could not reach to such an immense depth." To this spot, "whether in the body or out of the body" we cannot tell, Jesus was taken by the evil spirit. "Now," said his tempter, "if you really are what you seem to think, cast thyself down. You know what is written in the Divine writing, how the Eternal would give his angels charge concerning thee, they were to bear thee up, 'lest at any time thou dash thy foot against a stone.' If thou art he of whom all this is written, there will be no risk. *You* are *sure* that you are the Son of God: try this once, and see. If you triumphantly come out of this trial, all men will recognize you, and your reign as Messiah will commence forthwith." This temptation was of a more subtle nature than the other two. It appeals again to all ranks of men, and warns them of the sore danger of *selfishly* courting danger. The angels will ever watch over us with a tender care when, to accomplish a duty or to perform an act of self-denying love, we confront peril; not so when we presumptuously and for our own ends rush into danger.

Ver. 12.—**And Jesus answering said unto him, It is said, Thou shalt not tempt the Lord thy God.** It is remarkable that in these crowning instances of temptation, which no doubt were originally recounted by the Lord himself to the inner circle of the disciples, and from them passed into the regular course of instruction adopted by the Christian teachers of the first days, the Redeemer, in each of his three answers to the devil, uses words taken from two chapters (the sixth and eighth) of Deuteronomy. It has been suggested that the thoughts and expressions of this book were fresh in the mind of the tempted Christ, as he had probably, specially during his sojourn in the wilderness, used for his own study and meditation a book which told the story of Israel's wanderings in the desert for forty years. It seems, however, more likely that the Lord simply chose to frame his answers from a book with which every Israelite from his earliest years had been acquainted. The maxims and precepts of Deuteronomy were used in the education of every Hebrew child. Its devout and beautiful maxims were written on the phylacteries or frontlets which so many pious Jews were in the habit of wearing.

Ver. 13.—**And when the devil had ended all the temptation.**

"Thou Spirit, who ledd'st this glorious eremite
Into the desert, his victorious field,
Against the spiritual foe, and brought'st him thence
By proof the undoubted Son of God."
                                        (Milton.)

St. Matthew closes the story of the "victorious field" by telling us how, when every hellish suggestion had been made and repelled, the wearied and exhausted Jesus was visited and refreshed by the visible ministry of angels. The words of the Greek original translated "all the temptation" would be more accurately rendered by "every kind of temptation." The three great temptations, related by two of the evangelists in detail, are very varied and comprehensive in character, and appeal to most of the human passions and desires; but from the words with which St. Luke began his recital, "being forty days tempted of the devil," it is clear that Jesus was incessantly tempted the whole time by hellish whispers and suggestions, perhaps of the same kind, though with varied details, as the three we have recorded for us. Besides the uses of the temptation mystery in the development of the humanity of the blessed Son of God, the great scene has its deep lessons for all sorts and conditions of men in all times. Some eminent expositors would seem to wish to limit the area of the teaching of the temptation, and to regard it as mainly an experience preserved for the guidance of the disciples of the Master. They—so say these scholars—were, from this scene in the life of the great Teacher, to learn never to use their miraculous power for their personal advantage (first temptation); never to associate with wicked men for the attainment of good ends (second temptation); never to perform a miracle in an ostentatious spirit (third temptation). All this was doubtless contained in the Lord's story of his awful experience, and the lesson was never forgotten by the twelve and their own immediate followers. But the instruction was not meant to be confined to the little circle of his own; it was, like the whole of the gospel teaching, intended for all sorts and conditions of men. The common everyday lesson which every child may read in this story of his Master's trial, is that from the plain appointed path of duty, which very often too is the path of

suffering, no persuasion however skilfully worded, no sophistry however plausible, must be sufficient to turn him. **He departed from him for a season;** more accurately, *till a convenient season.* It is evident that all through the two years and a half of the public ministry, which succeeded the events just recorded, Jesus was exposed to the various trials and temptations to which suffering mortal flesh is exposed. So Bonaventura, in his 'Life of Christ,' says, "Many other were the occasions on which he endured temptation." Still there is no doubt but that the "convenient season" here pointedly alluded to referred to that other great epoch of temptation just before the cross, when our Lord prayed in the agony of the garden at the close of his earthly work. There the tempter tried if great suffering was not able to conquer that Sinless One.

Vers. 14—30.—THE PREACHING OF JESUS AT NAZARETH, AND ITS RESULT.

Ver. 14.—**And Jesus returned in the power of the Spirit into Galilee: and there went out a fame of him through all the region round about.** Between the events of the temptation and the preaching at Nazareth here related, some considerable time had intervened. St. John, in his Gospel, gives a somewhat detailed account of this period which St. Luke omits. Shortly after the temptation, took place the concluding incidents in the Baptist's career, which St. Luke summarized in his brief statement (ch. iii. 19, 20), when he tells us of the arrest and imprisonment of the fearless preacher by the Tetrarch Herod. St. John tells how the Sanhedrin sent some special envoys to the Baptist, asking him formally *who he really was.* After this questioning, John in his Gospel mentions the calling of Andrew, Simon, Philip, and Nathanael, and then records the first miracle of Jesus at Cana in Galilee, and how the Lord visited Capernaum. He then proceeds to relate some of the circumstances which took place at the Passover at Jerusalem, and how the Lord drove out the men who profaned his Father's house. He writes down, too, the particulars of Nicodemus the Pharisee's visit to Jesus by night. The Master then proceeded, as is here related by St. Luke, "in the power of the Spirit," who descended on him formally at his baptism, into Galilee, and on his journey thither tarried at Samaria, resting on the well there, and talking with the woman in those memorable words recorded by St. John at length in his fourth chapter (vers. 4—42). Rapidly the report of what he had done at Cana, the fame of his marvellous words at Jerusalem, Samaria, and other places, spread through all the central districts of the Holy Land.

Ver. 15.—**And he taught in their syna-**

gogues, being glorified of all. His miracles, his words touching and eloquent, perhaps too a dim memory of marvels which had happened years before at his birth, shed round the new Teacher a halo of glory. It was only when, instead of the Messianic hopes of conquest and power which they cherished, a life of brave self-denial and quiet generosity was preached, that the reaction against him set in. The men of Nazareth, with their violent antagonism, which we are about to consider, were only, after all, a few months in advance of the rest of the nation in their rejection of the Messiah.

Ver. 16.—**And he came to Nazareth, where he had been brought up: and, as his custom was, he went into the synagogue on the sabbath day.** This had been for years his practice in the little synagogue of the village where was his carpenter's shop. Children at the age of five years were admitted into the synagogue, and at thirteen attendance there was part of the legal life of the Jew. These synagogues were the regular places for religious gatherings every sabbath day, and also usually on Mondays and Tuesdays, besides on other special occasions. We hear of them after the return from the Captivity, and probably they existed long before. Some think that in Ps. lxxiv. 8 there is a reference to them. **And stood up for to read.** The holy books were always read standing. The ruler or elder presided over and directed the synagogue service. The priest and Levite had no recognized position in the synagogue. Their functions were confined to the temple and to the duties prescribed in the Law. It was not unusual for the synagogue officials, if any stranger was present who was known to be competent, to ask him to read and to expound a passage in the Law or Prophets. Our Lord was well known in Nazareth, and of late had evidently gained a great reputation as a preacher. It was, therefore, most natural that he should be asked to take a prominent part in the sabbath services.

Ver. 17.—**And there was delivered unto him the Book of the Prophet Esaias.** In the sabbath service there were two lessons read. The first was always taken from the Pentateuch (the Law). The five books of Moses were written on parchment, (usually) between two rollers, and the day's lesson was left unrolled for the reader's convenience. The Prophets were on single rollers, no special portion being left open. It has been suggested that the great and famous Messianic passage read by our Lord was the lesson for the day. This is quite uncertain; indeed, it is more probable that Jesus, when the roll of Isaiah was handed to him by the ruler of the synagogue, specially selected the section containing this passage.

Ver. 18.—**The Spirit of the Lord is upon me.** St. Luke here quotes, with a few unimportant variations, from the LXX. of Isa. lxi. 1, 2. The clause, "to set at liberty them that are bruised," does not occur in the present text of Isaiah. The bright, comforting words of the great prophet the Lord chose as giving a general summary of what he designed to carry out in his ministry. It could be no undesigned coincidence that the opening words of the passage contain a singularly clear mention of the three Persons of the blessed Trinity—the Spirit, the Father, and the Anointed (Messiah). **Because he hath anointed me to preach the gospel to the poor,** etc. The common interpretation referred this passage to the state of the people on the return from the Captivity. Nothing, however, that the people had yet experienced in any way satisfied the brilliant picture painted in the great prophecy. A remnant certainly had returned several centuries back from their distant exile, but the large majority of the chosen people were scattered abroad; their own land was crushed under what seemed a hopeless servitude; poverty, ignorance, universal discontent, reigned alike in Jerusalem, garrisoned with Roman legionaries, and in the most distant of the poor upland villages of Galilee. Only could deliverance come and a golden age of prosperity return with the promised Messiah. This was the interpretation which the choicest spirits in Israel applied to the great Isaiah prophecy read that sabbath day in the little synagogue of Nazareth. This was the meaning which Jesus at once gave to it, only he startled his hearers by telling them that in him they saw the promised long-looked-for Deliverer. We only possess, it is evident, the very barest abstract of the words of the Teacher Jesus on this occasion. They must have been singularly eloquent, winning, and powerful to have extorted the wonder and admiration alluded to in the twenty-second verse.

Ver. 20.—**And he closed the book, and he gave it again to the minister, and sat down.** This was the usual position adopted by a Jewish preacher. The chair of the preacher was placed near the spot where the lesson was read. These synagogues were built with the end pointed towards Jerusalem, in which direction the Jew ever loved to turn as he prayed (Dan. vi. 10). The men sat on one side of the building, the women on the other. There was always at the end of the chamber an ark of wood, a memory of the sacred ark of the covenant, which once, with its golden mercy-seat, hallowed now and again with the presence of the visible glory, was the chief treasure of the temple on Mount Zion. In the "ark" were kept the Law (the five books of Moses) and the rolls of the prophets.

Ver. 22.—**And they said, Is not this Joseph's Son?** Quickly the preacher caught the mind and feeling of his audience. Surprise and admiration soon gave place to a spirit of unbelief. Is not this who speaks to us such words, bright and eloquent with hope, often with a ring of sure triumph and certain victory in them—is it not the young Carpenter we have known so long in our village?

Ver. 23.—**Ye will surely say unto me this proverb, Physician, heal thyself.** "There is something interesting in our finding this proverb in the Gospel of the beloved physician. May we think of him as hearing the proverb casually, tracking out its application, and so coming on this history? It was, probably, so far as is known, a common Jewish proverb; but there is no trace of it in Greek writers, and it was therefore likely to attract his notice" (Dean Plumptre). **Whatsoever we have heard done in Capernaum, do also here in thy country.** Now, up to this time in Jesus' public career no miracles are recorded as having been done in Capernaum. After the miracle at Cana we know that the Lord resided for some time in Capernaum (John ii. 12); the miracles to which these men of Nazareth alluded were no doubt worked then. The memory of these early miracles, as Godet well observes, would have been effaced by more remarkable later events, as that at Cana would have been had not John, who required it in the plan of his Gospel, rescued it from oblivion. The Jews of Nazareth, after the first moment of surprise and admiration at Jesus' words, evidently looked at him with scorn and unbelief. That poor Carpenter their glorious expected Messiah! As for the marvellous deeds reported to have been done in Capernaum, they did not believe in them; at least why did he not here, in the neighbourhood of his own home, something of the same kind? If they could see with their eyes marvels worked by him, then perhaps they might accept him as Messiah.

Ver. 24.—**And he said, Verily I say unto you, No prophet is accepted in his own country.** But instead of gratifying their curiosity and supplying them with some more empty arguments why they should not listen to his words, the Lord quietly quotes a proverb well known to all people—Farrar calls it a curious psychological fact—the quoting prefaced by the solemn "verily." The Master was evidently looking far beyond the little prejudices of Nazareth. "His own country" meant far more than the narrow circuit bounded by the Nazareth hills. The Speaker was thinking of all the

chosen people—of the Jews, who as a nation he knew too well would not accept him. But if Israel would have none of him, he would reign in the hearts of that unnumbered multitude who peopled the isles of the Gentiles.

Vers. 25—27.—**But I tell you of a truth, many widows were in Israel in the days of Elias, when the heaven was shut up three years and six months, when great famine was throughout all the land; but unto none of them was Elias sent, save unto Sarepta, a city of Sidon, unto a woman that was a widow. And many lepers were in Israel in the time of Eliseus the prophet; and none of them was cleansed, saving Naaman the Syrian.** In support of these assertions, Jesus proceeds to quote two well-known incidents in the story of Israel. They must remember God's mercies in past times were not confined to Israel. There were many starving widows among the chosen people, not a few childless, desolate hearths; but their own great Elijah was sent to none of these, but to a despised Phœnician woman in Sarepta, hard by Sidon. Elisha, that loved man of God, who passed by the homes of the people continually, performed his famous miracle of healing on no child of Israel, though many a leper mourned his sad lot among the chosen people; but the one on whom Elisha worked his mighty miracle of mercy was the Syrian leper Naaman, the great foe of Israel.

Ver. 28.—**And all they in the synagogue, when they heard these things, were filled with wrath.** The Jews in the synagogue quickly caught the Master's meaning. Thoughts such as "Thou our Messiah, who talkest of Gentile, Syrian, and Zidonian in the same breath with us the chosen and elect of God, who hintest at the possibility of the accursed Gentile sharing in our promised blessings!" flashed through their minds, and as one man the congregation rose, and, seizing the Preacher, dragged him out of the synagogue, and hurried him through the little town to one of the rocky precipices close by.

Ver. 29.—**And rose up, and thrust him out of the city, and led him unto the brow of the hill whereon their city was built, that they might cast him down headlong.** The place now shown as the scene of the act of violence of the fanatics of Nazareth, known as the Mount of Precipitation, is some two miles from the town. It must be remembered that this happened on a sabbath day; this would therefore be beyond the limits of a sabbath day's journey. There is, however, close to Nazareth a cliff about forty feet high.

Ver. 30.—**But he passing through the midst of them went his way.** Not necessarily a miracle. There is nothing hinted here that our Lord rendered himself invisible, or that he smote his enemies with a temporary blindness. He probably quietly overawed these angry men with his calm self-possession, so that they forbore their cruel purpose, and thus he passed through their midst, and left Nazareth—as far as we know—for ever. The foregoing is probably the same visit very briefly alluded to by St. Matthew (xiii. 54—58) and by St. Mark (vi. 1—6), in both Gospels related in unchronological order. Most likely they were aware of the incident, but ignorant of the exact place it held among the early events of the Master's life. St. Luke, who gives it with far greater detail, inserts it evidently in its right place. Is it not at least probable that St. Luke derived *his* accurate knowledge of this Nazareth incident from Mary, or from some of her intimate circle, from whom he procured the information which he embodied in the earlier chapters of his Gospel? She, and others of her friends, would be likely to have preserved some accurate memories of this painful visit of Jesus to his old home.

Vers. 31—44.—AT CAPERNAUM.

Ver. 31.—**And came down to Capernaum.** Capernaum was the real home of the Master during the two years and a half of his public ministry. He chose this flourishing lake-city partly because his kinsmen and first disciples lived in it or its immediate neighbourhood, but more especially on account of its situation. It has been termed the very centre of the manufacturing district of Palestine; it lay on the high-road which led from Damascus and the Syrian cities to Tyre, Sidon, and Jerusalem. "It was, in fact, on 'the way of the sea' (Isa. ix. 1), the great caravan-road which led (from the East) to the Mediterranean. It was hence peculiarly fitted to be the centre of a far-reaching ministry, of which even Gentiles would hear" (Farrar). The evangelist speaks of "coming down" to the shore of the lake, in contrast with Nazareth, which was placed in the hills. We do not meet with the name Capernaum in the Old Testament; it therefore appears not to have been a city belonging to remote antiquity. Its name is generally interpreted as being compounded of two words, signifying "town of consolation," כפר נחום—a beautiful and significant derivation. It may, however, originally have taken its name from the Prophet Nahum. Josephus, the historian, tells us the name originally belonged to a fountain. He dwells also on the mildness of the climate; it would therefore seem as though, in the first place, Capernaum was used as a health resort, and then its admirable situation favoured its adoption as a convenient centre. The extensive ruins of *Tel-Hûm*,

on the lake-shore, are generally believed to be the remains of the once rich and populous Capernaum. **And taught them on the sabbath days.**

Ver. 32.—**And they were astonished at his doctrine : for his word was with power.** We have here again a picture which gives a general summary of Jesus' life extending over a considerable period. This is the fifth of these pictures of St. Luke. It represents the Master dwelling quietly at Capernaum, in the midst of his disciples, teaching and preaching; on the sabbath days gathering a considerable concourse drawn from the people at large, and generally surprising the listeners with his earnestness, freshness, and ability, which carried conviction into many a heart, Gentile as well as Jew. Although this period of the life of Jesus was signalized by many miracles, it does not seem that his *ordinary* preaching and teaching needed any such supernatural testimony to enable it to win its way. St. Luke especially tells us it was with power, and that the crowds heard it amazed and astonished. St. Matthew gives us (vii. 29) *one* reason, which helps us to understand something of this success which attended his teaching. It was "not as the scribes." In the Talmud we have many a fair specimen of the sacred instruction of the "schools" in the time of our Lord. Frivolous minutiæ, hair-splitting of texts, weary repetition of the sayings of the men of old, questions connected with the exact keeping of the sabbath, with the tithing of mint, anise, and cummin, a singular lack of all dealing with the weightier matters of the Law—justice, judgment, truth—were among the characteristics of the scribes' popular instruction. The practical heart-searching words of Jesus were in strong contrast with the curious but useless themes dwelt on by the official teachers of the day. It was with the thirty-first verse of this chapter that the great Gnostic heretic, Marcion (second century) began his Gospel, which, in the early days of Christianity, had a vast circulation. Marcion, while preferring St. Luke's Gospel, as emanating from St. Paul, before putting it out as the authoritative history to be used by his numerous followers, cut out the earlier chapters of our Gospel, which bore on the birth and infancy of the Lord, commencing here—prefixing, however, a note of time, thus : "In the fifteenth year of the government of Tiberius, Jesus went down" (Marcion probably intended it to be understood *from heaven*) "into the town of Galilee named Capernaum."

Ver. 33.—**And in the synagogue there was a man, which had a spirit of an unclean devil.** After the general picture of Jesus' life and work in Capernaum, St. Luke proceeds to give a detailed account of the way in which one sabbath day was spent, no doubt intending us to understand it as a specimen of the ordinary sabbath-day work of the Master. We meet with here, for the first time in our Gospel, one of those un-happy persons described as either "having a spirit of an unclean devil," or as "pos-sessed with a devil" or "devils," or in similar terms, generally signifying "de-moniacs," men or women—apparently a class by themselves, directly under the influence of some evil spirit. Who, now, were these unhappy beings with whom Jesus in his ministry of mercy seems often to have come in contact? Many of these "demoniacs" mentioned in the Gospels would nowadays certainly be classed under the ordinary category of the "sick." They seem to have been simply afflicted with disease of one kind or other; for instance, *the epileptic child* mentioned by St. Luke (ix. 39), or *dumbness* again (Matt. ix. 32), *blind-ness* (Matt. xii. 22), and *insanity*, among other instances, are ascribed to demoniac agency. Are we, then, simply to regard these cases, not as exceptional displays of dia-bolical power, but as instances of sickness and disease which still exist among us? and to suppose that our Lord, in speaking of devils possessing these sick ones, accom-modated himself to the popular belief, and spoke of these afflicted persons in the way men were able to understand? for it is in-disputable that Judaism in the days of Jesus of Nazareth ascribed to "demons," or "devils," much of the suffering and woe with which men are afflicted under the common name of disease. The Talmud, which well represents the Jewish teaching of that time, has endless allusions to evil spirits, or devils, who were permitted to work evil and mischief on the bodies and even on the souls of men. Josephus, the contemporary historian, narrates that a lamb grew at Machærus, the wool of which had the power of expelling devils; and he tells how he was the eye-witness of the cure of a man possessed of a devil by means of a ring containing a root which had similar pro-perties; this, he says, took place in the presence of the Emperor Vespasian ('Ant.,' viii. 2. 5; 'Bell. Jud.,' vii. 6. 3). Many be-lieved that these demons, or devils, were the souls of the wicked who returned to earth after death, and sought a new home for themselves in the bodies of the living. This popular belief in demoniacal agency is mentioned by Justin Martyr ('Apol.,' i.), and even seems to have lingered in some parts as late as Chrysostom. But such a theory—which represents Jesus in his mi-raculous cures accommodating himself to popular belief, and speaking of the sufferers

as possessed by devils which really had no existence save in imagination—is not only quite foreign to the transparently truthful character of all the Master's words and works, but is perfectly incompatible with the narratives given us by the evangelists of the cures in question. In these, in several instances, the devils are not only spoken to, but they speak themselves—they answer questions, they even prefer requests. Jesus, too, gives his own power to cast out devils (ch. ix. 1), and to tread on all the power of the enemy (ch. x. 19). He even, in St. Mark (ix. 29), is represented as distinguishing a special class of devils over whom a mastery could be obtained alone through prayer and fasting. Evidently the Holy Spirit, who guided the writers of those memoirs of the apostles we call the Gospels, intended that a marked distinction should be impressed upon the readers of the apostolic memoirs as existing between ordinary maladies of the flesh and those terrible and various scourges which the presence of devils inflicted upon those hapless beings in whose bodies, for some mysterious reason, they had been per-mitted to take up their habitation. The whole question is fraught with difficulties. Dean Plumptre suggests that perhaps we possess not the data for an absolutely certain and exhaustive answer. It seems, on the whole—while not denying the possible pre-sence of these evil spirits at different times of the world's history occupying the bodies and distracting the souls of men—best to assume that these devils possessed special and peculiar power over men at that period when Jesus walked among us. By this means, as Godet well says, Jesus could be proclaimed externally and visibly as the Conqueror of the enemy of men (and of his legions of evil messengers). That period, when the Lord taught among us, was a time when, it is generally conceded, moral and social evil had reached its highest point of development. Since that age the power of these unhappy spirits of evil has been, if not destroyed, at least restrained by the influence—greater, perhaps, than men choose to acknowledge—of the Master's religion or by the direct command of the Master himself.

Ver. 34.—**Let us alone; what have we to do with thee, thou Jesus of Nazareth? art thou come to destroy us?** This man, with his evil spirit, would have been looked on as unclean, and would not have been ad-mitted within the synagogue walls; he had probably crept in unseen. Something in the nearness to the holy Teacher we know compelled the demon to cry aloud. It is strange, this presence of God causing pain. It is the impossibility of the wounded eye bearing light. The cry rendered, "Let us alone," is scarcely the imperative of ἐάω, but an interjection, possibly the Greek reproduction of the Hebrew אֲהָהּ, ah! woe! There was evidently some deeper degree of misery possible for the unhappy spirit; hence its "Art thou come to destroy us?" The same dread appears in the case of the Gadarene demoniac (ch. viii. 31; Matt. viii. 29), where the spirits dreaded being driven into the deep, where such spirits await the judgment, that abyss, literally, "the bottomless place;" any doom seemed to these lost ones preferable to that. **I know thee who thou art; the Holy One of God.**

Ver. 35.—**And Jesus rebuked him, saying, Hold thy peace.** Jesus at once indignantly refuses this homage. He never allowed devils to proclaim they knew him. There is something very awful in the thought that to this whole class of created beings he is ever pitiless. In his dealings with these we never are allowed to catch sight of one ray of the Redeemer's tender pitiful love.

Ver. 37.—**And the fame of him went out;** more accurately rendered, *and there went out a rumour concerning him.*

Ver. 38.—**And he arose out of the synagogue, and entered into Simon's house. And Simon's wife's mother was taken with a great fever; and they besought him for her.** This abrupt mention of Peter (Simon) for the first time, without any explanatory notice, tells us that when St. Luke wrote his Gospel Peter was well known and honoured in all the Churches. The Lord's choice of one who was already married, the subsequent favour showed to him, the high position evidently accorded to him in the Church of the first days, is a perpetual protest against the exaggerated asceticism which later was so earnestly taught in ecclesiastical Christianity. The epithet "great," applied to the fever, was a well-known technical term; it was used by Galen of fevers. There are several expressions in this Gospel which remind us that the author was a trained physician.

Ver. 40.—**Now when the sun was setting, all they that had any sick with divers diseases brought them unto him; and he laid his hands on every one of them, and healed them.** The healing of the "possessed" in the synagogue that morning, followed by the cure of the fever of Simon's wife's mother, we know was rapidly noised abroad, and in great measure accounted for the crowds who brought their sick to him in the evening. It was evidently in the life of Jesus a notable occasion, and many a sick tortured one had occasion to bless the Master's presence then. It was so memorable an occasion that all the three evangelists notice it; their reports are recorded in almost the same words. No doubt, in the early days of the preaching of the faith, this evening's work was constantly alluded to by the first teachers. The note of time, "when the sun was setting," indicates that the moment in question had been waited for, for sunset ended the sabbath, and then those outside Capernaum and in its outlying suburbs were enabled to bring their sick and afflicted without infringing the strict sabbath rules. "The twilight scene, of Jesus moving about with word and touch of healing among the sick and suffering, the raving and tortured crowd (Matt. iv. 24), is one of the most striking in the Gospels, and St. Matthew quotes it as a fulfilment of Isa. liii. 4" (Farrar).

Ver. 41.—**Thou art Christ the Son of God.** The older authorities omit "Christ," and read simply, "Thou art the Son of God." **For they knew that he was Christ;** better rendered, *that he was the Christ,* or Messiah. After the Crucifixion, but not till then, "Christ" became a proper name. It was before simply a title, signifying "the Messiah," "the Anointed One." These words of the evil spirits do not seem to have been prompted by any design, as some have supposed, to excite the people either for or against the fresh Teacher; they are simply a cry of involuntary adoration. They knew who that poor Carpenter-Rabbi was; *they had seen him in his Divine glory!*

Ver. 42.—**And when it was day, he departed and went into a desert place.** For solitude, meditation, and prayer. The night, or at least most of it, must have been spent in these blessed works of mercy. It was very early in the deep, dark dawn that the Redeemer was up again seeking fresh strength from his Father. St. Mark tells us when he left the house "it was still very dark."

HOMILETICS.

Vers. 1—13.—*The temptation in the wilderness.* One of the most mysterious but most suggestive passages in the history of the Christ. Without attempting to indicate all the points presented for reflection (see homiletics on Matt. iv.), observe—

I. THE TEMPTATION IS NECESSARY TO THE PERFECTING OF JESUS AS THE SAVIOUR OF SINNERS. He is led by the Spirit into the wilderness—led for the purpose of being tried by the devil. In the solitudes and simplicities of the Nazareth life, he had not known, he could not know, this kind of trial. Now is to come the first distinct experience of the devil's power. God—may we so say?—carried him away from the scene of the baptism and the opened heavens and the Divine voice, and presented him to Satan, the prince of the power of the air : " This is my beloved Son : put forth thine hand, and touch him." Is this strange ? 1. It is a very real link of communion between the Lord and the life beset by sin and evil. " By thy fasting and temptation, good Lord, deliver me." 2. See in it a part, and an essential part, in the making of Jesus to us Wisdom, and Righteousness, and Sanctification, and Redemption. Let us not overlook that " the Son of God was manifested that he might destroy the works of the devil." Now begins the great pitched battle between the kingdoms of light and of darkness ; the wilderness-time is the girding of the sword on the thigh of the most Mighty. Do not think of the temptation as an isolated experience. At the end of all the temptations the devil departed from him only for *a season*, or *until* a season. He had been conquered, but he was not done with the Conqueror ; he only bided his opportunity. The whole earthly ministry was a conflict with that hell which had all but dominated over the world of man. And the conflict was concluded in victory only when the Head was bowed on the cross. " Through death he destroyed him that had the power of death, that is, the devil." Ah ! truly there is " an infinite more behind " all that is recorded.

II. TEMPTATION IS NECESSARY TO HUMAN PERFECTING. The hour of the leading into the wilderness is striking. St. Luke amplifies the account given by the earlier evangelist. The latter connects the event with the baptism and that which accompanied it ; the former tells us of what is subjective—of the conscious plenitude of life and power. Jesus, being full of the Holy Ghost, is led. When the sense of the mighty force is strong within him, when the chords of the heart are vibrating in response to the voice from heaven, when the soul feels straitened until it enters on the great mission given it ; when he is ready, lo ! this summons to the wilderness, this forcible taking of the anointed man, with the anointing fresh and full, to the dreary desert place over whose surface the wild beasts roam. But is not this a way of God ? Was not Saul of Tarsus, in the morning of his life in Jesus, sent for three years to Arabia ? Is not strength gathered, is not character compacted, through contact, direct and personal, with the forces alike of good and evil ? He who was " made in all things like to his brethren " must have that in his human history which corresponds to facts and necessities in ours. And the wilderness, with its struggle, its assaults on faith and obedience, its glimpse into the outer darkness, its resistance of the devil, is a necessity in the education of the man as the Son of God.

III. THE TEMPTATIONS OF CHRIST RECORDED ARE A MIRROR OF THE TEMPTATIONS OF HIS BRETHREN. Mark the word " recorded." St. Luke tells us that Jesus was led during forty days, tempted of the devil. What the forty days meant remains untold. Probably it could not be expressed in language intelligible to us. It was only at the end that " the Divine event becomes human enough to be made to appear." Until then the lower wants were in a condition of suspense ; the hunger is " the first sign of his coming back to us." Then the part of the temptation which we can understand begins. It will be remembered that we are dealing with a narrative of real transactions. It is not a poem, not a parable. Whether the acts were purely subjective, consisting only of suggestions to the inner spiritual sense, is a doubtful point ; but that there was a veritable tempting in the manner described, that we are regarding " a chronicle of events," cannot be doubted. Nor is it a mere likeness of temptation that is set before us. The gospel story would be nothing to the heart if we conceived of it as a series of visions which in no distinct way touched the citadel of the Lord's heart, was not to him what temptation is to us—the contact of the soul with some hour and power of darkness. If it be asked—How can this be if Jesus was without sin ? let it be recollected that sin does not consist in an impression of what is evil ; it consists in yielding to the impression, in receiving it. The sacred writers are careful to note that all suggestions come, not from the soul, but to the soul from a lying spirit outside the personality. When we speak of sinlessness, we do not mean that enticements to sin can never present themselves or be felt as enticements ; we mean that they are never yielded to or consented to—that there is a will so perfectly loyal to the Father that the wrong and the unchildlike are never in the purpose of Jesus. Note the three points or regions of the temptation recorded. The order is slightly different in the accounts of St. Matthew and St. Luke. That which is third in the one is second in the other, reminding us that too much stress is not to be laid on the mere sequence of the story. The first trial had reference to the urgent need; it came in the form of the subtle insinuation, " Son of God, you are hungry : why not use your power to satisfy the wants of nature ? You have not bread, you cannot buy bread : why not bid these stones become bread ? " So plausible, that the lie can scarcely be discerned. It is addressed to the man on the most pressing side of his necessity. And Jesus meets it as man. " Man's only life is not that by bread, but that by every word which proceedeth out of the mouth of God." God's Word had made the stone a stone. He would not say the stone is a loaf. He must be throughout in harmony with the eternal word and will. Then how subtle is the second attack ! Adhering to St. Matthew's order, " Thou art full of confidence in thy God. Thou dost trust him to the uttermost. Put thy faith to the proof. The Jews expect that their Messiah will descend from the clouds. Away to the top of yonder temple. Cast thyself down from thence. Do something striking; thou knowest it is written, ' He shall give his angels charge over thee.' " How plausible the appeal to the Son of God on the side of his faith ! And, once more— repelled by the counter-thrust, the counter-Scripture, " Thou shalt not try to the utter- most the Lord thy God, claiming a miraculous help for what is born of human pride and rashness "—mark the tact and the audacity in the final assault which the enemy makes. The love of power—that which is at once the strength and the weakness of every noble mind—shall be the wedge. " Son of God, look down on the kingdoms of the world and the glory of them. Thou art seeking the sovereignty of man. I can give it thee. The force is thine; use it at my instigation. The dominion of love is one of toil and pain. Take what I offer. Think what blessings to the world will be at once secured. The sole condition is to fall down and worship me. Am I not the real king of the world ? " It is the very climax of devilry. The temptation can go no further. " Then saith Jesus, Get thee behind me, Satan." It is the battle of man that is por- trayed in man's Lord. " For both he that sanctifieth and they that are sanctified are all of one." Here is *the tempter* who is tempting us, adapting the form of his solicita- tions to our tempers, our endowments, our circumstances. Here are the *characteristics of his approaches*, his doubts, his "*ifs*" (" if " is a devil-word which more than any other loosens the holdfasts of faith), his *quotations from Scripture* when it suits his pur- pose to do so, his *three great heads of temptation*—that which seeks us through bodily need or fleshly appetite, that which seeks us through even our purer and higher instincts, that which would draw us into the net by stirring up the pride of life. Ah ! there is no sleeping with this tempter. " Watch and pray, lest ye enter into temptation."

IV. THE VICTORY OF CHRIST IS OUR ENCOURAGEMENT. Blessed is the assurance contained in the words, " Get thee behind me, Satan." The devil is behind Jesus, the Captain of our salvation. What is our position towards our Captain ? Apart from him ? Ah, we may tremble ! With him, in him ? He is between us and Satan, and we can do all things through him strengthening. " Be of good cheer : I have overcome."

Vers. 14—30.—*The visit of Christ to Nazareth.* The Lord is in Galilee, slowly moving from place to place, always in the character of Teacher, and always winning the applause of those who throng the synagogues. It is the period of unbroken popu- larity, short but, so long as it lasts, complete. His face is towards his native place, foreseeing and, as we are reminded, foretelling that the tide will receive its first check there. The visit is in many ways significant.

I. IT REMINDS US OF A DUTY. " He came to Nazareth, where he had been brought up." He had testified, when leaving Samaria, that a prophet is without honour in his own country. But he will not turn from it. He makes it the place for the first unfolding of the blessed Messiah-mission. And, although cast forth from the city, he seems again to have visited Nazareth. " He does not give it up for a first sin, though that sin may have been a grievous one." Is not this a lesson for all ? The place of the upbringing, however far we may roam from it, has a claim on our special sympathy. Our own should never be neglected. It is easier sometimes to deal with strangers. We can speak more frankly and openly to them ; they meet us often more frankly and

openly than do our kindred or those directly related to us.   What is far-fetched is
frequently more esteemed than what is home-bred.   Nevertheless, the duty is to
witness for God to the circle which encloses our tenderest associations.   Yes, even to
repeat and repeat our message, and thus deliver our own soul.

II. IT SPEAKS TO US OF A GOOD HABIT.   "As his custom was, he went into the
synagogue on the sabbath day, and stood up to read."   Here was one, remember, who
knew more than the elders.   Might he not have said, " Why go to the place of meeting?   Can I not worship God, my Father, on mountain-side, or in my dwelling?   The
synagogue can give me nothing, no increase to my knowledge or to my devotion ; nay,
my meditation can be more free and sweet when my soul is alone with Heaven."   But
this he did not say.   It was his rule to be where the two or three met in the name of
God.   The sabbath day was God's ordinance ; therefore he kept it holy.   Social worship
has its authority, not only in the sanction which is implied in God's promises to those
who assemble together for his praise, but in the instincts of our common nature.
Therefore he kept rank with those who surrounded him, and when the call to the local
sanctuary was sounded, he was always responsive.   Surely in this he has left an
example on which may well be based the rule, " Forsake not the assembling of yourselves together."   Keep two things in view : (1) the honouring of God ; (2) our part as
members one of another.   And when these things are vivid, there will arise the sense,
not merely of benefit to be received by ourselves, but of duty, both to him who made
and redeemed us, and to those amongst whom we live and move.   No light excuse
will then be allowed to interfere with the custom.   Each worshipper will feel, "I
have my ministry, my place in the congregation ; this place vacant, this ministry not
rendered, there is a want for which I am responsible."   It is the absence of a feeling
of responsibility in regard to the services of the sanctuary, it is the presence of a mere
self-pleasing spirit, which explains much of the laxity of attendance which prevails.
Let Christians ponder the way of the Lord, whose custom was to enter the village
sanctuary, and contribute to the instruction of the village folk on the sabbath day.

III. IT SETS BEFORE US A REMARKABLE SERMON.   The first of the two lessons for
the day has been read ; the lesson which remains is from the prophets—it is from
Isaiah.   Jesus stands up to read it.   It is the passage which forms the sixty-first
chapter of the book.   The opening words of this chapter are his text.   He rolls up the
parchment, returns it to the attendant, and, as was the manner of the teacher, he sits
down.   Every eye is fastened on him as slowly and emphatically he declares, " This
day is this Scripture fulfilled in your ears."   And there follows the sermon, the substance
of which Luke records.   Concerning the sermon, note : 1. *Its thought and style.*   The
words are " gracious," literally, " words of grace."   Divine grace is the theme, and the
language befits the theme.   It is not in the fashion of ordinary teachers ; it shines,
and it burns.   It is beautiful, winning ; " grace is poured into the lips."   Such words
become the pulpit ; no other words become it.   2. *Its effect.*   At first the wonder,
the admiration, of the people is excited.   If they had only yielded to the teaching,
how mighty would have been the work of the day !   But, alas ! the small, petty
feelings of the village prevent the work.   The charm of the discourse is soon effaced
by the murmurs, " Is not this Joseph's Son?   Capernaum may shout in his
praise, but he is one of ourselves.   We know his parentage and early surroundings.
No, no ; Joseph's Son is not the Anointed of Jehovah."   And soon the countenance
changes from wonder into scorn, and from scorn into rage, as the Teacher, reading their
thoughts, charges home their guilt, and reminds them that the blessing passes from
those who account themselves unworthy of it.   Are these Nazarenes sinners above all
others because this is their treatment of the Holy One?   Have not we prejudices
and prepossessions sometimes quite as irrational as were theirs?   Has not the oscillation of feeling which we trace in them its counterpart in our own experience?   Have
not words sometimes seemed gracious to us until some little pride was touched, some
demand made on faith against which reason or inclination rebelled, and, in our secret
soul, Jesus was cast out?   May we not hear his love protesting, " How often would I
have gathered you, . . . and ye would not "?

Vers. 31—43.—*A sabbath day's work.*   "The despised and rejected " of Nazareth
comes down to Capernaum, henceforth the centre of his labour of love.   The evangelist

sets before us one of the sabbath days of this early Galilæan period, and bids us note the use made of the sabbath by the Son of man, who was also its Lord. He takes us to the synagogue, no doubt crowded by an expectant throng of fishermen, farmers, masters and workmen of busy Gennesareth. Jesus is the Teacher; and, as the discourse proceeds, we hear the sentence passing from one to another, " What a word ! " or, " What is this word ! "—so different from the speech to which they are accustomed, so strangely fascinating. Has not the exclamation of these simple folk been repeated, in circles ever widening ? Is it not, more than ever, the voice of the day in which we live ? Let us look to the incidents of the Capernaum sabbath for three illustrations of the abiding power of the Word of the Lord.

I. THERE IS THE POWER TO INSPIRE. We see this generally and specially. Generally, in the effect produced on the great body of the people. They had not yet been inflamed against Jesus by the emissaries of the Pharisees; and his preaching arrested the attention. It was not wild and startling, like that of John; it was calm, but intense. The pedantries of the scribes had no place in it; it spoke to the heart; it was the word of One in the light and love of God—the Son of God and the Son of man. " For a season " at least they rejoiced in it. There were responses in the conscience, deep answering " amens " in the soul. The word was with authority. Specially in the attitude of those by whom Jesus was accompanied. We are told by Mark that he is accompanied by Simon and Andrew, James and John. They are the elder sons of his special family. They have heard the word, " Follow me," and, obeying it, have left all to be his disciples. Oh, blessed power—the power of that Spirit who, in the beginning, moved on the face of the waters and said, " Let there be light ! " the power to awake the slumbering desire, to interpret the needs and thoughts of the heart, to stir up the longing to be better and nobler, to be the citizens of the kingdom of heaven and the sons and daughters of the Lord Almighty ! Who of us has felt the life-giving force of this heavenly spring ? Such a one will join in the cry, " What a word ! "

II. THERE IS THE POWER TO EXORCISE. One of the audience on the first of the Capernaum sabbaths is a miserable demoniac, " a man with the spirit of an unclean demon." Whether, by such an expression, we are to understand only a violent type of mania, there is no need to discuss. The language of the thirty-third and thirty-fourth verses seems to imply more than this. " It is utterly impossible," says Dean Alford, " to understand such a testimony as that of the sick person, still less of the fever or disease." Be this as it may, the multitude, spell-bound, is receiving the word which is with power, when suddenly a great scream is heard. " Ἔα, ἔα ! Let us alone; what have we to do with thee, thou Jesus of Nazareth ? I know thee who thou art; the Holy One of God." Calmly, firmly, the Preacher rebukes the spirit; there is a paroxysm, a convulsion, and the man rises up, the wildness all gone, a right spirit renewed in him. " What a word ! He commandeth the unclean spirits, and they obey him ! " Let us believe that this word of command and rebuke is still with us. Unclean spirits, demons in men, alas ! are legion, and sore havoc they make in human lives and homes. No demon is ever alone; it is always accompanied by evil powers, by manifold miseries. The only force adequate to the cleansing of the soul thus possessed is that of the Holy One of God. Welcoming all remedial legislation, all forms of philanthropic effort, with a view to raise the fallen, to cast out the devils which afflict society, let us remember that the innermost seat of the evil can be reached only by the gospel of the Holy One. With this gospel, let us never despair. " God is the God of hope; the devil is the spirit of despair."

III. THERE IS THE POWER TO HEAL. The mission of Jesus in Galilee was a great medical mission. The Preacher and the physician represent the two aspects of his ministry. Here is a thought which consecrates the art of the physician; he is a revelation of one side of the abiding power of Christ; it is for him to recognize the Master and acknowledge the supreme authority of the Word of the Lord. And turning to the physician and availing themselves of his skill, the sick and diseased may recall that it is Jesus Christ who maketh whole. This is the true faith-healing. See how the healing power of the words is illustrated. Read vers. 40, 41. What a hospital is before the eye of the Healer when the sun is setting ! And not one of the impotent and afflicted is without the touch; not one baffles the skill. For a more particular illustration, read vers. 38, 39. It is " a great fever," and they beseech him for that

precious life. He stands over her and "rebukes the fever." Another account is still
more touching: "He comes and takes her by the hand, and lifts her up." Is not this
a passage which makes all the Christian world kin? How many understand what is
meant by the beseeching for one laid low with "the great fever"! Ah! but some will say,
"It was not with my beloved as with her in the gospel story. I wept and fasted; I
cried, 'Oh, spare my dear one!' but there was no rebuke of the disease. The one for
whom I entreated was taken, and I was left, sitting alone and keeping silence." Peace,
thou bleeding heart! He allowed his beloved Lazarus to die; but in his own time and
way he stood beside the grave and bade Lazarus come forth. He told the sisters that
their faith was feeble; that the higher faith would not have been clamorous—it would
have felt, "His hand is holding that life; it is lifting it up; whosoever lives and believes
in him has been already lifted up, and never dies." So bethink thyself; not according
to thy way, but according to his own, he did come; he did take by the hand; he did
whisper, "Rise, my love, my fair one, and come; where I am thou shalt be also." In
the case of Simon's mother-in-law the answer is visible. Observe, not only is the fever
removed, but strength is infused—"immediately she rose up and ministered unto them."
A beautiful suggestion, that ministry to Christ always follows the sense of healing by
Christ. "What shall I render to the Lord for all his benefits toward me?"

HOMILIES BY VARIOUS AUTHORS.

Vers. 1, 2 (first part).—*Solitude and struggle.* We are not to suppose, even though
we read this statement as given by Matthew (iv. 1), that our Lord was led by the
Spirit into the wilderness for the express purpose of being tempted by the evil one:
to take that view would be to mistake the force of the Hebrew idiom. All that is
intended is that Jesus was constrained ("driven," Mark says) to retire into the solitude of the wilderness *where he would have to undergo* the temptation which did actually
befall him. He was led, by Divine direction, into retirement, and there, by Divine
permission, into spiritual struggle.

I. THE DIVINE DIRECTION. As Moses in Midian, as David around Bethlehem, as
Elijah at Horeb, as John in the wilderness of Judæa, as (afterwards) Saul in Arabia,
so Jesus prepared for his great work in the depth of "the solitary place." There we
can well believe that he held much *communion with God*; that he looked down into
the secret places of his own soul and communed carefully *with himself*; and that he
pondered long on the great work—*the Father's business*—which lay before him. We
may be sure that this period of solitude produced very rich fruit in after-days, not only
in the truth which was spoken, but in the life which was lived and the sorrow which was
endured. This period should find its counterpart in our history; if it does not find it
by our consent, it may do so without any choice of our own. For: 1. *God commends*
such retirement to us. He does so by the way in which he led the greatest and the
wisest of his servants (see above); by the faculties of devotion, introspection, and forecast which he has given us; by the example of our Lord. But: 2. *God compels us* to
such retirement. He does so by his holy providence, when he lays us aside, when he
takes us away from the busy scenes of toil, from "the strife of tongues," from the
excitements of society, and even from the distractions of the home circle; when he
shuts the door upon us and draws round the curtain and leaves us alone with himself.
Of that time, if we are wise, we shall make good use. It is a time for spiritual renovation; then we may learn lessons we should never gather even in the sanctuary; then
we may enter on an upward path which otherwise we should never take, and so
reach a goal we should otherwise never gain. It is a sacred opportunity, inciting to
(1) review; (2) introspection or self-examination; (3) onlook; (4) prayer, including
the solemn and determined rededication of our whole selves and our entire future to the
service of our Saviour.

II. THE DIVINE PERMISSION. By the permission of God the evil one came to our
Lord and tempted him (see following homilies). God allows the tempter to assail us
even as he did his "beloved Son." There are some temptations which are more likely
to beset us in the period of solitude than at any other time—temptations of the wilderness. They are: 1. *A morbid sensitiveness* as to (1) our own condition—a disposition

to look too much to our own feelings, and to dwell too little on the goodness and the love of God ; also as to (2) our own reputation, and the estimation in which we are held among men.   2. *Excessive disappointment* and consequent disheartenment concerning (1) the life we are living before God ; (2) the work we are doing for our fellow-men ; (3) the progress of the kingdom of God.   But though we may pass through these struggles we may come safely out of them.   The remedies are these : (1) An appeal to God for his guidance and inspiration ; (2) a resort to the promises of his Word ; (3) a timely return to the activities of daily work, of public worship, of active usefulness.—C.

Vers. 2—4.—*The temptation of the flesh.*   There can be no question as to the reality of the temptation.   Without contending for the strictly literal sense of the passage, we do maintain that the temptation was a very real thing to our Lord.   It constituted a serious struggle through which he went, out of which he came forth victorious, by passing through which he was our Exemplar.   We cannot afford to lose this aspect of his life, this view of our Lord himself ; but we must beware lest we do ; for " if we shrink from believing that he really felt the force of temptation . . . we make that Divine life a mere mimic representation of griefs that were not real, and surprises that were feigned, and sorrows that were theatrical.   But thus we lose the Saviour."   It was a real conflict that is here depicted ; and the first stage of it was that through which we have all, in our time, to pass—the stern contest with the temptation of the flesh.

I. THE SEVERITY OF THE TEMPTATION.   " He hungered " after long fasting.   Hunger, in its severer forms, is unknown to us.   In a country like this we have no experience of it.   We can only judge of it from the testimony of those who have endured it ; and, thus judging, we are sure that it is a very urgent, imperious, almost irresistible craving.   The extremities and inhumanities to which it has driven men who are not naturally inhuman tell their own tale with terrible force.   Our Master was suffering, we may well believe, from the most severe pangs of want.   There were stones of the size and colour of such a loaf as he would have given everything (it would be right to give) to obtain.   By an easy exertion of his miraculous power he could turn the one into the other.   Why not do so?   Because to do that would be to take himself out of the hands of that heavenly Father to whose care he was committed, and manifest distrust in his providential goodness.   Or because to do so would be to employ his Divine power first on his own behalf, instead of using it, as on the occasion of its first exercise it behoved him to employ it, on behalf of others.   Or because to do that would be to give present and bodily cravings precedence of the great concerns of the kingdom of God.   For some such reason our Lord thought that it would be wrong or, at any rate, undesirable for him to act on the suggestion, and he forbore.   Temptation of the fleshly kind comes to us in the shape of hunger, or thirst, or sexual passion. 1. These trials of our moderation and self-government are more or less severe according to (1) our temperament and (2) our circumstances.   2. They may lead us into errors and evils which are (1) mistakes to be avoided ; or (2) indiscretions to be condemned and regretted, and, of course, forsaken ; or (3) vices and sins which are shameful and deadly, which stain the conscience, which ruin the reputation, which lead down to swift destruction.

II. THE WAY OF VICTORY.   When the hour of conflict comes we must gird ourselves for the fight ; and though the peril may be great because the enemy is strong, yet have we great resources, and there is no reason why we should not win the battle.   We should call to our help our regard for : 1. The will of God as revealed in his Word ; that " sword of the Spirit, which is the Word of God," should be at hand with us as it was with our great Leader : " It is written."   2. The penalty of disobedience—a very heavy one in its ultimate issues.   3. The example of our Divine Master, calmly putting aside the false suggestion, preferring to suffer rather than to sin.   4. The consideration that sin excludes us from other and higher blessings.   Better far, in the thought of Christ, to rest in bodily hunger, committing himself to the faithfulness of the holy Father.   And how much better than any physical enjoyment is the satisfaction of spirit which attends purity and piety!   Not the bread of bodily comfort, but the sense of God's abiding favour, the continuance of the friendship of Christ, the cherishing of a heavenly hope,—that is the good thing to prize and to pursue.—C.

Vers. 5—8.—*Temptation : outward and inward grandeur.* Of course, literal exactness is necessarily excluded here; we must look for, and shall have no difficulty in finding, the sense and spirit of the words. We will look at—

I. THE APPEAL THAT WAS MADE TO OUR LORD, and the corresponding attack that is made on ourselves. Christ was tempted to seize " power and glory " for himself by an act of unholy submission. These were the prize which the worldly minded Jews of his age imagined to be within reach of their Messiah. To one of his humble circumstances but limitless capacity, and also of rightful and honourable ambition, there might very easily be presented a most powerful temptation to aim at a great and glorious supremacy—a throne like that of the Cæsar himself, on which imperial power might be exercised and human glory at its topmost height be enjoyed. And the force of this temptation would be very greatly intensified by the fact that such a throne as this would be gained by very different measures from those Jesus had been contemplating in his solitude. The collecting of multitudes by appealing to their national passions, the leading of armies and gaining of victories, the command of great bodies of men, the excitements of political strife,—all this is full of enjoyment to the ambitious soul. A vastly different experience this (and to all that was human in the mind of Jesus Christ immensely more attractive) from that of speaking unappreciated truth, living a life too noble to be understood, suffering from keen and malignant persecution, dying in the pangs and shame of martyrdom ! The price to be paid for surrendering the higher for the lower aim, and the distressing for the delightful means, was " worshipping " Satan ; in other words, declining the course which he most disliked, and adopting the course which he most desired. The attack which is now made on us, corresponding to this, is the suggestion that we should turn aside from the higher aspiration (whatever it may be) to the lower ambition. It may come to the Christian minister in his study, to the statesman in his cabinet, to the doctor in his consulting-room, to the author or editor at his table ; it is a suggestion to leave the straight line of duty, of faithfulness, of service, of truth, of loyalty to conviction, of moral and spiritual integrity, and take the lower path of popularity, of honour, of temporal success. To do this is to take a course which we may dignify by some fair name, but which, in Scripture language, is worshipping the devil.

II. THE SPIRIT IN WHICH IT WAS REPELLED BY HIM, and in which it should be defeated by us. This was one of holy indignation : " Get thee behind me," etc. Our Lord indignantly refused to entertain a suggestion so utterly opposed to his spirit of consecration, so subversive of all his high purposes and lofty hopes. He met it by the quotation of a word which demanded entire obedience to the will of God and full devotedness to his service. In this spirit of holy indignation let us repel the first advances of a temptation to leave the higher and the heavenly road of truth and service for the lower and the earthly one of mere temporal success. To take that lower course would be to play into the hands of the evil one ; to lose the commendation of our conscience and to live under the shadow of its rebuke ; to lower ourselves and to degrade our life in the estimate of all the true and wise on earth and in heaven ; to lose our true and high reward ; to break the word and depart from the will of the Lord our God.—C.

Vers. 9—12.—*Temptation to guilty haste.* One more attempt is made by the evil one on the integrity of our Lord's faithfulness. We note—

I. THE EVIL SUGGESTION. The idea conveyed to the mind of Jesus, now on the point of commencing his ministry, was this (as I understand it) : " Here is a glorious opportunity to make a most successful beginning ; alighting from this height among the assembled worshippers below, who are all ready to welcome the Messiah, you will gain such a prestige from so brilliant a miracle that the battle of conviction will be almost won by a single blow. There need be no fear ; the angels will sustain you," etc. But to act in this way would be to proceed along a line totally unsuited to the kind of work which Jesus came to do. It would be very gratifying, very stimulating, very agreeable to human feeling, but it would not be the *right* course to pursue. Christ came to build up a vast spiritual empire, and he was to lay its foundations carefully and steadily, and therefore deliberately and slowly, in the minds of men. This victory was not one to be snatched by a sudden impetuous charge ; there must be a long and a hard campaign. Everything could not be done by a brilliant stroke, appealing to the imagination ;

there must be a long, laborious process, by which the judgment and the conscience of mankind would be convinced. There would be fatal folly in an endeavour to force an issue. There would be Divine wisdom in " beginning at the beginning," in gradually working onwards, in toiling upwards amid fatigues and sorrows until the height was reached. Such are the victories before us now—triumphs over ignorance, over vice, over unbelief, over superstition, over indifference, over indecision, over spiritual languor. We should like to be working faster, to be winning the battle at a greater pace. Then cometh the evil one, and he says, " Leave these slow processes; mix a little error with the truth you preach; be more careful to produce an effect than to deliver the Divine message; sacrifice purity to power; introduce into the methods of the kingdom of Christ the principles and the weapons of the kingdom of the world; hasten to the goal and snatch the crown of success, instead of working so hard and waiting so long."

II. THE FIRM REFUSAL. Christ declined to adopt the suggestion; he said that to do so would be " tempting the Lord his God." It would be expecting God to work a miracle in order to gratify his unholy eagerness. We must not try to precipitate the cause of righteousness by an unholy impatience, which is a practical distrust of God's Word. To expect God to bless means which he has not sanctioned, to own and honour methods which are not in accord with the principles he has revealed,—this is to lose his favour and to draw down his condemnation; it is to invite discomfiture. " *He that believeth shall not make haste.*" Our wisdom as well as our duty, as " workmen together with God," is to (1) adopt God-given methods; (2) ask for the Divine help and inspiration; (3) confidently await the Divine blessing in God's own chosen time and way.—C.

Ver. 18.—*The poor and the gospel.* A most significant fact that the first work of the Messiah should be his " preaching the gospel to the poor." What is the significance of it?

I. BY THE POOR DIVINE TRUTH IS MOST NEEDED. Their life on earth is the hardest; it is often one of unremitting *toil;* often one of severe *privation,* almost destitute of comfort and enjoyment; often one of serious and hard•*oppression,* in which the strong will of another robs of all liberty of action. The past is sad, the present gloomy, the future dark. There are no pleasures in recollection, and there is no relief in hope. How precious, how necessary, to these are the joys which earth cannot give and cannot steal—the treasures which enrich the heart, the hopes which reach beyond the grave!

II. BY THE POOR DIVINE TRUTH IS MOST APPRECIATED. " How hardly do they that have riches enter the kingdom of heaven! " Their time is occupied, their minds are filled, with pursuits and pleasures which are on an earthly plane, and things higher and worthier are hidden from view. The poor, though they have indeed their own temptations and their own errors and failings, are yet more likely to see the Divine hand beckoning to them, and to hear the heavenly voice calling them to wisdom and service and eternal joy. And, as a fact, *they do.* The common people still hear Christ gladly, while the wealthy and the strong and the famous are sitting at the feet of " the world," to learn its wisdom and to seek its favour.

III. TO THE POOR DIVINE TRUTH IS CLEARLY AND MARKEDLY OFFERED. It was, in fact, a very great thing to say, " To the poor the gospel is preached." It was one of the " watermarks " of Christianity that our Master made his appeal, not, as philosophy and theology had done before him, and as science in our day is doing, to human learning and influence, but to the unlettered and the lowly, to the multitude and the millions among men, to the common human heart. Other systems had tried to reach the lower levels by affecting the heights of society first. The gospel of Jesus Christ " moves upward from below." It teaches, cleanses, raises *the people;* and so it purifies and exalts the nation. This is the Divine method, and must be ours. It is for the Church of Christ to follow its Divine Master, to see that the signs of truth are about its handiwork, and amongst them this leading sign, that " to the poor the gospel is preached." If this feature should be absent, it will be time for the Church to be considering where it stands—how near to or remote from its Master.—C.

Ver. 18.—*Healing the broken-hearted.* We have a supreme want, but we have a Divine remedy.

I. THE BROKEN HUMAN HEART.   There are two things which break hearts: 1. One is *intolerable shame*; the shame which comes from a crushing sense of sin; it may be of *flagrant* sin, such as commands the deep indignation and strong censure of our fellow-men, and involves the loss of our own self-respect; or it may be a sense of that *common* sin of which all the souls of men are guilty in the sight of God—the keeping back from him of all that has been due to him, all the reverence and love of our hearts and all the service of our lives.   Under a deep sense of sin, and therefore of condemnation, affected and afflicted with the consciousness of Divine disapproval and the fear of Divine punishment, the heart cries out for refuge.   2. The other is *overwhelming sorrow*; it may be some crushing disappointment, or it may be some wearing and trying sickness, or it may be some heavy and humiliating loss, or it may be some terrible bereavement and consequent loneliness of heart and life; under one or more of these overwhelming burdens the heart may be bowed down even to breaking.

II. THE ONE DIVINE REFUGE.   There is but one availing "Refuge of our soul" to whom we can flee with perfect assurance that in him we shall find what we need. Christ came "to heal the broken-hearted," and he does so by: 1. Offering us the *most tender sympathy*.   He is the High Priest who is "touched with a feeling of our infirmities, having been in all points tried even as we are," and therefore able to enter perfectly into our griefs, whether of mind, body, or estate.   2. Ministering to us *Divine comfort*.   By his Holy Spirit's ministry he comes to us, and dwells within us, and acts powerfully though graciously upon our hearts; thus he lets the gentle dews of his comfort cool the heats of our fevered spirit, making himself known to us as the "God of all comfort," as that "One who comforteth them that are cast down."   3. Granting us *effectual help*; enlightening our minds, energizing our spirits, making us capable of doing that which has to be done, animating and reviving us, fitting us to take our part and do our work.   In proportion as we are reverent and pure of heart in the time of our prosperity and joy, may we look for his indwelling and outworking in the "day of desperate grief" and of heart-brokenness.—C.

Ver. 18.—*Spiritual bondage and Christian freedom.*   Who does not pity the captive? Saddening to the sympathetic heart is the thought of the man who is confined within his lonely and dreary cell, shut in from the beauties and melodies of nature, excluded from the haunts of men, debarred from all the activities of busy life, unable to enter his own home, compelled to unwilling solitude and separation from those he loves!   There is no prayer that we breathe with a finer or fuller feeling than the petition, "Let the sighing of the prisoner come before thee."   Yet is there a bondage that is worse than any ever inflicted by stone walls and iron chains.   It is—

I. THE BONDAGE OF SIN.   Sin is at first a transgression, but it soon becomes a tyranny.   It grows into a power; and it becomes a power which holds the soul in its grasp, so that it is practically enslaved; it attempts to rise, to move, to do that which befits it and for which it was created, but it finds that it cannot; it is held down; its way is barred.   This is true of sin in all its forms, and it is true in a number of degrees, varying from an objectionable constraint down to an almost hopeless despotism.   It applies to: 1. *Error*, which becomes an inveterate prejudice through which no light will break.   2. *Folly*, such as that of procrastination, which in no length of time weaves itself round the soul.   3. *Vice*, such as intemperance, or profanity, or impurity (more especially in some of its forms).   There is no bondage more thoroughly deserving the name than this.   The victim of vice is, indeed, "holden with the cords of his sins" (Prov. v. 22); they have him fast in the saddest and most degrading thraldom in which a human being can be held.   4. *Vanity*.   How many a man is a wretched slave to the judgment of other men!   The fear of their condemnation, or still oftener of their ridicule, impels him in a direction in which he knows he ought not to be going, ties him to a position from which he is longing to break away.   5. *Rebellion* against God; disloyalty, estrangement, the withholding of the heart and life from God's service, so long maintained, that, when the soul thinks of repentance and return, it finds itself held to its wrong and sinful state.

II. THE FREEDOM WHICH IS IN CHRIST.   The gospel announces "deliverance to the captives."   And how does it effect this blessed emancipation?   1. By giving to the sinner a deep sense of his sin, and filling his soul with shame of himself and loathing of his iniquity. When men have come to hate sin they are well on the road toward its conquest. 2. By taking back the penitent to the favour and love of God. Through Christ sin is pardoned and the sinner is restored. As one that loves God, and seeks above all things to enjoy his favour, the man "cannot sin;" he has acquired a reason and motive for purity and integrity which gives him the victory over sin. How can he grieve his heavenly Father, his Divine Redeemer, the Holy Spirit of God? 3. By giving him access to a source of Divine power. God is ready to dwell effectually within, and to work mightily upon the soul that seeks his presence and asks his power. We can do "all things *in* Christ who strengtheneth us." He makes us to know "the exceeding greatness of his power to usward who believe," in snapping the bonds that bound us, and investing us with "the glorious liberty of the children of God."—C.

Ver. 18.—*Spiritual blindness.* "The recovering of sight to the blind." We think of—
I. THE BADNESS OF BLINDNESS, and its degrees. "It must be very bad to be blind," we say; probably we but faintly realize what it means. 1. It is bad to be *physically* blind—to look on no scenery, to read no book, to behold no countenance, to recognize no love in a human face, to grope our way in the thick darkness. 2. It is worse to be *mentally* blind—to see, and not to see; to open the eyes on the beauty and wonder and glory of the universe and to recognize nothing beautiful, wonderful, glorious, there; to be as lonely in a library as in a cell! 3. It is worse still to be *morally* blind—blind of soul, so that a man can see nothing degraded in drunkenness, nothing shameful in vice, nothing revolting in obscenity and profanity, nothing repelling in selfishness; so that a man can see nothing noble in generosity, nothing beautiful in beneficence, nothing regal in righteousness and duty, nothing sacred in human love. 4. It is worst of all to be *spiritually* blind—worst, because that is the root and source of all the others; blindness of spirit, a darkness in which the soul fails to see the Highest of all beings, the loftiest of all truths, the greatest of all facts; a darkness in which the soul fails to recognize the essential truth that in God we "live, and move, and have our being," and that to him we are responsible for all we are and have; in which it is blind to our sorrowful state of guilt and condemnation in the sight of God.
II. THE WORST FEATURE OF SPIRITUAL PRIVATION. That which is the best feature in physical is the worst in spiritual blindness. Under the merciful principle of accommodation, the blind became not only submissive, but contented and even cheerful in the darkness in which they dwell. They are able not only to speak of it, but to feel about it that it is "the shadow of God's wing." That is a very happy thing; but that is the very worst feature of spiritual blindness. It is spiritual insensibility that is the most deplorable—the fact that men don't know that they don't see; that they suppose themselves to know everything when they know nothing; that they are not aware what a world of truth and blessedness is around them and is accessible to them. Who shall reveal this to them?
III. CHRIST THE GREAT RESTORER of our spiritual vision. And how does he make us see that to which, but for him, we should have remained blind? 1. *By making quite plain and certain* that which would have remained shadowy and uncertain. Many truths of vital importance men would, in his absence, have speculated upon and discussed, but they would not have *known* them. Coming to us from God, the great Teacher has turned these uncertainties into living and sustaining *truth.* He tells us authoritatively and decisively that God is the one Divine Spirit, the righteous Ruler of all, the Father of souls, condemning them in their sin, pitying them in their estrangement, inviting them to return; that God has determined that when we die we *shall* live again, shall come forth to a resurrection of condemnation or of life. 2. By bringing the truth *close home to the eye of the soul.* When our Lord lived on earth he did this himself in his own Person; *e.g.* in the cases of the woman of Samaria, the rich young ruler, Nicodemus, he brought the truth of the kingdom home to the heart and the conscience. Those lips are closed to us now; Christ speaks not now as he spoke then. But his Spirit is with us still, speaking through his Word and through his faithful servants, and through his providence. 3. By more fully *enlightening the minds* of those who go in faith to seek and to serve him. Unto all seeking and trusting souls he manifests his truth in ever-enlarging fulness; them he leads "into all the truth" they

need to know; and to them it becomes gloriously true that the Spirit of the Lord has anointed him, their Saviour, for "the recovering of sight to the blind."—C.

Ver. 18.—*The bruised.* "To set at liberty them that are bruised." And who may they be who are thus characterized? and in what way does Jesus Christ meet their especial need?

I. BRUISED SOULS. We find these in: 1. Those who are *chafed* with the *worries* of life; whose disposition is such, or whose circumstances are such, that they are harassed and fretted by a multitude of minor conflicts with men and things; who are in danger of losing or have lost their mental equilibrium as the result of the perpetual strife. 2. Those who are *perplexed* with the *problems* of life; who want to be mentally satisfied and to see that their theories agree with the existing facts, and who, finding these two things in frequent antagonism, are troubled thereby in soul;—such men are never fixed in their convictions, but always thinking that these require readjustment. 3. Those who are *smitten* by the *persecutions* of life; who are continually coming into collision with men. They may have a combative habit, or they may be placed in human surroundings unfavourable to peace; but, from whatever cause, they are always in conflict, and are perpetually finding themselves the object of attack, of the ribaldry and the scorn of men; they bear a bruised feeling about them. 4. Those that are *worn* with excessive *toil.* 5. Those that are *wounded* by the *heavier sorrows* of life; from whom health, or reputation, or position, or fortune, or the object of strong and deep affection has been suddenly taken away.

II. THE REFUGE THEY HAVE IN CHRIST. Jesus Christ does not "set at liberty" bruised souls as a deliverer releases bruised prisoners; but he does emancipate them by taking from them their suffering, and giving to them a large measure of spiritual freedom. He blesses these bruised souls, and proves to them a Divine Refuge. 1. By his *sympathy.* In each one of their distresses they can feel sure of the tender sympathy of their High Priest, "touched with the feeling of their infirmities." 2. By his *example.* In all points he has been tempted, or *tried,* even as we are. We bear no cross which he has not carried before us, and his was heavier than ours. 3. By his *aid.* He is ready, at our appeal, to strengthen us by his indwelling Spirit, and to grant us such strong sustaining grace that, instead of groaning under our blows, we may even glory in them (2 Cor. xii. 9). 4. By his *promises;* those "exceeding great and precious promises," which not only cover the whole path of life, however long that may prove, but reach on beyond the horizon-line of death into the blessed and eternal future.—C.

Ver. 22.—*The graciousness of the words of Christ.* "The gracious words [words of grace] which proceeded out of his mouth." The "words of the Lord Jesus" were "words of grace" indeed. They were so whether we consider—

I. THEIR SUBSTANCE. They were not, indeed, without seriousness, and at times not without severity. Christ did say, when the occasion required it, things which startled his hearers, things which are well fitted to make us pause and even tremble if we are obnoxious to their severity. He is, as a Divine Teacher and Revealer of God, as far as possible removed from the easy good-naturedness which would represent it as a matter of indifference what men hold and how they live,—the "good God" will make it all right in the end. No man can listen attentively and reverently to Christ and settle down into comfortable unbelief or self-complacent sin. Yet were his words predominantly and pre-eminently "words of grace." By the truths he preached he made known to mankind that: 1. God is accessible to all; the Approachable One, who is always willing to receive his children, and who welcomes back those who have wandered farthest away. 2. That a noble life is open to all; we may be in character and spirit, as well as in name and in position, the children of God (Matt. v. 45—48); we are to be "the light of the world," "the salt of the earth." 3. That a glorious future is within the reach of all; "in the Father's house are many mansions." 4. That salvation is very near to all; the Scripture is fulfilled; the Redeemer is come; the blind may see; the captives may be delivered; this is "the acceptable year," "the accepted time;" "to-day is the day of salvation." Or whether we consider—

II. THEIR FORM. There is about the gracious words of Christ: 1. *An accent of persuasiveness.* He does not angrily threaten, he cordially invites us; he says, winningly,

"Come unto me ... I am meek and lowly;" "Abide in me, and I [will abide] in you;" "Behold, I stand at the door, and knock," etc. 2. *A note of considerateness.* "Come into a desert place, and rest awhile;" "I have many things to say unto you, but ye cannot bear them now;" "The spirit is willing, but the flesh is weak." 3. *A touch of tenderness.* "I will not leave you comfortless;" "Because I have said these things unto you, sorrow hath filled your heart."

1. It is perilous to abuse the grace of Christ. There is such a thing as "the wrath of the Lamb." 2. It is perfectly safe to trust in his grace. He means everything he says; the worst may obtain his mercy, the most diffident may confide in his redemption of his word.—C.

Vers. 32, 37.—*Fame and power.* "His word was with power;" "The fame of him went out." Fame and power are the objects of eager and arduous pursuit; they are supposed to be deserving of the expenditure of our strength, and to reward us for all our anxieties and toils. What is their worth, intrinsic and relative? What were they to our Lord? and what should they be to us?

I. THE WORTHLESSNESS OF FAME. 1. The fame of Jesus Christ, as a man, is remarkable indeed. Born in a little Judæan village, of humble parents, receiving a very scanty education, enjoying no patronage, teaching truths too deep to be understood by the multitude and too broad to be appreciated by the orthodox of his time, arousing the hatred of the powerful, and dying while yet a young man a death of utmost ignominy,—his name has become known, his doctrine has been received, he himself has been honoured and even worshipped by countless millions of mankind under every sky. This is fame of the first magnitude; there are very few names "under heaven given among men" that can aspire to stand in the same rank, on the ground of human fame. 2. Jesus Christ shunned rather than sought fame. "Jesus *straitly* charged them, saying, See that no man know it" (Matt. ix. 30; viii. 4; xii. 16; xvii. 9). "Great multitudes came together to hear and to be healed . . . and he withdrew himself into the wilderness" (ch. v. 15, 16; see also vers. 42, 43). 3. He appears to have been embarrassed by his fame rather than gratified, and his work seems to have been hindered rather than helped by it (see John vi. 15). And it is obvious that, as his great and high purpose was one which was far removed from the superficial and worldly hopes of the people, popularity or fame would not further but rather retard the work he had in hand. It is worth no man's while to be seriously concerned about his fame. To seek for and strive after an honourable reputation is what every man owes to himself, to his family, to his Church, to his Master. But no man need concern himself greatly about the acquisition of fame. (1) It is obvious that only a very small minority of mankind can attain it; therefore any extensive endeavour after it *must* end in disappointment. (2) It is of very slight intrinsic worth; for it is possessed and enjoyed by the bad as well as by the good, by the notorious as well as by the celebrated. (3) It does not usually crown its hero until he has gone where it will no longer affect him; useless to the martyred patriot himself, however valuable to his country, is the costly tomb, or the splendid monument, or the elaborate elegy contributed to his memory. (4) Its effect on living men is exceedingly doubtful; it may gladden and stimulate, but it may elate and injure.

II. THE EXCELLENCY OF POWER. "Power belongeth unto God" (Ps. lxii. 12). And power belonged to the Son of God. "Jesus returned in the power of the Spirit" (ver. 14). 1. Christ *possessed and exerted* power—the power of the prophet, speaking truth; "his word was with power" (ver. 32; Matt. vii. 28, 29); the power of the Son of God, working miracles; the power of holiness and innocency (John vii. 30; xviii. 6); the power of love and sympathy, attaching disciples, men and women, to himself with bonds of affection that no dangers or sufferings could break. 2. He *aspired after* other and still higher power than any he exercised—the power which could only be gained by a sacrificial death. "I, if I be lifted up, will draw all men unto me." That pure and holy aspiration has been and shall be gloriously fulfilled. It is well worth our while to seek after a true, living, spiritual power. (1) It is attainable by us all; it is within the reach of those who seek it in the fellowship and the service of Christ, and who ask it of the Spirit of God. (2) It is of real intrinsic worth; it is a Divine, a Christ-like, an angelic thing; it is a source of benefit and blessing to mankind. (3) It will enlarge our heritage both here and hereafter; for to every man God will give sacred and blessed opportunity of service "according to his several ability."—C.

Ver. 40.—*The healing Saviour.* This interesting picture had evidently been impressed upon the minds of the apostolic witnesses, for all the evangelists record the fact that the occurrence took place as the sun was setting, or in the evening of the day. It was, indeed, a sight to be long remembered. Who can imagine the gratitude and joy which filled the hearts of husbands and wives, parents and children, as they left that gracious presence and returned to their homes in health and strength?
I. THE SUPREME MALADY. The malady of maladies from which we suffer is *sin*. For sin is to the soul just what sickness is to the body. 1. *Its essential nature.* It is the radical disorder of the human spirit. The faculties of the soul, instead of doing that for which they were created, are helpless or are perverted, so that the man himself no longer walks with God, no longer speaks his praise, no longer works in his cause. The soul that was meant to find its life and its heritage in revering, honouring, rejoicing in, serving, glorifying God, is out of all happy relation with him, cannot do his will, may not even know who he is. Everything is in a state of disorder and helplessness. 2. *Its various forms.* As there are "divers diseases" of the flesh, as the sickness of the body takes a variety of forms—blindness, paralysis, fever, etc.—so does sin in the soul and in the life of man. It may appear as doubt, or disbelief, or even impious denial of God; or as the deliberate and determined rejection of his claims; or as a flagrant violation of his laws; or as a guilty inattention to his voice as he speaks to us in conscience, or in his Word, or in his Son; or as a prolonged and presumptuous procrastination, ever delaying to do what is recognized as the right and the wise thing.
II. THE ONLY CURE. As many of these sick ones knew not what else to do, to whom else they could apply; as they felt that the ordinary remedies and the human skill accessible to them must prove unavailing, and that, if this new and wonderful Healer did not help them, they must bear their burden of pain and helplessness through their future days; so may we feel respecting the supreme malady. Nothing merely human will prove to be a cure. Only a Divine hand can heal these deep wounds, these fatal ills. And how does Jesus Christ prove himself the one Healer of the heart? 1. By showing us our sin in its true light, as a grievous wrong done to our heavenly Father, and thus filling our souls with sorrow and shame concerning it. 2. By offering himself as that Divine One through whom it may be forgiven, and we be restored to the favour and friendship of God. 3. By leading us in every path of holiness and purity, and forming in us a righteous character and an obedient spirit.
III. AN EFFICACIOUS METHOD. "He laid his hands on every one of them." The touch of that Divine hand communicated health to the body, and at the same time hope and joy to the heart. It was not absolutely necessary that he should touch them; he could "speak the word only," and the patient would be healed. But he preferred to do so; it brought him, the Healer, into close and loving contact with those whom he was healing. We, too, in our way, are healers after Christ. We aspire to move through our life, dispensing health and happiness to them that are sick and sad of soul. If we fail in part to do this, may it not be because we do not get into close enough contact with those whom we are endeavouring to bless? We must learn to be like our Lord, and *lay our hands on every one of them,* and then shall we be most likely to heal them.—C.

Vers. 1—13.—*The temptation of Christ.* From the baptism of Jesus we now pass to his temptation. In the baptism he received, as we have seen, three gifts from the Father—the guarantee of a *perfect revelation* of the Father's will, of a *perfect inspiration* to do that revealed will, and of an *assurance of Sonship* during the trying ordeal. We are now to notice three temptations, corresponding very accurately to these three gifts, and so presenting in most artistic fashion the great drama of Messiah's life. But before taking them up as they are here presented by Luke, let us direct our attention to one or two preliminary matters. And first we must notice that Jesus was "led," or, as Mark puts it still more graphically, was "driven" of the Spirit into the wilderness (Mark i. 12). This clearly implies that our Lord did not "court temptation," nor rush with a light heart into it, nor shirk it, but accepted bravely what was *forced* upon him. It is only in such a spirit that we can hope successfully to resist it. There is no premise of Scripture to sustain any one who rushes madly into temptation. But, secondly, we observe that a great baptism of the Spirit is usually to prepare the recipient for some victoriously-to-be-met temptation. Jesus went to the wilderness filled with the Holy Ghost, and so was enabled to vanquish his tempter. Thirdly, the scene of the temptation is significant. While its exact location is not indicated, its general characteristics are. It was some *wilderness*, where nature affords no food or sustenance to man. What a contrast to the happy garden where the first Adam was tempted! Messiah meets the tempter in the most trying circumstances, and the tempter's defeat there is promise of his defeat everywhere. Moreover, Mark tells us he was "with the wild beasts" (Mark i. 13). It is a new Daniel braving the lions and subduing them. Fourthly, we must observe that he is here tempted in his *public* capacity, as Messiah. He had doubtless been tempted previously as a private individual; he had been urged by Satan most probably to leave the privacy of Nazareth for a more public position, and had put away all these temptations manfully. Now that he has dedicated himself as Messiah in the Jordan, he must undergo corresponding temptations.

I. Notice the temptation through appetite. (Vers. 3, 4.) After forty days' fast, during which time he was suffering temptation from Satan, he finds himself famishing. The spectacle in the wilderness and among the wild beasts is, therefore, that of a *famishing Messiah*. Never was he nearer death than on this occasion, except when death actually came. It is at this juncture that Satan first tempts him through his hunger. He claims to be the Son of God; this assurance was given him in his baptism; and as the Son he believes he possesses, though as yet he has not exercised, miraculous power. Let him, then, use his power for self-preservation, which is the first law of nature, and transform the stones of the wilderness into bread. The fallacy which underlies this temptation is one to which men are now most prone, viz. that "men must live," and then this false principle passes through degrees of comparison, and men say to themselves they must, if possible, *live well*, and, lastly, they must, if possible, live *very* well. But is it necessary that any of us should live? Who has given us this revelation? May not God's revelation be that the best thing we could do would be to *die* for truth and righteousness? Hence our Lord, instead of listening to the voice of appetite, declares his resolve to listen to the voice of God, and upon that revelation he will live. "It is written, That man shall not live by bread alone, but by every word of God." It is surely instructive in these times, when appetite is accepted by many as man's one certain revelation, to have our Lord directing our attention to a higher revelation and a more sustaining voice. Bread cannot sustain the whole man; it can only prop up the physical nature; but the spiritual needs other food and higher help, and finds it in God's Word alone! Amid the fierce struggle for bread, let us listen to him who speaks about the better bread which comes out of the mouth of God!

II. Notice the temptation through ambition. (Vers. 5—8.) Matthew puts this temptation last, instead of here, and in this is probably chronologically more accurate than Luke. But we need not transpose it in order to profit by it. Messiah, then, though famishing, abides by the revelation of God rather than make a miraculous banquet in the wilderness. But of the revelation the Father gave him this was a chief part—that he was to become Conqueror and Ruler of the world! Universal empire was, therefore, his legitimate ambition. It is here that Satan tempts him. Taking him to some mountain-top, he shows him, in some miraculous fashion, all the kingdoms of the inhabited world in a moment of time. Next he claims to be the rightful ruler of these kingdoms, but is willing to make a bargain with the ambitious Messiah that, if he will only acknowledge his sovereignty and pay him the homage due to earthly kings, all the kingdoms shall be made over to him. The temptation here is to gratify ambition at the cheapest rate. No self-denial, no self-sacrifice, no consuming spirit, shall be needful, but simply a little homage paid to the world's prince. It was such a bargain as a worldly mind would have welcomed eagerly. But Jesus refused the terms. He would not acknowledge Satan to be the world's rightful ruler. He regarded him as a usurper whom he had come to depose. Hence, in impatience with the arch-fiend, our Lord exclaimed, "Get thee behind me, Satan : for it is written, Thou shalt worship the Lord thy God, and him only shalt thou serve." The question in the first temptation was that of *revelation*, corresponding to the first of the baptismal gifts; the question in this temptation is that of *inspiration*, the spirit of service, and corresponding to the second of the baptismal gifts. Jesus will not render any homage to the world's betrayer, but will serve God alone! Once more may we see the grand spirit of self-sacrifice which this implies. Jesus will seek and obtain a universal empire, but by making no truce with the world; rather would he himself suffer unto death and be followed by myriads of martyrs, than gratify a poor ambition in Satan's suggested and worldly way.

III. NOTICE THE TEMPTATION TO PRESUMPTION AND OSTENTATION. (Vers. 9—12.) As Messiah Jesus must consider what plan would be best for beginning his public work. This must have been with him a distinct subject of thought. And now Satan suggests that if he precipitated himself from the pinnacle of the temple into the court, and did so with impunity as God's Son, the people could not but hail him as the promised Messiah. He should put his Sonship, the tempter suggests, to the test. He should test the promise about angels bearing up the believer and preventing him from dashing his foot against a stone. It was a temptation to carry faith into presumption, and becoming ostentatious in doing so. Our Lord, then, having resolved to live by faith, is as firmly resolved to avoid presumption. He will not tempt his Father by claiming support in ostentatious circumstances. And so he repels the insinuation, and resolves not to presume upon his Sonship. Hence we find that, instead of entering in any such spirit upon his work, he enters upon it publicly when he drives the traffickers from the temple. It was an amazing method of beginning Messianic work, and yet it was the best way.[1] These temptations have their little counterparts in our own experience. We are tempted through appetite, through ambition, and through presumption. We must resist the enemy in the Master's spirit. The apt quotations from the Divine Word show where the sword of the Lord lies, and it is for us not to let it rust in a napkin, like Goliath's at the tabernacle, but to have it in constant readiness for active service and faithful resistance.

And now, in conclusion, we have to notice the fact that angels came and ministered unto Jesus when the crisis was past. We know not what they brought to him— ambrosial food, the corn of heaven, perhaps; at all events the most delightful food of which he ever partook. Then, like Elijah, he went in the strength of the food received, not, indeed, *to* the mount of God and the wilderness, but *from* the wilderness to the busy haunts of men, and in the power of the Spirit. Satan, meanwhile, having "completed" the temptation, having done his worst to make him fall, leaves him for a season free. It must have been a heaven of happiness to be consciously free from his incessant wiles and snares, and to have *won* the freedom. So may we in our little measure win some respite from the enemy, if we faithfully follow our Lord in resisting temptation!—R. M. E.

Vers. 14—30.—*Christ's sermon in Nazareth.* The temptation of Christ strengthened all the graces within him, so that he felt himself prepared, on returning from the wilderness, for public work. Luke does not take us, as John does in his Gospel, back to the Jordan; nor does he take us to the marriage in Cana of Galilee, where the wonderful works began (John ii. 1—13). He prefers to sum up for us his early Galilæan ministry in two verses, before proceeding to a detailed account of his visit to Nazareth and his rejection by his countrymen. Let us consider—

I. THE ESTABLISHMENT OF HIS PUBLIC REPUTATION BEFORE APPEARING IN NAZARETH. (Vers. 14, 15.) Had he gone to his own city first without a reputation, he would not have received the attention he did. Jesus knew that a prophet has no honour in his own country; he knew that he need not go among his old companions without having achieved something remarkable; hence he made a name for himself in other parts of Galilee before advancing to the difficult task at his old home. And the method he pursued was significant. He did not create rival institutions to the existing Churches. He went into the synagogues and availed himself of the opportunities they offered.

---

[1] Woolsey's 'Religion of the Present and the Future,' pp. 24—41; cf. also Ullmann's 'Sinlessness of Jesus,' pp. 123—144, 261—291, etc.

He read the Word, expounded it, and made a reputation for himself as a popular *Teacher*. Of course, along with his teaching, there was a measure of miracle. But his wonderful works were merely to secure increased attention to his still more wonderful words. His expositions of truth were really the important element to which all else was but subsidiary. It was, therefore, with an established reputation that he advanced to Nazareth to test his countrymen as to their cordiality towards him.

II. LET US NEXT CONSIDER HIS VISIT TO NAZARETH. (Vers. 16—21.) We are not informed on what day of the Jewish week he came to Nazareth; but we are told what happened on the first sabbath day after his arrival. We shall notice the significant facts as they are told us by Luke. 1. *He shared in the public worship.* If any one ever had a right to absent himself on the ground of knowing more than others could tell him, it was surely Jesus. Yet we find him subjecting himself to family training, and putting all honour he could upon social and public worship. Moreover, it was his "custom." The habit of waiting upon God at the sanctuary has thus the highest warrant. In this, as in all else, our Lord is the perfect Example. But: 2. *He took part in public worship.* The Jews in their synagogues seem to have encouraged greater freedom than Church forms now admit of. They welcomed the help of young men as readers, and took exhortation from strangers when they happened to be present. Our Lord, then, took the place of reader on this occasion, and, as Isaiah's prophecy was handed to him, he selected as his text the notable passage about the mission of Messiah. The Anointed One was sent to "preach the gospel to the poor," etc. And here it is instructive to notice (1) the *class* Messiah gathers round him. Not those whom the world would choose, but the poor, the broken-hearted, the captives, the blind, the bruised, the imprisoned! What a policy to inaugurate! Again, (2) it is significant what *treatment* he gives them. He gives the gospel, not wealth, to the poor; healing, not freedom from trial, to the broken-hearted; freedom from sin to the captives; the recovering of sight to the blind; liberty to the bruised in spirit; and acceptance and jubilee joy to all imprisoned ones. In short, it is spiritual comfort over and above physical which he brings to them! It is here that the world's wisdom fails. It may do something to alleviate physical distress, but is as helpless as the doctor in *Macbeth* in "ministering to minds diseased." 3. *He embodied and illustrated his text.* When he had read the text he gave the book back to the minister and sat down before the congregation, and proceeded to expound the passage. He had to speak of himself. He was the Person referred to in it. No wonder the eyes of all were fastened on him. The Anointed One was in their midst, and he was ready to heal the broken-hearted and to work the wonders in the spiritual realm which were so important. The exposition was really the embodiment of blessing in his own Person. The Healer was there, the great Physician of souls.

III. LET US NEXT CONSIDER THE EFFECT OF HIS SERMON. (Vers. 22, 23.) The first effect was wonder and admiration. He had evidently interested them by his spiritual exposition. No such sermon had ever been heard before in Nazareth. It was a case of ministerial joy at the glad reception of a message.[1] But if these were the lights of joy in the picture, they were speedily followed by the shadows of ministerial disappointment. Their admiration gave way before familiarity. They began to say, "Is not this Joseph's Son?" They knew his antecedents, and so will put the worst construction possible upon his work. But the contempt of familiarity was not their only danger; they imagined that, as his countrymen, they were entitled to demand such miraculous credentials as he had given elsewhere. He had lived among them for the most of thirty years a sinless life, the greatest of all miracles in a sinful world; but they demand something more, and think that he will have but a sickly reputation if he does not accede to their request. The physician who cannot cure himself will not be in much demand to cure others; so if Jesus will not, by a miraculous display at Nazareth, establish his reputation which familiarity is undermining, they are prepared to say it is because he cannot. The mistake they make is in forgetting that Nazareth had no right to the treatment of Capernaum, since it had thirty years of the sinlessness of Jesus, which the seaside town had not.

IV. CONSIDER OUR LORD'S SOVEREIGN REFUSAL OF THEIR DEMAND. (Vers. 24—27.) The notion of the Nazarenes was that they had a *right* to a miraculous display from

[1] Cf. Gerok's 'Aus Ernster Zeit,' s. 147.

Christ. As Jews, and as his own townspeople, they fancied they had a claim which could not be got over. This self-righteous spirit must be put down. Hence our Lord declares, in the first place, that "no prophet is accepted in his own country." To this law of limited influence through familiarity Jesus himself has to bow. *It is the principle which secures a missionary enterprise.* Men are more influential away from home than they can ever be at home. Better leave the plain of Shinar than wait only to have one's tongue confounded and one's influence gone. But, besides, our Lord from history recalls two illustrations of God in his sovereignty passing all the Jews by and selecting Gentiles and outsiders for blessing. The first case was in Elijah's time, when many an Israelitish widow was famishing for want of bread ; but none of them was visited by the prophet, or got her barrel of meal miraculously replenished, as did the heathen widow at Sarepta. Again, there were many lepers in Israel in the time of Eliseus the prophet, but they were all passed over, and Naaman, the Syrian general, was cured. It was in both instances to show that Jews, as such, had no claim upon God's bounty, who could, if he pleased, pass them all by. This humiliation is one of the great lessons we must all learn if we are to profit by Christ's salvation. Divine sovereignty is to humiliate in order to exalt ; but if sovereignty is denied to God, the curse comes instead.

V. CONSIDER THE SAD ISSUE OF THE VISIT. (Vers. 28—30.) The Nazarenes are filled with wrath. They will not accept the invitation, but will contend for their rights, so called. So indignant are they as to meditate his destruction. Hence they take him towards the brow of the hill, with the intention of casting him headlong over it. It was a diabolical attempt. It was frustrated, however, by the majestic bearing of the Redeemer. He went through them by simple majesty of bearing, and they dare not touch him. Over the hills he passed in judicial separation from the misguided city. And now we are surely taught by this history not to be surprised if we are apparently unsuccessful in our work. It was the same with the Master. All, in such circumstances, we can do is to lay the truth of God before men's minds, and show them at once their *unworthiness to receive it*, and their *responsibility in rejecting it.* Moreover, if old acquaintances do not receive our testimony with that eagerness and respect we imagine it deserves, let us remember that our Master was subject himself to the same law, and accepted the situation. Patience under disappointment is the great lesson of comfort from such a passage.—R. M. E.

Vers. 31—44.—*Our Lord's labours at Capernaum.* As Nazareth knew not the day of her visitation, and had done her best to make away with Jesus, he had no alternative but to make another place his centre. Capernaum, a city situated on the lake of Galilee, and through which the Eastern caravans were accustomed to pass, is selected by him as the most suitable head-quarters for his Galilæan ministry. Accordingly, he came down from the uplands, where Nazareth lay, to this seaport, and there began his missionary enterprise. And here we have—

I. THE CHARACTER OF HIS PREACHING. (Vers. 31, 32.) Entering on the sabbath days into the synagogue, he taught with authority and with success. His teaching was a great contrast to that of the scribes. They seem to have contented themselves with quoting authorities. Unless they could back up their views by some great name, they were not sure about their doctrines. It was a prodigious use of commentators which they indulged in. But Jesus came and preached what he himself knew as a matter of certainty. There was a directness and "dead certainty" about his utterances which struck all the hearers as something new. And surely it is on this line that preachers still will find the path of safety. What we preach ought to be experience, the verities of our own spiritual life. And this preaching of certainties had its due effect in spiritual power. The word went home to the hearers' hearts—they had never heard truth so clearly presented before ; and so they were lost in wonder and astonishment. The secret of success lies here. It is not by radiating a series of uncertainties upon men ; it is not by bolstering men up in "honest doubt" and leaving them in the haze, that men will be won to what is high and holy. It is by telling them what we have learned ourselves—the glorious certainties of spiritual experience. Like the psalmist, we must gather men around us to tell them what God has done for our souls. "Out of the abundance of the heart the mouth speaketh," and speaketh well !

II. Our Lord demonstrated his power over devils as well as over men. (Vers. 33—37.) In the synagogue there happened to be an unfortunate man possessed by what is called an "unclean devil;" his "inspirations" from this unhappy source being perhaps of a lustful and sensual character. The possession of men by demons was a struggle upon the diabolical spirit's part for a physical instrument to bring him into relations with the sensible and material world. The humanity of the man became the slave or hack of the demon. He used the man's voice to utter his unholy thoughts, and reduced the poor subject to utter wretchedness. The presence of the holy Saviour aroused the demon's fears. He saw that his hour of judgment had come ; and so, as a last resort, he tried to injure the reputation of Jesus by bearing witness to his holy character. There are some people from whom it is not desirable to hold certificates or receive testimonials. And in this appeal to Jesus he speaks for the man as well as for himself, as if he had a commission to do so. "Let us alone ; what have we to do with thee, Jesus of Nazareth? Art thou come to destroy us?" etc. We have thus set before us : 1. The *separating power of sin.* The fellowship of the holy is not desired. 2. The *inherent dread of judgment.* The demon felt he deserved destruction. 3. The *overweening sense of success in sin.* The demon imagined that the poor possessed one would be involved in his own destruction. And now Jesus first *silences* the spirit, indicating that he desires no such witnesses ; and, secondly, commands him to come out of the possessed one. In this way the demon is bidden back to that spiritual realm which he seemed so anxious to escape. There is nothing for it but to obey Christ. In doing so, however, he does his *worst* upon the poor possessed one ; he throws him down, and to all appearance has once more the mastery over his prey. It is a last and unsuccessful effort. The man is found to have come unscathed through the ordeal. The restoration of human nature to freedom from demoniacal temptation is one great object of the Saviour's work. Clothing men in their right mind again, enabling them to think and act for themselves, and to resist the subtle temptations to impurity and sin,—this is a glorious function of the Holy One of God! The result of the miracle was the recognition of Jesus as the Sovereign of that spiritual world below man, from which he is liable to assault. His mighty word not only controlled human hearts, but extended to demons too. They had to obey his commands, no matter how loath they might be to do so. And this should comfort us in our temptations.

III. Our Lord carries on in Peter's household the healing work which he had exercised in the public congregation. (Vers. 38, 39.) Peter's mother-in-law was ill of a great fever ; and when he was come in they besought him for her. We are thus taught that our Lord likes to be asked for the blessings he is so ready to afford. Prayer is the *natural* cry of need, or of intercession, to One who is able to meet man's difficulties and bless him. And so our Lord, being besought, goes to the patient, rebukes the fever, takes her by the hand, and lo! it leaves her ; and she rose to the activities of health again. Her ministration showed the immediate and complete character of the cure, and also the gratitude which should characterize one who is saved by Jesus. And are we not thus taught that we should bring our fevered souls to Jesus as the great Physician? He can take away the fever instantaneously. There is nothing so wonderful as the way in which we regain spiritual health at the throne of grace. But let us see to it that it leads to ministration. He gives us back our health that we may use it for his glory and the benefit of those about us.

IV. Our Lord is next seen taking diseases and possessed ones by wholesale, and healing them. (Vers. 40, 41.) At sunset, when the sabbath ended, and when under the friendly shades of night the poor sick and deformed ones could conveniently be brought to him, he finds an immense opportunity confronting him. Peter's house is turned into a consulting hospital, and, like famous physicians, he is well-nigh overwhelmed with work. Possessed ones are also brought to him ; and the demons adopt the same plan as the one noticed already—they begin to testify to his Messiahship and Sonship. This mass of suffering humanity he takes in hand, and with infallible certainty heals them every one. He accomplishes the healing, too, in the most *sympathetic* fashion, laying his tender hand on each, and conveying through contact the needful blessing. It was truly "a night much to be remembered" by all these sons and daughters of affliction whom Jesus thus lovingly healed! As for the demons, on the other hand, they receive nothing from him but rebuke. He will not have their testimony to his nature or his mission. At the same time, he shows his sovereignty over them in dooming them to silence and solitude, at least so far as possessing men was concerned.

V. OUR LORD SHOWS US HIS NEED OF RETIREMENT AFTER LABOUR, AND ALSO WHAT HIS GREAT COMMISSION WAS. (Vers. 42—44.) After these mighty works he feels the need of retirement to commune with God, and keep his soul in proper tune for further work. If Jesus felt the need of prayer, how presumptuous in minor minds to excuse themselves from it! They seem to have given him an invitation to settle in Capernaum. And if he had, he would have had a famous physician's practice, doors besieged from morning to night, and no time for any other work. Hence he resolved to itinerate rather than settle down. His wandering from place to place secured him from overwork of a purely *physical* character, and enabled him to be the *Missionary* he was meant to be. It is an interesting question why he did not make Palestine a healthful land from end to end. He might have organized deputations and sought out all the sick, and made the land free from all disease and suffering. But while he healed all who came or were brought to him, and sent disciples forth on similar errands, he did not undertake this wholesale cure. And two answers may be given in the way of valid reason about it. In the first place, the people did not deserve such a blessing, and would not likely have been the better for it. A world of sinful men would not be improved if they were all made and kept healthy men. Health of soul and perfect health of body are to synchronize in the great future which lies before us. But secondly, if he had undertaken this *physical* work, he would have lost his opportunities of *purely spiritual* work, the preaching of the gospel, for which more especially he had come. Hence we must admire his resolve to be an itinerant Missionary rather than a settled and famous Physician. Preaching is really the highest work of man, if it is done conscientiously. The sphere is spiritual, and the results are for evermore. It is well to magnify the office as magnified by the Master.—R. M. E.

EXPOSITION.

CHAPTER V.

When St. Luke compiled his Gospel, many of the circumstances connected with the early relations of the leaders of Christianity with their Founder were so well known, and had been so often repeated, that it seemed unnecessary to rehearse them afresh; hence to us the seeming abruptness of the introduction of Simon (Peter), James, and John in the scene now about to be related. In the preceding, the healing of Simon's wife's mother of a great fever is related without any explanation, as though Simon Peter's connection with the Lord was a fact too well known to require any comment or explanation.

The association of Jesus and these chosen men seems to have commenced as follows: Simon (Peter) and his brother Andrew (sons of Jona), John and James (the sons of Zebedee and Salome), belonged to fisher families dwelling on the banks of the Lake of Gennesaret. They seemed to have been fast friends, at times even partners in their occupation. Sharers with many others of

the youth of Israel of their time, in a passionate hope that the hour of the long-promised deliverance from the yoke of their foreign oppressors was at hand, the four became disciples of the Baptist, and by him they were referred to Jesus, who in mysterious but exalted terms was pointed out by the great desert preacher, John, as "the Lamb of God," the Glorious, the Expected One (John i. 35—43). They joined the Master at the bidding of John, and for a time were associated with him. Still at first they were only with him apparently at times, leaving him and returning to their homes and occupations, waiting for some definite and imperative summons to join his cause permanently. The summons in question is related in this chapter. The time was now come when the Lord deemed it fitting that he should surround himself with a company of disciples or pupils who should be constant witnesses of his works, hearers of his words, and thus be trained up for the great task of continuing his mission when he should have returned to his home in heaven.

We read these Gospels as the story of the Master's life often without thinking how much of that life is never told. After all, we only possess a few representative incidents— the events which the twelve and their first friends had selected as the themes of their sermons and discourses in Jerusalem, Corinth, Ephesus, Rome, and the great centres of early Christian activity. Here, after the story of one sabbath day's blessed toil in Capernaum, follows a sentence which passes over, in a word or two, many days of quiet teaching in populous towns and villages of the once rich Galilee, and then the evangelist gives us with some detail the account of a morning by the lake, where he preached from a boat to the crowds on the shore, and then went out a-fishing, and, after the fishing, bade the fishermen leave all and come with him, and he would give them a new work.

Ver. 1.—**And it came to pass, that, as the people pressed upon him to hear the word of God.** His fame as a great Teacher was evidently now firmly established. If it were known that he intended speaking in public, a crowd of listeners would gather quickly round him, whether in the synagogues, or by the lake-shore, or in the market-place. **He stood by the Lake of Gennesaret.** On this occasion, as he taught by the quiet lake waters, the throng was so great that he borrowed the fishing-boat of one of his friends, and, just pushing out from the shore, spoke to the multitude from the little craft as it rocked on the wavelets of the lake. Dean Stanley calls it " the most sacred sheet of water which the earth contains." The rabbinical derivation is interesting: " *Gannesarim*, garden of princes ; " but it is more probable that *Gennesaret* is but a reproduction of the old Hebrew name *Chinneroth* (Josh. xii. 3), so called from its harplike shape. It is a beautiful sheet of water, twelve or thirteen miles long and nearly seven broad at one portion of the lake. The Jordan flows through it. In our Lord's time it was surrounded by the richest and most populous district of the Holy Land; large and flourishing towns were built along its shores. Capernaum, as has been said, was the junction of the great roads leading from Syria and the far East to the Mediterranean on the west, and Jerusalem and Egypt on the south. The lake was famous for its fish, and was crowded with all descriptions of craft. The whole scene is now changed. Scarcely a rude boat is ever seen on the blue silent waters. Desolate ruins fringe the deserted shores, with here and there a

crumbling mud village, inhabited by the poorest and least enterprising of peasants, so sadly changed is this beautiful and wealthy district, which the rabbis used to love to speak of as the one among the seven seas of Canaan which God had reserved for himself.

Ver. 3.—**And he sat down,** as in the synagogue of Capernaum—the usual attitude of the Jewish preachers.

Ver. 4.—**And let down your nets for a draught.** Not necessarily a miraculous draught ; it was probably a supernatural knowledge which the Lord had of a shoal of fish to be found in the spot indicated by him to the fishermen. Tristram (' Natural History of the Bible') says, " The thickness of the shoals of fish is almost incredible to any one who has not witnessed them. They often cover an area of more than an acre, and when the fish move slowly forward in a mass, and are rising out of the water, they are packed so close together that it appears as if a heavy rain was beating down on the surface of the water."

Ver. 5.—**Master.** The word in the original so rendered is not *Rabbi*, as in the other Gospels, but ἐπιστάτα, Teacher. The Jewish term would not have been understood by the Gentile reader for whom the story was especially intended.

Ver. 6.—**And their net brake.** Augustine beautifully compares the broken and torn net to *the Church that now is*, full of divisions and rents ; the net unrent and untorn will be the *Church of the future*, which will know no schisms.

Ver. 10.—**Fear not.** A feeling of intense overpowering awe on a sudden came on Simon after listening to the words and seeing this last act of power which so closely affected him. The very fish of his native lake, then, were subject to this strange holy Man ! This was no mortal, thought the fisherman, and he fell at the Master's feet. " Finding as it does its parallel in almost all manifestations of a Divine or even an angelic presence, it (this awful fear) must be owned to contain a mighty, because an instructive, witness for the sinfulness of man's nature, out of which it comes to pass that any near revelation from the heavenly world fills the children of men, even the holiest among them, with terror and amazement, yea, sometimes with the expectation of death itself" (Archbishop Trench, ' Introduction to the Epistles to the Seven Churches'). The same " Fear not " (" Be not afraid ") was uttered on like occasions to Isaiah (vi. 7), to Daniel (x. 12), and several times during the earthly ministry was said to the disciples, and for the last time the reassuring words were spoken by the Redeemer after the Ascension to his own dear follower, John, who could

not bear the sight of the glorious majesty
of his risen Lord. **Thou shalt catch men.**
The imagery contained in these words of
the Master to his fishermen-followers was,
of course, drawn from the late scene. Their
failure in catching fish, their Teacher's
marvellous success, the net bursting with
the great catch of silvery fish; the Lord's
strange prophetic words which accompanied
their call to his service,—all would in after-
years often come up before the disciples in
their hours of alternating failure and success
in the mighty task he had set them to do.
The great Fisherman, Christ; his imitators
and servants, fishers; the world of men
pictured as fish,—were ever favourite images
for the pencil, the graving tool, and the pen
of the Christian artist and writer of the
first ages of the faith. One of the earliest
extant hymns, for instance, of the Church,
by Clement of Alexandria, dwells on the
image. The words are addressed to Christ—

" Fisher of men, the blest,
Out of the world's unrest,
Out of sin's troubled sea,
Taking us, Lord, to thee;
Out of the waves of strife
With bait of blissful life;
Drawing thy nets to shore,
With choicest fish, good store."
(*Hymn of Clement of Alexandria.*)

The favourite Christian monogram of the
fish, carved on so many tombs in the Catacombs, belongs to the same imagery—the
ιχθυς

ιησους χριστος θεου υιος σωτηρ
ι   χ   θ   υ   σ

Vers. 12—16.—*The leper is healed in a
certain city.*

Ver. 12.—When he was in a certain city.
From the scene in the boat on the lake with
the fishermen, Luke abruptly passes to
another memorable incident which took
place probably soon after—memorable because it is the first recorded instance of
Jesus' contact with that most terrible of
earthly maladies, leprosy. The certain
city was probably the town of *Hattim*, for
we read in St. Matthew that the famous cure
took place as the Lord was coming down
from the mount of Beatitudes. (This will
be spoken of in its place in ch. vi.) **Behold
a man full of leprosy.** The expression
"behold" reproduces exactly the scene as
the eye-witness remembered it. There were
many apparently with the Master on that
occasion; but following him, suddenly, as he
went on before the crowd, one of those ghastly
victims of the frightful disease stood before
him, apparently having eluded observation,
for they were not allowed to appear in the
ordinary haunts of men. The unhappy man
fell down and knelt before the great Physi-

cian, of whom he may have heard so much,
and asks him to exercise his mighty power
on the dread malady which was eating away
his life. The leper evidently had no doubt
whatever of the *power* of Jesus; he was only
anxious as to whether he had the *will* to
cure him. The whole question respecting
the exact nature of the disease is a vexed
one. The word has been used with varying
extent of meaning. As far as we can gather,
the disease in its worst form seems to have
been a progressive decay arising from the
poisoning of the blood. The face and different members of the body were attacked
and gradually destroyed, till the sufferer
became a hideous spectacle, and literally
fell to pieces. It is much disputed whether
or not the malady in any of its varied developments and stages was contagious. The
strict separation which in well-nigh all
forms of the disease was rigidly insisted on
would seem at all events to point to the
conclusion that, in the popular estimation, it
certainly was so; some phases of the malady,
however, appear to have been considered as
perfectly free from contagious effect—for
instance, Naaman, the captain of the host
of Syria, was a leper. It is not conceivable
that one who was infected with so grave a
malady, considered incurable, would, if contagious, have been permitted to have exercised a function which would have brought
him into constant contact with masses of his
fellow-countrymen. These cases, however,
were apparently few in number, and those
afflicted with what was usually called
leprosy were rigidly separated from their
fellows, not only to dwell apart, but positively
forbidden to approach the dwellings of men.
In the Egyptian legends of the Exodus,
the Israelites were said to have been expelled *because they were lepers.*

**Ver. 13.—And he put forth his hand, and
touched him, saying, I will: be thou clean.
And immediately the leprosy departed from
him.** St. Mark adds here, "being touched
with compassion." The Redeemer, at the
sight of the man's awful wretchedness—wasting away, shunned by all men, dragging on a
hopeless, aimless, weary life—in his Divine
pity, with a sudden impulse tosses aside all
considerations of ceremonial uncleanness or
contagion, and lays his hand on the miserable sufferer from whom all shrank, with
his word of power exclaimed, "I will: be
thou clean." St. Ambrose writes here how
"Jesus, because he is the Lord of the Law,
does not obey the Law, but makes the Law."
"Here Jesus obeys that Divine eternal law
of compassion, in its sudden impulse, which
is older and grander than the written Law"
(Farrar). It is observable that in these sudden cases, in which the common brotherhood
of man was involved, the nobler spirits of

Israel ever rose above all consideration of law and custom, and, putting aside all legal, orthodox restriction, obeyed at once the sovereign dictates of the heart. So Elijah and Elisha, those true saints of God, shrank not from touching the dead.

Ver. 14.—**And he charged him to tell no man.** We find this desire of Jesus to check publicity after he had worked one of his great works, especially in the earlier part of his ministry. Chrysostom attributes this to the Master's regard for the one who had been healed, desiring that his gratitude to God for the mercy vouchsafed to him should not be frittered away in words, in idle talk with curious persons. It is, however, more likely that the Master wished to stem rather than to fan the tide of popularity which such mighty works would be sure to excite among the people. What he determined to check was a false and mistaken desire among the people to make him king.

Ver. 15.—**But so much the more went there a fame abroad of him: and great multitudes came together to hear, and to be healed by him of their infirmities.** It is evident that his wishes and commands were neglected, possibly out of a mistaken feeling of gratitude. The result was that his work of teaching was hindered by the crowds who resorted to him at once as a Physician of extraordinary power. But he had graver and much more important work before him than even the blessed task of relieving suffering. So he withdrew himself, says our evangelist, and again spent a short season in solitude and prayer.

Vers. 17—26.—*The healing of the paralyzed man.*

Ver. 17.—**And it came to pass on a certain day, as he was teaching, that there were Pharisees and doctors of the Law sitting by, which were come out of every town of Galilee, and Judæa, and Jerusalem.** Again an interval of time. The fame of the new Teacher had spread rapidly. One day, some time after the events told in the last section, the Master was sitting in the house apparently of some one of consideration in Capernaum, and, as usual, was teaching. Grouped round him were a different audience to the traders and fishermen of the lake-city; prominent men of the leading religious party in the state, not only from Galilee, but from Jerusalem and other Judæan cities, such as Hebron, as well as learned doctors of the Law. These had been drawn from curiosity, some doubtless by higher motives, to hear for themselves the teaching of this now famous Nazarene Carpenter. These do not appear to have been actuated with the jealous malignity of some of those later deputations from the Jerusalem Sanhe-

drin and schools. The house was thronged within and the crowd pressed round the doors. In the course of the quiet teaching, took place the incident which gave rise to one of the Lord's great sayings—an utterance so important that it evidently had been chosen by the apostles as a frequent theme or text in the preaching of the first days.

Vers. 18, 19.—**And, behold, men brought in a bed a man which was taken with a palsy: and they sought means to bring him in, and to lay him before him. And when they could not find by what way they might bring him in because of the multitude, they went upon the house-top, and let him down through the tiling with his couch into the midst before Jesus.** So far there was nothing very unusual in the incident. These healings must have been of common occurrence with our Lord. The poor sufferer and his friends, intensely anxious for an interview with One whom they justly regarded as the great Physician, were rightly confident that they had but to see the Master, to state their case, and to receive the blessing which they sought. On this occasion it seemed impossible to get at the merciful Healer. Now or never, they thought. He might, as he had done before, withdraw himself. The chance might never recur. So they accomplished their purpose in the way narrated by the evangelist. It was evidently nothing very extraordinary—an ingenious device, nothing more; only by it the friends of the sufferer showed that they were intensely in earnest, that they were confident that the Master had both the power and the will to do what they wanted. Much has been written on the device employed on this occasion by the friends of the paralytic. Delitzsch, in his 'A Day at Capernaum,' graphically describes what must have taken place. Two bearers ascend the roof by a ladder, and by means of cords they draw up by the same way the sick man after them, assisted by two other bearers. In the middle of the terrace was a square place, open in summer to give light and air to the house, but closed with tiles during the rainy season. Having opened this passage, the bearers let down the sick man into the large inner court immediately below, where Jesus was teaching, near the cistern fixed as usual in this court. The trap-stairs, which led down from the terrace into the court, would have been too narrow for their use, and would not have taken them into the court, but into the apartments which overlooked it from all sides.

Ver. 20.—**And when he saw their faith, he said unto him, Man, thy sins are forgiven thee.** For a moment the great Physician gave place to the Heart-reader; and the Lord spoke those strange, grand words to give comfort and peace to the suffering, silent, sick man. Jesus read what was in the heart of the poor paralytic; his sins distressed him more than his malady; very possibly the sad infirmity had been brought about by his old dissolute life. The soul, then, must be healed first. It was for *this*, we believe, that the story of the man taken with the palsy was told and retold by the first Christian preachers, and so found a place in the three Gospel narratives—this lofty claim of the Master to forgive sins; a claim so grandly supported by a miraculous act done in the open daylight in the presence of the people.

Ver. 21.—**And the scribes and the Pharisees began to reason, saying, Who is this which speaketh blasphemies? Who can forgive sins, but God alone?** It is very probable that some of those who stood by, had already, at Jerusalem, witnessed by the Bethesda Pool a wonder-work done by the same Jesus on the person of an impotent man lying there waiting for the troubling of the water (John v. 5, 9), and had taken part there in an angry expostulation with the Wonder-worker, who on that occasion, in his words, "made himself equal with God" (John v. 18). We know (see ver. 17) that some of the Jerusalem scribes were present that day in the Capernaum house. Again, thought these learned Jews, "this strange Man is uttering his dread blasphemies, but *now* in even more plain terms than *there*."

Ver. 23.—**Whether is easier, to say, Thy sins be forgiven thee; or to say, Rise up and walk?** The Heart-reader hears, perhaps, the murmur as it runs round the circle, and grasping in a moment all that was in the angry hearts of these men, said aloud, that all might hear, some such words as these, "See now what I am about to do. You, in your dim short-sighted wisdom, think my forgiving this poor repentant sinner his dark past, is but an empty, meaningless form of words. See now whether what I am about to do further for him is an empty meaningless boon."

Vers. 24, 25.—**That ye may know that the Son of man hath power upon earth to forgive sins, (he said unto the sick of the palsy,) I say unto thee, Arise, and take up thy couch, and go into thine house. And immediately he rose up before them, and took up that whereon he lay, and departed to his own house, glorifying God.** The lookers-on, the curious, the cavillers, the friendly, too, as the unfriendly, who crowded that Capernaum house, could not see with their eyes the Redeemer's remission of the palsied man's sins. The sufferer alone was conscious that the great burden which pressed on his soul was removed at the Master's word. But all could see the miracle which

followed. Any one of those present, had he dared, might have uttered the solemn absolution. None but he could surely risk, as he risked, such words which followed, and which challenged an instant and visible fulfilment. It was a strange, great claim the Master made that day, and we may be sure it and the mighty sign which followed sank deep into many a heart. We see why the memory of this day's work was treasured up so faithfully. *He took up that whereon he lay.* This could easily have been done. The bed or pallet would be nothing but a light portable framework covered with a blanket.

Ver. 26.—**We have seen strange things to-day.** The strange things (παράδοξα) alluded especially to the miracle which, as it were, solemnly authenticated the sublime claim to forgiveness of sins on the part of Jesus.

Vers. 27—29.—*The call of Levi (Matthew the publican), and the feast that followed.*

Ver. 27.—**And after these things he went forth, and saw a publican, named Levi, sitting at the receipt of custom: and he said unto him, Follow me.** Capernaum, as has been already noticed, had become, owing to its situation, a commercial centre of no small importance. It was on the great highway from the interior of Asia, and from Damascus to the seaboard Mediterranean cities, to Jerusalem, and to Egypt. The custom-house of Capernaum and the office of inland revenue there would naturally be under the control of officials of some importance. The local trade on the lake, too, we know at that period was very large. It has been frequently asked—What specially induced our Lord to select as one of his inner circle a man whose life-work was so hateful and unpopular to the Jewish people generally? why did he include in the twelve one who, from the nature of his detested office, had lost religious caste among the Jews, and who was compelled to consort with sinners, Gentiles, and persons who were considered, either from their birth or life and associations, outside the pale of the chosen people? Various replies to this question have been suggested, such as—by this open act he threw down the gauntlet to all that powerful Pharisee class who were beginning to suspect and to mistake his teaching and liberalism. Or was his apparently strange choice dictated by a simple desire to have, in the inner circle of his devoted friends, a business man—one who could manage the affairs and regulate the economy of the little growing society? but this seems to have been done by Judas; or was it simply done in obedience to a sudden impulse from on High? None of these seems satisfactory. Surely another motive, and that a deeper and a nobler one, suggested this enrolment of the despised publican in that glorious company of apostles. The Lord was determined to show, by this choice of his, that in his eyes all callings were equally honourable, all ways of life might lead to the city of the blessed. Never would the work ennoble the man, but only the way in which the work was done. The Baptist, as we have seen, first taught this Divine liberalism. The Baptist's Lord placed his seal of approval upon his servant's teaching by such acts as the calling of Matthew the publican, and feasting in his house with publicans and sinners.

Ver. 28.—**He left all, rose up, and followed him.** No doubt a hard and difficult bit of self-renunciation. He, at the bidding of the homeless, landless Teacher, gave up his lucrative employment, sacrificing all his life of promotion, of future wealth and position, exposing himself, doubtless, to sneers and calumny. With great truth could he re-echo his friend Peter's words, " Lo, *we* have left all, and followed thee."

Ver. 29.—**And Levi made him a great feast in his own house.** There is no doubt that this Levi was the same person as Matthew the publican (subsequently the evangelist), whose calling under precisely similar circumstances is related in the First Gospel (Matt. x.; and see Mark ii.). The name Matthew, " gift of God," was probably given to him, as that of Peter (or Cephas, " a rock ") was bestowed on Simon, after his association with Jesus. The words used, " a great feast," a great company, plainly indicate that Levi (Matthew) was a person of consideration and position. **And there was a great company of publicans and of others that sat down with them.** The great company was owing to the fact that the publicans and their friends, moved by the kindness and friendship of the new Teacher, assembled at the feast in numbers out of respect to him ; or, more likely, the assemblage was owing to the effort of Levi (Matthew) to bring into friendly relations his associates and friends and the new Master, for whose sake he had given up everything.

Ver. 30.—**But their scribes and Pharisees murmured against his disciples.** Many of the older authorities here omit " their " (αὐτῶν) before " scribes." The older authorities vary slightly in the position of the words here. The best reading and translation would give, " The Pharisees and the scribes among them "—" among them," that is, among the Capernaïtes ; in other words, " They among them who were Pharisees and scribes." These scribes (Hebrew, *sopherim*), under this appellation, first appear after the Exile. Their occupation was to copy and to expound the Law. They were

the recognized teachers of the Jews, and seem to have succeeded that great and influential class or order, the " sons of the prophets," originally founded by Samuel. These " sons of the prophets " are repeatedly mentioned in the books of the Old Testament which treat of the kingdoms of Israel and Judah. The scribes were succeeded, in the year 300 B.C., by the *tanaim* (repeaters), under which name the scribes were officially, though apparently not popularly, known until A.D. 220, after which date these scribes were termed *amoraim*. The Talmud (Mishna and Gemara) may be said to have been the work of this great and enduring teacher order. The Talmud was finally closed in A.D. 490, by Rabbina Abina, the last of the amoraim. **Why do ye eat and drink with publicans and sinners ?**

Vers. 31, 32.—**And Jesus answering said unto them, They that are whole need not a physician ; but they that are sick. I came not to call the righteous, but sinners to repentance.** This was one of those sayings of the Lord which sank very deep into the hearts of the hearers. All the three, Matthew, Mark, and Luke, repeat it with very slight variations ; it was evidently a favourite theme with the great first teachers who followed Christ. It has borne rich fruit in the Master's Church ; for this vindication of Jesus of his conduct in going so often into the society of the moral waifs and strays of the population has been the real " foundation of all those philanthropic movements which enlist the upper classes of society in the blessed work of bending down to meet in love the lower classes, so that the snapped circle of humanity may be restored ; it is the philosophy in a nutshell of all home and missionary operations " (Dr. Morrison, on Mark ii. 17).

Vers. 33—39.—*The teaching of the Lord concerning fasting.*

Ver. 33.—**And they said unto him, Why do the disciples of John fast often, and make prayers, and likewise** the disciples of **the Pharisees ; but thine eat and drink ?** We learn from the parallel passage in St. Mark that " they " who asked the Lord this question were the disciples of John the Baptist and the Pharisees, who united on this occasion. These disciples of John do not seem at first to have regarded Jesus with altogether friendly feelings. Such a jealousy was only too natural, and the rigid, unbending truthfulness of the evangelists compelled them to tell the story of the way the early foundations of the truth were laid without concealment of error or mistake. The Baptist himself practised the sternest asceticism, and required doubtless of his nearest followers that they should imitate his example. The Lord's way of life, his presence at feastings and merry-makings, his consorting with publicans, his choice of one of them as his disciple and friend, no doubt surprised and disturbed not a few of the followers of John ; hence such a question as the one we are now considering, and such a querulous complaining as we hear of in the Fourth Gospel (iii. 25, 26). The practice of fasting among the Jews was as follows : In the Law of Moses only one appointed fast in the year was enjoined—that on the solemn Day of Atonement (Lev. xvi. 29 ; Numb. xxix. 7). After the Exile the *one* fast was increased to *four*. But the prophets gave no sanction to this added ritual (see Zech. vii. 1—12 ; viii. 19). In the time of our Lord, rigid Jews used to fast twice a week (ch. xviii. 12)—on Monday and Friday (the day on which, according to tradition, Moses went up Mount Sinai). It is evident that our Lord himself never observed or even approved of these fasts of the Pharisee sect. In the well-known and often-quoted passages, Matt. xvii. 21 ; Mark ix. 29 ; Acts x. 30 ; 1 Cor. vii. 5—in many of the older authorities, *the word " fasting" does not occur at all.* In the Revised Version in each of these instances "fasting" does not appear in the new text. While, then, we must un-hesitatingly conclude that fasting is no rite commanded by the Blessed One, still the Church has practised it with signal advantage and profit on certain solemn occasions ; but it must ever proceed from the impulse of the sorrow-stricken heart, it must be no penance or duty imposed by authority, least of all must it be regarded as pleasing in the eye of the Almighty, or in any sense a substitute for the practice of the higher virtues really loved of God—justice, mercy, and truth.

Vers. 34, 35.—**And he said unto them, Can ye make the children of the bride-chamber fast, while the bridegroom is with them ? But the days will come, when the bridegroom shall be taken away from them, and then shall they fast in those days.** On this reply of the Lord Jesus Godet very beautifully writes, " In the midst of this feast of publicans, the heart of Jesus is overflowing with joy ; it is one of the hours when his earthly life seems to his feeling like a marriage-day. But suddenly his countenance becomes overcast : the shadow of a painful vision passes across his brow : 'The days will come,' . . . said he, in a solemn tone. At the close of this nuptial week, the Bridegroom himself will be suddenly smitten and cut off ; then will come the time of fasting for those who to-day are rejoicing ; there will be no necessity to enjoin it. In this striking and poetic answer Jesus evidently announces his violent death." The imagery of the bridegroom is

drawn from Hos. ii. 19, 20, and perhaps also from the more mystical Scripture, Ps. xlv. and the Song of Songs. Jesus here clearly regards himself as the Christ, as identical with the long looked-for Divine Deliverer ; but at this comparatively early stage of his public career he was fully conscious that in his Person, with the triumphant would be joined the suffering Messiah. The word rendered " shall be taken away from (them)," ἀπαρθῇ, only occurs here in the New Testament ; it points evidently to a death of violence. While the intimation given to Nicodemus (John iii. 14) was the first *private*, so this seems to have been the first *public* announcement of the last scene of the earth-life.

Ver. 36.—**And he spake also a parable unto them ; No man putteth a piece of a new garment upon an old ; if otherwise, then both the new maketh a rent, and the piece that was taken out of the new agreeth not with the old.** Oriental teaching has ever delighted in using these vivid and picturesque metaphors and parables taken from the everyday life of the people ; here the reference is, of course, to the question put by the Pharisees and John's disciples respecting fasting. This and the following little parable, and the curious simile which he added directly after, is part of the Lord's answer to his questioners. They charged him in their query with throwing (by the neglect of fasting) a slur on the time-honoured practices and observances of the most religious men of Israel. His reply acknowledged that, as far as he was concerned, they were right. He had quietly put aside the rigidly appointed fasts and other ceremonial rites by means of which the great Jewish teachers—to use their own expression—had put a hedge about the Law. They were right, too, in the conclusion they had come to, implied but not expressed, in their evidently hostile questioning. His *was* a totally new form of the old Hebrew religion—new altogether in the grandeur of its conception and in the breadth of its influence. His was a totally new garment that he was about to offer to the people ; now to patch up the beautiful new work with the old one would be surely to mar both. In the older authorities the text is slightly longer and more vivid than the text from which our own more corrupt Authorized Version was translated. It would run thus : " No one rending a patch from a new garment putteth it upon an old garment."

Vers. 37, 38.—**And no man putteth new wine into old bottles ; else the new wine will burst the bottles, and be spilled, and the bottles shall perish. But new wine must be put into new bottles ; and both are preserved.** In these two verses the Greek words rendered "bottles" properly signify "wine - skins." These leathern bottles throughout Syria and Palestine are generally made of goat-skins. They are still of universal use; the simile of the "old bottles" refers to "wine-skins" old and frail, which had been long in use, and hence nearly worn out; such "skins," after long usage, are in the habit of getting seamed and cracked. (Farrar, in an elaborate excursus, urges that must, and not wine in the ordinary sense, i.e. the fermented juice of the grape, is signified in the parable here, grape-juice in the form of unfermented must being much used as a favourite drink in the East. This suggestion, although ingenious and interesting, does not seem necessary to explain the imagery used; it seems more natural to understand wine in its ordinary meaning.) The "new wine" here represents the teaching of Jesus in all its freshness, originality, and power, and the "wine-skins" the men who are to receive from the Master the great principle of his doctrine. Now, the recognized teachers in Israel, termed scribes and rabbis, or doctors of the Law, were wedded to the old interpretation of the Law—were hampered by traditions, sayings of the Fathers, elaborate ritual observances, prejudices, narrowness, bigotry. The vast collection of the Talmud, where wise words on the same page are crowded out with childish sayings, well represents the teaching of these scribes and rabbis. Never would Jesus entrust to these narrow and prejudiced representatives of a worn-out religious school his new, fresh, generous doctrines. It would indeed be pouring new wine into old, decayed, worn-out wine-vessels. The new wine must be deposited in new wine-skins. His doctrine must be entrusted to no rabbi of Israel, fettered by a thousand precedents, hampered by countless prejudices, but to simple unprejudiced men, who would just receive his teaching, and then pass it on pure and unadulterated to other simple, truthful souls—men earnest, loyal, devoted, like his fisherfriends of Gennesaret, or his publican-follower of Capernaum. He needs, as Godet well phrases it—changing, though, the imagery of Jesus—"fresh natures, new men . . . fair tablets on which his hand may write the characters of Divine truth, without coming across the old traces of a false human wisdom. 'God, I thank thee because thou hast hidden these things from the wise and prudent, and hast revealed them unto babes.'"

Ver. 39.—**No man also having drunk old wine straightway desireth new: for he saith, The old is better.** St. Luke alone of the first three evangelists who related in detail this most important reply of Jesus when the disciples of John and the Pharisees came to question him, adds this curious simile. The meaning of the parable-pictures of the new patch being sewn on an old garment, and of new wine being poured into worn-out, decaying wine-skins, was very plain. Pitilessly severe it would ring in the ears of men brought up in the old rabbinic Jewish schools. The two first evangelists, conscious of the truth of their Master's words, were content to leave the stern teaching, which pronounced the old state of things among the religious Jews as utterly worn-out, in all its naked severity. But Paul, under whose guidance we believe Luke wrote his Gospel, with that tender and considerate love which so beautifies the earnest and impassioned nature of the apostle of the Gentiles, knew that Jesus had added a few words to the two seemingly harsh parables; these he bade Luke carefully insert in his narrative. They contain what may be termed an almost playful apology for the slowness and reluctance of the men trained in the rabbinic schools, or even of the pupils of John the Baptist, to accept the new, broad, generous view of truth which he (Jesus) was putting forth —it was an apology for a slowness and reluctance, shading too often into unveiled dislike and open hostility. (What experience Paul and Luke must have had of this hostility!) The Master, in his Divine wisdom, knew how hard it was to forsake long-cherished prejudices. Time must be given, allowance must be made, harsh judgment must be deprecated. These men, trained in the old system, are here compared to guests who, after the banquet, are suddenly asked to change the old wine, mellowed by age, of which they have been drinking, for new sweet wine. This new wine seems, in those days, generally to have been considered preferable, but to men who had been drinking the old, age-softened vintage, the new would seem fiery and even harsh. The Greek word rendered in the Authorized Version "better," in the older authorities is positive instead of comparative. The translation should therefore run, "the old is good." The argument would be the same: Why change what we have been drinking for something new? surely the old wine is good? Such passages as Neh. x. 35; Prov. iii. 10; Hos. iv. 11; Hag. i. 11, bear out the above statement, that in those days, among the Jews of Syria, Palestine, and the adjacent countries, new sweet wine was a favourite beverage among wine-drinkers.

HOMILETICS.

Vers. 1—11.—*The call to be fishers of men.* Each of the missionary circuits of Christ has its special features of interest. The first of these circuits is distinguished by three miracles significant of his work as the Christ of God. Look at the miracle of the draught of fishes, with the narrative to which it is related, as a record illustrative first of *personal conversion*, and secondly of the *ministry of the New Testament.*

I. AN ILLUSTRATION OF PERSONAL CONVERSION. 1. *There is already a faith.* The four men whom the Lord calls had heard his voice on the banks of Jordan (John i. 35—43), and had followed him. They had journeyed with him in Judæa, and even, it would seem, had baptized in his Name. But, after the return of Jesus to Galilee from the Passover-keeping noticed in John v., they had gone back to their homes and their usual callings. They believed in him, but they did not realize the constraint of a supreme influence. They did not hold themselves as solemnly engaged to him. It was this engagement to be his, going where he went, and dwelling where he dwelt, which was the work of the day by the Lake of Gennesaret. Now, see in this a reminder that there may be a belief, sincere and true so far as it goes, which prepares for, but which is not, the faith unto salvation. It establishes a certain intellectual relation to Christ, but nothing more. The effectual call is still wanting—the call, *i.e.*, to an entire self-surrender, leaving all and following him. 2. *There is a sovereignty of grace in this call.* Of this sovereignty there is much to remind us in the passage under review. The great crowd is before the Teacher as he stands by the lake. Of the many boats drawn up on the beach, he selects two; of the two he chooses Simon's. Another evangelist reminds us that out of the multitude he saw two brethren, and again he saw other two brethren. He saw and he spoke; there is the look and there is the word. "The Lord looked on Gideon, and said, Go in this thy might." All that is done is done so easily. Almost a chance, it might be said. There is he, and there are they; he at his work, and they at theirs. It was no chance. It was Christ's opportunity; it was their opportunity. "Follow me!" is the command of his royalty. Such was he then, such is he still. In the crowd he individualizes. The soul found by him asks, "Whence knowest thou me?" He knows his sheep, and is known of them. He calleth his own sheep by name. 3. *There is an instant response.* Christ's call is "Now;" "To-day if ye will hear his voice." The answer is "Now;" "To-day;" "Lord, here am I; send me"—an unreserved, uncalculating surrender, body, soul, and spirit, to Jesus. The net is left, and, mark, the net that has just been or is just being cast into the sea—the net on which so much had been spent. Net and father too. He will not come with them. "Farewell, then; not less do we love you; but he is nearer than father and mother, and his word is, 'Follow me!'" This is conversion —the turning of the face of the life to the eternal Lord; the acceptance of God's Beloved, in the consciousness of acceptance in the Beloved; the election, as the mark towards which to press, of the calling of God in Christ Jesus. "Thy people offer themselves willingly in the day of thy power."

II. But, secondly, see in the miracle which follows A PICTURE OF THE TRUTH OF CHRISTIAN MINISTRY. 1. *A conviction which gives intensity to it.* Simon Peter, in the light of Jesus' presence and power, falls down at his knees, crying, "Depart from me; for I am a sinful man, O Lord!" The cry in its matter was foolish, but the spirit which prompted it was true. For the first time he had realized his own unworthiness. Had he not all but given Jesus up? Had he not lived a poor, dull, earthly life? Who was he, that the Lord of glory should have sat in his boat, that he should have been in any way identified with him? It is not the "depart" of a will that refuses the Lord; it is the self-loathing heart-cry, "Lord, I am vile; what canst thou see in me?" The same heart-cry as that which burst from Isaiah when he saw the Lord and heard the antiphon of the seraphim, "Woe is me! . . . for mine eyes have seen the King, the Lord of hosts." It is in such prostration that the lips are touched by the seraph, and the live coal is laid on them, and the "Fear not; thine iniquity is taken away" is spoken, and the hitherto unprophetic tongue is loosed. In the service which springs out of this humility there is always the sign of the baptism with the Holy Ghost and with fire. 2. *An incident which declares the secret of ministry.* (1) Its *inspiration.*

"Nevertheless at thy word." Is not the word sufficient? The improbabilities are all on the one side. The time for fishing has passed. All night, and nothing; what could there be in the morning? "Nevertheless at thy word." "Lord, what wilt thou have me to do?" (2) Its *power*, not in the worker and not in the net. The worker had utterly failed; a charm might have been attributed to the net—the net *was broken*. No; the sufficiency is of God. The one human condition is an absolute self-resignation.

> "There is a Stay—and we are strong;
> Our Master is at hand."

"Ye shall receive power, after that the Holy Ghost is come on you." (3) Its *nature*. The fisher caught, and lying on the shore. This is the parable. The work is to catch men. The power is with the Spirit; but he calls for the hand to cast the net. This fishing for men is a holy art, in which the fishers must be trained. When the three thousand were added at Pentecost, Simon saw again the miracle of Gennesaret, heard anew the loving voice, "Fear not; from henceforth thou shalt catch men." (4) The *co-operation to which it summons*. When Simon's boat is full, he and Andrew beckon to James and John, *their partners* in the other ship, to come and help them. Is not this a hint as to the evangelical alliance which should distinguish all in the various boats that fish the sea? Why should they ply their task as rivals? Why should they envy the good estate, the success of any boat? Where Christ can be clearly seen, where the power is manifestly his, forbid that narrow jealousies hinder the recognition of the work. Verily there is need for all willing-hearted workmen, and there is enough and to spare for all the boats. If only the aim were simply to catch men, not for the boat, but through the boat for the Lord, how different would be the aspect of Churches and ministries! 3. Finally, an action *which manifests the eternal loving-kindness*. To obey the Master is no thankless service. Leave the net; yes; but we follow him to whom the spacious sea belongs. Could the brethren whom he called doubt that he was able to make all grace abound always in all things? Have not we the certainty that there is a love which sees us as

> "We watch our nets alone
> In drenching spray, and driving shower,
> And hear the night-bird's moan"?

We toil; let us ask our hearts if they have been satisfied. How many confess, even in the midst of abundance, that the toil has been only "vanity, and a striving after wind"! Nay; but let Christ enter the life, let him be the Leader and Commander, let him indicate whether the net should be cast; then shall the emptiness be filled out of an infinite fulness.

Vers. 12—26.—*The power present to heal.* In the setting forth of facts, there is another principle of guidance than chronology. We may group them around some thoughts with the view of illustrating the meaning and scope of the thought. On this principle let us regard the events related from the twelfth verse to the twenty-sixth. What they evidence is the power of the Lord that was working in Jesus as a power of healing. Strange, blessed things we shall see to-day.

I. THE WORK OF SALVATION AS REALIZED IN THE LEPER. (Vers. 12—14.) He is "full of leprosy," a mass of corruption, dying bit by bit. Notice the cry of this miserable outcast. When the father of the epileptic child met the Lord on his descent from the Mount of Transfiguration, the voice of his agony was, "If thou canst do anything, have mercy on us and help us." Jesus replied, "If thou canst believe, all things are possible to him that believeth." He had not yet got to the mountain of faith, and the father says with tears, "Lord, I believe; but oh, help me to that mountain-height, help thou mine unbelief." This wretched leper is already on the mountain height. It is not, "If thou canst," but "If thou wilt." The Jewish proverb was, "As God sends the leprosy, so God alone can heal it." God is in this Jesus; therefore he can. Such was the logic. How he had seen the secret of the Lord, we do not know; but the trust was his—it had been sown into his heart in the urgency of his need. Now, mark the response. Sometimes the Lord seems to tarry. But in this case the way is quite ready for the blessing. "We are never told," says Dr. Farrar, "that there was a

moment's pause when a leper cried to him." "If thou wilt." "I will." And *the touch.*
To touch a leper was an infraction of law. He had to withdraw into the wilderness
immediately afterwards. He did not wish to provoke any violent opposition. But he
broke the ceremonial law at the demand of a higher law—the law whose source is
the Divine compassion, and whose agent is the power present to heal. The foul body
could not pollute the hand; but the hand of the Infinite Purity could cleanse the foul
body. "Be thou clean. And immediately the leprosy departed from him." How
wonderfully this strange thing brings out what is characteristic of the Saviour in his
thoughts and ways to the sinner! None is beyond the reach of the love that could bid
away at once and for ever that leprosy. No cry can escape the ear of a love that has
the answering "I will" ready for the praying "If thou wilt." We have a High Priest
who has touched our sin in its exceeding sinfulness. For ever and ever there stands
the pledge of the world's Healer "I will: be thou clean."

II. But see THE SAME WORK REALIZED IN "THE MAN THAT WAS PALSIED." The
time is "one of those days that he was teaching." A crowd has gathered so great
that "there is no room to receive them, no, not so much as about the door." In this
crowd there are Pharisees and doctors of the Law sitting by. Significantly it is added,
"The power of the Lord was present to heal." A notable instance of this power is
supplied; its occasion being the letting down of the pallet-bed, on which was laid the
paralytic, through the tiles into the midst of the crowd before Jesus. There is no
resisting of such faith. Seeing it, the Healer says—what? "Man, thy sins are forgiven
thee." Now, as to this fulfilment of the imperial "I will," which proceeds from the
compassion of the Lord, remark: 1. *The work which represents the supreme Saviour—
blessing.* "That ye may know that the Son of man hath power on earth to forgive
sins." He will listen to the appeal made in behalf of the palsied man; but there is a
palsy hidden and spiritual with which first he must deal, for until it is dealt with there
can be no effectual healing. Yes; the true healing begins within. "Create a clean
heart." And the point at which the Redeemer lays hold of us is the need of forgiveness.
This action of Christ is the first in which he makes himself fully known, the first in
which his spiritual authority is declared. And from this moment the organized opposition of scribe and Pharisee dates. "His kingdom ruleth over all." All agencies of
relief and kindness are his, and are to be used in his name; but his kingdom is the
kingdom of heaven to all believers, because the Son of man has power on earth to forgive sins. 2. *The condition on which the power of Christ is realized.* "When he saw
their faith." Observe, not *his* faith. No one, it is true, can stand proxy for another as
to salvation. There must be the personal touch of Christ; and the narrative, when
attentively regarded, shows that Jesus secured this from the sufferer. He helped out
the sick man's trustfulness; he established a relation with himself. And then and
thus he did exceeding abundantly above all that could be asked. But he does attach
value to faith in friends for another friend, in the loving for the loved, in those who
have salvation for those who have not. Think of the four bearing the weak and wanting man, seeking the means to realize the blessing for him, their interest wholly unselfish, and unresting until the *doure man* is really brought to Jesus. Oh, is not this the
miniature of the Church of Christ in its intercession and labour for heathendom, for
the sick and perishing through lack of knowledge? Should it not indicate the truth
to be exemplified in the anxiety of parents as to their children? Should it not remind
us of the highest aim of all relatives of friendship or confidence? Jesus does "perceive"
this faith. It is the security of blessing unspeakable; for

> "So the whole round earth is every way
> Bound by gold chains about the feet of God."

Were there more of this faith, there would be more abundant sign of "the power of the
Lord present to heal." 3. *The hindrance and limitation of the power of the Lord.* "Pharisees and doctors of the Law sitting by," and the power present. It is always present with
the word of his grace. We never need to seek it as if it were sometimes here and sometimes there. But these Pharisees and doctors are not healed. The grace is present for them
too, but they do not realize it. They *sit by* as spectators, critics, censors, watching for
grounds of reproach and accusation. "The word of hearing did not profit them, because
they were not united by faith with them that heard." Is not this the limitation still?

Are there not many in our assemblies who, like these Pharisees, "sit by"?   They
scarcely believe what is said.   As old Matthew Henry writes, "It is to them a tale
that is told them, not a message that is sent them.   They are willing that we should
preach before them, not that we should preach to them."   It is this sitting by which
checks the work of grace.   More and more, as the ministry of Christ proceeds, does the
shadow of the Pharisees sitting by fall on it.   A withering, desolating shadow.   Thou
Pharisee of town and village, thou critic, sceptic, thy seat the seat of the scornful.
Mighty power to heal may be present, but mighty work of healing cannot be done in
thee until the story of the Pharisee of the Pharisees is repeated in thee, and thy self-
sufficiency smitten down, thou art cast to the earth, to ask, trembling and astonished,
"Who art thou, Lord?"

Vers. 30—39.—*The new and the old.*   Two classes of persons are amazed and
offended—those to whom old ways and recognized canons of respectability were of the
very essence of the religious life; and those whose minds occupied a sort of intermediate
position, who had so far broken from the old, but had not yet received the spirit of the
new time which had begun in Galilee.   Here is this Rabbi, whose fame has spread far
and wide, who is undoubtedly possessed of marvellous powers, associating with persons
whom every respectable Hebrew shunned, accepting a tax-gatherer's invitation, and
freely mingling with the worthless folk found at a tax-gatherer's table.   What an outrage on social and religious decency!   The scribes and Pharisees—the one of these two
classes—murmur (observe, against the disciples; they do not dare to the Lord himself),
"Why do ye eat and drink with publicans and sinners?"   The disciples, simple, guileless souls, were probably unable to explain or account for their Master.   He himself
replies by quoting an Old Testament Scripture—one of those great prophetic words
which express the spirit of all true religion, and prefacing and following this quotation
by sentences of searching irony.   "They that be whole need not a physician, but they
that are sick.   But go ye and learn what that meaneth, I will have mercy, and not
sacrifice: for I am not come to call the righteous, but sinners to repentance."   How significant is every clause!   "They that are whole."   Will the murmurers take that
description as appropriate to them?   Then the Jesus whom they surround has nothing
for them; his work is not for the self-righteous, but for the consciously sinful and
needy.   But "whoso" would be teachers of the people as they may be, let them go
and learn the first lesson of Divine wisdom, viz. that it is the delight of God's love to
find out fatherless souls; that he is satisfied, not by formal acts of worship, rendered in
mere obedience to usage, but by the seeking of poor outcasts from ordinance and
society, by such fellowship with them as reveals the purpose, "I will have mercy, and
not sacrifice."   Now comes the moment at which, along with the Pharisees, the other
of the two offended classes—those occupying an intermediate position between the old
and the new—appears on the scene.   Some disciples of the Baptist have been scanning
the movements of the Prophet of Nazareth, and the feast just held gives increased force
to their doubts and difficulties.   The joyous life which Jesus and his followers are
living contrasts with the sternly simple, ascetic life which they have been taught to
regard as the best.   Can the joyous life be right?   Why the disregard of the outward
signs of discipline?   Why is he so lax with those whom he has called?   The answer
returned has an abiding interest for the Church in all times.   First, observe Christ's
word with regard to the special issue raised; and, secondly, observe his setting forth of
the general truth as to his gospel and kingdom.

I. THE SPECIAL ISSUE IS FASTING.   Jesus does not deny its utility.   He fasted.
Moreover, in his sermon from the mount, he recognized fasting as one of the elements
of the religious life.   What his saying bears on is its observance as a fixed habit or
rule.   The time, the rule, Christ teaches, must come from within.   He goes to the
root of the matter when he asks, "Can the children of the bridechamber mourn?"
There is nothing if there *is* not mourning.   Mere non-eating is nothing; mere aus-
terities are nothing.   Self-denial for the sake of self-denial is nothing.   It is the
relation to spiritual ends, the power of interpreting and helping spiritual life, that
gives any service its value.   "How can you make these children mourn while I am
with them?   Their fasting, at present, would be wholly artificial.   It is the worship in
spirit and truth that I want.   When they can really mourn, they will.   Until then,

let them rejoice." The days did come. The Bridegroom was taken from them. And they mourned. And still, as then, there are, as one has called them, "fast-days which God appoints souls." Christ's disciples should have their *retreats*, when the round of pleasure or of care is given up, and the blessing of entire solitude with God is realized. Only, let these be, not because of a law made for them, but because of the law which the Lord, by the dealing of his Holy Spirit, writes within their own hearts. And, supposing the space for such *retreats* cannot be secured, remember there is a fasting which all can practise. All can abstain from self-pleasing and indulgence. All may consider whether it be not a duty to abstain from things lawful when the use of such things is an occasion of stumbling to their brethren. And all should recollect the grand old words, "Is not this the fast that I have chosen? to loose the bands of wickedness, to undo the heavy burdens, and to let the oppressed go free, and that ye break every yoke? is it not to deal thy bread to the hungry, and that thou bring the poor that are cast out to thy house? when thou seest the naked, that thou cover him; and that thou hide not thyself from thine own flesh?"

II. THE WORD AS TO FASTING BRINGS INTO SIGHT THE WHOLE QUESTION AS TO THE REQUIREMENTS AND THE NATURE OF THE TRUTH AS IT IS IN JESUS. Glance at the outstanding features of the ever-memorable parable between the thirty-sixth and the thirty-ninth verses. 1. *The bearing of the sentence as to patching.* The disciples of John and the Pharisees virtually ask that Jesus sew the new cloth, which is woven out of his Person and sacrifice, into an old rotten garment. The answer is "No; what has decayed and is waxing old is ready to vanish; let it go. When it comes to this, patching and mending is worthless policy. It does not benefit the old, whilst it spoils the new. The new will not hold to the seam of the old, and, when it gives way, not only is the rent made worse, but in the end the new must be rejected also." What is particularly meant by the similitude of the garment is the manner of life, that which forms the envelopment of the soul. As to this, Christ will have no patching. Christianity is not Judaism with something sewn on to it. It is not a conglomerate of religions. It comprehends all that is good anywhere. It destroys nothing. But it is a new robe. All that is old is made new. And so must it be with the character. It is not a mere amending at this point or at that that will suffice. Merely to sew a piece of the new cloth, to have a fragment of Christ's religion patched to the old self, will that suffice? Verily no. Put off the old man. Put on the new. "If any man be in Christ, he is a new creature." 2. *The bearing of the sentence as to wine.* By this, as it would seem, the Lord means the inward spiritual principle, the grace—"that best wine which goeth down smoothly, gliding through the lips of those that are asleep." This is not some compound of dregs of old wines; it has all the strength and flavour of the old, but it is new. It is the fruit of a grape which none but the Son of God could bruise; it is the product of a wine-press which none but he could tread; it has the power of a sustenance which none but he could infuse. And this new life must be put into new bottles. It demands forms of worship and action peculiar to itself—forms of worship adapted at once to the richness of the sentiments and the simplicity of its utterance, the natural and becoming vehicles of its own voice of prayer and praise; forms of action in harmony at once with its spirituality and its humanity. It is too living and strong for any receptacle of its influence except that which has been created for and by itself. New wine and new bottles. Let the hearer of the Word ponder this. Note the point of junction between liberty and discipline in the Christian life. "Where the Spirit of the Lord is, there is liberty." But to realize this liberty, the will presented to the Lord must be so opened and ordered that the movements of his love shall flow in, and the power of his grace shall be fulfilled. It is all of grace, but the new bottle is needed for the new wine. The Lord is very decided as to this. The principle of an entire subjection to God must be asserted over every impeding tendency. In our present state pains must go with prayers, that the heart be kept "believing, true, and clean," a wineskin fit for the new wine. Hereafter, in the eternal year of the Bridegroom-joy, it shall be otherwise. Then, they who wait upon the Lord shall "run, and not be weary; and walk, and not faint."

HOMILIES BY VARIOUS AUTHORS.

Vers. 4—6.—*Weary workers.* The passage is one of encouragement to those who have been labouring in the cause of truth and righteousness, and whose success has not been according to their hope. We have a picture of—

I. FRUITLESS TOIL. "We have toiled all the night, and have taken nothing;" words that have not only been on the lips of the unsuccessful fisherman, but often enough on those of the weary Christian workman—the pastor, the evangelist, the teacher, the philanthropist, the missionary. Weeks, months, even years, may go by, and nothing or little may have resulted. Especially is this the case in missionary labour among savages, or where venerable systems of superstition prevail. The workman goes through all stages, of lessened hope, of surprise at non-success, of disappointment, of despondency, until he may get down very near to despair.

II. THE COMMAND TO CONTINUE. Under discouragement and apparent defeat there frequently enters the thought of abandonment. The worker says, "I will lay down my weapon; it is useless to proceed. *I* must have better soil, or *it* must have a more skilful hand." But when this thought is being entertained there comes a manifestation of the Master, who by some means and in some language, says, "Go, labour on: toil on and faint not." To the "fisher of men" he says, "Let down your nets for a draught." This command to continue may cause us to reflect upon: 1. Our Lord's own example; for he laboured on most diligently and patiently under heavy and sore discouragements. 2. The ample means placed at our disposal with which to work for Christ and men; the glorious fulness and fitness of the gospel of the grace of God. 3. The near presence and promised aid of the Holy Spirit. 4. The inestimable value of the souls we seek to save. But whencesoever suggested, the voice we hear is imperative, Divine, "*Go, labour on.*"

III. THE SPIRIT AND ACT OF OBEDIENCE. 1. We may be indisposed to resume; we may feel, as Peter evidently did on this occasion, that there is nothing to be taken by our toil; that for all practical purposes we might as well leave the field. 2. But Christ's will is decisive. Against that there is no appeal. "At thy word I will let down the net." This is the true spirit of obedience. To work for Christ under every possible *encouragement* is easy and simple enough; perhaps it may not take high rank in heaven so far as its spiritual greatness is concerned. To continue at our post under every *discouragement*, because we believe it is the will of our Lord that we should still strive and sow—that is the trying, the honourable, the acceptable thing. It may be remarked that : 3. Obedience to our Lord is not inconsistent with a wise change of method. Launch out "into the deep." They were to cast their net into the likeliest waters.

> "Cast after cast, by force or guile,
>   All waters must be tried."
> (See Keble's hymn, "The livelong night we've toil'd in vain.")

If one method does not succeed, we must try another. We must not ascribe to God a failure which is due to our own inefficiency. We must not ask and expect his blessing unless we are doing our best in his Name and in his cause.

IV. THE LARGE REWARD. "When they had this done," etc. Patient, obedient work wrought for Jesus Christ will certainly meet with its recompense. "Refrain thine eyes from tears, and thy voice from weeping, for thy work *shall* be rewarded." We may "go forth weeping," but we shall doubtless "come again with rejoicing." The success may come : 1. After much labour and prayer and waiting. 2. In a way in which we did not expect it. 3. Only in part while we are here to rejoice in it; for often "one soweth and another reapeth." But sooner or later, in one form or another, here or hereafter, it will come; our net will "enclose a great multitude of fishes;" our hearts will be full, even to overflow, with joy and gratitude.—C.

Ver. 8.—*The soul shrinking from God.* It was the coming of God in the person of Jesus Christ that excited in the breast of the apostle such shrinking of soul. Peter perceived that he stood in the presence of One in whom was Divine power, of One who was in very close association with the Holy One of Israel; and, feeling his own unworthiness, he exclaimed, with characteristic candour of impulsiveness, " Depart from me ; for I am a sinful man, O Lord."

I. THE WAY IN WHICH GOD NOW MANIFESTS HIMSELF TO THE WORLD. That way is threefold. 1. *Nature* and *providence.* The heavens declare his glory, and so does this wonderful and beautiful and fruitful earth. Not less so do the souls and the lives of men, created with all their faculties, preserved and enriched with all their joys and blessings. "The invisible things of him . . . are clearly seen, being understood by the things that are made." But more than this was proved to be needed by the sad, dark history of mankind. Hence we have : 2. *Special revelation.* "At sundry times and in divers manners God spake unto our fathers" by Abraham, Moses, Samuel, David, etc.; but at a later time he spake unto us by his Son—by his life, his truth, his sorrow, his death, his resurrection. But this did not suffice. Divine love appeared, and human hatred slew it. Divine truth spake, and human error determinately rejected it. So God gives us what we need. 3. *The direct influences of his Holy Spirit,* to arouse, to quicken, to enlighten, to renew us.

II. THE FIRST EFFECT UPON THE SOUL OF THIS VISION OF GOD. What usually happens is that the soul is smitten with a sense of its sinfulness, and desires to withdraw from the Divine presence. At this we need not wonder. If conscious ignorance shrinks from great learning, poverty from great wealth, obscurity from high rank, human guilt from human purity, well may the consciously sinful soul of man shrink from the near presence of the thrice-holy God. As Adam and Eve hid themselves when they "heard the voice of the Lord God walking in the garden ; " as Isaiah exclaimed, " Woe is me ! I am a man of unclean lips," when he "saw the Lord" in the temple ;—so do we shrink from the felt presence of the Lord in view of our own unworthiness and guilt. Remembering our spiritual estrangement, our great undischarged indebtedness to God, our impurity of heart in his sight, our manifold transgressions of his righteous law,—our souls tremble before him ; and if we do not say, "Depart from me, O Lord ! " as Peter did, yet our first thought is to escape from his felt presence, to put some distance, in thought and feeling, between ourselves and that Holy and Mighty One in whose power we stand so absolutely, and whose Spirit we have grieved so greatly.

III. THE INTERPOSITION OF OUR SAVIOUR. The sacred record does not state what immediately ensued, but our instructed imagination will very readily supply the remainder of the incident. We are quite sure that our gracious Master, instead of acting on Peter's word, and leaving him, drew nearer to him, and "took him by the hand," and so reassured him. Thus does he treat us now. Instead of withdrawing from us when we know and feel our guilt, he comes nearer to us. Instead of saying to us, "Depart from me ! " he says, earnestly and emphatically, "Come unto me ! " He says to us, "If, in my teaching and in my life and in my death, there is (as there is) the strongest possible condemnation of sin, so is there also in all these things, in my words and my actions and my cross, the greatest possible hope for the sinner. Come unto me ; see in me the Propitiation for your sin, the Way back unto the Father, the Divine Friend and Helper of the sorrowing and struggling human soul. Do not leave me ; come to me, and abide in me ! "—C.

Vers. 12, 13.—*The cleansed leper.* Three points suggest themselves to our thoughts.
I. THE WAVERING OF A STRONG HUMAN HOPE. Outside the outer circumference of that congregation was a man to whom pity would have drawn us, but from whom an instinctive repugnance would have repelled us. He was one in whom were not only signs and spots of that dire plague of leprosy, but in whom it was seen in its most virulent form—he was "full of leprosy." Suffering in body, and afflicted far worse in mind by the terrible isolation which that disease imposed, there suddenly enters his heart a new and bounding hope ; in the dense darkness of his night there rises that morning star. A new Prophet has come to the people of God. He hears of his Name and fame (ch. iv. 37); he comes to see ; he witnesses the wonderful works which are wrought (ch. iv. 40). Will not this great Healer have mercy upon him ? Will not he who casts out the devil cure the leper ? If the poor paralytic, at his bidding, could rise and walk away with his friends, why should not he, at the command of that strong Voice, be healed of his foul disease, and go home to his family again ? So he comes where Jesus is, and listens as he speaks, and when he hears him say, " Ask, and it shall

be given you," he resolves that *he will* ask that a new life may be given *him;* he will seek: what if *he* should find? We have never made to man any request on which so much has hung as that which was now hanging on the answer he should receive at the lips of Jesus Christ. To him it was not success or failure merely; it was life or death that was at stake. How must the most eager expectation have wrestled in his heart with tremulous and agonizing fear! with what faltering voice must he have uttered those prayerful words, "Lord, if thou wilt, thou canst make me clean"!

II. The touch of the Divine hand. "Jesus put forth his hand, and touched him." All three evangelists record this significant fact. There were three reasons why he should not do this. 1. Strong instinctive human aversion. 2. The risk he ran in so doing. 3. The prohibition of the Law combined with social usage disallowing it. But our Lord set aside all these objections. Why? Was it not to show by instant action the kindness and compassion of his heart, to place himself practically by his side as One who felt deeply for and with him, and to teach us that, if we wish to heal the worst disorders, we must do that, not standing afar off, but, coming into close personal contact with the men we are seeking to save, by "laying our hand upon them"? We, too, must be ready, like our Lord, to do that which is distasteful, to run some risks, to disregard conventional proprieties, if we would remove from the land the leprosies which still afflict it.

III. The response of Divine love. That leper must have known, when Jesus laid his hand kindly upon him, that he meant to heal him; yet sweeter to his ear than are the most melting strains of music to the lover of melody and song were these words of the Lord when he said, "I will: be thou clean;" and then he who "speaks, and it is done," spoke the unheard word, and forces of nature came into play, and the life-blood leapt in the leper's veins, "and immediately his leprosy departed." Sin is the leprosy of the soul. 1 It is loathsome. 2. It is diffusive, spreading from faculty to faculty over the whole nature. 3. It exiles; it separates man from God, and man from man also. 4. It is deathful; it is death in life. When the sinful soul, though he be far gone in sin, "full of leprosy," makes his application to the great Physician, he has nothing to fear as to the result of his appeal. (1) Be not troubled, far less hindered, because hope is streaked with fear; there may be an "if" in the heart, as there was in that of this leper; the very intensity of the hope arising out of the magnitude of the issue at stake will perfectly account for that—such fear is only the shadow of a prevailing hope. (2) Be assured that you have no need to fear. Christ's readiness to save is beyond the shadow of a doubt; if we are only in real earnest to be saved from the leprosy of sin, it is certain that the hand of Divine love will be laid upon us, and that the voice of Divine mercy will address us, saying, "I will: be thou clean."—C.

Ver. 16.—*Christ at prayer.* The fact that our Lord did withdraw into the wilderness to pray, and that this was not at all a solitary instance of his devotion, may suggest—

I. That prayer becomes the strong and the holy as well as the weak and the guilty. Jesus prayed; the One who was holy, harmless, undefiled, he in whom was no sin. He had no guilt to confess, no mercy to implore, no cleansing of heart to seek of the Holy Spirit. *Yet he prayed;* and prayer was becoming in him because he could: 1. Render adoration to the God whom he reverenced and whom he revealed. 2. Offer gratitude to the Father who ministered unto him even as unto us. 3. Utter his love and his devotedness to him in whom he rejoiced and on whose great errand of mercy he had come. 4. Ask for the guidance and support he needed at the Divine hand for the future that was before him. For such purposes as these prayer will become us as much in the heavenly kingdom as it befits us now. When *we* have no sins to acknowledge and no forgiveness to obtain, we shall still need to approach the Divine Spirit to express our adoration, our gratitude, and our love; also to ask for the maintenance and the guidance of that strong hand on which, in every age and in every sphere, we shall be dependent as we are to-day.

II. That prayer is peculiarly appropriate before and after all special services. We have good reason to think that these were the circumstances under which our Lord spent much time in prayer. It is probable that he, under the limitations to which he stooped, found it highly desirable if not needful then. Certainly it is so for us. 1. Before special services we are in *greatest need*—need of strength and inspiration for the work immediately confronting us. 2. After special services we are in *greatest danger ;* for the human spirit is never so exposed to its spiritual adversaries as in that hour when it relaxes after great spiritual excitement.

III. THAT IT IS NEEDFUL TO SEEK AND TO FIND OPPORTUNITIES FOR PRAYER. Jesus Christ could not have poured out his heart to his Father as he did, and gained the refreshment and strength he gained in prayer, if he had remained in the midst of the curious and exacting throngs who waited upon him. He withdrew himself into the wilderness. We have intimation that he had to make a very strenuous effort to escape from the multitudes and to secure the seclusion he desired. *But he made it.* And we shall be wise if we do the same. If we only draw near to God and have fellowship with him when we happen to be left alone, and when occasions offer themselves to us, we shall be very lacking in our devotion ; the flame of our piety will languish on the altar of our heart. We must *make* occasion ; we must *seize* opportunity ; we must compel our life to yield the still hour, when, withdrawing ourselves into solitude, we are alone with God.

IV. THAT IF NEEDFUL TO OUR LORD, HOW MUCH MORE NECESSARY MUST SUSTAINED DEVOTION BE TO OURSELVES ! If purity needed to pray, how much more need has guilt ! if strength, how much more weakness ! if wisdom, how much more ignorance and folly ! If our Master did not go forth to great trials or temptations without first attuning his spirit and renewing his strength in the near presence of his Father, how much less shall we venture into the arduous and perilous future without first equipping ourselves at the sacred armoury, without first casting ourselves on God and drawing sustaining and overcoming vigour from his infinite resources !—C.

Ver. 17.—*Present power.* One of the noblest of the psalms commences with that verse which it would have been well worth while to have lived a long and stormy life to have written, " God is our Refuge and Strength, a *very present* Help in trouble." Who can estimate the thousands of thousands of tempest-tossed human souls to whom these words have brought help and comfort ! The latter part of this passage is in very close relation to our text. It brings before our minds—

I. THE COMPARATIVE NEARNESS OF GOD TO US. It may indeed be objected that the Omnipresent One, being everywhere, cannot be more truly in one place than in another. Doubtless that is so. But God may be more *manifestly* present, and therefore more present *to our consciousness*, in one place than in another. So the old Hebrew worshipper felt as he drew near Jerusalem, as he entered the precincts of the temple, as he went into the court of the Jews, as he saw the priests enter the sanctuary itself. And once in the history of mankind God did so visit us that he was "manifest in the flesh ; " he was " Emmanuel, God with us "—with us in a sense in which he was not before and has not been again. There is a sense in which God is nearer to us in the sanctuary and at the table of the Lord than elsewhere. He has promised to meet us there ; we go there on purpose to be in his presence ; therefore to our consciousness he is in a peculiar sense *present* with us—our *very present* Saviour.

II. THE PRESENCE OF HIS POWER. "The power of the Lord was present." Any Israelite of ancient time would have told you that God's power was present in the sky, in the sea, in the corn, in the rain. But he was most impressed with the power of God as manifested in the storm in harvest-time, or in the overthrow of Sennacherib's mighty host. Yet this was only in his imagination ; the power of God was as truly and as graciously present in the ordinary and the regular as in the miraculous. We are inclined to think that Divine power is most manifest in the shaking thunder or in the flashing lightning, or in the upheaving earthquake ; but the wiser we are, the more we " observe these things, and (consequently) understand the loving-kindness of the Lord," the more we perceive that God's power is as present in the common and the continuous as in the startling and the exceptional, is " very present " in the unfolding morning and the descending night, in the growing of the grass and the ripening of the corn and the blooming of the flowers. God's power is present with us always and everywhere, if we have but eyes to see it and hearts to feel it.

III. THE PRESENCE OF HIS HEALING POWER. 1. A very beneficent power is that of healing ; perhaps we never praise God quite so feelingly as when we bless him that

" he has healed our sicknesses." God has always been healing men. He has supplied us with the substances which are fitted to restore, and he has given us a bodily system of such a nature that it has great recuperative powers. There are but few among those who have reached manhood and womanhood who have not had occasion to know that the power of the Lord is present to heal us now. In the hour of convalescence they gave him the glory and offered their renewed life to him. What are they doing now that health has been restored and confirmed? 2. And this healing of the body is but the *picture* and the *promise* of the healing of the heart. When Jesus Christ went from village to village, healing all manner of diseases, it was partly, if not principally, to say to all men everywhere of every age, " Understand, ye blind souls that walk in darkness, I am the Light of the world; come to me, that you may see indeed ! Ye strengthless and sick ones in need of spiritual healing, I am the Divine Restorer; come unto me, that ye may be strong indeed ! Ye dying ones, I am the Resurrection and the Life; come unto me, that you may live indeed ! "—C.

Vers. 18—25.—*Superabounding kindness.* We learn from these words—
I. CHRIST'S CONSCIOUSNESS OF HIS OWN GREATNESS. He *assumes* the right to forgive men their sins (ver. 20), and, when this right is challenged by those present, he *asserts* it (ver. 24). And he does not dispute that this is a Divine prerogative. When it is claimed that only God can forgive sins (ver. 21), his reply is one that confirms rather than questions that doctrine. To a very large extent our Lord's Divinity was in abeyance. He was voluntarily accepting limitations which caused him to be numbered among the human and the finite. But his authority and power were *in him*, potentially; they were under a commanding restraint. Here and there, now and again, as on this occasion, it seemed fitting that they should be put forth. And it magnifies " the grace of our Lord Jesus Christ," that all the while that he was stooping to such lowliness, such poverty, such endurance, he was conscious of the fact that Divine right and Divine power were within him, to be exercised when he would. The Son of man had power on earth to forgive sins.
II. HIS AUTHENTICATION OF IT. His greatness was often questioned, sometimes denied; and often our Master allowed men to think of him as the Teacher or the Prophet whom they were to judge by his life or by his doctrine. But sometimes he vindicated his claims in a way that completely silenced, if it did not convince, his critics. He authenticated himself by some deed of mighty power. He did so now. Not that the exercise of healing power was one whit more Divine an act than the forgiveness of sin; not that an act of pity for bodily incapacity was greater or worthier than one of mercy and succour to the soul. That could not be. But that the working of the miracle was a more *obvious* and *signal* indication of the Divine than an act of forgiveness. And by this gracious and mighty work our Lord proved himself to be the One who had a right to say, " Thy sins be forgiven thee." We may say that the gospel of Jesus Christ is now authenticated *by its power.* We are sure that the message of grace and mercy which we preach does come from God because (among other reasons for our assurance) we witness the mighty power of Christian truth. We find it doing what nothing else ever tried to do—enlightening multitudes of dark minds, redeeming and restoring foul hearts, transforming evil lives, lifting men up from the dust and the mire of sin and shame and bidding them walk in the ways of righteousness.
III. OUR APPROACH TO THE SAVIOUR. It was the approach of this man to the Lord that led to Christ's words of mercy and then to his deed of power. The man could not and would not keep away from his presence; he was resolved to make his appeal to the great Healer, cost what it might to reach his ear. This is the approach that is successful—seeking the Lord with the whole heart, with a fixed intent to seek until he is found. Not a languid interest in Christ, not a pursuit of righteousness which may be turned aside by the first curiosity or indulgence that offers itself; but a holy earnestness which will not be denied, which, if one entrance is blocked, will find another, which knocks till the door is opened,—this is the search that succeeds. Not, indeed, that Christ is hard to find or reluctant to bestow; but that, for our sake, he does often cause us to continue in our seeking that our blessedness may be the fuller and our faith the firmer and our new life the deeper for our patience and our persistency.

IV. THE SUPERABUNDANCE WHICH IS IN CHRIST. This poor paralytic sought much of the Lord, but he found a great deal more than he sought; seeking healing for his body, he found that, and with that mercy for his soul. Christ has more to give us than we count upon receiving. Many a man has gone to him asking only for present relief from a burden of conscious guilt, and he has found that salvation by faith in Jesus Christ means vastly more than that. He finds that the forgiveness of sin is the initial step of a bright and blessed future, that it is the earnest of a noble inheritance. In Christ our Lord are "unsearchable riches;" and they who have received the most have only begun to find what a world of excellency and blessedness they have gained by hearkening to his voice and hastening to his side and entering his holy service.—C.

Vers. 27, 28.—*Following Christ.* Who can fail to be struck with—
I. THE COMMANDING AUTHORITY OF CHRIST. It will be observed that he speaks in the imperative; not "Wouldest thou," but "Do thou follow me!" He speaks, also, unconditionally, absolutely, not "Follow me if or when," but simply and without reserve, "Follow me!" Consider what large consequences would result from Matthew's choice—the complete breaking up of his old life, the forsaking of his old pursuits and of his old friends, the entering an entirely new sphere of thought and action. Yet Matthew appears to have recognized the right of Jesus Christ to make this demand of him. Must he not have acted under Divine illumination and guidance to decide so promptly and so wisely? So authoritatively and unconditionally the Saviour comes to us and summons us to his service. His claim rests on incontestable facts which prove him to be the Son of God who has a sovereign right thus to address us, to be the Son of man whose life of love and whose death of shame entitle him to ask the most and the best of us.
II. THE MEANING OF OUR SAVIOUR'S CALL. The form of service our Master desires of us when he bids us follow him is obviously different from that he asked of Matthew. What does he want of us? What is the precise thing he requires us to do? Taking, as we should take, one passage with another, we answer that he desires us to come into the closest possible union which a human spirit can sustain to the Divine; or, more specifically, he wants us *cordially to accept him for all that he offers to be to our soul*—to accept him as our Teacher from whom we learn all needful truth, as our Saviour in whose redeeming work we trust for God's abounding mercy, as our Lord to whom we dedicate our powers and our days, as our Divine Friend and Refuge in whom we hide.
III. THE EXCELLENCY OF AN IMMEDIATE RESPONSE. Matthew did well that he "left all, rose up, and followed him." Had he waited for another occasion, he would have been more entangled in human relationships and worldly interests; he might never have had so direct and personal an appeal made to him. As it was, by forsaking all to follow Christ, he lost a profitable calling and a company of friends; but what did he find instead? 1. The protection and friendship of Jesus Christ. 2. A new and nobler manhood, an exalted life. 3. The esteem and the gratitude of the Church of Christ for all time to come. 4. Eternal blessedness in the future. And so with us; when the Master comes and calls us, as he may do in one of a number of ways, we act most wisely when we *immediately* respond. (1) We lose the least that can be lost. (2) We *make sure* of the heritage which the truly wise are determined to gain. Jesus of Nazareth is "passing by;" we must avail ourselves of his offer while opportunity allows. (3) We gain immeasurable good—peace of mind, blessed consciousness of the favour and friendship of God, spiritual rectitude, a life that is worthy of our origin and our capacities, a hope that maketh not ashamed. That was a supreme hour to Matthew, the crisis of his life: who shall say how soon we may reach the supreme and critical hour of our career? Blessed are they who recognize it when it comes, and who come forth from it having "laid hold on eternal life."—C.

Vers. 29—32.—*Christian association.* On what principle shall we regulate our intercourse with men? How shall we follow Christ in the matter of associating with our fellow-men? Our answer, suggested by this incident, is—
I. THAT ASSOCIATION WITH BAD MEN ON THE GROUND OF FRIENDSHIP IS AN UNCHRISTIAN THING. The Pharisees would have been right enough if Jesus Christ had mingled with the mercenary and the vicious only to enjoy their company. His time

might certainly have been much better spent than in partaking of so doubtful a source of satisfaction, and he would have left an example that would have been better shunned than followed. For to mingle with the irreverent and the covetous, and, still more, to associate with the positively vicious, simply for the sake of passing gratification, is: 1. To spend time and strength where they are very ill applied. 2. To lend a sanction to those who need rather to be discouraged than sustained in their course of life. 3. To incur the serious danger of being lowered to their level. Some intercourse with the frivolous and the guilty we must have, and there is every reason why our conduct toward them should be as courteous and gracious as possible. But no wise man will establish an intimate friendship with another whose spirit is the spirit of worldliness, whose conduct is that from which purity and sobriety must shrink. Let the young especially remember that lifelong association with the unholy and the unworthy, in ninety-nine cases out of a hundred, means gradual moral degeneracy, continual spiritual decline.

II. THAT ASSOCIATION WITH THE GOOD IN THE SPIRIT OF CHRISTIAN FELLOWSHIP IS A WISE AND WORTHY THING. "The assembling of ourselves together," as those who are agreed on the same fundamental articles of faith, and who are animated by the same spirit and are promoting the same objects, is admirable for three reasons. 1. We gain spiritual strength ourselves. 2. We impart it to those with whom we unite. 3. We commend the common principles we hold to those who are without by the manifestation of our unity. Those who try to live a life of spiritual isolation not only make a *great mistake* by robbing themselves of a source of hallowed influence, but they neglect a *plain duty*, for they leave unemployed a weapon of usefulness by which truth and worth are materially advanced. But the main lesson of the passage is—

III. THAT ASSOCIATION WITH THE BAD FOR THEIR ELEVATION IS A DISTINCTLY CHRISTIAN THING. Those critics of Jesus Christ failed to see that the presence of a noble, unselfish motive made all the difference in the character of the act. It completely transformed it. It changed it from the unwise and the condemnable into the wise and meritorious. Our Lord mingled with publicans and sinners, not as a Companion to share their revelries, but as a Guide to lead them into other and better ways, as a Helper whose strong hand should raise them from the mire and place them upon the rock. And as he was here to seek and to save, where should he be found but among those who were lost? Where would you have the teacher? In the company of the mature and the literate, or in the schoolroom among the young and the ignorant? Where would you have the physician? In the homes of the healthy, or in the hospital and in the homes of the sick? And where should *they* be found who have truth to teach and restoration to impart such as no teacher of any human science can make known, no healer of bodily diseases can confer? We are never quite so Christian, we never reach a height so near the level on which our Lord was daily walking, as when we voluntarily and cheerfully forego the pleasanter security to which our character entitles us, and mingle freely and frequently with those whose spirit and whose tone is offensive to our taste and our judgment, in order that we may lift them up to a nobler life. And this is the one and only way in which to work out this great and beneficent reform. What legislation will not do, what literature will not effect, what art and science will leave unaccomplished if not untouched, that a holy and loving association on the ground of Christian kindness will secure. The actual and near presence of the pure and kind, the touch and the pressure of the hand of human love, the voice of invitation and of entreaty proceeding from those whose eyes are dim with the tears of a sorrowful sympathy,—this is the power which, coming, as it does, from Jesus Christ, and emanating from his Holy Spirit, will lead sinful souls, covetous men and erring women, into paths of penitence, and raise them to heights of holiness.—C.

Vers. 33—38.—*Christian naturalness.* We have here—
I. AN HONEST DIFFICULTY FAIRLY AND EFFECTUALLY MET. It was in no carping spirit that the disciples of John came to Jesus. We do not detect a trace of ill will in their question. It was a spirit of surprise and perplexity that dictated it. They had always thought that fasting was an essential feature of true piety. Their master John had encouraged them in this idea; but they looked in vain for this feature in

the doctrine of Christ. What could it mean? Our Lord met this inquiry in a very different way from that in which he might have done so. He might have said, "Where, in the books of Moses, is fasting enjoined on the people of God? On what day in all the year, excepting the Day of Atonement, is this practice prescribed? Is it not a tradition of men rather than a commandment of God?" But Jesus did not meet them thus. He said that his disciples did not fast because fasting on their part would be untimely, unsuitable, and therefore unacceptable. "Can the children of the bridechamber," etc.? "You would not have men fast when they have every reason for feasting? you would not have men show themselves miserable when there is every ground for gladness? you would not have my disciples do such violence to their spiritual nature? You do not act," Christ goes on to say, "with such unnaturalness and incongruity in other departments of life; you do not bring together things that do not agree with one another; you do not put unwrought cloth on an old garment; you do not put new unfermented wine in old skins that will not stretch; if you did, you would pay the penalty in spoiled clothes and spilled wine. Why should you do anything that is unfitting and incongruous in the realm of religion? If you do, you will have a serious penalty to pay. No; let my disciples rejoice while they have occasion to be glad; the days will come soon enough when they will have a heart for grieving: then will they fast in those days."

II. An indication of the true tone of Christian service. The disciples were glad of heart because their Master was "with them." To be the close companions of Jesus Christ is reason enough for a prevailing spiritual joy. As his disciples, indeed, there are certain special sources of sorrow—grief at the sin and misery of mankind, regret at our own slowness of growth and slackness of zeal, etc. But for us as his followers is (1) the joy of faith; (2) the joy of fellowship; (3) the joy of service, the delight of doing good, the blessedness of giving health and peace and hope to those in spiritual weakness and trouble; (4) the joy of hope, of immortal blessedness. Is it for us, with such a heritage in possession, and with such a prospect as this, to comport ourselves as if we were fatherless, friendless, portionless? Is it for us to go on our way homewards and heavenwards as if we were being conveyed to prison or were going into exile? Not gloom but gladness, not dreariness but delight, should be the prevailing note of our Christian life.

III. The importance of the fitting in the sphere of the sacred. We learn this, in the text, from the unwisdom of the unfitting in the sphere of the secular. "No man putteth," etc.; if he does, he spoils his garment, and he spills his wine. So in the sphere of the spiritual: if we force the sorrowful spirit to assume the tone of the happy; or if we reverse this unnatural process, and compel the happy to affect to be sorrowful; or if we require the young to manifest piety in the forms that are suitable to the mature; or if we insist on those who have been trained in godly and virtuous habits showing the same form of repentance which we demand of the vicious and the gross;—we may secure a result which gives us momentary satisfaction, but we shall have a penalty to pay further on. The unnatural is always a mistake. God does not desire to be served in ways which are not fitted to the spirit which he has made, or are not appropriate to the circumstances in which his providence has placed us. Let there be no forcing in the sphere of the sacred. Do the fitting, the congruous thing, and you will do the right and the acceptable thing. "Is any merry? let him sing psalms. Is any afflicted? let him pray." Is any filled with a sense of the value of this life? let him give himself heartily to holy usefulness. Is any weary and worn with the strife and burden of life? let him find cheer and comfort in anticipating the rest which remaineth for the people of God. Do not try to regulate your spiritual life by any calendar; let it flow on in joy or sorrow, in active service or patient waiting as the hand of God is laid on the springs of your human spirit, and is directing the course of your earthly life. Not the hard, cast-iron service of constraint, but the free, spontaneous service of the full and overflowing heart, is that for which our Lord is looking, and with which he is well pleased.—C.

Vers. 1—11.—*Fishers of men.* We left Jesus itinerating through Galilee and preaching in the synagogues. But his centre seems to have been the Lake of Gennesaret, and especially Capernaum. The synagogues have become too small for his audiences, and so he has to take to the seashore, and there meet popularity as best he can. The pressure of the people is great, and it is to hear the Word of God they have come. A great Prophet, they feel, has risen up among them, and so they are eager to know what are the latest tidings from the Most High. There are two ships floating near; they are empty, for the fishermen have returned after a fruitless night, and are washing their nets on shore. Into one of the ships he enters, which happens to be Simon's, and he sits down to teach the mighty multitude which rises tier upon tier above him on the land. We have thus presented to us—

I. THE GREAT FISHER OF MEN. (Vers. 1—3.) For out of this boat he is really casting his net to catch men. His word spoken is to draw souls into sympathy and service. The art of preaching as thus exercised by Jesus Christ was the fishing for men. The miracle of subsequent success was to throw light really upon this primary attitude of Jesus. Now, let us consider here: 1. *The substance of Christ's preaching.* It was doubtless about the kingdom of God, about membership in it, and about its prospects in the world. But we must remember besides that he could not, in the very nature of the case, *preach the cross.* Hence his preaching was *the purest morality* backed up by a perfect life. So that once, at all events, the preaching of morality got a chance of being most favourably tested. The success thereof we shall mention presently. But Jesus could preach *himself* as the Saviour of sinners. And this, indeed, is the sum and substance of all preaching. The people, however, did not understand the full meaning of his message at the time. 2. *The success of Christ's preaching.* There was interest and excitement. But the result of that day's preaching seems to have been very like the night's fishing on the part of the disciples. Ah! this is what illustrates the wonderful consideration of the Saviour. Some one must prepare the way, some one must do the pioneer work. The Baptist prepared the way for Jesus, and Jesus prepared the way for the disciples. It is at Pentecost, after the Crucifixion, when the full gospel can be proclaimed, that the real success begins. The miracle of the fishes subsequent to the preaching of the Master was the type of the order which the good Lord has ordained. The "greater works" done by believing disciples are the spiritual miracles which began in such numbers at Pentecost, and which have been happening ever since (John xiv. 12).

II. THE MIRACLE OF SUCCESS. (Vers. 4—7.) Our Lord, having been accommodated in Simon's boat, proceeds to show his gratitude for the obligation. He tells the fishermen to "launch out into the deep, and let down your nets for a draught." Simon honestly owns that they have toiled all the night, and taken nothing; still, though appearances are against it, he will at Christ's word let down the net. No sooner has he done so than success comes so overpowering in character that the net breaks. The result is that they have to beckon for the second boat, and both boats are filled, so that they begin to sink. Here, then, is success "exceeding abundantly above all they can ask or think" (Eph. iii. 20). This is to show them that success waits upon the word of Jesus. It is, of course, mere *temporal* success—success which in a few moments they are enabled to despise; yet it is success obeying Christ's word. We need not inquire into the nature of the miracle. It was most likely a miracle of *knowledge.* There are great shoals of fish manifesting themselves in inland lakes just in the way demanded by the narrative.[1] But Jesus, in giving the direction at the proper moment and securing the draught at the time that the fish were within reach, showed his command of all the circumstances. So that, as Robertson thought, this miracle, more perhaps than all others, shows the personality of God in Christ Jesus.[2] The laws of nature hold on their way, but the Author of them can calculate to a nicety their working, and accommodate himself or his people through their operation. He is King among his own arrangements, at home among his own laws. The "hierarchy of laws," as they have been called, acknowledge him as High Priest. But we should further notice how he arranges for the disciples' success rather than for his own. As already intimated, his spiritual success was not great, considering the splendid powers he exercised. As Bersier somewhere remarks, no one ever had so little proportional success as he. No wonder that such a passage as Isa. xlix. 4, " I have laboured in vain, I have spent my strength

---

[1] Cf. Tristram's 'Natural History of the Bible,' p. 285; also Godet, *in loc.*
[2] 'The Human Race, and other Sermons,' p. 127, by Rev. F. W. Robertson.

for nought and in vain," may have been often on his lips.[1] But he handed on the elements of success to his successors. They reaped the harvest of which his *apparent* failure and early death were the seed. The whole arrangement reflects glory on the consideration of the Master.

III. THE EFFECT OF THE SUCCESS UPON THE FISHERMEN. (Vers. 8—10.) They were all filled with *astonishment*. This is the prime effect of a miracle. It astonishes people. It brings them suddenly face to face with superhuman power. They stare. But after the astonishment comes, and it may be very swiftly, sober thought. It was so here. Peter is broken down at the sight. Goodness has led him to *repentance*. His sin is now uppermost, and he cries, "Depart from me; for I am a sinful man, O Lord." Did Peter wish to be separated from the Master? Nay; but he felt he *deserved* to be. And here we may notice how prayer is answered. Peter cries to be separated from his Saviour; but in heart he hopes to remain beside Jesus still. Hence Jesus answers the *heart*, and heeds not the literal meaning of his prayer.[2] The Lord does not depart from him, but abides with him; nay, more, arranges for Peter being always with him. Goodness is meant to break sinners' hearts (Rom. ii. 4). Success of all kinds should have this effect. It is sad when "Jeshurun waxes fat and kicks" (Deut. xxxii. 15). It is blessed when, like Peter, in presence of unexpected good fortune, we humble ourselves before him who has sent it, acknowledging that we do not in any wise deserve it.[3]

IV. THE CALL OF THE FISHERMEN TO THE MINISTRY. (Ver. 10.) Peter was not the only penitent on board the sinking ships, we may be sure. He was first and chief; but the sons of Zebedee and Andrew were, we may be quite sure, penitent too. Fear predominates; their notion is that they might justly be cast from Christ's presence for ever. This is just the spirit in which special work for God begins. And now let us see how Jesus deals with them. He says to Peter first, but the result shows that the others were included in his call, "Fear not; from henceforth thou shalt catch men." They are to be promoted from being fishermen to be "fishers of men." It is a call, not to the apostolic office which comes later, but to the ministry. 1. It is a call away *from a worldly occupation*. For the ministry is an order of men set apart from temporal concerns for spiritual work. Worldly occupations are incompatible with it. A minister cannot do his work well if compelled to dabble in business. 2. It is a call to *catch men*. Now, the fisherman uses every art and artifice to get the fish into his net. He toils during the night, that the fish may not see the net nor evade his wiles. In the same way the minister is to use every art, and even guile itself, as Paul confesses, to get souls into Christ's net. We may object to the methods some people employ to promote the gospel. They may be worldly arts—advertising, music, paraphernalia of all kinds. But, before condemning enthusiastic men, we should ask ourselves the question—Have *we* left "no stone unturned" to bring men, even by moral *compulsion*, under the power of Christ and his truth (cf. ch. xiv. 23)? But: 3. The instruction is *to catch men alive* (ζωγρῶν). It is here the fishing fails us as a figure. Fish are caught and, as a rule, in the catching are killed. They lose their lives in the process. But when souls are taken in the gospel net, they are taken alive—are taken to enjoy life abundantly. In truth, the greatest kindness we can confer on souls is to get them into the net. We never live in earnest till we have been brought to him who is the Life of men. Such, in brief terms, is the meaning of the ministry.

V. THE ACCEPTANCE OF THE MINISTERIAL CALL. (Ver. 11.) We would say, at first sight, that the success was singularly out of place. Why grant a shoal of fish, if the fishermen are to leave them without a moment's hesitation or delay? The purpose was to assure them that temporal success was Christ's gift; and secondly, that spiritual success must be preferred to the temporal, even when the latter is at its height. It was a greater surrender when they had been so successful at their fishing. But the noble men did not hesitate. They brought their ships to land, and then forsook all their "stock in trade" that they might follow Jesus. The fellowship with Jesus during his ministry was more precious than the world's wealth could ever be. He

---

[1] Cf. Bersier's 'Sermons,' tome ii. p. 351.

[2] Cf. Arndt's 'Leben Jesu,' zweiter theil, s. 88.

[3] Cf. Robertson, *ut supra;* also Martineau's 'Endeavours after the Christian Life,' 4th edit., p. 147.

was the great "Fisher of men," and it was from fellowship with him they were to learn their profession.   The training of the twelve was a most real and blessed thing.[1]   It was more than any theological learning could ever afford.   It was learning of Christ himself, who is the embodied Truth.   And yet to this same test every soul is sooner or later brought.   At death, if not before, we are all asked if we can forsake all to follow Christ into undiscovered lands.   May we all stand that test !—R. M. E.

Vers. 12—26.—*The healing of the leper and the paralytic.*   We noticed how Jesus called the fishermen to be fishers of men, and how they nobly responded to his call, and forsook the fish and boats and friends that they might follow him.   We have now before us two instructive miracles performed during his evangelistic work, and resulting in an extension of his influence.   Between them there is interposed a significant remark about our Lord's private prayer, so that the order of our thought is miracle, prayer, and more miracle.   It is thus that Divine work goes on.   We must, consequently, give ourselves unto prayer as well as the ministry of the Word if we would follow Jesus or his apostles.

I. CONSIDER THE CURE OF THE LEPROSY.   (Vers. 12—15.)   It was manifestly a very serious case—the man was "full of leprosy."   It was the disease in its worst stage.   Humanly speaking, it was incurable.   So far as man was concerned, the case was hopeless.   Now, in this respect, the leprosy is a type of *sin.*   Sin is leprosy in the soul.   It is so far incurable by man.   But further, the leper was isolated from his kind, not because the disease was infectious through contact, which seems to be quite disproved,[2] but because in this way God would show his abhorrence of sin and its essentially *separating* power.   The poor lepers, as they went up and down the land with rent garments, and crying, "unclean !" were virtually dead men mourning over their lost and hopeless condition.   But this poor leper had heard of Jesus, had come to him, convinced that he was able to save him.   He throws himself down consequently at Christ's feet, saying, "Lord, if thou wilt, thou canst make me clean."   He was convinced of the Saviour's power, and he threw himself upon his sovereign mercy in the matter of the willingness to save.   And it is just to this that every sinner must come.   Persuaded of Christ's ability to save, he must throw himself upon his sovereign clemency.   For the Saviour might *justly* refuse to save any, though, as a matter of fact, he is anxious to save all.   And now let us notice Christ's *method* in saving him.   He might have saved him by a word, but to show his sympathy and freedom from all fear of defilement, he heals him by a touch, saying, "I will : be thou clean."   And immediately the leprosy departed from him.   In the very same way can the Saviour heal the leprosy of sin.   If we only ask him, he will tenderly touch us, and instantaneously the soul's disease will depart.   But, when healed, the man has certain duties to discharge at the instigation of Jesus.   He is directed first to tell no man ; for Jesus wants to be something more than a physician of the body, and he might, through the patient's report, be so overwhelmed with physical cases as not to have sufficient time for the preaching and spiritual work which with him was paramount.   Secondly, he is directed to repair to the priest, and fulfil all that the Law of Moses required, "for a testimony unto them."   In this way our Lord desired to demonstrate that he had not come, as they basely insinuated, to destroy the Law and the prophets, but to fulfil them and to get them fulfilled.   Notwithstanding these precautions, his fame so spread that multitudes came flocking together to hear and to be healed of their infirmities.   We have thus presented to us the way of salvation and its results.   It is by coming to Jesus that we are saved from sin ; it is by doing what Jesus requires that we are made useful among men.   Let us test Jesus as the appointed Saviour, and live as our Lord directs.

II. CONSIDER OUR LORD'S RETIREMENT TO THE WILDERNESS FOR PRAYER.   (Ver. 16.)   There is a certain measure of exhaustion in such work as was performed by Jesus.   He bowed to the necessity of private communion with God.   Even Jesus could not be always in public ; solitude was as needful for his soul's health as society for his opportunity of usefulness.   Vinet, in a fine sermon on this passage, says, "We do not believe

---

[1] Cf. 'The Training of the Twelve,' by Dr. A. B. Bruce, *passim.*
[2] Cf. Archbishop Trench on 'The Miracles,' 7th edit., p. 214; Godet, *in loc.,* adheres to the old view of its contagious character.

that we exaggerate when we say that those who do not love solitude do not love truth." [1] It is in the secret place with God that we renew our spiritual strength and are fit for further service.   And what perfect prayers our Lord's must have been.   No personal sin to confess, but simply to confer with the Father about the salvation of the world and how best he could promote the welfare of men.   The time of solitude with God is the most fruitful time.   Without it how barren all else proves !

III. CONSIDER THE HEALING OF THE PARALYTIC.   (Vers. 17—26.) It was in Capernaum, it is believed, and in the house of Peter, that the miracle happened.   The audience was a *critical* one with whom Jesus was dealing, composed of Pharisees and doctors of the Law, out of every town of Galilee and Judæa and Jerusalem.   They had come to pass judgment on the new movement under Jesus.   And the Spirit was waiting there as the Agent to apply the healing Word of the Messiah to those not unwilling to be healed.   But alas ! these hard-hearted lawyers gave him no opportunity.   But four friends bring along the street a paralytic neighbour, in the hope that he may be healed by Jesus.   They cannot at first get near, and so they repair to the house-top, and proceed to tear up the tiles in sufficient numbers to allow of their lowering their helpless friend to the feet of Jesus.[2] Here was the Spirit's opportunity.   And here let us notice the twofold paralysis under which the poor man laboured—the one was the *paralysis of the soul*, the other the *paralysis of the body*.   Both appealed to the sympathy of Jesus.   Besides, he is pleased to notice the faith of the bearers.   We are not told that the paralytic at this time had faith in Jesus, but his friends had for him. They believed that if they could only get their friend before Jesus, they would not have to carry him home again.   And disinterested faith for a blessing upon others Jesus respects and rewards.   But which of the two paralyses will Jesus cure first ? The more serious—the paralysis of soul through sin.   Hence, in endearing accents he says, "Man, thy sins are forgiven thee."   It was a case of *absolution*, as Robertson boldly puts it in his sermon upon this passage.[3] And to absolution by one whom they regarded as a mere man the scribes and Pharisees secretly objected.   They rightly said that none but God alone could forgive sins as against God ; they wrongly concluded that Jesus was not Divine.   There was no blasphemy, for this was God incarnate.   Their objection was not publicly taken.   It was a mental note they took of the matter.   Jesus soon shows them that he can read their *thoughts*, by laying bare their objection, and putting his prerogative to the proof.   The demonstration he proposes is this : he has pronounced the absolution.   It may be deemed easy to do this, since no one can tell that it has not taken place.   But he is willing to rest his claim to absolving power by saying the harder word, " Rise up and walk."   According as this takes place or fails is he willing to be judged.   And so, before his enemies and to the palsied patient, he says, " Arise, and take up thy couch, and go into thine house."   Here was a *demonstration* of his ability to forgive sins as against God, for the paralysis departs and the powerless patient starts to his feet and reaches home with his bed as Jesus commands him.   In doing so, moreover, he glorifies God, doubtless, for the double blessing.   Now, these miracles are signs and symbols of spiritual things.   This healing of the body is a sign of what Jesus is willing and waiting to do for our souls.   Paralysis is what has seized on many.   What a living death it is !   It is only Jesus who can free our spirits from it.   If we look to him he will give us his Spirit to strengthen us with all might in the inner man, and to help us to earnestness and action.   And first we shall show to all about us that we are able to help ourselves, and will no longer be burdens upon others.   The four burden-bearers here were spared their hard work ever after.   This is the first manifestation of spiritual strength in the carrying honestly our own share of life's responsibilities !   Secondly, we shall glorify God through our spiritual powers.   We shall praise him for his loving-kindness and tender mercy towards us. And lastly, we shall lead others to fear and to glorify God too.   Hence the great importance of getting rid of spiritual paralysis and of rising into the exercise of spiritual power.   We should also learn distinctly from this miracle what possibilities lie await-

---

[1] 'Nouvelles Études Evangeliques,' p. 228.

[2] Cf. Delitzsch's ' Ein Tag in Capernaum,' ss. 40—46 ; Geikie's ' Life and Words of Christ,' vol. ii. p. 23.

[3] 'Sermons,' vol. iii. p. 69.

ing intercessory prayer and disinterested faith. We may do much in bringing helpless souls to Jesus, that they may be healed by him. He is able to do much for our friends as well as for ourselves, and the joy of bringing others to Christ is only exceeded by the joy of coming ourselves. Let us keep coming to Jesus for ourselves and with others, and strange and blessed experiences shall still be ours.—R. M. E.

Vers. 27—39.—*The call of Levi, and the subsequent banquet.* We noticed how, at the healing of the paralytic, there was a critical assemblage. Secretly did they impugn the absolution pronounced by the Master, and publicly were they refuted. Immediately after, it would seem from all the accounts, Jesus takes the bold step of calling a publican to become his disciple. It was a throwing down of the gauntlet to his enemies. It was taking up a man whom they had excommunicated and despised, and so bringing the kingdom of God into collision with the Jewish authorities. Let us, then, consider—

I. THE CALL OF LEVI, AND ITS ACCEPTANCE. (Vers. 27, 28.) Levi was a leading " custom-house officer," as we should now call him, situated at Capernaum, where the caravans from Damascus to the Mediterranean regularly passed. His office was, we have reason to believe, a lucrative one, so that he had every *worldly* reason for remaining in it. Doubtless he had no position in the Jewish Church, but, considering the Sadducean scepticism which flourished *within* the Church pale, the worldly advantages of the tax-gathering would reconcile Levi to excommunication. When Jesus found him he was busy at his tax-gathering. The piles of money were possibly before him. He was never more prosperously occupied before. But lo! this itinerant Preacher, who has no settled home, has not where to lay his head, comes along, and calls Levi from his business to become his follower. " Follow me," says Christ ; and for Levi it meant the surrender of his worldly calling, and becoming an itinerant preacher of the kingdom of God. The step for Levi was most serious. And here notice what Jesus demanded. It may be expressed in three words: it was *faith in himself*. In no way could he better test Levi's confidence than by asking him to surrender the comfort and certainty of his worldly calling for the uncertainty of the Christian ministry as carried on by the Master himself. It is the one demand which Jesus always makes, that men should *trust him*. And Levi surrenders at once. He leaves all, rises up, and literally follows him. It is a farewell to tax-gathering, that he may take service in the retinue of the Prince of peace. Such a surrender without reserve is what Christianity means. Jesus is put before every one and everything, and his command is our *law*. The following of Christ, moreover, includes the whole Christian morality. If we take his way and carry out his will, and do, day by day, what we believe he would in our circumstances, then we shall find ourselves holy and useful in increasing measure.

II. CONSIDER LEVI'S FIRST MISSIONARY EFFORT. (Ver. 29.) This was in the making of the great feast. Hospitality may be missionary in character. If its design is to bring friends into contact with Jesus, as was literally the case here, then it is distinctly a missionary enterprise. Levi felt that the best thing he could now do would be to get all his acquaintances together and to introduce them to Jesus. And ought not this to be the aim of hospitality still, apart from all cant and hypocrisy? Should not hosts inquire what their motives are in making feasts? Are banquets for display, for the advancement of worldly ends, or for the Master's sake? Moreover, this banquet of Levi shows us the *limits* of our work. All we can ever do for men is to introduce them to Jesus. We cannot do more for their salvation. It is the personal acquaintanceship with Jesus into which they must enter if eternal life is to be theirs. " This is life eternal, to know [*i.e.* to be acquainted with] thee the only true God, and Jesus Christ, whom thou hast sent " (John xvii. 3). The missionary enterprise through hospitality is only beginning to be realized. Hospitality needs to be redeemed, like many another good thing, from worldly uses. A loving heart will enable a faithful Christian to accomplish this.

III. PHARISAIC OBJECTIONS TO CHRIST'S NEW ASSOCIATIONS. (Vers. 30—32.) Eating and drinking in the East are the universal tokens of mutual confidence. After this, the parties will be true to each other until death. Hence the Pharisees with their scribes (so in Revised Version and best authorities)—the legal experts they had brought with them—object to Jesus and his disciples going in " hand and glove " with excommunicated men. From their standpoint it argued great laxity on the part of our

Lord. Really it only meant his freedom from Pharisaic pretence. And his defence was complete. He took the Pharisees on their own ground. He assumed that they were spiritually whole, as they supposed themselves to be. Of course, he knew how seriously they were in this matter deceiving themselves. But assuming they were whole, he would, as a Physician, have been losing his time and missing his opportunity had he associated only with them. It is the sick, these publicans and sinners, who need the Physician's care. Hence he hesitated not to enter into Levi's house and mix with Levi's guests. Now, association with others may, like hospitality, be a form of missionary enterprise. This should be our motive in associating with others. Why not be propagandists in all our contact with men? It is not necessary we should be "puritanical;" for that was exactly what Jesus in this case and in every case declined to be. But we may in all our hearty fellowship with others keep their spiritual good clear as a star in view. Our Lord's principle, too, as here stated, is impressive. He did not come to summon to his side the men of reputation, the men of good public character, the pharisaically righteous, but to call "sinners," those who despaired of themselves and needed help. In this he states his grand policy. It is for us to realize its meaning and to imitate him. As self-despairing ones, let us rally round the Saviour, as he calls us to him, and then let us vigorously publish the call to other sinners, that they too may be saved.[1]

IV. THE PHARISEES FURTHER OBJECTED TO CHRIST'S PRACTICE. (Vers. 33—35.) Having defended his association with publicans and sinners, he is next assailed because he did not teach the disciples to fast. The Baptist, in the spirit of the old *régime,* directed his disciples to fast, but Jesus took a different course altogether. And here we must remember that the Law of Moses prescribed fasting only on the great Day of Atonement, when sin was brought so powerfully to remembrance. The fasting twice a week, in which the Pharisees indulged, arose out of those "traditions of the elders" which in many respects overlaid the precepts of the Law. Against these traditions our Lord set himself firmly. Notice that: 1. *Fasting is a comparatively easy form of self-denial.* As Robertson has said in a sermon on ver. 33, "All can understand the self-denial of fasting, because hunger is a low want, known to all. But all cannot understand the self-denial of hard mental work, or that of associating with uncongenial minds, or that of honestly pursuing a disagreeable occupation or profession." [2] The coarse minds which proposed to criticize Jesus, therefore, took up fasting as the form of self-denial which they found themselves equal to, and sought to condemn Jesus for neglect of it. 2. *There is no good in fasting for its own sake.* The person who abstains from food merely to be able to say he has fasted and so fulfilled a human tradition, is not living a noble life. Asceticism had, therefore, no countenance from Jesus. 3. *The Divine life is essentially social.* The Trinity of Persons in unity declares this fact. God has been social from everlasting, and when he appeared incarnate it was as an eminently social Saviour. Hence he represents himself on this very occasion as a Bridegroom, and life with him as a bridal feast. Mourning would be as impertinent at a marriage-party as fasting would be when Jesus was present with his people. The sociality of the Christian faith endorses the propriety of the policy of Jesus. 4. *Fasting becomes appropriate when fellowship is interrupted.* Our Lord refers to his own departure as a being taken away from them, a violent operation—a prophetic note about the cross! In such days will the disciples fast. The felt *absence* of the Lord should so impress us that fasting would be only natural with us. Through fasting the soul regains its sovereignty over the body, and the gracious presence of the Master as an experience is regained.

V. OUR LORD'S SPIRIT OF INNOVATION. (Vers. 36—39.) The Pharisees expected he would conform to old customs, as unoriginal minds are wont to do. But they utterly mistook him. He came, as these twin parables tell us, with new cloth and new wine. This can only mean the *Christian spirit,* social and missionary in its very essence. Robertson is quite wrong, we believe, in making the new wine and new cloth "austere duties and doctrines," and the old bottles and old cloth as the weak novices in the shape of the new disciples (*ut supra,* p. 196). In what respect these "austere duties

[1] Cf. Gerok's 'Evangelien-Predigten,' s. 669.
[2] 'The Human Race, and other Sermons,' p. 192.

and doctrines," were *new* no one, we imagine, could tell us.   They were the old wine and the old garments, easy and palatable to the self-righteous mind, like *old* wine; but the Christian spirit of sociality and missionary enterprise was the new wine which the self-righteous do not particularly care for.   Hence our Lord resolved to initiate no such foolish policy as this, to tack on the free spirit of Christianity to the old pharisaic spirit of fasting frequently and being generally morose.   The two would not work, and so he courageously resolved to be an innovator, cost what it would, and to conduct his disciples to a better position than Pharisaism realized.[1]   The disciples are the new bottles, and the Christian spirit is the new wine.   The free, social spirit, which Christianity fosters, may not be palatable to the proud minds of men, but the humble appreciate aud preserve it as the disciples have done down to this day.   We ought to have the courage of our convictions, even when it leads us to take new courses for men's sake.—R. M. E.

EXPOSITION.

CHAPTER VI.

Vers. 1—11.—*The Lord's teaching on the question of the observance of the sabbath.*

Ver. 1.—**And it came to pass on the second sabbath after the first.**   The expression accompanying this note of time of St. Luke, "the second sabbath after the first," more literally, "the second-first sabbath," has always been a difficulty with expositors of this Gospel.   The word is absolutely unique, and is found in no other Greek author. Recent investigations in the text of the New Testament have proved that this word is not found in the majority of the more ancient authorities.   Of the modern critical editors, Alford and Lachmann enclose the disputed word in brackets; Tregelles and Meyer omit it altogether; but the Revisers of the English Version relegate it to the margin in its literal form, "second-first;" Tischendorf alone admits it in his text.   The question is of interest to the antiquarian, but scarcely of any to the theologian.   It was, perhaps, introduced at an early date into many of the manuscripts of St. Luke, owing to some copyist writing in the margin of his parchment in this place "first" to distinguish *this* sabbath and its scene from the *other* sabbath alluded to four verses further on; "second" was not unlikely to have been written in correctiou of "first" by some other copyist using the manuscript, thinking it better thus to distinguish this from the sabbath alluded to in ch. iv. 31; and thus the two corrections may have got confused in many of the primitive copies.   It can scarcely be imagined, if it really formed part of the original work of St. Luke, that so remarkable a word could ever have dropped out of the text of the most ancient and trustworthy authorities.   Supposing it to have been a part of the original writing, scholars have suggested many explanations. Of these the simplest and most satisfactory are : (1) The first sabbath of each of the seven years which made a sabbatic cycle was called first, second, third, etc., sabbath.   Thus the "second-first" sabbath would signify the first sabbath of the second year of the seven-years' cycle.   This is Wieseler's theory. (2) The civil year of the Jews began in autumn about mid-September to mid-October (month Tisri), and the ecclesiastical year in spring, about mid-March to mid-April (month Nisan).   Thus there were every year two first sabbaths—one at the commencement of the civil year, which would be called "*first-first;*" the other at the beginning of the ecclesiastical year, which would be called "*second-first.*"   The period here alluded to by St. Luke would perfectly agree with either of these explanations. The latter theory was suggested by Louis Cappel, and is quoted with approval by Godet.   **And his disciples plucked the ears of corn, and did eat, rubbing** them in their **hands.**   St. Matthew adds here that they "were an hungred."   This they might well have been in following the Master in his teaching in different places, even though some of their homes were nigh at hand. We have no need to introduce the question of their poverty—which, in the case of several of them at least, we know did not exist—here leading them to this method of satisfying their hunger.   They had probably been out for some hours with Jesus without breaking their fast, and, finding themselves in a field of ripe corn, took this easy, present means of gratifying a natural want.   The Law expressly permitted them to do this: "When thou comest into the standing corn of thy neighbour, then thou mayest pluck the ears with thine hand" (Deut. xxiii. 25).

Ver. 2.—**And certain of the Pharisees said unto them, Why do ye that which is**

---

[1] Cf. Gess's 'Christi-Selbstzeugniss,' s. 19.

not lawful to do on the sabbath days? It would seem that these Pharisees came from Jerusalem, and were no doubt privately commissioned to watch narrowly the acts of the new Teacher who was beginning to attract such general attention, and who already was openly setting at nought the numberless additions which the Jewish schools had added to the Law. Round the original "sabbath law" of Moses thirty-nine prohibitions had been laid down in the oral law; round these "thirty-nine" a vast number of smaller rules had grouped themselves. Amongst these greater and lesser sabbath restrictions were prohibitions against "reaping and threshing." Now, *plucking ears of corn* was defined to be a kind of " reaping," and *rubbing the ears in the hands* a kind of "threshing." "See," cried some of these spying Pharisees, "do thy disciples publicly break the sabbath, and dost thou not rebuke them?" The Lord's reply does not attempt to discuss what was and what was not lawful on the sabbath, but in broad terms he expounds the great doctrine respecting the significance, limits, and purpose of every law relating to outward acts, even in the event of that law having been given by God, which was not the case in the present alleged transgression. How rigidly the stricter Jews some fourteen or fifteen centuries later still kept these strained and exaggerated traditional sabbath-day restrictions, is shown in a curious anecdote of the famous Abarbanel, " when, in 1492, the Jews were expelled from Spain, and were forbidden to enter the city of Fez, lest they should cause a famine, they lived on grass; yet even in this state '*religiously avoided the violation of their sabbath by plucking the grass with their hands.*' To avoid this they took the much more laborious method of grovelling on their knees, and cropping it with their teeth!"

Vers. 3, 4.—**And Jesus answering them said, Have ye not read so much as this, what David did, when himself was an hungred, and they which were with him; how he went into the house of God, and did take and eat the shewbread, and gave also to them that were with him; which it is not lawful to eat but for the priests alone?** Their own loved David, said the new Teacher to his jealous accusers, scrupled not, when he "was an hungred," to set at nought the twofold ordinance of sacrilege and of sabbath-breaking. (The reference is to 1 Sam. xxi. 5. David's visit to the sanctuary at Nob took place evidently on the sabbath, as the fresh supply of shewbread had been apparently just laid out; he must, too, have violated another rule by his journey on that day. See Stier, 'Words of the Lord Jesus,' on Matt. xii. 3, 4.) The lesson which Jesus intended to draw from the example of the great hero-king and the high priest was that no ceremonial law was to override the general principle of providing for the necessities of the body. St. Matthew adds here a very forcible saying of the Lord's spoken on this occasion, which goes to the root of the whole matter, " But if ye had known what *this* meaneth, I will have mercy, and not sacrifice, ye would not have condemned the guiltless." These laws, as God originally gave them, were never intended to be a burden, rather they were meant to be a blessing for man. After ver. 5, Codex D—a very ancient authority, written in the fifth century, now in the University Library at Cambridge, but one which contains many passages not found in any other trustworthy manuscript or version—adds the following strange narrative: "The same day, Jesus seeing a man who was working on the sabbath, saith to him, O man, if thou knowest what thou art doing, blessed art thou; but if thou knowest not, thou art accursed, and a transgressor of the Law." As no other ancient authority of weight contains this remarkable addition to the recital of our Lord's teaching respecting the observance of the sabbath, it must be pronounced an interpolation. It belongs most likely to the very early days of the Christian story, and was probably founded on some tradition current in the primitive Church. The framework of the anecdote in its present form, too, shows a state of things simply impossible at this time. Any Jew who, in the days of Jesus Christ's earthly ministry, openly, like the man of the story, broke the sabbath in the daring way related, would have been liable to be arrested and condemned to death by stoning.

Ver. 5.—**And he said unto them, That the Son of man is Lord also of the sabbath.** The Master closed his reply to the Pharisee inquirers with one of those short assertions of his awful greatness which puzzled and alarmed his jealous foes. Who, then, was he, this poor unknown Carpenter of despised and ignorant Nazareth? He was either a blasphemer too wicked to be allowed to live, or——. The alternative must have been a very awful thought to some of the nobler spirits among those Jerusalem learned men. Across their minds must have flitted not once or twice in that eventful period some anxious questionings as to *who* and *what* was the strange and powerful Being who had appeared in their midst.

Ver. 6.—**And it came to pass also on another sabbath, that he entered into the synagogue and taught: and there was a man whose right hand was withered.** This was the second part of his sabbath teaching. The first had taken place in the open country, in one of the corn-fields near the Lake of Gennesaret. The second was given in a synagogue possibly in the city of Capernaum. St. Luke inserts this scene, which may have taken place several weeks after the one above related, because it completes in a way the teaching of the Lord on this important point of the ceremonial law.

Ver. 7.—**And the scribes and Pharisees watched him, whether he would heal on the sabbath day; that they might find an accusation against him.** The Pharisee emissaries from the capital were carefully watching him. The Master was perfectly aware of their presence, and well knew the spirit in which they listened to his words and marked his acts, and on this sabbath day he was evidently determined to let them see clearly what was in his mind respecting the present state of Jewish religious training.

Ver. 8.—**But he knew their thoughts, and said to the man which had the withered hand, Rise up, and stand forth in the midst. And he arose and stood forth.** When he perceived or was informed of the presence of the afflicted sufferer in the synagogue, who no doubt had come there with a view of seeing Jesus and asking his help as a physician, Jesus publicly bade the sufferer to stand out in a prominent place in the assembly, and then in the hush that followed proceeded with his public instruction, the poor man with the withered hand standing before him. The Gospel which Jerome found among the Nazarenes gives at length the prayer of this man with the withered hand. "I was a mason earning my livelihood with my own hands; I pray thee, Jesus, restore me to health, in order that I may not with shame beg my bread." This Nazarene Gospel was only used among a sect of early Jewish Christians, and has not been preserved. It possibly was one of those alluded to by the compiler of the Third Gospel in his preface (ch. i. 1).

Ver. 9.—**Is it lawful on the sabbath days to do good, or to do evil? to save life, or to destroy it?** The sum and substance of the Master's teaching here is—works of love done for the bodies and souls of men never mar or in any way interfere with the holiness of a day of rest. St. Matthew in his account of the plucking the ears of corn on the sabbath day (xii. 5), tells us, on that occasion Jesus asked how it was that the priests on the sabbath days profaned the sabbath and were blameless? The Jews in later days used to declare, perhaps in answer to Jesus Christ's famous question here, "that in the temple was there no sabbatism." Now, the Lord pressed home to those who listened to his voice the great truth that in all labours of love, of pity, and

of kindness, done anywhere, there was no sabbatism.

Ver. 10.—**Stretch forth thy hand!** It must have sounded a strange command to the people in the synagogue. How could he stretch out that withered, powerless limb? But with the command went forth the power. In other words, " Stretch forth that poor hand of thine; thou canst now, for, lo! the disease is gone." And we read that he did so, and as he stretched out the limb, so long powerless, the man discovered and the people saw that the cure was already performed.

Ver. 11.—**And they were filled with madness; and communed one with another what they might do to Jesus.** The storm was already gathering. From this time we gather from the words of SS. Matthew and Mark, that in the minds of others as well as in the mind of Jesus, the thought of his death was ever present. The thought-leaders of the Jews—the men whose position was secured as long as the rabbinic teaching held sway in the hearts of the people, but no longer—from this hour resolved upon the death of that strange mighty Reformer. He was, said they, an impostor, a fanatic; one who led men's minds astray. Had they no doubts, we ask; no qualms of conscience, no deep searchings of heart? Were these great ones of earth *really* persuaded that he was a deceiver?

Vers. 12—19.—*The choice of the twelve.*

Ver. 12.—**And it came to pass in those days.** That is to say, in the course of his ministry in Galilee, especially in the thickly populated district lying round the Lake of Genessaret, and after the events related in ch. v. and the first eleven verses of ch. vi., Jesus proceeded to choose, out of the company of those who had especially attached themselves to him, twelve who should henceforth be always with him. These he purposed to train up as the authorized exponents of his doctrine, and as the future leaders of his Church. Things had assumed a new aspect during the last few months. Jerusalem and the hierarchy, supported by the great teachers of that form of Judaism which for so long a period had swayed the hearts of the people, had, although not yet openly, declared against the views and teaching of Jesus. His acts—but far more his words—had gathered round him, especially in Galilee, in the north and central districts of Palestine, a large and rapidly increasing following. It was necessary that some steps should be taken at once to introduce among the people who had received his words gladly, some kind of organization; hence the formal choice of the twelve, who from henceforth stood nearest to him. We possess the following four lists of these twelve men :—

Matt. x. 2—4.	Mark iii. 16—19.	Luke vi. 14—16.	Acts i. 13.
Simon	Simon	Simon	Peter
Andrew	James	Andrew	James
James	John	James	John
John	Andrew	John	Andrew
Philip	Philip	Philip	Philip
Bartholomew	Bartholomew	Bartholomew	Thomas
Thomas	Matthew	Matthew	Bartholomew
Matthew	Thomas	Thomas	Matthew
James of Alphæus	James of Alphæus	James of Alphæus	James of Alphæus
Lebbæus	Thaddæus	Simon Zelotes	Simon Zelotes
Simon the Kananite	Simon the Kananite	Judas of James	Judas of James
Judas Iscariot	Judas Iscariot	Judas Iscariot	

He went out into a mountain to pray, and continued all night in prayer to God.

Ver. 13.—**And when it was day, he called unto him his disciples: and of them he chose twelve.** St. Luke frequently alludes to Jesus spending periods of time in prayer. He would have the readers of his Gospel never lose sight of the perfect humanity of the Saviour, and, while ever keeping in view the higher objects of his earthly mission, still is careful always to present him as the Example of a true life. This is why he mentions so often the prayers of Jesus. This time the Master continued in prayer all night. It was a momentous task which lay before him on the following morning— the choice of a few men, the measureless influence of whose life and work we, though we live eighteen centuries after the choice was made, and see already how the twelve have moved the world, are utterly unable to apprehend. In these solemn hours of communion with the Eternal, we may in all reverence suppose that the Blessed One took counsel with his Father, presenting, as Godet phrases it, one by one to the All-seeing, while God's finger pointed out those to whom he was to entrust the salvation of the world. **Whom also he named apostles.** The literal meaning of this term is "one who is sent," but in classical Greek it had acquired a distinct meaning as "envoy or ambassador" of a sovereign or of a state. These favoured men, then, received this as the official designation by which they were ever to be known. Unknown, unhonoured, and for the most part unlearned men, they with all their love and devotion for their Master who had called them, little recked that morning on the mountain-side to what they were called, and of whom they were the chosen envoys! The four lists of the apostles copied above vary very slightly. There was evidently in the matter of the holy twelve an unerring tradition at the time when Luke wrote these chronicles at Rome or Alexandria, at Ephesus or at Antioch,—all knew every detail connected

with the great first leaders of the faith. The bare list of names was enough. The Church of the first days knew a hundred facts connected with these famous men. The Church of the future needed no details of private history. These apostles, great though they were, were only instruments in the Master's hand; what they did and suffered was, after all, of little moment to those who should come after. In the four bare skeleton lists, though, certain points are noticeable. (1) Each catalogue falls into three divisions containing four names. In each of these divisions the same name always stands first, as though some precedence or authority was deputed to this one over the other three forming the division. This, in the absence of any further notice, must not be pressed. It is, however, a very probable inference. The names of these three are Peter, Philip, James. (2) The twelve were thus divided into three distinct companies, of which the first (this is clearly borne out by the gospel story) stood in the closest relation to Jesus. Of the twelve, the first five came from Bethsaida on the lake, and they all apparently—with the exception of Judas the traitor, who came from a town in Judæa— were Galilæans. The names are all Hebrew (Aramaic) with the exception of Philip and Andrew, which are Greek. It was, however, at that time by no means uncommon for Jews to possess Greek names, so widely did Hellenic influence extend over Egypt, Syria, and the Mediterranean-washed countries of Asia.

Ver. 14.—**Simon, (whom he also named Peter).** The Master had already, reading as he did the future, bestowed upon this often erring, but noble and devoted servant, the surname, *Cephas*, literally, a "mass of rock." **And Andrew.** One of the first believers, and reckoned among the four whose office placed them in closest relation to their Master, and yet for some—to us— unexplained reason, Andrew did not occupy that position of intimacy shared by Peter,

James, and John. He was apparently the intimate friend and associate of Philip, the first of the second "four." **James and John.** Well-known and honoured names in the records of the first days. Mark adds a vivid detail which throws much light on the character and fortunes of the brothers; he calls them Boanerges, "sons of thunder." The burning enthusiasm of James no doubt led to his receiving the first martyr-crown allotted to "the glorious company of the apostles," while the same fiery zeal in the loved apostle colours the Apocalypse. **Philip.** John vi. 5 may be quoted to show that the Lord was on terms of peculiar friendship with this first of the second four. **Bartholomew**; *Bar-Tolmai*: son of Tolmai, He therefore must have been known also by some other name. In St. John's Gospel Bartholomew is never mentioned, but Nathanael, whose name appears in the Fourth Gospel among the apostles, and who is not alluded to in the memoirs of Matthew, Mark, and Luke, evidently represents the same person. The real name of the son of Tolmai, then, would appear to have been Nathanael.

Ver. 15.—**Matthew.** In the list contained in the Gospel which unanimous Church traditions ascribe to this apostle, "the publican" (tax-gatherer) is significantly added. His brother evangelists, Mark and Luke, in their catalogues, omit the hated profession to which he once belonged. **Simon called Zelotes.** In SS. Matthew and Mark this apostle is called "Simon the Kananite." This epithet does not mean that Simon was a native or dweller in Cana of Galilee, but the epithet "Kananite" had the same signification as "Zelotes," the surname given by St. Luke, which is best rendered as "the Zealot." *Kananite* is derived from the Hebrew word קנא, zeal. "He had once, therefore, belonged to the sect of terrible fanatics who thought any deed of violence justifiable for the recovery of national freedom, and had probably been one of the wild followers of Judas the Gaulonite (Josephus, 'Bell. Jud.,' iv. 3. 9). Their name was derived from 1 Macc. ii. 50, where the dying Mattathias, father of Judas Maccabæus, says to the Assidæans (Chasidim, *i.e.* 'all such as were voluntarily devoted to the Law'), 'Be ye *zealous* for the Law, and give your lives for the covenant of your fathers'" (Archdeacon Farrar).

Ver. 16.—**Judas** the brother of James; more accurately, *Judas*, or *Jude, son of James*, or simply *James's Jude*. So this disciple is termed in both the writings ascribed to St. Luke (the Gospel and Acts). In St. Matthew's list we find a "Lebbæus," and in St. Mark's a "Thaddæus" occupy-

ing a position in the third division which in St. Luke's list is filled by "James's Jude." There is no doubt that Lebbæus and Thaddæus were surnames by which James's Jude, or Judas, was known generally in the Church. The necessity of some surname to distinguish this apostle was obvious. Already in the company of apostles there was a Judas, or Jude, who was afterwards known as "the betrayer." One, too, of the Lord's so-called brothers, a figure well known in the society of the Church of the first days, was also named Jude. The meaning of the two epithets is somewhat similar; they both were probably derived from the apostle's character —*Lebbæus* from the Hebrew לב (*lev*), the heart. Jude was probably so styled on account of his loving earnestness. *Thaddæus*, from *thad*, a word which in later Hebrew meant the female breast, was suggested possibly by his even feminine devotedness and tenderness of disposition. The addition in St. Matthew's catalogue to "Lebbæus, whose surname was Thaddæus," which we read in our Authorized Version, does not occur in any of the older authorities, "Thaddæus" being only found in St. Mark's list. **And Judas Iscariot, which also was the traitor.** Some scholars have derived "Iscariot" from *as-cara*, strangulation; or from *sheker*, a lie, *ish sheker*, the man of a lie; these derivations are, however, most improbable. The surname is evidently derived from the place whence this Judas came. Kerioth, possibly the modern town or village of *Kuryetein*, not far from Hebron in Judah. Kerioth is mentioned in Josh. xv. 25, *ish-Kerioth*, a man of Kerioth.

Ver. 17.—**And he came down with them, and stood in the plain.** Leaving the uppermost slopes of the hill—the modern *Kurm Hattin*, or "Horns of Hattîn"—where he had spent the night alone in prayer—Jesus probably descended a little and rejoined the band of disciples. Out of these he called the twelve above mentioned; and then, with the whole body of disciples—the twelve, no doubt, closest to his Person—he continued the descent for some way. On a level spot situate on the hillside, very likely a flat space between the two peaks of Hattîn, the Master and his followers came upon a crowd of inquirers, who had ascended thus far to meet him. These were composed, as we shall see, of various nationalities. Some came with their sick friends, seeking a cure; some were urged by curiosity; others by a real longing to hear more of the words of life from his Divine lips. It was to this crowd that, surrounded by the newly elected twelve, as well as by the larger company of disciples, that Jesus spoke the famous discourse known as the sermon on the mount. **A great multitude of people out of all Judæa and Jerusalem, and from the sea-coast of Tyre and Sidon, which came to hear him.** To the places here enumerated, St. Matthew adds Galilee, Decapolis, and the region beyond Jordan. St. Mark (iii. 8)—where the same period of our Lord's ministry is treated of—alludes to people from Idumæa forming part of the multitude which just then used to crowd round the Master as he taught. Thus the great sermon was addressed to men of various nationalities—to rigid and careless Jews, to Romans and Greeks, to Phœnicians from Tyre and Sidon, and to nomad Arabs from Idumæa.

Ver. 19.—**And the whole multitude sought to touch him: for there went virtue out of him, and healed them all.** The words here used are few, and we pass them over often without pausing to think of what they involve. It was, perhaps, the hour in the ministry of Jesus when his miraculous power was most abundantly displayed.

Vers. 20—49.—*St. Luke's report of the discourse of our Lord commonly termed the sermon on the mount.* We consider that the discourse contained in the following thirty verses (20—49) is identical with that longer "sermon on the mount" reported by St. Matthew (v.). Certain differences are alleged to exist in the framework of the two discourses.

In St. Matthew the Lord is stated to have spoken it on the mountain ; in St. Luke, in the plain. This apparent discrepancy has been already discussed (see above, on ver. 17). The "plain" of St. Luke was, no doubt, simply a level spot on the hillside, on the flat space between the two peaks of the hill.

The more important differences in the Master's utterances—of which, perhaps, one of the weightiest is the addition of St. Matthew to that first beatitude which explains *what* poor were blessed—the "poor in spirit "—probably arose from some questions put to the Master as he was teaching. In his reply he probably amplified or paraphrased the first utterance, which gave rise to the question ; hence the occasional discrepancies in the two accounts. It is, too, most likely that many of the weightier utterances of the great sermon were several times reproduced in a longer or shorter form in the course of his teaching. Such repetitions would be

likely to produce the differences we find in the two reports of the great sermon.

The plan or scheme of the two Gospels was not the same. St. Luke, doubtless, had before him, when he compiled his work, copious notes or memoranda of the famous discourse. He evidently selected such small portions of it as fell in with his design. The two discourses reported by SS. Matthew and Luke have besides many striking resemblances—both beginning with the beatitudes,.both concluding with the same simile or parable of the two buildings, both immediately succeeded by the same miracle, the healing of the centurion's servant. It is scarcely possible—when these points are taken into consideration—to suppose that the reports are of two distinct discourses. The theory held by some scholars, that the great sermon was delivered twice on the same day, on the hillside to a smaller and more selected auditory, then on the plain below to the multitude in a shorter form, is in the highest degree improbable.

No portion of the public teaching of the Lord seems to have made so deep an impression as the mount-sermon. St. James, the so-called brother of Jesus, the first president of the Jerusalem Church, repeatedly quotes it in his Epistle. It was evidently the groundwork of his teaching in the first days. Barnabas, Clement of Rome, Ignatius, and Polycarp, the nameless author of the recently found 'Teaching of the Apostles,' whose writings represent to us most of the Christian literature which we possess of the first century after the death of St. Paul, quote it often. It may be taken, indeed, as the pattern discourse which mirrors better and more fully than any other portion of the Gospels the Lord's teaching concerning the life he would have his followers lead.

It is not easy to give a *précis* of such a report as that of St. Luke, necessarily brief, and yet containing, we feel, many of the words, and even sentences, in the very form in which the Lord spoke them. What we possess here is, perhaps, little more itself than a summary of the great original discourse to which the disciples and the people listened. Godet has attempted, and not unsuccessfully, to give a *résumé* of the contents of St. Luke's memoir here. Still, it must be felt that any such work must necessarily be unsatisfactory.

There appear to be three main divisions in the sermon : (1) A description of the persons to whom Jesus chiefly addressed himself (vers. 20—26). (2) The proclamation of the fundamental principles of the new society (vers. 27—45). (3) An announcement of the judgment to which the members of the new kingdom of God will have to submit (vers. 46—49).

Ver. 20.—**Blessed be ye poor : for yours is the kingdom of God ;** better rendered, *blessed are ye poor,* etc. It is the exact equivalent of the well-known Hebrew expression with which the Psalms begin : אַשְׁרֵי הָאִישׁ, which should be rendered, " Oh the blessedness of the man," etc.! This was probably the exact form in which Jesus began the sermon : " Blessed are the poor." He was gazing on a vast congregation mostly made of the *literally* poor. Those standing nearest to him belonged to the masses—the fishermen, the carpenters, and the like. The crowd was mainly composed of the trading and artisan class, and they, at least *then*, were friendly to him, heard him gladly, came out to him from their villages, their poor industries, their little farms, their boats. The comparatively few rich and powerful who were present that day in the listening multitude were for the most part enemies, jealous, angry men, spying emissaries of the Jerusalem Sanhedrin, men who hated rather than loved the words and works of the Galilæan Teacher. The literally poor, then, represented the friends of Jesus ; the rich, his enemies. But we may conceive of some like Nicodemus, Joseph of Arimathæa, Gamaliel, or the wealthy patrician centurion, in that listening crowd, gently asking the Teacher as he taught, " Are only the poor, then, to be reckoned among thy blessed ones ? " Some such question, we think, elicited the qualifying words of Matthew, " Blessed are the poor *in spirit,*" with some such underlying thought as, " Alas ! this is not very often the character of the rich." It certainly was not while the Lord worked among men. While, then, the blessedness he spoke of belonged not to the poor *because* they were poor, yet it seemed to belong to them especially as a class, because they welcomed the Master and tried to share his life, while the rich and powerful as a class did not. It runs indisputably all through the teaching of Paul and Luke, this tender love for the poor and despised of this world ; full of warnings are their writings against the perils and dangers of riches. The awful parable of the rich man

and Lazarus gathers up, in the story form best understood by Oriental peoples, that truth of which these great servants of the Redeemer were so intensely conscious, *that the poor stand better than the rich for the kingdom of God. The kingdom of God.* Not here, not now. Just a few drops from the river of joy which flows through that kingdom will sprinkle the life of his blessed ones while they live and struggle to do his will on earth ; but the kingdom of God, in its full glorious signification, will be only enjoyed hereafter. It is an expression which includes citizenship in his city, a home among the mansions of the blessed, a place in the society of heaven, the enjoyment of the sight of God—the beatific vision.

Ver. 21.—**Blessed are ye that hunger now : for ye shall be filled.** A similar question probably to the one suggested above, brought out the addition reported in St. Matthew's account — " after righteousness." **Blessed are ye that weep now : for ye shall laugh.** There is a mourning which, as Augustine says, has no blessing from heaven attached to it, at best only a sorrow of this world and for the things of this world. What Jesus speaks of is a nobler grief, a weeping for our sins and the sins of others, for our weary exile here. This is "the only instance," writes Dean Plumptre, "in the New Testament of the use of 'laughter' as the symbol of spiritual joy. . . . The *Greek* word was too much associated with the lower forms of mirth. . . . It is probable that the Aramaic word which our Lord doubtless used here had a somewhat higher meaning. Hebrew laughter was a somewhat graver thing than that of Greek or Roman. Comedy was unknown among the Hebrew people." It is observable that we read of our Lord weeping. His joy is mentioned, and his sorrow. He sympathized with all classes and orders, talked with them, even ate and drank with them ; but we never read that he laughed. There was a tradition in the early Church that Lazarus, after he rose from the dead, was never again to smile.

Ver. 22.—**Blessed are ye, when men shall hate you, and when they shall separate you** from their company, **and shall reproach** you, **and cast out your name as evil, for the Son of man's sake.** An onlook into the yet distant future. These words would be repeated by many a brave confessor in the days when persecution, at the hands of a far stronger and more far-reaching government than that of Jerusalem, should be the general lot of his followers. We find from pagan writers of the next age that Christians were charged with plotting every vile and detestable crime that could be conceived against mankind (see, for instance, the historian Tacitus, 'Annal.,' xv. 44; Suetonius, 'Nero.,' 16).

Ver. 23.—**Rejoice ye in that day, and leap for joy: for, behold, your reward is great in heaven: for in the like manner did their fathers unto the prophets.** Well and faithfully did his followers in after-days fulfil their Master's prophetic charge. Not only did men like Paul and his brother apostles welcome persecution "for the Name" with joy, but long after Paul and his fellows had "fallen asleep," Christians in well-nigh every populous centre of the empire followed the same glorious lead. Indeed, we find the great teachers of the faith positively condemning the fiery zeal of men and women who even too literally obeyed this and other like charges of their adored Master, who positively courted a painful martyrdom, too willingly throwing away their lives, so deeply had words like these burned into their souls. The terrible persecutions which many of the old Hebrew prophets underwent were well known. These men of God endured this treatment during several generations, while evil princes sat on the thrones of Judah and Israel. Thus Elijah mourned the wholesale massacre of his brother prophets when Ahab and Jezebel reigned (1 Kings xix. 10). Urijah was slain by Jehoiakim (Jer. xxvi. 23). Jeremiah himself underwent long and painful persecution. Amos was accused and banished, and, according to tradition, beaten to death. Isaiah, so the Jews said, was sawn asunder by order of King Manasseh. These are only a few instances of the treatment which faithful prophets of the Lord had undergone.

Ver. 24.—**But woe unto you that are rich! for ye have received your consolation.** These "rich" referred to here signify men of good social position. These, as a class, opposed Jesus with a bitter and unreasoning opposition. Again the same warning cry to the so-called fortunate ones of this world is re-echoed with greater force in the parable of the rich man and Lazarus. "Thou in thy lifetime," said Abraham, speaking from Paradise to the poor lost Dives, "receivedst thy good things;" and yet the very characters represented in that most awful of the parable-stories of the pitiful Lord correct any false notion which, from words like these, men may entertain respecting the condemnation of the rich and great because they are rich and great. Abraham, who speaks the grave stern words, was himself a sheik of great power and consideration, and at the same time very rich. Prophets and apostles, as well as the Son of God, never ceased to warn men of the danger of misusing wealth and power; but at the same time they always represented these dangerous gifts as gifts from God, capable of a noble use, and, if nobly used, these teachers sent by God pointed out, these gifts would bring to the men who so used them a proportional reward.

Ver. 25.—**Woe unto you that are full! for ye shall hunger.** This saying points to men who used their wealth for self-indulgence, for the mere gratification of the senses. "The fulness," writes Dean Plumptre, "is the satiety of over-indulgence." **Woe unto you that laugh now! for ye shall mourn and weep.** These are they who, proudly self-satisfied, dreamed that they needed nothing, neither repentance in themselves nor forgiveness from God—a character too faithfully represented in the self-satisfied, haughty Pharisee of the time of our Lord, a character, alas! not extinct even when the hapless men to whom the Lord specially referred had paid the awful penalty of extinction of name and race, loss of home and wealth. The hunger, the mourning, and the weeping were terribly realized in the case of the men and their proud houses in the national war with Rome which quickly followed the public teaching of Jesus. When the Master spoke the words of this sermon the date was about A.D. 30-31. In A.D 70—that is, within forty years—Jerusalem, its temple, and its beautiful houses, were a mass of shapeless ruins. Its people, rich and poor, were ruined. Its very name, as a city and nation, blotted out. But from parables, and still more from direct words, we gather, too, that the hunger, the mourning, and the weeping point to the cheerless state of things in which those poor souls who have lived alone for this world will find themselves after death.

Ver. 26.—**Woe unto you, when all men shall speak well of you!** Dean Plumptre, with great force, remarks that these words "open a wide question as to the worth of praise as a test of human conduct, and tend to a conclusion quite the reverse of that implied in the maxim, *Vox populi, vox Dei.*" **So did their fathers to the false prophets.** A good instance of this is found in 1 Kings xviii. 19, where Queen Jezebel honours the false prophets. See, too, King Ahab's conduct to such men (1 Kings xxii.), and Jeremiah's bitter plaint respecting the popularity of these false men (Jer. v. 31). At this point, according to St. Luke's report, the Master paused. It would seem as though he was fearful lest the awful woes foretold as the doom of the rich, the powerful, and the persecutor, should impart a too sombre hue to the thoughts which his followers would in coming days entertain of the world of men about them. He would have his own think of the circle outside the little world of believers with no bitter and revengeful thoughts, but rather with that Divine pity which he felt and showed to all poor fallen creatures. " See now," the Master went on to say, "notwithstanding the woe which will one day fall on the selfish rich and great ones of earth, and to whom you, my people, will surely be objects of dislike and hate, while you and they are on earth together, the part you have to play with regard to these is steadily to return love for hate."

Ver. 28.—**Pray for them which despitefully use you.** Jesus himself, on his cross, when he prayed that his murderers might be forgiven, for they knew not what they were doing, and his true servant Stephen, who copied faithfully his Lord in his own dying moments, are beautiful though extreme examples of what is meant here. It is St. Luke alone who mentions this act of Jesus on the cross; it is St. Luke, again, who has preserved St. Stephen's words, uttered while they were stoning him to death. He would show how the Lord's command could be carried out.

Ver. 29.—**And unto him that smiteth thee on the one cheek offer also the other.** This and the following direction is clothed in language of Eastern picturesqueness, to drive home to the listening crowds the great and novel truths he was urging upon them. No reasonable, thoughtful man would feel himself bound to the letter of these commandments. Our Lord, for instance, himself did not offer himself to be stricken again (John xviii. 22, 23), but firmly, though with exquisite courtesy, rebuked the one who struck him. St. Paul, too (Acts xxiii. 3), never dreamed of obeying the letter of this charge. It is but an assertion of a great principle, and so, with the exception of a very few mistaken fanatics, all the great teachers of Christianity have understood it.

Ver. 30.—**Give to every man that asketh of thee ; and of him that taketh away thy goods ask** them not again. Here, again, it is clear that faithfully to cling to the literal interpretation would be utterly to ignore the true spirit of the Lord's words here, where he sets forth his sublime ideal of a charity which ignores its own rights and knows no limits to its self-sacrifice. Augustine quaintly suggests that in the words themselves will be found the limitation required. "'Give to every man,' but not *everything*," suggesting that in many cases a medicine for the hurt of the soul would better carry out the words of the Lord than the gift of material help for the needs of the body (' Serm.' ccclix.). But such ingenious exposition, after all, is needless. What the Lord inculcated here was that broad, unselfish generosity which acts as though it really believed those other beautiful words

of Jesus, that " it is more blessed to give than to receive."

Vers. 32, 33.—**For if ye love them which love you, what thank have ye ? for sinners also love those that love them. And if ye do good to them which do good to you, what thank have ye ? for sinners also do even the same.** There are three manners of return, as Augustine—quoted by Archbishop Trench in his ' Exposition of the Sermon on the Mount'—observes, which men may make one to another: the returning good for good and evil for evil,—this is the ordinary rule of man ; then beneath this there is the returning of evil for good, which is devilish ; while above it there is the returning of good for evil, which is Divine,—and this is what is commanded for the followers of Jesus here. On the words, " sinners also love those that love them," Augustine's words are singularly terse and quaint: " Amas amantes te filios et parentes. Amat et latro, amat et draco, amant et lupi, amant et ursi " (quoted by Archbishop Trench, ' Exposition of the Sermon on the Mount,' p. 234, note).

Ver. 35.—**And your reward shall be great, and ye shall be the children of the Highest.** It has been objected by the enemies of Christianity that, after all, Jesus offered his followers a reward by way of payment to them for their self-sacrificing lives on earth. What, however, is this reward? Is it not a share in that Divine and glorious life of God, who is all love; a hope of participation in that eternal work of his which will go from blessing to blessing, from glory to glory ; a certain expectation of dying only to wake up in his likeness, satisfied ? The Eternal had already made a similar promise to his faithful servant Abraham, when he bade him fear not, because here on earth God was his Shield, and after death would be his exceeding great Reward.

Ver. 36.—**Be ye therefore merciful, as your Father also is merciful.** " Yes," goes on the Master, "be ye kind, tender-hearted, merciful ; stop not short at the easier love, but go on to the harder ; and do this because God does it even to the unthankful and evil " (ver. 35). On this attribute of the mercy of the Most High, James, who had evidently drunk deep of the wisdom contained in this great discourse of his so-called brother, speaks of the Lord as " very pitiful, and of tender mercy " (Jas. v. 11).

Ver. 37.—**Judge not, and ye shall not be judged.** Jesus would have his followers avoid one great error which was too common in the religious Jewish life of his time—the habit of censoriously judging others. This uncharitable and often untrue censorship of the motives which led to the acts of others, was one of the practices of the day which stunted and marred all true healthy religious life. **Condemn not, and ye shall not be condemned.** That pitiless condemnation which, regardless of circumstances, condemned as sinners beyond the pale of mercy, whole classes of their fellow-countrymen, publicans, Samaritans, and the like. This haughty judgment of others in the case of the dominant sects of the Jews, resulted in an undue estimate of themselves. His disciples must be very careful how they judged and condemned others; their rule must be, not condemnation, but forgiveness of others.

Ver. 38.—**Give, and it shall be given unto you; good measure, pressed down, and shaken together, and running over.** The grand characteristic feature of the society of his followers must be generosity. They must be known among men as givers rather than judges. Boundless generosity, limitless kindness to all, saint and sinner—that is what he, the Master, would press home to those who would follow his lead (see 3 John 5, 6). Men would find out in time what generous friends they were, and would in their turn freely give to them. **Shall men give into your bosom.** The image is an Eastern one. In the dress then worn, a large bag-shaped fold in the robe above the cincture or girdle was used instead of a pocket.

Ver. 39.—**And he spake a parable unto them.** St. Luke closes his report of the great sermon with four little parables taken from everyday life. With these pictures drawn from common life, the Master purposed to bring home to the hearts of the men and women listening to him the solemn warnings he had just been enunciating. They—if they would be his followers—must indeed refrain from ever setting up themselves as judges of others. "See," he went on to say, "I will show you what ruin this wicked, ungenerous practice will result in: listen to me." **Can the blind lead the blind? shall they not both fall into the ditch?** It is not improbable that some of the links in the Master's argument here have been omitted by St. Luke; still, the connection of this saying and what follows, with the preceding grave warning against the bitter censorious spirit which had exercised so fatal an influence on religious teaching in Israel, is clear. The figure of *the blind man* setting himself up as a guide was evidently in the Lord's mind as a fair representation of the present thought-leaders of the people (the Pharisees). This is evident from the imagery of the beam and mote which follows (vers. 41, 42). Can these blind guides lead others more ignorant and blind too? What is the natural result? he asks; will not destruction naturally overtake the blind leader and the blind

led? Both will, of course, end by falling into the ditch.

Ver. 40.—**The disciple is not above his master: but every one that is perfect shall be as his master.** "Both," he went on to say, "will be lost hopelessly. You cannot expect the disciples of these mistaken men, surely, to be wiser than their teachers; for you know the oft-repeated saying, 'Every one that is perfect [better rendered, *that has been perfected*] shall be as his master;' in other words, the pupils of these censorious, evil-judging, narrow-minded, bitter men will grow up—as they become perfected in this teaching—in their turn equally narrow-minded and bitter as their masters." The conclusion, felt though not expressed, of course, is, "But *my* followers must be something different to these; another and nobler spirit, nobler because more generous, must rule in their hearts."

Ver. 41.—**And why beholdest thou the mote that is in thy brother's eye, but perceivest not the beam that is in thine own eye?** The thought-leaders of the day were in good truth hypocrites, proud, avaricious, in many cases self-indulgent, bigoted, and selfish; they were utterly unfit to be the moral teachers of the people—a position they had arrogated to themselves. The homely but well-known Jewish proverb of the mote and the beam picturesquely put before his listeners the position as it appeared to the Lord. The very defects among the people which the religious teachers professed to lecture upon and to discuss, disfigured and marred their own lives. They were—these priests and scribes and Pharisees—worse than self-deceivers; they were religious hypocrites. The now famous illustration of the mote and the beam is, as has been said, purely Jewish, and was no doubt a familiar one to the people. It is found in the Talmud (treatise 'Bava Bathra,' fol. 15. 2). Farrar quotes from Chaucer—

"He can wel in myn eye see a stalke,
   But in his owne he can nought see a balke."

The word "mote" translates the Greek κάρφος, a chip. In Dutch *mot* is the dust of wood. In Spanish *mota* is the flue on cloth.

Vers. 43, 44.—**For a good tree bringeth not forth corrupt fruit; neither doth a corrupt tree bring forth good fruit. For every tree is known by his own fruit.** For a religious teacher ever to work any real work of good, the first requirement is that he should be known as a faithful doer of the thing he advocates. He must be intensely in earnest, and to be in earnest he must be real. This is emphatically what the religious scribes of Israel were not. This portion of the report of the great sermon, at one period of the Church's history possessed a special importance. It was used as one of the foundations of the system of dualism taught in the once widespread Manichæan heresy, which apparently reached its culminating period of popularity in the fifth century. This heretical school taught that there were two original principles —one *good*, from which good proceeded; one *evil*, from which evil came; that there were two races of men, having severally their descent from the one and from the other. The Manichæan teachers, while rejecting many of the Christian doctrines, made much of the sermon on the mount, calling it the "Divine discourse," mainly on account of the statement we are here discussing. Yet here, when the words of Jesus are carefully considered, there is no assertion of Manichæan dualism, neither does the Master hint that there is anything irrevocably fixed in men's natures, so that some can never become good, and others never evil, but only that *,so long as a man is as an evil tree,* he cannot bring forth good fruit; that if he would *do* good he must first *be* good (see here Augustine, 'Contra Faust.,' xxxii. 7; and 'De Serm. Dom. in Mon.,' 11. 24; 'Contra Adimant.,' 26, etc., in Archbishop Trench's 'Exposition of the Sermon on the Mount,' pp. 309, 310). **For of thorns men do not gather figs, nor of a bramble bush gather they grapes.** This imagery is taken from what is a common sight in Palestine; behind rough hedges of thorn and of the prickly pear, fig-trees are often seen completely covered with the twining tendrils of vine branches.

Ver. 46.—**And why call ye me, Lord, Lord, and do not the things which I say?** It is evident from this heart-stirring appeal of Jesus that he had already obtained a large measure of recognition from the people. We should hardly be prepared to aver that any large number of the Palestinian inhabitants looked on him as Messiah, though probably some did; but that generally at this period he was looked on by the common folk, at all events, and by a few perhaps of their rulers, as a Being of no ordinary power, as a Prophet, and probably as One greater than a prophet. It is scarcely likely that even they who regarded him with the deepest reverence when he spoke the mount-sermon would have been able to define their own feelings towards him. But underneath the Lord's words lies this thought: "Those blind guides of whom I have been telling you, they with their lips profess to adore the eternal God of Israel, and yet live their lives of sin. You, my followers, do not the same thing."

Vers. 47—49.—**Whosoever cometh to me, and heareth my sayings, and doeth them,**

I will show you to whom he is like: he is like a man which built a house, and digged deep, and laid the foundation on a rock: and when the flood arose, the stream beat vehemently upon that house, and could not shake it: for it was founded upon a rock. But he that heareth, and doeth not, is like a man that without a foundation built a house upon the earth; against which the stream did beat vehemently, and immediately it fell; and the ruin of that house was great. "The surrounding scenery may, in this as in other instances, have suggested the illustration. As in all hilly countries, the streams of Galilee rush down the torrent-beds during the winter and early spring, sweep all before them, overflow their banks, and leave beds of alluvial deposit on either side. When summer comes their waters fail (comp. Jer. xv. 18; Job vi. 15), and what had seemed a goodly river is then a tract covered with *débris* of stones and sand. A stranger coming to build might be attracted by the ready-prepared level surface of the sand. It would be easier to build there instead of working upon the hard and rugged rock. But the people of the land would know and mock the folly of such a builder, and he would pass (our Lord's words may possibly refer to something that had actually occurred) into a byword of reproach. On such a house the winter torrent had swept down in its fury, and the storms had raged, and then the fair fabric, on which time and money had been expended, had given way and fallen into a heap of ruins" (Dean Plumptre). Augustine has some weighty and practical comments on this simile of the Master's, with which, as a picture of what they had no doubt seen with their own eyes, the listening multitude would be singularly impressed. The great Latin Father calls special attention to the fact that in this picture of our Lord's the declared rejecters of the truth do not appear mirrored. In *both* the cases here instanced there is a readiness to *hear* the truth. Both the men of the parable-story built their house, but in one case the building ends in terrible disaster. "Would it have been better," asks Augustine ('Serm.' clxxix. 9), "not to have built at all if the building is thus to perish?" He answers, "Scarcely so; that were not to hear at all—to have built nothing. The fate of such will be to be swept away naked, exposed to wind and rain and torrents. The doom is similar in both cases; the lesson of the Lord is one easy to grasp. The wise man will hear, and, when he hears, will do, that is, will translate his impressions into actions. This will be to build a house upon a rock" (see Archbishop Trench, 'Exposition of the Sermon on the Mount,' drawn from Augustine on Matt. vii. 24—27).

There is something very striking in the words with which our Master concluded his great sermon, " and the ruin of that house was great." " After all," men would say, "it was only the destruction of *one* human being." But our Lord's saying reminds us that in his eyes the ruin of *one* immortal soul is a thought full of unspeakable sorrow. " Jesus, in closing his discourse, leaves his hearers under the impression of this solemn thought. Each of them, while listening to this last word, might think that he heard the crash of the falling edifice, and say within himself, 'This disaster will be mine, if I prove hypocritical or inconsistent' " (Godet). In ver. 48 some, though not all, of the ancient authorities, instead of the words, " for it was founded upon a rock," read, " because it had been well built." This text is adopted in the Revised Version, the old reading, as less probably correct, being relegated to the margin.

HOMILETICS.

Vers. 1—11.—*Christ and the sabbath day.*   No feature of Christ's ministry is more striking than his attitude towards the sabbath of Israel. His first conflict with the Jewish authorities was associated with the sabbath. St. John tells us the story of this conflict in the fifth chapter of his Gospel. A man, paralyzed for thirty-eight years, had heard the voice, " Rise, take up thy bed, and walk ; " and, made instantly whole, he had gathered up the pallet which for so long had been stretched by the Pool of Bethesda, and had walked. " It is the sabbath day !" cried the narrow pedants who sat in Moses' chair; " it is not lawful for thee to carry thy bed." From that hour one of the things which spies and emissaries were instructed specially to watch was the conduct of Jesus on the sabbath. Behold the opportunity of accusation that is supplied in the incidents here related—two incidents, if not on the same sabbath, at least on sabbaths separated by a very short interval from each other. In these incidents —the plucking and rubbing of the ears of corn, and the healing of the man with the withered hand—there are presented lessons of permanent value. Two points in particular may be noticed.

I. The question—Is THE SABBATH OF THE FOURTH COMMANDMENT CONTINUED IN THE NEW TESTAMENT OF OUR LORD AND SAVIOUR ? In the light of Christ's teaching we can distinguish between what was dispensational and temporary and what is abiding because rooted in the fitness of things. The Christian sabbath is not merely the Jewish sabbath continued. It is a new day, reminding us of a new state of things, conjoining with the remembrance of the creation in the beginning the witness for the new creation, the new making of things in heaven and earth, through the resurrection of the Lord, calling us to acts of worship and praise and to offerings of love as the Israelitish sabbath did not. Ours is not the seventh, but the first day, and this first day is the Lord's day. To surround it with vexing and irksome restrictions is to take us back from the substance into the dim land of shadows. But, this said, the balancing and completing truth must not be omitted. It is urged by some that the fourth commandment is no longer our authority. But why is that commandment one of the ten great words ? Is it not because it is the expression of something essentially and therefore permanently right ? because behind it there is the original commandment of the Creator—that which is written in our human nature ? The sabbath—this is the testimony of Jesus—was no mere dispensational ordinance, no mere local or tribal arrangement. Grand and solemn is the word, " The sabbath was made for man." It is not by doing away with it, but by bringing into view its right proportions and its highest benefits, that he proves himself the Lord of the sabbath. What is the truth of the supremacy thus claimed ? Some persons take the sentence of the fifth verse, " The Son of man is Lord also of the sabbath," as implying that any one born of woman has authority to subordinate to the sense of his own need the sabbath which was made for man. Even supposing that this use of the word " Son of man " were allowable, is the conclusion drawn permissible ? Would the idea for an instant be tolerated that, because laws are imposed by the ruler for the benefit of his subjects, each subject might change them or dispense with them at his own convenience ? But there can be no doubt that the "Son of man " spoken of is Christ himself, the second Adam, the representative Man. He—realizing, on the one hand, the true purpose of the sabbath, and discriminating, on the other, between such a use as shall keep the institution subordinate to the end, the good of man, and such an abuse as practically inverts this order, making man a mere creature of the institution—gives the true note of the blessed sabbath-keeping.

II. WHAT IS THIS BLESSED SABBATH-KEEPING? Observe: 1. There is no disturbance of the primary conception—rest. That is implied in the very word "sabbath." Rest, undoubtedly, is the need to which the ordinance immediately refers. "Six days shalt thou labour" is part of the Divine injunction. "But on the seventh day thou shalt not do any work." What a blessing is the weekly cessation from weary toil! The experiment of a tenth-day rest has been tried, and has failed. The septennial period seems to be the proportion adapted to the human system. In our complex social life individuals must suffer for the general good; some must work that the greater number may rest. But can we too jealously guard the rights of the poorest, ay, of beast as well as man? Can we too earnestly demand that there shall be no causeless multiplication of labour on the day of the Lord? Yes; God's sabbath is for repose of body, brain, mind, spirit. What promotes a healthy rest is in harmony with it; what hinders is alien to it. A day of pleasure-seeking and excitement is not a help. Take two men—one spending his Sunday in search of mere enjoyment; the other spending it quietly in the midst of his family, at church, taking the quiet walk, doing some little service for Christ: which of the two is the more rested, soothed, fitted for the labour of the Monday morning? Rest but not torpor, repose but not inaction, is a want for which the sabbath was made. 2. But with this comes into view what is distinctive in Christ's theory of sabbath-keeping. Negatively, in the reply about the rubbing of the ears of corn. He reminds us that no dull uniformity must overbear pressing human necessities. These are not to be met by a categorical "It is not lawful." The consideration of human well-being must allow for a certain flexibility in all enactments. But, positively, remark what is shown in the case of the man with a withered hand. This—that a beneficent activity is the highest fulfilment of the sabbath. Therefore the activity of worship and instruction; therefore also the activity of kindness-doing, of seeking the good of our fellows, of having a part with God the Healer. The ideal of the rest-day is a day in which a due proportion of these two forms of well-doing is maintained—the assembly for the service of God in prayer and praise and mutual edification, and room for doing good in the home and in the world. Do we realize, or even attempt to realize, this ideal as we should? How listless, how wanting in brightness and usefulness, is the observance of Sunday by even religiously minded persons! Ah! the most lawful of lawful things is to do well on the sabbath day, and the holier and more refreshing will the day be the more that in it the opportunity is realized of doing good and saving life, and thus proving ourselves his brethren who, being the Son of man, is Lord also of the sabbath.

Vers. 12—49.—*The foundation of the kingdom.* The work set before us in this portion is great and solemn. It is the beginning of a new epoch of the earthly ministry. Hitherto Christ had been the Rabbi, the Prophet, the Healer. Now he is to "gird his sword on his thigh," to take to himself the power of the King. And for this work observe the preparation mentioned by the evangelist (vers. 12, 13), "All night in prayer to God." The hush breathed over nature; the silence unbroken except by the cry of the wild beast seeking, in its own way, its meat from God; the glories of the firmament above, united with the sabbath-quiet of the earth around,—these were the features which invited, not slumber to the eyelids, but prayer, meditation, conference with the Father in heaven. We cannot avoid the conclusion that the retreat and the "all-night prayer" were specially in view of the action of the morrow. Oh, what a rebuke on our listless, quickly dismissed intercessions! How impressive the reminder that, for the appointment of men to minister in the house of the Lord, to render any spiritual service, the right beginning is effectual fervent prayer! Would there not be more fruits of work, more blessing for workmen, if there were more diligent following of Christ's example? Compare this passage with Acts xiii. 3. Note the two points in the foundation-laying of the kingdom of heaven—the *personal agency,* and *the Law.*

I. "HE CALLED THE DISCIPLES"—the larger company, including those who had attached themselves to his Person, many, no doubt, of the healed, of those who had been delivered from demons and brought to their right mind; and " of them he chose twelve." Let us assume that the number is part of the ordering (see ch. xxii. 29, 30). And recollect also the significance attached to twelve—as the complete number of the Church—in the Book of Revelation. Do not exaggerate, but do not underrate, the significance of the numbers found in Scripture. The naturalist who would learn the differences, truths, and natures of things must take into account the curious parallels, the typical forms, the numbers which he discovers running through genera and species. It is the perception of these minute evidences of method, of purpose in details, which is part of the scientific man's paradise. And it is the same kind of perception, the " searching rapturous glance " into the hidden truth of Scripture, which carries the devout mind through the mere outer boundaries of the garden into the enjoyment of its delicacies and delights. Observe the *statement* as to the twelve. 1. *The Lord chose them.* " He called," it is said in St. Mark, " whom he would." This is the foundation of the apostolate for each and all. The choice is in his own hands, determined, not by any plan or rule of mere prudential wisdom, but because of that which, the night before, he had seen and heard of his Father. And to this same royalty all selection for spiritual office is evermore the witness. The action of the Church, through its officers, is only a supplementary or declarative action. The originating and efficient action is what we style the call of the Holy Ghost—an inward aptitude or anointing of Divine love and grace in the character so manifest that we can read the sentence, " Called because the Lord has willed." 2. *The Lord ordained.* This is expressly stated by St. Mark. It is included in St. Luke's " he named." Probably there was an outward act or symbol—that laying on of hands, which carried out well-known Hebrew associations, and, for designation to office, has been appropriated by the Christian Church from the earliest period of its history. Be this as it may, the ordination was also a disjunction; it was the final severance from the former calling; they were henceforth to give themselves wholly to the Word of God, the Master's meat their meat, the Master himself their all in all. Immediately before he suffered, Christ reminded the eleven of that transaction on the mountain-side, " I have chosen you, and ordained you, that ye should go and bring forth fruit." And, again, on the Resurrection morning, the fuller truth of the ordination symbol was realized when he said, " As the Father sent me, so have I sent you," and having so said, he breathed on them, and added, " Receive ye the Holy Ghost." 3. *What were the functions of the twelve?* Following the guidance of St. Mark, we reply: First, to be with Christ, his associates, sharing his temptations, eye-witnesses of his glory and majesty, depositaries of his words and of his inmost confidences. Second, to preach, to go forth declaring him and his gospel and his kingdom. Third, to exercise among men his own power of healing sickness and casting out devils. Keep hold of this sequence—this first, second, third. The first requirement is always life with Christ, communion with the personal Saviour: there is no real preaching, no real power, without that. A man must be taught before he can teach. And where and by whom shall he be taught? The university is well. Never more to be desired than now is a body of Christian instructors learned as well as godly. Experience of men is well: thence comes tact, the skill by which souls are attracted and won for higher things. But there is a graduation better still—one which is necessary to spiritual force—graduation in the school of Christ; the learning of Christ. And this can be realized only through day-by-day fellowship with him, beholding his beauty, and inquiring in his temple. Then the second demand is, preach him, speak out what he speaks in. And so also there is the third function, to work for him, to be in this world presences of healing and blessing, in Jesus' name " casting out devils, speaking with new tongues, taking up serpents, laying hands on the sick that they may recover." Thus were the twelve named apostles—the sent of the Lord. And, having been named, they were made ready by Christ himself for the day when they should do greater works than any which they had witnessed, because he had gone to the Father, and shed forth the promise of the Holy Ghost. A strange kingdom, indeed! The King, that lowly Man seated on one of the horns of Mount Hattîn, and his princes and companions these poor, uncouth-looking, unlearned men! Never, it might be thought, was such a burlesque of royalty seen. But that was, that is, the monarchy whose sceptre shall stretch from pole to pole, that at the name of Jesus every knee may bow.

II. HE CAME DOWN WITH THE TWELVE, it is added, and stood on the plain—the

King and the kingdom meeting the parliament of man. Yes, the King meek and lowly, but " the mighty God, the Lord, is about to speak, and call the earth from the rising of the sun to the going down thereof." He would not speak until he had constituted his Church. For the Man is before the Law, the Voice before the Scripture, the order before the ordering. This has been done, and he comes down to the great world with its fevers and diseases and spirits of uncleanness surging before him, and seeking to touch him from whom, as a great stream of healing, the power goes forth. The law, the manifesto of the kingdom, is published. What this law is admits of being more fully expounded in connection with the Gospel of St. Matthew. The differences between the reports in the two Gospels deserve to be studied. It is sufficient here to indicate the sum and substance of the legislation of Christ the King on the holy hill of Zion. Clearly the old Law, that delivered from Sinai, is fully in the mind of Jesus. It is quoted again and again. But how striking the contrast between that past and this present! That past, when

> " Around the trembling mountain-base
> The prostrate people lay ;
> A day of wrath and not of grace ;
> A dim and dreadful day ; "

this present, the soft grassy slope, the bright sky overhead, the rejoicing world around, the many sitting before him who had received the healing virtue; himself, in tones full of the music of love, declaring the truth for which the soul of man is made as the eye is made for the light. Not that the past is ruthlessly swept away. All is preserved —preserved because fulfilled. But his law-giving is a new law-making, because it penetrates to the innermost region of the life; it searches the spirit as with the candle of the Lord ; its dealing is not so much with the mere outer conduct as with the inner motive power. The man is right when the heart is right—this is the cardinal principle. And the sermon passes onward, from the beatitudes with which it begins, through the exposition of true soul-rectitude, to the sublime conclusion which may God help all to ponder. " Every one that cometh unto me, and heareth my words, and doeth them, I will show you to whom he is like . . . But he that heareth, and doeth not, is like," etc. From the great ruin foretold may the good Lord deliver us !

HOMILIES BY VARIOUS AUTHORS.

Vers. 6—11.—*Sin disabling, Christ restoring.* Being in the right place, our Lord found an opportunity of doing that for which he came, and much more besides. The doing of duty often leads to the finding of privilege and the exercise of power for good. We learn—

I. THAT SIN DISABLES US. This man came into the synagogue *with a withered hand.* That which was the natural instrument of power—his right hand—was powerless. Gradually its strength had been disappearing until it had completely gone ; and that with which God meant him to do his work, to greet his fellows, to make his mark in the world around him, had become an inefficient and useless member. The disease from which he was suffering, whatever it may have been, had by slow degrees wasted and worn away its vital power, and it could do nothing of all that it was created to do. Just such is the action of sin. It is a disabling spiritual disease. Its effect is to reduce and finally to remove those spiritual powers with which our Creator endowed us, and in the exercise of which our true life is found. Our human power, as we came forth from God, was that of worship, of contemplation, of recognizing and rejoicing in the truth, of delighting in God, of obedience to his commandments, of acquiescence in his will, of living in our sphere the life he lives in his, of reflecting his own likeness in our character and our deeds. But sin has been taking this away from us ; away from our race, away from the individual who allows it to reign over his soul. More and more it disables us from taking the part we were intended to take, and doing the work we were intended to do. It is the great and sad disabling force in the spiritual sphere.

II. THAT CHRIST COMES TO RESTORE US. He comes to say to us, " Stretch forth thy hand ; " resume thy power ; have again and use again those precious spiritual faculties which, under the grievous injury of sin, have lain dormant within thee.   And even as he wrought a cure in this afflicted man which was radical and thorough, making the life-blood to course through all his veins and nourish every nerve and muscle which had shrunk and withered, so does he heal our hearts by a process which is not super-ficial, which does not merely affect the extremities, but which goes to and proceeds from the heart.   *He shows us our true selves*—whence we came; what we were created to be; how far we have fallen from our right heritage and condition; what is our unworthiness and guilt; what we may yet become.   And *he reveals himself to us*—the Divine Mediator, Saviour, Lord, through whom we have access to God, in whom we are restored to God's favour, unto whom we dedicate, joyfully and unreservedly, all the faculties of our nature.   In Christ Jesus we enter on a new life; all the springs of our soul are touched and renewed; we regain our lost possession; we stretch forth the right hand of our spiritual power; we do our work in his world.

III. THAT CHRIST DEMANDS OF US AN IMMEDIATE, PRACTICAL RESPONSE.   That he may heal us, he summons us to act.   He said, "Stretch forth thy hand!" and in the act of obedience the cure was wrought.   To us he says, "Come unto me!"   "Abide in me!" and as we endeavour to comply we begin to be restored.

IV. THAT PRACTICAL KINDNESS IS A PRINCIPAL MANIFESTATION OF RENEWED POWER. The great Restorer was at the same time the great Teacher.   By the whole incident, and especially by his healing act, our Lord was making known to us for all time that, whatever may be the worth of religious observances—and they have their own great value—they are distinctly second in his sight to those acts of human pity and benefi-cence by which we lift a load from a brother's heart, and brighten the rest of his life on earth.—C.

Vers. 13—16.—*The designation of the twelve.*   Our Lord appears to have formally designated the twelve, on this occasion, to be his apostles.   He had called them singly before; now he appoints them to their post in a more formal manner.   This act of his suggests to us some thoughts upon—

I. THEIR LIKENESS TO ONE ANOTHER, and the consequent bond of union between one another.   This consisted in: 1. A common nationality, with all that meant to an intensely patriotic people.   2. A common faith, including a common hope that a new prophet would arise and accomplish all that was looked for from the expected Messiah. 3. Similar circumstances, education and social position; not the same, indeed, but of the same class.   4. A common attachment to Jesus Christ; in the case of most of them a trust and an affection that were to deepen every day, in the case of one of them a faith that was to slacken and to depart.

II. THEIR DIVERGENCES FROM ONE ANOTHER.   1. In the habits of mind and life formed by different occupations.   2. In mental constitution and moral disposition. How different Peter from John, and both from Thomas, and all three from James, etc.! 3. In reputation.   Of some of them we know nothing but their names; we do not know where they laboured or what was the kind or measure of their service.   Tradition has been busy with their names, but history tells us nothing.   Of others we have a con-siderable knowledge, and their reputation is great indeed and will be ever growing. 4. In their career: one ending in shame and gloom; the others in honour and in glory.

III. THEIR FUNCTIONS.   These, according to Mark (iii. 14, 15), were threefold. 1. Being with Christ, and witnessing his life; thus qualifying themselves to attest his purity, his power, his love.   2. Preaching the gospel; making known to their countrymen that the Promised One for whom they had so long been looking had come at last, and had come with the most gracious words on his lips that man had ever spoken.   3. Verifying the truth by acts of beneficent power—they were to exercise "power to heal."   And it is in no small or mean sense that our Lord summons us all to do these same things.   (1) To be with him; sitting at his feet and learning of him his heavenly truth; following him along his course, and becoming filled with a deep sense of his stainless purity and surpassing love; kneeling at his cross, and receiving all the benefit and blessing of his great salvation.   (2) Declaring to others all that we have thus learned of Christ, our Lord and Saviour; making known to the sad, the suffering, the sinful, what a Friend and Refuge they will find in him.   (3) Verifying the truth of our attestations by comforting stricken hearts, by enlightening darkened minds, by transforming evil lives, by lifting men up, God helping us, from the depths of wrong and of despair to the noble and blessed heights of holiness and joy and hope.—C.

Ver. 20.—*The blessedness of humility.* Acting on the established and valid principle that we must interpret the less by the more complete, we determine the meaning of this passage by the words as recorded in Matthew's Gospel, "Blessed are the *poor in spirit*," etc.; and thus taking it, we conclude—

I. THAT NARROWNESS OF MEANS IS NOT A DESIRABLE THING. Our Lord could not have intended to teach that the poor (in outward circumstances) were necessarily blessed, for poverty itself means privation, inability to command the various bounties and treasures our Creator has provided for our enjoyment and enrichment. Moreover, it by no means constantly or certainly leads to anything which can be called "the kingdom of God;" on the contrary, it frequently conducts to dishonesty, servility, demoralization (see Prov. xxx. 8, 9). Neither, therefore, in the present nor in the future can such poverty be pronounced blessed (see, however, homily on ch. iv. 18, "to preach the gospel to the poor").

II. THAT POOR-SPIRITEDNESS IS A DECIDEDLY UNWORTHY THING. A "poor-spirited" man, according to the common usage of the term, is a man no one can esteem, and he is a man who cannot respect himself. Christ could not have intended to commend *him* as the heir of the kingdom of God. He did indeed say much in praise of the meek, the enduring, the merciful, the forgiving; he did say much in deprecation of violence and retaliation. But meekness is a vastly different thing from meanness or cowardice; and a man may be nobly superior to mere violence who fights bravest battles for truth and righteousness. All struggle is not soldiership; and he who has most of what Christ meant when he blessed the poor in spirit may be very valiant and very aggressive at his post as the champion of all that is true and pure.

III. THAT HUMILITY OF HEART IS THE DESIRABLE THING FOR SINFUL MEN. Blessed are the men who have in their hearts a deep sense of their own unworthiness. And they are so because this is: 1. *The true and therefore the right thing.* Truth is always and under all circumstances to be preferred to error. It would make a man much more comfortable in his mind to persuade him that he is everything that is good, and that he had done everything that was required of him. But what a hollow and rotten thing such a satisfaction would be, if the man were wrong and guilty! How much better for him to know that he was guilty, in need of cleansing and of mercy! How pitiable (not enviable) the Church or the nation that supposes itself to be rich and strong when it is utterly poor and weak! How enviable (not pitiable) the man who has come to understand that he is in urgent need of those resources which he may have if he will seek them, and which—now that he knows his necessity—he will not fail to seek! To have a deep sense of our unworthiness before God is to *know ourselves as we are; it is to recognize our lives as they have been.* It is to perceive how far we have failed to be that which we should have been to our Divine Father; it is to realize how much there has been in our lives which God's Law condemns, how much there has been absent from them which his Word demands. It is to hold the truth in our hearts; it is, so far, to be in the right. It is a blessed estate as compared with its opposite—that of error and delusion. But it is also: 2. *The receptive and therefore the hopeful thing.* When a man imagines himself to be safe he admits no Saviour to his heart; when he knows and feels himself to be in danger and in difficulty he opens his door wide to one that will befriend him. The man in whose heart is a true humility, who finds himself to be wrong with God, who sees how far he is from perfect rectitude, is the very man who will welcome Jesus Christ in all his gracious offices. (1) Conscious ignorance will welcome the Divine Teacher. (2) Conscious guilt will rejoice in an all-sufficient Saviour. (3) Conscious weakness will lean on Almighty Power, and be ever seeking the upholding grace of a mighty Spirit. (4) Conscious error and insufficiency will yield itself to the guidance and direction of a Divine Lord and Leader. And surrendering ourselves to Christ, we enter the kingdom of God.—C.

Ver. 21.—*The blessedness of spiritual hunger.* On the same principle of interpretation as that which applies to the preceding verse (see preceding homily), we conclude that our Master is referring to those who hunger *after righteousness*, who are affected by a keen spiritual appetite. These are in a state of earnest religious inquiry; they are like the young man who ran eagerly and anxiously to "know what he must do to inherit eternal life" (ch. xviii. 18). In other words, they are earnestly desirous of gaining the *favour* and also the *likeness* of God; of being such that God will not condemn them as guilty, but count them as righteous; such also that they will in a very serious sense *be* righteous even as he is righteous, be "partakers of his holiness." Now, wherein consists the blessedness of this spiritual condition?

I. SEEKING GOD IS THE ONLY HONEST AND RIGHT THING TO DO. Those who believe of God what most men do believe—that he is the Author of their being and the Source of all their blessings, that he is more nearly and importantly related to them than any human being can be, that they owe everything they are and have to him—are most strongly and sacredly bound to seek his favour. To be blind when he is beckoning, deaf when he is calling, insensible when he lays his hand upon them,—this is to be wholly, sadly, shamefully in the wrong.

II. SEEKING GOD IS THE LOFTY AND NOBLE THING. To seek God, to hunger and thirst after him and his righteousness, is the true heritage of our manhood; it is that which, incalculably more than anything else, lifts us up to a high and noble level. Not to be a-hungred and athirst after the living God is to be forfeiting the very best portion for which our Creator called us into existence.

III. SEEKING GOD IS THE ONE SATISFYING THING. "Blessed are ye that hunger: for *ye shall be filled*;" and those who hunger after that which is lesser and lower are *not* filled. No earthly joy fills the soul; it leaves it still craving. 1. Not even the purer joys of earth fill the soul; not even beholding the beauties and glories of creation; "the eye is not satisfied with seeing" these. Not even listening to the sweetest melodies that can be heard; "the ear is not satisfied with hearing" them. 2. Much less with the grosser delights—making money, wielding power, receiving homage, indulging in bodily gratifications; certainly the tongue is not satisfied with tasting, and "he that loveth silver is not satisfied with silver" (Eccles. v. 10). But: 3. The love of God, the possession of the friendship of Jesus Christ, the spending of our days and our powers in the holy, elevating service of a Divine Redeemer,—this is that which fills the heart with a restful and abiding joy, and which brightens the life with a light that does not fade.

> "These are the joys which satisfy
> And sanctify the mind."

These are the joys which last; which live when the passions of youth have been burnt out, when the ambitions of manhood are dead, when life is lived through and death is waiting for its own; the joys which, as all else grows dim and worthless, become more and more precious still. "Blessed are they that hunger thus: for they shall be *filled*."—C.

Vers. 22, 23.—*The blessedness of martyrdom.* Using the word "martyrdom" in its broader sense, we have to consider the Lord's saying respecting it. It certainly is paradoxical enough. Yet his meaning is to be found for the looking. It is, indeed, true—

I. THAT THE ENMITY OF OTHERS IS A SORE TRIAL TO OUR SPIRIT. Other things bruise us beside bludgeons, and other things cut us beside whipcord. The manifest hatred of other hearts, the cruel reproaches of unsparing lips, banishment from the society of our fellow-men as being unworthy to remain, blighting a fair fame with unjust aspersions,—these things cut deep into the human soul, they bruise almost to breaking tender and sensitive spirits. Some, indeed, are so constituted that the roughest treatment on the part of others will not hurt them; they can throw it off, can cast it aside with indifference; it is to them "as the idle wind which they regard not." But these are the exception, and not the rule among men. God meant us to be affected by the judgment of our brethren and sisters, to be encouraged and sustained by their approval, to be discouraged and checked by their censure. It is a part of our humanity that, upon the whole, works for righteousness. But only too often its effect is evil; only too often the pure are pelted with reproaches, the faithful are condemned for their fidelity, the holy are exposed to the hatred and ribaldry of the profane. Then there is suffering which God never intended his children to endure,—that of the faithful witness to the truth, that of the brave, unyielding martyr to the cause of Jesus Christ. And many are they who would more readily welcome and more easily endure blows or imprisonment than bitter malignity of heart and cold severity of speech. But then it is also true—

II. THAT CHRISTIAN CONSIDERATIONS TRIUMPH OVER ALL. Our Master and Teacher would have our hearts to be so filled with the other and opposite aspect of the case, that our natural inclination to be saddened and stricken in spirit will be completely overborne, and that, instead of sorrow, there will be joy. "Our reward is great in heaven;" so great that we who are reproached for Christ's sake are "blessed;" we are, indeed, to "leap for joy." What, then, are these balancing, these overbalancing considerations? 1. That we are taking rank with the very noblest men: "In like manner . . . unto the prophets." We stand, then, on the same level with Moses, with Samuel, with Elijah, with Isaiah, with Jeremiah; with a noble company of men and women who, long since their day and their dispensation, have "gone without the camp, bearing his reproach;" men and women were these "of whom the world was not worthy," to be classed with whom is the highest honour we can enjoy. 2. That we take rank with One who was nobler than all; for did not he, our Lord himself, bear shame and obloquy? was not he crowned with the crown of thorns, because he was here "bearing witness unto the truth" (John xviii. 37)? 3. That we are serving our self-sacrificing Saviour. A modern missionary relates that when he and another were assaulted by a Chinese crowd, and when, putting his hand to his head where he had been hit, he found it moist with his blood, he felt a strange thrill of exceeding joy as he realized that he had been permitted to shed his blood for that Divine Saviour who had poured out his life for him. 4. That we are truly serving our race; for the truth to which we bear a rejected testimony to-day will, and partly as the result of our suffering witness, be accepted further on, and become the nourishment of the people. 5. That we are on our way to the highest heavenly honour. They who suffer shame "for the Son of man's sake" now shall one day be exalted in the presence of the holy angels. Great will be their reward in the heavenly kingdom.—C.

Vers. 27, 28, 32—35.—*Seeking the highest good from the highest motive.* In these words our Lord commends to us—

I. THE HIGHEST CONCEIVABLE MORAL EXCELLENCE. There are four gradations by which we may ascend from the devilish to the Divine, in spirit and in character. 1. We may hate those who love us. There are bad men bad enough, like enough to the evil one himself, to positively hate those who are trying to redeem them, who repay the devoted efforts of their truest friends with sneers and revilings. 2. We may hate those who hate us. Not only *may* we do this, *we do it.* As sin has perverted it, it is in the human heart to return hatred for hatred, blow for blow. 3. We may love those who love us. Most men are equal to that: "Sinners also love those that love them." 4. We may love those who hate us. "I say unto you, Love your enemies, do good to them which hate you," etc. Let us understand *whom Christ would have us consider our enemies*, and whom, as such, he would have us love. These are not only our *national* enemies; but they are certainly included. To allow ourselves to be carried into the current of bitter animosity against those with whom our country is at strife, so as to rejoice in their suffering and their death,—this is here rebuked by our Master. But our "enemies" are more often found at home. They include all those *whose relation to ourselves is likely to provoke ill feeling ; e.g.* those effectively opposing us in counsel or debate; those successfully contending with us in business; those engaged in vindicating their "rights" (as they seem to them) against us; those whose material interests clash with ours; those who have spoken against us or have taken any active steps to injure us. We must also understand *what Christ meant by our loving these.* Clearly he could not have intended that we should cherish toward them that full and complete friendship which is the very precious fruit of gratitude and esteem, and which can only be felt toward those to whom we owe great things, or for whom we have a real veneration. That is impossible in the nature of things. But it is not impossible, it is quite open to us, to extract from our heart every root of bitterness toward our enemies, to exclude all desire for their ill fortune; and, going much further than that, to nourish in our souls a positively kind feeling toward them, a readiness to serve them; nay, more, to form the habit of praying for them, and of looking out for an opportunity to show them kindness. Surely this is the supreme thing in human morality. No teacher has summoned us to climb higher than this; no learner has reached a loftier summit. And Christ asks us to do this—

II. From the highest conceivable motive. We might endeavour after this true nobility because: 1. God positively requires it of us (Mark xi. 26; Matt. xviii. 35) 2. It is the noblest victory over ourself. "He that ruleth his spirit is greater than he that taketh a city." 3. It is the greatest victory over others. "In so doing thou shalt heap coals of fire on his head." But there is an incentive higher than these—the highest of all; it is that which our Lord gives us in the text; because: 4. By so doing *we resemble God himself*. "Ye shall be the children of the Highest: for he is kind unto the unthankful and to the evil." Here is the loftiest aspiration cherished for the loftiest reason. Think kindly of those who are judging harshly of you; feel friendly toward those who are feeling bitterly about you; speak generously of those who are talking disparagingly of you; do deeds of kindness to those who are acting unhand-somely toward you; bend the knee in prayer on behalf of those who are persecuting you;—do this because then you will be breathing the very atmosphere of magnanimity which God breathes in heaven, because you will then be animated by the very spirit by which he is prompted in all he is doing there, because you will then be ruling your humble life by the very principles on which he is ruling his broad and boundless empire. "Love ye your enemies . . . and your reward shall be great;" indeed, you shall be "the children of the Highest;" the mind that is in him shall be in you, you shall then be perfected (Matt. v. 48), crowning every other virtue and grace of your character, even as God crowns all his other attributes, with the glorious, regal, trans-cendent excellency of an unquenchable, victorious love.—C.

Ver. 31.—*The golden rule*. We call this precept of Christ "the golden rule;" pro-bably we intend thereby to pay it the highest honour we can offer it. But it is the "precious metal," rather than the admirable precept, to which the compliment is paid by the association of the two. For if this rule of our Lord were only illustrated in the daily life of men, they would be enriched as no imaginable quantity of gold could enrich them. Then would such a revolution be effected as no statesman has ever dreamed of working; then would all social evils for ever disappear; then would human life wear another aspect from that which now saddens and shames us; for the golden rule, enacted in the lives of men, would soon inaugurate the "golden year." We look at—

I. Its surpassing excellency. 1. *It is within all men's apprehension*. It is no learned, erudite definition, requiring much culture to comprehend. The most simple-minded can understand it. 2. *It commends itself to all men's conscience*. It is not one of those commandments which require much thought and much practice to appreciate. It is obviously just and fair. It hardly admits of dispute. Every one can see, every one must feel—if "the light that is in him be not darkness"—that it is the *right* thing for him to do. 3. *It excludes all evasions*. No man can shield himself under any misrepresentation of the rule. He must know whether or not he is trying to act toward his neighbour as he would that his neighbour should act toward him. 4. *It covers the entire range of human life*, so far as our relations to one another are con-cerned. It covers: (1) Action, and also inaction; including in its sweep not only those things we do, but those we leave undone—the attention, the kindness, the considera-tion, the return we should render but may be withholding. (2) The judgment we form of others; the right they have to our patient, impartial, intelligent, charitable judgment; the claim they may fairly make that we should attribute the worthy rather than the unworthy, the pure rather than the impure, the generous rather than the mean motive. (3) Our speech; the utterance of the kind and true word *of* our neigh-bour, and also *to* him. (4) Conduct—all our dealings and doings, of all kinds whatso-ever, in all the varied relations in which we stand to our fellow-men. This one rule of Christ is a powerful test and solvent of all other prescriptions. If they can be carried out and yet leave us short, in our practice, of doing to others as they would like us to act toward them, these rules are imperfect. They leave something to be desired and to be attained.

II. The inspiration we need to fulfil it. This great precept of Christ is not to be translated into action like any ordinary military or municipal regulation. We must gain some inspiration from our Lord himself if we are to keep this great commandment. And we must be prompted by three things. 1. An earnest desire to follow Christ's own example. 2. A strong purpose of heart to do his holy will, that we may please and honour him. 3. A kind and Christian interest in our neighbours; a gracious pity for those whom he pitied, and for whom he suffered and died; a warm interest in their welfare; a firm faith that they can be raised and renewed and refined; a holy love for all those who love him.—C.

Ver. 37.—*Human judgment.* These words must be taken with discrimination; they must be applied in the exercise of our natural intelligence, distinguishing between things that differ. We must observe—

I. The truth which lies outside the thought of Christ. Our Lord could not possibly have meant to condemn the exercise of the individual judgment on men or things. By so doing, indeed, he would have condemned himself; for did he not say, "Why even of yourselves judge ye not what is right"? And almost in the same breath he intimates that men are to be judged by their actions as is a tree by its fruit (ver. 44). We are commanded by the Apostle Paul to "*prove* all things, and to hold fast that which is good;" and John exhorts us to "*try* the spirits whether they are of God." *Things* must be judged by us; new doctrines, new institutions, new methods of worship and of work, come up for our support or our condemnation, and we must judge them, by reason, by conscience, by Scripture, that we may know what course we are to pursue. *Men* must be judged by us also. We have to decide whether we will give them our confidence, our friendship; whether we will admit them into the family circle, into the society, into the Church. To decline to judge men is to neglect one of the most serious duties and most weighty obligations of our life. And knowing all that we do know from Jesus Christ what men and things should be, having learned of him the essential value of reverence, of purity, of rectitude, of charity, we are in a position to "judge righteous judgment," as he has desired us to do.

II. The sinful error which Christ condemns. The judging and the condemning which our Lord here forbids are those of a wrong and guilty order. They are, at least, threefold. 1. *Hasty judgment;* coming to unfavourable conclusions on slight and insufficient evidence; not giving to the inculpated neighbour any fair opportunity of explaining the occurrence; not waiting to think or to learn what has to be taken into account on the other side. 2. *Uncharitable judgment,* and therefore unjust judgment; for we are never so unjust as when we are uncharitable—as when we ascribe the lower motive, the ignobler purpose, the impure desire, to our neighbour. All uncharitableness is sin in the sight of Jesus Christ; and when the want of a kindly charity leads us to misjudge and so to wrong our brother, we fall under the condemnation of this his word, and under his own personal displeasure. 3. *Harsh condemnation;* taking a tone and using a language which are unnecessarily severe, which tend to crush rather than to reform, which daunt the spirit instead of inciting it to better things; condemnation which is not after the manner of him who "hath not dealt with us after our sins, nor rewarded us according to our iniquities," who "will not always chide, neither doth he keep his anger for ever;" condemnation which would be disallowed by him who rebuked his disciples when they rebuked those mothers who were bringing their children to his feet, and who forbade these disciples to forbid any one doing good in his name, even though he "followed not" with them.

III. The penalty we pay for our transgression. If we wrongly judge and wrongly condemn, we shall suffer for our mistake, for our sin. 1. God will condemn us for our injustice, or our undue and inconsiderate severity. 2. We shall have, some day, to reproach ourselves. But the most marked penalty will be found elsewhere. 3. Our fellow-men will treat us with the severity we impose on them. It is the universal habit among men to take up the attitude toward any neighbour which he assumes toward them. Toward the merciful *we* are merciful, even as our Father is; toward the severe we are severe. Again and again does the fact present itself to our observation that the men who have been relentless in their punishment of others have been held fast to the letter of the bond in the day of their own shortcoming; they who show no mercy will find none when they need it for their own soul. But if we judge leniently and condemn sparingly, we shall find for ourselves that men are just unto the just and generous unto the generous.—C.

Ver. 38.—*Human responsiveness.* This word of Christ may be taken with that other on the same subject, which none of the evangelists recorded, but which we could ill have spared, "It is more blessed to give than to receive." We may consider—

I. WHAT WE HAVE TO GIVE. We have much that we can draw from if we desire to benefit and to bless our fellow-men. 1. *Our possessions*—our money, our time, our books, our clothes, etc. 2. *Ourselves*—our thought, our affection, our sympathy.

II. WHO SHOULD BE OUR RECIPIENTS. These should be: 1. Our kindred according to the flesh. 2. Our kindred according to the spirit—our fellow-Christians, our fellow-members. 3. Our neighbours, those who, as the nearest and most within reach, should receive our kind thoughtfulness. 4. The children of want, of sorrow, of spiritual destitution, both at home and abroad. There is a sense, and that a truly Christian one, in which those who are in the saddest need and in the darkest error, aye, and even in the most deplorable iniquity, have the greatest claim on our pity and our help.

III. WHAT MAY BE OUR INCENTIVES. 1. That giving is that act which is most emphatically *Divine.* God lives to give—to bestow life, and health, and beauty, and joy on his creatures. Christ Jesus came to give himself for man. 2. That it is truly *angelic.* 3. That it is the *heroic* thing to do. Men have been true heroes in proportion as they have spent themselves and their powers on behalf of their kind. 4. That it is most *elevating* in its influence on ourselves and, when wisely directed, on those for whom it is expended.

IV. WHAT WILL BE OUR RECOMPENSE. 1. The Divine approval. "For God loveth a cheerful giver." 2. The unconscious and uncalculated reaction that will be received by ourselves, enlarging our heart and lifting us toward the level of the supreme Giver. 3. The response we shall receive from those we serve. This is the recompense which is promised in the text. "Give, and it shall be given unto you; good measure . . . shall men give into your bosom." There is far too much ingratitude in this world; more, perhaps, than we are willing to believe, until sad experience has convinced us. Nevertheless, there is also a very large measure of human responsiveness on which we may safely reckon. If we give to others, men will give to us; if we love them, they will love us. Do not even the publicans so? (Matt. v. 46). Even those whose hearts have been unchanged by the truth and grace of Christ will respond to genuine kindness. Patronage they will recognize and resent; officialism they will distinguish and may endure. But the help which comes straight from the heart they will appreciate, and to him who gives it they will give a free and gladdening response. To the really generous man, as distinguished from the formal "benefactor" or the professional philanthropist, there will flow a stream of warm-hearted gratitude and affection which will far more than repay all the time and treasure, and even all the sympathy and service, that have been expended. The generous giver will be the recipient of (1) the *regard*, (2) the *gratitude*, (3) the *affection*, and, (4) when it may be needed, the *substantial kindness* of those whom he has tried to serve, and of many others outside that circle. And to these may be added that which, if its worth be less calculable, yet may be even more valuable and more acceptable than any or all of these—the *prayers of the good.* Selfishness often misses its own poor mark, and it always fails to bless its author with an inward blessing; but beneficence is always blessed. God rains down his large benedictions from above, and below men offer their glad and free contribution. "Give, and it shall be given unto you . . . for with the same measure that ye mete withal it shall be measured to you again."—C.

Vers. 39, 40.—*Christian teaching.* We may learn from this parable some truths of the greatest consequence to all those who are teachers of religion; and this will include not only all Christian pastors and evangelists, but all those who are training the young, whether at school or at home.

I. That the wisdom of the world depends very largely on that of its religious teachers. The multitude have never yet been able to think great theological questions through; they have not attempted the settlement of them by their own examination. They have left that very largely indeed to their religious leaders. It is so in other departments of human knowledge, and so it has been and will be in the realm of religion. What our teachers teach the people will believe concerning the great and supreme questions affecting our relation to God, to our neighbours, to the future.

II. That blindness on the part of the teacher means disastrous error to the people. "Both will fall into the ditch." Religious truth is the most elevating of all knowledge; but error in religion is the most injurious of all errors. Men can make mistakes in the realms of literature, of physical science, of philosophy, and even of political economy, without fatal consequences. But serious errors in religion are nothing short of calamities. Teacher and taught fall into a deep ditch, from which they do not escape without much injury, both done and suffered. These evil consequences include: 1. Departure and distance of the mind from the thought of God, from truth and wisdom. 2. Superstitions which degrade and demoralize; or, on the other hand, unbelief which robs the soul of its true heritage, and leaves life without nobility and death without hope. 3. Morbid fancies which prey upon the mind, or shocking cruelties practised on the victim of error himself or on others. 4. Spiritual death.

III. That the teacher of truth is limited in his influence by his own attainments. "The disciple is not above his master." It is indeed true that a teacher may bring a disciple into connection with Jesus Christ; and from him and from his followers and his institutions he may gain help which his first teacher could not have imparted; but this is not derived from the *teacher himself*. This man, *as teacher*, can only render to his disciples the good which he has in himself—the *knowledge* he has in his own mind, the *worth* he has in his own character, the *wisdom* contained in the principles on which he is fashioning his own life. Let every teacher be impressed with the serious truth of this limitation. He cannot give what he has not gained. He has to say, "Follow me so far as I am following Christ,"—not a step further. If he ceases to acquire, if his path of progress in the knowledge or the likeness of God is arrested, there is stopped at the same hour his power of leading his disciples on and up those sacred and glorious heights. Therefore let him be always acquiring, always attaining.

IV. That the faithful teacher has a very noble opportunity. Every one that has been fully instructed "shall be as his master." If he is a "true philanthropist who makes two blades of grass to grow where only one grew before," what shall we not think of him who plants in the hearts of men true thoughts of God, of the human soul, of human life, of the future? This is the teacher's lofty function. And he can go beyond this. By the power of language, especially when that is illuminated by deep conviction and intense earnestness of spirit, he can pass on to his disciples so much of Divine truth, and he can communicate so much of heavenly wisdom, that they who "have been fully instructed," who are his mature or "perfect" disciples, will have in them the mind and temper which are in him. So that they will be "as he is," will think as he thinks, will feel what he feels, will live for the same objects for which he is living. Surely there is no nobler work that any man can do than this; it is well worth while the teacher's (1) most careful preparation, (2) most energetic effort, (3) most earnest prayer.—C.

Vers. 41, 42.—*Keenness and dulness of spiritual vision.* Of all the surprising things in this world there is nothing more wonderful than the way in which men mistake one another and misconceive themselves. Their vision is so seriously, so thoroughly distorted.

I. The keenness of spiritual vision some men exhibit. They have the nicest discernment of faults and failings in their brethren. There is nothing too minute to escape their notice and their condemnation. Censoriousness is a very great mistake in every light. Those who are guilty of "beholding the mote in their brother's eye" are wrong in four respects. 1. They do substantial injustice in their judgment and by their action; for they lay stress on the one small infirmity while they leave unregarded and unacknowledged many honourable acquisitions, many valuable virtues. 2. They are inconsiderate of the difficulties which the victims of their severity have had to contend with, and in doing battle with which they may have put forth the most commendable exertion. 3. They forget that every one of us is and will be subject to the judgment and (where it is due) the condemnation of God (see Rom. xiv. 4, 10). 4. They show a perverted ingenuity. It would be a most excellent quality to cultivate if they would only exert the same subtlety and patient observation in descrying the virtues and the beauties of those in whom they detect so many failures. This keenness of spiritual vision is a mistake in two other ways. (1) It is usually unprofitable; for it is more irritating than advantageous to those on whom it is expended. (2) It is odious to man, and it is unpleasing in the sight of God. Both in the human and in the Divine estimate, severity is the unattractive and charity is the becoming thing.

II. THE DULNESS OF SPIRITUAL VISION other men manifest. They do "not perceive the beam that is in their own eye." This fact in human experience is only too palpable. We see men whose souls are painfully charged with selfishness, or pride, or frivolity, or cruelty, or irreverence, or impurity, who have no conception that they are in grave spiritual delinquency and danger. There is not a mote but a beam in their eye, and they are blind to it altogether. They are not entitled to offer a judgment on the defects or transgressions of others, so far are they themselves from the straight line of truth. And any note of censure from their lips is utterly and even ludicrously misplaced.

III. OUR WISDOM IN VIEW OF THESE MISTAKES. It is to be far more concerned to be right and pure in our own hearts than to be keen in the detection and exposure of other people's shortcoming. Since men do so seriously and so fatally mistake their own spirit and condition, it behoves us to do these three things: 1. To examine our own hearts with impartial and anxious eye. 2. To welcome any friendly counsel or warning that may be offered us; and "it is lawful to learn *even from an enemy*." 3. To be often and earnestly asking God to show us what is wrong within, that we may see ourselves as he sees us. "Who can understand his errors? Cleanse thou me from secret faults!" (Ps. xix. 12, 13; and see Ps. cxxxix. 23, 24).—C.

Vers. 43—45.—*Being and doing.* The great Teacher here puts into figurative language the truth which was afterwards so tersely and forcibly expressed by his most appreciative disciple, "He that *doeth* righteousness *is* righteous." We have here—

I. THE FOUNDATION-TRUTH on which our Lord's word is built, viz. that life is the outcome of character; that as men *are* so they will *live*. "A good man out of the good treasure of his heart bringeth forth that which is good," etc. Granted that a man is sound at heart, it is certain that he will spend a good life, that he will shrink from the evil and pursue and practise the holy thing. Granted that a man is radically corrupt, it is certain that his life will be unworthy and sinful. Character must come forth into conduct; behaviour is the manifestation of the secret spring which is within the soul. "A good tree bringeth not forth corrupt fruit," etc.

II. THE APPARENT EXCEPTIONS, which are only apparent, and not real. If this be true, we want to know how it is, on the one hand, (1) that men we feel sure are bad at heart are found living lives that are blameless and even devout; and how it is, on the other hand, (2) that men we feel sure are sound at heart deviate so often from the straight line of propriety. The answer to this question is manifold. 1. It must be remembered that much of that which seems goodness of life, and which seems as if it must have come from a true heart, is not *real* goodness—it is only pretence. Hypocrisy, the affectation of piety and virtue, is not a good fruit, though it may look very much like it; it is no more "good fruit" in the garden of the Lord than poisonous berries are good fruit on the trees or shrubs of our visible garden. 2. And it must also be taken into account that much of that which seems like departure from moral excellence, and which seems as if it cannot have proceeded from the good heart, is not really "evil;" it is either mannerism that is only skin-deep, to be regretted indeed, but not to be confounded with essential moral evil; or it is undeveloped, struggling righteousness, the crude and imperfect attempt of a soul that is moving upwards from below; there is many a slip and many a false step, but then there is much honourable effort and much spiritual earnestness recognized and owned by the patient Father of spirits.

III. THE PRACTICAL CONCLUSION for which we must be prepared. "Every tree is known by his own fruit." "By their fruits ye shall know them." Men must form their judgment about us; and they must judge us by the lives they witness. If, therefore, we do not manifest a Christian temper and a loving spirit, if righteous principles are not visible in our daily dealings, if we do not give evidence of caring more for truth and for God and for the establishment of his holy kingdom on the earth than we care for our own temporal prosperity or present enjoyment,—we must not complain if men count us among the ungodly. Our godliness, our spirituality, our rectitude, ought to shine forth clearly and unmistakably from our daily life.

IV. THE PRACTICAL TRUTH which we must apply to ourselves—that, if we would live a life of uprightness in the sight of God, we must be *right at heart* in his esteem. It must be out of the fulness of our soul that we do right actions; it must be out of "the abundance of the heart that our mouth must speak" his praise and his truth; or our proprieties of behaviour and our suitableness of language will weigh nothing whatever in his balances. The first thing for every man to do is to become right in his own heart with God; to return in spirit unto him; to go to him in humility and in faith; to find mercy of him in Jesus Christ, and, having thus entered into sonship, to live the life of filial obedience to his Word; then and thus will the good tree bring forth good fruit.—C.

Vers. 46—49.—*Good and bad building.* In the moral and spiritual as well as in the material world there is good and bad, sound and unsound, safe and unsafe *building.* We are all builders; we are all planning, preparing, laying our foundation, erecting our walls, putting on our topstone.

I. THE FABRIC OF ENJOYMENT OR OF SUCCESS. That of *enjoyment,* of the gratification of indulgence, is indeed hardly worthy of the name of building; yet are there those who spend upon it a very large amount of thought and labour. To pursue this as the object of life is unworthy of our manhood, is to dishonour ourselves, is to degrade our lives; it is to expend our strength on putting up a miserable hovel when we might use it in the erection of a noble mansion; it is, also, to be laboriously constructing a heap of sand which the first strong wave will wash away. Worthier than this, though quite unsatisfying and unsatisfactory, is the pursuit of *temporal prosperity,* the building up of a fortune, or of a great name, or of personal authority and command. Not that such aims and efforts are wrong in themselves. On the other hand, they are necessary, honourable, and even creditable. But they are *not sufficient;* they are wholly inadequate as the aspiration of a human soul and the achievement of a human life. They do not fill the heart of man; they do not give it rest; they leave a large void unfilled, a craving and a yearning unsatisfied. Moreover, they do not stand the test of time; they are *buildings that will soon be washed away.* The tide of time will soon advance and sweep away the strongest of such edifices as those. Do not be content with building for twenty, or forty, or sixty years; build for eternity. "The world passeth away . . . but he that doeth the will of God abideth for ever."

II. THE FORTRESS OF CHARACTER. It is of this that our Lord is speaking in the text; and he says concerning it—Dig deep, build on the rock, erect that which the most violent storm cannot shake to its fall. What is that character which answers to this counsel? 1. Not that which is founded on *ceremony and rite.* Reason, Scripture, and experience all prove that this is a character built upon the sand. 2. Not that which is founded upon *sentiment or occasional emotion.* Many are they who like and who demand to be acted upon by powerful influences, and to be thus excited to strong feelings. In these moments of aroused sensibility they cry, "Lord! Lord!" with apparent earnestness. But if piety ends in sensibility "it is nothing;" it is worthless; it will be washed away by the first storm that breaks. 3. It is that which is established in *sacred conviction and fixed determination.* This is the rock to which we must dig down — sacred conviction passing into *real consecration;* the conviction that we owe everything to our God and Saviour, and the determination, in the sight and by the grace of God, to yield our hearts and lives to him. A character thus built, sustained by Christian services and ceremonies, will be strong against all assault. The subtlest influences will not undermine it, the mightiest earthly forces will not overturn it ; let the storms come, and it will stand.

III. THE EDIFICE OF CHRISTIAN USEFULNESS. Paul, in his first letter to the Church at Corinth, speaks of the wood, hay, and stubble, and also of gold, silver, and precious stones, *i.e.* of the combustible and the inflammable materials with which men construct their building in the field of holy service. And he says the fire will try every man's work ; so that we have apostolic warning also to take heed how we build. Let the Christian workman see to it that he too builds on the rock, that he effects that which will stand the waters and the fires that will try his work. Let him depend little on ceremonialism, little on excitement ; let him strive to produce deep, sacred convictions in the soul ; let him endeavour to lead men on to a whole-hearted dedication of themselves to Jesus Christ ; let him persuade men to the formation of wise habits of devotion and self-government ; so shall he be building that which the waters of time will not remove, and which the last fires will purify but not destroy.—C.

Ver. 49.—*The greatest ruin.* " The ruin of that house was great." Occasionally there occurs a panic in the commercial world. As the cause or, often enough, as the consequence of this, some great house is " broken ; " its liabilities are too great for its resources ; it cannot meet the claims that are falling due. And some morning it is found that when all other houses are open, its doors are closed—it has suspended payment ; it has fallen ; and it may be said, seriously enough, that " the ruin of that house is great." Great is the fall and sad is the ruin of (1) a great human *reputation ;* or of (2) a great human *hope.* With the fall of either of these there is bitter sorrow, keen humiliation, a dark shadow cast, not on one heart and home only, but on many. For we stand, in human society, not like detached houses in large grounds, but like houses that are close together, and when one falls it brings harm and injury to many that are connected with it. But *the* ruin, which is great indeed, compared with which all others are but small, is the ruin of a *human soul.*

I. THE SOUL IS ITSELF A BUILDING ; it is the main, the chief building which we are rearing. Whatever else we may be erecting—material, social, political—the one thing we do with which other things will not compare in seriousness and in consequence is to " *build up ourselves* " (see Jude 20). It is a daily, an hourly process ; it proceeds with every thought we admit into our mind, with every feeling we cherish in our heart, with every purpose we form in our soul. That which we are to-day in the sight of God is the whole result of all that we have been doing, of all our visible and invisible acts, up to the present hour.

II. IT IS A BUILDING WHICH MAY BE OVERTHROWN. We all know the man who is the wreck and ruin of himself. What he once was he is no more. Instead of devotion is impiety ; instead of purity is laxity ; instead of the beauty of holiness is the unsightliness of sin ; instead of honour is shame. The fair house of moral and spiritual integrity is down ; there is nothing left but the foundations ; and the ruin of *that* house is great indeed.

III. THIS OVERTHROW IS SAD BEYOND EXPRESSION. For consider : 1. *What it cost to build.* We do not mind if a hut or shanty is blown down ; that represents no great loss. But if a mansion or cathedral is destroyed, we grieve ; for the result of incalculable skill and toil is laid waste. And when a human soul is lost, what labour is thrown away, what experiences, what patience, what suffering, what discipline, what prayers and tears, both on the part of the man himself and of those who have loved him and watched over him and striven for him ! 2. *How intrinsically precious a thing it is.* We do not know the absolute value of a human spirit ; our language will not utter it ; our minds cannot estimate it. God alone knows that, and the Son of God has told us that it is worth more than all the material world (Mark viii. 36). 3. *How it drags down others with it.* As one large " house " in a great city drags down others in its fall, so does the house of a human spirit. What is it to the family when the father or the mother is morally lost ? for the neighbourhood when the minister or the magistrate sinks and perishes ? We do not fall alone ; we draw others down with us, and often those whom we are most sacredly bound to uplift or to sustain.

IV. THERE IS A WAY OF RECOVERY. " It is not the will of our heavenly Father

that one . . . should perish." "God so loved the world . . . that whosoever believeth
. . . should *not* perish." The fallen house may be down beyond recovery; not so the
human soul. In the gospel of Jesus Christ the way of restoration is revealed. By the
power of the Holy Spirit the soul that has fallen the furthest may be raised up again,
and be restored to the favour and the likeness and the service of God. By true
penitence and genuine faith we may lay hold on eternal life; and when the heart heeds
the voice of its merciful Father summoning it to return, and when it hastens to the
feet of Jesus Christ and seeks in him a Refuge and a Saviour, and when it lives a new
life of faith and love and hope in him, it is restored to all that it once was; and the
restoration of that soul is great.—C.

Vers. 1—19.—*The Lord of the sabbath, and his work.* We have just seen how Jesus
treated with deserved dishonour the tradition of the elders about *fasting.* He showed
his disciples a more excellent way. Fasting is not an end, but only a means to an end,
and this is the restoration of the soul to fellowship with its Saviour. In this way
should Christians use fasting. And now we pass on to notice how on sabbath-keeping
tradition again intruded itself and made cumbrous additions to the Mosaic commandment. Our Lord once more, as we shall see, set at nought the tradition, while he held
firmly by the Mosaic Law. The evangelist groups two sabbath-scenes for us in the
history here—the first in the corn-fields, the second in the synagogue, but both illustrating our Lord's sabbatic principle and practice. As the most interesting method of
considering the subject, let us notice—

I. THE PHARISAIC PRINCIPLE ABOUT SABBATH-KEEPING WAS THAT MAN WAS MADE
FOR THE DAY, NOT THE DAY FOR THE MAN. (Vers. 2, 7.) These reputedly religious
men had a certain idea about the day. They must have a holy day, and so it must be
so sacred that all work shall be deemed unlawful, lest it should be secularized. What
they objected to in the first case was not the plucking of the ears of corn, but the
rubbing of them in the hands. This was a violation of their tradition. In the second
case they objected to work on the sabbath day, even though it took the form of healing. Their ideal was, therefore, a day of such physical inactivity as would refuse to
minister to man's hunger or to man's healing. The fallacy underlying this idea was
that work is in its essence a secular thing, and that idleness is somehow sacred. To
declare this emphatically, they were ready to rebuke hungry men for satisfying themselves in the corn-fields, and to deny healing to the man with the withered arm because
he presented himself for it on the sabbath day. The day above the man, then, was
the Pharisees' notion. Hunger and helplessness must be endured in order that a day
of pretentious idleness may be presented to mankind. Healthy desire must be stifled,
longing for power and self-help must be denied, that a sufficiently idle sabbath may be
secured. The apotheosis of idleness, the vindication of indifference,—all this and more
is involved in the Pharisaic criticism of Christ and of his disciples. Now, it is
important to bring out clearly how contrary to God's idea all this is. Work is not
secularizing in itself. The infinite Father never ceases working, but his work is sacred
all through the year. Of course, men may secularize themselves by the selfishness of
their work, but they may secularize themselves as really by the selfishness of their
idleness. An idle day is not likely to be a holy one; a busy day may be most holy
if the glory of God and the good of souls be kept steadily in view.

II. CHRIST'S BETTER PRINCIPLE OF SABBATH-KEEPING IS THAT THE DAY IS MADE FOR
MAN. (Vers. 3—5, 9.) Hence necessity must be recognized as a law for the sabbath.
Even the ceremonial rite should give way before the needs of human nature, as the
case of David's hungry men being saved from famishing by a meal of shewbread indicates. Hence the hungry disciples, in rubbing the corn in their hands, were vindicated
by that sublime *necessity* which recognizes no higher law. Again, in the case of the
helpless fellow-man whose right hand was withered, our Lord is clear that the sabbath
should be a day for saving life, and not for allowing it to perish. In other words, Christ
would devote the day to man's salvation, while the Pharisees were prepared to sacrifice
the man to the peculiar sacredness which they thought belonged to an idle day. But
if the day is thus a means towards man's good, is he to employ it as he pleases? Is
every man to be lord of the sabbath by doing as he likes upon it? This would be a
dangerous prerogative to give to men. Not every one is fit to exercise it. The Phari-

sees, in fact, had taken the sabbath under their control and spoiled it altogether. Hence the sovereignty of the sabbath must be left in the hands of him who is called the Son of man. Christ is the Lord who can so order the sabbath that it shall be truly sanctified. It is, consequently, from Christ's sabbath-keeping that we learn what it ought to be. And we see from his life that he made the sabbaths his special opportunities for philanthropic effort. Most of his miracles were sabbath-day performances. He seems to have been busier on the sabbath than on any day of the week. We are safe in following along the lines of his most intelligent philanthropy. The sabbath is made for man. If Christ would have the hungry fed and the helpless healed, he would also have the souls fed with the bread of life and all spiritual helplessness removed. This is the purpose, therefore, of those means of grace which are presented with special earnestness on the Lord's day!

III. CHRIST DEMONSTRATED THE TRUTH OF HIS PRINCIPLE BY THE MIRACLE. (Ver. 10.) Now, this miracle, like the healing of the paralytic, was the test of a principle. In the former case Christ claimed the prerogative of absolution, and he demonstrated that he possessed the prerogative by telling the paralytic to rise and walk, and healing him. In the present case he has taken issue with the Pharisees as to the sabbath being a day for philanthropy. Healing is to be performed on it, if it is required. And now he singles out the patient with the withered hand, and by a word cures him. Thus he put their ideas on sabbath-observance to confusion. Instead, however, of rejoicing in the poor man's cure, they are filled with madness at their own discomfiture. Misanthropy in them is the contrast to the philanthropy of Jesus. But is not the miracle a sign of those miracles which are performed from sabbath to sabbath? Man comes in his weakness, his hand is withered, he can do nothing; but through the power of God he is enabled to stretch forth his hand, and enter into the sphere of spiritual power.

IV. THE SELECTION OF THE TWELVE WAS MADE BY CHRIST A MATTER OF VERY SPECIAL PRAYER. (Vers. 12—16.) We are told that he spent a whole night in prayer to God. This showed how important in his view the selection of the disciples was, and the establishment of his kingdom among men. He chose them in the morning after the prayerful view of the whole case before the Father. If Jesus realized the need of long-continued prayer before selecting them, how prayerfully should we go about our work for him! It is no easy matter to act wisely in our dealings with men and in our use of them. The persons selected were such as only Divine wisdom, as distinguished from worldly prudence, would have chosen. There was not an "influential" person among them; and it was not till after the Pentecost that any of them became what we should now call reliable. Into the analysis of the persons selected we do not enter. They have been divided into three groups: the first, containing the names of Peter and Andrew, James and John, gives us the chiefs of the apostolic band, the men of *insight*; the second, containing the names of Philip, Bartholomew, Thomas, and Matthew, are *reflective*, and, at first, *sceptical*, men; and the third and last contains the names of James the son of Alphæus, Jude, Simon the Zealot, and Judas Iscariot, all *practical* men.[1] Our Lord has thus use in his Church for all grades of men, and can even make use of traitors to serve his purpose.

V. THE HEALER IN THE MIDST OF THE MULTITUDE. (Vers. 17—19.) From the mountain-top of prayer he descends to the valley of opportunity, and there finds a vast multitude from the heathen parts of Tyre and Sidon, as well as from the Jewish districts of Judæa and Jerusalem, who have come to hear and to be healed of their diseases. Here were the two spheres—the sphere of mind, to which the ear is the great entrance; and the sphere of body, where disease may be checked and healing given. The mission of Jesus was to save men. Miracles were part of his message to mankind. The healing of the diseases of men was to tell how he can heal their souls and save them everlastingly. Moreover, they connected the cure with his Person. From him virtue or healing power radiated. His Person is the centre of healing influence. And for salvation this also holds good. It is to the Person of the Saviour we must come if we are to get really healed. It is surely well to have the source of all healing defined—it is the Person of our Saviour. To him, therefore, let us all come!—R. M. E.

[1] Cf. *Expositor*, vol. i. pp. 29—43.

Vers. 20—49.—*The Legislator on the mount.* We have seen how, after a whole night spent in prayer, our Lord proceeded to the important work of selecting his apostles. In this way he *organized* his kingdom. And now, having healed all who needed healing, and had been brought or had come to him, he has the ground cleared for legislative work. From this mountain-top in Galilee he publishes the laws of the kingdom, and thus gives to the world such a high-toned morality as has not been surpassed or superseded by any ethical speculations since. It may be safely said that all the Christless ethics which have been offered to the world in lieu of the Christian, contain nothing valuable which Christ's system has not in better form, and that they err by defect in many places. Christ is still, in the department of ethics, "the Light of the world."[1] The audience to whom the sermon on the mount was delivered was almost entirely Jewish, and they doubtless entertained the usual ideas about the kingdom of Messiah. This kingdom was, they hoped, to be one where they would enjoy immunity from trouble, and be in flourishing worldly circumstances. Theirs was a worldly dream. They wanted a golden age of wealth and worldly power. It was needful for our Lord, consequently, to correct these superficial notions, and to create a kingdom which could flourish in spite of the world's opposition and of all possible disadvantages. Accordingly, we find the Divine Legislator first quietly describing the members of his kingdom and distinguishing them from the worldly minded outside; secondly, laying down the policy his people should pursue; thirdly, pointing out the secret of true leadership among men; and lastly, the stability of the obedient. To these points let us devote ourselves for a little in their order.

I. CHRIST DIFFERENTIATES HIS SUBJECTS FROM THE WORLDLY MINDED OUTSIDE. (Vers. 20—26.) For the simple statement of the Beatitudes, and of the woes that constitute their contrast, really draws the line between his kingdom and the world. Matthew, in his fuller version of this sermon on the mount, gives eight Beatitudes and no woes; Luke balances the four Beatitudes by four contrasted woes. The teaching in both versions is, however, practically identical. And when we look into our Lord's declarations, we find, in the first place, that, in his kingdom, the poor, the hungry, the tearful, and the persecuted are enabled to realize blessedness. This is the paradox of Christian experience, that, in spite of poverty, and of hunger, and of sorrow, and of opposition, Christ enables his people to maintain a *blessed* spirit. The poor are "rich in faith;" the hungry, especially those whose appetite is keen for righteousness (cf. Matt. v. 6), are certain to be filled; the tearful have the assurance that God will wipe away all tears from their eyes, if not on earth, at all events in heaven (cf. Rev. vii. 17); and the persecuted for Christ's sake are enabled to rejoice in view of that great reward in heaven which awaits all Christ's faithful martyrs. This blessedness is maintained in all these cases in spite of everything which militates against it. On the other hand, our Lord shows the rich, and the satiated, and the laughter-indulging, and the popularity-hunting people that, having received their consolation in this life, there is nothing in the next life for them but disappointment, lamentation, and woe. This may easily be verified. Those who "trust in uncertain riches"—and it is to these our Lord refers, as parallel passages show—must be woefully disappointed when they have to cross the Stygian river without their gold. All that they trusted in shall then have failed them for evermore. Those, again, who are satiated with this world's pleasures, and who have contracted no higher appetite, will be terribly empty when this world and all its pleasures shall have passed away like a dream. Those, again, who lived for laughter— the sportsmen of the world—shall find no provision made in another life for such profitless people, and shall mourn and weep over the lost opportunities of life. And, lastly, the popularity-hunters, who made the good opinion of the populace their great ambition, and were satisfied when all men spoke well of them, will find, like the popular false prophets of the past, that the other life is constructed upon such lines as will assign to each his due, and to popularity-hunting the doom of those who love applause rather than principle. Upon the worldly minded and successful, so far as this life is concerned, there is cast, by the great Lawgiver, the shadow of doom. For such people there is no reserve fund in a future life; they have eaten up both capital and interest.

II. CHRIST LAYS DOWN THE POLICY HIS PEOPLE SHOULD PURSUE. (Vers. 27—38.) Now, one of the cardinal principles of worldly policy is to "give nothing for nothing."

---

[1] Cf. 'The Light of the World,' by A. S. Wilkins, M.A., *passim.*

The world insists on a *quid pro quo*. Hence the worldly minded will always ask the question about the course a person pursues, "What does he expect to gain by it?" To act without hope of recompense is what the world cannot understand. And in strict conformity with this, the world is prompted to "give as much as it gets" in the way of injury. Curse for curse, hatred for hatred, a blow for a blow, a counterplot for a plot. This is the gamut of the world's revenge. The great Legislator, on the other hand, sets his face against all this worldly policy. He ridicules doing good for the sake of getting good. Such speculative philanthropy is pure worldliness. He must have a better system within his kingdom. He can dispense with revenge and the *quid pro quo*, and work his kingdom upon purely philanthropic lines. God the Father is the great Philanthropist, and men, by entertaining love for its own sake, may become "children of the Highest" and the elements of a new kingdom. Hence our Lord directs his people to love their enemies, to do good to those that hate them, to bless those that curse them, to pray for their persecutors, to give a kiss for a blow, to suffer violence a second time rather than practise it revengefully; to give to the utmost of their power to all who ask. In short, they are to love and do good and lend, hoping for nothing again; they are to be merciful, like their Father in heaven; they are to be free from censoriousness, and forgiving; and they may rest assured that in another life they shall get a great reward. What Christ proposes, therefore, is a policy of patient philanthropy—a policy of consideration, doing always to others what we would like to receive were we in their circumstances. And it is this new policy of love which is sure to overcome the world.

III. Christ shows the secret of true leadership among men. (Vers. 39—45.) But if love is to regulate all our conduct, may not others suffer through the proverbial "blindness" of love? There is little danger from the blindness of real love, only from the blindness induced by selfishness. Our danger, as the Lord here shows, is always from exaggerated self-love; we are blind to our own faults; we see motes in a brother's eye, and forget the beam in our own. Hence he recommends here severe self-criticism, such self-criticism as will prevent all hypocrisy, and secure that our eyes be truly purged. When this is the case, then we can see the little faults in others, and deal with them after we have dealt honestly with the great ones of our own. And so heart-purity is the great secret of successful leadership among men. If our hearts are set right with God, if we are washed and cleansed from secret faults, if we are purged from an evil conscience and dead works,—then are we in a fit state to deal tenderly with erring brothers and lead them to a better way. And so our Saviour shows, by this part of his legislation, that only the purified in heart can become successful leaders of their fellows. It is he who knows his own heart's plagues that can tenderly and skilfully deal with the plagues of others, and put them, by God's blessing, on a better way.

IV. Christ finally brings out the stability of the obedient. (Vers. 46—49.) Now, it is important to recognize the position taken up here by the great Lawgiver. He claims *absolute sovereignty*. His word is to be law. Once we know his will, we have only got to do it. But the claim is not unreasonable, nor is it excessive. He understands the strain and stress of human temptations thoroughly. He not only understand these speculatively, but experimentally; for he "was in all points tempted like as we are, yet without sin" (Heb. iv. 15). He can consequently give to us the best advice, advice infallible. If we would stand like a rock amid the temptations of life, then we have got simply and cordially to obey Christ. He is the Rock of ages; nothing can shake him; and nothing can disturb those who have learned to trust him. But those who hear his advice and do it not, shall be swept away by the torrent of temptation and involved in a ruin that is great. Obedience is the secret, therefore, of stability. May it be our experience continually!—R. M. E.

EXPOSITION.

CHAPTER VII.

Vers. 1—10.—*The servant (or slave) of the centurion of Capernaum is healed.*
Ver. 1.—**Now when he had ended all his** sayings. This clearly refers to the sermon on the mount. That great discourse evidently occupied a position of its own in the public ministry of the Lord. Its great length, its definite announcement of the kind of reign

he was inaugurating over the hearts of men, its stern rebuke of the dominant religious teaching of the day, its grave prophetic onlooks,—all marked it out as the great manifesto of the new Master, and as such it seems to have been generally received. **He entered into Capernaum.** The residence of Jesus, as we have before pointed out, during the greater part of his public life. It was, as it were, his head-quarters. After each missionary tour he returned to the populous, favoured lake-city which he had chosen as his temporary home.

Ver. 2.—**And a certain centurion's servant;** literally, *slave.* The difference is important, as we shall see in the picture presented to us of the centurion's character. A centurion was an officer in the Roman army : the grade answers to the modern European captain—German, *hauptmann;* the command included a hundred soldiers. Scholars are not agreed respecting the special service of this particular officer. Some consider he was a Greek or Syrian holding a commission under the prince of the country, the tetrach Herod Antipas ; others, that he was in the service of the empire, with a small detachment of the garrison of Cæsarea, doing duty at the important lake-city, probably in connection with the revenue. It is clear that Roman garrisons at this period were dotted about the various centres of population in these semi-dependent states. At Jerusalem we know a considerable Roman force was stationed, professedly to keep order in the turbulent capital, but really, no doubt, to overawe the national party. **Was sick, and ready to die.** St. Matthew calls the disease paralysis, **and adds that the** sufferer was in extreme pain. The disorder was probably some dangerous form of rheumatic fever, which not unfrequently attacks the region of the heart, and is accompanied with severe pain, and proves in many instances fatal. The ordinary paralysis would scarcely be accompanied with the acute pain mentioned by St. Matthew.

Ver. 3.—**And when he heard of Jesus;** better rendered, *having heard about Jesus.* His fame as a good Physician, such as never had arisen before, coupled with his reputation as a Teacher, had now travelled far and wide. The devout centurion probably had watched with extreme interest the career of the strange and remarkable Teacher-Prophet who had risen up among the people, and had apparently (see note on ver. 7) made up his mind that this Jesus was no mortal man. **He sent unto him the elders of the Jews, beseeching him that he would come and heal his servant;** better rendered *elders* without the article ; that is, some of the official elders connected with his own synagogue. These would be able,

with more grace than himself, to plead his cause with the Master, telling him how well the centurion had deserved any assistance which a Jewish physician could afford him.

Vers. 4, 5.—**He was worthy for whom he should do this : for he loveth our nation, and he hath built us a synagogue.** There are several mentions of these Roman military officers in the Gospels and Acts, and in every instance the mention is a favourable one. Still more notable instances occur in the case of Cornelius—to whom Peter was specially sent (Acts x., xi.)—of the centurion who was on guard at the execution on Calvary, and of the centurion who conveyed Paul to Rome (Acts xxvii. 1—3). On these Gentile soldiers " the faith and life of Judaism (seen, we may well believe, to more advantage in the village life of Galilee than amid the factions of Jerusalem) had made a deep impression : he found a purity, reverence, simplicity, and nobleness of life which he had not found elsewhere, and so he loved the nation, and built a new one of the synagogues of the town " (Dean Plumptre). The centurion was apparently one of those foreigners who —without submitting to circumcision and other burdensome ceremonial rites which were incompatible with the exercise of his profession—had accepted the faith of Israel, and worshipped with the people in the position of one who, in another age, would have been termed a "proselyte of the gate." He was evidently one of those true-hearted men who translated a beautiful *creed* into *acts,* for it was specially urged by the elders, in their petition to Jesus, that he loved the people, no doubt emphasizing his generous almsgivings, and, as a crowning act of his kindness, had built a synagogue at Capernaum. Modern travellers tell us that among the ruins of this city of Jesus are the remains of a white marble synagogue of the time of the Herods. This may have been the Roman soldier's noble gift to Israel. The whole character of this nameless officer seems to have been singularly noble. In those selfish days of undreamed-of luxury, cruelty, and heartlessness, for a *master* to care for, much less to love, *a slave* was, comparatively speaking, rare. From his message to Jesus (ver. 7) it would seem as though he had a clearer conception who the poor Galilæan Teacher was than any one else at that period of the public ministry, not excluding the inner circle of disciples.

Ver. 6.—**Lord, trouble not thyself: for I am not worthy that thou shouldest enter under my roof.** Augustine's comment on these remarkable words is good : " By saying that he was unworthy, he showed himself worthy of Christ's entering, not within his walls, but within his heart."

Ver. 7.—**But say in a word, and my servant shall be healed.** The Gentile soldier's faith was really great. He had risen above the need of an outward sign, such as a touch or even the sound of a living voice. He needed no contact with the fringe of the Master's garment, asked for no handkerchief or apron that had touched his person (Acts xix. 12). The word the Master would speak would be enough; the result he willed would assuredly follow. "Do not come hither where my servant is, but only *speak here* where thou art." The centurion had a just notion of Christ's power. And our Lord greatly commended him, whereas Martha, who said, "I know whatsoever thou shalt ask of God he will *give it* thee" (John xi. 22) was reproved as having spoken amiss; and Christ thus teaches that he is the Source of blessings, which he could not be unless he were God (compare Bishop Wordsworth, in part quoting from St. Chrysostom).

Ver. 8.—**For I also am a man set under authority, having under me soldiers, and I say unto one, Go, and he goeth; and to another, Come, and he cometh; and to my servant, Do this, and he doeth it.** What the soldier really thought of Jesus is evident when we read *between the lines* of this saying of his: "If I, who am under many a superior—the chiliarch of my thousand, the tribunes of my legion, my emperor who commands at Rome—yet receive a ready and willing obedience from my soldiers, and have but to say to one, 'Go,' and he goeth, to another, 'Come,' and he cometh; how much more thou, who hast no one above thee, no superior, when *thou* commandest disease, one of thy ministers, will it not at once obey?" The same thought was in Archdeacon Farrar's mind when he wrote how the centurion inferred that Jesus, who had the power of healing at a distance, had at his command thousands of the "heavenly army" (ch. ii. 13; Matt. xxvi. 53), who would

"At his bidding speed
"And post o'er land and ocean without rest."
(Milton.)

Ver. 9.—**When Jesus heard these things, he marvelled at him.** Augustine strikingly comments here on the expression ἐθαύμασε, he marvelled: "Who had inspired that faith but he who now admires it?" In marvelling at it he intimated that we ought to admire. He admires for our good, that we may imitate the centurion's faith; such movements in Christ are not signs of perturbation of mind, but are exemplary and hortatory *to us* (St. Augustine, quoted by Bishop Wordsworth, on Matt. viii. 10). **I have not found so great faith, no, not in Israel.** St.

Augustine remarks here that "the Lord had found in the oleaster what he had not found in the olive."

Ver. 10.—**Returning to the house, found the servant whole that had been sick.** Farrar suggests "convalescent" as a more accurate rendering than "whole." The Greek equivalent is one of the medical words we find in this Gospel of St. Luke. The words, "that had been sick," do not occur in the other authorities. They are omitted in the Revised Version.

Vers. 11—17.—*The Master raises from the dead the only son of the widow of Nain.*

Ver. 11.—**And it came to pass the day after.** The Greek expression here, in the majority of the more ancient authorities, is vague as a note of time. The Revised Version renders it "soon afterwards." The incident that follows the raising from the dead of the widow's son is only mentioned by St. Luke. It is generally assumed that our Lord only raised three persons from the dead—this young man of Nain, the little daughter of Jairus the ruler, and Lazarus of Bethany. But such an assumption is purely arbitrary. We have before called attention to the vast number of miracles worked by Jesus during the two years and a half of the public ministry not reported by the evangelists at all, or only glanced at in passing. There were, most probably, among these unreported miracles several instances of men, women, and children raised from the dead. St. Augustine, in one of his sermons (xcviii.), specially calls attention to this in his words, "of the numerous persons raised to life by Christ, three only are mentioned as specimens in the Gospels." Each evangelist specially chooses one of the various examples, no doubt known to him—that peculiar instance or instances best suited to the especial teaching of his Gospel. St. John alone recounts the raising of Lazarus. St. Luke is the solitary reporter of the miracle performed on the dead son of the widow of Nain. We may reasonably infer, says Dean Plumptre, that this miracle, from its circumstances, had specially fixed itself in the memories of the "devout women" of ch. viii. 1, and that it was from them that St. Luke obtained his accurate and detailed knowledge of this, as well as of many other of the incidents which he alone relates in his Gospel. **He went into a city called Nain.** From the Hebrew נעים, *naim fair*, probably so called from its striking situation on a steep hill. It is on the slope of Little Hermon, near Endor, some twenty or more miles from Capernaum. The name *Nein* is still given to a small poor village on the same site. It is approached by a narrow, steep ascent, and on either side of the road are sepulchral caves. It was in one of these that the dead man was about to have been laid when the Master met the little mourning procession winding down the steep road as he and his crowd of followers were toiling up the ascent nearing the gate of the city.

Ver. 13.—**And when the Lord saw her.** It is rare in the Gospels to find the expression, "the Lord," used by itself, "Jesus" being the usual term. It agrees with the unanimous tradition in the Church respecting the authorship of this Gospel—neither Luke nor Paul had been with Jesus. These had always looked on Jesus, thought of him, as *the Lord* risen from the dead, enthroned in heaven. At the period when St. Luke wrote, not earlier than A.D. 60, this title had probably become the usual term by which the Redeemer was known among his own. **He had compassion on her.** In this instance, as in so many others, our Lord's miracles were worked, not from a distinct purpose to offer credentials of his mission, but proceeded rather from his intense compassion with and his Divine pity for human sufferings.

Ver. 14.—**And he came and touched the bier.** The young man was about to be buried in the Jewish manner, which differed from the Egyptian custom. The corpse was not laid in a coffin or mummy-case, but simply on an open bier, on which the dead lay wrapped in folds of linen; so Lazarus was buried at Bethany, and our Lord in his rock-tomb in Joseph of Arimathæa's garden. A napkin, or sudarium, was lightly laid over the face. It was pollution for the living to touch the bier on which a corpse was lying. The bearers, in their amazement that one so generally respected and admired as was Jesus, the Teacher of Nazareth, at this period of his career, should commit so strange an act, would naturally at once stand still to see what next would happen. **Young man, I say unto thee, Arise.** The Lord of life performed his miracle over death in a very different fashion to those great ones who, in some respects, had anticipated or followed him in these strange deeds of wonder. Before they recalled the dead to life, Elijah mourned long over the son of the widow of Sarepta, Elisha repeatedly stretched himself as he agonized in prayer upon the lifeless corpse of the Shunammite boy, Peter prayed very earnestly over the body of Dorcas at Lydda. The Master, with one solitary word, brings the spirit from its mysterious habitation back to its old earthly tenement—"*Kúm!*" "Arise!" St. Augustine has a beautiful comment on the three miracles of raising the dead related in the Gospels. He has been saying that all our Lord's works of mercy to the body have a spiritual reference to the soul; he then proceeds to consider

them "as illustrations of Christ's Divine power and love in raising the *soul*, dead in trespasses and sins, from every kind of spiritual death, whether the soul be dead, but not yet carried out, like the daughter of Jairus; or dead and carried out, but not buried, like the widow's son; or dead, carried, and buried, like Lazarus. He who raised himself from the dead can raise all from the death of sin. Therefore let no one despair" (St. Augustine, 'Sermon' xcviii., quoted by Bishop Wordsworth). Godet has a curious and interesting note on what he calls a difficulty peculiar to the miracle, owing to the absence of all moral receptivity in the subject of it. "Lazarus was a believer. In the case of the daughter of Jairus, the faith of the parents to a certain extent supplied the place of her personal faith. But here there is nothing of the kind. The only receptive element that can be imagined is the ardent desire of life with which this young man, the only son of a widowed mother, had doubtless yielded his last breath; and this indeed is sufficient, for it follows from this that Jesus did not dispose of him arbitrarily."

Ver. 16.—**And there came a fear on all: and they glorified God, saying, That a great prophet is risen up among us; and, That God hath visited his people.** With the exception of two or three like the centurion, whose sick servant was healed, this was the general conception which the people had of Jesus—a fear is mentioned in this place—the natural result of the marvellous works, especially those worked in the case of the already dead, but nothing more. The sublime humility of the great Wonder-worker failed to persuade the bulk of men and women with whom he came in contact. They could not look on this quiet Rabbi-Physician, who gently put all state and pomp and glory aside, as the Divine Messiah; but that in Jesus Israel possessed a great Prophet the people were persuaded—they recognized that at last, after four long centuries of absence, God again had visited his people. There had arisen in the coasts of Israel no prophet of the Highest since the far-back days of Malachi, some four hundred years before the days of the Lord and his forerunner John.

Vers. 18—35.—*John the Baptist sends messengers to ask a question of Jesus. The reply of the Master.*

Ver. 18.—**And the disciples of John showed him of all these things.** St. Luke, unlike St. Matthew, in the corresponding passage in his Gospel, does not specially mention that John was in prison; he evidently took it for granted that this would be known to his readers from the account of the Baptist's arrest and imprisonment by

Herod Antipas given in ch. iii. 19, 20. In the course of John's imprisonment, it is probable that very many of his disciples became hearers of Jesus. During the early period, at all events, of the Baptist's captivity it is clear that his friends and disciples had free access to his prison. There is no doubt but that, in reply to the anxious inquiries of John, his disciples told him of all the miracles they had witnessed, and the words they had heard, especially, no doubt, recounting to him much of the sermon on the mount which Jesus had lately delivered as the exposition of his doctrine. We can well imagine these faithful but impatient disciples, after detailing these marvels which they had seen, and the strange new words of winning power which they had heard, saying to *their* imprisoned master, "We have seen and heard these wondrous things, but the great Teacher gets no further; we hear nothing of the standard of King Messiah being raised, nothing of the high hope of the people being encouraged; he seems to pay no attention to the imperious rule of the foreigner, or the degrading tyranny of men like Antipas, the Herod who has wrongfully shut *you* up. He rather withdraws himself, and when the people, fired by his winning words and mighty acts, begin to grow enthusiastic, then this strange Man hides himself away. Can he be Messiah, as you once said?"

Ver. 19.—**And John calling unto him two of his disciples, sent them to Jesus, saying, Art thou he that should come? or look we for another?** What, now, was in John the Baptist's mind, when from his prison he sent his disciples to ask Jesus this anxious question? Disappointed in the career of Jesus, possibly himself partly forgotten, accustomed to the wild freedom of a desert-life, suffering from the hopeless imprisonment,—had his faith begun to waver? or was the question put with a view of re-assuring his own disciples, with the intention of giving these faithful followers of his an opportunity of convincing themselves of the power and real glory of Jesus? In other words, was it for *his own* sake or for *his disciples' sakes* that he sent to ask the question? Generally speaking, the second of these two conclusions — that which ascribed the question to a desire on the part of John to help his disciples (which we will call B)—was adopted by the expositors of the early Church. A good example of this school of interpretation is the following quotation from St. Jerome: "John does not put this question from ignorance, for he himself had proclaimed Christ to be 'the Lamb of God.' But as our Lord asked concerning the body of Lazarus, 'Where have ye laid him?' (John xi. 34),

in order that they who answered the question might, by their own answer, be led to faith, so John, now about to be slain by Herod, sends his disciples to Jesus, in order that, by this occasion, they who were jealous of the fame of Jesus (ch. ix. 14; John iii. 26) might see his mighty works and believe in him, and that, while their master asked the question by them, they might hear the truth for themselves" (St. Jerome, quoted by Wordsworth). To the same effect wrote SS. Ambrose, Hilary, Chrysostom, Theophylact. Among the Reformers, Calvin, Beza, and Melancthon contended for this opinion respecting the Baptist's message to Christ, and in our days Stier and Bishop Wordsworth. On the other hand, Tertullian among the Fathers, and nearly all the modern expositors, believe that the question of John was prompted by his own wavering faith—a faltering no doubt shared in by his own disciples. This conclusion (which we will term A) is adopted, with slightly varying modifications, by Meyer, Ewald, Neander, Godet, Plumptre, Farrar, and Morrison. This way—(A) generally adopted by the modern school of expositors — of understanding the Baptist's question to Jesus, is evidently the conclusion which would suggest itself to all minds who went to the story without any preconceived desire to purge the character of a great saint from what they imagine to be a blot; and we shall presently see that our Lord, in his answer to the question, where a rebuke is exquisitely veiled in a beatitude, evidently understood the forerunner's question in this sense. It is thus ever the practice of Holy Scripture; while it tenderly and lovingly handles the characters of its heroes, it never flinches from the truth. We see God's noblest saints, such as Moses and Elijah (John's own prototype) in the Old Testament, Peter and Paul in the New Testament, depicted in this book of truth with all their faults; nothing is hid. Only *one* flawless character appears in its storied pages—it is only the Master of Peter and Paul who never turns aside from the path of right.

Ver. 21.—**And in that same hour he cured many of their infirmities and plagues, and of evil spirits; and unto many that were blind he gave sight.** "He knew as God what John's design was in sending to him, and he put it into his heart to send at that very time when he himself was working many miracles which were the true answer to the question" (Cyril, quoted by Wordsworth).

Ver. 22.—**Tell John what things ye have seen and heard; how that the blind see, the lame walk, the lepers are cleansed, the deaf hear, the dead are raised.** These miracles which the messengers witnessed that day, striking though they were, were no novel ones in the work of our Lord. They were, too, precisely similar to those which had already been reported to him in his prison (ver. 18). But Jesus, pointing to these signs, bade the friends of the Baptist return and tell *their* master what they had seen in *these* words. The great Messianic prophet, whose writings were so well known to John, had said that Messiah's advent would be heralded by these very acts. John would in a moment catch the meaning of the reply. The passages in question are Isa. xxix. 18 and xxxv. 4, 6. Wordsworth, on these works wrought by the great Physician, very beautifully writes, " One of the most consolatory reflections produced by these mighty and merciful works of Christ on earth is the assurance they give that at the great day of resurrection he will remove all infirmities and blemishes from the bodies of his servants, and clothe them in immortal health, beauty, and glory, so as to be like his own glorious body, once marred on the cross, but raised by himself from the dead, and now reigning for ever in glory " (Bishop Wordsworth). **To the poor the gospel is preached.** John would be able to draw his inference, too, from this feature in Jesus' work. His messengers would have heard the Teacher's words, and would have marked from what class especially his hearers were drawn. It was a new experience in the world's story, this tender care for the poor. No heathen teacher of Rome or Athens, of Alexandria or the far East, had ever cared to make this vast class of unprofitable hearers the objects of their teaching. The rabbis of Israel cared nothing for them. In the Talmud we often find them spoken of with contempt. But John knew that this speaking to and consorting with the poor would be one of the marked characteristics of Messiah when he came.

Ver. 23.—**And blessed is he, whosoever shall not be offended in me.** Our Lord here shows that he understood that this question came from the Baptist himself. Dean Plumptre calls attention to the tender way in which our Lord dealt with the impatience which John's question implied. "A warning was needed, but it was given in the form of a beatitude, which it was still open to him to claim and make his own. Not to find a stumbling-block in the manner in which Christ had actually come, there was this condition of entering fully into the blessedness of his kingdom."

Ver. 24.—**And when the messengers of John were departed, he began to speak unto the people concerning John.** When the messengers of John were departed, the Lord, fearful lest the people who had been standing by and listening to the question which the Baptist had put, and his answer, should entertain any disparaging thought of a great and sorely tried saint of God, spoke the following noble testimony concerning that true, faithful witness. It has been termed the funeral oration of John; for not long after it had been spoken he was put to death by Herod Antipas. **What went ye out into the wilderness for to see? A reed shaken with the wind?** The imagery was taken from the scenery in the midst of which John the Baptist had principally exercised his ministry—the reedy banks of Jordan. It was surely to see an everyday sight—a weak vacillating man blown to and fro with every wind. John, though his faith failed him for a moment perhaps, was no wavering reed.

Ver. 25.—**But what went ye out for to see? A man clothed in soft raiment? Behold, they which are gorgeously apparelled, and live delicately, are in kings' courts.** Was it, again, to see one of earth's so-called great ones—a favourite of the reigning monarch, a courtier of the magnificent Herod? John was no court favourite, no powerful or princely noble. Dean Plumptre thinks that here a reference is made to the fact that, in the early days of Herod the Great, a section of the scribes had attached themselves to his policy and party, and in doing so had laid aside the sombre raiment of their order, and had appeared in the gorgeous raiment worn by Herod's other courtiers. "We may trace," adds the dean, "with very little hesitation, a vindictive retaliation for these very words in the 'gorgeous robe' with which Herod arrayed him in mockery, when the tetrarch and Christ stood for one brief hour face to face with each other" (ch. xxiii. 4).

Ver. 26.—**But what went ye out for to see? A prophet? Yea, I say unto you, and much more than a prophet.** The great Teacher proceeds in his discourse. From the scene and the surroundings—the reeds of the banks of Jordan—he went on to speak of the great Jordan preacher, so unlike, in spite of this one weak wavering hour, the reeds in the midst of which he preached. Jesus thus painted the grave, austere man, first in his stern enmity to the seductive magnificence of a court-life, then in his severe austerity as regards himself. Who, then, was he—this preacher to whom the people had resorted in such crowds to see and hear? Was he a prophet? was he one more of those men who in past ages had been the salt which preserved Israel from decay? Yes; that is what he was, that true great one—a prophet in the deepest, truest sense of the word. Ah! higher still, went on the Teacher, John was much more than a prophet. What then? and the by-standers marvelled; what *more* could he be? Was he, peradventure, the Messiah?

Ver. 27.—**This is** he, **of whom it is written, Behold, I send my messenger before thy face, which shall prepare thy way before thee.** He quietly answers the question surging up in the listeners' hearts. No; not Messiah, but his forerunner. Centuries ago the mission of this John was foretold, and exactly described by one of the well-known and honoured prophet line. They who were listening, many of them, knew the words well, as the Teacher quoted from the great Malachi. The old ring of the famous prediction was unchanged; perhaps few of the by-standers noticed the slight alteration which was made by Jesus as he quoted. But in after-days the deep significance of the seemingly trifling change, we may well imagine, was the subject of many a deep solemn hour of meditation among the twelve and the early leaders of the faith. The words in Mal. iii. 1 stand thus: " Behold, I will send my messenger, and he shall prepare the way before *me*." Our Lord so changes the text that, instead of " before me," it reads with this slight difference, " Behold, I send *my* messenger before thy face, which shall prepare thy way before thee." The *Lord* who speaks by the prophets in Malachi announces *himself* as the coming angel of the covenant: " *my* messenger shall prepare the way before *me*;" but *this*, the Lord who is come as the Son of man, may not as yet openly declare; it is enough that by the thrice-repeated σοῦ (" *thy* face," " thy way," " before thee "), he signifies that he is marked out and referred to by the Father. See how, without directly uttering it, he nevertheless announces his ἐγω εἰμι (" I am he ") in his sublime humility (so Stier, ' Words of the Lord Jesus '). Godet presents the same thought from another point of view: " In the prophet's eyes he who was sending, and he before whom the way was to be prepared, were one and the same Person, Jehovah. Hence the ' before me ' of Malachi. But for Jesus, who is speaking of himself, and never confounds himself with the Father, a distinction became necessary. It is not Jehovah speaking of himself, but Jehovah speaking to Jesus; hence the form ' before thee.'"

Ver. 28.—**For I say unto you, Among those that are born of women, there is not a greater prophet than John the Baptist: but he that is least in the kingdom of God is greater than he.** These striking words close the Master's splendid testimony to the great

pioneer. The usual explanation adopted by most if not all modern theologians of the last clause of the verse is, that, great as John was, yet he that is least among Christians who have been *born of God* and have accepted as an article of their faith the crucifixion and ascension of the Son of God, is greater than that great prophet; or, in other words, the humblest child of the new kingdom is superior to the greatest prophet of the old. But many of the wisest and best of the Fathers of the Church—amongst others Chrysostom, Augustine, Hilary, and Theophylact—find grave difficulty in accepting this too sweeping and facile explanation of a hard saying. They suggest what seems to the writer of this Exposition a more reverential meaning to the Lord's words here. By " the least " we prefer, then, with Chrysostom and other ancient Fathers, to understand *Jesus himself*. The literal meaning of the Greek μικρότερος is " the lesser," not " least " (in the Revised Version, in the text we find " he that is but little," but in the margin " lesser "). By " lesser" or "little" Chrysostom supposes that the Saviour refers to himself as *less than John in age and according to the opinions of many*. " Thus, then, among the sons of men no prophet greater than John the Baptist has arisen; yet there is one among you lesser in age and perhaps in public estimation,—in the kingdom of God, though, greater than he." Wordsworth strengthens the above interpretation by his comment on the words, "among those that are born of women." " No one among those born of human parents had appeared greater than this John the Baptist; but do not suppose that he is greater than I. I am not γεννητὸς γυναικῶν, but Θεοῦ, and though after him in the gospel because he is my precursor, yet I am greater than he." This great expositor, while on the whole preferring the usual interpretation, yet considers that the explanation which refers "he that is least" to Christ, is not lightly to be set aside. If this interpretation be adopted, the usual punctuation of the passage must be slightly altered thus: " He that is lesser, in the kingdom of God is greater than he."

Ver. 29.—**And all the people that heard him, and the publicans, justified God.** This is not, as many expositors have assumed, a statement of St. Luke's own as to the effect of John's preaching on varied classes of his hearers, but the words are still the words of Jesus; it is a continuation of his eulogy of the Baptist. He says here that the people, " the folk," listened gladly to him; they were persuaded in great numbers of the necessity of a changed life, and were in consequence baptized by him. The meaning of the term, "justified God," is that these, the common folk, by their actions and ready acceptance of the great reformer-preacher, thus publicly declared that they acknowledged the wisdom and goodness of God in this his work through the Baptist; *but*, as is stated in the next verse—

Ver. 30.—**But the Pharisees and lawyers rejected the counsel of God against themselves, being not baptized of him.** The ruling classes and the highly cultured in Israel, turned a deaf ear to the fervent preaching of the gospel; as a class, they came not to his baptism. The result of the refusal of these powerful and learned men to hear the reformer's voice was that John's mission failed to bring about a national reformation. *Rejected the counsel of God against themselves, being not baptized of him.* The English Version here is not happy, and might lead to a false conception of the words of the original. The Greek would be better and more accurately rendered, "rejected for themselves the counsel of God."

Ver. 31.—**And the Lord said, Whereunto then shall I liken the men of this generation? and to what are they like?** The Master evidently paused a moment here. He sought for some homely, popular simile which would drive home to the listeners' hearts his sad and solemn judgment of the conduct of the ruling Jews of this time. The generation he was then addressing had been singularly blessed with two great Divine messages — the one delivered by that eminent servant of God, John, about whom he had been speaking in such glowing, earnest terms; the other message was his own. He chose for his purpose one of those everyday scenes from the people's life, a scene which they had witnessed often, and in which, no doubt, in past days many of the by-standers themselves had taken a part—one of those child-games which the little ones in his day were wont to play in the summer evenings, and in which, likely enough, *he* in his boyish years had often shared in, as he played in the little market-place of Nazareth. He likened the wayward men of that generation to a group of children of the people in some open space of the city, now *playing at rejoicings*, such as take place at wedding festivities, now *at wailings*, which in Eastern countries accompany funerals; that is to say, the little group would divide itself into two companies, and one would say to the other, "Come, now we will play at a wedding; here are the pipers and the singers, do you come and dance and make merry;" but the others would not. Then the little company of would-be merry-makers would beat their breasts and cry with pretended sorrow; but the others still declined to join in the game of mourning—

would not play "at a funeral," just as they refused to join in the game of "rejoicing at a wedding." To such a band of imperious little ones, who were angry if the others did not at once comply with their demands, Jesus compared the wayward and evil generation in which he and John lived. Had they not found bitter fault with John because he had declined to have anything to do with their wicked self-indulgent feasting and luxury? How often had Pharisee and scribe railed with bitter railings against Jesus because he would have nothing to do with their false and hypocritical fastings, with their pretended shrinking from what they deemed unclean and unworthy of them! Dr. Morrison puts it rightly, and forcibly: "They were dissatisfied with John, and would have nothing to do with him. 'If we are to have reformers, commend us to such as come near us, and visit our houses, and sit at our tables, and are sociable like ourselves.' They pretended, on the other hand, to scorn Jesus, who, while making so lofty a profession, yet went about eating and drinking in people's houses, and even in the homes of publicans and sinners. 'He should have gone into the desert and lived an abstemious life. . . . Commend us to ascetic men for our reformers.'" The line of interpretation which seems to us simpler and fitted to the framework of the little parable is in the main thus adopted by Meyer, Dr. W. Bleek, Bishop Words-worth, and Dean Plumptre. "You men of this generation," writes Bishop Wordsworth, "are like a troop of wayward children, who go on with their own game, at one time gay, at another grave, and give heed to no one else, and expect that every one should conform to them. You were angry with John because he would not dance to your piping, and with me because I will not weep to your dirge; John censured your licentiousness, I rebuke your hypocrisy; you vilify both, and reject the good counsel of God, who has devised a variety of means for your salvation."

Ver. 33.—**For John the Baptist came neither eating bread nor drinking wine.** Referring to his austere life spent in the desert, apart from the ordinary joys and pleasures of men, not even sharing in what are usually termed the necessities of life. He was, in addition, a perpetual Nazarite, and as such no wine or fermented drink ever passed his lips. **And ye say, He hath a devil.** Another way for expressing their conviction that the great desert-preacher was insane, and assigning a demoniacal possession as the cause of madness. Not very long after this incident the curtain of death fell on the *earthly* scene of John's life. "We fools accounted his life madness, and his end to be without honour: how is he numbered among the children of God, and his lot is among the saints!" (Wisd. v. 4, 5). We may be quite sure that "in the fiery furnace God walked with his servant, so that his spirit was not harmed, and having thus annealed his nature to the utmost that this earth can do, he took him hastily away and placed him among the glorified in heaven" (Irving, quoted by Farrar).

Ver. 34.—**The Son of man is come eating and drinking; and ye say, Behold a gluttonous man, and a winebibber, a friend of publicans and sinners!** The reproach belonged to the general way of our Lord's way of living, consorting as he did with men and women in the common everyday life of man, sharing in their joys as in their sorrows, in their festivity as in their mourning. But the words specially refer to his taking part in such scenes as the feast in the house of Matthew the publican.

Ver. 35.—**But wisdom is justified of all her children.** One of those bright, wise sayings of the Son of man which belong not to the society of Capernaum and Jerusalem, but which are the heritage of all ages. The words find their fulfilment in all those holy and humble men of heart—rich as well as poor—who rejoice in goodness and purity, in self-denying love and bright faith, whether it be preached or advocated by a Fénélon or a Wesley.

Vers. 36—50.—*The nameless woman who was a sinner, and Simon the Pharisee.* As regards the incident about to be told, some commentators have believed that the anointing was identical with that related by St. John as having taken place at Bethany very shortly before the Crucifixion. Without detailing the several points of difference in the two recitals, it will be sufficient surely to call attention to the character of the Bethany family, Lazarus and his sisters, the intimate friends of Jesus, to show how monstrous it would be to attempt to connect the poor soul who followed the Master to Simon's house with the sweet Mary of Bethany. A widely spread and, in the Western Church, a very generally received tradition identifies this woman with Mary of Magdala—the Mary Magdalene mentioned in ch. ix. 2, and again after the Crucifixion, in company with the band of holy women (ch. xxiv. 10). Out of Mary Magdalene, we learn, had been cast seven devils. This, however, gives us no clue to identify the two; rather the contrary. It is scarcely likely that the apparently well-known courtesan of the touching story was a demoniac.

The earliest writers say nothing respecting the identity of the two. Gregory the Great, however, stamped the theory with his direct assertion, and that the Western Church generally accepted the identification of the two is clear from the selection of this narrative of St. Luke as the portion of Scripture appointed for the Gospel for the Feast of St. Mary Magdalene (this was one of the feasts omitted by the English Reformers from the calendar of the Prayer-book of 1552).

It is impossible to decide the question positively. One modern commentator of distinction quaintly pleads for Gregory the Great's rather arbitrary theory, by suggesting that there is no sufficient reason to disturb the ancient Christian belief which has been consecrated in so many glorious works of art; but, in spite of this, the opinion which considers "the woman which was a sinner" the same person as "the Magdalene," is really based on little else than on a mediæval tradition.

St. Luke alone relates this touching story. We can conceive the joy of Paul when this "memory of the Master" came across him. It so admirably illustrates what this great teacher felt was his Master's mind on the all-important subject—*the freeness and universality of salvation.*

It seems likely enough that Dean Plumptre's interesting conjecture respecting this scene in the Pharisee Simon's house is correct. "Occurring, as the narrative does, in St. Luke only, it is probable enough that the 'woman which was a sinner' became known to the company of devout women named in the following chapter (viii. 1—3), and that the evangelist derived his knowledge of the fact from them. His reticence—probably their reticence—as to the name was, under the circumstances, at once natural and considerate." No special note of time or of the locality is appended. If this *sinner* was one and the same with the *Magdalene*, then the city implied is certainly Magdala, the modern mud village of *El-Mejdel*, but at that time a populous wealthy town on the Lake of Galilee. If, as we believe, the two were not identical, the city is most probably Capernaum, the usual residence of our Lord.

Ver. 36.—**And one of the Pharisees desired him that he would eat with him. And he went into the Pharisee's house.** Up to this period the relations between our Lord and the dominant parties in the capital had not reached a state of positive hostility. The Pharisees, as the chief among these parties in the state, had taken the initiative, and were sharply watching One whose influence among the people they more than suspected was hostile to them. But they had not as yet declared him a public enemy and blasphemer. This wealthy Pharisee, Simon, was evidently, like others of his sect at this time, wavering in his estimate of Jesus. On the one hand, he was naturally influenced by the hostile views entertained at head-quarters concerning the Galilæan Teacher; on the other, personal intercourse with the Master, the acts he had witnessed, and the words he had heard, disposed him to a reverential admiration. Simon evidently (ver. 39) had not made up his mind whether or not Jesus was a Prophet. His soul, too—this we gather from ver. 42—had received some great spiritual good from his intercourse with the Master. But though he invited him to be a guest at his house, and evidently loved him (ver. 47) a little, still he received his Divine Guest with but a chilling and coldly courteous reception. Not unlikely Simon the Pharisee knew he was watched that day, and that among his guests were men who would report every action of his on that occasion to the leaders of his party in Jerusalem. His cold courtesy, almost lack of courtesy, towards the Master was thus probably the result of his fear of man and of man's judgment. **And sat down to meat;** literally, *reclined.* The Jews at that time followed in their repasts the Greek (or Roman) custom of reclining on couches; the guest lay with his elbows on the table, and his feet, unsandalled, stretched out on the couch.

Ver. 37.—**And, behold, a woman in the city, which was a sinner, when she knew that Jesus sat at meat in the Pharisee's house.** The text in the older authorities is more forcible: "a woman which was a sinner in that city." Her miserable way of life would thus be well known to Simon and other of the guests. This sad detail would serve to bring out the contrast in more vivid colours. In these Oriental feasts the houses were often left open, and uninvited strangers frequently passed in through the open court-yard into the guest-chamber, and looked on. *She* had heard Jesus already, perhaps often, and had drunk in his pleading words, begging sinners to turn and to come to him

for peace. Perhaps what had decided her to take this step of boldly seeking out the Master were words apparently spoken about this time (in St. Matthew's Gospel they follow directly after the discourse respecting the Baptist just related), "Come unto me, all ye that labour and are heavy laden, and I will give you rest," etc. (Matt. xi. 28—30). It was a bold step for one like her to press uninvited, in broad daylight, into the house of a rigid purist like Simon; but the knowledge that Jesus (though personally, as she *thought,* she was unknown to him) was there, gave her courage; she felt no one would dare to thrust her out of the presence of the strange loving Master, who so earnestly had bidden the sin-weary come to him, and he would give them rest! **Brought an alabaster box of ointment.** Pliny mentions alabaster as the best material for pots or vessels intended for these precious ointments. It was softer than marble, and easily scooped into pots or bottles. These costly unguents and cosmetics were much used by the wealthy Roman ladies. The precious ointment poured over the Redeemer's feet had probably been originally procured for a very different purpose. The word μύρον, translated "ointment," was used for any kind of sweet-smelling vegetable essence, especially that of the myrtle.

Ver. 38.—**And stood at his feet behind him weeping, and began to wash his feet with tears, and did wipe them with the hairs of her head, and kissed his feet, and anointed them with the ointment.** It had been, no doubt, with her a settled purpose for days, this presenting herself to the pitiful Master. She had been one of his listeners, without doubt, for some time previously, and that morning probably she made up her mind to approach him. He was a great public Teacher, and his movements would be well known in the city. She heard he was to be present at a feast in the house of the rich Pharisee Simon. It would be easier, she thought, to get close to him there than in the crowd in the market-place or in the synagogue; so taking with her a flask of perfumed ointment, she passed into the courtyard with others, and so made her way unnoticed into the guest-chamber. As she stood behind him, and the sweet words of forgiveness and reconciliation, the pleading invitation to all heavy-laden, sin-burdened ones to come to him for peace, which she in the past days had listened to so eagerly, came into her mind, unbidden tears rose into her eyes and fell on the Master's feet as he lay on his couch; and, after the manner of slaves with their masters, she wiped the tear-wet feet with her long hair, which she evidently loosed for this loving purpose, and then quietly poured the fragrant ointment on the feet where her tears had fallen. It was the perfume of the ointment which called the host's attention to this scene of sorrow and heartfelt penitence.

Ver. 39.—**Now when the Pharisee which had bidden him saw it, he spake within himself, saying, This Man, if he were a Prophet, would have known who and what manner of woman this is that toucheth him.** It is clear that it was no mere curiosity which prompted his asking the Master to be his Guest. Respect and love for the Galilæan Teacher alternated with dread of what the Pharisee order to which he belonged would think of his conduct. As we have said, he compromised the matter with his heart, by inviting Jesus publicly, but then only receiving him with the coldest formality. He seems half-glad of this incident, for it seemed in some measure to excuse his haughty unfriendly reception of One from whom he had undoubtedly received rich spiritual benefit, as we shall see further on. "Hardly a *great* Prophet, then, after all, else he would have known all about her." This was what at once occurred to Simon. **For she is a sinner.** Yes, in Simon's mind, and in the world's estimation, but before the throne of God she was differently viewed. She had heard the Master's loving call to repentance, and a new life and a change had taken place in her whole being since she had listened to his voice.

Ver. 40.—**And Jesus answering said unto him, Simon, I have somewhat to say unto thee. And he saith, Master, say on.** How accurately did the Master read Simon's heart. *Not* a real Prophet because he was in ignorance of the character and life of the woman whom he suffered without rebuke to pour the fragrant ointment over him! We almost *see* the half-sad smile flickering on the Teacher's lips as he turned and spoke to his host. Such a parable-story as Jesus was about to give utterance to was no uncommon form of teaching on such an occasion when a well-known Rabbi like Jesus was Guest at a festal gathering.

Vers. 41, 42.—**There was a certain creditor which had two debtors: the one owed five hundred pence, and the other fifty. And when they had nothing to pay, he frankly forgave them both.** The illustration was from the everyday life of the people. This lending and borrowing was ever a prominent feature in the common life of the Jews. Pointed warnings against greed and covetousness, and the habit of usury, and the love of perpetual trafficking, we find in all the Old Testament books, notably in Deuteronomy, and then centuries later in the Proverbs, besides repeated instances in the prophetic writings and historical books. The

character of the Jews in this respect has never changed from the days of their nomad life—from the times of their slavery under the Pharaohs to our own day. In this particular instance the two debtors were of the common folk, the sums in question being comparatively small; but in both cases the debtors could never hope to pay their creditors. They were alike hopelessly insolvent, both helplessly bankrupt. The larger sum, considering the relative value of money, has been computed only to have represented about £50 of our currency. And the two received from their creditor a free, generous acquittance of the debt which would have hopelessly ruined them. In the mind of Jesus the larger debt pictured the terrible catalogue of sins which the penitent woman acknowledged she had committed; the smaller, the few transgressions which even the Pharisee confessed to having been guilty of. They were both sinners before God, both equally insolvent in his eyes; whether the debt was much or little was to the almighty Creditor a matter of comparative indifference—he frankly forgave them both (better, "freely," the Greek word ἐχαρίσατο signifies "forgave of his generous bounty"). The Revisers simply translate "he forgave," but something more is needed to reproduce the beautiful word in the original. "Frankly," in the sense of "freely," is used by Shakespeare—

"I do beseech your grace . . .
. . . now to forgive me frankly."
　　　　('Henry VIII.,' act ii. sc. 1.)

Ver. 43. — **Thou hast rightly judged.** "Come, now, I will show thee what I meant by my little story, in thine answer. Thou hast judged thyself. *Thou* art the man with the little debt of sin, as thou thinkest, and the little love given in return for the cancelled debt; for see how *thou* hast treated me thy Guest, and how *she* has made up for thy lack of friendship and courtesy." The following contrasts are adduced by the Master: "Thou didst not provide me with that which is so usual to offer guests—I entered into thine house, thou gavest me no water for my feet" (in those hot dusty countries, after walking, water to wash the feet was scarcely a luxury, it was rather a necessity); "in thy house the only water which has touched my feet was the warm rain of this sad woman's tears."

Ver. 45.—**Thou gavest me no kiss: but this woman since the time I came in hath not ceased to kiss my feet.** "Thou gavest me no kiss of respect on entering, to which as a Rabbi I was surely entitled; she hath repeatedly kissed my feet."

Ver. 46.—**My head with oil thou didst not**

anoint: but this woman hath anointed my feet with ointment. "It never entered thy thoughts to pay me the homage—and yet I had helped thee, too, a little—of pouring oil on my head" (this was by no means an unusual mark of respect in the case of an honoured guest; to one who, under the burning sun of Palestine, had walked, perhaps, some distance, this pouring oil over the head was a great comfort and refreshment); "but *she* hath anointed, not my head, she shrank, poor soul! from doing this; but my feet. And, too, it was no common oil which she used, but precious, fragrant ointment. A cold, loveless welcome, indeed, my Pharisee friend, was thine! Thou thinkest it honour enough the mere admitting the carpenter's Son to thy table; no need of these special tokens of friendship for thy Guest—the water for the feet, the kiss for the face, the oil for the head. It were a pity, surely, for the great world at Jerusalem to look on thee as the friend of the Nazareth Teacher, as on the one Pharisee who loved to honour the Galilæan Reformer."

Ver. 47.—**Wherefore I say unto thee, Her sins, which are many, are forgiven.** Again, as in the synagogue, and no doubt on many other occasions, when these words were uttered, a thrill would run through the company present. Who was this, then, one would ask the other, who with this voice and mien dared to utter such things? Only *One* could forgive sins! Was, then, the Nazareth Rabbi, the great Physician, the Worker of awful miracles—was he the One whose Name was lost, but the echo of whose voice still lingered, they hoped, in that desecrated Holy Land? **For she loved much.** Are we, then, to understand by this that her love for Jesus was the cause of forgiveness? Many Roman and some Protestant expositors have believed this is the meaning of the Lord's words. But at once a contradiction is given to this interpretation by a reference to ver. 42, where, after the remission of the two debts—the great and the little—Jesus asks, "Which of these will love him most?" But had love been the cause of a forgiveness of either or both of the debts, the question should have run, "Which of the two loved him most?" not "will love him most." In addition to which the Master guards against any view of this kind being entertained, by his concluding words (ver. 50), "Thy faith hath saved thee; go in peace." The principle on which forgiveness was granted to the woman was *faith*, not *love*. Stier, in his comment here, writes that the expression of the Lord, "Her sins, which are many, are forgiven; for she loved much," is an *argumentum, non a causâ, sed ab effectu;* in

other words, "I say unto thee, Her *many* sins are forgiven, *and thou must infer from this* that she loved much, or, she loves much, for (that is, *because*) her sins are forgiven." Stier gives another example of the meaning of "for" (ὅτι) in this place : "The sun is risen [it must have risen], for it is day" (Stier, 'Words of the Lord Jesus:' Luke vii. 47). Some may ask—What great amount of sin is necessary in order to *loving much*? Godet well answers, "We need add nothing to what each of us already has, for the sum of the whole matter is—to the noblest and purest of us, what is wanting in order to love much, is not *sin*, but the *knowledge of it*. **But to whom little is forgiven**, the same **loveth little.** This saying refers to Simon the Pharisee; the first saying (in the former part of the verse) which we have been considering refers to the woman. The same principle exactly is presented as in the first instance, and viewed from the other side—*the less forgiveness, the less love results*. Our Lord is very tender in all this to Simon and men like Simon. This Pharisee had evidently tried to live up to his light, though his life was disfigured with censoriousness, narrowness, harshness, and pride —the many faults of his class. He too had heard Jesus, and had been moved and struck by his words, and, after a fashion, loved him; only the world—*his world*—came between him and his love, so that it was only a poor, pale reflection of the real feeling after all. But our Lord gives him full credit for that little love. He even excuses its poverty by saying that he, Simon, had only received a little forgiveness, and therefore only a little love was the result. Though the Lord implies in his sad irony that the *little* forgiveness which he had received was Simon's own fault, for he did not think, in his self-righteousness, that he had any need to be forgiven. "O Pharisæe, parum diligis, quia parum tibi dimitti suspicaris; non quia parum dimittitur, sed quia parum putas quod dimittitur" (St. Augustine, 'Serm.' xcix.). Godet has a deep reflection on this state of Simon's. He asks, "May forgiveness be only partial? Then there would be men half-saved, half-lost. . . . The real forgiveness of the least sin certainly contains in germ a complete salvation, but only in germ. If faith is maintained and grows, this forgiveness will gradually extend to all the sins of a man's life, just as they will then become more thoroughly known and acknowledged. The first forgiveness is the pledge of all the rest. In the contrary case, the forgiveness already granted will be withdrawn, just as represented in the parable of the wicked debtor (Matt. xviii.); and the work of grace, instead of becoming complete, will prove abortive."

Ver. 48.—**And he said unto her, Thy sins are forgiven.** Then, turning again to the woman, in her deep penitence, and at the same time in her deep joy—joy springing from her newly found peace—he formally renews to her the assurance of that pardon which she already was conscious of; but in renewing it the Lord mentioned no more "her many sins," as in the first place (ver. 47), but simply, "thy sins," thus reducing, as Stier remarks, at last both her and Simon to a common level.

Ver. 50.—**And he said to the woman, Thy faith hath saved thee; go in peace.** Then, with just one solemn word reminding the people assembled in that guest-chamber of faith, that firm trust in the goodness and mercy of God upon which her forgiveness rested, he dismissed the woman, rousing her at once from her dreamy ecstasy, sending her from his presence back again into the ordinary life of the busy world, but bearing along with her now his mighty priceless gift of a peace which passeth understanding.

HOMILETICS.

Vers. 1—10.—*The centurion.* He is a Roman, whose inclinations were naturally opposed to all that seemed Jewish. He is a heathen by birth, whose early education was wholly removed from the worship of the Father. He is a soldier with a charge in the garrison of Capernaum, tempted, therefore, to indulgence in a domineering spirit, and to the following of that voice which whispers, "Take thy fill ere death; indulge thee and rejoice." What is the portrait presented? A man deeply in earnest about religious things, seeking a fuller satisfaction for his need than heathenism can furnish; and on an occasion when human feelings are stirred, showing such kindliness, such gentleness, such deference along with his trust in Jesus, that, having regard to these qualities, the testimony is given, "I have not found so great faith, no, not in Israel." Notice some of the features of this great faith.

I. ITS HUMILITY. He does not himself go to Jesus. He is only a Gentile. He will not so far presume as personally to make a request. He sends the elders of the Jews. Nay, further still, as the time of Jesus' approach draws near, another feeling arises. Is it not too great an honour that the Son of the Highest should come to his house? Other messengers are despatched, begging the Master not to trouble himself; it is too much to ask him to come under the roof of one who is not worthy to come to him. "Say in a word, and my servant shall be healed." Great faith sees the greatness of its object. This heathen soldier has seen the hidden glory of Jesus. The disciples saw power; he saw, felt, holiness; and herein he is our teacher. On the very day of the preaching of the sermon, he is the illustration of its first Beatitude. What is the response of Christ? He entered under the roof of the Pharisee and sat at his table, but this to the Pharisee was condemnation. We do not know whether he entered the house of the centurion, but he came into his soul. As St. Augustine says, "In counting himself unworthy that Christ should enter into his door, he was counted worthy that Christ should enter into his heart." "To this man will I look . . . even to him that is humble and contrite in spirit."

II. ITS SIMPLICITY. "Say in a word, and my servant shall be healed." Observe how far he is in advance of the faith even of those who knew Christ best. The sisters of Bethany, *e.g.,* "If thou hadst been here, my brother had not died." His soldier experience and habits have come to his aid. Is not Christ the true King of Israel? Are not legions of angels at his bidding? Reasoning from himself, with soldiers under him, he argues—A sentence will suffice. The faith lies in his discernment of Jesus' real character, and his ready, implicit trust. Note two features in his word. *Law:* "I am under authority." *Will:* "I have under me soldiers, and I say to this one, Go, and he goeth; and to another, Come, and he cometh." These features are transferred to the conception of Jesus. Grand for its simplicity is this inner apprehension of Jesus' Person. The value of faith is that it opens the mind to the Lord. It is a poor, empty hand, but it lays hold of the law and the will. It is the "Amen" in which the soul appropriates the health of God's countenance.

III. ITS INFLUENCE. See the directions along which it wrought. 1. *Zeal for the worship of God.* "He loveth our nation." This of itself is sufficiently strange. But "he hath built us a synagogue." There was a spiritual want in his neighbourhood. What excuses he might have offered! "Help these Jews? I don't belong to their nation. I am here only for a time," etc. But he loved the God of the Jews; and the grace of God had educated the conviction that wherever the opportunity of usefulness opens there is the door of service. Faith is always evidenced by a similar zeal, by a desire to give as we have received, to witness for him to whom we owe ourselves. Andrew finds Simon. The woman of Samaria hastens to the city to preach Christ. The centurion builds the synagogue. "I have not hid thy righteousness within my heart : I have declared thy faithfulness and thy salvation. I have not concealed thy loving-kindness and thy truth from the great congregation." 2. *An affectionate interest in the slave.* "Dear to him." Cicero apologized in one of his noblest orations for being concerned about a slave. This soldier's heart is bound up in the menial who waits on him. May not this menial have been the instrument of the centurion's enlightenment? In the first Christian centuries the slaves were often thus blessed. If so, no wonder that he was grateful. Be this as it may, a true faith is a new bond of union with men. It gives a higher grace and character to every relation, because it invests the human life with a new sacredness, and reminds us of the equality of all in the love of God. In receiving God we receive one another. How does St. Paul write of the slave Onesimus? "A servant, but above a servant, a brother beloved." The sketch in the gospel is interesting, as a picture of both the good master and the good servant. "Dear to him," remarks Bengel, pointing to ver. 8, "because of his obedience." The master's interests are the servant's care. And to the master the dependent is more than "a hand." A nobler tenderness elevates the connection, and secures a place in the sympathies of the heart. Is there no homily in this touch of sanctified nature for our time?

Vers. 11—16.—*The widow's son.* We are indebted to St. Luke for the touching incidents recorded in these verses. Observe—

I. THE SPRING OF THE ACTION. "When the Lord saw her, he had compassion." Some of Christ's most notable words and works were associated with, grew out of, circumstances which presented themselves in the course of his journeyings. There was no attempt at miracle. There was neither show nor effort. Wl at was done was so spontaneous that it seemed as if he could not help doing it. Here a sad procession meets his eye. There are specialities in it which touch the fountains alike of Divine power and of brotherly sympathy. He is "moved with compassion." A beautiful phrase, which bids us not merely into but behind the humanity—into the light of such a sentence as "God so loved the world." What is redemption but the activity of Divine emotion? At Nain the compassion of Christ fulfilled itself by sparing an only son. The great love wherewith God has loved us has fulfilled itself by not sparing the only begotten Son. The compassion of Christ, as he approached the gate of the city, gave one son back to a mother. God's great love has, through the sacrifice of the cross, brought back many sons to the outstretched arms of a waiting Father. It is our faith in this infinite compassion that is the source of all our hopes for men. It cannot be a matter of indifference to the Father that one of even his little ones perish. There are problems, as bearing on this, which the facts we observe and some intimations of the meekest and lowliest himself suggest—problems so painful and awful that, in respect of them, we must hold our peace. But, against them, trust in a living God makes it almost a necessity to cling to this—that, in all possible states, God's compassion has a way towards the souls he has made. As regards this particular instance, the appeal to the compassion is threefold : a *mother* weeps behind the bier of an only son; a *widow* bewails the loss of her only comforter, the support and solace of her desolate heart; it is a son, a *young man,* with all the possibilities of use in this world cut off, who is being carried out. In response to this appeal, he is moved; and has he not, in thus yielding to a pure human impulse, left us an example? It is right to hold all impulses in obedience to reason. We must hold compassion with a firm rein; yet it is not to be restrained by irksome bit and bridle. The best teacher in all benevolences is the heart, like that of Jesus,

". . . at leisure from itself
To soothe and sympathize."

II. THE MANNER OF THE ACTION. Interesting, with regard, first, to the event related.

Note: 1. The whisper straight from the heart of the God-Man to the heart of the sufferer: " Weep not! " 2. The touch of the open coffin, causing ceremonial defilement, but expressive of the attitude of him who is the " Resurrection and the Life: " " He came and touched the bier." 3. Then, as the pall-bearers stand still, the word with power: " Young man, I say unto thee, Arise! " What a change is wrought in that moment, and by that word! " Death is swallowed up in victory." Suggestive and eloquent when accepted as a symbol of Saviour love and work. Behold in the action a *picture* and a *prophecy.* 1. Hearken to the voice of God, " Weep not! " " Cure sin," it has been said, " and you cure sorrow." He who was made sin for us, of whom the forerunner had testified, " Behold the Lamb of God, that taketh away the sin of the world! " could alone effectually wipe away the tear. The comfort of others plays on the surface; his comfort reaches into the hidden place, the hidden cause of all trouble—it is the cure of sin. Are there now only faint echoes—echoes becoming fainter and fainter as the ages roll on—of the sentence uttered at Nain? Nay; this sentence, now that he has ascended and is the Prince and Saviour, giving repentance and forgiveness of sins, is fuller in its volume and mightier in its force. All that can give strength, that can inspire with hope, is confirmed and sealed for evermore. " Weep not! " O bruised, broken heart, there is in the " strong Son of God, immortal love," an oil of joy for all your mourning, a garment of praise for every spirit of heaviness. 2. But the dead is there, with Christ; and the word for the dead is, " Arise! " Let us not think only of the physical death. The spiritual and the physical are always associated in the thought of Christ; and the work at Nain is a symbol of both. As special Christ-words conjoin " Weep not! " and " Arise! " " He saith," writes St. Paul, quoting no particular saying of God, but the substance of all God's sayings, " awake thou that sleepest, and arise from the dead, and Christ shall give thee light! "

III. A SPECIAL APPLICATION OF THE SCENE AND ACTION. " Young man, I say unto thee, Arise! " This is the key-note of sermons and addresses to young men. Brother, too often asleep to the higher meanings of thine own existence—asleep and unconscious of the presence of him who loves thee, self-indulgent, dead in the death of the self-seeking worldly mind, the Lord is touching thy bier; the Lord is calling, " Arise! " start from thy sad indifference. Give those who love thee the joy of the morning without clouds, the new, better life in God. Hear the voice of the Son of God, and thou too shalt live.

Vers. 18—35.—*The message of John Baptist, and the discourse occasioned by it.* Various answers, not now to be discussed, have been given to the question—Why did John send the two followers with the message recorded? The message does seem to imply that the confidence of the Baptist had become overcast by the sorrow of the passing hour. Would it have been strange if, hearing of Jesus in the flood-tide of popular enthusiasm, working and speaking in the power of the Lord, a moment's feeling of weariness stole over the ardent spirit? " He there, and I here, within the dismal walls of the prison! He, thinking of all else, and no thought apparently of me! He increasing more and more, like the sun advancing to the perfect day; I decreasing more and more, my sun setting in the thick darkness! Can it be all a reality? Has my witness been wholly true? What if—? what if—? Jesus of Nazareth, say, ' Art thou really he? Tell me, so soon to pass from this earthly scene, that I have followed no illusion—that verily there is none else to be looked for.' " Other thoughts may have filled the mind, other motives for the mission may have influenced; but it brings the passage very near to us when we trace in it the faltering of faith. For there are moments of faltering in the history of faith. The sky of our spiritual life is not always cloudless. All the while the soul may be thirsting for the living God, but it cannot see him; from within there come voices demanding, " Where is thy God? " If a tormenting scepticism visited the honest heart of John, we can understand it, and feel the more our kinship with him. The wonderful thing would have been if misgiving had never ruffled the face of his heart; if no such film had gathered over his eye as that signified in the question, " Art thou he that should come, or do we look for another? "

I. THE QUESTION HAS NOT YET RUN ITS COURSE. It expresses the attitude of the piety of the people, in the roll of whose greatest stands the Baptist's name. It is sad that so much of the culture of Israel has separated from Israel's hope, has declared its contentment with a mere barren pantheism; that so much of its piety is busied with the effort to explain away the obvious meaning of the old prophecies, or to deny their reference to the Anointed One. But the Jew still lives, and the land of the Jew still waits. Pray for the conversion and restoration of Israel, when the people that sit in darkness shall see the problem solved which has for so long been the stumbling-stone and rock of offence, "Jesus of Nazareth, art thou he who was promised to come, or must we continue to look for another?"

II. Now, OBSERVE THE LORD'S ANSWER. It is: 1. *A word to John.* The reply to the inquiry is given "in that hour." The messengers are charged to return and tell (vers. 22, 23) what things they saw and heard. The works of Christ are the credentials of his mission, not because they are miraculous, but because they are the kind of works appropriate to the Sent of God. Recognizing the supernatural efficacy of Christ's kingdom, the witness for him is chiefly what he does, what Christianity effects wherever it is truly received. We see it breathing a new life, inspiring with a new hope, awaking new powers, putting to flight the armies of the aliens—a power of God to salvation. *E.g.* Lady Barker, in her charming letters from South Africa, says, "I feel it incumbent on me to bear testimony, not only in this instance and in this colony, to the enormous amount of real, tangible, common-sense good accomplished among the black races all over the world by Wesleyan, Methodist, and Baptist missionaries." So, universally, it is the kind of life which Christ's teaching produces; it is the wondrous changes in man himself, and therefore in man's world, which the spirit of his life accomplishes, which, to all earnest inquirers, settles the issue, "Art thou he that should come?" "Blessed"—with gentle authority the Master adds—"blessed is he whosoever shall find none occasion of stumbling in me." 2. *A word concerning John after the messengers have departed.* "A word," says Farrar, "of rhythmic and perfect loveliness" (vers. 24—28). Mark the conclusion, however—Greater prophet than he now immured in Herod's gloomy prison never was born of woman. Yet this must be added, he who is really within the kingdom, who has really received the kingdom in receiving Jesus as the King, however inferior to him in gifts and force, is a partaker of fuller blessing and privilege than he. "With all my imperfections," said Bunsen, on his dying bed, "I have ever striven after the best. But the best and noblest is to have known Jesus Christ." 3. *A word to the unsympathetic and opposing Pharisees and lawyers.* The people endorse the eulogy passed on John; but the Pharisees and lawyers frown. It is with reference to their unreasonable petulance that the sentences vers. 31—35 are spoken. What could satisfy such carpers? Verily, their successors are to be found in our day. The mind that is enmity against God will make faults, will twist any evidence, will imitate the children who will not be pleased, no matter what is done to evoke their response. Poor pedants! "they must stay in the dark until they are tired of it." Very different from such are the children of the true wisdom. They recognize and honour her under different types and forms. Wherever they see the prints of her shoes, there they love to put their feet also. "Wisdom is justified of all her children."

Vers. 36—50.—*The woman who was a sinner.* It is a truly lovely story which the evangelist tells—one of those passages in the life of Christ which we are never tired of reading, and as full of meaning as it is full of beauty. We may regard it from many points, and present its didactic force in many ways. Perhaps we shall best ensure the reception of its various lights by studying the portraiture of character which it gives.

I. THERE IS SIMON THE PHARISEE—Jesus' host on the afternoon of the day whose earlier part had been signalized by the mighty work at Nain. The notable thing about this Simon is that he meets our view as the type of that anonymous, yet most powerful, influence which we call society. He is one of the priests of that goddess which society, everywhere and in every time, worships—Respectability. A Pharisee! that is as it should be. The Herodians were a base, courtly party, fawning on the Herodian dynasty, and therefore outside religious society. The Sadducees were latitudinarians. Some of them were clever, and had much to do with the intellectual life of the nation; but, on the whole, they were a cold-blooded sect which could not command the vote of society. The correct course was to be the Pharisee. That secured the social place, put one right with the Church and the world, for this life and the next. The odour of sanctity clung to the profession; it intimated a certain aristocratic position —a position among the elect of the heavenly kingdom. Simon the Pharisee is in society. And the desire that Jesus should eat with him, the entertainment which he offered Jesus, is in behalf of society. That must have its lion. It takes up one to-day and dismisses him to-morrow, but a lion it must have. Sometimes the lion is a religious person; a great preacher or a great author becomes, for the time, the fashion. Jesus of Nazareth was the hero of the hour. Everybody spoke of him, of what he did, said, was. This priest of society must give him a dinner. We need not suppose secret hostility. Simon seems to have been willing to know more of Jesus than he did know, to study him as a phenomenon with at least a measure of interest. But he is the patron. The courtesies which would have been extended to the privileged few are omitted. Is not this Jesus only a Peasant-Preacher? Further still, the conduct of the Pharisee is representative of the separatist side of society, not only toward Jesus, but toward the sinner. It is without generosity of feeling; it is narrow, bitter when its canons are broken. That horrid creature to come to his table and touch his guest!—is it not monstrous? He a Prophet? That he should let her go near him, that she should bestow her caresses on him—this is sufficient to dispose of the claim. He could not imagine any purpose of the visit except an evil one; and such a visit was a disgrace to his house. For Respectability, hard in its judgment, is always selfish, always thinking how a thing will look, what is becoming or proper, how it can be protected and preserved. Holiness seeks the sinner; it will give itself for him. Respectability bids the sinner away. Ah! this Simon is a figure most conspicuous in our life! Respectability is the Juggernaut-car which rolls through our midst; and, as it rolls, multitudes rush forward and lay themselves prostrate before it. It has a place for Jesus; it will patronize him. Jesus has a word for it, a terribly scathing word. "Simon, I have somewhat to say unto thee."

II. THERE IS THE WOMAN. Who she was we know not. There is really nothing to confirm the old tradition which identifies her with that Mary called Magdalene, referred to in the following chapter, out of whom seven devils were cast. Whoever she was, she is known by only one feature—she was a sinner, an abandoned woman of the city. Perhaps she had heard some word of the gentle Prophet as he passed through the street. In some way "the Dayspring from on high" had visited her. And—not so difficult a matter in an Eastern house—she forced her way to his presence. Poor, weary one, for whom, for many and many a day there had been no sunshine— a mere plaything of coarse and wicked men! Observe her action as recorded in vers. 37, 38. It is to her that the Lord turns; he has glances and words for her which he has not for the priests of Respectability. From her heart proceed the welcomes which the Pharisee had denied him (vers. 44—46). Yes, in the social outcast there is often a preparation for Christ, a power of self-abandoning, simple trust, which is wanting in the Pharisees of society, with their forms and phylacteries, the pomp and pride and circumstance of the be-worshipped Respectability.

III. THE DEALING OF JESUS is "a precious history, the sweet kernel of which poor sinners will never exhaust." Consider his words about the woman, and his words to the woman. 1. The word in the forty-seventh verse—let us see that we rightly apprehend it. The meaning is not, as might hastily be gathered, "forgiven because of her much love," as if the love were the reason of the forgiveness. That would be equal to putting the rill before the spring. There are two kinds of "for"—the "for" causal, and the "for" inferential. It is the "for" inferential which we find in Jesus' saying. "From the love which moved this sinner to me, which constrained her to lavish on me the signs of respect which thou, Simon, didst omit, thou canst infer that her sins, which are many, are forgiven. Even as the tree is known by its fruit, so her forgiveness is proved by the presence of its appropriate fruit—love." This is the view borne out by the short parable which was the something that Jesus had to say to Simon (vers. 41—43). Suppose that we insist on an interpretation of this parable which the terms employed in it might warrant, we are met by serious difficulties. For instance, it might seem to teach that the more, in amount, the debt remitted, the more will be the love realized; that the more of a sinner one has been, the more of a saint, after conversion, one will be. But we know that this could not be the meaning of Christ; and it was not. It is not the quantity of sins, but the conscience of sin, the sense of its sinfulness and bitterness and tyranny, which determines the question of the larger or smaller debtor. In the case before us, one steeped in iniquity represents the larger, the Pharisee the smaller. But, to prove that the consciousness of owing a great debt—the being, in one's own judgment, the five-hundred-pence debtor, yea, the chief of sinners—does not involve a wicked course of life, recollect the Apostle Paul, who had been zealous towards God above his equals. When he thinks of his "exceeding madness" against Jesus, he confesses, "I have nothing to pay. No debt could have been greater than mine, wretched man that I am." The much love is measured by the sense of there having been much forgiven. The love is *as* the knowledge of sin. If you think there is little to forgive, you will love only little. 2. There are two words to the woman herself (ver. 50). "He said to her, Thy sins are forgiven." An absolution, accepted by all who heard it, as full and authoritative. They are amazed : "Who is this that even forgives the sins?" Oh ! who is he? Hartley Coleridge finely says—

> " All the blame
> And the poor malice of the worldly shame
> To her were past, extinct, and out of date;
> Only the sin remained, the leprous state."

It was to this leprous state that the word went down. With the voice of a declared pardon, there was felt the power of a new purity. "Daughter, thy sins are sent away from between thy God and thee. They are blotted out, no more to be remembered. And lo! as thou art justified, thou art washed throughly from thine iniquity, and cleansed from thy sin. Thy faith hath saved thee" (ver. 50). The Lord gave no heed to the murmurs of those reclining at table. He answers these murmurs by not answering, or rather, by this additional word to the woman. The salvation was the entrance of forgiving love; and it was the trust in him that drew her to the Pharisee's house, which had opened her soul to his healing power. The power is only, is wholly, in him, but the faith is the condition and the means of the deliverance. "Saved, rejoicing sinner, go in peace." Wondrous, glorious gospel! his, hers, who wills to have it as the poor woman willed! Sinners of modern Christendom, you must be stripped of all the soft complacencies of Pharisaic righteousness; consciously poor and needy—sinners, and nothing else, you must get to the Christ of God. Until thus you have reached him, there is only a "something to say to you." The frank forgiveness, the fulness of the eternal life, is when he looks into the clinging soul, when he says, "Thy faith hath saved thee; go in peace."

HOMILIES BY VARIOUS AUTHORS.

Vers. 1—10.—*Faith in its fulness.* The greatness of the centurion's faith is attested by our Lord himself; he declared that it was superior to anything he had "found in Israel." We see evidence of its fulness in that—

I. IT TRIUMPHED OVER NATIONAL PREJUDICE. Here is a Roman exercising the most perfect confidence in a Jew—putting one in whom he was closely and deeply interested into the hands of an Israelite. We must remember all the pride of the Romans as such, and all their hatred as well as contempt of the Jews, to realize the fulness of this triumph.

II. IT WAS BASED ON COMPARATIVELY SLENDER EVIDENCE. "When he *heard of* Jesus, he sent." Clearly, then, he had not seen him, had not witnessed his works, had not listened to his wisdom; he was without the larger part of the evidence which was before the people of that neighbourhood. He had but "heard of" him, and yet he believed in him.

III. IT WAS CHERISHED IN SPITE OF CONSCIOUS UNWORTHINESS. He took a very humble view of himself. This we gather from his *action* in sending the elders of the Jews to intercede on his behalf (ver. 3), and from his *language* in stating that he was not worthy that Christ should "enter under his roof" (ver. 6). Yet had he such an assurance of our Lord's kindness of heart that he was persuaded he would pity and help him, notwithstanding this undeservedness on his part.

IV. IT ASSUMED THAT CHRIST WOULD RESPOND TO A RESPECTFUL AND EARNEST PLEA.

V. IT SHOWED A WONDERFUL CONFIDENCE IN HIS ABILITY TO HEAL. The sending of the deputation, in the first instance, showed the confidence of the centurion in the power of Christ. But the fulness of his faith in this direction was manifested in the sending of the second deputation—in charging them with that most striking message (vers. 6—8). It is interesting to notice how the soldierly profession, which might well seem to be most unlikely to help a man to discipleship to the Prince of peace, did, in fact, serve him in good stead. It enabled him to grasp fully the idea of Divine *authority*. He was, he said, a man who knew well what was meant by command and obedience. He was accustomed to obey implicitly those who were over him in position, and he was also in the habit of receiving the full and immediate obedience of those who were under him. To them he said, "Come," and they came; "Go," and they went. Whatever forces of nature this Divine Healer might wish to employ, he had only to do the like; he had but to command, and they would instantly obey. Thus his military training helped him to a faith in the authority and power of Christ which distinguished him above others, and which brought down the blessing he sought (ver. 10). We learn: 1. *That unbelief in Jesus Christ is wholly inexcusable in us* Consider how, in contrast with this centurion, we have no prejudice to overcome, but have been baptized into (or brought up in) the faith of Jesus Christ. Consider also how, in contrast with this man, we have had constant access to the Saviour, and are the children of privilege in the fullest sense of the word. And consider also what evidence we have had before us of Christ's willingness and power to save in all that we have heard, read, and seen. 2. *The validity of any sincere belief, weak or strong.* It may be that something in our spiritual constitution or in our religious training may make us incapable, at the beginning, of exercising so strong a faith as that here illustrated. This need not, and must not, keep us from making an appeal to the Saviour. Not all that sought his aid had faith like this; yet he healed them also. We must come as we are and as we can. He is One that "does not break the bruised reed." A faith that is feeble, but sincere, will not go home unblessed.—C.

Ver. 5.—*Patriotism and piety.* The mutual respect shown here by Jew and Roman is very pleasing, and the more so that it was so rare. Disdain rather than regard, hatred rather than affection, characterized both peoples; and it is a very agreeable change to find so different a state of mind. Here the Roman loves the Jewish nation, and the elders of the Jews come out to serve the Roman. The plea which they present to Christ, that out of attachment to their nation he had built them a synagogue, was very forcible, and it did not fail. The conjunction of the two clauses of the text suggests the close connection between piety and patriotism.

I. OUR INDEBTEDNESS TO THE RELIGION OF OUR NATIVE LAND. The centurion loved the nation, and why? The Jew had one thing to give the Roman, and that was a very great thing. Civilization, military science, and law, were of the Roman; but " salvation was of the Jews" (John iv. 22). This Roman, who probably saw many things in Galilee that he pitied, found something that first surprised, then convinced, then satisfied and ennobled him—he found a true theology and a pure morality. With this he found rest of soul, domestic purity, health and sweetness of life; he became another man, and lived another life. He was indebted to the religion of this country of his adoption. What do we owe to the religion of the land in which we were born? How much more do we owe to the Christianity we have learned in England than the centurion (of the text) owed to the Judaism he learned in Galilee! Our holy faith, taught us in childhood and impressed upon us through all our days, has brought into our view a heavenly Father, a Divine Saviour and Friend, a Holy Spirit and Comforter, a blessed service, a godly brotherhood, a noble life, a glorious hope of immortal blessedness. What shall we render to the country of our birth which has trained us in such truths as these?

II. OUR BEST ACKNOWLEDGMENT. This man "loved the nation and built them a synagogue." What better thing could he do than this? What kindlier or truer service could he render them? Those synagogues had been the homes of devotion and the sources of sacred instruction for four hundred years, and they had rendered inestimable service to the nation. The influences which radiated from them had kept the people loyal to their faith, and had preserved in them all the better qualities they possessed. And what can *we* do to serve the country which has nourished us in the faith of Christ? We can do all that lies in our power to promote its material prosperity, to secure its freedom, to extend its knowledge and intelligence. But, these not being left undone, there is one thing more which is greater than these—we can *promote its piety*. By so doing we shall serve it in the highest sphere; we shall be doing that which will gain for it the favour of Almighty God; we shall be indirectly serving it in all other ways, for the children of God will be the best citizens of their country in any and every department of human action. And how shall we best promote the piety of our land? 1. By living a devout and upright life in our own humble sphere. 2. By making known, in all open ways, the distinctive truths of the gospel of Jesus Christ. 3. By supporting the institutions which are closely connected with it—its edifices, its societies, its homes.—C.

Vers. 13—16.—*Christ visiting and abiding.* We cannot wonder that the people exclaimed as they did, "God hath visited his people," when they witnessed such a miracle as this. It was clear enough that One from the heavenly world was with them, manifesting Divine power and pity. We have here—

I. A TOUCHING PICTURE OF THE EXTREMES OF HUMAN JOY AND SORROW. The great darkness of *death* had overshadowed a human home; death had come to a *young man*, one who had passed through the perils of early life, and had qualified himself for the larger duties and weightier obligations of manhood; one, therefore, to whom life was peculiarly dear and precious. This young man was an *only son*, in whom all his mother's love had centred, on whom she leaned as her one support; and she was a *widow*, most needing the solace of affection, least able to dispense with the prop that was left her. A supreme sorrow was hers. Then came a sudden revulsion of feeling. Just at the very hour when grief was at its very depth, as the young man was being carried to his grave, he is restored to her. The inanimate form is quickened to a new life; there is "a light upon the brows" which is *not* "the daylight only," but the light of consciousness; the stilled tongue speaks again; the pallor of death gives place to the hue of health. Her son is hers again; her home is home again; she takes back her life with his. A more complete rebound from uttermost sorrow to intensest peace and joy can never have been known.

II. CHRIST'S CROWNING ACT OF AUTHENTICATION. When our Lord sent back his reply to John we are not surprised that he mentions, as the crowning instance of his power, that "the dead are raised" (ver. 22). Much as it was to give sight to the blind and hearing to the deaf and activity to the lame, much as it was to cleanse the lepers of their foul and terrible disease, it was very much more to restore the dead to life. That was the supreme and sovereign act, proving that Jesus did come forth from God, and was what he claimed to be. That was a power beyond all the skill of human science, beyond all the arts of necromancy; it bespoke the near presence of the Divine. Surely God *was* visiting his people.

III. A PROPHECY OF THE PRESENT AND THE LASTING MISSION OF THE DIVINE RESTORER. What Jesus Christ *visited* this world to do for the bodies of men he now *lives and reigns* to do for their souls—to restore them to newness of life. He is with us always, here on earth, "not to sojourn, but to abide" with us, exercising a far more glorious power than that he put forth at the gates of the city of Nain. That young man had another lease of life; to the days that he had spent on earth there were added a certain number more. Then he sickened again, and died; and death and the grave claimed their own. But when Jesus Christ, our Divine Saviour, now confers spiritual life, he awakens us to an existence (1) which is far higher than the mortal life we are living here, and (2) which is not limited by a few years. The great work of restoration which the risen Saviour is now accomplishing is that of which his work below was but the preparation and the promise. 1. The death to which this man succumbed was the type of the spiritual death which is the sad consequence of sin. 2. To those thus lost to God and man he speaks with sovereign voice, "Arise!" he bids them realize their guilt and danger; he summons them to repentance; he invites them to a whole-hearted trust in himself, the Almighty Saviour; he bids them walk thenceforth in the way of his commandments. 3. He restores them to their friends as those who, under his gracious hand, will be henceforth what they have never been before. 4. He calls forth deepest gratitude and reverence from all that witness the exercise of his power and grace.—C.

Vers. 19—22.—*Human goodness and the permanency of the gospel.* We have here—

I. A CONSTANT CHARACTERISTIC OF HUMAN GOODNESS. How came John to send this message? Was he really doubtful—he who had prepared the way of the Lord, who had baptized him, who had recognized in him the Lamb of God? Even so. Many ingenious theories account for it in some other way, but they do not satisfy. After all, was it surprising that John should begin to doubt? He had been lying in that lonely fortress by the Red Sea for some months; constitutionally active and energetic, he had been doomed to enforced idleness, and had had nothing to do but to form judgments of other people—a very perilous position; what he heard about Jesus may very well have seemed strange and unsatisfactory to him. Our Lord's method was very different from his own. He was living, as John had not done, in the very midst of the people; he was not drawing great crowds whom he excited to tempestuous feeling, but acting, with calm and deep wisdom, on smaller numbers; he was not living an ascetic life; he was not making any very great way according to ordinary human measurement; and John, writhing in captivity, and longing to be out and about in active work, allowed his mind to be affected, his belief to be disturbed, by what he heard and by what he did not hear. Nothing could be more natural, more human. This is human goodness all the world over. Nobility of spirit, self-sacrifice, devoutness, zeal, and infirmity, the partial subsidence of his faith. Who that knows the history of human goodness can be surprised at this? We must take this into the account in our estimate of good men. *Infirmity* is a *constant element* of human character. Perfection among the angels of God; perfection for ourselves further on among the glorified; meantime we may bestow our heartiest affection and our unstinted admiration upon those who are aspiring and endeavouring after the highest, but who sometimes fail to be all that they and we could wish that they were.

II. THE BEST PROOFS OF THE DIVINE POWER AND VIRTUE. Christ adduced two powerful proofs that he was indeed the "One that should come." 1. *The exercise of benignant power.* In that same hour he healed many that came to be cured, and he said to John's disciples, "Go and show your master what benignant power I am exercising; not smiting my enemies with blindness, but making the blind to see; not punishing the liar with leprosy, but pitying the poor leper and making him clean; not raining down fire from heaven on the obdurate, but calling back to life those who had entered the dark region of the dead; visiting the homes of men with health and life and joy." 2. *Love for the lowly.* "Go and tell John that I am caring much for those for whom men have not cared at all, instructing in heavenly wisdom those whom other teachers have left untaught, lifting up those whom other reformers have been content to leave upon the ground, making heirs of the outcast, making rich for ever the penniless and hopeless—say that 'the blind receive their sight, and the deaf hear,' etc., and forget not to add that 'to the poor the gospel is preached.'"

As these disciples came to our Master, so do some approach us now: they come with serious, earnest questioning. "Is the Christian system which we preach *the* system for our age? is it still the word we want? Or is not the world awaiting another doctrine, another method, another kingdom? Is Jesus Christ the Teacher for us, or do we look for another?" What is our reply? 1. Look at *the benignant power of the gospel of Jesus Christ.* Follow the broad, deep river of beneficence which took its rise at Bethlehem; see what it has been effecting through all these ages; consider what it has done, not only for the physical sufferer—for the blind, for the lame, for the leper, for the lunatic—but what it has done for the poor, for the slave, for the prisoner, for the savage, for the ignorant, for the little child, for woman; consider what it has done for the sorrowful, and for those laden and crushed with a sense of guilt; what it has done for the dying; consider how it has been enlightening and uplifting and transforming the minds and the lives of men; what a blessed beneficent power it has been exerting and is as capable as ever of exerting. 2. Look at *the care which the gospel takes of the lowly.*   Consider the fact that wherever the truth of Christ has been preached in its purity and its integrity, man as man has been approached; all human souls have been treated as of equal and incalculable worth, the poor as well as the rich, the slave as well as his master, the illiterate as well as the learned, the unknown and untitled as well as the illustrious. The gospel has gone among the people, it has made its appeal to the multitude; it is " the common salvation; " it does not content itself with imposing a faith and a cultus upon the nation; it does not rest until it has permeated the entire people with the knowledge and the love of God, and wrought in them the practice of its own pure and lofty principles. Surely this is not a system for Galilee or Syria; this is not a doctrine for one age of the world; it is the ever-living truth of God. Christ is *our* Teacher, our Saviour, our Lord; we do *not* look for another.—C.

Ver. 22.—*The leprosy of sin.* Why specify the fact that the lepers were cleansed ? Why single out this disease from others that might have been named ? Because it was peculiarly desirable that, when the Messiah came and gave credentials of his heavenly origin, he should exercise his power in this direction. For leprosy was *the chosen type of sin.* All disease is pictorial of sin ; it is to our bodily frame what sin is to the soul—it is *inward disorder showing itself in outward manifestation.* But leprosy was that peculiar form of sickness which the Divine Lawgiver selected as *the* type of sin. And surely it was perfectly fitted to be so regarded. We look at—

I. ITS LOATHSOMENESS. Why was the leper so rigidly excluded from society? We have no convincing evidence that this was a dangerous, contagious disorder. But the extreme loathsomeness of the leper's appearance fully accounted for the decree. It was not fitting that anything so terribly repulsive and shocking should be seen in the homes and in the streets. Sin is the most odious of all things ; it is " that abominable thing which God hates." God "cannot look" upon it. In its fouler forms it is infinitely offensive to the pure of heart.

II. ITS DIFFUSIVENESS. Leprosy was eminently diffusive. It was communicated from parent to child ; it spread from limb to limb, from organ to organ, until it covered the entire body. Sin is *a thing which spreads.* It, too, is communicable *by heredity*, and it also spreads *from faculty to faculty.* Sin leads to sin. " There's not a crime but takes its change out still in crime." Theft leads to violence, drunkenness to falsehood, impurity to deceit. Sin also spreads *from man to man*, from child to child, from friend to friend. You cannot circumscribe it ; it passes all bounds that may be set up.

III. ITS PITIFULNESS. Who could regard the leper, doomed to a long, perhaps a lifelong separation from his family and his business and all favourite pursuits, without heartfelt pity ? Life was worth nothing to him. Sin is condemnable enough ; but it is pitiable also. Blame the erring, reproach the faulty, remonstrate with the foolish, but do not fail to pity those whom sin is shutting out from all that is best below, and from all that is bright above. Pity these with a profound compassion, and help them with an uplifting hand.

IV. ITS SEPARATING INFLUENCE. As the leper was exiled from mankind and banished to a severe isolation, so does sin come in as a separating power. 1. It separates a man from God, opening the wide, deep gulf of conscious guilt. 2. It separates man from man. It is not high walls, or broad acres, or unmeasured seas, that divide man from man : it is folly, hatred, malice, jealousy, *sin.*

V. ITS DEATHFULNESS. In the leper the springs of health were poisoned; there was a process of dissolution going on ; it was death in life. *Sin is death.* " She that liveth in pleasure is dead while she liveth," wrote Paul. And our Lord's words imply the same : " Whoso believeth on me, though he were dead, yet shall he live." A man living apart from God and in rebellion against him is so far from answering the end of human life that he may be rightly regarded as dead while he lives.

VI. ITS INCURABLENESS BY MAN. The Jews did not bring the leper to the physician; they regarded him as incurable by the art of man. Sin is incurable by human methods. Regulations for conduct, vows of abstinence, parliamentary statutes, legal penalties, do not cure. They may be very valuable as accessories, but they will not heal. Only the Divine hand can accomplish that for the human heart. One there is who offers himself as the Divine Physician; he who sent back to John in prison the convincing message, "The lepers are cleansed." In him is all-forgiving grace and all-cleansing power. A living faith in him will lead to pardon and to purity. Instead of loathsomeness, there will be spiritual beauty; instead of isolation, communion; instead of a living death, eternal life.—C.

Ver. 23.—*Christ as an offence.* "Blessed is he, whosoever shall not be offended in me." It was simply inevitable that our Lord, if he laid himself out to do the very best and greatest that could be done, should be an offence to many. "Not to send peace, but a sword," was a purely incidental, but it was a necessary result of such faithfulness as he showed.

I. THE OFFENCE TO BE FOUND IN CHRIST. 1. *The offence of the Messiahship.* Our Lord offended John the Baptist (see preceding homily) by the quietness of his method and the slowness of his results. He offended Peter by foretelling the sorrows and the shame to which he was moving on (Matt. xvi. 22). He offended Nicodemus by the profundity of his teaching (John iii.). He offended the leaders of religion of his time by denouncing their formality and insincerity. He offended the people by preaching a doctrine too *broad* for their narrow-mindedness (ch. iv. 28), too *deep* for their shallow-mindedness (John vi. 52—66), too elevated for their earthly mindedness. 2. *The offence of the cross.* (1) The memory of a crucified Nazarene was a stumbling-block to the Jew, who expected something very different from this dishonour (1 Cor. i. 23). (2) The story of a crucified Jew was foolishness to the Greek. With his venerable mythology, his honoured philosophy, his pride of patriotism, he was not prepared to put his trust in a malefactor executed in Judæa. 3. *The offence of the kingdom.* In one sense, "the offence of the cross" has ceased. It has become the symbol of all that is beautiful in art, refined in culture, strong in civilization. Yet is there everywhere, yet will there always be, something in Christ that will offend the human soul. For he requires of us that (1) we empty our minds of preconceived ideas, and approach him with the docility of children (Matt. xviii. 3); (2) we surrender every evil habit, however dear or valuable it may seem to us (Matt. v. 29); (3) we give the first place in our thought and our affections to himself, making even our nearest and dearest human kindred occupy the second place (ch. xiv. 26); (4) we find our recompense for faithful service in the spiritual and the eternal, rather than in the material and the temporal; (5) we accept his Divine favour and enter his service as those who claim nothing and accept everything at his hand. Many are they who live in our land, who read our Christian literature, who sit in our sanctuaries, and who, for one of these reasons, are offended in Christ.

II. THE BLESSEDNESS OF THOSE WHO DO NOT FIND IT; who come to learn of him in all docility of spirit; who cheerfully part with all that he condemns that they may follow him; who offer to him their undivided heart; who accept his service that they may receive a spiritual and a heavenly recompense. Blessed, indeed, are they; for: 1. Their hearts will be the home of a heavenly peace, and a joy which no man taketh from them. 2. Their life will rise to a noble height of sanctity, of beauty, of usefulness. 3. On their checkered course will fall the sunshine of their Master's blessing—his consecration of their joy, his overruling of their sorrow. 4. Their life will end in a calm and peaceful hope, which will pass into glorious fruition. Blessed, indeed, is he whosoever is not offended in Christ, but cordially accepts him as the Saviour of his spirit and the rightful Lord of his life.—C.

Vers. 24—28.—*Christ's estimate of John; character and privilege.* It is pleasant to think that, immediately after John had intimated his doubt respecting the Christ, our Lord spoke in terms of unmeasured confidence concerning John. His language is strong and somewhat paradoxical, but it admits of a simple explanation. His first reference to John affirms—

I. HIS SUPERIORITY IN RESPECT OF CHARACTER. The nobility of John's character has already been illustrated (see ch. iii.). Its most marked features were: 1. His cheerful acceptance of privation; living on in the wilderness with nothing to gratify taste, and barely sufficient to sustain life, though his popularity as a teacher and prophet would have enabled him to make a very different provision for himself,

2. His incorruptible fidelity to the work committed to his charge (ch. iii. 15, 16)
3. His fearless, holy courage—a courage which was based on a sense of God's nearness
to him and his Divine faithfulness toward him; a courage manifested in public (ch.
iii. 7—9), and, what is more and what is worthier, shown in private also in an interview with one strong man who held his earthly destiny in his hand (ch. iii. 19).
4. His rare magnanimity.   Not merely accepting without resentment the fact that he
was to be supplanted by another, but going beyond that point in spiritual excellence,
and positively rejoicing in the elevation of that other Teacher; stepping down and
giving place gladly to one younger but greater than himself (John iii. 29).   We are
not surprised that he "who knew what was in man," who knew the strength and
the weakness of our human nature, said concerning John, "Among those that are born
of women," etc. (ver. 28).

II. His INFERIORITY IN RESPECT OF PRIVILEGE. " But he that is least *in* the kingdom
of God is greater than he." We must take the word "greater" as signifying *more
privileged* : it will not bear any other meaning. Most assuredly Jesus did not mean
to say that the man who, being within his kingdom, was lowest in moral worth, stood
higher in the favour of God than John. Such a sentiment is quite inconceivable,
perfectly incredible. But our Lord may very well have meant that any one, however
humble his position in the kingdom of grace, who yet stands *within* that kingdom, of
which John stood *outside*, has a distinct advantage over the great prophet. To know
what we, with all our obscurity and incapacity, do know ; to understand and enter into,
as we may do, the glorious purpose of God in Jesus Christ; to comprehend that, by
that death of shame upon the cross, the Redeemer of the world is drawing all men
unto him ; and not only to understand all this, but to enter into it by a personal, living
sympathy and co-operation ;—this is to stand on a height to which even John, though
he came in sight of it (John i. 36), did not attain. 1. We are the children of privilege ;
we are "the heirs of all the ages" of thought, of revealed truth. If we will read
reverently, and inquire diligently and devoutly, we may know the mind of God concerning us as the greatest of all the prophets did not know it. 2. Let us take care
that we are the children of God ; returned from the far country of estrangement and
indifference ; dwelling in the home of the Father's favour ; walking with God daily ;
finding a filial joy in doing and bearing his holy will ; entering by sympathy and effort
into his holy purpose.—C.

Vers. 31—34.—*Christian abstinence and participation.* These " children sitting in
the market-place" very well illustrate the perverse and contradictory of all generations.
Many are they, here and everywhere, who will neither dance at the wedding nor
mourn at the funeral, who will work neither along one line nor yet along its opposite,
to whom all ways are objectionable because their own spirit is out of tune with everything. But the special folly which these children are brought forward to condemn is
that of objecting to John because he was abstemious, and to Jesus because he partici-
pated in the good gifts of God. The right course to take is not that of objecting to
both, but rather that of accepting and honouring both. We shall find, if we care to
look for it—

I. CHRISTIAN ABSTEMIOUSNESS. John came "neither eating nor drinking." He
acted, no doubt, under Divine direction in so doing. But John was not our exemplar.
We are not called to follow John, but Christ ; and Christ came eating and drinking.
Is abstinence, then, a *Christian* course ? It is so ; it is justified by the language of our
Lord and by that of his apostles. He said that there were some celibates "for the
kingdom of heaven's sake" (Matt. xix. 12). And he urged upon men that they should
pluck out their right eye, or cut off their right hand, rather than perish in iniquity
(Matt. v. 29, 30). His apostle wrote that men should neither eat meat nor drink wine,
if by so doing they put a stumbling-block in the way of another (Rom. xiv. 21). And
it is certain that we are acting in a strictly and, indeed, an emphatically Christian
spirit when we: 1. Abstain because indulgence would be perilous to ourselves. This
may relate to food or drink, or to any kind of amusement or occupation, to anything
of any kind in which we find ourselves under a strong temptation to excess if we once
begin. 2. Abstain because our abstinence will make the path of virtue or piety more
accessible to others. Anything we can do, any privation we may accept, any habit

we may form, by which we help men upwards and Godwards, must be an essentially and radically Christian thing.

II. CHRISTIAN PARTICIPATION. "The Son of man came eating and drinking." He was no ascetic; he was present at the festivity; he accepted the invitation to the rich man's board; he did not choose the coarser garment because it was coarser, or the severer lodging because it was severer; he did not habitually and conscientiously decline the gifts of God in nature. He knew how to decline them when occasion called for it (see ch. vi. 12; ix. 58), but he did not do so regularly and as a sacred duty. Surely it was well for the world that he acted thus; for, had he sanctioned asceticism, we should have been continually oscillating, or everywhere divided, between an unamiable severity on the one hand and a degrading self-indulgence on the other hand. The wise and the true course is that of a Christian participation; this is a partaking of the gifts of God and of the sweets and enjoyments of earth, which is: 1. Sanctified by devout gratitude; by a continual and wholesome mindfulness that every good gift is from above, and calls for a grateful and reverent spirit. 2. Controlled by a wise moderation; so that nothing is indulged in which is in the smallest degree excessive; so that no injury of any kind is done to the spiritual nature. 3. Beautified by benevolence; the participation by ourselves being very closely and constantly accompanied by the remembrance of the wants of others. "Eat the fat and drink the sweet," but be careful to "send portions to them for whom nothing is prepared."—C.

Ver. 35.—*Our treatment of wisdom.* Whatever might have been expected to be the case, the fact is that wisdom has received but poor and sad treatment from the children of men. We perceive, without any search for it—

I. ITS REJECTION BY THE WORLD. 1. Up to the time of the coming of our Lord. The Eternal Wisdom uttered its voice by the constitution and course of nature, by the human reason and conscience, by occasional revelation. But that voice was unheard or unheeded. Few, indeed, in every age and land recognized and obeyed it in comparison with the vast multitudes that remained in ignorance and folly. The heavens declared the glory of God, but men knew not the hand Divine that moved the stars in their course. "The candle of the Lord" was kindled, and it shone within the soul, but men hid it under the bushel of their unholy habits and their perverting prejudices. Through those long, dark ages Wisdom spake, and (it might be almost said that) "no man regarded." 2. The coming of Christ. He who *was* the very "Wisdom of God" himself, he who *was* "the Truth," dwelt amongst us; and "he was despised and rejected of men." Those who should have been the first to appreciate and to welcome him were the first to dislike and to denounce him. "He came unto his own, and his own received him not." 3. From that time to our own day. Divine Wisdom, speaking in the gospel of Christ, has been summoning men to reconciliation with God, to peace, to virtue, to sacred joy, to immortal blessedness; and the world, upon the whole, has turned to it a deaf ear, has gone on its own way of folly, has refused to walk in its light, and to receive its benediction.

II. ITS RECOGNITION BY ITS OWN SONS. 1. There were some in the dark days before Christ who heard and heeded the voice of God. These may have been more numerous than we have supposed. "In every nation he that feared God and wrought righteousness was accepted of him." There may have been—we may rightly hope that there were—great numbers of the "children of wisdom" who recognized its voice and obeyed its teaching. 2. When our Saviour came there were those who recognized his voice and responded to it. Many of these were women, many of them "little ones," despised by the authorities of their day. *They* did not think him "possessed," nor charge him with self-indulgence (vers. 33, 34); they perceived in him a Divine Teacher, a true Friend, a gracious Saviour, and they "rose and followed him;" then, indeed, was "Wisdom justified of all her children." 3. Throughout these Christian ages the same truth has held. The psalmist prays, "Do good unto those that be good, and to them that are upright in their hearts" (Ps. cxxv. 4). And while it is true that men of the most perverse and froward spirit may be so mightily affected by Divine power and grace that the truth of God breaks through the thickest armour of opposition, yet is it generally true that it is only they who have the spirit of wisdom in them—"the children of wisdom"—who enter the kingdom of truth and righteousness. "Only the good discern the good," writes one of our truest poets and deepest thinkers. It is only they who are sincere seekers after the truth who reach the goal. It is "to the upright that there ariseth light in the darkness;" it is to the pure and the upright and the merciful that God shows himself to be such, and by them is seen to be such (Ps. cxii. 4; xviii. 25, 26). We cannot see the wisdom, the faithfulness, the kindness, the mercy of God, while our hearts are wrong with him. But when we ourselves are right with God, and we have so much of the spirit of goodness in us that we may be called the children of wisdom, then God's dealings with our race, with our Church, with our family, with ourselves, are recognized as the just and kind and faithful things they are, and in our experience "Wisdom is justified of all her children." (1) We need not be surprised if God's manifestations of himself in his Son or in his providence are misinterpreted. That is to be expected in the case of the children of error. (2) If we are pining and complaining under the hand of God, and are supposing ourselves ill treated, we may be sure that what is needed by us is not something done for us, but a change wrought within us. For that we must seek in humility and in prayer.—C.

Vers. 36—50.—*Loving and forgiving.* The peculiarity of Oriental customs, together with the earnestness and eagerness of this penitent, will account for her effecting an entrance into the house of this Pharisee, and gaining access to the feet of our Lord. The lessons we gain from this most touching incident are—

I. THAT THERE IS FREE AND FULL FORGIVENESS FOR THE WORST. It is somewhat striking that, although Old Testament Scripture abounds in passages which attest the greatness of God's mercy to the repentant, the Jews of our Lord's time had no place for such in their system or their practice. This could not be from unfamiliarity with the sacred record; it rather arose from ignorance of themselves. They did not acknowledge any sin in their own souls, any shortcoming in their own lives. Simon probably thought that Jesus was putting the debt which represented his obligation (fifty pence) at a high figure. And, thus mistaking themselves, it is not to be wondered at that they took a false view of their neighbours; that they looked upon those who were outwardly bad as hopelessly irrecoverable. But not so the Saviour. By action as much as by language he made it clear that the guiltiest of men and the worst of women might come in penitence and be restored. That is the valuable and lasting significance of his attitude on this occasion. His treatment of this woman, together with his gracious words to her (ver. 48), are to us, as they ever will be, the strong assurance that those whom we most unsparingly condemn and most scrupulously exclude may find mercy at his feet.

II. THAT NOT HER LOVE BUT HER PENITENCE WAS THE GROUND OF HER FORGIVENESS. When Christ said, "Her sins, which are many, are forgiven; for she loved much," he did not, could not, mean that her love was the *ground,* but that it was the *consequence* of her forgiveness. He meant to say, "You can see that she has been forgiven, for you see how she loves, and it is only they who have been forgiven what she has been forgiven that love as she loves. The fulness of her love is therefore the *proof* (not the ground) of her forgiveness." What led to her forgiveness was her penitence. Those bitter tears she shed (ver. 38) were the tears of a true contrition; they meant a holy hatred of her past sin, and a sincere determination to lead another life; and not being repelled, but accepted, by this Holy and Merciful One, deep and strong gratitude arose in her; and penitence, love, and a new and blessed hope surged and strove together in uncontrollable emotion within her heart. When God shows us our fault, we go at once to the merciful Saviour; trusting in him, we are received and restored; then a pure, deep, lasting love arises in our souls; it is the simple, natural, beautiful outgrowth of penitence and faith.

III. THAT THE SENSE OF GOD'S GRACE TO US WILL DETERMINE THE FULNESS OF OUR AFFECTION TOWARD HIM. "To whom little is forgiven, the same loveth little." If we have a very imperfect sense of our guilt, and therefore of God's mercy to us, our response in gratitude and love will be far below what it should be. It is, therefore, of the gravest importance that we should know and feel our own faultiness in the sight of God. For clearly it is not the magnitude of our past sin, but the *fulness of our sense of guilt,* which determines the measure of our feeling in the matter of gratitude and love. 1. It is for this that we must look. We shall find it as we dwell on the

greatness of God's goodness toward us in his providence and his grace; in the poverty
and feebleness of our filial return to him for all his love and care and kindness toward
us; in the fact that he has been requiring purity of thought and rectitude of soul and
sincerity of motive, as well as propriety of word and integrity of deed. 2. For this
also we must pray; asking for that enlightening Spirit who will show us our true
selves, and fill us with a due sense of our great unworthiness and our manifold
transgressions.—C.

Ver. 40.—*Christ and Simon: the correcting word.* There were some good points
about Simon. 1. He was an eminently respectable man; he was so in the true sense
of the word, for as a virtuous man he could respect himself, and his neighbours could
rightly respect him; he conformed his conduct to a high standard of morality. 2. He
was an open-handed, hospitable man. 3. He was an open-minded man. It was not
every Pharisee that would have invited Jesus Christ to supper, or would have given
him such freedom to speak his mind without resentment. But he was a much-mistaken
man. He was quite wrong in three important points.

I. His estimate of Jesus Christ. When he found that Jesus did not resent the
attention of "this woman," he came to the conclusion that he could not be a prophet,
or he would have known that she was a sinner, and, knowing that, he would have
repelled her. Here he was wrong in his conclusion; and he was also wrong in his
reasoning. His argument was this: a man as holy as a prophet would be certain to
repel such guilt as is present here; when *the* Holy Prophet comes, the Messiah, he
will be more scrupulously separate from sin and from sinners than any other has
been. Here he was completely mistaken. The Holy One came to be the Merciful
One; to say to guilty men and women, "Your fellows may despair of you and abandon
you. I despair of none, I abandon nobody. I see in all the possibilities of recovery;
I summon you all to repentance and to life. Touch me, if you will, with the hand of
your faith; I will lay my hand of help and healing upon you."

II. His view of that woman. A sinner she had been; but she was more, and
indeed other than a sinner now. That word did not faithfully describe her state before
God. She was a *penitent*. And what is a penitent? A penitent soul is one who
hates the sin that had been cherished, who has cast out the evil spirit from him, in
whom is the living germ of righteousness, who is on the upward line that leads to
heavenly wisdom and Divine worth, on whom God is looking down with tender grace
and deep satisfaction, in whom Jesus Christ beholds a servant, a friend, an heir of his
holy kingdom. This is not one to turn away from in scorn, but to draw nigh unto in
kindness and encouragement.

III. His estimate of himself. 1. He thought himself a very long way on in the
kingdom of God as compared with that poor woman; he did not know that, she being
poor in spirit and he being proud in spirit, she was much nearer to its entrance-gates
than he. 2. He thought himself in a position to patronize Jesus Christ, and consequently withheld some of the usual courtesies from his Guest; he did not know
that it was on himself the distinction was conferred. 3. He supposed himself to be
possessed of all the cardinal virtues: he did not know that he lacked that which is
the crowning excellence of all—love, the love that can pity, that can stoop to save.

We draw two main lessons. 1. *That Christ makes much of love.* Dwelling on the
various manifestations of this woman's feeling, he declares they are the signs of her
love, and he then traces her love to her deep sense of forgiven sin. God wants our
love, as we want the love of our children and of our friends, and cannot accept anything, however valuable, in its stead: so Christ wants the pure, deep, lasting affection
of our souls. No ceremonies, or services, or even sacrifices, will compensate for *its*
absence (see 1 Cor. xiii.). And the measure of our love will depend on the depth of
our sense of God's forgiving love toward us. Hence it is of the first importance that
we (1) should understand how much God has forgiven us, how great and serious
our guilt has been (see preceding homily); (2) should recognize how great and full is
the Divine forgiveness, how much it includes—how much in the sense of overlooking
the past, and in the way of granting us present favour and of promising us future
blessedness. Our wisdom and our duty, therefore, is to dwell on the greatness of God's
mercy to us in Jesus Christ, to rejoice much in it, to let our souls bathe in the thought

of it, be filled continually with a sense of it. For they who are (consciously) forgiven much will love much; and they who love much will be much beloved of God (John xiv. 23). 2. *That we should be ready to receive Christ's correcting word.* Simon was wholly wrong in his estimate of men and of things; but he was not unwilling to hear Christ's correcting word. "Master, say on," he replied, when the great Teacher said, "I have somewhat to say unto thee." Let us see to it that this is our attitude. Our Lord may have something very serious to say to us, as he had to those seven Churches in Asia Minor, which he addressed from his heavenly throne (Rev. ii., iii.). When, through his Word, his ministry, his providence, he does thus correct us, calling us to a renewed humility, faith, love, zeal, consecration, are we ready to receive his message, to bow our head, to open our heart, and say, "Speak, Lord; thy servants hear! Master, say on"?—C.

Vers. 1—17.—*The Saviour of sick and dead.* On returning to Capernaum after the sermon on the mount, the Saviour is confronted with a deputation from a centurion about his sick servant. To the miracle of *healing* in vers. 2—10 we turn first; and then we shall consider the miracle of *resurrection* (vers. 11—17), by which it is followed.

I. THE SAVIOUR OF THE SICK. (Vers. 1—10.) 1. *Let us observe the self-abasement of the centurion.* And in this connection we must notice the devotedness he had shown to the Jewish religion. As a proselyte, he had not only espoused Judaism, but built a synagogue to accommodate his fellow-worshippers. Hence he had an excellent reputation with the ecclesiastical authorities. But all this did not lead to any boasting on his part or exaltation of spirit. He remains the humble man before God after all his liberality. Hence he organizes no less than *two* deputations to Jesus Christ rather than obtrude himself upon him. And (1) he sends a deputation of *Jewish elders,* to ask from Jesus the cure of his sick servant. He esteems these ecclesiastical rulers as better than himself; he values them as highly almost as they do themselves! In reality he was spiritually far ahead of them; but he was unconscious of this, and conscious only of his great personal unworthiness. The elders come, and in their self-righteous spirit speak of his worthiness to Jesus. He was worthy, they declared, and had proved his worthiness by building the synagogue. They thought more of the centurion, and more of themselves, than the centurion did. Yet Jesus recognizes the humility which dictated the sending of the deputation, and responds to their entreaty by going with them towards the centurion's house. (2) He sends a second deputation of *friends* to entreat Jesus not to give himself so much trouble in the matter, seeing he was utterly unworthy of a visit from Jesus. His idea was that, as Christ could heal his servant without the trouble of coming to see him, could heal at any distance, then he *ought* to take things as easy as he could. So strong is his conviction on this subject, that he gives a military illustration in proof of it. "Evidently," says Robertson, "he looked upon this universe with a soldier's eye; he could not look otherwise. To him this world was a mighty camp of living forces, in which authority was paramount. Trained in obedience to military law, accustomed to render prompt submission to those above him, and to exact it from those below him, he read law everywhere; and law to him meant nothing unless it meant the expression of a personal will. It was this training through which faith took its *form.*"[1] Christ was, therefore, to the soldier's eye, the centurion of all diseases, and they obeyed him, so that he might have sent the disease of the servant away by a simple word of command, and so have saved himself all the trouble. Now, it is important to remember that our Lord did *not* take the easiest way always. He preferred to show his sympathy and thorough devotedness by taking sometimes the most irksome way. His idea was *not* to save himself trouble; "he spared not himself." He will not use his power to save himself trouble. 2. *Let us notice Christ's admiration of the centurion's faith.* We have seen how great humility is accompanied by great faith. The graces grow proportionally. There are no monstrosities in the spiritual world. And we have to notice what an eye Jesus has for faith. It is the most lovely product in this vale of tears. Hence he is wrapt in admiration of it. He recognizes it as greater in this Gentile than it has yet been in any Jew. The house of Israel had given him as yet no such believer as he had now

[1] 'Sermons,' second series, p. 132.

found in the simple soldier. Clearly faith is not always in proportion to opportunity and advantages. How weak the faith of many who have been all their lives long in the enjoyment of the means of grace! 3. *Christ responds to strong faith by a word of power.* Had he continued to press himself upon the centurion's attention and household, it might have led the humble believer to suspect the power of Jesus to save at a distance. In other words, if Jesus had advanced, it might have hurt the centurion's faith, instead of ministering to him any additional sense of sympathy. Hence he spoke, and the disease of the servant departed instantly. Now, this miracle is designed to show the beauty of Christian sympathy, the power of intercession, and the tender grace of the Saviour as he responds to the appeals of his servants. Let us take a similar interest in those who serve us, or are in anywise related to us; let us bring their case before the Lord, and he will help them for our sake, and for his own Name's sake too![1]

II. THE SAVIOUR OF THE DEAD. (Vers. 11—17.) We next turn to the *raising of the widow's son at Nain* (vers. 11—17). And here let us notice: 1. *The terrible sorrow which presented itself to Jesus.* (Ver. 12.) It was the death of a widow's only son. She stood before Jesus in all her loneliness—more lonely through the proximity of the crowd. Now, it is to a social Saviour she has come, One who lay in the bosom of the Father, a member of the " social Trinity," who enjoyed fellowship from all eternity. Hence her case did not appeal to him in vain. He does not need any intercession. His sympathetic heart takes up the case. Hence we have: 2. *The consolatory word our Saviour spoke.* " Weep not!" Sometimes, as Gerok has remarked, this word is spoken in a well-meant, yet unchristian sense, by many children of the world, as if weeping and mourning ought to be put away as out of place; in other cases, the word is spoken with a good Christian intention, but without much human tenderness; but Jesus shows us here when it ought to be spoken.[2] He wants the widow not to weep, for he can put all her sorrow away. Truly it is he who can wipe away the tears from off all faces (Rev. vii. 17). If we have such consolation to offer, well may we say, " Weep not." But if we only repeat the words, without offering any consolation, they are not likely to be of much avail. It is a striking contrast, our Lord's conduct on this occasion, and on the occasion of Lazarus's resurrection, where he wept himself, instead of commanding others not to weep (John xi. 35). 3. *The mighty word which backed up his consolation.* (Ver. 14.) This was, " Young man, I say unto thee, Arise!" He does so as the Prince of life. The result is that he that was dead first sat up, and then began to speak. Life was thus restored to him, and intercourse with others followed. Jesus thus demonstrated that he was " the Resurrection and the Life." 4. *The restoration of the young man to his mother.* (Ver. 15.) The purpose of the resurrection was the restoration of those relationships which death had so rudely severed. The bereaved mother is enabled to rejoice in her son again, and to see her home-circle restored. The great truth of recognition and restoration through resurrection is thus set before us.[3] 5. *The effect of the miracle upon the people.* (Vers. 16, 17.) They feared, because the miracle demonstrated that God was awfully near. Yet the fear inspired them to glorify God for the advent of such a Prophet, and the gracious visitation which he brought. They felt that the miracle was eminently worthy of God. An eminent scientific man, who doubts revealed religion, yet accepts spiritualism, has said, " Few, if any, reputed miracles are at all worthy of a God."[4] But in face of such a tender and touching work of grace as this at Nain, no such declaration could be made by an impartial mind. It was worthy of God, and tended to his glory. 6. *Consider, lastly, the type and promise it affords of what Christ will do in the world at last.* For, as a poet has suggested, this earth is the " bier whereon our race is laid," and to it will Christ at last come, and, arresting the long procession of the dead, will say, " Arise!" when lo! a race shall wake from clay, " young, deathless, freed from every stain." And the " Weep not!" shall also be heard then, for

[1] Cf. Gerok's 'Evangelien-Predigten,' s. 793, *seq.*
[2] Cf. Gerok's 'Aus Ernster Zeit,' s. 564.
[3] Cf. Dr. Macmillan's 'Our Lord's Three Raisings from the Dead,' pp. 75—129; Gerok's 'Evangelien-Predigten,' s. 710.
[4] A. R. Wallace, 'On Miracles and Modern Spiritualism,' p. 44.

from his people's faces every tear shall be wiped away.[1] The miracle thus throws a clear and steady light upon those last things which perplex so many people now.—R. M. E.

Vers. 18—35.—*The deputation from John.* Jesus pursued a policy of mercy and of salvation. He healed all who asked for healing or were brought to him ; he raised the dead; he was a Philanthropist rather than a Judge. The fame of his miracles was spread abroad, and made its way to the castle and its keep, where John the Baptist was now Herod's prisoner. The result is a deputation of two disciples sent by the illustrious prisoner to Jesus. We are to study the interview and the subsequent panegyric on John.

I. CONSIDER JOHN'S DIFFICULTY. John had preached about a coming One, according to such prophecies as that of Malachi. He had preached that Jesus was coming to judgment. His fan was to be in his hand; he was throughly to purge his floor ; he was to gather the wheat into his garner; and he was to burn up the chaff with unquenchable fire (ch. iii. 17). And in the spirit of the Old Testament, which was largely a dispensation of judgment, John looked for Messiah to be mainly a Messiah of judgment. The kingdom of Messiah was to be set up, John thought, like all world-kingdoms, by "the thunder of the captains and the shouting," by some remarkable series of judgments ; but now that Jesus is devoting himself to philanthropy pure and simple, John thinks that perhaps another messenger is to be looked for, who will make judgment his *rôle*. John's difficulty is what we all experience when we imagine that a more impressive and decisive method of advancing God's cause might be adopted. Human nature has great faith in *blows!*

II. OUR LORD'S RESPONSE. (Vers. 21—23.) This consisted of: 1. *Miracles of mercy.* All that needed healing in the crowd received it in presence of John's disciples. He cured many of their infirmities and plagues, and of evil spirits; and many blind ones received their sight. The Healer was there; philanthropy was in full swing. 2. He *preached the gospel* to the poor. He backed up the miracles by a message; he made his mercies to the body the texts from which he preached deliverance to the souls of men. 3. He directed the disciples to *report to John what they had seen and heard*, with the additional warning, "Blessed is he whosoever shall not be offended in me." His policy was one of love, of disinterestedness; and John was to study it more thoroughly and come to a better conclusion. We thus learn that the *best defence of a suspected work is the patient performance of it.* It will vindicate itself in due season, if it be good and genuine. Christ came not to wade through seas of blood to a temporal throne, but by persevering love to win men's hearts and rule over their lives from within !

III. HIS PANEGYRIC UPON JOHN. (Vers. 24—28.) It was after the deputation had departed that Jesus pronounced John's panegyric. Most people would have pronounced it in their hearing, that they might carry it to John; but Jesus says the good and noble things behind John's back, having given all the warning he needed before, so to speak, his face. It partakes, as Godet remarks, of the nature of a funeral oration. Like Jesus himself, John is anointed with considerate praise before his burial. And here we have to notice the order of the panegyric. 1. Christ describes John *negatively*. Borrowing his simile from the desert, where the reeds bow before the breeze and do not break, he insists that John was not like one of these. In other words, he was a man of unflinching integrity, who would break rather than bend before the breeze of opposition. He preferred to be Herod's prisoner in the dungeon rather than his fawning sycophant in the palace. Nor, again, was John a courtier gaily and silkenly clad. The camel's hair garment was a perpetual protest in the castle, before he was thrust down into the dungeon, against the effeminacy of the court. If he had come to be "court preacher" to Herod, he had come to be one in earnest. 2. He describes John *positively*. He was a "prophet." Great honour was it to be recipients and communicators of revelations. John was charged, like other Old Testament prophets, with messages from God. But he was more—he was the *forerunner of Messiah*. In applying to John the prophecy in Malachi, Jesus was asserting his own Messiahship and Divinity.[2] This was a great honour for John to be the immediate predecessor of the Lord. Still

[1] 'The Changed Cross, and other Poems : ' " The Widow of Nain."
[2] Cf. Gess's 'Christi-Selbstzeugniss,' s. 40.

further, our Lord asserts that of woman-born there has not been a greater prophet than the Baptist. This is unstinted praise. And it is just. When we consider all John attempted and the means he had at hand, when we consider that he attempted the regeneration of his country and asked no miraculous power to accomplish it,—then he comes before us in moral grandeur exceeding that of the first Elias. 3. He describes him *candidly.* The panegyric is judicious. Our Lord declares that, great though John undoubtedly is, he is surpassed by "the least in the kingdom of God." This may mean that the least Christian has greater insight into the nature of the kingdom than John. Or it may, perhaps, rather mean that he who is *consciously* the least in the kingdom of God, by whom we must understand the most advanced spiritually, is greater than John. The insight of a Paul, for instance, who felt himself to be less than the least of all saints, was greater than that of John, climax though he was of Old Testament prophecy. Or, finally, may it not mean Jesus himself, who was the meekest and lowliest in the Kingdom of God.

IV. THE CHARACTER OF JOHN'S SUCCESS WAS LIKE THAT OF JESUS. (Vers. 29, 30.) The evangelist seems to add the significant words that it was among the common people, the publicans and the poor, not among the Pharisees and lawyers, that he secured his penitents. So that John's revival was really among the humbler classes, where the work of Jesus was being now wisely prosecuted. The self-righteous rejected John's appeal for repentance; the common people and the publicans embraced it, and "justified God" by repenting before him. For we must acknowledge God's perfect justice in condemning us for our sins, before we can appreciate his justice and mercy in forgiving us for his Son's sake. Luke's observation, then, makes Christ's panegyric a perfect picture.

V. THE TWO ASPECTS OF TRUTH, AND THE GENERAL REJECTION OF BOTH. (Vers. 31—35.) Jesus, in these verses, contrasts John's ministry with his own. Little children at play sometimes find their fellows utterly intractable. Tried by a funeral, they will not join in the mournful procession; tried by a marriage, they will not join in the bridal party. They are too ill-natured to take part in either. Nothing pleases them. So was it with the Pharisees in their attitude to the preaching of John and to the preaching of Jesus. John presented the truth in its severe and mournful aspects. He was unsocial, to lead men to a sense of sin and to repent of it. But the Pharisees would not believe the self-denying preacher from the desert. Jesus presented the truth in all its winsomeness and attractiveness; but they found as much fault with Jesus as they did with John. John had a devil, and Jesus was a glutton and a wine-bibber. Neither could please these prim, self-satisfied ones. But the vindication of wisdom was on its way. The penitents of John and the joyful disciples of Jesus would yet justify the truth which John and Jesus preached.[1] The Pharisees might reject both missions, but the common people who received them justified the truth in both by lives and conversations becoming the gospel. We may in the same way leave our work with confidence to the verdict of the future, if we feel that it is true. Opposition from a self-righteous party is itself a vindication of the truth which we have embodied or declared.—R. M. E.

Vers. 36—50.—*Love the proof of pardon.* The generation to which Jesus had come with his social gospel thought him too "free and easy" with sinners. The Pharisees thought he had no right to associate with publicans and sinners, although he did so to save them. But the wisdom of his policy would be justified by the conduct of his converts, and here we have a justification ready to hand. One of the Pharisees invited him to eat with him. He accepts the invitation, and is reclining at his table, when, lo! a poor woman "off the streets" comes in behind him, and in her penitence and gratitude prepares to anoint with spikenard his blessed feet. She had heard him preach, she had received pardon for all her sins, she could not resist this exhibition of gratitude for it. But as she is about to anoint his feet, her pent-up grief refuses further restraint, and bathes them with copious tears, and, having no towel with her or offered to her, she unties her flowing hair, content to wipe with it the beautiful feet of him who had brought her glad tidings. Having thus washed and wiped them clean, she proceeds to anoint them with the ointment. To this conduct the Pharisee secretly objects, and

---

[1] Cf. Robertson's 'Human Race and other Sermons,' p. 182.

takes it as proof positive that Jesus is not the discerning Prophet he professes to be Our Lord's parable soon corrects the error and reveals the truth, and the poor sinner, so penitent and so grateful, is dismissed in peace.

I. GREAT SIN SHOULD NOT HINDER ANY OF US FROM COMING TO JESUS FOR PARDON. This is one of the difficulties which men make for themselves—they fancy that great sin may keep sinners from pardon. Now Jesus made it very plain that great sinners might receive pardon just as well as little sinners. The psalmist once prayed, " Pardon mine iniquity, for it is great " (Ps. xxv. 7), and some of the most notorious sinners ever seen have become monuments of mercy and joyful through pardon. This case before us is one in point. Jesus had so presented his message of salvation that this woman from the town embraced it and rejoiced in the thought of forgiveness. While, therefore, no one would recommend a sinner to sin in order to intensify his sense of guilt and qualify himself for receiving Christ's salvation, we would recommend every sinner to believe that the very enormity of his sins will move Christ's pity, and, when purged and pardoned, illustrate his saving power. Suppose a patient is brought to a hospital a mass of disease or of wounds and bruises : will not the very magnitude of his distress constitute such an appeal to pity as will secure his immediate admission ? In the same way, great sin is an argument with the Saviour in favour of mercy, rather than any obstacle to it. Besides, we should always remember that our sense of sin is always vastly below the reality, and that we in most penitent mood have really a better opinion of ourselves than the circumstances warrant.

II. WE OUGHT COURAGEOUSLY TO PROFESS CHRIST BEFORE MEN. This poor woman needed courage to profess Christ in Simon's house. Simon and his guests belonging to the Pharisaic party loathed her. It was a place where she was certain to be scorned and perhaps expelled. But her sense of obligation to Jesus and her love for his Person were so great that she could not forego her desire to make her way to his feet. And so she steals in and gets behind her Master, and proceeds to lavish her attention on his feet. So courageous is she, that she leisurely and most carefully washes his feet and wipes them with her hair and anoints them with the ointment; so that she actually, as Godet remarks, did the honours of the house, which Simon had neglected.[1] We need similarly to add to our faith courage (2 Pet. i. 4). We ought to give our hearts free play in their loyalty to Jesus. We must profess him before men, at whatever cost.

III. JESUS WILL ALWAYS TAKE OUR PART AGAINST THOSE WHO MISTAKE OUR MOTIVES OR DESPISE US. Jesus will acknowledge our profession of him in the next world, and even in this. In the case before us we see him taking the Pharisee to task for his mistake about the woman. Simon made several mistakes. 1. About the woman being unpardonable and unpardoned: she was neither. 2. About Jesus as being undiscerning and so ignorant of the woman's state : he was more thoroughly acquainted with her than she or Simon could be. 3. About himself, as nearer God's kingdom than she was: he was really further from Christ than she.[2] And Jesus consequently takes up the woman's cause and vindicates her character as a changed woman now and pardoned. This he does in parabolic language. The two debtors who are both forgiven have not the same sense of gratitude. Their gratitude is in proportion to their forgiveness. Hence the poor woman, feeling how much she has been forgiven, is proportionately grateful. The defence was triumphant. And in the same way will Jesus defend us if we are courageous in following him.

IV. LOVE IS THE PROOF OF PARDON. We are not pardoned because we love our Saviour, but we love him because he has pardoned us. Hence the stronger the love, the stronger must be our sense of the amount of sin we have been forgiven. Our love will grow just in proportion to our appreciation of our pardon.[3] Hence the man who comes to believe, with Paul, that he is " the chief of sinners," will love the Lord accordingly. He will feel constrained through his sense of obligation to love God with all his being.

---

[1] Cf. Saurin's 'Sermons,' tome iii. sermon ii.
[2] Cf. Ker's ' Sermons,' pp. 16—28.
[3] Cf. Maclaren's ' Sermons,' i. p. 28; Gerok's 'Evangelien-Predigten,' s. 751; Saphir's ' Conversion,' p. 253.

V. CHRIST'S ASSURANCE OF PARDON SECURES PEACE. The poor sinner's peace was threatened through the contempt of the Pharisees. But Jesus gives her special assurance, and sends her off in peace. So will it be in our own experience if we sincerely trust him.—R. M. E.

EXPOSITION.

CHAPTER VIII.

Vers. 1—3.—*St. Luke's brief notice of the women who formed part of the company of Jesus.*

Ver. 1.—**And it came to pass afterward.** St. Luke here notices an alteration in the Master's way of life. From this time forward Jesus ceased to make Capernaum "his city," his usual residence; he now journeys with his little band of followers from place to place. From this time there was also a distinct change in the tone of his teaching. The Greek word rendered "afterward" is the same as that translated "in order" in ch. i. 3. **Showing the glad tidings of the kingdom of God.** The public work of Jesus may be well arranged under three heads: his work as *Master*, as *Evangelist*, and as *Prophet.* The first had especial relation to his own immediate followers, women as well as men. In the second, as the Preacher of the grace, mercy, and the love of God, he peculiarly addressed himself to the general population;—this was the special side of the Lord's work which St. Luke loved to dwell on; this is what he alludes to here. In the third, as Prophet, the Master spoke generally to an evil generation, and especially to the political and religious leaders of the Jewish society of his day.

Ver. 2.—**And certain women.** It has before been noticed that St. Luke, in several places, especially notices the love and devotion of women to the Master. The present position of women is owing to the teaching of the Lord and his disciples. Fellow-heirs with men of the kingdom of heaven, it was obvious that they could no longer occupy on earth their old inferior and subordinate position. The sex, as a sex, has made a noble return to the Master. Much of the untold misery and suffering which tormented the old world has been at least alleviated in great measure by the labours of the women of Christianity. Several of these kindly grateful souls here alluded to evidently belonged to the wealthy class; some even occupied a high position in the society of that time. It was by their gifts, no doubt, that Jesus and his company were enabled to live during the thirty or more months of the public ministry. He had given up, as had also his companions, his earthly occupation, and we know that he deliberately refrained from ever using his miraculous power to supply his daily wants. The presence and loving interest of these and such like kindly generous friends answers the question—How did the Master and his disciples, poor men among poor men, live during the years of public teaching? **Mary called Magdalene.** The name Mary (Miriam) was a very favourite name among the Hebrew women; we meet with several in the gospel story. This one was called "Magdalene," or "of Magdala," to distinguish her from others bearing the same name. Magdala was a little town near Tiberias. There is nothing *definite* to connect her with the "sinner" of ch. vii. The early tradition which identified these two women was probably derived from Talmudic sources. There are many wild stories in these writings connected with one called Mary of Magdala, a grievous sinner. The "seven devils" probably allude to some aggravated form of demoniacal possession. Two sets of ecclesiastical legends busy themselves with the after-life of Mary of Magdala. The one represents her as coming with Lazarus and Martha to Marseilles; the other, as accompanying the Virgin and John to Ephesus.

Ver. 3.—**Joanna the wife of Chuza Herod's steward.** She must have been a person of wealth and high rank at the court of Herod Antipas. There were evidently not a few believers in that wicked and dissolute centre. Some years later we read of Manaen, the foster-brother of Herod, as a notable Christian (Acts xiii. 1). Even Herod himself, we know, at first heard John the Baptist gladly; and, after the terrible judicial murder, we find that unhappy prince fancying that his victim had risen from the dead. It has been suggested that this Chuza was the nobleman of Capernaum whose dying son was healed by Jesus (John iv. 46). If this be the case, there would be a special reason for the loving devotion of this Joanna to the Master. She reappears among the faithful women in the history of the Resurrection (ch. xxiv. 10). **Susanna.** The name signifies "lily." The Jews were fond of giving the names of flowers and trees to their girls; thus *Rhoda*, a rose (Acts xii. 13), *Tamar*, a palm (2 Sam. xiii. 2), among many instances. Of this Susanna nothing further is known.

Vers. 4—15.—*The parable of the sower, and the Lord's interpretation of it.*

Ver. 4.—**And when much people were gathered together, and were come to him**

out of every city, he spake by a parable. A great change, it is clear, took place in our Lord's way of working at this period. We have already (in the note on ver. 1) remarked that from henceforth he dwelt no longer in one centre, his own city Capernaum, but moved about from place to place. A new way of teaching was now adopted—that of the "parable." It was from this time onward that, when he taught, he seems generally to have spoken in those famous parables, or stories, in which so much of his recorded teaching is shrined. Hitherto in his preaching he had occasionally made use of similes or comparisons, as in ch. v. 6 and vi. 29, 48; but he only began the formal use of the parable at this period, and the parable of the sower seems to have been the earliest spoken. Perhaps because it was the first, perhaps on account of the far-reaching nature of its contents, the story of "the sower" evidently impressed itself with singular force upon the minds of the disciples. It evidently formed a favourite "memory" among the first heralds of the new faith. It is the only one, with the exception of the vine-dressers, one of the latest spoken, which has been preserved by the three—Matthew, Mark, and Luke. It is identical in structure and in teaching in all the three, which shows that they were relating the same story. It differs, however, in detail; we thus gather that the three did not copy from one primitive document, but that these "memories" were derived either from their own recollections or at least from different sources. Now, what induced the Master thus deliberately to change the manner of his teaching? In other words, why, from this time forward, does he veil so much of his deep Divine thought in parables? Let us consider the attitude of the crowds who till now had been listening to him. What may be termed the Galilæan revival had well-nigh come to an end. The enthusiasm he had evoked by his burning words, his true wisdom, his novel exposition of what belonged to human life and duty, was, when he left Capernaum and began his preaching in every little village (ver. 1), at its height. But the great Heart-reader knew well that the hour of reaction was at hand. *Then* the pressure of the crowds which thronged him was so great that, to speak this first parable, he had to get into a boat and address the multitude standing on the shore (Matt. xiii. 2); but the moment was at hand which St. John (vi. 66) refers to in his sad words, "From *that time* many of his disciples went back, and walked no more with him." It was in view of that moment that Jesus commenced his parable-teaching with "the sower." As regards the *great mass* of the people who had crowded

to hear his words and look on his miracles, the Lord knew that his work had practically failed. At the first he spoke to the people plainly. The sermon on the mount, for instance, contains little, if anything, of the parable form; but they understood him not, forming altogether false views of the kingdom he described to them. He now changes his method of teaching, veiling his thoughts in parables, in order that *his own*, to whom privately he gave the key to the right understanding of the parables, should see more clearly, and that those who deliberately misunderstood him—the hostile Pharisee and Sadducee, for instance—should be simply mystified and perplexed as to the Teacher's meaning; while the merely thoughtless might possibly be fascinated and attracted by this new manner of teaching, which evidently veiled some hidden meaning. These last would probably be induced to inquire further as to the meaning of these strange parable-stories. Professor Bruce, who has very ably discussed the reasons which induced Christ at this period of his ministry to speak in parables, says there is a mood which leads a man to present his thoughts in this form. "It is the mood of one whose heart is chilled, and whose spirit is saddened by a sense of loneliness, and who, retiring within himself by a process of reflection, frames for his thoughts forms which half conceal, half reveal them—reveal them more perfectly to those who understand, hide them from those who do not (and will not)—forms beautiful, but also melancholy, as the hues of forest in late autumn. If this view be correct, we should expect the teaching in parables would not form a feature of the *initial* stage of Christ's ministry. And such accordingly was the fact." As regarded the men of his own generation, did he use the parable way of teaching almost as a fan to separate the wheat from the chaff? "That he had to speak in parables was one of the burdens of the Son of man, to be placed side by side with the fact that he had not where to lay his head" (Professor Bruce, 'Parabolic Teaching of Christ,' book i. ch. i.). *And when much people were gathered together, and were come to him out of every city.* The impression of the witness who told the story to Luke and Paul evidently was that at this period of the Lord's ministry vast crowds flocked to listen or to see. St. Matthew expresses the same conviction in a different but in an equally forcible manner. Only the Lord knew how hollow all this seeming popularity was, and how soon the crowds would melt away. *He spake by a parable.* Roughly to distinguish between the parable and the fable: The fable would tell its moral truth, but its imagery might be purely fanciful; for instance, *animals*, or even *trees*, might be represented as reasoning and speaking. The parable, on the contrary, never violated probability, but told its solemn lesson, often certainly in a dramatic form, but its imagery was never fanciful or impossible.

Ver. 5.—**A sower went out to sow his seed.** The Master's words, in after-days, must often have come home to the disciples. They would feel that in each of them, if they were faithful to their work, the "sower" of the parable was reproduced; they would remember what they had heard from his lips; how he had warned them of the reception which their words would surely meet with; how by far the greater proportion of the seed they would sow, would perish. But though the disciples and all true Christian men in a greater or less degree reproduce the sower of the parable, still the great Sower, it must be remembered, is the Holy Spirit. Every true teacher or sower of the Word does but repeat what they have learned from him. **And as he sowed, some fell by the wayside.** Dean Stanley, on the scenery of the parable, thus writes : "Is there anything on the spot to suggest the images thus conveyed? So I asked as I rode along the tract under the hillside, by which the Plain of Gennesaret is approached. So I asked at the moment, seeing nothing but the steep sides of the hill, alternately of rock and grass. And when I thought of the parable of the sower, I answered that here at least was nothing on which the Divine teaching could fasten; it must have been the distant corn-fields of Samaria or Esdraelon on which his mind was dwelling. The thought had hardly occurred to me when a slight recess in the hillside, close upon the plain, disclosed at once, in detail, and with a conjunction which I remember nowhere else in Palestine, every feature of the great parable. There was the undulating corn-field descending to the water's edge; there was the trodden pathway running through the midst of it, with no fence or hedge to prevent the seed from falling here and there on either side of it, or upon it ; itself hard with the constant tramp of horse and mule and human foot" ('Sinai and Palestine,' ch. xiii.).

Ver. 6.—**And some fell upon a rock.** The picture here is not of a soil full of stones, but of a rocky portion of the corn-land where the rock is only covered with a thin layer of earth.

Ver. 7.—**And some fell among thorns.** "Every one who has been in Palestine must have been struck with the number of thorny shrubs and plants that abound there. The traveller finds them in his path, go where he may. Many of them are small, but some grow as high as a man's head. The rabbinical writers say that there are no less than twenty-two words in the Hebrew Bible denoting thorny and prickly plants" (Professor Hacket).

Ver. 8.—**And bare fruit an hundredfold.** This is by no means an unheard-of increase even in the West, where vegetation is less luxuriant. Herodotus, quoted by Trench ('Parables'), mentions that two hundredfold was a common return in the Plain of Babylon, and sometimes three hundredfold; and Niebuhr mentions a species of maize that returns four hundredfold. On the marvellous fruit-bearing which would take place in the days of the Lord's future kingdom on earth, Irenæus gives a quotation from Papias, who gave it on the authority of those who had heard St. John speak of the teaching of the Lord to that effect. Professor Westcott ('Introduction to the Study of the Gospels,' Appendix C, 21) thinks that the tradition was based on the real discourses of the Lord. It is, of course, allegorical, for is it not a memory of a conversation between Jesus and his disciples arising out of this parable of the sower? "The Lord taught of those days (of his future kingdom on earth) and said, *The days will come in which vines shall spring up, each having ten thousand stocks, and on each stock ten thousand branches, and on each branch ten thousand shoots, and on each shoot ten thousand bunches, and on each bunch ten thousand grapes, and each grape when pressed shalt give five and twenty measures of wine. And when any saint shall have seized one bunch, another shall cry, I am a better bunch ; take me ; through me bless the Lord.* Likewise also (he said) that *a grain of wheat shall produce ten thousand ears of corn, and each grain ten pounds of fine pure flour ; and so all other fruits, and seeds, and each herb according to its proper nature.* . . . And he (Papias) added, saying, Now, these things are credible to them that believe. And when Judas the traitor believed not, and asked—How, then, shall such productions proceed from the Lord? the Lord said, *They shall see who come to those times*" (Papias; see Irenæus, v. 33. 3).

Ver. 9.—**And his disciples asked him, saying, What might this parable be?** This is the only parable St. Luke gives as spoken by our Lord in this place. St. Matthew—who gives the additional detail that on account of the pressure of the crowd on the lake-shore it was spoken from a boat moored close to the bank—relates seven parables here in sequence. It is probable that the Master spoke some of these at least on this occasion, but St. Luke, possibly on account of its extreme solemnity, possibly because he wished to mark *this* parable as the first of this new kind of teaching, relates it and its interpretation only, saying nothing further respecting that day's parable-teaching. It is most probable that all these reported discourses, parables, expositions, or sermons, are simply a *résumé* of the original words. The disciples evidently by their question—which St. Mark tells us was put to Jesus when they were alone with him—were surprised and puzzled, first at the strange change which that eventful day inaugurated in the method of their Master's teaching, and secondly, at the peculiar character of this his first great parable-lesson. It was, indeed, a sombre and depressing announcement whatever way it was looked at—sombre as a picture of the results of his own past ministry, depressing if regarded as a prophecy of their future success as teachers.

Ver. 10.—**And he said, Unto you it is given to know the mysteries of the kingdom of God: but to others in parables; that seeing they might not see, and hearing they might not understand.** In St. Matthew we have the Lord's reply given at greater length; the same prophecy of Isaiah which here forms the basis of St. Luke's account of Jesus' reply is given in full. St. Mark weaves the Isaiah-words into the Master's answer. The thought, however, in each of the three accounts is exactly the same. The parable mode of teaching was adopted by Jesus who, as Heart-reader, was aware now by sad experience and still sadder foreknowledge, that his glorious news rather repelled than attracted the ordinary hearer. They did not *want* to be disturbed from their earthly hopes and loves and fears. They preferred *not* to be healed as God would heal them. The Master then spoke his parables with the intention of veiling his Divine story from the careless and indifferent. These, he knew, would for the most part be repelled by such teaching, while it would specially attract the earnest inquirer. "The veil which it (the parable) throws over the truth becomes transparent to the attentive mind, while it remains impenetrable to the careless" (Godet). It was therefore his deliberate wish that such hearers might neither see nor understand. Dr. Morrison ('Commentary on St. Mark') well and clearly puts the Lord's thought here: "It is the sinner's *deeply rooted wish* that he should *not* see and understand, and the sad explanation of this wish is given by St. Mark—the sinner is afraid lest he should be prevailed to turn. *Lest at any time they should be converted* (Mark iv. 12)."

Vers. 11—15.—*The Lord's interpretation of the parable of the sower.*

Ver. 11.—**The seed is the Word of God.** It was his own sad experience the Master was relating. The picture was of things, too, which had already happened in the case of many of his own true servants, the prophets. It mirrored, too, the many *future* failures and the few *future* successes of the listening disciples; it warned them not to be deluded by appearances, not to be discouraged by apparent failure. The Word, of course, in the first instance is his own teaching; it comprehends, however, any preaching or teaching, whether of prophet of the past or minister of the future, which tries faithfully to copy his own.

Ver. 12.—**Those by the wayside are they that hear; then cometh the devil, and taketh away the Word out of their hearts, lest they should believe and be saved.** The wayside hearers represent the great outer circle of men and women who more or less respect religion. It must be carefully borne in mind that in none of the four classes pictured in the parable are despisers of God, declared enemies of religion, portrayed. To these the gospel, with its warnings and its promises, rarely if ever speaks. These of "the wayside" are they whose hearts resemble a footpath, beaten hard and flat by the constant passing to and fro of wishes of the flesh, of thoughts concerning earthly things, mere sordid hopes and fears. Into these hearts the Word can never really penetrate. Momentary influence now and again seems to have been gained, but the many watchful agents of the evil one, with swift wings, like birds of the air, swoop down and snatch away the scattered seed which for a moment seemed as though it would take root. Judas Iscariot the Jew, and Pontius Pilate the Roman, might be instanced as types of this class. These—before their awful fate—both *appeared* to have been moved. The one for long months followed the Lord and was trusted by him; the other pitied, and for a moment in his—Pilate's case—pity seemed passing into love and admiration, and tried to find a way of escape for the innocent Prisoner. But the one betrayed, and the other delivered to death, the sinless Son of God!

Ver. 13.—**They on the rock are they, which, when they hear, receive the Word with joy; and these have no root, which for a while believe, and in time of temptation fall away.** These represent natures at once impressionable and excitable; impulsive men and women who, charmed with the beauty, perhaps (to them) the novelty, of the gospel message, receive the Word, take up the Master's yoke with joy, but without thought. These hastily make a religious profession, but they forget altogether to count what the real cost of such a profession amounts to. Upon these superficial but kindly natures come trouble, perplexity, discouragement, perhaps persecution; then quickly the once-loved religion withers away like corn growing on rocky places beneath the burning summer sun. John Mark, the would-be missionary companion of Paul and Barnabas, was one of this impulsive but little-enduring class; and Demas, once the friend of Paul, but who loved too well the present world. Another instance would be the man who offered to follow Jesus "whithersoever thou goest," as he phrased it, till he found, by the Lord's grave answer, that the Master he offered to follow had neither home nor resting-place; then he seems quickly to have turned back.

Ver. 14.—**And that which fell among thorns are they, which, when they have heard, go forth, and are choked with cares and riches and pleasures** of this life, and **bring no fruit to perfection.** There is something very sad in this, the thorn-choked class of believers. Each of them represents the *vie manquée*; the beautiful flower just spoiled as it was bursting into full bloom. These hear the Word, and, hearing it, grasp its deep solemn meaning, and for a *part* of each day honestly try to live the life which that Divine Word pressed home to them. But with these there is another life; side by side with the golden grain has grown up a crop of thorns, which, unless destroyed in time, will choke and utterly mar, as, alas, it often does, the true corn. Such men and women, the double-minded ones of St. James, try to serve two masters—God and the world. Dr. Morrison has a good note on the parallel passage in St. Mark, where, after suggesting that the cares, the riches, and the pleasures of this life in our time are such things as houses, land, works of art and *virtu*, posts of honour, gaiety of garments, grandeur of entertainments, and in general the myriad appliances of luxury, he goes on to say, "These come more or less in upon all men, but some men lay themselves peculiarly open to their influence, and allow them to twine and twist themselves like the serpents of Laocoon around every energy and susceptibility of their being." The rich young ruler whom Jesus loved is a fair instance of this not uncommon character, which perhaps is more often met with among the more cultured of society than among the poor and the artisan class. There must have been much that was really beautiful and true in that young man, or Jesus never had singled him out as one whom he especially loved, and yet in his case the thorns of riches and luxury had so twined themselves among the real corn that, as far as we know, it never brought fruit to perfection. Ananias and Sapphira may, too, be instanced. They had given up much for the Name's sake, associated themselves with

a hated and persecuted sect, sacrificed a large portion of their property to help the poor of the flock, and yet these apparently devoted ones were living a double life; the thorns had so grown up and twined about the corn that in their field nothing ever ripened.

Ver. 15.—**But that on the good ground are they, which in an honest and good heart, having heard the Word, keep it, and bring forth fruit with patience.** In this portraiture of the fourth class of our Lord's great life-picture of hearers of and inquirers concerning religion, the Greek words rendered in the Authorized Version "honest" and "good" ("in an honest and good heart") were words well known and in familiar use among the widely spread Greek-speaking peoples for whom especially St. Luke's Gospel was compiled. Professor Bruce ('Parabolic Teaching of Christ,' ch. i.) remarks that "the man who united the two qualities expressed by the term 'honest' (better rendered 'noble') and 'good,' represented the beau-ideal of manhood. He was one whose aim was noble, and who was generously devoted to his aim. The expression rendered 'honest' (better translated 'noble,' καλός) has reference to aims or chief ends, and describes one whose mind is raised above moral vulgarity, and is bent, not on money-making and such low pursuits, but on the attainment of wisdom, holiness, and righteousness. The epithet rendered 'good' (ἀγαθός) denotes generous self-abandonment in the prosecution of lofty ends; large-heartedness, magnanimous, overflowing devotion." Mary of Bethany, with her devoted love and her generous friendship; the centurion Cornelius, with his fervent piety and his noble generosity towards a despised and hated race; Barnabas, with his splendid liberality, his utter absence of care for self, his bright, loving trust in human nature, his true charity, "bearing all things, hoping all things;"—are good examples, drawn from different sexes and from varied races, and out of diverse paths of life, of these true inquirers, who not only hear the Word, but keep it.

Vers. 16—18.—*A solemn conclusion of the Lord's to his exposition of his first great parable.*

Ver. 16.—**No man, when he hath lighted a candle, covereth it with a vessel, or putteth it under a bed; but setteth it on a candlestick, that they which enter in may see the light.** The meaning of the Lord's saying here is—the disciples must not look on this parable-method of teaching, which from henceforth he purposed frequently to adopt, as mysterious, or as containing anything beyond ordinary human comprehension. The explanation of "the sower," which he had just given them, showed them how really simple and adapted to everyday life his teaching was. "No man," said the Lord, "when he hath lighted the candle of the true knowledge, really wishes to hide it— he rather displays it that men may see the light; and that is what I have been doing for you in my careful explanation of my story."

Ver. 17.—**For nothing is secret, that shall not be made manifest; neither anything hid, that shall not be known and come abroad.** "All will gradually become clear to them. Whilst the night thickens over Israel on account of its unbelief, the disciples will advance into even fuller light, until there is nothing left in the plan of God which is obscure or hidden. The heart of Jesus is lifted up at this prospect. This accounts for the poetical rhythm which always appears at such moments" (Godet). This is very good, but Godet scarcely goes far enough. The Master's words surely promise that, as the ages advance, more and ever more light on the subject of God's dealings with men will be vouchsafed to the humble, patient searcher after the Divine wisdom. This apophthegm seems to have been a very favourite one of our Lord; he evidently used it on several occasions (see, for instance, Matt. x. 26, where the same words are reported to have been spoken in a different connection).

Ver. 18.—**Take heed therefore how ye hear: for whosoever hath, to him shall be given; and whosoever hath not, from him shall be taken even that which he seemeth to have.** A grave warning to his disciples primarily, and then to all who take upon themselves any work, even the humblest, connected with teaching Divine truth. The real student, patient, humble, and restlessly industrious, he shall be endowed with ever-increasing powers; while the make-believe, lazy, and self-sufficient one shall be punished by the gradual waning of the little light which once shone in his soul.

Vers. 19—21.— *Interference of Christ's mother and his brethren.*

Ver. 19.—**Then came to him his mother and his brethren.** St. Mark, in his third chapter, gives us the reasons which led to this scene. It had been bruited abroad that a species of frenzy had seized upon that strange Man who had been brought up in their midst, and who had lately aroused such enthusiasm in all the crowded lake-district of Galilee. It is difficult to estimate aright the feelings of his own family towards him; admiration and love seem to have struggled in their hearts with prejudice and jealousy—not in the case of Mary, but in the case of the so-called brothers. They seem ever to have been close to him

during his public ministry, not among his "own," but still near him, watching him, and listening to him with a half-wondering, half-grudging admiration. But John tells us (vii. 5) that they did not believe in him. It needed the Resurrection to convert them. The crowd round the Master at this juncture was so great that they—his kinsmen—could not press through it to speak to him. They conveyed to him, however, a message. The Heart-reader knew well what were the motives which induced them to come to him just then; the brothers were so distrustful that they had suffered themselves to be carried away by the Pharisees' evil surmises, that Jesus was possessed by a devil. The mother, influenced by her earthly fears for her Son, was induced to accompany the brothers, no doubt hoping to induce him to withdraw himself from the scene of excitement, at all events for a season.

Ver. 21.—**And he answered and said unto them, My mother and my brethren are these which hear the Word of God, and do it.** The Master used the opportunity to send home into the hearts of the many listeners the stern, grave lesson that there was something more solemn even than family ties, and that these, holy and binding though they were, must not be allowed to stand in the way of plain, unmistakable duty.

Vers. 22—25.—*The lake-storm is stilled.*

Ver. 23.—**But as they sailed he fell asleep: and there came down a storm of wind on the lake; and they were filled with water, and were in jeopardy.** In the three Gospels of Matthew, Mark, and Luke, this and the three following incidents are closely united —the lake-storm; the devils sent into the herd of swine; the raising of the little daughter of Jairus; the healing of the woman afflicted with the issue of blood. Although this cycle of acts is always united by the three, yet they do not occupy the same position chronologically in the three Gospels. The explanation of this probably is that in the primitive apostolic teaching it was usual to relate these four incidents of the Master's work together. In St. Matthew, between the recital of the healing of the demoniac and the raising of the daughter of Jairus, are intercalated the healing of the paralytic, and the call of Matthew, and the feast which followed. These incidents, in a more extended primitive discourse, were no doubt joined to the other four recitals. Had they used a common document, the three would surely have placed them in the same connection with other events. They most likely were worked, with many other signs, somewhere in this period of public work, and were chosen by the first preachers of "the Name" as specially illustrative acts, showing the Lord's power over the elements, over the unseen spirits of evil, over death, over wearying chronic sickness. On the sudden storm, travellers remark how, without warning, winds from the snowy summits of the neighbouring Hermon rush down the mountain gorges into the warm tropical air of the lake-basin, and in a short space of time the calm Galilee sea is lashed into storm and foam. The graphic description of Mark is, as usual, the most vivid, and gives us, in a few master-touches, the aspect of the scene. The weary Master sleeping in the stern of the fishing-boat; the pillow beneath his head; the disciples, terrified by the sudden uproar of the waves surging round their frail bark, as the wild winds rushed down on the lake, hastily awaking their tired Master. The danger must have been very real to have alarmed these Gennesaret fishermen; the storm must have been something more than the usual lake-tempests. The very words the Lord used when he lifted up his head and saw the danger, St. Mark preserves for us. With his "Hush!" he silenced the wild roar of the winds and waters; with his "Be still!" he quieted the heaving waves. Some commentators, reasoning from the Master's personal address to the elements—the winds and the waters—suppose that, in the midst of the storm, was some evil presence, who, taking advantage of our Lord's helpless condition—asleep in that frail fisher's boat—raised up the wild storm, hoping, perhaps, to cut short his life. The idea of spirits thus blending with the elements is one by no means unknown to Scripture. "Who maketh his angels winds [rather than the usual, better-known translation, 'spirits'], his ministers a flaming fire" (Ps. civ. 4; Heb. i. 7; Job i. 12).

Vers. 26—39.—*The evil spirit in the Gergesene demoniac is dismissed into the herd of swine.*

Ver. 26.—**And they arrived at the country of the Gadarenes.** There is a perplexing difference in the reading of the older manuscripts here, but it is simply a question of the precise name of the locality where the great miracle was worked. In the three narratives of Matthew, Mark, and Luke the older manuscripts vary between "Gergesenes," "Gerasenes," and "Gadarenes." *Gadara* was a city of some importance, about three hours' journey distant from the southern end of the Lake of Gennesaret. Its ruins are well known, and are distinguished by the remains of two amphitheatres. *Gerasa* was also a place of mark, and was situate about fifty miles from the lake. These cities might in the days of our Lord have either given its name to a great district stretching to the borders of the lake. *Gergesa* was a small and very obscure town nearly opposite Capernaum. There are some ruins now on this spot still known by the very slight corruption of *Kerzha*. There is scarcely any doubt that the scene of the miracle on the poor demoniac, and of the subsequent possession of the swine, must be looked for on this spot. But it was an obscure, little-known spot, and in very early days the preachers who told the story of the great miracle may have often spoken of the country as the district of the *well-known* Gerasa or Gadara, rather than of the *unknown* village of Gergesa. Hence probably the variations in the name in the older manuscripts here.

Ver. 27.—**There met him out of the city a certain man;** better rendered, *there met him a man of the city.* He had been a dweller in Gergesa in old days before the terrible possession began. St. Matthew, in his account, tells us of two demoniacs. SS. Mark and Luke, however, both only mention one, the other for some reason or other had passed out of their thoughts—possibly the malady was much less severe, and the strange dialogue and its results had not taken place in his case. **Which had devils long time;** better, *dæmons (daimonia).* One of the current Jewish traditions was that these evil spirits were not fallen angels, but the spirits of wicked men who were dead (see Josephus, 'Bell. Jud.,' vii. 6. 3). The plural form "devils"—bitterly referred to later by the sufferer, when he was asked his name—seems in his case to speak of a very aggravated form of the awful malady. **And ware no clothes, neither abode in any house.** These were no uncommon features of the soul-malady—the horror at any bodily restraint, either connected with clothes or dwellings; a similar shrinking is not unusual even in the comparatively modified modern phases of madness. **But in the tombs.** Until the teaching and spirit of Jesus had suggested, even among men who had no faith in his Name, some thought and consideration for the helpless sufferers of humanity, neither hospital, nor home, nor asylum existed where these unhappy ones could find a refuge. In these gloomy tombs hollowed out of the rock on the mountain-side—polluted spots for the living, according to the Jewish ritual—these maniacs found the utter solitude they craved for.

Ver. 28.—**When he saw Jesus, he cried out, and fell down before him, and with a loud voice said, What have I to do with thee, Jesus?** "The sight of Jesus appears to have produced an extraordinary impression upon him. The holy, calm, gentle majesty, the tender compassion, and the conscious sovereignty which were expressed in the aspect of our Lord, awakened in him, by force of contrast, the humbling consciousness of his own state of moral disorder" (Godet). **Thou Son of God most high.** There seems some probability that this expression was frequently used in cases of exorcism of evil spirits; for again in Acts xvi. 17 the poor slave-girl, who we read had a Pythoness-spirit, which brought in no small gain to her masters, speaks of Paul and his friends, just before the apostle in his Master's Name cast the spirit out, as servants of the most high God. **I beseech thee, torment me not.** In this form of possession one remarkable and very terrible feature seems to have been the divided consciousness; the sufferer identifies himself with the demons, and now one speaks, now the other. St. Matthew adds a dread detail to this petition to the Lord, "*before the time :*" the evil spirits thus recognizing a period when certain torment would be their hapless destiny. The expression "torment" meets us in the parable of Lazarus; the dwelling-place of the rich man after death is *a place of torment.* In Matt. xviii. 34 the ministers of judgment are the *tormentors.* One very solemn reason why this special case of exorcism on the part of our Lord is related with so much detail and repeated by the three evangelists, SS. Matthew, Mark, and Luke, seems to be the glimpse which the dialogue between the evil spirits and the Master opens to us of the dread realities hidden in the future for those who sin *deliberately* against the will of God. The existence of the place or state of torment is affirmed very pointedly by our Lord and his disciples; but having done this they dwell but little on it. There is a striking and solemn quotation in Dr. Morrison's 'Commentary on St. Mark' on this clear but guarded reference to the final sufferings of those who will not be submissive to the moral will of God, " Further curiosity as to the *when,* the *where,* and the *how,* does not become beings whose main business and greatest wisdom is to fly from, not to pry too close into, these terrible secrets of the dark kingdom."

Ver. 30.—And Jesus asked him, saying, What is thy name? And he said, Legion: because many devils were entered into him The Master vouchsafed no reply to the demons' prayer, but puts a quiet suggestive question to their unhappy victim. The Lord's words, as Dean Plumptre suggests, would serve "to recall to the man's mind that he had once a human name, with all its memories of human fellowship. It was a stage, even in spite of the paroxysm that followed, in the process of recovery, in so far as it helped to disentangle him from the confusion between himself and the demons which caused his misery. But, at first, the question seems only to increase the evil.

'My name is Legion, for we are many.' The irresistible might, the full array of the Roman legion, with its six thousand soldiers, seemed to the demoniac the one adequate symbol of the wild, uncontrollable impulses of passion and of dread that were sweeping through his soul."

Ver. 31.—And they besought him that he would not command them to go out into the deep. This time the voice and the request apparently proceed from the terrible presence which had made the soul of the unhappy man their temporary habitation. The direful confusion in the state of the poor demoniac is shown by this request. By whom was it made? The bystanders could discern no difference between the possessed and the spirits dwelling in the afflicted human being. So St. Mark, in his relation, puts these words into the demoniac's mouth, "And *he* besought him much that he would not send *them* away out of the country;" apparently here partly conscious of his own personal being, and partly identifying himself with the demoniac forces which were afflicting him. The request is a strange one, and suggests much anxious thought. What is the abyss these rebel-spirits dreaded with so great a dread? It would seem as though, to use Godet's thought, that for beings alienated from God, the power of acting on the world is a temporary solace to their unrest, and that to be deprived of this power is for them just what a return to prison is for the captive. St. Mark's expression here is a curious one. He represents the spirits requesting Jesus "not to send them away out of the country." The two accounts put together tell us that these spirits were aware, if they were driven out of the country—whatever that expression signified, this earth possibly—they must go out into the deep, the abyss, what is called "the bottomless pit" in Rev. ix. 1, 2, 11. Any doom seemed to these lost ones preferable to *that.* The whole train of thought suggested by the incident and the words of the Lord is very terrible. We see at least one reason *why* the first preachers of the Word have selected *this* exorcism. It indeed lifts a bit of the curtain which hangs between us and the night of endless woe!

Ver. 32.—And there was there an herd of many swine feeding on the mountain: and they besought him that he would suffer them to enter into them. And he suffered them. For what end was this request? Was it simply the way they chose to enter the abyss by? We know that the lives of the creatures, after the permission was given, lasted but a few minutes at most. Was it a desire to do more mischief during their brief sojourn on earth? Theophylact (eighth century) suggests that the purpose of the evil spirits, in their request, was to injure Jesus in that part of the country by arousing fears among the covetous inhabitants lest they too might lose, in a similar way, their herds. But to the writer of this note it seems best to confess that no satisfactory answer can ever be given here. We know so little of these dread spirits of evil. The reason of the Lord's permission is more obvious. Some such visible proof as the sight of the evil and unclean forces that had mastered him so long, transferred to the bodies of other creatures and working their wild will upon them, was probably a necessary element in his perfect cure. It is likely also that Jesus wished to show his indignation at the flagrant disregard of the Mosaic Law, at the open disobedience to the Divine injunctions respecting swine, which was shown by the presence of so vast a herd of these animals pronounced unclean by the Mosaic Law under which these people were professedly living (St. Mark gives the number as two thousand). In this district the large majority of the inhabitants were Jews. The keeping or the rearing of swine was strictly forbidden by the Jewish canon law. Other Oriental peoples also held these animals as unclean. Herodotus (ii. 47) tells us that in Egypt there was a special class of swineherds, who alone among the inhabitants of the country were forbidden to enter a temple. This degraded caste were only allowed to marry among themselves. The eating of swine's flesh is referred to by Isaiah (lxv. 3, 4) as among the acts of the people which continually provoked the Lord to anger.

Ver. 33.—**And the herd ran violently down a steep place into the lake, and were choked.** Some exception has been taken at our Lord's action here in connection with the swine, but it has been well said "that the antedating of the death of a herd of unclean animals was as nothing compared with the deliverance of a human soul." But it seems better to see, in the permitted destruction of the herd, the Lord's grave rebuke to the open disregarders of the holy ritual law of Israel, for the sake of selfish lucre.

Ver. 34.—**When they that fed them saw what was done, they fled, and went and told it in the city and in the country.** The men who kept the swine had witnessed the whole transaction; and as the Master uttered the word "Go," they saw a change in a moment pass through the vast herd. A wild panic seemed to seize the creatures, *something* had filled them with a great fear,—they would hurry from the *unseen* but *felt* presence; the cool blue waters of the lake, clearly seen from the upland down where they were feeding, seemed to promise the best refuge; they

rushed from the plateau down a steep incline, which travellers since think they have identified, and the deep waters of Gennesaret put a quick end to the creatures' torments.

Vers. 35, 36.—**Then they went out to see what was done; and came to Jesus, and found the man, out of whom the devils were departed, sitting at the feet of Jesus, clothed, and in his right mind: and they were afraid. They also which saw it told them by what means he that was possessed of the devils was healed.** The swineherds told their story, quickly the news spread; a great concourse from all the country-side soon gathered round the scene of the catastrophe. It was quiet then; the waters of the lake had closed over the tormented creatures. The demoniac, so long the terror of the neighbourhood, now sane, clothed, too, like one of them, was sitting peacefully full of deep, awe-ful gratitude at the Master's feet; the disciples were standing round; Jesus was no doubt teaching them the deep import of the scene they had lately witnessed.

Ver. 37.—**Then the whole multitude of the country of the Gadarenes round about besought him to depart from them; for they were taken with great fear: and he went up into the ship, and returned back again.** The recital had no effect upon the headmen of the neighbouring towns and villages. They were probably for the most part owners of similar herds of swine, perhaps sharers in nameless sins, all specially hateful to the Rabbi Jesus, whom they no doubt knew well by repute. But he was, they saw, something more than a poor wandering moral Teacher; he possessed strange and awful powers: had they not had terrible experience of them? Which of them in that law-breaking, dissolute neighbourhood might not be the next victim whose unclean possessions were to be swept away? So they would have none of him: let him as quickly as possible depart from their coasts. They felt they could not keep both the Saviour and their swine, and of the two they preferred their swine! *And returned back again.* The chance, as far as the Gadarene district was concerned, was gone for ever. Jesus probably returned thither no more. Within forty years this district was the scene of one of the terrible calamities of the great Roman war. The sack of Gadara, and the desolation and ruin which was the hapless lot of this once wealthy but evilliving district, is one of the many melancholy chapters of the hopeless Jewish revolt (see Josephus, 'Bell. Jud.,' iii. 7. 1; iv. 7. 4). A modern traveller, Dr. Thomson, remarks, singularly enough, that the old district of Gadara at the present day is infested with wild, fierce hogs: "Everywhere," he writes, "the land is ploughed up by wild hogs in search of roots on which they live" ('The Land and the Book,' ii. ch. 25).

Ver. 38.—**Now the man out of whom the devils were departed besought him that he might be with him: but Jesus sent him away, saying.** The restored man longed to remain with his Deliverer, but this was not permitted—the great Teacher bade him stay behind in his own country. Perhaps, thought the Redeemer, "*some* of these hard-hearted Gadarenes will be won by his testimony—one of themselves, too, and so notorious a sufferer." His work, the Master told him, was *there* among his own people; so he stayed, and the next verse (39) tells us how he worked as a diligent evangelist. It is noteworthy how the Master referred the great act of deliverance to *God*. But to the restored, Jesus was at once his Deliverer and his God. The text of his preaching was "how great things Jesus had done unto him."

Vers. 40—56.—*The healing of the woman with the issue of blood, and the raising of the daughter of Jairus.*

Ver. 40.—**When Jesus was returned, the people gladly received him: for they were all waiting for him.** Allusion has already been made, in the notes which preceded the parable of the sower, to the enthusiasm for Jesus in the Galilee lake-cities and their neighbourhood. This, as the Master well knew, was only a temporary religious revival, but still while it lasted it gathered great crowds in every place where he visited. He had not been long in the Gadarene district, but his return was eagerly looked for in Galilee. This verse describes his reception on his return by the people, and introduces the recital of two famous miracles which he worked in this period of his ministry after his brief visit to the other shore of the lake. St. Matthew, before speaking of the request of Jairus that the Master would visit his dying child, relates the healing of the paralytic at Capernaum, and the calling of Matthew the apostle. It is scarcely possible now to arrange the events related, in their proper chronological order. The Gospel histories pretty faithfully represent the teaching of the first days, in which it was evidently the practice of apostles and apostolic men to group their accounts of particular incidents in the Lord's life with a view to teaching certain lessons connected with doctrine or with daily living, often disregarding the order in which these incidents really happened. Hence so many of the differences in detail in our Gospels.

Ver. 41.—**And, behold, there came a man named Jairus, and he was a ruler of the synagogue.** The public request, made too

with intense earnestness, of one holding such a position, is a clear proof that the Galilee enthusiasm for Jesus was by no means confined to the poorer part of the population, or even to the more careless and thoughtless; such a man as Jairus is a fair representative of the well-to-do, perhaps wealthy, orthodox Jew; strict and rigid in his ritual observances, and held in high honour by his fellow Jewish citizens. The name is only a form of the Hebrew *Jair* (Judg. x. 3).

Ver. 42.—**One only daughter.** This is not the only place where the same touching detail is recorded by this evangelist. Compare the story of the widow's son at Nain (ch. vii. 12), and the healing of the lunatic boy (ch. ix. 38). St. Luke's Gospel owes these and many similar touches of deep true sympathy to the great loving heart of the real author of the third Gospel, Paul.

Vers. 43, 44.—**And a woman having an issue of blood twelve years, which had spent all her living upon physicians, neither could be healed of any, came behind** him, **and touched the border of his garment.** It may be assumed that the disease from which she suffered made her, according to the Levitical Law, ceremonially unclean: this had separated her in a great measure for a very long period from all contact with the outer world. This would well account for her shrinking from any public appeal to the great Physician. The border of the Lord's garment which the woman touched was one of the four tassels which formed part of the Jewish tallith, or mantle; one of these was always arranged so as to hang down over the shoulder at the back; it was this one which the sufferer's fingers grasped. There was a certain sacredness about these tassels, as being part of the memorial dress enjoined by the Levitical Law, which, no doubt, induced the woman to touch this particular portion of the Saviour's dress. **And immediately her issue of blood stanched.** This is not the only instance of this kind of strange faith mingled with superstition being signally rewarded. The case of the miraculous efficacy of the handkerchiefs and aprons which had had contact with Paul's body (Acts xix. 12) is an interesting example. A still more startling one exists in the healing influence of the *shadow* of Peter falling on the sick as he passed along the street (Acts v. 15). The lesson evidently intended to be left on the Church of Christ by this and similar incidents is a very instructive one. Faith in Christ is a broad inclusive term: it is accepted and blest by the Master, as we see from the gospel story, in all its many degrees of development, from the elementary shape which it assumed in the case of this poor loving superstitious soul, to the splendid proportions which it reached in the lives of a Stephen and a Paul. Faith in him, from its rudest form to its grandest development, the Master knew would ever purify and elevate the character. It would, as it grew, be the best teacher and the truest monitor of the noble, generous life he loved. Therefore he watched for it, encouraged it, helped it; and his Church, if it would imitate its Master, would do well to follow his wise and loving example by fostering in every form, however crude, faith in Jesus Christ; for this incident in the Divine and perfect life which we have just dwelt on, teaches us with striking clearness that he can and will bless the dimmest, most imperfect faith, the faith of the little child, and of the poorest untaught one.

Ver. 45.—**Who touched me?** The Master's words here and the statement of ver. 46, " For I perceive that virtue is gone out of me," tell us something of the earnestness and faith of the suppliant. Many, as Peter said, in that crowd were touching Jesus as they pressed round him to look on his face or to listen to his words, but of them all none save this poor sufferer " touched " him in the true deep sense of touching, with the fixed idea that contact with his blessed Person would benefit or heal them.

Ver. 48.—**Daughter, be of good comfort.** This is the only place in the Gospels where our Lord is reported to have used this loving word to any woman. Eusebius preserves a curious legend in connection with this act of healing. In his time (fourth century) the house of this happy one who met Jesus in her sad life-journey, was shown at Paneas, a town in the north of Palestine. At the entrance of the house, on a stone pedestal, stood two brazen statues—one represented a woman kneeling; the other, a man with his cloak over his shoulder and his hand stretched out toward the kneeling woman. Eusebius relates how he had seen the house and statues and heard the legend (' Hist. Eccl.,' vii. 18). In the apocryphal Gospel of Nicodemus, a very early writing, though not one possessing much critical value, the name of the woman is stated to be Veronica. It was she, goes on the story to relate, who, on the Via Dolorosa, when the Lord, on his way to Calvary, stumbled and fell, gave the handkerchief to wipe the blessed face.

Ver. 49.—**While he yet spake, there cometh one from the ruler of the synagogue's house, saying to him, Thy daughter is dead; trouble not the Master.** This interruption, which must have occupied some time, was, no doubt, a sore trial to the ruler's faith. His little daughter was, he knew well, dying; and though he trusted that the famous Rabbi had power to arrest the progress of

disease, he never seems for a moment to have contemplated his wrestling with *death*; indeed, the bare thought of recalling the spirit to the deserted clay tenement evidently never occurred to any of that sad household, while the *hired* mourners (vers. 52, 53, and Mark v. 38), too accustomed to the sight of death in all its forms to dream of any man, however great a physician, recalling the dead to life, transgressing all courtesy, positively laughed him to scorn. It seems to us strange now that this supreme miracle should have seemed so much harder a thing to accomplish than the healing of blindness or deafness, or the creation of wine and bread and fish, or the instantaneous quieting of the elements, the waves, and the wind. While sufferers and their friends and the Lord's disciples, in countless instances, asked him to put forth his power in cases of disease and sickness, neither friend nor disciple ever asked him to raise the dead to life. To the last, in spite of what they had seen, none, till after the Resurrection, could persuade themselves that he was, indeed, the Lord of death as well as of life.

Ver. 50.—**But when Jesus heard it, he answered him, saying, Fear not: believe only, and she shall be made whole.** No shadow of hesitation crossed the Redeemer's mind; with unruffled calmness he whispered his words of cheer to the grief-stricken father, and bade him fear nothing, for that all would yet be well with the child. Then follows the well-known, often-read story told in such few words, yet are they so vivid, so dramatic, that we seem to be looking on the scene. The grief-stricken household, the hired mourners, the still death-room, the white motionless form of the dead girl—the ruler's only child—lying on her little bed, the group of the six with tear-dimmed eyes standing round; the loving Master bending over the little dead, his smile as for a moment he took back the all-power he had laid aside a little season *for our sakes;* the far-off look in his eyes as for a moment his vision ranged over his old home of peace and grandeur; and then the two words spoken in the familiar Aramaic (Hebrew), which Mark, or rather Mark's master, Peter, remembered so well, " Talitha, kumi!" and the dead child rose up again, the spirit had returned to its frail tenement.

Ver. 53.—**They laughed him to scorn.** These were, no doubt, the hired mourners. Familiar as they were with death, they ridiculed the idea of one whom they knew had passed away, awaking again as from a sleep. These public mourners were customary figures in all Jewish homes, even in the poorest where a death had occurred. They are still usual throughout the Levant. The expression, "laughed him to scorn," is found in Shakespeare—

"Our castle's strength
Will laugh a siege to scorn."
('Macbeth,' act v. sc. 5.)

The Aramaic words, *Talitha, kumi!* "Maid, arise!" were just homely words, spoken in the language which the little girl was in the habit of hearing and using. The Master's tender care for the child was shown not merely in the choice of the language and the words, but in his loving thought after her resurrection, for we read how—

Ver. 55.—**He commanded to give her meat.** She had been grievously ill, sick, we know, even to death; and now that the old strength and health had come back again, the Master felt she would at once, after her long abstinence, need food. Even the child's mother was not so motherly as Jesus.

Ver. 56.—**He charged them that they should tell no man what was done.** The enthusiasm in Galilee just then needed no extra spur. The crowds which followed him were increasing. The excitement, the Master felt, was unreal and evanescent; he wished rather to calm it than to increase it.

HOMILETICS.

Vers. 1—21.—*The evangelistic circuit.* Observe—

I. THE PLAN OF CIRCUIT. (Ver. 1.) "He went," or "went about," or "kept journeying." Hitherto Capernaum had been the centre from which short excursions were taken, the Lord always returning to it. Now he moves steadily on from place to place, "passing in patience until his work is done." "Through cities and villages." He will not omit any abode of man. If social influence and power had been the aim, this Prophet would have limited his operations to the chief centres of life; but his meat is to do the Father's will, and where there is even one soul waiting for the message, there is he. To the Father, to him, there is the same value in the soul of the peasant as in that of the prince. "Preaching and bringing the good tidings of the kingdom of God." The distinction between the words, "preaching and showing the good tidings"—or, to give the exact English rendering, "evangelizing"—is not to be pressed too far; but the latter word seems to mark an advance of thought on the former. The "preaching" was the more general proclamation, and the "evangelizing" was the presentation of the gospel thus proclaimed to the diversities of experience and need, the opening up of its several aspects of blessing, so that men from their different standpoints might realize the great love of God and behold the glories of his kingdom. Kings grant pardons, but they only send them; this King comes himself with the pardon, and deals personally with the sinner. "How beautiful upon the mountains are the feet of him thus bringing good tidings, and publishing peace; bringing good tidings of good, publishing salvation, saying unto Zion, Thy God reigneth!"

II. A NEW STYLE OF DISCOURSE. One which thenceforth becomes a marked feature of the teaching. He had frequently used comparisons, traced likenesses between the natural and the spiritual. But what had been an occasional trait now became a characteristic mode of conveying truth, and for the reason given by himself (ver. 10). To us, familiar with the sound and meaning of the parable, nothing can seem more apposite and happy as a means of communicating thought. By it the highest and deepest mysteries of the kingdom are most gently infused into the apprehension of the mind, whilst there is always a reserve of meaning on which we can draw. But the parable was not all this to those who heard it. It stimulated inquiry rather than imparted knowledge. It brought the disciples to Jesus, saying, "Expound to us;" "What might this story be?" Those who did not wish to learn were sent away with the feeling, "A dark saying has been uttered: who can hear it?" Jesus says that this defined his purpose in adopting it. He meant it to be a test of the spirit of the mind. Thus he laid his hearers in the balances. May we be of those "to whom it is given to know the mysteries of the kingdom of heaven"!

III. THE PARABLE OF THE SOWER. This is the only one of the famous seven given in Matt. xiii. which St. Luke places in our view. It falls more naturally to be considered at length in connection with the former of the accounts. Observe here—on this St. Luke is explicit—the point to which the discourse of Jesus looks (ver. 18), "Take heed therefore how ye hear." In this connection recall the four kinds of place in which the seed is sown: the *wayside*, where the seed is trodden down and devoured by the fowls; the *rock*, or *stony places*, where the seed springs up, but soon withers through want of moisture; the *thorny ground*, where the seed and the thorns grow together, and the thorns choke the seed; and the *good ground*, where the seed springs up and bears a hundredfold. These places are identified (vers. 12—15) with classes of hearers. There are the *wayside hearers*—those in whom there is no mental exercise on that which they hear, whose minds are thoroughfares for all sorts of thought. And what follows? As soon as they hear, the devil comes—some impish fancy or distracting influence, and takes away the word. "I never heard a sermon," said a man, who for years attended church, "I attended, but, whilst you were speaking, I reviewed the last week's task and arranged for the next." There are the *rocky-place hearers*—those who hear with interest, with emotion; you can see the response to the word in the animation of the countenance, in the tokens of lively feeling. But the message does not grasp the character, the centres of the life remain unchanged, and thus "in time of temptation they fall away." There are the *thorny-ground hearers*—those who have heard and yielded to the truth, but the busy, care-crowded, or pleasure-seeking world is waiting for them; the seed is not altogether lost, but the mind is choked with alien interests or pursuits. The poet Robert Burns compares himself to a lonely man walking where fragments of marble columns lie on the ground, overgrown by rank, tall weeds. There are the *good-soil hearers*—those in whom the earnest longing to know, to do, God's truth is a preparation for the word; who, having heard, hide the word in the heart, and patiently and habitually submit to it, and, through the blessing of the Holy Spirit, bring forth fruit abundantly. To which of these types of hearers does each of us belong? Oh the responsibility of hearing! Note the distinction, in ver. 18, between those who have and those who seem to have, or think they have. What is the warning? Whoso only thinks that he has, or is content with the appearance of having, is losing his possession. The life is really moving on other lines than those laid down in the word. The power of reception is diminishing: "Whosoever hath not, from him shall be taken even that which he thinketh he hath." "Take heed therefore *how* ye hear." It is the *manner* of hearing that is the main thing—the motive, the desire, the extent to which the heart and the soul are engaged whilst hearing. Persons are apt to blame the speaker, to lay the want of effect at his door. It may be so; no doubt it often is so. But what of these persons themselves? Let each examine himself. Eloquence, it has been said, is in the audience; and, undoubtedly, the sympathy of the audience has much to do with the power of the utterance. Christ reminds us that, where there is failure, the hearer at least divides the blame. He reminds us, too, that the life declares the quality of the hearing. Vers. 16, 17, "For nothing is hid, that shall not be made manifest; nor anything secret, that shall not be known and come to light."

IV. THE HELPERS AND THE HINDERERS IN THE MINISTRY. The twelve are with him. It is their university curriculum. Would to God that all who pass through universities and seminaries realized this curriculum also—"Eye-witnesses first, and then ministers of the Word"! But he has other companions than the apostles; and the noteworthy thing as to these other companions is that they ministered to him of their substance. "The Son of God," says Godet, "lived by the love of those whom his love had made to live." Who are they? *Women.* Three names are singled out. Mary of Magdala, "from whom seven devils had gone out" (*vide* previous section), once passionate, perhaps depraved, in her life; but henceforth the most loving and devoted; the one to whom the risen Saviour first appeared (John xx.). And with her are named the wife of Herod's steward, and Susanna, of whom nothing is known. "Many others," we are told. But we do not find, as Farrar has pointed out, the wives of Peter or of the married apostles; nor yet the mother of our Lord. The ministry of woman to Jesus! There is a deep sympathy between the true woman-heart and the Lord; the self-sacrificing love so pure and strong in the true woman-heart being the special attraction. Christianity has exalted woman, has raised her position, and purified her influence. But woman has more than paid back all that she owes to Christianity in respect of this. Who, indeed, that has been blessed by Christian mother, wife, sister, friend, does not know that God has created the ministry of his Word male and female?—giving to the female an even more winning beauty and a more spiritually educative service than the male. The apostles are with Jesus; but certain women minister to him of their substance. These are the helpers: who are the *hinderers?* *His mother and his brethren* (ver. 19). The Lord is compelled to say that, whilst the relation according to the flesh is respected, they are not at that moment connected with him by the affinities which alone are permanent. See how this bears on the idolatrous honour paid by the Roman Church to Mary. She has been prevailed on by her children, not to intercede with Jesus, but to join them in the effort—probably meant in kindness, but showing deficiency of insight—to prevent him from continuance in toils and prayers. And note, he distinctly declines to recognize any rights grounded on the motherhood with regard to his work; only spiritual relationships will he recognize. Even when he looks down from the cross and sees her standing, he says to the beloved disciple only, " Behold *thy* mother." But, apart from this, is it not suggestive, mournfully suggestive, that the hinderers are the nearest of relations—mother and brethren? So it has been often since. An unsympathetic home and circle of friends sometimes constitute the sorest trial which one must face who wills to have fellowship with the Son of God. " He goeth forth weeping, bearing the precious seed."

Vers. 22—25.—*Storm and calm.* " He entered into a boat, himself and his disciples." The association of Christ with the boat, with which we are so familiar in the gospel history, has been preserved in much of the poetry, the literature, and the art of the Church. A very old seal-ring represents the Church as a ship struggling against the winds, supported by a great fish in the sea beneath, and with two doves sitting on its mast and prow. The shape often given to Christian places of worship in the early ages was that of a boat. And the idea has entered into all Christian song and thought. Keble catches up the tone of centuries when he inserts the verse in the evening hymn—

> " Thou Framer of the light and dark,
> Steer through the tempest thine own ark :
> Amid the howling wintry sea
> We are in port if we have thee."

The key-note to all this symbolism is given in the incident reported in these verses.
I. IT IS A PICTURE OF LIFE. The sea was at rest when the disciples took Jesus as he was. As they sailed on the smooth waters the weary Prophet fell asleep. On a sudden down comes the squall—one of those furious hurricanes which sweep across a lake six hundred feet lower than the ocean, with gigantic funnels supplied by deep ravines cut by the action of wild watercourses. All is changed; there is heard now only the despairing cry, " Master, carest thou not that we perish?" Such is life: changeful, now the smiling sunshine with the clear blue sky, again the driving cloud and rain, with angry waves breaking over the craft. Job was at rest; his sons and daughters feasting together; he himself, with abundance and peace, fearing God and eschewing evil, when the one terrible day came on which messenger chased messenger, completing a tale of destruction and bereavement. How often does destruction fall as in a moment! The fitful weather of the inland lake is a type of the fitful climate, followed by the rapidly dissolving scenery, of the present time. How foolish to set the affection on things below! How sad when there is no Christ in the ship! when there is no fixture, among the sundry and manifold changes of this world, where the only true joys are to be found!
II. IT IS A SIGN OF CHRIST. The stilling of the tempest is a miracle. We seem to see the sleeping Master quietly raising himself, looking around, meeting the gaze of the all but frantic men, standing erect in the boat, sending forth the majestic, " Peace; be still!" " What manner of man is this, for he commandeth even the winds and the water, and they obey him?" Yes; what manner of man! He is himself the miracle, the One " made of God to us Wisdom, and Righteousness, and Sanctification, and Redemption." The work is the sign of himself in that deeper work in which he is manifest as the Saviour of sinners. What is that work but the rebuking of the storm of passion, and all the influences which are adverse to peace of mind and holiness of life? " Be still," is the Christ-word; " Peace to you," is the Christ-breath. In the world of man, " he maketh the storm a calm, so that the waves thereof are still. Then

are they glad because they are quiet; so he bringeth them unto their desired haven."
Is not this the experience of every truly converted life? Miss Havergal's verse
expresses it.

> " There were strange soul-depths, restless, vast and broad,
>   Unfathomed as the sea;
>   An infinite longing for an infinite stilling.
>   But now thy love is perfect filling:
>   Lord Jesus Christ, my Lord, my God,
>   Thou, thou art enough for me ! "

And so for all the days. "Let Christ be awakened," writes Augustine, "Though the
tempest beat into, yet it will not fill, thy ship; thy faith will now command the winds
and the waves, and thy danger will be over." Oh, see to it, that thou take Christ into
thy heart, even as he is. Blessed for thee, O needy sinner, when the Master is really
the occupant of thy life, thy "present Help in trouble."

III. IT IS A REPROOF OF LITTLE FAITH. "*Why* are ye so fearful?" is the part of
Jesus' word reported by Matthew. Why, when you know who is with you; when
you know that he is there, that it is not some enemy, some devil, that has the control
of elements, of circumstances? Why are ye so easily cast down? Why do ye give way
so readily? Why do ye fall into such despondencies, such paroxysms of grief? May
we not, in many an hour of shrinking, if not of terror, hear this "why" sounding in
our hearts? "Where is your faith?" is the part of the word reported by Luke.
Assume that you have it, that you are really trusting in Christ as your Master:
whither does the faith vanish when you are so fearful? Is it not the moment of trial
that proves the readiness and serviceableness of the faith? Do we not often need to
seek it when we have occasion for it? Verily a question most pertinent to us in the
varying circumstances and demands of our life. Think, think over the adverb, so
suggestive, "*Where* is your faith?"

Vers. 26—39.—*The demoniac whose name was Legion.* Two miserable creatures are
mentioned in Matthew. No sooner has Jesus come forth on the land than they rush
towards him. Human, yet without the mental attributes of humanity, shunned by
all, left in the lonely place, to rend the air with fearful cries, to dash themselves against
stones, wretched beyond all names of wretchedness. One of the two is singled out by
St. Luke, and described (vers. 27, 29). Observe the effect of Jesus' presence. Instantly
some long-silent chord was touched, some new sense of the awful misery into which
the man had been plunged was awakened, some conflict between a mind made
suddenly active, and the nameless power of darkness was originated. The maniac
falls down, and with a loud voice cries, as if some other one were crying through him,
"What have I to do with thee, Jesus, thou Son of the Most High God? I beseech
thee, torment me not." Marvellous confession! which, however, had been preceded by
a word of authority (ver. 29), and which is followed by a kind of confused perception.
"What is thy name?" What name had he? What personality? The only word
which seemed to describe the situation was the Roman name for a host, "My name
is Legion; for we are many." Poor Legion! there is in thee a groaning which cannot
be uttered; and that groaning, unawares to thyself, has the form of the old prayer,
"Unite my heart to fear thy Name!" Lo! he who knows the mind of the Spirit
has heard thee, and he has given a new song to thy mouth. Henceforth thou shalt
say, "I will praise thee, O Lord my God, with all my heart, and I will glorify thy
Name for evermore. For great is thy mercy toward me, and thou hast delivered
my soul from the lowest hell." Thus far, all, though wonderful, is beautiful and
Christ-like. But now comes the strange portion of the narrative. Jesus is described
as giving the demons which had laid waste the son of Abraham leave to possess the
herd of swine feeding on the mountain-side; the consequence being that the herd ran
violently down a steep place into the sea, and were choked. Against this destruction
many objections have been brought; it is a stone of stumbling and offence even to
believers. Even to faith it seems at variance with the mercifulness of the Lord, and
the transference of the evil power from the man to the herd of swine bristles with
things hard to be understood. Explanations offered, some of them ingenious, all
unsatisfactory, are not here to be dwelt on. It is assumed that we take the evangelist

to be a trustworthy guide as to events which are out of the plane of ordinary life. Somewhere, somehow, the work done is reconcilable with the true nature of things, with the mercy and the truth which are around all God's paths. Observe two points by way of practical improvement.

I. To THE DEMONIAC HIMSELF THERE WAS GIVEN A TESTIMONY NEVER TO BE FORGOTTEN OF THE SIN AND MISERY FROM WHICH THE STRONGER THAN THE STRONG ONE HAD DELIVERED HIM. The effect on character, the influence which some action or course of conduct would have in the establishment of trust in himself or in the education of the disciple, was always before the mind of Christ. Now, what an evidence—in a form which one whose shattered intellect was not yet fully restored could understand—was given of the awful waste of spiritual life, the awful force of an untrained, unsanctified nature, by the sight of that precipitate rush down the steep place into the sea! Recollect, too, that, according to the correspondences of Scripture, these swine represent the more bestial and corrupt propensities of our nature. Pascal, in one of his most cynical sayings, speaks of man as "half-beast, half-devil." There is something of the beast in men; and what happened that day is the token of what does happen when the lower animal is acted on by spirits of malignity or darkness—when, from some cause operating from without, that which is animal is acted on by that which is devilish. Is not that same violent rushing down steep places of poor animalized beings, their true life checked and destroyed, witnessed every day? Do we not constantly see infatuations similar to that portrayed in the herd of swine? In England more than a hundred and twenty thousand persons die every year directly in consequence of indulgence in strong drink. If, as has been asked, there was such a destruction of cattle or swine in the country, what attention would be called to it! what a host of remedies and measures with a view to its prevention would be propounded! But the matter passes with little notice. Undoubtedly, the event at Gergesa is a sign of what mere carnal appetite, when fed by some exciting cause, brings about; and, being so, it is a standing witness for the blessings of his salvation, whose gospel is a new order as well as a new life, who controls what is lawless by the law of liberty, and at whose feet the man from whom devils are departed sits clothed and in his right mind.

II. To ALL OF US THERE IS A SAD SIGNIFICANCE IN THE CONDUCT OF THE GADARENES. The two facts before them were—the swine lost, and the man gained. Which of the two was the greater? The *swine lost*. That spoke to them of a fearful power in the Man who had landed on their shore. Perhaps their consciences were uneasy. If they were Jews, and some of them must have been, they knew that, for the purpose of gain, they had broken Moses' Law. Why should he continue in their midst whose glance burnt like an oven? Anyhow, instead of remembering what attracted and spoke of healing in the cure of the man, they remember only what had caused them loss in the destruction of the swine. "Away!" they cry, "thou holy and terrible One! We don't wish to be disturbed in our way. Trouble us no longer!" Fearful prayer! But do not more than the Gadarenes pray it? Are there not many whose secret heart protests, "Let us alone, Lord God! Let us make money as best we can; eat, drink, and enjoy ourselves. Away with the spiritual—with Church, with God! Give us our swine, and let heaven go!" Fearful prayer, and fearful answer! "God answers sharp and sudden on some prayers, and flings the thing we have asked for in our face—a gauntlet with a gift in it." "He entered into a boat, and returned." There is only one of another spirit in the multitude. He who a few minutes before had cried, "What have I to do with thee?" now beseeches, like Ruth of old, "Entreat me not to leave thee: where thou goest I will go, and where thou dwellest I will dwell." Nay, he must remain—Christ's missionary and witness to his unbelieving countrymen. Not to luxuriate in him, but to live and work for him, is the call to the redeemed. "And he went his way, publishing throughout the whole city how great things Jesus had done for him."

Vers. 41—56.—*Jairus, and what happened on the way to his house.* A beautiful Scripture, whose beauty we feel all the more that, in this Gospel, it follows the rejection of Christ by the "witless Gadarenes." Its exact place in the history cannot with certainty be fixed; for the accounts of the three synoptists vary as to the time of the works. But whatever the precise period in the biography to which it belongs, the tale told is one which appeals to the more domestic affections of the heart; one too which gives a graciously full manifestation of Jesus the Resurrection and the Life. The transaction realized as he went illustrates chiefly Christ the Life ; that which was done in answer to the ruler's pleading illustrates chiefly Christ the Resurrection— the two aspects of the incarnate I Am.

With regard to the former of these events, consider the touch of the Lord by the woman who had found her way to his presence, and what came of the touch.

I. The touch represents THE ONLY HOPE. She had nothing else to which to cling. For twelve long years she had been a sick and weary woman. There is something interesting in the circumstance which Luke the physician records, that all her means had been spent on physicians, but that she could not be healed of any. Mark adds that she rather grew worse. The physician-evangelist has no such addition; but " he knew what human skill could do, and, still better, what it could not do, and he bowed himself humbly in the presence of Christ." Well, all the living has been spent. A little before the moment of Jesus passing, she might not have been so ready. A portion of her income would still have been left. The temptation would have been to try another doctor. But now there is only this chance. It is the energy of despair. " Thou must save, and thou alone." Ah ! sinner, if thou wouldst know the virtue that there is in the Son of God for thee, thou must come to an end with self, with all strivings after a righteousness of thine own. Thy living, all that is thine, must be wholly removed from thy sight. Jesus wholly ! Jesus only !

II. The touch represents AN IMMEDIATE ACT OF WILL. "When she had heard," says Mark, " the things concerning Jesus, she came." There is no delay over questions such as, " How can I reach his presence ? How can I get through this multitude ? Will he care for me ?" All such self-inquiry is at once dismissed. The true faith is busied only with its Object. The mind is too much in earnest to stop over problems concerning the act or the manner of faith. " If thou wert sick for want of God, how swiftly wouldst thou move !" Two things are seen—the need, and Christ the only answer to the need ; and, these things seen, the will is supreme over all that savours of intellectual doubt and difficulty. " If I may but get to him, I shall be whole."

III. The touch represents A PERSONAL CONTACT. " Only to put my hand on the clothes, or even the fringe of the garment." So she says to herself. Not, perhaps, a very lofty faith. A good deal in it, possibly, of the superstition to which she had been accustomed ; of an idea of magical charm, and so forth. But the real thing in it was the conviction that he was able to save to the uttermost ; that the cure was certain if she could get to him. The touch meant herself in her want laying hold of Christ himself, the Saviour and his salvation. And this is the vital force of faith. Notions may be confused, may be very poor and deficient ; the Lord will rectify that. The saving grace is such a confidence as will bring into direct relation to the love of God in Christ. And this touch is at once distinguished. Every one who has to do with multitudes understands, so far, the secret of the quick " Who touched me ?" He knows by intuition the souls that are really sympathetic with him. These touch ; the others only press around. In the crowd surging about Jesus there is only one who touches. The people have welcomed him, and are following him ; but their handling of him and her touch are quite different. Blessed among women ! type of the souls blessed eternally : " I perceived that power had gone forth from me."

IV. The touch is the way to THE CURE BOTH OF BODY AND SOUL. " Immediately she was healed." " Straightway," says Mark, " she felt in her body that she was healed." What a sensation that instant bound of health ! Observe that "immediately" or " straightway " in the reports of Jesus' works of healing in the Gospels. The health does not come as the end of a laborious discipline or regimen ; it is not the end, but the beginning of a new life. We do not work to salvation ; we work from it The moment a life is really surrendered to God and the affiance of the soul with the Redeemer is fulfilled, that moment it is healed, it is cleansed. There is a new life introduced—a life which is henceforth the power of God to salvation. It is not perfect, but it is there. This Divine life is the health of the soul. It is then in a healthy condition before God. And henceforth, according to his power that worketh in us, he completes and perfects the life which himself has imparted. Was it not so with the woman? After she was healed he brought her into the spiritual knowledge of himself and his will. She had stolen to Jesus, but she must not steal from him. He searches her out. She sees that she is not hid; and trembling, fearing, she falls down and tells him all the truth. Precisely what he desired. And what he desires evermore is frankness, openness to him. There must be no guile and no conceal-ment; there must be perfect truthfulness between the Lord and the soul. When any shadow comes in there, the cleansing of the conscience, the working out of the salvation, is hindered. Notice the word "daughter," the only woman who received this title from the Lord, and she the woman who was brought to tell all the truth. "For this let every one that is godly pray unto thee."

This interview, with its great work, is by the way. He who desires the opportunity of usefulness meets the opportunity even in travelling to the duty more immediately contemplated. All the while another work has been waiting. What parent does not enter into the feeling of the ruler of the synagogue? His only daughter, the darling, the desire of his eyes, is dying. And he must stand and listen to the talk which involves some delay. And then the message, "Thy daughter is dead: trouble not the Master!" We do not hear of any complaint or impatience, of any word of reproach like that which fell from the sisters of Bethany. Jesus meets a confidence such as this with loving frankness: "Fear not: only believe, and she shall be made whole." Look at the sign that is given of *Christ the Resurrection*.

I. IT HAS ITS SPECIALTY OF MEANING. Of the three acts of raising from the dead related by the evangelists, it is, adhering to the chronology of Luke, the second. The son of the widow of Nain was not only dead, but the body was being carried out to burial. Lazarus had been four days dead. The girl of twelve had only expired. The attendants *knew* that she was dead; Luke the physician is careful to add this. It was no trance; she was undoubtedly dead, but Death had only a short time before put his stamp on the countenance. Trench, writing on the miracle, beautifully speaks of "the fresh-trodden way between the body and the soul which has just forsaken it, and which lingers for a season near the tabernacle where it has dwelt so long. Even science itself," he adds, "has arrived at the conclusion that the last echoes of life ring in the body much longer than is commonly supposed; that, for a while, it is full of the reminiscences of life." Observe, when Christ says, "She is not dead, but sleepeth," the unbelieving mourners laugh; they have only *scorn* for such a saying. The sorrow is hard, cheerless sorrow, when there is no conception of death—as a sleep! "Asleep in Jesus;" "He fell on sleep;"—such words the Church has substituted for the cold, forbidding word "death." Look, O mourner in Zion, on the lifeless form of thy dear one, and as thou thinkest of "the fresh-trodden way between the body and the soul which has just forsaken it," remember the saying of him who is the Resurrection: "Not *dead, but sleepeth.*" Believest thou this?

II. NOTE THE WITNESSES OF THE WORK. It is the first occasion on which the three of the apostolic band are singled out—Peter and James and John. None except they and the parents are allowed to enter. There is a sacredness in great grief which demands protection from the rude gaze of mere curiosity. The hired mourners, with their shouts and cries, their ostentation and display, are abhorrent to the Lord. Sim-plicity and genuineness of emotion befit the house of the dead, and all connected with death and burial.

III. SEE THE GENTLE THOUGHTFULNESS OF CHRIST. When the maid arises, he com-mands that meat be given her. The life restored must be supported. He is sparing of the supernatural and extraordinary. Where the ordinary and natural come into play, there the call is to use them. The Church, in her spiritual work, must learn of her Lord. "Keep life living," said Bunsen. When the Divine life is bestowed, it must be nourished by the appropriate means of grace; it must be fed by food convenient to it, nourished through the Word, sacraments, and prayer, unto everlasting life.

IV. CONTEMPLATE THE WHOLE ACTION. How simple! how quiet! The touch of the hand, the head bent over the child; the voice soft yet clear in the familiar Aramaic, "Talitha cumi!"—these are the features of the action. Thus simple and quiet was the way of the Lord when, in the beginning, he "said, Let there be light! And there was light." Thus simple and quiet is his way when he comes to the human soul "as the rain, as the former and latter rain on the earth." The wind bloweth, indeed, where it listeth, sometimes with the fury of the hurricane tearing up the old refuges and joys of the life. But the hurricane prepares for the Lord. The Lord is in the still small voice which comes after. Wherefore he saith, in tones of imperial authority, but of thrilling tenderness, to thee, little maid, to thee, young man rejoicing in thy youth, to thee on whom the weight of years is resting, "Awake thou that sleepest, and arise from the dead, and Christ shall give thee light!"

HOMILIES BY VARIOUS AUTHORS.

Ver. 1.—*The gospel of the kingdom.* In a parallel passage in Matthew (iv. 23) we read that Jesus went about all Galilee, "preaching the gospel of the kingdom;" here we read of the same thing in a very slightly different form—"showing the glad tidings of the kingdom of God." It will clear away all possible confusion of thought respecting "the gospel" and "the kingdom," if we dwell upon the gospel (or the glad tidings) of the kingdom.

I. THE KINGDOM OF GOD. This kingdom of God, or of heaven, or of Christ (for our Lord sometimes spoke of it as his own), is something transcendently nobler than anything which the most pious or the most sanguine Jew ever hoped for in his heart or pictured in his imagination (see homily on ch. i. 31—33). As Jesus Christ conceived it, and as it will be when it has been fully and finally established, this glorious kingdom is or is to be : 1. A kingdom *of God* ; one in which God himself will be the one Sovereign, all men everywhere being his subjects, owning his sway and loyal to his will. 2. An essentially *spiritual* kingdom ; all the obedience and submission rendered being that of the heart and the will, as well as of the tongue and the hand. 3. A *righteous* kingdom ; in which every citizen will act in accordance with "the golden rule" (ch. vi. 31). 4. A *beneficent* kingdom ; the spirit of kindness, of practical helpfulness, animating every subject. 5. A *universal* kingdom ; coextensive with the human race. 6. An *everlasting* kingdom ; going down to the remotest generation. Such, in its purity, its nobility, its inherent greatness, its absolute uniqueness, is the "kingdom of God."

II. THE GOSPEL (THE GLAD TIDINGS) OF THE KINGDOM. The features of this kingdom which so much commend it to the hearts of erring, sinful, dying men, constituting "the glad tidings of the kingdom," are : 1. *That entrance into it is open to every child of man.* This is now so familiar to us as to be quite commonplace. But look at it in the light of the doctrine of Divine favouritism once prevalent ; in the light of the incident recorded in the fourth chapter of this Gospel (vers. 23—29) ;—then we cannot be too thankful that the gates of this blessed kingdom are open, stand *wide* open, to every comer—to the poor, to the despised, to the neglected, to the barbarous, to those whom men may consider irrecoverable or not worth redeeming. 2. *That its Divine Sovereign is actively seeking all souls*, that they may enter. It is not only that no one is excluded ; the good news, the glad tidings, is more and better than that—it is that every one is being individually, lovingly invited, nay, pressed and urged to enter ; it is that out into the "far country" of forgetfulness and dislike the heavenly Father goes in parental yearning, and bids each wandering child "Return ;" it is that away over hill and mountain of estrangement and guilt the good Shepherd goes, seeking and finding and bringing back the sheep which was lost ; it is that long and lovingly, at the door of each human soul, the patient Saviour stands and knocks, and cries, "If any man will open the door, I will come in to him, and sup with him." 3. *That admission is open to every humble and trustful soul at once.* If we have grieved some human friend and become estranged from him, and if there be a proposal to seek reconciliation, our decision will probably be determined by the consideration whether we shall be at once fully restored or whether there will be a long interval before full reconciliation is effected. It is the gospel (the glad tidings) of the kingdom of God that every penitent and believing soul is *immediately* and without any delay whatever taken into the favour of God. As soon as the submissive spirit of the man says, "Father, I have sinned," so soon is grace bestowed, so soon is the name entered on the roll of the heavenly citizenship. 4. *That citizenship now means citizenship for ever.* It is a large part of the gospel of Jesus Christ that this earth is only an antechamber of the Father's house, or only a small outlying province of his boundless empire. To be a faithful citizen here and now means being a happy citizen somewhere for evermore. Life under the benign sway of this heavenly King is not counted by years or decades; it is without a bound; it is continued, perpetuated, in other regions of his glorious domain. This is the "glorious gospel" of the kingdom. Is it well to wait for a better? Dare we hope that, if we reject these glad tidings, we shall ever hear any that we shall accept? "Behold, now is the accepted time."—C.

Vers. 2, 3.—*Christianity and woman.* We have seen (ch. ii. 36—38) that woman, in the person of Anna, welcomed the infant Saviour to the world; it was most fitting that she should do so, for Christianity and womanhood have had a very close relationship, and undoubtedly will have even to the end.

I. WHAT CHRISTIANITY OWES TO WOMAN. 1. Its Divine Author and the Object of its worship was, "as concerning the flesh," born of a woman (Gal. iv. 4). The Son of God was, in a true and important sense, the "Son of Mary." 2. He owed the care and the training of his childhood to a human mother. 3. He received, during his active life, the generous provision of ministering women (see text); these, out of "their substance," supplied his necessities. 4. He found some of his best disciples and of his most faithful attendants in women (Matt. xxvii. 65). 5. He had the comfort of the near presence of three devoted women in his last agonies (John xix. 25). Closer to him in that awful hour than the ruthless soldier and the taunting enemy, rendering him a silent and sorrowful but not unvalued sympathy, stood three women who loved him for all that he was in himself and for all he had been to them. 6. Last at the cross, women were first at the sepulchre (ch. xxiii. 55, 56; xxiv. 1). 7. Women were united with the apostles in the upper room, waiting and praying for the further manifestation of the Lord after his ascension (Acts i. 14). 8. The apostle of the Gentiles owed much to women in his abundant and fruitful labours (Phil. iv. 3). 9. From that time to this, women have been rendering valuable service to the cause of Jesus Christ: the mother of Augustine, the mother of the Wesleys, and many hundreds more have, by their holy and faithful motherhood, done signal service to the gospel. In these later days, moved by the Spirit of God, women have, by their writings and by their "prophesyings," effected great things for the furtherance of the truth as it is in Jesus Christ. And it is right that it should be so; for we have to consider—

II. WHAT WOMAN OWES TO CHRISTIANITY. 1. We know what barbarism does, and fails to do, for woman. 2. We know also what Greek and Roman civilization did, and failed to do, for her; in how unsatisfactory a condition it left her; how completely it failed to raise her to her true spiritual dignity. We know what Christianity has done and is doing for her. (1) Jesus Christ taught and enforced the transcendent value of every human soul. (2) He admitted women into his kingdom on the same terms on which he received men: "In him is neither male nor female." (3) He gave to women a sphere of honourable service in his kingdom; not only (as above) accepting their loving ministry for himself, but for his disciples also. (4) Influenced increasingly by these ideas, the Church of Christ has been giving to woman a place of growing honour and usefulness; it has made her the full helpmeet and equal companion of man; it has opened for her the gateway of knowledge and influence; it has placed her on the highest seat to receive its respect, its affection, its service. We may look at—

III. THE SPECIAL CONTRIBUTIONS WHICH WOMAN MAY RENDER. 1. When not bound by domestic ties, she can offer, as these women did, of her worldly substance. 2. She can minister, as man cannot, to the sick and suffering; she has a gentle touch of hand and a tenderness and patience of spirit for which we look to man in vain. 3. She can train the child in the home, and, by giving to him or her the earliest and deepest impressions concerning Divine love, prepare for noblest work in after-years in various fields of holy service.—C.

Vers. 4—8.—*Failure and success in hearing.* The produce of our spiritual fields does not always answer to our hopes or reward our labours; there is much sowing, but little reaping. How do we account for it?

I. THE ACCOUNT OF THE FAILURE. 1. *Inattention* on the part of the hearer. The truth is spoken faithfully, but so little heed is given to it that it is no sooner uttered and heard than it has disappeared from view. Sown on the hard wayside (ver. 5), it does not enter into the soil, and is readily borne away. They who do not know *how to listen* when God speaks to them, need not be surprised if they are of those who are " ever learning, and never coming to a knowledge of the truth." " Give earnest heed " as the Word is being spoken. 2. *Want of reflection.* (Ver. 6.) Many listen with delight, and consider themselves the better for their present gladness. But they do not reflect on what they have heard; there is nothing to nourish the feeble life—no " moisture," no " earth," no thoughtfulness and prayer; and the end is that the emotion that was aroused as the hearer listened withers away. 3. *Incapacity to stand tests.* (Ver. 7.) There may be earnest attention, and this may be followed by some consideration and even prayer; but the root of conviction does not go down far enough to become resolute consecration, and the result is that the " thorns " choke the corn as it is growing. There are two kinds of thorn which are of a deadly influence in the spiritual field— one is that of *worldly cares,* and the other that of *unspiritual pleasure.* These are not evil things in themselves, but, just as the weeds in the field draw up and into themselves the nourishment which should be given to the useful plant, so do these lower anxieties and gratifications absorb the time, the thought, the energy, which should go to the maintenance of the new spiritual life, and, being unfed and unsustained, it languishes and perishes.

II. The conditions of success. What is the good ground? What is the honest and good heart (vers. 8—15)? It is that of: 1. *Sincere inquiry.* The hearer goes to learn what is the will of God concerning him—to " inquire in his temple." The question of his heart is, " Lord, what wilt thou have me to do? " Hence he listens eagerly and continuously. 2. *Devout meditation.* He ponders, he dwells upon, he prays over, the truth he has been receiving. 3. *Intelligent, deliberate dedication.* The man takes all things into his mind that must be taken; he counts the cost; he considers what the service of Christ means, and how much it involves in the way of surrender and of activity, and he solemnly devotes himself to the service, or, as the case may be, to the work of the Lord.

Jesus *cried,* " He that hath ears to hear, let him hear." He spoke that word in a striking, impressive, emphatic voice. He would say to us: 1. Your privilege in having access to the gospel is very great, and as is your privilege so also is your responsibility. 2. Many are the children of opportunity who are not heirs of the kingdom of God; many go into the " house of God " who remain outside the Church of Christ; who hear but do not heed, or who listen but do not ponder and pray, or who pray but do not determine and devote; who at some point or other fall short of the kingdom. It is a sad thing to be " in the way of salvation," and yet to be unsaved. 3. Very blessed are the children of wisdom. When the Word of God takes deep root and brings forth fruit, its fertility is great indeed; the increase may be " an hundredfold " (ver. 8). In the *heart itself* in which it is sown, it may produce all the graces of the Spirit of God; and in the *better life* thus called forth there may shine all the excellences which are in Christ Jesus our Lord and Exemplar; and *from that life* there may flow forth influences for good, of which the number and the nature and the duration only God can tell.—C.

Ver. 16.—*Covered character.* If we have a large object immediately before us in the daytime, and yet are unable to see it, we are driven to the conclusion that, if we are not blind, there must be something opaque between the object and our eye. Now: 1. *There is much of solid goodness in Christian men.* All who name the name of Christ are under bond to depart from all iniquity; their life is a life of holy endeavour after the character of their Lord; they are seeking daily the aid and inspiration of the Divine Spirit; they must be wiser and worthier than those who are living for themselves. 2. This light of Christian character is shining straight before the eyes of unholy men. In the great field of the human world the wheat and the tares grow together. Here we meet together, good and bad, the irreverent and the profane, under the same roof, at the same table and hearth, in the same shop and warehouse. We witness one another's lives. Christian character is near enough to be seen by all. 3. We are sometimes asked to be shown the light of Christian worth. Men say, " Where is this excellency, this supposed superiority of spirit and conduct, these fruits? we should like to see them." What shall we say to this challenge? That they who thus complain do not see what they look for because there is something the matter with their vision, because it is distorted by prejudice? Or shall we say that where no goodness is seen it is because there is none to see; that piety, being popular, is simulated, and they are looking at those who are only pretending to be Christian men, and that godliness is no more accountable for hypocrisy than the good coin is answerable for the counterfeit? We might often make one of these two replies, with right and reason on our side. But that would not meet the case; it would leave the question partially unanswered. The fact is that goodness is often unseen in consequence of *the intervening of some surface faults which hide it from view.* There is—

I. THE COVERING OF RETICENCE. Many a man is right at heart, sound in faith, well fitted by his knowledge and intelligence to render essential service; but he is so reserved, so self-contained, so inaccessible, lives so much in the inner circle of his own familiar friends, that he is far less forcible and influential than he is capable of being;—he is hiding the light of his character under the covering of reserve, instead of setting it on the candlestick of open-heartedness and expressiveness.

II. THE COVERING OF RESENTFULNESS. Other men are warm-hearted, good-natured, diligent, and devoted in every good work, capable of rendering admirable service; but they are quick-tempered, irascible, ready to take offence; so hasty and resentful that they are shunned when they would otherwise be approached;—they hide the light of their character under the vessel of ill temper.

III. THE COVERING OF SELF-ASSERTION. Some men are upright, honourable, zealous, resolute, forcible, well fitted to effect great things, but they hide their light under the bushel of self-assertion; they insist on everything being done in the way they prefer; they make co-operation impossible; they cut their influence in twain by their want of conciliation and concession.

IV. THE COVERING OF DISCOURTESY. There are those who are honest, and even earnest and hardworking Christian men, acting along the lines of holy usefulness; but they cover their character with the vessel of bluntness, or ignorance, or positive rudeness, instead of putting the light of piety and zeal on the candlestick of courtesy.

Now, it has to be remembered that our children and our neighbours, all with whom we have to do, judge of our character not only by its solid and essential elements, but also (and rather) by its superficial features; they will be affected and influenced, not more by that in us which is deep and decisive than by those outside qualities which are visible to them just because they *are outside.* Hence, if we care, as we are bound to do, that our character should be telling on those with whom we are connected, and for whom we are responsible, we shall strive and pray to be not only pure and just and true, but also frank and amiable and courteous. If we would not go through our life with our Christian character covered over and lost by some superficial failing, if we would have it fixed on the candlestick on which it will "give light to all that are in the house,"—we must not only think on the things which are true, honest, just, and pure, but also on those things which are "lovely and of good report."—C.

Ver. 17.—*Revelation—a duty, a fact, a certainty.* These words of our Lord may have been a familiar aphorism of his time, or they may have been a sententious saying of his own, having many applications. Certainly they are significant of many things. They may be regarded as expressing for us—

I. A SACRED DUTY WE ARE CALLED UPON TO DISCHARGE. It is in this sense our Lord used them on the occasion reported by Matthew (x. 25—27). What was then hidden in the minds of the disciples they were to reveal to the world in due time; the truth which the Master was making known to them "in the darkness" they were to "speak in the light." And this duty is of universal obligation. What God reveals to us and what is, at first, hidden in our own soul we are bound to bring forth into the light of day. It may be any kind of truth—medical, agricultural, commercial, economical, moral, or directly and positively religious; whatever we have learned that is of value to the world we have no right to retain for our own private benefit. Truth is common property; it should be open to all men, like the air and the sunshine. When God, in any way, says to us, "Know," he also says, "Teach; pass on to your brethren what I have revealed to you; 'there is nothing secret that shall not be made manifest, nor hid that shall not be known.'"

II. A SERIOUS FACT WE DO WELL TO CONSIDER. Guilt loves secrecy. "Every one that doeth evil hateth the light . . . lest his deeds should be reproved." Men that sin against God and their own conscience would be only too glad to know that their deeds were finally buried and would never reappear. But no man may take this consolation to his soul. Secret things are disclosed; there is an instinctive feeling expressed in the common belief that " murder will out," that flagrant wrong will sooner or later be exposed. We may not say that no crimes have ever been successfully concealed ; but we may safely say that no man, however careful and ingenious he may be in the art of concealing, can be at all sure that his iniquity will not be laid bare. And this will apply to lesser as well as larger evils. Habits of secret drinking, of impurity, of dishonesty, of vindictive passion, will sooner or later betray themselves and bring shame on their victim. Indeed, so closely allied are the body and the spirit, so constantly does the former receive impressions from the latter, that there is no emotion, however deep it may be within the soul, which will not, after a time, reveal itself in the countenance, or write its signature in some way on " the flesh." If illegible to the many, it is still *there*, to be read by those who have eyes to see, and to be seen of God. There is a very true sense in which " *nothing* is secret that shall not be made manifest " even here. But this is more perfectly and strikingly true of the future.

III. A CERTAINTY IN THE FUTURE WE SHALL WISELY ANTICIPATE. There is a " day when God shall judge the secrets of men " (Rom. ii. 16), when he " will bring to light the hidden things of darkness, and will make manifest the counsels of the hearts " (1 Cor. iv. 5). Then shall these words be indeed fulfilled. Then may we know how : 1. This language will prove a terrible prediction; our buried and forgotten iniquities being brought back to us, God " reproving us, and setting them [our sins] before our face " (Ps. l. 21). 2. This warning may be met and modified ; our sins, having been repented of and forgiven, will be buried in those depths of Divine mercy whence they will never be brought back (Ps. ciii. 11, 12; Micah vii. 18, 19). 3. These words may constitute a blessed promise—all acts of pity, of patience, of kindness, of mercy, of magnanimity, of self-sacrifice, reappearing for Divine approval and award. " Then shall every man have praise of God."—C.

Vers. 19—21.—*Christ's one relationship.* How is Christ related to us? And is he related to us in a way other than that in which he was related to men and women during his life on earth? The answer to this question is that there is only one way in which he has been or will be permanently related to mankind. We look at—

I. THE VERY TEMPORARY CHARACTER OF HIS FLESHLY RELATIONSHIP. He was, of course, most intimately associated, in purely human bonds, with " his mother and his brethren." But he gave the clearest intimation that this was only to last during his sojourn on the earth, and that it was not to be relied upon as a source of life even then. 1. He checked his mother in her eagerness at the very first miracle he wrought (John ii. 4). 2. He intimated in the text that his human connections were already merging in those of a higher, a spiritual kind. 3. He disengaged himself, tenderly but decidedly, from his human, filial obligations as he was about to consummate his redemptive work (John xix. 26). 4. He declined the demonstrativeness of his warm-hearted disciple as partaking too much of the fleshly, and intimated that all approach thenceforward must be of a heavenly and spiritual character (John xx. 16, 17). 5. He instructed his apostle to declare that all further knowledge of Jesus Christ must not be " after the flesh," but spiritual (2 Cor. v. 16). 6. He gave no position in his Church to his mother or his brethren because they had been such. They did not derive anything, in their after-relation to him, from the fact of their motherhood or brotherhood ; they stood related to him just as all other souls did, by their reverence, their trust, their love, their service, and by these alone.

II. THE PERMANENT AND INTIMATE CHARACTER OF HIS SPIRITUAL RELATIONS WITH US. " My mother and my brethren are these which hear the Word of God and do it." " Whosoever shall do the will of my Father who is in heaven, the same is my brother, and sister, and mother " (Matt. xii. 50). From these words of truth and grace we gather : 1. That what unites us to Christ is *practical godliness*. It is reverent attention followed by obedient life ; hearing and doing the will of God. It is well to place ourselves where the will of God is made known ; better to listen attentively when it is revealed ; better still to be excited to solemn and earnest feeling concerning it ; but we do not become Christ's, we are not numbered amongst *his own*, until we so hear and heed and feel that we resolve to be and strive to do what we know is his holy will concerning us. We may fail frequently to realize our own intention; we may strive upwards and Godwards with many a stumble on our way ; but if there be an honest and earnest effort towards the good and the true, animated and inspired by the fear and the love of God, then Christ acknowledges us as his, we are citizens of his kingdom. We are something more than that; for we learn from the text : 2. That those who are truly united to Christ are in very close affinity with him. So much are they to him that the nearest and dearest human relationships are called in to express it. Dear as the mother is to her child, as the sister to her brother, so dear are all true and earnest souls to their Divine Lord. With filial, with brotherly love will he watch and guard them, will he provide for their necessities, will he sympathize with them in their sorrows, will he attend their steps, will he secure their lasting interest in the Father's home.—C.

Vers. 22—25.—*Christ the Lord of nature.* We shall find two things concerning the miracles of Jesus Christ—that he never *refused* to put forth his power if by its exercise he could do an act of pure pity and kindness; and that he never *consented* to do so for the mere purpose of display. Hence there is a most marked difference between his "works" and the pretences of the impostor. The perfect suitableness of the occasion and the moral character of the action are the signature of Divinity. Yet it was fitting that the strong desire on the part of the Jews to see a miracle wrought "in the heavens" should, if occasion offered, have at least one fulfilment. And such it certainly had in this stilling of the storm. And in this incident we have—

I. AN IMPRESSIVE ILLUSTRATION OF CHRIST'S DIVINE COMMAND. It would only be right, we may argue, that our Lord should give to his disciples one illustration of his Divine power that would be *exceedingly impressive*, and therefore convincing and permanently effective. There was no more virtue or force in the stilling of the storm on the lake than in the expulsion of the demon on the other side of the water ; to control the elements of nature did not require more Divine power than to control the will of an evil spirit ; *perhaps less.* But the moral effect upon the observer's mind was much greater in the former instance than in the latter. It appealed most influentially to the imagination as well as to the reason. And considering all that these disciples would be called upon to pass through in his cause, remembering the severity of the trial of their faith, it was surely well that, in addition to many other proofs of their Lord's Divinity, they should be able to recall this scene upon the lake, and be assured that he whom the winds and the waves obeyed was the Christ of God indeed.

II. AN ASSURANCE THAT HE IS LORD OF THE CIRCUMSTANCES OF OUR LIFE. As we ply our little bark across the lake of our life, we shall find storm as well as calm, rough adverse winds as well as favourable breezes. It will help us to think that the Divine will which subdued that tempest is the will that is ruling wind and wave beneath every sky ; that Christ is Lord of the circumstances of our life; and that if only we have him on board as our chief Passenger, we may count on his controlling power in the time of danger or of trouble. But we must be sure that Christ *is* with us ; for the promises of gracious guidance and merciful interposition can only be pleaded by those who are loyal to him and to his cause.

III. A PICTURE OF THE PRESENT CHRIST IN THE TRIAL-HOUR OF HIS CHURCH. In that little boat was the Christian Church : if that vessel had sunk, the Church would have perished with it. But the Church that has Christ with it cannot sink. The question of questions, therefore, is this—*Is Christ with us or not?* And the answer to that question will be found, *not in the shape of the vessel*, but in the *character of the crew* ; not in the peculiarity of the ecclesiastical structure, but in the spirit and character of those who compose and who direct the Church. Is his truth, is he himself, preached and taught in our sanctuaries and our schools? Are his principles inculcated in our homes and illustrated in our lives? Is his spirit breathed by us in our intercourse with one another, and with "them that are without"? These are the questions we must answer satisfactorily if we would reply in the affirmative to that one vital question—Is Christ with us or not?

IV. A REMINDER OF THE DIVINE PEACE-BRINGER TO THE HUMAN SOUL. There is something unspeakably grand in a storm in nature; we are affected, awed, subdued, by it.   But in the estimate of Divine wisdom there is something of profounder interest in the unrest and perturbation of a human soul.   Jesus Christ cares more to speak peace to one troubled human heart than to produce the most striking change in the whole face of nature.   There are many sources of spiritual disquietude; but the most constant and the worst of all is *guilt*, the sin with which we have sinned against the Lord and the sense of his condemnation we carry iu our hearts.   It is that which takes the light out of our skies, the joy out of our homes, the beauty and the brightness out of our lives.   The deepest question that wells from the human soul is this—

"Oh ! where shall rest be found—
Rest for the weary soul ? "

And in reply—

" The voice of Jesus sounds o'er land and sea ; "

a voice which has brought and will ever bring peace to the aching, burdened, stricken heart; "Come unto *me*, all ye that labour and are heavy laden, and I will give you rest."—C.

Ver. 23.—*The sleep of Christ.* "As they sailed he fell asleep."   Christ asleep!   Christ asleep in the daytime!   Christ asleep in the storm!   Christ asleep with his disciples in danger and distress!   What have we here?

I. THE SON OF MAN ASLEEP IN THE HOUR OF HIS OWN BODILY WEARINESS.   A hard and long day's work had the Master had that day.   He had thought much, taught much, wrought much ; and each one of these had been laborious and exhausting to One who was what he was and felt as he felt.   He was completely spent with his strenuous and sustained exertion.   And as they sailed he fell asleep ; so fast asleep that, though the winds raged round him and the spray fell upon him, he did not awake.   The incident points to : 1. *The devoted diligence of his life.*   Other things might have accounted for this simple fact of being overcome, but *that* was *the true account of it.*   How laboriously he *must* have worked to do all that he did in the few months at his command! we might well argue ; how devotedly he *did* labour the memoirs of the evangelists assure us. 2. *The generous impulse which he allowed himself* in the conduct of his life.   That life was not without plan, arrangement.   But our Lord permitted himself to be guided by the conduct and attitude of others ; he went back when repelled (ver. 37), he went on when invited (ver. 41).   On this occasion he allowed the importunity of the people to hold him longer in teaching and healing than he would otherwise have remained ; thus he left room in his life for the play of generous impulse.   By all means let us be methodical, laying out our time intelligently and wisely ; but let us leave room also for an unselfish responsiveness in the structure of our life, even as our Lord did. 3. *The thoroughness of his humanity.*   Who but the Son of God could, of his own will and in his own name, command the mighty elements of nature ?   Who but a veritable Son of man could be overcome by weariness, and sleep in the midst of the raging of the storm?   He was one of ourselves—walking wearied him, teaching tired him, healing exhausted him ; he expended himself as he wrought day by day ; his manhood was real and true.

II. THE MASTER ASLEEP IN THE HOUR OF THE DISCIPLES' DANGER AND DISTRESS.   Christ sleeping when the boat was sinking!   It looked like negligence!   "Carest thou not that we perish ? "   That negligence was only apparent ; there was no real danger.   As it was right for him to sleep under such exhaustion, he could with perfect safety commit himself and his cause to the care of the unsleeping Father.   As it was, the greatness of the apparent peril brought about an illustration of Divine power which otherwise they would have missed.   That was not the last time that the Master *seemed* negligent of his own.   To his Church in its storm of terrible persecution, to his people (in their individual lives) in the tempests of temptation or adversity through which they have passed, Christ may often, indeed has often, seemed to be heedless and indifferent.   But he has always been at hand, always ready for action at the right moment.   We have but to make our earnest appeal to him, and if the right time has come for the manifestation of his power—though on this point we may be mistaken (**see John ii. 4; Acts i. 6, 7**)—he will most effectually respond ; he will say to the mightiest forces with which we are in conflict, "Peace, be still!" and there will be "a great calm."—C.

Vers. 38, 39.—*Our return for God's greater kindnesses.* The outcasting of a demon from a man was certainly one of the greater miracles Christ wrought, and the greater benefits he bestowed. It required special power, and it conferred a boon of the highest order. We look at—

I. THE GREATER KINDNESSES WE RECEIVE FROM GOD. It might be argued that all God's mercies are great, inasmuch as (1) coming from his heart, all his kindnesses are loving-kindnesses; and (2) they are all so thoroughly undeserved. God sends us a gift when he might send us a blow, a blessing when we deserve a rebuke (Gen. xxxii. 10). Yet some of God's gifts to us are greater than others, and we may ask which they are that might fairly draw such words as these from Christ concerning them, "how great things God hath done for thee." And it is worthy of remark: 1. *That some of them are little marked by us.* Among these are: (1) Our *being* itself, our intelligent, immortal nature, with all its illimitable capacities. We so gradually awaken to the realization of this, that the boundless value of the gift does not impress us as it should. (2) Our *health*. We accept this as a matter of course, little affected by it until we lose it. (3) Our *kindred*. So does the mantle of parental, filial, fraternal love wrap us round from our infancy, that its beauty and its blessedness do not strike us as they might well do, and we live on for years, failing to appreciate all the mercies which are associated with the one word "home." (4) Our *education*; all those educational influences and privileges which build and shape our mind and character. But it is clear: 2. *That there are special kindnesses we cannot fail to note.* Of these are (1) deliverance from sudden peril, from the railway accident, from death by drowning, etc.; (2) recovery from dangerous sickness; (3) rescue from the grasp of some fell temptation; (4) special Divine influences, those which make the truth of God clear to our understanding, and bring it home to our heart and conscience, thus placing eternal life within our reach.

II. THE RETURN WHICH WE MAKE TO GOD for these greater kindnesses. Jesus Christ bade this man to whom he rendered such signal service return and show his friends what great things he had received; and he did so freely and fully. What is our response to our heavenly Father, our Divine Saviour? 1. What are we *being* to him? What is the measure of our *thought* concerning him who never for one moment forgets us, and who, in so full and deep a sense, "remembered us in our low estate"? of our *feeling* toward him who has spent on us such generous, such self-sacrificing love? of our *service* of him whose we are and to whom we owe everything we are and have? 2. What *testimony* are we bearing to him—what testimony concerning the goodness, the patience, the faithfulness of God are we bearing in *the home* in which we live? Are parents impressing on their children by their whole bearing and demeanour that, in their deliberate judgment, the service of Christ and likeness to Christ are things of immeasurably greater concern to them than the making of money or the gaining of position? Are elder brothers and sisters doing their best to commend the truth they have come to appreciate to the understanding and the affection of those who are younger, and who are taking their cue from them? What testimony are we bearing in the *shop* and the *factory*, to our fellow-workers, to those whom we are employing? What testimony in the *Church*? Are we avowing our faith, our love, our hope, our joy? Are we, who have received greater kindness by far than even this poor demoniac, so acting that as much is ascribed to us in God's book of account as is here recorded of him, that "he published throughout the whole city how great things," etc.?—C.

Vers. 37, 40.—*Jesus Christ: rejection and welcome.* We have in these two passages a very striking contrast; we have in the one a very deliberate and consentaneous dismissal, and in the other a very cordial and unanimous reception of our Lord,—it is illustrative of the treatment he is now receiving at the hands of men.

I. THE REJECTION OF JESUS CHRIST. 1. It may be *deliberate and determined.* In the case of the Gadarenes it was emphatically so. They all came together to seek him and to entreat of him that he would leave their neighbourhood. Their request was unqualified with any condition; it was decisive, absolute. It is not often that men suddenly arrive at the conclusion that they will not have the Son of man to reign over them; but the long postponement of his claims leads on and down to a decisive rejection; at length the mind is fully made up, the soul resolved that it will seek its good elsewhere, that the patient Saviour may knock but he will wait in vain. 2. It may *proceed from motives that are distinctly unworthy.* It was a procedure on the part of these Gadarenes that was simply shameful; they preferred their swine to a Divine Restorer; they would rather keep their property than entertain One who would bring health to their homes and wisdom to their hearts. When men reject Christ, they seldom put before their minds the alternative as it really is in the sight of God; but traced far enough, seen in the light of truth, viewed as it will have to be one day regarded, it is an unholy and an unworthy preference of the human to the Divine, or of the present to the future, or of the fleshly to the spiritual; it is a preference which God condemns, and for making which the soul will one day reproach itself. 3. It may be *only too successful.* It was so here. Jesus did not contest the point; he did not assert his right to go where he pleased and labour where he liked. He yielded to their urgency; "He went up into the ship, and returned back again." Man has a power which may well make him tremble, of resisting and rejecting the Divine; of sending away the messenger and the message which come from God himself; of silencing the voice which speaks from heaven. "How often would I! . . . but ye would not;" "Ye shall not see me until," etc. (ch. xiii.). This is the record of many a soul's history in its relation to Christ. We send away from our hearts and homes the Lord that would heal and save and enrich us.

II. The welcome of Christ. "The people gladly received him" (ver. 40); they welcomed him, "for they were all waiting for him"—were in expectation of his coming. 1. The *spirit in which* it is offered. We cannot suppose that every one then present had the same feeling about our Lord's return. Probably there were those who were influenced by a legitimate but unspiritual curiosity; others by a desire to be healed, or to secure his services as Healer of sickness for their friends; others by a wish to learn more of his wondrous wisdom; others by a reverent thankfulness and a desire to manifest their gratitude to him. Many motives take men into the presence of Christ. Some are low and very near the ground, that may or may not go unblessed. Others are higher and more hopeful. And yet others are certain to be recompensed. They who receive Christ's word in the love of it, who go to him to learn of him and to be healed by him, or who want to be employed by him in his cause, may make sure of a full-handed welcome by him. 2. *Its reception* by our Lord. We know that this is cordial and full of blessing. "If any man . . . open the door, I will come in to him, and will sup with him, and he with me." If, when Jesus Christ offers himself to us as our Teacher and Saviour, we heartily welcome him as such, there will be for us an enrichment of soul surpassing all that we can imagine—reconciliation to the living God; his own blessed and unfailing friendship; a life of sacred service, holy usefulness, and abiding joy; a death of peace and hope; an immortality of glory.—C.

Vers. 45, 46.—*Christ's discriminating notice.* Who can help being interested in the woman who is the subject of this sacred story? She has suffered long; she has wasted her substance in vain endeavours to be healed. Now a new hope springs up in her heart; though excited by this hope she shrinks from the publicity which she fears is necessary for its fulfilment. At last faith and hope triumph over timidity, and she comes into the presence of Christ. We are sympathetically present in that crowd; we see her stealing into it, pushing her way nearer and nearer to the Master, at length timidly stretching out her hand and touching the sacred fringe of his garment. We almost pity this trembling woman, albeit we know that she is healed, as Jesus turns and says, "Who touched me?" We know that it is only by a great spiritual effort that she tells her story to the Master in the presence of the people, and our hearts draw yet nearer in trust and love to that Divine Healer, to our Divine Lord, as we hear him say, "Daughter, be of good comfort: thy faith hath made thee whole; go in peace." The incident may speak to us of—

I. The difference between bodily and real spiritual contact. "There are times when hands touch ours, but only send an icy chill of unsympathizing indifference to the heart; when eyes gaze into ours, but with a glazed look that cannot read our souls; when the multitude throng and press us, but we cannot say, 'Somebody hath touched me,' for the contact has not been between soul and soul, but only between form and form." We are very much thronged in this modern life we live, but we are not very often touched to newness of thought and feeling; and except we live a life of prayer and genuine human sympathy, we must not expect to "touch" other souls so as to quicken and inspire them.

II. THE USELESSNESS OF ANY REMEDY BUT THE GOSPEL FOR OUR SPIRITUAL NEED. This woman in her helplessness is a picture of humanity. It is sick with the worst of all maladies—sin. It is suffering all the wretched consequences of guilt—weariness, restlessness, misery, remorse. It often spends its resources on things which have no healing virtue, and which leave it ill as ever. At length it repairs unto him in whom is no disappointment, in the shelter of whose cross, and in the shadow of whose love, and in the sunshine of whose service is pardon for every sin, comfort for every sorrow, rest for every soul.

III. THE DUTY OF DECLARING WHAT GOD HAS DONE FOR US. That sensitive heart, trying to screen herself from the observation of the crowd, and wishing to come and go unnoticed, was not rejected. Nevertheless, the Lord, by his repeated questioning, constrained her to come forward and acknowledge the blessing she had received. Christ does not wish for an ostentatious piety; he hates all pretence; but he approves and desires a suitable and grateful avowal of our indebtedness to him. Though we come with a trembling heart, yet we are to come and tell our friends what great things the Lord has done for us.

IV. THE DISTINGUISHING NOTICE CHRIST TAKES OF US. "Who touched me?" asked the Lord. "Master, the multitude throng thee; is it wonderful that somebody should touch thee? Anybody might chance to touch thee in such a crowd; can it matter who it was?" urges Peter. "Ah! but that is not enough. Somebody, *some one*, hath touched me; there is one individual, whom I distinguish from the others, that has laid an appealing hand upon me. You see nothing in that touch but an accidental encounter. I see much more than that—the approach of a human mind, the appeal of a human heart, the contact of a human soul with mine." This is the spirit of our Lord's reply. And it conveys to us the important truth that *we are not lost in the crowd*. It is not so true to say, "God loves man," as to say, "God loves *men*." "He tasted death for *every man*;" "He loved *me*, and gave himself for *me*." There are no limitations in the Infinite One. The fact that he controls the universe is no reason why he should not watch the workings of each humblest human soul. The vastness of the range of his observation does not diminish the fulness of his knowledge of every member of his family. Disciples see only a pressing, pushing throng; but the Master singles out the woman who has come to see whether her last chance will fail her. The crowd may hide us from one another, but not from our Lord. God sees us, every one; follows us; pursues us with his watchful and redeeming love; guides us with his hand; leads us into his kingdom. But we must see that our touch is one that will call forth such a response as this. Christ discriminates between the touch of this woman and that of the unmannerly crowd. It is not necessary for us to have a full and perfect understanding of his nature, or even a perfect, unwavering assurance of the success of our appeal. This woman had neither of these. It *is* necessary that we should have what she had—*earnestness of spirit*, and a measure of *genuine faith* in him. Then will he say to us, as to her, "Be of good comfort . . . go in peace."—C.

Ver. 49.—*A needless anxiety concerning Christ.* "Trouble not the Master." This ruler of the synagogue showed a commendable desire not to give useless trouble to the Prophet of Nazareth; he could not expect that his power would extend so far as to raise the dead, and he wished to save him fruitless trouble. Equally creditable was the behaviour of the centurion whose action is recorded in a previous chapter (vii. 6). He felt that the Lord could accomplish in the distance the object of his perhaps toilsome journey, and he sent to say, "Trouble not thyself: for I am not worthy that thou shouldest enter under my roof." It was right that, by considerate kindness, the Son of man should be saved all that those who loved and honoured him could save him from. And the same is true enough to-day of the Son of God. There are—

I. WISE AND RIGHT SOLICITUDES CONCERNING HIM. We are bound to refrain most carefully and conscientiously from troubling the Master by: 1. Doing in his name that which he would disown; *e.g.* carrying on a cruel, though it may be a refined, persecution of those who "follow not with us" in the mode of our worship, or the method of our Christian work. 2. Asking his blessing on that which he disapproves; *e.g.* on the war which is an unrighteous one, on the cause which is an unsound one, on the business which is not conducted on principles he can acknowledge as his own. 3. Misrepresenting him by the spirit which we manifest; instead of breathing the spirit of graciousness and self-sacrifice toward those who are weaker or younger or less cultured or less privileged than ourselves, adopting a tone of haughty superiority, or doing that which "causes them to offend." 4. Failing to approach him in prayer, to seek his aid and his influence, to apply for his redeeming touch. Christ may be much troubled by our distance and neglect; he is not likely to be burdened by our earnest approaches and appeals.

II. NEEDLESS ANXIETIES CONCERNING HIM. 1. *Inviting him to stay too long with us.* The centurion, modestly and properly enough, felt that he was not worthy that Christ should come under his roof. We may feel that also, and especially that we are not worthy that he should make our hearts his home, as he has promised us. But we must not refrain from inviting him to come and to stay with us. We must ask him earnestly to "abide with us from morn till eve," not "to sojourn, but *abide* with us." He will not count that a trouble; he will honour our faith and appreciate our welcome. "Abide in me, and I [will abide] in you." 2. *Going to him too often.* He places no limit on our spiritual approach to him. He says ever to us, "Come unto me;" "Draw nigh unto me;" "Seek ye my face." We shall not burden him by our fellowship; we may grieve him by our absence and by our preference of the society of those who are his enemies. 3. *Asking too much of him*—either for ourselves or for others. There is no magnitude or multitude of sins we may not ask him to forgive; no depth of evil we may not ask him to eradicate; no severity of disease we may not ask him to undertake. The maiden may be dead (text), the cause may be very low, the heart may be very cold, the character may be very corrupt, the life may be very base, the case may seem very hopeless; but do not shrink from "troubling the Master;" his touch "has still its ancient power;" to the lifeless form he can say, "Arise!" and into the cause that seems wholly gone, and the soul that seems utterly lost, he can infuse newness of life. 4. *Doing too much in his cause for him to watch and bless.* The more often we ask him to crown our holy labours with his energizing touch, the better we shall please his yearning and loving spirit.—C.

Vers. 1—21.—*Incidents in evangelistic work.* We have now to contemplate Jesus as fairly loosed from Capernaum as the centre of his mission work, and as making systematically the tour of the province of Galilee. The "beloved physician" gives to us here just such an insight into the material conditions of Christ's evangelistic work as we naturally desire. Let us, then, notice—

I. THE SPIRITUAL AND TEMPORAL SIDES OF OUR LORD'S EVANGELISTIC WORK. (Vers. 1—3.) Twelve men and a number of holy women form Christ's band—a choir, so to speak, of joyful evangelists. The substance of the message was "the glad tidings of the kingdom of God." Christ himself was Preacher. None of the others could enter into the nature of this coming kingdom. But it was to be a kingdom of peace and of joy to all who became members of it. Hence the preaching was "glad tidings." The *spiritual* side of the work was, therefore, joy-inspiring. The temporal conditions of the work are here revealed. Our Lord lived on charity, or, as we should put it, on *love*. Hospitality, especially to every one who professed to be a rabbi, would supply Christ with much; but it could not cover the whole case; consequently, certain women, who had been delivered from demoniacal possessions, and who were correspondingly grateful to their Deliverer, were proud to follow him and minister to him of their substance. Joanna, whose husband seems to have looked after Herod's housekeeping, transfers her attentions to a greater King, and becomes chief minister, we may believe, to her Master's wants. The twelve disciples were candidates for the ministry under training; the holy women were the caterers for the college; and so our Lord, as President, received the help of men and women in their respective spheres.

II. THE ELEMENT OF JUDGMENT IN PARABOLIC TEACHING. Before noticing briefly the parable of the sower, we must ask attention to the change in our Lord's method of ministration. It would seem that up to this time he had preached less figuratively, but as the Pharisees had taken up their position of hostility, it was absolutely necessary for him to exercise what may be called intermediate judgment (cf. Godet, *in loc.*). This was by taking to parabolic teaching. While to a docile and childlike spirit a parable sets truth in its most attractive aspect, to a proud, self-sufficient spirit it veils and hides the truth. It is light or darkness according to our spiritual attitude. Hence the change in the Preacher's method heralded a new stage in his work. The common people would still hear him gladly, but the proud would be kept at a convenient distance through the veiled character of the truth presented in parables.

III. THE PARABLE OF WARNING. (Vers. 4—8, 11—15.) This, according to all the evangelists, was the first parable. It was breaking ground in the delivery of parables. Hence its character as a warning. Its subject is the hearing of the Word. Its warning is that there are three bad ways of hearing as against one good way. These are : 1. *Careless hearing*—represented by wayside seed devoured by the birds before it can fall into the earth and bear any fruit. The devil visits careless hearers, and takes the Word out of their hearts, lest they should believe and be saved. 2. *Rapturous hearing* —represented by seed falling into rocky soil and springing up suddenly, only to wither away. Hence the danger of hearing with rapture and resting in the rapture. It is the religion of feeling, of happy times, and such superficialities. Something deeper is needed than this. 3. *Careworn and preoccupied hearing*—represented by seed falling into soil that is not cleansed of roots and thorns, and where the seed is choked. We cannot hear to advantage if we put anything before the Word. Unless it is put before worldly concerns, there will not be much fruit. 4. *Honest and good-hearted hearing*—represented by the seed falling into good and cleansed ground. In this case there is fruit-bearing, in some cases up to an hundredfold. Hence the warning voice, "He that hath ears to hear, let him hear." Unless the multitude hearing Jesus, unless in particular the disciples, took the Word of God ministered by Jesus patiently and honestly into their consideration, they could not bring forth fruit unto perfection.

IV. THE APPLICATION TO THE TWELVE. (Vers. 16—18.) The disciples had received Jesus' explanation of the first parable. And now he further applies it to their case. They are intended, he tells them, to be lights in the world ; and he has no intention of putting them under a bushel or bed, where the light would be lost and useless, but on a candlestick to illuminate all who enter the house. In this beautiful and figurative way our Lord indicates the position he means to give them in his Church. Consequently, they must remember that every secret thing is on its way to manifestation (ver. 17), and so their lives, no matter how secret and apparently insignificant, are *public* lives. By this thought all hearing will be intensified with a new sense of responsibility. Besides, he tells them that the law of *capital* obtains in hearing as well as in everything else. This is the law by which the person, who has something to start with, gets something more. For example, if we bring to the contemplation of the truth a "good and honest heart," then its goodness and honesty will be intensified and increased by the truth ; whereas, if we bring a vacant heart, an inattentive mind, then our heart will be still more vacant, and our mind still more inattentive. We lose power by indifferent hearing, just as we gain power by attentive and honest hearing. This was a most important lesson for the candidates about him. Doubtless they profited by it.

V. BLOOD-RELATIONSHIP VERSUS SPIRITUAL RELATIONSHIP. (Vers. 19—21.) We learn from the parallel passages that this incident occurred in consequence of our Lord's enthusiasm. His relatives thought him mad, and that he ought to be put under restraint. His reply to their message is most significant. As Gess says, " He draws his true disciples the more closely around him as the hostility of his own relatives increases, and calls *them* his family." [1] We have thus, as Saurin puts it, the family of Jesus Christ according to the flesh contrasted with the family of Jesus Christ according to the Spirit. The spiritual relationship is put before the blood-relationship, other things being equal.[2] It is not that Jesus loved his brothers and mother less, but that he regarded the Father's will and those who obeyed it as more to him than they can be. His conduct on this occasion most likely conduced to the conversion of his kindred to believe upon him. It enabled them to see exactly the principle of his work.

---

[1] 'Christi Selbstzeugniss,' s. 48.
[2] Cf. Saurin's 'Sermons,' tome vi. pp. 227—264.

And in this loyalty to members of God's family we must follow our Lord. We must not allow others to usurp their rights under any pretence of relationship or authority. —R. M. E.

Vers. 22—56.—*A group of miracles.* The mother and brethren of Jesus had tried in vain to interfere with the important work in which he was engaged; he clung to his disciples as the real members of his Father's family. And so we find his career as a merciful Miracle-worker continuing. We have here a group of notable miracles; it was, as Godet suggests, the culmination of his miraculous work. Nature, human nature, and death yield to his authority in their order.

I. SAFETY IN THE SOCIETY OF JESUS. (Vers. 22—25.) The disciples and Jesus had embarked to visit the country of the Gadarenes. His object in doing so, as we shall presently see, was to rescue from diabolical possession a single soul. But to rescue this soul they had all to pass through storms in crossing. It was surely worth all the risk they ran! The weary Saviour fell asleep soon after embarking, and it was while he was sleeping the storm arose in nature, and the storm of fear in the souls of the disciples. It argued little faith on their part to suppose that they were in danger when beside them is the sleeping Christ. Yet so it was. Jesus may lead his people into danger, but he always shares it with them, and leads them in due time out of it. No sooner do they appeal to him to save them from perishing, than he arises, rebukes the wind and the wave, so that, contrary to custom, there is an immediate calm; and then proceeds to rebuke the storm within their souls, and make all these also to be peace. In this way our Lord showed his sovereignty over nature, and his sovereignty over man. He can rebuke "the noise of their seas, the noise of their waves, and the tumult of the people" (Ps. lxv. 7). No wonder that the strangers who were in the boat with the disciples were astonished at One who could command wind and wave, and they obeyed him!

II. JESUS THE MINISTER TO MINDS DISEASED. (Vers. 26—40.) In the greatest peace the disciples and their Master approached the shore. But here a more terrible storm confronted him—the mania of the poor possessed one. "The beloved physician," who writes this Gospel, brings out the characteristics of the mania as a physician would.[1] No sooner does the case present itself to Jesus, than he commands the devil to depart from him. No protest on the part of the unclean tenant avails; the spirit and his companions are compelled to prepare for departure. They bargain hard not to be sent "into the abyss" (εἰς τὴν ἄβυσσον), where their final doom awaits them, and, as an alternative, ask to be permitted to enter into an adjoining herd of swine. This association of evil spirits with animals is illustrated in the Edenic temptation, and it may account for the reign of terror in the geologic times.[2] The possession of the animals may be different from that of a moral being like man, as Godet suggests; yet it shows surely the sensualism into which evil spirits can descend. The prodigal son only *desired* to satisfy himself with the swinish life; but these demons actually made the experiment (cf. ch. xv. 16). But now the swine, reinforced by the devils, rush madly onwards to the sea, and perish in the waters. The result is that one human being is delivered from his mania, while a herd of swine are sacrificed. If such an alternative is presented, there can be no doubt as to the decision. Better that all the swine in the world should perish, if as the result a single human soul is delivered from his mental disease. Hence the wretched souls, who came from the city and lamented the loss of the swine instead of rejoicing in the cure of the demoniac, show thereby that they deserved the judgment which had overtaken them. Jesus can "minister to minds diseased;" he can bring the maniac to his right mind again; and he can cure us of the insanity of sin and have us sitting clothed at his feet and anxious to be with him evermore. When, besides, the Gadarenes desire his departure, he can make arrangements for witness-bearing, so that when he returns after a time, the unwilling people shall be found to have renounced their unwillingness and to gladly welcome him. So may we all witness among our friends to the power of our Lord.

III. THE TOUCH OF FAITH. (Vers. 43—48.) We have next to notice the healing of the

---

[1] Cf. Hobart's 'Medical Language of St. Luke,' pp. 13, 14; also Trench on 'The Miracles,' p. 171, etc.

[2] Cf. Bersier's 'La Solidarité,' p. 119.

woman with the issue of blood. This was the solitary miracle where faith anticipates our Lord's consent, and finds healing through the touch of his garment. Having presented herself so often to the physicians, she in this case refuses to obtrude upon his notice, but thinks she will escape in the crowd. But our Lord, perceiving that from his sacred Person healing power had flowed, inquires for the patient, who in due season comes and confesses all. But she has been brought before him that he might convey to her the lesson that it was her faith, and not a mere physical touch, which had saved her. That is to say, the process was moral, and not merely physical. And surely this case of the issue of blood is to represent certain aspects of sin. It is a drain upon the moral system which man cannot staunch. But once we look to Jesus by faith and touch the hem of his garment, we are instantly healed, and power begins again to rise within us. We ought not to let our vital power be undermined when such a Saviour is at hand to heal us!

IV. THE AWAKENING OF THE DEAD. (Vers. 41, 42, 49—56.) This case of resurrection-power presents Jesus in the culmination of his miraculous work. The command of nature and of human nature is important, but still more magnificent is the command of death, the power to enter into the gloomy realm, and there assert one's authority. This is what Jesus does. He is humbly asked by Jairus to come to his dying daughter. He finds that he has to face the little daughter already dead. The father, ready to despair, is told to " believe only, and she shall be made whole." He believed, and lo ! he found in Jesus One who could awake the dead ! The resurrection is witnessed by the parents and three disciples—chosen witnesses. And after she is raised, he gives directions that she should be fed, and then that they should be silent about the miracle. He did not desire to be overwhelmed by the miraculous part of his work, but that he might be able to give a due proportion of his attention to teaching.[1] Similarly may each of us experience Christ's resurrection-power in our souls now, and in our bodies afterwards.—R. M. E.

EXPOSITION.

CHAPTER IX.

Vers. 1—6.—*The Master sends out the twelve on a mission.*

Ver. 1.—**Then he called his twelve disciples together.** The Galilee ministry was just over ; *outwardly* it had been a triumphant success; vast crowds had been gathered together. The Master was generally welcomed with a positive enthusiasm ; the people heard him gladly. Here and there were visible, as in the cases of the woman who touched him and the synagogue ruler who prayed him to heal his little daughter, just related (ch. viii.), conspicuous examples of a strange or mighty faith; but the success, the Master knew too well, was only on the surface. The crowds who to-day shouted "Hosanna !" and greeted his appearance among them with joy, on the morrow would fall away from him, and on the day following would reappear with the shout " Crucify him !" It was especially to warn his Church in coming ages of this sure result of all earnest devoted preaching and teaching, that he spoke that saddest of parables, " the sower " (ch. viii.). But before he finally brought this Galilæan ministry to a close, he would gather in some few wavering souls,

whose hearts he knew were trembling in the balance between the choice of life and good, and death and evil. To help these he sent out this last mission. The word rendered " called together " indicates a solemn gathering. **And gave them power,** etc. This and the further detail of the next verse (2) roughly describe the work he intended them to do, and the means bestowed on them for its accomplishment. Very extraordinary powers were conferred on them— powers evidently intended to terminate with the short mission on which he now despatched them.

Ver. 2.—**And to heal the sick.** St. Mark (vi. 13), in his brief notice of this mission of the twelve, mentions the special instrument of their power over sickness—*the twelve anointed the sick with oil, and healed them.* It is probable that the early Christian custom alluded to by St. James (v. 14), of anointing the sick with oil, arose from our Lord's direction to his apostles on the occasion of this mission. The practice was continued, or possibly was revived, long after the original power connected with it had ceased to exist. It still survives in the Roman Catholic Church in the sacrament of extreme unction, which, singularly enough,

---

[1] Cf. Macmillan's ' Our Lord's Three Raisings from the Dead,' pp. 3—72.

is administered when all hope of the patient's recovery from the sickness is over. Anointing the sick with oil was a favourite practice among the ancient Jews (see Isa. i. 6 and ch. x. 34). It was to be used by the twelve as an ordinary medicine, possessing, however, in their hands an extraordinary effect, and was to be, during this mission, the visible medium through which the Divine influence and power to heal took effect. We never read of Jesus in *his* miracles using oil; his usual practice seems to have been simply to have used words. At times he touched the sufferer; on one occasion only we read how he mixed some clay with which he anointed the sightless eyes.

Ver. 3.—**Take nothing for your journey.** Dr. Farrar well sums up the various directions of the Master to these his first missionaries: "The general spirit of the instructions merely is, 'Go forth in the simplest, humblest manner, with no hindrances to your movements, and in perfect faith;' and this, as history shows, has always been the method of the most successful missions. At the same time, we must remember that the *wants* of the twelve were very small, and were secured by the free open hospitality of the East."

Ver. 4.—**And whatsoever house ye enter into, there abide, and thence depart.** On entering any new place they were to select, after due and careful inquiry (Matt. x. 11), a family likely and able to assist them in their evangelistic work. This "house" they were to endeavour to make the centre of their efforts in that locality. This rule we find continued in the early years of Christianity. In the history of the first Churches, certain "houses" in the different cities were evidently the centres of the mission work there. We gather this from such expressions in St. Paul's letters as "*the Church which is in his house*" (comp., too, Acts xvi. 40, where the house of Lydia was evidently the head-quarters of all missionary work in Philippi and its neighbourhood).

Ver. 5.—**And whosoever will not receive you, when ye go out of that city, shake off the very dust from your feet for a testimony against them.** It was the custom of the Jews when they returned from foreign (Gentile) lands, as they crossed the frontiers of the Holy Land, to shake the dust from off their feet. This was an act symbolizing that they had broken, now on their return to their own land, all communion with Gentile peoples which a residence among them had necessitated for a season. The bitter hatred and loathing of the Jews, after their return from the Captivity, for all Gentile races can only be understood by the student of the Talmud. So comprehensive and perfect a hatred, enduring, too, for centuries, has never been witnessed in the case of any other peoples. This accounts in great measure for the retaliative persecution which more or less has been carried on all through the Christian era against this marvellous race. In our day—the day of a liberalism possibly exaggerated and unreal —in many parts of Europe the untrained sense of the *masses* strangely revolts against this spirit of toleration; and wild excesses, massacres, and bitter persecution—the *Judenhetz*, hatred of the Jews in Germany and in Russia—are among the curious results of the liberality and universal toleration of the time.

Vers. 7—9.—*Herod's terror.*

Ver. 7.—**Now Herod the tetrarch heard of all that was done by him.** This was Herod Antipas; he was a son of Herod the Great; his mother's name was Malthace. After his father's death he became tetrarch or prince-ruler of Galilee, Peræa, and of a fourth part of the Roman province of Syria. His first wife was daughter of Aretas, a famous Arabian sheik spoken of by St. Paul as "king of the Damascenes" (2 Cor. xi. 32). This princess he divorced, and contracted a marriage at once incestuous and adulterous with his niece Herodias, the beautiful wife of his half-brother Philip. Philip was not a sovereign prince, and it was probably from motives of ambition that she deserted Philip for the powerful tetrarch Herod Antipas. It was owing to his fearless remonstrances against this wicked marriage that John the Baptist incurred the enmity of Herodias, who was only satisfied with the head of the daring preacher who presumed to attack her brilliant wicked life. What Herod now heard was the report of the widespread interest suddenly aroused by the mission of the twelve—a mission, we know, supported by miraculous powers, following close upon the Galilæan ministry of the Lord, which, as far as regarded the numbers who thronged his meetings, and the outward interest his words and works excited, had been so successful. Rumours of all this at last reached the court circle, wrapped up in its own selfish and often wanton pleasures and false excitement. **Because that it was said of some, that John was risen from the dead.** Herod Antipas was probably inclined to the Sadducee creed, which believed in neither angel nor spirit. But Sadduceeism and the easy doctrines of Epicurus, which no doubt found favour in the luxurious palace of Herod, are but a flimsy protection at best against the ghastly reminiscences and the weird forebodings of a guilty conscience. The murder of John had been, Herod knew, strongly condemned by the public voice.

He would not believe it was his old monitor risen, but yet the prince was anxious and perturbed in his mind. The murmur that the great prophet was Elias (Elijah) disquieted him, too. Herod could not help recalling to his mind the lifelong combat of that great and austere servant of God against another wicked sovereign and his queen, Ahab and Jezebel, whose great crime was that *they*, too, had slain the Lord's prophets. That history, Herod felt, had to some extent been reproduced by himself and Herodias. There was a rooted expectation among the Jews that Elijah would reappear again on earth, and that his appearance would herald the advent of the Messiah. There are numberless references in the Talmud to this looked-for return of the famous Elijah.

Ver. 8.—**One of the old prophets.** Jeremiah and also Isaiah, though to a lesser degree than Elijah, were looked for as heralds of the coming Messiah (see 2 Esdr. ii. 10, 18, and 2 Macc. ii. 4—8; xv. 13—16). It was expected that Jeremiah would reveal the hiding-place of the long-lost ark and of the Urim.

Ver. 9.—**And he desired to see him;** that is, Jesus. The desire of Herod was gratified, but not then. He saw him the day of the Crucifixion, when Pilate sent him to Herod for judgment; but the tetrarch, weak and wicked though he was, declined the responsibility of shedding *that blood*, so he sent him back to the Roman governor. Here, in SS. Matthew and Mark, follows the dramatic and vivid account of the death of John the Baptist. St. Luke probably omits it, as his Gospel, or rather Paul's, was derived from what they heard from eye-witnesses and hearers of the Lord. As regards SS. Matthew and Mark, the latter of whom was probably simply the amanuensis of St. Peter, the awful event was woven into their life's story. It was most natural that, in their public preaching and teaching, they should make constant mention of the tragedy which so personally affected Jesus and his little company. St. Luke and his master, Paul, on the other hand, who were not *personally* present with the Lord when these events took place, would be likely to confine their memoirs as closely as possible to those circumstances in which Jesus alone occupied the prominent place.

Vers. 10—17.—*The Lord feeds the five thousand.*

Ver. 10.—**And the apostles, when they were returned, told him all that they had done. And he took them, and went aside privately into a desert place belonging to the city called Bethsaida.** This, perhaps the most famous and oftenest told of the Lord's miracles, was worked directly after the return of the twelve from their mission. He and they were no doubt very weary of the crowds which continually now thronged them. The excitement of the multitude about Jesus was now at its height. Directly after the discourse at Capernaum (John vi.), which immediately followed the great miracle we are about to discuss, the popular enthusiasm began to wane. Intensely weary, dispirited too at the story of the murder of John the Baptist, which was told the Master by the disciples and the friends of John on their return from their mission, Jesus determined for a brief space to withdraw himself from the public gaze. He crossed the Lake of Gennesaret in one of his friends' fishing-boats to a town lately identified by modern research as Bethsaïda Julias, a small city recently beautified by Herod Philip, and named Bethsaïda Julias, after the daughter of Augustus. Bethsaïda, "house of fish," was a name attached evidently to several of these fishing centres on the shores of the lake. Many of the multitude of whom we read subsequently in the account of the miracle, had watched his departure in the boat for the neighbourhood of Bethsaïda Julias, and had gone on foot round the head of the lake to join the popular Teacher again. The distance round the north end of the lake from the point of embarkation, most likely Capernaum, to Bethsaïda Julias is not very considerable. The crowd which soon joined him in retirement would be considerably swelled by many of the Passover pilgrims just arrived at Capernaum on their way to Jerusalem to keep the feast. These would be anxious, too, to see and to hear the great Galilæan Prophet, whose name just then was in every mouth. Not very far from Bethsaïda Julias there is a secluded plain, *El Batihah;* thither Jesus no doubt went after leaving his fishing-boat, purposing to spend some time in perfect rest. Soon, however, the usually quiet plain becomes populous with the crowds following after the Galilæan Master. Though longing intensely for repose so necessary for himself and his disciples, he at once, moved by the eagerness of the multitude to hear and see him again, gives them his usual loving welcome, and begins in his old fashion to teach them many things, and to heal their sick.

Ver. 12.—**And when the day began to wear away, then came the twelve, and said unto him, Send the multitude away, that they may go into the towns and country round about, and lodge, and get victuals: for we are here in a desert place.** Simple consideration for the crowds, among whom we know were women and children, probably dictated this remark of the twelve, though it has been with some ingenuity suggested that the advice of the disciples was owing to their fear that, as darkness would soon creep over the scene, some calamity might happen which would give a fresh handle against Jesus to his many enemies.

Ver. 13.—**But he said unto them, Give ye them to eat.** Godet here beautifully observes that this reply, and the great miracle that followed, was the result of a loving thought of the Redeemer. "John has disclosed it to us (vi. 4). It was the time of the Passover. He could not visit Jerusalem with his disciples, owing to the virulent hatred of which he had become the object. In this unexpected gathering, resembling that of the nation at Jerusalem, he discerns a signal from on high, and determines to celebrate a feast in the desert as a compensation for the Passover Feast." **We have no more but five loaves and two fishes; except we should go and buy meat for all this people.** The main lines of this story are the same in each of the four accounts which we possess of this miracle; but each of the four evangelists supplies some little detail wanting in the others. It is clear that there was no original written tradition from which they all copied. St. John tells us it was a little boy who had this small, rough provision. The boy probably was in attendance on the apostles, and this was no doubt the little stock of food they had provided for their own frugal meal. The barley loaves were the ordinary food of the poorest in Palestine, and the two fish were dried, as was the common custom of the country; and such dried fish was usually eaten with the bread.

Ver. 14.—**They were about five thousand men.** St. Matthew adds, "besides women and children." The multitude generally had come from a considerable distance, we know; there would not be, comparatively speaking, many women and children among them. These were grouped together apart, and, of course, fed, but were not counted among the five thousand. **And he said to his disciples, Make them sit down by fifties in a company.** "Jesus has no sooner ascertained that there are five loaves and two fishes, than he is satisfied. He commands them to make the multitude sit down. Just as though he had said, 'I have what I want; the meal is ready; let them be seated!' But he takes care that his banquet shall be conducted with an order worthy of the God who gives it. Everything must be calm and solemn; it is a kind of Passover meal. By the help of the apostles, he seats his guests in rows of fifty each (St. Matthew), or in double rows of fifty, by hundreds (Mark). This orderly arrangement allowed of the guests being easily counted. St. Mark describes

in a dramatic manner the striking spectacle presented by these regularly formed companies, each consisting of two equal ranks, and all arranged upon the slope of the hill. The pastures at that time were in all their spring glory. SS. John and Mark both bring forward the beauty of this natural carpet. 'Much grass' (St. John); 'on the green grass' (St. Mark)" (Godet). St. Mark's vivid picturesque details show the observant eye-witness. The words rendered "in ranks" ("they sat down in ranks") literally mean they were like flower-beds set in the green grass. The bright-coloured Eastern robes of these men, as they sat in long rows, suggested the happy comparison.

Ver. 16.—**Then he took the five loaves and the two fishes, and looking up to heaven, he blessed them, and brake, and gave to the disciples to set before the multitude.** The blessing was the usual introduction of a pious Jewish family to a meal. It was pronounced by the head of the household. An ordinary formula was, "May God, the Ever-blessed One, bless what he has given us!" The Jewish barley loaves were broad, thin cakes; these were usually *broken*, not cut—hence the expression, "and brake." In SS. Mark and Luke the tense of the verb rendered "gave," in the original Greek, is an imperfect, and signifies, "he gave, and kept on giving." This supplies a hint as to the way of working the miracle. Each disciple kept coming to him for a fresh supply of bread. It was, however, as it has been well said, a miracle of the highest order, one of creative power, and is to us inconceivable. The evangelists make no attempt to explain it. They evidently did not care to ask. They beheld it, and related it to us just as they saw it in its simple grandeur. Neither disciples nor crowds seem at first to have grasped the stupendous nature of the act. St. John tells us of its effect on the crowds, who, when they came to see what had been done, wished to take him by force and make him king. For a brief space they were convinced that in the poor Galilee Rabbi they had found King Messiah—none but he could have done this great thing. They were right.

Ver. 17.—**And they did eat, and were all filled: and there was taken up of fragments that remained to them, twelve baskets.** A very impressive lesson from the Creator himself against waste or extravagance. St. John expressly tells us that this order to gather up the fragments of their meal emanated from Jesus himself. Carefulness, thrift, and economy in small things as in great, form part of the teaching of the loving Master. From such passages as Mark vi. 37 and John xiii. 29, it seems probable that the disciples, acting under their Master's direction, were in the habit of distributing, out of their comparative abundance, food to those persons in the villages who were poorer than themselves. It was, no doubt, for some such hallowed object as this that the careful collection of the fragments which filled twelve baskets was made. The "baskets" (*cophinus*) were usually carried by travelling Jews to keep their food from contracting Levitical pollution in Gentile places. Juvenal, in a well-known passage ('Sat.,' iii. 14), writes of the Jews travelling about Italy with no baggage save a little bundle of hay to serve as a pillow, and this cophinus, or basket, for their food. So abundant had been the provision created by Jesus, that the fragments collected far exceeded the original stock of food which the disciples gave to Jesus to bless, to break, and to distribute among the five thousand and upward who were fed that memorable afternoon. This miracle is the only one in the entire Galilæan ministry which is told by all the four evangelists. It evidently had a very prominent place in the teaching of the first days. Rationalizing interpretation in the case of this miracle is singularly at fault. After eighteen centuries of unremitting hostility to the teaching of Jesus Christ, not even a plausible explanation of this miraculous multiplication of the loaves and fishes has been found by adverse critics. In our own days, Renan, following the ancient interpretation of Paulus, simply suggests that the multitudes were fed by materials provided by themselves. "Every one took his little store of provision from his wallet; they lived on very little"—an explanation, as it has been happily termed, "ludicrously inadequate."

After the relation of the great miracle of feeding the five thousand, St. Luke omits in his Gospel a variety of incidents and several discourses told at greater or lesser length by the other evangelists. For instance, the reverential amazement of the people when the nature of the stupendous miracle in connection with the creation of the loaves and fishes flashed upon them, —they wished to recognize him as King Messiah; the walking on the sea; the long and important discourse on the true Bread at Capernaum, the text of which was the late great miracle of the loaves; the journey among the heathen as far as Tyre and Sidon; the meeting with the Syrophœnician woman; the feeding of the four thousand, etc. These incidents are related in Matt. xiv.—xvi. 12; Mark vi. 45— viii. 30; John vi. No commentator has

satisfactorily explained the reason of this omission of important portions of our Lord's public ministry. The reason for St. Luke's action here probably will never be guessed. We must, however, in all theories which we may form of the composition of these Gospels, never lose sight of this fact, that while SS. Matthew and Peter (Mark) were eyewitnesses of the events of the life, St. Luke, and his master, Paul, simply reproduced what they had heard or read. We may, therefore, suppose that St. Luke exercised larger discretionary powers in dealing with materials derived from others than the other two, who desired, no doubt, to reproduce a fairly general summary of their Divine Master's acts. On such a theory of composition, a gap in the story like the one we are now alluding to, in the more eclectic Gospel of St. Luke, would seem scarcely possible in the first two Gospels. We, of course, make no allusion here to the Fourth Gospel; the whole plan and design of St. John was different to that upon which the first three were modelled.

Vers. 18—27.—*Jesus' question to his own: Who did they think he was? He tells them of a suffering Messiah, and describes the lot of his own true followers.*

Ver. 18.—**And it came to pass, as he was alone praying, his disciples were with him: and he asked them, saying, Whom say the people that I am?** With these abrupt words, St. Luke changes for his readers the time and scene. Since the miracle of feeding the five thousand at Bethsaïda Julias, Jesus had preached at Capernaum the famous sermon on the "Bread of life" (reported in John vi.); he had wandered to the north-east as far as the maritime cities of Tyre and Sidon; had returned again to the Decapolis region for a brief sojourn; and then once more had turned his footsteps north; and it was in the extreme confines of the Holy Land, in the neighbourhood of Cæsarea Philippi, and close to the great fountain, the source of the sacred Jordan, at the foot of the southern ridge of Hermon, where he put the momentous question here chronicled, to his listening disciples. Much had happened since the five thousand were fed. The defection which the Master had foreseen when he commenced his parable-teaching with the sad story of the "sower," had begun. After the great Capernaum sermon (John vi.), many had fallen away from him; the enthusiasm for his words was rapidly waning; the end was already in sight. "Well," he asks his own, "what are men saying about *me*? Whom do they think that I am?"

Ver. 19.—**They answering said, John the Baptist; but some say, Elias; and others say, that one of the old prophets is risen again.** It was a strange answer, this report of the popular belief concerning Jesus. There had been for a long period among the people expectations more or less defined, that certain of the great national heroes were to reappear again to take up their incomplete work, and to play the part in Israel, of heralds of the looked-for glorious King Messiah. The popular belief respecting Jesus was that he was one of these. Some thought of Elijah. The two miracles of creating the loaves and fishes for a great famishing crowd especially suggested this idea. There was a shadowy, but not an unreal resemblance here to the well-remembered miracle of Elijah, worked for the Sarepta widow and her son, with the cruse of oil and the barrel of meal which failed not (1 Kings xvii. 14). The words of Malachi (iv. 5) pointed in the same direction. The image of the recently murdered Baptist was present with some. Herod's words, already commented on, point to this, perhaps, widespread belief. Jeremiah would be a likely instance of "one of the old prophets." Tradition had already asserted that the spirit of that great one had passed into Zechariah; surely another similar transmigration was possible. Jeremiah, popular tradition said, had safely hidden the ark and the tabernacle and the altar of incense somewhere in the mountain where Moses died by the "kiss of God." Already had he appeared to the brave and patriotic Judas Maccabæus in a vision as a man grey-haired and exceeding glorious, as one praying for the people as their guardian-prophet, and had given the gallant Maccabæan hero a golden sword from God. It was one of these old heroic forms, so loved of Israel, once more in the flesh, that the people believed Jesus to be.

Ver. 20.—**But whom say ye that I am? Peter answering said, The Christ of God.** And the Master listened, apparently without comment, to this reply, which told him what the people said of him, and then went on, "But you, my disciples, who have been ever with *me*, what say, what think *you* about *me*?" Peter, as the representative of the others in that little chosen company, answers, "*We* believe that thou art more than any prophet or national hero or forerunner of the Messiah; *we* think that thou art the Messiah himself." Dr. Morrison very beautifully pictures the disciples' state of mind at this juncture. "No doubt the true light on the subject had often gleamed through the darkness of their minds (see

John i. 29, 33, 34, 41, 45, 49, etc.). But, though gleam succeeded gleam, in flashes that revealed the Illimitable, the darkness would ever, more or less, close in again. They could not altogether help it. They were witnesses of a 'humiliation' which they could not reconcile with the notions they had inherited in reference to the power and pomp of the Messiah. And yet it was evident that he was entirely unlike all other rabbis. He was the Master of masters, and a mystery over and above. An inner lustre was continually breaking through. It was glorious; it was unique. His character was transcendently noble and pure. He had not, moreover, obtruded self-assertions on them. He had left them, in a great measure, to observe for themselves; and they *had been* observing." It was, indeed, on the part of these feeble disciples a pure and lofty expression of the effect produced on their hearts by Jesus Christ's teaching. But though these men, afterwards so great, had attained to this grand conception of their adored Master, though they alone, among the crowds, through the sad coloured veil of his low estate, could see shining the glory of Divinity, yet *they* could not grasp yet the conception of a suffering Messiah, and in spite of all the teaching of the Master, the cross and the Passion made them unbelievers again. It needed the Resurrection to complete the education of faith.

Ver. 21.—**And he straitly charged them, and commanded them to tell no man that thing.** It would have been no hard task for the disciples to have gone about with an expression of their earnest conviction that the great Prophet was indeed the long looked-for King Messiah, and thus to have raised the excitable crowds to any wild pitch of enthusiasm. It was only a very short time back that, moved by the miracle of the loaves, the multitudes wished to crown him King by force. *That* was not the kind of homage Jesus sought; besides which, any such enthusiasm thus evoked would quickly have died away, and a hostile reaction would have set in when the high hopes excited by the idea of King Messiah were contradicted by the life of suffering and self-denial which Jesus sternly set himself to live through to its bitter end. This life he sketched out for them in the severe language of the next verse.

Ver. 22.—**Saying, The Son of man must suffer many things, and be rejected of the elders and chief priests and scribes, and be slain, and be raised the third day.** "See how," as Riggenbach, quoted by Godet, says ('Vie de Jésus,' p. 318), "Jesus was obliged, in the very moment of self-revelation, to veil himself, when he had lighted the fire to cover it again." This dark and terrible prediction came upon the disciples evidently as something new. It was their Master's reply to their confession of faith in him. It said in other words, " You are right in your conception of me and my work. I am the promised King Messiah; but this part of my reign will be made up of affliction and mourning and woe. The great council of the people will reject me, and I shall only enter into my grand Messianic kingdom through the gate of suffering and of death. But do you, my own, be of good cheer. Three days after that death I shall rise again." The enumeration of "elders, chief priests, and scribes" is simply a popular way of describing the great council of the Jewish nation, the Sanhedrin, which was composed of these three important and influential sections of the people.

Ver. 23.—**And he said to them all, If any man will come after me, let him deny himself, and take up his cross daily, and follow me.** Before sketching out the life which the true disciples of a suffering King Messiah must lead on earth, our Lord seems to have given notice of one of his public discourses. Even though his great popularity was now on the wane, to the last he was evidently listened to by crowds, if not with enthusiasm, certainly with eager and impatient curiosity. The sermon, of which we have the outline in the next five verses, and the subject-matter of which was, " No cross, no crown," was preached evidently to the masses. This is plain from the opening words of ver. 23. The sermon was evidently a hard saying, and, no doubt, gave bitter offence to many of the hearers. "If any man *will*," that is, *wishes* to, " come after me, to follow me where I am going" (Jesus was going to his kingdom), " let that man be prepared to give up earthly ease and comfort, and be ready to bear the sufferings which will be sure to fall on him if he struggle after holiness." This readiness to give up ease, this willingness to bear suffering, will be a matter, they must remember, of everyday experience. The terrible simile with which the Lord pressed his stern lesson home was, of course, suggested to him by the clear view he had of the fearful end of his own earthly life—an end then so near at hand, though the disciples guessed it not. *The cross* was no unknown image to the Jews who that day listened to the Master. The gloomy procession of robbers and of rebels against Rome, each condemned one bearing to the place of death the cross on which he was to suffer, was a sadly familiar image then in their unhappy land.

Ver. 24.—**For whosoever will save his life shall lose it: but whosoever will lose his life for my sake, the same shall save it.** The Greek word here rendered "life"

signifies the natural animal life, of which the main interests are centred in the earth. If a man grasp at this shadowy, quickly passing earthly life, he will assuredly lose the substantial enduring heaven-life. If, on the other hand, he consents, "for my sake," to sacrifice this quickly fading life of earth, he shall surely find it again in heaven, no longer quickly fading, but a life fadeless, eternal, a life infinitely higher than the one he has for righteousness' sake consented to lose here. The same beautiful and comforting truth we find in that fragment, as it is supposed, of a very early Christian hymn, woven into the tapestry of St. Paul's Second Epistle to Timothy—

" If we be dead with him,
 We shall also live with him:
 If we suffer,
 We shall also reign."
    (2 Tim. ii. 11, 12.)

Ver. 25.—**For what is a man advantaged, if he gain the whole world, and lose himself, or be cast away?** Godet's comment here is pithy and quaint: " Jesus supposes, in this twenty-fifth verse, the act of *saving one's own life* accomplished with the most complete success . . . amounting to a gain of the whole world. But in this very moment, the master of this magnificent domain finds himself condemned to perish! What gain to draw in a lottery a gallery of pictures . . . and at the same time to become blind!" " O flesh," writes Luther (quoted by Dr. Morrison), " how mighty art thou, that thou canst still throw darkness over those things, even to the minds of the holy!"

Ver. 26.—**For whosoever shall be ashamed of me and of my words, of him shall the Son of man be ashamed, when he shall come in his own glory, and in his Father's, and of the holy angels.** Here follows the punishment in the world to come. It consists in the Judge's solemn award to the man who has succeeded in saving his life in this world. The award is, " Depart from me : I know you not." Of such a selfish soul, who here has loved his own ease, and has declined all self-sacrifice, will the Son of man, in the day of his glory, be justly ashamed. The suffering Messiah thus completed his vivid picture of himself. Not always was he to suffer, or to wear the robe of humiliation. The Despised and Rejected would assuredly return with a glory indescribable, inconceivable. His assertion, advanced here, that *he* will return as Almighty Judge, is very remarkable. In the parallel passage in St. Matthew (xvi. 13) it is put even more clearly. There Jesus asks his disciples, " Whom do men say that *I, the Son of man*, am?" In ver. 27 Jesus goes on to say, "*The Son of man* shall come in the glory of *his* Father, with *his* angels, and then *he* shall reward every man according to his works." The lesson was very clear. His own might surely be content. Only let them be patient. Lo! in the poor rejected Rabbi now before them, going to his bitter suffering and his death, they were looking really on the awful form of the Almighty Judge of quick and dead. These words, very dimly understood *then*, in days to come were often recalled by his hearers. They formed the groundwork of many a primitive apostolic sermon.

Ver. 27.—**But I tell you of a truth, there be some standing here, which shall not taste of death, till they see the kingdom of God.** This magnificent promise has always been more or less a difficulty to expositors. Two favourite explanations which (1) in the Transfiguration mystery, (2) in the fall of Jerusalem and destruction of the Jewish state, see the fulfilment of this great prediction, must be put aside as inadequate, as failing utterly to satisfy any idea of the kingdom of God. Concerning (1), it must be borne in mind that the words were addressed, not only to the disciples, but to a mixed multitude; the expression then, "there be *some* standing here," etc., would seem to point to more than *three* (Peter, James, and John were alone present at the Transfiguration) who should, while living, see the kingdom of God. Concerning (2), those who were witnesses of the great catastrophe which resulted in the sack of Jerusalem and the ruin of the Jewish polity, can scarcely be said to have looked on the kingdom of God. It was rather a great and terrible judgment; in no way can it fairly be termed the kingdom, or even its herald; it was simply an awful event in the world's story. But surely the Lord's disciples, the holy women, the still larger outer circle of loving followers of Jesus, who were changed by what happened during the forty days which immediately succeeded the Resurrection morning—changed from simple, loving, fearful, doubting men and women, into the brave resistless preachers and teachers of the new faith—the five hundred who gazed on the risen Lord in the Galilæan mountain,—*these* may in good earnest be said to have seen, while in life, " the kingdom of God." These five hundred, or at all events many of them, after the Resurrection, not only looked on God, but grasped the meaning of the presence and work of God on earth. The secret of the strange resistless power of these men in a hostile world was that their eyes had gazed on some of the sublime glories, and their ears had heard some of the tremendous secrets of *the kingdom of God.*

Vers. 28—36.—*The Transfiguration.*

Ver. 28.—**And it came to pass about an eight days after these sayings, he took Peter and John and James, and went up into a mountain to pray.** Some eight days after this question asked in the neighbourhood of Cæsarea Philippi, and its reply, and the sermon to the people on the subject of "No cross, no crown," which immediately followed, our Lord summoned the three leading disciples and took them up into a mountain to pray. They had spent the last few days apparently in quiet converse together. SS. Matthew and Mark speak only of six days. St. Luke gives the period in round numbers, counting portions of the first and last days as whole days. We may well imagine that this was a period of intense depression in the little company of Jesus. Their Master's popularity was fast waning among the people. His powerful enemies seemed gathering closer and closer round the Teacher whom they were determined to crush. The late utterances of Jesus, too, whether spoken to them alone, or publicly to the people, all foreshadowed a time of danger and suffering in the immediate future for him and for them—a time which, as far as he was concerned, would close with a violent death. To raise the fainting spirits of his own, to inspire them with greater confidence in himself, seems to have been the *immediate* purpose of that grand vision of glory known as the Transfiguration. It is true that to only three was vouchsafed the vision, and silence was enjoined on these, but the three were the leading spirits of the twelve. If Peter, James, and John were brave, earnest, and hopeful, there was little doubt that their tone of mind would be quickly reflected in their companions. Tradition, based on the fairly early authority of Cyril of Jerusalem, and of Jerome (fourth century), speaks of the mountain as Tabor, but the solitude evidently necessary for the manifestation would have been sought for in vain on Mount Tabor, a hill which rises abruptly from the Plain of Esdraelon, not very far from Nazareth to the south-east, for the summit of Tabor at that time was crowned with a fortress. The mountain most probably was one of the lower peaks of Hermon, at no great distance from the fountain source of the Jordan and Cæsarea Philippi, in which district we know Jesus and his companions had been teaching only a few days before.

Ver. 29.—**And as he prayed, the fashion of his countenance was altered,** etc. The marvellous change evidently passed over Jesus *while* he was in prayer, probably *because* of his intense prayer. Real, close communion with God ever imparts to the countenance of the one who has thus entered into communion with the High and Holy One, a new and strange beauty. Very many have noticed at times this peculiar and lovely change pass over the faces of God's true saints as they prayed—faces perhaps old and withered, grey with years and wrinkled with care. A yet higher degree of transfiguration through communion with God is recorded in the case of Moses, whose face, after he had been with his God-Friend on the mount, shone with so bright a glory that mortal eye could not bear to gaze on it until the radiance began to fade away. A similar change is recorded to have taken place in the case of Stephen when he pleaded his Divine Master's cause in the Sanhedrin hall at Jerusalem with such rapt eloquence that to the by-standers his face then, we read, "was as the face of an angel." Stephen told his audience later on, in the course of that earnest and impassioned pleading, that to him the very heavens were opened, and that his eyes were positively gazing on the beatific vision. Yet a step higher still was this transfiguration of our Lord. St. Luke tells us simply that, "as he prayed, the fashion of his countenance was altered." St. Matthew tells us *how* it was altered when he writes that "his countenance shone as the sun." **And his raiment was white and glistering;** literally, *lightening forth*, as if from some inward source of glorious light. The earthly robes were so beautified by contact with this Divine light that human language is exhausted by the evangelists to find terms and metaphors to picture them. St. Matthew compares these **garments** of the Blessed One to light; St. Mark, **to** the snow; St. Luke, to the flashing lightning.

Ver. 30.—**And, behold, there talked with him two men, which were Moses and Elias;** literally, *there were talking*. Evidently these two glorified beings had been conversing with Jesus some time before the three apostles, heavy with sleep, had noticed their presence; wearied and tired, slumber had overtaken them; we are not told how long they slept. The glorious light which environed them and the murmur of voices probably roused them, and in after-days they recounted what, after they were awake, they saw, and something of what they heard.

Ver. 31.—**Who appeared in glory.** Why were these two chosen as the Lord's companions on that solemn night? Probably (1) because they were what may be termed the two great representative men of the chosen race of Israel. The one was the human author of the Divine Law which for so many centuries had been the guide and teacher of the covenant people. The other had been the most illustrious of that great order of prophets who, during the centuries of their eventful history as a nation, had,

under the commission of the Most Highest, kept alight the torch of the knowledge of the one true God. And (2) because these men alone of the race of Israel apparently had kept their earthly bodies as the shrines of their immortal spirits. *Elijah*, we know, was translated *alive* into the other and the grander world; and as for *Moses*, God, his heavenly Friend, closed his eyes, and then hid his body from mortal sight, and, the mysterious words of Jude (ver. 9) would seem to tell us, from mortal corruption. **And spake of his decease which he should accomplish at Jerusalem.** Why was *this* the chosen subject of the august conference between the Lord and the heavenly pair? (1) In all reverence we may feel that one reason for the visit of these blessed spirits on that solemn night was the strengthening the sinless Sufferer himself. The vista which lay immediately before Jesus, of rejection, desertion, the death of agony, and the dreadful sufferings which preceded it, —all this had been very present before him lately. He had dwelt upon these things, we know, to his own. He had pondered over them, no doubt, often when alone. It was not only in Gethsemane that his "soul was sorrowful even unto death." As in the garden-agony "appeared to him an angel from heaven strengthening him," so here on the mount came to him these glorified spirits for the same blessed purpose of ministering. And (2) it was to help the three disciples. Their wavering faith would surely be strengthened if the words which they heard from those heavenly visitants dwelt with reverent awe and admiration on the circumstances of their Master's self-sacrificing career of agony and suffering. It must be remembered that a few days earlier they had listened to him, when he spoke to them of these things, with shrinking terror and incredulous amazement. They would now know what was thought of all this in the courts of heaven.

Ver. 32.—**And the two men that stood with him.** It has been asked—How did the disciples know the names which those glorified ones had once borne? Three replies are at least probable. (1) They may have heard their Master address them by their old earthly names. (2) In subsequent conversations the Lord may have disclosed them to the three. (3) Is it not a very *thinkable* thought that the blessed bear upon their spirit-forms their old individuality transfigured and glorified? Were such a vision vouchsafed to us, should we not in a moment recognize a Peter, a Mary, or a Paul?

Ver. 33.—**And it came to pass, as they departed from him, Peter said unto Jesus, Master, it is good for us to be here: and** let us make three tabernacles ; one for thee, and one for Moses, and one for Elias: not knowing what he said. The three evangelists who relate the Transfiguration scene, with trifling variations repeat this remark of Peter's. It is valuable to us when we remember that the tradition of the marvellous event comes from Peter, James, and John ; and that they repeat the strange inconsequent words uttered by one of themselves—their acknowledged spokesman. No thought of self-glorification evidently tinged this strange memory of theirs. They simply wished to record the plain truth just as it happened, and in the course of the narrative they had to repeat their own poor, babbling, meaningless words—for the remark of Peter is nothing else. Their own remark, which immediately follows, is the best comment upon them, "not knowing what he said." There was a deep feeling that in such a company, bathed, too, in that glorious and unearthly light, *it was well with them.* But they saw the heavenly visitants preparing to leave them. They would stay their departure if they could, so they stammered, "Let us build some shelter; let us erect some temple, however humble, to do honour, Lord, to thee and thy companions."

Ver. 34.—**While he thus spake, there came a cloud, and overshadowed them : and they feared as they entered into the cloud.** This luminous cloud, bright though it was, yet veiled the more intolerable brightness within. That such a bright cloud had the power of overshadowing and concealing, is not strange, for light in its utmost intensity hides as effectually as the darkness would do. God dwells in light inaccessible, whom therefore "no man hath seen, nor can see" (1 Tim. vi. 16). Milton writes—

"Dark with excess of light."

Philo speaks of the highest light as identical with darkness. Anselm thus understands the cloud here, quoting the words of 1 Tim. vi. 16, referred to above, and then the words of Moses, "And Moses drew near unto the thick darkness where God was" (Exod. xx. 21), and then this passage from the Transfiguration, and comments thus : "Illa caligo et ista nubes, atque illa lux idem sunt" (see Archbishop Trench on "Transfiguration," in 'Studies in the Gospels,' 8). The fear which these eye-witnesses remember as one of their experiences that memorable night was a very natural feeling. As the cloud stole over the mountain ridge, and the glory-light gradually paled and waned, the sensation of intense pleasure and satisfaction, which we may assume to be the natural accompaniment of such a blessed scene, would give place to awe and amazement.

Ver. 35.—**And there came a voice out of the cloud, saying, This is my beloved Son: hear him.** The reading here of the older authorities must be adopted. Instead of the voice out of the cloud saying, "This is my beloved Son," we must substitute, "This is my Elect." As SS. Matthew and Mark both read, "my beloved Son," we have here another of the many proofs that each of the three records of the Transfiguration is a distinct and separate memory of itself. The voice was evidently for the disciples—one more help for them in their present and future struggle against the cold and chilling doubts which ever and again would be suggested to them by the enemy of human souls, with a view to marring their present training, their future mighty missionary work.

Ver. 36.—**And they kept it close, and told no man in those days any of those things which they had seen.** The reasons of this silence for the present have been already discussed. The scene, doubtless, had done its work in the education of the three. Without telling their companions what they had seen and heard on the mount, we may assume that the sight of the serene confidence and renewed trust on the part of Peter, James, and John did its effectual work in strengthening their brethren. No doubt directly after the Resurrection, possibly during the days of darkness and gloom which followed the day of the cross, the chosen three related at length their experience of the Transfiguration mystery. The narrative of the Transfiguration and its attendant circumstances, as might have been expected, has been a favourite subject for hostile criticism. It does not, however, lend itself to any probable, or even possible, explanation which refers the story to some exaggerated report of a mistaken natural phenomenon. The whole story, as we have it thrice—with very slight variation in the details—repeated in the synoptical Gospels, must stand as we have it, or else must be wholly rejected as a myth. But, if a myth, whence did it spring? for nothing in the Jewish expectation of Messiah could possibly have suggested the "legend." The strange and even childish interruption of Peter could never have been *invented.* No one *friendly* to the apostle would have chronicled such a saying had there been any doubt resting on its authenticity; and a writer *hostile* to the apostle would scarcely have invented a narrative which treated of the Divine glory of the apostle's adored Master. If it be an invention, whence comes it? in whose interest was it composed? and how did it find its way into the very heart of the three synoptical Gospels? for there we find it woven into that marvellous tapestry of revelation and teaching which has at once charmed and influenced so many millions of men and women now for more than eighteen hundred years. Something of the purpose which the Transfiguration was intended to serve in the education of the twelve has been already discussed in the foregoing notes. Dr. Lange, who has made this difficult passage in the story of Jesus a subject of deep and earnest study, has given us some beautiful thoughts on the real signification of the Lord's transfiguration. This scholar and divine considers that, just at this period of his public ministry, Jesus had reached the zenith of his power. This is indicated by the grandeur of his recent miracles. There was nothing higher and more sublime to be reached by him. From this moment, therefore, earthly existence became too narrow a sphere. There only remained death; but death is, as St. Paul says, *the wages of sin.* For the sinless Man the issue of life is not the sombre passage of the tomb, rather is it the. royal road of a glorious transformation. Had the hour of this glorification struck for Jesus? and was the Transfiguration the beginning of the heavenly renewal? Gess, quoted by Godet —from whose *précis* of Lange's note these observations are derived—gives expression to Lange's thoughts in these words : " This event (the Transfiguration) indicates the ripe preparation of Jesus for immediate entrance upon eternity." " Had not Jesus himself," goes on Godet to say, thus concluding this very beautiful and suggestive, if somewhat fanciful note, " voluntarily suspended this change which was on the point of being wrought in him, this moment, the moment of his glorious transfiguration would have become the moment of his ascension."

Vers. 37—45.—*The scene at the foot of the hill of Transfiguration. The healing of the demoniac boy.*

Ver. 37.—**On the next day, when they were come down from the hill.** The Transfiguration had taken place in the late evening or night. It probably lasted for a much longer period than the brief account, preserved by the eye-witnesses, seems to speak of. How long the three disciples slept is not mentioned. Wearied and exhausted, deep slumber overtook them while the Master was praying. When they awoke, Jesus was bathed in glory, and the two heavenly spirits were conversing with him. They only tell us generally that the subject which occupied the blessed ones was their Master's speedy departure from earth ; no mention is made of the time all this consumed. It was morning when they rejoined their company. **Much people met him.** St. Mark, whose account here is more de-

tailed—evidently Peter preserved a very vivid memory of these events—tells us that the crowds, "when they beheld him, were greatly amazed." Without concluding that any lingering radiance of the last night's glory was still playing about his Person, we may well imagine that a holy joy just then lit up that face over which for some time past a cloud of deep sadness had brooded. The heavenly visitants; the words he had been listening to, which told him of his home of grandeur and of peace, voluntarily left by him that he might work his mighty earthwork ;—had no doubt strengthened with a strange strength the Man of sorrows; and when the crowds gazed on his face they marvelled, as St. Mark tells us, at what they saw there.

Ver. 38.—**A man of the company cried out, saying, Master, I beseech thee, look upon my son: for he is mine only child.** The tender sympathy of St. Luke is shown in this little detail. He is the only evangelist who mentions that the poor tormented boy was an *only child.*

Ver. 40.—**And I besought thy disciples to cast him out; and they could not.** This appears to have been a case of the deadliest kind of epileptic lunacy. Our Lord distinctly assumes here that the disease in this case was occasioned by an unclean spirit who had taken possession of the suffering child. The whole question of demoniacal possession, its extent, its cause, whether or no it still survives in some of the many mysterious phases of madness, is very difficult. It has been discussed elsewhere (see notes on ch. iv. 33 and following verses).

Ver. 41.—**And Jesus answering said, O faithless and perverse generation, how long shall I be with you, and suffer you?** This grave and mournful expression of the loving but just Master was addressed to the entire crowd, in whose midst he now found himself. *The people,* swayed hither and thither, now enthusiastic in his favour, when some sweet promise, or noble sentiment, or marvellous work touched their hearts, now coldly indifferent or even hostile, when his teaching seemed to exact some painful sacrifice of self at their hands,—these were looking on with quiet indifference at his disciples' failure in the case of the poor possessed child, and listened to their scribes as they wrangled with the Lord's dismayed and perplexed followers. These followers, trying to imitate their Master in his wonderworks, but failing because, after all, their faith in him wavered. The father of the child, confessing his unbelief, but utterly wretched at the sight of the suffering of his boy. The ghastly spectacle of the insane boy writhing and foaming on the ground, and then lying all bruised and dishevelled, with the pallor of death on the poor, pain-wrung face, and this sorely afflicted one *a child*, one of those little ones whom Jesus loved so well. Poor child-sufferer, on whose comparatively innocent life the sin of mother and father weighed so heavily ! What a contrast for the Lord between the heavenly hours he had just been spending on the mount, and this sad sight of pain and suffering, of jealousy and wrangling, of doubts and indecision, in the midst of which he now stood ! "O faithless and perverse," cried the pitiful Lord with a burst of intense sorrow, "how long shall I be with you, and suffer you?" One word, he knew, and for him all *this* might be exchanged for the scenes of heaven, for the company of angels and of blessed spirits, for the old home of grandeur and of peace; only it was just to heal this bitter curse that he had left his heaven-home. But the contrast between the glory of the Transfiguration mount and the memories which they evoked, and the present scene of pain and woe unutterable, of human passions and weakness, called forth from the Lord this bitter, sorrowful expression.

Ver. 42.—**And Jesus rebuked the unclean spirit, and healed the child, and delivered him again to his father.** A word of the great Master was sufficient, and the spirit which had brought the cruel curse of disease and madness into the boy was cast out, and the strange cure was complete. St. Peter supplied St. Mark with fuller details here, and especially adds one priceless gem of instruction in the Christian life. The Lord told the father of the suffering child that the granting of the boon he craved for his son depended on his own faith. Then the poor father, won by the Divine goodness manifest in every act and word of Jesus, stammered out that pitiful, loving expression, re-echoed since in so many thousand hearts, "Lord, I believe ; help thou mine unbelief." If he accepted and rewarded *that* trembling, wavering faith in him, will he reject mine ?

Ver. 43.—**And they were all amazed at the mighty power of God. But while they wondered every one at all things which Jesus did, he said unto his disciples.** Once more were kindled the disciples' hopes of an earthly royalty in the Person of that strange Messiah. For was he not Messiah after all, who with a word worked such stupendous works as the miracle they had just witnessed? But Jesus read their thoughts, and again tells them (in ver. 44) of the terrible doom which awaited him. They must remember there was no earthly crown or human sovereignty for him.

Ver. 45.—**And they feared to ask him of that saying.** The "saying" was to them so utterly distasteful, perhaps inconceivable. It is possible that they thought this betrayal

and death simply veiled for them some bit of teaching to be explained hereafter; it is possible they at once dismissed it from their minds, as men often do painful and mournful forebodings. At all events, they dreaded asking him any questions about this dark future of suffering which he said lay before him.

Vers. 46—48.—*How the Lord answered the question which arose among the disciples as to which was the greatest.*

Vers. 46, 47.—**Then there arose a reasoning among them, which of them should be greatest. And Jesus, perceiving the thought of their heart.** Somewhere on their journey back to the south, between the neighbourhood of Cæsarea Philippi and the old scene of his labours, Capernaum, this dispute must have taken place. Shortly after their arrival at Capernaum, the Master called them together, and gave them the following lesson on human greatness. **Took a child, and set him by him.** St. Mark mentions that this teaching was "in the house," and commentators have suggested, with some probability, that the house was St. Peter's, and the child one of his. Clement of Alexandria ('Stromata,' iii. 448, B) especially mentions that this apostle had children. St. Matthew relates this incident at greater length, and, still dwelling upon the text of "the little one," gives us another and different sketch of the Master's teaching on this occasion. St. Mark tells us how Jesus folded his arms round the little creature in loving fondness. If the child, as above suggested, was Peter's own, such an incident as that embrace would never have been forgotten by the father, and would, of course, find a place in the memoir of his faithful disciple Mark. A (late) tradition of the Eastern Church identifies this child with him who afterwards became the famous Ignatius, Bishop of Antioch, a martyr. Ignatius styled himself Theophoros; this, understood in a *passive* sense, would signify "one who had been carried by God." But in this Father's own writings we find the name used by himself in an *active* sense, as "one who carries God within himself." *And Jesus, perceiving the thought of their heart, took a child.* The dispute "which of them should be greatest," which no doubt had taken place among themselves in their last journey from the north of the Holy Land to Capernaum, was still a leading thought in the hearts of the twelve, so little had they really understood their Master's teaching, and especially his later solemn words which pointed the *way of the cross* as the only way to heaven and to *real greatness*. The Lord reads these poor sinful hearts; then, calling them together, he takes a child in his arms, and sets him by him. *By this action* the Lord answers the silent questioning thought of the worldly twelve. "The child stands as the type of the humble and childlike disciple, and (the dispute having been about the comparative greatness of the disciples) such a disciple is the greatest; he is so honoured by God that he stands on earth as the representative of Christ, and of God himself (ver. 47), since "he that is [willingly] least among you all, the same shall be [truly] great' (ver. 48)" (Meyer).

Ver. 48.—**Whosoever shall receive this child in my Name receiveth me.** The general lesson here—and it is one that has gone to the heart more or less of *all* professing Christians—is that all the followers of Jesus should practise humility before, and show tenderness to, the weak. It is one of the great sayings of the Master which has stirred that practical charity which has ever been one of the great characteristic features of Christianity. But while the general lesson is clear, the particular reminder still claims attention. Singular and touching was the affection of Jesus for children. Several marked instances of this are noted in the Gospels. To this passage, however, and to the sequel as reported in St. Mark (ix. 42), may be especially referred the thought which has founded the countless child-homes, schools, and hospitals in all lands in different ages, and in our own time the institution of the Sunday school, not the least beautiful of Christian works done in the Master's Name.

Vers. 49, 50.—*A question put by John.*

Ver. 49.—**And John answered and said, Master, we saw one casting out devils in thy Name; and we forbad him, because he followeth not with us.** The character of John is a strangely interesting one. With the exception of his forming one of the chosen three who were in a peculiar manner received into their Master's confidence, John seldom appears, during the public ministry of Christ, to have played a prominent part. Many years had to elapse before he attained that unique position of influence in the early Church which no one seems to have disputed. In the mean time, his character was slowly forming. Fiery and impetuous, although reserved and retiring, it seemed in these first days scarcely probable that such a nature would ever deepen or ripen into that John who became the world-teacher of his Master's love. St. Luke here records two circumstances which suggested some of the Master's important teaching, in both of which John plays the prominent part. The question of John was evidently suggested by Jesus' words spoken in connection with his teaching respecting little ones. "Whosoever," said the Master, "shall receive this child in *my Name*." But John and others had just been sternly rebuking some one not of their com-

pany, who had been using, to some effect evidently, that same Master's Name, which possessed, as John saw, wondrous power. Had he and his friends been doing right in rebuking the comparative stranger for using a Name which Jesus, in his words just spoken, seemed to regard as the common property of kindly devout men? Meyer remarks here "that outside the company of disciples of Jesus there were, even then, men in whose hearts his teaching and acts had evoked a higher and even a supernatural power. Certain sparks which had fallen here and there beyond the little circle of his own, kindled flames occasionally away from the central fire." Those who were ever close to the Master seemed to dread lest, if these were allowed unchecked to teach and to work in the *Name*, grave error might be disseminated. Some natural jealousy of these outsiders no doubt influenced men like John in their wish to confine the work in the limits of their own circle.

Ver. 50.—**And Jesus said unto him, Forbid him not: for he that is not against us is for us.** The older authorities, manuscripts, and the more venerable versions here read for the last clause, "He that is not against you is for you." Exegetically as well as critically this amended reading is to be preferred. The offence of the stranger, if it were an offence, was not against Jesus, whose Name had evidently been used reverently and with faith, but against the disciples, whose rights and privileges were presumably infringed upon. The Master's reply contained a broad and far-reaching truth. No earthly society, however holy, would be able exclusively to claim the Divine powers inseparably connected with a true and faithful use of his Name. This is the grand and massive answer which stretches over a history of eighteen centuries, and which will possibly extend over many yet to come; the answer which gives an ample reason why noble Christian work is done whether emanating from Churches bearing the name of Protestant, or Roman, or Greek.

THE SO-CALLED JOURNEYINGS TOWARDS JERUSALEM. The great characteristic feature in St. Luke's Gospel, distinguishing it especially from the other two synoptical Gospels of SS. Matthew and Mark, are the events in the public ministry of Jesus dwelt on in the next ten chapters of this Gospel. Many incidents in the succeeding chapters are recorded by this evangelist alone. Two questions suggest themselves.

1. To what period of the Lord's public work does this large and important section of our Gospel refer?

2. (1) Why is this period, comparatively speaking, so little dwelt on by the other two synoptists SS. Matthew and Mark? (2) Where did St. Luke probably derive his information here?

1. Commentators frequently, and with some accuracy, speak of this great section of St. Luke's work as "the journeyings towards Jerusalem." Three times does this writer especially tell us that this was the object and end of the journeys he was describing; in ch. ix. 51, "He steadfastly set his face *to go to Jerusalem;*" in ch. xiii. 22, "He went through the cities and villages . . . *journeying toward Jerusalem;*" in ch. xvii. 11, "And it came to pass, *as he went to Jerusalem.*"

These journeyings to Jerusalem were evidently just before *the end.* They were the close of the public life. They immediately preceded the last Passover Feast, which all the four evangelists tell us the Lord kept at Jerusalem, and in the course of which he was crucified. They fill up, then, the last six or seven months of his earth-life—that period, roughly speaking, from the Feast of Tabernacles (alluded to in John vii.), which falls in October, until the Passover Feast in the following spring. These last months were occupied by the Master in a slow progress from Capernaum, through those parts of Galilee hitherto generally unvisited by him, gradually making his way toward the capital, which we know he reached in time for the Passover Feast, during which he was crucified.

In the course of this period it seems, however, likely that, in St. Luke's account of Mary and Martha (ch. x. 38—42), we have an allusion to a short visit to Jerusalem of the Lord, undertaken in the course of these journeyings, at the Dedication Feast (John x. 22).

2. (1) In these last journeyings it appears that the Lord was in the habit of constantly sending out by themselves small companies of his disciples as missionaries in the neighbouring districts, thus accustoming his followers, in view of his own approaching death, to act alone and to think alone. It is, therefore, extremely probable that SS. Matthew and Peter (the real author of St. Mark's Gospel) were, during this period of our Lord's work, constantly absent from

their Master's immediate neighbourhood. These apostles would naturally choose, as the special subjects of their own teaching and preaching, those events at which they *personally* had been present. Much of what was done and said by the Master during these last six months was done during the temporary absence, on special mission duty, of these two evangelists.

(2) When we consider the probable sources whence St. Luke derived his detailed information concerning this period, we are, of course, landed in conjecture. We know, however, that the whole of his narrative was composed after careful research into well-sifted evidence, supplied generally by eyewitnesses, of the events described.

Thus, in the earlier chapters, we have already discussed the high probability of the Virgin-mother herself having furnished the information; so here there is little doubt that SS. Paul and Luke, in their researches during the composition of the Third Gospel, met with men and women who had formed part of that larger company which had been with Jesus, we know, during those last months of his ministry among us. Nor is it, surely, an unreasonable thought for us to see, in connection with this important portion of our Gospel, the hand of the Holy Spirit, who, unseen, guided the pen of the four evangelists, especially throwing Luke and his master, Paul, into the society of men who had watched the great Teacher closely during that period of his work, when the other two synoptists, SS. Matthew and Peter (Mark), were frequently absent.

From the language employed in this portion of the Gospel, there seems a high probability that many of the notes or documents supplied to SS. Luke and Paul were written or dictated in Aramaic (Hebrew).

Vers. 51—56.—*The Samaritan insult to the Lord. The Master's reception of it.*

Ver. 51.—**And it came to pass, when the time was come that he should be received up, he steadfastly set his face to go to Jerusalem.** This is a very solemn introduction to this great section of St. Luke's writing. It at once marks off all that now follows as a winding-up of the earthly ministry. The expression, "that he should be received up," is simply the rendering of one Greek word, which signifies "ascension." The Passion, the cross, and the grave are passed over here, and the glorious goal alone is spoken of. What a lesson of comfort is here suggested! The words in the Greek original, " he steadfastly set his face," are evidently literally translated from a well-known Aramaic (Hebrew) expression.

Ver. 52.—And sent messengers before his face. Probably, as the sequel shows, these were John and James. This was necessary at this period of the Lord's life. A numerous company now usually followed the Lord; it is probable that many of those most devoted to him, both men and women, scarcely ever left him, now that the popular enthusiasm was waning, and the number of his deadly enemies increasing. **And they went, and entered into a village of the Samaritans, to make ready for him.** These Samaritans were the descendants of a mixed race brought by Esarhaddon (eighth century B.C.) from Babylon, Cuthah, Ava, Hamath, and Sepharvaim, to replace the ten tribes carried captive to the East. These became worshippers of Jehovah, and, on the return of Judah and Benjamin from captivity, sought to be allowed to share in the rebuilding of the temple, and then to be admitted as Jews to share in the religious privileges of the chosen race. Their wishes, however, were not complied with. They subsequently erected a rival temple on Mount Gerizim, and henceforward were known as a schismatical sect, and continued in a state of deadly enmity with the orthodox Jews. This bitter hatred is noticed in the New Testament (see John iv. 9), where it is stated that the Jews "had no dealings with the Samaritans," whom they looked on as worse than heathen. In the synagogues these Samaritans were cursed. The Son of Sirach named them as a people that they abhorred (Ecclus. i. 25, 26); and in the Talmud we read this terrible passage, " Let not the Samaritans have part in the resurrection!" This hatred, however, we know, was not shared in by our Lord, and on more than one occasion we find him dealing gently and lovingly with this race.

Ver. 53.—And they did not receive him, because his face was as though he would go to Jerusalem. Here the kindly overtures were rejected by the inhabitants of the Samaritan village in question. The reason alleged by them was that this Teacher, who wished to come among them, was on his way up to worship at the rival temple at Jerusalem.

Ver. 54.—And when his disciples James and John saw this, they said, Lord, wilt thou that we command fire to come down from heaven, and consume them, even as Elias did? The natural fiery temper and burning zeal of these highly favoured and loved brethren—who, we know, received,

perhaps in half-playful rebuke from their Master, the epithet Boanerges, sons of thunder—flamed forth at this insult offered to their adored Master in return for his tender, loving consideration for this hated people. Possibly, what these two had lately witnessed on the Transfiguration mount had deepened their veneration for their Lord, and caused them the more bitterly to resent an insult levelled at him. So they prayed him—him whom they had so lately seen radiant with the awful fire of heaven—prayed him to call that fire down, and so wither in a moment those impious despisers of his gracious goodness. The words, " even as Elias did," form a very appropriate historical instance, but they are of doubtful authenticity—the older authorities have them not.

Ver. 55.—But he turned, and rebuked them. " Christ wrought miracles in every element except fire. Fire is reserved for the consummation of the age" (Bengel). **And said, Ye know not what manner of spirit ye are of.**

Ver. 56.—For the Son of man is not come to destroy men's lives, but to save them. This entire clause is absent in a large majority of the older authorities. On every principle of criticism it must be, if not struck out, at least marked as of doubtful authenticity. Commentators are, however, very loth to part with the words, which breathe, as has been remarked, "a spirit far purer, loftier, and rarer than is usually discernible in ecclesiastical interpolations." They are certainly very old, as old almost as the apostolic age, being found in the Italic and Peshito, the most venerable of versions. Many, therefore, of the contemporaries of apostolic men must have read these words as a genuine utterance of our Lord. **And they went to another village.** The Greek word translated " another" suggests that our Lord, after the insult offered by the Samaritans, quietly turned his steps to a Jewish community.

Vers. 57—62.—*Three would-be disciples. The Lord, in plain terms, tells them what is required of men who seek his service.* The first two of these incidents in the life of Jesus are related by St. Matthew (vii. 19—22), but he places them in an earlier period. They evidently did not occur together, but most probably they took place about this time in the ministry. They are placed in one group as examples of the way in which the Master replied to numerous offers of service made to him under different conditions.

Vers. 57, 58.—Lord, I will follow thee whithersoever thou goest. And Jesus said unto him, Foxes have holes, and birds of the air have nests; but the Son of man hath not where to lay his head. St. Matthew tells us that the " certain man" who made this offer of service was a scribe. This detail is useful, as showing that those who were attracted by our Lord's teaching were by no means confined to the peasant and artisan class. If we look a little below the surface of the gospel story, we find numberless indications of this. In the Master's reply it is probable that the depression, naturally the result of the churlish refusal of the Samaritan villagers to receive him (ver. 53), coloured the sad but true reflection. The wise Master distrusted the too-ready enthusiasm of his would-be disciple. He saw it would never stand the test of the severe privation or the painful self-sacrifice which would be the sure lot of any one, especially at that juncture, really faithful to him.

Vers. 59, 60.—**And he said unto another, Follow me. But he said, Lord, suffer me first to go and bury my father. Jesus said unto him, Let the dead bury their dead : but go thou and preach the kingdom of God.** In this case the Master was the Summoner. Something he read in this man's heart, or words he had heard him speak, moved the Redeemer's great love, so he gave him a special call. This was a very different character from the last. Whereas *that* seeker for work from Jesus was impulsive, and even thoughtless in his enthusiasm, one who would begin to act without counting the cost, *this* one was over-cautious, cold and calculating to an ungenerous excess ; yet there was evidently sterling stuff in the character, for Jesus argues and remonstrates with him ; there was, too, much gold mingled with the earth of that man's disposition, for the Lord lightly to let it go. It is thus that the Spirit pleads still with the selfishness which disfigures many a noble and devoted servant of high God. He seems to say, "My call is too imperative to yield to any home duties, however orderly and respectable." During the official days of mourning (in the case of a funeral, these were seven) the impression now made by his summoning

words would have worn off. It is noticeable that the home duties, which Jesus suggested should give place to other and more imperative claims, were in connection with *the dead.* It was not the *living* father who was to be left to hirelings, only the inanimate corpse. It was rather a *society* call than a *home* or *family* duty which was to give place to work for the Master. St. Chrysostom makes some quaint, but strikingly practical, remarks here. "He might need, if he went to the funeral, to proceed, after the burial, to make inquiry about the will, and then about the distribution of the inheritance, and all the other things that followed thereupon ; and thus waves after waves of things coming in upon him in succession might bear him very far away from the harbour of truth. For this cause, doubtless, the Saviour draws him, and fastens him to himself."

Vers. 61, 62.—**And another also said, Lord, I will follow thee ; but let me first go bid them farewell, which are at home at my house. And Jesus said unto him, No man, having put his hand to the plough, and looking back, is fit for the kingdom of God.** There is an implied reproach in our Lord's reply to what, on first thoughts, would seem a reasonable request. The offer in this case came from the man himself. It would appear that this would-be disciple, on thinking the matter over, considered it might be desirable to hear what his family and friends thought about his project. At all events, one thing is clear—his first ardour was cooled, his first love left. The Master, in his pithy but striking comment, shows when such is the case, that there is little or no hope of any real noble work being carried out. The simile is drawn from agricultural imagery. Jesus was evidently very familiar with all the little details of rural life. We find a similar saying in Hesiod, "He who would plough straight furrows, must not look about him" ('Works and Days,' ii. 60).

HOMILETICS.

Vers. 1—22.—(See afterwards in connection with ch. x.)

Ver. 24.—*The life saved, and the life lost.* The martyr, then, is the type of the true Christian. Christ (ver. 22) predicts his own fate. And immediately afterwards (ver. 23) he announces to all that whosoever will come after him must, through the gate of suffering, pass into glory ; must "deny himself, take up his cross daily, and follow him." This is the essence of martyrdom. The martyr is not necessarily one who is burned at the stake, or slain by the sword, or left to rot in damp prison-cells ; he is one who, in will, surrenders the life to God, and daily bears the cross of Jesus. Let not the variations of the meaning attached to the words "save" and "lose" be overlooked. In the first clause, "Whosoever *wills to save* shall lose ; " *i.e.* whosoever is bent on preserving the life may in a sense preserve it, but, in the nobler sense, he shall lose his real being, or as in the verse following, "he shall lose *himself.*" In the second clause,

" Whosoever *wills to lose* his life for Christ's sake "—to subordinate all considerations merely personal to the command of a supreme affection—may incur shame, may suffer many things, but, in the nobler sense, he shall realize the truth of his existence, he shall receive the crown of his life. Ah! wonderfully suggestive are the sharp antitheses of Jesus' saying. What, then, is the abiding reality of the Christian type of manhood? of the true martyr-life? Shall we say that the abiding reality is *a capacity of self-forgetfulness?* Undoubtedly, there is this capacity. We recognize the man of genuine goodness at once. With him there is no part-acting. He is not one who stands before mirrors, studying attitudes and effects; in what he does there is the absence of the feeling of self. "Whither the spirit that is in him is to go, he goes straight forward." A great enthusiasm always removes the action, if not from the shadow, at least from " the corrosive power," of selfishness. Certainly, Christ looked forward to a love that could hold the closest affections as only second to it; that could sacrifice all in which the self is most bound up; that, as against the very pleadings of nature, would close with a higher vision, " Here am I; send me." And, more or less, this is always a characteristic of the martyred soul. "If," says Thomas à Kempis, " a man should give all his substance, yet is it nothing. And if he should practise great repentance, still it is little. And if he should attain to all knowledge, he is still afar off. And if he should be of great virtue, and of fervent devotion, yet there is much wanting; especially one thing which is most necessary for him. And what is that? That leaving all, he forsake himself, and go wholly from himself, and retain nothing out of self-love." But, when we speak of self-forgetfulness, we speak of only half the truth. The question remains—Whence the *inward pressure* which causes this self-forgetting spirit? We cannot be self-denying by the mere resolution to be so. We may subject ourselves to the most rigid of disciplines, and the result only be that we assert self in one aspect to deny self in another aspect. There must be some force in the soul, some obligation which, once discerned, becomes an irresistible spiritual power. Take, *e.g.*, one of the purest forms of self-devotion. The mother's love is not an affair of reasoning. There is no calculation of quantity in it. When the child is stricken with sickness she watches by the bed and ministers to the wants of the sufferer, denying herself by day and night, and never stopping to ask what is the limit to be observed. The action is the consequence of an obligation inlaid in the relation of mother to child. This relation takes her out of self. She "goes wholly from herself, and retains nothing out of self-love." She loses her life in the child. And thus with self-sacrifice, through its diversity of forms. Its root is, some relation into which one mind enters with another, or with a higher and vaster issue whose vision has dawned on it. The relation supplies at once the motive, and the food which nourishes the motive. It is in the mind an omnipotent " *I must.*" Remember, self-sacrifice may be a power for evil as well as good. The devil's martyrs far outnumber God's martyrs. For what is evil, or for ends that are "not of the Father, but of the world," persons spend themselves with a zeal and persistence which may well put Christians to shame. Self-consecration is not necessarily a Christian virtue. It is the character of the alliance into which the soul enters which makes the virtue. "He that loseth his life *for my sake* the same shall save it." This was the new thing which came into the world through Jesus Christ. Truthfulness as between man and man was no new thing. The sanctions of morality were no new thing. Through the religions and philosophies of paganism there came gleams of an ethic pure and spiritual. But an obligation to One unseen, yet ever-present, One to whom the life was bound, and in whom the life was hidden; an obligation that regulated all aims, that was sovereign over all the action, to deny which, or be false to which, was the soul's damnation;—that was the new thing. And that new thing was the secret of the Christian martyr-life. And it was this Christian martyr-life which lifted the individual man from his obscurity, as a mere unit in the mass of humanity, and invested him, be he bond or be he free, with the inalienable glory of the calling—" an heir of God, and a joint-heir with Christ." And from that day to this there has echoed back, from a great multitude which no man can number, the sweetly constraining " For my sake." The cross of Jesus has really gone before the ages. Its spirit has entered into the conditions of human life, has influenced the minds and hearts of men far more widely than we can estimate. We trace its witness far outside the circle of his professing followers. But where the response to him is conscious, where there is a real personal relation to him, where the adoring cry of Thomas, "My Lord and my God!" is felt,—in this supreme spiritual affiance we recognize the pressure which constrains to live not to self, in Jesus' love to lose the life for Jesus, sake. It is this pressure which bestows a beauty quite unique on the career of a man who has a place in the foremost rank of Christian heroes. Exploits brilliant and daring are associated with the name of Gordon. And whether we think of him in China, or in Egypt, or in the quiet garrison town, or speeding on the swift dromedary across the desert, or shut up in Khartoum, waiting for the succours that arrived too late, and facing death as one who had learned to regard it without quailing,—there is always an unmistakable and lofty individuality. But the crown of the glory is the spiritual elevation of the soul, the enthusiasm for God and good which filled the heart. How he believed in God!—not to him a mere sign of some unknown quantity, but the Living One, the Father in heaven. How he believed in Christ!—not a mere "apotheosis of humanity," but Jesus Christ who is to-day what he was yesterday, and of whom he writes, "There would be no one so unwelcome to come and reside in this world as our Saviour, while the world is in the state it now is." How he believed in the government of the world by a loving and righteous will! To reveal this will; to work out its purpose with all his might; to raise the down man; to strike the fetter from the slave; to make God's universe a little better, happier, wholesomer;—for this he lived, for this he died. Died? Nay, verily, "the immortal dead live again in minds made better by their presence." He who loses his life for Jesus' sake, he only has saved it. Let this, then, be accepted as the lesson of Jesus' saying: We find the true life, the great, wide, everlasting Christ-life, only by losing, for his sake, the narrow, small, merely self-life. Shall it be said by any that to speak thus is to speak in parables? that heroics are not for ordinary Christian people living in quiet, ordinary ways? There is no parable. The words bear on all in all sorts and conditions. Every person is called to settle on what plan his life shall be built, what manner of person he shall be. He who has no ideal of conduct is little better than a creature drifting through his days. The Christian ideal is sketched in this word of the Lord. If any one will come after Christ, let him know this; and let him know further that it is not the circumstances that make the man—he makes his place, works his ideal out in different kinds of circumstances. General Gordon, in an obscurer lot, in a humbler sphere, might not have developed the same *amount* of force; but, given the grace of God with him, he would have developed the same *kind* of force, he would have been the same type of man. And it is faithfulness to this type in the place we occupy, there not elsewhere, that Christ demands. Are we confessing him before men? Day by day, do we take his cross and follow him? Then, no matter what the scene of the life-work may be, we are losing our life for his sake. This is the obligation of that life "which martyred men have made more glorious for us who strive to follow."

Vers. 28—36.—*The Transfiguration.* "When, in the desert, he was girding himself for the work of life, angels of life came and ministered to him. Now, in the fair world, when he is girding himself for the work of death, the ministrants come to him from the grave, but from the grave conquered—one from that tomb under Abarim which his own hand had sealed long ago, the other from the rest into which he had entered without seeing corruption. 'There stood by him Moses and Elias, and spake of his decease.' And when the prayer is ended, the task accepted, then first since the star passed over him at Bethlehem the full glory falls on him from heaven, and the testimony is borne to his everlasting Sonship and power—'Hear him!'" Thus beautifully and truly writes Ruskin of the solemn transaction in Jesus' history recorded by the synoptical evangelists. It is a new anointing of Jesus as the Christ of God, his installation into the last part of his ministry on the earth. At the baptism, the Spirit descended, and the voice came from heaven, "My beloved Son, in whom I am well pleased." This was the general inauguration of the Messiahship. Now there comes the special inauguration of Christ as "the End of the Law for righteousness to every one that believeth." "Moses and Elias appear to hold converse on that sublime event which had been the great central subject of all their teaching, and solemnly to consign into his hands, once and for all, in a symbolical and glorious representation, their delegated and expiring power." Now the voice is, "Hear" *not* Moses and Elias, but "my beloved Son!"   A wondrous, awe-striking hour!   The hush over nature, the darkness illumined by an inexpressible radiance, the face of the Man of sorrows then and there shining as the sun, the raiment penetrated by the glory "white and glistering" as the light, and the conversation of the three shining ones,—these, the features of the scene, left an indelible impression on the chosen witnesses.   Peter, ever ready, though not ever wise, has some foolish speech about erecting three booths.   But by-and-by they realize the significance of that which they saw.   "We were eye-witnesses of his majesty," cries the same Peter.   "This voice we heard, when we were with him in the holy mount." Not, indeed, that such a momentary illumination of Christ is to be held as a proof of first authority.   He proceeds, "We have also a *more sure word* of prophecy; whereunto ye do well that ye take heed, as unto a light that shineth in a dark place."   But it was a hint as to the "power and coming of the Lord Jesus," confirming the "more sure word," and helping into the understanding of the truth that, with the decease at Jerusalem, the old was finished and the new began.   "God had reconciled all things to himself."   Now, with regard to the vision, observe—

I. IT WAS ON A MOUNTAIN.   The hill or upland scene occupies a prominent place in the history of our Lord.   It seems to have been a craving of his human heart to get "where beyond the voices there is peace."   There he could breathe more freely; there he found a nourishment and invigoration which were welcome.   On the high ground he preached his famous sermon.   To the mountain he was wont to retire for prayer. When all went to their own homes, he went to the Mount of Olives.   On the hill of Golgotha he died.   The mountain in Galilee was the meeting-place with his apostles after the Resurrection.   From the slope of Olivet he ascended to heaven.   Now, for this brief moment of glory, the place chosen is "the high mountain apart."   Do we not need an upland scene in our life?   No hill, no transfiguration.   The face never shines. It is a dull, dreary toil.   The holy mount, on whose top one can leave the carking care and the weary plod, where the air is always pure—the hill that is commanded only by the heights of God's presence—ah! this is the secret worth possessing.

II. IT IS AS HE PRAYS THAT THE FASHION OF THE COUNTENANCE IS ALTERED.   He goes up to the mountain, not to meet Moses and Elias, nor to have a *séance* with spirits, but to pray—to meet his Father, that, out of the Father's heart, he might fill the fountains of his spirit.   As he prays he passes into that blessed light of God which "enwrapped him in such an aureole of glistering brilliance, his whole presence breathed so Divine a radiance, that the light, the snow, the lightning, are the only things to which the evangelist can compare that celestial lustre."   Christian! the lesson thereby suggested thou needst not that any teach thee.   It is the same lesson, but in a higher form, that was shadowed forth in Jacob's Peniel, in the wrestling by the brook Jabbok. Through the wrestling of the angel the heart of the supplanter was plucked out of him; in his prayer which prevailed he found the new name—the Israel, the prince with God and man.   Hast thou never found it so?   Hast thou never, in some great sorrow, poured out thy heart before God, and realized that, when thou didst kneel, thou wast only the worm, and no man—weak and spiritless; when thou didst rise from thy knees, thou wast the man, and no worm—the fashion of thy countenance had been altered?   Let the sons of pride speak as they choose, the children of quietness know that "more things are wrought by prayer than the world dreams of."

III. THERE IS CONFERENCE WITH THE DEPARTED.   The two shining presences are spoken of as invested with the properties and functions of life.   "Two men, which were Moses and Elias."   We know little about the world of the dead, about the possibilities of intercommunion—they with us, and we with them.   There is a feeling, widely diffused, that some kind of intercourse there is.   Even the negro, in his African platoon, lays aside a little rice each day as the share of his departed kindred.   Through all times, everywhere, the human heart is found asking, speculating over the question, "Is there no bridge between the dead and the living?   Is all speech, all fellowship, for ever broken?"   Well, in this Scripture we read of two men, who for long generations had been removed from this earthly scene, profoundly interested in events to be transacted on this globe of ours on which depended the salvation of the world.   May not this be a glimpse into the hidden economy?   May not that which we see in them during this moment of sight into the unseen, be the picture of what is going on even now in the home of the blessed and holy dead?   Is not the talk on Hermon an illustration of the communion of saints; reminding us that heaven and earth are nearer than we think of, that it is given to us in prayer to

> ". . . join hands
> With those who went before,
> And greet the blood-besprinkled bands
> On the eternal shore"?

"Ye are come . . . to the spirits of just men made perfect."

IV. THE GLORY IS TRANSIENT. A brief moment, and then the vision fades into the light of common day. Moses was forty days and forty nights on the mount. Jesus is on the Mount for only a short hour. Even while the foolish apostle spoke, there came a cloud that overshadowed them. The Lord cannot afford to luxuriate on the mountain-top. There is a universe to be reclaimed; there are shapes of disease and sin and want waiting for him below. More than ever is he straitened until his bloody baptism is done. And so with the disciple. It is good to have the retreat, the mountain, the sabbatical hour each day, the sabbatical day each week. But the purpose of the rest is to refit for the labour. And, after all, the highest transfiguration is not that of the dazzling outward light, but that of the beauty shining through the common ordinary things, and investing them with a heavenly grace and truth. The teaching given the apostles next after the transaction on the mountain is the taking of a little child, and saying, "Whosoever shall receive this child in my Name receiveth me."

Vers. 46—50.—*Humility and charity.* Were these apostles sinners above all ecclesiastics because of this reasoning which arose among them? Were their controversies about precedence one whit more foolish and unseemly than the controversies with which the air of councils and courts is laden, and by which passions are often enkindled to fever heat? Alas! is it not the earthenness of the vessel in which the heavenly treasure is deposited which is made manifest in the strife, "Who shall be greatest"? Jesus' action is a symbol to be read, marked, learned, and inwardly digested by all. "He took a little child, and set him by his side," as if to say, "See, there is the greatness of the kingdom of heaven;" nay, as may be gathered from St. Matthew, as if to say more strongly still, "There is no other greatness recognized in the heavenly kingdom than that of character. Except you are fashioned according to the character delineated in childhood, you cannot even enter the kingdom." Reflect on the import of this saying, this symbol. Does it seem strange that (Matt. xviii. 4) Christ should distinguish *humility* as the characteristic of the child? But is not the essence of humility unconsciousness of self? And is not this unconsciousness the trait conspicuous in a truly childlike child? The little one has a will, a temper, but there is not much of the feeling of self. Watch the caresses and endearments; they are less love seeking to be loved, than love merely loving, absorbed in loving. Observe the play; the costly toy is seldom the most prized; the pleasure found in toy or romp is the outgoing of self. Nature is spontaneous, free. Therein, says Jesus, we have a revelation of heaven, a sign of the real greatness. The image likest God, the fact, in this universe, nearest God, with most in it of the stamp of the high and holy One, is the little child whom Christ has called. The everlasting love humbles itself as the little child. It loves, it is absorbed in loving. The Incarnation only makes us see what is hidden in the very being of God—self-emptying, making self of no reputation. The King of kings is the Servant of servants. He is among us the one that serveth. "Be ye therefore imitators of God as the children of his love." For it is pride that stands between us and the true greatness. We are great only in the measure in which we lose ourselves, in which we find our life, in a cause or truth which is higher than ourselves. The world has three chief patterns of greatness. *Culture*—the development, through science and art, of a certain inward sweetness and light. *Power*—the ability to use men as pawns on a chess-board, to project far and near the image of self. *Luxury*—imbedding the years in the voluptuous comfort which money commands. That which is common to all these forms, from the most gross to the most refined, is that the supreme reference of the mind is to *having* rather than *being*, getting rather than giving, being served rather than serving. Christ's idea is in sharp antagonism to this. To be of use, to be free from that self-love which is always akin to self-idolatry, to be men in understanding but children in heart and spirit,—this is the mark which he presents when, in answer to the reasoning in the heart, he says, pointing to the child, " He that is least among you all, the same shall be great." A sentence ever to be pondered, implying (Matt. xviii. 3) that the soul has been *turned* to the right law of its being. " He restoreth my soul." With this lesson of humility there is joined at this time a lesson of *charity and forbearance.* How this lesson was occasioned is explained in ver. 49. The expression used by the Lord, " in my Name," seems to have suggested to John an incident, perhaps the circumstance which somehow gave rise to the reasoning, " Master, we saw one casting out devils in thy Name, and we forbade him, because he followeth not with us." Interdict honestly enough meant! But one wholly foreign to the law of the spirit of Christ's life. His greatness is that he is not confined to any circle; his gospel is " the presence of a good diffused." There is a virtue in even the hem of his garment. The communion of God with men is always wider than the communion of men with God. He is in contact with minds which do not even consciously surrender to him. Beware of identifying the bestowment of spiritual grace with the acknowledgments of belief according to any set of words, or with adherence to any particular company of believers. " The Spirit divideth to every man severally as he wills." It is not for any to forbid another " because he followeth not with us." No; in the next chapter we shall find Christ protesting, " He that is not with me is against me." That is the one side of his mind. But it is balanced by the other (ver. 50), " He that is not against us is for us." The two sentences are not mutually contradictory. The one establishes that there is no middle course between Christ and Satan; that those who will not join Christ in his warfare against Satan must, directly or indirectly, aid Satan against Christ. In the other it is shown that the man whom John and his brethren forbade was really with Christ in his warfare, and had received from him the faith which was mighty against the kingdom of darkness. The miracle in Christ's Name was the proof that he was really on Christ's side, gathering with him. " Try the spirits," such is practically the rejoinder of Jesus; " do not forbid simply because one has not complied with what you consider necessary or right; look at the character of the deed, at the motive present to him; if that bear the mark of my Name, account him with me, although he follows not with you." John would have been justified in going to the man who cast out devils, and expounding the way of God more perfectly to him; he was not justified in prohibiting. Most difficult of graces is the grace of charity; charity as distinguished from the toleration which is the outcome of a mind that has no positive conviction of its own, and regards all views as alike to it; charity which has its hand firm in definite truth, but recognizes that Christ, not any man or any system, is the Truth; " Thou, O Lord, art more than they; " and because of this reverence, this feeling of the infiniteness of truth, allows for many forms of apprehension, welcoming the Name of the Lord, howsoever it is revealed in character and life, and, when there cannot be fellowship, sorrowing rather than denouncing. Humility and charity God has joined together. They are the two inseparable features of the childlike character. Where humility reigns, there is always the desire to be fair, to acknowledge the excellences even of doctrines and opinions to which the mind is opposed; most of all, of persons from whom it may differ. " O Lord, who hast taught us that all our doings without charity are nothing worth; send thy Holy Ghost, and pour into our hearts that most excellent gift of charity, the very bond of peace and of all virtues, without which whosoever liveth is counted dead before thee."

Vers. 51—62.—*The face steadfastly set.* Very pathetic and sublime is the announcement of the fifty-first verse. The bright, joyous spring-time has gone. The cornfields and gardens, the hill and dale, the " lake's still face sleeping sweetly in the embrace of mountains terraced high with mossy stone "—all the scenery which the Son of man so dearly loved, must now be left behind. No more for him the crowds of simple fisher-folk hanging on his words; no more for him the circuits from village to village, returning to the quiet Capernaum home; no more for him the happy work which marked the earlier years of the Prophet of Nazareth. Now there are only the deepening opposition of scribe and Pharisee, and the lengthening shadow of the cross. He is the Man of men. Not without pain must he have left Nazareth in the distance, and taken his way through the Plain of Esdraelon, past Nain and Shunem, bound for Jerusalem. But this is sublime: " He steadfastly set his face." It implies that there were solicitations, temptations in another direction. The Christ of God needed to gird up all his energies. Flesh and blood cried, "Stay a little longer at least." The mind of the Son made answer, " Nay, how am I straitened until the baptism be accomplished!" It is of an hour in this journey that Mark speaks, when he says that " Jesus went before the disciples : and they were amazed ; and, as they followed, they were afraid." Why they were afraid, we are not told ; but we may well conceive that there was the print of a secret agony on his brow, that there was something in his aspect, as he walked a little way ahead of them, which awed and silenced. His face was "steadfastly set." And would that we better knew the secret of this steadfast face! How we shrink from the duty which our Father lays on us ! How we withdraw our gaze from the cups of suffering, from the cross-bearing, which our Father assigns us! How we run away from what is irksome! or, when we must do it, how often we meet it with a countenance awry ! Lord, we cannot penetrate the mystery of thy way. At times even thy presence seems dreadful. But lead us in the truth of thy steadfastness, and keep us following thee, even although amazed and afraid ! Two features of the beginning of the journey are set before us in the passage under review.

I. THE ONE, THE REJECTION OF THE LORD BY A VILLAGE OF THE SAMARITANS. And this for a reason which suggests to us many similar mistakes and misjudgments. Bigotry dethrones reason, and stirs up what is worst against what is best in the heart. To these rude villagers, the one condemning circumstance is that his face is towards Jerusalem. If he had been only going in the other direction, they would have been forward with welcomes, and in return would have received unspeakable blessings. Let us not be too ready to cast the stone. We are all apt to be carried away by the appearance of a person or thing, and, in advance of rational considerations, to judge, sentence, or condemn. Thus many a time the messengers of the Lord, with blessings in their hand, seeking to make ready for him a place in human charities and kindnesses, are repelled. "What wonder," says an old Latin Father, "that the sons of thunder wished to flash lightning !" (ver. 54). There have been many such Boanerges since the days of James and John. They are the exponents of a tendency too frequently illustrated in the ecclesiastical world, to meet Samaritan disdain and rebuke by the terrors of the Lord, by the mere force of authority, in mistaken zeal to denounce and excommunicate. Ah! how often has the voice of the Gentlest repeated the rebuke in the ears of his followers, " Ye know not what manner of spirit ye are of; for the Son of man is not come to destroy men's lives, but to save them."

II. THE OTHER FEATURE (though it does not seem clear when it occurred) is, THE WORD BEARING ON DISCIPLESHIP GIVEN IN REPLY TO THE THREE MEN WHO ARE INTRODUCED TO US AT THE CLOSE OF THE CHAPTER. These three men are types of classes whose representatives we need not go far to seek. 1. *There is the hasty disciple.* (Ver. 57.) " Lord, I will follow thee whithersoever thou goest." There is no discernment of what is implied in the "whithersoever." There is no counting of the cost. He is the man of impulse and fresh warm feeling, who has "received some word of Jesus with joy, yet has no root in himself." The "I will" stands forth in its own strength, which is but weakness. Observe how the Lord deals with him. He does not reject the offer made; only he sends the man to prayer and self-review, giving him, in one far-reaching sentence, to see what in his rashness he had been undertaking. "Follow me whithersoever I go? Knowest thou not that I am the poorest of all; that, in my Father's world, I am the One 'despised and rejected. No throne, no royalties, no kingdom as thou conceivest of a kingdom? The fox has its hole, the bird has its nest, the Son of man hath not where to lay his head. Think, then, on that to which thou wouldst pledge thyself." A word still called for ! The will which is eager to follow is sometimes slow to receive the Law of the spirit of the life which is in Christ Jesus. 2. As the hasty disciple passes out of sight, lo ! another appears, he who may be called the *dilatory.* Notice the difference between the two. In the former, the initiative is taken by the man ; in the latter, the initiative is taken by Jesus, with the short, peremptory, "Follow me." The one has no misgivings ; the other desires to follow but has not courage enough to express his convictions. And the mind is not decided. Secretly there is the attraction to the Lord, but there is also the home, the aged father, the circle in the quiet village. No; he is nearly, but not quite, ready. It is on him that the Lord looks. He sees him trembling at the word that is working in his soul, and forth comes the calling, empowering, "Follow!" Was it not so natural (ver. 59), "Lord, suffer me first to go and bury my father"? And will not he whose commandment is, "Honour thy father and mother," at once consent? No; the Lord's need, the Lord's call, sets the private and domestic claims aside. Hence the enigmatical reply of ver. 60. "Thou hast neighbours, brethren, who have not received the life that is pulsing in thee; to them may be left such a charge as that which thou hast named. But thou, with that life in thee, hast something else to do. Life must live; go thou, the living, and fulfil the living man's charge—preach the kingdom of God." 3. Finally, there comes into view *the tender-hearted disciple*. (Ver. 61.) "I will follow thee"—only first let me say farewell at home; a last look, a last adieu is all. Ah! this may not be. The rejoinder is somewhat stern (ver. 62). Now, what is the lesson? It is this. On the rocks and reef of the seashore we find creatures rooted to them. Scarcely can we separate the anemone from its reef. How terrible it would be for a human being, with a human soul, to be doomed, like that zoophyte, to cleave to that rock, with no variety except what is caused by the ebb and flow of the sea! Yet, is the life actually lived by many much better? Day following day, and always the monotone of a mere worldly life; no higher end, no higher reference; all of the earth, earthy! O piteous sight—a soul cleaving to the dust! Have we not seen a nobler truth? Looking into the face of Christ, is there not a voice bidding us higher? What but death and darkness could be if this earth of ours moved only in its own little diameter, around its own axis? Is it not the recipient of life and light because of its higher orbit as a member of the great solar system? And have we not spiritual life and light because the centre of our being is God? Then, disciple of Jesus, as he who has put his hand to the plough is intent on guiding it to the end of the furrow, ploughing on though the clod be hard and the work severe, be thou steadfast, thy face set with thy Lord toward his Jerusalem; no looking back, precursor of going back; this the prayer of all thy praying, "Lord, unite my heart, that I may love and fear thy Name."

HOMILIES BY VARIOUS AUTHORS.

Vers. 1—6.—*Lessons from the first commission.* We learn from this commission and these instructions—

I. THAT CHRIST HAS DIVINE RESOURCES FOR SPECIAL NECESSITIES. He gave to the twelve "power and authority over all devils," etc. If he had such resources at his command then, when he was stooping so low and laying aside so much of heavenly rank and authority, of what is he not possessed now—now that he is enthroned, now that "all power is given unto him in heaven and on earth"? His Church may be very bitterly assailed; it may fall very low in consequence of the slackness and unfaithfulness of its own members; it has thus fallen more than once since he ascended: but in his hand are great reserves; his Divine resources are illimitable. He can equip and send forth men endowed with wonderful power, with marvellous faculty of persuasion or of organization; he can send forth those whose influence shall be felt even "where Satan's seat is," in the depths of spiritual evil and moral wrong, and thus he can establish or re-establish his kingdom.

II. THAT WE MAY COMMIT OURSELVES TO WORKS OF USEFULNESS though conscious of much insufficiency. We may be surprised that our Lord should send out the twelve to "preach the kingdom of God" (ver. 2) at a time when they had so very imperfect an idea as they then had of the character of that kingdom. Their views of it were very elementary; they had yet to learn concerning it facts and truths which seem to us of the first importance. But still he sent them; there was something, and something of substantial value, they could teach; and they were (all of them, at that time) genuinely attached to their Divine Master. If we wait until we know everything it would be well to know before we begin our ministry, we shall be postponing the time until our chance is gone. We should begin the work of holy usefulness *early*, even when there is very much to learn; we shall acquire knowledge, tact, wisdom, power, as we go on our way of service. The one requisite thing is that we shall be thoroughly sincere, and do all that we do out of a true and faithful heart.

III. THAT CHRIST MAY CALL ON US TO CAST OURSELVES ENTIRELY ON HIS PROVIDING AND PROTECTING CARE. This he did with his apostles now (ver. 3). Usually it is our duty to take every precaution for our bodily necessities; not to expose ourselves to needless perils or to injurious privations. But there are times when it becomes our duty—especially that of the Christian minister, or evangelist, or missionary—to cast aside all prudential considerations, to run all risks, to commit himself absolutely to the care of the Divine Father.

IV. THAT THERE IS A LIMIT WHICH EVEN HOLY PERSISTENCY MAY NOT PASS. (Ver. 5.) It is well to work patiently on under discouragement. It is our sacred duty to do this; we are quite unfitted for the nobler spheres of service if we are not prepared to do so. We admire and applaud those who cannot tear themselves away from work which they have set their hearts on accomplishing. Let patient persistency have abundant scope for its exercise, but there *is* a point where it must stop; to exceed a certain measure is to be disregardful of those who would not reject the Word of life, on whom Christian service would not be spent in vain.

V. THAT PRACTICAL KINDNESS TO BODILY WANTS goes well with earnest attention to spiritual necessities (ver. 6).—C.

Vers. 7—9.—*The tetrarch and the Teacher.* Our Lord had very little to do with the "kings and rulers of the earth," but they did occasionally cross his path. At such times he bore himself as we should expect he would—he who was so far below and yet so much further above them. His relations with Herod, as suggested by the text, were these—

I. THE TEACHER CAUSING TROUBLE TO THE TETRARCH. Herod "was perplexed" by all that he heard concerning Christ : his own wonderful works and those which he commissioned and enabled his apostles to perform (vers. 1—6) made an impression which entered and disturbed the palace. We have reason to think that in Herod's case the fame of Jesus brought not only mental perplexity, but moral perturbation also (see Matt. xiv. 2; Mark vi. 14). He could not understand who this new, great prophet could be, and he consulted his court respecting him. But it was his own apprehension, if not his conviction, that the man whom he had so guiltily slain " was risen from the dead." His carefully trained judgment told him that he had nothing more to fear from that faithful spokesman of the Lord. But his conscience, that struck deeper than his judgment, compelled him to fear that he had not seen the last of that beheaded prisoner. It is a very easy thing to take a human life, but it is a very difficult thing to escape from responsibility for a human death. 1. Christ's coming to us has caused and will cause a large amount of intellectual perplexity. The world has for eighteen centuries been asking who he is, and what is the true and full account of him. In this mental perplexity there is nothing to be regretted; there is no better subject on which the human intelligence could be employed. 2. Christ's coming to man has occasioned much trouble of soul. The truths he taught, the life he lived, the claims he makes upon us,—these have stirred the human conscience to its depth; they have awakened a sense of sin and ill desert; they have turned a strong light upon the guilty past and the perilous future; they have called forth much self-condemnation and self-reproach. It is well that they have done, it is right that they should do so.

II. THE TETRARCH DESIRING TO SEE THE TEACHER. "He desired to see him," perhaps to have his mental curiosity set at rest; perhaps to have his conscientious fears appeased; perhaps for both these reasons. Certainly not in the hope of hearing heavenly truth, of hearing that Divine wisdom which would enable him to be a better man and to live a nobler life. And his motive being low, it proved, as we might have expected, that when he did see him, the interview gave him no gratification, but only added to his guilt (ch. xxiii. 8—11). It is well, indeed, to wish to come into the presence of Christ, but whether the fulfilment of our desire will end in good or evil depends mainly upon our motive. 1. A selfish spirit is almost sure to be unblessed, is most likely to have its guilt increased thereby. 2. A spirit of mere curiosity will probably return unrewarded, though it may meet with a gracious benediction. 3. A spirit of devotion and inquiry will certainly gain a blessing from his holy hand. We may look at—

III. The Teacher and the tetrarch in their strong contrasts. 1. Of present position. 2. Of moral character and the purpose of their life. 3. Of their destiny.—C.

Ver. 11.—*The healing hand of Christ.* "And healed them that had need of healing." And who are they to whom these words do not apply? In a world as full of sin as ours is, there is nothing of which we have greater need than a Divine Healer. For sin means sickness, disease, derangement, pain—both spiritual and corporeal. *Every* human ear wants to hear those gracious words, "I am the Lord that healeth thee;" *every* human heart has occasion to plead, "Heal me, O Lord, and I shall be healed;" *every* soul is again and again in need of the great beneficent Physician.

I. As those liable to disease and pain. Considering the extreme intricacy of our bodily structure, and considering also the irregularities and evils of which we are guilty, it is wonderful that there is as much health and as little sickness as we find. But he is an exception to his fellows who goes for many years without ailment and, indeed, without illness. And we have all of us reason to bless the Lord of our lives that he heals us so readily and so often. He heals in two ways. 1. By conferring on us a nature which has recuperative powers, so that without any medical aid the wound is healed, the organ recovers its power and fulfils its functions. 2. By giving us medicinal herbs which our science can discover and apply, the nature of which is to heal and to restore. In both these cases it is the Lord of our human body and of nature who "works" (John v. 17) for our benefit. Our art, where it is exercised, only supplies one condition out of many; it alone would be utterly insufficient. Whenever we are healed of any malady, slight or serious, we should join in the exclamation of the psalmist (ciii. 3), and feel that we have one reason more for gratitude and devotion. Let those who have been brought back from the gates of the grave by Christ's pitiful and healing kindness consider whether they are paying him the vows which they made in the hour of suffering and danger (Ps. lxvi. 14).

II. As the children of sorrow. Possibly we may know nothing of serious sickness—there are those who escape it—but we all know what sorrow means. Trouble is a visitor that knocks at every door, that finds its way to every human heart. It may be some gradually approaching evil, which at length culminates in disaster; or it may be some sudden blow, which badly bruises if it does not break the heart. It may be the heavy, entangling loss; or the grave, oppressive anxiety; or the lamentable failure; or the sore and sad bereavement. How precious, then, beyond all price, the healing of the Divine Healer! In these dark hours our Divine Lord comes to us with ministering hand. 1. He impels all those who are dear to us to grant us their tenderest and most sustaining love; and human kindness is a very healing thing. 2. He grants us his own most gracious sympathy; he is touched with a feeling of our infirmity; we know and feel that he is with us, watching over us, "afflicted in our affliction;" and the sympathy of our Saviour is a precious balm to our wounded spirit. 3. He comes to us in the office and the Person of the Divine Comforter, directly soothing and healing our torn and troubled hearts. Thus he heals us according to the greatness of our need.

III. As those who suffer from a wounded character. A wounded spirit is worse than a bodily infirmity (Prov. xviii. 14); but a wounded character is worse than a wounded spirit, for that is a spirit that has *injured itself*. There are those who present to their friends and neighbours the spectacle of bodily health and material prosperity; but what their Master sees when he regards them is *spiritual infirmity*. They are weak, sickly, inwardly deranged. Their hearts are very far from being as he would like to see them; instead of ardent love is lukewarmness; instead of reverence is flippancy of spirit; instead of a holy scrupulousness and a wise restraint is laxity if not positive disobedience; instead of zeal is coldness and indifference to his cause and kingdom. Of all men living, these are they who have most "need of healing." And Christ both can and will heal them. To such as these he says, "I will heal thy backsliding;" "Wilt thou be made whole?" And if they will but go to him in a spirit of humility, of faith, of reconsecration, they will receive power from his gracious touch, they will rise renewed; and as they rise from the couch of spiritual langour and indifference to walk, to run in the way of his commandments, to climb the heights of close and holy fellowship with God, a deeper note of joy will sound from the depth of their hearts than ever comes from the lips of bodily convalescence, "I will extol thee, O Lord; for thou hast lifted me up, and hast not made my foes to rejoice over me."—C.

Vers. 12—17.—*The Divine provision for the world's need.* This miracle of our Lord, meeting as it did the present bodily necessities of the multitude about him, stands for ever as a picture and parable of the far more wonderful and the gloriously bountiful provision which the Saviour of mankind has made for the deeper necessities of our race.

I. OUR HOLY SOLICITUDE FOR THE SPIRITUALLY DESTITUTE. There is a note of true sympathy in the language of the disciples (ver. 12; see Mark vi. 35, 36). They were concerned to think of that great number of people, among whom were "women and children" (Matt. xiv. 21), having gone so long without food, and being "in a desert place" where none could be obtained. How strong and keen should be our sympathy with those who are spiritually destitute; who have received from God a nature with immeasurable capacities, with profound cravings for that which is eternally true and divinely good, and who "have nothing to eat"! No solicitude for hungering human hearts can be extravagant; it is only too common to be guiltily and pitifully unconcerned. And if the stage of spiritual hunger and thirst should have passed into that of spiritual unconsciousness, that is one degree (and a large degree too) more deplorable, for it is one stage nearer to spiritual death. We do well to pity the multitudes at home and abroad who might be and who should be living on Divine and everlasting truth, but who are pining and perishing on miserable husks,—on errors, on superstitions, on morbid fancies, on low ambitions, on unsatisfying and perhaps demoralizing pleasures.

II. THE APPARENT INADEQUACY OF THE DIVINE PROVISION. Well may the disciples, not yet enlightened as to their Master's purpose, regard "five loaves and two fishes" as hopelessly inadequate to the occasion. So to human judgment they seemed. Not less strikingly disproportioned must the Divine provision for man's higher necessities have seemed to those who first regarded it. What was it? It was, in the language of our Lord recorded a few verses on in this chapter (ver. 22), "the Son of man suffering many things, being rejected . . . and slain, and being raised the third day." A crucified and restored Messiah was to be offered as the Bread of life to a hungering world! Would this satisfy the needs of all mankind—of Jew and Gentile, of barbarian and cultured, of bond and free, of man and woman? Could One that seemed to fail, whose cause was all but extinguished in obloquy and desertion, be the Redeemer of mankind? It was unlikely in the last degree; speaking after the manner of men, it was impossible! And the machinery, too, the instrumentality by which this strange provision was to be conveyed to all human souls everywhere and through all generations, was that not equally inadequate? A few "unlearned and ignorant men," a few earnest and true but obscure and uninfluential women,—could they establish and perpetuate this new system? could they pass on these scanty provisions to the waiting and perishing multitude? How hopeless! how impossible! Yet see—

III. ITS PROVED SUFFICIENCY. As those five loaves and two fishes, under the multiplying hand of Christ, proved to be far more than enough for the thousands who partook of them, so is the provision in the gospel of Christ for the needs of man found to be all-sufficient. In a once-crucified and now exalted Saviour we have One in whom is found: 1. Pardon for every sin and for every repentant sinner. 2. Admission, instant and full, to the presence and favour of God. 3. A source of purity of heart, and excellency, and even nobility, of life. 4. Comfort in all the sorrows and privations of our earthly course. 5. Peace and hope in death. 6. A glorious immortality. Well does this great Benefactor say, "I am come that ye might have life, and . . . *have it more abundantly.*" The provision is more than equal to the necessity; there is a marvellous overflow of truth and grace.—C.

Vers. 23, 24.—*Life gained by losing it.* These strong and sententious words may teach us three truths which are of vital importance to us.

I. THAT THE VOLUNTARY SURRENDER OF OUR LIFE TO GOD IS OUR ENTRANCE UPON LIFE INDEED. *What is it for a man to live?* We speak truly but superficially when we say that any one is a living man from whom the breath of life has not yet departed. But there is deep truth in the objection of our English poet, "As though to breathe were life." Human life, as its Divine Author regards it, means very much more than this. And, taught of Christ, we understand that we then attain to our true life when we live unto God, in his holy service, and for the good of those whom he has committed to our care. The thoughts of sinful men concerning life are utterly false; they are the exact contrary of the truth. Men imagine that just as they gain that which will minister to their own enjoyment, and keep that which, if parted with, would benefit other people, they make much of their life. This is not even a caricature of the truth; it is its contradiction. The fact is that just as we *lose* ourselves in the love of God, and just as we *expend* our powers and possessions in the cause of mankind, we enter upon and enjoy that which is the "life indeed." For all that is best and highest lives, *not to gain, but to give.* As we pass from the lowest of the brute creation up an ascending line until we reach the Divine Father himself, we find that the nobler being exists, not to appropriate to himself, but to minister to others; when in our thought we reach the Divine, we see that God himself is receiving the least and is giving the most. He finds his heavenly life in giving freely and constantly of his resources to all beings in his universe. This is the supreme point that we can attain; we surrender ourselves entirely to God, to be possessed and employed by him; we enter upon and we realize the noble, the angelic, the true life. Whosoever will save his life by retaining his own will and withholding his powers from his Redeemer, *by that very act* loses it; but whosoever will freely surrender his life to God and man will, *by that very act,* find it. To live is not to get and to keep; it is to love and to lose ourselves in loving service.

II. That the full service of Christ means habitual self-denial. 1. It means the abandonment of all that is vicious; *i.e.* of all that is positively hurtful to ourselves or others, and that, as such, is condemned of God as sinful. 2. It means the avoidance of that which is not unlawful in itself, but which would be a hindrance to usefulness and the service of love (see Rom. xiv.). Of the rightness and desirableness of this, every man must be a judge for himself, and no man may "judge his brother." That life must be a narrow one which does not afford scope for the frequent forfeiture of good which might lawfully be taken, but which, for Christ's sake, is declined. 3. It involves struggle and sacrifice at the first, but the sense of personal loss is continually declining, and the consciousness of Divine approval is a counterbalancing gain.

III. That to secure eternal blessedness it may be necessary to lay down our mortal life. Many are they who have been called upon to put the most literal interpretation on the twenty-fourth verse; who have had to choose between parting with everything human and earthly on the one hand, and sacrificing their fidelity to Christ and their eternal hopes on the other hand. For that hour of solemn crisis the Lord has granted abounding grace, and from every land and age a noble army of martyrs have made the better choice, and now wear the crown of life in the better land.—C.

Ver. 25.—*The priceless.* Our Lord has taught us as no other teacher ever has—

I. The transcendent worth of our human nature. When he came that was held in very small esteem. Men showed what they thought of human *nature* by the use they made of it, and of human *life* by the readiness with which they threw it away. There was no thought of the inviolable sacredness of a human spirit. Jesus Christ has taught us to think of it as precious beyond all price. Man's body is only the vesture of his mind; man, like God, is spirit, but he is spirit clothed in flesh. He is a spirit (1) accountable to God for all he thinks and feels, as well as for all he says and does; (2) capable of forming a beautiful and noble character resembling that of the Divine Father himself; (3) capable of living a life which, in its sphere, is a reproduction of the life God is living in heaven; (4) coming into close contact and fellowship with God; (5) intended to share God's own immortality.

II. The temptation to lose sight of this great truth. There are two things that often have such a deteriorating effect upon us that it is practically erased from the tablet of our soul. 1. *The love of pleasure;* whether this be indulgence in unholy pleasure, or the practical surrender of ourselves to mere enjoyment, to the neglect of all that is best and highest. 2. *The eager pursuit of gain.* Not that there is any radical inconsistency between profitable trading and holy living; not that a Christian man may not exemplify his piety by the way in which he conducts his business; but that there are often found to be terribly strong temptations to untruthfulness, or dishonesty, or hardness, or unjust withholdment, or a culpable and injurious absorption in business. And under the destructive influence of one of these two forces the soul withers or dies.

III. THE CALAMITOUS MISTAKE THAT IS SOMETIMES MADE. It is not only a grievous sin, but a disastrous error to gain worldly wealth, and, in the act of gaining it, to lose the soul. That is the worst of all possible bargains. The man who makes many thousands of pounds, and who loses conscientiousness, truthfulness, spirituality, all care for what God thinks of him and feels about him, sensitiveness of spirit—in fact, *himself*, is a man over whom Heaven weeps; he has made a supreme mistake. Gold, silver, precious stones, are of *limited* worth. There are many of the most important services we want which they have no power to render; and the hour is daily drawing near when they will have no value to us whatever. But the soul is of *immeasurable* worth; no sum of money that can be expressed in figures will indicate its value; that is something which absolutely transcends expression; and time, instead of diminishing, enhances its importance—it becomes of more and more account "as our days go by," as our life draws toward its close. Jesus Christ not only put this thought into words, —the words of the text—he *put it into action*. He let us see that, in his estimation, the human soul was *worth suffering and dying for*—worth suffering for as he suffered in Gethsemane, worth dying for as he died at Calvary. Then do we wisely enter into his thought concerning it when we seek salvation at his cross, when, by knowing him as our Divine Redeemer, we enter into eternal life.—C.

Ver. 28.—*The Transfiguration*. This incident is one that stands quite by itself; it is wholly unlike everything else in our Lord's history. It was miraculous enough, yet we do not count it amongst the miracles of Christ. It may be viewed in many lights; it may illustrate—

I. THE CLOSE RELATION BETWEEN OUR SPIRITUAL AND OUR BODILY NATURE. This manifested glory was not altogether outward; it was more than a radiance thrown around or imposed upon him, which might just as readily have occurred to any Jewish rabbi. It does not correspond with the illumination of the wall of a building or the face of a cathedral. It was the glory of his Divine nature, usually hidden, now shining through and revealing itself in his form and countenance. We are sure that the appearance of our Lord at all times answered to his character and his spirit. We gather this from the charm which he exerted over his disciples and over little children; from the confidence which he inspired in the social outcasts of his day; in the occasional flashings forth of his Divine sovereignty (John ii. 15; Mark x. 32; John xviii. 6). The Transfiguration was by far the most striking instance of his bodily nature being lighted up and irradiated by his indwelling glory; there was as much of the spiritual as of the material about it; it could not have happened to any other than to our Lord. And this opens the question how far our spiritual experiences may and should glorify our personal appearance. The spirit does act powerfully upon and manifest itself through the body which is its organ. We know how love gleams, how indignation flashes, how scorn and hatred lower, how hope shines, how disappointment pales, how all the passions that breathe and burn in the human breast come forth and make themselves felt in the eye, the lip, the countenance of man. We may and should see a kind or a pure heart in a kind or pure countenance, as we do see avarice or indulgence in a keen or a bloated visage. We bear about in our body the marks of our association with the Lord Jesus, and other marks also which are not derived from such fellowship as that. Holiness has its transfiguring influence, as sin has its debasing effect, upon the human form and figure—the one refines and glorifies, as the other disfigures and degrades. There are two things to be heeded here. 1. We must not draw hasty and unjust inferences; there are those who, so far as appearance goes, are victims of misfortune or are vicarious sufferers. 2. We must endeavour to let a holy character be visible in our bodily persons. Inward excellence is *the* source of outward beauty. No tailoring or millinery, no cosmetics or perfumery, will make beautiful the face and form behind which is an ugly heart; selfishness and pride and envy will never look anything but unsightly and forbidding. The thoughts that breathe, the feelings that glow, the spirit that animates, the character that shines through—it is this which beautifies, which adorns, which makes attractive, which wins confidence and love. These are the things to care for, to cultivate, to cherish; it is thence that our influence for good will spring.

II. THE CARE WHICH GOD TAKES OF HIS OWN IN THEIR TIME OF SPECIAL NEED. What was the purpose of this wonderful scene? It was to prepare the disciples (and perhaps the Master) for the last scenes of all. Those two celestial visitants spake of "the decease which he should accomplish," etc. A terrible ordeal was that through which he and they would pass. Therefore it seemed well to the Father to give to him and to them the most imposing, the most impressive, the most convincing proof that he was well pleased with his Son, and that he was, indeed, the Messiah of their hopes. We know from Peter's Epistle (2 Pet. i. 16, 17) how strong a confirmation of their faith it was and continued to be. Thus God cared for his own, and thus he still cares. Our lives glide on like peaceful rivers; but most human lives prove to be rivers with cataracts in their course. Times of grave trial and peril come, when there is a great strain on our faith and patience; when we have to draw on our last resources; critical trial-hours they are, like those which came to the Master and to his faithful band. How shall we be assured of calmness, fortitude, fidelity, when we pass through them? If we are loyal to our Lord in the days of sunshine and prosperity, if we "abide in him" now, he will not fail us then. As our day his grace will be. He will prepare us for the trial-hour; he will be with us in its darkest moments; he will lead us out into the sunshine on the other side.—C.

Ver. 35.—*The wisdom of hearing Christ.* Three things are clear to us, preliminarily. 1. *Jesus Christ is addressing us.* From his home and throne on high our Saviour stoops to call us, to instruct us, to bless us. He is saying to *us*, "Come unto me;" "Abide in me;" "Follow me." 2. *We need not hear him if we choose not to do so.* As in a room where many groups of people are conversing, we only hear the voice of that company to which we join ourselves and listen, so in the large room of this world there are many voices speaking and it rests with each of us to determine which we will regard. Shall it be the voice of ambition? or that of appetite? or that of human learning? or that of Christ? 3. *Our heavenly Father urges us to give our best attention to Jesus Christ.* "This is my beloved Son: hear *him*." We shall see, if we consider, how and why God presses on us this act of hearing.

I. BECAUSE OF OUR URGENT NEED OF A VOICE THAT IS DIVINE. There are two things we urgently require, but which, apart from Jesus Christ, we cannot have. 1. One is *a knowledge of what is true.* We are "strangers on the earth," and know but very little. Like the little bird (of the ancient story) that flew from the darkness into the dimly lighted room and out into the darkness on the other side, so from the darkness of the past we enter and stay for a brief time in the dimly lighted present, and forth we pass into the darkness of the future. 2. The other is *the power to do what we know to be right.* Truly pathetic is the Roman's confession, "I see the better course, and approve; I follow the worse." What men everywhere have wanted is the inspiration and the power to be and to do that which they perceive to be good and right. Whence shall we gain this? Only from a Divine Saviour, from One who has lived and died for us, to whom we offer our hearts and our lives, the love of whom will constrain us toward all that is good and pure, and restrain us from all that is bad and wrong.

II. BECAUSE OF HIS INTIMATE RELATION TO HIS DIVINE FATHER. "This is my beloved Son," *therefore* should we "hear him." For one of the deepest and most practical questions we can ask is—What is God's thought, feeling, purpose, toward us? If there were any human being who sustained toward us a relation which at all approached in intimacy and importance that which God sustains to us, we should be eager indeed to know what was his feeling and intention concerning us. How eagerly, then, should we inquire of him "in whom we live, and move, and have our being," "with whom we have everything to do," on whose will we are absolutely dependent for our future here and hereafter! What does God think about us? On what conditions will he receive and bless us? Christ, "the beloved Son," who came forth from God, and who knows his mind as none other can (Matt. xi. 27), can answer this supreme question for us.

III. BECAUSE OF HIS CLOSE AND INTIMATE RELATION TO OURSELVES. We want some one to speak to us who knows us well, who understands us altogether; one about whom we can feel that this is true. To whom, then, should we listen, if not to the Son of God, our Maker; to the Son of man, our Brother? "He knew what was in man," as the evangelist testified, and again and again he showed that he knew his disciples far better than they knew themselves. Such is his knowledge of us. We may think that we know ourselves and what is best for ourselves. But we may be utterly mistaken. We find that our neighbours display lamentable and ruinous ignorance on these great matters. Who are we that *we* should be full of wisdom where others err? Let us distrust ourselves: "There is a way which seemeth right unto a man, but the end thereof are the ways of death." Ignorant presumption is a foe that "hath slain its ten thousands." The truly wise will seek the great Teacher's feet, and say, "Lord, what wilt *thou* have me to do?"—C.

Vers. 37—42.—*The healing of the lunatic child.* From this most interesting story we may gather the truths—

I. That from the very fangs of defeat a great victory may be secured. More than once in the history of war there has occurred such an incident as that which is related concerning the great struggle in the United States (1860—1864). A severe and successful attack is made by one army on the other; the enemy is driven back, his guns and his camp captured. As his regiments are in full retreat, the general of the defeated force, who has been unfortunately absent, arrives on the scene; he arrests the tide of retreat, gathers his soldiers about him, stops the pursuing host in their career, leads a triumphant attack upon them, drives them beyond his own camp, recaptures his guns, and chases the once-conquering but now defeated army for miles to the rear of its first position. Such a victory snatched from the jaws of humbling defeat took place on this occasion. The returning Saviour found his disciples driven before the hostile attack of his enemies, but his presence soon availed "to restore the day," and before long transformed humiliating failure into joyous triumph. In the Master's actual, *spiritual* absence the cause of the Church may be brought very low indeed, and a complete and crushing disaster may impend; but let the Lord return, let his presence and his power be felt, and from the very teeth of threatened calamity there shall be secured a glorious victory. Let no heart despond so long as there is a present Captain; failure is never irretrievable when he is "on the field;" under his leadership even "death is swallowed up in victory."

II. That human affection is meant to lead to spiritual attachments. It was *his son's* sickness that led this man to seek Jesus; but for that he would not have sought and found him. It was his strong *parental* love that would not be denied, that led him to urge his plea, that enabled him to overcome his fears and to gain that valuable victory. God employs many instrumentalities to lead his children into his kingdom. We ought to be influenced by our sense of what is *right* and of what is *wise* in the matter; but, if not won by these, let the consideration of the deep and tender interests of those who are dear to us convince and determine us. For the sake of those children of ours, whom we love so profoundly, and who have such a vital interest in Christian truth, let us sit at the feet of Christ, and be subject to his sway.

III. That the very worst case will yield to the touch of the Divine hand. There could not well be a worse case of possession than this (see vers. 39, 42). If the malignant forces could have triumphed over the benevolent Spirit, they would have triumphed here. But everything was accomplished when "Jesus took him by the hand" (Mark ix. 27). So is it with the worst spiritual maladies. They may seem so bad as to be incurable; it may be the general opinion that the case is utterly hopeless. But there is a power in reserve against which the most virulent and the most violent evils are not able to stand. For

". . . many of whom all men said,
'They've fallen, never more to stand,'
Have risen, though they seemed as dead
When Jesus took them by the hand."

The most stricken souls will be healed, the most sorrowing ones comforted, the most despondent filled with a new and blessed hope, the most fallen and sunk in sin lifted up to purity and even to beauty and nobility of spirit and of life, when the Divine voice is heard bidding to be comforted, when the Divine hand is laid on the broken heart or the defiled and guilty soul.

IV. That the earnest soul need not let anything keep him back from

CHRIST AND HIS SALVATION. This father had much to overcome—the natural reluctance he would have to bring the poor demoniac into such publicity; the failure of the
disciples to effect a cure, well calculated as that was to discourage and dishearten him;
his own imperfect faith (Mark ix. 22, 24). But he overcame all these, and gained his
plea. Many may be the obstacles in the way of our salvation; they may be circumstantial, or they may be inward and spiritual; but if there be a thoroughly earnest
spirit, they will not prevail over us; we shall triumph over them, and go on our way
with our cause gained and our hearts gladdened.—C.

Vers. 46—48.—*The Church and the child.* The scene is well worthy the genius of
the artist: the disciples together, but still at variance with one another, with cold or
averted look; the Master with a little child in his arms (Mark ix. 36), either turning a
reproachful glance on his disciples, or a look of tenderness upon that little one; the child
himself with a trustful but wondering expression in his countenance. The scene is
suggestive of the thought—*What is the child to the Church?* (For homily on the contention between the apostles, see ch. xxii. 24.) We may consider—

I. WHAT THE CHILD WAS TO THE DISCIPLES. The answer to this question is—*not
much.* They were devout and worthy men; but they were Jews, and they shared the
mental habits of their countrymen. To them the little child was of small account—one
to be kept carefully out of sight; one to be taken charge of by parent or teacher, but
superfluous in society; one too many when a great man was present, when a great prophet was speaking, or a great healer was healing. This we know from their conduct on
a memorable occasion (ch. xviii. 15).

II. WHAT THE CHILD IS TO THE CHURCH. The poor, our Lord said, we have
"always with us." So is it with the children. Whoever are absent, they are present;
whoever fail, they abound. The child is in the midst of us, and we have to decide what
he shall be to us. Taught by our Lord's teaching, led by his example, imbued with
his Spirit, we have to take up a very different attitude from that of the disciples. The
Christian Church no longer regards the child as one that has to be carefully kept out
of the way lest he should be troublesome. It welcomes him cordially; like its Master,
it takes him into the embrace of its affection and its care. 1. It regards the children
as the *Church of the future.* It remembers that "death and change are busy ever,"
that the fathers and mothers are passing on and away, and that others will soon be
needed to take their place. When a few more years have come, the place which knows
us now will know us no more; who then, but the children about our feet, will bear the
flag we bear, will speak the truth we speak, will do the work we do? 2. It regards the
children as a *present valuable heritage.* For the little child (1) can be a recipient of
Divine truth, and not only can he be this, but his natural open-mindedness and trustfulness make him a peculiarly apt learner in Christ's great school; (2) can be a true
follower of the Divine Master—to him also Jesus says, "Follow me," and not only can
he "rise and follow" him, but his disposition to trust and love and obey makes him
to be a close and a very acceptable follower of his Lord; (3) can illustrate in his own
way the excellences of the Christian life, by the exhibition of those virtues and graces
which most become childhood and youth. The Church of Christ should find in the
little child its most interesting and its most valuable disciple. And this a great deal
the more because of—

III. WHAT THE CHILD IS TO THE SAVIOUR HIMSELF. This is *very much indeed.*
For Christ knows, as we do not, all the possibilities of the little child—the height to
which he may rise, or the depth to which he may sink; the good he may live to do, or
the evil he may live to work; the blessedness to which he may attain, or the shame
and woe which may be his end. He is more deeply interested in the young than we
are, and however earnest and eloquent our voice of invitation or of warning may be,
more earnest far is the voice of the Lord himself, as he says, "Come unto me, take my
yoke upon you, . . . my yoke is easy, my burden is light."—C.

Vers. 49, 50.—*Exclusiveness and neutrality—the forbidden and the impossible thing.*
We do well to take together this passage and that of ch. xi. 23. For one is the complement of the other. "He that is not against us is for us;" "He that is not with
me is against me; and he that gathereth not with me scattereth." There is not the

slightest inconsistency between these two declarations of our Lord. One states one truth, and the other a different one. They teach successively—

I. THAT WE ARE IN DANGER OF COUNTING AMONG OUR OPPONENTS THOSE WHOM WE SHOULD RECKON AS ALLIES. It did not seem to be a service of any particular account that a man should use the name of Jesus to exorcise demons, even though he may have had a measure of success in his attempts. But Christ said he was not to be " forbidden " as an outsider, but rather hailed as a friend and as an ally. What, then, would he not say now of those who go so far towards the fullest declaration of his truth as many thousands do, but who remain outside the particular Church with which we may be connected? Would he have us blame and brand these because they "follow not with us"? The spirit of persecution is cruel, foolish, and emphatically unchristian. Rather let us rejoice that there are found so many who, while not feeling it right to connect themselves with our organization, are yet loving the same Lord and serving the same cause. These are not our enemies; they are our allies.

II. THAT WE CANNOT WITHHOLD OUR EARNEST THOUGHT AND DELIBERATE CHOICE FROM CHRIST without being counted by him as his enemies. " He that is not with me is against me," etc. There is no neutrality in the great campaign now being fought out between sin and righteousness. In great European wars it is customary for generals and correspondents from other countries, not involved in the strife, to attend the movements and watch the operations of the armies; they, of course, are strictly neutral. But in this great spiritual campaign we cannot be mere spectators; *we must be soldiers fighting* on one side or on the other. For we are all deeply involved; we are implicated in what is past; we are interested in the issue; we have great responsibilities resting on us; we have great things at stake. God is addressing himself to every one of us, and it is not open to any of us to refuse to take up a decisive attitude in regard to the subjects of his address. 1. *He speaks to us of himself.* He makes himself known to us as our Creator, our Preserver, our generous Benefactor; he makes his appeal to us as our Divine Father, who earnestly desires our return to his home that he may bless us with his parental love. Can we possibly remain unaffected by this? Is not our very silence a most grievous offence and injury? Not to respond to him is to sin grievously against him. 2. *He comes to us in the Person of his Son Jesus Christ.* And he offers himself to us as the Redeemer who at the greatest possible price has wrought out our redemption, as the Divine Friend in the shelter of whose love and power we may spend our days, as the Source of our eternal life. Can we possibly take up a position toward him in which we are neither one thing nor another—neither enemy nor subject? Can we do other than either accept him or reject him? 3. *He summons us to his service,* and to the service of our kind. We are to be "living epistles," making known his truth, revealing to men the goodness of God, the grace of Christ, the excellency of his service. We are to bear witness unto him. Either our life is witnessing for him and for his truth, or our influence is thrown into the other scale. Those who know us are either being attracted toward Christ through all they see and know about us, or they are being repelled. We cannot be cyphers, try how we may. Our lives are telling on one side or on the other. Either we gather with Christ or we scatter abroad. We *must* make our choice.—C.

Vers. 51—55.—*Wisdom, duty, danger.* Among the various difficulties in this passage that have been the subject of exegetical debate, we may clearly discern three important lessons.

I. OUR WISDOM IN FRONT OF APPARENT EVIL. At this time our Lord had before him the dark days which would bring his ministry to a close. The contemplation of them had evidently gone down deep into his own mind, but he found none to share the thought or to sympathize with him in the prospect. He asked his disciples to let these things "sink down into their ears" (ver. 44), but they understood him not. He was the sole possessor of the great secret of his coming sorrow, struggle, and death. How did he face it? With an immovable resoluteness of soul. "He *steadfastly* set his face to go up to Jerusalem." What reason have we to be thankful for that holy and noble tenacity of spirit! Could anything less strong than that have carried him, unscathed, through all that followed? And if there had been any, even the slightest failure, what would have been the consequences to our race? When we have to face a future of *pain*, or of *separation* and attendant loneliness and single-handedness of struggle, or of strong and sustained *temptation*, in what spirit shall we face that? In the temper of calm and devout resoluteness; with a full and fixed determination to go bravely and unfalteringly through, shrinking from no suffering, enduring the worst that man can inflict, yielding nothing to the enemy of our soul. An unflinching resoluteness will do great things for us. 1. It will *save us from much suffering*; for cowardice and apprehension do not simply *add* to human wretchedness; they *multiply* it. 2. It will *save us from the chief peril and go far to secure us the victory*. The greatest of all perils before us is that of recreancy, unfaithfulness to our own convictions. An unstable mind is only too likely to be guilty of it. A resolute spirit is almost certain to escape it. 3. It will *place us by the side of our Divine Leader and of the noblest of his followers*. We shall be treading in the footsteps of him who "steadfastly set his face," etc., and who went up to that city of martyrs and gloriously triumphed there.

II. OUR DUTY IN THE PRESENCE OF A PROFESSED PROPHET. "They did not receive him;" "They went to another village." How much is contained, in these simple words, of human folly and privation! These villagers were profoundly prejudiced against Christ, and declined absolutely to see what he could do, to hear what he would say. They would not "judge for themselves" on the evidence ready to be furnished. And consequently they suffered a great privation. The great Healer and Teacher of mankind went another way; their sick went unhealed, their souls went unenlightened, while Divine tenderness and truth found other hearts and homes. Often since then has Christ gone, in the person of some one of his prophets or spokesmen, to the city, to the village, to the home, to the individual heart, and offered his truth, his grace, his salvation. But deep-seated prejudice, or strong material interests, or keen love of pleasure, has barred the way. He has not been received. And as he does not force an entrance anywhere, he has gone elsewhere; he has passed by, and all the treasure of his truth has been unpossessed, all the blessedness of his salvation unknown. Of what unimaginable good, of what highest heritage, does human folly deprive itself!

III. OUR DANGER OF MISTAKING THE LOWER FOR THE HIGHER FEELING. The apostles, James and John, gave vent to a burst of strong resentment, and proposed to have a severe punishment inflicted. They supposed themselves to be actuated by an honourable and acceptable indignation. But Jesus "turned, and rebuked them;" they were entirely mistaken; their feeling was not that of pure indignation, it was tainted by an unholy irritation against men who would not receive *them* and *their* Master; moreover, the desire for immediate punishment was to give place, under Christian teaching, to a determination to win to a better way. Not extinction but reformation, not the infliction of the death which is due but the conferring of the life which is undeserved, not rigorous exaction but patient pity, not the folded fist of law but the open and extended hand of helpfulness, is the Christian thing. When we find ourselves giving way to wrath and proposing punishment, we do well to ask ourselves whether we are sure we know the "spirit we are of," and whether there is not a "more excellent way" for Christian feet to tread.—C.

Ver. 61.—*Decision and indecision.* "Lord, I will follow thee; but," etc. Two trains may leave the same platform and travel for a while along the same lines, and they may look as if they would reach the same terminus; but one of them diverges slightly to the right and the other to the left, and then the further they go the greater is the distance that separates them. Two children born under the same roof, brought up under the same religious conditions, are baptized into the same faith, receive the same doctrines, are affected by the same influences;—they should reach the same home. But they do not. One makes a resolution to serve God outright, unconditional, without reserve; he says simply, deliberately, "I will follow thee;" but the other makes a resolution under reserve, with conditions attached—he says, "Lord, I will follow thee; but," etc. The one of these two goes on, goes up, in the direction of piety, zeal, devotedness, sacred joy, holy usefulness; the other goes down in that hesitation, oscillation between wisdom and folly, and finally of impenitence and spiritual failure. We will look at—

I. THE MAN OF INDECISION ALONG THE LINE COMMON TO HIMSELF AND THE MAN OF

RELIGIOUS EARNESTNESS. 1. They both receive instruction in the common faith; they learn and admit the great fundamental truths of the gospel—the life, death, resurrection, teaching of Jesus Christ. 2. They are both impressed by the surpassing excellence of Christ; for there is in him now, as there was when he lived among men, that which constrains admiration, reverence, attraction. 3. They both feel the desirableness of availing themselves of the blessings of the gospel of grace—of the pardon, peace, joy, worth, hope, immortality, which it offers to the faithful. And when Christ's voice is heard, as it is in many ways, each of these men is prepared to say, "Never man spake, Lord, as thou speakest to me; no one else will give me what thou art offering; evermore give me this living bread, this living water. Lord, I will follow thee."

II. THE MAN OF INDECISION AT THE POINT OF DIVERGENCE. He says not, simply and absolutely, "I will;" he says, "I will follow thee; but," etc. One word *more*, but how much *less* in fact and in truth? What is in that qualifying word? 1. But *I am young, and there is plenty of time.* I am a long way off the "three score and ten years;" and all along the road of life there are paths leading into the kingdom; let me go on unburdened by such serious claims as these of thine. "I will," etc., but not yet. 2. But *I have a bodily as well as a spiritual nature,* and I must satisfy *its* claims. These hungerings and thirstings of the sense are very strong and imperious; let me drink of this cup, let me lay by those treasures first. 3. *I am waiting for some decisive intimation* from Heaven that my time has come. I do not wish to act precipitately or presumptuously; I am looking for the prompting of the Divine Spirit, the direction of the Divine hand; when the Master says distinctly, "Follow thou me," I will arise at once. 4. *I am in embarrassed circumstances,* and am waiting until they clear away. The claims of the business or the home are so urgent, so near, so practical, that they consume my time, and I have none to spare for thee; there are bonds I have formed which I do not know how to break, but which must be broken if thy friendship is to be made and kept. 5. But *I am old and unable.* I have heard thy voice in my ear in earlier days; but I am old and spiritually blind; old and deaf; old and insensitive. I do not expect thee to come this way again; I would follow thee if I felt once more the touch of thy hand upon me.

III. THE GREATNESS AND SADNESS OF HIS MISTAKE. A grievous thing it is for a man to buoy himself up with such false imaginations, to build his house of hope on such shifting sands, to rest the weight of his destiny on such a sapless, strengthless reed. 1. Does death never lay his cold and hard hand on youth? and does not Christ command our strength and our beauty as well as our feebleness and our unsightliness? 2. Does Christ ask us to give up one *rightful* pleasure? and had we not better sacrifice all *wrongful* ones? And has he not promised all we need if we do but take the one true step into his kingdom (Matt. vi. 33)? 3. No man is waiting for God; but God is waiting for many halting and hesitating human souls. Behold, he stands at the door and knocks! 4. We are not more embarrassed than thousands have been, or more than we shall continue to be. If it is hard to *find* time, then for a purpose so *supreme* as this time *must be made*; if evil friendships are in the way, they must be made to stand out of the way. The voice that speaks from heaven is commanding; the case of our eternal destiny is critical in the very last degree. 5. It is true that long disuse is dangerously disabling, and spiritual capacity wanes with neglect; but men are not too deaf to hear the sovereign voice of Christ, not too blind to find their way to his cross, his table, his kingdom.—C.

Vers. 61, 62.—*The workman's qualification.* What more natural, we are inclined to say, than that, before setting out on an unknown future, a man should wish to say farewell at home? How do we account for this strictness, this disallowance of our Lord? First, however, let us remark—

I. WHAT CONSCIOUSNESS OF POWER AND OF ULTIMATE SUCCESS the Saviour shows! How eager we are to secure followers, how pleased and proud to add to our ranks! Especially when a cause is yet young are we desirous of making converts and counting new disciples. At this time the cause of Christianity was very far from being an assured success; yet Jesus did not *hurry* to be successful, to crowd his Church. He said to the *scribe*—not an ordinary disciple—"Foxes have holes," etc. (Matt. viii. 19,

20; ver. 58). He risked the attachment of another (ver. 60); and again of this man (text). How was this? It was that he had such absolute confidence in the rectitude of his cause, in the support of his Divine Father, and therefore in the triumph of his truth and grace. It is never well to hurry even good issues; we should only work with right instruments, content to wait for the result. "He that believeth will not make haste." To the too-anxious workman there needs to come the remembrance of his Master's holy confidence; it says to such a one, "Be still, and know that I am God." We shall better understand our Lord's reply if we consider—

II. WHAT SUPERHUMAN KNOWLEDGE OF INDIVIDUAL HEARTS the Saviour shows! He did not commit himself to men; "for *he knew what was in man.*" This is the key which unlocks the difficulty in many instances. It is this which explains how it was that he encouraged or accepted, how it was that he tested or declined, the services of men. And it is this which explains the differences in his treatment of us now ; how it is that to one man he sends so many more trials and sufferings than to another ; how it is that he withholds from one man so many bounties or privileges which he gives to another. He knows both perfectly; he knows their nature and their need, and he treats them accordingly.

III. THE FACT THAT CHRIST REQUIRES SPECIAL QUALIFICATIONS FOR SPECIAL WORK. There is a faith that "removes mountains" of difficulty; but there is also a faith, much more common, which will do good work, though it will not accomplish such great things. Christ had work for the contemplative John which that man of speech and action, Peter, could not have done; work for the many-sided and devoted Paul which John could not have done. To "follow Christ" as this scribe (of our text) proposed to do was work which meant many and great things—the severance of old and strong ties, the endurance of privation, exposure to hatred and violence, readiness to look death in the face, self-immolation on the altar of a sacred cause. Jesus probably knew that this man had not the spiritual qualifications for such a sacrificial post as this. Even the common labourer must have concentration of mind; he must not have his hand on the plough while his eye is off the field. And the workman in his field of holy service must be a man of unflinching steadfastness, of unwavering resoluteness of soul. No other would be fit for such work as he had on hand. Surely it is far kinder of the Master to keep back, even by strong and apparently hard words, the unfit servant from the sphere in which he would fail miserably, than to let him go on and reap all the bitter fruits of failure; and surely it is wiser far, on our part, to reckon well before-hand, and see whether our mental and spiritual resources will carry us through a proposed service and to retire if we find ourselves unequal to it, than to go blindly forward and to have to come back with something else upon our brows than the crown of honour and success. We may also learn—

IV. WHAT ARE THE PRESENT, CONSTANT REQUIREMENTS which Jesus Christ makes of those who work for him. He is saying to us, "Follow me into the vineyard of holy usefulness." It is in our hearts to say, "Lord, I will follow thee." What must we have in order that he will readily engage us in his active service? We must have that spirit of self-surrender which will make us willing to give up to our Lord all that he asks us to part with; we must be whole-hearted, single-eyed. We must be work-men that have the hand on the plough and the eye on the field. We must be *thorough* in all that we do for him, contributing all our strength and energy in his cause. And there is every reason why we should be. 1. Our Master is worthy of the very best we can bring to him. 2. The sinful, suffering world around us is crying for our pity and our help. 3. It is well worth our while to do our utmost. In full-hearted service is the present recompense of sacred joy as we warm to our work and spend ourselves in it, while in the future there await us those "many cities," that enlarged sphere of influence which will reward the faithful followers of their Lord.—C.

Vers. 1—17.—*The mission of the twelve.* After the group of miracles, we have our Lord next conferring the power of working miracles upon the twelve. This was miraculous power in its highest form. It is important to work well one's self; but it is a still greater feat to get all about one's self into working order too. Jesus was training his disciples to be workers like himself. Let us, then, consider—

I. THE CONDITIONS OF THE MISSION OF THE TWELVE. (Vers. 1—6.) And here we have to notice : 1. The power delegated was *healing and exorcising power*. That is to say, their miraculous power was to change the sick and the insane into able-bodied members of society. The aim of our Lord's philanthropy and of theirs was to enable men to become useful *workers*. When men can help themselves, then are they in the happiest of all conditions. This is infinitely better than spoon-feeding and pauperizing people. 2. The disciples were *not* to use miracle to *make themselves independent of the hospitality of the people*. Christ never used miracle to make life easier for himself; nor did he allow his delegates to do so. It would seem to some a wiser arrangement to make them independent of random hospitalities. But it was better for all parties that hospitality should be looked for. Rabbis were hospitably entertained, and so should these disciples be. They were also to accept of hospitality as it came, and not to be choosers of the grand and pretentious houses which might be opened to them. There may be as much magnanimity in accepting hospitality as in extending it.[1] 3. In case of rejection, they were *simply to symbolize their separation* by shaking off the dust of their feet against them. This was the symbol of hostility and war ; but there was no further outward act to be undertaken. The war was spiritual, and the judgment of the rejectors must be left with God. Toleration was thus made consistent with faithfulness to their convictions; and was freed from all laxity. 4. Their career of *preaching and of accompanying philanthropy* was continued throughout the towns of Galilee. The gospel they brought to men was one of trust in the Saviour who had come and of devotion to him. It was a gospel of work inspired by that faith which operates through love. Hence it carried philanthropy with it, and this philanthropy was of the most useful and stimulating character.

II. HEROD'S FEARS AND CURIOSITY. (Vers. 7—9.) The mission of the twelve had proved sufficiently influential to attract the notice of Herod. It led him to consider his sin and danger in murdering the Baptist. The miracles of which he heard, however, were merciful, and not wrathful; and so, though he was perplexed about the Saviour, he was curious to see him. Most likely he thought he would get Jesus into his power, as he had got John. But John's ideas about the kingdom and its coming were essentially different from those of Jesus. Hence Herod is left in isolation ; his curiosity and desire to see Jesus are alike unsatisfied.

III. THE RETIREMENT INTO WHICH JESUS TAKES THE DISCIPLES AFTER THEIR CAREER OF SUCCESS. (Ver. 10.) The disciples, as we learn from the other Gospels, returned with joy, highly elated with their success. It was on this account doubtless that our Lord deemed retirement so needful for them. There is nothing so wholesome for us when dangerously elated as solitude and prayer. In this way the true character of success is appreciated, and all undue elation about it overcome.

IV. THE INCONVENIENCES OF POPULARITY. (Ver. 14.) The seasons of retirement so salutary for public men are apt to be invaded, and more work forced upon them than they would themselves desire. The disciples and Jesus had most likely secured some fellowship with God before the popular invasion ; for our Lord anticipated both friends and foes, and wrought out his beautiful plan in spite of interruption. So when the people came crowding around him, he was able to receive them with unruffled spirit, and to give them the counsel and the healing they needed. It was the same policy which the disciples had pursued by his directions which he here pursues. Miracle is used to heal and render useful, but not to minister to self-indulgence or render life easier to men. He made the multitude hopeful through his preaching, and healthy through his miraculous power.

V. THE FEEDING AND DISMISSAL OF THE PEOPLE. (Vers. 12—17.) This miracle is narrated by all the evangelists. The sending of the multitude away is urged by the disciples. They have got the healing, and should expect no more. As for hospitality, the five thousand should have entertained Jesus and the disciples, rather than be entertained by them. But our Lord would go beyond his previous limitations, and become the Host instead of the Guest of men. For after all, he is really men's Host, and we all sit at his board, though he condescends to be our Guest and to take of what we provide. Hence he shows by this miracle how all men may really depend upon his bounty and are fed from his hand. The multiplication of the five loaves and two fishes, that is, of *cooked* food, cannot be assigned to any natural law, and could only have been miraculous.

---

[1] Cf. Emerson's ' Essays,' vol. ii., No. v., on ' Gifts.'

It was not quantitatively so great a miracle as the feeding of the Israelites with the manna for forty years; yet it was a sufficient miracle to show that the Sustainer of the world was among them.   Upon him they should depend, and, if they fed by faith on him, they would always be strengthened.   It was at the same time sufficiently *moderate* in its size and duration to show that he was *not* going to keep lazy men in idleness by spreading a gratuitous feast for them every day.   They are dismissed by him that very evening, that they might not be able to go through the *selfish ceremony* of making him a king.   He did not want to be a king over idlers, over men who would like to eat without the trouble of working; and so he defeated their worldly plans.   His lesson of *frugality* also was most significant.   He wanted no waste in his kingdom. He would not prostitute miraculous power to minister either to idleness or to wastefulness.   Very clear light is thus cast upon the *economy* of Jesus.   He kept miracle in its place.   It ministered to usefulness; it was not allowed to minister to idleness or waste.   It would be well if all learned the wholesome lesson which Christ thus conveys.—R. M. E.

Vers. 18—36.—*The Saviour's secret revelations.*   After the miracle of the loaves Jesus resumes his season of devotion, and in the course of it he asks the disciples who had just returned from their mission-tour what reports are being circulated about him. They tell him that some say he is John Baptist, some Elias, some one of the prophets risen again.   This shows that they regarded his present life as *preliminary* only.   The idea of his being the real Messiah, "the Christ of God," was not entertained by any of the outsiders at all.   It is then he asks them what their idea is, when Peter answers unhesitatingly, "The Christ of God."   And now we must inquire—

I. The reason for this secrecy about the Messiahship. (Vers. 18—22.) Though the disciples believed in his Messiahship, they are directed *not* to make it known.   Now, we must remember how different the Jewish ideas of the Messiahship were from the reality presented by Christ.   Even such a noble-minded man as John Baptist had doubted the propriety of the course Jesus took.   How much more liable to mistake would the common people be, if it had been blazed abroad that he was Messiah!   It was needful, therefore, to wait till the picture was nearer completion before people were asked to look upon it.   In fact, it was only his intimates who could at such a stage realize his magnificence at all.[1]   To give the people time to form a proper opinion, to prevent them from rising into premature opposition, to allow them no valid excuse if they rejected him at last, was the purpose of his secrecy and patience. He saw clearly that he "must suffer many things, and be rejected of the elders and chief priests and scribes, and be slain," but he would not provoke the crisis by publishing his Messianic claims.   His modesty and secrecy in this matter are in striking contrast to the manners and methods of the world.

II. Personal salvation through self-sacrifice.   (Vers. 23—27.)   While predicting his death, he also predicts his resurrection.   This is salvation through self-sacrifice.   He immediately indicates that we are under the same law.   The man alone saves himself who dedicates himself even unto death to Jesus.   There are two policies pursued. 1. The *selfish policy*.   People think they are so very valuable that they must save themselves at every turn.   Hence they give the strength of their time and attention to *self-preservation*.   This is their first law of nature.   In doing so, they think that if they can only gain as much of the world and worldly things as possible, the better.   They think it wise to win the world.   But now Jesus shows that such a course only ends in utter loss of self.   What does the self-centred, self-preserving soul become?   What is the fate of the grasping, worldly mind?   Such a soul shrivels up, becomes a nonentity, a mere derelict or castaway on the sea of existence.   Such a life is "not worth living."   2. Notice the *self-sacrificing policy*.   This is the policy pursued by the soul which is devoted to Jesus as supreme.   It is no trial to carry the cross; such a soul is ready to die any day for Jesus.   He cannot be ashamed of Jesus, or of his words, but prizes him and them as beyond all price.   And what is such a soul's experience?   He feels that he is self-possessed and the subject of a grand development. He really has gained himself.   His powers of mind and of heart grow into luxuriance, and he feels enriched in all the elements of being as he goes onward.   And if perchance

---

[1] Cf. Kahnis' ' Der Gang der Kirche,' s. 23.

he becomes a martyr for the faith and lays down, as these disciples did, his life for Jesus, he finds in an immortal future of further dedication all his best being carried forward. Death may cripple him in working powers here, but promotion awaits him beyond the shadows, and he finds that " he is himself again" after the death-experience is over. Jesus thus presents the case in the proper light—self-sacrifice is real *salvation of self* if our self-sacrifice is for the sake of Jesus.

III. THE PRIVATE GLIMPSE OF GLORY. (Vers. 28—36.) Eight days after the noble confession of Christ by the disciples, Jesus takes Peter, James, and John up to a mountain-top, that he might have another season of prayer. Though so busy, he never became prayerless. A most useful lesson! And here we have to note: 1. That *transfiguration came through prayer*. (Ver. 29.) There is nothing changes people's appearance so suddenly and so satisfactorily as being on the mountain-top of prayer. Jesus in transfiguration-glory is but a type of his people who come radiant from the secret places too. If there were more prayer on the part of God's people, there would be more transfiguration and less scepticism about its efficacy. 2. *Transfigured ones are attractive to the heavenly world*. (Vers. 30, 31.) Moses and Elias from their abodes of bliss are but indications of a perpetual interest in transfigured men. A new star is not more attractive to the astronomer than is a transfigured and radiant soul to the inhabitants of heaven. And further, the decease to be accomplished at Jerusalem is the supreme topic with the men from the heavenly city. For to this did the Law and the prophets point, and in the abodes of bliss other interests have not superseded this. If the cherubim were represented as gazing rapturously upon the mercy-seat and its baptism with blood, so may we believe the whole society out of which Moses and Elias came concentrate their interest upon the salvation which comes through the death of Jesus. 3. *Transfigured ones attract attention from the inhabitants of earth*. (Ver. 32.) The disciples had fallen asleep, but the glory awoke them, as a candle will when brought before a sleeper. They saw the Master's glory, and Moses and Elias at his side, and they regarded the Messianic kingdom as having in this triple glory dawned. 4. *There is a natural desire to retain the rapturous vision*. (Ver. 33.) As soon as the disciples became watchful witnesses, Moses and Elias appear to have moved away. Their converse has now been interrupted by unspiritual auditors, and so they prepare for their departure. It is in these circumstances that Peter proposes to retain the visitors by making "tabernacles" in the mount. With such a reinforcement, he thinks, as Moses and Elias, in radiance bright, the victory of Messiah will be assured. It is thus we dream. We read the history of the heroes who are gone, and we imagine that if we were only reinforced from the past we should be triumphant all along the line. Their spirit and their history may well inspire us, but they cannot take our burden. 5. *The rapture may pass away in cloud, but Jesus abides with us for ever.* (Vers. 34—36.) There can be little doubt about this bright cloud being the Shechinah.[1] It came to indicate the true manifestation of God in the incarnate Son, and to withdraw the possible competitors. The disciples feared as they entered the cloud. But a gracious paternal voice assured them, "This is my beloved Son: hear him." And when the cloud cleared away, they saw no man, but Jesus only. To the teaching of Jesus, consequently, they would yield intenser attention. Besides, they kept it secret what they had seen. It was one of those glorious visions which could not wisely be yet revealed. Let us enjoy Jesus, no matter how rapturous associations may fade away.—R. M. E.

Vers. 37—62.—*The secret of successful work.* We saw that the Transfiguration was the result of prayer; but it was not the *end* of the prayer. This was preparation for further service. The glory is not the end, but only an incidental accompaniment, of devotedness of spirit. It is work for God, further service in his kingdom, which is the aim of all means of grace. And now these verses bring out in different aspects the secret of successful work. Let us notice——

I. SUCCESSFUL WORK MUST BE PRAYERFUL. (Vers. 37—42.) We have here a case of failure on the part of the nine disciples, and of success on the part of the descended Christ. The difference between the two cases was that Christ had been praying on the mountain while they had been prayerless in the valley. Prayerlessness and powerlessness

---

[1] Cf. Arndt's 'Leben Jesu,' vierter theil, s. 112.

go hand-in-hand.   Work done in a prayerless spirit cannot succeed as it ought to do. The transfigured ones alone can meet the emergencies of Christian work, and succeed where others fail.   Some cases are doubtless more difficult than others, and some demons make a harder fight of it than others; but there are none of them who can stand a prayerful Christian who faithfully follows Jesus in his line of attack.

II. SUCCESSFUL WORK MUST BE IN SPITE OF MALIGNANT OPPOSITION.   (Vers. 43— 45.)   Our Lord, as the crowd are wondering at his success, tells the disciples plainly that he is destined to be delivered into the hands of men.   This is a sufficient set-off to his success.   Men will take and kill him, notwithstanding all his philanthropy and exorcising power.   This crucifixion of Jesus is but the type of the world's recognition of the best work done by human hands.   A long line of noble workers have followed Jesus along the path of martyrdom.   Let no worker, then, be surprised at the world's malignity.

III. SUCCESSFUL WORK MUST BE DIVESTED OF BASE AMBITIONS.   (Vers. 46—48.) Notwithstanding recent failure through want of prayer, the disciples are soon selfishly contending about the first places, and who is to be greatest.   It is wonderful how soon we forget our failures and betake ourselves to our ambitions.   Now, one characteristic of base ambition is pride about work.   Certain lines of work are thought to be beneath our dignity and worth.   To correct this in the disciples, our Lord sets a little child before them, and shows that such a child might be received in such a spirit as would be recognized by God himself.   The nursing of a little child may be done for the sake of Jesus Christ, and in such a case it is such a work as he will regard, and the Father who sent him also.   It is not a great work, therefore, that is needed, but a *great heart* carried into the smallest work.   *We* think of quantity; Christ thinks of quality.   We will not "take our coats off," so to speak, unless it is some work eminently creditable; Christ could throw his great spirit into the fondling of a little child, and do the little one everlasting good.   Hence we must do any work clearly laid to our hand with large-heartedness, and we shall find it successful in the best sense. It is the meek ones who are ready to put their hand to anything who are great in the kingdom of God.

IV. SUCCESSFUL WORK DEMANDS, BESIDES, A TOLERANT SPIRIT.   (Vers. 49—56.) John and James, after the Transfiguration privileges, seem to have got very excited and ardent in Christ's service.   Two cases in particular show how heated and hasty they were.   The first was a case of *exorcism through Christ's Name.*   Some Jew had witnessed the exorcisms of Christ, and, abandoning the Jewish methods and traditions, had tried the new plan, and proved the power of "the Name which is above every name."   But because he did not join the disciples, and so preserve their monopoly of delegated power, he is forbidden by them to do such work.   This was intolerance misplaced.   The worker, though not uniting with the disciples, was promoting the Master's glory by showing the power of his Name.   He was an ally, though not a disciple of the same set.   Hence Jesus instructs them always to act on the tolerant principle that " he that is not against us is for us." [1]   The second case in which the sons of Zebedee exhibited unholy zeal was in a certain Samaritan village, during Jesus' journeys to Jerusalem.   The last journey has begun (ver. 51), and nothing will keep him from accomplishing it.   The Samaritans would have liked him to linger with them, and avoid his enemies and theirs.   But he would not listen to their syren voice, but insisted on going up to Jerusalem.   Taking umbrage at this, one Samaritan village denied him the usual hospitalities when his forerunners sought it.   Incensed at this, John and James inquire if they should not call down fire from heaven to consume the inhospitable Samaritans, as Elijah had done.   Samaria was the scene of that fiery ministry.   But Elijah's spirit would not suit the Saviour's times.   Had the prophet descended from the Mount of Transfiguration, he would not have insisted on any such policy as this. He had doubtless got less fiery in the peaceful abodes above!   As a destructive force, he had served his generation, but the disciples were to remember that saving men, not destroying them, was to be their mission.   From both these cases we learn that the true evangelical spirit must reject all intolerance if it is to secure the highest success.

[1] Cf. Vinet, on ' La Tolerance de l'Evangile,' in ' Discours sur quelques Sujets Religieux, p. 225.

V. SUCCESSFUL WORK REQUIRES FAITHFUL DEALING WITH INDIVIDUAL CASES. (Vers. 57—62.) As Jesus was moving upwards to the capital, the people perceived that a crisis was at hand. Hence the desire of some on insufficient grounds to cast in their lot with him who is to be the conquering King. Here is a case in point. A man comes and professes his willingness to be a follower of Jesus wheresoever he goeth. But Jesus undeceives him by indicating that he is not going to be sure of any lodging in this world. Perhaps the man was hoping to reach a palace by following him; but Jesus shows that the birds and beasts have more certain lodgings than he. He thus laid bare the man's danger, and prevented a rash decision. The second case is an invitation to the individual by Jesus himself. It is a case of bereavement, and Jesus seizes on it to secure a disciple. He knew that the best thing this broken-heart could do would be to become a herald of his kingdom. The bereaved one naturally enough asks leave to go and bury his father, but Jesus assures him that there are sufficient dead hearts at home to pay due respect to his father's remains, and the formalities of the funeral may only change his promptitude into delay and neglect; and so he urges him to become a preacher at once. A third case is that of one who is ready to follow Christ, but wishes to bid those at home farewell. Our Lord tells him the *danger of looking back.* The farewells at home might have resulted in a farewell for ever to Jesus. It is thus Jesus shows the importance of dealing faithfully with individual souls. We have the secret of successful work laid clearly before us.—R. M. E.

EXPOSITION.

CHAPTER X.

Vers. 1—24.—*The mission of the seventy. The Lord's words to them of instruction and direction and warning.*

Ver. 1.—**After these things the Lord appointed other seventy also.** That is to say, after the events just related which had taken place in the north of the Holy Land. "After these things" formally began the solemn marches in the direction of Jerusalem, which ended, as we have stated, in the last Passover. Roughly speaking, the seventy were first sent out about the October of the last year of the public ministry. The manuscripts vary between seventy and seventy-two. The preponderance of authority is in favour of seventy. The Sanhedrin numbered seventy-one. The elders appointed by Moses were seventy. There was a Jewish saying also that the number of peoples on earth were seventy or seventy-two. Fourteen descended from Japhet, thirty from Ham, twenty-six from Shem. In the 'Clementine Recognitions,' a writing of the first half of the third century, the number of peoples is given as seventy-two. The Fathers dwell on the sacred symbolism of the desert-wanderings especially mentioned at Elim—"twelve wells and seventy palm trees," alluding to the two groups of Christ-sent missionaries, the twelve apostles and the "seventy" here mentioned. **Two and two.** As in the case of his apostles sent forth previously, for mutual help and comfort. **Before his face into every city and place, whither he himself would come.** By their means, as the time left him was now so short, all the need-

ful preparations should be made before he personally visited the place. Villages and towns, too, where his presence was found, as in the case of the Samaritan village, unwelcome, would be thus carefully noted, and no time would needlessly be lost.

Ver. 2.—**Therefore said he unto them, The harvest truly is great, but the labourers are few: pray ye therefore the Lord of the harvest, that he would send forth labourers into his harvest.** This and many of the sayings reported on this occasion had been said apparently before, when the twelve had been sent out on a similar mission. It seems almost certain that, on several occasions, the Lord repeated the same expressions containing great truths, with scarcely any variation in language. The harvest simile was evidently a favourite one of the Master. "The field is the world" he told them in the parable of the sower. It is reproduced by St. John (Rev. xiv. 14—19).

Ver. 3.—**Go your ways: behold, I send you forth as lambs among wolves.** These *first* missionaries were to go forth unarmed and unprovided. They were to be a type of the strange, *seemingly* weak Christian preachers of the next two hundred years, before whose simple words and unarmed presence the great system of paganism was to go down. One of the rare but beautiful *traditional* sayings of the Lord is referred to the first occasion of his speaking the words of this third verse. Peter is said to have asked him, "But how, then, if the wolves tear the lambs?" And the Lord said, "Let not the lambs fear the wolves, when the lambs are once dead;" and then added again the words of Matt. x. 28, "Fear not them which kill the body," etc.

Ver. 4.—**Carry neither purse, nor scrip, nor shoes.** They were to burden themselves with no useless baggage, nor were they to be careful for ways and means of livelihood. Dean Plumptre very beautifully writes, on the similar words reported in Matt. x. 10, "Experience (and, we may add, the spirit that teaches by experience) has led the Christian Church at large to look on these commands as binding only during the mission on which the twelve were actually sent. It is impossible not to admire the noble enthusiasm of poverty which showed itself in the literal adoption of such rules by the followers of Francis of Assisi, and, to some extent, by those of Wickliffe; but the history of the mendicant orders and other like fraternities forms part of that teaching of history which has led men to feel that in the long-run the beggar's life will bring the beggar's vices. Yet here, as in the case of the precepts of the sermon on the mount, the spirit is binding still, though the letter has passed away. The mission work of the Church has ever prospered in proportion as that spirit has pervaded it." **And salute no man by the way.** This especially refers to the length and tediousness of Eastern salutations, often very unreal, and which would consume much valuable time. Men were to see that one absorbing interest possessed them, and that to them was no time given for the ordinary useless amenities of life.

Ver. 5.—**Peace be to this house.** The original of the words used in the Church of England Office for the Visitation of the Sick.

Ver. 6.—**The son of peace.** An Aramaic (Hebrew) expression. Although the language here is pure and fairly classical Greek, yet the presence of such expressions as this shows that the basis of this part of St. Luke's narrative was probably an Aramaic document.

Ver. 7.—**And in the same house remain. . . . Go not from house to house.** Similar instructions were given in the case of the sending out of the twelve as missionaries. One house and family were to be selected as the centre of their work (see note on ch. ix. 4). **Eating and drinking such things as they give : for the labourer is worthy of his hire.**

Ver. 8.—**Eat such things as are set before you.** Most commentators have simply seen in this charge (1) an instruction to be content with whatever their host should set before them, avoiding even the appearance of caring or wishing for dainties; (2) that his servants should look upon such maintenance in the light of a fairly earned wage, rather than as an alms bestowed upon a beggar. In other words, his servants, while perfectly content with the most frugal fare,

at the same time should preserve their manly independence. The bare austere sustenance, the simple lodging,—*these* things they had surely earned. But in addition to this meaning, true and appropriate though it be, there seems a quiet recommendation not to be rigid in inquiring as to the cleanness or uncleanness of the viands. One very able commentator (Godet) remarks that of this there is no question, for we are yet in a Jewish world. But remembering only in the last chapter a mission was specially sent to a Samaritan village, such an assertion can scarcely be maintained. It seems probable that extreme rigidness in this particular, now that mission work on a broad scale had commenced, here began to be relaxed; and that in this charge of Jesus we have, at least, the basis of that yet broader commandment set out by St. Paul in 1 Cor. x. 27.

Ver. 9.—**And heal the sick that are therein.** These were strangely great powers to confer upon poor weak men—men, too, only in the very dawn of faith—and their naïve surprise and joy (see ver. 17) show how little they believed in their possession of such powers, even after their Master's words announcing to them the gift. But this prodigality of miraculous energy was needful then. The first beginning of so stupendous a work as laying securely the ground stories of Christianity—what Renan, with all his enmity to revealed religion, calls "l'événément capital de l'histoire du monde"—required this special aid from another sphere.

Ver. 12.—**But I say unto you, that it shall be more tolerable in that day for Sodom, than for that city.** Such a rejection implied that they would have nothing to do with the Master of these preachers, the pitiful, loving, Galilæan Teacher. These were days of possible mighty blessings, of proportional terrible punishments. The woe of Sodom, that well-known swift destruction, most probably through sudden volcanic agency, was tolerable in comparison with the far more awful doom reserved in the immediate future, at the hands of Rome, for these guilty cities of Palestine (see a further note on this on ver. 15).

Ver. 13.—**Woe unto thee, Chorazin! woe unto thee, Bethsaida! for if the mighty works had been done in Tyre and Sidon, which have been done in you, they had a great while ago repented, sitting in sackcloth and ashes.** In St. Matthew's Gospel (xi. 20), where the woe of the fair lake-cities is announced in similar language, the "woe" is introduced with the words, "Then began he to upbraid the cities wherein most of his mighty works were done." Now, we have no record of any miracles having been worked at Chorazin, the first mentioned. But these cities were in the immediate vicinity of Capernaum, where for a length-ened period our Lord principally resided. He was, no doubt, during the Galilæan ministry, constantly in one or other of those bright, busy cities built on the shores of the Lake of Gennesaret. This bears out St. John's statement (xx. 30) concerning the many unrecorded miracles of Christ, and gives us some notion of the numerous events in the life left without mention; much must have happened in Chorazin to have called forth this stern saying. Late research thinks it probable that the site of Chorazin has been discovered near Capernaum; the ruins, however, at a little distance, look but a mere rough heap of stones. A great theo-logical truth is urged in this saying of the Master. Men will be judged not only for what they have done or failed to do, but their opportunities, their circumstances, their chances in life, will be, before they are judged, strictly taken into account.

Ver. 14.—**But it shall be more tolerable for Tyre and Sidon at the judgment, than for you.** Tyre and Sidon, those represen-tative examples of the luxury and vileness of the great cities of the old pagan world, will, when the dreadful awards are made, *be beaten with few stripes*, while the cities of the lake will *be beaten with many*, because these last listened unrepentant to the sweet and tender words, and gazed unmoved at the mighty works of mercy, of the pitiful Jesus of Nazareth. This is one of the passages in the New Testament where the doctrine of degrees in punishment is plainly set forth, and in words which fell from the lips of the Redeemer himself!

Ver. 15.—**And thou, Capernaum, which art exalted to heaven, shalt be thrust down to hell.** When the Lord came to speak of the woe of Capernaum, his own chosen city, his favourite earthly home, his words grew even more solemn. The simile he uses, "hell," better rendered *Hades*, is chosen to paint the contrast between the glorious destiny this beautiful lake-city might have chosen, and the tremendous woe which she had voluntarily brought on herself. The present state of the Plain of Gennesaret is indeed so desolate and miserable that we can scarcely picture to ourselves that it was once a populous, crowded district, the blue lake covered with fishing and trading vessels, its shores and the plain inland highly culti-vated, a very garden in that part of Asia. Rich towns and thriving villages in that favoured neighbourhood are described by contemporary writers in such glowing terms that we, who are spectators of the dreary and melancholy shores of the Gennesaret lake, are puzzled as we read, and should suspect an exaggeration, only an exagge-ration would have been purposeless (see

Josephus, 'Bell. Jud.,' iii. 3. 2). Some thirty years after the woe had been uttered, in the terrible wars in which Rome avenged herself on the Jewish hatred and scorn, the garden of Gennesaret was changed into a ruin-covered solitude. Josephus, who had been dwelling on the loveliness of the place, describes the state of the shore strewn with wrecks and putrefying bodies, "insomuch that the misery was not only an object of commiseration to the Jews, but even to those that hated them and had been the authors of that misery" ('Bell. Jud.,' iii. 10. 8; and see Dr. Farrar's 'Life of Christ,' ii. 101).

Ver. 17.—**And the seventy returned again with joy, saying, Lord, even the devils are subject unto us through thy Name.** How wavering and hesitating the faith of the chosen followers of Jesus was, even at this late period of his public ministry, is clear from this frank confession of surprise at their powers. They were contrasting the present with what had lately happened at the foot of the Mount of Transfiguration, where the disciples were utterly unable to heal the possessed boy. What a contrast do these true writers of the gospel story paint between themselves and their Master! They never seem to tire in their self-depreciatory de-scriptions. They describe with the same careful, truthful pen their slowness to understand what afterwards became so clear to them—their mutual jealousies, their cove-tous hopes of a brilliant future, their shrink-ing from pain and suffering, their utter failure when they try to imitate their Master; and now we find them marvelling at their own—to them—unexpected success in their imitation of him.

Ver. 18.—**And he said unto them, I beheld Satan as lightning fall from heaven.** The Lord's words here were prophetic rather than descriptive of what had taken, or was then taking place. The seventy were telling him their feelings of joy at finding that his Name in their mouths enabled them to cast out evil spirits from the possessed. Their Master replied in an exalted and exultant strain—strange and rare sounds on the lips of the Man of sorrows—telling them how he had been looking—not on a *few* spirits of evil driven out of unhappy men, but on the king and chief of all evil falling from his sad eminence and throne of power like a flash of lightning. Jesus Christ saw, in the first success of these poor servants of his, an earnest of that wonderful and mighty victory which his followers, simply armed with the power of his Name, would shortly win over paganism. He saw, too, in the dim far future, many a contest with and victory over evil in its many forms. He looked on, we may well believe, to the final defeat which at length his servants, when they should have learned the true use and the resistless power of that glorious Name of his, should win over the restless enemy of the souls of men.

Ver. 19.—**Behold, I give unto you power to tread on serpents and scorpions, and over all the power of the enemy.** The older authorities read here, "I have given." The only recorded instance of a literal fulfilment of this promise was in the case of Paul at Melita, after the shipwreck (Acts xxiv. 3—5). A similar promise was made during the "forty days" (Mark xvi. 17, 18). It seems, however, best, in the case of this peculiar promise, to interpret the Lord's words as referring to spiritual powers of evil, taking the serpent and scorpion as symbols of these. It should be remembered that the subject of conversation between the Master and his servants was the conflict with and victory over these awful powers restlessly hostile to the human race (see Ps. xci. 13).

Ver. 20.—**But rather rejoice, because your names are written in heaven.** "After all," went on the wise and loving Master, "though you have made the glad discovery of the power you possess, if, as my servants, you use aright my Name, after all, your real reason for joy is, not the possession of a new, mighty power, but the fact of your name having been written in the book of life as one of my servants commissioned to do my work." Many commentators here cautiously point out that even this legitimate joy should be tempered with fear and trembling, for even this true title to honour might be blotted out of that golden book of heaven (see Exod. xxxii. 33; Jer. xvii. 13; Ps. lxix. 28; Rev. xxii. 19). In *this* deep legitimate joy men and women of all callings, who try to follow the Master, in every age, may share.

Ver. 21.—**In that hour Jesus rejoiced in spirit.** More than "rejoiced;" the Greek word rather signifies "exulted." Very rarely in the holy story of the life of lives is a hint given us of any gleam of gladness or of joy irradiating the spirit of the Man of sorrows. The exultation of the Blessed here was based upon his conviction that this first success of his own was but the *commencement* of a long and weary, but yet, in the end, of a triumphant campaign against the spirits of sin and evil. What *these*, in their mortal weakness by the aid of their poor imperfect faith in his Name, had been able to accomplish, was an earnest, a pledge, of the mighty work which his followers would, in the power of the same Name, be enabled to effect in the coming ages. In that solemn hour did Messiah see, in the *far future*, of "the travail of his soul," and was satisfied. The absence of all sign of joy in

the life of our Lord is well brought out in that touching legend which we find in the spurious letter of P. Lentulus to the senate, that he wept often, but that no one had ever seen him smile. **That thou hast hid these things from the wise and prudent, and hast revealed them unto babes.** Looking upon his servants after their return from their successful mission, a group made up certainly for the *most* part of poor untutored men—fishers, artisans, and the like, children of the people, without rank or position—Jesus thanks the Father that, in the persons of the men chosen to be the instruments of his work, he has looked away from all the ordinary machinery of human influence. As he gazes upon the band of successful missionaries, Jesus thanks the Father that henceforth his servants, if they would be successful, must owe the powers which gave them success entirely to *his* training, and not to the world's. **Even so, Father; for so it seemed good in thy sight.** This is "the only record, outside St. John's Gospel, of a prayer like that which we find in John xvii. For the most part, we may believe, those prayers were offered apart, on the lonely hillside, in the darkness of night; or, it may be, the disciples shrank in their reverence, or perhaps in the consciousness of their want of capacity, from attempting to record what was so unspeakably sacred. But it is noteworthy that in this exceptional instance we find, both in the prayer and the teaching that follows it in St. Matthew and St. Luke, turns of thought and phrase almost absolutely identical with what is most characteristic of St. John. It is as though this isolated fragment of a higher teaching had been preserved by them as a witness that there was a region upon which they scarcely dared to enter, but into which men were to be led afterwards by the beloved disciple, to whom the Spirit gave power to recall what had been above the reach of the other reporters of his Master's teaching" (Dean Plumptre).

Ver. 22.—**All things are delivered to me of my Father.** These words, spoken late in the public ministry, evidently refer to the Almighty power possessed and frequently exercised by the incarnate Son of God. During the days of his humiliation, Jesus Christ exercised the power of Creator, Lord of the elements, Lord of the secrets of health and disease, Lord of life and death. Dean Mansel, comparing this statement, recorded both by SS. Matthew and Luke, with the language of St. John, remarks "that there is no substantial difference between the different evangelists in their views of our Lord's Person and nature, and that the Gospel of St. John, far from being the representative of a later theology, does but more fully expound what is implicitly contained in the earliest of the Gospels." St. Matthew (xi. 28—30) here gives us that sublime invitation of the Master's to the weary and heavy-laden. In the consciousness of his possession of all power, Jesus, with infinite compassion, offers to the great army of sufferers that rest which he alone can give.

Vers. 23, 24.—**And he turned him unto his disciples, and said privately, Blessed are the eyes which see the things that ye see: for I tell you, that many prophets and kings have desired to see those things which ye see.** Alluding, especially, to such prophets and their words as Balaam (in Numb. xxiv. 17) and Jacob (in Gen. xlix. 18). Keble has a quaint verse here, striking, as is usual with him, the central truth—

" Save that each little voice in turn
Some glorious truth proclaims ;
*What sages would have died to learn,
Now taught by cottage dames.*"

These last words, the evangelist expressly says, were spoken *privately*. In fact, such a statement could only have been addressed to the inner circle—to those men (not exclusively the twelve) who had been much under the immediate influence of the Lord's teaching about himself. Gradually their sense as to who and what he was was becoming more acute. Glimpses of his Divinity ever and anon flashed before their eyes. But, to the last, their faith was very weak and wavering. Such words as these, after what had gone before, must have sunk deep into many of the listeners' hearts.

Vers. 25—37.—*The question of the lawyer. The Lord answers with the parable of the good Samaritan.*

Ver. 25.—**And, behold, a certain lawyer.** It seems (as has already been noticed) probable that in St. Luke's general account of our Lord's teaching during the six months which immediately preceded the last Passover, certain events which took place at a short visit which Jesus paid to Jerusalem at the Feast of the Dedication are noticed. This question of the lawyer was probably asked on the occasion of this visit, and the little episode connected with the Bethany family of Lazarus took place at the same period. The "lawyer" is sometimes termed "scribe." There is little difference between these appellations. They were professional teachers and expounders of the Mosaic Law and of the vast complement of traditional sayings which had gathered round it. As the whole life of the people at this period was ruled and guided by the Law, written and traditional, this profession of scribe and lawyer was an important and influential one. **Stood up.** The Master was evidently

teaching in a house or a courtyard of a house. Many were sitting round him. To attract his attention, this lawyer stood up before putting his question to Jesus. This scene, as we have said, took place most likely in or near Jerusalem, not improbably, as the Bethany episode follows, in that suburb of the city, and perhaps in the house of Lazarus. **And tempted him**; that is to say, tested him and his skill in answering questions out of that Law which then was the rule and guide of daily life in Israel. It is not unlikely that the lawyer hoped to convict the broad and generous Rabbi of some unorthodox statement which would injure his reputation as a Teacher. It was a hard and comprehensive question, this query how eternal life was to be won, and possibly one carefully prepared by the enemies of Jesus,

Ver. 26.—**He said unto him, What is written in the Law?** The Lord replied, perhaps pointing to one of the phylacteries which the lawyer wore on his forehead and wrist. These phylacteries were little leather boxes (the dimensions of these varied from the size of an ordinary hazelnut, to that of a large walnut, and even in some cases much larger). In these leather boxes were little parchment rolls containing certain texts from the Pentateuch. Certainly the first of the two great rules, that concerning *God*, was one of these texts (Deut. vi. 5); possibly, but not certainly, the second concerning the neighbour formed another text.

Ver. 28.—**This do, and thou shalt live.** The learned Jew was evidently confounded at the Galilæan Rabbi's first answer referring him to the sacred Mosaic Law. His perplexity is increased by the Lord's quiet repartee when he had rehearsed the two duties, to his God and his neighbour, " This do, and thou shalt live." It seems as though the clever, unfriendly critic of Jesus of Nazareth now forgot the hostile purpose with which he stood up to question, and, really conscience-stricken, willing to justify himself, in real good faith put the query which called out the famous parable.

Ver. 29.—**And who is my neighbour?** The self-righteous, but probably rigidly conscientious, Jewish scholar, looking into the clear, truthful eyes of the Galilæan Master he had been taught to hate as the enemy of his own narrow, lightless creed, was struck, perhaps for the first time, with the moral beauty of the words of his own Law. Of the first part, *his duty towards God*, as far as his poor distorted mind could grasp the idea, he was at ease in his conscience. The tithe, down to the anise and cummin, had been scrupulously paid; his fasts had been rigidly observed, his feasts carefully kept, his prayer-formulas never neglected. Yes; as regards *God*, the Pharisee-lawyer's conscience was at ease! But his neighbour? He thought of his conduct towards that simple, truthful-looking Galilæan Rabbi, Jesus, that very day; trying to trip him up in his words, longing to do him injury—*injury* to that worn-looking, loving Man who had never done *him* any harm, and who, report said, was only living to do others good. Was *he*, perchance, his neighbour? So, vexed and uneasy— but it seems in perfect honesty now, and in good faith—he asks this further question, "Master, tell me, who do you teach should be included in the term 'neighbour'?"

Ver. 30.—**And Jesus answering said.** For reply the Master told him and the listening by-standers the parable-story we know so well as the "good Samaritan"—the parable, which has been "the consolation of the wanderer and the sufferer, of the outcast and the heretic, in every age and country." (Stanley). The story was one of those parables especially loved by Luke (and Paul), in which instruction is conveyed, not by types, but by example. It was very probably a simple recital of a fact which had happened, and at some period in the Lord's life had come under his own observation. The local scenery, the characters of the story, would all lead to the supposition that the parable was spoken in or near Jerusalem. **A certain** man **went down from Jerusalem to Jericho, and fell among thieves, which stripped him of his raiment, and wounded** him, **and departed, leaving him half dead.** We are not told who the traveller was, Jew or Gentile; not a word about his rank, descent, or religion; simply that he was a man, a human being. It seems, however, from the whole tone of the story, most probable that the wounded traveller was a Jew. The way he was travelling was the road leading down from Jerusalem to Jericho, a distance of twenty-one miles—not the only way, but the most direct. It was a rugged, rocky pass, well adapted for the purposes of thieves and desperadoes, and was known, owing to the many dark deeds of which it had been the scene, as "The Way of Blood." The Lord's words tell the story. The traveller, likely enough a Jew pedlar, had fallen among thieves, who had robbed him, and then had left their victim—dying or dead, what cared they?—lying in the pass.

Ver. 31.—**There came down a certain priest that way: and when he saw him, he passed by on the other side.** Both the priest and Levite were frequent travellers along this road between the capital and Jericho. Jericho was especially a city of priests, and when the allotted service or residence time at the temple was over, these would return

naturally to their own homes. It has been remarked that the grave censure which this story levels at the everyday want of charity on the part of priests and Levites, fills up what would otherwise have been a blank in the Master's many-sided teaching. Nowhere else in the gospel narrative do we find our Lord taking up the attitude of censor of the priestly and Levitical orders. We have little difficulty in discovering reasons for this apparently strange reticence. They were still the official guardians and ministers of his Father's house. In his public teaching, as a rule, he would refrain from touching these or their hollow, pretentious lives. Once, and once only, in this one parable did he dwell—but even here with no severe denunciations, as in the case of scribes and Pharisees—on the shortcomings of the priestly caste. The bitter woe was fast coming on these degenerate children of Aaron. In less than half a century, that house, the glory and the joy of Israel, would be utterly destroyed, not to be raised again. No woe that the Christ could pronounce could be as crushing in its pitiless condemnation. *The very reason for the existence of priest and Levite as priest and Levite would exist no longer.* The selfish life of the doomed order, in which holiness seemed effectually to have been divorced from charity, is portrayed in the lifelike picture of the parable of the good Samaritan.

Ver. 32.—**And likewise a Levite, when he was at the place, came and looked** on him, **and passed by on the other side.** They both, priest and Levite, shrank from the trouble and expense of meddling with the poor victim of the robbers; perhaps a cowardly fear of being identified with the robbers was mixed with these feelings. The whole of their conduct was inhuman, but not unnatural; alas! how faithfully is it copied by multitudes of men and women professing Christianity now! The Levite's conduct was better and worse than his official superior's—better, in that he did feel a little pity, and stopped to look, no doubt compassionately, on the sufferer; and worse, because he selfishly strangled the noble impulse in its birth, and passed on to his own place without so much as throwing a cloth over the poor maimed body to shelter it from the scorching sun, or the cold night dew.

Ver. 33.—**But a certain Samaritan, as he journeyed, came where he was: and when he saw him, he had compassion** on him. Now, for the sake of strong contrast, Jesus paints on his canvas the figure of one who, as a Samaritan, was as far removed as possible from being a neighbour to the sufferer (who, most probably, was a Jew) in the sense in which the austere Jewish lawyer would of himself understand the term "neighbour." The Samaritan, hated of the Jews, and most probably, in common with the rest of his nation, hating them—he, in his turn, was journeying along the ill-omened "Way of Blood;" he too sees, like the priest, the form of the man, wounded perhaps to death, lying by the way, and, like the Levite, draws near to look on the helpless sufferer; but, unlike priest and Levite, stays by the wounded man, and, regardless of peril, trouble, or expense, does his best to help the helpless.

Vers. 34, 35.—And went to him, and bound up his wounds, pouring in oil and wine, and set him on his own beast, and brought him to an inn, and took care of him. And on the morrow when he departed, he took out two pence, and gave them to the host, and said unto him, Take care of him; and whatsoever thou spendest more, when I come again, I will repay thee. All these little tender details of the Samaritan's pitiful love are sketched in by a master-hand. There is first a noble, generous impulse, at once crystallized into a kindly brotherly act. Not satisfied with merely carrying out the first impulse, the Samaritan puts himself to inconvenience, perhaps to peril, and, after dressing the wounds, takes the wounded one along with him, provides lodging for him, and even takes care of the sick and friendless man's future. The wounded man was no rich and powerful merchant or noble—that is clear from the necessity of the little provision which the Samaritan made for him at the inn when he went on his journey; probably just an itinerant Jew pedlar. There were many of these always travelling about the East, we know. The piled-up acts of kindness were all clearly done to a poor stranger, without hope of recompense or reward. The life of that kindly man was evidently one which finds its high but secret guerdon in the blessedness of its own deeds. The Master had been called by his bitter foes, in their blind rage, a "Samaritan." Was he in any way picturing himself? *To an inn.* The Greek word is not the same as the "inn" of ch. ii. 7. It reminds us that, besides the open khan or caravanserai spoken of at Bethlehem, and which was crowded with travellers, in Palestine at this period was to be found the Greek type of inn, where a host or landlord entertained the guests. The khan was simply a group of empty buildings kept up for the use of travellers, who provided furniture and food for themselves. Throughout the Levant, Greek customs were gradually being introduced.

Vers. 36, 37.—Which now of these three, thinkest thou, was neighbour unto him that fell among the thieves? And he said, He that showed mercy on him. The deep pathos of the little story, the meaning of which the trained-scholar mind of the lawyer at once grasped, went right home to the heart. The Jewish scribe, in spite of prejudice and jealousy, was too noble not to confess that the Galilæan Master's estimate of a neighbour was the true one, and the estimate of the Jerusalem schools the wrong one; so at once he replies, "*He that showed mercy on him.*" Even then, in that hour of the noblest confession his lips had ever made, the lawyer trained in those strange and mistaken schools, the outcome of which is the Talmud, could not force himself to name the hated Samaritan name, but paraphrases it in this form. The scene closes with the Lord's charge, "Then imitate *that* act." **Go, and do thou likewise.** The parable thus answers the question—Who is my neighbour? Any one, it replies, who needs help, and whom I have power and opportunity to help, no matter what his rank, race, or religion may be. Neighbourhood is made coextensive with humanity; any human being is my neighbour who needs aid, or to whom I can render aid. But it answers the other and the still larger and deeper question with which the scene which called the parable out began. "Master," asked the lawyer (ver. 25), "what shall I do to inherit eternal life?" Or in other words, "What is the virtue which saves?" The Scriptures teach that without holiness no one shall see the Lord, that is, shall inherit eternal life; and in this parable two kinds of holiness are set before us—the one spurious, the other genuine. The spurious holiness is that of the priest and Levite, two officially holy persons;—spurious holiness is sanctity divorced from charity. In the person of the Samaritan the nature of true sanctity is exhibited; —we are taught that the way to please God, the way to genuine holiness, is the practice of charity. Another and a very different exposition of this great and loving parable treats it as a Divine allegory. It commends itself to the present generation less than the plain matter-of-fact exegesis adopted in the foregoing notes. In the allegory, the wounded traveller represents mankind at large, stripped by the devil and his angels; he is left by them grievously wounded, yet not dead outright. Priest and Levite were alike powerless to help. "Many passed us by," once wrote a devout mediæval writer, "and there was none to save." Moses and his Law, Aaron and his sacrifices, patriarch, prophet, and priest,—these were powerless. Only the true Samaritan (Christ), beholding, was moved with compassion and poured oil into the wounds. Among the ancients, Chrysostom and Clement of Alexandria and Augustine might be cited as good examples of these allegorical expositors. Among mediæval Churchmen, Bernard and his devout school. Although this method of exposition has not been adopted here, still an exegesis which has commended itself so heartily to learned and devout Churchmen in all the Christian ages deserves at least a more respectful mention than the scornful allusion or the contemptuous silence with which it is nowadays too often dismissed. Godet, for instance, describes this allegorical interpretation adopted by the Fathers as rivalling that of the Gnostics.

Vers. 38—42.—*The sisters of Bethany.* The following points are noticeable. A close intimacy evidently existed between the brother and his two sisters and Jesus. They evidently were prominent friends of the Master, and during the years of the public ministry were on many occasions associated with Jesus of Nazareth, and yet a singular reticence evidently existed on the part of the writers of the first three Gospels in respect of the brother and sisters. His name is never mentioned by them. Here, for instance, Bethany is simply alluded to as "a certain village."

There was some reason, no doubt, why the three synoptical evangelists exercised this reticence. We have before explained that these Gospels more or less represent the "texts," so to speak, upon which the first preachers of the religion of Jesus based their sermons and instructions.

The long recital of John xi. gives us the clue. For the disciples of Jesus publicly to call attention in their sermons and addresses to *Lazarus,* on whom the Master's greatest miracle had been worked, would have no doubt called down a ceaseless, restless hostility on the Bethany household; for it must be remembered that for years after the Resurrection the deadly enemies of Jesus and his followers were supreme in Jerusalem and the neighbourhood.

There were reasons, no doubt, now unknown to us, which rendered it important to the welfare of the early Church that the Bethany family should remain undisturbed and in comparative privacy. The peculiar and unique position of Lazarus. *During those four days what had he seen and heard?* Much curiosity, no doubt, existed to question the risen one: what fierce hostility, what morbid useless speculation, might not have been easily aroused?

St. John's Gospel was not written for long years after the event. It probably represents no public preaching, rather a private and esoteric teaching. The home of St. John, too, for years prior to putting forth his Gospel, was far distant from Jerusalem. Probably Jerusalem had ceased to exist as a city and the Jews as a nation well-nigh a quarter of a century before St. John's writing was given to the Church. There were no reasons *then* for any silence. Jerusalem and Bethany were a heap of ruins. Lazarus and his sisters and well-nigh all their friends had probably then been long in the presence of the loved or hated Master.

Ver. 38.—**Now it came to pass, as they went, that he entered into a certain village.** The scene here related took place, no doubt, at Bethany, and, most probably, during that short visit to Jerusalem, at the Feast of Dedication, in the month of that December which preceded the Passover " of the Crucifixion." This visit to Jerusalem, as has been suggested above, was made in the course of that solemn progress the account of which fills up the long section of St. Luke's Gospel, beginning at ch. ix. 51. The characters of the sisters here mentioned exactly correspond, as do their names, with the well-known Bethany family of that Lazarus for whom the great miracle, related at length by St. John, was worked. There are several mentions of this family in the synoptical Gospels, besides the long and important notice in St. John. **A certain woman named Martha.** The name is rather Aramaic than pure Hebrew. It is equivalent to the Greek *Kyria,* and signifies "lady." It has been suggested that the Second Epistle of St. John was addressed to this Martha. It was written, we know, to the elect *kyria,* or "lady" (2 John 1). Various identifications, more or less probable, have been attempted in the persons of the Bethany family. Martha has been supposed to be identical with the wife of Simon the leper (Matt. xxvi. 6; Mark xiv. 3). One hypothesis identifies Lazarus with the "young ruler" whom Jesus loved (see Dean Plumptre, in Bishop Ellicott's Commentary); another, with the saintly Rabbi Eliezer (or Lazarus) of the Talmud. These are, however, little more than ingenious, though perhaps not quite baseless, fancies.

Ver. 40.—**Came to him.** Dr. Farrar very happily seizes the tone and temper of Martha. He renders the Greek words here, " but suddenly coming up." We see in this inimitable touch the little petulant outburst of jealousy in the loving, busy matron, as she hurried in with the words, "Why is Mary sitting there doing nothing?" **Bid her therefore that she help me.** "We almost seem to hear the undertone of 'It is no use for *me* to tell her.' Doubtless, had she been less 'fretted,' she would have felt that to leave her (Martha) alone and withdraw into the background while this eager hospitality was going on, was the kindest and most unselfish thing which Mary could do."

Ver. 41.—**And Jesus answered and said unto her, Martha, Martha.** There are several notable instances of this repetition of the name by the Master in the New Testament story, and in each case apparently in pitying love. So "Simon, Simon," in ch. xxii. 31, and "Saul, Saul," in Acts ix. 4.

Ver. 42.—**But one thing is needful.** Jesus had been saying to this kindly but over-fussy friend, "Are you not *too* anxious about these household cares of yours?" and then he adds, "See, only one *thing* is really needful." Now, what is the exact meaning of these last words? Some expositors have taken the expression to mean "a single dish is sufficient" for my entertainment; so much careful, anxious thought is thrown away. A curious variation in the reading occurs here in some, though not in all the oldest, authorities. It seems as though some of the early copyists of the text of the Gospel were wishful to make the words, which they possibly understood as a lesson of the Master's on *simplicity* of *food*, clearer and more emphatic. This other reading is, "There is need of few things, or of one only." In other words, "Few things are enough for me and my friends to sit down to, or even one dish only." The teaching contained in ver. 7 gives a little colour to this quaint interpretation of the Master's words here, which sees in them a general warning against taking thought for the pleasures of the table. But, on the whole, the old reading contained in the received text is preferable, and the old interpretation, too, viz. that the true life of man needs but *one* thing, or, if the other reading be adopted, needs but few things. If we must specify the *one*, we would call it "love," or "charity." So John, we know, in his old days, summed up all man's duties in this "love." If, on the other hand, we are asked to name the *few*, then we would add to love, *faith* and *hope*. The parable of the "good Samaritan," that practical lesson of the love or charity the Master was alluding to, had just been spoken; it was still, we may reverently assume, fresh in the Divine Teacher's mind. **And Mary hath chosen that good part, which shall not be taken away from her.** And Mary, his dear Bethany friend, had made *her* happy choice of the *one* thing, that love or charity which never fails; or, perchance, had made her choice of the *few* things needful (if we prefer the longer reading of those old manuscripts we have spoken of)—the few things would then mean that faith, hope, and charity which abide both *now* and in the ages of ages yet to come!

HOMILETICS.

Ch. ix. 1—6 and ch. x. 1—11.—*The mission of the twelve, and the mission of the seventy.* The differences between the two missions can be easily distinguished. The scene of the mission related in the ninth chapter is Northern Galilee; the scene of the mission related in the tenth chapter is Southern Galilee. The one speaks of a power delegated to the twelve apostles; the other, of an office and of gifts delegated to seventy—"other seventy also"—the two numbers of completeness, seven and ten multiplied. And these seventy are sent before the Lord's face, while the twelve are kept near to his Person. The one, although actually exercised for only a short time, is the sign of a work which, in its design and consequences, is coextensive with the world and its ages; the other refers to a merely temporary work—to objects local and immediate. But, different as the two missions are, they are connected in this homily because they set before us the great principles and features of Christian work in every time. The instructions in the ninth and tenth chapters are similar; and this, as we may conclude, because the instructions contain hints and suggestions to be embodied in ministries and services for Christ. No portion of the evangelical narrative more deserves to be attentively considered in connection with all that the hand of love finds to do. Let us regard some of its more salient features.

I. Observe, first, THE EVER-ABIDING CHARACTER OF TRUE CHRISTIAN WORK. Ch. ix. 2 and x. 9 give us the word "heal." And the meaning of this word "heal" may be learned from the life and sacrifice of Christ himself. In both the sending of the twelve and the sending of the seventy, the spring of the action is the perception of a harvest waiting to be reaped (cf. Matt. ix. 36—38). He sees the multitude around him tired and worn out, like sheep exhausted and scattered over a plain, with no shepherd. "The harvest truly is plenteous." It is the emotion thus expressed which always beats within his breast. "I am come," he cries, "that they might have life, and have it more abundantly." His presence is that of the Healer in a charnel-house of corruption. Before him evil spirits exclaim, "What have I to do with thee?" Foul shapes of sin and want are expelled by his touch. His works are more than wonders; they are signs of redemption, of healing—the overflow of that fountain of life which was enclosed in his Person. Now, it is in this, the sphere of the Lord's love and power, that the servant is to labour. He is sent to save. He is to calm the troubled. He is to exorcise the demons which prey on the life of man. He is to be a channel of the love which is neighbour to man in all man's need.

> "The world's a room of sickness, where each heart
>   Knows its own anguish and unrest;
> The truest wisdom there and noblest art
>   Is his who skills of comfort best."

Notice what this healing includes. The apostles (ver. 1) were endowed with authority over all devils, and power to cure diseases. "Go and preach," commands Jesus; but also, "Go and heal the sick." The clergyman and the medical man represent the two halves of the Christian ministry. We shall never rise to the height of the Church's calling until we realize more systematically the conjunction of these aspects. To some extent we do. In our medical missions we do. In the increased care of Christian communities as to sanitary regulations, nursing, and so forth, we do. But much remains to be developed. And what we need, as the sustaining spirit of all work, is the conviction that Christ has given his Church power to heal, to cure diseases. Those who magnify "faith-healing" have hold of a truth, though they press it unduly, and indeed often give it a twist which makes it practically an untruth. They are right in the contention that it is Jesus Christ who makes whole, that the power of the cure is with him, and that, in respect of the cure, as of all else, the way of blessing is the way of prayer. He is able to do exceeding abundantly above all that we ask or think. On this, undoubtedly, faith should build. But why oppose this to the use of means? Or why suppose that there is a higher faith in trusting him and dispensing with ordinary means, than in trusting him and availing ourselves of the medicinal properties with which he has endowed things in nature, or of the knowledge and skill which also are gifts of God? God answers prayer as really in making the means effectual, as in restoration without the application of surgeon's or physician's art. The essential point is that the power over body and soul is his, and delegated by him to men. Let the Church's devotion be, not less theological, but less polemical; more emphatic, first in the requirement of personal righteousness, and next in such work as "shall deliver the poor and him that crieth, the fatherless, and him that hath none to help him."

II. Now, this general position assumed, observe, secondly, THE CONDITIONS WHICH CHRIST LAYS DOWN AS REGULATIVE OF ALL TRUE CHRISTIAN WORK. Putting ourselves alongside of the twelve and the seventy, let us listen to our marching orders, our code of instructions. *Condition the first*: "Begin at the point next you." The twelve (ch. ix. 6) are sent through the towns preaching the gospel. The seventy (ch. x. 1) are sent "into every city and place, whither the Lord himself would come." Let us not mistake. These are special embassies. By-and-by the word is, "Witness in Jerusalem, and Judæa, and Samaria, and unto the uttermost part of the earth." The principle is this—there are times when attention should be concentrated on the field that is at our own door. And generally, the beginning, though not the end, of all work, is with our own. We are to work outwards from the circle that is next us; thence are to be extended, outwards, ever outwards, the golden pipes through which the healing oil empties itself. *Condition the second*: "Proclaim, The kingdom of heaven is at hand." The twelve (cf. Matt. x. 6, 7) are to speak this to the lost sheep of the house of Israel. The seventy (ch. x. 9) are to stand by the sick, and, while they heal, preach the advent of the kingdom. They are to raise a supreme expectation. Not halting to give elaborate courtesies. As men hastening, full of a great word, they are to sound in the ear, now in trumpet-tones, now in gentle whispers, "God's kingdom is come close to you." To tell poor weary men and women of the Christ who is behind them, of the love that is seeking them; to hold before their gaze the reality of a kingdom which is, not a name in a book, not a Utopia of priest or poet, but a living fact, a kingdom which "is not meat and drink, but righteousness, and peace, and joy in the Holy Ghost,"—this is the burden of the preaching—the free giving of that which they have freely received. *Condition the third :* " Willingly, wholly, give yourselves to the work, trusting in the Lord whose it is." The pith of the Master's charge is, Be not anxious as to worldly provision—'purse, scrip, shoes.' Confer not with flesh and blood. Lo! I have sent you." Let us distinguish between the letter and the spirit. To act on the mere letter, in the conditions of nineteenth-century civilization, would be fanaticism. "The sterility of missionary labour," writes Dr. Farrar, "is a constant subject of regret and discouragement among us. Would it be so if all our missions were carried out in this wise and conciliatory, in this simple and self-abandoning, in this faithful and dauntless spirit? Was a missionary ever unsuccessful who, being enabled by the grace of God to live in the light of such precepts as these, worked as St. Paul worked, or Francis Xavier, or Henry Martyn, or Adoniram Judson, or John Eliot, or David Schwartz?" Undoubtedly not; yet, are Christian people to demand of missionaries what they are not, in some measure, practising themselves? Are they to insist that the missionary shall have all the self-denial whilst they take all the ease? Is it not better for each person to aim at levelling up to the mark required of the missionary? to ask what his or her Christianity amounts to? what is given for it? what living, working force is in it? what of self-sacrifice is really prompted by it? Oh for a more heroic trust in the King, and devotion to the kingdom! "Lord, here am I." And *condition the last :* "Your whole conduct in the discharge of your mission is to be marked by courtesy." "Into whatsoever house ye enter, first say, Peace be to this house" (ch. x. 5). First—before the character of its inmates is declared. The house is the home of men and women. No matter what it may prove to be, it is to be treated with respect. Christ's disciples are to be pre-eminent for the kindly courtesies which are the beauty of Eastern life. Contrast the sketch in the Book of Ruth, of Boaz coming to the reapers, "The Lord be with you," and the reapers answering, "The Lord be with thee;" with the picture of our worlds of capital and labour, each too often addressing the other in tones suspicious, if not defiant. All that is rude and bitter in speech and thought should be alien to the followers of the meek and lowly Jesus. There is a time to be firm. "The wisdom which cometh from above is first pure, then peaceable." He who commands the gracious politeness tells the seventy that against the city which will not receive them, they are to testify, "The very dust of your city, which cleaveth on us, we do wipe off against you." But first, and always, let the Christian see that the name of gentleman is not, in service for Christ, soiled by any "ignoble use."

So much for the nature and conditions of Christian ministry. Note, in conclusion : 1. *The twelve and the seventy go in the strength of the Lord God.* They are solemnly appointed to the work. God is a God of order; and ordinance is always honoured. But, with the ordination, they receive the power; and the power is in Christ for them, and from Christ into them. Let *us* recollect that Christ is risen. He has received of the Father the promise of the Holy Ghost. The Church is his body—"the fulness of him who filleth all in all." The strength which inspired apostle and evangelist in the first days is waiting for all who will to serve the Lord. 2. *The seventy are sent, two and two, before his face.* Economy and helpfulness in ministry are thus secured. The order of the "two and two" in the ranks of the apostles is given by St. Matthew—Simon and Andrew, James and John, Philip and Bartholomew, Thomas and Matthew, James and Jude, Simon and the son of Carioth. By some law of affinity these companionships were formed. In the Church there are alliances also. For two are better than one, and mutual sympathy and tenderness are Christ's rule.

Ch. ix. 10—23 and ch. x. 17—24.—*Utterances on the return of the twelve, and of the seventy.* These passages are separated by an interval of time. But as the missions of the apostles and of the seventy were considered together, tracing in them the great laws and principles of Christian ministry, so let us connect the utterances called forth by the reports of the two companies, tracing in them the expression of all that is to be most vividly realized by those who yield to the command, "Go work to-day in my vineyard." A threefold lesson seems to be conveyed. 1. A lesson as to the spirit of mind proper to the servant of Christ. 2. A lesson as to the ministry appointed to the servant of Christ. 3. A lesson as to the confession of him demanded from the servant of Christ.

I. THE SPIRIT OF MIND PROPER TO THE TRUE SERVANT OF CHRIST. Turn, for guidance as to this, to the words contained between the seventeenth and twenty-fourth verses of the tenth chapter. The seventy have returned triumphant. They have succeeded far beyond their expectation. Healing of the sick? "Even the devils are subject to us through thy Name." What a strange new sensation! Men, hitherto utterly obscure, the custodiars of a power so marvellous, beholding, at the word which passes from them, the most marvellous results in the lives and characters of men! There is no such jubilation in the tone of the twelve when they return; perhaps the issue had fallen below their expectations. But the seventy, the special and temporary executive of Jesus, are filled with the supreme joy of the conqueror—"the devils are subject to us." Now, there is no rebuke of this spirit. On the contrary (ver. 19), they are told that, in Christ's strength, they shall tread on all sorts of evil spirits—on the serpent and the scorpion, opposing them in serpent and scorpion-like natures—on "all the power of the enemy." And the Lord shares their elation. In their tidings (ver. 18) he sees the presage of the complete victory of the good over the evil. He pours forth (ver. 21) a fervent stream of praise that, at length, and through these poor babe-like souls, his holy love has been declared as victorious over the kingdom of darkness. Was not the message brought (ver. 22) a new sign of the Father's acceptance of the Man Christ Jesus, and of the universal sovereignty which had been assigned to him? But mark the "notwithstanding" of ver. 20. It is the interposition of a great check. Undoubtedly, nothing is more thrilling than the sense of strength. It may be tyrannous to use, but it is great to have, a giant's strength. But there is nothing more hurtful than a complacent resting on the evidences and results of power. Many a good man is spoiled by the overweening consciousness of force; he becomes inflated with pride; and, as he does so, he loses rank before God; he is not far from the loss of power even with men. Therefore the importance of Christ's "Notwithstanding, rejoice not that the spirits are subject to you, but rather rejoice because your names are written in heaven." "Not, i.e. in the tokens of command, but in the capacity of service; not that you rule, but that you are ruled; that God in his grace has called you to work with him, has written your name in the register of the citizenship of heaven, has allowed you a part in the heavenly life and ministry." Both in what he thus said, and in the glimpse into his own mind (vers. 21, 22), he indicates that the true disciple finds his joy, not in what *he* does, but in what God does by him; not in trophies of power, but in signs of Divine acceptance and anointing; not in the subjection of spirits to him, but in the subjection of his own life to, and his sympathy with, the eternal Father and the purpose of his love.

II. This being the spirit of the mind, look back to the narrative from vers. 10—17 of ch. ix., and recognize in it A SYMBOL OF THE TRUE DISCIPLE-WORK—the work in which Master and scholar are at one. This work is set forth in *its essential character*, and its *Divine order, or method*. 1. *Its essential character is giving.* (Ver. 13.) "Give ye them to eat." The most typical pictures of the Divine love are those which most purely bring out the relation of the Giver—man wanting, God supplying; man's argument, "I need," God's argument, "I have." The babe cries, settles at once to the kindly bosom—the argument being the need. The mother has, and her abundance is the life of the child. This is a reflection of God and man. So, on that grassy plain near Bethsaida, we are introduced to a scene and work most significant of the love of God in Christ. All the evangelists relate it. It is the occasion of one of the most memorable of Jesus' discourses—that concerning the Bread of life. Altogether, it is a notably royal act, the picture of the ministry of the kingdom of God. How it came about we are told (vers. 10—12). The compassionate heart of Jesus is moved with pity by the sight of the great multitude which has followed him. "Send them away, Master," is the whisper. "We are here in a lonely place. They are hungry; they may become furious; let them go into the towns and villages, and lodge, and get victuals." The answer is, "Give ye them to eat." This is the manifestation of God in the flesh—God in his power, no less than his will. "What! Master," exclaims Philip, "all our store

consists of five loaves and two fishes: shall we go and buy meat for all the people?"
Oh, it is the unbelief, the slow-heartedness of man, which thus speaks out. "Can God
furnish a table in the wilderness?" Does not faith need to be reminded that the little
brought to Christ is multiplied a hundredfold? "Not by might, nor by power, but by
my Spirit, saith the Lord of hosts." 2. Notice *the order or method of the work.* Christ
is always orderly. He sent the twelve, and the seventy, two by two, giving them their
rules of procedure. Here, again (ver. 14), "Make the men sit down in companies of
fifties." Dr. Farrar reminds us of the expression of Mark, "reclined in parterres, like
a multitude of flower-beds in some well-cultivated garden." Organization is thus
implied. And yet the life, the strength, is not in the organization. It is "the blessing
of the Lord that maketh rich" (ver. 16). The outstretched arm, the food held up to
heaven, the look, the blessing, the breaking, the giving to the Church, and, through
the Church, to the world,—every part of the action is sacramental, every part is
expressive of some aspect of the truth as to the dispensation of the Bread of life.
And then note, in ver. 17, the care as to the fragments—the teaching of thrift even in
the midst of abundance. The transaction, from beginning to end, is inlaid with suggestions which admit of endless applications to the changing circumstances and the
varying conditions of the world and the Church.

III. Finally (in vers. 18—22) we have THE RECORD OF A PRIVATE INSTRUCTION—
one given "as he was alone, praying, his disciples with him"—TO THOSE WHOM THE
LORD HAD CALLED INTO HIS MINISTRY. It is the instruction which gives the third of
our lessons—that as to the confession of Christ which is demanded of the disciple.
Observe: 1. There is *the confession* (vers. 18—21) which is a secret between the soul
and the Lord himself—that which is apart from all that men say, which is the expression of the personal loyalty and devotion. "Whom say *the people* that I am?"
"Whom say *ye* that I am?" Parent, teacher, worker, pastor, is thy labour, is thy
life, built on Peter's noble testimony, "The Christ of God"? 2. There is *the living out
of that inward life*—the bold and fearless testimony for that preference as dominating
all the action (vers. 22, 23). The Master lays a cross on the back of his disciple, and
bids him carry that cross daily, in token of his being grafted into a suffering, sacrificed
Son of man. Solemn and searching are the words about the willing to come after him,
and all which this involves. May our hearts answer, "Amen!"—"amen" to the daily
following, "amen" to the losing of life for Christ's sake, "amen" to the sturdy witnessing
for him in the midst of the crooked and perverse nation; our "amen," rising upwards
to receive his when he shall come "in his own glory, and in the Father's, and of the
holy angels."

Vers. 25—37.—*The parable of the good Samaritan.* The second of the parables
peculiar to St. Luke, and one of the loveliest and most suggestive of the matchless
pictures of him who "spake as never man spake." Notice—
I. ITS OCCASION. Our Lord is in Judæa, not, as we infer from what follows, at a
great distance from Bethany. He and his disciples, we may suppose, are resting, when
a lawyer—*i.e.* a person who made the Law both oral and written his study—proposes a
question with which, or its likeness, we meet at six different times in the ministry of
Jesus. "Tempting him" is the phrase descriptive of the motive for the question;
probably the phrase means nothing more than putting the Rabbi to the proof, submitting a question, the answer to which would, in the lawyer's view, settle his right to be
heard as a Teacher from God. Jesus meets his interviewer as one not far from the
kingdom of God, yet in a way which proved that, in regard to the issue presented, mere
dialectics were of little avail. "What shall I do to inherit eternal life?" The mind
is at once referred to the underlying reality of the Law. "What is written therein?
thou who dost profess to know, how readest thou? That which thou hast read, that
which thou dost find there—the love, in its two great aspects, upward and outward—
that is the eternal life." Ah! this is not quite according to the jurist's expectation.
"He came to catechize Christ that he might know him, but Christ will catechize him,
and make him know himself." Seeking to parry the thrust, there comes forth the
next question (ver. 29), "Who is my neighbour?" This question is the occasion of
the parable. Note, before passing, the clause, "willing to justify himself." The true
heart casts itself on the Lord, "Lord, save, help! lighten my darkness!" The proud

heart wills some self-justification, and, thus willing, produces some excuse, some word by which to turn aside the arrow of conviction.

II. THE SCENE AND THE PERSONS OF THE DRAMA. 1. *The scene.* The wild road, proverbial for deeds of blood, which Jesus and the disciples had just traversed. 2. *The persons.* The traveller, who had been attacked by the Bedouins, had fallen among them, and been spoiled, mutilated, left half dead. The priest, coming that way by chance, or rather "by a coincidence;" it was natural that he should be there, since Jericho was a station of the priests. When the priest saw the half-dead man, afraid of any defilement, "he passed by on the other side." Next, the Levite. Observe, "he came and looked on him," with the life ebbing away, and he too moved to the other side. And then, finally, the Samaritan. (1) Look at him in contrast with the other two. Of them the kindness might have been expected. The traveller, we may suppose, is their co-religionist. They, at least, are fresh from the sanctuary—from the reading of Moses and the prophets. They hide themselves from their own flesh. The desire is to get home, and they pass by. The one not expected is "he who shows mercy." Is it not often so ? Recall the word used concerning the Roman centurion, "I have not found so great faith, no, not in Israel." (2) Who is the Samaritan ? Priest and Levite denied him a share in the kingdom. He was a heretic, a descendant of the half-heathen stock, "the men from Babylon and Cuthah, whom the King of Assyria placed in the cities of Samaria instead of the children of Israel." Cursed in the synagogues, the people were taught that to entertain a Samaritan was to lay up judgments for a house. This is the man. If it had been a Jew approaching a Samaritan, the Jew would have left him in his blood. The Samaritan stops, compassionates, binds the wounds, pours in the oil and the wine, puts him on his own beast, tends him, pays for him, provides for him. Brave, tender-hearted Cuthite that he is ! Thus the Lord answers the inquiry, "Who is my neighbour?" Neighbourhood is dissociated from the range marked out by co-religionism ; it is constituted by the fact of need. "Where you can be helpful, to whom you can be helpful, there, in him, is the neighbour." There are circles within circles. To love them that love us is not wrong ; but, if that is all, what do we more than others ? Humanity is neighbourhood. Do not ask what the man is. Enough that he is there, and in want. Sad, and worse than sad, when the representative of religion is not also the representative of humanity ! After all, who is man's neighbour? Like the traveller in the parable, man has left the heavenly city, and has fallen among thieves. To man the sinner the love of God in Christ is the neighbour. He has showed mercy ; he is our Example : "Go, and do likewise." "Be imitators of God, as dear children ; and walk in love as Christ also loved us."

Ver. 27.—*The love of the neighbour.* Fixing, then, on Christ's definition of the sphere of neighbourhood, we are called to give a length and a breadth to his rule, which make it equivalent to the assertion, "Your neighbour is, not your blood-relation only, not the circle of your acquaintance only, not your countryman or co-religionist only ; but he or she whom you can help in any way whatsoever—the wretched tatterdemalion from the slightest contact with whom you shrink ; the besotted and degraded ; even your enemy, who hates you and despitefully uses you ; him, her, mankind, you are to love." "Thou shalt love thy neighbour as thyself." A very searching word indeed. God help us ! how far are we from realizing it ? Here some may will to justify themselves, and assume the defensive in some such manner as this : "It is impossible. We may cherish a feeling of benevolence towards all men in virtue of their common humanity ; but how can we love them? Love requires the perception of what is lovable ; it requires, too, that there shall be some link connecting one personally with another. But to summon us to love the neighbour, in Christ's sense of the phrase, is to insist on love before the discovery of any such link, or notwithstanding the discovery that such a link is wholly wanting." Or, again, "This is a commandment to love. Now, we cannot love by commandment ; we cannot go beyond the prompting of our own natures. Some we can embrace with affection, but from others we turn away. We have tried the law that is announced on a limited scale, and the result of the trial was this—So long as we thought of the world in a general, ideal way, we felt, in a measure, ardent ; but as regards the persons actually crossing our path as neighbours, before the selfishness and greediness and ugliness which confronted us, we were forced to retreat, and to

confess that we cannot love because we are told to love our neighbour as ourselves."
Now, let it be acknowledged that these and similar difficulties are real difficulties.
But, in the mean time, see whether Christ, in commanding, has not indicated the way
of assistance; whether a more spiritual exposition of his teaching may not lead us into
a region of thought in which the solution of the difficulties lies. Such a region seems
to be opened up in the sentence reported by St. Matthew, "The second commandment
is *like to* the first." To the first, "Thou shalt love the Lord thy God with all thine
heart, and with all thy soul, and with all thy mind," we must look for the full truth of
the love enjoined in the second, and for the significance of the measure which the second
proposes, "Thou shalt love thy neighbour as thyself."

I. For, to show that the love enjoined in the two commandments is really one grace,
WHAT DO WE MEAN WHEN WE SPEAK OF LOVING GOD? Surely we mean a delight in
God for what he is; for his righteousness, his goodness, his holy and loving will; we
mean that surrender of ourselves to him in which our spirits respond to the Father of
spirits. Now, in the first moment of such self-surrender, is it not the longing of the
mind that he be glorified? Such a longing necessarily takes beyond self. It embraces
the desire that the Eternal Name be hallowed, the eternal will be done in earth as it is in
heaven, and the eternal kingdom of the Father come; that God be honoured in all, and
all find their true life in God. The pulse of this longing beats in friendship like that
of Mr. Erskine of Linlathen. To his friend, the cold, astute lawyer, Rutherford, Mr.
Erskine writes, "I love you. I could die for you to bring you to your true Centre,
God." In the love of God, his love for his friend had been quickened and intensified.
Yes; when Christ revealed God as our Father, he gave us men as our brethren; when
the Spirit of the Son is sent into the heart, the spirit of the brother is formed in the
heart. However we may distinguish in speech, in the working of the eternal life, there
is no distinction between the love of God and the love of man. Each is implied in the
other. They are the two sides of the one grace, the one life—love. And in this we
have the solution of the difficulty already referred to. If there is no higher prospect
than the neighbour, it is not to be wondered at that persons cry out, "Impossible!
where the special links fail, there love must stop." But, observe, when we have gained
the second commandment through the first; when the love of the neighbour proceeds
out of the love whose first and greatest is God; such links are always at hand; there
are interests and sympathies which serve as points of approach to all, to any one. Our
love is God's love extending through us. All sorts and conditions of men are within
the reach, before the vision, of God's love. Even beneath the hateful we can discern
that which, to the Creator who is also the Redeemer, is immeasurably precious.

> ". . . . who loves the Lord aright,
> No soul of man can worthless find;
> All will be precious in his sight,
> Since Christ on all hath shined."

We are, then, partners in the Divine interest in man. We clothe the neighbour
with this interest. "Thy Father is my Father; my Saviour is thy Saviour too, and
thou art precious in his sight. As he loves, so would I love thee—'as myself.'"

II. BUT WHAT OF THE MEASURE, "AS THYSELF"? Let it be answered, "Thyself,
after the first and great commandment has been fulfilled in thee—thyself loving the
Lord thy God with all thy heart, and soul, and strength, and mind." There is a true
self-love, and what the true self-love is is thus defined. Recollect, Christ's phrase is,
"as thyself." In his teaching there is no place found for the pretentious altruism
which strives

> ". . . . to wind itself too high
> For mortal man beneath the sky,"

which insists that the love of man shall swallow up, shall annihilate, all self-feeling; that
it shall involve the renunciation of all that is individual for the sake of a universal good,
of humanity. The teaching of Jesus is too practical, has too keen a sight of "what is in
man," for this humanitarianism. He recognizes a love of self as right and natural;
but it is the self when truly consecrated to God. "There is no need," says one, "of a
heart of supernatural texture in order to the love of our brother. What is needed is only
the heart of flesh instead of the heart of stone." Yes; but this heart of flesh is a new

heart. It is described in the Scriptures as the gift of God. It is "a heart of super-natural texture"—part of that new ordering of the life which is realized when the wayward will is offered to the consuming fire of God, and the inner man is born from above. See, then, what this pure self-love, which is the measure of love to the neigh-bour, represents. It represents *a power of sacrifice.* "Hereby perceive we the love of God, because he laid down his life for us: and we ought to lay down our lives for the brethren." Not only so; the principle which illustrates the direction of the love of our neighbour exhibits that which is to be sought for in it. He who prays that his self shall be in harmony with God's thoughts and ways, loving his brother with the same love, will discriminate between that which only serves the flesh, and that which tends to promote the righteousness which God reckons the permanent well-being; he will strive against the things in internal life and external condition which hinder this well-being; he will study the ways through which the greatest good may be realized for the neighbour. Thus, given the love of God poured out in the heart, the love of self, instead of separating, unites the man to his world. It is the dynamic of a holy and enlightened philanthropy.

Let the two commandments, then, be kept in the order which our Lord has marked—the first, as the first and greatest; and the second, as the second which is like to the first. Let them, in this order, abide in us; and, though the keeping of them may be to the flesh a cross, possible only through the slaying of that in the flesh which objects, the external nature of the commandments will gradually disappear; from laws outside us they will be changed into states of life, each finding its congenial nourishment in the other. The love of God will be fed by the love of the neighbour; the love of the neighbour will be fed by the love of God. So thought, so wrote St. John, in his own profound yet simple manner, "Beloved, let us love one another: for love is of God; and every one that loveth is born of God, and knoweth God." "If a man say, I love God, and hateth his brother, he is a liar; for he that loveth not his brother whom he hath seen, how can he love God whom he hath not seen? And this commandment have we from him, that he who loveth God love his brother also."

Vers. 38—42.—*Christ's sermon in the house of Martha.* A very short sermon, its substance being given us in the two last verses. But it is a sermon whose teaching goes far down into the truth of our hope and faith. Let us trace it, first, in the reve-lation made in Christ's word of the differences which the heavenly life comprehends; and, secondly, in the counsel with regard to this life which Christ's word conveys.

I. How INTERESTING IS THE SKETCH OF THE TWO SISTERS AT BETHANY! They are so lifelike that we feel as if we had seen and known them. And, indeed, we have, because they portray familiar types of character and temper. No person of candour will regard the elder sister as only the embodiment of worldly mindedness in contrast with the younger as the embodiment of spiritual-mindedness. When we look more closely into the narrative, we see the injustice of this view. It is Martha who receives Jesus; it is she who provides for his comfort. If she is bustling and busy, this is only the sign of her devotion. Nor does Jesus say that, in her anxiety about many things, she had lost the one thing needful, and that she had no share in the good part which could not be taken away. He is defending Mary against the temporary petu-lance of Martha, and, in so doing, he cautions her against the temptations incident to her activity. "Jesus," says St. John, "loved Martha, and her sister, and Lazarus." Assume, then, that each of the two has a place in the communion of saints, and see what this place is and wherein each is fulfilled in the other. 1. The usefulness of the Martha character is at once suggested. It bears the impression of the liberal soul who deviseth liberal things, who will take any amount of pains to oblige, who is eager to serve. Honour to those who have the readiness to do, and the knack of business! In such persons there is generally a vast amount of self-denial. You will find them toiling when there might be many excuses for resting. Prompt, energetic, shrewd, they go straight on, their activity being in a high state of development. All honour to the housekeepers! They enable the quiet and thoughtful to think and write. Erasmus and Melancthon can study when Luther and Farel are up and doing; the Leightons can preach for eternity because the Melvilles and Hendersons preach to the time. Your Marys could not sit at Jesus' feet unless the Marthas were going about the house.

But the Marys, too, have their place. Busy business people are apt to underrate them. They exhibit something of the elder sister's impatience: "We are left to do all; these dreamers do not help." Not help? It is Mary who sees into the truth of Jesus' sacrifice. It is she who, sitting and listening, divines the joy and the sorrow which meet in the heart of the Lord. By-and-by, when Martha makes a feast, she feels that the hour has come, and she brings the alabaster box of ointment which she has been keeping for the hour. "Against the day of my burying," says Christ, "has she kept this box . . . this that she hath done shall be spoken of for a memorial of her." The prophetic spirit belongs to the meditative. Martha is the worker, but Mary is the seer. 2. The conclusion, therefore, is, "Let the Marthas and the Marys abide together in peace and mutual self-respect. Let the world of action and the world of letters recognize, each in the other, the balancing, completing half. God has created minds male and female—the active and the contemplative, the communicative and the receptive, the objective and the subjective. The Church of Christ, the progress of humanity, demands both; if the one is the guide, the other is the inspirer, of movement; and, for permanent effect, as well as for the discovery of truth, the Johns outrun the Peters. Let each person ascertain which of the two sides is predominant in him, and seek the balance supplied by the other. Whoso is Martha-like should cultivate the Mary temper. Unless he sit at Jesus' feet, he will be cumbered about the serving. It is not enough to get all right for the Lord; the first thing is to be right with and in the Lord. Whoso is Mary-like should recollect that gymnastic is needful to health; that he must work as well as enjoy quietly. He must not eat all the fat and drink all the sweet. The sitting at Jesus' feet must be with a view to the following in Jesus' steps. The real moral strength is found when this balance is found. So, from the Martha side it was found by St. Paul, who laboured more abundantly than all the apostles, yet all the while sat at Jesus' feet. From the Mary side it was found by St. John, who, although the one who leant on Jesus' bosom, was the one named Boanerge—Son of thunder. To serve much, without being cumbered about it, "inquiring in the temple;" to be the thinker, with the liberty of the seat at the Master's feet, and yet the doer of the Word;—this is the beautiful proportion of the heavenly life. This life is love; and love must first see as did Mary; then, but in a sweeter and wholesomer spirit, it can work as did Martha.

II. Consider now THE TRUTH OF THE HEAVENLY LIFE WHICH IS INDICATED IN THE COUNSEL GIVEN BY CHRIST. It is a counsel administered under the twofold form of a *caution* and a *commendation*. 1. *The finger of caution is pointed to Martha.* (Ver. 41.) Observe the antithesis—the "many things," the "one thing." The good, kind soul is distracted by a multitude of concerns. Who does not know the worry which comes through the pressure of many littles? May it not be added that there is nothing which more wears the energy out than attention to the details of home-management? The whole sentence of Jesus is most expressive. First, the "careful, or anxious,"—this is the inward fault; and then the "troubled,"—this includes the external, the "restless turning and bustling hither and thither." Is it not eminently characteristic of what we notice in others and sometimes feel in ourselves? And note the mistake. It is not the serving; it is the being "cumbered" about the serving—the serving imped- ing the movement heavenward, as a heavy garment impedes the one who runs a race. The "many things" run away with both the peace and the strength of the mind. We may not absolutely forget; in a kind of way we recollect; but we cannot really con- centrate our attention on the one thing which is needful. "Martha, the feast over which thou art exercised is good in its way. The intention is kind. But this day salva- tion has come into thy house. There is no need of all these dishes, all this cooking and preparing. But there is need of thine acceptance of the gift of God. If thou knewest that gift, and who it is that speaks to thee, thou wouldst feel that the one thing need- ful is to ask life of him, to learn what the life is from him, to receive the gift of the life eternal. O Martha-like souls, of every type and shade, 'why do ye spend money on that which is not bread, and your labour on that which satisfieth not'? The heart hearkening for Christ is the one thing, and you cannot have that without an inward collection and repose of spirit, without peace and liberty in God. Why be so greedy of the unneedful? Why pursue it with such impetuous eagerness that there are only odd times, fragments of thought, for that which is needful to health of mind, to the wants and desires of an immortal nature?" 2. *The finger of commendation is pointed to Mary.* (Ver. 42.) "She hath chosen that good part, which shall not be taken away from her." The good part is a *place*, a *nourishment*, and a *choice*. The *place*—Jesus' feet. Oh the blessedness of sitting there! When the Gadarenes went out to see what had been done in their country, they saw the man who had devils long time—the devils now departed—"sitting at Jesus' feet, clothed, and in his right mind." To find that place is the sign that the strong one who binds with chains and fetters has been bound by the Stronger One, who has come into the heart. The *nourishment*—"She heard his word." That is the meat which endures to life everlasting. What cares she for the feast about which Martha is so busy, whose care is—

> "Oh, take away whate'er has stood
> Between me and the highest good!
> I ask no better boon than this—
> To find in thee my only bliss"?

The *choice*—"She has chosen." Behold the way of deliverance from the Martha carefulness and trouble. Choose your portion. Have within you, as the centre of your life, a fixed, supreme determination. In this there is force. It keeps a united heart among the competitions of the "many things." The part is good, because it interprets the voice of reason; it expresses the wedding of the actual life to the truth and calling of God. It is good, because it confers a real spiritual independence, so that a man is not mastered by things, but can be the master of things. It is good, because it never can be taken away. Your banquets last for only a short time. The most satisfying food, apart from God, must one day fail and forsake you. Whatever is *yours* will be taken away. This part alone is *you*. It is you hidden with Christ in God—hidden where death can obtain no entrance. "He asked life of thee, and thou gavest it him, even length of days for ever and ever ... Thou hast made him most blessed for ever: thou hast made him exceedingly glad with thy countenance." It is good, to sum up all, because it is not, as was the part of Martha, a moving about and around Christ, but "a seeking, laying hold of, and enjoying Christ himself." Thus one of the poets of the German Fatherland has sung—

> "As Mary once devoutly sought
> The eternal truth, the better part,
> And sat, enwrapt in holy thought,
> At Jesus' feet with burning heart,
> For naught else craving, yearning for the word
> That should be spoken by her Friend, her Lord,
> Losing her all in him, his word believing,
> And through the One all things again receiving;
>
> "Even so is.all my heart's desire
> Fix'd, dearest Lord, on thee alone.
> Oh, make me true and draw me higher,
> And make thyself, O Christ, my own!
> Though many turn aside to join the crowd,
> To follow thee in love my heart is vowed,
> Thy Word is life and spirit. Whither go?
> What joy is there in thee we cannot know?"

HOMILIES BY VARIOUS AUTHORS.

Ver. 2.—*Spiritual husbandry.* I. THE LARGENESS OF THE FIELD. "The harvest truly is great." It is not a few human families, or a few small populations; it is not one large nation; it is not even one great continent; it is the entire human race, which Jesus Christ proposed and which he still purposes to redeem—this great human race; with all its nationalities, with all its creeds and all its doubts and denials, with all its pride and all its degradation, with all its profound estrangement from Divine truth and the living God. The harvest is great indeed; the task is tremendous; the victory, if it be gained, will make all other victories sink into utter insignificance;

they will be but the small dust in the balance. There is encouragement in the thought of—

II. THE CHARACTER OF THE SEED WHICH IS SOWN. That seed was in course of preparation as Jesus Christ was speaking and working and suffering. It was his whole life; it was, indeed, *himself* in all his relations with men, in all the aspects in which he could be regarded, whether as Teacher, or Friend, or Exemplar, or Divine Sufferer. This was the seed which should be sown, the fruits of which would be the great harvest of God. "I, if I be lifted up," etc. But, on the other hand, there has to be taken into account—

III. THE CHARACTER OF THE AGENTS at work in the broad field of the world. 1. Their *infirmity*. They are men; good men, but "the best of men are but men at the best;" all (they should be) renewed by the Spirit of God and fired with the love of Christ and of human souls; but all (they are) "compassed about with infirmity," all bound with limitations of understanding, of character, of wisdom. 2. Their *paucity*. "The labourers are few"—few in comparison with the agents of evil and the sources of error; few, regarded in their proportion to the multitude on whom they are to act. In this light they are lamentably insufficient. There are great breadths of the field scarcely worked and other vast districts positively untouched. What, then, is—

IV. THE HOPE OF THE FAITHFUL? When we survey the greatness of the harvest and the fewness of the labourers in the field, where does our hope lie? In the providing power of the great Lord of the harvest. He who moves the stars in their spheres can create human souls, can endow them with noble faculties, can inspire them with generous aims, can send them forth on glorious and triumphant missions. We cannot tell the possibilities which are hidden in one great human soul whose heart God has touched, whose hand God has strengthened. One such man may be instrumental in turning a whole tract of barrenness into fertility: what, then, may not a number of such souls accomplish? When the Lord of the harvest speaks the word, great will be the company of the preachers, the number of the labourers. Wherefore let us pray the Father of spirits to put forth his creative power and send mighty workers into his waiting fields.—C.

Ver. 7.—*Our due.* "The labourer is worthy of his hire." What is it that we deserve? The answer depends entirely on the light in which we regard the question. We may look at it in three aspects.

I. OUR UNWORTHINESS OF ANYTHING. If God were to give to us exactly what we deserve, everything of every kind being taken into account, we should receive nothing more. For, weighing in one scale all that we owe to him for everything he has been to us and wrought for us and bestowed upon us, and in the other scale what response we have made to him in gratitude, love, service, we should "be found wanting," and could claim nothing. We are *not* worthy the least of all his mercies. All that he gives us is so much beyond our desert.

II. OUR OBLIGATIONS TO ONE ANOTHER. It is well that we do not make these a "matter of account," as tradesmen do with the articles they supply to one another, only paying the balance now and then. For who would decide on which side that balance lay? And of how much beauty and excellence would our daily life be divested! The true and wise course is to make acknowledgment of every kindness received, the warmer gratitude for the greater favour, but some thanks for the least indebtedness, not waiting to consider who is the greater debtor of the two. We are to "owe no man anything" only in the sense that we are to be ever paying and therefore ever cancelling our debts. But we are to be constantly indebted to one another. Poor and small indeed would that human life be which did not owe much to the service of others. What we are to seek after is not a life without obligation, but a life in which we are very freely placing our neighbours in our debt by the kindness we show them, and in which we are making very free acknowledgment of all that we owe to the love and the service we receive. Every labourer should receive his hire, his due reward, and among others the Christian workman should be rightly recompensed. 1. It is a matter of righteousness, as between man and man; faithful service should have its meet reward; and this reward should be in (1) affectionate honour, and (2) substantial, material support. 2. When rightly rendered, the reward received will be an incentive to fuller labour and more energetic service. 3. The payment of the reward will react beneficially on him that pays it—he will appreciate more highly the ministry he receives.

III. GOD'S GRACIOUS AND GENEROUS OFFER.   Though (as said) we can claim nothing from God as our right, yet he is pleased to offer us much. Our Lord has told us (1) that the humblest service, done in a true and loyal spirit, shall certainly be rewarded (Matt. x. 41, 42); and (2) that the reward we shall hereafter receive will be in proportion to the fidelity of our service here (ch. xix. 16—19). Our tone and spirit will be that of men who are not conscious of deserving anything (Matt. xxv. 37). But his spirit and action will be that of a magnanimous Master, and he will make the most of all that we have done (Matt. xxv. 40), and count us worthy of a large reward.—C.

Vers. 12—15.—*Guilt and punishment.* These very solemn words of our Lord demand our attention the more, because his thought is so fully illustrated. They suggest or convey to us three truths.

I. THAT GREAT INIQUITY MAY LOOK FOR SIGNAL PUNISHMENT AT THE HAND OF GOD. Jesus does not intimate that Tyre and Sidon suffered any more than they deserved, that Sodom had a retribution which was in the smallest degree out of proportion to its guilt. These cities deserved their doom; they sowed the wind, and reaped the whirlwind. That which happened to them was exactly what they might have expected; and it is just what such cities as they were may always look for. It does not require a desolating army or a miraculous storm to bring disastrous evil upon the head of shameful wrong. Without such particular instruments as these, the blow which slays and buries will certainly descend. If destruction comes not on the wings of one wind, it will come on those of another; whether we think of the vicious city or the profligate man, we may be sure that great guilt will, sooner or later, work out the downfall and extinction of the evil-doer. By human history and the record of the lives of men, as well as by the sacred page, "the wrath of God is revealed against all unrighteousness of men;" they cannot and will not "escape the judgment of God."

II. THAT NEITHER SWIFTNESS NOR APPARENT SEVERITY IN PUNISHMENT IS A SURE CRITERION OF THE MAGNITUDE OF THE CRIME. Destruction had come down suddenly and terribly on Sodom; Capernaum, Chorazin, and Bethsaida were still existing, and were still rejoicing in outward prosperity. Was the ancient city so much guiltier in God's sight than the (then) modern towns of Galilee? No, replied the great Teacher. Had these ruined cities of a former age enjoyed such privileges as the citizens of his own time were possessing but neglecting, they would have repented and would have been spared. We must take care how we argue from sudden and severe evils to the *relative* guiltiness of the sufferers. These evils may clearly indicate wrong; they *may* (though in some cases they do *not*) indicate very great wrong-doing; but they do not prove that those on whom they descend are more guilty than others who are spared. 1. God may think well, in one case, to manifest his holiness by severe visitation, and in another case to illustrate his patience by delaying long the stroke of justice. 2. God may punish one city (or man) by physical and visible inflictions; he may chastise another by letting his moral laws do their appointed work, and bring down the *men themselves* to that low spiritual estate which is the saddest and direst consequence of sin.

III. THAT PRIVILEGE IS VERY PRECIOUS, BUT IT IS ALSO VERY PERILOUS. Capernaum was "exalted to heaven," raised very high indeed in privilege. There the Son of God abode; there he wrought his mightiest works; there he lived his holy, patient, loving life; there he spake his deep, broad, ever-living truths; there God was manifested in power and grace. It was favoured above all cities in the height of its spiritual privileges. But it knew not the day of its visitation; it drew not nigh in reverence to its Lord; it rejected his doctrine; it remained afar off from God and heavenly wisdom. And it incurred thereby the Saviour's strong condemnation; it accumulated guilt, and laid up for itself wrath against the day of wrath; it was "thrust down to hell" in reproach and retribution. We learn, more particularly: 1. That humility of spirit, rather than reproachfulness of tone, becomes us. 2. That the children of special privilege have great reason for devout heart-searching, lest they should find themselves the heirs of Divine condemnation.—C.

Ver. 16.—*The largeness of our life.* Jesus Christ is sending his disciples, two and two, to prepare his way; it is certain that by some towns and villages they will be well received, and equally certain that by others they will be repelled. He tells them that those who received them would be doing more and better than barely receiving *them*,—they would be entertaining *him;* but those who rejected them would do more and worse than repulsing them,—they would be despising *him*, nay, even the Father himself. That there is more in our acts, and so in our lives, than appears on the surface was a frequent doctrine of our Lord. In his first sermon he intimated that those who cherished a causeless anger or spoke a contemptuous word against their brethren were guilty of a very serious offence in the sight of God; and so also they who imagined themselves chargeable with nothing more than a hasty word (see Matt. v. 22, 34—36). He told his disciples that that "poor widow" was making a very much larger offering than the rest—a much greater one, we may be sure, than she herself suspected (ch. xxi. 1—4; see also ch. xxiii. 34). Christ saw more in men's actions, both for good and evil, than they saw themselves at the time. It is the wisdom of the wise to recognize much in words and deeds, in decisions and in actions, which seem small to those that do them. Our human life is larger than we think as we live it; its several actions have more seriousness in the sight of God, and from our life greater issues will proceed than any we can estimate. This main underlying principle will apply to—

I. THE MESSENGERS AND THE MESSAGES THAT COME TO US FROM JESUS CHRIST. There may come to speak to us concerning the habits or the purpose of our life, or the character we are forming, or the good we are doing or leaving undone, or the prospects that are before us, some messenger that appears in very humble form, not delegated by any high authority, not sustained by any learning, not armed with any eloquence; there may be nothing more about the outward spokesman than a plain or even a blunt man, nothing better about the form of the message than a periodical which has no worth in the market at all; and yet the message which comes through that very common, through that vulgar medium, may come from above, may come from Christ himself, to warn or to arrest us, to lead us out of the dark shadows we were entering, into the path of life. And in repelling that message we should be rejecting the very truth of God; in accepting and heeding it we should be welcoming our Lord himself, and taking his Divine influences into our soul. This principle of the greater value and seriousness of our life finds an illustration in—

II. THE STUDIES OF YOUNGER DAYS. They who have to go through the daily task in the school or home see nothing more in their work than the laborious gratification of their teacher. But there is much more in it than that. There is obedience to parents; there is the consequent pleasing of God, and the reward of filial behaviour; there is the serving and honouring of Jesus Christ by diligence and dutifulness, by doing the right thing as in his presence and as unto him; there is the mental and moral growth which prepares for an honourable and useful manhood. Life at home or at school, in our earlier days, is really a larger thing, with larger and greater issues, than it seems to be at the time. The same is true of—

III. STRUGGLES FOR HONOURABLE MAINTENANCE. The Christian man who thinks he is doing nothing more than "paying his way," is or may be doing a very great deal more than that. He is illustrating in his sphere the very principles which the Lord himself taught and lived when he was here; he is translating godliness, Christliness, into busy human life; he is preparing for some broader sphere in that higher kingdom where, if not before, he that has been found faithful in that which is least will be proved to be faithful in much. We not only speak in the spirit and strain of our Lord's words, but we pursue the same subject when we refer to—

IV. ENDEAVOURS TO SERVE OUR FELLOW-MEN; and this, whether in the way of common philanthropy, or of distinctively religious service. Do we ask of those whom we find in the school, or the mission-room, or the church, "What are you doing here?" And do they reply, "We are only teaching some children, only feeding some poor people, only trying to gather some wanderers into the fold"? Then shall we reply to them, and say, "Nay, but you are doing much more than that: you are serving them; and you are rendering the very highest service you can to yourselves, for you are sowing seed of which you shall one day reap a glorious harvest of joy and power; and you are also serving your Saviour, and that in a way in which he most delights to be served.   He is saying to you, 'If you had eyes to see, you would recognize *me* in those pinched faces and ill-clad forms; if you had ears to hear, you would recognize *my* voice in those plaintive tones; it is *my* need that you are supplying, it is *my* heart that you are gladdening: inasmuch as you are carrying succour, strength, hope, life, to one of the least of these, you are doing it unto *me*.'"—C.

Ver. 20.—*Better things.*   When Jesus said, "Rejoice not, . . . but rather rejoice," he did not mean to condemn the satisfaction which the seventy were expressing in their triumph over the evil spirits.   There was nothing wrong in such gratification. To exercise power, especially a newly acquired power, and more especially a power that is possessed by few,—this is simply natural; and to rejoice in the exercise of beneficent power is not only not wrong, but is distinctly and positively right and worthy.   But there are other sources of joy that are more excellent; it is a question of the relatively rather than the absolutely good.   We conclude from our Master's words—

I. THAT IT IS BETTER TO BUILD ON CHARACTER THAN ON CIRCUMSTANCE.   This was a very pleasing incident in the life of the seventy; they would always look back to it with pleasure, and speak of it with interest to themselves and others.   But it was *only an incident*.   It was decisive of nothing.   It did not determine their future course, their final destiny.   They might have done what they did and yet have gone downward and reached an evil end.   To have "their names written in heaven" meant to be right at heart, to be reconciled to God, to be loyal citizens of the spiritual and heavenly kingdom, to be sound and true within.   It is this which is to be desired and to be sought and to be built upon.   Life may have a large number of interesting episodes, of gratifying circumstances, and may yet be a miserable failure, may have to be looked back upon with pain and shame.   To be right with God, to have "truth in the inward parts," to be such a one on earth as that those who live in heaven will recognize us as their kindred,—that is the thing to be concerned about, that is the goal to be gained at all costs, the true source of human joy.

II. THAT IT IS BETTER TO ENJOY THE ABIDING FAVOUR OF GOD THAN THE SHORT-LIVED THANKS OF MAN.   Doubtless one part of the satisfaction which the seventy enjoyed was the gratitude they received from those whom they relieved; but better than human gratitude is the favour of the living God.   The thankfulness of a sensitive and responsive human soul is by no means to be despised or disregarded, but it is a very precarious basis of human happiness.   It is sometimes denied where it is most due; it is sometimes very slight and transient when it should be deep and lasting. But God's favour abides.   "Having loved his own, he loves them to the end;" "In his favour is life."   If we are upheld in our integrity, and God sets us before his face for ever (Ps. xli. 12), we can afford to part with other things.

> " Better to walk the realm unseen
> Than to watch the hour's event
> *Better the smile of God alway*
> Than the voice of man's consent."

III. THAT IT IS BETTER TO EXERT A LASTING INFLUENCE FOR GOOD UPON THE SOUL THAN TO CONFER A TEMPORARY GOOD UPON THE BODY.   The bodily service rendered by the seventy was great as far as it went and so long as it lasted.   But the eyes then and by their means opened, and the ears then unstopped, were soon closed again in death; and the feet then made to walk were soon motionless in the grave.   But to have their names written in heaven, and to be thus prepared to enlighten the minds and to quicken the souls of men, was to be in a position to render lasting, even everlasting good; that was to confer immeasurable benefit on those whom they sought to bless.   1. Are our names written in that book of life?   2. Are we appreciating its inestimable value? 3. Are we making use of the qualifications it implies to serve our fellow-men in the highest ways?—C.

Ver. 21.—*The gladness of gratitude, etc.*   Our thought is directed to—
I. THE GLADNESS OF GRATITUDE.   "Jesus rejoiced in spirit, and said, I thank thee,

O Father." Joy and thankfulness are here united, as indeed they are everywhere. It is gratitude that holds the key to happiness of heart and life. Who are the miserable? Not the poor; they are often the most contented. Not the afflicted; they are often very cheerful under great privation. Not the lonely; they are found happy in their solitude, conversing with the departed great or communing with the Highest. It is the ungrateful who are the unhappy; it is they who take every kindness shown them by their fellow-men in a spirit of surliness, as if they deserved more than they have received; it is they who accept innumerable mercies and the "unspeakable Gift" at the hand of God without response, unmindful of the one, unappreciative of and ungrateful for the other. Who are the happy? Not the rich because they are rich; not the strong because they are strong; not those who have many friends because they have them. These may be burdened, wearied, wretched, and their life be darkly shadowed. It is the grateful who are the happy souls; it is they who receive with appreciation and thankfulness whatever man may give them, whether of love, of confidence, of sympathy, of practical help; it is they who have a deep sense of the kindness of the heavenly Father, and of the grace of the Lord Jesus Christ. The heart that is full of gratitude is the heart that is full of joy; and such joy is both pure and lasting.

II. THE HERITAGE OF THE HUMBLE-HEARTED. "Thou hast hid these things from the wise, . . . and revealed them unto babes." 1. In our Lord's time the scribes and lawyers "rejected the counsel of God;" they refused the wisdom of the Wisest; and the supercilious Sadducees stood aloof from the kingdom of Divine truth, from the kingdom of God. The "wise and prudent" were too haughty of heart to part with their beloved prejudices and to welcome the new truth which the great Teacher brought them. But the "common people heard him gladly;" all "the people" were "very attentive to hear him." The fishermen of Galilee left their nets and their ships to follow him. 2. In the time of the apostles the same results were found (see 1 Cor. i. 26—28). 3. In our own time we find that they who have gathered together a little human learning are apt to think that they are competent to solve, unaided, all the great problems of their being and their destiny, and they close the gates of their mind against the great verities of the Christian faith. But they who know how little they have grasped of all that is to be acquired, and who stand as "babes," as very little children, before the Divine Father, are ready to welcome to their souls all that he is ready to reveal to them, and theirs is the blessed heritage of spiritual truth, of heavenly wisdom, of eternal life.

III. THE REFUGE OF THE PERPLEXED. "Even so, Father; for so it seemed good in thy sight." We have our perplexities now, and they may weigh upon our spirit with crushing power. We cannot understand God's doings or his inaction in the wide human world, or in the Church of Christ, or in the more limited sphere where our own interests and efforts lie. The more we think the more we are assured that we are baffled and beaten. The various solutions proposed do not reach the heart of the difficulty. What, then, can we do? Just retreat to that safe refuge—the strong, immovable assurance that all things are in the hands, and are subject to the guidance, of a holy, wise, loving Father.—C.

Vers. 23, 24.—*Apostolic advantage and disadvantage.* Our Lord compares the position of his apostles with that of the great and enviable of past times. We may follow his thought and may also pursue the same line of comparison in our own times. We look at their position—

I. AS RELATED TO DISTINGUISHED MEN BEFORE THE ADVENT. 1. It was one of some *disadvantage*; they were men in a very much *humbler* position than many of the great in past days. Great kings had lived in a social state and with pleasant surroundings to which they could lay no claim; in society they were nowhere; of this world's luxuries and trappings they had nothing. Moreover, they were in a much *less powerful* position than some of the great men that had gone. Prophets had made or unmade kings; or they had delivered laws or changed customs, materially affecting the civil, social, moral, and religious life of the nation; witness Moses, Samuel, Elijah, Elisha, Nehemiah, John. The apostles of our Lord were not doing anything of this kind when he spoke to them; they had done very little of a public character thus far; their influence had not been felt in the life of their countrymen. 2. It was one of glorious *advantage* in one respect. They had the most distinguished honour of being the personal attendants upon the Messiah himself. They not only *saw* his face and *heard* his words, but they ministered to his wants; they rendered him service; and, by rendering him service, they contributed largely and importantly to the well-being of all later generations. 3. It was one of *greater honour* than they themselves supposed; for he at whose feet they sat and of whose truth they drank was One very much higher than they imagined even their Messiah would be; and he wrought a greater good for a larger world than they conceived it possible even for the Anointed of God to work.

II. As RELATED TO OURSELVES. 1. Their position was one of supreme privilege in one great particular—they attended upon and they served Jesus Christ himself, *in his own Person*. That was an honour which stands by itself; it is unique; of its kind it is unapproachable. Let any disciple of the later time reach any imaginable position; he must feel that in actually ministering to our Lord, supplying his necessities, being sympathetically as well as bodily present "with him in his trials," helping him in his supreme and critical work, the apostles of our Lord stand pre-eminent. 2. And in being *the first to publish the gospel* after our Lord's ascension they also stand in the very front rank. 3. It was also a very distinct advantage to receive Christian truth *direct*, without intervening media, with nothing to subtract from it or to add to it; they had truth at the fountain source, uncorrupted by the channels through which it passed. 4. But they were subject to some disadvantage also. (1) Jesus Christ was not, in his *Divine Person*, so fully revealed to them as he has been to us; that would have made free and full fellowship utterly impossible. (2) His *doctrine* was not as complete at the time of our text as it afterwards became; for his death, resurrection, and ascension constitute a very large part of Christian truth. (3) They had not the advantage of Christian *experience* we possess. All the thoughts of wise Christian thinkers during many centuries; all the recorded experience of multitudes of Christian lives; all the moral and spiritual workings and triumphs of Christian truth and principle under many skies and through many ages;—these are ours as they were not theirs. Our privilege, even as compared with theirs, is very great indeed. Perchance our Lord would tell us, if he spake to us to-day, that it is *as* great as theirs, and that our responsibility answers to our privilege.—C.

Vers. 25—27.—*Our love of God.* It is the glory of the gospel that it has made common to the multitude of mankind that which was once dimly seen by a few solitary men ; that it has put into the mouth of the little child that which once was stammeringly spoken by a few philosophers; that the truths which once were only found upon the summit by a few hardy climbers are the fruits which are now gathered by thousands as they walk the King's highway. Here is one of these—the duty, binding on us all, of *loving God*. 1. If to those Greeks who came to see Jesus (John xii. 20), he had said that the greatest obligation, or, as they would have put it, the most fitting thing, was for man to love God, they would have been amazed. They would have been prepared to render services and sacrifices to their deities, but to love God with all the heart was beyond their most active imagination. 2. If Christ had uttered this truth to the Roman procurator before whom he appeared, he would have been equally astonished. 3. This truth was far in advance of the Jew, as well as of the Greek and the Roman. It is true that it was to be found in his Law (see Deut. vi. 4, 5; x. 12; xxx. 20). But it was not in his mind, in his heart, in his cherished convictions, in his life. He "tithed mint and rue and all manner of herbs, but passed over . . . the love of God" (ch. xi. 42). Even the worthies of Old Testament times were men who were more constantly and profoundly affected by the sentiment of holy fear than fervent love. "I fear God," rather than "I love God," was the summary of their religious character. How do we account for this?

I. THE JEW HAD REVERENCE ENOUGH FOR GOD TO BE ABLE TO LOVE HIM. The Roman, the Greek, had not. We must respect those whom we love, and the beings they worshipped could not be respected; they were unworthy of regard. Not so he whom the Jew worshipped. He was the Just, the Righteous, the Faithful, the Holy One. The Jew honoured, he revered, God enough to be able to love him.

II. HE HAD A VERY CONSIDERABLE KNOWLEDGE OF THE GRACE AND MERCY OF GOD.

For we find in Old Testament Scripture passages affirming the kindness, the pity, the patience, the mercy, of God, well worthy to be placed by the side of any we find in the New (Exod. xxxiv. 6, 7 ; Ps. ciii. 8—14 ; cxlv. 8, 9 ; Micah vii. 18, etc.). It was surely possible for him to let reverence ascend to love.

III. To some extent the Jew did love God. Abraham was "his friend." David could exclaim, "Oh, love the Lord, all ye his saints!" "I love the Lord, because," etc. Yet it was not love but fear that was the central, commanding, regulating element of his inner life. This need not surprise us when we consider—

IV. The Jew did not know God as revealed in Jesus Christ. 1. He had not heard Jesus speaking of the Divine Father hating sin but pitying and yearning over the sinner, determining at his own great cost to redeem him, as we have done. 2. He had not witnessed the Saviour's life as we have followed it ; had not seen the Father's character and spirit reflected in that of the Son, with his tender affection, his inexhaustible patience, his matchless condescension, his generous forgiveness. 3. He did not know the story and the meaning of his death ; had not had, like us, a vision of the love of God paying that great price for our redemption, bearing that burden on our behalf, pouring itself out in pain and shame and sorrow for our sake. It is at Calvary, far more than elsewhere, that we learn the blessed secret of the love of God—his love for us, our love for him. We learn : (1) *That to love God is the highest heritage of our manhood.* "As a man thinketh in his heart, so is he ; " *as we think, we are ;* a man is great or small, noble or ignoble, according as he thinks and feels ; the height of our love is the stature of our soul, is the measure of ourselves. God invites us to love him, the Highest One, and by so doing he immeasurably enriches and ennobles us. If he filled our house with gold he would only give us something pleasant *to have ;* but in inviting us to love him he confers on us that which is blessed and noble *to be.* (2) *That not to have loved God is the most condemning fact of our lives.* Do we say, "All these [prohibitions] have we kept from our youth up : what commandment have we broken ? " We reply, "The first and great commandment. Have you loved God with all your heart ? " We may well bow our head in shame as we realize the poor and pitiful response we have made to the Fatherly love of God. (3) *That the fact that we can at once return to God,* in filial devotion, is the *best of all glad tidings.* Our return to him begins in humility, goes on in faith, is completed and perfected in love. (4) That the fact that we shall continue to love God is the *brightest of all good prospects.* Other things will fail us sooner or later, but "the love of God which is in Jesus Christ" in our hearts will take us everywhere, will be our refuge and defence in all emergencies, will sanctify our joy and our prosperity, will be with us at the last scenes, will cross the river with us and will be with us and in us on the other side, will be our passport to and our qualification for the brightest and broadest spheres in the heavenly kingdom.—C.

Ver. 29.—*Who is our neighbour?* This was a very pertinent question, by whatsoever motive prompted. None better could possibly have been asked, for it drew forth Christ's own interpretation of his own Law. And, like the Jews of his time, we are in no little danger of limiting the Divine thought. "Who is *our* neighbour?"—in *our* thought, in *our* feeling and practice? Who are those we feel bound to love and help? Our kindred, those of our fellow-citizens from whom we want the interchange of civilities, our countrymen,—do we draw the line there? If so, we "have not the faith of our Lord Jesus Christ" in this matter ; we are falling out of rank as his disciples. There is nothing especially Christian about the affection we feel or the kindness we show to these. Going thus far, we go no further than pagans have gone before us. We must transcend this if we are to be worthy of the name we bear. In order to be that, we must find our neighbour everywhere and in every one, but more especially in the man who has need of us. The Christian conception of "our neighbour"—

I. Oversteps the limit of race. It is painful to think that men have been taught to look upon those who inhabit other lands with positive enmity, so much so that even Cicero could say that the natural relation of neighbouring nations was that of enmity ; that whole peoples (like the Greeks and the Chinese) should treat the outer world as "barbarians" to be despised and avoided. It is foolish and illogical enough, but it has been all too common. Nothing but the prevalence of Christian principle and the permeating force of the Christian spirit will avail to lead us to love those beyond our borders, without the pale of our own civilization.

II. REMOVES THE LIMIT OF SPACE. The simple and common notion of a neighbour is that of one locally near to us. But that idea, under Christ, has been very greatly enlarged. 1. It is true that, since he spoke, we have seemed to be further off, in space, from one another. For those to whom he spoke had no notion of the width of the world, no idea that there were fellow-men living twelve thousand miles away from them. 2. But it is also true that, since he spoke, we have been brought near to one another. (1) Christian civilization has given us an intimate knowledge of one another, so that we know more of what is happening in India than the "dwellers in Jerusalem" knew then of the events occurring in Nazareth; and (2) Christian zeal has made possible to us a genuine sympathy and a practical kindness. We can, by putting a coin in a plate, help to send the light of Divine truth to men of every colour, in every latitude and longitude of the habitable globe. Who is our neighbour? All men beneath all skies, and it is open to us all to do something to help the wounded pilgrim on life's highway, even in remotest lands, to health and joy and life.

III. TRANSCENDS THE LIMIT OF CHARACTER. If that lawyer had answered his own question, it is certain that he would have given a reply which would have excluded the ungodly and the immoral. But in Christ's view the neighbour we should commiserate and rescue is not only the poor traveller who has fallen among thieves, but the erring soul who has lost his way in the search of truth, and that pitiable one who has fallen into the mire of guilt and shame; those who have been smitten by the worst of all strokes, and have descended into the darkest of all shadows. Our neighbour, in the view of our Lord, is not the man who is up and who can assist us on our way, but he that is down and whom we can help to rise; he is the man who is most in need of our sympathy and our succour; he is the man who has a bruised and bleeding heart that patient, sacrificial love alone can heal. If we will go to him and help and bless him, and make ourselves "neighbour unto" him, we shall thus "fulfil the law of Christ;" and we shall thus be not only "keeping his commandment," but living his life.—C.

Vers. 38—42.—*Christ at Bethany.* There are few places at which we so much like to think of our Lord's presence as Bethany. We like to think that there the Son of man, who had not where to lay his head, did find a home; that there, away from the conspiracies of those who hated him, he found a refuge with those who loved him. We like to think that there he found a diligent disciple in one sister, and an assiduous and eager ministrant in the other. We must carefully consider—

I. THE COMPARISON WHICH OUR LORD WAS MAKING. (Ver. 42.) For it *was* a comparison, not a contrast—a comparison between the choice that was good but was not the best, and the choice that was *the good one.* It was not a contrast between the absolutely bad and the positively good; it was a comparison between the good that was insufficient and the good that sufficed. There are those who choose the positively bad —pleasures which are unlawful, profits which are dishonest, a life that is ungodly. Christ condemns this elsewhere; but here (in the text) he is condemning another thing. He condemns the too-absorbing pursuit of that which is not supreme, which is good only up to a certain point, and beyond that is powerless. Christ was comparing the woman who was absorbed in doing a right but an inferior thing with her sister who was intent on the highest and best of all.

II. THE INFERENCE HE WAS DRAWING. That many good things, however many they may be, do not constitute *the good thing,* and that they will disappear and disappoint. Health, home comforts, worldly position, literary delights, art,—these are good in their measure; but they will not together make up our human requirement; they are not "the bread of life" and "the water of life;" they do not satisfy, and they will not last; sooner or later they break down and leave us portionless and hopeless.

III. THE POINT WHICH HE WAS PRESSING. There is one thing which is so surpassingly excellent that it may be considered *the one good thing*—"that good part which shall not be taken away." To Mary this was Divine truth as it came to her in the Person and in the words of Jesus Christ. And to us it is also heavenly wisdom, as we gain it direct from our Divine Lord. She drank in that immortal truth as she "sat at his feet, and heard his word." We also receive it into our hearts as we " go unto him " and " learn of him," as we follow him, and as we abide in him. Of him we learn the way to God, the way to the light and the peace and the life which are in him. From him we gain forgiveness, friendship, purity, usefulness, a hope that does not make ashamed. This is the " good part," the intrinsically precious, the invaluable thing, of which no figures can indicate the worth; it is the good part which can never be lost. For there is no power on earth that can touch it to harm it. Disease will not waste it, fire will not consume it, force will not crush it, fraud will not steal it, time will not enfeeble it, death will not destroy it, the grave will not hold it. It lives ever and out-lives everything which the eyes can see, on which the hand can rest. This is the one thing which is above high-water mark; all other, all earthly good things will be washed away by the incoming tide; but this portion, this heritage, no wave will reach in the mightiest storm. This is the " part " to choose. 1. We all *can* choose it. God is opening his hand to offer it; we can open ours to take it if we will; our destiny is in our choice. 2. We *must* choose it. If we fail to do so, we shall not only shut ourselves out from all that is most worth having and being, but we shall shut ourselves in to loss, to shame, to death.—C.

Vers. 1—24.—*The mission of the seventy.* Jesus, as we have seen, is now going up on his last journey to Jerusalem, and he is anxious that the places he is to visit for the last time, and some possibly for the first as well as last, should be ready to receive him. On this account he organizes the mission of the seventy in addition to that of the twelve already noticed. They are to be forerunners, going to announce his advent in the different cities and villages. Let us study the mission as here presented to us. And—

I. THEY ARE TO GO FORTH IN A SPIRIT OF PRAYER FOR ADDITIONAL LABOURERS. (Ver. 2.) The desire in the world to limit and regulate the number of labourers, to keep up wages, is to have no counterpart in the Church of Christ. The needs of men are so great, the harvest of souls is so enormous, that as many reapers as can possibly be equipped are needed and should be prayed for. Narrow-mindedness and jealousy are, therefore, out of place in Christian work. Those already labouring for God are to be the chief intercessors for more workers, and it is the inspiration of God which can alone fit men for such work.

II. THEY ARE TO GO FORTH PREPARED FOR OPPOSITION EVEN UNTO DEATH. (Ver. 3.) It seems at first a foolish policy to send lambs among wolves. Will they not be torn to pieces instantly? Is it not to court defeat and failure? But it so happens that it is the manifestation of a meek and lamblike spirit among ravenous and wolfish men which wins the battle for Christ and conquers the world. Were it not for such exhi-bitions of meekness the world would never be won. Hence the martyr-spirit is the safety of the Church.

III. THEY ARE TO DEPEND UPON THE PEOPLE FOR SUPPORT. (Vers. 4—8.) Some of the seventy, like some of the twelve, might have taken some provision or money with them. They were not all absolutely poor. The Lord himself might have brought from heaven or furnished miraculously all that he needed during his ministry on earth, but he preferred to depend upon his Father in heaven, and to accept of the loving ministrations of his friends on earth. The same rule he prescribes for his servants. They are to receive their support from those among whom they labour. And in the reception of support, they are to be content with whatever hospitality comes first. Peacefully are they to dwell in the house of their host, and they are not to be choosing some better hospitality and showing a mean and worldly spirit.

IV. THEY ARE TO GIVE THEMSELVES UNRESERVEDLY TO THE KING'S BUSINESS. (Ver. 4.) The instruction, " Salute no man by the way," does not advise any dis-courtesy, but as the Eastern salaams are protracted pieces of etiquette, they are to show so clearly that their " King's business requireth haste," that such cumbrous formalities must be dispensed with. It is a great thing gained if the Lord's servants are so con-centrated upon their work that nothing is allowed in the least degree to interfere with it. God's work must be paramount.

V. THEY ARE TO HEAL THE SICK AND ANNOUNCE THE KINGDOM. (Ver. 9.) It is the advent of salvation to these cities and villages of Palestine; hence the healing of the sick is performed as a sign of the higher salvation which is included in the coming of the kingdom. Physical miracles are spiritual signs. The health of the soul is to follow that of the body, if the people will only trust the King. The delegated miraculous power is the sign and announcement of coming spiritual power and salvation.

VI. The penalties attached to the rejection of these ambassadors. (Vers. 10—16.) The Lord directs them, as in the case of the twelve, to simply shake off the dust of their feet against them. This was the sign of separation complete and final. But he indicates that in the judgment it shall be more tolerable for such cities as Sodom, Tyre, and Sidon, than for the cities which reject them. Now, the doom of Sodom and of Tyre was terrible. In the one case God destroyed the cities of the plain by fire; in the other case by siege and bombardment. But for Sodom and for Tyre— meaning, of course, for their inhabitants—there yet remains a judgment in the great day. Yet their sin, though heinous, was not so great as that of rejecting Jesus and his ambassadors. Chorazin, Bethsaida, and Capernaum will experience a deeper doom than even Tyre and Sodom, because they repented not. The solemn position of an ambassador of Christ cannot be over-estimated. To speak for Christ, in his Name, in some way worthy of him, is surely a great commission. What an altitude in ministration should we reach before we can conscientiously adopt the attitude of the apostles! [1]

VII. The joy of the seventy at their success. (Ver. 17.) They delighted in the thought that the devils had become subject unto them through the Name of Jesus. How natural it is to rejoice in the success the Lord grants! But as Jesus here shows, it is dangerous. While assuring them of triumph over Satan and all the power of the enemy, he also would have them to rejoice rather in this, that their names are written in heaven. The meaning of this seems to be that they should rejoice in *what the Lord has done for them rather than what they have done for the Lord*. In the one case, they are liable to be puffed up and to think highly of themselves; in the other case, they are kept in wholesome humility. Let the Lord's work and the Lord's part of the work, rather than ours, be the source of our spiritual joy.

VIII. The joy of Jesus about the arrangements of his kingdom. (Vers. 21— 24.) While Jesus advised them to rejoice in God's salvation of them, he himself proceeds to rejoice in their successful work. His reason for this was: 1. That it *put to confusion the wise and prudent, through the revelation being made to babes.* Those who are proud and self-confident miss the meaning of the gospel and the kingdom, while those who are babelike in their docility get an apprehension of both. 2. It is in *virtue of his mediatorial commission.* The Father has committed all things to Jesus, and he proceeds, as Son, to reveal the Father to whomsoever he will. Without such a revelation we should never know the Father. 3. Christ's joy is also because of *the distinguished privileges enjoyed by the disciples.* Many prophets and kings desired to see such things as they saw, but the prophets and kings had been passed by, and these weak ones selected. Hence it is that Jesus rejoices in such God-glorifying arrangements. The more humble we are in heart, the fuller shall be the revelation which God will make to us through Jesus Christ.[2]—R. M. E.

Vers. 25—42.—*The good Samaritan, and the good part.* From the success of the seventy we now pass to the temptation of the Master. The tempter is a lawyer, one who, therefore, professed special acquaintance with the letter and spirit of the Divine Law. He thinks he may find accusation against Jesus by inquiring from him the way of life. His question implies the belief on the lawyer's part that he can win his own way to heaven. But Jesus, when he asks, "Master, what shall I do to inherit eternal life?" puts it to himself to answer, eliciting from the lawyer the reply, "Thou shalt love the Lord thy God with all thy heart," etc. Jesus then drives home the arrow of conviction by saying, "Thou hast answered right: this do, and thou shalt live." The lawyer, if he will only analyze his life fairly, must admit that he has failed to fulfil the Law. This suggests—

I. The experience of Christ in fulfilling the Law. When our Lord said to the lawyer, "This do, and thou shalt live," he was giving forth his own experience. He was himself loving God with all his heart, and all his soul, and all his strength, and

---

[1] Cf. Bruce's 'Training of the Twelve,' pp. 113, 114.
[2] Cf. Martineau's 'Hours of Thought,' vol. i. p. 114.

all his mind; he was also loving his neighbour as himself; and he found and felt that this was life, and life everlasting too. Doubtless he might have to die, but beyond death there was the compensation of resurrection. He was entitled to life on the ground of law, since he had kept it in every particular. What the lawyer imagined he could do, Jesus had actually done. He had acquired the right, not on his own behalf merely, but also on behalf of all who trust in him, to the life everlasting. The obedience of Jesus to Law was the perfect obedience required.

II. The attempt at self-justification on the lawyer's part. He seems to have thought that his attitude to God was unimpeachable; but he was not so clear about having fulfilled his duty by his neighbour. Hence he asked Jesus to define "neighbourhood." The Jew had the notion that, because he belonged to the chosen people, he had to show neighbourliness only to those of his own nation; all the rest were "dogs." And this lawyer had been as proud and as contemptuous as any of his tribe. Hence he wants from Jesus some definition of who his neighbour is, that he may estimate his own duty and the patriotism of Christ. The excuses in which selfish men indulge are marvellous. They are ready on any pretext to defend their selfishness.

III. Jesus defines "neighbourhood" by the precious parable of the good Samaritan. And here we have four characters brought before us. Let us look at them in order. 1. *The half-murdered traveller.* The road from Jerusalem to Jericho has been from time immemorial infested by robbers. It is so still. This poor traveller has met the cruel fate of many before and since Christ's time. The highwaymen have robbed him of all he had, and almost of his life too. It is a case of unmistakable need. There is no possibility of deception in the circumstances. 2. *The heartless priest.* Coming down from the holy services at the temple, he so far forgets himself as to ignore the half-murdered man's wants, and pass by on the other side. The aristocratism of office has steeled his heart against those charitable impulses which the case should have evoked. 3. *The heartless Levite.* The sole difference between these two officials was that the Levite seems to have crossed the road, to have looked upon him, and then, judging it a hopeless case, or one in which he could render no help, passed by, like the priest, on the other side. 4. *The good Samaritan.* This man might have said, "This poor fellow is one of those Jews, who will have no dealings with us Samaritans; he has often, most likely, called us dogs; he deserves no care." But instead of looking for excuses for neglecting the sufferer, he gives his heart free play, and owns the poor man as a brother in distress. The result is he dismounts, and pours into his wounds oil and wine—the best remedies, the one to keep down inflammation, and the other to heal; and, having carefully bound up his wounds, he sets him on his own beast and brings him to the nearest inn and has him comfortably lodged. The next day he pays the bill, and becomes the innkeeper's security for anything more the patient may require until he is sound and well. Here is neighbourliness. Our neighbour is whoever is laid in our path by Providence and really needs our help. If we look carefully into the case, as the Samaritan here did, and conclude that it is a case of real need, then we should recognize in the needy one our neighbour, and have mercy on him. As Jesus dismisses the lawyer with this ideal neighbourliness before him, the self-justification must have passed completely away.[1] Now, we have here the cosmopolitan spirit which Christianity fosters, and which is above and beyond the fellow-citizenship and patriotism which alone earlier civilizations fostered. Christ taught his people to be "citizens of the world," and to recognize in every needy human being a "man and a brother." It was in this spirit our Lord himself lived, and so he was able to inculcate it powerfully upon his people.

IV. The good part as defined at Bethany. (Vers. 38—42.) And here we have to notice the two types of character presented to the Lord. 1. *Martha, to whom life is a perpetual worry and weariness.* She was a Christian in the real sense, for she loved her Lord; but she was a Christian who had not escaped from the fuss and weariness which make up the life of so many. Besides, all her bustle was really under a false impression, that the greatest compliment she could pay her Master was to give

---

[1] Cf. Trench on the Parables, p. 296; Arndt's 'Gleichniss-Reden Jesu Christi,' zweiter theil, s. 112; Gerok's 'Aus Ernster Zeit,' s. 529.

him a good physical feast.   She never fancied that a good listener like Mary complimented the Master more than any repast could.   Hence Martha's fret and weariness.
2. *Mary, to whom life is a calm fulfilment of her Master's will.*   The good part Mary
chose was that of a scholar at Christ's feet, whose word is deemed Mary's law.   This
one idea made life simple and supremely blessed.   Let us make sure of it, and the
fret and worry of life shall cease, and an orderly and blessed procession of duties will
make us experience a foretaste of heaven.   The following poem expresses as beautifully as possible the thought of this passage ; it is entitled " Cumbered about much
Serving : "—

> " Christ never asks of us such busy labour
>   As leaves no time for resting at his feet ;
> The waiting attitude of expectation
>   He ofttimes counts a service most complete.
>
> " He sometimes wants our ear—our rapt attention,
>   That he some sweetest secret may impart ;
> 'Tis always in the time of deepest silence
>   That heart finds deepest fellowship with heart.
>
> " We sometimes wonder why our Lord doth place us
>   Within a sphere so narrow, so obscure,
> That nothing we call work can find an entrance
>   There's only room to suffer—to endure !
>
> " Well, God loves patience !   Souls that dwell in stillness,
>   Doing the little things, or resting quite,
> May just as perfectly fulfil their mission,
>   Be just as useful in the Father's sight,
>
> " As they who grapple with some giant evil,
>   Clearing a path that every eye may see !
> Our Saviour cares for cheerful acquiescence
>   Rather than for a busy ministry.
>
> " And yet he does love service, where 'tis given
>   By grateful love that clothes itself in deed ;
> But work that's done beneath the scourge of duty,
>   Be sure to such he gives but little heed.
>
> " Then seek to please him, whatsoe'er he bids thee !
>   Whether to do—to suffer—to lie still !
> 'Twill matter little by what path he led us,
>   If in it all we sought to do his will."

> (From Randolph's ' At the Beautiful Gate.')
> R. M. E.

EXPOSITION.

CHAPTER XI.

Vers. 1—13.—*The Lord's teaching on the
subject of prayer.*   Again the scene is far
away from Jerusalem ; no special note of
time or *place* enables us to fix the scene or
date with any exactness.   Somewhere in
the course of the last journeyings towards
Jerusalem, related especially in this Gospel,
did this scene and its teaching take place.

Ver. 1.—**Lord, teach us to pray, as John
also taught his disciples.**   It seems as
though some of his disciples—we know at
this period many were with him besides the
twelve—heard their Master praying.   It

appeared to them—no doubt, as they caught
here and there a word and expression as he
prayed, perhaps partly alone, partly to himself—as though a friend was speaking to a
friend ; *they* would pray like that : would
not the Master teach them his beautiful
secret ?   In reply, Jesus repeats to them, in
rather an abbreviated form, what, at an earlier
period of his ministry, he had taught to the
multitudes and the twelve.   It was very
likely one of the seventy who made this
request, who had not been present on the
first occasion, when the Lord gave his
prayer of prayers to the people.   We have
already remarked that at this time the
twelve, who *had* heard it, were probably
often absent on mission work.   It was a

usual practice among the more famous rabbis to give prayer-formulas to their pupils. We have no tradition extant of John the Baptist's prayer here alluded to.

Ver. 2.—And he said unto them, When ye pray, say. The older authorities leave out the clauses erased. The prayer, as originally reported by St. Luke, no doubt stood as follows. The erased clauses were filled in by early scribes from the longer formula supplied by St. Matthew, and spoken at an earlier period by the Master :—

" Our Father which art in heaven,
Hallowed be thy Name.
Thy kingdom come.
Thy will be done, as in heaven, so in earth.
Give us day by day our daily bread.
And forgive us our sins;
for we also forgive every one
that is indebted to us.
And lead us not into temptation;
but deliver us from evil."

It has been said that our Lord has derived from the Talmud the thoughts embodied in this prayer. If this could be shown to be the case, it would in no way detract from its admitted value and beauty. Indeed, the earthly training of Jesus would naturally lead him to make use of whatever was true and practical in the teaching of the schools of his people. There is no doubt that in the New Testament many a gem of exquisite beauty could be found, drawn from that strange, weird Talmud, where the highest wisdom is mingled with the wildest errors and conceits. But in the matter of the " Lord's Prayer," it must be borne in mind that only a comparatively small portion of its thoughts can be traced to Talmudical sources, and there can be no positive certainty as to their priority, since the Mishna was not committed to writing before the second century of the Christian era, and the Gemara later still. The Lord's Prayer, in the report of St. Luke, contains five petitions. Two have reference to the love of God, and three to human needs. Our Father which art in heaven. It was not now uncommon in Jewish liturgies and prayers to invoke the Eternal of Israel under the dear name of " Father." " Thou, O Lord, art our Father." Hallowed be thy Name. Not only do we pray that the Name of God may be to us a sacred precious thing, not lightly used in trivial speech, still less in bitterness and anger, only in holy reverent prayer; but we include in these words a prayer, too, that all our thoughts of God may be pure, lofty, holy. Thy kingdom come. No Messianic kingdom, in the old Jewish meaning of the word, is signified here. It is a far onlook to the close of this dispensation, which close, we believe, is hindered by human sin and perversity. It is the prayer for the end, when there will be no more tears and partings, no more sorrow and sin. It tells of the same feeling which John, at the close of the Revelation, expressed in " Even so, come, Lord Jesus." Instead of these words, Gregory of Nyssa, in his manuscript of St. Luke, appears to have read, " Thy Holy Spirit come upon us, and purify us."

Ver. 3.—Give us day by day our daily bread. There would need no comment upon this—at first sight—quite simple prayer, but for the word ἐπιούσιος, rendered " daily." This word, in all Greek literature, occurs only in these two evangelists, in SS. Matthew and Luke's report of the Lord's Prayer. Now, does this strange word mean " daily," as our translation gives it ; or is it the rough Greek rendering of some Aramaic word of a loftier signification ? Most probably our Lord was speaking Aramaic in this place, far away from the capital, in the heart of Palestine. Jerome attempts to Latinize literally the Greek compound word with *supersubstantialis;* hence the Rheims Version renders it " supersubstantial," and Wickliffe " over other substance." Generally speaking, the patristic expositors interpret this famous word in such a way that the petition prays, not for the *common bread* of everyday life, but for a spiritual food, even the Bread from heaven, which giveth life unto the world. So, with unimportant differences, interpret Origen, Tertullian, Cyril of Jerusalem, Athanasius, Ambrose, and Augustine. Among the moderns who adopt the same view may be cited Olshausen, Stier, and Dean Plumptre. The last-named scholar's words are an admirable answer to any who would abandon this higher and nobler meaning, for the sake of preserving the reference to the commonplace of everyday life. " So taken, the petition . . . raises us to the region of thought in which we leave all that concerns our earthly life in the hands of our Father, without asking him even for the supply of its simplest wants, seeking only that he would sustain and perfect the higher life of our spirit." If, however, the interpretation (on the whole unlikely) of *common, everyday bread*, be accepted, and the simple reference of ch. x. 42 to the necessity for only one dish at table be adopted, then, with the charge to the seventy contained in ch. x. 7, to eat and drink " such things as they give," and the further instruction to " take no thought . . . what ye shall eat " (ch. xii. 22), we have, in this last period of our Lord's public life, clear expressions on the part of the Master of his wish that his followers should ever content themselves with the simplest human food, avoiding not only all excess, but all extravagance, and even consideration and thought, in providing for anything beyond the simplest daily sustenance.

Ver. 4.—**And forgive us our sins; for we also forgive every one that is indebted to us.** Unforgiving is unforgiven. Nothing apparently more easy to frame with the lips, and to desire intensely with the heart, than this petition that the Father would forgive us our sins, only, in praying the prayer, how many forget, or at least slur over, the condition of that forgiveness—a condition they impose themselves! We forget the ten thousand talents as we exact the hundred pence, and, in the act of exacting, we bring back again the weight of the great debt on ourselves. **And lead us not into temptation.** The simple meaning of this concluding petition in St. Luke's report of the prayer is, " Thou knowest, Father, how weak I am; let me not be tempted above that I am able."

Vers. 5—13.—*Prayer continued. The wisdom of perseverance in prayer is pressed. The Lord introduces his argument by the short parable of the selfish neighbour.*

Ver. 5.—**And he said unto them, Which of you shall have a friend, and shall go unto him at midnight, and say unto him, Friend, lend me three loaves.** This whole passage follows naturally the Lord's own formula of prayer. The teaching contained in vers. 1—13 may be well summarized as the Master's *lesson on prayer*. The disciples, when they heard Jesus pray, asked him to instruct them in the holy art. The Lord then suggested to them a series of short *subjects* for constant prayer, and further gave them *words* in which they could embody these subjects, and then proceeded to press upon them that this constant seeking help from God should never be interrupted; no discouragements were ever to prevent their praying. " See," said the Master, " *this* " (telling them the little parable) " is what God appears to be when prayer receives no answer." Of course, he is not what he appears to be (see ver. 9). The truth concerning *God* does not really come out before the words of ver. 9; but the parable, grotesque and quaint, and picturing a common scene of everyday life, arrested the attention *then* as it has done in many a million cases since, and told men out of heart and despairing of receiving any answer to their prayers, to think. Well, here is a case in point; but is God like this? The Lord replies shortly to this mute heart-query. *At midnight.* The whole picture is drawn from a poor man's house—children and parents sleeping in one room. " With me in bed " probably suggests what is common in an Eastern house, where a divan or raised platform (rendered here " bed ") often filled well-nigh half the room. The hour

midnight has nothing strained in it—it was frequently the practice in the East to travel by night, and so to escape the great heat of the day.

Ver. 8.—**Because of his importunity, he will rise.** The one idea left upon the minds of the hearers of this little quaint homely parable is—*importunity is completely successful.* The borrower had only need to keep on knocking to get all he wanted.

Vers. 9, 10.—**And I say unto you, Ask, and it shall be given you; seek, and ye shall find; knock, and it shall be opened unto you. For every one that asketh receiveth; and he that seeketh findeth; and to him that knocketh it shall be opened.** Then the Lord—taking advantage of the state of mind into which his strange words had brought his hearers—made, as Professor Bruce well points out, the solemn declaration on which, and not on the parable, he desired the tried soul to lay the stress of its faith : " And *I* say unto you, Ask, and it shall be given you," etc. Jesus here pledges that those who act in accordance with this counsel shall find the event justify it. This statement, that those who pray to God shall surely be heard, rests absolutely on Christ's authority. It is not given as a fact which is self-evident, but as a fact which he, the Speaker, knows to be true. The man in bed is pictured in the parable as utterly selfish, regardless of his poorer neighbour's wants and sufferings. So God *seems* to us often, as we pray to him day after day, month after month, and our prayer receives no answer; he merely appears to us then as a passionless Spectator of the tragedies and comedies of time. "Children," said the Saviour, " the selfish man of my story yields to constant importunity. Think ye God, who only *seems* to be deaf to man's pleading voice that he may deepen his faith and educate his soul—think ye God is not listening all the while, and will not in the end, in all his glorious generosity, grant the prayer? Only pray on."

Ver. 11.—**If a son shall ask bread of any of you that is a father, will he give him a stone? or if** he ask a fish, **will he for a fish give him a serpent?** The Master keeps on adducing instances of the loving Fatherhood of God. All the while men were thinking hard things of him and his sovereignty. "Children," urged the Saviour, "such things, such a cruel part as you would in your dark sad thoughts ascribe to the loving heavenly Father, is simply unthinkable in the case of *earthly* parents. *They* never really turn a deaf ear to their children's pleading; think you that your Father which is in heaven will refuse to listen to *you* when you indeed call on him?"

Ver. 13.—**How much more shall your heavenly Father give the Holy Spirit to them** that ask him? In St. Matthew we find the last portion of this teaching related as having taken place at a much earlier period of the Lord's ministry. It is more than probable that much of Jesus Christ's general instruction was repeated on more than one occasion. There is an important difference between the words reported by the two evangelists. St. Matthew, instead of the "Holy Spirit," has the more general expression, "good things." In both accounts, however, is the Master's assurance that prayer, if persisted in, would ever be heard and granted, and there is the all-important limitation that the thing prayed for must be something "good" in the eyes of the heavenly Father. How many requests are made by us, poor, short-sighted, often selfish men, which, if granted, would be harmful rather than a blessing to the asker! Here the Lord, the Reader of hearts, having taken notice of some of the deep earnest longings, perhaps scarcely crystallized into prayer, of his own disciples, of a John or a James, pictures the case of one who deserves a special deepening of the spiritual life, and prays some prayer for the presence of the Holy Spirit. Such a prayer, says Christ, *must* be granted.

Vers. 14—36.—*The bitter attack of the Pharisees. Their accusation of the Lord that he was in league with the evil one. His reply.* The grave and terrible charge which was formally made by persons evidently of rank and position sent down from the capital to watch, and if possible to entrap, the hated Galilæan Teacher, was a charge no doubt brought against the Lord on more than one occasion. Of this we have clear evidence in the Gospel narratives. Puzzled and dismayed by the marvellous acts of power worked by Jesus, it was only too easy to say that he had friends and helpers among those spirits of evil which the Jew knew well were working unseen on earth.

The circumstances under which the accusation was made, and the reply of the Lord spoken, were as follows: The scene is still in the provinces, the time somewhere in the period between October and the spring of the last Passover—the period which the Master spent in that slow solemn progress, through as yet unvisited places, towards Jerusalem. Learned and experienced members of the Pharisee party, scribes and doctors of the Law, had been told off to watch the dangerous and popular Galilæan Teacher, and, whenever it was possible, to lessen his influence among the people.

Jesus (ver. 14) had been occupied in one of his (probably) daily works of healing. He had expelled an evil spirit from a sufferer whose malady had assumed the grave form of insanity which refused to speak. The people around were wondering at this gracious act of power; then broke in voices of accusation, voices to challenge him to show them some sign from heaven, saying that his power was only derived from evil sources. To this the Master replies with consummate skill, knowing the trained minds with whom just then he had to do. He is interrupted by murmurs of approval from the crowd (vers. 27, 28). He notices these for a moment, and then proceeds in detail to reply to that subtle request that he would prove his claims by showing them some sign from heaven.

Ver. 14.—**And he was casting out a devil, and it was dumb.** Some very terrible and apparently helpless form of possession which manifested itself in a mute, possibly in a motionless, melancholy insanity. **And the people wondered.** Not improbably the professional exorcists had tried here and signally failed; hence the special *wonder* of the people.

Ver. 15.—**But some of them said, He casteth out devils through Beelzebub the chief of the devils.** The accusation seems to have been whispered among the people by the Pharisee emissaries from the capital; the words of the charge were evidently not addressed to Jesus. These men could not deny the reality of the work of healing, so they tried to suggest that the great Healer had dealings with some great evil angel, whom they call, from some old Jewish tradition, Beelzebub. In 2 Kings i. 3 we read that this idol-deity was the god of Ekron. The name signifies "lord of flies." He was very likely worshipped in the low-lying cities of the sea-coast of Philistia as a god who would be likely to avert the plague of flies and insects which infested that locality. So Zeus was adored as Apomuios (the averter of flies), and Apollo as Ipuktonos (the slayer of vermin).

Ver. 16.—**And others, tempting** him, **sought of him a sign from heaven.** As in the case of Manoah or Elijah. Some such sign as the pillar of fire these cavilling Jews probably referred to. No doubt, in the course of the public teaching, in the presence of his mighty acts, Jesus was asked for such a sign on several occasions. His questioners would argue after this fashion: "We suspect that these great works of yours, especially your strange power over spirits of evil, are derived from the realm of darkness; now, show us that our suspicion is baseless by some splendid sign of the visible approval of Heaven."

Ver. 18.—**If Satan also be divided against himself, how shall his kingdom stand? because ye say that I cast out devils through Beelzebub.** Throughout this argument Jesus assumes the existence of a kingdom of evil, all armed and thoroughly organized to carry out its dread purposes. He concedes, too, in language which admits of no questioning, the existence of a chief of this evil confederacy. Throughout his reply, the Master, while carefully bearing in mind the ability and skill of his enemies who had suggested this questioning to the people, addresses himself to the common sense of the mixed multitude who were present on this occasion. The argument is perfectly simple. It is not thinkable that the prince of evil would fight against himself, which he would be doing if he put such mighty weapons into Jesus' hands.

Ver. 19.—**By whom do your sons cast them out? therefore shall they be your judges.** But he goes further in his skilful line of argument. " I am not the only one," said Jesus, "who claims to cast out devils. There are those in the midst of you, your sons, who make a similar assertion. Have *they* too entered into a league with this evil angel?" A question has been raised respecting these professed exorcists of evil spirits whom Jesus here styles "your sons." Who were they? Some, notably the older patristic expositors, have supposed that our Lord here alluded to his own apostles, to whom a measure of this power over unclean spirits was certainly given. Others, that they are identical with the "pupils of the wise," disciples of the great rabbinical schools, such as were presided over by the famous doctors of the Talmud. This is quite possible; but we have no proof that professional exorcists were pupils in any of the known rabbinical schools. It is more likely that by this general term Jesus alluded to the exorcists. These were, at this period of Jewish history, numerous. They are alluded to in Acts xix. 13; by Josephus ('Ant.,' viii. 2, 5); mention of them is also specially made in the Talmud, which even describes something of their mode of procedure. Our Lord seems to affirm in some cases, to a certain extent, the efficacy of the power of these exorcists. "These, Jews like yourselves," argued Jesus, "some of them, you know, belonging to your own Pharisee sect,—these have in certain cases apparently driven out the evil spirit of insanity: you do not accuse them, do you, of working with an evil angel?" Godet, in the next seven verses, has suggested a new line

of interpretation, which, while generally preserving the traditional exposition of the various details, supplies the connecting thought between ver. 23 (" He that is not with me is against me," etc.) and the verses which precede and follow. This, apparently, has never been done satisfactorily by any commentator. Indeed, some, *e.g.* De Wette and Bleek, are frank enough to confess that they abandon the attempt. In these seven verses Jesus draws two pictures, in which he contrasts one of those expulsions of evil spirits which he works with that of a cure worked by an exorcist.

Ver. 20.—**But if I with the finger of God cast out devils, no doubt the kingdom of God is come upon you.** Here Jesus points to a fact well known and thoroughly established. There was no question here; the most obstinate cases of possession had yielded to that "finger" he spoke of here; the fiercest of the, alas! (then) great company of the insane, at the bidding of that quiet, humble Rabbi, for ever shook off the spirit of madness, in whatever form of terrible possession it had been dwelling in his body. There was no question here; the only point raised by his enemies—*how* had that quiet Rabbi done these strange, mighty works—Jesus had answered; and now draws a picture of one of these acts of his. The "finger of God" in St. Matthew, where the same or a similar discourse is related, is called the "Spirit of God." The expression is strange, but is one not unusual in ancient Hebrew phraseology. So the Egyptian magicians said to Pharaoh, "This *is* the finger of God" (Exod. viii. 19). The ten commandments are described as written on the two tables of stone with the "finger of God." "You have seen by what power the devils obey *me*; yea, the kingdom of God, for which you are waiting and looking, lo, it is come upon you."

Vers. 21, 22.—**When a strong man armed keepeth his palace, his goods are in peace: but when a stronger than he shall come upon him, and overcome him, he taketh from him all his armour wherein he trusted, and divideth his spoils.** The exegesis is easy here. *The strong man* is the devil; *his palace* is the world; *his goods* especially here the poor possessed; *the stronger than he* is Jesus himself, who, as he paints this feature in the picture, is thinking of the scenes of the temptation, when in good earnest he overcame his ghostly adversary, then he took from him all his armour wherein he trusted, and now he, the Conqueror, *divideth his spoils*, among which are these unhappy possessed ones now being rescued from the power of their tormentor.

Ver. 23.—**He that is not with me is against me; and he that gathereth not with me** scattereth. Our Lord here is referring to the exorcists, and contrasting *their* imperfect work with *his*, showing how hopeless a task it was to attempt to combat the evil one and his satellites apart from him—Christ. It is particularly to be noticed that Jesus neither here nor elsewhere charges these with imposture. Pretence and ridiculous spells and incantations were doubtless constantly mixed up with their attempts to exorcise; indeed, the term used to describe them in Acts xix. 13 is one of contempt; but Jesus assumes in his argument here, what was no doubt the fact, that in these cases there was often, in the person of the physician-exorcist, earnestness and prayer mingled with the deepest pity for the unhappy sufferer, and before these there is no doubt that, in the less severe cases of possession, the evil influence or spirit yielded, and for a time at least let go his victim. "See," said the Master, "he that is not with me is against me in this dire conflict against evil;" for these would-be exorcists were utterly unable, even in those instances where they expelled the devil, to render him powerless to do mischief for the future. "*My* power sent these dread beings to the abyss, there to wait. The would-be exorcists were unable to replace the hellish tenant which they expelled by another and a holier influence. *I* bring back the once-tormented soul to its old relations with its God-Friend, and replace the unclean spirit by the Holy Spirit." He goes on to say—

Vers. 24, 25.—When the unclean spirit is gone out of a man, he walketh through dry places, seeking rest; and finding none, he saith, I will return unto my house whence I came out. And when he cometh, he findeth it swept and garnished. The devil, expelled for a season, watches his opportunity and quickly returns; the exorcist-physician was powerless without the aid of Christ to accomplish anything more than a half-cure; the relapse, as we shall see, was worse than the original malady. The imagery of the "dry place" through which the devil walked during his temporary absence from the afflicted soul, was derived from the popular tradition that spirits of evil frequented ruins and desert places (see the Talmud, 'Treatise Berachôth,' fol. 3, *a*; and Tobit viii. 3).

Ver. 26.—Then goeth he, and taketh to him seven other spirits more wicked than himself; and they enter in, and dwell there: and the last state of that man is worse than the first. As instances of such a terrible possession, not improbably the result of a relapse such as is above portrayed, might be cited the cases of Mary Magdalene, out of whom we are told went seven devils, and of the Gergesene demoniac, who was possessed by a swarm or legion of these unclean spirits. There is another well-known historical reference contained in these words of Jesus, which speak of the triumphant return of the temporarily banished devil. In this, the chosen people represent the one possessed; the expelled devil was the one besetting sin which from the time of the Exodus to the Captivity—that fearsome idolatry with its attendant mischief — exercised over Israel a strange and horrible fascination. After the return from exile, idolatry seemed driven out for ever. But the house was only empty; there was no indwelling Presence there of the Holy Spirit of the Lord, only an outward show of ceremonies and of rites, only a religion of the lips, not of the heart; and so the old state of possession returned under the form of hypocrisy, envy, narrowness, jealousy, covetousness. The Jewish historian, Josephus, has dared to paint the picture of national degradation which closed in the sack and burning of the city and temple (A.D. 70). But this striking application belongs to St. Matthew, who represents our Lord closing his sad sketch of the return of the devils with the words, "Even so shall it be also unto this wicked generation." It may have been that Jesus prolonged on this occasion the terrible sermon, and drew out lesson upon lesson suggested by his words; but it is more likely that St. Matthew is writing of another occasion, when, taunted with working with the aid of the devil, the Master spoke similar words, drawing from them other lessons. The general lesson to be learned—if the above exegesis be in the main followed—is the utter hopelessness of attempting any work which has as its object the amelioration of the human race *without the aid of Christ*. Earnestness and imposture will alike in the end fail here. The case of the one of whom the disciples complained to their Master as casting out devils, but who followed not with them, was very different. *Here* the Lord said, "Forbid him not: he that is not against us is for us." The good work in this case was done, we read, *in the Name of Christ*: hence the Divine approval.

Ver. 27.—And it came to pass, as he spake these things, a certain woman of the company lifted up her voice, and said unto him, Blessed is the womb that bare thee, and the paps which thou hast sucked! This woman seems to have expressed the popular feeling. The crowds who had seen the great miracle, had listened to the cavilling suspicions, and then heard the Master's wise and skilful reply, were evidently impressed with the wisdom as with the power of the famous but hated Teacher, for they no doubt echoed the lofty and sublime blessing of the woman here. She, perhaps, had in her own person experience of the two kinds of healing just contrasted by the Master; at all events, she had rightly comprehended his words. "How many women have blessed the holy Virgin, and desired to be such a mother as she was! What hinders them? Christ has made for us a wide way to this happiness, and not only women, but men may tread it—the way of obedience; this it is which makes such a mother, and not the throes of parturition" (St. Chrysostom). It has been ingeniously noticed that this is the first direct fulfilment of the "Magnificat"—"all generations shall call me blessed."

Ver. 28.—**But he said, Yea rather, blessed are they that hear the Word of God, and keep it.** As was invariably his practice, he declines to enter into any discussion respecting the peculiar blessedness which earthly relationship to him might bring. It was not for public discussion. The Lord, in his reply, tells her, however, that there was something even more blessed than that earthly relationship to which she was alluding, and to that something all, if they pleased, might attain.

Vers. 29, 30.—**And when the people were gathered thick together, he began to say, This is an evil generation: they seek a sign; and there shall no sign be given it, but the sign of Jonas the prophet. For as Jonas was a sign unto the Ninevites, so shall also the Son of man be to this generation.** Jesus now proceeds—the crowd was, we read, become denser—to reply to the unbelieving suggestion that he should show by a sign from heaven that it was not by the help of Satan and the powers of hell that he was enabled to exercise so mighty a power over the spirits of evil. No sign of the startling nature demanded would be given to the Jews of his day. Evidence in support of his high claims and lofty assertions was then in process of being supplied. What were their eyes beholding day by day, and their ears hearing? Evidence still more complete would yet be given them, but it would avail nothing! Lo, the solemn sign of the Prophet Jonas, who preached to wicked Nineveh after his strange resurrection—*that* would be given them. It is clear that St. Luke's account of our Lord's words is abbreviated. To make the symbolism of the resurrection-sign complete, we must compare St. Matthew's report (xii. 39, 40), where in plain terms the Lord's death, and the resting in the tomb, and subsequent resurrection is foretold, and compared to the well-known story of the entombment of Jonah at sea for three days. This simile of the Master's was no doubt one repeated on several occasions. It is likely enough that it was so well-known a comparison when St. Luke wrote his memoir of the life that the evangelist felt it was not needful to go into all the details of the comparison; to mention the simile was enough;

no Christian individual, household, or congregation but could at once fill up the details originally spoken by the Lord here. In the catacombs the Jonah-story is, owing to its use by our Lord, an oft-repeated and very favourite representation on those long galleries of tombs of Christian men and women of the first three centuries.

Ver. 31.—**The queen of the south shall rise up in the judgment with the men of this generation, and condemn them: for she came from the utmost parts of the earth to hear the wisdom of Solomon; and, behold, a greater than Solomon is here.** The Queen of Sheba, her visit to King Solomon, and its subsequent results made a lasting impression throughout the East; probably the immediate consequence was that a great commerce was opened up between Yemen, of which she was queen, and other parts of Arabia and the far East. The Talmud and Koran, for instance, have various legends respecting this Eastern queen who was so dazzled and impressed by the magnificent Israelitic sovereign. Such a simile would be singularly attractive to the common folk who were then, we know (from ver. 29), crowding round Jesus. King Solomon's wisdom charmed and attracted from far countries the famous queen. Lo! One wiser than Solomon was in their midst: can we not hear from the honest, plain folk around him a murmur of assent here? Hadn't they been just listening to his wise words when the Pharisees tried to prejudice them against him? Hadn't they burst out, in the person of the woman of vers. 27, 28, with an irrepressible sign of admiration? Lo! the great Arabian queen, when at the day of judgment she arose, would condemn Israel for their blind folly.

Ver. 32.—**The men of Nineve shall rise up in the judgment with this generation, and shall condemn it: for they repented at the preaching of Jonas; and, behold, a greater than Jonas is here.** And these poor sinners of the wicked city of Nineveh, they, too, will join in approval of the sad condemnation of the chosen people. In Nineveh, when Jonah appeared among them and bade them repent, they obeyed the solemn warning voice. Lo! a greater Preacher far than Jonah was in their midst; but, alas! Israel was deaf.

Ver. 33.—**No man, when he hath lighted a candle, putteth it in a secret place, neither under a bushel, but on a candlestick, that they which come in may see the light.** The Lord continues his reply to those who asked him to support his claims by a visible sign from heaven, "Do not think for a moment that the sign I speak about, and which was prefigured in the story of the Prophet Jonah, will be an obscure or secret thing.

No man lights a lamp to hide : so will it be with that sign which will be given to you." Jesus was speaking all the while of the mighty sign of his resurrection.

Vers. 34, 35.—**The light of the body is the eye: therefore when thine eye is single, thy whole body also is full of light; but when thine eye is evil, thy body also is full of darkness. Take heed therefore that the light which is in thee be not darkness.** He goes on, though, with his solemn warning words. Plainly visible though the *sign* would be—shining bright as a lighted lamp set on high—still it, too, was possible to miss seeing it. If the eye, the organ of the body which perceives the light, be sound and healthy, then the illumination given by the lamp is seen, and the whole body, so to speak, is full of light; but if the eye was diseased, purblind, no bright shining light would be seen—the body then would be full of darkness. The word rendered "single" denotes the eye in its natural healthy state; that translated "evil" speaks of the eye as diseased, as incapable of perceiving the rays of light. The imagery to those Orientals, accustomed to parable and allegory in the stories and poems they had listened to from their childhood, was easily translated into the language of everyday life. If they gave way to passion, jealousy, prejudice, impurity, lawlessness in its hundred forms, then for them the spiritual eye of the soul would become diseased, and therefore incapable of rightly discerning any heavenly sign. It was this danger that the Master was pointing out to the crowd. "Ah!" he seems to say, "you ask a heavenly sign which will substantiate my lofty claims; that sign, in a grander and more stately form than ever you have dreamed of, shall, indeed, be given you. Have no fear on *that* score; rather dread that blindness, the punishment of a hard and evil heart, will come upon you, and render you incapable of seeing the sign you ask for, and which I mean to give you." *He was speaking still of his resurrection.* Alas, for them! the blindness of which he warned them was the unhappy lot, we know, of very many of those listening then.

Ver. 36.—**If thy whole body therefore be full of light, having no part dark, the whole shall be full of light, as when the bright shining of a candle doth give thee light.** The Lord here completes his allegory, still preserving the same images, with a sketch of the condition of a holy and humble man of heart, who with a " single eye," that is, honestly, trustfully, lovingly, has looked upon the sign and believed. Godet's comment on this hard and mystic saying of the Blessed is very beautiful : " When, through the fact of the clearness of thine eye, thy

whole body shall be penetrated with light, without there being in thee the least trace of darkness, then the phenomenon which will be wrought in thee will resemble what takes place on thy body when it is placed in the rays of a luminous focus. Jesus means that from the inward part of a perfectly sanctified man there rays forth a splendour which glorifies the external man, as when he is shone upon from without. It is glory as the result of holiness. The phenomenon described here by Jesus is no other than that which was realized in himself on the occasion of his transfiguration, and which he now applies to all believers." There is little doubt that this teaching had been spoken by the Master on one, if not on more than one, previous occasion. In St. Matthew's report, in almost identical language (v. 15 and vi. 22), the immediate application was different, and the reference of the lamp put in a prominent place was not to the Resurrection.

Vers. 37—54.—*In the Pharisee's house. The Lord's stern denunciation of the Pharisee teaching and life.* The day was not far advanced, and the Master was probably weary and faint after the long and exciting discussion just related; taking advantage, probably, of this evident weariness, some of the Pharisee emissaries from the capital, to whose presence we have before alluded, suggested to one of their friends, who had a residence in the town where the events just related had taken place, that he should invite the Master to come in and rest awhile and partake of a repast. They wished, no doubt, to get him away from the fast increasing crowd, and, when alone with him, they hoped to entangle him in a fresh discussion, and entrap him into some statement which they would be enabled subsequently to make use of, when they formally accused him of heretical, blasphemous teaching. There is no doubt that at this period of his ministry a deep-laid plot had been formed to compass in some way or other the death of this Teacher, whose words and acts were beginning so deeply to compromise their position and influence in the nation.

Ver. 38.—**He marvelled that he had not first washed before dinner.** An elaborate system of utter meaningless ablutions, each carried out with particular gestures, had been instituted by the rabbinical schools. All these senseless forms and ceremonies had been developed out of the original simple directions to secure cleanliness in the Levitical Law. It is probable that our Lord, intending to bring about this discussion, pointedly abstained from even the ordinary ablution on this occasion. The language of ver. 37 seems to point to his entering the house and at once sitting down at the table. The Talmud has many references to these practices. R. Akhibha, it proudly relates, died of thirst rather than pass over these preliminary washings. In the same compilation we read that it was currently supposed that a demon sat on hands unwashed.

Vers. 39, 40.—**And the Lord said unto him, Now do ye Pharisees make clean the outside of the cup and the platter; but your inward part is full of ravening and wickedness.** Ye fools, did not he that made that which is without make that which is within also? Many of the words spoken on this occasion had been uttered by the Master previously. The variations in them, slight though they be, necessitate often quite a different interpretation. This helps us to come to the conclusion that in these cases the Lord must have spoken such sayings on different occasions. In this place, for instance, in the report of a similar accusation levelled against the Pharisees reported by St. Matthew (xxiii. 25), the second clause of the verse, which treats of the outside of the cup and the platter, reads thus: "but within they are full of extortion and excess." The meaning of this is—while every care had been taken to purify the cup and the dish, *no pains whatever had been paid to the source whence came the contents of these.* They were too often the proceeds of extortion, they were too frequently consumed with self-indulgence. But here, in St. Luke, the second clause reads, "your inward part is full of ravening and wickedness." The meaning of these words is, "In spite of your extreme care for the vessels of your table, *your whole moral life is unclean and defiled.* Are you not," argues the Master, "fools to lay down such strict rules to avoid *outward* defilement, while within, in the soul, you allow all manner of wickedness? Surely God, who created the things we see and touch, created the soul also!"

Ver. 41.—**But rather give alms of such things as ye have; and, behold, all things are clean unto you.** The translation here should run, *but rather give the things that are in them as alms,* etc. The thought of the *contents* of these cups and dishes—a thought which came out, as we have seen, so prominently in St. Matthew—here is evidently in the Lord's mind. "Ah!" he seems to say, "what you Pharisees and your schools of formalism indeed want is the knowledge of that great law of love" (the

law Jesus was ever teaching in such parables, for instance, as that of the good Samaritan). "I will tell you how really to purify, in the eyes of God, these cups and dishes of yours. *Share their contents with your poorer neighbours."* "Let them do one single loving, unselfish act, not for the sake of the action itself, not for any merit inherent in it; but out of pure good will towards others, and their whole inward condition would be different" (Bishop Basil Jones, in the 'Speaker's Commentary').

Ver. 42.—**But woe unto you, Pharisees! for ye tithe mint and rue and all manner of herbs, and pass over judgment and the love of God: these ought ye to have done, and not to leave the other undone.** Probably the primitive Law of Moses, which directed that a tenth of every income in Israel should be given up to the service of the invisible King alone, referred to such important products as corn, and wine, and oil, and the like; but the present elaboration of the Law and the Pharisee schools had extended the primitive obligation to the smallest garden herbs, such as mint and rue. The Talmud even condescends to discuss whether, in tithing the seeds of these garden herbs, the very stalk too ought not to be tithed! The Master, ever tender and considerate, does not blame this exaggerated scrupulosity, if it were done to satisfy even a warped and distorted conscience; what he does find fault with, though, and in the bitterest terms language can formulate, is the substitution of and the clear preference for these infinitely lower duties for the higher.

Ver. 43.—**Ye love the uppermost seats in the synagogue.** These seats were in a semicircle round the pulpit or lectern of the reader; they faced the congregation. **And greetings in the markets.** The love of these Jews in the time of our Lord for exaggerated titles of respect and honour is well known.

Ver. 44.—**Ye are as graves which appear not, and the men that walk over** them are not **aware** of them. Here and in St. Matthew the same imagery was present in the great Teacher's mind—the whitewashed tombs of a cemetery. But in the report of St. Matthew the Master's picture drew a sharp contrast between the fair outward appearance of the clean white tomb, and the decaying, loathsome mass of what represented poor humanity within! When Jesus spoke the saying related by St. Luke here, the imagery was still drawn from the graves in a cemetery; but now he compared his hosts and their school of thought to graves, from the wood and stones of which the whitewash was worn off, and passers-by would walk over them, thus touching them and contracting ceremonial defilement, without being conscious *what* they were walking over and touching. All contact with sepulchres involved ceremonial defilement; hence the fact of their being constantly whitewashed in order to warn passers-by of their presence. This silent warning of the graves has been compared to the leper's cry, "Unclean, unclean!" with which he warned passers-by of his sad defiling presence. These tombs were whitewashed usually yearly on the fifteenth day of the month Adar (about the beginning of March). Tiberias on the lake was built partly on the site of an old unsuspected cemetery; no true Jew would reside there in consequence.

Ver. 45.—**Then answered one of the lawyers, . . . Master, thus saying thou reproachest us also.** It did not follow that all these professed jurists were of the Pharisee sect; some, doubtless, were Sadducees. It seems, however, probable that the greater proportion of these professional teachers and expounders of the Law did belong to the Pharisees. The oral and written Law, based upon the comparatively simple Mosaic code, had now become the absolute guide and director of the whole life of the people in all its smaller details. The various copyists, lecturers, teachers, and casuists, who debated the many doubtful points constantly arising in the perplexing and elaborate system, were all known under the general term "scribes." The *lawyer* was the scribe who had especially devoted his attention to the unravelment of the difficult and disputed questions which arose in the daily life of the people. This lawyer was certainly, considering the company he was associated with, of the strictest sect of Pharisees. This person could not believe that this able Rabbi from Galilee—for that they must all, after the morning's discussion, have allowed Jesus to be—could include him and his holy order in his terrible denunciations, the truth of which the learned scribe not improbably dimly discerned.

Ver. 46.—**Ye lade men with burdens grievous to be borne, and ye yourselves touch not the burdens with one of your fingers.** Then the Lord turned to the accomplished Jerusalem scholar, and with withering emphasis pronounced upon his famous and influential order those scathing reproaches which for eighteen centuries have been the woeful inheritance of all hypocritical self-deceivers. How true was the expression, "burdens grievous to be borne," a very superficial study of the Talmud will amply show; for although even the earliest parts of that stupendous compilation were not committed to writing until some time after, yet very much of what we now peruse in those strange, weary

treatises existed then in the *oral tradition.* which it was the life-work of scholars and pedants, like the lawyer to whom Jesus was then speaking, to learn, to expound, and to amplify; and these vexatious and frivolous ordinances which the lawyers and scribes pressed home upon the people with such urgency were often shirked and avoided by the learned and cultured scribe-class as a body.

Vers. 47, 48.—**Ye build the sepulchres of the prophets, and your fathers killed them. Truly ye bear witness that ye allow the deeds of your fathers: for they indeed killed them, and ye build their sepulchres.** There are still existing four singular tombs at the foot of Olivet, in the Valley of Jehoshaphat. Remarkable objects now to the modern traveller at Jerusalem, in all their fresh beauty they would be still more striking in the days of our Lord. The peculiar composite nature of the architecture of these great tombs has decided antiquaries to ascribe the building of these to the days of the later Herods. It is, therefore, not improbable that these conspicuous objects in the landscape, seen from the temple platform, and possibly others like them, which have since perished, were the tombs and sepulchres especially in our Lord's mind when he was speaking to the lawyer, and later at Jerusalem, when he repeated, with some slight variations, the same awful woe (Matt. xxiii. 29). It was, indeed, a speech of awful and cutting irony, these words of Jesus. "Your fathers," he said, "killed the prophets; *you* complete their evil work by building tombs for these slain men of God. In other words, you pretend to make amends for the crimes of past generations by this show of ostentatious piety; but if you really differed from your wicked fathers in spirit, if you indeed honoured, as you profess to do by this gorgeous tomb-building, the holy men of God whom *they* slew, would you be acting as you now are doing—trying, as you know you are, to take my life? Is not *my* life like the lives of those old murdered prophets? are not *my* words resembling theirs?"

Ver. 49.—**Therefore also said the wisdom of God, I will send them prophets.** "'Therefore'—in other words, 'Because of the determined, irreconcilable hatred of you Pharisees, and the people whom you guide, to all that is noble and true and real; because, in spite of your seeming piety, you are fast rooted in impiety'—'*Therefore* said the wisdom of God, I will send.'" The expression, "wisdom of God," has been a difficulty to commentators. The words have been referred (1) to a quotation of the Lord's from a lost apocryphal book of that name; but we have no instance of Jesus ever quoting from an apocryphal book, known or unknown. (2) St. Luke is here quoting from the similar passage in St. Matthew's Gospel, which, when he was compiling his Gospel, lay before him, and alludes to the earlier memoir as "The Wisdom of God." Against this we have no proof that St. Luke ever saw St. Matthew's Gospel, but a strong probability exists to the contrary; besides which, the expression is never used by an apostolic writer in such a sense. (3) A reference is here intended to the Book of Proverbs, which in the early Church was known by the title of "The Wisdom of God," and the passage referred to is ch. i. 20 and 31. Putting aside all these, it seems best to consider the expression simply as a solemn utterance of the Lord, in which he identifies himself with the "Wisdom of God." And this certainly is borne out by a comparison with the report of St. Matthew of a similar announcement made by Jesus on another occasion (Matt. xxiii. 34). There we read that the Master said, "Behold, *I* send unto you prophets," etc. The *I* is emphatic, and betrays the Divine self-consciousness of Jesus. For a moment the poor Rabbi of Galilee is forgotten, and in his lofty indignation, in his profound sorrow over the stubborn heart of Israel, on both the occasions in which he is reported to have spoken these words of awful prophecy, the Redeemer identifies Himself with *God.* St. Matthew, "Wherefore, behold, *I* send unto you prophets," etc.; St. Luke, "Therefore also said *the Wisdom of God,* I will send them prophets," etc. The form of the prediction and the original thought were both, no doubt, derived by Jesus from the solemn passage in 2 Chron. xxiv. 19, "Yet he sent prophets to them, to bring them again unto the Lord; . . . but they would not give ear," etc. This was followed immediately by the account of the preaching of Zechariah (the instance chosen here by the Lord, ver. 51), and how the faithful witness was stoned by the people in the court of the house of the Lord (2 Chron. xxiv. 20, 21). **And apostles, and some of them they shall slay and persecute.** The title "apostle" is joined here with the well-known title of "prophet." The earthly reward that these *his* servants, the apostles, will meet with at the hands of the people of Israel will be the same as that meted out to those old martyr-prophets, viz. persecution and death.

Ver. 50.—**That the blood of all the prophets, which was shed from the foundation of the world, may be required of this generation.** He looked on to his own bloody death; to the day of the last witness of Stephen and of James; to the long series of persecutions which his servants would cease-

lessly suffer at the hands of the Jews;—he looked on to the state of Israel growing worse and worse, till the day when the storm of Divine anger at last burst over Jerusalem, and overwhelmed the city and the temple and the nation. That terrible day came in less than forty years.

Ver. 51.—**From the blood of Abel unto the blood of Zacharias, which perished between the altar and the temple.** The reason, probably, why these two are selected out of the long red list of the noble army, must be sought for in the special position which the recital of these two deaths occupies in the Jewish canon of Scripture; the death of Abel being related in Genesis, the first book of the canon, that of Zacharias in the Second Book of Chronicles, which occupies the last place in the sacred volume (in the Jewish canon). They were simply two martyrdoms of illustrious men at the beginning and at the close of the long many-coloured story of the chosen race. There is no doubt that the Zacharias here alluded to was Zechariah, the son of Jehoiada the high priest—a prophet and preacher of righteousness, who at the commandment of the king was stoned in the court of the house of the Lord. This is related in 2 Chron. xxiv. 20—22, in the same passage which was evidently in the Lord's mind when he pronounced the awful woe upon the generation then living. This martyrdom of Zacharias was to his Jewish listeners a very familiar and painful memory. It evidently ranked among the most terrible crimes committed by their fathers, and was the subject of some wild strange legends in the Talmud. The martyr's blood would not dry up; it was still bubbling when Nebuchadnezzar and the Chaldeans took the temple. No sacrifices availed to stop the awful flow. Tradition assigns one of the four great sepulchral monuments at the foot of Olivet, alluded to above, to the murdered Zacharias.

Ver. 52.—**Woe unto you, lawyers! for ye have taken away the key of knowledge: ye entered not in yourselves, and them that were entering in ye hindered.** The Talmud gives us the clue to the Master's words of bitter reproach here. There were very many, in that restless age of inquiry, waiting for the consolation of Israel, who longed to enter into the real meaning of psalm and prophecy; but the scribe, the lawyer, and the doctor, with their strange and unreal interpretations, their wild and fantastic legends, their own often meaningless additions, effectually hindered all real study of the Divine oracles. The Talmud—in the form we now possess it—well represents the teaching of these schools so bitterly censured by the Lord.

Ver. 53.—**And as he said these things unto them.** The older authorities here, instead of these words, read, *and when he was gone out from thence.* Thus, after uttering the last "woe," Jesus appears abruptly to have risen and left the house of his Pharisee entertainers. A crowd of angry men, composed of scribes and lawyers and friends of the Pharisee party, appear to have followed the Galilæan Teacher, whose words just spoken had publicly shown the estimation in which he held the great schools of religious thought which then in great measure guided public Jewish opinion. From henceforth there could be only one end to the unequal combat. The bold outspoken Teacher must, at all hazards, be put out of the way.

HOMILETICS.

Vers. 1—13.—*Christ teaching his disciples to pray.* "He was praying in a certain place." Might not *he* have dispensed with the special season and act of prayer? Was not *his* whole life one continuous act of prayer? Did he not always realize that communion with the Father to which praying is the means? Yes; but even he needed the time and the place of prayer. "Made in all things like to his brethren," he, too, required to recruit the energy; he, too, for power with God and men, must lift up his eyes to heaven. Those who say that they can dispense with the particular form and the definite act; that all places are their oratories, and all words and deeds the form of their conference with the Unseen; have realized a spirituality sublimated beyond Christ's, and, it may safely be said, beyond the truth and limits of our human nature. Is it private or is it social prayer of which the evangelist informs us? It would seem that the disciples heard the "strong crying" of their Master; it may be that he and they were united in prayer—he speaking with them and for them, as the Father of the family, as the Head of the household. Be this as it may, one of his followers, impressed with the action, expresses the desire that such instruction should be given them as the Baptist had given to his proselytes. And the request, by whomsoever proffered, occasions an answer which is full of meaning. Notice its two points—*what* to pray for, and *how* to pray.

I. WHAT TO PRAY FOR. This is set forth in the words which are so familiar to the Christian ear. The same words, slightly modified, are found in the sermon from the mount. There they are presented in opposition to the repetitions and much speaking of the Pharisees' prayers; here they are presented as the brief but comprehensive summary of the desires of a true disciple of Christ. "When ye pray, say," etc. Notice two points. 1. A good deal has been made of supposed parallels between the Lord's Prayer and some devotional utterances in Jewish and even in heathen scriptures. Supposing, for the sake of argument, that our Lord appropriated sentences in use by his countrymen: what matters it? Did he not express his innermost feeling on the cross in the words of the Psalter? The affectation of novelty is one of the poorest kinds of affectation. What could have been more worthy of the Divine Teacher than the selection of that which was fitted to nurture the soul-life from the devotional literature which his followers already had, or which had moulded the sweetest elements of the religious consciousness of his nation? And for the rest, if he is the Truth, I should expect to find traces of his thought, rays of the light by which he has lightened all men, in every quarter and age of his world. Truth is always Catholic. The finder of truth unites scattered fragments, and, as he unites, he creates a new thing, a new unity. The thoughts of many generations might be gathered into the prayer which Christ taught his disciples; but not the less on that account would it be a new and blessed fact. 2. Observe, further, there are slight differences in the form of the fourth and the fifth petitions in the prayer as rendered in Luke, and the prayer as rendered in Matthew. May we not infer from this that, whilst the prayer is to be used, whilst it is more than a mere outline, whilst it is indeed the Breviary of the Christian Church, it is not pressed on us as a hard-and-fast rule. For the same reason that rendered it fitting that Christ should teach words, it may well be argued that it is expedient, so far, to prescribe words when the wants of many are to be interpreted, sometimes even when the wants of individual worshippers are to be expressed. But there is an elasticity, a freedom, which is an essential element of spiritual worship. Christ's prayer is not to be slavishly used. His own deviations in the second from the first giving of it are suggestive of flexibleness. And so also his commands. In the Third Gospel we read, "say ye;" but in the first, "After this manner pray ye." Have these sentences in the heart; let the mind realize the fulness that is in them; at times speak them forth; yet take your liberty. As those who have confidence as to their entering into the holiest in the blood of Jesus, let the cry of the Spirit of adoption freely ascend, "praying always with all prayer and supplication in the Spirit."

II. For in teaching to pray, we need instruction, not so much in *what* to say as in HOW TO SAY IT. "It is the Spirit that quickeneth; the flesh profiteth nothing." Therefore, no sooner has Christ expounded the rule, or form, than he proceeds to exhibit the spirit of prayer, the right mental attitude, the faith without which the most perfect words are no prayer at all. And this he does, according to his wont, first in the shape of a simple parable, and next through an appeal to and from the heart of Fatherhood. The parable (vers. 5—8) is very short, referring to things of commonplace life. A great many meanings have been fastened on every point in this little story. Take it, however, as it is wiser to do, as bringing out the one feature—that if, as between friend and friend, importunity overcomes reluctance; if it triumphs even over surliness; much more effectual will it be when reluctance to give is only seeming—when, indeed, that of which it takes hold is the willingness of eternal love! Therefore ought we to pray, and not to faint. Augustine (quoted by Trench) has some good sayings on this. "When God sometimes gives tardily, he commends his gifts; he does not deny them. Things long desired are more sweet in their attainment . . . God for a time withholds his gifts, that thou mayest learn to desire great things greatly." It is this great desiring of great things that is the moral of the story. Prayer is not a mere isolated act; it is, as typified in the story of Jacob with whom the angel wrestled, as proved in the history of the Lord himself, an energetic, prolonged dealing with God: "I will not let thee go, except thou bless me." An old Greek writer calls it "the silence of the soul;" and there is in it the silence of the soul that ceases from the will of self, and worships only the sweet will of God. But there is another view taken in the word of Jesus. In this word it is described (vers. 9, 10) as an asking; beyond this, as a seeking; beyond this even, as a knocking—"an ascending scale of earnestness." To this earnestness the promise is given. Mark how full and unqualified the promise is. The relation of friend to friend can teach much; but there is the relation more intimate still of child to parent, and this can teach more. For here we come into the inner circle of the thoughts which are connected with prayer. Therefore the Lord proceeds to illustrate what it is in his heart to teach by a reference to this analogy. What is it in his heart to teach? Surely, that the Father's good things are open to all his children, and, as the Crown of all, as the Gift of gifts, his own Holy Spirit. This is the climax of all childlike desire. Even in what is lower, the child stretches forth to this as his highest. "Father, give me the Holy Spirit." Is it possible to conceive a refusal? Would a parent who has bread meet the cry of a hungry child with the offer of a stone? Would he torment him by giving a serpent when he asked a fish? or by giving him a scorpion when he asked an egg? If it is so with us imperfect men, if we wish to share our good things with our children, how much more (ver. 13) shall our heavenly Father give his Holy Spirit to them who ask him? His Fatherhood must be the fountain-light of his children's day. "Fear not," says Christ, "to appeal to it." "Blessed is the man that maketh the Lord his trust." Thus the Lord answers the request of the disciples. Is it not a request as pertinent to us in the nineteenth as to them in the first century? There is a secret in prayer which only the Lord can teach. We may recall a remarkable passage in the life of Coleridge which suggests this: "Shortly before his death he was conversing, solemnly, although familiarly, on his own history and thoughts. 'I have no difficulty,' he said, 'as to forgiveness. Indeed, I know not how to say with sincerity the clause in the Lord's Prayer which asks forgiveness as we forgive. I feel nothing answering to it in my heart. Neither do I find or reckon the most solemn faith in God as a real object the most arduous act of the reason and will. Oh no, my dear, it is to pray—to pray as God would have us: this is what at times makes me turn cold to my soul. Believe me, to pray with all your heart and strength, with the reason and will, to believe vividly that God will listen to your voice through Christ, and verily do the thing he pleases thereupon—this is the last, the greatest, achievement of the Christian's warfare on earth. Teach us to pray, O Lord ! ' And then," adds his biographer, " he burst into a flood of tears, and begged me to pray for him. Oh, what a sight was there ! "

Vers. 14—26.—*Christ and his adversaries.* Observe—

I. THE CONTRAST. " He was casting out a devil, and it was dumb." This was his work. As the Redeemer, he was ever intent on setting the human nature free from its manifold evil by acting on the hidden cause of the evil. It is to be noted that the dumbness is traced to a demon—to the possession of the inner nature by a spirit whose fettering of the man was evidenced in the fettering of the organ of speech. " To cure sorrow by curing sin " is the special service of Christ's Church. In this deeper reference —the reference to sin and the evil one—it is distinguished from mere philanthropy. Philanthropy contemplates the evil, and seeks to remove its occasions in social life or in the personal history. Christianity reaches to the springs of the evil. It contemplates sin ; and it sees in sin an enslavement from which the soul is to be delivered by the One stronger than Satan. But see the attitude of the world. There is wonder (ver. 14) on the part of some when the long silence is broken, and the dumb speaks. There is (ver. 15) the tempting or provocation of the Holy One by the demand for some flaming portent. And there is the devilish opposition of the Pharisees, who always hung on his rear, and who, unable to deny facts, insinuated that there was a league between the Lord and Beelzebub. So it is still. The darkness which will not receive the light has degrees of guilt. The blackest form of the guilt is that which cannot but admit the force that is active amongst men, which sees the results of that force, and yet refuses to acknowledge it to be light, closes the soul against it.

> " The deaf may hear the Saviour's voice,
>   The fettered tongue its chain may break ;
> But the deaf heart, the dumb by choice,
>   The laggard soul, that will not wake,
> The guilt that scorns to be forgiven,—
> These baffle e'en the spells of Heaven.
> In thought of these, his brows benign
> Not e'en in healing, cloudless shine."

II. THE LORD'S DISCOURSE IN REPLY TO THE THOUGHTS WHICH HE READS. The three " *ifs* " in vers. 18, 19, 20, may well be studied. The first exposes the absurdity of the supposition that he is possessed by Beelzebub. Beelzebub *in* him divided against Beelzebub without him ! the one destroying the works of the other ! How could such a power stand ? The second takes another ground. Before him there are heads of the state ; now, their sons claimed to exorcise spirits by repeating formulas of incantation : would they allow that such exorcism was by Beelzebub ? They pointed to it as an evidence of Divine favour ; how inconsistent and absurd to see the hand of the devil in his work, and the finger of God in theirs ? The third drives the argument home. If the same finger as that which they recognized in their so-called exorcisms is being really put forth, as they themselves can discern, is it not clear that the kingdom of God is come on them, and that to resist this kingdom is their condemnation ? The parable and the words which follow (vers. 21—26) relate to this. A strong man, fully armed, guards his own court, and all his goods are secure ; he and his will stand or fall together. How can the goods be taken ? Only by overcoming the strong man, by proving that there is Another stronger than he. It is only through this personal conflict that the possessions can be abstracted. So in the Lord's holy wars, a symbol of which had been given that day. Satan had been holding the afflicted person in his grasp ; and the wasted life could be restored only by the mightier power of love—the love incarnated in Christ—" coming upon him, and overcoming him, and taking from him his whole armour wherein he trusted." This he had done ; the departure of the malignant spirit, and the restoration of the man, were the sign of his victory to be fulfilled through all the ages.

III. And then follow TWO WORDS CONSTANTLY TO BE PONDERED. 1. In respect of this, Christ's holy war, there can be no neutrality. The eye, perhaps, is directed to the groups of the people " wondering," and of those tempting him. They had not actually taken part with the scorners ; they are now reminded, as all in all times are reminded,

that a negative attitude is virtually an attitude of hostility.   It is, by so much, a sub-
traction of the strength to be utilized against the enemy.   It is an occasion of stumbling
to others.   More than this, it withdraws from the attraction of his presence and love,
and lays the heart open to alienating influences.   Ever to be insisted on is the sentence,
"He that is not with me is against me."   There is another saying of Christ, one uttered
a short time before (ch. ix. 50), which may seem to be at variance with the tone of this
saying, "He that is not against us is for us."   But a glance at the context shows
the difference between the circumstances in which the words are spoken, and the
references which they bear.   The case brought before us in the ninth chapter is this:
John mentions that he and his brethren had seen a man casting out demons in Christ's
Name, and that they had forbidden him, because he was not one of their company.
This was the only offence.   The man acknowledged the authority of Jesus, was really
receiving the power from Jesus.   He wanted only in knowledge of the Lord; the affection and will were right.   And the charge of the Master is, "Do not forbid such a one;
no one can do a miracle in my Name who will lightly speak evil of me; he that is not
opposing me is, in such a ministry, on our part."   In the case introduced in the eleventh
chapter Christ is alluding to the attitude of the affections and will.   The one sentence
is a reproof of exclusiveness of spirit; it is virtually—and truly the lesson is most
necessary to-day—"Do not ban one who is seeking the same ends as yourself, who is
acknowledging me as you do, because his methods are not yours, or his orders seem of
doubtful validity, or he stands apart from your fellowship."   The other sentence is a
reproof of indecision, of colourlessness in the religious life, of the absence of vital sympathy
with the Lord.   Virtually it is, "Let every one take his side, and stand by it; be out and
out with me; have his share in my war with the devil: for all purposes, the unsympathetic or faint-hearted is my enemy; he whose life by its influence, whose action
by its tone and aims, is not gathering with me, is practically scattering."   We hear
the old cry, sounding ever on, "Who is on the Lord's side?"   2. The picture of moral
deterioration in vers. 24—26 is most graphic.   Those around Christ had been witnesses
to the exodus of an unclean spirit.   Let them suppose that such a spirit is impelled by
a ceaseless activity; "it passes through waterless places, seeking rest, but finding none."
It must have some embodiment.   It resolves to return to the old home—"the house
whence he came out."   "How can a devil find rest which the creature can find only
in God?   He has lost it for ever; he seeks it in vain in all waste places, which otherwise
please him; he seeks it especially in vain there where God, the Lord of creation, will
have his rest, and where, therefore, the devil, if he can force an entrance, finds himself
relatively best—namely, in man.   Therefore the desire soon returns upon him to look
after his own more peculiar house" (Stier).   He finds the old home "swept and garnished."   "Empty" is a word added—and an expressive word it is—by Matthew.
Good the sweeping would have been, if the house had not been empty.   God is not
there; it is open to the evil one.   There is his opportunity.   He comes to it, resumes
possession, but with reinforcements.   "Seven other spirits more evil than himself.
And the last estate is worse than the first."   Verily, a sketch awfully true!   It was
applied by the Lord to the generation whom he addressed.   Israel had indeed been
swept from the corruption of idolatry; it had been garnished by the traditions of the
elders, by the scrupulosities of the Pharisees; but it was empty—a living faith in
God had been crushed out.   And the attitude of its wise men towards the Truth was
the token of an occupation by a spirit of darkness, sevenfold more virulent than in the
earlier days.   But its applications reach to all.   "He that hath an ear, let him hear."

Vers. 27, 28.—*The voice out of the crowd.*   The preacher never knows how far his
words reach, what responses they elicit, or what chords they cause to vibrate.   Here
is one "out of the crowd," a witness for the emotion of many hearts which had felt
the mighty power of the Prophet.   That she had any real insight into the mission of
Jesus, or that she was really attracted to the truth uttered by him, cannot be affirmed.
It was, perhaps, only a passing excitement, "a most artlessly unintelligent outcry of
mere womanly feeling."   But the soul had been stirred; "while it had mused, the
fire burned, then spake she with her tongue."   A woman's word!—the idea with which
it is charged being the honour which had been put on her whose relation to the Prophet was that of mother.   She was the echo of the angel in his salutation, the pioneer

of the generations who should call Mary blessed.   The answer of Christ is very striking in respect of—

I. THAT WHICH IT IMPLICITLY CONDEMNS. We see, in this incident, the germ of Mariolatry.   A natural interest in the one who had been so highly favoured grew, and corrupted as it grew, into a veneration for her person, and the supposed influence of her motherhood.   Instead of recognizing the sacredness which had been put on motherhood, and dwelling on the very and real humanity of the Lord, the reverence of the mind was gradually transferred to the image of the woman, as that rose before the imagination of the nameless one of the crowd, nursing the babe.   And the mother and her motherhood became, like Gideon's ephod, a snare to the Israel of God.   Observe how constantly and expressively Christ bids away from the region of such veneration. His silence as to his mother implicitly condemns it.   He recognizes her, not as mother, but in the title "Woman."   His last earthly care was for her, but the sentence which conveyed it was, "Woman, behold thy Son!" and to John, "Behold thy mother!"   And his declinature to allow the praise to pass unchallenged, his call to consider something else as the only legitimate blessedness, confirms the reproof (see the parallels, Matt. xii. 46—50; Mark iii. 31—35).   "What is the preaching of the Reformation more than the word which the Lord here speaks?   In the Council of Trent they heard not that voice, but repelled it with anathema—for a maranatha to themselves" (Stier).

II. THAT WHICH IT OPPOSES TO THE CRY OUT OF THE CROWD.   Mark the "yea rather."   The woman's saying is not denied, but thought is directed to the only legitimate cause of blessedness.   The mother herself was blessed because she had given herself entirely to the Word of God.   She had felt herself the Lord's handmaiden when the salutation came at which she was troubled; and when the Divine Son, even as a Child, spoke, she kept his sayings in her heart.   This, then, is singled out as the "yea rather, blessed are they that hear the Word of God, and keep it."   It is a word both of encouragement and of searching.   There is a tinge almost of jealousy in her who accosts him.   One had been selected for the honour which she might have coveted. "Nay," is the encouragement, "this is the honour which thou canst share with her.   If she had it not, whilst thou hadst it, she would have no lasting honour, whilst thou wouldst have praise evermore.   If thou hast this honour, thou art near me as she is."   The vital question is—What is the relation of the life to the Word of God?   To have heard it is well, but there must be both the hearing and the keeping.   "He that hath my words, and keepeth them, he it is that loveth me."   The only relationships which Christ recognizes are spiritual relationships.   They are the blood-relationships in the family of heaven.   "He stretched forth his hand toward his disciples, and said, Behold my mother and my brethren!"

Vers. 29—36.—*Truth; the conditions of its reception, and our responsibility with regard to it.*   We are on trial, placed in a scene of conflict between good and evil, and called to make our election.   Our whole life is such an election; every day, every action, goes to complete that solemn probation on which depend issues of unspeakable moment.   Such has always been the contention of Christian teachers.   There is a higher aspect of life than that.   To say that life is a Divine education is to give the fuller and nobler conception of God's purpose concerning us.   He is not merely testing us; he is training us, disciplining our character, seeking to perfect our moral being.   This world is his school, and the influences of which we are conscious, the events which mark our days, the varieties in befalling and condition, are the schoolmasters through which he is stimulating or correcting, guiding or controlling, the natures with which we are endowed.   But it is wrong to set this higher, as against the other aspect referred to.   The two—that which regards probation and that which regards education—are not opposed.   Our part is to refuse the evil and to choose the good, and to stand by our choice.   In respect of this we are on trial.   We are called to work out our own salvation with fear and trembling.   Yet, in all, God is working in us to will and to do; educating the response of our will to his, that as his dear children we may walk before him in love.   In this passage the Lord reminds all to whom he speaks of the relation of the human mind to the truth that looks down from heaven.   His discourse bears on the test of inward state supplied by the attitude of the mind to the truth.   Let us listen to it as reminding us (1) of *the proper and characteristic force of truth*; (2) of *the spiritual condition in which this force is realized ;* (3) *of the responsibility with regard to it which rests on us individually.*

I. THE PROPER AND CHARACTERISTIC FORCE OF TRUTH. Christ is grieved with the generation whose representatives are with him. He had wrought in their presence the works of God; he had spoken to them the words of God. And what did they aver? That he was secretly leagued with Beelzebub; in the ministry of love they saw the malignities of hell, the finger, not of God, but of Satan. Those who shrank from such wilful misconstruction clamoured for a sign—some portent in the skies, some miracle so striking as to prove the Divine Source of his mission. And, feeling the pain of this contradiction of sinners, he says (vers. 29—32), "Sign, more than the preaching itself? What Jonah was to the Ninevites—the testimony against them—that the Son of man shall be. Sign, more than the preaching itself? The heathen Queen of Ethiopia shall condemn them; for her the preaching of Solomon was enough, and the Greater than Solomon is here. The people of heathen Nineveh shall condemn them, for they repented when the prophet preached; and yet this generation repents not, though the Son of God is himself speaking to it. Sign? The truth is its own sign. It is open; it may be known and read of all men. It is light (ver. 34), not covered by a bushel, but set as a candle on a candlestick, that all who come into the house may see it." This is the abiding characteristic of truth. It is light. Pharisees with cabbalistic lore, so-called philosophers, with their doctrine for the initiated, their pretentious knowledge, are not the light-givers. "Whatsoever doth make manifest is light." When the soul is interpreted or helped; when God in nature, in providence, or in thought, is declared; when the relations and proportions of facts are discerned; when the order of the universe is apprehended and felt; when, if puzzle and problem are not seen through, the light pierces into what is beyond, and the heart is enabled to say, "I cannot understand, I love;"—when thus the truth is known, the truth that is known makes free. It is the freedom of light before which the darkness passes. Let us realize the self-evidencing nature of truth. Signs outward and carnal it does not need. What speaks of Christ in miracle is not the mere wonder. That only called attention to the real sign, the object and the manner of the work. The claim of truth consists, not in what adheres to it, but in what it is. We do not need a sign to tell us that the sun shines; the shining is the sign. We do not need a sign to tell us that a candle is lit; the candlestick shows that. And so with regard to Christianity. As it has eloquently been said, " The central unquestionable miracle is Jesus himself—One from the cradle to the grave, walking in spotless purity, through all temptation wearing a conscience without a scar, treading the great deep of human life and never wetting his feet with the spray; equally at home with saints in the glory of the mount, and with men writhing in misery at its base; elect to wipe away the tear of humanity, to bear it undwarfed and undimmed to the heavenly places, yet to whom we can go when the shame burns in the cheek, and the sweat stands on the brow." Ah! yes; and this *miracle* is still writing its mark on the conscience and life of man. Persons speak dolefully about the decadence of the evangelical faith, and indeed the signs are mixed; but the evangel of the living Christ is still the power of God—never more than now

> " The presence of a good diffused,
> And in diffusion ever more intense."

Not less, but all the more, as the world waxes old, and the needs of men become more urgent and complicated, is this evangel " the light shining in the darkness, and the darkness will never overtake it."

II. But now observe THE CONDITIONS ON WHICH THE FORCE OF THE TRUTH IS REALIZED. These conditions, as stated by the Lord, are two. 1. There is the *quality of the receptive organ*. " The light of the body is the eye " (ver. 34). Whatever affects the eye affects the impression of the object beheld. For example, the very common defect known as *colour-blindness* necessarily vitiates the discernment. Any injury to the eye, any disturbance of the wondrously delicate mechanism, mars the vision. All this has its moral counterpart. " As a man thinketh in his heart, so is he." The truth presented to the soul may yet not be apprehended as truth by the soul, and the fault lies in the soul itself. The moral necessarily acts on the intellectual. The intellectual life that springs out of or develops in harmony with a developing spiritual life is the light of the soul. All is then beheld in its real force and its right proportions. But not otherwise. And therefore the great Teacher emphasizes the need of "the *single eye*," the mind purely intentioned to know God and his will and truth, and this intention undisturbed by appetite of sense, or by prejudice closing against the evidence of the light. Ah, the single eye! The tiniest mote may confuse and becloud. One cunning bosom sin, one aberration from the right, so small as scarcely to be thought of, may yet impair the organ. And once let the eye become evil, "thy body also is full of darkness." 2. There is, as the second condition, *a complete enlightenment of mind* (ver. 36). See to it that every part of the thinking, willing, activity is submitted to the light. The whole being must be yielded to it. "Search me, O God, and know my heart: try me, and know my thoughts: and see if there be *any wicked way* in me, and lead me in the way everlasting." It is the partial illumination which we have so often to deplore. The prophet describes Ephraim as "a cake *not turned*"—one part of it under the influence of the fire, burned; the other part uninfluenced and doughy. So there is often to be noticed an imperfect sanctifying of character, an imperfect acquaintance with the way of the Lord. Men are always apt to measure what is due to God, what is to be kept for themselves. The apostle says, "The God of peace sanctify you *wholly*." We are often pained by a narrowness of view in Christians, by their failure in learning the lesson suggested by the evangelist, when he speaks of Christ "looking round about on all things." We are often pained, again, by a so-called breadth of view—no height in it, no mountain, forgetful that in the city which lieth foursquare, the length and the breadth and the height of it are *equal*. Oh, how needful is the prayer to increase in the knowledge of his will *in all wisdom and spiritual understanding*! Offer all, conscience, intellect, emotions, affections, will, all to the light; make an unreserved surrender. "If the whole be full of light, having no part dark, that whole is full of light." Not like a candle burning dimly, flickering and feeble, but as "when by its bright shining it giveth light."

III. Here, then, is THE RESPONSIBILITY WITH REGARD TO THE TRUTH. Men discuss whether we are responsible for our faith. We are responsible for ourselves, and what we are individually will greatly determine what, individually, we believe. This seems most obvious. "Take heed therefore that the light which is in thee be not darkness" (ver. 35). There is a light, a capacity of receiving and verifying the light, in every man—unless, indeed, in rare cases, or in those who are described as "past feeling." In speaking to men, in preaching the gospel to every creature, we assume this. And it is this which defines the responsibility resting on all. For the state of this receptive faculty, for its exercise, we must answer. "Take heed," says the Master. How solemn and expressive his sentence! Not merely "that the light shine," or "lest the light be extinguished," but more strongly still, "that this inner light be not darkness itself"— that what should lead to God does not take from God and become an angel, a power, of darkness. This was the catastrophe already fulfilling in the Pharisees, the catastrophe which he had declared (see parallel passage, Matt. xii.) to be the sin against the Holy Ghost. And the word of warning still confronts us. Take care of all that savours of sophisticating the conscience. Take care of all that cuts off from the light. Take care lest your prayers lose tone, your desires lose fervour, your soul loses interest in Divine things. Take care lest any way of thought, through companions, or literature, or otherwise, blight what is best and holiest in yourselves. The life of God in a soul is very sensitive. It needs to be guarded; it needs to be kept open to all Heavenward influence; it needs to be ever filled anew out of the fulness of God. A very little may destroy the organ, may separate from the vision. "The little rift within the lute by-and-by will make the music mute." Walk in the light. As the Light of God is ever seeking you, so let the light in you be ever seeking him. "Feed daily on Christ in your heart by faith, with thanksgiving." Do God's will with all the strength. Then the life is a beauteous order. Apart from the Light, the life is a chaos, a darkness *how great*!

HOMILIES BY VARIOUS AUTHORS.

Ver. 1.—*The influence of devout example*, etc. The fact which is stated in the first verse of this chapter suggests—

I. The influence of a devout example. "As he was praying . . . one of his disciples said unto him, Lord, teach us to pray." It was the sight of his Master in the act of prayer which prompted this disciple to make his request. Thus devotion in him begat devotion in them. All actions, good and bad, are contagious. Bad actions entice the evil, and good ones attract and inspire the holy and the pure. An oath is an encouragement to the profane, a prayer is an incentive to the devout. Only infinite wisdom can tell whether we produce the greater effect by the unconscious influence of our life, or by the result of direct, verbal persuasion. But we can all see that they go well together; that persuasion to piety with the drawback of a prayerless life would be of very small account. But to be a man of prayer, to be (without ostentation) known to be such, to be evidently "at home" with God, to be felt to be one that continually seeks Divine guidance in the daily conduct of life,—this is to be influential for good. It is to be saying in the most effective way, "It is good for me to draw near to God," and indeed to be saying most forcibly also, "It is good for you to draw near to God." The man of sustained piety, of devout habits which he never lays down, who compels men to feel that in his view God is not to be forgotten or his service relegated to the second place, is a power for good; he is living a truth of vital consequence, he is a blessing to the society in which he moves.

II. The highest function of a religious teacher. "Lord, teach us to pray." 1. Not to instruct in sacred truth, high as that is, enlightening the mind on the greatest of all subjects. 2. Not even to cause disciples to meditate on their spiritual condition, and to consider how they are themselves affected by the truth they have learned. 3. But to lead to God in direct and immediate devotion: the teacher or religious friend who helps another to unburden his heart in prayer to God, to pour out his spirit in submission or in dedication to the Divine Saviour, is rendering the highest possible service one human being can render to another.

III. The office of the Divine Teacher. This is not only or chiefly to instruct or to cause us to inquire, but rather to lead us to God in direct, spiritual communion. This Jesus does by: 1. Opening the way to God; becoming the one and only Mediator between God and man, through whom we have constant and perfect access to the Holiest One. 2. Showing us the efficacy of prayer; and this he does (1) by his own most strong and satisfying assertion (vers. 9—13); and (2) by revealing God to us as a Father who distinguishes each one of his children from all others, earnestly desires the return of each absent child, and purposes to renew and transform every son and daughter into his own likeness. Such a Father could not but listen and respond when his children cry to him. 3. Giving to us a deep sense of the need of prayer; and this he does by his own example, and also by his teaching. In this he so impresses us with the value of each human soul, with the sinfulness of sin, with the possibilities of spiritual worth and sacred usefulness, and with the grand opening for the faithful soul in the higher spheres beyond, that we are impelled to come to God for his redeeming, sanctifying, strengthening grace.—C.

Vers. 2—4.—*The true service of the Lord's Prayer.* It is a very painful and pitiful thing that words which came from the lips of the great Master of the spiritual and the living should have been allowed to degenerate into an unspiritual and lifeless form. That this has been the case to a large extent with the "Pater-noster" is a lamentable fact. It is very doubtful whether Jesus Christ ever intended these words which he gave to his disciples to be a permanent formula for the Christian Church. It is clear that the true obedience to his Word is not found in a number of correct and regular repetitions of the phrases, but in the devotion which is rendered in the *strain and spirit* of the "prayer." The true service to be gained from "the Lord's Prayer" is to gather from it the way in which to draw nigh to God, not only in the worship of the sanctuary, but in the quiet, unseen fellowship of the chamber. What Christ would say to us is this, that in our prayer to God—

I. We should give a prominent place to the progress of his spiritual kingdom. Out of six petitions the first three are devoted to the growth of the glory and the kingdom of God. This is surely a very significant fact. It rebukes all selfishness and short-sightedness in the presence of God. It invites us, and indeed it summons us, to make the object of our first and deepest solicitude the cause of Jesus

Christ, the exaltation of our Divine Father in the minds and in the lives of men. It suggests to us the consideration whether we are as much concerned as our Master would have us be for this great issue. How much do we care that God's Name is profaned as it is, his will left undone and violated as it is, his claims disregarded as they are, by the irreverent, by the disloyal, by the disobedient children of men? In prayer our mind should turn readily and frequently to this theme.

II. THAT WE SHOULD ASK FOR GOD'S HELP IN THE CONDUCT OF OUR TEMPORAL AFFAIRS. "Give us day by day our daily bread" is a petition that not only warrants, but requires, that we make our bodily necessities and all matters pertaining to our world-life the subject of prayer. It is right to ask for strength and skill, for wisdom and guidance, that we may discharge our daily duties and earn our livelihood honestly in the sight of all men. It is wrong to leave this out of our daily devotion. Jesus Christ would have us look to God for the supply of temporal needs, and ask his blessing and aid in securing it. We shall work all the more worthily, honourably, uprightly, through the day for asking God's guidance at its commencement; we shall make a better use of what we earn if we continually seek strength of God to earn it.

III. THAT WE SHOULD SEEK EARNESTLY FOR THE DIVINE FAVOUR. "Forgive us our sins," etc. It should be a matter of vital interest to us that we are walking in the light of God's loving favour, our sins forgiven, and ourselves regarded as his beloved children, reconciled to him in Jesus Christ. God's abiding favour should be the very sunshine of our soul, the presence of which makes all things bright, the absence of which throws everything into dark shadow.

IV. THAT WE SHOULD PRAY FOR DIVINE HELP IN OUR SPIRITUAL STRUGGLE. "Lead us not," etc. We should be daily recognizing the fact that our condition here is that of men that are fighting a hard battle against powerful enemies; that we need continual deliverance from evils which beset us; that the worst foes that assail us are those which would lead us into sin and down to shame and death. In this supreme struggle we need the arm of the Almighty on our side. If he be on our side, we shall conquer; if not, we shall be defeated. Therefore let us seek daily help from our heavenly Father for the daily conflict through which we pass on our way homeward.

V. THAT THERE ARE TWO SPIRITUAL CONDITIONS under which alone we can expect to find favour with God. 1. That we breathe a forgiving spirit in our relations with our fellow-men (ver. 4). 2. That we shun the path where perilous temptation lurks; for how can we ask God to "lead us not" thither, when we deliberately walk into it?—C.

Ver. 2.—*The will of God.* "Thy will be done, as in heaven, so in earth." A few very short words with a very large meaning. We may ask what doing God's will here on earth as in heaven—

I. WOULD MEAN TO OUR RACE. It would mean very much more than the triumph of the Strong One. 1. It would mean the rule of the absolutely *Holy One*—of that One who only wills that which is pure, just, good, in every possible relation. It would mean, therefore, the abolition of all wrongs of every kind, and the establishment of the right and the true in every scene and sphere. 2. Also the guidance of the perfectly *Wise One*—of that One who chooses the very best means to secure the right ends. It would bring about the adoption of the wisest course in the pursuit of every worthy aim. 3. Also the supremacy of the altogether *Benevolent One*—of him who desires the perfect welfare of all his creatures, of all his children—their temporal prosperity, their spiritual well-being.

II. WOULD MEAN TO OURSELVES. The light in which it would present itself to our minds would, perhaps, be this—that *our* Divine Father was exalted to the throne of humanity; that he whom we worship and whom we love and obey had become the object of the reverence, the affection, the obedience, of all mankind; that he who, in our heart's deepest convictions, is alone worthy to receive the homage of the race, was receiving it; and in that crowning triumph we should find our victory and our joy.

III. DEMANDS OF US THAT IT MAY BE REALIZED. 1. And the first demand is that we ourselves become subject to his holy will. And to do this we must (1) accept his Son as our Divine Teacher, Redeemer, Lord (John vii. 29; 1 John iii. 23); (2) live in daily obedience to his will as revealed in his Word; (3) bow in meekness of spirit to his will, whatever he may ordain for us. 2. And the second is that we seek, in prayer for his transforming influence, that the will of evil men may be overthrown, and his holy will be done; that he would send forth noble workers into the great harvest-field (ch. x. 2); that he would greatly bless the labours of those who are sowing the seed of the kingdom, and cause it to multiply a hundredfold. 3. And that by our lives and by our lips we commend the truth of his Word, the gospel of his grace, to the understanding and the conscience of all whom we can affect.—C.

Vers. 5—10.—*Continuance in prayer.* These words of our Lord are not intended to present God to us as one that is reluctant to respond to our prayer, and that, consequently, has to be besought and entreated with growing energy and ardour, as Baal's prophets imagined to be the case with the deity they worshipped (1 Kings xviii.). Rather should we think of him as of a Divine Father who, *for our sake,* delays his answer to our prayer, in order that we may be disciplined in devotion, and in order that he may give us what we ask, with a fuller blessing in the bestowal.

I. THE FACT OF UNANSWERED PRAYER. It is a fact attested by the common, if not the universal, experience of the devout, that prayer is often presented to God without any answer being presently and consciously received. And this is not only true of prayer that is not worthy of the name—of mere sacred formalities which proceed only from the sense and not from the soul; it is true of genuine, spiritual devotion. Men honestly and earnestly pray God to give them blessings, and he withholds them. The sickness is not removed, the life not spared, the burden not lightened, the son not reclaimed, the friend not reconciled, the cause not blessed, the wrong not stayed, the faithful not delivered; and the hearts of the people of God are filled with sorrow and dismay; the question that rises to their lips is, "How long, O Lord, how long dost thou not respond?"

II. THE MEANING OF GOD'S SILENCE. 1. It may mean that we ask for the *wrong thing*—for that which we think will help us, but which God knows will harm us; which (he knows) will do us much more of lasting, spiritual harm than confer on us present bodily or temporal relief. 2. It may mean that we are expecting the answer in the *wrong way*. Like Naaman, we may have laid down, in our own thought, the precise way in which God is to help or heal us, and it may be with us, as it was with him, that God is purposing to respond in another way altogether—perhaps by some simple means (as in his case), which we are disposed to consider unworthy of the occasion; perhaps by some way in which we shall be taught a lesson in humility or in some other grace. 3. It may mean that we are expecting the answer *at the wrong time*, much sooner than it would be wise for God to give it, or well for us to receive it.

III. THE REWARD OF CONTINUANCE IN PRAYER. We find, as our Lord teaches us in the parable, that while our friend will not always give us our request at once, yet he will grant it if we do but persevere (ver. 8). And so with our Divine Friend; he may not answer our prayer at once; he may delay long to respond to us. He may know that if we received immediately everything we desired of him, we should become unduly confident or be otherwise injuriously affected. He may know and may wish us to learn by disciplinary experience that

> " His help is always sure,
> His methods seldom guessed ;
> Delay will make our pleasure pure,
> Surprise will give it zest."

But sooner or later, in one way or in another, in his own good time, God will reward our persevering prayer with his effectual blessing. We must ask, and go on asking, and we *shall* certainly receive; must knock, and go on knocking, at the door of his mercy and his power, and it *will* assuredly be opened to us. This will be found in our seeking: 1. Conscious and joyous acceptance with God through faith in Jesus Christ. 2. Our spiritual growth. 3. Our usefulness in that especial sphere in which we are engaged for him.—C.

Vers. 11—13.—*The argument from the human fatherhood to the Divine.* Jesus Christ revealed the Father *to* men, and he revealed him *as* the Father *of* men. He taught us to address him as such (ver. 2), and to feel toward him as such. He would have us realize that God sustains to us a relationship very closely indeed corresponding to that which a human father sustains to his child. In the text he teaches us that this analogy is so close and so real that we may draw practical inferences from the lower to the higher one. The particular conclusion which our Lord draws is—

I. FROM OUR GIVING TO HIS. No human father would give his son a stone when appeal was made to him for bread, etc.; would put him off with a response which would only be a bitter disappointment. Such a one would be not only an exception to his kind, but would be guilty of an act that would be simply monstrous in general regard. If, then, we, "being evil," cannot withhold "good gifts" from our children, how much less will the heavenly Father deny his blessings to us, his sons and daughters! What we, with our finite and limited love, could not refuse, it is certain that he, in his infinite goodness and boundless pity, will readily bestow. There are two blessings which we particularly want of God our heavenly Father—*provision* for our *temporal* well-being, and *succour* for our *soul*. We cannot live without these. Our bodily nature craves the one, our spiritual nature needs the other. Bread we must have, and all that "bread" stands for, that we may live happily and serviceably as those that tread the path of mortal life. But "man cannot live on bread alone;" he needs those higher and holier gifts which nourish the soul, which feed the flame of piety and zeal, which strengthen him for spiritual conflict, and give him the victory over his worst enemies. For these two great blessings we may confidently ask God, and he will assuredly grant them. It is much more certain that God our Father will provide for our real necessities, and will strengthen our souls with all needful Divine influences, than it is certain that the kindest human father will not mock his beloved children when they appeal for his bounty. With holy boldness, then, may we go to the throne of grace, and pray for all those things that are requisite alike for the body as for the soul. But we may carry this argument with which our Lord has supplied us into other spheres, and may thus "assure our hearts" concerning him.

II. FROM OUR FORGIVING TO HIS. We may have a difficulty in realizing the great truth that God is willing to forgive us all our sin and to reinstate us fully in his favour. But if as sons we have been forgiven by our parents, or if as parents we have forgiven our children and taken them back into the fulness of our favour, we may argue safely from the human fatherhood to the Divine. If we, "being evil," with such small and scanty magnanimity as we possess, can forgive freely, how much more can he—he whose ways of mercy are as much higher than ours as the heaven is higher than the earth!

III. FROM OUR GUIDANCE TO HIS. How impossible it is for any of us that is a father to refuse guidance to one of our children when he comes to ask it of us! Only the most heartless, the most unfatherly, could think of declining it. And since that is so with us, in all our human imperfection, how positive it is that the Divine Father will guide us by the shaping of his providence, or by the prompting of his Spirit, when we see not our way, but make known our request unto him to "lead us all our journey through"!

IV. FROM OUR SOLICITUDE TO HIS. One of the very greatest questions we propose to ourselves is this—Does God care enough for each one of us to renew our life in another realm when we leave this world? Jesus Christ's declaration is *the* answer to this question (John v. 24—29). But we find strong, reassuring help here. How much do we care for the continuance of the life of our children? How much do we *not* care? What words will express our parental solicitude that death should not strike them down, that they should *live*, and that their life should be large, free, blessed? If that is our concern for them, what will not God our Father desire for us? What will he not care that we do not perish in the arms of death, but have everlasting life in the embrace of his own heavenly love?—C.

Ver. 20.—*Christianity the benignant power.* Lasting *power* shows solid worth. The corrupt empire falls; the false system is exploded; the demoralizing custom is discarded. That which, under all changes, shows itself strong and enduring, is proved to be sound and good. But add the element of *benignity*. Jesus Christ adduces his beneficent power in the expulsion of evil spirits from the bodies of men as a convincing evidence of the Divine presence; that being done, "no doubt the kingdom of God is come." Power for good, for healing, for restoring, for transforming, such power continuing for many generations and acting under all skies,—"no doubt" that is from above; it is of God. If we find that Christianity has proved itself to be the one great benignant power in the world, exerting a gracious, redeeming, elevating influence on humanity, then "no doubt the kingdom of God is come" upon us. We shall see that this is so if we consider—

I. THE STATE OF SOCIETY WHEN JESUS CAME. And we have to take into our account the *parental tyranny*; the position of *woman* in her state of inferiority and even degradation; the universal sentiment toward the *stranger* or the foreigner, spoken of and treated as a "barbarian" and an enemy; the prevalence of *war*, and its conduct with every imaginable cruelty and the most shocking recklessness of life; the prevalence of *slavery* under a system in which the slaves were regarded and treated as absolutely without any rights or claims whatsoever; the existence of *gladiatorial shows*, in which the lives of hundreds of strong men in the midst of life were sacrificed for sport to men and even to women; the common usage of *infanticide*; the abundance of *pauperism*, existing to such an extent that in the time of Cæsar "nearly three-fourths of the whole population of the city of Rome were on the roll of public succour;" the institution of *torture*; the practice of licentious *shows*, and of unnatural and unnameable vices. We have here no more than a bare outline of the evils which existed in the world when "Jesus was born at Bethlehem."

II. WHAT AMELIORATION CHRISTIANITY HAS WROUGHT AND IS WORKING. Three things have to be mentioned—one to be admitted, and the other two to be maintained. 1. That there have been one or two auxiliary forces in the field, which have contributed towards the elevation of mankind; but theirs has been very much indeed the smaller share. 2. That Christianity was prevented from doing all it would have done by being bitterly opposed. 3. That its action has been most pitifully weakened by its truth having been so greatly corrupted. But what, notwithstanding, has it accomplished? (1) It has cast out the demon of parental tyranny, and made the child to be the object of respect and kindness. (2) It has raised woman, and made her the helpmeet, in every way, of her husband, causing her to be treated with deference and consideration. (3) It has mitigated the terrible severities of war, carrying its red cross of succour into the very midst of the battle-field, and, to a large extent, removing its hideous savagery. (4) It has gone far towards exorcising the demon of slavery. (5) It has abolished the shameful scenes of the old Roman arena. (6) It has extinguished infanticide and torture wherever it has authority to legislate. (7) It is carrying on a stern and victorious campaign against impurity and intemperance. (8) It has built hospitals, lunatic asylums, reformatories, orphanages, almshouses, by the hundred, by the thousand. (9) It has opened the school-door in which youth everywhere is prepared for the duties, the joys, and the conflicts of life. (10) It has sent forth its many hundreds of heralds to carry light, peace, love, purity, wisdom, into the haunts of superstition, violence, and vice. (11) It is penetrating the worst slums of our great cities, seeking out the profane, the abandoned, the criminal; and with its touch of holy pity, which surely proceeds from "the finger of God," it is casting out the demons of sin and shame. At the present rate of progress, another half-century will see a most wonderful and glorious change in the aspect of the human world.

III. THE CONCLUSION THAT WE DRAW. If Christianity has done, is doing, will do, all this, then "no doubt" in its advent we have the coming of the "kingdom of God." No doubt Christ has *that to say to us* which it is infinitely worth our while to know; that *to do for us* it is our highest privilege to have done on our behalf; that *to be to us* which it is immeasurably desirable he should be. Let us learn of him; be led by him into paths of sacred service; and invite him to become our personal Lord and Saviour.—C.

Vers. 24—26.—*Spiritual failure.* These words apply to—

I. THE JEWISH CHURCH. Delivered of the demon of idolatry, and having a house "swept and garnished," perfected with all external religious proprieties, it became possessed of the worse demon of hypocrisy—worse in that it was more hopeless. For the idolater may be and often is convicted of his folly and is led into wisdom and piety; but the formalist and hypocrite is scarcely ever, if ever, won from his unreality and spiritual pride.

LUKE.

II. Many a Christian Church. Delivered from worldliness, from vanity, from vice, in the first instance, many a Church has cherished the cruel demon of persecution, or the evil demon of pride, or the dangerous demon of formality. And it proves to be harder to awaken the sinful Church, living under its Lord's condemnation, to a new repentance and a revival of religious earnestness, than it was at first to conduct it into his kingdom. Its last state is less hopeful than the first.

III. Many a human soul. 1. Men go a very long way in the direction of heavenly wisdom. They listen, they understand, they feel, they purpose, they pray, they profess, they preach or teach Divine truth to others, they conform their conduct to the requirements of the Word of God. 2. In this good course they are arrested, and they return on their way. Their devotedness slackens; their habits of worship become less regular; their habits of life become less scrupulous; the "spirit of their mind" grows secular, and indeed profane; they fall out of the ranks of the earnest, and, at last, even of the reverent; perhaps they descend to the unworthy, and even to the criminal. Not literally, but metaphorically speaking, there are "evil spirits" in them. They "are gone away backward." 3. Thus returning, they have almost hopelessly separated themselves from Christ; the "last state of that man is worse than the first" (see Heb. vi. 4—6). Not that renewal is *absolutely* "impossible," but it is so spiritually difficult and so exceedingly rare that it may be said to be *morally* impossible. You cannot restore elasticity to the spring that has been overbent. You cannot make pungent again the salt that has lost its savour. You cannot infuse new force into truths which an emasculating familiarity has deprived of their virtue and their interest. Far more hopeless is the condition of the human soul that has drifted away from Christ than the one that has never heard of his Name or never been impressed with his claims. Therefore what? (1) Let the Christian teacher see that his work is deep as well as broad; that the roots of sacred conviction are well planted in the soil; let him not be satisfied with his "converts" when they only manifest feeling; let him be assiduous in his attention, earnest in his prayer, until he is well assured that the soul for whom he is watching (Heb. xiii. 17) has yielded himself, fully and whole-heartedly, to the Lord his Saviour. (2) Let the Christian disciple be on his guard; let him "watch and pray" lest he come under the power of some insidious temptation, lest he "lose that which he has wrought," lest the powers and principles that are from God and that have entered and touched his soul should depart from him, lest evil influences that are from beneath should take possession of him; for in that sad event he will be in a far worse spiritual state, more hopeless and pitiable, than if he had never heard the voice of Christ, and never risen at his call.—C.

Vers. 31, 32.—*Christ and Solomon.* It is one of the strong arguments in favour of our Lord's Divinity that, while there was that about him which made him free to claim for himself the attribute of meekness (Matt. xi. 29), and which saved him from the charge of immodesty, yet was there in him a wonderful and wholly exceptional consciousness of greatness. On appealing to his own consciousness, he found himself anterior in existence to Abraham (John viii. 58); greater (of more consequence to the nation) than the very temple itself, that object of boundless veneration (Matt. xii. 6); living in heaven even while dwelling on the earth (John iii. 13); associated in the most intimate way possible and (to us) inconceivable with the Divine Father (John v. 19; vi. 46; x. 30); wiser and worthier than the "wise man" himself (text). It may not be surprising that One claiming to be a Prophet should believe himself to be superior in worth and work to Jonah; for there was nothing remarkably great either in the moral character or in the professional course of that erratic prophet. But in respect to Solomon? It may be said that only One who could claim to be highest among the highest was entitled to say, "I am greater than he." But the actual superiority of Christ to Solomon is apparent enough if we consider—

I. The dignity of his Person. The Son of David was great, as such; but nothing in comparison with the Son of God. The King of Israel was great, as such; but nothing when compared with the Prince of peace, with him "who sitteth on the throne" of heaven.

II. The character of his wisdom. Solomon was very learned in the knowledge of his age (1 Kings iv. 29—34); he was also very skilled in the intellectual conflicts of his time (1 Kings x.); he had, moreover, a very keen discernment of the ways and wants and weaknesses of human nature (Proverbs). And he had (what Jesus Christ had not) an acquaintance, gained by his own experience, of the hollowness of earthly greatness, of the pitiful consequences of human folly. But the wisdom of Christ was the wisdom of God. For such he had, and such indeed he was. He *was* "the Truth" (John xiv. 6); he *was* "the Wisdom of God" (1 Cor. i. 24, 30). He knew and taught mankind, as Solomon could not do, the nature and the will of God (ch. x. 22); the capacities and the possibilities of man (John ii. 25); the way home to God (John xiv. 6); the secret of spiritual triumph (Matt. x. 39); the glory and the shame awaiting the faithful and the unfaithful in the future (Matt. xxv.).

III. THE BEAUTY AND EXCELLENCY OF HIS LIFE. Beginning admirably (1 Kings iii. 5), and continuing well for a season, Solomon gave way to dangerous luxury, to selfish and exacting legislation, and at last to moral corruption (1 Kings xi. 1—10). The surpassing beauty of the character of Jesus Christ became more manifest as his life continued, and it culminated in a supreme act of self-sacrifice which is the crowning glory of his life.

IV. THE GLORY OF HIS CAREER. Solomon's career began in brilliance, it remained bright for many years; but its light waned as his character declined, and it was concluded in sombre shadows. The career of Jesus Christ began in lowliest obscurity, it continued in struggle and in sorrow for a while; but it has risen into the light, it becomes ever more blessed as his influence grows ever wider and deeper; it will not be complete until all the kingdoms of the earth are in subjection to his holy will. 1. Are we wise in the wisdom of Christ? 2. Are we the subjects of his benignant rule?—C.

Ver. 32.—*Comparative guilt.* The main truth of the text, that the weight of our guilt depends on the measure of our privilege, rests on the solid foundation of—

I. MAN'S MORAL FREEDOM. However much character may be affected by circumstance, it remains true that man is a free agent. When we condemn ourselves or others, as we continually do; when we distinguish between misfortune and sin, between calamity and crime; whenever we apply the word "ought" to our own or to another's behaviour;—we practically assent to the doctrine that man is spiritually free; otherwise such action on our part is unjust or illogical, such language improper. But, in truth, a sense of our moral freedom is inwrought in our deepest convictions; we cannot extricate it from our nature, however much we try.

II. OUR ACCOUNTABLENESS TO GOD FOR OUR CHARACTER AND LIFE. 1. God is requiring great things of us—thought, reverence, affection, submission, obedience. 2. He is marking at every moment the life we are living, the character we are forming; he is looking upon us and into us. 3. He is recording all our actions, including among these the thoughts of our mind, the feelings of our heart, the purposes of our will. 4. He will one day call us to give an account of "*all* the things done in the flesh."

III. A REVEALED PRINCIPLE OF DIVINE JUDGMENT. The men of Nineveh, the great Teacher tells us, will be a source of condemnation to those of Judæa, for with slighter privilege they repented, while the contemporaries of our Lord remained impenitent at the preaching of Christ himself. 1. There is to be punishment in the future. 2. This will be comparative—some guilty servants will be "beaten with few stripes," others with "many." 3. This, again, will depend on the degree of condemnation, whether it will be less or more severe. 4. And on what, then, will God's condemnation hang? Surely on two things. (1) On the *guiltiness of the character* and life; for of the condemned there will be those in whom there was the "some good thing," or even many good things; and there will be those in whom there was no good thing toward God, but in whom were shameful things of many kinds. (2) On the *character of God's requirement;* for God will require much less of some men than he will of others. What he will require of us depends on the measure of spiritual capacity he has conferred upon us, and also (and very largely) on the measure of the privilege he has granted to us. From those to whom Christ had preached he would require far more than from those to whom Jonah had delivered his brief warning message. And if we reject the gospel of the grace of God, how guilty shall *we* be in comparison with the men of our Master's own time! Surely we shall be at least as guilty as they. For though, indeed, we do not actually behold the countenance of the Son of man, nor hear the tones of his voice, yet we do " sit at his feet ; " we are his disciples ; we know the thoughts of his mind ; we understand his will ; we are familiar with his overtures of love.   Indeed, we have certain great advantages which those to whom our Lord was speaking did not possess.   (a) We have the light that shines not only from the whole of his completed life, but also from his death and resurrection.   (b) We have Christ's own commentary, through the writings of his inspired apostles, upon his life and death.   (c) We have freedom from the national prepossessions which misguided those, his hearers.   (d) We have the accumulated experience of the Christian Church through eighteen centuries.   If we heed not his Word, and range not ourselves on his side, if, "gathering not" with him the sheaves of righteousness, we scatter abroad the seeds of sin and death, who will there not be "to rise up in the judgment" and condemn us!—C.

Vers. 34—36.—*Spiritual sight.*   "The light of the body is the eye ; " *i.e.* the eye is the organ through which light enters so that the mind perceives ; and if our eye is "single," if it is sound, and does not give a double or distorted or coloured impression, then the "whole body is full of light," then the man knows exactly what is about him and how to use his hands and direct his feet ; but if the eye be diseased, if it be "evil," giving false impressions, then all is confusion in the mind, and it is as if "the whole body were full of darkness," no member of the body can take its proper part— the hands do not know how to handle, nor the feet to walk.   Here we have a parable, very easily understood.   "The spirit of man is the candle [lamp] of the Lord."   God has given truth to the mind as he has prepared light for the body ; he has also given us a spiritual eye, an organ through which Divine truth enters the mind.   We may call it mind, conscience, reason, the soul ; it is of no consequence what we call it ; it is that in us which distinguishes between right and wrong, righteousness and unrighteousness, truth and falsehood, nobility and baseness ; it is that which gives us the place we occupy in God's creation.   If the light we receive into us is sound, pure, healthy, then our whole soul is full of light, then we "see light in God's light."   But if this inward light be confused, disordered, discoloured, our whole spirit is "full of darkness ; " that is to say, if our understanding be darkened, if we are habitually judging unrighteous judgment, if our conscience be condemning what is good and be approving what is evil, if our reason be misconceiving and misinterpreting, how hopeless is our condition!   When that which should lead is misleading, when that which should be guiding us into wisdom is betraying us into deadly error, when the light that is in us is darkness, "how great is *that* darkness" (Matt. vi. 23)!   But if, on the other hand, our reason is directing us to right conclusions, and our conscience is "approving things that are excellent," then our whole soul is walking and rejoicing in the light of the Lord, our spirit is full of light, it is a house wherein the bright shining of the lamp of truth does give us light.   What, then, brings about bad spiritual sight?   What are the diseases of the inward eye?

I. PREJUDICE.   How that warps the judgment and blinds the eyes of men!   Determined to recognize one object only, men can see no other, however it may stand before them in bold relief.   It was prejudice that made the men of Christ's time fail to perceive that the kingdom of God had come among them.   His wisdom, his worth, his power, everything was distorted and misconceived by them ; their inward eye was diseased, and how great was the darkness that resulted!

II. PRIDE.   How many men there are walking, strutting, across the stage of life, confident, complacent, contemptuous, that have been too proud to learn!   Pride has bent their judgment, has affected for evil the inward eye ; the truth has become distorted ; there is darkness in the soul.   Well does the apostle say, "If a man think himself to be wise, let him become a fool [in his own opinion], that he may be wise."   Pride blocks the path, while humility opens the gates of the kingdom of truth.   "The meek will he guide in judgment, the meek will he teach his way."

III. SELFISHNESS.   The worst of all diseases spoiling the spiritual sight.   The man who lives under its evil dominion "sees double," is mentally confused, wanders in bewildering error.   The slave-owner could not see the iniquity of slavery when his temporal interests covered the eyes of his mind with a thick film of falsity.   Present prospects, worldly advantages, fleshly indulgences,—do these not form *thick* scales which cover the eyes of the children of men, leaving them in the darkness of error and of sin? Who can understand his errors? Who of us can be sure that he is not allowing some folly, some unworthy habit of the body or the mind, to intervene between the pure truth of Christ and his own spiritual understanding? The thought of Jesus Christ calls upon us to be humble, vigilant, prayerful, that "the thoughts of our hearts may be cleansed by the inspiration of his Spirit," so that instead of great darkness, or even an imperfect and ineffectual light within us, the whole house of the soul may be illumined with purest heavenly wisdom, "as when the bright shining of a candle does give us light."—C.

Vers. 37—42.—*Piety out of perspective.* We have seen pictures in which no regard whatever has been paid to the laws of perspective, and in which, as the consequence, the mountain has appeared as small as the men, the men as large as the mountain. These have been objects of amusement, but not of admiration. Unfortunately, there was nothing either amusing or admirable in these practical pictures of piety which the Pharisees were drawing, wholly out of perspective, in the time of our Lord. In them were—

I. OBJECTS OF GROSS EXAGGERATION. Our Lord pointed out the exaggerated import-ance which they attached to the outward, to the bodily, to the minute. They made everything of religious observances and customs. To wash the hands after coming from market, before eating bread, was to them quite a serious obligation, which they would on no account neglect; to tithe the small herbs that grew in their garden was to them a sacred duty, which they took pains to observe; to make the outside of their culinary vessels clean was a rule by no means to be forgotten; to carry no smallest stick on the sabbath day was a very sacred law, etc. These things, and such things as these, were made the staple of their religion; their piety was composed of small observances, of conformity to prescriptions and proscriptions which only touched the outside and not the inner sanctuary, which only affected the body and not the soul; they made everything of that which was only of very slight importance; they exag-gerated the minute until these became misleading and practically false.

II. OTHER OBJECTS FATALLY OVERLOOKED OR SLIGHTED. These were: 1. *Inward purity.* What did it matter if some cups were not quite clean? Something certainly, but very little comparatively; it was a matter of infinitesimal consequence. But it mattered much that their "inward part," their soul, was "full of ravening and wicked-ness." If they were themselves corrupt, no ceremonial cleanness would avail them. It is of infinite consequence to any man that he should be "all glorious within;" that there should be truth and purity "in the inward parts," in the deep recesses of the soul. It is the pure in heart alone that can see God and that can enter his kingdom. 2. *Charity;* a kind heart showing itself in a generous hand. Whoso has this disposition to pity, to heal, to help; whoso spends himself in endeavours to do good, to lighten the burdens of the afflicted, to brighten the path that lies in shadow;—this man is one to whom "all things are clean." He who is earnestly concerned to mitigate the sorrow of some bleeding heart, or to extricate some fallen spirit from the cruel toils of vice, or to lead some weary wanderer from the desert of doubt into the bright and happy home of faith and love,—he is not the man to be "greatly moved" because he carries a speck of dust upon his hands, or because a utensil has not been washed the proper number of times in a day. 3. *Rectitude.* The Pharisees passed over "judgment;" but they should have given to this a front place. To recognize the righteous claims of men on our regard, on our considerateness, on our fidelity, on our truthfulness,—is not this a very large part of any piety that is of God, commended by him and commending us to him? 4. *The love of God.* This also the Pharisees slighted. But it was of the very first importance. Their Law laid stress upon it (Deut. vi. 4, 5). It is the heritage and glory of manhood (see homily on ch. x. 27). To make little of this was so to misrepresent as to lead into ruinous error. Purity, charity, rectitude, the love of God,—these are the precious things which make man great, worthy, dear to God his Father.—C.

Vers. 1—13.—*Lessons on prayer.* Luke takes us from "the one thing needful," which Mary's loving waiting on her Lord illustrates, to a kindred subject, viz. the lessons on prayer which Jesus gave his disciples. He had been enjoying what we should now call a "retreat" with them, and had himself led the devotions of the little band. Struck by the beauty of his petitions, one of his disciples asked him to teach them to pray, as John had taught his disciples. To this appeal Jesus responds at once, and in doing so gives them first a *form*, which was also meant to be a *model*; and secondly, a *theory* of prayer, in which we shall have little difficulty in finding its true philosophy. Let us look at these two matters in their order.

I. THE FORM AND MODEL OF PRAYER COMMONLY CALLED THE LORD'S PRAYER. (Vers. 2—4.) Jesus is represented here as saying to the disciples, "When ye pray, *say*," while in Matt. vi. 9 it is "*After this manner* therefore pray ye." It is evident from this that he meant the words to answer the double purpose—to be a form in constant use, and to be a model constantly imitated. It is consequently most important to look carefully into its contents. And here we have to notice that it sets *intercession* before petition for *personal benefits*. Prayer thus becomes a great instrument for rendering us disinterested and unselfish. When modelled on this peerless prayer of Christ, it carries us at once into the wide interests of God's kingdom before we devote any consideration to petty personal interests. The genius of prayer is thus seen to be the *subordination of self to the universal interest.* The hallowing of the Father's precious Name comes first, then the coming of his kingdom, and then the doing of his will on earth as in heaven. What a statesmanlike view we are thus led to take of the general problem before we even think of the particular and personal problem! The moment we have in our closet entered intelligently and heartily into these three petitions, we have got out of the narrowness of petty cares and troubles into the broad expanse of the Divine love. We are taken to mountain-tops at once, and from the sublime heights of Divine compassion we are led to intercede for the world below us, that it may be as speedily as possible transmuted into something like what heaven happily is. Then as for the minor personal petitions, these refer to daily bread, and daily pardon, and daily deliverance from evil—the personal blessings, in fact, which fit the individual for aiding the wider interest and subserving the universal blessing. We are thus warranted in asking for bread to sustain the body, for pardon to relieve the heavy-laden soul, for deliverance amid the further temptations to which we may be exposed. And in the petition for pardon, it is clearly implied that forgiveness can only be realized by a forgiving spirit. The soul which will not forgive a brother who asks for forgiveness shows that forgiveness has not been and cannot be realized. In fact, the unforgiving spirit is, as far as we can judge, the unpardonable sin (cf. Matt. xviii. 21—35).

II. OUR LORD'S THEORY OF PRAYER. (Vers. 5—13.) When we analyze our Lord's argument here, we find it to be *analogical*; and the truth is that we are shut up in this matter to analogical reasoning. It can be shown that it is to analogy we owe our knowledge of human beings, of the lower animals, and finally of God above us. In order to any other than analogical knowledge, we should require to become incarnated, so to speak, in the other being whose condition we desire to know. Seeing that this is impossible, we are shut up to the argument from analogy upon such a subject.[1] Our Lord, then, looked around him, and saw that *efficacious prayer* was embedded as a fact in the very constitution of society. Petition is the form which conscious need assumes in social intercourse; and a response comes forth with more or less promptitude and grace, and demonstrates that the prayer has proved efficacious. It is further to be noticed that our Lord, in pointing out efficacious prayer as existing in the society of his time, gives us first an example of efficacious *intercession*, and then an example of efficacious *personal petition*. His illustrations consequently follow the lines laid down in his prescribed form of prayer. To encourage intercession, he presents the picture of the importunate friend begging successfully a supper for an unexpected and hungry guest; to encourage personal petition, he presents the picture of hungry children crying to their father for food; and he would have us to reason from the efficacious prayer among men to the certainty of prayer being efficacious when presented unto God. Let us look at the illustrations in the order given. A kindly, hospitable man is about to retire to rest with his household, having in the last meal consumed the small stock of

---

[1] We have discussed this subject in the *Christian Monthly* for July, 1882; also in the 'Theological Handbook' upon the subject of prayer, published by Hodder and Stoughton.

food which his humble house contains; when, lo! to his surprise, a friend arrives after a long journey, hungry as well as weary—a most fitting object, therefore, of hospitality. What is to be done? He quickly decides. Having most probably arranged for the washing of the guest's feet, he passes out into the darkness, and seeks the door of a friend who can, he believes, lend him as many loaves as he needs. It is not a personal want he is about to urge, but the need of a hungry and weary friend. He stands before the door, consequently, in the simple majesty of disinterestedness. He begins to knock, but at first receives no encouragement. "Trouble me not," says his friend within: " the door is now shut, and my children are with me in bed; I cannot rise and give thee." Nothing daunted, however, and pocketing all his pride, for he knows well it is no selfish plea he is urging, he resolves to knock on till his beleaguered friend capitulates. At length importunity triumphs; the friend in bed sees plainly that the only chance of rest that night for himself and his children is to give in as soon as possible, and let the importunate petitioner have his way; and so he rises and gives him as many loaves as he needs. Here, then, according to our Lord, is a case of efficacious intercessory prayer as between men. It may not receive an immediate answer, but importunity secures an ultimate answer. We are warranted, therefore, in rising from efficacious intercessory prayer among men to the assurance that intercessory prayer will prove efficacious with God. God may keep us waiting, not certainly from any selfish consideration, but for our own good, but ultimately he will respond to every unselfish intercession. Hence our Lord reaches the assurance, " And I say unto you, Ask, and it shall be given you; seek, and ye shall find; knock, and it shall be opened unto you," etc. The second case brought before us by Christ is efficacious prayer in the family circle. Hungry children present prayers to parents for food, for bread, for fish, for eggs, as among the humbler classes in Palestine; and the fathers who are asked for such things never think of mocking the hungry ones with a stone, a serpent, or a scorpion. The earthly parent hears and answers the children's prayer; the prayer is efficacious. So will it be, argues our Lord, as we appeal for the needful blessings to our Father in heaven. "If ye then, being evil, know how to give good gifts unto your children: how much more shall your heavenly Father give the Holy Spirit to them that ask him?" It is surely instructive to think that earthly parents, in the midst of a "reign of law," which they only partially understand, can yet know how to give good things to their children. Be the times ever so hard, they can generally manage to give the little ones bread and keep them off the parish. Is it not reasonable to argue that the heavenly Father, who knows *all* " the reign of law," because its Author and Lord, can give the Holy Spirit, or any minor and needful blessing his children crave, unto the prayerful? We have only, in conclusion, to emphasize the fact that the Holy Spirit is the great need of human souls. Let us ask him as God's supreme Gift, and we shall assuredly receive him even in Pentecostal power. It is this Gift which individuals and Churches need to make them truly useful!—R. M. E.

Vers. 14—36.—*Inspirations.* Our Lord had just held out the possibility of Divine inspirations for prayerful disciples, and the evangelist next takes up and contrasts *diabolical* inspirations with this. Unless we notice the artistic treatment by the accomplished author of the Third Gospel, we shall miss much of his meaning. The circumstance which led to the question of infernal inspiration was the healing of a man who was possessed by a dumb devil. Here was a case, then, where a demon, entering into and possessing a human being, had sealed his lips so that he could not speak. Our Saviour expelled the demon, and the man immediately recovered the power of speech. At this the people wondered. But the wise men among his enemies had a theory to meet the case; they insisted that it was because Beelzebub, the chief of the devils, dwelt in Christ that he was able to expel the inferior demon. Others insisted on a sign from heaven to supplement these " signs " on earth. To both classes he gives due answer. Let us look at the two theories, and the interlude which separates Christ's treatment of them, in their order.

I. THE THEORY THAT JESUS WAS POSSESSED BY BEELZEBUB. There was something plausible in this. Assuming that demons are subject to their superiors, the hostile spirits insinuated that Jesus had got the chief of the devils in him, and so was able to order the inferior demons. In the theory there was the admission that the devil, who had made the poor possessed one dumb, had obeyed Christ's command and left his victim. But so far from this demonstrating Christ's goodness to their suspicious souls, it only demonstrated his league with the chief of the devils. It is truly wonderful how unholy hearts can twist the clearest demonstrations into the foulest suspicions and insinuations. The question of infernal inspirations is thus raised, as a set-off and contrast to the Divine inspirations which Jesus showed his disciples were possible for them, and which he illustrated in perfection himself. Let us see how our Lord meets the insinuation of his enemies. 1. *Christ shows that in expelling the dumb devil he had been so far breaking up Satan's kingdom.* Although, therefore, it must be acknowledged that Satan and his emissaries do often take *suicidal courses,* and by fancied wisdom really undermine their kingdom, yet it could not be supposed that the chief of the devils would deliberately restore a man to sanity and the power of speech. This would be too insane a course for the arch-fiend to take. When souls are rendered sane and social, we may conclude at once that it is *not* Satan's work. Hence in the fact that the kingdom of Satan was being broken up by the philanthropic policy of Jesus, there was proof positive that their theory was false. 2. *Christ reminds them of Jewish exorcism, and asks if they have considered the suspicion their theory casts on their own exorcists.* By certain incantations and tedious processes the Jews had been accustomed to expel the demons and cure the demented ones. The difference between the Jewish exorcisms and this one of Jesus was that his was simpler and speedier. Hence if it was Beelzebub that enabled him to exorcise the demon, it must be some other form of diabolic inspiration which enabled their own exorcists to succeed. Our Lord thus used a crushing *argumentum ad hominem,* which they could not resist. 3. *Jesus insists on the victorious character of the spiritual inspiration of which he was at once an Embodiment and the Source.* It was by "the finger of God" he expelled the demons, and in his Person the triumphant kingdom of God had come nigh to them. For, as he here shows, there is a contention between two opposing parties for the palace of the human heart. The devil may for a time usurp possession. There is peace throughout the palace; there may even be silence, as in the present case, when the devil had made the possessed one dumb. But the Stronger One comes, the Spirit of Christ enters, overcomes the devil, robs him of his armour in which he trusted, and divides the spoil. Thus graphically does our Lord represent the conquest of the soul and the glorious result of the victory. It is the Mightiest overcoming the strong, and claiming his rights in the palace of the soul. Thus does God's kingdom come within us! 4. *Jesus shows the dangers of a vacant soul.* Referring possibly to the Jewish exorcisms, wherein the demons were expelled, but no stronger occupant introduced to the palace of the soul, our Lord shows how the vacant soul becomes a prey to demons once more. And the result of reoccupation is generally worse than the first occupancy. How often is it seen that superficial reform is followed by a backsliding worse than any previous sin! The last state of the man is worse than the first. It is essential, therefore, that when a soul is freed from one spirit, it should be tenanted by another and a better. Only the radical change which the indwelling of the Divine Spirit secures can make the soul safe amid the temptations of Satan and his hosts.

II. THE INTERLUDE UPON THE BLESSEDNESS OF OBEDIENCE. (Vers. 27, 28.) As Jesus spake these wise words about inspiration, a woman in the crowd, touched by their beauty and faithfulness, exclaimed, "Blessed is the womb that bare thee, and the paps which thou hast sucked!" Her idea was that it must have been a great privilege to be related to such a Person, especially to have been his mother. And the blood-relationship, of course, could have no wide radius; only a select few could stand around him in actual relationship. But Jesus interposes at once to show that there is a blessedness which all may realize, a blessedness which his mother or brethren could not monopolize, and this is the blessedness of obedience to God's Word. Motherhood involved many trials in the case of Mary, as well as many privileges; but obedience is an open door into which all may enter. In the keeping of God's commandments there is a great reward. Thus he forbade all discontent and all envy, and put the woman and the audience generally upon the true track in which to realize blessedness. Receiving God's Word in humble faith, trying to keep it in dependence upon God's grace,—this is the secret of true blessedness. Such spiritual relationship is better than blood-relationship. At it all of us should aim.

III. The theory of insufficient signs. (Vers. 16, 29—36.) The miracles of healing, it would seem, were insufficient to convince Christ's enemies that he was from God. They demanded more—a sign from heaven; something, that is, which would connect him with the heavenly world. 1. Now, the way our Lord meets this unreasonable demand is by *denying their right to such a sign.* It was most unreasonable, and to unreasonable clamour our Lord never yielded. His miracles were of such a character, were so numerous, and so instructive, that nothing but wilful blindness could prevent the demonstration from being final and conclusive. 2. *Jesus declares that in the history of Jonah they would have a sign.* (Vers. 29, 30, 32.) Now, in what respect was Jonah a sign to the Ninevites? Accepting as historic the narrative of his flight, his imprisonment in the fish, his release from it, and his subsequent preaching to the Ninevites, we see a striking parallel between it and the history of Christ. As Jonah was buried in the fish, and so the endangered seamen were saved, so Jesus was buried in the tomb, and through his death saved endangered sinners. Again, as Jonah was cast forth from his imprisonment to land and life again, so Jesus by resurrection passed from the imprisonment of the tomb into the newness of immortal life. And as Jonah became a witness to the Ninevites of the truth of God's threatenings and God's mercy, so Jesus, in the persons of his apostles, and in Pentecostal power, became a witness to his generation. Moreover, the Ninevites repented at the preaching of Jonah, and in so doing they would be a standing rebuke and condemnation to Christ's contemporaries, who resisted his preaching and would not repent of their sins. In the light of Christ's subsequent fate, the sign of the Prophet Jonah must have proved striking in the extreme. 3. *Jesus declares that the Queen of Sheba would condemn his contemporaries, as she was attracted by the wisdom of Solomon, while a greater than Solomon was here.* (Ver. 31.) The wisdom of Solomon was not associated with any miracle. It stood alone. It was rendered impressive by a halo of worldly glory; but this was all. Yet it commanded the queen of the south, who came from her distant land and learned wisdom at Solomon's feet. The worth of wisdom is the lesson of her long journey. But Christ's contemporaries, who have more wisdom by far in his discourses, and who have the miracles backing up the whole, are refusing the matchless testimony. Their condemnation shall be all the greater considering the noble conduct of the queen. How prone we are to despise the present opportunity, and to imagine that the former days were better than these, when the truth may be that now the most magnificent opportunity of all the ages is lying to our hands! 4. *The great necessity he shows is singleness of eye.* (Vers. 33—36.) This is the practical lesson with which our Lord closes his answer to his enemies. There is a light in the world, and it is not hidden. As the Light of the world, he was himself occupying a sufficiently elevated candlestick, and illumining all within the house. But if his hearers and interviewers had duplicity and not singleness of aim, they would miss the illumination and be filled with darkness. This was their danger. Hence he urges singleness of eye. If they but gazed on him with the proper motive, they would find their whole lives illumined, and glory waiting upon their work. He was anxious for this result—hence his warning. We learn, then, the necessity of singleness and simplicity of aim. In such a case we shall need no theories to account for Christ's power, but acknowledge its Divine and gracious character at once. Then shall our whole heart go forth in sympathy to him, and we shall be with him in co-operation and in success.—R. M. E.

Vers. 37—54.—*Pharisaism and legalism rebuked.* Our Lord, who was eminently social in his habits, accepts an invitation to dine with one of the Pharisees, and meets many Pharisees and lawyers there as guests. Such scenes were, to his pure and philanthropic mind, important opportunities, and as such he entered upon them. In this case he breaks ground at once by deliberately neglecting the usual preliminary ablutions. This was through no slovenliness in his personal habits, we may be sure; for if cleanliness is next to godliness, we may be pretty certain Jesus practised it. But as it is quite possible for men to put cleanliness in place of godliness, to be scrupulous about outward cleansing and careless about the heart, it was necessary that Jesus should expose the Pharisees' error and danger in this particular. Accordingly, we find him at this dinner-table exposing with great power first, Pharisaic hypocrisy, and, secondly, legalized impositions. Let us look at these in their order.

I. Christ's exposition of Pharisaic hypocrisy. (Vers. 37—44.) Pharisaism was a supreme regard for appearances. Long garments, phylacteries, multiplied ablutions, long prayers in public places, ostentatious tithing of little things, combined to make up Pharisaism, a reputation based upon externals. One who looked upon the heart, like our Lord, could easily see that all this outward decorum was quite compatible with wickedness of heart. And so he told his host deliberately, "Now do ye Pharisees make clean the outside of the cup and the platter; but your inward part is full of ravening ['extortion,' Revised Version] and wickedness." The cure is suggested when he leads him to think of God as alike the Author and Observer of what is without and within. "Ye fools ['foolish ones,' Revised Version], did not he that made that which is without ['the outside,' Revised Version] make that which is within ['the inside'] also? But rather give alms of such things as ye have ['Howbeit give for alms those things which are within,' Revised Version]; and, behold, all things are clean unto you." In this way he tries to lead his Pharisaic host to spirituality of life, to the expenditure of sympathy, of love, of brotherly kindness upon others, instead of indulging in outward acts behind which there was no real heart, but only a desire for personal reputation. Following up this line, he charges them with tithing pot-herbs, "the mint, anise, and cummin," while the weightier matters, "judgment and the love of God," matters that were within and spiritual, were left undone. Their preference for appearances, for the uppermost seats in the synagogues, for greetings in the markets, and all that goes to form a reputation, showed that they had not weighed aright the matters of the heart. No wonder that he concludes by comparing them to graves—"tombs," Revised Version—that appear not, over which men unwittingly tread. Whited sepulchres they were, beautiful outwardly, but within were dead men's bones and all uncleanness. It was a manly and terrible indictment for our Lord to make against them. And in doing so he exposed the principle of hypocrisy. It rests on appearances, on superficial judgments, on a forgetfulness that God searcheth the heart. It can be got rid of only by our getting down to first principles, and remembering that God "searcheth the hearts and trieth the reins of the children of men, even to give to every one according to his ways, and according to the fruit of his doings" (Jer. xvii. 9, 10).

II. Christ's exposure of legalized impositions. (Vers. 45—54.) A lawyer in the company, seeing his Pharisaic friends so severely handled by Christ, complains that his special department was involved also in the reproach. This leads our Lord to handle the lawyers more severely still. Their position was one of *monopoly of the Law.* To sustain their profession they had to make a great mystery of the meaning of the Law. Though it was largely plain enough for a runner to read and understand, it would have swept away all their privileges and profits to have left such an impression on the common people. Hence they took the Law into their own especial keeping, and interpreted it for the people as they pleased. The result of this was the imposition of heavy burdens upon the ignorant people. This has been the temptation of legal experts always; they increase the burdens of the common people—burdens which they leave the people to carry alone. Not only so, but the lawyers were manufacturing reputations out of the shortcomings of their fathers. Their fathers had murdered the prophets; the sons were now busy building their sepulchres, and so far pretending to dissent from their fathers' murderous spirit. But our Lord shows that this policy is a simple hypocrisy, for, in seeking the life of Jesus, they were demonstrating that the old spirit was still within them. It is easier to serve on a building committee than to entertain kindly feelings towards the Saviour. All this hypocrisy, however, will receive judgment in due season. Upon the generation that murdered Christ will descend the judgment which the murderous spirit of so many generations deserved. Our Lord in this way brings out how we may, by our conduct in the present, become involved in the responsibilities of the past. We cannot isolate ourselves from the past; we are not only heirs of all the ages, but share the responsibilities of all the ages by reason of our attitude towards them. History is thus brought into the field of responsibility, and we are either for or against the good in the olden time. It would be well for us to treat history in a sympathetic fashion, and have our hearts in proper training as we review the past. We may sin by hating an old martyr's memory just as really as by despising his counterpart to-day. Our Lord concludes by denouncing the dog-in-the-manger policy of the lawyers, pretending to knowledge, while at once they had lost the key and kept others effectually from finding it. No wonder that, when our Lord came out from the banquet, he found himself violently beset on every side by those he had so exposed, in hope that some such statement would form the basis of his accusation. But they found themselves baffled by his limitless knowledge of human nature. Instead of contending with him, it will be better for us all to submit to his superior judgment and gracious pleasure.—R. M. E.

EXPOSITION.

CHAPTER XII.

Vers. 1—59.—*The Lord, after leaving the Pharisee's house, speaks at great length to a numerous crowd waiting for him, addressing his words principally to his own disciples.* The foregoing scene (ch. xi.), when the Master addressed his bitter reproaches to the learned and cultivated of the great Pharisee party, took place in a private house belonging to an apparently wealthy member of this, the dominant class. The name of the large village or provincial town where all this happened is unknown. The crowd who had been listening to the great Teacher before he accepted the Pharisee's invitation still lingered around the house. Many from the adjoining villages, hearing that Jesus was in this place and was publicly teaching, had arrived; so, when the Lord came out from the guest-chamber into the street or market-place, he found a vast crowd—literally, myriads of the multitude—waiting for him. The words descriptive of the crowd in ver. 1 indicate that a vast concourse was gathered together. His fame then was very great, though his popularity was on the wane.

Ver. 1.—**Beware ye of the leaven of the Pharisees, which is hypocrisy.** In dwelling on this and similar expressions used by our Lord in respect to the life and work of this famous section of the people who were generally so bitterly hostile to him and his teaching, we must not condemn their whole character with a condemnation more sweeping than the Master's. Utterly mistaken in their views of life and in their estimate of God, whom they professed to know, our Lord here scarcely charges them with deliberate hypocrisy. These mistaken men dreamed that they possessed a holiness which was never theirs; unconscious hypocrites they doubtless were, without possibly even suspecting it themselves.

Vers. 2, 3.—**For there is nothing covered, that shall not be revealed; neither hid, that shall not be known. Therefore whatsoever** ye have spoken in darkness shall be heard in the light. The day would come when his estimate of this now popular teaching of the Pharisees would be found to have been correct. Its real nature, now hid, would be revealed and fully known and discredited; while, on the other hand, the words and teaching of his disciples, now listened to but by few, and those of seemingly little account, would become widely and generally known and listened to. **Upon the house-tops.** These were flat, terrace-like roofs, and, the houses generally being low, one who spoke from them would easily be heard in the street beneath. "These words have a strong Syrian colouring. The Syrian house-top (in Matt. x. 27 and here) presents an image which has no sense in Asia Minor, or Greece, or Italy, or even at Antioch. The flat roofs cease at the mouth of the Orontes; Antioch itself has sloping roofs" (Renan, 'Les Evangiles,' p. 262, note 1).

Ver. 4.—**And I say unto you my friends, Be not afraid of them that kill the body, and after that have no more that they can do.** All this the Master knew was true and would shortly happen. His words were verified before fifty years had passed. The triumphant success of the great Christian preachers and the discredited condition of the old rabbinic schools is testified to by such words as we find in St. Paul's letters. "Where is the wise? where is the scribe?" (1 Cor. i. 20). But this success the Master well knew would be accompanied with many a suffering on the part of the heralds of his message. Persecution in its many dreary forms would dog their footsteps; a death of agony and shame not unfrequently would be their guerdon. It was, for instance, we know, the earthly recognition of that devoted servant of the Lord (Paul) who, we believe, guided the pen of Luke here. This painful way, which his disciples must surely tread, had already been indicated in no obscure language by the Master ("*some* of them"—my apostles—"they shall slay and persecute," ch. xi. 49). A triumph, greater than any which had ever been given to the sons of men, would surely be theirs, but the Master would not conceal the *earthly* price which his chosen servants must pay for this splendid success. There was a point, however, beyond which human malice and enmity were utterly powerless; he would have his servants turn their thoughts on that serene region where men as men would have no power.

Ver. 5.—**But I will forewarn you whom ye shall fear: Fear him, which after he hath killed hath power to cast into hell;** literally, *into Gehenna.* This is simply *Gee-hinnom,* "valley of Hinnom," translated into Greek letters. This valley was situated in the neighbourhood of Jerusalem, and originally was noted for the infamous rites practised there in the worship of Moloch, in the times of the idolatrous kings of Judah. King Josiah, to mark his abhorrence of the idol-rites, defiled it with corpses; fires were subsequently kindled to consume the putrefying matter and prevent pestilence. The once fair valley, thus successively defiled with hideous corrupting rites, by putrefying corpses, and then with blazing fires lit to consume what would otherwise have occasioned pestilence, was taken by rabbinical writers as a symbol for the place of torment, and is used not unfrequently as a synonym for "hell." The translators of the Authorized Version have done so here. The reminder is, after all, we need not fear *men.* When they have done their worst, they have only injured or tortured the perishable body. The One whom all have good reason to fear is God, whose power is not limited to this life, but extends through and beyond death. Some have strangely supposed, not *God*, but the *devil*, is intended here to be the real object of human fear. The devil can be no object of fear to the Master's disciples.

Vers. 6, 7.—**Are not five sparrows sold for two farthings, and not one of them is forgotten before God? But even the very hairs of your head are all numbered. Fear not therefore: ye are of more value than many sparrows.** Though persecution and bitter suffering, even death, may be the guerdon of the Lord's true servants here, none of these things can happen without the consent of God. This thought will surely give them courage to endure. Suffering undergone in God's service, inflicted, too, with his entire consent, so that the suffering becomes part of the service,—what an onlook is afforded to the brave, faithful servant by such a contemplation! Oh the welcome from God he is sure to meet with when such a death has been endured! These extreme instances of God's universal care—his all-knowledge of everything, however little and insignificant, belonging to his creatures—are chosen to give point to the Master's words. If he knows of the death of these little, almost valueless, birds—ay, even of the falling of one of the many hairs of your head—surely you cannot doubt his knowledge of, his caring for, the life or death of one of his proved and gallant followers. These little sparrows were sold in the markets, strung together, or on skewers.

Ver. 8.—**Also I say unto you, Whosoever shall confess me before men, him shall the Son of man also confess before the angels of God.** The great Teacher pursues the subject of the future of his disciples. It is by no means only to a wise *fear* of that God, whose hand stretches beyond this life, that he appeals as a mighty inducement for his servants utterly to disregard all dangers which may meet them in the course of their service; he tells them, too, of a splendid recompense, which will assuredly be the guerdon of all his true followers. Before that glorious throng of heavenly beings, whose existence was a part of the creed of every true Jew; before the mighty angels, the awful seraphim; before that countless crowd of winged and burning ones who assisted at the awful mysteries of Sinai, would they who witnessed for him, and suffered because of him, be acknowledged by him. Their sufferings in the service of the King of heaven, whom they knew on earth as the poor Galilee Teacher, would be recounted before the angels by the same King of heaven, when he returned to his home of grandeur and of peace in heaven.

Ver. 9.—**But he that denieth me before men shall be denied before the angels of God.** Splendid as would the recompense be to the faithful and the loyal, equally shameful would be the guerdon meted out to the cowardly and faint-hearted. Before the same glorious throng would the King detail the failure, through slavish fear, of those whom he had chosen for so royal a service. Such an announcement as this proclamation of glory and of shame before the holy angels, in which stupendous scene *he*, the poor Galilæan Rabbi, was to play the part of the Almighty Judge, could only have been made in the last weeks preceding his Passion. All reticence was then laid aside. Before friend and foe, in public and in private, in these last solemn weeks Jesus tore away the veil of reticence with which he had been pleased hitherto in great measure to shroud his lofty claims, and the Master now declared before all that he was the King of kings, the Lord alike of angels and of men. In the face of such an announcement, his prosecution by the priests and the Pharisee party for blasphemy naturally follows. He was either a daring impostor or ——. In the latter case, to the poor Galilee Rabbi belonged the *Name of names* which no Jew dared to pronounce.

Ver. 10.—**And whosoever shall speak a word against the Son of man, it shall be forgiven him.** And yet even *that* offence, which consisted in playing the renegade and the coward; which refused to suffer for him here; which, out of slavish fear of man, consented to abandon his pure and righteous cause;—*that* offence, which would be proclaimed before the angels of heaven, would in the end find forgiveness. Some commentators point, as an illustration of this, to the fact of the dying Lord praying on the cross for his murderers; but the offence alluded to here, which should in the end be blotted out, was of far deeper dye. He prayed on his cross for those Romans who sinned, but sinned in the face of little light. But this forgiveness was to be extended to men who, through fear of men and love of the world, should deny him whom they knew to be their Redeemer. This is one of the most hopeful passages which treats of sin eventually to be forgiven, in the whole New Testament. But even here there is no so-called universal redemption announced, for in the next sentence the Lord goes on to speak of a sin which he emphatically said shall *never* have forgiveness. **But unto him that blasphemeth against the Holy Ghost it shall not be forgiven.** What is *this* awful sin? We have only to speak of its connection in this place. Here there is no possibility of mistake; it was that determined hatred of holiness, that awful love of self, which had induced the Pharisee leaders to ascribe his beneficent and loving works to the spirit of evil and of darkness. The accusation was no chance one, the fruit of impulse or of passion. They who accused him knew better. They had heard him teach, not once, but often; they had seen his works; and yet, though they knew that the whole life and thoughts and aspirations were true, who were conscious that every word and work was holy, just, and pure, in order to compass their own selfish ends, simply because they felt his life and teaching would interfere with them, *they dared to ascribe to the devil what their own hearts told them came direct from God.* This sin, now as then, the merciful Saviour tells us *has no forgiveness.*

Ver. 11.—And **when they bring you unto the synagogues, and** unto **magistrates, and powers, take ye no thought how or what thing ye shall answer.** The Master comes back again to his old calm, and continues his loving instructions to his disciples; and turning again to the little group of his friends, he says to them, "*When* they bring you before hostile tribunals, special help, you will find, will be given you. Have no fear, then, that you will be wanting in wisdom or courage; the Holy Spirit of God will be your Advocate, and will whisper to you words for your defence." The best example of this supernatural aid to the accused

followers of Jesus which we possess is the grave and stately apology of Stephen before the Sanhedrin. Peter's speech before the same tribunal, and Paul's before Felix and Festus, are also fair instances.

Ver. 13.—And one of the company said unto him, **Master, speak to my brother, that he divide the inheritance with me.** Apparently there was a pause here in the Lord's teaching. The Master was about to enter on a new subject, and at this juncture one of the crowd, waiting for such a break in the Master's discourse, came forward with a question. It was purely connected with his own selfish interests. He seems to have been a younger brother, discontented with the distribution of the family property, of which, most likely, in accordance with the usual Jewish practice, a double portion had been taken by the elder brother. This was likely enough the point which he submitted to the Lord. Such a reference to a scribe and rabbi of eminence was then not uncommon. Jesus, however, here, as on other occasions (see John viii. 3—11), firmly refuses to interfere in secular matters. His work was of another and higher kind. The word he addresses to the questioner has in it a tinge of rebuke. The utter selfish worldliness of the man, who, after hearing the solemn and impressive words just spoken, *could* intrude such a question, comes strongly into view. Was not this poor unimpressionable Jew, so wrapped up in his own paltry concerns that he had no thought or care for loftier things, perhaps a specimen of most of the material upon whom the Lord had to work? Is he an unknown figure in our day and time?

Ver. 15.—And he said unto them, **Take heed, and beware of covetousness: for a man's life consisteth not in the abundance of the things which he possesseth.** The older authorities read, "beware of every kind of covetousness." No vice is more terribly illustrated in the Old Testament story than this. Prominent illustrations of ruin overtaking the covetous man, even in this life, are Balaam, Achan, and Gehazi. Has not this ever been one of the besetting sins of the chosen race, *then as now, now as then?* Jesus, as the Reader of hearts, saw what was at the bottom of the question: greed, rather than a fiery indignation at a wrong endured. "A man's life." *His true life,* would be a fair paraphrase of the Greek word used here. The Master's *own* life, landless, homeless, penniless, illustrated nobly these words. *That* life, as far as earth was concerned, was his deliberate choice. The world, Christian as well as pagan, in each succeeding age, with a remarkable agreement, utterly declines to recognize the great Teacher's view of life here. To make his meaning perfectly clear, the Lord told them the following parable-story, which reads like an experience or memory of something which had actually happened.

Ver. 16.—**The ground of a certain rich man brought forth plentifully.** The unhappy subject of the Lord's story was a common figure in Palestine in an ordinarily prosperous time. We have the portrait of a landowner whose farms do not seem to have been acquired by any unjust means. This man, after years of successful industry, having acquired great wealth, wholly devotes himself to it and to its further increase. He does not give himself up to excess or profligacy, but simply, body and soul, becomes the slave of his wealth; utterly, hopelessly selfish, he forgets alike God and his neighbour.

Vers. 17, 18.—**And he thought within himself, saying, What shall I do, because I have no room where to bestow my fruits? And he said, This will I do: I will pull down my barns, and build greater.** "No place to bestow my fruits." Well answers St. Ambrose, "Thou *hast* barns—the bosoms of the needy, the houses of the widows, the mouths of orphans and of infants." Some might argue, from the sequel of the story, that God looks with disfavour on riches as riches. St. Augustine replies to such a mistaken deduction, "God desires not that thou shouldest lose thy riches, but that thou shouldest change their place" ('Serm.,' xxxvi. 9). The Greek word rendered "barns" (ἀποθήκας—whence our word "apothecary") has a broader signification than merely barns; it signifies store or warehouses of all kinds, thus suggesting that the hero of the story was more than a mere wealthy farmer—he was probably also a trader. **And there will I bestow all my fruits and my goods.** As he grew richer, he grew more covetous. Absolutely no care or thought for anything save his loved possessions seems to have crossed the threshold of that poor mistaken heart of his. This strange hunger after riches for riches' sake is, alas! a very usual form of soul-disease. Can it be cured? Alas! it is one of the most hopeless of soul-maladies. This unhappy love in countless cases becomes a passion, and twines itself round the heart, and so destroys all the affections and higher aspirations.

Ver. 19.—**And I will say to my soul, Soul, thou hast much goods laid up for many years.** "What folly!" writes St. Basil. "Had thy soul been a sty, what else couldst thou have promised to it? Art thou so ignorant of what really belongs to the soul, that thou offerest to it the foods of the body? And givest thou to thy *soul* the things which the draught receives?" *Many years.* How little did that poor fool, so

wise in all matters of earthly business, suspect the awful doom was *so* close to him! He forgot Solomon's words, "Boast not thyself of to-morrow" (Prov. xxvii. 1). **Take thine ease, eat, drink, and be merry.** "Extremes meet," suggests Dean Plumptre; "and the life of self-indulgence may spring either from an undue expectation of a lengthened life" (as was the case here), "or from unduly dwelling on its shortness, without taking into account the judgment that comes after it. The latter, as in the 'carpe diem' of Horace ('Odes,' i. 11. 8), was the current language of popular epicureanism" (see St. Paul's reproduction of this thought, 1 Cor. xv. 32); "the former seems to have been more characteristic of a corrupt Judaism."

Ver. 20.—**But God said unto him, Thou fool, this night thy soul shall be required of thee.** The literal rendering of the Greek here is more solemn and impressive in its awful vagueness: *This night they require thy soul of thee.* Who are meant by *they?* Most likely the angels: not necessarily "avenging," as Trench would suggest; simply those angels whose special function it was to conduct the souls of the departed *to their own place.* So we read in the parable of Lazarus and Dives how angels carried the soul of Lazarus into Abraham's bosom. On the words, "they require," Theophylact writes, "For, like pitiless exactors of tribute, terrible angels shall require thy soul from thee unwilling, and through love of life resisting. For from the righteous his soul is not *required,* but he *commits* it to God and the Father of spirits, pleased and rejoicing; nor finds it hard to lay it down, for the body lies upon it as a light burden. But the sinner who has enfleshed his soul, and embodied it, and made it earthy, has so prepared it to render its divulsion from the body most hard; wherefore it is said *to be required* of him, as a disobedient debtor that is delivered to pitiless exactors." **Then whose shall those things be, which thou hast provided?** Our Lord here reproduced the thought contained in passages with which no doubt he had been familiar from his boyhood. "Yea, I hated all my labour which I had taken under the sun: because I should leave it unto the man that shall be after me. And who knoweth whether he shall be a wise man or a fool?" (Eccles. ii. 18, 19). "He heapeth up riches, and knoweth not who shall gather them" (Ps. xxxix. 6). The parallel in the apocryphal book, Ecclus. xi. 18, 19, is very close.

Ver. 21.—**And is not rich toward God;** better rendered, *if he is not.* And this slight change helps us, too, in drawing the right lesson. The *being rich* is never condemned by Jesus Christ; nor even the *growing richer*. Among the saints of God in both Testaments are many notable rich men, whose possessions seem to have helped rather than hindered their journey to the city of God. The lesson which lies on the forefront of this parable-story is the especial danger which riches ever bring of gradually deadening the heart and rendering it impervious to any feeling of love either for God or man.

The directions which immediately followed upon this parable were addressed to the inner circle of disciples. The general instruction, it will be seen, belongs to all who in any age wish to be " of his Church ; " but several of the particular charges cannot he pressed as *general* commands, being addressed to men whose work and office were unique.

Ver. 22.—**And he said unto his disciples, Therefore I say unto you, Take no thought for your life, what ye shall eat ; neither for the body, what ye shall put on.** A better rendering for "Take no thought" is *Be not anxious about*. This, too, suggests a more practical lesson. "What ye shall eat." How repeatedly in the Master's sermons do we find the reminder against the being careful about eating! We know from pagan writers in this age how gluttony, in its coarser and more refined forms, was among the more notorious evils of Roman society in Italy and in the provinces. This passion for the table more or less affected all classes in the empire.

Vers. 24—27.—**Consider the ravens: for they neither sow nor reap ; which neither have storehouse nor barn ; and God feedeth them. . . . Consider the lilies . . . they toil not, they spin not: and yet I say unto you, that Solomon in all his glory was not arrayed like one of these.** What a contrast between the life of the rich and prosperous landowner just related, whose whole heart and soul were concentrated on a toil which should procure him dainty food and costly raiment, and these fowls fed by God so abundantly, and those flowers clothed by God so royally! The ravens knew nothing of the anxious care and the restless toil of the rich man in the midst of which he died, and yet they lived. The lilies simply grew, and God's hand painted the rich and gorgeous clothing for each golden-jewelled flower; Solomon, the splendid Jewish king, the example of all that was magnificent, was never arrayed, men knew, like one of these lilies. With such a God above them, who surely loved each one as he never loved a bird or flower, was it worth while

to wear a life away in toiling for less than what God simply *gave* to raven and to lily ? Such was the Master's argument, adorned, we may well conceive, with all the beauty and force of Eastern illustration. We possess, after all, but a scant *résumé* of these Divine sermons. To apostle and chosen missionary his words had a peculiar interest. He bade them, in coming days of poverty and abandonment, never to lose heart. They would remember *then* their loved Teacher's words that day when he spoke of the fate of one whose life had been wasted in filling his storehouses and his barns; would remember how he turned from the foolish, toiling rich man, and told them of the birds and flowers, and how God tenderly cared even for such soulless things. Did they think he would ever lose sight of them, his chosen servants? They might surely reckon on the loving care of that Master to whose cause they were giving their life-service. Yet have these and other like words of the great Teacher been often misunderstood; and St. Paul's earnest and repeated exhortations to his converts—not to neglect honest toil, but by it to win bread for themselves, and something withal to be generous with to those poorer than they—were his protest against taking the Master's words in too literal a sense, and using them as a pretext for a dreamy and idle life. Paul's teaching, and perhaps still more Paul's life—that life of brave, simple toil for himself and others—were *his* comment upon this part of the Master's sermon. *The lilies.* It is a little doubtful whether our Lord meant to speak of the red anemone, a very common but beautiful flower, with which the meadows throughout all Palestine are enamelled (*Anemone coronaria*), or the great white lily (*Lilium candidum*), or the exquisite red lily (*Lilium rubrum*); these latter are more rare. The Saviour, probably, had each of these and other specimens of the flora of Palestine in his mind, when he spoke of the inimitable beauty and the matchless splendour of these flowers of God.

Ver. 29.—**And seek not ye what ye shall eat, or what ye shall drink.** Again, after the moving, touching words we have been commenting on, does the Lord return to the pressing injunction with which he began his lessons to his disciples upon the parable of the " rich fool." Trouble not yourselves about your eating and drinking. This repeated insistence of the Master upon this point in the future lives of his disciples has evidently a deeper significance than a mere injunction to cast all their care on him, and not to be over-anxious about their poor earthly maintenance. This was, of course, the first lesson they had to learn from these words; but beneath all this they could, and no doubt often in later days did, read in the words a clear expression of their dear Lord's will in favour of the utmost simplicity in all matters of food and drink. His own must be marked men here, ever frugal and temperate even to abstemiousness. It is a grave question whether his Church has ever fully grasped the Master's meaning here. **Neither be ye of doubtful mind**; literally, *do not toss about like boats in the offing* (so Dr. Farrar very happily). The word is not found elsewhere in New Testament writers, but it is known in classic writers. Its use here is one of the many signs of St. Luke's high culture.

Ver. 32.—**Fear not, little flock.** Another term of tender endearment addressed to his own who were grouped near him. In the earlier part of this discourse (ver. 4) he had called them "my friends." He had told them of the troublous life which awaited them, but at the same time wished to show them how dear they were to him. It was as though he said, "Endure the thought of these necessary trials *for my sake;* are you not my chosen friends, for whom so glorious a future, if ye endure to the end, is reserved?"

Ver. 33.—**Sell that ye have, and give alms; provide yourselves bags which wax not old, a treasure in the heavens that faileth not.** "Those of you who *have* riches, see, this is what I counsel you to do with them." In considering these much-disputed words of the Master, we must remember (1) *to whom* they were spoken: they were addressed to men and women who, if they would follow him, *must* set themselves free from all worldly possessions; they must literally forsake *all* to follow him. (2) We must bear in mind (*a*) that the only community which attempted, as a community, to obey this charge *literally* was the Church of Jerusalem, and the result was that for long years this Church was plunged into the deepest poverty, so that assistance had to be sent even from far-distant Churches to this deeply impoverished Jerusalem community. [This we learn from Paul, the real compiler of this very Gospel, where the charge is reported. See many passages in his letters, notably the Second Epistle to the Corinthians, *passim.*] (*b*) The mendicant orders in the Middle Ages, with no little bravery and constancy, likewise attempted to carry out to the letter this direction. The impartial student of mediæval history, while doing all justice to the aims and work of these often devoted men, can judge whether or no these mendicant orders can be reckoned among the *permanently* successful agencies of the cross. We conclude, then, that these words had a *literal* meaning only for those to whom they were

specially addressed, viz. the disciples. While to the Church generally they convey this deep, far-reaching lesson, a lesson all would-be servants of Christ would do well to take to heart—it is the Master's will that his followers *should sit loose* to all *earthly possessions, possessing them as though they possessed not.* Thus living, the heart will be free from all inordinate care for earthly treasure, and will, in real earnest, turn to that serene region where its real and abiding riches indeed are—even to heaven.

Vers. 35, 36.—**Let your loins be girded about, and your lamps burning; and ye yourselves like unto men that wait for their lord, when he will return from the wedding; that when he cometh and knocketh, they may open unto him immediately.** The Master goes on with his teaching on the subject of covetousness, still addressing himself primarily to the disciples. "There is another reason why my chosen followers should treat the amassing of earthly goods with indifference; no man knows *when* the end of this state of things may come; their hearts must be fixed on something else than perishable things. They must act as servants on the watch for the return of their lord. See now, my own," Jesus proceeds to say; "your attitude in life must be that of servants, at once loyal and devoted, whom their employer has left in his house while he is absent at a great wedding-feast. The day of his absence passes into evening, and evening shades into night; and even the night wears slowly and tediously away, and still the master of the house comes not back from his festival." But the *faithful* servants all this while never slumber, or even lie down to rest. All the time of his absence, with their loose flowing Eastern robes taken up, and the skirt fastened under the girdle, with their lamps all trimmed and burning, these watchers wait the coming of their lord, though he tarry long, that they may be ready to receive him and serve him the moment he arrives. All kinds of busy house service, too, carried on during the long night of watching, is implied by the girt-up robes and the lit lamps of the tireless watchers.

Ver. 37. — **Blessed are those servants, whom the lord when he cometh shall find watching: verily I say unto you, that he shall gird himself, and make them to sit down to meat, and will come forth and serve them.** The title "blessed," when used by our Lord, is ever a very lofty one, and implies some rare and precious virtue in the one to whom this title to honour is given. It seems as though the house-master of the parable scarcely expected such true devotion from his servants; so he hastens to reward a rare virtue with equally rare blessedness and honour. He raises the slaves to a position of equality with their master. These true faithful ones are no longer his servants; they are his friends. He even deigns himself to minister to their wants. A similar lofty promise is made in less homely language. The final glorious gift to the faithful conqueror in the world's hard battle appears in the last of the epistles to the seven Churches: "To him that overcometh will I grant to sit with *me* in my throne" (Rev. iii. 21).

Ver. 38.—**And if he shall come in the second watch, or come in the third watch, and find** them **so.** Among the Jews at the time of our Lord, the old division of the night into three watches had given place to the ordinary Roman division into four. They were reckoned thus: from six to nine, from nine to midnight, from midnight to three, and from three to six. In this parable the second and third watches are mentioned as necessary for the completeness of the picture; for the *banquet* would certainly not be over before the end of the first watch, and in the fourth the *day* would be breaking. The second and third watches, then, represent the still and weary hours of the night, when to watch is indeed a task of difficulty and painfulness; and here again the Lord repeats his high encomium on such devoted conduct in his second "blessed are those servants." It is perfectly clear that in this parable the master's return signifies the coming of Christ. The whole tone, then, is a grave reminder to us, to all impatient ones, that the great event *may* be long delayed, much longer than most Christian thinkers dream; but it tells us, too, that this long delay involves a test of their loyalty. "The parousia does not come so quickly as impatience, nor yet so late as carelessness, supposes" (Van Oosterzee).

Vers. 39, 40.—**And this know, that if the goodman of the house had known what hour the thief would come, he would have watched, and not have suffered his house to be broken through. Be ye therefore ready also: for the Son of man cometh at an hour when ye think not.** The Lord abruptly changes the scene of his parable imagery, and with another striking and vivid example enforces his teaching on the subject of the urgent necessity of his servants keeping a sleepless and diligent watch and ward against his coming again in judgment. Very deeply must this image of the Lord's sudden return, as a thief breaks into the house in the still hours of the night, have impressed itself on the hearts of the awe-struck, listening disciples, for we find in the case of SS. Paul and Peter the very words and imagery, and in the case of St. John the imagery again made use of (see 1 Thess. v. 1, 2; 1 Pet. iii. 10; Rev. iii. 3; xvi. 15). The meaning of the simile is obvious. The disciples and all followers of Jesus would do well to remain always on the watch for the second advent of the Lord. The time of that awful return was unknown, never could be known; men, however, must not be deceived by the long tarrying; the day of the Lord would surely come on the world as a thief in the night.

Ver. 41.—**Then Peter said unto him, Lord, speakest thou this parable unto us, or even to all?** Peter's question here referred evidently to the longer and more important parable-story, where the reward which the faithful watchers were to receive is mentioned (ver. 37). The grandeur of that reward seems deeply to have impressed the impulsive apostle. Some true conception of the heaven-life had entered into Peter's mind; we know, too, that now and again dimly Peter seemed to grasp the secret of his Master's awful Divinity. What meant, then, thought the faithful, loving man, the figure in the parable of the lord? Who was that lord—*himself serving* his faithful followers? The same curious perplexity evidently passed through Peter's mind when, on the evening before the death, in a symbol-act the Master repeated the words of the great promise made here, and washed his disciples' feet. Then we read how Peter said to him, "Lord, dost *thou* wash *my* feet?" Were *all* who followed Jesus to share in that strange, mighty promise; or only a few, such as Peter and his companions, called for a special purpose?

Vers. 42—44.—**And the Lord said, Who then is that faithful and wise steward, whom his lord shall make ruler over his household, to give** them their **portion of meat in due season? Blessed is that servant, whom his lord when he cometh shall find so doing. Of a truth I say unto you, that he will make him ruler over all that he hath.** Jesus goes on with his discourse. *Apparently* he pays no heed to Peter's question, but *really* he answers it fully, giving in fact more details on the subject of rewards to the faithful in the life to come than even Peter's question required. "Who then," asks the Lord, "is that faithful and wise steward, whom *his* lord shall make ruler over his household?" Who? Peter must answer the question. *This* steward should be Peter himself and each of Peter's chosen companions. *This* high position of steward in the household of the Lord should be filled by those whom Jesus had specially chosen. If, when he came again, the Lord found *these* faithful to their solemn trust, then *these* should receive a still higher and grander recompense even than that inconceivably splendid reward (mentioned in ver. 37) which had so struck Peter; and the higher recompense which these, the faithful and wise stewards, should then receive would be *the being made rulers over all that the Lord hath*. The answer of the Master then told Peter that *all* his followers, if found true and loyal, should receive the reward promised (in ver. 37) to the watching servants, who in the world to come would be not the *servants* but the *friends* of God. While the *few*, the chosen apostles of the Lord, if *they* endured to the end, if *they* were found wise and faithful, to them would be given in the new life a yet more glorious recompense; they would be set in some special position of government and dominion in the glorious city of God. This teaches, too, indirectly, but with great clearness, that in the heaven-life all Christ's redeemed will enjoy in the friendship of God a perfect blessedness. Still, in that perfect blessedness which will be the heritage of all the redeemed, there will still be degrees in glory.

Vers. 45, 46.—**But and if that servant say in his heart, My lord delayeth his coming; and shall begin to beat the menservants and maidens, and to eat and drink, and to be drunken; the lord of that servant will come in a day when he looketh not for him, and at an hour when he is not aware.** "But," continued the Master, "although certain of my servants have onlooks to higher degrees of glory than the great mass of their fellows, these seemingly favoured ones have at the same time more perilous responsibilities; and only if in these graver responsibilities they are faithful to the end, will they receive their high and peculiar reward." If, on the other hand, they fail in their perpetual watch for the coming of their Lord, and instead of the restless toil which the Master has assigned to these stewards, these servants, weighted with higher responsibilities, give themselves up to worldly pleasures and passions, terrible will be their doom. Again the excesses of the table are specially mentioned. If, instead of spending themselves in the cares of their high office, they make a profit out of that office, if they live as oppressors of the flock rather than as shepherds, then to these unfaithful stewards will the Lord suddenly come, as pictured in the parable imagery, a thief in the night. **And will cut him in sunder, and will appoint him his portion with the unbelievers.** The terrible punishment here specified was not unknown among the ancients (see Herodotus, vii. 39; and Heb. xi. 37). Isaiah was said to have been sawn asunder. Bengel's comment is curious: " Qui cor *divisum* habet, *dividetur*." It has been suggested, to bring the punishment into harmony with the statement immediately following, which speaks of a definite and, perhaps, of an enduring position for the guilty one, a "portion with

the unbelievers," to understand the word as an equivalent for scourging; so in the Latin we find *flagellis discindere*, to scourge the back with the rod. There is, however, no known instance of the Greek word διχοτομεῖν being used in this sense. The expression is, however, used as simply implying that a terrible doom is surely reserved in the life to come for those who have so sadly misused their high opportunities and neglected their great responsibilities. "The image of the parable itself is blended with the reality which the parable signifies; this thought of the human master who can punish his slaves with temporal death passes into that of the Divine Judge who can punish with spiritual death" (Dean Mansel).

Vers. 47, 48.—**And that servant, which knew his lord's will, and prepared not himself, neither did according to his will, shall be beaten with many** stripes. **But he that knew not, and did commit things worthy of stripes, shall be beaten with few** stripes. **For unto whomsoever much is given, of him shall be much required.** These verses are easy to understand. They explain the broad principles upon which the foregoing statements, in parable and in direct teaching, are based. Rewards and punishments will be allotted in the coming world with strict justice. To some, great knowledge of the Divine will is given and splendid opportunities of work are afforded; to such, if only they are faithful and true, will indeed a high place in the city of God be allotted; but alas for them in the life to come if they fail, if they miss the splendid chance of being true toilers with and for God! Their portion will be the *many stripes*. To others a knowledge of the Divine will, scanty compared with those just spoken of, is given, and opportunities of doing high and noble work are here comparatively few; if these use the little knowledge and seize the few opportunities, they will, while occupying a lower grade in the hierarchy of heaven, still enjoy the perfect bliss of friendship with God. The punishment for failure here is designated by the *few stripes*. In this solemn passage it is notable that degrees or grades in punishment as well as degrees or grades in glory are distinctly spoken of.

Ver. 49.—**I am come to send fire on the earth.** It is still the same train of thought that the Master pursues—a train which had been only slightly diverted by Peter's question. The text, so to speak, of the whole discourse was "the strange attraction which riches possess for men, and the palsying effect which this attraction, when yielded to, exercises over the whole life." The Master's argument was as follows: "Beware of covetousness; let your attachment to earthly possessions sit very lightly on you all; and as for *you*, my disciples, do you have *nothing* to do with these perishable goods." And here, with an abrupt solemnity, probably the voice changing here, and ringing with an awful emotion, he enforces his charge to the disciples with the words, "I am come to send fire on the earth." "My stern, sad work is to inaugurate a mighty struggle, to cast a firebrand on the earth. Lo, my presence will stir up men—you will see this in a way none now dream of; a vast convulsion will rend this people asunder. In the coming days of war and tumult, what have you, my disciples, who will be in the forefront of this movement,—what have you to do with earthly goods? Toss them away from you as useless baggage. The pioneers of the army of the future, surely *they* must be unencumbered in the war, which is about to break out; for remember, 'I am come to send fire on the earth.'" **And what will I, if it be already kindled?** better rendered, *how I would that it had been already kindled!* That is to say, "How I wish that this fire were already burning!" (so Olshausen, De Wette, Bleek, and Farrar). Through all the woe, however, the Redeemer could see, shining as it were through a dark cloud, the unspeakable glory and blessedness of his work. But this fire could not be kindled into a flame until something had happened. The cross must be endured by him; till then his work was not finished; and in his pure human nature—it is with stammering tongue and trembling pen we speak or write here— he felt, we believe, the bitter stinging pain of dread expectation of what was coming. With this onlook he was weighed down, we know, at times; witness especially the Gethsemane agony. He goes on to say—

Ver. 50.—**But I have a baptism to be baptized with; and how am I straitened till it be accomplished!** The baptism he here speaks of was the baptism of pain and suffering and death—what we call the Passion of the Lord. He knew it must all be gone through, to bring about the blessed result for which he left his home in heaven; but he looked on to it, nevertheless, with terror and shrinking. "He is under pressure," says Godet, "to enter into this suffering because he is in haste to get out of it, mournfully impatient to have done with a painful task." This passage of the discourse of Jesus here has been called "a prelude of Gethsemane."

Ver. 51.—**Suppose ye that I am come to give peace on earth? I tell you, Nay; but rather division.** But the Master quickly leaves himself and his own sad forebodings. He puts by for a season his own holy impatience and continues his warnings. "I have been dwelling on the troublous times quickly coming on. Do not deceive your-

selves, my disciples; the great change about to be inaugurated will only be carried out in war and by divisions in the individual house as in the nation. I bring not peace, but a sword, remember." And then follows a curious picture of a home torn asunder by the conflict of thought which would spring up as the result of the cross and of the preaching of the cross.

Ver. 54.—**And he said also.** A note of the compilers, SS. Luke and Paul, which seems to say, "Besides all the important sayings we have just written down, which were spoken on this occasion, the Master added as a conclusion the following words." It is probable that the expressions used in the next seven verses were called out by the general apathy with which his announcement of the coming woes was received by the listening multitude. Possibly he had noticed a smile of incredulity on the faces of some of the nearer by-standers. The words had already been used on other occasions in a different connection. Here he used them as a last appeal, or rather as a remonstrance. He seems to say to the people, "O blind, blind to the awful sins of the times! You are weather-wise enough, and can tell from the appearance of the sky and the sighing of the wind whether a storm is brewing or no: why not use the same faculty of discernment in higher and more important matters? Ah! be wise; make your peace with God without delay; it will soon be too late; there is an awful judgment close at hand!" **When ye see a cloud rise out of the west, straightway ye say, There cometh a shower; and so it is.** To the *west* of Palestine lay the great Mediterranean Sea, from which, of course, came all the rains which fell on that country.

Ver. 55.—**And when ye see the south wind blow, ye say, There will be heat; and it cometh to pass.** To the south of Palestine lay the desert; when the wind blew from that direction, it was usually a time of heat and drought.

Ver. 56.—**Ye can discern the face of the sky and of the earth; but how is it that ye do not discern this time?** *These* things had an interest for them. Heat and drought, wind and rain, affected materially the prospect of their wheat-harvest and vintage, the fruitfulness of their orchards and olive-yards, therefore they gave their whole mind to the watching of the weather; but to the awful signs of the time in which they were living they were blind and deaf. What were these signs? (1) *The low state of morality among public men.* Did none of them notice how utterly corrupt were priests and scribes and people, how hollow and meaningless their boasted religious rites, how far removed from them was the presence of the God of their fathers? (2) *Political situation*. Did none of them notice the terribly strained relations between the Roman or Herodian, and the great national party? Were they blind to the bitter, irreconcilable hatred to mighty Rome which was seething scarcely beneath the surface of Jewish society? Were they deaf to the rumbling noises which too surely heralded a fierce and bloody war between little Palestine, split up into parties and sects, and the mighty world of Rome which had seized them in its own grip? What could be the result of such a war? Were they devoid of reason as well as blind and deaf? (3) *Heavenly warnings*. What had they done with John the Baptist? Many in Israel knew that man was indeed a great prophet of the Lord. His burning words had penetrated far and wide; vast crowds had heard the awful sounds with breathless awe; but no one heeded, and the people watched him die. And now—they had listened to him who was speaking to them. He had told them all; no sign of power was wanting to his ministry, and it was just over, and the people had not repented.

Vers. 58, 59.—**When thou goest with thine adversary to the magistrate, as thou art in the way, give diligence that thou mayest be delivered from him; lest he hale thee to the judge, and the judge deliver thee to the officer, and the officer cast thee into prison. I tell thee, thou shalt not depart thence, till thou hast paid the very last mite.** And then the Master passed into one of those parable illustrations with which his hearers were now familiar, and which in a homely way taught the crowd the same grave truth which he had been dwelling upon — the impending terrible judgment which was coming on the people. The lesson, " be reconciled to God while it is yet time," is, of course, applicable to all lives, precarious and hanging seemingly on a

thread as they all are, but it was especially spoken to that generation in view of the awful ruin which he knew was so soon to fall on every Jewish home. The general meaning of the parable illustration was obvious; no hearer could fail to understand the Lord's meaning. It is *before* arriving at the judgment-seat that you must be reconciled with the one who accuses you, otherwise it will be too late, and nothing would remain for the guilty accused but the eternal prison-house. At *that* moment, when the Master was speaking, individual or nation might have turned to the Lord and lived. There was no time, however, for hesitation. The sands in the hour-glass, which marked the duration of God's long-suffering with Israel, were just running out. Theologians in different ages and of varied schools have made much of the concluding sentence (ver. 59). Roman Catholic divines see in it a strong argument in favour of the doctrine of purgatory, arguing that after death condemnation would be followed by liberation, when a certain payment had been made by the guilty soul; strange ways of paying this debt by means of others we know have been devised by the school of divines who teach this doctrine of purgatory. But the Lord's words here are terribly plain, and utterly exclude any payment of the debt of the soul *by others*. The Master emphatically says, "till *thou* hast paid the very last mite." The advocate who pleads for universal redemption, and shrinks from a punishment to the duration of which he can see no term, thinks that in the words, "till thou hast paid," he can discern the germ at least of eternal hope. But the impenetrable veil which hangs between us and the endless hereafter prevents us, surely, from even suggesting that any suffering which the soul may endure in the unseen world will ever pay "*the very last mite*," and so lead to pardon and peace.

HOMILETICS.

Vers. 1—12.—*An evil to be shunned, and a virtue to be cultivated.* Jesus had been partaking of the light forenoon meal with a Pharisee. In this Pharisee's house he proclaimed war to the death with the bigots who had been dogging his steps. A small fire may kindle much wood. For some reason unknown to us, he had omitted the washing of hands before sitting down to meat. Instantly the whole company turned on him with scowl and sneer and shrug. And the action of the Truth incarnate, in reply to this, was the utterance of the six "woes"—scathing thunderbolts—which St. Luke has recorded between vers. 42 and 52 of the previous chapter. His utterance was the signal for something like a riot (vers. 53, 54). Ah! thou Son of Mary, thou Meekest and Lowliest, the column has turned. Hitherto thy progress has been, not without contradiction of sinners, but for the most part one of sweet poetries—unbounded the wonder and generous the admiration of the people. Thine enemies have been kept back; they have been held in restraint by the lightning which has flashed from thee.

But now thou must enter on a new phase of thy ministry; henceforth the issues towards which thou hast been looking will be hastened.

> " Ride on, ride on in majesty!
> The wingèd squadrons of the sky
> Look down with sad and wondering eyes
> To see the approaching sacrifice."

"In the mean time," whilst the dinner with its tumultuous conversation is proceeding, the crowd has so accumulated that "many thousands are gathered together." They are so eager to hear the Prophet that some persons are trodden down. To this seething mass Christ comes forth, his heart stirred by the controversy, vehement and provocative, which single-handed he had sustained. Most natural, in view of the circumstances related, is the discourse which follows, addressed immediately to his followers, but reaching the ear of "the many thousands." 1. First, there is the word as to "*the leaven of the Pharisees, which is hypocrisy*" (vers. 1—3). Hypocrisy was the evil which permeated and vitiated their action. What is meant by hypocrisy? The hypocrite is "the man who has to play a part, to maintain a reputation, to keep up a respectable position, to act consistently with the maxims of the party to which he is allied, or the profession to which he belongs." As thus interpreted, is not the "beware!" of the afternoon long ago, a "beware!" for this day as well? "Pharisee" and "Sadducee" are words which no longer distinguish classes; but when the classes which they once designated are studied, it is found that, for what was most characteristic of each, there are correspondents among us. Let it not be supposed that the Pharisee was nothing else than a sanctimonious charlatan, a mere pretentious formalist. He was the representative of the more earnest religious spirit. The Sadducee was generally a wealthy man, one belonging to the ruling order. Content with easy and low standards, the worldly or rationalistic Jews belonged to the party comprehended by the name. The Pharisee disowned such a conception of religion. He would not have any fellowship with such latitudinarianism. To him the Law was the Law of God, and he was bent on keeping it to its minutest point. In over-zeal he even added, to the observances enjoined, observances which might be inferred or which had been added by rabbins. The traditions of the elders were, in his view, a supplement to the Law and the prophets. "It is needless," as has well been observed, "to show that there was something in Pharisaism worthy of admiration, for this is implied in the charge brought against the Pharisees of our Lord's time. They were accused of being hypocrites, of not being what they pretended to be; in which it is implied that, if they had really been what they seemed, they would have deserved the praise they claimed. And doubtless there were some whose goodness was more than outside show, both in the first original of the sect, and in those later times when Pharisaic culture prepared the soil on which the seeds of the gospel most readily flourished; for to this sect belonged the majority of the first converts, and the many thousands who believed are all described as 'zealous for the Law.'"[1] Any one playing the hypocrite will prefer the Pharisee type. The scanty clothing of the Sadducee will not suit; the fitting dress is the long robe and the well-phylacteried garment of the Pharisee. The devil's homage to truth, which hypocrisy has been declared to be, is more becomingly rendered in such a garb. A *part-actor!* Ah! we need to be reminded that this is a character still to be found in the religious world. Bunyan introduces us to persons who are not mere fictions—My Lord Turn-about, my Lord Fair-speech, Mr. Smoothman, Facing-both-ways, the parson Mr. Two-tongues; the points in which all agree being "that they never strive against wind and tide, and that they are always most zealous when religion goes in his silver slippers." A *part-actor!* Almost unconsciously, we play a part which marks an excess of what we have ourselves verified—a part beyond, if not covering, the very thought of the soul. "Beware of the leaven!" Milton describes hypocrisy as "the only evil that walks invisible except to God alone." To be real, not to be a Mr. Facing-both-ways, is one of the great lessons of the life of Christ. In any diagnosis of human nature, we must remember the mixture to be found in character. Few persons intend, deliberately and systematically, to lie to God

[1] 'Non-Miraculous Christianity,' pp. 263, 264, by Professor Salmon, D.D., of Dublin.

and man. The Pharisees whom our Lord condemned were not—at least we may in charity so suppose—intentionally false. If they prayed to be seen of men, we need not imagine that they secretly mocked at and disbelieved in the duty of prayer. The *leaven* was the endeavour to maintain a reputation with which they were credited; so much had this endeavour gained on them, that they were far more anxious about it than about their possession of truth in the inward parts. And thus they became part-actors. Now, so with regard to ourselves and our fellow-men. A person is observed doing, in some directions or at some times, what is inconsistent with his conduct at other times or in other directions. And worldly minded people, always eager to scent blemishes, cry out, "Hypocrite!" This is a harsh, and may be a wrong, judgment. A lapse from the standard aimed at does not evidence insincerity. Nay, those who observe most closely the facts of life, can often trace what seems a twofoldness of self. The Apostle Paul in a most striking passage (Rom. vii.) has described the struggle in his own heart, the contending laws, the spiritual and the carnal, the oppositions and thwartings of the sin that dwelt in him—oppositions so fierce that it seemed as if he were sold under sin. "O wretched man that I am!" he cries. His hope, his triumph, is, "I thank God through Jesus Christ our Lord." Looking up to Jesus Christ, he saw his right and higher self; looking down on the evil ever present with him, on the body of death in which he appeared to be enslaved, he saw the lower and the wrong self. "I myself with the mind serve the Law of God; but with the flesh the law of sin." The one feature in this portrait is the determination of the will. That was God's; the deflections from it were the signs of an alien force from which he wished to be free. So long as this feature is predominant, the sanctification may be imperfect, but the life is true. What constitutes hypocrisy is appearing to be what one is not; concealing the want of piety in the heart under the cloke of piety in the action; such a study of outward effect that the conduct gradually becomes a tissue of dishonesties. This *posing* to be something and this anxiety about the *pose* rather than the truth, constitute the leaven of hypocrisy. "Be no part-actor," says Christ (vers. 2, 3); "be no whisperer in darkness, be no mutterer in the ear in inner chambers. Be not one thing in secret, and another thing in public. Keep clear of pretences of all sorts. Remember, concealment cannot avail. Walls have ears. The universe has its libraries on which all that is whispered is written. And there is an Eternal Truth to whom ' all hearts be open, all desires known, and from whom no secrets are hid.'" 2. Next, there is the word as to *courage*. Is it not the word which we might expect from him who had defied the most compact order in the land? Listen to the Christian's "Fear *not*," and the Christian's "Fear." "Fear not man, having power only over the body" (ver. 4). Have the courage of your convictions. Trust in God and do the right. Fear *God* (ver. 5). Fear not to speak the truth; fear to tell the lie. "Yea, I say unto you, fear the Eternal Righteousness." The lesson is enforced by three considerations. (1) The value to God of every true and honest life (vers. 6, 7). Not one sparrow is forgotten, not one of the tiniest and least valued of God's creatures is outside his care. Every hair on your head is numbered. You are dear to God. He is waiting for you to work with him. The life of each of you is of value to him. Fear not. (2) The danger of trifling with conviction (vers. 8—10). Do not refuse, for some fear of man, to give effect to it. You may possibly, says the Lord, quench the Holy Spirit. This was the sin of the Pharisees. This is the unpardonable sin. A word against Jesus may be spoken "ignorantly in unbelief;" and the Redeemer says, "Father, forgive; for they know not what they do." But to shut the eye to the light, to refuse to see light as light, to sophisticate the voice of God's Spirit speaking through reason and conscience, this is to destroy the possibility of spiritual health. Christ says to the disciples, "To confess me before men, no matter what the consequences to yourselves, is to deliver your souls, is to realize the confession in heaven; to deny me is to lose the fellowship of the holy angels, is to approach the confines of the sin which shall not be forgiven." (3) The support assured for all testimony to him (vers. 11, 12). God is ever on the side of the true. Christ bids those who confess him dismiss anxiety when brought to "synagogues, magistrates, and powers." They are never alone. Moses, the stammering, had his Aaron with him when he went in unto Pharaoh. A Mightier than Aaron is with the most timid and stammering of the confessors of the kingdom of God. "The Holy Ghost shall teach you in the same hour what ye ought to say."

Vers. 13—31.—*Worldliness.*　To the earnest teacher nothing can be more irritating than a half-attentive attitude or a remark which indicates preoccupation of mind with other and inferior things.　Think of Christ, towards the close of a day of controversy with the Pharisees, and in the midst of solemn speech as to the duty of a true man, invited on a sudden to decide in a family quarrel, to settle a dispute about some money or some acres of soil.　We know nothing about the person who appealed to him (ver. 13)—"one out of the multitude."　But it is evident that, while the discourse pro-ceeded, he had been engrossed with the consideration of his own rights and interests; like many who may be in the multitude thronging around Jesus, but are secretly busied with their own concerns—earth-grubs, intent only on getting all they can get from others for themselves.　The abrupt reply (ver. 14) shows the displeasure of the Lord.　It is a reply of reproof; it is a reply of instruction also.　God has a great variety of spheres and ministries for men, and the Son of God will not contravene his Father's ordering.　The judge, the measurer, the arbiter as to property, is a Divine calling.　Those who are entrusted with it are God's servants.　The State is no less sacred than the Church.　Let each realize its own place, and each respect the other— the State looking to the Church as the expounder of the eternal principles, the Church looking to the State as charged with government and the settlement of the issues between man and man.　"My kingdom," says the Christ, "is not of this world."　The incident gives a new direction to the teaching of Jesus.　It is a disclosure of the mind against which he must warn his followers.　And then follows one of the most solemn and beautiful of expositions—that in which the Lord conveys his great lesson as to worldliness.　Observe (1) *the more public instruction* between vers. 15 and 21; and (2) *the more private instruction*, specially addressed to the disciples, between vers. 21 and 32.　The more public is the admonition concerning *covetousness;* the more private is the admonition concerning *carefulness.*　The two types of the one spirit—worldliness.

I. The former instruction is enforced by a parable, by observing the point of which we discern THE MEANING WHICH CHRIST GIVES TO THE WORD "COVETOUSNESS," AND THE PRINCIPLE IN RELATION TO IT WHICH HE LAYS DOWN.　Notice, it is the most insinuating, therefore the most dangerous, form of the temptation which is presented.　The ground (ver. 16) of a man already rich brings forth plentifully.　There is no dis-honesty charged; there is no financial *finesse* suggested; it is in the natural course of things.　The money makes money, and good soil and good harvests aid.　The covetous-ness is the greed of *having* rather than *getting;* it is manifest in the thought as to that which has been already got.　The anxiety is to treasure up for self.　Existing barns are insufficient (vers. 17, 18).　What is to be done?　There never enters the thought of any stewardship of the substance with which the man is enriched; never the feeling, "What I have God has given me.　The labour of others, too, has helped me to acquire it.　I am the custodian of so much of a commonwealth.　God wills that I enjoy richly, but not that I keep all to myself.　I enjoy in the measure in which the use of the gifts unites me to the will of him who is the Giver."　Bengel remarks, "Not a word of the poor in all his self-communion."　It is simply a hard, selfish "greater barns."　Covetousness is not the desire to enjoy so much as the desire to have.　First, the having of a great store; then, not until then (ver. 19), "Soul, thou hast much goods laid up for many years; take thine ease, eat, drink, and be merry."　Very delicate is the Master's touch.　The happiness in the wealth is a thing future, and the *future never comes.*　Do we not often see abundance going about with a load of care on its back— fear about losses, anxiety about investments, etc.?　The wealthy are often prevented from getting the full good of their wealth.　They are possessed by their money more than they are possessors of their money.　"The increase serves not as water to quench, but as fuel to feed the fire; he that loveth silver shall not be satisfied with silver."　Christ is not condemning wealth or denouncing abundance of things.　"The filling of the barns with plenty, and the bursting out of the vats with new wine," is represented (Prov. iii. 9, 10) as the blessing prepared for those who honour the Lord with their sub-stance.　What he condemns is the vice which specially threatens the rich—the tendency to identify the life with the possessions (ver. 15), to love the money, to hoard it, and regard it all as a treasure to be devoted to self.　And truly the words of the Truth are most needful for our time.　"The desire to accumulate is the source of all our greatness and of all our baseness."　The baseness begins when the barn, with its "much goods" is regarded as the soul's portion; when that is the man's main interest; and, looking on to some day when the pile will be complete, he says in himself, " Then eat, drink, and be merry." Very striking the sentence (ver. 20). " *God* says, Thou fool!" Folly indeed! Thomas Adams quaintly says, " The competency of earthly things is a blessing; but what is this to abundance? Is not he as warm that goes in russet as another that rustles in silk? Has not the poor labourer as sound a sleep in his flock bed as the epicure on his down bed? Doth not quiet lie oftener in cottages than in glorious mansions? And, for a good appetite, we see the toiling servant feed savourly of one homely dish when his surfeited master looks loathingly on his far-fetched and dearly bought dainties. This gentleman envies the happiness of his poor hind, and would be content to change states with him on condition he might change stomachs. It is not the plenitude, but the competency of these things that affords even content; so that a man's estate should be like his garment, rather fit than long." Folly indeed! What stupidity to contemplate the many years! " This night thy soul shall be required." Thy soul, thyself, without all the goods. " When I die, let my hands be outside my shroud," said the emperor, " that all may see they are empty." And what is to become of the " much goods"? Pass into the hands of others, possibly only to do them harm, neither the accumulator nor his kind made the better for all the gathering. " Fool, fool! this thou art, O man, who, without generosity of heart or liberality of hand, day by day scrapest the dust of earth to thy store, oblivious of the celestial crown above thy head, rich in man's estimation, but (ver. 21) a pauper, a bankrupt, towards God."

II. THE MORE GENERAL INSTRUCTION SOUNDS THE WARNING. " Take heed, and keep yourselves from all covetousness." The more *special and private instruction* to the disciples is joined to the preceding parable by a " therefore " (ver. 22). It, too, is an admonition against *worldliness*. It presents that aspect of the worldly spirit which more immediately tempted the disciples of Jesus; it gives also the key-note for that higher life which, as those joined to the Lord, they are called to live. The two parts of the discourse illustrate the meaning of St. Paul's saying as to " the new man created, after God, in righteousness and true holiness [or, 'holiness of truth'] " (Eph. iv. 24). The righteousness which is incumbent on all, from the very nature of their existence and their relation to God and men, is represented in the part already considered; " the holiness of truth "—that *plus* which is because of our place in the body of Christ, and our relation to him as the Head of the body—is represented in the beautiful words which are prefaced by the injunction, " Be not anxious for your life, what ye shall eat, nor yet for your body, what ye shall put on." With some variations, a part of the sermon from the mount is repeated (see homiletics on the sermon). One or two remarks will here suffice. 1. The life which marks the holiness of the new man created in Christ Jesus consists in *a supreme preference* (ver. 31). What distinguishes this life is that it has a " rather " or a " howbeit " at its heart. Its first concern is the kingdom of the Father; its second is (ver. 30) the things which the nations of the world seek after. " These things "—eating, drinking, clothing, etc., have their value. But the mind is not in search of them. They are not its good or portion. Its sympathies and craving are towards the eternally right and true. To realize that in self, and aid its fulfilment everywhere, is the highest aim and object of the being. The property of the soul rich towards God is, indeed, a vast property; but it has heights as well as lengths; it is the threefold estate—" all things are yours, and ye are Christ's, and Christ is God's." The things which the nations of the world seek after are given into the bargain, so to speak, as far as they are necessities, to all who seek the Father's kingdom. 2. For those in whom this life is formed, *a rule is laid down* (ver. 22), " Be not anxious as to these things." The rendering of the Greek word in the Authorized Version might mislead. Christ himself has taught us to take thought for our life—to provide for the morrow. He bade his disciples gather up the fragments, that nothing might be lost. He had a bag, of which Judas was the bearer, from which things needful were purchased. It is a sign of the savage, not the civilized man, to live only for the present hour, wasting what he does not immediately consume. The teaching is that, living the true life, and preferring what is right to what is merely politic, we may reckon on God for the supply of all our need. As to eating and drinking, we will not ask the satiety of abundance, we will ask only sufficiency; and on this we may rely. He who feeds the ravens will not forget those who faithfully serve him (vers. 23, 30). We are to labour constantly and diligently whilst we have strength, to sow and reap, to " provide things honest ; " for labour is God's appointed means of feeding and clothing—as even the raven witnesses, which God feeds, but which yet is ever picking what it can find ; as even the lily witnesses, which is faithful to the conditions of its growth. But we are to toil with a free heart, delivered from carking and worrying care, turning ever trustfully to the love of our Father in heaven. Matthew Henry puts it thus : " As in our stature, so in our state, it is our wisdom to take it as it is, and make the best of it ; for fretting and vexing, carking and caring, will not mend it." " Do not live in suspense ; do not cherish the doubting, doubtful mind," says the Lord to his followers. " Do not fear. A little flock you may seem ; but the shepherding is perfect. Live generously, self-denyingly, self-sacrificingly (ver. 31). The purses which hold good deeds never wax old. The treasure bestowed on that which is out of sight is laid up in the heavens (ver. 33), and no thief can abstract it, and no moth can destroy it. Living in the unseen, in God's kingdom of grace as its subjects, your heart (ver. 34) will settle towards its treasure ; you will be prepared and fitted to be the princes of your Father's kingdom of glory."

HOMILIES BY VARIOUS AUTHORS.

Vers. 2, 3.—*Hidden things.* Our Lord's affirmation implies that there is a great deal which has been long beneath the surface, and we naturally ask—*Does God hide?* And the answer is—Yes, truly, " thou art a God that hidest thyself." He hides his own glory, that we may not be dazzled thereby ; he hides the bliss of the beatified, that we may not be discontented thereby. Like as a father hides from his children many things which they will better learn a little later on, or had better make out for themselves, so God hides many things from us for the very same reasons. But he has so hidden treasures of truth and wisdom from us, that we have every possible inducement to search for them, and full capacity to find them.

I. THE PROVISION MADE FOR OUR TEMPORAL WELFARE. Did he not hide the coal, the copper, the iron, the lead, the silver, the gold, that we might discover, might raise, might refine, might shape them to our use ? And the corn which he gives us to eat, the raiment to wear, the music to enjoy,—these are only to be had by searching, by inquiry, by study, by endeavour. The powers of steam, of electricity, were long hidden from the knowledge of mankind, but they, with the other secrets of the world, are being known.

II. HIS SAVING AND SANCTIFYING TRUTH. Paul speaks much of "the mystery hidden from the generations," *i.e.* God's great purpose to redeem, not a nation from political bondage, but the whole human race from spiritual servitude and degradation ; his purpose to accomplish this by coming to the world in the Person of his Son Jesus Christ. This was hidden in Old Testament promises, and in the Law given by Moses ; it was there, undiscovered by any but a few discerning souls ; and it was "not revealed unto the sons of men " until, enlightened by the Spirit of God, the apostles made known the riches of his grace. There are still some things in connection with Christian doctrine which may be said to be hidden, but which sooner or later will be revealed and known.

III. HUMAN CHARACTER AND HUMAN LIFE. There are depths of secrecy in these human hearts of ours. Evil thoughts may hide there unknown to any but to those that entertain them ; nay, may lurk and work within the soul unsuspected even by that soul itself. For men are both better and worse than they know themselves to be. What purity and gentleness and self-sacrificing love may steal silently through life, and may pass and be forgotten ! what deeds of truest heroism may be wrought which no pen records and no tongue recites ! Yet the wrong shall be exposed, and the right be understood and honoured ; human character shall be read in the light of truth ; the guilty shall be humbled and the upright be exalted "in that day." 1. *Our duty.* It is that of : (1) Exposure. Tear the mask from the hypocrite ; let the covering be torn off the false man, the charlatan, the betrayer of the soul, with a firm and fearless hand ; make him stand out before his fellows stripped of his pretences ; *make* it true that " there is nothing covered," etc. (2) Disclosure. Live to teach, to enlighten, to enlarge.

Let the secret of health, of wisdom, of usefulness, be published on every hand.   Tell all you can reach—the children in the school, the sick by the bedside, the loiterers by the wayside, the congregation in the cottage, or the hall, or the church—the secret of pure and lasting joy, of real and true success.   2. *Our danger.*   Since God *will* cause the hidden things to be known, since he will "bring to light the hidden things of darkness, and make manifest the counsels of all hearts," since he "will judge the secrets of men," well may the guilty shudder, well may we all ask—Who shall abide that solemn hour?   But there is an alternative.   "The blood of Jesus Christ cleanses from all sin."   True penitence and genuine faith will secure for us such a covering that *nothing* shall be revealed.   There is a Divine forgiveness which swallows up and hides for ever the wrong that we have done.   3. *Our hope.*   "And then"—at that day—"shall every man have praise of God;" *i.e.* every man who is, in the true sense, praiseworthy ; every man to whom Christ will be free to say, "I was hungry, and ye gave me meat; for inasmuch," etc.   He who does good "to be seen of men" *has* his reward now; his recompense is exhausted here.   But he who works for Christ and for men in the spirit of his Master has *not* his reward now; he has only a foretaste of it. The best of it has yet to come.   And it will come; for there is nothing hidden that shall not be revealed.   Blessed is the quiet, humble life of unpretending goodness, which is like the silent spring that makes the meadows green ; from such lives as these come deeds of loveliness and usefulness to be made mention of by the lips of the Lord himself, when the things that are covered now shall be revealed, and the things which man overlooks God will own and honour.—C.

Vers. 4, 5.—*The power to hurt and bless.*   We are admonished of—
I. THE POWER WHICH MAN HAS TO HURT US.   1. He can *wound our body.*   He can smite, can wound, can slay us.   The sad story of human persecution contains only too many illustrations of this fact.   2. He can *wound our spirit.*   This is a course he can, and still does very often take; he can mock, can sneer, can indulge in heartless ribaldry, can hold up our most sacred convictions to ridicule, and thus he can inflict on us a very deep wound.   For words, though they may be the slightest, are yet the keenest of weapons, and "a wounded spirit who can bear?"   3. He can *tempt us to evil.*   This is the worst thing he can do ; he can make the evil suggestion, can give the perilous invitation, can make the guilty overture, which leads down to sin and to spiritual failure.   There is no measure of pain he can inflict, or loss he can cause us to suffer, which equals in shamefulness this act of dark temptation.   That is the *deadly* thing to do.
II. THE LIMITATION OF HIS POWER.   Beyond these lines our worst enemies cannot go.   1. No man can *follow us into the unseen realm.*   Beyond the veil we are safe from the questions of the inquisitor, the blows of the tyrant, the suggestions of the tempter.   These may hunt us to very death, but "after that have no more that they can do."   Truly, if this life were the sum of our existence, that would be much indeed —it would be everything.   But since we know that it is not so, but only its first short term, only its initial stage, only its brief introduction, we may console our hearts with the thought that it is no great harm that the strongest potentate, with the sharpest sword, can do us.   2. No man can *compel us to sin.*   A sinful deed includes the consent of the agent ; and all the forces of iniquity and error can never compel a true and brave soul to assent to an evil act.   The only great harm that can be done us is that which we do ourselves when we "consent to sin" when men *tempt* us to sin,—after that there is no more that they can do ; if more is done, if the line is crossed, it is of our own accord ; the tempting is theirs, the sinning is ours.
III. THE ONLY ONE OF WHOM WE HAVE TO BE AFRAID.   "Fear him," etc.; *i.e.* shrink from the disfavour of that Divine Lord of the human spirit who can punish according to our desert.   To shrink from the condemnation of God is not an unworthy act on our part.   It is both right and wise; for his condemnation is that of the Righteous One, and of the Mighty One also.   It is only the guilty that are lost to all sense of obligation, and the foolish that are dead to all sense of prudence, who will be indifferent to the anger of God.   Fear God's solemn displeasure, for if he rebukes it is certain that you are grievously in the wrong; fear it, for if he inflicts penalty there is none to deliver out of his hand, and, what is more, even death, that *does* deliver from the hand

of man, is no shield from his power. Beyond the veil we are as much within his reach as we are on this side of it. There is every reason why we should seek and find his Divine favour, and live in the light of his countenance. We may go on in our thought, and be reminded by our Lord's words of—

IV. THE ONE WHOSE FRIENDSHIP WE SHOULD SEEK. "I say unto you, *my friends*." We do not simply want to escape the wrath of an offended Judge; we aspire to his favour and his love. Jesus Christ is offering us his friendship (see John xv. 14, 15). If we will cordially accept him for all that he desires to be to us, we shall find in him the Friend in whom we shall implicitly confide, whom we shall gladly and happily love, by whose side and in the shelter of whose guardian care we shall walk all the way till the gates of home are reached.—C.

Vers. 8, 9.—*Confessing Christ.* From these solemn words we gather—

I. THAT CHRISTIANITY CENTRES IN THE PERSON OF JESUS CHRIST. Our Lord taught us much concerning *ourselves*—the inestimable value of our spiritual nature; the real source and spring of evil in our own souls; the true excellency of a human life; whom we should regard as our neighbour, etc. But he taught us still more of *himself*—of his relations with the Divine Father; of his essential superiority even to the greatest among mankind; of his sorrow and his death on behalf of the human race; of his mission to enlighten, to redeem, to satisfy the souls of men. And he not only affirmed, but frequently and emphatically urged, the doctrine that, if we would enter into life, we must come into the very closest personal relation with himself—trusting in him, loving him, abiding in him, following him, making him Refuge of the heart, Sovereign of the soul, Lord of the life. Not his truth, but himself, is the Source of our strength and our hope.

II. THAT JESUS CHRIST DEMANDS AN OPEN CONFESSION OF OUR FAITH IN HIM. More than once (see Mark viii. 38) he insisted upon a clear recognition of his authority and regal position. He will have us "confess him before men." How shall we do that? 1. In a heathen country, by avowing the Christian faith, renouncing Hinduism, Buddhism, Confucianism, etc., and declaring before all that Jesus Christ is the one Teacher of truth and Lord of man. 2. In a Christian country, by making it clear that we have accepted him as the Lord whom we are living to serve. We shall probably think it right to do this by attaching ourselves to some particular Christian community ; also by regular, public worship of Christ ; but certainly, in all cases, (1) by paying honour to his Name; (2) by upholding against his enemies the truth and worth of his religion; (3) by translating his will into active human life in all its departments— domestic, social, commercial, political, ecclesiastical.

III. THAT COMPLIANCE WITH HIS DEMAND WILL SOON PROVE TO BE AN ACT OF THE FIRST IMPORTANCE. The day draws on when we shall meet our Master : then will he tell us what he thinks of us. Then, if we have failed to honour him, he will refuse to honour us "before the angels of God." What is involved in that denial? The worst of all exclusions—exclusion from the favour, from the home, of God. And then, if we have honoured him, he will acknowledge us as his own. And what will that include? 1. Acceptance with the Judge of all. 2. The expression of his Divine approval—the "well done" of the Lord. 3. Admission to the heavenly kingdom, with all its advancing glory, its deepening joy, its extending influence, its enlarging life.—C.

Ver. 15.—*A man's life.* What is the worth of a man's life? Clearly that does not depend merely on *duration*. For while to the insect the term of seventy years would seem a most noble expanse, on the other hand, compared with the age of a mountain or the duration of a star, it is an insignificant span. The truth is that the value of human life depends on *what is done within its boundaries*. Here quality is of the chief account. To the insensible stone all the ages are as nothing ; to the dormant animal time is of no measurable value. To a thinking, sensitive spirit, with a great capacity for joy and sorrow, one half-hour may hold an inestimable measure of blessedness or of woe. There are three things it may include ; we take them in the order of value, beginning at the least.

I. HAVING WHAT IS GOOD. "The things which a man possesseth" are of value to him. "Money is a defence," and it is also an acquisition, for it stands for all those necessaries and comforts, all those physical, social and intellectual advantages which it will buy. But it is a miserable delusion—a delusion which has slain the peace and prospects of many a thousand souls—that the one way to secure the excellency of life is to gain amplitude of material resources. 1. Muchness of money does not even ensure human happiness. The wealth that lives in fine houses and sits down to sumptuous tables and moves in "good circles" is very often indeed carrying with it a heavy heart, a burdened spirit, an unsatisfied soul. This is not the imagination of envy; it is the confession of sorrowful experience, uttered by many voices, witnessed by many lives. 2. Muchness of money does not constitute the *excellency of human life*. In a country where "business" means as much as it does in England, we are under a strong temptation to think that to have grown very rich is, *by so doing*, to have succeeded. That is a *part* of some men's success; but it does not *constitute* success in any man's life. A man may be enormously rich, and yet he may be an utter and pitiable failure. "In every society, and especially in a country like our own, there are those who derive their chief characteristics from what they have; who are always spoken of in terms of revenue, and of whom you would not be likely to think much but for the large account that stands in the ledger in their name. . . . So completely do they paint the idea of their life on the imagination of all who knew them, that, when they die, it is the fate of the money, not of the man, of which we are apt to think. Having put vast prizes in the funds, but only unprofitable blanks in our affections, they leave behind nothing but their property, or, as it is expressly termed, their effects. Their human personality hangs as a mere label upon a mass of treasure" (Dr. Martineau). A *man's life* should rise higher than that.

II. DOING WHAT IS JUST AND KIND. Far better is it to *do* the just and kind action than to *have* that which is pleasant and desirable. Life rises into real worth when it is spent in honourable and fruitful action. In sustaining right and useful relationships in the great world of business, carrying out our work on principles of righteousness and equity; in ruling the home firmly and kindly; in espousing the cause of the weak, the ignorant, the perishing; in striking some blows for national integrity and advancement —in such a healthful, honourable, elevating action as this "a man's life" is found. But this, in its turn, must rest on—

III. BEING WHAT IS RIGHT. For "out of the heart are the issues of life." Men may do a large number of good things, and yet be "nothing" in the sight of heavenly wisdom (see 1 Cor. xiii. 1—3). The one true mainspring of a worthy human life is "the love of God which is in Christ Jesus our Lord." To love God, and therefore to love all that is good; to love God, and therefore to interest ourselves in and try to help all those who are so nearly related to him; to love God, and therefore to be moving on and up in an ever-ascending line toward Divine wisdom and worth;—this is the one victorious and successful thing. Without this, "a man's life" is a defeat and a failure, hold what it may; with it, it has the beginnings of a true success—it is already, and will be more than it now is, *eternal life.*—C.

Ver. 20.—*Sudden death.* The parable which Jesus Christ delivered in rebuke of covetousness puts in striking and even startling form the facts on which God's providence requires us to look. For we know—

I. THAT SUDDEN DEATH IS AN EVENT WHICH MAY OCCUR TO ANY ONE OF US. Human science has done much for us; and much in the direction of preserving and prolonging life. It has given to us a considerable knowledge of disease, and therefore an increased sense of danger. But it has not *materially* diminished the fact of a sudden and unanticipated end of our mortal life. It is probable that with the advance of civilization and the growing intricacies, complications, and obligations of human life, diseases of the heart have increased, and it is quite open to doubt whether sudden death is less frequent than it was. Certainly it is an ordinary rather than an extraordinary event. It is probable that these two words will be found at the head of at least one paragraph in any newspaper we may chance to be reading. Little as we realize it, it is a stern fact that it is quite possible that any man, enjoying the most robust health and in the midst of the most pressing and weighty duties, may be dead within the day on which we speak to him; that to this possibility there is absolutely no exception. Just now life may be to us and to those related to us of the greatest value; there may be a thousand reasons why, as it seems to us and to them, our life should be spared; and yet it may be of us that the word is passed in that realm where there is none to hinder, "This night thy soul shall be required of thee." It may be very trite, but it is most seriously true, that sudden death may come to any one *of us*.

II. THAT SOME SUDDENNESS IN DEATH IS AN EXPERIENCE WE ARE ALL LIKELY TO SHARE. Few remarks are more often made than that death was "sudden at the last." Even the sick man thinks that he will live; that there are months, or at least weeks, before him. They who are clearly and even loudly admonished, either by serious illness or by advanced age, that their end is drawing on will think and talk of the days that are coming, of the things they will accomplish. It is usually with a start of surprise that the patient learns from his attendant that he must die. Such is our human nature that, even when death comes gradually and kindly, the Master's words are applicable: "In such an hour as ye think not, the Son of man cometh."

III. THAT AMIDST HUMAN UNCERTAINTIES WE MAY HOLD FAST SOME DIVINE AND EVER-LIVING TRUTHS. 1. That it matters little whether our life be long or short, if only it be given to the service of Christ. Our Lord died a young man, and the term of his active public life is counted by months rather than by years; but what did he achieve! 2. That temporal success is not the true or the wise aim to set before the soul. There are far higher things we can do, and therefore should do; besides, our material achievements and possessions may be taken from our grasp at any hour. 3. That the right and wise course to take is to be ready for death whenever it may come. Readiness for death will secure us a true peace when the hour of trial arrives; it will also give us calmness of spirit, and therefore capacity for service and for pure enjoyment in the midst of life.—C.

Ver. 21.—"*Rich toward God*." Jesus Christ is here drawing a contrast between the inward and the abiding on the one hand, and the outward and the perishing on the other hand. When he disparages the act of "laying up treasure for ourselves," he does not mean to say either (1) that *material wealth* is not of God, for it is he who gives us "power to get wealth" (Deut. viii. 18); or (2) that the *spiritual treasure* a man secures is not "for himself,"—indeed, that is the only treasure he can make permanently his own; he that is wise is wise for himself (Prov. ix. 12), and he has "rejoicing in himself alone, and not in another." But Christ would have us regard material acquisitions as of very small account indeed in comparison with the enrichment of the soul in God, with spiritual wealth. To be rich toward God may include—

I. A WEALTH OF RIGHT FEELING TOWARD GOD. There are certain thoughts and feelings which every intelligent being ought to cherish toward his Creator, in the absence of which he himself is poor, and in the presence of which he is rich. The more we have in our hearts of reverence for God; of trust in his Word of promise; of gratitude for his goodness and faithfulness; of love for him, our Father and our Saviour; of filial submission to his holy will; of consecration to his cause and interest in the advancement of his kingdom,—the more "rich we are toward" him.

II. WEALTH IN QUALITIES WHICH ARE DIVINE, or being rich in the direction in which God himself is rich. We cannot, indeed, hope to be rich in some of his attributes—in majesty, in power, in wisdom. But there are qualities in him in which we may have a real and a valuable share. As God is rich in righteousness, in truth and faithfulness, in goodness and kindness, in mercy and magnanimity, so may we hope, and so should we strive and pray, that we may be "partakers of the Divine nature" in these things also. Illumined by his truth, guided by his example, and inspired by his Spirit, we may have a goodly share in these great and noble qualities.

III. WEALTH IN GOD HIMSELF; in the enjoyment of his Divine favour and friendship; in the indwelling of his Holy Spirit in our souls, being thus enriched with his abiding presence and his gracious influence; in the enlarging and elevating contemplation of his character and worship of himself. 1. *Have we any treasure at all in God?* As the Church at Laodicea imagined itself to be spiritually rich when it was miserably poor (Rev. iii. 17), so may any Christian society of our own time; so may any individual member of a Church of Christ. If, in a searching and devout examination, we find that we are poor, there is nothing for us but to go to Jesus Christ anew, in humblest penitence and simplest faith and whole-hearted surrender. 2. *Are we rich toward God?* There are many degrees between beggary and wealth. We may not be absolutely destitute, and yet we may be far from *rich* toward God. We should aspire to "abound," to "be enlarged," to have a good measure of those qualities which constitute spiritual wealth. We must "buy of Christ" (Rev. iii. 18), that we "may be rich;" we must abide in him, and so "bring forth much fruit" (John xv. 5). 3. If we are rich toward God *we may thankfully rejoice.* The man who is "laying up treasure for himself" may be essentially and radically poor; he may be securing that which will give him no happiness, but only be a burden and a bane to him; he must part with it all soon. But he who is "rich toward God" has that which is wealth indeed; has a treasure which will gladden his heart and brighten his life; has a joy and an inheritance which are his for ever.—C.

Vers. 22—30.—*Anxiety or trustfulness?* We read of "care-encumbered men;" and truly we see more than we could wish of them. As we look into the faces of those we meet daily, we are saddened with the thought that a great weight of care rests on our race as a heavy burden. And when we see, as we do, a few faces that wear the look of a sweet serenity born of holy trust in God, we ask—Is it necessary that such an oppressive burden should be borne by the children of men? Jesus Christ answers this question in the negative. He says that anxiety is quite needless to the children of God; he says, "*Trust and rest;* believe in God, and be at peace; recognize the power and the love of your heavenly Father, and do not be 'greatly moved' by temporal necessities." And he reasons with us on the subject; he desires to prove to us the needlessness of anxiety in the presence of such a God and Father as is he whom we worship. He argues this—

1. FROM GOD'S GREATER KINDNESS TO OURSELVES. (Ver. 23.) Any one of our friends who would do us a very great kindness would certainly be prepared to render us a very small favour. To one who has done us a valuable service we should look with perfect confidence to do some slight office for us. The love which is equal to the one will be more than equal to the other. Now, God has given us life, and has been sustaining us in being by his constant visitation; he has given us our wonderfully constituted body, and he has been preserving it in health and strength for years. Will he who has conferred these great boons upon us withhold from us blessings so simple and so slight as food and raiment? "Is not the life more than meat [food], and the body than raiment?" Will he who grants the greater refuse the less?

II. FROM GOD'S CARE OF THINGS THAT ARE OF LESS ACCOUNT THAN WE ARE. (Vers. 24, 27, 28.) "Consider the ravens"—birds of the air, creatures that are interesting in their degree, but unintelligent, unaccountable, perishable: God feeds *them.* "Consider the lilies, how they grow;" they do nothing for their clothing; and not only are they unintelligent and irresponsible like the birds, but they are unconscious, insentient *things;* yet they are exquisitely fair: God clothes *them.* If he takes thought for such creatures and for such things as these; if he concerns himself with that which is so much lower in the scale than are we, his own beloved children, created in his image and formed to share his own immortality, how certain it is that he will provide for us! The Divine wisdom that expends so much upon the lower will not neglect the higher.

III. THE COMPLETENESS OF OUR DEPENDENCE ON GOD. (Ver. 25.) So completely are we in the hands of our Creator that we cannot, by any amount of thinking, "add one cubit to our stature." Do what we may, try what we can, we are still absolutely dependent on God. It rests with him to decide what shall be the length of our days, what shadow or sunshine shall fall on our path, whether our cup shall be sweet or bitter. We are in his Divine hands; let us be his servants; let us ask his guidance and blessing; and then let us trust ourselves to his power and his love. And this the more that we should remember—

IV. THE UNWORTHINESS OF GREAT CONCERN FOR SUCH TEMPORALITIES. To be greatly troubled about what we shall eat, or what we shall wear, or in what house we shall live,—this is pagan, but it is not Christian; leave that to "the nations of the world" (ver. 30).

V. THE RELATION IN WHICH GOD STANDS TO US. (Ver. 30.) This is that of an all-wise Father. "Our Father knows." We are in the power of One who is perfectly acquainted with our circumstances and with ourselves; he will not deny us anything we need because he is ignorant of our necessity; he will not give us anything that would be hurtful, for his fatherly love will constrain him to withhold it. We are immeasurably safer in his hands than we should be in those of the kindest of our human friends, or than we should be if it rested with our own will to shape our path, to fill our cup.—C.

Ver. 31.—*Service and sufficiency.* It has been much debated whether God should be represented as the Sovereign or the Father of mankind. It has been but a foolish strife; it has been another case in which both disputants have been right and both wrong. God *is* the Sovereign of the world, and a great deal more than that; God *is* the Father of men, and a great deal beside. He is a royal Father, or a fatherly King. The Lord's Prayer might have taught us this: "Our Father . . . thy kingdom come." God is to us all and much more than all *both* these human relationships represent, only that one presents him in one aspect and the other in another. Here Christ invites us to think of him as a Sovereign; and we look at—

I. THE KINGDOM OF GOD, of which we may become citizens. "Seek ye [the citizenship of] the kingdom of God." Jesus Christ launched a perfectly new idea when he spoke of this kingdom. In his mind that was nothing less than a universal spiritual empire; a kingdom of peace, righteousness, and joy, wide as the world and lasting as time; a kingdom to be established without forming a regiment, or shaping a sword, or fashioning a crown; a kingdom of God, in which all men of every land and tongue should own him as their rightful Sovereign, should cheerfully obey his righteous laws, should dwell together in holiness and in love.

II. THE ALLEGIANCE WHICH IS OUR SACRED DUTY. Christ summons us to citizenship. He says imperatively, "Seek ye the kingdom;" and he bids us seek entrance into it "rather" than pursue any earthly objects, rather than be anxiously concerning ourselves about temporal supplies. He indicates that this is something which has the first claim on our thought and on our endeavour. And so, indeed, it has. For God is that King (1) without the exercise of whose sovereign power there would be no other kingdom, no subjects, no liberties, no riches, no honours, in fact, no being; (2) to be disloyal to whom is the lowest depth of ingratitude, is the deliberate abandonment of the most bounden duty, the guilty severance of the most sacred tie. Being what he is to all men, and having done what he has wrought for all men, he rightly demands of us, through Jesus Christ, our fealty, our loyal service. To respond to this summons of the Saviour and to become citizens of the kingdom of God, we must offer him something more than the honour of the bended knee, or the tribute of the acclaiming voice, or the service of the dutiful hand; we must bring the homage of the reverent spirit, the affection of the loving heart, the submission of the acquiescent will. And out of this inward and spiritual loyalty will proceed the praises of the tongue and the obedience of the life. Seeking the kingdom means a real returning of soul unto God and a consequent devoting of the rest of our life to his service.

III. CHRIST'S PROMISE OF SUFFICIENCY to all loyal subjects. "All these things shall be added unto you." It is well for the world that there is not attached to the service of Christ any very valuable and attractive treasures which are of this earth. If there were, we should have the Church choked with insincere and worldly minded members, paying as little devotion as they thought necessary for as much enjoyment and prosperity as they could reap. Christ has mercifully saved us from this calamity; but he has not found it needful to leave us without a provision for our need. 1. He has made present happiness an attendant upon virtue, and virtue is an appanage of piety. 2. But he has given us a promise and a pledge in our text. He assures to those who enter his holy kingdom not, indeed, luxury, not a large measure of prosperity and enjoyment on an earthly ground, but *sufficiency.* They who yield themselves to him and who live in his service may be well assured that they will want "no good thing;" nothing that would really make for their well-being will he withhold. All resources are at his disposal, and he will see that his children are supplied. (1) Let none be kept out of the kingdom because they dread social or pecuniary evils; God will shield and save them. (2) Let none who are in the kingdom despond, though circumstances are against them; at the right moment God will appear on their behalf; "goodness and mercy will follow them all the days of their life," and attend them right up to the gates of the heavenly city.—C.

Vers. 35—40.—*Death a Divine visitation.* To us the coming of the Son of man means the hour of death; that is the practical view and therefore the wise view of the subject. And we may well regard our departure from this world as a coming of God to us.

I. DEATH AS A DIVINE VISITATION. 1. At death God comes to us all in judgment. Death is the appointed penalty of sin. It is true that the burden of that penalty is spiritual rather than material, and that God grants us a kind reprieve before he executes it; but still, in conformity with it, the accidents of death have to occur to us; that ancient sentence has to be fulfilled; the shadows of the last hour must fall around us; and whenever and however that may happen, with whatever mitigations, God will come to us then in solemn penalty, saying, "My child, thou hast sinned, and thou must die." 2. At death God comes to us in providence. (1) God has given to us a perishable frame, one that is only constructed to last for a term of years, that after a certain point begins to waste and wane. (2) He suffers, if he does not send, the special circumstances which lead up to death; at the least, he withholds the interposing act or suggestion which would prolong the life that is taken. Man never "goes to his long home" but we may say, "Thou turnest man to destruction; and sayest, Return, ye children of men." On each such occasion the Son of man comes and says, "Put off thy tabernacle, and come within the veil." 3. At death Christ comes to us in sacred summons. In life God's voice should be daily heard saying, "Put out those powers; use those opportunities; cultivate that spiritual nature I have entrusted to thee; serve thy brethren; glorify my Name." But at death Christ comes to us and summons us to his presence; then we hear him say, "Give account of thy stewardship;" "Reap what thou hast sown."

II. READINESS FOR DEATH A PART OF HUMAN WISDOM. "Let your loins be girded about . . . be like men that wait for their Lord . . . the Son of man cometh at an hour when ye think not." 1. It is true that there is usually less suddenness than there seems in cases of sudden death; on inquiry, it is nearly always found that there were premonitory signs of danger, kindly warnings from the Author of our nature, that the end was not far off. 2. But it is also and equally true that death is unexpected when it does arrive. (1) So do we cling to life, that we are not willing to acknowledge concerning ourselves the fact which is obvious to every one else respecting us. (2) It is our mental habit to expect continuance where we ought to look for severance and cessation. The oftener we have crossed the decaying and breaking bridge, the more confidently we do cross it, though we know well that it is nearer than ever to its fall. We may be almost sure that, in whatever form and at whatever hour the Son of man comes to us, we shall be surprised at his appearance. 3. It will be a terrible thing to be unready; to have to do, if we can, in a few brief hours that for which a long life is not a day too long. 4. It will be a blessed thing to be ready for this vision of our Lord; not merely, nor chiefly, because we shall thus be enabled to cross, with calm hopefulness, into the other country, but because we shall then be ready for those high services and celestial honours which our gracious and generous Master intends to confer upon us (ver. 37).—C.

Vers. 49, 50.—*Spiritual strenuousness.* Our Lord's life deepened and enlarged as it proceeded, like a great and fertilizing river. And as conflict became more frequent and severe, and as the last scenes drew on, his own feeling was quickened, his spirit was aflame with a more ardent and intense emotion. We look at the subject of spiritual strenuousness—

I. IN VIEW OF OUR LORD'S PERSONAL EXPERIENCE. In these two verses we find him passing through some moments of very intense feeling; he was powerfully affected by two considerations. 1. *A compassionate desire* on behalf of the world. He came to the world to kindle a great fire which should be a light to *illumine*, a heat to *cleanse*, a flame to *consume*. Such would be the Divine truth of which he came to be the Author, especially as it was made operative by the Divine Spirit whose coming should be so intimately associated with and should immediately follow his life-work (see ch. iii. 16; Acts ii. 3). As he looked upon the gross and sad darkness which that light was so much needed to dissipate, upon the errors that heat was so much required to purify, upon the corruption that flame was so essential to extinguish, his holy and loving spirit yearned with a profound and vehement desire for the hour to come when these heavenly forces should be prepared and be freed to do their sacred and blessed work. 2. *A human longing to pass through the trial* that awaited him. " *But* "—there was not only an interval of time to elapse, there was a period of solemn struggle to be gone through, before that fire would be kindled. There was a baptism of sorrow and of conflict for himself to undergo, and how was he " straitened " in spirit until that was accomplished! Here was the feeling of a son of man, but it was the feeling of the noblest of the children of men. He did not desire that it should be postponed; he longed for it to come that it might be passed through, that the battle might be fought, that the anguish might be borne. Truly this is none other than a holy human spirit with whom we have to do; one like unto ourselves, in the depth of whose nature were these very hopes and fears, these same longings and yearnings which, in the face of a dread future, stir our own souls with strongest agitations. How solemn, how great, how fearful, must that future have been which so profoundly and powerfully affected his calm and reverent spirit!

II. IN VIEW OF OUR OWN SPIRITUAL STRUGGLES. We cannot do anything of very great account unless we know something of that spiritual strenuousness of which our Lord knew so much. 1. We should show this in our concern for the condition of the world. How much are we affected by the savagery, by the barbarism, by the idolatry, by the vice, by the godlessness, by the selfishness, which prevail on the right hand and on the left? How eagerly and earnestly do we desire that the enlightenment and the purification of Christian truth should be carried into the midst of it? Does our desire rise to a holy, Christ-like ardour? Does it manifest itself in becoming generosity, in appropriate service and sacrifice? 2. We may show this in our anxiety to pass through the trial-hour that awaits us. Whether it be the hour of approaching service, or sorrow, or persecution, or death, we *may*, like our Master, be straitened until it be come and gone. Let us see that, like him, we (1) await it in calm trustfulness of spirit; and (2) prepare for it by faithful witness and close communion with God in the hours that lead up to it.—C.

Ver. 57.—*Individual responsibility.* " Why even of yourselves judge ye not what is right?" Those to whom our Lord was speaking were men of intelligence, education, religious privilege. They exercised their mental faculties with great keenness on some subjects (vers. 54, 55): why could they not recognize the supreme fact of their time, viz. that the Messiah was before them (ver. 56)? why did they not employ their powers to discern between the false and the true, between the evil and the good?

I. THAT WE MAY NOT DEVOLVE OUR ACCOUNTABILITY FOR HOLDING THE TRUTH on any one or any body of men. It has not been merely " the *right* of private judgment " which has been in question, which some have striven so hard to withhold, and which others have suffered so much to obtain or to preserve. It has been the sacred *duty* of determining for ourselves what is the mind and the will of God, the solemn obligation to put into use the talents he has committed to our care. We are to discharge this duty under all circumstances and whoever may propose to relieve us of it. We may not delegate it: 1. To *the State*. The State may prescribe Islamism in one region, Confucianism in another, Catholicism in a third; but we are not at liberty to make our religious creed depend on the latitude and longitude where we reside. 2. To *the Church;* or Jesus Christ himself would have been criminal, for he entirely disregarded the decision of the " council," and the Christian Church has, in its collective capacity, spoken differently in different times and places. 3. To *society;* that is frequently at fault. 4. To *the parent*. For a time this is necessary, right, becoming, praiseworthy; but the time comes when the son must no longer shield himself behind his filial obedience, he must think and must decide for himself. If we are possessed of ordinary human powers and privileges we must " of ourselves judge what is right." It is a solemn burden, a sacred duty, which our Creator has laid on each human spirit he has called into being.

II. THAT GOD HAS GIFTED US WITH A SPIRITUAL NATURE for this very purpose. He has endowed us with *reason*, or with that faculty which intuitively perceives the great and deep truths which are presented to it; with *conscience*, the faculty which commends and condemns, filling with inward joy or inward pain; with *judgment*, the faculty that compares and concludes, and arrives at just decisions as to the thing that should be done, the way that should be taken. It is, indeed, only too true that a long course of sin will warp and degrade this spiritual nature of ours; but where there is as much enlightenment as the Jews of our Lord's time had, and as we ourselves possess, we ought to be able by its means "to judge what is right."

III. THAT THE HEALTHFUL ACTION OF OUR SPIRITUAL NATURE IS ONE LARGE PART OF OUR PROBATION. If "the light that is in us be darkness," if our conscience is misdirecting us, it is because we have been wrong, it is because we have not been true to ourselves. Sin has weakened or even distorted our faculty of spiritual discernment. But if we are true to ourselves, if we (1) honestly seek to know what the will of God is concerning ourselves and others; (2) faithfully endeavour to do what we believe to be his will; (3) earnestly ask for Divine guidance in our pursuit of wisdom;—we shall be "led into the truth." We may not see everything in the light in which other true-hearted people see it, but we shall recognize those great leading truths which bring us into right relation to God, which constrain us to take a right attitude toward our brethren, which light up our earthly path and conduct us to our home. 1. We may not refuse our responsibility under any plea, not even that of humility. It would be pleasant to say, "We will leave to others who can do it better the work of deciding what is true, which message is from God, which path leads heavenwards." But we may not say this without declining the sacred duty our heavenly Father devolves on each one of his children. 2. Accepting our post as truth-seekers, we must do our work conscientiously, thoroughly, without prejudice. 3. We may be sure that Christ will grant us all the Divine aid we need if we honestly endeavour and devoutly pray.—C.

Vers. 58, 59.—*The inexorable.* From the lips of such a parabolic teacher as Jesus Christ we expect to have some striking illustration of a general principle, our duty being to detect that principle and to make our own practical applications of it. Here the great Teacher adduces an illustration drawn from the legal practice of his time; the general truth underlying it is evidently this—that *law* is a *rigorous* thing, a broken law a terribly exacting thing; that, if we are in any danger of coming under its power, we should refrain from so doing with the greatest carefulness; that, if we do not act thus prudently, we must be prepared to pay a very heavy penalty a little way on. The principle applies to—

I. A BREACH OF THE LAW OF PEACE. We are here in this world to sustain toward one another interesting and important relationships. It is the will of God that, in all of these, we should be actuated by the spirit and be ruled by the law of love, of kindness, of charity, of peace. But in this world of sin the Divine Law is continually broken, and the broken Law exacts a terrible penalty. What wretched homes it makes! what lamentable feuds in families! what miserable ruptures of friendship! what deplorable contentions even in Christian Churches! what social dissensions! what national and international strife! The violated law of love exacts "the uttermost farthing" from those who break it. Christ's word of wisdom is this—Look to it at once; do not lose a day; fill up that little crack; tear up that small root; let everything, even devotion itself (Matt. v. 24), give place to the sacred work of reconciliation; do your best, your quickest, your utmost, to heal the breach before it widens into a gulf, or the slight difference, the small suspicion, the trivial offence will grow and deepen, and hearts that once were the home of trust and love will become the haunts of doubt and enmity. Therefore agree with thine adversary *quickly.* The same principle applies to—

II. A BREACH OF THE LAW OF VIRTUE. We owe it to ourselves to be temperate, truthful, pure, industrious; we owe it to others to be just, fair, kind, considerate; we are under law to be all this—the sacred Law of God. This Law we break, and it becomes our "adversary;" it arraigns us as its debtors, and it makes us pay the penalty that is due. *And what a penalty!* In the *body*—disease, pain, weakness, shattered nerves, death; in *circumstances*—loss, poverty, beggary; in *reputation*—humiliation and disgrace; in *heart*—compunction, agony of soul; in *character*—deterioration, baseness, ruin. Christ says, "Beware of the first step; if tempted to violate any law of virtue of any kind, consider what you will have to pay a little further on; think how that broken law will rise against you and condemn you, and you will not escape until the last farthing has been paid." If there should be any breach, however minute it may be, hasten to repair it.

III. A BREACH OF THE LAW OF PRIVILEGE. Privilege and peril, opportunity and obligation go together, like substance and shadow; they cannot be dissociated. From those to whom much is given will much be required (see vers. 47, 48). It is a constant law, and its violation will be rigorously attended with penalty. If we neglect our privilege, if we abuse our opportunity, we must expect "many stripes," the uttermost farthing of condemnation and retribution. We are the firstborn children of privilege; ours is the dispensation, the period, the land, the home of privilege. Ill will it fare with us if we pass on to the last tribunal and stand before the great Judge, not having repaired this breach, not having sought and found forgiveness for this great transgression.—C.

Vers. 1—12.—*A call to courage.* The commotion between the scribes and Pharisees and our Lord seems to have increased his audiences, as we find "an innumerable multitude," as the Authorized Version has it, or "the many thousands of the multitude," as the Revised has it, treading on one another in eagerness to hear him. And his subject at this time is important—a denunciation of Pharisaic hypocrisy and a call to courage under their certain opposition. And here we have to notice—

I. THE CURE FOR HYPOCRISY. (Vers. 1—3.) Our Lord brings this out in a distinct revelation that everything is yet to be dragged into the light of day. These are his words: "There is nothing covered ['covered up,' Revised Version], that shall not be revealed; neither hid, that shall not be known." There is nothing in nature which would lead us to such a wonderful truth; it is a matter of distinct revelation. Everything, it appears, is constructed on the *public* principle. We are all living *public lives* if we only knew it. All attempts at secrecy are destined to prove failures; consequently, hypocrisy is a mistake. It can impose only for a time; sooner or later it will be exposed and despised. Hence our Lord recommends the people to speak, if they have to do so, in the darkness only what they are willing should be heard in the light, and to whisper in closets only such things as may be proclaimed on the housetops. By God's arrangement secrecy is impossible, and publicity the inevitable destiny of all and of everything. It is consequently this persuasion of ultimate publicity which constitutes the Divine remedy for hypocrisy. All hypocrisy proceeds from forgetfulness or disbelief of this.

II. THE EXPULSIVE POWER OF GODLY FEAR. (Vers. 4, 5.) Our Lord wishes to guard the people from the leaven of the Pharisees, which is hypocrisy, and also from cowardly fear of Pharisaic opposition. Accordingly, he points out that the Pharisees could at the very most kill the body; they have, after that, "no more that they can do." But there is another One who can cast into "Gehenna" after he hath killed, and him they should fear. We discard the idea suggested by Stier and others that this is the devil; especially as courage is not likely to be created by substituting, for fear of diabolical men, the fear of the devil himself. This would be a poor basis for the martyr-spirit. We believe that the fear of man is to be expelled and supplanted by the fear of God, who can consign the soul to Gehenna after death. And our Lord shows here that the fear of God begins in *dread* of his infinite power. No soul, we suppose, ever turns to God without passing through this stage, however brief may be the sojourn in it. God's vaster power makes the hostile power of mere men appear trifling, and we wisely resolve to have men for our enemies rather than God. But once this sense of God's great power has overcome our craven fear of man, we begin to realize that we may have all his power on our side. He will pardon us and take us under his protection, and enable us to fear no evil. Godly fear, consequently, gets modified in our experience, and passes from slavish fear and dread into reverential and filial fear of God as an almighty Father.

III. GOD'S MICROSCOPIC AND PRESENT PROVIDENCE. (Vers. 6, 7.) The sparrows may be cheap in man's estimation—five for two farthings—but "not one of them is forgotten before God." He caters for them. His providence is minute enough to take them under his wings. Men ought, therefore, to take courage from the assurance that, in God's sight, they "are of more value than many sparrows." And God's oversight is so microscopic that he counts the very hairs of our head. Hence the contest with their Pharisaic and worldly foes is to be conducted under the sweet assurance that greater is he who is for them than all who are against them, and that his care is so minute as to extend to the numbering of the hairs of their head. A great Being on our side, so minute and careful in his interest, is fit to inspire with dauntless courage every one who realizes his presence by faith and trusts him.

IV. THE IMPORTANCE OF CONFESSING CHRIST. (Vers. 8, 9.) Our Lord further shows how important it is to confess him; but in the other life there is to be another confession—the confession before the angels of the courageous souls who have confessed Christ here. On the other hand, there is to be a denial of the cowards who denied Christ here. Out of the publicity of the future life, therefore, our Lord draws such considerations as are fitted to rally souls around him in courageous confession. And there can be no doubt that this great publicity which our Lord locates in the future life is a fountain-head of courage for souls struggling with opposition. The highest type of courage can undoubtedly be produced through the doctrine of a future life with its rewards and punishments.

V. THE DANGER OF BLASPHEMY AGAINST THE HOLY GHOST. (Ver. 10.) The introduction of the Holy Ghost in connection with the Pharisaic opposition seems to have been suggested in this way: the Pharisees, not content with libelling and defaming Christ, professed to trace his power over demons to its source. This, they asserted, was not the Holy Ghost, but Beelzebub within him. That is to say, they attributed spiritual results to a diabolic origin. In this way they blasphemed the Holy Ghost. Now, our Lord, in his meekness and lowliness of mind, declares that there is forgiveness for unfair words against *him*, but warns those who are misinterpreting the Spirit's work, that blasphemy against him if continued cannot be forgiven. Now, this subject of the unpardonable sin has given rise to much discussion, but, perhaps, the best view is that adopted by such men as Stier, Tholuck, Olshausen, Hahn, Julius Muller, and Hoffmann—" an internal state of the highest sinfulness which cannot be changed, and shows itself in speech or action, resisting or deliberately setting the soul against the influences of the Holy Ghost." Its practical value is immense. It should lead every thoughtful soul to guard against all trifling with or grieving of the good Spirit whose agency within us alone secures the victory over evil. The Pharisees were treading on the confines of the terrible sin in their denunciation of Christ, and the multitude Christ was addressing and all who have the offer of spiritual help should guard against all offence offered to the all-important Spirit.

VI. THE INSPIRATIONS TO BE EXPECTED FROM THE GOOD SPIRIT. (Vers. 11, 12.) The calumniated Spirit would sustain the confessors of Christ before their enemies, so that all the tried men had got to do was to rely on his inspirations, and they would never fail them. The Holy Ghost would prompt such words and thoughts as would secure on their part a good confession. And a similar aid is to be expected by all Christ's witnesses as they confront the world. If we but rely on his help, he will never fail us. Of course, this does not encourage idleness and want of preparation for the emergencies of life. The Spirit is more likely to inspire a studious, careful, prayerful man than a self-reliant idler. But reliance on the Spirit's inspirations must never be rendered needless or doubtful by any prudent forethought we entertain. We are to be organs of the Spirit, and ought to act worthy of our high calling.—R. M. E.

Vers. 13—21.—*A warning against covetousness.* Amid the important teaching of our Lord there comes an interlude by reason of a brother, who had been wronged out of his share of the inheritance, appealing for redress to Christ. He wanted our Lord to play the part of a small attorney and get conveyed to him some share. This our Lord deliberately declines to do, indicating that he has come into the world for higher work than worldly arbitration. This aspect of the subject has been well handled by Robertson of Brighton, and, following him, by Bersier of Paris.[1] But our Lord does far better for the poor brother than if he had become arbitrator for him. He warns him against covetousness, and indicates that " a man's life consisteth not in the abundance of the things which he possesseth." To back up the lesson, he relates a parable about a certain rich man whose whole concern was to multiply his possessions, but who is surprised by death while doing so. He leaves his wealth behind him, and enters the other world utterly poor. If by this timely warning our Lord succeeds in

---

[1] Robertson's 'Sermons,' second series, p. 1; and Bersier's 'Sermons,' tome iv. p. 3.

leading the claimant to the possession of better riches, then all will be well. And here we notice—

I. A MAN CAN NEVER BE SATISFIED WITH THINGS. (Ver. 15.) This is the great mistake men are making. They imagine that things can satisfy their hearts; whereas we are so constituted, with our affections and emotions, that fellowship with persons is indispensable to any measure of satisfaction, and to *full* satisfaction with no less a Being than God himself. All the effort, consequently, to be satisfied with things, with gifts, when the Giver is left out, proves vain.[1] No abundance can satisfy the craving of the heart. And the feverish desire for more and more wealth on the part of worldly men demonstrates simply that they are on the wrong track altogether, and that satisfaction can never be found in things. Covetousness, consequently, as the idolatry of things, is a total mistake. It misinterprets human nature, and is doomed to terrible disappointment.

II. SUCCESS MAY DOOM MEN TO LIFELONG WRONG. (Vers. 16—18.) The rich fool, as the man in the parable has been generally called, is overwhelmed by success. It outgrows his calculations. His barns are too small; they must be pulled down to allow of bigger barns being built, so that years of anxious labour are provided out of his inordinate success. He gets steeped to the lips in care. His life becomes a ceaseless worry. His grasping only secures his misery. It is truly lamentable to witness the self-inflicted wrong which worldly minds experience as they try to garner more and more of this world's goods to the neglect of better things. How well our great dramatist understood this ! In his poems Shakespeare says—

> " The profit of excess
> Is but to surfeit, and such griefs sustain,
> That they prove bankrupt in this poor-rich gain.
> The aim of all is but to nurse the life
> With honour, wealth, and ease, in waning age;
> And in this aim there is such thwarting strife,
> That one for all, or all for one, we gage,
> As life for honour in fell battle's rage,
> Honour for wealth ; and oft that wealth doth cost
> The death of all, and altogether lost."

III. IN THE CAREER OF SUCCESS THERE IS ONLY A VAIN DESIRE FOR REST. (Ver. 19.) The soliloquy betrays the utter weariness of the man. After his bigger barns are built, away down the fretful years he will reach, he hopes, a time when he will be in a position to say to his soul, " Soul, thou hast much goods laid up for many years; take thine ease, eat, drink, and be merry." He longs for rest, but it will be years yet before he can think of it. All the worry and the fret of the interval must be passed before rest can come. His idea is to *win* rest by wealth; to buy it up by a certain measure of success. And the experience of all men is that rest is never got on this line at all. It is something that cannot be purchased, but must be God-given.[2] How often do we see men who have retired with a competency at a loss how to kill time, and as weary and restless as ever !

IV. DEATH CUTS THE SOUL OFF AT ONCE FROM HIS WORLDLY POSSESSIONS. (Vers. 20, 21.) We never hear of millionaires carrying their money-bags with them. A moment after death Crœsus is no richer than the beggar. The *things* which were so anxiously amassed remain to be divided among the heirs, while the owner goes out into another world absolutely penniless. The state to which death reduces him is pitiful indeed. Having forgotten God the Giver through occupation with his gifts, he faces his Judge without a single feeling or aspiration which, in God's sight, is valuable at all. A miserable and wretched soul receives dismissal from the gracious God whose bounty was ignored and whose Being was despised.

V. HOW ALL-IMPORTANT IN THESE CIRCUMSTANCES TO ACCEPT OF CONTENTMENT AND REST AS THE SAVIOUR'S OFFERED GIFT. If the young man had accepted of contentment in place of cherishing covetousness, he would have been at ease at once. Rest of spirit and growth of spirit would thus have been secured, and he would have been on

---

[1] Cf. Gerok's ' Evangelien-Predigten,' s. 690.
[2] Cf. Goebel's ' Osterbeute,' s. 272.

not only equal terms with, but most probably superior terms to, his more grasping brother. It is thus that Jesus deals with us. He can give us a present rest from sin, from worry, from care of all kinds, and make us rich in the sight of God. With the riches of the soul in graces and gifts, we may hope to pass into the Divine presence and enjoy the Divine society and escape being castaways.—R. M. E.

Vers. 22—40.—*Lessons from the fowls and lilies.* Our Lord, having related the parable against covetousness, or the selfish use of money, proceeds in the present section to show how foolish the anxious thought is about these temporal things. And here we have to—

I. CONSIDER HOW POOR THE LIFE IS WHICH MAKES EATING AND DRESSING THE CHIEF THOUGHT. (Vers. 22, 23.) A man's life is intended to be much more assuredly than this; and yet are there not some who have no thought beyond this? The weight of anxiety is purely secular and physical. The devotees of the table and of the fashions make eating and dressing all. Now, the idea of the passage is that no one is so circumstanced as to be compelled to think only or chiefly of food and raiment. There is not a poor man but may feel that he was born for higher thoughts and things than to "keep the pot boiling" and to have something seemly to wear! He can think of the government of the world, and gain insight into it. He can rise into the thought of the government of God's kingdom, and the noble ideas it embodies. He can make ends meet without being the slave of circumstances and the creature of a day. He can walk among the eternities like others of his kind. Hence we must be on our guard against such a low view of life as this purely secular and temporal one.[1]

II. CONSIDER THE LESSON ABOUT FOOD FURNISHED BY THE FOWLS. (Vers. 24—26.) The fowls of the air are not "gentlemen at large," but most patient gatherers of their food. Life is not a sinecure with them, but a season of continual work. True, they do not become anxious farmers, sowing seed or reaping harvests, or building and stocking barns. They are spared a world of anxiety, but they accept the world of provision as God gives it to them. That which he gives they on unwearied wing gather. "God feedeth them" in the wisest way, and they accept it as he sends it. Moreover, the feeding of themselves is not their whole labour. There is much more in the bird's day than the quest of food. Whether they appreciate the beauty about them or no; whether their thoughts are like ours as from dizzy heights we see magnificent landscapes or stretches of sea, we cannot of course tell; but one thing seems certain, that the birds realize something more in the make-up of life than the mere satisfaction of their appetites. Their lesson is, therefore, one about a busy life, a thoughtful life, not always occupied with the satisfaction of the flesh. Let us trust God more in temporal matters, and think more of eternal things; and then life will be more thoughtful and more happy. No amount of thinking will add a cubit to our stature; and no amount of anxiety will deliver us from life's burdens. It is better to let God reign, and accept the conditions which in his wisdom he assigns.

III. CONSIDER THE LESSON ABOUT RAIMENT FROM THE LILIES. (Vers. 27, 28.) Here again we are face to face with nature. The purple lilies which deck the spring fields are gorgeously apparelled. Even Solomon in all his glory was not arrayed like one of them. So that when God is allowed to work, he weaves a more splendid texture in his loom than ever was produced by man. The lilies are evidences of his microscopic care of the flower of the grass, how worthy he regards it of beautiful raiment. But then he values his children more than his plants. Men may go the length of lavishing more attention upon their exotics and their flowers than upon their children. But this is not God's order. He has taken more thought for his human children than for all his gardens and their magnificent contents. He loves a family more than a conservatory; a school more than a forest; a population more than a deer-park or prairie. Hence we may trust him about raiment; it will come in due season and order. He will not give it to us like *paupers' clothing*, for we should hardly like it in that way; but to honest work there will come substantial reward.

IV. CONSIDER THE NOTORIOUS SECULARITY OF THE NATIONS. (Vers. 29—32.) Now, the analysis of heathenism will show that at heart heathen are *secular*. There is no better way of seeing this than by looking into their prayers. As one has said, "Idola-

[1] Cf. Martineau's 'Hours of Thought,' vol. i. pp. 17—44.

trous nations have in all places and in all ages prayed with unanimous voice that their god would give them health and physical force, riches, honour, pleasure, success ; for it is indeed for these the pagans pray."[1] This is what composed the life of paganism for the most part, and does so still. There is all the more reason why the Lord's little flock should trust him about the kingdom he has promised, and give themselves fearlessly to the bringing in of the kingdom from above. If we seek God's kingdom and glory first, we shall find a sufficient amount of food and raiment stored for us by no niggard and no pauperizing hand.

V. CONSIDER THE BENEFIT OF ALMSGIVING. (Vers. 33, 34.) Now, by almsgiving we are to understand enlightened and not lackadaisical charity. It is the investment of love, the expenditure of money for God's sake and for his kingdom. It is truly wonderful how *all* may become almsgivers. Is this not proof positive that God is a bountiful Provider ? How is it that there is hardly one in this hard world but could give if he only tried ? And what a transference of the heart's affections this will secure ! The heart no longer grovels amid the secular and temporal, but passes outward to the spiritual and eternal. Then the people whom we have tried to help, on the principle of giving " the greatest amount of needful help with the smallest encouragement to undue reliance on it," will form for us a bright and wholesome field for thought and hope, and the building up of God's kingdom shall be the result.

VI. CONSIDER THE DUTY OF WAITING FOR THE ADVENT. (Vers. 35—40.) From almsgiving our Lord proceeds to the duty of diligence in expectation of his advent. He has gone to attend a wedding, and will return when the marriage is complete. This has surely an instructive bearing upon the advent as *subsequent* to the completed plan about the bride, the Church. But what we have to notice is his readiness to serve the servants who are found faithful and diligent in his work. He has had a sufficiency at the wedding-feast ; he can consequently wait at the supper-table of the servants. And what an honour it will be to receive such attention from the Lord himself ! Let us, then, be *semper paratus*, and then, whether his advent be soon or late, we shall be overtaken by no surprise ![2]—R. M. E.

Vers. 41—59.—*The glories and responsibilities of the Christian ministry.* The previous parable attracts Peter by reason of its glorious promise, and he accordingly wonders if it can apply to all believers or to the apostles only. Having asked our Lord, he receives light upon the responsibilities and glories of the ministerial office. From our Lord's words we learn—

I. IT IS CHRIST'S WILL THERE SHOULD BE STEWARDS IN HIS CHURCH, WHOSE DUTY IT IS TO GIVE HIS PEOPLE MEAT IN DUE SEASON. (Vers. 42—44.) This is the great design of the ministry—to feed the flock of God. All other duties are subsidiary to this. For souls need to be as regularly fed with truth as the body with food. To this end the Christian ministry should, therefore, direct all its effects, that the people may be fed. And need it be said that the truth which nourishes men's souls is the truth as it is in Jesus ? When Jesus is presented in the glory of his Person and offices, then the famished souls are saved and satisfied. Now, our Lord declares that the ministry will continue for such a purpose until his advent. The household of God will always need the food furnished by the ministry. No time will come when the ministry shall be superseded. And the ministers who are diligently employed at their teaching and feeding of souls when our Lord comes will find themselves blessed (1) in their own experience, and (2) in the magnificent promotion awaiting them. Christ promises the faithful minister no less than *universal influence.* He is to be ruler over all he has. Others may have some influence, but a faithful minister will, in the world made new, have universal sovereignty. Ministerial influence is often incomparably the grandest and widest exercised among men in this life : how much more in the life and order which will be ushered in by the advent !

II. OUR LORD AT HIS ADVENT WILL MAKE SHORT WORK OF SPIRITUAL DESPOTS. (Vers. 45, 46.) Some in the ministry, it would seem, instead of living in expectation of the advent, will live as if the long-delayed advent would never come. In such a case selfish tyranny over the people committed to them will soon manifest itself; and

---

[1] Rougemont's 'La Vie Humaine,' p. 279.
[2] Cf. Gerok's 'Pilgerbrod,' s. 787; also 'Aus Ernster Zeit,' s. 10.

upon the self-indulgent despot our Lord shall come suddenly, to appoint him his portion with the unbelievers. A ministry that is not earnest, but self-indulgent and tyrannical, has before it a terrible doom.[1]

III. HE ALSO SHOWS THAT JUDGMENT IN THE WORLD TO COME SHALL BE GRADUATED ACCORDING TO DESERT. (Vers. 47, 48.) The difficulties about the Divine judgment have been partly owing to the forgetfulness of the fact that sinners are not to be cast indiscriminately into some common receptacle, but subjected to a series of graduated punishments of the most carefully adjusted character. The rhapsodies which are so plentiful against any thoroughness in punishing the impenitent are based mainly upon the false assumption of indiscriminating punishment. According to a person's opportunities will be his doom.

IV. OUR LORD DECLARES THAT HIS PRESENT ADVENT MUST GENERATE OPPOSITION. (Vers. 49—53.) The fire which our Lord came to kindle is that of spiritual enthusiasm; such a fire as burned in the disciples' hearts as he spoke to them on the way to Emmaus; such a fire as was promised in the baptism with the Holy Ghost.[2] Such incendiarism is just the blessed commotion the world needs. But in the kindling of the holy flame our Lord will have to pass through a bloody baptism. He sees how inevitable this dread experience is, and yet he pants for the cross which is to crown his work and revolutionize the world.[3] The cross of Christ is really the great divider of mankind; by its instrumentality families are divided into different camps, and the battle of the truth begun. But the division Christ creates is infinitely better than the unity without him. Better far that we should have to fight for truth than that we should live, like lotus-eaters, through indifference towards or ignorance of it. The battle for Christ is wholesome exercise, and the victory at last is assured.

V. HE CHARGES THEM WITH MISUNDERSTANDING THE SIGNS OF THE TIMES, WHILE THEY CAN APPRECIATE THE SIGNS OF THE WEATHER. (Vers. 54—56.) He is now speaking to the people, and not to the apostles. He points out how they can anticipate shower and heat by certain signs on the face of nature. People become "weather-wise," and can often show wonderful predictive power. And yet the *times* were providentially more significant than the weather. And before their eyes were hung the signs of a great contest between good and evil, between Christ and the world; and yet their hypocritical hearts would not allow them to appreciate the signs or take the proper side. It is a curious fact that many will study the laws of physical nature with intense interest and success, and yet neglect utterly those laws of the Divine government which involve the mightiest of revolutions. The hypocrisy of the heart is, our Saviour here says, the secret of such inconsistent apathy.

VI. HE DECLARES THE URGENCY OF RECONCILIATION WITH GOD. (Vers. 57—59.) The adversary, magistrate, and officer, are three individuals needful for the initiation and execution of human judgment. But the context shows that Jesus here refers to the Divine judgment which these hypocrites are courting. In this case—as Godet, *in loco*, observes—the adversary, judge, and officer are united in the Person of God. He is the Adversary to charge us with our defaults; he is the Judge to decide our guilt; he is the Officer to execute due vengeance on us in case we incur it. Christ consequently urges reconciliation with God without delay upon these hypocrites. To secure this he appeals to their conscience. They can surely come to this conclusion themselves, that, in opposing and persecuting him, they are not doing right. Their own inward monitor must witness to the guilt of their present course. Let them see to it, then, that they are delivered from their doom. Only one way is open, and that is by throwing themselves upon his mercy manifested in Christ. In this appointed way our Lord leaves them without excuse. There is surely a hopeless air about the terms of this judgment. The payment of the last mite is surely impossible in the prison-house of eternity, and current remedial programmes about the future life are but " will-o'-the-wisps " to lure thoughtless minds onwards towards doom! May we calculate upon no *post-mortem* reformation, but enter upon the pardon and spiritual progress God offers to us now! —R. M. E.

[1] Cf. Urwick on 'The Second Advent,' pp. 46, 47.
[2] Cf. Tholuck's 'Werke,' band iii. s. 304.
[3] Cf. Hull's 'Sermons preached at King's Lynn,' vol. iii. p. 70.

THE

GOSPEL ACCORDING TO ST. LUKE

VOL. II.

EXPOSITION

CHAPTER XIII.

Vers. 1—9.—*Signs of the times. The Lord continues his solemn warnings. Israel pictured in the parable of the barren fig tree.*

Ver. 1.—There were present at that season some that told him of the Galilæans, whose blood Pilate had mingled with their sacrifices; better rendered, *now there were present at that particular time;* namely, when the Master was discoursing of the threatening signs of the times, and urging men to repent and to turn and make their peace with God while there was yet time, for a terrible crisis was impending on that doomed land. Some of those then present, probably Jerusalem Jews, specially told off to watch the great Teacher, struck with his grave foreboding tone, when he spoke of the present aspect of affairs, quoted to him a recent bloody fray which had taken place in the temple courts. "Yes, Master," these seemed to say, "we see there is a fierce hatred which is ever growing more intense between Jew and Roman. You know, for instance, what has just taken place in the city, only the victims in this case were Galilæans, not scrupulous, righteous Jews. Is it not possible that these bloody deeds are simply punishments of men who are great sinners, as *these* doubtless were?" Such-like incidents were often now occurring under the Roman rule. This, likely enough, had taken place at some crowded Passover gathering, when a detachment of soldiers came down from the Castle of Antonia and had dealt a red-handed "justice" among the turbulent mob. Josephus relates several of the more formidable of such collisions between the Romans and the Jews. At one Passover he relates how three thousand Jews were butchered, and the temple courts were filled with dead corpses; at another of these feasts

two thousand perished in like manner (see 'Ant.,' xvii. 9. 3; xx. 5. 3; and 'Bell. Jud.,' ii. 5; v. 1). On another occasion disguised legionaries were sent by Pilate the governor with daggers among the Passover crowds (see 'Ant.,' xviii. 31). These wild and terrible collisions were of frequent occurrence in these sad days.

Vers. 2, 3.—And Jesus answering said unto them, Suppose ye that these Galilæans were sinners above all the Galilæans, because they suffered such things? I tell you, Nay: but, except ye repent, ye shall all likewise perish. "Yes," answered the Master, "these, you are right, are among the dread signs of the times I spoke of; but do not dream that the doom fell on those poor victims because they were *special* sinners. What happened to *them* will soon be the doom of the *whole nation*, unless a great change in the life of Israel takes place."

Ver. 4.—Or those eighteen, upon whom the tower in Siloam fell, and slew them, think ye that they were sinners above all men that dwelt in Jerusalem? "You remember," goes on the Master, "the catastrophe of the fall of the tower in Siloam; the poor sufferers who were crushed there were not specially wicked men." The Lord used these occasions, we see, for something more than the great national lesson. Men are too ready, now as then, to give way to the unloving error of looking at individual misfortune as the consequence of individual crime. Such human uncharitable judgments the Lord bitterly condemns. Ewald's conjecture in connection with this Siloam accident is ingenious. He supposes that the rigid Jews looked on the catastrophe as a retribution because the workmen who perished were paid by Pilate out of the sacred corban money (see Josephus, 'Bell. Jud.,' ii. 9. 4). The works were no doubt in connection with the aqueduct to the Pool of Siloam.

Ver. 5.—Except ye repent, ye shall all likewise perish. The words were indeed prophetic to the letter. Thousands of Jews perished in the last terrible war by the swords of the Roman legionaries, like the Galilæans of ver. 1; not a few met their death in the capital among the ruins of the burning fallen houses. We know that Jerusalem in its entirety was destroyed, and the loss of life in the siege, and especially in its dread closing scenes, was simply incalculable. Within forty years all this happened.

Ver. 6.—He spake also this parable: A certain man **had a fig tree planted in his vineyard.** And then, without any further prelude, Jesus spoke this parable of the barren fig tree, which contained, in language scarcely veiled at all, warnings to Israel as a nation—the most sombre and threatening he had yet given utterance to. "Hear, O people," said the Master. "In the vineyard of the Lord of hosts is a fig tree, long planted there, but utterly unfruitful. It is now on its last trial; indeed, were it not for the intercession of the Gardener, the Lord of the vineyard had already pronounced its final doom." "The very intercession, though, is ominous; the Vinedresser shows his mercifulness by deprecating immediate cutting down, but the careful specification of conditions, and the limitation of the period within which experiments are to be made, intimate that peril is imminent. . . . The restriction of the intercession of the Vinedresser for a single year's grace indicates Christ's own sympathy with this Divine rigour. . . . The Vinedresser knows that, though God is long-suffering, yet his patience as exhibited in the history of his dealings with men is exhaustible, and that in Israel's case it is now all but worn out. And he sympathizes with the Divine impatience with chronic and incurable sterility " (Professor Bruce). **A fig tree planted in his vineyard; and he came and sought fruit thereon, and found none.** It is not an uncommon practice to plant fig trees at the corners of vineyards, thus utilizing every available spot of ground. Still the Lord's choice of a fig tree as the symbol of Israel, the chosen people, is at first sight strange. This image was no doubt selected to show those Pharisees and other Jews, proud of what they considered their unassailable position as the elect of the Eternal, that, after all, the position they occupied was but that of a fig tree in the corner of the vineyard of the world—planted there and watched over so long as it promised to serve the Lord of the vineyard's purpose; if it ceased to do that, if it gave no further promise of fruit, then it would be ruthlessly cut down.

Ver. 7.—Behold, these three years I come seeking fruit on this fig tree, and find none. Some expositors see in this period of three years an allusion to the storied past of Hebrew life, and in the number 3 discern the three marked epochs, each lasting several centuries, of the high priests, judges, and kings. This, however, is a very doubtful reference, owing to the impossibility of separating the first two periods of the rule of high priests and judges, as these interchange and overlap each other. Another school of interpreters sees a reference to the three years of the public ministry of Jesus. A better reference would be God's successive calls to Israel by the Law, the prophets, and by Christ. It is, however, safer, in this and in many of the Lord's parables, not to press every little detail which was necessary for the completion of the picture. Here the period of three years in which the Lord of the vineyard came seeking fruit, represents by the number 3 the symbol of completeness—a period of full opportunity given to the tree to have become fruitful and productive. **Cut it down; why cumbereth it the ground?** better rendered, *why doth it make the ground useless?* It is an unproductive tree, and occupies the place which another and a fertile tree might fill.

Ver. 8.—And he answering said unto him, Lord, let it alone this year also, till I shall dig about it, and dung it. The last year—the year of grace *they* who listened to him then were living in. It was the last summons to repentance, the final reminder to the old covenant people that to their high privileges as the chosen race there were duties attached. They prided themselves on the privileges, they utterly forgot the duties. The period represented by this last year included the preaching of John the Baptist, the public ministry of Jesus Christ, and the forty years of apostolic teaching which followed the Crucifixion and Resurrection. The last chance was given, but in the Vinedresser's prayer to the Lord of the vineyard there is scarcely a ray of hope. The history of the world supplies the sequel to this parable-story.

Vers. 10—17.—*A miracle of mercy. The Lord's teaching on certain strict observances of the sabbath day then practised by the more rigid Jews.*

Ver. 10.—And he was teaching in one of the synagogues on the sabbath. We hear little of our Lord's public teaching in the synagogues of the towns and villages through which he was then passing in this his last long journey. In the earlier months of the ministry of Jesus he seems to have taught frequently in these houses of prayer, very possibly every sabbath day. It has been suggested, with considerable probability, that owing to the persistent enmity of the hierarchy and dominant class at Jerusalem, he was excluded from some at least of the synagogues by what was termed the "lesser excommunication."

Ver. 11.—**And, behold, there was a woman which had a spirit of infirmity eighteen years, and was bowed together, and could in no wise lift up** herself. The description of the sufferer, so accurate in its details, marks the medical training of the compiler here. The malady was evidently a curvature of the spine of a very grave character. Her presence in the synagogue that day gives us a hint, at least, that this poor afflicted one loved communion with her God. Doubtless the faith and trust on her side necessary to the cure were there. Her first act, after she was sensible of the blessed change wrought in her poor diseased frame, was an outpouring of devout thanks to God.

Ver. 14.—**And the ruler of the synagogue answered with indignation, because that Jesus had healed on the sabbath day.** The people, as usual, were stirred to enthusiasm by this glorious act of power and mercy. Afraid, before the congregation of the synagogue, to attack the Master personally, the "ruler," no doubt influenced by members of the Pharisee party who were present, attempted to represent the great Physician as a deliberate scorner of the sacred Law. The sabbath regulations at this time were excessively burdensome and childishly rigorous. The Law, as expounded in the schools of the rabbis, allowed physicians to act in cases of emergency, but not in chronic diseases such as this. How deep an interest must such a memory of the Master's as this sabbath day's healing have had for that beloved physician who has given his name to these memoirs we call the Third Gospel! Often in later years, in Syrian Antioch, in the great cities of Italy and Greece, would he, as he plied his blessed craft among the sick on the sabbath day, be attacked by rigid Jews as one who profaned the day. To such would he relate this incident, and draw *his* lessons of mercy and of love.

Ver. 15.—**The Lord then answered him, and said, Thou hypocrite, doth not each one of you on the sabbath loose his ox or his ass from the stall, and lead him away to watering?** The older authorities here read "hypocrites," and thus join the cavilling synagogue ruler with the whole sect of men who taught an elaborate ritual in place of a high, pure life. The Lord, in a few master-touches, exposes the hollowness of such sabbath-keeping. Every possible indulgence was to be shown in cases where their own interests were involved; no mercy or indulgence was to be thought of, though,

where the sick poor only were concerned. He vividly draws a contrast between the animal and the human being. The ox and the ass, though, were personal property; the afflicted daughter of Abraham was but a woman, friendless and poor.

Vers. 18—21.—*The Lord, in two little prophetic parables tells the people how strangely and mightily his religion would spread over the earth.*

Ver. 18.—**Then said he, Unto what is the kingdom of God like? and whereunto shall I resemble it?** In the seventeenth verse —after the Lord's words spoken to his enemies, who took exception at his miracle of healing worked for the poor woman who had been bent for eighteen years, because he had done it on the sabbath day—we read how "all his adversaries were ashamed; and all the people rejoiced for all the glorious things that were done by him." This discomfiture of the hypocrites, and the honest joy of the simple folk over a noble and Divine deed of mercy, accompanied by brave, kind words, seem to have suggested to the Master the subject of the two little parables of the mustard seed and the leaven, in which parables the growth of his glorious kingdom was foreshadowed from very small beginnings. The very small beginning he could discern in what then surrounded him.

Ver. 19.—**It is like a grain of mustard seed, which a man took, and cast into his garden; and it grew, and waxed a great tree; and the fowls of the air lodged in the branches of it.** The simile was a well-known one in the Jewish world. "As small as a grain of mustard seed" was a proverb current among the people in those days. In Eastern countries this little seed often becomes a tree, and stories are even told of mustard trees so tall that a man could climb up into their branches or ride beneath them on horseback. Such instances are possibly very rare, but it is a common sight to see a mustard plant, raised from one of these minute grains, grown to the height of a fruit tree, putting forth branches on which birds build their nests. It was with sorrowful irony that the great Teacher compared the kingdom of God in those days to this small grain. The kingdom of God on earth then was composed of Jesus and his few wavering followers. To the eye of sense it seemed impossible that this little movement could ever stir the world, could ever become a society of mighty dimensions. "See," said the Master, taking up a little mustard seed; "does *this* seem as though it would ever become a tree with spreading branches on which the birds might rest? The kingdom of God is like this seed."

Ver. 21.—**It is like leaven, which a woman took and hid in three measures of meal, till** the whole was leavened. The *first* of these two little parables of the kingdom, "the mustard seed," portrayed its strangely rapid growth. The *second*, "the leaven," treats of the mighty inward transformation which the kingdom of God will effect in the hearts of men and women. Chemically speaking, leaven is a lump of sour dough in which putrefaction has begun, and, on being introduced into a far greater mass of fresh dough, produces by contagion a similar condition into the greater bulk with which it comes in contact. The result of the contact, however, is that the mass of dough, acted upon by the little lump of leaven, becomes a wholesome, agreeable food for men. It was a singularly striking and powerful simile, this little commonplace comparison, and exactly imaged the future progress of "the kingdom." Quietly, silently, the doctrine of the Master made its way into the hearts and homes of men. "He shall not strive, nor cry; neither shall any man hear his voice in the streets" (Matt. xii. 19). None on earth would have dared hint at the future success of the doctrine of the Master during the Master's life, and his death seemed as though it would effectually crush out the last feeble spark of life. The apparent result of his work was the devotion of a few simple hearts, mostly of fishermen, artisans, and the like, and yet, though men suspected it not, the secret and powerful influence was already at work among men. The story of the years succeeding the cross and the Resurrection, on a broader stage and with more actors, was a story of similar silent, quiet working. In a century and a half after the strange leaven-parable had been spoken, the whole civilized world knew something of the Master's history and doctrine. His disciples then were counted by tens of thousands. No city, scarcely a village, but contained some into whose hearts the teaching had sunk, whose lives the teaching had changed. *In three measures of meal.* Perhaps referring here to the well-known division of man into body, soul, and spirit. More likely, however, the number 3 is used as the symbol of completeness, signifying that the Divine purpose was then influencing the whole mass of mankind. *Till the whole was leavened.* It would seem as though the Master looked on to a definite time when all nations should come and worship him, and acknowledge his glorious sovereignty. If this be the case, then a very long period still remains to be lived through by the world; many kingdoms must rise and fall, new civilizations spring up, before that day of joy and gladness dawns upon the globe— that is, reasoning on the analogy of the past. Be this, however, as it may, the drift of both

these parables of the kingdom distinctly points to a slow yet a progressive development of true religion. Very different, indeed, was the Jewish conception of Messiah's kingdom. They expected a rapid and brilliant metamorphosis of the then unhappy state of things. They never dreamed of the slow and quiet movement Messiah's coming was to inaugurate. One thing is perfectly clear—the Speaker of these two parable-stories never contemplated a speedy return to earth. With strange exactness the last eighteen hundred and fifty years have been fulfilling the conditions of the two similes, and as yet, as far as man can see, they are not nearly complete.

Ver. 22.—**And he went through the cities and villages, teaching, and journeying toward Jerusalem.** This note of the evangelist simply calls attention that the last solemn progress in the direction of the capital was still going on. The question has been discussed at length above. St. Luke, by these little notes of time and place, wishes to direct attention to the fact that all this part of the Gospel relates to one great division of the public ministry—to that which immediately preceded the last Passover.

Vers. 23—30.—*Jesus replies to the question of "Are there few that be saved?"*

Ver. 23.—**Then said one unto him, Lord, are there few that be saved?** The immediate circumstance which called out this question is not recorded, but the general tone of the Master's later teaching, especially on the subject of his kingdom of the future, had disturbed the vision of many in Israel, who loved to dwell on the exclusion of all save the chosen race from the glories of the world to come. The words of the Second Book of Esdras, written perhaps forty or fifty years after this time, well reflect this selfish spirit of harsh exclusiveness, peculiarly a characteristic of the Jew in the days of our Lord. "The Most High hath made this world for many, but the world to come for few" (2 Esdr. viii. 1). "There be many more of them which perish, than of them which shall be saved: like as a wave is greater than a drop" (2 Esdr. ix. 15, 16). Other passages breathing a similar spirit might be quoted. What relics we possess of Jewish literature of this period all reflect the same stern, jealous, exclusive spirit. The questioner here either hoped to get from the popular Master some statement which might be construed into an approval of this national spirit of hatred of everything that was not Jewish, or, if Jesus chose to combat these selfish hopes, the Master's words might then be quoted to the people as unpatriotic.

Ver. 24.—**Strive to enter in at the strait**

gate: for many, I say unto you, will seek to enter in, and shall not be able. The Master, as was frequently his custom, gave no direct answer to his questioner, but his teaching which immediately follows contained the answer to the query. The older authorities, in place of "at the strait gate," read "through the narrow door." The meaning of the image, however, is the same, whichever reading be adopted. The image was not a new one. It had been used before by the Lord, perhaps more than once (see Matt. vii. 13, 14), and not improbably had been suggested by some town or fortress hard by the spot where he was teaching— a fort on a hill with a narrow road winding up to a narrow door. In the rabbinical schools he frequented in his youth, he might, too, have heard some adaptation of the beautiful allegory known as the 'Tablet' of Cebes, the disciple of Socrates: "Dost thou not perceive a narrow door, and a pathway before the door, in no way crowded, but few, very few, go in thereat?" The teaching of the Master here is, that the door of salvation is a narrow one, and, to pass through it, the man must *strive* in real earnest. "See," he seems to say; "if only few are saved, it will not be because the Jews are few and the Gentile nations many, but because, of the Jews and Gentiles, only *a few* really strive. Something different from race or national privileges will be the test at that narrow door which leads to life. "Many will seek to enter in, and shall not be able." The reason for the exclusion of these many is to be sought in themselves. They *wished* to enter in, but confined themselves to wishes. They made no strong, vigorous efforts. Theirs was no life of stern self-surrender, of painful self-sacrifice. To wish to pass through that narrow door is not enough.

Ver. 25.—When once the master of the house is risen up, and hath shut to the door, and ye begin to stand without, and to knock at the door, saying, Lord, Lord, open unto us; and he shall answer and say unto you, I know you not whence ye are. The great Teacher here slightly changes the imagery. The narrow door no longer is the centre of the picture; one, called the "master of the house," becomes the principal figure. The door now shut may still be, most probably is, the narrow fort or hill-city entrance, and the one called the master is the governor of the Place of Arms, into which the door or gate led. It is now too late even for the earnest striver to enter in. Sunset probably —the shades of night, had the Divine Painter furnished the imagery—would have been the signal for the final closing of the door of the fortress. Death is the period when the door of salvation is shut to the

children of men. It has been asked—To what time does the Master refer in the words "when once"? It cannot be the epoch of the ruin of Jerusalem and the breaking up of the Jewish nationality, for then there was nothing in the attitude of the doomed people to answer to the standing without, to the knocking at the door, and to the imploring cries, "Lord, Lord, open unto us," portrayed here. It cannot be the second coming of the Lord; surely then his people will not call on him in vain. It refers, without doubt, to the day of judgment, when the dread award will be pronounced upon the unbelieving, the selfish, and the evil-liver.

Vers. 26, 27.—Then shall ye begin to say, We have eaten and drunk in thy presence, and thou hast taught in our streets. But he shall say, I tell you, I know you not whence ye are; depart from me, all ye workers of iniquity. A very stern declaration on the part of Jesus that in the day of judgment no special favour would be granted to the souls of the chosen people. It was part of the reply to the question respecting the "fewness of the saved." The inquirer wished to know the opinion of the great Teacher on the exclusive right of Israel to salvation in the world to come, and this statement, describing salvation as something independent of all questions as to race, was the Master's reply.

Ver. 28.—There shall be weeping and gnashing of teeth, when ye shall see Abraham, and Isaac, and Jacob, and all the prophets, in the kingdom of God, and you yourselves thrust out. No less than six times is this terrible formula, which expresses the intensest form of anguish, found in St. Matthew's Gospel. St. Luke only gives us the account of one occasion on which they were spoken. They indicate, as far as merely earthly words and symbols can, the utter misery of those unhappy ones who find themselves shut out from the kingdom in the world to come. "Abraham, and Isaac, and Jacob." In his revision of St. Luke's Gospel, Marcion, the famous Gnostic heretic, in place of these names, which he strikes out, inserts "all the just." He did this with a view to lower the value of the Old Testament records.

Ver. 29.—And they shall come from the east, and from the west, and from the north, and from the south, and shall sit down in the kingdom of God. Instead of "shall sit down," a clearer and more accurate rendering would be, *shall recline as at a banquet.* This image of the heaven-life as a banquet, at which the great Hebrew patriarchs were present, was a well-known one in popular Hebrew teaching. There is an unmistakable reference to Isa. xlv. 6 and xlix. 12

in this announcement of comers to the great banquet of heaven from all the four quarters of the globe. This completes the answer to the question. It forbids any limitation to the numbers of the saved. It distinctly includes in those blessed ranks men from all parts of the far isles of the Gentiles.

Ver. 30.—**And, behold, there are last which shall be first, and there are first which shall be last.** This expression, which apparently was more than once used by the Lord, in this place clearly has an historical reference, and sadly predicts the rejection of Israel, not only in this present world.

"There above (on earth)
How many hold themselves for mighty kings,
Who here like swine shall wallow in the mire,
Leaving behind them horrible dispraise!"
(Dante, 'Inferno.')

Vers. 31—35.—*The message of Jesus to Herod Antipas, and the lament over the loved city of Jerusalem, the destined place of his own death.*

Ver. 31.—**The same day there came certain of the Pharisees, saying unto him, Get thee out, and depart hence: for Herod will kill thee.** Very many of the older authorities read here, instead of "the same day," "in that very hour." This incident connected with Herod Antipas, which is only related by St. Luke, not improbably was communicated to Luke and Paul by Manaen, who was intimately connected with that prince, and who was a prominent member of the primitive Church of Antioch in those days when Paul was beginning his work for the cause (see Acts xiii. 1). This curious message probably emanated from Herod and Herodias. The tetrarch was disturbed and uneasy at the Lord's continued presence in his dominions, and the crowds who thronged to hear the great Teacher occasioned the jealous and timorous prince grave disquietude. Herod shrank from laying hands on him, though, for the memory of the murdered friend of Jesus was a terrible one, we know, to the superstitious tetrarch, and he dreaded being forced into a repetition of the judicial murder of John the Baptist. It is likely enough that the enemies of the Lord were now anxious for him to go to Jerusalem and its neighbourhood, where he would be in the power of the Sadducean hierarchy, and away from the protection of the Galilæan multitudes, with whom his influence was still very great. The Pharisees, who as a party hated the Master, willingly entered into the design, and under the mask of a pretended friendship warned him of Herod's intentions.

Ver. 32.—**And he said unto them, Go ye, and tell that fox;** literally, *that she-fox.* The Lord saw through the shallow device, and, in reply to his false friends, bade them go to that intriguing and false court with a message which he would give them. The epithet "she-fox" is perhaps the bitterest and most contemptuous name ever given by the pitiful Master to any of the sons of men. It is possible it might have been intended for Herodias, the influence of that wicked princess being at that time all-powerful at court. **Behold, I cast out devils, and I do cures to-day and to-morrow, and the third day I shall be perfected.** "Tell Herod or Herodias that I have a work still to work here; a few more evil spirits to cast out, a few more sick folk to heal. I am going on as I have begun; no message, friendly or unfriendly, will turn me from my purpose. I have no fears of his royal power, but I shall not trouble him long; just to-day and to-morrow—this was merely (as in Hos. vi. 2) a proverbial expression for a short time—and on the third day I complete my work." This completion some have understood by the crowning miracle on dead Lazarus at Bethany, but it is far better to understand it as referring to the Passion, as including the last sufferings, the cross, and the resurrection. The τελειοῦμαι here was supplemented by the utterance with which the blessed life came to its close on the cross— Τετελέσται! Τελείωσις became a recognized term for martyrdom.

Ver. 33.—**Nevertheless I must walk to-day, and to-morrow, and the day following: for it cannot be that a prophet perish out of Jerusalem.** He reflects, "Yes, I must go on with my journey for the little space yet left to me;" and then turning to the false Pharisee friends, with the saddest irony bids them not be afraid. Priest and Sanhedrin, the unholy alliance against him of Sadducee and Pharisee, would not be balked of the Victim whose blood they were all thirsting after. Their loved city had ever had one melancholy prerogative. It had ever been the place of death for the prophets of the Lord. That sad privilege would not be taken from it in his case.

Ver. 34.—**O Jerusalem, Jerusalem, which killest the prophets, and stonest them that are sent unto thee!** This exquisite and moving apostrophe was uttered in similar language in the Passion-week, just as Jesus was leaving the temple for the last time. It was spoken here with rare appropriateness in the first instance after the promise of sad irony that the holy city should not be deprived of the spectacle of the Teacher-Prophet's death. "O Jerusalem, Jerusalem!" It was a farewell to the holy city. It was the sorrowful summing-up of the tenderest love of centuries. Never had earthly city been loved like this. There the anointed of the Eternal were to fix their home. There the stately shrine for the service of the invisible King of Israel was to keep watch and ward over the favoured capital of the chosen race. There the visible presence of the Lord God Almighty, the Glory and the Pride of the people, was ever and anon to rest. And in this solemn last farewell, the Master looked back through the vista of the past ages of Jerusalem's history. It was a dark and gloomy contemplation. It had been all along the wicked chief city of a wicked people, of a people who had thrown away the fairest chances ever offered to men—the city of a people whose annals were memorable for deeds of blood, for the most striking ingratitude, for incapacity, for folly shading into crime. Not once nor twice in that dark story of Israel chosen messengers of the invisible King had visited the city he loved so well. These were invested with the high credentials which belong to envoys from the King of kings, with a voice sweeter and more persuasive, with a power grander and more far-reaching than were the common heritage of men; and these envoys, his prophets, they had maltreated, persecuted, murdered. **How often would I have gathered thy children together, as a hen doth gather her brood under her wings!** God's great love to Israel had been imaged in the far back days of the people, when Moses judged them, under a similar metaphor. *Then* it was the eagle fluttering over her young and bearing them on her wings; now it is slightly altered to one if possible more tender and loving, certainly more homely. How often in bygone days would the almighty wings, indeed, had Israel only wished it, have been spread out over them a sure shelter! Now the time of grace was over, and the almighty wings were folded. **And ye would not!** Sad privilege, specially mentioned here by the Divine Teacher, this freedom of man's will to resist the grace of God. "Ye would not," says the Master, thus joining the generation who heard his voice to the stiffnecked Israel of the days of the wicked kings.

Ver. 35.—**Behold, your house is left unto you desolate.** The older authorities omit "desolate." The sentence will then read, "your house is left unto you." *Their* house from henceforth, not *his*. **Ye shall not see me, until** the time **come when ye shall say, Blessed** is **he that cometh in the Name of the Lord.** "Ye shall not see me." Van Oosterzee comments here: "Their senses are still blinded. The veil of the Talmud that hangs over their eyes is twice as heavy as the veil of Moses." The promise which concludes this saying of the Master can only refer to the far future, to the day of the penitence of Israel. It harmonizes with the voice of the older prophets, and tells us that the day will surely come when the people shall look on him whom they pierced, and shall mourn. But *that* mourning will be turned speedily into joy.

HOMILETICS.

Vers. 1—9.—*The barren fig tree.* "At that season," or "at that particular time"—whilst the pleading, warning words which follow from the forty-ninth verse of the previous chapter are ringing in the ears of those around the Lord—some bystanders tell him of judgments which had actually been fulfilled, of Galilæans whose blood Pilate had mingled with their sacrifices. We have no information as to the particular event referred to. Riots, small insurrections, revolts from Roman authority, were by no means uncommon, and we know that Pilate was cruel in his repression of them. Probably these Galilæans had been rioting, and the procurator had profaned the holy things of the sanctuary by casting their blood over the offering made by fire. And the thought simmering in the minds of the superstitious speakers was, "These wretched people had not given the diligence which had been spoken of. They died unreconciled and impenitent. They were great offenders, therefore they endured great punishment." It was a prevalent belief among the Jews that signal calamity to individuals was the token of signal Divine displeasure. This was the inference of Job's companions when they saw him in the day of his sore grief. This was the inference of the men near Christ as to the victims of the dark catastrophe. And he who knows what is in man at once finds the place of their thought, rebukes their hasty reasoning, and summons them, instead of reflecting on others, to try their own ways and remember, "Except ye repent, ye shall all likewise perish." The parable which follows enforces this appeal to the conscience. It is a short but wonderfully expressive parable. "Everything is involved in it," says Stier, "which a mission of repentance to a people demands."

I. Observe, the truth on which Jesus insists is THE NEED OF PERSONAL REPENTANCE

ON THE PART OF ALL. In contrast with his audience, this was the application of the calamities related which he made. These were to him the prophecy of the doom awaiting every one who continued in his sins. Archbishop Trench emphasizes the "likewise." "Ye shall all *likewise* perish, *i.e.* in a manner similar to that in which both the Galilæans and the eighteen on whom the tower in Siloam fell perished. So, in the destruction of Jerusalem years afterwards, multitudes of the inhabitants were crushed beneath the ruins of their temple and their city, and, during the last siege and assault, numbers were pierced through by the Roman darts, or, more miserably yet, by those of their own frantic factions in the courts of the temple, in the very act of preparing their sacrifices. So that, literally, their blood, like that of the Galilæans, was mingled with their sacrifices, one blood with another." All befallings of judgment which men witness should be, not occasions of criticism or of harsh stricture on others, but voices bidding to humility and self-examination. The sin which I can trace in my neighbour should chiefly remind me of the sin which has dominion over myself. If I have been kept from his transgression, let me thank the grace which has kept me, recall how great perhaps was the difference between his circumstances and mine, and ask whether, in some other form, I may not have been a transgressor as great as he. Reflections such as these will save from all Pharisaic exaltation, will send us to our knees for the erring brother, ay, and send us to our knees for ourselves—the word of the Lord sounding within, "Thinkest thou that he is a sinner above thee, because he suffers such things? I tell thee, Nay: except thou repent, thou shalt likewise perish."

II. Now see in the parable BOTH THE GOODNESS AND THE SEVERITY WHICH LEAD TO REPENTANCE. The details—who owns the vineyard? what the vineyard represents? who is the Dresser or the Gardener? for what the three years and the one year of grace stand?—need not here be discussed. The parable is a picture of Almighty God in his dealings with his Church, Jewish or Gentile, in the desire of his love, in the responsiveness of his heart to the intercession of the Mediator whom he has appointed, in the deferring of his judgment so that a fuller opportunity may be given to men to confess his presence and seek him with their whole heart, and flee from the wrath to come. Notice three of the salient features. 1. *The fruit which is sought*— sought year by year with increasing disappointment; fruit, the legitimate product of the tree, growing out of its life, marking its use and value. We hear the astonished "What more could I do to my vineyard that I have not done?" And nothing—"nothing but leaves." Herein we recognize the longing of the love of God. He gives to men that men may give of his, one to another. As his own goodness is "a flowing life-fountain," so is the goodness which is the expression of the new heart and the right spirit. The fruitless tree keeps a certain energy to itself. There is a power in it which remains undeveloped. It draws the moisture away from the surrounding soil, it receives the rain and sunshine of heaven; it is all an *in*-come, there is no *out*-come. Is it not the type of the kind of person who is a stranger and foreigner to the life of the Eternal—a person who is fed, but does not feed; who claims to be ministered to, but does not seek the bliss of ministering; whose character has no distinct influence for good; who is not what, in his place and according to his opportunity, the Lord of the vineyard expects him to be? God comes to men for his harvest. Is he receiving it from us? "Herein," says Christ, "is my Father glorified, that ye bear much fruit." Remember, "*much* fruit"—the well-matured, well-ripened godliness of the one in whose heart are God's ways. Resemblances cannot impose on him whose eyes are as a flame of fire. Why did he curse the tree which he beheld on his way to Bethany? Not because it was barren, but because it was false. In the fig tree the fruit should appear before the leaves. He saw leaves where there had been no fruit. Profession is nothing. A routine of religious offices is nothing. Appearance before God is nothing. All this may be only an extra assumed for an occasion, and then taken off. The tree which produces is the tree that is sound at the core. The conscience right produces the life right. Repentance, the way of making the tree good; holiness, the life of repentance —for this God comes to each of us, seeking, expecting. 2. *What as to the intercession?* There appears on the scene the one who has been charged with the care of the vineyard. The first reference, no doubt, is to the Lord Jesus Christ himself, into whose hand the Father has given all things, and in whom is substantiated the craving of the old patriarch for the Interpreter—"the one among a thousand to whom the Eternal is gracious, and saith, Deliver from going down into the pit: I have found a ransom." It is he who ever liveth, the God-Man, to make intercession. "Yet not," as has been remarked, "as though the Father and the Son had different minds concerning sinners, not as though the counsels of the Father were wrath, and of the Son mercy: for righteousness and love are not qualities in him who *is* Righteousness and who *is* Love; they cannot, therefore, be set the one against the other, since they are his essential Being." Yes, "if any man sin, we have an Advocate with the Father, Jesus Christ the Righteous." But there is a secondary reference not to be overlooked. Before Jesus left the world to go to the Father, he promised to send the Holy Ghost as another Advocate; not another in the sense that he would be a different Person, but in the sense that he would be his other self—a Divine presence inhabiting the Church which is his body, and revealing and glorifying him. All faithful souls, anointed with the sevenfold gifts of this Paraclete, are joined with him in intercession for the unfaithful and unfruitful. The prayer of the Church is the voice of the Holy Ghost—Christ's voice echoing from human hearts. And the whole Bible is charged with the thought that, for the sake of the elect, because of their life and work and cry to heaven, judgments impending over the earth are stayed. Intercession is not a merely beautiful and becoming function; it is the power which binds "the whole round earth by golden chains about the feet of God." "Cut it down; why mischieveth it the ground? . . . Lord, let it alone this year also." 3. Finally, *God's times and spaces—what are they?* "These three years I come." The three years have been supposed to signify the epoch of the natural law, the epoch of the written Law, and, finally, the epoch of grace; Moses, the prophets, the acceptable year of the Lord's coming; the three years of Christ's ministry; childhood, manhood, old age. Whatever may be the value we attach to these explanations, the fact denoted is the long-suffering of God. Notice the two aspects of the waiting: to judge, but be gracious, and to judge and condemn. The latter is the "strange work." In grace, God comes silently; for condemnation, he comes, first crying aloud by his threatenings, "I am coming quickly," that the opportunity for the Intercessor may be given. First, the axe is laid at the root of the tree; there it lies, ready, yet the blow is deferred. "Cut it down;" yet a little longer—"this year also."

Vers. 22—30.—*The question and the answer.* "He went through the cities and villages." The circuits into which the ministry of Jesus was divided are most interesting. "He went about doing good." One feature is suggested by the evangelist's sentence. The *village* is not overlooked. If the desire had been merely to gain influence, he would have limited the teaching to the city. "Win the great centres of the populations; thus you will establish your reputation; thence the light will radiate to the obscurer places;"—this would have described the method of the action. Christ had another method. The small hamlet, no less than the crowded town, was the scene of his labour. It was the passion for souls which inspired him. The human soul, under all outward conditions, was one and the same to him. "The Son of man came to seek and to save that which was lost." Note *the direction of the face.* He is "journeying *towards* Jerusalem." The shadows of Gethsemane and Golgotha are lengthening. Ever before him, and now pressing on his heart, is the thought of the decease that he should accomplish. It is the occasion at once of the Saviour's sorrow and the Saviour's joy. The teaching would have been little without the forecast of the sacrifice; apart from the sacrifice, it loses its power. Jerusalem and its cross is the reference ever present to the Christian minister, whether in city or in village. In one of the places visited, the Lord is accosted by a person of whom the only notice is, "Then said one unto him." But the incident is instructive. It reminds us of (1) *a kind of question that is to be discountenanced;* and (2) *a kind of practical exhortation that is to be enforced.*

I. A KIND OF QUESTION THAT IS TO BE DISCOUNTENANCED. There is no reason to doubt the good faith of the interrogator. He is reverent in his inquiry, "Lord." There is nothing captious in his tone. He is the type of many earnest minds, puzzled over the problems of human life and destiny—minds that feel the pressure of the things which circumscribe the opportunity of multitudes, the bars which seem to interpose between men's souls and salvation, the limitations arising from imperfect knowledge and untoward condition; and, looking far and near over the ever-pouring throng, ask,

"Lord, what will this man and that man do? What is the extent to which the purpose to save will be realized?" He answers by not answering. The absence of a direct reply is itself a reply. It intimates that speculations and inquiries in the line of the word addressed to him are not to be encouraged. There was the wisdom which he emphasizes in the response once given by a child of quietness to the question, "What are the decrees of God?" "He knows that best himself," was the response. There are secrets which belong to the Lord our God, and these we must be content to leave with him. The things revealed belong to us; and these are expressed in the assurances that God loved the world, that whosoever believeth in the only begotten Son shall not perish, that him who comes to Christ he will in no wise cast out. They forget Christ's silence on the occasion before us who dogmatize either Calvinistically or Arminianistically. What can poor human nature do, in view of all that relates to the ultimate state of men, but simply trust him who is absolute Righteousness and Infinite Love? We may "faintly trust" larger hopes; we can, not faintly, but fully, trust him who will do what is best for all, who "hateth nothing that he hath made."

> "Wait till he shall himself disclose
> Things now beyond thy reach,
> And be not thou meanwhile of those
> Who the Lord's secrets teach.
>
> "Who teach thee more than he has taught,
> Tell more than he revealed,
> Preach tidings which he never brought,
> And read what he left sealed."

II. A KIND OF PRACTICAL EXHORTATION THAT IS TO BE ENFORCED. Withdrawing the mind of the inquirer from vague speculations, the matter which the Lord places next before him is this, "*Agonize* to enter in at the strait gate." How urgent, how solemn is the entreaty! The strait gate! Is it not a wide and ever-open one? Yes, in one sense it is. None who come with a true heart, in full assurance of faith, will be, can be, excluded. There is room for the east, and for the west, and for the north, and for the south; all nations, kindreds, peoples, and tongues. Christ's aim is, a universal religion. He throws his arms wide to all who labour and are heavy laden. But, in another sense, it is a strait gate. It is too narrow to admit any one in his sins. It is too narrow to admit the Pharisee in his Pharisaism, or the Sadducee in his Sadduceeism, or the Herodian in his Herodianism; too narrow to admit any one in his "*-ism*," in his self-righteousness, in anything on which he rests with satisfaction as a ground of distinction or superiority. All who enter, enter as sinners looking for the mercy of God, and desiring to be cleansed from all unrighteousness.

> "Nothing in my hand I bring,
> Simply to thy cross I cling."

The entrance into the strait gate is the first of all interests, is the most pressing of all concerns. Instead of scattering energy over secondary issues, energy is to be concentrated on this. Put your whole strength into the accomplishment of the one end. Christ insists, "Strive [or, 'agonize'] to enter." "Faith is a very simple thing." Yet there is a discipline which is not a very simple thing. Evangelical, especially the phase which is called evangelistic, preaching too often overlooks the discipline. It is frequently an exclusive repetition of the cry, "Believe, and you receive; believe, and you shall live." It forgets that the beginning of the gospel of Christ was "Repent!" It has not a distinct enough place for repentance. It is so occupied with the endeavour to make the way easy, that it fails to urge, with the intensity of Jesus' preaching, the necessity of a thorough self-repression, of a real taking of the cross, of the fighting of the good fight of faith. Let none overlook the *agonistic* side of the Christian life. Let the preacher echo and illustrate the sharp, stern, "Agonize to enter in"—not, indeed, a joyless and weary, but always, to flesh and blood, a real *agony*. There are three enforcements of the exhortation. 1. *Many are unable to enter* : unable when the desire becomes active. The door was open when the desire was torpid, when the heart was listless. They might have heard the beseechings of grace, but there was only a feeble response. Perhaps they intended, at some time, to enter; like Augustine, who prayed for his conversion, and added, "But not yet." Anyhow, the hour is coming when the impotence of unfulfilled intentions will be made manifest. Jesus' language passes (ver. 25) into the familiar form of parable. He imagines the Master of the house allowing the door to stand open—the invitation to all free and full. But at length he rises and shuts the door, and then those who had thought that any time would do, that there was no call to make haste, rush forward, clamouring for the entrance of which they had thought little—their clamour to be met only with the retort, "I know you not whence ye are." "My sheep hear my voice, and I know them." These had not heard his voice. It is not the attraction of his voice to which they confess; it is only the sense of their danger. And the word goes forth for judgment: "I know you not; you are not mine." The parable is not to be unduly strained; but the point which it tends to illustrate is the necessity of *instant*, as well as *earnest*, agonizing. There is a "too late, too late!" From its unutterable darkness may the good Lord deliver us! 2. *Enjoyment of privilege will not avail as a plea.* (Vers. 26, 27.) To have had the teaching of the Lord in street and house, to have lived in the marvellous light of his gospel, to have realized his fellowship and the influences of his grace,—this is much. But the vital matter is, what is the use which has been made of privilege, of opportunity, of instruction, of means of grace? That the Lord displayed his tokens in our midst may only add to our condemnation. Negligence, hardness of heart, the contempt of his Word and commandments, which is evidenced in the refusal to yield ourselves wholly to him who speaks from heaven, is iniquity; and most solemn is the protestation, "Depart from me, all ye workers of iniquity." 3. *Grace unavailed of is blessing lost.* (Vers. 28—30.) The Jew assured himself that in the kingdom of God, when declared, he would share the everlasting banquet with Abraham and Isaac and Jacob, and that part of the zest of this feast would be the consciousness that the hated Gentiles were excluded. The Lord warns his audience that the picture might be, would be, reversed. The grace which they would not use would be transferred to others, coming from the east, and the west, and the north, and the south. And he concludes with the sentence, which at other times also he utters, "There are last which shall be first, and there are first which shall be last." Verily it may here be added, "He that hath an ear, let him hear."

Vers. 31—35.—*The composure and the emotion of Jesus.* I. THE COMPOSURE IN THE FACE OF A MESSAGE WHICH MIGHT HAVE AGITATED. The message may have been a concoction of the Pharisees, who, wishing to have him removed from the district, used the name of Herod to alarm him ; or it may have been inspired by Herod himself, who, although desiring to see Jesus, was jealous of his popularity, and was fearful lest in some way an uproar might be excited among the people. The latter seems the more likely supposition. The circumstance that Jesus sends his reply to the king, and that in so doing he singles him out as crafty and subtle, trying to do by intrigue what he could not do openly—"that fox"—gives weight to the view that, in saying what is recorded, certain of the Pharisees obeyed the command of the human tyrant. Be that as it may, the message was calculated to disturb the mind with secret terrors. For, of all the persons who pass before us in the life of our Lord, none was more capable of doing "the hellish thing" by mean ways than this petty ruler of Peræa. His character has been thus described : "He was false to his religion, false to his nation, false to his friends, false to his brethren, false to his wife—the meanest thing the world had ever seen." What could not such a man do? Would it not be well at once to take the hint, "Get thee out and depart thence"? But how perfectly calm is Jesus! No word like that could throw his soul off from its centre. The only phrase expressive of sheer scorn and contempt which ever fell from his lips belongs to this occasion (ver. 32). "Go tell that fox"—that human embodiment of deceit and cunning—"I shall take my time; *he* cannot frighten me; he cannot hasten me. My work in his country will be done. I must work to-day, and to-morrow, and the day following; for it cannot be that a prophet perish out of Jerusalem." Notice some characteristic points in this reply. 1. *The three days.* Is it a definite space of time that is marked out? If so, does it point to the remaining portion of the Galilæan ministry? or to the time which would elapse before his departure from Herod's territory? I incline to the

latter view. But it may be better to accept the saying as an intimation that, deliberately and without hurry, he would accomplish his task—" not to-day nor to-morrow,
but on a third day he would be perfected, or finished." 2. *The clause, " it cannot be
that a prophet perish out of Jerusalem."* Ah! there is a sad irony in it. " Herod kill
me here? No; I must reach the holy city. That is the slaughter-house of the
prophets. It would never do that I, the Prophet of Galilee, should perish elsewhere."
Sublime, serene, we have the sentences, "Behold, I cast out devils, and do cures"
(ver. 32); "I must walk to-day and to-morrow, and the day following" (ver. 33).
A good man's mission is a concern of God; God will take care of it and of him, so far as
he is essential to it. It may be said that no person is indispensable; yet, to a certain
extent, persons are indispensable. And every one who is consciously striving after the
best and noblest, and who is giving himself to some labour of love, may be sure that
there is a Divinity hedging him around through which no fox can break. The Herods
of the world, with all their scheming, cannot shorten the times of God. As he wills,
and while he wills, we must walk. Until he wills that we walk no longer, we are
immortal. Reposing in his heavenly Father's love, straitened until his baptism of
blood is accomplished, "journeying towards Jerusalem," the Christ of the Eternal is
lifted above the region of selfish fears. Tyrant cannot harm him, threat cannot ruffle
him: "Walk and work to-day and to-morrow, and a third day to boot, I must and
shall."

II. BUT OBSERVE HOW AND WHY THE EMOTION OF "THAT SAME HOUR" BURSTS
FORTH. These Pharisees could not scare him from his purpose, but they touched
the fountain of a Divine sensibility in his breast. And now, as at a later stage, a
cry of intense sorrow escapes him—the sorrow of wounded, but agonizing love. The
feeling of patriotism combines with the tenderness of Saviour-longing in the wail, more
than wail, which begins (vers. 34, 35), "O Jerusalem, Jerusalem, that killest the
prophets, and stonest them that are sent to thee!" The cry naturally follows the
sadly ironical reference to Jerusalem as the slaughter-house of the prophets! What are
the thoughts which fill the mind of Christ as he utters it? 1. *The conscious opposition
between a love that would save and an obstinate dulness that will not be saved.* Note
the figure, so often employed in the Psalms and prophetical books of the Old Testament—the wings stretched out for the shelter and warmth, the peace and safety, of the
brood (see Deut. xxxii. 11, 12). "How often," says the Lord Jesus (ver. 34), " would
I have gathered thy children together, as a hen gathereth her brood under her wings,
and ye would not!" Is this, "How often would I!" merely a reference to previous
visits to the capital and ministrations in it? Nay, it is the Lord of the prophets who
is speaking; the allusion, in its full meaning, is to the often-made effort to gather the
children together through the prophets whom Jerusalem killed, the messengers whom
Jerusalem stoned. It is the truth afterwards brought out in the parable of the wicked
husbandmen (see ch. xx). The protest is wrung from the patient, seeking, yet often
baffled will to save and bless. It is the protest which reverberates through infinite space
concerning men—the protest whose subject-matter is, slighted overtures, unheeded
calls, grace resisted, gifts sent away, knocks heard yet doors unopened; the "I would"
of God defied by the "I will not" of men. 2. *The knowledge of opportunity for ever
gone.* "If thou hadst known even in this thy day the things that belong to thy
peace! but now they are hid from thine eyes." This is spoken on the same day, at
the same hour, as that in which the warnings connected with the entering in at the
strait gate were uttered. Observe the connection with ver. 25. Solemn, awful
words! The things were open to the eyes during the day, the time of Divine visitation; then the eye would not regard them. It was fixed on other things—the black
dust of earthly care, or the glittering dust of earthly vanity. Now the story is
reversed. The eye would fain behold. Oh for a day of the Son of man! Oh for
the moments that have been thrown away! But the Master of the house has risen up,
and has shut to the door. The vision now (ver. 35) is a desolate house—a house left
to itself, God-forsaken. "O Jerusalem, Jerusalem, all thy palaces swallowed up, thy
strongholds destroyed, thy solemn feasts and sabbaths forgotten, thine altar cast off,
thy sanctuary abhorred, thy gates sunk, thy bars broken; thou that wast called the
perfection of beauty, the joy of the whole earth, abandoned, as it might seem, by him
who sought to gather thee, and thou wouldst not! O Jerusalem, Jerusalem, bleak,

bare, stripped! dost thou not sit in thy lonely place among the silent lonely hills, spreading forth thy hands, but there is none to comfort thee; yet ever in thy desolation witnessing, 'The Lord is righteous, for I have rebelled against his commandments'?" Jesus weeps! My soul, are these tears wept over thee? Dost thou know the things that belong to thy peace? Hast thou received the One who seeks to gather thee, and whose goodness and severity urge thee to repentance? O my soul, remember that he who shed tears, from the same fountain of love and mercy shed blood also. Let the tears of compassion and remonstrance send thee to the blood of cleansing.

> " Foul, I to the fountain fly;
> Wash me, Saviour, or I die."

HOMILIES BY VARIOUS AUTHORS.

Vers. 1—5.—*The significance of suffering.* What does it mean, that all men suffer? and what is signified by the great calamities which some men endure? The Jews of our Lord's time were drawing inferences which were common and natural enough; but they were not the safest nor the wisest that might have been drawn. In the light of the Master's teaching, we conclude—

I. THAT SUFFERING IS ALWAYS SIGNIFICANT OF SIN. Whenever we see any kind of suffering, whether it be ordinary sickness and pain, or whether it be of such an extraordinary character as that referred to here (vers. 1—4), we safely conclude that there has been sin. And this for two reasons. 1. That all sin tends toward suffering; it has the seeds of weakness, of decline, of dissolution, in it. Give time enough, and sin is certain, " when it is finished, to bring forth death." It carries an appropriate penalty in its own nature, and, except there be some merciful and mighty interposition to prevent it, the consequences will be felt in due time. 2. That it is certain there would have been no suffering had there been no sin. A good and holy man may be experiencing the results of other men's iniquity, and his troubles may be directly traceable to any wrong or even any imprudence in himself. Yet were he not a sinful man, to whom some penalty for some guilt is due, he would not have been allowed to be the victim of the wrong-doing of others. We bear the burden of one another's penalty; and there is no injustice in this, because, though we all suffer on account of other men's actions, we suffer no more than is due to our own delinquency. The fact that a man is suffering some evil thing is therefore a proof that, whether or not he brought this particular trial on himself, he has offended, he has broken Divine law, he has come under righteous condemnation.

II. THAT GREAT CALAMITY IS SUGGESTIVE OF GREAT GUILT. There are two considerations which suggest this conclusion. 1. One is a logical inference. We argue that if sinners suffer on account of their guilt, the greater sinners will be the greater sufferers. 2. The other is the result of observation. We do often see that men who have been guilty of flagitious crimes are compelled to endure signal sorrows; the tempest of human indignation bursts upon them, or the fires of a terrible remorse consume them, or the retribution of a righteous Providence overtakes and overwhelms them.

III. THAT WE ARE BOUND TO TAKE CARE LEST WE DO OUR NEIGHBOUR WRONG in this conclusion of ours. 1. For the heinousness of individual guilt and the measurable magnitude of present punishment do not always correspond with one another. We do not always know how much men are suffering; they may be experiencing inward miseries we know not of; and it is most likely that they are undergoing inward and spiritual deterioration which we cannot estimate—a consequence of sin which is immeasurably more pitiful than any loss of property or of health. 2. And the calamities that have overtaken a man may be due to the fault of others, and they may be *disciplinary* rather than *punitive* in their bearing upon him. They may rather indicate that God is cleansing his heart and preparing his spirit for higher work, than that God is visiting him with penalty for past iniquity. We must therefore be slow to act on the principle on which the Jews based the conclusion of the text. There is one thing which it is always right to do. We may be sure—

IV. THAT THE WISE THING IS TO MAKE HONEST INQUIRY ABOUT OURSELVES. What about our own sin ? *It is certain that we have sinned.* Biblical statements, our own consciences, the testimony of our neighbours,—all affirm this. We have sinned against the Lord, and deserve his condemnation and retribution. *Is it certain that we have repented ?* Have we turned away from the attitude and the actions of selfishness, of ungodliness, of insubmissiveness, of disobedience ? And are we resting and rejoicing in the mercy of God which is in Jesus Christ our Lord ? If not, we shall perish ; for impenitence means death.—C.

Vers. 6—9.—*Fatal fruitlessness.* We have to consider—
I. THE PRIMARY SIGNIFICANCE OF THE PARABLE. What did the great Teacher intend his hearers to understand by his words ? It was this (as I read it): 1. The *vineyard* is the kingdom of God—that realm of truth and righteousness which he has been, from the beginning, establishing on the earth. 2. Israel is the *fig tree* which God planted in his vineyard—a fig tree in a vineyard ; there not by any natural right, but at the option and discretion of the Divine Owner ; there " only so long as it served the purpose of him who planted it." 3. Sufficient time was given to Israel to show whether it would prove fruitful or fruitless, the " *three years* " standing for its day of probation, perhaps for the three periods represented by the judges, the kings, and the high priests. 4. Israel is found to be barren ; to be without real loyalty, real piety, solid worth. 5. Thus fruitless, it is only in the way ; it is failing to render the service which another " people of God," another Church, would render ; it is thwarting the holy and beneficent purpose of its Creator. Not only is it useless, therefore ; it is positively noxious and hurtful to the world ; it is a tree that must be cut down, for it cumbers the ground. 6. Jesus Christ, the Vinedresser, intercedes for it and obtains a merciful reprieve ; he will expend upon it the faithful toil of a gracious ministry. 7. But he recognizes the fact that persistent barrenness must meet its appropriate fate —banishment from the kingdom of God.
II. ITS APPLICATION TO OURSELVES. 1. God is founding a broad and blessed kingdom here—a kingdom wherein dwelleth righteousness and peace ; a spiritual, universal, benignant empire. 2. In it he places us, as the children and heirs of the most precious privileges, seeing and hearing (as we do) what kings and prophets saw not, nor heard ; enlightened as to some most valuable points, in regard to which the disciples themselves were necessarily in the dark (see homily on ch. x. 23, 24). 3. From us, thus advantaged, the Divine Husbandman demands good fruit. He may well expect that we should "yield much fruit" (John xv. 8), much reverence, purity, love, joy, service, usefulness. He is correspondingly disappointed and grieved when he finds but little, or even none at all. 4. The unfruitful are not only the guilty, but they are the *intolerably wasteful;* they receive without returning, whilst others in their place would receive and return. (1) As those who are *wrought upon* by Christian truth and influence, they remain unblessed, where others in their place would hearken and heed, would obey and live. (2) As those who are professing to work on and for others, they are holding some post uselessly, where others would be scattering benefit and blessing on every hand. They cause a deplorable and unendurable *waste* in the kingdom of God. 5. Christ offers us a merciful reprieve. Under his patient rule we are allowed another year, another period for repentance, for reformation, for renewal of heart and life. It is a sacred and a solemn time, an opportunity which we must not by any means neglect. For if we do, the word of Divine condemnation will be spoken, and we shall lose our place in the kingdom of our Lord.—C.

Vers. 11—13.—*The opportunity of love.* Jesus found himself, on the sabbath day, in the synagogue ; and being in the right place, he found something more than he presumably went to seek (see next homily). We have our minds directed to—
I. OUR LORD'S OPPORTUNITY, and the use he made of it. 1. He found this in *the presence of human infirmity.* There he saw a woman who had been afflicted in body for eighteen years ; she was " bowed together," etc. Not only was she subject to very considerable *privation,* but, as one whose figure was uncomely, she was exposed to the *ridicule* of the flippant and the heartless ; and this without break for a very large proportion of human life. Here was a most fitting object of tender pity and, if the

way were clear, of Divine help. 2. We mark the ready *manifestation of his sympathy.* He instantly *spoke* to her words of cheer and kindliness, awakening such hopes as she had not cherished for many a long year; and then he laid upon her a *healing touch :* " he laid his hands on her." It means much when God " lays his hand upon us." It meant everything to this woman with the new hope in her heart, that this kind, strong Prophet laid his hand of love and power upon her person; then she felt how near he had come to her, how close at hand was the delivering hour. 3. Then came *the exercise of his benignant power.* A great as well as a good work was wrought. (1) The injury by long disease was undone in a single moment; the rigidity of eighteen years was " immediately " relaxed (see Acts iv. 22). (2) The great Healer raised to the full stature and to the dignity and capacity of perfect womanhood one who had been helplessly and hopelessly disfigured and crippled. (3) And he called forth from her, and from all who witnessed his work, reverent and grateful joy; she and they rejoiced and glorified God.

II. OUR OWN OPPORTUNITY. 1. *The presence of human wrong,* and its manifold consequences. Around us are ignorance, unbelief, vice, crime, *sin ;* around us, therefore, are poverty, want, suffering, shame, degradation, death. No man who has an open eye for the condition of his kind can fail to see, day by day, some pitiful object that may well excite his deepest and tenderest compassion—men and women, all too many, whom sin has " bowed down," and who can " in no wise lift themselves up." 2. *The manifestation of our sympathy.* And how shall we show our feeling of regret and of desire? (1) By our *voice ;* by speaking the kind, true, enlightening, hope-giving word. (2) By our *touch ;* we shall not succeed without this. To take a man by the hand, or to lay a brotherly hand upon his shoulder, is to come into healing contact with him. It is to " come near " to the one we are seeking to bless; it is to give him the sense that, instead of " standing aloof," we feel and own and claim our brotherhood with him; it is to stand on the same level with him—the level of our common humanity, our erring, striving, suffering, aspiring humanity; it is to be where the healing and restoring power can be exercised and received. 3. *The result of our healing touch.* We exert the *influence that elevates.* The first result is enlightenment concerning himself; then faith in a Divine Saviour; then *uprightness* of character and *erectness* of spirit. The man is " made straight." He is no longer bowed down in spiritual bondage, with eyes directed to the earth; he stands erect in spiritual freedom, in purity of heart, in a large and blessed hopefulness; he has attained, through the influence of Christian love, a noble elevation; henceforth he will walk in the way of life, with all true dignity, in all gladness of soul, giving glory to the great Healer.—C.

Vers. 14—16.—*Suggestions from the synagogue.* The fact that this work of our Lord (see previous homily) was wrought in a synagogue on the sabbath day, and that it led to an outburst of fanaticism on the part of the ruler, which was followed by the severe rebuke of Christ, may suggest to us—

I. THAT EARNEST SEEKERS AT THE SANCTUARY MAY FIND MORE THAN THEY SEEK. We may class this woman amongst the earnest seekers; for the fact that, with such a bodily infirmity as hers, she was found in her place in the house of God is evidence of her devotion. She went there, we may assume, to seek the ordinary spiritual refreshment and strength which are to be found in worship, in drawing near to God and in learning his will. She found this as usual, and a *great deal more ;* she found immediate and complete restoration from her old complaint; she found a new life before her; she found a new Teacher, a Lord of love and power, in whose Person and in whose ministry God was most graciously manifesting himself to her. If we go to the sanctuary in an entirely unspiritual mood, with no hunger of soul in us, we shall probably come empty away; but if we go there to worship God and to inquire of his will, desirous of offering to him the service he can accept, and to gain from him the blessing he is willing to impart, then is it not only possible, but likely, that we may secure more than we seek. God will manifest himself to us in ways we did not anticipate; will show us the path we had never seen before; will take away the burden we thought we should bring home on our heart; will fill us with the peace or the hope that passes all our understanding; will open to us gates of wisdom or joy we never thought to enter.

II. THAT NOTHING BETTER BEFITS THE DAY OF THE LORD than doing the distinctive work of the Lord. Jesus Christ completely disposed of the carping and censorious criticism of the ruler. If it was right, on the sabbath day, to discharge a kindly office of no very great value and at some considerable trouble to a brute beast, how much more must it be right to render an invaluable service, by the momentary exercise of a strong will, to a poor suffering sister-woman who was one of the children of Abraham, and one of the people of God? And how can we better spend the hours which are sacred, not only to bodily rest, but to spiritual advancement, than by doing work which is peculiarly and emphatically Divine—by helping the helpless; by relieving the suffering; by enriching the poor; by enlightening those who are in darkness; by extricating those who are in trouble; by lifting up them that are bowed down? When, on the sabbath day, we forget our own exertions in our earnest desire to comfort, or to relieve, or to deliver, we may be quite sure that the Lord of the sabbath will not remember them against us, but only to say to us, " Well done."

III. THAT A FORMAL PIETY WILL NOT PRESERVE US FROM THE SADDEST SINS. This ruler was probably regarded as a very devout man, because his ceremonialism was complete. But his routine observances did not save him from making a cowardly, because indirect, attack upon a beneficent Healer; nor from committing an act of gross inhumanity—assailing the woman he should have been the first to rejoice with; nor from falling into an utter misconception of the mind of God, thinking that evil which was divinely good. We may hold high positions in the Church of Christ, may habitually take very sacred words into our lips, may flash out into great indignation against supposed religious enormities, and yet may be obnoxious to the severe rebuke of the final Judge, and may stand quite outside and even far off the kingdom of heaven. Let us be sure of our own position before we undertake the office of the accuser; let us beware lest over our outward righteousness Divine Truth will at last inscribe that terrible word " hypocrisy." Formal piety proves nothing; the only thing we can be sure about is the love of God in the heart manifesting itself in the love of men.—C.

Vers. 18, 19.—*The growth of the kingdom of God.* When we think of it we cannot fail to be impressed with the confidence, amounting even to the sublime, which Jesus Christ cherished in the triumph of his sacred cause. For consider—

I. THE UTTER INSIGNIFICANCE of " the kingdom " at its commencement. At first it was represented by one Jewish Carpenter, a young Man born of very humble parents, unlearned and untravelled, without any pecuniary resources whatever, regarded with disfavour by the social and the ecclesiastical authorities of his time, teaching doctrines that were either above popular apprehension or that ran counter to popular prejudices, unable to find a single man who thoroughly sympathized with him in his great design, moving steadily and fearlessly on toward persecution, betrayal, an ignominious and early death. Here was *a grain* indeed, something which, to the eye of man, was utterly insignificant and destined to perish in a very short time. Had we lived then and exercised our judgment upon the prospects of the nascent faith called by its Founder " the kingdom of God," we should certainly have concluded that in fifty years at the utmost it would have disappeared as a living power, and would only have remained, if it survived in any form at all, as a tradition of the past. But let us glance at—

II. ITS MARVELLOUS GROWTH. Truly the least of all seeds has become the greatest of all herbs; the grain has grown and become a "great tree." In spite of (1) the determined opposition of other faiths, which resented and resisted its claim to supplant them; (2) the sanguinary violence of the civil power, which almost everywhere strove to drown it in the blood of its adherents; (3) the hostility of the human heart, which has opposed itself continually to its purity, its spirituality, its unselfishness; (4) the deadly injury done to it by the inconsistency, the unfaithfulness, the dissensions of its own disciples;—it spread with wonderful rapidity. In three centuries it triumphed over the paganism of the known world; it has become the accepted faith of Europe and of (the greater part of) America, and of many "islands of the sea;" it has gained a firm foothold in the other continents, in the midst of the most venerable systems of religious error. Since the purification of its creed and the awakening of its members to their high privileges, it has made an immense advance toward the goal of a complete triumph; it has proved itself to be a benign and elevating power wherever it has been planted; it is the refuge, the strength, the hope, of the human world. What are—

III. ITS PROSPECTS? 1. It has numerous enemies who predict that it will decline and die. They regard it as a spent force that must give place to other powers. But this prediction has been often made before, and it has been falsified by the event. 2. Its friends are more numerous, and they are more intelligent, and they are more energetic and self-denying than they ever were at any former period in its history. 3. It holds truth which ministers to the wants of the human world—its sorrows, its sins, its aspirations—such as no other doctrine can pretend to. There is but one Jesus Christ in the history of the human race; but one Saviour from sin, one unfailing Refuge and Friend in life and in death. 4. God is with us in our work of faith and our labour of love. The crucified Lord will "draw all men unto him," and his salvation shall cover the earth, because the power which prevails against all finite forces is on its side. "All power is given unto me in heaven and in earth. Go ye *therefore*, and teach all nations," etc. (Matt. xxviii. 18, 19).—C.

Vers. 20, 21.—*The peaceableness and diffusiveness of Christian truth.* The words of Christ may properly suggest to us—

I. THE QUIET PEACEABLENESS OF THE CHRISTIAN METHOD. The starting and the spreading of "the kingdom of God" is like a woman taking and hiding leaven in some meal. How impossible to imagine any of the founders of the kingdoms or empires of this world thus describing the course of their procedure! The forces they employed were forces that shone, dazzled, smote, shattered; that excited wonder and struck terror; that crushed and clanged and conquered. Those which the Son of man employed were such as fittingly reminded of a *woman hiding leaven in some meal*—silently but effectually penetrating to the depth; quietly, peaceably spreading on every hand. He did not "strive nor cry," etc.; his gospel "came not with observation," with beat of drum, with dramatic display; shunning rather than seeking celebrity, he lived, taught, suffered, witnessed, died, leaving behind a penetrating power for good that should renew and regenerate the race. There may be occasion, now and then, to say and do that which astonishes or alarms or otherwise arouses; but that is not *the* Christian method. The influence which steals into the soul, which insinuates itself into the whole body, which noiselessly communicates a right spirit and diffuses itself without ostentation or pretence from centre to circumference,—that is the method of the Master.

II. THE DIFFUSIVENESS OF DIVINE TRUTH FROM WITHIN OUTWARDS. "Leaven, which a woman . . . hid;" not spread over the surface, but put into, placed in the heart of it, there to spread, to permeate, working from the centre towards the surface. This is the method of the gospel as distinguished from that of the Law. The Law exerts its power in the opposite direction—*from without inwards*; it acts directly on behaviour, leaving behaviour to become habit and habit to become principle. 1. Jesus Christ places the leaven of Divine truth in the *mind*, in the understanding, teaching us how *to think* of God and of ourselves, of sin and of righteousness, of the present and the future. 2. Then Divine truth affects our *feelings*, producing awe, reverence, fear, hope, trust, love. 3. Thence it determines the desires and convictions, leading to choice, decision, full and final determination. 4. And thence, moving towards the surface, it decides behaviour and ends in rectitude of action, excellency of life; so "the whole man," the complete nature, is leavened. Similarly, Divine truth is placed in the heart of the community, and, once there, it communicates itself from man to man, from home to home, from circle to circle, until "the whole" nation is leavened. But a man may ask, How is my entire nature to be thoroughly leavened with Christian principle— perfectly sweetened, purified, renovated, as it is not now? *Have we enough of the sacred leaven hidden within us?* It is true that "a little leaven leaveneth the whole lump," but there is a quantity, less than which is insufficient for the work. Have we enough of the truth of Christ lodged in our minds for this great and high purpose? Are we thinking, as Christ meant us to think, of our Divine Father, of our human spirit, of our human life, of the needs and claims of our neighbour, about giving and about forgiving, and about eternal life? Is our Master's thought on these great, decisive, determining themes *hidden in our hearts,* doing its sweetening and renewing work within us ? Christ says, "Come to me ; " he also says, " *Learn of me.*" Are we diligently, meekly, devoutly learning of Christ, receiving more and more of his hallowing and transforming truth into our mind, to stir our feeling, to regulate our choice, to beautify and to ennoble our life ?—C.

Vers. 23, 24.—*Vain inquiry and spiritual strenuousness.* There is all the difference in the world between the question that is general and speculative and that which is personal and practical; between asking, " Are there few that be saved ? " and asking, " What must I do to be saved ? " A great many unspiritual people show no small concern respecting matters that pertain to religion. It may be that they are curious, or that they are imaginative, or that they are visionary, and that religion provides a wide field for investigation, or for romance, or for mysticism. This speculative and unpractical piety may be: 1. A vain and unrewarded curiosity. It was so in this instance ; the applicant was moved by nothing more than a mere passing whim, and he received no gratification from Christ (see ch. xxiii. 8, 9 ; John xxi. 21, 22). It will be found that, on the one hand, Jesus always answered the questions of those who were in earnest, however humble might be the applicant ; and, on the other hand, that he never answered the questions of the irreverent, however distinguished the inquirer might be. And it is found now by us that if we go to his Word or to his sanctuary to inquire his will, we shall not go away unblessed ; but that if we go to either for mere gratification, we shall be unrewarded. 2. The retreat of irreligion and unworthiness (see John iv. 18—20). It is convenient to pass from personal and practical considerations to those of theological controversy. 3. The act of mistaken religiousness (see John xiv. 8). We act thus when we want to see the *Divine side* of God's dealings with us, or are anxious to know "the times and seasons which the Father hath put in his own power." Our Lord's reply suggests—

I. THE SUPREME IMPORTANCE OF PERSONAL RELIGION. "Are there few that be saved? . . . Strive to enter in," etc. ; *i.e.* the question for you to be concerned to answer is, whether you yourself are in the kingdom of God ; that is preliminary to all others ; that is the thing of primary importance ; *that* is worth your caring for, your seeking after, your diligent searching, your strenuous pursuit. Surely the most inconsistent, self-condemning, contradictory thing of all is for men to be thinking, planning, discussing, expending, in order to put other people into the right way when they themselves are taking the downward road. Shall we not say to such, " Go and learn what *this* meaneth, 'Let every man prove his own work, then shall he have rejoicing in himself alone, and not in another ; for every man shall bear his own burden' of responsibility to God "? The first duty a man owes to God and to his neighbour is the duty he owes to himself—to become right with the living God by faith in Jesus Christ his Saviour.

II. The fact that ENTRANCE INTO THE KINGDOM OF GOD DEMANDS GREAT STRENU-OUSNESS OF SOUL. 1. It is the great crisis of a man's career, and may well be attended with much spiritual disturbance. When a human soul first hears and heeds his Father's call and rises to return to his true spiritual home, he may well be affected with profound spiritual solicitude, and may well count that the goal he is seeking is worth all the labour and all the patience he expends to reach it. 2. There are occasions when special strenuousness of soul is demanded. Such are these: (1) When a man by long neglect has lost nearly all his sensibility. (2) When the earnest seeker cannot find the consciousness of acceptance which he yearns to attain. (3) When a man finds himself opposed by adverse forces ; when " a man's foes are they of his own household ; " when he has to act as if he positively " hated " father and mother, in order to be loyal to his Lord ; when downright earnestness and unflinching fidelity bring him into serious conflict with the prejudices and the practices of the home, or the mart, or the social circle ; and when to follow the lead of his convictions means to suffer, to lose, to endure much at the hands of man. Then comes the message of the Master— Strive, wrestle, agonize to enter in ; put forth the effort, however arduous ; make the sacrifice, however great ; go through the struggle, however severe it may prove to be. *Strive* to enter in ; it will not be long before you will have your reward in a pure and priceless peace, in a profound and abiding joy, in a heritage which no man and no time can take from you.—C.

Ver. 30.—*First and last.* There are many beside those to whom these words were first applied by Jesus Christ to whom they are applicable enough. They were originally intended to denote the positions of—

I. THE JEW AND THE GENTILE. The Jew, who prided himself on being the first favourite of Heaven, was to become the very last in God's esteem; he was to bear the penalty due to the guilty race that " knew not the day of its visitation," but imbrued its hands in the blood of its own Messiah. The scenes witnessed in the destruction of Jerusalem are commentary enough on these words of Christ. But this truth has a far wider meaning; it is continually receiving illumination and illustration. It applies to—

II. THE OUTWARDLY CORRECT AND THE ILL-BEHAVED. The Pharisee of every age and land is first in his own esteem, but he stands, in sullen refusal, far off the kingdom, while " the publican and the sinner " are found at the feet of Christ, asking for the way of life, for the waters of cleansing, for the mercy of God.

III. THE LEARNED AND THE IGNORANT; the astute and the simple-minded. Still we ask, "Where is the wise? where is the scribe? where is the disputer of this world?" Still may we, after the Master himself, give God thanks that he has " hidden these things from the wise and prudent, and revealed them unto babes." Human learning, in its unholy and foolish pride, still closes its ear to the voice that speaks from heaven. Lowly minded simplicity still listens to the truth and enters the open gate of the kingdom of God.

IV. THE PRIVILEGED AND THE UNPRIVILEGED. The children of privilege may be said to be among " the first." We congratulate them sincerely and rightly enough; yet are they too often found among the last to serve and to shine. For they build upon their privileges, or they reckon confidently on turning them some day to account, and they fail to use them as they should; and the end of their presumption is indifference, hardness of heart, insensibility, death. The first has become the last. On the other hand, the ear that never before heard " the music of the gospel " is ravished by the sound of it; the heart that never knew of the grace of God in Jesus Christ is touched by the sweet story of a Saviour's dying love, and is won to penitence and faith and purity; the last is first. Let presumption everywhere tremble; it stands on perilous ground. Again and again is it made to humble itself in the dust, while simplicity of spirit is lifted up by the hand of God.—C.

Ver. 34.—*Divine emotion, etc.* These words are full of—

I. DIVINE EMOTION. They are charged with sacred feeling. The heart of Jesus Christ was evidently filled with a profound and tender regret as he contemplated the guilt and the doom of the sacred city. Strong emotion breathes in every word of this pathetic and powerful lament. And manifesting to us the Divine Father as Jesus did, we gather therefrom that our God is not one who is unaffected by what he witnesses in his universe, by what he sees in his human children. The infinite Spirit is one in whom is not only that which answers to our intelligence, but that also which answers to our emotion; and this, of course, in a manner answering to his Divinity. He rejoices in our return to his side and his service; he is gladdened by our spiritual growth, by our obedience and activity; he is pleased with our silence and submissiveness when we do not understand his way but bow to his holy will; and he is pained by our spiritual distance from him, is grieved by our slackness and our lukewarmness and our withdrawal, is saddened by our sin. He looks with a deep, Divine regret on a Church or on a child of his that is rejecting his grace as Jerusalem did, and over whom, as over it, there impends a lamentable doom.

II. DIVINE PERSISTENCY. " How often would I have gathered," etc.! The Saviour desired and endeavoured to gather the children of Jerusalem under his gracious guardianship, not once, nor twice, nor thrice; his effort was a frequent act of mercy; it was repeated and prolonged. God " bears long " with us, forbearing to strike though the stroke be due and overdue; he is " slow to anger and of great mercy." But he does more than that, and *is* more than that; he continues to seek us that he may save us. He follows us, in his Divine patience, through childhood, through youth, through early manhood, through the days of prime, or unto declining years, with his teaching and his influence. He speaks to us by his Word, by his ministry, by his providence, by his Spirit. He seeks to win us, to warn us, to alarm us, to humble, and thus to

save us.   At how many times and in how many ways does our Saviour seek us!
How often does he endeavour to gather us under the shadow of his love!

III. HUMAN FREEDOM.   "How often would I!" "Ye would not!" It is quite vain
for us to attempt to reconcile God's omnipotence with our freedom, his right and
power over us with our power to act according to our own will.   The subject is
beyond our comprehension, and it is true wisdom to leave it alone, as an inaccessible
mountain peak which we cannot climb; there is danger, if not death, in the attempt.
But the *facts* are before us, visible as the mountain itself.   God has power over us,
and exercises that power benignantly and patiently.   But he does not interfere with
our freedom ; that, indeed, would be to unman us, to put us down from the level of
children into that of irresponsible creaturedom.   He leaves us free; and we are free
to oppose his sovereign will, to resist his Divine grace, to be deaf to his pleading voice,
to shake off his arresting hand.   He "would" that we should be reclaimed, be raised,
be enlarged, be ennobled ; and too often we "will not."   A solemn, awful thing it is
to share a human heritage, to live a human life, to incur human responsibility.

IV. HUMAN OBDURACY.   Jerusalem "often" refused to be drawn to its Redeemer.
Not only can we and do we resist the grace of God ; we can continue to do so; and
we *do* continue.   We can spend our life in a long contest with redeeming love; we
can repel the overtures of mercy and go on rejecting our Father's offer of eternal life
through all the years and periods of a long life of privilege.   Men do this, and to them
the words of Jesus are applicable in all their force; over them, also, his lament has to
be uttered.   1. It is well for those to whom it may apply to awake and to return before
he says to them, "Your house is left unto you desolate."   2. It is better, for it is safer
for us all to heed his inviting voice and place ourselves under the wings of his blessed
friendship long before such words as those of our text are anywise applicable to us.—C.

Vers. 1—21.—*The grace and progress of God's kingdom.*   We saw at the close of last
chapter how urgent a matter it is to get reconciled to God.   Luke, in constructing his
Gospel, introduces us next to a cognate thought—the necessity of repentance if judgment is to be escaped.   Let us take up the orderly thoughts as they are laid before
us in this passage.

I. JUDGMENT EXECUTED UPON OTHERS IS A CALL TO REPENTANCE ADDRESSED TO US.
(Vers. 1—5.)   There was a disposition then, as there is still, to set down special judgment as the consequence of some special sin.   Job's comforters simply expressed the
fallacy to be found in every heart.   When Christ's attention was, therefore, directed
to the Galilæan *émeute,* and to the bloody way in which Pilate had put it down, he
directed his hearers to discern in it a providential warning and call to repentance.
The accident at the tower of Siloam had the same significance.   It was a call to survivors to repent lest a judgment as severe should overtake them.   The fate of the
dead was no proof of special sin, but it was a clear call to repentance addressed to the
survivors.[1]   The warning was singularly appropriate.   The cruelty of Pilate and
the overturning of the tower of Siloam had their counterparts in the siege of Jerusalem
forty years after, when the people had demonstrated their impenitence.   Hence we
should learn the practical lesson from every judgment of the imperative necessity of
personal repentance.   These terrible calamities are allowed to occur, not that we may
uncharitably criticize the conduct of the dead, but that we may carefully review the
conduct of ourselves who survive, and repent before God.[2]

II. BEFORE MEN BECOME FINALLY IMPENITENT AND INCORRIGIBLE THEY GET A
LAST CHANCE OF AMENDMENT AND REFORM.   (Vers. 6—9.)   The siege of Jerusalem
has been before the prophetic eye of Christ, and, to impress the necessity of personal
amendment and reform upon the people, he tells the parable of the fig tree.   It is a
history of care without any return.   Orientals dig about their fruit-trees, and manure
the roots, and encourage fruitfulness in every way.[3]   Fruitless trees they burn, after a
three-years' probation.   Now, the Jews were as a nation represented by this fig tree.

[1] Cf. Geikie's 'Life and Words of Christ,' vol. i. p. 279; also Wolfe's 'Remains,' 6th edit.,
pp. 318—329.
[2] Cf. Gerok's 'Pilgerbrod,' s. 764; Gerok's 'Aus Ernster Zeit,' s. 687; and Saurin's
'Sermons,' tome i. p. 375.
[3] Cf. Van Lennep, p. 136.

Through long years the heavenly Husbandman had given it every chance of bearing fruit. His long-suffering is nearly exhausted, and but for the dresser of the vineyard—by whom Jesus means himself—it would have been cut down as a cumberer of the ground. His intercessions saved the nation for other forty years. And what tender care was expended on it in the closing ministry of Christ, and in the ministry of the apostles ! Truly the tears of our Lord over Jerusalem, the self-sacrificing zeal of Paul and Peter and the rest for the conversion of their own countrymen, and the series of significant providences with which the forty years were filled, unite to show that the national annihilation was deserved. A fruitless nation must make way for others. Let this last chance of the Jewish nation, the forty years of respite between Christ's death and Jerusalem's doom, admonish sinners of their solemn responsibility amid similar respites still. The Lord's long-suffering, though great, is not infinite ; upon it sinners need not eternally presume; a day comes round in every case, when he who will be filthy and unholy is allowed to be so still (Rev. xxii. 11).

III. THE SABBATH SHOULD BE THE SEASON OF SPECIAL UPLIFTING TO INFIRM SOULS. (Vers. 10—17.) How should a Divine day be spent ? This was the controversy Christ had with the chief priests and Jewish rulers. The rabbinical idea was that it should be a day of purely physical rest, and that even healing should be postponed to the succeeding and secular days. Our Lord, on the contrary, held that the sabbath was a day for special philanthropies, a day of opportunities such as the other days, with their secular routine, cannot afford. Hence the sabbaths were days of special miracle. Meeting a poor woman whose infirmities had been of eighteen years' standing, he took her, laid his hands upon her, and healed her. It was a glorious uplifting which the poor bent woman received. But the ruler of the synagogue, where this happened, indignantly objected to such a work being done on the sabbath day; only to draw upon him, however, the rebuke of Jesus, " Ye hypocrites, doth not each one of you on the sabbath loose his ox or his ass from the stall, and lead him away to watering ? And ought not this woman," etc. ? (Revised Version). His argument is unanswerable. They were accustomed to deal mercifully with their own beasts, but were ready most inconsistently to deal unmercifully with human beings, who should have been more valued, but are often, alas ! less cared for than dumb animals. Such hypocrisy found in Jesus a constant foe. His adversaries were thus put to shame, and the common people rejoiced and praised God for the glorious sabbath services which Jesus rendered to the poor and needy. Ought we not, then, to look for special upliftings of our infirm souls on the holy days? Jesus is waiting to heal us, and to raise us up to spiritual power.[1] As Gerok daintily puts it, we should expect to pass from work-day worry to sabbath rest; from earthly grief to heavenly joy; from the yoke of sin to the service of the Lord. We do not utilize our Lord's days aright, if such experiences are not enjoyed.

IV. THE KINGDOM OF GOD IS A WIDENING PHILANTHROPY. (Vers. 18, 19.) After the philanthropy extended to the infirm woman, it was natural for our Lord to pass to the parable of the mustard seed. This represents an insignificant beginning, followed by growth to such an extent, that under the branches of the mustard tree the birds of heaven find fitting shelter. In the same way the kingdom of God began around Jesus, apparently an insignificant Person, and eventually passed on to afford shade to many. In a word, the kingdom of God is an extending philanthropy. It widens its arms and embraces more and more in its shadow. In the same way, we may be sure that it has no true lodgment within us, unless it is making our philanthropy a growing and extending power. We are not Christ's unless we have his beautiful and philanthropic spirit.

V. THE KINGDOM OF GOD IS A THOROUGHLY TRANSFORMING POWER. (Vers. 20, 21.) From mustard seed and its growth, Christ proceeds to speak of leaven. It is hid in the three measures of meal, and works its way onwards until the whole mass is leavened. There is thus indicated how thorough and gradual the work of Christianity is. We are not true Christians unless every portion of our nature feels its transforming power ; nor will Christianity pause until it has penetrated to the utmost extent the population of the world. The great idea of the parable is *thoroughness*. Let this characterize us always in our connection with the kingdom.—R. M. E.

---

[1] Cf. Gerok's ' Evangelien Predigten,' s. 582.

Vers. 22—35.—*Christ's farewell words to the theocracy.* As Jesus was journeying steadily towards Jerusalem, the people saw that a crisis was at hand. Hence their anxiety to know how many would be saved in the new kingdom. They consequently inquire if the number of the saved shall be few. To this speculation the Lord returns a very significant answer; he tells them that many shall strive to enter in on false grounds, and that they should strive to enter in on true ones.

I. THOSE WHO SPECULATE ABOUT NUMBERS ARE USUALLY PEOPLE WHO PLUME THEMSELVES UPON THEIR PRIVILEGES. (Ver. 26.) It is wonderful how men deceive themselves. Here we find our Saviour asserting that at the last people shall come maintaining that because they have eaten and drunk in his presence, and because he has taught in their streets, they should be accepted and saved. We should naturally imagine that these privileges should lead souls to inquire anxiously how they have profited by them, whereas they are made the ground of claim and the hope of salvation. The Jews thought that, because they were possessed of privileges beyond other nations, they should be accepted before God; and self-righteous people to-day think that, because they have regularly gone to church and sacrament, and the various privileges of the sanctuary, they should for this reason be accepted and saved at last. So far from privileges constituting a ground of salvation, they are certain to prove a ground of increasing condemnation, if not faithfully used. People may be sinners all the time that they are associating with saints. They may be sitting at groaning tables provided by God, they may be listening to the lessons which he has furnished in his holy gospel, and yet their hearts may be homes of vanity, waywardness, and sin.

II. OUR LORD DIRECTS THEM TO STRIVE TO ENTER IN AT THE STRAIT GATE INSTEAD OF SPECULATING ABOUT NUMBERS. (Ver. 24.) Many are more addicted to speculation and religious controversy than to decision of character. They would rather argue a point than make sure of their personal salvation. Now, what was the strait gate in our Lord's time? It was attachment to himself as the humiliated Messiah, just as the wide gate and broad way were the expectation of a glorious and worldly Messiah (cf. Godet, *in loc.*). It is easy to attach one's self to a winning, worldly cause; it needs no spiritual preparation. But it was not easy, but took an effort of self-denial, to stick to the despised Saviour through all his sad and humiliating experience. And the same struggle is still needed. The cause of Christ is not a winning, worldly cause. You might do better in a worldly sense without identifying yourself with Jesus. But no man will ever have reason to regret identifying himself with the Saviour. No matter what self-denial it entails, it is worth all the struggle.

III. THE LAST JUDGMENT SHALL BE A REVERSAL OF HUMAN JUDGMENTS. (Vers. 25—30.) The current notions of Christ's time accorded to the Pharisees and religious formalists the chief seats in the new order of things which Messiah was to introduce. But Christ showed plainly that the Pharisaism and formalism of sinners will not save them or their sins in the day of the revelation of the righteous judgment of God. The first shall then be last; while the last in the world's estimation shall be the first in God's.[1] Abraham, Isaac, and Jacob would have received scanty recognition from the Pharisees of Christ's time; the patriarchs were men of a meek and quiet spirit, who did not seek to exalt themselves. Hence our Lord represents the despised ones getting to their bosom at the last, while the bustling Pharisees shall find themselves cast out.

IV. WE HAVE NEXT TO NOTICE CHRIST'S CONTEMPT FOR HEROD. (Vers. 31, 32.) It was thought by some of the poor spirits in the crowd that Christ would quail before the murderous king Herod, and that the sooner he got out of his jurisdiction the better. But no sooner do they suggest this to Christ, than he bursts into contemptuous terms about the cunning king. He calls him fox, and tells them to tell him, if they like, "Behold, I cast out devils, and I do cures to-day and to-morrow, and the third day I shall be perfected." The perfection of which he speaks is that which is reached through experience. Christ was sinless, but he had to go through the whole gamut of human trial, including death itself. He had to experience all the "undertones" of human experience before he could be perfect. Hence he was "made perfect through suffering." Contempt of others may be the very finest proof of our healthy moral state. It is the antipodes of that despicable flattery which is generally extended to kings.

[1] Cf. Mozley's 'University Sermons,' No. iv.

V. LASTLY, WE MUST NOTICE HIS LAMENT OVER JERUSALEM, BECAUSE THE MURDERER OF THE PROPHETS. (Vers. 33—35.) Our Lord was going to perish at Jerusalem. The reason was that there the policy of the nation was carried out, and all the prophets had found there their fate, and yet Christ had offered his protection to the doomed city. As easily as ever hen gathered her tiny brood beneath her wings could he gather the whole cityful under his wings. It is a beautiful and indirect proof of his Divinity. No mere man would have expressed himself thus.[1] But Jerusalem would not accept his protection. Instead thereof, it resolved to murder him, as the last in the line of the prophets. No wonder, therefore, that their house was left desolate, and that the murdered Messiah would withdraw himself until better times! He takes his "adieu of the theocracy," to use the words of Godet, and speaks of a welcome being his when the new views of a better time shall prevail. How important that we all should accept the proffered protection of the Saviour, and not imitate Jerusalem in her obstinacy and her doom!—R. M. E.

EXPOSITION.

CHAPTER XIV.

Vers. 1—6.—*The Pharisee's feast on a sabbath day. The healing of the sick with dropsy.*

Ver. 1.—**And it came to pass, as he went into the house of one of the chief Pharisees to eat bread on the sabbath day.** Still on the same journey; the Lord was approaching gradually nearer Jerusalem. The house into which he entered this sabbath belonged to one who was a leading member of the Pharisee party, probably an influential rabbi, a man of great wealth, or a member of the Sanhedrin. "To eat bread on the sabbath day," as a guest, was a usual practice; such entertainments on the sabbath day were very usual; they were often luxurious and costly. The only rule observed was that all the viands provided were cold, everything having been cooked on a previous day. Augustine alludes to these sabbath feasts as including at times singing and dancing. They watched him. This explains the reason of the invitation to the great Teacher, on the part of a leading Pharisee, after the Master's bitter denunciation of the party (see ch. xi. 39—52). The feast and its attendant circumstances were all arranged, and Jesus' watchful enemies waited to see what he would do.

Ver. 2.—**And, behold, there was a certain man before him which had the dropsy.** This was the scheme of the Pharisee host. The sick man was not one of the invited guests; with the freedom which attends a feast in a large Oriental house, the afflicted man was introduced, as though by chance, with other lookers-on. The skilful plotters stationed him in a prominent position, where the eyes of the strange Guest would at once fall on him. The situation is described by the evangelist with dramatic clearness: "And, behold, there was a certain man before him which," etc. In an instant Jesus grasped the whole situation. It was the sabbath, and there before him was one grievously sick with a deadly chronic malady. Would he pass by—contrary to his wont—such a sufferer? Would he heal him on the sabbath day? *Could* he? perhaps thought the crafty foes of the great Physician-Teacher. The disease was a deadly one, utterly *incurable*, as they thought, by earthly means.

Ver. 3.—**And Jesus answering spake unto the lawyers and Pharisees, saying, Is it lawful to heal on the sabbath day?** And the Heart-reader read their thoughts, and in a moment he saw all and understood all, and answered the unasked question of his host and the assembled guests by putting to them another query, which went to the root of the whole matter which they were pondering in their evil hearts.

Ver. 4.—**And they held their peace.** What could they say? If they had pressed the absurd restrictions with which they hedged round the sabbath day, they felt they would be crushed by one of the Master's deep and powerful arguments. They had hoped he would have acted on the impulse of the moment, and healed the sufferer or else failed; but his calm question confused them. **And he took** him, **and healed him, and let him go.** With one of his majestic exercises of Divine power—so slight a task to Christ —the deadly disease was cured in a moment, and then, with quiet crushing contempt, the Physician passed into the Rabbi, and to the awe-struck guests he put a question; it was his apology for the late infringement of the traditions of the sabbath day. What had they to say?

Ver. 5.—**And answered them, saying,**

[1] Cf. Brown's 'Divine Glory of Christ,' pp. 9, 10.

Which of you shall have an ass or an ox fallen into a pit, and will not straightway pull him out on the sabbath day? Most of the older authorities here, instead of "an ass or an ox," read "a *son* or an ox." The difference here in the reading without doubt arises from the perplexity which was felt in very early days over the strangeness of the collocation of "a son and an ox." This is the reading, however, which, according to all the acknowledged principles of criticism, we must consider the true one. The meaning is clear. "If thy son, or even, to take a very different comparison, thy ox, were to fall into a pit, wouldn't you," etc.? How the sophistries of the scribes and the perplexing traditions of the Jerusalem rabbis on their sabbath restrictions must have been torn asunder by the act of mercy and power performed, and the words of Divine wisdom spoken by the Physician-Teacher of Galilee! The noble instincts even of the jealous Pharisees must have been for a moment stirred. Even they, at times, rose above the dreary, lightless teaching with which the rabbinical schools had so marred the old Divine Law. Dr. Farrar quotes a traditional instance of this. "When Hillel"—afterwards the great rabbi and head of the famous school which bore his name—"then a poor porter, had been found half-frozen under masses of snow in the window of the lecture-room of Shemaiah and Abtalion, where he had hidden himself, to profit by their wisdom, because he had been unable to earn the small fee for entrance, they had rubbed and resuscitated him, *though it was the sabbath day*, and had said that he was one for whose sake it was well worth while to break the sabbath."

Vers. 7—14.—*At the Pharisee's feast. The Master's teaching on the subject of seeking the most honourable places. Who ought to be the guests at such feasts.*

Ver. 7.—**And he put forth a parable to those which were bidden, when he marked how they chose out the chief rooms; saying unto them.** The scene with the sufferer who had been healed of his dropsy was now over. The Master was silent, and the guests proceeded to take their places at the banquet. Jesus remained still, watching the manœuvring on the part of scribes and doctors and wealthy guests to secure the higher and more honourable seats. "The chief rooms;" better rendered "first places."

Vers. 8, 9.—**When thou art bidden of any man to a wedding, sit not down in the highest room.** The pretensions and conceit of the Jewish doctors of the Law had been for a long period intolerable. We have repeated examples in the Talmud of the exaggerated estimate these, the scholars and doctors of the Law, formed of themselves,

and of the respect they exacted from all classes of the community. One can well imagine the grave displeasure with which the Divine Teacher looked upon this unholy frame of mind, and upon the miserable petty struggles which constantly were resulting from it. The expositors of the Law of God, the religious guides of the people, were setting an example of self-seeking, were showing what was their estimate of a fitting reward, what was the crown of learning which they coveted—the first seats at a banquet, the title of respect and honour! How the Lord—the very essence of whose teaching was self-surrender and self-sacrifice—must have mourned over such pitiful exhibitions of weakness shown by the men who claimed to sit in Moses' seat! **Lest a more honourable man than thou be bidden of him; and he that bade thee and him come and say to thee, Give this man place.** As an instance of such unseemly contention, Dr. Farrar quotes from the Talmud how, "at a banquet of King Alexander Jannæus, the rabbi Simeon ben Shetach, in spite of the presence of some great Persian satraps, had thrust himself at table between the king and queen, and when rebuked for his intrusion quoted in his defence Ecclus. xv. 5, 'Exalt wisdom, and she . . . shall make thee sit among princes.'"

Ver. 12.—**Then said he also to him that bade him, When thou makest a dinner or a supper, call not thy friends, nor thy brethren, neither thy kinsmen, nor thy rich neighbours; lest they also bid thee again, and a recompense be made thee.** This remark of Jesus took place somewhat later in the course of the feast. Those present were evidently mostly, if not all, drawn from the upper ranks of Jewish society, and the banquet was no doubt a luxurious and costly entertainment. Godet's comment is singularly interesting, and well brings out the half-sorrowful, half-playful sarcasm of the Master. He was the rich Pharisee's Guest; he was partaking of his hospitality, although, it is true, no friendly feelings had dictated the invitation to the feast, but still he was partaking of the man's bread and salt; and then, too, the miserable society tradition which then as now dictates such conventional hospitality, all contributed to soften the Master's stern condemnation of the pompous hollow entertainments; so he "addresses to his host a lesson on charity, which he clothes, like the preceding, in the graceful form of a recommendation of intelligent self-interest." The μήποτε, *lest* (ver. 12), carries a tone of liveliness and almost of pleasantry. "Beware of it; it is a misfortune to be avoided. For, once thou shalt have received human requital, it is all over with Divine recompense." Jesus did not mean to forbid our entertaining those whom we love. He means simply, "In view of the life to come, thou canst do better still."

Vers. 13, 14.—**But when thou makest a feast, call the poor, the maimed, the lame, the blind: and thou shalt be blessed; for they cannot recompense thee.** Great pagan moralists, sick at heart at these dreary, selfish society conventionalities, have condemned this system of entertaining those who would be likely to make an equivalent return for the interested hospitality. So Martial, writing of such an incident, says, "You are asking for gifts, Sextus, not for friends." Nehemiah gives a somewhat similar charge to the Jews of his day: "Eat the fat, and drink the sweet, and send portions unto them for whom nothing is prepared" (viii. 10). **Thou shalt be recompensed at the resurrection of the just.** There is no doubt that Jesus here was alluding to that first resurrection which would consist of the "just" only; of that resurrection which St. John speaks of in rapt and glowing terms: "Blessed and holy is he that hath part in the first resurrection" (Rev. xx. 6). This was a doctrine evidently much insisted on by the early teachers of Christianity (see John v. 25; Acts xxiv. 15; 1 Cor. xv. 23; 1 Thess. iv. 16; Phil. iii. 11; and compare our Lord's words again in ch. xx. 35).

Vers. 15—24.—*In reply to an observation of one of the guests, Jesus relates the parable of the great supper, in which he shows how few really cared for the joys of God's kingdom in the world to come.*

Ver. 15.—**And when one of them that sat at meat with him heard these things, he said unto him, Blessed is he that shall eat bread in the kingdom of God.** One of those who were partaking of the banquet, and had witnessed the whole scene, now speaks to the Stranger Guest. He had looked on the miracle performed for the afflicted man; he had heard the wise words spoken by the Galilæan Rabbi; he had listened to the gentle and yet pungent rebuke to the Pharisee for his ostentatious hospitality to the rich and great; he had marked the quiet reminder as to the many sufferers who really stood in need of the viands so plentifully spread for those who wanted them not; he had been specially struck by the mention of the recompense which the just who remembered the poor would receive at the resurrection. This quiet observer, noticing that the Master's remarks were touching upon the recompense of the just in the world to come, now breaks in with a remark on the blessedness of him who should eat bread in the kingdom of God. The words do not seem to have been spoken in a mocking spirit, but to have been the genuine outcome

of the speaker's admiration of the Guest so hated and yet so wondered at. There is, no doubt, lurking in the words a certain Pharisaic self-congratulation—a something which seems to imply, "Yes, that blessedness to which you, O Master, are alluding, I am looking forward confidently to share in. How happy will it be for us, Jews as we are, when the time comes for us to sit down at that banquet in the kingdom of heaven!"

Ver. 16.—**Then said he unto him.** The parable with which the great Teacher answered the guest's remark contains much and varied teaching for all ages of the Church, but in the first instance it replies to the speaker's words. "Yes," said the Master, "blessed indeed are they who sit down at the heavenly feast. You think you are one of those whom the King of heaven has invited to the banquet; what have you done, though, with the invitation? I know many who have received it who have simply tossed it aside; *are you of that number?* Listen now to my story of the Divine banquet and of the invited thereto." **A certain man made a great supper, and bade many.** The kingdom of heaven, under the imagery of a great banquet, was a picture well known to the Jews of that age. The guests in the Pharisee's house for the greater part were probably highly cultured men. At once they would grasp the meaning of the parable. They knew that the supper was heaven, and the Giver of the feast was God. The many—these were Israel, the long line of generations of the chosen people. So far strictly true, they thought; the Galilæan Teacher here is one with the rabbis of our Jerusalem schools. But, as Jesus proceeded, a puzzled, angry look would come upon the self-satisfied faces of Pharisee, scribe, and doctor; whispers would run round, "What means the Galilæan here?"

Vers. 17—20.—**Come; for all things are now ready. And they all with one consent began to make excuse.** The excuses, viewed as a whole, are paltry, and "if," as it has been well said, "as a mere story of natural life it seems highly improbable, it is because men's conduct with regard to the Divine kingdom is not according to right reason. . . . The excuses are all of the nature of pretexts, not one of them being a valid reason for non-attendance at the feast." The fact was, the invited were pleased to be invited, but there the matter ended with them. The banquet, which they were proud to have been asked to share in, had no influence upon their everyday lives. They made their engagements for pleasure and for business without the least regard to the day or the hour of the banquet: indeed, they treated it with perfect indifference. The key to the parable is easily found. The Jews were "solemn triflers in the matter of religion. They were under invitation to enter the kingdom, and they did not assume the attitude of men who avowedly cared nothing for it. On the contrary, they were pleased to think that its privileges were theirs in offer, and even gave themselves credit for setting a high value on them. But in truth they did not. The kingdom of God had not by any means the first place in their esteem. . . . They were men who talked much about the kingdom of heaven, yet cared little for it; who were very religious, yet very worldly—a class of which too many specimens exist in every age" (Professor Bruce, 'Parabolic Teaching'). **I have bought a piece of ground. . . . I have bought five yoke of oxen. . . . I have married a wife**, etc. These excuses, of course, by no means exhaust all possible cases. They simply represent examples of usual every-day causes of indifference to the kingdom of God. To all these excuses one thing is common—in each a present good is esteemed above the heavenly offer; in other words, temporal good is valued higher than spiritual. The three excuses may be classed under the following heads. (1) The attraction of property of different kinds, the absorbing delight of possessing earthly goods. (2) The occupations of business, the pleasure of increasing the store, of adding coin to coin, or field to field. (3) Social ties, whether at home or abroad, whether in general society or in the home circle; for even in the latter case it is too possible for family and domestic interests so completely to fill the heart as to leave no room there for higher and more unselfish aims, no place for any grander hopes than the poor narrow home-life affords. The primary application of all this was to the Jews of the Lord's own time. It was spoken, we must remember, to a gathering of the *élite* of the Israel of his day. In the report of the servant detailing to the master the above-recorded excuses, it has been beautifully said, "we may hear the echo of the sorrow-ful lamentation uttered by Jesus over the hardening of the Jews during his long nights of prayer." The invitation to the feast was neglected by the learned and the powerful among the people.

Ver. 21.—**Then the master of the house being angry said to his servant, Go out quickly into the streets and lanes of the city, and bring in hither the poor, and the maimed, and the halt, and the blind.** The invitations to the great feast, seeing that those first bidden were indifferent, were then sent out far and wide—through broad streets and narrow lanes, among wealthy publicans (tax-collectors) and poor artisans.

The invitations were distributed broadcast among a rougher and less cultured class, but still the invitations to the banquet were confined to dwellers *in the city;* we hear as yet of no going *without the walls.* Here the invitation seems generally to have been accepted. All this in the first instance referred to the Galilæan peasants, to the Jewish publicans, to the mass of the people, who heard him, on the whole, gladly.

Ver. 22.—**And the servant said, Lord, it is done as thou hast commanded, and yet there is room.** While these words are necessary to complete the picture, still in them we have a hint of the vast size of the kingdom of God. The realms of the blessed are practically boundless. Here, again, in the first instance, there was a Jewish instruction intended to correct the false current notion that that kingdom was narrow in extent, and intended to be confined to the chosen race of Israel. It is very different in the Lord's picture.

Ver. 23.—**And the lord said unto the servant, Go out into the highways and hedges.** Hitherto the parable-story has been dealing with the past and the present of Israel; it now becomes prophetic, and speaks of a state of things to be. The third series of invitations is not addressed to inhabitants of a city. No walls hem in these far-scattered dwellers among the high-ways and hedges of the world. This time the master of the house asks to his great banquet those who live in the isles of the Gentiles. **And compel** them **to come in.** A greater pressure is put on *this* class of out-siders than was tried upon the favoured first invited. The indifferent ones were left to themselves. *They* knew, or professed to know and to appreciate, the nature of that feast in heaven, the invitation to which they treated *apparently* with so much honour, and *really* with such contempt. But *these* outsiders the Divine Host would treat differently. To them the notion of a pitying, loving God was quite a strange thought; *these* must be compelled—must be brought to him with the gentle force which the angels used when they laid hold of the hand of lingering Lot, and brought him out of the doomed city of the plain. Thus faithful men, intensely convinced of the truth of their message, *compel* others, by the bright earnest-ness of their words and life, to join the company of those who are going up to the feast above. Anselm thinks that God may be also said to *compel* men to come in when he drives them by calamities to seek and find refuge with him and in his Church. **That my house may be filled.** In ver. 22 the servant, who knew well his master's mind and his master's house too, and its capabilities, tells his lord how, after many had accepted the invitation and were gone in to the banquet, "yet there was room." The master of the house, approving his servant's words, confirms them by repeating, "Bring in more and yet more, that my house may be filled." Bengel comments here with his quaint grace in words to which no translation can do justice : "Nec natura nec gratia patitur vacuum." Our God, with his burning love for souls, will never bear to contemplate a half-empty heaven. "Messiah will see of the travail of his soul, and be satisfied." "The love of God," says Godet, "is great; it requires a multitude of guests; it will not have a seat empty. The number of the elect is, as it were, determined beforehand by the riches of the Divine glory, which cannot find complete reflection without a certain number of human beings. The invitation will, therefore, be continued, and consequently the history of our race prolonged, until that number be reached."

Ver. 24.—For I say unto you, That none of those men which were bidden shall taste of my supper. Whose words are these? Are they spoken by the host of the parable-story ; and if so, to whom does he address them? For in the original Greek it is not "I say unto *thee*" (singular), the servant with whom throughout he has been holding a colloquy, but "I say unto you" (plural). Who does he mean by "you"? The assembled guests? or especially the already introduced poor of ver. 21 (so Bengel)? But what conceivable purpose, as Stier well asks, would be served by addressing these stern words to the guests admitted? Would *their* bliss be increased by a side-glance at those who had lost what they were to enjoy? How inharmonious a close would this be of a parable constructed with such tender graciousness throughout! It is better, therefore, to understand it as spoken with deep solemnity by the Master himself to the assembled guests in the Pharisee's house, with whom he was then sitting at meat, and for whose special instruction he had spoken the foregoing parable of the great supper. "I say unto you, that none of *those* who were bidden in the parable-story (and ye know full well that you yourselves are included in that number) shall sit at my table in heaven." This identification of himself as the Host of the great heavenly banquet was quite in accordance with the lofty and unveiled claims of the Master during the last period of his public ministry. Throughout this exposition of the great supper parable, the idea of the primary reference to the Jewish people has been steadily kept in view. It was a distinct piece of teaching, historic and prophetic, addressed to the Jew of the days of our Lord. As years passed on, it became a saying of the deepest interest to the Gentile missionaries and to the rapidly growing Gentile congregations of the first Christian centuries. In time it ceased to be used as a piece of warning history and of instructive prophecy, and the Church in every succeeding age has recognized its deep practical wisdom, and is ever discovering in it fresh lessons which belong to the life of the day, and which seemingly were drawn from it and intended for its special instruction, for its warning and for its comfort.

Vers. 25—35.—*The qualifications of his real disciples. Two short parables illustrative of the high price such a real disciple must pay if he would indeed be his. The half-hearted disciple is compared to flavourless salt.*

Ver. 25.—And there went great multitudes with him. These great multitudes were made up now of enemies as well as friends. Curiosity doubtless attracted many; the fame of the Teacher had gone through the length and breadth of the land. The end, the Master well knew, was very near, and, in the full view of his own self-sacrifice, the higher and the more ideal were the claims he made upon those who professed to be his followers. He was anxious now, at the end, clearly to make it known to all these multitudes what *serving him* really signified—entire self-renunciation; a real, not a poetic or sentimental, taking up the cross (ver. 27). Even his own chosen disciples were yet a long way from apprehending the terrible meaning of this cross he spoke of, and which to him now bore so ghastly a significance.

Ver. 26.—If any man come to me, and hate not his father, and mother, and wife, and children, and brethren, and sisters, yea, and his own life also, he cannot be my disciple. The Lord's teaching throughout, in parable and in direct saying, pressed home to his followers that no home love, no earthly affection, must ever come into competition with the love of God. If home and his cause came ever into collision, home and all belonging to it must gently be put aside, and everything must be sacrificed to the cause. Farrar quotes here from Lovelace—

"I could not love thee, dear, so much,
    Loved I not honour *more*."

Vers. 28—30.—For which of you, intending to build a tower, sitteth not down first, and counteth the cost, whether he have sufficient to finish it? Lest haply, after he hath laid the foundation, and is not able to finish it, all that behold it begin to mock him, saying, This man began to build, and was not able to finish. The imagery was not an unfamiliar one in those days. The magnificent Herodian house had a passion for erecting great buildings, sacred and profane, in the varied cities under their sway. They would doubtless be often imitated, and no doubt many an unfinished edifice testified to the foolish emulation of some would-be imitator of the extravagant royal house. Now, such incomplete piles of masonry and brickwork simply excite a contemptuous pity for the builder, who has so falsely calculated his resources when he drew the plan of the palace or villa he was never able to finish. So in the spiritual life, the would-be professor finds such living harder than he supposed, and so gives up trying after the nobler way of living altogether; and the world, who watched his feeble efforts and listened with an incredulous smile when he proclaimed his intentions, now ridicules him, and pours scorn upon what it considers an unattainable ideal. Such an attempt and failure injure the cause of God.

Vers. 31, 32.—Or what king, going to make war against another king, sitteth not down first, and consulteth whether he be able with ten thousand to meet him that cometh against him with twenty thousand? Or else, while the other is yet a great way off, he sendeth an ambassage, and desireth conditions of peace. It is not improbable that this simile was derived from the history of the time. The unhappy connection of the tetrarch Herod with Herodias had brought about the divorce of that sovereign's first wife, who was daughter of Aretas, a powerful Arabian prince. This involved Herod in an Arabian war, the result of which was disastrous to the tetrarch. Josephus points out that this ill-omened incident was the commencement of Herod Antipas's subsequent misfortunes. Our Lord not improbably used this simile, foreseeing what would be the ultimate end of this unhappy war of Herod. The first of these two little similes rather points to the *building* up of the Christian life in the heart and life. The second is an image of the warfare which every Christian man must wage against the world, its passions, and its lusts. If we cannot brace ourselves up to the sacrifice necessary for the completion of the building up of the life we know the Master loves; if we shrink from the cost involved in the warfare against sin and evil—a warfare which will only end with life—better for us not to begin the building or risk the war. It will be a wretched alternative, but still it will be best for us to make our submission at once to the world and its prince; at least, by so doing we shall avoid the scandal and

the shame of injuring a cause which we adopted only to forsake. The Swiss commentator Godet very naturally uses here a simile taken from his own nationality: "Would not a little nation like the Swiss bring down ridicule on itself by declaring war with France, if it were not determined to die nobly on the field of battle?" He was thinking of the splendid patriotism of his own brave ancestors who had determined so to die, and who carried out their gallant purpose. He was thinking of stricken fields like Morgarten and Sempach, and of brave hearts like those of Rudolph of Erlach, and Arnold of Winkelried, who loved their country better than their lives. This was the spirit with which Christ's warriors must undertake the hard stern warfare against an evil and corrupt world, otherwise better let his cause alone. The sombre shadow of the cross lay heavy and dark across all the Redeemer's words spoken at this time.

Ver. 33.—So likewise, whosoever he be of you that forsaketh not all that he hath, he cannot be my disciple. "We must live in this world as though the soul was already in heaven and the body mouldering in the grave" (St. Francis de Sales). There was much unreasoning, possibly not a little sentimental enthusiasm, among the people who crowded round Jesus in these last months of his work. The stern, uncompromising picture of what ought to be the life of his real followers was painted especially with a view of getting rid of these useless, purposeless enthusiasts. The way of the cross, which he was about to tread, was no pathway for such light-hearted triflers.

Vers. 34, 35.—Salt is good: but if the salt have lost his savour, wherewith shall it be seasoned? It is neither fit for the land, nor yet for the dunghill; but men cast it out. Here "salt" stands for the spirit of self-sacrifice, self-renunciation. When in a man, or in a nation, or in a Church, that salt is savourless, then that spirit is dead; there is no hope remaining for the man, for the people, or the Church. The lesson was a general one—it was meant to sink into each listener's heart; but the Master's sad gaze was fixed, as he spoke the sombre truth, on the people of Israel whom he loved, and on the temple of Jerusalem where his glory-presence used to dwell. *Men cast it out.* Jesus could hear the armed tramp of the Roman legions of the year 70 as they cast out his people from their holy land.

HOMILETICS.

Vers. 1—24.—*The great supper.* The feast of which Christ was partaking had been carefully prepared, and was an event of some consequence in the town. This may be inferred not only from the tone of the Lord's remarks, but also from the intimations of the evangelists. Thus from ver. 12 it appears that the Pharisee had gathered together the *élite* of the place, along with his more intimate friends and his kinsmen. From ver. 7 we learn that there had been an eager scramble on the part of the guests for the chief places, the precedencies, and dignities. It was the observation of this which called forth the saying (ver. 11), "Whosoever exalteth himself shall be abased; and he that humbleth himself shall be exalted." Notice, too, as proving the care which had been bestowed on the entertainment, that there was an understanding among the more prominent guests that the movements and words of the invited Prophet should be closely watched. In fact, the supper was a trap laid. To complete the scheme, a man was introduced (ver. 2) who laboured under a severe illness— dropsy; a man whose presence might be a temptation to the loving-hearted Healer to violate the sacredness of the sabbath. Jesus, we are told (ver. 3), "answering," *i.e.* knowing the intention of the lawyers and Pharisees, put a question to them which revealed the thoughts of the heart, whilst it so vindicated his work of mercy that it reduced his hypocritical friends to silence : "they could not answer him again to these things ". (ver. 6). This great supper is the text of one of the most beautiful of our Lord's parables. The introduction of the parable is very simple. He had taught his host a lesson of charity (vers. 12—14), when one of the company, catching at the last clause, "recompensed at the resurrection of the just," and giving this the accepted Pharisee-meaning—a banquet at which the elect of the nation would sit down with Abraham, Isaac, and Jacob (presuming, of course, that he would have a place at that banquet)—exclaims, "Blessed is he that shall eat bread in the kingdom of God" (ver. 15). "Yes," virtually replies the Prophet, "only recollect that this kingdom of God is not the blessedness which you imagine; nay, since the call to it has been rejected by those who were bidden—*i.e.* the covenant-people—that call will be extended, in the fulness of its glory, to the publicans and sinners whom you reject—the people of the streets and lanes; it will be extended further still, even to the ignorant heathen— the people of the highways and hedges. For (representing in these words the giver of the festival) "None of those men that were bidden shall taste of my supper" (ver. 24). Such was the primary application of the parable. In its details it is entirely within the circle of prophetic ideas. The supper is an Old Testament symbol of the day of Christ, the Messiah (see Isa. xxv. 6). The "many bidden" were those who, having Moses and the prophets, were possessors both of the Word heard outwardly with the ear, and of the grace through which it is grafted inwardly in the heart. The servant at the supper-time denotes that preaching of the kingdom which began with John the Baptist, and was carried on by our Lord and those whom "he sent before his face into every city and place, whither he himself would come." The excuses intimate the pleas on which the invited, with one consent, turned away from the call. And the further missions of the servant, first keeping within the city, to the streets and lanes, and, secondly, quitting the precincts of the city, to the highways and hedges, denote, as has been said, the inclusion of the excluded classes of the Jews, along with the Samaritans, and the bidding of the Gentiles to the light of the gospel. "I said," thus ancient prophecy expressed it (Isa. lxv. 1), "Behold me, behold me, unto a nation that was not called by my Name." Passing from the first relations of the parable to those which more directly concern us, every part of it is suggestive of some aspect of Christian truth or life. Notice three points—

I. THE HOSPITALITY OF GOD. God is the Presence shadowed forth in the "man who makes the great supper." In the notion of such a supper we see the Divine hospitality. A supper carries with it the thought of an abundant provision, of satisfaction for all want, of an infinite and various fulness. And is not this associated in the Scriptures with the very name of God? Take, *e.g.*, one of the most beautiful utterances of the Psalter, Ps. xxxvi. 5—9. Indeed, the manifold revelation of God in nature, providence, grace, in the firmament above us, the earth around us, the great and wide sea,

our own consciousness, the Word who in the beginning was with God and was God—
God himself in every form of his communication, is the exceeding joy of the pure
in heart. His greatness is so hospitable. It makes room for all our littleness and
weakness " in its lap to lie." As Faber, in verses of sweetest music, has sung—

> " Thus doth thy grandeur make us grand ourselves ;
>   'Tis goodness makes us fear;
> Thy greatness makes us brave, as children are
>   When those they love are near.

> " Great God ! our lowliness takes heart to play
>   Beneath the shadow of thy state ;
> The only comfort of our littleness
>   Is that thou art so great.

> " Then on thy grandeur I will lay me down ;
>   Already life is heaven for me ;
> No cradled child more softly lies than I :
>   ' Come soon, Eternity.' "

It is this hospitality that is declared in the Son of the Eternal Love. Christ is the
Great Supper. In him God has " abounded towards us in wisdom and prudence."
St. Paul speaks of " the love of Christ which passeth knowledge," of Christ " the All in
all; " and, more particularly defining the supper-making, he says, " Christ, of God
made to us Wisdom, Righteousness, Sanctification, Redemption." All that we need as
men, all that is salvation for sinners, is ours in him. And how is it ours? " If any
man hear my voice, and open the door, I will come in to him, and will sup with him,
and he with me."

II. THE CHURLISHNESS OF MEN. This is God, with the door thrown wide open, the
table prepared, the life eternal given, the grand, ever-urgent " Come!" " Ho, every
one that thirsteth, . . . and he that hath no money, come!" But what is the reception ?
Strange, wonderful, but still too true, " They all with one consent began to make
excuse" (ver. 18). Look at the excuses. They are pictures of states of mind, of attitudes
of thought, as real now as at any time. Three such pictures are sketched. The first
(ver. 18), a mind which rejoices in a good realized. The man has the desire of his
heart. He is the lord of broad acres. " Soul, take thine ease; what need for thee of
the supper?" The second (ver. 19), a mind still immersed in business, with its cares
and anxieties. The man has just concluded an important purchase; before all else he
must prove it. The third (ver. 20), a mind absorbed in earthly delights and social
relationships—he " cannot come." We can trace, in the three pictures, a climax like
that of the parable reported in Matt. xxii., which closely resembles this. There is an
ascending scale in the rejection. The first is covetous to a degree; he would go with
all his heart—only that little estate; he must needs " pray let me be excused." The
second is polite, but more abrupt; there is a graceful wave of the hand, a gentlemanly
" Pray let me be excused;" but there is no " I must needs." The third is rude
and flat in his denial; there is a quick " No, I cannot." Is it not the climax of
worldliness in every period ? And what is worldliness? The celebrated Robert
Hall one day wrote the word " God" on a slip of paper. " You can read that?" he
said, as he passed the slip to a friend. " Yes." He covered the name on the slip
with a sovereign. " Can you read it now?" The sovereign was above, was nearer the
gaze than *God*. That is worldliness. It is not the having, not the purchasing, of the
ground or the oxen. It is the having the earthly thing in the first place, the setting
of the " must needs" over against it. And it is the mind which does this, to which
the heavenly kingdom is second to the earthly good, which is fruitful of excuses. Oh,
how often it puts off! how often there comes even the rude " I cannot"! Has the
Giver of the supper found such a mind in any of us?

III. THE COMMISSION OF THE SERVANT. It is to bear the Master's call, to declare
that " all things are ready;" that salvation is full and is present; life now, life for
ever, given with God's " yea" and " amen" to even the chief of sinners. The word
of the reconciliation is " Come!" the ministry of reconciliation implies, " Go, ever out

and out." The house of the Lord must be filled; he is bent on the winning of souls. A supper, and none to eat; a great supper, and only a few guests!

> "Salvation! O salvation!
> The joyful sound proclaim,
> Till earth's remotest nation
> Has learnt Messiah's Name."

"Compel them" is the voice of the Everlasting Love. Use, *i.e.*, all means of moral suasion; circle around their wills; plead, beseech, entreat, persuade, "instant in season and out of season;" draw them, watch over them; establish such links between the messenger and them that they shall feel that they must come with you, since God is with you of a truth. "Now then we are ambassadors for Christ, as though God did beseech you by us: we pray you in Christ's stead, be ye reconciled to God."

HOMILIES BY VARIOUS AUTHORS.

Vers. 7—11.—*Christ's word on modesty.* The remark which the conduct of these guests called forth from Christ suggests to us—

I. OUR LORD'S INTEREST IN THE HUMBLER DETAILS OF OUR DAILY LIFE. We might have imagined, judging antecedently, that the great Teacher would not concern himself with a matter so trivial as this; or that, if he did, we should not find a record of his remark in a narrative so brief as are our evangels. We know that he had occasion to rebuke the Pharisees for letting religious faith lose itself altogether in minute and infinitesimal prescriptions (ch. xi. 42; Mark vii. 4). And there is a very remarkable absence from our Master's teaching of petty regulations. He sought not to prescribe particulars of behaviour, but to convey Divine principles and to impart a holy and a loving spirit; he knew that these would spontaneously and invariably issue in appropriate conduct. But Jesus Christ would not have us think that he is indifferent to the way in which we act on small occasions. He could be "much displeased" by an act of small officiousness (Mark x. 13, 14); and he could be deeply moved by an act of simple generosity (ch. xxi. 2, 3). And we may learn from this incident that it is not a matter of indifference how we behave in the common occurrences of our daily life: to what homes we go, what place in the house we take, how we act at the table (1 Cor. x. 31), what is the tone of our conversation (Matt. xii. 37), with what raiment we are clothed (1 Pet. iii. 3), whether we encourage or discourage the weak and timid disciple (Matt. x. 42; xviii. 6). These things, and such things as these, are occasions when, by manifesting a kindly and humble spirit, we may greatly please our Divine Lord, or when, by an opposite spirit, we may seriously offend him.

II. THE PREFERENCE OF MODESTY TO SELF-ASSERTION. Jesus Christ here plainly and emphatically commends modesty of spirit and behaviour, and as decidedly condemns an immodest self-assertion. To take a lower place than we might claim to do is often found to be the prudent and remunerative course. Self-assertion frequently goes too far for its own ends, and is discomfited and dishonoured. Every one is pleased when the presumptuous person is humiliated. But modesty is frequently recognized and honoured, and every one is gratified when the man who "does not think more highly of himself than he ought to think" is the object of esteem. But when, in a more worldly and diplomatic sense, such modesty does not answer; when a strong complacency and a vigorous self-assertion do, as they often will, pass it in the race of life, and snatch the fading laurel of "success;"—still is it the becoming, the beautiful thing; still is it worth possessing for its own sake. To *be lowly-minded* is a far better portion than to *have* all the honours and all the gains which an ugly assertiveness may command.

III. THE VITAL VALUE OF HUMILITY. (Ver. 11.) Lowliness of mind, penitence, may be of small account in the eyes of men, but, on the part of those as guilty as we are, it is everything in the sight of God: "Blessed are the poor in spirit: for theirs is the kingdom of heaven." Spiritual pride is utterly offensive to God, and draws down his most serious condemnation; if we exalt ourselves we shall be abased by him. But a sense of our own unworthiness is what he looks to see in children that have forgotten their Father, in subjects that have been disloyal to their King; and when he sees it he is prepared to pardon and to restore. If we humble ourselves before him and plead his promise of life in Jesus Christ, he will exalt us; he will treat us as his children; he will make us his heirs; he will raise us up to "heavenly places in Christ Jesus."—C.

Vers. 12—14.—*Moderation; disinterestedness; patience.* We find in these words of our Lord—

I. THE CORRECTION OF A COMMON FAULT. Jesus Christ did not, indeed, intend to condemn outright all family or social gatherings of a festive character. He had already sanctioned these by his own presence. The idiomatic language, "do not, but," signifies, not a positive interdiction of the one thing, but the superiority of the other. Yet may we not find here a correction of social, festive extravagance; the expenditure of an undue measure of our resources on mutual indulgences? It is a very easy and a very common thing for hospitality to pass into extravagance, and even into selfish indulgence. Those who invite neighbours to their house in the full expectation of being invited in return may seem to themselves to be open-handed and generous, when they are only pursuing a system of well-understood mutual ministry to the lower tastes and gratifications. And it is a fact that both then and now, both there and here, men are under a great temptation to expend upon mere enjoyment of this kind a degree of time and of income which seriously cripples and enfeebles them. Thus that is given to display and indulgence which might be reserved for benevolence and for piety; thus life is lowered, and its whole service is reduced; thus we fail to reach the stature to which we might attain, and to render to our Master and his cause the service we might bring. In the matter of indulgence, direct or (as here) indirect, while we should keep away from asceticism, it is of still greater consequence that we do not approach a faulty and incapacitating selfishness.

II. AN INVITATION TO A NOBLE HABIT. "Call the poor . . . and thou shalt be blessed; for they cannot recompense thee." An act of disinterested kindness carries its blessing with it. 1. It is an intrinsically excellent thing. "To do good and to communicate" is honourable and admirable; and to do this with no thought of return from those who are benefited, is an act of peculiar and exceptional worth. It takes very high rank in the scale of spiritual nobleness. 2. It allies us with the highest and the best in all the universe; with the noblest men and women that ever lived in any land or age; with the angels of God (Heb. i. 14); with our Divine Exemplar (Mark x. 45); with the eternal Father himself (Matt. v. 45). 3. It leaves a benign and elevating influence on our own spirit. Every man is something the better, is so much the worthier and more Christ-like, for every humblest deed of disinterested benevolence.

III. THE PROMISE OF A PURE REWARD. If the idea of recompense is admitted, everything turns upon the character of the reward, so far as the virtue of the action is concerned. To do something for an immediate and sensible reward is unmeritorious; to act in the hope of some pure and distant recompense is an estimable because a spiritual procedure. Our life is, then, based upon faith, upon hope, and especially upon patience. To do good and to be content to wait for our recompense until "the resurrection of the just," when we shall reap the approval of the Divine Master and the gratitude of those whom we have served below,—this is conduct which our Lord approves; it bears the best mark it can bear—that of his Divine benediction.—C.

Ver. 18.—*Excusing ourselves.* There are two things which seem as if they could not exist together, but which we continually confront. One is the felt obligation and value of religion, and the other is the mournful commonness of irreligion. Where shall we find an explanation of the coexistence of these two things? We find it in *the habit of self-excuse.* With one consent men excuse themselves. Now, an excuse is one of two things.

I. A PRETEXT which men invent, so as to shun, without self-reproach, a plain but painful duty. A tradesman is not prospering in business; he is aware that he is losing money; he feels sure that an examination of his books will show a serious deficit at the end of the year; he knows that he ought to acquaint himself with his actual financial position; but he is reluctant to see how far he is behind; he would much rather escape that scrutiny, and he consequently looks about for a reason that he can place before his own mind for postponing it. He easily discovers one. He could make better use of the time; he ought not to neglect an opportunity that offers of making a good bargain—or anything else. What does it matter? Anything will serve; one pretext is as good as another. Here is a human soul that owes much to its Creator; has received everything, and has paid nothing or scarcely anything—owes "ten thousand talents," and "has nothing to pay." One comes to him from God, and says, "See how things stand between you and your Maker; 'acquaint thyself with him, and be at peace.'" But the man shrinks from the scrutiny; he is in debt, and knows that he is; he would much rather enter into any other account than that. So he searches for some plausible reason for putting it off to another time. And he easily finds one. Excuses are in the air, at every one's command. He has no time for religious inquiry; so many people speak in God's Name, he is not sure who holds the truth; he will be under more favourable spiritual conditions further on—or something else. What does it matter? One excuse serves as well as another. It is nothing but a screen put up between the eye and the object. This is a course of action to be ashamed of. It is not manly; it is not right; it is perilous; it is delusive, and leads down to destruction.

II. A PREFERENCE of that which is second-rate to that which is of supreme importance. Here the particular illustrations of the parable serve us. These men are invited to be present at that which they ought to attend; but they allow something of inferior urgency to detain them. God is inviting us to partake of a most glorious spiritual provision; he is offering eternal life to his human children. He is sending his servants to say, "Come, for all things are ready!" But how many decline! and they decline because they "make excuse;" they put into the first place that which should come second. It is the demands of business; or it is the cares of the household; or it is the sweets of literature, of art, of family affection; or it is the claims of human friendship; or it is the hope of political influence or renown. It is something human, earthly, finite, on the ground of which the soul is saying, "Ambassador of Christ, I pray thee have me excused!" But it is wrong and it is ruinous to act thus. 1. Nothing will ever justify a man in placing first in his esteem that which God has placed second, in keeping behind that which has such sovereign claims to stand in front. The claims of God the eternal Father of spirits, of Jesus Christ our Divine Saviour, of our own priceless spirit, of those whom we love and for whose immortal well-being we are held responsible by God,—these cannot be relegated to a secondary and inferior position without serious *guilt*. 2. Nothing will make it other than *foolish* for a man to leave unappropriated the immeasurable blessings of godliness; to prefer any passing earthly good to the service of Jesus Christ, the service which hallows all joy, sanctifies all sorrow, ennobles all life, prepares for death, and makes ready for judgment and eternity. How can such folly be surpassed?—C.

Ver. 23.—*Spiritual breadth.* The parable presents the gospel as a sacred feast prepared by the Divine Lord for the hungering hearts of men. The invitation is declined by one and another, who have inclinations for other and lower good than that which is thus provided. Hence the measures taken to supply their room. The text suggests—

I. THE LARGENESS OF GOD'S LOVING PURPOSE. God wills that his house "shall be filled." This house of his grace is built on a large scale; in it are "many mansions," many rooms. The magnitude of it answers to the greatness of his power and to the boundlessness of his love. The number of the ultimately redeemed will be vast indeed. To this point: 1. The hopes of all holy and generous souls. 2. The terms of predictive Scripture. 3. The attributes of the wise, strong, benignant Father of men. 4. The duration of the redemptive scheme. 5. The character of the redemptive work —the Incarnation, the sorrow, the shame, the death, of the Son of God. God's loving purpose is to gather a multitude which no man can number into the heavenly home, into the eternal mansions.

II. THE FULNESS OF THE DIVINE COMMISSION. Those who represent the Lord of the feast are to "go into the highways and hedges, and *compel* men to come in." No people are to be excluded; no efforts are to be spared; no "stone is to be left unturned" to win men to the feast. There is to be a sacred compulsion used rather than the efforts of the "servants" should be unsuccessful. Here is no warrant for persecution. No two things can conceivably be further apart from one another than the use of violence and the spirit of Christ. To employ cruelty in order to compel men into Christianity is worse than a senseless solecism; it is a flagrant and guilty contradiction. There are other and nobler ways of "compelling men to come in" to the kingdom and the Church of Christ—ways which are not discordant but harmonious with the spirit and the teaching of the Lord of love. They are such as these: 1. The constant and irresistible beauty of our daily life. The "waters" of spiritual loveliness "wear" the hardest stones of spiritual obduracy. 2. Occasional magnanimity of Christian conduct. Men are often *compelled* to bow down in admiration and even in reverence before some deed of noble self-sacrifice, of lofty heroism. 3. Convincing presentation of the Christian argument. The truth of Christ may be presented so cumulatively, so forcibly, so directly, so practically, so winningly, so affectionately, that the most defiant are abashed, the most prejudiced are convinced, the most impervious are penetrated, the most insensible are moved and won; they are compelled to come in. 4. Earnest persistency of Christian zeal. There is a blind, imprudent zeal, which is worse than worthless, which only teases and torments, which does not allure but drives to a greater distance. But there is also a wise, holy, Divine persistency, which will not be refused, which employs every weapon in the sacred armoury, which knows how to wait in patience as well as how to work in ardour, which, like the patient Saviour himself, "stands at the door, and knocks." This is the zeal which continues to plead with men for God, and ceases not to plead with God for men, until the barriers are broken down, until the indifference is broken up, until the heart looks up to heaven and cries, "What shall I do that I may inherit eternal life?"—C.

Vers. 25—33.—*The time and the room for calculation in religion.* What room is there in the religion of Jesus Christ for calculation? What amount of reckoning before acting is permissible to the disciple of our Lord? When and in what way should he ask of himself—Can I afford to do this? Have I strength enough to undertake it?

I. THE CIRCUMSTANCE WHICH SUGGESTED THE IDEA. It was the temporary popularity of Christ that led him to the strain of remark we have in the text. "There went great multitudes with him" (ver. 25), fascinated by his presence and bearing, or struck by his teaching, or marvelling at his mighty works. And these men and women were far from entering into his spirit or sharing his high purpose; it was necessary that they should understand what discipleship to Jesus meant, what absolute self-surrender it involved. So the Master gave utterance to the strong and trenchant words recorded in the context (vers. 26, 27). And the words of the text itself are explanatory of this utterance. Their import is this: "I say this because it is much better you should know what you are doing by following me than that you should enter upon a course which you will find yourselves obliged to abandon, than that you should undertake a duty to which you will find yourselves unequal. All wise people, before they definitely commit themselves to any policy carefully consider whether they can carry it through. Every wise builder calculates the cost before he begins to build; every wise king estimates his military strength before he declares war. So do you consider whether you are prepared to make a full surrender of your will to my will, of your life to my service, before you attach yourselves to my side; for whoever is not able to 'forsake all that he hath' at my bidding, 'cannot be my disciple.' Ponder the matter, therefore; weigh everything before you act, count the cost, decide deliberately and with a full understanding of what it is you are doing."

II. THE PLACE THERE IS FOR CALCULATION IN PERSONAL RELIGION. 1. At the entrance upon a Christian life. It would seem as if there could be no room for reckoning here. We may well ask—When God calls us to himself, when Christ invites us to come unto him, what time should we allow ourselves before responding to his summons? Should not our response be immediate, instantaneous? We reply—Time enough to understand what we are undertaking to be and to do; time enough to take the Divine message into our full and intelligent consideration; so that our choice may be not the impulse of an hour, but the fixed and final purpose of our soul. God would not have us act in ignorance, in misconception. In malice we may well be children, but in understanding we should be men. There is no step any man can take which is comparable in importance with that which is taken when a human soul enters the kingdom of God: on that hang everlasting issues. Let men, therefore, diligently and reverently inquire until they understand what it means to have a living faith in Jesus Christ, to enter his spiritual kingdom, and become one of his subjects; let them understand, among other things, that it means the cheerful and full surrender of themselves to the Saviour himself, with all that such surrender involves (ver. 33). 2. At the entrance on a public profession of personal religion. Here is a visible "Church" which we are invited to join, taking upon ourselves the Christian name, and openly avowing our attachment to our Lord; thus honouring him before men. This is a step to be taken deliberately. Before taking it, a man should certainly ask himself whether he is prepared to act in accordance with his profession *everywhere,* in all circles and in every sphere; not only where he will be encouraged to do the right, but where he will be solicited to do the wrong thing; not only in the midst of genial influences, but in the throng of perilous temptations. But while these things are to be carefully taken into account, there must be reckoned, on the other side, the assurance which genuine piety may always cherish of *needed Divine succour.* If we go forth in the Name and in the strength of our Lord to do that which is his own command, we may confidently count on his support; and with him at our right hand we shall not be moved from the path of integrity and consistency. Look the facts in the face, but include *all* the facts; and do not forget that among these are the promises of the faithful Friend. 3. Before undertaking any post of sacred service. It would be worse than foolish for a Christian man to go forth to any enterprise requiring an amount of physical strength, or of intellectual capacity, or of educational advantages, which he knows well he does not possess. That would be to begin to build and to be unable to finish, to declare war with the certainty of defeat. At all times, when we are thinking of Christian work, we must carefully consider our qualifications. A wise and modest refusal is a truer sacrifice than an indiscreet and unwarrantable acceptance. But, again, let our judgment include the great factor of the Divine presence and aid, and also the valid consideration that competency comes with exercise, that to him that hath (uses his capacities) is given, and he has abundance (of power and of success).—C.

Ver. 26.—*Christ and kindred.* The circumstances under which these words were spoken will explain the strength of the language used. Jesus Christ said that he came "not to send peace on earth, but a sword," by which he meant that the first effect of the introduction of his Divine truth would be (as he said) to set the members of the same family "at variance" against one another, and to make a man's foes to be "they of his own household" (Matt. x. 34—36). By honouring and acknowledging him as the Messiah of the Jews and as the Redeemer of mankind, his disciples would excite the bitterest enmity in the minds of their own kindred; they would be obliged to act *as if they hated them,* causing them the keenest disappointment and the severest sorrow. They would be compelled to act as if they *hated their own life* also, for they would take a step which would remove all comfort and enjoyment from it, and make it valueless if not miserable. On the relation of Jesus Christ and his gospel to human kindred, it may be said that Christianity—

I. DISALLOWS PARENTAL TYRANNY. Such unmitigated authority as the Roman law gave to the parent over the child is not sanctioned, but implicitly condemned, by Jesus Christ. No human being is wise enough or good enough to exercise such prerogative; and to yield such deference is to cede the responsibility which our Creator has laid upon us, and which cannot be devolved.

II. DISALLOWS FILIAL WORSHIP. Such idolatrous homage as the children of the Chinese render to their parents is also distinctly unchristian; it is giving to the creature what is due only to the Creator. It is to elevate the human above its lawful level.

III. SANCTIONS AND ENJOINS FILIAL DEVOTEDNESS. Our Lord himself severely condemned the perversity of the Pharisees, who contrived to evade filial obligations by sacred subtleties (Mark vii. 9—13). And amid the physical agonies and the spiritual struggles and sufferings of the cross he found time to commend his mother to the care of "the beloved disciple." His apostles explicitly enjoined filial obedience (Eph. vi. 1). And entering into the profounder spirit of our Lord's teaching, we are sure that he desires of children that they should not only be formally obedient to their parents' word, but that they should be careful to render to them all filial respect in manner; should have regard to their known will, whether uttered or unexpressed; should render the service of love and of cheerfulness rather than of constraint; should make their filial ministry to abound as parental health and strength decline.

IV. RESERVES ABSOLUTE OBEDIENCE FOR THE DIVINE REDEEMER. When Christianity is assailing a false faith, as in the first century, as in heathen lands to-day, it very frequently happens that disciples have to choose between their attachment to the earthly parent and their obligations to Christ. Then the words of Jesus Christ have a literal application; then the convert has to pass through the most severe and trying of all conflicts; he has to weigh one authority against another; he has to make a decision which will cause grief and wrath to one whom he would fain please and honour. But much as the human parent may have been to him, and strong as are his claims, the Divine Redeemer is more, and his claims are stronger still and stronger far. The Lord who created him (John i. 3; Col. i. 16); who redeemed him with his own blood; who sought and found and restored him; who has made him an heir of eternal life;—this Lord, who has been upholding him by his power, and who is the one Hope and Refuge of his soul, has claims upon his obedience to which even those of a human parent are utterly unequal. And when the choice has to be made, as it sometimes has even here and now, there can be but one course which he recognizes as right; it is to choose the side and the service of the holy Saviour; *meekly bearing* the heavy cross of domestic severance; *earnestly praying* for the time when the human authority will be reconciled to the Divine; *faithfully believing* that the sacrifice which is thus entailed will bring with it, in Christ's own time and way, a large and abundant recompense (Mark x. 28—30).—C.

Vers. 34, 35.—*Ourselves as salt.* It is hardly possible to mistake the meaning of Christ here. We know that salt is the great preservative of animal nature, the antidote of putrefaction and decay. We know also that the great Teacher intended that his disciples should *be* the salt of the earth, doing in the human the same purifying work which salt does in the animal world.

I. THE PRESERVING POWER OF THE GOOD IN THE SOCIETY IN WHICH THEY ARE FOUND. 1. As those who act directly on God, and so on behalf of men. Had there been ten righteous men in Sodom, they would have preserved it from destruction. Similarly, the presence of a few righteous men would have saved the cities of Canaan. Is it not the presence of the righteous men and women in our modern cities which averts the retribution of God? 2. As those that act directly on man, and thus on God. As there is a tendency in animal nature, when life is extinct, towards putrefaction, so is there a tendency in human nature, when spiritual life is extinct, towards degeneracy and corruption. It is the function of salt in the economy of nature to prevent this result, to preserve sweetness and wholesomeness; it is the part of moral goodness to prevent corruption in society and to preserve purity and excellency there. And this it does. Purity, sobriety, uprightness, reverence, self-control,—these are powers for subduing, for restraining; they are powers that permeate, that sweeten, that preserve. This is eminently true of *Christian discipleship*: for it has (1) *truth* to *propound* which is most cleansing in its character; and it has (2) a *life* to *live* which is eminently purifying in its influence—the distinctive truth of the gospel of Jesus Christ, and the life of the great Exemplar, which every follower of his is charged and is empowered to live again.

II. THE DANGER THAT THIS POWER WILL BE LOST. "Salt is good: but *if the salt have lost its savour!*" It may do so. The salt, by exposure to sun and rain, may lose its pungency and its virtue while retaining its appearance. 1. And so Christian truth may lose its distinguishing force. Men may use Christian forms of speech in their teaching, and yet the doctrine they declare may be an enfeebled and emasculated Christianity, from which all that is distinctive and all that is redeeming is extracted: it is salt without its savour. 2. And so Christian life may lose its excellency and its virtue. These may be blurred and blemished lives, or they may be spotted and stained lives, or they may be lives with nothing in them beyond mere conventional propriety —lives not animated by the love of Christ, not filled with the Spirit of Christ, not governed by the principles of Christ; not blamable, but not beautiful; not wicked, but worldly; not criminal, but not Christian: the salt has lost its savour.

III. THE EXTREME UNLIKELIHOOD OF RESTORATION. "If the salt have lost . . .

wherewith shall it be seasoned?" That is an impossibility. Salt that has lost its virtue is useless for all ordinary purposes, and is "cast out." It is not *absolutely* impossible for the soul that has lost its Christian spirit and character to regain its worth, but it is very difficult and it is very rare. The recovery of lost feeling is a spiritual marvel. 1. It is so improbable that no man who loves his soul will expose himself to the peril; if he does, he most seriously endangers his spiritual life, he most gravely imperils his eternal future. 2. It is not *so* impossible that any unfaithful soul need despair. True penitence and genuine faith will bring back the wanderer from the fold to the shelter of the good Shepherd's love.—C.

Vers. 1—24.—*Table-talk of Jesus.* We have now brought before us an interesting conversation which Jesus had with certain guests at an entertainment in the house of "one of the chief Pharisees." It was a sabbath-day feast, indicating that sociality was not incompatible even with Jewish sabbath-keeping. Into the guest-chamber had come a poor man afflicted with the dropsy, and, to the compassionate eye of our Lord, he afforded an opportunity for a miracle of mercy. But, before performing it, he tests their ideas about sabbath-observance. They were sufficiently merciful to approve of sociality among themselves, but the healing of neighbours was another matter. They could even be merciful to cattle if they were their own; but to be merciful to a brother-man would have shown too much breadth of sympathy. The sick man might wait till Monday, but an ass or an ox might die if not delivered out of its difficulty, which would be so much personal loss. In spite of their narrow-mindedness, our Lord took the poor man and healed him, and then proceeded to give the guests very wholesome advice.

I. LET US LOOK AT THE PARABLE ABOUT THE WEDDING. (Vers. 7—11.) To the Lord's eye the feast became the symbol of what is spiritual. The wedding of the parable is the consummation of the union between God and his people. The invitation is what is given in the gospel. Hence the advice is not instructive as to the prudential temper, but as to our spirit in coming before God. Shall it be the spirit which claims as right the highest room, or that which accepts as more than we deserve the lowest room? In other words, shall we come before God in a spirit of self-righteousness or in a spirit of self-abasement? Now, our Lord points out, from the collisions of social life, the absolute certainty of the self-important and self-righteous being abased among men: how much more in the righteous administration of God! The self-righteous under his administration shall be abased, how deeply and terribly we cannot conceive. On the other hand, those who have learned to humble themselves under the mighty hand of God shall be exalted in due season, and have glory in the presence of the celestial guests! Jesus thus attacked the self-righteousness of the Pharisees, not as a social, but as a spiritual question. God would at last cast it away from his presence and society with loathing and contempt.[1] On the other hand, self-abasement is the sure sign of grace and the sure earnest of glory. He who takes with gratitude the lowest room in God's house is certain of speedy promotion!

II. OUR HOSPITALITY SHOULD BE DIVINE IN ITS SPIRIT AND CHARACTER. (Vers. 12—14.) Having improved the conduct of the guests, and shown its spiritual bearings, he next turns to the host, and gives him an idea of what hospitality should be. It should not be *speculative*, but disinterested—something, in fact, which can only be recompensed at the resurrection of the just. In no clearer way could our Lord indicate that hospitality should be exercised in the light of eternity; and the bearing of it upon spiritual interests should constantly be regarded. And here we surely should learn: 1. How important it is to be social. God is social. His Trinity guarantees the sociality of his nature. We are to be God-like in our sociality. 2. It may be most helpful to lonely spirits upon earth. Many a lonely heart may be saved for better things by a timely social attention. 3. There is great blessing in giving attention to people who cannot return it. It is a great field of delight that those with large hearts may have. "It is more blessed to give than to receive." We are following

---

[1] Suggestive discourses on this passage may be found in Gerok's 'Pilgerbrod,' s. 669; Gerok's 'Aus Ernster Zeit,' s. 574; Hofacher's 'Predigten,' s. 670; Beck's 'Christliche Reden,' i. s. 290.

God's plan in the attentions we bestow. 4. At the final arrangement of God's kingdom, all such disinterested hospitality shall be recompensed. How? Surely by opportunity being afforded of doing the like again! The hospitable heart, which keeps eternity in view in all its hospitality, shall have eternity to be still more hospitable in.

III. THE PARABLE OF THE GREAT SUPPER. (Vers. 15—24.) Jesus proceeds from the question of hospitalities to present the gospel in the light of a supper provided by the great Father above, and to which he invites sinners as his guests. And here we have to notice: 1. The *greatness of the supper*. The preparations were long and elaborate. How many centuries were consumed in preparing the feast which we have in the gospel! It was to be the greatest "feast of reason and flow of soul" the world has seen. And so it is. Nowhere else does man get such food for his mind and heart as in the gospel of Christ. 2. The *freedom of the invitations*. Many were bidden. No niggardliness about the invitations. They are scattered so freely that, alas! they are not by many sufficiently prized. 3. The *supplementary summons by the faithful servant*. It is not an invitation by ink and pen merely that God sends, but he backs the written revelation by personal persuasion by the mouth of faithful servants. Here is the sphere of the gospel ministry. These true ministers tell what a feast is ready in the gospel, and what their own experience of it has been. 4. The *triviality of the excuses*. To the invitations sent out by God men make excuses. There is something peculiarly sad and significant in refusals upon insufficient grounds. Our Lord gives us three examples of the excuses men make for refusing salvation and the gospel. (1) The first man puts a *piece of ground* before salvation. "Real property" keeps many a man out of the kingdom of heaven. (2) The second puts *cattle* before salvation. Many men are so interested in good "stock," and all the mysteries of breeding and work, as to have no time for their eternal interests. A few chattels keep multitudes out of God's kingdom. (3) The third puts *social concerns* before spiritual. He has married a wife, and so cannot attend to the claims of God. Society, its attractions and allurements, is keeping multitudes out of the kingdom above. These are but specimens of the trivialities which are monopolizing men's attention, and preventing their giving good heed to the things of the gospel. 5. The extension of the invitation to *those who are sure to accept it*. The poor, maimed, halt, and blind represent the souls who feel their spiritual poverty and defects, and who are sure to appreciate God's gracious invitation. When the self-righteous spurn it, the abased and humiliated greedily receive it. 6. The *abundant room, and the difficulty in getting the places filled*. There is no possibility of any one coming and being refused admittance. There is room for all who care to come. Those who will not taste of the supper are those who thought themselves better employed. In compelling men to come in, we must do our best in persuading them to accept the gospel. May we leave nothing undone that the Divine table may be filled.[1]—R. M. E.

Vers. 25—35.—*The cost of discipleship.* The Pharisee's banquet being over, our Lord continues his journey towards Jerusalem, and, as a crisis is evidently at hand, he has a goodly multitude of expectant followers. Have they any notion of the cost of discipleship? Are they prepared for all which it involves? Jesus determines to make this unmistakable, and so he gives them the admonition contained in the present section. He gives point to his advice by mentioning the folly of beginning to build a tower without calculating the cost of finishing it, or of beginning a war without calculating the reasonable chances of success. Each follower would have a costly tower to build in the devoted life he must lead, and a costly war to wage in the contest for the faith. It was every way desirable, therefore, that they should go carefully into the meaning of discipleship, and undertake it intelligently.

I. NOTHING LESS THAN THE FIRST PLACE IN THE HEART MUST BE OFFERED UNTO JESUS. (Ver. 26.) He insists on being put before father and mother, before wife and children, before brothers and sisters. All relations are to be put below him. He must be more than them all. It is a great demand, and yet a most reasonable one. For: 1. The love of Jesus anticipated all *parental* love. In fact, the love of our parents is only the latest expression of his far-seeing and foreseeing love. The generations to whom we owe so much have only mediated for us the love of Jesus. 2. The unity of

[1] Cf. Gerok's 'Evangelien-Predigten,' s. 806.

marriage only feebly illustrates the *intensity* of Christ's love. Husband owes much to wife, and wife to husband. The marriage union is a close and intimate one; but Jesus comes closer to our hearts than husband or wife can. He is nearer, and should be dearer, than either. 3. The *rising generation* does not lay so much love and hope at our feet as Jesus. Children are dear; the promise of their young lives and hearts is precious; they come as pledges for the future; they are prophecies of the world about to be; but "the holy Child Jesus" comes closer to our hearts than even they. He is the prophecy of all coming time, the goal and ideal at which, not the rising generation only, but generations yet unborn, are to aim. 4. He gives us a more profound *brotherhood* than brothers or sisters can. The brotherhood of Jesus, "the elder Brother born for all adversity, and who can never die," is an experience which brothers and sisters can only help us to understand.[1] Jesus consequently claims first place, because in his manifold relations he is not only more than each, but more than all combined.

II. WE MUST PRIZE CHRIST MORE THAN LIFE ITSELF. (Ver. 26.) Life is another precious benefit which we naturally prize. Satan, in the trial of Job, imagined that Job would give all that he had rather than lose his life (Job ii. 4). He fancied that the patriarch, who would not curse God under the loss of children and property, would break down if God touched his bone or his flesh. But Job was so spiritually minded as to be ready to trust God, even should he, for some mysterious and hidden reason, slay him (Job xiii. 15). Now, Jesus comes and insists on being put before life itself. When the two come into competition there must be no question about yielding the palm to Christ. Jesus is more to us than physical life, because he is our spiritual life (John xiv. 6). We can never forfeit blessed existence so long as we trust in Christ, and the mere existence of the body is but a bagatelle in comparison.

III. SELF-SACRIFICE IS THE MARCHING ORDER OF THE REDEEMED. (Ver. 27.) The idea of cross-bearing is often interpreted as if it simply meant enduring those "crosses" to which life is heir. But much more is meant than this. In the Revised Version it is put, "Whosoever doth not bear *his own* cross." Now, as Christ carried his cross to to die upon, so must we take our lives in our hands, and be ready at any moment to sacrifice them for Jesus. He was crucified for us: are we ready to be crucified for him, or to die in any other way he wishes? It is the *martyr-spirit* which Christ here insists upon. He is surely worthy of such self-sacrifice.

IV. WE MUST FORSAKE ALL AS A GROUND OF CONFIDENCE IF WE WOULD FOLLOW JESUS. (Ver. 33.) Christ, having insisted on disposing of our lives as he pleases, nexts insists on disposing of our property. He comes in with his *right* to tell us, as he told the rich young ruler, that we must give up our all for his sake. Not, of course, that he exercises this right often. Voluntary poverty has been an *exceptional* way of serving him. But we may all show plainly that our property is his, and that, when Christ and our possessions come into competition, all must give way to him. If we prize property more than Jesus, then he is nothing to us. We must be ready to put him before everything which we have, and to sacrifice everything when he claims it from us. In this way we make Christ first and all in all.

V. THE WORLD NEEDS SUCH PRINCIPLES IN PRACTICE TO KEEP IT FROM CORRUPTION. (Vers. 34, 35.) Were it not for the self-sacrifice of souls, the world would become utterly corrupt. Now, it is this heroic element which Christ's cause has *par excellence* supplied. Only by the martyr-band, whose pure self-sacrifice was unmistakable, has the world been kept from utter selfishness and corresponding corruption. It was mindful of this martyr-spirit which his gospel ensures, that Jesus told his servants they were "the salt of the earth" (Matt. v. 13). Unless this wholesome antidote to natural selfishness be supplied, society must go to pieces. It cannot be built on selfishness. The economics which assume no higher ethical element than each man looking after himself, may give expression to tendencies; but they must be overpassed by realities if the world is to keep moderately sweet and habitable.[2] But suppose that Christ's servants make a mere profession of self-sacrifice, and do not carry out the spirit of their Master, then they become but insipid salt, which can only be trodden underfoot of men on the highway, where nothing is meant to grow. In other words,

---

[1] Cf. Hull's sermon at King's Lynn, on "The Christian Brotherhood of Man:" 'Sermons,' i. p. 121.

[2] Cf. Cairnes's 'Logical Method of Political Economy.'

the Christians who are not genuine are sure to be despised. They are trodden down by a world whom they have vainly tried to deceive. A *false* professor is the most contemptible of all men.—R. M. E.

EXPOSITION.

CHAPTER XV.

Vers. 1—32.—*The Lord speaks his three parable-stories of the "lost," in which he explains his reason for loving and receiving the sinful.*

Vers. 1, 2.—**Then drew near unto him all the publicans and sinners for to hear him. And the Pharisees and scribes murmured, saying, This Man receiveth sinners, and eateth with them;** more accurately rendered, *there were drawing near to him.* This was now, in the last stage of the final journey, the usual state of things. The great outside class came in crowds to listen to Jesus. These were men and women who, through home and family associations, through their occupations, which were looked upon with disfavour by the more rigid Jews, often no doubt through their own careless, indifferent character, had little or nothing to do with their religious and orthodox countrymen. Poor wanderers, sinners, thoughtless ones, no one cared for them, their present or their future. Do not these in every age make up the majority? The religious, so often Pharisees in heart, despising them, refusing to make allowances for them, looking on them as hopelessly lost ones. But at no time was this state of things so accentuated as when Jesus lived among men. Now, among such careless irreligious men and women, are many whose hearts are very tender, very ready to listen if the teacher of religion has any kind, wise words for them. The grave and severe, yet intensely pitiful and loving, doctrines of the Galilæan Master *found* such. His words were words of stern rebuke, and yet were full of hope, even for the hopeless. No man had ever spoken to them like this Man. Hence the crowds of publicans and sinners who were now ever pressing round the Master. But the teachers of Israel, the priestly order, the learned and rigid scribes, the honoured doctors of the holy Law,—*these* were indignant, and on first thoughts not without reason, at the apparent preference felt for and special tenderness shown by Jesus to this great outside class of sinners. The three parables of this fifteenth chapter were the *apologia* of the Galilæan Master to orthodox Israel, but they appeal to an audience far greater than any enclosed in the coasts of the Holy Land, or living in that restless age.

Vers. 3—5.—**And he spake this parable unto them, saying, What man of you, having an hundred sheep, if he lose one of them, doth not leave the ninety and nine in the wilderness?** Now, there are two leading ideas in the three stories—one on the side of the Speaker; one on the side of those to whom the parable-stories were spoken. (1) *On the side of the speaker.* God's anxiety for sinners is shown; he pities with a great pity their wretchedness; he sets, besides, a high value on their souls, as part of a treasure belonging to him. (2) *On the side of the listeners.* Their sympathy with him in his anxiety for sinners is claimed. He has sought it hitherto in vain. The imagery of the first story is very homely—easy, too, to understand. A small sheep-master pastures his little flock of a hundred sheep in one of those wide uncultivated plains which fringe portions of the land of promise. This is what we must understand by "the wilderness." The hundred sheep represent the people of Israel. The lost sheep, one who had broken with Jewish respectability. *One* only is mentioned as lost, not by any means as representing the small number of the outcast class—the contrary is the case—but as indicative of the value in the eyes of the All-Father of *one* immortal soul. **And go after that which is lost, until he find it? And when he hath found it, he layeth it on his shoulders, rejoicing.** This diligent search after the lost one, the tender care shown by the shepherd when the object of his search was found, and the subsequent joy, pictured in a humble everyday figure the mode of acting of which the orthodox Jews complained. They said, "He receiveth sinners, and eateth with them."

Ver. 6.—**And when he cometh home, he calleth together his friends and neighbours, saying unto them, Rejoice with me; for I have found my sheep which was lost.** And here the shepherd craves for *sympathy* from his fellows; he would have others share in his joy in finding the perishing, suffering sheep. This sympathy with his effort to win the lost the Galilæan Master had looked for among the rulers and teachers of Israel in vain. Now, sympathy, it must be remembered, is not merely sentiment or courtesy. True sympathy with a cause means working in good earnest for the cause. This, however, the ruling spirits in Israel, in every sect, coldly refused. They not only declined their sympathy with the acts of Jesus; they positively condemned his works, his efforts, his teaching.

Ver. 7.—I say unto you, that likewise joy shall be in heaven over one sinner that repenteth, more than over ninety and nine just persons, which need no repentance. "But," the Master went on to say, "what I looked for in vain on earth, see, I have found in heaven. What men coldly refused me, the celestials have joyfully given. These understand *me*. *They* love both *me* and *my* work, do the holy angels." This coldness, even opposition, on the part of the Pharisees and the religious men of Israel to himself and his works, to his teachings of mercy and love, seems certainly to be the reason why Jesus emphasizes, both here and in the next parable, the sympathy which he receives, not on earth from men, but in heaven from beings, inhabitants of another world. Men, have, however, asked —Why do these heavenly beings rejoice over the one more than over the ninety and nine? It is utterly insufficient to say that this joy is occasioned by the getting back something that was lost. Such a feeling is conceivable among men, though even here it would be an exaggerated sentiment, but in heaven, among the immortals, no such feeling *could* exist; it partakes too much of the sentimental, almost of the hysterical. This higher joy must be due to another cause. Now, the shepherd, when he found the wanderer, did not bring it back to the old fold, or replace it with the rest of the flock, but apparently (ver. 6) brought it to his own home. This would seem to indicate that sinners whom Jesus has come to save, and whom *he has saved*, are placed in a better position than that from which they originally wandered. This gives us the clue to the angels' joy over the "found one" more than over those who were safe in the old fold. The Talmudists have taught— and their teaching, no doubt, is but the reflection of what was taught in the great rabbinical schools of Jerusalem before its ruin—that a man who had been guilty of many sins might, by repentance, raise himself to a higher degree of virtue than the perfectly righteous man who had never experienced his temptations. If this were so, well argues Professor Bruce, "surely it was reasonable to occupy one's self in endeavouring to get sinners to start on this noble career of self-elevation, and to rejoice when in any instance he had succeeded. But it is one thing to have correct theories, and another to put them into practice. . . . So they found fault with One (Jesus) who not only held this view as an abstract doctrine, but acted on it, and sought to bring those who had strayed furthest from the

paths of righteousness to repentance, believing that, though last, they might yet be first."

Ver. 8.—Either what woman having ten pieces of silver, if she lose one piece, doth not light a candle, and sweep the house, and seek diligently till she find it? Another and very homely picture is painted in this parable. This time the chief figure is a woman, a dweller in a poor Syrian village, to whom the loss of a coin of small value out of her little store is a serious matter. In the story of the lost sheep the point of the parable turns upon the suffering and the sin of man, under the image of a lost sheep searched for and restored by the Divine pity. Here, in the second parable-story, the ruined soul is represented as a lost coin, and we learn from it that God positively misses each lost soul, and longs for its restoration to its true sphere and place in the heaven life and work for which it was created. In other words, in the first parable the lost soul is viewed from man's standpoint; in the second, from God's. If, then, a soul be missed, the result will be, not only missing for itself, but something lost for God.

Vers. 9, 10.—And when she hath found it, she calleth her friends and her neighbours together, saying, Rejoice with me; for I have found the piece which I had lost. Likewise, I say unto you, there is joy in the presence of the angels of God over one sinner that repenteth. Again, as in the parable of the lost sheep, we find this longing for sympathy; again the finding of this sympathy in heavenly places, among heavenly beings, is especially recorded. There is a slight difference in the language of rejoicing here. In the first parable it was, "Rejoice with me; for I have found my sheep *which was* lost;" here, ". . . for I have found the piece *which I had* lost." In the first it was the anguish of the sheep which was the central point of the story; in the second it was the distress of the woman who had lost something; hence this difference in the wording. "What grandeur belongs to the picture of this humble rejoicing which this poor woman celebrates with her neighbours, when it becomes the transparency through which we get a glimpse of God himself, rejoicing with his elect and his angels over the salvation of a single sinner!" (Godet).

Ver. 11.—And he said, A certain man had two sons. It seems probable that this and the two preceding shorter parables were spoken by the Lord on the same occasion, towards the latter part of this slow solemn journeying to the holy city to keep his last Passover. The mention of the publicans and sinners in ver. 1 seems to point to some considerable city, or its immediate vicinity, as the place where these famous parables were spoken. This parable, as it is termed, of the prodigal son completes the trilogy. Without it the Master's formal *apologia* for his life and work would be incomplete, and the rebuke of the Pharisaic selfishness and censoriousness would have been left unfinished. In the *apologia* much had still to be said concerning the limitless love and the boundless pity of God. In the *rebuke* the two first parables had shown the Pharisee party and the rulers of Israel how they ought to have acted; this third story shows them how they did act. But the Church of Christ—as each successive generation read this exquisite and true story—soon lost sight of all the temporal and national signification at first connected with it. The dweller in the cold and misty North feels that it belongs to him as it does to the Syrian, revelling in his almost perpetual summer, to whom it was first spoken. It is a story of the nineteenth century just as it was a story of the first. We may, with all reverence, think of the Divine Master, as he unfolded each successive scene which portrayed human sin and suffering, and heavenly pity and forgiveness, man's selfish pride and God's all-embracing love, passing into another and broader sphere than that bounded by the Arabian deserts to the south and the Syrian mountains to the north, forgetting for a moment the little Church of the Hebrews, and speaking to the great Church of the future—the Church of the world, to which, without doubt, this Catholic parable of the prodigal, in all its sublime beauty and exquisite pathos, with all its exhaustless wealth of comfort, belongs.

Vers. 12, 13.—**And the younger of them said to his father, Father, give me the portion of goods that falleth to me. And he divided unto them his living. And not many days after the younger son gathered all together.** The subject of the story this time is not derived from humble life. The family pictured is evidently one belonging to the wealthy class. There was money to be distributed; there were estates to be cultivated; means existed to defray the cost of feasting on a large scale; mention, too, is made incidentally of costly clothing and even of gems. Like other of the Lord's parable-teachings, the framework of the story was most likely founded upon fact. The family of the father and the two sons no doubt had been personally known to the Galilæan Teacher. This imperious demand of the younger seems strange to us. Such a division, however, in the lifetime of the father was not uncommon in the East. So Abraham in his lifetime bestowed the main body of his possessions on Isaac, having pre-

viously allotted portions to his other sons. There was, however, no Jewish law which required any such bestowal of property in the parent's lifetime. It was a free gift on the part of the father. But to the young son it was a hapless boon.

"God answers sharp and sudden on some prayers;
And flings the thing we have asked in our face,
A gauntlet—with a gift in it."
(E. B. Browning.)

And took his journey into a far country. The youth, who probably in the Master's experience had suggested this part of the story, after receiving his share of money, started with unformed purposes of pleasure, perhaps of trade. The man, who was a Jew, left his home for one of the great world's marts, such as Carthage or Alexandria, Antioch or Rome. **And there wasted his substance with riotous living.** This is an extreme case. Few probably of the publicans and sinners whose hearts the Lord touched so deeply, and who are examples of the great class in every age to whom his gospel appeals so lovingly, had sinned so deeply as the young man of the story. Indecent haste to be free from the orderly quiet home-life, ingratitude, utter forgetfulness of all duty, the wildest profligacy,—these were the sins of the prodigal. It has been well remarked that the line runs out widely to embrace such a profligate, that every sinner may be encouraged to return to God and live. There is a grave reticence in sparing all details of the wicked life—a veil which the elder son with pitiless hand would snatch away (ver. 30).

Ver. 14.—**And when he had spent all.** True of many a soul in all times, but especially in that age of excessive luxury and splendour and of unbridled passions.

"On that hard Roman world, disgust
And secret loathing fell;
Deep weariness and sated lust
Made human life a hell."
(Matthew Arnold.)

There arose a mighty famine in that land; and he began to be in want. The "mighty famine" may be understood to represent difficult times. War or political convulsions, so common in those days, may have speedily brought about the ruin of many like the prodigal of our story, and his comparatively small fortune would quickly have been swallowed up. Selfish evil-living, excesses of various kinds, had gained him no real friends, but had left him to meet the ruin of his fortune with enfeebled powers, homeless and friendless; hence the depth of the degradation in which we speedily find him. Not an unusual figure in the great world-drama, this of the younger son—the man who had sacrificed everything for selfish pleasure, and soon found he had absolutely nothing left but suffering. Very touchingly the greatest, perhaps, of our English poets writes of this awful soul-famine. In *his* case fortune and rank still remained to him, but everything that can really make life precious and beautiful had been wasted.

" My days are in the yellow leaf;
   The flowers and fruits of love are gone;
The worm, the anguish, and the grief,
      Are mine alone.

" The fire that on my bosom preys
  Is lone as some volcanic isle;
No torch is kindled at its blaze—
      A funeral pile ! "
        (Byron.)

Ver. 15.—**And he went and joined himself to a citizen of that country.** " That citizen," says St. Bernard, quoted by Archbishop Trench, " I cannot understand as other than one of the malignant spirits, who in that they sin with an irremediable obstinacy, and have passed into a permanent disposition of malice and wickedness, are no longer guests and strangers, but citizens and abiders in the land of sin." This is a true picture of the state of such a lost soul, which in despair has yielded itself up to the evil one and his angels and their awful promptings and suggestions; but the heathen citizen is well represented by the ordinary sordid man of the world, who engages in any infamous calling, and in the carrying on of which he employs his poor degraded ruined brothers and sisters. **To feed swine.** What a shudder must have passed through the auditory when the Master reached this climax of the prodigal's degradation ! For a young Israelite noble, delicately nurtured and trained in the worship of the chosen people, to be reduced to the position of a herdsman of those unclean creatures for which they entertained such a loathing and abhorrence that they would not even name them, but spoke of a pig as *the other thing !*

Ver. 16.—**And he would fain have filled his belly with the husks that the swine did eat: and no man gave unto him.** So low was this poor lost man reduced, that in his bitter hunger he even came to long for the coarse but nutritious bean with which the herd was fed. These swine were of some value when fattened for the market; but he, the swineherd, was valueless—he might starve. The husks in question were the long bean-shaped pods of the carob tree (*Caratonia siliqua*), commonly used for fattening swine in Syria and Egypt. They

contain a proportion of sugar. The very poorest of the population occasionally use them as food.

Ver. 17.—**And when he came to himself.** This tardy repentance in the famous parable has been the occasion of many a sneer from the world. Even satiety, even soul-hunger, did not bring the prodigal to penitence; nothing but absolute bodily suffering, cruel hunger, drove him to take the step which in the end saved him. There is no doubt it would have been far more noble on the young man's part if, in the midst of his downhill career, he had suddenly paused, and, with a mighty and continued effort of self-control, had turned to purity, to duty, and to God. Certainly this had been heroic conduct—a term no one would think of applying to anything belonging to the life of the younger son of our story. But though not heroic, is not the conduct of the prodigal just what is of daily occurrence in common life ? The world may sneer; but is not *such* a repentance, after all, a blessed thing ? It is a poor mean way, some would tell us, of creeping into heaven; but is it not better to enter into God's city even thus, with bowed head, than not at all ? Is it not better to consecrate a few months, or perhaps years, of a wasted life to God's service, to noble generous deeds, to brave attempts to undo past mischief and neglect, than to go sinning on to the bitter end ? There is something intensely sorrowful in this consecrating to the Master the end of a sin-worn life; but there is what is infinitely worse. What a deep well, too, of comfort has the Church-taught teacher here to draw from in his weary life-experiences ! **How many hired servants of my father's have bread enough and to spare, and I perish with hunger !** Among the bitternesses of his present degradation, not the least was the memory of his happy childhood and boyhood in his old home.

" For a sorrow's crown of sorrows
  Is remembering happier things."

The family of the prodigal, as we have already remarked, was certainly possessed of wealth, and was probably one of high rank. In the old home there was nothing wanting.

Vers. 18, 19.—**I will arise and go to my father . . . make me as one of thy hired servants.** The repentance of the prodigal was real. It was no mere sentimental regret, no momentary flash of sorrow for a bad past. There was before him a long and weary journey to be undertaken, and he—brought up in luxury—had to face it without means. There was the shame of confession before dependents and relatives and friends, and, as the crown of all, there was the position of a servant to be filled in the home where once he had been a son, for that was all he hoped to gain even from his father's pitying love.

Ver. 20.—**And he arose, and came to his father.** And so he came safe home; sad, suffering, ragged, destitute, but still safe. But, in spite of this, the parable gives scant encouragement indeed to sin, poor hope indeed to wanderers from the right way, like the hero of our story; for we feel that, though he escaped, yet many were left behind in that sad country. We dimly see many other figures in the picture. The employer of the prodigal was a citizen, but only one of many citizens. The prodigal himself was a servant—one, though, of a great crowd of others; and of all these unhappy dwellers in that land of sin, we only read of *one coming out*. Not an encouraging picture at best to any soul purposing deliberately to adventure into that country, with the idea of enjoying the pleasant licence of sin for a season and then coming home again. Such a home-coming is, of course, possible—the beautiful story of Jesus tells us this; but, alas! how many stay behind! how few come out thence! **But when he was yet a great way off, his father saw him, and had compassion, and ran, and fell on his neck, and kissed him.** But although many who wander never escape from that sad country, it is not because they would be unwelcomed should they choose to return. The whole imagery of this part of the parable tells us how gladly the eternal Father welcomes the sorrowful penitent. The father does not wait for the poor wanderer, but, as though he had been watching for him, sights him afar off, and at once takes compassion, and even hastens to meet him, and all is forgiven.

Ver. 21.—**Father, I have sinned against heaven, and in thy sight, and am no more worthy to be called thy son.** Many, though not all, of the older authorities add here (apparently taking them from ver. 19) the words, "make me as one of thy hired (servants)." The selfsame words of the original resolution are repeated. They had been stamped deep into the sad heart which so intensely desired a return to the old quiet, pure home-life; but now in his father's presence he feels all is forgiven and forgotten, therefore he no longer asks to be made as one of the servants. He feels that great love will be satisfied with nothing less than restoring him, the erring one, to all the glories and happiness of the old life.

Ver. 22.—**But the father said to his servants, Bring forth the best robe, and put it on him; and put a ring on his hand, and shoes on his feet.** The older authorities add "quickly" after the words "bring

forth." Everything is done by the father to assure the wanderer of full and entire forgiveness. Not only is a welcome given to the tired, ragged son, but he is invested at once, with all speed, with the insignia of his old rank as one of the house. But it is observable not a word is spoken of reply to the confession; in grave and solemn silence the story of the guilty past is received. Nothing can excuse it. He forgives, but forgives in silence.

Vers. 23, 24.—**And bring hither the fatted calf.** There was a custom in the large Palestinian farms that always a calf should be fattening ready for festal occasions. **And let us eat. . . . And they began to be merry.** Who are intended by these plurals, *us* and *they*? We must not forget that the parable-story under the mortal imagery is telling of heavenly as well as of earthly things. The sharers in their joy over the lost, the servants of the prodigal's father on earth, are doubtless the angels of whom we hear (vers. 7, 10), in the two former parables of the lost sheep and of the lost drachma, as rejoicing over the recovery of a lost soul.

Ver. 25.—**Now his elder son was in the field.** The broad universal interest of the parable here ceases. Whereas the story of the sin and the punishment, the repentance and the restoration, of the prodigal belongs to the Church of the wide world, and has its special message of warning and comfort for thousands and thousands of world-workers in every age, *this* division of the story, which tells of the sour discontent of the prodigal's elder brother, was spoken especially to the Pharisees and rulers of the Jews, who were bitterly incensed with Jesus being the Friend of publicans and sinners. They could not bear the thought of sharing the joys of the world to come with men whom they had despised as hopeless sinners here. This second chapter of the great parable has its practical lessons for every-day common life; but its chief interest lay in the striking picture which it drew of that powerful class to whom the teaching of Jesus, in its broad and massive character, was utterly repulsive. Now, while the events just related were taking place, and the lost younger son was being received again into his father's heart and home, the elder, a hard and selfish man, stern, and yet careful of his duties as far as his narrow mind grasped them, was in the field at his work. The rejoicing in the house over the prodigal's return evidently took him by surprise. If he ever thought of that poor wandering brother of his at all, he pictured him to himself as a hopelessly lost and ruined soul. The Pharisees and rulers could not fail at once to catch the drift of the Master's parable. They too, when the

Lord came and gathered in that great harvest of sinners, those firstfruits of his mighty work—they too were "in the field" at work with their tithings and observances, making hedge after hedge round the old sacred Hebrew Law, uselessly fretting their lives away in a dull round of meaningless ritual observances. They—the Pharisee party—when they became aware of the great crowds of men, whom they looked on as lost sinners, listening to the new famous Teacher, who was showing them how men who had lived their lives too could win eternal life— they, the Pharisees, flamed out with bitter wrath against the bold and daring Preacher of glad tidings to such a worthless crew. In the vivid parable-story these indignant Pharisees and rulers saw themselves clearly imaged.

Ver. 28.—**Therefore came his father out, and entreated him.** The disapprobation of Jesus for Pharisee opinions was very marked, yet here and elsewhere his treatment of them, with a few exceptional cases, was generally very gentle and loving. There was something in their excessive devotion to the letter of the Divine Law, to the holy temple, to the proud traditions of their race, that was admirable. It was a love to God, but a love all marred and blurred. It was a patriotism, but a patriotism utterly mistaken. The elder brother here was a representative of the great and famous sect, both in its fair and repulsive aspect, in its moral severity and correctness, in its harshness and exclusive pride. The father condescended to entreat this angry elder son; and Jesus longed to win these proud mistaken Pharisees.

Vers. 29—32.—**Lo, these many years do I serve thee.** Bengel quaintly comments here, "Servus erat." This was the true nature of this later Jewish service of the Eternal. To them the eternal God was simply a Master. They were *slaves* who had a hard and difficult task to perform, and for which they looked for a definite payment. **Neither transgressed I at any time thy commandment.** We have here repro-

duced the spirit, almost the very words, of the well-known answer of the young man in the gospel story, who was no doubt a promising scion of the Pharisee party : "All these things have I kept from my youth up." The same thought was in the mind, too, of him who thus prayed in the temple : "God, I thank thee that I am not as other men are," etc. (ch. xviii. 11, 12). **Yet thou never gavest me a kid. . . . All that I have is thine.** Thy brother has the shoes, the ring, the robe, the banquet; thou the *inheritance*, for all that I have is thine. Why grudge to thy brother an hour of the gladness which has been thine these many years? **As soon as this thy son was come, . . . For this thy brother was dead.** The angry elder son will not even acknowledge the prodigal as *his* brother; with bitter scorn and some disrespect he speaks of him to his father as "*thy* son." The father throughout the scene is never incensed. He pleads rather than reproaches, and to this insolence he simply retorts, "*Thy* brother was dead to us, but now—It was meet that we should make merry, and be glad." What was the end of this strange scene? The last words, breathing forgiveness and joy, leave a sweet sense of hope upon the reader that all would yet be well in that divided household, and that the brothers, friends again, would clasp hands before the loving father's eyes. But when Jesus told the parable to the crowds, the story was not yet played out. It depended on the Pharisees and rulers how the scene was to end. What happened at Jerusalem a *few weeks later*, when the Passion-drama was acted, and some *forty years later*, when the city was sacked, tells *us* something of what subsequently happened to the elder son of the Lord's parable. But the end has yet to come. We shall yet see the brothers, Jew and Gentile, clasp hands in loving friendship before the father, when the long-lost elder son comes home. There will be joy then indeed in the presence of the angels of God.

HOMILETICS.

Vers. 11—32.—*The parable of the prodigal son.* This parable is at once a history, a poem, and a prophecy. A history of man in innocence, in sin, in redemption, in glory. A poem—the song of salvation, whose refrain, "My son was dead, and is alive again, was lost, and is found," is ringing through the courts of the Zion of God. A prophecy, speaking most directly and solemnly, in warning and meditation, emphasis of reproof or of encouragement, to each of us. It is beyond the reach of the scalpel of criticism. Its thoughts, its very words, have enriched every speech and language in which its voice has been heard. It stands before us "the pearl of parables," "the gospel in the gospel" of our Lord and Saviour Jesus Christ. It is the last of three stories, illustrative of Divine grace, which were spoken especially to the Pharisees, and to them with reference to their cavil as expressed in ver. 2. Without minutely analyzing the three, the progress of the teaching may be indicated. Bengel has, with his usual felicitousness of touch, indicated this progress. The silly sheep represents the sinner in his foolishness. The sinner lying in the dust, yet still with the stamp of Divinity on him, is figured by the piece of money. Finally, the younger of the two sons is the representation of the sinner left to the freedom of his own will, and falling into an estate of sin and misery. We can trace, too, a progress in the setting forth of the Divine love. The journey of the shepherd into the far wilderness speaks to us of the infinite compassion of highest God; for the sheep's own sake he goes after it until he finds it; and the recovery is the occasion of the joy of heaven. The aspect specially illustrated by the search for the piece of silver is the infinite value to God of every soul. Not one will he lose; for his righteousness' sake he will seek until he finds. The last of the parables combines the two former, with a glory superadded : Infinite Compassion recognizing the infinite preciousness of the human life, but this, now, in the higher region of Fatherhood and sonship. Let us discard all stiffening exposition of Christ's words; *e.g.* that which takes as its key-thought that the younger son is the Gentile world, the elder son the Jewish Church. Let us regard it in the width of its generosity, as the picture of him whose love is reflected in the " Man who receiveth sinners, and eateth with them." The two words of the parable are " lost" and " found." Let us try to open up the wealth of meaning in them.

I. Lost. 1. *Whence?* There is a glimpse into the sweet home-life—the father with the two sons. The joy of the father's home is the communion of his children. It was what he saw in the Father which moved the prayer of Jesus, " That they whom thou gavest me may be with me where I am." The joy of the child's home is the communion of the Father, and is realized when the Father's life—not the Father's living—is the desire, and the word of the psalm is fulfilled, " In thy presence is fulness of joy, and in thy right hand are pleasures for evermore." So we think of the days speeding on— musical, blessed days, such as we recollect, perhaps, in the home of our childhood, when, as we look back, the sun seemed to shine far more brightly than now, and the day was longer, and all was peace. Parents and children together! For it is man's home to abide with God as Father. By-and-by there comes the far country, because there is no Father. 2. *How?* The younger son demands the portion of goods that falleth to him. Mark how the tone has lowered, how the eye has drooped. " Father, give me!" is the cry of the filial heart. " Give me my daily bread!" is a true prayer, because it waits on God; it sees the living in the life which he gives. But "my portion of goods" is the voice of a sinful independence. It separates " what is mine " from what is " my Father's; " it conceives of his as being, by some right or title, mine. Himself, as the good, is no longer the all. This is the serpent's lie. " Ye shall not surely die, for God doth know that in the day ye eat thereof your eyes shall be opened, and ye shall be as gods, knowing good and evil." Such was the seductive whisper in the beginning. As if (1) God was keeping to himself a God-dom, in jealousy preventing the enjoyment of a blessedness which was the man's right. And as if (2) the way to know good is through the experience of evil—good discerned as the opposite of that which we have tasted, instead of evil being felt only as the darkness seeking to overtake the light in which we are abiding. The serpent's lie repeats itself in many forms, not the least familiar that which insinuates, " Let the young man sow his wild oats; the good oats will come afterwards. Let him take his fill of enjoyment; there will come the sober days and the quiet time." It works in us all; it is the tendency of the sinful mind to withdraw from the authority of Heaven, from the rule of duteous love, to appropriate for self, and in mere self-will, the living of God. The father does not deny the son. He respects the sovereignty in the son which is derived from himself. " He who suffers us to go our way takes care indeed that it be hedged with thorns." But a son cannot be forced as a slave. If go he will, go he must. The father divides the living. 3. *Whither?* Not at once, possibly, does the separation in will show itself. It is not always easy to trace the first moment of the apostasy. Many a one continues, for a time, in the semblance of piety, even after he has ceased to desire spiritual things. But " not many days after" the rift in the lute appears. " He gathers all together." Now the purpose of the will is active; no advice will stand in the man's path. The father's tear, the father's smile, avails not;

not the sight of the old roof-tree, or the remembrance of the sweet life that lies behind. There is an eager "farewell;" he rushes forward—*Whither?* "To a far country." Yes; yield to appetite, to fleshly lust, it will take the soul on and on, away from the fences of religion, away to the far-off Nod, bidding it, as Cain did, build there the city of habitation, yet bidding only to mock, since he who would put miles between him and the face of his Father in heaven must be a sorry fugitive and vagabond. "A far country!" That is wherever God is forgotten, is dishonoured as the Father. No ship is needed to bear one to the uttermost parts of the earth; the distance is measured not by oceans or continents, but by tracts of affection and sympathy. "Alienated from the life of God"—this is the far country. Observe the two stages of the existence in the far country—the *fulness* and the *famine.* (1) There is *fulness*— a season of apparently inexhaustible happiness: "riotous living." The life of the youth is like a mountain-torrent that has been pent up and bursts forth. The Greek word has the force of "prodigally." And prodigal the wanderer is in the earlier period. Fill high the bowl; loud let the revel swell; eat, drink; there is more to follow, there is more behind.

> "Such is the world's gay garish feast
>   In her first charming bowl,
> Infusing all that fires the breast,
>   And cheats th' unstable soul."

But—what? "The substance is wasting;" literally, is "scattering abroad;" for so it is. As has well been said, "All creaturely possession consumes itself in the using; all wealth must turn itself into poverty, either by its actual dissipation or in consequence of the folly of covetousness, which the more mammon increases is the less satisfied by it. Thus man, in his sin, consumes first of all his earthly goods, so that he can no more find comfort or satisfaction in them; and then, alas! the true and real possessions which his heavenly Father communicated to him are also consumed." What a description of substance scattered (Prov. v. 7—14)! (2) Then comes in the second stage. All which had been gathered together spent; then arises the *famine.* For one who has nothing there is always a famine in that land. The world will give you so long as you have to give it; when you can bring nothing, when you are used up; ah, the fields which seemed golden become the bleakest of moors. There is no sight more pitiful than a worn-out, used-up worldling.

> "The fire that on my bosom preys
>   Is lone as some volcanic isle;
> No torch is kindled at its blaze—
>   A funeral pile!"

Alas! the pleasure has died out; the soul, the immortal self, not yet dead, is in want in a famine-stricken land. How is this want to be met? 4. *Wherein?* It is an evil and bitter thing to forsake the Lord. The son's own wickedness is correcting him, and his backslidings are reproving him. In want, but not yet in poverty blessed with desire. Here is the witness. Hitherto the son has been the son, wicked, reckless, but still not naturalized in that far country. The day of this separation has passed; and, oh! the double degradation! "He *joins* himself"—"*pins* himself" is the word— becomes wholly, abjectly dependent on, "a citizen of that country." He began by being his own master; he ends by being the slave of the citizen. The world uses for its pleasure the one who uses the world for his pleasure. A man's passion is his minister for a time; by-and-by it becomes his tyrant. A very hard tyrant! The devil has no respect for the freedom of the will: "I was your companion, your Mephistopheles, your slave. Now I have you, you are mine; get out and feed these swine." It was an employment which conveyed the idea of utter wretchedness to a Jew. Strong, thickly laid, is the colouring; it is not one whit too strong or too thickly laid for fact. How do we behold this prince, this son of the Father? Toiling in the fields, with no shelter except the rude hut which he makes, and his only companions—the herd of swine! And all the while the hunger gnawing! Were not these swine, wallowing in the mire, picking the carobs, eating the scanty grass, happy as compared with him? They got what they wanted; he provided their food for them, but there is none to give him. He had rejected his father's hand, and there is no hand in all the world outstretched to him. In Oriental lands there grows a tree whose fruit is like the bean-pod, though larger than it, with a dull, sweet taste; the swine would take of it; and the longing eye of the swineherd is cast on it. It is all he can get, for there is no food in that far country suited to him. The soul starves, whether in riotous living or in want, until it looks upwards and learns the old home-cry, "Father, give me!"

II. FOUND. Consider the return, the welcome, the supper. "It is meet," says the father, "that we should make merry and be glad." 1. Mark *the steps of the return.* The hopeful feature about the poor swineherd is that, although *pinned* to the citizen of the country, he is yet a person distinct. He has sold himself; but himself is more than, other than, the citizen. There is an inalienable nobility which even "riotous living" cannot stamp out. There are "obstinate questionings," "blank misgivings," "fugitive recollections of the imperial palace whence he came." Ponder the record of the finding of the conscience, and the Litany first, and the Jubilate afterwards, which followed the finding. "He comes to himself." He has never been the right true self from the moment when he demanded the portion. The right self is sonship. This wallowing in the sty with swine, this bound-overness to tyrant appetite and earthliness ah! as one awaking from a horrid dream he recognizes the *reality.* And wherein does the conscience, now awakened, become articulate? (1) There is the sense of an awful discord and wrong. The menial of that citizen left to starve. How different are the menials in his father's house! *They* have bread enough and to spare. "Whatever is orderly is blest. I, the disorderly, the one out of place, out of my right mind, am the unblest, the one perishing with hunger." It was this feeling which came over the wild student when, in the solemn sweet moonlight, he gazed from the height on one of the fairest scenes of nature. And the cry was evoked, "All lovely, all peaceful, except myself!"—a cry that bade him back to another and nobler life. Who is there that in calmer moments does not understand the inward glance of the vision—the peaceful father's house, and the misrule, unrule, of the self-willed and undutiful? (2) There succeeds a higher thought: "The menial in that house, and I, the son!" Gradually there emerges the feeling of the heaven—the authority from which the soul has broken, the order it has contravened, and more still, "against heaven, and *before thee.*" The recollection of the father rushes in, bringing tides of holy ardour. *His* eye, the son feels, has been following him in the journey, in the wasting of the substance; it has been all "*before him.*" "O my father, my father! to have grieved and wounded thee! I will weep no longer. I will arise and go. I will throw myself on thee. I will ask for a place anywhere, if only it is near thee; if I may be again in thy sight, and no longer *the* sinner!" It is a repentance not to be repented of. The matter of it is not, "I have played the fool exceedingly;" it is ever and throughout "I have sinned." What causes the will to arise is the longing to be again with the father, to pour out the broken and contrite spirit on his bosom. And he arises and goes. "The best and most blessed said and done" that can be in heaven or on earth. 2. And now for *the welcome.* The love that descends is always greater than the love that ascends. The love of the child is only a response to the love of the parent. And as to this father! Most touchingly explicit is the word of Jesus. "When yet a great way off, the father saw him." A very great way off! Even in the far country he had been near. The seeing expresses the knowing all about the misery, and the earnestness of the return—a seeing that is a drawing also, a drawing through the need, and all along the journey forming an atmosphere of love that compassed him about. To come to the love of God is to realize that he was first; it is to find that which found us when yet a great way apart. What more? A reproach? A reproof? The arms are at once thrown around the neck, and the kiss of reconciling fatherliness is printed on the cheek. The forgiveness, observe, comes before all confession. In confessing the sin we meet the blessing that has already covered us. But there is a confession. "The truest and best repentance," as it has been said, "follows, and does not precede, the sense of forgiveness; and thus too, repentance will be a thing of the whole life long, for every new insight into that forgiving love is as a new reason why the sinner should mourn that he ever sinned against it." Only, note, beneath the pressure of that fatherly heart there is no mention of the hired servant's place. The "Father, I have sinned," is sobbed forth on the father's heart, and the son leaves himself to the father's will. And how the expression of the welcome rises! The best robe is ordered out; a sonship higher than that of mere birth. " The adoption of children by Jesus Christ to the Father " is the best robe. And the ring is to be put on the hand—the ring with the seal of the spirit of adoption. And shoes are provided for the torn and weary feet, that henceforth they may walk up and down in the Name of the Lord. And hasten, complete the tokens of the rejoicing— make ready the supper in which the father can rejoice over his child with joy, and rest in his love. 3. The fulfilment of the welcome is *the supper*, with the slain fatted calf, and the dancing and music. It denotes the free festal joy of God, of heaven, in the found, repenting sinner. It denotes also the festal blessedness of the sinner himself when the great Object of all need and longing is found, when he is at home with his God. There is a representation of the supper in Rom. v. We hear the music and dancing in Rom. viii. They express the truth of the new existence. There had been, in the past, a living, but not a fellowship, with the Father; henceforth it is fellowship : God is the soul's Good, and the life is lived in and out of him. Oh the swellings of harmony, of poetic triumphant raptures, now ! " My son was dead ; and is alive again ; was lost, and is found." So much for the younger son and the father. But we must not over- look the elder son. And we must not misjudge him. He was not bad ; he is not a mere churl. He is faithful, if he is not free ; he is just, if he is not generous. He had never transgressed a command ; if his life had no heights, it had no depths ; it had been even and calm. And he had been blessed, for he had been ever with the father, and all that was the father's had been his. We need not fix on any particular repre- sentation of the elder son. The Pharisee-heart is, no doubt, castigated in the picture. But it touches many who would resent being associated with the Pharisee. Krum- macher was once asked his opinion of the elder son. He quietly said, " I well know now, for I learned it only yesterday." Being asked further, he laconically remarked, " Myself," and confessed that yesterday he had fretted his heart to find that a very ill-conditioned person had suddenly been enriched with a remarkable visitation of grace. The sketch supplies the foil to the love of God. It brings out, also, his patience and gentleness in the dealing with the elder son. How the father bears even with the foolish wrath ! How he reasons and expostulates, and invites to a share in the joy ! " Meet that *we* should make merry, and be glad—I over my son, thou over thy brother." Two things notice. 1. The one as *bearing on the elder son*. He comes *out of the fields*, punctual and orderly in all his ways. He cannot understand the merry-making ; he never had received a kid. That son's life had been a wholesome one. The prodigal had his ecstasies ; but the elder son had had his lifetime. He is the man of habit—habit which is to us better than instinct. The danger to the man of habit is that he becomes mechanical, doing his part steadily, but without the oil of gladness. 2. The other as *bearing on the younger son*. Let not Christ's teaching be misapplied. Do not think that it is a higher thing to be first irreligious and then religious ; to spend the best part of the life in self-gratification, and give God only the remnants. Ah! years of godlessness leave their record. They write their impression on brain and heart ; and, free and full as is God's forgiveness, the impression cannot be obliterated. What a man sows, he reaps.

HOMILIES BY VARIOUS AUTHORS.

Vers. 1, 2.—*A bitter charge the highest tribute.* The great Teacher himself said that the things which are highly esteemed among men may be abomination in the sight of God ; and we may safely assume that the converse of this proposition is true also. Certainly, in this bitter charge brought against our Lord we now perceive the very highest tribute which could be paid him.

I. A BITTER CHARGE AGAINST THE SAVIOUR. It is not easy for us to realize the intensity of the feeling here expressed. The Jews, arguing from the general truth that holiness shrinks from contact with guilt, supposed that the holier any man was, the more scrupulously would he avoid the sinner ; and they concluded that the very last thing the holiest man of all would do was to have such fellowship with sinners as to " eat with them." Their patriotic hatred of the publican, and their moral repugnance toward "the sinner," filled them with astonishment as they saw him, who claimed to be the Messiah himself, taking up a positively friendly attitude toward both of these intolerable characters. Their error was, as error usually is, a perversion of the truth. They did not understand that the same Being who has the utmost aversion to sin can have and does have the tenderest yearning of heart toward the sinner; that he who utterly repels the one is mercifully pitying and patiently seeking and magnanimously winning the other. So the men of acknowledged piety and purity in the time of our Lord failed completely to understand him, and they brought against him the charge which might well prove fatal to his claims—that he was having a guilty fellowship with the outcast among men and the abandoned among women.

II. THE HIGHEST TRIBUTE TO THE SAVIOUR. In that attitude and action of his which seemed to his contemporaries to be so unworthy of him we find the very thing which constitutes his glory and his crown. Of course, association with sinners, on the basis of spiritual sympathy with them, is simply shameful; and to break up their association with the intemperate, the licentious, the dishonest, the scornful, is the first duty of those who have been their companions and have shared their wrong-doings, but whose eyes have been opened to see the wickedness of their course. It is for such to say, "Depart from me, ye evil-doers; for I will keep the commandments of my God." But that is far from exhausting the whole truth of the subject. For Christ has taught us, by his life as well as and as much as by his Word, that to *mingle with the sinful* in order to *succour and save* them is the *supreme act of goodness*. When a man's character has been so well established that he can afford to do so without serious risk either to himself or to his reputation, and when, thus fortified, well armed with purity, he goes amongst the criminal and the vicious and the profane, that he may lift them up from the miry places in which they are wandering, and place their feet on the rock of righteousness, then does he the very noblest, the divinest thing he can do. It was this very thing which Jesus Christ came to do: "He came to seek and to save that which was lost." It was this principle which he was continually illustrating; and nothing could more truly indicate the moral grandeur of his spirit or the beautiful beneficence of his life than the words by which it was sought to dishonour him: "This Man receiveth sinners, and eateth with them." It is this which will constitute the best tribute that can be paid to any of his disciples now. "There is nothing of which any true minister of Jesus Christ, whether professional or not, ought to be so glad and so proud, as to be such that the enemies of the Lord shall say tauntingly, while his friends will say thankfully, 'This man receiveth sinners.'"

III. THE GREATEST POSSIBLE ENCOURAGEMENT TO OURSELVES. There are men who know they are sinners, but care not; there are those who do not know that they are guilty in the sight of God; and there are others who do know and who do care. It is to these last that the Saviour of mankind is especially addressing himself. To them all he is offering Divine mercy; restoration to the favour, the service, and the likeness of God; everlasting life. On their ear there may fall these words, intended for a grave accusation, but constituting to the enlightened soul the most welcome tidings—"This Man receiveth sinners."—C.

Vers. 3—7.—*The parable of the lost sheep.* Of these three parables, illustrative of the grace of Christ shown to lost human souls, the first brings into view—
I. THE GREAT FOOLISHNESS OF THE WANDERING SOUL. It goes from God as a foolish sheep strays from the fold. So doing, it leaves *security for peril.* In the fold is safety; in the wilderness are many and serious dangers. At home with God the soul is perfectly safe from harm; its life, its liberty, its happiness, is secure; but, apart and astray from God, all these are not only gravely imperilled, they are already forfeited. It also leaves *plenty for want.* In the fold is good pasture; in the wilderness is scarcity of food and water. With God is rich provision for the spirit's need, not only satisfying its wants, but ministering to its best and purest tastes; at a moral distance from him the spirit pines and withers. To go from God is an act of uttermost folly.
II. THE STRAITS TO WHICH IT IS REDUCED. 1. It is on the point of perishing. Without the interposition of the seeking Shepherd, it would inevitably perish. 2. It is reduced to such utter helplessness that it has to be carried home, "laid upon his shoulders." (1) Under the dominion of sin the soul draws nearer and nearer to spiritual destruction;

and (2) it is often found to be reduced to so low a state that it can put forth no effort of its own, and can only be carried in the strong arms of love.

III. THE LOVE OF THE DIVINE SHEPHERD. The strong and keen interest taken by the human shepherd in a lost sheep is indicative of the tender interest which the Father of our spirits takes in a lost human soul. The former is more occupied in his thought and care with the one that is lost than he is, for the time, with the others that are safe; the latter is really and deeply concerned for the restoration of his lost child. And as the shepherd's sorrow leads him to go forth and search, so does the Father's tender care lead him to seek for his absent son. Christ's love for us is not general, it is particular; it reaches every one of us. He cares much that each one of the souls for whom he suffered should enjoy his true heritage, and when that is being lost he desires and he "seeks" to restore it.

IV. HIS PERSISTENCY IN SEEKING. "Until he find it." The shepherd, in pursuit of the lost sheep, is not detained by difficulty or danger; nor does he allow distance to stop his search; he goes on seeking until he finds. With such gracious persistency does the Saviour follow the wandering soul; year after year, period after period in his life, through several spiritual stages, the good Shepherd pursues the erring soul with patient love, until he finds it.

V. HIS JOY IN FINDING IT. The shepherd's joy in finding and in recovering, shown by calling his friends and neighbours together, saying, "Rejoice with me," etc., is pictorial of the Saviour's joy when a soul is redeemed from sin and enters into the life which is eternal. He rejoices not only, not chiefly, because therein does he "see of the travail of his soul," but because he knows well from what depth of evil that soul has been rescued, and to what height of blessedness it has been restored; he knows also how great is the influence, through all ages, which one loyal and loving human spirit will exert on other souls.—C.

Ver. 10.—*The joy of the angels.* Our first thought may be—What do the angels know about us? But our second thought should be—How likely it is that the angels would be deeply interested in us! For, granted that there are "heavenly hosts" who are in supreme sympathy with God, and who are therefore careful to watch the workings of his holy will in the broad realm he rules, what is there more likely than that they would be profoundly interested in the recovery of a lost world, in the restoration of a rebellious and ruined race? We could well believe that it would be *the* study of the angelic world, the practical problem that would engage their most earnest thought, if it did not occupy their most active labours. And this being so, we can understand the greatness of their joy "over one sinner that repenteth." For—

I. THEY KNOW, BETTER THAN WE, THE STERN CONSEQUENCES OF SIN. Not, indeed, by experience. Experience is not the only teacher, and it does not at all necessarily follow that one who has had some experience of a course of conduct knows more about it than another who has had no experience at all; otherwise we should be driven to the absurd conclusion that guilty man knows more about sin than God does. Many of the inexperienced are a great deal wiser than many who have had "part and lot in the matter," because those learn from all they witness, and these do not learn from anything they do and suffer. The "angels of God" witness the commission and also the fruits of sin; they see what lengths and depths of wrong and wretchedness it brings about from year to year, from age to age; they see what evil it works within and without, in the sinner himself and on all with whom he has to do. As they live on through the centuries, and as they learn Divine wisdom from all that they behold in the universe of God, they must acquire a hatred of sin and a pity for sinners which is beyond our own emotion and which passes our reckoning. How great, then, their joy when they witness the emancipation of one human soul from spiritual bondage, the birth of a spirit into the life eternal!

II. THEY KNOW, BETTER THAN WE, THE BLESSED FRUITS OF OBEDIENCE. Here they have their own angelic experience to guide and to enlighten them. With added years of loyalty to the King of heaven; with the spiritual enlargement which (we can well believe) comes with a holy and stainless life, they rejoice in God and in his service with ever-deepening delight; their heritage becomes ampler, their prospects brighter, as the celestial periods pass away; and when they think what it means for one holy intelligence to be filled with the fulness of Divine life and of heavenly blessedness, we can comprehend that they would rejoice "over one sinner that repenteth."

III. THEY ARE DEEPLY INTERESTED IN THE PROGRESS OF THE KINGDOM OF GOD, and they know, better than we, how limitless is the influence one soul may exercise. 1. Because they earnestly, supremely desire the honour of God, the glory of Christ on the earth, they rejoice that one more spirit is brought into loyal subjection to his rule. 2. Because they desire that everything may be put under his feet, they rejoice that all that one man can do—which means more in their measurement than it means in ours—will be done to further his cause and exalt his Name.—C.

Ver. 11.—*The Father's home.* By the Father's home we commonly mean the heavenly home, the sphere where the nearer and more immediate presence of God is realized. But heaven once included earth—earth was once a district of heaven. God meant this world to be a part of his own home; this, but for the separating force of sin, it would be now; and this, when sin has been cast forth, it will be again. And it is properly regarded as a home because *the* relation in which God wished its inhabitants to stand toward himself was that (and *is* that) of children to a Father. The truest picture, the nearest statement, the least imperfect representation of that relationship, is not found in the words, " A certain king had subjects," or " A certain proprietor had servants (or slaves)," but in those of our text, " *A certain man had sons.*" Nothing *so* adequately represents God's position toward us as fatherhood, or our true position toward him as sonship, or the sphere in which we live before him as the Father's home. This family relationship means—

I. HIS DWELLING WITH US. God's dwelling with us or in us is very closely associated with his Fatherhood of us (see 2 Cor. vi. 16—18). The ideal human father is one who dwells under the roof where the family resides; who is at home with his children, maintaining a frequent and a close and intimate intercourse with them. Such is God our Father's desire concerning us. He wishes to be near us all and near us always; so near to us that we have constant access to him; that our free, full, happy, unconstrained "fellowship is with the Father;" that it is the natural and instinctive thing for us to go to him and make our appeal to him in all time of need.

II. HIS CONTROL OF OUR LIVES. God's purpose is to direct the lives we are living, to choose our way for us, even as a father for his children; so that we shall be going where he sends us, be doing his work, be filling up his outline, be walking in the path his own hand has traced.

III. HIS EDUCATION OF OUR SPIRITS. Our children come to our home with great capacities, but with no power. It is our parental privilege to educate them, so that their various faculties—physical, mental, spiritual—shall be developed, so that they shall gain knowledge, acquire wisdom, exert influence, be a blessing and a power in the world. God places us here, in this home of his, that he may educate us; that, by all we see and hear, by all we do and suffer, we may be taught and trained for noble character, for faithful service, for an ever-broadening sphere.

IV. HIS PARENTAL SATISFACTION WITH US. Perhaps the most exquisite satisfaction, the very keenest joy which fills and thrills the human heart, is that which is born of parental love; it is the intense and immeasurable delight with which the father and the mother behold their children as these manifest not merely the beauties of bodily form but the graces of Christian character, and as they bring forth the fruits of a holy and useful life. God meant and still means to have such parental joy in us; to look on us, the children of his home, and be gladdened in his heart more than when he looks on all the wonders of his hand in field and forest, in sea and sky. It is our docility, our affection, our obedience, our rectitude and beauty of character and of spirit, that constitute *the* source of his Divine satisfaction. The children of the Father's home are dearer and more precious far than any marvellous things in all the breadth of his universe. Thus God's thought concerning our race was to establish *a holy family,* himself the Divine Father; we his holy, loving, rejoicing, human children; this world a happy home. That *was* his thought in creation, that *is* his purpose in redemption. To its blissful realization the best contribution each one of us can make is to become his true and trustful child, reconciled to him in Jesus Christ, living before him every day in filial love and joy.—C.

Vers. 12, 13.—*Departure; the far country.*   We all know only too well that God's
gracious purpose concerning us (see previous homily) has been diverted by our sin;
the holy and happy home-life which he designed and introduced has been broken up
by our unfilial attitude and action.   From the Father's home we have wandered away
into "the far country."   The strict parallel to this picture we find in the disobedience
of our first parents and in the gradual departure of our race from God and from his
righteousness to a great distance from him.   As to ourselves, there never was a time
when we were not outside the home; yet we may speak of—

I. THE NEARNESS OF CHILDHOOD.   For not only does a great poet speak of "heaven
lying about us in our infancy," but One from whom there is no appeal tells us that
"of such [as the little child] is the kingdom of heaven."   In childhood are those qualities which are most favourable to the reception of the truth and grace of God.   And if in
our childhood we did not stand actually within the door, we did stand *upon the threshold*
of the Father's house.   Then God spoke to us, whispered his promises in our ear, laid
his hand upon us, touched the chords of our heart, drew forth our thought, our wonder,
our hope, our yearning, our prayer.   And well is it for us, blessed are we among the
children of men, if, thus hearing that voice and feeling that hand Divine, we chose
the good part, entered in at the open door, and have been thenceforth inmates of that
home of faith and love!   But perhaps it was not so; perhaps, like the prodigal son,
we were dissatisfied with the heritage of the Father's favour, of a Saviour's love;
perhaps we wanted a "portion of goods" quite different from this, and went away and
astray from God.   And there came—

II. A DEPARTURE FROM THIS NEARNESS OF CHILDHOOD.   We opened the Bible with
less interest and closed it with less profit; we neglected the throne of grace; we began
to shun the sanctuary; we became less careful of our speech and our behaviour; God
was less and still less in our thought; our hold upon Christian principle became
relaxed, and the cords of the temporal and the material were wound around us.   Then
we dwelt in—

III. THE FAR COUNTRY OF SIN.   For sin *is* a "far country."   1. *It is to be a long
way off from God himself*; to be separated from him in spirit and in sympathy; to be
willing to spend our time without his society; to be satisfied with his absence.   The
soul, instead of continually looking up for his guidance and his good pleasure, shuns
his eye and tries to shake itself free from his hand; instead of placing itself under his
elevating teaching and enlarging influence, the soul sinks into lower conditions, and
loses its grasp of truth and power and goodness; instead of sharing his likeness, the
soul goes down into folly and wrong.   2. *It is to be a long way from his home.*   For
God's home is the home of righteousness, of wisdom, and of blessedness; and to be
living under the dominion of sin is to be dwelling in a sphere of unrighteousness; it is
to be spending our days and our powers in an element of folly; it is to be cutting ourselves off from the sources of true joy, and to be where all the roots of sorrow are in the
soil.   Surely there is no epithet anywhere applied to sin which so truly and so powerfully
characterizes it as this—it is *the far country of the soul*; under its sway the human
spirit is separated by a measureless distance from all that is worthiest and best.   Why
should any soul continue there, when God is ever saying, "Return unto me, and I will
return unto you;" when Christ is ever saying, "Come unto me, and I will give you
rest"?—C.

Vers. 13—15.—*Life in the far country.*   When the prodigal son had attained his
wish and was free to do as he liked without the restraints of home, how did he fare?
He found, as in our distance from God we shall find, that life there meant three evil
things—

I. A TWOFOLD WASTE.   He "wasted his substance in riotous living."   He misspent
his powers, devoting to frivolous and unremunerative enjoyment those bodily and
mental faculties that might have been put to profitable use, and he scattered the
material resources with which he started.   Sin is spiritual waste.   1. *It is the waste of
consumption.*   The "substance" of the soul includes: (1) *Spiritual understanding;* a
noble capacity to perceive Divine truths and heavenly realities—the thoughts, the
wishes, the purposes of God.   Under the dominion of sin this capacity becomes
enfeebled; in disuse it rusts and is eaten away: "From him that hath not [uses not

what he has] is taken away that [unused capacity] which he has." (2) *Spiritual sensibility*; the capacity of feeling the force of things Divine, of being sensibly and practically affected by them, of being moved and stirred by them to appropriate decision and action. No man can live on in conscious sin without continually losing this sacred and precious sensibility. Neglected and unapplied, it withers away, it wastes. 2. *It is the waste of perversion.* Man was made for the very highest ends—made for God; to study, to know, to love, to serve, to rejoice in God himself. And when he spends his powers on himself and on his own animal enjoyment, he is "wasting his substance," turning from their true Object to one immeasurably lower the faculties and the opportunities with which he came into the world.

II. PITIABLE WANT. "He began to be in want." Indulgence is expensive, and unfits for work; sinful companions are happy to share the treat, but they are slow to refill the purse. Sin leads down to destitution; it takes away a taste for all pure enjoyment, and provides nothing lasting in its stead. The man who yields himself to the power of sin loses all joy in God, all relish for spiritual enjoyments, all gratification in sacred service, all capacity for appreciating the fellowship of the good and great, all sense of the sacredness and spiritual worth of life. What has he left? He is beggared, ruined. "No man gives unto him;" no man *can* give unto him. You cannot give to a man what he is not capable of receiving; and until he is radically changed he cannot receive anything truly precious at your hands.

III. GRIEVOUS DEGRADATION. He was "sent into the fields to feed swine." This was bad enough; yet was there one thing worse—"he was fain to fill his belly with the husks the swine did eat." He went down to the lowest grade imaginable. The degradation of the soul is the very saddest thing under the sun. When we see a man who was made to find his heritage in God's likeness and service satisfying himself with that which is bestial, degrading himself to the drunkard's song, to the impure jest, to the part of astute roguery, and finding a horrible enjoyment in these shameful things, then we see a human heart satiating itself with "husks that the swine do eat," and then we witness the most lamentable of all degradations.

Such is life in the "far country." Distance from God means waste, want, degradation. Its full and final outworking may take time, or it may hasten with terrible rapidity. But it comes sooner or later. 1. There is a way of return even from that "strange land," that evil estate (see succeeding homilies). 2. How wise to place ourselves out of danger of these dire evils by connecting ourselves at once with Jesus Christ!—C.

Vers. 17—19.—*The soul's return.* Out in the far country, living a life of guilty waste, of dreary want, of shameful degradation, the prodigal son was in truth a man "beside himself;" he was lost to himself; he had taken leave of his own better self, of his understanding, of his reason; from his own true self he was afar off. But now there is—

I. A RETURN TO HIMSELF. 1. He regains his wisdom as he gains a sense of his folly. He returns to his right mind; he loses his infatuation as he perceives how great is his foolishness to be in such a state of destitution when he might "have all things and abound." What insensate folly to be starving among the swine when he might be sitting down at his father's table! The soul comes to itself and regains its wisdom when it perceives how foolish it is to be perishing with hunger in its separation from God when it might be "filled with all the fulness of God." Our reason returns to us when we refuse to be any longer misled by the infatuation, by "the deceitfulness of sin," and when we see that the pining and decay of our spiritual powers is a poor exchange indeed for the wealth and health of spiritual integrity. 2. He is restored to sanity of mind as he obtains a sense of his sinfulness. To be able to say, as he is now prepared to say, "I have sinned," is to come back into a right and sound spiritual condition. We are in a wholly unsound mental state when we can regard our disloyalty and disobedience to God with complacency and even with satisfaction. But when our ingratitude, our forgetfulness, our unfilial and rebellious behaviour towards God, is recognized by us as the "evil and bitter thing" it is, as the wrong and shameful thing it is, and when we are ready, with bowed head and humbled heart, to say, "Father, I have sinned," then are we in our right mind; then have we *returned to ourselves*.

II. A RESOLVE TO RETURN TO GOD. This return on the part of the prodigal:
1. Arose from a sense of the greatness of his need. 2. Was based on a sound confidence, viz. that the father, whose disposition he knew so well, would not reject but
receive him. 3. Included a wise and right determination, viz. to make a frank
confession of his sin and to accept the humblest position in the old home which the
father might allot him. (1) Out of the greatness and soreness of our need we come to
the conclusion that we will return unto God. Our state of guilt and shame is no
longer tolerable; we must turn our back on the guilty past and the evil present; there
is no refuge for our soul but in God—"in God, who is our home." (2) We may hold
fast the firm conviction that we shall be graciously received. Of this we have the
strongest assurance we could have in the character and the promises of God, and in
the experience of our brethren. (3) Our resolution to return should include the wise
and right determination: (a) To make the fullest confession of our sin; meaning by that
not the use of the strongest words we can employ against ourselves, but the full outpouring of all that is in our heart; for, above all things, God "desires *truth* in the
inward parts." (b) To accept whatever position in God's service he may appoint us.
Not that we are expecting that he will make us "as a hired servant;" we may be sure
(see next homily) that he will place us and count us among his own children; but so
humble should our spirit be, such should be our sense of undeservedness, that we
should be ready to be anything and to do anything, of however lowly a character it may
be, which the Divine Father may assign us in his household.—C.

Vers. 20—24.—*The welcome home.* Having seen the younger son of this parable
dissatisfied with his estate, having followed him into the far country of sin, having
seen how there he frittered or flung everything away in his guilty folly and was reduced
to utmost want and degradation, and having been with him in the hour of self-return
and wise resolve, we now attend him on his way home to his father. We look at—
I. THE WISDOM OF IMMEDIATE ACTION. "He said, I will arise . . . *and he arose.*"
"Most blessed said and done," as has been well remarked. What if he had lingered
and given room for vain imaginations of things that would "turn up" on his behalf
where he was, or for needless fears as to the reception he would have at home! How
many more sons and daughters would there be now in the Father's home if all who
said, "I will arise," had *at once* arisen, without parleying, without giving space for
temptation and change of mind! Let there be no interval between saying and doing;
let the hour of resolution to return be the hour of returning.
II. THE ABOUNDING GRACE OF HIS FATHER'S WELCOME. 1. He eagerly desired his
son's return; he was looking out for it; when he was *yet a great way off* he saw him,
and recognized him in all his rags and in all his shame. 2. He went forth to meet
him; did not let his dignity stand in the way of his giving his son the very earliest
assurance of his welcome home; he "put himself out," he "ran" to receive him back.
3. He welcomed him with every possible demonstration of parental love. He tenderly
embraced him; he had him at once divested of his livery of shame and clad with
the garments of self-respect and even honour; he ordered festivities to celebrate his
return. As if he would say, "Take from him every sign and token of misery and
want; remove every badge of servitude and disgrace; clothe him with all honour;
enrich him with all gifts; ring the bells; spread the table; wreathe the garlands;
make every possible demonstration of joy; we will have music in our hall to utter the
melody in our hearts, 'for this my son,' etc." It all means one thing; every stroke
in the picture is intended to bring out this most precious truth—the warm and joyous
welcome which every penitent spirit receives from the heavenly Father. (1) We do
not wonder at the misgivings of the guilty heart. It is natural enough that those who
have long dwelt at a great distance from God should fear lest they should fail to find
in God *all* the mercy and grace they need for full restoration. (2) Therefore we bless
God for the fulness of the promises made to us in his Word—promises made by the
lips of the psalmist, of the prophet, and of his Son our Saviour. (3) And therefore we
thankfully accept this picture of the prodigal's return; for as we look at it and dwell
upon it we gain a sense and a conviction, deeper than any verbal assurances can
convey, of the readiness, the eagerness, the cordiality, the fulness, of the welcome with
which the Father of our spirits takes back his erring but returning child. If any

wandering one comes to us and says, "Will God receive *me* if I ask his mercy?" we reply, "Look at that picture, and decide; it is a picture drawn by the eternal Son to indicate what the eternal Father will do when any one of his sons comes back to him from the far country of sin. Look there, and you will see that it is not enough to say, in reply to your question, 'He will not refuse you;' that is immeasurably short of the truth. It is not enough to say, 'He will forgive you;' *that* also is far short of the whole truth. That picture says, 'O children of men, who are seeking a place in the heart and the home of the heavenly Father, know this, that your Father's heart is yearning over you with a boundless and unquenchable affection, that he is far more anxious to enfold you in the arms of his mercy than you are to be thus embraced; he is not only willing, but waiting, ay, longing, to receive you to his side, to give you back all that you have lost, to reinstate you at once into his fatherly favour, to confer upon you all the dignity of sonship, to admit you to the full fellowship of his own family, to bestow upon you the pure and abiding joy of his own happy home.'"—C.

Ver. 31.—*Ungrateful recipiency and ample heritage.* The "elder brother" is by no means so unpopular out of the parable as he is in it. As he is seen in the picture every one is ready to throw a stone at him. In actual life there are many Christian people who pay him the high compliment of a very close imitation. We are in danger of setting up a certain type of Christian character as a model, and if one of our neighbours should show any serious departure from that type, we are disposed to be shy of him and to shun him. Is the returned penitent whom Christ has received into his love always cordially welcomed into our society and made to feel at home with us? But let us look at this young man as—

I. A TYPE OF THE UNGRATEFUL RECIPIENTS OF THE CONSTANT KINDNESS OF GOD. He complained of his father's partiality in that for his brother there had been killed a fatted calf, while not even a kid had been slain for himself and his friends. But the reply was that, without any intermission, he had been enjoying the comfort of the parental hearth and the bounty of the parental table; that one extraordinary feast granted to his brother was nothing in comparison with the constant and continued manifestations of fatherly love and care he had been receiving day by day for many years. "Thou art ever with me, and all that I have is thine." It is for us to remember that our Divine Father's continual loving-kindnesses are much more valuable than one interposition on our behalf. A miracle is a much more brilliant and imposing thing than an ordinary gift, but one miracle is not such evidence of fatherly love as we have in an innumerable series of daily and hourly blessings. A greater gift than the manna in the wilderness were the annual harvests which fed many generations of the people of God. A more valuable gift than the water that issued from the rock in the desert were the rains, the streams, and the rivers that fertilized the soil from year to year. Kinder than the providential rescue from threatening embarrassment or impending death is the goodness which preserves in peaceful competence and unbroken health through long periods of human life. It is a sad and serious mistake; it is indeed more and worse than a mistake when we allow the very constancy of God's kindness, the very regularity of his gifts, to hide from our hearts the fact that he is blessing us in largest measure and in fullest parental love. He is saying to us the while, "Children, ye are ever with me, and all that I have is yours."

II. A TYPE OF OUR COMMON SONSHIP. In the parable the father says to his son, "My property is thine—thine to use and to enjoy; there is nothing I have made that is within your view and your reach which you are not free to partake of and employ; all that I have is thine." Is not that our goodly estate as the sons of God? This world is God's property, and he shares it with us. He interdicts, indeed, that which would do us harm or do injury to others. Otherwise he says to us, "Take and partake, enrich your hearts with all that is before you." 1. And this applies not only to all material gifts, but to all spiritual good—to knowledge, wisdom, truth, love, goodness; to those great spiritual qualities which are the best and most precious of the Divine possessions. 2. It has also a far-reaching application; it is a promise as well as a declaration. Of "all that God has" we only see and touch a very small part now and here. Soon and yonder we shall know far more of what is included in his glorious estate, and still and ever will it be true that what is his is ours; for he lives to share with his children the blessedness and the bounty of his heavenly home.—C.

Vers. 1—10.—*Murmurs on earth, and joy in heaven.*   Our blessed Lord, in his progress towards Jerusalem, had shown the same kindly interest in the outcast classes which had always characterized him, and his love was beginning to tell.   Publicans and sinners gathered eagerly around him to hear his tender, saving words; while the reputable Pharisees and scribes eyed him from a distance with self-righteous suspicion. Their murmurs, however inaudible to mere man, were audible to him to whom all things are naked and open, and he exposes their criticisms by a *trinity* of parables which are without peers in literature.   Stier thinks that the trinity of parables is intended to present the Persons of the adorable Trinity in their respective relations to our salvation.   The first would thus represent the Son's shepherd-care; the second, the Spirit's maternal solicitude for the restoration of lost souls to the heavenly treasure; and the third, the Father's yearning that prodigal sons might come home.[1]   This view is certainly commendable, and not too artistic for such a weighty Preacher as the Lord Jesus Christ, and such a reporter as St. Luke.   Leaving the third and greatest of the parables for separate treatment, let us, in this homily, discuss the other two; and as they are so similar, we need not separate them in our treatment.

I. WE ARE HERE TAUGHT BY CHRIST WHAT UNFALLEN BEINGS THINK ABOUT THEM-SELVES.   (Ver. 7.)   A door is opened by these parables into heaven, and we have glimpses of the celestial world.   Jesus is here testifying about heavenly things (John iii. 12).   Now, we must know, in the first place, who are meant by the ninety and nine sheep which never went astray, and by the nine pieces of silver which were never lost.   They cannot mean self-righteous souls such as the Pharisees and scribes.   For they needed repentance, and over them no celestial ones would think of rejoicing. Hence they can only refer to *unfallen* beings.[2]   Now, the parables imply that there is joy over the unfallen.   Why should there not be?   To us who are fallen it appears but right that the most intense joy should be taken in the unfallen and sinless.   They are a new type of beings to us.   We have only had one of them in this world.   The sinless Saviour broke the law of continuity, and constitutes the marvel of human history.[3] Ninety and nine unfallen beings would seem to us a marvellously interesting group. A sinless city, such as the new Jerusalem is, appears to our comprehension such a novelty, such a new notion and thought amid the sad monotony of sin, that we almost wonder how those who have got within the city could ever think of aught beyond it. And yet to the unfallen ones themselves—sinlessness being the rule, and no exception being found within the celestial city—there must come over the joy with which they contemplate each other a certain monotony, which must keep the joy down to a certain uniform level.   Where everything is exactly as it should be, and no tragedy is possible, the joy of contemplation must be so uniform as to partake almost of what is common. The sinless ones contemplate one another with rapture, doubtless, but the joy is not of the *intensest* type by reason of the monotony and sameness associated of necessity with it.   We may make sure of this by simply contrasting the complacency of the self-righteous with the consciousness of the sinless that they never can be more than unprofitable servants, for they can never rise above the sphere of duty.   Nothing corresponding to the self-satisfaction of the Pharisee, who thanks God that he is not as other men, can be entertained by the celestial world.   They are not absorbed in self-admiration.   That is only possible with lost men!   So that the joy of unfallen beings over one another is modified by the thought that their sinlessness is nothing more than should be expected from those possessed of such privileges as they.   Unlost sheep and money receive but moderate admiration.

II. WE ARE HERE TAUGHT WITH WHAT INTENSE INTEREST UNFALLEN BEINGS CONTEMPLATE THE CAREER OF LOST SOULS.   (Vers. 4, 8.)   The problem of sin comes upon the sinless as an exception to the rule.   They contemplate the career of the lost as a

[1] Cf. 'Words of the Lord Jesus' (Clark's edition of 1864), vol. iv. pp. 109, 110.

[2] Cf. Nettleton's 'Sermons and Remains,' p. 62; also Arndt's 'Gleichniss-Reden,' erster theil, s. 97; Gerok's 'Aus Ernster Zeit,' s. 400; and Beck's 'Christliche Reden,' band i. s. 128.

[3] Cf. Mozley's Essay 'Of Christ alone without Sin.'

tragedy added to the monotony of life. They hover over the lost ones with intense interest. They follow their career and study its issues. We must not regard the celestial world as walled out from the tragedies of this earth. All, according to Christ's idea, is open to the celestial side. We may not see with our dull eyes the city of the Apocalypse; but the celestials can follow our terrestrial careers and note the lessons of our different destinies. "The bourne from whence no traveller returns" is the celestial country. The lack of tidings is *here*, not there! The majority beyond the shadows may seem all silent, like the grave, to us; but the din of our voices reaches across the void to them, and constitutes a study of unfailing interest.

III. THE UNFALLEN ONES HAVE SENT FORTH MESSENGERS TO SAVE THE LOST. (Vers. 4—6, 8, 9.) Angels hover around us, and with intensest interest contemplate our sin-burdened, sin-stained careers. But the celestial world did not contemplate the problem from a distance, and allow the wanderers to die. Two, at all events, came forth from heaven in the interests of lost men—the shepherd Son of God, and the Spirit, with all womanly tenderness. The Second and Third Persons of the adorable Trinity have come forth as messengers to save lost men. In addition, there are multitudes of ministering angels who exercise a mysterious but real ministry, and aid the heirs of salvation in their pilgrimage home. To the celestial visitants, however, who are set before us in these parables, we must meanwhile give our attention. 1. *The good Shepherd.* He follows the lost sheep over the mountains into the wilderness, up the rocky steeps, wherever lost souls wander and are waiting to be found. It was arduous work. It involved the exchange of Paradise for this wilderness-world, and a life of privation and trouble of many kinds, and all that the lost sheep might be found and brought home. Christ's work was self-denial and self-sacrifice in the highest degree. He had to lay down his life for the rescue of the sheep. 2. *The painstaking Spirit.* Like the house-wife who searched so thoroughly the dust of the house until she found the lost piece of money, so the Spirit comes down and searches in the dust of this world for lost souls, that he may restore them to the heavenly treasure. There is no work too severe or too searching for the Spirit to undertake in the rescue of our lost souls. As Gerok puts it, "No trouble is too great for God to undertake in seeking out a soul."

IV. THE JOY OF THE CELESTIAL WORLD OVER REPENTANT SOULS IS GREATER THAN THEIR JOY OVER THE UNFALLEN. (Vers. 7, 10.) Our Lord represents the joy of heaven over *one* repentant sinner as greater than the joy over even *ninety and nine* unfallen beings. No angel of light amid his sinless glory ever caused such rapture to the heavenly world as does a sinner repenting and returning to God. "Gabriel," says Nettleton, "who stands in the presence of God, never occasioned so much joy in heaven. We may number ninety and nine holy angels and then say, 'There is joy in heaven over one sinner that repenteth, more than over those ninety and nine just persons.' The creation of the world was a joyful event, when 'the morning stars sang together, and all the sons of God shouted for joy.' But this is not to be compared with the joy over one sinner that repenteth. . . . The joy of angels is most sensibly felt every time one more is added to the company of the redeemed. The ninety and nine already redeemed seem to be forgotten, when, with wonder and joy, they behold their new companion with whom they expect to dwell for ever. Could we know, as well as angels do, the reality of a sinner's repentance, we should know better how to rejoice." How important, consequently, should we regard the repentance of a sinner! Instead of our indulging in Pharisaic suspicion and murmuring, should we not join the joyful companies above in their ecstasy over the lost being found? And does it not further help us to understand why evil has been permitted, seeing that grace can translate it into so much joy? In all the assemblies of the saints we have reason to believe angels are present, watching with intense interest the exercises and noting what repentances result. The interest we take in such services is, we must believe, as nothing to the interest of the heavenly world. How they must wonder at so much indifference on our part! How they must wonder at the cool and matter-of-fact way we receive tidings of credible conversions to God! The joy of heaven over penitent sinners is a standing rebuke to our murmurings or apathy! May the thought of it lead to a better feeling and a better life!—R. M. E.

Vers. 11—32.—"*From home, and back.*" The two previous parables which our

Lord related in defence of his conduct are really but introductory to what has been with justice called " the pearl of parables," that of the prodigal son. To it we will now devote ourselves, under the title recently given to it as " From home, and back." It brings out in a most interesting way the attitude of God the Father towards lost souls. It is necessary before setting out, however, to notice that, according to the ancient Law, the division of the family inheritance was *not* conditioned by the parent's death. If a son insisted on his share, the father publicly declared to his household his testamentary intentions, and the son entered at once into possession.[1] What our Lord's parable supposes, therefore, is what constantly occurred. The father did not keep his testamentary intentions a secret to be revealed only at his death, but got up and declared publicly how the inheritance was to be allotted, and the impatient son entered at once into possession. Death, as a matter of fact, does not enter into the case at all. There is another preliminary point which we had better distinctly state, and that is that historically the younger son is intended to cover the case of the " publicans and sinners " Jesus was receiving into the kingdom of God; while the elder son covers the case of the " Pharisees and scribes " who murmured at Christ's policy. If we keep this clearly in view, it will help us greatly in our interpretation. We shall take up the two sons in the order presented in the parable.

I. THE PRODIGAL LEAVING HOME AND COMING BACK. (Vers. 11—24.) Imagining he could not enjoy life with his father and amid the restraints of home, he clamours for his share of the inheritance, turns it into money, and sets out. We cannot do better than take up the stages in the history one by one, and interpret them as we proceed. We have, then: 1. *The emigration.* (Ver. 13.) Now, if this younger son represents historically " the publicans and sinners," we must remember that they did not leave Palestine or even Jerusalem when separated from the Jewish Church. The emigration pictured in the parable was, therefore, not emigration to a *locally* distant land, but to a *morally* distant land; in other words, by the " far country " is not meant a foreign country, but the country of *forgetfulness of God.* The soul that lives at a distance from God, that never considers that he is near, has by that forgetfulness of him emigrated to the " far country," and gone from home. In strict accordance with this principle of interpretation, the " substance " which was gathered and wasted in the far country was *moral wealth,* not monetary. As a matter of fact, the publicans, or tax-gatherers, were in many cases careful, money-gathering men, and not spendthrifts in the vulgar sense. What was squandered, therefore, in the far-off land of forgetfulness of God was moral wealth, the wealth of the heart and mind. The waste was moral waste. And it is just here that we have to notice what may be called the *defamation of the prodigal,* in that painters and expositors have represented his " riotous living " as including actually the deepest immorality. This was the line adopted, too, by the elder brother, who represented his brother as having devoured the father's living with harlots (ver. 30), although, as a matter of fact, he had no evidence of such " excess of riot " in the case at all. The most careful expositor of this parable has accordingly pointed out that the prodigal did not reach the sphere of sensuality until he envied the swine, and then only entered it by the mental act.[2] It is when we note how carefully our Lord constructed the parable, that we can see how the moral character of the publicans was appreciated in the picture, and they were not confounded with sinners of the more sensual type. The far-off country, then, and the waste which took place there, represent the land of forgetfulness of God, and the waste of mind and heart that a God-forgetting life is certain to experience. 2. *The famine.* (Ver. 14.) This is the second stage. It represents the hunger of the heart and mind which comes over the soul that has forgotten God and taken to worldly courses. The famine is the utter vacancy of heart that settles down upon the moral emigrant. He begins to realize what he has lost by leaving God. 3. *The effort after recovery.* (Vers. 15, 16.) The famished worldling betakes himself to work; becomes a swineherd—an unlawful occupation for a Jew—our Lord touching thus gently on the question of the farming of the taxes for Rome by the publicans; and finds that there is no real regeneration to be found in work. He, in his utter want of satisfaction, wishes he could satisfy his soul

---

[1] Cf. Maine's ' Ancient Law,' 4th edit., pp. 198—214.
[2] ' La Parabole de l'Enfant Prodigue,' par D. Chantepie de la Saussaye, p. 46.

as the swine satisfy their nature, upon husks. Sensuality is seen by the famished one
to be as unsatisfying as work. And then the last experience is the utter helplessness of
man. "No man gave unto him;" no one could minister to his mental trouble. It is
through a similar experience the soul comes. Self-recovery turns out to be a delusion,
and man is found to be of no avail. 4. *The return of reason.* (Vers. 17—19.) In
his isolation he begins to see that all the past forgetfulness of God was a mistake; that
he was insane to take the course he did; and that in his right mind he must act
differently. Accordingly he begins in sane moments to reflect on the Father's house,
how good a Master God is, how his hirelings have always enough and to spare, and that
the best thing for him to do is to return, confess his fault, and get what place in God's
house he can. This is repentance—the remembrance of God and how we have sinned
against him. 5. *Coming back.* (Ver. 20.) The resolution to come home must be put
in practice. The hope may only be for a servant's place, yet it is well to begin the
return journey and test the loving-kindness of God. 6. *The welcome home.* (Vers.
20, 21.) The father has been on the look-out for the son, and, the moment he begins
the journey, the father's compassion becomes overpowering, and he runs and falls on
the prodigal's neck and kisses him. And when the broken-hearted son pours forth his
penitence, and that he is no more worthy to be called a son, he is met by the father's
welcome and passionate embrace. In this most beautiful way does our Lord bring out
God's yearning for lost souls, and his intense delight when they return to him. 7. *The
feast of joy.* (Vers. 22—24.) Orders are given to the servants to take away his rags,
and put upon him the best robe, and a ring on his hand, as signs of his rank as his
father's son, and shoes on his feet, and to prepare the fatted calf and have a merry feast.
In this way does our Lord indicate the joy which fills God's heart and that of the
angels and that of the returned soul himself when he has come home to God. It is
indeed "joy unspeakable and full of glory." These are the stages, then, in a soul's
history as it passes into the far-off land of forgetfulness of God, and then gets back to
his embrace.

II. THE ELDER SON STAYING AT HOME, BUT NEVER HAPPY. (Vers. 25—32.) We
now turn to our Lord's picture of the Pharisees and scribes, under the guise of the elder
brother. Although these men had not left the Church, although they put in their
appearance at the temple, they never were happy in their religion. 1. *Nominally at
home, the elder son is yet from home.* (Ver. 25.) The elder son was always at work
in the fields, happiest away from the father. The self-righteous spirit is after all an
isolating spirit. The elder son was really as forgetful of God as the younger, only
the forgetfulness took a different form. 2. *The merry-making at home distresses him.*
(Vers. 26—30.) He first asks an explanation of the unusual mirth, and then, when he
gets it, bursts into a fit of censoriousness of the most exaggerated character, in which
he accuses the father of favouritism in receiving his penitent child, and refuses to be
any party to such merry-making. How it exposes the gloomy, Pharisaic spirit which
with some passes for religion! 3. *The godless spirit manifests itself within him.* (Ver.
29.) He has been a faithful and faultless servant, he believes, and yet he has never
got even a kid to make merry with his friends. His whole idea of joy is away from
the father. He is still in the first stage of the younger brother, from which he happily
has escaped. 4. *He is unable to realize how meet it is to rejoice over the return of the
lost.* (Vers. 31, 32.) The father's expostulations are vain, although they ought to
have been convincing. Joy over the recovery of the lost is one of the necessities of an
unwarped nature. It was this great sin of which the scribes and Pharisees were guilty,
that they would not rejoice at the recovery of fallen fellows by the ministry of Christ.
May the broken-heartedness of the prodigal be ours, and never the heartlessness and
censoriousness of the elder brother!—R. M. E.

EXPOSITION.

CHAPTER XVI.

Vers. 1—31.—*The Lord's teaching on the
right use of earthly possessions with regard*
to the prospect of another world, in the form
of the two parables of the unjust steward, and
Dives and Lazarus.

Vers. 1, 2.—**And he said also unto his**

disciples. There is no doubt that this important teaching belongs to the last portion of our Lord's life, and it is probable that it is closely connected with the parable of the prodigal son just related. It is not likely that two such weighty sermons had been preached at the same time, but in the evening, or on the following day, or at least on the next sabbath, the same auditory that listened to the prodigal son we believe were startled and enthralled by the story of the unjust steward, and then, or very shortly after, by the awful and vivid picture of life beyond the grave in the parable of the rich man and Lazarus. There is a close link of thought between the parable of the unjust steward and that of the prodigal. The heroes of both these narratives, in the first instance, had a considerable share of this world's goods entrusted to their charge, and by both, in the early portions of the story, these goods were misused and wasted. The Greek words used of the " wasting " of the prodigal and of the steward were in both cases the same (ch. xv. 13; xvi. 1). No parable in the New Testament has been so copiously discussed or has received so many and such varying interpretations at the hands of ex-positors. We will at once put aside all the ingenious, but from our point of view mis-taken, interpretations which see in "the steward" the Pharisees, the publicans, Judas Iscariot, or Satan. The parable has a broader, a more direct, a more universally interesting, meaning. It contains a deep and important teaching for *every* man or woman who would wish to rank among the followers of Jesus Christ. Now, our Lord would have all men look forward gravely and calmly to the certain event of their death, and, in view of that event, would have them make careful and thoughtful prepara-tion for the life which was to come after death. To press this most important lesson home, the Master, as his custom was at this late period of his ministry, conveyed his instruction in the form of a parable. The sketch of a steward about to be dismissed from his office, and who thus would be stripped of his income, was a fit emblem of a man about to be removed from this world by death. The steward in the parable-story felt that, when dismissed, he would be as it were alone, stripped of all, and destitute. The soul of such a man, when dead, would be also stripped of everything, would be alone and destitute. The question here might be asked—Why take for the principal figure of the parable so immoral a character as an *unjust* steward? The answer is well suggested by Professor Bruce, " For the simple reason that his misbehaviour is the natural explanation of the impending dis-missal. Why should a *faithful* steward be

removed from office? To conceive such a case were to sacrifice probability to a moral scruple." Roughly, then, two things all-important to us are taught here: (1) that dismissal, death, will certainly come; (2) that some provision certainly ought to be made for the life that lies beyond—the life that comes *after* the dismissal, or death. **There was a certain rich man, which had a steward; and the same was accused unto him that he had wasted his goods. And he called him, and said unto him, How is it that I hear this of thee? give an account of thy stewardship; for thou mayest be no longer steward.** The story of the parable contains little incident. There is the rich man, clearly a noble of high rank, whose residence is at a distance from his estates, the scene of the little story. Over these he has placed, as administrator or factor, the one called here a steward; the revenues of the lands this official has wasted; he appears to have been generally a careless if not a dishonest servant. The owner of the estates, when he becomes aware of the facts of the case, at once gives notice of dismissal to the steward, desiring him, however, before yield-ing up his office, to give in his accounts. Appalled at the sudden and utter destitution which lay before him, the steward occupies the short time of office yet remaining to him in devising a plan by which he would secure the good offices of certain persons who were in debt to his master. He (the steward) had yet a little time of power remaining before he was turned adrift; he would turn this to account, and would do a good turn to these men, poor neighbours of his, and debtors to his lord, while he was in office, and so win their friendship, and, on the principle that one good turn deserves another, would be able to reckon on their gratitude when all else had failed him. With the immorality of the act by which he won the good will of these debtors of his master we have nothing to do; it is simply a detail of the picture, which is composed of figures and imagery chosen for their fitness to impress the lesson intended to be taught. *Give an account of thy stewardship; for thou mayest be no longer steward.* This taking away the position and privileges of the man represents the act of death, in which God takes away from us all the varied gifts, the possessions, and the powers large or small with which we are entrusted during our lifetime. Our day of dismissal will be the day of our passing away from this life.

Ver. 3.—**What shall I do? for my lord taketh away from me the stewardship.** This day of dismissal *must* be prepared for; very carefully, very anxiously, the man who has received the sentence of doom ponders over his future. The lesson of the Master is spoken to all; it is a solemn warning to each of us to see what we can do by way of providing for the inevitable day when we shall find ourselves alone and naked and perhaps friendless in the great, strange world to come. The hero of the parable seems suddenly, after a life of carelessness and thoughtlessness, to have awakened to a sense of his awful danger. So the voice of the *real Owner* of the goods, which we have so long deluded ourselves into thinking were our own, comes to us, bidding us make ready to give them back again to him, their Owner, and at the same time to render an account of our administration of them. The voice comes to us in the varied forms of conscience, sickness, misfortune, old age, sorrow, and the like; well for us if, when we hear it, we at once determine, as did the steward of the parable, to make a wise use of the goods in our power for the little time they are still left to us to dispose of as we will.

Ver. 4.—**I am resolved what to do.** The first part of the parable teaches, then, this great and all-important lesson to men—that they will do well to provide against the day of dismissal from life. The second part points out very vividly how kindness, charity, beneficence, towards those poorer, weaker, more helpless than ourselves is one way, and that a very sure and direct way, of so providing against the inevitable dismission, or death. Vers. 5, 6, and 7 simply paint in the details of the interesting picture of the parable. This singular plan of providing for himself by becoming a benefactor of the debtor, remarks Professor Bruce, was by no means the only possible one under the circumstances; but the Speaker of the parable made his hero make choice of it as the aim of the imaginary narrative was to teach the value of beneficence as a passport into the eternal habitations. Various explanations have been suggested to account for the difference in the gifts to the debtors. It is probable that when our Lord spoke the parable, reasons for these varied gifts were given, such as the circumstances of the debtors. It is scarcely now worth while to frame ingenious guesses respecting the details, which apparently do not affect the grand lessons which the story was intended to teach.

Ver. 8.—**And the lord commended the unjust steward, because he had done wisely.** This, again, is a detail which has little bearing on the main teaching. It is a graphic and sarcastic eulogy which a good-humoured man of the world would pronounce upon a brilliant and skilful, although unprincipled, action, and it completes the story as a story. It seems evident that the intentions of the steward in regard to

the debtors were carried out, and that they were really indebted to him for the release of a part of their indebtedness, and that the owner of the property did not dispute the arrangement entered into by his steward when in office. **For the children of this world are in their generation wiser than the children of light.** This was a melancholy and sorrowful reflection. It seems to say, "I have been painting, indeed, from the life. See, the children of this world, men and women whose ends and aims are bounded by the horizon of this world, who only live for this life, how much more painstaking and skilful are *they* in their working for the perishable things of this world than are the children of light in their noble toiling after the things of the life to come. The former appear even more in earnest in their search after what they desire than do the latter. There is underlying the Lord's deep and sorrowful reflection here, a mournful regret over one feature that is, alas! characteristic of well-nigh all religious life—the unkindness which religious professors so often show to one another. One great division of Christianity despises, almost hates, the other; sect detests sect; a very slight difference in religious opinion bars the way to all friendship, often to even kindly feeling. With truth Godet remarks here " that the *children of this world* use every means for their own interest to strengthen the bonds which unite them to their contemporaries of the same stamp, but, on the other hand, the *children of light* neglect this natural measure of prudence; they forget to use God's goods to form bonds of love to the contemporaries who *might* one day give them a full recompense, when they themselves shall want everything, and these shall have abundance."

Ver. 9.—**And I say unto you, Make to yourselves friends of the mammon of unrighteousness.** Then, with his usual solemn formula, " I say unto you," the Lord gave out his moral interpretation of the parable. His words were addressed to possessors of various degrees of wealth. " You will soon have to give up all your worldly goods; be prudent in time, make some real friends out of the mammon of unrighteousness; by means of that money entrusted to your care, do good to others who are in need." *The mammon of unrighteousness.* This word " mammon " does not denote, as some have supposed, the name of a deity, the god of wealth or money, but it signifies " money " itself. It is a Syriac or Aramaic term. The words, " of unrighteousness," are added because in so many cases *the getting* of money is tainted with unrighteousness in some form or other; and, when possessed, it so often hardens the heart, as the Lord himself said in another place (ch. xviii. 25), that it was easier for a camel to pass through the eye of a needle than for a rich man to enter the kingdom of God. "What the steward of my story," said the Master, "did to men of *his* world, see that you with your money do toward those who belong to *your* world." **That, when ye fail, they may receive you into everlasting habitations.** So that when you shall be dismissed from being stewards of God's possessions, that is, when ye shall die, "when ye suffer the last eclipse and bankruptcy of life," that then others, your friends, may receive you (welcome you) into everlasting dwellings. The majority of the older authorities here, instead of "when ye fail," read, "when it (money) shall fail you" (by the event of your death). The sense of the passage, however, remains the same, whichever reading be adopted. But now a deeply interesting question arises—When the Lord speaks of *friends* receiving us after death into eternal homes, to what *friends* is he alluding? Great expositors, Ewald and Meyer, for instance, tell us that he means *the angels*. But the plain sense of the parable points, not to angels, but to poor, weak, suffering persons whom we have helped here; these, then, must be the friends who will receive us, or welcome us, in the world to come. A further query suggests itself—*How* will these be able to receive us? To such a question no definite reply can be given. We know too little of the awful mysteries of *that* world to be able even to hazard a surmise as to the help or the comfort which grateful, blessed spirits will be able to show to their brethren the newly arrived, when they receive them. His word here must suffice us; well will it be for us, if one day we practically discover the holy secret for ourselves. Godet has a weighty note with which he concludes his exposition of this difficult but most instructive parable : "There is no thought more fitted than that of this parable, on the one hand to undermine the idea of merit belonging to alms-giving (what merit could be got out of that which is another's? and is not all money, are not all goods out of which we bestow our alms, God's?); and on the other, to encourage us in the practice of that virtue which assures us of friends and protectors for the grave moment of our passing into the world to come." One beautiful and exquisitely comforting thought is shrined in this playful and yet intensely solemn utterance of Jesus. The eternal tents, the "many mansions," as John calls them, will have among their occupants, it is certain, many a one whose life on earth was hard and sorrowful. These are now enjoying bliss indescribable, these poor Lazaruses, to whom this world was so sad, so dreary a habitation. And perhaps

a portion of their blessedness consists in this power, to which the Lord makes allusion here, of assisting others—*the helped here becoming the helpers there.* Although the teaching of Christ and his chosen servants here and elsewhere shows us distinctly that no *merit* can attach to almsgiving, seeing that our alms are only given out of property entrusted to us for a short time by God for this and other similar purposes, yet the same authoritative teaching informs us that God *has* regard to almsdeeds done in the true spirit of love, in determining our eternal destiny. Thus a message direct from heaven informs the Roman legionary Cornelius that his prayers and alms were come up for a memorial before God. Paul writes to Timothy to charge the Ephesus Christians "that they do good, that they be rich in good works, ready to distribute, willing to communicate ; laying up in store for themselves a good foundation against the time to come, that they may lay hold on eternal life." In the parable of Lazarus and Dives we shall find this principle yet more clearly illustrated. These are only a few out of the many passages where this generosity and almsgiving is commended to the believer with peculiar earnestness.

Ver. 10.—**He that is faithful in that which is least is faithful also in much : and he that is unjust in the least is unjust also in much.** This and the next three verses are closely connected with the parable of the unjust steward. Our Lord no doubt continued speaking, and these four verses contain a general *résumé* of what may be called his reflections on the important piece of teaching he had just delivered. We have here the broad rule, upon which God will decide the soul's future, laid down. If the man has been faithful in his administration of the comparatively unimportant goods of earth, it is clear that he can be entrusted with the far more important things which belong to the world to come. There is, too, in these words a kind of limitation and explanation of the foregoing parable of the unjust steward. The conduct of that steward, regarded in one point of view, was held to be wise, and we, though in a very different way, were advised to imitate it; yet here we are distinctly told that it is fidelity, not unfaithfulness, which will be *eventually* rewarded—the just, not the unjust steward.

Ver. 11.—**The unrighteous mammon.** As above in the parable, "mammon" signifies money. The epithet "unrighteous" is used in the same sense as in ver. 9, where we read of the "mammon of unrighteousness."

Ver. 12.—**And if ye have not been faithful in that which is another man's.** Here we have our earthly possessions plainly spoken of as the goods of another, that is, of God, and of these goods we are but the temporary stewards. **Who shall give you that which is your own?** We have here a very magnificent promise. Although on earth man can possess nothing of his own —here he is but a steward for a time of property belonging to another—yet a prospect is held out to him that, if he be found faithful in the trust while on earth, in the world to come something will be given to him really and truly his own. There will be no dismissal or death there.

Ver. 13—**No servant can serve two masters. . . . Ye cannot serve God and mammon.** Very vividly is this experience brought out in the great parable which immediately follows. There the rich man was evidently one who observed the sacred ritual of the Law of Moses : this we learn without doubt from his conversation after death with Abraham. Thus he tried, after his light, to serve God, but he also served mammon : this we learn, too, clearly from the description given to us of his life, from the mention of the gorgeous apparel and the sumptuous feeding. The service of the two was incompatible, and we know from the sombre sequel of the story to which master the rich man really held, and whom—alas for him!—in his heart he despised.

Ver. 14.—**And the Pharisees also, who were covetous, heard all these things : and they derided him.** This shows that many of the dominant sect had been present and had listened to the parable of the unjust steward. Although scrupulous, and in a way religious men, these Pharisees were notorious for their respect and regard for riches, and all that riches purchase, and they felt, no doubt deeply, the Lord's bitter reproach of covetousness. *They*, the rulers and leaders of Israel, the religious guides, were evidently attacked in such teaching as they had been lately listening to, not the common people whom they so despised. The scornful words alluded to in the expression, "they derided him," were no doubt directed against the outward poverty of the popular Galilæan Teacher. " It is all very well," they would say, " for one springing from the ranks of the people, landless, moneyless, to rail at wealth and the possessors of wealth ; we can understand such teaching from one such as *you*."

Ver. 15.—**And he said unto them, Ye are they which justify yourselves before men ; but God knoweth your hearts.** The part the Pharisees played in public imposed upon the people. The great influence which they exercised was in great measure due to the respect generally felt for their strict and religious lives. The hypocrisy of this famous sect—it was probably in many cases unconscious hypocrisy—and the false colour-

ing which it gave religion, contributed not a little to the state of things which led to the final disruption of the Jewish nation as a nation some forty years after these words were spoken. It is only a student of the Talmud who can form any notion of the Pharisee mind ; a superficial study even of parts of this strange, mighty collection will show why our Lord was so seemingly hard in his rebukes of these often earnest and religious men ; it will show, too, why the same Divine Master at times seemed to change his words of bitter wrath into accents of the tenderest sympathy and love. **For that which is highly esteemed among men is abomination in the sight of God.** Especially alluding to that haughty pride of men in wealth and money, which, after all, is not theirs.

Ver. 16.—**The Law and the prophets were until John: since that time the kingdom of God is preached, and every man presseth into it.** Some expositors discern so little connection between the sayings contained in these verses which intervene between the two great parables of the unjust steward and the rich man and Lazarus, that they consider them as a number of sayings of the Master collected by Luke and inserted here. A clear thread, however, runs through the whole piece between the two parables. Probably, however, here, as in many parts of the Gospel, we only have just a bare sketch, or *précis*, of what the Lord said ; hence its fragmentary character. Here (in the sixteenth verse), the Master went on speaking to the Pharisees who derided him (ver. 14). " Up to the period of John the Baptist," said the Master, " the old state of things may be said to have continued in force. With him began a new era ; no longer were the old privileges to be confined to Israel exclusively ; gradually the kingdom of God was to be enlarged, the old wall of separation was to be taken down. See, every man is pressing into it ; the new state of things has already begun ; you see it in the crowds of publicans, sinners, Samaritans, and others pressing round me when I speak of the kingdom of God."

Ver. 17.—**And it is easier for heaven and earth to pass, than one tittle of the Law to fail.** " Yet think not," went on the Master, " that, though things are changing, the Divine Law will ever fail. The mere temporary and transitory regulations will, of course, give place to a new order, but not the smallest part of one letter of the Divine moral Law will fail." " One tittle." This is the rendering of a Greek word the diminutive of " horn," which denoted the horn or extremity of a Hebrew letter, by the omission or addition of which—to give an instance —the letter *d* becomes the letter *r* ; thus with the horn it is ר, daleth, *d*; without the horn ר, resh, *r*. The heresiarch Marcion (second century) here, in his recension of St. Luke, changes the text thus: "It is easier for heaven and earth to pass, than for one *tittle of my sayings* to fail." Marcion, who refused to allow the Divine origin of any part of the Old Testament, was afraid of the testimony which this assertion of our Lord would give to the Divine authority of the Pentateuch. In illustration of his saying that the moral Law given to the Jews was changeless, and while earth endured would never fail, the Master instances one grave chapter of the Law with which there had been much tampering—that of divorce. "See," he said, " the new state of things which I am now teaching, instead of loosening the cords with which the old Law regulated human society, will rather tighten them. Instead of a laxer code being substituted, I am preaching a yet severer one. My law of divorce is a severer one than that written down by Moses."

Ver. 18.—**Whosoever putteth away his wife, and marrieth another, committeth adultery: and whosoever marrieth her that is put away from her husband, committeth adultery.** The teaching of the rabbis in the time of our Lord on the question of the marriage tie was exceedingly lax, and tended to grave immorality in the family life. In the late unlawful marriage of Herod Antipas with Herodias, in which so many sacred and family ties were rudely torn asunder, no rabbi or doctor in Israel but one had raised his voice in indignant protest, and that one was the friend and connection of Jesus of Nazareth, the prophet John the Baptist. Divorce for the most trivial causes was sanctioned by the rabbis, and even such men as Hillel, the grandfather of that Gamaliel whom tradition speaks of as the rabbi whose lectures were listened to by the Boy Jesus, taught that a man might divorce his wife if in the cooking she burnt his dinner or even over-salted his soup (see Talmud, treatise 'Gittin,' ix. 10).

SS. Luke and Paul, different to the great masters of profane history, like Thucydides, or Livy, or Xenophon, were evidently at no pains to round off their narratives. They give us the account of the Lord's words and works very much as they had them from the first listeners and eye-witnesses. When the notes and memories were very scant and fragmentary, as appear to have been the case in the Lord's discourse which St. Luke interposes between the parable of the steward and that of Dives and Lazarus, the fragmentary notes are reproduced without any

attempt to round off the condensed, and at first sight apparently disconnected, utterances. So here, directly after the fragmentary report of certain sayings of Jesus, the great parable of Lazarus and Dives is introduced with somewhat startling abruptness; nothing of St. Luke's is added—simply the original report as Luke or Paul received it is reproduced.

The following is probably the connection in which the famous parable was spoken.

When the Lord spoke the parable-story of the unjust steward, he pressed home to the listeners, as its great lesson, the necessity of providing against the day of death, and he showed how, by the practice of kindness here towards the poor, the weak, and the suffering, they would make to themselves friends who would in their turn be of use to them —who would, in their hour of sore need, when death swept them out of this life, receive them into everlasting habitations.

We believe that the Master, as he spoke these things, purposed—either on that very occasion, or very shortly after, when his listeners were again gathered together—supplementing this important teaching by another parable, in which the good of having friends in the world to come should be clearly shown. The parable of Lazarus and Dives, then, may be regarded as a piece of teaching following on to and closely connected with the parable of the unjust steward.

Nine verses, however, as we have seen are inserted between the two parables. Of these, vers. 10—13 are simply some reflections of the Master on the parable of the steward just spoken. Then comes ver. 14— a scornful interruption on the part of the Pharisee listeners. Our Lord replies to this (vers. 15—18), and then goes on, either then or very soon after, to the same auditory, with the parable of Lazarus and Dives, which is, in fact, a direct sequel to the parable of the unjust steward, and which St. Luke proceeds to relate without any further preamble.

Ver. 19.—**There was a certain rich man.** He is thus introduced by the Lord without any details respecting his age or place of residence—*nameless, too!* Seems he not to have been reading from that book where he found the name of the poor man written, but found not the name of the rich; for that book is the book of life?" (Sermon 178. 3 of St. Augustine). Tradition says his name was Nimeusis, but it is simply a baseless tradition. **Which was clothed in purple and fine linen.** The words which describe the life of Dives were chosen with rare skill; they are few, but enough to show us that the worldly hero of the story lived a life of royal magnificence and boundless luxury. His ordinary apparel seems to have been purple and fine linen. This purple, the true sea purple, was a most precious and rare dye, and the purple garment so dyed was a royal gift, and was scarcely used save by princes and nobles of very high degree. In it the idol-images were sometimes arrayed. The fine linen (byssus) was worth twice its weight in gold. It was in hue dazzlingly white. **And fared sumptuously every day.** With this princely rich man banquets were a matter of daily occurrence. Luther renders the Greek here, "lebte herrlich und in Freuden." Thus with all the accompaniments of grandeur this nameless mighty one lived, his halls ever filled with noble guests, his antechambers with servants. Everything with him that could make life splendid and joyous was in profusion. Some have suspected that our Lord took, as the model for his picture here, the life of the tetrarch Herod Antipas. The court of that magnificent and luxurious prince would certainly have well served as the original of the picture; but Herod was still living, and it is more likely that Jesus was describing the earth-life of one who had already been "dismissed" from his earthly stewardship, and who, when he spoke the parable, was in the world to come.

Vers. 20, 21.—And there was a certain beggar named Lazarus, which was laid at his gate, full of sores, and desiring to be fed with the crumbs which fell from the rich man's table. In striking contrast to the life of the rich man, the Master, with a few touches, paints the life of the beggar Lazarus. This giving a name to a personage in the parable occurs nowhere else in the evangelists' reports of our Lord's parabolic teaching. It probably was done in this case just to give us a hint, for it is nothing more, of the personal character of the poor sufferer who in the end was so blessed. The object of the parable, as we shall see, did not include any detailed account of the beggarman's inner life; just *this* name is given him to show us why, when he died, he found himself at once in bliss. Among the Jews the name very often describes the character of him who bears it. The Greek name *Lazarus* is derived from two Hebrew words, *El-ēzer* ("God-help"), shortened by the rabbis into *Leazar*, whence *Lazarus.* He was, then, one of those happy ones whose confidence, in all his grief and misery, was in

God alone. Well was his trust, as we shall see, justified. The gate at which he was daily laid was a stately portal (πυλών). Lazarus is represented as utterly unable to win his bread. He was a constant sufferer, covered with sores, wasting under the dominion of a loathsome, incurable disease. This representative of human suffering has taken a strange hold on the imagination of men. In many of the languages of Europe the name of the beggar of the parable appears in the terms "lazar," "lazar-house," and "lazaretto," "lazzaroni." Unable himself to walk, some pitying friend or friends among the poor—the poor are never backward in helping others poorer than themselves, thus setting a noble example to the rich—brought him and laid him daily close by the splendid gates of the palace of Dives. The crumbs signify the broken fragments which the servants of the rich man would contemptuously, perhaps pityingly, toss to the poor helpless beggar-man as he lay by the gate. **Moreover the dogs came and licked his sores.** These were the wild, homeless pariah dogs so common in all Eastern cities, who act as the street-scavengers, and are regarded as unclean. This mention of the dogs clustering round him does not suggest any contrast between the pitying animals and pitiless men, but simply adds additional colour to the picture of the utter helplessness of the diseased sufferer; there he lay, and as he lay, the rough homeless dogs would lick his unbandaged wounds as they passed on the forage.

Ver. 22.—And it came to pass, that the beggar died, and was carried by the angels into Abraham's bosom. At last kind death came, and relieved Lazarus of his sufferings. His *dismissal*, as might have been expected, preceded that of the rich man; for he was enfeebled by a deadly disease. We must not, of course, press too much the details we find in parables; still, from our Lord's way of speaking of the great change in the cases of both Lazarus and Dives, it would seem as though there was absolutely no pause between the two lives of this world and the world to come. The rich man evidently is pictured as closing his eyes upon his gorgeous surroundings *here*, and opening them directly again upon his cheerless surroundings *there*. Lazarus is described as being borne at once into Abraham's bosom. Indeed, some interpret the words as signifying that the body as well as the soul was carried by angels into Paradise. It is, however, better, with Calvin, to understand the expression as alluding only to Lazarus's soul; of the body of the pauper nothing was said, as *men* probably contemptuously, if not carelessly, buried it with the burial rites which such homeless, friendless ones too often receive. The place whither the blest Lazarus went is termed "Abraham's bosom." This term was used by the Jews indifferently, with "the garden of Eden," or "under the throne of glory," for the home of happy but waiting souls. **The rich man also died, and was buried.** There is a terrible irony here in this mention of burial. This human pageantry of woe was for the rich man what the carrying by the angels into Abraham's bosom was for Lazarus—it was *his* equivalent; but while these empty honours were being paid to his senseless, deserted body, the rich man was already gazing on the surroundings of his new and cheerless home. After the moment's sleep of death, what an awakening!

Ver. 23.—**And in hell he lift up his eyes, being in torments**; more accurately, *in Hades* (the unseen world of the dead) *he lift up his eyes.* The idea of *suffering* does not lie in these first words, but in the participle "being in torments," which immediately follows. It is noticeable that, in this Divine picture of unhappy life in the other world there is no coarse, vulgar word-painting such as we meet with so often in mediæval human works. The very fact of the man's being *unhappy* is gently represented. The graver aspect of the torments we learn from the hapless one's own words. Still, it is all very awful, though the facts are so gently told us. "Being in torments:" How could it be otherwise for such a one as Dives? The home of the loving, where Abraham was, would be no home for that selfish man who had never really loved or cared for any one save himself. What were the torments? men with hushed voices ask. A little further on the doomed one speaks of a flame and of his tongue apparently burning, owing to the scorching heat; but it would be a mistake to think of a material flame being intended here. There is nothing in the description of the situation to suggest this; it is rather the burning never to be satisfied, longing for something utterly beyond his reach, that the unhappy man describes as an inextinguishable flame. Were it desirable to dwell on these torments, we should remind men how lustful desires change rapidly into torture for the soul when the means for gratifying them exist not. In the case of Dives, his delight on earth seems to have been society, pleasant jovial company, the being surrounded by a crowd of admiring friends, the daily banquet, the gorgeous apparel, the stately house,—these details more than hint at the pleasure he found in the society of courtier-friends; but in the other world he seems to have been quite alone. Whereas among the blessed there appears to be a sweet companionship. Lazarus is in the company of Abraham, who, of course, only represents a great and goodly gathering. "Abra-

ham's bosom" is simply the well-known expression for that feast or banquet of the happy souls judged worthy of an entrance into Paradise. But in that place where the rich man lifted up his eyes there seems a strange and awful solitariness. A total absence of everything, even of *external* causes of trouble, is very noticeable. He was *alone;* alone with his thoughts. **And seeth Abraham afar off, and Lazarus in his bosom.**

Ver. 24.—**And he cried and said, Father Abraham, have mercy on me, and send Lazarus, that he may dip the tip of his finger in water, and cool my tongue; for I am tormented in this flame.** His intense longing seems to be for companionship. "Oh for a friend," he seems to say, "who could speak to me, comfort me, give me the smallest alleviation of the pain I suffer!" What picture of a hell was ever painted by man comparable to this vision of eternal solitude, peopled alone by remorseful memories, described by Jesus? As the Divine Speaker advanced in his thrilling, melancholy description of the rich man's condition in the world to come, how vividly must the listeners have recalled the Master's earnest advice to them, in his former parable of the steward, to make to themselves *while here* friends who would receive them into everlasting habitations! They saw the meaning of that detail of the parable then. Were *they*, in their luxurious abundance, were *they* making friends here who would help them there in the eternal tents? Were they not, perhaps, making the same mistake as the rich man of the story? The question might be asked—Why is Abraham, the father of the chosen race, the centre of this blessed life in Hades? In reply, *firstly*, it must be remembered that the whole colouring of this parable is peculiarly rabbinic, and in the schools of the rabbis the life of the blessed in Paradise is represented as a banquet, over which, until Messiah come, Abraham is represented as presiding. And, *secondly*, when the parable was spoken, the Saviour was actually on earth; his great redemption work had still to be accomplished. There was truth as well as error mingled in that strange rabbinical teaching. Messiah, *as Messiah*, when the parable was being probably acted, had not entered that realm where Abraham and many another holy and humble man of heart were in the enjoyment of exquisite bliss.

Ver. 25.—**But Abraham said, Son, remember that thou in thy lifetime receivedst thy good things, and likewise Lazarus evil things: but now he is comforted, and thou art tormented.** Abraham here simply bids the tortured man to call to his memory the circumstances of the life he had lived on earth, telling him that in these circumstances he would find the reason for his present woeful state. It was no startling record of vice and crime, or even of folly, that the father of the faithful calls attention to. He quietly recalls to the rich man's memory that on earth he had lived a life of princely splendour and luxury, and that Lazarus, sick and utterly destitute, lay at his palace gate, and was allowed to lie there unpitied and unhelped. And because of the studied moderation of its language, and the everyday character of its hero Dives—for he, the rich man, not Lazarus, is the real hero, the central character of the great parable-lesson — the lesson of the parable goes home necessarily to many more hearts than it would have done had the hero been a monster of wickedness, a cold calculating or else a plausible villain, a man who shrank not from sacrificing the lives and happiness of his fellowmen if their lives or happiness stood in his way. Dives was merely a commonplace wealthy man of the world, with self-centred aims, and the sin for which he was condemned to outer darkness was only that everyday sin of neglecting out of the mammon of unrighteousness—in other words, out of his money—to make for himself friends who should receive him into the eternal tents.

Ver. 26.—**And beside all this, between us and you there is a great gulf fixed: so that they which would pass from hence to you cannot; neither can they pass to us, that would come from thence.** Although the whole thought which runs through this parable is new, and peculiar to Christ, yet the colouring of the picture is nearly all borrowed from the great rabbinic schools; one of the few exceptions to this rule being this chasm or gulf which separates the two regions of Hades. The rabbis represented the division as consisting only of a wall. "What is the distance between Paradise and Gehenna? According to R. Johanan, a wall; according to other teachers, a palm-breadth, or only a finger-breadth" ('Midrash on Koheleth'). What, asks the awestruck reader, is this dreadful chasm? why is it impassable? will it be for ever there? will no ages of sorrow, no tears, no bitter heartfelt repentance succeed in throwing a bridge across it? Many have written here, and kindly souls have tried to answer the stern question with the gentle, loving reply which their souls so longed to hear. What is impossible to the limitless love of God? Nothing, wistfully says the heart. But, when interrogated closely, the parable and, indeed, all the Master's teaching on this point preserves a silence complete, impenetrable.

Vers. 27, 28.—**Then he said, I pray thee therefore, father, that thou wouldest send** him to my father's house: for I have five brethren; that he may testify unto them; lest they also come into this place of torment. The condemned acquiesces in this dread fact; convinced of the utter impossibility of any interchange of sympathy between him and the dwellers in the realms of bliss, he ceases to pray for any alleviation of his own sad and wretched state. But another wail of woe quickly rises from the awful solitude. What means this second prayer of the doomed man? Are we to read in it the first signs of a new and noble purpose in the lost soul, the first dawning of loving thoughts and tender care for others? It seems, perhaps, unkind not to recognize this; but the Divine Speaker evidently had another purpose here when he put these words into the mouth of the lost rich man—he would teach the great lesson to the living that a selfish life is inexcusable. On first thoughts, the rich man's request to Abraham appears prompted alone by his anxiety for the future of his brothers who were still alive; but on examination it would seem, to use the striking words of Professor Bruce, that he wished rather to justify his own sad past by some such reflection as this: "Had only some one come from the dead with the calm, clear light of eternity shining in his eyes, to inform me that this life beyond is no fable, that Paradise is a place or state of unspeakable bliss, and Gehenna a place or state of unspeakable woe, I should have renounced my voluptuous, selfish ways, and entered on the path of piety and charity. If one had come to me from the dead, I had surely repented, and so should not have come to this place of torment."

Ver. 29.—**Abraham saith unto him, They have Moses and the prophets; let them hear them.** The reply of Abraham was especially addressed to those Jews who were standing round him and even asking for a sign. They had all read and heard again and again the Books of Moses and the records of the prophets; if these guides had failed to show them the right way, a special messenger sent to them would be quite useless.

Vers. 30, 31.—**And he said, Nay, father Abraham: but if one went unto them from the dead, they will repent. And he said unto him, If they hear not Moses and the prophets, neither will they be persuaded, though one rose from the dead.** The Master not only wished to drive home this momentous truth to the hearts of the group of varied ranks and orders listening to him then; his words were for a far larger auditory, so he prolongs the dialogue between Dives and Abraham. "If Lazarus from the dead would only go to them," pleaded the lost soul. "Even if I send," replied Abraham, "and Lazarus goes, they will not be persuaded." They would see him, listen to him, perhaps, and then, when the first feelings of amazement and fear were dying away, would find some plausible reasons for disregarding the messenger and his message. Criticism would discuss the appearance; it would be disposed of by attributing it to an hallucination, or others would suggest that the visitant from the other world had never been really dead, and these pleas would be readily taken up by others who cared not to examine the question for themselves, and so life, careless, selfish, thoughtless, would go on as it had done aforetime. A striking example of what the Lord asserted through the medium of the shade of Abraham took place within a few days from that time. *Another* Lazarus *did* come back again from the dead into the midst of that great company of friends and mourners and jealous watchers of Jesus gathered round the sepulchral cave of Bethany, and though some true, faithful hearts welcomed the mighty sign with awful joy, still it served not to touch the cold and calculating spirit of Pharisee, scribe, and Sadducee, thirsting for the blood of the Master, whom they feared and hated, and whose word had summoned back the dead into their midst. The mighty wonder wrought no change there. One went unto them from the dead, and yet their hard hearts only took counsel together how they might put Lazarus again to death.

And so the parable and this particular course of teaching came to a close. Perhaps it is the deepest, the most soul-stirring of all the utterances of the Master. Expositors for eighteen centuries have drawn out of its clear, fathomless depths new and ever new truths. It is by no means yet exhausted. This voice from the other side of the veil charms and yet appals, it terrifies and yet enthrals all ages, every class, each rank of men and women. There are many other important items of special teaching which have been scarcely touched on in the notes above. Among the more interesting of these is the brief notice of the life which the blessed lead in Paradise. The happy dead are represented as a wide family circle. Abraham is pictured with Lazarus in his bosom. The image is taken from the way guests used to sit at a banquet. John at the Last Supper occupied a similar position with regard to the Master (John xiii. 23, 25) to that occupied by Lazarus with regard to Abraham here. The two extremes of the social scale are thus represented as meeting in that blessed company on terms of the tenderest friendship. With these were Isaac and Jacob and all

the prophets (ch. xiii. 28). "All the just," as Marcion gives it in his recension of St. Luke. And while the Paradise-life for the blessed dead is described as a holy communion of saints, there is evidently no corresponding communion in the case of the *unhappy* dead. The selfish rich man finds himself in an awful solitude. The suffering is rather represented by the image of the void; there are no external causes of pain apparently; hence his longing to speak a word with Lazarus, to feel the touch of a friendly sympathizing hand, if only for a moment, to distract his burning remorseful thoughts. There was nothing to live for *there*, nothing to hope for, but he felt he must go on living —*hopeless*. As no special crime, no glaring sin of lust or wanton excess or selfish ambition, is laid to the rich man's charge, and yet when dead he is represented as lifting up his eyes, being in torments, many, especially men belonging to those schools which are generally unfriendly to the religion of Jesus Christ, have endeavoured to show that the condemned was condemned on account of his riches, while the saved was saved because of his deep poverty. Nor is this error alone common to the Tübingen school, and to brilliant free-lances in religious literature like M. Renan. Some such mistaken notion doubtless materially aided the rise and the popularity of the mendicant orders, who played so important a part in the Christianity of the Middle Ages in so many lands. But the burden of our thrilling parable emphatically is not *"Woe to the rich! blessed are the poor!"* The crime of the life to which so awful a punishment was meted out as the guerdon, was *selfish inhumanity*, which Christ teaches us is the damning sin. (See his words in his great picture of the final judgment, Matt. xxv. 41—46.) Lazarus was no solitary individual; he was one of the many suffering poor who abound in this world, and to find whom the rich need not go far from their own gates. Lazarus represents here the *opportunity* for the exercise of Dives's humanity. Of this, and doubtless many like opportunities, Dives cared not to avail himself. He was apparently no ill-natured, cruel man, he was simply self-centred, delighting in soft living, generous wines, costly fare, sumptuous clothing, good society. He loved to be surrounded with applauding, pleasant guests; but the Lazaruses of the world, for him, might pine away and die in their nameless awful misery. Professor Bruce, with great force, puts the following words into the beggar Lazarus's mouth; these words tell us with startling clearness what was the sin of Dives: "I was laid at this man's gate; he knew me; he could not pass from his house into the street without seeing my condition, as a leprous beggar, yet as a beggar I died." Dives here was endowed richly with all the materials of human happiness, but he kept all his happiness to himself, he took no trouble whatever to diffuse his joy and gladness, his bright and many-coloured life among that great army of weak, poor, woe-begone brothers and sisters who go far to make up the population of every great city. That riches are not in themselves a ground for exclusion from the blessed life is plainly shown by the position occupied by Abraham in that happy family circle of the blessed. For Abraham, we know, was a sheik possessed of vast wealth. Then, too, in the latter part of the parable, when the imminent danger which the five brothers of the lost Dives ran of being similarly lost, was discussed, the danger is represented as springing from their careless disregard of the Law and the prophets, and not from the fact of their being rich men. When Ezekiel sought for examples of the most righteous men that had ever lived, he chose, it must be remembered, as exemplars of mortals living the fair, noble life loved of God, three men distinguished for their rank and riches—Noah, Daniel, and Job (Ezek. xiv. 14, 20).

HOMILETICS.

Vers. 1—13.—*The unjust steward.* Whereas the three preceding parables were spoken to the Pharisees, this is spoken to the disciples. It is not quite certain whether all the parables were uttered at or about the same time; but the use of the word "also" (ver. 1) suggests that they were. Anyhow, the saying before us has reference to a different kind of wasting from that of the younger son—a wasting against which the followers of Jesus are solemnly warned. We are called to listen to the Master as he indicates temptations and enforces duties within the special circle of discipleship. This parable is a saying hard to be understood. Many explanations have been given. A very learned commentator, appalled by the difficulties connected with the interpretation, abandoned the attempt, declaring that the solution of the problem is impossible. And truly, if we canvassed all the schemes of exposition which have been proposed, all the inferences which have been founded on clauses, and all the speculations which have been raised, we should find "no end in wandering mazes lost." Let our aim be less ambitious; let us try to get hold of some plain, practical instruction which shall help us to be better disciples of Jesus Christ. The outline of the story is simple. The *dramatis personæ* are not numerous. A wealthy landowner has a steward who, in the management of his estates, possesses a large discretionary power. He is informed that this steward has, not stolen or wrongfully applied, but by neglect or want of skill has squandered, the estate entrusted to him. He is called to account and is dismissed peremptorily. Now comes into view the adroitness of the man. He wishes to have some friends who can do him a good turn when he is out of a situation; and so, before news of his dismissal reaches any, while it is supposed that he has full power, he calls together those who are in arrears of rent or are otherwise indebted to his lord. We can imagine the trembling with which they obey the summons. How bland and smiling is the factor! What kind inquiries as to wife and children and belongings! And then, "By the way, what is the amount of your obligation?" Two specimens are given. One person owes a hundred measures of oil. "Take your pen," says the factor, "score out the hundred, and make it fifty." Another owes a hundred measures of wheat. "Take your pen, write down eighty." All retire charmed, loud in the steward's praise. Had he not secured a warm place in their regard? When told of his downfall, would not they all cry, "Shame!" and speak of him as the tenants' friend, and welcome him to their houses? The point of the lesson which Christ would teach is this—separate the energy from the dishonesty, the foresight from the fraud, and as he, for his own wrong ends, was wise and calculating, so, for your right ends, practise a wisdom like his, though nobler than his: "Make to yourselves friends of the mammon of unrighteousness, that when ye die, or fail, they may receive you into everlasting habitations." Now, without puzzling ourselves over the details of the parable, consider the lessons inculcated as to (1) *Christian responsibility;* (2) *Christian administration;* and (3) *Christian service.*

I. CHRISTIAN RESPONSIBILITY. In the relation of the steward to the rich man we have a foreshadowing of the relation in which we stand to God. "Steward" is the word which indicates this relation. To every one of us is given a charge of goods whose Owner is God. Our own constitution—physical, mental, moral—is a trust; all our endowments—talents, powers of whatsoever kind—are a property of which we are farmers; and he who thinks that he can do as he likes with these, that he can dissipate his substance by intemperance, or alienate his strength from higher ends, is false to his Maker and false to himself. So with regard to all our influence—direct and indirect—it is a power delegated to us by the Almighty, and to be realized under the sense of the account to be rendered to him. Money, relationships, social positions,—all are items of the estate over which we are set. Do we all realize this as we should? Do we not sadly forget this fact of stewardship? Christ speaks of "the mammon of unrighteousness." Here is an explanation which has been given. "The ears of Jesus must have been repeatedly shocked by the kind of rashness by which men speak, without hesitation, of '*my* fortune,' '*my* land,' '*my* house.' He who felt keenly the dependence of man on God perceived that there was in this feeling of property a sort of usurpation, a forgetfulness of the real owner; in hearing such language he seemed to see the tenant changing into the master." Ah! does he not hear such language every day? Is it not in the air? Is it not in our own feeling? Are we not, in many ways, changing the tenant into the master, the steward into the owner? taking the goods, and using them without giving praise to him whose they are? Would that the answer given to the first question in an old Catechism were written into the texture of every life—"Man's chief end is to glorify God, and to enjoy him for ever."

II. Connected with Christian stewardship is THE TRUTH OF CHRISTIAN ADMINISTRATION. And may it not be said that this is a truth far too little studied and practised? When we hear of depressions of trade, of hard, dull times, we may well reflect on the saying of the Prophet Haggai (i. 5, 6), "Consider your ways. Ye have sown much, and bring in little; ye eat, but ye have not enough; ye drink, but ye are not filled with drink; ye clothe you, but there is none warm; and he that earneth wages, earneth wages to put it into a bag with holes." In regard to Christian objects, is there not much to learn from such tact and prudence as the steward's in the parable? Do we not need them much in the conduct of benevolent enterprises? Competition may be healthy; but a competition which, in a limited area, or on mere windmills, spends a force which should be far more diffusive, is not only not healthy, it is a loss and a scandal. Is not this the kind of competition which is too prevalent in ecclesiastical and in charitable spheres? Otherwise must we not confess that, through our want of inventiveness or wisdom in management, our want of skill to turn opportunities to the best advantage, of the sagacity which is exercised in worldly matters, we lay ourselves open to the reproach, "The children of this age are wiser in their generation than the children of light" (ver. 8)? Realize that, whether there is much or little, faithfulness is demanded of the steward—such a disposal or investment of all wealth as that the Lord's interests are furthered. To each of us is given the charge, "So allocate the mammon of unrighteousness, the uncertain, unstable wealth which you possess, that it shall not hinder, but help you to the everlasting habitations." How many does that mammon hinder! How few of us so use our money as to advance not only Christ's cause but our own holiness! But should it not be rendered a means of spiritual gain? It is concerning this fidelity to God in the laying out of the perishable riches that Christ hints that they in whom it abounds will not want the friendly welcome when the tent of this tabernacle is dissolved, and the spirit passes into the everlasting habitations.

III. A word as to CHRISTIAN SERVICE. This mammon, which was meant to be an instrument for the accomplishment of our stewardship, is apt to assume the bearing of a master. At first it is the slave, the most obedient, until, by constant trafficking with it and by taking it into the region of our affections, it becomes our love; and when it is the love of a man, the consideration which to him is first, the supreme point of his interest, then it ascends from the kitchen into the parlour, and claims the self as its own. This mammon-rule, mammon-worship, is one of the most distinct features of the day, and few of us know how deep is its mark in our souls. Here is the choice—this mammon, or Christ with the thorn-crowned brow; this mammon, or God himself. One or other we may serve; Christ insists we cannot serve both (ver. 13). "That usurping lord has a will so different from God's will, gives commands so opposite to his, that occasion must speedily arise when one or other will have to be slighted, despised, and disobeyed, if the other be regarded, honoured, and served. God, for instance, will command a scattering, when mammon will urge to a further keeping and gathering; God will require spending on others, when mammon or the world will urge a spending on one's own lusts. Therefore, the two Lords having characters so different and giving commands so opposite, it will be impossible to reconcile their services : one must be despised if the other is held to; the only faithfulness to the one is to break with the other; 'ye cannot serve God and mammon.'" "Choose ye this day whom ye will serve." There is to be no playing at religion. A saintly voice (Augustine) has thus interpreted the election : may the " amen " to his words arise from our souls ! " O my God, thou sweetness ineffable, make bitter for me all carnal comfort which draws me away from the love of eternal things, and in evil manner allures me to itself by the view of some present delightsome good. Let me not be overcome, O Lord, by flesh and blood. Let not the world and the brief glory thereof deceive me. Let not the devil and his subtle fraud supplant me. Give me strength to resist, patience to endure, and constancy to persevere. Give me, instead of all the comforts of the world, the most sweet unction of thy Holy Spirit and the love of thy blessed Name."

Vers. 19—31.—*The rich man and Lazarus.* A parable so striking and solemn that, as has been said, "they must be fast asleep who are not startled by it." It is in several respects unique. Figure is so blended with reality, so rapidly passes into reality, that we are doubtful where and how far to separate between the form of truth and the truth itself. Indeed, it has been questioned whether the discourse is to be regarded as a parable at all; whether it is not to be regarded as the record of facts and experiences. Alone, too, of all the pictorial sayings of Jesus, it carries thought into the region behind the veil; it gives us a glimpse into the hidden economy. He who has access to the invisible takes us whither the eye of man has never pierced. And yet it is most difficult to settle on what principle we shall interpret the mysterious conversations reported, and what signification we are to attach to the words concerning the world of the dead. Let us not strain the sentences beyond the meanings which they are fairly entitled to bear; let us aim at a calm, truthful, practical application of Christ's teaching to heart and conscience.

I. Consider THE RELATION OF THE PARABLE TO THE WORDS WHICH PRECEDE, AND TO THE CIRCUMSTANCES WHICH SURROUND, IT. The Pharisees, we are told in ver. 16, had derided the teaching as to "the mammon of unrighteousness," their opposition having been intensified by the declaration, " Ye cannot serve God and mammon." The reply of Christ contains an indictment with two counts, in respect of which their mammon-worship was made apparent. 1. *Their self-justifying spirit before men.* Their piety was so disposed as to attract the observation and win the applause of men. It was the covering of covetousness, because it indicated a dependence on men, a wish to make gain of godliness. The parable which follows illustrates the same state of mind and heart under another phase of the same world-worship. Certainly the portrait of the rich man resembles the Sadducee rather than the more severe and abstemious Pharisee. But extremes often meet. Pharisee and Sadducee have this in common—man and the present are more than God and the future : to look well, to stand well with society, is really the horizon of the aim and the prize of the ambition. 2. *Their merely outward and legal righteousness.* In their casuistry (as, *e.g.*, about marriage, glanced at in ver. 19) they tampered with the eternally right and good; and their essential unbelief was proved by the failure to see that Moses and the prophets prepared men for that kingdom of God to which John had pointed, and into which he had called every one to press. They were so imbedded in their respectabilities that they felt no need of this kingdom, and did not receive it. The parable presents a man who, having Moses and the prophets, had never awakened out of a false, carnal security, had never seen his real poverty and wretchedness. And all, in the latter part of the tale, which brings out his awakenment when too late—the torments of his conscience, his appeal, his cry, his pleading for his brethren—is intended to vivify the worthlessness and worse than worthlessness of the trust on which the Pharisee was built up, and to declare that, before the judgment-seat of the Eternal, Moses and the prophets would witness against him for his rejection of the Light that had come into the world.

II. Now, having seen its root in moral conditions which Christ intended to lay bare, REGARD THE SALIENT FEATURES OF THE SKETCH BEFORE US. 1. There is *a rich man*. No particulars as to his estate are given; no judgment is passed on his character. It is not said that he had amassed his wealth by unfair means, or that he was unjust, or that he was harsh; he is simply presented as rich, fond of show and glitter and good living. Now and again a monarch might assume his robe of costly purple, but purple and fine linen are the ordinary dress of this Dives, and the appointments of his table are always splendid. A jovial, magnificent personage, to whom menials in gorgeous array do homage, and whom all the flunkeydom of his city silently reverences. There is only one drawback. At the entrance to his palace, a beggar—a miserable creature, full of sores—is laid; one so reduced that he is glad of the crumbs which fall from the table. Such crumbs are dainties to him. Clearly, no effort is made to relieve this beggar; none is employed to heal his diseases; his only guardians and mediciners are the curs which prowl about Eastern cities. The "inhumanity of man" is condemned by the action of these curs. 2. The rich man has no name, *the beggar has*—Lazarus, or Eleazar, "God's help." Beautifully Augustine asks, "Seems not Christ to you to have been reading from that book where he found the name of the poor man written, but found not the name of the rich; for that book is the book of life?" Thus day by day, the millionaire, reclining on his couch, his table groaning with delicacies, elegantly sipping at this, and taking that, and withal complaining of indigestion, occasionally sallying forth and dazzling all by his splendour, is yet offended by the loathsome thing at the gate, from which the eye is withdrawn. Day by day the gaunt form of haggard poverty obtrudes on the rights of wealth; squalor, in all its hideousness, stares into the face of wealth. Is it not the contrast which, instead of lessening, becomes more intense as the curious complexity which we call civilization develops?—civilization, with its heights separated only by hand-breadths from its depths. Day by day it is so, until—— 3. *"Died."* Ah! a word which it is impossible to expunge, which gathers up the fears and tears, which crowns or crushes the hopes of men. First the beggar. To him death is a message of relief, bidding away from sores which dogs have licked to joys in which angels share, from the flagged pavement, hard and cold, of the palace of the rich man harder and colder still, to the embrace and warmth and fulness of Abraham's bosom. "It is well," says Dives, when he misses the bundle of rags and disease; "it is the best thing which could happen to that Lazarus!" But the clock moves on; the "purple and fine linen" begin to hang about the limbs; the viands come and go untasted; there is the sickness, the sick-bed, the muffled knocker, the bated breath of physicians and attendants. Oh, horror of horrors! it is *death!* All must be left. The hands which used to be so full are now still, starched, and empty! The poor to die,—that is good; but the rich man also to die! What is the difference between the two? Of the one the burial is noted; no doubt a grand affair, for which, possibly, he had himself arranged. I have heard of a Dives, who, afraid that he might not have a sufficiently splendid coffin, procured a sarcophagus from Egypt, and lay down in it to be sure that it would fit. The burial; yes, but something more! Beggar and millionaire are in Hades—the *sheôl* of the Old Testament—the unknown place, the unseen region which contains the departed until the coming of the Lord. What of the beggar? While he was on earth man in pity carried him to the palace gate, and laid him there to starve and rot unless the crumb was thrown to him. When he dies angels carry him to the place of bliss, though not yet heaven, which was signified sometimes by the word "paradise," sometimes by the phrase "under the throne," sometimes by "Abraham's bosom." For the millionaire there is only Hades; no purple robe and fine linen, no sumptuous feast; the robe and the linen are now only a garment of fire, the sumptuous feast only a reminiscence continued in torments. To him Hades is only the reservation to the judgment of the great day. 4. And *there is the awakenment*. The Lord describes it in sentences which it is better only to summarize. The eyes of Dives are lifted up, and lo! near, yet far off, is Abraham, and—can it be?—with him Lazarus; no rags now, no sores now; his now the "purple and fine linen" and the sumptuous living, for he is in the bosom of Abraham. And through these distances there rings a cry—no cry to the Father in heaven, no cry for repentance; only to "Father Abraham," and only a respite from the pain, even a moment's respite; a cry which is still charged with the old *hauteur*,

"Send that beggar to serve me." To this he has come; there is no thought of banquet or wines; only the tip of the erstwhile beggar's finger dipped in water and cooling the tongue. Alas! the reply sounds the knell of all hope; mild, yet awful, it is, "Son, remember!" What? The good things are exhausted. He had got all that he had lived for; he had, in the bygone existence, a choice of things, and he had made his choice. His reward was drained. Lazarus had no portion in the world which was gone from sight. His election had been outside of it. He has come to his choice; he has entered on his reward. "He is comforted, but thou art tormented." For the rest, even supposing the will to grant the request, it cannot be. "There is a great gulf fixed" (ver. 26), and no passage may be between the upper and lower sides of the Hades of the dead. "Without God, and without hope." Is it a touch of still surviving humanity, or is it lest the misery be aggravated, that the petition of Dives proceeds, "Then send him where there is no gulf fixed; send him to my father's house, to my five brethren" (vers. 27, 28). "They have Moses and the prophets" (ver. 29). "Nay, but if one went to them from the dead, they will repent" (ver. 30). "If they hear not Moses and the prophets, neither will they be persuaded, though one rose from the dead" (ver. 31).

CONCLUSION. What a variety of "instruction in righteousness" is suggested by this parable! It invites thought in the direction of the most awful questions which connect themselves with human destiny. 1. As to *the Hades*—the condition, or place, of the dead. Dean Alford proposes a good rule of interpretation : "Though it is unnatural to suppose that our Lord would, in such a parable, formally reveal any new truth respecting the fate of the dead, yet, in conforming himself to the ordinary language current on these subjects, it is impossible to suppose that he whose essence is truth could have assumed as existing anything which does not exist. It would destroy the truth of our Lord's sayings if we could conceive him to have used popular language which does not point at truth." What is that, then, in the figures, in the symbols employed, as to which we can say, "Here is matter to be pondered and believed in"? Christ seems to put the stamp of his approval on these things. (1) That there is a conscious personal life after death. If this is not true, he would have started from a falsehood. (2) That in this future life the identity of the self is preserved. All references imply this. The rich man lifts up his eyes. He sees Lazarus. He cries, "Father Abraham!" He recalls his father's house and his five brethren. The I who *was* is the essential *I* for ever. (3) That in the other world, the intermediate Hades, there is a separation between the evil and the good. We should not unduly strain the meaning of "the great gulf fixed." It is in Abraham's reply to a soul in which there is no sign of a turning to God ; which is as far from the faith of the patriarch as hell is from heaven. Between a soul thus godless, and the holy dead who are at rest in the Lord, there is a great gulf fixed. But to press this into an argument for a hell of endless torment is to overstep the limits of parabolic interpretation. Yet, undoubtedly, a most solemn warning is conveyed—the warning that, in the world to come, the distinctions of character are sharp, clear, and fixed; that then the real tendencies of mind are manifested, and find their natural affinities. As to the torment of this Dives in Hades, Luther hit on the right explanation when, in one of his sermons, he exclaims, "It is not corporeal. All is transacted in the conscience as he perceives that he has acted against the gospel. Nothing was actually spoken by him, but only internally felt." It is in view of this that we apprehend the scope of the recorded conversation. That is the outward form in which the emotion, the terror, of the conscience is portrayed. For, the retribution, whose fire is not quenched, is pointed to in the saying, "Son, remember!" "It is not necessary to imagine anything beyond the stroke, stroke, stroke, ever repeating, of a scorpion-conscience," recalling, revivifying all the past, the real character of actions being made evident, as with the force of a fire from whose heat nothing can be hidden. To perceive the awful vengeance-taking on every soul of man that doeth evil, it is not necessary to suppose more than the quickening of conscience into full energy, than the continual accusation of the soul which forgets nothing, or finds all preserved, eternized for it, "when the roaring cataract of earthly things is still." 2. To return to the most pressing instruction of the parable; *life or death is the choice before every one of us.* Death; if to any one comforts are more than duties, if the plane of the existence is a merely worldly one—good things of one kind or another, and the kingdom of God left out of the reckoning. The rich man is not condemned because of his riches; the poor man is not carried into Abraham's bosom because of his poverty. The riches were the temptation, and the soul had been mastered; but one may be rich and yet simple in heart as a child, not trusting in the riches, willing to distribute, and recognizing the stewardship to God for all. One may be poor, yet greedy, showing covetousness by the fierceness with which the sense of want is expressed, by the bitter envying of the more fortunate, by the utter absence of poverty of spirit. But, "Son, remember!" if thou livest for good things, thou mayest have them; but then, the greater the prosperity, the greater the curse, the more fatal will the possession be to the true life—the life in God. By-and-by, for even the hardest and dullest there is an awakenment—to shame and everlasting contempt. Here, messages of love, the very pleading of the one risen from the dead may fail to reach the heart; there, where the ever-shifting scenes of this world disappear for ever, shall be heard the voice of conscience, speaking only for doom.

HOMILIES BY VARIOUS AUTHORS.

Vers. 1—9.—*Cleverness and sagacity.* There is a wide difference between worldly cleverness and spiritual sagacity; of these two acquisitions, the former is to be questioned if not avoided, the latter to be desired and attained. Christ's teaching here will be entirely misunderstood if we fail to discriminate between them.

I. THE EMPLOYER'S COMMENDATION OF HIS STEWARD'S CLEVERNESS. "*His* lord" (not *our* Lord) commended the unjust steward because he had acted "shrewdly" (not "wisely") (ver. 8). What does this commendation amount to? It cannot be a justification of his action upon the whole,—that idea cannot be entertained, for this action on the steward's part was wholly adverse to the employer's interests. It was simply a compliment paid to his keenness; it was equivalent to saying, "You are a very clever fellow, a very sharp man of the world; you know how to look after your own temporal affairs;" only that, and nothing more than that, is meant.

II. OUR LORD'S COMMENDATION OF SPIRITUAL SAGACITY. 1. Jesus Christ could not possibly praise cleverness *when devoid of honesty.* He could not do that for two reasons. (1) Because mere cleverness without honesty is a criminal and a shameful thing; no amount of imaginable "success" would compensate for the lack of principle; he who pays truthfulness for promotion, conscientiousness for comfort, purity for gratification, self-respect for honour or applause, pays much too high a price, does himself an irreparable wrong, sins against his own soul. (2) Because mere cleverness does not succeed in the end. It did not here. The steward of the text would have been better off if he had shown less sharpness and more fidelity; if he had been faithful he would not have been reduced to a dishonourable shift to secure a roof above his head. It does not anywhere. No one is more likely to outwit himself than a very clever man of the world. Unprincipled dexterity usually finds its way to desertion and disgrace. Success begets confidence, confidence runs into rashness, and rashness ends in ruin. No wise man would bind up even his earthly fortunes with those of his clever, unscrupulous neighbour. 2. Jesus does praise sagacity *in connection with integrity.* He would like the "children of light" to show as much forethought, ingenuity, capacity, in their sphere as the "children of this world" show in theirs. He counsels them, for instance, to put out their money to good purpose, so as to secure much better results than it is often made to yield. *Make friends with it,* he suggests. What better thing can we buy than friendship? Not, indeed, that the very best fellowship is to be bought like goods over the counter or like shares in the market; but by interesting ourselves in our fellow-men, by knowing their necessities and by generously ministering to them, we can win the gratitude, the blessing, the benediction, the prayers of those we have served and succoured. And how good is this! What will personal comforts, bodily gratifications, luxuries in dress and furniture, any visible grandeurs, weigh against this? Nay, more, our Lord suggests, we may make even money go further than this; it may yield results that will pass the border. It, itself, and all the worldly advantages it secures, we know that we must leave behind; but if by its means we make friends with those who are "of the household of faith," we relieve them in their distress, help

them in their emergencies, strengthen them as they pass along the rough road of life,
—then even poor perishable gold and silver will be the means of helping us to a fuller,
sweeter, gladder welcome when our feet touch the other shore of the river that runs
between earth and heaven. This is true sagacity as compared with a shallow shrewdness. It is to make such of our possessions, and of all our resources of every kind,
that they will yield us not only a passing gratification of the lower kind, but rather a
real satisfaction of the nobler order, and even lay up in store for us a " treasure in the
heavens," enlarging the blessedness which is beyond the grave. (1) Is our wisdom
limited to a superficial cleverness? If so, let us " become fools that we may be wise "
indeed. (2) Are we making the *best* use of the various faculties and facilities God has
committed to our trust? There are those who turn them to a very small account
indeed, to whom they are virtually worth nothing; and there are those who are compelling them to yield a rich harvest of good which the longest human life will be too
short to gather in.—C.

Ver. 5.—*Our indebtedness to our Lord.* " How much owest thou unto my Lord? "
Taking these words quite apart from the context to which they properly belong, we
may let them suggest to us the very profitable question, how much we, as individual
men, owe to him who is the Lord of all.
I. WE OWE HIM FAR MORE THAN WE CAN ESTIMATE. Who shall say how much we
owe our God when we consider: 1. *The intrinsic value of his gifts to us.* How much
are we indebted to him who gave us our being itself; who gave us our physical,
mental, and spiritual capacities; who has been preserving us in existence; who has
been supplying all our wants? 2. *The wisdom of his gifts;* their moderation, not too
large and liberal for our good; the conditions under which he grants them—in such
wise that all manner of virtues are developed in us by our necessary exertions to obtain
them. 3. *The love which inspires them.* The value of a gift is always greatly enhanced
by the good will which prompted its bestowal. God's gifts to us his children should
be very much more highly valued by us because all that he gives to us is prompted
by his Fatherly interest in us; all his kindnesses are loving-kindnesses. 4. *The costliness of one supreme Gift.* " He spared not his own Son, but delivered *him* up for us
all." The costliness of that surpassing Gift is such as we have no standards to compute,
no language to express.
II. EACH ONE OF US HAS HIS OWN SPECIAL INDEBTEDNESS. " How much owest *thou*
unto my Lord? " 1. One man has been long spared in sin, and has been reclaimed at
last; he owes peculiar gratitude for long patience and merciful interposition at the
last. 2. Another has had his rebelliousness suddenly and mightily broken down; he
is under peculiar obligation for God's redeeming and transforming grace. 3. A third
has been led almost from the first by the constraining influences of the home and the
Church; he owes very much for the earliness and the constancy and the gentleness
of the Divine visitation. Which of these three owes most to the heavenly Father, to
the Divine Saviour, to the renewing Spirit? Who shall say? But we can say this, that—
III. WE ALL OWE MORE THAN WE CAN HOPE TO PAY. We are all in the position of
him who "owed ten thousand talents," and *had not to pay* (Matt. xviii.). When we
consider the unmeasured and practically immeasurable amount of our indebtedness to
God, and also consider the feebleness of our power to respond, we conclude that there
is but one way of reconciliation, and that is a generous cancelling of our great debt.
We can only cast ourselves on the abounding mercy of God in Jesus Christ our Lord,
and accept his forgiving love in him. For his sake he will forgive us " all that debt,"
will treat us as those who are absolutely free and pure: then will uprising and overflowing gratitude fill our hearts, and the future of our lives will be a holy and happy
sacrifice, the offering of our filial love.—C.

Ver. 10.—*The wisdom of fidelity.* Between the text and the verse that precedes it
there is some interval of thought. There may have occurred a remark made by one
of our Lord's apostles: or we may supply the words,—"as to the supreme importance
and obligatoriness of fidelity, there is the strongest reason for being faithful at all times
and in everything;" for "he that is faithful in that which is least," etc. This utterance of our Lord is seen to be profoundly true, if we consider—

I. THE LAW OF INWARD GROWTH. The Lord of our nature knew that it was "in man" to do any act more readily and easily the second time than the first, the third than the second, and so on continually; that every disposition, faculty, principle, grows by exercise. This is true in the physical, the mental, and also in the spiritual sphere. It applies to acts of submission, of obedience, of courage, of service. One who is faithful to-day will find it a simpler and easier thing to be faithful to-morrow. The boy who faithfully studies at school, scorning to cheat either his teacher or his fellows, will be the apprentice who faithfully masters his business or his profession; and *he* will be the merchant on whom every one may rely in large transactions in the market; and *he* will be the minister of state who will be trusted with the conduct of imperial affairs. Fidelity of habit will grow into strong spiritual principle, and will form a large and valuable part of a holy and Christ-like character. "He that is faithful in that which is least will," in the natural order of spiritual things, "be faithful also in much." Of course, the converse of this is equally true.

II. THE PRINCIPLE OF DIVINE REWARD. God blesses uprightness in the very act, for he makes the upright man something the better and the stronger for his act of faithfulness. That is much, but that is not all. He holds out to faithfulness the promise of a reward in the future. This promise is twofold: 1. It is one of *heavenly wealth*, or wealth of the highest order. The proprietor of the estate (ver. 1) would remove the unfaithful steward altogether; but he would treat faithfulness very differently—he would be prepared to give him something so much better that it might even be called "true riches" (ver. 11); nay, he might even go so far as to give him lands, vineyards, which he should not farm for another, but for himself, which he should call "his own" (ver. 12). The Divine Husbandman will reward fidelity in his service by granting to his diligent servants "the *true* riches;" not that about which there is so much of the fictitious, the disappointing, the burdensome, as there is about all earthly good, but that which really gladdens the heart, brightens the path, ennobles the life—that noble heritage which awaits the "faithful unto death" in the heavenly country. 2. It is *inalienable wealth*, that will not pass. Here a man points to his estate and says complacently, "This is mine." But it is only his in a secondary sense. He has the legal use of it, to the exclusion of every other while he lives. But it is alienable. Disaster may come and compel him to part with it; death *will* come and undo the bond which binds it to him. It is only his in a certain limited sense. Of nothing visible and material can we say strictly that it is "our own." But if we are faithful to the end, God will one day endow us with wealth with which we shall not be called to part; of which no revolution will rob us, of which death will not deprive us—the inalienable estate of heavenly honour and blessedness; that will be "our own" for ever.

III. THE GROUND FOR PRAISE AND PATIENCE. 1. Bless God that he is now righteously endowing and enlarging his faithful ones. 2. Live in the well-assured hope that the future will disclose a much larger sphere for spiritual integrity.—C.

Ver. 11.—*The true riches.* We must gain our idea of the sense in which the word "true" is to be taken by our knowledge of Christ's use of it. And we know that he used it as distinguishing, not the correct from the incorrect, or the existing from the imaginary, but the valuable from the comparatively unimportant, the substantial from the shadowy, the essential from the accidental, the abiding from the transitory. It is in this sense that he says of himself, "I am the *true* Light;" *i.e.* "I am not that which renders the smaller service of revealing outward objects and the outward path, but that which renders the supreme service of making clear Divine and heavenly truth, and the way that leads home to God himself." Thus he speaks also of himself as "the *true* Bread;" *i.e.* not the food which sustains for a few hours, but that inward and spiritual nourishment which satisfies the soul and makes it strong for ever. Similarly he declares that he is "the *true* Vine;" *i.e.* the Divine Author of the soul's refreshment, strength, and joy. We shall, therefore, find in "the true riches" those treasures which are truly valuable, which permanently endow their possessor, in opposition to those other treasures which are of inferior worth. We glance at—

I. THE INFERIOR CHARACTER OF EARTHLY TREASURE. No doubt these riches, which are not entitled to be called the "true riches," have a worth of their own which is far from contemptible. Indeed, they render us services which we cannot help calling valuable; they provide us with shelter, with food, with raiment, with instruction, and even (in the sense of ver. 9) with friendship. But they neither supply to us nor secure for us lasting satisfaction. 1. *They do not supply it* in themselves. The possession of wealth may give, at first, considerable pleasure to the owner of it; but it may be doubted whether there is not more pleasure found in the pursuit than in the possession of it. And it cannot be doubted that the mere fact of ownership soon ceases to give more than a languid satisfaction, often balanced, often indeed quite outweighed, by the burdensome anxiety of disposing of it. 2. *They do not ensure it.* They can command a large number of pleasant things; but these are not happiness, much less are they well-being. That life must have been short or that experience narrow which has not supplied many instances in which the riches of this world have been held by those whose homes have been wretched, and whose hearts have been aching with unrest or even bleeding with sorrow.

II. The supreme value of spiritual good. 1. *There are true riches in reverence.* To be living in the fear of God; to be worshipping the Holy One; to be walking daily, hourly, continually, with the Divine Father; to have the whole of our life hallowed by sacred intercourse with heaven;—this is to be enriched and ennobled indeed. 2. *There is real wealth in love.* Our best possession at home is not to be found in any furniture; it is in the love we receive, and in the love we have in our own hearts: "The kind heart is more than all our store." And to be receiving the constant loving favour of a Divine Friend, and to be returning his affection; to be also loving with a true and lasting love those for whom he died;—this is to be really rich. 3. *There are true riches in the peace, the joy, the hope, of the gospel of Christ.* The peace that passes understanding; the joy that does not pall, and which no man taketh from us—joy in God and in his sacred service; the hope that maketh not ashamed, that is full of immortality;—these are the true riches. To be without them is to be destitute indeed; to hold them is to be rich in the sight of God, in the estimate of heavenly wisdom.—C.

Ver. 13.—*The dividing-line.* Ingenuity is an excellent thing in its way; it counts for much in the conduct of life; it renders valuable aid in our "taking possession of the earth and subduing it;" it has its place and function in the spiritual sphere. A holy love will press it into its service and make it further its benign and noble aims. But there is a dividing-line, which is such that no ingenuity will enable us to stand on both sides of it. We must elect whether we will take our place on this side or on the other of it. That line is found in the service of Jesus Christ. To be his servant is to have withdrawn from the service of the world; to remain in the latter is to decline "to serve the Lord." We may be loyal enough to this present world, may be animated by its spirit, governed by its principles, numbered amongst its friends, and—

I. Yet make a loud profession of piety; or

II. Yet enjoy a good reputation for religion,—witness the Pharisees of our Lord's time and the false prophets of an earlier age; or—

III. Still count ourselves among the people of God; for many of those whom God "knoweth afar off" are persuaded of themselves that they are quite near and very dear to him. In nothing do men make greater mistakes than in the estimation that they form of their own moral and spiritual worth. But no man can live under the dominion of any one sin or with his heart yielded to the objects and interests of time, and—

IV. Yet be a true servant of Christ. For to be the servant and follower of Christ is: 1. To have surrendered self to him, and the spirit of selfishness is the essential spirit of worldliness. 2. To have sworn undying enmity to all the false doctrines and pernicious habits which abound in "the world," and which both characterize and constitute it. 3. Not to be living for time, but to be building for eternity.—C.

Ver. 14.—*The explanation of false judgment.* "Herein is a marvellous thing," that the men who were reputed to be the best and wisest among the people of God went so far astray in their judgment and their behaviour that they treated with positive contempt the Good and the Wise One when he lived before their eyes and spoke in their hearing. It demands explanation.

I. An apparently unaccountable fact. Here we have: 1. Heavenly wisdom derided by those who were divinely instructed. The Pharisees had the Law of God in their hands. Moreover, they had it in their minds and memories; they were perfectly familiar with it; they knew it well to the last letter. They had the great advantage of the devotional Scriptures following the legal, and the didactic and the illuminating prophetic Scriptures added to both. Then, to crown all, came the enlightening truths of the great Teacher himself; yet they failed to appreciate and even to understand him. Nor did they simply turn from him without response; they took up the position of acute and active opposition—"they derided him;" they sought to bring his doctrine into popular contempt. 2. *Divine goodness derided by those who were exceptionally devout.* No man could impeach the devoutness of the Pharisees, that is to say, so far as manner and habit were concerned. Their outward behaviour was reverent in the extreme; their habit of life was regulated by rules that brought them into frequent formal connection with God and with his Word. Yet with all their exterior piety they saw the Holy One of God living his transcendently beautiful, his positively perfect life before them, and, instead of worshipping him as the Son of God, instead of honouring him as one of the worthiest of the sons of men, they actually judged him to be unholy and unworthy, and they endeavoured to bring him under the contempt of all good men! Such was their moral perversity, their spiritual contradictoriness.

II. THE TRUE EXPLANATION OF IT. That which accounts for this radical and criminal mistake of theirs was *spiritual unsoundness.* They were all wrong at heart; they loved the wrong thing, and a false affection led them, as it will lead all men, very far astray. Everything is explained in the parenthetical clause, "who were covetous." For covetousness is an *unholy selfishness.* It is a mean and a degrading carefulness about a man's own circumstances, a small and a withering desire for an enrichment at other men's expense; it is an affection which lowers and which enslaves the soul, ever dragging downwards and deathwards. And it is also a *guilty worldliness.* It is not that ambition to make the most and best of the present, which may be a very honourable aspiration; for "all things are ours [as Christian men], things present" as well as things to come (1 Cor. iii. 22); it is rather the moral weakness which allows itself to be lost and buried in the pursuits and pleasures of earth and time; it is the narrowing of the range of human attachment and endeavour to that which is sensuous and temporal, excluding the nobler longings after the spiritual and the eternal. This worldliness is not only a guilty thing, condemned of God; but it is a disastrous thing, working most serious evils to mankind. 1. It distorts the judgment. 2. It leads men into wrong and mischievous courses of action; it led the Pharisees to take such an attitude and to initiate such proceedings against Christ as culminated in his murder. 3. It ends in condemnation—such severe judgment as the Lord passed on these blind guides (see Matt. xxiii.). If we would be right at heart and in the sight of God, it is clear that "our righteousness *must* exceed the righteousness of the scribes and Pharisees." (1) Multiplied ceremonialism will not suffice. (2) Perfected proprieties will not avail. (3) Only a humble, trustful, loving heart will make us right. A true affection, the love of Christ, will lead us into truth and wisdom, will commend us to God, will land us in heaven.—C.

Ver. 15.—*Divine and human judgment.* This declaration of Christ was a judgment in a double sense. It was drawn down upon themselves by the Pharisees, who had been doing their worst to bring into derision the doctrine and the character of our Lord. This reply was not indeed a retort, but it was of the nature of a judgment. It declared the mind of Christ, and it declared it in strong disapproval of evil-doing and strong condemnation of an evil spirit. It brings before us three subjects of thought.

I. OUR DESIRE TO STAND WELL WITH OUR BRETHREN. "Ye . . . justify yourselves before men." The desire to be justified of man is almost universal. 1. It may be a right and worthy sentiment. When the approval of man is regarded in the light of a confirmation of God's acceptance of us or of the commendation of our own conscience, then is it right and honourable. 2. But it may be of very little value indeed; it is so when it is sought merely as a matter of gratification, irrespective of the consideration of its true moral worth. For the approval of man is often a very hollow and always a transient thing; change the company, and you change the verdict; wait until a later day, and you have a contrary decision. The hero of the past generation is the criminal of the present time. And it may be that the man or the action the multitude are praising is the one that God is most seriously condemning. Of what value, then, is "the honour that cometh from man"? (1) Care nothing for the opinion of the selfish and the vicious. (2) Care little for the judgment of those whose character you do not know. (3) Be desirous of living in the esteem of the good and wise.

II. GOD'S SEARCHING GLANCE. "God knoweth your hearts." Men do not see us as we are; we do not know ourselves with any thoroughness of knowledge; the power we have and use to impose on others reaches its climax when we impose on ourselves, and persuade ourselves that those things are true of us which are essentially false. Only God "knows us *altogether*;" for it is he alone that "looketh upon the heart," that is "a Discerner of the thoughts and intents of the heart." His glance penetrates to the innermost chambers of our soul. He sees: 1. *The motives* by which we are actuated in our deeds; seeing often that apparently good deeds are inspired by low or even bad motives, and that deeds which society condemns are relieved by unselfish promptings. 2. *The feeling* that accompanies our expression; whether it is slight or whether it is deep; often perceiving that it is more or that it is less than we imagine it to be. 3. *The purpose of our heart* toward himself; determining whether, in the presence of much profession, there is genuine devotedness; whether, in the absence of profession and even of assurance, there is not true godliness in the soul.

III. THE DIVINE REVERSAL. "That which is highly esteemed," etc. Of those things concerning which these strong words are true, there are: 1. *Assumed and also unpractical piety.* The *hypocrite* is hateful in the sight of Absolute Purity; we know what Christ thought of him. Less guilty and yet guilty is the *mere cere-monialist*—he who has no more piety than is found in a multitude of sacred ceremonies, who has not learned to regulate his life or to regard the claims of others. To frequent the sanctuary on one day, and the next to take a mean advantage of some weak brother, is odious in the sight of the common Father. 2. *Self-seeking philanthropy*—the show of doing good to others which is nothing more than a profitable pretence, a course of conduct which has a benevolent aspect but which is secretly aiming at its own enrichment. 3. *Irreverent activity.* Men often yield great admiration to those whose lives are full of successful labour, who build up large fortunes or rise to great eminence and power by much energy and unremitting toil. But if those men are living godless lives, are excluding from the sphere of their thought and effort that Divine One, "with whom they have [everything] to do," and whose creative, preserving, and providing love has everything to do with their capacity, must we not say that the lives of these men are so seriously defective as to be even "abomination in the sight of God"?—C.

Vers. 19—26.—*The sin and doom of selfish worldliness.* This parable, taken (as I think it should be), not in connection with the immediately preceding verses (16—18), but with those that come before these (with vers. 1—15), is a very striking confirmation of the doctrine delivered by Christ concerning selfishness and worldliness. He brings its sinfulness and its doom into bold relief.

I. WHERE THE RICH MAN WAS WRONG. 1. Not in being rich. He is not brought forward as the type of those whose very possession of wealth—because ill-gotten—is itself a crime and a sin. He may be supposed to have entered on his large estate quite honourably. 2. Not in being vicious. There is no trace of drunkenness or debauchery here. 3. Not in being scandalously cruel. It is not a monster that is here depicted; not one that took a savage and shameful pleasure in witnessing the sufferings of others. He was so far from this that he consented to the beggar being placed at his gate, and (it may be taken) that he allowed his servants to give the suppliant broken pieces from his table; he was not at all unwilling that the poor wretch outside should have for his dire necessity what he himself would never miss. This is where he was wrong. 4. He was *living an essentially selfish and worldly life.* God gave him his powers and his possessions in order that with them he might glorify his Maker and serve his brethren. But he was expending them wholly upon himself, or rather upon his present personal enjoyment. If he parted with a few crumbs which he could not feel the loss of, that was an exception so pitifully small as to serve no other purpose than that of "proving the rule." It went for nothing at all. His spirit was radically and utterly selfish; his principles were essentially worldly. It was nothing to him that outside his gates was a world of poverty, of which poor Lazarus was only one painful illustration; that sad fact did not disturb his appetite or make his wines lose anything of their relish. It was nothing to him that there were treasures of a better kind than those of house and lands, of gold and silver; that there was an inheritance to be gained in the unseen world; enough for him that his palace was his own, that his income was secure, that his pleasures there was no one to interrupt. Selfishness and worldliness characterized his spirit; they darkened and degraded his life, and they sealed his doom.

II. THE SEVERITY OF HIS DOOM. "In hell he lift up his eyes, being in torments;" "There is a great gulf fixed." Jesus Christ was not now unveiling the future world for curious eyes; he was simply using current language and familiar imagery to intimate to us that the man who has lived a selfish and worldly life will meet with severe condemnation and grievous penalty in the next world; a penalty in regard to which he has no right to expect either mitigation or release.

1. Are our lives governed *by the spirit of active benevolence?* To throw the crumbs to Lazarus is far from "fulfilling the law of Christ" (Gal. vi. 2). We must go a very long way beyond that infinitesimal kindness. We must have a heart to pity the poor and needy; a soul to sympathize with them and share their burdens (Matt. viii. 17); a generous hand to help them (ch. x. 33—37). The sorrow and the sin of the world must be upon our heart as a serious and heavy weight, and we must be ready to make an earnest effort to soothe the one and to subdue the other. 2. Have we regard to the *day of trial and the future of retribution* (see Matt. xxv. 41—46)?—C.

Vers. 19, 20.—*Poverty at the gate of wealth.* Here is a picture which we recognize in England in this nineteenth century quite as readily as it would be recognized in Judæa in the days of our Lord; it is that of poverty and wealth in very close association. It is not only a picture to look upon but a problem to solve, and one of much urgency as well as great difficulty.

I. POVERTY AND WEALTH IN CLOSE JUXTAPOSITION. As the rich man of the parable could not enter his house without seeing Lazarus lying in rags and sores at his gate, so are we unable to pass our days without being impressed with the fact that "the poor [even the very poor] we have with us," and indeed all around us. *Lazarus lies at our gate.* Not only have we the *professional beggar,* who has adopted "begging" as his means of livelihood, but we have the whole army of *the unfortunate,* who have been incapacitated by some means, and who cannot "work that they may eat;" and we have also another large and equally pitiable multitude of *the ill-paid,* who cannot earn enough by the honest industry in which they are employed to sustain themselves and their families. And so it comes to pass that in England to-day, side by side with competence, with wealth, with inestimable affluence, is poverty walking in rags, lying in loneliness, shivering with cold and hunger, working without reward that is worthy of the name. It is a sad sight in a Christian land; and it is not sad alone, it is alarming; for such extremes are full of evil and of peril.

II. THE PAINFUL ASPECT OF THIS FEATURE OF OUR MODERN LIFE. For who can doubt: 1. *The dangers attending great wealth?* It leads to luxury, and luxury favours sloth, indulgence, a false standard of the worth and purpose of life, a proud heart, and a haughty bearing. In circumstances where there is no necessity for energetic and patient labour, and where there is every opportunity of enjoyment, many evil weeds grow fast, and there the best flowers that grow in the garden of the Lord too often languish. Or who can doubt: 2. *The perils of extreme poverty?* These lead down by a straight and steep path to servility, to craftiness and cunning, to falsehood, to dishonesty, to envy and hatred. And who can fail to see: 3. *The evil influence on the State* of these two extremes? Here there can be no true brotherhood, no proper association and co-operation; here is separation from one another, a division as great as that which is interposed by the high mountain range or the broad sea; nay, greater than that! Many English people see more and know more of the inhabitants of Switzerland than they see and know of the denizens of the streets of another part of their own parish. It is the uninteresting and objectionable poor at their gate who are the "strangers."

III. ONE MITIGATING FEATURE. This juxtaposition of poverty and wealth provides an opportunity for the exercise of sincere benevolence and of the highest Christian wisdom. To the Christian heart there is a plaintive plea which cannot be unheard or disregarded, even though Lazarus be kept out of sight and hearing by judicious arrangements. And to the honest patriot there is an inviting and urgent problem to which, far more than to the questions of fortifications and armaments, he will give earnest heed, viz. how to bring about an approachment, an intermingling, of all classes and conditions of men, a better distribution of the great resources of the land.

IV. THE TRUE HOPE OF ADJUSTMENT. Whither shall we look for a better distribution of the riches of the land? 1. *Almsgiving* can only touch the fringe of the difficulty. 2. *Economic changes* may have a valuable part to play in the matter; but we are not yet agreed as to the best course to take. 3. *Beneficent legislation* will certainly bring its large contribution; it can do two things: it can (1) educate the whole nation, and so provide every citizen with necessary weapons for the battle of life; and it can (2) do much to remove temptation from the path of the weak. But it is: 4. *Spiritual renewal* which must prove the main source of social reconstruction. Change the character, and you will change the condition of men. And the one force which will effect this is the redeeming and regenerating truth of God, made known by the holy lives and in the loving words of the disciples of Jesus Christ.—C.

Vers. 27—31.—*A dangerous delusion.* The rich man found himself undergoing the penalty of a selfish and worldly life, and, bethinking himself of his five brethren, he desired for them the advantage which he himself had not possessed; he prayed that a visitant from the unseen world might appear to them and warn them of the danger in which they stood. He thought this extraordinary privilege would accomplish for them what the ordinary influences around them had not wrought. He was assured that in this notion he was mistaken; if they were not hearing "Moses and the prophets, neither would they be persuaded though one rose from the dead."

I. THE ONE HOPE FOR ERRING AND SINFUL MEN—that they may *be persuaded*. They are living in sin; for selfishness and worldliness are such in the sight of God that they may be said to be sin itself; they are the soul turning from the living God to find its centre, its sphere, its satisfaction, in its own poor self, in the material and transitory good of this present world. And living in sin, men are living under God's high displeasure, under his solemn and awful condemnation, in peril of final banishment and penalty in the future. The one hope for them is that they will *be persuaded*: 1. *To consider.* To consider whence they came, whose they are, unto whom they owe their powers and their possessions, what is the true end and aim of human life, their accountableness to the God whom they have neglected and displeased, the nearness of death, the greatness of eternity. 2. *To repent.* That is, not to be convulsed with a strong and passing agony of soul, nor to use the current and approved language of contrition, but to change their minds, their views, their feelings; to have in their hearts a deep sense of shame and of regret that they should have so sadly misspent their powers and lost their opportunities. 3. *To resolve.* To come to a deliberate and fixed resolution to live henceforth unto God their Saviour.

II. THE REFUGE OF THE DISOBEDIENT. There are many who, when they thus recognize their duty, are "not disobedient to the heavenly vision;" they say, "Lord, what wilt thou have me to do?" and proceed without delay to do his holy will. But there are others who weakly and wrongly postpone the hour of decision and of return. They think that the time will come for them to enter the kingdom of God, but it has not yet arrived. There has not happened to them any great visitation. God has not appeared in any striking and overwhelming form. There will come an hour when it will be made manifest to them that they must no longer delay; when they will be mightily constrained to yield themselves to the service of the Supreme; *then* they will freely and gladly respond; meantime they will pursue the old path of selfishness and worldly pleasure.

III. THE VANITY AND THE FOLLY OF THIS RESORT. 1. *The vanity of it.* Jesus Christ taught that men, if they were unmoved by the sacred truths they learned in Deuteronomy and Isaiah, would not be stirred to newness of life even by an apparition from the unseen world; that it was not by the extraordinary and the startling, but by the *divinely true*, that souls were to be saved. And this doctrine is in conformity with the known facts of our human experience. Men that know their Lord's will but delay to do it will find some excuse for disobedience when the unusual or even when the supernatural is before them. The disobedient heart goes on in sinful procrastination, with a vague and feeble hope that this hour will come; but it does not arrive. He has a vision of sudden death, but he rises from the sick-bed to pursue the old path; he loses some companion and is powerfully admonished of his own mortality, but he returns from his friend's grave the same man that he was before; he goes to hear the wonderful preacher and listens with admiration not unmixed with fear or even trembling, but he awakes on the morrow with a closed mind, with an unbroken heart. Some great trouble overtakes and overthrows him, but his soul is hardened, and the "sorrow of the world worketh death" and not life in his case. His hope is a vain one. 2. *The folly of it.* Why should he wait for the extraordinary, the supernatural? Has he not at hand everything he needs to convince him and to induce him to take the step of spiritual decision? Why want some one from heaven to bring down the word of truth or the Saviour himself (Rom. x. 6)? All that we want we have. (1) Our conscience is urging us to a life of holy service. (2) Our reason tells us that our present and eternal welfare is bound up with the forgiveness and the favour of the living God, in whose power we stand and who holds all our future in his sovereign hand. (3) Our Divine Father is summoning us to his side, to his hearth, to his table, and is waiting to welcome us. (4) Our gracious Saviour is inviting us to an immediate and to an absolute trust in himself. (5) The Holy Spirit of God is pleading and striving with us. There is no reason, there is no excuse, for a single day's delay. Every one to whom it is right to listen, everything to which it is wise to yield attention, says, "Come." It is only the evil voices around us and from below that say, "Wait." Delay means the doom of Dives; immediate obedience leads along the paths of heavenly wisdom and holy service to the home of the blessed.—C.

Vers. 1—13.—*Money as a means of grace.* The previous chapter was spoken against the *pride* of the Pharisaic party, who were too exclusive to welcome publicans and sinners to the same feast of privilege as themselves. The parable now before us was spoken against their *covetousness.* It will be found that, as the graces are to be found and grow together, so do the vices of mankind. The idolatry of wealth goes hand-in-hand with pride. In warning his disciples, however, against the vice, our Lord inculcates positive truth, and brings out in his parables the important fact that money may either be a means of grace to men, or a temptation and a snare. The first parable, about the unjust steward, shows us one who was wise in time in the use of money; the second parable, about the rich man and Lazarus, shows us one who became wise when it was too late and his doom was sealed. The story need be no moral difficulty to us. The all-important point is the deprivation of his stewardship. It was taken from him on the ground of injustice of some kind. In view of his exodus from the stewardship, he prudently makes his lord's debtors his debtors too, by largely reducing their liabilities. Having thus made friends with them all, he awaits his dismissal with confidence, and expects befriendment when out of his situation. It is his *prudence*, not his motives, that our Lord commends. Now, to our Lord's spiritual eye, this was a beautiful representation of what a soul may do in prospect of dismissal from his earthly stewardship at death. He may take the money he happens to possess, and, feeling that it is not his own absolutely, but God's, and that he is only a steward of it, he can use it liberally, making the troubles of his brethren lighter, so that, having laid them under obligations to him, he can calculate with certainty upon their cordial sympathy in the world beyond the grave. A prudent outlay may make hosts of friends among the immortals beyond; in a word, money may be utilized as a very important means of grace.

I. MAMMON IS A BAD MASTER. (Ver. 13.) We start with this thought as a kind of background to the more comforting teaching which our Lord here emphasizes. The soul that is enslaved by mammon becomes miserable. Is not this implied in the term "miser," which designates the slave of money? The poor slave is kept grinding away, amassing more and more, and yet never getting any benefit from all the lust of gold. Nothing seems more foolish and insane than the race for riches; nothing more ruinous than the snares into which the runners fall. When life's end comes and the accumulated hoard has to be left behind, the condition of the soul is pitiful indeed.

II. ON THE OTHER HAND, MONEY MAY BE MADE A VERY USEFUL SERVANT. (Vers. 1—9.) For nothing is gained by denying that money is a great power. How much it can accomplish! Every department of enterprise regards money as the "one thing needful." So powerful is it, that people by the use of it may become thoroughly *hated*, as many selfish speculators and covetous people are every day. On the other hand, it may be so wisely laid out as to increase our friends to troops. A judicious use of money can gather friends around us by the thousand. It may serve us by increasing our list of friends.

III. MONEY CAN BE USED BY US TO SERVE GOD. (Vers. 10—12.) This is the gist of Christ's teaching in the parable before us; and we never use money aright until we have got this idea driven home of serving God by it. And to emphasize this, let us notice : 1. *Money is God's, and we are never more than stewards of it.* This truth underlies the whole parable. The very rich man who has the steward is God. We are all his stewards, faithful or unfaithful, as the case may be, in our use of *his* money. It is never ours apart from God; it is ours only as his stewards. Other things are held far more surely—for example, education, thoughts, culture. They enter our being and become ours, we have reason to believe, for evermore. But money is only ours for a time—a loan from God to be put out to a proper use. 2. *We are faithful in our stewardship when we give ungrudingly to those who are in real need.* God gives us "enough *and to spare*" for the purpose of laying the needy under obligation. In this way we transmute our money into gratitude. The gratitude of the assisted is better than the money, for it abides and can be enjoyed when money cannot. 3. *God guarantees the gratitude and the reward.* Some of the recipients may turn out to be ungrateful, but "he that giveth unto the poor lendeth unto the Lord," and "Inasmuch as ye have done it unto one of the least of these my brethren, ye have done it unto me." We are, therefore, sure of the highest recognition when for the Lord's sake we help our fellows.

IV. THE TRULY GENEROUS AND LIBERAL SOUL HAS A WELCOME AWAITING HIM IN THE ETERNAL TABERNACLES. (Ver. 9.) The expression, "eternal tabernacles," to adopt the Revised Version, seems to indicate everlasting *progress* to be realized in the next life. We shall be moving onwards even there to higher and higher attainment. Those we have befriended here will receive us into their eternal tents. There will be recognition and fellowship and its accompanying progress. What a judicious outlay to have all this awaiting us in the world to come! What a means of grace money may thus become! and what a help to glory! Let the so-called unjust steward, then, admonish us to make the most of our capital on earth, that we may have the best heavenly return from it when we have left the money behind us for ever.—R. M. E.

Vers. 14—31.—*The misuse of money.* The possibility of making "friends of the mammon of unrighteousness" has been clearly set before us by our Lord in the preceding parable. The "eternal tents" may afford us warmest welcome if we have conscientiously used our money. But the Pharisees who needed the warning against covetousness only derided him for his pains. It is supposed that it was his poverty which they thought took away his right to speak as he did of riches. He is consequently compelled to turn upon them a severer rebuke, and he does so in the sentences preceding, as well as in the substance of, the next parable. The intermediate sentences need not long detain us. Christ charges the Pharisees with *self-justification.* Now, this can only take place "before men." It is an appeal to a mere human tribunal—to those who can only judge by the appearance, but cannot search the heart. God, he tells them plainly, will not endorse this justification. He will reverse the sentence of self-complacency. He follows up this by stating the *permanence of the Law.* The reputation of the Pharisees may wither and decay, but not one tittle of the Law shall fail. And in present circumstances he declares that the Divine kingdom is being stormed by anxious men who have learned to humble themselves in penitence and pass into exaltation through pardon. They ought to see to it that they are not induced by lust to play fast and loose with the unchanging Law, and to imagine that they can divorce their wives on the usual pretexts, and be guiltless. But now we must proceed to the striking parable of the rich man and Lazarus. Upon the details of the story we do not tarry. It is an exquisitely powerful picture. The artist is here at his best. The rich man in his " purple and fine linen, faring sumptuously every day ; " the poor man " laid at his gate, full of sores," and thankful for the crumbs that fall from the rich man's table and for the attention of the dogs ; then two deaths, when lo ! the positions are reversed, and the poor man finds himself in the bosom of Abraham and with his good things all about him, while the rich man finds himself in utter poverty, in need of everything and sure of nothing. The picture closes, too, all hope for such a selfish soul as the rich man proved himself to be. The following lessons are here taught us.

I. EVERY ONE WITH MEANS HAS AMPLE OPPORTUNITY IN THIS LIFE OF BEING GENE-ROUS. (Ver. 20.) The friends of the poor man laid him, or, as the word ($\epsilon\beta\epsilon\beta\lambda\eta\tau o$) may mean, " threw him down " at the rich man's gate.[1] There could be no doubt about the rich man's opportunity ; it was pressed upon his notice. And amid all the artificial separations which civilization makes between rich and poor, there is always some friendly hand to force opportunity upon us. " The poor we have with us always." They appear, do what we may, at the feast of life, and we cannot exclude them from our considerations. It requires an effort to be utterly ungenerous. Now, we ought to bless God that he has not left us with any excuse for hard-heartedness. He brings the world's needs to our very gates. He emphasizes opportunity. He gives us outflow for our generosities. He will not leave us in our hard-heartedness, but calls us evermore to nobler things.

II. SELF-INDULGENCE MAKES PEOPLE ABSOLUTELY PITILESS. (Ver. 21.) Mosheim, in a suggestive discourse from this parable, reminds us at the outset of the words of Peter about " fleshly lusts warring against the soul." [2] It is wonderful how hard-hearted luxurious living can make people. The rich man in the parable can find in his heart to pass out and in and never once to relieve his poor brother. The latter may have got crumbs from the rich man's table, but if he did, it was more likely by the servants' charity than by the master's orders. From the self-indulgent worldling he got no consideration. He is ignored, for the selfish soul has become pitiless. When self is supreme, it can shut out all consideration of others from one's thoughts. When they obtrude themselves or are obtruded upon our attention, we say, alas ! that they have no claim upon us, forgetting that they are our brothers. Against such hard-heartedness we should all be upon our guard.

III. DEATH, IN DEPRIVING THE SELFISH SOUL OF HIS GOOD THINGS, LEAVES HIM NECES-SARILY IN TORMENT. (Vers. 22, 23.) Good living is a most dangerous habit when it constitutes any man's *all*. A soul, to be confined to this tariff, is in danger of dying *into* utter want. The round of sensual indulgence goes on day after day, the appetites are gorged, and man sinks down into the animal pure and simple. Now, if the world beyond makes no provision for such gross indulgences ; if it has no venison and cham-pagne ; if the appetites are left without a larder and the famine of the senses has come ;— what kind of life must the poor soul have ? It needs no furnace of actual fire to secure his torment. The burning desire, within which nothing can quench, leaves him of necessity in torment. If God has made no provision for the intemperate, for the gourmand, for the dissolute, in their environment beyond the grave, must not their lusts, denied satisfaction, be perpetual torment ? The torment of unsatisfied desire, the hunger of a self-centred spirit, must be terrible !

IV. UNBELIEF IS INEXCUSABLE, AND MAY BE INVINCIBLE. (Vers. 27—31.) The selfish worldling had evidently been living without regard to a future life. In his torment he realizes that his five brethren are living the same heedless life. Lest, therefore, they should come and *increase his torment*, he asks that Lazarus be sent on a special mission to warn them about their doom. Now, it is plain that, with Moses and the prophets in their hands, they were without excuse. What, then, did Moses and the prophets teach ? They do *not* teach with great distinctness the doctrine of a future life. They undoubtedly *imply* that doctrine. But the question is—Did the rich man or his brethren need that doctrine to guard them against inhumanity of life ? Must I tremble before prospective torment ere I am convinced that I ought to be

---

[1] Cf. Bruce's ' Parabolic Teaching of Christ,' p. 388.
[2] ' Heilige Reden,' erster theil, s. 65, etc.

generous and considerate? [1] Nay, do I not know by the law of conscience that such conduct as is inhuman must incur the curse of God? Even the pagans are inexcusable when they live inhuman lives. Besides, we must not, with the rich man, imagine that a prescribed miracle may overbear all unbelief. Unbelief may be invincible. No miracle may be strong enough to defeat self-will. May we all be kept from such a hardened state!

V. ABRAHAM, AS HE CHERISHES LAZARUS IN THE OTHER LIFE, SHOWS US HOW A RICH MAN MAY PERPETUATE HIS KINDLY OFFICES AND INFLUENCE. (Vers. 23—25.) It has been very properly observed that in Abraham we have a rich man in blessedness, as a set-off to the other rich man in torment. Abraham was very probably the richer of the two while in life, but he had used his wealth for the good of his fellows. He had cherished the poor and needy. And so it is to good-hearted, faithful Abraham that the consolation of Lazarus is committed. Here the habits of helpfulness which the patriarch had cultivated upon earth find exercise in the better world. What a prospect is thus opened up to the large-hearted! Heaven will be full of opportunity for ministration. Those whose lot has been a hard one in this world will be taken to the bosom of the patriarchs of God—those who have become "seniors" in his house of many mansions —and receive from them the compensation which God has in store for all who have learned to love him.—R. M. E.

EXPOSITION.

CHAPTER XVII.

Vers. 1—37.—*The Master's teaching on the subject of the injury worked on the souls of others by our sins. The disciples pray for an increase of faith that they may be kept from such sins. The Lord's reply. His little parable on humility. The healing of the ten lepers. The ingratitude of all save one. The question of the Pharisees as to the coming of the kingdom. The Lord's answer, and his teaching respecting the awful suddenness of the advent of the Son of man.*

Vers. 1, 2.—**Then said he unto the disciples, It is impossible but that offences will come: but woe unto him, through whom they come! It were better for him that a millstone were hanged about his neck, and he cast into the sea, than that he should offend one of these little ones.** The thread of connection here is not very obvious, and many expositors are content with regarding this seventeenth chapter as simply containing certain lessons of teaching placed here by St. Luke without regard to anything which preceded or succeeded them in the narrative, these expositors regarding the contents of this chapter as well authenticated sayings of the Master, which were repeated to Luke or Paul without any precise note of time or place, and which appeared to them too important for them to omit in these memoirs of the Divine life. Notwithstanding this deliberate opinion, endorsed by Godet and others, there does seem a clear connection here with the narrative immediately preceding. The Divine

Master, while mourning over the sorrowful certainty of offences being committed in the present confused and disordered state of things, yet pronounces a bitter woe on the soul of the man through whose agency the offences were wrought. The "little ones" whom these offences would injure are clearly in this instance not children, although, of course, the words would include the very young, for whom Jesus ever showed the tenderest love; but the reference is clearly to disciples whose faith was only as yet weak and wavering—to men and women who would be easily influenced either for good or evil. The offences, then, especially alluded to were no doubt the worldliness and selfishness of professors of godliness. The sight of these, professedly serving God and all the while serving mammon more earnestly, would bring the very name of God's service into evil odour with some; while with others such conduct would serve as an example to be imitated. The selfish rich man of the great parable just spoken, professedly a religious man, one who evidently prided himself on his descent from Abraham the friend of God, and yet lived as a heartless, selfish sinner, who was eventually condemned for inhumanity, was probably in the Lord's mind when he spoke thus. What fatal injury to the cause of true religion would be caused by one such life as *that! It were better for him that a millstone were hanged about his neck, and he cast into the sea.* This was a punishment not unknown among the ancients. The ancient Latin Version, and Marcion in his

[1] Cf. Bruce, *ut supra.*

recension of St. Luke, read here, "It were better for him that he had never been born, or that a millstone," etc. The awful sequel to a life which apparently had given the offence to which the Lord referred, endorses this terrible alternative. Yes; better indeed for him had that evil life been cut short even by such a death of horror as the Master pictures here, when he speaks of the living being cast into the sea bound to a millstone.

Ver. 3.—**Take heed to yourselves: If thy brother trespass against thee, rebuke him; and if he repent, forgive him.** "But do you take heed," the Lord went on to say, "my disciples; you too are in danger of committing deadly sin yourselves, and of doing my cause irreparable injury. Soft living in selfish luxury, about which I have been speaking lately, is not the only wrong you can commit; there is sore danger that men placed as you are will judge others harshly, even cruelly, and so offend in another way 'the little ones' pressing into the kingdom: this is your especial snare." Things Jesus had noticed, perhaps congratulatory, self-sufficient comments he had heard them make on the occasion of the lately spoken parable of Dives, very likely had suggested this grave warning. So here he tells them, the future teachers of his Church, how they must act; while ever the bold, untiring, fearless rebukers of all vice, of every phase of selfishness, they must be never tired of exercising forgiveness the moment the offender is sorry. The repentant sinner must never be repelled by them.

Ver. 5.—**And the apostles said unto the Lord, Increase our faith.** The disciples, moved by the severe and cutting rebuke of their Master—a rebuke they probably felt their *harsh*, self-congratulatory state of mind had well merited—come to him and ask him to give them such an increased measure of faith as would enable them to play better the difficult and responsible part he had assigned them. They evidently felt their weakness deeply, but a stronger faith would supply them with new strength; they would thus be guided to form a wiser, gentler judgment of others, a more severe opinion too of themselves.

Ver. 6.—**And the Lord said, If ye had faith as a grain of mustard seed, ye might say unto this sycamine tree, Be thou plucked up by the root, and be thou planted in the sea; and it should obey you.** The Lord signifies that a very slight *real* faith, which he compares to the mustard seed, that smallest of grains, would be of power sufficient to accomplish what seemed to them impossible. In other words, he says, "If you have any real faith at all, you will be able to win the victory over yourselves

necessary for a perpetual loving judgment of others." The sycamine tree here mentioned in his comparison is not the sycamore; he was probably standing close by the tree in question as he spoke. The sycamine is the black mulberry, *Morus nigra*, still called *sycamenea* in Greece.

Vers. 7, 8.—**But which of you, having a servant ploughing or feeding cattle, will say unto him by-and-by, when he is come from the field, Go and sit down to meat? and will not rather say unto him, Make ready wherewith I may sup, and gird thyself, and serve me, till I have eaten and drunken; and afterward thou shalt eat and drink?** And here we have the Lord's answer to his disciples' request to increase their faith. They were asking for a boon he would not, nay, could not, grant them yet. A small measure of *real* faith was sufficient to teach them that God would give them strength enough to keep themselves from committing this offence against love and charity of which he warned them so solemnly; but they prayed for more. "They were asking for faith, not only in a measure sufficient for obedience, but for a faith which would exclude all uncertainty and doubt. They were looking for the crown of labour *before* their work was done, for the wreath of the conqueror *before* they had fought the battle. . . . In other words, the 'increase of faith' for which the apostles prayed was only to come through obedience to their Master's will" (Dean Plumptre). The little parable was to teach them that they were not to look to accomplishing great things by a strong faith given to them in a moment of time, but they were to labour on patiently and bravely, and *afterwards*, as in the parable-story, *they too should eat and drink.* It was to show them that in the end they should receive that higher faith they prayed for, which was to be the reward for patient, gallant toil. *And gird thyself, and serve me.* It is scarcely wise, as we have before remarked, to press each separate detail of the Lord's parables. Zeller, quoted by Stier, "makes, however, an application of this to the 'inner world of the heart,' in which there is no going straightway to sit down at table when a man comes from his external calling and sphere of labour, but we must gird ourselves to serve the Lord, and so prepare ourselves for the time when he will receive us to his supper." This is interesting, but it is doubtful if the Lord intended these special applications. The general sense of the parable is clear. It teaches two things to all who would be, then or in the ages to come, his disciples—*patience* and *humility*. It reminds men, too, that his service is an arduous one, and that for those really engaged in it it not only brings hard toil in the fields during the day, but also further duties often in the evening-tide. There is no rest for the faithful and true servant of Jesus, and this restless work must be *patiently* gone through, perhaps for long years.

Vers. 9, 10.—Doth he thank that servant because he did the things that were commanded him? I trow not. So likewise ye, when ye shall have done all those things which are commanded you, say, We are unprofitable servants: we have done that which was our duty to do. And for the loyal, patient, unwearied worker there must be no saying, "What shall we have therefore?" (Matt. xix. 27). No spirit of self-complacency and of self-satisfaction must be allowed to brood over the faithful servant's thoughts. In much of the Lord's teaching at this period of his life the position of man as regards God seems to have been dwelt on. God is all; man is nothing. In God's great love is man's real treasure; man is simply a steward of some of God's possessions for a time; man is a servant whose duty it is to work ceaselessly for his Master, God. There are hints of great rewards reserved for the faithful steward in heaven, promises that a time should come when the unwearied servant should sit down and eat and drink in his Master's house; but these high guerdons were not *earned*, but were simply *free, gracious gifts* from the Divine Sovereign to his creatures who should try to do his will. This patient, unwearied toil; this deep sense of indebtedness to God who loves man with so intense, so strange a love; this feeling that we can never do enough for him, that when we have taxed all our energies to the utmost in his service, we have done little or nothing, and yet that all the while he is smiling on with his smile of indescribable love; —this is what will increase the disciples' faith, and only this. And in this way did the Lord reply to the disciples' prayer, "Increase our faith."

Ver. 11.—And it came to pass, as he went to Jerusalem. Just a note of time and place inserted by St. Luke to remind the reader that all these incidents took place, this important teaching and the momentous revelations concerning man's present and future were spoken, during those last few months preceding the Crucifixion, and generally in that long, slow progress from the north of Palestine through Galilee and Samaria to the holy city.

Vers. 12, 13.—And as he entered into a certain village, there met him ten men that were lepers, which stood afar off: and they lifted up their voices, and said, Jesus, Master, have mercy on us. These met him somewhere outside the village, separated, by the fact of their unhappy malady, leprosy,

from their fellows, in accordance with the old Mosaic Law of Lev. xiii. 46, "He is unclean: he shall dwell alone; without the camp shall his habitation be." These had no doubt heard of the many lepers who had been healed by the Galilæan Teacher who was then drawing nigh the village. They did not venture to approach him, but they attracted his attention with their hoarse, sad cry. The legal distance which these unfortunates were compelled to keep from passers-by was a hundred paces. He does not seem to have touched them, or talked with them, but with an impressive majesty bids them go and return thanks for their cure, which his will had already accomplished. They evidently believed implicitly in his healing power, for without further question they went on their way as he had commanded, and as they went the poor sufferers felt a new and, to them, a quite strange thrill of health course through their veins; they felt their prayer was granted, and that the fell disease had left them. They were not sent to the capital city; any priest in any town was qualified to pronounce on the completeness of a cure in this malady (Lev. xiv. 2—32).

Ver. 16.—And he was a Samaritan. Apparently nine of these lepers were Jews, and only one a Samaritan. This man would not have been allowed to associate with Jews but for the miserable disease with which he was afflicted, and which obliterated all distinction of race and caste. It is the same now at Jerusalem; in the leper-houses, termed "Abodes of the Unfortunate," Jews and Mohammedans will live together. Under no other circumstances will these hostile peoples do this.

Ver. 17.—Where are the nine? It has been suggested that the priests, in their hostility to Jesus, hindered the return of the nine. The one who was a Samaritan would naturally pay little heed to a remonstrance from such a quarter. From the terms of the narrative it is, however, more likely that the strange Samaritan, as soon as he felt he was really cured, moved by intense, adoring gratitude, at once turned back to offer his humble, heartfelt thanks to his Deliverer. The others, now they had got what they so earnestly required, forgot to be grateful, and hurried off to the priests to procure their certificate of health, that they might plunge at once again into the varied distractions of everyday life—into business, pleasure, and the like. The Master appears especially moved by this display. He seems to see in the thanklessness of the nine, contrasted with the conduct of the one, the ingratitude of men as a whole, "as a prophetic type of what will also ever take place" (Stier).

Ver. 19.—Thy faith hath made thee whole.

This was something more than the first noble gift, which he, in common with his nine fellow-sufferers, had received. A new power was his from that day forth. Closely united to his Master, we may think of the poor unknown Samaritan for ever among the friends of Jesus here and in the world to come. There are degrees in grace here. The nine had faith enough to believe implicitly in the Master's power, and in consequence they received his glorious gift of health and strength; but they cared to go no further. The one, on the other hand, struck with the majesty and the love of Jesus, determined to learn more of his Benefactor. From henceforth we may consider the Samaritan was one of "his own." SS. Luke and Paul gladly recorded this "memory," and no doubt not once or twice in the eventful story of their future lives used the incident as a text for their teaching when they spoke to the stranger Gentiles in far cities. Being a hated Samaritan, they would say, argued no hardness of heart, nor was it any bar to the bestowal of Jesus' most splendid gifts, first of life here, and then of life glorious and full in the world to come.

Ver. 20.—**And when he was demanded of the Pharisees, when the kingdom of God should come.** The following discourse of the Lord in reply to the Pharisee question, "When cometh the kingdom?" was delivered, clearly, in the closing days of the ministry, probably just before the Passover Feast, and in the neighbourhood of Jerusalem. The query was certainly not put in a friendly spirit. The questioners had evidently caught the drift of much of our Lord's late teaching, and had seen how plainly he was alluding to himself as Messiah. This seems to have been the starting-point of their bitter, impatient inquiry. We must remember that the great rabbinic schools in which these Pharisees had received their training connected the coming of Messiah with a grand revival of Jewish power. If in reality this Galilæan Rabbi, with his strange powers, his new doctrines, his scathing words of reproach which he was ever presuming to address to the leaders in Israel,—if in reality he were Messiah, when was that golden age, which the long looked-for Hope of Israel was to introduce, to commence? But the words, we can well conceive, were spoken with the bitterest irony. With what scorn those proud, rich men from Jerusalem looked on the friendless Teacher of Galilee, we know. We seem to hear the muttering which accompanied the question: "*Thou* our King Messiah!" **The kingdom of God cometh not with observation.** This answer of our Lord's may be paraphrased: "The kingdom of God

cometh not in conjunction with such observation and watching for external glorious things as now exist among you here. Lo, it will burst upon you suddenly, unawares." The English word "observation" answers to the signification of the Greek as meaning a singularly anxious watching.

Ver. 21.—**Neither shall they say, Lo here! or, lo there! for, behold, the kingdom of God is within you.** That kingdom will be marked out on no map, for, lo, it is even now in your midst. It may be asked—How "in your midst"? Scarcely not as Godet and Olshausen, following Chrysostom, think, *in your hearts.* The kingdom of God could not be said to be in the hearts of those Pharisees to whom the Master was especially directing his words of reply here. It should be rather understood *in the midst of your ranks;* so Meyer and Farrar and others interpret it.

Ver. 22.—**And he said unto the disciples.** The Master now turns to the disciples, and, basing his words still upon the question of the Pharisees, he proceeds to deliver a weighty discourse upon the coming of *the kingdom* which will be manifest indeed, and externally, as well as internally, exceeding glorious, and *for which* this kingdom, now at its first beginning, will be for long ages merely a concealed preparation. Some of the imagery and figures used in this discourse reappear in the great prophecy in Matt. xxiv. (a shorter report of which St. Luke gives, ch. xxi. 8—36). Here, however, the teaching has no reference to the siege of Jerusalem and the destruction of the Jewish polity, but only to "the times of the end." **The days will come, when ye shall desire to see one of the days of the Son of man, and ye shall not see it.** In the first place, our Lord addressed these words to the disciples, who, in the long weary years of toil and bitter opposition which lay before them, would often long to be back again among the days of the old Galilæan life, when they could take their doubts and fears to their Master, when they could listen without stint to his teaching, to the words which belonged to the higher wisdom. Oh, could they have him only for one day in their midst again! But they have a broader and more far-reaching reference; they speak also to all his servants in the long Christian ages, who will be often weary and dispirited at the seemingly hopeless nature of the conflict they are waging. Then will these indeed long with an intense longing for their Lord, who for so many centuries keeps silence. These will often sigh for just one day of that presence so little valued and thought of when on earth.

Ver. 23.—**And they shall say to you, See here; or, See there: go not after them, nor** follow them. Again addressed to the disciples in the first instance, but with a far more extended reference. In the early days of Christianity such false reports were exceedingly frequent; false Messiahs, too, from time to time sprang up; unhealthy visions of an immediate return disturbed the peace and broke into the quiet, steady work of the Church. Nor have these disturbing visions been unknown in later ages of Christianity. Dean Alford has a curious comment here. He sees in the words of this verse a warning to all so-called expositors and followers of expositors of prophecy who cry, "See here! or, See there!" every time that war breaks out or revolutions occur.

Ver. 24.—**For as the lightning, that lighteneth out of the one part under heaven, shineth unto the other part under heaven; so shall also the Son of man be in his day.** "Yes," went on the Master, "let not delusive expectations interrupt you or turn you aside out of the narrow way of patient faith, for my coming will, like the lightning, be sudden, and will gleam forth on every side. There will be no possibility of mistake *then.*"

Ver. 25.—**But first must he suffer many things, and be rejected of this generation.** But, and here again he repeats "as a solemn refrain to all his teaching," the warning to his own of the fearful end fast coming on him. If he is to come again with glory, he must first go away with shame, persecuted, forsaken, by the generation then living. *The suffering Messiah must precede the glorified Messiah.* After this rejection and suffering would begin the period alluded to above (ver. 22) as the time when men should long to have him only for one day in their midst. During this period Messiah should continue invisible to mortal eye. How long this state was to continue, one century or—— (eighteen have already passed), Jesus himself, in his humiliation, knew not; but he announced (vers. 26—30) that a gloomy state of things on earth would be brought to a close by his reappearance. Ah! "when the Son of man cometh, shall he find faith on the earth?"

Vers. 26—28.—**As it was in the days of Noe (Noah) . . . as it was in the days of Lot.** The prominent sin of the antediluvian, he reminds them, was *sensuality* in its varied forms. The torch of religious feeling will have waned in that unknown and possibly distant future when Messiah shall reappear, and will be burning with a pale, faint light. The bulk of mankind will be given up to a sensuality which the higher culture then generally reached will have been utterly powerless to check or even to modify. Men, just as in the days when the ark was building and Noah was preaching,

as in the days when the dark cloud was gathering over the doomed cities of the plain and Abraham was praying, will be entirely given up to their pursuits, their pleasures, and their sins. They will argue that the sun rose yesterday and on many yesterdays; of course it will rise to-morrow. Perfect security will have taken possession of the whole race, just as, on a smaller scale, was the case in the days of Noah and of Lot, when the floods came and the fire, and did their stern, pitiless work; so will that day of the second coming of Messiah, with its bloody and fiery dawn, assuredly come on man when he is utterly unprepared.

Ver. 30.—**Even thus shall it be in the day when the Son of man is revealed.** "Is revealed," that is to say, he has been present all along, through those long ages of waiting; only an impenetrable veil has hid him from mortal eyes. In that day will the veil be lifted, "and they shall look upon me whom they have pierced" (Zech. xii. 10).

Vers. 31, 32.—**In that day, he which shall be upon the house-top, and his stuff in the house, let him not come down to take it away: and he that is in the field, let him likewise not return back.** Remember Lot's wife. The Lord, with this striking imagery, describes, not the attitude which men who would be saved must assume when he appears with power and great glory—there will be no time then to shape any new way of life—but it pictures the attitude they must always maintain, if they would be his servants, towards the things of this world. His servants must be ready to abandon all earthly blessings at a moment's notice; none but those who have been sitting loosely to these will be able, when the sudden cry comes, at once to toss away all, and so to meet the long-tarrying Bridegroom. The reminder of Lot's wife—a very familiar story to Jews—warned all would-be disciples of the danger of the double service, God and the world, and how likely the one who attempted it would be to perish miserably.

Ver. 33.—**Whosoever shall seek to save his life shall lose it; and whosoever shall lose his life shall preserve it.** Very deep must have been the impression which this saying made upon the early Church. So literally did many interpret it, that the wiser and more thoughtful men in the congregations during the days of persecution had often to prevent persons of both sexes recklessly throwing away their lives in the conflict with the Roman authorities. Very many in the first three centuries positively *courted* martyrdom.

Vers. 34, 35.—**I tell you, in that night there shall be two men in one bed; the one shall be taken, and the other shall be left. Two women shall be grinding together; the one**

shall be taken, the other left. How taken?
Not, as some scholars have supposed, *taken
only to perish*, but taken away by the Lord
in the way described by St. Paul in 1 Thess.
iv. 17, where he paints how the faithful
servant who is living when the Lord returns
in glory, will be caught up in the clouds, to
meet the Lord in the air. The *other* will
be left. Thus, as it has been strikingly
observed, " the beings who have been most
closely connected here below shall, in the
twinkling of an eye, be parted for ever."

Ver. 36 is wanting in nearly all the oldest
authorities. It was subsequently inserted
in this place by copyists from Matt. xxiv. 40
—a passage in which much of the imagery
here used was repeated by the Master. In
one important feature this discourse differs
from that delivered at Jerusalem a little
later, and reported at length by St. Matthew
in his twenty-fourth chapter. There is no
reference here (in St. Luke) to the siege of
Jerusalem; the whole teaching is purely
teleological, and deals exclusively with what
will take place at the close of this age.

Ver. 37.—**And they answered and said
unto him, Where, Lord?** The disciples were
still unable to grasp the full meaning of
their Master's words when he spoke of his
second advent being visible in all parts of
the world, comparing it to a flash of lightning
which gleams at the same instant in every
point of the horizon. " Where, Lord, will
all this take place which thou hast been
telling us about?" **And he said unto them,
Wheresoever the body is, thither will the
eagles be gathered together.** The imagery
is taken from Job xxxix. 30, " Where the

slain are, there is she " (the eagle); the bird
intended being most probably the great
vulture, well known in Syria. It is seen,
for instance, travellers tell us, in hundreds
on the Plain of Gennesaret; it is a hideous-
looking bird, equal to the eagle in size and
strength, and acts as a scavenger to purify
the earth from the putrid carcases with
which it would otherwise be encumbered.
" Do you ask where all this will take place?
As the curtain of the future rolls up before my inward eye, I see the vultures of
Divine vengeance flying in flocks athwart
the whole area of the earth; the sky is
darkened with their numbers; far as my
eye can reach, I still see them. Alas! for
the habitable earth, my Father's goodly
world . . . it is rank everywhere with corruption . . . wheresoever the carcase is, there
the vultures will gather together" (Dr.
Morrison). The Lord's answer to the
question—" Where?" was that his words applied to the whole earth. The terrible and
awful scenes he had pictured would take
place everywhere. The carcase, as Godet
phrases it, is " humanity, entirely secular and
destitute of the life of God. . . . The eagles
(vultures) represent punishment alighting
on such a society." There is another interpretation of these words, which, although
many great expositors favour it, must be
rejected as improbable, being so alien to the
context of the whole passage." The dead
body (the carcase), according to these interpreters, is the body of Christ, and the eagles
are his saints, who flock to his presence, and
who feed upon him, especially in the act of
Holy Communion.

HOMILETICS.

Vers. 1—10.—*The Addition Besought.* We are not informed of the circumstances
which called forth the discourse condensed in the first ten verses of the chapter. An
occasion was, by some incident, provided for a solemn warning against the sin of an
unforgiving and uncharitable spirit. And this warning apparently intensified a conviction which had been simmering in the minds of the disciples, and led to the prayer,
" Lord, Increase [or, 'add to us'] faith." Have we not a part in this cry? Are there
not some of us who feel that, although we live in the light of Christ's Word and
kingdom, we yet need one great addition—faith?—

> " The childlike faith that asks not sight,
> Waits not for wonder or for sign."

I. THE PRAYER SUPPOSES A WANT. Trace this want from two or three positions. 1.
Reflect how sorely we *are wanting in a lively sense of the great truths of our holy faith.*
These truths are not mere opinions; they are facts. The seat of the doctrine is the fact;
it is with the facts that faith has primarily to do. Are we receiving the facts with our
whole mind and strength? That God is; that Jesus Christ is; that the Holy Spirit
of God is witnessing with our spirits and helping our infirmities;—what of these
fundamental verities? Realize what a thorough grasp of these facts would involve;
what manner of persons they ought to be to whom they are matters of experience and
consciousness. And what are we? Alas! is it not too certain that, between the

truths in which we declare our belief, and the affections and attitudes of our minds, there is a sad disproportion; that whilst we say, "Lord, I believe," we have need of the addition, "Help our unbelief; add to us faith"? 2. Reflect again, how *constantly we are reminded that the words of Christ are "too deep, too high," for us.* Even when we follow him as our Master, how dim are our apprehensions of his truth! Perhaps this was the immediate reason of the apostles' prayer. They had been listening to wonderful teaching—*e.g.* the cycle of parables in the fourteenth and fifteenth chapters—and, after hearing all, how poor was the vision of the realities with which the sayings were charged! And the demand made on them in respect of forgiveness, how could they meet such a demand in a world like this? "O Lord, thy thoughts are very deep, thy commandment is exceeding broad; add faith!" Can we not sympathize? Do we not often feel that Christ's doctrine is pitched on a note far above the level of our mind? We think that it will not do to interpret it too literally, that we must take only broad and general views. The teaching as to conduct seems too fine, too pure and other-worldly for the state of things about us. How can we realize it? "Lord, add to us faith." 3. Reflect, once more—when we look around, *what is one of the chief wants of the time?* Is it not faith? How much of the instruction given in Christian churches is halting and confused!—the sceptic too evidently looking over the shoulder! Religion is a thing talked about rather than lived in. And when we scrutinize the countenances of the "anonymous many-sided" force which we call society, what furrows appear in it! what lines betokening the absence of trust—man in man, having its root in the absence of trust; man in the living God! Is not this signified in the conflict of interests—labour and capital, class against class. To bridge the yawning social chasms, oh for a new spirit of faith! We need a chasm-bridging Church—a Church presenting, with a new force, the ideal of Christian brotherhood. "Lord, add to those who call on thy Name the faith by which the just live, through which 'they work victories, obtain promises, stop the mouths of lions'!" It is because of the lack of an heroic trust in the living God and his government that so few sycamine trees are plucked up by the root, so few mountains of sin and pride are cast into the sea. "Lord, bid us stretch forth our palsied hand, that we may take the fulness of thy grace! Add to us *faith!*"

II. So much for the want which the prayer supposes. Consider THE SCOPE AND IMPORT OF THE PRAYER ITSELF. First, it suggests the *way of the addition;* secondly, it reminds us of the *conditions on which the increase sought is realized.* 1. *The way of the addition.* "The apostles *said unto the Lord.*" It is the only example of a common appeal, the only instance of the apostles, as distinct from the disciples, having a special concerted supplication. Sometimes there was a holy restraint on them, and they durst not ask him. But this is a matter on which they could speak; it came out of the sense of their relation to him that they should go, with their great weakness, direct to his presence. Sometimes, when the hard saying was uttered, they reasoned one with another. But this is not a matter for conference. Only the hand of the Lord opened wide can supply the needed addition. For so it is. In pressing with the little we have to the Lord himself, we get the addition, we have the faith. Any faith, any trust whatsoever in the eternal love and righteousness, is a gift of God, a hold which God has on you, and which, if you only go whither it would lead, will bear you to a confidence more complete and unreserved. The one thing is, do not stop, mourning over what you have not; use what you have; it is enough to lead you to the Lord. Little-faith, at least thou canst cry. Cry the more, the more that the noisy world within or without bids thee hold thy peace. Cry the more, the less thou dost seem to have. "To them that have no might, he increaseth strength." "This poor man cried, and the Lord heard him." 2. Further, connecting the apostles' prayer with the Lord's reply, we see *the condition on which the increase sought is realized.* The reply is given in vers. 8—10. There is a twofold type, with a twofold promise. (1) The mustard seed, smallest of all seeds, which yet grows into the tallest of trees. Let there be faith, even of the dimensions of this seed, any measure whatsoever, then be sure of a Divine power co-operating, which is able to do exceeding abundantly above all that can be asked. As the seed is the promise of the tree, so is this your small faith the promise of a greater and ever greater. "Not by might, nor by power, but by my Spirit, saith the Lord of hosts." (2) Nay, says the Lord, pointing to some mulberry tree at hand, "does that seem strong? Strength which may be compared to that of tearing the tree up by the roots and casting it into the sea is, through Divine co-operation in that grain-like faith. It can tear up by the roots and cast into the sea the selfishness against which the commandment of love has struck." But now follows the condition. What I take the words from ver. 7 to mean is, "If you would have that faith, if you would have more faith, you must cease from all self-trust, you must renounce all self-complacency, you must be as nothing before God. The highest possible excellence is only the fulfilment of an obligation. You are only unprofitable servants. Your life is a bright life only when, instead of thinking of what you are to get from God, or of thanks from God for service, you take the servant's place, and are only and wholly God's. Do not aim at accomplishing great things. Let your one point be an unwearied continuance. Work now, and rest afterwards when all is done. The less there is of self and self-feeling, the more you are busied with him as his servants and sons, the purer, larger, and more victorious will be your faith. All true faith has the certainty of addition; and this addition will be in the measure in which the faith leaves the heart alone with God, worshipping and obeying his holy will.

> "So in the darkness I may learn
>   To tremble and adore,
> To sound my own vile nothingness,
>   And thus to love thee more.

> "To love thee, and yet not to think
>   That I can love so much,
> To have thee with me, Lord, all day,
>   Yet not to feel thy touch."

Vers. 11—19.—*The ten lepers.* Our minds have been so occupied by the fulness of teaching contained in the three last chapters, that we have almost lost sight of the progress of our Lord to the capital. Now the evangelist recalls our attention. He presents the little party, followed no doubt by many who were attracted from one motive or from another, as "passing through the midst of," or rather "between Samaria and Galilee"—Samaria on the right, Galilee on the left, and before them the river Jordan. It is in the immediate neighbourhood of a certain village, no name given, that the company are met by the fellowship of misery. A sad spectacle indeed, but one not unfrequent in the sunny isles of Southern seas, and in Eastern cities and thoroughfares. "Sauntering down the Jaffa road," says Dr. Thomson, "on my approach to the holy city, in a kind of dreamy maze, with, as I remember, scarcely one distinct idea in my head, I was startled out of my reverie by the sudden apparition of a crowd of beggars, without eyes, nose, hair. They held up to me their handless arms, unearthly sounds gurgled through throats without palates; in a word, I was horrified." It is a group of these miserables which clamours to Jesus as he nears the village walls. Those with him had heard the wild "Tamé, tamé! Unclean, unclean!" when suddenly the cry was exchanged for "Jesus, Master, have mercy on us!" These ten, each a homeless man; some with the recollection, perhaps, of happy homes, of other days, of the solaces of human love,—all drawn together by virtue of that gregarious instinct which acts on even the wretched. Class distinctions, even the estrangement of opposite nationalities, are forgotten in the one uniting circumstance—a common woe. No man would have allowed the dust of the Jew to have the same place of sepulture as the dust of the Samaritan; but these men, dead while they live, may herd as they please. Oh, what a sight to that heart in whose consciousness there survived the feeling of the morning stars and the triumph of the sons of God over the creation on which God had pronounced his "Very good"! What resistless eloquence in the cry, "Jesus, Master, have mercy"! He hears, and he answers in his own way; for in the Gospels there is a striking variety in the dealings of the Lord with those who call on him. Each person is a specialty to him. His way with these ten is not to respond as he did to the leper who knelt to him, beseeching, "If thou wilt, thou canst." To them he gives no direct answer; he bids them at once go and show themselves to the priests. This was the trial of their faith. The priests could only pronounce a person cured; for the ten to obey was equivalent to a trust that the power of the cure lay with Jesus the Master. They go; and shortly the limbs no longer drag, the sensations of health, as of new fresh currents coursing through the frame, tell them that they are cleansed. And now for the point of the incident. One, and only one, turns back, and he a Samaritan; and with a loud voice he gives God the glory, and, falling down before his Benefactor, renders thanks and praise. "Were there not the ten cleansed? Where are the nine? There are not found that returned to give glory to God, save this stranger." It is the old story of the thankless heart. Note some of the lights and shadows of the picture of ingratitude.

I. ALL HAD BEEN EARNEST UNDER THE PRESSURE OF THE GREAT WANT AND IN THE PRESENCE OF THE DELIVERER. There was faith enough for prayer, not for praise. Is this uncommon? We have heard that, overtaken by unexpected calamity—fire, shipwreck, etc.—knees which for long years refused to bow, have bowed, and lips that uttered the adorable Name only in blasphemy have uttered the most fervent pleadings for mercy. The record of the great plague in London is a most graphic description of a new earnestness which nearly the whole population manifested, so that there were not clergy enough, services enough, to meet the demand for prayer. Have we not the tokens of this same state of feeling in ourselves? Oh, there is no difficulty in a cry when the life hangs in doubt, when the shadow of death creeps up the wall of the home and lies across the bed of the dearly beloved. The heart needs no book then to teach to pray; it will cling to any plank; somehow, anyhow, the voice must rise like a fountain, "Jesus, Master, have mercy!"

II. WHERE ARE THE NINE WHO WERE EARNEST?

> "Even he who reads the heart—
> Knows what he gave and what we lost,
> Sin's forfeit, and redemption's cost—
> By a short pang of wonder crost,
> Seems at the sight to start."

They are cleansed. The need is relieved. They are so far on their way. Perhaps there had been some discussion between the one and the nine, and they may have argued, "Let us get to our homes. Grateful to him? Certainly; but he will never miss us." Have we not all illustrated the reasoning? How did the writing of Hezekiah when he was sick condemn him when he was well! "I will go softly all my days" was part of the writing which contained the reflections and purposes of the recovery. How did that harmonize with his pride and ostentation to the messengers of Baladan? Alas! how quickly is the love which special moments originate overborne by the return of the old things, or the influence of new scenes and circumstances?

> "Not showers across an April sky
> Drift when the storm is o'er,
> Faster than those false drops and few
> Fleet from the heart, a worthless dew."

Most of all is this true when the record borne is of blessings bestowed, when the prayer which brought to the feet of Jesus has been answered even in a manner which can be traced. What healings are received! and yet there is no turning back of the soul to glorify the Healer! What plenteousness of redemption! and yet there is no loud voice to confess the Redeemer! The proportion is the nine thankless to the one thankful. And is not ingratitude among the most common of vices?—the Aaron's rod which swallows up and comprises in itself all the baser vices? Archdeacon Farrar quotes the lines of Wordsworth—

> "I've heard of hearts unkind
> Kind deeds with coldness still returning:
> Alas! the gratitude of men
> Hath left me oftener mourning."

And he adds, "If Wordsworth found gratitude a common virtue, his experience must have been exceptional." "Give thanks unto the Lord at the remembrance of his holiness. Give unto the Lord the glory due unto his Name. Bring an offering, and come into his courts."

Vers. 20—37.—*The kingdom and the day of the Son of man.* This passage is not to be isolated as if it were a definition complete in itself of Christ's view of the kingdom of God. Some, doing this, have found in it a justification of the teaching that God's kingdom has no external character, that the coming of the Lord is only a revelation of truth in and to the heart of man. This is to do violence to the language of Jesus. In what he says afterwards to his own, in the solemn discourse reported two chapters hence, he refers to the coming of the Son of man as a fulfilment which would have its outward signs and effects, and for which his people are to wait. On the occasion before us he sets his Word in the sharpest possible antagonism to the carnal and unworthy notions which prevailed among the Pharisees who had demanded a statement from him as to how the kingdom should come. *E.g.* the Pharisees conceived of this kingdom as a victorious world-power. "Not so," is the assertion (ver. 20); "God's kingdom does not come with observation, does not lend itself to such outwardness as your vision contemplates." The Pharisees separated the citizenship in the Divine kingdom from character. The right to partake of its glories was a political right. It measured the extravagance of their social caste. It was not a chastening and purifying expectation. It was a dream of conquest and outward abundance which kept their minds on the stretch, which made them dupes of those who claimed to be Messiahs or forerunners of Messiahs. "The kingdom of God," says Jesus, "is not heralded by loud professions, by cries of, 'Lo here! or, lo there!' Unobserved, often unthought of, are its marches and movements, its surprises and its conquests" (ver. 21). As the concluding touch of the answer, Jesus warns against a restless asking "when the kingdom shall come," as if it were a prospect wholly future. He reminds us (ver. 21) that the kingdom is here and now, that it is verily and indeed among us. And the caution is as timely for us to-day as it was for the Pharisee then. For we are all apt to associate God's kingdom with some distant prospect or some condition removed from the world in which we live. And the doctrine of the Lord's advent is too often mixed up with schemes of prophecy, with calculations of catastrophes and the like, which men profess to expound or to forecast, crying, "Lo here! or, lo there!" Not, therefore, without meaning for more than the old Hebrew separatists is the counsel, "Look into the region of character for the reality of the kingdom. Where the King is, there is the court. If God has possessed your souls, his kingdom is among, is in you." Observe the solemn discourse to the disciples suggested by the demand which he has met. The words which follow from ver. 22 may be regarded either as an epitome of longer addresses, or as an address in itself complete. Look on it as an instruction preliminary, and preparatory, to the fuller opening up of the time of the end. The shadows are getting longer and longer; Jerusalem is not far ahead; the night is at hand in which, under the form of his first appearing, the Son of man cannot work. The look forward in the verses before us is to (1) a day of distress; (2) a day calling for patient faith; (3) a day of retribution and judgment.

I. A DAY OF DISTRESS. When (ver. 22) the mind would cast a regretful retrospect on the time when the Lord was with them—their Sun and Shield. Ah! would that he, the Bridegroom of our souls,

> "Our Shepherd, Husband, Friend,
> Our Prophet, Priest, and King,"

were going before us as in the days of old! But no; the shadow on the dial of time cannot be put back. The Church must face perplexities and follow its path through them. It hears voices crying, "Lo here! and lo there!" and the voices are so delusive that even the elect are often bewildered. The Master's word is, "Onwards!" He bids us look up where Stephen beheld him—standing, bending forward in sympathy and help. In the struggle, through the din, although it seems as if he were not, he is with his Church until the end of the age.

II. A DAY CALLING FOR PATIENT FAITH. There are incertitudes and excitements which sometimes almost suspend the action of faith. There are complications in the Church and the world which induce a feverishness of tone. What the Lord enjoins (ver. 25) is a calm, although wakeful, vigilance. He reminds his followers that the way to the crown is by the cross, that the offence of the cross must be exhausted, and then the end shall come. Thus, whilst the sentence is (vers. 26—30), "The coming may be at any moment, it will be, as was prefigured in the days of Noah and Lot, when men are least expecting it," the balancing thought is added, that a testimony must be given to all the nations. And the right kind of waiting is that which seeks to fill up what remains of his sufferings, so that, when he shall appear, his people may be found "not sleeping in sin, but diligent in his service, and rejoicing in his praises." It is in this connection that the reference is made (ver. 29) to the tradition concerning the wife of righteous Lot. "She looked back, and became a pillar of salt." The world-clinging heart was stiffened into a very column of worldliness. Remember, there are to be no regrets, no glances behind. A heart single, and free for the Lord, is the condition of the disciple who shall escape all these things that shall come to pass, and stand before the Son of man. "Whosoever shall seek to save his life shall lose it; and whosoever shall lose his life shall preserve it" (ver. 33).

III. A DAY OF JUDGMENT. The revelation of Christ is a judgment—in the fuller meaning of the word, a making manifest, a bringing to light of the hidden bents of mind and separation of the true from the false. Whenever Christ is presented, the judgment is set and the books are opened. The end is simply the full apocalypse of the judgment which is now proceeding. The lightning (ver. 24) "that lighteneth out of the one part of heaven, shining to the other," is the manifestation of the electricity with which the atmosphere is charged. What of this day of judgment? It is (vers. 27, 28) the condemnation of the world as to its worldliness in both its more sensual and its more cultured aspects—the *sensuality* typified in the days of Noah; the *culture*, with coarseness, typified in the wealthy citizen of Sodom. It is (vers. 34, 35) the disjunction of the closest of life's fellowships—the two in the bed, the two at the mill, the two in the field. The issues that, unobserved by many, are being adjusted and completed will be set forth in their reality. What men would not believe men will be brought to know. "The Lord cometh; he cometh to judge the earth." "Where?" ask these simple men, affrighted—"where, Lord?" and the enigmatical response (ver. 37) is given. Wherever there is corruption, wrong, death, there is the scene of the judgment of God. Jerusalem was the carcase more immediately in view, and the eagle, sign of the Roman empire, that was raised over its battlements was the sign of other eagles that were already gathering. But may we not ask whether the Jerusalem that is in bondage, the Christendom that is, is not ripening for judgment? "Receiving the kingdom which cannot be moved, let us have grace whereby we may serve God acceptably, with reverence and godly fear: for our God is a consuming fire."

HOMILIES BY VARIOUS AUTHORS.

Vers. 1, 2.—*Spiritual resistance.* Our Lord here delivers very weighty truth of a practical kind to the whole body of his adherents—to "the disciples." It is truth which remains as appropriate and as necessary as it was when it was uttered.

I. OUR NEED OF THE POWER OF SPIRITUAL RESISTANCE. "It is impossible but that offences will come." Knowing the human world as Christ knew it, he perceived that his disciples would, through many generations, be subjected to continual and severe trial of their faith. With such error, such selfishness, such despotism, such heartlessness, such iniquity in the world, it was inevitable that temptations should abound. The path of Christian life must lie through a country beset with moral evil; the journey home must be attended by the most serious perils. 1. *The aim of the enemy.* This would be, as it is still, to lead the disciples of Christ into (1) doubt, disbelief, denial, apostasy; (2) indecision and irreligion; (3) half-heartedness in worship, in sacred service, in domestic and individual devotion; (4) worldliness of tone and spirit; (5) unworthy and (ultimately) injurious and even fatal methods of presenting the truth and advocating the cause of Christ; (6) laxity of speech and of behaviour, leading down to positive and destructive sin. 2. *The weapons of his attack.* These are (1) evil suggestion; (2) bad example; (3) specious argumentation; (4) commandment and constraint. 3. *Our resources of resistance.* These are (1) a simple sagacity; such a knowledge of the evil that is in men as will ensure vigilance, a wise carefulness, a hesitation to commit ourselves to every plausible spokesman, to every inviting and well-sounding doctrine (1 John iv. 1). (2) A spirit of fidelity; a steadfastness of purpose and earnestness of spirit that is born of pure devotedness to a Divine Saviour, and that is sustained by intimacy of fellowship with him. (3) Strength in God—that strength which comes from God's own indwelling in the soul and direct action upon it (Isa. xl. 29—31).

II. OUR LORD'S REGARD FOR HIS DISCIPLES OF HUMBLER RANK. "Woe unto him" through whom it results that the stumbling-block is in the way and the weak disciple falls! "It were better for him" that the worst disaster should befall him than that he should contract such guilt as that and be open to such condemnation. Nothing could more strongly mark the deep interest our Lord takes in his humbler disciples than the severity of this his indignation against those who wrong them. The intensity of his wrath is the measure of the depth and tenderness of his love. Among his followers are those who occupy high places—in ecclesiastical position, in social honour, in mental equipments, in constitutional strength. But there are also those who take the lower place; not the children only—the "little ones" in years and size—but the inexperienced, the unsophisticated and unsuspecting, the mentally weak, the spiritually feeble; those who are much at the mercy of the strong; those who, for some cause and in some one respect, are unendowed and unequipped with the ordinary means of defence. These "little ones" are often : 1. The object of disregard. Many pass them by as unworthy of consideration ; they will not repay attention ; they will not contribute anything considerable to the cause in hand. 2. The mark at which iniquity aims. For it is one that can be easily hit; it is a victim ready for the blow. 3. But it is for us to remember that they are always the object of our Lord's peculiar interest and affection. He cares for them the more that men care for them so little. He remembers them in "their low estate;" and as a mother lets her heart go most freely to her weakest child, so does he bestow upon these members of his Church all the fulness and all the tenderness of his Divine love. He indicates to us here how he feels toward those that do them harm ; and, conversely, it is safe for us to infer that he is peculiarly pleased with those who, entering into his own spirit, love and guard and guide these disciples of lowlier rank.

III. CHRIST'S ESTIMATE OF SIN AND SUFFERING. "It were better," etc. We have sometimes to choose between sinning and suffering; e.g. the martyr in time of persecution ; the son or servant commanded to do that which to him would be sin because "not of faith." This word of our Lord reminds us that any physical suffering, any bodily evil, any temporal misfortune, of whatever magnitude it be, is much to be preferred to any serious sin. Be sunk in the sea, be utterly extinguished, let the worse come to the worst, but do not descend to anything which is mean, which is unholy or impure, which would stain your own conscience or injure and perhaps slay a brother's or a sister's character, which would grieve the Father and Saviour of us all.—C.

Vers. 3, 4.—Our duty when wronged. The opening words of this passage, "Take heed to yourselves," point to our Lord's sense of the great difficulty we are likely to experience in learning the forthcoming truth, or to the great stress he lays upon its illustration in our lives—it might well be either or both of these. For it is a difficult lesson to learn well ; and our Master does make much, as other passages show, of this particular grace.

I. OUR OPENNESS TO INJURY. 1. We come into the world with a strong sense of what is due to us. We all feel that there is due to us a certain measure of respect as human beings, as those made in the image of God; also that we can claim just and equitable treatment. Men may not withhold or remove from us that which we consider to belong to us. If they do we are aggrieved; we have a sense, more or less deep, of having been wronged—our sense of injury rising and falling with the sensitiveness of our nature and the character of the offence. There is neither virtue nor vice, honour nor shame, in this. It is an instinct of our nature which we have in common with our kind. 2. There are many possibilities of offence. In our present condition we touch one another at so many points that there is great likelihood of offence being given and taken. At home; in all the complications of our business life; in all our social relations; in the Church of Christ and the worship of God; in the field of philanthropy ;—in all these domains we "have to do" with one another ; and it is improbable in a very high degree, it is almost impossible, that we should always comport ourselves as our neighbours would expect; it is inevitable that we should occasionally differ as to what *is* due from one to another.

II. OUR DANGER UNDER A SENSE OF INJURY. 1. The *mistake* we are likely to fall into when we have a sense of injury is that of instantly concluding that we have been wronged; we are apt to hurry to the conclusion that some one has slighted or injured us. But before we give way even to a strong feeling, we should make quite sure that things are as they seem to be. There are many possibilities of mistake in this world of error and misunderstanding. 2. The *sin* into which we are tempted to fall is that of giving way to unbecoming anger and unchristian retaliation—a *feeling* of bitter resentment, vindictive, passionate, such as does not become the children of God; and *action* which is intended to result in suffering on the part of the wrong-doer; we proceed to " avenge ourselves."

III. OUR DUTY WHEN WRONGED. 1. *Direct communication,* and, where it is necessary, *friendly remonstrance.* Matthew tells us that Christ enjoined upon us that, under a sense of injury, we should " go and tell our brother his fault between ourselves and him alone." This is surely most wise. Instead of *dwelling upon* it and magnifying it in our own mind; instead of *talking about* it and causing it to be spread abroad and discoloured and misrepresented,—the one right thing to do is to go at once to our offending neighbour and tell him our grievance. It is very likely he will explain everything, and there will be no need of any overlooking on our part; or, if wrong has been done, it is very likely he will appreciate our fairness and friendliness in coming straight to him, and will make the apology that is due on his part. Then must come: 2. *Free and full forgiveness.* " If he repent, forgive him." If he should refuse to repent, we must pity him and pray for him, that his eyes may be opened and his action amended, and himself raised by doing the right and honourable thing. But if he repent, then it is our high and Christian duty *to forgive.* And how shall we forgive? Even as God, for Christ's sake, forgives us (Eph. iv. 32). (1) *Immediately.* (2) *Frankly and heartily*; reinstating the one who has wronged us in the place he occupied before in our confidence, affection, kindness. (3) *Uncalculatingly.* " Seven times in a day." However often our child, our servant, our neighbour, may offend, if there be sincere penitence on his part, and therefore an honest effort to amend, we do well to forgive. The more of this grace we have in our heart and life, the closer is our resemblance and the fuller is our obedience to our forgiving Saviour.—C.

Vers. 5, 6.—*Effective faith.* It is the part of a wise teacher to endeavour both to elevate and to humble his disciples. He will not discharge his whole duty nor realize his full opportunity unless he imparts elevating aspirations and unless he promotes a deep humility of heart; he will thank God and congratulate himself when he knows that his hearers are happily sensible of progress, and also when he learns that they are profoundly dissatisfied with their attainments. Both these results ensued from the teaching of our Lord.

I. THE DISCIPLES' DISSATISFACTION WITH THEMSELVES. Evidently the apostles of our Lord felt that there was something lacking in their souls which they would gladly possess. The doctrine of the great Teacher, perhaps, was not so clear to them as they could have wished; or perhaps they felt themselves a painfully long distance behind their Leader in their spirit and bearing; or it may be that they found themselves unable to do such works as they judged they ought to be able to do, in and through the Name of the great Healer. But whencesoever their source of dissatisfaction, they agreed that they were in spiritual want.

II. THEIR CONCLUSION AS TO THE REMEDY THEY NEEDED. They agreed that what was wanted was an increase of faith. And they were perfectly right in their judgment. 1. They wanted to believe in Christ in a way *not then open to them.* They became " greater in the kingdom of heaven" afterwards, more enlightened, more spiritual, more devoted, more useful, because afterwards they had a deep and a firm faith in Jesus Christ as their almighty Saviour, as their Divine Lord. But they did not know him yet as such; for as such he had only begun to reveal himself to them. 2. But they needed a fuller faith in him *as they did then know him.* A more complete and implicit confidence in him (1) would have led them to eject from their minds all their own old prejudices and prepossessions, and so have made way for the reception of his truth in its fulness and in its power; (2) would have evoked a profounder reverence and a more fervent affection, and thus have led to a nearer likeness to him in spirit and in character; (3) would have given them power over the forces of evil outside them, and made them equal to the emergencies to which they were unequal (see Matt. xvii. 19, 20). They did well, therefore, to make of their Lord the request they made, " Increase our faith."

III. THE TRUTH CONTAINED IN OUR LORD'S REPLY. "If ye had faith as a grain of mustard seed," etc. This truth is surely *not* that the possession of a faith *as slight* as the mustard seed is small will suffice, *but* that the faith which *is full* as is the mustard seed *of life and power of appropriation* will avail for all occasions. For it is not true that a slight and feeble faith does suffice. It failed the apostles on one memorable day (ch. ix. 40). It has been failing ever since. Only a faith which is a living and a growing power, like the mustard seed in the soil, will triumph over the difficulties to be met and mastered. The fact is that: 1. A formal faith is worth nothing at all; indeed, less than nothing, for it deludes and misleads. 2. A feeble faith will accomplish little. It sinks in the hour of trial (Matt. xiv. 30); it shrinks from open avowal, and makes feeble fight in the hour of battle (John iii. 1; vii. 50; xix. 38); it enters upon, but abandons, the goodly enterprise (Acts xiii. 13). 3. A living, appropriating faith is the only effective power. A faith that, like the mustard seed in the soil, puts forth the power of life, and appropriates to itself the riches that are around it in order that, further on, it may bear fruit—this is a power that will be felt. It will accomplish great and even wonderful things; it will surprise the unbelieving as much as if it actually did the very thing which the Master speaks of in his illustrative language. (1) It will uproot great evils in God's Name and strength. (2) It will upraise noble structures of good, when inspired at the same source.

1. Is there anything seriously lacking in our spirit, character, life, work? 2. May it not be traced to the absence or to the feebleness of our faith? If we believed more truly in Jesus Christ, if we realized more thoroughly what we accept, should we not be more to God and do more for him? 3. Shall we not come to our Saviour, unhesitatingly, earnestly, perseveringly, with this prayer of the apostles?—C.

Vers. 7—10.—*The spirit of Christian service.* The hardest nut may have the sweetest kernel; the least inviting and most difficult parable may have the most strengthening and stimulating truth beneath the surface. So with this passage. We may be even repelled from treating it because it seems to represent our Father in a light in which we do not like to look at him. It *seems* as if we were required to regard him as a hard taskmaster, indifferent to the past labour and present weariness of his servants, accepting their service without sign or token of recognition. We don't recognize the portrait in this picture. But when we look longer and see more, we understand that Jesus Christ *did not* for a moment *intend to convey this impression* of his Father and ours. 1. It is inconsistent with the revelation of God which Christ gave us both in his doctrine and in his own Person and life. For in both of these God is revealed to us as a Father who gives rather than receives. Jesus Christ himself was "amongst us as he that serveth;" he "came not to be ministered unto but to minister, and to give his life;" it is not from him that we can receive the impression that God is one that exacts everything and makes no response. 2. Christ's method of teaching does not require us to interpret the parable in this sense. He argued not only from comparison, but from contrast; not only from the less to the more worthy, but also from the unworthy to the excellent. He said, "If an *unjust* judge for a *bad* reason will do right, how certainly will the *just* Judge for a *high* one!" He said, "If an ungracious neighbour, prompted by a selfish consideration, will listen and comply, how much more surely will the gracious God, from beneficent considerations!" So here. The slave, when he returns from his day's laborious duties, prepares, unthanked, for his master's comfort before he thinks of his own necessities; and he does this unquestioningly, uncomplainingly. How much more ready, more eager, should *we* be to serve our God!—*we* who are not slaves, but children; to serve *him*, who is no unresponsive and inconsiderate taskmaster, but who is Considerateness itself, who is Responsiveness itself, who is Encouragement itself. We should be ready and eager to serve him to the uttermost, and when we have done everything we can do, be prepared to say, "It is nothing of all that we should do and would do for thee." Now, there are certain *occasions to which this more particularly applies*; and here we have a touch of *resemblance* in the parable. As the master there requires of his slave something over and above his day's work in the field, so does our Lord sometimes ask of us *more than we thought he would* when he first said to us, "Follow me," and we said, "Lord, I will." This may be in the way—

I. OF ACTIVE SERVICE; *e.g.* when parents have clothed and fed, taught and trained their own children, they may be directed, in God's providence, to take charge of the children of others; or when the minister, superintendent, missioner, teacher, finds that the duty he has undertaken involves a great deal more of costly work than he had counted upon—more time, trouble, patience, self-mastery, self-sacrifice.

II. OF SACRIFICE; *e.g.* when the young man leaves home or college for work in the foreign field, he finds that the privations he has to endure, the scenes he has to witness, the discouragements he has to bear, the parting with his children he has to go through, are a great deal more than he realized when he started on his way.

III. OF SUBMISSION. When life seems to have been lived through, its strength spent and its work done, the weary human spirit craves rest, the rest of the heavenly home; but God may allot many months or even years of patient waiting before the summons is sent to "come up higher." And in whatever way, or to whatever degree, the heavenly Father may ask of his children the service which they did not look for, such should be and may be their spirit of (1) *perfect trustfulness*, and of (2) *fervent love*, that they will gladly and faithfully respond; doing with alacrity and bearing with cheerfulness all his holy will, and quite disposed at the end to say, "All is not half enough to give unto the 'Lamb that was slain,' who is worthy to receive the *riches* of our hearts and of our lives."—C.

Vers. 11—19.—*The commonness of ingratitude, etc.* Under the guidance of this narrative, we think of—

I. THE COMMONNESS OF INGRATITUDE. Only one of these ten men had a sufficient sense of indebtedness to return to Christ to offer thanks. The ingratitude of the remaining nine touched, smote, wounded our Lord, and he used the reproachful words of the text (ver. 17). This ingratitude was not a remarkably exceptional illustration of our nature; it is one of those things in respect of which "he that increaseth knowledge increaseth sorrow." For that which youth refuses to believe, experience obliges us to acknowledge, viz. that to accept a great boon from the hand of love, and to show no proper sense of gratitude, is not a rare but a common thing. It is likely enough that we may go much out of our way to do a man a kindness, and that when we look for his response we shall be disappointed. What then? Shall we be diverted from the path of beneficence by this unlovely fact? Shall we say, "Since it is very likely that my services will not be appreciated, they shall not be rendered"? Certainly not. For: 1. There *is* gratitude to be gained and to be enjoyed. This proportion is not representative. It is not the case that nine men out of ten are insensible to kindnesses shown them. It is as likely as not, perhaps more likely than not, that if we do help our brother in his hour of need, if we do sustain him in sorrow, succour him in distress, stand by him in temptation, lead him into the kingdom of God, we shall win his gratitude, and we *may* secure the profound, prayerful, lifelong affection of a human heart. And what better reward, short of the favour and friendship of God, can we gain than that? 2. If we fail to obtain this, we shall stand by the side of our Divine Master; we shall share his experience; we shall have "fellowship with the sufferings of Christ." He knew well what it was to serve and be unappreciated, to serve and be disparaged. To be where he stood, to

> "Tread the path our Master trod,
> To bear the cross he bore,"

—this is an honour not to be declined. 3. If man our brother does not bless us, Christ our Saviour *will*. The most heroic deed of love may go, has gone, unrewarded of man. But the smallest act of kindness rendered to the humblest child will *not* go unrewarded of him. "Whosoever shall give to drink unto one of these little ones a cup of cold water only . . . shall *in no wise* lose his reward."

II. THE UNCOUNTED DEBT DUE TO JESUS CHRIST. These nine men having received the greatest good one man could receive from another—deliverance from a living death—failed to recognize their obligation, did not stop to consider it. They were not the last to be guilty in this respect. 1. How much more do many owe to Christ *than they think they do!* They say, "We do not choose to range ourselves under him and call him 'Master;' we can construct our own character, can build up rectitude and purity and benevolence of spirit apart from his truths or his will; we can do without Christ." But suppose we subtract from the elevating and purifying influences which have made these men what they are all those elements which are due to Christ, how much is left? How *little* is left? The influences that come from him are in the air these men are breathing, in the laws under which they are living, in the literature they are reading, in the lives they are witnessing; they touch and tell upon them at every point, they act silently and subtly but mightily upon them; they owe to Jesus Christ the best they are and have; they ought to come into direct, living, personal relations with the Lord himself. 2. How much more do some men owe to Christ *than they stay to consider!* These nine men would not have disputed their obligation had they been challenged, but they were so anxious to get home to their friends and back to their business that they did not stay to consider it. Have we *stayed to consider* what we owe to him who, though he has not indeed cured us of leprosy, has at infinite cost to himself prepared for us a way of recovery from that which is immeasurably worse —from sin and death? to him who, "though he was rich, for our sakes became poor, that we through his poverty might be rich"?

III. THE PERIL OF EARLY PRIVILEGE. It is significant enough that the tenth leper who did return to give glory to God was a Samaritan—was "this stranger." Taking this fact with that concerning the Roman soldier whose faith surprised our Lord, and that of the Syro-Phœnician woman whose importunity prevailed over every obstacle, we may conclude that the Hebrew mind was so familiarized with "signs and wonders," that those outside the sacred circle were far more impressed by what they witnessed than the people of God themselves. It is well to be the children of privilege; but there is one grave peril connected with it. We may become so familiar with the greatest of all facts as to become insensible to their greatness. The Swiss peasant who lives on the Alpine slopes sees no grandeur in those snow-clad summits on which his eyes are always resting; the sailor who lives by the sea hears no music in "old ocean's roar." We may become so familiar even with the story of the cross that our minds are unaffected by its moral grandeur, by its surpassing grace. It behoves us to take earnest heed that we fall not into this fatal snare; lest many should come "from the north, and the south, and the east, and the west, and sit down in the kingdom of God," and we, the children of the kingdom, be excluded. We must do our utmost to *realize* the great truths which have so long been uttered in our hearing.—C.

Vers. 20, 21.—*Radical mistakes respecting the kingdom of God.* Pharisaism took its hostile attitude toward Christianity because it entirely failed to understand it. It made two radical mistakes which completely misled it.

I. THE MISTAKES WHICH PHARISAISM MADE. 1. As to the *character of the coming kingdom.* It thought it was to be outward, earthly, political, temporal; it was looking and longing for the time when another David, another Judas Maccabæus, should come, should liberate the Holy Land from the grasp of the pagan power, and make Jerusalem the metropolis, the centre and glory of the earth. 2. As to the *evidences and signs of its coming.* It looked for a grand display of power, for overwhelming evidences that would strike every eye and startle and convince every mind that One was at hand who should assume the sovereignty awaiting him. And so it came to pass that when Jesus was born at Bethlehem, a Babe cradled in a manger; when he grew up to be a Carpenter at Nazareth; when he gathered no army, and struck no blow for national deliverance; when there was no ostentation about his method; when he lived to bless and teach individual men and women, and wrought his work quietly and unpretendingly;—Pharisaism decided that he was not the Coming One, and that his reign was not to prove the kingdom of God. Pharisaism entirely mistook God's purpose, and fatally misinterpreted his procedure.

II. THE MISTAKES INTO WHICH WE ARE LIABLE TO FALL. Not, of course, the same but similar, and equally disastrous. 1. When we look for blessedness in outward circumstances instead of in inward peace. We say, " If I could but win that prize, gain that post, secure that friendship, earn that income, how bright would be my lot, how glad my heart, how radiant my life! " But we are wrong. Gladness of heart and excellency of life are not to be found in sunny circumstances, but in a pure heart, a heart that is at rest, a heart at home with God. " Out of the heart are the issues of life; " the fountain of lasting joy rises from our own breast; the kingdom of God is *within* us. 2. When we look for blessedness in the time that is beyond. "Man never *is*, but always *to be* blessed." There is even an unchristian longing for the heavenly future. When " to abide in the flesh" is more needful for those for whose welfare we are largely responsible, then the "kingdom of God" for us is not in the distance; it is in the present sphere of duty; it is in present peace, present joy, present service, in the blessedness which Christ gives to his servants

> " Before they reach the heavenly fields,
>   Or walk the golden streets,"

in those "heavenly places" of holy service and happy fellowship in which he "*has* made them to sit" (Eph. ii. 6). 3. When we wait for heavenly influences to fall upon us instead of availing ourselves of those we have. Not only is there no need for any soul to wait for some remarkable and overwhelming influences before entering the kingdom, not only is it *wholly unnecessary*, but it is *positively wrong* to do so. It is in those quiet influences which are now working within your heart that God comes to you. He will never be nearer to a human soul than when his Spirit fills it with a holy longing, and makes it eager to know what it must do to enter into life. Wait not for anything that is coming: act on the promptings that are within you, and your feet shall then surely stand within the kingdom of God.—C.

Vers. 22—25.—*The brief day of opportunity.* The thought of our Master in this passage (as I understand it) is this: " I have been asked when the kingdom of God will come: my reply is that it has come already; that you have not to look about in this and that direction; here, in the midst of you, impersonated in him that speaks, *is* the kingdom. It is present in the Present One. But," he says to his disciples, " he is present in a very strict sense. The time will soon be here when you will greatly long for his fellowship, and you will not be able to possess it. Do not believe those who will tell you that the Son of man is still on earth; it will not be true. His life below will be of the very briefest; it will be but as a lightning-flash which passes through the darkened heavens in a moment, and is gone again; so brief will be his stay, so soon will he be gone. But before he goes he must suffer many things; much must be done, for much must be endured, before his short day is done."

I. THE BRIEF DAY OF OUR LORD'S OPPORTUNITY. When we think of the long centuries that preceded, and of those that have already succeeded, the day of Christ, we may well regard his short visit to our world as a mere flash of light for transitoriness. What were those few months of his short stay among men compared with all those dark ages, and to all those that have been illumined by the light which his truth has shed upon them! But, transient as it was, it sufficed. It does not take long to utter or to illustrate the most Divine and the most vital truths; it did not take long to undergo the most mysterious and the most availing sorrows—it took but a few agonizing hours to die the death of atonement. Into that short day of opportunity our Divine Redeemer compressed: 1. The utterance of all needful truth—all the truth we need for our guidance into the kingdom of God, and for our passage through life and death into the kingdom of glory. 2. The illustration of every human grace; the living of a human life in all its perfect loveliness and grandeur. 3. The endurance of sorrow such as constituted him for ever the Man of sorrows, and the High Priest of human nature, touched with the feeling of our infirmities (Heb. iv. 15). 4. The dying of that death which is the all-sufficient sacrifice for sin. A few months of time sufficed to complete his work and make him the Divine Teacher, Leader, Friend, Saviour, of the whole race of man for all time to come.

II. OUR BRIEF DAY. 1. Measured by hours, our day is very brief. Human life is short at the longest. We are "but of yesterday," and to-morrow we shall not be.

The rocks and even the trees look down on many generations. And in all the bustle and battle, in all the pursuits and pleasures of our life, the little time we have hastens away and is gone far sooner than we thought it would go. It is not only our poetry that sings, but our experience that testifies of the swiftness of our course beneath the sun. 2. Yet it holds manifold and precious opportunities of regaining our position as the children and heirs of God; of doing "many things" that shall tell even in future years for truth and God; of "suffering many things" after Christ our Lord, and in holy and noble fellowship with him (Phil. iii. 10). 3. Its transiency is an urgent reason for (1) immediate decision, and (2) constant and earnest action in the cause of righteousness. Whilst we have the light that shines, let us walk and let us work in the light.—C.

Vers. 26—30.—*The unlearnt lesson.* Man differs from the brute creation in that he learns and profits by experience—he advances. He passes through stage after stage toward the perfection of his life upon the earth. He is the hunter at one period, then the shepherd, then the agriculturist. From the lowest barbarism he reaches, in time, the most refined civilization. But he is very slow indeed to learn, if he does learn at all, moral and spiritual truths. The excellency of thrift, of temperance, of purity, of patience,—how long a time it is taking man to acquire these virtues! Our text opens to us the truth of the danger of spiritual trifling, and indicates that what men were long ages ago, that they still are in this respect.
I. SPIRITUAL TRIFLING. The men of the time of Noah were living in a state of utter worldliness and impiety. They were not without remonstrance and rebuke; Noah was himself "a preacher of righteousness" unto them. But they hearkened not, nor heeded; they made light of his admonitions and his warnings. They found some pretext under which they could easily hide the truth he reminded them of, and they went on their way of materialism and enjoyment. The same with the people of Sodom, and the character and instruction of Lot. And so with us. 1. Men are living in sinful selfishness and worldliness—many in crime, many more in vice; but a very large multitude in practical godlessness. God is not in all, he is not in many if in any of their thoughts. His will is not *the* object of their inquiry, is not *the* rule of their life. 2. The religious teacher comes and admonishes; he says, "Man cannot live by bread alone;" the claims of the Divine Father, of the holy Saviour, are the supreme claims, etc. 3. But still the same course is pursued; the better thoughts that are momentarily stirred in the heart are silenced; sacred truths are extinguished; the truth of God is treated lightly; the world and the things that are in the world are uppermost and are victorious.
II. THE PALPABLE FOLLY OF SUCH TRIFLING AS THIS. 1. It is attended with immediate and certain injury. For it is impossible for a human soul to reject the truth or to quench the Spirit of God, and not be seriously the worse for such an act. 2. There is the grave peril of a great disaster. The generation is eating and drinking and marrying, and behold! the Flood sweeps them away. The cities are trading and feasting, and lo! the fires of heaven come down and consume them. They who trifle with the most sacred things are sure to find that, suddenly, in such an hour as they think not, the end arrives. The business plans are all broken off; the brilliant career is concluded; the flow of pleasures is arrested. Death suddenly appears, and deals his fatal blow. These sacred opportunities which have been so little prized, so much disparaged, recede with terrible rapidity and disappear. Opportunity that waited by the side, and waited all in vain, melts and vanishes in a moment. The soul awakes from its long lethargy to see that its powers have been wasted and that its chance is gone!
III. THE ELUSIVENESS OF THIS SOLEMN LESSON. Men have always known this, and they have always acted as if they were ignorant of it. "As it was . . . so shall it be." So is it to-day. By spiritual trifling men fritter away the golden chance that Divine love puts into their hands. Be wise in time. Realize what you are doing, what injury you are working, what risk you are running.—C.

Vers. 34—36.—*Accidents.* "The one shall be taken, and the other left." And who or what is it that decides which one shall be taken and which left? Events are often occurring which convey to us the impression of—

I. THE LARGE AMOUNT OF ACCIDENT which enters into the fabric of human life. Take, for example, a bad railway accident. How accidental it seems that one man should just miss that train and be saved, and that another should just catch it and be killed; that one should take a seat in the carriage which is crushed, and another in the carriage which is left whole; that one should be sitting exactly where the bent and twisted timber pierced him, and another exactly where no injury was dealt, etc.! It is the same with the battle-field, with the thunderstorm, with the falling house. One is taken, and another left; and the taking of the one and the leaving of the other seems to be pure accident—not the result of reason or forethought, but entirely fortuitous.

II. OUR CORRECTED THOUGHT CONCERNING IT. 1. Of accident in the sense of *chance* we know there is nothing. Everything is "under law;" and even where there is no law apparent, we are assured, by the exercise of our reason, that there must be the operation of law, though it is out of our sight. In this world of God's, pure chance has not an inch of ground to work upon. 2. There is usually much more play of reason and habit in "accidental events" than seems at first sight. Things result as they do because habit is stronger than judgment, or because foolish men disregard the counsel of the wise; because thoughtful men take the precautions which result in their safety, and because thoughtless men take the action which issues in their suffering or death. 3. The providence of God covers the entire field of human life. May we venture to believe that the hand of God is in the events and issues of life? I think we may. (1) It is clearly within the range of the activities of an Infinite Being to whom nothing is small as nothing is great. (2) His Fatherhood would lead him to follow the course of every one of his children with parental interest, and to interpose his hand wherever he saw it was wise to do so. (3) Scripture warrants the conclusion: "Precious in the sight of the Lord is the death of his saints;" "The way of man is not in himself; it is not in man that walketh to direct his steps;" "Not a sparrow falleth to the ground without your Father: ye are of more value than many sparrows."

III. THE LARGE MEASURE OF UNCERTAINTY THAT REMAINS AND MUST REMAIN. Human science has introduced many safeguards, but it has also introduced new perils. The "chapter of accidents" is as long as it ever was in the contemporary history of mankind. God is supreme, but he lets many things happen we should antecedently have supposed he would step in to prevent; he lets good men take the consequence of their mistakes; he permits the very holy and the very useful to be overtaken by sad misfortunes and even by fatal calamities. We cannot guarantee the future; we cannot ensure prosperity, health, friends, reputation, long life. To one that seems to be heir to all these good things they will fall; to another who seems equally likely to inherit them they will be denied: one is taken, the other left. Therefore let us turn to—

IV. THE ONE GOOD THING ON WHICH WE CAN ABSOLUTELY COUNT. There is "a good part which shall not be taken away." This is a Christian character; its foundations are laid in repentance and faith; it is built up of reverent study, of worship, of the obedience of love. Its glory is in resemblance to Jesus Christ himself. This is within every man's reach, and it *cannot* be taken; it *must* be left. He who secures that is safe for ever. No accident can rob him of his heritage. His treasure and himself are immovable; for "he that doeth the will of God abideth for ever."—C.

Vers. 1—19.—*Graces stimulated and strengthened.* The preceding chapter urges most powerfully, by precept and parable, consideration for others. Money is to be used for this end. But consideration may be shown in many other ways. And want of consideration may be one of those "occasions of stumbling" (so in Revised Version) to the Lord's little ones which shall be visited with such overwhelming retribution. Our Lord consequently begins by teaching—

I. THE GREAT DANGER OF CAUSING A LITTLE ONE TO STUMBLE. (Vers. 1, 2.) In this way he urges his disciples to watchfulness. He plainly implies that defenceless individuals who fall through stumbling-blocks placed in their path shall have in God a most terrible Avenger. Better the most fearful physical death than the fate of those who cause them to stumble. Of Judas it was expressly stated it would have been better if he had never been born; and the same might be said of every one who, like him, throws stumbling-blocks in his brother's way. The ruin of the innocent, through exposing them to temptation, will be visited by God's most terrible indignation.

II. THE DISCIPLES OF CHRIST MUST GUARD AGAINST AN UNRELENTING AND UNFORGIVING TEMPER. (Vers. 3, 4.) The disciples are to take heed to themselves. *They are not to be avengers.* They have not the solidity of judgment or of character to exercise vengeance. It is to be left to God. If, therefore, a brother trespass against us, we are to pursue such a path as will result in forgiveness and reconciliation. We are to rebuke him courageously; then, if he repents, if he shows signs of sorrow and confesses his fault, even though it should be repeated seven times a day, we are to forgive him. Now, this forgiving spirit is Divine. It is God-like. It is the spirit God has manifested in Christ, and which we should cultivate most diligently.

III. OUR LORD'S EXHORTATIONS LED THE DISCIPLES TO SEEK AN INCREASE OF FAITH. (Vers. 5—10.) When we have discovered how small our forgiving spirit is, we then begin to see how small other graces are, and to cry, "Lord, Increase our faith." It is most instructive to notice how our Lord responds to the disciples' desire. And: 1. *He shows them how very small their faith is.* His statement implies that it was less than a grain of mustard seed, for, if they had even so little a measure of genuine faith, they could remove any difficulty out of their path. Even a sycamine tree might be plucked up by the roots, or any difficulty which such an obstacle would represent, and be cast by faith into the sea. The first lesson we have got to learn is how small our faith is, and then it will soon increase. 2. *He impresses on them the cultivation of a sense of their own unprofitableness to God.* He likens them to a farm-servant who, when he has finished in the field, comes home and is then put to wait at table on his lord. His work is never done. He turns from one occupation to another; and only laments at the close that he could not do more and better. Now, this sense of unprofitableness really arises out of the magnificence of the Christian ideal. The Christian system sets before us such incomparable excellency, that we are always coming short of it. All Christian progress is just conditioned upon this sense of unprofitableness. Our faith will grow exceedingly when this sense of unprofitableness has been secured and is maintained. Of course, this teaching of our Lord is quite consistent with the reward promised in his grace, of "Well done, good and faithful servant." The servant looks at his labours in the light of strict justice, and acknowledges his shortcoming. The Master looks at them in the light of grace and love, and rewards them with overflowing bounty. Even when receiving the reward at last, it will be with surprise, and with the consciousness that we have been but unprofitable servants.

IV. THE DISCIPLES ARE INSTRUCTED AT THE SAME TIME REGARDING HUMAN INGRATITUDE. (Vers. 11—19.) It so happened that ten lepers cross the Saviour's path, and their cry for mercy meets with immediate response. But their cure is given on their way to the priests, who could only give them a certificate of cure. The sense of cure came upon the ten, we may believe, at the same time. But only one, and he a Samaritan, returned to express his gratitude. The other nine, all Jews, passed on to the priest with a joyful sense of cure, but little sense of gratitude. It was such ingratitude as called for the animadversion of Jesus, while the Samaritan's gratitude led our Lord to say his faith hath made him whole. It seems clear that he became attached to Jesus in a way the others did not. The expression of his gratitude led to an assurance of faith. Now, this was a wholesome lesson for the disciples, as it is also for us. How many blessings have we all got from the hands of Christ, for which we have returned no thanks at all! And, if we have been ungrateful to our Lord, should we not put up with a good deal of ingratitude? It is a sense of personal ingratitude which will stimulate the grace within us, and make us less surprised when we are the objects of ingratitude on the part of others we have befriended. In this plain and practical fashion our Lord stimulated and strengthened the graces of his disciples, and indicates how our graces may be stimulated likewise.—R. M. E.

Vers. 20—37.—*The advent of the kingdom and the King.* Jesus was on journey to Jerusalem when the ingratitude of the nine lepers, just noticed, took place, and this gave rise to speculation as to the near approach of his kingdom. His enemies, the Pharisees, put the sarcastic question when the kingdom of God should come, as much as to say, " We have heard of it long; we should like to see it." [1] This leads our Lord to unfold the nature of his kingdom's advent and of his own.

I. His KINGDOM COMES IN THE HEARTS OF MEN. (Vers. 20, 21.) The characteristic of worldly kingdoms has always been *ostentation*. They try to impress the senses by noisy advents, brag, advertisement, the blare of bugle and roll of drum. And some think that there is nothing worth talking about which can come in any milder way. The Jews expected a kingdom of God to supersede the Roman, and that its advent would be seen in the defeat and expulsion of the conquerors of Canaan. But, no; the kingdom was coming in men's hearts; it was there it had its sphere and home. 1. *How superficial is the sovereignty which is not founded in the heart!* This is the world's experience daily. The outward sovereignty is a name and based on fear. 2. *How noble is the sovereignty which is based upon people's hearts!* It is here Jesus reigns. We love him. We would die for him. Thus his kingdom progresses wherever a heart is touched by Christ's love. His triumph is over the selfishness of mankind. He conquers them by self-sacrificing love.[2]

II. THE KING HIMSELF IS TO COME AS SUDDENLY AS THE LIGHTNING-FLASH. (Vers. 22—24.) He is not to give warning of his approach. There will be no need to go here or there under the impression that he has come quietly and privately, to prepare for his public manifestation; but suddenly like the lightning-flash, and publicly like its heaven-enlightening beam, is he to come for judgment. Hence the awful sudden-ness of his advent is distinctly implied. He will give no premonitory warnings, but overwhelmingly sudden and awful will be his approach. No wonder in such circum-stances that many shall desire to see one of the days of the Son of man, one of those seasons of quiet philanthropy such as the Saviour was now leading among men. The Pharisees were mistaking altogether the significance of his present mission.

III. THE RESULTS OF THE PRESENT MISAPPREHENSIONS. (Vers. 25—30.) 1. The *first* sad result will be the rejection and martyrdom of Jesus (ver. 25). Misapprehending the significance of his meek and lowly philanthropic life, his generation united in rejecting him, and secured his crucifixion on the tree. They would not have the King when actually among them in flesh and blood. 2. Men will act like the *antediluvians* and *Sodomites* up to the very time of our Lord's advent. A sense of *carnal security* characterized these sinners. They thought in Noah's day that no harm would over-take them. There was no sign of the Deluge except Noah's precautions against it, and they would not act upon such signs. In Sodom it was the same. The inhabitants thought no change would come over their selfish, sensual dream. But the Deluge came, and the fire and brimstone descended, notwithstanding. So will it be with the advent of Christ—it will come as a sudden, unexpected judgment upon many. And this carnal security is a present danger with many. They fancy they are safe, that nothing will interfere with their security; but the Saviour makes his advent suddenly, and they are overwhelmed.

IV. THE REALITIES OF THE ADVENT. (Vers. 31—37.) Now, the truth is clearly brought out that some shall be saved and others lost at the advent. 1. Let us look at *the lost*. They are brought under our notice here in several ways. Thus *Lot's wife is taken as a type of the lost*. Now, we know that she was lost through looking longingly back to her worldly things. God, by his angels, had set the family's faces towards the mountains and himself. Were they prepared to take him and his favour as their portion, and give up all their property in Sodom? If they looked longingly behind them, it would show that the world was still more to them than God. The poor wife could not resist the temptation, and so she was changed into a pillar of salt. She is, then, the type of those who are almost saved, but worldliness gets the better of them, and they are lost. Again, the lost ones are represented as *food for eagles* (ver. 37). This brings out the *corruption* characterizing them. They have become moral carrion, which only the eagles can consume. There is, doubtless, a reference to the Roman invasion under Titus, and to the destruction of corrupt Jerusalem. The Roman armies were God's scavengers to destroy a corrupt people. This was one way in which Christ made an advent to judgment. Lastly, we have the lost described as those who are *continually seeking to save themselves* (ver. 33). Those whose one aim in life is self-

---

[1] Robertson's ' Human Race and other Sermons,' p. 63.
[2] Cf. Liddon's ' Church Troubles,' serm. i.

preservation, the saving of themselves at every turn, who think of self as the supreme concern, are only *losing themselves*. The curious paradox is that those who save themselves at every turn lose themselves; while those who do not count their lives dear, but Christ's concern as supreme, find themselves safe at last. Let us see to it, therefore, that we are neither worldly minded, nor corrupt, nor given up to selfishness, else we are among the lost. 2. But let us look at the *saved ones*. These are those who have kept Christ before them as their Lord and Master, whose interests should be supreme (ver. 33). They value him more than life, and so he saves them. The nature of salvation is thus plainly unfolded. The saved ones are those with whom Christ is all in all. They prefer him to everything else. The instinct of self-preservation has in them given place to an instinct to preserve the honour and promote the kingdom of the Master. And those who have trusted him and honoured him so thoroughly shall find that he will not disappoint them. Let us wait for his appearing, then, and *love* it; and when it flashes across the world, we shall be allowed to escape the judgments that come upon the earth, and to stand before the Son of man.—R. M. E.

EXPOSITION.

CHAPTER XVIII.

Vers. 1—14.—*The Lord speaks the two parables on prayer—the importunate widow, and the Pharisee and publican.*

Ver. 1.—**And he spake a parable unto them to this end, that men ought always to pray, and not to faint.** The formula ἔλεγε δὲ καί, literally, "and he spake also," calls attention to the fact that the parable-teaching immediately to follow was a continuation of what had preceded. Indeed, the connection between the first of the two parables, which urges restless continued prayer, and the picture which the Lord had just drawn of men's state of utter forgetfulness of God, is obvious. "The Son of man has been rejected; he has gone from view; the masses are plunged in gross worldliness; men of God are become as rare as, in the days of Abraham, they were in Sodom. What, then, is the position of the Church? That of a widow whose only weapon is incessant prayer. It is only by means of this intense concentration that faith will be preserved. But such is precisely the disposition which Jesus fears may not be found in the Church at his return" (Godet).

Ver. 2.—**There was in a city a judge, which feared not God, neither regarded man.** Probably enough the whole scene was a sketch from life; under such a rule as that of Herod Antipas there were, doubtless, judges of the character here portrayed.

Ver. 3.—**And there was a widow in that city; and she came unto him, saying, Avenge me of mine adversary.** The petitioner was a woman and a widow, the latter being in the East a synonym for helplessness. With no one to defend her or plead her cause, this widow was ever a prey to the covetous. Not once nor twice in the noble generous words of the chivalrous Hebrew prophets we find this readiness on the part of those in power

to neglect, if not to oppress these helpless widow-women, sternly commented upon. So in Isaiah we read (i. 23), "They judge not the fatherless, neither doth the cause of the widow come unto them." While Jesus (Matt. xxiii. 14) includes this cowardly sin among the evil deeds of the rulers of the Israel of his day: "Ye devour widows' houses, and for a pretence make long prayer." A more desperate situation, as regards any hope of obtaining the object of her earnest prayer, could not well be pictured—a careless, corrupt judge of the lawless Herod period for the tribunal in Israel, and a poor helpless widow for the suppliant. The forlorn woman of the parable represents the Church or people of God in dire straits, overborne by an unbelieving world and seemingly forgotten even of their God. The story is a reminder that there is hope even in that extreme situation sketched in the parable, if the petitioner only continues persistent in her prayer. The argument which lies on the surface of the parable-teaching is obvious: if such a judge will in the end listen to the prayer of a suppliant for whom he cares nothing, will not God surely listen to the repeated prayer of a suppliant whom he loves with a deep, enduring love? Such is the argument of the story. Importunity, it seems to say, must inevitably triumph. But underlying this there is much deep teaching, of which, perhaps, the most important item is that it insists upon the urgent necessity for us all to continue in prayer, never fainting in this exercise though no answer seems to come. "The whole life of the faithful," as Origen once grandly said, "should be one great connected prayer." That is the real moral of the story; but there are a number of minor bits of Divine teaching contained in this curious parable setting, as we shall see. *Avenge me of mine adversary.* We must not suppose that mere vengeance in the vulgar sense is what the widow prayed for; *that* would be of no use to her; all she wanted was that the judge should deliver her from the oppression which her adversary exercised over her, no doubt in keeping from her the heritage to which she was lawfully entitled. Of course, the granting her prayer would involve loss and possibly punishment to her fraudulent oppressor.

Ver. 7.—**And shall not God avenge his own elect, which cry day and night unto him?** The Master tells us that God permits suffering among his servants, long after they have begun to pray for deliverance. But we are counselled here to cry day and night unto him, and, though there be no sign of reply, our prayers shall be treasured up before him, and in his own good time they will be answered. **Though he bear long with them.** With whom does God bear long? With the wrong-doers, whose works and words oppress and make life heavy and grievous to the servants of God; with *these* who have no claim to consideration will God bear long. And this announcement gives us some clue to the meaning of the delay we often experience before we get an answer to many of our prayers. The prayer is heard, but God, in the exercise of mercy and forbearance, has dealings with the oppressors. It were easy for the Almighty to grant an immediate answer, but only at the cost often of visiting some of the oppressors with immediate punishment, and this is not his way of working. God bears long before his judgments swift and terrible are sent forth. This has ever been his way of working with individuals as with nations. Was it not thus, for instance, in his acted towards Egypt and her Pharaohs during the long period of the bitter Hebrew bondage? We who would be God's servants must be content to wait God's time, and, while waiting, patiently go on pleading, sure that in the end "God will avenge his own elect, which cry day and night unto him."

Ver. 8.—**I tell you that he will avenge them speedily.** "Non *bientôt*, mais *bien vite*" (Godet). It means that God will act in accordance with his servant's prayer, not soon, but suddenly; sure and sudden at the crisis the action of Divine providence comes at the last "as a thief in the night." **Nevertheless when the Son of man cometh, shall he find faith on the earth?** These difficult words seem to point at least to a fear lest the second coming being long delayed, true faith would have died out of the hearts even of the godly. Such a *fear* might be Jesus'; for we know, from his own lips, that to him, while on earth and wearing the body of humiliation, the day and hour of the second advent was not known. Was not our Lord speaking with the same sad

onlook in his parable of the virgins, when he said, "they *all* slumbered and slept," wise virgins as well as foolish (Matt. xxv. 5)? "It is often the case that God's action as a Deliverer is delayed until his people have ceased to hope for deliverance. So it was with Israel in Egypt; so was it with her again in Babylon. 'Grief was calm and hope was dead' among the exiles when the word came that they were to return to their own land; and then the news seemed too good to be true. They were 'like them that dream' when they heard the good tidings. This method of Divine action—long delay followed by a sudden crisis—so frankly recognized by Christ, is one to which we find it hard to reconcile ourselves. These parables help us so far, but they do not settle everything. They contain no philosophy of Divine delay, but simply a proclamation of the fact, and an assurance that, in spite of delay, all will go well at the last with those who trust in God" (Professor Bruce).

Ver. 9.—**And he spake this parable.** With this parable, "the Pharisee and the publican," St. Luke concludes his memories of the last journeyings toward Jerusalem. The incidents which directly follow took place close to Jerusalem; and here St. Luke's narrative rejoins that of SS. Matthew and Mark. No note of time or place assists us in defining exactly the period when the Master spoke this teaching; some time, however, in these last journeyings, that is, in the closing months of the public ministry, the parable in question was certainly spoken.

Ver. 10.—**Two men went up into the temple to pray; the one a Pharisee, and the other a publican.** This parable constitutes an important chapter in Jesus' apology or defence—if we may dare use the word—for loving the sinful, for consorting with publicans and sinners. It tells men, in very simple language, how they are saved; not by works of righteousness which they have done, but of grace; in other words, by God's free mercy. Jewish religious society in the time of our Lord, as represented by the great Pharisee sect, totally misunderstood this Divine truth. They claimed salvation as a right on two grounds: (1) because they belonged to the chosen race; (2) because they rigidly and minutely obeyed the precepts of a singular code of laws, many of them devised by themselves and their fathers. Upon these two grounds they claimed salvation, that is, eternal blissful life. Not content with this claim of their own, they condemned, with a sweeping, harsh condemnation, all other peoples, and even those of their own race who neglected rigidly to observe the ordinances and ritual of a law framed in great measure in the schools of their own rabbis. Two extreme instances are here chosen—a rigid, exclusive, self-satisfied member of the religious society of Israel; and a Jewish officer of the hated Roman government, who knew little or nothing of the Law, but yet who longed after a higher life, and craved for an inward peace which he evidently was far from possessing. These two, the Pharisee and the publican, both went up to God's holy house, the temple, with a view of drawing near to the eternal King.

Ver. 11.—**The Pharisee stood and prayed thus with himself, God, I thank thee that I am not as other men are.** How closely drawn from the life is this picture of a Pharisee will be seen by a comparison of the prayer here with the prayer of a rabbi contained in the Talmud. When Rabbi Nechounia Ben Hakana left his school, he used to say, "I thank thee, O Eternal, my God, for having given me part with those who attend this school instead of running through the shops. I rise early like them, but it is to study the Law, not for futile ends. I take trouble as they do, but I shall be rewarded, and they will not. We run alike, but I for the future life, while they will only arrive at the pit of destruction" (from the treatise 'Berachôth').

Ver. 12.—**I fast twice in the week.** There was no such precept in the Law of Moses. There only a single fast-day in the year was enjoined, *the Day of Atonement* (Lev. xvi. 29). By the time of Zechariah the prophet (viii. 19) the one fast-day had grown into four. But this fasting twice every week was a burthensome observance imposed in the later oral Law. Thursday and Monday were the appointed fasting-days, because tradition related how, on those days, Moses ascended and descended from Sinai. Compare the Talmud (treatise 'Bava Khama,' fol. 82. 1). **I give tithes of all that I possess.** Here, again, the Mosaic ordinance only enjoined tithes of corn, wine, oil, and cattle. The later rabbinic schools directed that everything should be tithed, down to the mint and anise and cummin. And so this poor deluded Pharisee dreamed he had earned his eternal salvation, *forgetting* that the tithes he so prided himself on paying were merely tithes of goods of which he was steward for a little time, tithes, too, given back to their real Owner—God. Could this be counted *a claim* upon God? He boasted, too, that he was no extortioner: did he forget how often he had coveted? He was no adulterer: what of those wicked thoughts which so often found a home in his heart? He rejoiced that he was not like the publican and others of that same class: did he think of the sore temptations to which these and the like were exposed, and from which he

was free? He gloried in his miserable tithes and offerings : did he remember how really mean and selfish he was? did he think of his luxury and abundance, and of the want and misery of thousands round him? did his poor pitiful generosity constitute *a claim* to salvation? All this and more is shrined in the exquisite story of Jesus, who shows men that salvation—if it be given to men at all—must be given entirely as a free gift of God.

Ver. 13.—**And the publican, standing afar off, would not lift up so much as his eyes unto heaven, but smote upon his breast, saying, God be merciful to me a sinner!** Utterly sad and heart-broken, the publican neither recounts nor thinks of good kind deeds done, or special sins committed; no thoughts came into that poor heart, such as, "I have done some fair deeds; I am not altogether vile and sinful." He felt that with him evil so far overbalanced good that he could make no plea for himself, and yet he, too, longed for salvation, so he threw himself wholly upon God's mercy and love in his sad prayer, "God be merciful to me *the* sinner!" for so the words should be rendered. Different to the Pharisee, who thought himself better than his neighbours, this man, in his sad humility, evidently thought other men better than himself, but still he so trusted in God that he felt even for him, the sinner, there might be mercy.

Ver. 14.—**I tell you, this man went down to his house justified rather than the other: for every one that exalteth himself shall be abased; and he that humbleth himself shall be exalted.** And the publican was right; there was mercy even for him, all sin-stained though he was. The words with which the Lord closes his teaching are full of comfort. *That* prayer he tells us was heard and granted. The "I tell you" of Jesus here means, as Stier well puts it, "*I tell you*, for I know, I have seen, I have heard all this in many such a case, and in many such prayers." With this example of prayer favourably heard, there is surely no sin-burthened soul on earth who may not take courage in seeking God's face. One great object of this parable, we may believe, was to suggest some such thoughts, to embolden sorrowful, heart-broken sinners simply to go to God, trusting in his great pitying love. It should not be forgotten that the publican's prayer was heard *in the temple;* a silent approval seems given to his having thus sought out the appointed consecrated place of prayer.

Vers. 15—30.—*Jesus and the children. The young ruler refuses to give up his riches. The Lord speaks of the reward of them that leave all for his sake.*

Ver. 15.—**And they brought unto him also**

infants, that he would touch them. Our Lord's noticing children is several times alluded to in the Gospels. There was something evidently in his look and manner which singularly attracted little ones to him. SS. Matthew and Mark both recount this blessing of the children immediately after the teaching on divorce. Our Lord thus sanctifies the bond of marriage and its legitimate offspring. It was a silent but powerful reply to the mistaken inference which his disciples had drawn from his words. They had said, "It is not good to marry" (Matt. xix. 10). **But when his disciples saw it, they rebuked them.** Something of what the Master had said concerning the marriage state affected the disciples. Had he not just (see Matt. xix. 10—12) been claiming high honour for the solitary life where there were no family ties to claim attention? Surely, then, these women and their children had better stand aloof: what had that grave and earnest Teacher of theirs to do with these? He had higher and more important matters on his mind!

Ver. 16.—**But Jesus called them** unto him, **and said, Suffer little children to come unto me, and forbid them not: for of such is the kingdom of God.** St. Mark, who gives us here the memories of a faithful eye-witness —St. Peter—records how much displeased Jesus was when he saw them pushing back the mothers and their little ones, eager to win a smile or perhaps a touch from him whom the people justly regarded as the children's Friend. It seems also to have been the practice for Jewish mothers to bring their babes to famous rabbis, and to ask these teachers to bless their little ones. Christ's "interest in the little children was real, *and for their own sakes*. It was primary; not merely secondary, and because of the childlikeness of his subjects. *If they who are like little children belong to the kingdom of heaven, why should we for a moment doubt that the little children themselves belong to the kingdom?* Doubtless they all do. And if that change which men call *death* happen to them while they are still little children, we may rest assured that it will be to the little ones *life everlasting*. They will not be shut out from the higher province of the kingdom of heaven when they are snatched away from the lower" (Dr. Morrison). St. Mark's account, being that of an eye-witness, is fuller and more graphic. It is read in the Office of the Church of England for the Baptism of Infants, wherein young children are in like manner presented to Christ. It is considered that the Master's words and act here justify the Church in commending infants, as such, to the blessing of their Father. Surely if little ones were capable of spiritual blessings then, they are so now. It is noticeable that these children were not brought to the Lord to be taught, but "that he should put his hands upon them, and bless them" (Mark x. 16).

Ver. 17.—**Whosoever shall not receive the kingdom of God as a little child shall in no wise enter therein.** Jesus here reminds men that if they hope to enter the kingdom, it must be in the spirit of children, who never think of putting forward any claim of merit or paying any price for kindness showed them. His late parable of the Pharisee and publican was evidently in the Master's mind when he said this.

Ver. 18.—**And a certain ruler asked him, saying, Good Master, what shall I do to inherit eternal life?** This incident is related in the three synoptical Gospels. St. Matthew speaks of him as the young man. St. Luke here styles him a ruler; by some the title is supposed simply to denote that he was the ruler of a synagogue or congregation; others, however, consider that it denotes that the subject of the narrative was a ruler of the Jews, and possibly, but this is of course doubtful, a member of the Sanhedrin. His youth (Matt. xix. 20) is not at variance with this inference. Youth is defined by Philo as including the period between twenty-one and twenty-eight. All the three evangelists mention his great wealth. Dean Plumptre suggests that his large possessions and evident devotion had probably opened to him, at a comparatively early age, a place in the great council. His question concerning eternal life indicates that he was a Pharisee, and he evidently represented the noblest phase of this religious party. He had sedulously followed out the precepts of the best rabbinic schools of his day, but there was something lacking, he felt, and his intercourse with Jesus and the influence of the Master's words led him to take this question point-blank to the famous Teacher, who he felt—alone of any master whom he had met—was able to satisfy this longing desire of his heart.

Ver. 19.—**And Jesus said unto him, Why callest thou me good? none is good, save one,** that is, God. The title "good" was a singular one for the young ruler to have used. It was never used to the most famous rabbis by their pupils. It implied an intense reverence, but nothing more. The young man distinctly did not *then* believe the Master was Divine, else he had never made the great refusal recorded directly afterwards. "To be a good man is impossible. . . . God alone could have this honour" (Plato, 'Phæd.' 27). "*You* are looking at me," said the Master, "as a man: why give me this strange, lofty title? You are looking on me only as an earthly

Teacher." The great Heart-reader was reading the young man's thoughts, thoughts which soon crystallized, as we shall see, into the *refusal* to do what he, whom he chose to style " good," directed him to carry out.

Ver. 20.—Thou knowest the commandments. The report in St. Matthew is somewhat fuller. There the ruler, when directed to the commandments, replies by asking " which ?" expecting most likely to be referred to some of the elaborate traditional laws of the rabbinic schools, which were difficult to keep even by men in the position of a wealthy Pharisee; but to his surprise Jesus mentions the most general and best-known of the ancient ten.

Ver. 21.—And he said, All these have I kept from my youth up. He listens to the Master with something like impatient surprise. There is a ring of concealed indignation in his " All these have I ever kept. What do you take me for? I am a religious, God-fearing Jew; from my child-days have I kept these." Kept these! How little the poor questioner knew the secrets of his own heart! Yet he had answered Jesus in the true spirit of a Pharisee trained carefully in the rabbinic schools. We read, for instance, in the Talmud how " when Rabbi Chaninah was dying, he said to the angel of death, ' Go and fetch me the book of the Law, and see whether there is anything in it which I have not kept.' "

Ver. 22.—Now when Jesus heard these things, he said unto him, Yet lackest thou one thing. St. Mark (x. 21), who had St. Peter's memories to draw from, adds here a very touching detail. " Jesus beholding him [looking earnestly at him] loved him." There was something noble and true in that life, struggling in the imperfect light of the rabbinic teaching after eternity and heaven, and feeling that in all its struggles some element was surely wanting; and Jesus, as he gazed on the young earnest face, loved him, and proceeded to show him how far removed his life was as yet from the perfect life he dreamed of attaining to. He would show him in a moment how selfish, how earthly, were his thoughts and aims; how firmly chained to earth that heart of his, which he thought only longed for heaven. **Sell all that thou hast, and distribute unto the poor, and thou shalt have treasure in heaven: and come, follow me.** " Well," the Master said, " I will test you. You say you have from your child-days kept your whole duty to your neighbour; you say that you hunger after the higher righteousness. Do you really? Will you indeed be perfect (Matt. xix. 21)? Then I will tell you what you lack. Go, sell those great possessions which I know you love so dearly, and give

all to the poor, and come, take up the cross (Mark x. 21), and follow me, the homeless, landless Teacher whom you call by the Divine title ' good.' " The " cross " of St. Mark only Jesus understood then in all its dread significance. It was coming then very near; and the great Teacher saw that his true servants, if they would indeed follow him, must follow him along that lonely road of suffering he was then treading. " Via crucis, via lucis." The young ruler, with his great wealth, thought he had from his youth done his whole duty to his neighbour. The Galilæan Master, whom he so reverenced and admired, reminded him that out of those wide domains, those stored-up riches, out of the mammon of unrighteousness, he had forgotten to make to himself friends who, when he died, should receive him into the eternal tents of heaven. This is what he lacked. He had probably heard the Lord's teaching in the parables of the unjust steward and of Lazarus.

Ver. 23.—And when he heard this, he was very sorrowful: for he was very rich. St. Mark adds (a memory of Peter's) that when he heard this the ruler went away frowning, with a lowering look. *This* was too much. He could not, even at the bidding of that loved Teacher, give up the pleasant life he loved so well, the things he prized so highly; so silently and sadly he turned away. The ' Gospel of the Hebrews,' a very ancient document, dating from the first days of the faith, a few fragments only of which have come down to us in quotations in the Fathers, thus describes the scene: " Then the rich man began to scratch his head, for that was not to his mind. And the Lord said to him, How then canst thou say, I have kept the Law; for it is written in the Law, Thou shalt love thy neighbour as thyself; and, lo! many of thy brethren, children of Abraham, live in the gutter, and die of hunger, while thy table is loaded with good things, and nothing is sent out to them ? " (quoted by Origen, in Matt. xix.). Dante calls this " The Great Refusal," and represents the shade of the young ruler among the throng of the useless, of those who faced both ways (' Inferno,' x. 27). It is worthy of notice that there was no angry retort from the wealthy ruler, no scornful, cynical smile of derision, as we read of among the covetous, wealthy Pharisees (ch. xvi. 14). Still, in the heart of this seeker after the true wisdom there was a sore conflict. Grieving, sorrow-stricken, with gloomy looks, he turned away in silence.

Ver. 24.—And when Jesus saw that he was very sorrowful, he said, How hardly shall they that have riches enter into the kingdom of God! The temptations which beset a rich man are so many and so various.

The poor, indeed, with all their trials, stand fairer for the kingdom than do their envied richer brothers and sisters.

Ver. 25.—**For it is easier for a camel to go through a needle's eye, than for a rich man to enter into the kingdom of God.** This simile, taken in its plain and obvious sense, appears to many an exaggerated one, and various explanations have been suggested to soften it down. The best is found in Lord Nugent's 'Lands Classical and Sacred,' who mentions that in some modern Syrian towns the narrow gate for foot-passengers at the side of the larger gate by which waggons, camels, and other beasts of burden enter the city, is known as the "needle's eye." It is, however, very uncertain whether this term for the little gate was known in ancient times. But the simile was evidently a common one among the Jews. The Talmud, for instance, gives us the parallel phrase of an elephant passing through a needle's eye. The Koran repeats the very words of the Gospel. It is the object of the proverb to express human impossibility.

> "I would ride the camel,
> Yea leap him flying, through the needle's eye
> As easily as such a pampered soul
> Could pass the narrow gate."
>
> (Southey.)

It seems strange that the three evangelists, SS. Matthew, Mark, and Luke, who tell this story of the young questioner and the Master's conversation with him, do not mention his name. And yet he must have been a conspicuous personage in the society of the time. First of all, his riches were evidently remarkable. One account tells us that he was "very rich." Two of the Gospels mention his "great possessions." St. Luke tells us that he was "a ruler." He was, then, certainly a very wealthy Jew holding a high official position, not improbably a member of the Sanhedrin council. Why is he nameless in the three Gospels? Dean Plumptre has a most interesting theory that the young wealthy ruler was *Lazarus of Bethany.* He bases his hypothesis upon the following data: He begins by stating that "there is one other case in the first two Gospels which presents similar phenomena. In the narrative of the supper at Bethany, St. Matthew and St. Mark record the passionate affection which expressed itself in pouring the precious ointment of spikenard upon our Lord's head as the act of ' a woman' (Matt. xxvi. 7; Mark xiv. 3), leaving her unnamed. In John xii. 3 we find that the woman was Mary, the sister of Lazarus. The train of thought thus suggested points to the supposition that here

also there may have been reasons for suppressing in the records a name which was familiar to the narrator. What if the young ruler were Lazarus himself? The points of agreement are sufficiently numerous to warrant the conjecture. The household of Lazarus, as the spikenard ointment shows, were of the wealthier class. The friends who came to comfort the bereaved sisters were themselves, in St. John's language, ' of the Jews,' *i.e.* of the chief rulers (John xi. 19). The young ruler was obviously a Pharisee, and the language of Martha (John xi. 24) shows that she, too, believed in eternal life and the resurrection of the dead. The answer to the young ruler, ' One thing thou lackest' (as given by St. Mark and St. Luke), is almost identical with that to Martha, ' One thing is needful ' (ch. x. 42). In such a case, of course, nothing can be attained beyond conjectural inference; but the present writer must avow his belief that the coincidences in this case are such as to carry the evidence to a very high point of probability."

Ver. 26.—**And they that heard it said, Who then can be saved?** This hard saying appeared to the disciples to be terribly comprehensive in its scope; the longing to be rich was confined to no one class or order, it was the universal passion. Were *they* guiltless here? Were *they* not looking for riches and glory in the Messianic kingdom of the immediate future? And of all peoples the Jews in every age have been credited with the blindest devotion to this idol, wealth. In St. Mark (x. 24) we find certainly an explanatory statement: "How hard is it for them that *trust* in riches to enter into the kingdom of God!" But this explanatory and softened statement is not found in the older authorities; these read instead, in Mark x. 24, simply the words, "How hard is it to enter the kingdom of God!" Hard alike, the Master meant, for rich and poor, though harder for the former.

Ver. 27.—**And he said, The things which are impossible with men are possible with God.** Yes, impossible, the Divine Teacher repeated, from a man's point of view; impossible from the platform of legal obedience on which the young ruler (ver. 21) had taken his stand, or the Pharisee in his prayer (vers. 11, 12); but it was not impossible with God. *He* might give this salvation as a perfectly free gift, utterly undeserved, perfectly unmerited, as he did to the *prodigal son* when he returned, or to the *publican* when he beat his breast in almost voiceless mourning, or still more conspicuously, not many days later, to the *penitent thief* dying on the cross.

Ver. 28.—**Then Peter said, Lo, we have left all, and followed thee.** Again the question of Peter, evidently acting as spokes-man of the twelve, is repeated by the first three evangelists. Strangely faithful in their accounts of their own dealings with their adored Master, they never veil or hide any human weakness or error of their own which led to an important bit of teaching from their Lord. Now, in this place, they, in the person of Peter, gave utterance to a very worldly, but a very natural, thought. The ruler had failed when the test was applied to him; he was a conspicuous ex-ample of failure in the rich to enter the kingdom. But *they* had not failed when the test had been applied to them; they had given all up for his sake: what would be their reward?

Vers. 29, 30.—**And he said unto them, Verily I say unto you, There is no man that hath left house, or parents, or brethren, or wife, or children, for the kingdom of God's sake, who shall not receive manifold more in this present time, and in the world to come life everlasting.** Evidently, from the reports of the three evangelists, the reply of Jesus was a lengthy one, and contained much deep teaching. St. Luke only gives us, however, one section, so to speak, of the great discourse which followed upon Peter's question. Here and in St. Mark Peter and the twelve receive a quiet rebuke in this general promise. The Master seems to say, "My promises are not especially to you, my first followers, but to all who, not for any selfish hope of recompense or reward, but for the kingdom of God's sake, give up what they hold dearest; there will be real, true happiness for them even in this world, and in the world to come unspeakable joy will be their portion; theirs will be the life that knows no ending." St. Mark adds, with rare truth, that the happiness which his faithful are to enjoy in this world will be accompanied *with persecutions*. It is the same beautiful thought which the Master had put out before, only the gem now is set in different words. "Blessed are they which are persecuted for righteousness' sake: for theirs is the kingdom of heaven" (Matt. v. 10; see, too, vers. 11, 12). St. Matthew deals especially with another division of the Lord's discourse. Here Jesus speaks of the future of the twelve; and, looking forward to the generally noble and self-devoted lives he saw these would live, he tells them of the great destiny surely reserved for them if they remained faithful to the end. But even here, in his words, "the first shall be last" (Matt. xix. 30), and still more point-edly in the parable of the labourers which followed (Matt. xx. 1—16), he warned these devoted but often mistaken men of the danger of self-complacency. It was only because he foresaw that in these really great

ones this spirit would in the end be over-come (at least in eleven of them) that he made the grand and mysterious promise of Matt. xix. 28.

The narrative here, in the three synopti-cal Gospels, is not continuous; at this point there is a break. There is little doubt but that the sickness and death of Lazarus of Bethany, and the summons of the sisters to Jesus, took place about this period. The three synoptical evangelists are silent here for reasons we have discussed elsewhere.

Between vers. 30 and 31 there probably should be inserted the hasty journey to Bethany. The Master was not far when the news of his friend's death reached him. Immediately after the miracle there appears to have been a meeting of the Sanhedrin, when it was decided to put Jesus to death, though not during the ensuing Passover, with such precautions as were possible. The terrible decision became known. Jesus then retired to Ephraim, an obscure village about twenty miles from the city. Here a very short time was spent in absolute retire-ment and seclusion. But the Passover Feast was nigh at hand. In company with some of the crowded pilgrim caravans, and secure under their protection till his last few days of work were accomplished, Jesus journeys to Jerusalem. At this point the three synoptical Gospels take up the story again. The eleventh chapter of St. John fills up this gap in the connected story.

Vers. 31—42.—*Jesus again tells them of his Passion. The healing of the blind at Jericho.* Ver. 31.—**Then he took unto him the twelve, and said unto them.** St. Mark (x. 32) prefaces this announcement with the words, "And they were in the way going up to Jerusalem; and Jesus went before them: and they were amazed; and as they followed, they were afraid." There was something unusual, evidently, in the man-ner and behaviour of the Master; silently, wrapped up in his own lofty meditations, he strode on in front of the company of his followers. A feeling of awe and fear stole over them as they watched the silent Master with the shadow of the coming cross falling, perhaps, across his countenance. Much had happened lately: the teaching growing more and more solemn as the end drew near; the raising of Lazarus; the intense enmity of the great men of the nation; the fixed determination to put the Master to death; his short retirement; then the announcement that he was going up to face his enemies at the great feast in Jerusalem; and now alone and silent he walked at their head. What was coming? thought the twelve and their friends. He read their thoughts, and, calling them round him, told them what was about to happen. **Behold, we go up to Jerusalem, and all things that are written by the prophets concerning the Son of man shall be accomplished.**

Vers. 32, 33.—**For he shall be delivered unto the Gentiles, and shall be mocked, and spitefully entreated, and spitted on: and they shall scourge** him, **and put him to death: and the third day he shall rise again.** The outlines of the Passion he had sketched for the disciples before on two occasions, but never so clearly as now. He even tells them the manner of his end, and how his own countrymen would give him up to the Romans, and how these Gentiles, amidst every conceivable circumstance of horror, would do him to death. And the Master closed his dread revelation by predicting his speedy resurrection.

Ver. 34.—**And they understood none of these things: and this saying was hid from them, neither knew they the things which were spoken.** But they listened all dazed and confused; they could not take it in, neither the shame of the death of their loved Leader, nor the glory of the Resurrection which was to follow immediately after. They could not persuade themselves that the hopes of an earthly Messianic glory in which they were to share must positively be given up. "We must learn to *love* Divine truths before we can understand them," said Pascal. "Toward everything which is contrary to natural desire," wrote Riggenbach (in Godet), "there is produced in the heart a blindness, which nothing but a miracle can heal."

Ver. 35.—**And it came to pass, that as he was come nigh unto Jericho.** Jericho was once called "the City of Palms," afterwards "the City of Perfumes." It was about eighteen miles from Jerusalem. In the Herodian times it became a popular resort, owing to the affection the great Herod entertained for it. Its palm-groves and balsam-gardens were a present from Antony to Cleopatra. Herod the Great bought them from her, and made it one of his royal cities, and adorned it with many stately buildings, and eventually died there. It is now a miserable village. **A certain blind man sat by the wayside begging.** An apparent discrepancy exists in the three accounts given of this act of our Lord. St. Luke speaks of one blind man who was healed as our Lord was *entering* the town. St. Matthew and St. Mark mention that the miracle took place as our Lord was leaving the place,

and St. Matthew mentions that two blind men received their sight at the bidding of Jesus. Several solutions of this little difficulty have been proposed. Perhaps the most probable is that the sufferers were sitting near the town gates as the Lord entered. They, hearing who was passing by, eagerly called to him for help. Surrounded by the crowd, he probably did not hear the cry, or possibly wished to test the earnestness of their faith by allowing them to wait. They follow him through the place, and in the open space outside the city they attract his attention, and he heals them. Or, in the words of Dr. Morrison, "the case seems to have begun as he entered into the city, but it culminated in all likelihood as he departed." A later explanation, apparently preferred by Godet and Farrar, is that, as Josephus and Eusebius distinguish between the old and the new Jericho—the old town on the ancient site, and the new Herodian town which had sprung up at a little distance from it—the blind man might, according to some traditions, have been healed as Jesus was leaving old Jericho; according to others, as he was entering the new town. The fact of SS. Mark and Luke only mentioning one blind man is easily explained. There was one evidently (as we shall suggest further on), a well-known character in Christian story—Bartimæus. Two of the evangelists recorded his cure, as being of special interest to the Church, leaving the second among the numberless unrecorded miracles of healing of Jesus. *A certain blind man.* St. Mark names him Bartimæus. It may be inferred that, as St. Mark specially names him, this man was well known in early Christian story. We know that after the cure he joined the company as one of the followers of Jesus.

Ver. 37.—**And they told him, that Jesus of Nazareth passeth by.** The Lord's name was by this time a household word in Palestine, and among the sick and afflicted a most precious and welcome sound.

Ver. 38.—**Jesus, thou Son of David.** This form of address distinctly shows that the idea that the Rabbi of Nazareth, the great Wonder-worker, the wise kind Teacher, was in some way or other the long looked-for Deliverer, was now taking possession of the people's mind. "Son of David" was distinctly a Messianic salutation.

Ver. 39.—**And they which went before rebuked him.** It must be remembered that our Lord was surrounded by a great host of Passover pilgrims, by many of whom he was reverenced as "some great One," perhaps the King Messiah. Such a low wailing cry on the part of a blind beggar, asking to be brought into the presence of him they wondered at and admired and hoped so much from, seemed a great presumption: hence these rebukes.

Vers. 40, 41.—**And Jesus stood, and commanded him to be brought unto him.** St. Mark here adds, " And they call the blind man, saying unto him, Be of good comfort, rise; he calleth thee." These kindly sympathizing words of the disciples to the beggar, doing their loving Master's behest, were one of Peter's own memories of the scene under the walls of Jericho. **And when he was come near, he asked him, saying, What wilt thou that I shall do unto thee?** Many besides the governor Pilate, who a few days later put the query to him, " Art thou a King, then?" during this period must have often asked silently the same question. We shall soon see the whole multitude carried away with enthusiasm, giving him a royal welcome as he entered the city. Here, with a majesty truly royal, as Godet well remarks, Jesus seems to open up to the beggar the treasures of Divine power in " What wilt thou that I shall do unto thee?" and to give him, as it were, *carte blanche.* **And he said, Lord, that I may receive my sight.** There is a curious variation in the terms of this request in that ancient Syriac Version known as " the Curetonian," in the account of St. Matthew, " That our eyes might be opened, and we shall see thee:"

Ver. 42.—**And Jesus said unto him, Receive thy sight.** "Magnifique aumône du Christ" (Pressensé). **Thy faith hath saved thee.** The American Longfellow has united the cry for mercy of the blind, the kindly sympathizing words of the disciples (reported by St. Mark), and the gift of Jesus Christ, in his exquisite poem of ' Blind Bartimæus.'

" Those mighty voices three—
'Ιησοῦ, ἐλέησόν με !
Θάρσει, ἔγειρε· φωνεῖ σε !
'Η πίστις σου σέσωκέ σε !"

HOMILETICS.

Vers. 1—8.—*The importunate widow.* The importance which Christ attaches to prayer is evidenced by the frequency with which he recurs to it in his teaching, and the variety of his illustration of its duty and blessedness. The sermon on the mount enforces it as one of the cardinal virtues of the perfect disciple. In the eleventh chapter of this Gospel both the manner after which we are to pray, and the assurance on which faith should rest, are presented. Again, towards the close of the ministry we are introduced to two parables bearing on it, each with the lesson which the Master would teach clearly defined. The former of these two has this as its object (ver. 1), " that men ought always," *i.e.* unremittingly, " to pray, and not to faint ; " *i.e.* not to be scared by hindrances, or induced to desist by the sickness which comes through hope deferred. The structure of the parable is very simple. There is a judge who neither fears God nor regards man. A poor widow, who has been wronged, claims his interposition. He pays no regard to her suit. But she importunes him ; day by day she presents herself, until, though he has no regard to the justice of her case, he listens to her pleading in order that he may be relieved of her solicitations. If man, unjust and selfish, thus yields to unceasing prayer, how much more, argues Jesus, will he, who is the Absolutely Just and the Infinitely Loving, yield to the cry, day and night, of his own people ! Notice three features in the delineation.

I. GOD IN CONTRAST WITH THE HUMAN AVENGER. The latter consults his own ease. He acts in mere selfishness. The Eternal Righteousness is ever consistent with itself. " To this man will I look, even to him that is humble and contrite in spirit."

II. GOD'S PEOPLE IN CONTRAST WITH THE WIDOW. They resemble her in one thing —in the sense of need, of helplessness. But the widow stands in no special relation to the judge. God's people are his own elect. They are part of the blood-bought, ransomed family. " As many as are led by the Spirit of God, they are the sons of God ; " and " the secret of the Lord is with them that fear him." Each of them is in the most intimate relation to the Eternal. " I am poor and needy, yet the Lord thinketh on me."

III. THE LONG-SUFFERING OF GOD IN CONTRAST WITH THE LONG-SUFFERING OF MAN. The long-suffering of man is in consequence of the indisposition to act; if in the end it is dispelled, if the action after a lengthened interval follows, it is only that repose may be purchased by the effort, and that the mind may be free to carry out its unloving projects. God bears long with his elect, not because he is unwilling to bless, but that he may draw them closer to himself, that he may prepare them for fuller measures of blessing, that he may chasten their wills into completer union with his will, and so ultimately bestow the higher gifts of his Fatherhood. When they cry, there is much that needs to be corrected; they desire only what they regard as the best or what will relieve them from some pressure. There is still a distance between their will and his; he delays the answer that they may be brought in true self-emptiness to his heart, and that, their faith being purified, they may be enriched out of his exceeding abundance. So the Lord bore long with Job; in him patience had its perfect work; he learned to "abhor himself, and repent in dust and ashes;" he was "attuned also to finer issues" by the charity which led him to pray for his friends. And the Lord turned his captivity when his prayer was thus disciplined and enlarged, and he received "twice as much as he had before." So, too, the woman of Canaan cried, and "the Lord answered her not a word" (Matt. xv.). Then came she "and *worshipped* him." She bowed her whole soul before him, and she received the reward of the "great faith." "Therefore," says the Lord, "*faint not.*" "Pray without ceasing." The heavens above are not brass. There is a flexibility in the ordering of the universe which admits of the answer, direct and real, to prayer. "More things are wrought by prayer than the world dreams of." "O thou that hearest prayer, unto thee shall all flesh come." The Lord anticipates a decadence in the belief as to the efficacy of prayer, for he adds a "nevertheless" (ver. 8). Is this loss of faith true of the Church and of Christians in this day?

Vers. 9—14.—*The Pharisee and the publican.* The lesson as to prayer is continued. The parable which follows exhibits the spirit and conditions of effectual prayer. Mark the two features of the audience specially addressed. He speaks to certain (1) who trusted in themselves as being righteous; (2) who, as the outcome of this trust, despised others. He spoke in the previous parable of "God's own elect." Now, the Pharisees accounted themselves the elect of God. They were puffed up by this confidence. They regarded themselves as the righteous, who kept the Law, both oral and written. And, indeed, they were most scrupulous as to every requirement; nay, they were willing to burden themselves with minute and vexatious observances. And the sin which beset them was the pride shadowed forth in one of the two who went up to pray. As the illustration of the elect, the Lord chooses a tax-gatherer, one of a hated class, for whom, in Pharisee-thought, there was no place in the kingdom of heaven. The instruction is suitable to every time. Pharisee separation and pride are features to be recognized in the Church of this day, as they were prominent in the Jewish Church of our Lord's day. Ever to be studied is the antithesis—*respectability* in the Pharisee, non-*respectability* in the publican. See the two. The one, with his broad phylactery, his supercilious bearing, his Pharisaism reflected in every feature of his sallow countenance, as with measured step he proceeds to the temple. In its inner court he stands erect; he arranges his prayer-robe, he looks around, the face darkened by a scowl as he observes the publican in a distant corner of the sacred building. And then he lifts his eye. No prayer trembles in any tone; no pleading escapes through any word; he "speaks with himself" rather than with God. It is a soliloquy, a self-gratified recital of his own piety. If he says, "God, I thank thee" (vers. 11, 12), it is not for any grace that he has received, it is not in acknowledging that only through a higher mercy and strength he is what he is; nay, with something of familiarity in the address, he bids the Almighty join him in admiration of his virtues, on account of which he is lifted above other men. Only by certain averages of his own striking does he measure his excellence, the climax being reached, when there comes the contemptuous "even as this publican." Oh, what a superior person, to be sure! With what satisfaction must highest Heaven regard one who fasted twice in the week, and gave tithes of all he possessed! The other, with hurried gait, as one intent only on pouring out his heart before God, takes his place far off. He has no wish to disturb the complacency of his fellow-worshipper. He claims nothing; self-assertion in every form is absent from his heart. The only presence with him is the Holy One of Israel. Beneath the vision of his holiness all that is of the earth must keep silence. He will not even lift up his eyes. He has not much to record; human righteousness even is but a filthy rag when held up to the light of that Perfect Holiness. And as for him, oh, there can be only the one prayer, "God be merciful to me a sinner!" (ver. 13). He is overpowered with the conviction of sin. His only refuge is the mercy of the Eternal. " I tell you " (ver. 14), concludes Christ, " this man is manifested to be one of God's elect. He, not the other, returns to his house the one accepted and justified." The parable is most suggestive.

I. It is the EXPOSURE OF SPIRITUAL PRIDE IN ITS ROOT AND FRUIT. Its root, the measurement of self by " other men." God is not in the thought. The song of the seraphim, " Holy, holy, holy, Lord God of hosts," sounds faintly in the ear. The mind is not occupied with him and his holiness. It looks around rather than above. The standard is a social one. There is " a zeal for the Law, but not according to knowledge." Having settled the constituents of righteousness, and having in conduct realized these constituents, it looks from the legal vantage-ground on others. And, seeing the many below the elected level, it whispers within itself, " I thank thee that I am not as they." The *I* struts abroad with a distinct sense of superiority. This pride is the parasite of religiosity. And religiosity is the whole religion of many. Religiosity means the performance, punctilious and sincere, of acts and offices, functions and services. It may comprehend a wide area of the existence. It may fill up much of time and much of thought, and he who abounds in it is held to be a religious man. But it is a morality untouched by the emotion of the broken and contrite spirit. There is no distinctively evangelical motive force. On an earlier occasion, the contrast between the routine religiosity and the warm religion of the heart was presented at the dinner-table where Simon the Pharisee presided, and the woman washed the Lord's feet with her tears. Of her he said, " She hath loved much." Here the Pharisee is in opposition to the publican, who had the inner spirit of poverty. Now, one who has the religiosity, not the religion, is apt to rest on the duties which he discharges, on the zeal which he manifests. He trusts in himself as being righteous, and, wherever there is this trust, there creeps around it a feeling of superiority. " I am not as other men are." It engenders the separatist's haughty spirit. It brings in the sentiment of a caste. The " I " belongs to the religious world, " others " are without. Let us beware lest we rest satisfied with a righteousness like that of the Pharisee, lest we substitute the outward for the inward—what we do for what we are. Let us beware of that which always develops with this tendency—the habit of comparison of self with others on levels lower than our own, instead of realizing " the vision splendid " of that righteousness which demands the entire self. It is this trust, this self-elevation, this pride of righteousness, which vitiates the sacrifice of many who go up to the temple to pray.

II. It is the COMMENDATION OF HUMILITY, IN ITS ESSENTIAL NATURE AND BLESSEDNESS. What is humility ? It is not so much a self-consciousness as a God-consciousness; not so much a mean thinking of ourselves as a thrilling, penetrating consciousness of him who is perfect holiness and truth. There is a self-abhorrence, but that follows the seeing of God with the opened inner eye. The Pharisee had no conviction of sin, because he had no real discernment of the Eternal. His god was the property of his caste, one on whom he had a claim because of his belonging to the caste and doing what was required by it. The publican felt God at his heart; and the sight awoke the longing to be holy as God is, and the longing to be holy called out the sense of wrongness. Oh, how he had offended ! how selfish and grasping and wicked he had been ! All else fades into indistinctness; in that temple there are to him but the two presences, God and his soul, and the soul cries, " God be merciful ! " It is the first cry of the soul which God has appropriated. There is no real prayer until that cry. A genuine earnest pleading is evoked. The beginning of all prayer, Christ reminds us, is the taking of the sinner's place, and the simple appeal to mercy. And as it is the first, so it is the cry ever pulsing through prayer. It is never wanting from the justified. The pardon has been received. The blood cleanses from all sin; but not the less, all the more, is the knowledge of sin and the need of the ever-renewed application of mercy. This is humility—sinful self cast on Divine mercy, and, forgiven much, loving much. There is no measurement with other men, for God is the all in all. And this is blessed. The Pharisee returns—his pride more deeply written into his nature, its blight and curse; no spring in the heart, no visitation of any day-spring from on high. Remaining in his pride, he was truly abased. The publican returns— a burden rolled off from his heart, a new elasticity in his step, a new light in his countenance. "The winter is past, . . . the flowers appear on the earth." He is at peace with God, justified, sanctified, righteous in the communion of the Righteous One. "I, yet not I, for he lives in me." In his humility he was exalted.

Vers. 18—25.—*The ruler who refused the crown.* It is a certain ruler, a young man, who accosts our Lord. And the question which he asks represents one of the deepest cravings of the human breast. Is it only in the Gospels that we find this question? It is written into all the religions, into the best of all the philosophies, the poetries, the guesses at truth, which have commanded the thought of the ages. It is as old as human nature, as manifold in its complexion as the human experience, as abiding in its persistence as the human need. It is our question—one compared with which the hundred things which claim our attention are only as strivings after wind. Let us listen. The eternal life: what is it? and how is it realized?

I. WHAT DID THE YOUNG MAN MEAN when he came running and kneeling and asked, "What shall I do to inherit eternal life?" The answer may indicate the essential features of the desire that has haunted the breast. Clearly he meant three things: 1. *A real, personal existence*—one implying distinct consciousness and activity. He is too prosaic, too selfishly in earnest, to mean less than this. 2. *An existence removed from the imperfections of the present time.* His notions of immortality may have been crude; but he certainly desired a life which, as contrasted with the changeful and limited, is an eternal life. 3. *A life in relation to a moral or spiritual system.* He has possessions. Sirens are ever luring him to the fateful shores of pleasure. Against them "the categorical imperative" of conscience is ever dominant. It says, "Root thy conduct in the everlastingly true. The eternal life is not mere endlessness. It is endless goodness, truth. And to be in harmony with this is to live eternally." Now, such being the contents of his thought, the burden which he brings to the Master is—how it comes that, although the harmony of his conduct with this system is complete, he is still unsatisfied; nay, that the more he seems to approach the ideal the more conscious he is that it is far ahead of him. "Explain it to me" is the passionate entreaty; and who does not love him for this sublime passion? "What is the missing quantity? What is the *plus* yet to be possessed that I may have eternal life?"

II. Turning to THE ANSWER OF CHRIST, and connecting it with words elsewhere, WHAT IS CHRIST'S EXPOSITION OF THE ETERNAL LIFE? The question is, "What shall I do?" And to this the specific reply is, "Be free. Your life does not consist in the abundance of your possessions. Can you part with them, that you may the more unreservedly obey the vision which has dawned on you?" (ver. 22). Thus the truth probed him. He might not have been called actually to sell his estate, any more than Abraham was called to offer up Isaac. But the trial of his will was made; and, in the trial, he was found wanting (ver. 23). Do we blame him?—we whom the truth is proving every day, only to find that we are caught up by all kinds of vanities! He turned away; and, alas! what of us? But the demand of the Lord reminds us of the requirement essential to the eternal life. Life, we are told by scientists, consists in an adaptation of organism to surrounding. When the adaptation is complete, and the surrounding nourishes the organism, there is health. When it is impaired, there is sickness; when it is broken, there is death. Human life has both a spiritual and a material environment. As the ruler rightly supposed, the eternal life implies correspondence to the spiritual environment. Where there is no such correspondence, where, in Scripture phrase, the life is "without God," there is death. Where the correspondence has been formed, and the inner life is nourished by the system which surrounds it, there is spiritual, eternal life. But are not the phrases, "systems," "environments," too vague and abstract? Do we not need something more concrete, something nearer us, than such abstractions? *This* is more concrete, *this* is nearer us, "Take up the cross; come, follow me" (ver. 22). A perfect Man has walked this earth—One in whom the correspondence with the heavenly environment was complete, who lived in and with a Father in heaven, and whose meat was to do his will. His existence, in its details, we cannot copy; but his life, in its principles, inspirations, in all that gave it its beauty and glory, we can realize, under varying conditions. To be joined to him; to live in his light; to be the manner of person that he was; to be affianced to him as the Lord and Friend and Brother of our perfect choice; and have his flesh as meat indeed, and his blood as drink indeed;—this is the way to the eternal life. But what is this life whose way is thus defined? It must be kept always in view that *eternal* is not merely another name for *endless*. Endless time would not be eternity. The eternal is the timeless. Everlasting existence may be involved; but this is because the life is what it is—Divine, and therefore imperishable. Christ has supplied many unfoldings of this Divine life (see John iii. 1—13; vi. 32—53; xvii. 3). May the guidance of the Holy Spirit illumine this teaching! and may we all realize the secret of St. John: "He that hath the Son hath the life!"

III. THIS RULER INTERESTS US. The narrative concerning him suggests reflections which may be dwelt on with profit. 1. *The difficulty, the hindrance, to salvation that is interposed by riches.* (Vers. 24, 25.) Great possessions, Christ declares, increase the risk of losing the true spiritual health, are apt to stand in the way of the eternal life. It is not the riches themselves that are evil; it is, as one of the evangelists explains, the trust in them, the sensation of them, that is the evil. And may there not be a trust in riches, even when they are not actually possessed? We may have very little, and yet have such a craving for more as proves that the ungotten wealth stands for our best. More than this, with little there may be as much of earthliness and love of the world as when there is much. It is a wretched slavery which one often sees, and the feeling of which one often detects in one's own breast. Persons are miserably ruled over by the sense of wealth. Neither do they get the good, nor does the world get the full good, of what they have. On the other hand, the poor cannot rise to the real dignity of their being because they set possessions on the height which they regard as the *summum bonum.* Social life is honeycombed by that trust in riches. "How hard it is," says Christ, "for those that have riches to enter into the kingdom of God!" (ver. 24). 2. *A crown is refused.* Who the ruler was we cannot tell. On a sudden he appears, on a sudden he disappears. Is he wrecked, like a ship with full sail, at the harbour-bar? It is noticeable that Jesus "loved him;" in this distinction he is bracketed, in the Gospels, with Martha and Mary and Lazarus. For a moment the crown hangs over his head. Did he finally reject it? But he waves it aside. Oh, not the last who has missed the flood-tide—the blessing offered to the man, and the man turning from it! Young men, all, reflect!

Vers. 35—43.—*Bartimæus.* Here are two noises suggestive of the human life with which we are all familiar. There is the tramp, tramp, tramp, of the swaying multitude, the din of the many minds, many experiences, many mouths, all moving in obedience to a common impulse. Men and women, when they become mere units of a crowd, forget for the time their personal histories. They are swept on by the current, sharing and adding to its excitement. There is nothing more unaccountable sometimes than the impulses which are communicated from person to person, and pass by infection to the multitude. Different days have their different idols. Those who are shouting themselves hoarse with their hosannahs at Jericho will shout themselves hoarse with the cry, "Away with him! Crucify him!" at Jerusalem. Oh, fickle popularity! The Lord knew what the applause of the crowd was worth. The children crying in the temple were far more to him than the loud voice and the tremendous enthusiasm of the thousands who had swelled the triumph of the entry into the city of David. But through that tumult, in the midst of that noise, there is another—that which always reaches the ears of the Lord of Sabaoth. Only one voice, at most two voices, shrill and clamorous—the voice of misery and want and prayer! Had he not heard that same voice in highest heaven? Had it not pierced through the praises of angel and archangel, of cherubim and seraphim—the cry of a sinful and weary world? A little one only in the system of the universe, but the least in need has a special way of access to the Eternal Love. Far off the great Shepherd hears the bleat of the sheep that has strayed into the wilderness. He who heard the sigh of the world from the excellent glory will not turn from the piteous pleading of the poor and needy. God's tenderness individualizes. "*This* poor man cried, and the Lord heard him, and saved him out of all his troubles."

I. REGARD THIS POOR MAN. Perhaps we shall realize that he is our near kinsman. 1. *He has been sitting by the wayside begging.* And what are we all but beggars at the world's wayside? Even the mind most richly endowed, the heart most wealthy in love and imagination, needs "the life more and fuller." Is there no begging from heaven? no consciousness of a fountain of living waters? This Bartimæus, taking his place day by day on the thoroughfare and asking an alms, is only too faithful a picture of me, wanting, desiring, and, alas! too often trying to satisfy my soul with some dole of happiness or excitement thrown to me—a beggar all the while, blind. 2. *What is this?* An unusual bustle and din. What does it mean? We can imagine the question addressed, with only a languid interest, to some person at hand—a languor which vanishes when the answer is given, "It is Jesus of Nazareth who is passing by." Ah! the newness of cry, sign of newness of life! What and how he had heard of this Jesus we know not; but he had heard enough to open the gates of the soul. The one argument is need, the one reasoning, "I am here; he is there. Son of David, have mercy on me!" It is the great hour of a human life when speech is begun between the soul and heaven. Such speech arrests the love of God in the way. "We enter heaven by prayer." 3. *Those around bid the one who cries hold his peace.* So speak the many to the one in earnest. Notice how often in the Gospels the disciples are represented as keeping back from Christ instead of helping to him (see ver. 15). They did not know the heart of God. And men do not know it still. There is often a "send away" in the minds of even the well-disposed. Earnestness meets discouragements where it least expects them. Cry on, thou who hast felt the breath of the passing Saviour. If those about thee are unsympathetic, throw thyself the more on thy Lord; the more they protest, cry thou the more, "Son of God, they will not take me up. Father and mother even forsake me. Thou, thou only art my hope. Make no tarrying, O my God."

II. THINK OF THE SAVIOUR, IN WHOM THE LIVING GOD IS REVEALED. 1. There is *the Christ-commandment.* "Bring him hither to me." It is the commandment to an often misunderstanding and misinterpreting Church. Christ has much to bear at the hand of the world; he has much also to bear at the hand of his Church. How frequently those who are his repel rather than attract, send away rather than bring! "Bring"—there is no gainsaying this charge. Instantly the tone of the multitude changes. Now it is, "Rise, be of good comfort; he calleth thee." And what alacrity in the Bartimæus-obedience! The old tattered garment connected with the past time of, it may have been, a sinful life is thrown away. There is no stopping to inquire how the blind can reach that blessed presence. He has called. In the call there is the pledge of a sufficient grace. O mirror of Divine condescension! O word, preparing for work, of power! "The blind, the poor, bring to me!" 2. There is *the Christ-question.* "What wilt thou that I shall do unto thee?" The question is put when the presence is reached. The presence is the help to the answer. Now, the great underlying want is expressed, "Lord, that I may receive my sight." Is it not the prayer of the human heart when the quickening presence of God is realized? It is to prepare for the revelation that the will is gently besieged. He cannot force; he can only draw. Stooping to thee, the person thou art, and as thou art, the word of grace and truth is, "What wilt thou?" 3. And then *the Christ-action.* "He touched the eyes," says St. Matthew. "Receive thy sight: thy faith hath saved thee," says St. Luke. His faith had been a trust in the dark. He could not make the light, but he could call for it. And he had called, he had pressed to Christ, awfully in earnest, unboundedly confident. The faith saved through what it did. It brought him to the Lord; and that is salvation. The first use of the new sight was to behold the Deliverer. The first face that wrote its image in the heart was the face of God in Christ. Saved, whole, because that face was formed in the heart of hearts, never more to fade from it. "I was blind; now I see." "Go thy way," says the Lord. "Nay, dearest Master, where thou goest I will go. Where thou dwellest I will dwell. Thy way is mine. Mine the new song which thou hast given. Thou hast touched my eyes—

"'And in that light of life I'll walk
Till travelling days are done.'"

HOMILIES BY VARIOUS AUTHORS.

Vers. 1—7.—*Continuance in prayer: Divine delay.* We have first to consider what is—

I. The ARGUMENT IN THE TEXT. It is one from the less to the greater, or rather from the unworthy to the worthy. If a bad man will, for a poor reason, accede to the request of one for whom he cares nothing, how much more certainly will the Righteous One himself, for a good reason, espouse the cause of those who are so dear to him! The reasons for confidence in God's faithfulness and interposition are therefore threefold. 1. If an unprincipled judge amongst men will finally do justice, assuredly the righteous Judge of all the earth will do so. His character is something which cannot fail; we may build on that as on the most solid rock. 2. If justice is granted by us for so poor a reason as that of fearing vexatious annoyance, surely God will listen and will respond to reverent and believing prayer. He is far more certain to be won by that in us which pleases him than is an unjust judge by that in his appellant which annoys him. And our approach to him in prayer, our reverent attitude, our faith in his goodness, our trust in his Word,—all this is very pleasing unto our Father. 3. If a man will yield a demand made by one to whom he does not feel himself related, and in whom he is absolutely uninterested, how confident we may be that God will interpose on behalf of those who, as his own sons and daughters, are dear to his parental heart, and who, collectively, constitute "his own elect"—those who are most tenderly and intimately related to him in Jesus Christ his Son!

II. The SERIOUS FACT OF THE DIVINE DELAY. "Though he bear long with them" (ver. 7), or, "and he delays [to interpose] in their cause" (Dr. Bruce). It is certain that, *from our point of view*, God does delay to vindicate his people; his answer does not come as soon as we expect it; it is held back so long that we are ready "to faint" (lose heart). Thus was it many times in the history of Israel; thus has it been frequently in the history of the Church of Christ. How many times have suffering bands of noble martyrs looked up piteously and despondently to heaven as they cried, "How long, O Lord, holy and true, dost thou not judge and avenge our blood?" Thus has it been in multitudes of individual instances; men have been oppressed, or they have been embarrassed, or they have been disappointed, or they have been otherwise afflicted; they have appealed to God for his delivering grace; and they have looked long in vain for the Divine response. They say, "O my God, I cry, . . . but thou hearest not" (Ps. xxii. 2).

III. The EXPLANATION THAT WILL BE FOUND. The time will come when we shall understand why God did delay to answer us. But we may be quite sure that when it comes it will be seen: 1. That it was not in him—not in his absence from us, nor his indifference to us, nor his unreadiness to help us. 2. That it was in us—in our unreadiness to receive his interposition, or in the misuse we should make of it, or in the greater and truer good to be gained by our patience than by our relief; and thus in the ultimate gain to our own well-being by his withholding.

IV. The BLESSED FACT THAT IT IS ONLY A DELAY. "I tell you that he will avenge them speedily." 1. It is probable that when God does manifest his power he will work speedy and overwhelming destruction to the guilty; he will avenge "speedily," *i.e.* quickly, instantaneously. "How are they brought into desolation, as in a moment! they are utterly consumed with terrors. As a dream when one awaketh; so, O Lord, when thou awakest, thou shalt despise their image" (Ps. lxxiii. 19, 20). 2. It is certain that in his own time and way God will defend his people, that he will relieve his children, that he will redeem and bless his "own elect." His faithfulness to his Word; his love for them that love him; his intimacy of relation to those who are "in Jesus Christ;"—this is a sure and absolute pledge that the appeal to him cannot be and will not be in vain. Men ought continuously, perseveringly, to pray, and never to lose heart. The day of Divine appearing is entered in the books of God.—C.

Ver. 8.—*Our unbelief.* "Nevertheless when the Son of man cometh, shall he find faith on the earth?" These words have no special reference, if they have any at all, to the condition of the world at the "second coming" of Christ. In order to understand and appreciate them, we must consider—

I. WHAT IS THE FORCE AND RANGE OF THIS EXPRESSION, "the coming of the Son of man." And it will be found on investigation that it signifies any special manifestation of God's power or any special appearance of Christ either in Person or in providence. This may be: 1. *In mercy;* including the Incarnation, when the Son of man came "not to destroy but to save" the world; the Resurrection, when he came in power and triumph from the other world; the Day of Pentecost, when he came in marvellous outpouring of Divine influence upon the world. 2. *In judgment;* including the destruction of Jerusalem; the day of death to each human being; the day of judgment itself, when "before him shall be gathered all nations."

II. WHAT IS THE APPLICATION OF IT IN THE TEXT. A widow appeals for redress against "her adversary" (the defendant) to an unprincipled judge. He puts her off until her importunity makes him listen and respond in order to save himself from annoyance. Arguing *à fortiori,* our Lord contends that God, the righteous Judge, will most certainly grant to his own people (children) the requests they make of him (see previous homily). But, continues the great Teacher, who had such a perfect insight into our nature, when he *does* that, and "comes" in judgment to his foes and in mercy to his friends, will he find his friends expecting him? will they be looking for his appearing? will their attitude be one of holy expectation, of instant recognition, and of devout thankfulness? or will they not, after all their asking, be positively surprised and even incredulous at his manifestation? He *will* come most assuredly, but when he comes, will he find faith on the earth?

III. WHAT ILLUSTRATIONS WE HAVE OF THE TRUTH OF IT. 1. We have two striking *scriptural* illustrations. (1) Christ's own coming, after his resurrection, to his disciples. Instead of looking for him and welcoming him, according to his word (ver. 33), they were astounded and incredulous (ch. xxiv. 11, 22, 23, 37). He did not "find faith" in them. (2) His coming in providential deliverance to Peter. When the Church had been praying without ceasing for him, they should have been hoping for a Divine visitation in response to their prayer. Nevertheless, when it came, were they not found unbelieving and astonished (Acts xii. 5, 15)? Are we much better than they? 2. Christ's coming *in judgment.* Such narrow and false interpretations as the Jews were apt to put upon sudden and sad calamities (ch. xiii. 1—4) we must scrupulously avoid. But when we see a man who has defied all laws, human and Divine, brought down into shame and ruin, or when we see a guilty empire which was founded on violence, sustained by force, and nourished in corruption, stricken down by defeat and reduced to dishonour and disaster, shall we be surprised as if a strange thing had happened? or shall we not rather feel that this is precisely what we had every reason to expect from the righteousness of the Divine Ruler? 3. Christ's coming *in grace and mercy.* When the Christian family, in answer to earnest and continued prayer, is just saved from serious embarrassment and perhaps from disgrace; when the Christian Church, after much pleading for God's Spirit, receives marked and manifest tokens of the presence and power of God in the midst of it; when the Christian teacher or preacher, as the issue of much devout and faithful work, finds many souls to be seeking the life which is of God;—is the attitude of that family, that Church, that teacher, one of calm expectation and devout acquiescence? or is it not rather one of surprise, if not even of incredulity? When we have been imploring the Son of man to come, and he comes at our appeal, does he find us awaiting and expecting him? Surely, with fuller and deeper faith on our part, there would be a more frequent coming on the part of our gracious Lord in life-giving power and blessing.—C.

Vers. 9—14.—*The Pharisee and the publican.* The scene indicated by our Lord's opening sentences is easily realized. We readily picture to our minds the place and the two persons in whom we are interested—the haughty Pharisee and the humble-minded publican. We readily imagine their demeanour as they enter, their posture as they pray, their reception as they pass through the courts going and returning. But we ask how and why was it that the Pharisee was rejected and the publican accepted. And in reply we say: 1. In some respects the two men stood on the same ground. Both were free from the taint of idolatry and were worshipping God; both appreciated the privilege of prayer; both came to the same building, and, using the same invocation, each uttered the uppermost thought in his mind. 2. In some aspects the Pharisee seemed to have the advantage. (1) He had the respect of the public, the good and God-fearing public, of the respectable people of his day; (2) he had lived the worthiest life in all social and political relations; (3) he was much the more "religious" of the two, in the sense that his habit of life was devout and charitable, while that of the publican had been godless and avaricious. 3. The terms of their respective prayers are not decisive of their acceptableness in the sight of God. (1) A truly humble man might speak to God in the strain, though not in the spirit, of the Pharisee. It is quite right to thank God for being preserved from presumptuous sins and being kept in the path of rectitude and devotion (see Ps. xli. 12, 13). (2) A thoroughly formal worshipper might present the petition of the publican. How often, since then, have these or very similar words been used by "penitents" who have been impenitent, by those who have taken the language of humility on their lip while they "have regarded iniquity in their heart"! A modern writer (T. T. Lynch) represents these two men as going up again to the temple; but this time the Pharisee, adopting the publican's form of words in hope of acceptance, is again rejected; while the publican, giving thanks to God for his reconciliation and renewal, is again accepted—

"For sometimes tears and sometimes thanks,
But only *truth* can please."

How, then, do we explain the fact that "this man went down to his house justified rather than the other"?

I. THE PHARISEE HAD FORMED A RADICALLY FALSE ESTIMATE of his own character, and the publican a true one of his. The Pharisee thought he was everything God wished him to be, and was miserably wrong in his estimate; he was reckoning that God cared chiefly if not exclusively for the outside in religion, that his favour was secured by ceremonies, by proprieties, by punctualities, by utterances of prescribed forms. He failed to understand that this was only the shell and not the kernel, and that the shell of correct behaviour is nothing without the kernel of a reverent and loving spirit. The publican, on the other hand, believed that he was very far from right with God; that he had been living a guilty life, and was condemned of God for so doing; and his thought was true.

II. THE PHARISEE'S FALSE ESTIMATE LED HIM INTO SELF-FLATTERY; the publican's true estimate into frank, penitential acknowledgment. Under the cover of gratitude, the one man paid himself handsome compliments, and held on high his great meritoriousness, thus confirming in his own mind the delusion that he was a favourite of Heaven; the other, moved by a deep sense of personal unworthiness, made honest confession of sin, and sought the mercy he knew he needed.

III. GOD HATES THE PROUD, AND HONOURS THE HUMBLE-HEARTED. Old and New Testaments may be said to be full of this truth. God has said and has repeated, he has most plainly and emphatically declared, that pride is odious and unpardonable in his sight; but that humility shall live before him (ver. 14; see also Ps. xxxii. 5; cxxxviii. 6; Prov. xxviii. 13; Isa. lvii. 15; Matt. v. 3; 1 Pet. v. 6; 1 John i. 8, 9). Here is: 1. *A message of solemn warning.* It concerns those who are the spiritual descendants of the Pharisee; who are satisfied with their spiritual condition but have no right to be so; who are building the hope of their hearts on things which are external, but in whom the love of God does not dwell. And here is: 2. *A message of gracious encouragement.* It concerns those who are burdened with a sense of sin and need not remain so. The way of mercy is open to every penitent soul. Jesus Christ is the "Propitiation for the sins of the whole world," and the grace of God in him far more than suffices for every guilty heart. In him we have forgiveness of sins; in him we have peace and hope and joy, even eternal life.—C.

Vers. 15, 16.—*Christ and the children: a sermon to children.* This familiar and attractive scene is well conceived and described in the lines commencing, "Over the hills of Jordan." It contains valuable lessons for the young.

I. THE KINDLINESS OF JESUS CHRIST. Some kind men are not kindly. They will do a great deal for you, will give much to you, will run serious risks or even make serious sacrifices on your behalf; but they are not gracious, genial, winning. They are not *approachable*; you are not drawn to them; you are not inclined to address them and make friends with them; they rather repel than invite you. Such was *not* Jesus Christ. He was not only kind at heart, but kindly in manner and in bearing. The children of his day went freely and gladly to him. That "he was never seen to smile" is a wholly unauthorized and, we may be quite sure, an entirely false statement. Did he not take those infants into his arms with a smile upon his face? Did he not frequently, ay, *constantly*, smile as he looked upon innocency, upon hopefulness, upon childhood? Think of Jesus Christ as not only the kind but the kindly One, as not only the good but the gracious One, as not only the wise but the winning One. Think of him as that One to whom, if he were with us now as he was with men of old, you would be drawn with an irresistible attraction, and to whom you could, without any effort, unburden your heart. And believe that just what he was on earth he is in heaven.

II. Jesus Christ still receives us to the shelter of his loving power. He took them up into his arms. The arms of the parent are the place of shelter to the child; to them in all time of danger or of distress he naturally and eagerly resorts. It is the place of strength, of defence, of succour. But youth needs more than human sympathy and help; it needs a refuge in Divine tenderness and power. It does so always; but more particularly when parental care is lost, because the parents themselves have "passed into the skies." Very seriously is this need felt when parental care is *left behind*, when youth or young manhood goes forth from the shelter of the home. Then how priceless is the shelter of the loving power of the Divine Friend! In that unknown "world" which lies beyond the home-life are perils that cannot be anticipated, and that are all unknown. Take care to secure the invaluable refuge of the Divine arm; for only in the protection of the all-wise Leader and almighty Friend will safety be found.

III. Jesus Christ still lays his hand upon us. Mark tells us (x. 16) that he "put his hands upon them, and blessed them." You still sing, "I wish that his hands had been laid on my head." It is a right and becoming thought. But the laying of the hand of flesh on those children's heads may not have wrought any great spiritual change in them; they may have grown up to reject him. Of far more consequence is it that Christ should now lay the hand of his Divine power and grace upon your heart; that he should so act upon you by his Divine Spirit that your mind should be illumined, and that you understand what is the good and the wise thing to do; that your heart should be touched so that you will live to love him who is worthiest of all that is best. "His touch has still its ancient power." Yes; and more than the healing touch which gave sight to the blind and wholeness to the poor leper is that benignant power which opens the closed mind and cleanses the unholy heart.

IV. Jesus looks and waits for your submission. He says that it is *you* who, of all people, can most readily enter his holy kingdom. He must have your free and full consent. When he made the world, and sent the sun on its course, and gave to the sea its bounds, "he spake, and it was done; he commanded, and it stood fast." He *compels* all things in nature to do his bidding; but he *asks*, he *invites* your trust, your worship, your love. He cannot bless you as he would unless you consent to receive him as your own personal Lord and Saviour and Friend. But he assures you that this is open to you as it is not to others; the young can readily give their attention, their docility, their love, their obedience. Fewer and slighter hindrances are in your way than are in the path of those who have travelled further. Of such as you are now "is the kingdom of God." This is the golden chance of your life.—C.

Ver. 17.—*The child of man and the kingdom of God.* Jesus Christ not only opened the gate of his kingdom to the little child as he opened his arms to the little children whom the mothers of Judah brought to him; he also took the little child as a type of the true disciple. He taught us that if we wish to enter his kingdom, our spirit must be the child-spirit. "Whosoever shall not receive the kingdom of God *as*," etc. And what is this spirit? It is that of—

I. Docility, or readiness to accept what is told us. The ideal child is teachable; it will learn because it is ready to receive; it has not found out the way of distrust and of rejection; it takes in the light, the truth, which is offered and it grows thereby. Men of mature years and powers, who have had all the advantages of Christian privileges, often stand without the kingdom because they will not receive the truth that is offered them; their mind is preoccupied with theories, systems, imaginations, of their own. They seem to know much; they believe they know much, for they are familiar with some things of which many (perhaps most) are ignorant; they could easily puzzle their neighbours by asking questions which these could not answer; they have a number of facts and laws, and a much larger number of names at their command; they "seem to be wise" (1 Cor. iii. 18). But their knowledge is very small in comparison with all that has to be acquired; it is partly (largely) local, temporary, evanescent (1 Cor. xiii. 8); it is nothing to the wisdom of God. It becomes them, as it becomes us all, to feel toward God as our little children feel towards us—to cherish a spirit of docility. How much more he has to tell us than we have to teach them! How much greater is our ignorance in his sight than theirs is in ours! He who will not accept the doctrine of the Divine Fatherhood; he who will not yield himself to a Divine Saviour; he who will not pursue the path of holy service, hoping to find at the end of it a heavenly home,—because this does not square with some favourite theories, or because it transcends the range of some intellectual faculties, cannot enter the kingdom of truth, and therefore shuts himself out of the kingdom of God. We shall fail to stand on the first rung of the ladder that reaches heavenly wisdom unless we realize that we are all of us but very little children in the presence of our Father, and unless with docile spirit we come to his feet and say, "Lord, we are very ignorant; wilt thou teach us?"

"Lead us, O Father, in the path of truth;
Unhelped by thee, in error's maze we grope."

II. SIMPLICITY. The little child (of our thought and our affection) is simple, transparent, sincere; he says just what is in his mind, does not pretend he is naughty when he believes himself to be good—is *real*. This God demands of us—"truth in the inward parts," sincerity of spirit. It does not further our cause with him to affect a piety that is not genuine; to simulate a penitence of which our heart knows nothing; to use the language of humility while pride is reigning within. He would rather we tell him just what we feel, just what we are, than adopt the most appropriate confessions or petitions. We must be like the children of our home; we must mean what we say when we draw nigh to him.

III. TRUSTFULNESS. Christianity is a religion which centres in a Person, in one Divine Being. "He that believeth in me," "that abideth in me,"—that is the prevailing note. Trust in Jesus Christ as the Teacher, Saviour, Sovereign of the human soul, is the way of life. He who has that stands within "the kingdom of God." Where shall we learn *to trust*? Is it not of the little child? As the child flees for refuge to its parent's arms, confides itself and all it has or hopes for to its parent's wisdom and love, so the human soul is invited to commit itself and all its everlasting interests to the Almighty Saviour, to say with implicit, childlike confidence and self-surrender—

"Jesus, Refuge of my soul,
Let me to thy bosom fly."

C.

Vers. 18—22.—*The golden chance: a sermon to the young.* Many features combine to make this incident one of peculiar interest.

I. THE PRINCIPAL ACTOR IN THE SCENE A YOUNG MAN. Matthew tells us this quite incidentally (xix. 22), but it adds great interest to the occurrence. For our hearts are drawn towards youth. Youth is innocent, ingenuous, frank, trustful, hopeful, loving. There is, moreover, some mystery about it. We know what the old man has been; we know what the man of middle life will be; but of youth we cannot tell; it may accomplish great things; it is covered with the delicate buds, with the beautiful flowers of promise.

II. A YOUNG MAN OF WEALTH AND INFLUENCE. This might not make him more interesting to Christ; but it does to us. The rich young heir may be of no more intrinsic worth than the beggar by the wayside; but because he is the heir of fortune, we care about him, we watch his career; we are specially glad if he takes a wise course, and are specially grieved if he goes astray.

III. A YOUNG MAN WITH SOME OF THE NOBLER QUALITIES OF YOUTH. 1. We note *his reverence.* Youth should be reverent. Ignorance and inexperience should pay to knowledge and wisdom the regard which is their due. We like this young man because he saw in that homeless Teacher a wisdom superior to his own, and came and prostrated himself before him in becoming homage. 2. We note *his ardour.* He came running (Mark x. 17) to meet and to learn of Christ. Youth should be, as in the person of this inquirer it was—eager, ardent, enthusiastic, sanguine of good things. 3. We note *his religiousness.* "Heaven lies about us in our infancy," etc. Youth is the time when heavenly visions are most and best seen; when Divine claims, spiritual realities, are strongest and clearest to the soul; then "life eternal" has the deepest meaning. So was it with him. To him life held something larger and better than all his lands and houses; other and higher voices than those of debtors and stewards reached his ear; he had a vision of a holy service in which he might be engaged; of a Divine life he might be living; and running in his eagerness, and kneeling in his reverence, he looked up into the face of Christ and said, "Good Master, what good thing shall I do, that I may have eternal life?"

IV. A YOUNG MAN IN THE PRESENCE OF CHRIST, exciting his special interest. A young man, with his life before him and a soul not yet stained by the evil which is in the world, standing in the very presence of him who knew what human life might include and what the human soul was worth, who could tell him how to enlarge the one and how to ennoble the other, and who (Mark x. 21) took a tender and loving interest in this earnest spirit,—what could we have more profoundly interesting than this?

V. JESUS CHRIST REVEALING TO HIM THE TRUE STATE OF HIS HEART. Our Lord's treatment of inquirers differed much; it was, no doubt, determined by the state of their heart, *as he alone knew it.* He replied to this young man as he did, because he wished him to know where he actually stood; he wished to show him that, in order to be prepared to lay hold on eternal life, it was not only necessary to have such sincerity as he had, and such earnestness as he had, but such earnestness as would make him ready to yield everything to the Lord of his life; *and that this he had not.* So, after leading him up to the point, he said, "Sell all that thou hast," etc. And then the inquirer knew that he lacked one thing—one essential thing; he wanted that thoroughness of purpose toward God which made self-surrender possible to him. It was a glorious, golden chance, then used or then lost when this interview was held. It must have been *the crisis of his career,* on which everything hung for all the future. Similar in its nature, though not alike in its circumstances, is the opportunity offered to each one of us. 1. All the life of Christian privilege is the golden chance of our existence. "Now is the accepted time," the period when everything is open to us, when a noble and immortal future stretches out before us and is within our power. 2. Youth is the golden chance of life. It is in the days that are now passing, when the heart is warm, and the mind is open, and the conscience tender, and the life unburdened and unembarrassed, that Christ should be approached and his lasting friendship gained. 3. The day of Divine visitation is the golden chance of youth—that day when the truth and the grace of Jesus Christ are most powerfully felt, and a voice from heaven is heard saying of the path of life, "This is the way: walk ye in it."—C.

Ver. 24.—*Wealth and piety.* Wherein lies *the* difficulty of a rich man entering the kingdom? This young ruler shrank from parting with his property; but Jesus Christ does not ordinarily ask men of wealth to "sell all that they have, and give to the poor." His difficulty, therefore, is not the common one. 1. It is not that the rich man is not as welcome to the friendship of Christ as the poor man. He does not make distinctions in his invitation, or in his desire that men should come to him. In him in whom is neither male nor female, bond nor free, there is neither rich nor poor. The poor as much as the rich, and also *the rich as much as the poor,* are the objects of his love and of his seeking. The Lord of our nature regards us, and concerns himself for us, not on account of our circumstances, but because he knows the value of our souls. 2. Not because the rich man cannot illustrate the distinctive graces of Christianity.

The sale and distribution of property in apostolic times was an expedient which was adopted for the occasion; but it was not insisted upon as necessary even then (Acts v. 4), and it was very soon abandoned. Paul, writing to Timothy, wrote on the supposition that the Christian Church included many wealthy men (1 Tim. vi.). Every age and every country has witnessed the lives of wealthy Christian men, who have illustrated every grace that the great Teacher has commended. It is clear that a rich man *may be* as humble, as generous, as temperate, as pure, as devout, as any poor man can be; and he sometimes *is* so. The explanation of our Lord's language is found in the fact that *riches are apt to put a serious obstacle* in the way of entrance into the kingdom. If we would find our way into that holy and blessed kingdom, it is necessary that we should have a sense of our personal emptiness and need. We come to Christ to be filled with his fulness, to be enriched by his grace and love. He is a Physician, and it is they who feel that they are sick that are likely to apply for his healing power. He is the Divine Source of all wealth and enrichment (Rev. iii. 18), and they must know themselves to be poor who come to buy of him gold that they may become rich. Hence the difficulty. It is for this reason that—

I. A MAN WHOSE MIND IS FULL OF KNOWLEDGE finds it hard to receive distinctive Christian truth. He is rich, as compared with his fellows, in the acquisition of knowledge. He is proud of this possession of his, and is bent on making the most of it. Jesus Christ comes to him, and says that he must lay aside his own views and notions, and sit at his feet and receive the truth he brings to him from God. Then the "rich" man has to sacrifice his favourite theories, has to make nothing of his learning, that he may admit to his mind the wisdom that is from above; and he finds it very "hard" to do this.

II. A MAN WHO IS CLOTHED WITH HONOUR finds it hard to take a very humble view of himself. For honour is an order of wealth, and one that is highly prized. But the natural and common effect of it is to lead those who are the objects of it to form a flattering view of themselves; it is hard to get them to believe that in God's sight they may be as sinful as those held in very much less regard by their fellow-men. But the ground on which human souls must come to Christ is that of humility. "Blessed are the poor in spirit : for *theirs* is the kingdom of heaven."

III. A MAN WHOSE CHAMBERS ARE FULL OF TREASURE is tempted to seek his satisfaction in the lower good. We have to make our choice, as Divine truth is presented to us, whether we will live for the service of Christ or for our own personal enjoyment and aggrandizement. To the poor, to the afflicted, to the suffering, to those who know they have not long to live, the temptation to live for this present world is not so strong; on their ear the overtures of the gospel of grace fall as that very thing they need for their comfort and their peace; they have little to surrender, they have much to gain. But to those to whom every avenue of enjoyment is open; to those who may look hopefully, perhaps confidently, for place, for power, for society, for pleasure, for honour,—the inducement is very strong and urgent to cast in their lot with those "whose portion is in this life." Many voices very close to their ear, very clear and convincing, call for their strength to be given to the material rather than the spiritual, to the temporal rather than the eternal, to the human rather than the Divine; and it is "hard" for them to resist and to overcome. 1. Let poverty find its ample consolation in the accessibility of the riches that always satisfy and never flee. 2. Let those who know neither poverty nor riches thank God for the happy mean in which his providence has placed them—not subjecting them to the temptations of either. 3. Let wealth beware lest it make a sad, a supreme, mistake; lest, in the great spiritual strife, it—

"Clutch the tinsel gilding, and let go the crown of life."

C.

Vers. 28, 29 (comp. Mark. x. 29, 30).—*Christ's estimate of a Christian life.* It is certain that no literalist could ever understand Jesus Christ. Men of this order of mind utterly failed to understand him in his own time (see particularly John vi. 41—46), and they are equally at fault to-day. It is clearly impossible to give a literal interpretation to these words of the Lord; the facts of the case do not permit it. But going to the heart of this Divine utterance, we understand that any one who for Christ's sake suffers the loss of kindred and of worldly goods, shall have that which, in the sight of

God and in the light of his truth, *is worth* a hundred times more than any human or earthly blessings can be. We shall better see the truthfulness of this declaration if we approach the main thought from a little distance, and consider that *human life is something the value of which depends not on the quantity but on the kind of it.* A small quantity of human life outweighs in value a large amount of animal life. A very small portion of the higher human life transcends in value a large extent of lower human life. "Better fifty years of Europe than a cycle of Cathay." Bailey has well written—

> "Life's more than breath and the quick round of blood ;
> It is a great spirit and a busy heart.
> We live in deeds, not years ; in thoughts, not breaths;
> In feelings, not in figures on a dial.
> We should count time by heart-throbs. He most lives
> Who thinks most, feels the noblest, acts the best."

And there is wisdom as well as strength in the lines—

> "One crowded hour of glorious life
> Is worth an age without a name."

Lifting up this truth to the spiritual level of the teaching of Jesus Christ, we find that in such a life as that which is *of* him and *in* him—for the attainment of which we may have to make very great sacrifices—

I. THERE IS AN ELEVATED AND TRANSPORTING JOY experienced in the very endurance of persecution; and this alone goes far towards fulfilling the Saviour's word. This statement is simply historical. The apostles returned from the council, condemned and severely scourged, "rejoicing that they were counted worthy to suffer shame for his Name." Paul and Silas sang the praises of God in the darkness and foulness of a Philippian dungeon. And under every sky since then, men and women, old and young and in the midst of life, have gone to the dungeon and to the stake and to the open grave in which they were to be buried alive, not with tears in their eyes and lamentations on their tongues, but with songs of praise upon their lips, and with keen, exultant triumph in their hearts. To-day there is far more of real and lasting joy to be found under the roof of the missionary compound than in the palatial buildings of European capitals, profounder and more lasting satisfaction in the self-sacrificing labours of the evangelist than in the lounging idleness of the sons and daughters of fashion and of pleasure.

II. IN TRUE DISCIPLESHIP THERE ARE SOURCES OF JOY which altogether outweigh any losses that may be entailed by fidelity. Some people know just enough of "religion " to find it a weariness, a burden, an anxiety. This is neither piety nor policy ; it does not secure God's favour, and it gives no satisfaction to them. But the true and thorough servant of Jesus Christ, heartily surrendering himself to his Divine Redeemer, and devotedly engaging in his service, has "manifold more " of blessedness than he loses by anything with which he parts. He has (1) the favour, the forgiving and abiding love of God his Father; his lifelong, his unfailing friendship; (2) happy, holy fellowship with Jesus Christ, and, through him, with the true and pure and good amongst men ; (3) a share in that holy service, outside of which is no rectitude for man, in which is rightness and wisdom, and therefore peace and joy; (4) the luxury, the blessedness of usefulness, of doing good and communicating, of being a source of strength and healing to the poor and needy ; (5) "And in the world to come *eternal life:* " not the lingering and lasting shadows into which Greek and Roman shrank from descending ; not the uninviting *sheôl* of the Hebrews; but everlasting day, eternal life—life in its fulness, its freedom, its blessedness, its glory, life never ceasing but enlarging and unfolding evermore. What commanding, convincing, constraining reasons are here for choosing the Master's service ! What is it that he asks us to surrender for his sake ? Anything in the way of profit, or pleasure, or companionship? Perhaps something in these ways. But what we gain by accepting him as Saviour and Friend is a thousand times more precious than all that we can be called upon to renounce. Even here and now God gives to us *far* more than he takes from us ; and, beside this, in the world to come is "eternal life." We may well do as Peter said he and his associates had done —leave all to follow Christ.—C.

Vers. 31—34.—*God's concealing kindness, etc.* The clear prevision which the Lord Jesus Christ had of the future which was before him may suggest to us the thought—

I. GOD'S KINDNESS IN CONCEALMENT. We often try to forecast the future, and sometimes wish that we could do so less imperfectly than we can. But our very inability to do this is to us a valuable shield that saves us from great unhappiness. For who of us would care to proceed at all if he knew all the sorrowful experiences through which his path would lie? We sometimes feel a humane satisfaction that the sheep and cattle that browse so contentedly to-day in the field have not their short enjoyment marred by any expectation of the slaughter-house they are to enter to-morrow. And we may well be thankful that so thick a veil hangs over our future, that we cannot possibly tell what are the troubles that will befall us, or where our life will be darkened with its deeper shadows. Even when, as with Paul, we know that "bonds and afflictions abide us," still, like him, we do "*not* know the things that will befall us" then. And whilst, on the one hand, we very commonly have enough of premonition to make desirable preparation for coming evil, on the other hand our life is so ordered that we go happily and hopefully on our way, untroubled by the evils which are in front of us but which are mercifully hidden from our view.

II. OUR LORD'S LEADERSHIP IN THE EXPERIENCE OF APPREHENSION. Our happy inability to anticipate the future is not the whole of the truth, though it is a large part of it. It remains true that there is a considerable amount of apprehension in the structure of our life. There are times when we clearly foresee some trial ahead of us. We may not know precisely the time of its arrival, nor the elements of which it will be composed. But we can tell that "our hour is coming." Before us, at no great distance, is suffering, is separation, is loss, is loneliness, is heart-ache. The road we are travelling along will soon descend, and we shall go down into the darkly shaded valley. Of that we have no doubt; and our spirit trembles, our heart is full of foreboding and, perchance, misgiving. How shall we pass through that dark valley? How bravely or how weakly, how worthily or how unbecomingly, shall we undergo that experience when it comes? There are many sources of encouragement to which we might resort. But this passage speaks to us of one of the best of them. Christ has gone this way before us—this way of keen and anxious apprehension. He knew that the most trying experiences were only a little way in front of him. He knew that the last extremity of human hatred and of human cruelty would be visited upon him. The Jews would condemn him with all their malignity, and the Gentiles would maltreat him with all their disdainful and powerful heartlessness. The sad and shameful future immediately before him stood clear to his sight, clearer far than any coming sorrow can shape itself to us. Therefore we may feel that: 1. We are treading in the footsteps of our Lord, and it is enough for the disciple to be as his Master. 2. We may be confident of his tenderest and fullest sympathy. He has suffered just what we are suffering now. 3. He will help us in our time of need. As he himself sought of man the succour he did not find, and was glad to receive from heaven the comfort he did not ask (Mark xiv. 34, 37; and ch. xxii. 43), we may be well assured that he will not refuse us all the aid we need and ask of him when the trial-hour of our experience shall have come.

III. THE DIFFICULTY OF DISCIPLESHIP—TO LEARN UNWELCOME TRUTH. There was no inherent incomprehensibleness in the words Christ here employed; yet "they understood none of these things." Why did they not comprehend such intelligible language? Because the truth conveyed was so exceedingly unwelcome. It cut across all their cherished hopes respecting the Messiah; it dashed their natural expectations to the ground; and it went sorely against all that their affection prompted them to believe and cherish. "It could not, must not, did not mean *that*," they said in their hearts. It is not the strangeness nor the profundity of truth which is too much for us; it is its *remoteness from that on which we have set our heart.* We do not understand that which clashes with our prejudices, or our passions, or our affections. The apostles of Christ would have saved themselves from many hours of awful sorrow and abject hopelessness and painful incredulity, if their feelings had allowed them to understand the truth which their Master put so plainly and so repeatedly before them (Matt. xvi. 21; xvii. 22; xx. 17). Can it be that Jesus Christ is saying something to us which we ought to understand, but do not because it is unwelcome to our hearts, or because it is at variance with all our old and strong habits of thought? Is it possible that he is calling us to repentance, to self-surrender, to a full confession of our faith, to a nobler life, to some field of active work, and we do not understand what he is saying to us? Where his own apostles so greatly failed, may not we be found at fault? Shall we leave it to future darkness and a great surprise and a mortifying discovery of error to set us straight? Or shall we not rather recognize in time our liability to mistake; seek to have an open mind to receive all his holy will concerning us; ask God to help us to remove the bandages of prejudice and of earthly attachments from the eyes of our understanding; seek by docility and devoutness of spirit to be such disciples of the Master that, when he speaks even unwelcome truth to us, we shall understand him and obey?—C.

Ver. 37.—*Present but passing opportunity.* Pathetic stories are told of those who, in circumstances of the greatest danger or distress, have suddenly found themselves almost within reach of blessed deliverance, but who just failed to realize their hope. It is the captive knight past whose dungeon a friendly host is filing, and the sound of the clarion drowns his pleading cries; or it is the shipwrecked sailor on the lonely island whose laboriously constructed signal the ship that is homeward bound does not descry, and who sees his one chance of rescue vanishing away. Those who have never known a supreme misfortune, together with a possibility, which was only a possibility, of deliverance, cannot realize the thrilling and all but intolerable suspense of such moments of present but passing opportunity as Bartimæus now knew. He was blind, helpless, shut out from all the sights and nearly all the enjoyments of human life; his lot was of the darkest and the saddest; and there was passing by One who could turn darkness into day, dreariness and gloom into blessedness and beauty, if only he could win his ear and make his plea. This glorious Healer was within a few paces of him, would soon be actually in front of him, would all too soon be gone beyond his call. "Jesus of Nazareth was *passing by!*" We see here—
I. THE SORENESS OF OUR SPIRITUAL NEED. We are blind, helpless, suffering the worst privations, under the dominion of sin. We recognize not our Father, our brethren, our true selves, our true opportunities, our chief perils, our real interests; and our blindness is not only immeasurably reducing the value of our present life, but is leading us to that which is darker still and sadder far.
II. THE NEAR PRESENCE OF JESUS CHRIST. A Divine Deliverer is at hand. Quite near to us, within reach of our voice, within touch of our hand, is One who can open our eyes and make us see clearly all that we need to know. At our very door is One who is not only ready at our entreaty, but even prepared already and eager to supply all our need. Here is One who offers to: 1. Enlighten our mind. 2. Restore the relationship to God our Father we have lost by our sin. 3. Constitute himself our almighty and unchanging Friend and Guide through all our life. 4. Conduct us and receive us to a heavenly home.
III. THE PASSING OF PRESENT OPPORTUNITY. This priceless chance is ours to-day; but how long will it remain within our reach? Jesus of Nazareth is near, but he is passing. 1. We know nothing of Christian privilege beyond the grave, and our life is hastening on; it may close at any hour, and it is hurrying away on the swift wings of duty and of pleasure. 2. The favoured period of youth is still more transient. Christ is very near us in the golden days of youth, when the spiritual nature is so open and so responsive; but how fast these days are fleeing! how soon will they be gone! 3. The hour of special grace and of rare privilege is but an hour—that time when Heaven puts forth its most constraining influences, and we see and feel that the gates into the kingdom of God are opened wide for our entrance. We cannot afford to delay when Jesus of Nazareth is near us. When eternal life is within our grasp, we must compel every other interest to take the second place; and this, not only because it is of such transcendent value, but because we may never have so golden an opportunity again. There is "a tide" in the history of every man which leads on to something more than "fortune;" it leads *unto life*—the life that is Divine and everlasting. On no account whatever must *that* be "omitted." Foolish beyond all reckoning, as well as guilty before God, is the soul that lets Jesus of Nazareth pass by without seeking his feet and finding his favour.—C.

Ver. 41.—*What we want of Christ.* Our hearts are drawn towards blind Bartimæus; we compassionate him for his long-continued blindness; we enter into his feeling of keen hopefulness when he hears of the passing of Jesus Christ; we like the importunity of the man, his sturdy refusal to be put down by popular clamour; we like also his manly directness in reply to the question asked him, "Lord, that I may receive my sight!" We owe him some gratitude in that it was his necessity which provided our Lord with one more opportunity of illustrating his power and his pity, and of carrying on the great redemptive work he came to accomplish. For these miracles he wrought were a part, and a valuable part, of that work of his. If apprised of less value than they once were, they are very far indeed from being valueless. And amongst other things they illustrate Christ's *personal* dealing with men. As he did not heal in troops and companies but addressed himself to each individual man or woman that was sick or suffering, blind or lame, so does he now make his appeal to each individual heart, and say to this man and to that man, "What wilt *thou* that I shall do unto thee?" And what *do* we want of him, as he thus approaches us?

I. THOSE WHO WANT NOTHING IN PARTICULAR. They meet with their neighbours to worship him and to hear about him, but they have no sense of need in their hearts; their souls are not suffering and smarting under a painful sense of sin; their hearts are not athirst for the living God and Saviour. They wish for "bread enough," but it is not the bread of life for which they hunger; they would like much to be wealthy, but they are not careful to be "rich toward God."

II. THOSE WHO WANT NOTHING OF CHRIST NOW. The time will come when they will be glad of a Saviour and Friend—some future hour of sorrow, or difficulty, or loneliness, and certainly the hour of death; they would like to keep open the line of communication, but at present they do not feel that they want anything of the great Healer of hearts. But let us look rather at—

III. WHAT WE ALL DO REALLY WANT OF HIM. If our Divine Father is not to be disappointed in us, if our lives on earth are not to be miserable failures, then may we all urge, with this blind man, "Lord, that we may receive our sight!" For it is essential to the life of our life that we should be enlightened upon: 1. The transcendent value of the human spirit, and thus understand of how much more value we ourselves are than any of our earthly surroundings, or than the body which is our temporary residence. 2. The intimate and tender relation in which we stand to God. That God is the one Being with whom we have to do, from whom we cannot withhold our love and service without doing him and ourselves the greatest wrong, who is "earnestly remembering" and patiently seeking us in our distance and estrangement. 3. The supreme and abiding blessedness of the service of Christ; that this is the soul's only true rest and portion, its peace and its inheritance. We want that these great saving truths should stand out before the eyes of our soul as *the* solid and living facts, in comparison with which all other things are of small account; we want to recognize in them *the* great verities which alone will satisfy and save us. If we would that Christ should do this for us, we must remember that what he is saying to us is this: (1) "Learn of me;" (2) "Believe in me;" "Have faith in me;" (3) "Abide in me;" (4) "Follow me."—C.

Vers. 1—14.—*Lessons in prayer.* Our Lord, in the two parables composing the present passage, gives the disciples encouragement to pray. The one brings out the need of perseverance and importunity in prayer; the other brings out the spirit of self-abasement which should be cultivated in prayer. They are thus linked together as twin lessons in the art of prayer.

I. LET US NOTICE THE NEEDFUL IMPORTUNITY OF GOD'S ELECT AS ILLUSTRATED BY THE IMPORTUNATE WIDOW. (Vers. 1—8.) The story is about an earthly judge of unscrupulous character, to whom a widow in her weakness, but with a deep sense of injury, appeals for redress. The weak woman is able by her importunity to extort from the heartless judge the redress which he would give on no other conditions. He even becomes facetious and humorous over it, and declares that he will avenge her, lest "by her continual coming she *strike* me." Having related this story, our Lord makes certain deductions from it. And: 1. *He declares that at his coming there will be little faith in his advent.* (Ver. 8.) Now, this unbelief about his advent can be accounted for on several grounds. (1) The procession of nature is so uniform. All things seem to continue as they were from the creation. Nature is on so large and grand a scale that we do not appreciate the real progress, and imagine that we are in the midst of a standstill. Uniformity, however, is *not* standstill. (2) Hope deferred will make many hearts sick. And so what has been so long talked of and yet has never appeared will be thought at last as never to appear. And (3) stoicism will lead many just to take things as they are, and entertain no concern about any change. It is astonishing how easy-going people tolerate manifest wrongs rather than take the trouble either to pray about them or to work for their removal. But: 2. *Our Lord acknowledges the wrong to which his elect ones have been exposed.* Their cry is for justice, for redress, like the widow. Now, our Lord admits that his people have not got justice from the world. The world has not been worthy of them. The world has made them time after time martyrs. It is a great assurance that the Lord acknowledges his servants' wrongs. 3. *He intimates at the same time that, like the widow, they will need importunity.* The one weapon must be wielded and wielded incessantly. He keeps us waiting doubtless for our good. If we got all the moment we asked it, how should we ever learn patience? But: 4. *He promises a sudden redress.* The idea seems to be not "speedily" but "suddenly" he will avenge them. It will be a sharp and decisive deliverance when it comes. We thus see that all life's discipline is planned to stimulate prayer. And when we have least taste for it, we should, like Luther, pray on. This is the importunity the Lord loves and will answer.

II. LET US NOTICE THE SPIRIT OF SELF-ABASEMENT WHICH SHOULD CHARACTERIZE OUR PRAYER AS ILLUSTRATED IN THE PARABLE OF THE PHARISEE AND THE PUBLICAN. (Vers. 9—14.) And in this second story we have a Pharisee first presented whose prayer is an outburst of self-confidence. He thanks God that he is so much better than his neighbours. For in these he recognizes extortioners, unjust men, and adulterers. A self-righteous spirit is censorious; its prayer is a criticism; even a publican's modesty in standing afar off, and his contrition in smiting on his breast, are set down to his disparagement. Then the Pharisee can congratulate himself on fasting twice a week, and on giving tithes of all he possesses. But he was not a bit the better for all this so-called prayer, this bit of blatant self-praise. On the other hand, the publican, though he remained afar off and hardly ventured to look up, but smote on his breast and cried, "God be merciful to me a sinner!" went down to his house a happier and better man. For the important point is not their *consciousness*, but God's attitude towards their respective spirits. To the one spirit God responds by justification and a sense of acceptance. The other is sent empty away. Hence the principles Jesus deduces are twofold. 1. *Self-exaltation always precedes abasement.* The proud will sooner or later get his fall. The Pharisaic spirit is always humiliated in the end. The man who is filled with self-satisfaction is only demonstrating his own self-ignorance and distance from God and his great ideal. 2. *Self-abasement always leads to exaltation.* It is when we feel "as a beast" before God, like Asaph in the seventy-third psalm, that we are on the way to spiritual rapture. For God has provided for the abased sinner the *pardon* he needs, and, besides the pardon, *sanctification and everlasting progress.* Let us, then, pray in the penitential key continually, and let us pray determined not to be denied; and heights of spiritual exaltation and rapture will be seen rising from our very feet, and inviting us to sit down on them with Jesus.— R. M. E.

Vers. 15—30.—*The children of the kingdom.* During the progress of the King towards Jerusalem, his personal influence and benediction were greatly valued. It would seem that mothers brought their children to him to be blessed, and ended by producing the very little ones. The disciples thought the line should be drawn somewhere, and so ventured to forbid the anxious mothers, only, however, to receive the significant rebuke from him, "Suffer little children to come unto me, and forbid them not: for of such is the kingdom of God." We are thus introduced to the important principle that—

I. CHILDLIKENESS IS THE QUALIFICATION FOR GOD'S KINGDOM. (Vers. 15—17.) Now, that is only another way of stating that God's government is paternal, and that his subjects are sons. It is, in fact, "a mighty family" of which he is himself the Head.

It is when we recognize in him our Father, and are prepared to accept as little children all he sends, and to do all he commands, that we truly belong to his kingdom. Hence the two characteristics specially brought out are (1) *trust*, and (2) *obedience*. It is thus we are to test ourselves. Do we *trust* God our Father as little children trust their fathers according to the flesh? and do we *obey* our heavenly Father as little ones obey their earthly parents? Then are we in the kingdom.

II. CHRIST EXPECTS THE RICHEST RULER TO TRUST AND TO OBEY HIM LIKE A LITTLE CHILD. (Vers. 18—27.) We have here an interesting case of anxiety, and how Christ dealt with it. And here we have to notice that: 1. *Neither his wealth nor his position satisfied the young ruler.* Something more was needed. The heart cannot content itself with either rank or gold. Hence his anxiety to lay hold on eternal life, which he felt was something more than he had yet obtained. 2. He fancied he could *entitle himself to it by a stroke of public service.* Hence his inquiry, "Good Master, what shall I *do* to inherit eternal life?" His notion was that he could claim it as a right, if he could only find out the additional duty he felt able to discharge. 3. *Jesus destroys with a single stroke his overestimate of human nature.* The flattery of human nature coincides with self-esteem. The young ruler believed in his own goodness and capabilities, and he complimented Jesus as "good Master," because he believed in the existence of any number of good men—himself, of course, included. Now, Jesus will not accept a false compliment. Human nature is *not* good; and it is not as a mere man that he is going to receive such flattery. Hence he tells the ruler that there is no mere man good; that God alone is good. There is here no repudiation of goodness as belonging to himself, but simply a repudiation of goodness as an attribute of unaided humanity. 4. Jesus insists on *examination of past conduct in the light of the Divine Law.* He asks the young ruler if he has kept the second table of the Decalogue, and been dutiful to his fellow-men. Looked at from without, the self-sufficient mind imagines it is a simple thing to keep the Law. But when for "law" we substitute "love," the self-examination does not so assure us. Meanwhile the young ruler is strong in the belief that he has kept the whole Law. 5. *Jesus now demands, as a test of his trust in him, the surrender of his riches to the poor, and the subsequent following of him.* The demand was for faith. When we consider that Jesus was apparently but a poor artisan, then, unless the young ruler would absolutely and implicitly trust him, he would never think of obeying his demand. The result proved that he was not yet ready to trust Jesus. He trusted his money more! Hence his sorrow as he leaves the Lord. And herein lies the money-danger. It bids for the trust of the soul. Moneyed men find it hard to trust any one more than money. They think it only natural that they should feel independent. But if money leads men away from Jesus, it is a curse, and not a blessing. When tempted to be covetous, let us remember that money has its special dangers, and makes it harder and even impossible for some to enter into God's kingdom. 6. *Jesus, while stating the difficulty which rich men find in entering God's kingdom, shows that God manifests his great power in saving some of them.* Money is such a barrier that we might well despair of the salvation of any rich men. Poor men have a chance. They have so little that they dare not trust in it, but in God only. But the rich man is tempted to trust in the uncertain riches, and leave God out of the account. But for this very reason God magnifies his grace in saving some rich men—in saving some in spite of all their temptation to trust in their abundance. A rich yet real believer is a splendid illustration of the grace of God. He sees through his riches and forbids them to come between his soul and his Saviour.

III. CHRIST INDICATES THE RECOMPENSE AWAITING ALL THOSE WHO HAVE SACRIFICED THEIR ALL FOR HIM. (Vers. 28—30.) Peter, as spokesman for the others, asks Christ what they shall have, seeing they have sacrificed their worldly positions to follow him. They thought that they should have some recompense. Nor were they mistaken; for Christ shows that they shall have: 1. *A recompense in kind in this world.* Often when a home is left for the sake of Jesus, a happier home is found in the midst of the Lord's work. When rich prospects are renounced for the Saviour's sake, unexpected recompense comes round in the shape of riches. When relatives are resigned that Christ's cause may be promoted, new relations spring up around the devoted soul and bring compensation. And the spirit of loving appreciation which appropriates all things makes ample amends for all our self-denial for our Saviour (1 Cor. iii. 21—23).

2. *A recompense in the world to come in the shape of eternal life.* So that self-denial, self-renunciation, becomes the path to the life eternal. The opportunity of living in God and for God awaits all sincere souls in the other life, and satisfies them. Let us consequently rejoice in hope of the glory, and have grace to fear no evil.—R. M. E.

Vers. 31—43.—*Blindness, mental and physical.* Having spoken to the disciples about recompense, he balances his consolation by giving them fair warning of his own approaching humiliation and death. But they were so infatuated about the honours that they were totally blind to the humiliation. Christ's words were no better than idle tales to them. It suggests—

I. THE ONE-SIDED WAY IN WHICH PEOPLE MAY READ THE BIBLE. (Ver. 31.) What was about to happen to Jesus was prophesied ages before. The Old Testament presented a suffering as well as an exalted Messiah. But the Jews totally overlooked the humiliating aspect. And in the very same way people go still to God's Word, and find there only what they want to find. It needs great trials oftentimes to expound some passages of the Divine Word to us. We are partial students; we do not enter into the wide meaning of the Word as God would have us!

II. GREAT TRIALS ARE NEEDED TO OPEN OUR EYES TO THE OVERLOOKED REALITIES. (Vers. 32—34.) It is plain that they did not take in Christ's meaning until he was actually taken from them and crucified. In the terrible suffering which seemed to extinguish all their fond hopes, the overwhelmed men got the spiritual vision, and were enabled to see a suffering as well as an exalted Messiah revealed in the Divine Word. And do we not often, when crushed and broken by trial, come to appropriate passages of God's Word which formerly were blank to us? We ought to bless God for the opened eye, even though the process of opening it be painful.

III. THE RESURRECTION OF CHRIST MADE AMENDS FOR ALL THE PREVIOUS SUFFERING. (Ver. 33.) For resurrection was exaltation; it was glory which could only be reached through the tomb. No possibility was there of Jesus being raised if he had never died. It is an experience cheaply purchased, perhaps, through death and the grave.

IV. LET US CONTRAST WITH THIS THE CURE OF BLIND BARTIMÆUS. (Vers. 35—43.) From blind disciples—mentally blind—Luke proceeds to speak of the blind beggar and his physical cure. Jesus was proceeding to Jerusalem to enter it as King. It was a royal progress. Here was one of the splendid accompaniments of it. 1. *The condition of the poor blind beggar.* He was blind, and, as he could not keep himself by work, he had to beg. He was thus perfectly helpless and dependent. And he knew his deficiencies. There was no unconsciousness of them or indifference to them. 2. *The knowledge he possessed of Jesus.* He had heard of Christ's miracles, how he had cured several blind men previously. He knew he was the Son of David, and regarded him as true Messiah. Hence his knowledge of Christ was sufficient to lead him to throw himself upon his mercy as soon as he had the chance. 3. *The visit of Jesus to his neighbourhood.* Jesus was passing on, and the crowd surged mightily around him. The noise fell upon the blind man's acute ear, and led him to ask what it all meant. Then, as soon as he learned that Jesus was passing by, he began to cry, "Jesus, thou Son of David, have mercy on me!" Noble example! Should not all who feel their need of mercy cry as Bartimæus did? 4. *Discouragement only intensifies his eagerness for blessing.* The crowd rebuked him, but Bartimæus persevered. The more discouragement, the more importunity. So let it be with us in our seasons of discouragement. 5. *The call of Jesus.* The importunate one is summoned to the Saviour's presence. Those who once discouraged him now urge him forward. 6. *The inquiry of Jesus.* Bartimæus is asked what mercy he desires; and his whole soul goes forth in the words, "Lord, that I may receive my sight!" It is surely well when we clearly know our need and desire its supply. 7. *The cure conferred and its consequences.* Bartimæus is thrown upon his faith; according to this is his cure. But his faith was strong enough for the occasion. He consequently sees plainly, and his fresh sight is used to guide him after Jesus. So is it with us if we receive from Jesus our spiritual healing. Then we see the Saviour plainly, and we learn and are proud to follow him. The people, too, in seeing us follow Christ, will learn to glorify the God of grace who has enabled us to do so.—R. M. E.

EXPOSITION.

CHAPTER XIX.

Vers. 1—10.—*Jesus lodges in the house of Zacchæus, "the chief among the publicans" at Jericho.* This episode, which took place at Jericho just before the Lord's entry into Jerusalem the last time, is peculiar to this Gospel. That the source was Hebrew (Aramaic) is clear from the wording of the narration. Some brief Hebrew (Aramaic) memoir was given to St. Luke, whence he derived his information of this most interesting and instructive incident of the last journey of the Master.

Vers. 1, 2.—**And Jesus entered and passed through Jericho. And, behold, there was a man named Zacchæus, which was the chief among the publicans, and he was rich.** Jericho, under the Herods, had become again an important centre of trade. It lay on the road from Peræa to Judæa and Egypt, and had, of course, an important custom-house. The balm which came especially from the Gilead district was sent through there into all parts of the world. Zacchæus was at the head of this customs department at Jericho. The exact position of such an official in those days is not known. He probably farmed the customs revenue under some great Roman capitalist of the equestrian order. In such an appointment it was easy to commit even involuntary injustices. The temptations to such an official to enrich himself at the expense of others, besides, were sadly numerous. *Named Zacchæus. Zakkai* signifies "pure" (see Ezra ii. 9; Neh. vii. 14). It is curious that we find in the Talmud a man named Zakkai, the father of the famous rabbi Jochanan, living at Jericho.

Ver. 3.—**He was little of stature.** Such a curious detail comes, of course, from some memoir written just at the time.

Ver. 4.—**Into a sycomore tree.** *Ficus sycomorus,* the fig-mulberry, is here meant. It grew in the Jordan valley to a considerable height; the low, spreading branches were easy to climb. "We can picture the scene to our mind's eye. The eager, wistful, supplicating face looking down from the fresh green foliage—it was early spring—and meeting the gaze of Jesus as he passed" (Dean Plumptre).

Ver. 5.—**Zacchæus, make haste, and come down; for to-day I must abide at thy house.** Jericho was one of the cities of the priests, and yet our Lord, setting public opinion at defiance, passed over their houses, and

announced his intention of lodging for the night with one whose life's occupation was so hateful to the Jewish religious world. The Master recognized in the intense eagerness of Zacchæus to get a sight of him, and possibly a word from him, that it was in the chief publican's house where lay his Father's business for him in Jericho.

Ver. 7.—**They all murmured.** This very inclusive statement, "they all," shows the general intensely Jewish spirit of the age, narrow and sectarian. The people could not imagine goodness, or earnestness, or generosity in one who served the hateful Roman power. Probably in priestly Jericho this stern exclusive spirit was especially dominant.

Ver. 8.—**And Zacchæus stood, and said unto the Lord; Behold, Lord, the half of my goods I give to the poor; and if I have taken anything from any man by false accusation, I restore him fourfold.** Zacchæus's memorable speech was addressed not as an *apologia* to the murmuring, jealous crowd, either in the room or the courtyard of the house, but to his Divine Guest, who, he felt, understood him, whose great heart, he knew, sympathized with him in that life of his, so tempted and yet so full of quiet, noble acts; for the chief publican's words do not refer to a *future* purpose, but they speak of a *past* rule of life which he had set for himself to follow, and probably had followed for a long period. So Godet, who paraphrases thus: "He whom thou hast thought good to choose as thy host is not, as is alleged, a being unworthy of thy choice. Lo, publican though I am, it is no ill-gotten gain with which I entertain thee." In a profession like his, it was easy to commit involuntary injustice. There may, too, have been, probably was, many a hard if not an unjust act worked by the chief of the tax-gatherers and his subordinates in their difficult employment.

Ver. 9.—**And Jesus said unto him, This day is salvation come to this house.** This solemn announcement on the part of the Redeemer was something more than a mere comforting assurance to a man who, in spite of difficulties and temptations, had striven manfully to lead a brave and generous life, helping, it is clear, the very multitude who were so ready to revile him. It is an assurance to the world that men might work in *any* profession or calling, and at the same time live a life pleasing to God. It repeats with intense emphasis—and this is the great lesson of this striking scene—that it is never the work or the position in life which ennobles the man in the sight of

God, but only the way in which the work *is done*, and the position *used*, which are of price in his pure eyes. The hated publican at the receipt of custom—the servant of Rome, might so live as to win the smile of God, as well as the priest in the sanctuary, or the rabbi in his theological school. **He also is a son of Abraham.** That is to say, a spiritual son—a son in the highest and most real sense. Zacchæus was a faithful follower of Abraham, in his life and in his faith.

Ver. 10.—**For the Son of man is come to seek and to save that which was lost.** A quiet rebuke to the Pharisees and priests and their followers, who would limit the redeemed. Surely the "publicans" and the great tempted mass of mankind needed him more than the happy privileged class. It was for the sake of *these* poor wandering sheep that he left his home of grandeur and peace. But there was a vein of sad irony running through these words of the Master. Between the lines we seem to read some such thoughts as these: "You know, O priests and Pharisees, *you* do not want me. You think you are safe already. But these poor despised ones, *they* want, they welcome me, like this Zacchæus." This, too, was a lesson for all time. This scene probably took place the evening of the Lord's arrival at Zacchæus's house at Jericho, after the evening meal, when the room and court of the house were filled with guests and curious spectators. Dean Plumptre has an interesting suggestion that Zacchæus the publican was one and the same with the publican of ch. xviii. 10—14, who in the temple "smote upon his breast, saying, God be merciful to me a sinner!" "Is it too bold a conjecture that he who saw Nathanael under the fig tree (John i. 48) had seen Zacchæus in the temple, and that the figure in the parable of ch. xviii. 14 was in fact a portrait?"

Vers. 11—27.—*The parable of the pounds.*
Ver. 11.—**And as they heard these things, he added and spake a parable.** The words which introduce this parable-story indicate its close connection with the events which had just taken place. "He added, and spake (προσθεὶς εἶπε)." **Because he was nigh to Jerusalem, and because they thought that the kingdom of God should immediately appear.** Thus were briefly stated the reasons which determined the Master to speak the following parable. First, "he was nigh to Jerusalem," only at most a few hours' journey from the holy city—his last solemn, awful visit, when the mysterious act of stupendous love would be accomplished. So he determined to give a veiled parabolic picture of himself and of his chosen people. Second, "they thought that the kingdom of God should immediately appear." In his parable

he proposed to moderate the wild romantic enthusiasm of his immediate followers and of the Passover crowds by painting for them a quiet picture of the future of work and waiting which lay before them. The parable contains three sets of lessons. (1) The varieties of reward apportioned to different degrees of zeal and industry in the Master's service. (2) The eternity of loss and shame which will be the portion of the slothful and unfaithful servant. (3) The terrible doom of his enemies.

Ver. 12.—**He said therefore, A certain nobleman went into a far country to receive for himself a kingdom, and to return.** There was a singular fitness in the Master's choice of a framework for his parable, which at first sight would seem strange and unreal. Two nobles, Herod and Archelaus, in that age had literally gone from Jericho, where the Speaker of the parable-story then was, to a far country across the sea—to Rome, to receive a kingdom from Cæsar (Josephus, 'Ant.,' xiv. 14; xvii. 9). And one of these two nobles, Archelaus, had rebuilt the stately royal palace of Jericho, under the very shadow of which the Speaker and the crowds were perhaps standing.

Ver. 13.—**And he called his ten servants, and delivered them ten pounds, and said unto them, Occupy till I come.** No doubt when our Lord spoke these parables he considerably enlarged the details, made many parts of the framework clearer than the short reports which we possess can possibly do. The meaning of the great noble's action here is that he wished to test his servants—to try their various capabilities and dispositions, intending, when he should return from his long journey, having received his kingdom, to appoint them to high offices in the administration, to such positions, in fact, as their action in regard to the small deposit now entrusted to them should show themselves capable of filling. The Greek verb rendered "occupy" (πραγματεύσασθε) occurs here only in the New Testament: a compound form of it is rendered (ver. 15) by "gained by trading."

Ver. 14.—**But his citizens hated him.** Again history supplies the framework. This was what the Jews had done in the case of Archelaus. They had sent a hostile deputation to complain of their future king before the emperor's court at Rome. In the parable, in these "citizens who hated him" a thinly veiled picture is given of those Jews who utterly rejected the mission of Jesus, and by whose designs the Crucifixion was brought about.

Ver. 16.—**Thy pound.** At first the smallness of the sum given to each of the servants is striking. Was it not a sum unworthy of a noble about to receive a kingdom?

The Attic pound was in value somewhat less than £4 sterling. In the parable of the talents (Matt. xxv. 14—30), where although very different lessons are inculcated, yet the imagery is somewhat similar, the amounts, however, are vastly larger, varying from five talents, which would represent about £1000. Here the very smallness of the sum entrusted to the servants has its deep meaning. The "nobly born" one who is about to receive a kingdom, represents our Lord, who *here* is in a state of the deepest poverty and humiliation. The little sum in one sense represents the work he was able *then* to entrust to his own. Again, the paltriness of the sum given them seems to suggest what a future lay before them. No sharing in what they hoped for—the glories of a Messianic kingdom on earth. No rest in repose under the shadow of the mighty throne of King Messiah. The "very little" (ver. 17) told them—if they would only listen—that their future as his servants would be a life of comparatively obscure inglorious activity, without rank or power, landless, homeless, well-nigh friendless. But the sequel of the parable told more than this. It proclaimed that their Master was able to estimate the moral worth of those who had been faithful and true in a "very little;" ay, more, was in a position to reward the faithful servant. And the recompense, a city for a pound, just hints at the magnificent possibilities of the heaven-life, just suggests the splendour of its rewards.

Ver. 17.—**Well, thou good servant.** It is noticeable that, in the bestowal of the "five cities" upon the servant who had with his one pound gained five, no expression of praise like this "good servant" is used by the King on his return. Now, what does this omission teach us? Christ, we know, was very careful and very sparing in his use of moral epithets. "Why callest thou me good?" was his stern address to the young ruler who used the expression, not because he was convinced of its applicability, but because he was desirous of paying a flattering compliment to the wise Rabbi from whom he desired information. We may safely conclude that, from the second servant in the story, the one who had earned but five pounds, he withheld the noble appellation "good" because he felt he had not deserved it. He had done *well*, it is true, and was splendidly recompensed, but he might have done *more*. He had won a high and responsible place in the kingdom; he was appointed the ruler over five cities; but he had not earned the noble title, ἄγαθος, "good." Very accurately, indeed, it seems, will places and names and power be awarded in the heaven-life, exactly in proportion to merits and deserts.

Vers. 20, 21.—**And another came, saying, Lord, behold, here is thy pound, which I have kept laid up in a napkin: for I feared thee, because thou art an austere man; thou takest up that thou layedst not down, and reapest that thou didst not sow.** This is the third class into which the servants who knew their Lord's will are roughly divided. We have, first, the devoted earnest toiler, whose whole soul was in his Master's work —great, indeed, was his reward. And, second, we have the servant who acquitted himself fairly respectably, but not nobly, not a hero in the struggle of life; he, too, is recompensed magnificently, far above his most ardent hopes, but still his reward is infinitely below that which the first brave toiler received at his Lord's hands. The third falls altogether into a different catalogue. He is a believer who has not found the state of grace offered by Jesus so brilliant as he hoped; a legal Christian, who has not tasted grace, and knows nothing of the gospel but its severe morality. It seems to him that the Lord gives very little to exact so much. "Surely," such a one argues, "the Lord should be satisfied with us if we abstain from doing ill, from squandering our talent." The Master's answer is singularly to the point: "The more thou knowest that I am austere, the more thou shouldest have tried to satisfy me!" The Christian who lacks the experience of grace ought to be the most anxious of workers. The punishment here is very different from that awarded to the enemies (ver. 27). We hear nothing of darkness and gnashing of teeth; it is simply *deprivation*. Still, even this modified penalty seems to tell of an eternity of regret and loss. Instead of the ten cities, or even the five, there is not even the poor pound left to the hapless condemned one, unworthy even to retain that little heritage.

Ver. 23.—**Wherefore then gavest not thou my money into the bank, that at my coming I might have required mine own with usury?** Many in "the bank" have seen mirrored those Christian societies and religious organizations to which every believer may entrust the resources which he is uncertain how best to use himself. Without particularizing, however, it seems better to understand the Lord here simply intending to teach, by his image of the bank, that no man in this world is doomed to inactivity or uselessness, but that there will be opportunity afforded to every one who is willing to use his talent in a humble and obscure, if not in a heroic and conspicuous, way.

Ver. 27.—**But those mine enemies, which would not that I should reign over them, bring hither, and slay them before me.** An obvious reference to the Lord's dealings with the chosen people, and an unmistakable reference to the awful ruin and disaster which was so soon to overwhelm the city and temple and the whole nationality. But behind this temporal reference there looms in the background the vast shadow of a terrible eternal doom reserved for the enemies of the Redeemer. Godet has a beautiful and suggestive note on the signification of the ten and five cities, the reward of the faithful toiler here. "They," the "cities," "represent mortal beings in a lower state of development, but whom the glorified faithful are commissioned to raise to their Divine destination."

Vers. 28—48.—*Jesus enters Jerusalem as King Messiah* (vers. 29—44). *His work in the temple* (vers. 45—48). St. Luke here passes over in silence the events which happened after the episode at the house of Zacchæus at Jericho and the speaking the great parable of "the pounds." This parable may have been spoken in the house of Zacchæus before leaving Jericho, but it seems better to place it somewhere in the course of the walk from Jericho to Bethany, a distance of some twelve miles.

St. John fills up the gap left in the narrative of St. Luke.

The main body of pilgrims to the feast, with whom Jesus and his company were travelling, left him on the Jericho road at Bethany: they going on to their caravanserai in the holy city, he remaining for two nights with his friends at Bethany—the next evening Jesus was entertained at Bethany in the house of Simon the leper (Matt. xxvi. 6—13; Mark xiv. 3—9)—the feast at which Lazarus the risen sat a guest and Martha served, and to which Mary brought her precious ointment and her contrition (John xi. 1—9).

Jesus must have arrived at Bethany before sunset on Friday, Nisan 7, and therefore before the sabbath began.

The sabbath was spent in quiet. The supper probably took place directly after the end of the sabbath. The next morning (Palm Sunday) the Lord started for Jerusalem, and entered the holy city in the triumphant way as King Messiah related by St. Luke in our Gospel.

Ver. 29.—**And it came to pass, when he was come nigh to Bethphage and Bethany.** Bethphage is never mentioned in the Old Testament, but in the Talmud we find it specified in some interesting ceremonial

directions. It was evidently an outlying suburb of Jerusalem. Bethphage, which lay between the city and Bethany, was by the rabbis legally counted as part of Jerusalem. Bethany signifies "House of Dates," no doubt so called from its palm trees. Bethphage, "House of Green Figs," from its fig-orchards. The modern Bethany is known as *El-Azarieh* or *Lazarieh*, the name attaching to its connection with the history of Lazarus.

Ver. 30.—**Ye shall find a colt tied, whereon yet never man sat: loose him, and bring him hither.** The account of this transaction is less circumstantial in St. Luke than in the other evangelists. The reference to the prophecy of Zech. ix. 9 is here left out. This prophecy is, however, necessary for the full understanding of the mystic act of riding upon an ass's colt. St. Luke, compiling especially for Gentile readers, would feel that such a reference to the old Hebrew story would scarcely interest a foreigner, and would serve to distract such a one's interest in the progress of the great recital. For us, however, the meaning of the scene, read in the light of the Zechariah (ix. 9) words and of Hebrew story generally, is as follows : The disciples and multitude wished their Master to claim a kingdom. At this moment in his eventful history, aware that death awaited him in the course of the next few days, he chose to gratify them; so he claimed his kingdom, but a kingdom utterly unlike what *they* longed for. He came to his royal, sacred city in the strange guise foreshadowed by Zechariah, as a Prince of Peace, not with chariot and horse, but meekly riding on an ass's colt, claiming, too, a dominion from sea to sea, from the river to the ends of the earth (Zech. ix. 10). *Whereon yet never man sat.* For this reason specially adapted for a sacred use (see Numb. xix. 2; Deut. xxi. 3; 1 Sam. vi. 7).

Ver. 31.—**And if any man ask you, Why do ye loose** him ? **thus shall ye say unto him, Because the Lord hath need of him.** Had he not right here ? surely the cattle on a thousand hills were his ! St. Matthew not only mentions the colt, but also the ass. This little detail is unnoticed by St. Luke. Probably the colt, though not broken in, would go the more quietly accompanied by its mother. But the reason of St. Matthew's special mention of the ass as well as of the colt was the reference to Gen. xlix. 11, in which Justin Martyr, in a curious chapter of the 'Dialogue with Trypho,' finds a direct reference to the ass and the foal (see Justin Martyr, 'Dialogue with Trypho,' c. liii.).

Ver. 35.—**They cast their garments upon the colt.** "An extemporized housing in default of the purple trappings. Doubtless the fittest of the proffered robes would be selected by the disciples" (Morrison).

Ver. 36.—And as he went, they spread their clothes in the way. A common act of homage to a king or royal personage. So in the case of Jehu, the officers of the army offered him this tribute (2 Kings ix. 13). So Agamemnon walked on costly carpets and tapestry when he entered his palace at Mycenæ. Clytemnestra, in the 'Agamemnon' of Æschylus, says—

" But, my loved lord,
Leave now that car ; nor on the bare ground set
That royal foot, beneath whose mighty tread
Troy trembled. Haste, ye virgins, to whose care
This pleasing office is entrusted, spread
The streets with tapestry ; let the ground be covered
With richest purple, leading to the palace,
That honour with just state may grace his entry."

(905—911.)

Ver. 37.—At the descent of the mount of Olives, the whole multitude of the disciples began to rejoice and praise God with a loud voice for all the mighty works that they had seen. At this point on the Bethany road the city of Jerusalem comes into view. Here a crowd of pilgrims to the Passover Feast, many of whom were well acquainted with Jesus, came out to meet and welcome him with their branches of palm. These joined his friends who accompanied him from Bethany. This enthusiasm was excited among the Passover pilgrims in great measure owing to the report which by this time had got abroad of the raising of Lazarus (see John xii. 17, 18). Many had already gone out from the city to Bethany to see Jesus and Lazarus. Of the Messianic shouts of welcome which sounded in the crowd, St. Luke does not mention the "Hosanna ! " of St. Matthew, no doubt because this peculiar Hebrew cry would not have conveyed any meaning to the Gentile readers to whom his story was especially addressed. The two incidents which follow—the crying out of the stones, and the weeping of the Master over his beautiful doomed city (vers. 39–44)—occur only in St. Luke. His source of information here was evidently quite different to the other two synoptists or St. John.

Vers. 39, 40.—And some of the Pharisees from among the multitude said unto him, Master, rebuke thy disciples. And he answered and said unto them, I tell you that, if these should hold their peace, the stones would immediately cry out. These Pharisees were probably some of that great and influential sect who had all along listened

with respect and attention to the Master, looking upon him as a most able and powerful Rabbi, but refusing to entertain any of the growing Messianic conceptions respecting his person. Godet graphically paints the scene in his suggestion that the words, "Rebuke thy disciples," were accompanied with an irritated and anxious look towards the frowning citadel of Antonia, where the Roman garrison of Jerusalem lay. It was there in full view of Jesus and the crowds. The anxious look seemed to say that the Romans were on the watch for any signs of disaffection on the part of the hated and suspected Jews. The answer of Jesus, continues the same writer, has a terrible majesty. "If I could silence all these," looking round on the impassioned faces of the multitude as they waved their palm branches in homage to their King, " the very stones on the ground would cry aloud." This striking imagery was a memory of our Lord of the prophecy of Habakkuk : " The stone shall cry out of the wall, and the beam out of the timber shall answer it " (ii. 11).

Ver. 41.—He beheld the city. It was a very different view to what the traveller of the present day would see from the same spot. Though Jerusalem, when Jesus Christ was teaching on earth, was subject to the stranger Herodian, and the Herodian to the great Italian power, yet the beauty and glory of the city were remarkable. Still glittered in the midst of the great city that " mass of gold and snow " known as the temple. The far-extending suburbs were covered with the gardens and palaces of the wealthy Jews. But the mighty memories which hung so thickly round the sacred city and the glorious house of God after all constituted its chief charm. What might not that city have been ! what splendid and far-reaching work might it not have done ! and now the cup of its iniquities was just brimming over ; only a few more short years, and a silence the most awful would brood over the shapeless ruins of what was *once* Jerusalem and her house on Zion, the joy of the whole earth. **And wept over it.** No merely silent tears of mute sorrow, but ἔκλαυσεν, he wept aloud. All the insults and the sufferings of the Passion were powerless to elicit from the Man of sorrows that expression of intense grief which the thought of the ruin of the loved city called forth.

Ver. 42.—If thou hadst known, even thou, at least in this thy day. The emphatic repetition of the "thou," and the broken form of the sentence, tell of the intense feeling of the Divine Speaker. "In this thy day." There was still time, still one day left, before his terrible trial-time began, which filled up the measure of Jerusalem and her people's iniquity. *Still one day* in which, had they only known "the things which belonged to their peace," they might have won a forgiveness for all the past centuries of sin.

Vers. 45, 46.—**And he went into the temple.** The recital of St. Luke here is more general and less precise than that of the other two synoptists. The Lord on that "Palm Sunday" evening simply went into the temple, "and when he had looked round about upon all things" it was then evening, and he returned to his lodging at Bethany with the twelve (Mark xi. 11). The expulsion of the money-changers, mentioned in the next verse (46), took place on the following day. St. Matthew adds another interesting detail respecting the excitement caused by the presence of Jesus in the city. "When he was come into Jerusalem, all the city was moved, saying, Who is this?" (Matt. xxi. 10). **And he went into the temple, and began to cast out them that sold therein, and them that bought; saying unto them, It is written, My house is the house of prayer: but ye have made it a den of thieves.** This visit of the Lord to the temple, in which he spoke

and acted as King Messiah, was a fulfilment of Mal. iii. 1, 2. In the outer court of the temple stalls had been erected in which money-changers were located (*geld-wechsel comptoir — change de monnaies*), in order that pilgrims from foreign lands might be able to exchange their foreign coins for the purchase of sacrificial victims. These also seem to have been sold in the precincts. All this made the courts of the Lord's house a scene of noise and tumult, and, from the Master's stern words, a scene often of cheating and overreaching. The words of Jesus were taken from Isa. lvi. 7 and Jer. vii. 11.

Ver. 47.—**And he taught daily in the temple.** This and the following verses give, after the manner of St. Luke, both in his Gospel and in the Acts, a general picture of the Lord's life in these last days of his public ministry in Jerusalem; and of the effect of his last teaching (1) upon the priests and scribes, etc., and (2) upon the mass of the people. The Greek word rendered "very attentive to hear (him)" is an expressive one, and describes the intense attention with which the people generally listened to the last solemn public utterances of the Master. It means literally, "they hung upon his lips."

HOMILETICS.

Vers. 1—10.—*Zacchæus.* Very pleasant was the city of Jericho when our Lord passed through it; and very pleasant is the Scripture which records the visit of Jesus to it. It has a fragrance like that of the roses and palms in which the gardens of Jericho were luxurious; its verses remind us of the cells of the many honeycombs for which it was famous. Each verse is full of sweet and holy thought. A child can understand it; an angel will desire to look into it. One of the two incidents which have made Jericho memorable in connection with the life of the Saviour of men has been already considered. That which is told in the verses before us points to a different series of circumstances, a different and perhaps fuller illustration of the more Catholic aspect of Christ's mission. Consider three points.

I. The incident illustrates A PURPOSE TRIUMPHANT OVER HINDRANCES. These hindrances connect with social position, with wealth, with personal disqualifications. 1. *He was a tax-gatherer.* His place was usually filled by Roman knights, who farmed the taxes that they might replenish their empty coffers. It was a calling which aroused the hostility of the Jews. And to be a social Ishmael is hurtful to all that is generous and noble in the breast. He was "chief among the publicans"—a great man to whom many deferred; with the temptation, therefore, to imagine that the crowd was a vulgarity to be shunned, and so to isolate himself from the enthusiasms of the townsfolk. 2. *He was rich.* Almost insensibly a kind of pride grows in the person who is wealthy. He is conscious of his means. And the comfort with which they surround him tends to dull the edge of more spiritual feeling, to withdraw the interest from truths which imply the sense of need and poverty. He might have said to himself, "This Jesus of Nazareth, what is he to me? I have all that heart can desire: why should I make an ado about this travelling Prophet?" 3. *He was short of stature.* A little man: what hope was there that he would obtain a glimpse of the passing Nazarene? Why should he expose himself to the risk of being laughed at, especially when the chances were against his obtaining even a glimpse of the Stranger? Against all such hindrances the purpose to see Jesus is supreme. He must; the necessity of his soul makes him quick in invention. He forces his way through the crowd, climbs the small sycamore tree, and there he waits. He knows, confusedly enough, but by a kind of intuition, that the Poorest of all who on foot treads the street is his Lord; that with him is the wealth wanting which a man has no real inheritance. When the fountains of the inner deep are broken up, when any one is in earnest about the kingdom of God and his righteousness, the mere accidents of position and circumstance are forgotten. The Princess Alice of England, on her dying-bed, acknowledged her debt to a Scotsman in humble life for the help he had given in bringing her soul back to its rest in Christ. Zacchæus, chief among the publicans, heeds not appearances, thinks not of dignity, runs before the multitude, perches himself on the branch of the fig tree that he might see him whom his soul loved.

II. The incident illustrates THE MEETING BETWEEN A SUPREME PURPOSE IN MAN AND THE PURPOSE OF THE LOVE OF GOD. It may be said that the publican's motive was mere curiosity. Supposing that it was, it brought about the sight of the Lord. Curiosity impelled Augustine to the church of Ambrose in Milan, and there Christ found him. It is a gain to get people, even from an inferior desire, within the reach of the gospel of grace: who knows whether the one who came to scoff may not remain to pray? But was there not a cause deeper than mere curiosity at work in Zacchæus? He may not have had the same kind of plea as blind Bartimæus, but he had his own plea; and what Christ asks from each of us is that, as we are, in the specialties of our need and condition, we come to him. Faith carries an " I must " in its bosom. It always presses: "To-day I must see thee who thou art." That day the two "I musts," the one in the sinner, the other in the Saviour's heart, meet and touch. " Zacchæus, to-day I must abide at thy house " (ver. 5). What a journey that " *I must* " of Jericho represents! Has it not come from the heaven of heavens, out from the bosom of the great God himself? The fig leaves and branches cannot hide from Christ. The eyes of the two are seeking each other. He looks up; the one for whom he is in search receives the gaze. That one knows that he is looked into; he is understood; he is named. And the fellowship is formed from which neither things present nor things to come can separate.

III. The incident illustrates THE PURPOSE OF A MIND RENEWED IN ITS SPIRIT. What is the response to the Lord's " make haste "? " He made haste, and came down, and received him joyfully " (ver. 6). The whole heart opens to this new Master. There is no further asking who he is. That has been answered by the heart itself; and the welcome to his home, to all, immediately follows. If Christ will take one such as he,

> " Love so amazing, so Divine,
> Demands the soul, the life, the all."

There is more than this. We need not discuss whether the noble speech recorded in ver. 8 is the vindication of the publican as against the calumnies of those around him, indicating that he had not been the unjust extortioner whom they took him to be; that he had been in the habit of giving half of his goods to the poor. The latter part of the verse at least is the expression of a solemn purpose formed in Christ's presence. It indicates a change of character. " Is his *pocket* converted? " was a question put, when the conversion of one who had been greedy and selfish was announced. Hitherto this Zacchæus had lived to make money; now he will live to use it. Hitherto he had lived for himself; now he will live for God. Henceforth he will aim, not only at being just, but at making others the better and happier for him. When Christ is received joyfully, the narrow becomes the broad, the hard becomes the generous; the levels of the life are altered : " Old things pass away, and all things become new."

IV. Reflecting on the incident, two points are to be noted—its revelation of Christ, and its enforcement of the solemn word " opportunity." 1. *Christ the Brother and Saviour.* (1) It is interesting to observe that, on the same day, poor and rich were visibly embraced within the love of God. That love stretches from pole to pole in human experience and condition. Christ's sympathies are not with class as against class; for he is the Son of man. When the beggar comes he is so polite: " What wilt thou? " As to Zacchæus, he turns to the Jews (ver. 9). Everywhere he recognizes a something of God—a jewel to be snatched from among the ruins. " He is not afraid of consorting with the rich lest people should say he cares too much for money, any more than he is of consorting with the poor lest they should say he cares too little for respectability. He will dine with the Pharisee, if invited; and he will dine with a publican, even when uninvited, if the man's heart be indeed a guest-chamber." The most brotherly of hearts is the heart of God. (2) *The Brother and the Saviour.* See the sentence in which the conjunction is realized (ver. 10). It was spoken with immediate reference to Zacchæus. He was lost, for he had lived alone; and whoso lives alone, away from the light of God, out of sympathy with his brethren, an outside person, is really one lost. And is not Christ among us to bring the outsiders in, to awaken up dead worldly souls, and restore them to communion with the Father in heaven and the Father's children on earth? Christ is the Saviour because he is the Brother, and he is the Brother because he is the Son. Look at the Saviour in his work of love. The royalty of his grace shines marvellously forth. Note the *self*-invitation: "I love him because he first loved me." Note also the joy of salvation—not a passing glimpse —"I *must abide.*" There is a new rule, a new companionship, a new mirth. 2. *The word "opportunity" is enforced.* That word contains the lesson most obviously taught in every part of the story. Jesus is passing; to-day and to-day only. There is no time to trifle. "Make haste, and come down."

Vers. 11—27.—*The parable of the pounds.* This parable closely resembles that reported in Matt. xxv. 14—30. The two are undoubtedly different, but they have much in common. We cannot rightly understand each without balancing it by the other. Certainly we realize the full effect of their application when, to borrow an expressive figure, we look on them "as twin parables, resembling one of those trees whose main trunk separates just above the earth into two equal towering stems." Thus connecting them, let us extract a portion of the instruction conveyed, our topics these: (1) *The endowments bestowed;* (2) *the trading recommended;* and (3) *the dealing of the Master with his servants presented.*

I. Observe the two principles which run in parallel lines as THE PRINCIPLES OF GOD'S DISTRIBUTION OF ENDOWMENTS. 1. *The parable of the talents* suggests an inequality in the gifts or faculties with which God enriches men: one gets five talents, another two, and another one. And this description is entirely consistent with fact. It is true as to even the commonest things; it is true as to higher qualities of intellect and will. There is no dead level. There are hills and plains; there are gardens and deserts in man's world as well as in the physical universe. God takes fact into account. He distributes according to ability; he imposes responsibility according to ability. He does not demand that the one with two talents make the ten—only the four. Let the vessel, according to its possibilities, be full; the smaller vessel is not required to hold the amount of the larger. One farm may not be as extensive as another, but it is still a farm. Cultivate to the measure of the farm; make full use of the capital such as it is. "What but this, O man, does the Lord thy God require of thee?" 2. But *observe the teaching in the parable of the pounds.* If talents are unequally bestowed, remember every one has his pound. The pound was of very small value as compared with the talent—£3 or a little more as compared with £160. The ten servants get each one pound—the same sum in every case. We have varying capacity, but we have all some capacity—"a little knowledge, a little love, a little experience, a little money, a little favour with men, a little conscience, a little pity, a little time, a little opportunity." We have one mina, one pound. Work, my brother, with thy pound, rather with the pound that the Lord has given thee. It may be increased tenfold, and the gain is (ver. 17) a city for every added pound—a blessing in possession, and rule, wholly unmerited by, yet graciously corresponding to, the servant's faithfulness.

II. WHAT MEANS THE OCCUPYING OR TRADING WHICH THE LORD ENJOINS ON ALL TO WHOM HE GIVES HIS GOODS? Let it be remembered that, in the olden time, the relation between master and servant was different from that in our time. It is not usual to leave sums of money to the servant to be put out by him in his master's behalf when he takes a journey into the far country. But it was a common practice to make such arrangements as allowed the slave to transact business, either on condition of paying a yearly sum to his master, or on the footing of a man with so much of another's wealth committed to his charge to be invested for the other's benefit. To this custom our Lord refers. "Occupy [or, 'trade'] till I come." The two persons opposed are the trader and the idler; and the striking feature is that the idler is denounced as "the slothful and wicked servant." All start with some advantages; they are not persons just hired; they have been in his service, they know his character, and they know what he wants. The one who does not trade is lying when he excuses himself; his slothfulness (ver. 22) is sheer wickedness. The point of the exhortation can very readily be apprehended. God wants his interest, as the merchant wants his. How is this interest to be gained? The purpose and destination of life must be kept steadily in view—

> " Not enjoyment, and not sorrow,
> Is our destined end and way;
> But to act that each to-morrow
> Find us farther than to-day."

Recollect that the self in each of us connects with two factors—God who made us; and our brother, whose good is to be as sacred to us as our own. We cannot be making increase unless we are true to him whose we are, and to every one who is near us; unless both God and man are benefited, and benefited the more the greater our means and ability are. Consider how we can best lay out our influence, whatever that may be; how we can best use our time; how we can get the best percentage for whatever capacity, whatever force, we possess. As it is essential to a prosperous business that there be a good administration, reflect how we are administering the affairs with which, in one sphere or another, we are entrusted—in a word, on what plan, with what aim, and by what methods, our life is being fulfilled. Give two men five pounds each; in the hands of the one they may remain five pounds neither more nor less, or they will gradually melt away; the other will spend the sum wisely, will so invest it that it will increase to him tenfold. We have read the story of the successful merchant of Bristol—the beginning of whose merchant life was the horseshoe that he picked up one day on his way to school, and carried for three miles and sold to the blacksmith for a penny. That penny was the foundation of a business pronounced, after his death, the largest in the West of England, turning nearer millions than thousands in the course of the year. All was the result of the judicious use of that which he had. In our Christian life and service this is the lesson which we most need to learn. Is there not comfort in the thought that, whilst the talents increase only twice, the pounds increase ten times? The more ordinary gifts which we all have, when faithfully applied, are capable of indefinite increase. We cannot keep unless we add; and it is God's law that to him who, thus adding, has, much is given. In spiritual, as in every other kind of commerce, much always tends to the making of more. The trader and the idler! Notice, neither the talent nor the pound is absolutely lost. It is not a spendthrift who is held up to contempt. It is the awfully careful man. It is the one who hoards. "There is that scattereth, and yet increaseth; and there is that withholdeth, . . . and it tendeth to poverty." Here is the one who withholds. And a distinction is delicately hinted at. The pound is carefully wrapped in the napkin; the man intends to do something with it when the convenient season comes; in the mean time it is safe in the napkin. But the talent is not in a napkin; it is hidden in the earth—" a precious thing," as it has been said, " made worthless because abandoned to be useless. And within how many a man's earthiness is there a talent hidden and wasted?" Take that thought home—the Master's antipathy to the idler. Who of us, in these harvest-days of God, is standing all the day idle?

III. Consider THE DEALING OF THE LORD WITH HIS SERVANTS. That is very striking and solemn as it is set before us in both the parables, especially the one as to the talents. In that of the pounds we are told only that the unused, napkin-hidden, pound is taken from the unprofitable servant and given to the one who has ten pounds. "Lord," his hearers exclaim, " he hath ten pounds" (ver. 25). The thriftiest, the most diligent, will get the addition. Why not? He has proved himself the ablest, the one who has given the most abundant guarantee that it will not be wasted. But in that of the talents the judgment is, " Let the unfaithful be bound hand and foot, and cast into the outer darkness." The wasted life, the life that has buried its force in mere earthiness, is that for which the outer darkness is reserved. The soul consigns itself to an unspeakable loneliness that, by indolence and engrossment with what is perishing, loses the grace of God. Abiding alone is the second death—the outer darkness. Most note-worthy are the scathing sentences to the poor trembling idler! How he stammers out his lame and impotent excuses (vers. 20, 21)! The very words are sent back. The mouth is the witness against the man. He might have known, should have known, if he had done right would have known, that his excuse was a falsehood. Hard thoughts of the Lord are certain if the Lord's work is shirked. The man would not be foolish if he were not wicked. O man, woman, with thy pound kept, but not traded with, who shall abide the day of his coming? who shall stand when he appeareth? Very different are the sentences on the nine who have been faithful, who have seen in their pound the Lord's pound, and traded with it for him. Humbly, joyfully, the first and the second meet the Master's eye (vers. 16, 18). What is the award? It is so gracious (ver. 17): "Thou hast been faithful *in a very little.*" To faithful service, rule is given. The one who can best serve is the one who can best rule.

> "Strive, man, to win that glory;
>   Toil, man, to gain that light;
> Send hope before to grasp it,
>   Till hope be lost in sight."

Vers. 28—44.—*From Jericho to Jerusalem.* The last glimpse which we obtain of Moses presents him wending his way up the slope of Mount Nebo, thence to give one fond gaze towards the land he might not enter, and, having so done, then to lay himself down and die. Imagination has often attempted to portray the working of the great lawgiver's mind, the emotion of his heart, the thoughts which must have crowded on him as he took that last solitary journey to the sepulchre which no man must know, in which the Lord alone was to bury him. Jesus Christ, by whom came grace and truth, is now facing the hill of sacrifice. He has begun the ascent to Mount Calvary, not alone and yet alone; the people crowd behind, but of the people there is none with him in the region of consciousness and desire. Only the Father knows the Son. Let us not attempt to draw aside the veil. Words to be pondered, but not commented on, are these (ver. 28): "When he had thus spoken, he went before, ascending up to Jerusalem." Coming near the capital, Jesus and his apostles made for Bethany. It was Friday evening. He must spend the last sabbath on earth in the quiet of the rural village. We can suppose what that sabbath was—not so much to him, for now he is moving in a sphere beyond our vision, but to those with whom he passed the hallowed hours. When the sun sets and the sabbath is over, a family feast is made in the house of Simon, once a leper. Lazarus, the man raised from the dead, one of the party, Martha for the time resuming her old ways, and Mary filling her heart with his love, until, swayed by an irresistible impulse, she pours on him the contents of an alabaster box of ointment—the preparation against the approaching burial. It was on the Sunday morning that the Lord set out for Jerusalem, at first in the ordinary guise of a pilgrim. People were hovering around the home, waiting for him, and at every step of the journey the number increased. Then occurred the transaction mentioned in vers. 29—35. From a place not now to be identified, but not far from Bethany, called Bethphage, or "the house of figs," the Saviour "in lowly pomp rides on to die." Verily, the King comes, "meek and lowly." His state, his pageant, at best is humble. And yet its simplicity is its royalty; its want of the poor tinsel and trapping of earthly greatness is the sign of the kingdom which is in the world, yet not of it. "Behold the Man!" "Behold your King!" The procession sweeps onward, along the southern shoulders of Olivet, until the road, having gained the summit of the hill, turns north-ward and begins the descent. And there the stream that had poured out from Jerusalem when the news was borne that the Prophet was on his way to the city met the stream pouring towards Jerusalem, and the disciples, inspired by an enthusiasm which was caught up and prolonged by the multitude, rent the air with songs (ver. 38) of joy and praise to God, and rock and cave and peak sent it back in gladsome echoes. Truly, a soul-stirring entry! The whole city is moved as Jesus of Nazareth rides through its gate, and passes towards Mount Zion and the holy and beautiful house which glitters on its heights. Before we think of him there, pause over two characteristic signs of the King given in his journey on that day.

I. THE KING'S WORD OF POWER. (Ver. 31.) "Say, The Lord hath need of him." We do not believe that there was any secret agreement between Christ and the owner of the colt. But he was a man prepared for the announcement; he was at least in the outer circle of believers. He understood who was meant by "the Lord," and the Lord's need was the one irresistible argument. So should it be. That the Lord needs, that there is a use for us and ours, should be enough. First, the King's word has its bond over us personally. Man, woman, it is for thee that Jesus calls. He needs thy heart, for he redeemed it; thy life, for it is his; thyself, for "he is thy Lord, and worship thou him." Shall not the response "straightway" be, "Now to be thine, for ever thine"? And then the possessions. Art thou ready to give him what thou hast, however dear it may be? Ah! the life is a new life when Christ's voice, as the voice of the life's true Master, is heard, and the answer is returned, "Here am I; for thou didst call me."

II. THE KING'S SORROW. (Ver. 41.) "He beheld the city, and wept over it." It has been noticed that "at the grave of Lazarus he had dropped silent tears, but here he wept aloud. All the shame of his mockery, all the anguish of his torture, was powerless to extort from him a single groan, or to wet his eyelids with one trickling tear, but here all the pity that was in him overmastered his human spirit, and he not only wept, but broke into a passion of lamentation in which the choked voice seemed to struggle for its utterance." It was the agony of the Saviour over the lost. There had been the time of the visitation, and Jerusalem had not known it. Now was the day, the hour, the last offer, the last opportunity; and it was to be rejected. The city was hardened in ignorance. It was blinded by its own deceived heart, and all that remained was ruin. And thus he weeps still; for still men hear their own passions and inclinations, not the voice of the prophets whom he rises early and sends.

> "Ye hearts that love the Lord,
> If at this sight ye burn,
> See that in thought, in deed, in word,
> Ye hate what made him mourn."

Ver. 45—ch. xx. 18.—*Passion Week.* The last of the old Hebrew prophets, Malachi (iii. and iv.), had announced that the Lord, the Sought One, would come "suddenly" into his temple, and manifest himself there in a threefold character—that of Judge, that of the Purifier and Refiner, and that of the swift Witness of the kingdom of heaven. It is in this threefold character that Christ is presented during the week in which he suffered. *The Judge.* St. Mark, with his usual delicacy of touch, informs us that, after the procession which swept through the gates of the city halted at the foot of Mount Moriah, Jesus advanced to the temple, walked through its courts, and looked round about on all things (Mark xi. 11). Every part of the building, every arrangement, every feature, was comprehended in that gaze. It was the act of the Judge. The survey completed, the *Purifier and Refiner* disposes his crucible. At the beginning of the ministry he cleansed the house of his Father, which had been rendered a den of merchandise; at the end of the ministry he repeats the cleansing (vers. 45, 46). Jerusalem was crowded; outside the city wall there was a vast city of pilgrims' booths. For the sale of victims for sacrifice, and no doubt for the vending of many wares besides, the temple precincts were for the time a huge holy fair. One could scarcely distinguish that its real purpose was an asylum for weary hearts, a refuge for sin-stricken consciences, a place for quiet meditation and prayer. Where, amid the hubbub of buyer and seller, could the pious Israelite "dwell in the courts of Jehovah, beholding his beauty and inquiring in his temple"? It is this that kindles the wrath of the Son of God, and incites to the action portrayed by the synoptic evangelists. "Who shall stand when he appears who is like a refiner's fire, and like fuller's soap?" This purging of the holy house of that which made it like a cave of brigands was the work of that first day, which has been called Palm Sunday. The night which followed was spent in Bethany, perhaps on the slope of Olivet. On the second day we find the Lord again in the temple, and now in the third of Malachi's characters—as the *swift Witness* against the enemies of God. This was the aspect of his countenance on the days which remained until the night came on which, in the form of his human presence, the Lord could no more work. "He taught daily in the temple" (ver. 47). The events of the Monday would seem to be these: In the keen-aired early morning, Jesus, on his way to the temple, is hungry. He sees (Matt. xxi. 19; Mark xi. 12—14) a fig tree, evidently a conspicuous one, which, rich in leaves, gave the promise of fruit. There is nothing but leaves, a mere *simulacrum*, the semblance without the reality of goodness. As a lesson to all the ages, a swift witness against all part-acting, he pronounces over it the curse of the Eternal Truth, and leaves it to wither and rot. The temple gained, again the dense crowd gathers around the Prophet of Nazareth. The phrase is most expressive: "The people were very attentive to hear him" (ver. 48). The tide had not yet turned. He was still engirt by the hosannahs of the multitude; when, lo! cries are heard, "Make way for the chief priest!" and, followed by a retinue of priests and scribes, the head of the temple-worship confronts the Teacher. Poor, purblind souls! they do not look for his authority to the truth with which he is filled, to the works which he does. To bigots like them the certificates which the truth supplies are unintelligible; their only point is a formally expressed delegation of power (ch. xx. 2). Had not Jesus met similar cavils at the Feast of Tabernacles two years before? Had he not argued (John v. 32—47) that it is impossible for minds brimful of prejudice, loving and courting the honour of men, to understand him, to know whose he is, whence he comes, and by what right he speaks? But now he will not thus argue. They are there to browbeat and overawe him; they shall themselves be silenced by a thrust impaling them on the horns of a dilemma from which they will escape only in confusion and chagrin. Question is replied to by the question of ch. xx. 3, 4. They cannot answer. Then, rejoins the Truth, "Neither tell I you by what authority I do these things" (ver. 8). And there follows a series of parables bearing on and bringing out the obstinacy which had just been exemplified: the two sons; the wicked husbandmen; and the marriage of the king's son. Only the second of these is quoted by St. Luke (xx. 9—16). The parable is in harmony with well-known prophetic symbols; *e.g.* Isa. v. 1—7. The vineyard is the kingdom of God, which had been planted in Israel; the husbandmen are the priests and scribes to whom had been committed the care of the vineyard; the servants sent—first one, then another, and then a third—to demand the fruit, represent the prophets, ending with John the Baptist; and the climax of the wickedness of the husbandmen is the rejection and death of the beloved Son. "What will the owner do with such men?" Christ demands. He pauses for the reply; and, not perceiving that it is pronouncing its own judgment, his audience answers, "He will miserably destroy them, and give the vineyard to others." Ah! priest and Pharisee, out of your own mouth are you condemned. "The kingdom of heaven shall be taken from you, and given to a nation bringing forth the fruits thereof." And from startled consciences comes back the shuddering, "God forbid!" He has not done with them. The eye, flashing its holy fire, fastens on the crouching multitude, and, resuming the discourse, he sends straight home the words of Ps. cxviii. 22, 23. Solemn, memorable words! Pause and ponder them. The spurning of the Incarnate Love and truth by those amongst whom he came often seems to us a miserable infatuation, a double-dyed sin against the Holy Ghost. Are we sure that Christ, coming as the swift Witness, would be welcomed even in the house of his friends to-day? The late General Gordon said, "*No;* he would be a Stranger, rejected, if not despised, by the society which is professedly Christian." One thing, at all events, is strange; and that is that men and women should live in such marvellous light as that into which we are called, and remain the men and women they are, unmoved by, unresponsive to, the voice of God, willing to live apart from him whose service is their perfect freedom. May we not summon ourselves before the great white throne of truth, and ask whether God is receiving from us the fruit of his own vineyard; whether we are consciously and really living to him; whether our attitude towards the Son of his love is that of a whole-hearted and loyal acceptance; or only like that which has been strikingly compared to "some fever-reduced patient, lifting himself up for an instant from the bed on which he is lying, and putting out a hand, and then falling back again, the vacillating, fevered, paralyzed will recoiling from the resolution, the conscience having power to say, 'Thou oughtest,' but with no power to enforce the execution of its decrees, and the heart turning away from the salvation that it would have found in the love of God to the loss that it finds in the love of self and earth." That vacillation, that impotence, is the strange, sad thing. Reflect intensely, prayerfully, on the house which the builders rejected. Which of the two ways is it, will it be : this House taken as the Head of the corner, the reconciling centre of all the days—pride, wilfulness falling on it, and through the fall broken ? or, the house rejected, and the Corner-stone falling on the disobedient soul, grinding its very strength to powder ? Love rejected—the wrath of the Lamb : who can measure that force ?

HOMILIES BY VARIOUS AUTHORS.

Vers. 1—9.—*Zacchæus ; the triumph of earnestness.* The incident here recorded provides a very good opportunity for the imagination. We can picture the scene before us quite vividly ; it is a subject for the sacred artist. But let us look at *the triumph of earnestness* as illustrated in the story of Zacchæus.

I. It triumphed over THE PERIL WHICH ATTENDS WEALTH. This man was rich (ver. 2). Riches are unfavourable to religious earnestness ; we have Christ's own word for it (ch. xviii. 24 ; see homily). They present a very strong inducement to their owner to forsake the fountain of living waters, and to quench his thirst in the lower streams. Far too often they lead to luxury, to indulgence, to spiritual indifference. But Zacchæus did not suffer this calamity to befall him, this fatal injury to be wrought upon him. His spiritual solicitudes won the victory over his temporal circumstances.

II. It triumphed over THE DEMORALIZING CALLING IN WHICH HE WAS ENGAGED. Our daily vocation must necessarily have a very great influence over us for good or evil ; and if it be one that tends to lower and degrade a man, he is placed in the greatest possible peril. Much wisdom of mind, much resoluteness of soul, and much devoutness of spirit must be required to withstand the adverse powers. But though Zacchæus was engaged in a pursuit that invited avarice and oppression, still he did not lose his religious earnestness.

III. It triumphed over AN EVIL REPUTATION. Few things are more degrading than a bad name. Men quickly become what they are supposed to be and what they are called. Let all his neighbours consider and call a man a rogue, and it will be strange indeed if he maintains his integrity. Yet, although Zacchæus was denominated and dismissed as "a publican," spoken of by a term which was full of the strongest reproach, he did not descend to that level.

IV. It triumphed over THE OBSTACLES WHICH STOOD BETWEEN HIM AND CHRIST. He could not venture to solicit an interview with this holy Prophet ; that he knew was completely barred by his vocation. He found it difficult to secure even a view of him as he passed along ; his smallness of stature was against him. But such was his determination that he disregarded all considerations of dignity and decorum, and ran any risk of popular derision and affront, and climbed up, as if he had been a boy, into a tree to command a view of Jesus of Nazareth. So he prevailed.

V. IT WON WHOLLY UNEXPECTED GOOD. 1. The honour of entertaining this great Prophet at his own house ; thus securing a standing to which he had long been a stranger. 2. The advantage of a protracted interview, an extended privilege, in which he could not only secure a few sentences from the great Teacher, but could unburden his heart to him and learn his holy will.

VI. IT LED TO NEWNESS OF LIFE. (Vers. 8, 9.) Zacchæus from that day forth was a new man. His character was thenceforth determined : whatever selfishness or wrongness there had been, it should be renounced, and, where possible, reparation should be made. Character and life were to be cleansed and renewed ; and Christ took him up into his favour and friendship. He was to be perfectly restored to the position he had lost. By his pursuit and practice he had become an alien, disinherited, no longer admitted to the services of the sanctuary. But now he was to be, in the fullest and deepest sense of the word, " a son of Abraham," a far truer son of his than many who prided themselves on their descent from the " father of the faithful."

Thus *earnestness* of spirit completely prevailed. 1. *Only earnestness* will prevail. *Indifference* will go down to the death from which it is already not far removed. *Half-heartedness* will go only a very little way towards the goal ; it will have to take some trouble and to suffer some pains, but it will not win the prize. Even *impulsiveness,* which bears a considerable resemblance to earnestness, but is not the same thing, will fail before the way is trodden and the end secured. Only earnestness wins. 2. *It always must.* Whatever comes in the way; whatever inward or outward obstacles present themselves; whatever personal or social hindrances intervene; however victory be delayed; notwithstanding that the case may again and again seem hopeless;— still in the end earnestness will succeed. Jesus Christ will manifest himself; he will be found in the home; his presence and his grace will fill the soul with joy; he will declare sonship and heirship to his devoted and determined follower.—C.

Ver. 9.—*Forfeiture and recovery.* Our Lord's words refer in the first instance to—
I. THE LOSS AND RECOVERY BY ZACCHÆUS of his place in the commonwealth of Israel. 1. He had forfeited this. It was by no means inalienable. Only they were the true children of Abraham who did the deeds, who lived the life, who were possessed with the spirit, of Abraham. So our Lord taught himself (see John viii. 39). This was Paul's doctrine also (Rom. ii. 28, 29; ix. 7; Gal. iii. 7). The true child of Abraham was he who walked by faith, who was the servant and the friend of God (Isa. xli. 8). But Zacchæus had lost this true, this real and effectual sonship. For he had been living the life of sense, and not of faith; he had departed from the service of God, and engaged in the practice of extortion and corruption. He had ceased to be the friend of God, and made friendship with an evil world. 2. But now he was in the path of restoration. He was penitent; he was a seeker after heavenly wisdom in Jesus Christ; and this meant renewal of heart and life; it meant rising into a new and elevated region, breathing the pure air of devotion, of service, of righteousness; it meant the recovery of the forfeited birthright. Salvation had come to himself and his household; once more he was " a son of Abraham." We are thus led to look at—
II. THE SAD POSSIBILITIES OF FORFEITURE open to all the children of men. God made us to be heirs of all that is good and blessed—of liberty, of truth, of honour and of love, of himself and of his kingdom. But sin comes in and spoils our heritage; under its evil ban we lose our good estate; our inheritance is forfeited; instead of being the " sons of God" and the " children of wisdom," we become rather the " children of wrath." We may forfeit: 1. *Our liberty.* We may become, how many do become, enslaved by some evil habit which holds them fast in its strong coils—some bodily or mental habit! 2. *Our hold upon the truth.* We may lose our faith in, and our appreciation of, the leading and vital doctrines which bring us into close and conscious fellowship with God. 3. *Our very manhood.* For there are many who suffer themselves to sink so low in the moral scale that they forfeit all claim to be accounted men; their lives are simply brutal. 4. Our rightful place *in the estimate of our fellow-men.* We may lose all the esteem, the confidence, and (consequently) the affection of our neighbours. 5. *The friendship of Jesus Christ.* Too often those who once walked with him and worked for him stand aside, and " walk no more " by his side; they leave his service, they lose his loving favour, they cannot be any longer counted among his friends. And with all this there must be the sad and grievous forfeiture of: 6. *The hope of eternal life.* For when fidelity is lost, hope is lost also.
III. THE BLESSED OPENING FOR RESTORATION provided by the Saviour of souls. There is no " house," however fallen, to which " salvation " may not come; no human being, however sunk in sin and wrong, who may not be restored in the mercy of God by the power of Jesus Christ the Saviour. It is when *he* is admitted to the home and to the heart that recovery is attained. In him, for all earnest seekers, is escape from bondage and from error and unbelief; in his service is found the gradual but effectual return of the trust and the love of man; he offers the renewal of his friendship, and opens again the closed door of hope to the penitent and the believing spirit. The slave of sin becomes the son of God; the companion of the evil-doer becomes the friend and co-worker of Christ; the candidate for condemnation becomes the heir of heaven.—C.

Ver. 10.—*The great purpose of Christ.* Mankind had lost its way utterly, its way from the home of God, from the fields of truth, from the path of holiness, from the fountains of joy; was wandering, blind and miserable, in forbidden ways; was stumbling on the dark mountains of error and sin. And the Son of man came to seek this erring and lost race, to lead it back again, to restore it to its heritage in wisdom, in righteousness, in God. This great and most beneficent purpose is enough of itself to explain such action as he took on this occasion ; it covers the propriety of the conduct which seemed at the time so inexplicable to the good people of his day. For on what more fitting errand could the Saviour be engaged than on that of saving another human soul from its sin and its shame, and lifting it up into the light and liberty of the truth ? But there are three reasons which we gain from the words or the actions of our Lord which perfectly justified him (and would justify us) in seeking out and saving a lost human soul.

I. An appeal to our finer and nobler instincts. If you have a hundred sheep, and of these all but one are safely sheltered from the cold and protected from every peril, but that one is shut out, is away shivering in the blast, is exposed to the attack of the wild beast, is nearing the deadly precipice,—your heart prompts you to leave those that are safe, and to go and seek and rescue the one that is lost. Christ's heart prompts him to find that human soul which is lost in the mazes of error, or caught in the meshes of vice, or starving on the barren plains of unbelief. The most generous instincts of our nature will help us to understand his action when he went to the house of the publican, or suffered the daughter of shame to come in penitence to his feet.

II. An appeal to our higher interests. We should put forth that labour in the field of sacred usefulness which is most remunerative. But which answers best— attention to the pretentious Pharisee, or to the shamefaced publican ? To forgive fifty shillings to him who will first dispute the claim and then think nothing of your readi- ness to forego it will not be so satisfactory as to forgive five hundred pounds to him who is constrained to acknowledge the indebtedness, and is filled with gratitude to you for cancelling it. To endeavour to convince the scribe and the Pharisee of sin would have proved vain and fruitless work ; but to lead some guilty ones to penitence and purity was to earn unbounded gratitude, and to unloose streams of devoted love that should refresh the parched and thirsty soil.

III. An appeal to our sense of duty. The physician has several patients ; some of them are not very ill, and these have the idea that they know what ails them and what remedies will do them good ; but there are two or three that are dangerously, perhaps desperately ill, who do not know what they should do for recovery, and who will gladly take his advice and adopt his measures. To whom should he go but to those who need him most and will receive him best ?

1. *Let us enter more into the pitifulness of spiritual degradation.* Sin is to be con- demnèd, and strong indignation is often a duty and even a grace. But it is also very *pitiful.* Whether we find it in publican or harlot, in the covetous man or in the degraded woman, it is a thing to grieve over, even as Christ our Lord did, with a generous compassion ; to affect our hearts with a pure and even deep distress. And if we should feel thus as we contemplate the condition of *one* lost human being, what should our emotion be in view of the multitudes who are sunk in superstition, in wrong- doing, in utter hopelessness and helplessness ! When we "see these multitudes," should we not, like the Master, be "moved with compassion for them, because they are as sheep without a shepherd " ? May we not well exclaim—

> " My God, I feel the mournful scene,
> And my heart bleeds for dying men,
> While fain my pity would reclaim
> And snatch the firebrands from the flame " !

2. *Let us avail ourselves of every means for seeking and saving the lost :* whether it be individual effort, or action in combination with others, or liberal contribution to the missionary institution, let every opportunity be taken to follow in the path of love once trodden by "those sacred feet."—C.

Ver. 10.—*Saving the lost.* It has been questioned whether there can be mentioned one word which is more pathetic than any other. It might be well maintained that this word would be found in our text. What truly and profoundly pathetic pictures are called up before us by the sound of the word, "lost"! It speaks to us of the *vessel* far out of its track and drifting toward the rocks where it will find its ruin; it speaks of the *traveller* lost among the mountains, moving toward the precipice over which he is bound to fall and perish; it speaks of the *firm* whose affairs have been growing serious and have now become desperate, before which there is no other prospect than the closed door and a place in the gazette; and it speaks of the sad story, old as sin but young as yesterday, of one that has been deceived and led astray, over whose character and over whose future the darkest shadows rest. But our text reminds us of—

I. THE LOST WORLD WHICH CHRIST CAME TO SAVE. 1. There was a day in the history of heaven when it was announced that a new world was lost; that a race created in its Divine Maker's image was lost, had departed from the truth and wisdom of God, had left its home in his love, and had wandered away in guilt and wrong. 2. Only God himself could comprehend what *that* meant; what evil, what sorrow, what error, what darkness of soul, what wretchedness of life, what degradation of character, what death-fulness. 3. But the Son of God determined to restore it; ordered everything in his holy providence that would prepare for his own personal intervention; in due time manifested himself in the flesh, spake, wrought, lived, suffered, died, arose, reascended; left behind him the great work of redemption in all its fulness and fitness—the gospel of the grace of God.

II. THE LOST SOUL WHICH HE IS EVER SEEKING AND SAVING. 1. *The sense in which each sinful human soul is lost.* (1) It has lost *its way*; it is a traveller going in the wrong direction, away from his home toward the perilous precipice. (2) It has lost *its treasure*, its heritage; for it has lost its peace, its harmony, its accordance with all those beings to whom it is most nearly and vitally related; it has lost its hopes. (3) It has lost *its worth*, its likeness to the Holy One; it has been brought down to folly, to that which is unbeautiful and unworthy. 2. *The fact that Christ is seeking it.* (1) *He is tenderly interested in every human soul.* At all stages in its history. When it is in the far country he is regarding it with infinite compassion and Divine yearning; when the first thought of returning is kindled in the heart and the beginnings of penitence are seen; when there is earnestness which makes toward, but does not amount to, actual repentance (see Mark x. 21); when the soul is seeking its Saviour. (2) *He is endeavouring to win it.* He is coming to it by various approaches, laying a loving hand upon it at many points, addressing it in many tones, returning again and again to it in patient solicitude. "Behold, he stands at the door, and knocks." (3) *Our only possible response.* Not, indeed, that we *cannot* reject and refuse him; *we can*; it is open to us to do that. But, then, *how can we?* If we would not be shamefully and guiltily ungrateful, if we would not make his dying and ever-living love to be of no avail to us, if we have any regard for our own present and immortal blessedness, if we would win the prize and enjoy the heritage of eternal life, the only possible response we can make to the seeking Saviour is to open wide the door of our hearts and bid him enter and take full possession of our grateful and loving spirit.—C.

Vers. 12—27.—*Probation and award.* Jesus Christ here invites us to do two things.

I. TO TREAT THIS LIFE AS A TIME OF SACRED OPPORTUNITY. The "nobleman" of the parable gave to his servants a certain sum, of which they were to make good use during his absence. His charge was this: "Occupy till I come." 1. The time of the nobleman's absence stands for our mortal life. Whether it be long or short, our present life is a period during which we have to be preparing for another of far greater consequence. It is a probationary period, that on which the larger and more serious future depends. This is in harmony with our experience; for one part of our life is a preparation for another, and the nature of the succeeding period depends upon the character of that which precedes it—childhood for youth, youth for young manhood, etc. 2. The "pound" of the parable stands for God-given opportunity—for the constitutional capacity with which we are endowed; for the favouring circumstances and facilities by which we are surrounded; for the Christian privileges with which we are blessed. 3. The smallness of our endowment affords no escape from responsibility. Only "one pound." It seems a very small sum for a nobleman to give in charge; but clearly it was large enough for a righteous requirement. No plea could be found in the littleness of the sum; it is not even urged. No man is entitled to say that his human spirit is worth nothing to God, his life worth nothing to the cause of righteousness; only God knows how valuable one human spirit, one earthly life, is. 4. No slavish timidity will excuse the most faint-hearted (vers. 21, 22). Our God is not a Being from whose service we have to turn because we shrink from his severity (Ps. ciii. 8—14; Isa. xl. 29; lvii. 16; 2 Cor. viii. 12).

II. To LOOK FORWARD TO A DAY OF ACCOUNT AND OF AWARD. 1. There will be a day of judgment. The nobleman will return and call his servants before him (ver. 15). This may stand for some one great day, or we may still better look upon it as the day, when our earthly life terminates, and when.we shall, as individual souls, stand before the Judge. 2. God will require of us the use we have made of our opportunity; what we have gained; what we have done in the direction (1) of self-culture, ministering to the growth of our spiritual faculties; (2) of the service of our kind, enlightening and aiding and blessing them; (3) of magnifying the Name of our Divine Lord. 3. He will express his Divine judgment concerning us—his warm approval of those who have been most faithful (ver. 17); his acceptance of those who have not been unfaithful (ver. 19); his displeasure with the unworthy (ver. 22). We are to look for the clearly and fully expressed decision of Jesus Christ upon the character of our life-work, upon the comparative excellency or faultiness of our Christian life. 4. He will determine the measure of our award by the degree of our fidelity (see vers. 17, 19). The more faithful and devoted the life on earth, the larger the recompense, the brighter the crown, the broader the sphere, in the heavenly kingdom. The doctrine of Matt. xx. 14, 15 does not contradict this; it simply teaches that those to whom God gives a smaller share of bounty and of grace are not to complain because there are those to whom he grants a larger one. God is righteous, and he not only will not forget our work and labour of love (Heb. vi. 10), but he will not allow those of his servants who have devoted their powers to his cause with the greatest energy, constancy, and self-sacrifice to miss the most generous and gracious recognition at his loving hand.—C.

Vers. 12—24.—*Life a sacred opportunity.* We may bring out the main thought of our Master in this parable if we consider the four points of—
I. GOD'S SOVEREIGNTY OF OUR LIFE. He is the Divine Lord of our life. It came from him; it is continued by him; it is enriched perpetually and liberally from his bountiful stores; and it is subject to his sway. He has a sovereign right to determine what it shall be—what shall be its aim and its issue. He is the "nobleman;" we are "his servants." If we do think of objecting to his claim (ver. 14), we shall only be disappointed and defeated in our rebelliousness of heart. He cannot be dethroned; against his right to rule there can be no appeal. Submission is our true wisdom, as it is our first and last obligation.
II. THE SACRED CHARGE HE LAYS UPON US. He gives to each of us money (silver)—a talent (Matt. xxv.), a "pound" (text), and he says to each of us, "Occupy till I come." 1. The time of the nobleman's absence represents our mortal life, or (more correctly) the period between our first sense of responsibility and the last hour of consciousness. 2. The pound (talent) represents the opportunity of service which he places within our reach. This opportunity is compounded of (1) our natural capacity—bodily, mental, spiritual; and of (2) all the favourable circumstances by which we are attended as we pass through our life—education, home influence, capital, facilities for entering a sphere of activity, etc. And this sacred opportunity looks out in three directions: (1) the cultivation of our own nature; (2) the service of mankind; (3) the worship of God, and work in his broad field. The Lord of our life is saying to us, "Occupy till I come;" *i.e.* put out this pound, employ this sacred opportunity now within your reach, turn it to good account, use your capacities and your circumstances for high and noble ends—for your own spiritual enlargement, for the good of your brethren, for the glory of Christ.
III. THE REWARD OF FAITHFULNESS. (Vers. 16—19.) Here are two principles on which we may depend as guiding the Divine hand when the day of account arrives. 1. Those who have done well will receive God's gracious commendation and reward. To them he will express his good pleasure, and to them he will give an award. 2. They who have been more faithful will receive the more gracious approval and the larger sphere. He who turns his one pound into ten has a warmer welcome and a more

liberal reward; to him are those most gladdening words addressed, and to him are entrusted not five but ten cities over which to rule (ver. 17). "Then shall every man have praise of God." But then shall those who have striven hard and toiled long and suffered much in the cause of Jesus Christ have a full measure of benediction; and to such will be apportioned a crown that will be bright indeed, a sphere that will be broad indeed.

IV. THE PENALTY OF NEGLIGENCE. (Vers. 20—24.) The slothful servant may make excuses, but they will be brushed aside; he himself will be severely condemned; he will be divested of what he has left him; he will be sent into saddest exile (Matt. xxv. 30). It is not the atheist, or the criminal, or the perpetrator of vicious deeds; it is not the outward and flagrant transgressor, who is here condemned and sentenced; it is the man who *made nothing of his life*; it is the man who had no sense of sacred responsibility; it is he who withheld his powers from the service of God;—it is he who is pronounced to be so guilty. To let our lives go by without making them a service and a blessing, to let our powers and our opportunities rust in mere disuse, is to be accumulating a debt which we shall not be able to discharge, and which will make us to appear bankrupt at the great account.—C.

Ver. 26.—*The law of spiritual increase.* Here we have one of those paradoxes of Jesus Christ into the heart of which many have failed to find their way. Why, it is asked, should one who *has* have more? will he not have too much? Why should he who *has but little* lose the little he has? will he not be still worse off than ever? Where is the wisdom, where the righteousness of this course? This criticism arises from a pure misunderstanding of Christ's meaning. We shall see what he meant if we consider—

I. THE VIEW CHRIST TOOK OF POSSESSION. When may a man be said *to have* anything? When he has legal documents to prove that it belongs to him? Or when it is securely locked up in a box or buried in the earth? Not at all. It is when *he is using it*, when he is turning it to account, when he is making it answer the purpose for which it exists. If a man lets an object rust in disuse, remain unemployed, he has it not, virtually and practically. It is not his at all; it does him no good, renders him no service, is to him as if it were not; he has it not, in truth. This accords perfectly with Christ's usage in Matt. xxv. There the men who put out their talents *had* them; the man who hid his latent *had it not*. He who does not make use of that which is at his command only "seemeth to have" (or thinketh he has) it (ch. viii. 18). It is use that really constitutes possession. This is not a mere fancy or conceit; it is the language of truth, it is the verdict of experience. The miser does not really possess his gold; it answers to him none of the ends which make it the valuable thing it is. He might as well own as many counters. He seems to have (thinks he has) money, but in truth he *has* it not. It is thus with men of great intellectual capacity which they do not employ; their faculties, unused, are of no value to themselves or to others; they might as well be non-existent. According to the wise and true usage of the great Teacher, we have the things we use; those we use not we have not. Now we can understand—

II. THE DIVINE LAW OF INCREASE AND DECLINE. For this is not a mere action done on one particular occasion; there is nothing exceptional or arbitrary about it. It is a Divine method invariably adopted; a Divine principle running through the whole econony; a Divine law with illustrations on every hand. It affects us at every turn of our life, in every part of our nature. It applies to us considered: 1. *Physically.* The muscle that is used is developed; that which is neglected shrinks, and in time becomes wholly powerless. To him that has is given; from him that hath not is taken away. 2. *Mentally.* The boy who cultivates his intellectual capacities becomes mentally strong; every acquisition of knowledge is an increase of power; the more he knows the better he can learn: to him that has is given. But the boy who does not study, but wastes his youth in idleness, not only does not acquire knowledge; he loses the faculty of acquisition: from him that has not is taken away that (capacity) which he has. 3. *Spiritually.* (1) *Spiritual perception.* The little child can readily understand the elements of the Christian faith, and, apprehending them, go on to master "the deep things of God." But the aged man who has learnt nothing of Divine truth through a long life of godlessness, is quite unteachable ; he is dull of apprehension : from him has been taken away, etc. ; his faculties have become shrivelled. (2) *Christian work.* Every one has a certain capacity for usefulness ; and he is bound to put it out at once ; if he waits until his capacity has grown into a power, he will find that not only will he not gain the skill he is waiting for, but he will lose the capacity he now has. But if, on the other hand, he uses what he has, the exercise of his humblest talent will bring increase, and he will soon acquire the strength and facility he is eager to possess. What, therefore, we wish to be able to do—teach, preach, pray, etc.—we must set about doing ; every intelligent, devout effort to do good means not only a little good done, but a little power gained. What we do poorly to-day we shall do fairly well to-morrow ; be ourselves to-day, we shall surpass ourselves to-morrow. Aptitude comes with effort and exercise : to him that has is given. (3) *Spiritual sensibility.* The little child is open to impression, and, if he yields to the truth he knows, that truth will always be effective ; but if he rejects it his heart becomes hardened, and he becomes increasingly unresponsive : from him that *has not*, etc. Thus God's holy Law engirts us on every side ; we cannot step outside it. It is determining our character and our destiny. We must act upon it, must turn it to good account. We must see to it that we really have what we seem to have, that we are using the talent, the opportunity, that is at our command. Then to us will be given—here, on the earth, in the shape of increased faculty and multiplied usefulness ; there, in the heavens, in the way of a far broader sphere of celestial service.—C.

Vers. 28—38.—*Christ's royalty.* Something like a royal procession is here described. On the foal of an ass, on which it comported as well with Oriental ideas of *honour* as with Christian ideas of *peace* that he should ride, the "King came, meek," but not without attention and acclaim, into Jerusalem. A large company of the curious, the devout, and even the enthusiastic, welcomed him as "the King that came in the Name of the Lord." At last, thought his disciples, his hour is come ; at last their Master was entering on his heritage, was assuming his kingdom ; at last their long-delayed hopes were to be fulfilled. Gladly they accepted and sustained the greetings of the multitude, and fondly, we may be sure, they hoped that a triumphant issue was at hand. But it had no such ending as they looked for. Jesus went into the temple, healed the sick, received the adoration of the children, whose voices (as we can well believe) were the last to sink into silence, and went quietly back to Bethany. What, then, did it mean ? What was the service and significance of the scene?

I. A VALUABLE REMINDER OF HIS POWER OF SELF-RESTRAINT. He had been moving among men as "one that serveth," as one that "ministered." He had moved as a very humble traveller along the path of human life. But how easy it would have been for him to call forth the honour of the people, and to live amid the excitements of popularity, and to reach the high places of power ! But this he resolutely declined to do, choosing deliberately the lowlier but the nobler path of humble, holy service.

II. A STRIKING INDICATION OF HIS ACCEPTANCE WITH THE PEOPLE. No one can say that Christ's teaching was not profound ; it was deep as the very fountains of truth. No philosophy went further ; he went down into the deep places of the human soul. Yet, while the philosophers made their appeal to the cultured, Christ addressed himself to the multitude, to the common human heart. And "all the people were very attentive to hear him." So here, while the men who prided themselves on their knowledge looked on with angry disdain (ver. 29), the people and the children were enthusiastic in his favour—they recognized in the Prophet of Nazareth the true Teacher that had come from God. Better be numbered among the simple-hearted who can appreciate the Divine than among the wise and learned who misread the providence of God, and stand sullen and silent while everything is inviting to joy and praise. Better be the ignorant cottager whose heart is full of reverence, or the little child who has the songs of Zion on his lips and the love of Jesus in his heart, than the learned critic who never bends the heart in homage to the true and the eternal.

III. A HINT OF CHRIST'S TRUE ROYALTY. The Messiah of the Jews was to be a King. To that conclusion prophecy pointed with unfailing finger, and on that event Jewish faith rested with gathering hope. The Son of David was to occupy his father's throne ; the daughters of Jerusalem were to rejoice because "her King was coming."

Claiming the Messiahship, Jesus was bound to claim this sovereignty, but how do this without encouraging the current fallacy as to his temporal and visible royalty? Is not this simple scene the answer? Christ then and thus said, "I am the King you are awaiting." But its extreme simplicity and its transiency showed that he did not intend to wear the trappings and be surrounded with the common grandeurs of earthly royalty; it showed that he came not for pomps and pageantries and outward triumphs, but to seek a sovereignty of another kind in another realm altogether. That very simple and passing regal state was only an emblem of the spiritual sovereignty which was immeasurably higher and more to be desired. Sweet to his ear may have been the acclaim of the populace and the hosannas of the children; but how much sweeter is the voice of man or woman or of little child who goes in glad submission to his feet to offer loyal service to the Divine Redeemer, to place heart and life beneath his gracious and benignant sway!

IV. A PROPHECY OF FAR FUTURE GLORY. Never on this earth will that scene be re-enacted; but there is an hour coming when, in another realm, it will be amplified and perpetuated. Christ will be acknowledged King by all the hosts celestial and terrestrial. The transient gladness of the sacred city will be nothing to the everlasting joy of the new Jerusalem; the passing enthusiasm of that happy demonstration to the abiding blessedness of the life in the heavenly land. Yet may we take that one hour of Jerusalem's acceptance of her King as a prelude and a prophecy of the adoration which the redeemed of every kindred and tribe shall pay him when they cast their crowns at his feet.

> "Oh that with yonder sacred throng
> We at his feet may fall," etc.!

PRACTICAL LESSONS. We gather: 1. That Jesus Christ is now claiming the real, spiritual sovereignty of ourselves. He is calling upon us not to strew his path with palm branches, but to offer him the first place in our heart; to yield him our perfect trust, our unfailing and unfading love, our cheerful and constant obedience. 2. That the rest of soul which follows such surrender of ourselves is incomparably better than the passing exultation of a triumphal entry. 3. That by loyal and devoted service in his cause we shall gain a place in the acclaiming company that will praise the King in his celestial glory.—C.

Ver. 28.—*Eagerness in the upward path.* "He went before, ascending up to Jerusalem." "To go to Corinth" once meant to give way to dissipation. What did it mean to "go to Jerusalem"? To the Jews generally it meant to go to some sacred service, to visit the temple of Jehovah, to enter the sacred precincts where sacrifice was offered to God. To Jesus Christ, now, it meant to go on to martyrdom and to death. But still to go thither was to "go up," was to "ascend," and in his progress to that sacred city he did not lag behind, nor even walk abreast; he "went before," he showed great eagerness in that upward and most honourable path. Such was his eagerness of soul that the disciples were astonished and even awed as they beheld it (Mark x. 32); they were profoundly impressed with the ardour and intensity of his spirit: "As they followed they were afraid." We may share the Saviour's spirit of holy ardour and elevation as we tread—

I. THE PATH OF HOLY PRIVILEGE. When may we be said to be on the upward road so far as our activities are concerned? When we are presiding? or when we are ruling? or when we are winning? or when we are rejoicing? It may be so. But assuredly we are then on the way that slopes upward and heavenward when we are in the path of sacred privilege, when we are "on our way to God"—to his nearer presence, to the worship of the Holy and the True One, to communion with the righteous Lord of all, to fellowship with Christ, to gathering at his table of love, to work in his vineyard. Then are we in the high places—"in the heavenly places;" then are we engaged in an exercise of human power which is most worthy of our highest faculties and reflects dignity on our human nature; then are we "ascending" in spirit; and we do well to feel that it is not a time for slackness of speed, for exhaustion of spirit, for signs of weariness. We should show a sacred ardour, a holy eagerness, like unto him who "went before" as he ascended to Jerusalem.

II. THE WAY OF WITNESS-BEARING. To go to Jerusalem was, to our Lord, to go where he should " bear witness to the truth" (John xviii. 37); should bear witness by *words*, of which many would be utterly misunderstood, and many treated with high disdain; should bear witness by *suffering*, by calm, brave, patient endurance of wrong. And to do this was to go up, to ascend; as it is to-day, and will always be. Where shall we find the martyr-witnesses among mankind? Not as we look down, but as we look up—up to the very loftiest altitudes that human foot has ever trodden. Kings and statesmen walk not along such lofty, such truly celestial paths as do they who speak amid derision or suffer without flinching to attest the living truth of God. When we go forward toward self-sacrifice for Christ's sake we "ascend up" to the high places of the kingdom of God. It may well be with no faltering or lingering step, but with a free and forward movement, like him who now "went before," that we move to those sacred and noble levels.

III. THE MOUNT OF TRANSLATION. Jesus went up to Jerusalem, to Calvary, to that wondrous redeeming death which is the world's great sacrifice. We may well say that he ascended to that. That was the culminating point of his career; that not only concluded, but crowned his course. And after receiving all the light which he has shed upon it, we need not be ever speaking of death as a dark valley down which we must descend; we may rather regard it as a mount of translation up which we move. In all things physical, indeed, we descend to die; our powers become lower, our life grows less. But we walk by faith in Christ Jesus. And by faith we regard ourselves as going up to the gateway which admits to the celestial glories. In view of that which immediately afterwards awaits us, we need not lag behind; we may press forward, like our Master, as we draw toward the close, and may eagerly pass on the way which ends in death and victory.—C.

Vers. 39, 40.—*Suppression and expression.* It is not difficult to find the meaning of our Lord in this hyperbolical utterance of his. "Why should I silence my disciples?" he says. "Of what use would it be to suppress such strong feelings as theirs? Feeling will always find its vent. If suppressed in one form, it will express itself in another; if driven underground in one spot, it will only come up in another; if these human beings whose hearts are so filled with exultation were silenced, the very stones would cry out." It is useless, and worse than useless, to try to extinguish enthusiasm by a hard repressive commandment. The folly of suppression and the wisdom of allowing and inviting, indeed of providing, the means of suitable expression will apply to many things.

I. YOUTHFUL CURIOSITY. Curiosity is an irrepressible thing; it will be satisfied. Age cannot extinguish it, try how it may. It may have occasion to check it, but its true wisdom is to guide it—to take the necessary trouble to satisfy it in the best possible way. Curiosity is not a plant of the evil one; it is rooted in the soul by the heavenly Father; it is a main source of knowledge; it ought to be wisely but amply nourished. If we endeavour to suppress it we shall find that it will *not be* suppressed, but will find other ways of satisfaction than those we disallow.

II. THE LOVE OF LIBERTY. A desire for freedom and independence is a strong sentiment of the human soul. Where intelligence exists there it will arise and assert itself. It will not be put down; it cannot be put out. Authority may "rebuke" it, as the Pharisees wanted Christ to act on this occasion; but the Lord of our nature knows that it will be heard and must be respected. Neither domestic, nor social, nor national, nor ecclesiastical despotism can survive beyond a certain time. The aspirations of the human soul for freedom will not be denied. If not permitted a wise and rightful form of action, they will take improper and harmful ones.

III. THE RELIGIOUS SENTIMENT IN MAN. Philosophy has tried to silence the voice of faith; it has undertaken to rebuke the disciples; and it has temporarily and superficially succeeded. But it has found that so deep and so strong is the religious sentiment in man that when religion is driven down below the surface it comes out again in superstition in some form or other. The sense of the Supreme, a yearning of the human heart for the living God, is not to be erased from the soul, is not to be removed from the life of man.

IV. DEFINITE RELIGIOUS CONVICTIONS. These also are not to be suppressed. Men have taken very various views of the doctrines of the Christian faith; and, as we know too well, opponents have not only "rebuked," but tried arrogantly and forcibly to silence, those who have differed from them. But they have not succeeded. Religious conviction is an inextinguishable force; slain in the persons of its champions, it rises again and reappears, often in tenfold power.

V. RELIGIOUS ENTHUSIASM. To this the words of our Lord primarily and most properly apply. Religious fervour may frequently be disposed to take a form which we do not think the best, or even the suitable and becoming. But we must take care how we deal with it. It is not a thing to be suppressed; it is to be encouraged and enlightened and guided. It is, or it has within it, a true, living power; this power is of God, and is for good. Abruptly and harshly rebuked and silenced, it will only assert itself in other and probably still more questionable forms. Treated with Christian sympathy and encouragement (see ch. x. 49, 50), informed and enlightened by superior intelligence, directed into wise channels, it may do a noble work for the Master and mankind. 1. Let not a young enthusiasm be mindful only of its own exuberance; let it be regardful of the judgment and feeling of experience. 2. Let experience be tolerant of eager-hearted enthusiasm, and be prepared to count it amongst its friends.—C.

Ver. 41.—*The tears of Christ.* We are touched by the tears of a little child; for they are the sign of a genuine, if a simple, sorrow. Much more are we affected by the tears of a strong and brave man. When a man of vigorous intelligence, accustomed to command himself, gives way to tears, then we feel that we are in the presence of a very deep and sad emotion. Such were the tears of Christ. Twice, at least, he wept; and on this occasion we understand that he gave free vent to an overpowering distress. The tears of Christ speak of two things more especially.

I. HIS TENDER SYMPATHY WITH HUMAN SORROW. The grief which now overwhelmed the Saviour was (as we shall see) very largely due to his sense of its past and its approaching guilt. But it was also due, in part, to his foreknowledge of the sufferings its inhabitants must endure. An intense sympathy with human woe was and is a very large element in the character and life of Jesus Christ. 1. It was his compassion for our race that brought him from above—that we by his poverty might become rich. 2. It was this which, more than anything else, accounts for the miracles he wrought. He could not see the blind, and the lame, and the fever-stricken, and the leprous without tendering them the restoring grace it was in his power to bestow. He could not see mourning parents and weeping sisters without healing the heart-wounds he was able to cure. 3. It was this which drew to himself the confidence and affection of loving hearts. It was no wonder that pitiful women and tender-hearted children, and men whose hearts were unhardened by the world, were drawn in trust and love to the responsive Son of man, whose step was always stopped by a human cry, to whose compassion no stricken man or woman ever appealed in vain. 4. It is this feature of his character which makes him so dear to us now as our Divine Friend. For in this world, where sorrow treads so fast on the heels of joy, and where human comforters so often fail us, of what priceless value is it to have in that Everlasting One, who is the Ever-present One, a Friend who is "touched" with our griefs, and who still carries our sorrows by the power of his sympathy! (1) Let us thank God that we *have* such a Friend in him; and (2) let us resolve before God that such a friend will we seek and strive *to be.*

II. HIS PROFOUND REGRET FOR THOSE WHO ARE IN THE WRONG. With what eyes do we look upon human sin when we see it at its worst? How are we affected by the sight of a drunkard, of a thief, of a foul-mouthed and fallen woman? Are we filled with contempt? Many bad things are indeed contemptible; but there is a view to be taken which is worthier and more Christ-like than that; a view which is more humane and more Divine—a feeling of profound pitifulness and sorrowful regret. It was this which filled the heart of Christ when he looked upon Jerusalem, and that called forth his tearful lamentation. Much was there about that city that might well move his righteous anger, that did call down his strong, unsparing indignation (Matt. xxiii.)— its spiritual arrogance, its religious egotism, its fearful pretentiousness, its deep-seated hypocrisy, its heartless cruelty, its whitewash of ceremony *without* with all its corruptness and selfishness *within.* But Jesus forebore to denounce; he stopped to weep. He was most powerfully affected by the thought that Jerusalem might have been so much to God and man, and was—what she was. Jesus Christ was not so much angered as he was saddened by the presence and the sight of sin. He might have withered it up in his wrath, but he rather wept over it in his pity. This is the Christian spirit to be cherished and to be manifested by ourselves. We must contemn the contemptible; but we rise to higher ground when we pity the erring because they are in error, when we mourn over the fallen because they are down so low, when we grieve for those who are afar off because they are astray from God and blessedness. But we must not only *weep* for those who are in the wrong because they are in the wrong. We must *do* our utmost to set them right. "How often" did Christ seek to gather those sons and daughters of Jerusalem under the wings of his love! How often and how earnestly should we seek to reclaim and to restore!—C.

Vers. 41, 42.—*Judæa and England.* Did Jesus Christ grieve over Jerusalem as a patriot over his own country? Was there an element of patriotic sorrow in that touching and tearful lament? Did he love that land any the more because, as concerning the flesh, he was the Son of David, was born at Bethlehem, and regarded the Jews as his fellow-citizens? The idea is open to one objection. To be a patriot seems to put a man under limitation. To love our own country more than others is to love others less than our own. We shrink from associating with him anything that even looks like partiality or partisanship. On the other hand, we must take care that we do not lose the human in our desire to preserve the Divine. Might not the same consideration be urged against our Lord cherishing a peculiar regard and affection for his mother, his sisters, his brothers, his personal friends? But who can doubt that there was especial love in his heart for these? There was then, probably, something of patriotic grief in those tears of Christ, an additional pang in his heart, as he thought that it was Jerusalem itself, the city round which so many associations gathered, whose guilt and doom stood in clear, sad vision before him. However that may be, he felt deep compassion as he looked forward to—

I. THE FUTURE OF THE HOLY LAND. We speak of the land or country, though it was the city of Jerusalem over which he wept. But in the sense in which "Paris is France" Jerusalem was Judæa, was Israel itself. It was the strength, the light, the glory, of the land; it was the centre to which all the inhabitants looked and journeyed; it was the source of the people's habits and beliefs. The capital taken, everything was well-nigh gone, the fate of the country was settled. Concerning this people, this nation, Jesus Christ felt, as he beheld the city: 1. That it had been *enriched with peculiar privilege.* (1) Commencing with a signal and glorious deliverance from bondage; (2) continued with the granting of a Law and a system admirably fitted to save them from surrounding superstitions and impurities; (3) multiplied by the coming of psalmist and of prophet with inspiring song and elevating speech and life, uplifting their imagination and cleansing their conscience; (4) enhanced by the strong and severe, but yet kind and merciful, discipline through which they were made to pass; (5) culminating in the presence, the teaching, the life, of him, in whom One wiser than Solomon, mightier than David, devouter than Samuel, nobler than Elijah and John, "was there." 2. That it was *charged with a high and sacred mission.* It was designed by God to be the depository and guardian of his Divine truth, to hold fast and to hold high those great verities which are the strength, the life, and the glory of our manhood. Just what part it was to have played, and what exact service it would have rendered our race had it been loyal and true, may be questioned by us. But it would undoubtedly have played a very great part, and been, as a nation, the great factor in the restitution of mankind. 3. That it had now *missed its chance,* and was *hastening to its doom.* (1) The Hebrew faith had become a hollow formality, a mere ritual, from which true reverence, love, charity, earnestness, were all absent; and (2) the nation was in the very act of rejecting and was about to slay its Messiah, thus going down into the darkest crime and then going on to the saddest disaster. We glance at—

II. THE FUTURE OF OUR OWN COUNTRY. There is no little parallelism between Judæa and England. 1. God has enriched our land with *peculiar privileges.* We have (1) a large share of religious liberty; (2) a good measure of spiritual enlightenment, not indeed without some dark shadows of ignorance and superstition; (3) numerous and strong organizations covering the land, whose function is to teach, to guide, to guard, to rescue, and redeem. May *we* not say, "He hath not dealt so with any nation; as for his statutes and commandments, they have not known them" as we have known them? 2. God has given us a high and a *great mission* to perform. Responsibility goes with privilege; it is, indeed, the obverse side of the same thing. We have not only to present to his view "a holy nation" within our own borders, to raise our own community to the height of Christian knowledge, of social purity, of national well-being in all its forms; but also to diffuse the light of Divine truth far and wide, and to make our influence tell for peace, righteousness, and truth in every quarter of the globe. 3. We have to consider whether we are *declining* that *mission* or are *fulfilling it*. That is a question which cannot be determined by public professions; nor by the number or character of our sanctuaries; nor by the number or constitution of our Churches. It can only be determined by the actual spiritual and moral condition of our people, of the multitudes and millions of our citizens; and by the earnestness and devotedness of Christian men and women in the field of sacred work. By these criteria we stand or fall.—C.

Ver. 44.—*The time of visitation.* "This thy day;" "The time of thy visitation." What is it that makes man, everywhere and under all conditions, so deeply interesting? He is found on savage shores in nakedness and barbarism, in idolatrous lands living in saddest superstition, in the slums and purlieus of great cities as debased and vicious as the brutes of the field, yet still most interesting. It is because God made man for himself, and, far as he has wandered from his side, it is still open to him to return. It is because man was created to move along the loftiest levels, and, low as he has fallen, *it is in him to rise.* Bring to bear the right influences upon him, and from the very lowest depths of debasement and dishonour he may attain to noble heights of excellency and power. Again and again in the history of mankind and of individual men has this been proved to be true. Illustrative and reassuring instances can be adduced in which whole tribes, or even nations, and in which particular men and women, have been visited with "the truth and grace of Jesus Christ," and have been lifted up to knowledge, to virtue, to piety, to spiritual beauty, to preparedness for the heavenly sphere. But the serious aspect of this truth is that which is here suggested, viz. that God's dealings with us *may reach a climax which is ignorantly and fatally neglected.* We know how true this was of the Hebrew people. God's dealings with them (see previous homily) were long-continued, varied, gracious; they culminated in the coming of the King's Son. Then Divine Wisdom uttered its voice in their hearing; then Divine Power wrought its marvels of mercy before their very eyes; then Divine Purity lived its life of loveliness; and Divine Love manifested itself in a hundred forms of kindness and of pity in the very midst of them. But "this their day," this "time of their visitation," they did not know. Israel missed its golden chance, and went down, as a nation, to rise no more. But looking at God's redemptive dealing with ourselves, as individual spirits, we see—

I. How OFTEN GOD VISITS US in his redeeming love. In childhood, by a mother's tenderness; in youth, by a father's wisdom; in young manhood (womanhood), by many voices of the home and of the Church, uniting to say, "Thy God hath commanded thy strength;" in prime, by some chastening providence, laying his hand upon us and constraining us to listen and to understand.

II. How HIS DEALINGS WITH US CULMINATE in some day of grace. There comes a time in the history of souls—it may come in any period of life—when "the powers of the world to come" are most strongly felt, when God's nearness is most vividly realized, when the claims of Christ most forcibly touch and move the soul, when the kingdom of God is very near, and its gates are seen to stand wide open. It is "this thy day," it is the "time of visitation" to such a human heart.

III. How WISE, THEN, IS IMMEDIATE ACTION! How wise and well for us to *know* the time of our visitation, to recognize our great and priceless opportunity, to flee to the seeking Saviour "swift as the morning light," lest the golden chance be gone, the gates of opportunity be closed!—C.

Ver. 46.—*The house of prayer.* The strong indignation of our Lord shown on this occasion is a plain indication of the importance he attached to right thought concerning the sanctuary, and to the right use of it. He brought into prominence the act of prayer as that which should, above all things, characterize the house of God. We enter into his thought if we consider—

I. THE SENSE IN WHICH SACRIFICE WAS PRAYER. The temple existed primarily and pre-eminently for sacrifice. There, and there alone, might sacrifices be offered to the Lord. It was the one place in all the land where the sin offerings and the burnt offerings could be presented. Was it not, then, essentially, the *place of sacrifice*? Truly; but sacrifice, when rightly viewed, was a *form of prayer*. In it and by it the offerer drew near, consciously, to the loving God; in it he made confession of sin to God; in it he made acknowledgment of his continual indebtedness to God; in it he supplicated the mercy and the grace of God. But *this is* prayer; it is prayer in the form of offering rather than in words. Less than this—this conscious approach, this confession, thanksgiving, and supplication—is not prayer at all. Inasmuch, then, as the temple was the place of sacrifice, it was the place of prayer.

II. THE FACT THAT THERE WAS ROOM IN THE TEMPLE FOR PRAYER AS WE ORDINARILY UNDERSTAND IT. We gather from our Lord's own words that the temple was the place commonly chosen by the people for the offering of prayer (ch. xviii. 10). It was toward the temple that the exiled Jews looked when they knelt down to pray in distant lands; and it was in the temple that they stood to pray when that sacred building was within reach. It was, no doubt, regarded as of all places in the world the very fittest in which to realize the presence of Jehovah, and to spread forth the soul's desires and aspirations before him. There were many places for prayer, but that was *the* place of prayer.

III. THE PLACE OF PRAYER IN THE CHRISTIAN SANCTUARY. By what, above all things else, should the Christian sanctuary be characterized? 1. It should be the place of *common assembly*. Where all classes of the people meet together, the rich and the poor, and feel that the Lord is the Maker of them all (Prov. xxii. 2); where the learned and the unlearned worship and bow down together, and "kneel before the Lord their Maker" (Ps. xcv. 6); it is the place where human spirits meet, and where earthly circumstances are of no account whatever—where wealth does not weigh, and rank creates no distinction. 2. It should be the place of *spiritual enlightenment.* (1) Where the Word of God is read, and should be read (as it may be) impressively and effectually; for there is nothing in literature which is more fitted to attract and interest a miscellaneous assembly; (2) where the will of God is faithfully delivered, and the gospel of Christ expounded and enforced; (3) where the cause of the Master and of mankind is fully and earnestly pleaded. But most especially is it: 3. The place of *prayer*. Here, either in sacred psalmody, or through some prepared formula, or led by the extemporaneous thought and aspiration of the minister, the worshippers draw nigh to God in every way in which he is approached by man—in adoration, in communion, in thanksgiving, in confession, in supplication, in consecration. No worshipper in the house of the Lord can reach a higher level of spiritual attainment than when he pours out his heart in prayer to God in these various utterances; and no minister in the house of the Lord can render to the people gathered together a truer or higher service than when he helps them thus to approach the Father of spirits, and thus to come into direct communion with him. Then is the house of God put to its noblest and worthiest use when it is made by those who meet within its walls "the house of prayer."—C.

Ver. 46.—*Desecration.* Our Lord was touched and troubled with a holy indignation as he saw the temple of Jehovah turned into a place of traffic; that which was intended for the approach of the human spirit to God made to serve the purpose of hard bargaining, and even, as we judge from the language of the text, of dishonest dealings. It was a shocking, an intolerable desecration, and, exerting the authority which always resided in him and which he occasionally put into exercise, he drove these hucksters from the sacred place which they were desecrating by their presence and their practices. What places are we now tempted to desecrate?

I. THE SANCTUARY. When, instead of making it a place of worship, of drawing near to God, of speaking to him or for him, of learning something more of his holy will, we make it a place for distinguishing ourselves, or for advertising our respectability, or for gaining enjoyment which is wholly unspiritual.

II. THE HOME. When that which should be the abode of peace, of love, of purity, of fellowship, of tenderness, of gracious ministry, of quiet growth and joy, is turned into a scene of bitterness, of recrimination, of estrangement, of deterioration, of unhappiness.

III. THE PLACE OF BUSINESS. That might be a sphere where valuable virtues and most acceptable graces are manifested and are strengthened—truth, equity, courtesy, honour, courage, sagacity; too often it is nothing better than a sphere in which deceit, low cunning, dishonesty, a mean and miserable selfishness, are sown and reaped bountifully.

IV. THE HUMAN BODY. In our treatment of this bodily frame, so skilfully and so wonderfully made, so nicely adjusted to receive and convey impressions from and to the outside world of man and nature, we may and we should act as if we were dealing with a very sacred thing. By cleanliness, by moderation, by purity; by entertaining through the ear and the eye God's own truth and wisdom; by employing the tongue to speak his love and to sing his praise; by letting the graces of Christian character write themselves, as they will, in lineaments of beauty upon our countenance; by letting our bodies be, as they may be, the very temples of the Holy Ghost (1 Cor. vi. 19),—we may make them worthy and sacred in the sight of God. But when we regard them as mere instruments of gratification, and make them the ministers of sinful and even shameful pleasure, how great is such desecration before God!

V. HUMAN LIFE. It is here that the Holy One most often sees with Divine regret a pitiful desecration. He gave us our life that it might be spent, through all its stages, in sacred service, in spiritual growth, in elevating joy, in excellent preparation for the larger and fuller life beyond. How grievously is it desecrated when it is turned into a time for mere pecuniary acquisition, or for mere fleshly enjoyment, or for mere emptiness and aimlessness of existence! 1. What a pitiful waste is this! and how it will one day be deplored as absolutely irreparable! 2. How perilous to form such evil habits of the soul, every day becoming more fixed! how wise to hear the Master's voice summoning us to noble service, "Why stand ye all the day idle? go, work in my vineyard"!—C.

Ver. 48.—*Christ's popularity.* That Jesus Christ, as a Teacher, had no small share of popularity is beyond all question. "The people were astonished at his doctrine; for his word was with power;" "He taught them as one that had authority." His hearers wanted to know "whence hath this Man this wisdom?" The officers of the Sanhedrin declared that "Never man spake like this Man." His enemies' purpose was defeated: "They could not find what they might do: for all the people were very attentive to hear him." Large companies of men and women flocked to hear him; he had not to seek an audience; he had to seek shelter from their curiosity and intrusion. "Whence had this Man" this popularity? What was the source and the secret of it? There were—

I. THREE THINGS IN SPITE OF WHICH HE WAS POPULAR WITH THE PEOPLE. 1. *The depth of his doctrine.* Many gain a ready audience with the people by carefully restricting themselves to those truths which their hearers can easily understand: superficialities are generally acceptable. Not so with the great Teacher. He struck far below the surface, and was frequently announcing and enforcing truths which the majority of his hearers must have found "hard to be understood." Many of his utterances were "hard sayings" (John vi. 60). 2. *The height of his purpose.* Christ would have "got on" with the multitude much further and faster if he had but brought down his teaching to the level of their national aspirations. But when they were thinking of something as shallow and as transitory as a political revolution, he was laying broad and deep the foundations of a spiritual, universal, everlasting kingdom of God. His lofty purpose was high as the heavens above their hopes. His and their aims were altogether diverse and inconsistent with one another. 3. *The strength and straightness of his charge.* "Do you suppose these men were extraordinary sinners? I tell you, Nay; but except ye repent," etc.; "Except ye be converted, and become as little children, ye cannot *enter* the kingdom;" "Except your righteousness exceed the righteousness of the scribes," etc. (ch. xiii. 2, 3; Matt. xviii. 3; v. 20).

II. TWO THINGS WHICH CONTRIBUTED TO, WITHOUT ACCOUNTING FOR, HIS POPULARITY.
1. The *illustrativeness* of his style. He called to his aid all visible nature, all homely occupations, the familiarities of social and domestic life.

> " He talked of grass and wind and rain,
> And fig trees and fair weather,
> And made it his delight to bring
> Heaven and the earth together.
> He spoke of lilies, vines, and corn,
> The sparrow and the raven;
> And words so natural, yet so wise,
> Were on men's hearts engraven."

2. The *fearless front* he showed to those who were the worst enemies of the people. He denounced in unsparing terms the selfishness and rapacity as well as the pretentiousness and actual impiety of those who were fastening the bonds of a merciless and oppressive legality on the necks of their victims; and the people looked on with approval and with enjoyment. Men always listen with delight when oppression is unsparingly denounced. They always like to see the mask torn off the face of falsehood. But it is not here that *the* secret of the popularity of Jesus is to be found.

III. FOUR THINGS WHICH MADE CHRIST'S TEACHING ACCEPTABLE TO THOSE WHO HEARD HIM, and may well make his doctrine acceptable to us to-day. 1. He spoke of those things the *truth of which* the people *most wanted to know*. They did not want to know a number of legal niceties and small social and domestic proprieties of which the scribes spoke to them. They wanted to know what God thought of them, and how he felt toward them, and what was the way by which they could gain and claim his favour; what was the meaning and the purpose and the possibility of human life; what followed death; and what was the true hope for the after-time. On such themes Jesus spoke to men, and we need not wonder that " all the people listened attentively " as he spake. 2. *He spoke as one that knew.* He spoke "with authority, and not as the scribes; " "His word was *with power.*" He did not indulge in hair-splitting argumentations, nor in vague and dreamy imaginings, nor in doubtful and unreliable guesses. He spake as one that knew; as one who could speak about God, because he came forth from him, and dwelt with him; about prayer, because he was in constant communion with Heaven; about righteousness, because he himself was pure in heart; about love, because his whole life was one act of self-denial. Out of the depths of a living soul he gave the known facts of experience, the certain truths of God. 3. His teaching was that *of helpfulness and hopefulness.* He saw men "as sheep without a shepherd, tired out and lying down," wandering, smitten, dying. He grieved over the multitudes that were being misled, and he longed to do them good, to lead them back; he knew that he could help, that he could rest-re them. So he announced himself as that One who came " to preach good tidings to the poor, to heal the broken-hearted, to preach deliverance to the captive; " he offered himself as One to whom all the heavy-laden might repair, and in whom they would find rest unto their souls. He stretched forth an uplifting hand to those who were thought by every one else to have fallen beyond recovery. He breathed hope and life into despairing and dying ears. 4. His doctrine was *sustained by his character and his life.* Men listened to him, not only because he " spake as never man spake," but because he lived as never man lived before—in such perfect purity, in such constant devotion, in such self-forgetting love, with such gracious and tender sympathy in his heart and upon his countenance. They listened to him with such wrapt attention because they loved him for his goodness and for his love. (1) Such popularity as springs from such sources as these we may desire and seek to obtain. (2) For these same reasons we should be as attentive to hear the Master as were "the common people who heard him gladly " when he lived amongst us.—C.

Vers. 1—10.—*A son of Abraham found in Zacchæus the publican.* The healing of blind Bartimæus was not the only saving act done by Jesus at Jericho. A notable publican, called Zacchæus, becomes the object of our Lord's compassion and the subject of his grace. He was at the head of the custom-house, as we should now call it, and in his important post he had become rich. Having heard of Jesus and seen the advancing crowd, his curiosity prompted him to have a look at him if possible; but, being little of stature, he could not from the ground obtain the view he wished. Accordingly he ran before, climbed up into a sycamore tree, one of whose branches it has been supposed may have extended across the road, and, perched upon this, he awaited the advent of Jesus. How astonished he must have been to find Jesus pausing below his perch, looking up, naming him, and telling him, "Zacchæus, make haste, and come down; for to-day I must abide at thy house"! Thus invited, he came down with all haste, and received Christ joyfully. Doubtless the Pharisees will murmur at Christ becoming the publican's guest; but what does it matter when Zacchæus is gathered into the kingdom of God, makes his declaration about future conduct, and receives the Lord's assurance of being Abraham's son? Let us notice the points of interest as they present themselves in this case.

I. ZACCHÆUS NEEDED A SAVIOUR. For success is not sufficient for any man. He needs besides, salvation from sin, that is, from selfishness, and often from success itself. It is well when even curiosity leads a man to the Saviour, and to a sense of his great need. Zacchæus's case is instructive for us all. His need of a Saviour ought to emphasize our need.

II. HIS HINDRANCES IN SEEKING THE SAVIOUR. And of these we shall only mention three. 1. *His riches.* These are often a great hindrance to souls. They compete with Christ as a ground of trust. Men are tempted to trust in uncertain riches instead of in the living God. Zacchæus had, however, got over this hindrance, and, rich man though he was, he was not ashamed to climb the sycamore to get a sight of Jesus. 2. *His business.* For the tax-farming had been denounced and excommunicated by the Jewish authorities, so that Zacchæus, because of his business, did not enjoy the means of grace in the measure and amount he might otherwise have done. Jesus had, however, overcome this hindrance by his own manly and merciful policy, and insisted on associating with publicans and sinners to save them. Every one should ask himself the question, however, if his business is a hindrance or a help to his salvation. Can we ask Christ to meet us in it and save us in it? or can we only expect him to save us *from* it? 3. *His physical state.* His stature hindered him for a time from seeing Jesus, as the physical state of others often hinders them. But when one is thoroughly in earnest, he can overcome all hindrances as Zacchæus did by climbing the sycamore. Hindrances may be changed by energetic action into helps and spiritual gains.

III. SALVATION MEANS HEARTFELT SYMPATHY WITH A PERSONAL SAVIOUR. For salvation comes to us clothed in loving personality, and the advent of Jesus to our souls, as in the case of Zacchæus, is the advent of salvation. What we are asked in the gospel to do is to trust a Person, and to accept of safety in his blessed society. There is no abstract and confusing process to be passed through, but a concrete and real fellowship to be entered on and enjoyed.

IV. THE SAVED SOUL PROVES HIS SALVATION BY LIBERALITY AND RESTITUTION. As soon as Zacchæus enters into sympathy with Christ, he makes a public profession. Here is his resolve deliberately made to Christ, "Behold, Lord, the half of my goods I give to the poor; and if I have wrongfully exacted aught of any man, I restore four-fold" (Revised Version). His riches are now to be made a means of grace, enabling him, in the first place, liberally to make restitution to all wronged ones; and secondly, to dedicate largely to the poor. Contact with Christ has opened his heart and made him open-handed. Murmuring Pharisees might restrict their ostentatious almsgiving to a tenth, but converted Zacchæus will dedicate a half to the wants of the poor! A rich man may thus make his wealth the basis of princely generosity, and reap a reward in the gratitude of God's poor people.

V. JESUS GIVES ZACCHÆUS A BLESSED ASSURANCE OF SONSHIP. For Zacchæus, if originally a Jew, had forfeited through his tax-gathering his position in the Jewish Church. No longer would the Jewish authorities regard him as a son of Abraham or heir of the promises. But Jesus interposes and reinstates him in his position of privilege. He declares before the guests that Zacchæus has been saved by his visit to his house, and that this salvation-visit is because the publican is also a son of Abraham. In this beautiful way the selecting love of God in Christ is set before the people and the assurance of Abrahamic sonship conveyed to the new convert. It is thus the Lord comforts those who trust in him.

VI. CHRIST THUS DEMONSTRATES HIS MISSION TO SEEK AND SAVE THE LOST. Not by the parables of the fifteenth chapter merely does he demonstrate the merciful character of his mission, but also by such a missionary act as the salvation of Zacchæus. As "the Son of man" he is interested in the welfare of his race, and finds in the lost the sphere of his gracious operation. It is thus he comforts the lost ones, by enabling them to see that they are the proper objects of his compassion.—R. M. E.

Vers. 11—27.—*The law of capital in Christ's kingdom.* Zacchæus's conversion and all the stir on leaving Jericho led many in the crowd to imagine that Christ was immediately to assume a visible kingdom. To remove misapprehension, therefore, he proceeds to tell them a parable which would at once rouse them to the necessity of working instead of indulging in lackadaisical waiting. Comparing himself to a nobleman who is going into a far country to receive a kingdom and to return, he compares his disciples to servants left to make the best of what is entrusted to them. The worldly minded as distinct from the servants are called his citizens, whose spirit is manifested in the message transmitted to him, "We will not have this man to reign over us." Then the return of the crowned king is to be celebrated by the distribution of rewards and punishments as the case may be. Out of this significant parable we may learn the following lessons.

I. IT IS IN HEAVEN, AND NOT ON EARTH, OUR LORD IS TO RECEIVE HIS KINGDOM. This is the great mistake many have made about Christ's kingdom and reign. They localize head-quarters on earth instead of in heaven. It is not by a democratic vote, by a *plébiscite*, our Lord is to receive his kingdom, but by donation from the Father. When he went away by death, resurrection, and ascension, therefore, it was to receive a kingdom that he might return crowned. Hence we are to regard him as now reigning over his mediatorial kingdom. He is on the throne. His government is administered from the heavenly places.

II. IT IS PERILOUS TO REFUSE TO ACKNOWLEDGE HIS PRESENT REIGN. The citizens that hate the absent King will be slain before him when he returns for judgment. Hostility, enmity, to Christ, if continued, must lead to utter discomfiture at last. Rebellion of spirit is, therefore, to be diligently uprooted if we would have any share in Christ's kingdom. It is at our peril if we refuse his loving and righteous reign.

III. CHRIST'S SERVANTS LIVE UNDER A LAW OF CAPITAL IN HIS KINGDOM. In this parable we have "pounds," and not "talents," referred to. The question is, therefore, of some equal endowment which all receive in common, not of unequal endowment distributed in sovereign wisdom. In the parable of the talents, given in another Gospel, we have equal diligence exhibited in the use of unequal endowments; and the reward is righteously equalized in the completed kingdom. Here, on the other hand, we have an unequal use of equal endowments, with the unequal reward attached in proportion to the diligence. We discern in the arrangement, therefore, that law of increase which has been denominated the law of capital. But first we have to settle the signification of the pounds. We shall not be far astray if, with Godet, we regard them as indicating those donations of Divine *grace* which are offered to the Lord's servants, we may suppose, in equal measure. These endowments are put to use in some cases, utterly neglected in others. It will be found at last that the law of capital has obtained in the Lord's arrangements. One man, by judicious use of what the Lord has given, finds his grace growing tenfold, so that by the time the Lord returns he is ready to undertake the government of ten cities. Another man, by diligence, but not so persevering as the former, finds his graces growing fivefold, so that in the final arrangement he is equal to the oversight of five cities. A third is represented as making no use whatever of his endowment, under the impression that the Lord is a grasping speculator, who wants to make the most he can out of men. He ventures to return his trust just as it was. He finds, however, that his selfish idleness is visited with utter ruin. He has the misused endowment recalled and made over to the better trader. "To him that hath shall be given." Accumulated capital tends to increase in proper hands, and it is right it should do so. It follows, then, from this law of capital as thus applied: 1. *That we should use diligently every means to increase our Christian graces.* Sanctification should be our life-work, and all action, meditation, prayer, should be utilized for the one great object of becoming the best servants of our

Master our circumstances admit of. 2. *We shall find ourselves thereby becoming rulers of men.* It is wonderful the influence exercised by consecrated lives. It is easy understanding how we may become kings and priests unto God the Father. As consecrated by his grace, we begin immediately to influence others for good and to reign. 3. *The influence on earth will have its counterpart in the reign enjoyed by us in heaven.* For heaven will be the home of order. It will be no happy, musical mob. It will be a great society, with recognized kings of men, under the gracious authority, of course, of him who is "King of kings, and Lord of lords." Influence, character, all that is gracious, is destined to be continued and to abide. Those who have done men most good, and made the most of their opportunities here, shall be rewarded with corresponding influence in the well-ordered commonwealth above. 4. *Wrong views of Christ's character may also be perpetuated, with their corresponding judgments.* The pitiful servant who thought his Master austere, hard, grasping, was only attributing his own hard character to his superior. He failed to understand him. So is it with some souls. They insist on misunderstanding God, and the result is that their misunderstanding continues and is its own punishment. How important, therefore, that we should have correct views of God our Saviour! It will save us from misuse of his gifts and graces, and from the doom awaiting all faithless souls.—R. M. E.

Vers. 28—48.—*The advent of the humble King.* To illustrate still more thoroughly the character of his kingdom as one not of ostentation and worldly glory, but of humility, our Lord directed two of his disciples to procure for him a colt, the untrained foal of an ass, that he might ride into Jerusalem thereon. The marvellous way in which the ass was lent to him indicated preternatural knowledge. Upon this colt, then, he sat, and passed amid the hosannas of the people into the sacred city. But his advent was in tears, and his terminus was not a palace, but the temple. The whole character of the procession and its termination tended to upset all vulgar Messianic hopes and lead thinking minds to reflection. Let us look at the different stages of the royal progress and such lessons as they suggest.

I. THE HUMBLE CHARACTER OF THE PROCESSION. (Vers. 28—40.) For it was on an *ass*, not on any royal mule, he rode; to fulfil the prophecy of Zechariah, "Rejoice greatly, O daughter of Zion; shout, O daughter of Jerusalem; behold, thy King cometh unto thee: he is just, and having salvation; lowly, and riding upon an ass, and upon a colt the foal of an ass" (Zech. ix. 9). The very fact of his selecting such a lowly and despised animal indicated his humility. At the same time, his perfect command of the untrained colt revealed his sovereignty in animated nature—that, like an unfallen Adam, he was lord of the lower creatures. It was akin to his being with the wild beasts and unscathed in the wilderness. But secondly, the *extemporized character of the procession was humiliating.* A great king gets the parade organized, and knows what will for the most part compose his escort. But this King of kings rests his escort upon the extemporized enthusiasm of the crowd, and values at its proper figure the measure of enthusiasm that is evoked. He knew that the same people who then shouted, "Hosanna; Blessed be the King that cometh in the name of the Lord: peace in heaven, and glory in the highest!" would a few days after cry out, "Crucify him!" And so he was humiliated rather than honoured by the shallow enthusiasm of the motley crowd. Thirdly, *the unseemly interruptions of the Pharisees rendered it humiliating.* So irritated were they that they urged him to rebuke the disciples for crying out as they were doing. But the Lord only declared that, if the disciples were silent, the very stones would get tongues to sound his praise. This Pharisaic jar, this unseemly interruption, must have been humiliating to the Lord. To bear it as he did demonstrated the humility and meekness of his spirit. Truly he was "meek and lowly in heart."

II. THE TEARS OF THE ADVANCING KING ARE NOTABLE. (Vers. 41—44.) For instead of a city welcoming him, instead of this city of the great King recognizing the day of her visitation, and opening her arms for her Deliverer, there was apathy and scorn for his methods and aims. No wonder, therefore, that he had to speak about the siege of Titus, which he saw plainly must come. Pursuing their poor worldly policy, they must be encompassed ultimately by the Roman eagles. And so he wept those tears of deepest sorrow over the impenitence of Jerusalem. How different from the processions of earthly monarchs or great captains! The very last thing looked for on such occasions would be tears. The sympathy of this Saviour for Jerusalem sinners was deep indeed when it led him to such a weeping-time as the processionists witnessed.

III. His SECOND PURIFICATION OF THE TEMPLE WAS THE CULMINATION OF THE PROCESSION. (Vers. 45, 46.) The tempter wanted him to begin his Messianic work by a harmless descent from the temple-pinnacle; he began his work by entering into the temple and casting out the traffickers. And now he has to finish his work by repeating the purification. Usually the processions of kings end at palace gates and in palace halls; but the procession of Christ ends at the temple and in its court. He must convert it from a den of thieves to a place of prayer. The meaning of his kingdom could not be better represented. It was really the sphere of religion and of worship that he made his own; in the regulation thereof he was supreme, and exercised his influence.

IV. He TAUGHT DAILY IN THE TEMPLE UNTIL THE END. (Vers. 47, 48.) He was surrounded by his enemies. They were on the *qui vive* to secure him and put him away. But now that his hour of self-sacrifice is near, he feels himself immortal till his work is done. It is the interests of others that occupy him. He must teach to the last. And so from Bethany he comes in morning by morning to instruct the interested crowds. What solemn lessons they must have been, those closing ones of Jesus! And they attracted great attention, and their popularity restrained his enemies, although it must have intensified their determination to put him out of the way. Thus we have seen how this humble King entered Jerusalem to work reformation there, and, if possible, save the people by enlightening and teaching them. If his mission failed with most, it succeeded with some, and inaugurated the new kingdom, which is " righteousness and peace and joy in the Holy Ghost."—R. M. E.

EXPOSITION.

CHAPTER XX.

Vers. 1—8.—*Question of the priests and scribes as to the nature of the authority under which Jesus was acting.*

Vers. 1, 2 —**And it came to pass, that on one of those days, as he taught the people in the temple, and preached the gospel.** We are now in the midst of the so-called Passion week. Probably the events related in this chapter took place on the Tuesday. The first day of the week, Palm Sunday, was the day of the public entry into the city. The purification of the temple took place on the Monday, on which day also the barren fig tree was cursed. We are now considering the events of the Tuesday. The Greek word εὐαγγελιζομένου is especially a Pauline word; we find it rarely used save in his writings, and of course in those of St. Luke. St. Paul uses it twenty times, and St. Luke twenty-five. **The chief priests and the scribes came upon him with the elders, and spake unto him, saying, Tell us, by what authority doest thou these things?** This appears to have been a formal deputation from the supreme council of the Sanhedrin. The three classes here specified represented probably the three great sections of the Sanhedrin—(1) priests, (2) scribes and rabbis, (3) Levites. These came upon him evidently with hostile intent, and surrounded him as

he was walking in the temple. The jealous anger of the rulers of the Jews had been lately specially excited by the triumphant entry on Palm Sunday, and by the stir and commotion which the presence of Jesus had occasioned in the holy city. And in the last two or three days Jesus had evidently claimed especial power in the temple. He had publicly driven out the money-changers and vendors of sacrificial victims who plied their calling in the sacred courts. He had, in addition, forbade the carrying vessels across the temple (Mark xi. 16), and had allowed the children in the temple, probably those attached to its choir, to shout " Hosanna!" to him as the Messiah. From the point of view of the Sanhedrin, such a question might well have been looked for. His interlocutors made quite sure that Jesus, in reply, would claim having received a Divine commission. Had he made openly such a formal claim in reply to their question, then he would have been cited before the supreme court to give an account of himself and his commission. Then, as they thought, would have been their opportunity to convict him out of his own mouth of blasphemy.

Vers. 3—6.—**And he answered and said unto them, I will also ask you one thing; and answer me: The baptism of John, was it from heaven, or of men? And they reasoned with themselves, saying, If we shall say,**

From heaven; he will say, Why then believed ye him not ? But and if we say, Of men ; all the people will stone us: for they be persuaded that John was a prophet. The reply of Jesus was one of strange wisdom. He—Jesus—as was well known, had been introduced to the people by this very John. If the Sanhedrin acknowledged John the Baptist as a divinely accredited messenger, then surely they could not question the claims of one borne special witness to by him, brought forward and introduced to public notice by him! If, on the other hand, the Sanhedrin refused to acknowledge the authority of John as a Heaven-sent messenger, which would have been the course they would have preferred, then the popularity and influence of the Sanhedrin would have been sorely imperilled, for the people generally held firmly that John the Baptist was really a prophet of the Lord. They even feared—as we read, " All the people will stone us "—personal violence on the part of the people whose favour they so zealously courted.

Ver. 7.—And they answered, that they could not tell whence it was. The reply of Jesus, which so perplexed the Sanhedrin, really inflicted a grave blow to their prestige, thus compelling the grave doctors of the Law, who claimed the right of deciding all momentous questions, to decline to pronounce a judgment on so grave a question as "the position of the Baptist," that mighty preacher who had so stirred and roused Israel and who had with his life paid the forfeit of his boldness in rebuking crime in high places, thereby no doubt enormously enlarging his already vast popularity with the people.

Ver. 8.—And Jesus said unto them, Neither tell I you by what authority I do these things. Jesus, on hearing their plea of ignorance, now contemptuously declines to answer the Sanhedrists' question in the direct way they desired, but at once proceeds to speak a parable which unmistakably contains the reply.

Vers. 9—19.—Parable of the wicked husbandmen in the vineyard, and the simile of the corner-stone.

Ver. 9.—A certain man planted a vineyard, and let it forth to husbandmen. Under a very thin parabolic veil, Jesus foretells the awful tragedy of the next few days. He adopts a well-known imagery, and seems to say, " Listen to Isaiah's well-known story of the vineyard, the vineyard of the Lord of hosts, which is the house of Israel. I will expand it a little, that I may show you how it stands with you as regards this matter of 'authority,' that we may see whether you have as much respect for the ascertained will of God as ye pretend, so that ye should

be sure to submit to me if only ye were satisfied that I was an accredited Messenger of God" (Professor Bruce). For a long time. Representing the nearly two thousand years of Jewish history.

Vers. 10—12.—He sent a servant to the husbandmen, that they should give him of the fruit of the vineyard. After the pains and care bestowed upon the vineyard, that is, after the many mighty works done in Israel's behalf, the Lord of hosts looked for fruits of gratitude and fidelity in some proportion to the mighty favours which it had received from him. The people were intended to be the example to, and the educators of, the world, and, instead of carrying out these high functions, they lived the poor selfish life so sadly depicted in the long story contained in the historical and prophetical books. " He looked that it [his vineyard] should bring forth grapes, and it brought forth wild grapes " (Isa. v. 2). But the husbandmen beat him, and sent him away empty. And again he sent another servant: and they beat him also, and entreated him shamefully, and sent him away empty. And again he sent a third: and they wounded him also, and cast him out. These represent the prophets, those faithful servants of the Lord, whose toils and trials and fate are painted in the Epistle to the Hebrews (xi.) in such glowing and eloquent language. And again he sent. In vers. 11 and 12, προσέθετο πέμψαι, literally, "he added to send another"—a Hebraism. This shows St. Luke here based his account on a Hebrew (Aramaic) original. Professor Bruce well puts the thoughts which possessed the wicked husbandmen thus: "When the servants came for fruit, they were simply surprised. 'Fruit! did you say? We have occupied the position of vine-dressers, and have duly drawn our wages: what more do you want?' Such was the actual fact in regard to the spiritual heads of Israel. They were men who never thought of fruit, but only of the honour and privilege of being entrusted with the keeping of the vineyard. They were triflers, men utterly devoid of earnestness, and the practical purpose of the property committed to their charge they habitually forgot. Generally speaking, they had utterly lost sight of the end of Israel's calling." Their anger flamed forth when accredited messengers of the Lord visited them and reminded them of their forgotten duties ; they vented their furious wrath by persecuting some and killing others of these faithful men.

Ver. 13.—Then said the lord of the vineyard, What shall I do? I will send my beloved son. The guilt of the husbandmen who acted as vine-dressers here reached its highest measure. The words represented here by Jesus as spoken by God, possess the deepest doctrinal value. They, under the thin veil of the parable-story, answer the question of the Sanhedrin (ver. 2), "By what authority doest thou these things?" The deliberative words, "What shall I do?" recall the Divine dialogue alluded to in Gen. i. 26. St. Luke here represents the Father as calling the Son, "*my Beloved.*" St. Mark adds that he was *an only Son.* Such sayings as this, and the remarkable prayer of Matt. xi. 25—27, are a clear indication of the Christology of the synoptists. Their estimate of the Person of the blessed Son in no wise differed from that given us by St. John at much greater length and with fuller details.

Ver. 14.—**But when the husbandmen saw him, they reasoned among themselves, saying, This is the heir: come, let us kill him, that the inheritance may be ours.** The husbandmen are represented as knowing the son and heir. Nor can we resist the conclusion that some at least of those grave learned men who sat in the Sanhedrin as priests or scribes well knew who the Speaker of the awful words claimed to be, and, in resisting him and seeking his destruction, were deliberately sinning against the voice of their own hearts.

Vers. 15, 16.—**So they cast him out of the vineyard, and killed** him. The parable-story *of itself* was an improbable one. The conduct of the husbandmen, the long patience of the owner of the vineyard, his last act in sending his beloved and only son,—all this makes up a history without a parallel in human experience. Yet this is an exact sketch of what did actually take place in the eventful story of Israel! **What therefore shall the lord of the vineyard do unto them? He shall come and destroy these husbandmen, and shall give the vineyard to others.** Again a hint of a solemn deliberation in heaven, a prophetic picture of the future of the Jewish race fulfilled with terrible exactness. **And when they heard it, they said, God forbid!** Well understood they the Speaker's meaning here. He foreshadowed, in no veiled language, the utter ruin of the Jewish polity. When they heard this, forgetting to be scornful, they exclaimed, in deprecation of the ominous and terrible prediction, Μὴ γένοιτο! which we render accurately, though not literally, "God forbid!"

Vers. 17, 18.—**And he beheld them, and said, What is this then that is written, The stone which the builders rejected, the same is become the head of the corner? Whosoever shall fall upon that stone shall be broken; but on whomsoever it shall fall, it will grind him to powder.** In spite of the deprecating expression, the severity of the tone of Jesus increases in his next words, when, looking at them with grave anger (ἐμβλέψας), he proceeds to speak of himself under the figure of the rejected stone. Quoting a well-known psalm (cxviii. 22), and using the imagery of Isa. viii. 14, 15 and Dan. ii. 44, he describes his fortunes under the image of a corner-stone—that stone which forms the junction between the two most prominent walls of a building, and which is always laid with peculiar care and attention. In ch. ii. 34 of our Gospel Simeon refers to the same well-known prophetic saying. The husbandmen who had just been described as vine-dressers are now described as builders, and the murdered son is reproduced under the image of a corner-stone tossed aside as useless. In the first part of the picture, the earthly humiliation of Messiah is portrayed when the stone is laid in the earth. In the second, the stone falling from the top of the building represents the crushing of all earthly opposition by Messiah in his glory. Woe to the builders, then, who had scornfully rejected him!

Ver. 19.—**And the chief priests and the scribes the same hour sought to lay hands on him; and they feared the people: for they perceived that he had spoken this parable against them.** Again the Sanhedrin take counsel. They long to arrest him on some capital charge; but they dared not, for the people, joined by the Passover pilgrims, had exalted him to the rank of a hero. Not a few evidently looked on him at that period as King Messiah. But the feeling of the great council was intensely bitter. They felt *their* power and influence was slipping away from them. These last parables were scarcely veiled attacks on them. In the last spoken words he had calmly announced that he was to die, and *their* hands were to carry out the bloody work. And then, in the simile of the corner-stone, he, in no ambiguous terms, told them that in killing him they will not be done with him, for that in the end they will be utterly crushed by his power.

Vers. 20—26.—*The question of the tribute money.*

Ver. 20.—**And they watched** him, **and sent forth spies, which should feign themselves just men, that they might take hold of his words, that so they might deliver him unto the power and authority of the governor.** In their intense hatred, conscious that the populace were on the whole in sympathy with Jesus, the Sanhedrin, to carry out their design on his life, determined to avail themselves of the hated Roman military police. Their hope henceforward is to substantiate a charge of treason against him. This was, in those troublous times, when insurrection against the detested Gentile rule was ever being plotted, a comparatively easy matter. The incident of the tribute money, which immediately follows, was part of this new departure in the Sanhedrin policy respecting the murder they so longed to see carried out.

Vers. 21, 22.—**And they asked him, saying, Master, we know that thou sayest and teachest rightly, neither acceptest thou the person of any, but teachest the way of God truly: Is it lawful for us to give tribute unto Cæsar, or no ?** SS. Matthew and Mark both tell us that in this plot the Herodians were united with the Pharisees (and Sanhedrin). The great Nazareth Reformer was equally hateful to both these hostile parties; hence their union in this matter. It was a well and skilfully laid question. This "tribute" was a capitation tax—a denarius a head assessed on the whole population, the publicans who farmed it being answerable for it to the Roman treasury. As a direct personal tax it was most unpopular, and was looked on by scrupulous legalists and the more zealous Jews as involving a greater humiliation than the ordinary import or export customs dues. It occasioned at times popular tumults, as in the case of Judas of Galilee (Acts v. 37). If Jesus answered the question in the affirmative: " Yes, it is lawful for the Jews to give this tribute to Cæsar," then the Pharisees would use this decision of his as a means of undermining his credit with the zealous populace. " See, after all," they would say, " this pretended Messiah of yours is but a poor-hearted traitor. *Think of King Messiah paying tribute to a Gentile.*" If, on the other hand, the Master had said such payment of tribute was unlawful, then the Herodians, who were watching him, hoping for some such expression of opinion, would at once have denounced him to their Roman friends as One who taught the people— only too ready to listen to such teaching— lessons of sedition. In the latter case Pilate and the officials of Rome would have taken good care that the Galilæan Master had troubled the Sanhedrin no more.

Ver. 24.—**Show me a penny**; literally, *a denarius*, a coin of the value of 7½d., but really representing a larger sum in our money. It seems probable, from the language of Mark xii. 15, 16, that his interrogators had to borrow the Roman coin in question from some of the neighbouring money-changers. These Jews would scarcely carry any but Jewish coins in their girdles. That the Roman denarius, however, was evidently a coin in common circulation in those days, we gather from the parable of the labourers in the vineyard. **Whose image and superscription hath it ? They answered and said, Cæsar's.** " On one side would be

the once beautiful but now depraved features of Tiberius; the title ' Pontifex Maximus' was probably inscribed on the obverse" (Farrar).

Ver. 25.—**And he said unto them, Render therefore unto Cæsar the things which be Cæsar's, and unto God the things which be God's.** As regarded the immediate issues the Lord's answer was in the affirmative : " Yes, it is lawful under the present circumstances to pay this tribute." The Roman money current in the land, bearing the image and title of the Cæsar, bore perpetual witness to the fact that the rule of Rome was established and acknowledged by the Jewish people and their rulers. It was a well-known and acknowledged saying, that " he whose coin is current is king of the land." So the great Jewish rabbi Maimonides, centuries after, wrote, "Ubicunque numisma regis alicujus obtinet, illic incolæ regem istum pro Domino agnoscunt." The tribute imposed by the recognized sovereign ought certainly to be paid as a just debt; nor would this payment at all interfere with the people's discharging their duties God-ward. The tithes, tribute to the temple, the offerings enjoined by the Law they revered,—these ancient witnesses to the Divine sovereignty in Israel might and ought still to be rendered, as well as the higher obligations to the invisible King, such as faith, love, and obedience. Tribute to the Cæsar, then, the acknowledged sovereign, in no way interfered with tribute to God. What belonged to Cæsar should be given to him, and what belonged to God ought to be rendered likewise to him. Godet, in a long and able note, adds that Jesus would teach the turbulent Jewish people that the way to regain their theocratic independence was not to violate the duty of submission to Cæsar by a revolutionary shaking off of his yoke, but to return to the faithful fulfilment of all duties toward God. "To render to God what is God's was the way for the people of God to obtain a new David instead of Cæsar as their Lord. To the Pharisees and Zealots, ' Render unto Cæsar ;' to the Herodians, ' Render unto God.' " Well caught the great Christian teachers their Master's thought here in all their teaching respecting an institution such as slavery, in their injunctions concerning rigid and unswerving loyalty to established authority. So St. Paul : " Be subject to the powers . . . not only from fear of punishment, but also for conscience' sake " (Rom. xiii. 1 and 1 Timothy).

Vers. 27—40.—*The scornful question of the Sadducees bearing on the doctrine of the resurrection, and the Lord's reply.*

Vers. 27, 28.—**Then came to him certain of the Sadducees, which deny that there is** any resurrection; and they asked him, saying, Master, Moses wrote unto us, If any man's brother die, having a wife, and he die without children, that his brother should take his wife, and raise up seed unto his brother. This is the only occasion related in the Gospels where our Lord comes in direct conflict with the Sadducees. They were a small but very wealthy and powerful sect. The high priests at this period and their families seem to have belonged generally to this party. They acknowledged as Divine the books of Moses, but refused to see in them any proof of the resurrection, or indeed of life after death. To the prophets and the other books they only attached subordinate importance. Supercilious worldliness, and a quiet indifference to all spiritual things, characterized them at this period. They come, comparatively speaking, little in contact with Jesus during his earthly ministry. While the Pharisee hated the Galilæan Master, the Sadducee professed to look on him rather with contempt. The question here seems to have been put with supercilious scorn. SS. Matthew and Mark preface the Lord's answer with a few words of grave rebuke, exposing the questioners' utter ignorance of the deep things involved in their query.

Vers. 29—33.—There were therefore seven brethren: and the first took a wife, and died without children. And the second took her to wife, and he died childless. And the third took her; and in like manner the seven also: and they left no children, and died. Last of all the woman died also. Therefore in the resurrection whose wife of them is she? for seven had her to wife. The question here put to the Master was a well-known materialistic objection to the resurrection, and had on several occasions been asked by these shallow Epicureans—as the Talmud calls them—to the great rabbis of the schools of the Pharisees. Their usual answer was that the woman in question would be the wife of the first husband.

Vers. 34—36.—And Jesus answering said unto them, The children of this world marry, and are given in marriage: but they which shall be accounted worthy to obtain that world, and the resurrection from the dead, neither marry, nor are given in marriage: neither can they die any more. How different are the few rare pictures which our Master draws of the heaven-life to those painted by the great founders and teachers of other world-wide religions! In his world beyond the grave, while he tells us of a continuing existence, of varied and ever-increasing activity, in contradistinction to the Nirvâna of Buddha, in these pictures of Jesus the sensual paradise of Mohammed,

for instance, finds no place. Marriage is, according to our Lord's teaching, but a temporary expedient to preserve the human race, to which death would soon put an end. But in the world to come there will be no death and no marriage. We may assume from his words here that the difference between the sexes will have ceased to exist. They are equal unto the angels. Equal with the angels in being immortal; no death; no marriage. Jesus in this place asserts that angels have a body, but are exempt from any difference of sex. The angels are here introduced because our Lord was speaking with Sadducees, who (Acts xxiii. 8) denied the existence of these glorious beings. He wished to set the seal of his teaching on the deeply interesting question of the existence of angels.

Vers. 37, 38.—Now that the dead are raised, even Moses showed at the bush. You Sadducees, in your own arbitrary fashion, set aside the authority of the prophets and all sacred books save the Pentateuch; well, I will argue with you on your own, comparatively speaking, narrow ground—the books of Moses. Even he, Moses, is singularly clear and definite in his teaching on this point of the resurrection, though you pretend he is not. You are acquainted with the well-known section in Exodus termed 'the Bush:' what read you there?" When he calleth the Lord the God of Abraham, and the God of Isaac, and the God of Jacob. For he is not a God of the dead, but of the living; more accurately rendered, not a God of dead beings, but of living beings. The meaning of the Lord's argument is, "God would never have called himself the God of Abraham, of Isaac, and of Jacob, if these patriarchs, after their short lives, had become mere crumbling dust. God cannot be the God of a being who does not exist." So Josephus—who, however, no doubt drew his argument from these words of Christ, for this strong and conclusive argument from the Pentateuch for the immortality of man does not appear to have occurred to rabbis before the time of our Lord—so Josephus writes: "They who die for God's sake live unto God as Abraham, Isaac, and Jacob, and all the patriarchs." The expression, "at the bush," should be rendered "in the Bush," that is, in that division of Exodus so named. So the Jews termed 2 Sam. i. and following verses "the Bow;" Ezek. i. and following section, "the Chariot."

Vers. 39, 40.—Then certain of the scribes answering, said, Master, thou hast well said. And after that they durst not ask him any question at all. "This prompt and sublime answer filled with admiration the scribes, who had so often sought this decisive word in Moses without finding it; they cannot restrain themselves from testifying their joyful surprise. Aware from this time forth that every snare laid for him will be the occasion for a glorious manifestation of his wisdom, they give up this method of attack " (Godet).

Vers. 41—44.—*The question respecting Christ's being David's Son.*

Ver. 41.—**And he said unto them, How say they that Christ is David's Son?** St. Matthew gives us more details of what went before the following saying of Jesus in which he asserts the Divinity of Messiah. Jesus asked the Pharisees, " What think ye of Christ? whose Son is he? They say unto him, *The Son* of David. He saith unto them, How then doth David in spirit call him Lord, saying, The Lord said unto my Lord," etc.? (Matt. xxii. 42—44). This is one of the most remarkable sayings of our Lord reported by the synoptists; in it he distinctly claims for himself Divinity, *participation in omnipotence.* Unmistakably, lately, under the thinnest veil of parable, Jesus had told the people that he was Messiah. For instance, his *words* in the parable of the " wicked husbandmen; " in the parable of " the pounds; " in his late *acts* in the temple—driving out the sellers and buyers, allowing the children in the temple to welcome him with Messianic salutation, receiving as Messiah the welcome of the Passover pilgrims and others on Palm Sunday as he entered Jerusalem. In his later *parables,* too, he had with startling clearness predicted his approaching violent death. Now, Jesus was aware that the capital charge which would be brought against him would be blasphemy, that he had called himself, not only the Messiah, but Divine, the Son of God (John v. 18; x. 33; Matt. xxvi. 65). He was desirous, then, before the end came, to show from an acknowledged Messianic psalm that if he was Messiah— and unquestionably a large proportion of the people received him as such—he was also Divine. The words of the psalm (cx.) indisputably show this, viz. that the coming Messiah was Divine. This, he pointed out to them, was the old faith, the doctrine taught in their own inspired Scriptures. *But this was not the doctrine of the Jews in the time of our Lord. They, like the Ebionites in early Christian days, expected for their Messiah a mere "beloved Man."* It is most noticeable that the Messianic claim of Jesus, although not, of course, conceded by the scribes, was never protested against by them. *That* would have been glaringly unpopular. So many of the people, we know, were persuaded of the truth of these pretensions; Jesus had evidently the greatest difficulty to stay the people's enthusiasm in

his favour. What the scribes persistently repelled, and in the end condemned him for, was *his assertion of Divinity.* In this passage he shows from their own Scriptures that whoever was Messiah *must be Divine.* He spoke over and over again as Messiah; he acted with the power and in the authority of Messiah; he allowed himself on several public occasions to be saluted as such: who would venture, then, to question that he was fully conscious of his Divinity? This conclusion is drawn, not from St. John, but exclusively from the recitals of the three synoptists.

Ver. 42.—**And David himself saith in the Book of Psalms, The Lord said unto my Lord, Sit thou on my right hand.** The Hebrew runs thus: " Jehovah said to my Lord (*Adonai*)." The Eternal is represented as speaking to David's Lord, who is also David's Son (this appears clearer in St. Matthew's account, xxii.. 41—46). The Eternal addresses this Person as One raised to sit by him, that is, as *a Participator in his all-power,* and yet this one is also David's Son! The scribes are asked to explain this mystery; alone this can be done by referring to the golden chain of Hebrew Messianic prophecy; *no scribe in the days of our Lord would do this.* Such passages as Isa. ix. 6, 7; Micah v. 2; and Mal. iii. 1, give a complete and exhaustive answer to the question of Jesus.

Ver. 44.—**David therefore calleth him Lord, how is he then his Son?** That Jesus was the acknowledged descendant of David during his earthly ministry, is indisputable; we need but refer to the cries of the populace on Palm Sunday, the words of the woman of Canaan, of blind Bartimæus, and others. History bears its witness to the same fact. The Emperor Domitian, it is well known, summoned the kinsmen of Jesus, the sons of Jude, his so-called brother, to Rome as " the sons of David."

Vers. 45—47.—*St. Luke's brief summary of the Lord's denunciation of the scribes and others.*

Vers. 45, 46.—**Then in the audience of all the people he said unto his disciples, Beware of the scribes.** Here, in St. Matthew, follows the great denunciation of the Sanhedrist authorities with the other rabbis, Pharisees, and public teachers and leaders of the people. It fills the whole of the twenty-third chapter of the First Gospel. The details would be scarcely interesting to St. Luke's Gentile readers, so he thus briefly summarizes them. **Which desire to walk in long robes.** " With special conspicuousness of fringes (Numb. xv. 38—40). ' The supreme tribunal,' said R. Nachman, ' will duly punish *hypocrites who wrap their talliths round them* to appear, what they are not, true Pharisees ' " (Farrar).

Ver. 47.—**Which devour widows' houses.** Josephus specially alludes to the influence which certain of the Pharisees had acquired over women as directors of the conscience. **For a show**; rather, *in pretence.* "Their hypocrisy was so notorious that even the Talmud records the warning given by Alexander Jannæus to his wife on his death-bed against *painted* Pharisees. And in their seven classes of Pharisees, the Talmudic writers place '*Shechemites*,' Pharisees from self-interest; '*Stumblers*,' so mock-humble that they will not raise their feet from the ground; '*Bleeders*,' so mock-modest that, because they will not raise their eyes, they run against walls, etc. Thus the Jewish writers themselves depict the Pharisees as the Tartuffes of antiquity" (Farrar). **Shall receive greater damnation**; rather, *judgment.* The translators of our beautiful English version are most unhappy in their usual rendering of κρίμα.

HOMILETICS.

Ver. 19—ch. xxi. 38.—*The last working day.* It is Tuesday, the last of the Lord's working days; for Wednesday and the early part of Thursday were spent apparently in the quiet of his Bethany home. A busy, trying day, crowded with events in which we see the Son of God enduring against himself the contradiction of sinners. Let us gather up a part of its teaching. When, in the early morning, Christ entered the outer courts of the temple, he encountered a deputation of persons secretly commissioned by the Pharisees to entrap him into admissions which might be used against him (vers. 19, 20). The deputation consisted (Matt. xxii. 16) of some of the more prominent scholars of the rabbis, and some politicians who were attached to the Herodian dynasty. For so it often is—a common hatred will unite those whose positions, mental or moral, are antagonistic. This has been frequently exemplified in religious and religio-political movements. The emissaries of priest and politician, thus leagued together, submit their question with ceremonious politeness (vers. 21, 22). He to whom they speak knows what is in man (ver. 23). And, demanding the penny, with the coin held before them he returns the famous sentence on which so much has been spoken and written, which has been rendered the catchword of heated ecclesiastical controversy (ver. 24), "Whose image and superscription hath this penny?" It is the image and superscription of the proud Tiberius. "Then," is the reply, "if you use his coin, give back to him what is his due, and to God, whose is the image and superscription on the human soul, give back what is God's" (ver. 25). The confusion of the spies is complete. "They marvelled at his answer, and held their peace" (ver. 26). As the day passes, another deputation appears on the scene. This time the Sadducees (ver. 27) measure the sword of their wit against the Witness for God. The Sadducee mind, cold, cynical, cavilling, pronouncing all earnestness fanaticism, with no definite views as to a life beyond the present, but willing enough to toy over the subject —faith and the things of faith being only a matter to be talked about—has its representative in all ages. And it has some trafficking with Christ. It has its problems, its questions, its discussions. Behold an illustration of their kind in the problem submitted as to the seven brothers (vers. 28—33). A more foolish issue than that raised it is scarcely possible to conceive, and it might have been treated with contemptuous silence. But truth may be taught even though the occasion of the teaching is unworthy. And, by the incident related, a weighty, suggestive instruction is elicited, one which gives, as by a lightning flash, not only a glimpse into the invisible, but a discernment of the spirit of the old Mosaic economy. First of all, disabusing the thought of his hearers of their carnal conceptions of the resurrection-life (vers. 34—36), he reminds them (ver. 37) of the character which, by their own admission, belonged to God; of the great covenant word which Moses uttered when he called the Eternal "the God of Abraham, Isaac, and Jacob." Could they conceive him (ver. 38) the God of mere empty names? Does not the word imply that Abraham, Isaac, and Jacob are not mere dust and ashes, but still living persons, heart to heart with him? It is not wonderful that the quickness and keenness of the reply, and the light which it shed on human destiny, impressed all who were present; so that the multitude hearing were astonished at his doctrine, and from the admiring crowd (Matt. xxii. 23) came the approbation, echoed (ver. 39) by certain of the scribes, "Master, thou hast well said." But not yet does the temptation cease. A jurist, or student of the Law, accustomed to hair-splitting distinctions and controversies over mere pin-points, exclaims, "Master, which is the great command-ment in the Law?" (Matt. xxii. 35). In the school to which he belonged, the precepts of the moral and ceremonial law were reckoned to be more than six hundred, although the great Rabbi Hillel reminded his pupils that, after all, the word, "Do justly, love mercy, and walk humbly with God," is the essence of the Law, the rest being only commentary. "Which commandment," asks this lawyer, "is the greatest, Master? What sayest thou?" Let us thank the tempting jurist whose question evoked the golden wisdom of the emphatic enforcement of the two sentences to which all obedience returns and from which all worthy conduct departs—the first commandment bidding us love God with all the heart, and the second, which is like to it, bidding us love our neighbour as ourselves (Matt. xxii. 37—40). Pharisee, Sadducee, and scribe have all been defeated in their trial of Jesus. It is his turn to try them. He will not let them go until he has shown them the slowness of their minds, and left with them a question to be afterwards inwardly digested. He puts the query, "What think ye of Christ?" (Matt. xxii. 42). And when they answer, "He is the Son of David," he reminds them (vers. 41—44) of the language of the psalmist, implying that there is another than the merely filial relation: "If David call him Lord, how is he then his Son?" Who can abide the thrusts of Jesus? No more questions are asked. No; and pointing to his discomfited tormentors, he preaches the terrible denunciation epito-mized in vers. 45—47, given at fuller length in the eight crushing woes of Matt. xxiii. It is a scene that beggars description—the grandest moment in the ministry of Christ, the Prophet and King. The evangelist, guided, perhaps, by the sense of fitness to that scene, represents the tone of the speech as changing, at the close of the commination, from indignation hot and strong to the moaning, saddened cry of a heart breaking with grief—the cry, already considered, over impenitent, hard-hearted Jerusalem. So the Lord moves towards the gate of the temple. It is on his way thither that he observes (ch. xxi. 1—4) the action of the poor widow, who cast into one of the chests which were placed in the temple courts her poor little all. How calm was the soul which, even in the heat of that day of temptation, could pause, observe, and speak of a deed apparently so insignificant! It is observable that the last word of Christ in the temple should be one concerning the love and the love-offering, which are better than formal sacrifices. Ever to be remembered, too, is the sentence, "He looked up, and *saw* the gifts cast into the treasury." The gifts that men and women furtively cast, thinking that none will observe the meanness, or the ostentatiously cast money expecting that all will applaud the munificence, he sees. He is always looking to the treasury; he estimates the real value of the offering. What is the principle of the commendation? "One coin," says an old Father, "out of a little is better than a treasure out of much; for it is not con-sidered how much is given, but how much remains behind." "He went out and departed from the temple." It is the "Ichabod," the departing of the glory. Thirty-five years later the holy and beautiful house was left desolate; the prediction (ver. 6) as to the great costly stones was fulfilled. The ploughshare of a fearful retribution was driven through Israel's palace, as through Israel itself. The quitting of the temple by the Son of God was the beginning of the end. Thenceforth it was the whited sepulchre, beau-tiful in appearance, but within full of the dead bones of religion and all spiritual uncleanness. Lo! the house is left to these Pharisees desolate. As the closing feature of that great Tuesday, we behold Christ and his apostles seated on the slope of Olivet. The golden radiance of the setting sun is flung over the glorious city. The pinnacles of the temple, the palaces, and massive buildings and endless houses of the Jews are, one by one, bathed in the georgeous reflection. There, in the vale below, are Gethsemane and the Kedron, and around are the well-known features of the landscape so dear to the Israelite. It is with this prospect full in his view that Jesus gives the instruction as to the end of the age in those mysterious intimations in which the downfall of the city of the great King is so blended with other and greater catastrophes that it is difficult to distinguish what relates specially to the one and what relates specially to the others. Oh, how urgent the exhortation to vigilance! How real and solemn for all the injunction "to pray always, that we may be accounted worthy to escape all these things that shall come to pass, and to stand before the Son of man" (ver. 36)!

HOMILIES BY VARIOUS AUTHORS.

Vers. 1—8.—*The great Teacher's silence.* The refusal of Jesus Christ to answer the question proposed to him demands explanation and suggests remark.

I. THE DIFFICULTY WE FIND IN HIS SILENCE. Had not the Sanhedrin a right to ask this of him? It was a legally constituted body, and one of its functions was to guide the people of the land by determining who was to be received as a true Teacher from God. John had recognized their right to formally interrogate him (John i. 19—27). As Jesus was claiming and exercising authority (ch. xix. 45), it seems natural and right that this council of the nation should send a deputation to ask the question in the text; and, if that be so, it seems only right that our Lord should give them a formal and explicit answer. Why did he not?

II. ITS EXPLANATION. There was: 1. *A formal justification.* The Sanhedrin had not yet declared its mind on the great Prophet who had been before the public, and in regard to whom an official decision might well be demanded. Jesus Christ, as a Jew, had a right to ask this question concerning one whose ministry commenced before his own, and had already been concluded. If they were unwilling or unable to pronounce a judgment, they ruled themselves unfit or incompetent to do what they undertook to do. As the event proved, they declined to say, and their refusal justified Jesus in withdrawing his own case from a tribunal which confessed its own incompetence. But there was also: 2. *A moral ground* on which our Lord might base his action. The Sanhedrin was not solicitous to guide the people in the ways of truth and righteousness; they wanted to *entrap their enemy* (see ch. xix. 47). Their aim was not holy, but unholy; not patriotic, but malevolent. They were not seeking the public good, but their own personal advantage; they desired to crush a rival, and so to maintain their own position of authority. Such an object as this deserved no regard; it was one not to be respected, but to be defeated; and our Lord, with Divine wisdom, adopted a course which cut the ground completely from beneath their feet.

III. ITS SIGNIFICANCE TO OURSELVES. Jesus Christ will not always answer our questions. Whether or not he will do so depends on the spirit in which he is approached by us. 1. *Mere curiosity* has nothing to expect of him (see ch. xiii. 23, 24; Acts i. 6, 7). 2. *Unmeaning and unspiritual utterance* makes no way with him (see ch. xiv. 15). The formalities and proprieties of religious language fall on his ear, but they do not touch his heart or move his hand. 3. *Malevolent activity* can look for nothing but defeat from his wisdom and his power (see text and following verses of this chapter). 4. *Presumption* will be turned away unrewarded. To see the Father as he is in himself is an impossible and impracticable desire; our wisdom is to understand him as he is revealed in his Son (John xiv. 8, 9). We may not ask of Christ those things which are beyond the range of our powers. 5. *Impatience* must be postponed, and must wait the fitter time (John xvi. 12). Christ will sometimes, perhaps often, be silent when we would that he should speak to us. But there is—

IV. ONE CONDITION UNDER WHICH HE WILL SPEAK TO US. *Practical, spiritual earnestness* will draw down his blessing, will command his gracious and life-giving word. If we earnestly and perseveringly seek our own spiritual well-being or that of others, we shall not fail to hear him say, "According to your faith be it unto you."—C.

Ver. 16.—*Deprecation and doom.* We may regard—

I. THE FORCE OF THESE WORDS AS ORIGINALLY APPLIED. The people who listened to this parable: 1. *Deprecated a guilt in which they were to be partakers.* "God forbid," said they, "that we should do such shameful things as these, that we should be in any way involved in such crimes as these! Whosoever hands may be dyed with the blood of the Husbandman's Son, ours shall be stainless." Yet were they moving on to the last and worst enormity, and already were they doing their best to bring about the guilty consummation. 2. *Deprecated a doom to which they were descending.* "God forbid," said they, "that we should be subjected to the Divine wrath, and that we should lose that place of privilege we have so long enjoyed! May Heaven avert from us the calamity of having to yield to another nation or kingdom the post of honour, the place of privilege, which our fathers handed down to us!" But they were then pursuing the course which led inevitably to this very doom. If they only walked on in the path along which they were then hurrying, they were bound to reach that "miserable" end.

II. ITS APPLICATION TO OUR OWN HEARTS AND LIVES. 1. We may be supposing ourselves incapable of wrong-doing the seeds of which are already sown in our heart. Hazael proved to have "dog" enough in him to do the worst things he shuddered at when he spoke (2 Kings viii. 13). David discovered that he was capable of a selfishness which he was condemning to death in another (2 Sam. xii. 5—7). These Jews shrank from an action which was described to them, as a thing too base for them to commit; and yet they were in the very act of committing it. We little know what possibilities of evil are within us; we cannot estimate aright our own capacity for wrong-doing. Probably every man has in his heart something of which sin may lay hold in some dark hour, and by which he may conceivably be led down to guilt and shame. The declension and fall of those who once stood among the worthiest and the most honoured speaks to us in earnest tones of the possible wandering of our own souls from God and goodness. Even Paul realized this stern possibility, and acted upon it (1 Cor. ix. 27). The histories of the erring and ruined souls of men who once seemed beyond the reach of wrong and crime, but who became entangled in their meshes and were slain by them, call upon us to be (1) watchful with a constant vigilance, and (2) prayerful with an unflagging earnestness, lest we too fall under the power of temptation (Matt. xxvi. 41). 2. We may be supposing ourselves safe from a doom which lies straight in front of us. How many a youth imagines himself secure from a degradation and a darkness toward which he has, in the sight of God, already set his foot! How many a man considers himself safe from a low and dishonourable level, when he is already on the slope that leads down to it! What if we could see the goal to which the path we tread is tending! "God forbid," we say, "that this should be our destiny!" and all the while our face is turned in that direction. There is "an earnest need for prayer" that God would show us what is the way in which we are walking; that, if we are in the wrong road, he would "apprehend" us even as he apprehended his chosen messenger (Phil. iii. 12), and turn our feet into the way of his testimonies (Ps. cxxxix. 23, 24).—C.

Ver. 17.—*The rejection and exaltation of Christ.* We look at—

I. THE REJECTION OF JESUS CHRIST. *Its strangeness.* 1. From an *evidential* point of view. How came the builders to reject that valuable Stone? How was it that all the *miracles* of Jesus, so wonderful, so beneficent, so simple, and so credible as they were; that the *life* of Jesus, so holy and so beautiful, so gracious and so winning as it was; that the *truth* spoken by Jesus, so profound, so original, so lofty, so satisfying to the deepest wants of man as it was;—how came it to pass that all this left him the "despised and rejected of men"? 2. From a *providential* point of view. How do we account for it that there should have been such a long and complicated preparation for the coming of the Messiah of the Jews, and of the Redeemer of mankind, and that he should fail to be recognized when he came? Does not all that Divine arrangement of Law and ritual and prophecy, of privilege and discipline, seem to have been attended with failure? Of what use was all that elaborate preparation, when the people of God rejected the Son of God? when he to whom everything pointed, and of whom everything foretold, was not welcomed and honoured, but denounced as a deceiver and slain as a criminal?

II. CONSIDERATIONS WHICH ACCOUNT FOR IT; or which, if they do not account for it, lessen our surprise concerning it. 1. As to the *evidential* difficulty. We need not wonder that the very strongest evidence failed to convince those who were unconvinced. What evidence *can* prevail against bigotry (or prejudice) and selfishness combined? Our knowledge and experience of mankind must have abundantly proved that either of these can repel the clearest and weightiest proofs; much more can both of them. And surely prejudice and self-interest never found a firmer seat than they found in the minds of the "chief priests and the scribes" who led the opposition to our Lord. 2. As to the *providential* difficulty. We must take into our consideration (1) the fact that God's dealings with our race include such apparent failures as this, and oblige us to wait the issue before we judge; (2) the fact that the long preparation of Israel was by no means wholly an *apparent* failure. There is evidence of much fulfilment of prophecy; there is the valuable contribution of all that is contained in Old Testament Scripture, which is a rich and precious heritage to the human race; and there is, above all, the formation of a pure and reverent people, distinguished from and raised above all surrounding nations in the supreme element of moral character, which supplied the human material for the first great missionary epoch. Moreover, the very rejection of Jesus Christ has proved to be the beginning and foundation of ultimate success, and of a success far deeper and larger than any contemporary and national triumph would have been. It has led up to—

III. HIS EXALTATION. 1. *Notwithstanding his humiliation.* That Stone was rejected indeed; that Teacher was silenced, that Prophet slain, that cause covered with infamy; those hopes, cherished by a few disciples, were laid in the tomb and covered from sight; yet, notwithstanding all that apparent defeat and discomfiture, that "Stone has become the Head of the corner," that Teacher the great Teacher of Divine wisdom, that Prophet the acknowledged Saviour of mankind, that cause the kingdom of God upon earth. 2. *As the reward of his humiliation.* "Wherefore also God hath highly exalted him" (Phil. ii. 6—11; Heb. ii. 9, 10). 3. *As the result of his humiliation.* "I, if I be lifted up, will draw all men unto me." The cross has been the great loadstone which has been attracting the world. It is to a crucified Saviour, once slain for our sins, dying in mercy toward our race, that we are drawn in faith and love. It is he "who loved us, and gave himself for us" unto such shame and sorrow and death—it is he whom we rejoice to make the Friend of our heart and the Sovereign of our life.

1. Learn the *place of privilege.* It is well for us that we stand where we do stand— at a point in time where we can recognize the Corner-stone. The mountain is best seen afar off, the city or the sea is best seen from above, the character of the generation is best understood after some interval of time. We know Jesus Christ better than we should have done had we lived when he was the Stone rejected of the builders. We could not be better placed than we are by the providence of God for understanding him and rejoicing in his worth. 2. Know the *day of opportunity.* Recognizing the true character of that once-slighted "Stone," knowing Jesus Christ as we know him now, it is for us to accept him without delay as our personal Redeemer, and to commend him, with all devotedness, to the estimation and trust of all beholders.—C.

Ver. 18.—*Contact and conflict with Christ.* There is one thing which, as a stone or rock, Christ is willing and waiting to be to us; there is that also which, in spite of his own desire concerning us, we may compel him to be to us. I. THE ROCK ON WHICH WE MAY BUILD. 1. Christ desires to be as the Corner-stone or Foundation-stone on which the whole structure of our character and of our destiny is resting. 2. If we exercise a living faith in him, we shall find him to be all this to us. (1) Building on him, our confidence in the forgiving love of God will be well grounded and our peace of mind will be secure; (2) building on him, our character will be strong and saintly, our life will be useful and noble; (3) resting on him, our souls will be sustained in hours of trial; (4) abiding in him, we shall have peace at the last. II. THE ROCK AGAINST WHICH WE ARE BRUISED OR EVEN BROKEN. We cannot come, in any sense or degree, into *conflict* with Christ without being injured by the act. 1. To turn from him is to deprive ourselves of the best; it is to rob ourselves of the highest motives to rectitude and spiritual worth, of the deepest springs of goodness and of beauty, of the heavenliest influences that can breathe upon the soul, of the purest and most elevating joys that can fill the heart, of the noblest activities that can occupy and crown our life. 2. To reject him, whether by deliberate and determined refusal or by a foolish and guilty procrastination, is to do conscious wrong to ourselves; it is to injure our conscience, to weaken our will, to suffer constant spiritual deterioration, to be moving along that downward slope which ends in darkness of mind and in self-despair. 3. To disobey the commandments of Christ is to come into collision with those laws of God which are also laws of our spiritual nature, any and every infraction of which is attended with inward and serious injury; *e.g.* to hate our brother without a cause, to look with lustful eye, to love our own life rather than the cause of God and righteousness,—this is to suffer harm and damage to the spirit. 4. To work against Christ and his gospel is to be constructing that which will be destroyed, is to be

delving and building on the sand with the tide coming in which will wash everything away.   In no way can we take up an attitude of resistance to Jesus Christ
without "wronging our own soul;" it may be by a cruel renunciation of all that is best,
or it may be by incurring the judgment which must fall and does fall upon folly
and sin.

III. THE ROCK WHICH MAY CRUSH US IN ITS FALL.   "On whomsoever it shall fall,"
etc.   The snow-drift and the glacier are magnificent objects on which to gaze; but how
terrible is the descending, destructive avalanche!   It is simply inevitable that the
brightest light should cast the deepest shade; that fullest privilege and most abounding
opportunity should, in the case of the guilty, end in deepest condemnation and severest
penalty (John iii. 19; Heb. vi. 4—8; Phil. iii. 18, 19).   "When God arises to judgment,"
when the rock of Divine dissatisfaction falls, when the "wrath of the Lamb" is revealed,
then must there be made known what God intends by "everlasting destruction from
his presence."   All that is meant by that we do not know: we may well resolve that,
by timely penitence and loving faith, we will never learn by the teaching of our own
experience.—C.

Vers. 19—26.—*The sacred and the secular.*   There are three preliminary truths
which may be gathered before considering the proper subject of the text.   1. *The
worthlessness of heartless praise.*   What value do we suppose Jesus Christ attached to
the eulogium here pronounced (ver. 2)?   How worthless to him now are the epithets
which are uttered or the praises which are sung by lips that are not sincere!   2. *The
evil end of a false attitude* toward Christ.   The attitude of hostility which his enemies
had definitely taken up led them to resort (1) to shameful deceit (ver. 20), and (2) to a
malign conspiracy against the one Teacher who could and would have led them into
the kingdom of God.   3. *The final discomfiture of guilt.*   (Ver. 26.)   It is silenced and
ashamed.   Respecting the principal subject before us, we should consider—

I. TWO NOTIONS THAT FIND NO COUNTENANCE IN OUR LORD'S REPLY.   1. When Jesus
answered, "Render unto Cæsar," etc., he did *not* mean to say that the spheres of the
secular and the sacred lie so apart that we cannot serve God while we are serving the
state.   Let none say, "Politics are politics, and religion is religion."   That is a
thoroughly unchristian sentiment.   If we ought to "eat and drink," if we ought to do
everything to the glory of God, it is certain that we ought to vote at elections, to speak
at meetings, to exercise our political privileges, and to discharge our civil duties, be
they humble or high, to the glory of God.   A man may be, and should be, serving
Christ as truly and as acceptably in the magistrates' court, or in the lobby of the House
of Commons, as he can be in the school or the sanctuary.   2. Nor did Christ mean to say
that these spheres are so apart that a man cannot be serving the state while he is engaged
in the direct service of God; for, indeed, there is no way by which we render so true
and great a service to the whole body politic as when we are engaged in planting
Divine truth in the minds and hearts of men; then are we sowing the seeds of peace, of
industry, of sobriety, of every national virtue, of a real and lasting prosperity.   3.
Nor yet that there are no occasions whatever when we may act in opposition to the
state.   Our Lord encouraged his apostles in their refusal to obey an unrighteous
mandate (Acts v. 28, 29).

II. THE LEADING TRUTH WHICH CHRIST'S WORDS CONTAIN, viz. that our obligation
to God does not conflict with our ordinary allegiance to the civil power.   If the latter
should enjoin apostasy, or blasphemy, or positive immorality, then disobedience would
become a duty, and might rise into heroism, as it has often done.   But ordinarily, we
can serve God and be loyal citizens at the same time, and this none the less that the
rulers whom we serve are Mohammedans or pagans.   To be orderly and law-abiding
under the rule of an infidel is as far as possible from being unchristian.   On the contrary, it is decidedly Christian (see 1 Tim. ii. 2; Rom. iii. 1—7).   Indeed, service rendered to "the froward" has a virtue not possessed by service to "the good and gentle;"
and faithful citizenship in "a strange land" may be a more valuable and acceptable
service than in a Christian country.   Our duty, in the light of Christ's teaching, is not
that of discovering conscientious objections to the support of the civil government; it
is rather that of rendering a hearty obedience to the Divine will, and also of conforming
in all loyalty to the requirements of human law.—C.

Vers. 27—38.—*Foundations of Christian hope.* On what foundation do we build our hope for the future? Not now on any philosophical deductions; these may have a certain measure of strength to some minds, but they are not firm enough to carry such a weight as the hope of immortality. We build on the Word that cannot be broken—on the promise of Jesus Christ. Our future depends upon the will of our Divine Creator, on the purpose of our God, and only he who came from God can tell us what that purpose is. Here, as elsewhere, we have—

I. THE FIRM GROUND OF CHRISTIAN PROMISE. Our Lord tells us, from his own knowledge, that there is a future for the sons of men. And he indicates some features of this future. 1. Our life will be one *of perfect purity.* There is to be nothing of the grosser element that enters into our social relations here (ver. 35). Great founders of great faiths have promised to their disciples a paradise of enjoyment of a lower kind. Christ leads us to hope for a life from which everything that is sensual will be removed. Love will remain, but it will be spiritual, angelic, absolutely pure. 2. It will be a life *without end,* and therefore *without decay.* "Neither can they die any more" (ver. 36). How blessed the life that knows no fear of interruption, of dissolution, of sudden cessation, and, more particularly, that is free from the haunting consciousness of passing on to a time when faculty must fade, or the sadder sense of decline already commenced or even hastening to its end! What will it be to live a life that becomes ever brighter and fuller as the periods of celestial service pass away! 3. It will be a life *of highest honour and elevation.* "They are equal unto the angels; and are the children of God, being the children of the resurrection" (ver. 36). "*Now* are we the sons of God," and when the future life is disclosed our sonship will mean yet more to us—it will be life on a loftier plane, in a deeper and fuller sense; we shall be nearer to God, and more like him in our faculty and in our spirit and our character.

II. THE ADDITIONAL SUPPORT OF CHRIST'S INFERENCE. To be "the God of Abraham," he argued, meant to be the God of a living soul; he whose God was the living God was a living man in the fullest sense. For God to be *our* God includes everything we need. The living God is the God of living men; the loving God of loving men; the blessed God of happy men; the holy God of holy men. All the highest good for which we long in our noblest hours is guaranteed to us in that "the everlasting God," the righteous and the faithful and the loving One, is *our God.* 1. The heritage of the future is not promised unconditionally; there are "those accounted worthy to obtain" it; therefore there are those who are not worthy, and who will miss it. 2. The condition that is implied is that of a living personal connection with God himself. Those who can truly claim him as "their God" may confidently look forward to an eternal home in his presence and in his service. To us, to whom he has revealed himself in his Son, this means a living union with Jesus Christ our Saviour. To know *him,* to live unto him, to abide in him,—this is life eternal.—C.

Vers. 40—44.—*The lowliness and the greatness of Jesus Christ.* This is *the* subject of these verses; but they are suggestive of minor truths. We have—

I. A PROOF OF UTTER FALSITY. (Ver. 40.) How came these men to be afraid to ask questions of Christ? Others did not shrink from him, or fear to ask things of him. The children were not afraid of him; nor were "the strangers"—those not of Israel: nor were the women who waited on him and learned of him; nor the simple-hearted and genuine inquirers. It was only the men who sought his overthrow, because they dreaded his exposure; it was only those who shrank from his heart-searching gaze and his truth-telling words, that dared not approach him and ask questions of him. No man however ignorant, no child however young, need shrink from the Lord of love, from asking of him what he needs; it is only the false who are afraid.

II. THE TIME FOR AGGRESSIVE ACTION. The successful general may act long on the defensive, but he waits and looks for the moment of attack. Jesus bore long with the questionings of his enemies, but the time had come for him to ask something *of them.* We may well *bear* long *with* the enemies of Christ, but the hour comes when we must *bear down upon* them with convincing and humbling power.

III. THE OCCASIONAL DUTY OF PUTTING MEN INTO A DIFFICULTY. On this occasion our Lord placed his hearers in a difficulty from which he did not offer to extricate them. His prophetic function was to enlighten, to liberate, to relieve. But here was an occasion when he best served men by placing them in a difficulty from which they found no escape. Such service may be rare for a Christian teacher, but it does occur. There are times when we cannot render a man a better service than that of humbling him, of showing him that there are mysteries in presence of which he is a little child.

IV. THE WISDOM OF FURTHER INQUIRY. These Pharisees imagined that they knew everything about the Scriptures that could be known. They were learned, but they were unwise; they had a large verbal and literal acquaintance with their sacred books, but they had missed their deepest meaning. They had not inquired humbly, intelligently, reverently enough. How much more is there in our New Testament than we have yet found! What depth of wisdom in the words of Christ! What enlightenment in the letters of his apostles! Though we may not have missed our way so grievously as the scribes had done, yet may there be very much of Divine truth we have not yet discovered, which patient and devout inquiry will disclose.

V. THE LOWLINESS AND THE GREATNESS OF JESUS CHRIST. He is the Son of David, and he is also his Lord. We understand that better than the most advanced and enlightened of his disciples could at that point. "As concerning the flesh" he was "born of a woman, made under Law;" yet is he "exalted to be a Prince and a Saviour;" Son of man and Son of God. Only thus could he be what he came to be: 1. Our Mediator between God and man. 2. Our Divine Saviour, in whom we put our trust and find mercy unto eternal life; our Divine Friend, of whose perfect sympathy we can be assured; our rightful Lord, to whom we can bring the offering of our hearts and lives.—C.

Vers. 45—47.—*Character and precept, etc.* These verses suggest five truths of practical importance.

I. THAT CHARACTER IS OF MORE CONSEQUENCE THAN PRECEPT. "Beware of the scribes;" they "sit in Moses' seat, and teach things that you should do" (Matt. xxiii. 2); but their conduct is such that they are to be avoided rather than sought after. Beware of the bad man, though he be a good teacher; the influence of his life will be stronger than the effect of his doctrine; the one will do more harm than the other will do good. In a religious teacher, character is the principal thing; if that be unsound, proceed no further; seek some one else, one that you can respect, one that will raise you by the purity of his heart and the beauty of his behaviour.

II. THAT UNGODLY MEN FALL INTO A FOOLISHNESS THE DEPTH OF WHICH THEY DO NOT SUSPECT. How childish and even contemptible it is for men to find gratification in such display on their own part and in such obsequiousness on the part of others as is here described (ver. 46)! To sink to such vanity is wholly unworthy of a man who fears God, and who professes to find his hope and his heritage in him and in his service. They who thus let themselves down do not know how poor and small is the spirit they cherish and the behaviour in which they indulge; they do not suspect that, in the estimate of wisdom, it is at the very bottom of the scale of manliness.

III. THAT FAMILIARITY WITH DIVINE TRUTH IS CONSISTENT WITH THE COMMISSION OF THE WORST OFFENCES. The scribes themselves, familiar with every letter of the Law, could descend to heartless misappropriation in conjunction with a despicable hypocrisy (ver. 47). Guilt and condemnation could go no further than this. It is a solemnizing thought that we may have the clearest view of the goodness and the righteousness of God, and yet may be very far on the road to perdition. Paul felt the solemnity of this thought (1 Cor. ix. 27). It is well that the children of privilege and the preachers of righteousness should take this truth to heart and test their own integrity.

IV. THAT THE AFFECTATION OF PIETY IS A SERIOUS AGGRAVATION OF GUILT. The "making long prayers" entailed a "greater condemnation." Infinitely offensive to the Pure and Holy One must be the use of his Name and the affectation of devotedness to his service as a mere means of selfish acquisition. The fraud which wears the garb of piety is the ugliest guilt that shows its face to heaven. If men will be transgressors, let them, for their own sake, forbear to weight their wrong-doing with a simulated piety. The converse of this thought may well be added; for it is truth on the positive side, viz.—

V. THAT DEVOUT BENEVOLENCE IS GOODNESS AT ITS BEST. To serve our fellow-men because we love Christ, their Lord and ours, and because we believe that he would have us succour them in their need, is to do the right thing under the purest and worthiest prompting; it is goodness at its best.—C.

Vers. 1—19.—*Christ's collision with the Sanhedrin.* We have studied Christ's triumphal entry into Jerusalem and his cleansing of the temple. And now we have to notice the interruptions to which he was subjected as he improved his last days of ministration in the temple-court. He had exercised authority in God's house, he was also teaching with authority the people; hence the Jewish rulers came, demanding from him the sign of his authority to do so. As with many still, there is great demand for signs, certificates, orders. In these circumstances Jesus throws them back on John the Baptist, and asks if they had made out *his* authority. This so "cornered" them that they decline giving an opinion, and Jesus consequently is warranted in declining to tell them by what authority he takes the course he does. Now, here it is to be noticed—

I. THE MINISTRY OF JESUS WAS BOUND UP HISTORICALLY WITH THE CLAIMS OF JOHN. It was to the Baptist he went for baptism. It was when being baptized by John that he received the gifts of the opened heaven, descending dove, and assurance of Sonship. It was from John he received the first start in securing disciples, when the Baptist pointed to him and said, "Behold the Lamb of God, which taketh away the sin of the world!" How natural, therefore, that Jesus should take the chief priests back to John! It was no able manœuvre on the Master's part, but *simple historic defence.* "John recognized my authority and mission; he set his seal upon them: should this not satisfy you?" And surely this course taken by our Lord has deep significance. If ever one in this world might have stood in his own individual right and said, "My work and teaching are surely self-evidently Divine," he was the Man; but no, he takes his questions along the historic line, and shows how he stands on prophetic ground, as successor of the last of the prophets. It was the recognition of the prophetical succession rather than any independent assumption.

II. FEAR OF MAN WILL INCAPACITATE MEN FOR THE SIMPLEST ACT OF JUDGMENT. What Jesus asks these rulers to decide is whether John the Baptist, in introducing baptism, was taking a Heaven-inspired course or not. "The baptism of John, was it from heaven, or of men?" Instead of facing the question like men, they fenced with it. They saw clearly that in either case their answer would put them in a difficulty. If they said that John's baptism was from heaven, Jesus would immediately say, "Why then believed ye him not?" but if they declared it was a mere human innovation, they would come into such collision with the people as to run the risk of being stoned. In fear of man they decline judgment. Now it is instructive here to notice that such temporizers never can be martyrs. They have no notion of *dying* for their conviction about John. Why should they be stoned? They prefer being silent on the whole subject. As long as we fear man more than God, as long as we value man's esteem more than truth, we are unfit for judgment. We only become *impartial* when we are ready to take truth with all its consequences upon us.

III. THE INCOMPETENT DO NOT DESERVE TO BE TREATED AS JUDGES. These rulers have demonstrated their utter incompetency to undertake any decision upon a prophet's claims. They are consequently treated by Jesus as undeserving of the position of judges. It were well if this rule were faithfully observed. Men are treated often as if they had the judicial spirit, capacity, and temper, when they are simply *man-fearing partisans.* It is lost time putting such people in the judgment-seat. Better far to spend the time in teaching the common people, as the Master did, than in trying to convince the partisans who interrupt good work and do none themselves.

IV. BY A PARABLE OF JUDGMENT HE REVEALS TO THESE PARTISANS THEIR DANGER. The vineyard indicates the theocratic people, the husbandmen the men who exercised government among them, and the naturally expected fruit was the loyalty and spiritual service which prophets called for but seldom secured for their Master in heaven. Instead of rendering the fruits, the rulers of the Jewish people subjected the line of prophets to increasing indignities. Last of all, the only Son is sent; but, instead of reverencing him and yielding to Divine demands, they cast him out of the Jewish Church and kill him. How clearly does Jesus thus claim Sonship to God, and indicate his approaching and dreadful doom! The result of this murder of God's Son is to be the transference of the theocracy from the Jews to other husbandmen. The chief priests and scribes are to be supplanted by apostles; and Judaism to give place to Christianity. Seeing that the parable was spoken against them, they cry, "God forbid!" but Jesus clinches his argument by apt quotation from their own Scriptures. He asks, " Is not the stone rejected of the builders to become the head of the corner? And will not all who collide with it be either broken or ground to powder?" In this way he claims to be the test of men, and his rejection to be fatal and final.—R. M. E.

Vers. 20—40.—*Christ supreme in debate.* We have seen in the last section how our Lord told a parable whose bearing was unmistakably against the Jewish rulers. They are determined, in consequence, to so entrap him in discussion as, if possible, to bring him within the grasp of the Roman governor. But in entering the doubtful field of debate with a base purpose such as this, it was, as the sequel shows, only to be vanquished. Jesus proves more than a match for the two batches of artful men who try to entrap him. Let us look at the victories separately, and then at Jesus remaining Master of the field.

I. HIS VICTORY OVER THE REVOLUTIONARY PARTY. (Vers. 21—26.) This party was composed mainly of Pharisees. They corresponded to the modern revolutionary party in settled or conquered states. They were constantly fomenting sedition, plotting against the Roman power, the sworn enemies of Cæsar. They come, then, with their difficulty about tribute. But notice: 1. *Their real tribute to Christ's character in their pretended flattery.* (Ver. 21.) They own to his face that he was too brave to make distinctions among men or to accept their persons. In other words, their testimony clearly is that, like God his Father, Jesus was " no respecter of persons." No one is fit to be a teacher of truth who panders to men's tastes or respects their persons. Only the impartial mood and mind can deal with truth truthfully. In the hollow flattery of the Pharisees we find rich testimony to the excellency of Jesus. 2. Notice their *scruple about paying tribute.* (Ver. 22.) The law of the nation might possibly be made to teach the duty of being tributary to none. It was this they wished to elicit from him, and so hand him over to the governor as seditious. They wished a pretext for revolution, and if he furnished them with one and perished for it, so much the better, they imagined. The baseness of the plot is evident. Their hearts are hostile to Cæsar, but they are ready to become " informers " against him for the sake of getting rid of him. 3. Notice *how simply he secured a victory.* Showing them at once that he knew their designs, he asks them to show him a penny. In his poverty he hardly possessed at this time a spare penny to point his teaching. Having got the penny, he asks about the image on the currency, and receiving for answer that it was Cæsar's, he simply instructs them to give both Cæsar and God their due. Cæsar has his domain, as the currency shows. He regulates the outward relations of men, their barter and their citizenship, and by his laws he makes them keep the peace. But beyond this civil sphere, there is the moral and the religious, where God alone is King. Let God get his rights as well as Cæsar, and all shall be well. These words of Christ sounded the death-knell of the Jewish theocracy. They point out two mutually independent spheres. They call upon men to be at once loyal citizens and real saints. We may do our duty by the state, while at the same time we are conscious citizens of heaven, and serve our unseen Master in all things.[1]

II. HIS VICTORY OVER THE SADDUCEES. (Vers. 27—38.) The Pharisees having been confounded by his subtle power, he is next beset by the rival party, the party of sceptical and worldly tendencies. They have given over another world as a no-man's land, the region of undoubted difficulty and puzzle. Especially do they think it impossible to settle the complicated relations into which men and women enter here in any hereafter. Accordingly they state a case where, by direction of the Mosaic Law, a poor woman became successively the wife of seven brothers. In the other life, ask they, whose wife shall she be? Christ's answer is again triumphant through its simplicity. In the immortal life to which resurrection leads there shall be no marrying or giving in marriage. All shall be like the angels. No distinction in sex shall continue. All are to be " sons of God, being sons of the resurrection " (Revised Version). The

---

[1] Cf. Bersier's 'Sermons,' tome iv. p. 239, etc.

complicated earthly relations shall give place to the simplicity of *sonship*. God's family shall embrace all others. His Fatherhood shall absorb all the descending affections which on earth illustrate feebly his surpassing love, and our sonship to him will embrace all the ascending affection which his descending love demands. The simplicity of a holy family, in which God is Father and all are brethren, and the angels are our high-born elder brethren, will take the place of those complex relationships which sometimes sweeten and sometimes sadden human love. But, in addition, our Lord renders Sadduceeism ridiculous by showing from the Scriptures these sceptics revered that the patriarchs had not ceased to be, but were still living in the bosom of God. For God, in claiming from the burning bush to be the God of Abraham, Isaac, and Jacob, revealed the reality of life beyond death. It was a demonstration of the resurrection. The patriarchs must have been living worshippers when God was still their God, and this life unto him demands for its perfection the resurrection. The plenitude of life is guaranteed in the continued and worshipful life beyond the grave. In this simple and perfect fashion Jesus silences the Sadducees.

III. HE REMAINS COMPLETE MASTER OF THE FIELD. (Vers. 39, 40.) They are beaten in the field of debate. Jesus is Victor. There is no question now which they can ask him. All is over on the plane of intellectual and moral argument. Not even a Parthian arrow can be shot against him. But treachery and brute force remain, and they can have him betrayed and crucified whom they cannot refute. Resort to weapons like these is always proof of weakness. Victory has always been really with the persecuted party. Persecution on the part of any cause or organization demonstrates its inherent weakness. Hence we hail the Christ in the temple as the supreme Master and Conqueror of men. The very men who put unholy hands upon him must have felt that they were doing the coward's part after ignominious defeat. The weapons of our warfare should always be spiritual; with carnal weapons we only confess defeat and court everlasting shame.—R. M. E.

Ver. 40—ch. xxi. 4.—*Vindications and judgments.* We saw on the last occasion how Christ had vanquished all who had tried with him the fortunes of debate. And now we find him putting a pertinent question to them about himself, and effectually puzzling them. Not, of course, that he had this in view in presenting it. His purpose was always a clear and pure one; it was, as Godet suggests, to vindicate beforehand those claims to Divine Sonship on the ground of which they are so shortly to condemn him to death.

I. CONSIDER CHRIST AS DAVID'S SON AND LORD. (Vers. 41—44.) It is clear from the Gospels and from the Targums that the Messiah wanted by the Jews was not necessarily to be Divine. It was a temporal prince, a military Messiah, they longed for; and no Divinity was needful to play the *rôle* of "conquering hero" which they desired. A merely human Messiah would have suited them admirably. When they got one, therefore, who claimed to be Divine, they condemned him for blasphemy, and never stopped until they had made away with him by crucifixion.[1] Our Lord's question in the temple was to arouse them to a sense of Messiah's proper claims. This suggests: 1. *How prone we are to be satisfied with mere human saviours.* The Jews wanted a Messiah to collect armies, to deliver them from Roman bondage, and to give them all good situations in the new kingdom. They wanted nothing that a clever leader could not do for them. And there are plenty of people whose only desired salvation is from hunger and thirst and discomfort of a physical kind. They have no real longing after deliverance from sin and covetousness and discontent. Their one thought is to find somebody who can help them on a bit. 2. *David's royal line produced a Prince who was also David's Lord.* Now, it is plain from the psalm (cx.) which Jesus quotes that David realized in the Messiah his present Lord. He ruled over David, and was recognized by David as his Lord. When we add to this the fact that David was the greatest monarch of his time, we see that the only interpretation of this Lordship is the Divinity of Messiah. This Messiah is made by the Most High to sit at his right hand until his enemies are made his footstool. The whole picture involves and implies Christ's Divinity. Now, if these scribes and Pharisees had acted honestly, they would have said, "Here is a point which escaped us; this Lordship over David is a claim which

[1] Cf. Treffry, on 'The Eternal Sonship,' 4th edit., pp. 77—99.

the sonship does not cover; there must be more in the Messiahship than we suspect; we must reconsider our attitude towards Jesus, and do him justice." But instead of this, they deliberately ignored the difficulty, and went on with their persecution of the Divine Messiah. Now, this is surely to show us that we need a Divine Saviour, for the salvation must be from the power and guilt of sin. We need a Saviour who will be our Lord; to whom we not only owe allegiance, but give it cheerfully. It is a Divine Lord of the ages, the King of kings, the Lord of lords, the infinite Majesty, whom we need to give us the emancipation which can alone profit our souls.

II. Consider Christ's condemnation of the scribes. (Vers. 45—47.) Seeing how they reject the scriptural evidence of his claims, Jesus proceeds to warn his disciples against them. He knows them thoroughly. And: 1. He charges them with *skilfully manufacturing a religious reputation.* They wore peculiar garments; the man-milliners of the day had been brought into requisition. They welcomed recognition from the people in the markets; they took, as their right, the highest seats in the synagogue and the chief rooms at social feasts. They manufactured such a reputation as secured them abundant honour. 2. *They traded upon their reputation.* Widows got their advice and intercession, and paid them well for giving it. In fact, our Lord charges them with devouring widows' houses in their greed. Instead of the widows inspiring pity, they seemed eligible because defenceless victims. 3. *Their condemnation shall be proportionally great.* Professions which are traded upon will ultimately procure a deeper condemnation. How needful that the genuineness of our profession should be tested! If it is for God's dear sake, and not for the sake of worldly advantage, it will stand the test at last.

III. Consider Christ's encomium upon the poor widow. (Ch. xxi. 1—4.) Sitting over against the treasury, our Lord saw both rich and poor depositing their gifts. Some of the rich gave largely out of their abundance, and Jesus noted doubtless the proportion. But one poor widow came along, and she deposited in the temple-chest a single farthing. It was little, but it was her all. Behind her sackcloth Jesus discerned the biggest heart in all the company. Now, we are taught by this circumstance: 1. That *all our gifts are deposited in sight of Christ.* As Divine Saviour he sits, so to speak, over against every treasury, and notes what the people deposit there. There is no such thing as secret giving so far as Jesus is concerned. We may give so that the right hand knows not what the left is giving, but Jesus knows all the same. 2. It is *the heart which determines the character of our liberality.* It is not the quantity of money, but the quality of the act, which is important. A farthing from a widow is more in the sight of God than thousands from a millionaire. Hence we ought to examine ourselves, and see clearly what our motives may be. 3. *Hence it is possible even for the poorest to be liberal.* It is this which we require to have driven home. When poor as well as rich give with large-heartedness, the Church's "golden age" shall come. It is to this that our Lord would lead us.—R. M. E.

EXPOSITION.

CHAPTER XXI.

Vers. 1—4.—*The widow's mite.* We find this little sketch only here and in St. Mark (xii. 41—44). The Master was sitting—resting, probably, after the effort of the great denunciation of the scribes and Pharisees—in the covered colonnade of that part of the temple which was open to the Jewish women. Here was the treasury, with its thirteen boxes in the wall, for the reception of the alms of the people. These boxes were called *shopheroth,* or trumpets, because they were shaped like trumpets,

swelling out beneath, and tapering upward into a narrow mouth, or opening, into which the alms were dropped. Some of these "trumpets" were marked with special inscriptions, denoting the destination of the offerings.

Ver. 1.—**And he looked up, and saw the rich men casting their gifts into the treasury.** It is not improbable that a special stream of almsgivers were just then passing through the temple court, many being specially impressed by the solemn words they had just been listening to.

Ver. 2.—**And he saw also a certain poor widow casting in thither two mites.** The

mite (λεπτόν) was the smallest current coin.
Two of these little pieces were the smallest
legal offering which could be dropped into
the "trumpet." But this sum, as the
Heart-reader, who knew all things, tells us
(ver. 4), was *every particle of money she had
in the world;* and it was this splendid
generosity on the part of the poor solitary
widow which won the Lord's praise, which
has touched the hearts of so many generations since, which has stirred up in so many
hearts an admiration of an act so strangely
beautiful, but well-nigh inimitable.

*Vers. 5—7.—The temple—its impending
ruin. The disciples' questions.*

Ver. 5.—**And as some spake of the temple.**
After the Lord's remark upon the almsgiving of the rich men and the poor widow
to the treasury of the temple, the Master
left the sacred building for his lodging outside the city walls. As far as we know,
his comment upon the widow's alms was
his last word of public teaching. On their
way home, while crossing the Mount of
Olives, they apparently halted for a brief
rest. It was then that some of his friends
called attention to the glorious prospect
of the temple, then lit up by the setting
sun. It was, no doubt, then in all its perfect beauty, a vast glittering mass of white
marble, touched here and there with gold
and colour. Whosoever had not gazed on
it, said the old rabbis, had not seen the
perfection of beauty. It is possible that the
bystander's remark was suggested by the
memory of the last bit of Divine teaching
they had listened to. "Lord, is not the
house on Zion lovely? But if only such
gifts as those you have just praised with
such unstinting praise had been made, never
had that glorious pile been raised in honour
of the Eternal King." More probable, however, the sight of the great temple, then
bathed in the golden glory of the fast-setting
sun, recalled some of the Master's sayings
of that eventful day, notably such as,
"Your house is left unto you desolate,"
which occurred in the famous twice-spoken
apostrophe, "O Jerusalem, Jerusalem, thou
that killest the prophets!" (Matt. xxiii. 38;
ch. xiii. 35). "What, Lord! will *that*
house, so great, so perfect in its beauty, so
loved, the joy of the whole earth,—will *that
house* be left desolate and in shapeless
ruins?" **With goodly stones.** The enormous
size of the stones and blocks of marble with
which the temple of Jerusalem was built
excited the surprise of Titus when the city
fell. Josephus mentions ('Bell. Jud.,' v. 5)
that some of the levelled blocks of marble
or stone were forty cubits long and ten
high. **And gifts;** better rendered, *sacred
offerings,* such as the "golden vine," with
its vast clusters, the gift of Herod—which

probably suggested the discourse, "I am
the true Vine" (reported in John xv.)—such
as crowns, shields, vessels of gold and silver,
presented by princes and others who visited
the holy house on Zion. The temple was
rich in these votive offerings. The historian
Tacitus, for instance, calls it "a temple of
vast wealth" ('Hist.,' v. 8).

Ver. 6.—**There shall not be left one stone
upon another.** There is a remarkable passage in 2 Esdr. x. 54, "In the place wherein
the Highest beginneth to show *his* city, there
can no man's building be able to stand."
The Lord's words were fulfilled, in spite of
the strong wish of Titus to spare the temple.
Josephus, writing upon the utter demolition
of the city and temple, says that, with the
exception of Herod's three great towers and
part of the western wall, the whole circuit
of the city was so thoroughly levelled and
dug up that no one visiting it would believe
that it had ever been inhabited ('Bell.
Jud.,' vii. 1. 1).

Ver. 7.—**And they asked him, saying,
Master, but when shall these things be? and
what sign** will there be **when these things
shall come to pass?** St. Mark (xiii. 3) tells
us that these questioners were Peter and
James, John and Andrew. They said to
their Master, "When shall these things be,
and what sign shall precede them?" They
asked their question with mingled feelings
of awe and gladness: *of awe,* for the ruin
of their loved temple, and all that would
probably accompany the catastrophe, was a
dread thought; *of gladness,* for they associated the fall of city and temple with
the manifestation of their Lord in glory.
In this glory they would assuredly share.
But they wished to know more respecting
the times and seasons of the dread event.
Of late the disciples had begun dimly to
see that no Messianic restoration such as
they had been taught to expect was contemplated by their Master. They were re-
casting their hopes, and this solemn prediction they read in the light of the late
sad and gloomy words which he had spoken
of himself and his fortunes. Perhaps he
would leave them for a season and then
return, and, amid the crash of the ruined
city and temple, set up his glorious kingdom.
But they longed to know when this would
be; hence the question of the four.

The Lord's answer treated, in its first
and longer portion, exclusively of the destruction of Jerusalem and its temple—the
fair city and the glorious house on which
they were then gazing, glorified in the
light of the sunset splendour; then, as he
spoke, gradually the horizon widened, and
the Master touched upon the fortunes of

the great world lying beyond the narrow pale of the doomed, chosen people. He closes his grand summary of the world's fortunes by a sketch of his own return in glory. The disciples' hearts must have sunk as they listened; for how many ages lay between *now* and *then!* Yet was the great prophecy full of comfort, and in later days was of inestimable practical value to the Jerusalem Christians. The discourse, which extends from ver. 8 to ver. 36, has been well divided by Godet into four divisions. (1) The apparent signs of the great catastrophe, which must not be mistaken for true signs (vers. 8*b*—19). (2) The true sign, and the destruction of Jerusalem, which will immediately follow it, with the time of the Gentiles, which will be connected with it (vers. 20—24). (3) The coming of the Lord, which will bring this period to an end (vers. 25—27). (4) The practical application (vers. 28—36).

Vers. 8—19.—*The apparent signs which would show themselves, but which must not be mistaken for the true signs immediately preceding the catastrophe.*

Ver. 8*b*.—**Many shall come in my name, saying, I am** Christ. Many of these pretenders appeared in the lifetime of the apostles. Josephus mentions several of these impostors ('Ant.,' xx. 8 §§ 6—10; 'Bell. Jud.,' ii. 13. § 5). Theudas, one of these pretenders, is referred to in Acts xxi. 38 (see, too, Josephus, 'Ant.,' xx. 5. § 1). Simon Magus announced that he was Messiah. His rival Dositheus, his disciple Menander, advanced similar pretences. Mr. Greswell (quoted by Dean Mansel, 'Speaker's Commentary,' on Matt. xxiv. 5) has called attention to the remarkable fact that, while many of these false Messiahs appeared in the interval between the Lord's ascension and the Jewish war, there is no evidence that any one arose claiming this title before the beginning of his ministry. It was necessary, he infers, that the true Christ should first appear and be rejected by the great body of the nation, before they were judicially given over to the delusions of the false Christs.

Vers. 9, 10.—**Wars and commotions . . . nation shall rise against nation, and kingdom against kingdom.** Josephus the Jewish, and Tacitus the Roman, historian—the former in his 'Jewish Wars,' and the latter in his 'Annals'—describe the period which immediately followed the Crucifixion as full of wars, crimes, violences, earthquakes. "It was a time," says Tacitus, "rich in disasters, horrible with battles, torn with seditions, savage even in peace itself."

Ver. 11.—**Great earthquakes.** These seem to have been very frequent during the period; we hear of them in Palestine, Italy, Greece, Asia Minor, Crete, Syria. **Famines and pestilences.** The Jewish and pagan historians of this time—Josephus, Suetonius, Tacitus, and others—enumerate several memorable instances of these scourges in this eventful time. **Fearful sights and great signs.** Among the former may be especially enumerated the foul and terrible scenes connected with the proceedings of the Zealots (see Josephus, 'Bell. Jud.,' iv. 3. § 7; v. 6. § 1, etc.). Among the great signs "would be the rumour of monstrous births; the cry, 'Woe! woe!' for seven and a half years of the peasant Jesus, son of Hanan; the voice and sound of departing guardian-angels; and the sudden opening of the vast brazen temple gate which required twenty men to move it" (Farrar).

Ver. 12.—**But before all these, they shall lay their hands on you, and persecute you.** The Master continues his prophetic picture. From speaking generally of wars, and disasters, and tumults, and awful natural phenomena, which would mark the sad age in which his hearers were living, he proceeded to tell them of things which would surely befall *them*. But even then, though terrible trials would be their lot, they were not to be dismayed, nor to dream that the great catastrophe he had been predicting was yet at hand. Some doubt exists as to the meaning of "before" ($\pi\rho\delta$) in this twelfth verse. It usually has been understood in a temporal sense, *i.e.* "Before all the wars, etc., I have been telling you of, you will be persecuted." A more definite sense is, however, produced by giving the word $\pi\rho\delta$ (before) the signification of "before," equivalent to "more important"—"more important for you as signs will be the grave trials you will have to endure: even *these* signs must not dismay you, or cause you to give up your posts as teachers, for the end will not be heralded even by these personal signs." **Delivering you up to the synagogues, and into prisons, being brought before kings and rulers for my Name's sake.** What may be termed instances of many of these special persecutions are detailed in the Acts (see, for instance, Acts v. 40; and portions of vi., vii., viii., xii., xiv., xvi., xxi., and following).

Ver. 15.—**For I will give you a mouth and wisdom, which all your adversaries shall not be able to gainsay nor resist.** Instances of the splendid fulfilment of this promise are supplied in the "Acts" report of St. Stephen's speech (vii.), and St. Paul's defence spoken before the Roman governor Felix (xxv.) and before King Agrippa (xxvi.).

Ver. 16.—**And ye shall be betrayed both by parents, and brethren, and kinsfolk, and friends.** His disciples must be prepared to pay, as the price of their friendship with him, the sacrifice of all home and domestic life and peace. How often in the records of the early Christians are these terrible sufferings added to public persecution! Literally, his own would have very often to give up mother, father, friends, for his sake. **And some of you shall they cause to be put to death.** This was literally true in the case of several of those then listening to him.

Ver. 17.—**And ye shall be hated of all men for my Name's sake.** All the records of early Christianity unite in bearing witness to the universal hatred with which the new sect were regarded by pagans as well as Jews. The words of the Roman Jews reported in Acts xxviii. 22 well sum this up, "As concerning this sect, we know that everywhere it is spoken against" (see, too, Acts xxiv. 5 and 1 Pet. ii. 12). The Roman writers Tacitus, Pliny, and Suetonius, bear the same testimony.

Ver. 18.—**But there shall not an hair of your head perish.** Not, of course, to be understood literally; for comp. ver. 16. Bengel's comment accurately paraphrases it: "Not a hair of your head shall perish without the special providence of God, nor without reward, nor before the due time." The words, too, had a general fulfilment; for the Christian community of Palestine, warned by this very discourse of the Lord's, fled in time from the doomed city, and so escaped the extermination which overtook the Jewish people in the great war which ended in the fall of Jerusalem (A.D. 70).

Ver. 19.—**In your patience possess ye your souls.** Quiet, brave patience in all difficulty, perplexity, and danger, was the attitude pressed upon the believers of the first days by the inspired teachers. St. Paul constantly strikes this note.

Vers. 20—24.—*The true signs which his people are to be on the watch for.*

Ver. 20.—**And when ye shall see Jerusalem compassed with armies, then know that the desolation thereof is nigh.** This is to be the sign that the end has come for temple, city, and people. Wars and rumours of wars, physical portents, famine and pestilence succeeding each other with a terrible persistence, all these will, in the forthcoming years, terrify and perplex men's minds, presages of something which seems impending. But his people are to bear in mind that these were not the immediate signs of the awful ruin he was foretelling. But when the holy city was invested, when hostile armies were encamped about her—then this would surely come to pass, and some of these very bystanders would be-

hold it—*then*, and not till then, let his people take alarm. Let them at once and at all cost flee from temple and city, for there would be no deliverance, God had left his house, given up the chosen people. "Jerusalem shall be trodden down of the Gentiles" (ver. 24). It is probable that these solemn words of the Master, becoming, as they did, at a comparatively early date, the property of the Church, saved the Christian congregations in Palestine from the fate which overtook the Jewish nation in the last great war. Clearly warned by Jesus that the gathering of the Roman armies in the neighbourhood of Jerusalem was the unmistakable sign of the end of the Jewish polity, the Christian congregations fled to Pella beyond Jordan. The Jews never ceased to the last trusting that deliverance from on high would be vouchsafed to the holy city and temple. The Christians were warned by the words of the Founder of their faith—words spoken nigh forty years before the siege—that the time of mercy was hopelessly past.

Ver. 24.—**And they shall fall by the edge of the sword, and shall be led away captive into all nations.** It is computed that 1,100,000 Jews perished in the terrible war when Jerusalem fell (A.D. 70). Renan writes of this awful slaughter, "that it would seem as though the whole (Jewish) race had determined upon a rendezvous for extermination." **Jerusalem shall be trodden down of the Gentiles.** After incredible slaughter and woes, Titus, the Emperor Vespasian's son, who commanded the Roman armies, ordered the city (of Jerusalem) to be razed so completely as to look like a spot which had never been inhabited (Josephus, 'Bell. Jud.,' v. 10. § 5). The storied city has been rebuilt on the old site—*but without the temple*—and since that fatal day, more than eighteen centuries ago, no Jew save on bare sufferance has dwelt in the old loved and sacred spot. In turn, Roman and Saracen, Norseman and Turk, have trodden Jerusalem down. Literally, indeed, have the sad words of Jesus been fulfilled. **Until the times of the Gentiles be fulfilled.** These few words carry on the prophecy past our own time (how far past?)—carry it on close to the days of the end. "The times of the Gentiles" signify the whole period or epoch which must elapse between the destruction of Jerusalem and the temple, and the beginning of the times of the end when the Lord will return. In other words, these "times of the Gentiles" denote the period during which they—the Gentiles—hold the Church of God in place of the Jews, deposed from that position of favour and honour. These words separate the prophecy of Jesus which belongs solely to the ruin of the city and temple from the eschatological portion of the same prophecy. *Hitherto the Lord's words referred solely to the fall of Jerusalem and the ruin of the Jewish race. Now begins a short prophetic description of the end and of the coming of the Son of man in glory.*

Vers. 25—27.—*The prophecy of the coming of the Son of man in glory. The signs which shall precede this advent.* **And there shall be signs in the sun, and in the moon, and in the stars; and upon the earth distress of nations, with perplexity; the sea and the waves roaring; men's hearts failing them for fear, and for looking after those things which are coming on the earth: for the powers of heaven shall be shaken. And then shall they see the Son of man coming in a cloud with power and great glory.** The Lord continues his solemn prophecy respecting things to come. Now, the question of the four disciples—to which this great discourse was the answer—was, When were they to look for that awful ruin of city and temple of which their loved Master spoke? *But they, it must be remembered, in their own minds closely connected the temple's fall with some glorious epiphany of their Master, in which they should share.* He answers generally their formal question as to the temple, describing to them the very signs they are to look for as heralding the temple's fall. He now proceeds to reply to their real query respecting the glorious epiphany. *The temple's ruin,* that belonged to the period in which they were living; but the glorious epiphany, *that* lay in a far distance. "See," he said, "city and temple will be destroyed; this catastrophe some of you will live to see. The ruin will be irreparable; a new epoch will set in, an epoch I call 'the times of the Gentiles.' These once despised peoples will have their turn, for I shall be their Light. Ages will pass before these 'times of the Gentiles' shall be fulfilled, but the end will come, and then, and not till then, will the Son of man come in glory. Listen; these shall be the signs which shall herald this glorious advent: *Signs in the sun, and in the moon, and in the stars.*" St. Matthew (xxiv. 29) supplies more details concerning these "signs." The sun would be darkened, and the moon would not give her light; the stars would fall from heaven. These words are evidently a memory of language used by the Hebrew prophets to express figuratively the downfall of kingdoms. So Isaiah (xiii. 10) speaks thus of the destruction of Babylon, and Ezekiel (xxxii. 7) of the fall of Egypt (see too Isa. xxxiv. 4). It is, however, probable that our Lord, while using language and figures familiar to Hebrew thought, foreshadowed a literal fulfilment of his words.

So Godet, who picturesquely likens our globe just before the second advent to "a ship creaking in every timber at the moment of its going to pieces." He suggests that "our whole solar system shall then undergo unusual commotions. The moving forces (δυνάμεις), regular in their action till then, shall be, as it were, set free from their laws by an unknown power, and, at the end of this violent but short distress, the world shall see him appear" (see 2 Pet. iii. 10—12, where it is plainly foretold that tremendous physical disturbances shall precede the second coming of the Lord). *The Son of man coming in a cloud.* The same luminous cloud we read of so often in the Pentateuch: the flames of the desert-wanderings; the pillar of cloud and fire; the same bright cloud enveloped the Lord on the Mount of Transfiguration; it received him as he was taken up (Acts i. 9). Nothing is said in this place as to any millennial reign of Christ on earth. The description is that of a transitory appearance destined to effect the work upon quick and dead—an appearance defined more particularly by St. Paul in 1 Cor. xv. 23 and 1 Thess. iv. 16, 17.

Vers. 28—36.—*Practical teaching arising out of the foregoing prophecy respecting the fall of Jerusalem and the "last things."*

Ver. 28.—**And when these things begin to come to pass, then look up, and lift up your heads; for your redemption draweth nigh.** There is no doubt that the first reference in this verse is to the earlier part of the prophecy—the fate of the city and the ruin of the Jewish power. "Your redemption" would then signify "your deliverance" from the constant and bitter hostility of the Jewish authority. After A.D. 70 and the fall of Jerusalem, the growth of Christianity was far more rapid than it had been during the first thirty or forty years of its existence. It had no longer to cope with the skilfully ordered, relentless opposition of its deadly Jewish foe. Yet between the lines a yet deeper meaning is discernible. In all times the earnest Christian is on the watch for the signs of the advent of his Lord, and the restless watch serves to keep hope alive, for the watcher knows that that advent will be the sure herald of his redemption from all the weariness and painfulness of this life.

Ver. 29.—**And he spake to them a parable.** "It is certain," went on the Lord to say, "that summer follows the season when the fig tree and other trees put forth their green shoots. It is no less certain that these things—the fall of Jerusalem, and later the end of the world—will follow closely on the signs I have just told you about."

Ver. 32.—**Verily I say unto you, This generation shall not pass away, till all be** fulfilled. In the interpretation of this verse, a verse which has occasioned much perplexity to students, any non-natural sense for "generation" (γενεά), such as being an equivalent for *the Christian Church* (Origen and Chrysostom) or *the human race* (Jerome) must be at once set aside. Γενεά (generation) denotes roughly a period of thirty to forty years. Thus the words of the Lord here simply asserted that within thirty or forty years all he had been particularly detailing would be fulfilled. Now, the burden of his prophecy had been the destruction of the city and temple, and the signs they were to look for as immediately preceding this great catastrophe. This was the plain and simple answer to their question of ver. 7, which asked "when these things should come to pass." The words he had added relative to the coming of the Son of man did not belong to the formal answer, but were spoken in passing. This mighty advent the Lord alluded to as probably a very remote event—an event certainly to be postponed, to use his own words, "until the times of the Gentiles be fulfilled." Not so the great catastrophe involving the ruin of Jerusalem and the temple, the prophecy concerning which occupied so much of the Lord's reply. *That* lay in the immediate future; *that* would happen in the lifetime of some of those standing by. Before forty years had elapsed the city and temple, now lying before them in all its strength and beauty, would have disappeared.

Ver. 33.—Heaven and earth shall pass away: but my words shall not pass away. A general conclusion to the whole prophecy. "No word of mine," said the Master, "will ever pass away unfulfilled. Some of you will even live to see the terrible fulfilment of the first part of these utterances. All that mighty pile of buildings called Jeru-

salem will pass away, but my words which told of their coming ruin will remain. All this vast creation, earth, and stars will disappear in their turn, but these sayings of mine, which predict their future passing away into nothingness, will outlive both earth and heaven."

Ver. 34.—And take heed to yourselves. The Master ended his discourse with an earnest practical reminder to his disciples to live ever with the sure expectation of his return to judgment. As for those who heard him then, conscious of the oncoming doom of the city, temple, and people, with the solemn procession of signs heralding the impending ruin ever before their eyes, no passions or cares of earth surely would hinder *them* from living the brave, pure life worthy of his servants. As for coming generations—for the warning voice of Jesus here is equally addressed to them—they too must watch for another and far more tremendous ruin falling upon their homes than ever fell upon Jerusalem. The attitude of his people in every age must be that of the "watcher" *till he come.*

Ver. 37.—And in the daytime he was teaching in the temple; and at night he went out, and abode in the mount that is called the Mount of Olives. This brief picture of the last days of public work is retrospective. This was how our Lord spent "Palm Sunday" and the Monday and Tuesday of the last week. The prophetic discourse reported in this twenty-first chapter was, most probably, spoken on the afternoon of Tuesday. After Tuesday evening he never entered the temple as a public Teacher again. Wednesday and Thursday were spent in retirement. Thursday evening he returned to the city to eat the last Passover with his own.

HOMILIES BY VARIOUS AUTHORS.

Vers. 1—4.—*Worth in the estimate of wisdom.* What is the real worth of a human action? Surely, to us who are acting every wakeful hour of life, a very serious question. How shall we decide that an action of ours is worthy or unworthy, and what is the standard by which we shall estimate the comparative excellence of worthy deeds? Our text gives us one principle by which to judge. There are, however, two others which are essentially Christian, that should be placed in the foreground. Acts are worthy—

I. AS THEY ARE USEFUL; as they tend to promote well-being. And here we should note that their usefulness is greater: 1. As they affect character rather than circumstance. 2. As they are free from drawback; for the usefulness of many a course of action is the difference between the intentional good and the incidental evil that is wrought. 3. As they are permanently influential and therefore reproductive. Many a deed, being done, is *done with*; it has no appreciable results; but many another is as seed in the soil—there is a fruitful harvest to be reaped from it in the after-time.

II. ACCORDING TO THE SPIRIT IN WHICH THEY ARE DONE. If useful things are done in the spirit of rivalry, or for the purpose of display, or in the hope of social or material remuneration, their worth in God's sight is nothing or next to nothing. If they are done to honour and to please Jesus Christ, or prompted by pure benevolence, or in the spirit of filial obedience, they have a real worth and are the objects of Divine approval. But the teaching of our text is that actions are worthy—

III. MEASURED BY THEIR UNSELFISHNESS. If at heart they are selfish, then in the judgment of God they are without virtue; in proportion to their generosity, and that is to say, to their costliness, they are beautiful, and even noble. 1. *The gift of money.* The widow's mite was more in the sight of God than the rich men's gold; and it was so because they gave of their abundance a sum the loss of which they would not feel—a sum that entailed no reduction of their comfort and constituted no sacrifice at all; but she gave all that she had—a sum she would miss much, a truly generous sacrifice. How often we applaud the donation of some hundreds of pounds, when the ten shillings contributed by some struggling worker has a higher place in the heavenly ledger! 2. *The gift of time.* The man whose easy circumstances allow him to give much time to religion or philanthropy may be less worthy and may be making a really smaller contribution than he who, pressed hard by pecuniary obligations and having a heavy burden of family responsibility to carry, yet squeezes a few hours from toilful days to lend a helping hand to the cause of Christ and of man. The *horæ subsecivæ* are of more account than many leisure days. 3. *Active service* in the field of Christian labour. Some men are so constituted that they can render service in the pulpit, on the platform, in the class-room, *almost without cost;* they can speak without previous preparation and without subsequent exhaustion. But others can only serve at much cost to themselves; their strength is taxed to be ready for the hour of opportunity, they expend themselves freely in the act of utterance or in the outpouring of sympathy, and they know what the miseries of prostration mean. A slight service, as reckoned by the time-table or the census, on the part of these latter may be more than equal to very prominent and much-appreciated work rendered by the former. 4. *The sacrifice of life.* It might seem that those who gave their life for their Lord or for their kind were all offering a gift of the same value. But not so. Life has very different values at different stages. It is comparatively little for the man who has spent his days and his powers to surrender the short and uninteresting remainder; it is much for the young man who has all the pleasures and prizes of life within his reach to part with the bright, inviting future in order to serve his fellows; the deed is nobler, for the sacrifice is greater. (1) Let us take care that we do not judge by the appearance only, or we shall be unjust. (2) Let us be sure that every true act of worthy service is appreciated and will be owned of Christ.—C.

Vers. 5, 6.—*The destructible and the indestructible.* We have our Lord's own authority for comparing the temple with a human being (John ii. 19). He, however, compared it with his body; we may without any impropriety make the comparison with a human spirit—with the man himself. We look at it in regard to its destructibleness.

I. THE BUILDING ITSELF, AND OUR BEING ITSELF. The temple was the pride and the delight of every Jew. Among other things that gratified him, he rejoiced in its strength; he felt that it was secure. Generations of men would come and go, but that building would remain. Built of the most durable materials, it would defy the action of the elements; placed in the strong city and guarded with such ramparts, the enemy would assail it in vain. Where it then stood, there after many centuries it would be found. But the Jew was wrong; already those elements were at work which would bring on the fatal conflict, and that generation was not to pass (ver. 33) until that glorious fabric should be cast down and " not one stone left upon another." A very slight thing in comparison with such a great and imposing structure seems a human being How easily destroyed! " crushed before the moth; " " destroyed between the morning and the evening." Yet is there within the compass of the smallest and feeblest man that which is more lasting than the temple, that which will survive the strongest structure that art or nature ever reared. Not that the human soul is absolutely indestructible: " *He* can create and he [can] destroy it." But it is created and intended for immortality. And if only it be on the side of truth and in the service of God—*in* Christ Jesus, it is *destined* for immortality; it will survive the strongest temples and the most impregnable castles; no wrath of man, no lapse and wear of time, no shock of material forces, can destroy it; it is indestructible.

II. ITS STRENGTH AND BEAUTY, AND OUR OWN. The temple was "adorned with goodly stones and gifts." But strong as these massive stones were, and carefully as those gifts were guarded, the day came, and came in the experience of that very generation, when not one stone was left upon another, and nothing of the exquisite offerings was preserved; everything perished in the fire or was ploughed up by the ruthless share. Now, there is one thing which no fire can consume and no violence shatter —*a spiritually strong and spiritually beautiful character;* a holy and lovely character rooted in Christ and sustained by his indwelling Spirit. Buildings massive and solid, fortunes large and brilliant, kingdoms fortified by great armies and costly navies,—these may be broken to pieces and perish. But the character of a Christian man, who is simply loyal to his Master, cannot be broken. Character that is not rooted in faith and that is not sustained by devotion may fall and be broken, and great and sad is the fall of it. But (1) let a man build on the foundation which is laid for it, even Jesus Christ; (2) let him abide in Christ by a living faith; (3) let him seek the continual sustenance of the Spirit of God;—and no opposing or wasting forces will touch him to harm him. The strength and beauty of his character will remain, will become stronger and fairer with the passing years, will be the object of commendation when the eye of the great Judge shall rest upon them at last.—C.

Ver. 13.—*Afterwards.* "No chastening for the present seemeth to be joyous, but grievous: nevertheless *afterward* it yieldeth the peaceable fruit of righteousness." Concerning any course we take the question *how it affects us now* is not so important as is the question *to what it leads,* or, in the words of the text, "to what it turns." And while that which is very pleasant often "turns to" much that is painful and bitter, or even shameful (see Rev. x. 10), on the other hand, that which is very trying and even saddening at the time often "turns to" an issue that is full of honour and of joy. The context suggests that—

I. PERSECUTION TURNS TO TESTIMONY—to a most valuable proof of sincerity and faithfulness. When a man endures the blows and buffetings of the cruel hand of the persecutor, "we know the proof of him;" we write him down a true, loyal, noble servant of Christ. To how many men, not of the earliest age only but of all ages, has this steadfastness in the hour of trial been accepted by us as a "testimony" of the very greatest worth, so that their names are treasured by us as those of men that have done highest honour to their race! And their martyr-sufferings have turned to a testimony in the heavenly country; they have gained for them there the commendation of their Lord and the greeting of their glorified brethren. When, from "wandering in deserts, and in mountains, and in dens and caves of the earth," the persecuted Christians of Madagascar came forth to be welcomed by those who were then living under a kindly rule, they were greeted as such faithful and heroic men deserved to be; their persecution had turned into a testimony. In a similar way we may say that—

II. TOIL TURNS INTO ACHIEVEMENT. The toil of the desk, of the field, of the shop, of the factory, may be hard and wearisome; our back may bend beneath our burden; our mind may be strained to its utmost capacity of continuance; but let us take courage and work on at our task; further on is the precious goal of achievement; after a while we shall look with unspeakable satisfaction on the work that has been done, the result that has been reached.

III. PRIVATION TURNS INTO ENRICHMENT. Sad and serious indeed are the privations, the losses, which are suffered when men are suddenly reduced in their temporal possessions, or when they are bereaved of near relatives or most intimate friends. Yet is there something more than compensation when the loss of the one leads, as it has often led, to the enrichment of the soul, by its finding refuge in God and in his service; or when the loss of the other has brought to the soul the fulness of the sympathy and friendship of Jesus Christ; privation has turned to enrichment.

IV. SERVICE TURNS INTO RULE. The soldier in the ranks becomes an officer of the army; the apprentice becomes the master; by long and faithful service in any one of the fields of human activity we prepare to rule. Thus is it in the spiritual realm. Obedience to Divine law turns into a perfect self-command, which is another name for liberty. And a lifelong service of Jesus Christ will turn to an occupancy of that heavenly sphere for which our fidelity shall have fitted us; the "faithful and wise servant" his Lord will "make ruler over all his goods" (Matt. xxiv. 45—47). Faithful service here "turns to" happy and helpful rule hereafter.

V. PATIENT WAITING TURNS TO BLISSFUL PARTICIPATION. Some souls have much waiting for the hour of deliverance, for "the redemption of our body;" it is a weary and a trying time. To "learn to wait" is the hardest of all lessons. But though the night seem very long, the morning will come in time; and if the steadfast soul wait patiently the holy will of God, the long endurance shall turn to a full and joyous participation in the glory that is to be revealed—the "glorious liberty of the children of God."—C.

Vers. 14—19.—*Inevitable trial and unfailing resources.* Here we have one more illustration of the faithfulness of Jesus Christ toward his apostles. So far was he from encouraging in them the thought that their path would be one of easy conquest and delightful possession, that he was frequently warning them of a contrary experience. It was not his fault if they failed to anticipate hardship and suffering in the near future; he told them plainly that his service meant the cross, with all its pain and shame. In reference to the apostles of our Lord, we have here—

I. THE SEVERITY OF THE TRIALS THAT WERE BEFORE THEM. Jesus Christ had already indicated the fact that fidelity to his cause would entail severe loss and trial; here he goes into detail. He says that it will include: 1. *General execration.* They would be "hated of all men." This is a trial of no small severity; to move among men as if we were unworthy of their fellowship; to be condemned, to be despised, to be shunned by all men; to be the object of universal reprobation;—this is a blow which, if it "breaks no bones," cuts into the spirit and wounds the heart with a deep injury. Fidelity to their Master and to their mission would entail this. 2. *Desertion and treachery* on the part of their own friends and kindred. (Ver. 16.) Very few sorrows can be more piercing, more intolerable, than desertion by our own family, than betrayal by our dearest friends; it is the last and worst calamity when "our own familiar friend lifts up *his* heel against us." Those who abandoned the old faith, or rather the Pharisaic version of it, and who followed Christ had to be prepared for this domestic and social sorrow. 3. *Death.* (Ver. 16.)

II. THE UNFAILING RESOURCES ON WHICH THEY COULD DEPEND. 1. Everything they suffered would be endured for the sake of Jesus Christ; all would be "for my Name's sake" (ver. 17). We know how the thought that they were experiencing wrong and undergoing shame for Christ's sake could not only alleviate, not only dissipate sorrow, but even turn it into joy (see Acts v. 41; Phil. i. 29). To suffer for Christ's sake could give a thrill of sacred joy such as no pleasures could possibly afford. 2. They would have the shield of the Master's power (ver. 18). Not a hair of their head should perish until he allowed it. That mighty Friend who had kept them in perfect safety, though enemies were many and fierce, would be as near to them as ever. His presence would attend them, and no shaft should touch them which he did not wish to hurt them. 3. They should have the advantage of his animating Spirit (vers. 14, 15). Whenever wisdom or utterance should be needed, the Spirit of Christ would put thoughts into their mind and words into their lips. His animating power should be upon them, should dwell within them. 4. They should triumph in the end; not, indeed, by martial victories, but by unyielding loyalty. "In patience" (in persistency in the right course) "they would possess their souls." *Losing* their life in noble martyrdom, they would *save* it (ch. ix. 24); loving their life, they would lose it; but "hating their life in this world, they would keep it unto life eternal" (John xii. 25). The bright promise of an unfading crown might cheer them on their way, and help them to pursue without flagging the path of devoted loyalty.

APPLICATION. 1. *Similar trials await the faithful now.* The dislike, the aversion, the opposition, of some, if not the active and strong hatred of all; the opposition, perhaps quiet enough, and yet keen and injurious enough, of our own friends or relatives; loss, struggle, suffering, if not fatal consequences of enmity. Downright loyalty to Jesus Christ, tenacity and intensity of conviction, usually carry persecution and trial with them. 2. *We have the same resources* the apostles had. (1) The constant, sustaining, inspiring sense that we are enduring all for Christ our Saviour—for him who suffered all things for us. (2) His protecting care. (3) His indwelling, upholding Spirit. (4) The strong assurance that he will cause us to triumph, that he will help us to be faithful unto death, and will then give us the crown of life; that by "patient continuance in well-doing" (patience, perseverance) we shall have "eternal life" (shall possess our souls).—C.

Ver. 28.—*The second redemption.* "Lift up your heads; for your redemption draweth nigh." Jesus Christ led his disciples to think that beyond the redemption which he was working out for them, and subsequent to it in time, was another great deliverance which should prove of unspeakable value to them. This is true now of our discipleship; we look for and we sorely need a second redemption.

I. ITS CHARACTER. It is not, like the first, distinctively and purely spiritual. *That was;* men were yearning for a political revolution and redemption. But the kingdom of heaven was not to be "of this world;" it was to be wholly inward and spiritual; it was to be our redemption from sin and restoration to the favour and the likeness of our Divine Father. But the second redemption is not distinctively and primarily that of the soul; it is to be "the redemption of our body" (Rom. viii. 23). It will have a gracious and beneficent effect, a redeeming and elevating influence, upon the soul; but in the first instance it is a redemption from a troublous and trying condition; it is being taken away, by the appearance of Christ, in the providence of God, from a state in which happy service is almost impossible; it is a removal from storm to calm, from hostile to friendly forces, from turbulence to serenity; from hard conflict, or tense anxiety, or painful suffering, to "the rest which remaineth for the people of God." It is a blessed and merciful change from unfavourable to favourable conditions.

II. OUR HUMAN NEED OF IT. We are not *of* this world, we who have been redeemed by Jesus Christ and renewed by the Spirit of God. And we may be nobly, even grandly, victorious over it, being "always caused to triumph" by that Divine Spirit that dwells within us, and "strengthens us with all might." Yet are we actually, and by universal experience, seriously affected by it, and we suffer many things as we pass through it. We may suffer, as the early Christians did (to whom these words were addressed), from persecution, and thereby be made "most miserable" (1 Cor. xv. 19). Our life may be made worthless, or worse than worthless, to us by the cruelties of our fellow-men. Or we may suffer so much from privation of privilege, or from the struggles of daily life, or from grief and disappointment, or from a steadily advancing decrepitude, that we may earnestly long for this second redemption, the redemption of our body. We may be in sore need of its approach, of its presence.

III. ITS KINDLY SHADOW. It will then be much to us, perhaps everything, that our redemption *draweth nigh.* 1. It is *something* that at any moment we may be within a step of the heavenly sphere; for anything we know, Christ may be about to say concerning us, "This day ye shall be with me in Paradise." 2. It is *more* that we may be confident that a life of holy activity will rapidly pass away and bring us to the day of rest and of reward. 3. It is very much indeed that the duration of the blessed future will prove to be such that any number of years of earthly trouble will be nothing in comparison. 4. It is also a truth full of hope and healing that every day spent in faithful service or patient waiting brings us that distance nearer to the blessedness that lies beyond.

> "We nightly pitch our moving tent
> A day's march nearer home."

Beneath the varied and heavy burdens of time we are fain to bow our heads; but we shall lift them up with strength and eager-hearted expectation as we realize that every step forward is a step onward to the heavenly horizon.—C.

Ver. 33.—*The immortality of Christian truth.* These striking words suggest to us—

I. CHRIST'S CONSCIOUS CONNECTION WITH THE ETERNAL FATHER. Had there not been in him a profound and abiding consciousness that, in a sense far transcending our own experience, God dwelt in him and he in God, these words would have been wholly indefensible; they would have been in the last degree immodest. Proceeding from any other than the Son of God himself, they would have simply repelled us, and would have cast grave discredit on every other utterance from the same lips. It was because he was Divine, and felt the authority which his Divinity conveyed, that he could and did use such words as these without any trace of assumption; without violating that "meekness and lowliness of heart" which he claimed to possess—the possession of which neither friend nor enemy has attempted to dispute.

II. THE PERMANENCE OF TRUTH COMPARED WITH THE TRANSITORINESS OF MATTER. It is only in a limited and figurative sense that we can speak of material things as eternal. The hour will come when they will perish; indeed, they are perishing as we speak. The immovable rocks, the everlasting hills, are being disintegrated by sun and rain; the fixed earth rises and falls; the "changeless rivers" are cutting new courses for their waters. Only truth abides; it is only the words in which the thought of the Eternal is expressed that do not pass away. Fashions do not touch it with their finger; revolutions do not overthrow it; dispensations leave it in its integrity. We look particularly at—

III. THE IMMORTALITY OF THE THOUGHTS OF CHRIST. 1. We have found him a true Prophet. Events have happened according to his word. 2. We are finding him to be the Divine Teacher of truth to-day. He has that to say to us which, in our better moods and worthier moments, we hunger and thirst to hear. In his deathless words there are still treasured for us salvation from our sin, comfort in our sorrow, sanctity in our joy, strength in our struggle, companionship in our loneliness, and peace and hope in our decline and death. Unto whom shall we go if we sit at his feet no longer? 3. We shall find him the Source of truth in the after-life. Death will not make his words less true, even if it makes some of them less applicable than they are here and now. His thoughts will never lose their hold upon our heart, never cease to affect and shape our course. The truths which Jesus spake eighteen centuries ago will beautify our life and bless our spirit in the furthest epochs and the highest spheres of the heavenly world. (1) If we would render the truest service to ourselves, we shall do our utmost to fill our minds with the thoughts of Christ; for these will prepare us for any and every condition, here or hereafter, in which we can possibly be placed. (2) If we would serve our race most effectively, we shall consider in how many ways we can impress his thoughts upon the minds of men and weave them into the institutions of the world. And we shall find, at any rate, these three: (a) The testimony of a Christian life. (b) The utterance, in public or in private, of Christian doctrine. (c) The support of Christian institutions.—C.

Ver. 34.—*Christian and unchristian carefulness.* Take care not to be overtaken and overweighted by care is the simple and intelligible paradox of the text; in other words, have a wise care lest you have much care that is unwise. There is a carefulness that is eminently godly and worthy, the absence of which is not only faulty and dangerous, but even guilty and fatal; but there is another carefulness which is an excess, a wrong, an injury in the last degree.

I. A WISE ORDINATION OF GOD. Surely it is in pure kindness to us that God has ordained that if we will not work neither shall we eat; that possession and enjoyment involve thoughtfulness and activity on our part. To be provided with everything we could wish for without the necessity for habitual consideration as well as regular exertion is found to be hurtful, if not positively disastrous to the spirit. The necessity for care, in the sense of a thoughtful provision for this life, involves two great blessings. 1. The formation of many homely but valuable virtues—the cultivation of the intellect, forethought, diligence, sobriety of thought and conduct, regularity of daily habits, the practice of courtesy, and the avoidance of offence, etc. 2. The practice of piety; there is perhaps no better field in which we can be serving God than in that of our daily duties as citizens of this world. Whether it be the counting-house, the desk, the factory, the shop, the home, the school,—in each and in all of these there is a constant opportunity for remembering and doing the will of God; there will true and genuine godliness find a field for its exercise and its growth.

II. OCCASION FOR FILIAL TRUST. Care, in the sense of anxiety, about our temporal affairs is an evil to be met and mastered by Christian thought. Christ has said to us,

"Take no thought [be not anxious] for your life" (Matt. vi. 25); Paul writes, "Be careful [anxious] for nothing," etc. (Phil. iv. 6); Peter says, "Casting all your care upon him; for he careth for you" (1 Pet. v. 7). Clearly our Christian duty is to do our best with head and hand, by thoughtfulness and diligence, to ask for God's direction and blessing, and then to put our trust in him, resting humbly but confidently on his Word of promise. This is a promise where there is much occasion for filial trustfulness. When the way is dark we must not yield to an unspiritual anxiety, but rise to a holy, childlike faith in our heavenly Father.

III. A SPHERE FOR DETERMINED LIMITATION. The great and the growing temptation is to fill our lives and hearts with the affairs of time. No more needful or seasonable counsel could be given us than this of our Lord, "Take heed to yourselves, lest your hearts be *overcharged* with ... the cares of this life." Undue and unwise carefulness about these mundane interests does two evil things: *it wears out that which is good*—good health, good spirits, good temper; and *it shuts out that which is best*—for it excludes the worship and the direct service of God; it leaves no time for devout meditation, for profitable and instructive reading, for religious exercises, for Christian work. It shuts men up to the lesser and lower activities; it dwarfs their life, it starves their soul; they "lose their life itself for the sake of the means of living." Two things are requisite, requiring a very firm and vigorous hand. 1. To resist the temptation to enlarge our worldly activities when such enlargement means spiritual shrinkage, as it very often does. 2. To insist upon it that the cares of life *shall not* exclude daily communion with God and the culture of the soul. If we do not exhibit this wise care against the unwise carefulness, we shall (1) displease our Divine Lord by our disobedience; (2) sacrifice ourselves to our circumstances; (3) be unready for the advancing future; "that day will come upon us unawares," and we shall not be "worthy to stand before the Son of man" (see next homily).—C.

Ver. 36.—*Standing before Christ.* "Watch ... and pray that ye may be accounted worthy ... to stand before the Son of man." What is involved in this worthiness? It must include our being—

I. PREPARED TO GIVE ACCOUNT TO HIM. We know that we shall have to do that (Rom. xiv. 10; 2 Cor. v. 10); and we must expect, when we do stand before the Judge, to account to Jesus Christ for (1) the relation which we have voluntarily sustained to himself—how we have received his invitation, and with what fulness we have accepted him as the Redeemer, the Friend, the Lord of our heart and life; (2) the way in which we have served him since we called ourselves by his Name— *i.e.* how closely we have followed him, how obedient we have been to his commandments, how earnest and faithful we have showed ourselves in his cause; in fact, how true and loyal we have proved to be as his servants here.

II. CONFORMED TO HIS LIKENESS. Will not our Lord expect to find those who professed to be his disciples, who had access to so many and such great privileges, stand before him *such as he lived and died to make them?* We know what that is. "He gave himself for us, to redeem us from all iniquity;" he has "called us to holiness;" he came and wrought his work in order that he might make us to be in our spirit and character the children of God, bearing our heavenly Father's image. He will therefore look to those who stand before him as his redeemed ones for: 1. *Purity of heart;* the abhorrence of all that is evil, and love for that which is good and true and pure. 2. *A loving spirit;* a spirit of unselfishness, of devotedness, of generosity, of tender solicitude for the well-being of others. 3. *Reverence and consecration of heart to God.*

III. READY FOR THE HEAVENLY SPHERE. To "stand before" the king meant to be ready to fulfil his royal behest, prepared to do at once and to do effectively whatever he might require. To stand before our Divine Sovereign means to be ready to do his bidding, to execute his commandments as he shall employ us in his heavenly service. We naturally and rightly hope that he will entrust us with the most honourable errands, will appoint us to elevated posts, will charge us with noble occupations that will demand enlarged ability and that will contribute great things to his cause and kingdom. We may be sure that the devoted and faithful discharge of our duties here will prove the best preparation for celestial activity and usefulness. He that is faithful in a few things now will be made ruler over many things hereafter. He who puts out his talents here will be found worthy to stand before the King, and to be employed by him in broad and blessed spheres of service there. If we would be " accounted worthy " to do this, we must "watch and pray." 1. We must spend much time with God—in the study of his will and in supplication for the quickening influences of his Spirit. 2. We must often examine our own hearts, observing our progress or retrogression, ready for the act of penitence, or of praise, or of reconsecration as we find ourselves declining. We must also observe the forces that are around us, and distinguish carefully between the hostile and the friendly, between those which make for folly and for sin and those which lead up to wisdom and to righteousness.—C.

Vers. 5—38.—*Preliminaries of the second advent.* It would seem that, as an interlude amid his diligent teaching in Jerusalem, Jesus and the disciples, on their way back to Bethany, had paused on the Mount of Olives and contemplated the temple. The building was a superb one, and so well put together that the disciples and people generally believed it would last till doomsday. Hence, amid their admiration for the gorgeous pile, came their question about the end of the world, which would, they believed, synchronize with that of the temple. Now, our Lord, while prophesying its destruction, warns them not to be mistaken about times and signs.

I. OUR LORD WARNS THE DISCIPLES AGAINST FALSE ALARMS. (Vers. 7—9.) He indicates that many false Messiahs will arise, declaring their Messiahship and the speedy approach of the end. They are to be for the most part of the military type, for this was the kind of Messiah Israel wanted. The result will of necessity be "wars and tumults." But the disciples ought not to be alarmed at these mere preliminaries. The end would *not* be "immediately" (Revised Version). It is well known that between our Lord's time and the destruction of Jerusalem quite a number of military and mushroom Messiahs arose, "making confusion worse confounded." They were only the outcome of the people's false hopes, and of no prophetic import.

II. THE DISCIPLES, AS THEIR LORD'S WITNESSES, WOULD EXPERIENCE BOTH PERSECUTIONS AND INSPIRATIONS. (Vers. 10—19.) And here the Lord states that persecution of his people would precede national and natural troubles. War, earthquake, and pestilence would be the providential judgment upon unrighteous persecution. But the persecuted witnesses should receive the inspiration needful to speak resistlessly. They might be betrayed and martyred, but no real injury would overtake them. "There shall not an hair of your head perish." In this remarkable deliverance of our Lord about persecution he implies that his people are really imperishable. The world might do its best to annihilate them by fire and sword; their bones might be scattered, no marble tells whither; but the Lord who loves and prizes his people's dust will reorganize the scattered remains, and demonstrate how absolutely imperishable his people are. Hence he urges patience. "In your patience," he declares, "ye shall win your souls." So that it was a most wonderful preparation of these marked men for martyrdom and all preceding tribulation. Were we more dependent on Divine inspirations, we should be more calm and influential before a hostile world.

III. THE DESTRUCTION OF JERUSALEM IS DISTINCTLY FORETOLD AS AN INSTANCE OF DESERVED VENGEANCE. (Vers. 20—24.) And here the Lord gives his people directions to escape from the doomed city as soon as they should see the armies gathering round it. The siege was drawn upon it by no misconduct of theirs, but by the misconduct of their enemies: why, therefore, should the Christians lay down their lives for a false policy and cause? Their duty was, if possible, to escape. He also hints at the horrors of the siege, and how mothers with their infant children would suffer terribly. The issue of the investment would be the slaughter of multitudes and the exile of the rest. The Jews became wanderers and exiles from that moment.

> " Tribes of the wandering foot and weary breast,
>   How shall ye flee away and be at rest !
>   The wild dove hath her nest, the fox his cave,
>   Mankind their country—Israel but the grave ! "

IV. REDEMPTION MAY BE DISCERNED AS DRAWING NIGH. (Vers. 25—33.) Our Lord indicates that distress of nations, perplexity, and faint-heartedness through fear will precede his second coming. But his people need be no sharers in this fear. So far from this, as soon as the judgment-signs begin they are to lift up their heads, assured that redemption is drawing nigh. The outlook may be wintry for the world, but it is summer for the saints of God. And here we may notice: 1. *The parable of the spring trees.* (Vers. 29, 30.) Our Lord reminds the disciples that every spring, in the buds and shoots of the various trees there is the promise of the summer. The progress is gradual, yet noticeable. In the same way his people are to look for the signs of coming summer, and to manifest a hopeful spirit in beautiful contrast to the despairing spirit of the world. 2. *The imperishable character of the Christian stock.* (Vers. 31—33.) All the world's opposition and persecution will not annihilate the Christian stock. As the martyrs fall before their persecutors, it is only to summon fresh witnesses for the Master from the ranks of their enemies. The Christian stock abides. There need be no fear. Let this be left to the unbelieving world.

V. THE LORD'S PEOPLE OUGHT CONSEQUENTLY TO BE WATCHING AND PRAYING FOR THE ADVENT. (Vers. 34—38.) And in the conclusion of this discourse our Lord clearly indicates: 1. *That it is possible to escape the judgments which are coming on the earth before the advent.* For there is no merit in allowing one's self to be involved in judgments which others by their unbelief have invited. It is our duty to escape, if possible, the catastrophe. 2. *It can only be by a watchful and prayerful spirit.* Self-indulgence, everything that would dull our sense of the impending advent, must be avoided. It is to come as a thief and a snare upon those that dwell on the face of the whole earth. Hence the imperative necessity of watching. And it is prayer which will help us in our watching. We must wrestle with the coming King, that he may count us worthy to escape the world's judgments and to stand before him. 3. *How great a privilege it will be to be permitted to stand in the presence of the Son of man!* No such privilege is afforded even by the greatest of earthly kings. It becomes us, therefore, to be in downright earnest about this privilege, and by persevering prayer to secure it.

VI. OUR LORD GAVE THE DISCIPLES THE EXAMPLE OF THE WATCHFUL PRAYER REQUIRED. (Vers. 37, 38.) For it would seem that, in the closing days, the people came so early to the temple to be taught, that he could not go as far as Bethany to spend the night. He went out, therefore, at nightfall to the Mount of Olives, and spent the night-watches more in prayer than in sleep. He was showing what persevering prayer in the crises of history must be. Let our Lord's Gethsemane habits call each of us to privacy and patient prayer such as will alone secure the proper public spirit.—R. M. E

EXPOSITION.

CHAPTER XXII.

Ver. 1—ch. xxiii. 56.—THE LAST PASS-OVER.

Vers. 1, 2.—*Short explanatory introduction.*

Ver. 1.—**Now the Feast of Unleavened Bread drew nigh, which is called the Passover.** These words show that many of the readers for whom this Gospel was intended were foreigners, who were unacquainted with Jewish terms such as the "Passover." *Passover* (τὸ πάσχα, חֹסֶפ) means, literally, "a passing." The feast so named commemorated the manner in which the chosen people were spared in Egypt when the destroying angel of the Lord passed over all Israelitish houses, which had been sprinkled with the blood of the lamb, *without* slaying the firstborn. Dr. Farrar suggests that the Greek word πάσχα is a

transliteration, with a sort of alliterative allusion to the Greek πάσχω, "I suffer." This greatest and most important of the Jewish feasts, which ever brought a great host of pilgrims to Jerusalem, was kept in the first month of the Jewish year (Nisan), from the 15th of the month, the day of full moon, to the 21st. Roughly, this corresponded to the end of our March.

Ver. 2.—**And the chief priests and scribes sought how they might kill him; for they feared the people.** The determination, long maturing, had, during the last few days of public teaching, been come to on the part of the Sanhedrin. They had determined to put the dangerous public Teacher to death. The bitter hatred on the part of the Jewish rulers had been gradually growing in intensity during the two years and a half of the public ministry of Jesus of Nazareth. The raising of Lazarus seems to have finally decided the governing body with as little delay as possible to compass the Reformer's death. The temporary withdrawal of the Lord after the great miracle deferred their purpose for a season; after, however, a retirement for a few weeks, Jesus appeared again, shortly before the Passover, and taught publicly in the temple, at a season when Jerusalem was crowded with pilgrims arriving for the great feast. Never had his teaching excited such interest, never had it stirred up such burning opposition as at this juncture. This decided the Jewish rulers to carry out their design on the life of the Galilæan Teacher with as little delay as possible. The only thing that perplexed them was *how* this could safely be accomplished, owing to the favour in which he was held by the people, especially by the crowds of pilgrims from the provinces then in Jerusalem.

Vers. 3—6.—*Judas Iscariot betrays his Master.* **Then entered Satan into Judas surnamed Iscariot, being of the number of the twelve. And he went his way, and communed with the chief priests and captains, how he might betray him unto them. And they were glad.** This was their chance. In the very heart of the Galilæan Teacher's own company a traitor showed himself, one who knew well the plans of his Master. With his help the Sanhedrin and the priestly party would be enabled to effect the arrest privately. They then must trust to Roman jealousy to help them to carry out their evil design. The expression, "Then entered Satan into Judas," is a strong one, and definitely shows that, in the opinion of these inspired compilers of the Gospels, there was *a person* who bore rule over the powers of evil. The character and history of the faithless friend of Jesus is mournfully interesting. For one to whom such splendid chances were offered to fall so low, is an awful mystery. It is clear that the betrayal was no sudden impulse. He set up self as the one object of all his thoughts, and followed Jesus because he believed that, in following him, he could best serve his own interests. His ambition was cruelly disappointed by his Master's gradual unfolding his views respecting his kingdom, *which was not to be of this world.* He was still further shocked by the undisguised announcement on the part of his Master, whose greatness and power Judas recognized from the first, that he would be rejected by the nation, and even put to death. It has been suggested, as an explanation of the betrayal, that at the last he seems to have fancied that he could force the manifestation of Christ's power by placing him in the hands of his enemies; but the acceptance of a reward, miserable though it

was, seems to point to vulgar greed, and to the idea of making friends with the dominant party in the state now that his Master evidently looked forward to a violent death, as the real motives of the betrayal. The question has been asked whether Christ, in his choice of Judas as one of the twelve, read the inmost depths and issues of his character. Canon Westcott, in a profound note on John xiii. 18, writes "that the records of the gospel lead us to believe that the Lord had perfect human knowledge realized in a human way, and therefore limited in some sense, and separable in consciousness from his perfect Divine omniscience. He knew the thoughts of men absolutely in their manifold possibilities, and yet as man, not in their actual future manifestation." These mysteries "underlie all religious life, and, indeed, all finite life—for finite being includes the possibility of sin and the possibility of fellowship between the Creator and the creature. . . . Thus we may be content to have this concrete mystery as an example—the most terrible example—of the issues of the two fundamental mysteries of human existence."

Vers. 7—13.—*The disciples Peter and John are directed to prepare for the last Passover.* Ver. 7.—**Then came the day of unleavened bread.** This was the Thursday, Nisan 13. On this afternoon all leaven was carefully and scrupulously put away; hence the name.

Ver. 8.—**Go and prepare us the Passover, that we may eat.** The three synoptists unite in describing this solemn meal, for which Peter and John were sent to prepare, as the ordinary Paschal Supper. But, on comparing the record of the same Supper given by St. John, we are irresistibly led to a different conclusion; for we read that on the following day those who led Jesus into the Prætorium went not in themselves, "lest they should be defiled; *but that they might eat the Passover*" (John xviii. 28); and again it is said of the same day, that "it was the preparation of the Passover" (John xix. 14). So the time of the Supper is described by St. John (xiii. 1) as "before the Feast of the Passover." It appears that our Lord was crucified on the 14th of Nisan, *on the very day of the sacrifice of the Paschal Lamb*, a few hours before the time of the Paschal Supper, and that his own Last Supper was eaten the night before, that is, twenty-four hours before the general time of eating the Passover Supper. The most venerable of the Fathers preserved this as a sacred tradition. So Justin Martyr: "On the day of the Passover ye took him, and on the day of the Passover ye crucified him"

('Dial. cum Trypho,' ch. iii.). To the same effect write Irenæus ('Adv. Hær.,' iv. 23) and Tertullian ('Adv. Judæos,' ch. 8). Clement of Alexandria is most definite: "The Lord did not eat his last Passover on the legal day of the Passover, but on the previous day, the 13th, and suffered on the day following, being himself the Passover" (Fragment from 'Chron. Paschal.,' p. 14, edit. Dindorf). Hippolytus of Portus bears similar testimony. The question—as to whether the famous Last Supper was the actual Passover Supper, or the anticipatory Paschal Feast, which we believe it to have been—is important; for thus the language of St. Paul (1 Cor. v. 7), "Christ our Passover is sacrificed for us," is justified. "The apostle regarded not the Last Supper, but the death of Christ, as the antitype of the Paschal sacrifice, and the correspondence of type and antitype would be incomplete unless the sacrifice of the Redeemer took place at the time on which alone that of the Paschal lamb could legally be offered" (Dean Mansel).

Ver. 9.—**And they said unto him, Where wilt thou that we prepare?** It is probable that the disciples, in asking this question, concluded that the Passover was to be eaten by them and their Master at the same time with the rest of the Jews on the following day; but our Lord gave directions for its being eaten the same evening.

Ver. 10.—**And he said unto them, Behold, when ye are entered into the city, there shall a man meet you.** The name of the man who should meet them was omitted—purposely, think Theophylact and others, lest the place of meeting should be prematurely known to Judas. **Bearing a pitcher of water.** This would be an unusual sight in an Oriental city, where the water is drawn by women. It is probable that the "man" whom the Master foretold John and Peter would meet, was the master of the house, who, according to the Jewish custom on the 13th of Nisan, *before the stars appeared in the heavens,* had himself to go to the public fountain to draw the water with which the unleavened bread for the Passover Feast was kneaded.

Ver. 12.—**And he shall show you a large upper room furnished: there make ready.** The house which possessed so large an upper chamber must have been one of considerable size, and evidently belonged to a man of some wealth and position, possibly to Nicodemus or Joseph of Arimathæa. That it perhaps belonged to St. Mark's family has also been suggested. It had evidently been prepared beforehand for the purpose of the feast, in obedience to a previous direction of Jesus. "Furnished" (ἐστρωμένον) applies specially to carpets spread over the couches for the reception of guests. "In this large upper chamber thus prepared," said the Lord, "make the necessary arrangements for the Paschal Supper; procuring and preparing the lamb, the unleavened bread, the herbs, and other customary dishes." It seems probable that this "large upper room," evidently belonging to a disciple, or at least to one friendly to Jesus, was the same room which, in the happier hours *after* the Resurrection, witnessed the appearance of the Risen to the eleven, and, later, the descent of the Holy Ghost at Pentecost.

Vers. 14—38.—*The Last Supper.*

Ver. 14.—**And when the hour was come, he sat down, and the twelve apostles with him.** The preparation had been made in the "large upper room," and the Lord and the twelve sat down, or rather reclined on the couches covered with carpets, the tables before them laid with the dishes peculiar to the solemn Passover Supper, each dish telling its part of the old loved story of the great deliverance. There was the lamb the Paschal victim, and the bitter herbs, the unleavened bread and the reddish sweet conserve of fruits—commemorating, it is said, by its colour the hard labours of brick-making, one of the chief burdens of the Egyptian bondage—into which the Master dipped the sop, and gave it to the traitor-apostle (John xiii. 26). The Lord reclined, probably, at the middle table; St. John next to him; St. Peter most likely on the other side; and the others reclining in an order corresponding more or less closely with the threefold division of the twelve into groups of four. The Supper itself had its special forms and ceremonies, which the Lord transformed as they proceeded in such a way as to change it into the sacred Supper of the New Testament.

Ver. 15.—**And he said unto them, With desire I have desired to eat this Passover with you before I suffer.** This peculiar expression, "with desire," etc., is evidently a reproduction by St. Luke of the Lord's very words repeated to him originally in Aramaic (Hebrew). They seem to be a touching apology or explanation from him to his own, for thus anticipating the regular Passover Supper by twenty-four hours. He had been longing with an intense longing to keep this last Passover with them: *First* as the *dear human Friend* who would make this his solemn last farewell. (Do not *we,* when we feel the end is coming, long for a last communion with our dearest ones?) And, *secondly,* as the *Divine Master* who would gather up into a final discourse his most important, deepest teaching. We find this teaching especially reported by St. John in his Gospel (xiii.—xvii.). And *thirdly,* as the *Founder of a great religion*, he purposed, on this momentous occasion, transforming the most solemn festal gathering of the ancient Jewish people, which commemorated their greatest deliverance, into a feast which should—as age succeeded age—commemorate a far greater deliverance, not of the old chosen race only, but of every race under heaven. These were three of the reasons why he had desired so earnestly to eat this Passover with them. "To-morrow, at the usual hour, when the people eat their Passover, it will be too late for us." This he expresses in his own sad words, "*before I suffer.*"

Vers. 16—18.—**For I say unto you, I will not any more eat thereof, until it be fulfilled in the kingdom of God.** There was yet one other reason for the Master's special desire once more to eat the solemn Passover with his chosen disciples. He would, by some significant action and word, show that the great Jewish feast, for so many centuries the central act of the ritual observances under the Mosaic Law, from henceforth would be superseded by a new and a yet more solemn religious rite. The Jewish Passover was to give place to the Christian sacrament. He, their Master, would with them share in the Passover meal that evening for the last time. The next time that he would partake would be still with them, but it would be in the kingdom of God, that is to say, in the Church of God, which was to be founded after his resurrection. The kingdom of God commenced with the resurrection of Jesus. The constant celebration of the Holy Eucharist commenced from that time; it is more than probable that our Lord partook of it, after his resurrection, with his own (see ch. xxiv. 30; Acts x. 41). **I will not any more eat thereof, until . . . I will not drink of the fruit of the vine, until**, etc. These statements, which speak of a final partaking (eating and drinking), are closely parallel to the command contained in vers. 19, 20. The first statement seems solemnly to close the celebration of the Passover Feast; the second, to institute with equal solemnity a new feast in its place—

" *With desire I have desired to eat this passover with you before I suffer* " (ver. 15); for—

The Passover Feast is solemnly put an end to.	The Holy Eucharist is solemnly instituted.
" I will not any more *eat* thereof, until it be fulfilled in the kingdom of God " (ver. 16).	" He took *bread*, . . . and brake it, and gave unto them : . . . This do in remembrance of me " (ver. 19).

" I will not *drink* of the fruit of the vine, until the kingdom of God shall come " (ver. 18).

" Likewise also the *cup* after Supper " (ver. 20).

It was in the course of the great ritual Supper on some of the occasions when the cup was passed round, and the unleavened bread formally broken or dipped in one of the Passover dishes, that the Lord found his opportunity solemnly to announce the formal abrogation of the old Paschal Supper and the institution of the new communion feast. The above *literal* interpretation of the Lord's mystic words, "until that day when I drink it new with you in my Father's kingdom " (Matt. xxvi. 29), or, as St. Luke reports them, " I will not drink of the fruit of the vine, until the kingdom of God shall come "—which literal interpretation in the main is that preferred by Dean Mansel (Commentary on Matt. xxvi. 29); see, too, St. Chrysostom in Matt. Hom. lxxii., who adopts the same literal interpretation—does not exclude a yet deeper and more spiritual meaning which lies beneath the surface, and which speaks of another and spiritual banquet in the heavenly realm, which not only the Redeemer, but also his redeemed, will partake of. Heaven-life under the form of a banquet was imagery well known and often painted by the Jewish masters in the old rabbinic schools before and contemporary with the earthly life of Christ. The New Testament writers in several places have adopted the similar imagery, notably in Matt. viii. 11; ch. xxii. 30; Rev. xix. 9. How widespread and well loved was this Jewish representation of the heaven-life under the form of a banquet is clear from the three above-quoted references taken from SS. Matthew, Paul (Luke), and John.

Vers. 19, 20.—**And he took bread, and gave thanks, and brake it, and gave unto them, saying, This is my body which is given for you : this do in remembrance of me. Likewise also the cup after supper, saying, This cup is the new testament in my blood, which is shed for you.** Around these words, and the parallel passages in SS. Matthew and Mark, for more than a thousand years fierce theological disputes have raged. Men have gone gladly to prison and to death rather than renounce what they believed to be the true interpretation. Now, a brief exegetical commentary is not the place to enter into these sad controversies. It will be sufficient here to indicate some of the lines of thought which the prayerful earnest reader might wisely follow out so as to attain certain just ideas respecting the blessed rite here instituted—ideas which may suffice for a practical religious life. Now, we possess a Divine commentary on this sacrament instituted by our Lord. It is noticeable that St. John, whose Gospel was the latest or well-nigh the latest of the canonical writings of the New Testament, when at great length he relates the story of the last Passover evening and its teaching, does not allude to the institution of that famous service, which, when he wrote his Gospel, had become part of the settled experience of Church life. He *presupposes* it; for it had passed then into the ordinary life of the Church. In another and earlier portion of his Gospel, however, St. John (vi. 32—58) gives us a record of the Lord's discourse in the synagogue of Capernaum, in which Jesus, while speaking plainly to those who heard him at the time, gave by anticipation a commentary on the sacrament which he afterwards instituted. The truth which was taught in this discourse is presented in a specific act and in a concrete form in the Holy Communion. In the fifty-third verse of that sixth chapter we read, "Verily, verily, I say unto you, Except ye eat the flesh of the Son of man, and drink his blood, ye have no life in you." How is this now to be done? We reply that our Lord has clothed these ideas and brought them near to us in this sacrament; while, by his teaching in the sixth chapter of St. John, he guards this sacrament from being regarded on the one hand as an end in itself, or on the other as a mere symbol. Certain truths, great *landmarks* laid down in this discourse, have to be borne in mind. (1) The separation of the flesh of the Son of man into flesh and blood (John vi. 53) presupposes a violent death submitted to for the sake of others (John vi. 51). (2) Both these elements, the flesh and the blood, are to be appropriated individually by the believer (John vi. 56). (3) How appropriated? St. Bernard well answers the question which he asks: "What is it to eat his flesh and to drink his blood, but to *share in his sufferings and to imitate the life he lived when with us in the flesh?*" (St. Bernard, on Ps. iii. 3). "If ye suffer with him, ye shall also reign with him." The Holy Eucharist is from one point of view a great truth dramatized, instituted for the purpose of bringing before men in a vivid manner the great truths above alluded to. *But it is something more.* It brings to the believer, to the faithful communicant, to the one who in humble adoring faith carries out to the best of his ability his Master's dying charge—it brings a blessing too great for us to measure by earthly language, too deep for us to fathom with human inquiry. For the partaking of this Holy Communion is, first, the Christian's solemn public confession of his faith in Christ crucified; his

solemn private declaration that it is his deliberate wish to suffer with his Lord and for his Lord's sake; that it is, too, his firm purpose to imitate the earthly life lived by his Lord. The partaking of this Holy Communion, too, is the Christian's most solemn prayer for strength thus to suffer and to live. It is, too, his fervent expression of belief that this strength will be surely given to him. Further, the partaking of this Holy Communion is, above all, the Christian's most solemn prayer for living union with Christ—"that Christ may dwell in his heart by faith." It is, too, his fervent expression of belief that "then we dwell in Christ, and Christ in us; we are one with Christ, and Christ with us." This confession, declaration, and prayer he constantly renews in obedience to the dying command of his Master. It is difficult to understand how any belief in a physical change in the elements of bread and wine, such as is involved in the theory of transubstantiation held in the Roman Church, or of consubstantiation in the Lutheran community, can be supposed to enhance the reverence of the communicant, or to augment the blessing promised. The words of the Lord, "This is my body . . . my blood," cannot surely be pressed, seeing that the same Divine Speaker was in his discourses in the habit of using imagery which could not literally be pressed, such as "I am the Bread of life," "I am the Door of the sheep," "I am the true Vine," etc. Nothing that can be conceived is more solemn than the simple rite, more awful in its grandeur, more Divine and far-reaching in its promises to the faithful believer. Human imaginings add nothing to this Divine mystery, which is connected at once with the Incarnation and the Atonement. They only serve to envelop it in a shroud of earth-born mist and cloud, and thus to dim if not to veil its Divine glory.

Vers. 21—23.—*The Lord's sorrowful allusion to Judas the traitor.*

Ver. 21.—**But, behold, the hand of him that betrayeth me is with me on the table.** This is the second mention of the traitor in St. Luke's account of the Last Supper. From St. John's recital, we gather that Jesus returned several times in the course of that solemn evening to this sad topic. That one of his own little inner circle, so closely associated with him, should so basely betray him, was evidently a very bitter drop in the Lord's cup of suffering. In his dread experience of human sorrow it was needful that the Christ should fulfil in his own experience what even the noblest of the children of men—David, for instance—had felt of the falseness of friends. What suffering can be inflicted on a generous heart comparable to it? Surely he of whom it was written, "Whose sorrows are like unto my sorrows?" must make trial of *this* bitterness. Chrysostom thinks that the Master, in some of these repeated allusions during the "Supper," tried to win Judas over to a better mind.

Ver. 22.—**Woe unto that man by whom he is betrayed!** We seem to hear a wailing in this woe, although the denunciation was so firmly pronounced. St. Matthew, in his account, here adds some more words spoken by the Master, "It had been good for that man if he had not been born." Dean Plumptre, on this saying of Christ, very suggestively remarks, "Awful as the words were, they have their bright as well as their dark side. According to the estimate which men commonly form, the words are true of all except those who depart this life in the faith and fear of God. In his applying them to the case of the traitor in its exceptional enormity, there is suggested the thought that for others whose guilt was not like his, existence even in the penal suffering which their sins have brought upon them may be better than never to have been at all."

Ver. 23.—**And they began to inquire among themselves, which of them it was that should do this thing.** That all the disciples, on hearing this statement of their Master, should at once question their own hearts with the "Is it I?" (of St. Matthew's Gospel), shows with what cunning skill the arch-traitor must have concealed not merely his plans but his very sentiments. No suspicion on their parts ever seems to have fallen on Judas, their companion for so long a time. The direct colloquy of the Lord with the traitor, reported at length in the other Gospels on the occasion of dipping the sop into one of the Paschal dishes, was most probably carried on in a whisper (see John xiii. 26—29, where mention is specially made of the disciples' ignorance of the dread meaning of their Master's words to Judas).

Vers. 24—30.—*The jealousy among the disciples.*

Ver. 24.—**And there was also a strife among them, which of them should be accounted the greatest.** The Lord's words in these verses are peculiar to St. Luke. The strife among the disciples which suggested the Lord's corrective sayings was evidently no mere dispute as to precedence in their places at the supper, but some question as to their respective positions in the coming kingdom of which their Master had said so much in the course of his later instructions. It is closely connected with the "feet-washing" related at length by St. John (xiii. 4—17). This has been well described as a parable in action, exhibited to illustrate forcibly the novel and sublime truth which

he was teaching them, the world-teachers of the future, that in self-sacrifice consisted the secret of true greatness. In the kingdom of heaven this would be found to be conspicuously the case.

Ver. 25.—**Are called benefactors** (εὐεργέ-ται). Those who were listening knew well how utterly false these high-sounding human titles often were. Εὐεργέτης (*Euergetes*), Benefactor, was the well-known title appropriated by Ptolemy Euergetes and other hated royal tyrants well known to the Jewish people.

Ver. 28.—**Ye are they which have continued with me in my temptations.** But after the gentle rebuke of their jealous ambition, which rebuke was veiled in the great instruction, their Master, with the tenderest grace, referred to their unswerving loyalty to him. Their faithfulness stood out at that hour in strong contrast with the conduct of Judas. It is always thus with their Master and ours. Every good deed, every noble thought, each bit of generosity and self-forgetfulness on our part, is at once recognized and rewarded a hundredfold *now* as *then.*

Ver. 29.—**And I appoint unto you a kingdom, as my Father hath appointed unto me.** This promise refers to earth and this life. *They* and their successors in his Church would bear sway over men's hearts. His kingdom would be administered by them. With strangely literal accuracy has this promise been fulfilled. From the hour when the despised Master, already doomed to a shameful death, uttered this seemingly improbable prediction, his kingdom over men's hearts has been extending. *Then* at most the kingdom numbered a few hundreds; *now* it can only be reckoned by millions. For centuries the story of the civilized world has been the story of this kingdom.

Ver. 30.—**That ye may eat and drink at my table in my kingdom, and sit on thrones judging the twelve tribes of Israel.** While the words just considered (ver. 29) referred to a success and a reward, the scene of which was to be this world, the Master now continues his promises of reward to his chosen faithful followers—a reward which will be their blessed portion in eternal life, which will follow this. *First*, the endless bliss to be shared with him is pictured under the old favourite Jewish image of the heavenly banquet; and *second*, in that heavenly realm a special place of honour and a distinct work is promised to these his chosen faithful servants.

Vers. 31—38.—*The Lord foretells Simon Peter's fall. He tells the disciples of the hard times coming on them.*

Ver. 31.—**And the Lord said, Simon, Simon, behold, Satan hath desired to have** you, that he may sift you as wheat. The majority of the more ancient authorities omit the words, "and the Lord said." These words were possibly inserted at an early date to obviate the abruptness of this sudden change in the subject-matter of the Lord's discourse. The more accurate translation would be, "Satan obtained you by asking that he," etc. Bengel comments with "*not content with Judas.*" This saying of Jesus is a very mysterious one; it reveals to us something of what is going on in the unseen world. A similar request was made by the same bitter, powerful foe in the case of Job (i. 12). Are we to understand that these are examples of what is constantly going on in that world so close to us, but from which no whisper ever reaches our mortal ears? Such grave thoughts lend especial intensity to those words in the prayer of prayers, where we ask "our Father which is in heaven" *to deliver us from evil*, or *the evil one*, as so many of our best scholars prefer to translate ἀπὸ τοῦ πονηροῦ. Satan asks that he may test and try the apostles. Judas he had already tempted, and he had won him. Possibly this signal victory emboldened him to proffer this request. We may imagine the evil one arguing thus before the Eternal: " These chosen ones who are appointed to work in the future so tremendous a work in thy Name, are utterly unworthy. Let me just try to lure them away with my lures. Lo, they will surely fall. See, *one* has already."

Ver. 32.—**But I have prayed for thee, that thy faith fail not.** The prayer of Satan *apparently* was not refused. Jesus, however, says, that *for one* of that loved company, who he knew from his peculiar temperament was in especial peril, *he had prayed*. The prayer was answered thus: the temptation came to all the apostles; all fell; Peter, though, more disastrously by far than his brethren, but the result of the fall was not hopeless despair as in the case of Judas, but bitter remorse and a brave manly repentance. "It is said by Roman divines (*e.g.* Maldonatus, à Lapide, and Mai, here) that this prayer and precept of our Lord extends to all bishops of Rome as St. Peter's successors, and that in speaking to St. Peter our Lord spoke to them. Would they be willing to complete the parallel, and say that the bishops of Rome specially need prayer, because they deny Christ? Let them not take a part of it and leave the rest" (Bishop Wordsworth). **When thou art converted.** "Converted" must not be understood here in its technical sense; it should rather be translated, "And thou, when thou hast turned (*i.e.* to God) strengthen thy brethren."

Ver. 33.—**And he said unto him, Lord, I am ready to go with thee, both into prison, and to death.** This kind of confident enthusiasm is usually a sign of weakness. Jesus, *the Heart-reader*, knew too well what such a wild protestation was worth, and went on at once to predict his friend's and servant's awful fall, *that very night*.

Vers. 35, 36.—**And he said unto them, When I sent you without purse, and scrip, and shoes, lacked ye anything? And they said, Nothing. Then said he unto them, But now, he that hath a purse, let him take it, and likewise his scrip; and he that hath no sword, let him sell his garment, and buy one.** The Lord speaks one more word to his own before leaving the upper room. More occupied with the future trials of his disciples than with his own tragic destiny, which he knew was about to be fulfilled, he reminds his friends of the comparatively quiet and serene existence they had been spending during the last two years and a half with him. In that period, generally speaking, they had been welcomed and kindly entertained by the people, sometimes, they would remember, even with enthusiasm. But they must prepare now for a different life—cold looks, opposition, even bitter persecution, would be their lot for the future. They must order themselves now to meet these things. No ordinary prudent forethought must be omitted by them. He had more than hinted that this future lay before them in his words, " Behold, I send you forth as lambs in the midst of wolves;" now he plainly tells them what kind of life awaited them in the immediate future. Of course, the advice as to the sword was not meant to be taken literally. It was one of those metaphors the Lord used so often in his teaching. For a similar metaphor still more elaborately developed, see Eph. vi. 17, and following verses.

Ver. 37.—**For I say unto you, that this that is written must yet be accomplished in me, And he was reckoned among the transgressors.** Here he shows them what he meant. They, as disciples of One treated as a malefactor, had surely nothing to expect but hatred and persecution. Stier remarks that this is the first time that the Lord himself directs us to the fifty-third chapter of Isaiah, that most pre-eminent and complete text of the Passion. **For the things concerning me have an end.** The tragic end of his earthly ministry is close at hand. The prophetic description of the suffering Servant of the Lord will soon be found to have been terribly accurate.

Ver. 38.—**And they said, Lord, behold, here are two swords. And he said unto them, It is enough.** As so often, the disciples took their Master's words with curious literalness, and, as a reply, produced two swords, as if these two poor weapons *could* help them in the coming times of sore need. If they were to stand firm in the long trial-season which lay before them, they must surely provide themselves with very different weapons to these; their arms in the campaign of the future must be forged in no earthly workshop. But our Lord sadly declined then to enter into further explanation. His meaning would be all clear to them soon, so he closed the dialogue with the words, " It is enough." This verse was curiously perverted in the famous Bull of Pope Boniface VIII., " Unam sanctam," to prove his possession of both secular and spiritual power: " Dicentibus apostolis, *ecce gladii duo*, in Ecclesiâ scilicet, quum apostoli loquerentur, non respondit Dominus *nimis esse*, sed *satis*. . . . Uterque ergo in potestate est Ecclesiæ, spiritualis scilicet gladius et materialis."

Vers. 39—46.—*The agony in the garden.* This eventful scene is recounted in detail by all the three synoptists. St. Matthew's account is the most complete. St. Mark adds one saying of the Lord's containing a deep theological truth, " Abba, Father, all things are possible unto thee." These remarkable words, occurring as they do in the midst of the most solemn scene of prayer in the Redeemer's earth-life, tell of the vast *possibilities* of prayer. What may not be accomplished by earnest supplication to the throne of grace?

St. Luke's account is the shortest, but it contains the story of the angelic mission of help, and the additional detail of the " bloody sweat."

St. John alone of the four omits the scene; but, as in other most important recitals where he refrains from repeating the story of things thoroughly known in his Master's Church at the period when he committed his Gospel to writing, he takes care, however, often to record some hitherto unrecorded piece of the Lord's teaching, which is calculated to throw new light upon the momentous twice and thrice told incident, the story of which he does not deem it necessary to repeat. So in ch. ii. he throws a flood of light upon Christian baptism. Ch. vi. is a Divine commentary on the Holy Eucharist. While in ch. xii. 23—28 he gives us, in his Master's words, a new insight into that awful sorrow which was the source of the agony in Gethsemane.

Canon Westcott suggests that the succession of the main events recorded by the four evangelists was as follows :—

Approx. time.

1 a.m.........The agony.
The betrayal.
The conveyance to the high priest's house, probably adjoining " the Booths of Hanan."

2 a.m.........The preliminary examination before Annas in the presence of Caiaphas.

About 3 a.m...The examination before Caiaphas and the Sanhedrin at an irregular meeting at " the Booths."

About 5 a.m...The formal sentence of the Sanhedrin in their own proper place of meeting— Gazith or Beth Midrash (ch. xxii. 66; Matt. xxvii. 1, πρωΐας γενομένης; comp. Mark xv. 1; ch. xxii. 66, ὡς ἐγένετο ἡμέρα).
The first examination before Pilate at the palace.

5.30 a.m....The examination before Herod.
The scourging and first mockery by the soldiers at the palace.

6.30 a.m. ...The sentence of Pilate (John xix. 14, ὥρα ἦν ὡς ἕκτη).

7 a.m.........The second mockery of the condemned " King " by the soldiers.

9 a.m.........The Crucifixion, and rejection of the stupefying draught (Mark xv. 25, ἦν ὥρα τρίτη).

12 noon......The last charge.

12—3 p.m...The darkness (Matt. xxvii. 45; Mark xv. 33; ch. xxiii. 44, ἦν ὡσεὶ ὥρα ἕκτη . . . ἕως ὥρας ἐννάτης).

3 p.m.........The end.

Ver. 39.—**And he came out, and went, as he was wont, to the Mount of Olives.** In the other evangelists we find the place on the Mount of Olives described as Gethsemane. The word *Gethsemane* signifies " oil-press." It was a garden; one of the many charming gardens which Josephus tells us old Jerusalem abounded with. It perhaps belonged to a friend of Christ, or else was with others of these gardens, or " paradises," thrown open at the great festival seasons to the faithful pilgrims who on these occasions crowded the holy city and its suburbs. There is at the present day just beyond the brook Kedron, between the paths that go up to the summit of the mount, about three quarters of a mile from the Jerusalem wall, an enclosed garden called Gethsemane. It belongs to the Latin community in Jerusalem. In it are eight very ancient olive trees. When Henry Maundrell visited the spot, in 1697, these eight aged trees were believed to be the same that stood there in the blessed Saviour's time. Bové the botanist, in Ritter's 'Geography of Palestine,' vol. iv., quoted by Dean Mansel, says these venerable olive trees are two thousand years old. Josephus, however, relates that in the great siege the soldiers of Titus cut down all the trees in the Jerusalem suburbs. Even if this be assumed, these soldiers, from some feeling of awe stirred up by the tradition which hung, of course, round this hallowed spot, might have spared this little sacred grove; or they might at the time have been still young saplings, of no use for the purpose of the siege operations. "In spite of all the doubts that can be raised against their antiquity, the eight aged olive trees, if only by their manifest difference from all others on the mountain, have always struck even the most indifferent observers. They will remain, so long as their already protracted life is spared, the most venerable of their race on the surface of the earth. Their gnarled trunks and scanty foliage will always be regarded as the most affecting of the sacred memorials in or about Jerusalem —the most nearly approaching to the everlasting hills themselves in the force with which they carry us back to the events of the gospel history" (Dean Stanley, 'Sinai and Palestine,' p. 455).

Ver. 40.—**Pray that ye enter not into temptation.** The temptation in question was the grave sin of moral cowardice into which *so* soon the disciples fell. Had they prayed instead of yielding to the overpowering sense of weariness and sleeping, they would never have forsaken their Master in his hour of trial and danger.

Ver. 42.—**Saying, Father, if thou be willing, remove this cup from me: nevertheless not my will, but thine, be done.** The three synoptists give this prayer in slightly varying terms; "but the figure of *the cup* is common to all the three; it was indelibly impressed on tradition. This cup, which Jesus entreats God to cause to pass from before (παρά) his lips, is the symbol of that terrible punishment, the dreadful and mournful picture of which is traced before him at this moment by a skilful painter with extraordinary vividness. The painter is the same who in the wilderness, using a like illusion, passed before his view the magical scene of the glories belonging to the Messianic kingdom" (Godet). *If thou be willing.* He looked on in this supreme hour, just before "the Passion" really began, to the Crucifixion and all the

horrors which preceded it and accompanied it—to the treason of Judas; the denial of Peter; the desertion of the apostles; the cruel, relentless enmity of the priests and rulers; the heartless abandonment of the people; the insults; the scourging; and then the shameful and agonizing lingering death which was to close the Passion; and, more dreadful than all, the reason why he was here in Gethsemane; why he was to drink this dreadful cup of suffering; the memory of all the sin of man! To drink this cup of a suffering, measureless, inconceivable, the Redeemer for a moment shrank back, and asked the Father if the cross was the only means of gaining the glorious end in view—the saving the souls of unnumbered millions. Could not God in his unlimited power find another way of reconciliation? And yet beneath this awful agony, the intensity of which we are utterly incapable of grasping—beneath it there lay the intensest desire that his Father's wish and will should be done. That wish and will were in reality his own. The prayer was made *and answered.* It was not the Father's will that the cup should pass away, and the Son's will was entirely the same; *it was answered* by the gift of strength—strength from heaven being given to enable the Son to drink the cup of agony to its dregs. How this strength was given St. Luke relates in the next verse.

Ver. 43.—**And there appeared an angel unto him from heaven, strengthening him.** The Lord's words reported by St. Matthew were no mere figure of rhetoric. "My soul is exceeding sorrowful, even unto death." The anguish and horror were so great that he himself, according to his humanity, must have before the time become the victim of death had he not been specially strengthened from above. This is the deep significance and necessity of the angel's appearance. So Stier and Godet, the latter of whom writes, "As when in the wilderness under the pressure of famine he felt himself dying, the presence of this heavenly being sends a vivifying breath over him,—a Divine refreshing pervades him, body and soul, and it is thus he receives strength to continue to the last the struggle."

Ver. 44.—**And his sweat was as it were great drops of blood falling down to the ground.** Some (for instance, Theophylact) understand this "as it were" to signify that the expression, "drops of blood," was simply parabolic; but it is far better to understand the words in their literal sense, as our Church does when it prays, "By thine agony and bloody sweat." Athanasius even goes so far as to pronounce a ban upon those who deny this sweat of blood. Commentators give instances of this blood-sweat under abnormal pathological circumstances. Some, though by no means all, of the oldest authorities omit these last two verses (43, 44). Their omission in many of these ancient manuscripts was probably due to mistaken reverence. The two oldest and most authoritative translations, the Itala (Latin) and Peshito (Syriac), contain them, however, as do the most important Fathers of the second century, Justin and Irenæus. We have, then, apart from the evidence of manuscripts, the testimony of the earliest Christianity in Italy and Syria, Asia Minor and Gaul, to the genuineness of these two famous verses. They are printed in the ordinary text of the Revised English Version, with a side-note alluding to their absence in some of the ancient authorities.

Vers. 45, 46.—He found them sleeping for sorrow, and said unto them, Why sleep ye ? rise and pray, lest ye enter into temptation. The events of the past evening; the long excitement stirred up by listening to such words as their Master had been speaking to them during the sad hours of the Last Supper; the sure consciousness of coming sorrow; then the walk through the silent city:—all predisposed them to sleep. Commentators are never weary with pressing these excuses for the slumber of the eleven at that awful moment. But all these things, though they may well have predisposed them to slumber, are not sufficient to account for that strange heavy sleep which seems to have paralyzed the eleven in Gethsemane. In spite of their Master's solemn injunction to watch and pray, he finds them, several times during that dreadful watch of his in the garden, asleep, in spite of his asking them for sympathy and prayer, in spite of his evident longing for their sympathy—each time he cast his eyes on them, he sees them, not watching, but sleeping! Many a time in their work-filled lives those fishermen he loved so well, John and Peter and Andrew, had toiled all night with their nets; but on this night of sorrow, when their pleading voices were listened for, possibly their hand-press waited for, their silent sympathy certainly longed for, they slept, seemingly forgetful of all save their own ease and comfort. Surely on this night of temptation they were influenced by some invisible power, who lulled them to sleep during those precious moments when they should have been agonizing with their Master in prayer, and so arming themselves against the supreme moment of temptation just coming upon them. But swayed by the power of evil of whom the Lord had been warning them, but in vain, they let the moments slip by, and the hour of temptation came on them unawares. We know how grievously they all fell.

"'Forsake the Christ thou sawest transfigured! him
Who trod the sea and brought the dead to life?
What should wring this from thee?'—ye laugh and ask.
What wrung it? Even a torchlight and a noise,
The sudden Roman faces, violent hands,
And fear of what the Jews might do! Just that;
And it is written, 'I forsook and fled:'
There was my trial, and it ended thus."
(Browning, 'A Death in the Desert.')

Vers. 47—53.—*The arrest of the Redeemer.* All the four evangelists tell the story of the last hours, in the main the same, though the language is often quite different, and fresh and important details appear in each memoir.

The general effect on the thoughtful reader is that the Crucifixion and the events leading up to it were very far from being the result of the counsels of the Jewish leaders, the outcome of their relentless enmity. The death and all the attendant circumstances took place in their solemn order, then, when the public teaching of the Redeemer was finished, *because* it had been determined by some higher and grander power than was possessed by Jerusalem Sanhedrin or Roman Senate.

So St. Matthew, in his account, twice (xxvi. 54, 56) gives the ground for the arrest, "That the Scriptures might be fulfilled." And the Scriptures were but the echoes of that other and grander power.

Ver. 47.—And while he yet spake, behold a multitude. Different to his disciples, their Master, who had prayed and received as an answer to his prayer the angel's visit, was now, when the hour of mortal danger struck, in possession of the profoundest calm. Nothing disturbed his serenity any more. With calm majesty he advanced to meet the traitor as he guided his Master's deadly enemies into the garden. From this hour Jesus welcomes the cross, from which for a brief moment he had seemed to shrink. The company who was thus guided to Gethsemane to effect the arrest in the dead of the night was composed of Roman legionaries detailed for this duty from a cohort on guard in the Antonia Fort by the temple, and of Levitical guards belonging to the temple—an armed force of police, part of the temple watch at the disposal of the priests. **He that was called Judas, one of the twelve.**

Each of the evangelists mention the presence of the traitor. It was evidently a strange and startling detail for the writers of these memoirs that one of the chosen twelve should have been the betrayer! **And drew near unto Jesus to kiss him.** This was the sign agreed upon between Judas and his employers. They knew that it would be night, and that Gethsemane was shaded with olives, and that therefore some conspicuous sign would be necessary to indicate to the guards which of the company of twelve was the Master whom they were to seize. But the signal was superfluous, for, as St. John tells us, Jesus of his own accord advanced before the others, telling those who came for him who he was. Because of this kiss the early Christian Church discontinued the customary brotherly kiss on Good Friday.

Ver. 50.—**And one of them smote the servant of the high priest, and cut off his right ear.** The name of the disciple who smote the servant of the high priest is given by St. John: it was Peter. He gives, too, the servant's name, Malchus. John wrote many years later, when Jerusalem had long ceased to exist; Peter, too, had passed away. Before this incident, St. John relates how the Roman and Jewish guards "went backward, and fell to the ground." *What* overawed the party of armed men is uncertain—whether some supernatural or merely a natural cause; possibly something of majesty in the Lord's appearance impelled these men to retire and reverently to salute him they were ordered to seize. St. John mentions this to show that it was of his own free will that he rendered himself up.

Ver. 51.—**Suffer ye thus far.** The exact meaning of these words has been much debated. They probably were addressed to the company of armed men, and contained a plea for the mistaken zeal of his disciple Peter. "Excuse this resistance." **And he touched his ear, and healed him.** This miraculous cure of the wound inflicted by the zealous disciple is related by the physician Luke.

Ver. 53.—**When I was daily with you in the temple, ye stretched forth no hands against me: but this is your hour, and the power of darkness.** These words of the Lord may signify, "It was from a cowardly fear of the people whom you felt were my friends that you did not dare to arrest me in the full light of day." But it is better to take the last clause as possessing a deeper meaning: "I have often been in your power before, when, without concealment, I taught publicly in that sacred house where you are the appointed guardians; you never dared to lay hands on me *then*. But this, I know, is *your* hour, the moment God has

given up to you to effect this sad triumph, and this (*i.e.* the power by which you work) is the power of darkness (*i.e.* the power of the spirit of darkness)."

Vers. 54—62.—*The denial of Peter.*

Ver. 54.—**Then took they him, and led him, and brought him into the high priest's house. And Peter followed afar off.** There has been some discussion here on the question of harmonizing the separate accounts. There is, however, no real difficulty if the following historical details be borne in mind. The actual high priest at this juncture was Caiaphas, son-in-law to Annas, who was the legal high priest, but had been deposed by the Roman power some time before. Annas, however, although prevented by the Roman government from bearing the high priestly insignia, was apparently looked upon by the people as the rightful possessor of the dignity, and evidently exercised the chief authority in the Jewish councils. It seems that he and his son-in-law Caiaphas, the Roman nominee, occupied together the high priest's palace. There were three trials of our Lord by the Jews: (1) Before Annas (John xviii. 12—18). (2) Before Caiaphas and what has been termed a committee of the Sanhedrin (John xviii. 24; Matt. xxvi. 59—68; Mark xiv. 55—65). (3) Formally before the whole Sanhedrin at dawn (ch. xxii. 66—71; Matt. xxvii. 1; Mark xv. 1). The thrice-repeated denial of Peter took place: (1) On his first going in (he was admitted through the influence of John, who was known to the officials) to the court-yard of the high priest's palace, in answer to the female servant who kept the door (John xviii. 17). (2) As he sat by the fire warming himself, in answer to another maid (Matt. xxvi. 69) and to other bystanders (John xviii. 25; ch. xxii. 58), including the kinsman of Malchus (John xviii. 26). (3) About an hour later (ch. xxii. 59), after he had left the fire to avoid the questioners, and had gone out into the porch or gateway leading into the court-yard, in answer to one of the maids who had spoken before (Mark xiv. 69; Matt. xvi. 71), and to other bystanders (ch. xxii. 59; Matt. xxvi. 73; Mark xiv. 70).

Ver. 55.—**And when they had kindled a fire in the midst of the hall, and were set down together, Peter sat down among them.** We know that the arrest in Gethsemane was followed by the flight of the eleven apostles. John and Peter, however, once out of reach of the armed band, seem in some way to have recovered from their first panic, and to have followed their Master and his guards into the city. Arrived at the high priest's house, John, who was known to the high priest, had no difficulty in procuring admission for himself and his companion. Peter's motive in pressing into what he knew for him was a locality full of peril, is given by St. Matthew (xxvi. 58), "to see the end." There was no doubt there was in the heart of the impulsive, loving man, sorrowful anxiety and deep sorrow for his dear Master's fate. But, alas! with the feverish sad expectation to see what he felt would be the end, there was no earnest prayer for guidance and help. The fire is mentioned because, generally speaking, the nights in the Holy Land about the Passover season are warm. The cold on this night appears to be spoken of as something unusual. *Peter sat down among them.* "St. John (it must be supposed) had passed on into the audience-chamber, so that St. Peter was alone. St. John, who remained closest to the Lord, was unmolested; St. Peter, who mingled with the indifferent crowd, fell" (Westcott).

Ver. 56.—**But a certain maid beheld him as he sat by the fire, and earnestly looked upon him, and said, This man was also with him.** Comparing the several accounts of the evangelists together, we see how naturally the incidents followed each other. As he entered, the portress first thought she recognized him as one of the followers of the well-known Teacher just arrested on a capital charge. Then as, weary and chilled, he drew near the fire, the firelight shone on his face, a face known to many who had listened during the last few days to his Master as he taught, with his disciples grouped round him in the temple-courts before crowds of listeners. Thoroughly alarmed, he drew aside from the friendly warmth of the fire into the outer shade of the gateway; yet he could not tear himself away from the neighbourhood of the spot where his dear Master was being interrogated by his deadly foes; and even there, while lurking in the shadow, he was recognized again, and then, just as he was in the act of fiercely denying, with oaths and curses, his friendship for and connection with Jesus, came the Master by, after the second examination before Caiaphas and certain members of the Sanhedrin, being conducted by the guard to another and more formal court. And as the Master passed, he turned and looked upon his poor cowardly disciple.

Ver. 59.—**For he is a Galilæan.** The strong provincial dialect of the fisherman of the Lake of Galilee at once told these Jerusalem Jews, accustomed to the peculiar pronunciation of the Galilee pilgrims at the Passover Feast, that the man whom they suspected certainly came from the same province as Jesus the Accused.

Ver. 61.—**And the Lord turned, and looked upon Peter.** As he was passing from the interrogation before Caiaphas to be examined before the Sanhedrin assembled in solemn council, he heard his servant's well-known voice raised and accompanied with oaths and curses, assuring the by-standers he had no connection with and knew nothing of Jesus of Nazareth. Then, as he passed, the Master turned and looked on his old friend, that disciple who so lately had declared that even if all others deserted the Lord, he never would! The glance of Jesus was full of the tenderest pity; it was not angry, only sorrowful; but it recalled Peter to his better, nobler self. SS. Matthew and Mark (Peter's own Gospel) record how, when he heard the cock crow, which St. Luke tells us happened as our Lord turned to look on the recreant disciple, he remembered all, and burst into bitter weeping. We meet him again on the Resurrection morning in company with St. John (John xx. 3), whence, it would seem, that in his bitter sorrow he had turned to his old friend, who had probably heard his denial. St. John, who briefly in his narrative touches upon the "denial," omits to mention the repentance, but, according to his custom, specially illustrates it in the scene by the lake (John xxi. 15, and following verses).

Vers. 63—65.—*After the second examination, the officials of the Sanhedrin mock and ill treat Jesus as one doomed to death.*

Ver. 63.—**And the men that held Jesus mocked him, and smote him.** The position of the Redeemer when the cruelties took place, described in this and the two following verses, was as follows: After the arrest in Gethsemane, the guards, Jewish and Roman, escorted the Prisoner to the palace of the high priest in Jerusalem. There both Annas and Caiaphas apparently lodged. In the first instance, Jesus was brought before Annas, who was evidently the leading personage of the Sanhedrin of that day. Details of the preliminary examination are given apparently by John xviii. 13, 19—24. In this first and informal trial Caiaphas was evidently present, and took part (ver. 19). At the close of this unofficial but important proceeding, Annas sent him to Caiaphas. The true reading in John xviii. 24 is ἀπέστειλεν οὖν, "Annas therefore sent him." That is, at the close of the first *unofficial* examination, which took place in Annas's apartments in the palace of the high priest, Annas sent him to be examined *officially* before Caiaphas, the reigning high priest, and a committee of the Sanhedrin. This, the second trial of Jesus, is related at some length by St. Matthew (xxvi. 59—66) and St. Mark (xiv. 55—64). The priests on that occasion sought false witnesses, but their witness did not, we know, agree. Jesus kept silence until Caiaphas arose, and with awful solemnity adjured him to say whether he was the Christ, the Son of God. So adjured, Jesus answered definitely in the affirmative. Then Caiaphas rent his robe, and appealed to the assembly, who answered the appeal by a unanimous cry, " He is guilty of death." After this hearing before Caiapnas and a committee of the Sanhedrin, the condemned One was conducted before the full assembly of the Sanhedrin. While being led across the court, he heard Peter's third denial. It was during the interval which elapsed before the great council assembled, that the mocking related in these verses (63—65) took place.

Ver. 64.—**And when they had blindfolded him, they struck him on the face, and asked him, saying, Prophesy, who is it that smote thee?** The Jews, in this terrible scene (see, too, for further details of the outrages, Matt. xxvi. 67; Mark xiv. 65), were unconsciously working out a literal fulfilment of Isaiah's picture of the righteous Sufferer (Isa. l. 6; liii. 3—7).

Vers. 66—71.—*The third trial before the Sanhedrin.*

Ver. 66.—**And as soon as it was day.** The Sanhedrin as a council could only meet by day; all the preliminaries had been settled and the course of procedure fully arranged when the legal time for the meeting of the state council arrived. **The elders of the people and the chief priests and the scribes came together, and led him into their council.** These were the three constitutional parts of the Sanhedrin. The name of the famous Sanhedrin, curiously enough, is a Greek, not a Hebrew or Aramaic word, being derived from συνέδριον, an assembly. We first come on the word, says Dr. Farrar, when this state council summoned before them Hyrcanus II., son of Alexander Jannæus. In the time of our Lord, the Roman government had taken from them the power of carrying out capital sentences; hence their bringing Jesus before Pilate. There is a remarkable tradition that the council left their proper place of assembly, Gazith, and sat in another chamber (forty years before the destruction of the temple). Now, it was forbidden to condemn to death except in Gazith (see ' Avoda Zara,' pp. 61, etc.). Dr. Westcott quotes from Dérenbourg ('Essai sur l'Histoire et la Géographie de Palestine'), who suggests the probability of the night sitting of Annas and Caiaphas and the members of the Sanhedrin favourable to their policy (the second trial) being held at " the Booths of the Sons of Hanan" (Annas). These booths, or shops, were under two cedars on the Mount of Olives (Jerusalem Talmud, 'Taanith,' iv. 8). There were four of these booths, which were for the sale of objects legally pure. In one of these

pigeons were sold for the sacrifices of all Israel. Dérenbourg conjectures that these booths on the Mount of Olives were part of the famous Booths of the Sons of Hanan (Annas), to which the Sanhedrin retired when it left the chamber Gazith.

Ver. 67.—**Art thou the Christ? tell us. And he said unto them, If I tell you, ye will not believe.** In his answer Jesus evidently refers to something which had preceded this interrogation on the part of the Sanhedrin. He referred, no doubt, to that night examination before Caiaphas and certain chosen members of the council—the meeting passed over by St. Luke, but recounted by SS. Matthew and Mark. In this earlier trial, which we (see above) term the second, a similar question had been put to Jesus, but, as Lange and Stier point out, *now* the political significance of the charge, the claim to Messianic royalty, is brought into prominence. They were desirous to formulate an accusation which they could bring before the Roman tribunal of Pilate. The words, " *Son of God*," which the fury of jealous anger had wrung from Caiaphas (Matt. xxvi. 63), is here left out of sight, and is only brought forward again by the fierce Jewish wrath excited by the Lord's quiet words telling of his " session at the right hand " (vers. 69, 70). *If I tell you, ye will not believe.* If you, who have seen my life, have heard my words, and seen my works, believe not, to what end is it to say it again now?

Ver. 68.—**And if I also ask you, ye will not answer me.** The Lord here especially refers to those public questions of his put to members of the Sanhedrin and others in the last days of his public ministry, such as we find in Matt. xxii. 45, to which the rulers had attempted to give no answer.

Ver. 69.—**Hereafter shall the Son of man sit on the right hand of the power of God.** Jesus decided to put an end to this weary and useless trial, and supplied his judges with the evidence they were seeking to extort from him. The Master's words would recall to the teachers of Israel, sitting as his judges, the words of their loved prophet Daniel (vii. 13, 14). These solemn words of his were, and they perfectly understood them as such, a claim on the part of the Prisoner who stood before them—*a direct claim to Divine glory.*

Ver. 70.—**Then said they all, Art thou then the Son of God?** Now bringing forward the loftier title formerly suppressed (in ver. 67). "And *art* thou, then, dost *thou*, poor Man, vain in thy imagining, dost thou assert thyself to be the Son of God?" So Stier. **And he said unto them, Ye say that I am.** This form of reply is not used in Greek, but is frequent in rabbinic. By such an answer the one interrogated accepts *as his own* *affirmation* the question put to him in its entirety. We have, then, here, in the clearest possible language: (1) A plain assertion by our Lord of his Divinity. (2) The reply of the Sanhedrists, showing that *they* for their part distinctly understood it as such, but to make it quite clear they asked him if that *was* his meaning, *i.e.* the assertion of his Divinity. (3) We have the Lord's quiet answer, " Yes, that was his meaning." The next verse (71) shows that they were satisfied with the evidence which they proceeded without delay to lay before the Roman governor, Pilate.

HOMILETICS.

Vers. 1—30.—*Wednesday and Thursday of Passion Week.* Look at *that* picture— the Son of God awaiting the hour; spending the last day before the arrest and the trial in the deep seclusion of the Bethany home. Over that day the veil of an impenetrable secrecy hangs. One thing only is certain—it was a time in which the shrinking spirit, whilst feeling even unto death the shadow of the exceeding heaviness, nevertheless drank of the brook by the way, the comforting " I am not alone, for the Father is with me." Look at *this* picture — the priests and scribes, defied and denounced in the temple and in the presence of the people, have resolved that, by fair means or by foul, they must get rid of this " Swift Witness " against them. These men, united by a common hatred, consult (ver. 2) how they may kill him. We can imagine the conferences in the dimly lighted chamber—the partial light only casting deeper shadows, and bringing into fuller relief the lines of fierce resentment on the faces of the councillors. There is no debate as to the object; the only and the long debate is simply as to the means of accomplishing the object. Their deliberations are unexpectedly aided. The evangelist informs us of the satisfaction which lightens their countenances as they conclude the bargain with Judas of Karioth, and receive from him the assurance that he will find " the opportunity to betray him to them " (ver. 6) without the risk of exciting a tumult. Thus, whilst heaven is calm, hell is agitated at its depths; whilst love is directing its prayer and looking up, pride and envy are laying their plots and meditating the darkest crime which blots the page of history. " Mark the perfect, and behold the upright; for the end of that man is peace." " But the wicked are like the troubled sea, when it cannot rest, whose waters cast up mire and dirt." The early hours of Thursday swiftly pass. The next day is the great Passover day; and the disciples have begun to press the inquiry, " Where shall we keep it? " In the forenoon (ver. 8) Jesus gives Peter and John his instructions. A place is in the Lord's view. That the one to whose house the apostles are directed was a believer may be inferred (1) from the word which the three synoptists represent the Lord as using, " The Master saith " (ver. 11); and (2) from the confidential character of the message. The two are commanded to go in advance of the party, and have all in readiness for a celebration of the Paschal meal, which probably anticipated by one day the usual celebration of the Lord's Passover. Christ and the remaining ten apostles follow in the evening. Nothing is told us of that journey, whether, *e.g.*, it was private, or whether, as usual, Jesus was accompanied by a multitude of people. It is the last time on which the feet of the Christ who had been known after the flesh shall press the grassy slope of the hill he loved. But he had spoken to his own of another day, that foretold in prophecy, when " his feet shall stand on the Mount of Olives, which is before Jerusalem on the east . . . the day when the light shall not be clear nor dark, but one day known to the Lord. And living waters shall go out from Jerusalem; half of them toward the former sea, and half of them toward the hinder sea; . . . and the Lord shall be King over all the earth " (Zech. xiv. 4—9). All that is reported is this: " When the hour was come, he sat down, and the twelve apostles with him " (ver. 14). The details of that memorable evening are full of interest; and, regarding them, the narratives of the evangelists are singularly explicit. " The four streams that go forth to water the earth in that tale meet in a common channel; the four winds of the Spirit are in it, united and one." The scene is (vers. 11, 12) " a large upper room "—the guest-chamber of the house. (For distinction, emphasize " the *guest-chamber.*") 1. *Its object.* To receive and entertain the Friend, the one to be honoured. Is not Christ the Guest (Rev. iii. 20)? 2. *Its characteristics.* The *best room.* Is he not entitled to the best? A *large room.* The whole breadth of the life's aims, the whole strength of the heart's love, is due to him. An *upper room*. Poor and sorry is the life that has no upper room; blessed is the life whose upper room is reserved for him. A *furnished room*, all in readiness for his presence—a heart and will furnished for every good work. 3. *Its consecration.* How realized? On *our* side, by an *unreserved* surrender: "The Master saith;" and by the ready-making of faith and love, as symbolized in Peter and John. On *his* side, by the coming as the Lamb of God with the gospel of forgiveness, and as the Bread of life to have communion with us and we with him. When Jesus enters the room there is a strife for precedence, for the places nearest him. St. Luke places the strife (ver. 24) along with the questioning among themselves who would be false to Christ; but his language, "there was also," is inexact, and it seems consistent with the fitness of things that the contention should occur when seats were being taken. The Master, observing it, administers the rebuke recorded in vers. 26, 27; and, having so done, he proceeds to comply with the ceremonial of the feast. It was wont to begin with the passing of a cup of wine, blessed and hallowed. The word recorded in vers. 15, 16 is spoken before the dispensation of the cup; the word in vers. 17, 18 accompanies the dispensation; both words intimating the declinature to partake of the shadowy rite when the substance is so soon to be realized. "Suffer it to be so *now*," said Jesus to John at the baptism. The *now* is exhausted. "I will not any more" is the sentence of the supper-table. As they divide the cup, he rises. He is minded to give them the lesson never to be forgotten, as his sharpest rebuke of all their contentions for priority— the lesson so graphically related in John xiii. 1—17. Resuming his place at the table, lo! a troubled look flits across the countenance. A little later in the evening he can no longer refrain. There is one seated near him over whom the heart yearns, though it recoils from his baseness (ver. 21). The hand of the betrayer is with him. " *One of you.*" Startled, deeply moved, the question passes from one and another, "Lord, is it I?" Simon whispers to John, "Ask who it is;" and John, leaning forward, his head close to Jesus, puts the question. He gets the sign by which the one will be identified—a morsel to be dipped in the dish that is before the Lord will be given to him. It is given to Judas, hitherto silent, something of the better self still struggling within. But, after the sop, the Satanic spirit gains in boldness. He has the effrontery to ask, "Is it I?" What is the answer? "Thou hast said . . . That thou doest do quickly." O Judas, there is no need to linger; thou art detected. "The Son of man goeth, as it is written: but woe unutterable to thee!" It is difficult to determine the precise stage in the keeping of the feast at which the sacrament of the Lord's Supper was instituted. Matthew makes the departure of the traitor precede the appointment of the ordinance. Luke seems to place the institution of the Supper at an earlier period than the departure. But the fact of the institution is beyond doubt (vers. 19—21). The Christian Church, in all ages, has obeyed the command of her beloved Lord, spoken in the guest-chamber when keeping the Passover with his disciples: "This do in remembrance of me." The central point of the interest attaching to the Thursday evening is this consecration of the bread and the cup as the abiding pledges of redeeming love. It is sad to think that over the gracious words of Christ in the consecration so many controversies should have been waged. Why cannot men recognize the language of figure and symbol? Those who insist that in the sentence, "Take, eat; this is my body," there is implied the transubstantiation of the cake of bread held in the hand, claim for that sentence a narrow literalism which they themselves do not observe when they read, "I am the true Vine," or "I am the Door." Let us receive, with all possible oblation of praise, the earthly creatures as, in sacramental use, the hallowed representations to the eye and pledges to the soul of the never-failing nourishment of the body that was broken and the blood that was shed for us. Let all who would feed on Jesus in their heart with thanksgiving reflect on the words of the Thursday evening which mirror his consciousness, and let them examine themselves in the light of this consciousness. "With desire I have desired" (ver. 15). O my Lord, if thy desire was thus vehement; if, because of it, thou didst overlook all that lay in the immediate future; if thou didst so long to share thy feast with men, why the want of desire in me? why the backwardness and slowness of my soul to receive thee in the mysteries of thy love? Lord, lead me in thy truth, and teach me. "Until the kingdom of God shall come" (ver. 18). O my Lord, how vivid to thee was the future consummation of thy sacrifice! As, in perspective, the distant is often near, the intervening spaces being lost to sight, so was it with thee. Thou didst behold thy kingdom in glory as at hand, and thy soul stretched forward whither thy prayer afterwards pointed,—" Father, that which thou hast given me, I will that where I am they also may be with me." Why beats my pulse so slow and feeble in response to the hope of thy kingdom? Why is my Lord's Supper so much of a mere commemoration, so little of a prophetic joy, of a prayer, as already in the vision of the kingdom? "Come, Lord Jesus, come quickly."

> " Thou strong and loving Son of man,
>   Redeemer from the bonds of sin,
>   'Tis thou the living spark dost fan
>   That sets my heart on fire within.
> Thou openest heaven once more to men—
>   The soul's true home, thy kingdom, Lord;
> And I can trust and hope again,
>   And feel myself akin to God."

Vers. 31—34.—*The special word to Simon.* Its solemnity is indicated by the twice-repeated " *Simon.*" Observe, when the warning is given, this is the name used; afterwards (ver. 34), in reply to the disciple's protestation, " I am ready to go both to prison and to death," the name is changed, " I tell thee, *Peter.*" How gentle, how pathetic, the irony! Of the Peter, the rock, it is to be said, " The cock shall not crow until thou shalt thrice deny that thou knowest me." Note three points in the word of Christ.

I. THE TEMPTATION. To him the personality of the tempter is always real. Real, in respect of his own temptations: " Get thee hence, Satan;" "The prince of this world cometh." Now we are reminded that it is real in respect of the temptations of men. Beware of foolish speaking and jesting in connection with the actual existence of the Satan. " Behold!" says Jesus. All is vividly present to him; he would have the agency of the adversary vividly present to his follower. The expression employed is very striking (see the Revised Version, " Satan asked to have you"). The phrase recalls the scene in Job ii. But this is memorable—the tempter recognizes the proprietary of the Lord. Of Judas it is said, " Satan entered into him." Of Simon it is said, " He asked to have you." This is one over whom he has no right. He belongs to the Son of God—a man given him by the Father. And he makes request that the disciple be sifted. In the margin of the Revised Version it is put as an alternative reading: " He obtained you by asking." All is so suggestive. The Christian Father speaks of the Christian's *fasting-days.* Such days are often part of the experience of God's people. The sieve, as if with God's permission, is applied. The tempter obtained the Lord himself by asking, and the sieve was applied to him. It was similarly applied to his apostle; it is similarly applied, in one form or another, to those who are his. God will have his wheat winnowed. Remember, there is the sieve: " Watch and pray."

II. THE INTERCESSION. It is spoken of (ver. 32) as *past,* and as a transaction accomplished in the invisible world. And who knows what transactions are there realized? How blessed is the assurance that

> " Where high the heavenly temple stands,
>   The house of God, not made with hands,
>   A great High Priest our nature wears,
>   The Guardian of mankind appears"!

" I *made intercession* for thee." Ah! in the day when all secrets are declared, with what marvellous light will this word be illumined! Ye Simons of all ages, thyself, O my soul, what a reflection it is that between the one tempted and the outer darkness there is the intercession of the ever-living and ever-mighty One, who is able to " save to the uttermost"! What is the intercession? Not that the sieve be withdrawn, that the sifting fail? It is needful. Simon would not have been the Peter he became without the sieve and without the discipline. The tempter and the trial are used as discipline. He who would not pray that his own be taken out of the world, will not pray that the Satan-request be refused. No; but he intercedes that the " faith fail not " (ver. 32). The great feature of Simon was his confidence in Christ. Why should he have been selected as the Rock-man, who was so often rash, and who so weakly denied his Master? Through all there was still the faith. He had quicker insight into the secrets of his Master's power and presence than any of his fellows; he had a higher and fuller perception of and trust in him. Were this to fail, all would fail. And the fruit of the intercession was evidenced in the springing back of his faith— nay, in its rising to a still higher measure of knowledge on the ruins of the old self-confidence; there was created the new heart that by-and-by was ready to go to prison and death.

III. THE EXHORTATION. Simon will turn again. When the Lord turns, in the day of the trial, and looks on the apostate disciple, there is born a godly sorrow which works repentance not to be repented of. Out of this repentance there comes the earnest, "Lord, thou knowest all things; thou knowest that I love thee." And the charge is, "Do thou, when once thou hast turned again, stablish thy brethren" (ver. 32, Revised Version). The most helpful man is he who has himself been tempted, who has passed, not without scars, through the fight of faith. It is the sympathy of the soul that has come through great tribulation that has the delicate touch, the magnetic force, the faculty of establishing the brethren. All discovery of the Lord is to be utilized in the way of strengthening, cheering, building up human souls in the kingdom of God. What we receive we hold in trust for others, and, in giving as we receive, what we have gained becomes doubly ours.

> "Heaven does with us as we with torches do,
> Not light them for themselves."

Experience of God and his love is the best teacher. What we learn, even through falls and failures, turns most to the profit of poor human nature. Simon, after the sifting, through the turning again, was the confirmer of the brethren.

Vers. 39—46.—*Gethsemane.* It is now dark. On the way to the Mount of Olives, the customary retreat of Jesus (ver. 39), at the point where the upward slope begins, there is a shady place, belonging, perhaps, to one of those who believed in him, whither "Jesus had often resorted" (John xviii. 2). The site of the garden of Gethsemane may, with sufficient accuracy, be identified. It may not have been the exact spot, over-shadowed by the eight venerable trees, which immemorial tradition has distinguished as the scene of the lonely vigil, but it must have been close to that spot. It was a place where there were many olives, and, as the name suggests, an oil-press; a place of perfect quiet and seclusion, where, beyond the voices of rude men, there was the peace of heaven. To this place he who had uttered the high-priestly prayer brought the high-priestly sacrifice; and there he began the walk through the valley of the shadow of death. The tale of the sore amazement and exceeding heaviness is told, with more fulness of detail, by the Evangelists Matthew and Mark (see homiletics *in loc.*). Here, without enlarging on the meaning and scope of the features of the narrative, note—

I. THE AGONY. (Ver. 44.) It has always been felt that in this there is immeasurably more than a mere revolt from imminent pain and death. The anguish is marked by an intensity for which this revolt cannot account. A brave man, however sensitive, can face, with unflinching fortitude, a high enterprise, even though its fatal consequence is evident. "The sweat becoming as it were great drops of blood," speaks of a conflict in the soul for which the impending physical dissolution cannot account. Some references supply us with suggestions. 1. The announcement made at the Supper-table (John xiv. 30), of the coming of the prince of the world, speaks to us of a temptation, intensified by the circumstances of the hour, in the line of the wilderness-temptation, to grasp the power of the Messiah otherwise than through the suffering of the cross (see, in this connection, Matt. xxvi. 53). 2. The sorrow which cast its shade over his countenance when the betrayal was mentioned (John xiii. 21); the horror with which he regarded the perfidy (ver. 22; Matt. xxvi. 24); the utterance by which he awoke the disciples, marking out the betrayal as the bitterness of the hour at hand (Matt. xxvi. 45); the appeal to Judas (ver. 48);—these things indicate the *amazement* and pain caused by the action of the son of perdition. 3. The word of the Son to the Father as to the cup so full of woe that he humbly besought its removal, reminds us of a region beyond all that our thought can trace, in which the Christ of God was treading the wine-press alone. Better, in view of this, a holy reticence than a zeal which is eager with explanations. If we must speak of the special fearfulness and trembling of Gethsemane, let us simply say that there, in all its crushing weight, was realized the bearing of the sin of the world.

II. THE PRAYER. 1. *Observe its characteristics.* (1) *Humility.* "He kneeled down." More strongly still St. Mark says (xiv. 35), "He fell on the ground." It was the attitude of deepest reverence, of entire prostration. In the high-priestly prayer, "he lifted up his eyes to heaven;" but now, in human weakness and dependence, he is prostrate before his Father. Sign of the "godly fear" (Heb. v. 7) for which he was heard. (2) *Importunate repetition.* Thrice he prayed, "saying the same words" (Matt. xxvi. 44). It is not the eloquence, but the sincerity of desire in the prayer which God regards. (3) *Increasing earnestness.* "Being in an agony, he prayed more earnestly." The greater the pressure on the soul, the more fervent became the cry. The sorrow of the disciples sent them to sleep; his sent him to the Father. "Love overmasters agony," not agony love. Let the disciple learn of the Master. 2. *Observe its subject-matter.* (Ver. 42.) "Remove this cup from me;" or (as in Matt. xxvi. 30), "Let this cup pass from me." It was the pleading of the sensitive human soul. And we may be assured that to plead for the removal of a cup of pain, for relief from burdens which seem greater than we can bear, is in the way of the child's privilege; only there must be the spirit of entire dependence. "If thou be willing." There is to be no "if" where God's promise is absolute. We do not need to say, "If thou be willing, make thy grace sufficient." His pledge as to this is distinct and unequivocal: "My grace *is* sufficient." From this, on this resting, we pray. But when we desire that concerning which we have no definite assurance of the Father's mind, then all is to be subordinated to him. This is to abide in the Son as he is revealed in Gethsemane. "If we ask any thing according to God's will, he heareth us." The godly McCheyne spoke of getting into tune for prayer. We get into tune when we learn Christ's "If it be possible;" "If thou be willing."

> "Renew my will from day to day;
> Blend it with thine," etc.

3. *Observe its answer.* The answer is manifest: (1) In the *righting* "*Nevertheless.*" (Ver. 42.) In the prayer the soul realized "God my Rock." From what might have been self-seeking, it was delivered.

> "Do thou thy holy will:
> I will lie still; I will not stir,
> Lest I should break the charm."

"In the day when I cried, thou answeredst me, and strengthenedst me with strength in my soul." (2) In the *comforting angel.* (Ver. 43.) The holy one, sign of the sympathy in heaven above. For to the one who prays in an agony the heavens are not brass. There are ministries of love. God's angels are all ministering spirits. In visible form the angel may not appear; but we know that he is with us in the comfort and peace. Have we not the Comforter himself?—

> "A gracious, willing Guest,
> While he can find one humble heart
> Wherein to rest."

And thus, though the cup does not pass, the will of the Son is strengthened into perfect harmony with the will of the Father. He rises up from prayer, ready, "strong in the Lord, and in the power of his might."

III. Observe, finally, THE REMONSTRANCE. Very touching the *word to Peter* (Matt. xxvi. 40). The one hour never again to come, the one hour of watching, lost in sleep! And now (ver. 46). May not the pathetic question ring in the ears of the Christian? Why do *we* sleep—we whom the Son of man has associated with himself in his prayers and pains? We asleep, and he toiling! We asleep, and the world lying in darkness! Ah! in the solemn light of Gethsemane, what is the utmost Christian activity but a slumber? and how many who claim to be Christ's are fast asleep, not for sorrow, but in self-indulgence and sin! Oh that the gentle, reproachful "why?" may be as an alarum-clock to conscience, a continual incitement to will and heart! The spirit may be willing, but the flesh is ever weak. "Rise and pray, lest ye enter into temptation!"

Ver. 47—ch. xxiii. 46.—*Thursday night to Friday evening.* It is time to be going. The footfall of the coming host has already been heard, and the gleam of the lanterns and the flashing of the swords have been detected at no great distance. Guiltily, under shadow of night, the conspirators have approached. "While Jesus is yet speaking." (ver. 47), the traitor is bending forward to give the salute of friendship. Note the question, so full of gentle dignity, "Companion, wherefore art thou come? Betrayest thou the Son of man with a kiss?" Note what follows down to the flight of the apostles, when to them it seems that the end has come. "We trusted that it had been he who should have redeemed Israel;" and now? Betrayed into the hands of sinners, he is "led as a lamb to the slaughter, and as a sheep dumb before her shearers." Priest, Pharisee, scribe, he who scourged you with the whip of his holy indignation is now the Prisoner on whose bleeding body the furrows of your scourge may be made long. No legion of angels will interpose. The Son of God only waits to die. There are: (1) *a precognition by Annas;* (2) *an arraignment before Caiaphas and the Sanhedrin;* and, finally (3), *the deliverance to the judicature of the governor.* Briefly trace the narrative.

I. THE PRECOGNITION BY ANNAS. Annas, or Hanan, to whom first the fettered Jesus is borne, occupied at the time a peculiar position. His son-in-law, Joseph Caiaphas, was the actual high priest. But Annas, having been deposed by the Roman governor, was still regarded as the priest *jure divino,* and his influence seems to have been immense. Five of his sons and his son-in-law were raised to the pontifical throne. It was under the last of his five sons that James, the brother of our Lord, was put to death. He was an unscrupulous intriguer. A Sadducee, who had been mixed up in foul plots and conspiracies, the head of "a viper brood," as a Jewish chronicler says, which amassed wealth by unlawful gains. Farrar has called attention to the fact that, when the capture of Jesus is determined, the Pharisees disappear from the scene; his implacable enemies are the chief priests and scribes. Before this Annas Jesus stands (John xviii. 13—23). Some questions are put as to his disciples and doctrine. And these, as has well been remarked, Jesus answers "with dignified repulsion"—a repulsion so sharp that the first blow inflicted on that sacred face was bestowed by one of the menials of the court. "Answerest thou the high priest so?" How complete the self-restraint expressed in the only action which followed—the reply, "If I have spoken evil, bear witness of the evil; but if not, why strikest thou me?"

II. THE ARRAIGNMENT BEFORE CAIAPHAS AND THE SANHEDRIN. All that Annas could do was to order his Prisoner to be still more tightly bound, and to send him to the portion of the temple court which was occupied by the priest, his son-in-law, Caiaphas. The morning had not yet dawned, and until dawn no meeting of council could be convened. It was during this interval that the predicted denial of the Lord by Peter occurred (vers. 54—62). The clock marks the hour of six, when Caiaphas and his assessors confront the Nazarene. Their object is to establish a charge of blasphemy, and suborned witnesses are cited. They are clumsy perjurers, who contradict one another and contradict themselves. And the evidence breaks down. Then the tactics are changed. The high priest, directly addressing the Prisoner, demands a "yea" or "nay" to the interrogation, "Art thou the Christ?" Jesus has been silent, but now (vers. 60—71), calmly and solemnly, he answers, "Thou hast said;" and adds that, by-and-by, they should see "the Son of man sitting on the right hand of the power of God." It is enough. "Blasphemy!" is the shout, and he is condemned as worthy of death. And there ensues a scene of brutal ferocity. The wretches in attendance spit on the face, buffet, strike him with the palms of their hands, and rend the air with ribald cries. For the world shows its baseness when a man is down; then the many rush forward to have their fling and kick.

III. JESUS IS DELIVERED TO THE JUDICATURE OF THE GOVERNOR. What priests and elders could do has been done. The procurator alone could inflict the sentence of death. Their next movement must be to coerce him into the carrying out of their plan. And they know that in Pontius Pilate, stained with violences the report of which to his imperial master would cost him his government, if not his life, they have the ruler whom they can rule. Two appearances (ch. xxiii.) of our Lord before the governor are recorded, and between them stands the episode with which the name of Herod is associated. There is nothing more sad than the record of the expedients, the shufflings to and fro, the efforts to save One whom Pilate felt to be guiltless, whilst yet he dared not give effect to his convictions. A record most sad, but most instructive. Is it not a portrait, many of whose features suggest cowardly concessions, timidities, struggles between conscience and policy in which conscience is worsted, with which, in one form or another, too many of us are familiar? A character-sketch, like that of Pilate in the trial, gauges the directions and the possibilities of the human nature which is common to us all. In the afternoon of Friday the Saviour of sinners was crucified. An incident on the way to Calvary is related by the evangelist, which is touching in itself, and which reminds us of the attitude of mind, the kind of feeling towards him, the Crucified, which he denies and accepts. We are told that he was "followed by a great company of women, who bewailed and lamented him" (vers. 27—31). Observe his saying, most tenderly prefaced by the phrase, "Daughters of Jerusalem." Virtually, he declines tears and cries, which express only sorrow over his fate. He wishes those who bewail to estimate the significance of the spectacle, to realize what it foreboded for them and theirs; to weep not *for* him, but *with* him in his sadness concerning Jerusalem, in his baffled longing to gather its children together, in his thwarted purpose to save and bless. The events of that day were the prophecy of a doom not to be long delayed: in his thought and emotion as to this doom, and in this alone, he sought their sympathy. And so, remember, Christ desires not a luxury of sentiment, which ends in lamentations on account of his suffering. He desires partnership in his suffering. His cross is to be our cross. We are to hold ourselves identified with him in it. The apostle's words are the interpretation of the genuine Christian sentiment: "I was crucified with Christ: nevertheless I live; yet not I, but Christ liveth in me: and the life which I now live in the flesh I live by the faith of the Son of God, who loved me, and gave himself for me;" "God forbid that I should glory, save in the cross of our Lord Jesus Christ, through which the world has been crucified to me, and I to the world."

HOMILIES BY VARIOUS AUTHORS.

Ver. 2.—*Piety, pedantry, and formalism.* Of all those who in any and every way were responsible for the death of Jesus Christ, the largest share of guilt lies at the door of the religious leaders of the time. The Roman soldiers were only the *immediate instruments* of it; the Jewish populace were only the *blind agents* of it; but these scribes and chief priests were the *guilty instigators of it*: they brought it about. It was they who first conceived the idea; it was they who suggested and urged it; it was they who ceased not to agitate and direct until the dark deed was done. How came they to go so far astray? How came it to pass that while "all the people came early in the morning to him in the temple for to hear him" (ch. xxi. 38), thus bearing witness to the sincerity of their discipleship and their desire to know the truth he taught, *they*, the leaders of the land—scribes who were familiar with every letter of the Law, priests who were daily occupied in the services of the sanctuary, learned doctors, and pious ministrants—were actively and earnestly compassing his death? The fact is that—

I. RELIGIOUS PEDANTRY MAY BE VERY LEARNED, AND YET WHOLLY WRONG. These men knew their Scriptures with a fulness and nicety of detail that surpasses the knowledge we have of our sacred writings; and they had also a perfect familiarity with the teachings of traditional lore. They despised the ignorance of the common people in these respects (see John vii. 47). Yet they were not wise with the wisdom of God; they entirely failed to understand the Divine will and the way to eternal life. The religion they taught and lived was utterly heartless; it was a service without any soul in it, a mechanism without any life in it; it was an elaborate error, a great and sad misconception of the mind of God; it was a surrender of freedom that did man no good and gave God no pleasure; it was a toilsome and torturing imposition that neither satisfied the intellect, nor cleansed the heart, nor elevated the life. And it so perverted the judgment that, when the Truth himself came to reveal the Father, these learned but unwise leaders, instead of being eager to hear him like the people (ch. xxi. 38), were "seeking how they might kill him."

II. RELIGIOUS FORMALISM WILL GO TO GREAT LENGTHS OF WRONG-DOING. If the scribes were men of pedantry, the chief priests represented the evil and error of religious formalism; and the latter were in no way behind the former in either spiritual blindness or malevolence. They, too, failed to recognize their Messiah, and were actively engaged in compassing his murder. In every age and land religious formalism has been blind and cruel; it has failed to recognize the reformer when he has come to speak in God's name; and it has been forward to accuse and to slay him. Such has been its spirit and its course, that the home of love and mercy has been converted into the hotbed of hatred and of cruelty. It is another illustration of the truth that the corruption of the best becomes the worst of all; the piety that runs into ordinances, utterances, abstinences, formalities, will in time degenerate into utter error and shameful wrong. This is a truth which applies to many more Churches than one; it is, indeed, more or less applicable to all religious circles. There lies a deep-seated tendency in our nature which accounts for the facts in our Lord's time and in every age since then. Let us, therefore, learn that—

III. TRUE PIETY IS FOUND IN RECTITUDE OF HEART AND LIFE. Not in holding and professing certain correct formulæ; not in going through certain ceremonies or observing a number of rules and regulations. These have their place in the kingdom of God, but they do not by any means assure us of our place in it. It is rightness of heart toward God our Father and our Saviour, and consequent integrity of life, which make us to "stand before God" as his loyal subjects now, and will make us "worthy to stand before the Son of man" when he shall call us to his nearer presence.—C.

Vers. 3—6.—*The deepest wound, etc.* When everything has been allowed for Judas that the most ingenious and the most charitable have begged us to consider, we must judge him to be a man whose conduct is to be solemnly and seriously condemned. It is Divine Love itself that decides this question (see ver. 22; Matt. xxvi. 24; John xvii. 12). The text suggests to us—

I. THAT OUR DEEPEST WOUNDS ARE THOSE WE RECEIVE AT THE HAND OF OUR NEAREST FRIENDS. How much force is there in the parenthesis, "*being of the number of the twelve*"! What deep pathos is in those sad words of the Lord, "Verily I say unto you, that *one of you* shall betray me" (Matt. xxvi. 21)! This was a "sword that entered into his soul," a keen distress, one of the very bitterest of all the sorrows of the Son of man. That one whom he had admitted to his intimate fellowship, of whom he had made a friend, who had partaken of his confidence and shared his strong affection,—that *he* should be the one to betray him to his foes! There is no trouble possible to us so great as that which lies open to us on the side of our purest and strongest affections. It is not our avowed enemy, nor the man to whom we are indifferent, but it is our dearest friend, who has it in his power to lacerate our soul with the sharpest thrust, and to spoil our life by throwing over it the darkest shadow (see Ps. xli. 9). 1. Be slow to admit to the inner sanctuary of the heart; for he who has entrance there holds your happiness in his own right hand. 2. Realize the responsibility of intimate friendship; it is not only a privilege, but an obligation; it gives you power to gladden and to bless, but also opportunity to mar and to destroy.

II. THAT MONEY PLAYS A LARGE PART, FOR GOOD OR EVIL, IN HUMAN LIFE. They "covenanted to give him money." It seems hardly credible that any man who had lived in the society of Jesus Christ, and had witnessed his kindness and his purity, should take money for betraying him. Other motives—those of resentment or ambition—are far less shocking and revolting than this mercenary one. To betray his Master, his Friend, for thirty pieces of silver, fills us with wonder and excites the deepest reprobation. But for what has not money been responsible in human history? How large a part it plays in the great drama! What untold good it is instrumental in effecting! What admirable virtues it is the means of illustrating! To what deeds of folly and even of infamy the desire to obtain it has conducted! It is clear that men who have been trained to hate immoral and criminal behaviour with an intense hatred have been induced to part with every principle they have honoured, and to do the worst deeds they have denounced, in order to obtain money, when they have *found themselves pressed* for its possession. Probably no man who has not felt it knows the deadly force of the temptation. Who shall say that he is safe from this powerful snare? It is probable that to obtain money more evil deeds have been done than under any other inducement whatever. Therefore let every man beware lest he subjects himself to this strong and fell temptation. Let neither an overweening ambition nor extravagance of habit lead where the possession of more money becomes an imperative demand. Moderation in desire and economy in habit save men from a temptation in which, it may be, their souls would be entangled and their very life taken away.

III. THAT EARNESTNESS IS SURE TO SEEK ITS OPPORTUNITY UNTIL IT FINDS IT. He " *sought opportunity* to betray him." By whatever motives inspired, Judas was intent on compassing the act he had undertaken. And he did not wait idly until an opportunity offered itself. He *sought it*. If evil is thus in earnest, how much more so should righteousness and mercy be! *These* should surely be about their holy and loving work "with both hands earnestly." Opportunity to raise, to help, to redeem, to restore,—this is not to be passively waited for, but to be actively sought out. There is a very marked difference between readiness to work when we are invited and even urged to do so, and that noble zeal which will not be contented without finding material for activity. It is the difference between a goodness that you do not blame and a goodness that you admire; between a life that will not stand condemned and a life that will be crowned with victory and honour. If there are those who, in the interest of error and of evil, will set about diligently to promote these ends, shall we not put forth our utmost energy on behalf of truth and heavenly wisdom? If men can be found who will "seek opportunity" to *betray*, shall not we with deeper devotedness "seek opportunity" to *honour* our Lord?—C.

Vers. 15, 16.—*The Passion, from two standpoints.* I. AS IT LOOKED TO OUR LORD WHEN HE WAS APPROACHING IT. It was to him a terrible trial, which he was eager to reach and pass through. "With desire he desired" the time to arrive when he should suffer and should complete his work. He did not wish to escape it; he was not looking about for an alternative; he knew that he could not save himself if he would save the world; and he longed for the trial-time to come and to be passed. Here was the heroic, and here was also the human. Here was the determination to endure, and, at the same time, the natural, human anxiety to know the worst and to exchange an almost intolerable suspense for the suffering that awaited him. 1. Having chosen the path of self-sacrifice, and having entered upon and pursued it, it behoved him to continue and to complete his appointed work. He could not turn back without suffering defeat; he accepted the dark future that was before him as a sacred duty. From it there must be no turning aside to other ends; and *there was none*. He never wavered in his purpose from beginning to end. "This shall not be unto thee," from Peter, appears to have been a strong shock of temptation to him (Matt. xvi. 21—23). But nothing induced him to turn aside by a single step from the path of sacrificial service. 2. Yet we have here a glimpse of the extreme severity of the trial he underwent. He knew that his "suffering" would immediately follow this Passover, and he "earnestly desired" that Passover to come, that the sufferings might follow. With perfect reverence we may say that he could not realize what they would include, for they had never before been experienced; they stood absolutely by themselves, and could not be known until they were actually felt. And this element of suspense and uncertainty must have added a great weight of trouble to the sorrows of our Lord. "How bitter that cup no heart can conceive;" not even *his* heart did conceive until it was in his hands. (1) Like our Lord, we should go on without faltering to the darkest future which we feel it becomes us to face. (2) As with him, the uncertainty of the actual elements of our grief may oppress our spirit and fill us with eager desire for its coming (see also ch. xii. 50). (3) We shall find, as he found, all needful Divine help when the hour does actually arrive.

II. AS HE WOULD HAVE US REGARD IT NOW. That is, as a completed work of redeeming love. That last Passover has been "fulfilled in the kingdom of God." All that the Passover prophesied has been fulfilled. The "Lamb of God" has been slain—that Lamb "which taketh away the sin of the world." Everything in the way of sacred endurance, of Divine preparation, is now completed, and the way into the kingdom is open. Those sufferings to which Jesus was so eagerly looking forward, to which he had now come, with nothing between them and him but that Passover Feast, had to be endured (see ch. xxiv. 26); and now *they have been* endured. Everything predicted in sacred rite or solemn utterance has been "fulfilled," and we wait for nothing more. We sit down to no predictive Passover Feast, because "Christ, our Passover, *is* slain for us." What we have to do is gratefully and eagerly to avail ourselves of the "finished" work of our redeeming Lord; to let that suffering, that death, that sacrifice, (1) evoke our humility; (2) call forth our faith; (3) kindle our love and command our obedience; (4) inspire us with sacred and abiding joy, inasmuch as his "sorrow unto death" is the source of our eternal life.—C.

Vers. 19, 20.—*The Lord's Supper.* A very simple rite as first observed was the Lord's Supper. But for certain passages in the Acts of the Apostles and in the Epistles, we should not have known that Jesus Christ intended to create a permanent institution. But though the simpler the ceremony is the more scriptural it is, yet are the ideas associated with it and suggested by it many and important. They are these—

I. THE NEAR PRESENCE OF OUR LORD. Not in the elements but presiding over the company. It is a table at which he entertains his friends; and can he, the Divine Host, himself be absent?

> " Around a table, not a tomb,
> He willed our gathering-place should be;
> When going to prepare our home,
> The Saviour said, ' Remember me.' "

And at that table, meeting and communing with his friends, we may feel sure and can realize forcibly that our living Lord is, in spirit and in truth, "in the midst of us."

II. CHRIST OUR STRENGTH AND OUR JOY. The chosen elements are bread and wine, the sources of strength and of gladness. He, our Lord, is the one constant Source of our spiritual nourishment and strength, of the joy with which our hearts are for ever glad.

III. CHRIST OUR PROPITIATION. The *broken* bread, the *outpoured* wine—of what do these speak to our hearts? Of the "marred visage," of the weariness, of the poverty and privation, of the toilfulness and loneliness of that troubled life, of the griefs and pains of that burdened and broken heart, of the shame and the darkness and the death of the last closing scene. We stand with bowed head and reverent spirit at that cross and see—

> " Sorrow and love flow mingled down."

And our hearts are full as we ask—

> " Did e'er such love and sorrow meet;
> Or thorns compose so rich a crown? "

And we realize that that sorrow was borne, that death died, *for us.* "This is my body, 'given for you;' my blood, 'shed for you.'" It is the Propitiation for *our* sins.

IV. OUR INDIVIDUAL APPROPRIATION OF OUR LORD'S GREAT WORK. Each one eats of that bread and drinks of that cup. As he does so, in and by that act he declares his own personal need of a Divine Saviour; he affirms his conviction that the sacrifice was offered for him; he renews his faith in the Divine Redeemer; he recognizes the claim of him that loved him unto death; he rededicates himself to Jesus Christ and to his service; he rejoices, in spirit, in his reconciled Father, in his Divine Lord and Friend.

V. HAPPY AND HOLY COMMUNION WITH ONE ANOTHER. Gathered round one table, in the felt presence of our common Lord, *all* invited to drink of the same cup (Matt. xxvi. 27), we are drawn to one another in the bonds of Christian love. We realize our oneness in him as a strong bond which triumphs over all the separating influences of the world. Faith, joy, love, are kindled and "burn within us;" and we are strengthened and sanctified, built up, enabled to "abide in him."—C.

Vers. 21, 22.—*Jesus and Judas; our Lord and ourselves.* The ordinance of the

Lord's Supper was closely connected, not only in time but in apostolic thought, with the act of the betrayal (see 1 Cor. xi. 23)—the institution of the greatest privilege with the commission of the darkest crime. Our Lord's demeanour on this occasion is well worthy of our most reverent thought.

I. JESUS AND JUDAS. 1. *His length of sufferance.* After knowing that Judas was seeking to betray him (ver. 6), Jesus might well have expelled him from his society. He might have done so, acting *judicially*, as being no longer worthy to be classed among his apostles. He might have done so, acting *prudentially*, as one (1) whom it was not wise to admit to his counsels and his plans; and as one (2) whose association with the eleven would be a source of evil. He might very appropriately have declined to acknowledge him as an officer and a friend. But Jesus did not press his right. On the contrary, he let him continue as one of the twelve, he let him come under the same roof with himself, he permitted him to share the Paschal feast: the hand of him that was betraying him was "with him on the table." To such a length as that his long-suffering went. 2. *His dignity in rebuke.* He did not break forth into passionate invective; he did not use words of natural and permissible vehemence; he quietly said, "Woe unto that man," etc.! Matthew tells us that he added, "It had been good for that man if he had not been born." What a transcendent calmness and serenity of spirit we have here! What a contrast between two children of men! One man preparing to betray his Teacher, his Friend, his Master; the other compassionating his betrayer for the depth of his fall and the sadness of his doom. Jesus went on to his sacrificial death and to his throne; Judas went out into the night (John xiii. 30)—into the dark night of guilt, of shame, of despair, of death.

II. OUR LORD AND OURSELVES. 1. The wrong against our Lord it is still open to us to commit. We cannot betray him *as* Judas did; yet may we do that which answers to, and is almost if not quite as deplorable as that sad and shameful act. Let us consider that: 1. We know more about Jesus than Judas then did; for we have all the light of his resurrection and of the teaching of his apostles. 2. He has granted to us mercies as many and as great in intrinsic value as those he bestowed on Judas. 3. Owing him as much as Judas did, we may do even greater injury to his cause than the traitor did. The act of Iscariot ultimately issued in the all-sufficient sacrifice; this did not extenuate or lessen his guiltiness by a simple grain; but it nullified the *mischief* of the crime. We may do incalculable and irreparable mischief to the cause of our Master by our unfaithfulness, our infidelity, our disobedience, our criminal negligence. 4. By such disloyalty we may wound and grieve his Spirit almost as severely as his betrayer did. Wherefore let us: (1) *Be humble-minded.* "Let him that thinketh he standeth," etc. If we could find the man who has smitten Christ and his cause the severest blow that was ever struck, it is probable that we might easily find an hour in that man's history when he would have shrunk with holy horror from such a guilty act. (2) *Be prayerful;* ever looking heavenward with the supplication, "Hold thou me up," etc. (3) *Be diligent* in the field of earnest Christian work. It is the idler in the vineyard whom the tempter will assail. It is the faithful workman who is in a position to say, after his Lord and Leader, "The prince of this world cometh, and hath nothing in me" (John xiv. 30).—C.

Vers. 24—27.—*Greatness after Christ.* Three things claim our attention.

I. APOSTOLIC FAILURE. When the apostles of our Lord came to look back on this most memorable evening, how pained and how ashamed they must have felt as they recollected this unseemly contest (ver. 24)! At the very hour when their Lord was manifesting his love and his forethought for his Church in two most striking and touching ways—at the very hour when his heart was torn with distracting sorrow by the desertion and treachery of one of his chosen band, and when he might well have been looking for some consolation in the attachment and the obedience of the others, they must needs show their unlikeness to himself and their unworthiness of their position by an untimely dispute about their own importance! In connection with that condescending service of their Lord's, how small such a controversy seems! And in connection with such a trial as that through which he was passing, how unbecoming and ill-timed was any anxiety about their own affairs! It was in their power to render to Jesus Christ a most helpful sympathy, and, instead of doing that, they grieved him by the exhibition of a contentious and an ambitious spirit. It was a sad failure on their part. How often do his disciples fail him now! How often do they let the opportunity of loving and effective service pass unused! When the hour strikes for faithfulness, or for courage, or for self-sacrifice, or for humility, or for energetic action, is there not found unfaithfulness, or timidity, or selfish time-serving, or pride, or a culpable inactivity, that loses everything and leaves behind nothing but failure and regret?

II. WORLDLY VANITY. (Ver. 25.) What a poor thing indeed is mere official dignity, or even arbitrary power, or servile flattery! *Official dignity* without moral worth is a miserably hollow thing. *Arbitrary power*, exercised in caprice and apart from a pure desire to do good and to enrich, is an evil thing; it is injurious to the possessor and it is burdensome to the objects of it. *Servile flattery* is a false thing. It is simply contemptible on the part of those who pay it; it is morally ruinous to those who accept it. Let the "Gentiles" act thus if they must; but "*ye* shall not be so." Ye who care to be true, to be loving, to be humble—ye shall not sit on *that* seat of honour, ye shall not run into that serious temptation, ye shall not pursue such a worthless prize. Other and better things are within your reach; for you there is—

III. CHRISTIAN GREATNESS. (Vers. 26, 27.) 1. Jesus Christ, the greatest One, was the Servant of all. He *came* to serve; it was his holy, heavenly errand; he came to seek and to save the lost. He *lived* to serve. That act of menial service in which he had just been engaged (John xiii. 1—5) was only a picture and illustration of the whole spirit and substance of his life; to bear the burden of others was the law of his life (Gal. vi. 2). He lived to heal, to help, to comfort, to enlighten, to redeem; his life from end to end was a loving ministry, a gracious and generous service (Mark x. 45). He *suffered* to serve. He *died* to serve. He had a perfect right to say, "I am among you as he that serveth." 2. We are nearest to our Lord as we live to serve; we rise towards the spiritual stature of Jesus Christ as we are filled with this his spirit and as we live this his life. There *is* a path for ambition to tread in the kingdom of Christ; but it is not the path that leads to high office and official dignity and popular applause: these things may come unsought, and be used for good. But the one road along which true Christian greatness travels is the way of self-forgetting service. To be touched and moved by the sorrows and the sins of our fellow-men; to be stirred to helpful, earnest, sacrificial effort on their behalf; to pity the poor and needy; to seek and to save the lost; to breathe the air and to do the work of an unpretentious but effective kindness, to have the right to say, "I am among you as he that serveth;"—*that* is greatness after Christ himself.—C.

Vers. 28—30.—*Fidelity and its reward.* The lesson of the text is the bountiful reward of faithfulness to Jesus Christ; but taking these words of his in connection with the position in which he well knew himself to be, they speak to us of—

I. THE MAJESTIC CONFIDENCE OF OUR LORD. "I appoint [bequeath] unto you a kingdom . . . that ye may sit on thrones." And who is this thus calmly disposing of kingdoms and thrones?—a reigning emperor, a brilliant conqueror? Only a poor, homeless, soldierless Prophet! One who knew that he was about to be taken, tried, convicted, scourged, crucified! Yet he meant it all. What majestic confidence in God, in the power of his gospel, in his own integrity! With what reverent homage shall we bow before him who could make such royal offers when the shadow of the cross already rested on his path! And what nobler sight is there to be seen among men than that of one (missionary, minister, teacher, reformer, etc.) calmly going on his way when every one and when everything is against him, confident in the triumph of the cause for which he pleads! Taking these words of Christ in connection with the preceding verses, we see—

II. THE QUICKNESS WITH WHICH HE PASSED FROM CORRECTION TO COMMENDATION. Seeing that his apostles were not only silenced, but humbled by the rebuke he had administered to them (vers. 24—26), and wishing to reassure and revive them, our Lord turned to the fidelity they had shown toward himself, and spoke words of praise and of promise. "You are wrong altogether in your spirit and behaviour in this matter; I blame you for this. But be not cast down; I do not forget your constancy toward me in all my times of trial, and I will reward you." Such was, such is, the gracious, considerate, generous Master.

> " His anger is so slow to rise.
> So ready to abate."

It is the flying shadow which the wind-driven cloud casts upon the field, chased by the hastening sunshine. " O slow to strike and swift to spare ! " might well have been written of him. Can it be said or sung of us, in our relations with one another? But the main truth here is—

III. The reward of fidelity in the Master's service. Our Lord wished to assure his disciples that he was by no means unmindful or unappreciative of their faithfulness; and he found the best proof of this in their constancy toward himself in his times of trouble. Through all poverty, all persecution, all desertion, all apparent failure, they had been true and loyal—they had shared his sorrows, had kept step with him through the dark shadows; they had ministered to his bodily necessities (John iv. 8), and (so far as they could) had sympathized with him in his spiritual conflicts. " Ye are they who have *continued with me* in my trials." And what a reward he was prepared to give them (vers. 29, 30)! Not understanding these words literally, we take it that their Lord held out before them : 1. *Fulness of joy.* "Eat and drink at my table." 2. *Signal honour.* "Sit on thrones." 3. *Large and abiding power* and influence. "I appoint unto you a kingdom." This promise has been already fulfilled, though in a different form from that which they then expected—in the exalted privilege of being the first to publish the gospel of his grace to mankind; in the glorious work of writing those memorials and letters which show no sign of age and are esteemed the one *absolutely invaluable* literature of the world; in the celestial joy, dignity, influence, which they have long inherited. (1) What are the best proofs of loyalty *we* can give? These are (*a*) showing tender sympathy and untiring helpfulness towards his people (see Matt. xxv. 40); (*b*) having continual regard to his will in all the duties and details of our life (see John xiv. 15, 21, 23); (*c*) being practically concerned for the progress of his kingdom. (2) What is the reward he will grant *us?* A goodly measure *of joy,*—of sacred joy in worship, fellowship, work, life; *of honour,*—the esteem which purity and love rarely, if ever, fail to win; *of quiet power,*—the holy and blessed influence which spiritual beauty and earnest testimony exert on heart and life, which they transmit from generation to generation. This reward *here;* and hereafter joy, honour, power, such as we must wait to see and must resolve to experience.—C.

Vers. 31, 32 (first part).—*The worth of man.* These verses afford incidental but valuable evidence of the surpassing worth of the human spirit, and should help us to feel of how much greater account are we ourselves than anything that merely belongs to us. This is brought out by—

I. The designs that are laid against us. It was evidently in a very solemn and earnest strain that Jesus said, " Satan desired to have you [plural], that he may sift," etc. The evil one longed with eagerness, and strove with strength, to pass the apostles of Christ through the sieve of temptation, that he might compass their overthrow. And Peter, at a later hour, tells us that that is his attitude and habit in regard to all Christian disciples (1 Pet. v. 8). We may take it that: 1. All the unholy intelligences of the spiritual realm are bent on securing our overthrow. 2. In this malign intention they are supported by human agents. And this, not only because evil naturally propagates evil, and because the wicked feel stronger and more secure as they are more numerous, but because they recognize the value of one human spirit and the advantage secured by gaining it to their side. Hence there is a deliberate and determined design often made upon the individual man by the forces of evil. This is a fact by no means to be overlooked. As we go on our heavenward way there may be an ambush laid for us at any point; at any time strong spiritual foes may do their utmost to contrive our fall. The possibilities of evil and of ruin are manifold. We may fall by error and unbelief, by pride, by selfishness, by worldliness and vanity, by intemperance or impurity, by departure in spirit from the fear and love of God. There is room, there is reason, for vigilance on the part of him who believes himself well on the way toward or even nearing the gates of the celestial city.

II. THE SOLICITUDE OF OUR SAVIOUR ON OUR BEHALF. "I have prayed for thee." The strain of our Lord's address, "Simon, Simon," and the fact of his interceding on Peter's behalf, speak of a tender solicitude on his part for his disciple. Jesus knew well all Peter's infirmities; but he also knew how ardently he could love, how devotedly he could serve, *how much he could be.* Hence the intensity of his desire that he would not be overcome. And for this reason we may be sure that our Lord is regarding us all with a Divine interest. He knows the worth of any and every human spirit—how much it can know and can enjoy; whom and what it can love; what graces it can illustrate, and what truth adorn; what influence it can instil; what good, and even great, work it can accomplish for God and man. He knows also what sorrow it may bring upon itself, what shame, what ruin; and also what irreparable injury it may do. We need not hesitate, but should accustom ourselves to think that Jesus Christ is regarding us with a very tender interest; is following the choices we are making and the course we are pursuing with holy and loving solicitude; is grieved when he sees us wander from the way of wisdom, rejoices in us and over us when he sees us take the upward path.

III. THE REALITY OF OUR HUMAN RESPONSIBILITY. Jesus Christ prayed that Peter's faith might not fail. And it did not—we should naturally expect. But in part *it did.* It did not utterly break down as that of Judas did, but it failed to keep him loyal in a very trying hour. It did not save him from the act of denial and from the sorrow which succeeded the sin. It did not in any way relieve the apostle of his individual responsibility. He continued to "bear his own burden," as every man must. Not the very highest privilege, not even the intercession of the Lord himself, will relieve us of that. It must rest with us, in the last resort, whether we will strive and win, or whether we will yield and be lost.—C.

Ver. 32 (latter part).—*The privilege of spiritual maturity.* "When thou art converted, strengthen thy brethren." This forward-looking injunction of Christ reminds us of—

I. OUR NEED OF STRENGTHENING POWER. Such are the manifold and effective forces opposed to us, invisible as well as visible and human (see Eph. vi. 12); so strong and so subtle are the temptations that beset us on every side; that we urgently need, not only the presence of resisting principles within us, but the aid of friendly and helpful auxiliaries around us. We want, indeed, the help which is from above; *that* is the first thing to seek. And, having besought that, we do well to avail ourselves of all the strength we can gain from other sources. For the battle is severe, and we are often hard pressed by our vigilant and relentless foes.

II. THE HELP WE CAN FIND IN MAN. God is, as stated, *the* Source of spiritual strength. He renews our strength by the direct communications of his Divine Spirit. But man helps us also. "*A man* shall be as an hiding-place . . . as rivers of water . . . as the shadow of a great rock." Paul went through the region of Galatia, "strengthening the disciples" (Acts xviii. 23). Peter was to "strengthen his brethren." We can and we should do much to strengthen one another, to build one another up on our holy faith. We can do this: 1. By the force of a beautiful and attractive example. 2. By the utterance of invigorating truth. 3. By the inspiration of a cheerful, hopeful, loving spirit.

III. THE INCOMPETENCE OF INEXPERIENCE. Peter was not in a position to afford spiritual strength then. He was too inexperienced. He had not yet learned what the fierceness of the fire of temptation meant. He did not then understand where his true strength lay. He had not yet graduated in the school of experience. It is they, and only they, who know what spiritual struggle means who can impart to others the help they need. We must have passed through the waters before we can undertake to teach others how to swim the strong stream of trial and temptation.

IV. THE UNFITNESS OF UNFAITHFULNESS. Peter was about to fall. A few hours would find him in the power of the adversary. Before another day dawned he would have to reproach himself as a disloyal disciple. He was about to rest under the shadow of great guilt, and he would have to wait until he came forth from that shadow. Not until he "was converted," not until the spirit of overweening self-confidence had given place to that of humble trust in God, not until the knowledge of Christ "after the flesh" had passed, had risen into a knowledge of him that was truly spiritual and real, —not till then would he be fitted to "strengthen his brethren." His case was strikingly parallel with that of David (see Ps. li. 11—13). We have similar experiences now. When the Christian disciple loses ground spiritually and morally, it becomes him to "return unto the Lord" himself, and "*then* to teach transgressors" the way of God; it becomes him to undergo a change of spirit, to be "renewed in the spirit of his mind," and then to speak the helpful and sustaining truth of Christ. Unfaithfulness to our Lord, departure and distance from him,—this has no teaching function; its first duty is penitential; then it may think of useful work. But we should understand that all true usefulness rests on the foundation of spiritual integrity; it can find no other footing.

V. The privilege of Christian maturity. Peter was to look forward to a not distant future. when, having learnt truth by what he suffered, he should strengthen his brethren in all that was true and wise and good. This he did, and in this he found a noble heritage. To this we may look forward as the reward of spiritual struggle, as the goal of earthly good. What better portion can we ask for than to be the source of spiritual strength to our brethren and sisters as they bear the burdens and fight the battles of their life?—C.

Vers. 33, 34 (with 55—62).—*The apostle's fall.* From this most memorable incident, recorded with noticeable candour by all the evangelists, many lessons spring.

I. How ignorant of himself even a good man may prove! (Ver. 33.) Peter believed himself to be capable of daring and enduring the very last extremity in the cause of his Master. He would have utterly ridiculed the idea that the sneer of a servant-girl could draw from him a denial of his Lord. The event showed how entirely he mistook himself. We ought to know ourselves well; but, in fact, we do not. We suppose ourselves to be strong and steadfast, when we are feeble and unreliable; or to be humble-minded, when we are proud of heart; or to be generous, when we are essentially self-seeking; or to be devout, when we are really unspiritual; to be near to God, when we are afar off (Rev. iii. 17; 1 Cor. x. 12; Ps. xix. 12, 13; cxxxix. 23, 24).

II. How perfect the knowledge our Master has of our heart and life! (Ver. 34.) Jesus knew how weak his disciple was, and he foresaw his speedy failure. He knows us altogether. He knows *our heart;* how sincere is our purpose, how frequent are our efforts, how many our disappointments, how faulty is our nature, how wounded and weak is our spirit. He knows also *our life.* He sees it as it lies before his all-beholding eye; he "knows the way we take," the path we are about to pursue. It is to One who has a thorough and complete knowledge of us that we belong, and it is to him we draw nigh in our best hours.

III. From what a height a good man may fall! This erring one is no other than the Apostle Peter, the very man who had made the great confession, and upon whom or upon whose testimony Christ would build his Church (Matt. xvi. 13—19). It is he who had been admitted to such close fellowship with Christ, and been allowed the high privilege of rendering him constant personal service. There is no office, however high it may be in the Christian Church, which will ensure to its occupant spiritual integrity. And even he who has been "raised up to heavenly places," and has known even the raptures of an exalted spiritual experience, may fall under the power of temptation. It is not the lofty but the lowly that stand on safe ground in the kingdom of God.

IV. How steep is the descent of sin! From a presumptuous and blind self-confidence Peter fell to a half-hearted following (ver. 54); from that he fell to untruthfulness and denial of his Lord (ver. 57); from that to a more deliberate and repeated denial (vers. 58, 59), accompanied even (as Matthew tells us) with profanity. Sin is a slope which seems slight at the summit, but it becomes steeper and yet steeper as we go on our downward way. And it too often happens that we reach a point where we cannot arrest ourselves, but are compelled against our own desire to continue. Shun the first step in the downward course!

V. How merciful is Christ's method of conviction! (Ver. 61.) Not a blow that smote him to the ground; not even burning words of condemnation that should sound ever afterwards in his soul; but one reproachful glance—the look of wounded love. So merciful and so pitiful is our Lord when we are unfaithful or disloyal to him now. He bears long with us; he seeks to win us back through added privilege and multiplied mercy; he deals very patiently and gently with us; only when other and milder methods fail does he mercifully afflict us, that in some way and by some means he may redeem us from folly and from ruin.

VI. WHITHER CHRIST SEEKS TO LEAD THE ERRING. (Ver. 62.) He seeks to lead us, as by his reproving glance he led his fallen disciple, to a pure and saving penitence. He would have our hearts filled with a worthy and a cleansing shame, with a purifying sorrow; that this may lead us into a condition of (1) abiding humility, of (2) living faith, of (3) thorough reconsecration to himself and to his cause.—C.

Vers. 35—38.—*Misunderstanding Christ.* There is no teacher who has been so well heard, and none that has been so much honoured and obeyed, as Jesus Christ. Yet there can have been few who have been so much misunderstood as he has been. We have our attention drawn by the text to—

I. CONTEMPORARY MISUNDERSTANDING. 1. *By the apostles themselves.* (1) On this occasion their Lord wished to intimate to them, in strong and forcible language, that to whatever perils and straits they had been exposed before, the time was now at hand when, he himself being taken from their side and the saddest foreshadowings being fulfilled, they would be subjected to far severer trials, and would be (in a sense) cast on their own defences. The apostles, mistaking his meaning, put a literal interpretation on his words, and produced a couple of swords, as perhaps meeting the emergency! (2) On a previous occasion (Matt. xvi. 5—8) the Lord warned them against "the leaven of the Pharisees;" and they supposed him to refer to their neglect in forgetting the bread! (3) They completely failed to apprehend his meaning when he foretold his own sufferings and death (ch. xviii. 31—34). 2. *By his disciples generally.* (1) They could not comprehend what he meant by "eating his flesh and drinking his blood" (John vi. 60). (2) They completely misunderstood the end he had in view, the character of that "kingdom of heaven" of which he spoke so much. (3) They did not enter into the great redeeming purpose for which he came. 3. *By his enemies.* (1) In so small a matter as his saying recorded in John ii. 19; (2) in so great a matter as that recorded in John xviii. 37.

II. SUBSEQUENT MISUNDERSTANDING. In how many ways has the Church of Christ, since apostolic days, misunderstood its Lord! It has done so in regard to the meaning of particular words; and in regard to the great end he had in view (the nature of his kingdom); and in regard to the means and methods he would have his friends employ. How pitifully and how painfully has it misunderstood him when it has interpreted his reference to the sword of the text (ver. 36), and his use of the word "*compel*" (ch. xiv. 23) as justifying every conceivable cruelty in the furtherance of his cause!

III. MODERN MISUNDERSTANDING. Judging from what we know has been, we conclude that it is likely enough that we also misunderstand our Master. 1. We may fail to reach the true significance of his words; we may find out, further on, that they have another and a larger meaning than that we have been ascribing to them. 2. We may mistake his will as to the object we should work for, or as to the right and the wise methods we should adopt to secure our end. 3. We may be wrong in our judgment of what Christ is doing with ourselves and with our life; we may misread his Divine purpose concerning us. There are three principles which we shall do well to keep in mind in our endeavour to understand the Divine Teacher. The thought of Christ is (1) profound rather than superficial: (2) spiritual rather than sensuous; (3) comprehensive and far-seeing (reaching through time to immortality) rather than narrow and time-bounded.—C.

Vers. 39—45.—*Gethsemane.* As we enter "the place which is called Gethsemane," we pass into the "holy place," the nearest of all to "the holy of holies"—that is, to Calvary itself. Thither our Lord went on this most memorable evening; and "his disciples followed him"—the eleven who remained faithful to him. But even of these only three were counted worthy to attend him into the secret place of prayer and struggle, and to witness his agony. Such sorrow as he was then to know seeks the secret place and chooses only the very closest and dearest friendship for its ministry. Then fell upon our Divine Lord a sorrow and a temptation; an agitation and agony of soul for which our language has no name, our heart no room, our life no experience. We ask—What *was* that intolerable and overwhelming anguish, which the Saviour asked might pass from him, and which had so marvellous and so terribly significant an effect on his bodily nature (vers. 42—44)? Our completest answer leaves much to be said, much to be explained. 1. We barely touch the outer line of the whole circle of truth when we speak of the *apprehension of coming torture and death* as events in the natural, physical sphere. It is an irreverent and wholly unworthy conception that what many men—many who have not even been good men —have faced without flinching, our Lord and Master shrank from with an over-mastering dread. 2. We come nearer to the centre of the truth when we think that the *whole shadow of the cross,* with its spiritual darkness and desolation, then began to rest upon him. Something of that shadow had been darkening his path before (Mark x. 38; ch. xii. 50; John xii. 27). And this shadow darkened and deepened as he drew near to the dread hour itself. At this point the cross immediately confronted him in all its awful severity, and he knew that this was the time when he must finally resolve to endure everything or to retrace his steps. This, then, was the critical hour; then was "the crisis of the world." Great and terrible was the temptation to decline the fearful future now at hand; it was a temptation he struggled against with a spiritual violence that showed itself in the drops of blood; it was a temptation he only overcame by tearful supplications to the Eternal Father for his prevailing succour (Heb. v. 7). 3. But we miss our true mark if we do not include the thought that he was then bearing *something of the burden of human sin.* Whatever was intended by "bearing our sins in his own body," by "making his soul an offering for sin," and by expressions similar to these, we believe that Jesus Christ was then in the very act of fulfilling these predictions when he thus strove and suffered in the garden. As we look upon him there we see "the Lamb of God taking away the sin of the world." The scene may teach us very varied lessons and affect us in many ways; but it is certainly well fitted to be—

I. AN ATTRACTION TO SOULS STILL DISTANT FROM THE SAVIOUR. It says, "Behold how he loved you!"

II. AN INVITATION TO PRAYER FOR FAITHFULNESS IN THE HOUR OF TRIAL. Both before and after, the Master exhorted his disciples to pray that "they entered not into temptation" (vers. 40, 46). He himself triumphed through the strong efficacy of prayer (ver. 41). Prayer, appropriate at all times, is urgently needed as we enter the shadow of temptation; but it is positively indispensable when the greater trials of our life assail us.

III. A SUMMONS TO STRENUOUS AND UNFALTERING PERSEVERANCE. Christian pilgrim, Christian workman, do you weary of your way or of your work? Does the one seem long and thorny, or the other tedious and unsuccessful? Do you think you must sleep as the disciples did, or that you must put down the cup as their Master did not? Do you talk about giving up the journey, about retiring from the field? Consider him who went quite through the work the Father gave him to do, who strove and suffered to the very last; consider him, the agonizing but undaunted, the suffering but resolving Saviour; consider him, lest ye be wearied and faint in your minds.

> "Go, labour on, spend and be spent,
> Thy joy to do the Father's will;
> It is the way the Master went,
> Should not the servant tread it still?"

C.

Ver. 42 (latter part).—*Self-surrender.* "Not my will, but thine, be done." These words are suggestive as well as expressive. They suggest to us—

I. THE ESSENTIAL NATURE OF SIN. Where shall we find the root of sin? Its manifold fruits we see around us in all forms of irreligion, of vice, of violence. But in what shall we find its root? In *the preference of our own will to the will of God.* If we trace human wrong-doing and wrong-being to its ultimate point, we arrive at that conclusion. It is because men are not willing to be what God created them to be, not willing to do what he desires them to do; it is because they want to pursue those lines of thought and of action which he has forbidden, and to find their pleasure and their portion in things which he has disallowed,—that they err from the strait path and begin the course which ends in condemnation and in death. The essence of all sin is in this assertion of our will against the will of God. We fail to recognize the foundation truth that we are his; that by every sacred tie that can bind one being to another we are bound, and we belong to him from whom we came and in whom we live, and move, and have our being. We assume to be the masters of our own lives and fortunes, the directors of our own selves, of our own will; we say, "My will, not thine, be done." Thus are we radically wrong; and being radically wrong, the issues of our hearts are evil. From this fountain of error and of evil the streams of sin are flowing; to that we trace their origin.

II. THE HOUR AND ACT OF SPIRITUAL SURRENDER. When does the human spirit return to God, and by what act? That hour and that act, we reply, are not found at the time of any *intellectual apprehension* of the truth. A man may understand but little of Christian doctrine, and yet may be within the kingdom of heaven; or, on the other hand, he may know much, and yet remain outside that kingdom. Nor at the time of *keen sensibility*; for it is possible to be moved to deep and to fervent feeling, and yet to withhold the heart and life from the Supreme. Nor at the time of *association with the visible Church of Christ*. It is the hour at which and the act by which the soul *cordially surrenders itself* to God. When, in recognition of the paramount claims of God the Divine Father, the gracious Saviour of mankind, we yield ourselves to God, that for all the future he may lead and guide us, may employ us in his holy service; when we have it in our heart to say, "Henceforth thy will, not ours, be done;"—then do we return unto the Lord our God, and then does he count us among the number of his own.

III. THE HIGHEST ATTAINMENT OF CHRISTIAN ENDEAVOUR. When do we reach our highest point? Not when we have fought our fiercest battle, or have done our most fruitful work, or have gained our clearest and brightest vision of Divine truth; but when we have reached the point in which we can most *cheerfully* and most *habitually* say, after Christ our Lord, "Not my will, but thine, be done;" when under serious discouragement or even sad defeat, when after exhausting pain or before terrible suffering, when under heavy loss or in long-continued loneliness, or in prospect of early death, we are perfectly willing that God should do with us as his own wisdom and love direct.—C.

Vers. 47—52, 63.—*Christianity and violence.* The use of the sword by Peter, and the presence of "swords and staves" in the hands of the officers, suggest to us the connection between Jesus Christ (and his disciples) and the employment of violence; and this both by them and against them.

I. THE UNSEEMLINESS OF VIOLENCE USED AGAINST JESUS CHRIST AND HIS DISCIPLES. It is true that there was something worse than the weapons of violence in that garden; the traitor's kiss was very much worse. We may be sure that Jesus was conscious of a far keener wound from those false lips of Judas than he would have been from the hands of those armed men had they struck him with their strength. The subtle schemes and the soft but treacherous suggestions of false friends are deadlier in their issue, if not in their aim, than the hard blows of open adversaries. But: 1. How unseemly was open violence shown *to Jesus Christ!* To come with sword and stick against the Gentle One from heaven; against him who never used his omnipotence to harm a single adversary; against him who "would not break the bruised reed" among the children of men; against him who had been daily employing his power to relieve from pain, to raise from weakness, to remove privation, to restore from death! 2. How unseemly is such violence shown to *Christ's true disciples!* His true disciples, those who are loyal and obedient to their Lord, are men and women in whom a patient and loving spirit is prevailing; they are peace-makers among their brothers and sisters; they have "put away bitterness, wrath, anger, clamour, railing;" they walk in love; they seek to win by a gentle manifestation and by a gracious utterance of the truth. How entirely inappropriate and unseemly is violence shown to them! And it may be added, how *useless* is such violence employed against the cause they advocate! It has never happened yet that sword and stave have crushed the living truth. They have smitten its champions to the ground, but they have only brought out into the light the heroic courage and noble unselfishness which that truth inspires. "So that those things [those persecutions] have fallen out rather unto the furtherance of the gospel." Cruelty strikes at its enemy, and smites itself.

II. THE UNLAWFULNESS OF VIOLENCE EMPLOYED ON BEHALF OF CHRISTIANITY. How vain and how foolish the act of "smiting with the sword" (ver. 49)! It was an act of intemperate and ill-considered zeal; it was calculated to do much more harm than good. Its effects had to be undone by the calm interposition and the healing power of Christ (ver. 51). It was rebuked by the Master in decided terms (Matt. xxvi. 52). And from that hour to the end of apostolic history the use of physical violence disappears. Well would it have been for the cause and kingdom of our Lord if it had never been revived. The sword and the stave have no place in the Christian armoury. The weapons of its warfare are not carnal. Such instruments do not, they cannot, serve it; they gain a momentary victory at the sad and great expense of entirely misrepresenting the spirit and the method of Jesus Christ. Compulsion is utterly out of place in connection with the Church of Christ; it loses immeasurably more than it gains by that resource. Let the disciples of Christ be assured that (1) the utterance of Divine truth, especially the truth that relates to the redeeming love of the Saviour himself; (2) living a life of blamelessness and beauty, of integrity and kindness; (3) dependence on the aid of the Divine Spirit to make the spoken Word and the living influence effectual and mighty;—that these are the weapons which will conquer the enemies of Christ, and will place him upon the throne of the world.—C.

Ver. 53.—*The power of spiritual darkness.* As our Lord, declining to avail himself of the physical forces at his command, surrendered himself to the will of his assailants, he used an expression which was full of spiritual significance. "This is your hour," he said, "and the power of darkness." By this he intimated (1) that the hour of his enemies' triumph had arrived—the brief hour of their outward success and inward exultation, the dark hour of his humiliation and visible defeat; and (2) that this passing hour was simultaneous with the prevalence of the power of darkness. Wicked men were to triumph because the forces of guilty error were for the time prevailing. We look at—

I. THE POWER OF DARKNESS. 1. *Its spiritual nature.* It is a state of spiritual blindness. We may not, with a great Greek philosopher, resolve all evil into error; but we may say that sin is continually, is universally, springing from inward blindness. Men do not see the truth; they call good evil, and evil good; they have the most false imaginations concerning all objects, from the Divine Being himself to the lowliest human duty; and hence they go far astray. 2. *Its most glaring manifestations.* It lays its unholy hand on innocence, on Divine Love itself, and leads it away to trial and crucifixion. It conducts the devoted servant of Christ to the brutal judge, to the shameful scaffold, to the devouring flame. It arms a vast multitude of men and leads them forth to a vain and useless strife, shedding human blood and wasting human labour, as if Christ would be pleased or could be served by such means as these. It covers with the sacred name of religion a system that holds millions of human beings in a degrading bondage. It sanctions all the sinful institutions the world has seen and suffered from. 3. *Its most deplorable effects.* These are not found in the deeds and the sufferings of men, but rather in their souls; the worst issue of spiritual misconception is in the utter darkness of spirit in which it ends. "If the light that is in us be darkness, how great must that darkness be!" It means: (1) *False thoughts.* Here were men who should have known better thinking the worst things of Jesus Christ—judging him to be a criminal, to be a traitor, to be a blasphemer; and there are men amongst us who, under the power of error, think altogether wrong thoughts of God and of the Saviour—thoughts which do him wrong, which misrepresent him to the mind, which repel rather than attract the soul. (2) *Bad feelings.* Here were men indulging in feelings of positive and perfect hatred against Jesus Christ; and there are men, misled by the power of darkness, hating instead of loving the Father of spirits, repelled from instead of being drawn towards good and true souls whom they have grievously misunderstood. (3) *Wrong purposes of heart.* Under this malignant influence men are purposing to injure their fellow-men. Instead of resolving to rescue, to raise, to ennoble them, they determine to put them down or to hold them down, to lay a hard hand upon them and keep them harmless because helpless. It is in the blinding, misleading, deteriorating effects upon the soul itself that the very worst results of darkness are to be seen.

II. OUR HOPE CONCERNING IT. The "power of darkness" was coincident with "the hour" of the enemies of our Lord. And that was *but an hour*; it was limited to the brief period of the Passion. Then came Christ's glorious hour—the hour of his resurrection; the hour of his ascent to the right hand of Power. The prevalence of this evil power of darkness is limited in time; it will not last for ever. Innocence, purity, truth, love, righteousness, may be led away to trial and death, as they were then in the Person of Jesus Christ; but the hour of their resurrection and their triumph will arrive. Let *faithful labour* do its noble part, and let calm and Christian *patience* bring its priceless contribution, and another hour will strike than that of the foes of Christ, and another power than that of moral darkness will take the sceptre and rule the world.—C.

Ver. 54.—*Distant discipleship.* "Peter followed afar off." 1. In this we find something that was *commendable.* The impulsive and energetic Peter did not exhaust his zeal in that unfortunate sword-stroke of his; nor was it quenched by the rebuke of his Master. Though it was far from an ideal discipleship to "follow afar off," it *was* discipleship still. We do not read that the others did as much as that; they probably sought their own safety by complete retirement. Peter could not do that; his attachment to Christ did not allow him to disconnect himself any further than was involved in a *distant* following. But: 2. In this we find something that was incomplete. The disciple desired to be near enough to his Master to know what the end would be, but he wished to be far enough off to be secure from molestation. He took counsel of his fears, and was so far from the scene that he was showing no sympathy with his Friend, and was running no risk from his enemies. It is not at all unlikely that this timidity, from which he succeeded in partially and momentarily shaking himself, was the beginning and the explanation of his subsequent failure.

I. GENUINE DISCIPLESHIP. This is found in *following Christ.* 1. Owning his claim as Lord and Leader of the soul; owning it by a willing and entire submission of our will to his will, a consecration of our life to his service, a perfect readiness of heart to say, "Lord, I will follow thee." 2. Endeavouring to walk even as he walked—in *reverence*, in *righteousness*, in *love.* 3. Striving to live this Christian life not only *after* him, but *unto* him.

II. DISTANT DISCIPLESHIP. We follow "afar off" when we are: 1. *Lacking in devotion.* He who is only found irregularly and infrequently with God, in the attitude of praise and prayer, and in the act of studying his holy will, must be at a great distance from that "beloved Son" who spent so much time with his Father, and found so much strength in his conscious presence and loving sympathy. 2. *Wanting in purity.* He whose spirit is much entangled with the cares, absorbed in the pursuits and prizes, hungering and thirsting for the pleasures of this world, and certainly he whose soul is to any considerable degree affected and tainted by the lower temptations of the flesh,—is a long way behind the holy Saviour; is far off from him who was "holy, harmless, undefiled, separate from sin," from him "in whose mouth *no* guile was found." 3. *Failing in generous and practical kindness.* He who is only sparingly offering his resources, spiritual or material, to the cause of human comfort and elevation, who is drawing the line of his service at the point of self-sacrifice, and declines to go across it,—is surely a very distant follower of that gracious and generous Friend of man who suffered the very last and the very worst that he might redeem us from sin and restore us to truth, to holiness, to God. This distant discipleship is, in every aspect, to be deplored. (1) It is *unfaithfulness to ourselves.* A departure from the position we took when we first "yielded ourselves unto God, as those alive from the dead." (2) It is *perilous to our own souls.* *That* way failure lies; and failure here means utter and disastrous defeat; it means suffering and shame; it may even mean death. (3) It is *disappointing to our Divine Lord.* He looks for a close following on our part; he wants us to be at his side, to be serving him with all our strength, to be like him in spirit and in character and in life. And when he sees us "afar off," he is grieved with us instead of rejoicing in us. (1) Let those who have been abiding in him, and therefore following him closely, be watchful and prayerful that they do not "drift away" and lag behind; (2) and let those who have to reproach themselves as distant disciples draw near to their Lord in renewed penitence and devotedness of spirit.—C.

Ver. 61.—*The look of our Lord.* "And the Lord turned, and looked upon Peter." What was there then, and what is there now, in the glance of Jesus Christ?

I. HIS LOOK OF PENETRATION. We read of one of the earliest disciples being convinced by our Lord's discernment of him under the thick foliage of the fig tree; he was then told to look for greater things than that (John i. 50). And surely one of those greater things was found in that penetration which saw through the thicker covering of the human flesh and of human speech and demeanour to the very thought of the mind, to the very desire of the heart, to the inmost secrets of the soul. He knew what was *in man.* It was his knowledge of men that directed him in his varying treatment of them; it *is* his penetrating insight into men now that determines his dealing with us all.

II. HIS LOOK OF COMPASSION. What did the sick and the suffering, the fevered and the paralyzed and the leprous, the men and women who had left afflicted ones behind them at their homes—what depths of tender compassion did these sons and daughters of Israel see in the eyes of Jesus Christ? And what inexhaustible fulness of pity, what unbounded sympathy, may not the stricken and the sorrowing souls who are badly bruised and wounded on life's highway still find in "the face of Jesus Christ"!

III. HIS LOOK OF SAD REPROACH. Sometimes there was that in the glance of Jesus Christ from which the guilty shrank. When "he looked round about on them with anger," we may be sure that his baffled enemies quailed before his glance. And when "the Lord turned, and looked upon Peter," what keen sorrowful reproach was then apparent in the face of Jesus Christ! how that look gathered up all possible words and tones of solemn expostulation, of sad disappointment, of bitter sorrow! It was a look which wrought great things in the apostle's soul, the remembrance of which, we may be sure, he carried with him to the end. Christ has all too many occasions now to turn toward us that reproachful glance. 1. When we fail to keep the promises we made him at the time of our self-surrender. 2. When we fail to pay the vows we made him in some hour of discipline. 3. When we fall seriously short of the allegiance which all his disciples owe to him—in reverence, in obedience, in submission. Let us, who are professing to follow him, ask ourselves what we should see in his countenance if we stood face to face with him to-day. Would it be the benign look of Divine commendation? or would it be the pained look of sorrowful reproach? To those who are inquiring their way to life it is a source of blessed encouragement that they will see, if they regard their Lord—

IV. HIS LOOK OF TENDER INTEREST. When the rich young man came and made his earnest inquiry of the great Teacher, he was not yet in the kingdom, and was not yet fully prepared to enter it; but he was a sincere and earnest seeker after God, and "Jesus, beholding him, loved him" (Mark x. 21). With such tender regard, with such loving interest, does he look down on every true suppliant who looks up to him with the vital question on his lips, "Good Master, what shall I do that I may inherit eternal life?"—C.

Vers. 63, 64.—*The patience of Christ.* In these touching words, which we cannot read without a sentiment of shame as members of the human race, we have—

I. A PICTURE OF SUPREME ENDURANCE. How much our Lord was called upon to endure, we shall be best able to realize when we consider: 1. The greatness of which he was conscious (see ver. 70). He knew and felt that he had a right to the most reverent homage of the best and highest, and was thus treated by the worst and lowest. 2. The power which he knew he wielded: with what perfect ease could he have extricated himself from these cruel insults! 3. The character of the men who were maltreating him—the lowest amongst the low. 4. The nature of the indignities to which they subjected him; these went from bad to worse—from binding him to beating him, from beating him to spitting upon him, from this most shameful indignity to the yet more cruel sneer at his holy mission, "Prophesy unto us," etc. They vented upon him the very last extremes of human contumely and shame.

II. A PICTURE OF SUBLIME PATIENCE. He bore it all with perfect calmness. Here shone forth in its full lustre "the meekness of Jesus Christ." "When he was reviled, he reviled not again; when he suffered, he threatened not;" "As a sheep before her shearers," etc. And wherein shall we find the source and explanation of this sublime patience? 1. He was bent on bearing, to the full and to the end, his Father's will. 2. He was determined to complete the work he had undertaken, and of that work those sufferings were a part. He was then "wounded for our trangressions," then was he "bruised for our iniquities," and by *those* "stripes were we healed."

APPLICATION. 1. Like our Divine Master, *we are called upon to endure.* In doing those things we believe to be right of which others do not feel the obligation, also in abstaining from those things we feel to be wrong, which other people allow, we come into conflict, we excite displeasure, we incur odium, we suffer censure, opposition, ridicule; we "bear his reproach." Thorough loyalty to our Lord and to our own convictions means exposure to the assaults and indignities of the world. 2. We have *the highest incentives to endure.* (1) As with our Master, it is *the Father's will* that we should suffer. (2) As with Christ, it is an important part of the testimony we are to bear and the work we are to do in this world. (3) Only thus can we completely follow our great Leader; he who does not go with Christ into the valley of humiliation does not follow him all the way he trod. (4) So doing, we are building up a strong Christian character, and are thus preparing for fuller and higher service. (5) Then are we especially pleasing our Master, and "great is our reward in heaven" (Matt. v. 10—12).—C.

Vers. 1—23.—*The last Passover of our Lord.* After the significant survey of Jerusalem's fate which is given in the previous chapter, Jesus seems to have remained quietly at Bethany, or in the Mount of Olives, until the time for the Passover. The season of solitude was brief, but all the more important in consequence. Every moment was utilized by our Lord that he might be ready for his great ordeal. But if he was making preparations, so were his enemies. Accordingly, we have an account here of the treason which led up to his sacrifice. We have, consequently, to consider—

I. THE TREASON OF JUDAS. (Vers. 1—6.) The Sanhedrin was in session, anxious to seize on Jesus and get him removed; for they feared that an attached populace would declare for him rather than for the old leaders. It was a vain fear. The people were fickle, and as ready to cry out for his crucifixion as they had been to cry "Hosanna!" Yet the fear of losing popularity goaded the Church leaders to desperation. Being beaten in debate by the Master-Mind who tabernacled among them, they can only expect by treachery to secure their purpose. They find their ready instrument in Judas. And here consider: 1. *The worldliness of Judas.* He had evidently joined the cause of Jesus in hope of a place in a world-kingdom. But our Lord's prophecies of his speedy suffering and death have blighted all these hopes. How can he best make his peace with the world, which is getting the upper hand, and before which Jesus is going down? Judas believes that he can best do this by betraying Jesus to his enemies, and, to make the transition the easier for himself, he consents to do the shameful work for thirty pieces of silver—the mean price of the life of a slave! It was not covetousness pure and simple which led Judas to such a bargain, but astute worldliness. He was making his peace with the world on the most liberal terms. 2. Notice *the Satanic inspiration under which Judas acted.* It is evident that Scripture represents the sphere of evil as under the domination of a great personality called Satan. He can enter into men and take possession of them. But we are not to suppose that he has the same intimate access to the human spirit which God the Holy Ghost enjoys. We have reason to believe that Satan moves men by presenting in all their attractiveness the worldly motives such as we have noticed. Further, the Satanic impulse is such as in no way to relieve the subject of it from responsibility. No one will be able to plead "not guilty" on the ground of Satanic temptation. 3. Notice *the mean prudence under which the traitor acted.* Had the band come in open day, when the entranced populace hung upon the lips of Jesus, there would have been a dangerous *émeute*, and life been lost. Accordingly, Judas seeks to betray Jesus "in the absence of the multitude." There is a meanness and cowardice about most of the diabolic wickedness which goes on in the world; a cowardice, moreover, which is generally overtaken by just and terrible retribution.

II. PREPARATIONS FOR THE LAST PASSOVER. (Vers. 7—13.) Jesus meanwhile directs the two disciples, Peter and John, to make ready the Passover. He so times the celebration as to have it over on the Thursday night of the Passover week, and without haste, to secure the further preparation which his spirit required. And here we have the facts set before us (1) that he owed accommodation to the consideration of a stranger; and (2) that his supernatural knowledge guided the disciples in their quest of a guest-chamber. There, then, in the guest-chamber of a stranger, without taking the lamb to the temple, but in the primitive fashion, the two faithful men made ready for their Master. It was a recurrence to the primitive ritual.

III. THE PASSOVER FEAST. (Vers. 14—18.) With the twelve accordingly he comes at the appointed hour, and sits down to the significant feast. He tells them with what desire he had contemplated this last Passover before he should suffer. He will not again eat of it till it is fulfilled in the kingdom of God. The order of celebration was first the passing round of the wine-cup; next, the bitter herbs, dipped, as salad would be, in a red sauce made of almonds, nuts, figs, and other fruits; next, another wine-cup, after which the father of the family explained the nature of the rite; then came the morsel of unleavened bread and the piece of the roast lamb, made palatable by the aforesaid sauce; the last act was the passing round of a third wine-cup (cf. Godet, *in loc.*). It must have been a touching and tender type in the eyes of him who was so soon to be offered. We should have listened to his explanations on that occasion with peculiar interest. His references must have been somewhat veiled in presence of the betrayer, yet sufficiently explicit to have broken ordinary hearts. It was a marvellous feast—the Paschal Lamb himself partaking of the Passover; the Antitype experiencing a special benefit through the study of the type! What a solemnity, moreover, is thrown over the whole scene through his indication that it is all shortly to be fulfilled!

IV. THE INSTITUTION OF THE LORD'S SUPPER. (Vers. 19, 20.) Upon the more formidable feast, which is to pass away on fulfilment, Jesus founds a simpler feast, to be celebrated till he comes again. It is to consist of bread and wine, two of the elements there at the table. The bread is to represent his body, which is to be broken for his people; and the wine his blood, which is for them to be shed. In this way a memorial more lasting than brass or marble is to be reared, and his gracious presence is to be experienced in the Christian Church. The new institution was a promise of the most gracious kind, regarding the season when he would be absent from them.

V. THE INTIMATION OF THE BETRAYAL. (Vers. 21—23.) Along with the solemn joy there is dashed profoundest sorrow at the intimation of betrayal by one of the apostolic band. A traitor is there, and they should know it. Good sign in that each man suspects himself! They all, except Judas, ask Christ if it is he. Last of all, it would seem, came the inquiry of the real traitor. But this unearthing of the false one does not shake him from his foul purpose. Christ could not do more for him than he here does, even though it does not save him. How salutary is self-suspicion! How dangerous self-confidence!—R. M. E.

Vers. 24—38.—*The proper Christian spirit.* Through our Lord's faithful dealing the disciples had been led to wholesome self-suspicion. They cried out at the possibility of a betrayal of the Master, "Lord, is it I?" But no sooner have their minds been relieved through the singling out of Judas than they swing round again to self-confidence and even base ambition. There, at the table of the Lord, in spite of the hallowed associations, they speculate who is to be greatest in the coming kingdom. Jesus has consequently to check this nascent ambition. He does so by ennobling—

I. THE SPIRIT OF SERVICE. (Vers. 24—27.) Now, the world's idea is that it is noble to exercise authority, to be able to order people about. In fact, the world has come to call men "benefactors" who have done nothing but command other people. What tributes are paid to princes, who have done nothing all their lives but issue orders and receive the homage and service of other people! A blear-eyed world is ready, as Christ here shows, to pronounce such princes the benefactors of their age and country. But he has come into the world to *ennoble the opposite idea.* Here at this very feast he has been as one that serveth. His whole life, moreover, has been a public service. Everywhere he has just considered how he could serve others. To minister, not be ministered unto, was his continual care. To make the service of others glorious in the eyes of discerning men was one great purpose of his earthly life. This reveals also the very spirit of the Divine life.[1] God is Lord of all because Servant of all. He sustains all, as he has created all; and his greatness is the greatness of ministration. It is only Oriental barbarism which supposes greatness to consist in indolent and luxuriant state. Here, then, is the field of genuine ambition. Let us try to be *first in the field of service*; let us do our best and most for the benefit of all about us; and then alone shall we become noble and Christ-like.

II. CHRIST INDICATES THE RESULTANT INFLUENCE. (Vers. 28—30.) To these disciples, who continue with Christ in his temptations, he appoints a kingdom. In this kingdom they are to have thrones, and to be judges of the twelve tribes of Israel. In this way our Lord indicates the influence which these men, who entertain his spirit of service, will acquire. And when we consider the history of Christianity, we see that even in the world of humanity these humble servants of God and mankind have become kings and judges. It is by their deliverances in the primitive age that men are judging themselves and being judged. The apostles are pre-eminently the *sovereigns of this new and better time.* And this posthumous influence on earth is only a faint reflection of their influence in heaven. Now, is not this to encourage every serviceable soul? Let each of us be only content to serve, to do whatever a brother needs, and by our service we acquire influence and kingship. The world is really ruled by obliging, serviceable, meek, and earnest men.

III. CHRIST NEXT POINTS OUT TO PETER HIS DANGER, RECOVERY, AND CONSEQUENT USEFULNESS. (Vers. 31—34.) For, strange to say, temptation is overruled as well as service to the creation of influence. There is in Peter's nature a good deal of pride and vain-glory to be winnowed out. There is wheat within him, but also chaff. Now, Satan had set his mind upon the fall of Peter; but Jesus has already prayed for him that his faith may not fail. Here was Peter's safeguard in the timely intercession of his Master.[2] How watchful the Lord was and is for souls! Oh, how our want of watchfulness stands rebuked! Yet Peter was permitted to fall under temptation; but he was won back again, converted the second time, so to speak, by the loving look of Jesus; and thus destined to become a strengthener of the brethren. So that our Lord's prayers for us may be that, through permitted humiliations and tears and penitence, we may pass on to power. It is only when self-confidence, as in Peter's case, has been purged out of us by humiliating discoveries of our personal weakness, that we are in a position to undertake the care and strengthening of brethren. Broken-hearted Simon becomes, after Pentecost, the reliable Rock-man, worthy of the new name, Peter.

IV. THE CONTRASTED POLICIES OF CONFIDENCE AND OF PRUDENCE. (Vers. 35—38.) In sending the disciples out on their first missions, Jesus relied on the hospitality of the people as a fitting support for his agents. Going to the people as philanthropists, working miracles, preaching the advent of Messiah, they would meet with such support as would be all-sufficient. This was the policy of confidence—the reliance on the people for entire support. But when the world turned against Christ, and realized how opposed he was to its worldliness, then the disciples would require to exercise all possible prudence. They would require to look out for themselves, and even to fight for their own hand. That is to say, there are times when we may trust the world, and times when we are warranted in distrusting it. When is it, we are inclined to ask, that the prudential temper must take the place of confidence? When the world is determined on injustice. Thus at this time the world is about to reckon Christ among the transgressors, and to do him manifest injustice. The *fit of unfairness* was upon it, and the disciples should then stand in self-defence. But other days would dawn again, when disciples will be warranted in pursuing a policy of public confidence, and thus giving the world the chance of compensation. Let us wisely consider the "signs of the times," and act accordingly. Christ will guide us to the policy which is best, if we prayerfully ask him.—R. M. E.

[1] Cf. Dr. Dykes's noble sermon on ver. 27: 'Sermons,' p. 291.
[2] Cf. Vinet's 'Nouvelles Etudes Evangeliques,' p. 238; also Woolsey's 'Religion of the Present and the Future,' p. 186; and Dykes's 'Sermons,' p. 263.

Vers. 39—53.—*Gethsemane.* After the Passover and the address given in John xiv., he led the disciples out through the vineyards, where most likely John xv. was delivered to them, and John xvi., until he reached his usual rendezvous in Gethsemane, part of the Mount of Olives. Here let us suppose the high-priestly prayer given in John xvii. took place, which being ended, he retired to an adjacent and secluded place for further prayer. Gethsemane was thus his preparation for suffering and death, as the Transfiguration had been for work. And here we have to notice—

I. His dread of the denouément was not a dread of physical pain and death. His cry for escape, if possible, was not prompted by physical fear. He always showed himself brave before danger of a mere physical kind. Socrates seems the braver man before he drank the hemlock, but this was because Socrates could not see the issues that were before him as Christ foresaw his fate. The cup he shrank from was not like that of Socrates. It was no literal cup, but the apprehension of isolation from his Father. Not the trial, nor the mockery, nor the physical pain, but the isolation from God, the sense of forsakenness, the constraint to cry, "My God, my God, why hast thou forsaken me?" which prompted the cry to escape. Now, the very elevation of his being rendered the dread of separation even for the shortest season from his Father intensely painful. Vulgar souls can take separation from others quietly, but the elect souls pass through deepest pains in consequence. That darkness which came on when Son was separated from Father because of the sin-bearing was what Jesus dreaded, and would gladly have escaped. Want of fellowship with the Father seemed to this holy Child Jesus something to be escaped if at all possible.

II. The intensity and efficacy of his prayer. Just as Jacob had to wrestle at Peniel to obtain the blessing, so had the Saviour in the garden. He was in an agony of earnestness, and was in consequence bathed in a bloody sweat. Time after time he prayed thus earnestly. And we are expressly told, "He was heard in that he feared" (Heb. v. 7). His prayer was efficacious. Now, let us consider what he prayed for. It was for deliverance from isolation from God—deliverance from death without a sense of the Divine fellowship. And when we consider the sequel, we find that he was heard, and his prayer answered. For (1) he enjoyed an *angelic visit* and was strengthened by it (ver. 43); (2) he was granted *light and fellowship with the Father before death* supervened; and (3) he was saved from death by *resurrection.* In these ways the Father undoubtedly heard and answered the cry of Christ in Gethsemane.

III. Notice the disciples' sleep of sorrow. For sorrow often induces sleep, while at other times it makes sleep impossible. In the present case the disciples ought to have been praying for Jesus, for themselves, seeking preparation for the trial he had forewarned them was at hand. Instead of doing so they slept. Here we have to notice: 1. *Opportunity for showing spiritual sympathy was missed.* Jesus, as we know, was most anxious they should watch with him. He needed and he sought their sympathy; but they, in thoughtlessness, denied it to him. It would be well if deepest consideration were exhibited for noble souls that are greatly tried. 2. *Opportunity for private preparation was missed.* They themselves needed spiritual help more than Christ. They could less afford than he to meet the crisis prayerlessly. Yet this was their condition when the trial fell upon them. 3. *Physical effort was their only resource when the crisis came.* They could lay on with the sword. It does not take much prayer to help men to fight. But other and better weapons were needed than Peter's sword, but they could only be taken out of the armoury by prayer.

IV. The betrayal. Judas and his band were upon them before the sleepy disciples had time to pray. He had planned the capture as only a coward can. He betrays Christ with the semblance of friendship, trying to give the Master the usual kiss. To this offer Jesus simply replies, "Judas, betrayest thou the Son of man with a kiss?" Force behind deceit is apparently overpowering the spirituality which had its home in that place of prayer.

V. The defence of the disciples and the miracle of the Master. The disciples, spiritually off guard, betake themselves to the carnal weapon, and Peter lays round him with the sword. He succeeds in cutting off the right ear of the high priest's servant. Here is fresh trouble created. If this servant has to go back thus wounded, a warrant will soon be out for the disciples, and the whole issue thrown into perplexity. Our Lord accordingly interposes, heals the sufferer's ear, and advises Peter to put up his sword. In this way Jesus rescues the disciples from the liability incurred through their own imprudence. It was a wonderful consideration manifested when his own troubles were rising to their height.

VI. THE REBUKE ADMINISTERED TO HIS ENEMIES. Why had they come out against him as against a thief? Had he not confronted them time after time in open day? They had not dared to lay hands upon him then. He thus convicted them of cowardice. It was "their hour, and the power of darkness." A deed of darkness dare not be done in open day. Thus was it that our Lord bravely met his adversaries. He was prepared, though the disciples were not.—R. M. E.

Vers. 54—71.—*Christ's trials in the high priest's palace.* The agony of Gethsemane is over, and our Lord has met his enemies in the calmness of real courage. He allows himself to be led to the palace of the high priest, and we have now to consider all the trials through which he passed there. The first of these is from Peter. Love to the Master keeps the disciple in the train of the procession, and even leads him to linger without until through John's good offices he gets into the hall. But, alas! instead of keeping near the Master, he lingers near the fire which was kindled in the hall to keep the cold at bay. And here let us notice—

I. PETER'S TEMPTATION. (Vers. 54—60.) It was identification with a lost cause. Here is Jesus down; no hope apparently lingers about him; he cannot now be saved. What use is there in further identifying himself with Jesus? Instead of responding boldly to the challenge and confessing Christ, he is tempted to deny him. And the denials are repeated, the last time with an oath. Peter's distant view of his Master and of his cause leads him to the fatal conclusion that it is safest to cut the connection and deny that he has ever known him. It is, alas! the temptation of men still. In the blazing light of society, when worldliness seems so strong and comfortable, it is convenient to ignore the Master and his cause. Peter's temptation is constantly repeated, and his fall has its counterpart continually in the cowardice of souls.

II. PETER'S RECOVERY AND REPENTANCE. (Vers. 61, 62.) The Master in warning him had given him a sign, that of the cock-crow. It acts as an alarum upon the dull ear of Peter. Along with this there comes the look ineffable of the loving Lord. The great heart is broken, and Peter passes out to weep bitterly. We have a great contrast between the sorrow of Peter and that of Judas. It is the sorrow of the world which worketh death in the one case; it is the sorrow which is godly and saving in the other. As Gerok, in an admirable discourse upon the subject, says, (1) *Peter's sorrow proceeds upon his sin,* Judas's upon the *consequences of his sin;* (2) Peter's sorrow turns him *from* the world, Judas's turns him *towards* the world; and (3) Peter's sorrow leads him *to life,* Judas's leads him *to death.*[1] Peter's repentance was thus the consequence of his Master's love, and the sign of his recovery. How sensible he must have been of the mighty wrong he had done the Master! Jesus knew when Peter slunk away out of the palace that he was safe in his bitter sorrow, and that he would come forth from it a better man. Our Lord's trial through Peter's faithlessness terminated when the disciple's heart was broken.

III. THE BUFFET-GAME. (Vers. 63—65.) The heavy hours till morning must be spent, and so the soldiers determine to get some amusement out of their notable Prisoner. They make Jesus, consequently, the centre in what is now known as the buffet-game. Blindfolding him, they proceed to strike him, and call upon him to tell who has inflicted the blows. They are terrible liberties they thus take with the Son of God. But they are unable to irritate this meek and lowly Man. Their blows are lost upon his magnificent meekness. They must have been struck at the majestic carriage of the Prisoner under their brutal horse-play. Yet the blows of the soldiers were less a trial, we may be sure, than the faithlessness of the disciple. But we are surely taught how essentially degrading it is to manufacture mirth out of the humiliation of others! The soldiers never were so *brutal* as when they treated Jesus in the style they did.

IV. HIS TRIAL BEFORE THE SANHEDRIN. (Vers. 66—71.) In the morning the Jewish authorities assembled, and their line of examination was as to the nature of his Messiahship. As we have seen, it was not a Divine, but a *military Messiah* the Jews

[1] Gerok's 'Evangelien-Predigten,' s. 276.

desired. To their question he replies first that they will not believe him if he answers them truthfully. They will only believe what they *like*. In other words, faith is largely a matter of the will as influenced by emotion. They were not prepared to accept truth and follow it to its consequences. After this preliminary, Jesus goes on to declare, "From henceforth shall the Son of man be seated at the right hand of the power of God" (Revised Version). That is to say, his Messiahship is to be a heavenly reign, not an earthly and temporal one. At once they saw in this a claim to Divine Sonship. Hence they challenge him upon the point, and get his manly reply that he is. On this ground they condemn him. It is plain, therefore, that this *Divine* Messiah was not what suited their fancy. It was not deliverance from such impalpable foes as sin and anxiety and suffering they desired, but from the Romans. They wanted a military leader—a pasha; and when God gave them his Son as their heavenly King, they condemned him to an ignominious death. It is thus that men despise their greatest blessings, and do their best to put them out of the way.—R. M. E.

EXPOSITION.

CHAPTER XXIII.

Vers. 1—4.—*The trial before Pilate: First examination.*

Ver. 1.—And the whole multitude of them arose, and led him unto Pilate. The Sanhedrin had now formally condemned Jesus to death. They were, however, precluded by the Roman regulations then in force from carrying out their judgment. A capital sentence in Judæa could only be inflicted as the result of a decision by the Roman court. The Sanhedrin supposed, and as we shall see rightly, that the judgment they had pronounced would speedily be confirmed by the Roman judge. The Sanhedrin condemnation to death was, however, from the Jewish standpoint, illegal. In capital cases judgment could not be legally pronounced on the day of trial. But in the case of Jesus, the Accused was condemned without the legal interval which should have been left between the trial and the sentence. The Prisoner was then at once hurried before the Roman tribunal, in order that the Jewish sentence might be confirmed and carried out with all the additional horrors which accompanied Gentile public executions in such cases of treason. Dérenbourg ('Histoire de la Palestine,' p. 201) attributes the undue illegal precipitancy of the whole proceeding to the overwhelming influence exercised in the supreme council by Annas and Caiaphas with their friends who were Sadducees, a party notorious for their cruelty as well as for their unbelief. Had the Pharisees borne sway in the Sanhedrin at that juncture, such an illegality could never have taken place. This apology possesses certain weight, as it is based upon known historical facts; yet when the general bearing of the Pharisee party towards our Lord during the greater part of his public ministry is remembered, it can scarcely be supposed that the action of the Sadducee

majority in the Sanhedrin was repugnant to, or even opposed by, the Pharisee element in the great assembly. **Pilate.** Pontius Pilate, a Roman knight, owed his high position as Procurator of Judæa to his friendship with Sejanus, the powerful minister of the Emperor Tiberius. He probably belonged by birth or adoption to the gens of the Pontii. When Judæa became formally subject to the empire on the deposition of Archelaus, Pontius Pilate, of whose previous career nothing is known, through the interest of Sejanus, was appointed to govern it, with the title of procurator, or collector of the revenue, invested with judicial power. This was in A.D. 26, and he held the post for ten years, when he was deposed from his office in disgrace. His government of Judæa seems to have been singularly unhappy. His great patron Sejanus hated the Jews, and Pilate seems faithfully to have imitated his powerful friend. Constantly the Roman governor appears to have wounded the susceptibilities of the strange, unhappy people he was placed over. Fierce disputes, mutual insults arising out of apparently purposeless acts of arbitrary power on his side, characterized the period of his rule. His behaviour in the one great event of his life, when Jesus was brought before his tribunal, will illustrate his character. He was superstitious and yet cruel; afraid of the people he affected to despise; faithless to the spirit of the authority with which he was lawfully invested. In the great crisis of his history, from the miserably selfish motive of securing his own petty interests, we watch him deliberately giving up a Man, whom he knew to be innocent, and felt to be noble and pure, to torture, shame, and death. **Ver. 2.—And they began to accuse him, saying, We found this fellow perverting the nation, and forbidding to give tribute to Cæsar, saying that he himself is Christ a King.** To understand this scene perfectly we must read St. John's account in his eighteenth chapter (ver. 28 and following). From the place of meeting of the Sanhedrin, Jesus was led to the palace of Pilate, the Prætorium. The Roman governor was evidently prepared for the case; for application must have been made to him the evening before for the guard which arrested Jesus in Gethsemane. St. John tells us that the delegates of the Sanhedrin entered not into the hall of judgment, "lest they should be defiled; but that they might eat the Passover." Pilate, who knew well from his past experience how fiercely these fanatics resented any slight offered to their religious feelings, wishing for his own purposes to conciliate them, went outside. These Jews, prior to eating the Passover, would not enter any dwelling from which all leaven had not been carefully removed; of course, this had not been the case in the palace of Pilate. The governor asks them, in St. John's account, what was their accusation against the Man. They replied that they had three charges: (1) he had perverted the nation; (2) he had forbidden that tribute should be given to Cæsar; (3) he had asserted that he was Christ a King.

Ver. 3.—And Pilate asked him, saying, Art thou the King of the Jews? Pilate then went again into his judgment-hall, where he had left Jesus, but before going back he could not resist addressing an ironical word to the accusing Jews: "Take ye him, and judge him according to your Law" (John xviii. 31), to which the Sanhedrists replied that they were not allowed to put any man to death, thus publicly confessing the state of comparative impotence to which they were now reduced, and also revealing their deadly purpose in the case of Jesus. Pilate, having gone into the judgment-hall again, proceeds to interrogate Jesus. The first two accusations he passes over, seeing clearly that they were baseless. The third, however, struck him. Art thou, poor, friendless, powerless Man, the King I have been hearing about? And he answered him and said, Thou sayest it. St. Luke gives only this bare summary of the examination, in which the prisoner Jesus simply replies "Yes," he was the King. St. John (xviii. 33—38) gives us a more full and detailed account. It is more than probable that John was present during the interrogatory. In the sublime answers of the Lord, his words explanatory of the nature of his kingdom, which "is not of this world," struck Pilate and decided him to give the reply we find in the next verse.

Ver. 4.—Then said Pilate to the chief priests and to the people, I find no fault in this Man. The Roman was interested in the poor Prisoner; perhaps he grudgingly admired him. He was so different to the members of that hated nation he had been brought into such familar contact with; utterly unselfish, noble with a strange nobility, which was quite unknown to officials and politicians of the school of Pilate; but as regards Rome and its views quite harmless. The Roman evidently was strongly opposed to harsh measures being dealt out to this dreamy, unpractical, generous Enthusiast, as he deemed him.

Vers. 5—12.—*Pilate sends Jesus to be tried by Herod.*

Ver. 5.—And they were the more fierce, saying, He stirreth up the people, teaching throughout all Jewry, beginning from Galilee to this place. On hearing the Roman governor's declaration that in his opinion the Prisoner was innocent, the Sanhedrists became more vehement, repeating with increased violence their accusation that Jesus had been for a long time past a persistent stirrer-up of sedition, not only here in the city, but in the northern districts of Galilee.

Vers. 6, 7.—When Pilate heard of Galilee, he asked whether the Man were a Galilæan. And as soon as he knew that he belonged unto Herod's jurisdiction, he sent him to Herod, who himself also was at Jerusalem at that time. Now, Pilate dreaded lest these Jews should make his clemency towards the Prisoner a ground of accusation against him at Rome. Pilate had enemies in the capital. His once powerful patron Sejanus had just fallen. His own past, too, he was well aware, would not bear examination; so, moved by his cowardly fears, he refrained from releasing Jesus in accordance with what his heart told him was just and right; and yet he could not bring himself to condemn One to whom he was drawn by an unknown feeling of reverence and respect. But hearing that Jesus was accused among other things of stirring up sedition in Galilee, he thought he would shift the responsibility of acquitting or condemning, on to the shoulders of Herod, in whose jurisdiction Galilee lay. Herod was in Jerusalem just then, because of the Passover Feast. His usual residence was Capernaum.

Ver. 8.—And when Herod saw Jesus, he was exceeding glad: for he was desirous to see him of a long season, because he had heard many things of him; and he hoped to have seen some miracle done by him. This was Herod Antipas, the slayer of John the Baptist. He was at that time living in open incest with that princess Herodias concerning whom the Baptist had administered the public rebuke which had led to his arrest and subsequent execution. Godet graphically sums up the situation: "Jesus was to Herod Antipas what a juggler is to a sated court—an object of curiosity. But Jesus did not lend himself to such a part; he had neither words nor miracles for a man so disposed, in whom, besides, he saw with horror the murderer of John the Baptist. Before this personage, a monstrous mixture of bloody levity and sombre superstition, he maintained a silence which even the accusation of the Sanhedrin (ver. 10) could not lead him to break. Herod, wounded and humiliated, took vengeance on this conduct by contempt."

Ver. 11.—**And Herod with his men of war set him at nought, and mocked him, and arrayed him in a gorgeous robe, and sent him again to Pilate.** He treated him, not as a criminal, but as a mischievous religious Enthusiast, worthy only of contempt and scorn. The "gorgeous robe," more accurately, "bright raiment," was a white festal mantle such as Jewish kings and Roman nobles wore on great occasions. It was probably an old robe of white tissue of some kind, embroidered with silver. Dean Plumptre suggests that we might venture to trace in this outrage a vindictive retaliation for the words which the Teacher had once spoken—with evident allusion to Herod's court—of those who were gorgeously apparelled (ch. vii. 25). It was this Herod of whom the Lord had spoken so recently with for him a rare bitterness, "Go ye, and tell that fox [literally, 'she-fox'] Herod" (ch. xiii. 32).

Ver. 12.—**And the same day Pilate and Herod were made friends together.** This union of two such bitter enemies in their enmity against Jesus evidently struck the early Church with sad wonderment. It is referred to in the first recorded hymn of the Church of Christ (Acts iv. 27). How often has the strange sad scene been reproduced in the world's story since! Worldly men apparently irreconcilable meet together in friendship when opportunity offers itself for wounding Christ!

Vers. 13—25.—*The Lord is tried again before Pilate, who wishes to release him, but, over-persuaded by the Jews, delivers him to be crucified.*

Vers. 13—16.—**And Pilate . . . said unto them . . . behold I . . . have found no fault in this Man . . . No, nor yet Herod : . . . lo, nothing worthy of death is done unto him;** more accurately rendered, *is done by him.* This was the Roman's deliberate judgment publicly delivered. The decision then announced, that he would scourge him (ver. 16), was singularly unjust and cruel. Pilate positively subjected a Man whom he had pronounced innocent to the horrible punishment of scourging, just to satisfy the clamour of the Sanhedrists, because he dreaded what they might accuse him of at Rome, where he knew he had enemies! He thought, wrongly as it turned out, that the sight of

Jesus after he had undergone this dreadful and disgraceful punishment would satisfy, perhaps melt to pity, the hearts of these restless enemies of his.

Ver. 17.—**(For of necessity he must release one unto them at the feast.)** Probably, however, before the scourging was inflicted, the attempt to liberate Jesus in accordance with a custom belonging to that feast was made by Pilate. We know it failed, and a condemned robber called Barabbas was preferred by the people. The more ancient authorities omit this verse (17). It probably was introduced at an early period into many manuscripts of St. Luke as a marginal gloss, as an explanatory statement based on the words of Matt. xxvii. 15 or of Mark xv. 6. As a Hebrew custom, it is never mentioned save in this place. Such a release was a common incident of a Latin Lectisternium, or feast in honour of the gods. The Greeks had a similar custom at the Thesmophoria. It was probably introduced at Jerusalem by the Roman power.

Vers. 18, 19.—**And they cried out all at once, saying, Away with this Man! and release unto us Barabbas: (who for a certain sedition made in the city, and for murder, was cast into prison).** Barabbas, whose release the people demanded at the instigation of the influential men of the Sanhedrin, was a notable leader in one of the late insurrectionary movements so common at this time. St. John styles him a robber; this well describes the character of the man; a bandit chief who carried on his lawless career under the veil of patriotism, and was supported and protected in consequence by many of the people. The meaning of his name *Bar-Abbas* is "Son of a (famous) father," or possibly *Bar-Rabbas*, "Son of a (famous) rabbi." A curious reading is alluded to by Origen, which inserts before Barabbas the word "Jesus." It does not, however, appear in any of the older or more trustworthy authorities. Jesus was a common name at that period, and it is possible that "when Barabbas was led out, the Roman, with some scorn, asked the populace whom they preferred—Jesus Bar-Abbas or Jesus who is called Christ!" (Farrar). That this reading existed in very early times is indisputable, and Origen, who specially notices it, approves of its omission, not on critical, but on dogmatic grounds.

Ver. 23.—**And they were instant with loud voices, requiring that he might be crucified.** The Roman governor now found that all his devices to liberate Jesus with the consent and approval of the Jews were fruitless. After the clamour which resulted in the release of Barabbas had ceased, the terrible cry, "Crucify him!" was raised among that fickle crowd. Pilate was determined to carry out his threat of scourging the Innocent. *That* might satisfy them, perhaps excite their pity. Something whispered to him that he would be wise if he refrained from staining his life with the blood of that strange quiet Prisoner.

St. Luke omits here the "scourging;" the mock-homage of the soldiers; the scarlet robe and the crown of thorns; the last appeal to pity when Pilate produced the pale, bleeding Sufferer with the words, "Ecce Homo!" the last solemn interview of Pilate and Jesus, related by St. John; the sustained clamour of the people for the blood of the Sinless. "*Then he delivered Jesus to their will*" (ver. 25). (See Matt. xxvii., Mark. xv., and John xix., for these details, omitted in St. Luke.)

Of the omitted details, the most important piece in connection with the "last things" is the recital by St. John of the examination of Jesus by Pilate in the Prætorium. None of the Sanhedrists or strict Jews, we have noticed, were present at these interrogatories. They, we read, entered not into the judgment-hall of Pilate, lest they might be defiled, and so be precluded from eating the Passover Feast.

St. John, however, who appears to have been the most fearless of the "eleven," and who besides evidently had friends among the Sanhedrin officials, was clearly present at these examinations. He too, we are aware, had eaten his Passover the evening before, and therefore had no defilement to fear.

The first interrogatories have been already alluded to, in the course of which the question, "Art thou a King, then?" was put by Pilate, and the famous reflection by the Roman, "What is truth?" was made. Then followed the "sending to Herod;" the return of the Prisoner from Herod; the offer of release, which ended in the choice by the people of Barabbas. The scourging of the prisoner Jesus followed.

This was a horrible punishment. The condemned person was usually stripped and fastened to a pillar or stake, and then scourged with leather throngs tipped with leaden balls or sharp spikes.

The effects, described by Romans, and Christians in the 'Martyrdoms,' were terrible. Not only the muscles of the back, but the breast, the face, the eyes, were torn; the very entrails were laid bare, the anatomy was exposed, and the sufferer, convulsed with torture, was often thrown down a bloody heap at the feet of the judge. In our Lord's case this punishment, though not proceeding to the awful consequences described in some of the 'Martyrologies,' must have been very severe: this is evident from his sinking under the cross, and from the short time which elapsed before his death upon it. "Recent investigations at Jerusalem have disclosed what may have been the scene of the punishment. In a subterranean chamber, discovered by Captain Warren, on what Mr. Fergusson holds to be the site of Antonia—Pilate's Prætorium—stands a truncated column, no part of the construction, for the chamber is vaulted above the pillar, but just such a pillar as criminals would be tied to to be scourged" (Dr. Westcott).

After the cruel scourging came the mocking by the Roman soldiers. They threw across the torn and mangled shoulders one of those scarlet cloaks worn by the soldiers themselves—a coarse mockery of the royal mantle worn by a victorious general. They pressed down on his temples a crown or wreath, imitating what they had probably seen the emperor wear in the form of laurel wreath—Tiberius's wreath of laurel was seen upon his arms (Suetonius, 'Tiberius,' c. 17). The crown was made, as an old tradition represents it, of the *Zizyphus Christi*, the *nubk* of the Arabs, a plant which is found in all the warmer parts of Palestine and about Jerusalem. The thorns are numerous and sharp, and the flexible twigs well adapted for the purpose (Tristram, 'Natural History of the Bible,' p. 429). "The representations in the great pictures of the Italian painters probably come very near the truth" ('Speaker's Commentary').

In his right hand they placed a reed to simulate a sceptre, and before this sad, woe-begone Figure "they bowed the knee, saying, Hail, King of the Jews!"

Hase ('Geschichte Jesu,' p. 573) is even moved to say, "There is some comfort in the fact that, even in the midst of the mockery, the truth made itself felt. Herod recognizes his innocence by a white robe; the Roman soldiery his royalty by the sceptre and the crown of thorns, and that has become the highest of all crowns, as was fitting, being the most meritorious."

It was *then* and *thus* that Pilate led Jesus out before the Sanhedrists and the people, as they shouted in their unreasoning fury, "Crucify him!" while the Roman, partly sadly, partly scornfully, partly pitifully, as he pointed to the silent Sufferer by his side, pronounced "Ecce Homo!"

But the enemies of Jesus were pitiless. They kept on crying, "Crucify him!" and when Pilate still demurred carrying out their bloody purpose, they added that "by their Law he ought to die, because he made himself the *Son of God.*"

All through that morning's exciting scenes had Pilate seen that something strange and mysterious belonged to that solitary Man accused before him. His demeanour, his words, his very look, had impressed the Roman with a singular awe. Then came his wife's message, telling him of her dream, warning her husband to have nothing to do with *that just Man.* Everything seemed to whisper to him, "Do not let that strange, innocent Prisoner be done to death: he is not what he seems." And now the fact, openly published by the furious Jews, that the poor Accused claimed a Divine origin, deepened the awe. Who, then, had he been scourging?

Once more Pilate returns to his judgment-hall, and he says to Jesus, again standing before him, "Whence art thou?"

The result of this last interrogatory St. John (xix. 12) briefly summarizes in the words, "From thenceforth Pilate sought to release him."

The Sanhedrists, and their blind instruments, the fickle, wavering multitude, when they perceived the Roman governor's intention to release their Victim, changed their tactics. They forbore any longer to press the old charges of blasphemy and of indefinite wrong-doing, and they appealed only to Pilate's own dastardly fears. The Prisoner claimed to be a King. If the lieutenant of the emperor let such a traitor go free, why, that lieutenant emphatically was not Cæsar's friend!

Such a plea for the Sanhedrin to use

before a Roman tribunal, to ask for death to be inflicted on a Jew because he had injured the majesty of Rome, was a deep degradation; but the Sanhedrin well knew the temper of the Roman judge with whom they had to deal, and they rightly calculated that his fears for himself, if properly aroused, would turn the scale and secure the condemnation of Jesus. They were right.

Ver. 24.—**And Pilate gave sentence that it should be as they required.** This sums up the result of the last charge of the Sanhedrin. Pilate's selfish fears for himself overpowered all sense of reverence, awe, and justice. There was no further discussion. Bar-Abbas was released, and Jesus was delivered up to the will of his enemies.

Vers. 26—32.—*On the way to Calvary. Simon the Cyrenian. The daughters of Jerusalem.*

Ver. 26.—**And as they led him away.** Plutarch tells us that every criminal condemned to crucifixion carried his own cross. There was borne in front of him, or else hung round his own neck, a white tablet, on which the crime for which he suffered was inscribed. Possibly this was what was afterwards affixed to the cross itself. **Simon, a Cyrenian.** Cyrene was an important city in North Africa, with a large colony of resident Jews. These Cyrenian Jews had a synagogue of their own in Jerusalem. It is probable that Simon was a Passover pilgrim. St. Mark tells us he was the father of "Alexander and Rufus;" evidently, from his mention of them, these were notable persons in the early Christian Church. Very likely their connection with the followers of Jesus dated from this incident on the road to Calvary. **Coming out of the country.** He was probably one of the pilgrims lodged in a village near Jerusalem, and met the sad procession as he was entering the city on his way to the temple. **On him they laid the cross.** Our Lord was weakened by the trouble and agitation of the past sleepless night, and was, of course, faint and utterly exhausted from the effects of the terrible scourging. The cross used for this mode of execution was (1) either the *Crux decussata* X, what is usually known as St. Andrew's cross; or (2) the *Crux commissa* ┬, St. Anthony's cross; or (3) the ordinary Roman cross ✝, *Crux immissa.* Our Lord suffered on the third description, the Roman cross. This consisted of two pieces, the one perpendicular (*staticulum*), the other horizontal (*antenna*). About the middle of the first was fastened a piece of wood (*sedile*), on which the condemned rested. This was necessary, else, during the long torture, the weight of the body would have torn the hands, and the body would have fallen. The cross was not very high, scarcely twice the height of an ordinary man. Strong nails were driven through the hands and feet. The victim usually lived about twelve hours, sometimes much longer. The agonies endured by the crucified have been thus summarized : " The fever which soon set in produced a burning thirst. The increasing inflammation of the wounds in the back, hands, and feet; the congestion of the blood in the head, lungs, and heart; the swelling of every vein, an indescribable oppression, racking pains in the head; the stiffness of the limbs, caused by the unnatural position of the body ;— these all united to make the punishment, in the language of Cicero (' In Verr.,' v. 64), *crudelissimum teterrimumque supplicium.* From the beginning Jesus had foreseen that such would be the end of his life."

Ver. 27.—**And there followed him a great company of people, and of women, which also bewailed and lamented him.** The great company was made up of the usual concourse of curious lookers-on, of disciples, and others who had heard him in past days, and now came, with much horror, to see the end. *The women* specially noticed consisted mostly, no doubt, of holy women of his own company, such as the "Maries," together with some of those kindly Jerusalem ladies who were in the habit of soothing the last hours of these condemned ones—unhappily in those sad days so numerous—with narcotics and anodynes. These kindly offices were apparently not forbidden by the Roman authorities. This recital respecting the women is peculiar to St. Luke.

Ver. 28.—**But Jesus turning unto them said, Daughters of Jerusalem.** This address to them by the Lord indicates that the majority at least of this company of sympathizing women belonged to the holy city. **Weep not for me, but weep for yourselves, and for your children.** Again here, as on the cross, the utter unselfishness of the dying Master comes out. His thoughts in his darkest hour were never of himself. Here, apparently, for the first time since his last interrogation before Pilate does our Lord break silence. Stier beautifully calls this the first part of the *Passion sermon of Christ.* The second part consisted of the "seven words on the cross." "Weep," said our Lord here. It is noticeable that it is the only time in his public teaching that he is reported to have told his listeners to weep. "The same lips whose gracious breath had dried so many tears now cry on the way to the cross, 'Weep for yourselves, and for your children.'"

Ver. 29.—**Blessed are the barren.** A strange beatitude to be spoken to the women of Israel, who, through all their checkered history, so passionately longed that *this* barrenness might not be their portion !

Ver. 30.—**Then shall they begin to say to the mountains, Fall on us ; and to the hills, Cover us.** The allusion, in the first place, was to the awful siege of Jerusalem and to the undreamed-of woes which would accompany it; and in the second place, to the centuries of misery and persecution to which the children of these "daughters of Jerusalem" would, as Jews, be subjected in all lands.

Ver. 31.—**For if they do these things in a green tree, what shall be done in the dry ?** Bleek and others interpret this saying here thus : The *green wood* represents Jesus condemned to crucifixion as a traitor in spite of his unvarying loyalty to Rome and all lawful Gentile power. The *dry wood* pictures the Jews, who, ever disloyal to Rome and all Gentile authority, will bring on themselves with much stronger reason the terrible vengeance of the great conquering empire. Theophylact, however, better explains the saying in his paraphrase, " If they do these things in *me,* fruitful, always green, undying through the Divinity, what will they do to *you,* fruitless, and deprived of all life-giving righteousness?" So Farrar, who well summarizes, "If they act thus to me, the Innocent and the Holy, what shall be the fate of these, the guilty and false ?"

Ver. 32.—**And there were also two other, malefactors, led with him to be put to death.** Many commentators suppose that these were companions of that Bar-Abbas the robber who had just been released. They were not ordinary thieves, but belonged to those companies of brigands, or revolted Jews, which in those troublous times were so numerous in Palestine.

Vers. 33—49.—*The Crucifixion.*

Ver. 33.—**And when they were come to the place, which is called Calvary ;** literally, *unto the place which is called the skull.* The familiar name " Calvary " has its origin in the Vulgate translation, *Calvarium,* a skull. The name "Place of a skull," *Golgotha* (properly *Gulgoltha,* an Aramaic word גלגלתא, corresponding to the Hebrew *Gulgoleth,* גלגלת, which in Judg. ix. 53 and 2 Kings ix. 35 is translated "skull"), does not come from the fact that the skulls of condemned persons remained lying there, but it is so called from being a bare rounded mound like a skull in form. Dean Plumptre suggests that the spot in question was chosen by the Jewish rulers as a deliberate insult to one of their own order, Joseph of Arimathæa, whose garden, with its rock-sepulchre, lay hard by. A later legend derives the name from its being the burying-place of Adam, and that as the blood flowed from the sacred wounds on his skull, his soul was translated to Paradise. A tradition traceable to the fourth century has identified this spot with the building known as the Church of the Holy Sepulchre. St. Cyril of Jerusalem alludes to the spot repeatedly. In the time of Eusebius there was no doubt as to the site. The Bordeaux Pilgrim (A.D. 333) writes thus: "On the left side (of the original Church of the Holy Sepulchre) is the hillock (*monticulus*) Golgotha, where the Lord was crucified. Thence about a stone-throw distance is the crypt where his body was deposited." Recent research confirms this very ancient tradition, and scholars are generally now agreeing that the evidence in support of the *traditional site* is strong and seemingly conclusive. **And the malefactors, one on the right hand, and the other on the left.** St. John adds, "and Jesus in the midst," as holding the position of preeminence in that scene of uttermost shame. Even in suffering Christ appears as a King. Westcott thus comments on the next detail recorded by St. John (xix. 19), where the accurate rendering is, "And Pilate wrote a title *also*." This title (see further, ver. 38) was drawn up by Pilate, who caused it to be placed on the cross. The words, "wrote a title also," perhaps imply that the placing of the Lord in the midst was done by Pilate's direction.

Ver. 34.—**Then said Jesus, Father, forgive them; for they know not what they do.** These words are missing in some of the oldest authorities. They are found, however, in the majority of the most ancient manuscripts and in the most trustworthy of the old versions, and are undoubtedly genuine. These *first* of the seven words from the cross seem, from their position in the record, to have been spoken very early in the awful scene, probably while the nails were being driven into the hands and feet. Different from other holy dying men, *he* had no need to say, "Forgive *me*." Then, as always, thinking of others, he utters this prayer, uttering it, too, as Stier well observes, with the same consciousness which had been formerly expressed, "Father, I know that thou hearest *me* always." "His intercession has this for its ground, though in meekness it is not expressed: 'Father, I will that thou forgive them.' " In the same sublime consciousness *who he was*, he speaks shortly after to the penitent thief hanging by his side. These words of the crucified Jesus were heard by the poor sufferer close to him; they—with other things he had noticed in the One crucified in the midst—moved him to that piteous prayer which was answered at once so quickly and so royally. St. Bernard comments thus on this first word from the

cross: " Judæi clamant, 'Crucifige!' Christus clamat, 'Ignosce!' Magna illorum iniquitas, sed major tua, O Domine, pietas!" **And they parted his raiment, and cast lots.** The rough soldiers were treating the Master as already dead, and were disposing of his raiment, of which they had stripped him before fastening him to the cross. He was hanging there naked, exposed to sun and wind. Part of this raiment was torn asunder, part they drew lots for to see who was to wear it. The garments of the crucified became the property of the soldiers who carried out the sentence. Every cross was guarded by a guard of four soldiers. The coat, for which they cast lots, was, St. John tells us, without seam. "Chrysostom," who may have written from personal knowledge, thinks that the detail is added to show "the poorness of the Lord's garments, and that in dress, as in all other things, he followed a simple fashion."

Ver. 35.—**And the people stood beholding.** A hush seems to have fallen over the scene. The crowd of by-standers were awed as they at first silently gazed on the dying form of the great Teacher. What memories must have surged up in the hearts of many of the gazers—memories of his parables, his mighty miracles, his words of love; memories of the raising of Lazarus, and of the day of palms! Such a silent awe-struck contemplation was dangerous, the rulers felt, so they hastened to commence their mockery—"to clear," as Stier remarks, "the stifling air, and deafen the voice which was stirring even in themselves." "Look now," they would cry, "at the end of the Man who said he could do, and pretended to do, such strange, unheard-of things!" They seem soon to have induced many to join in their mocking cries and gestures, and so to break the awful silence.

Ver. 36.—**And the soldiers also mocked him, coming to him, and offering him vinegar.** Three times in the Crucifixion scene we find a mention of this vinegar, or the sour wine of the country, the common drink of the soldiers and others, being offered to the Sufferer. (1) Matt. xxvii. 34. This was evidently a draught prepared with narcotics and stupefying drugs, no doubt by some of those compassionate women addressed by him on his way to the cross as "daughters of Jerusalem," a common work of mercy at that time, and one apparently permitted by the guards. This, St. Matthew tells us, "he tasted of," no doubt in courteous recognition of the kindly purpose of the act, but he refused to do more than taste of it. He would not dull the sense of pain, or cloud the clearness of his communion with his Father in that last awful hour. (2) The second, mentioned here by St. Luke, seems to imply that the soldiers mocked his agony of thirst—one of the tortures induced by crucifixion—by lifting up to his parched, fevered lips, vessels containing their sour wine, and then snatching them hastily away. (3) The third (John xix. 28—30) relates that here the Lord, utterly exhausted, asked for and received this last refreshment, which revived, for a very brief space, his fast failing powers, and gave him strength for his last utterances. The soldiers, perhaps acting under the orders of the compassionate centurion in command, perhaps touched with awe by the brave patience and strange dignity of the dying Lord, did him this last kindly office.

Ver. 38.—**And a superscription also was written over him in letters of Greek, and Latin, and Hebrew, THIS IS THE KING OF THE JEWS.** The older authorities omit "in letters of Greek, and Latin, and Hebrew," but the fact is indisputable, for we read the same statement in John xix. 20, where in the older authorities the order of the titles is, "in Hebrew, in Latin, and in Greek." Such multilingual inscriptions were common in the great provincial cities of the empire, where so many nationalities were wont to congregate. The four reports of the inscriptions slightly differ verbally, not substantially. Pilate probably (see note on ver. 33, on effect of accurate rendering of John xix. 19, "and Pilate wrote a title also") wrote a rough draft with his own hand, "Rex Judæorum hic est." One of the officials translated freely into Hebrew and Greek the Roman governor's Latin memorandum of what he desired to have written in black on the white gypsum-smeared board to be affixed to the upper arm of the cross.

ישו הנצרי מלך היהודים (John).

'Ο βασιλεὺς τῶν 'Ιουδαίων (Mark).

Rex Judæorum hic est (Luke).

Dr. Farrar suggests that the title over the cross was as above. St. Matthew's is an accurate combination of the three, and was not improbably, *as a combination of the three inscriptions,* the common form reproduced in the first oral Gospel.

Vers. 39, 40.—**And one of the malefactors which were hanged railed on him, saying, If thou be Christ, save thyself and us. But the other answering rebuked him, saying, Dost not thou fear God?** In the first two synoptists we read how, shortly after they were nailed to their crosses, both thieves "reviled" Jesus. The Greek word, however, used by SS. Matthew and Mark is ὠνείδιζον (reproached). The word used by St. Luke in this place of the impenitent one is ἐβλασφήμει, "began to use injurious and

insulting language"—a much stronger term. Farrar suggests that at first, during the early hours of the Crucifixion, in the madness of anguish and despair, they both probably joined in the reproaches levelled by all classes alike at One who might seem to them to have thrown away a great opportunity. They, no doubt, knew something, possibly much, of Jesus' career, and how he had deliberately prevented more than once the multitude from proclaiming him King. Watching him as he hung bravely patient on his cross, only breaking the dread silence with a low-muttered prayer for his murderers to his Father, one of these misguided men changed his opinion of his fellow-Sufferer, changed his opinion, too, of his own past career. There, dying with a prayer for others on his lips, was the Example of true heroism, of real patriotism. *If thou be Christ.* The more ancient authorities read, *Art thou not the Christ? But the other.* In the Apocryphal Gospel of Nicodemus the names of the two are given as Dysmas and Gysmas, and these names appear still in Calvaries and stations in Roman Catholic lands. **Seeing thou art in the same condemnation.** His words might be paraphrased, "How canst thou, a dying man, join these mere lookers-on at our execution and agony? we are undergoing it ourselves. Dost thou not fear *God?* In a few hours we shall be before *him.* We have at all events deserved our doom; but not this Sufferer whom you revile. What has he done?"

Ver. 42.—**And he said unto Jesus, Lord, remember me when thou comest into thy kingdom.** The majority of the older authorities omit "Lord." The translation should run thus: *And he said, Jesus, remember me when thou comest in thy kingdom—in,* not *into.* The penitent looked forward to the dying Jesus coming again in (arrayed in) his kingly dignity, surrounded with his power and glory. Very touching is this confidence of the dying in the Dying One who was hanging by his side, his last garment taken from him; very striking is this trust of the poor penitent, that the forsaken Lord will one day appear again as King in his glory. He, and he alone, on that dread day read aright the superscription which mocking Pilate had fixed above the cross, "*This is the King of the Jews.*" He read "with Divine clear-sightedness in this deepest night" (Krummacher). He asks for no special place in that kingdom whose advent he sees clearly approaching; he only asks the King not to forget him then. On this knowledge of the thief concerning the second advent of Christ, Meyer well writes, "The thief must have become acquainted with the predictions of Jesus concerning his coming, which may very easily have been the case at Jerusalem, and does not directly presuppose any instructions on the part of Jesus; although he may also have heard him himself, and still remembered what he heard. The extraordinary character of his painful position in the very face of death produced as a consequence an extraordinary action of firm faith in those predictions."

Ver. 43.—And Jesus said unto him, Verily I say unto thee, To-day shalt thou be with me in paradise. No strengthening angel could have been more welcome to the dying Redeemer than these words of intense penitence and strong faith. Very beautifully Stier suggests that the crucified King "cannot see these two criminals, cannot direct his glance to this last without adding to his own agony by movement upon the cross. But that he forgets, and turns with an impulse of joy as well as he can to the soul that speaks to him, thus making the nails more firm." With those solemn words, "Verily I say unto thee," with which he had so often in old days begun his sacred sayings, he replied to the sufferer by his side. One at least, St. John, of his disciples would have heard the well-known words from the well-known voice. What memories must they not have recalled to that disciple whom Jesus loved, as he stood hard by the cross with the Mother of sorrows! The Lord's answer was very striking. Remember him, who could call on him with such reverent faith at the moment of his deepest humiliation! Remember him! yes; but not in the far-off "coming," but on that very day, before the sun then scorching their tortured bodies set; he would not be remembered by him only, but would be in closest companionship with him, not, as he prayed, in some far-off time in the midst of the awful tumult of the bloody and fiery dawn of the judgment advent, but almost directly in the fair garden, the quiet home of the blessed, the object of all Jewish hopes. There would he be remembered, and there, in company with his Lord, would the tortured condemned find himself in a few short hours. Are we right in thinking that there was no fulfilment of the words till death had released the spirit from its thraldom? May there not even then have been an ineffable joy, such as made the flames of the fiery furnace to be as a "moist, whistling wind" (Song of the Three Children, ver. 27), such as martyrs have in a thousand cases known, acting almost as a physical anæsthetic acts? (Dean Plumptre).

"Non parem Paulo veniam requiro,
  Gratiam Petri neque posco, sed quam
  In crucis ligno dederis latroni
    Sedulus oro."

This striking verse is engraved on the tomb of the great Copernicus, and alludes to this prayer and its answer. Paradise. This is the only instance we have of our Lord's using this well-known word. In the ordinary language used by the Jews, of the unseen world, it signifies the "Garden of Eden," or "Abraham's bosom;" it represented the locality where the souls of the righteous would find a home, after death separated soul and body. The New Testament writers, Luke and Paul and John, use it (Acts ii. 31; 1 Cor. xv. 5; 2 Cor. xii. 4; Rev. ii. 7). To Luke and Paul, probably, this was a memory of the word spoken on the cross, which they alone record in their Gospel. It may have been told Luke by the Mother of sorrows herself. John, who uses it in his Revelation, doubtless heard it himself as he stood at the foot of the cross. Paradeisos is derived from the Persian word pardes, which signifies a park or garden.

Ver. 44.—The time of the Crucifixion. And it was about the sixth hour. We have before given (see note on ch. xxii. 47) the approximate hours of the several acts of the last night and day. This verse gives us the time of the duration of the "darkness"—from the sixth to the ninth hour; that is in our reckoning, from 12 noon to 3 p.m. With this date the other two synoptists agree (comp. Matt. xxvii. 45; Mark xv. 33). Our Lord had then been on the cross three hours (see Mark xv. 25, where it is stated that he was crucified in the third hour, i.e. 9 a.m.). But while the three synoptists are in perfect harmony, we are met with a grave difficulty in St. John's account, for in ch. xix. 14 of his Gospel we read how the final condemnation of our Lord by Pilate took place about the sixth hour. At first sight, to attempt here to harmonize St. John with the three synoptists would seem a hopeless task, as St. John apparently gives the hour of the final condemnation by Pilate, which the three give as the hour when the darkness began, i.e. when the Sufferer had already hung on the cross for three hours. Various explanations have been suggested; among these the most satisfying and probable is the supposition that, while the three synoptists followed the usual Jewish mode of reckoning time, St. John, writing some half a century later in quite another country, possibly twenty years after Jerusalem and the temple had been destroyed, and the Jewish polity had disappeared, adopted another mode of reckoning the hours, thus following, probably, a practice of the province in which he was living, and for which he was especially writing. Dr. Westcott, in an additional note on John xix. 14, examines the four occasions on which St. John mentions a definite hour of the day; and comes to the conclusion that the fourth evangelist generally reckoned his hours from midnight. The Romans reckoned their civil days from midnight, and there are also traces of reckoning the hours from midnight in Asia Minor. "About the sixth hour" would then be about six a.m. Before touching upon the strange darkness which at the sixth hour seems to have hung over the land like a black pall, we note that somewhere in the first three hours, possibly *after* the words spoken to the dying penitent, must be placed the incident of the entrusting the virgin-mother to St. John (xix. 25, etc.). There is no doubt that on the surface of this, his third word from the cross, lay a loving desire to spare his mother the sight of his last awful suffering. Hence his command to John to watch over from henceforth the mother of his Lord. We may assume, then, that, in obedience to his Master's word, John led Mary away before the sixth hour. So Bengel, who comments here, "Great is the faith of Mary to be present at the cross; great was her submission to go away before his death." **And there was a darkness over all the earth until the ninth hour.** St. Matthew gives us additional particulars respecting this phenomenon. He says that besides this darkness there was also an earthquake, and that several graves were opened, and the dead during those hours of solemn gloom appeared to many in the holy city. Early Christian writers of high authority, such as Tertullian ('Apol.,' ch. 21) and Origen ('Contra Cels.,' ii. 33), appeal to this strange phenomenon as if attested by heathen writers. It was evidently no slight or imaginary portent, but one that was well known in the early Christian years. The narrative does not oblige us to think of anything more than an indescribable and oppressive darkness, which like a vast black pall hung over earth and sea. The effect on the scoffing multitude was quickly perceptible. We hear of no more cries of mocking and derision; only just at the end of the three dark hours is the silence broken by the mysterious and awful cry of the Sinless One related by SS. Matthew and Mark, "My God, my God, why hast thou forsaken me?" Godet's comment is remarkable: "The darkness, the rending of the veil of the temple, the earthquake, and the opening of several graves, are explained by the profound connection existing on the one side between Christ and humanity, on the other between humanity and nature. Christ is the Soul of humanity, as humanity is the soul of the external world." The darkness, he suggests, was perhaps connected with the earthquake with which it was accompanied, or it may have resulted from an atmospherical or cosmical cause. The phenomenon need not necessarily have extended over all

the earth; it probably was confined to Palestine and the adjacent countries.

Ver. 45.—And the veil of the temple was rent in the midst. This was the inner veil, which hung between the holy place and the holy of holies. It was rich with costly embroidery, and very heavy. Before the willing surrender of life told of in the next verse (46), our Lord spoke twice more. These fifth and sixth words from the cross are preserved by St. John (xix. 28, 30). The first of these, "*I thirst*"—an expression of bodily exhaustion, of physical suffering—was predicted as part of the agony of the Servant of God (Ps. lxix. 21). The second, "*It is finished!*" tells that "the earthly life had been carried to its issue. That every essential point in the prophetic portraiture of Messiah had been realized. The last suffering for sin had been endured. The end of all had been gained. Nothing was left undone or unborne" (Westcott).

Ver. 46.—And when Jesus had cried with a loud voice, he said. This is better rendered, *and Jesus cried with a loud voice and said.* The cry with the loud voice is the solemn dismissal of his spirit when he commended it to his Father. The object of the receiving the refreshment of the vinegar—the sour wine (John xix. 30)—was that his natural forces, weakened by the long suffering, should be restored sufficiently for him to render audible the last two sayings—the "It is finished!" of St. John, and the commending his soul to his Father, of St. Luke. **Father, into thy hands I commend my spirit.** St. John (xix. 30) has related now already Jesus had uttered the triumphal cry, Τετέλεσται! "It is finished!" This was *his farewell to earth*. St. Luke records the words which seem almost immediately to have followed the "It is finished!" This commending his spirit to his Father has been accurately termed *his entrance-greeting to heaven*. This placing his spirit as a trust in the Father's hands is, as Stier phrases it, an expression of the profoundest and most blessed repose after toil. "It is finished!" has already told us that the struggling and combat were sealed and closed for ever. Doctrinally it is a saying of vast importance; for it emphatically asserts that the soul will exist apart from the body *in the hands of God*. This at least is its proper home. The saying has been echoed on many a saintly death-bed. Stephen, full of the Holy Ghost, in his great agony shows us the form of this blessed prayer *we* should properly use for ourselves at that supreme hour, when he asked the *Lord Jesus* to receive his spirit, and then fell asleep. Thus coming to the Son, we come through him to the Father. Huss, on his way to the stake, when his enemies were triumphantly giving over his soul to devils, said with no less theological accuracy than with sure, calm faith, "But I commit my spirit into thy hand, O Lord Jesus Christ, who hast redeemed it." **And having said thus, he gave up the ghost.** This setting his spirit free was his own voluntary act. He had already told his disciples of his own independent power to lay down and take up his life (John x. 17, 18). The great teachers of the early Church evidently lay stress on this (see Tertullian, 'Apol.,' ch. 21). Augustine's words are striking: "Quis ita dormit quando voluerit, sicut Jesus mortuus est quando voluit? Quis ita vestem ponit quando voluerit, sicut se carne exuit quando vult? Quis ita cum voluerit abit, quomodo ille cum voluit obiit?" and he ends with this practical conclusion: "Quanta speranda vel timenda potestas est judicantis, si apparuit tanta morientis?" "Under these circumstances," writes **Dr. Westcott,** "it may not be fitting to speculate on the physical cause of the Lord's death, but it has been argued that the symptoms agree with a rupture of the heart, such as might be produced by intense mental agony."

Ver. 47.—Now when the centurion saw what was done, he glorified God, saying, Certainly this was a righteous Man. This was the Roman officer who was in command of the detachment on guard at the three crosses. St. Paul—who, if he did not absolutely put together the Third Gospel and the Acts, had much to do with the compilation and arrangement of these writings—on his many journeys and frequent changes of residence in different parts of the empire, had many opportunities of judging the temper and spirit of the Roman army, and on several occasions speaks favourably of these officers (ch. vii. 2; xxiii. 47; Acts x. 1; xxii. 26; xxvii. 43). *Certainly this was a righteous Man.* The noble generosity, the brave patience, and the strange majesty of the Sufferer; the awful portents which for three hours had accompanied this scene—portents which the centurion and many of the bystanders could not help associating with the crucifixion of him men called "the King of the Jews;" then the death, in which appeared no terror;—all this drew forth the exclamation of the Roman. In St. Matthew, the words of the centurion which are reported are "the Son of God." Twice in those solemn hours had the centurion heard the Crucified pray to his Father. This may have suggested the words, "Son of God;" but this change in the later Gospel of St. Luke to "a righteous Man" seems to point to the sense in which the Roman used the lofty appellation.

Ver. 48.—And all the people that came
together to that sight, beholding the things which were done, smote their breasts, and returned. We must remember that the condemnation of the Christ was no spontaneous deed of the multitude. Their miserable share in the act was suggested to them by their rulers. In the multitude very quickly revulsion of feeling sets in, and they often regret the past with a bitter, useless regret. The wave of sorrow which seems to have swept across those wavering, unstable hearts, which induced them to smite their breasts in idle regret, was a dim and shadowy rehearsal of the mighty sorrow and true penitence which will one day, as their prophet told them, be the blessed lot of the once-loved people when "they shall look upon *me* whom they have pierced, and they shall mourn for him, as one mourneth for his only son" (Zech. xii. 10).

Ver. 49.—Stood afar off. Disciples open and secret, friends and acquaintances among the Jerusalem citizens and Galilæan pilgrims (with the exception of the little group of which Mary and John were the centre till the dying Lord bade them leave him), all alike lacked courage and devotion, all feared to stand by their Master and Friend at that awful season. *He trod the winepress alone* (see Isa. lxiii. 3). None possessed the heroic faith which through the sombre cloud of seeming failure could see the true glory of the Sun of Righteousness, which *so soon* was to arise and shine.

Vers. 50—56.—*The entombment.* The sequence of events which immediately followed the death of Christ appears to have been as follows.

Our Lord expired apparently soon after 3 p.m. The "even" alluded to by St. Matthew and St. Mark began at 3 p.m. and lasted till sunset, about 6 p.m., when the sabbath commenced. Some time, then, between 3 p.m. and 6 p.m. Joseph of Arimathæa went to Pilate to ask for the body of Jesus. The governor was surprised, not at the request, but at hearing that Jesus was dead already (Mark xv. 44), and, to assure himself of the fact, sent to inquire of the centurion on duty at the crosses. Somewhere about the same time, probably a little later in the "evening," but still before 6 p.m., the Jews, *i.e.* the Sanhedrin leaders, came to Pilate with a request that the death of the three crucified might be hastened by their legs being broken, in order that their bodies hanging on the crosses might not pollute the very sacred day which followed.

(It would be the sabbath, and the day of the Passover.)

This terrible, but perhaps merciful, end to the tortures of the cross seems not to have been uncommon in Jewish crucifixion inflicted by the Roman authority.

Crucifixion with this and all its attendant horrors was abolished by the first Christian emperor Constantine in the fourth century.

The two thieves apparently expired under this treatment. The soldiers, however, when they looked on the form hanging on the central cross, found the Crucified, as we know, dead already. To make sure of this, one of the executioners thrust his spear deeply into the side of the motionless body of Jesus, "and forthwith came there out blood and water" (John xix. 33, 34). Upon this, in accordance with the permission of the governor already obtained, the body of the Lord was delivered to Joseph of Arimathæa and his friends.

Vers. 50, 51.—And, behold, there was a man named Joseph, a counsellor; and he **was a good man, and a just: (the same had not consented to the counsel and deed of them;) he was of Arimathæa.** This Joseph was a member of the Sanhedrin, a personage of high distinction in Jerusalem, and evidently of great wealth. It is especially mentioned that his vote in the supreme council was not given when the death of Jesus was determined on. Nicodemus and his costly offering of spices for the entombment is only mentioned by St. John (xix. 39). Arimathæa, the place whence this Joseph came, is famous in Jewish history, being identical with Ramathaim Zophim, the "Ramah of the watchers," the native town of Samuel. Each evangelist speaks of Joseph in high terms, and each in his own way. "Luke styles him 'a counsellor, good and just;' he is the καλὸς κἀγαθός, the Greek ideal. Mark calls him 'an honourable counsellor,' the Roman ideal. Matthew writes of him as 'a rich man:' is not this the Jewish ideal?" (Godet). And St. John, we might add, chooses another title for this loved man, "being a disciple of Jesus:" this was St. John's ideal. In Joseph of Arimathæa and Nicodemus we have specimens of a class of earnest and devout Jews, perhaps not uncommon at that time—men who respected and admired our Lord as a Teacher, and half believed in him as the Messiah (the Christ), and yet from many mixed and various motives shrank from confessing him before men till after the cross had been endured. It was not only

the Resurrection which so enormously increased the number and raised the character of the followers of Jesus. When he was gone, men reflected on the inimitable life, on the deep, heart-searching teaching, on the confirmatory works of power; and when the news of the Resurrection came, the little wavering, half-hearted band of followers and hearers became in a few months a great host, and in a few years they had spread over the then civilized world. There is a strange but interesting tradition which tells how this Joseph of Arimathæa came to Great Britain about A.D. 63, and settled in Glastonbury, and there erected a humble Christian oratory, the first in England. The miraculous thorn of Glastonbury, long supposed to bud and blossom every Christmas Day, was reported to have sprung from the staff which Joseph stuck in the ground as he stopped to rest himself on the hill-top.

Ver. 53.—And he took it down, and wrapped it in linen. The last sad rites of love seem all to have been performed by friendly hands. Joseph and Nicodemus, and those with them, reverently took down the pierced and bleeding body; then, after the usual ablution, the sacred head was covered with the napkin, the *soudarion* (St. John), and the holy body was wrapped tenderly and carefully in broad bands of the finest linen, covered with thick layers of the costly aromatic preparation of which Nicodemus had laid up such ample store (St. John). This was to preserve the loved remains of the Master from any corruption which might set in before they could proceed with the process of embalming, which was delayed necessarily until after the sabbath and Passover day were passed. St. John adds, "as the manner of the Jews is to bury," probably marking the Jewish custom of embalming and thus preserving the body, as contrasted with burning, which was the Roman usage. **And laid it in a sepulchre that was hewn in stone.** St. John tells us the sepulchre was in a garden. This seems not to have been an unusual practice with "the great" among the Jews. Josephus relates of Kings Uzziah and Manasseh that they were buried in their gardens ('Ant.,' ix. 10 and x. 3. 2). "He made his grave with the rich" (Isa. liii. 9). **Wherein never man before was laid.** St. John styles it "a new sepulchre." These details are given to show that the Lord's sacred body was not brought into contact with corruption.

Ver. 54.—And that day was the preparation, and the sabbath drew on. It was the preparation for the sabbath, but more especially for the great Passover Feast. St. John, for this reason, calls the coming sabbath "a high day." *Drew on;* literally *began to dawn;* although the sabbath began at sunset, the whole time of darkness was regarded as anticipatory of the dawn. The evening of Friday was sometimes even called "the daybreak."

Vers. 55. 56.—And the women also, which came with him from Galilee, followed after, and beheld the sepulchre, and how his body was laid. And they returned, and prepared spices and ointments. The real process of embalming, the women who were of the company of Jesus—the Maries, Salome, and others—proposed to undertake as soon as the sabbath was passed, that is, on the first day of the coming week—the Sunday. How little even his nearest and dearest friends dreamed of a resurrection of the body! It seems probable that they expected, at least some of them, a glorious reappearance of Jesus, *but when, but how,* they had evidently formed no definite conception. None, however, seemed to have thought of the bodily resurrection which took place on the first day of the week—on that Sunday morning. St. Matthew (xxvii. 62—66) relates how, after the entombment, the chief priests and Pharisees went to Pilate and asked that the sepulchre might, "until the third day," be made sure; and how the Roman governor bade them take such precautions as seemed good to them. These —his bitter opponents—were more clear-sighted than his friends. They had some dim fears of *something* which might still follow, while his disciples, in their hopeless sorrow, thought all was over. **And rested the sabbath day according to the commandment.** "It was the last sabbath of the old covenant. It was scrupulously respected" (Godet).

HOMILETICS.

Vers. 47—56.—*Friday night until Sunday morning.* "*It is finished!*" But there are witnesses to the solemnity of the moment and the significance of the word, whose testimony gives weight to the voice of conscience. The rumble and reel of the earthquake are felt. When "the loud voice" is uttered, the veil which separates the most holy from the holy place is torn in two; an ominous darkness covers the city; there is a crash as of rending rocks and opening tombs, and strange forms, as of those who were dead, flit before the vision. Three hours are marked by portents (vers. 44, 45), beneath whose impression even the officer in charge of the Roman soldiery exclaims (ver. 47), "Certainly this was a righteous Man. He must have been a Son of God." And when, besides, the multitude, hushed and solemnized, gazes on the countenance now calm and still in the repose of death, and the recollection of the life so pure and noble becomes vivid in the mind, the reaction from intense excitement sets in, and (ver. 48) smiting on their breasts in unavailing sorrow, they steal away from the scene of death. Only two groups remain—the soldiers, who must watch until the crucified are dead, and their bodies are removed; and "the acquaintance of Jesus, and the women who had followed him from Galilee, far off, in speechless amazement beholding these things" (ver. 49). All that remains is the burial. He whose cross was erected between the malefactors is dead. The priests and scribes had begged that the closing act of the death by crucifixion, that called the *crucifragium*—the smiting or breaking of the legs—might be hastened and the corpses removed, so that no offence to decency might be felt on the high day, "the double sabbath," at hand. Pilate had acceded to the request; and the forms of the two malefactors had been smitten. Not the form of Jesus. No spark of life, it was said, remained. Only, to make assurance sure, a spear is thrust into the side; the spear, it may be, pierced the pericardium of the heart, or that had already been ruptured; anyhow, a mixture of blood and water flows out. St. John is emphatic as to this, no doubt to silence the suggestion that Jesus had only seemed to die, or that the seeming death had been only a swoon. No, says the evangelist (John xix. 35), "I saw it myself." It is the symbolic meaning of that effusion which we set before us when we sing—

"Let the water and the blood,
From thy riven side which flowed,
Be of sin the double cure—
Cleanse me from its guilt and power."

Is the Lord buried in the sepulchre reserved for those who had been doomed to capital punishment? No. Here there comes into view the beautiful and striking incident recorded in vers. 50—53. And, in connection with it, we light on a word which is used at the hour when we should least have expected to find it. One of the Sanhedrists—a man universally esteemed for piety and prudence—Joseph of Arimathæa—had not consented to the counsel and deed of his colleagues. Hitherto he had never dared to avow the attraction which he felt. Why should he now risk his reputation, it may be his life, by an acknowledgment which he had withheld in his earlier days? Every dictate of worldly wisdom bade him be wholly silent. What do we read in Mark xv. 43? It is the death of Christ that dispels the fear, that at last prompts to decision. He goes in *boldly* to Pilate, and craves the body of Jesus. And the demand of the senator is granted. And as he bears away the sacred frame, he is joined by another (John xix. 39), the Nicodemus of whom we read at the beginning of the ministry (John iii.), who brings with him a princely offering of myrrh and aloes. The reverent and loving hands thus joined together wrap the body (ver. 53) in linen, and hastily and partially embalm it, laying it in the tomb which Joseph had scooped out for himself as his own last resting-place. What happened between this time and the third, the appointed day? Let us ask, first, *What, as it concerns our Lord?* secondly, *What, as it concerns the disciples?* and, thirdly, *What, as it concerns the world which crucified him?*

I. WHAT HAPPENED AS IT CONCERNS OUR LORD? Two or three words give us some hints concerning our Lord after his death and before the Resurrection. First, his own assurance given to Mary on the resurrection-day (John xx. 17), "I am not yet ascended to my Father." The place and condition into which he passed, in dying, were intermediate between the life on earth and the life in glory. He was not then, as the Man Jesus, in the glory of the Father. And, as bearing on this, we further recall the promise to the dying malefactor (ver. 43). "Lord, remember me," he had said, "when thou comest into thy kingdom." "To-day," was the reply, "shalt thou be with me in Paradise." Paradise, then, received the soul of Christ. Thither he bore with him the one who, in penitence and faith, had cast himself on his mercy. And Paradise meant the region in the under-world of the dead set apart for the faithful as their rest until the resurrection—a blessedness real, though incomplete; a garden with the tree of life in it, but not the full enjoyment of the beatific vision. This is the meaning of the clause in the Apostles' Creed, "He descended into hell," *i.e.* into Hades, the state of the dead. It is true that this clause has not the antiquity which may be claimed for other clauses; but it expresses the belief of all times that our Lord submitted to the conditions of the holy dead—that he was truly and verily numbered among them. The soul was actually in Hades, or Sheôl. What part in the great redemptive work was fulfilled by this descent? Had he a ministry in this short but significant period? There is a passage in 1 Peter too obscure to allow of being pressed as an answer to this question, but suggestive of interesting lines of thought (1 Pet. iii. 18—20). To many it has seemed that the preaching to the spirits in prison mentioned there was the work of the Hades-state; that he proclaimed his gospel to those who were kept in ward—not the righteous only, but those who were disobedient, *e.g.* the antediluvian generations to which Noah had preached in vain. And the inference drawn from this view of the passage has appeared "to throw light on one of the darkest enigmas of Divine justice—the cases where the final doom seems infinitely out of proportion to the lapse which has incurred it." No argument can be built on a passage whose interpretation is doubtful; but the exposition hinted at falls in with convictions which have been cherished from the time of the apostles. We are, at all events, on solid Scripture ground when we suppose that, in the world of the dead, the triumph over him that had the power of death, *i.e.* the devil, was completed. The descent was the following of the enemy into his innermost citadel; it was the spoiling of the principalities and power of darkness; it was the opening of the way through death into life by him who has the keys of Hades. Is not Paradise all the sweeter that Christ has been there? Is not the inheritance all the surer that through death he went to the Father? Is not this the symbol of our faith and hope—that "the Lord has set his cross in the midst of Hades, which is the sign of victory that will remain to eternity"?

II. WHAT HAPPENED AS IT CONCERNS THE DISCIPLES. But what of those who weep and lament whilst the world is rejoicing—the sorrow-stricken, orphaned company of disciples? The last to leave the place where the body of Jesus was laid, as the first to hasten to the tomb when the sabbath is past, are the holy women (vers. 55, 56). We see them on Friday evening watching the tomb, and observing how the lifeless form was attended to, and then hastening into the city, that they may make ready the spices and ointments for embalming before the sabbath began. Their love is stronger than their faith. The heart's yearning is sometimes more than the heart's believing. A very dreary sabbath that was to all the disciples. "They rested according to the commandment" (ver. 56). A commandment—rest, and nothing more. What conflicts of thought and affection! What desolation of spirit! Peter—what a strange sabbath it must have been to him! Only one thing for all. The sense of relation to the crucified Jesus can never be effaced; but it has no glow of hope, it has only the darkness of a memory, the gloom of a despair. "They rested on the sabbath; *but*" (the first word of the twenty-fourth chapter should be "but" rather than "now"); but the running of the spirit, the movement of the love, is only towards the garden and its sepulchre. Is it not the type of Church, of Christian, wanting the power of the Holy Ghost? Work for Christ, loyal but cheerless, without sight of his glory, or waiting for his advent— this is suggested by the preparation of the spices and ointments, and the sabbath-keeping but without the true spiritual sabbath, the joy of the Lord; ordinances observed, but with no inner alacrity, only because of the commandment. This is suggested by the unrestful resting on that seventh day. Not yet is there the anointing of the Holy Ghost, the power of the Resurrection.

III. WHAT HAPPENED AS IT CONCERNS THE WORLD WHICH CRUCIFIED HIM. Is it not strange that what was absent from faith as a hope was present to unbelief as a fear? Those who had crucified the Lord have their memory wonderfully quickened. They recall (Matt. xxvii. 62—64) some words which he uttered nearly three years before, about a temple which he would raise in three days, and their dread gives a force to these words. Sabbath though it be, the chief priests and Pharisees seek an audience of Pilate, and beg him to "make the sepulchre sure until the third day, lest his disciples come by night, and steal him away, and say to the people, He is risen from the dead: and so the last error be worse than the first." They are told to go their way and do as they choose; and hence the sealing of the great stone and the setting of the watch. Is not all now secure? Have they not for ever dispelled the illusions as to the Deceiver? So thought the Jewish authorities; so men think still. They are always crying out that the Christian religion is effete, that the Christian's Christ has been slain. "Are there any Christians still?" asked a notable sceptic some years ago. O purblind souls! What avail your watch and seal? He whom you call Deceiver is yet alive; and there are compunctions of heart, convictions of guilt and wrong-doing, and needs of spiritual restoration and inward rectitude, which will assert themselves against all your philosophies! Pentecost days are never far distant days when a mighty remorse rolls over the minds of men, and the cry which never can be silenced, because it is the cry of the human soul in its most solemn hours, and with reference to its deepest wants, bursts through lips which are quivering with a genuine earnestness, "What shall we do to be saved?" On that sabbath the world religious and irreligious holds its rest. It cannot altogether forget; but it holds its Paschal feasts, and complies with all the etiquette of these feasts, as if there were no Calvary, as if no Jesus had lived and died. And is not this the feature of all times? Do not men push their ambitious projects, scheme and toil, spend their strength, and hold their sabbaths without the living consciousness of the Christ who died for their sins? May not we ourselves say—

> "I sin; and heaven and earth go round
>   As if no dreadful deed were done,
> As if Christ's blood had never flowed
>   To hinder sin or to atone"?

There is no word more solemn than that (Heb. vi. 4—6) in which the sacred writer reminds us that if those who have tasted the Word of God and the powers of the world to come fall away, they pass from the fold of the Church into the ranks of Christ's enemies, seeing "they crucify to themselves the Son of God afresh, and put him to an open shame."

HOMILIES BY VARIOUS AUTHORS.

Vers. 1—3.—*The Divine kingdom.* Deeply interesting is this interview between the Nazarene and the Roman, the Jewish Prisoner and the Roman judge; the *one* then brought forth as a malefactor and now seated on the throne of the world, the *other* then exalted on the seat of power and now sunk to the depth of universal pity if not of universal scorn. "Art thou a King?" asks the latter, in the tone of lofty superiority. "I am," replies the former, in the tone of calm and profound assurance. What, then, was this kingdom of which he spoke? What was that kingdom of God, that kingdom of heaven, that "kingdom of the truth" (John xviii. 37) which he foretold, which he came to this world and which he laid down his life to establish? It was *the sovereignty of God over all human souls.* God's claim—which is not founded on *prescription*, nor upon *force*, but upon *righteousness*—is his claim on the reverence, the affection, the obedience, of those whom he has created, preserved, enriched, who owe to him all that he demands of them. With us, who have revolted from his rule, this means nothing less than the restoration of our loyalty, and thus our return to his likeness and to his favour as well as to his sway. We look at—

I. THE ORIGINALITY OF THE CONCEPTION. We plume ourselves upon the originality of our ideas, upon our "creations." But when did the mind of man launch on the sea of human thought such a conception as this kingdom of God? Men had entertained the idea of founding by force a widely extended empire which should command the outward homage and tribute of hundreds of thousands of men, and should last for many generations. But who ever designed a creation like this glorious "kingdom of heaven"—a world-wide sway embracing all living souls whatsoever, exercised by an unseen King, in which the service of the lip, and even that of the life, would be of no account at all without the homage of the heart and the willing subjection of the spirit, characterized by universal righteousness, and crowned by abounding peace and lasting joy?

II. THE IMMENSITY OF THE WORK TO BE ACCOMPLISHED. For what would be involved in the establishment of such a kingdom as this? Not only the formation and maintenance of a new religion that should hold up its head and keep its course amid surrounding faiths, but the utter intolerance and complete subversion of every other creed and *cultus;* the emptying of all the temples and all the synagogues in every land; the dissolution of all the venerable religious institutions which were rooted in the prejudice, fixed in the affections, wrought into the habits and the lives of men; it meant the establishment in the convictions and in the conscience of mankind of a faith which came into direct collision with all its intellectual pride, with all its social selfishness, with all its powerful passions.

III. ITS SUBLIMITY AS A PURPOSE AND A HOPE. Not merely to ameliorate the circumstances and conditions of a country, or of the world at large. That would have been a noble purpose; but that would have been slight and small in comparison with the aim of Jesus Christ. His view was to put away *the source* of all poverty and sorrow and death; to "put away sin by the sacrifice of himself;" to found in the hearts and therefore in the lives of men a kingdom of holiness, and therefore of true and lasting blessedness; to restore to God his rightful heritage in the love of his children, and, at the same time, to restore to men everywhere their high and glorious portion in the favour and friendship, in the likeness and glory, of God. Was ever scheme, was ever hope like this—so divinely new, so magnificently great, so unapproachably sublime? 1. The *way into* this kingdom is by a humble, living faith. 2. The way *on* to its higher places is the service of sacrificial love. The path which takes us to the cross is the way to the throne.—C.

Vers. 4—12.—*The majesty of meekness, etc.* Beautiful in the last degree, as a moral spectacle, is the sight of the meek but mighty Saviour in the presence of the scornful human sovereign. But there are many lessons which we may gather on our way to that striking scene.

I. HOW PITIFUL HUMAN AUTHORITY MAY PROVE TO BE! Poor Pilate, occupying his high seat of authority and power, is "driven with the wind and tossed," as if he were a leaf upon the ground. He "finds no fault in Jesus" (ver. 4), but he dares not acquit him; he is afraid of the men he is there to govern. He casts about for a way of escape; he at lasts hits upon the poor expedient of shifting the difficulty to other shoulders. He presents to us a very pitiable object as a man who sits in the chair of office, and dares not do his duty there. Authority divested of a manly courage and shaking with fear of consequences is a deplorable thing.

II. How FEEBLE IS MERE PASSIONATE VEHEMENCE! The people, led by the priests, were "the more fierce" (ver. 5), insisting that Pilate should not release the Prisoner of whose innocence he was convinced. We see them, with hatred flashing from their eyes, indulging in frantic gestures of deprecation and incitement, loudly clamouring for the condemnation of the Holy One. Their urgency did, indeed, prevail for the moment, as vehemence frequently does. But into what a dire and terrible mistake it led them! to what a crime were they hastening! what awful issues were to spring from their success! How truly were they sowing the wind of which they would reap the whirlwind! Earnestness is always admirable; enthusiasm is often a great power for good; but passionate vehemence is nothing better than a noisy feebleness. It is not the presence of real power; it is the absence of intelligence and self-control. It leads men to actions which have a momentary success, but which end in a lasting failure and in sad disgrace.

III. How UNFRUITFUL IS IDLE CURIOSITY. (Vers. 8, 9.) Herod congratulated himself too soon. He reckoned on having a keen curiosity fully gratified; he thought he had this Prophet in his power, and could command an exhibition of his peculiar faculty, whatever that might prove to be. But he did not want to arrive at truth, or to be better able to do his duty or serve his generation; and Jesus Christ declined to minister to his royal fancy. He was silent and passive, though urged to speech and action. Christ will speak to our hearts, and will work for our benefit and blessing when we approach him in a reverent and earnest spirit; but to a worldly and irreverent curiosity he has nothing to say. It must retire ungratified, and come again in another mood.

IV. How INCONSTANT IS UNSPIRITUAL FRIENDSHIP! Herod had very little to thank Pilate for, on this occasion; he appears to have mistaken a cowardly attempt to evade duty for a mark of personal respect or a desire to effect a reconciliation (ver. 12). A friendship that had to be renewed, and that was patched up in so slight a way and on such mistaken ground, would not last long and was worth very little. Friendship that is not built on thorough knowledge and on mutual esteem is exceedingly fragile and of small account. It is only common attachment to the same great principles and to the one Divine Lord that binds together in indissoluble bonds. Sameness of occupation, similarity of taste, exposure to a common peril, or the possession of a common hope,—this is not the rock on which friendship will stand long; it rests on character, and on the character that is formed by close, personal intimacy with the one true Friend of man.

V. How WRONG AND EVEN WICKED IS UNENLIGHTENED SCORN! (Ver. 11.) Quite unimaginable is the uproarious laughter and the keen, low enjoyment with which the actors went through this wretched ribaldry, this (to us) most painful mockery. How little did they think that he whom they were so mercilessly insulting *was* the King he claimed to be, and was immeasurably higher than the highest of them all! Wrong and wicked is human scorn. Often since then has it mocked at truth and wisdom, and poured its poor ridicule on the head of holiness and true nobility! It is not only the "stranger" who may prove to be the "angel unawares entertained;" it is also the man whom we do not understand, whom we may think entirely in the wrong, whom we are tempted to despise. Many are the mockers who will be fain, one day, to receive a gracious pardon from the object of their derision.

VI. How MAJESTIC IS SPIRITUAL MEEKNESS! (Ver. 11.) We know well how our Lord bore this cruel trial. "A silent Man before his foes" was he. Able at any moment to bring them into utmost humiliation, to turn the mocking glance of triumph into the countenance blanched with unspeakable fear, and the brutal laugh of mockery into a cry for mercy, he stood without a blow, without a word on his own behalf, enduring as one that saw the invisible and the eternal. There is nothing more majestic than a calm endurance of wrong. To accept without return the strong buffeting of cruelty, to take without reply the more keen and piercing utterance of falsehood, because stillness or silence will advance the cause of truth and the kingdom of God,—

this is to be very "near the throne" on which it is our highest ambition to be placed; it is to be carrying out, most acceptably, the commandment of the meek, majestic Saviour as he says to us, "Follow me!"—C.

Ver. 16.—*Guilty compromise.* Twice (see ver. 22) Pilate made this offer to the Jews. He would chastise Jesus and release him; he would thus gratify them by putting the Object of their hatred to pain and humiliation, and he would satisfy his own conscience by saving an innocent man from the last extremity. It was a poor and a guilty compromise he proposed as a solution. If Jesus were as guilty as they claimed that he was, he deserved to die, and Pilate was in duty bound to condemn him to death; if he were innocent, he certainly ought not to have been subjected to the exposure and agony of scourging. It was a cowardly and ignoble endeavour to save himself at the expense either of public or of individual justice. Compromises are of very different character. There are compromises which are—

I. JUST, AND THEREFORE HONOURABLE. Two men in business have claims one against the other, and one cannot convince the other by argument; the proposal is made to adjust their respective claims by a compromise, each man consenting to forego something, the concession of the one being taken as a fair equivalent to that of the other: this is honourable to both. It very probably results in each man getting what is his due, and it saves both from the misery and expense of litigation, and preserves good will and even friendship.

II. WISE, AND THEREFORE COMMENDABLE. A society—it may be of a distinctly religious character—is divided by its members holding opposite opinions. Some advocate one course, the others urge a different one. The idea is suggested that a third course be adopted, which includes some features of the two; there is no serious principle involved, it is only a matter of procedure, a question of expediency. Then it will probably be found to be the wisdom of that society to accept the proposed compromise. Every one present has the double advantage of *securing something* which he approves, and (what is really better, if it could but be realized) that of *yielding something* to the wishes or the convictions of other people.

III. GUILTY, AND THEREFORE CONDEMNABLE. Such was that of the text. Such have been innumerable others since then. All are guilty that are effected: 1. At the *expense of truth.* The teacher of Divine truth may bring his doctrine down to the level of his hearers' understanding; he may make known the great verities of the faith "in many portions" (πολυμερῶς); but he may not, in order to "please men," distort or withhold the living truth of God. If he does that he shows himself unworthy of his office, and he exposes himself to the severe condemnation of his Divine Master. 2. At the *expense of justice.* However anxious we may be to preserve outward harmony, we may not, for the sake of peace, do any one man a wrong; may not asperse his character, injure his prospects, wound his spirit. Rather than do that, we must face the storm, and guide our bark as best we can. 3. At the *expense of self-respect.* If Pilate had been less hardened than he probably was, less accustomed to the infliction of human pain and shame, he would have gone back to the interior of his house ashamed of himself, as he thought of the lacerating scene that immediately followed that mockery of a trial. If we cannot yield without inflicting on our own soul a real spiritual injury, without doing (or leaving undone) an action the remembrance of which will not only shame but weaken us, then we must not compromise the matter in dispute. We must tell our tale, whatever it may be; we must make our motion, whomsoever it may offend; we must walk straight on in the road of rectitude, in the path of humanity.—C.

Ver. 24.—*The character of Pilate.* It is true that Pilate's opinion concerning Jesus of Nazareth was very different indeed from that of his accusers; but he little imagined that it would be to that poor suffering Prisoner that he would owe such immortality as he is to enjoy. Yet so it is; it is only because we are disciples of Jesus Christ that we care to ask who and what was Pilate. He is nothing but the gold upon the altar. In considering the elements of his character, we note—

I. THAT HE WAS POSSESSED OF ENERGY AND ENTERPRISE. He would hardly have reached the station he occupied, or held it as long as he did, if he had not had these two qualities in his character.

II. THAT HE WAS NOT DEVOID OF SPIRITUAL DISCERNMENT. It is clear that he was much impressed by all that he saw of Jesus. The calmness, patience, and nobility of our Lord called forth from Pilate a sincere respect. There was genuine admiration in his heart as he led forth the Divine Sufferer and exclaimed, "Behold the Man!" He was affected, and even awed, by the moral greatness he was witnessing. He may also have been moved to pity.

III. THAT HIS WORLDLINESS HAD WORN OUT HIS FAITH. He had probably had his visions, in earlier days, of the sacredness and supremacy of truth; he had indulged his idea of what was morally good and sound, more to be desired than riches, more to be pursued than honour or authority. But a life of worldliness had done for him what it will do for any of its votaries—it had eaten away his early faith; it had caused his fairest views and noblest purposes to melt and to disappear; it had left his spirit "naked to his enemies," without any assured belief in any one or in anything. "To bear witness to the truth." "What is truth?" asks the poor sceptic, whose soul was empty of all sustaining trust, of all ennobling hope.

IV. THAT HE HAD COME TO SUBORDINATE RIGHTEOUSNESS TO POLICY. That Prisoner on his hands was innocent : of that he was well assured. He would not condemn him to a cruel death unless he was obliged to do so. But he must not push his preference for righteousness too far. He must not seriously endanger his own position; he must not put a handle into the power of his enemies. No; rather than that, this pure and holy One must be scourged, must even die the death. As the trial proceeds, it appears that he is exciting a very strong hostility to himself. Let the poor Man go, then, to his doom; one more act of injustice, however regrettable in itself, will not make much difference. "And Pilate gave sentence that it should be as they required."

APPLICATION. 1. Outward circumstances prove very little. It is the judge whom we pity now; it is the bound and buffeted, the maltreated and maligned Prisoner whom we now honour and emulate. 2. Real strength is in righteousness and in love. Unrighteousness and selfishness, in the person of Pilate, resorted to shifts and expedients, and vacillated again and again between obligation and self-interest. Flawless integrity and abounding love for man, in the person of Jesus Christ, wavered not for an instant, but pursued its holy and gracious purpose through pain and shame. Policy prevails for a very little while; it goes back to its palace, but its end is exile and suicide. Poverty and love go through the deep darkness of earth to the unshadowed glory of the skies.—C.

Ver. 26.—*Compulsion and invitation; the human and the Divine methods.* Here we have an illustration of—

I. HUMAN VIOLENCE. "They laid hold upon" one Simon, and "him they compelled" (Matt. xxvii. 32) to bear his cross. What right had these Roman soldiers to impress this stranger into their service? What claim had they upon him? By what law of rectitude did they arrest him as he was entering the city, and insist on his bearing a burden, and going whither he would not? What justified them in laying hands upon him and violently enforcing this service? None whatever; nothing whatsoever. It was only another instance of the unscrupulousness of human power. Thus has it been everywhere and always. Let men but feel that they have the mastery, that theirs is the more powerful mind, the firmer will, the stronger hand, and they will ask no leave, consult no law, be restrained by no consideration of conscience. The history of man, where not under special Divine direction, has been the history of the assertion of strength over weakness; that has been the course of national, of tribal, of family, of individual life. The strong man, well armed, has "laid hold upon" the weak man, and laid some burden upon him to carry. He has virtually said, "I can command your labour, serve me; if you refuse to do so, you shall pay some penalty of my own choosing." Human violence (1) is essentially unrighteous, for it is based on no claim that can be properly so called; (2) has been found to be shamelessly unmerciful; (3) has been gradually, though slowly, subjected to the great rule of Christ (Matt. vii. 12); (4) is destined in time to make way for the rule of righteousness.

II. DIVINE PERSUASIVENESS. God does not compel us to serve him. He may, indeed, so wisely overrule all things as to make the life deliberately withheld from him or the action directed against him (*e.g.* the act of betrayal by Judas) contribute to the final issue; but he does not force the individual soul to serve him. Jesus Christ does not compel us to his service. It is true that his invitations have the authority of a command; but his commands have the sweetness of invitations. 1. He *invites us to approach* him and seek his favour. " Come unto me all ye that labour " is not a severe command; it is a most gracious invitation. " Whosoever believeth on me hath everlasting life " is not a peremptory injunction; it is a welcome and generous announcement. And while it is indeed true that Christ says, imperatively " Follow me ! " it is also true that he does not force any one into his company; he makes his appeal to our conscience and conviction; he will not have any in his service who do not freely and whole-heartedly consent to come. 2. *He graciously influences us,* that we may see and follow the true light. Paul, indeed, does speak of Christ as " apprehending," or laying hold of, him (Phil. iii. 12). But this referred to the very exceptional manifestation of his Divine power, and the language is strongly figurative. The Spirit of God does illumine our understanding and affect our heart; but he does not compel us to decide without the consent of our own will. In the last resort we have to " choose life" or death. 3. He summons us to a *full discipleship by following him* as one that bore a cross (ch. ix. 23; Matt. xvi. 24). He lets us know that we shall not meet with his full approval if we do not bear the cross after him, if we do not follow him in the path of sacrificial love. But there is truest kindness, both of substance and manner, in this his urgent challenge. 4. He *promises us inward rest* here, and a *large reward* hereafter, if we do hear his voice and do thus follow him. Between human compulsion and Divine invitation or Divine constraint, there is exceeding breadth : the one is an intolerable tyranny; the other *is* essential righteousness, and *introduces* to true liberty, to spiritual rest, to abiding joy.—C.

Vers. 27—31.—*Sympathy and solicitude.* Before reaching Calvary an interesting and instructive incident occurred. Among the tumultuous crowd that surged round the soldiers and their victims were many women. These were better away, we are disposed to think, from a scene so brutal and so harrowing as this. But we will believe that something better than curiosity, that gratitude, that affection, that womanly pity, drew them, spite of their natural shrinking, to this last sad ending. By whatever motives impelled, they were certainly moved to strong compassion as they saw the Prophet of Nazareth, the great Healer and Teacher, led forth to die. Their loud laments did not fall on the ear of One too occupied with his own impending doom to hear and heed them. Our Lord made to these weeping women the reply which is here recorded, longer and fuller than we should have supposed the circumstances would allow. It suggests to us—

I. THAT HUMAN DISTRESS NEVER FAILS TO REACH AND TOUCH HIM. If there were any moments in his life when he might have been preoccupied, and might not have noticed the sounds of sorrow, it was this hour of his agony, this hour when the weight of the world's sin rested on his soul, when the great sacrifice was in the very act of being offered. Yet even then he heard and stopped to console the troubled. An appeal to Jesus Christ in circumstances of sorrow is never ill-timed.

II. THAT SUCH SYMPATHY WITH JESUS CHRIST IS ENTIRELY OUT OF PLACE. " Weep not for me." Some men speak and act as if it were appropriate to express sympathy with the Saviour on account of his sufferings. It is, indeed, impossible to read the story of his last hours, and *realize* what it all *meant,* without having our sympathetic feeling very keenly quickened; but Jesus Christ does not ask that we should express to him, or to one another, our sympathy with him as One that then suffered. These sufferings are past; they have placed him upon the throne of the world; they have made brighter than ever his celestial crown, deeper than ever his heavenly joy. So far as *we* are concerned, and so far as they speak of our sin, they may well humble us; in so far as *he* is concerned, we *rejoice with him* that he " was perfected through suffering."

III. THAT A HOLY SOLICITUDE FOR OURSELVES AND OURS IS OFTEN THE MOST APPROPRIATE SENTIMENT. " Weep for yourselves, and for your children." We know well what reason these Jewish women had, both as patriots and as mothers, to be concerned for the fate that threatened their country and their homes. Our Lord certainly would not condemn, would not disparage, an unselfish sympathy. He who wept at Bethany, and whose law of love was the law that covered and inspired a gracious burden-bearing

(Gal. vi. 2), could not possibly do that. Indeed, we seldom stand nearer to his side than when we "weep with them that weep." But there are many times when we are tempted to be troubled by our brother's smaller difficulty instead of being concerned about our own much greater one. Do not be blind to the bodily pains or the circumstantial struggles of your neighbour; but look eagerly and earnestly to the rent which is opening in your own reputation, to the gap that is increasingly visible in your own consistency, to the fact that you are palpably descending the slope which leads down to spiritual ruin.

IV. THAT THERE ARE SAD EXTREMITIES OF EVIL WHEN NOTHING IS LEFT BUT A HOPELESS CRY. (Ver. 30.)

V. THAT SIN AND PUNISHMENT BECOME DEEPER AND NEARER AS TIME GOES ON. The green tree is exposed to the consuming fire; but the green tree in time becomes the dry, and how much more certain and more fierce then will be the devouring flame! The nation goes from bad to worse, from the worse to the worst; from dark to darker guilt, from condemnation to calamity. So does a human soul, unguided by heavenly truth and unguarded by holy principle. At any and every time in danger, its peril becomes continually greater as its guilt becomes constantly deeper. Go not one step further in the course of sin, in the way of worldliness, into the "far country" of forgetfulness. Each step is an approach to a precipice. Return on thy way without a moment's lingering.—C.

Ver. 34.—*Magnanimity an attainment.* "*Then* said Jesus, Father, forgive them; for they know not what they do." When—at what particular point did he say that? It is commonly believed that he uttered this most gracious prayer just at the time of the actual crucifixion. Just when the nails were driven into those hands, the hands that had constantly been employed in some ministry of mercy; into those feet that had been continually carrying him on some errand of kindness; or just when the heavy cross, with its suffering Victim fastened upon it, had been driven into the ground with unpitying violence;—just *then*, at the moment of most excruciating pain and of intolerable shame, he opened his lips to pray for mercy on his executioners. We have here—

I. A RARE INSTANCE OF HUMAN MAGNANIMITY. 1. Conscious, not only of perfect innocence, but of the purest and even the loftiest aims, Jesus Christ found himself not only unrewarded and unappreciated, but misunderstood, ill treated, condemned on a totally false charge, sentenced to the most cruel and shameful death a man could die. What wonder if, under those conditions, all the kindliness of his nature had turned to sourness of spirit! 2. At this very moment he was the object of the most heartless cruelty man could inflict, and must have been suffering pain of body and of mind that was literally agonizing. 3. At such a time, and under such treatment, he forgets himself to remember the guilt of those who were so shamefully wronging him. 4. Instead of entertaining any feeling of resentment, he desired that they might be forgiven their wrong-doing. 5. He did not haughtily and contemptuously decline to condemn them; he did not hardly and reluctantly forgive them; he found for them a generous extenuation; he sincerely prayed his heavenly Father to forgive them. Human magnanimity could hardly go further than that.

II. A BEAUTIFUL EXAMPLE OF HIS OWN LOFTY DOCTRINE. When in his great sermon (Matt. v.—vii.) he said, "Love your enemies ... pray for them which despitefully use and persecute you, that ye may be the children of your Father which is in heaven," he urged upon us to cherish and to illustrate the loftiest virtue on the highest grounds. This he now beautifully, perfectly exemplified. He was literally and truly praying for those who were using him despitefully. As the greatest generals and captains have proudly and honourably claimed that they "never bade men do that which they were not willing to do themselves," so this our glorious Leader, he who came to be the "Leader and Perfecter of the faith" (Heb. xii. 2: Alford), never desired of us any virtue or grace which he did not possess and did not himself adorn. He could and did say to his disciples, not only, "Go thither in the way of righteousness," but also, "Follow me in every path of purity and love." We may well love our enemies, and pray for those who despitefully use us, that we may be the children of our Father in heaven, and that we may be followers of our patient, magnanimous Master. And it is here, truly, that we have—

III. A CHALLENGE TO A GREAT ATTAINMENT. 1. To pray sincerely for those who do us wrong is one of the very highest points, if not actually the very loftiest, of human magnanimity. To dismiss all vindictive purpose, all resentful thought; to look at our enemy's procedure in a kindly light, and to take, as Christ did here, a generous view of it; to cherish a positive wish for his good; to put this wish into action, into prayer;—by these stages we reach the summit of nobility. 2. This is an attainment we should sedulously and devoutly pursue. There are those of noble nature, men and women whom God endows with a most "excellent spirit," to whom this may be plain and easy; to them it is not a steep ascent to be laboriously climbed, but a gentle slope along which they can walk without difficulty. But to most men it is an *attainment* and not an endowment. It is an attainment which can only be secured by earnest and continued cultivation. But we have for this great end the most effectual means: (1) the realization of the near presence of God, and the knowledge of his Divine approval; (2) the sense that when we succeed we win the greatest of all victories; (3) the efficacy of prayer—its *subjective* influence, and the aid which it brings us *from above;* (4) the inspiration of our Lord's example, and that of his most faithful followers (Acts vii. 60; 2 Tim. iv. 16).—C.

Ver. 34.—*Sin greater than it seems.* "They know not what they do." There is more in our actions, and therefore in our life, than there seems to be to ourselves (see "The largeness of our life," homily on ch. x. 16). There is more of good; more also of evil. These soldiers imagined that they were doing nothing more than executing a malefactor. They *were* murdering a Messiah; they were putting to death the Son of Man, the Saviour of mankind. They knew not what they did; they did not recognize the extreme seriousness, the actual awfulness, of the crime they were committing. Thus is it constantly. We suppose ourselves to be doing something of very little consequence; but he who knows the realities and the issues of all things sees in our action something far more serious than we see. We know not what we do when we err from the straight line of moral and spiritual rectitude. We do not know—

I. HOW WE HURT A HUMAN SPIRIT WHEN WE WOUND IT. Whether this be by something said or done, by a glance of the eye, by the withholding of the expected word or action, we often wound more deeply than we think. We suppose we have caused a momentary irritation. If we knew all, we should know that we have produced a soreness of feeling, a keenness of disappointment, or (it may be) a depth of distress, which it will take weeks or months to heal.

II. HOW WE WRONG OURSELVES WHEN WE SIN AGAINST OUR CONSCIENCE. It is, we assure ourselves, a very slight deviation from rectitude; it is a negligence for which we can easily make up a little further on. But, in truth, we have begun a slow, steady, spiritual descent, which will take us to the bottom. We know not what we do when we take the first step in moral laxity. We have started our soul on an evil course; we have done ourselves a wrong which we quite fail to measure.

III. HOW WE DAMAGE ANOTHER'S CHARACTER WHEN WE INJURE IT. We have only induced our neighbour to take a step which will open his eyes to that which he ought to know. So we say, and perhaps think. But, in fact, we have done much more than that. We have led him to do that which has injured his conscience, which has weakened his self-respect, which has enfeebled his character. He will be less strong, henceforth, in the evil hour of temptation; he will be more open to attack, less likely to resist and to conquer his adversary. When we lead into temptation and sin, we "know not what we do."

IV. HOW WE GRIEVE OUR SAVIOUR WHEN WE DISOBEY OR DISHONOUR HIM. We do not know how much he expects of his disciples, especially of those who have such opportunities as we have of knowing and doing his will—how much attachment, how strong an affection, how quick an obedience, how full and patient a submission, he has a right to look for, and does wait to receive. And we do not know the fulness and intensity of his feeling of disappointment and sorrow when we fail him. The disciples did not know what they did, how grievously they failed, when they slept in that hour through which they should have watched. What depth of touching, tenderest pathos we hear in these words of gentle remonstrance: "Could ye not watch with me one hour?"

V. How WE HINDER THE CAUSE OF CHRIST when we discredit it. We think, perhaps, that the evil impression we have conveyed by our inconsistency will soon be forgotten, lost entirely in the current of human affairs. But more harm is done than we know or think. Some souls are shocked, scandalized, injured; their faith is lessened, perhaps pierced; they will not count for Christ what they would have counted. Springs of anti-Christian influence are started: who shall say whither they will flow?

VI. How WE SIN AGAINST GOD WHEN WE WITHHOLD FROM HIM OURSELVES AND OUR SERVICE. We may imagine that we are only delaying till a more suitable or convenient time the duty we intend to discharge. But we are really disobeying a Divine command; we are refusing a Divine invitation; we are continuing in open rebellion, in unfilial estrangement. We are seriously sinning against our heavenly Father, our merciful Saviour, our rightful and righteous Sovereign. 1. Our ignorance of "what we do" is, in part *a necessity of our finite nature;* for we cannot possibly look down into the depth of things; nor can we look on to the final issues. This is beyond the compass of our powers. 2. But it is in part also *the fault of our character.* We do not think, we do "not consider" (Isa. i. 3), we do not inquire. We do not use as we might our spiritual faculties. More patient, prayerful consideration of "what we do" would save us from many errors, many wrongs, and also from many painful memories and much self-reproach.—C.

Ver. 35.—*A sad spectacle and the supreme vision.* "And the people stood beholding." "Sitting down they watched him there" (Matt. xxvii. 36). Shall we envy those spectators the scene they then witnessed? Shall we wish that we had lived when, with our mortal eyes, we could have seen the Saviour crucified on our behalf? I think not. With this distance of time and space between us, we have a better, truer standpoint where we are. No doubt we lose much by that distance; but we gain at least as much as we lose. To those who "stood beholding," or who "sat and watched," there was—

I. AN EXCEEDINGLY SAD SPECTACLE. They saw: 1. A human being suffering the last extremity of pain and shame. Some among that company could look upon that scene with positive enjoyment, some with stolid indifference; but those of whom we think, the disciples, would witness it with intense, heart-piercing sympathy, with utmost agitation of spirit. His suffering must, in a large degree, have been theirs also —theirs in proportion to the love they bore him. 2. A Prophet who had failed to be appreciated, and was now a martyr nobly dying in attestation of the truth. 3. A sacred cause losing its Chief and Champion; a cause being wounded and almost certainly slain in the person of its Founder and Exponent. For who could hope that there would be found amongst his disciples any that would take the standard from his hands, and bear it on to victory? For Christ to die was for Christianity to perish. Such was the spectacle on which his disciples looked as they gathered about his cross. The scene was more vivid, more impressive, more powerfully affecting, as thus enacted before their eyes; but we see in reality more than they did. We have before us—

II. THE SUPREME VISION on which we can gaze on earth. We see: 1. *One who once suffered and died,* but whose agony is over; whose pain and sorrow are not now to him sources of evil, but, on the other hand, the ground and the occasion of purest joy and highest honour (see homily on vers. 27—31). Had we been present then, we must have shrunk from the spectacle before us as too painful for sensitiveness to endure. Now we can bear to dwell on his dying and his death, because the element of overwhelming and blinding sympathy is happily withdrawn. 2. *A grand spiritual victory.* We do not see in the crucified prophet One that was defeated; we see One that told us all that he came to tell, communicating to us all the knowledge we need in order to live our higher life on earth, and to prepare for the heavenly life beyond; that was not prevented from delivering any part of his Divine message; that completed all he came to do; that was amply entitled to say, as he did before he died, "It is *finished!*" 3. *A Divine Redeemer ensuring,* by his death, *the triumph* of his cause. Had he *not* died as he did, had he saved himself as he was taunted and challenged to do, had he not gone on to that bitter end and drunk that bitter cup even to the dregs, *then* he would have failed. But because he suffered unto death, he triumphed gloriously, and became "the Author of eternal salvation to all them that believe."

This is the supreme vision of human souls. We do well to gaze on nobility as we see it illustrated in human lives around us. We do well to look long and lovingly on human virtue as manifested in the lives and deaths of the glorious army of martyrs. But there is no vision so well worthy of our view; of our frequent, our constant, our protracted and intense beholding, as that of the merciful and mighty Saviour dying for our sins, dying in wondrous love that he might draw us to himself and restore us to our Father and our home. Before our eyes Christ crucified is conspicuously set forth (Gal. iii. 1); and if we would have forgiveness of sin, rest of soul, worthiness of spirit, nobility of life, hope in death, a blessed immortality, we must direct our eyes unto him who was once "lifted up" that he might be the Refuge, the Friend, the Lord, the Saviour of the world to the end of time. Better than the saddest spectacle man ever saw is that supreme vision which is the hope and the life of each looking and trusting human heart.—C.

Vers. 35—37.—*Self-saving and self-sacrifice.* We have two things here of which the latter is much the more worth looking at.

I. INHUMANITY AT ITS LOWEST. There are many degrees of inhumanity. 1. It is bad for men or women deliberately to shut themselves out of the society of the wrong and miserable, in order that, without distraction, they may minister to their own comfort or consult their own well-being. 2. It is worse to look on the wounded traveller as he lies within sight and reach of us, and to pass him coldly by "on the other side." 3. It is worse still to regard the overthrow of human greatness or prosperity with positive satisfaction of spirit, to find a guilty enjoyment in the humiliation of another. 4. It is worst of all to do as did these men at the cross—to mock at human misery, to taunt it in the hour of its agony, to add another pang to the keen sufferings that already lacerate the soul. Alas! what may not men become! what positively awful possibilities of evil are wrapt up in every human soul! that tiny hand, so soft and delicate, so beautiful, so harmless, what blow may it not possibly strike, some day, against all that is most sacred and most precious! It makes all the difference whether, under Christian principles, we are steadily climbing *up* toward that which is holy and Divine; or whether, under the dominion of evil forces, we are slowly sliding *down* toward all that is wrong and base. What an argument for ranging ourselves, while yet young, under the guidance of Jesus Christ, the Righteous and the Gracious One!

II. MAGNANIMITY AT ITS HIGHEST. 1. *The extremity of evil* to which our Lord was then submitting; the most excruciating bodily pain; the most terrible and almost intolerable mental distress; the apprehension of approaching death. 2. *The powerful temptation* presented to him to deliver himself from it all. By one volition of his will he could have descended from the cross, thus releasing himself and confounding his enemies. He had (1) the strongest possible *inducement* to do this from the instincts of the nature he had assumed; (2) the strongest possible *provocation* to do this in the bitter and cruel taunts of his enemies. 3. *His most magnanimous refusal* to exert his power in his own favour. He heard those derisive cries, but he heeded them not. He let those revilers think that he *was* unable to save himself; he knew that if he did save himself he could not save others (Matt. xxvii. 42). So he voluntarily continued to endure all that torture of body, to bear all that burden of shame and agony of spirit, to go on and down into the deepening shadow of death. Surely spiritual nobility could never strike a higher note than that, could never reach a loftier summit than that. How far can we follow our Lord along this upward path? There have been men who, at a certain point in their career, have clearly foreseen a dark and deathful ending, who have been entreated by their friends to go no further, to stand aside, to "save themselves" and think no more about the salvation of others (see Acts xxi. 12). And it is quite possible that, though we shall never be placed in a position just like that of our Master, we may have the choice offered us which was then offered him—we may have to choose between *saving ourselves and leaving others to their fate* on the one hand, or *sacrificing ourselves and saving our fellows* on the other hand. If that choice should be presented to us, what should we do? The answer depends very much on the measure of the *spirit of unselfishness* we are cherishing and practising continually. (1) Before us is a noble opportunity—that of teaching, enlightening, (instrumentally) redeeming men; but (2) we cannot use this opportunity to any extent without self-sacrifice. If we are determined to "save ourselves," we shall do but very little in the work of saving others. (3) We must choose between the two : either we must resolve to spare ourselves expenditure and endurance, and let the work of human elevation go on without our help; or we must resolve *not* to spare ourselves, not to save time or money, or trouble, or health, not to spare ourselves uncongenial acts or unpleasant endurances, that men may learn what they know not, may see that to which they are yet blind, that they may be led out of exile into the kingdom of God.   If we are keeping our Master well in view, especially if we are beholding him on the cross refusing to save himself though challenged with utmost bitterness to do so, we also shall make the nobler choice.—C.

Vers. 39—43.—*True penitence.* These verses narrate what we may call a standard fact of the gospel of Christ—a fact to which appeal will always be made, as it has always been made, in reference to a late repentance. We have to consider—

I. THE BREVITY WITH WHICH A GREAT SPIRITUAL REVOLUTION MAY BE WROUGHT IN A HUMAN MIND. Twelve hours before, this man was a hardened criminal, habituated to a life of rapacious and murderous violence; his counterpart is to be found to-day in the cells of a penal establishment.   And now, after a short companionship with Jesus, after hearing him speak and seeing him suffer, his heart is purged and cleansed of its iniquity, he is another man, he is a child of God, an heir of heaven.   There are great capacities in these human souls of ours, which do not come often into exercise, but which are actually within us.   Powerful speech, imminent peril, great emergencies, sudden inspiration from God,—these and other things will call them forth; there is a brilliant flash of remembrance, or of emotion, or of realization, or of conviction and resolution.   And then that which is ordinarily wrought in many days or months is accomplished in an hour.   The movements of our mind are not subject to any time-table calculations whatsoever.   No man can define the limit of possibility here.   Great revolutions can be and have been wrought almost momentarily.   Not slowly toiling upward step by step, but more swiftly than the uprising of the strongest bird upon fleetest wing, may the human soul ascend from the darkness of death into the radiant sunshine of hope and life.

II. THE THOROUGHNESS OF THIS MAN'S CHANGE AS EVIDENCED BY HIS WORDS. 1. He recognizes the existence and the power and the providence of God (ver. 40). 2. He has a sense of the turpitude of his own conduct, a due sense of sin (ver. 41). 3. He recognizes the innocence and excellence of Jesus Christ (ver. 41). 4. He believes in his real royalty, though it is so hidden from sight, and though circumstances are so terribly against it (ver. 42). 5. He believes in the pitifulness as well as the power of this kingly Sufferer, and he makes his humble but not unhopeful appeal to his remembrance. 6. He does the one thing for Christ he can do as he is dying on the cross—he remonstrates with his companion in crime, and seeks to silence his cruel taunts.   Here is penitence, faith, service, all springing up and in earnest exercise in this brief hour.

III. A SUDDEN TRANSITION FROM THE LOWEST TO THE HIGHEST ESTATE.   (Ver. 43.) "What a day to that dying man! How strange a contrast between its opening and its close, its morning and its night! Its morning saw him a culprit condemned before the bar of earthly judgment; before evening shadowed the hill of Zion he stood accepted at the bar of heaven. The morning saw him led out through an earthly city's gates in company with One who was hooted at by the crowd that gathered round him; before night fell upon Jerusalem the gates of another city, even the heavenly, were lifted up, and he went through them in company with One around whom all the hosts of heaven were bowing down as he passed to take his place beside the Father on his everlasting throne" (Hanna).   In view of this most interesting fact we gather two lessons. 1. *One of hopefulness.* It is never too late to repent; in other words, repentance, when real, is never ineffectual.   None could be more undeniably impenitent until within a few hours of his death than this malefactor, and no man's penitence could be more decisively availing than his.   It was real and thorough, and therefore it was accepted.   It is a great thing for those who speak for Christ to be warranted, as they are, in going to the dying and despairing, and telling these departing ones, that true penitence, however late, avails with God; that his ear is not closed against the sigh of the contrite, even at the last hour of the day; that up to the last there is mercy to be had by them who truly seek it. But there is another lesson to be learnt. 2. *One of warning and of fear.* There is every reason to hope that true though late repentance is always accepted; but there is grave reason to fear that late repentance is seldom real and true. How often does experience prove that men in apparently dying hours have believed themselves to be penitent when they have only been apprehensive of coming doom! The dread of approaching judgment is far from being the same thing as repentance unto life. Not the last hour, when a selfish dread may be so easily mistaken for spiritual conviction, but the day of health and strength, when conviction can pass into action and honest shame into faithful service, is the time to turn from sin and to seek the face and the favour of the living God. Let none despair, but let none presume.—C.

Ver. 44.—*The shelter of the darkness.* The darkness which fell upon Jerusalem at midday and enshrouded the scene of the Crucifixion was a phenomenon for which it is impossible to account physically, and which it is not easy to explain morally. It is a matter for reverent conjecture, for thoughtful and devout inference, for sacred and solemn imagination. We are on sure ground when we say that it came from the Divine Father, and came on behalf of his beloved Son. We do not venture much when we suggest that it came in response to that Son's appeal in this dark "day of his flesh" (Heb. v. 7). We may do well to consider what was the probable impression it made on those who were concerned in that sad and sacred scene.

I. ON THE LEADERS OF THE PEOPLE. Surely they were smitten with consternation. One would suppose that, as these men witnessed the wonderful works of Christ, *some doubts* as to the rightness of their antagonism to him must have darted into their minds, and that beneath their confident and defiant attitude of enmity there must have lain some secret misgivings as to the course they were taking. Probably they were not without their fears that something would happen at the last to disappoint them. But as the day wore on, and Jesus actually hung upon the cross, and his strength was certainly going, and the people quietly acquiesced if they did not possibly "assist," all seemed to be satisfactory, to be indeed triumphant. When, lo! a strange, unaccountable darkness, an impenetrable obscurity! The sun refuses to shine at midday. No man sees his fellow, or sees him only in the faintest light. The Crucified One is screened from view. The scoffs and shouts are silenced, and there is a terrible stillness and solemnity. What can that mean? God is speaking in his own chosen way, and is rebuking their guilty deed. There is a quaking at the proud Pharisee's heart, a trembling in the soul of the scribe; there are no more taunts from *their* bitter lips; an unspeakable terror invades even their closed hearts which no casuistry can bar. Is it, then, the blood of their Messiah that they have been shedding?

II. ON THE MULTITUDE. How must they have been subdued with awe, if not agitated with wild alarm! How overwhelming to their less cultured minds must so astounding an event have been! "Whither," we hear them say, "have our rulers led us? Surely there is something sacred and Divine in this Galilæan Prophet! Heaven is pronouncing in his favour. Have we crucified our King? Will his blood be upon us?" and the daughters of Jerusalem already begin to weep for themselves and for their children, as they think that some great calamity impends.

III. ON THE ROMAN SOLDIER. Trained to face peril and to be calm even in the presence of overshadowing death, he probably remained quiet and firm, the least moved of all the throng. Nothing could be *done*, and he would lean on his spear, waiting the centurion's command when light should break; though exceedingly astonished and awe-struck, he would stand to his post with unmoved purpose and well-mastered fear.

IV. ON THE DISCIPLES. To them it must have come as a relief, if not a promise. Believing in their Lord, wondering with great amazement at his capture and crucifixion, they would feel that any miraculous interposition was not unlikely, was quite probable. It raised their hopes a few degrees above despair; possibly many degrees. If God interposed thus far, he might restore everything. At the least, this welcome darkness screened themselves, who were too near the cross for security, though too far from their Master for service; perhaps it quieted their fear while it comforted their conscience.

V. ON THE SAVIOUR HIMSELF. To him we may be well assured that it was a most welcome succour. 1. It was a verdict from heaven attesting his innocency. It brought confusion to his enemies and confirmation to himself. It was "a sign from heaven" distinctly in his favour.   The sun refused to shine on so guilty a crime as that then perpetrated; the darkness that wrapped them round was God's attestation of the darkness of the deed then being enacted.   2. It effectually shut the mouth of ribaldry and reproach.   "It stopped each wagging head, it silenced each gibing tongue."   We cannot tell how painful and how piercing to his sensitive spirit those cruel mockings were; nor can we, therefore, tell how much of a relief was the stillness that came with the darkness.   3. It screened him from shame.   "Men would leave the Crucified exposed in shame and nakedness to die, but an unseen hand was stretched forth to draw the drapery of darkness round him and hide him from vulgar gaze."   4. It gave him a desired privacy for sorrow and for prayer.   Sorrow and prayer always seek solitude; they desire to be alone with God.   We do not like any others, except it be one that is most beloved, to witness the deeper griefs, or the sadder and sterner wrestlings of our soul.   We seek the shade of some Gethsemane for such sacred experiences as these. What awful sorrow now rested upon Christ, now agitated his soul to its very depths, we may never understand.   But we know that the burden he bore for us was at its very heaviest, that the sorrow he endured for us was at its extremest point just at this time, for it culminated in that terrible cry of desolation (Matt. xxvii. 45, 46) which we do not try to fathom, which silences all speech and subdues every spirit.   Such sacred sorrow, accompanied, as it certainly was, with the most close communion and fervent prayer, was not for the curiosity of that heartless crowd.   It needed the most perfect privacy.   And so the Divine Father, in this supreme hour of his Son's great work and of the redemption of mankind, "made darkness, and it was night;" shut the Saviour round with the merciful folds of thick darkness, that he might be alone with that Father in whose sole presence the great sacrifice was to be completed.—C.

Ver. 45.—*The rent veil.*   At the time when Jesus died it is exceedingly probable that there would be priests in the "holy place."   It was now afternoon, it was drawing toward the time of evening sacrifice; they would be in attendance rendering the service of the sanctuary; they would certainly be aware of what was happening just outside Jerusalem, and would be powerfully affected by the fact.   Suddenly, as if grasped and rent by unseen hands, that most sacred veil interposing between the antechamber and the reception-room of God himself, was torn in twain, "from the top to the bottom."   The incident was undeniably miraculous.   No Jew would have dreamed of daring to do an act that would have been so impious in a man.   A Divine hand must have been there, and when they entered into the mysterious darkness and felt the earthquake, must not these priests have asked themselves whether the rending of the veil did not signify a new epoch in the kingdom of God?   May not the conversion of a "great company of the priests" (Acts vi. 7) be partly accounted for by this striking and significant event? But what did it symbolize?

I. That God had adopted a new method of asserting his holiness and impressing it on the mind and heart of the world.   That veil was an essential part of a system of carefully graduated approach to God.   It divided the "holy" from the "most holy" place, and beyond it none might pass but the high priest, and he only once a year.   It was intended to teach the absolute holiness of God—that it was only as men were prepared, and as they were separated from sin that they could be admitted to his presence.   It was not without effect on the Jewish mind; that nation had thus grasped the idea of the purity and perfection of God.   But now his character was so revealed that all such symbolism was no longer needed.   The death of Jesus Christ his Son, as the Sacrifice for the sin of the world, was an expression of Divine holiness incomparably superior to the symbolism of the temple and for ever superseding it. Henceforth, when men wanted to know what God felt about sin—how he hated it, what he thought it worth while to do and to suffer in order to expel it—they would look to that cross at Calvary, and there read his mind and know his will.   Holy places were no longer needed.

II. That God had now provided another and better way of mercy for mankind.   Behind the veil was the innermost chamber; and of this chamber *the* furniture was the ark with the two tables of the Law, *and the mercy-seat above it*; we read of this compartment thus: "within the veil before the mercy-seat."   *Mercy was thus resting on Law.*   Mercy always must be founded on holiness; for without holiness there can be no mercy worthy of the name. And on the great Day of Atonement the high priest entered this "holy of holies," and sprinkled blood upon the mercy-seat for the cleansing of the sins of the nation. But the cross of Jesus Christ spoke of the Divine mercy as no temple furniture could do; there needed nothing to teach the supremacy of mercy above Law after the dying love of the Redeemer of mankind, and there needed no more sprinkling of blood upon a mercy-seat after *this* great Day of Atonement, when " by one sacrifice of himself for ever" the spotless Lamb of God presented "a Propitiation for the sins of the world." The temple rites then became obsolete; its services were past; there need be no more guarding of one sacred place from another; let the sacred curtain be taken down or rent in twain.

III. THAT THE WAY TO THE HOLY ONE HIMSELF IS NOW OPEN TO ALL MANKIND. That veil was an instrument that not only secluded, but excluded; through it no eye might venture to glance, no intruding hand might reach, no presumptuous feet might step. To pass that limit was to incur the heaviest penalty; "the Holy Ghost this signifying, that the way into the holiest of all was not yet made manifest." But now "the good High Priest is come, supplying Aaron's place," and having offered up the one all-sufficient sacrifice, having obtained thereby "eternal redemption," that excluding veil is rent in twain, that barrier is broken down; there are no more limitations, no more distinctions; there is access for every child of man to the mercy-seat of God— to the Holy One himself, to seek his grace and find his favour. Are we drawing nigh? Are we entering in? Are we availing ourselves of this priceless privilege, this glorious provision for our spirit's need? In many words and ways God invites us to draw nigh to himself: he did so when his invisible hand rent in twain that separating veil. "Having therefore boldness to enter into the holiest by the blood of Jesus . . . let us draw near with a true heart in full assurance of faith."—C.

Ver. 46.—*How to die and to live.* Our text treats of the dying of our Lord. We may distinguish between death and dying. All men die, but all men have not a dying experience. Those who are killed instantaneously in war or by accident, those who are attacked by fatal apoplexy, those who die in their sleep, have no such experience. It is probable that we shall have *to face the fact* that we are passing away from life, that when a few more hours have come and gone we shall have entered the unseen world. It is therefore of no small value to us that our great Exemplar underwent not only death, but the conscious act of dying, and that in this respect also he "left us an example that we should follow his steps." We look at—

I. THE DYING OF OUR LORD IN THE LIGHT OF THESE WORDS. The words he uttered just as his end drew near indicate: 1. *Deep serenity of spirit.* They show nothing of agitation or anxiety; they breathe a calm stillness of soul; they are fragrant of peace and tranquillity. They begin with that word, "Father," which all along had been a name of strength and peace; he was evidently resting in the assurance of parental love. And the words that follow are in a strain of entire spiritual composure. 2. *True and living faith.* Jesus was resigning his spirit to God's gracious charge, knowing that in his holy and mighty keeping it would be safe and blessed. Here was fullest confidence in God and in immortality. 3. *Holy resignation.* As a Son of man, Jesus felt still subject to the Divine Father of all; and as he came to do and bear his will, and had done and had borne it perfectly in every hour and act of life, so now in this last volition he yielded himself to God. Thus with a soul tranquil to its profoundest depths, realizing the unseen and eternal world, resigning his spirit to the Divine Father, he bowed his head in death.

II. OUR OWN DEPARTURE. Having found in the death of Jesus Christ that which is the ground of our pardon, our peace, our life before God; having lived in the love and in the service of a once crucified and now ever-living Saviour;—there is no reason to doubt that we shall die as he died, breathing the spirit he breathed, if we do not use the very language that was upon his lips. 1. Our departure will be *tranquil.* We shall not be terrified, alarmed, agitated; our spirit will look calmly forward to the moment of departure from this world and of entrance into another. We shall face the very near future with a smile. 2. For we shall be sustained by a *living faith.* (1) We shall feel that we are only going into the nearer presence of our own Father—of him before whom we have been living and in whom we have been rejoicing; only passing from one room to another in our Father's house. (2) We shall have faith in Jesus Christ himself. That death upon the cross constitutes him a Divine Saviour, in whom we hide; and we shall die in the calm assurance that we shall be "found in him," and accepted through him. We shall say, with deeper and fuller meaning than the psalmist could, "Into thine hand I commit my spirit: *thou hast redeemed me, O Lord God of truth*" (Ps. xxxi. 5). (3) *We shall yield ourselves to God in the spirit of consecration*, assured that in that new and unknown realm which we are entering we may spend our time and our powers, liberated and enlarged, in his holy and blessed service: and the spirit of consecration is the spirit of confidence and hope. And while these words are particularly appropriate to dying lips, and very probably suggested the last utterance of the first Christian martyr (Acts vii. 59), they need not be held in reserve for that occasion; they admirably express our true attitude in—

III. OUR DAILY LIFE. So David evidently felt (Ps. xxxi. 5), and so we may feel. In faith and in self-surrender we should be continually commending our spirit to our heavenly Father's charge: 1. When the day is done and we enter the nightly darkness and unconsciousness, during which we can take no charge of ourselves. 2. As we go forth each morning to duties, trials, temptations, opportunities, to which our own unaided strength is quite unequal. 3. If we feel that we are entering some dark cloud of adversity and trial in which we shall have peculiar need of Divine support. 4. When we are called to new spheres and weightier responsibilities, wherein other graces will be required than any that have yet been demanded of us. At all such times should we, in faith and consecration, commit the keeping of our souls to our heavenly Father, to be sheltered in his faithfulness, to be enriched by his love and his power.—C.

Ver. 48.—*Sacred impressions.* There was a considerable company of spectators at the Crucifixion. They were attracted not only by the spectacle of a triple execution, but, far more, by the fact that the Prophet whose fame had filled the land was to be led forth to die. It was not the riffraff of Jerusalem merely that "beheld the things that were done." The sense of impropriety in attendance at such sanguinary and harrowing scenes is quite modern. It did not prevail there and then. Probably the leading citizens were present—the well-to-do, the educated, the refined—male and female. All classes and all characters were there—the devout and the profane, the rough and the gentle, the selfish and the sympathetic. And of that large company of people there would be present men and women very variously affected toward Jesus Christ. We may say, without hesitation, that the eleven were there; though it is more than likely that, for a time at any rate, they stood afar off, we cannot doubt that they were there, waiting and wondering; hoping with a faint hope, fearing with a terrible and mastering dread. Many true and loyal disciples were there, among whom, truest among the true, were the women who had followed him and "ministered to him" (Matt. xxvii. 55). Besides these were the fickle, doubled-minded multitude, who cried, "Hosannah!" one day, and a few days later shouted, "Crucify him!" And beyond these in spiritual distance were his implacable and bitter enemies. What may we suppose to have been the effect of the Crucifixion on the minds of "the people that came together to that sight"?

I. IMMEDIATE EFFECTS PROBABLY PRODUCED. 1. There were *physical elements* sure to excite their wondering imagination. When an unnatural darkness brooded over the entire scene for three long dread hours, when the earth trembled, when the loud death-cry of the suffering Saviour pierced the air, there was a combination of strange marvels and unusual experiences which must have shaken their souls and filled them with a great awe. 2. And there were *moral elements* there fitted to touch their hearts. There was the presence of *death*—death, "the great reconciler," that quenches strong animosities, that awakens an unwonted pity, that subdues the hardened soul to a surprising softness. There was the death of a Man still young, of a Man who had rendered undeniably great services to many hearts in many homes. There was death met with heroic fortitude, undergone with a calmness, a magnanimity, a moral greatness, such as their eyes had never seen before. These two elements together powerfully affected the people that drew to that sight; and with whatsoever thought in their mind they "came together," it is certain that a very great majority of them went home astonished, if not ashamed and alarmed; they returned "smiting their breasts." But what were—

II. THE ULTIMATE EFFECTS PRODUCED? 1. Some effects were permanently good. Surely it was partly, if not largely, the remembrance of what they had seen and done and felt on this great day that led to the "pricking of heart" they experienced when Peter spoke so faithfully, and led them to Christian baptism (Acts ii. 22, 23, 37—41). Was not the "smiting of the breast" more than an antecedent in time to that being smitten in heart when they listened and responded? 2. Others, we may be sure, were *evanescent and unfruitful.* It would have been a very singular case if there were not many who felt much agitation that day, and the next, and, perhaps, the day after; but who soon allowed pressing cares or passing pleasures to drive convictions from the soul. They "smote their breasts, and returned;" but, instead of returning to God, they went back to the old routine and the old formalism and unspirituality. It is well to be affected by the facts of God's providence, whether these be simple and ordinary, or whether unusual and startling. It is well indeed to be affected by the view of a Saviour's death, however that death may be presented to our souls. But let no man rest contented with such emotion as was in the breast of the people who "came together to that sight." It is wholly undecisive; if it lead not to something better than itself, it will bring forth no fruit of life. It must pass, and should pass quickly, into an intelligent conviction of sin, into a real and living faith in him who was then the Crucified One, and so into newness of life in him and unto him.—C.

Vers. 1—25.—*Jesus vindicated by his enemies.* We pass now from the ecclesiastical to the secular sphere. The charge brought forward in the Sanhedrin is *blasphemy*; before Pilate and Herod the charge must be *sedition* and *treason.* Yet amid his unscrupulous enemies unimpeachable testimony is forthcoming of his innocence.

I. THE TESTIMONY ELICITED BY PILATE. (Vers. 1—7.) The accusation made against Christ was twofold: (1) forbidding to pay tribute; (2) assuming royalty. Now, the first part of the accusation was totally false. Jesus, when asked about the tribute, had expressly advised the people to "render unto Cæsar the things that are Cæsar's." There could be no conflict of interests between the emperor and Christ so far as tribute was concerned. Doubtless upon this first point Pilate received ample assurance that it was groundless. When, again, he inquired about Christ's *royalty,* he was told that his kingship was not earthly, but *spiritual.* Although Pilate could not grasp its exact meaning, he saw sufficient to assure him that it was on a different plane from that of Cæsar's. Hence Pilate declared his innocence before his accusers. Upon this the chief priests and scribes were reduced to the complaint that he was stirring up the people from Galilee to Judæa. Strange complaint, that Jesus was rousing up his fellows! He was troubling Israel very much as Elias had done. Men are in desperate need of an accusation when they resort to this one, which merely means that the accused one is in downright earnest![1] As soon as Pilate hears of Christ's earnestness in Galilee, he inquires if he belongs to Herod's jurisdiction, and is happy to hand him over for trial to the Idumean.

II. THE TESTIMONY BORNE BY HEROD. (Vers. 8—12.) We have next to notice how Herod has unconsciously to testify to Christ's innocence. The murderer of the Baptist thinks, now that Jesus is brought before him, that he has only to express a wish for a miracle, and it will be gratified. To his great surprise and humiliation he receives no answer to his numerous questions; nor do the fierce calumnies of the Jews elicit from the meek Messiah a single word in mitigation or defence. The treatment of Herod was that of *silent contempt.* The wicked king deserved no other fate. And his only revenge was to mock Christ and set him at naught. So they array him in a robe such as the high priests wore, white and brilliant, indicating at once what he pretended to be and how innocent he really was. Herod, in sending him back in this scornful fashion, conveyed to Pilate's mind clearly that he had no more fault to find with him than the Roman governor had.[2] This was the second testimony to the innocency of Jesus.

III. THE TESTIMONY IMPLIED BY THE DEMAND FOR BARABBAS. (Vers. 13—19.) In no clearer way could the chief priests have shown the utter groundlessness of their first charge than in demanding Barabbas in preference to Jesus. Here was a real rebel,

[1] Cf. Saurin's 'Sermons,' tome xi. p. 236.
[2] Cf. Godet, *in loc.*; also Gerok's 'Evangelien-Predigten,' s. 319.

who had committed murder in the insurrection, and he is made the idol of the Jewish
populace.   They show in this their *sympathy with sedition*.   They show clearly to
Pilate that Jesus must be thwarting in some way their seditious designs, else they
would not clamour so eagerly for his blood.   Instead of substantiating their accusation
against Jesus, therefore, they really formulate an accusation of treason against themselves.   They were guilty ; he was innocent.   They were the dangerous class ; Jesus
occupied a region altogether outside the interests of Cæsar.

IV. Jesus sacrificed to popular clamour. (Vers. 20—25.) There is no show
of justice in condemning Christ.   All accusation against him fails, and all which can
be done is to *shout him down*.   If Jesus be not crucified, Jerusalem will go into revolt.
Will not an *émeute* be worse than the death of an individual?   And so the worldly
governor, charged by Rome to keep the peace in the province at all hazards, prefers to
deliver the innocent to the will of the guilty than to brave their wrath.   It is clamour
that secures his condemnation.   The judge, who should be the protector of the innocent, unites with the populace in doing him to death.   Alas! that men should be so
bent on peace as to be ready to sacrifice the innocent to secure it! And yet our Lord's
character never shone with so bright a lustre as when he submitted to such wrongs as
these.   He was truly meek and lowly in heart when he bore so quietly the wrath of
the Jews and the time-serving policies of Pilate and Herod.   This friendship of Herod
and of Pilate, resting on a common indifference to Jesus, is the emblem of those worldly
truces which men make who wish to enjoy immunity from trouble; but they do not
wear well.—R. M. E.

Vers. 26—46.—*The merciful Saviour on the cross.*   Delivered unto the will of the
Jews by the indecision of Pilate, Jesus accepts the cross, and proceeds under its crushing
weight towards Calvary.   But seeing him fainting under it, they press Simon the
Cyrenian into service, and he has the everlasting honour of carrying the end of the
beam after Jesus.   Thus is it in all life's burdens—the weighty end of them is carried
by the sympathetic Master, while the lighter end he allows his people to carry after
him.   And here we must notice—

I. His consideration for Jerusalem's weeping daughters. (Vers. 27—31.)
The victim of Rome's cruelty, he has enlisted the sympathy of many weeping women.
They see in his death the departure of their best earthly Friend.   It is the moment
of their deepest sorrow.   But Jesus tells them to reserve their tears for themselves.
This death of his will lead inevitably to the destruction of Jerusalem and to the dire
calamities of the nation.   These will be much more lamentable than any sorrows through
which he is now to pass.   Why, then, does he call upon them to weep?   Manifestly
that their timely repentance may ensure their escaping the troubles which are so surely
coming upon the earth.   But the *self-forgetful* attitude of Jesus is surely most instructive.   He thinks not of himself, but of their hard case, even though on his journey to
the cross.   It is the most perfect consideration for others' welfare, and the most beautiful
forgetfulness of one's own, that he here exhibits.

II. He was numbered with the transgressors. (Vers. 32, 33.) There was
something peculiarly contemptuous in the arrangement of Jesus between two notable
criminals.   They were robbers—perhaps had been associates of Barabbas.   They had
committed, most probably, murder in the insurrection, so that the cross was the rightful
end of such careers.   But to number Jesus, the innocent, with them, to make him one
with the greatest criminals then available, was diabolical!   And yet he does not
protest.   Nay, he is willing to be thus identified that he may save even one of his
associates.   And yet, is not this arrangement, which numbered him with the transgressors, simply the outward expression of the great fact which is the foundation of our
salvation?   If Jesus had not voluntarily taken up the position of substitute, and identified himself with sinners, we should never have been redeemed.

III. Intercession from the cross. (Ver. 34.) It was ignorance on the part of
many which led to this great crime, but *culpable* ignorance.   They should have known
better.   They needed forgiveness for it.   They are the subjects of his intercession.   He
prays, "Father, forgive them ; for they know not what they do."   There never had
been such a forgiving spirit manifested since the world began.   No wonder that the
dying scenes took on ever after a new halo, and that martyrs were able, in spite of

suffering, to forgive their murderers and intercede for their salvation! It was the glory of patience which was manifested upon the cross.

IV. THE CHARGE OF SELF-NEGLECT. (Vers. 35—38.) As they walk round the cross in their selfishness, the Jews charge Jesus with self-neglect. He had saved others, but now he does not try to save himself. If he would only show that he can take care of "number one," they would believe on him. Assuredly we have here the self-revelation of the world. The world believes in the selfish, self-seeking leaders of men. A Napoleon or Cæsar, who is willing to sacrifice millions of men to gratify his ambition, is believed in—at all events for a time! But Jesus, who sacrifices himself, is derided. Yet in the end the kingship of the self-sacrificing Saviour is acknowledged. The true King of the Jews is he who could lay down his life for his subjects, and so redeem them.

V. THE FIRST RECOGNIZER OF CHRIST'S KINGSHIP. (Vers. 39—43.) One in the vast assemblage, however, sees below the surface, and recognizes the sovereignty of self-sacrifice. At first reviling Christ, he had come to see, beneath the meek exterior of the Saviour, the real regal spirit. Hence he changes sides, begins to rebuke the other malefactor who continues his unholy maledictions, and then quietly implores the Lord to remember him when he comes in his kingdom. The poor robber, who had perhaps fought under some false Messiah, and knew what Jewish hopes were, believes that this meek and suffering One upon the cross beside him will yet come to his kingdom. When that advent is to be he knows not. But even in the far-off time it will be well for him to be remembered by him. Thus he prays, and is answered. But "To-day shalt thou be with me in Paradise," is the blessed hope set before him. Paradise is part of his kingdom, and the dying robber will be with Jesus in its peaceful bowers that very day. What a hope to be opened up to the dying man! What comfort it gave him, and should give to us!

VI. THE CONSUMMATION. (Vers. 44—46.) After these preliminaries are settled, the dealing of Jesus with the Father himself comes on. It was meet that a veil of darkness should surround the suffering Son and the righteous Father. The Priest and the Victim, who offered himself without spot to God, should in deep darkness pass through the act of unexampled worship. No wonder also that the veil of the temple was rent in the midst; for it was exactly this which his death secured—a way into the holiest through the rent veil of his flesh. And then, when the cry of desolation, that loud and bitter cry, " My God, my God, why hast thou forsaken me?" had given place to quiet assurance, and amid returning light the last cry from the cross went up to heaven, " Father, into thy hands I commend my spirit!" it was meet that he should quietly surrender his life and give up the ghost. There is much to encourage and strengthen us in this consummation on the cross.—R. M. E.

Vers. 47—56.—*The consequences of our Saviour's death.* Our Lord died in the light. The disappearance of the darkness before his decease was an outward symbol of the light and serenity which came across his spirit. His departure exercised a powerful influence upon all around the cross. Let us notice the consequences of the death, as detailed by Luke.

I. THE ROMAN CENTURION WAS CONVINCED OF CHRIST'S RIGHTEOUSNESS AND DIVINE SONSHIP. (Ver. 47.) In Matthew the exclamation of the centurion is given as, "Truly this was the Son of God;" while here in Luke it is, "Certainly this was a righteous Man." The one conclusion had reference to the Roman trial. His death was so glorious and triumphant as to vindicate his character from every aspersion. He was no malefactor, but a benefactor of mankind. The other conclusion had reference to the Jewish trial, which was on the ground of his claim of Sonship. Now, his last cry was in the light of Sonship, and " Father, into thy hands I commend my spirit!" was so tenderly and yet firmly uttered as to convince the centurion that the Lord's claim was real. In the same way, should not our death as believers constitute some vindication of our character and claims? It should show that our righteousness and sonship were not pretences, but glorious realities.

II. THE PEOPLE WERE CONVINCED OF THEIR SIN IN HAVING CLAMOURED FOR HIS CRUCIFIXION. (Ver. 48.) The smiting on the breast was a sign of perplexity and penitence. They were evidently humiliated that they had so treated One who could so nobly die. If the conviction of the centurion was an earnest of the conversion of the pagan world, this was an earnest of the conversion of the Jewish (cf. Godet, *in loc.*). The meek and quiet spirit with which Christ died broke down their hard-heartedness more than any other course could have done; so that its effect was a manifest preparation for the triumphs of the Pentecost. And should not a Christian's death strike alarm into the heart of unbelievers, suggesting to them the possibility of their being unable to meet death with becoming courage?

III. His acquaintance and the women from Galilee are petrified with astonishment. (Ver. 49.) "They stood," we are told, "afar off." They were so unmanned that they could not venture nigh. To them the death was inexplicable. It was apparently the defeat of all their hopes. It was a crushing blow. No mystery in providence had ever appeared to them exactly like this. They were ready to say, with Jacob, "All these things are against us." Is this not the position of God's people often? They have entertained bright hopes about the Master and his cause, but have found them fading away like summer flowers, so that they stand perplexed and afar off before God's providences. Is it not the dark hour before the dawn? Is it not the travail-hour before the jubilance of birth? The disciples experienced this, and so may we. Before apparent defeat, let us always exclaim by faith, "It is real victory."

IV. Joseph of Arimathæa is led by Christ's death to real decision. (Vers. 50—52.) Joseph, a good and just man, had been for some time, we know not how long, a "secret disciple" of Jesus. Nicodemus and he seemed to be in the same category, and perhaps they were led into faith about the same time. In the Sanhedrin they had done all that timid men could to prevent the crime of the Crucifixion; but popular feeling was always too strong for them. They had not as yet taken the bold step of professing to belong to Christ. But, strange to say, the death of Jesus, the apparent defeat of his cause, determined them both to be professors. Joseph accordingly goes and boldly begs the body from Pilate, that he may lay it in his own new tomb, while Nicodemus goes off to procure the needful spices. And here have we what seems a law in God's kingdom. Successors always appear to carry on his work. Christ's death induces two at least to join his cause at once. As the apparently important pass away, it is only to be succeeded by others, and perhaps a larger number, to take up the fallen banner and prove their faithfulness. Apparent calamities are splendid tests of character—they call forth the brave!

V. Christ's funeral could only be a temporary interment. (Vers. 53—56.) It was necessary that the body should be put away before the sabbath began. Now, if he died a little after three o'clock, there were less than three hours to complete the interment. There could not be the customary embalmment. All that was possible was to wrap the dear remains in linen with spices, and then, if nothing prevented, to complete the embalmment on the first day of the week. It was a hurried burial, therefore, and by compulsion a temporary one. Yet "with the rich was his tomb." It was in a virgin sepulchre, so to speak, he lay for a season, just as he had lain in the Virgin's womb. It was so far private also that none apparently but the immediate friends and acquaintances followed the funeral. All the circumstances combined to make the funeral and interment most singular. It was well known where they laid him; it was known that they intended completing the embalmment on the first day of the week; his enemies had every opportunity, therefore, to prevent any imposture about a resurrection. All was above-board, like everything in our Lord's life. Consequently there was in the burial of Jesus a noble foundation laid for that crowning hope of resurrection. We shall see that there was every advantage offered to those who wished to expose duplicity about his rising again. It was the most important burial and most hopeless, so far as the mourners were concerned. They above all others seemed oblivious of all promise of resurrection.—R. M. E.

EXPOSITION.

CHAPTER XXIV.

Vers. 1—49.—THE RESURRECTION. All the four evangelists give an account of the Resurrection. None of the four, however, attempt to give a *history* of it simply from a human point of sight. Each Gospel probably reproduces the special points dwelt on in certain great centres of Christian teaching, in what we should now term different schools of thought. (Attempts have been made by theological scholars to *classify* these as Jewish, Gentile, Greek, Roman; but only with indifferent success).

The teaching which St. Matthew's Gospel represents, evidently in the Resurrection preaching dwelt with peculiar insistence on the great Galilæan appearance of the Risen. St. Luke confines himself exclusively to the appearance, in Judæa. St. John chooses for his Resurrection instruction scenes which had for their theatre both Galilee and Judæa. St. John, as his central or most detailed piece of teaching, dwells on a fishing scene on Gennesaret, the actors being the well-known inner circle of the apostles. While St. Luke chooses for his detailed Resurrection narrative a high-road in a Jerusalem suburb; and for actors, two devoted, but historically unknown, disciples.

Then there is no question of *discrepancies* in this portion of the great history. It is not easy to frame a perfectly satisfactory harmony of all the events related by the four, after the Lord had risen; for, in fact, we possess no detailed account or history of what took place in that eventful period in presence of the disciples. We simply have memoranda of eye-witnesses of certain *incidents* connected with the Resurrection selected by the great first teachers as specially adapted to their own preaching and instruction.

The events of the first Easter Day have been tabulated by Professor Westcott, in what he terms a provisional arrangement, as follows :—

Approx. time.
Very early The Resurrection, followed by
on Sunday the earthquake, the descent of the angel, the opening of the tomb (Matt. xxviii. 2—4).

Approx. time.

5 a.m......Mary Magdalene, Mary the [mother] of James and Salome, probably with others, start for the sepulchre in the twilight. Mary Magdalene goes before the others, and returns at once to Peter and John (John xx. 1, etc.).

5.30 a.m. ...Her companions reach the sepulchre when the sun had risen (Mark xvi. 2).
A vision of an angel.
Message to the disciples (Matt. xxviii. 5, etc.; Mark xvi. 5, etc.).

6 a.m. ......Another party, among whom is Joanna, come a little later, but still in the early morning (ch. xxiv. 1, etc.; comp. Mark xvi. 1, note).
A vision of "two young men." Words of comfort and instruction (ch. xxiv. 4, etc.).

6.30 a.m. ...The visit of Peter and John (John xx. 3—10).
A vision of two angels to Mary Magdalene (John xx. 11—13).
About the same time the company of women carry their tidings to the apostles (ch. xxiv. 10, etc.).

7 a.m. ......The Lord reveals himself to Mary Magdalene (John xx. 14—18; Mark xvi. 9).
Not long after he reveals himself, as it appears, to the company of women who are returning to the sepulchre. Charge to the brethren to go to Galilee (Matt. xxviii. 9, etc.).

4—6 p.m...The appearance to the two disciples on the way to Emmaus (ch. xxiv. 13, etc.; Mark xvi. 12).

After 4 p.m...An appearance to St. Peter (ch. xxiv. 34; comp. 1 Cor. xv. 5).

8 p.m.......The appearance to the eleven and others (ch. xxiv. 36, etc.; Mark xvi. 14; John xx. 19, etc.).

In the above table one point must be specially noticed: *two companies* or separate groups of women are mentioned as going to the sepulchre with the same pious object of assisting in the final embalming of the sacred body.

If this be assumed to be the fact, there will be nothing improbable in the supposition that both these groups of women, all doubtless intimate friends belonging to the little company of the Master, but living probably some distance apart in Jerusalem, came together some time on the sabbath day, and then arranged to meet early on the first day at the sepulchre. Probably the spices purchased in some haste *just before the sabbath commenced* were judged inadequate.

(1) For in ch. xxiii. 56 we read of a company of women, most probably including all, *i.e.* both groups, of holy women, who, after beholding the sepulchre, "returned, and prepared spices and ointments; and *rested the sabbath day."*

(2) In Mark xvi. 1 we read, " *When the sabbath was past,* Mary Magdalene, and Mary the mother of James, and Salome, bought [not ' *had* bought] sweet spices, that they might come and anoint him." This company (alluded to in Mark xvi. 1) arrives *the first* at the sepulchre, and sees the vision of one angel (Mark xvi. 5). The other company (alluded to in ch. xxiv. 1) arrives not long after at the sepulchre, and sees the vision of two angels (ch. xxiv. 4).

In considering the accounts of the Resurrection, the following memoranda will be found suggestive:—

(1) *The holy women* are the principal actors in all the four accounts of the circumstances connected with the tomb. But their assertions were not believed by the disciples until their statements were confirmed by the Lord's personal appearance.

(2) When St. Paul (1 Cor. xv. 5—8) sums up the great appearances of our Lord, the basis of our faith, he makes no reference to his appearance to Mary Magdalene (John xx. 14, etc.; Mark xvi. 9) or to the women (two Maries mentioned Matt. xxviii. 9, 10).

(3) No evangelist describes the Resurrection—no earthly being having been present. St. Matthew is the evangelist who, in his narrative, goes furthest back. He mentions the shock of the earthquake, the awful presence of the angel, the benumbing terror which seized the guards who were watching. Most probably these signs accompanied the Resurrection.

(4) The risen Lord appeared only to his own.

(5) That no future doubt should be thrown on the *reality* of the appearances of the Risen, he showed himself not only to solitary individuals, but to companies, *i.e.* to two, to the eleven (repeatedly), and to above five hundred brethren at once. And these manifestations took place (*a*) at different hours of the day; (*b*) in different localities—in Judæa, in Galilee, in rooms of houses, in the open air.

Vers. 1—12.—*The Resurrection. At the sepulchre.*

Ver. 1.—**Now upon the first day of the week, very early in the morning, they came unto the sepulchre, bringing the spices which they had prepared, and certain others with them.** In the foregoing general note on the Resurrection, the probability has been discussed of the holy women having been divided into two companies who separately came to the sepulchre. St. Luke's notice here refers to the party who arrived the second at the tomb.

Ver. 2.—**And they found the stone rolled away from the sepulchre.** The tomb in which the body of the "King's Son" was laid was in a garden close by the scene of the Crucifixion. It had been recently hewn out of a rock, the low ridge opposite the slight ascent of Calvary. " In front of a tomb belonging to a rich family there was generally a vestibule open to the air, then a low entrance sometimes, as in this case, on the side of a rock, leading into a square chamber of moderate dimensions, on one side of which was a place for the body, either cut some seven feet into the rock, or lengthways, three feet deep, with a low arch over it. . . . The tomb had been lately made, and the door which closed the entrance, the only aperture into the tomb, was a large stone " ('Speaker's Commentary,' on Matt. xxvii. 60). Recent investigations in Jerusalem serve to confirm the accuracy of the original traditional sites. (comp. Williams, 'Holy City,' ii. 240; Professor Willis, 'Treatise on the Holy Sepulchre,' etc.). We find the following passage in the Bordeaux Pilgrim (A.D. 333): "On the left side (of the original Church of the Holy Sepulchre) is the hillock Golgotha, where the Lord was crucified. Thence about a stone-throw distance is the crypt where his body was deposited." St. Cyril of Jerusalem makes several references to the spot. In the days of Eusebius (first half of the fourth century) there was no doubt as to the site.

Ver. 4.—**And it came to pass, as they were much perplexed thereabout, behold, two men stood by them in shining garments.** To one company of women one angel appeared: to another, two. Mary Magdalene, a little later, saw two angels in white sitting, as it were keeping watch and ward over the sepulchre for a short time after the sacred form had left it. The words which these beings from another sphere spoke to the mourning women were slightly different, but the teaching was the same in each case: "He is not here, but is risen. Do you not remember what he told you when he was yet with you?" Van Oosterzee and Farrar repeat a beautiful passage from Lessing on this: "Cold discrepancy-mongers, do you not, then, see that the evangelists do not count the angels? . . . There were not only two angels—there were millions of them. They appeared not always one and the same, not always the same two; sometimes this one appeared, sometimes that; sometimes on this place, sometimes on that; sometimes alone, sometimes in company; sometimes they said this, sometimes they said that."

Vers. 6, 7.—He is not here, but is risen. These words were repeated in each of the angelic communications at the sepulchre. Remember how he spake unto you when he was yet in Galilee, saying, The Son of man must be delivered into the hands of sinful men, and be crucified, and the third day rise again. The angels here call to the women's memory the Master's former promises of the Resurrection. In SS. Matthew and Mark the angel bids them tell the disciples not to forget the appointed place of meeting in Galilee, referring to the Lord's words on the way from the "Last Supper" to Gethsemane (Matt. xxvi. 32; Mark xiv. 28).

Ver. 9.—And told all these things unto the eleven, and to all the rest. The account of the scenes at the sepulchre in St. Luke are the least vivid and detailed of the four evangelists. It must be remembered that Matthew, Mark (the amanuensis of Peter), and John relate their own memories here, as well as what they had heard from the holy women. Peter and John, we know, were present themselves at the sepulchre. St. Luke received his less detailed and more summarized account of that early morning, years after, most probably from the lips of one of the holy women who had formed part of one of the "two companies" who carried spices for the embalming.

Ver. 11.—And their words seemed to them as idle tales, and they believed them not. The utter incredulity of the friends of Jesus when these reports of his resurrection were brought to them is remarkable when contrasted with the evident dread of the Sanhedrin that something of grave moment would happen after three days had elapsed. The disciples were evidently amazed at their Master's rising from the dead. The

chief priests and Jewish leaders would apparently have been surprised if something startling had not happened (see Matt. xxvii. 63, etc., where an account is given of the measures these able but unprincipled men took, in their short-sighted wisdom, to counteract any fulfilment of the Crucified One's word—a fulfilment *they* evidently looked forward to as to no improbable contingency). The utter surprise of the disciples at the Resurrection, which in their Gospels they truthfully acknowledge, is no small side-proof of the genuineness of these records of the event.

Ver. 12.—Then arose Peter, and ran unto the sepulchre; and stooping down, he beheld the linen clothes laid by themselves, and departed, wondering in himself at that which was come to pass. This verse is omitted in some of the ancient authorities. It is, however, no doubt genuine, and is, in fact, a condensed report (omitting all mention of John) of the narrative given at length in St. John's Gospel (xx. 3—10).

Vers. 13—35.—*The meeting with the risen Jesus on the way to Emmaus.*

Ver. 13.—And, behold, two of them. This long piece, which relates in a singularly vivid and picturesque manner one of the earliest appearances of the Risen, is peculiar to St. Luke. St. Mark (xvi. 12, 13) mentions it, but as it were only in passing. This Gospel, written probably after the Gospels of SS. Matthew and Mark, holds a middle place between the earliest apostolic memoirs represented by the first two Gospels and the last memoir, that of St. John, which was probably put out in its present form by the apostle "whom Jesus loved" some time in the last fifteen years of the first century. Writers of varied schools unite in expressions of admiration for this singularly beautiful "memory of the Lord." Godet styles it one of the most admirable pieces in St. Luke's Gospel. Renan, belonging to another, perhaps the most cheerless of all schools of religious thought, writes thus: "L'épisode des disciples d'Emmaus est un des récits les plus fins, les plus nuancés qu'il y ait dans aucune langue" ('Les Evangiles,' p. 282). Dean Plumptre speaks of "the long and singularly interesting narrative peculiar to St. Luke." He says, "It must be looked upon as among the 'gleaning of the grapes,' which rewarded his researches even after the full vintage had apparently been gathered in by others" (*i.e.* SS. Matthew and Mark). The "two of them," although doubtless well known in the apostolic age, seem to have held no distinguished place in early Christian history (see note on ver. 18, where Cleopas is mentioned). That same day. The first day of the week—the first Easter Day. The events of the early morning of the Resurrection have been already commented upon. **To a village called Emmaus.** This Emmaus, the narrative tells us, was about sixty furlongs—some six miles and a half—from the holy city. It was situated east-south-east from Jerusalem. The name is connected with the modern Arabic term *Hammâm* (a bath), and indicates probably, like the Latin *Aquæ*, or the French *Aix*, and the English "Bath," or "Wells," the presence of medicinal springs; and this may possibly account for St. Luke the physician's attention having in the first instance been drawn to the spot. This Emmaus is now called *Kulonieh.* A curious Talmudical reference, quoted by Godet, belongs to this place Emmaus, now Kulonieh: "At Maûza they go to gather the green boughs for the Feast of Tabernacles" (Talmud, 'Succa,' iv. 5). Elsewhere it is said that "Maûza is Kulonieh."

Ver. 15.—**While they communed together and reasoned, Jesus himself drew near, and went with them.** One, if not the first, fulfilment of the comforting promise, "Where two or three are gathered together in my Name, there am I in the midst of them." Compare also the words of Malachi, "Then they that feared the Lord spake often one to another: and the Lord hearkened, and heard it" (iii. 16).

Ver. 16.—**But their eyes were holden, that they should not know him.** So Mary Magdalene looked on and failed to recognize at first the Person of her adored Master (John xx. 15). So by the lake-shore, as he stood and spoke to the tired fishermen, they who had been so long with him knew him not. Some mysterious change had been wrought in the Person of the Lord. Between the Resurrection and the Ascension, men and women now looked on him without a gleam of recognition, now gazed on him knowing well that it was the Lord. "It is vain," writes Dr. Westcott, "to give any simply natural explanation of the failure of the disciples to recognize Christ. After the Resurrection he was known as he pleased, and not necessarily at once. . . . Till they who gazed on him were placed in something of spiritual harmony with the Lord, they could not recognize him." The two on their walk to Emmaus, and Mary Magdalene in the garden, were preoccupied with their sorrow. The fisher-disciples on the lake were preoccupied with their work, so that the vision of the Divine was obscured. The risen Christ will surely fulfil his own words, "The pure in heart, they shall see God"— *but only the pure in heart.*

Ver. 17.—**What manner of communications are these that ye have one to another, as ye walk, and are sad?** The older authorities make the question stop at "as ye walk,"

and then add, "and they stood still, looking sad." This change is, of course, of no great importance, but it considerably adds to the vividness of the picture.

Ver. 18.—**And the one of them, whose name was Cleopas.** This name is a Greek contraction of *Cleopatros*, and points to Alexandrian antecedents. Dean Plumptre suggests that this may in part, perhaps, account for this Cleopas, not improbably a Jew of Alexandria, imparting to St. Luke what had not found its way into the current oral teaching of the Hebrew Church at Jerusalem, as embodied in the narratives of SS. Matthew and Mark. **Art thou only a stranger in Jerusalem?** better translated, *dost thou alone sojourn in Jerusalem, and not know*, etc.? That is to say, "Art thou the *only* stranger in Jerusalem who does not know about the wonderful events which have just taken place in the holy city?"

Ver. 19.—**And they said unto him, Concerning Jesus of Nazareth, which was a Prophet mighty in deed and word before God and all the people.** To the Stranger's question, "What things have so lately excited Jerusalem?" they both probably burst out with "the Name," then doubtless on all lips in the holy city, "Jesus of Nazareth," the hated and adored Name. And then they went on with a further explanation to One who seemed a stranger just arrived: they explained who this Jesus was supposed to have been. "He was a Prophet mighty in deed and word before God and all the people," which Lange happily paraphrases "equally great in secret contemplative holiness and in public acts of beneficence." But then the "two" explained, "*This he was;* for he is no more. Our chief priests and rulers have done him to death. They have crucified him."

Ver. 21.—**But we trusted that it had been he which should have redeemed Israel.** And *we* who were his friends and followers, we thought we had found in him the Redeemer of Israel, King Messiah! Think! the *Redeemer crucified!* Although the Redeemer, in the sense they probably understood the word, was something very different to the sense we give to it, the idea was still something very lofty and sublime. It included, no doubt, much of earthly glory and dominion for Israel, but in some definite sense the Gentile world, too, would share in the blessings of Messiah. And to think of the shameful cross putting an end to all these hopes! **And beside all this, to-day is the third day since these things were done.** But yet terrible and despairing as was the story of Cleopas and his friend, their tone was not quite hopeless; for they went on, "And now we have come to the third day since they crucified him." No doubt they dwelt a short space on the expression, "third day," telling the Stranger how their dead Master, when alive, had bade his friends watch for the third day from his death. The third day, he had told them, would be the day of his triumphant return to them; and, strangely enough, on the early morning of this third day, something *did* happen which had stirred, excited, and perplexed them. Certain women of their company, who had been early to the grave of the Master, meaning to embalm the corpse, found the sepulchre empty, and they came back reporting how they had seen a vision of angels there, who told them their Master lived. What did it all mean?

Ver. 24.—**And certain of them which were with us went to the sepulchre, and found it even so as the women had said: but him they saw not.** Tholuck writes, "Does not their word sound as the language of those in whose heart the smoking flax yet glimmers, though nigh to extinction?"

Ver. 25.—**Then he said unto them, O fools, and slow of heart to believe all that the prophets have spoken!** better translated, *O foolish men, and slow of heart to believe in all that the prophets have spoken!* The Stranger now replies to the confused story of sorrow and baffled hopes just lit up with one faint ray of hope, with a calm reference to that holy book so well known to, so deeply treasured by every Jew. "See," he seems to say, "in the pages of our prophets all this, over which you now so bitterly mourn, is plainly predicted: you must be blind and deaf not to have seen and heard this story of agony and patient suffering in those well-known, well-loved pages! When those great prophets spoke of the coming of Messiah, how came it about that you missed seeing that they pointed to days of suffering and death to be endured by him before his time of sovereignty and triumph could be entered on?"

Ver. 26.—**Ought not Christ to have suffered these things, and to enter into his glory?** better translated, *ought not the Christ*, etc.? "St. Luke dwells on the Resurrection as a spiritual necessity; St. Mark, as a great fact; St. Matthew, as a glorious and majestic manifestation; and St. John, in its effects on the members of the Church. . . . If this suffering and death were a necessity (οὐχ ἔδει), if it was in accordance with the will of God *that the Christ should suffer*, and so *enter into his glory*, and if we can be enabled to see this necessity, and see also the noble issues which flow from it, then we can understand how the same necessity must in due measure be laid upon his brethren" (Westcott). And so we obtain a key to some of the darkest problems of humanity.

Thus the Stranger led the "two" to see the true meaning of the "prophets," whose burning words they had so often read and heard without grasping their real deep signification. Thus he led them to see that the Christ must be a *suffering* before he could be a *triumphing* Messiah; that the crucifixion of Jesus, over which they wailed with so bitter a wailing, was in fact an essential part of the counsels of God. Then he went on to show that, as his suffering is now fulfilled—for the Crucifixion and death were past—nothing remains of that which is written in the prophets, but the entering into his glory.

Ver. 27.—**And beginning at Moses and all the prophets, he expounded unto them in all the Scriptures the things concerning himself.** The three divisions, the Pentateuch (Moses), the prophets, and all the Scriptures, cover the whole Old Testament received then in the same words as we possess them now. The Lord's proofs of what he asserted he drew from the whole series of writings, rapidly glancing over the long many-coloured roll called the Old Testament. "Jesus had before him a grand field, from the Protevangelium, the first great Gospel of Genesis, down to Malachi. In studying the Scriptures for himself, he had found himself in them everywhere (John v. 39, 40)" (Godet). *The things concerning himself.* The Scriptures which the Lord probably referred to specially were the promise to Eve (Gen. iii. 15); the promise to Abraham (Gen. xxii. 18); the Paschal lamb (Exod. xii.); the scapegoat (Lev. xvi. 1—34); the brazen serpent (Numb. xxi. 9); the greater Prophet (Deut. xviii. 15); the star and sceptre (Numb. xxiv. 17); the smitten rock (Numb. xx. 11; 1 Cor. x. 4), etc.; Immanuel (Isa. vii. 14); "Unto us a Child is born," etc. (Isa. ix. 6, 7); the good Shepherd (Isa. xl. 10, 11); the meek Sufferer (Isa. l. 6); he who bore our griefs (Isa. liii. 4, 5); the Branch (Jer. xxiii. 5; xxxiii. 14, 15); the Heir of David (Ezek. xxxiv. 23); the Ruler from Bethlehem (Micah v. 2); the Branch (Zech. vi. 12); the lowly King (Zech. ix. 9); the pierced Victim (Zech. xii. 10); the smitten Shepherd (Zech. xiii. 7); the messenger of the covenant (Mal. iii. 1); the Sun of Righteousness (Mal. iv. 2); and no doubt many other passages. Dr. Davison, in his book on prophecy, pp. 266—287, shows that there is not one of the prophets without some distinct reference to Christ, except Nahum, Jonah (who was himself a type and prophetic sign), and Habakkuk, who, however, uses the memorable words quoted in Rom. i. 17. To these we must add references to several of the psalms, notably to the sixteenth and twenty-second, where sufferings and death are spoken of as belonging to the perfect picture of the Servant of the Lord and the ideal King. His hearers would know well how strangely the agony of Calvary was foreshadowed in those vivid word-pictures he called before their memories in the course of that six-mile walk from Jerusalem to Emmaus.

Ver. 28.—**And they drew nigh unto the village, whither they went: and he made as though he would have gone further.** This was no feint or deception. The Lord would have left them then to themselves had they not prayed him with real earnestness to abide with them. "How many are there," says Stier, "*to* whom he has drawn near, but *with* whom he has not tarried, because they have suffered him to 'go away again,' in his living and heart-moving words! How comparatively rare is it for men to reach the full blessing they might receive (see, for example, the striking historical instance, 2 Kings xiii. 14, 19)!" But these were not content to let the unknown Teacher pass on, and see no more of him, and hear no more of his strange powerful teaching. It is the words of, and the thought contained in, this verse which suggested the idea of the well-known hymn—

"Abide with me; fast falls the eventide."

Ver. 29.—**And he went in to tarry with them.** Some have supposed that one at least of the two had a dwelling at Emmaus; but the position which the strange Teacher assumed as "Master of the household," in the solemn act recorded in ver. 30, seems to indicate that it was an inn where they sojourned.

Ver. 30.—**And it came to pass, as he sat at meat with them, he took bread, and blessed it, and brake, and gave to them.** There was a deep significance in the concluding act of this memorable appearance of the risen Lord. This taking the bread, and blessing it, and breaking it, and then giving it to them, was no ordinary act of courtesy, or welcome, or friendship, which, from a master or teacher might be shown to his disciples. It resembles too closely the great sacramental act in the upper room, when Jesus was alone with his apostles, for us to mistake its solemn sacramental character. The great teachers of the Church in different ages have generally so understood it. So Chrysostom in the Eastern, and Augustine in the Western Church; so Theophylact, and later Beza the Reformer all affirm that this meal was the sacrament. It taught men generally, even more plainly than did the first sacred institution teach the twelve, that in this solemn breaking of bread the Church would recognize their Master's presence. So generally, in fact, has this Emmaus "breaking

of bread" been recognized by the Catholic Church as the sacrament, that later Romanist divines have even pressed it as a scriptural demonstration for the abuse which administered the elements under one form (compare, for instance, the 'Refutation of the Confession of Augsberg,' quoted by Stier, in his comment on this passage of Luke, 'Words of the Lord Jesus'). How unnecessary and forced such a construction is, Bishop Wordsworth points out in his note on ch. xxiv. 30, "It may be remembered that *bread* (ἄρτος) was to the Jews a general name for *food*, including drink as well as meat. . . . Thus *bread* became spiritually an expressive term for all the blessings received from communion in Christ's body and blood, and the κλάσις ἄρτου, or 'breaking of bread,' was suggestive of the source from which these blessings flow, (viz.) Christ's body (κλώμενον) broken (1 Cor. xi. 24); hence κλάσις ἄρτου in Acts ii. 42 is a general term for the Holy Eucharist."

Ver. 31.—**He vanished out of their sight.** Not *here*, not *now*, can we hope to understand the nature of the resurrection-body of the Lord; it is and must remain to us, in our present condition, a mystery. Certain facts have, however, been revealed to us : (1) The Resurrection was a reality, not an appearance ; for on more than one occasion the Lord permitted the test of touch. He also ate before his disciples of their ordinary food. (2) Yet there was a manifest exemption from the common conditions of bodily (corporeal) existence ; for he comes through a closed door; he could *withdraw himself* when he would from touch as well as from sight; he could vanish in a moment from those looking on him; he could, as men gazed on him, rise by the exertion of his own will into the clouds of heaven. (3) He was known just as he pleased and when he pleased ; for at times during the "forty days" men and women looked on him without a gleam of recognition, at times they gazed at him, knowing well that it was the Lord. On the words, "he vanished out of their sight," Godet writes, "It must be remembered that Jesus, strictly speaking, *was* already *no more with them* (ver. 44), and that the miracle consisted rather in his appearing than in his disappearing." Dr. Westcott expresses the same truth in different language, "What was natural to him before was now miraculous, what was before miraculous is now natural."

Ver. 32.—**And they said one to another, Did not our heart burn within us, while he talked with us by the way?** better rendered, *was not our heart burning within us, while,* etc. ?

Vers. 33, 34.—**And they rose up the same hour, and returned to Jerusalem.** "They fear no longer the night-journey from which they had dissuaded their unknown Companion" (Bengel). **And found the eleven gathered together, and them that were with them, saying, The Lord is risen indeed, and hath appeared to Simon.** Late that evening Cleopas and his friend arrived from Emmaus at Jerusalem. Hastening to the accustomed meeting-place of the disciples of Jesus, to tell their wondrous story of the meeting with the risen Master, they find the eleven together full of joy. Peter *had seen* and had no doubt conversed with his Master. What a meeting must that have been! The once eager and devoted apostle had probably not gazed on that form in life since he caught the sorrowful look bent on him in the court-yard, when Jesus, bound, passed through and heard his servant denying him with oaths and curses. This appearance to Peter is not recorded in the Gospels. It is, however, placed first of all by St. Paul in his records of the manifestation of the Risen (1 Cor. xv. 4—8).

Ver. 35.—**And they told what things were done in the way, and how he was known of them in breaking of bread.** The two travellers now relate to the eleven their wondrous story. The words used by Cleopas and his friend in their narration, ἐν τῇ κλάσει τοῦ ἄρτου, which should be rendered, "in the breaking of the bread," are significant. It is an expression which, at the time when St. Luke wrote his Gospel, had acquired a definite meaning in the language of the Christian Church, and was applied to breaking bread in the "Supper of the Lord" (see Acts ii. 42, 46; 1 Cor. x. 16). While they were speaking together, the personal appearance of the Lord was vouchsafed to them; for, of a sudden, he stood in the midst and spoke to them!

Vers. 36—49.—*The Lord appears to the apostles as they were gathered together on the evening of the first Easter Day.*

Ver. 36.—**And as they thus spake, Jesus himself stood in the midst of them.** St. John, who also gives an account of this appearance of the Risen, adds the detail, "when the doors were shut." The eleven and their friends were gathered together for counsel, probably too in hope that something more would happen after what had already taken place that Easter Day—the report of the holy women of the repeated vision of angels, their own verification of the empty sepulchre, and above all the testimony of Peter that he had seen the Lord. Into this anxious, waiting assembly the two "Emmaus" disciples enter with their wondrous story. In the act of their mentally comparing notes, *Jesus himself stood in the midst of them.* This sudden presence there is evidently supernatural.

He "stood in the midst of them," though the doors were carefully closed and barred "for fear of the Jews" Rumours of the Resurrection, no doubt, had already spread through the city, and it was uncertain whether such rumours might not be followed by the arrest of the chief followers of the Crucified. **Peace be unto you.** This was the ordinary Jewish greeting, but on this occasion, spoken by the Lord, possessed more than the ordinary meaning. This "peace" was his solemn, comforting greeting to his own, just as "his peace" which he left with them on the sad Thursday eve was his solemn farewell to the eleven, spoken, perhaps, in the same "upper room" just before he went out to the garden of the agony.

Ver. 37.—**But they were terrified and affrighted.** They spoke one to another of the Master; they discussed the empty sepulchre, the angelic vision, the recital by Peter of his interview with the Risen, and were listening to the details of the quiet Emmaus meeting, all hoping for something more; but this sudden, mysterious appearance of their crucified Master in their midst was not, after all, what they had looked for. *It terrified them.* **And supposed that they had seen a spirit.** How else could they explain his presence in their midst, when the doors were shut? The evangelists make no attempt to explain his sudden appearance. *He was simply there* as they spoke of him. It is clear that his presence could be accounted for in no ordinary, natural way. His disciples felt that; hence their supposition that they were looking on a spirit. We can, with our present limited knowledge, form no adequate conception of this resurrection-body of the Lord. It was a reality, no phantasm or appearance; of that the scene about to be described gives us ample evidence. Still, it is clear that his resurrection-body was not bound by the present conditions of material existence of which we are conscious. Epiphanius ascribes to the body of the risen Lord λεπτότης πνευματική, "a spiritual subtilty." Euthymius uses similar language when he speaks of "his body being now subtile, thin, and unmixed." He could *come* into a closed, barred room. He could be visible or invisible, known or unknown, as he pleased and when he pleased.

Ver. 38.—**And he said unto them, Why are ye troubled? and why do thoughts arise in your hearts?** He had just given them his peace. He proceeds further to allay their fears. Before showing them his pierced hands and feet and side, before eating in their presence, he addresses these comforting words to them: "See," he seems to say, "I give you my peace: why are ye troubled? why do you allow perplexing, harassing thoughts to arise in your hearts?

The past is forgiven and forgotten." "I come not," as Stier beautifully sugests, "as a wrathful Judge to reckon with you for your unbelief and unfaithfulness. I bring to you (and all the world) from my sepulchre something very different from upbraidings."

Ver. 39.—**Behold my hands and my feet, that it is I myself.** "See," he says, inviting the terror-stricken disciples to a calm, unaffrighted contemplation—" see my hands and my feet pierced with the nails which fastened them to the cross; *it is I myself.*" **Handle me, and see; for a spirit hath not flesh and bones, as ye see me have.** The first words quietly told the awe-struck ones to look closely at him, and to ascertain from the dread marks he bore that what they looked upon was Jesus their Master. Then he proceeded to bid them *touch* him, handle him, and so assure themselves that it was no phantom, no bodiless spirit, that stood before them. These words of the Lord, and the invitation, " handle me, and see," made the deepest impression on the hearers. These, then, were proofs of the Resurrection that admitted of no shadow of doubt. These words, this sight, changed their lives. What cared they afterwards for men and men's threatenings? Death, life, to them were all one. They had *seen* the Lord, they had handled with their hands "that which was from the beginning" (see 1 John i. 1). Browning forcibly puts this thought which so influenced the first great teachers. The dying St. John is dwelling on the thought that when he is gone there will be none left with men who *saw* and *touched* the Lord.

" If I live yet, it is for good, more love
Through me to men : be nought but ashes
  here
That keep awhile my semblance, who was
  John.
Still, when they scatter, there is left on
  earth
No one alive who knew (consider this !),
Saw with his eyes, and handled with his
  hands,
That which was from the first, the Word
  of life.
How will it be when none more saith, ' I
  saw ' ? "

('A Death in the Desert.')

Ver. 40.—Some (but not the majority) of the older authorities omit this verse. **And when he had thus spoken, he showed them his hands and his feet.** It has been suggested that the Risen simply pointed to those parts of his body which were not covered with clothing, and invited the disciples to touch *these*, and so to assure themselves that he had actually flesh and bone.

Von Gerlach has an interesting suggestion that the feet were especially referred to " because there was in the feet something more convincing and touching than even in the hands, on account of the wonder that One who had been so grievously wounded could move." The real reason, however, of the Lord calling attention to *the hands and feet* comes out from St. John's account of this appearance of the Risen, for he adds that Jesus also showed them *his side.* Thus he pointed to the *wounded members* of his blessed body to show that in the resurrection-body he retained these marks of his wounds. That he retained them now and for ever we know from the glorious vision of the Revelation, where the wounded humanity of the Lord appears throned and adored in the highest heaven : " Lo, in the midst of the throne and of the four beasts [living creatures], and in the midst of the elders, *stood a Lamb as it had been slain* " (Rev. v. 6). Our Master and God retains these as the glorious tokens of his victory and atonement. Augustine very strikingly deduces from this that perhaps we shall see the same with respect to the wounds of the martyrs (' De Civ. Dei,' lib. xxii. cap. 19).

Vers. 41, 42.—**And while they yet believed not for joy.** The awful joy of the disciples *now* was something too deep for words, even for calm belief. St. John records it, too, with simple pathos. "Then were the disciples glad, when they saw the Lord." This was the fulfilment of his promise to them, when, full of sadness, they were listening to him that last solemn Passover evening in the upper room. " Ye now therefore have sorrow : but I will see you again, and your heart shall rejoice, and your joy no man taketh from you " (John xvi. 22). In after-days, as John preached and taught in his old age, how the remembrance of *that hour* must have stirred in his heart when he thus wrote of it ! **Have ye here any meat ? And they gave him a piece of a broiled fish, and of an honeycomb.** The Master would not permit this state of wondering ecstasy to continue ; so he changes the current of their thoughts by thus descending into the region of everyday life, at the same time powerfully demonstrating by this further proof that, though changed, his resurrection-body was no mere Docetic semblance, no phantom, but that he could eat if he chose. The next sentence (ver. 43) tells simply how he took the food, and ate before them. The fish and honeycomb which they gave him no doubt formed the staple of their evening meal. Fish was part of the common food of the disciples—we see this from the miracles of the five thousand and the four thousand, and also from the narrative of John xxi. 9. Honey, we know, in

Canaan, the land flowing with milk and honey, was common enough to enter into the diet of the poor (compare, among many passages, Exod. iii. 8, 17; Deut. xxvi. 9, 15; Jer. xi. 5; Isa. vii. 15, 22; Matt. iii. 4).

Vers. 44—49.—*A summary of some of the Lord's last words.* The next six verses do not record sayings uttered the same first Easter evening. They are, in fact, a very brief summary of instructions given by the Master on different occasions during the forty days which elapsed between the Resurrection and the Ascension.

In considering the reasons of the omission of any special reference to the Galilæan appearances of the risen Lord, two points must be borne in mind.

(1) Neither Luke nor Paul had any personal reminiscences, like Matthew, or Mark (who wrote down, we believe, St. Peter's memories), or St. John. Luke was dependent on other sources altogether.

(2) Luke, when he wrote the Gospel bearing his name, probably proposed to complete his recital of the close of the earthly ministry of the Lord in his second work, the Acts of the Apostles. His knowledge of what took place after the Resurrection was evidently derived from a source unfamiliar with the Galilæan manifestations of the risen Lord.

St. Luke's knowledge of the Ascension seems to have been most precise. He evidently lays great stress upon the importance of this last scene, both as a piece of evidence and as a theme of teaching; for he not only concludes his Gospel with it, but commences his book of the Acts with the same recital, accompanied with further details.

Ver. 44.—**And he said unto them, These are the words which I spake unto you, while I was yet with you, that all things must be fulfilled, which were written in the Law of Moses, and in the prophets, and in the Psalms, concerning me.** The words, "while I was yet with you," plainly show that, in the Master's mind, the period of his sojourn with men was, in the human sense of the expression, *past.* His abode now was elsewhere. This and the next verse (45) probably refer to what the Master said that first Easter evening to the assembled disciples, but the exact fixing the time in the forty days (the time specially mentioned by St. Luke in the Acts as elapsing between the

Resurrection and the Ascension, Acts i. 3) is of comparatively small importance. What is, however, of real moment is the weight Jesus showed that he attached to Old Testament words and types and prophecies by this repeated mention. The remarks of Meyer and Van Oosterzee on this subject are well worthy of being quoted : "If the exegete should read the Old Testament Scriptures without knowing to whom and to what they everywhere point, the New Testament clearly directs his understanding, and places him under an obligation, if he would be a sound Christian teacher, to acknowledge its authority and interpret accordingly. Doubt as to the validity of our Lord and of his apostles' method of expounding, involves necessarily a renunciation of Christianity " (Meyer). "They who consult the teaching of Jesus and his apostles with respect to the prophecies concerning the Messiah, need not grope in uncertainty, but should, nevertheless, remember that the Lord probably directed the attention of the disciples, on this occasion (he is referring to the walk to Emmaus), less to isolated Scriptures than to the whole tenor of the Old Testament in its typical and symbolical character" (Van Oosterzee).

Ver. 45.—**Then opened he their understanding, that they might understand the Scriptures.** Assuming (as is most probably the case) that vers. 44 and 45 refer to words spoken by Jesus on the first Easter evening to the eleven and to Cleopas and his friend, then *the way* in which he opened their understanding is described by St. John (xx. 22) thus : " He breathed on *them,* and saith unto them, Receive ye the Holy Ghost." Among the new powers bestowed on them by this Divine gift, St. Luke especially dwells on the spiritual insight henceforth possessed by these men into the Scriptures of the Old Testament, hitherto only partly understood. This power was doubtless one of the great instruments of their success as preachers.

In the next four verses (46—49) St. Luke evidently briefly summarizes the Master's great sayings, some probably spoken in the course of the walk to Emmaus, some on that first Easter evening, some on other occasions during the forty days which elapsed between the Resurrection and the Ascension. The introductory words, "and said unto them" (ver. 46), seem the commencement of. this summary.

Ver. 46.—**Thus it is written, and thus it behoved Christ to suffer, and to rise from the dead the third day.** The majority of the older authorities omit the words, "and thus it behoved." The verse should be read thus: "Thus it is written that Christ should suffer," etc. These words probably were spoken on that first Easter evening. They were apparently repeated on several occasions during the forty days. The Old Testament—they would see now with the new light cast upon it—showed the necessity of an *atoning* Redeemer, from the *sin* which it everywhere reveals, and of a *dying* Redeemer, from the *death* which it proclaims as the consequence. While the same Scriptures no less authoritatively proclaim that through this suffering the Redeemer-Messiah should attain to his glorification.

Ver. 47.—**And that repentance and remission of sins should be preached in his Name among all nations.** This is more definitely expressed in Matt. xxviii. 19 and Mark xvi. 15, where the universality of his message, here summarized, is found in the form of a definite command. **Beginning at Jerusalem.** St. Luke enlarges the thought contained in these words in his Acts (i. 8). Ps. cx. 2, contains the prophecy that from Zion should first proceed the proclamation.

Ver. 48.—**Ye are witnesses of these things.** This personal *witness* of the first preachers of Christianity was the secret of their great power over men's hearts. What Dr. Westcott wrote of St. John was true of the rest of the eleven. "*We have seen, and do testify.* He (John) had no laboured process to go through; he saw. He had no constructive proof to develop; he bore witness. His source of knowledge was direct, and his mode of bringing conviction was to affirm."

Ver. 49.—**And, behold, I send the promise of my Father upon you.** Promised on the last Passover evening (John xiv.—xvi; see especially John xiv. 16—26; xv. 26, 27; xvi. 7, etc.), and fulfilled partly on the first Easter evening, when he breathed on them (John xx. 22), and completely on the first Pentecost (Acts ii. 1, etc.). **But tarry ye in the city of Jerusalem, until ye be endued with power from on high.** These words apparently were spoken on the day of his ascension (see Acts i. 4).

Vers. 50—53.—THE ASCENSION. In considering the questions which suggest themselves in connection with the ascension of our blessed Lord, we are met on the threshold with the fact that only St. Luke, in his Gospel in this place, and in the Acts (i.), has given us a detailed account of the scene. But the fact is referred to *plainly* by St. John (iii. 13; vi. 62; xx. 17) and by St. Paul (Eph. iv. 9, 10; 1 Tim. iii. 16). A vast number of passages besides, in the Epistles of SS. Paul, Peter, and James, and

in the Revelation of St. John, presuppose the Ascension, when they describe the heavenly glory of Jesus and of his session at the right hand of God.

St. John's triple mention of the Ascension (see above) is exactly in accordance with his constant practice in his Gospel; he avoids rewriting a formal narrative of things which, when he wrote, were well known in the Churches; yet he alludes to these things in clear and unmistakable language, and draws from them his lessons and conclusions.

Notably this is the case in the Fourth Gospel with regard to the sacraments. "It contains," says Dr. Westcott, "no formal narrative of the institution of sacraments, and yet it presents most fully the idea of sacraments."

Neander writes with great force on this apparent omission of the Ascension: "We make the same remark upon the ascension of Christ as was before made upon his miraculous conception. In regard to neither is prominence given to the special and actual *fact* in the apostolic writings; in regard to both, such a fact is presupposed in the general conviction of the apostles, and in the connection of Christian consciousness. Thus the end of Christ's appearance on earth corresponds with its beginning. Christianity rests upon supernatural facts—stands or falls with them. By faith in them has the Divine life been generated from the beginning. Were this faith gone, there might indeed remain many of the *effects* of what Christianity has been; but as for Christianity in the true sense, as for a Christian Church, there could be none."

Ver. 50.—**And he led them out as far as to Bethany;** more accurately, *and he led them out until they were over against Bethany.* The scene of the Ascension could scarcely have been the central summit of the Mount of Olives (*Jebel-el-Tur*), according to ancient tradition; but it is more likely that it took place on one of the remoter uplands which lie above the village. "On the wild uplands which immediately overhang the village, he finally withdrew from the eyes of his disciples, in a seclusion which, perhaps, could nowhere else be found so near the stir of a mighty city; the long ridge of Olivet screening those hills, and those hills the village beneath them, from all sound or sight of the city behind; the view opening only on the wide waste of desert-rocks and ever-descending valleys, into the depths of the distant Jordan and its mysterious lake" (Dean Stanley, 'Sinai and Palestine,' ch. iii.). **He lifted up his hands, and blessed them.** In Acts i. 4 we read how Jesus, having assembled (συναλιζόμενος) the apostles, gave them some last commands before he left them. It is not expressly stated that only the eleven were present on this occasion.' When he had finished speaking, "he lifted up his hands, and blessed them." There is *now* no laying on of hands. "Jam non imposuit manus," comments Bengel. Those hands, as they were lifted up, were already separated from them, the space between the Risen and those he was blessing grew greater every moment.

Ver. 51.—**And it came to pass, while he blessed them, he was parted from them, and carried up into heaven;** more accurately rendered, *while he blessed them, he parted from them, and was carried up into heaven.* The last clause, "was carried up into heaven," is absent from some, but not from the majority of the older authorities. The Acts (i. 9) describe the act of ascension thus : " As they were looking, he was taken up ; and a cloud received him out of their sight." The eleven and those chosen to witness the last earthly scene of the Lord's ministry came together, in obedience probably to some command of their Master, to some meeting-place in Jerusalem, possibly the well-known upper room. Thence he led them forth from the sacred city, past the scene of the agony and the scene of the weeping, on to some quiet spot hard by loved Bethany, talking to them as they went; and as he spoke, suddenly he lifted up his pierced hands and blessed them; and in the very act of performing this deed of love, he rose, they still gazing on him—rose, as it appears, by the exercise of his own will into the air, and, while they still gazed, a cloud came and veiled him from their sight. *He was parted from them, and carried up into heaven.* Among the appearances of the Risen to his followers during the forty days (ten of these distinct appearances are related in the Gospels and Epistles), this last notably differs from all that preceded it. As at other times when he showed himself to his friends during these forty days, so on the " Ascension " day Jesus apparently came forth suddenly from the invisible world ; but not, as on former occasions, did he suddenly vanish from sight, as if he might shortly return as he had done before. But on this fortieth day he withdrew in a different way ; as they gazed he rose up into the air, and so he parted from them, thus solemnly suggesting to them that not only was he "no more with them" (ver. 44), but that even those occasional and

supernatural appearances vouchsafed to them since the Resurrection were now at an end. Nor were they grieved at this final parting ; for we read—

Ver. 52.—**And they worshipped him, and returned to Jerusalem with great joy.** This " great joy," on first thoughts, is singular till we read between the lines, and see how perfectly they *now* grasped the new mode of the Lord's connection with his own. They *knew* that henceforth, not for a little time as before the cross, not fitfully as since the Resurrection, but that for ever, though their eyes might not see him, would they feel his blessed presence near (see John xiv. 28 ; xvi. 7). One question more connected with the Ascension presses for an answer. Much modern criticism regards this last scene simply as one of the ordinary disappearances of the forty days, and declines to admit any external, visible fact in which the Ascension was manifested. But St. Luke's description, both in his Gospel and in the Acts, is plainly too circumstantial to admit of any hypothesis which limits the Ascension to a purely spiritual elevation. At the end of his earthly ministry, the evening before the cross, Jesus asked back his glory : " Now, O Father, glorify thou *me* with thine own self, with the glory which I had with thee before the world was " (John xvii. 5). The Ascension and consequent session at the right hand was the answer to the prayer of Christ. It was necessary for the training of the first teachers of Christianity that the great fact should be represented in some outward and visible form. "The physical elevation," writes Dr. Westcott, " was a speaking parable, an eloquent symbol, but not the truth to which it pointed, or the reality which it foreshadowed. The change which Christ revealed by the Ascension was not a change of place, but a change of state; not local, but spiritual. Still, from the necessities of our human condition, the spiritual change was represented sacramentally, so to speak, in an outward form. . . . He passed beyond the sphere of man's sensible existence to the open presence of God " (' The Revelation of the Risen Lord '). *The session at the right hand of God* (Mark xvi. 19) cannot designate any particular place. The ascension, then, of Jesus is not the exchange of one locality, *earth*, merely for another we term *heaven.* It is a change of state; it is a passing from all confinement within the limits of space to *omnipresence.*

Ver. 53.—**And were continually in the temple, praising and blessing God. Amen.** These last words of the Gospel just alluded to the life of the first teachers, which is dwelt upon with considerable detail in the Acts. In the early days which succeeded the Ascension, the temple and its courts were the principal resort of the teachers of the new " way." We know that in an extraordinarily short time the numbers of adherents to the crucified and risen Jesus, in Jerusalem only, were counted by thousands. The temple and its vast courts, from its storied past, from its having been the scene of much of the Master's last teaching, was the natural centre for these leaders of the new " way." When Luke wrote the words, " were continually in the temple," it is almost certain that he proposed continuing his great narrative in the book we know as the Acts of the Apostles, in which, guided by the Divine Spirit, he relates to us how the Lord Jesus continued to work on earth—in and by his Church—from his glory-throne in heaven. The early chapters of the Acts take up the thread of the gospel story, and describe the life and work of the friends of Jesus in the great Jerusalem temple, the dangers they had to encounter, and the splendid success which rewarded their brave, faithful toil. These same Acts, in the first lines of their thrilling story, take up again the Ascension scene, which is described with fresh and vivid details From these details we learn

how, when the disciples' eyes were fixed on that cloud which veiled their ascending Master, they became aware of two stranger-forms with them, clad in white and glistening garments. They knew these belonged to no earthly company. They were two among the thousands of thousands of angels, possibly the angels of the Resurrection, who sat in the empty garden-tomb. These angels tell the awe-struck friends of the ascended Jesus that their adored Master will one day (Acts i. 2) come back to *earth* in like manner as they had seen him go to heaven. " O earth, thou grain of sand on the shore of the great ocean of the universe of God, thou Bethlehem among the princes of the regions of heaven, thou art and thou ever wilt be, among ten thousand times ten thousand suns and worlds, the loved one, the elect of the Lord; thee will he visit again; thou shalt provide him a throne, even as thou gavest him a manger; thou shalt rejoice in the splendour of his glory, even as thou drankest his blood and his tears, and mournedst at his death. On thee he hath a great work yet to accomplish " (Häfeli, quoted by Stier).

HOMILETICS.

Vers. 1—12.—*The Resurrection-morning.* Who are the witnesses to the Resurrection? What is the evidence on which it was believed by the first disciples?—on which it is received by all Christians still?

I. THE WITNESSES ARE THE HOLY WOMEN AND THE APOSTLES. It is (ver. 1) the very early morning: " while it was yet dark," says St. John; " as the day began to dawn," says St. Matthew; " at the rising of the sun," says St. Mark. Then the women hasten towards the sepulchre. How many formed the company, or, as seems to be implied, the two companies, of women we know not. The names of five are given, and the rest are grouped under the phrases, the " others that were with them," and " the others from Galilee." They quickly pass through the silent streets. Jerusalem is still asleep; neither memory of what had happened, nor fear of what might happen, has disturbed its repose. They have only one care (ver. 1)—the complete embalming of the body which had been hastily laid in the rock-hewn sepulchre of Joseph. There is no idea beyond this; there is no hope even against hope that, on this the third day, he would rise again. With the eagerness characteristic of woman's nature, they proceed, the question never suggesting itself until they near the tomb, " Who shall roll away the stone from the mouth of the cave? " It would seem that they did not know of the guard which had been commanded to watch or of the sealing of the stone, for that had been done on the sabbath morning; but some of them had observed the setting of the stone—a block three or four feet in height, and two or three in breadth, requiring several men to move it. " How shall it be moved? how shall we find an entrance? " is the question before them as they press towards the holy place. Now, what are the facts? In the dawn, half-clear and half-dark, as the east begins to lighten, Mary of Magdala, the foremost of the company, sees the cave standing wide open—the stone having been rolled aside. Horror-struck, she turns to her companions, and, yielding to the moment's impulse, she speeds back to the city to communicate her fears to Peter and John (John xx. 1, 2). In the mean time, her companions venture forward. Timidly they enter the tomb, or the vestibule of the tomb, to search for the body. Lo, there (Matt. xxviii. 2, 3), on the stone which had been pushed into a corner, sits one

" whose countenance is like lightning, and his raiment white as snow," and prostrate on the ground are the Roman sentries. The women start, but the assuring word, " Fear not ye," is spoken, and the invitation (Matt. xxviii. 6) is given to " come and see the place where the Lord lay." Yes, guardians, and only guardians, are these—one where the head, another where the feet, of Jesus had been—token of the complete, protecting care of his Father. And these guardians ask (vers. 5—7), " Why do you seek the living among the dead ? " and repeat the testimony, " He is not here : he is risen," bidding them remember his own words, and bear the news of the Resurrection to the sorrowing company. It is with fear and great joy that they depart, running to bring the disciples word. They encounter scepticism. Their hot, eager sentences (ver. 11) seem to the apostles "as idle tales, and they believe them not." Peter and John, however, have already obeyed the importunate pleading of Mary. And there, to be sure, as they reach the sepulchre, is the open door. John, who is first, looks in without entering ; Peter, coming up, enters at once. " John," observes Matthew Henry, " could outrun Peter, but Peter could out-dare John." Undoubtedly the tomb is empty. Examining it, they discover (ver. 12) the linen clothes laid by themselves ; and the napkin which had surrounded the head laid by itself. There had been no haste. Not thus would any have acted who had borne away the sacred form. Peter, after minute examination of the surroundings, " departed, wondering in himself at that which had come to pass." John, with the quick intuition of love, not only wondered, but believed—felt sure that these grave-clothes were the sign of a victory. Such is the account of that ever-memorable morning. The arrangement of its events may not be absolutely accurate ; in the ignorance of all that occurred, it is impossible to supply every link in the chain of narrative. The evangelists are so filled with the one reality, " He is risen," that they are not careful as to the minutiæ of the circumstances. On the Resurrection, as personal, as real, the structure of Christian life and doctrine is reared. By the effect of the Resurrection the apostles were transformed. The foolish and slow-hearted fishermen of the past became the princes of a new and heavenly kingdom. " With great power they gave witness to the resurrection of the Lord Jesus, and great grace was upon them all."

II. But WITHOUT FURTHER DWELLING ON THE EVIDENCES OF THE RESURRECTION AS AN HISTORICAL FACT, CONSIDER IT AS A MIGHTY SPIRITUAL FORCE. Consider what the apostle calls " the power of the Resurrection." What is the central truth of the forty days between the Resurrection and Ascension ? Study the brief account of these forty days, and you see at once a change in the manner and conditions of the revelation of Christ. He shows himself only to chosen witnesses. St. Mark says that he appeared to the disciples " in another form." The eyes of the disciples are declared to be so held (ver. 16) that they do not know him. It is the same Jesus, but much is altered. " He came and he went as he pleased ; material substances such as the fastened doors were no impediment to his coming ; when he was present his disciples did not, as a matter of course, know him." These forty days were what the sunrise is to the day ; they were the beginning of the relation in which he stands to his Church now. All his self-revelations are pictures of the way and truth of his presence as we are called to realize it. Men had seen him without knowing him ; now they know him without seeing him. We behold him, as Newman has finely said, " passing from his hiding-place of sight without knowledge to that of knowledge without sight." As a transition-time, giving us intimations of the glory in which he is abiding and of the grace in which he is dealing with us, regard the period that was ushered in by the early morning of the first day of the week. It was a great day. Four appearances are noted. The first (John xx.), to Mary of Magdala, followed or preceded, perhaps, by an appearance to the other women (Matt. xxiii.) ; the second (vers. 13—35), to the two brethren journeying to Emmaus ; the third, to Simon Peter (ver. 35) ; and the fourth (John xx. 19—23), to the disciples assembled at night when the doors were shut for fear of the Jews. Each of these appearances is significant. St. Luke relates the second. One remark only as to Mary of Magdala. Renan has asserted that the glory of the Resurrection belongs to her ; that, " after Jesus, it is Mary who has done the most to the founding of Christianity." There can be nothing more contrary to the explicit statements of the evangelists than much that is contained in the brilliant Frenchman's statement. But the message of Mary is indeed the basis of the faith of the

Church, the basis of the faith of humanity. "If Christ is not risen, our hope is vain; we are yet in our sins." And the commandment which sent her to the disciples is the inspiration of all Christian hearts. "Go, tell my brethren." Tell the message of the risen Lord in the light with which the countenance is irradiated; tell it in the glad obedience by which the life is sanctified; tell it through all that you do and are; tell—let your teaching cease only with your breathing—that Christ has risen, that the imprisoning stone has been rolled away, and the kingdom of heaven is open to all believers, its gates being closed neither by day nor by night, for there is no night there.

Vers. 13—35.—*Emmaus.* (For a beautiful paraphrase of this Scripture, see the passage in Cowper's poem 'Conversation,' beginning, "It happened on a solemn even-tide." The incident is presented by him as an illustration of converse "such as it behoves man to maintain, and such as God approves." And it is impossible to resist the appropriateness of the lesson which is enforced.) The time of the memorable appearance is the afternoon, probably between four and six; and its prominent persons are two disciples, not apostles, whom it is impossible to identify. The one is called Klopas or Cleophas, supposed by many to be Alphæus, the brother of Joseph of Nazareth, and father of James; but the name being a contraction of Cleopatrus, the supposition is scarcely admissible. The other is not mentioned by name, and many conjectures concerning him have been framed. A worthy German pastor once said, "The learned cannot come to any agreement who the other was, and I will give you this good counsel—let each of you take his place." Look at these two men as they journey. "The sun of the Resurrection was enveloped in thick clouds of despondency and sorrow, scarcely penetrated by a ray of light." It would seem that they had left the gathering of disciples before Mary had brought her tale. What they dwell on is, "True, the body was not in the tomb; but then he was not seen;" and one risen from the dead was a thought which they could scarcely credit. They are not sure even that the women really saw angels; it was, perhaps, only a vision of angels, and, having the notions of their time as to ghosts and apparitions, they incline to the belief that there was no reality in the presence of whom the Maries and Salome and others had spoken. No; he is dead, and the third day has come and gone, and he has not been seen. Let this state of mind be noted. There was no predisposition in Christ's followers to accept the Resurrection. Far from this, the evidence made way against doubtings, against scepticisms, we might say, of the most obstinate nature. These foolish and slow-hearted men were almost the last people likely to credit the tale. How was it that this temperament, incredulous, despondent, so quickly gave way to one full of worship and great joy? How was it that such men gave up all, travelled hither and thither with the one message ever on their lips, many of them suffering death because they would maintain that the Christ who was crucified did rise, had been seen by them, and is alive for evermore? I can find only one answer to the question—They witnessed to truth. "The Lord is risen indeed." But regard the incident in the light of the thought that the forty days in which Christ showed himself alive after his Passion were intended as a time of preparation for that new form of his presence which began when the day of Pentecost was fully come. Studying the forty-days' period, we can find many hints and suggestions as to the manner of Christ's intercourse with us, of his coming to us in the Comforter whom he promised until the end of the age. The special teaching of this journey to Emmaus, and all that befell the two, may be gathered under three points: (1) *Christ with us, but unrevealed;* (2) *Christ teaching, but personally unrecognized;* (3) *Christ revealed and recognized.*

I. CHRIST WITH US, BUT UNREVEALED. A Stranger asks the cause of the dejection of the two travellers, and, by his sympathy and courtesy, draws out their confidence. Two reasons for not discerning him are given. The one is (Mark xvi. 12), that "he appeared in another form" than that with which they were familiar. Not the form of the Shepherd going before them, but that of the Companion in walking and working clothes travelling by their side. But there is the other reason (ver. 16)—"Their eyes were holden that they should not know him." They were not at that time in spiritual light; their vision was narrowed by their great sorrow. Are not these still the reasons why so often we do not see the Christ who is with us as we travel along the thoroughfares of life? He is not in the form in which we expect him. Sometimes he hides himself, that he may get the more fully into our hearts. He is with us, wanting the halo, wanting all that would at once declare him, that he may be more intimately our Friend, "familiar, patient, condescending, free." And we miss or mistake him, because we cannot see beneath the form, because our minds are self-occupied, or, when intent on higher things, are wanting in the elevation, in the pure sweet light, of the spiritual mind. Only when the spiritual eyes are opened do we know who has been and is with us. But he is with us as we toil on our toilsome way, bearing the heat and burden of the afternoon. It is he who is touching the springs of our thought and action. It is he who is speaking to us. Fear not, thou weary and heart-sore disciple; when thy comforts seem to be gone, he, the Comforter, is close to thee. Thy tears are falling; he is nigh with his "Why weepest thou?" Thou art seeking thy God, but thy soul is unresting, because it cannot find the Rock; he is nigh with his "Whom seekest thou?" Thou hast left the city's din behind thee, and art alone with thyself; he is nigh, assuring thee that the fairest vineyards are those which are received from the valley of troubling. Thou art in communion with some kindred spirit, exchanging the fears and joys of the mind that turns to heaven; he is nigh, rejoicing to add himself to the two or three. The story of Emmaus is indeed a figure of the life-pilgrimage. Bear from it the pledge that whosoever is true to the light, is, though halting and uncertain may be his steps, the neighbour to Jesus Christ—Jesus himself near and in fellowship with all communing and reasoning.

II. And how? TEACHING, ALTHOUGH PERSONALLY UNRECOGNIZED. What Christ was in his dealing with the two, he has been in his dealing with his Church. During the past centuries he has been "teaching and expounding the things concerning himself." Did he not promise that the Holy Ghost would be the Guide into all truth, through the glorifying of him, the receiving of his and showing it to his own? What is the witness for the fulfilment of this office? It is the history of the past eighteen centuries. The text from which the Holy Ghost has been preaching is that which Jesus sounded (ver. 26); and the way of the sermon is the very way of Christ (ver. 27). Moses and the prophets, apprehended in New Testament light, have, for these centuries, been read, opened up, as the treasury of the things of Christ. Thought and culture, devotion and obedience, stand to-day where they stood yesterday—before the mighty "Ought not Christ to have suffered these things, and to enter into his glory?" Is there not progressiveness in the teaching of the Holy Ghost? There is development in Christianity. It has its permanent, but it has its progressive, element also. It is only by little and little that the higher truth of the kingdom enters the hearts of men. Precept must be on precept, line on line, until the dispensation of the opening, when the Church, gathered fully into the house of the Lord, will receive from the pierced hand the bread of the eternal life. So in personal history and experience. There is One teaching us, even when we do not recognize who he is. Life is the school in which the Holy Ghost is the Instructor. Christ and Christ's love, and the meaning of our existence as interpreted in Christ's cross, is the lesson in which we are taught. We pass from standard up to standard, the book which regulates all the teaching being the Scriptures. Many are the forms which the Holy Ghost, the Teacher, assumes; many are the agencies through which he draws near. But if, with receptive minds, we are yielded to him, he is taking us step by step along the path of the manifold education meant for the disciple of Jesus; expounding as we are able to bear, stooping to our immaturities and weaknesses; a presence in us rather than external to us, stimulating thought and desire, enkindling into fuller flame the smoking flax; so that by-and-by we are able to say, "Did not our heart burn within us, while he talked with us by the way, and while he opened to us the Scriptures?" (ver. 32).

III. Behold CHRIST REVEALED AND RECOGNIZED. The village is reached. Must the delightful companionship end? Courteously saluting them, the Stranger apparently is going on. Nay, the sun is about to set; they entreat him not to leave them (ver. 29). He would have gone on if there had been no prayer. The personal desire is essential to the tarrying. But that desire never pleads in vain. How many never plead for the tarrying—indeed, do not want it! For the drawing near and journeying with us, no desire from us is needed. Christ does that of his own will. But the tarrying is another matter. He cannot force an entrance; he will be forced. "They constrained him." He receives sinners *for* salvation; their reception of him *is* salvation (Rev. iii. 20). At meat with them he is revealed. What it was that disclosed him we cannot exactly say. The whole manner is solemn and striking. At once he takes the head of the table. The Master's place is conceded to him. And that always prepares for revelation. When the heart is truly yielded to Christ, the moment of the showing of himself is near. He takes the bread; he blesses; he breaks, and gives it to the two. And their eyes are opened, and they know him. There is the voice, the blessing, and I think, the sight of the pierced hands—the sight that I expect to have in glory. The meal may not have been a full sacrament. But Christ's presence and blessing made, the meal sacramental; for that presence and that blessing elevate whatever is ordinary. And the action before us is a consecration of ordinance as well as Word as the means of revelation. The Word prepares for the ordinance; in the ordinance Christ is revealed. Is not this a forecast of the future? Is it not Christ's will to make himself known to those who sit at meat with him—they having first constrained him and being thus spiritually susceptible—in the breaking of bread? Observe the signs of the revelation. A new sight (ver. 31); a new energy (ver. 33); a new sympathy (vers. 33, 34); a new eloquence (ver. 35). Joy, joy to the disciples who have seen the Lord. But he has vanished out of their sight. He must not hinder, by his bodily presence, the lifting of the consciousness into the region of the spiritual presence. That on which afterwards they dwell is, not the glimpse they have had of face and hand, but the power of his Spirit, the life-giving force of his Word (ver. 32). The clouds were dispelled by the rising of the Day-star in the heart. That is the sign of Christ with us here. By that we know that it is he who has been talking with us. One day, but not in this present time, we shall see him as he is; he will bless and break and give to us himself, the Bread of life. And then he will not vanish out of our sight.

> "Oh, then shall the veil be removed,
>   And round me thy brightness be poured;
> I shall meet him whom absent I loved,
>   I shall see whom unseen I adored.'

Vers. 36—43.—*Christ and his Church.* I. THE CHURCH. It is found in miniature in the upper room—"The eleven, and them that were with them." 1. *Its separation.* It is isolated from the outer world. A new bond, a new manner, of union is already realized. It is not of the world, as Christ himself was not. There is a door shut between the little flock and the Jews. A supreme attraction to him whom the world sees not, an affiance of soul of which the world knows not, unites the company, and, in thus uniting, separates it. It has a secret with which the world does not inter-meddle. 2. *Its unity.* (1) That stands in Christ, "Ye have not chosen me, but I have chosen you" (John xv. 16). The Church is not a mere voluntary association; it is a spiritual organism rooted and grounded in the Man Christ Jesus—in what he is and has done, in his Divine-human Person, and the offices which he executes as Redeemer. (2) It is realized through continuance in the apostles' doctrine and fellow-ship. "The eleven, and those with them." Christ had looked through the ages down to the end of the time, and thus had spoken: "I pray for those who shall believe on me through the word of the men whom thou didst give me." Here the eleven form the centre of the company. There is a definite word on which the Church is built. It has not a mere collection of "memoranda;" it is not an institution of "hazy outlines." It has a distinct testimony—that of the apostles and prophets. And there is a social life, a fellowship, by which it "makes increase to self-edifying in love"—the fellowship which continues that which is witnessed to in the assembly of the eleven and those with them. Remember, it is *fellowship*, all holding themselves to be fellows in Christ, exchanging their experiences, imparting the gift which each has received, that it may tend to quicken the faith and love of all. "As *they thus* spake, Jesus himself stood in the midst" (ver. 36).

II. CHRIST. He had promised, "I will not leave you comfortless: I will come to you." Behold the fulfilment and the way of the fulfilment of this promise. Behold him present in his Church. 1. *The sovereignty of the presence.* On a sudden he stands in the midst. They are not expecting him. He comes through barred doors. It is the day of his power. Christ prescribes means; he ordains channels of grace; and, where there is the obedience of faith in the use of the means, there is blessing. "Where two or three are gathered together, there am I in the midst of them." But in all that speaks of spiritual life, there is the witness for a spiritual sovereignty, for reserves of power in the hands of the Lord himself. The new birth is a secret and a surprise (John iii. 7, 8). 2. It is *the personal Jesus who is present to bless—"Jesus himself."* (Ver. 36.) Above and beyond the mere teaching and fellowship, there is *the Lord*. Christianity is Christ. The full blessing, that which wholly fills the soul, is himself in felt relation with each self. "Of him are ye in Christ Jesus, who of God is made to us Wisdom, Righteousness, Sanctification, Redemption" (1 Cor. i. 30). 3. The *announcement of the presence is peace.* (Ver. 36.) One of the last words before he suffered was "peace." It was the legacy of the dying Saviour. The salutation of the risen Saviour is, "Peace *to* you!"—the customary salutation transformed and glorified. His immanence in the Church is evidenced by the breathing of peace over human souls. "Peace with God through the Lord Jesus Christ;" "The peace of God which passeth all understanding." 4. The *complete benediction of the presence.* (1) Fears and doubts are scattered. The disciples are terrified and affrighted (ver. 37). They are afraid at his tokens. Scepticisms reassert themselves. A Church, a Christian, wanting in spiritual enthusiasm, with a low spiritual temperature, is subject to the fogs of doubt. Its action is crippled by a subtle scepticism. When he is realized as truly in the midst, the fogs are dispelled. There is a counteracting *why* (ver. 38). In the psalms (Ps. xlii.) the soul, dark and doubtful, asks, "Why hast thou forgotten me?" Its questioning is dispelled through another *why:* "Why art thou cast down, O my soul?" The blessed Jesus-question to poor confused humanity is, "*Why* art thou troubled? and *why* do thoughts arise in thy heart?" As the Sun of Righteousness shines into the soul, the melancholy, perplexing thoughts scatter, the clouds whose banks lie so low on the heart's horizon flee away. (2) The *evidence of the sacrifice establishes the faith.* (Vers. 39, 40.) He shows the pierced hands and feet—the wounds whence comes the healing, the death whence has come the life. And, even in the glory into which he has entered, the print of the nails is seen. The gaze of the redeemed who share that glory is ever towards the Lamb that was slain. "Worthy is the Lamb!" (3) The *full revelation is the Divine humanity.* (Vers. 41—43.) While they believe, and yet can scarcely believe, for the joy seems too great and too wonderful, he eats the fish and honeycomb before them. It is no ghost who is in that room; it is very man of very man. And this is the abiding consciousness and strength of the Church. It presents the true humanity. It has the true humanitarianism. The Christ is he "who liveth and was dead, and is alive for evermore." And in him humanity is fulfilled, represented, and redeemed. This is the truth of the social life of the Church. The Church is not a mere institute for instruction and worship; it is a social state built up in the ever-abiding humanity of Jesus Christ. Thus, in the upper room at Jerusalem, on the first Easter night, there is an apocalypse of the great mystery, Christ and the Church.

Vers. 44—49.—*The instruction of the apostles.* The words contained in these verses are a summary of the instruction given by the risen Lord during the forty days in which he showed himself alive after his Passion. They are not to be regarded as the outline of only one discourse, following the appearance to the eleven recorded in the previous verses; they are rather the heads of the teaching which was imparted in the great period between the Resurrection and the Ascension. "We must suppose the evangelist to be hurrying to a close in this portion of his history, and to be giving us a brief sketch of the words and actions of our Lord which are summed up in the expression in the first chapter of the Book of Acts, "Jesus had given commandment unto the apostles." Note the points in this instruction.

I. THE SWORD WHICH HIS CHURCH IS TO WIELD. (Vers. 44, 45.) As St. Paul afterwards said, "The sword of the Spirit, which is the Word of God." The Lord gives the treasury from which the Church is to draw—the Law, the prophets, the psalms, the Scriptures; but these writings, with the key to their inner meaning, to their saving force—"all things in them *concerning* me." The great word spelt through all the books—each book, as De Quincey put it, forming as it were a letter of the word—is

"Christ." And not only so; these Scriptures are to be expounded and enforced in the light and through the skill of the opened understanding. This is the secret of the effect; it is this that makes them the sword. Only when they are thus the weapon of the Spirit, illuminating the mind of the teacher, as well as acting on the conscience of the hearer, are they quick and powerful. The opening of the understanding is spoken of as a definite action at a definite time. " *Then* opened he their understanding." What a new light is then shed on the sacred page! What a blessed "Eureka!" is then realized! The foolish and slow in heart go forth with the sword of the Spirit, "conquering and to conquer."

II. THE MESSAGE WHICH THE CHURCH IS TO DELIVER. (Ver. 46.) The message is: the Christ whom God has sent, and the world needs—the *historical* Christ, incarnate, suffering, crucified, risen; and this Christ presented as the fulfilment of all Scripture, the consummation of Divine thought and purpose, "the Lamb slain from the foundation of the world," the Prophet, Priest, and King, by whom man is redeemed, in whom the nature and want, the hope and desire, of all nations are interpreted. The Church is called to teach that "thus it *behoved* Christ to suffer, and to rise from the dead the third day." Wide is the environment of truth, and the Church must sweep this environment in its vision; but this is the centre of all the circle.

III. THE CONDITIONS OF FELLOWSHIP IN THE KINGDOM OF GOD WHICH IT IS TO DECLARE. (Ver. 47.) The beginning of the gospel preached by Christ was the word "repent" (Matt. iv. 17). Now he solemnly and emphatically urges that repentance is to be the great fact in New Testament preaching. The end to be ever before the Church is "to open the eyes, and turn men from darkness to light, and from the power of Satan to God." And with this repentance is to be associated the blessing of the kingdom, "remission of sins;" *i.e.* the sending of the guilt and power of sin away from between the soul and God, and thus making the inner vision clear, inspiring with the consciousness of the spirit of adoption and the spirit of brotherhood, confirming in the liberty wherewith Christ makes free. In the name of Christ, all nations are to be summoned to repent, and receive this remission; the voice lifted up with strength, "There is none other Name given under heaven among men whereby we must be saved."

IV. THE WITNESS WHICH THE CHURCH IS TO REALIZE. (Ver. 48.) 1. Its *range*. "Among all nations." The universality and catholicity of the Christian word, of the Christian Church, are asserted, with regal authority, at the conference on the mountain in Galilee (Matt. xxviii. 18—20). 2. Its *course*. "Beginning at Jerusalem." There, where the Lord of glory was crucified, the first call to repentance is to be sounded, the first offer of the Christ for the remission of sins is to be made. So it was (Acts ii.). But, from Jerusalem, the course of the witness is ever outward—"to Judæa, Samaria, the uttermost parts of the earth." We are first to find our own; but the love which begins, is never to stop, at home. 3. Its *power*. (Ver. 49.) Not in the witnessing man or woman; not in the things witnessed to; not in word, ordinance, ministry; no, the power is from on high. Christ reasserts what he taught in the last discourse before he suffered. The great consolation then was the promise of the Father—that in which his Fatherly love and will are expressed, his great promise to his Son—the Holy Ghost. It is the Holy Ghost who testifies of him. He is not the accompaniment of the Church; the Church is his accompaniment. "He shall testify of me: and ye *also* shall bear witness" (John xv. 26, 27). Now, in the forty days' instruction, he repeats this word. He reminds us that *the* power of witnessing is a descent from on high, the anointing of the man by the Holy Spirit. Two things are said—the one, the declaration that the promise is imminent, "I am sending it;" and the other, the injunction to wait in the city, to attempt nothing, until the promise is made good, and they are endued with the power. Let the Church, let every Christian, remember the injunction; let eternal thanksgiving arise because the promise of the Father has been sent, and the Holy Spirit now dwells with the Church.

Vers. 50—53.—*The farewell and the Ascension.* Once more the old relation is resumed. The Shepherd of Israel goes before his little flock. They see him, as in the former time, at their head. The well-known route is taken, the well-known place is reached. And the crowning memory of Bethany is imprinted on their hearts. It is the scene of the last adieu, of the Ascension (ver. 50). In the earlier history of Israel (2 Kings ii.) there was a day when the sons of the prophets, referring to Elijah, said to Elisha, "Knowest thou that the Lord will take away thy master from thy head to-day?" And his answer was, "Yea, I know it; hold ye your peace." There were no sons of prophets thus speaking to the eleven. But whispers, no doubt, in their hearts raised shadows of some coming event. Something like the old amazement and fear (Mark x. 32) would he felt as, in silence, they followed their Leader. He is to be taken from their head; but better far than the mantle thrown on Elisha from the vanishing prophet is to be their portion. Observe Christ as he is revealed in the concluding verses of the Gospel; observe those whom he is to leave behind.

I. OBSERVE CHRIST AS HE IS HERE REVEALED. See: 1. *The action of the Lord towards them.* "He lifted up his hands" (ver. 50). Before he suffered he had lifted up his eyes to heaven, and the voice of intercession had been raised for them (John xvii.). As the high-priestly prayer closed, the voice had passed from the tones of earnest but humble pleading into those of the Sovereign expressing his will: "I will that they also whom thou hast given me, be with me where I am." Now the Priest, about to ascend to his throne, extends those hands in which is the print of the nails. It is the first time in which we are introduced to this attitude in the Gospels. The uplifted hands are the sign of the accepted sacrifice ever potent to cleanse. They are the sign of the righteousness ever ample to clothe. They are the sign of the protection ever sufficient to overshadow his Church. The uplifted hands constituted the last recollection of the Christ whom the disciples had seen; they mark the abiding truth of the Christ whom the eye sees not. And, as the hands are lifted, the lips are opened to bless. What were the words of the blessing? Perhaps the benediction (Numb. iv. 24) which the sons of Aaron were commanded to pronounce was included in it. But who can measure all that it comprehended—all the wealth of grace and truth with which it was charged? Let us say rather, with which it *is* charged for the Church until the end of the age. "Lo, I am with you alway, blessing and keeping, my face shining on you, my will gracious to you, the light of my countenance lifted on you, my peace possessing you." 2. *The ascending Lord.* "While blessing" (ver. 51). While the accents of his tenderness are flowing over the soul, lo! he moves from the soil on which he and his have been standing. Upward, ever upward, he is borne; they gaze in wonder as the form in which they have beheld him is sublimated and passes whither their adoring vision can no longer follow. The apostle who was "born out of due time" completes, as far as thought of mortal can, the account of the evangelist (Eph. i. 20—23), when he describes the ascent "far above all principality, and power, and might, and dominion, and every name that is named, not only in this world, but in that which is to come;" all things put under the feet of the glorified Man, "Head over all things to the Church, which is his body, the fulness of him that filleth all in all." He is "parted from them;" but only to be more nearly and entirely with them; only to bear with him the humanity through which Highest God is in touch with the whole life of man; only that, in the unchangeable Priesthood, he may ever live to make intercession; only to make good the word as to the promise of the Father. When ten more days have passed, the gates which had opened that the King of glory might enter, shall open again, and the Paraclete, Christ's other self, shall descend from the heaven into which he has gone, to fill the little company with his presence. And in that day they shall know that he is in the Father, and they in him, and he in them.

II. OBSERVE THE DISCIPLES. 1. *The new worship.* They had followed him, and had called him Master. His appearances during the forty days had prepared them for something higher still. Now, in deepest reverence, they kneel before the Lord. Thomas learns the whole reality of his answer, "My Lord and my God." Mary learns that which is higher and holier than the touch with which, on the resurrection-morning, she had sought to detain him. John learns the word which afterwards he wrote, "This is the true God, and the Eternal Life." Peter learns that which moves him to interpret the consciousness of faith, "Whom having not seen ye love." Then first sounds the music which burst forth, in later years, in the sublimest hymn of the Church: "We praise thee, O God; we acknowledge thee to be the Lord. . . . Thou art the King of glory, O Christ." And this worship is the true life of the Church. It is the outcome of the faith in the Resurrection. "Christ died, yea rather, is risen again, and is even

at the right hand of God, making intercession for us." Wanting this, there may be such
an apostrophe as that with which Renan concludes his ' Life of Jesus ;' but worship full
and adoring there cannot be. It is this worship which is the spring of all energy, the
pledge of all victory, the bond of union between heaven and earth. "Salvation to our
God who sitteth on the throne, and unto the Lamb for ever and ever." 2. *The new
joy.* "They returned to Jerusalem" (ver. 25). But what a difference ! They had left
it dispirited, weighed down by many thoughts. Now "they come again rejoicing,
bringing their sheaves with them." "Parted from them !" Might they not feel as
sheep without a Shepherd? Nay ; for they know that their Shepherd is with them.
Their hope had been sealed and confirmed, and they are flushed with "a great joy."
Should not this joy thrill the Church? Enthusiasm is essential to its vitality. To
be strong, it must be sanguine, triumphant. Times of worshipful faith are always
times of great joy. "We triumph in God through our Lord Jesus Christ, in whom
we received the reconciliation." 3. *The new life.* "They were continually in the
temple" (ver. 53). But the temple had a new meaning to them. Rite and offering,
house of prayer and songs of praise, were all clothed with a new character. It was
their Father's house, and he had given a new song to their lips. Continually are they
"praising and blessing God." This is the life; for they are sitting in the heavenly
places, and partaking of the heavenly things. "Day by day we magnify thee."
Beautiful as the first days of summer is this picture of the waiting Church. Would
that the impression of this life of praise and blessing were more evident in the Church,
witnessing, working, and still waiting. May the Church be "found unto praise, and
honour, and glory, at the appearing of Jesus Christ "!

HOMILIES BY VARIOUS AUTHORS.

Vers. 1—12.—*Side-lights from the Resurrection.* The simple, unpretending story of
the Resurrection, as here narrated, brings into view other truths than that great and
supreme fact of the rising of our Lord. We have our attention called to—

I. THE CONSTANCY AND THE EAGERNESS OF TRUE AFFECTION. (Ver. 1.) No thought
had these women of deserting him whom they loved but whom the world hated and
had now slain. On the contrary, the enmity of those that maligned and murdered him
made their affection to cleave all the more firmly to him. It attended him right up to
the very last; it followed him to the grave ; it came to bestow those final ministries
which only devoted affection would have cared to render. And it showed itself as
eager as it was constant. "Very early in the morning they came unto the sepulchre."
True love to our Lord will stand these tests. It will survive the enmities and oppositions of an indifferent or a hostile society ; it will be unaffected by these except,
indeed, to be strengthened and deepened by them ; moreover, it will show its loyalty
and its fervour by the eagerness of its service, not waiting for the last hour of necessity,
but availing itself of the first hour of opportunity.

II. THE DISAPPEARANCE OF DIFFICULTIES AS WE GO ON OUR WAY OF FAITHFUL
SERVICE. We know from Mark (xvi. 3) that these women were full of apprehension
lest they should be unable to get the stone rolled away from the door. But they went
on their way to do their sacred office ; and when they reached the spot they found
their difficulty vanished (ver. 2). This is the common experience of the seeker after
God in Christ, of the man desirous of discharging his duty in the fear of God, of the
Christian worker. "Who will roll away that intervening stone ?" we ask timidly and
apprehensively. "How shall we get over that insurmountable barrier? How will our
weakness prevail against such solid obstacles ?" Let us go on our way of faith, of
duty, of loving service, and we shall find that, if some angel has not been on the
scene, the hindrance has disappeared, the way is open, the goal within our reach,
the service within the compass of our powers.

III. THE SURPRISES THAT AWAIT US AS WE PROCEED. These women found an
empty grave, visitants from the unseen world, a most unexpected though most
welcome message ; instead of a mournful satisfaction, they found a new hope, far too
good and far too great to be held all at once within their heart (vers. 4—7). Peter,
too, found himself the subject of a great astonishment (ver. 12). God has his merciful

surprises for us as we proceed on our Christian path. He may surprise us with a sudden fear or a sudden sorrow; but he also surprises us with an unanticipated peace; with an unlooked-for joy; with a new, strange hope; before long he will introduce us to the blessed surprise of the heavenly realities.

IV. THE NEARNESS OF THE HEAVENLY TO THE EARTHLY SPHERE. (Ver. 4.) Angels were always at hand to render service in the great redemptive work. Why should we think of heaven as "beyond the stars"? Why should we not think of it as encompassing us on every side, only separated from us by a thin veil, through which our mortal senses cannot pass to its glorious spectacles and its blessed harmonies?

V. THAT GOD HAS MUCH BETTER THINGS IN STORE FOR US THAN WE THINK POSSIBLE. Neither the wondering women nor the incredulous apostles could believe in such a happy issue as they were assured of, though they had been carefully prepared to expect it (ver. 11). In the feebleness of our faith we say to ourselves, "Surely God is not going to give me *that*, to place me *there*, to bestow on me such a heritage as *this!*" But why not? For him to make all grace, all power, all life, to abound, is for him to do what he has promised, and what he has been doing since he first opened his hand to create and to bestow.—C.

Vers. 5, 6.—*The Resurrection and the Life.* No smallest touch of censure can we trace in the words of these angels. On their errand of faithful love these women would not be greeted thus. It was but a strong, awakening appeal, calling them to consider that, while they had come in the right spirit, they had come on a superfluous mission, and were looking in the wrong place for their Lord. Not there in the tomb among the dead, but breathing the air of a life that would never be laid down, was he whom they sought. The words attest—

I. THE RESURRECTION OF OUR LORD. This was: 1. Here attested by the angels. It was, at the same time, indicated by the empty tomb. The latter, of course, would not of itself prove such a fact; but it strongly sustained the word of the heavenly visitants. But beyond this, weightier than this, was: 2. The repeated and unmistakable evidence of the apostles and the women. Ten several times, at least, the risen Saviour was seen by those who knew him best. These were so thoroughly assured of the fact of his rising again, that they not only testified it, but risked and even sacrificed their lives to propagate a faith of which it was the corner-stone. And they not only undoubtedly believed it themselves, but they spoke as men who could be and who were credited by those who heard them. Then we have here: 3. The twofold buttress of a *Divine promise* and of *human incredulity.* Jesus "spake, saying, . . . the third day he should rise again." This was the fulfilment of the promise of One who gave such convincing proof that he could do what he willed. Moreover, it was believed in spite of the strongest incredulity. The apostles ought to have expected it, but they did not; we might almost say that it was the last thing they were looking for. They had given up their Lord and their cause as utterly lost; and when the tidings came, they refused to believe (ver. 11). So far from the Resurrection being the figment of a diseased expectation, it was a fact forced upon minds strongly predisposed to discredit it. The second clause of the angels' sentence was as true as the first: he was not there; *he had risen.* He had kept his word; he who had commanded the winds and the waves, and who showed himself Master of the elements of nature, now proved that the keys of death were in his royal hand, and proved himself to be the Son of God, the Lord of life. And with his "glorious resurrection" comes the fact of—

II. OUR OWN IMMORTALITY. The resurrection of Jesus Christ is the sure sign, proof, forerunner, of our own life beyond the grave. Without that supreme and crowning fact, we could have had no certain hope, no assurance; without that he could not have been to us "the Resurrection and the Life." With that he can be and is. Now we have in him a *living Lord,* who can carry out his kindest promises and be to us all that, during his ministry, he undertook to be. Wherefore let us: 1. Seek and find spiritual life in the once-crucified and ever-living Saviour. "He that believeth in him, though he were [spiritually] dead, yet shall he live," live in very deed and truth, *i.e.* live before God, unto God, and in God—partake of the life which is spiritual and Divine. 2. Be assured, then, of a blessed immortality; for "whoso liveth [in him] and believeth in him shall never die." His outward, bodily dissolution will be a mere incident in his career; so far from its being a termination of it, it will prove to be the starting-point of another and nobler life than the present, one nearer to God and far fuller of power, of usefulness, of blessedness. 3. Realize this truth concerning the departed. We may go to the grave and weep there like the sorrowing sisters of Bethany; we may tend their tomb with the carefulness which is the simple prompting of pure and deep affection; but let us learn to dissociate our thoughts of our departed friends from the grave. *They* are not there; let us not be seeking the living among the dead. There rest their mortal remains, but they themselves are with God, with the Saviour whose presence and friendship are exceeding gladness, with the holy and the true who have passed into the skies. *They* are in the light and the love and the joy of home. Let us dwell on this, and comfort ourselves and comfort one another with these thoughts.—C.

Vers. 13—32.—*Privilege; unconscious companionship; incredulity.* In this most interesting narrative, beside a very pleasing and attractive picture, we have a variety of lessons. We may gather instruction respecting—

I. OUR LORD'S ELECTIVE LOVE. It was a very great favour he granted to these two men. Why, we ask, was it rendered *to them?* Of one we do not even know his name, and of the other nothing but his name. Why was so rare and high a privilege accorded to these obscure disciples, and not rather to those more prominent and active? In truth, we find ourselves quite unable to decide who are the fittest to receive special favours from the hand of God, or on what grounds he wills to manifest his presence and his power. His selections, we are sure, cannot be arbitrary or irrational. God must have not only a reason, but the best reason, for everything he does. But into the reasons for his choice we often may not enter; they lie beyond our reach. It is not to the acknowledged leaders of the Church that God often chooses to manifest especial privilege, but to those who are simple, unexpectant, unknown. He grants illuminations of his Spirit, peculiar joy and gladness of heart in him, remarkable success in the utterance of his truth, anticipatory glimpses of heavenly glory, to whom he will. And these are quite likely to be found amongst the humbler members of his Church. If there is any law which will guide our judgment it is this—that it is to the "pure in heart," to those who have most perfectly conquered the fleshly passions and are most freed from worldly ambitions and anxieties, who have the simplest and purest hope in him and desire toward him, that he vouchsafes his presence and grants the teaching and inspiration of his Spirit. But Christ's elective love is fully as much of a *fact* as it is of a *doctrine.*

II. UNCONSCIOUS COMPANIONSHIP WITH CHRIST. These two men were walking and talking with Christ, receiving his truth and responding to his appeal, their hearts "burning within them" as they held sweet and sacred intercourse with him; yet they did not recognize him; they had no idea that they were having fellowship with the Lord. There is much unconscious companionship with Jesus Christ now. Men are led into belief of the truth, are impressed with the sovereign claims of God upon their service, and of Jesus Christ upon their love; they ask, they inquire, they come to the feet of Christ to learn of him; they come to the cross of Christ to trust in him; they shun what they believe to be offensive, and pursue what they think is right and pleasing in his sight; and yet they are not at rest. They think they may be in a good way or in a fair way to find life; but they do not realize that they are *in* the *right* way. The fact is ofttimes that they are walking in the path of life with Christ, but "their eyes are holden that they do not know him." A Divine One has joined himself to them, as familiarly and unpretendingly as to these two disciples, ingratiating himself into their favour, wooing and winning their trust and their love; but because there has been no period of well-recognized revolution, no sudden remarkable convulsion, they have failed to perceive that the work wrought within them has been that of his own kind and holy hand. Such souls need to learn that oftenest it is not in the wind, or in the earthquake, or in the fire, but in the still small voice of familiar truth and gracious influence, that Christ comes to the soul in renewing power. If it is in Christ we are trusting, if it is in *his* service we are most willing to live, if it is *his* will we are most concerned to do, then it is *he* himself by whose side we are walking day by day.

III. THE STRANGE INCREDULITY OF CHRISTIAN DISCIPLESHIP. Our Master, who was so gentle and so considerate, here employs a very strong expression (ver. 25). This is the language of serious reproach; it is a weighty rebuke. The disciples of Christ ought to have read their Scriptures better, and they ought to have heeded the reiterated warning and promise he had himself given them of his death and his rising again. But while we wonder at what seems to us their slowness to learn and to believe, are we not as obtuse and as incredulous as they were? Do we not fail to grasp the promises of God as they are written in his Word, as they were spoken by his Son our Saviour? When those things happen which we should expect to happen in connection with the teaching of Divine truth; when the Spirit of God works mightily and mercifully in the souls of men; when hard hearts are broken and stubborn wills are subdued to the obedience of Christ; when wrong and shameful lives are changed into pure and holy ones; when the kingdom of God comes amongst us;—are we not surprised, incredulous? Are we not tempted to ascribe these issues to other than heavenly sources? And yet *ought not* this very result to happen? Is it not precisely what we should have been looking for, and wondering that it did not occur? We shall probably find abundant illustrations of Christian incredulity to match anything of which we read in our New Testament. "Slow of heart" are we to believe all that the Master has said of the presence and the power and the promises of God.—C.

Vers. 13—32.—*Further lessons by the way.* Other lessons beside those already gleaned (see preceding homily) await our hand in this instructive story.

I. THE THREAD OF TRIAL WHICH RUNS THROUGH THE FABRIC OF OUR LIFE. On one occasion our Lord asked a question of one of his disciples, and of that question it is said, "This he said to prove him" (John vi. 6). There were other occasions, *e.g.* that of the blind beggars by the wayside, and that of the Syro-phœnician woman, when Jesus said things to *prove* or to *try* those who came to him. We have the same thing here. He drew near to these two disciples in the guise of a stranger; he chose to remain unknown to them; he drew them out as if he were one unacquainted with the events which were filling their minds and hearts; he induced them to discover themselves freely and fully both to his own eyes and to theirs; moreover, he was in the act of passing on, and would have gone beyond Emmaus if they had not availed themselves of the opportunity of persuading him to remain. And thus he tried them. The "trial of our faith," and of our love and loyalty, forms a great part of our Master's dealing with ourselves. It explains many otherwise inexplicable things in our life. God appears to us other than the kind, gracious, pitiful, considerate Father that he is; Christ seems to be other than the present, strong, faith-rewarding Master that he is. Why does God let such things happen to us? Why does not Christ bring to pass that for which we labour and pray so earnestly? It may be that, in these cases, he is trying us; proving the sincerity and deepening the roots of our faith and love and zeal. We shall be the stronger, and our lives will be the more fruitful, for his action or his lingering, a little further on.

II. THE TRUE WAY TO MAKE THE SABBATH A DELIGHT. It was fitting that on the first sabbath of the Christian era there should be recorded an instance in which the day was spent as Christ would have it be. What a pleasant picture this of communion with Christ, of searching the Scriptures, of sitting down at the same table with him! We have here: 1. *Communion with our Lord.* About one-fourth of the whole day these favoured men were conversing with Christ, opening their minds and outpouring their hearts to him, telling him their hopes and their fears, and receiving kind and illuminating responses from his lips. So should our "fellowship be with the Father, and with his Son Jesus Christ," on the "day of the Lord." And as we may be sure that the way to Emmaus was marvellously shortened that afternoon, and the village houses showed themselves long before they were looked for, so will earnest and loving communion with our living Lord, so will our walking with Christ, make the hours go swiftly by on the wings of holy and elevated joy, and we shall "call the sabbath a delight." 2. *Sacred study.* (Vers. 27, 32.) How wonderful these Scriptures which contain the record of Divine revelation! So short as to be capable of being committed to the memory, and yet so full as to contain all that is needful for our enlightenment and enrichment, for guidance to God and heaven; so dull to the unquickened conscience, and so delightful to the awakened and renewed; holding mysteries insoluble to human learning, and yet intelligible and instructive from Genesis to Revelation to the earnest inquirer after truth and life; valueless in the market, and yet precious beyond all price to all who want to know how to live and how to die. As Christ and the two learners walked and talked, new light shone on the old passages, and the way was too short and the time too soon gone for their interest and their eagerness to be expended. 3. *Meeting the living Lord at his table.* (Ver. 30.) This was not, strictly speaking, a "sacramental" meal to which they sat down. It was not the "Lord's Supper" of which they partook. But there was about it so much of reverence, of religious earnestness, of holy communion, of sacred joy, that it may well suggest to us that most excellent way of spending some part of "the Lord's day."

III. THE WORTH OF ALL TRUE CHRISTIAN LABOUR. Possibly those who teach may sometimes ask themselves whether it is worth their while to conduct so small a class, to preach to so poor a congregation. Here is the answer to that questioning. If the risen Lord of glory thought it worth his while to walk seven miles and spend two hours in enlightening the minds and comforting the hearts of two humble and obscure disciples; if he was content to spend a good part of his first sabbath in taking a class of two, and pouring from the rich treasury of his truth into their minds, we may not think it unworthy of us to spend time in enlightening or comforting *one* human heart that craves the succour it is in our power to give. The disciple is not above his Master.

IV. THE SECRET OF SPIRITUAL INTEREST. Do we devoutly wish that we knew more of that sacred gladness of which these disciples were so happily conscious as he "talked with them by the way, and opened to them the Scriptures" (ver. 32)? Then: 1. Let us see that we are, as they were, earnestly desirous of knowing more of Jesus Christ. Let us go to our Bible and go up to the house of the Lord with that end *distinctly* and prominently in view. 2. Let us seek and gain the same Divine illumination. It is still to be had, though *that* voice is not now heard in our ear. The "Spirit of truth" is with us still, waiting to illumine and to enlarge our hearts; if we seek his aid and open our minds to his entrance, he will "guide us into all the truth" (John xvi. 13).—C.

Ver. 29.—*The exigency of old age.* The disciples "constrained" our Lord to abide with them; for, they said, "It is toward evening, and the day is far spent." This act of theirs and their words taken together are suggestive of the truth that those whose life is fast waning—with whom it is "toward evening," whose day is "far spent"—have urgent need that Jesus Christ should "abide with" them. We have before us the special spiritual necessities of old age. It has—

I. ITS SPECIAL RESPONSIBILITY. We look to advanced religious experience to set us a particularly blameless example, to show us most clearly the spirit and the complexion of a distinctly Christian life, to lead us in the direction of spirituality and purity. For this high service the near presence of the Saviour is needed, and the constant exercise of his gracious power.

II. ITS SPECIAL TEMPTATION. The temptation of age is to querulousness, to an illiberal criticism of the present and to an undue and partial preference of the past, to an unjust and unwise severity in judging the eccentricities and irregularities of the young, to a dissatisfaction with the comparative obscurity to which it is itself descending. To prevail against this temptation, and to preserve equanimity, sweetness, cheerfulness of spirit and hopefulness of heart, age has urgent need of a constant renewal from above.

III. ITS SPECIAL PRIVATIONS. There are a few who live to a "good old age" without any or without much consciousness of loss. But these are only a few. With old age usually comes privation. In respect of sight, of hearing, of power of locomotion, of facility in speaking, of memory, of intellectual grasp, the aged are painfully conscious that "they are not what they were; they speak with diminished fire, they act with a lessened force." Their life is lower, is narrowed; they are less to their contemporaries than they used to be. They need comfort under the sense of loss; they need another source of satisfaction and of joy. In whom, in what, shall they find it, but in the Person and the presence of the Divine Friend and Saviour?

IV. ITS SPECIAL LONELINESS. Age is often lonely. It misses the companions of its youth and its prime. Most of these, perhaps nearly all, have fallen, and they are as the last leaf upon the wintry bough. "They are all gone, the old familiar faces," is the plaintive strain of their discourse; and some who still live have drifted away from them in space or in spirit. There is no one left who can go back with them in thought and sympathy to the old times, the memory of which is so pleasant, and which they would fain revisit with the friends of youth and childhood. Age is apt to be very lonely, and it has great need of a Divine Companion who does not pass away, who "abides," who is "the same yesterday, and to-day, and for ever."

V. ITS SPECIAL LIMITATION. We all know that there *may* not be many days left in which we can bear witness for our Lord and his gospel. But the aged know that there *can* not be many more left to them. So much the more, therefore, as they see the night approaching when they can work no more for their Master, may they well desire to *be* and to *do* all that still lies in their power. Every hour is golden to him to whom but few remain. And because the opportunities of serving men here on earth are narrowing perceptibly day by day, the aged may earnestly entreat their Lord to be near to them, and to let his grace rest upon them, that their last days may be full of fruitfulness as well as of peace and hope.

VI. ITS NEARNESS TO DEATH. We wish not only to "*live*" unto the Lord," but also to "*die* unto the Lord;" to honour him in the manner of our death as well as by the spirit of our life. They who feel that the evening shadows are gathering, and that the night of death is near, may well wish for the near presence of the upholding Saviour, with whom they will go tranquilly and hopefully through the last darkness. "Abide with us," they say; "be with us as we take the last steps of our earthly journey, go down with us into the deep waters, attend us till we reach the heavenly shore."

> "Oh, meet us in the valley,
> When heart and flesh shall fail,
> And softly, safely, lead us on,
> Until within the veil:
> When faith shall turn to gladness,
> To find ourselves with thee,
> And trembling Hope shall realize
> Her full felicity."

C.

Vers. 33—43.—*Sense and spirit: the Resurrection.* The story of the Resurrection in its relation to the disciples of our Lord suggests to us thoughts concerning—

I. THE TRIUMPH OF THE SPIRIT OVER THE FLESH. These two disciples who had walked from Jerusalem to Emmaus, and who persuaded the mysterious Stranger to remain because the day was far gone, and subsequently spent some time in earnest converse with him, now *hastened back to Jerusalem* (ver. 33). This was quite contrary to their intention when they set out from the city; it was not in the natural order of things to start out again on a long two-hours' walk after the fatigues of that eventful day. But their minds were so enlarged, their hearts so filled with joy, their souls so stirred with animating and vivifying hope, that they could not remain where they were; they must impart the transporting and transforming tidings to the crushed and sorrowing brethren they had left behind them that afternoon. It was late and dark, and (when they thought of it) they were tired. But what were these considerations? They were things not to be entertained for a moment, they were a mere feather's weight in the scale; and we may be certain that they set off to Jerusalem with a much lighter step in the evening, and far more alacrity of spirit, than they left that city in the afternoon of the day. In one sense "we are but dust and ashes," but "animated clay;" our soul is subject to certain limitations from its close connection with the body. Yet can the spirit triumph nobly over the flesh. Let but the kindling truth come down from heaven, let the Divine hand but touch the secret springs of the soul, and all our bodily sensations and our lower instincts go down and disappear. Fatigue, loss, danger, death itself, is nothing to a soul alight with the celestial fire. A new hope, a new faith, a new purpose, can carry the weary frame along the dusty road of duty, or up the steep ascent of arduous or dangerous achievement, better than angels' wings. Our true self is not the tabernacle of the flesh, but the indwelling and victorious spirit.

II. THE ESSENTIAL SERVICE WHICH THE FLESH RENDERS TO THE SPIRIT.   Christianity is essentially spiritual.   It makes its *appeal* to the spiritual nature; its *aim* is spiritual; and the *weapons* of its warfare are also spiritual—the efforts of the spirit of man and the energies of the Spirit of God.   But it rests largely on a basis of facts attested by our senses—the fact of the Incarnation, "God manifested in the flesh," the "Word made flesh;" the fact of the miracles of Christ, miracles wrought before the eyes of men, and assured by their sensible observation of them; the fact of a blameless life lived in the bodily presence of eye-witnesses; the fact of the death at Calvary, borne witness to by those who actually beheld it; and the great crowning fact of the Resurrection, the return of Jesus Christ *in the flesh* to his disciples.   The entire fabric of our religion rests upon the history of the Man Christ Jesus; and the acceptance of him as a Divine Teacher, whose word can be trusted and whose character can be honoured, stands or falls with the truth of the Resurrection.   For if he did not rise again, he certainly was not the One he claimed to be.   Of what service to us, then, these physical facts here recorded—his eating with the two at Emmaus; the sound of the familiar voice in many words of intercourse; the sight of his hands and feet with the imprint of the cruel nails; the sight and feeling of the "flesh and bones," which a spirit has not but which they found he had; and the act of sitting down at the table and eating of the fish and honeycomb before their eyes?   The sight of his face, the sound of his voice, the style of his speech, the handling of his limbs ("handle me, and see," ver. 39), supplemented by his eating and drinking before them,—all this at length convinced their incredulity that it was indeed the risen Lord himself, returned according to his word.   And all this accumulated evidence of all the senses is as good for us as it was for them.   We are thankful for this multiplication of the material evidence, for, taken with other considerations, it substantiates the great fact of facts, and gives to us not only a marvellously original Thinker, but an unmistaken and faultless Exemplar, a Divine Lord and Master.   The human senses never rendered to the human soul so great a service as when they attested the supreme fact of the resurrection of Jesus Christ.   But they still do render very valuable service in every Christian life. 1. The control and regulation of our senses for Christ's sake and in obedience to his word is a continual tribute to the power of his truth.   2. Our feet can carry us forth on errands of Christian charity.   3. Our hands can be put daily to deeds of righteousness, of justice, of excellency.   4. Our lips can sing the praises of our Lord, and can speak words of kindness to the young, of sympathy to the suffering and sorrowing, of hope to the dying.   5. Our eye can read, our ears can hear, the truths which impart or which sustain the inner life of the spirit.   Through our bodily senses God's own living truth, and with his truth himself also, comes continually into our soul; and through these same senses there go forth from us all healing, all helpful, all saving influences to the world; and thus we enrich and are enriched.—C.

Ver. 36.—*The peace of Christ.*   It is true that these words, "Peace be unto you!" were the ordinary Jewish salutation.   But remembering that our Lord used these words a second time in this interview (see John xx. 21), and having in mind the way in which he made these words his own, and gave to them not merely a formal but a profound significance (John xiv. 27), we may find much meaning in them.   We recognize the fact that they were—

I. SPECIALLY APPROPRIATE TO THE CIRCUMSTANCES.   The minds of his apostles had passed through the deepest *distress*.   They had lost their Lord and their Friend; and with him they had lost, as they thought, their cause and their hopes; they were, therefore, afflicted with an overwhelming grief.   And now they were filled with the liveliest *agitation*.   They were in a mental state in which blighted hopes were struggling with darkest fears; their soul was stirred to its very depths; and what, above all things, they needed was One that could come and say, "Peace be unto you!"   It was the very word that was wanted to be breathed into their ear, to be spoken to their heart.

II. ADMIRABLY DESCRIPTIVE OF HIS ABIDING MISSION.   It is true that Jesus once said, "I came not to send peace, but a sword."   But it will be found, on referring, that then he simply meant to say that division and strife would be an inevitable incident of the course of his gospel; he did not mean that this was its deep purpose or its long and last result.   It was the back-water, and not the main current, of the truth he preached. Christ came to give peace to a world profoundly disturbed and disquieted by sin. "Come unto me," he said, " and I will give you rest." Not as the world gives rest or peace does he give. (1) Not mere comfort or gratification that is very short-lived; (2) nor satisfaction that is based on ignorance of ourselves, and must before long be exposed; (3) nor the quiet of indifference or unbelief that must soon be broken up. Not of this order is the peace of Christ. It is: 1. *Rest to the burdened conscience.* He shows us our sin and makes us ashamed of it; he fills our heart with a true and righteous sorrow for it; he awakes within us a just and honourable concern for the consequences of it. And then he offers himself as the One who bore the burden upon himself, through whom we may find forgiveness and acceptance. And "being justified by faith, we have peace with God through our Lord Jesus Christ." 2. *Abiding gladness to the hungering heart.* "In the world" is unsatisfiedness of soul, emptiness and heart-ache; a sense of disappointment. But in him is a true and lasting satisfaction. "How happily the days in his blest service fly!" To live heartily and wholly unto him who loved us and gave himself for us, to expend our powers in his praise and in his service, —this is the secret of lifelong peace. All the lower springs will fail, but this never. To "lose our life" *unto him* is to "find it" and to keep it for ever. 3. *Comfort to the troubled spirit.* When darkness falls upon the path, when losses come, when bereave-ment makes a gap in the home and in the heart, when some heavy disappointment blights the prospect,—then the felt presence, the realized sympathy, and the unfailing succour of that Divine Friend give a peace which is deeper than our disturbance, a thrice-blessed calm to the tempest-tossed soul. 4. *Peace in death.* For many centuries the dying have departed in peace because they have hoped for everything through the Divine Saviour; they have calmly "slept in Jesus;" and those who now look forward to death as a passage through which they will be passing can find no better wish or prayer than that "the music of his Name" may "refresh their soul in death."—C.

Ver. 45.—*The Divine Spirit and the human understanding.* It may be that we do not sufficiently recognize the very intimate connection between our human intelli-gence and the action of the Spirit of God. We may be seriously in danger of coming short in gratitude for all that God has wrought for us in this respect, and in prayer for his continued and especial help in the future.

I. THE DIVINE ENDOWMENT WITH WHICH HE STARTS US ON OUR COURSE. We receive from his creative hand a kind and a measure of intellectual power which may be said to vary with each individual of the human race. To one he giveth five talents, to another two, to another one. And it is not only difference in measure, but also in kind. The human spirit has many faculties, and one man has a large share of one and another a goodly share of another, "as it pleaseth him." Most happily for us, there is every possible variety of human understanding resulting from the different capacities and dispositions with which our Creator endows us.

II. THE BENEFICENT LAW OF EXPANSION HE HAS ORDAINED FOR US. The law under which we live, and under which our understanding grows, is this—" to him that hath is given." We observe, we hear and read, we reflect, we reason, we construct and produce; and as we do this, we grow—our intelligence is opened and enlarged. Thus by the operation of one of his wise and kind laws God is "opening our understanding" every day, but more particularly in the earlier days of curiosity and of study. Youth has but to do its rightful and proper work, and God will do his gracious, enlarging work; and thus he will "build up" a mind, well stored with knowledge and wisdom, capable of great and noble service.

III. THE SPECIAL ILLUMINATIONS HE HAS GRANTED AND IS WILLING TO IMPART. 1. God has given to members of our race illumination or expansion of mind which we pronounce *miraculous,* i.e. not in accordance with known laws. Such was the inspira-tion he gave to Moses when he inspired him to write his books; or that he gave to Samuel, to Elijah, to Isaiah, to Zechariah, when he moved these prophets to remonstrate with or to exhort their contemporaries, or to write words that should live for all time on the sacred page; or that he gave to these two disciples when he opened *their* understand-ing that they might understand the Scriptures as they had never understood them before; or that he gave to the Apostles Peter and Paul and John when he prompted them to speak as they spoke and to write as they wrote. Here was an altogether unusual and supernatural enlightenment and enlargement of mind granted for the special purpose of making known his mind and will to the race of man. 2. God still imparts special illumination to us according to our need and in response to our prayer. The "age of miracles" may be past, but assuredly the age of Divine illumination is not passed. God remains, and will remain, in constant communication with his human children; he has, and ever will have, access to their understanding; he can touch and quicken us, can enlarge and equip our minds for special service in his Name and cause, can make clear to our minds those things which have been obscure, whether in his Word or in his providence, so that we can "understand the Scriptures," and also interpret his dealing with ourselves and his fashioning of our lives. Three things become us. (1) *A sense of our own insufficiency*—insufficiency both for *comprehending* what we are called upon both to consider and (as far as may be) to understand, and for *doing* the work of explanation and enforcement which is required of us. (2) *Faith in God*—in his observation of us; in his interest in our humble endeavours to take our part and do our work; in his power over us to "open our understanding" as well as to "open our heart" (Acts xvi. 44; see Eph. i. 18; 2 Tim. ii. 7). (3) *Prayer for Divine illumination.* Lacking wisdom, let us ask of God, "who giveth to all men liberally, and upbraideth not" (Jas. i. 5; see Col. i. 9; Eph. i. 16, 17). Whenever we read the Scriptures that we may learn the "mind of Christ," whenever we stand up to speak in his Name, whenever we set ourselves to any effort that requires spiritual wisdom, we do well to pray in the spirit, if not in the language, of our great poet—

"Thou, O Spirit, that dost prefer
Before all temples the upright heart and pure,
Instruct me; for thou know'st: . . . What in me is dark,
Illumine! What is low, raise and support!"

C.

Ver. 47.—*The solemn charge.* It is an allowable curiosity to wonder how the apostles of our Lord received this "their solemn charge." 1. They must have been greatly impressed by its extreme seriousness; they were to preach repentance and remission of sin "among *all nations.*" And although they did not know as we do what that meant, and how wide was the range of the Saviour's purpose, they could realize as we cannot how deep and bitter would be the enmity which a gospel of the crucified Nazarene would encounter, more especially in Jerusalem. 2. But they may have been powerfully sustained by the presence of the Lord himself. The "power of his resurrection" was then upon their souls; they were to go forth in *his* Name, who had just triumphed over man's last and greatest enemy—death. What could they not do through him? If we ask what was the message, in its fulness, which they were charged to deliver, we reply—

I. REPENTANCE AS CHRIST HAD PREACHED IT. They were to preach repentance *in his Name.* Therefore of the kind which he demanded. And this was no mere outward amendment; it was not found in the external habits of devotion; no amount of almsgiving, fasting, prayers, would constitute it. It meant: 1. *Self-condemnation.* Not necessarily the exhibition of overwhelming emotion, but the decided and deep conviction of our own unworthiness, and real regret for wrong done and for service withheld in the past. 2. *The return of the heart to God.* The coming back from the far country of estrangement, or forgetfulness, or denial and open enmity, and the seeking anew the Father's face and favour. 3. *The outcasting from the soul* of all tolerance of evil, so that sin is not only shunned but hated. 4. *The pursuit of all moral excellency;* to be attained by the study and the love of the great Exemplar himself. And this repentance, real and thorough, was to be *immediate.* There was to be no guilty and dangerous postponement; as soon as the soul recognized its duty it was to start on the true and right course.

II. REMISSION AS CHRIST OFFERED IT. And this was: 1. *Full.* It was a forgiveness without reserve. The son (of the parable, ch. xv.) was not relegated to the servants' hall, though he had thought of asking for no more than that. He was admitted to the full honour of sonship; he was to wear the best robe and the ring, and he was to sit down to the table which was loaded in his honour. The mercy we receive through Christ, and which is to be offered "in his Name," is no imperfect thing;

it is full, entire, complete. All past transgressions are absolutely forgiven, so that they will never be alleged against us or stand between us and the love of God. We ourselves are taken into the gracious favour of our heavenly Father, admitted to his family, counted among his own children, constituted his heirs, having freest access to his presence, welcome to call him by the most endearing name. 2. *Immediate.* There is no probation or apprenticeship to be served; we have not to wait to approve ourselves; we are not sentenced to any form of expiation by menial service before we gain our childhood. At once, so soon as we return in spirit unto God, that moment we are welcomed to the side and to the home of our Father. 3. *In faith.* We are to seek and to find forgiveness "in Christ's Name," *i.e.* in the exercise of a simple but living faith in him as in our Divine Saviour. So the apostles evidently understood their Master (see Acts x. 43; xiii. 38, 39; 1 Pet. i. 8, 9; 1 John ii. 12). Thus the ascended Saviour instructed the "abortive-born apostle" (Acts xxvi. 18), and thus that faithful witness continually taught (see Acts xx. 21). Those who speak for Christ are to invite all sinful men to put their trust in him, the Saviour of mankind, the "Propitiation for the sins of the world," and, accepting him as such, to take the full, free mercy of God unto eternal life.

Such was the message which the apostles were solemnly charged to deliver. There was in this great instruction: 1. One charge which they were more particularly to observe—they were to begin at Jerusalem. It was right they should begin there, for it was there that all "these things" (ver. 48) were known and could be attested; and, beginning there, the grace and the magnanimity of the Crucified One would be more abundantly manifested. 2. Another, which more particularly affects ourselves—this message of mercy is to be carried to "all nations." It is "the common salvation," needed by all and fitted for all, to work out and send forth which the Lord Jesus lived and died.—C.

Ver. 48.—*Bearing witness.* These brief words, "Ye are witnesses," being among the very last which Jesus spoke to his apostles, must have lingered in their ear for the rest of their life. In moments of doubt, or of depression, or of danger, the remembrance that their Lord and Leader had charged them to be his witnesses may well have stirred and strengthened them to fresh courage and to renewed activity. They are words that may well stimulate us also to duty and self-sacrifice.

I. THE UNIQUE SERVICE RENDERED BY THE APOSTLES. They were witnesses of "those things," the greatest things that were ever seen and ever attested in the history of mankind; things they were on the full and true statement of which, on the cordial and practical acceptance of which, depended the life and the hope of the world. They could face all with whom they came in contact, and declare that they saw with their own eyes, heard with their own ears, witnessed in their own persons: 1. A perfectly beautiful, a spotless human life, in which, though they saw it under all possible circumstances and when under least constraint or reserve, they could find no flaw at all (1 Pet. ii. 22). 2. Works of power, which were invariably works of pity and of kindness, of such a nature that there was no possibility of mistake. 3. Words of truth and grace such as mortal lips had never spoken, and such as met the deepest wants of man's hungering heart, of his yearning and aspiring soul. 4. Sufferings and sorrows beyond what others knew, borne with a patience that was sublime. 5. A death undergone in shame and pain, amid natural wonders and with more than human nobility. 6. A glorious resurrection from the grave. 7. A message of mercy and hope to be delivered to all mankind in the name of this great Teacher, Healer, Sufferer, Conqueror.

II. THE VALUABLE SERVICE WHICH IS OPEN TO US ALL. 1. We also can testify, in word, to "these things." We leave, and are content to leave, some mysteries which belong to the Christian faith; we do not try, as we need not try, either to explain or to understand them. But "these things," which the world needs to know for its inward peace and its true prosperity, we can speak. We are familiar with the holy and beautiful life of Jesus Christ. We know the thought, we "have the mind of Christ" on all the deepest and highest subjects with which our character and our destiny are bound up. We are conversant with the sufferings and the sorrows of the Saviour; for the story of his Passion is better known by us than any other history whatsoever—it is not only in our memory, it is in our heart. We can speak of his death and of his triumph over the grave. We know well what is the message of truth and grace he desires to be declared to the whole world. We can speak of him and for him. 2. And we can find an audience. There are many who will not listen to us, but there are those who will. The *young*, who have a spirit of docility and inquiry; the *sick* and the *sad*, to whom " the consolation which is in Christ " is the one thing that heals and calms; the *poor*, to whom the pearl of great price is welcome, and who are willing to be made " rich toward God; " the *disappointed* and the *weary*, who are glad to know of One who can give " rest unto the soul; "—these will receive our testimony. 3. We can bear the best and truest witness of the life. What men want to be convinced of is that Christianity is a living power; that it not only has very fine sentiments to teach —these can be found elsewhere—but that it is a moral and spiritual power that can save the lost, can cleanse the foul, can soften the hard-hearted, can humble the proud, can arouse the indifferent and obtuse, can infuse cheerfulness and joy into the heart of the poor and lowly, can give rest of spirit to those who are encompassed by the cares of time, can fill the soul with tender sympathy and prompt to generous and self-denying succour, can substitute a forgiving for a vindictive spirit in the wronged, can enable its possessors to gain a victory over themselves and over the world and to crown a victorious life by a death of calm tranquillity and joyful hope. Here is scope for witness-bearing; and, as every Christian man has the truth of Christ on which to feed, the example of Christ to follow, and the Holy Spirit of Christ to whom to look for his indwelling power, it is open to every disciple to be a witness, whose testimony shall be valuable on earth and acceptable in heaven.—C.

Ver. 49.—*The secret of spiritual strength.* How came it to pass that the apostles of our Lord became such strong men and did such noble work for their Master and for mankind *so soon after* they manifested such weakness as they did? We consider—
I. THEIR INSUFFICIENCY UP TO THE TIME OF THE ASCENSION. They had been receiving for many months the inestimable advantage of Christ's own teaching for their mental enlightenment, and his own influence for their spiritual ennoblement. And this teaching and training cannot have been—we may confidently say *was not*—without very great value throughout their subsequent course. Yet they undoubtedly lacked something which would complete them for the great task before them. They showed but scant determination (Matt. xxvi. 41, 43), but feeble courage (Matt. xxvi. 56), but little understanding of their Master's aim (Acts i. 6); and this, too, at the very close of his ministry, when their great and special privilege was expiring. Something more they sadly needed to prepare them for their work.
II. THE PROMISED POWER. 1. Its announcement and its confirmation. It was first predicted by the prophets who preceded our Lord (Isa. xliv. 3); and more particularly Joel (ii. 28, 29). It was renewed and confirmed, at first more indefinitely, and here more definitely, by our Lord (John xiv. 16, 26; xv. 26, 27; xvi. 7; text). 2. Its historical fulfilment (Acts ii. 1—11). 3. Its permanent results. These men, whose character and whose fitness for their grand and lofty mission left much to be desired, " endued with power from on high," became wonderfully equipped for and admirably adapted to the noble mission to which Christ appointed them. They became strong (1) to stand in the evil hour of temptation, defying the authority of Jewish council and the sword of Roman ruler; they became strong (2) to suffer, rejoicing that they were " counted worthy to suffer shame " for the Master's sake and Name; they became strong (3) to testify, " with great power " giving witness to the Resurrection, and great grace being on them all; they became strong (4) to grasp the great central and saving truths of the gospel, making known to their own compeers by their speech, and to all time by their letters, the " mystery which was hidden from the generations," the great and gracious purpose of God to the whole race of men; they became strong (5) to build and work, to lay the foundation-stone of the gospel of Christ (Eph. ii. 26), of that Church of the future which has already endured for eighteen centuries, and is more than ever bent on the conversion and conquest of the world. We know what made these weak men strong, these failing men to triumph. It was the power of the Holy Ghost resting upon them, opening their eyes that they might see, quickening their souls that they might feel, nerving their hearts that they might stand, strengthening their hands that they might labour and achieve.

III. ITS LASTING LESSON. It is this which, if anything does, will make us strong also. What the Christian workman wants is *the power which comes immediately from God*, the inspiration of the Divine Spirit; in truth, the same bestowal as that which the apostles were now promised and afterwards received. The miraculous endowments which accompanied the gift of the Holy Ghost were but the accidents of the bestowal. The power to heal without failure or to speak without error was nothing to the power to testify without fear and to live without reproach.

> " Though on our heads no tongues of fire
>   Their wondrous powers impart,"

we need, as much as they did then, the illuminating, sanctifying, empowering influences of Heaven—" God's Spirit in our heart." Without that, our most heroic efforts will fail; with it, our humblest endeavours will succeed. To gain that we must have (1) purity of heart and aim; (2) earnest and believing prayer.—C.

Ver. 50.—*The Ascension.* Many thoughts offer themselves to us as we think upon this last scene.

I. THE FITNESS OF THE PLACE WHENCE JESUS ASCENDED. Not, indeed, that Jerusalem could claim to be worthy of such an honour—Jerusalem that had but lately dyed its hands in the blood of its Messiah. But as the ancient dwelling-place of God, as the seat and source of heavenly truth, as the metropolis of religion upon the earth, as the place that furnishes the name and type of the city of our hope, as the joyous gathering-place of the good,—it was well that, from without *its* walls, he whose presence makes the home and the joy and the glory of his people should pass to his throne. For from that moment " Jerusalem " meant another thing to mankind. Christ took up its meaning as he rose. All the associations of love and hope, of grandeur and gladness, which had belonged to the earthly are transferred to the heavenly city, where he dwells in glory, where he reigns in power. There is a transference, not formal but actual, of the centre and metropolis of religious thought from the Jerusalem below to the Jerusalem above.

II. THE NATURE OF THE LAST SCENE. " They climb the hillside; they cross its summit; they are approaching Bethany. He stops; they gather round. He looks upon them; he lifts his hands; he begins to bless them. What love unutterable in that parting look! What untold riches in that blessing! His hands are uplifted, his lips engaged in blessing, when slowly he begins to rise. Earth has lost her power to keep him; the waiting up-drawing heavens claim him as their own. He rises, but still, as he floats upward through the yielding air, his eyes are bent on those uplooking men; his arms are stretched over them in the attitude of benediction, his voice is heard dying away in blessings as he ascends. Awe-struck, in silence they follow him with straining eyes as his body lessens to sight, till the commissioned cloud enfolds, cuts off all further vision, and closes the earthly and sensible communion between Jesus and his disciples " (Dr. Hanna).

III. THE RECEPTION THE SAVIOUR HAD IN HEAVEN. There have been " triumphant entries " in this little world of ours, and in the history of our human race, the pouring forth in loud acclaim of the pride and joy of many thousands of hearts. But to what a vanishing point do they sink when placed by the side of this entry of the conquering Saviour into heaven! Though unable to form any conception that can approach the glorious reality, yet we may well love to linger in imagination over that blessed scene. His struggle over, his sorrows borne, his temptations met and mastered, his work finished, his great battle fought and his victory won,—the victorious Lord passes through all the ranks of the angelic host, amid their reverent worship and adoring acclamations, to his throne of power and glory.

> " Look, ye saints! the sight is glorious:
>   See the Man of sorrows now
>   From the fight returned victorious;
>   Every knee to him shall bow."

IV. THE EFFECT IMMEDIATELY PRODUCED ON THE MINDS OF THE DISCIPLES. Blank dismay, inconsolable sorrow, should we think? So thinking, we should be wrong.

They "returned to Jerusalem with great joy." Yet their Master was gone from them to return no more till that uncertain and distant day of which the angels spoke (Acts i. 11). How do we account for this? The explanation is found here—they were *now perfectly assured of the Divine mission* of Jesus Christ. His death had cast a dark shadow of doubt and dread over their hearts. His resurrection had revived their confidence and their hope. But this final manifestation, this "sign in the heavens," this act of being taken up, like Elijah, into heaven, swept away the last fragment of doubt that may have been left behind; they were now absolutely sure, without any reserve or qualification whatever, that the Master they had loved and served was indeed their true Messiah, the Sent of God, worthy of their deepest veneration and their strongest attachment; so they "worshipped him" reverently, and went back to Jerusalem with the joy of faith and love filling their souls. There is no misery so unendurable as doubt, and there is no blessedness so sweet as rest of heart after spiritual disquietude.

V. ITS PERMANENT EFFECT ON THE APOSTLES' MINDS. This was unreservedly good. It *was* "expedient for them that he should go away." His bodily absence changed the complexion of their dependence upon him. It had been that of childhood; it was now to be that of manhood. With him by their side, as he had been, they would not have become the "men in him" they did become after he left them. The deeper and fuller knowledge of him they gained by his departure led to an enlargement of faith and to a deepening of love, and also to that fulness of attachment and consecration we recognize and rejoice in during their later life. They came to know him and love him and serve him as the Divine Saviour of mankind, and this made them worthier men and truer servants of their Lord. All earthly ambitions respecting the right and left hand of the throne were transformed into a noble consecration to the invisible Lord.

VI. ITS PRICELESS VALUE TO OURSELVES. 1. Christ is *accessible* to us all. Had he lived and reigned at Jerusalem, or some other sacred metropolis, he would only have been accessible to those who dwelt or journeyed there. But now he is "with us all." For heaven is everywhere; the throne of grace is within the reach of the faintest whisper that comes from every burdened heart, from every seeking soul, wheresoever it may be breathed. A living faith can now realize the constant nearness of its living Lord; it has not to take even a sabbath day's journey to find itself in his presence and to make known its request. 2. He is seated on the *throne of power*. To him who has passed into the heavens we can realize that "all power is given" (Matt. xxviii. 18). We can well believe that our Master in heaven can do for us what we ask of him; that his arm is one of glorious might; that his hand has plenteousness of bounty and of blessing. And in all our time of need we can go to him, with holy confidence, to ask of him the help, the guidance, the blessing, we require. 3. He has *all rightful authority*. If he still dwelt on earth, we might be dubious of this; but to the heavenly Saviour we unanimously and cordially ascribe all headship; to him we yield our willing and unquestioning obedience; and we rejoice to believe that he is ruling and governing the affairs of his Church, and reigning in the interests of the whole human race; that it is his hand that is at the helm, and that will safely guide the tempest-ridden vessel to the harbour. 4. He is our *constant and ever-living* Lord. With all that is earthly we associate change and death; with the heavenly we connect the thought of continuance and life. Of our heavenly Lord we can think, and we delight to think, that whoever changes he is evermore the same, "yesterday, and to-day, and for ever;" that while human ministers "are not suffered to continue by reason of death," he hath "an unchangeable priesthood," and is able to save *evermore* ("to the uttermost") all those "that come unto God by him." And as we look forward to the future, and realize our own mortality, we cherish the joyous thought that, if we do but "abide in him" until the evening shadows gather and "life's long day" passes into the darkness of death, we shall, in heaven's eternal morning, open our eyes to see the "King in his beauty," to "behold his glory," and shall "sit down with him on his throne," sharing for ever his own and his saints' everlasting rest.—C.

Vers. 1—12.—*The Resurrection discovered.* When the women and the other mourners left the Lord's tomb on the evening of the Crucifixion, it was with the intention, after the sabbath was past, of completing the embalmment. This office of love seems to have been left largely to the women; for it is they who make their way, in the early morning of the first day of the week, to the sepulchre. They seem to have had no knowledge, for they had no apprehension, of the Roman guard, which was manifestly placed at the sepulchre on the Jewish sabbath, when the disciples and the women were keeping the sad day in strictest privacy. Their one apprehension was how to roll away the stone; but, like so many apprehended difficulties, it was found to vanish away—some hands stronger than women's had been before them and had rolled away the stone, and left them no difficulty in *discovering* an empty tomb. The narrative of John about Mary Magdalene's visit is quite consistent with Luke's narrative; for, as Gilbert West has pointed out in his admirable analysis of the Resurrection-history, Mary rushes off alone to tell the disciples, "They have taken away the Lord out of the sepulchre, and *we* know not where they have laid him"—implying that others had been with her at the tomb. Without any misgivings, therefore, about the reliable character of the history, let us point out the instructive steps in the discovery of our Lord's resurrection.

I. THE WOMEN WITH THE SPICES DISCOVER AN EMPTY TOMB. (Vers. 1—3.) They had employed the evening after the sabbath was past in preparing all that was needful for embalming thoroughly and finally the Saviour's body. It was with this fragrant burden they made their way in the twilight towards the tomb, to find their fears groundless and the stone already removed. But a new fear now laid hold on them. There is no body in the tomb; it is empty. They do not appear to have taken in the significance of the grave-clothes carefully put aside because never to be needed more, as John did at his subsequent visit; their whole anxiety was about what had become of the dear body which they had come to embalm. The empty tomb was a discovery. The first impression, as indicated by Mary's message (John xx. 2), was that their enemies had seized the body and disposed of it to defeat all their ideas of embalming. One thing is certain from the history, that neither the women nor the disciples could have been parties to the removal of the body.

II. THE WOMEN THAT WAITED GOT EXPLANATIONS FROM THE ANGELS. (Vers. 4—7.) Mary Magdalene, acting on impulse, seems to have hurried off to tell Peter and John about the discovery of the empty tomb, while her companions wait longer to get some explanation, if possible, regarding it. And the waiting women are not disappointed. Angels appear in shining garments, and, as the women sink before them in terror, they proceed to reassure them with the glad tidings, "Why seek ye the living among the dead? He is not here, but is risen: remember how he spake unto you when he was yet in Galilee, saying, The Son of man must be delivered into the hands of sinful men, and be crucified, and the third day rise again." It was the angels that reminded them of the promise of resurrection, and how it was now fulfilled. This is the second stage, therefore, in the discovery of the Resurrection. The fear of the women had been that the Jews had got the body. But there could have been no such plot carried out, for the very simple reason that, if they had got the body and it had not risen, they could have produced such evidence at the Pentecost as would have overturned the apostolic testimony, and prevented the inauguration of the Christian society. The angelic explanation, based as it was on our Lord's previous promises, was the only satisfactory one. The Resurrection was the fulfilment of Christ's deliberate plan.

III. THE REPORT OF THE WOMEN TO THE ELEVEN AND THE REST. (Vers. 8—11.) It is quite reasonable to suppose that Mary Magdalene was the forerunner of the rest, and through her report induced Peter and John to start at once for the sepulchre, while the main body of the women, consisting of Joanna, Mary the mother of James, and others, returned more leisurely to make their report. At all events, the narrative of Luke implies all that is given by Matthew and by John. For the disciples who went to Emmaus distinctly say that certain of the disciples "went to the sepulchre, and found it even so as the women had said; but *him they saw not*" (ver. 24)—implying that the women, in their report, had spoken of having seen the Master.[1] The testimony of the women was based upon a threefold foundation—first, the assurance of the angels; secondly, the promise of resurrection given in Galilee by the Lord; thirdly, according to

[1] Cf. Gilbert West's 'Observations on the History and Evidences of the Resurrection of Jesus Christ'—a work which received favourable recognition from Lessing, in his remarks appended to the 'Wolfenbüttel Fragments.'

Matthew's account, an interview with the risen Lord himself (Matt. xxviii. 9, 10). It was a remarkable testimony certainly, but at the same time it had ample warrant.

IV. THE BEST-ATTESTED FACTS MAY SEEM, TO DAZED MINDS, THE IDLEST FANCIES. (Ver. 11.) The poor disciples are, however, so overpowered with grief and disappointment that they are utterly unprepared for the announcement of the Resurrection. Here the suppler mind of woman is revealed in contrast to the more plodding, sifting, logic-demanding mind of man. The women enjoy the consolations of the Resurrection much sooner than the men. They take in the evidence at a glance. They do not question. They simply accept. But the disciples will not believe in a hurry. And so the messengers of the best tidings ever related unto men are at first in the position of the Master himself, and constrained to cry, "Who hath believed our report?" And the unbelieving criticism of to-day is more unreasonable than the disciples were before the women. Because the resurrection of Christ may break in upon the ideas of nature's absolute uniformity which the critics have adopted, the whole evidence of resurrection-power continued through the ages is to be treated as an idle tale! Minds may be so dazed with grief or with success on certain lines as to discredit the completest evidence ever offered to the world. Before prejudice, the strongest facts get resolved into the idlest fancies. We should earnestly seek an impartial mind.

V. PETER'S FIRST ATTEMPT TO DEAL WITH THE EVIDENCE OF THE RESURRECTION. (Ver. 12.) Peter, as we learn from John's account, accompanied by John, rushes off to see the sepulchre. He reaches it after John, but pushes past him, and goes into the sepulchre. There he sees the linen clothes laid by themselves, yet departs without reaching anything but perplexity. To John's keener intellect the grave-clothes, so neatly deposited and the napkin laid in a place by itself, show that Jesus had risen, and laid aside his sleeping-clothes, as we do our night-dresses in the morning, because he had entered on the day of resurrection. John becomes a believer in the Resurrection on *circumstantial evidence*. Peter, it would seem, cannot make it out, and has to get a personal interview somewhat later on that day (cf. ver. 34), before he can take it in. It thus appears that one mind may handle the Resurrection evidence successfully, while another may only stumble through it into deeper perplexity. But when a soul like Peter is in earnest, the Lord will not leave him in the darkness, but will grant such further light as will dispel the gloom and dissipate all perplexity. Meanwhile the discovery of Christ's resurrection is but the interesting first stage in the remarkable evidence to part of which we have yet to proceed.—R. M. E.

Vers. 13—35.—*The risen Christ the best Escort on the pilgrimage of life.* We left Peter in perplexity, but he and John must have returned to the rest of the disciples, and reported the emptiness of the sepulchre, but that they had not seen the Risen One (ver. 24). John does not seem to have communicated his own convictions unto the others. Most likely he is turning the matter over in his mind, as contemplative and deep-thinking men will do before giving a public pronouncement. Meanwhile there is a dispersion of some of the disciples that very afternoon. Thomas seems to have gone away, and to have remained away that night. And two of them proceed seven or eight miles into the country to Emmaus, where their home seems to have been. It is these two pilgrims that we are now to follow. They leave the city, and their conversation is sad. They are discussing the bright hopes which have been so lately quenched by the crucifixion of their Lord. It is while so sad that Jesus joins them; for he who had been the "Man of sorrows" and "acquainted with grief" is ever breaking in upon men's troubles to relieve them. His treatment of these "unwilling sceptics," as they have been lately called, is most instructive.[1] He probes their sorrow, gets an insight into its cause, gets them to state their hopes, their disappointments, and the rumours they had heard of his resurrection. On this basis, although apparently an unknown Stranger, he proceeds to show them their error and slowness in not believing all that the prophets have spoken about Messiah. Beginning, therefore, at Moses, he expounds to them from all the prophets that Messiah must first suffer, and then enter into his glory. The exposition was so brilliant and interesting, that they felt their hearts burning within them during the process. Then, under compulsion, he enters their lodging at Emmaus, sits down as Guest, then proceeds as Host to distribute the food as

---

[1] Cf. Munger's 'Appeal to Life,' p. 25.

at the sacramental meal. Not till then did they recognize their risen Lord in the devout Being who graced their board. Once recognized, and thus dispelling all their doubt, he vanishes into the invisible. Such experience could not be quietly kept at Emmaus. They resolve to return that very night to Jerusalem, to report their interview, and how blessed an Escort Jesus had been in their pilgrimage. They are in time for the manifestation of the Risen One to the assembled disciples. We may learn from the narrative such lessons as these.

I. JESUS MAKES HIS ADVENT TO US WHEN OUR SOULS ARE SAD. This is the very spirit of the dispensation. Thus he cried, "Come unto me, all ye that labour and are heavy laden, and I will give you rest" (Matt. xi. 28). And as the risen Saviour he prefers, we may well believe, the house of mourning to the house of mirth. Not only so, but when souls are in sad perplexity, when they are "unwilling sceptics," it is his delight to come and be their Escort along life's way, and lead them out of gloom and difficulty into real peace and joy. Now, when we know how accessible he is through prayer, we should never undertake any pilgrimage without securing the companionship of Jesus.

II. WE LEARN THAT JESUS IS OFTEN WITH US WHILE WE KNOW IT NOT. Here was he with these two pilgrims, taking step by step with them to Emmaus, and yet their eyes were so holden that they did not know him. He was near them, but they did not know him. Is not this the case with all of us? He is at our side, he takes every step with us, but we are so blinded with care and preoccupation that we fail to see him or enjoy his society as we should. The omnipresence of Jesus should be the believer's constant consolation.

III. JESUS IS HIMSELF AT ONCE THE GREAT SUBJECT AND THE GREAT EXPOSITOR OF SCRIPTURE. Here we find him, after listening so sympathetically to all the difficulties of the disciples, proceeding to expound to them, "in all the Scriptures, the things concerning himself." "The testimony of Jesus is the spirit of prophecy." And here it is well to notice what is the substance of the whole revelation. It is put in these words of the risen Saviour, "Ought not Messiah to have suffered these things, and to have entered (εἰσελθεῖν) into his glory?" The Authorized and Revised Versions have alike failed to give the proper rendering here. Our Lord declares that he has entered already into his glory, just as he has already passed through his sufferings. We believe it can be made out from this and other passages that our Lord ascended—of course invisibly—without disciples as spectators, to heaven, and reported himself on high immediately after telling Mary, "I ascend [not 'will ascend'] unto my Father and your Father, to my God and your God" (John xx. 17; cf. also Bush on 'The Resurrection.') This supposition of an ascension on the very day of the Resurrection enables us to understand his movements during the rest of the day, and his bestowal of the Spirit, which was conditioned on his glorification, in the evening (John xx. 22; cf. John vii. 39). It also enables us to regard heaven as his head-quarters during the forty days before his *visible* ascension from Olivet. Upon this interesting subject we cannot now dwell, however; but we content ourselves by pointing it out, and emphasizing the fact of Jesus as the suffering and glorified Messiah being the Hero, the Substance, and the great Expositor of revelation. It is when we look for him in the Word that it becomes luminous and delightful.

IV. THE ENTERTAINMENT OF JESUS IS SURE TO LEAD TO SPECIAL BLESSING. These two men insisted on Jesus sojourning with them, because it was towards evening and the day was far spent. And as he sojourned, he was transmuted from Guest to Host, and gave them a sacramental instead of common feast. It is when devoutly asking a blessing on the bread that he is recognized, only, however, to vanish like a vision from their sight. Now we may pass through an analogous experience. Is not this what is meant by the Master when he says, "Behold, I stand at the door, and knock: if any man hear my voice, and open the door, I will come in to him, and will sup with him, and he with me" (Rev. iii. 20)? If we are open-hearted, and welcome Jesus, he will enter our hearts and sup with us, taking whatever we have to give him, and delighting in it, and enable us to sup with him. He will change into a *Host* from being our *Guest*. It was thus he acted at the marriage of Cana; it was thus he acted at Emmaus; it was thus he acted on the shore of the Galilæan lake. He may be Guest, but he will soon show himself to be our Host, and give us a feast of fat things.

V. LIFE IS LARGELY A LIVING UPON HAPPY MEMORIES. As soon as the Risen One had vanished, they began to compare notes about the burning heart, and all the happy memories of their journey from Jerusalem. And as they plodded in that night through the dark to report their great discovery, they lived upon the happy memory. But, had they only known it, the risen Jesus was in some way making that return journey to Jerusalem too, making for the same upper room, to reveal himself to the disciples, and their fellowship with him might have been repeated. At all events, we need not live on happy *memories*, but may enjoy Christ's spiritual presence and his escort all through the pilgrimage of life. It is this which will make the present life a heaven, not by anticipation merely, but in actual enjoyment; for fellowship with Christ, even though he be unseen, is the chief element of heaven. May we have the great Escort with us all the way!—R. M. E.

Vers. 36—53.—*Infallible proofs and inevitable partings.* The Emmaus pilgrims have hardly entered the upper room and reported their interview with Jesus, receiving the intelligence that perplexed Peter has got his perplexity resolved, when, notwithstanding that the doors are barred for fear of the Jews, the Risen One appears in the midst of them, and says, "Peace be unto you!" They are at first terrified at such an advent, seeing that it sets aside the ordinary laws of matter, and shows all precaution unavailing when Jesus is determined to get in. But he soon disabuses their minds and dismisses their troubles. Although he can get through barred doors, he is not a disembodied spirit, but a Person with flesh and bones. This he proceeds to demonstrate to their sense-perceptions. Having given them infallible proofs, he next proceeds to expound the Scriptures in detail to them, just as he had done on the way to Emmaus. On these sure foundations he bases their faith, and sends them forth, commissioned to preach repentance and remission of sins. He concludes his interview with the promise of the Father, for which they were to wait at Jerusalem after his visible ascension. And so he is carried up to heaven from Bethany, and the disciples return to wait at Jerusalem in joy until they receive power from on high. And here we have to notice—

I. THE MESSAGE OF THE RISEN SAVIOUR TO DISTRACTED SOULS IS PEACE. The salutation of the East received new depth and meaning when employed by the risen Saviour, when for the first time he appeared among his assembled disciples. He only could pacify them. He is the same "Peacemaker" still. It is his advent which drives away distractions, and secures a peace which passeth all understanding.

II. THE RISEN JESUS SUPPLIES INFALLIBLE PROOFS OF HIS RESURRECTION TO THE PACIFIED DISCIPLES. When pacified by him, they were then fitted for judgment. To place the proofs before worldly, distracted souls would have been throwing pearls before swine.[1] It is before the disciples whose fears have been dispelled that he places the proofs. He urges calm investigation. Here are his hands and feet and side. Handle him, use sense-perception to the utmost. Make out that he has a body, and the same one which was crucified. Their joy at the proofs overpowered them for the moment, so that they could hardly credit it. Then he asked them for meat, and was content to eat before them a piece of a broiled fish. The honeycomb addition is not supported by the best manuscripts, and has been omitted in the Revised Version. The last doubt must depart before such proofs. It is the same Saviour who had been crucified, and he is among them in a body, able to partake of food, and perform all the functions assigned to a body dominated by a healthy spirit. Now, although we cannot see or handle the Risen One, we have yet the evidence of his Resurrection so set before us that only criminal partiality can resist it. Dr. Arnold, so accomplished an historian, declares that there is no fact of history sustained by better evidence.[2] If we made sure of impartial and fearful minds to begin with, the infallible proofs would be recognized in their full power.

III. THE RISEN SAVIOUR HELPS HIS SERVANTS TO UNDERSTAND THE SCRIPTURES. We learn from John's account that "he breathed on them," and so conveyed to them the Holy Ghost. Along with the outward exposition, therefore, of the Scripture refer-

[1] Cf. on this important point a sermon by Bishop Reichel on 'The Necessary Limits of Christian Evidences.'
[2] 'Sermons on Christian Life: its Hopes, its Fears, and its Close,' 4th edit., pp. 15, 16.

ences to himself, there is given the inward inspiration. It is this which made these men such masters of the sacred oracles so far as they indicate Christ's mission. With opened understandings, with inspired hearts, the once sealed book became an open secret, and the fountain-head of missionary enterprise. And the witnesses need similar enlightenment still. By waiting on the Master prayerfully and studiously we shall obtain the key to interpretation, and have the fairy palaces unlocked for us.

IV. A GOSPEL OF REPENTANCE AND REMISSION OF SINS OF A UNIVERSAL CHARACTER IS TO BE PREACHED IN HIS NAME. For Christ comes to make men sorry for their sins, while at the same time they enjoy the sense of their pardon. As risen Saviour, he is the outward Guarantee of our justification from all things from which we could not be justified by the Law of Moses. He was "delivered for our offences, and raised again for our justification" (Rom. iv. 25). And to these benefits all nations are to have access. The proofs of resurrection, the understanding of the Scriptures, and the inspiration of the Holy Ghost, were with a view to a practical issue in the publication of glad tidings to all nations.

V. POWER IS GUARANTEED IF THEY WAIT PRAYERFULLY AT JERUSALEM. They had got the Spirit as zephyr-breath. They had still to get him in Pentecostal and fiery power. Hence they are encouraged by the Lord to wait for this at Jerusalem, for work without spiritual power would be useless. And they waited, and were made world-conquerors by the gift of power. So ought the Lord's people to wait for power still.

VI. THE ASCENSION WAS THE NECESSARY COMPLEMENT OF RESURRECTION, AND THE GUARANTEE OF ULTIMATE VICTORY. We have already seen reason for believing that, on the day of resurrection, Jesus *privately* ascended to the Father, reported himself there, and made heaven his head-quarters during "the great forty days." But a *public* ascension before the assembled disciples was necessary to establish their faith and joy. And so they were permitted to see their beloved Lord ascending, in spite of gravitation, up into the blue heavens, and speeding towards the centre of the universe at the right hand of God. Yet the inevitable separation did not prevent them from returning to Jerusalem with great joy, and continuing there until the Pentecost. They divided their time between the upper room and the temple. They waited in joyful anticipation of the promised power, and they got it in due season. And the Ascension ought to be to all believers a matter of definite experience. It is to this St. Paul refers when he speaks, in the Epistle to the Ephesians, of being "raised up together with Christ, and made to sit together in heavenly places in Christ Jesus." There is an ascension-experience as well as a resurrection-experience—an experience in which we feel that we have risen superior to all earthly attractions, and that we, setting our affections, indeed, on things above, are sitting by faith among them with our Lord. It is this ecstatic state which heralds the advent of spiritual power. May it belong to all of us!—R. M. E.

HOMILETICAL INDEX

TO

THE GOSPEL ACCORDING TO ST. LUKE

VOLUME I.

CHAPTER IX.

CHAPTER X.

CHAPTER XI.

CHAPTER XII.

HOMILETICAL INDEX

TO

THE GOSPEL ACCORDING TO ST. LUKE

VOLUME II.

INDEX.